SYMPHONIC CATALOG
1977
3RD EDITION

R. R. BOWKER COMPANY
New York & London

Published by R. R. Bowker Co.
1180 Avenue of the Americas, New York, N.Y. 10036
Copyright © 1977 by American Society of Composers,
    Authors and Publishers
ASCAP Building, One Lincoln Plaza
New York, N.Y. 10023

International Standard Book Number: 0-8352-0910-5
International Standard Serial Number: 0145-5265
Library of Congress Catalog Card Number: 77-133

Printed and bound in the United States of America

The American Society of Composers, Authors and
Publishers (ASCAP) and the R. R. Bowker Company
have used their best efforts in collecting and preparing
material for inclusion in the *ASCAP Symphonic Catalog 1977*, 3rd Edition, but do not assume and hereby
disclaim any liability for omissions or errors in this
work.

CONTENTS

PREFACE

This is the third edition of the Symphonic Catalog of the American Society of Composers, Authors and Publishers, the first and foremost U.S. music licensing organization. ASCAP has grown dramatically since the second edition of 1966, and this is reflected in the 26,000 symphonic, chamber orchestra, chamber ensemble (10 instruments or more) and choral works listed—an increase of some 9,000 twentieth-century compositions and arrangements of earlier classics.

Since its birth as America's performing rights society in 1914, ASCAP has always been proud to license the works of men and women of many races, creeds, tastes and dreams. The gifted creators who have made memorable realities of these dreams include ASCAP's numerous Pulitzer Prize winners and many others of global repute.

The sophistication, diversity and internationally recognized talents of ASCAP's more than 20,000 members—well represented among the creators and publishers of the extraordinary treasure trove this catalog encompasses—are reflected in the great variety of works. It is no exaggeration to state that every form of contemporary composition, from the most avant garde to the most traditional, is well represented here.

This catalog also lists the works of many distinguished foreign composers whose U.S. performances are licensed by ASCAP as a result of arrangements with music publishers and sister societies in literally dozens of other countries in every part of the world. Not only are East German works appearing for the first time, but the catalog includes many more Yugoslav, Finnish, Canadian and Swiss compositions than ever before.

The established and the young, the traditional and the ground-breakers, are side by side in this volume. The past, the present and the future are all represented in this volume—one which we see as both a catalog and a challenge.

We know that it will be useful, probably invaluable, to today's international music community. It reflects the labors of thousands of composers and publishers plus an ASCAP editorial team guided by Dr. Rudolf Nissim, with extensive preliminary editing by Doris and Gerald Deakin and with all complete copyright verification and final editing by James Cohn assisted by Delmar Brown. We are indebted to all of them for this unique volume.

This book tells us that musical creativity is greater than ever, that an ASCAP license brings access to more and more varied works than ever before and that the "symphonic" community is a healthy and dynamic one. The dream is a live one and we are proud to have this opportunity to share its celebration with you.

STANLEY ADAMS
President, ASCAP

NOTES REGARDING
INSTRUMENTATION
AND MOVEMENTS

KEY TO INSTRUMENTATION

Since the customary numerical listing of instrumentation does not indicate clearly whether or not the piccolo, English horn, bass-clarinet and contrabassoon are used, this catalog employs an asterisk to indicate that these parts are present and require extra performers. Thus,

    *3,*3,*4,*3 - 4,2-3,3,1 - timp., perc.(5) - str.

      means

    2 flutes & piccolo, 2 oboes & English horn, 3 clarinets & bass-clarinet,
    2 bassoons & contrabassoon; 4 horns, 2 to 3 trumpets, 3 trombones, tuba;
    5 percussion players, incl. timpani; and string

Please note that the asterisk does not indicate doubling. Wherever doubling occurs, the catalog so specifies.

Instruments which are very rare or not generally employed in the orchestra are not abbreviated, but are spelled out in full. For example,

Ondes-martenot	An electronic instrument
Pressure horn	An arrangement of tubes operated by a valve and a cylinder of compressed air or carbon dioxide
Tarogato	A single-reed conical wood instrument not unlike a saxophone
Theremin	An electronic instrument
Trautonium	An electronic keyboard instrument

Electronic instruments and other electronic devices (including tape-playing equipment) are indicated after the percussion, and before nonelectric keyboard instruments and stringed instruments.

NOTE REGARDING MOVEMENTS

Tempo indications are shown for movements of works in sonata form (e.g., symphonies, concerti) in most cases only when such indications and the order in which the movements appear are known to be a departure from the expected and customary. In most cases the opening movement and finale are fast, or fast but preceded by a short slow introduction.

INSTRUMENT ABBREVIATIONS

picc.	piccolo	cymb.	cymbals
fl.	flute	glock.	glockenspiel
ob.	oboe	mar.	marimba
Eng.hn.	English horn	trgl.	triangle
heck.	Heckelphone	vibra.	vibraphone
cl.	clarinet	xyl.	xylophone
b.-cl.	bass-clarinet	acc.	accordion
sax.	saxophone	cemb.	cembalo (keyboard part playable on either a harpsichord or a piano)
bn.	bassoon		
c.-bn.	contrabassoon		
sarr.	sarrusophone	guit.	guitar
hn.	horn	harm.	harmonium
tpt.	trumpet	hp.	harp
cnt.	cornet	hpsc.	harpsichord
flg.-hn.	flügel-horn	org.	organ
trb.	trombone	pf.	piano
bar.	baritone	str.	strings
euph.	euphonium	vln.	violin
tu.	tuba	vla.	viola
timp.	timpani	c.	cello
perc.	percussion	d.-b.	double-bass
cel.	celesta		

NOTICE REGARDING PERFORMANCES

Dramatic works are indicated by the % symbol after the title. These, and all other works in the Society's repertory, are available for *nondramatic performance only*, in the United States, under an ASCAP license. Users of this catalog outside of the United States will want to consult their local Performing Right society. A list of those societies is included in this volume on the inside front cover.

ASCAP SYMPHONIC CATALOG

A

AALTOILA, Heikki
—— MUSIC TO AESCHUYLUS' PLAY "AGAMEMNON" (1962)
    1,1,1,1 - 0,1,1,0 - timp.,perc. - hp. - str.   24:00 FinnMICtr.
—— MUSIC TO ALEXIS KIVI'S PLAY "KULLERVO" (FOR SATB CHORUS AND ORCH.) (1972)
    2,1,2,1 - 1,1,3,1 - timp.,perc.(3) - str.   FinnMICtr.
—— MUSIC TO ARISTOPHANES' PLAY "THE CLOUDS" (WITH WOMEN'S CHORUS) (1952)
    1,0,3,0 - 0,3,3,0 - timp.,perc.,cel. - banjo,mandolin - hp.
                         27:00 FinnMICtr.
—— MUSIC TO CARLO GOZZI'S PLAY "L'AUGELLINO BELVERDE" (WITH SOLO VOICES) (1952)
    3,2,3,2 sax.,2 - 3,1,1,1 - timp.,perc.(3),cel. - pf. - d.-b.
                         54:00 FinnMICtr.
—— MUSIC TO E. LEINO'S PLAY "TARQUINIUS SUPERBUS" (1954)
    1,2,0,1 - 2,1,1,0 - timp.,perc. - d.-b.   16:00 FinnMICtr.
—— MUSIC TO EURIPIDES' PLAY "IPHIGENIA IN AULIS" (1957)
    1,2,0,1 - 0,0,0,0 - timp.,perc.(5) - hp. - pf.   18:00 FinnMICtr.
—— MUSIC TO GHELDERODE'S PLAY "BARRABAS" (WITH SOLO VOICES) (1951)
    1,2,2,1 - 3,2,3,0 - timp.,perc. - str.   27:00 FinnMICtr.
—— MUSIC TO GOETHE'S PLAY "FAUST" (WITH TENOR, BARITONE, BASS AND SATB CHORUS) (1966)
    1,1,1,1 - 2,1,1,0 - timp.,perc. - guit. - hp. - org. - d.-b.
                         16:00 FinnMICtr.
—— MUSIC TO GRILLPARZER'S PLAY "SAPPHO" (1945)
    2,1,0,1 - 3,3,3,0 - timp.(2) - str.   18:00 FinnMICtr.
—— MUSIC TO HUUGO JALKANEN'S PLAY "NIGHT SOUL" (WITH BASS-BARITONE AND MALE CHORUS) (1958)
    1,2,0,0 - 2,1,0,0 - timp.,perc. - vla.,c.   14:00 FinnMICtr.
—— MUSIC TO JEAN ANOUILH'S PLAY "BECKET" (WITH MEZZO-SOPRANO) (1962)
    0,2,0,2 - 2,1,1,0 - perc. - guit. - org. - hpsc. - str.
                         16:00 FinnMICtr.
—— MUSIC TO KASMUNK'S PLAY "NIELS EBBESEN" (1946)
    1,1,2,1 - 0,2,1,0 - 2 vla.,2 c.   18:00 FinnMICtr.
—— MUSIC TO KUA MO JO'S PLAY "TSHU YUAN" (WITH SOLO VOICES AND SATB CHORUS) (1959)
    1,2,0,1 - 0,2,0,0 - timp.,perc.(5) - domra - pf.(prepared) - vla.
                         28:00 FinnMICtr.
—— MUSIC TO L. KOKKONEN'S PLAY "STORM BIRD" (1962)
    2,1,2,1 - 0,2,2,0 - perc. - hp. - str.   20:00 FinnMICtr.
—— MUSIC TO LENORMAND'S PLAY "ASIA" (FOR SOLO VOICES, BOYS' CHORUS AND ORCH.) (1942)
    1,1,2,sax.,1 - 3,2,1,0 - timp.,perc. - org.   20:00 FinnMICtr.
—— MUSIC TO M. FRISCH'S PLAY "ANDORRA" (1962)
    1,2,0,2 - 0,2,0,0 - perc. - vla.,c.,d.-b.   15:00 FinnMICtr.
—— MUSIC TO MAXWELL ANDERSON'S PLAY "ANNE OF THE THOUSAND DAYS" (WITH SOPRANO, MEZZO-SOPRANO, TENOR AND BARITONE) (1951)
    2,2,2,2 - 3,2,2,1 - timp.,perc. - hp. - vla.   28:00 FinnMICtr.

—— MUSIC TO MEREŽKOWSKY'S PLAY "DEATH OF THE CZAR" (1938)
    2,0,0,2 - 4,2,0,1 - timp.,perc.(3) - hp. - str.   16:00 FinnMICtr.
—— MUSIC TO MOLIÈRE'S PLAY "LE BOURGEOIS GENTILHOMME" (1963)
    1,1,1,1 - 2,1,1,0 - timp.,perc. - str.   28:00 FinnMICtr.
—— MUSIC TO MOLIÈRE'S PLAY "LE MALADE IMAGINAIRE" (1953)
    0,2,0,2 - 2,0,0,0 - timp. - str.   20:00 FinnMICtr.
—— MUSIC TO NESTROY'S PLAY "THE TALISMAN" (1961)
    1,1,2,1 - 2,1,1,0 - timp.,perc. - guit. - acc. - str. 42:00 FinnMICtr.
—— MUSIC TO PETER WEISS' PLAY "MARAT" (WITH SOLO VOICES AND SATB CHORUS) (1965)
    2,2,0,2 - 0,2,0,0 - timp.,perc. - harm.   30:00 FinnMICtr.
—— MUSIC TO RACINE'S PLAY "PHAIDRA" (1959)
    1,*2,*3,1 - 0,0,2,0 - timp.,perc. - d.-b.   8:00 FinnMICtr.
—— MUSIC TO RAUL ROINE'S PLAY "THE FOOL'S COURT" (WITH SOLO VOICES) (1946)
    1,1,2,1 - 2,2,1,0 - timp.,perc.(3),cel. - hp. - pf. - str.
                         42:00 FinnMICtr.
—— MUSIC TO ROSTAND'S PLAY "CYRANO DE BERGERAC" (1958)
    1,1,0,0, - 2,2,1,0 - timp.,perc. - str.   25:00 FinnMICtr.
—— MUSIC TO SHAKESPEARE'S PLAY "JULIUS CAESAR" (WITH MEZZO-SOPRANO) (1959)
    1,1,0,1 - 3,2,3,1 - timp.,perc.(3) - hp.   18:00 FinnMICtr.
—— MUSIC TO SHAKESPEARE'S PLAY "MACBETH" (FOR 3 ALTOS, SATB CHORUS AND ORCH.) (1964)
    1,1,3,1 - 0,1,3,0 - timp.,perc. - hp. - str.   25:00 FinnMICtr.
—— MUSIC TO SHAKESPEARE'S PLAY "THE MERCHANT OF VENICE" (FOR SOPRANO, ALTO, TENOR, BARITONE, SATB CHORUS AND ORCH.) (1955)
    2,1,1,1 - 2,2,1,0 - timp.,perc. - hp. - str.   25:00 FinnMICtr.
—— MUSIC TO SHAKESPEARE'S PLAY "THE TAMING OF THE SHREW" (1963)
    2,2,2,2 - 2,1,1,1 - timp.,perc. - hp. - d.-b.   32:00 FinnMICtr.
—— MUSIC TO STRINDBERG'S "A DREAM PLAY" (FOR ALTO, TENOR, BARITONE, BASS, SATB CHORUS AND ORCH.) (1959)
    2,2,2,2 - 2,0,0,0 - timp.,perc.,cel. - hp. - org. - pf. - str.
                         32:00 FinnMICtr.
—— MUSIC TO STRINDBERG'S PLAY "MISS JULIE" (WITH SATB CHORUS) (1948)
    1,1,1,1 - 0,2,1,0 - perc. - mandolin - acc. - harm. - pf. - vla.,c.
                         23:00 FinnMICtr.
—— MUSIC TO STRINDBERG'S PLAY "THE GREAT HIGHWAY" (1967)
    1,1,1,1 - 2,1,0,0 - timp. - str.   16:00 FinnMICtr.
—— MUSIC TO STRINDBERG'S PLAY "THE ROAD TO DAMASCUS" (1954)
    0,*3,*3,1 - 0,0,0,0 - timp.,perc. - str.   16:00 FinnMICtr.
—— MUSIC TO THE CHILDREN'S PLAY "THE MAGIC BONNETS" (FOR MEZZO-SOPRANO, 2 ALTOS, 2 BARITONES, BASS, CHILDREN'S VOICES, SATB CHORUS AND ORCH.) (1964)
(Text: Pirkko Karppi)
    1,1,2,1 - 2,0,0,0 - timp.,perc. - d.-b.   28:00 FinnMICtr.

—— MUSIC TO THE CHILDREN'S PLAY "THROUGH THE SKIES" (WITH SOLO VOICES AND WOMEN'S CHORUS) (1945) (Text: Toini Aaltonen)
    2,1,2,1 - 3,2,1,0 - timp.,perc.,cel. - hp. - pf. - str.
                  34:00 FinnMICtr.

—— MUSIC TO THE MARIA JOTUNI'S "KLAUS, THE LORD OF LOUHIKKO" (1942)
    2,2,2,2 - 2,2,1,1 - timp.,perc.,cel. - hp. - str.   25:00 FinnMICtr.

—— MUSIC TO THE PLAY "A STREETCAR NAMED DESIRE" (1950) (Text: Tennessee Williams)
    3,2,3,4 sax.,2 - 4,3,3,1 - timp.,perc.(4),cel. - hp. - pf.
                  45:00 FinnMICtr.

—— MUSIC TO THE PLAY "CAT ON A HOT TIN ROOF" (FOR SOPRANO, ALTO, TENOR, BARITONE, BASS, CHILDREN'S CHORUS, SATB CHORUS AND ORCH.) (1956) (Text: Tennessee Williams)
    1,0,3,4 sax.,1 - 0,3,3,0 - perc. - guit. - pf. vln.,d.-b.
                  34:00 FinnMICtr.

—— MUSIC TO THORNTON WILDER'S PLAY "OUR TOWN" (WITH SOLO VOICES, BOYS' CHORUS AND SATB CHORUS) (1939)
    2,2,2,2 - 2,0,0,0 - perc. - hp. - org. - str.   20:00 FinnMICtr.

—— MUSIC TO VILHO HELANEN'S PLAY "BERENIKE" (FOR ALTO, TENOR, BARITONE, 2 BASSES, SATB CHORUS AND ORCH.) (1954)
    1,1,2,1 - 2,1,1,1 - timp.,perc. - str.   25:00 FinnMICtr.

—— THE VILLAGE DANCE (1934)
    2,2,2,2 - 4,2,3,0 - timp.,perc.(3) - str.   6:00 FinnMICtr.

—— WOODEN WAGON (SUITE) (1936)
    2,2,2,2 - 4,2,3,0 - timp.,perc.(3) - str.   7:00 FinnMICtr.

AALTONEN, Erkki
—— THE COBBLERS ON THE HEATH (BALLET) % (1963) (TENOR AND VIOLIN)
    2,1,3,2 - 2,2,2,0 - timp.,perc. - hp. - str.   75:00 FinnMICtr.

—— CONCERTO FOR VIOLIN AND ORCH. (1966)
    2,1,2,1 - 3,3,2,0 - timp.,perc. - hp. - str.   22:00 FinnMICtr.

—— CONCERTO NO. 1 FOR PIANO AND ORCH. (1948)
    2,3,2,3 - 4,3,3,1 - timp.,perc. - pf. - str.   27:00 FinnMICtr.

—— CONCERTO NO. 2 FOR PIANO AND ORCH. (1954)
    3,2,2,2 - 4,3,3,1 - timp.,perc.(3) - pf. - str.   32:00 FinnMICtr.

—— FOLK MUSIC FOR ORCHESTRA (SUITE) (1960)
    3,2,2,2 - 4,3,3,0 - timp.,perc. - str.   20:00 FinnMICtr.

—— FOLK MUSIC FROM HÄME (1941)
    2,2,2,2 - 4,3,3,0 - timp.,perc. - str.   9:00 FinnMICtr.

—— HÄMEENLINNA (SUITE) (1945) (In 4 movements)
    2,3,3,2 - 4,2,3,0 - timp.,perc. - hp. - str.   18:00 FinnMICtr.

—— LAPPONIA NO. 1 (BALLET SUITE) (1956)
    3,2,2,2 - 4,3,3,0 - timp.,perc. - hp. - str.   10:00 FinnMICtr.

—— LAPPONIA NO. 2 (BALLET SUITE) (1959)
    2,2,3,2 - 4,3,3,1 - timp.,perc. - str.   18:00 FinnMICtr.

—— LITTLE BALLET SUITE FOR ORCH.
    3,2,2,2 - 4,3,3,0 - timp.,perc. - str.   FinnMICtr.

—— MACBETH (SUITE) (1958)
    2,3,3,2 - 4,3,3,0 - timp.,perc. - hp. - str.   16:00 FinnMICtr.

—— SUITE FROM THE FILM "THE COBBLERS ON THE HEATH" (1957)
    2,1,2,1 - 2,2,1,0 - timp.,perc. - hp. - str.   35:00 FinnMICtr.

—— SYMPHONY NO. 1 IN C MAJOR (1947)
    3,2,2,3 - 4,3,3,1 - timp.,perc. - str.   23:00 FinnMICtr.

—— SYMPHONY NO. 2 ("HIROSHIMA") (1949)
    3,3,4,3 - 6,4,3,1 - timp.,perc.(3) - 2 hp. - str.   37:00 FinnMICtr.

—— SYMPHONY NO. 3 ("POPULAR SYMPHONY") (1952)
    3,3,4,3 - 4,3,3,1 - timp.,perc.(3) - str.   25:00 FinnMICtr.

—— SYMPHONY NO. 4 (1959)
    3,2,3,2 - 4,3,3,1 - timp.,perc.(3) - str.   25:00 FinnMICtr.

—— SYMPHONY NO. 5 (1964)
    3,2,3,2 - 4,3,3,1 - timp.,perc.(3),cel. - hp. - pf. - str.
                  27:00 FinnMICtr.

AATZ, Michael
—— CONVERGENCES (FOR TROMBONE, PERCUSSION AND STRINGS)
    trb. - perc. - str.   11:00 Presser.

—— MORDFELD
    1,0,2,2 - 2,2,2,0 - timp. - str.(no vlns.,no d.-b.)   11:30 Presser.

ABBADO, Marcello
—— VARIATIONS ON A THEME OF MOZART
    2,1,1,1 - 2,1,0,0 - perc.(4),bells,cel.,vibra.,xyl. - str.   18:00 Leeds.

ABBOTT, Alain
—— MUSIC FOR ACCORDION AND STRINGS
    acc. - str.   19:00 Presser.

—— LES NOMBRES INVISIBLES
    3,4,4,3 - 5,4,3,1 - timp.,perc.(3),cel. - 2 hp. - str.   14:00 Presser.

ABEL, Karl Friedrich - HOECKNER
—— SHORT SYMPHONY IN F MAJOR, OP. 1, NO. 5
    2 ob.(or 2 fl.) - 2 hn. - cemb. - str.   Henmar.

—— SHORT SYMPHONY IN G MAJOR, OP. 1, NO. 6
    2 ob.(or 2 fl.) - 2 hn. - cemb. - str.   Henmar.

ABEL, Karl Friedrich - PETERS, Gerhard-Ewald
—— CONCERTO IN C MAJOR FOR FLUTE AND STRING ORCH.
    fl. - str.   18:00 Henmar.

ABENDROTH, Walter
—— CONCERTANTE FANTASIE, OP. 23
    1,2,0,2 - 0,3,2,0 - timp. - hpsc. - str.   16:00 Sikorski.

—— CONCERTO FOR VIOLIN AND ORCH., OP. 35
    2,2,2,3 - 4,3,3,0 - timp.,perc. - str.   25:00 Belw-Mills.

—— DIVERTIMENTO FOR CHAMBER ORCH., OP. 24
    1,1,1,1 - 1,1,1,0 - perc. - str.   16:00 Belw-Mills.

—— SINFONIE (IN C MAJOR)
    1,2,0,2 - 0,3,3,0 - timp.,perc. - hp. - str.   26:00 Sikorski.

—— SINFONIE (IN F MAJOR), OP. 19
    2,2,2,2 - 4,3,3,0 - timp.,perc. - str.   30:00 Sikorski.

—— SINFONIETTA, OP. 32
    1,2,1,2 - 1,2,2,0 - timp.,perc. - str.   19:00 Belw-Mills.

—— SYMPHONY NO. 5, OP. 34
    2,3,3,2 - 4,2,2,0 - timp.,perc. - hp. - str.   32:00 Belw-Mills.

ABESHOUSE, Warren Alan
—— COLORATIONS, OP. 8 (1974)
    *3,2,Eꞥcl.,1,0 - 2,2,1,1 - timp.,perc.(5, incl. 4 on timp.),glock.,xyl. - org. - pf. - str.   6:30 A.P.R.A.

ABRAHAMSEN, Hans
—— FOAM (FOR CHAMBER ORCH.)
    14:00 K.O.D.A.

—— SYMPHONY
    3,3,3,3 - 4,3,3,1 - str.   9:00 K.O.D.A.

ABRAMSON, Robert M.
—— AGES OF TIME (MUSIC FROM THE FILM OF THE SAME NAME)
    *2,1(alt. with Eng.hn.),2(2nd alt. with b.-cl.),2 - 2,2,3,0 - timp.,perc.(2),bells,xyl. - hp. - pf. - str.   25:00 Composer.

—— DANCE VARIATIONS (FOR PIANO AND ORCH.)
    *3,*3,*3,2 - 4,3,3,1 - timp.,perc. - hp. - pf. - str.   16:25 General.

—— THE PSYCHIATRIST (A FARCE BALLET) %
    *3,2,2,2 - 2,2,2,1 - timp.,perc.(2),bells,xyl. - pf. - str.
                  22:00 Composer.

ABRAVANEL, Claude
—— FOUR PSALMS (FOR HIGH VOICE, 5 WOODWINDS, HARP AND STRINGS)
    8:00 IsMuPublns.

ABSIL, Jean
—— CONCERTINO FOR CELLO AND ORCH., OP. 42
    2,2,2,2 - 4,2,2,1 - timp.,xyl. - hp. - str.   13:00 CBDM.

—— CONCERTO FOR PIANO AND ORCH., OP. 30
    2,2,2,2 - 4,2,2,1 - timp.,perc.,xyl. - pf. - str.   14:00 CBDM.

—— CONCERTO FOR VIOLA AND ORCH., OP. 54
    2,2,2,2 - 3,2,0,0 - timp.,cel.,xyl. - hp. - str.   16:00 CBDM.

—— CONCERTO FOR VIOLIN AND ORCH., OP. 11
    2,2,4,3 - 3,1,1,1 - timp.,perc.,cel.,xyl., - hp. - str.   22:00 CBDM.

—— CONCERTO GROSSO, OP. 60 (FOR WIND QUINTET AND ORCH.) (1944)
    2,2,2,2 - 2,0,0,0 - str.   11:00 H. Elkan.

—— CONCERTO NO. 2 FOR PIANO AND ORCH., OP. 131 (1967) (IN 3 MOVTS.)
    2,2,2,2 - 4,2,2,1 - timp.,perc. - pf. - str.   22:00 H. Elkan.

—— CONCERTO NO. 3 FOR PIANO AND ORCH., OP. 162 (1973) (IN 3 MOVTS.)
    2,2,2,2 - 4,2,2,1 - timp.,perc. - pf. - str.   H. Elkan.

—— DÉITÉS, OP. 160 (1972) (IN 5 MOVTS.)
    2,1,2,1 - 3,1,1,0 - timp.,perc. - str.   22:00 H. Elkan.

—— DIVERTIMENTO, OP. 86 (FOR 4 SAXOPHONES AND ORCH.) (1955)
    1,1,0,4 sax.,0 - 3,1,0,0 - timp.,perc. - str.   20:00 H. Elkan.

—— FANTAISIE CONCERTANTE, OP. 99 (FOR VIOLIN AND
ORCH.) (1958)
   2,2,2,2 - 4,2,2,1 - timp.,perc. - str.   13:30 H. Elkan.
—— HOMMAGE À LEKEU, OP. 35-B (1939)
   2,2,2,2 - 4,2,2,1 - timp.,perc. - hp. - str.   6:00 H. Elkan.
—— INTRODUCTION ET VALSES, OP. 89 (1955)
   2,1,2,1 - 3,2,1,0 - timp.,perc.,xyl. - hp. - str.   12:00 H. Elkan.
—— MYTHOLOGIE (SUITE), OP. 84 (1954)
   2,2,2,2 - 4,2,2,1 - timp.,perc.,cel.,xyl. - hp. - str.   20:00 H. Elkan.
—— PEAU D'ÂNE, OP. 26 (SUITE) (1937)
   1,1,1,1 alto sax.,0 - 1,1,1,0 - timp.,perc. - pf. - str.
   15:00 H. Elkan.
—— RHAPSODIE BRÉSILIENNE, OP. 81 (1953)
   3,2,3,alto sax.,3 - 4,2,2,1 - timp.,perc.,bells,mar.,xyl. - hp. - str.
   15:00 H. Elkan.
—— RHAPSODIE FLAMANDE, OP. 4
   3,3,2,3 - 3,2,2,1 - timp.,perc.,glock.,xyl. - str.   12:00 CBDM.
—— RHAPSODY NO. 2
   15:00 CBDM.
—— SERENADE, OP. 44 (1940)
   2,2,2,2 - 2,2,0,0 - timp.,perc.,cel.,glock.,xyl. - hp.(ad lib.) - str.
   18:00 H. Elkan.
—— SUITE BUCOLIQUE, OP. 95 (1957) (IN 5 MOVTS.)
   str.   16:00 S.A.B.A.M.
—— SUITE D'APRÈS LE FOLKLORE ROUMAIN, OP. 92 (1956)
   2,1,2,1 - 3,1,1,0 - timp.,perc.,xyl. - str.   18:00 H. Elkan.
—— SYMPHONY NO. 2, OP. 25
   3,3,4,3 - 4,2,2,1 - timp.,perc.,cel.,xyl., hp. - str.   23:00 CBDM.
—— SYMPHONY NO. 3, OP. 57
   3,3,4,3 - 4,3,3,1 - timp.,perc.,cel.,glock.,xyl. - hp. - str.
   22:00 CBDM.
—— SYMPHONY NO. 4, OP. 142 (1969) (IN 4 MOVTS.)
   2,2,3,2 - 4,2,2,1 - timp.,perc. - str.   22:00 H. Elkan.
—— SYMPHONY NO. 5, OP. 148 (1970) (IN 4 MOVTS.)
   2,2,2,2 - 4,2,2,1 - timp.,perc. - str.   16:00 H. Elkan.
—— TROIS AIRS DE BALLET (FROM "PEAU D'ÂNE", OP. 26)
   1,1,1,1 alto sax.,0 - 1,1,1,0 - perc.,xyl. - pf. - str.   9:00 H. Elkan.
—— VARIATIONS SYMPHONIQUES, OP. 50
   3,3,4,3 - 4,2,2,1 - timp.,perc.,glock.,xyl. - hp. - str.   20:00 CBDM.

ACHRON, Isidor
—— CONCERTO IN B♭ MINOR FOR PIANO AND ORCH.
   3,3,2,2 - 4,3,3,1 - timp.,perc. - hp. - pf. - str.   30:00 C. Fischer.
—— SUITE GROTESQUE, OP. 7
   3,2,2,2 - 4,3,0,0 - timp.,perc.,xyl. - hp. - str.   9:00 Composer.

ACHRON, Joseph
—— CONCERTO NO. 2 FOR VIOLIN AND ORCH., OP. 68
   *3,2,2, alto sax., 2 - 4,2,0,0 - perc. - pf. - str.   25:19 Composer.
—— CONCERTO NO. 3 FOR VIOLIN AND ORCH., OP. 72
   *3,2,2,2 - 4,2,3,1 - timp.,perc.(3) - hp. - pf., - str.
   21:47 Composer.
—— DANCE IMPROVISATION, OP. 37
   *3,*3,*3,2 - 4,2,3,1 - timp.,perc. - hp. - str.   2:00 Composer.
—— ELEGY (FOR STRING ORCHESTRA)
   str.   Composer.
—— EPITAPH (IN MEMORY OF SCRIABINE) OP. 38 (WITH
OPTIONAL CHORUS)
   *3, alto fl.,*3,*3,*3 - 8,4,3,1 - timp.,perc.(2) - 2 hps. - str.
   9:00 Composer.
—— IMPROVISATION ON RAMEAU'S "TAMBOURIN"
   str.   3:00 G. Schirmer.
—— SINFONIETTA
   str.   Composer.
—— SUITE FROM "THE GOLEM" (IN 5 MOVTS.)
   *2,*2,*2,*2 - 2,3,1,1 - perc.(1) - hp. - pf. - str.(6 c., 6d.-b.)
   10:00 Composer.
—— TABLEAUX FROM THEATER MUSIC TO "BELSHAZZAR",
OP. 58 (IN 2 MOVTS.)
   *3,*3,D cl., *3,4 sax.,*3 - 4,3,3,1 - timp.,perc. (8) - pf. - str.
   16:00 Composer.

ACKER, Dieter
—— TEXTURES I (FOR LARGE ORCH.)
   Hans Gerig.
—— TEXTURES II (FOR CHAMBER ORCH.) (1972)
   Hans Gerig.

ADAIR, Dorothy
—— A CHRISTMAS WREATH (FOR CHORUS AND ORCH.)
   2,*3,2,2 - 4,3,3,1 - timp.,perc.,bells,cel.,glock. - org. - pf. - str.
   20:00 Composer.

ADAM, Adolphe - HOROVITZ, Joseph
—— BEATRIX (BALLET)(AFTER "LA JOLIE FILLE DE GAND") %
   2,2,2,2 - 4,2,3,0 - timp.,perc.(4) - hp. - str.   P.R.S.

ADAM, Adolphe - SCHMID, Adolf
—— GISELLE FANTASIA
   2,2,2,2 - 4,2,3,0 - timp.,perc. hp. - str.   9:00 Bo. Hawkes.

ADAM, Adolphe - SWANSON, Walter Donald
—— GISELLE (BALLET) %
   2,2,3,2 - 4,2,3,1 - timp.,perc. - str.   70:00 S.A.M.R.O.

ADAM, Adolphe - WILSON, Don
—— OVERTURE TO "LE ROI D'YVETOT" ("THE KING OF
YVETOT")
   8:00 Remick.
—— OVERTURE TO "QUEEN FOR A DAY"
   3:45 Remick.

ADAM, Adolphe - WINTER, Aubrey
—— OVERTURE TO "IF I WERE KING"
   8:00 Bo. Hawkes.

ADAM, Claus
—— CONCERTO FOR CELLO AND ORCH.
   1(alt. with picc.),*2,*2,1 - 0,1,0,0 - timp.,cel.,glock. - str.
   23:00 G. Schirmer.

ADAMS, Ernest Harry
—— BOURREE IN G
   str.   10:00 Composer.
—— CONCERTO NO. 1 FOR PIANO AND ORCH. (IN 3
MOVEMENTS)
   2,2,2,2 - 2,2,2,1 - timp.,perc. - pf.   20:00 Composer.

ADASKIN, Murray
—— ADAGIO FOR CELLO AND ORCH. (1975)
   2,2,2,2 - 2,2,0,0 - perc.(2) - st.   5:40 CanMusCtr.
—— BALLET SYMPHONY (1950-51) (IN 6 MOVTS.)
   *3,*3,*3,*3 - 4,3,3,1 - timp.,perc. - hp. - pf. - str.
   24:25 CanMusCtr.
—— CAPRICCIO FOR PIANO AND ORCH. (1961)
   3,2,2,2 - 4,3,3,1 - timp.,perc.(3) - pf. - str.   18:10 CanMusCtr.
—— CONCERTO FOR BASSOON AND ORCH. (1960) (IN 3
MOVTS.)
   *3,2,2,1 - 2,2,2,0 - timp. - str.   14:55 CanMusCtr.
—— CONCERTO FOR VIOLIN AND CHAMBER ORCH.
   17:00 C.A.P.A.C.
—— CONCERTO FOR VIOLIN AND ORCH. (1956) (IN 3 MOVTS.)
   *2,*3,2 - 2,2,1,0 - perc. - str.   17:15 CanMusCtr.
—— CORONATION OVERTURE
   3,3,3,2 - 4,3,3,1 - timp.,perc. - str.   9:00 C.A.P.A.C.
—— DIVERSION FOR ORCH. (1969)
   2,2,2,2 - 2,2,0,0 - perc. - str.   8:15 CanMusCtr.
—— DIVERTIMENTO NO. 4 (WITH SOLO TRUMPET AND
PICCOLO TRUMPET) (1970)
   2(2nd alt. with picc.),2,2,2 - 2,4,0,0 - timp.,perc. - str.
   12:45 CanMusCtr.
—— ESSAY FOR STRINGS (1972)
   str.   5:30 CanMusCtr.
—— FANFARE (1970)
   2,2,2,2 - 4,3,3,1 - timp.,perc.(5) - str.   4:45 CanMusCtr.
—— FUGUE, OSTINATO AND FINALE
   str.   10:00 C.A.P.A.C.
—— IN PRAISE OF "CANADIAN PAINTING IN THE THIRTIES"
(1975) (IN 3 MOVTS.)
   hpsc. - str.   16:50 CanMusCtr.
—— NOOTKA RITUAL (1974) (IN 1 MOVT.)
   2,2,2,2 - 2,2,2,0 - perc.(4) - str.   8:00 CanMusCtr.
—— QALALA AND NILAULA OF THE NORTH (1969) (IN 1
MOVT.)
   1,1,1,1 - 1,0,0,0 - perc.(2) - str.   17:25 CanMusCtr.
—— RONDINO (1964)
   *4,2,3,2 - 4,3,3,1 - timp.,perc.(3) - pf. - str.   5:30 CanMusCtr.
—— SUITE FOR ORCHESTRA (IN 3 MOVTS.)
   14:00 C.A.P.A.C.
—— SUITE FOR STRING ORCHESTRA (IN 3 MOVEMENTS)
   str.   14:00 C.A.P.A.C.
—— SUITE FOR STRINGS
   str.   14:00 C.A.P.A.C.
—— THERE IS MY PEOPLE SLEEPING (IN 1 MOVT.)
   2(2nd alt. with picc.),2,2,2 - 2,2,0,0 - timp.,perc.(4) - str.
   13:20 CanMusCtr.

ADDINSELL, Richard
—— SMOKY MOUNTAINS
                                13:30 Chappell.
—— WARSAW CONCERTO (FOR PIANO AND ORCH.)
    2,1,2,2 - 4,3,3,0 - timp. - pf. - str.   8:30 Chappell.

ADDISON, John
—— CARTE BLANCHE (BALLET SUITE)
    2,2,2,3 - 4,2,2,0 - timp.,perc.,cel. - hp. - pf. - str.   16:00 Oxford.
—— CONCERT OVERTURE
                                7:00 Oxford.
—— CONCERTINO FOR PIANO AND ORCH.
                             15:00 Oxford.
—— CONCERTO FOR TRUMPET AND STRINGS
    tpt.-str.   18:00 Galaxy.
—— CONVERSATION PIECE (FOR PIANO AND ORCH.)
    2,2,2,2 - 4,2,3,0 - timp.,perc. - hp. - pf. - str.   12:00 Oxford.
—— HEROUM FILLII (SONS OF HEROES) (OVERTURE)
                             9:00 P.R.S.
—— PARTITA
    str.   16:00 Oxford.
—— SUITE FROM THE OPERA "DEIRDRE OF THE SORROWS"
                         22:00 Oxford.
—— THREE TERPSICHOREAN STUDIES
                         14:00 P.R.S.
—— VARIATIONS FOR PIANO AND ORCH.
                         12:00 Galaxy.
—— WELLINGTON SUITE
    2 hn. - timp.,perc. - pf. - str.   16:00 Oxford.

ADLER, Hugo Charles
—— OVERTURE TO THE BIBLICAL CANTATA "BALAK AND BILAM", OP. 17
                         6:00 Transcon.

ADLER, James R.
—— THE ORIGINAL RAG-TIME SUITE (ON THEMES OF SCOTT JOPLIN)
    2,2,3,2 - 4,2,3,1 - timp.,perc. - banjo - str. 10:00 Chappell.
—— A SUITE FOR STRINGS (1975) (IN 4 MOVTS.)
    str.   13:00 Fleisher.

ADLER, Samuel
—— BE-SHAARAY TEFILAH (SACRED SERVICE)
    3,*3,3,*3 - 4,3,2,1 - timp.,perc.(6,incl. 5 on timp.) - str. Transcon.
—— THE BINDING (ORATORIO) (1967) (FOR SOLO VOICES, MIXED CHORUS AND ORCH.) (Text: Dr. Albert Friedlander)
    2(2nd alt. with picc.),2(2nd alt. with Eng. hn.),2,2 - 4,3,3,1 - timp.,perc.(3),bells,glock.,xyl. - str. 50:00 Oxford.
—— CITY BY THE LAKE (A PORTRAIT OF ROCHESTER N. Y.)
    2(2nd alt. with picc.),2,2,2 - 2,3,1,0 - timp.,perc. - hp. - str.
                           8:00 G. Schirmer.
—— CONCERTINO (IN THE FIRST POSITION)
    str.   8:00 G. Schirmer.
—— CONCERTO FOR ORCHESTRA
                        20:00 Bo. Hawkes.
—— CONCERTO FOR ORGAN AND ORCH.
    3,3,3,3 - 4,3,3,1 - timp., perc. - org. - str. 20:00 C. Fischer.
—— ELEGY FOR STRINGS
    str.   7:30 Presser.
—— THE FEAST OF LIGHTS (A HANUKKAH SUITE)
    2,2,2,1 alto sax.,1 ten. sax.,2 - 2,2,0,1 - timp. - pf. - str.
                         6:00 G. Schirmer.
—— FINALE (A POSTLUDE FOR ORCH.)
                        Composer.
—— MUSIC FOR ELEVEN (SUITE FOR WOODWINDS AND PERCUSSION)
    2(1 alt. with picc.),1,*2,1 - 0,0,0,0 - timp.,perc.(5),glock,xyl.
                         16:00 Oxford.
—— THE OUTCASTS OF POKER FLAT (1-ACT OPERA) % (Text: J. Stampfer)
    2,2,2,2 - 2,2,0,0 - timp.,perc. - str. 60:00 Oxford.
—— REQUIESCAT IN PACE (A POEM FOR SYMPHONY ORCH.)
    *3,*3,3,3 - 4,3,3,1 - timp.,perc. - hp. - str. 13:30 Oxford.
—— RHAPSODY FOR VIOLIN AND ORCH.
    2(2nd alt. with picc.),2,2,2 - 2,2,3,1 - timp.,perc.(1) - str.
                         13:30 Oxford.
—— SONG AND DANCE (FOR VIOLA AND ORCH.)
    2(2nd alt. with picc.),2,2,2 - 2,2,2,0 - timp.,perc. - hp. - str.
                         13:00 Oxford.
—— SYMPHONY NO. 1 (IN 3 MOVTS.)
    *3,*3,*2,*3 - 4,3,3,1 - timp. - hp. - str. 27:00 Presser.

—— SYMPHONY NO. 2 (IN 3 MOVTS.)
    *3,*3,*3,*3 - 4,3,3,1 - timp., perc.(2),glock.,xyl. - pf. - str.
                         29:00 Presser.
—— SYMPHONY NO. 4 (GEOMETRICS)
    2 picc.,2,*3,3 - 4,3,3,1 - timp.,perc. - pf. - str. 17:00 Oxford.
—— THE VISION OF ISAIAH (FOR BARITONE, MIXED CHORUS AND ORCH.)
    2,2,2,2 - 2,2,2,0 - timp.,perc.(2),glock. - str. 15:00 SouthernTx.
—— WISDOM COMETH WITH THE YEARS (FOR SATB CHORUS AND ORCH.)
    1,1,1,1 - 0,3,1,0 - timp. - str. 11:00 Southern.
—— THE WRESTLER (1-ACT OPERA) % (Text: Judah Stampfer)
    *3,1,1,1 - 1,2,2,0 - perc.(2) - org. - pf.(alt. with cel.) - str.(4,2,2,1)
                         40:00 Oxford.

ADOMIAN, Lah
—— SUITE FOR ORCHESTRA (IN 5 MOVTS.)
                        17:00 General.

ADORIAN, Andrew
—— THE DIARY (4 PIECES)
    2,2,2,2 - 2,2,3,0 - timp.,perc. - hp. - str. 10:00 P.R.S.
—— HUNGARIAN SUITE
    2,1,2,1 - 2,3,3,0 - timp.,perc. - hp. - str. 11:00 P.R.S.
—— THREE PIECES, AFTER LA FONTAINE (THE TWO COCKS, THE LION AND THE OYSTER)
    0,0,0,sax.,0 - 0,1,0,0 - perc. - guit. - pf. - str. 38:00 P.R.S.
—— A TRIFLING INCIDENT
    3,2,2,2 - 4,3,3,1 - timp.,perc. - hp. - str. P.R.S.

AGABABOV, Arkadij A.
—— CONCERTO FOR ORGAN AND STRING ORCH.
    org. - str.   G. Schirmer.

AGAY, Denes
—— CANDLELIGHT CONCERTO (FOR PIANO AND ORCH.)
    2,2,2,2 - 2,3,3,0 - timp.,perc. - hp. - pf. - str. 5:30 MCA Music.
—— INTRODUCTION AND CONTRADANCE
    *3,2,2,2 - 4,2,3,0 - timp.,perc. (1) - hp. - pf. - str. 6:20 Composer.
—— OVERTURE TO A MARIONETTE PLAY
    2,2,2,2 - 4,2,0,0 - timp.,perc. (2) - str. 3:35 Composer.
—— SUITE DE BALLET (FOR CHAMBER ORCH.) (IN 3 MOVTS.)
    1,0,2,0 - 1,1,0,0 - timp.,perc. (1) - hp. - pf. 8:50 Composer.

AGER, Klaus
—— REFLEXIONS
    2,0,1,0 - 1,1,2,0 - perc.(4) - pf. - str.(2,0,1,2) 14:00 Modern.

AGOSTINI, Lucio
—— SERENADE FOR ALTO FLUTE AND ORCH.
                        13:00 C.A.P.A.C.
—— SUITE FOR FLUTE AND ORCH.
                        20:00 C.A.P.A.C.

AHERN, David Anthony
—— HILO (1975)
    0,0,0,0 - 0,6,0,4 - perc.(4) - hp. - pf. - str.(16,0,0,8) 8:00 A.P.R.A.

AHLBERG, Gunnar
—— DYNAMICS (1969)
    2,2,2,sax.,2 - 4,2,3,0 - timp.,perc. - guit. - pf. - str. 18:00 Fleisher.
—— ENTRATA (1971)
    1,0,0,0 - 0,1,0,0 - perc. - pf. - str. 5:00 Fleisher.
—— PARENTES (1969)
    2,2,2,2 - 2,2,0,0 - timp.,perc. - str. 9:00 Fleisher.

AHN, Eaktay
—— KANGTEUNSUNGGOK (MUSIC COMING FROM HEAVEN) (SYMPHONIC POEM)
    3(3rd alt. with picc.),*3,*3,3 - 4,3,3,1 - perc. - hp. - str.
                        30:00 G.E.M.A.
—— KOREA (SYMPHONIC FANTASIA, WITH OPTIONAL CHORUS)
    3(3rd alt. with picc.),*3,*3,3 - 4,3,3,1 - perc. - hp. - str.
                        30:00 G.E.M.A.

AHNELL, Emil
—— ADAGIO FOR STRING ORCHESTRA (1963)
    str.   4:00 Composer.
—— DISCOURSE FOR ORCHESTRA (1956)
    *3,2,0,2 - 4,3,3,0 - timp.,perc. - str. 15:00 Composer.

—— IN THE CITY OF THE DEAD (1951) (FOR NARRATOR AND ORCH.) (Text: K. Gibran)
2,2,2,2 - 4,2,0,0 - timp. - str.   18:00 Composer.
—— SYMPHONY PASTORALE (1952)
2,2,2,2 - 4,2,2,0 - str.   11:00 Composer.
—— TRILOGY FOR ORCHESTRA (1971)
2,2,2,2 - 4,3,3,0 - timp.,perc. - str.   15:00 Composer.
—— UNISONG (1970) (FOR SATB CHORUS AND ORCH.)
2,2,2,2 - 4,3,3,0 - timp.,perc.(2) - str.   20:00 Composer.

AHO, Kalevi
—— SINFONIA CONCERTANTE, FOR VIOLIN AND ORCHESTRA (1972)
3,2,3,3 - 4,4,3,1 - timp.,perc.(4) - str.   30:00 FinnMICtr.
—— SYMPHONY CONCERTANTE FOR VIOLIN AND ORCH. (SYMPHONY NO. 3)
1. Andante; 2. Prestissimo; 3. Lento
3,2,3,3 - 4,3,3,1 timp.,perc.(4) - str.   35:00 FinnMICtr.
—— SYMPHONY NO. 1 (1969)
2,2,2,2 - 2,2,2,0 - perc. - hp. - str.   25:00 FinnMICtr.
—— SYMPHONY NO. 2 (1970)
3,3,4,3 - 4,6,3,1 - timp.,perc.(3) - str.   24:00 FinnMICtr.
—— SYMPHONY NO. 4 (1972)
3,2,3,3 - 4,6,3,1 - timp.,perc.(3) - str.   55:00 FinnMICtr.

AHREND, Karl
—— JOHNNY APPLESEED
2,1,2,1 - 2,3,2,0 - timp.,perc. - str.   11:00 C. Fischer.

AHRENS, Joseph
—— CONCERTO FOR ORGAN AND WINDS
0,0,0,0 - 2,4,4,0 - org.   Henmar.
—— CONCERTO IN E MINOR FOR ORGAN AND ORCH.
                                                    Anton Böhm.

AHROLD, Frank
—— BALLET: "548-56-8037" % (1968)
*3,2,2,2 - 2,2,3,0 - timp.,perc.bells,glock.,xyl. - tape-recorder - str.
                                                    20:00 Composer.
—— BEHOLD THE JOY (CANTATA) (FOR SATB CHORUS AND ORCH.)
2,2,2,2 - 2,2,2,1 - timp.,perc. - hp. - str.   35:00 Belw-Mills.
—— CONCERTO FOR STRING ORCH. (1969) (IN 3 MOVTS.)
str.   15:00 Composer.
—— IT MAY NOT ALWAYS BE SO (FOR SOPRANO AND ORCH.) (1969) (Text: e. e. cummings)
*3,2,2,2 - 4,2,3,1 - timp.,perc.(3),bells,glock. - hp. - str.
                                                    8:00 Composer.
—— SECOND COMING (FOR DRAMATIC TENOR AND ORCH.) (1972) (Text: William Butler Yeats)
*3,2,2,*3 - 4,2,3,1 - timp.,perc.(3),bells,cel.,glock.,xyl. - str.
                                                    14:00 Composer.
—— THE SPIDER AND THE FLY (BALLET) % (WITH SATB CHORUS) (1965)
*2,1,1,1 - 1,1,1,0 - timp.,perc.,bells,glock. - hp. - d.-b.
                                                    30:00 Composer.
—— STAR JOURNEY (BALLET) %
*3,2,2,*3 - 4,2,3,1 - timp.,perc.(4),bells,cel.,glock.,vibra.,xyl. - hp. - pf. - str.
                                                    14:00 Composer.

AITKEN, Hugh
—— CANTATA NO. 5, OP. 37 (FOR SOPRANO AND ORCH.) (1962) (Text: Rainer Maria Rilke)
1(alt. with picc.),2,*2,0 - 2,0,0,0 - str.   12:00 Oxford.
—— CHAMBER CONCERTO, OP. 4 (1949) (FOR PIANO AND SMALL ORCH.)
1,1,1,1 - 0,2,2,0 - pf. - str.   9:00 Composer.
—— CONCERTO FOR PIANO AND ORCH., OP. 12 (1953)
2,2,2,2 - 4,2,2,0 - timp. - pf. - str.   20:00 Composer.
—— MASS, OP. 6 (FOR SOPRANO, ALTO, TENOR AND BASS SOLI, SATB CHORUS AND ORCH.) (1950)
2,2,*3,2 - 4,2,3,0 - pf. - str.(2,2,2,2)   30:00 Composer.
—— THE MOIRAI ("THE FATES"), OP. 33 (BALLET) % (1961)
1(alt. with picc.),1,1,1 - 1,1,1,0 - timp.,perc.(3) - str.
                                                    30:00 Composer.
—— PARTITA FOR PIANO AND STRING ORCH., OP. 30 (1960)
pf. - str.   8:00 Composer.
—— PARTITA FOR STRING QUARTET AND ORCH., OP. 42 (1964)
1(alt. with picc.),2(2nd alt. with Eng. hn.),1(alt. with E♭ cl.),1 - 2,1,1,1 - timp.,perc.(1) - str.
                                                    13:00 EV.
—— PARTITA I FOR ORCH., OP. 18 (1957)
3(3rd alt. with picc.),*3,*3,*3 - 4,2,3,1 - timp.,perc.(4) - str.
                                                    9:00 Composer.

—— PARTITA II FOR ORCH., OP. 28 (1959)
*3,*3,*3,*3 - 4,3,3,1 - timp.,perc.(5) - str.   15:00 Composer.
—— PARTITA III FOR ORCH., OP. 43 (1964)
2,2,2,2 - 4,2,2,1 - perc.(5) - str.   3:00 Composer.
—— PARTITA IV FOR ORCH., OP. 44 (1964)
*3,*3,*3,*3 - 4,3,3,2 - perc.(5) - str.   4:00 Composer.
—— SERENADE, OP. 24 (1958) (FOR CHAMBER ORCH.)
1,1,1,1 - 1,0,0,0 - str.   8:00 Composer.
—— SEVEN PIECES FOR CHAMBER ORCH., OP. 20 (1957)
2,2,1,1 - 1,2,0,0 - perc.(2) - str.   6:00 Composer.
—— SHORT SUITE, OP. 16 (1954)
pf. - str.   5:00 Oxford.
—— TRIOS FOR 11 PLAYERS
1,1,1,1 - 1,1,1,0 - str.(1,1,1,1)   23:00 EV.

AJEMYAN, A.
—— SYMPHONY NO. 3
                                                    G. Schirmer.

AKERS, Howard E.
—— LITTLE CLASSIC SUITE (IN 3 MOVTS.)
str.   3:30 C. Fischer.

AKPABOT, Samuel
—— OVERTURE FOR A NIGERIAN BALLET
2,0,1,2 - 2,2,0,0 - timp. - str.   6:00 Oxford.
—— SCENES FROM NIGERIA
2,0,2,2 - 0,2,0,0 - timp. - str.   12:00 Oxford.
—— THREE NIGERIAN DANCES
str.   9:00 Oxford.

AKUTAGAWA, Yasushi
—— MUSIC FOR ORCHESTRA
2,*3,*3,*3 - 4,3,3,1 - timp.,perc. - pf. - str.   15:00 Fema.
—— TRIPTYQUE FOR STRINGS
str.   13:00 Presser.

ALAIN, Jehan - GALLOIS-MONTBRUN, Raymond
—— TROIS DANSES
3,3,3,3 - 4,3,3,1 - timp.,perc,cel.,vibra.,xyl. - 2 hps. - org. - str.
                                                    21:00 Baron.

ALBENIZ, Isaac - STOKOWSKI, Leopold
—— FÊTE DIEU À SEVILLE
                                                    7:00 Arranger.

ALBERSTÖTTER, Karl
—— KONZERTSTÜCK (BALLADE), OP. 3 (FOR HARP AND ORCH.)
2,2,2,2 - 4,2,3,0 - hp. - str.   12:00 Henmar.

ALBERT, Karel
—— ANANKEE (OVERTURE FOR A GREEK TRAGEDY)
2,2,2,2 - 3,3,3,1 - timp.,perc. - str.   H. Elkan.
—— DANSENDE BEELDEKENS (SUITE) (1959)
2,2,2,2 - 2,2,1,0 - timp.,perc. - pf. - str.   15:45 H. Elkan.
—— DRIE CONSTRUCTIES (FOR STRING ORCH.) (1959)
str.   12:00 H. Elkan.
—— HETLAND (1937)
3,3,3,3 - 4,3,3,1 - timp.,perc. - str.   12:00 H. Elkan.
—— HUMORESKE (BALLET FOR ORCHESTRA) (1929)
2,2,2,2 - 3,3,3,1 - gong - hp. - pf.   H. Elkan.
—— IMPULSEN (1939)
3,3,3,3 - 4,3,3,1 - timp.,perc. - str.   H. Elkan.
—— LENTEWANDELING (FOR CHAMBER ORCH.) (1935)
1,1,2,1 - 1,1,1,0 - str.   H. Elkan.
—— DE NACHT (1956)
2,2,2,2 - 2,2,1,0 - timp.,perc. - str.   15:00 H. Elkan.
—— SIMFONIETTA (1969)
2,2,2,2 - 2,2,1,0 - timp.,perc. - str.   H. Elkan.
—— SUITE (1958)
2,2,2,2 - 2,2,1,0 - timp.,perc. - str.   24:00 H. Elkan.
—— SYMPHONY NO. 1 IN E (1941)
2,2,2,2 - 4,2,3,1 - timp.,perc. - str.   33:00 H. Elkan.
—— SYMPHONY NO. 2 IN G (1943)
2,2,2,2 - 4,2,3,1 - timp.,perc. - str.   38:00 H. Elkan.
—— SYMPHONY NO. 3 IN B (1945)
2,1,2,1 - 3,2,1,0 - timp.,perc. - str.   28:00 H. Elkan.
—— SYMPHONY NO. 4 (1966)
3,3,3,3 - 4,3,2,1 - timp.,perc. - str.   27:30 H. Elkan.
—— TORNOOI (BALLET FOR ORCH.) (1953)
3,3,3,3 - 4,3,3,1 - timp.,perc. - str.   20:00 H. Elkan.

—— DE TOVERLAHTAARN (SUITE FOR BALLET) (1954)
   2,2,2,2 - 2,2,1,0 - timp.,pf. - str.   H. Elkan.

ALBERT, Stephen
—— BACCHAE (A CEREMONY IN MUSIC) (FOR BASS, SATB
   CHRORUS, ELECTRIC GUITAR, DOUBLE BASS,
   SAXOPHONES AND ORCH.)
                                                 G. Schirmer.
—— CATHEDRAL MUSIC (CONCERTO FOR FOUR QUARTETS)
   2(amplified),0,0,0 - 2,1,1,0 - perc.(2) - electric guit. - hp. - org. - 2
   pf.,elctric pf. - 2 c.   20:00 C. Fischer.
—— ORCHESTRA BOOK
   3,3,3,2 alto. sax.,bar.,sax.,3 - 4,3,3,2 - timp.,perc.,cel. - electric
   guit.,electric d.-b. - hp. - pf. - str.   C. Fischer.
—— SUPERNATURAL SONGS (CYCLE FOR SOPRANO AND
   ORCH.)
   1,2,2,0 - 0,0,0,0 - perc.,cel. - hp. - pf. - str.   C. Fischer.
—— VOICES WITHIN (FOR INSTRUMENTAL GROUP AND
   ORCH.)
   *3,3,E^b cl.,2,alto sax.,3 - 4,cnt.,2,3,1 - timp.,perc., - hp. - pf. - str.
                                                 C. Fischer.
—— WINTER SONGS (CYCLE FOR TENOR AND ORCH.)
   3,2,3,3 - 4,2,2,1 - timp.,perc.,cel. - 2 hp. - pf. - str.   C. Fischer.
—— WOLF TIME (FOR SOPRANO AND ORCH.)
   1(amplified),0,1(amplified),0 - 1,1,1,0 - perc.(6) - electric
   guit.,electric d.-b. - electric hpsc. - hp. - pf. - str.   C. Fischer.

ALBERTI, Giuseppe Matteo - DESDERI
—— CONCERTO IN E MINOR, OP. 1, NO. 7 (FOR VIOLIN,
   CEMBALO AND STRINGS)
   cemb. - str.   Henmar.
—— CONCERTO IN G MAJOR, OP. 1, NO. 3 (FOR VIOLIN,
   CEMBALO AND STRINGS)
   cemb. - str.   Henmar.

ALBICASTRO, Henricus - ZULAUF, Max
—— CONCERTO A QUATTRO IN B MINOR, OP. 7, NO. 7
   cemb. - str.   10:00 G. Schirmer.
—— CONCERTO A QUATTRO IN F MAJOR, OP. 7, NO. 6
   cemb. - str.   10:00 G. Schirmer.

ALBIN, Roger
—— CONCERTINO FOR CELLO AND CHAMBER ORCH.
   1,1,1,1 - 1,1,0,0 - timp. - str.   20:00 Presser.
—— SYMPHONY NO. 1
   3,3,3,3 - 4,3,2,1 - timp.,perc.(3),cel.,xyl. - hp. - str.   40:00 EV.
—— SYMPHONY NO. 2
   str.   18:00 EV.

ALBINONI, Tomaso - BONELLI
—— CONCERTO NO. 7 (FOR STRING ORCH.)
   str.   Henmar.

ALBINONI, Tomaso - FAGOTTO, Virginio
—— CONCERTO A CINQUE NO. 2, IN G MINOR (FOR VIOLIN,
   STRINGS AND CONTINUO)
   cemb. - str.   7:00 Presser.

ALBINONI, Tomaso - GIAZOTTO, Remo
—— CONCERTO IN D MINOR, OP. 9, NO. 2
   ob. - str.   14:00 MCA Music.

ALBINONI, Tomaso - KNEUSSLIN
—— CONCERTO IN A MINOR FOR 2 VIOLINS, CEMBALO AND
   STRINGS, OP. 5, NO. 5
   cemb. - str.   15:00 Henmar.
—— CONCERTO IN C MAJOR, OP. 7, NO. 5
   2 ob. - cemb. - str.   Henmar.
—— CONCERTO IN D MINOR, OP. 9, NO. 2
   ob. - cemb. - str.   Henmar.

ALBINONI, Tomaso - OUBRADOUS, Fernand
—— ADAGIO (FOR ORGAN AND ORCH.)
   1,1,2,1 - 2,0,0,0 - org. - str.   8:00 Presser.

ALBINONI, Tomaso - PAUMGARTNER, Bernhard
—— CONCERTO IN B FLAT FOR OBOE AND STRINGS, OP. 7,
   NO. 3
   ob. - str.   9:00 Bo. Hawkes.
—— CONCERTO IN D FOR OBOE AND STRINGS, OP. 7, NO. 6
   ob. - str.   8:30 Bo. Hawkes.

—— CONCERTO IN D, OP. 7, NO. 1 (FOR CONTINUO AND
   STRINGS)
   cemb. - str.   Bo. Hawkes.
—— SONATA A CINQUE, OP. 5, NO. 9 (FOR CONTINUO AND
   STRINGS)
   cemb. - str.   Bo. Hawkes.

ALBINONI, Tomaso - THILDE, Jean
—— CONCERTO IN A MINOR, FOR TRUMPET AND STRINGS
   tpt. - str.   Presser.
—— CONCERTO IN D MAJOR, FOR TRUMPET AND STRINGS
   tpt. - str.   10:00 Presser.
—— CONCERTO IN D MINOR, FOR TRUMPET AND STRINGS
   tpt. - str.   8:00 Presser.

ALBINONI, Tomaso - UPMEYER
—— CONCERTO IN C MAJOR, FOR VIOLIN, CEMBALO AND
   STRINGS
   cemb. - str.   Henmar.

ALBRECHTSBERGER - SOMFAI, László
—— CONCERTO FOR ORGAN AND STRINGS
   org. - str.   Bo. Hawkes.

ALBRECHTSBERGER, Johann Georg - NAGY, Oliver - VÉCSEY, Jenö
—— CONCERTO FOR HARP
                                                 Bo. Hawkes.

ALBRIGHT, William
—— ALLIANCE (MASCULINE-FEMININE) (1968)
   3(3rd alt. with picc.),*3,*3,*3 - 4,3,3,1 -
   timp.,perc.(5),bells,cel.,glock.,mar.,vibra. - hp. - pf.   16:00 EV.
—— FOILS (1963) (FOR WINDS AND PERCUSSION)
   3,*3,3(3rd alt. with b.-cl.),3 - 3,3,3,1 - timp.,perc.(3-6),mar.,vibra.
                                                 10:30 EV.
—— GOTHIC SUITE (1973) (IN 3 MOVTS.)
   perc.(1) - org. - str.   14:00 EV.
—— MARGINAL WORLDS (1970) (FOR CHAMBER ORCH.)
   1,0,1,1 - 0,1,1,0 - perc.(2) - pf. - str.(1,1,1,1)   18:00 EV.
—— NIGHT PROCESSION (1972)
   1,2,1,2 - 2,0,0,0 - perc.(1) - pf. - str.(8,2,2,1)   11:00 Composer.

ALCALAY, Luna
—— IDENTIFICATIONS
   str.   10:00 Modern.
—— IN MEMORIAM OSSIP MANDELSTAM (FOR SPEAKING
   VOICE, TAPE AND ORCH.)
   4(2 alt. with 2 picc.),4,*5,alto sax.,4 - 4,4,4,1 -
   perc.(4),cel.,glock.,vibra.,xyl. - tape-recorder - electric org. - hp. -
   str.   15:00 Modern.
—— NEW POINT OF VIEW
   2,2*2,1 - 1,2,1,0 - perc.(3),cel.,glock.,vibra.,xyl. - hp. - str.
                                                 15:00 Modern.
—— NUMÉROTAGE ACTIONNÉ
   2(2nd alt. with picc.),2(2nd alt. with Eng. hn.),0,2(2nd alt. with
   c.-bn.) - 1,1,1,1 - perc.,cel.,glock.,vibra.,xyl. - pf. - str.(9,4,2,2)
                                                 28:00 Modern.
—— ORGANIZATIONS
   1,1,1,1 - 1,1,1,0 - perc.(2) - str.(2,2,1,1)   8:00 Modern.
—— SIGNALS
   1,2(2nd alt. with Eng. hn.),2(2nd alt. with b.-cl.),2(2nd alt. with
   c.-bn.) - 1,1,1,0 - perc.(2),cel.,vibra.,xyl. - hp. - str.(2,1,1,1)
                                                 7:00 Modern.
—— UNA STROFA DI DANTE (FOR SATB CHORUS AND ORCH.)
   4(2 alt. with 2 picc.),4(4th alt. with Eng. hn.),5(5th alt. with
   b.-cl.),4(4th alt. with c.-bn.) - 4,4,4,1 - perc.(4) - str.
                                                 13:00 Modern.

ALDERIGHI, Dante
—— CONCERTO NO. 2 FOR PIANO AND ORCH.
   3,3,3,3 - 4,3,3,1 - timp.,perc.(2) - hp. - str.   33:00 Leeds.
—— DIVERTIMENTO
   pf. - str.   18:00 Leeds.
—— OUVERTURE BREVE
   2,2,2,2 - 4,3,2,1 - timp. - str.   8:00 Leeds.

ALETTE, Carl
—— LARGO CANTABILE (1966)
   3(3rd alt. with picc.),2,2,2 - 4,2,3,1 - timp. - hp. - str.
                                                 5:00 Composer.

—— RESURGENCE (1965) (TONE POEM)
  3(3rd alt. with picc.),2,3(3rd alt. with b.-cl.),0 - 4,2,3,1 -
  timp.,perc. - hp. - str.   18:00 H. Elkan.
—— SYMPHONY FOR CHAMBER ORCH. (1954) (IN 3 MOVTS.)
  1,1,1,1 - 0,0,0,0 - str.   19:00 H. Elkan.

ALEXANDER, Haim
—— ARTZA (CONCERT OVERTURE)
  3,3,3,3 - 4,3,3,1 - timp.,perc. - hp. - str.   10:00 Mills.
—— SIX ISRAELI DANCES
  2,2,2,2 - 2,2,0,0 - timp.,perc. - str.   12:00 IsMuPublns.
—— SIX ISRAELI DANCES
  2,2,2,2 - 2,2,0,0 - timp.,perc. - str.   12:00 IsMuPublns.

ALEXANDER, Josef
—— THE ANCIENT MARINER (SYMPHONIC POEM)
  *4,*3,1 E♭cl.,*3,*3 - 4,3,3,1 - timp.,perc.(3-4),cel. - 2 hp. - str.
                                                        30:00 AmMuCtr.
—— ANDANTE AND ALLEGRO
  str.   Composer.
—— CANTICLE OF NIGHT (FOR MEDIUM VOICE AND ORCH.)
  (Text: Rabindranath Tagore)
  3(3rd alt. with picc.),*3,2,*3 - 4,3,3,1 - timp.,perc.(4) - hp. - str.
                                                        12:00 AmMuCtr.
—— CELEBRATION OVERTURE (PEACE OVERTURE)
  *3,*3,2,*3 - 4,3,3,1 - timp.,perc.,glock. - str.   8:30 General.
—— CHALLENGE (AMERICAN RHAPSODY)
  *4(3rd alt. with 2nd picc.),*3,1 E♭cl.,*3,*3 - 4,3,3,1 -
  timp.,perc.(3) - str.   AmMuCtr.
—— CLOCK WORK FOR STRING ORCH.
  str.   23:00 C. Fischer.
—— CONCERTINO FOR TRUMPET AND STRING ORCHESTRA
  tpt. - str.   6:00 Templeton.
—— CONCERTO IN C MINOR FOR PIANO AND ORCH. (IN 3
  MOVTS.)
  2,2(2nd alt. with Eng. hn.),2,2 - 4,2,3,1 - timp.,perc.(2) - pf. - str.
                                                        21:00 Fleisher.
—— DIALOGUES SPIRITUELS (IN 2 MOVTS.)
  *3,*3,*3,*3 - 4,3,3,1 - timp.,perc.(2) - hp. - org. - str. 13:00 Gray.
—— DITHYRAMB FOR ORCHESTRA (BACCHANALIAN
  DANCES)
  3(3rd alt. with picc.),*3,*3,*3 - 4,3,3,1 - timp.,perc.(3) - 2 hp. - str.
                                                        16:00 AmMuCtr.
—— DOINA (ROUMANIAN FANTASY)
  *3,*3,0,2 - 4,3,2,0 - timp.,perc.(3),xyl. - pf. - str. 14:00 AmMuCtr.
—— DUO CONCERTANTE (FOR TROMBONE, STRINGS AND
  PERCUSSION)
  trb. - perc. - str.   12:00 General.
—— EPITAPHS
  3,3,3,3 - 4,3,3,1 - timp.,perc. - pf. - str.   23:00 C. Fischer.
—— A NEW ENGLAND OVERTURE
  3(3rd alt. with picc.),*3,2,2 - 4,2,3,0 - timp.,perc.(3),xyl. - str.
                                                        12:00 AmMuCtr.
—— QUIET MUSIC FOR STRINGS
  str.   12:00 General.
—— SYMPHONY NO. 2 (IN 4 MOVTS.)
  3(3rd alt. with picc.),*3,*3,*3 - 4,3,3,1 - timp.,perc.(3),glock. - str.
                                                        22:00 C. Fischer.
—— SYMPHONY NO. 3
  3(3rd alt. with picc.),2(2nd alt. with Eng.hn.),2(2nd alt. with
  b.-cl.),0 - 4,3,3,1 - timp.,perc. - pf. - str.   24:00 General.
—— THREE SYMPHONIC ODES (FOR MEN'S CHORUS AND
  ORCH.)
  3(3rd alt. with picc.),2,2,2 - 4,3,3,1 - timp.,perc. - str.
                                                        18:00 General.
—— WILLIAMSBURG SUITE
  3,2,2,2 - 2,2,1,0 - timp.,perc. - hp. - str.   19:00 C. Fischer.

ALEXANDERSSON, Helmer
—— AFTON VID SJÖN (FOR PIANO AND STRING ORCH.)
  pf. - str.   Gehrmans.
—— SYMPHONY IN G MINOR
  2,2,2,2 - 4,2,3,0 - timp. - str.   40:00 S.T.I.M.

ALEXANDERSSON, Helmer - MALM, A.
—— CONCERTO IN C MINOR FOR HORN AND ORCH.
  1,1,2,2 - 1,0,0,0 - perc. (2) - hp. - str.   11:00 S.T.I.M.
—— CONCERTO IN D MINOR FOR HORN AND ORCH.
  2,2,2,2 - 2,0,0,0 - timp. - hp. - str.   12:00 S.T.I.M.
—— RHAPSODY (SVENSKA FOLKVISOR OCH DANSER)
  1,1,2,1 - 2,1,1,0 - timp.,perc. - pf. (ad lib) - str. 10:00 S.T.I.M.

ALEXANDROV, Anatole N.
—— CLASSICAL SUITE, OP. 32 (IN 7 MOVTS.)
  *3,2(2nd alt. with Eng. hn.),2,2 - 2,1,0,0 - timp.,perc.,glock. - str.
                                                        18:00 G. Schirmer.
—— OVERTURE ON RUSSIAN FOLK THEMES, OP. 29
  *3,3,3,3 - 4,3,3,1 - timp.,perc. - str.   7:30 G. Schirmer.
—— SUITE ROMANTIQUE (WITH OPTIONAL CHORUS), OP. 16
  (IN 5 MOVTS.)
  2,2,2,2 - 4,3,3,1 - timp. - str.   18:00 G. Schirmer.
—— THIRTEEN (SUITE FROM THE FILM) OP. 47 (FOR TENOR
  AND ORCH.) (IN 6 MOVTS.)
  3(3rd alt. with picc.),2(2nd alt. with Eng hn.),2,2 - 4,3,3,1 -
  timp.,perc.,cel. - hp. - pf. - str.   22 G. Schirmer.

ALFANO, Franco
—— IL DOTTOR ANTONIO (DR. ANTONIO) (OPERA) %
  3,3,3,2 - 4,3,3,1 - timp.,perc.,cel. - hp. - pf. - str. Leeds.
—— DUE CANTI NAPOLETANI (2 NEAPOLITAN SONGS) (FOR
  VOICE AND ORCH.)
  2,2,2,2 - 2,2,0,0 - timp.,perc. - hp. - pf. - str.   10:00 Leeds.
—— TRE LIRICHE (3 SONGS FOR MEZZO-SOPRANO AND
  ORCH.) (Text: Miranda Bona)
  2,2,2,2 - 2,2,0,0 - timp. - pf. - str.   11:30 Leeds.
—— VESUVIUS (SYMPHONIC POEM)
  3,3,3,2 - 4,3,3,1 - timp.,perc.(2),glock.,xyl. - 2 hp. - pf. - str.
                                                        25:00 Leeds.

ALFIDI, Joseph
—— CONCERTO NO. 2 FOR PIANO AND ORCH.
                                                        20:00 Gate.
—— RONDO BRILLANTE
                                                        Gate.

ALFVÉN, Hugo
—— ANDANTE RELIGIOSO (FOR SMALL ORCH.)
  cel. - hp. - str.   5:00 Gehrmans.
—— BERGAKUNGEN SUITE, OP. 37 (IN 4 MOVTS.)
  4,4,4,4 - 6,4,3,1 - timp.,perc. (4), cel. - 2 hps. - str.
                                                        14:00 Gehrmans.
—— DALA (SWEDISH RHAPSODY NO. 3), OP. 47
  3,3,3,Sax. 3 - 4,2,3,1 - timp.,perc. hp. - str.   18:00 G. Schirmer.
—— DRAPA (SYMPHONIC PIECE), OP. 27
  3,3,4,4 - 6,4,3,1 - timp.,perc. (5) - 2 hps. - str.   10:00 S.T.I.M.
—— ELEGI (VID EMIL SJOGRENS BÅR), OP. 38
  3,3,4,3 - 4,3,3,1 - timp.,perc.,cel. - hp. - str.   10:00 Lundquists.
—— EN BYGDESAGA (A COUNTRY TALE) (SUITE), OP. 53
  3,2,2,2 - 2,2,1,1 - timp. - str.   33:00 Bo. Hawkes.
—— FESTIVAL OVERTURE, OP. 52
  3,3,3,3 - 4,3,3,1 - timp.,perc. (2) - str.   10:00 Bo. Hawkes.
—— DEN FÖLORADE SONEN ("THE PRODIGAL SON") (BALLET)
  %
  4,4,4,1 alto sax.,4 - 6,4,3,1 - timp.,perc.(4) - 2 hp. - str.
                                                        40:00 S.T.I.M.
—— DEN FÖRLORADE SONEN ("THE PRODIGAL SON")
  (BALLET SUITE)
                                                        17:00 S.T.I.M.
—— FYRA LÅTAR FRÅN LEKSAND (SUITE) (IN 4 MOVTS.)
  2,2,2,2 - 2,0,0,0 - pf. - str.   9:00 Gehrmans.
—— GUSTAV II ADOLF, OP. 49 (SUITE) (IN 8 MOVTS.)
  3,3,3,3 - 4,3,3,1 - timp.,perc. (5), cel. - str.   36:00 Gehrmans.
—— SWEDISH RHAPSODY NO. 2 (UPPSALARAPSODI), OP. 24
  2,2,2,2 - 4,3,3,1 - timp.,perc. (2) - str.   11:00 Lundquists.
—— SYMPHONIC POEM: EN SKÄRGÅRDSSÄGEN (LEGEND OF
  SKERRIES), OP. 20
  3,3,4,4 - 4,2,3,1 - timp.,perc.(2) - 2 hps. - str.   16:00 Bo. Hawkes.
—— SYMPHONY NO. 1 IN F MINOR, OP. 7
  3,2,2,2 - 4,2,3,1 - timp.,perc. - str.   37:00 Bo. Hawkes.
—— SYMPHONY NO. 3 IN E MAJOR, OP. 23
  3,3,4,3 - 6,3,3,1 - timp. - str. or   34:00 Bo. Hawkes.
  3,3,3,0 - 4,3,3,1 - timp. - str.
—— SYMPHONY NO. 5 IN A MINOR, OP. 55
  3,3,3,3 - 4,3,3,1 - timp.,perc. (3) - str.   50:00 S.T.I.M.
—— SYNNÖVE   SOLBAKKEN (SUITE), OP. 50 (IN 6 MOVTS.)
  2,2,2,2 - 2,0,0,0 - hp. - str.   22:00 Nordiska.

ALGAZI, Leon
—— COL NIDRÉ (LARGO)
  2,2,2,2 - 4,3,3,1 - timp.,perc. - hp. - str.   7:00 Belw-Mills.
—— LARGO
  2,2,2,2 - 4,3,3,1 - timp.,perc. - hp. - str.   5:00 Salabert.

ALIPRANDI, Paul
—— ESQUISSES PYRÉNÉENNES
  2,2,2,2 - 1,2,1,0 - timp.,perc.(3) hp. - str.   8:30 Presser.
—— FANTAISIE (FOR VIOLIN AND ORCH.)
  2,2,2,2 - 3,3,3,0 - perc.(2) - hp. - pf. - str.   6:50 Presser.

ALIX, René
—— CONCERTO FOR PIANO AND ORCH.
                                                  30:00 Henmar.
—— MESSE POUR NOTRE-DAME DE L'ASSOMPTION (FOR MIXED CHORUS AND ORCH.)
  3,2,2,2 - 4,3,3,1 - timp.,perc.,bells,cel.,glock. - hp. - org. - str.
                                                  Henmar.
—— REVENANTS (BALLADES SYMPHONIQUES)
                                                  8:00 Henmar.

ALKAN, Charles-Henri Valentin - AUSTIN, Richard R.
—— ALKAN SUITE NO. 1 (FROM 25 PIANO PRELUDES)(ARR. 1967)
  2,2,3,3 - 4,2,3,1 - timp.,perc. - str.   15:00 P.R.S.
—— ALKAN SUITE NO. 2
  1,1,1,0 - 2,0,0,0 - hp.(ad lib.) - str.   6:00 P.R.S.

ALKAN, Charles Henry Valentin - CHISHOLM, Eric
—— SYMPHONY, OP. 39 (FOR STRING ORCH.)
  str.   23:00 S.A.M.R.O.

ALLAN, Cameron Beck
—— MADRIGALS (1974)
  cel. - hp. - str.(8,4,4,2)   10:00 A.P.R.A.

ALLAN, Harold
—— FUGUE FOR STRINGS (1964)
  str.   7:00 P.R.S.
—— INTRODUCTION AND ADAGIO FOR STRINGS (1965)
  str.   8:30 P.R.S.
—— OVERTURE
  str.   7:00 P.R.S.

ALLANBROOK, Douglas
—— CONCERTO FOR CHAMBER ORCH. AND HARPSICHORD (1950) (IN 3 MOVTS.)
  1,1,1,1 - 2,1,0,0 - timp. - hpsc. - str.   29:00 Bo. Hawkes.
—— CONCERTO FOR VIOLIN AND ORCH. (1962)
  3(3rd alt. with picc.),3(3rd alt. with Eng. hn.),*3,*3 - 4,2,3,1 - timp. - hp. - str.   17:00 Composer.
—— ETHAN FROME (LYRIC OPERA IN 3 ACTS AND AN EPILOGUE) (1952) % (Text: John Hunt, after the novel of Edith Wharton)
  3(3rd alt. with picc.),2,2,2 - 4,2,3,0 - hp. - str.   105:00 Composer.
—— FOUR ORCHESTRAL LANDSCAPES (SYMPHONY NO. 3) (1967)
  3(3rd alt. with picc.),3(3rd alt. with Eng.hn.),3(3rd alt. with b.-cl.),*3 - 4,3,3,1 - timp.,perc.(4),bells,cel.,glock.,xyl. - 2 hp. - str.   21:00 Bo. Hawkes.
—— NIGHTMARE ABBEY (COMIC OPERA) % (Text: Composer, after novel by Peacock)
  2(2nd alt. with picc.),2(2nd alt. with Eng. hn.),2(2nd alt. with b.-cl.),2(2nd alt. with c.-bn.) - 4,2,3,0 - timp.,perc.(2) - hp. - str.   107:00 Composer.
—— THE SEVEN LAST WORDS (1969) (FOR MEZZO-SOPRANO, BARITONE, CHORUS AND ORCH.) (Text: Biblical)
  2,3(3rd alt. with Eng.hn.),3(3rd alt. with b.-cl.),*3 - 4,2,3,1 - timp.,perc.(2),xyl. - hp. - str.   55:00 Composer.
—— SYMPHONY NO. 1 (SYMPHONY IN 3 MOVTS.) (1960)
  3(3rd alt. with picc.),3(3rd alt. with Eng.hn.)3(3rd alt. with b.-cl.),*3 - 4,3,3,1 - timp. - str.   23:00 Composer.
—— SYMPHONY NO. 2 ("AN ELEGY") (1964) (IN 1 MOVT.)
  3(3rd alt. with picc.),3(3rd alt. with Eng.hn.),*3,*3 - 4,3,3,1 - timp.,perc.(4),cel.,xyl. - hp. - str.   20:00 Composer.
—— THREE NOBLE LOVE SONGS (FOR BARITONE AND ORCH.) (1960) (Texts: Raliegh, Wyatt, Campion)
  3(3rd alt. with picc.),3(3rd alt. with Eng.hn.),3(3rd alt. with b.-cl.),*3 - 4,3,3,1 - timp.,perc.(2) - hp. - str.   16:00 Composer.
—— THREE SONGS TO SHAKESPEARE SONNETS (FOR MEDIUM VOICE AND ORCH.)
  2(2nd alt. with picc.),2,2,2 - 2,2,0,0 - hp. - str.   13:00 Composer.
—— THE TRIUMPH OF REASON (OVERTURE) (1956)
  *3,2,2(2nd alt. with b.-cl.),2 - 4,3,3,0 - timp.,perc.(2) - hp. - pf. - str.   12:00 Composer.

ALLDAHL, Per-Gunnar
—— KNAVERLEK (FOR HURDY-GURDY AND STRINGS) (1974)
  Hurdy-gurdy - str.   Fleisher.
—— NULLA ARS (1966)
  str.   10:00 Fleisher.
—— PLAY (1970)
  3,3,3,3 - 4,3,3,1 - perc.(3) - hp. - str.   10:00 Fleisher.

ALLEN, Harold
—— POEM (1965)
  1,1,1,1 - 0,1,1,0 - str.   3:00 P.R.S.

ALLEN, Robert E.
—— CONCERTO FOR PIANO AND ORCH., OP. 10 (IN 3 MOVEMENTS)
  3(3rd alt. with picc.),2,2,2 - 4,3,3,1 - timp.,perc.(2) - pf. - str.   21:00 Composer.
—— INTRODUCTION AND RONDO CAPRICCIOSO, OP. 12 (FOR ACCORDION AND ORCH.)
  2,2,2,2 - 2,2,2,1 - timp. - acc. - str.   7:00 Composer.
—— SYMPHONIC MOVEMENT OP. 6
  3(3rd alt. with picc.),2,*3,2 - 4,3,3,1 - timp.,perc. (2) - hp. - str.   12:00 Composer.

ALLENDE SARÓN, (Pedro) Humberto
—— CONCERTO FOR CELLO AND ORCH. (1915)
                                                  Fleisher.
—— SYMPHONIC CONCERTO IN D (FOR VIOLIN AND ORCH.) (1941)
  2,2(2nd alt. with Eng. hn.),2,2 - 4,2,0,0 - timp. - hp. - str. Fleisher.
—— TROIS TONADAS DE CARACTÈRE POPULAIRE CHILIEN (WITH OPTIONAL WOMEN'S CHORUS)
  3,3,3,3 - 4,3,3,1 - timp.,cel. - 2 hps. - str.   12:00 Salabert.
—— LA VOZ DE LAS CALLES (SYMPHONIC POEM ON STREET-CRIES) (1920)
  3(3rd alt. with picc.),3,3,3 - 4,3,3,1 - timp.,cel. - hp. - str. Fleisher.

ALLESANDRO, Raffaele d'
—— DIVERTISSEMENT FOR CHAMBER ORCH.
  1(alt. with picc.),1,1,1 - 0,0,0,0 - perc. - str.   13:50 Modern.

ALLGÉN, Claude L.
—— CONCERTO FOR VIOLIN AND ORCH. (1957)
  3,3,2,3 - 4,3,3,0 - timp.,perc. - hp. - str.   63:00 Fleisher.
—— FANTASIA (1960)
  3,3,3,alto sax.,3 - 4,3,4,0 - timp.,perc.(4),xyl. - 2 hp. - str.
                                                  60:00 Fleisher.

ALLWORTH, Robert Cooper
—— AUSTRALIA SUITE, OP. 126 (1974)
  2(alt. with 2 picc.),2,2,2 - 2,4,4,2 - timp. - hp. - str.
                                                  22:00 A.P.R.A.
—— HAZE OF AUTUMN, OP. 22 (1970) (FOR PIANO AND STRINGS)
  pf. - str.   10:00 A.P.R.A.
—— PALE MOON IN A BLUE SKY, OP. 37 (1971)
  2,2,2,2 - 4,2,3,0 - str.   18:00 A.P.R.A.
—— PLATEAU, OP. 59 (1972)
  2,2,2,2 - 2,2,0,0 - timp.,perc. - hp. - pf. - str.   15:00 A.P.R.A.
—— SUITE FOR ORCH., OP. 130 (1975)
  2,2,2,2 - 4,2,3,1 - timp. - hp. - str.   16:00 A.P.R.A.
—— TRANSIENT, OP. 23 (1970)
  cel. - pf. - str.   7:00 A.P.R.A.

ALNAES, Eyvind
—— CONCERTO FOR PIANO AND ORCH., OP. 27
  2,2,2,2 - 4,2,3,1 - timp. - pf. - str.   33:00 G. Schirmer.

ALPAERTS, Flor
—— AVONDINDRUK (SYMPHONIC POEM) (1928)
  3,3,3,3 - 4,2,3,1 - timp.,perc.,cel. - hp. - str.   9:00 H. Elkan.
—— CAPRICCIO (1953)
  3,3,2,2 - 4,3,3,1 - timp.,perc. - str.   7:00 H. Elkan.
—— CONCERTO FOR VIOLIN AND ORCH. (1948)
  2,2,2,2 - 3,0,0,0 - timp.,perc. - str.   25:00 H. Elkan.
—— HUMOR (1936)
  3,3,3,2 - 4,2,3,0 - timp.,perc.,glock - hp. - str.   7:00 H. Elkan.
—— JAMES ENSOR SUITE
  3,3,3,3 - 4,3,3,1 - timp.,cel.,xyl. - hp. - str.   24:00 CBDM.
—— KLEINE SUITE (1947)
  str.   15:00 H. Elkan.

—— PALLIETER (SYMPHONIC POEM IN 3 PARTS)
3,3,3,3 - 6,4,3,1 - timp.,perc., cel.,glock.,xyl. - hp. - acc. - str.
35:00 CBDM.
—— SERENADE FOR CELLO AND ORCH. (1936)
2,2,2,2 - 2,0,0,0 - timp. - str.   5:00 H. Elkan.
—— SUITE NO. 1 FOR ORCHESTRA (1932)
2,2,2,2 - 2,2,0,0 - timp.,perc. - str.   15:00 H. Elkan.
—— SUITE NO. 2 FOR ORCHESTRA (1932)
2,2,2,2 - 2,2,0,0 - timp.,perc.,glock. - pf. (or hp.) - str.
12:00 Henmar.
—— THYLUILENSPIEGEL (SYMPHONIC POEM IN 3 PARTS)
3,3,3,3 - 4,3,3,1 - timp.,perc., cel.,glock. - hp. - str. 15:00 CBDM.
—— VLAAMSE IDYLLE (1920)
2,2,2,2 - 4,4,3,1 - timp.,perc. - hp. - str.   12:00 H. Elkan.
—— ZOMERIDYLLE (SYMPHONIC POEM) (1928)
3,3,2,3 - 4,3,3,1 - timp.,perc.,cel. - hp. - str.   10:00 H. Elkan.

ALTMAN, Ludwig
—— PSALM 13 (FOR ALTO, SATB CHORUS AND ORCH.)
0,2,0,2 - 2,2,0,0 - timp. - str.   5:00 Law-Gould.

ALWYN, William
—— AUTUMN LEGEND
Eng. hn. - str.   11:00 Lengnick.
—— CONCERTO FOR OBOE (WITH HARP AND STRINGS)
ob. - hp. - str.   18:00 Lengnick.
—— CONCERTO GROSSO NO. 1 (FOR SMALL ORCH.)
10:30 Lengnick.
—— CONCERTO GROSSO NO. 2 (FOR STRING ORCH.)
str.   14:30 Bo. Hawkes.
—— DERBY DAY (OVERTURE)
*3,2,2,2 - 4,0,3,0 - timp.,perc. - str.   9:00 Lengnick.
or:
*3,2,2,2 - 4,2-3,3,1 - timp.,perc. - str.
—— ELIZABETHAN DANCES
2,2,3,2 - 4,3,3,0 - timp.,perc.,cel.xyl. - hp. - str. 16:00 Lengnick.
—— LYRA ANGELICA
30:00 Lengnick.
—— THE MAGIC ISLAND (SYMPHONIC PRELUDE)
3,3,2,2 - 4,3,3,1 - timp.,perc.,cel. - hp. - str.   10:00 Lengnick.
—— SUITE OF SCOTTISH DANCES
*2,1,2,0 - 2,1,1,0 - timp.,perc. - str.   7:00 Oxford.
—— SYMPHONY
35:00 Lengnick.
—— SYMPHONY NO. 2
3,2,2,2 - 4,3,3,1 - timp.,perc. - hp. - str.   26:00 Lengnick.
—— SYMPHONY NO. 3
31:40 Lengnick.
—— SYMPHONY NO. 4
2(2nd alt. with picc.),2(2nd alt. with Eng. hn.),2,2 - 4,3,3,1 - timp.
- str.   28:00 Lengnick.

AMATO, Bruno
—— BASSES AND BRASS (1969)
0,0,0,0 - 4,4,0,0 - 3 d.-b.   10:00 Seesaw.

AMBROSI, Alearco
—— ELEGIA (BALLET) %
3,3,3,3 - 4,4,3,1 - timp.,perc.(4),cel.,mar.,xyl. - 2 hp. - pf. - str.
50:00 MCA Music.
—— RITMOLOGICA
2,2,2,2 - 2,2,0,0 - timp.,perc. - hp. - pf. - str.   Leeds.

AMELLER, André
—— AUBADE POUR LA SAINT JEAN D'ÉTÉ
str.   25:00 Presser.
—— CONCERTINO FOR DOUBLE BASS AND ORCH.
2,1,2,1 - 2,1,0,0 - timp. - str.(no vlns.)   13:00 Presser.
—— HETERODOXES (FOR STRING QUARTET AND CHAMBER
ORCH.)
2 fl. - 2 tpt. - perc. - str.   6:00 Presser.
—— TRIPTYQUE SYMPHONIQUE
3,3,3,3 - 4,4,3,1 - timp.,perc. - hp. - str.   15:00 Belw-Mills.

AMELUNG, Julian
—— GLORIA IN EXCELSIS (FROM COMMUNION SERVICE IN G,
OP. 8) (1928)
0,0,0,0 - 2,2,1,0 - timp.,perc(1) - org. - pf. - str. 10:00 Composer.

AMEND, Erwin
—— CONCERTO IN C FOR TRUMPET AND STRING ORCH.
tpt. - str.   15:00 Mannheimer.

—— VARIATIONS ON A THEME OF RAMEAU
2(2nd alt. with picc.),2(2nd alt. with Eng.hn.),2,2 - 3,2,3,0 -
timp.,perc. - hp. - str.   17:00 AhnSimrock.

AMFITHEATROF, Daniele
—— REQUIEM (FOR SATB SOLO VOICES, CHORUS AND ORCH.)
(1961)
78:00 Composer.

AMIRAN, Emanuel
—— NACHAMU AMI (CANTATA) (FOR MIXED CHORUS AND
ORCH.)
1,1,2,1 - 2,1,1,0 - timp.,perc. - str.   9:00 Bo. Hawkes.

AMIROV, Fikret
—— TWO AZERBAIJAN MUGAMS
18:00 G. Schirmer.
I. KYURD OVSHARI
3,3,3,2 - 4,3,3,1 - timp.,perc. - hp. - pf. - str.
II. SHOUR
3,3,3,2 - 4,3,3,1 - timp.,perc.,xyl. - str.

AMMANN, Benno
—— TRIODION (DREI STUCKE FUR STREICHORCHESTER)
str.   16:00 S.U.I.S.A.

AMY, Gilbert
—— ANTIPHONIES FOR 2 ORCHESTRAS
3,3,5,4 sax.,3 - 6,2,3,1 - timp.,perc.(4),cel. - guit. - 3 hp. - pf. - str.
20:00 Presser.
—— CETTE ÉTOILE ENSEIGNE À S'INCLINER (FOR TAPED
MENS CHORUS AND INSTRS.)
3 trb. - vibra. - tape-recorder - guit. - 2 hp. - 2 pf. - 3 c.,3 d.-b.
15:00 Presser.
—— CHANT (1958)
4,4,4,4 - 6,5,4,1 - timp.,perc.(6),cel. - 2 hp. - pf. - str.
25:00 Presser.
—— DIAPHONIES (FOR 2 ORCHESTRAS)
2,2,2,2 - 2,4,4,0 - perc.(6) - 2 hp. - str.   8:00 Presser.
—— MOUVEMENTS (FOR 17 SOLO INSTRS.)
1,1,2,1 - 0,1,1,0 - perc. - 2 hp. - pf. - str.(5)   10:00 Presser.
—— STROPHE (FOR SOPRANO AND ORCH.)
4,3,4,3 - 6,4,3,1 - perc. - hp. - str.   22:00 Presser.
—— TRAJECTOIRES (FOR VIOLIN AND ORCH.)
0,0,0,0 - 6,4,4,0 - perc. - hp. - str.   22:00 Presser.
—— TRIADE (WITH FILM) (Text and Film: Henri Michaux)
3,1,4,b.-sax.,1 - 1,2,2,0 - perc.(2) - hp. - pf. - str.   11:30 Presser.

ANCELIN, Pierre
—— CONCERTO FOR PIANO AND SMALL ORCH., OP. 14
ob. - pf. - str.   14:00 Henmar.
—— POEMES DE GUERRE (FOR BARITONE AND ORCH.)
1,1,1,1 - 2,1,1,0 - perc.,cel. - hp. - str.   12:00 Presser.
—— SYMPHONY NO. 2, OP. 18
1,1,1,1 - 1,1,1,0 - perc.(2) - hp. - str.   22:00 Henmar.

ANCELIN, Pierre - RAMPAL, Jean-Pierre ed.
—— CONCERTO GIOIOSO (FOR FLUTE, PIANO AND STRINGS)
fl. - pf. - str.   Presser.

ANDERBERG, Carl-Olof
—— ACROAMA I, OP. 57 (1965)
2,2,2,2 - 4,2,2,1 - timp. - str.   16:30 S.T.I.M.
—— ACROAMA II, OP. 58 (1966)
3,2,2,2 - 4,3,3,1 - timp.,perc(2) - hp. - str.   22:00 S.T.I.M.
—— BARABBAS (SYMPHONIC SUITE, AFTER THE BOOK BY PÄR
LAGERKVIST)
2,2,2,2 - 4,2,1,1 - timp.,perc. (4) - str.   26:00 S.T.I.M.
—— CONCERTO FOR A BALLET, OP. 70 (FOR PIANO AND
ORCH.) (1970)
2,3,3,alto sax.,bar. sax.,2 - 1,2,2,1 - timp.,perc.(2) - pf. - d.-b.
25:00 Fleisher.
—— CYCLUS STELLARUM NO. 1 (SUITE FOR STRINGS AND
PERCUSSION)
perc. - str.   19:00 S.T.I.M.
—— CYCLUS STELLARUM NO. 2 (SUITE FOR STRING ORCH.)
str.   24:00 S.T.I.M.
—— EAST AND WEST (OVERTURE) (1956)
2,2,2,2 - 4,2,3,1 - timp.,perc.(3) - pf. - str.   7:30 S.T.I.M.
—— FOR PIANO AND ORCHESTRA, OP. 66 (1968)
2,2,3,2 - 0,3,2,1 - perc.(4) - hp. - pf. - str.   22:00 S.T.I.M.
—— KONSERTMUSIK (FOR ORCH., WITH PIANO OBBLIGATO)
0,0,0,0 - 2,2,2,0 - timp.,perc.(2) - pf. - str.   22:00 S.T.I.M.

—— LITEN BALLETTMUSIK (SUITE FOR STRING ORCH.)
 str.   11:00 S.T.I.M.
—— LITEN MÅRTENGÅSMUSIK (SUITE FOR STRING ORCH.)
 str.   12:00 S.T.I.M.
—— LITEN SVIT (LITTLE SUITE)
 2,2,2,2 - 0,2,0,0 - timp. - str. 11:00 S.T.I.M.
—— LUSTSPELSSVIT (SUITE FOR ORCH.)
 2,2,2,2 - 2,2,1,1 - timp.,perc. - str. 14:00 S.T.I.M.
—— MUSIC FOR CHAMBER ORCH., NO. 1 (APRIL 1947)
 1,1,1,1 - 2,0,0,0 - str. 18:00 S.T.I.M.
—— MUSIC FOR CHAMBER ORCH., NO. 2 (RADHUSKONSERT)
 1,1,1,1 - 2,0,0,0 - str. 17:00 S.T.I.M.
—— MUSIK FÖR BARN (SUITE FOR ORCH.)
 1,1,2,1 - 2,2,1,0 - perc. - str. 12:00 S.T.I.M.
—— ORKESTERSPEL II, OP. 68 (1970)
 2,2,2,2 - 4,2,2,0 - timp.,perc.(3) - str. 15:00 Fleisher.
—— PASTORAL À DANSER (SUITE FOR ORCH.)
 2,2,2,2 - 2,1,0,0 - perc. - str. 14:00 S.T.I.M.
—— SAXOFONKONSERT (CONCERTO FOR SAXOPHONE AND ORCH.)
 2,2,2, sax.,2 - 2,2,0,0 - timp.,perc. - str. 20:00 S.T.I.M.
—— SERENADE FOR STRING ORCH. (SUITE) (1958)
 str.   15:00 S.T.I.M.
—— STOCKHOLMSBILDER (SUITE FOR ORCH.)
 1,1,2,1 - 2,2,1,0 - perc. - str. 8:00 S.T.I.M.
—— SUITE UR MUSIKEN TILL KAJ MUNKS "PUZZLESPEL"
 1,1,2,1 - 2,2,0,0 - timp.,perc. - str. 16:00 S.T.I.M.
—— SYMPHONIC FANTASIE
 2,2,2,2 - 4,2,3,0 - timp.,perc. (2) - str. 17:00 S.T.I.M.
—— SYMPHONY NO. 1
 2,2,2,2 - 4,3,3,1 - timp.,perc.(2) - str. 25:00 S.T.I.M.
—— TEATER (SUITE) (1958)
 1,1,2,1 alto sax.,1 - 1,1,1,1 - timp.,perc.(3) - pf. - str.
      20:00 S.T.I.M.
—— TROIS ESTAMPLES (SUITE FOR STRINGS, PIANO, TIMPANI AND PERCUSSION)
 timp.,perc. - pf. - str. 13:30 S.T.I.M.
—— VAJANG (MUSIK TILL ETT JAVANESIST SKUGGSPEL)
 3,3,2,3 - 4,2,0,0 - timp.,perc. (4),xyl. - hp. - pf. - str.
      19:00 S.T.I.M.
—— VIER UNABHANGIGE STUCKE, OP. 63 (1968)
 str.   17:00 S.T.I.M.
—— VIOLAKONSERT (CONCERTO FOR VIOLA AND ORCH.)
 1,1,1,1 - 2,0,0,0 - str. 18:00 S.T.I.M.

ANDERS, Erich (Baron Wolff von Gudenberg)
—— ROMANTISCHE OUVERTÜRE, OP. 41
 2,2,2,2 - 4,2,2,0 - timp.,perc. - h.p. - str. 6:00 Henmar.

ANDERSEN, Arthur Olaf
—— FIVE MINIATURES (CHARACTER SKETCHES)
 2,*3,*3,0 - 4,2,3,1 - timp.,perc. - hp. - str. 10:00 Composer.
—— LAND OF LIGHT (CANTATA FOR SOLOISTS, CHORUS AND ORCH.)
 3 (3rd alt. with picc.), 2,*4,3 sax., 2 - 4,3,3,1 - timp.,perc. (6) - str.
      18:00 Composer.
—— A ROMAN HOLIDAY (SYMPHONIC POEM)
 *3,2,*3,3 sax.,*3 - 4,2,3,1 - timp.,perc. - str. 20:00 Composer.
—— THEME AND VARIATIONS
 *3,2,2,2 - 4,3,3,1 - timp.,perc (1) - str. 12:00 Composer.

ANDERSEN, Karl
—— FESTFORSPELL (FESTIVAL PRELUDE)
 3,3,3,2 - 4,3,3,1 - timp.,perc. - str. 11:00 T.O.N.O.
—— SUITE IN FOUR MOVEMENTS
 1,1,1,1 - 2,2,1,1 - timp.,perc. - str. 30:00 T.O.N.O.
—— SYMPHONY IN FOUR MOUVEMENTS
 1,1,1,1 - 1,1,1,1 - str. 28:00 T.O.N.O.

ANDERSEN, Michael
—— CHAMBER SYMPHONY (1965) (IN 3 MOVTS.)
 1,1,1,1 - 1,1,1,0 - timp.,perc.(1),xyl. - pf. - str. 19:00 Composer.
—— CONCERT OVERTURE (1964)
 2,2(2nd alt. with Eng.hn.),2,2 - 4,2,3,0 - timp.,perc.(2),xyl. - hp. - pf. - str. 8:30 Composer.
—— CONCERTO FOR TRUMPET AND ORCH (1959) (IN 3 MOVTS.)
 1(alt. with picc.),1,1,1 - 1,1,1,0 - timp.,perc.(1),xyl. - hp. - str.
      12:37 Composer.
—— SEVEN HOUSEMAN SONGS (FOR VOICE AND ORCH) (1961) (Text: A. E. Houseman)
 2(2nd alt. with picc.),2,2,2 - 4,3,3,0 - timp.,perc.(2),glock.,xyl. - str. Composer.

—— SYMPHONY IN A (COMMEMORATING CARL SANDBURG) (1967) (IN 5 MOVTS.)
 3(3rd alt. with picc.),3(3rd alt. with Eng.hn.)3(3rd alt. with b.-cl.),3(3rd alt. with cbn.) - 4,3,3,1 - timp.,perc.(3),glock.,xyl. - hp. - str. 28:03 Composer.

ANDERSON, Florence
—— ALICE IN WONDERLAND (BALLET SUITE)
 3,3,3,2 - 4,3,3,1 - timp.,perc., cel. - hp. - str. 16:45 C. Fischer.
—— TWO SKETCHES (FOR STRING ORCH.)
 str.   4:00 Composer.

ANDERSON, John Maxwell
—— CANTERBURY TALES (FOR BASSOON AND ORCH.) (1969) (IN 4 MOVTS.)
 2(2nd alt. with picc.),2,2,3 - 4,3,3,1 - timp.,perc.(3),bells - hp. - str. 28:00 Composer.
—— CONCERTO FOR CELLO AND ORCH. (1966) (IN 1 MOVT.)
 *3,*3,2,2 - 4,3,3,1 - timp.,perc.(3),cel. - hp. - pf. - str.
      35:00 Composer.
—— CONCERTO FOR ORGAN AND ORCHESTRA (1972) (IN 3 MOVTS.)
 *3,2,2,2 - 4,3,3,1 - timp.,perc.(3) - hp. - org. - str.(16,6,8,6)
      30:00 Composer.
—— CONCERTO NO. 3 FOR PIANO AND ORCH. (1965) (IN 1 MOVT.)
 2(2nd alt. with picc.),2,2,2 - 4,3,3,1 - timp.,perc.(3) - hp. - pf. - str.
      23:00 Composer.
—— THE RED LAUGH (TONE POEM) (1973)
 2(1 alt. with picc.),2,2,2 - 4,3,3,1 - timp.,perc.(3) - str.(16,6,8,6)
      Composer.
—— SYMPHONY NO. 1 (1967) (IN 3 MOVTS.)
 *3,2(2nd alt. with Eng. hn.),*3,2 - 4,3,3,1 - timp.,perc.(3) - pf. - str. 21:00 Composer.

ANDERSON, Leroy
—— ALMA MATER (SCENES FOR ORCHESTRA) (IN 4 MOVTS.)
 *3,2,2,2 - 4,3,3,1 - timp.,perc. (3), 2 electric auto horns - str.
      6:00 Mills.
—— CONCERTO IN C MAJOR FOR PIANO AND ORCH.
 *3,*3,2,2 - 4,3,3,1 - timp.,perc. (2) - pf. - str. 16:00 Composer.
—— IRISH SUITE (IN 6 MOVTS.)
 3(3rd alt. with picc.),2,2,2 - 4,3,3,1 - timp.,perc. (4) - str.
      19:50 Mills.
—— SCOTTISH SUITE (IN 4 MOVTS.)
 3(3rd alt. with picc.),2,1 Eng. hn. (ad lib.),2, b. - cl. (ad lib.),2 c.-bn. (ad. lib.) - 4,3,3,1 - timp.,perc.,bells,glock. - hp. (ad lib.) - str. 11:00 Mills.

ANDERSON, Olive Jennie Paxton
—— ELEGY, OP. 42 (1975)
 2,1,2,1 - 2,1,2,0 - timp. - str. 7:00 A.P.R.A.

ANDERSSÉN, Alfred
—— CANTATA FOR THE NATIVE DISTRICT (FOR SATB CHORUS AND ORCH.) (1925) (Text: A. Tokolander)
 0,0,0,0 - 2,2,2,0 - str. 15:00 FinnMICtr.
—— CHURCH CANTATA AT VÖYRI (FOR SATB CHORUS AND ORCH.) (Text: Jacob Tegengren)
 2,2,2,2 - 2,2,1,0 - timp. - org. - str. 25:00 FinnMICtr.
—— DESTINY ON BOARD (OPERA) % (1932) (Text: Jarl Hemmer)
 2,2,2,2 - 2,2,1,0 - str. FinnMICtr.
—— DESTINY (1934)
 3,3,2,2 - 2,2,1,0 - timp. - hp. - str. 22:00 FinnMICtr.
—— FESTIVE CANTATA (FOR SATB CHORUS AND ORCH.)(1934)
 org. - str. 8:00 FinnMICtr.
—— SYMPHONY NO. 1 IN A MINOR, OP. 17 (1927)
 2,2,2,2 - 4,2,3,1 - timp.,perc. - hp. - str. 40:00 FinnMICtr.
—— SYMPHONY NO. 2 IN D MINOR (1938)
 2,2,2,2 - 3,2,3,0 - timp. - hp. - str. 30:00 FinnMICtr.

ANDERSSON, Kjell
—— WALKIN' (1968)
 1,0,2,1 - 1,1,2,0 - timp.,perc.(3) - pf.(or cel.) - str. 15:00 Fleisher.

ANDREAE, Volkmar
—— CONCERTINO FOR OBOE AND ORCH.
 2,1,2,2 - 2,2,0,0 - timp.,perc. - str. 14:00 Bo. Hawkes.
—— LI-TAI-PE (ACHT GESÄNGE FÜR TENOR AND ORCH.), OP. 37
 3,*3,*3,*3 - 4,3,3,0 - timp.,perc. - hp. - str. 18:00 Hug.
—— MUSIC FOR ORCHESTRA, OP. 35
 *3,*3,*3 - 4,3,3,1 - timp.,perc. - pf. - str. 14:00 Hug.

—— RHAPSODIE FOR VIOLIN AND ORCH., OP. 32
2,2,2,2 - 3,2,3,0 - timp.,perc. - str.　　14:00 Hug.

ANDRÉ-BLOCH
—— GUIGNOL (BALLET FROM THE OPERA) % (1949)
2,1,2,1 - 2,2,1,0 - timp. - hp. - str.　　10:30 Presser.

ANDRESS, Walter
—— CONCERTINO FOR CLARINET AND ORCH.
1,*1,1,1 - 0,2,0,0 - perc. - str.　　16:00 Modern.
—— CONCERTINO FOR VIOLIN AND ORCH.
　　9:00 Hawlik.
—— CONCERTO IN D MINOR FOR VIOLIN AND ORCH., OP. 72
(IN 3 MOVTS.)
　　21:00 A.K.M.
—— DREI ORCHESTER-STÜCKE, OP. 69
　　16:00 A Tempo.
—— LITTLE SUITE FOR STRINGS
str.　　14:00 Modern.
—— SYMPHONY IN F MAJOR
　　40:00 A.K.M.
—— SYMPHONY NO. 1, OP. 3 (IN 2 MOVTS.)
　　20:00 A.K.M.
—— SYMPHONY NO. 2 IN A MINOR, OP. 71 (IN 4 MOVTS.)
　　42:00 A.K.M.
—— SYMPHONY NO. 3 IN E♭ MAJOR, OP. 77 (IN 4 MOVTS.)
　　40:00 A.K.M.

ANDRICU, Mihail
—— SINFONIA NO. 2
3,3,3,3 - 4,3,3,1 - timp.,perc.,cel. - hp. - str.　　Templeton.

ANDRIESSEN, Hendrik
—— L' ATTENTE MYSTIQUE (FOR SOPRANO AND ORCH.)
(1920) (Text: L. Le Cardonnel)
2,2,2,2 - 4,0,0,0 - str.　　20:00 Henmar.
—— L' AUBE SPIRITUELLE (FOR MEZZO-SOPRANO AND
ORCH.) (1916) (Text: Charles Baudelaire)
2,2,2,2 - 2,0,0,0 - str.　　6:00 Henmar.
—— BALLET SUITE
3,2,2,2 - 4,3,3,1 - timp.,perc., cel. - hp. - str.　　18:00 Henmar.
—— CAPRICCIO
2,2,2,2 - 4,3,3,0 - timp. - str.　　12:00 Henmar.
—— CONCERTO FOR ORGAN AND ORCH.
2,2,2,2 - 4,3,3,1 - timp. - hp. - org. - str.　　17:00 Henmar.
—— IL PENSIERO (1965)
str.　　7:00 Henmar.
—— L' INVITATION AU VOYAGE (FOR MEZZO-SOPRANO AND
ORCH.) (1918) (Text: Charles Baudelaire)
2,2,2,2 - 2,0,0,0 - str.　　6:00 Henmar.
—— LIBERTAS VENIT (RHAPSODIE)
2,2,2,2 - 4,2,3,1 - timp.,perc. - str.　　13:00 Henmar.
—— LUX JOCUNDA (FOR SOLO VOICE, MIXED CHORUS AND
ORCH.) (1968)
　　14:00 Henmar.
—— MASCHERATA (SYMPHONIC FANTASY) (1962)
3,2,2,3 - 4,3,3,1 - timp.,perc.,xyl. - hp. - str.　　21:00 Henmar.
—— MIROIR DE PEINE (FOR SOPRANO AND STRING ORCH.)
(1923) (Text: H. Ghéon)
str.　　15:00 Henmar.
—— PSALM IX (FOR TENOR, CHOIR, ORCH.) (Text: Biblical and
Gabriel Smit)
　　25:00 Henmar.
—— RICERCARE
3,2,2,2 - 4,3,3,1 - timp.,perc. - hp. - str.　　9:00 Henmar.
—— SYMPHONIE CONCERTANTE (1962) (IN 3 MOVTS.)
3,2,2,2 - 4,3,3,1 - timp. - hp. - str.　　25:00 Henmar.
—— SYMPHONIE NO. 1
2,2,2,2 - 4,2,3,0 - timp. - str.　　17:00 Henmar.
—— SYMPHONIE NO. 2
2,2,2,2 - 4,3,3,0 - timp. - str.　　20:00 Henmar.
—— SYMPHONIE NO. 3
3,2,2,2 - 4,3,3,1 - timp. - hp. - str.　　25:00 Henmar.
—— SYMPHONIE NO. 4
3,2,2,2 - 4,3,3,1 - timp.,perc. - str.　　25:00 Henmar.
—— SYMPHONISCHE ETUDE
3,2,2,2 - 4,3,3,1 - timp.,perc. - hp. - str.　　10:00 Henmar.
—— TE DEUM LAUDAMUS (FOR MIXED CHORUS AND ORCH.)
(1946)
3,2,2,2 - 4,3,3,1 -timp. - str.　　12:00 Henmar.
—— TE DEUM LAUDAMUS II (1968) (FOR MIXED CHORUS AND
FULL ORCH.)
　　10:00 Henmar.

—— TROIS PASTORALES (FOR VOICE AND ORCH.) (1966) (Text:
Arthur Rimbaud)
　　9:00 Henmar.
—— VARIATIONS AND FUGUE ON A THEME BY KUHNAU
str.　　12:00 Henmar.
—— VARIATIONS ON A THEME BY COUPERIN (FOR SOLO
FLUTE, HARP AND STRINGS)
1,0,0,0 - 0,0,0,0 - hp. - str.　　Henmar.
—— WILHELMUS VAN NASSOUWE (RHAPSODIE)
2,2,2,2 - 4,3,3,1 - timp.,perc. - hp. - str.　　9:00 Henmar.
—— DE ZEE EN HET LAND (DECLAMATORIUM) (FOR
SPEAKER, MIXED CHORUS AND ORCH.) (1953) (Text: B.
Aafjes)
3,2,2,2 - 4,3,3,1 - timp.,perc. - str.　　20:00 Henmar.

ANDRIESSEN, Jurriaan
—— ANTIFONA DELL AJA (1969)
　　6:00 Henmar.
—— ANTIFONA E FUSIONE (FOR WIND QUINTET, BRASS
QUARTET AND TIMPANI) (1966)
　　9:00 Henmar.
—— BERKSHIRE SYMPHONY (SYMPHONY NO. 1)
3,2,3,2 - 4,3,3,1 - timp.,perc. - str.　　30:00 Henmar.
—— LES BRANSLES EROTIQUES (1968) (IN 6 MOVTS.)
　　9:00 Henmar.
—— CONCERTINO FOR BASSOON, WINDS AND BRASS
2,2,2,3 - 2,0,0,0　　Henmar.
—— CONCERTINO FOR PIANO AND ORCH.
2,2,2,2 - 0,0,0,0 - pf. - str.　　12:00 Henmar.
—— CONCERTINO FOR SOUSAPHONE (OR TUBA) AND ORCH.
(1967)
1. Alla Breve; 2. Adagio; 3. Allegro scherzando; 4. Cadenza
　　15:00 Henmar.
—— CONCERTO FOR FLUTE AND ORCH.
　　Henmar.
—— CONCERTO FOR PIANO AND ORCH.
3,3,3, Sax,3 - 4,3,3,1 - timp.,perc.,cel. - hp. - pf. - str.
　　17:00 Henmar.
—— CONTRA-BANDE (RAPSODIA INTERROTTA) (1968)
　　11:00 Henmar.
—— HOMMAGE À MILHAUD
1,1,1,sax.,1 - 1,1,1,0 - str.　　Henmar.
—— INNO DELLA TECNICA INTRODUZIONE AND SCHERZO
FOR ORCHESTRA
3,2,2,2 - 4,3,3,1 - timp.,perc. cel. - str.　　8:00 Henmar.
—— MAGNIFICAT (FOR SOPRANO SOLO, CHORUS AND ORCH.)
　　Henmar.
—— MOURNING BECOMES ELECTRA ("ROUW PAST ELECTRA")
(SYMPHONIC SUITE FOR 11 WIND INSTRUMENTS AND
PERCUSSION)
1,2,1,2 - 1,2,2,0 - timp.,perc.　　20:00 Henmar.
—— MOVIMENTI (FOR TROMBONE AND SMALL ORCH.)
0,0,0,0 - 1,1,1,0 - timp. - str.　　16:00 Henmar.
—— OMAGGIO A SWEELINCK (1968)
cemb. - str.　　17:00 Henmar.
—— LES OTARIES (THE SEALS) (BALLET FANTASIE
CLASSIQUE)
3,2,2,2 - 4,3,3,1 - timp.,perc. - hp. - str.　　17:00 Henmar.
—— OUVERTURE "CYMBELINE"
3,2,2,2 - 4,3,3,1 - timp.,perc., xyl. - hp. - str.　　9:00 Henmar.
—— RITRATTO DI UNA CITTÀ (OUVERTURE DEN HAAG) (1957)
2,2,2,2 - 4,3,3,0 - timp.,perc. - str.　　13:00 Henmar.
—— SYMPHONIETTA CONCERTANTE (CONCERTO FOR 4
TRUMPETS AND ORCH.)
2,2,2,sax.,2 - 4,4,3,1 - timp.,perc.,cel.,xyl. - hp. - str.
　　12:00 Henmar.
—— HET WONDERLIJK UUR: SUITE NO. 1 (1948)
3,3,3,3 - 4,3,3,0 - timp.,perc.,xyl. - pf.- 6 c.,4 d.-b.　　18:00 Henmar.

ANDRIESSEN, Louis
—— CONTRA TEMPUS (1968)
　　18:00 Henmar.
—— ITTROSPEZIONE NO. 2 PER. ORCH. (1963)
4,3,3,3 - 4,4,3,1 - timp.,perc.,vibra.,xyl. - hp. - pf. - str.
　　12:00 Henmar.
—— ITTROSPEZIONE NO. 3
　　12:00 Henmar.

ANDRIESSEN, Willem
—— CONCERTO FOR PIANO AND ORCH.
2,2,2,2 - 4,2,3,0 - timp., - pf. - str.　　30:00 Henmar.

—— DRIE LIEDERIN (3 SONGS FOR MEZZO - SOPRANO AND
ORCH.) (1911)
2,2,2,2 - 4,2,0,0 - timp. - str.   12:00 Henmar.
—— MASS (MISSA IN ES KL.TERTS.) (FOR SATB SOLI, SATB
CHORUS AND ORCH.) (1916)
2,2,2,2 - 4,3,3,1 - timp. - org. - str.   22:00 Henmar.
—— OUVERTURE IN C
2,2,2,2 - 4,3,3,1 - timp., - str.   Henmar.

ANGERER, Paul
—— BALLETT (1952) (FOR CELLO AND CHAMBER ORCH.)
20:00 A.K.M.
—— CONCERT POUR LA JEUNESSE
18:00 A.K.M.
—— MUSIK (FOR PIANO AND STRING ORCH.)
pf. - str.   26:00 A.K.M.
—— MUSIK (1950)
20:00 A.K.M.
—— MUSIK (1950) (FOR STRINGED INSTRUMENTS)
str.   8:00 A.K.M.
—— SINFONIA IN A (1951)
19:00 A.K.M.

ANGYAL, Laszlo
—— VALSE MACABRE
3(3rd alt. with picc.),*3,3(3rd alt. with b.-cl.),0,2 c.-bn. - 4,3,3,1 -
timp.,perc.,cel. - pf. - str.   16:00 Modern.

ANNESSA, Luigi
—— NOTTURNO FIABESCO
2,2,2,2 - 2,0,2,0 - timp.,perc.,cel. - hp. - str.   10:00 S.I.A.E.
—— NOTTURNO NOSTALGICO
2,2,2,2 - 2,0,2,0 - timp.,perc.,cel. - hp. - pf. - str.   18:00 S.I.A.E.

ANREP-NORDIN, Birger
—— DIVERTIMENTO FOR STRINGS
str.   S.T.I.M.
—— KRAKEBOSERENADEN (PIECE FOR STRINGS)
str.   11:00 S.T.I.M.

ANROOY, Peter Van
—— PIET HEIN (SYMPHONIC POEM)
11:00 Alsbach.

ANSELL, John
—— CHILDREN'S SUITE (IN 2 PARTS)
2,1,2,1 - 2,2,3,0 - perc. - harm. - str.   28:30 Bo. Hawkes.

ANSON, George
—— CONCERTINO FOR PIANO AND ORCH.
1. Rather slowly; 2. Slow, song-like; 3. Fast
1,1,2(1 alt. with Eng. hn.),1 - 4,2,3,0-1 - timp. - pf. - str.
14:00 Composer.
—— CONCERTINO FOR TWO PIANOS AND ORCH. (IN 3
MOVTS.)
1,1,2(1 alt. with Eng. hn.),1 - 4,2,3,1 - timp.,perc.(2),glock. - 2-pf.
- str.   10:00 Composer.
—— SUITE FOR PIANO AND ORCH. (IN 6 MOVTS.)
*3,*2,2,1 - 4,2,3,1 - timp.,perc.,bells,cel.,glock.,xyl. - hp. - pf. - str.
20:00 Composer.

ANSON, Hugo
—— CONCERTO FOR TWO PIANOS AND STRINGS
2pf. - str.   Novello.

ANTHEIL, George
—— ARCHIPELAGO (RHUMBA)
3,3,3,2 - 4,3,2,1 - perc. (4) - hp. - pf. - str.   10:00 Composer.
—— CABEZA DE VACA (CANTATA) (FOR MIXED CHORUS AND
ORCH.)
52:00 Templeton.
—— CAPITOL OF THE WORLD (BALLET SUITE)
*2,2,2,2 - 4,3,2,1 - timp.,perc. (2) xyl. - hp. - pf. - str.
30:00 G. Schirmer.
—— CONCERTO NO. 1 FOR PIANO AND ORCH.
2,2,2,2 - 4,2,0,0 - perc. (3) - pf. - str.   25:00 Composer.
—— CONCERTO NO. 1 FOR VIOLIN AND ORCH.
2,2,2,2 - 4,2,2,0 - perc. (3) - str.   27:00 Composer.
—— DECATUR IN ALGIERS (NOCTURNE)
2,2,2,2 - 4,2,3,1 - timp.,perc. (4) - hp. - str.   3:00 Weintraub.
—— DREAMS (BALLET SUITE)
2,2,2,2 - 4,2,0,0 - perc. (3) - pf. - str.   25:00 Composer.

—— GOLDEN SPIKE OVERTURE
*3,2,2,2 - 4,2,2,1 - timp.,perc. (2) - str.   5:00 Composer.
—— HELEN RETIRES (OPERA) %
*3,*3,*3,*3 - 4,3,3,1 - timp.,perc., bells, cel.,glock.,xyl. - hp. - pf. -
str.   Composer.
—— HEROES OF TODAY (ODE)
*4,*3,*3,*3 - 4,3,3,1 - perc. (4) - str.   7:00 Composer.
—— MCKONKEY'S FERRY (CONCERT OVERTURE)
*3,*3,*3,*3 - 4,3,3,1 - timp.,perc. (3), glock. - str.   7:00 Weintraub.
—— OVER THE PLAINS
2,*3,*3,2 - 4,2,2,1 - perc. (4) - hp. - str.   7:00 Weintraub.
—— SERENADE FOR STRING ORCHESTRA
str.   15:00 Weintraub.
—— SERENADE NO. 2 (IN 3 MOVEMENTS)
2,1,1,0 - 2,1,1,0 - perc.(1) - pf. - str.   18:00 Composer.
—— THE SPECTRE OF THE ROSE (SUITE)
2,1,*3,2 - 3,2,2,1 - perc. (3) - 2 pf. - str.   18:00 Weintraub.
—— SUITE FOR ORCHESTRA
2,2,2,0 - 4,1,1,0 - perc. (2) - str.   8:00 Composer.
—— SYMPHONY NO. 1
3,3,3,2 - 4,3,3,0 - perc. (4) - hp. - str.   30:00 Composer.
—— SYMPHONY NO. 2 IN F (REVISED VERSION)
*4,*4,*3,*3 - 4,3,2,1 - perc. (4) - hp. - str.   30:00 Composer.
—— SYMPHONY NO. 3 ("AMERICAN") (IN 4 MOVTS.)
2,2,2,2 - 4,3,3,1 - perc. (4) - hp. - str.   25:00 Composer.
—— SYMPHONY NO. 4 (1942)
*4,*3,*3,*3 - 4,3,3,1 - timp.,perc. (4) - hp. - pf. - str.
25:00 Bo. Hawkes.
—— SYMPHONY NO. 5 ("THE JOYOUS") (IN 3 MOVEMENTS)
*3,*3,*3,*3 - 4,3,3,1 - timp.,perc. (3), glock.,xyl. - pf. - str.
20:00 Leeds.
—— SYMPHONY NO. 6 (AFTER DELACROIX)
*3,*2,*3,*3 - 4,3,3,1 - timp.,perc. (3), glock.,xyl. - pf. - str.
24:00 Weintraub.
—— TOM SAWYER (A MARK TWAIN OVERTURE)
*3,*3,*3,*3 - 4,3,3,1 - timp.,perc. (1) - pf. - str.   7:00 Composer.
—— VENUS IN AFRICA (OPERA) %
Weintraub.
—— VOLPONE (OPERA) %
120:00 Weintraub.
—— THE WISH (OPERA) %
1,1,1,1 - 2,2,1,0 - timp.,perc. (1-2), bells,cel.,glock.,xyl. - hp. - pf. -
str.   60:00 Composer.

ANTILL, John
—— CONCERTO FOR HARMONICA AND ORCH.
A.P.R.A.
—— CORROBOREE (SUITE FROM THE BALLET) (IN 4 MOVTS.)
3,3,3,3 - 4,2,3,0 - timp.,perc.,cel. - hp. - pf. - str.
20:00 Bo. Hawkes.
—— CORROBOREE (THE COMPLETE BALLET SUITE)
3,3,3,3 - 4,2,3,1 - timp.,perc.,cel. - hp. - pf. - str.
45:00 Bo. Hawkes.
—— FIVE AUSTRALIAN LYRICS (FOR VOICES AND STRINGS)
(Text: H. Allen)
hp. - str.   12:30 Bo. Hawkes.
—— G'DAY DIGGER (BALLET) %
30:00 A.P.R.A.
—— HAGAR (ORATORIO) (FOR MALE CHOIR, BOYS' CHOIR
AND ORCH.)
35:00 A.P.R.A.
—— AN OUTBACK OVERTURE
3,2,2,2 - 4,2,2,1 - timp.,perc., cel. - hp. - str.   Bo. Hawkes.
—— OVERTURE FOR A MOMENTOUS OCCASION
5:00 A.P.R.A.
—— SENTIMENTAL SUITE (SYMPHONIC BALLET)
40:00 A.P.R.A.
—— SNOWY (BALLET) (FOR SOPRANO VOICES AND ORCH.) %
30:00 A.P.R.A.
—— SYMPHONY ON A CITY
37:00 A.P.R.A.

ANTONINI, Alfredo
—— THE GREAT CITY
Mills.
—— NURSERY RHYMES (SMALL FRY OVERTURE)
2(2nd alt. with picc.),2,2,3 sax.,2 - 4,3,3,0 - timp.,perc. - pf. - str.
2:00 Mills.
—— PARIS - A VIEW OF THE EIFFEL TOWER (1962)
*3,*3,*3,2 - 4,3,3,1 - timp.,perc.(4),bells,cel.,glock.,xyl. - hp. - str.
7:00 Composer.
—— SARABANDE (FROM "SUITE IN ANCIENT STYLE")
str.   4:30 Leeds.

—— UNITED STATES OF AMERICA, CIRCA 1790 (SUITE OF
EARLY AMERICAN MUSIC)
Fox.

ANTONIOU, Theodore
—— ANTITHESEN, OP. 18A (1962)
1,0,1,1 - 0,1,0,0 - perc. - hp. - str.   18:00 G. Schirmer.
—— CASSANDRA (SOUND-ACTION) (WITH DANCERS, ACTORS,
CHORUS OF ALTOS AND BASSES, TAPES, LIGHTS AND
PROJECTIONS) (1969) %
3(3rd alt. with alto fl.)2,*2,2 - 4,3,3,1 - perc.(4) - tape-recorders -
pf. - str.   45:00 G. Schirmer.
—— CHEIRONOMIAI (GESTURES) (1971) (FOR ANY
COMBINATION OF INSTS.)
G. Schirmer.
—— CLYTEMNESTRA (SOUND-ACTION) (WITH ACTRESS,
DANCERS AND TAPE) (1967) %
2,1,0,0 - 0,0,3,1 - perc.(2) - tape-recorder - hp. - d.-b.'s
25:00 G. Schirmer.
—— CONCERTINO, OP. 16B (FOR PIANO, STRINGS AND PERC.)
(1962)
perc. - pf. - str.   13:00 G. Schirmer.
—— CONCERTINO, OP. 21 (FOR PIANO, 9 WINDS AND PERC.)
(1963)
1,1,2,2 - 2,1,0,0 - perc. - pf.   13:00 G. Schirmer.
—— CONCERTO FOR VIOLIN AND ORCH., OP. 28 (1965)
1,1,1,1 - 1,1,1,1 - perc.(3),cel. - hp. - str.   20:00 G. Schirmer.
—— EVENTS I (FOR VIOLIN, PIANO AND ORCH.) (1968)
2,2,2,2 - 4,2,3,1 - perc.(3) - hp. - hpsc. - pf. - str.
20:00 G. Schirmer.
—— EVENTS II (1969)
4(4th alt. with picc.),*4,*4,*4 - 6,4,4,1 - perc.(5) - hp. - pf. - str.
15:00 G. Schirmer.
—— EVENTS III (WITH TAPES AND SLIDES) (1969)
1,1,1,1 - 0,0,0,0 - perc.(2) - tape-recorder - pf. - str.
12:00 G. Schirmer.
—— JEUX (FOR CELLO AND STRINGS) (1963)
str.   13:00 G. Schirmer.
—— KATHARSIS (FOR FLUTE AND ORCH., WITH TAPES AND
PROJECTIONS) (1968)
0,1,2,0 - 0,0,2,1 - tape-recorder - Hammond org. - pf. - str. (c. and
d.-b. only)   12:00 G. Schirmer.
—— KINESIS ABCD, OP. 31 (1966)
str.   15:00 G. Schirmer.
—— KONTAKION, OP. 27 (FOR SOPRANO, ALTO, TENOR, BASS,
OPTIONAL SATB CHORUS AND STRINGS) (1965)
str.   12:00 G. Schirmer.
—— MELOS, OP. 17 (CANTATA FOR MEDIUM VOICE AND
ORCH.) (1962) (Text: Sappho)
1(alt. with picc.),0,1,1 - 0,1,1,0 - perc.(2) - guit. - str.
15:00 G. Schirmer.
—— MICROGRAPHIES, OP. 24 (1964)
3,*3,*3,*3 - 6,3,3,1 - perc.(5),cel. - hp. - pf. - str.
15:00 G. Schirmer.
—— NENIKIKAMEN (WE HAVE TRIUMPHED) (CANTATA) (FOR
MEZZO-SOPRANO, BARITONE, SPEAKER, MIXED CHORUS
AND ORCH.) (Text: T. S. Tolia)
3,3,3,3 - 4,3,3,1 - perc.(4-6) - hp. - pf. - str.   25:00 G. Schirmer.
—— OP OVERTURE (FOR ORCHESTRA AND TAPE, WITH
THREE GROUPS OF LOUDSPEAKERS) (1966)
1,1,*2,0 - 2,2,2,1 - perc.(3) - tape-recorder - 2 pf. - str.
11:00 G. Schirmer.
—— PROTEST II (FOR MEDIUM VOICE, ACTORS ORCH., TAPE
AND LIGHTS) (1971)
1,1,*2,0 - 1,1,2,1 - perc. - tape-recorder - Hammond org. - pf. -
str.(no d.-b.)   15:00 G. Schirmer.
—— STIMMUNG DER ABWESENHEIT (FOR MEDIUM VOICE
AND ORCH.) (1968)
1,1,1,1 - 0,0,0,0 - perc. - pf. - str.   9:00 G. Schirmer.
—— THRENOS (FOR WIND ORCH.) (1972)
2,1,*3,*3 - 2,2,3,1 - perc. - pf. - (d.-b.'s)   12:00 G. Schirmer.

ANTUNES, Jorge
—— CATASTROPHE ULTRA-VIOLETTE (FOR MEN'S CHORUS, 3
TAPES AND ORCH.)
3(3rd alt. with picc.),3(3rd alt. with Eng.hn.),3(3rd alt. with
b.-cl.),3(3rd alt. with c.-bn.) - timp.,perc.(8, incl. 4 on timp.),cel. -
3 tape-recorders - 2 hp. - pf. - str.   20:00 Salabert.

APERGHIS, Georges
—— ASCOLTARE STANCA
1(alt. with picc.),2,0,0 - 2,0,0,0 - hpsc. - pf. - str.   10:00 Salabert.

—— B.W.V. (FOR SOPRANO, MEZZO-SOPRANO,
COUNTER-TENOR, TENOR, 2 BARITONES AND
INSTRUMENTS)
2 recorders,0,0,*4,0 - 0,0,4,0 - perc.(2) - hpsc. - org. - pf. -
str.(0,1,1,4)   Salabert.
—— JACQUES LE FATALISTE (OPERA) %
4 recorders,1,*2,*2,0 - 1,1,1,1 - perc.(4),cel. - hpsc. - régal - org. -
pf. - str.(0,0,4,3)   Salabert.
—— SYMPLEXIS (FOR 5 INSTRUMENTAL GROUPS, INCLUDING
2 JAZZ ORCHESTRAS)
3 picc..,3,*4,5 sax.,3 - 5,8,5,1 - perc.(2) - electric org. - pf. -
str.(3,0,3,2)   20:00 Presser.
—— VARIATIONS FOR 14 INSTRUMENTS
1,1,1,1 - 1,0,0,0 - perc. - guit. - hp. - pf. - str.(2,1,1,1)
12:00 Salabert.
—— DIE WÄNDE HABEN OHREN ("THE WALLS HAVE EARS")
3(3rd alt. with picc.),3,3,3 - 4,3,3,1 - timp.,perc.,xyl. - str.
17:00 Salabert.

AP IVOR, Denis
—— BLOOD WEDDING, OP. 23 (1953)
3,2,2,3 - 4,2,3,1 - timp.,perc.,(3),cel. - hp. - pf. - str.   30:00 P.R.S.
—— CONCERTO FOR PIANO AND ORCH., OP. 13 (1948)
2,2,2,2 - 4,2,2,1 - timp.,perc.(3),cel. - hp. - pf. - str.   20:00 P.R.S.
—— CONCERTO FOR VIOLIN AND 15 INSTRUMENTS, OP. 16
(1950)
1,1,1,1 - 1,1,1,0 - perc.(2) - hp. - pf. - vln.,d.-b.   17:00 P.R.S.
—— CORPORAL JAN, OP. 42 (1967)
4,0,0,0 - 0,2,2,0 - perc.(4) - acc. - org. - pf. - str.   37:00 P.R.S.
—— THE GOODMAN OF PARIS, OP. 18 (1951)
2,2,2,2 - 2,2,2,0 - timp.,perc. - pf. - str.   20:00 P.R.S.
—— THE HOLLOW MEN (FOR BARITONE VOICE, MEN'S
CHORUS AND ORCH.)
*2,0,1,2 alto sax.,*2 - 0,3,3,0 - timp.,perc.(2-3) - pf. - str.
16:00 Oxford.
or:
*2,*1,2,*2 - 0,3,3,0 - timp.,perc.(2-3) - pf. - str.
—— A MIRROR FOR WITCHES, OP. 19 (BALLET) % (1951)
3,3,3,3 - 4,3,3,1 - perc.(3),cel. - hp. - pf. - str.   45:00 P.R.S.
—— OVERTONES, OP. 33 (9 ORCHESTRAL PIECES ON WORKS
OF PAUL KLEE) (1961)
2,2,3,1 - 1,1,2,1 - perc.(3),cel. - guit.,mandolin - hp. - pf. - str.
17:00 P.R.S.
—— SAUDADES, OP. 27 (1955)
2,2,2,2 - 4,2,2,0 - perc.(3),cel. - hp. - pf. - str.   30:00 P.R.S.
—— STRING ABSTRACT, OP. 43. (FOR VIOLIN, VIOLA, CELLO
AND STRINGS)(1967)
str.   18:00 P.R.S.
—— SYMPHONY NO. 1, OP. 22 (1959)
3,3,3,3 - 4,3,3,1 - timp.,perc.(3),cel. - hp. - 2 pf. - str. 21:00 P.R.S.
—— SYMPHONY NO. 2, OP. 36 (1963)
1,1,1,1 - 2,1,2,1 - perc.(3) - guit.,mandolin - hp. - pf. - str.
13:30 P.R.S.
—— TAROT, OP. 46 (1969)
2,1,2,1 - 0,2,1,0 - perc.(3) - hp. - pf. - str.   30:00 P.R.S.

APONTE-LEDEE, Rafael
—— LA VENTANA ABIERTA
1,0,1,0 - 0,1,0,0, - perc.(2) - pf. - str.   18:00 Seesaw.

APOTHÉLOZ, Jean
—— CALENDRIER (FOR MIXED CHOIR AND CHAMBER ORCH.,
WITH TWO PIANOS)
2,1,1,1 - 1,1,0,0 - 2 pf. - str.   10:00 S.U.I.S.A.
—— LITURGIE POUR LE TEMPS PASCAL (FOR MIXED CHOIR,
BARITONE SOLO AND STRING ORCH., WITH TWO
PIANOS)
2 pf. - str.   35:00 S.U.I.S.A.
—— PASTORALE FOR CHAMBER ORCHESTRA
2,1,1,1 - 1,1,0,0 - timp. - str.   13:00 S.U.I.S.A.

APPLEBAUM, Edward
—— CONCERTO FOR VIOLA AND ORCH (1967)
2(2nd alt. with picc.),2(2nd alt. with Eng.hn.),2(1 alt. with E♭ cl.
and 1 alt. with b.-cl.),2(2nd alt. with c.-bn.) - 2,1,1,0 - 1 vla.,3 plus
c.,1 plus d.-b.   15:00 G. Schirmer.
—— SYMPHONY NO. 1 (1969)
3(3rd alt.with picc.),3(3rd alt.with Eng. hn.),*3(1 alt.with E♭
cl.),sopr.sax.,*3 - 5,3,3,1 - timp.,perc.(3),bells,cel.,glock.,vibra.,xyl. -
guit. - hp. - pf. - str.   16:00 G. Schirmer.

—— VARIATIONS FOR ORCHESTRA (1966)
    3(3rd alt.with picc.),3(3rd alt.with Eng.hn.),*3(1 alt.with E♭cl.),*4 -
    6,4,4,1 - timp.,perc.,(4),bells,cel.,vibra.,xyl. - hp. - str.
            15:30 G. Schirmer.

APPLEBAUM, Louis
—— ACTION STATIONS
    1,1,2,1 - 1,2,2,0 - timp.,perc. - hp. - str.   15:00 C.A.P.A.C.
—— BALLET IN NINE SCENES (DARK OF THE MOON)
    (BARBARA ALLEN)
    1,1,2,1 - 1,2,1,0 - timp.,perc. - pf. - str.   50:00 C.A.P.A.C.
—— CHRISTMAS OVERTURE
    2,1,1,1 - 1,3,2,0 - timp.,perc. - str.   5:00 C.A.P.A.C.
—— CONCERTANTE (FOR SMALL ORCHESTRA)
    2,2,2,2 - 2,2,0,0 - perc. - str.   17:00 C.A.P.A.C.
—— EAST BY NORTH (SEA SKETCHES)
    2,2,2,2 - 2,2,1,0 - timp.,perc. - hp. - str.   13:00 C.A.P.A.C.
—— HOMAGE (CEREMONIAL BALLET) % (1969)
    *3,2,2,2 - 4,4,3,1 - timp.,perc. - hp. - pf. - str.   6:30 CanMusCtr.
—— PIECE FOR CHRISTMAS
    1,1,1,1 - 1,2,1,0 - timp. - str.   10:00 C.A.P.A.C.
—— PLACE SETTING (1973) (IN 1 MOVT.)
    2,2,2,2 - 4,3,3,1 - timp.,perc.(3) - str.   7:30 CanMusCtr.
—— REVIVAL MEETING AND FINALE FROM "BARBARA
    ALLEN" (1960)
    2,2,2,2 - 2,2,2,0 - perc. - hp.(ad lib) - pf. - str.   13:00 CanMusCtr.
—— SEVEN MINIATURE DANCES FOR "ALL'S WELL THAT
    ENDS WELL"
    1,2,1,1 - 0,2,0,0 - perc. - hp.   10:00 C.A.P.A.C.
—— THREE GREEK DANCES
    1,1,2,1 - 1,2,2,0 - timp.,perc. - hp. - str.   7:00 C.A.P.A.C.

APPLEBAUM, Stanley
—— CONCERTO NO. 1 FOR PIANO AND ORCH. (1951)
            Composer.

APPLETON, Jon H.
—— AFTER "NUDE DESCENDING A STAIRCASE" (1965)
    *3,*3,*3,2 - 2,2,2,0 - timp.,perc.(2),cel. - str.   8:00 Composer.
—— THE DEVIL-IN-LAW (MUSIC-DRAMA, AFTER A SPANISH
    FOLK TALE) % (1961) (Text: William Bain)
    1,1,1,1 - 1,1,1,0 - timp.,perc.(1),bell - str.   90:00 Composer.
—— THE EMPEROR'S NEW CLOTHES (MUSIC-DRAMA) % (Text:
    Willard Bain)
    1,1,1,1 - 1,1,1,0 - timp.,bell - pf. - str.   60:00 Composer.
—— THREE AMERICAN SONGS (FOR TENOR AND ORCH.)
    (Texts: Hart Crane and Emily Dickinson)
    *3,*3,*3,*3, - 2,2,2,0 - timp.,perc.(2) - str.   9:00 Composer.

ARAKASHVILI, D.
—— SHOTA RUSTAVELLI (SUITE)
    3,3,2,2 - 4,2,3,1 - timp.,perc. - hp. - str.   10:00 G. Schirmer.

ARÁMBARRI Y GÁRATE, Jesús
—— FANTASIA ESPAÑOLA
    3,3,3,0 - 4,3,3,1 - timp.,perc. - hp. - pf. - str.   S.G.A.E.
—— FOUR IMPROMPTUS
    3,2,2,2 - 2,2,0,0 - timp.,perc.,cel. - hp. - str.   S.G.A.E.
—— IN MEMORIAM
    3,2,3,2 - 4,2,3,1 - timp.,perc., - hp. - str.   S.G.A.E.
—— OFRENDA A FALLA
    Eng.hn. - str.   S.G.A.E.

ARANYI, György
—— VARIATIONS FOR PIANO AND STRINGS
    pf. - str.   Bo. Hawkes.

ARDEVOL, José
—— CONCERTO FOR PIANO, WINDS AND PERCUSSION
    1,2,1,1 - 2,2,2,1 - timp.,perc. - pf.   24:00 Southern.
—— CONCERTO GROSSO NO. 1
    1,1,0,1 - 0,2,0,0 - pf. - str.   15:30 Southern.
—— CONCERTO GROSSO NO. 2
    0,2,2,2 - 0,2,1,0 - pf. - str.   20:30 Southern.
—— MUSIC FOR SMALL ORCHESTRA
    2 hn. - timp.,perc.,cel. - hp. - hpsc. - pf. - str.   25:00 Southern.
—— NINE LITTLE PIECES (HOMAGE TO ERIK SATIE)
    3,*3,4, alto sax.,3 - 4,4,3,1 - timp.,perc., cel.,glock. - 2 hp. - pf. -
    str.   22:30 Southern.
—— SUITE CUBANA NO. 1
    3,3,3,3 - 4,3,3,1 - timp.,perc. - pf. - str.   26:00 Southern.
—— SUITE CUBANA NO. 2
    2,2,2,2 - 2,2,2,1 - timp. - pf. - str.   12:00 Southern.

—— SYMPHONIC VARIATIONS (FOR CELLO AND ORCH.)
    3,2,3,3 - 4,3,3,1 - timp.,perc., cel. - hp. - str.   16:30 Southern.
—— SYMPHONY NO. 2
    4,4,4,4 - 6,4,6,2 - timp.,perc., cel.,glock. - 2 hp. - hpsc. - 2 pf. - str.
         35:00 Southern.
—— SYMPHONY NO. 3
    4,3,2, Eng. hn., 5,5 - 8,6,5,2 - timp.,perc. - 2 pf.   37:00 Southern.
—— TRIPTICO DE SANTIAGO
    3,3,4,3 - 4,4,4,1 - timp.,perc., cel.,glock. - 2 hp. 2 pf. - str.
         29:30 Southern.

AREL, Bülent
—— SIX BAGATELLES FOR STRING ORCH.
    str.   8:30 Presser.

ARENSKY, A. - KRAMER, A. Walter
—— SUITE IN CANON FORM, OP. 65 (FOR STRING ORCH.)
    str.   Witmark.

ARGENTO, Dominick
—— THE BOOR (1-ACT OPERA-BUFFA, AFTER THE CHEKHOV
    PLAY) % (1957) (Text: John Olon-Scrymgeour)
    1(alt. with picc.),1(alt. with Eng. hn.),2(2nd alt. with b.-cl.),1 -
    2,1,0,0 - perc. - pf. - str.   55:00 Bo. Hawkes.
—— BRAVO MOZART (AN IMAGINARY BIOGRAPHY) (1969)
    1(alt.with picc.),1,2(2nd alt. with b.-cl.),0 - 1,2,2,0 -
    timp.,perc.(1),bells,cel.,glock.,xyl. - pf. - str.   30:00 Bo. Hawkes.
—— CHRISTOPHER SLY (2 SCENE COMIC OPERA) % (Text: John
    Manlove)
         Bo. Hawkes.
—— COLONEL JONATHAN, THE SAINT (OPERA) % (Text: John
    Olon)
    2(2nd alt. with picc.),2(2nd alt. with Eng. hn.),2(2nd alt. with
    b.-cl.),2 - 3,2(2nd alt. with cnt.),1,0 - timp.,perc. - hp. - pf. - str.
         135:00 Bo. Hawkes.
—— DIVERTIMENTO FOR PIANO AND STRINGS (IN 3 MOVTS.)
    pf. - str.   17:00 Bo. Hawkes.
—— FROM THE ALBUM OF ALLEGRA HARPER, 1867 (SUITE
    FROM "COLONEL JONATHAN, THE SAINT")
    2(2nd. alt. with picc.),2(2nd alt. with Eng. hn.),2(2nd alt. with
    b.-cl.),2 - 3,2(2nd alt. with cnt.),1,0 - timp.,perc.(2) - hp. - pf. - str.
         9:00 Bo. Hawkes.
—— THE MASQUE OF ANGELS (1-ACT OPERA) % (1963) (Text:
    John Olon-Scrymgeour)
    0,2(2nd alt.with Eng.hn.),0,1 - 0,2,1,0 - perc.(1) - hp. - 2 vla.,1 c.
         70:00 Bo. Hawkes.
—— ODE TO THE WEST WIND (CONCERTO FOR SOPRANO
    AND ORCH.) (Text: Shelley)
    3,3,3,3 - 4,3,3,1 - timp.,perc. - str.   28:00 Bo. Hawkes.
—— OVERTURE TO "THE BOOR"
    1,1,2,1 - 2,1,0,0 - perc. - pf. - str.   5:00 Bo. Hawkes.
—— THE RESURRECTION OF DON JUAN: (BALLET) %
    2,2,2,2 - 4,2,2,1 - timp.,perc. - hp. - str.   45:00 Bo. Hawkes.
—— THE RESURRECTION OF DON JUAN: BALLET SUITE
    2(2nd alt. with picc.),2,2(2nd alt. with b.-cl.),2 - 4,2,2,1 -
    timp.,perc.(2),glock. - hp. - str.   22:00 Bo. Hawkes.
—— THE REVELATION OF ST. JOHN THE DIVINE (FOR TENOR,
    MALE CHORUS, BRASS AND PERCUSSION) (1966)
    0,0,0,0 - 3,2,2,0 - perc.(2) - hp. - pf.   40:00 Bo. Hawkes.
—— A RING OF TIME
    4,4,4,4 - 4,3,3,1 - timp.,perc.,cel. - hp. - pf. - str.
         28:00 Bo. Hawkes.
—— ROYAL INVITATION (OR, HOMAGE TO THE QUEEN OF
    TONGA) (Text: John Olon)
    1,2,2,0 - 2,0,0,0 - str.   23:00 Bo. Hawkes.
—— SEBASTIAN'S DREAM (3-ACT OPERA) %
         Bo. Hawkes.
—— SONGS ABOUT SPRING (CYCLE FOR SOPRANO AND
    CHAMBER ORCH.) (Text: e. e. cummings)
    2,2,2,2 - 2,1,1,0 - timp.,perc.,cel. - hp. - str.   12:00 Bo. Hawkes.
—— VARIATIONS FOR ORCHESTRA ("THE MASK OF NIGHT")
    (WITH SOPRANO OBLIGATO)
    2(2nd alt. with picc.),2,2(2nd alt. with b.-cl.),2 - 4,3,3,1 -
    timp.,perc. - hp. - str.   27:00 Bo. Hawkes.
—— THE VOYAGE OF EDGAR ALLAN POE (OPERA) %
    2,2,2,2 - 3,2,2,1 - timp.,perc.,cel. - hp. - pf. -str.   Bo. Hawkes.

ARIAS, Luis
—— POLARRIZACIONES
    3,0,3,1 sax.,2 - 2,3,3,0 - perc.(7), cel. - electric guit. - 2 hp. - pf. -
    str.(12,6,4,4).   16:00 Bo. Hawkes.

ARISTAKESYAN, Emil
—— PROMETHEUS (BALLET) %

G. Schirmer.

ARLEN, Albert
—— THE ALAMEIN CONCERTO (FOR PIANO AND ORCH.)
2,1,2,2 sax.,1 - 2,3,3,1 - perc. (3) - hp. - pf. - str.   7:30 Chappell.
—— KINGS CROSS SUITE

8:00 A.P.R.A.
—— THE PAGODA OF JADE (CHINESE SUITE)

8:00 Southern.
—— SONG OF ENGLAND (FOR BARITONE, CHORUS AND
ORCH.)

15:00 A.P.R.A.

ARLEN, Harold - MATOVSKY, Samuel
—— SYMPHONIC SUITE FROM "BLUES OPERA"

27:00 Chappell.

ARMA, Paul
—— DEUX TRANSPARENCES (FOR FLUTE AND STRINGS)
fl. - str.   16:00 Presser.
—— DIVERTIMENTO DE CONCERT NO. 1 (FOR FLUTE OR
VIOLIN SOLO WITH STRS.)
fl.(or vln.) - str.   15:00 Presser.
—— DIVERTIMENTO DE CONCERT NO. 4 (FOR CELLO AND
CHAMBER ORCH.)
1,1,1,1 - 0,0,0,0 - timp.,perc. - str.   16:00 Presser.
—— DIVERTIMENTO DE CONCERT NO. 6 (FOR CLARINET OR
VIOLA, WITH STRINGS)
cl.(ad lib.) - str.   16:00 EV.
—— HUIT RESONANCES
2,2,2,3 - 4,2,3,1 - timp.,perc.,cel. - pf. - str.   22:45 Presser.
—— IMPROVISATION, PRÉCÉDÉE ET SUIVIE DE SES
VARIATIONS
2,3,3,3 - 0,0,0,0 - timp.,perc.(3),cel.,xyl. - electronic tape - str.
32:00 S.A.C.E.M.
—— PETITE SUITE
str.   12:00 Mills.
—— SEPT RESONANCES
2,2,2,3 - 4,2,3,1 - timp.,perc. - pf. - str.   19:00 Presser.
—— SIX RESONANCES
2,2,2,2 - 4,2,3,1 - timp.,perc.(3) - pf. - str.   16:00 Presser.
—— SIX TRANSPARENCES (FOR OBOE AND STRINGS)
ob. - str.   19:00 Presser.
—— SUITES DE DANSES (FOR FLUTE AND STRINGS)
fl. - str.   EV.
—— SYMPHONY IN 4 MOVTS. (FOR STRINGS)
str.   24:00 Presser.
—— TRANSPARENCE
2,3,3,2 - 2,4,3,0 - timp.,perc. - pf. - str.   11:30 Presser.
—— TRENTE-ET-UN INSTANTANÉS (31 SNAPSHOTS)
3,3,3,3 - 0,0,0,0 - timp.,perc.,cel.,xyl. - pf.   21:00 S.A.C.E.M.
—— VARIATIONS FOR STRINGS
str.   7:45 Eds. Fran.

ARMANDO, Gualterio
—— NIGHT IN THE EXCURIAL

15:00 B.U.M.A.
—— OLLANTAY (SUITE IN 4 MOVTS.)
2,2,2,2 - 2,0,0,0 - timp.,perc. - str.   20:00 Schuberth.
—— SPANISCHE LUSTSPIEL-OUVERTÜRE
2,2,2,2 - 2,2,0,0 - timp.,perc. - str.   10:00 Schuberth.

ARMBRUSTER, René
—— CONCERTO DA CAMERA (POUR VIOLIN ET ORCHESTRE À
CORDES)
str.   19:00 S.U.I.S.A.
—— FANTASIA (PER FLAUTO E ORCHESTRA D'ARCHI)
fl. - str.   18:00 S.U.I.S.A.

ARMBRUSTER, Robert
—— VARIATIONS IN MINIATURE (ON "CHOPSTICKS")
2,2,*3,2 - 2,3,2,1 - perc. - hp.(or pf.) - str.   3:15 C. Fischer.
—— WE THE PEOPLE (FOR SATB CHORUS AND ORCH.) (BASED
ON THE PREAMBLE TO THE CONSTITUTION)
2,2,*3,2 - 3,3,3,0 - timp.,perc.(2) - hp. - str.   3:15 C. Fischer.

ARMENIAN, Raffi
—— PASSION CANTATA (FOR TENOR, MIXED CHORUS AND
ORCH.) (1969)
*3,*3,*3,*3 - 4,3,3,1 - perc.(4) - str.   15:00 CanMusCtr.

—— SUITE DÉCOMPOSÉ (1969) (IN 3 MOVTS.)
2(2nd alt. with picc.),2(2nd alt. with Eng. hn.),2,2(2nd alt. with
c.-bn.) - 2,2,1,1 - timp.,perc. - hp. - str.   15:00 CanMusCtr.

ARNATT, Ronald
—— CONCERTO NO. 1 IN A MINOR, OP. 5, FOR PIANO AND
ORCH. (IN 3 MOVTS.)
2,*3,2,1 alto sax.,2 - 4,3,3,1 - timp.,perc.(4),cel. - hp. - pf. - str.
25:00 Composer.
—— GREENSLEEVES SUITE (FOR NARRATOR, SSA CHORUS
AND CHAMBER ORCH.) (IN 5 MOVTS.)
fl. - hp. - str.   10:15 Composer.
—— A PRAYER OF ST. FRANCIS OF ASSISI (FOR BARITONE,
SSAATTBB CHORUS AND ORCH.) (1954)
2,2,2,2 - 2,1,0,0 - timp. - str.   20:00 Composer.
—— RHAPSODY, OP. 6 (ON THE MALVERN HILLS)
2,2,2,2 - 2,1,0,0 - timp. - str.   6:00 Composer.
—— A SERVICE OF PSALMS (FOR NARRATOR, MIXED CHORUS
AND SMALL ORCH.) (IN 5 MOVTS.)
fl. - hn. - str.   25:00 Composer.
—— SUITE FOR FLUTE AND STRINGS (IN 3 MOVTS.)
fl. - str.   8:00 Composer.

ARNE, Thomas - BEECHEY, Gwilyn
—— OVERTURE TO "THE GUARDIAN OUTWITTED"
2,0-1,2,0 - 0,0,0,0 - cemb. - str.   10:00 Oxford.

ARNE, Thomas - BUSH, Geoffrey
—— SINFONIETTA (FROM THE SONATA NO. 5 FOR
HARPSICHORD)
1,1,1,1 - 2,1,0,0 - timp. - str.   Galaxy.

ARNE, Thomas - CARSE, A.
—— THE JUDGMENT OF PARIS: OVERTURE
2 ob. bn. - str.   6:00 Galaxy.
—— SYMPHONIA (OVERTURE) NO. 4 IN F
1. Conspirito; 2. Con spirit., allegro moderato; 3. Andantino
2 ob. - 2 hn. - str.   5:00 Galaxy.

ARNE, Thomas - COLLINS, Anthony
—— SUITE OF 6 DANCES
1,1,1,1 - hn. - str.   16:00 Skidmore.

ARNE, Thomas - HERBAGE, Julian
—— COMUS - A MASQUE (OPERA) %
2,2,0,1 - 2,2,0,0 - timp. - cemb. - str.   Galaxy.
—— OVERTURE TO "COMUS"
2,2,0,1 - 0,2,0,0 - timp. - cemb. - str.   Galaxy.

ARNE, Thomas - PLATT, Richard
—— SYMPHONY NO. 1 IN C MAJOR
0,2,0,1 - 2,0,0,0 - cemb. - str.   8:00 Oxford.
—— SYMPHONY NO. 2 IN F MAJOR
0,2,0,1 - 2,0,0,0 - cemb. - str.   9:00 Oxford.
—— SYMPHONY NO. 3 IN E FLAT MAJOR
0,2,0,2 - 2,0,0,0 - timp. - cemb. - str.   8:00 Oxford.
—— SYMPHONY NO. 4 IN C MINOR
2,2,0,2 - 2,0,0,0 - cemb. - str.   11:00 Oxford.

ARNE, Thomas - WARRACK, Guy
—— OVERTURE TO "ARTAXERXES"
2 ob., 2 bn. - str.   6:30 Bo. Hawkes.

ARNE, Thomas A. - CARSE, Adam
—— CONCERTO NO. 4 IN B-FLAT, FOR CEMBALO AND ORCH.
2 ob.(ad lib.) - cemb. - str.   11:00 Galaxy.
—— CONCERTO NO. 5 IN G MINOR, FOR CEMBALO AND
ORCH.
2 ob.(ad lib.) - cemb. - str.   10:00 Galaxy.
—— OVERTURE TO THE MASQUE "BRITANNIA"
1,1,1,1 - 2,1,0,0 - timp. - str.   7:00 Galaxy.

ARNE, Thomas A. - HERBAGE, Julian
—— OVERTURE IN B♭
2 ob., bn. - str.   6:00 Bo. Hawkes.

ARNE, Thomas A. - LEBELL
—— A SUITE OF THREE PIECES (FOR STRING ORCH.)
str.   Oxford.

ARNE, Thomas A. - TOMLINSON
—— GEORGIAN SUITE

Oxford.

ARNE, Thomas A. - WHITTAKER, W. G.
—— THE DANCES IN "COMUS"
fl. 2 ob. - pf. (ad. lib) - str.   8:00 Oxford.

ARNE, Thomas Augustine - MASKE, Hans Herbert Adolf Engelbert
—— DIE KUIPER (OPERA) % (Afrikaans Text: Arranger)
2,2,3,2 - 4,2,3,1 - timp.,perc. - str.   60:00 S.A.M.R.O.

ARNELL, Richard
—— CANZONA AND CAPRICCIO, OP. 37 (FOR VIOLIN AND
STRINGS)
str.   Presser.
—— SONATA, OP. 18 (FOR CHAMBER ORCH.)
1,1,1,1 - 2,0,0,0 - str.   Presser.

ARNESTAD BJAEKE, Finn Oluf
—— CONCERTO FOR VIOLIN AND ORCH. (IN 3 MOVTS.)
2,0,2,2 - 2,2,0,0 - str.   25:00 T.O.N.O.

ARNESTAD BJAERKE, Finn Oluf
—— THE BLACKSMITH AND THE BAKER (SMEDEN OG
BAGEREN) (FOR BARITONE AND CHAMBER ORCH.) (Text:
Johan Herman Wessel)
1,1,0,0 - 0,0,0,0 - cemb. - str.(7,3,2,1)   35:00 T.O.N.O.
—— CAVATINA CAMBIATA
2,2,2,2 - 3,2,2,1 - perc. - str.   7:30 T.O.N.O.
—— CONSTELLATION (INTERMEZZO FOR ORCH.)
2,2,2,2 - 4,2,2,0 - timp.,perc. - hp. - str.   7:00 T.O.N.O.
—— CONVERSATION (INTERMEZZO FOR PIANO AND ORCH.)
2,2,2,2 - 2,2,0,0 - timp.,perc. - pf. - str.   4:00 T.O.N.O.
—— I.N.R.I. (2 CONCERT SUITES, FROM A SYMPHONIC
MYSTERY PLAY)
3,3,3,3 - 4,3,3,1 - timp.,perc. - hp. - str.   T.O.N.O.
SUITE NO. 1
                                        14:00
SUITE NO. 2
                                        12:00
—— I.N.R.I. (2 CONCERT SUITES, FROM A SYMPHONIC
MYSTERY PLAY)
3,3,3,3 - 4,3,3,1 - timp.,perc. - hp. - str.   T.O.N.O.
(SUITE NO. 1)
                                        14:00
SUITE NO. 2
                                        12:00
—— MEDITATION (INTERMEZZO FOR ORCH.)
1,1,2,2 - 4,2,2,0 - timp.,perc. - hp. - str.   5:00 T.O.N.O.
—— SUITE IN OLD DANCE RHYTHMS
1,1,0,0 - 0,0,0,0 - hpsc. - str.   20:00 T.O.N.O.

ARNIČ, Blaž
—— CONCERTO FOR VIOLA AND ORCH., OP. 75
2(2nd alt. with picc.),2,2,2(2nd alt. with c.-bn.) - 4,3,3,1 -
timp.,perc.(5) - str.   15:00 Hans Gerig.
—— CONCERTO NO. 1 FOR VIOLIN AND ORCH.
2(2nd alt. with picc.),2,2,2 - 4,3,3,1 - timp.,perc. - str.
                                        37:00 Hans Gerig.
—— CONCERTO NO. 3 FOR VIOLIN AND ORCH.
2(2nd alt. with picc.),2,2,2(2nd alt. with c.-bn.) - 4,3,3,1 -
timp.,perc.(3) - str.   35:00 Hans Gerig.
—— EXPECTATION, OP. 26 (SYMPHONIC POEM)
2(2nd alt. with picc.),2,2,2 - 4,3,3,1 - timp.,perc.(4) - str.
                                        14:00 Hans Gerig.
—— FIRST SPRING, OP. 52 (PRVI POLET) (SYMPHONIC POEM)
(FOR PIANO AND ORCH.)
1,0,2,0 - 0,2,2,0 - timp. - pf. - str. 12:00 Hans Gerig.
—— THE FORESTS SING, OP. 27 (SYMPHONIC POEM)
2(2nd alt. with picc.),2,2(2nd alt. with b.-cl.),3 - 4,3,3,1 -
timp.,perc.(3) - hp. - str.   18:00 Hans Gerig.
—— OVERTURE TO A COMIC OPERA, OP. 11
*2,2,2,2 - 4,2,3,1 - timp.,perc.(4) - hp. - str.   7:00 Hans Gerig.
—— PASTORAL, OP. 64 (SYMPHONIC POEM, FOR CELLO AND
ORCH.)
2(2nd alt. with picc.),2,2,2 - 4,3,3,1 - timp.,perc. - hp. - str.
                                        30:00 Hans Gerig.
—— THE SEDUCER, OP. 19 (SYMPHONIC POEM)
2(2nd alt. with picc.),2(2nd alt. with Eng. hn.),2(2nd alt. with
b.-cl.),3 - 4,3,3,1 - timp.,perc.(3) - hp. - str.   24:00 Hans Gerig.
—— SONG OF THE HIGHLANDS, OP. 20 (SYMPHONIC POEM)
2(2nd alt. with picc.),2(2nd alt. with Eng. hn.),2(2nd alt. with
b.-cl.),2(2nd alt. with c.-bn.) - 4,3,3,1 - timp.,perc.(3) - hp. - str.
                                        17:00 Hans Gerig.

—— SYMPHONY NO. 1, OP. 10 (TE DEUM) (FOR CHORUS,
ORGAN AND ORCH.)
2(2nd alt. with picc.),2,2,2 - 4,2,3,1 - timp.,perc.(4) - org. - str.
                                        17:00 Hans Gerig.
—— SYMPHONY NO. 2, OP. 12 (PSALM 160) (A SYMPHONIC
RHAPSODY)
2(2nd alt. with picc.),2,2,2 - 4,2,3,1 - timp.,perc.(4) - hp. - pf. - str.
                                        18:00 Hans Gerig.
—— SYMPHONY NO. 3, OP. 17-24 (DUMA) (FOR BARITONE,
SATB CHORUS AND ORCH.)
2(2nd alt. with picc.),2,2,2(2nd alt. with c.-bn.) - 4,2,3,1 -
timp.,perc.(5) - str.   75:00 Hans Gerig.
—— SYMPHONY NO. 4, OP. 15 (RESURRECTION)
0,0,2,0 - 2,2,2,0 - timp.,perc.(3) - org. - str.   15:00 Hans Gerig.
—— SYMPHONY NO. 5, OP. 22 (PARTIKULARNA)
2(2nd alt. with picc.),2,2,2(2nd alt. with c.-bn.) - 4,3,3,1 -
timp.,perc.(5) - str.   35:00 Hans Gerig.
—— SYMPHONY NO. 6, OP. 36 (SAMORASTNIK)
2(2nd alt. with picc.),2,2,3 - 4,3,3,1 -timp.,perc.(4) - str.
                                        35:00 Hans Gerig.
—— SYMPHONY NO. 7, OP. 35 (DELA) (FOR CHAMBER ORCH.
WITH PIANO)
1,1,1,0 ⌐ 0,1,1,0 - timp.,perc.(3) - pf. - str.   18:00 Hans Gerig.
—— SYMPHONY NO. 8, OP. 40 ("ON NATIVE SOIL")
2(2nd alt. with picc.),2,2,2(2nd alt. with c.-bn.) - 4,3,3,1 -
timp.,perc.(5) - hp. - str.   35:00 Hans Gerig.
—— SYMPHONY NO. 9, OP. 63 (WAR AND PEACE) (FOR
SOPRANO, ALTO, BASS, SATB CHORUS AND ORCH.)
2(2nd alt. with picc.),2,2,2(2nd alt. with c.-bn.) - 4,5,5,1 -
timp.,perc.(6) - str.   70:00 Hans Gerig.
—— THE TEMPEST, OP. 72 (SYMPHONIC POEM)
2(2nd alt. with picc.),2,2,2(2nd alt. with c.-bn.) - 4,4,3,1 -
timp.,perc.(4) - hp. - str.   27:00 Hans Gerig.
—— TEMPORALNA, OP. 78 (SYMPHONIC POEM, FOR
TROMBONE AND ORCH.)
2(2nd alt. with picc.),2,2,2(2nd alt. with c.-bn.) - 4,3,3,1 -
timp.,perc.(5) - str.   15:00 Hans Gerig.
—— THE WATER-SPRITE, OP. 38 (BALLET) %
2(2nd alt. with picc.),2,2,3 - 4,3,3,1 - timp.,perc.(4) - hp. - str.
                                        Hans Gerig.
—— WITCHES' DANCE (SYMPHONIC POEM)
1(alt. with picc.),2,2,2(2nd alt. with c.-bn.) - 4,2,3,1 - timp.,perc.(4)
- zither - str.   18:00 Hans Gerig.
—— Z VLAKOM, OP. 48 (WITH TRAIN) (CANTATA) (FOR SOLO
VOICES, CHORUS AND ORCH.)
(2nd alt. with picc.),2,2,2 - 4,3,3,1 - timp.,perc.(4) - str.
                                        25:00 Hans Gerig.

ARNOLD, Hubert E.
—— SCHERZO FOR PIANO AND ORCH.
                                        7:00 Composer.

ARNOLD, Malcolm
—— ANNIVERSARY OVERTURE, OP. 99
2,2,2,2 - 4,2,3,0 - timp.,perc. - str. 4:00 G. Schirmer.
—— BECKUS THE DANDIPRATT (COMEDY OVERTURE)
3,2,2,2 - 4,3,3,1 - timp.,perc. - str. 8:30 Lengnick.
—— CARNIVAL OF ANIMALS, OP. 72
3,2,2,2 - 4,3,3,1 - timp.,perc.(3) - hp. - str.   15:00 P.R.S.
—— COMMONWEALTH CHRISTMAS OVERTURE, OP. 64
3,2,2,2 - 4,3,3,1 - timp.,perc.(4),cel.,mar. - 4 guit. - hp.
                                        14:30 P.R.S.
—— CONCERTO FOR CLARINET AND STRINGS
cl. - str.   17:00 Lengnick.
—— CONCERTO FOR FLUTE AND STRINGS, OP. 45
fl. - str: 12:30 C. Fischer.
—— CONCERTO FOR GUITAR AND SMALL ORCH., OP. 67
1,0,1,0 - 1,0,0,0 - guit. - str.   21:00 C. Fischer.
—— CONCERTO FOR HARMONICA AND ORCH., OP. 46
0,0,0,0 - 4,3,3,1 - timp.,perc.,glock. - harmonica - str .
                                        9:00 C. Fischer.
—— CONCERTO FOR OBOE AND STRINGS, OP. 39
Ob - str.   6:00 C. Fischer.
—— CONCERTO FOR ORCHESTRA
                                        12:00 G. Schirmer.
—— CONCERTO FOR ORGAN AND ORCH., OP. 47
*1,0,0,0 - 0,3,0,0 - timp. - org. - str.   C. Fischer.
—— CONCERTO FOR PHYLLIS AND CYRIL, OP. 104 (FOR TWO
PIANOS, 3-HANDS AND ORCH.)
3,2,2,2 - 4,3,3,1 - timp.,perc.(2) - hp. - 2 pf. - str.
                                        13:00 G. Schirmer.
or:
2,2,2,2 - 2,2,1,1 - timp.,perc. - 2 pf. - str.

—— CONCERTO FOR PIANO DUET AND STRINGS
  pf. (4 hands) - str.   21:00 Lengnick.
—— CONCERTO FOR TWO VIOLINS AND STRING ORCH., OP. 77 (1962) (IN 3 MOVTS.)
  str.   18:00 G. Schirmer.
—— CONCERTO FOR VIOLA AND CHAMBER ORCH., OP. 108
  1,2,2,2 - 2,0,0,0 - str.   20:00 G. Schirmer.
—— CONCERTO FOR 28 PLAYERS, OP. 105
  1,2,0,1 - 2,0,0,0 - str.   15:00 G. Schirmer.
—— CONCERTO NO. 1 FOR HORN AND ORCH.
  3,2,2,2 - 1,0,0,0 - timp. - str.   22:00 Lengnick.
—— CONCERTO NO. 2 FOR CLARINET AND ORCH.
  *2,2,1,2 - 2,0,0,0 - timp.,perc.(1) - str.   17:00 G. Schirmer.
—— CONCERTO NO. 2 FOR FLUTE AND ORCH., OP. 111
  1,2,0,0 - 2,0,0,0 - str.   14:00 G. Schirmer.
—— DIVERTIMENTO NO. 1, OP. 1
  3,2,2,2 - 4,3,3,1 - timp.,perc.(3) - str.   10:30 P.R.S.
—— DIVERTIMENTO NO. 2
  3,2,2,2 - 4,3,3,1 - timp.,perc. - hp. - str. 9:00 C. Fischer.
—— ELECTRA, OP. 79 (BALLET) %
  3,2,2,2 - 4,3,3,1 - timp.,perc.(4) - hp. - str.   25:00 P.R.S.
—— ENGLISH DANCES, SET 1
  3,2,2,2 - 4,3,3,1 - timp.,perc. - hp. - str.   8:00 Lengnick.
—— ENGLISH DANCES, SET 2
  3,2,2,2 - 4,3,3,1 - timp.,perc.,cel. - hp. - str.   9:00 Lengnick.
—— FESTIVAL OVERTURE, OP. 14
  2,2,2,2 - 2,2,0,0 - timp. - str.   6:00 P.R.S.
—— FOUR CORNISH DANCES
  3,2,2,1 - 4,3,3,1 - timp.,perc. - hp. - str.   10:00 G. Schirmer.
—— FOUR SCOTTISH DANCES, OP. 59
  2,2,2,2 - 4,2,3,0 - timp.,perc. - hp. - str.   9:00 C. Fischer.
—— GRAND CONCERTO GASTRONOMIQUE, OP. 76 (FOR EATER, WAITER AND LARGE ORCH.)
                                          20:00 P.R.S.
—— A GRAND, GRAND OVERTURE, OP. 57
  3,2,2,2 - 4,3,2,1 - timp.,perc.(5),bells - 3 vacuum cleaners,1 floor-polisher, 4 rifles - org. - str.   8:00 C. Fischer.
—— HOMAGE TO THE QUEEN
                                          20:00 C. Fischer.
—— LARCH TREES, OP. 3 (TONE POEM)
  3,2,2,2 - 4,0,0,0 - str.   8:30 P.R.S.
—— LITTLE SUITE NO. 1 FOR ORCHESTRA, OP. 53 (IN 3 MOVTS.)
  2,2,2,2 - 4,3,3,1 - timp.,perc. (3) - str.   9:00 C. Fischer.
—— LITTLE SUITE NO. 2 FOR ORCH., OP. 78
  2,2,2,2 - 4,3,2,1 - timp.,perc. - str. 10:00 C. Fischer.
—— OVERTURE: "THE FAIR FIELD", OP. 110
  *3,2,2,2 - 4,3,3,1 - timp.,perc.(2) - str.   7:00 G. Schirmer.
—— PETERLOO, OP. 97 (OVERTURE FOR ORCH.)
  3,2,2,2 - 4,3,3,1 - timp.,perc. - hp. - str. 9:30 G. Schirmer.
—— RINALDO AND ARMIDA, OP. 49 (BALLET) %
  3,2,2,2 - 4,3,3,1 - timp.,perc.(3),cel. - hp. - str.   23:00 P.R.S.
—— SERENADE (FOR SMALL ORCH.)
  2,2,2,2 - 2,2,0,0 - timp. - str.   12:00 Lengnick.
—— SINFONIETTA NO. 1, OP. 48
  2 ob. - 2 hn. - str.   12:00 C. Fischer.
—— SINFONIETTA NO. 2, OP. 65
  2 fl. - 2 hn. - str.   13:00 C. Fischer.
—— THE SMOKE (OVERTURE)
  3,2,2,2 - 4,3,3,1 - timp.,perc. - hp. - str. 5:00 Lengnick.
—— SONG OF SIMEON (NATIVITY MASQUE) % (FOR MIMERS, SATB SOLO VOICES, MIXED CHORUS AND ORCH.) (Text: Christopher Hassall)
  0,0,0,0 - 0,3,3,1 - timp.,perc.,cel. - hp. - str.   30:00 Oxford.
  or:
  Recorders,0,0,0,0 - 0,0,0,0 - timp.,perc. - pf. 4-hands - str.
—— A SUNSHINE OVERTURE, OP. 83
  2,2,2,2 - 2,2,1,0 - perc. - str.   6:00 P.R.S.
—— A SUSSEX OVERTURE
  3,2,2,2 - 4,3,3,1 - timp.,perc. - str. 9:00 Lengnick.
—— SWEENEY TODD, OP. 68 (BALLET) %
  2,2,2,2 - 2,2,3,0 - pf. - str.   23:00 P.R.S.
—— SYMPHONIC STUDY FOR BRASS, PERCUSSION AND STRINGS, OP. 30
  0,0,0,0 - 4,3,3,1 - timp.,perc.(4) - str.   6:00 P.R.S.
—— SYMPHONIC SUITE, OP. 12
  3,2,2,2 - 4,3,3,1 - timp.,perc(3) - str.   15:00 P.R.S.
—— SYMPHONY FOR STRINGS
  str.   22:00 Lengnick.
—— SYMPHONY NO. 1
  3,2,2,2 - 4,3,3,1 - timp.,perc. - hp. - str. 29:00 Lengnick.
—— SYMPHONY NO. 2, OP. 40
  3,2,2,3 - 4,3,3,1 - timp.,perc. - str. 30:00 C. Fischer.

—— SYMPHONY NO. 3, OP. 63
  3,2,2,2 - 4,3,3,1 - timp. - str.   33:00 C. Fischer.
—— SYMPHONY NO. 4, OP. 71
  *3,2,2,*3 - 4,3,3,1 - timp.,perc.(4),cel. - hp. - str.   30:00 C. Fischer.
—— SYMPHONY NO. 5
  3,2,2,2 - 4,3,3,1 - timp.,perc.,cel. - hp. - str.   33:00 C. Fischer.
—— SYMPHONY NO. 6, OP. 95
  3,2,2,2 - 4,3,3,1 - timp.,perc.(4) - str.   26:00 G. Schirmer.
—— TAM O'SHANTER OVERTURE, OP. 52
  3,2,2,2 - 4,3,3,1 - timp.,perc. - str. 7:30 C. Fischer.
—— TOY SYMPHONY, OP. 62
                                          C. Fischer.
—— WATER MUSIC, OP. 82-B
  3,2,2,2 - 4,3,3,1 - timp.,perc. - str. 10:00 C. Fischer.

ARRIEU, Claude
—— CONCERTO FOR FLUTE AND ORCH.
  1,2,2,1 - 2,1,0,0 - timp.,perc. - str. 13:00 E.C.Kerby.
—— CONCERTO IN C, FOR 2 PIANOS AND ORCH.
  2,2,2,2 - 2,2,0,0 - timp.,perc.(3) - 2 pf. - str.   14:00 Presser.
—— CONCERTO NO. 2 IN D MINOR, FOR VIOLIN AND ORCH.
  2,2,2,2 - 2,2,0,0 - timp.,cymb. - hp. - str.   22:30 Presser.
—— MASCARADE (SUITE) (IN 3 MOVTS.)
  2,3,2,2 - 4,3,3,0 - timp.,perc.,cel. - pf. - str.   7:00 Presser.
  or:
  1,1,1,1 - 1,1,0,0 - timp.,perc. - pf. - str.
—— MYSTÈRE DU CIEL
  *1,*2,*2,0 - 0,0,0,0 - timp.,perc.,cel. - str.   24:10 Presser.
—— PETITE SUITE EN 5 PARTIES
  2,1,2,1 - 2,3,2,0 - timp.,perc.,cel. - hp. - pf. - str.   8:00 Henmar.
—— SUITE FOR STRINGS (IN 4 MOVTS.)
  str.   13:00 F. Colombo.
—— SUITE FUNAMBULESQUE (FOR 12 PERFORMERS)
  1(alt. with picc.),0,0,1 sopr. sax.,1 alto sax.,1 - 0,1,1,1 - timp.,perc.(2),cel.,glock.,vibra.,xyl. - hp. - pf. - d.-b.
                                          7:25 Eds. Fran.

ARRIGO, Girolamo
—— THUMOS (FOR WINDS AND PERCUSSION)
  3,3,4,2 sax.,3 - 4,4,3,1 - perc.(2) - hp. - pf.   14:00 Presser.
—— TRE OCCASIONI (FOR SOPRANO AND ORCH.)
  2,1,2,1 - 2,1,1,1 - perc.(4),bells,cel.,vibra.,xyl. - guit. - hp. - mandolin - pf. - 6 vla.,6 c.,2 d.-b.   14:00 Presser.

ARUTUNIAN, Alexander
—— CONCERTO FOR TRUMPET AND ORCH.
  2,2,2,2 - 4,2,3,1 - timp.,perc. - hp. - str.   13:00 G. Schirmer.

ASCHAFFENBURG, Walter
—— BARTLEBY, OP. 10 (OPERA IN A PROLOUGUE AND TWO ACTS) % (Based on the Story by Herman Melville; Text: Jay Leyda)
  2(2nd alt. with picc.),2,2(2nd.with b.-cl.),2 - 2,2,1,0 - timp.,perc.(2),xyl. - hp. - pf. - str.   85:00 Presser.
—— ELEGY FOR STRINGS, OP. 12 (IN MEMORIAM DAVID ROBERTSON) (1961)
  str.   4:30 Presser.
—— OZYMANDIAS, OP. 5 (SYMPHONIC REFLECTIONS FOR ORCH.) (1952)
  3(3rd alt. with picc.),*3,*3,2 - 4,3,3,1 - timp.,perc.(3) - hp. - str.   13:00 Composer.
—— THREE DANCES FOR ORCHESTRA, OP. 15 (1966)
  *3,3,1 E♭cl.,*3,3(3rd alt. with c.-bn.) - 4,3,3,1 - timp.,perc.(6),glock.,xyl. - hp. - str.   10:45 Presser.

ASCHENBRENNER, Johannes
—— CONCERTO FOR VIOLA AND ORCH.
                                          Sikorski.
—— DIVERTIMENTO FOR STRING ORCH.
  str.   21:00 Modern.
—— DIVERTIMENTO FOR VIOLIN AND ORCH.
                                          R.Eichmann.
—— DIVERTIMENTO FÜR KLAVIER UND KAMMERORCH
  2,1,1,1 - 1,0,0,0 - timp. - hp. - pf. - str.   25:00 H & G.
—— DIVERTIMENTO FÜR STREICHORCHESTER
  1. Largo - Andante; 2. Larghetto; 3. Langsames Menuettempo; 4. Allegro
  str.   21:00 Modern.
—— JAHRMARKTSMUSIK (MUSIC AT A FAIR)
  *2,2,2,2 - 4,3,3,1 - timp.,perc. - str. 12:00 Modern.

—— DAS MAGNETISCHE KARUSSELL (SUITE AUS DEM BALLETT)
*3,2,*3,*3 - 4,3,3,1 - timp.,perc. - rautonium - hp. - hpsc. - pf. - str.　　　　15:00 Modern.

—— SYMPHONY 1953
　　　　R.Eichmann.

—— VIER ORCHESTERSTÜCKE (NACH BILDERN VON PABLO PICASSO)
2,2,2 b.-cl.(ad lib.),2 - 3,2,2,0 - timp.,perc. - hp.(or pf.) - str.　　　　25:00 Modern.

—— WELCOME, MR. TARZAN (SUITE AUS DEM BALLETT)
2(or picc.),2,2(or b.-cl.),*3 - 0,3,3,1 - perc. - pf. - str.　　　　17:00 Modern.

—— ZWEITE FRANZÖSISCHE SUITE (NACH VOLKSLIEDERN AUS FRANKREICH)
1(or picc.),1,1,1 - 3,1,1,0 - timp.,perc. - str.　　　　16:00 Modern.

ASCONE, Vicente
—— CANTOS DEL ATARDECER (SONGS OF EVENTIDE) (SYMPHONIC IMPRESSIONS)
3(3rd alt. with picc.),3,3,1 sopr.sax., 1 alto sax.,4 - 4,3,3,1 - timp.,perc.,cel. - hp. - pf. - str.　　　　14:00 Fleisher.

—— OVERTURA PARA SANTOS VEGA
3,3,3,3 - 3,3,3,1 - timp.,perc.,cel. - hp. - str.　　　　5:00 Southern.

ASHRAFI, Mukaddima
—— DILARAM (4-ACT OPERA) %
　　　　G. Schirmer.

—— SYMPHONY NO. 1
1. Maestoso molto sostenuto - Allegro con brio; 2. Andante cantabile; 3. Allegro vivace
*3,*3,3(3rd alt. with b.-cl.),2 - 4,3,3,1 - timp.,perc.,xyl. - hp. - str.　　　　34:00 G. Schirmer.

—— SYMPHONY NO. 2 (IN 1 MOVT.)
3,3,3,2 - 4,3,3,1 - timp.,perc. - hp. - str.　　　　19:00 Leeds.

ATANACKOVIĆ, Slobodan
—— POEMA ETERICO (FOR FEMALE CHORUS AND ORCH.)
3,0,0,1 - 0,0,0,0 - timp.,perc.,cel.,vibra.,xyl. - pf. - str.　　　　14:00 MIC,Zagreb.

ATTERBERG, Kurt
—— ALLADIN (OPERA) %
　　　　S.T.I.M.

—— ÄLVEN (DER FLUSS), (SYMPHONIC POEM), OP. 33
3,2,2,2 - 4,3,3,1 - timp.,perc. - hp. - str.　　　　22:00 S.T.I.M.

—— BÄCKAHÄSTEN (OPERA) %
　　　　S.T.I.M.

—— BERGSLAGSSERENAD, OP. 23 (SUITE FOR STRING ORCH.)
str.　　　　12:00 Nordiska.

—— CONCERT OVERTURE IN THE POPULAR STYLE, OP. 41
2,2,2,2 - 4,2,3,0 - timp.,perc.,glock. - org.(ad lib.) - str.　　　　11:00 S.T.I.M.
str.
2,1,2,1 - 2,2,2,0 - timp.,perc.,glock. - org.(ad lib.) - str.

—— CONCERT OVERTURE, OP. 4
2,2,2,2 - 2,2,1,0 - timp. - str.　　　　12:00 S.T.I.M.

—— CONCERTO FOR HORN AND ORCH., OP. 28
0,0,0,0 - 1,0,0,0 - perc. - str.　　　　23:00 AMP.

—— CONCERTO FOR VIOLIN, CELLO AND ORCH., OP. 57
2,1,2,1 - 2,0,0,0 - hp.(ad. lib.) - str.　　　　17:00 S.T.I.M.

—— FANAL (OPERA) %
　　　　S.T.I.M.

—— DE FÅVITSKA JUNGFRURNA, (SWEDISH RHAPSODY), OP. 17
2,1,2,1 - 3,0,0,0 - str.　　　　18:00 Gehrmans.

—— FIVE PIECES FROM THE OPERA "ALADDIN", OP. 43
2,2,2,2 - 4,3,3,1 - timp.,perc.(4),cel. - hp.,pf. - str.　　　　S.T.I.M.

—— FYRA NOKTURNER UR "FANAL"
2,2,3,2 - 4,3,3,1 - timp.,perc.(4) - hp. - str.　　　　26:00 S.T.I.M.

—— HÄRVARD HARPOLEKARE, OP. 12 (OPERA) %
　　　　S.T.I.M.

—— INDIAN TUNES, OP. 51 (SYMPHONIC PIECE)
2,2,2,2 - 4,3,3,1 - timp.,perc.(2) - str.　　　　13:00 S.T.I.M.

—— INTERMEZZO (FROM "HÄRVARD HARPOLEKARE") (FOR MEZZO SOPRANO AND ORCH.)
3,3,3,2 - 4,3,3,1 - timp.,perc. - hp. - str.　　　　10:00 S.T.I.M.

—— OVERTURE TO "ALADDIN", OP. 44
2,2,2,2 - 4,2,3,1 - timp.,perc. - str.　　　　6:00 S.T.I.M.
or:
2,2,2,2 - 2,2,2,1 - timp.,perc. - str.

—— PER SVINAHERDE SUITE
2,2,2,2 - 2,2,3,1 - timp.,perc. - hp. - str.　　　　45:00 S.T.I.M.

—— PRELUDE TO ACT TWO OF "FANAL"
3,2,2,2 - 2,2,3,1 - timp.,perc. - str.　　　　4:00 S.T.I.M.

—— PRELUDE TO "HÄRVARD HARPOLEKARE"
3,3,3,2 - 4,3,3,1 - timp.,perc. - hp. - str.　　　　10:00 S.T.I.M.

—— PRELUDE TO "PER SVINAHERDE", OP. 9
2,2,2,2 - 2,2,0,0 - timp. - hp. - str.　　　　9:00 S.T.I.M.

—— PRELUDE TO THE DRAMA "PERSEUS"
2,1,2,1 - 2,2,0,0 - timp. - str.　　　　5:00 S.T.I.M.

—— RHAPSODY FOR PIANO AND ORCH., OP. 1
2,2,2,2 - 4,2,3,1 - timp.,perc. - pf. - str.　　　　S.T.I.M.

—— RONDEAU - OUVERTURE, OP. 55 (PA MELODIER AV BIRGER SJÖBERG)
2,2,2,2 - 2,2,0,0 - str.　　　　4:00 S.T.I.M.

—— RONDEAU CARACTERISTIQUE, OP. 42
3,2,2,2 - 2,2,3,1 - timp.,perc. - hp. - str.　　　　11:00 S.T.I.M.

—— RONDEAU-RÉTROSPECTIF, OP. 26
3,2,2,2 - 4,2,3,1 - timp.,perc. - hp. - str.　　　　12:00 S.T.I.M.

—— SÅNGEN (DER BARDE) (SYMPHONIC POEM), OP. 25
2,2,2,2 - 2,2,0,0 - timp.,perc. - pf. - str.　　　　22:00 S.T.I.M.

—— SÅNGENS LAND (SYMPHONIC POEM), OP. 32
1,1,2,1 - 2,2,1,0 - timp. - hp. - str.　　　　6:00 S.T.I.M.

—— SINFONIA VISIONARIA, OP. 54 (FOR ALTO OR BARITONE SOLO, MIXED CHORUS AND ORCH.)
3,2,2,2 - 4,3,3,1 - timp.,perc.(3) - hp. - pf.(or org.) - str.　　　　36:00 S.T.I.M.

—— STORMEN (OPERA) %
　　　　S.T.I.M.

—— STORMEN SUITE
2,1,2,1 - 2,2,2,0 - timp.,perc. - pf. - str.　　　　22.00 S.T.I.M.

—— SUITE NO. 1 (ORIENTAL SUITE)
1,1,2,1 - 2,2,1,0 - timp.,perc. - hp. - pf. - str.　　　　11:00 S.T.I.M.

—— SUITE NO. 2 ("MATS OCH PETTER")
1,0,1,0 - 0,0,0,0 - str.　　　　9:00 Nordiska.

—— SUITE NO. 6 (ORIENTAL LEGEND), OP. 30
1,1,1,0 - 0,0,0,0 - perc. - pf. - str.　　　　22:00 S.T.I.M.

—— SUITE NO. 9 (SUITE DRAMMATICA), OP. 47
1,1,1,0 - 0,2,1,0 - timp. - pf. - str.　　　　16:00 S.T.I.M.

—— SYMPHONY NO. 1 IN B MINOR, OP. 3
3,2,2,2 - 4,3,3,1 - timp.,perc. - pf. - str.　　　　41:00 AMP.

—— SYMPHONY NO. 2 IN F MAJOR, OP. 6 (1913)
3,2,2,2 - 4,2,3,1 - timp.,perc. - pf. - str.　　　　40:00 Nordiska.

—— SYMPHONY NO. 7 (SINFONIA ROMANTICA), OP. 45
2,2,2,2 - 4,3,3,1 - timp.,perc. - hp. - str.　　　　47:00 S.T.I.M.

—— SYMPHONY NO. 8 (PA SVENSKA FOLKMOTIV), OP. 48
2,1,2,1 - 2,2,1,0 - timp. - str.　　　　36:00 S.T.I.M.

—— SYMPHONY NO. 9, OP. 54 (1956)
2,2,2,2 - 4,3,3,2 - timp.,perc.(2) - hp. - str.　　　　36:00 S.T.I.M.

—— THREE DANCES FOR ORCHESTRA
2,2,2,2 - 2,2,3,1 - timp.,perc. - hp. - str.　　　　12:00 S.T.I.M.

—— VITTORIOSO, OP. 58 (1962)
2,2,2,2 - 4,3,3,1 - timp.,perc.(2) - hp. - str.　　　　12:00 S.T.I.M.

—— THE WISE AND FOOLISH VIRGINS
2,2,2,2 - 3,0,0,0 - str.　　　　18:00 Bo. Hawkes.

AUBE, Lucien-Marie
—— PETITE SUITE "1830"
2,2,2,2 - 2,2,3,0 - timp.,perc. - hp. - str.　　　　11:00 Henmar.

AUBER - WINTER, Aubrey
—— OVERTURE TO "FRA DIAVOLO"
　　　　Bo. Hawkes.

—— OVERTURE TO "MASANIELLO" ("LA MUETTE DE PORTICI")
　　　　8:00 Bo. Hawkes.

—— OVERTURE TO "THE BRONZE HORSE"
　　　　7:30 Bo. Hawkes.

—— OVERTURE TO "THE CROWN DIAMONDS"
　　　　7:00 Bo. Hawkes.

—— OVERTURE TO "ZANETTA"
　　　　8:00 Bo. Hawkes.

AUBERT, Louis
—— CAPRICE FOR VIOLIN AND ORCH.
2,2,2,2 - 2,2,0,0 - timp.,perc. - str.　　　　6:30 EV.

—— CINEMA (TABLEAUX SYMPHONIQUES) (IN 6 MOVTS.)
3,*3,3, alto sax.,3 - 4,3,3,1 - timp.,perc.,cel. - 2 hp. - str.　　　　25:00 EV.

—— FANTASIE IN B MINOR (FOR PIANO AND ORCH.), OP. 8
2,2,2,2 - 4,2,3,1 - timp. - str.　　　　EV.

—— FEUILLE D'IMAGES (5 PIÈCES ENFANTINES)
　　　　12:00 EV.

—— LA FORÊT BLEUE (THE BLUE FOREST) (OPERA) %
2,*3,2,3 - 4,3,3,1 - timp.,perc.,cel. - 2 hp. - str.　　　　EV.

—— HABANERA
    3,3,3,2,sar.(or c.-bn.) - 4,3,3,0 - timp.,perc. - 2 hps. - str.
          12:00 EV.
—— OFFRANDE
    2,*3,2,2 - 4,3,3,0 - timp.,perc. - str.   7:00 EV.
—— SAISONS (FOR MEZZO SOPRANO SOLO, MIXED CHORUS
    AND ORCH.)
    2,2,2,2 - 4,3,3,1 - timp.,perc. - hp. - org. - str. 18:00 EV.
—— SUITE BRÈVE, OP. 6
    2,2,2,2 - 4,2,3,1 - timp.,perc.(4) - hp. - str. 10:00 EV.
—— LE TOMBEAU DE CHATEAUBRIAND
    3,*3,3,3 - 4,3,3,1 - timp.,perc.,cel. - 2 hp. - str. 14:00 EV.

AUBERT, Louis Jaques - BOULAY, L.
—— SYMPHONY NO. 1 FOR STRINGS
    str.   11:30 Bo. Hawkes.

AUBIN, Tony
—— LA CHASSE DU CHEVALIER PÉCOPIN
          12:00 Baron.
—— LES DEMOISELLES DE LA SEINE (SUITE FROM THE
    BALLET "AU FIL DE L'EAU")
    2,2,2,3 - 2,2,2,1 - timp.,perc.,cel. - hp. - str. 16:00 Presser.
—— FRANÇOIS VILLON
          17:00 Henmar.
—— LA JOCONDE
    2,2,2,2 - 2,2,3,1 - timp.,perc.(3),cel. - hp. - str. 7:25 Presser.
—— SUITE DANOISE (IN 4 MOVTS.)
    2,2,2,2 - 2,2,1,1 - timp.,perc. - pf. - str. 14:00 Baron.
—— SUITE ÉOLIENNE (IN 4 MOVTS.)
    1,0,1,0 - 0,0,0,0 - str.   20:00 Baron.
—— SYMPHONY NO. 2
    2(2nd alt. with picc.),2,2,2 - 2,2,3,1 - timp.,perc. - hp. - str.
          50:00 Baron.

AUCLERT, Pierre
—— CONCERTO FOR PIANO AND ORCH.
    3,3,2,2 - 4,2,0,0 - timp.,perc.,cel. - pf. - str. 16:00 Baron.
—— QUATRE AIRS À DANSER
    3,2,2,2 - 2,2,0,0 - timp.,perc. - hp. - str. 14:00 Presser.

AURIC, Georges
—— LA CHAMBRE (SYMPHONIC SUITE FROM THE BALLET)
    2,1,2,1 - 2,2,1,1 - timp.,perc. - pf. - str. 18:00 F. Colombo.
—— LES ENCHANTEMENTS D'ALCINE (MUSIC FROM THE
    BALLET)
    3,3,2,2 - 4,3,4,0 - timp.,perc.(3),cel. - 2 hp. - pf. - str.
          30:00 Presser.
—— LES FÂCHEAUX (BALLET AFTER THE COMEDY BY
    MOLIERE) %
    3,3,3,3 - 4,3,3,1 - timp.,perc.,xyl. - hp. - str. 26:00 Salabert.
—— LE MARIAGE DE LA TROUHADEC
    1,1,1,1 - 1,1,0,0 - pf. - str. 19:30 Presser.
—— LES MATELOTS (THE SAILORS) (BALLET) %
    *3,*3,*3,4 - 4,4,3,1 - timp.,perc. (2),xyl.,cel. - 2 hp. - str. Mercury.
—— MUSICAL CHAIRS (SYMPHONIC SUITE FROM THE
    BALLET)
    2,1,2,1 - 2,2,1,0 - perc. - hp. - pf. - str. 17:00 F. Colombo.
—— OUVERTURE ET RITOURNELLE (FROM "LES MARIÉS DE
    LA TOUR EIFFEL")
    2,2,2,2 - 4,3,3,1 - timp.,perc. - hp. - str. 5:15 Salabert.
—— OVERTURE
    2 picc.,2,*3,3,3 - 4,3,3,1 - timp.,perc.,cel. - 2 hp. - str. 8:00 Leeds.
—— LA PASTORALE (MUSIC FROM THE BALLET)
    3,3,2(2nd alt. with. E♭cl.),0 - 3,4,4,4 - timp.,perc.,cel. - 2 hp. - str.
          40:00 Presser.
—— LE PEINTRE ET SON MODÈLE (BALLET SUITE)
    2,2,2,2 - 2,2,1,0 - timp.,perc. - pf. - str. 15:00 Salabert.
—— PHÈDRE (BALLET SUITE)
    3,3,3,3 - 4,4,3,1 - timp.,perc. (2),cel.,vibra.,xyl. - 2 hp. - str.
          20:00 Salabert.
—— QUATRE CHANTS DE LA FRANCE MALHEUREUSE (FOR
    MEZZO-SOPRANO AND ORCH.)
    3,3,3,3 - 4,3,3,1 - timp.,perc.(7) - 2 hp. - str. 13:00 Salabert.
—— QUATRE CHANTS DE LA FRANCE MALHEUREUSE (FOR
    MEZZO-SOPRANO AND ORCH.) (Texts: Louis Aragon, Jules
    Supervielle)
    3,3,3,3 - 4,3,3,1 - timp.,perc.(6) - 2 hp. - str. 12:30 Salabert.

AUSTIN, Ernest
—— VICAR OF BRAY VARIATIONS, OP. 35
    str.   18:00 Novello.

AUSTIN, Frederick
—— PALSGAARD (4 DANISH SKETCHES)
    3(3rd alt. with picc.),*3,2,2 - 4,2,3,1 - timp.,perc. - hp. - pf. - str.
          14:00 G. Schirmer.
—— PRELUDE FOR A CHURCH FESTIVAL
    timp. - org. - str.   8:00 Bo. Hawkes.
—— THE SEA VENTURES (OVERTURE)
    3,3,3,2 - 4,3,3,1 - timp.,perc.,cel. - 1-2 hp. - str.
          10:00 Bo. Hawkes.
—— SPRING (SYMPHONIC RHAPSODY)
    3,3,3,2 - 4,3,3,1 - timp.,perc. - hp. - str. 12:30 Bo. Hawkes.

AUSTIN, Richard R.
—— D'URFREY'S PILLS (1968)
    2,2,2,2 - 4,4,2,1 - timp.,perc. - str. 15:00 P.R.S.
—— LECLAD DANCES (1967)
    2,2,2,3 - 4,2,2,2 - timp.,perc. - str. 11:00 P.R.S.

AUSTIN PHILLIPS, Eric
—— THE COMET VENUS (1973)
    2,2,2,2 - 4,3,3,1 - timp.,perc.(3) - hp. - str. 9:00 A,P,R,A.
—— THE HOBBISON SUITE (1972)
    perc.(2) - 2 hp. - str.   10:00 A.P.R.A.
—— VARIATIONS AND FUGUE (1968)
    2,2,2,2 - 4,2,3,0 - timp.,perc.(3) - str. 26:00 A.P.R.A.

AVIDOM, Menahem
—— ALEXANDRA (OPERA IN 3 ACTS AND 6 SCENES) % (Text:
    Aharon Ashman)
    3,3,3,3 - 4,3,3,1 - timp.,perc. - hp. - pf. - str. 120:00 Bo. Hawkes.
—— ALEXANDRA (3-ACT OPERA) %
    2,2,2,2 - 2,2,3,7 - timp.,perc. - str. 120:00 Bo. Hawkes.
—— CONCERTO FOR FLUTE AND STRINGS
    fl.,str.   16:00 IsMuPublns.
—— THE CROOK (COMIC OPERA IN 2 ACTS AND 5 SCENES)
    (FOR SSATBB SOLO VOICES AND CHAMBER ORCH.) (Text:
    E. Kishon)
    1,1,1,1 - 1,0,0,0 - perc. - pf. - str. 70:00 A.C.U.M.
—— A FESTIVAL SINFONIETTA (SYMPHONY NO. 8)
    2,2,2,2 - 4,2,3,1 - timp.,perc. - str. 20:00 A.C.U.M.
—— IN EVERY GENERATION (3-PART OPERA) %
          90:00 A.C.U.M.
—— JUBILEE SUITE
          20:00 A.C.U.M.
—— MEDITERRANEAN SINFONIETTA
    2,2,2,2 - 4,2,3,1 - timp.,perc. - hp. - pf. - str. 16:00 IsMuPublns.
—— MUSIC FOR STRINGS
    str.   22:00 IsMuPublns.
—— SUITE 1962, ON THE NAME OF "B-A-C-H"
    1,1,1,1 - 0,0,0,0 - gong,vibra.,xyl. - pf. - str. 18:00 IsMuPublns.
—— SYMPHONY NO. 1 (SYMPHONIE POPULAIRE)
    1,1,1,1 - 2,2,1,0 - timp.,perc. - str. 18:00 IsMuPublns.
—— SYMPHONY NO. 2 ("DAVID")
    3,3,3,3 - 4,3,3,1 - timp.,perc.,cel.,xyl. - hp. - pf. - str.
          27:00 IsMuPublns.
—— SYMPHONY NO. 4
    2(2nd alt. with picc.),2(2nd alt. with Eng.hn.),2,2 - 4,2,3,1 -
    timp.,perc.,cel. - hp. - pf. - str. 20:00 Mills.
—— SYMPHONY NO. 5 ("THE SONG OF EILAT") (WITH
    MEZZO-SOPRANO OR BARITONE)
    2,2,2,2 - 4,2,3,1 - timp.,perc. - str. 28:00 IsMuPublns.
—— SYMPHONY NO. 6
    2,*3,2,2 - 4,2,3,1 - timp.,perc.,cel. - hp. - pf. - str.
          24:00 IsMuPublns.
—— SYMPHONY NO. 7 ("THE PHILHARMONIC")
    2(2nd alt. with picc.),2,2,2 - 4,2,3,1 - timp.,perc.,cel. - pf. - str.
          20:00 Mills.
—— TRIPTYQUE SYMPHONIQUE
          15:00 A.C.U.M.

AVISON, Charles - BOWIE
—— CONCERTO IN A, OP. 9, NO. 2
    cemb. - str.   Oxford.

AVISON, Charles - MILNER, Arthur
—— CONCERTO GROSSO NO. 1 IN G MINOR (FOR STRING
    ORCH.)
    str.   Oxford.
—— CONCERTO GROSSO NO. 13 IN D (FOR STRING ORCH.)
    str.   Oxford.

AVISON, Charles - WARLOCK, Peter
—— CONCERTO IN E MINOR (FOR STRING ORCH.)
    str.   7:00 Galaxy.

AVNI, Tzvi
—— MEDITATIONS ON A DRAMA
    2,1,1,1 - 1,0,0,0, - perc. - pf. - str.   14:00 A.C.U.M.
—— TEFILA (PRAYER) (FOR STRING ORCH.)
    str.   9:00 Mills.

AVRAMOVSKI, Risto
—— BIBLIOFONIJA
    3,3,3,3 - 4,3,3,1 - timp.,perc. - hp. - pf. - str.   12:00 S.O.K.O.J.
—— PSIHOFONIJA I
    1,1,1,1 - 1,1,1,1 - timp.,perc. - tape-recorder - pf. - str. S.O.K.O.J.
—— VARIATIONS
    1(alt. with picc.),1,1,1 - 2,1,1,0 - timp.,perc.,cel. - hp. - pf. - str.   25:00 S.O.K.O.J.

AVSHALMOV, Aaron
—— CONCERTO FOR FLUTE AND ORCH.
    1,2,2,2 - 2,2,3,1 - timp.,perc. - hp. - str.   15:00 Ricordi.
—— CONCERTO IN D FOR VIOLIN AND ORCH. (ON CHINESE THEMES)
    2,2,2,1 - 2,2,0,0 - timp.,perc.,cel. - hp. - str.   30.00 Ricordi.
—— CONCERTO IN G FOR PIANO AND ORCH.
    3,2,2,2 - 4,3,2,1 - timp.,perc.,cel.,xyl. - hp. - pf. - str.
                                   32:00 Ricordi.
—— PEIPING HUTUNGS (TONE POEM ON CHINESE STREET CRIES)
    3,3,4,3 - 4,3,3,1 - perc.,cel.,xyl. - hp. - pf. - str.   12:00 Ricordi.
—— SOUL OF THE CHI'N (SUITE FROM THE BALLET "KINSEI")
    2,2,2,2 - 4,3,3,1 - timp.,perc.,xyl. - hp. - str.   30:00 Ricordi.
—— SYMPHONY NO. 1 IN C
    3,3,2,2 - 4,3,3,1 - timp.,perc.,cel.,xyl. - hp. - pf. - str.
                                   36:00 Ricordi.
—— SYMPHONY NO. 2 IN E
    3,3,3,3 - 4,3,3,1 - timp.,perc.,cel. - hp. - pf. - str.   34:00 Ricordi.
—— SYMPHONY NO. 3 IN B
    3,3,3,3 - 4,3,3,1 - timp.,perc.,cel. - hp. - pf. - str.   26:00 Ricordi.

AXMAN, Emil
—— MORAVIAN DANCES: SUITE NO. 1
    2,2,2,2 - 2,2,1,0 - timp.,perc. - pf. - str.   18:00 Bo. Hawkes.
—— MORAVIAN DANCES: SUITE NO. 2
    2,2,2,2 - 2,2,1,0 - timp.,perc. - pf. - str.   17:00 Bo. Hawkes.

B

BAAREN, Kees van
—— CONCERTINO FOR PIANO AND ORCH.
    1,1,1,sax,0 - 1,0,0,0 - pf. - str.   13:00 Henmar.
—— CONCERTO FOR PIANO AND ORCH. (1964)
                                    13:00 Henmar.
—— THE HOLLOW MAN (FOR SOLOISTS, CHOIR AND ORCH.)
                                      Henmar.
—— MUSICA PER ORCHESTRA
    3,3,3,3 - 4,3,3,1 - timp.,perc.,cel. - hp. - pf. - str.   18:00 Henmar.
—— MUSICA PER ORCHESTRA (1966)
    1. Lento non troppo; 2. Sostenuto
                                    17:00 Henmar.
—— SINFONIA (1957)
    2,2,2,2 - 2,2,0,0 - timp. - str.   16:00 Henmar.
—— VARIAZIONI PER ORCHESTRA (1959)
    3,2,2,2 - 3,4,3,1 - timp.,cel.,vibra.,xyl. - pf. - str.   8:00 Henmar.

BABADZHANJAN, Arno
—— CONCERTO FOR CELLO AND ORCH.
    3,2,3,2 - 4,1,0,0 - timp.,perc.,cel. - pf. - str.   18:00 G. Schirmer.
—— HEROIC BALLAD (SYMPHONIC VARIATIONS FOR PIANO AND ORCH.)
    3,2,3,2 - 4,3,3,1 - cel.,xyl. - str.   21:00 G. Schirmer.

BABIĆ, Konstantin
—— PRELUDE
    2(2nd alt. with picc.),2(2nd alt. with Eng.hn.),2(2nd alt. with b.-cl.),2(2nd alt. with c.-bn.) - 4,3,3,1 - timp.,perc.,xyl. - hp. - str.
                                  10:00 MIC,Zagreb.

—— TRILLING
    2(2nd alt. with picc.),2(2nd alt. with Eng.hn.),2(2nd alt. with b.-cl.),2(2nd alt. with c.-bn.) - 4,3,3,1 - timp.,perc.,xyl. - hp. - str.
                                  8:00 MIC,Zagreb.

BABIN, Stanley
—— CONCERTO FOR PIANO AND ORCH. (IN 3 MOVTS.)
    *3,*3,0,*3 - 4,3,3,0 - timp.,perc.(3) - pf. - str. 21:00 MCA Music.

BABIN, Victor
—— ARIA AND CAPRICCIO
    *3,2,*3,2 - 2,3,1,0 - timp.,perc. (3),xyl. - hp. - str. 8:30 Composer.
—— CAPRICCIO FOR ORCHESTRA
    *3,*3,*3,*3 - 4,3,3,1 - timp. - hp. - str.   13:00 Bo. Hawkes.
—— CONCERT PIECE FOR VIOLIN AND ORCH. (IN 1 MOVT.)
    2,2,*3,2 - 4,0,0,0 - 1 timp. - str.   15:30 Composer.
—— CONCERTO DA CAMERA (1965) (IN 4 MOVTS.)
    pf.4-hands - str.   29:00 Composer.
—— CONCERTO FOR TWO PIANOS AND ORCH.
    1. Allegro con fuoco; 2. Passacaglia; 3. Intermezzo; 4. Rondo (Presto)
    2,2,2,2 - 4,2,3,1 - timp.,perc. (2) - 2pf. - str.   29:00 Composer.
—— CONCERTO NO. 2 FOR TWO PIANOS AND ORCH. (IN 4 MOVEMENTS)
    2,(2nd alt. with picc.),2,2,2(2nd alt. with c.-bn.) - 4,2,3,1 - timp.,perc. (3) - 2pf. - str.   23:00 Composer.

BABITS, Linda
—— WESTERN STAR (CONCERTO FOR PIANO AND ORCH.)
    *4,*3,*3,*3 - 4,3,2,1 - timp.,perc.(2) - pf. - str.   16:00 Mills.

BACARISSE, Salvador
—— CONCERTINO FOR HARP AND STRINGS
    hp. - str.   13:00 Salabert.
—— LE SANG D' ANTIGONE (THE BLOOD OF ANTIGONE) (OPERA) %
    3,3,3,3 - 4,3,3,1 - timp.,perc. - hp. - pf. - org. - str.   Salabert.
—— TRES MARCHAS BURLESCAS
    3,2,2,2 - 2,2,2,0 - timp.,perc. - str.   8:00 Salabert.

BACH, Carl Philipp Emanuel - CASADESUS, H.
—— CONCERTO FOR VIOLIN AND ORCH. (IN 3 MOVEMENTS)
    2,2,0,2 - 2hn. - str.   12:00 G. Schirmer.
—— SUITE FOR STRING ORCH. (WITH OPTIONAL DOUBLE BASSES) (IN 3 MOVEMENTS)
    str.(d-b ad lib.)   12:00 G. Schirmer.

BACH, Carl Philipp Emanuel - DUBENSKY, A.
—— LA COMPLAISANTE (FOR STRING ORCH.)
    str.   Ricordi.

BACH, Carl Philipp Emanuel - EDEL, Oliver
—— CONCERTO NO. 2 IN B FLAT MAJOR, FOR CELLO AND STRING ORCH.
    cemb. - str.   Fema.

BACH, Carl Philipp Emanuel - JACOBI, Erwin R.
—— DOUBLE CONCERTO IN E FLAT MAJOR (FOR HARPSICHORD, PIANO AND ORCH.)
    2,0,0,0 - 2,0,0,0 - hpsc. - pf. - str.   18:00 G. Schirmer.

BACH, Carl Philipp Emanuel - LANDSHOFF
—— CONCERTO IN D MAJOR FOR CEMBALO AND SMALL ORCH.
    2,0,0,0 - 2,0,0,0 - cemb. - str.   Henmar.
—— CONCERTO IN D MAJOR FOR HARPSICHORD (OR PIANO) AND CHAMBER ORCH.
    2 fl. - hpsc.(or pf.) - str.   15:00 Henmar.

BACH, Carl Philipp Emanuel - LAUSCHMANN
—— CONCERTO NO. 1 IN B FLAT MAJOR, FOR OBOE, CEMBALO AND STRINGS
    ob. - cemb. - str.   Henmar.

BACH, Carl Philipp Emanuel - OBERDOERFFER
—— SINFONIA IN C MAJOR (POTSDAM, 1755)
    2 fl. - 2 hn. - cemb. - str.   Henmar.

BACH, Carl Philipp Emanuel - POLLAIN, F.
—— CONCERTO NO. 3 IN A MAJOR FOR CELLO AND STRING ORCH. (IN 3 MOVEMENTS)
    str.   13:00 Salabert.

BACH, Carl Philipp Emanuel - SCHMID, Ernst Fritz
—— SINFONIA IN B MAJOR
    cemb. - str.   10:00 G. Schirmer.
—— SINFONIA NO. 3 IN C MAJOR
                        Nagel.

BACH, Carl Philipp Emanuel - STEINBERG, Maximilian
—— CONCERTO IN D
    1,3,0,1 - 1,0,0,0 - str.   14:00 Bo. Hawkes.

BACH, Carl Philipp Emanuel - WENZIGER, August
—— SINFONIA IN D MAJOR
    2,2,0,0 - 2,3,0,0 - timp. - cemb. - str.   12:00 G. Schirmer.
—— SINFONIA IN E FLAT MAJOR
    0,2,0,1 - 2,0,0,0 - str.   15:00 G. Schirmer.

BACH, Erik
—— THE BALLAD OF THE BLACK SORROW, OP. 15-B
    fl. - str.   11:00 K.O.D.A.
—— FESTIVAS AROSIENSIS, OP. 19 (OVERTURE)
    3 tpt.,4 cnt.,3 trb.,1 tu. - perc.   10:00 K.O.D.A.
—— PROFILE
                    16:00 K.O.D.A.
—— RÉFLEXIONS DES PRÉLUDES, OP. 13 (FOR CLARINET AND
CHAMBER ORCH.)
                    19:00 K.O.D.A.
—— SYMPHONY, OP. 12 ("TEMPTATIONS IN FOREIGN
LANDSCAPES") (IN 1 MOVT.)
                    24:00 K.O.D.A.
—— VIKINGS, OP. 22 (FOR MALE CHORUS AND
INSTRUMENTAL ENSEMBLE)
                    10:00 K.O.D.A.

BACH, Jan
—— BURGUNDY VARIATIONS (ON A 16TH-CENTURY FOLK
TUNE) (1968)
    *3,*3,*3,2 - 4,3,3,1 - timp.,perc.(4) - pf. - str. 17:00 Composer.
—— TOCCATA FOR ORCHESTRA (1959)
    *3,2,2,2 - 4,3,3,1 - timp.,perc.(5) - str. 13:00 Composer.

BACH, Johann Christian - BEVERIDGE, Lowell P.
—— THE CHILDHOOD OF CHRIST (FOR SATB CHORUS AND
CHAMBER ORCH.)
    2,0,0,0 - 2,0,0,0 - org. - str.   Belw-Mills.

BACH, Johann Christian - BODART, Eugen
—— OVERTURE IN D MAJOR
    0,2,0,0 - 2,0,0,0 - str.   11:00 Mannheimer.

BACH, Johann Christian - CARSE, A.
—— OVERTURE IN B♭
    2,2,0,2 - 2tpt. - timp. - str.   5:00 Galaxy.
—— SYMPHONY IN B♭, OP. 21, NO. 3 (IN 3 MOVEMENTS)
    2ob. - 2hn. - pf. - str.   8:00 Galaxy.

BACH, Johann Christian - CARSE, Adam
—— CONCERTO, OP. 13, NO. 2, FOR CEMBALO AND ORCH.
    cemb. - str.   14:00 Galaxy.
    or:
    0,2,0,0 - 2,0,0,0 - cemb. - str.
    or:
    2,0,0,0 - 2,0,0,0 - cemb. - str.

BACH, Johann Christian - CASADESUS, Henri - CASADESUS, Francis
—— CONCERTO IN C MINOR (FOR VIOLIN, VIOLA OR CELLO
AND ORCH.) (IN 3 MOVEMENTS)
    2,2,0,2 - 2,2,0,0 - timp. - str.   15:00 Salabert.
    or:
    fl., ob. - str.

BACH, Johann Christian - HOFMANN, Wolfgang
—— CONCERTO FOR PIANO AND ORCH., OP. 12, NO. 3
    2,0,0,0 - 2,0,0,0 - pf. - str.   13:00 Mannheimer.

BACH, Johann Christian - KNEUSSLIN
—— SINFONIA IN B FLAT MAJOR, OP. 3, NO. 4
    2 ob. (or 2 fl.) - 2 hn. - str.   13:00 Henmar.

BACH, Johann Christian - ORMANDY, Eugene
—— SINFONIA IN D MAJOR, OP. 18, NO. 3, FOR DOUBLE ORCH.
    2,2,2,2 - 2,0,0,0 - str.   13:30 Arranger.

BACH, Johann Christian - TALMADGE, Arthur S.
—— THE CHILDHOOD OF CHRIST (FOR SSA OR SSAA CHORUS
AND CHAMBER ORCH.)
    2,0,0,0 - 2,0,0,0 - org. - str.   Belw-Mills.

BACH, Johann Christian - WARRACK, Guy
—— OVERTURE TO "ORIONE"
    2,2(or 2Eng. hns.),2,2(ad lib.) - 2,0,0,0 - str. 10:00 Oxford.

BACH, Johann Christian - WOJCIECHOWSKI, Johann
—— CONCERTO IN B FLAT MAJOR, FOR BASSOON AND ORCH.
    0,2,0,1 - 0,0,0,0 - str.   F. Colombo.
—— CONCERTO IN E FLAT MAJOR, FOR BASSOON AND ORCH.
    0,2,0,1 - 2,0,0,0 - str.   F. Colombo.

BACH, Johann Christian - WURTZLER, Aristid von
—— CONCERTO IN D MAJOR ("GOD SAVE THE KING") FOR
HARP AND STRING ORCH. (ARR. 1967) (With original cadenza
by A. von Wurtzler) (IN 3 MOVTS.)
    hp. - str.   10:30 Lyra.

BACH, Johann Sebastian
—— THE PASSION ACCORDING TO ST. JOHN (Engl. Text: Robert
Shaw)
                    Law-Gould.
—— THE PASSION OF OUR LORD ACCORDING TO ST.
MATTHEW (Engl. Text: Robert Shaw)
                    G. Schirmer.

BACH, Johann Sebastian - ABBADO, Marcello
—— CIACCONA (FROM SOLO VIOLIN PARTITA NO. 2)
    str.   15:00 Leeds.

BACH, Johann Sebastian - ABERT, J. J. - DASCH, George
—— PRELUDE, CHORALE AND FUGUE
                    C. Fischer.

BACH, Johann Sebastian - ADLER, Samuel
—— PRELUDE, CHORALE AND FUGUE (FOR 32 CELLOS)
    32 c.   13:00 Arranger.

BACH, Johann Sebastian - AKON, Alfred
—— PRELUDE AND FUGUE IN A MINOR (ORIGINALLY FOR
ORGAN)
    3,3,3,3 - 4,3,3,1 - timp. - str.   10:00 Belw-Mills.

BACH, Johann Sebastian - ATKINS, Ivor - DIACK, J. Michael
—— PSALM 121 (FOR SATB CHORUS AND ORCH.)
    2,2,0,1 - 0,3,0,0 - timp. - str.   C. Fischer.

BACH, Johann Sebastian - BAKER, Harry Edgar
—— THE PEASANT CANTATA (FOR SOLO VOICES, SATB
CHORUS AND ORCH.) (Engl. Text: J. Michael Diack)
    1,1,1,1 - 0,0,0,0 - str.   45:00 C. Fischer.
    Or
    1,1,1,1 - 1,1,1,0 - timp., - str.

BACH, Johann Sebastian - BALES, Richard
—— FUGUE IN D MAJOR (FROM "WELL-TEMPERED
CLAVICHORD")
    *3,2,2,2 - 4,3,3,1 - timp.,perc. (2) - str.   Arranger.

BACH, Johann Sebastian - BANTOCK, Granville
—— SHEEP MAY SAFELY GRAZE
    pf.(ad lib.) - str.   6:00 Mills.

BACH, Johann Sebastian - BARBIROLLI, John
—— CHORALE PRELUDE: "WENN WIR IN HÖCHSTEN NÖTEN
SEIN" (IN OUR HOUR OF DEEPEST NEED)
    4 hn., tpt. - str.(no vlns.)   Oxford.
—— SHEEP MAY SAFELY GRAZE
    4 fl.,2 Eng. hn.,2 bn. - str.   4:30 Oxford.

BACH, Johann Sebastian - BAUER, Harold
—— CONCERTO NO. 2 IN C MAJOR, FOR 3 PIANOS AND
STRING ORCH.
    3 pf. - str.   G. Schirmer.

BACH, Johann Sebastian - BAUMGARTNER, Rudolf
—— CONCERTO IN D MAJOR, FOR 3 VIOLINS AND STRING
ORCH.
    str.   Hug.

BACH, Johann Sebastian - BECKETT, W.
—— TOCCATA AND FUGUE IN D MINOR
    *3,2,2,2 - 4,2,3,1 - timp.,perc. (2) - str.   8:00 Oxford.

BACH, Johann Sebastian - BEN-HAIM, Paul
—— CHORALE PRELUDE: "VOR DEINEM THRON TRET' ICH
HIERMIT"
    1,*2,1,0 - 1,1,1,0 - cel.,glock. - hp. - str.   4:00 IsMuPublns.

BACH, Johann Sebastian - BERKOWITZ, R.
—— CAPRICCIO ON THE DEPARTURE OF A BELOVED
BROTHER
    2,2,2,2 - 2,2,0,0 - timp. - str.   11:00 EV.
—— TOCCATA IN C MINOR (ARR. 1948)
    2,2,2,*3 - 4,2,3,0 - timp. - str.   12:00 Arranger.
—— TOCCATA IN E MINOR (ARR. 1950)
    2,2,*3,2 - 4,2,3,0 - timp. - str.   10:00 Arranger.

BACH, Johann Sebastian - BIGGS, E. Power
—— SHEEP MAY SAFELY GRAZE (FOR ORGAN AND STRINGS,
WITH 2 FLUTES AD LIB)
    2 fl.(ad lib) - org. - str.   5:00 Gray.

BACH, Johann Sebastian - BLACK, Norman
—— SARABANDE AND BOURRÉE (FROM PARTITA NO. 1 IN B
MINOR)
    str.   9:00 C. Fischer.

BACH, Johann Sebastian - BLOOMFIELD, T.
—— TOCCATA AND FUGUE IN C
    *3,3,3,*3 - 4,3,3,1 - timp.,perc. - str.   16:00 Hargail.

BACH, Johann Sebastian - BOESSENROTH, H.
—— CHORALE PRELUDE: "WIR GLAUBEN ALL' AN EINEN
GOTT"
    3,3,3,3 - 4,4,2,1 - timp. - org. (ad lib) - str.   3:00 EV.
—— PASSACAGLIA AND FUGUE IN C MINOR
    3,3,3,3 - 4,4,3,1 - timp.,perc. - hp. - str.   13:00 EV.
—— PRELUDE (FROM VIOLIN SONATA NO. 6)
    3,3,3,3 - 4,3,3,1 - timp. - hp. - str.   3:00 EV.

BACH, Johann Sebastian - BOUTNIKOFF, Ivan
—— FANTASIA AND FUGUE IN G MINOR
    *3,*3,*3,*3 - 4,2,3,1 - timp. - str.   12:00 Arranger.
—— PRELUDE AND FUGUE IN A MINOR
    *4,*4,*4,*4, - 4,3,3,1 - timp. - str.   9:00 Arranger.
—— PRELUDE AND FUGUE IN G MINOR
    *3,*3,*3,*3 - 4,2,3,1 - timp.,perc.(2),glock. - 2 hp. - str.
    8:00 Arranger.

BACH, Johann Sebastian - BRANT, Henry
—— AUS TIEFER NOT SCHREI ICH ZU DIR
    4,2,0,4 - 4,1,0,0   8:00 C. Fischer.
—— KYRIE GOTT, HEILIGER GEIST
    4,0,4,2 - 0,3,3,2 bar.,1 - timp. - pf.   6:00 C. Fischer.

BACH, Johann Sebastian - BROWN, James
—— SONATA IN G (FOR STRING ORCH.)
    str.   Galaxy.
—— TWO SONATAS
    str.   Galaxy.

BACH, Johann Sebastian - BRUSSELS, Iris
—— THREE DANCES
    str.   7:00 Arranger.

BACH, Johann Sebastian - BUSONI - STEINBERG, M
—— CHACONNE (FROM THE SECOND VIOLIN PARTITA)
    2,2(2nd alt. with Eng. hn.),2,2 - 4,2,3,1 - timp. - str.
    13:00 Bo. Hawkes.

BACH, Johann Sebastian - CAILLIET, Lucien
—— CHORALE: "HERZLICH THUT MICH VERLANGEN"
    2,*3,*3,3sax.(ad lib.),*3 - 4,3,3,1 - timp. - pf.(ad lib) - str.   EV.
—— CHORALE PRELUDE: "JESU, JOY OF MAN'S DESIRING"
    *3,*3,*3,*3 - 4,3,3,1 - timp., - hp. - str.   Arranger.
—— CHORALE PRELUDE: "SLEEPERS AWAKE"
    Arranger.
—— FERVENT IS MY LONGING
    SouthernTx.
—— FUGUE IN D MINOR ("GIANT")
    2,3,4,3 - 4,2,3,1 - timp. - str.   3:00 Arranger.

—— FUGUE IN G MINOR ("THE LITTLE")
    3,3,3,3 - 4,3,3,1 - timp.,perc. - hp. - str.   3:00 C. Fischer.
—— PASTORALE (FROM CHRISTMAS ORATORIO)
    Arranger.
—— PRELUDE AND FUGUE IN E-FLAT MINOR (ARR. 1955)
    2,*3,*3,1 d.-b.cl.,*3 - 4,3,3,1 - timp.,glock. - hp. - str.   H. Elkan.
—— PRELUDE AND FUGUE IN F MINOR
    *3,*3,*3,*3 - 4,3,3,1 - timp. - hp. - str.   Arranger.
—— PRELUDE AND FUGUE IN G MINOR (FROM THE "EIGHT
SHORT PRELUDES AND FUGUES" FOR ORGAN)
    2,3,3,3 - 4,3,2,1 - timp.,perc. - hp. - str.   4:00 C. Fischer.
—— PRELUDE, CANON AND FUGUE
    *3,*3,*3,*3 - 4,3,3,1 - timp.,perc.(2),glock. - hp. - str.
    7:00 Arranger.
—— PRELUDE IN E MAJOR
    2,2,3,3 - 4,2,3,1 - timp.,perc. - hp. - str.   5:00 Arranger.
—— PRELUDE IN Eb MINOR
    2,2,3,2 - 4,2,3,1 - timp. - hp. - str.   H. Elkan.
—— SHEEP MAY SAFELY GRAZE
    *3,*3,*3,*3 - 4,3,3,1 - timp.,perc.(3),glock. - hp. - str.
    5:00 Bo. Hawkes.
—— STRONG IN THY STRENGTH ("KOMM' SÜSSER TOD")
    *3,*3,*3,*3 - 4,3,3,1 - timp.,perc.(3),glock. - hp. - pf.(ad lib.) - str.
    Belwin.
—— TOCCATA AND FUGUE IN D MINOR
    *3,*3,*3,*3 - 4,3,3,1 - timp.,perc.(3),glock. - hp. - str.
    8:40 C. Fischer.

BACH, Johann Sebastian - CAMPBELL-WATSON, Frank
—— CHORALE PRELUDE: "WE ALL BELIEVE IN ONE GOD"
(FOR STRING ORCH.)
    str.   Witmark.
—— PASSACAGLIA AND FUGUE (FOR STRING ORCH.)
    str.   Witmark.

BACH, Johann Sebastian - CASELLA, Alfredo
—— CIACONNA
    *4,*3,*3,*3 - 4,3,4,0 - timp. - org. - str.   18:00 Bo. Hawkes.

BACH, Johann Sebastian - CASTELNUOVO-TEDESCO, Mario
—— PARTITA IN B MINOR (FOR STRING ORCH.) (IN 4 MOVTS.)
    str.   20:00 Leeds.
—— SUITE NO. 6 IN D (FOR CELLO AND STRING ORCH.) (IN 6
MOVTS.)
    str.   25:00 Arranger.

BACH, Johann Sebastian - CAZDEN, Norman
—— TOCCATA IN D MAJOR (FOR HARPSICHORD)
    3,2,2,3 - 3,2,2,0 - str.   MCA Music.

BACH, Johann Sebastian - COOPERSMITH, J. M.
—— SARABANDE (FOR STRING ORCH.)
    str.   Ricordi.

BACH, Johann Sebastian - DAMROSCH, Walter
—— A MIGHTY FORTRESS IS OUR GOD (FOR CHORUS AND
ORCH.)
    *3,*3,*3,*3 - 4,3,3,1 - timp.,perc.(2) - str.   4:00 Witmark.
—— PASTORALE IN F
    2,*3,*3,2 - 0,0,0,0 - str.   12:00 Arranger.

BACH, Johann Sebastian - DAVID, H. T.
—— SIX-PART RICERCAR (FUGUE) (FROM "THE MUSICAL
OFFERING")
    cemb. - str.   7:00 G. Schirmer.

BACH, Johann Sebastian - DAVID, Hans T.
—— THE MUSICAL OFFERING (FOR FLUTE, VIOLIN, CELLO,
PIANO AND STRING ORCH.)
    fl. - pf. - str.   50:00 G. Schirmer.

BACH, Johann Sebastian - DAYMOND, Emily
—— OVERTURE (IN 5 MOVTS.)
    str.   Oxford.
—— THREE MOVEMENTS
    str.   Oxford.

BACH, Johann Sebastian - DE FILIPPI, Amedeo
—— CHORALE PRELUDE: "IN DULCI JUBILO"
    2,2,2,2 - 4,2,3,1 - timp. - str.   3:30 Arranger.
—— CHORALE PRELUDE: "WACHET AUF" (SLEEPERS, AWAKE!)
    2,*2,2,2 - 4,2,3,1 - timp. - str.   5:20 Arranger.

—— PRELUDE AND FUGUE
    *3,*3,*3,2 - 4,3,3,1 - timp.,perc. - str.   10:00 Arranger.

BACH, Johann Sebastian - DEFOSSEZ, René
—— TOCCATA AND FUGUE (1956)
    3,3,3,3 - 4,3,3,1 - timp. - str.   9:00 Cousins.

BACH, Johann Sebastian - DE LAMARTER, Eric
—— BRANDENBURG CONCERTO NO. 3
    str.   Arranger.
—— CHORALE PRELUDE: "DAS ALTE JAHR VERGANGEN IST"
(FOR STRING ORCH.)
    str.   Ricordi.
—— CHORALE PRELUDE: "HERZLICH THUT MICH
VERLANGEN" (FOR STRING ORCH.)
    str.   4:00 Ricordi.
—— CHORALE PRELUDE: "O MENSCH BEWEIN DEIN SÜNDE
GROSS"
        Arranger.
—— CHORALE PRELUDE: "VALET WILL ICH DIR GEBEN" (FOR
STRING ORCH.)
    str.   Ricordi.

BACH, Johann Sebastian - DEMAREST, Clifford
—— FUGUE IN G MINOR (THE "LESSER")
    2,*3,*3,2 - 4,2,3,1 - timp.,perc. - str.   3:15 Remick.
—— PRELUDE AND FUGUE IN D MINOR
    2,2,2,2 - 2,2,3,1 - timp.,perc. - str.   3:30 Witmark.

BACH, Johann Sebastian - DE TAR, Vernon
—— CANTATA NO. 141 ("FOR US A CHILD IS BORN") (FOR
SOLO VOICES, CHORUS AND ORCH.)
    2,2,0,0 - cemb. - str.   20:00 Galaxy.
    or:
    str.

BACH, Johann Sebastian - DIACK, J. M.
—— TEN DANCE MOVEMENTS FROM THE SUITES
    fl.,ob.,cl.,bn. - str.   Arranger.

BACH, Johann Sebastian - DIACK, J. Michael - BAKER, Harry Edgar
—— THE COFFEE CANTATA (FOR SOPRANO, TENOR,
BARITONE, SATB CHORUS AND ORCH.)
    1,1,1,1 - 0,0,0,0 - pf. - str.   30:00 C. Fischer.
—— A FESTIVAL CANTATA (ON MUSIC OF BACH AND
HANDEL) (FOR SA CHORUS AND ORCH.)
    1,1,1,1 - 0,0,0,0 - timp.,perc. - str.   21:00 C. Fischer.
—— THE FOUR SEASONS (SCHLEICHT, SPIELENDE WELLEN)
(CANTATA) (FOR SATB CHORUS AND STRINGS)
    str.   40:00 C. Fischer.
—— PSALM 100 (FROM CANTATA 195) (FOR CHORUS AND
ORCHESTRA)
    0,2,0,0 - 3,0,0,0 - timp. - cemb. - str.   C. Fischer.
—— PSALM 121 (FROM CANTATA 37) (FOR CHORUS AND
ORCHESTRA)
    2,2,0,1 - 0,3,0,0 - timp. - str.   C. Fischer.
—— THE ST. LUKE PASSION (FOR SOPRANO, TENOR, BASS,
SATB CHORUS AND ORCH.)
    2 ob. - str.   50:00 C. Fischer.

BACH, Johann Sebastian - DI BONAVENTURA, Mario
—— JESU, JOY OF MAN'S DESIRING
        S.A.C.E.M.

BACH, Johann Sebastian - DUBENSKY, Arcady
—— OUR FATHER IN HEAVEN
    str.   5:00 AMP.

BACH, Johann Sebastian - DUNHILL, T. F.
—— ANNA MAGDALENA SUITE (FOR STRING ORCH.) (IN 5
MOVTS.)
    str.   Oxford.

BACH, Johann Sebastian - EHRET, Walter
—— SANCTUS NO. 4 IN G (FOR MIXED CHORUS AND SMALL
ORCH.)
    2ob. - cemb. - str.   3:00 Bo. Hawkes.

BACH, Johann Sebastian - ELGAR, E.
—— FANTASIA AND FUGUE IN C MINOR
    3,3,3,3 - 4,3,3,1 - timp.,perc.,glock. - 2hp. - org. (ad lib.) - str.
      9:30 Novello.

BACH, Johann Sebastian - ELGAR, Edward - ATKINS, Ivor
—— THE PASSION OF OUR LORD ACCORDING TO ST.
MATTHEW
      210:00 Novello.

BACH, Johann Sebastian - ELKAN, Henri
—— COME, SWEET DEATH (FOR STRING ORCH.)
    str.   4:00 EV.

BACH, Johann Sebastian - ESPOSITO, Michele
—— BRANDENBURG CONCERTO NO. 6 (FOR STRING ORCH.)
      Oxford.
—— WACHET AUF (FROM CANTATA NO. 140)
    1,1,1,1 - 2,1,0,0 - str.   Oxford.

BACH, Johann Sebastian - ESSER, H. - ELGAR, E.
—— TOCCATA IN F (WITH A CODA BY ELGAR)
    3,2,2,2 - 4,3,3,1 - timp.,perc. - str.   12:00 Novello.

BACH, Johann Sebastian - FARINA, G.
—— CIACONNA
    2,*3,2,*3 - 4,3,4,1 - timp.,perc. - hp. - org. - str.
      18:00 Bo. Hawkes.

BACH, Johann Sebastian - FERGUSON, Howard
—— FUGA RICERCATA (FROM THE "MUSICAL OFFERING")
(FOR STRING ORCH.)
    str.   6:30 Bo. Hawkes.

BACH, Johann Sebastian - FISCHER
—— CONCERTO IN D MAJOR FOR THREE VIOLINS AND
STRINGS (A RECONSTRUCTION FROM BWV 1064)
    cemb. - str.   11:00 G. Schirmer.
—— LITTLE CHRISTMAS CONCERTO (FROM CANTATA 142)
    2 recorders (or 2 fl.) - cemb. - str.   Henmar.
—— PASTORAL MUSIC (FROM CANTATA 175)
    3 recorders (or 3 fl.) - cemb. - str.   Henmar.

BACH, Johann Sebastian - FOSTER
—— FUGUE IN A MINOR
    str.   Galaxy.

BACH, Johann Sebastian - FRANKO, S.
—— ARIOSO
    str.   4:00 G. Schirmer.

BACH, Johann Sebastian - FREDERICK, Donald R.
—— ANDANTE (3RD MOVT. FROM THE SONATA IN A) (1941)
    1,2,2,2 - 4,2,3,1 -timp.,perc.(2) - str.   3:45 Arranger.

BACH, Johann Sebastian - FRIEDMAN, S. P.
—— BIST DU BEI MIR (FOR STRING ORCH.)
    str.   3:30 Arranger.
—— BOURREE (FROM VIOLIN SONATA NO. 2) (FOR STRING
ORCH.)
    str.   2:00 Arranger.
—— GAVOTTE EN RODEAU (FROM VIOLIN SONATO NO. 6)
(FOR STRING ORCH.)
    str.   3:00 Arranger.

BACH, Johann Sebastian - FROST, Thomas T.
—— LITTLE SUITE (FROM THE ANNA MAGDALENA
NOTEBOOK) (1969) (IN 4 MOVTS.)
    2,2,0,2 - 2,1,0,0 - timp.,perc.(1) - str.   7:27 Tetra.
—— LITTLE SUITE NO. 2 (ARR. 1973) (IN 5 MOVTS.)
    2,*3,0,2 - 2,2,0,0 - timp. - str.   12:25 Tetra.
—— SHEEP MAY SAFELY GRAZE (FOR SATB CHORUS AND
SMALL ORCH.)
    2,0,0,0 - 0,0,0,0 - str.   4:34 Tetra.

BACH, Johann Sebastian - FROTSCHER
—— SINFONIA IN B MINOR (FROM THE CANTATA "NON SA
CHE SIA DOLORE")
    fl. - cemb. - str.   Henmar.

BACH, Johann Sebastian - FRY, Tommy J.
—— ARIOSO, FROM KANTATE 156 (ARR. 1968)
    str.   3:00 C. Fischer.

BACH, Johann Sebastian - GALLIERA
—— PRELUDE AND FUGUE IN G
    2,2,2,2 - 4,2,0,0 - timp. - str.   10:00 Bo. Hawkes.

BACH, Johann Sebastian - GAUL, H. B.
—— ARIOSO (FOR VIOLIN AND STRING ORCH.)
    str.   Volkwein.
—— ARRIETTA (FOR STRING ORCH.)
    str.   Volkwein.
—— BACH WROTE ON B-A-C-H (PRELUDIUM AND FUGUE FOR STRING ORCH.)
    str.   8:00 Arranger.
—— CHORALE PRELUDE: "SHEEP MAY SAFELY GRAZE"
    fl., cl. - str.   Volkwein.
—— CHRISTMAS CHORALE PRELUDE (FROM THE CHRISTMAS ORATORIO) (FOR STRING ORCH.)
    str.   Volkwein.
—— CHRISTMAS SUITE (FOR STRING ORCH.)
    str.   Volkwein.
—— FORTY DAYS AND FORTY NIGHTS ("AUS DER TIEFE RUFE ICH") (FOR STRING ORCH.)
    str.   3:00 Volkwein.
—— JESUS SUFFERED PAIN AND DEATH ("JESU LEIDEN PEIN UND TOD") (FOR STRING ORCH.)
    fl. - str.   3:00 Volkwein.
—— MYSTICAL ADORATION ("JESU MEINE FREUDE") (FOR STRING ORCH.)
    str.   Volkwein.
—— OVERTURE TO CHRISTMAS CANTATA (FOR STRING ORCH.)
    str.   Volkwein.
—— PASSIONTIDE CHORALE ("O SACRED HEAD SURROUNDED") (FOR STRING ORCH.)
    str.   3:00 Arranger.
—— SYMPHONY, ON THE SECOND DAY OF THE FESTIVAL OF CHRISTMAS (FOR STRING ORCH.)
    str.   Volkwein.

BACH, Johann Sebastian - GEORGE, Thom Ritter
—— PRELUDE AND FUGUE IN E MAJOR
    1,1,1,1 - 2,0,0,0 - str.   Arranger.
—— PRELUDE AND FUGUE IN G MINOR (NO. 16 FROM VOL. 2 OF "THE WELL-TEMPERED CLAVICHORD")
    *3,*3,*3,*3 - 4,2,3,1 - timp. - str.   Arranger.

BACH, Johann Sebastian - GESENSWAY, Louis
—— CHACONNE
    *3,*3,*3,*3 - 4,3,3,1 - timp. - 2 hp. - str.   18:00 Presser.
    or:
    *3,2,*3,*3 - 4,4,4,1 - timp. - 2 hp. - str.

BACH, Johann Sebastian - GHEDINI, G. F.
—— THE MUSICAL OFFERING (L'OFFERTA MUSICALE)
    3,3,2,2 - 0,3,3,0 - hpsc. - 2 hp. - str.   70:00 Leeds.

BACH, Johann Sebastian - GOEDICKE, A. F.
—— ORGAN FANTASY AND FUGUE IN G MINOR
    3(3rd alt. with picc.), 3,*3,*3 - 4,3,3,1 timp.,perc. - str.   G. Schirmer.
—— PASSACAGLIA
    *3,2,*3,*3 - 4,3,3,1 - timp.,perc.,glock. - str.   20:00 G. Schirmer.

BACH, Johann Sebastian - GOOSSENS, Eugene
—— SUITE IN G (IN 7 MOVTS.)
    3,2,2,2 - 2,3,0,0 - timp. - str.   18:00 G. Schirmer.

BACH, Johann Sebastian - GOUNOD, Charles - SAAR, Louis Victor
—— MEDITATION ("AVE MARIA") (FOR SSA WOMEN'S CHORUS, VIOLIN, ORGAN AND STRINGS)
    org. - str.   C. Fischer.

BACH, Johann Sebastian - GRAINGER, Percy
—— BLITHE BELLS ("SHEEP MAY GRAZE IN SAFETY") (FROM CANTATA 208)
    2(2nd alt. with picc.),1,2,1(or 2) - 2,1(or 2)1(ad lib.),0 - cel.(ad lib.),glock.,vibra.(ad lib.) - hp.(ad lib.) - pf.(4-hands) - harm. or org. (ad lib.) - str.   G. Schirmer.

BACH, Johann Sebastian - GRANT, Francis H.
—— ADAGIO
    str.   5:00 Studio PR.
—— FUGUE IN G MINOR
    str.   5:00 Studio PR.

BACH, Johann Sebastian - GUI, Vittorio
—— ARIOSO
    2,3,0,2 - 2,0,0,0 - str.   4:00 Bo. Hawkes.

—— CANTATA NO. 151, "MEIN SÜSSER TROST" (FOR 4 SOLO VOICES, CHORUS AND ORCH.)
    2fl.,2ob. - org. - str.   Bo. Hawkes.
—— CANTATA NO 161, "KOMM, DU SÜSSE TODESSTUNDE" (FOR CONTRALTO, TENOR, CHORUS AND ORCH.)
    2fl.,2bn. - 2hn. - str.   23:00 Bo. Hawkes.
—— CANTATA NO. 170. "VERGNÜGTE RUH" (FOR CONTRALTO AND ORCH.)
    2fl.,ob. d'amore(or ob.), 2Eng.hn. - org. - str.   Bo. Hawkes.
—— DUE CORALI (TRANSCRIBED FROM THE ORGAN)
    2,3,0,2 - 4,0,0,0 - str.   5:00 Bo. Hawkes.
—— THREE CHORALE PRELUDES
    1. Lento, calmo; 2. Lento mistico; 3. Maestoso
    2,*3,*3,*3 - 4,3,3,1 - timp. - str.   7:00 Bo. Hawkes.

BACH, Johann Sebastian - HARRISON, J.
—— PRELUDE AND FUGUE IN G MINOR (FROM "WELL-TEMPERED KLAVIER", BOOK 2)
    str. (d.-b- ad lib.)   Novello.

BACH, Johann Sebastian - HARTMANN, Thomas de
—— CONCERTO D'APRÈS UNE CANTATE DE BACH, OP. 73 (FOR CELLO AND STRING ORCH.)
    str.   18:00 Bo. Hawkes.
—— TWO ORGAN FUGUES OF BACH, OP. 48
    3,2,3,2 - 4,2,3,1 - timp. - str.   11:00 Bo. Hawkes.

BACH, Johann Sebastian - HERFURTH, C. Paul
—— ARIOSO (FROM CANTATA NO. 156)
                       C. Fischer.

BACH, Johann Sebastian - HERMANN, F.
—— SARABANDE (FROM SONATA NO. 2 FOR VIOLIN)
    fl. - str.   Galaxy.

BACH, Johann Sebastian - HODGE, H.
—— SIX ORGAN CHORALE PRELUDES
    str.   Oxford.

BACH, Johann Sebastian - HOLST, Gustav
—— FUGUE À LA GIGUE
    2,2,2,2 - 2,2,2,1 - str.   3:00 Bo. Hawkes.

BACH, Johann Sebastian - HOWORTH, Wayne
—— JESU, JOY OF MAN'S DESIRING
                       Belwin.

BACH, Johann Sebastian - ISAACS, Leonard
—— THE ART OF FUGUE (DIE KUNST DER FUGE)
    1(alt. with alto fl.),1(alt. with Eng.hn.),1 ob. d'amore,0,2 - 0,0,0,0 - hpsc. - str.   80:00 Galaxy.

BACH, Johann Sebastian - JACQUES, Reginald
—— A BACH SUITE FOR STRINGS (IN 5 MOVTS.)
    str.   12:00 Oxford.
—— JESU JOY OF MAN'S DESIRING (CHORALE FROM CHURCH CANTATA NO. 147)
    str.   Oxford.
—— SANCTIFY US BY THY GOODNESS (CHORALE FROM CHURCH CANTATA NO. 22)
    str.   Oxford.
—— SHEEP MAY SAFELY GRAZE (ARIA FROM SECULAR CANTATA NO. 208)
    str.   Oxford.

BACH, Johann Sebastian - JAMES, Philip
—— CHORALE PRELUDE: "WE ALL BELIEVE IN ONE GOD" ("WIR GLAUBEN ALL' AN EINEN GOTT")
    *3,2,2,*3 - 4,3,3,1 - timp.,perc.(3) - org.(ad lib.) - str.   4:00 Mercury.

BACH, Johann Sebastian - JOACHIM, Henry
—— FOUR CHORAL PRELUDES
    pf.(ad lib.) - str.   10:00 Mills.

BACH, Johann Sebastian - JOSEPHSON, Harry D.
—— CHORALE: VOM HIMMEL HOCH (FROM HEAVEN ABOVE)
    0,1,0,0 - 2,0,0,0 - timp. - str.   12:00 Arranger.

BACH, Johann Sebastian - KALLSTENIUS, Edvin
—— BACH MINIATURES SUITE (BACH-MINIATYRER)
    1,1,1,0 - 0,0,0,0 - cemb. - str.   13:00 Bo. Hawkes.
    or:

fl. - str.

BACH, Johann Sebastian - KIPNIS, Igor
—— CONCERTO NO. 8 IN D MINOR FOR HARPSICHORD AND
ORCH. B.W.V. 1059 (FROM A 9-MEASURE FRAGMENT OF
THE CONCERTO PLUS PORTIONS OF CANTATA NO. 35)
(1970) (IN 3 MOVTS.)
ob. - hpsc. - str.   19:50 Arranger.

BACH, Johann Sebastian - KLAUSS, Noah
—— PRELUDE AND FUGUE NO. 22 (FROM VOL. 1 OF
"WELL-TEMPERED CLAVIER")
2,2,2,1 alto sax.,1 ten.sax.,2 - 2,2,3,0 - timp. - str.
                                                      5:00 Summy-Bir.

BACH, Johann Sebastian - KLEMPERER, Otto
—— BIST DU BEI MIR
                                                      P.R.S.
—— NUN KOMM DER HEIDEN HEILAND
                                                      P.R.S.

BACH, Johann Sebastian - KLENOVSKY, pseud.
—— TOCCATA AND FUGUE IN D MINOR
4(4th alt. with picc.),4,4,4 - 6,4,4,1 - timp.,perc.,cel.,glock. - 2hp. -
org. - str.   8:00 Oxford.

BACH, Johann Sebastian - KODALY - DUBENSKY, Arcadi
—— CHORALE: "CHRISTUS DER UNS SELIG MACHT" (FOR
STRING ORCH.)
str.   8:00 Arranger.

BACH, Johann Sebastian - KODALY, Zoltan
—— THREE CHORALE PRELUDES (FOR CELLO AND ORCH.)
                                                      16:00 Presser.

BACH, Johann Sebastian - KOSCHINSKY, Fritz
—— PRELUDE AND FUGUE IN D MINOR (FOR VIOLIN AND
STRING ORCH.) (Originally for Organ)
str.   9:00 Henmar.

BACH, Johann Sebastian - KOUGUELL, Arkadie
—— CHORALE FROM CANTATA 147 ("JESU, JOY OF MAN'S
DESIRING")
str.   3:00 Arranger.

BACH, Johann Sebastian - KOUTZEN, Boris
—— RICERCAR A 6 (FROM "THE MUSICAL OFFERING")
2,*2,2,1 - 2,2,0,0 - str.   Arranger.

BACH, Johann Sebastian - KRAMER, A. Walter
—— CHACONNE
2,2,2,2 - 4,2,3,1 - timp. - hp. - str.   16:00 J. Fischer.
—— CHORALE PRELUDE: "O MAN, LAMENT THY GRIEVOUS
SIN" (FOR STRING ORCH.)
str.   Witmark.
—— FUGUE IN A MINOR (FOR STRING ORCH.)
str.   Galaxy.
—— PRELUDE AND FUGUE IN D (FROM THE
"WELL-TEMPERED CLAVIER") (FOR STRING ORCH.)
str.   G. Schirmer.
—— PRELUDE (FOR STRING ORCH.)
str.   Arranger.

BACH, Johann Sebastian - LA ROTELLA
—— LARGO (FROM THE TOCCATA AND FUGUE IN C)
1,1,2,2 - 2,2,3,0 - str.   4:00 Bo. Hawkes.

BACH, Johann Sebastian - LEIBOWITZ, René
—— TOCCATA AND FUGUE IN D MINOR (FOR DOUBLE
ORCHESTRA)
Orch. I: - 2,1,2,2 - 2,2,1,1 - str.   Boelke-Bo.
Orch. II: - 2,2,2,2 - 2,2,1,1 - str.

BACH, Johann Sebastian - LEONARDI, Leon
—— CHACONNE (FOR 9 SOLO INSTRUMENTS AND ORCH.)
3(3rd alt. with picc.),alto fl.,*3,*4,*4 - 4,3,3,1 - timp. - 2hp. - str.
                                                      17:00 EV.
Solo instruments: fl., alto fl., ob., Eng. hn., bn., str. quartet
—— OVERTURE FROM CANTATA 26 ("ACH WIE FLUCHTIG")
2,2,3,2 - 4,3,3,1 - timp. - str.   4:00 EV.
—— PRELUDE AND FUGUE IN E MINOR ("THE CATHEDRAL")
2,*3,*3,*3 - 4,3,3,1 - timp. - hp. - str.   5:00 EV.

—— TOCCATA AND FUGUE IN D MINOR
3(3rd alt. with picc.),*3,*4,*3 - 4,3,3,1 - timp.,cel. - hp. - str.
                                                      9:00 EV.

BACH, Johann Sebastian - LOTH, L.
—— TWO-PART INVENTIONS NO. 3 AND 14 (FOR STRING
ORCH.)
str.   Arranger.

BACH, Johann Sebastian - LOTTER, A.
—— CONCERTO IN C MAJOR (FOR STRING ORCH.)
str.   7:00 Bo. Hawkes.

BACH, Johann Sebastian - LOVELOCK, William
—— FOUR CHORALE PRELUDES (ARR. 1961)
2,2,2,2 - 4,3,3,1 - perc. - str.   10:00 A.P.R.A.
—— PRELUDE AND FUGUE IN B MINOR (ARR. 1961)
2,2,2,2 - 4,3,3,1 - perc. - str.   12:00 Chappell.
—— PRELUDE AND FUGUE IN G MAJOR (ARR. 1962)
2,2,2,2 - 4,3,3,1 - perc. - str.   10:00 A.P.R.A.

BACH, Johann Sebastian - LUBIN, Ernest
—— PASSACAGLIA AND FUGUE IN C MINOR (ARR. 1969)
2,2,2,2 - 2,2,1,0 - timp. - str.   14:00 Arranger.

BACH, Johann Sebastian - MCDONALD, Harl
—— CHORALE: "ACH GOTT VOM HIMMEL SIEH' DAREIN"
str.   4:00 EV.
—— GOTT, DER DU SELBER BIST DAS LICHT (FOR
WOODWINDS, BRASS AND TIMPANI)
2,*3,*4,3 - 0,*3,3,1 - timp.   2:00 EV.

BACH, Johann Sebastian - MACLEAN, Quentin
—— PRELUDE AND FUGUE IN E^b
                                                      18:00 C.A.P.A.C.

BACH, Johann Sebastian - MACMILLAN, Ernest Campbell
—— TWO CHORALE PRELUDES
                                                      C.A.P.A.C.

BACH, Johann Sebastian - MAEKELBERGHE, August
—— PRELUDE IN B MINOR
*3,*3,*3,2 - 4,2,3,1 - timp.,perc. - str.   8:00 Arranger.

BACH, Johann Sebastian - MAGANINI, Quinto
—— LAMENT (FOR STRING ORCH.)
str.   6:00 Musicus.

BACH, Johann Sebastian - MAHLER, Gustav
—— SUITE (IN 4 MOVTS.)
1,2,0,1(ad lib.) - 3tpt. - timp. - pf. - org. - str.   8:00 G. Schirmer.

BACH, Johann Sebastian - MARCELLI, Nino
—— CHORALE FUGUE: "ALL GLORY BE TO GOD ON HIGH"
3(3rd alt. with picc.),2,2,2 - 4,3,3,1 - timp.,perc.(3) - str.
                                                      3:30 C. Fischer.

BACH, Johann Sebastian - MARKEVITCH, Igor
—— THE MUSICAL OFFERING (DAS MUSIKALISCHE OFFER)
(FOR SOLO OCTET AND STRING ORCH.)
1,*2,0,1 - pf. or hpsc. - str.   55:00 Bo. Hawkes.

BACH, Johann Sebastian - MARTIN, Vernon
—— LITTLE FUGUE IN G MINOR
tu. - str.   4:00 Arranger.

BACH, Johann Sebastian - MARTINOTTI, Bruno
—— L' OFFERTA MUSICALE (FOR WOODWINDS,
HARPSICHORD, STRING TRIO AND DOUBLE STRING
ORCHESTRA)
1,2,01 - 0,0,0,0 - hpsc. - str.(13,7,5,2)   46:00 MCA Music.

BACH, Johann Sebastian - MARX, Burle
—— CHACONNE
*3,2,2,2 - 4,2,3,0 - timp. - str.   16:00 Fleisher.
—— IN MEMORIAM (AFTER THE SINFONIA NO. 9)
1,2 recorders,1,1,1 - 0,0,0,0 - str.   Fleisher.

BACH, Johann Sebastian - MASSIS, Amable
—— CONCERTO FOR VIOLA AND ORCH.
2 fl. - 2 hn. - str.   19:45 Presser.

BACH, Johann Sebastian - MELICHAR, Alois
—— TOCCATA AND FUGUE IN D MINOR (Originally for Organ)
3,2(2nd alt. with Eng. hn.),2(2nd alt. with b.-cl.),2(2nd alt. with
b.-cn.) - 4,3,3,1 - timp.,perc. - hp. - str.   9:00 Henmar.

BACH, Johann Sebastian - MENDEL, Arthur
—— THE PASSION ACCORDING TO ST. JOHN
2,2,0,2 - 0,0,0,0 - cemb. - str.   134:00 G. Schirmer.

BACH, Johann Sebastian - MILES, Maurice
—— JESU, MY DEAREST FRIEND ("JESU, JOY OF MAN'S
DESIRING")
1,1,2,1 - 1,2,0,0 - str.   5:00 Galaxy.

BACH, Johann Sebastian - MILLS, Alvin
—— PRELUDE AND FUGUE IN C MINOR (ARR. 1974)
str.   7:00 Arranger.

BACH, Johann Sebastian - NABOKOFF, Nicholas
—— ORCHESTRA SUITE (FROM THE "GOLDBERG"
VARIATIONS)
S.A.C.E.M.

BACH, Johann Sebastian - NACHEZ, Tivadar
—— CONCERTO IN G MINOR FOR VIOLIN AND STRING ORCH.
org. - str.   G. Schirmer.

BACH, Johann Sebastian - NICHOLSON, Ralph
—— FUGUE IN A MINOR
str.   3:30 Oxford.

BACH, Johann Sebastian - NIELSON, Riccardo
—— CIACCONA
str.   18:00 Bo. Hawkes.

BACH, Johann Sebastian - ORMANDY, Eugene
—— CHORALE PRELUDE: "IN THEE IS JOY"
str.   Bo. Hawkes.
—— CHORALE PRELUDE: "JESU JOY OF MAN'S DESIRING"
str.   Bo. Hawkes.
—— CHORALE PRELUDE: "O MENSCH BEWEIN DEIN SÜNDE
GROSS"
str.   Bo. Hawkes.
—— CHORALE PRELUDE: "SLEEPERS AWAKE" ("WACHET AUF
RUFT UNS DIE STIMME")
2,2,2,2 - 4,3,3,1 - timp.,perc. - str.   4:30 Bo. Hawkes.
or:
2,2, picc.,*3 - *3,*3 - 4,4,3,1 - timp.,perc. - str.
—— FROM HEAV'N ABOVE (VOM HIMMEL HOCH)
2,2,2,2 - 4,0,2,1 - str.   4:00 Bo. Hawkes.
or:
3,*3,1,2 - 4,0,3,1 - str.
—— KOMM SÜSSER TOD
Arranger.
—— ORGAN SONATA NO. 1 IN E♭ MAJOR (IN 3 MOVEMENTS)
3,2,2,2 - 2,0,0,0 - timp. - str.   Arranger.
—— PASSACAGLIA AND FUGUE IN C MINOR
3(3rd alt. with picc.),*3,3(3rd alt. with b.-cl.),3(3rd alt. with c.-bn.)
- 4,4,3,1 - timp.,perc. - str.   13:05 Arranger.
—— PRELUDE AND FUGUE IN C MINOR
3,*3,*3,*3 - 4,3,3,1 - timp. - str.   Phil or Assn.
—— RICERGARE
4,*3,*3,*3 - 4,3,3,1 - timp. - str.   Arranger.
—— TOCCATA, ADAGIO AND FUGUE IN C MAJOR
*4,*3,*4,3(3rd alt. with c.-bn.) - 4,4,3,1 - timp.,perc. - str.
15:45 Arranger.
—— TOCCATA AND FUGUE IN D MINOR
3,*3,*3,*4 - 4,4,3,1 - timp.,perc. - str.   8:30 Arranger.
—— VATER UNSER IM HIMMELREICH
3,*3,*3,*3 - 4,3,3,1 - timp.,perc. - str.   Arranger.

BACH, Johann Sebastian - PALMER - BEST
—— FOUR INVENTIONS (FOR STRING ORCH.)
str.   Oxford.

BACH, Johann Sebastian - PARELLI, A.
—— TOCCATA IN F
*3,*3,*3,*3 - 4,2,3,1 - timp. - str.   8:00 Bo. Hawkes.

BACH, Johann Sebastian - PARELLI, Attilio
—— TOCCATA IN F
3,3,3,3 - 4,3,3,1 - timp. - str.   8:00 Bo. Hawkes.

BACH, Johann Sebastian - PERESS, Maurice
—— WACHET AUF (CHORALE VERSE FROM CANTATA NO.
140) (ARR. 1966)
*3,2,*3,2 - 4,3,3,1 - org.(ad lib.) - str.   5:00 Arranger.

BACH, Johann Sebastian - PILLNEY, Karl Hermann
—— THE ART OF THE FUGUE (DIE KUNST DER FUGUE)
(TRANSCRIBED FOR CHAMBER ORCH.)
97:00 G.E.M.A.

BACH, Johann Sebastian - RAPEE, Erno
—— ARIOSO
Arranger.

BACH, Johann Sebastian - READ, Gardner
—— PRELUDE AND FUGUE IN B MINOR
3,alto fl.,3,3,3 - 4,3,3,1 - timp. - str.   12:00 Arranger.
or:
3,alto fl.,3,3,3 - 4,4,4,1 - timp. - str.

BACH, Johann Sebastian - RESPIGHI, Ottorino
—— SONATA IN E MINOR FOR VIOLIN AND CONTINUO
Org - str.   9:30 C. Fischer.

BACH, Johann Sebastian - RISSLAND, K.
—— GAVOTTE (FROM VIOLIN SONATA NO. 6) (FOR STRING
ORCH.)
pf. - str.   Ditson.

BACH, Johann Sebastian - ROBERTS, Charles J.
—— HEAR MY CRY, O GOD ("O HERZENSANGST")
C. Fischer.
—— JESU, JOY OF MAN'S DESIRING (FROM CANTATA NO. 147)
C. Fischer.
—— LORD OF GLORY ("ES IST GEWISSLICH AN DER ZEIT")
C. Fischer.

BACH, Johann Sebastian - ROBINSON, Stanford
—— ADAGIO (FROM BRANDENBURG CONCERTO NO. 3 IN G.)
str.   5:00 Oxford.

BACH, Johann Sebastian - ROPER, E. Stanley
—— FLOCKS IN PASTURES GREEN ABIDING (FROM CANTATA
208) (FOR CHORUS AND ORCH.) (Engl. Text: Phyllis James)
Oxford.

BACH, Johann Sebastian - ROSE, Bernard
—— FIVE CHORALE PRELUDES
str.   Oxford.

BACH, Johann Sebastian - RUSS, Isidor
—— EIGHT ORGAN PRELUDES AND FUGUES
str.   Kalmus.

BACH, Johann Sebastian - SAGUER, Louis
—— CONCERTO GROSSO FOR STRINGS AND CONTINUO
(Attributed to J. S. Bach)
cemb. - str.   8:00 Presser.

BACH, Johann Sebastian - SANFORD, R. C.
—— FUGUE IN G MINOR ("THE GREAT") (FOR STRING ORCH.)
str.   Witmark.

BACH, Johann Sebastian - SCHENKMAN, E.
—— CHORALE PRELUDE: "COME NOW, THOU SAVIOUR" ("NUN
KOMM', DER HEILAND")
str.   Galaxy.
—— CHORALE PRELUDE: "DAS ALTE JAHR VERGANGEN IST"
fl.,2ob.,2cl.,2bn. - str.   G. Schirmer.
—— CHORALE PRELUDE: "IN DIR IST FREUDE"
3,3,3,3 - 4,3,3,1 - timp.,perc. - str.   G. Schirmer.

BACH, Johann Sebastian - SCHOENBERG, Arnold
—— ORGAN PRELUDE AND FUGUE IN E FLAT MAJOR (ARR.
1928)
4,4,6,4 - 4,4,4,1 - perc.,cel. - hp. - str.   13:00 Belmont.
or:
4,3,4,3 - 4,4,4,1 - perc.,cel. - hp. - str.
—— PRELUDE AND FUGUE IN E FLAT MAJOR (THE ST. ANNE
ORGAN-PRELUDE AND FUGUE) (ARR. 1928)
4,4,6,4 - 4,4,4,1 - perc.,cel. - hp. - str.   13:00 Belmont.
or:
4,3,4,3 - 4,4,4,1 - perc.,cel. - hp. - str.

—— TWO CHORALE PRELUDES (ARR. 1922)
4,4,6,4 - 4,4,4,1 - perc.,cel. - hp. - str.   7:00 Belmont.

BACH, Johann Sebastian - SCHROEDER, W. A.
—— TWO FUGUES
2,1,2,1 - 2,2,2,0 - timp.,perc.(2) - str.   5:00 Arranger.

BACH, Johann Sebastian - SCOTT, C. Kennedy
—— CANTATA NO. 161 ("COME, THOU LOVELY HOUR OF DYING") (FOR ALTO, TENOR, MIXED CHORUS AND ORCH.) (Text: Beatrice E. Bulman)
    Oxford.
—— INVENTION IN F
1,1,1,1 - 2,1,1,1 - str.   Novello.

BACH, Johann Sebastian - SEVITZKY, Fabien
—— ARIA (FOR STRING ORCH.)
str.   4:00 Arranger.
—— CHORALE PRELUDE: "HERZLICH THUT MICH VERLANGER"
str.   4:00 C. Fischer.
—— CHORALE PRELUDE: "SLEEPERS AWAKE"
2,*3,*3,3 - 4,3,3,1 - timp.,perc. - hp. - str.   3:30 Arranger.
—— FANTASY AND FUGUE IN G MINOR ("THE GREAT")
*3,*3,*3,*3 - 4,3,3,1 - timp.,perc. - hp. - str.   12:00 Arranger.
—— THE GIANT FUGUE (CHORALE PRELUDE: "WIR GLAUBEN ALL' AN EINEN GOTT")
2,*3,*3,2 - 4,3,3,1 - timp. - str.   8:00 Arranger.
—— JESU, JOY OF MAN'S DESIRING (FOR STRING ORCH.)
str.   3:30 Arranger.
—— KOMM' SÜSSER TOD
2,*3,*3,*3 - 4,3,3,1 - hp. - str.   7:00 Arranger.
—— A MIGHTY FORTRESS IS OUR GOD
2,*3,E♭cl.,1,1 - 0,0,0,0, - str.   3:00 Arranger.
—— PASSACAGLIA AND FUGUE IN C MINOR
*3,*3,*3,*3 - 4,3,3,2 - timp.,perc. - hp. - str.   11:00 Arranger.
—— PRELUDE (FROM "THE WELL-TEMPERED CLAVICHORD")
2,3,3,2 - 4,3,3,1 - perc. - hp. - str.   F. Colombo.
—— TOCCATA AND FUGUE IN D MINOR
*3,*3,*3,*3 - 4,3,3,1 - timp.,per.,cel. - hp. - str.   12:00 Arranger.
—— YE ARE NOT OF THE FLESH (FOR CHAMBER ORCH.)
str.   4:00 Arranger.

BACH, Johann Sebastian - SHAW, Robert - PARKER, Alice
—— THE CHRISTMAS ORATORIO (FOR CHORUS AND ORCH.)
    120:00 Arranger.
—— SINGET DEM HERRN EIN NEUES LIED (FOR CHORUS, ORGAN AND SMALL ORCH.)
    Law-Gould.

BACH, Johann Sebastian - SHEPHERD, Arthur
—— GAVOTTE IN E MAJOR
    Arranger.

BACH, Johann Sebastian - SILOTI, A.
—— ADAGIO (FROM TOCCATA IN C) (FOR STRING ORCH.)
str.   C. Fischer.

BACH, Johann Sebastian - SKROWACZEWSKI, Stanislaw
—— TOCCATA AND FUGUE IN D MINOR
    10:00 G. Schirmer.

BACH, Johann Sebastian - SONTAG, Wesley
—— ALLEGRO (FROM "DRAMA PER MUSICA")
    2:00 Leeds.
—— PRELUDE AND FUGUE IN B FLAT MINOR
str.   6:00 Galaxy.
—— SUITE FOR STRING ORCH. (IN 5 MOVTS.)
str.   G. Schirmer.

BACH, Johann Sebastian - SONZOGNO, G. C.
—— ADAGIO E FUGA (FROM THE TOCCATA IN C)
2,2,2,2 - 4,2,2,1 - hp. - str.   4:00 Bo. Hawkes.

BACH, Johann Sebastian - SOPKIN, Henry
—— CHACONNE
*3,*3,*3,*3 - 4,3,3,1 - timp. - hp. - str.   C. Fischer.
—— CONCERTO FOR 2 VIOLINS AND STRING ORCHESTRA
hp. - str.   Arranger.
—— PRAELUDIUM
2,2,2,2 - 4,2,3,0 - timp. - str.   4:30 C. Fischer.

BACH, Johann Sebastian - STANFORD, C. V.
—— CANTATA NO. 140, "SLEEPERS AWAKE" ("WACHET AUF") (FOR CHORUS AND ORCH.)
    Bo. Hawkes.

BACH, Johann Sebastian - STANGER, Russell
—— EIN FESTE BURG IST UNSER GOTT (CHORALE) (ARR. 1973)
    4:30 Arranger.
—— MACH'S MIT MIR, GOTT, DEINER, GUT (ARR. 1973)
    4:30 Arranger.

BACH, Johann Sebastian - STEINBERG, M.
—— CHACONNE
2,2,2,2 - 4,2,3,1 - timp., - str.   13:00 Bo. Hawkes.

BACH, Johann Sebastian - STOCK, F.
—— ANDANTE (FROM SOLO VIOLIN SONATA IN A MINOR) (FOR STRING ORCH.)
str.   G. Schirmer.

BACH, Johann Sebastian - STOESSEL, A.
—— CHORALE AND CHORALE PRELUDE (FOR STRING ORCH.)
str.   C. Fischer.
—— FANTASIA IN G MAJOR
str.   G. Schirmer.
—— PASSACAGLIA AND FUGUE
    Arranger.
—— PRELUDE (FROM VIOLIN SONATA IN E) (FOR STRING ORCH.)
str.   G. Schirmer.
—— TWO GAVOTTES: (FROM THE SUITE IN D) (FOR STRING ORCH.)
str.   C. Fischer.

BACH, Johann Sebastian - STOESSEL, Albert
—— CHORALE PRELUDE: "BY THE WATERS OF BABYLON"
str.   G. Schirmer.
—— FESTIVE SONG OF PRAISE (3 EXTENDED CHORALES)
    Summy-Bir.

BACH, Johann Sebastian - STOKOWSKI, Leopold
—— ADAGIO (FROM THE TOCCATA AND FUGUE IN C)
3,*3,*2,*3 - 4,4,4,1 - timp.,perc.(2),glock. - hp. - str.   4:00 Broude.
—— ANDANTE SOSTENUTO (FROM VIOLIN SONATA NO. 2)
4,3,3,3 - 2,0,0,0 - str.   Henmar.
—— ARIA (FROM OVERTURE IN D MAJOR)
    Broude.
—— ARIA (FROM SUITE IN D)
str.   5:45 Broude.
—— ARIOSO (FROM THE CONCERTO A CEMBALO CERTATO)
2,0,3,2 - 2,0,0,0 - 2 hp. - str.   Henmar.
—— AUS DER TIEFE RUFE ICH (PSALM 130)
fl.,ob. - str.   Henmar.
—— AUS TIEFER NOT
0,0,0,0 - 8,0,4,1 - str.   Henmar.
—— BOURREE
    Henmar.
—— CHACONNE
    Henmar.
—— CHORALE (FROM THE EASTER CANTATA)
4,*4,*3,*3 - 6,4,4,1 - timp. - str.   5:00 Broude.
—— CHORALE PRELUDE: "CHRIST LAG IN TODESBANDEN"
    Henmar.
—— CHORALE PRELUDE: "ICH RUF ZU DIR"
    Arranger.
—— CHORALE PRELUDE: "NUN KOM' DER HEIDEN HEILAND"
    Henmar.
—— ES IST VOLLBRACHT
    Arranger.
—— FUGUE IN C MINOR
    Arranger.
—— FUGUE IN G MINOR ("THE SHORTER")
2, alto fl.,*3,E♭cl.,*3,*3, - 5,4,4,2 - timp.,perc. - 2 hp. - str.   8:00 Broude.
—— GIANT FUGUE ("WIR GLAUBEN ALL' AN EINEN GOTT") (CHORALE PRELUDE)
3,*3,E♭cl.,*3,*2 - 4,3,3,2 - timp. - str.   6:00 Broude.
—— JESU, JOY OF MAN'S DESIRING ("WOHL MIR, DASS ICH JESUM HABE") (FROM CANTATA NO. 147)
1,2,0,3 - 3,1,0,1(bar. or euph.) - str.   Henmar.
—— KOMM' SÜSSER TOD
3,*3,*1,*2 - 4,3,4,1 - timp. - hp. - str.   4:00 Broude.

—— MEIN JESU (FOR STRING ORCH.)
  str.   4:00 Broude.
—— MY SOUL IS ATHIRST
                                              Henmar.
—— NUN KOMM'DER HEIDEN HEILAND
  1,2,0,1 - 0,0,0,0 - str.   Henmar.
—— PASSACAGLIA AND FUGUE IN C MINOR
  *5,alto fl.,*4,*4,*4 - 8,4,4,1 - timp. - str. 13:00 Broude.
—— PASSACAGLIA IN C MINOR
                                              Broude.
—— PRELUDE AND FUGUE IN E MAJOR
  4,3,3,4 - 5,4,3,1 - str.   Henmar.
—— PRELUDE: "EIN FESTE BURG"
                                              Henmar.
—— PRELUDE IN B MINOR (FROM "WELL-TEMPERED
  CLAVIER")
  str.   4:00 Broude.
—— PRELUDE IN E FLAT MINOR
  0,0,0,4 - 3,0,3,0 - glock. - 2 hp. - str.   6:00 Broude.
—— SARABANDE
                                              Henmar.
—— SARABANDE IN C MINOR (FROM PARTITA NO. 1)
  4,2,1,0 - 0,0,0,0 - 2 hp. - str.   Henmar.
—— SARABANDE IN G MINOR
  2,*1(or ob. da caccia) 0,0 - 0,0,0,0 - 2 hp. - str.   Henmar.
—— SHEEP MAY SAFELY GRAZE (FROM CANTATA NO. 208)
  2,2,0,0 - 0,0,0,0 - str.   Henmar.
—— SICILIANO (FROM SONATA NO. 4 IN C MINOR FOR
  CEMBALO AND VIOLIN)
  str.   3:15 Broude.
—— SINFONIA (FROM "ICH HATTE VIEL BEKUMMERNIS")
  (CANTATA NO. 21)
                                              Arranger.
—— SINFONIA (FROM "ICH STEH MIT EINEM FUSS IN GRAB")
  (CANTATA NO. 156)
                                              Arranger.
—— SONATA IN E FLAT MAJOR FOR PIANO: FIRST MOVT.
  1,2,1,2 - 1,1,0,0 - str.   Henmar.
—— TOCCATA AND FUGUE IN D MINOR
  4,*4,*4,*4 - 6,3,4,1 - timp.,2cel. - 2hp. - str.   9:00 Broude.
—— WACHET AUF
  4,3,4,1 alto(or ten.)sax.,3 - 5,4,3,5 (incl. 4 euph. or bar.) - hp. - str.
                                              Henmar.

BACH, Johann Sebastian - STRAVINSKY, Igor
—— CHORAL VARIATIONEN: "VOM HIMMEL HOCH" (FOR
  MIXED CHORUS AND ORCH.)
                                              12:00 Bo. Hawkes.

BACH, Johann Sebastian - SUTHERLAND, Margaret
—— SUITE IN E MINOR
  str.   A.P.R.A.

BACH, Johann Sebastian - SZIGETI, Josef - DAHL, Ingolf
—— CONCERTO IN D MAJOR, FOR VIOLIN AND STRING
  ORCH.
  str.   24:00 Bo. Hawkes.

BACH, Johann Sebastian - THAULOW, L.
—— PRELUDE IN E MINOR (FOR STRING ORCH.)
  str.   5:00 Leeds.

BACH, Johann Sebastian - THILDE, Jean
—— CONCERTO IN G MINOR, FOR TRUMPET AND STRINGS
  tpt. - str.   9:00 Presser.
—— SUITE IN B MINOR, FOR TRUMPET AND STRINGS
  tpt. - str.   Presser.

BACH, Johann Sebastian - TOCH, Ernst
—— PRELUDE AND FUGUE (ARRANGED FREELY FROM THE
  SOLO VIOLIN SONATA NO. 3) (FOR STRING ORCH.)
  str.   11:00 Mills.

BACH, Johann Sebastian - TÖTTCHER - MÜLLER, Gottfried
—— CONCERTO IN F MAJOR, FOR OBOE, STRINGS AND
  CONTINUO
  ob. - cemb. - str.   F. Colombo.

BACH, Johann Sebastian - TOVEY, Donald F.
—— THE ART OF FUGUE
                                              Oxford.

—— INVERTIBLE FUGUE (COMPLETING "THE ART OF THE
  FUGUE")
  str.   15:00 Oxford.

BACH, Johann Sebastian - VAN AMELSVOORT, F.
—— MAGNIFICAT
                                              14:00 Harmonia.

BACH, Johann Sebastian - VAN HOESEN, Karl D. - HUNT, Frederick
—— FANTASIA CON IMITAZIONE
  2,2,2,2 - 4,2,3,0 - timp. - pf. - str.   C. Fischer.

BACH, Johann Sebastian - VARDI, Emmanuel
—— CHACONNE (FROM THE VIOLIN PARTITA NO. 2 (ARR.
  FOR STRINGS)
  str.   MCA Music.

BACH, Johann Sebastian - VAUGHAN WILLIAMS, R. - FOSTER, A.
—— THE GIANT FUGUE (CHORALE PRELUDE: "WIR GLAUBEN
  ALL' AN EINEN GOTT") (FOR STRING ORCH.)
  str.   Oxford.

BACH, Johann Sebastian - VENE, R.
—— PRELUDE IN E♭ MINOR (FROM THE "WELL-TEMPERED
  CLAVIER") (FOR STRING ORCH.)
  str.   5:00 G. Schirmer.

BACH, Johann Sebastian - VOLKEL, George
—— FUGUE IN G (FOR STRING ORCH.)
  str.   G. Schirmer.
—— PRELUDE AND TOCCATA (FOR STRING ORCH.)
  str.   Witmark.

BACH, Johann Sebastian - VON KREISLER, Alexander
—— PRELUDE AND FUGUE
  str.   SouthernTx.

BACH, Johann Sebastian - WAGNER, R. - SEVITZKY, Fabien
—— TEN CHORALES FOR BRASS ENSEMBLE
  0,0,0,0 - 4,2,3,1   Arranger.

BACH, Johann Sebastian - WALTON, William
—— SHEEP MAY SAFELY GRAZE (ARIA FROM CANTATA 208)
  1,*2,1,1, - 1,0,0,0 - hp. - str.   7:00 Oxford.
—— THE WISE VIRGINS (BALLET SUITE) (IN 6 MOVTS.)
  2,2,2,2 - 4,2,3,0 - timp. - hp. - str.   16:00 Oxford.

BACH, Johann Sebastian - WERNER, Jean Jacques
—— CANZONA
  1,1,1,1 - 1,0,0,0 - str.   10:00 Presser.

BACH, Johann Sebastian - WETZLER, H. H.
—— SONATA IN E♭
  2,2,2,2 - 2,3,3,0 - timp. - str.   10:00 Novello.

BACH, Johann Sebastian - WHITNEY, Maurice C.
—— SARABAND (FROM SUITE NO. 6 IN G MAJOR FOR
  VIOLONCELLO)
  str.   3:15 Bourne.

BACH, Johann Sebastian - WHITTAKER, W. G.
—— ANNA MAGADALENA SUITE
  str.   Oxford.
—— AWAKE US, LORD, AND HASTEN (CHORALE NO. 2) (FOR
  CHORUS AND ORCH.) (Engl. Text: C. S. Terry)
                                              Oxford.
—— CANTATA NO. 26 ("AH, HOW FLEETING") (FOR ALTO,
  TENOR, BASS, MIXED CHORUS AND ORCH.) (Engl. Text: W.
  G. Whittaker)
                                              Oxford.
—— CANTATA NO. 50 ("NOW HATH THE GRACE AND THE
  STRENGTH") (FOR MIXED CHORUS AND ORCH.) (Engl.
  Text: W. G. Whittaker)
                                              Oxford.
—— CONCERTO (FROM CANTATA NO. 142) (FOR 4 VIOLINS OR
  WOODWINDS AND STRING ORCH.)
  (2fl. and 2ob. ad lib.) - str.   Oxford.
—— CONCERTO (FROM CANTATA NO. 152)
  (fl. and ob. ad lib.) - str.   Oxford.
—— FIVE STRING SUITES
  str.   Oxford.
—— JESU, JOY OF MAN'S DESIRING
  2tpt. - str.   4:00 Oxford.

—— JESU, JOY OF MAN'S DESIRING (FROM CANTATA 147)
(FOR CHORUS AND ORCH.) (Engl. Text: Robert Bridges)
4:00 Oxford.
—— MARCH (FROM "DRAMA PER MUSICA") (CANTATA NO.
212)
fl.,ob.,cl(or 3tpt.) - timp. - str. 1:50 Oxford.
—— PASTORAL SYMPHONY (FROM CHRISTMAS ORATORIO)
(FOR STRING ORCH.)
str. 8:00 Oxford.
—— SHEEP MAY SAFELY GRAZE (AIR FROM SECULAR
CANTATA NO. 208) (FOR STRINGS, WITH 2 OPTIONAL
FLUTES AND PIANO)
2fl.(ad lib.) - pf.(ad lib.) - str. Oxford.
—— A SHORT PASSION (FROM ST. MATTHEW'S GOSPEL) (FOR
SOLO VOICES, MIXED CHORUS AND ORCH.) (Engl. Text: C.
S. Terry)
90:00 Oxford.
—— SINFONIA (FROM THE EASTER ORATORIO) (1ST MOVT.)
2ob.,bn.,3tpt. - str. 5:00 Oxford.
—— SINFONIA (FROM THE EASTER ORATORIO) (2ND MOVT.,
FOR OBOE OR VIOLIN AND STRING ORCH.)
ob.(ad lib.) - str. 4:00 Oxford.
—— SINFONIA NO. 1 (FROM CANTATA NO. 35)
2ob.,Eng. hn. - org. - str. Oxford.
—— SINFONIA NO. 2 (FROM CANTATA NO. 35)
Eng. hn. - org. - str. Oxford.
—— SINFONIA TO CANTATA NO. 18 (FOR 2 FLUTES OR
VIOLINS AND STRING ORCH.)
2fl.(ad lib.), bn. (ad lib.) - str. 4:00 Oxford.
—— SINFONIA TO CANTATA NO. 29
6tpt. - timp. - str. Oxford.
—— SINFONIA TO CANTATA NO. 42 (FOR 2 OBOES AND
BASOON, OR 2 VIOLINS AND CELLO, AND STRING ORCH.)
2ob. and bn. (ad lib.) - str. Oxford.
—— SINFONIA TO CANTATA NO. 75
Tpts. - str. 3:00 Oxford.
—— SINFONIA TO CANTATA NO. 76
ob. (ad lib.) - org. - str. 3:00 Oxford.
—— SINFONIA TO SECULAR CANTATA NO. 209 (FOR FLUTE
OR VIOLIN AND STRING ORCH.)
fl.(ad lib.) - str. 3:00 Oxford.
—— SINFONIAS TO CANTATAS NO. 12, 21, AND 156 (FOR OBOE
OR VIOLIN AND STRING ORCH.)
ob.(ad lib.) - str. 8:00 Oxford.
—— SINFONIAS TO CANTATAS NO. 150 AND 196 (FOR STRING
ORCH.)
org. - str. Oxford.
—— SONATA (FROM CANTATA NO. 182) (FOR 2 FLUTES OR
VIOLINS AND STRING ORCH.)
2fl. (ad lib.) - str. 3:00 Oxford.
—— SONATA (FROM CANTATA NO. 31)
3ob.,Eng.hn.,2bn. - 3tpt. - timp. - str. 5:00 Oxford.
—— SONATINA (FROM CANTATA NO. 106) (FOR 2 FLUTES OR
VIOLINS AND STRING ORCH.)
2fl. (ad lib.) - str. 2:00 Oxford.
—— WHO HOPES IN GOD (CHORALE NO. 20) (FOR CHORUS
AND ORCH.) (Engl. Text: C. S. Terry)
Oxford.

BACH, Johann Sebastian - WILLIAMS, G.
—— BACH SUITE (IN 6 MOVTS.)
fl.,ob.,cl.,bn.,tpt. and timp., ad lib. - str. Oxford.
—— PRELUDE (FROM ENGLISH SUITE NO. 5)
fl.,ob.,cl.,bn. and tpt., ad lib. - str. Oxford.

BACH, Johann Sebastian - WOOD, Henry J.
—— BRANDENBURG CONCERTO NO. 1 IN F MAJOR
3ob.,bn. - 2hn. - cemb. - str. 17:00 Chappell.
—— BRANDENBURG CONCERTO NO. 3 IN G MAJOR
cemb. - str. Bo. Hawkes.
—— SUITE NO. 6 FOR ORCHESTRA (IN 6 MOVTS.)
3,3,4,3 - 4,3,3,1 - timp. - hp. - org. - str. 17:00 Chappell.

BACH, Johann Sebastian - WOOD-HILL, Mabel
—— AN WASSERFLUSSEN BABYLON (BY THE WATERS OF
BABYLON)
1,1,1,2 - 1,0,0,0 - hp. - str. 7:00 Mills.

BACH, Johann Sebastian - WOODHOUSE, Charles
—— FOUR PIECES (FROM SUITE IN D MAJOR)
pf.(ad lib.) - str. 10:30 Bo. Hawkes.
—— GIGUE AND FUGUE
pf. (ad lib.) - str. 8:30 Bo. Hawkes.

—— SUITE OF SIX PIECES
pf. (ad lib.) - str. 13:30 Bo. Hawkes.

BACH, Johann Sebastian - ZADOR, Eugene
—— PRELUDE AND FUGUE IN F MINOR
*3,*3,*3,*3 - 4,3,3,1 - timp. - str. 6:00 Arranger.

BACH, P. D. Q. (Peter Schickele)
—— CANINE CANTATA: "WACHET ARF" ("SLEEPING DOGS
AWAKE") (FOR DOG OR HOUNDENTENOR AND ORCH.)
0,0,0,2 - 2,2(in D),0,0 - timp. - str. 9:00 Presser.
—— CHORALE PRELUDE: "SHOULD" (FOR THE NEW YEAR)
(FOR VOICES AND SMALL ORCH.)
2 tpt. - timp. - str. 3:00 Presser.
—— CONCERTO FOR BASSOON VS. ORCHESTRA
2,2,2,3 - 2,2,0,0 - timp. - str. 20:00 Presser.
—— CONCERTO FOR HORN AND HARDART, S. 27
hn. - hardart(special instrument invented by composer) - str.
11:00 Presser.
—— CONCERTO FOR PIANO VS. ORCHESTRA
2,2,2,2 - 2,2,0,0 - timp. pf. - str. 25:00 Presser.
—— GROSS CONCERTO (FOR DIVERSE FLUTES, 2 TRUMPETS
AND STRINGS)
12:00 Presser.
—— HINDENBURG CONCERTO
*3,0,0,0 - 1,0,1(ten.-b.),1 - perc.(2) - str. 8:00 Presser.
—— IPHIGENIA IN BROOKLYN, S. 53162 (CANTATA) (FOR
BARGAIN-COUNTER TENOR AND CHAMBER ORCH.) (Text:
Composer)
Wine-bottle,3 double-reeds - tpt.-mouthpiece - hpsc. - str.(2,1,1,0)
10:00 Presser.
—— MISSA HILARIOUS (FOR BARGAIN-COUNTER TENOR,
BASSO-BLOTTO, SATB CHORUS AND ORCH.)
2 recorders,0,0,0,0 - 2,2,1,0 - timp.,perc. - str. 19:00 Presser.
—— OVERTURE TO "THE CIVILIAN BARBER"
0,2,0,2 - 2,0,0,0 - str. 2:45 EV.
—— PERUCKENSTUCKE (HAIRPIECE, FROM "THE CIVILIAN
BARBER") (FOR SOPRANO AND CHAMBER ORCH.) (Text:
Composer)
Pumpflute**, double-reed hookah** - police-trombone** - str.
11:00 Presser.
**Special instrument; invented by the composer
—— PERVERTIMENTO
Bagpipes - bicycle, balloons - str. 10:00 Presser.
—— THE SEASONINGS (ORATORIO) (FOR SATB SOLO VOICES,
CHORUS AND CHAMBER ORCH.) (Text: Composer)
2 slide-whistles,2 kazoos,tromboon and windbreaker(special
instruments invented by composer),shower-hose - fog-horn, 2 tpt. -
timp. - str. 20:00 Presser.
—— SERENUDE
2 slide-whistles, 2 kazoos, tromboon**, windbreaker**,
shower-hose - str. 10:00 Presser.
**Special instrument; invented by the composer
—— SINFONIA CONCERTANTE
Left-handed sewer flute(special instrument invented by
composer),ocarina,dougle-reed slide music stand(special instrument
invented by the composer),bagpipes - balalaika,lute- str.
8:00 Presser.
—— THE STONED GUEST (HALF-ACT OPERA) % (FOR
OFF-COLORATURA SOPRANO, MEZZANINE-SOPRANO,
BARGAIN-COUNTER TENOR, BASSO-BLOTTO, DOG AND
CHAMBER ORCH.) (Text: Composer)
1,1,0,1 - 1,1,1,0 - hpsc. - str. 30:00 Presser.
—— SUITE FROM "THE CIVILIAN BARBER"
0,0,0,2 - 2,2,1,0 - timp. - str.(no vlns. or vlas.) 9:00 Presser.

BACH, Wilhelm Friedemann - SMIGELSKI, Werner
—— CONCERTO IN F MINOR, FOR HARPSICHORD, STRING
ORCH. AND BASSO CONTINUO
hpsc. - cemb. - str. F. Colombo.

BACH, Wilhelm Friedrich Ernst - TOWNSEND, Douglas
—— CONCERTO BUFFO ("THE MUSIC MAKERS") (Text: Oscar
Brand)
Arranger.

BACHELET, Alfred
—— BALLADE FOR VIOLIN AND ORCH.
3,3,2,2 - 4,2,3,1 - timp.,perc.(3) - hp. - str. 18:00 EV.
—— UN JARDIN SUR L'ORONTE: DANCES FROM THE OPERA
(1931)
3,2,2,2 - 4,3,4,0 - timp.,perc.,cel.,xyl. - 2 hp. - str. 16:00 Presser.

—— QUAND LA CLOCHE SONNERA (1-ACT OPERA) % (1922)
2,2(2nd alt. with Eng.hn.),2,2 - 4,2,3,1 - timp.,perc.,cel.,glock - 2
hp. - str.   60:00 Presser.
On Stage: band

BÄCK, Sven-Erik
—— APERIO (FOR ORCH., TAPE AND ELECTRONIC
INSTRUMENTS)(1973)
                                                                 50:00 Tetra.
—— ARKITEKTUR - 60 (MUSIC FOR 2 WIND-ORCHESTRAS AND
PERCUSSION)
                                                                 S.T.I.M.
—— THE BANQUET ("GÄSTABUDET") (2-ACT CHAMBER
OPERA) % (FOR SOLO VOICES, MIXED CHORUS AND
SMALL ORCH.)
1,0,1,1 - 1,1,1,0 - timp.,perc. - pf. - str.   105:00 G. Schirmer.
—— CHAMBER SYMPHONY
1,1,1,1 - 1,1,1,0 - timp.,perc.(2) - str.   13:00 S.T.I.M.
—— CONCERTO FOR CELLO AND ORCH.
                                                    16:00 G. Schirmer.
—— CONCERTO FOR VIOLIN AND ORCH. (1957)
2,0,0,2 - 2,0,0,0 - timp.,perc.(3),cel. - pf. - str. 17:00 G. Schirmer.
—— THE CRANE ("TRANFJÄDRARNA") (RADIO OPERA IN 5
SCENES) % (FOR 4 SOLO VOICES, MIXED CHORUS,
CHILDREN'S CHORUS AND SMALL ORCH.)
1(alt. with picc.),0,0,1 - 1,0,0,0 - timp.,perc. - str.(no. vlns.)
                                                   55:00 G. Schirmer.
—— FANTASY ON "DIES SIND DIE HEIL'GEN ZEHN GEBOT"
1,1,1,1 - 2,1,1,0 - timp.,perc. - str.   13:00 G. Schirmer.
—— FÅGELN (THE BIRDS) (RADIO OPERA) % (FOR 3 SOLO
VOICES, MIXED CHORUS AND 20 INSTRS.)
                                                   60:00 S.T.I.M.
—— A GAME AROUND A GAME (CONCERTO FOR STRINGS
AND PERCUSSION)
timp.,perc.(5),cel. - pf. - str.   15:00 G. Schirmer.
—— INTRADA
                                                   10:00 G. Schirmer.
—— KÖPMANNEN I VENEDIG ("THE MERCHANT OF VENICE")
(INCIDENTAL MUSIC TO SHAKESPEARE'S DRAMA) (FOR
WOMEN'S CHORUS AND CHAMBER ORCH.)
1,1,0,1 - 0,1,1,0 - perc.(1),cel. - str.(no vlns.) 15:00 S.T.I.M.
—— LUSTSPELMUSIK (SUITE)
1,0,1,1 - 0,2,1,0 - perc.(2),cel. - pf. - str.   S.T.I.M.
—— MOVEMENTS (MUSIC FOR BALLET) % (1965)
1,0,1,0 - 0,1,1,0 - timp.,perc.,cel. - hp. - pf. - str.
                                                   21:00 G. Schirmer.
—— MOVIMENTO II (RUOLI PER ORCH.) (1966)
*3,3(3rd alt. with Eng.hn.),*3,*3 - 4,3,3,1 - timp.,perc.(4),cel. - 2
hp. - org. - pf. - str.   15:00 G. Schirmer.
—— O, ALTITUDO II (1966)
*3,3,2(2nd alt. with b.-cl.),3(3rd alt. with c.-bn.) - 4,3,3,1 -
timp.,perc.(4) - 2 hp. - org. - pf.(alt. with hpsc.) - str.
                                                   10:00 G. Schirmer.
—— A PLAY ABOUT MARY, MOTHER OF JESUS (ETT SPEL OM
MARIA, JESU MODER) (ORATORIO) (FOR SOLO VOICES,
CHILDREN'S CHORUS, MIXED CHORUS AND ORCH.)
2,2,0,0 - 0,2,2,0 - timp.,perc.(2) - hp. - org. - pf. (or cel.) - str.
                                                   85:00 G. Schirmer.
—— ROLES (MOVEMENT II) (CONCERT VERSION OF
"MOVEMENTS") (1966)
3,3,3,3 - 4,3,3,1 - timp.,perc.(4),cel. - pf. - str. 15:00 G. Schirmer.
—— SINFONIA FOR STRINGS
str.   23:00 S.T.I.M.
—— TROJANSKORNA (THE TROJAN WOMEN) (THEATER
MUSIC TO EURIPEDES' DRAMA) (FOR WOMEN'S CHORUS
AND CHAMBER ORCH.)
0,2,0,2 - 0,2,2,0 - perc.(1) - org. - pf.   30:00 S.T.I.M.
—— VARIATIONS ON A LUTHERAN HYMN
1,1,1,1 - 2,1,0,0 - timp.,perc.(2) - str.   12:00 S.T.I.M.

BACKER LUNDE, Johan
—— PRELUDES SYMPHONIQUES
3,3,2,2 - 4,2,3,1 - timp. - hp. - str.   T.O.N.O.
—— RONDO
3,2,2,2 - 4,2,3,1 - timp.,perc.,cel. - hp. - str. Norsk Mfl.
—— SYMPHONY IN D MINOR
3,3,2,2 - 4,2,3,1 - timp. - hp. - str.   T.O.N.O.
—— THREE SKETCHES, OP. 22
str.   Norsk Mfl.

BACON, Ernst
—— BLACK AND WHITE SONGS (5 FOLKSONGS) (FOR LOW
VOICE AND ORCH.)
2,2,2, alto sax.,2 - 4,2,3,1 - cel. - hp. - str.   12:00 Arranger.
—— THE ECCLESIASTES (A CANTATA) (FOR SOPRANO, BASS
AND ORCH.)
                                                   35:00 Composer.
—— ELEGY (VARIANTS ON A VENETIAN MELODY)
ob. - str.   9:00 Composer.
—— ERIE WATERS (SUITE) (BASED ON UPSTATE NEW YORK
FOLKSONGS) (IN 4 MOVTS.)
2,2,2,2 - 4,3,3,1 - perc.(1) - str.   14:00 Composer.
—— FABLES (FOR NARRATOR AND ORCH.) (IN 6 MOVTS.)
1,1,1,1 - 1,0,0,0 - perc. - pf. - str.   25:00 Composer.
—— FROM EMILY'S DIARY (FOR WOMEN'S CHORUS AND
SMALL ORCH.) (Text: Emily Dickinson)
*2,1,1,1 - hn. - perc. - pf. - str.   25:00 G. Schirmer.
—— GREAT RIVER (THE RIO GRANDE) (SUITE) (FOR
NARRATOR AND ORCH.)
                                                   30:00 Composer.
—— MIDNIGHT SPECIAL (4 FOLKSONGS) (FOR MEDIUM OR
HIGH VOICE AND ORCH.)
2,*3,2,1 - 1,2,0,0 - perc.,cel. - hp.,guitar - str. 7:00 Arranger.
—— MY RIVER (5 SONGS ON POEMS OF EMILY DICKENSON)
(FOR VOICE AND ORCH.)
2,1,2,2 - 2,0,0,0 - hp. - str.   12:00 Composer.
—— PLACES TO PAUSE (A PIANO CONCERTO IN TEN MOVTS.)
2,2,2,2 - 4,3,3,1 - perc.(3) - pf. - str.   25:00 Composer.
—— SONATA FOR STRINGS (IN 4 MOVTS.)
str.   21:00 Composer.
—— SONGS OF ETERNITY (FOUR SONGS FOR MEDIUM VOICE
AND ORCH.)
                                                   12:00 Composer.
—— SYMPHONY NO. 3 (IN 5 MOVTS.)
                                                   26:00 Composer.
—— A TREE ON THE PLAINS (2 ACT OPERA) % (REV. 1961)
(Text: Paul Horgan)
1,1,2,1 - 2,2,2,0 - perc.(2) - pf. (4-hands)   135:00 Composer.
—— TWILIGHT (THREE SONGS FOR LOW VOICE AND ORCH.)
(Text: Walt Whitman)
2,2,2,1 - 3,2,0,0 - perc.,cel. - str.   9:00 Composer.
—— VARIATIONS ON "THE MUFFIN MAN"
*2-*3,2,2,2 - 4,3,3,1 - timp.,perc.(2),bells,cel.,glock.,xyl. - hp.(ad
lib.) - str.   5:00 G. Schirmer.

BADEN, Conrad
—— CANTATA FOR SKIEN'S 600TH ANNIVERSARY (FOR SOLO
VOICES, MIXED CHORUS AND ORCH.) (Text: Halvor J.
Sandsdalen)
2,2,2,2 - 4,3,3,1 - timp.,perc. - org.   60:00 T.O.N.O.
—— CANTATA FOR STRØMSØ CHURCH'S 300TH ANNIVERSARY
(1967) (FOR SOLO VOICES, CHORUS AND ORCH.)
                                                   T.O.N.O.
—— CONCERTINO FOR CLARINET AND STRINGS (IN 3
MOVTS.)
cl. - str.   12:00 Henmar.
—— CONCERTO PER ORCHESTRA
2,2,2,3 - 4,3,3,1 - timp.,perc.,bells,cel.,xyl. - hp. - str.
                                                   13:00 T.O.N.O.
—— DIVERTIMENTO (IN 3 MOVTS.)
2,2,2,2 - 4,3,3,0 - timp. - str.   15:00 Ed. Lyche.
—— FAIRY-TALE SUITE (EVENTYRSUITE) (IN 6 MOVTS.)
3,2,2,3 - 4,3,3,1 - timp.,perc. - hp. - pf. - str. 14:00 Ed. Lyche.
—— FANTASIA BREVIS
3,2,2,3 - 4,3,3,1 - timp.,perc.,cel. - hp. - str. 10:00 T.O.N.O.
—— MASS (MESSE) (FOR SOLO VOICES, MIXED CHORUS AND
ORCH.)
2,2,2,2 - 4,3,3,1 - timp. - org. - str.   60:00 T.O.N.O.
—— OVERTURA GIOIA
2,2,2,2 - 4,2,3,1 - timp.,perc. - str.   6:00 Henmar.
—— PASTORALE E FUGA (FOR CHAMBER ORCH.)
1,1,1,1 - 2,0,0,0 - str.   12:00 Henmar.
—— SYMPHONY NO. 1 (IN 3 MOVTS.)
2,2,2,2 - 4,3,3,1 - timp.,perc. - str.   25:00 Ed. Lyche.
—— SYMPHONY NO. 2 (IN 3 MOVTS.)
2,2,2,2 - 4,3,3,1 - timp.,perc. - str.   27:00 Henmar.

BADGER, Harold
—— CONCERTANTE FOR PIANO AND ORCH.
                                                   12:30 A.P.R.A.
—— FIVE SHAKESPERIAN SONGS (FOR SOPRANO AND ORCH.)
                                                   11:00 A.P.R.A.

—— OVERTURE FOR ORCHESTRA

8:00 A.P.R.A.

BADINGS, Henk
—— APOCALYPS (ORATORIUM OP TEKSTEN UIT DE
OPENBARING VAN JOHANNES) (FOR SATB SOLO VOICES,
MIXED CHORUS AND ORCH.) (1948)
  3,3,3,3 - 4,4,3,1 - timp.,perc.,cel. - hp. - pf. - str.   100:00 Henmar.
—— ARIA TRISTA AND RONDO GIOCOSO (1948)
  1,0,1,0 - 0,0,0,0 - hp. - pf. - str.   12:00 Henmar.
—— ASTERION (RADIO OPERA) (1957) (WITH SOPRANO, ALTO,
TENOR, BASS AND CHORUS)
  2,3,2,0 - 3,2,2,1 - perc. - tape recorder - hp. - pf. - str.
75:00 B.U.M.A.
—— ATLANTISCHE DANSEN (CONCERTO NO. 2 FOR PIANO
AND ORCH.) (1955)
  1,1,2,1 - 1,2,2,0 - timp.,perc.,xyl. - pf. - str.   12:00 Henmar.
—— AVE MARIS STELLA (HYMNUS) (FOR FEMALE CHORUS
AND ORCH.) (1965)
10:00 Henmar.
—— BALLADE (SYMPHONIC VARIATIONS II)(ON "THERE WERE
TWO ROYAL CHILDREN")
  2,2,2,2 - 4,3,3,0 -timp.,perc. - hp. - str.   9:00 Henmar.
—— BALLETTO SERIOSO (L'APPARECCHIO MIN-ACCIANTE)
  2,2,3,2 - 4,3,3,1 - timp.,perc.,cel. - pf. - str.   25:00 Henmar.
—— CANTATA NO. 4 (FOR MIXED CHORUS AND ORCH.) (1954)
  2,2,2,2 - 4,3,3,1 - timp.,perc. - str.   12:00 Henmar.
—— CONCERTINO (TRIPLE CONCERTO) FOR VIOLIN, CELLO,
PIANO AND SMALL ORCH. (1942)
  3,2,3,2 - 3,1,1,0 - timp.,perc.,cel. - pf. - str.   20:00 Henmar.
—— CONCERTO FOR HARP AND ORCH. (1968)
  1. Lento; 2. Grave; 3. Presto
  2,2,2,2 - 4,2,2,0 - timp.,perc.,cel. - hp. - str.   20:00 Henmar.
—— CONCERTO FOR SAXOPHONE AND ORCH. (1951)
  2,2,2,alto sax.,2 - 3,3,3,1 - timp.,perc. - str.   18:00 Henmar.
—— CONCERTO FOR TWO PIANOS AND ORCH.
  3,2,2,2 - 3,3,1,1 - timp.,perc.,cel. - 2 pf. - str.   24:00 Henmar.
—— CONCERTO FOR TWO VIOLINS AND ORCH. (DOUBLE
CONCERTO NO. 1) (1954)
  2,2,2,2 - 4,3,3,1 - timp.,perc.,cel. - pf. - str.   24:00 Henmar.
—— CONCERTO FOR VIOLA AND STRING ORCH.
  str.   18:00 Henmar.
—— CONCERTO FOR VIOLIN, VIOLA AND ORCH. (1965)
  3,2,2,2 - 3,2,0,0 - timp.,perc.,cel. - pf. - str.   21:00 Henmar.
—— CONCERTO NO. 1 FOR CELLO AND ORCH. (1930)
  1. Allegro moderato; 2. Largo; 3. Allegro non troppo
  1,1,1,1 - 1,1,1,0 - perc. - str.   18:00 Henmar.
—— CONCERTO NO. 1 FOR FLUTE AND ORCH. (1956)
  3,1,2,1 - 2,1,1,0 - timp. - pf. - str.   23:00 Henmar.
—— CONCERTO NO. 1 FOR ORGAN AND ORCH. (1952)
  2,2,2,2 - 3,3,3,1 - timp.,perc. - org. - str.   24:00 Henmar.
—— CONCERTO NO. 1 FOR PIANO AND ORCH. (1939)
  2,2,3,2 - 4,3,3,1 - timp.,perc.,cel. - pf. - str.   20:00 Henmar.
—— CONCERTO NO. 1 FOR VIOLIN AND ORCH. (1928)
  2,1,2,1 - 3,2,3,1 - timp.,perc. - str.   20:00 B.U.M.A.
—— CONCERTO NO. 2 FOR CELLO AND ORCH. (1954)
  2,2,3,2 - 3,2,2,0 - timp.,perc. - str.   22:00 Henmar.
—— CONCERTO NO. 2 FOR ORGAN AND ORCH. (1966)
  1. Lento; 2. Tranquillo; 3. Allegro
  2,2,2,2 - 3,3,2,0 - timp.,perc.,cel. - org. - str.   18:00 Henmar.
—— CONCERTO NO. 2 FOR VIOLIN AND ORCH.
  3,3,3,3 - 2,2,2,1 - timp.,perc. - str.   22:00 Henmar.
—— CONCERTO NO. 2 FOR 2 VIOLINS AND SMALL ORCH.
  (Written in 31-tone system)
  4 trb. - timp.,perc.(6) - str.   20:00 Henmar.
—— CONCERTO NO. 3 FOR VIOLIN AND ORCH.
  2,2,2,2 - 3,2,0,0 - timp. - str.   30:00 Henmar.
—— CONCERTO NO. 4 FOR VIOLIN AND ORCH.
  3,1,1,1 - 2,0,0,0 - timp. - str.   26:00 Henmar.
—— DANSVARIATIES (DANCE VARIATIONS)(SYMPHONIC
VARIATIONS III) (1956)
  3,2,3,3 - 4,3,3,1 - timp.,perc. - pf. - str.   17:00 Henmar.
—— DIVERTIMENTO FOR SYMPHONY ORCHESTRA (AT THE
COURT OF CHINON: SCENE FROM THE LIFE OF JEANNE
D'ARC)
  3,3,3,3 - 4,3,3,1 - timp.,perc.,vibra. - str.   12:00 Henmar.
—— DRIE KERSTLIEDEREN (3 SACRED SONGS) (FOR SOPRANO
AND ORCH.) (1939)
  2,2,2,1 - 3,2,1,0 - timp.,perc.,cel. - hp. - str.   10:00 Henmar.
—— LES ELFES (FOR NARRATOR AND ORCH.) (1948)
  3,2,2,2 - 3,3,3,0 - perc.,cel. - hp. - str.   8:00 Henmar.
—— EPISODE FOR STRING ORCH.
  str.   5:00 B.U.M.A.

—— FANFARE 1492 FOR JEANNE D'ARC (FOR 4 TRUMPETS
AND ORCH.) (1944)
  3,3,3,3 - 4,4,3,1 - timp.,perc. - hp. - str.   7:00 Henmar.
—— FESTIVAL CANTATA (CANTATA NO. 1) (FOR SOLO
VOICES, MIXED CHORUS AND ORCH.) (1936)
  3,3,3,3 - 6,6,3,2 - timp.,perc. - hp. - org. - str. 30:00 B.U.M.A.
—— GIJSBREGHT VAN AEMSTEL (INCIDENTAL MUSIC TO
VONDEL'S PLAY) (WITH ALTO SOLO AND CHORUS) %
(1937)
  2,2,2,2 - 4,2,2,1 - timp.,perc. - str.   85:00 Henmar.
—— HONESTUM PETIMUS USQUE (CANTATA NO. 2) (FOR
SOPRANO, MIXED CHORUS AND ORCH.) (1937)
  2,0,3,0 - 2,2,1,0 - timp.,perc.,cel. - pf. - str.   24:00 Henmar.
—— IRISH OVERTURE (IERSE OUVERTURE) (OVERTURE NO. 6)
(1961)
  3,3,3,2 - 4,3,3,1 - timp.,perc.,cel.,xyl. - hp. - pf. - str.
10:00 Henmar.
—— JONAH (ORATORIO) (FOR SOLO VOICES, MIXED CHORUS
AND ORCH.) (1963)
  6,1,3,0 - 2,2,2,0 - timp.,perc.,cel. - tape recorder - pf. - str.
30:00 Henmar.
—— LANCELOET (INCIDENTAL MUSIC TO THE PLAY) % (1950)
  1,1,1,0 - 1,0,0,0 - str.   15:00 Henmar.
—— LAUS PACIS (CANTATA NO. 5) (FOR SOPRANO, MALE
CHORUS AND WINDS) (1956) (Text: D. Erasmus)
  2,1,3,1 - 2,3,3,1 - timp.,perc.,cel. - pf. - d.-b.   30:00 Henmar.
—— LAUS STULTITIAE (CANTATA NO. 6) (FOR MIXED CHORUS
AND ARBITRARY-SIZED ORCH.) (1961)
  Minimum: 4 woodwinds or brass (obbligato) - perc. - 2 pf. - vlns.
  (obbligato)   25:00 Henmar.
  or:
  Maximum: 8 woodwinds or brass (4 obbligato) - perc. - 2 pf. - str.
—— LIEDEREN VAN LEVEN EN DOOD (SONGS OF LIFE AND
DEATH) (4 SONGS FOR TENOR AND ORCH.) (1940) (Text: P.
C. Boutens)
  2,2,3,2 - 3,2,3,0 - timp.,perc.,cel.,vibra. - hp. - str.   18:00 Henmar.
—— LOUISVILLE SYMPHONY (SYMPHONY NO. 7)
  2,2,3,2 - 4,2,3,1 - timp.,perc. - hp. - pf. - str.   25:00 Henmar.
—— LOVE'S RUSES (LIEBSRÄNKE) (COMIC CHAMBER OPERA)
% (1945) (Sopr. Alt. Ten. Bar. and Bass solo voices)
  3,2,2,1 - 3,1,0,0 - perc. - str.   120:00 Henmar.
—— MARTIN KORDA, D. P. (DRAMATIC CHORAL OPERA) %
(1960) (WITH S.A.T.B. SOLO PARTS)
  3,2,2,2 - 4,3,3,1 - timp.,perc.,cel. - tape recorder - str.
150:00 Henmar.
—— NEDERLANDSE DANSEN
  2,2,2,2 - 4,2,3,0 - timp.,perc. - str.   12:00 Henmar.
—— ORESTES (RADIO OPERA) (1954) (WITH SOPRANO, TENOR,
NARRATOR AND CHORUS)
  4,3,4,2 sax.,3 - 4,4,3,1 - timp.,perc.,cel. - tape recorder - hp. - pf. -
str.   60:00 B.U.M.A.
—— OVERTURE NO. 5 (OVERTURE TO A HOLLAND FESTIVAL)
(1954)
  2,2,2,2 - 4,3,3,1 - timp.,perc. - str.   12:00 Henmar.
—— PREDILCOVA (1935)
  1,1,1,1 - 1,1,1,0 - perc. - pf. - str.   5:00 Henmar.
—— PSALM 147 (FOR CHILDREN'S CHORUS, MIXED CHORUS
AND ORCH.) (1959)
  3,2,3,2 - 4,3,3,1 - timp.,perc.,cel. - pf. - str.   30:00 Henmar.
—— PUPAZZETTI AZZURRI (1950)
  1,1,2,1 bar. sax.,0 - 0,2,2,0 - perc. - guit. - pf. - str. 9:00 Henmar.
—— SERENADE
  2,2,2,2 - 4,3,3,1 - timp.,perc. - str.   18:00 Henmar.
—— SYMPHONIC OVERTURE (OVERTURE NO. 3) (1942)
  3,3,3,3 - 4,4,3,1 - timp.,perc. - str.   12:00 Henmar.
—— SYMPHONIC VARIATIONS IV, ON A SOUTH AFRICAN
THEME (1960)
  3,3,3,3 - 4,4,3,1 - timp.,perc.,cel.,vibra.,xyl. - str. 21:00 Henmar.
—— SYMPHONY NO. 1, FOR 16 SOLO INSTRUMENTS (1932)
(1932)
  2,2,2,2 - 2,1,0,0 - str.(2,1,1,1)   20:00 Henmar.
—— SYMPHONY NO. 2
28:00 B.U.M.A.
—— SYMPHONY NO. 4 (1943)
  3,3,3,3 - 4,3,3,1 - timp.,perc.,cel. - str.   32:00 Henmar.
—— SYMPHONY NO. 6 (PSALMENSYMPHONIE) (FOR MIXED
CHORUS AND ORCH.) (1953) (IN 4 MOVTS.)
  2,2,3,2 - 4,3,3,1 - timp.,perc.,cel. - str.   32:00 Henmar.
—— SYMPHONY NO. 8 (HANNOVER-SINFONIE) (1956)
  3,2,3,2 - 4,3,3,1 - timp.,perc.,cel. - pf. - str.   18:00 Henmar.
—— SYMPHONY NO. 9 (SYMPHONY FOR STRING ORCH.)
(1959) (IN 3 MOVTS.)
  str.   17:00 Henmar.

—— SYMPHONY NO. 10 (1961)
3,2,3,2 - 3,2,3,1 - timp.,perc.,cel. - str.   22:00 Henmar.
—— SYMPHONY NO. 11 (SINFONIA GIOCOSA) (1964)
3,2,3,2 - 4,3,3,1 - timp.,perc. - str.   8:00 Henmar.
—— SYMPHONY NO. 12 (SINFONISCHE KLANGFIGUREN) (1964)
4,3,4,3 - 4,3,3,1 - timp.,perc.,cel. - hp. - pf. - 18:00 Henmar.
—— THREE DUETS (FOR SOPRANO, CONTRALTO AND STRING
ORCH.) (1936) (DREI DUETTE)
str.   7:00 Henmar.
—— VARIATION ON A THEME OF RICHARD STRAUSS (FOR 2
VIOLINS AND ORCH.) (1958)
2:00 Henmar.
—— VIER WIEGELIEDJES (4 CRADLE SONGS) (FOR SOPRANO
AND STRING ORCH.) (1936)
str.   5:00 Henmar.
—— DE WESTEWIND (FOR NARRATOR AND ORCH) (1936)
2,2,2,1 - 4,2,2,1 - perc.,cel. - hp. - pf. - str.   9:00 Henmar.

BAERVOETS, Raymond
—— CONCERTO FOR VIOLA AND ORCH. (1968)
3,3,3,3 - 4,3,3,1 - timp.,perc. - str.   16:00 H. Elkan.
—— CONSTALLATIONS (FOR 23 PERFORMERS, IN 4 GROUPS)
(1966)
1,1,*1,alto. sax.,1 - 0,1,1,0 - perc.(6),cel.,vibra.,xyl. - 2 hp. - pf. -
str.(2,2,2,1)   8:30 H. Elkan.
—— ESPRESSIONI (1966)
3,3,3,3 - 4,3,3,1 - timp.,perc. - str.   8:00 H. Elkan.
—— IMMAGINI (FOR 14 INSTRUMENTS)
1,1,1,0 - 1,0,0,0 - perc. - hp. - pf. - str.   H. Elkan.
—— MUSICA (FOR CHAMBER ORCH.) (1972)
2,2,2,2 - 2,2,2,0 - timp.,perc. - str.   10:00 H. Elkan.
—— NOTTURNO (1971)
2,2,2,2 - 2,2,2,0 - timp.,perc. - str.   12:00 H. Elkan.

BAEYENS, August
—— ARKADIA (CHAMBER SYMPHONY FOR 19 SOLOISTS) (1951)
2,2,2,2 - 1,1,1,0 - perc. - pf. - str.   25:00 H. Elkan.
—— CONCERTO FOR VIOLA AND ORCH.
2,2,2,2 - 2,2,2,0 - timp.,perc. - str.   23:00 H. Elkan.
—— NOTTURNO
2,2,2,2 - 4,2,3,1 - timp. - hp. - str.   10:00 CBDM.
—— SINFONIA BREVE (1928)
2,2,2,2 - 2,2,1,0 - timp.,perc. - str.   10:00 H. Elkan.
—— SYMPHONY NO. 2 (1939)
2,2,2,alto sax,2 - 4,2,3,1 - timp.,perc. - str.   25:00 H. Elkan.
—— SYMPHONY NO. 3
3,2,2,2 - 4,3,3,1 - timp.,perc. - str.   30:00 CBDM.
—— SYMPHONY NO. 4 (1952)
4,3,4,4 - 4,4,3,1 - timp.,perc. - 2 hp. - str.   80:00 H. Elkan.
—— SYMPHONY NO. 5
2,2,2,2 - 4,2,3,1 - str.   29:00 CBDM.
—— SYMPHONY NO. 6 (1955)
3,2,3,3 - 4,3,3,1 - timp.,perc. - hp. - str.   40:00 H. Elkan.

BAFARK, Bálint - DARVAS, Gábor
—— THREE LUTE FANTASIES
2,2,0,2 - 0,1,0,0 - 2 cymb. - hp. - str.   9:00 Bo. Hawkes.

BAGRINOWSKY, M.
—— CONTES RUSSES (MINIATURES FANTASTIQUES), OP. 1
3,3,2,2 - 4,4,3,1 - timp.,perc. - hp. - str.   15:00 Bo. Hawkes.
—— LE MATIN (FROM "CONTES RUSSES")
3,3,2,2 - 4,3,3,1 - timp.,perc. - str.   5:00 Bo. Hawkes.

BAILEY, Judith M.
—— CORNISH OVERTURE ("PENMORVAH")
1,1,2,1 - 2,1,0,0 - timp. - str.   10:00 P.R.S.

BAILLY, Jean-Guy
—— LES MUTATIONS
3,3,3,2 - 4,3,1,0 - timp.,perc. - 2 hp. - str.   34:00 Presser.
—— ZENITH
3,2,3,2 - 3,3,3,1 - timp.,perc. - hp. - str.   20:00 Presser.

BAINTON, Edgar L.
—— A HYMN TO GOD THE FATHER (FOR CHORUS AND
ORCH.)
*3,*3,3,2 - 4,3,3,1 - timp.,perc. - str.   Oxford.
—— PAVANE, IDYLL AND BACCHANAL (FOR STRING ORCH.)
fl.(ad lib.) - str.   P.R.S.

BAIRD, John
—— CAPRICCIO FOR ORCH.
2,2,2,2 - 4,2,3,0 - timp.,perc. - str.   15:00 P.R.S.

BAIRD, Tadeusz
—— FOUR NOVELETTES
2,1,2,1 - 1,1,1,0 - timp.,perc.,cel. - hp. - pf. - str.
12:00 G. Schirmer.
—— FOUR SONGS (A SONG CYCLE) (FOR MEZZO-SOPRANO
AND ORCH.)
3,1,2,1 - 1,1,1,0 - timp.,perc.,cel. - guit. - hp. - str.
11:00 G. Schirmer.
—— SINFONIA BREVIS
3,1,3,3 - 4,3,3,1 - perc.(5) - 2 hp. - hpsc. - pf. - str.
15:00 G. Schirmer.
—— SYMPHONY NO. 3 (1969)
4,3,3,3 - 6,4,3,1 - perc.(6),cel. - 2 hp. - hpsc. - pf. - str.
15:00 G. Schirmer.

BAIRSTOW, Edward C.
—— THE PRODIGAL SON (FOR SATB CHORUS AND SMALL
ORCH.) (Text: Biblical)
Oxford.

BAKALEINIKOFF, Vladimir
—— CONCERTO FOR VIOLA AND ORCH. (IN 3 MOVEMENTS)
2,2,2,2 - 2,2,0,0 - timp. - str.   16:00 Composer.
—— LITTLE SYMPHONY (IN 3 MOVEMENTS)
*3,2,2,*3 - 4,3,1,0 - timp.,perc.(3),glock - str.   16:00 F.E.M.A.
—— THREE ORIENTAL DANCES
*3,*3,*3,*3 - 4,3,3,1 - timp.,perc.(4),cel.glock. - str.
12:00 Composer.

BAKER, Claude
—— CONCERTINO FOR 3 QUINTETS, PIANO AND PERCUSSION
(1970)
1,1,1,1 - 2,2,1,1 - timp.,perc.(3),glock.,vibra.,xyl. - pf. - str.(2,1,1,1)
8:00 Composer.
—— REST, HEART OF THE TIRED WORLD (FOR SOPRANO AND
CHAMBER ORCH.) (1973) (Text: Kenneth Patchen)
1,1,1,1 - 0,1,1,0 - timp.,perc.(3),cel.,glock.,vibra.,xyl. - str.
6:00 Composer.
—— SPECULUM MUSICAE, PARS II (1976)
1,1,1,1 - 1,1,1,0 - timp.,perc.(3) - pf. - str.(no d.-b.)
18:00 Composer.
—— STROPHES FOR STRING ORCH. (1972)
str.   5:00 Composer.
—— THREE SONGS FOR SOPRANO AND ORCHESTRA (1973) (1.
WHERE; 2. BEAUTIFUL YOU ARE; 3. AN EASY DECISION)
(Text: Kenneth Patchen)
1(alt. with picc.),1,1,1 - 0,1,1,0 -
timp.,perc.(3),cel.,glock.,vibra.,xyl. - str.   8:00 Composer.

BAKSA, Robert F.
—— ARIA DA CAPO (OPERA) % (Text: Edna St. Vincent Millay)
2(2nd alt. with picc.),2(2nd alt. with Eng. hn.),2(2nd alt. with
b.-cl.),2 - 1,1,1,0 - perc. - hp. - str.   60:00 Tetra.
—— THE BURGERMEISTER'S BRIDE (SUITE) (IN 3 MOVTS.)
3(3rd alt. with picc.)*3,*3(1 alt. with E♭ cl.),2 - 4,3,3,0 -
perc.(2),xyl. - str.   11:00 Shawnee.
—— CHAMBER CONCERTO
1,1,1,1 - 0,0,0,0 - str.   Tetra.
—— CONCERTINO FOR WIND QUARTET AND STRINGS (IN 3
MOVTS.)
1,1,1,1 - 0,0,0,0 - str.   11:00 Composer.
—— THE GOLDEN NUGGET (OVERTURE)
3,2,2,2 - 4,3,3,0 - timp.,perc. - pf. - str.   6:00 Shawnee.
—— THE KRESS COLLECTION SUITE (RENAISSANCE SUITE) (IN
4 MOVTS.)
3,3,3,2 - 4,3,3,1 - timp. - str.   20:00 Shawnee.
or:
2,2,2,2 - 4,3,3,1 - timp. - str.
—— MEDITATION FOR ORCH.
2-3,1,2,2 - 4,0,3,0 - str.   7:00 Shawnee.
—— RED CARNATIONS (OPERA) %
1,1,2,1 - 0,0,0,0 - pf. - str.(3,1,2,1)   35:00 Tetra.
—— SERENADE FOR STRING ORCH.
str.   18:00 Tetra.
—— THREE OPTIMISTIC PIECES
2,2,1 E♭ cl.,3,2 - 3,2,3,0 - perc. - pf. - str.   9:00 Shawnee.

BALADA, Leonardo
—— AURORIS
    3,3,3,2 - 6,4,3,1 - timp.,perc.(4) - hp. - pf. - str. 14:00 Belw-Mills.
    or:
    3,3,3,2 - 4,3,3,1 - timp.,perc.(4) - hp. - pf. - str.
—— CONCERTO FOR BANDONEON AND ORCH.
    0,0,0,0 - 3,3,3,0 - perc.(3) - bandoneon - str. 14:00 General.
—— CONCERTO FOR CELLO AND 9 PLAYERS (1962)
    1(alt. with picc.),1(alt. with Eng. hn.),1(alt. with b.-cl.),1 - 1,2,1,0 -
    perc.(1) - 1 c. 15:00 General.
—— CONCERTO FOR GUITAR AND ORCHESTRA (1965) (IN 3 MOVTS.)
    2(2nd alt. with picc.),1,2(2nd alt. with b.-cl.),2 - 2,2,0,0 -
    perc.(2),vibra. - guit. - str. 18:00 General.
—— CONCERTO NO. 1 FOR PIANO AND ORCH. (1964)
    2(2nd alt. with picc.),2(2nd alt. with Eng.hn.),*3,2 - 3,3,3,1 -
    timp.,perc.(3),glock.,xyl. - pf. - str. 21:00 General.
—— GUERNICA (1966)
    2(2nd alt. with picc.),2,2(2nd alt. with b.-cl.),2 - 2-3,2-3,2-3,1 -
    timp.,perc.(4),glock.,vibra. - str. 12:00 General.
—— HOMMAGE A CASALS
    2(2nd alt. with picc.),2(2nd alt. with Eng.hn.),2,2 - 4,4,3,1 -
    timp.,perc.(4) - hp. - pf. - str. 8:00 G. Schirmer.
—— HOMMAGE A SARASATE
    2(2nd alt. with picc.),2(2nd alt. with Eng.hn.),2,2 - 4,4,3,1 -
    timp.,perc.(4) - hp. - pf. - str. 8:00 G. Schirmer.
—— MARIA SABRINA (SUITE) (FOR NARRATOR, SATB CHORUS AND ORCH.)
    2(2nd alt. with picc.),2(2nd alt. with Eng.hn.),2,0 - 2,3,1,1 -
    timp.,perc.(5) - org. - pf.(amplified) - str. 33:10 General.
—— MUSICA TRANQUILLA (1959)
    str. 7:00 General.
—— NO-RES (1975) (FOR NARRATOR, TAPE, SATB CHORUS AND ORCH.)
    *2-3,2-3,*3,*3 - 4,3,3,1 - timp.,perc.(5) - tape-recorder - acc. -
    hpsc. - org.(electric) - pf.(electric) - str. 40:00 G. Schirmer.
—— PONCE DE LEON (FOR NARRATOR AND ORCH.)
    4,3,3,4 - 6,4,4,1 - timp.,perc.(4) - pf. - str. Belw-Mills.
    or:
    3,2,2,3 - 4,3,3,1 - timp.,perc.(4) - pf. - str.
—— SINFONIA EN NEGRO (SYMPHONY IN BLACK)
(HOMENAJE A MARTIN LUTHER KING) (1968)
    2(2nd alt. with picc.),2,2(2nd alt. with b.-cl.),2(2nd alt. with c.-bn.)
    - 2,3,2,1 - timp.,perc.(3),xyl.,vibra. - pf. - str. 20:00 General.
—— STEEL SYMPHONY (SINFONIA DEL ACERO) (1972)
    *3,2,2,*3 - 4,3,3,1 - timp.,perc.(4),bells,vibra.,xyl. - pf. - str.
    20:00 Belw-Mills.

BALAKIREV, M. A. - CASELLA, A.
—— ISLAMEY
    3,3,3,*4 - 4,4,3,1 - timp.,perc. - 2hp. - str. Leeds.

BALAKIREV, M. A. - LIAPUNOV
—— ISLAMEY
    4,2,3,2 - 4,4,3,1 - timp.,perc. - 2hp. - str. 12:00 G. Schirmer.

BALANCHIVADZE, Andre
—— SYMPHONY
    3,3,3,2 - 4,4,3,1 - timp.,perc.,cel. - 2hp. - str. 41:00 G. Schirmer.

BALASSA, Sándor
—— IRIS, OP. 22
    3,*3,*3,*3 - 4,4,3,1 - timp.,perc.,cel. - cimbalom - hp. - pf. - str.
    12:00 Bo. Hawkes.
—— REQUIEM FOR LAJOS KASSÁK, OP. 15
    *4,*4,*4,*4 - 4,4,3-4,1 - perc.,cel. - cimbalom - hp. - str.
    23:00 Bo. Hawkes.
—— TABULAE, OP. 25 (FOR CHAMBER ORCH.)
    *2,*1,*2,*1 - 1,0,0,0 - perc.,cel. - cimbalom - pf. - str.
    12:00 Bo. Hawkes.

BALDWIN, Samuel
—— SYMPHONIC RHAPSODY NO. 4
    3,3,3,3 - 4,3,3,0 - timp. - hp. - str. 22:00 J. Fischer.

BALES, Richard
—— COMMUNION SERVICE (FOR SATB CHORUS AND ORCH.)
    2 ob. - 2 tpt. - timp. - org. - str. 13:00 Composer.
—— THE CONFEDERACY (CANTATA ON MUSIC OF THE
SOUTH DURING THE YEARS 1861-1865)
    2,2,2,2 - 2,2,1,0 - timp.,perc. (2), glock.,xyl. - hp. - pf. - str.
    35:00 Arranger.

—— FITZWILLIAM SUITE (ON 18TH CENTURY VIRGINAL
PIECES) (FOR STRINGS) (ARR. 1972) (IN 5 MOVTS.)
    str. 10:00 Southern.
—— GATE OF THE YEAR (FOR MIXED CHORUS AND ORCH.)
    0,2,0,0 - 0,3,0,0 - timp. - org.(optional) - str. Novello.
—— A LINCOLN BALLET (SUITE OF EPISODES FROM THE
COMPLETE WORK) (FOR NARRATOR AND ORCH.)
    1(alt. with picc.),0,2,1 - 2,2,1,0 - timp.,perc.(1) - pf. - str.
    15:00 Composer.
—— MUSIC FOR STRINGS
    str. 5:00 Composer.
—— NATIONAL GALLERY SUITE NO. 1
    1,1,1,1 - 2,2,1(ad lib.),0 - timp.,perc.(2) - str. 13:00 Composer.
—— NATIONAL GALLERY SUITE NO. 2 (AFTER 3 PAINTINGS
IN THE KRESS COLLECTION) (IN 3 MOVTS.)
    1,1,*3,1 - 2,2,1,0 - timp.,perc.(1),xyl. - pf. - str. 10:00 Composer.
—— NATIONAL GALLERY SUITE NO. 4 (SUITE OF EARLY AND
TRADITIONAL MUSIC) (IN 8 MOVTS.)
    2(alt. with 2 picc.),2,2,2 - 4,4,1,1 - timp.,perc.(3),2 glock. - hp. -
    str. 22:00 Tetra.
—— PRIMAVERA
    1,1,2,1 - 2,2,1,0 - timp.,perc.(1),glock. - str. 5:00 Composer.
—— THE REPUBLIC (PATRIOTIC CANTATA ON MUSIC AND
DOCUMENTS OF THE AMERICAN REVOLUTION AND
EARLY DAYS OF THE REPUBLIC)
    1(alt. with picc.),1,2,1 - 2,2,1,0 - timp.,perc. (2), glock.,xyl. - hpsc.
    - str. 56:00 Arranger.
—— A SET OF JADE (8 SONGS FOR MEZZO-SOPRANO AND
ORCH.) (ON ANCIENT CHINESE POEMS, TRANSLATED
INTO ENGLISH) (1968)
    1,1,1,1 - 2,2,1,0 - timp.,perc.(3),bells,cel.,glock.,xyl. - hp. - str.
    15:00 Composer.
—— STONY BROOK SUITE FOR STRINGS (ON 19TH-CENTURY
AMERICAN TUNES) (1968) (IN 6 MOVTS.)
    str. 14:00 Arranger.
—— STONY BROOK (SUITE) (IN 6 MOVTS.)
    str. 10:00 Southern.
—— THEME AND VARIATIONS
    str. 10:00 Composer.
—— THE UNION (CANTATA ON MUSIC OF THE NORTH
DURING THE YEARS 1861-1865)
    1(alt. with picc.),1,2,1 - 2,2,1,0 - timp.,perc. (2), glock.,xyl. - hp. -
    str. 50:00 Arranger.

BALISSAT, Jean
—— CONCERTINO POUR PERCUSSION ET ORCHESTRE
    2,2,2,2 - 2,2,2,0 - perc. - str. 14:00 S.U.I.S.A.
—— INTRODUCTION ET MARCHE (POUR TROMPETTE ET
ORCHESTRE)
    5:30 S.U.I.S.A.
—— SINFONIA BREVE
    2,2,2,2 - 2,2,2,0 - perc. - str. 13:00 S.U.I.S.A.
—— VARIATIONS CONCERTANTES (POUR 3 PERCUSSIONS ET
ORCH. DE CHAMBRE)
    1,1,2,1 - 2,2,1,0 - perc.(3) - str. 15:00 S.U.I.S.A.

BALLANTINE, Edward D.
—— VARIATIONS ON "MARY HAD A LITTLE LAMB"
    Humphries.

BALLARD, Louis W.
—— DEVIL'S PROMENADE
    *3,*3,2,2 - 4,3,3,1 - timp.,perc.(7) - str. 15:00 New SW MuP.
—— THE FOUR MOONS (A BALLET PAS DE QUATRE) %
    1. Overture; 2. Intr'acte; 3. Dance of the Four Moons; 4. Four
    Solo Dances; 5. Pas De Quatre; 6. Finale
    *3,2,2,2 - 4,3,3,1 - timp.,perc.(2),bells,glock.,xyl. - hp. - str.
    30:00 New SW MuP.
—— INCIDENT AT WOUNDED KNEE (IN 4 MOVTS.)
    1,1,1,2 - 2,0,0,0 - perc.(ad lib.) - str. 15:00 Belw-Mills.
—— ISHI (AMERICA'S LAST CIVILIZED MAN) (1975)
    2(2nd alt. with picc.),2(2nd alt. with Eng. hn.),2,0 - 4,2,2,0 -
    timp.,perc.(2),glock.,xyl. - str.(24,10,10,8) 15:45 New SW MuP.
—— JI-JO-GWEH, THE WITCH WATER GULL (3-ACT BALLET) %
(1962)
    2,2,2,2 - 4,3,2,0 - timp.,perc.(3),audio oscillator - pf. - str.
    30:00 New SW MuP.
—— KATCINA DANCES (FOR CELLO AND ORCH.) (1969)
    20:00 Bourne.
—— KOSHARE (2-ACT BALLET, ON THE HOPI INDIAN MYTH
OF CREATION) % (1964)
    *3,flageolets,2,2,2 - 4,3,3,1 - timp.,perc.,glock.,xyl. - str.
    31:00 New SW MuP.

—— PORTRAIT OF WILL ROGERS (FOR NARRATOR, SATB
SOLO VOICES, SATB CHORUS AND ORCH.) (Text: Will
Rogers)
    3,3,3,2 - 4,2,3,1 - timp.,perc. - hp. - pf. - str.   25:00 Belw-Mills.
—— SCENES FROM INDIAN LIFE (SUITE) (1966)
    2(2nd alt. with picc.),2,2,2 - 4,2,2,0 - timp.,perc.,bells,xyl. - hp. -
    str.   4:45 Bourne.
    I. TWO INDIANS; ONE NAVAJO, ONE TAOS
    II. BUILDING A WALL; ADOBE HOUSE
    III. INDIAN FRIENDS FINISH THE WALL
—— WHY THE DUCK HAS A SHORT TAIL (FOR NARRATOR,
ORCH. AND AUDIENCE) (Text: Ruth Ballard, after an old
Navajo legend (1969)
    2(2nd alt. with picc.),2,2,2 - 4,2,3,1 - timp.,perc.(2),xyl. -
    tape-recorder - hp. - pf. - str.   15:00 Bourne.

BALLERINO, Gregory R.
—— METANOIA
    *3,*3,*3,*3 - 4,2,3,1 - timp.,perc.(4),bells,2 vibra. - hp. - str.
    12:00 Composer.

BALLIF, Claude
—— À COR ET À CRI
    Presser.
—— LOVECRAFT
    Presser.
—— SIXIÈME IMAGINAIRE (FOR 11 STRINGS)
    str.   Presser.

BALMA, Mauro
—— PERIODI (1969)
    2,2,2,2 - 2,2,0,0 - timp. - str.(14,4,4,0)   11:00 MCA Music.
—— VARIAZIONI SU UNA TEMA DI BERG (1968)
    1,1,1,1 sax.,1 - 1,1,1,0 - timp.,perc.,cel. - hp. - pf. - str.(6,2,2,1)
    10:00 MCA Music.

BALMER, Luc
—— BALLETTMUSIK AUS DER SPIELOPER "DIE GEFOPPTEN
EHEMÄNNER" (FÜR GROSSES ORCHESTER)
    6:00 S.U.I.S.A.
—— BRIENZERSEE-SUITE (TRIPEL-KONZERT FÜR 3 BLÄSER
UND STREICHORCHESTER)
    15:00 S.U.I.S.A.

BALOGH, Erno
—— DANSE INFERNALE (FOR STRING ORCH.)
    str.   5:00 Composer.
—— DIVERTIMENTO
    1. Andante non troppo; 2. Allegro energico; 3. Andante - Presto
    str.   14:00 Composer.
—— PORTRAIT OF A CITY FROM MORNING TO MIDNIGHT
(SUITE FOR PIANO AND STRING ORCH.) (IN 8 MOVTS.)
    pf. - str.   24:00 Composer.

BALTIN, Aleksandr A.
—— CONCERTINO FOR HARP AND ORCHESTRA
    1,1,2,1 - 2,2,0,0 - timp.,perc. - hp. - str.   9:00 MCA Music.
—— CONCERTO FOR MEZZO-SOPRANO AND ORCH.
    G. Schirmer.

BAMERT, Matthias
—— CAPRICCIO (FÜR FLÖTE, OBOE, HORN UND
STREICHORCHESTER)
    fl.,ob. - hn. - str.   12:30 Composer.
—— CIRCUS PARADE
    *3,2*3,2 - 4,2,2,0 - timp.,perc.(3) - hp.(ad. lib). - pf. - str.
    12:00 G. Schirmer.
—— CONCERTINO FOR ENGLISH HORN AND STRINGS
    Eng. hn. - hpsc. - str.   18:00 G. Schirmer.
—— MANTRA-JANA
    10:00 G. Schirmer.
—— ONCE UPON AN ORCHESTRA (WITH OPTIONAL PARTS
FOR NARRATOR, MIME AND DANCERS)
    *3,*3,*3,2 - 4,3,3,1 - timp.,perc. - hp. - str.   50:00 G. Schirmer.
—— RHEOLOGY (FOR STRINGS)
    str.   10:00 G. Schirmer.
—— SEPTURIA LUNARIS (SUITE) (IN 7 MOVTS.)
    *2,*2,*2,*2 - 2,2,2,1 - perc.(3) - hp. - hpsc. - str.
    20:00 G. Schirmer.

BANCQUART, Alain
—— L' ARBRE AU REGARD DE CHANT (FOR 12 STRINGS)
    str.   Presser.

—— BROQUES (FOR VIOLA AND ORCH.)
    3,4,4,3 - 4,3,3,1 - perc. - str.   18:20 Presser.
—— CONCERTO FOR VIOLA AND ORCH.
    2,2,2,2 - 4,2,2,0 - timp.,perc.(3),cel.,xyl. - str.   20:00 EV.
—— ETUDE POUR 15 (FOR VOICE, ELECTRONIC TECHNICIAN,
INSTRUMENTS AND CONDUCTOR)
    0,0,0,0 - 2,2,2,0 - pf. - str.(2,1,1,1)   17:00 Presser.
—— ÎLES (FOR VIOLIN AND ORCH.) (WITH MICROPHONE AND
AMPLIFICATION)
    3,3,3,4 - 4,3,3,1 - perc. - pf. - str.   27:00 Presser.
—— JEUX POUR LUMIÈRE (FOR STRING TRIO AND ORCH.)
    4,0,0,0 - 0,2,2,0 - perc.(4) - 2 hp. - str.   18:00 Presser.
—— LA NAISSANCE DU GESTE (FOR PIANO AND STRING
ORCH.)
    pf. - str.   15:30 EV.
—— OMBRE ECLATÉE (FOR FEMALE VOICE AND ORCH.)
    3,3,3,3 - 4,3,3,1 - perc.(3) - str.   14:00 Presser.
—— PALIMPSESTES (FOR 22 INSTRUMENTALISTS)
    2,2,2,2 - 4,2,3,0 - perc.(2),vibra. - 2 hp.   11:40 Presser.
—— PASSAGES
    3,3,3,3 - 4,4,3,1 - perc.(4) - 2 hp. - pf. - str.   17:00 Presser.
—— SYMPHONY IN 3 MOVEMENTS
    3,3,3,3 - 4,3,3,1 - timp.,perc.(2),cel.,vibra.,xyl. - pf. - str.
    24:30 EV.

BANDO, Gyula
—— CONCERTO FOR VIOLIN AND ORCH.
    2,2,2,2 - 4,3,3,1 - timp. - str.   30:00 Presser.

BANFIELD, Rafaello de
—— FOUR SONGS OF RILKE (1967) (FOR SOPRANO AND
ORCH.) (Text: R. Maria Rilke)
    2,1,2,2 - 2,2,2,1 - perc. - hp. - org. - str.   30:00 Salabert.

BANG, Elling
—— THE TOWER GUARD'S SONG (TARNVAEGTERSANG) (FOR
VOICE AND ORCH.) (Text: I. P. Jacobsen)
    2,2,2,2 - 3,2,2,0 - timp. - hp. - str.   7:00 T.O.N.O.

BANGERT, Emil
—— CONCERT OVERTURE, OP. 7 ("APRIL I CHOOSE")
    2,2,2,2 - 4,2,3,1 - timp.,perc. - str.   7:00 Henmar.

BANKS, Don
—— EPISODE FOR CHAMBER ORCH.(1958)
    1,1,*2,0 - 1,1,1,1 - cel. - hp. - str.   4:00 A.P.R.A.

BANKS, Harry C.
—— THE CHRISTMAS STORY (FOR BARITONE, SATB CHORUS,
TIMPANI, ORGAN AND STRINGS)
    timp. - org. - str.   Belw-Mills.

BANTOCK, Granville
—— ELEGIAC POEM (FOR CELLO AND ORCH.)
    2,2,2,2 - 2,0,0,0 - str.   10:00 Galaxy.
—— FIFINE AT THE FAIR
    4,2,4,4 - 6,3,3,1 - timp.,perc. - 2hp. - str.   30:00 Novello.
—— THE FROGS (OF ARISTOPHANES) (COMEDY OVERTURE)
    *3,1,2,2,c.-bn.(or tu.) - 4,2,0,0 - timp. - str.   12:00 G & T.
—— HAMABDIL (FOR CELLO AND ORCH.)
    timp. - hp. - str.   G. Schirmer.
—— HEBRIDEAN SYMPHONY
    *3,*3,*3,*3 - 4,3,3,1 - timp.,perc.,cel. - hp. - str.   28:00 Novello.
—— KING SOLOMON (FOR NARRATOR, CHORUS AND ORCH.)
    *3,*3,*3,*3 - 4,3,2,6(bar.,euph.,2B♭basses,2E♭basses) - timp.,perc. -
    2hp. - str.   12:00 G & T.
—— OLD ENGLISH SUITE
    2,2,2,2 - 4,2,0,0 - timp. - str.   11:00 Novello.
—— PIBROCH (FOR CELLO AND ORCH.)
    G. Schirmer.
—— PRELUDE TO "THE BACCHAE"
    7:00 Galaxy.
—— SAPPHIC POEM (FOR CELLO AND ORCH.)
    2,2,2,2 - 2,1,0,0 - timp.,perc. - str.   Novello.
—— SUITE FROM "THE BACCHAE"
    30:00 Galaxy.
—— WITCH OF ATLAS (TONE PICTURE NO. 5, AFTER
SHELLEY)
    3,2,3,3 - 4,3,3,1 - timp.,perc. - hp. - str.   15:00 Novello.

BARAB, Seymour
—— CHANTICLEER (1-ACT COMIC OPERA, AFTER A TALE BY CHAUCER) % (Text: M. C. Richards)
    Bo. Hawkes.
—— A CHILD'S GARDEN OF VERSES (FOR MEDIUM HIGH VOICE AND CHAMBER ORCH.)
    0,1(or tpt.),1,1 - 0,0,0,0 - pf. - str.   35:00 Bo. Hawkes.
—— CONCERTO FOR HORN AND STRINGS
    hn. - str.   12:00 Bo. Hawkes.
—— A GAME OF CHANCE (1-ACT COMIC OPERA) % (1960) % (Text: Evelyn Manacher)
    1,1,1,1 - 1,1,1,0 - timp.,perc. - hp. - str.   35:00 Bo. Hawkes.
—— HOW FAR TO BETHLEHEM (1-ACT OPERA) % (1963) (Text: Susan Otto)
    Bo. Hawkes.
—— LITTLE RED RIDING HOOD (COMIC OPERA) %
    1,1,2,1 - 2,1,1,0 - perc. - str.   50:00 Bo. Hawkes.
—— LITTLE STORIES IN TOMORROW'S PAPER (1-ACT OPERA) % (1966) (Text: Composer)
    Composer.
—— THE MALETROIT DOOR (CHAMBER OPERA IN 1-ACT) % (1963) % (Text: Martha England)
    2,2,2,2 - 2,2,2,0 - timp.,perc. - hp. - str.   30:00 Bo. Hawkes.
—— A MATTER OF TIME (1-ACT OPERA) % (1959) (Text: Composer)
    Composer.
—— PHILIP MARSHALL (2 ACT OPERA) % (1967) (Text: Composer)
    Presser.
—— A PIECE OF STRING (2-ACT OPERA) % (1965) (Text: Composer)
    Composer.
—— THE RAJAH'S RUBY (1-ACT COMIC OPERA) % (Text: Composer)
    1,1,1,1 - 1,1,1,0 - timp.,perc. - str.   45:00 Bo. Hawkes.
—— ROLAND THE MINSTREL (BALLET) % (1971) (Text: William Steig)
    Composer.
—— SYLVESTER (BALLET) % (1970) (Text: William Steig)
    Composer.
—— TALES OF RHYME AND REASON (FOR NARRATOR, DANCERS AND ORCH.) (1967) % (Text: Composer) (IN 5 MOVTS.)
    75:00 Bo. Hawkes.
—— TENNYSON SONGS (LUTE SONGS) (6 SONGS FOR SOPRANO AND STRINGS) (Text: Alfred Lord Tennyson)
    hp. - str.   Bo. Hawkes.
—— THREE SKETCHES (1968)
    Bo. Hawkes.
—— WHO AM I (1-ACT OPERA) % (1966) (Text: Composer)
    Bo. Hawkes.

BARANOVIĆ, Krešimir
—— GORAN (SYMPHONIC POEM) (FOR SPEAKING VOICE, SOLO VOICES, SATB CHORUS AND ORCH.)
    3(3rd alt. with picc.),2(2nd alt. with Eng.hn.),2(2nd alt. with b.-cl.),2 - 4,3,3,1 - timp.,perc. - str.   37:00 MIC,Zagreb.
—— ODA AVNOJ-U (ODE TO AVNOJ-U) (CANTATA) (FOR BARITONE, SATB CHORUS AND ORCH.)
    3,3,3,3 - 4,3,3,1 - timp.,perc. - str.   MIC,Zagreb.
—— U IME DOMOVINE (IN THE NAME OF THE HOMELAND) (CANTATA) (FOR SOPRANO, BARITONE, NARRATOR, SATB CHORUS AND ORCH.)
    3,3,3,3 - 4,3,3,1 - timp.,perc. - str.   MIC,Zagreb.

BARBE, Helmut
—— CANTICUM SIMEONIS (CANTATA) (FOR SOLO VOICE, SATB CHORUS AND SMALL ORCH.)
    cel. - org. - str.   Hänssler.
—— CONCERTO FOR VIOLIN AND ORCH.
    Sikorski.

BARBER, Samuel
—— ADAGIO FOR STRINGS, OP. 11
    str.   6:30 G. Schirmer.
—— ANDROMACHE'S FAREWELL, OP. 39 (FOR SOPRANO AND ORCH.) (Text: John Patrick Creagh, after the Greek of Euripides' "The Trojan Women")
    *3,*3,*3,2 - 4,3,3,1 - timp.,perc.(3) - hp. - str.   12:00 G. Schirmer.
—— ANTHONY AND CLEOPATRA (OPERA) % (Text: Franco Zeffirelli, after Shakespeare)
    G. Schirmer.
—— ANTONY AND CLEOPATRA: TWO SCENES FROM THE OPERA (OP. 40). (FOR SOPRANO AND ORCH.)
    3,3,3,3 - 4,3,3,1 - timp.,perc. - 2 hp. - pf. - str. 15:00 G. Schirmer.
—— CAPRICORN CONCERTO, OP. 21 (FOR FLUTE, OBOE, TRUMPET AND STRINGS)
    1,1,0,0 - tpt. - str.   14:00 G. Schirmer.
—— CHORALE PRELUDE ON "SILENT NIGHT" (FROM "DIE NATALI", OP. 37)
    1,2,2-3,0-1 - 4,0,3,1 - cel. - hp. - str.   G. Schirmer.
—— CONCERTO FOR CELLO AND ORCH. (IN 3 MOVEMENTS)
    2,*2,2(2nd alt. with b.-cl.),2 - 2,3,0,0 - timp. - str.   20:00 G. Schirmer.
—— CONCERTO FOR PIANO AND ORCH., OP. 38 (IN 3 MOVTS.)
    *3,*3,*3,2 - 3,4,3,0 - timp.,perc. - hp. - pf. - str.   26:00 G. Schirmer.
—— CONCERTO FOR VIOLIN AND ORCH., OP. 14
    2,2,2,2 - 2,2,0,0 - timp.,perc.(2) - pf. - str.   22:00 G. Schirmer.
—— DIE NATALI (CHORALE PRELUDES FOR CHRISTMAS), OP. 37
    *3,*3,*3,2 - 4,3,3,1 - timp.,perc.,bells,cel.,xyl. - hp. - str.   16:00 G. Schirmer.
—— DOVER BEACH (FOR BARITONE AND STRING ORCH.)
    str.   7:00 G. Schirmer.
—— ESSAY FOR ORCH., OP. 12
    2,2,2,2 - 4,3,3,1 - timp. - str.   7:00 G. Schirmer.
—— FADOGRAPH OF A YESTERN SCENE
    *3,*3,*3,2 - 4,3,3,1 - timp.,perc.,cel. - 1-2 hp. - str.
    7:00 G. Schirmer.
—— FOUR SONGS (FOR VOICE AND ORCH.)
    1,2,3,2 - 3,2,2,0 - timp. - hp. - str.   G. Schirmer.
—— A HAND OF BRIDGE (OPERA) % (FOR 4 SOLO VOICES AND CHAMBER ORCH.) (Text: Gian Carlo Menotti)
    1,1,1,1 - 0,1,0,0 - perc. - pf. - str.   9:00 G. Schirmer.
—— INTERMEZZO FROM THE OPERA "VANESSA"
    3,3,3,2 - 4,2,3,1 - timp.,perc. - hp. - str.   4:00 G. Schirmer.
—— KNOXVILLE: SUMMER OF 1915, OP. 24 (FOR SOPRANO AND ORCH.)
    1,1,1,1 - 2,1,0,0 - trgl. - hp. - str.   16:00 G. Schirmer.
—— THE LOVERS (FOR BARITONE, SATB CHROUS AND ORCH.)
    4,3,3,2 - 4,3,3,1 - timp.,perc.,cel. - hp. - pf. - str.
    31:00 G. Schirmer.
—— MEDEA (BALLET SUITE), OP. 23 (IN 7 MOVTS.)
    *2,2(2nd alt. with Eng.hn.),2,2 - 2,2,2,0 - timp.,perc.(3),xyl. - pf. - str.   22:00 G. Schirmer.
—— MEDEA'S MEDITATION AND DANCE OF VENGEANCE, OP. 23A
    3(3rd alt. with picc.),*3,1Eᵇcl.,*3,*3 - 4,3,3,1 - timp.,perc.(3),xyl. - hp. - pf. - str.   13:00 G. Schirmer.
—— MUSIC FOR A SCENE FROM SHELLEY, OP. 7
    3,*3,*3,3 - 4,3,3,1 - timp.,perc.(2),glock. - hp. - str.
    8:00 G. Schirmer.
—— NIGHT FLIGHT, OP. 19A
    *3,*3,1 Eᵇcl.,*3,2 - 4,3,3,1 - cymb. - pf. - str.   7:30 G. Schirmer.
—— OVERTURE TO "THE SCHOOL FOR SCANDAL", OP. 5
    *3,*3,*3,2 - 4,3,3,1 - timp.,perc.(4),cel. - hp.   7:30 G. Schirmer.
—— PRAYERS OF KIERKEGAARD (FOR CHORUS AND ORCH.), OP. 30
    *3,*3,*3,2 - 4,3,3,1 - timp.,perc.,xyl. - hp. - pf. - str.
    18:00 G. Schirmer.
—— SECOND ESSAY, OP. 17
    *3,*3,2(2nd alt. with b.-cl.),2 - 4,3,3,1 - timp.,perc.(3) - str.
    9:30 G. Schirmer.
—— SERENADE, OP. 1 (FOR STRING ORCH.)
    str.   10:00 G. Schirmer.
—— SOUVENIRS, OP. 28 (IN 6 MOVTS.)
    1(alt. with picc.),1(alt. with Eng.hn.),2,2 - 4,3,3,0 - timp.,perc.,cel. - hp. - str.   19:00 G. Schirmer.
—— SYMPHONY NO. 1, OP. 9 (IN 1 MOVT.)
    *3,*3,*3,*3 - 4,3,3,1 - timp.,perc.(2) - hp. - str.
    18:30 G. Schirmer.
—— SYMPHONY NO. 2, OP. 19
    3,3,4,3 - 4,3,3,1 - timp.,perc. - str.   27:00 G. Schirmer.
—— TOCCATA FESTIVA, OP. 36 (FOR ORGAN AND ORCH.)
    3,3,3,2 - 4,3,3,1 - timp.,perc. - org. - str.   14:00 G. Schirmer.
    or:
    tpt. - timp. - org. - str.
—— VANESSA (OPERA) % (Text: Gian Carlo Menotti)
    3,3,3,2 - 4,3,3,1 - timp.,perc. - hp. - str.   G. Schirmer.

BARBER, Samuel - HOIBY, Lee
—— PRAYERS OF KIRKEGAARD, OP. 30 (FOR SATB CHORUS AND ORCH.) (Reduced Orchestration)
    1,1,2,1 - 2,1,1,0 - timp.,perc. - org. - str.   16:00 G. Schirmer.

BARBIER, René
—— ADAGIO, OP. 82 (1947)
    2,1,2,1 - 2,2,1,0 - timp.,perc. - str.   6:00 H. Elkan.
—— CONCERTINO FOR 2 GUITARS AND STRING ORCH., OP. 116 (1971)
    2 guit. - str.   12:00 H. Elkan.
—— CONCERTINO NO. 1 FOR PIANO AND ORCH., OP. 28 (1922)
    3,3,3,2 - 4,2,3,1 - timp.,perc. - pf. - str.   30:00 H. Elkan.
—— CONCERTO FOR CELLO AND ORCH., OP. 54 (1938)
    2,2,2,2 - 4,3,3,1 - timp.,perc. - hp. - str.   20:00 H. Elkan.
—— CONCERTO FOR ORGAN, STRING ORCH., AND TIMPANI, OP. 113 (1967)
    timp. - org. - str.   20:00 H. Elkan.
—— CONCERTO NO. 2 FOR PIANO AND ORCH., OP. 43 (1934)
    2,2,2,2 - 4,3,3,1 - timp.,perc. - pf. - str.   40:00 H. Elkan.
—— DIPTYQUE, OP. 68 (1941)
    3,2,2,2 - 4,3,3,1 - timp.,perc.,bells,cel.,glock. - hp. - org.(ad lib.) - pf. - str.   26:00 H. Elkan.
—— LES ELEMENTS, OP. 64 (SUITE PLATONICIENNE) (1935)
    3,2,2,2 - 4,3,3,1 - timp.,perc. - hp. - str.   28:00 H. Elkan.
—— EPITAPHE SYMPHONIQUE (1945)
    3,3,3,3 - 4,3,3,0 - timp.,perc.,cel. - hp. - str.   7:00 H. Elkan.
—— EVOCATION SONORE DE L'ARDENNE, OP. 115 (1971)
    3,2,2,2 - 4,3,3,1 - timp.,perc. - str.   20:00 H. Elkan.
—— FANTAISIE CONCERTANTE, OP. 51 (FOR VIOLIN AND ORCH.) (1937)
    2,2,2,2 - 4,2,3,1 - timp.,perc. - hp. - str.   14:00 H. Elkan.
—— LES GENIES DU SOMMEIL, OP. 29 (SYMPHONIC POEM) (1923)
    3,3,3,3 - 4,3,3,1 - timp.,perc.,bells,cel.,xyl. - hp. - pf. - str.   40:00 H. Elkan.
—— INTRODUCTION ET ALLEGRO SYMPHONIQUE, OP. 112 (1967)
    3,2,2,2 - 4,3,3,1 - timp.,perc. - str.   12:00 H. Elkan.
—— INTRODUCTION ET FANTAISIE RHAPSODIQUE (SUR 2 AIRS WALLONS), OP. 72 (1946)
    2,1,2,1 - 2,2,1,0 - timp.,perc.,glock. - str.   12:00 H. Elkan.
—— INTRODUCTION (FANFARE, OP. 90) ET 3 ESQUISSES SYMPHONIQUES
    2,1,2,1 - 4,3,3,1 - timp.,perc.,cel.(or glock), xyl. - pf. - str.   19:00 H. Elkan.
—— LA MUSIQUE DE PERDITION, OP. 75 (SYMPHONIC POEM) (1947)
    3,2,2,2 - 4,3,3,1 - timp.,perc. - hp. - str.   24:00 H. Elkan.
—— OUVERTURE CONCERTANTE, OP. 114 (1969)
    3,2,2,2 - 4,3,2,1 - timp.,perc. - str.   14:00 H. Elkan.
—— PETITE SUITE, OP. 86 (1955)
    2,1,2,1 - 2,2,1,0 - timp.,perc. - pf(ad lib.) - str.   12:00 H. Elkan.
—— PÉGASE, OP. 97 (OVERTURE) (1955)
    2,1,2,1 - 2,2,1,0 - timp.,perc. - pf. - str.   7:00 H. Elkan.
—— LES PIERRES MAGIQUES, OP. 94 (BALLET) (1957) %
    3,2,2,2 - 4,3,3,1 - timp.,perc.,bells,cel.,glock.,xyl. - guit. - hp. - pf. - str.   43:00 H. Elkan.
—— PIÈCE CONCERTANTE, OP. 95 (FOR VIOLIN OR ALTO SAXOPHONE AND ORCH.) (1958)
    1,1,2,1 alto sax.(ad lib.),1 - 2,0,0,0 - timp. - str.   10:00 H. Elkan.
—— POCO ADAGIO ET ALLEGRO BRILLANTE, OP. 66 (FOR CLARINET AND ORCH.) (1940)
    1,1,3,1 - 2,2,1,0 - timp.,perc. - str.   12:00 H. Elkan.
—— POÈME, OP. 14 (FOR CELLO AND ORCH.) (1936)
    2,2,2,2 - 4,2,3,0 - timp. - hp.(or pf.) - str.   12:00 H. Elkan.
—— SINFONIETTA, OP. 111 (FOR CHAMBER ORCH.) (1966) (IN 3 MOVTS.)
    2,1,2,1 - 2,2,1,0 - timp.,perc. - str.   15:00 H. Elkan.

BARBIROLLI, John
—— AN ELIZABETHAN SUITE
    4 hns. - str.   12:00 Oxford.

BARCLAY, Robert
—— ALASKAN OVERTURE, OP. 16
    8:30 B. Barclay.
—— BALLET SUITE
    20:00 C.A.P.A.C.
—— SEAPORT TOWN OVERTURE
    6:30 B. Barclay.
—— SYMPHONIC POEM, OP. 24 (1954)
    15:00 C.A.P.A.C.
—— SYMPHONY IN ONE MOVT.
    2,2,2,2 - 2,2,0,0 - timp. - str.   15:00 Bo. Hawkes.
—— VARIATIONS, OP. 25 (1955)
    10:00 C.A.P.A.C.

BARDWELL, William
—— CONCERTO FOR HARPSICHORD AND SMALL ORCH. (1954)
    1,2,1,0 - 1,0,0,0 - hpsc. - str.   15:00 P.R.S.
—— CONCERTO FOR MANDOLIN AND SMALL ORCH. (1965)
    0,2,0,2 - 2,0,0,0 - mandolin - str.   18:00 P.R.S.
—— INVENTIONS (1967)
    3,3,2,2 - 2,2,2,0 - perc. - hp. - str.   14:00 P.R.S.
—— NOCTURNE (REV. 1967)
    str.   7:00 P.R.S.
—— SYMPHONY (1966)
    3,3,2,3 - 4,2,3,1 - timp.,perc. - hp. - str.   26:00 P.R.S.

BARILLER, Robert
—— LE MARTYRE DE MARSYAS (FOR FLUTE AND ORCH.)
    1,*2,0,2 - timp.,perc. - hp. - str.   12:00 Baron.
—— RAPSODIE BRETONNE (FOR ALTO SAXOPHONE AND ORCH.)
    2,2,2,alto sax,2 - 4,3,3,1 - timp.,perc.,bells - str.   12:00 Baron.

BARK, Jan
—— METAKRONISMER FÜR ORKESTER
    3,3,3,3 - 4,4,4,0 - timp. - str.   20:00 S.T.I.M.
—— MISSA BASSA (1964) (WITH 7 CONDUCTORS, 6 PERFORMING VOCAL PARTS)
    1,1,1,1 - 1,0,0,0 - str   20:00 S.T.I.M.
—— PYKNOS (1962)
    3,3,3,3 - 4,4,3,1 - timp.,perc.(2) - hp. - str.   14:00 S.T.I.M.

BARLOW, David
—— FIVE PRELUDES (1965)
    1,2,0,2 - 2,0,0,0 - str.   11:30 P.R.S.
—— HOMAGE TO JOHN CLARE (1966)
    1,2,0,2 - 2,0,0,0 - str.   9:00 P.R.S.
—— MICROCOSMS (1964)
    str.   7:00 P.R.S.
—— PASTORALE AND VARIATIONS (1957)
    0,2,0,0 - 2,0,0,0 - str.   11:45 P.R.S.
—— SYMPHONY IN E MINOR (1950) (IN 1 MOVT.)
    2,2,2,2 - 4,2,3,0 - timp.,perc. - str.   17:30 P.R.S.
—— SYMPHONY NO. 2 (1959)
    2,2,2,2 - 4,2,3,0 - timp.,perc. - str.   20:00 P.R.S.
—— THREE MOODS (1957)
    2,2,2,2 - 4,2,3,0 - timp.,perc. - str.   11:30 P.R.S.
—— WUTHERING HEIGHTS (1958)
    2,2,2,2 - 2,2,0,0 - timp.,perc. - str.   13:00 P.R.S.

BARLOW, Wayne
—— LENTO AND ALLEGRO
    2(2nd alt. with picc.),2,2,2 - 4,2,3,1 - timp.,perc.(2),xyl. - hp. - str.   11:00 Composer.
—— LYRICAL PIECE FOR CLARINET AND STRINGS
    0,0,1,0 - 0,0,0,0 - str.   4:55 C. Fischer.
—— MASS IN G (FOR CHORUS AND ORCH.)
    2,*3,*3,*3 - 4,2,3,1 - timp.,perc.(1) - hp. -str.   30:00 Composer.
    or:
    0,0,0,0 - 4,2,3,1 - str.
—— NOCTURNE (FOR CHAMBER ORCH.)
    2,2(2nd alt. with Eng.hn.),2,2 - 2,2,0,0 - hp. - str. 6:00 C. Fischer.
—— PSALM 23 (FOR CHORUS AND ORCH.)
    2,2,2,2 - 2,2,0,0 - str.   5:00 J. Fischer.
—— RONDO OVERTURE
    Composer.
—— SINFONIA DA CAMERA (IN 5 MOVTS.)
    18:00 Composer.
—— SINFONIETTA IN C
    2,2,2,2 - 4,2,3,1 - timp.,perc.,xyl. - hp. - str.   15:00 Composer.
—— SOUNDSCAPES (FOR ORCH. AND ELECTRONIC TAPE) (1972) (IN 4 MOVTS.)
    3(1 alt. with picc.),*3,*3,2 - 4,3,3,1 - timp.,perc.(3),bells,cel.,glock.,vibra. - tape-recorder - str.   16:00 Composer.
—— THREE SONGS FROM THE SILENCE OF AMOR (FOR VOICE AND ORCH.) (Text: William Sharp)
    2,2,2,2 - 2,2,0,0 - perc.(1) - hp. - str.   10:00 Composer.
—— VISTAS
    2,*2,2,2 - 4,2,3,0 - perc.(1),bells - hp. - str.   8:00 Composer.
—— THE WINTER'S PASSED (FANTASY ON AN APPALACHIAN FOLK TUNE)
    ob. - str.   4:00 C. Fischer.

BARNEA, Aviasaf
—— ISRAELI SUITE
    3,3,E♭cl.,*4,3 - 4,3,3,1 - timp.,perc.,xyl. - pf. - str.
                                  18:00 IsMuPublns.

BARNES, Milton
—— AMBER GARDEN (BALLET SUITE) (1972)
    1,1,1,1 - hn. - str. - (no d-b.)   23:20 CanMusCtr.
—— THE CHILDREN'S SUITE (1966) (IN 6 MOVTS.)
    2(2nd alt. with picc.),2,2,2 - 4,3,3,0 - perc. - str. 7:50 CanMusCtr.
—— CLASSICAL CONCERTO, FOR PIANO AND ORCH. (1973) (IN 3 MOVTS.)
    2,2,2,2 - 2,2,0,0 - timp. - pf. - str.   23:20 CanMusCtr.
—— CONCERT OVERTURE (1973)
    3,2,3,2 - 4,3,3,1 - perc. - str.   7:30 CanMusCtr.
—— CONCERTO FOR SAXAPHONE AND STRINGS (1975) (IN 3 MOVTS.)
    alto sax. - str.   20:00 CanMusCtr.
—— CONCERTO FOR VIOLIN AND STRINGS (1975) (IN 3 MOVTS.)
    str.   20:00 CanMusCtr.
—— INVOCATIONS FOR ORCHESTRA (1962) (IN 4 MOVTS.)
    2(2nd alt. with picc.),2(2nd alt. with Eng. hn.),2,2(2nd alt. with c.-bn.) - 4,2,3,1 - timp., perc.(3) - str. 10:35 CanMusCtr.
—— PINOCCHIO (SYMPHONIC POEM) (1966) (IN 2 PARTS; 4 MOVTS. EACH)
    *3,2,2,2 - 4,2,3,1 - timp.,perc.(4) - str. 16:50 CanMusCtr.
—— PSALMS OF DAVID (FOR MEZZO-SOPRANO, BARITONE, MIXED CHORUS AND ORCH.) (1973)
    2,2(2nd alt. with Eng.hn.),2,2 - 4,4,3,1 - timp.,perc. - hp. - str.
                      70:00 CanMusCtr.
—— SHEBETIM (12 TABLEAUX FOR STRINGS) (1974)
    str.   27:30 CanMusCtr.
—— SONATA FOR FLUTE AND STRING ORCH. (1970) (IN 4 MOVTS.)
    Fl - str.   14:00 CanMusCtr.
—— SYMPHONY NO. 1 (1964)
    *3,*3,2,2 - 4,2,3,1 - perc. - str.   30:00 CanMusCtr.
—— THREE MOVEMENTS FOR STRING ORCH. (1958)
    str.   18:00 CanMusCtr.
—— TWO MOVEMENTS FOR STRING ORCH (1958)
    str.   14:40 CanMusCtr.

BARON, Maurice
—— AMERICAN GOTHIC (FOR CLARINET AND ORCH.)
    1,1,1,1 - 2hn. - str.   5:00 Baron.
—— BLOOD, SWEAT AND TEARS
    *3,*3,*3,*3 - 4,4,3,1 - timp.,perc.(4),xyl. - 2hp. - org.(ad lib.) - str.
                      12:00 Baron.
—— CONCERTO ROMANTICO IN G MINOR (FOR ALTO SAXOPHONE AND ORCH.)
                      22:00 Baron.
—— FOSTERIANA (RHAPSODY ON MELODIES OF STEPHEN COLLINS FOSTER)
    *3,2,2,2 - 4,3,3,1 - timp.,perc.(3),xyl. - hp. - pf. - str. 16:00 Baron.
—— ODE TO DEMOCRACY (CANTATA FOR BARITONE OR NARRATORS, OPTIONAL MIXED CHORUS AND ORCH.)
    *3,2,2,2 - 4,3,3-5,1 - timp.,perc.(4) - hp. - str. 8:00 Baron.
—— PRAYER: "THE BLESSED DAMOZEL" (FOR STRING ORCH.)
    str.   Baron.
—— SUSAN AT THE ZOO (CHOREOGRAPHIC SUITE) (IN 6 MOVTS.)
    2,2,2,2 - 2,2,2,0 - perc.(2),cel. - hp. - str.   17:00 Baron.
—— THESE HONORED DEAD (A SYMPHONIC TRIBUTE FOR GRAND ORCH., WITH ORGAN AD LIB.)
                      Baron.
—— VARIATIONS ON "L'AMOUR DE MOY"
    3,3(2nd ad lib.),3,b.-cl.(ad lib.),3,c.-bn.(ad lib.) - 4,3,3,1 - timp.,perc.(3),cel. - hp. - str.   18:00 Baron.

BARR, Ray
—— A STUDY IN TRANQUILITY (TONE POEM) (FOR PIANO AND ORCH.) (1971)
    2,1,2,2 b.-cl.,2 - 4,3,3,1 - timp.,perc.(3),bells,glock.,xyl. - hp. - pf. - str.   11:00 Composer.
—— SWEET COUNTRY SUITE (FOR PIANO AND ORCH.) (1969) (IN 4 MOVTS.)
    2,2,2(alt. with 2 alto sax.),2 b.-cl.(alt. with 2 ten. sax.),*3(cbn. alt. with bar. sax) - 4,4,4,1 - timp.,perc.(3),glock.,xyl. - hp. - pf. - str.   16:20 Composer.

—— THEME AND VARIATIONS IN E FLAT (FOR PIANO AND ORCH.) (1966)
    2,2,3(1 alt. with b.-cl.),2 - 4,4,4,1 - timp.,perc.(3),glock. - hp. - pf. - str.   9:20 Composer.

BARRAINE, Elsa
—— CHRISTINE (OPERA) % (Text: J. Supervielle)
    0,1,1,0 - 0,2,2,0 - perc.,bells,cel.,vibra. - ondes Martenot - hp. - str.
                      26:40 Eds. Fran.
—— LA MISE AU TOMBEAU
    2,2,2,2 - 2,2,2,0 - timp.,perc. - hp. - pf. - str.   7:20 Presser.
—— OUVRAGE DE DAME (FOR 5 WOODWIND AND 5 STRING INSTRUMENTS)
                      SouthernTx.
—— LES PAYSANS (OPERA) % (Text: A. Frénaux)
    cel. - str.   26:30 Eds. Fran.
—— SYMPHONY NO. 2
    3,2,2,2 - 4,3,3,1 - timp.,perc. - str.   16:00 Leeds.

BARRATT, Carol Ann
—— CANZONA FOR ALTO FLUTE AND STRING ORCH., OP. 17 (1969)
    alto fl. - str.   4:00 P.R.S.
—— PASSACAGLIA FOR STRING ORCH. (1964)
    str.   8:00 P.R.S.

BARRAUD, Henri
—— CONCERTO FOR FLUTE AND STRING ORCH.
    fl. - str.   Bo. Hawkes.
—— CONCERTO FOR PIANO AND ORCH. (IN 3 MOVTS.)
    2,2,2,2 - 2,2,2,0 - timp.,perc.,cel. - hp. - pf. - str. 20:30 Baron.
—— DIVERTIMENTO FOR ORCHESTRA
    2,2,2,2 - 2,2,2,0 - timp.,perc.(3),cel. - hp. - pf. - str.
                      21:00 Bo. Hawkes.
—— LA FARCE DU MAITRE PATHELIN (1-ACT COMIC OPERA) % (Text: Gustave Cohen; Engl. trans.: Robert Gay)
    2,2,2,2 - 2,2,1,0 - timp.,perc.,cel. - hp. - str. 40:00 Bo. Hawkes.
—— HOMMAGE A RAMEAU ("PANGE LINGUA") (FOR SOPRANO, BARITONE, CHORUS AND ORCH.)
                      Bo. Hawkes.
—— IMAGES POUR UN POÈTE MAUDIT
    1,0,1,1 - 0,1,0,0 - timp.,perc.,cel. - hp. - str. 20:00 Salabert.
—— LA KERMESSE (SUITE SYMPHONIQUE)
    3,3,3,3 - 4,3,3,1 - timp.,perc.,cel.,xyl. - hp. - str.
                      20:30 Bo. Hawkes.
—— LAVINIA (OPERA) %
    1,1,1,1 - 1,1,1,0 - timp.,perc.,cel. - hp. - pf. - str.   Bo. Hawkes.
—— LAVINIA: OVERTURE
    1,1,1,1 - 1,1,1,0 - timp.,perc.,cel. - hp. - pf. - str.   Bo. Hawkes.
—— LE MYSTERE DES SAINTS INNOCENTS (ORATORIO) (FOR SOLI, CHORUS AND ORCH.)
    3,3,3,3 - 4,3,3,1 - timp.,perc.,cel. - 2hp. - pf. - str.
                      54:00 Bo. Hawkes.
—— L' OFFRANDE À UNE OMBRE
    2,2,2,2 - 4,3,2,0 - timp.,perc. - hp. - str.   10:00 Baron.
—— LES PETITS MÉTIERS
    1,1,1,alto sax.,1 - 0,1,0,0 - timp.,perc. - hp. - str. 13:00 Salabert.
—— POÈME
    3,3,3,3 - 4,3,3,1 - timp.,perc. - hp. - str.   9:00 Henmar.
—— PRÉLUDES (FOR STRING ORCH.)
    str.   9:00 Baron.
—— RAPSODIE CARTÉSIENNE
    3,3,3,3 - 4,3,3,1 - timp.,perc.(3),cel. - 2 hp. - pf. - str.
                      14:00 Bo. Hawkes.
—— RAPSODIE DIONYSIENNE
    3,3,3,3 - 4,3,3,1 - timp.,perc.(3),cel.,xyl. - 2 hp. - pf. - str.
                      13:00 Bo. Hawkes.
—— SINFONIE CONCERTANTE (FOR TRUMPET AND ORCH.)
    3,3,3,3 - 4,3,3,1 - timp.,perc.,cel. - hp. - pf. - str.
                      21:00 Bo. Hawkes.
—— SUITE FOR A COMEDY OF ALFRED DEMUSSET (IN 5 MOVTS.)
    1,1,1,1 - 1,1,0,0 - timp.,perc. - pf. - str.   15:30 Baron.
—— SYMPHONY DE NUMANCE
    3,3,3,3 - 4,3,3,1 - timp.,perc. - hp. - str.   27:00 Bo. Hawkes.
—— SYMPHONY FOR STRINGS
    str.   25:00 Bo. Hawkes.
—— SYMPHONY NO. 3
    3,3,3,3 - 4,3,3,1 - timp.,perc. - hp. - pf. - str. 25:00 Bo. Hawkes.
—— TE DEUM (FOR MIXED CHORUS AND ORCH.)
    2,2,2,2 - 2,2,2,0 - d.-b.   20:00 F. Colombo.
—— TROIS ETUDES FOR ORCHESTRA
    3,2,2,2 - 4,3,3,1 - timp.,perc.(6),cel. - hp. - pf. - str. 11:15 Presser.

BARRELL, Bernard
—— CONCERTINO FOR SOLO INSTRUMENT AND STRINGS, OP. 29 (1961)
    Harmonica (or fl.,ob.,cl.,sax. or vln.) - str.   12:00 P.R.S.
—— DIVERSIONS ON AN ORIGINAL THEME, OP. 2 (1938)
    str.   6:00 P.R.S.
—— EPITAPH FOR ZOLTAN KODALY, OP. 49
    Descant recorder - perc. - str.   5:00 P.R.S.
—— FOUR STUDIES FOR STRINGS, OP. 8 (1951)
    str.   6:30 P.R.S.
—— FUGUE FOR STRINGS, OP. 11 (1954)
    str.   5:00 P.R.S.
—— A HOLIDAY OVERTURE, OP. 14 (1956)
    1,1,1,1 - 1,1,1,0 - timp. - str.   4:30 P.R.S.
—— HOMMAGE À RAVEL, OP. 1-A (1939)
    1,1,1,0 - 0,0,0,0 - hp. - str.   7:00 P.R.S.

BARRELL, Joyce
—— NORFOLK MUSIC, OP. 17 (1961)
    str.   12:00 P.R.S.
—— SATURDAY MUSIC, OP. 13 (1956)
    1,1,1,0 - 0,1,0,0 - str.   5:00 P.R.S.

BARRYMORE, Lionel
—— FUGUE FANTASIA
    Composer.
—— INTRODUCTION AND SCHERZO
    6:00 Composer.
—— PARTITA (IN 3 MOVTS.)
    13:30 Composer.
—— PIRANESI SUITE
    20:00 Fox.
—— PRELUDIUM AND FUGUE
    13:00 Composer.
—— THEME AND VARIATIONS
    6:00 Composer.

BARSAM, Yizhak
—— TOCCATA AND CAPRICCIO
    0,0,0,0 - 4,2,0,0 - str.   12:00 IsMuPublns.

BÁRTA, Lubor
—— CONCERTO FOR PIANO AND ORCH.
    2,2,2,2 - 4,3,3,1 - timp.,perc. - pf. (solo) - str.   18:00 Bo. Hawkes.
—— CONCERTO FOR VIOLIN AND ORCH.
    2,2,2,2 - 4,3,3,1 - timp.,perc.,trgl. - hp. - str.   26:00 Bo. Hawkes.
—— DRAMATIC OVERTURE
    3,3,3,3 - 4,3,3,1 - timp.,perc. - 2 hp. - str.   16:00 Bo. Hawkes.
—— SYMPHONY NO. 1
    3,3,3,3 - 4,4,3,1 - timp.,perc. - 2 hp. - str.   33:00 Bo. Hawkes.

BARTEL, Hans-Christian
—— CONCERTO FOR ORCH.
    2,2,2,2 - 3,3,2,1 - timp.,perc. - pf. - str.   25:00 Tetra.
—— CONCERTO FOR VIOLA AND CHAMBER ORCH.
    1,1,2,1 - 1,1,0,0 - timp.,perc. - str.   20:00 Tetra.

BARTH, Hans
—— CONCERTO FOR PIANO AND ORCH., OP. 11
    2,2,2,2 - 4,2,3,0 - timp.,glock. - pf. - str.   19:00 Composer.
—— CONCERTO FOR QUARTER-TONE PIANO AND STRING ORCH., OP. 15
    pf.(special model) - str.   8:00 Composer.
—— PEACE SYMPHONY, OP. 25 (IN 3 MOVTS.)
    1(alt. with picc.),2,2,2 - 4,4,3,0 - timp.,perc.,cel. - hp. - str.   30:00 Composer.
—— TEN ETUDES FOR PIANO AND ORCH., OP. 26
    2,2,2,2 - 4,2,3,0 - timp. - pf. - str.   30:00 Composer.

BARTHELSON, Joyce H.
—— CHANTICLEER (1-ACT COMIC OPERA, AFTER CHAUCER) % (1966)
    *3,1-2,2,1-2 - 2,2,2,0 - timp.,perc.(3),bells,cel.,glock.,xyl. - str.   45:00 C. Fischer.
—— CONCERTO DA CAMERA (FOR OBOE AND STRING ORCH.) (1962) (IN 3 MOVTS.)
    ob. - str.   15:00 Composer.
—— FEATHERTOP: OVERTURE TO THE OPERA
    2(1 alt. with picc.),2,2,2 - 2,2,2,0 - timp.,perc.(3),cel.,glock. - pf. - str.   10:00 C. Fischer.

—— FEATHERTOP (2-ACT OPERA BUFFA, AFTER NATHANIEL HAWTHORNE) % (1965) (Text: Composer)
    *3,1,2,1 - 2,2,2,0 - timp.,perc.(3),cel.,glock.,xyl. - pf. - str.   120:00 C. Fischer.
—— ODE TO FRANKLIN D. ROOSEVELT
    3,3,3 - 4,3,3,1 - timp.,perc. - hp. - str.   18:00 Composer.
—— WEATHER REPORT
    3,2,2,2 - 4,3,3,1 - timp.,perc. - str.   15:30 C. Fischer.

BARTLES, Alfred H.
—— BALLAD FOR CELLO AND STRING ORCH. (1969)
    str.   8:00 Composer.
—— ENGADINE OVERTURE (1970)
    *3,*3,1 E^{b}cl.,2,*3 - 4,3,3,1 - timp.,perc.(3),glock. - str.   6:00 Composer.
—— MUSIC FOR SYMPHONY ORCHESTRA AND JAZZ ENSEMBLE, OP. 3 (1966) (IN 3 MOVTS.)
    3(3rd alt. with picc.),3(3rd alt. with Eng.hn),3(3rd alt. with b.-cl.),2 alto sax.,2 ten.sax.,1 bar.sax.,3(3rd alt.with c.-bn.) - 4,7,7,1 - timp.,perc.(3-4),glock. - pf. - str.   20:00 Third Stream.

BARTÓK, Béla
—— BLUEBEARD'S CASTLE (OPERA) %
    Bo. Hawkes.
—— CANTATA PROFANA (FOR TENOR, BARITONE, CHORUS AND ORCH.)
    3,3,3,3 - 4,3,3,1 - perc. - hp. - str.   17:00 Bo. Hawkes.
—— CONCERTO FOR ORCHESTRA
    1. Andante non troppo - Allegro vivace; 2. Allegro scherzando;
    3. Elegy (Andante non troppo); 4. Intermezzo interrotto - Allegro;
    5. Finale (Presto)
    3,3,3,3 - 4,3,3,1 - timp.,perc. - 2hp. - str.   38:00 Bo. Hawkes.
—— CONCERTO FOR TWO PIANOS, PERCUSSION AND ORCH.
    2,2,2,2 - 4,2,3,0 - cel. - 2pf. - str.   24:30 Bo. Hawkes.
—— CONCERTO NO. 1 FOR PIANO AND ORCH.
    2,2,2,2 - 4,2,3,0 - timp.,perc. - pf. - str.   23:00 Bo. Hawkes.
—— CONCERTO NO. 1 FOR VIOLIN AND ORCH., OP. POSTH.
    2,3,2,2 - 4,2,2,1 - timp.,perc. - 2 hp. - str.   21:00 Bo. Hawkes.
—— CONCERTO NO. 2 FOR PIANO AND ORCH.
    3,2,2,3 - 4,3,3,1 - timp.,perc. - pf. - str.   25:00 Bo. Hawkes.
—— CONCERTO NO. 2 FOR VIOLIN AND ORCH.
    1. Allegro non troppo; 2. Theme and variations; 3. Rondo
    2,2,2,2 - 4,2,3,0 - timp.,perc.,cel. - hp. - str.   32:00 Bo. Hawkes.
—— CONCERTO NO. 3 FOR PIANO AND ORCH.
    2,2,2,2 - 4,2,3,1 - timp.,perc.,xyl. - pf. - str.   23:00 Bo. Hawkes.
—— DANCE SUITE
    2,2,2,2 - 4,2,2,1 - timp.,perc.,cel. - hp. - str.   16:00 Bo. Hawkes.
—— DANCES OF TRANSYLVANIA
    2,2,2,2 - 2,2,2,1 - timp.,perc. - hp.(or pf.) - str.   4:00 Bo. Hawkes.
—— DIVERTIMENTO
    str.   22:00 Bo. Hawkes.
—— FIVE HUNGARIAN FOLKSONGS (FOR MEDIUM VOICE AND ORCH.)
    2,2,2,2 - 2,2,2,1 - perc. - hp. - pf. - str.   11:00 Bo. Hawkes.
—— FOUR ORCHESTRAL PIECES, OP. 12
    4,3,4,4 - 4,4,4,1 - perc.,cel. - hp. - pf. - str.   25:00 Bo. Hawkes.
—— HUNGARIAN PEASANT SONGS
    2,2,2,2 - 2,2,2,1 - timp.,perc. - hp. - str.   9:00 Bo. Hawkes.
—— HUNGARIAN SKETCHES (BILDER AUS UNGARN)
    2,2,2,2 - 2,2,2,1 - timp.,perc. - hp. - str.   11:00 Bo. Hawkes.
—— KOSSUTH, OP. POSTH. (SYMPHONIC POEM)
    Bo. Hawkes.
—— KOSSUTH SYMPHONY, OP. POSTH. (ORIGINAL VERSION)
    Bo. Hawkes.
—— THE MIRACULOUS MANDARIN (BALLET) %
    3,3,3,3 - 4,3,3,1 - timp.,perc.,cel. - hp. - org. - pf. - str.   60:00 Bo. Hawkes.
—— MUSIC FOR STRINGS, PERCUSSION AND CELESTA
    1. Andante tranquillo; 2. Allegro; 3. Adagio; 4. Allegro molto
    timp.,perc.,cel.,xyl. - hp. - pf. - str.   25:30 Bo. Hawkes.
—— RHAPSODY NO. 1 FOR CELLO AND ORCH.
    2,2,2,2 - 2,2,2,1 - cemb.(or hp, or pf.) - str.   12:00 Bo. Hawkes.
—— RHAPSODY NO. 1 FOR VIOLIN AND ORCH.
    2,2,2,2 - 2,2,1,1 - perc. - cimbalom(or hp. or pf.) - str.   11:00 Bo. Hawkes.
—— RHAPSODY NO. 2 FOR VIOLIN AND ORCH.
    2,2,2,2 - 2,2,1,1 - perc.,cel. - hp. - pf. - str.   12:00 Bo. Hawkes.
—— RUMANIAN FOLK DANCES
    2,0,2,2 - 2hn. - str.   6:00 Bo. Hawkes.
—— RUMANIAN FOLK DANCES (FOR STRING ORCH.)
    str.   3:30 Bo. Hawkes.
—— SCHERZO FOR PIANO AND ORCH., OP. 2 (POSTH.)
    4,3,4,4 - 4,2,3,1 - timp.,perc. - 2 hp. - pf. - str.   29:00 Bo. Hawkes.

—— SIX PART - SONGS FOR CHORUS AND ORCH.
2,2,2,2 - 4,2,0,0 - timp.,perc. - pf. - str.   11:00 Bo. Hawkes.
—— SUITE FROM "THE MIRACULOUS MANDARIN"
3,3,3,3 - 4,3,3,1 - timp.,perc.,cel. - hp. - pf. - str.
20:00 Bo. Hawkes.
—— SUITE FROM "THE WOODEN PRINCE", OP. 13
4,4,4,2sax.,2 - 4,4,2cnt.,3,1 - perc.,cel. - str.   30:00 Bo. Hawkes.
—— SUITE NO. 2 FOR ORCH., OP. 4 (REVISED 1943)
1. Commodo; 2. Allegro vivace; 3. Andante; 4. Commodo
2(2nd alt. with picc.),2(2nd alt. with Eng. hn.),2(1 alt. with E♯cl.;
2nd alt. with b.-cl.),2(2nd alt. with c.-bn.) - 3,2,0,0 - timp.,perc. -
2hp. - str.   25:00 Bo. Hawkes.
—— THREE VILLAGE SCENES (SLOVAK FOLK SONGS) (FOR
WOMEN'S VOICES AND CHAMBER ORCH.)
2,1,2,sax.,1 - 1,1,1,0 - perc. - hp. - pf. - str.   10:00 Bo. Hawkes.
—— THE WOODEN PRINCE (PANTOMIME) %
4,4,4,2 sax.,4 - 4,6,3,1 - timp.,perc.,cel. - 2 hp. - str.
40:00 Bo. Hawkes.

BARTÓK, Béla - DORATI, Antal
—— SUITE OP. 14
2,2,1,2 - 2,0,0,0 - hp.   9:00 Bo. Hawkes.

BARTÓK, Béla - ORMANDY, Eugene
—— SIX ROUMANIAN FOLK DANCES
*3,2,2,2 - 4,2,3,0 - timp.,perc.,glock. - hp. - str.   Arranger.

BARTÓK, Béla - SERLY, Tibor
—— BARTÓK SUITE (FOR SMALL ORCH.) (IN 4 MOVTS.)
Southern.
—— CONCERTO FOR CELLO AND ORCH. (ADAPTATION OF
VIOLIN CONCERTO)
20:30 Bo. Hawkes.
—— CONCERTO FOR VIOLA AND ORCH., OP. POSTHUMOUS
3,2,2,2 - 3,2,2,1 - timp.,perc. - str. 20:30 Bo. Hawkes.
—— SUITE FOR "MIKROKOSMOS" (IN 8 MOVTS.)
3,2,2,2 - 4,3,3,1 - timp.,perc.,cel. - hp. - str.   16:00 Bo. Hawkes.

BARTÓK, Béla - WEINER, Leo
—— TWO ROUMANIAN DANCES, OP. 8A
2,2,2,2 - 4,2,3,0 - timp.,perc. - hp. - str.   9:00 Bo. Hawkes.

BARTÓK, Béla - WILLNER, A.
—— FIVE ROUMANIAN FOLK DANCES (FOR STRING ORCH.)
str.   6:00 Bo. Hawkes.

BARTOLOZZI, Bruno
—— CONCERTO FOR ORCHESTRA
3,3,3,2 - 4,3,3,1 - timp.,perc.,xyl. - hp. - pf. - str.   27:00 Leeds.
—— CONCERTO FOR VIOLIN, HARPSICHORD AND STRING
ORCH.
hpsc. - str.   18:00 Leeds.
—— CONZERTAZIONI
bn. - perc. - str.   Leeds.
—— DIVERTIMENTO
1,1,1,1 - 1,1,0,0 - hp. - str.   12:00 Leeds.
—— TUTTO CIO'CHE ACCADE TI RIGUARDA (DRAMATIC
REPRESENTATION IN 1 ACT, WITH PROLOGUE, ON
GÜNTHER EICH'S "TRAÜME") % (1970)
1,2,2,2 - 3,3,3,1 - timp.,perc.(4),mar.,vibra.,xyl. - tape-recorder -
org. - str.   35:00 MCA Music.

BARTON-ARMSTRONG, John
—— THE ANDES (TONE POEM) (1962)
1,1,1,1 - 4,1,3,1 - perc. - str.   19:00 P.R.S.
—— SUITE OF INCIDENTAL MUSIC (1968)
1,1,1,1 - 2,2,2,0 - perc. - str.   12:00 P.R.S.
—— SYMPHONY (1968)
2,2,2,2 - 4,2,3,1 - timp.,perc. - str.   35:00 P.R.S.

BARTOŠ, František
—— MUSIC FOR BROADCASTING, OP. 12 (IN 3 MOVTS.)
1,1,1,1 - 1,1,1,0 - perc. - str.   12:00 Bo. Hawkes.

BARTOŠ, Jan Zdeněk
—— SYMPHONY NO. 1, OP. 65
3,3,2,3 - 4,3,3,1 - timp.,perc. - hp. - str.   37:00 Bo. Hawkes.
—— SYMPHONY NO. 2 (CHAMBER SYMPHONY)
2,2,2,2 - 4,2,3,1 - timp. - str.   23:00 Bo. Hawkes.

BARTOW, Nevett
—— MASS, OP. 4 (FOR 4 SOLO VOICES, CHORUS AND SMALL
ORCH.)
4 hn. - timp.,glock. - org. - str.   40:00 Composer.
—— SUMMERSHADOW (ELEGY FOR ORCH.) (1968)
2(2nd alt. with picc.),1,*2,2 - 4,2,2,1 - timp. - hp. - str.
8:00 Shawnee.

BARVIK, Miroslav
—— DIMITROV (SYMPHONIC PICTURE) (1953)
Bo. Hawkes.
—— GOTTWALD CANTATA (1952)
Bo. Hawkes.
—— OLD CZECH LEGENDS (ORATORIO) (1951)
Bo. Hawkes.
—— PRAGUE SPRING (CANTATA) (FOR MIXED CHORUS AND
ORCH.) (1950)
Bo. Hawkes.
—— SERENADE FOR STRING ORCH. (1948)
str.   Bo. Hawkes.
—— SYMPHONIETTA (FOR ORCH., MIXED CHORUS, ORGAN
AND CONTRALTO SOLO) (1948)
Bo. Hawkes.
—— SYMPHONY NO. 1 (1948)
Bo. Hawkes.

BASHMAKOV, Leonid
—— CANZONA NO. 1 (FOR SATB CHORUS AND ORCH.) (1969)
2,1,1,1 - 1,1,1,0 - perc.(4) - pf. -str.   23:00 FinnMICtr.
—— CANZONA NO. 2 (FOR SOPRANO AND ORCH.) (1971)
2,2,2,2 - 2,2,2,0 - perc.(3) - pf. - str.   17:00 FinnMICtr.
—— CONCERTO FOR ORCHESTRA (1969)
3,3,2,2 - 4,3,3,1 - timp.,perc.(4) - str.   22:00 FinnMICtr.
—— CONCERTO FOR VIOLIN AND ORCH. (1966)
1,1,2,2, - 2,2,3,0 - timp.,perc.(3),cel. - pf. -str. 18:00 FinnMICtr.
—— CONCERTO PER FLAUTI E ORCHESTRA ("IMPRESSIONI
MARINE")
1. Calmo; 2. Allegro; 3. Lento; 4. Agitato
20:00 FinnMICtr.
—— FANTASTIC PICTURES (SUITE) (1953)
3,3,3,3 - 4,3,3,1 - timp.,perc. - str.   15:00 FinnMICtr.
—— SINFONIETTA (1971)
2,0,2,2 - 2,2,0,0 - timp.,perc.(4) - pf. - str.   15:00 FinnMICtr.
—— SYMPHONY NO. 1 (1963)
3,2,3,2 - 4,3,3,1 - timp.,perc.(3),cel. - hp. - str. 23:00 FinnMICtr.
—— SYMPHONY NO. 2 (1965)
3,2,2,3 - 4,4,4,0 - timp.,perc.(3),cel. - hp. - pf. - str.
16:00 FinnMICtr.

BASINSKAS, Justinas J.
—— REQUIEM (FOR BASS, SATB CHORUS AND ORCH.) (Text: K.
Stanishev; Eng. trans.: T. Dambrauskene)
G. Schirmer.

BASS, Warner S.
—— ADAGIO FOR STRING ORCH. ("TAPS")
str.   5:15 C. Fischer.
or:
tpt. - perc.(1) - str.
—— LARGHETTO FOR OBOE AND STRING ORCH.
ob. - str.   6:00 Composer.
—— MUSIC FOR STRING ORCH.
str.   C. Fischer.
—— SERENATA CONCERTANTE (FOR VIOLA AND STRING
ORCH.) (IN 6 MOVTS.)
str.   22:10 Composer.
—— SONG OF HOPE (OVERTURE AND FUGUE)
2(2nd alt. with picc.),2(2nd alt. with Eng. hn.),2(2nd alt. with
b.-cl.),2 - 3,2,3,0 - timp.,perc.(4),bells,glock.,xyl. - str.
11:00 Transcon.
—— SUITE FOR STRING ORCH. (IN 3 MOVTS.)
str.   10:00 Composer.
—— TAPS (ADAGIO)
tpt. - perc. - str.   7:30 C. Fischer.
or:
str.

BATE, Stanley
—— CONCERTO FOR HARPSICHORD AND ORCH.
1,1,1,1 - 0,0,0,0 - hpsc. - str.   Lengnick.
—— CONCERTO GROSSO
pf. - str.   Lengnick.

—— CONCERTO NO. 2 FOR PIANO AND ORCH., OP. 28
2,2,2,2 - 4,3,3,1 - timp. - pf. - str.   21:00 Lengnick.
—— CONCERTO NO. 3 FOR PIANO AND ORCH.
3,2,2,2 - 4,3,3,1 - timp.,perc. - 2 hp. - pf. - str.   31:00 Presser.
—— SINFONIETTA NO. 1, OP. 22
2,2,2,2 - 4,2,2,0 - perc. - str.   16:00 Lengnick.
—— SYMPHONY NO. 3, OP. 29
2,2,2,2 - 4,3,3,1 - perc. - str.   28:00 Lengnick.
—— SYMPHONY NO. 4
3,2,2,2 - 4,3,3,1 - timp.,perc. - hp. - pf. - str.   32:00 Lengnick.

BATH, Hubert
—— CORNISH RHAPSODY (FOR PIANO AND ORCH.)
*2,*2,2,2 - 4,3,2,1 - timp.,perc.(2) - pf. - str.   8:00 Fox.
—— LEGEND OF NERBUDDA (DRAMATIC CANTATA FOR
SOLI, CHORUS AND ORCH.)
     80:00 Bo. Hawkes.

BAUDO, Serge
—— TROIS DANSES PAÏENNES
2,*2,3,2 - 2,2,2,0 - timp.,perc.,bells.,vibra,xyl. - d.-b.   6:55 Baron.

BAUDRIER, Yves
—— CREDO ADJUVA (FOR SOLO VOICES, CHILDREN'S
CHORUS, MIXED CHORUS AND ORCH.)
3,3,3,3 - 4,3,3,1 - timp.,perc. - hp. - pf. - str.   35:00 Eds. Fran.
—— ELEONORA
1,1,1,1 - 0,1,0,0 - Ondes-martenot(or sax.) - hp. - pf. - str.
     11:00 Presser.
—— LE MUSICIEN DANS LA CITÉ
2,2,2,2 - 4,3,3,1 - timp.,perc.(4),cel. - hp. - str.   22:30 Presser.

BAUER, Harold
—— SICILIANO (BY PURCELL), THREE VARIATIONS AND
FINALE (FOR STRING ORCH.)
str.   G. Schirmer.

BAUM, Alfred
—— CONCERTINO FÜR SCHLAGZEUG UND KLEINES
ORCHESTER
     15:00 S.U.I.S.A.
—— DIVERTIMENTO FÜR OBOE UND KLEINES ORCHESTER
     12:00 S.U.I.S.A.
—— SERENADE (FÜR 13 BLASER, VIOLA, KONTRABASS UND
SCHLAGZEUG)
     15:00 S.U.I.S.A.
—— TANZSUITE
3,2,2,2 - 3,3,3,0 - timp.,perc. - str.   15:00 S.U.I.S.A.

BAUMANN, Herbert
—— ALLEGRO CAPRICCIOSO (FOR PIANO AND ORCH.)
2,2,2,2 - 4,2,3,1 - timp.,perc. - pf. - str.   9:00 F. Colombo.
—— AS YOU LIKE IT (SUITE) (AFTER SHAKESPEARE'S PLAY)
1,1,2,1 - 2,0,0,0 - perc. - str.   12:00 F. Colombo.
—— BROOKLYN BRIDGE
3,2,2,2 - 4,2,3,1 - timp.,perc. - hp. - str.   7:00 F. Colombo.
—— CONCERTO FOR GUITAR AND STRINGS
guit. - str.   20:00 F. Colombo.
—— THE HUNT (JAGDOUVERTÜRE)
2,2,2,2 - 3,2,2,0 - timp.,perc. - str.   7:00 F. Colombo.
—— ITALIAN SUITE (IN 3 MOVTS.)
2,2,2,2 - 4,2,3,1 - timp.,perc. - hp. - str.   10:00 F. Colombo.
—— MEXICAN SUITE
3,2,2,2 - 4,3,3,1 - timp.,perc. - str.   20:00 F. Colombo.
—— NORDIC IMPRESSIONS (SUITE FOR STRING ORCH.)
str.   8:00 F. Colombo.
—— ROBIN HOOD (OVERTURE-FANTASY)
3,2,2,2 - 4,3,3,1 - timp.,perc. - str.   5:00 F. Colombo.
—— ROTOR (AN OVERTURE)
3,2,2,2 - 4,3,3,0 - timp.,perc. - pf. - str.   6:00 F. Colombo.

BAUMANN, Max
—— CONCERTO FOR ORGAN, TIMPANI AND STRINGS, OP. 70
timp. - org. - str.   22:00 Henmar.
—— DEUTSCHE VESPER, OP. 64 (FOR SOPRANO, SPEAKER,
MIXED CHORUS AND ORCH.)
1,1,1,1 - 1,1,0,0 - timp. - str.   35:00 Sirius.
—— ORCHESTER-VARIATIONS, OP. 29
2,2,2,2 - 4,2,3,0 - timp.,perc. - hp. - str.   15:00 Sirius.
—— THE PASSION, OP. 63 (FOR SOPRANO, BARITONE,
NARRATOR, SPEAKING-CHORUS, MIXED CHORUS AND
ORCH.)
4,0,0,0 - 0,2,0,0 - timp.,perc. - hp. - 2 pf. - str.   71:00 Sirius.

—— PERSPECTIVES II (IN 1 MOVT.)
2(2nd alt. with picc.),2,2,2 - 4,3,3,1 - timp.,perc. - str.
     13:00 Henmar.
—— PETITE SUITE, OP. 38 (IN 4 MOVTS.)
1,1,1,1 - 0,0,0,0 - pf.(ad lib.) - str.   8:00 Henmar.
—— SINFONIA PICCOLA, OP. 65 (IN 3 MOVTS.)
0,2,0,0 - 2,0,0,0 - str.   15:00 Sirius.

BAUMGARTNER, Walter
—— MUSIK ZU EINEM ALTJAPANISCHEN MÄRCHENSPIEL
3,3,3,3 - 4,3,3,1 - perc.,cel. - 2hp. - pf. - str.   6:00 Modern.

BAUTISTA CACHAZA, Julián
—— FANTASÍA ESPAÑOLA (FOR CLARINET AND ORCH.)
2,2,3,2 - 4,2,0,0 - timp.,perc. - hp. - str.   16:00 Bo. Hawkes.
—— OBERTURA GROTESCA
3,2,2,2 - 4,3,3,1 - timp.,perc. - str.   10:00 Bo. Hawkes.
—— SINFONIA BREVE
2,2,2,2 - 2,1,2,0 - timp. - str.   20:00 F. Colombo.
—— SINFONIA NO. 2 ("RICORDIANA")
3,2,2,2 - 4,2,3,1 - timp. - pf. - str.   32:00 F. Colombo.
—— SUITE ALL'ANTICA (FOR SOLO STRINGS AND ORCH.)
1,1,1,1 - 1,1,1,0 - timp., perc. - str.   18:00 Bo. Hawkes.
—— SUITE DE DANZAS (FROM THE BALLET "JUERGA")
3,2,2,2 - 4,2,2,1 - timp.,perc. - hp. - str.   12:00 Bo. Hawkes.

BÅVEUDDE, Sven
—— EN LITEN GRIPSHOLMSMUSIQUE (SUITE)
2,2,2,2 - 2,2,0,0 - timp. - str.   21:00 S.T.I.M.
or:
1,1,2,1 - 2,2,0,0 - timp. - str.
—— FRÅN SVERIGE - NORRÖVER, OP. 11
3,3,3,3 - 4,2,3,1 - timp. - hp. - str.   10:00 S.T.I.M.
—— KLUBBA GROTTA (SUITE)
3,3,3,3 - 4,2,3,1 - timp. - str.   12:00 S.T.I.M.
or:
2,2,2,2 - 2,2,1,0 - timp. - str.
—— NYMPHAEA (NÄCKROSORNA) (BALLET
DIVERTISSEMENT)
2,2,2,2 - 2,2,1,0 - timp. - str.   17:00 S.T.I.M.
—— PRELUDE TO "ARVET"
4,3,4,3 - 6,3,3,1 - timp.,perc. - hp. - str.   10:00 S.T.I.M.
—— PRELUDE TO "BOHUS"
4,3,3,3 - 4,4,3,1 - timp.,perc. - hp. - str.   8"00 S.T.I.M.
—— SWEDISH RHAPSODY NO. 1 (SWEDISH SUMMER NIGHT)
2,3,2,2 - 4,2,3,0 - timp. - str.   17:30 S.T.I.M.
or:
2,2,2,2 - 2,2,1,0 - timp. - str.
—— SWEDISH RHAPSODY NO. 2 (TILL EN SVENSK SPELMANS
KÄRESTA)
3,3,3,3 - 4,2,3,1 - timp. - str.   13:00 S.T.I.M.
or:
2,2,2,2 - 2,2,1,0 - timp. - str.
—— SWEDISH RHAPSODY NO. 3 (SÖDERTÖRN)
3,3,3,3 - 4,2,3,1 - timp. str.   12:00 S.T.I.M.
or:
2,2,2,2 - 2,2,1,0 - timp. - str.
—— SWEDISH RHAPSODY NO. 4 (WINGÅKER)
3,3,3,3 - 4,2,3,1 - timp. - str.   16:00 S.T.I.M.
or:
2,2,2,2 - 2,2,1,0 - timp. - str.
—— SWEDISH SUITE NO. 9
2,2,2,2 - 2,2,1,0 - timp.,perc. - str.   16:00 S.T.I.M.
or:
1,1,2,1 - 2,2,1,0 - timp.,perc. - str.
—— SYMPHONY NO. 1 IN E MINOR, OP. 7
3,3,3,3 - 4,2,3,1 - timp. - hp. - str.   37:00 S.T.I.M.

BAVICCHI, John
—— A CONCERT OVERTURE, OP. 29
*3,2,*3,*3 - 4,3,3,0 - timp.,perc.(3) - str.   10:00 Oxford.
—— CONCERTANTE, OP. 44 (FOR OBOE, BASSOON AND
STRING ORCH.) (IN 3 MOVTS.)
0,1,0,1 - 0,0,0,0 - str.   15:00 BKJ.
—— CONCERTO FOR CLARINET AND STRING ORCH., OP. 11
(IN 3 MOVTS.)
cl. - str.   20:00 Oxford.
—— FANTASIA ON KOREAN FOLK TUNES, OP. 53 (1966)
2,1,*3,1 - 2,2,3,1 - timp.,perc. - str.   8:00 BKJ.
—— FANTASY, OP. 36 (FOR HARP AND CHAMBER ORCH.)
1,1,1,1 - 1,0,0,0 - hp. - str.   10:00 BKJ.

—— FAREWELL AND HAIL, OP. 28 (FOR SOPRANO AND
CHAMBER ORCH.) (Text: Norma Farber)
tpt. - str.   11:00 BKJ.
—— FIREWORKS, OP. 48 (1962) (With optional Baritone voice)
1,0,1,0 - 1,0,0,0 - timp.,perc.(1) - pf. - str.   19:30 BKJ.
—— FOUR SONGS FOR CONTRALTO AND CHAMBER
ORCHESTRA, OP. 6
2,1,*2,0 - 2,0,0,0 - str.   14:00 BKJ.
—— SUITE NO. 1 FOR ORCH., OP. 19 (IN 5 MOVTS.)
*3,*3,*3,*3 - 4,3,3,1 - timp.,perc.(4) - str. 20:10 Oxford.
—— SUMMER INCIDENT, OP. 34 (1959)
2,2,2,2 - 2,0,0,0 - timp.,perc. - pf.   20:00 BKJ.
—— THREE PSALMS, OP. 50 (1963) (FOR SOLO VOICE, CHORUS
AND CHAMBER ORCH.)
0,0,0,0 - 0,2,0,0 - str.   13:00 BKJ.
—— TOBAL, OP. 5 (A FANTASY CONCERT PIECE)
2,2,*3,2 - 4,3,3,0 - timp.,perc. - str.   11:00 BKJ.

BAX, Arnold
—— CONCENTRATE FOR 3 SOLO INSTRUMENTS AND ORCH.
                                               25:00 Chappell.
—— CONCERTO FOR BASSOON, HARP AND STRINGS
(THRENODY AND SCHERZO)
bn. - hp. - str.   12:00 Chappell.
—— CONCERTO FOR CELLO AND ORCH.
1. Allegro Moderato; 2. Nocturne; 3. Molto vivace
3,3,2,3 - 4,2,0,0 - timp. - hp. - str.   33:00 Chappell.
—— CONCERTO FOR PIANO LEFT HAND AND ORCH.
                                               22:30 Chappell.
—— CONCERTO FOR VIOLIN AND ORCH.
3,3,2,3 - 4,2,0,0 - timp. - hp. - str.   31:00 Chappell.
—— THE GARDEN OF FAND (TONE POEM)
4,3,4,3 - 4,3,3,1 - timp.,perc.,cel.,glock. - 2 hp. - str.
                                               17:00 Chappell.
—— GOPAK
3(3rd alt. with picc.),2,2,2 - 4,2,3,1 - timp.,perc. - hp. - str.
                                               6:00 Galaxy.
—— THE HAPPY FOREST (NATURE POEM)
3,3,4,3 - 4,3,3,1 - timp.,perc.,cel.,glock. - hp. - str. 10:00 Chappell.
—— IN THE FAERY HILLS
3,3,4,2 - 4,3,3,1 - timp.,perc.,cel.,glock. - 2 hp. - str.
                                               15:00 Chappell.
—— MEDITERRANEAN (A FANTASY)
2,3,2,2 - 4hn. - timp.,glock. - hp. - str.   3:05 Chappell.
—— MORNING SONG (FOR SOLO PIANO AND ORCH.)
                                               7:30 Chappell.
—— NOVEMBER WOODS
4,3,4,3 - 4,3,3,1 - timp.,perc.,cel. - 2hp. - str. 15:00 Chappell.
—— OVERTURE, ELEGY AND RONDO
3(3rd alt. with picc.),*3,*3,*3 - 4,3,3,1 - timp.,perc.,glock.,xyl. -
hp. - str.   22:00 Chappell.
—— OVERTURE TO A PICARESQUE COMEDY
4,3,4,3 - 4,3,3,1 - timp.,perc.,cel. - hp. - str. 10:00 Chappell.
—— OVERTURE TO ADVENTURE
                                               9:00 Chappell.
—— PHANTASY FOR VIOLA AND ORCH.
3(3rd alt. with picc.),*3,2,2 - 4,2,0,0 - timp.,perc. - hp. - str.
                                               16:00 Chappell.
—— ROMANTIC OVERTURE
2,1,2,2 - 2,1,0,0 - pf. - str.   10:00 Chappell.
—— SAGA FRAGMENT
tpt. - perc. - pf. - str.   10:00 Chappell.
—— SUMMER MUSIC
3,2,2,2 - 4,1,0,0 - timp. - hp. - str.   9:00 Chappell.
—— SYMPHONY NO. 1, IN E♭ (IN 3 MOVEMENTS)
4(3rd alt. with alto fl.;4th alt. with picc.),*3,heck.,*4(3rd alt. with
E♭cl.),2,c.-bn.(or sarr.) - 4,3,3,1 - timp.,perc.,cel.,glock.,xyl. - 2hp. -
str.   30:00 Chappell.
—— SYMPHONY NO. 2
1. Molto moderato; 2. Andante; 3. Poco largamente
3(3rd alt. with picc.),*3,*4,*3 - 4,3,3,2 - timp.,perc.,cel.,glock. -
2hp. - pf. - org. - str.   35:00 Chappell.
—— SYMPHONY NO. 3 (IN 3 MOVEMENTS)
3(3rd alt. with picc.),*3,*4,*3 - 4,3,3,1 - timp.,perc.,cel.,glock.,xyl.
- 1-2hp. - str.   30:00 Chappell.
—— SYMPHONY NO. 4 (IN 3 MOVEMENTS)
3(3rd alt. with picc.),*3,*4,*3 - 6,3,3,2 - timp.,perc.,cel. - hp. - org.
- str.   35:00 Chappell.
—— SYMPHONY NO. 5 (IN 3 MOVEMENTS)
3(3rd alt. with picc.),*3(3rd alt. with E♭cl.),*4,*3 - 4,3,3,1 -
timp.,perc. - hp. - str.   43:00 Chappell.

—— SYMPHONY NO. 6 (IN 3 MOVTS.)
3(3rd alt with picc.),*3,*4,*3 - 4,3,3,1 - timp.,perc.,cel. - hp. - str.
                                               35:00 Chappell.
—— SYMPHONY NO. 7
3,3,4,3 - 4,3,3,1 - timp.,perc. - hp. - str.   Chappell.
—— THE TALE THE PINE TREES KNEW
3,3,4,3 - 4,3,3,1 - timp.,perc. - 2hp. - str. 18:00 Chappell.
—— TINTAGEL (TONE POEM)
3,3,3,3 - 4,3,3,1 - timp.,perc.,glock. - hp. - str. 12:00 Chappell.

BAYER, Friedrich
—— COMEDY OVERTURE
3,2,2,2 - 4,3,3,0 - perc. - str.   7:00 Modern.

BAYER-VETESSY, Georg
—— CONCERTO FOR PIANO AND ORCH.
2,2,2,2 - 4,3,3,1 - timp.,perc. - pf. - str.   21:00 Modern.
—— SUITE NO. 1 FOR ORCH.
2,2,2,2 - 4,3,3,1 - timp.,perc.,cel. - hp. - str. 14:00 Modern.

BAZELAIRE, Paul
—— RAPSODIE DANS LE STYLE RUSSE (FOR CELLO AND
ORCH.)
3,2,2,2 - 4,2,0,0 - timp.,perc.(3) - hp. - str. 8:30 EV.

BAZELON, Irwin A.
—— ADAGIO AND FUGUE FOR STRINGS
str.   Weintraub.
—— BALLET 17 (CONCERT BALLET - "CENTAURI 17") %
1(alt. with picc.),1,*2(1 alt. with E♭cl.),1 - 1,2,0,1 - timp.,perc.
(2),bells,glock.,Javanese gamelan,vibra,xyl. - theremin - pf. -
str.(no vlns.)   23:00 Bo. Hawkes.
—— CHURCHILL DOWNS CONCERTO (FOR SOLO WOODWINDS
AND INSTRUMENTS)
*2,0,1,alto sax.,0 - 1,3,2,0 - timp.,perc.,cel - electric guit., electric
b.-guit - electric hpsc. - electric org. - electric pf.
                                               23:00 Bo. Hawkes.
—— CONCERT OVERTURE
                                               10:00 Bo. Hawkes.
—— DRAMATIC MOVEMENT FOR ORCH.
2(2nd alt. with picc.),2,1 E♭cl.,*3,*3 - 4,3,3,1 -
timp.,perc.(5),vibra,xyl. - pf. - str.   18:00 Bo. Hawkes.
—— DRAMATIC MOVEMENT FOR ORCH.
3,2,4,3 - 4,3,3,1 - timp. - pf. - str.   18:00 Bo. Hawkes.
—— EXCURSION FOR ORCHESTRA
1-3,2,2,2 - 4,3,3,1 - timp.,perc. - str.   12:00 Bo. Hawkes.
—— EXCURSION FOR ORCHESTRA (1965)
*3,*3,1 E♭cl.,2,*3 - 4,3,3,1 - timp.,perc.(4),glock.,vibra.,xyl. -
pf.(ad lib.) - str.   12:00 Bo. Hawkes.
—— HUMORESQUE FOR ORCHESTRA
3(2nd and 3rd alt. with 2 picc.),2,D cl.,2,*3 - 4,3,3,1 -
timp.,perc.(2),cel.,glock.,xyl. - pf. - str.   10:00 Composer.
—— AN ORCHESTRAL FANTASY (POEM FOR ORCHESTRA)
3(3rd alt. with picc.),2,2,2 - 4,3,3,1 - timp.,perc. (2),bells,cel.,glock.
- pf. - str.   15:00 Composer.
—— OVERTURE TO SHAKESPEARE'S "THE TAMING OF THE
SHREW"
1(alt. with picc.),1,1(alt. with E♭cl.),1 - 2,2,1,0 -
timp.,perc.(2),glock.,vibra.,xyl. - pf. - str. 10:00 Bo. Hawkes.
—— A QUIET PIECE FOR A VIOLENT TIME
2,1,2,1 - 3,2,2,1 - perc. - hp. - str.   20:00 Bo. Hawkes.
—— A QUIET PIECE (FOR A VIOLENT TIME) (1975)
*2,1,*2,1 - 3,2,2,1 - perc.(3),bells,glock.,mar.,vibra. - hp. - str.
                                               12:00 Bo. Hawkes.
—— SUITE FOR SMALL ORCH. (IN 5 MOVTS.)
1,1(alt. with Eng.hn.),1,1 - 1,1,0,0 - timp. - str. 17:00 Weintraub.
—— SUITE FROM SHAKESPEARE'S "THE MERRY WIVES OF
WINDSOR" (IN 7 MOVTS.)
1(alt. with picc.),1,1(alt. with E♭cl.),1 - 2,2,0,1 -
timp.,perc.(2),glock.,vibra.,xyl. - pf. - str. 20:00 Composer.
—— SYMPHONIC ETUDES
3(3rd alt. with picc.),2,2,2 - 4,3,3,1 - timp.,perc.(2),bells,glock. -
hp. - str.   25:00 Composer.
—— SYMPHONIC VARIATIONS ON AN OLD ENGLISH FOLK
THEME
3(3rd alt. with picc.),2,2,2 - 4,3,3,1 -
timp.,perc.(2),bells,cel.,glock.,xyl. - pf. - str. 25:00 Composer.
—— SYMPHONY NO. 1 (IN 1 MOVT.)
3,3,3,2 - 4,3,3,1 - timp.,perc. - pf. - str.   28:00 Bo. Hawkes.
—— SYMPHONY NO. 2 (A SHORT SYMPHONY) (TESTIMONIAL
TO A BIG CITY)
1,1,*2,1 - 2,2,1,0 - timp.,perc.(2),bells,glock.,vibra.,xyl. - pf. - str.
                                               14:00 Bo. Hawkes.

or:
  2,2,2,2 - 2,3,2,1 - timp.,perc.,cel. - pf. - str.
—— SYMPHONY NO. 3 (FOR BRASS, PERCUSSION, PIANO AND SOLO SEXTET)
  1,0,2,0 - 4,6,4,2 - timp.,perc.,cel. - electric guit. - pf. - vla.,c.
  27:00 Bo. Hawkes.
—— SYMPHONY NO. 4 (SYMPHONY IN THREE MOVEMENTS)
  2(2nd alt. with picc.),*3,1 E♭cl.,*3,*3 - 4,3,3,1 - timp.,perc.(5),cel.,glock.,vibra.,xyl. - pf. - str.   34:00 Bo. Hawkes.
—— SYMPHONY NO. 5 (1968)
  3(3rd alt. with picc.),*3,1 E♭cl.,*3,*3 - 4,3,3,1 - timp.,perc.(4-5),bells,glock.,mar.,vibra.,xyl. - pf. - str.
  30:00 Bo. Hawkes.
—— SYMPHONY NO. 6 (IN 4 MOVTS.)
  *3,ten.recorder,2,1 E♭cl.,*3,*3 - 4,3,3,1 - timp.,perc.(4-5),glock.,mar.,vibra.,xyl. - accord.(amplified) - pf.(amplified) - str.   27:00 Bo. Hawkes.

BEACH, Bennie P.
—— NATURE HAS FOUR CHILDREN (FOR SATB CHORUS AND ORCH.) (1952) (IN 6 MOVTS.) (Text: Composer)
  1,1,1,1 - 1,0,0,0 - str.(no d.-b.)   19:00 Composer.
—— SOLILOQUY (1951) (FOR CHAMBER ORCH.)
  1,2,2,1 - 2,0,0,0 - str.   3:30 Composer.

BEACH, Bruce
—— PLAZA (BALLET IN FORM OF 4 MOVT. SYMPHONY) %
  3,2,2,2 - 4,2,3,1 - timp.,perc. - hp. - str.   27:00 EV.

BEACH, Mrs. H. H. A.
—— THE CANTICLE OF THE SUN, OP. 123 (FOR SOLOISTS, CHORUS AND ORCH.)
  2,2,2,2 - 4,2,3,1 - timp. - str.   25:00 Composer.
—— CHRIST IN THE UNIVERSE, OP. 133 (CANTATA) (FOR SOLOISTS, CHORUS AND ORCH.)
  2,1,2,2 - 4,2,0,0 - timp. - pf. - str.   25:00 Gray.

BEADELL, Robert
—— IMPROVISATION AND DANCE (FOR SYMPHONY ORCH. AND JAZZ ENSEMBLE) (1974)
  *3,2,2,5 sax,(2 alto,2 ten.,1 bar.)2 - 4,8,7,1 - timp.,perc.,bells,vibra.,xyl. - guit. - pf. - str.   15:00 Composer.
—— NAPOLEON (2-ACT OPERA) % (1972) (Text: Dean Tschetter and William Wallis)
  *3,2,*3,2 - 4,3,3,1 - timp.,perc.(3),bells,glock. - org. - pf. - str.
  120:00 Composer.
—— NEW FRONTIER (AN OVERTURE) (1961)
  *3,2,*3,2 - 4,3,3,1 - perc.,bells,xyl. - str.   9:00 Composer.

BEALL, John
—— ESSAY FOR ORCHESTRA. (1965)
  *3,2,2,2 - 4,3,3,1 - timp. - str.   12:00 CAP.
—— LAMENT FOR THOSE LOST IN THE WAR (1972)
  *3(picc. alt. with alto fl.),2,2,2 - 4,3,3,1 - timp.,perc.(4) - pf. - str.
  10:00 Composer.
—— SONGS OF AUTUMN (SONG CYCLE FOR TENOR AND ORCH.) (1966) (Texts: Various Classical Chinese Poets)
  *3,*3,2,2 - 4,3,3,1 - timp.,perc.(4),glock. - pf. - str.   30:00 CAP.

BEAUMONT, Adrian
—— FANFARE, CHORALE AND TOCCATA
  3,3,3,3 - 4,3,3,1 - timp.,perc. - pf. - str.   15:00 P.R.S.
—— SYMPHONY NO. 1, IN A
  2,2,2,2 - 4,2,3,1 - timp.,perc. - pf. - str.   25:00 P.R.S.

BECAUD, Gilbert
—— L' ENFANT À L'ÉTOILE (FOR BARITONE, CHILDREN'S CHORUS, MIXED CHORUS AND ORCH.)
  3,3,3,3 - 4,3,3,1 - timp.,perc. - 2 hp. - org. - str.   17:00 Salabert.
—— OPERA D'ARAN (LYRIC DRAMA IN 2 ACTS AND 7 SCENES) % (Text: Jacques Emmanuel)
  3,2,3,2 - 3,3,3,0 - timp. - hp. - str.   Salabert.

BECERRA SCHMIDT, Gustavo
—— CONCERTO FOR FLUTE AND STRINGS
  fl. - str.   18:00 Oxford.
—— SINFONIA NO. 1
  3,3,3,3 - 4,3,3,1 - perc.,cel. - pf. - str.   11:00 Oxford.
—— SINFONIA NO. 2 (DE PROFUNDIS)
  3,3,3,3 - 4,3,3,1 - perc.,cel. - pf. - str.   17:00 Bo. Hawkes.

BECK, Conrad
—— MOUVEMENTS LYRIQUES (FÜR VIOLINCELLO UND KAMMERORCHESTER)
  2,2,2,0 - 2,2,0,0 - str.   19:00 S.U.I.S.A.

BECK, John N.
—— CANTICLE OF PRAISE (FOR CHORUS AND ORCH.)
  1,1,1,1 - 2,3,3,1 - perc. - str.   Presser.
—— VISIONS OF ST. JOHN (FOR CHORUS AND INSTRS.)
  0,0,0,0 - 4,4,3,bar.,1 - perc.(3) - hp. - pf.   Presser.

BECK, Martha
—— FANTASY FOR CHAMBER ORCHESTRA (1960)
  1,1,1,1 - 1,1,1,0 - timp.,perc.(1) - hp. - str.   9:00 Composer.
—— A LEGEND OF TAMARAC (CANTATA) (FOR SATB CHORUS AND SMALL ORCH.) (1966) (Text: Composer)
  1,1,1,1 - 1,1,1,0 - perc. - 7 vlns.,2 c.   27:00 Composer.
—— MICHAEL AND CORNELIA (A SAGA OF THE HUDSON VALLEY DUTCH) (CANTATA) (1975) (Text: Composer)
  *2,1,1,1 - 1,2,2,0 - timp.,perc.(1),bells,xyl. - pf. - str.(2,1,1,0)
  70:00 Composer.

BECK, Thomas
—— ARNLJOT GJELLINE (SYMPHONIC CANTATA) (FOR MIXED CHOIR, TENOR, BASS AND ORCH.) (Text: B. Bjornson)
  2,2,2,2 - 4,2,3,1 - timp.,perc. - hp. - str.   65:00 Musikk-Hu.
—— BALLAD ON A NORWEGIAN FOLK TUNE
  2,2,2,2 - 4,2,3,1 - timp.,perc.,cel. - hp. - str.   8:00 T.O.N.O.
—— HOLY FUTURE (HEILAG FRAMTID) (CANTATA) (FOR MIXED CHORUS AND ORCH.) (Text: Arne Garborg)
  1,1,2,1 - 2,2,2,0 - timp.,perc. - str.   15:00 T.O.N.O.
—— IN THE MOUNTAINS (HOIFJELL) (CANTATA) (FOR SOPRANO, BARITONE, NARRATOR, MIXED CHOIR AND ORCH.)
  3,2,2,2 - 4,3,3,1 - timp.,perc. - hp. - str.   45:00 T.O.N.O.
—— KING OLAV ON STIKLESTAD (FROM "ARNLJOT GJELLINE") (FOR NARRATOR AND ORCH.) (Text: B. Bjornson)
  2,2,2,2 - 4,2,3,1 - timp.,perc. - hp. - str.   10:00 Musikk-Hu.
—— THE MOUNTAIN BROOK (FROM THE CANTATA "IN THE MOUNTAINS") (FOR CHORUS AND ORCH.) (Text: Leif S. Rode)
  5:00 Musikk-Hu.
—— NORWEGIAN HYMN (NORSK HYMNE) (FROM THE CANTATA "HOLY FUTURE") (FOR MIXED CHORUS AND ORCH.) (Text: Arne Garborg)
  1,1,2,1 - 1,0,0,0 - str.   6:00 T.O.N.O.
—— OLAVADRAPA (FROM "ARNLJOT GJELLINE") (FOR BARITONE, MIXED OR MALE CHORUS AND ORCH.) (Text: B. Bjornson)
  2,2,2,2 - 4,2,3,1 - timp.,perc. - hp. - str.   22:00 Musikk-Hu.
—— THREE DANCES FROM GUDBRANDSDAL
  3,2,2,2 - 2,2,2,1 - timp.,perc. - str.   10:00 Musikk-Hu.

BECKER, Alfred
—— MUSIC FOR 2 OBOES AND STRINGS
  2ob. - str.   23:00 Mannheimer.
—— SONATINA FOR STRINGS
  str.   12:00 Mannheimer.

BECKER, Frank W.
—— PHILIAPAIDEIA
  *4,3,3,3 - 4,3,3,0 - perc. - pf. - str.   16:00 Salabert.

BECKER, Günther
—— ATTITUDE FOR ORCH. (1973)
  Hans Gerig.
—— CONCERTO FOR ELECTRONICALLY MODULATED OBOE AND ORCH. (1974)
  Hans Gerig.
—— CORRESPONDENCES I (FOR CLARINET AND CHAMBER ORCH.)
  Hans Gerig.
—— NACHT-UND TRAUMGESÄNGE (FOR SATB CHORUS AND ORCH.)
  Hans Gerig.
—— STABIL - INSTABIL (FOR LARGE ORCH.) (1965)
  Hans Gerig.
—— TRANSFORMATIONS (WITH AMPLIFICATION AND TAPE) (1970)
  Hans Gerig.

BECKERATH, Alfred von
—— CONCERTO FOR HORN AND SMALL ORCH. (IN 3 MOVTS.)
    1,1,2,1 - 1,0,0,0 - perc. - str.   14:00 Henmar.
—— DOUBLE CONCERTO FOR FLUTE, CLARINET AND SMALL
    ORCH.
    1,0,1,0 - 2,0,0,0 - timp.,glock.,trgl. - str.   16:00 Noetzel.
—— VIER SÄTZE FÜR STREICHORCHESTER
    perc. - str.   20:00 Noetzel.

BECKETT, Wheeler
—— BY THE LAKE (DEDICATION TO INDONESIA NO. 1) (FOR
    WORDLESS SOPRANO, 13-PIECE GAMELAN ENSEMBLE
    AND ORCH.)
    *3,*3,2,2 - 4,0,0,0 - timp.,perc.(7),cel.,glock., - hp. - Indonesian
    Gamelan ensemble (native gongs, 1 saron, 6 kempul, 6 kenong) -
    str.   6:30 Composer.
—— CARMEL (A SEA-SCAPE)
    1(alt. with picc.),*3,2,2 - 4,3,3,1 - timp.,perc.(3) - str.
        10:00 Composer.
—— CINDERELLA FANTASY (THEME AND 8 VARIATIONS)
    *3,*3,*3,*3 - 4,3,3,1 - timp.,perc.(2),cel. - hp. - str.
        16:00 Composer.
—— INTERMEZZO FROM AN IRISH PLAY
    *3,*3,2,2 - 2,0,0,0 - timp.,perc.(2),cel. - hp. - str. 8:00 Composer.
—— LITTLE PRELUDE FOR WINDS
    2,2,2,2 - 2,2,0,0 - timp.,glock.   4:00 Composer.
—— MOONLIGHT ON A NEW HAMPSHIRE LAKE (1967)
    2,2(2nd alt. with Eng. hn.),2,2 - 4,3,3,1 - timp.,perc.(2),cel.,glock. -
    hp. - str.   6:00 Composer.
—— THE MYSTIC TRUMPETER (FOR HIGH VOICE, CHORUS
    AND ORCH.) (IN 4 MOVT.)
    *3,*3,*3,*3 - 4,3,3,1 - timp.,perc.(3) - hp. - str. 35:00 C. Fischer.
—— THE OPEN ROAD ("AFOOT AND LIGHT-HEARTED I TAKE
    TO THE OPEN ROAD")
    *3,2,2,2 - 4,2,3,1 - timp.,perc.(2) - str.   5:00 Composer.
—— PRELUDE TO ACT III OF "THE QUEEN'S MIRROR" (1940)
    *2,*3,2,2 - 4,2,3,1 - timp.,perc. - str.(30,8,8,5) 5:00 Composer.
—— REVERIE
    2,2,2,2 - 4,2,3,1 - timp. - str.   5:00 Composer.
—— REVERIE FOR STRINGS
        Composer.
—— SYMPHONY IN C MINOR (IN 3 MOVEMENTS)
    *3,*3,*3,*3 - 4,3,3,1 - timp.,perc.(3) - str. 26:00 Composer.

BECKHELM, Paul
—— CANTILENA (FOR FLUTE AND CHAMBER ORCH.)
    1,2,2,2 - 2hn.,perc. - hp. - str.   4:00 Composer.
—— CONCERT OVERTURE IN D MINOR
    2,2,2,2 - 4,2,3,0 - timp.,perc.,glock.,xyl. - str. 8:00 Composer.
—— COW COUNTRY SUITE (IN 4 MOVTS.)
    3,3,2,2 - 4,2,3,0 - timp.,perc. - hp. - str. 14:30 Composer.
—— FUNERAL MARCH FOR A HERO
    2,3,3,2 - 4,2,3,0 - timp.,perc. - hp. - str.   Composer.

BECKMAN, Bror
—— DIVERTIMENTO GIOCOSO
        21:00 Henmar.
—— FOLKDANSMOTIV, OP. 4
        7:00 S.T.I.M.
—— I SOMMÄRNATTER (TWO PIECES FOR STRING ORCH.)
    str.   16:00 S.T.I.M.
—— OM LYCKAN (SYMPHONIC PIECE)
        15:00 Lundquists.
—— SVIT UR MUSIKEN TILL "HARALD MOLANDERS EN
    LYCKORIDDARE"
    2,1,2,0 - 2,2,1,0 timp. - str.   25:00 S.T.I.M.
—— SYMPHONY IN F MAJOR
    2,2,2,2 - 4,2,3,0 - timp. - str.   40:00 Nordiska.

BECKMAN, Frederick - HEILAKKA, Edwin
—— SYMPHONY OF BELLS (FOR BELL ENSEMBLE AND ORCH.)
    2(1st alt. with picc.),2,2,2 alto sax.(ad lib.),1 ten. sax.(ad lib.), 1
    bar. sax(ad lib.),2 - 4,3,3,1 - timp.,perc.(6),bells - pf. - str.
        8:00 EV.

BEDELL, Robert Leech
—— CHORALE PRELUDE: "O WORLD I E'EN MUST LEAVE
    THEE"
    2,1,1,2 - 2,2,2,0 - str.   4:00 EV.

BEECHAM, Thomas
—— CONCERTO FOR PIANO AND ORCH. (BASED ON THEMES
    BY HANDEL) (IN 4 MOVTS.)
    2,2,2,2 - 4,2,0,0 - timp. - pf. - str.   22:00 Mills.

BEECROFT, Norma
—— FANTASY FOR STRINGS (1958)
    str.   6:00 CanMusCtr.
—— FROM DREAMS OF BRASS (FOR NARRATOR, MIXED
    CHORUS AND ORCH.) (1963-4)
    0,0,0,0 - 4,2,3,1 - timp.,perc. - tape-recorder - hp. - str.
        20:00 MCA Music.
—— IMPROVISAZIONI CONCERTANTI: (FOR FLUTE AND
    ORCH.) (1961)
    1,0,0,0 - 2,2,3,0 - timp.,perc.,vibra. - hp. - str.(minimum 6 d.-b.)
        7:00 MCA Music.
—— IMPROVVISAZIONI CONCERTANTI NO. 2 (FOR CHAMBER
    ORCH.) (1971)
    2,2,2,2 - 2,2,0,0 - timp.,perc.,xyl. - str. 8:05 MCA Music.
—— IMPROVVISAZIONI CONCERTANTI NO. 3 (FOR FLUTE, 2
    TIMPANISTS AND ORCH.) (1973)
    3,2,2,2 - 4,2,2,1 - timp.,perc.(4) - str. 9:00 CanMusCtr.
—— PIECE CONCERTANTE NO. 1 (1966)
    2,2,2,2 - 2,2,1,0 - timp.,perc.(3) - hp. - org. - pf. - str.
        4:00 CanMusCtr.
—— TWO MOVEMENTS FOR ORCHESTRA (1958)
    *3,*3,*3,*3, - 4,3,3,1 - perc. - hp. - str.   CanMusCtr.

BEEKHUIS, Hanna
—— CHI-KING (3 SONGS) (FOR MEZZO-SOPRANO AND ORCH.)
    (1939) (Text: Klabund)
    2,2,2,2 - 4,2,3,1 - timp.,perc.,cel. - str.   8:00 Henmar.
—— FIVE MINIATURES FOR ORCH.
    2,2,1,1 - 2,1,0,1(ad lib.) - timp.,perc. - pf. - str. 7:00 Henmar.
—— KERSTKANTATE (FOR MEZZO-SOPRANO, BARITONE,
    WOMEN'S CHORUS, MALE CHORUS AND ORCH.) (1938) (IN
    3 PARTS)
    2 fl. - hp. - str.   20:00 Henmar.
—— KERSTMUZIEK (FOR WOMEN'S OR CHILDREN'S CHORUS
    AND ORCH.)
    1,0,1,0 - 0,0,0,0 - trgl.(ad lib.) - pf. - str. 11:00 Henmar.
—— SCHOUWBURGHDICHTEN (FOR ALTO, BARITONE, MIXED
    CHORUS AND ORCH.) (1933) (Text: J. van den Vondel)
    3,2,2,2 - 4,2,2,1 - timp.,perc. - hp. - str. 15:00 Henmar.
—— THREE SERENADES (FOR MEZZO-SOPRANO AND ORCH.)
    (1939)
    2,2,2,2 - 2,0,0,0 - timp.,perc. - hp. - str. 15:00 Henmar.
—— VIER LIEDEREN (NAAR AANL, VAN OUD-HOLLANDSCHE
    MELODIEËN (FOR ALTO VOICE AND ORCH.)
    3,2,2,2 - 4,2,3,1 - timp.,perc.,cel. - hp. - str. 18:00 Henmar.

BEERS, Jacques
—— CONCERTO FOR SOPRANO VOICE, SAXOPHONE, PIANO
    AND ORCH.
    1,1,1,1 alto sax.,1 - 1,1,1,0 - pf. - str. 28:00 Henmar.
—— MANYANAS LIEBESLIEDER (ROMANTIC SONG CYCLE)
    (FORSOPRANO AND ORCH.)
    3,1,3,2 - 3,2,2,0 - timp.,perc.,vibra - str. 17:00 Henmar.
—— QUODLIBET SERIA (FOR ALTO, WOMEN'S CHORUS AND
    ORCH.) (1938)
    ob. - str.   Henmar.
—— THREE PSALMS (FOR ALTO OR BARITONE AND ORCH.)
    3,3,3,3 - 2,2,2,0 - timp.,perc. - hp. - str. 12:00 Henmar.

BEESON, Jack
—— CAPTAIN JINKS OF THE HORSE MARINES (3-ACT OPERA)
    % (1975) (A ROMANTIC COMEDY IN MUSIC) (Text: Sheldon
    Harnick, after a play by Clyde Fitch)
    2(alt. with 2 picc.),2(2nd alt. with Eng. hn.),2(2nd alt. with E♭cl.
    and b.-cl.),2 - 2,2 cnt.,0,0,1 bar.,1 - timp.,perc.(3),cel.,glock.,xyl. -
    hp. - pf. - str.   120:00 Bo. Hawkes.
—— HELLO OUT THERE (CHAMBER OPERA IN 1 ACT) % (1953)
    (Text: William Saroyan)
    1(alt. with picc.),1,1,1 - 1,1,0,0 - perc.(1) - pf.(alt. with harm.) -
    str.(2,1,1,1)   40:00 Mills.
—— HYMNS AND DANCES, FROM THE OPERA "THE SWEET
    BYE AND BYE" (IN 3 MOVTS.)
    3(3rd. alt. with picc.),3(3rd alt. ad lib. with Eng.hn.),3(2nd. alt.
    with E♭cl.,3rd alt. with b.-cl.),3(3rd. alt. ad lib. with c.-bn.) -
    4,3,3,1 - perc.,cel.,glock.,xyl. - hp. - pf.(4-hands, alt. with harm) -
    str.   15:15 Bo. Hawkes.

—— JONAH (AN OPERA TO BE PLAYED, DANCED AND SUNG)
% (1950) (Text: Paul Goodman)
2(alt. with 2 picc. and 1 alto fl.),1,2(2nd alt. with b.-cl.).2 - 2,2,1,0
- perc.(2) - hp. - pf.(alt. with harm.) - str.   Composer.
—— LIZZIE BORDEN (A FAMILY PORTRAIT IN 3 ACTS)
(OPERA) % (1965) (Text: Kenward Elmslie)
2(2nd alt. with picc.),2(2nd alt. with Eng. hn.),2(2nd alt. with
b.-cl.),2 - 2,2,2,2 - perc.(2) - harm. - str.   120:00 Bo. Hawkes.
—— MY HEART'S IN THE HIGHLANDS (2-ACT CHAMBER
OPERA) % (1969) (Text: William Saroyan)
2(alt.with 2 picc. and 1 alto fl.),2(2nd alt.with Eng.hn.)2(alt.with 1
b.-cl.and 1 ten.sax.),0 - 2,1 cnt.,0,0 - perc.(1) - pf.(alt.with acc.,cel.
and harm.) - str.   Bo. Hawkes.
—— THE SWEET BYE AND BYE (2-ACT OPERA) % (1956) (Text:
Kenward Elmslie)
2(alt. with 2 picc.),1,2(2nd alt. with b.-cl.),1 - 3,1,1,0 - perc.(1),cel.
- hp. - 2 pf. - str.   120:00 Bo. Hawkes.
—— SYMPHONY NO. 1 IN A (IN 3 MOVTS.)
2(alt. with 2 picc.),2(2nd alt. with Eng.hn.),2(2nd alt. with
b.cl.),2(2nd alt. with c-bn.) - 4,2,3,0 - timp.,perc.(4),cel.,2 glock., 2
xyl. - hp. - str.   20:00 MCA Music.
—— TRANSFORMATIONS
3(3rd alt. with picc.),3(3rd alt. with Eng.hn.),3(3rd alt. with
b.-cl.),3(3rd alt. with c-bn.) - 4,3,3,1 - timp.,perc.,glock. - hp. - str.
10:00 MCA Music.
—— TWO CONCERT ARIAS (FOR HIGH VOICES AND ORCH.)
2,2,2,2 - 3,2,1,0 - timp.,perc. - hp. - str.   8:00 Composer.

BEETHOVEN - DORATI, A.
—— MOONLIGHT SONATA (IN 3 MOVEMENTS)
2,2,2,2 - 3,2,0,0 - timp. - str.   15:00 Mills.

BEETHOVEN - EVANS, Archibald
—— OVERTURE TO "CORIOLANUS", OP. 62
7:00 Bo. Hawkes.
—— OVERTURE TO "FIDELIO", OP. 72B
6:30 Bo. Hawkes.
—— OVERTURE TO "KING STEPHEN", OP. 117
8:00 Bo. Hawkes.

BEETHOVEN - FOSS, Lukas
—— MILITARY MARCHES FOR WINDS
3,2,3,3 - 4,4,2,1 - perc.   C. Fischer.

BEETHOVEN - HESS, Willy
—— SCENE FROM "VIESTA'S FEUER" (Engl. Text: John and
Barbara Bitter)
12:00 Henmar.

BEETHOVEN - MARTINON, Jean
—— GRANDE FUGUE, OP. 133 (ARR. FOR STRING ORCH.)
str.   Presser.

BEETHOVEN - ORMANDY, Eugene
—— GRAND FUGUE IN B♭ MAJOR, OP. 133
str.   15:00 Arranger.

BEETHOVEN - ROBERTS, Charles J.
—— OVERTURE TO "EGMONT"
C. Fischer.

BEETHOVEN - SEREDY, J. S.
—— OVERTURE TO "PROMETHEUS"
C. Fischer.

BEETHOVEN - SKORNICKA, Joseph
—— OVERTURE "EROICA"
Belwin.

BEETHOVEN - SMITH, Julia
—— VOICES OF VICTORY (ADAPTATION OF THE FIFTH
SYMPHONY, FOR CHORUS AND ORCH.)
1(alt. with picc.), 1,2,1 - 2,2,1,0 - timp. - str.   15:00 Mowbray.

BEETHOVEN - SOPKIN, Henry
—— OVERTURE TO "EGMONT"
C. Fischer.
—— SONATINA IN G MAJOR
C. Fischer.
—— THEME AND VARIATIONS (FROM TRIO, OP. 44)
1,1,2,1 - 2,2,1,0 - timp. - hp. - str.   4:00 C. Fischer.

BEETHOVEN - STRAVINSKY, Igor
—— MEPHISTOPHELES' LIED VOM FLOH (MEPHISTO'S SONG
OF THE FLEA), OP. 75, NO. 3 (FOR BASS AND ORCH.)
2,2,2,2 - 2,0,0,0 - str.   3:00 Bo. Hawkes.

BEETHOVEN - TOBANI, Theo M. - SEREDY, J. S.
—— OVERTURE TO "CORIOLAN"
2,2,2,2 - 2,2,3,0 - timp. - str.   C. Fischer.

BEETHOVEN - TOSCANINI, Arturo
—— SEPTET, OP. 20
cl.,bn. - hn. - str.   25:00 Guild Cal.

BEETHOVEN - TRANCHELL, Peter
—— BEETHOVEN DANCES (1963)
3,2,1,1 - 0,3,cnt.,1,0 - timp.,perc.(3) - pf. - str.   8:00 P.R.S.

BEETHOVEN - WINTER, Aubrey
—— OVERTURE TO "LEONORE" NO. 3, OP. 72A
14:00 Bo. Hawkes.
—— OVERTURE TO "THE RUINS OF ATHENS," OP. 113
6:00 Bo. Hawkes.
—— SYMPHONY NO. 5 IN C MINOR, OP. 67
32:00 Bo. Hawkes.

BEETHOVEN - ZIPPER, Herbert
—— ELEGY, OP. 118 (FOR SATB CHORUS AND ORCH.)
5:00 Galaxy.

BEGLARIAN, Grant
—— DIVERSIONS FOR ORCHESTRA
Piedmont.
—— DIVERSIONS FOR VIOLA, CELLO AND ORCH. (1972)
2(2nd alt.with picc.),2,2,2 - 2,2,2,0 - timp.,perc.(2) - str. Composer.
—— DIVERTIMENTO FOR ORCHESTRA (1958) (IN 4 MOVTS.)
2,2,2,2 - 4,2,3,0 - timp.,perc.(2) - str.   Piedmont.
—— NURSES' SONG (FOR CHORUS AND ORCH.) (1960) (Text:
William Blake)
2,2,2,2 - 2,2,2,0 - perc.(1),xyl. - str.   12:00 Composer.
—— SINFONIA FOR ORCHESTRA (1961) (IN 3 MOVTS.)
2(2nd alt. with picc.),2,2,2 - 4,3,3,1 - timp.,perc.(2) - str.
18:00 CMP.
—— TWELVE HUNGARIAN SONGS (FOR CHILDREN'S UNISON
CHOIR AND ORCH.) (ARR. 1958)
*3,2,2,2 - 4,2,3,1 - timp.,perc.,cel. - hp. - str.   25:00 Arranger.

BEHÁR, György
—— CONCERTO PER TROMBONE E ARCHI
trb. - str.   10:20 Bo. Hawkes.
—— SCÈNES HONGROISES (SUITE)
3,3,2,2 - 4,3,3,0 - timp.,perc.(6),xyl. - hp. - str.   13:00 Belw-Mills.

BEHREND, Jeanne
—— FROM DAWN UNTIL DUSK - A CHILD'S DAY (SUITE) (IN 7
MOVTS.)
*3,*3,*3(1 alt. with e♭cl.),*3 - 2,2,2,1 - timp.,perc.(4),bells,cel.,xyl.
- 2 harmonicas - 2 hp. - str.   22:00 Composer.

BEHREND, Siegfried
—— LEGNANIANA (ON THEMES OF L. LEGNANI)
fl. - guit. - str.   18:00 Henmar.

BEHRENS, Jack
—— ANDANTE CANTABILE, OP. 1 (1955)
ob.(or tpt.) - str.   6:00 Composer.
—— COLLOQUY (FOR PIANO AND ORCH.)(1964) (IN 1 MOVT.)
2,2,2,2 - 4,2,2,1 - timp. - pf. - str.   8:45 Composer.
—— CONCERTO FOR CLARINET, VIOLIN, PIANO AND ORCH.
(TRIPLE CONCERTO) (1971) (IN 3 MOVTS.)
2(2nd alt. with picc.),2,2,2 - 4,2,2,1 - timp.,perc.(2-3),bells,xyl. - pf.
- str.   16:00 Composer.
—— CONCERTO FOR TROMBONE AND CHAMBER ORCH., OP.
30 (1962)
1,0,1,1 - 1,0,1,0 - str.(no d.-b.)   14:00 Composer.
—— DECLARATION, OP. 43 (1963)
2,2,2,2 - 4,0,0,0 - perc. - str.   13:30 Composer.
—— FANTASIA, OP. 12 (1959)
str.   7:15 Composer.
—— GREEN CENTER, OP. 45 (AFTER A PAINTING OF KEN
LOCHHEAD) (1963)
1,1,3,2 sax.,1 - 3,3,2,bar.,euph.,1 - perc.   6:00 Composer.

—— HOT YELLOW, OP. 46 (AFTER A PAINTING OF KEN
LOCHHEAD) (1963)
1,1,3,2 sax.,1 - 3,3,2,bar.,euph.,1 - perc.   5:00 Composer.
—— I AM HE THAT WALKS WITH THE TENDER AND
GROWING NIGHT, OP. 23 (FOR MEZZO-SOPRANO AND
STRINGS) (1961) (Text: Walt Whitman)
str.   8:00 Composer.
—— INTROSPECTION, OP. 3 (1956)
str.   5:15 Composer.
—— LAMENT, OP. 13 (FOR BRASS AND PERCUSSION) (1959)
0,0,0,0 - 2,4,3,1 - timp.,perc.,glock.   8:00 Composer.
—— THE LAY OF THRYM (OPERA) % (1968) (FOR 3 SOLO
VOICES, CHORUS AND ORCH.) (Text: Keith Cockburn)
1(alt. with picc.),1,1(alt. with b.-cl. and ten. sax.),1 - 1,1,1,0 -
timp.,perc. - pf. - str.   Composer.
—— THE SOUND OF MILO (FOR NARRATOR AND ORCH.)
(1970) (Text: Jack Wassermann)
*3,2,2,2 - 4,2,2,1 - timp.,perc.(2),xyl. - str.   24:00 Composer.
—— SUITE FOR ORCHESTRA, OP. 6 (1958) (IN 5 MOVTS.)
2,2,2,2 - 2,1,1,0 - perc. - pf. - str.   20:00 Composer.
—— SUITE FOR STRINGS, OP. 18 (1960) (IN 3 MOVTS.)
str.   9:00 Composer.
—— THERE I MET AN OLD MAN, OP. 16 (1960) (FOR CHAMBER
ORCH. AND TENOR) (Text: Bruce Haack)
1,0,2,1 - 0,0,0,0 - cel. - pf. - 2 vln.,2 vla.   12:45 Composer.
—— TRANSFIGURED SEASON, OP. 19 (BALLET) %
1,1,1,1 - 0,0,0,0 - str.   20:00 Composer.

BEKKU, Sadao
—— DEUX PRIÈRES
3,3,3,0 - 4,3,3,1 - timp.,perc.(4) - hp. - pf.(or cel.) - str.
15:00 Presser.
—— SYMPHONIETTA FOR STRINGS
str.   16:00 Presser.
—— SYMPHONY NO. 1
3,3,3,3 - 4,3,3,1 - timp.,perc.(6) - hp. - pf.(or cel.) - str.
34:00 Presser.

BELAUBRE, Louis Noël
—— CONCERTO FOR FLUTE AND STRINGS
fl. - str.   Presser.
—— CONCERTO NO. 1 FOR PIANO AND ORCH.
1,1,1,1 - 1,1,0,0 - timp.,perc. - pf. - str.   Presser.
—— CONCERTO NO. 2 FOR PIANO AND ORCH.
1,1,1,1 - 1,1,1,0 - perc.(2) - pf. - str.   Presser.

BELFIORE, Turi
—— DIMENSIONI
1,1,2,2 sax.,2 - 1,1,1,0 - timp.   6:00 Leeds.
—— IDEAZIONI (IMAGININGS): DISCORDIA CONCORS
2,2,3,1 - 3,3,3,0 - timp.,perc.,cel.,vibra. - pf. - str.   15:00 Leeds.
—— PARADIGMI (PARADIGMS)
2,1,3,1 - 3,2,2,0 - perc.(2),xyl. - pf.   14:00 Leeds.

BELINFANTE, Daniel
—— CONCERTO FOR VIOLIN AND ORCH.
3,3,3,3 - 4,0,2,1 - timp. - str.   Henmar.
—— CONCERTO FOR 2 VIOLINS AND ORCH.
2,1,0,1 - 0,0,0,0 - hp. - str.   23:00 Henmar.

BELL, W. H.
—— FOUR MEDIEVAL SONGS (FOR WOMEN'S CHORUS AND
STRING ORCH.)
pf. - str.   Oxford.
—— MOTHER CAREY
3,3,3,3 - 4,2,3,1 - timp.,perc. - org. - str.   26:00 Novello.

BELLINI, Vincenzo - DI STEFANO
—— SINFONIA BREVE IN D MAJOR
0,0,2,0 - 2,0,0,0 - str.   6:00 Henmar.

BELLINI, Vincenzo - LELOIR, Edmond
—— CONCERTO FOR HORN AND STRINGS
hn. - str.   7:00 Presser.

BELLINI, Vincenzo - RICHTER, Clifford G.
—— SALVE, REGINA (FOR SATB CHORUS AND ORCH.)
2,2,2,2 - 2,0,0,0 - str.   5:15 Tetra.

BELLINI, Vincenzo - THILDE, Jean
—— CONCERTO FOR TRUMPET, HARPSICHORD AND STRINGS
tpt. - hpsc. - str.   8:30 Presser.

BELOV, Gennady
—— CONCERTO FOR ORGAN, STRINGS AND PERCUSSION, OP.
4
perc. - org. - str.   29:00 G. Schirmer.

BELTI-PILINSZKY, Geza
—— UNGARISCHE RHAPSODIE
2,2,2,2 - 4,3,3,1 - perc. - hp. - pf. - str.   8:30 Finale.

BENARY, Peter
—— APHORISMEN (FÜR FLÖTE, SCHLAGZEUG UND
STREICHER)
fl. - perc. - str.   23:00 Hans Gerig.
—— CONCERTINO FÜR KLAVIER, 9 BLÄSER UND
SCHLAGZEUG
12:00 S.U.I.S.A.
—— CONCERTO FOR HARPSICHORD AND STRING ORCH.
hpsc. - str.   11:00 Mannheimer.
—— KONZERTANTE VARIATIONEN (FÜR BRATSCHE, KLAVIER
UND ORCH.)
2,2,2,2 - 0,4,2,0 - timp. - str.   26:00 S.U.I.S.A.
—— SINFONIE NR. 1
3,2,2,2 - 4,3,3,1 - timp. - str.   24:00 S.U.I.S.A.
—— SINFONIE NR. 2
3,3,3,3 - 4,3,3,1 - timp. - str.   15:00 S.U.I.S.A.
—— SINFONIE NR. 3
2,2,2,2 - 2,2,0,0 - str.   22:00 S.U.I.S.A.
—— SONATE FÜR STREICHORCHESTER
str.   16:00 S.U.I.S.A.
—— TRACTUS (FÜR STREICHORCHESTER)
str.   6:00 S.U.I.S.A.

BENAVENTE, Regina
—— KRONOS
4,3,3,3 - 4,4,4,0 - perc.,cel.,vibra.,xyl. - hp. - pf. - str.
9:00 Bo. Hawkes.
—— MUSICA PARA ORQUESTRA DE CUERDA
str.   Bo. Hawkes.
—— PASTORAL AND DANCE (PASTORAL Y DANZA)
3,3,3,3 - 4,3,3,1 - timp.,perc.,cel. - 2hp. - pf. - str.
9:00 Bo. Hawkes.
—— SINFONIETTA
3,3,3,2 - 4,3,3,1 - timp.,perc. - hp. - pf. - str.   15:00 S.A.D.A.I.C.
—— SINFONÍA DE PRIMAVERA
3,3,3,3 - 4,3,3,1 - timp.,cel. - hp. - pf. - str.   21:00 Bo. Hawkes.

BENDA, Friedrich Ludwig - FENDLER, Edvard
—— SINFONIA TO "THE BARBER OF SEVILLE"
2 fl. - 2 hn. - str.   Bo. Hawkes.

BENDALL, W.
—— SONG DANCES (ORCHESTRAL SUITE)
2,2,2,2 - 2,2,0,0 - timp. - str.   Novello.

BENGER, Richard
—— AUTOLYCUS (1965)
3,2,3,2, - 4,3,3,1 - timp.,perc. - str.   8:00 P.R.S.
—— DIVERTIMENTO FOR STRING ORCH. (1966)
str.   12:00 P.R.S.
—— OVERTURE FOR STRINGS (1965)
str.   5:00 P.R.S.
—— SYMPHONIA (1967)
3,2,3,2 - 4,3,3,1 - timp.,perc. - pf. - str.   20:00 P.R.S.
—— VARIATIONS FOR STRING ORCH.
str.   8:00 P.R.S.

BENGTSSON, Gustav
—— ÄLVEN SJUNGER (VÄRMLÄNDSK RAPSODI)
2,2,2,2 - 2,2,1,0 - timp. - hp. - str.   12:00 S.T.I.M.
—— CANONE CONCERTANTE IN G MAJOR (FOR VIOLIN,
VIOLA AND CHAMBER ORCH.)
1,1,2,2 - 2,2,0,0 - timp. - str.   11:00 S.T.I.M.
—— CONCERTO IN A MINOR FOR CELLO AND ORCH.
2,2,2,2 - 4,2,3,0 - timp. - str.   28:00 S.T.I.M.
or:
2,2,2,2 - 2,2,1,0 - timp. - str.
—— CONCERTO IN B MINOR FOR VIOLIN AND ORCH.
2,2,2,2 - 4,2,3,0 - timp. - str.   30:00 S.T.I.M.
or:
2,2,2,2 - 2,2,0,0 - timp. - str.
—— I WADSTENA KLOSTER (3 TONMÅLNINGAR)
2,2,2,2 - 2,0,0,0 - perc.(2) - str.   21:00 S.T.I.M.

—— ORKESTERSVIT NO. 1 (IN 5 MOVTS.)
2,2,2,2 - 2,2,1,0 - timp. - str.   22:00 S.T.I.M.
—— SINFONIETTA CONCERTANTE IN A MINOR (FOR VIOLIN, VIOLA AND ORCH.)
2,2,2,2 - 2,2,0,0 - timp. - str.   17:00 S.T.I.M.
or:
1,2,2,1 - 2,2,0,0 - timp. - str.
—— SYMPHONY NO. 1 IN C MINOR
2,2,2,2 - 4,3,3,1 - timp. - str.   23:00 S.T.I.M.
or:
2,1,2,1 - 2,2,3,0 - timp. - str.
—— SYMPHONY NO. 2 IN D MINOR
2,2,2,2 - 4,3,3,1 - timp. - str.   36:00 S.T.I.M.
or:
2,1,2,1 - 2,2,3,0 - timp. - str.
—— SYMPHONY NO. 3 IN C MINOR
2,2,2,2 - 4,2,3,1 - timp. - str.   30:00 S.T.I.M.
or:
2,2,2,1 - 2,2,2,0 - timp. - str.
—— VETTERN (SYMPHONIC POEM)
2,2,2,2 - 2,2,3,0 - timp.,perc. - hp. - str.   13:00 S.T.I.M.
or:
2,2,2,2 - 2,2,1,0 - timp.,perc. - hp. - str.

BENGUEREL, Xavier
—— CONCERTO FOR TWO FLUTES AND STRINGS (1961)
2fl. - str.   20:00 G. Schirmer.
—— CONCERTO FOR VIOLIN AND ORCH. (1965)
2,2,2,2 - 2,2,2,0 - timp.,perc.,cel. - str.   20:00 Seesaw.
—— FESTSINFONIE
3(3rd alt. with picc.),2,3(3rd alt. with b.-cl.),3(3rd alt. with c.-bn.) - 4,2,0,0 - timp.,perc.,cel.,vibra. - str.   16:00 Modern.
—— NOCTURNO DE LOS AVISOS (FOR SOPRANO, SATB CHORUS AND ORCH.) (Text: Pedro Salinas)
2,2,2,2 - 4,2,3,1 - timp.(2),vibra. - str.(2,1,1,1)   20:00 Modern.

BEN-HAIM, Paul
—— CAPPRICCIO FOR PIANO AND ORCH.
2,2,2,2 - 4,2,0,0 - timp.,perc. - hp. - pf. - str.   12:00 IsMuPublns.
—— CONCERTO FOR CELLO AND ORCH.
IsMuPublns.
—— CONCERTO FOR PIANO AND ORCH.
3,2,2,2 - 4,2,3,0 - timp.,perc.,cel. - hp. - pf. - str.(viola d'amore solo in 2nd movement)   32:00 IsMuPublns.
—— CONCERTO FOR STRINGS
str.   18:00 IsMuPublns.
—— CONCERTO FOR VIOLIN AND ORCH.
2,2,2,2, - 2,2,0,0 - timp.,perc.,cel. - hp. - str.   22:00 IsMuPublns.
—— DANCE AND INVOCATION
3,*3,*4,3 - 4,3,3,1 - cel. - hp. - str.   12:00 IsMuPublns.
—— THE ETERNAL THEME
3,3,2,3 - 4,6,0,0 - timp.,perc. - 2 hp. - hpsc. - str.   20:00 IsMuPublns.
—— EVOCATION (YISKOR) (POEM FOR VIOLIN AND ORCH.)
3,2,2,2 - 4,2,3,0 - timp.,perc. - hp. - str.   18:00 IsMuPublns.
—— FANFARE TO ISRAEL
2,2,2,2 - 4,3,3,1 - timp.,perc. - str.   4:00 IsMuPublns.
—— FROM ISRAEL (SUITE FOR ORCH.)
2,1,2,2 - 2,2,0,0 - timp.,perc. - hp. - hpsc. - str.   18:00 IsMuPublns.
—— HYMNS FROM THE DESERT (FOR SOPRANO, BARITONE, MIXED CHORUS AND ORCH.) (Text: From the Dead Sea Scrolls)
3,3,3,2 - 4,3,3,1 - timp.,perc. - hp. - str.   15:00 IsMuPublns.
—— KABBALAT SHABBAT (FOR SOLO VOICES, CHORUS AND ORCH.) (1968),(Text: Traditional)
45:00 Seesaw.
—— LITURGICAL CANTATA (FOR BARITONE, SATB CHORUS AND ORCH.)
2,1,2,1 - 2,2,2,0 - timp.,perc. - hp. - str.   32:00 IsMuPublns.
—— MUSIC FOR STRINGS
str.   15:00 IsMuPublns.
—— MYRTLE BLOSSOMS FROM EDEN (SONG CYCLE FOR SOPRANO AND ORCH.)
15:00 IsMuPublns.
—— PASTORAL VARIÉE (FOR CLARINET SOLO, HARP AND STRINGS)
cl. - hp. - str.   14:00 IsMuPublns.
—— PSALM 23 (FOR CONTRALTO OR BARITONE, WITH STRING ORCH.)
str.   5:00 IsMuPublns.
—— THE SWEET PSALMIST OF ISRAEL (IN 3 MOVTS.)
3,3,3,2sax.,3 - 4,4,0,0 - timp.,perc. - hp. - hpsc. - str.
26:00 IsMuPublns.

—— SYMPHONY NO. 1
3,3,3,3 - 4,3,3,1 - timp.,perc. - hp. - str.   30:00 IsMuPublns.
—— SYMPHONY NO. 2
3,3,3,3 - 4,3,3,1 - timp.,perc.,xyl. - hp. - str.   35:00 IsMuPublns.
—— THREE PSALMS (FOR SOPRANO, BARITONE, SATB CHORUS AND ORCH.)
2,2,2,2 - 2,2,2,0 - timp.,perc., cel.,vibra. - hp. - str.
15:00 IsMuPublns.
—— THREE SONGS WITHOUT WORDS
2,*3,2,2 - 2,0,0,0 - hp. - str.   10:00 IsMuPublns.
—— TO THE CHIEF MUSICIAN (METAMORPHOSIS FOR ORCHESTRA)
2,2,2,2 - 3,2,2,1 - perc. - hp. - hpsc. - str.   15:00 IsMuPublns.
—— THE VISION OF A PROPHET (FOR SOLO VOICES, SATB CHORUS AND ORCH.)
2,2,2,ten.,sax.,2 - 4,3,2,1 - timp.,perc.,cel.,xyl. - hp. - pf. - str.   20:00 IsMuPublns.

BENJAMIN, Arthur
—— BALLADE (FOR STRINGS)
12:00 Bo. Hawkes.
—— CONCERTO FOR HARMONICA AND ORCH.
2,0,2,2 - 2,2,0,0 - xyl.,cel. - harm. - str.   17:30 Bo. Hawkes.
—— CONCERTO FOR VIOLA AND ORCH. (IN 3 MOVTS.)
2,2,2,2 - 4,2,3,1 - timp.,perc. - hp. - pf. - str.   17:00 Bo. Hawkes.
—— CONCERTO FOR VIOLIN AND ORCH.
2,2,2,2 - 4,2,3,1 - timp.,perc. - pf. - str.   25:00 Bo. Hawkes.
—— CONCERTO QUASI UNA FANTASIA (FOR PIANO AND ORCH.)
2,2,2,2 - 4,2,3,1 - timp.,perc. - str.   26:00 Bo. Hawkes.
—— COTILLION (SUITE OF 9 ENGLISH DANCING TUNES)
2-3(1alt. with picc.),2,2,2 - 4,2,3,1(ad lib.) - timp.,perc. - hp. - str.   11:00 Bo. Hawkes.
—— THE DEVIL TAKE HER (1-ACT OPERA) % (Text: A. Collard and John Gordon)
2,2,2,2 - 4,2,3,1 - timp.,perc. - pf. - str.   60:00 Bo. Hawkes.
—— DIVERTIMENTO ON THEMES BY GLUCK
ob. - str.   14:30 Bo. Hawkes.
—— DIVERTISSEMENT (FROM "STEPS OF THE BALLET")
2,2,2,2 - 4,2,3,1 - timp.,perc.,cel. - hp. - pf. - str.
9:00 Bo. Hawkes.
—— LIGHT MUSIC (SUITE IN 4 MOVTS.)
2,1,1,1 - 2,2,1,0 - perc.,cel. - pf. - str.   13:30 Bo. Hawkes.
—— NORTH AMERICAN SQUARE DANCE (SUITE)
2,2,2,2 - 4,2,3,1 - timp.,perc. - pf. - hp. - str.   11:00 Bo. Hawkes.
—— OVERTURE TO AN ITALIAN COMEDY
2,2,2,2 - 4,2,3,0 - timp.,perc. - hp. - str.   6:00 Bo. Hawkes.
or:
2,2,2,2 - 2,2,0,0 - timp.,perc. - hp. - str.
—— PRELUDE TO "HOLIDAY"
3,2,2,2 - 4,2,3,1 - timp.,perc.,cel. - hp. - str.   10:30 Bo. Hawkes.
—— PRIMA DONNA (1-ACT COMIC OPERA) % (Text: Cedric Cliffe)
2,2,2,2 - 4,2,3,0-1 - timp.,perc.,cel.(optional) - guit. - hp.(optional)-pf. - str.   60:00 Bo. Hawkes.
or:
1,1,1,1 - 2,1,1,0 - timp.,perc.,cel. - pf. - str.
—— ROMANTIC PHANTASY (FOR VIOLIN, VIOLA AND ORCH.) (IN 3 MOVTS.)
2,2,2,2 - 4,2,0,0 - timp.,perc. - pf. - str.   23:00 Bo. Hawkes.
—— SONATINA (FOR CHAMBER ORCH.)
fl.(alt. with picc.),ob.,cl. - perc. - hp.(or pf.) - str.
11:00 Bo. Hawkes.
—— SYMPHONY NO. 1
3,3,2,3 - 4,3,3,1 - timp.,perc.,cel. - hp. - pf. - str.
42:00 Bo. Hawkes.
—— A TALE OF TWO CITIES (MELODRAMA) % (IN 6 SCENES) (Text: Cedric Cliffe)
3,2,2,2 - 4,3,3,1 - timp.,perc.,cel. - hp. - pf.(optional) - str.
Bo. Hawkes.
On Stage: fl. - guit. - vln.

BENJAMIN, Thomas
—— EPODE (FOR CHAMBER ORCH.)
9:00 Composer.

BENNETT, George John
—— SUITE IN D MINOR
3,2,2,2 - 4,3,3,1 - timp.,perc. - hp. - str.   23:00 Novello.

BENNETT, Richard Rodney

—— THE APPROACHES OF SLEEP (FOR SOPRANO, ALTO, TENOR, BASS AND CHAMBER ORCH.)
1,1,1,1 - 1,1,0,0 - hp. - str.(no c.)   12:00 Mills.

—— CALENDAR FOR CHAMBER ENSEMBLE (1960)
2,0,1,1 - 0,1,1,0 - timp.,perc.(3),glock.,xyl. - pf. - vln.,vla.,c.
10:00 Belw-Mills.

—— CONCERTO FOR ORCHESTRA
3,3,2(2nd alt. with b.-cl.),3 - 4,3,3,1 - timp.,perc. - hp. - pf.(or cel.) - str.   23:00 Novello.

—— CONCERTO FOR VIOLA AND SMALL ORCH.
1,1,1,1 - 2,0,0,0 - str.   20:00 Novello.

—— JAZZ CALENDAR (1965)
1,0,0,3 sax.,0 - 1,2,1,1 - perc. - pf. - d.-b.   30.00 P.R.S.

—— JOURNAL FOR ORCHESTRA
2(2nd alt. with picc.),1,2,1 - 2,1,1,1 - timp.,perc.,cel. - hp. - str.   12:30 Mills.

—— THE LEDGE (OPERA) %
1(alt. with picc.)1,1,1 - 2,1,2,1 - timp.,perc. - hp. - pf. - str.   35:00 Mills.

—— LONDON PASTORAL (FOR TENOR AND ORCH.)
2(2nd alt. with picc.),1,1,1 - 1,1,1,0 - perc., - hp. - str.(no d.-b.)   14:00 Mills.

—— NOCTURNES (FOR CHAMBER ORCH.)
1,1,1,1 - 1,0,0,0 - hp. - str.   12:00 Belw-Mills.

—— SUITE FRANÇAISE
2,1,2,1 - 2,1,1,0 - timp.,perc.,glock.,cel.,xyl. - hp. - str.   12:30 Belw-Mills.

BENNETT, Robert Russell

—— ABRAHAM LINCOLN (A LIKENESS IN SYMPHONY FORM) (IN 4 MOVTS.)
4(3rd alt. with picc. 4th alt. with alto fl.),3(3rd alt. with Eng.hn.),4(4th alt. with b.-cl.),*4 - 6,4,3,1 - timp.,perc.(4),cel. - 2hp. - str.   30:00 Harms, Inc.

—— A CHARLESTON RHAPSODY
1,1,1,1 - 1,1-2,1,0 - timp.,perc.(1) - pf. - str.   14:00 Composer.

—— CLASSIC SERENADE FOR STRINGS ("PORTAITS OF THREE FRIENDS") (IN 3 MOVTS.)
str.   12:00 Composer.

—— A COMMEMORATION SYMPHONY: STEPHEN COLLINS FOSTER (WITH MIXED CHORUS)
3,3,3,2 - 4,3,3,1 - timp.,perc.(2) - hp. - str.   21:30 Chappell.

—— CONCERT VARIATIONS FOR VIOLIN AND ORCH.
2,*2,2,2 - 4,2,3,1 - timp.,perc.(2),cel.(alt. with pf.) - str.   14:00 Composer.

—— CONCERTO FOR VIOLIN, PIANO AND ORCH.
2,2,2,2 - 4,2,3,0 - timp. - pf. - str.   24:00 Chappell.

—— CONCERTO GROSSO FOR WIND QUINTET AND WIND ORCH.
Henmar.

—— DRY-WEATHER LEGEND (FOR FLUTE AND ORCH.)
*2,*2,*2,1 - 2,2,1,0 - timp.,perc.,mar.,xyl. - hp. - str.   5:30 Composer.

—— EIGHT ETUDES
2,2(2nd alt. with Eng.hn.),*3,1 - 3,3,2,0 - timp.,perc.(2) - hp. - str.   20:00 Composer.

—— THE FOUR FREEDOMS SYMPHONY
2(2nd alt. with picc.),2,*3,1 - 4,3,3,1 - timp.,perc.(3) - str.   19:00 Robbins.

—— THE FUN AND FAITH OF WILLIAM BILLINGS - AMERICAN (FOR SATB CHORUS AND ORCH.)
3,3,3,2 - 4,3,3,1 - timp.,perc. - hp. - str.   33:00 Chappell.

—— THE GREY FLUTE SONG (BASED ON A HOPI INDIAN SONG)
2,2,*3,1 - 2,3,2,0 - perc.(1) - hp. - pf. - str.   5:30 Composer.

—— HOLLYWOOD (INTRODUCTION AND SCHERZO)
*3,*3,*3,2 - 4,3,3,1 - timp.,perc.(2) - 2pf. - str.   14:00 Composer.

—— KANSAS CITY ALBUM (SEVEN SONGS FOR ORCH.)
3(3rd alt. with picc.),2(2nd alt. with Eng.hn.),*3,2 - 4,3,3,1 - timp.,perc.(3),xyl. - hp. - str.   25:00 Composer.

—— MARIA MALIBRAN (FRAGMENTS FROM THE OPERA)
2,*3,*3,2 - 4,3,3,1 - timp.,perc.(2-3) - hp. - pf. - str.   30:00 Composer.

—— NOCTURNE AND APPASSIONATA (FOR PIANO AND ORCH.)
2,2,2,2 - 2,3,2,0 - timp.,perc.(2) - hp. - pf. - str.   13:00 Composer.

—— OVERTURE TO AN IMAGINARY DRAMA
2,2,*3,1 - 4,3,3,1 - timp.,perc.(2-3) - hp. - str.   7:00 Composer.

—— OVERTURE TO THE MISSISSIPPI
2(1alt. with picc.),*2,*3,2 - 4,3,3,1 - timp.,perc.(3) - hp. - str.   9:00 Chappell.

—— PAYSAGE (LANDSCAPE)
3(3rd alt. with picc.),*3,*3,2 - 4,3,3,1 - timp.,perc.(1-2) - hp. - str.   15:00 Composer.

—— SIGHTS AND SOUNDS (AN ORCHESTRAL ENTERTAINMENT) (IN 7 MOVTS.)
2picc.,2,*4,*4,4sax.,*4 - 6,4,3,2 - timp.,perc.(4),cel. - hp. - pf. - str.   28:00 Harms, Inc.

—— SIX VARIATIONS ON A THEME BY JEROME KERN
1,1,2,1 - 2,2,1,0 - timp.,perc.(1) - pf. - str.   10:30 Composer.

—— SUITE FOR CLARINET AND ORCH. (IN 5 MOVTS.)
1,1,1,4 sax.,1 - 2,3,2,0 - timp.,perc.(2),cel.(alt. with pf.) - str.   12:00 Composer.

—— SUITE OF OLD AMERICAN DANCES (IN 5 MOVTS.)
2(1 alt. with picc.),2(1 alt. with Eng.hn.),*3,2 - 4,3,3,1 - timp.,perc.(2-3),xyl.,vibra. - str.   15:25 Chappell.

—— SYMPHONY IN D FOR THE DODGERS (IN 4 MOVTS.)
2,2,2,2 - 2,3,2,0 - timp.,perc.(2) - hp. - pf. - str.   19:00 Composer.

—— UNITED NATIONS ALL FAITH PRAYER FOR PEACE (FOR CHORUS AND ORCH.) (Text: John Golden)
2,2,3,2 - 4,3,3,1 - timp. - hp. - str.   Chappell.

BENSON, Warren F.

—— AEOLIAN SONG (FOR SAXOPHONE AND ORCH.)
2(2nd alt. with picc.),1,1,sax.,1 - 1,0,0,0 - bells - str. MCA Music.

—— THE BEADED LEAF (FOR BASSO AND WIND ENSEMBLE)
3,3,3,3 - 4,3,3,0 - perc. - hp. - d.-b.   11:00 C. Fischer.

—— CHACONNE FOR VIOLA AND STRING ORCH.
str.   4:50 Composer.

—— CHANTS AND GRACES
picc. - perc.,mar. - str.   7:00 C. Fischer.

—— CONCERTINO FOR SAXOPHONE AND ORCH.
0,0,0,1 alto sax.,0 - 4,4,3,1 barritone,1 - timp.,perc.(4)bells,glock. - str.   12:00 MCA Music.

—— CONCERTO FOR HORN AND ORCH.
3,3,3,3 - 5,3,3,1 - timp., perc. - pf. - str.   22:00 C. Fischer.

—— DELPHIC SERENADE
2(2nd alt. with picc.),2,2,2 - 4,3,3,1 - timp.,perc.(3) - hp. - str.   12:00 C. Fischer.

—— ELEGIAC PRELUDE
2,2,2,2 - 4,3,3,1 - timp.,perc.(2) - str.   4:00 Fema.

—— FIVE BRIEF ENCOUNTERS
2,2,0,0 - 2,1,1,0 - perc. - str.   5:30 C. Fischer.

—— POLYPHONIES FOR PERCUSSION (FOR 4 PERCUSSIONISTS AND ORCH.)
*3,*3,*3,*3 - 4,3,3,1 - timp.,perc.(4) - str.   5:30 Leeds.

—— PRELUDE AND PIPER'S TUNE
1,1,2,1 - 0,1,0,0 - str.   6:00 C.H.Hansen.

—— PSALM 24 (FOR WOMEN'S CHORUS AND STRING ORCH.)
str.   11:30 C. Fischer.

—— THEME AND EXCURSIONS (FOR STRING ORCH.)
str.   4:00 Fema.

—— VIGNETTES FOR SMALL ORCH. (IN 7 MOVTS.)
2,0,2,0 - 2,1,1,0 - timp.,perc.(1) - str.   9:00 Composer.

BENTON, Daniel

—— THREE LITTLE PIECES (1973)
1,1 alto fl.,1,*2,2 - 2,2,0,0 - electric pf. - str.   4:00 Composer.

BENTZ, Cecil

—— INTRODUCTION AND FUGUE FOR STRING ORCH. (1954)
str.   7:36 Composer.

—— SYMPHONY IN THREE MOVEMENTS (1955)
*3,2,2(2nd alt. with b.-cl.),1 alto sax.,1 - 4,3,3,1 - timp.,perc.(3),cel.,xyl. - str.   17:35 Composer.

BENTZON, Jørgen

—— CHAMBER CONCERTO NO. 3, OP. 39 (FOR CLARINET AND CHAMBER ORCH.)
Henmar.

—— CHAMBER CONCERTO 1945
K.O.D.A.

—— CONCERTINO FOR FLUTE AND ORCH.
K.O.D.A.

—— CYKLEVISE-RHAPSODY, OP. 29
G. Schirmer.

—— DRAMATIC OVERTURE, OP. 5
K.O.D.A.

—— EVENING MUSIC FOR RECORDERS AND STRINGS, OP. 20-B
K.O.D.A.

—— FOTOMONTAGE, OP. 27 (OVERTURE)
G. Schirmer.

—— INTERMEZZO EXPRESSIVO (CHAMBER CONCERTO NO. 2)
(1930)
Henmar.
—— INTRODUCTION, VARIATION AND RONDO (1939)
sax. - str.   K.O.D.A.
—— MORNING AND EVENING MUSIC (FOR RECORDERS,
LITTLE DRUM AND STRINGS) (1931)
K.O.D.A.
—— MORNING MUSIC, OP. 20-A (FOR RECORDERS, DRUM
AND STRINGS)
K.O.D.A.
—— SINFONIA BUFFO, OP. 35
tpt. - b. drum - pf. - str.   G. Schirmer.
—— SINFONIA SERIA, OP. 33
fl. - perc. - str.   G. Schirmer.
—— SINFONIETTA NO. 1, OP. 41
str.   14:00 G. Schirmer.
—— SYMPHONIC TRIO, OP. 18 (CHAMBER CONCERTO NO. 3)
(FOR 3 INSTRUMENTAL GROUPINGS)
12 hn. - str. (39,0,12,6)   25:00 Henmar.
—— SYMPHONY NO. 1, OP. 37
G. Schirmer.
—— SYMPHONY NO. 2 (1947)
K.O.D.A.
—— VARIATIONS FOR CHAMBER ORCH., OP. 28
Skand. & Bo.
—— VARIATIONS ON A DANISH FOLKTUNE, OP. 17
perc. - pf. - str.   Möseler.

BENTZON, Niels Viggo
—— BONJOUR MAX ERNST, OP. 138 (CANTATA) (FOR CHORUS
AND ORCH.) (Text: Composer)
3,3,3,3 - 4,3,3,1 - timp.,perc.,cel. - 2 hp. - pf. - str.
19:00 G. Schirmer.
—— BUSONISM, OP. 267
*3,*3,*3,*3 - 4,3,3,1 - timp.,perc.(4),vibra.,xyl. - hp. - str.
29:00 G. Schirmer.
—— CHAMBER CONCERTO FOR 11 INSTRUMENTS, OP. 52
0,0,1,1 - 0,2,0,0 - timp.,perc.(3),vibra. - 3 pf. - d.-b.
18:00 G. Schirmer.
—— CHORUS DANIENSIS NO. 2, OP. 247
*3,*3,*3,*3 - 4,3,3,1 - timp.,perc. - str.   10:00 G. Schirmer.
—— CONCERTO FOR ACCORDION AND ORCH., OP. 146
2,2,2,2 - 2,0,0,0 - acc. - str.   17:00 G. Schirmer.
—— CONCERTO FOR CELLO AND ORCH., OP. 106
2,2,2,2 - 2,0,0,0 - str.   22:00 G. Schirmer.
—— CONCERTO FOR CLARINET AND ORCH., OP. 269
*3,*3,*3,*3 - 4,3,3,1 - timp.,perc.(4),vibra.,xyl. - hp. - str.
29:00 G. Schirmer.
—— CONCERTO FOR FLUTE AND ORCH., OP. 147
1,2,2,2 - 2,0,0,0 - str.   21:00 G. Schirmer.
—— CONCERTO FOR OBOE AND STRING ORCH., OP. 74
ob. - str.   18:00 G. Schirmer.
—— CONCERTO FOR ORCH., OP. 148
*3,*3,*3,*3 - 4,3,3,1 - timp.,perc.,xyl. - hp. - pf. - str.
17:00 G. Schirmer.
—— CONCERTO FOR PIANO AND ORCH., OP. 49 (1948)
2,2,2,2 - 2,0,0,0 - timp.,perc. - pf. - str.   29:00 G. Schirmer.
—— CONCERTO FOR PICCOLO AND STRING ORCH., OP. 69-A
picc. - str.   11:00 G. Schirmer.
—— CONCERTO FOR STRING ORCH., OP. 114 (CONCERTO PER
ARCHI)
str.   15:00 G. Schirmer.
—— CONCERTO FOR TUBA AND ORCH., OP. 373
3,*3,3,3 - 4,3,3,2 - timp.,perc.,vibra. - str.   G. Schirmer.
—— CONCERTO FOR VIOLA AND ORCH., OP. 303 (1973)
2,2,2,2 - 4,3,3,1 - timp.,perc. - vla.   33:00 G. Schirmer.
—— CONCERTO FOR VIOLIN AND ORCH., OP. 70
2,2,2,2 - 4,2,3,0 - perc.,cel. - hp. - str.   37:00 G. Schirmer.
—— CONCERTO NO. 2 FOR VIOLIN AND ORCH., OP. 136
*3,*3,*3,*3 - 4,3,3,1 - timp.,perc. - hp. - str.   30:00 G. Schirmer.
—— CONCERTO NO. 4 FOR PIANO AND ORCH., OP. 96
3,2,2,2 - 2,0,0,0 - timp.,perc. - pf. - str.   34:00 G. Schirmer.
—— CONCERTO NO. 4 FOR VIOLIN AND ORCH., OP. 374
3,*3,3,3 - 4,3,3,1 - timp.,perc.,cel. - 2 hp. - vln.   G. Schirmer.
—— CONCERTO NO. 5 FOR PIANO AND ORCH., OP. 149
2,2,2,2 - 4,3,3,1 - timp. - pf. - str.   25:00 G. Schirmer.
—— CONCERTO NO. 6 FOR PIANO AND ORCH., OP. 195
2,2,2,2 - 2,2,0,0 - timp.,perc. - pf. - str.   25:00 G. Schirmer.
—— CONCERTO NO. 7 FOR PIANO AND ORCH., OP. 243
*3,*3,*3,*3 - 4,3,3,1 - timp.,perc. - pf. - str.   23:00 G. Schirmer.
—— COPENHAGEN CONCERTO NO. 1, OP. 167
1,0,0,0 - 1,1,0,0 - hpsc. - str.   18:00 G. Schirmer.

—— COPENHAGEN CONCERTO NO. 2, OP. 168 (WITH SOLO
STRINGS)
ob. - hpsc. - str.   18:00 G. Schirmer.
—— COPENHAGEN CONCERTO NO. 3, OP. 169 (WITH SOLO
VIOLA)
bn. - hpsc. - pf. - str.   G. Schirmer.
—— COPENHAGEN CONCERTO NO. 4, OP. 170 (WITH SOLO
CONTRABASS)
cl. - trb. - hpsc. - str.   18:00 G. Schirmer.
—— COPENHAGEN CONCERTO NO. 5, OP. 171
1,1,1,1 - 1,0,0,0 - hpsc. - str.   18:00 G. Schirmer.
—— COPENHAGEN CONCERTO NO. 6, OP. 172 (WITH SOLO
STRING QUARTET)
hpsc. - str.   18:00 G. Schirmer.
—— THE COURTISAN, OP. 89 (BALLET) %
60:00 G. Schirmer.
—— DIVERTIMENTO, OP. 19
str.   20:00 G. Schirmer.
—— THE DOOR, OP. 141 (BALLET) %
60:00 G. Schirmer.
—— EASTERN GASWORKS NO. 2, OP. 244
*3,*3,*3,*3 - 4,3,3,1 - timp.,perc. - str.   10:00 G. Schirmer.
—— FAUST III, OP. 144 (OPERA) %
120:00 G. Schirmer.
—— FEATURE ARTICLE ABOUT RENÉ DESCARTES, OP. 357
26:00 G. Schirmer.
—— FIVE MOBILES, OP. 125
2,2,3,2 - 4,3,3,1 - timp.,perc. - pf. - str.   17:00 G. Schirmer.
—— FORMULA, OP. 261
*4,*4,*4,*4 - 5,3,3,1 - timp.,perc.,cel.,vibra.,xyl. - hp. - pf. - str.
15:00 G. Schirmer.
—— INTRADA, OP. 64
2,2,2,2 - 4,3,3,1 - timp.,perc. - str.   5:00 G. Schirmer.
—— LEIPZIGER TAGE, OP. 383
pf. - str.   G. Schirmer.
—— MEET THE DANES, OP. 153
*3,2,*3,2 - 4,3,3,1 - timp.,perc.(3 incl. 2 on timp.) - guit. - str.
10:00 G. Schirmer.
—— METAPHOR, OP. 58 (BALLET) %
30:00 G. Schirmer.
—— MUTATIONS, OP. 123
2,3,3,2 - 4,3,3,1 - timp.,perc.,cel.,vibra.,xyl. - pf. - str.
10:00 G. Schirmer.
—— OSTINATO
K.O.D.A.
—— OVERTURE, OP. 137
2,2,2,2 - 4,0,0,0 - timp.,perc. - str.   8:00 G. Schirmer.
—— PASTORALE, OP. 107
2,2,2,2 - 4,3,3,1 - timp. - str.   5:00 G. Schirmer.
—— PEZZI SINFONICI, OP. 109
2,2,2,2 - 4,3,3,1 - perc. - hp. - str.   14:00 G. Schirmer.
—— PRELUDE AND RONDO, OP. 56
2,2,2,2 - 2,0,0,0 - timp. - str.   9:00 G. Schirmer.
—— PREMIERE, OP. 151 (BALLET) %
30:00 G. Schirmer.
—— RHAPSODY FOR PIANO AND ORCH., OP. 131
3,3,3,3 - 4,3,3,1 - timp.,perc.,xyl. - hp. - pf. - str.
31:00 G. Schirmer.
—— SINFONIA CONCERTANTE, OP. 100
0,0,1,0 - 0,3,3,1 - timp. - str.(no d.-b.)   39:00 G. Schirmer.
—— SINFONIA CONCERTANTE, OP. 178 (FOR 6 ACCORDIONS
AND ORCH.)
2,2,2,2 - 4,3,3,1 - timp.,perc. - 6 acc. - str.   20:00 G. Schirmer.
—— SINFONIA DA CAMERA, OP. 139 (WITH SOLO STRINGS)
1,1,1,1 - 1,1,1,1 - timp.,perc.,vibra.,xyl. - pf. - str.
20:00 G. Schirmer.
—— SONATA FOR FLUTE AND STRING ORCH., OP. 27
fl. - str.   20:00 G. Schirmer.
—— SONATA FOR 12 INSTRUMENTS, OP. 257
1,1,1,1 - 1,1,1,0 - pf. - str.   10:00 G. Schirmer.
—— SUITE FOR FOREIGNERS, OP. 154 (WITH JAZZ GROUP)
2,2,2,3 sax.(1 alto,1 ten.,1 bar.),3 - 4,5,4,1 - timp.,perc. - guit. - hp.
- 2 pf.   14:00 G. Schirmer.
—— SUITE FOR STRING ORCH., OP. 60
str.   20:00 G. Schirmer.
—— SYMPHONIC FANTASY FOR 2 PIANOS AND ORCH., OP. 119
3,3,3,2 - 4,3,3,1 - timp.,perc. - 2 pf. - str.   12:00 G. Schirmer.
—— SYMPHONIC SUITE, OP. 101
3,3,3,2 - 4,3,3,1 - timp.,perc.,cel. - str.   16:00 G. Schirmer.
—— SYMPHONIC VARIATIONS
3,2,3,2 - 4,3,3,1 - timp.,perc.,cel. - hp. - str.   17:00 G. Schirmer.
—— SYMPHONY NO. 3, OP. 46
2,2,2,2 - 4,3,3,1 - timp.,perc. - str.   37:00 G. Schirmer.

—— SYMPHONY NO. 4 ("METAMORPHOSES")
2,2,2,2 - 4,3,3,1 - timp.,perc. - hp. - str.   33:00 G. Schirmer.
—— SYMPHONY NO. 5 ("ELLIPSEN")
2,2,2,2 - 4,3,3,1 - timp.,perc.,cel. - hp. - str.   33:00 G. Schirmer.
—— SYMPHONY NO. 6, OP. 66
2,2,2,2 - 2,0,0,0 - timp.,perc. - str.   30:00 G. Schirmer.
—— SYMPHONY NO. 7, OP. 83 ("THE THREE VERSIONS")
3,3,3,2 - 4,3,3,1 - timp.,perc.,cel. - hp. - str.   27:00 G. Schirmer.
—— SYMPHONY NO. 8, OP. 113 (SINFONIA DISCREZIONE)
(SINFONIA DISCREZIONE)
2,2,2,2 - 4,3,3,1 - timp.,perc. - str.   40:00 G. Schirmer.
—— SYMPHONY NO. 9, OP. 126
3,3,3,3 - 4,3,3,1 - timp.,perc. - str.   33:00 G. Schirmer.
—— SYMPHONY NO. 10, OP. 150
*3,*3,*3,*3 - 4,3,3,1 - timp.,perc.,vibra.,xyl. - hp. - pf. - str.
27:00 G. Schirmer.
—— SYMPHONY NO. 11, OP. 158
2,2,2,2 - 2,0,0,0 - timp.,perc. - str.   22:00 G. Schirmer.
—— SYMPHONY NO. 12, OP. 166 ("TUNIS")
2,2,2,2 - 2,0,0,0 - timp.,perc. - str.   18:00 G. Schirmer.
—— SYMPHONY NO. 13, OP. 181 ("MILITARY")
2,2,2,2 - 4,3,3,1 - timp.,perc. - str.   18:00 G. Schirmer.
—— TORQUILLA, OP. 132 (ORATORIO) (Text: Composer)
3,3,3,3 - 4,3,3,1 - timp.,perc. - hp. - hpsc. - pf. - str.
55:00 G. Schirmer.
—— TRIPLE CONCERTO, OP. 94, FOR OBOE, CLARINET,
BASSOON AND STRINGS
ob.,cl.,bn. - str.   22:00 G. Schirmer.
—— VARIAZIONE BREVE
3,3,3,2 - 4,3,3,1 - timp.,perc. - hp. - str.   12:00 G. Schirmer.

BEREZOWSKY, Nicolai
—— BABAR THE ELEPHANT (CHILDREN'S OPERA), OP. 40 %
1(alt. with fl.),2,2,2 - 3,2,1,1 - timp.,perc.(3),glock.,xyl. - pf. - str.
C. Fischer.
—— CIRCUS MUSIC
3,2,2,2 - 3,2,1,1 - perc. - pf. - str.   3:00 C. Fischer.
—— CONCERTO FOR CLARINET (OR VIOLA) AND ORCH., OP.
28 (IN 4 MOVEMENTS)
*3,2,0,2 - 2,2,1,1 - timp.,perc.(2) - str.   23:00 Bo. Hawkes.
—— CONCERTO FOR HARP AND ORCH., OP. 31
1. Moderato; 2. Adagio; 3. Allegro non tanto
*3,2,*3,2 - 4,2,3,0 - timp.,perc. - hp. - str.   22:00 EV.
—— CONCERTO FOR VIOLIN AND ORCH., OP. 14
2,2,2,2 - 2,2,0,0 - timp.,perc. - str.   20:00 Bo. Hawkes.
—— CONCERTO LIRICO FOR CELLO AND ORCH., OP. 19
1. Lento; 2. Allegro; 3. Andante
1,1,*2,1 - 2,2,1,1 - timp.,perc.(2) - hp. - pf. - str.
23:00 Bo. Hawkes.
—— GILGAMESH (BABYLONIAN EPIC POEM FOR QUARTET OF
SOLOISTS, CHORUS, NARRATOR AND ORCH.), OP. 32
*3,*3,E♭cl.,*3,2 - 4,3,3,1 - timp.,perc.(4),cel.,glock.,xyl. - hp. - pf. -
str.   70:00 W-Levant.
—— PASSACAGLIA FOR THEREMIN AND ORCH. (IN 1 MOVT.)
*3,2,*3,2 - 4,2,3,1 - timp.,perc.(2) - theremin - str.
9:30 Composer.
—— SINFONIETTA, OP. 17 (IN 3 MOVEMENTS)
*3,2,2,2 - 4,2,3,1 - timp.,perc.(2) - str.   12:00 AmerMusEd.
—— SUITE HEBRAIQUE (IN 5 MOVTS.)
*3,*3,*3,*3 - 4,2,3,1 - timp.,perc.,cel. - hp. - str.
11:00 Bo. Hawkes.
—— SYMPHONY NO. 1, OP. 12
*3,3(3rd alt. with Eng.hn.),3(3rd alt. with b.-cl.),2 - 4,2,3,1 -
timp.,perc.(3),xyl. - hp. - str.   20:00 Bo. Hawkes.
—— SYMPHONY NO. 2, OP. 18 (IN 4 MOVEMENTS)
*3,*3,D cl.,*3,*3 - 6,4,3,1 - timp.,perc.(4),cel. - str.
35:00 Bo. Hawkes.
—— SYMPHONY NO. 3, OP. 21
3,3,3,3 - 4,3,3,1 - timp.,perc. - str.   25:00 Bo. Hawkes.
—— SYMPHONY NO. 4
*3,*3,*3,E♭cl.,*3 - 4,4,3,1 - timp.,perc.(4),cel.,glock.,xyl. - str.
35:00 Bo. Hawkes.
—— TOCCATA, VARIATIONS AND FINALE, OP. 23 (FOR STRING
QUARTET AND ORCH.)
3,2,3,2 - 4,2,3,1 - timp.,perc. - str.   23:00 Bo. Hawkes.

BERG, Gottfrid
—— DIVERTIMENTO FOR STRING ORCH. (IN 4 MOVTS.)
str.   10:00 S.T.I.M.
—— PARTITA BREVIS
Recorder - str.   5:00 S.T.I.M.
—— PÅ STRÖVTÅG (SUITE IN 4 MOVTS)
2,1,2,2 - 2,2,0,0 - timp.,perc. - str.   12:00 S.T.I.M.

—— SERENADE FOR STRING ORCH. (IN 5 MOVTS.)
str.   13:00 S.T.I.M.

BERG, Gunnar
—— FRISE (FOR PIANO AND CHAMBER ORCH.) (1961)
Henmar.

BERG, Irenee Marius
—— SYMPHONETTE
Belwin.

BERG, Natanael
—— ALLES ENDET WAS ENTSTEHET (SYMPHONY)
3,4,4,3 - 4,4,4,1 - timp.,perc.(4) - 2hp. - str.   39:00 S.T.I.M.
—— ÅRSTIDERNA (SYMPHONY)
4,3,4,3 - 4,3,4,1 - timp.,perc.(2) - str.   25:00 S.T.I.M.
—— CONCERTO IN C# MINOR FOR PIANO AND ORCH.
3,3,3,3 - 4,2,3,1 - timp. - pf. - str.   30:00 S.T.I.M.
—— CONCERTO IN E MINOR FOR VIOLIN AND ORCH.
2,3,2,2 - 4,2,3,1 - timp. - hp. - str.   25:00 Nordiska.
—— MAKTER (SYMPHONY IN 2 MOVTS.)
3,3,3,3 - 4,3,3,1 - timp.,perc.(3) - hp. - str.   25:00 S.T.I.M.
—— PEZZO SINFONICO (IN 4 MOVTS.)
2,3,2,2 - 4,2,3,1 - timp.,perc.(3) - str.   22:00 Nordiska.
—— PRELUDE TO ACT 2 OF THE OPERA "ENGELBREKT"
3,3,3,3 - 4,2,3,1 - timp.,perc. - str.   S.T.I.M.
—— PRELUDE TO THE OPERA "ENGELBREKT"
3,3,3,3 - 4,2,3,1 - timp.,perc. - str.   9:00 Suecia.
or:
2,2,2,2 - 2,2,1,0 - timp.,perc. - str.
—— REVERENZA (HYLLINGSMUSIK)
2,2,2,2 - 4,2,3,1 - timp.,perc. - hp. - str.   7:00 S.T.I.M.
—— SERENADE FOR VIOLIN AND ORCH.
2,2,2,2 - 2,0,0,0 - hp. - str.   10:00 S.T.I.M.
—— SUITE FOR ORCHESTRA
2,2,2,2 - 4,0,0,0 - str.   15:00 S.T.I.M.
—— SUITE FROM "BIRGITTA" (IN 4 MOVTS.)
3,3,3,3 - 4,2,3,1 - timp.,perc. - hp. - str.   29:00 S.T.I.M.
—— SVITA UR HERTIGINNANS FRIARE
3,3,2,3 - 4,2,3,1 - timp.,perc.(2) - hp. - pf. - str. 30:00 Nordiska.
—— TRAUMGEWALTEN (SYMPHONIC POEM)
4,4,4,3 - 4,3,3,1 - timp.,perc.(2) - 2hp. - str.   13:00 Gehrmans.
—— TRILOGIA DELLE PASSIONI
2,3,2,2 - 4,2,3,1 - timp.,perc. - hp. - str.   41:00 S.T.I.M.
—— TWO DANCES FROM THE BALLET "ÄLVORNA"
2,2,2,2 - 4,2,3,1 - timp.,perc. - hp. - str.   S.T.I.M.
—— TWO DANCES FROM THE OPERA "JUDITH"
2,2,2,2 - 4,0,0,0 - timp. - str.   S.T.I.M.
—— VARDE LJUS (SYMPHONIC POEM)
5,3,5,4 - 6,4,4,2 - timp.,perc.(4) - 2hp. - str.   25:00 S.T.I.M.

BERGE, Sigurd
—— A FOR ORCHESTRA
3,3,3,3 - 4,3,3,1 - timp.,perc. - str.   11:00 T.O.N.O.
—— B FOR ORCHESTRA (1966)
3,3,3,3 - 4,3,3,0 - timp.,perc. - str.   6:00 T.O.N.O.
—— CHROMA (PICTURES FOR ORCHESTRA) (IN 1 MOVT.)
3,3,3,3 - 4,3,3,0 - timp.,perc. - str.   12:30 T.O.N.O.
—— DANCES FROM GUDBRANDSAL (1956) (IN 3 MOVTS.)
2,2,2,2 - 4,2,2,0 - timp.,perc. - str.   25:00 T.O.N.O.
—— PEZZO ORCHESTRALE (IN 2 MOVTS.)
3,2,2,2 - 4,3,3,1 - timp.,perc. - str.   11:00 T.O.N.O.
—— RAGA (FOR OBOE AND ORCH.)
2,2,2,2 - 4,3,3,0 - timp.,perc. - str.   18:00 T.O.N.O.
—— SINE (SINUS)
timp.,perc. - str.   9:00 T.O.N.O.
—— TAMBURO PICCOLO
timp.,perc. - str.   5:00 T.O.N.O.

BERGEL, Bernd
—— DIVERTIMENTO
2,2,2,2 - 1,2,0,0 - str.   12:00 IsMuPublns.
—— JA'AKOB'S TRAUM (OPERA) % (Text: Richard Beer-Hofmann)
3,*3,*3,*3 - 4,3,3,0 - timp.,perc.,cel.,xyl. - org.(4-hands) -
pf.(4-hands) - str.   180:00 IsMuPublns.
—— TWO MOVEMENTS FOR STRINGS
str.   17:00 IsMuPublns.
—— VARIATIONS FOR ORCHESTRA
2,2,2,2 - 4,2,3,1 - timp.,perc.,cel. - str.   15:00 IsMuPublns.

BERGEL, Paul
—— DIVERTIMENTO FOR SMALL ORCH.
2,2,2,2 - 1,2,0,0 - str.   12:00 IsMuPublns.

BERGEN, Hans Willy
—— MUSIK ZU EINEM SCHACHSPIEL (MUSIC FOR A GAME OF CHESS)
2(2nd alt. with picc.),2(2nd alt. with Eng.hn.),2,2 - 4,3,3,0 - perc.,cel. - hp. - pf. - str.   10:20 Modern.
—— THREE SKETCHES (FOR PIANO AND ORCH.)
2(2nd alt. with picc.),2(2nd alt. with Eng. hn.),2,2 - 4,2,3,0 - timp.,perc. - hp. - pf. - str.   8:30 Modern.

BERGER, Arthur
—— CHAMBER CONCERTO
2,1,2,1 - 1,1,0,0 - perc.,cel.,glock. - pf. - str.   12:00 Boelke-Bo.
—— CHAMBER MUSIC FOR 13 PLAYERS
1,1,1,1 - 1,1,0,0 - cel. - hp. - str.(2,1,1,1)   8:00 Henmar.
—— IDEAS OF ORDER
3,2,3,2 - 4,2,2,0 - timp., perc. - hp. - str.   12:00 Henmar.
—— POLYPHONY
2,2,2,2 - 4,2,2,0 - timp.,perc.,cel.,glock. - hp. - str.   14:00 Boelke-Bo.
—— SERENADE CONCERTANTE (FOR WOODWIND QUARTET, VIOLIN AND ORCH.)
1,1,1,1 - 2,1,0,0 - str.   9:00 Henmar.
—— THREE PIECES FOR STRING ORCH.
str.   10:00 Boelke-Bo.

BERGER, Jean
—— BOULDEROLLICKS (SUITE) (1963) (IN 3 MOVTS.)
pf.(ad lib.) - str.   8:00 J. Boonin.
—— CARIBBEAN CONCERTO (FOR HARMONICA AND ORCH.) (IN 3 MOVEMENTS)
2(1 alt. with picc.),3,*3,*3 - 4,3,3,1 - timp.,perc.(3),mar. - harmonica - str.   14:00 Composer.
—— CONCERT PIECE FOR TWO FLUTES AND STRING ORCH.
2 fl. - str.   10:00 G. Schirmer.
—— CONCERTINO FOR PIANO AND CHAMBER ORCH. (IN 3 MOVEMENTS)
1,1,1,1 - 2,1,0,0 - pf. - str.   13:00 Mannheimer.
—— DIVERTISSEMENT
str.   10:50 G. Schirmer.
—— ELEGY FOR STRINGS
str.   4:00 J. Boonin.
—— THE EXILES (FOR LOW VOICE AND STRING ORCH.) (IN 4 MOVTS.)
3tpt. - hp. - str.   13:00 Composer.
—— INTRADA
2(1 alt. with picc.),2,2,2 - 4,3,3,1 - timp.,perc.(1)glock. - str.   12:00 Composer.
—— PETITE SUITE (1952) (IN 3 MOVTS.)
pf.(ad lib.) - str.   9:00 J. Boonin.
—— PSALM NO. 13
5:30 J. Fischer.
—— PSALMS OF PENITENCE (FOR MIXED CHORUS AND ORCH.)
20:00 J. Fischer.
—— SHORT OVERTURE FOR STRINGS
str.   6:00 G. Schirmer.
—— A SHORT SYMPHONY (1952) (IN 1 MOVT.)
2(1 alt. with picc.),2,2,2 - 4,3,0,0 - timp,perc.(2),glock.,xyl. - str.   12:00 J. Boonin.
—— SONATA DA CAMERA (FOR OBOE AND STRING ORCH.) (IN 4 MOVTS.)
ob. - str.   13:00 Broude.
—— TWO PSALMS (FOR SATB CHORUS AND STRING ORCH.)
str.   25:00 Augsburg.

BERGER, Theodor
—— CAPRICCIO, OP. 3-A (FOR 2 VIOLINS AND ORCH.)
2(2nd alt. with picc.),2(2nd alt. with Eng. hn.),2(2nd alt. with b.-cl.),2 - 2,2,0,0 - perc. - str.   5:00 Henmar.
—— CONCERTO MANUALE
perc.,metallophon,marymbaphon - pf. - str.   16:00 Sikorski.
—— HOMERISCHE SINFONIE
4,4,4(or 4b.-cl.),4 - 8,4,4,1 - perc. - hp. - str.   37:00 Sikorski.
—— MALINCONIA, OP. 5
str.   Henmar.
—— LA PAROLE
3,3,3,3 - 4,3,3,1 - timp.,perc. - hp. - str.   12:00 Belw-Mills.
—— RHAPSODIC DUO, OP. 9 (FOR VIOLIN, CELLO AND ORCH.)
2,2(2nd alt. with Eng. hn.),2(2nd alt. with b.-cl.),2 - 2,2,0,0 - perc. - str.   14:00 Henmar.
—— RONDINO GIOCOSO, OP. 4
str.   Henmar.

—— SCHUBERT-LEGENDE (HOMMAGE A SCHUBERT)
3,2(or 2Eng.hn.),3,3 - 4,3,3,1 - perc. - str.   10:00 Sikorski.
—— THE SEASONS
3,3,3,3 - 4,3,3,1 - timp.,perc. - hp. - str.   32:00 Belw-Mills.
—— SINFONIA PARABOLICA
3,3,3,3 - 4,3,3,1 - timp.,perc. - hp. - str.   25:00 Sikorski.
—— SYMPHONIC TRIGLYPH
3,3,3,3 - 4,3,3,1 - timp.,perc. - str.   16:00 Belw-Mills.
—— VOCALISES (FOR WOMEN'S CHORUS AND ORCH.)
3,2,3,2 - 0,0,0,0 - perc.,cel.,glock.,2 mar. - 2 hp. - str.   25:00 Belw-Mills.

BERGH, Arthur
—— THE CONGO (FANTASY FOR CHORUS AND ORCH.)
3,alto sax. - 0,3,3,1 - perc.(2-3) - org.(ad lib.) - 2pf.   20:00 Ditson.
—— HONOR AND GLORY (CONCERT OVERTURE, WITH OPTIONAL CHORUS), OP. 30
*3,*3,*3,2 - 4,3,3,1 - timp.,perc. - hp. - str.   5:30 Remick.
—— THE INTRUDER (FOR NARRATOR AND ORCH.)
fl.,ob.,cl. - timp.,perc.,vibra. - novochord - pf. - str.   21:00 Composer.
—— THE RAVEN (FOR NARRATOR AND ORCH.)
2,*3,2,2 - 4,2,3,1 - timp.,perc.(2) - hp. - str.   20:00 Composer.
—— SCHERZO-TARANTELLA
2,2,2,2 - 4,3,3,1 - timp.,perc.(3) - str.   5:00 Composer.

BERGH, Roger
—— LES FUNAMBULES (BALLET SUITE) (IN 5 MOVTS.)
2,1,2,sax.,1 - 2,2,1,0 - timp.,perc. - str.   25:00 Modern.

BERGH, Rudolph
—— TRAGISCHE SINFONIE, OP. 50
3,3,2,3 - 4,2,3,1 - perc. - str.   35:00 T & J.

BERGH, Sverre
—— CANTATA FOR HAMAR'S 100TH ANNIVERSARY (FOR SOPRANO, BARITONE, CHORUS AND ORCH.) (Text: Einar Skjaeraasen)
2,2,2,1 - 3,2,3,0 - timp.,perc. - str.   35:00 T.O.N.O.
—— CONCERTINO FOR CLARINET AND STRINGS
cl. - str.   12:00 T.O.N.O.
—— DEVIL'S DANCE (FANITULLEN) (FOR CHORUS AND ORCH.)
3,3,3,3 - 4,3,3,1 - timp.,perc. - str.   13:00 T.O.N.O.
—— A FUGUE FOR FUN (KONTRAPUNKT I GRUKKEDALEN)
2,2,2,2 - 4,3,3,0 - timp.,perc. - str.   3:08 T.O.N.O.
—— INN TE VEGG (BERGEN NURSERY RHYMES)
2,2,2,2 - 4,2,3,0 - timp.,perc. - str.   4:00 T.O.N.O.
—— KA SA EG?! (A BERGEN OVERTURE)
2,2,2,2 - 2,2,2,0 - timp.,perc. - str.   5:49 T.O.N.O.
—— KRISTIN LAVRANSDATTER: SUITE (IN 7 MOVTS.)
str.   18:00 T.O.N.O.
—— SKETCHES FROM A SMALL TOWN (SMÅBYSKISSER) (SUITE) (IN 4 MOVTS.)
2,2,2,2 - 2,2,2,0 - timp.,perc. - str.   15:00 T.O.N.O.

BERGHMANS, José
—— CONCERTINO FOR TROMBONE AND ORCH.
2,*2,2,*2 - 2,2,2,1 - timp.,perc.,xyl. - pf. - str.   13:30 Baron.
—— CONCERTO GROSSO (FOR HORN, TRUMPET, TROMBONE, PERCUSSION AND STRING ORCH.)
0,0,0,0 - 1,1,1,0 - timp.,perc. - str.   18:00 Baron.
—— CONCERTO LYRIQUE (FOR ALTO SAXOPHONE AND ORCHESTRA)
14:00 Presser.
—— LA JEUNE FILLE AU GRENIER (BALLET) %
Baron.
—— TABLEAUX FORAINS (SUITE)(FOR SOLO WIND INSTRS. AND CHAMBER ORCH.) (IN 7 MOVTS.)
1,1,1,1 - 1,1,1,0 - timp.,perc.,xyl.(ad lib.) - str.   23:00 Baron.

BERGHORN, Alfred
—— KONZERTANTE SINFONIE, OP. 34
1,1,1,1 - 1,1,1,0 - timp. - str.   32:00 Ries-Erler.

BERGMAN, Erik
—— ATON, OP. 49 (FOR NARRATOR, BARITONE, SATB CHORUS AND ORCH.) (1959) (Text; Ikhnaton)
2,2,2,2 - 3,3,3,0 - timp.,perc.(3),cel. - str.   22:00 FinnMICtr.
—— AUBADE, OP. 48 (1958)
3,2,3,2 - 4,3,3,0 - timp.,perc.(4),cel. - str.   13:00 Fazer.
—— BURLA, OP. 31 (1948)
2,2,2,2 - 3,3,0,0 - timp.,perc.(4) - str.   9:00 FinnMICtr.

—— CANTICUM FENNICUM, OP. 62 (FOR SOLO VOICES, MALE CHORUS AND ORCH.) (1968)
2,2,2,2 - 4,2,2,0 - timp.,perc. - str.　　　　22:00 Fazer.
—— CIRCULUS, OP. 58
2,2,2,2 - 4,2,2,1 - timp.,perc(5),cel. - hp. - str.　11:00 FinnMICtr.
—— COLORI ED IMPROVVISAZIONI
3,3,3,3 - 4,3,3,1 - timp.,perc.(4) - hp. - str.　19:00 FinnMICtr.
—— THE RUBAIYAT, OP. 41 (FOR BARITONE, MALE CHORUS AND ORCH.) (1953)
3,2,2,2 - 3,3,0,0 - timp.,perc.(4) - guit. - str.(no vlns.)
　　　　21:00 FinnMICtr.
—— SELA, OP. 55 (FOR BARITONE, SATB CHORUS AND ORCH.) (1962) (Text: Martin Buber)
1,2,2,0 - 0,2,1,0 - timp.(2),cel. - str.(no vlns.)　19:00 FinnMICtr.
—— SIMBOLO, OP. 52 (1960)
2,2,3,2 - 4,3,3,0 - timp.,perc.(4),cel. - hp. - str. 11:00 G. Schirmer.
—— SONGS OF SOLITUDE, OP. 27 (FOR MEZZO-SOPRANO OR BARITONE AND ORCH.) (1947) (Swedish text: Edith Södergran; Finnish text: Kyllikki Solanterä)
2,2,2,2 - 4,2,3,0 - timp.,perc. - hp. - str.　14:00 FinnMICtr.
—— SUITE FOR STRINGS, OP. 2 (1938)
str.　　　　18:00 FinnMICtr.
—— TRE ASPETTI D'UNA SERIE DODECAFONICA, OP. 46 (1957)
2,2,2,2 - 3,2,2,0 - timp.,perc.(4) - str.　11:00 FinnMICtr.

BERGMANN, Robert H.
—— CANTIQUE DES TROPIQUES (FOR PERCUSSION ENSEMBLE AND ORCH.)
　　　　10:00 EV.

BERGSMA, William
—— A CAROL ON TWELFTH NIGHT
*2,2,2,2 - 4,2,3,1 - timp. - hp. - str.　　7:00 Galaxy.
—— CHAMELEON VARIATIONS
3(3rd alt. with picc.),2,3(3rd alt. with b.-cl.),2 - 4,3,3,1 - timp.,perc.(3),glock.,xyl. - hp. - pf. - str.　12:00 Galaxy.
—— CHANGES (FOR SOLO WIND QUINTET AND CHAMBER ORCH.)
1,1,1,1 - 1,0,0,0 - timp., perc. - hp. - str.　9:00 Galaxy.
—— A CHRISTMAS SONG (FOR ALTO, CHORUS AND ORCH.)
2hn.,2tpt.,2trb. - timp. - org. - str.　5:00 Composer.
—— CONCERTO FOR VIOLIN AND ORCH.
1(alt. with picc.),2,1(alt. with b.-cl.),2 - 2,2,0,0 - perc. - hp. - str.
　　　　21:00 Galaxy.
—— CONCERTO FOR VIOLIN AND ORCHESTRA (1966) (IN 3 MOVTS.)
2(2nd alt. with picc.),2,*2,2 - 2,2,0,0 - timp.,perc.(3),glock.,xyl. - hp. - str.　22:00 Galaxy.
—— CONFRONTATION (FROM THE BOOK OF JOB) (FOR CHORUS AND 22 INSTRS.) (Text: Biblical)
2(2nd alt. with picc.),0,*2, alto sax.,0 - 2,2,2,1 - timp.,perc.(4),bells, glock.,xyl. - pf. - str.(no vlns., or vlas.)
　　　　26:00 Galaxy.
—— DANCES FOR JOSÉ (IN 3 MOVTS.)
1(alt. with picc.)1,1(alt. with b.-cl.),0 - 2,2,3,1 - timp.,perc.(2),glock.,xyl. - 2 pf. - str.　10:00 Composer.
—— DANCES FROM A NEW ENGLAND ALBUM, 1856
1,1,1,0 - 0,1,1,0 - melodeon - str.　8:00 Galaxy.
—— DOCUMENTARY I: PORTRAIT OF A CITY (SUITE) (IN 4 MOVTS.)
2(2nd alt. with picc.),*2,2(2nd alt. with b.-cl.),2 - 4,2,2,1 - timp.,perc.(3),glock.,xyl. - str.　17:00 Galaxy.
or:
2(2nd alt. with picc.),*2,2(2nd alt. with b.-cl.),1 - 2,2,2,1 - timp.,perc.(3),glock.,xyl. - str.
—— DOCUMENTARY II: BILLIE'S WORLD
2(2nd alt. with picc.),2,2(2nd alt. with b.-cl.),2 - 4,3,3,1 - timp.,perc. - pf. - str.　10:00 Galaxy.
—— THE FORTUNATE ISLANDS (FOR STRING ORCH.)
str.　　　　19:00 C. Fischer.
—— GOLD AND THE SEÑOR COMMANDANTE (SUITE)
2(2nd alt. with picc.),1,2,2 - 2,2,2,0 - timp.,perc. - pf. - str.
　　　　11:00 Galaxy.
—— GOLD AND THE SEÑOR COMMANDANTE (BALLET) %
　　　　11:00 Galaxy.
—— HIGH BARBAREE (VARIATIONS ON A SEA-CHANTY)
3(3rd alt. with picc.),*3,3(2nd alt. with b.-cl.),2 - 4,3,3,1 - timp. - str.　9:00 Composer.
—— IN CELEBRATION: TOCCATA FOR THE SIXTH DAY
*3,2,*3,2 - 4,2,3,1 - timp.,perc. - pf. - str.　11:00 Galaxy.

—— THE MURDER OF COMRADE SHARIK (OPERA) % (Text: Mikhail Bulgakov; Engl. Text: Mirra Ginsburg)
1(alt. with picc.),1,1(alt. with b.-cl.),1 - 1,0,0,0 - perc. - pf. - str.(2,1,1,1)　105:00 Galaxy.
—— MUSIC ON A QUIET THEME
2,2,2,2 - 4,2,3,1 - timp.,perc. - str.　7:30 Bo. Hawkes.
—— PAUL BUNYAN (BALLET) (FOR PUPPETS AND SOLO DANCERS) %
3,3,3,2 - 4,2,3,1 - timp. - pf. - str.　30:00 C. Fischer.
—— PAUL BUNYAN SUITE (IN 3 MOVTS.)
3,2,3,2 - 4,3,3,1 - timp. - str.　8:00 C. Fischer.
—— SERENADE TO AWAIT THE MOON ("BECAUSE, OF COURSE, SHE MIGHT NOT COME") (1965)
2(2nd alt. with picc.),2,*2,2 - 2,0,0,0 - perc.(1),glock.,vibra. - hp. - str.　10:30 Galaxy.
—— SIESTA AND HAPPY DANCE (FROM THE BALLET, "GOLD AND THE SEÑOR COMMANDANTE")
2(2nd alt. with picc.),1,2,2 - 2,2,2,0 - timp.,perc.(2) - pf. - str.
　　　　4:00 Galaxy.
—— SUITE FROM A CHILDREN'S FILM (IN 4 MOVTS.)
2(2nd alt. with picc.),1,2,1 - 2,2,2,0 - timp.,perc.(2) - pf. - str.
　　　　8:00 G. Schirmer.
—— SYMPHONY FOR CHAMBER ORCH. (IN 3 MOVTS.)
1(alt. with picc.),0,1,0 - 2,1,0,0 - timp.,perc.　15:00 Composer.
—— SYMPHONY NO. 1
3,3,3,2 - 4,3,3,1 - timp.,perc. - str.　25:00 C. Fischer.
—— SYMPHONY NO. 2 ("VOYAGES") (FOR SOLO VOICES, CHORUS AND ORCH.)
2(1 alt. with picc.),2,*2,2 - 4,2,3,1 - timp.,perc. - pf. - str.
　　　　25:00 Galaxy.
—— TRUMPET SING JUBILEE
2(2nd alt. with picc.),2,2(2nd alt. with b.-cl.),2 - 4,2,3,1 - timp.,perc.(2) - str.　8:00 Composer.
—— THE WIFE OF MARTIN GUERRE (THREE-ACT OPERA) % (Text: Janet Lewis)
2(2nd alt. with picc.),1,1(alt. with b.-cl.),1 - 1,1,0,0 - perc.(1),glock.,xyl. - hp. - str.　103:30 Galaxy.

BERIO, Luciano
—— ALLELUJAH
4,2,4,2 sax.,3 - 8,5,3,1 - timp.,perc.(4),bells,cel.,glock.,mar.,vibra.,xyl. - 2 hp. - pf. - str.
　　　　9:30 Leeds.
—— ALLELUJAH NO. 2
4,2,3,4 sax.,2 - 8,6,6,1 - perc.,bells,cel.,glock.,mar.,vibra,xylorimba. - guit. - 2 hp. - pf. - str.　19:00 Leeds.
—— ALLEZ HOP (PANTOMIME) %
3,3,4,3 sax.,3 - 4,4,3,1 - timp.,mar.,vibra - electric guit. - hp. - pf. - str.　Leeds.
—— MIMUSIQUE NO. 2 (BALLET) %
3,2,3,3 - 4,4,3,0 - timp.,perc.(4),cel.,glock.,vibra.,xyl. - hp. - str.
　　　　Leeds.
—— NONES
3,2,2,1 sax.,3 - 4,4,3,1 - timp.,perc.(6),cel.,glock.,vibra.,xyl. - electric guit. - hp. - pf. - str.　10:00 Leeds.
—— SERENATA (FOR FLUTE AND 14 INSTRS.)
1,*2,2,1 - 1,1,1,0 - hp. - pf. - str.　11:00 Leeds.
—— VARIOZIONI
2,1,2,2 - 2,2,1,0 - str.　11:35 Leeds.

BERIO, Luciano - MADERNA, Bruno
—— DIVERTIMENTO
3,3,4,5 sax.,3 - 2,5,3,1 - timp.,perc.(6),cel.,glock.,mar.,vibra.,xyl. - electric guit. - hp. - pf. - str.　12:00 Leeds.

BERKELEY, Lennox
—— CONCERTO FOR FLUTE AND ORCH.
1,2,0,2 - 2,0,0,0 - timp. - str.　20:00 G. Schirmer.
—— CONCERTO FOR PIANO AND ORCH.
2,2,2,2 - 2,2,1,0 - timp. - pf. - str.　25:00 G. Schirmer.
—— CONCERTO FOR TWO PIANOS AND ORCH.
　　　　30:00 G. Schirmer.
—— CONCERTO FOR VIOLIN AND CHAMBER ORCH., OP. 36
0,2,0,0 - 2,0,0,0 - str.　15:00 G. Schirmer.
—— A DINNER ENGAGEMENT (OPERA IN 2 SCENES) (7 SINGERS) % (Text: Paul Dehn)
1(alt. with picc.),1,1(alt. with b.-cl.),1 - 2,0,0,0 - perc. - hp. - pf. - str.　60:00 G. Schirmer.
—— DIVERSIONS
0,1,1,1 - 1,0,0,0 - pf. - str.(no d.-b.)　G. Schirmer.
—— DIVERTIMENTO
2,2,2,2 - 2,2,1,0 - timp.,perc. - str.　18:00 G. Schirmer.

—— DOMINI EST TERRA
2,2,2,2 - 0,3,3,1 - timp.,perc. - hp. - pf. - str.   9:00 G. Schirmer.
—— FOUR POEMS OF SANTA TERESA OF AVELA (FOR CONTRALTO AND STRINGS)
str.   12:00 G. Schirmer.
—— FOUR RONSARD SONNETS (FOR TENOR AND ORCH.)
2,2,2,2 - 4,2,3,1 - timp.,perc. - hp. - str.   18:30 G. Schirmer.
—— INTERLUDE (FROM THE OPERA "NELSON")
*3,2(2nd alt. with Eng.hn.),2,2 - 4,3,3,1 - perc. - hp. - str.
5:00 Schirmer.
—— JONAH (ORATORIO) (FOR CHORUS AND ORCH.)
3,3,3,3 - 4,3,3,1 - timp.,perc. - str.   60:00 G. Schirmer.
—— THE JUDGEMENT OF PARIS (BALLET) %
2,2,2,2 - 4,2,3,0 - timp. - hp. - str.   Bo. Hawkes.
—— NOCTURNE
2,2,2,2 - 4,2,3,0 - timp.,perc. - hp. - str.   10:30 G. Schirmer.
—— OVERTURE
*3,*3,2,*3 - 4,3,3,1 - timp. - str.   8:00 G. Schirmer.
—— PARTITA (1965)
1,1,2,1 - 2,1,1,0 - timp.,perc. - str.   13:00 G. Schirmer.
—— SERENADE (FOR STRING ORCH.)
1. Vivace; 2. Andantino; 3. Allegro moderato; 4. Lento
str.   14:00 G. Schirmer.
—— SIGNS IN THE DARK
str.   20:00 G. Schirmer.
—— SINFONIETTA
2,2,2,2 - 2,0,0,0 - timp. - str.   13:00 G. Schirmer.
—— STABAT MATER (FOR 6 SOLO VOICES AND CHAMBER ORCH.)
1,2,2,1 - 1,0,0,0 - perc. - hp. - str.   G. Schirmer.
—— SUITE FROM THE OPERA "NELSON"
*3,2,2,2 - 4,3,3,1 - timp.,perc.,cel. - hp. - str.   16:00 G. Schirmer.
—— SYMPHONY NO. 1
2,2,2,2 - 4,2,3,1 - timp.,perc. - hp. - str.   33:00 G. Schirmer.
—— SYMPHONY NO. 2
*3,2,2,*3 - 4,3,3,1 - timp.,perc. - str.   29:00 G. Schirmer.
—— SYMPHONY NO. 3 (1969) (IN 1 MOVT.)
3,3,2,3 - 4,3,3,1 - timp.,perc.(3) - hp. - str.   25:00 G. Schirmer.
—— VARIATIONS ON A HYMN BY ORLANDO GIBBONS (FOR ORGAN AND STRINGS)
org. - str.   18:00 G. Schirmer.
—— VOICES OF THE NIGHT
2,2,2,2 - 4,3,3,1 - timp.,perc.,vibra. - hp. - str.   10:00 G. Schirmer.
—— WINDSOR VARIATIONS (1969)
1,2,0,2 - 2,0,0,0 - str.   13:00 G. Schirmer.
—— THE WINTER'S TALE (SUITE)
*3,2,2,2 - 4,2,3,1 - timp.,perc. - hp. - str.   16:00 G. Schirmer.

BERKOWITZ, Leonard
—— CONCERTO FOR PIANO AND WINDS
3,2,4,2 - 4,3,3,1 - timp.,perc. - pf. - d.-b.   MCA Music.

BERKOWITZ, Ralph
—— A TELEPHONE CALL (ARIA FOR SOPRANO AND ORCH.) (1950) (Text: Dorothy Parker)
1,1,1,1 - 2,0,0,0 - timp. - pf. - str.   15:00 Composer.

BERKOWITZ, Sol
—— DANCE SUITE FOR STRINGS
str.   17:00 Presser.

BERLIN, David
—— STRUCTURES FOR CHAMBER ORCH., OP. 29 (1975) (IN 3 MOVTS.)
1(alt. with picc.),1,1,1 - 1,1,1,0 - timp.,perc.(2),glock.,vibra.,xyl. - str.(2,1,1,1)   10:00 Composer.
—— VARIANTS FOR ORCHESTRA (1975)
2(2nd alt. with picc.),2,2,2 - 3,3,3,0 - timp.,perc.(3),vibra.,xyl. - str.
13:48 Mss.Publs.

BERLINSKI, Herman
—— CONCERTO DA CAMERA (REV. 1975) (IN 3 MOVTS.)
1,1,1,1 - 0,0,0,0 - timp. - pf. - str.   22:00 Composer.
—— CONCERTO FOR ORGAN AND ORCH. (1964)
Composer.
—— DAVID AND GOLIATH (1946) (FOR BARITONE AND ORCH.)
2(2nd alt. with picc.),2(2nd alt. with Eng.hn.),2,2 - 3,2,2,1 - timp.,perc.(4) - hp. - pf. - str.   19:00 Presser.
—— FOR THE PEACE OF MIND (1952)
1. Allegro moderato; 2. Adagio; 3. Presto; 4. Andante moderato
ob. - pf. - str.   23:00 Presser.

(ORATORIO) (REV. 1975) (FOR SATB SOLI, SATB CHORUS AND ORCH.)
3(3rd alt. with picc.),3(3rd alt. with Eng.hn.),3(3rd alt. with b.-cl.),3(3rd alt. with c.-bn.) - 4,3,3,1 - timp.,perc.(4),cel. - hp. - pf. - str.   90:00 Composer.

BERLIOZ, Hector
—— BEATRICE AND BENEDICK (OPERA) % (Engl. Text: Geoffrey Dunn)
2,2,2,2 - 4,2,2 cnt.,3,0 - timp.,perc.(3) - 2 guit. - 2 hp. - str.
120:00 Oxford.

BERLIOZ, Hector - CARTER, Anthony
—— THE MARCH TO THE SCAFFOLD (FROM THE "SYMPHONIE FANTASTIQUE")
2(2nd alt. with picc.),2,3,2 - 4,3,2,1 - timp.,perc. - org. - pf. - str.
6:00 Oxford.

BERLIOZ, Hector - CLEMENTS, John
—— BENEVENUTO CELLINI: CHORAL SUITE (FOR MIXED CHORUS AND ORCH.) (English Translation by Arthur Jacobs)
2,2,2,2 - 4,2,3,0-1 - timp.,perc. - hp.(opt.) - str.   13:00 Oxford.

BERLIOZ, Hector - ROBINSON
—— BALLET MUSIC FROM "THE TROJANS" (SUITE)
Minimum: 1,1,2,1 - 2,0,0,0 - perc. - str.   15:00 Oxford.

BERNAOLA, Carmelo A.
—— SUPERFICIE NO. 1
1,1,1,1 - 0,0,0,0 - perc. - pf. - str.   12:00 Modern.

BERNARD, Filip
—— SCHERZO (FOR STRINGS)
str.   7:00 Hans Gerig.

BERNARD, Robert
—— POÈME SYMPHONIQUE (FOR STRINGS)
str.   23:00 Presser.

BERNAUD, Alain
—— CONCERTO LYRIQUE (FOR CLARINET AND ORCH.)
2,*2,2,2 - 2,2,1,0 - timp.,perc.,xyl. - str.   20:00 Baron.

BERNERS, Lord
—— ADAGIO AND VARIATIONS
str.   G. Schirmer.
—— ADAGIO, VARIATIONS AND HORNPIPE (FROM "THE TRIUMPH OF NEPTUNE")
5:00 G. Schirmer.
—— FANTAISIE ESPAGNOL
*3,*3,*4,*4 - 4,3,3,1 - perc. - hp. - str.   7:00 G. Schirmer.
—— FUGUE IN C MINOR
*4,2,2,*3 - 4,2,2,0 - perc. - hp. - str.   5:30 G. Schirmer.
—— LUNA PARK (BALLET SUITE)
1,1,2,1 - 2,2,1,0 - perc. - hp. - str.   17:00 G. Schirmer.
—— SUITE FROM THE BALLET "THE TRIUMPH OF NEPTUNE"
*4,*3,*3,*3 - 4,3,3,1 - perc.,cel. - pf. - hp. - str.
25:00 G. Schirmer.
—— THREE ORCHESTRAL PIECES
*3,*3,*3,*3 - 4,3,2,1 - perc.,cel. - hp. - str.   8:00 G. Schirmer.

BERNIER, Nicolas - CELLIER, A.
—— CONFITEOR TIBI DOMINE (FOR 4 SOLO VOICES, MIXED CHOIR AND ORCH.)
30:00 Salabert.

BERNIER, Nicolas - CHAILLEY, J. ed.
—— ACCURITE (MOTET FOR VOICE AND ORCH.)
fl. - hpsc. - str.   25:00 Presser.

BERNIER, René
—— LE BAL DES OMBRES (DANSES PARODIQUES) (SUITE DE BALLET) (1954)
3,3,3,2 - 4,2,3,0 - timp.,perc.,bells,cel.,glock.,xyl. - hp. - str.
17:00 BizetMuPrd.
—— HOMMAGE À SAX (DIPTYQUE CONCERTANT) (FOR ALTO SAX, AND ORCH.) (1958)
2,*2,2,1 alto sax.,1 - perc.,cel.,glock.(ad lib.),xyl. - hp. - str.
11:00 Baron.
—— LITURGIES (FOR ALTO AND STRING ORCH.)
str.   13:00 Salabert.

—— MÉLOPÉES ET RYTHMES (DIPTYQUE SYMPHONIQUE)
(1932)
    3,3,3,2 - 4,3,3,1 - timp.,perc.,cel.,glock.,xyl. - hp. - str.
                                              12:00 H. Elkan.
—— NOTTURNO (FROM "VARIATIONS ON A THEME OF
ROLAND DE LASSUS") (1955)
    2,2,2,2 - 4,2,2,0 - timp.,perc.,cel.,glock.,slide-flute(ad
    lib.),vibra.,xyl. - hp. - str.   6:00 H. Elkan.
—— ODE À UNE MADONE (1938)
    2,2,2,2 - 3,2,0,0 - cel. - hp. - str.   9:00 Cranz.
—— POUR UNE DANSEUSE ANTIQUE (1947)
    2,1,2,1 alto sax.,1 - 2,1,1,0 - timp.,perc.,cel. - hp. - str.
                                              4:00 H. Elkan.
—— SYMPHONIETTE (1957)
    str.   12:00 Cranz.
—— TANAGRAS (1975) BALLET FOR ORCH. (IN 9 MOVTS.)
    2,2,2,2 - 2,2,1,0 - timp.,perc. - hp. - str.   28:00 H. Elkan.
—— THRENE POUR UNE OMBRE AIMÉE (FOR STRING
ORCHESTRA)
    str.   H. Elkan.
—— LE TOMBEAU DEVANT L'ESCANT (SUITE SYMPHONIQUE)
                                                  Baron.

BERNSTEIN, Leonard
—— THE AGE OF ANXIETY (SYMPHONY NO. 2 FOR PIANO
AND ORCH.) (IN 2 MOVTS.)
    *3,*3,*3,*3 - 4,3,3,1 - timp.,perc.(5),cel.,glock.,xyl. - hp. - pf. -
    pianino(or barrel organ) - str.   30:00 G. Schirmer.
—— CHICHESTER PSALMS (FOR CHORUS AND ORCH.) (IN 3
MOVTS) (1965)
    0,0,0,0 - 0,3,3,0 - timp.,perc.,bells,glock.,xyl. - 2 hp. - str.
                                              10:00 G. Schirmer.
—— DYBBUK VARIATIONS (FOR BARITONE, BASS AND ORCH.)
    2,3,4,3 - 4,3,3,1 - timp.,perc. - hp. - pf. - str.   50:00 Bo. Hawkes.
—— DYBBUK VARIATIONS: SUITE NO. 1 (FOR BARITONE, BASS
AND ORCH.)
    2,3,4,3 - 4,3,3,1 - timp.,perc. - hp. - pf. - str.   30:00 Bo. Hawkes.
—— DYBBUK VARIATIONS: SUITE NO. 2
    2,3,4,3 - 4,3,3,1 - timp.,perc. - hp. - pf. - str.   20:00 Bo. Hawkes.
—— JEREMIAH (SYMPHONY, NO. 1 WITH MEZZO-SOPRANO)
(IN 3 MOVTS.)
    3(3rd alt. with picc.),3(3rd alt. with Eng.hn.),E♭cl.(alt. with
    b.-cl.),2,3(3rd alt. with c.-bn.) - 4,3,3,1 - timp.,perc.(3) - pf. - str.
                                              23:00 Harms, Inc.
—— MASS (A THEATRE PIECE FOR SINGERS, PLAYERS AND
DANCERS) % (FOR SOLO VOICES, MIXED CHORUS, BLUES
BAND, ROCK BAND AND ORCH.) (Text from Liturgy of the
Roman Mass, with additional texts by the composer and Stephen
Schwartz)
    2(2nd alt. with picc.),2(2nd alt. with Eng.hn.),3(3rd alt. with
    b.-cl.),2 - 4,4,3,1 - timp.,perc.(2),glock.,vibra.,xyl. - 3 guit. - Fender
    electric d.-b. - hp. - 2 cemb.(alt. on pf.,org.,Rock-org.,etc.) - str.
                                              115:00 G. Schirmer.
—— OVERTURE TO "CANDIDE"
    3,2,4,3 - 4,2,3,1 - timp.,perc. - hp. - str.   4:30 G. Schirmer.
—— SERENADE FOR VIOLIN AND ORCH. (AFTER PLATO'S
"SYMPOSIUM") (IN 5 MOVEMENTS)
    timp.,perc.(5),glock.,xyl. - hp. - str.   30:00 G. Schirmer.
—— SUITE FROM "FACSIMILE"
    2,2,2,2 - 4,2,cnt.,2,1 - perc.(4) - pf. - str.   21:00 Harms, Inc.
—— SUITE FROM "FANCY FREE" (IN 6 MOVTS.)
    1(alt. with picc.),2,2,2 - 4,3,3,1 - timp.,perc. - pf. - str.
                                              20:00 Harms, Inc.
—— SYMPHONIC DANCES (FROM "WEST SIDE STORY")
    3,2,4,1 alto sax.,2 - 4,3,3,1 - timp.,perc. - hp. - pf. - str.
                                              22:00 G. Schirmer.
—— SYMPHONIC SUITE FROM "ON THE WATERFRONT"
    3,3,4,alto sax.,3 - 4,3,3,1 - timp.,perc. - hp. - pf. - str.
                                              23:00 G. Schirmer.
—— SYMPHONY NO. 3 (KADDISH) (FOR SOPRANO SOLO,
NARRATOR (WOMAN), BOYS' CHORUS, MIXED CHORUS
AND ORCH.) (Text: Composer, also Trad. Hebrew and Aramaic)
    4(2 alt. with picc. and alto fl.),*3,1 E♭cl.,*3,1 alto sax.,*3 - 4,3,3,1
    - timp.,perc.(6),bells,cel.,glock.,vibra.,xyl. - hp. - pf. - str.
                                              43:00 G. Schirmer.
—— THREE DANCE EPISODES FROM "ON THE TOWN"
    *2,1(alt. with Eng. hn.),1(alt. with E♭cl. and b.-cl.),0 - 2-4,3,3,0 -
    timp.,perc.(1-2),glock.,xyl. - pf. - str.   9:30 Witmark.
—— TROUBLE IN TAHITI (OPERA IN 7 SCENES) % (5 SINGERS)
(Text: Composer)
    2,2,2,2 - 2,2,2,1 - perc. - hp. - str.   40:00 G. Schirmer.

BERNSTEIN, Leonard - PERESS, Maurice
—— OVERTURE TO "WEST SIDE STORY"
    2,2,2,2 - 4,3,3,1 - timp.,perc. - guit.(opt.) - hp. - pf. - str.
                                              5:00 G. Schirmer.

BERRY, Wallace Taft
—— THE ADMIRABLE BASHVILLE (ONE-ACT OPERA, ON A
VERSE COMEDY OF SHAW) % (1954) (Text: George Bernard
Shaw)
    1,1(alt. with Eng. hn.),1,1 - 1,1,1,0 - timp.,perc.,cel.,xyl. - pf. -
    str.(2,1,1,1)   65:00 Composer.
—— CANTICLE ON A JUDAIC TEXT (FOR TENOR AND ORCH.)
                                                  Composer.
—— CONCERTO FOR PIANO AND ORCH.
    *3,*3,2,3(3rd alt. with c.-bn.) - 4,2,3,1 - timp.,perc.,bells,xyl. - pf. -
    str.   20:00 C. Fischer.
—— FIVE PIECES FOR SMALL ORCH.
    1,1,1,1 - 1,1,1,0 - timp.,cymb. - hp. - str.   18:23 C. Fischer.
—— FOUR MOVEMENTS FOR CHAMBER ORCH.
    2,2,2,2 - 2,2,1,0 - timp.,perc. - str.   21:00 C. Fischer.
—— ORCHESTRAL FANTASY IN D
                                                  Composer.
—— SPOON RIVER (6 SONGS FOR SOPRANO, BASS AND ORCH.)
(Text: Edgar Lee Masters)
    2,1,2,1 - 2,2,1,0 - timp.,perc.(1),glock. - pf. - str.   19:50 Composer.
—— SYMPHONY IN ONE MOVEMENT (1953)
                                                  Composer.

BERTEN, Walter M.
—— INTRADA
    2,2,2,2 - 4,3,3,1 - timp.,perc. - hp. - str.   10:00 Alkor.

BERTINI, Garry
—— CONCERTO FOR HORN, STRINGS AND TIMPANI
    hn. - timp. - str.   16:00 IsMuPublns.

BERTONCINI, Mario
—— SEI PEZZI PER ORCHESTRA (1962) (SIX PIECES FOR ORCH.)
    *3,2,2,3 sax.,3 - 3,3,2,1 - timp.,perc. - str.   9:10 Seesaw.

BERTONI, Ferdinando - BONELLI, Ettore
—— SINFONIA IN C (FOR 2 OBOES, 2 TRUMPETS AND
STRINGS)
    0,2,0,0 - 0,2,0,0 - str.   Henmar.

BERTOUILLE, Gérard
—— ANDANTE (1955)
    str.   7:00 H. Elkan.
—— ARIA ET DIVERTIMENTO (FOR FLUTE AND ORCH.) (1958)
    3,1,2,2 - 2,2,1,0 - timp. - hp. - str.   11:00 H. Elkan.
—— CONCERTINO FOR CLARINET AND STRING ORCH. (1970)
    cl. - str.   11:00 H. Elkan.
—— CONCERTO FOR CHAMBER ORCH. (1942)
    1,1,2,1 - 2,1,0,0 - str.   16:30 H. Elkan.
—— CONCERTO FOR HORN AND STRING ORCH.
    hn. - timp. - pf. - str.   H. Elkan.
—— CONCERTO FOR STRING ORCH. (1974)
    1. Adagio; 2. Adagio come sopra; 3. Allegro
    str.   17:00 H. Elkan.
—— CONCERTO FOR TRUMPET AND STRINGS
    tpt. - str.   22:00 CBDM.
—— CONCERTO FOR VIOLIN AND ORCH. (1942)
    2,2,2,2 - 2,2,0,0 - timp. - str.   20:00 H. Elkan.
—— CONCERTO NO. 2 FOR PIANO AND ORCH. (1953)
    2,2,2,2 - 2,2,0,0 - timp. - pf. - str.   17:00 H. Elkan.
—— CONCERTO NO. 2 FOR TRUMPET AND STRINGS (1973) (IN
3 MOVTS.)
    tpt. - timp. (ad lib.) - str.   15:00 H. Elkan.
—— CONCERTO NO. 2 FOR VIOLIN AND ORCH.
    2,2,2,2 - 4,3,3,1 - timp. - hp. - str.   20:00 H. Elkan.
—— FANTAISIE
    2,2,3,2 - 0,2,0,0 - timp.,perc.,cel. - pf. - str.   13:00 CBDM.
—— FANTAISIE LYRIQUE (1969)
    3,3,3,3 - 4,3,3,1 - timp.,cel. - pf. - str.   H. Elkan.
—— MUSIQUE (1972)
    3,2,2,2 - 4,3,3,1 - timp. - pf. - str.   13:00 H. Elkan.
—— OVERTURE POUR TRIO D'ANCHES ET ORCH. À CORDES
(1956)
    0,1,1,1 - 0,0,0,0 - timp. - pf. - str.   10:00 H. Elkan.
—— PETITE MUSIQUE (FOR STRING ORCH.)
    str.   6:00 H. Elkan.

—— PRELUDE AND SCHERZO (FOR FLUTE AND STRING
ORCH.) (1958)
fl. - str.   10:00 H. Elkan.
—— SINFONIA DA REQUIEM (1957)
3,2,3,2 - 4,3,3,1 - timp.,perc. - str.   18:00 H. Elkan.
—— SINFONIETTA (1942)
2,1,2,1 - 2,2,1,0 - timp. - pf. - str.   15:00 H. Elkan.
—— SYMPHONIE PICTURALE
2,2,3,2 - 4,3,3,1 - timp.,bells,perc.,cel. - str. 18:00 CBDM.
—— SYMPHONY NO. 2 (1955)
3,2,3,2 - 4,3,3,1 - timp.,cel. - str.   20:00 H. Elkan.
—— VARIATIONS DIDACTIQUES (1954)
str.   12:00 H. Elkan.

BERWALD, Franz - BLOMSTEDT, Herbert
—— SINFONIE SINGULIERE
2,2,2,2 - 4,3,4,1 - timp. - str.   28:00 G. Schirmer.

BERWALD, Franz - HEDWALL, Lennart
—— SINFONIE SÉRIEUSE
2,2,2,2 - 4,2,3,0 - timp. - str.   G. Schirmer.

BERWALD, William
—— DRAMATIC OVERTURE
3,*3,*3,*3 - 4,4,3,1 - timp.,perc. - hp. - str.   10:00 Composer.
—— HYMN OF PRAISE (FOR SOPRANO SOLO, CHORUS AND
ORCH.)
2,2,2,2 - 4,3,3,1 - timp. - hp. - str.   10:00 Composer.
—— NIGHT'S FROLICS (SUITE) (FIVE IMPRESSIONS)
*3,2,*3,2 - 4,3,3,1 - timp.,perc. - hp. - str.   15:00 Composer.
—— OVERTURE HEROIC (WALTHARI)
3,*3,*3,*3 - 4,3,3,1 - timp.,perc. - hp. - str.   10:00 Composer.
—— PRELUDE AND TOCCATA
3,*3,*3,*3 - 4,3,3,2 - timp.,perc. - hp. - str.   6:00 J. Fischer.
—— SCHERZO FANTASTIC
*3,2,2,2 - 4,3,3,1 - timp.,perc. - hp. - str.   8:00 Composer.
—— SYMPHONIC LEGEND
*3,*3,*3,2 - 4,3,3,1 - timp.,perc. - hp. - str.   10:00 Composer.
—— SYMPHONIC PRELUDE FOR ORGAN AND ORCH.
2,2,2,2 - 4,3,3,1 - timp.,perc. - org. - str.   12:00 Composer.
—— THE WAY OF THE CROSS (CANTATA) (FOR CHORUS AND
ORCH.)
2,2,2,2 - 4,2,3,1 - timp.,perc. - hp. - str.   60:00 Gray.

BESARD, Jean Baptiste - SEIBER, Matyas
—— BESARDO SUITE NO. 1 (DANCE TUNES FROM BESARD'S
"THESAURUS HARMONICUS", 1603) (IN 6 MOVTS.)
2,2,2,2 - 2-4,2,2,0 - perc. - hp. - str.   16:00 Galaxy.

BESSEM, Saar
—— DE ZEE (FOR MIXED CHORUS AND ORCH.) (1952) (Text: H.
Marsman)
1,2,1,1 - 2,1,0,0 - pf. - str.   10:00 Henmar.

BETTARINI, Luciano
—— TRE LIRICHE DE G. PASCOLI (FOR VOICE AND ORCH.)
3,3,3,2 - 4,1,3,0 - perc.,cel. - pf. - str.   Leeds.

BETTINELLI, Angelo
—— CAROVANE NOTTURNE
3,3,2,2 - 4,2,3,1 - timp.,perc.,cel. - hp. - str. 6:00 Bo. Hawkes.
—— SARABANDA
3,2,2,2 - 4,2,3,1 - timp.,perc. - hp. - str.   6:00 Bo. Hawkes.

BETTINELLI, B.
—— FANTASIA CONCERTATA (FOR STRING QUARTET AND
ORCH.)
3,2,2,2 - 4,2,2,0 - timp.,perc. - str.   19:00 Bo. Hawkes.
—— LAUDI DEL 1200 (FOR SOPRANO, MEZZO-SOPRANO,
MIXED CHORUS AND ORCH.)
hp. - str.   19:00 Bo. Hawkes.
—— MOVIMENTO SINFONICO
3,2,3,2 - 4,3,3,1 - timp.,perc. - pf. - str.   8:00 Bo. Hawkes.

BETTS, Lorne M.
—— CONCERTINO FOR SOPRANO SAXOPHONE AND ORCH.
(1972) (IN 1 MOVT.)
2,0,2,sop.sax.,0 - 2,0,0,0 - perc. - hp. - str.   9:00 CanMusCtr.
—— CONCERTO NO. 1 FOR PIANO AND ORCH. (1955)
2,*2,2,2 - 2,2,0,0 - perc. - pf. - str.   20:00 CanMusCtr.
—— CONCERTO NO. 2 FOR PIANO AND ORCH.
2ob. - 2hn. - pf. - str.   15:00 C.A.P.A.C.

—— A CYCLE OF THE EARTH (FOUR SONGS FOR SOPRANO
AND ORCH.) (1967) (Text: Bliss Carman)
2,2,2,2 - 2,0,0,0 - perc. - hp. - str.   11:30 CanMusCtr.
—— DAVID (FOR NARRATOR, MIXED CHORUS AND ORCH.)
(1949) (Text: Earle Birney)
*2,*2,2,2 - 2,2,2,0 - timp.,perc.,cel. - str.   15:00 CanMusCtr.
—— DIVERTIMENTO
2,2,2,2 - 2,2,0,0 - perc. - str.   12:30 CanMusCtr.
—— ELEGY (1949)
Eng.hn. - str.   5:30 CanMusCtr.
—— FANTASIA CANADIANA (1955)
2,2,2,2 - 2,2,2,0 - perc. - hp. - str.   CanMusCtr.
—— FIVE SONGS FOR HIGH VOICE AND STRING ORCH. (1949)
(Text: Ezra Pound)
str.   12:30 CanMusCtr.
—— JOE HARRIS, 1913-1942 (FOR MALE CHORUS, MALE
NARRATOR AND 13 INSTRUMENTS) (Text: Earle Birney)
2,2,2,2 - 2,2,2,0 - perc. - str.   18:00 C.A.P.A.C.
—— KANADARIO (MUSIC FOR A FESTIVAL OCCASION) (1966)
(IN 3 MOVTS.)
*3,2,2,2 - *3 - 4,2,3,1 - perc.(3),cel. (ad lib.) - str.
                                                   13:00 CanMusCtr.
—— MARGARITA SORORI (FOR WOMEN'S CHORUS AND
ORCH.) (1975) (Text: W. H. Henley)
2,2(2nd alt. with Eng. hn.),2,2 - 2,0,0,0 - hp. - str.
                                                   10:00 CanMusCtr.
—— MUSIC FOR ORCHESTRA (1963)
*2,2,2,2 - 4,2,3,1 - perc. - str.   8:00 CanMusCtr.
—— RIDERS TO THE SEA (1-ACT OPERA) (1955) % (Libretto: J. M.
Synge)
1,*2,1,1 - 2,1,1,0 - perc.(1) - hp. - str.   30:00 CanMusCtr.
—— SONATA FOR ORCHESTRA (1949)
1. Slow; 2. Lightly; 3. Slow, lyrical; 4. Vigorous
*3,*3,*3,2 - 4,3,3,1 - timp.,perc.,cel. - hp. - str. 20:00 CanMusCtr.
—— SUITE DA CHIESA (IN 3 MOVTS)
2,2,2,2 - 2,2,0,0 - perc. - str.   10:00 C.A.P.A.C.
—— SUITE FOR SMALL ORCH.
2,2,2,2 - 0,0,0,0 - perc. - str.   11:00 C.A.P.A.C.
—— SUITE FOR STRINGS (1948) (IN 3 MOVTS.)
str.   9:30 CanMusCtr.
—— SUITE IN THREE MOVEMENTS (1975)
2,2,2,2 - 4,3,2,1 - timp.,perc.(5) - str.   8:30 CanMusCtr.
—— SYMPHONY NO. 1
3,3,2,2 - 4,3,2,1 - perc.(2) - hp. - str.   20:00 C.A.P.A.C.
—— SYMPHONY NO. 2 (1961)
1. Broadly, fast; 2. Slow; 3. Lightly; 4. Slow
*3,3,*3,*3 - 4,3,2,1 - timp.,perc. - 2 hp. - str. 18:00 CanMusCtr.
—— TWO ABSTRACTS FOR ORCH. (1961)
2,2,2,2 - 4,2,2,1 - timp.,perc. - str.   7:45 CanMusCtr.
—— TWO DANCES FOR ORCH. (1950)
*2,*2,2,2 - 2,2,2,0 - timp.,perc.,vibra. - hp. - str. 7:00 CanMusCtr.
—— VARIANTS FOR ORCHESTRA (1969) (IN 1 MOVT.)
2(2nd alt. with picc.),2,2,2 - 4,2,3,0 - perc.(2) - str.
                                                   5:00 CanMusCtr.

BEUGNIOT, Jean-Pierre
—— CONCERTINO FOR CLARINET AND STRINGS
cl. - str.   15:00 Presser.
—— CONCERTO FOR TRUMPET, PIANO AND STRINGS
tpt. - pf. - str.   23:00 Presser.

BEURDEN, Bernard van
—— INTERPRETATIE
                                                   6:00 Henmar.
—— MUSIC FOR RECORDER AND CHAMBER ORCH.
                                                   7:00 Henmar.

BEURLE, Jürgen
—— STATISCH-DYNAMISCH
2(2nd alt. with picc.),*2,*2,2(2nd alt. with c.-bn.) - 0,2,2,1 -
perc.,xyl. - hp. - pf.(or cel.) - str.   14:00 AhnSimrock.

BEVERIDGE, Thomas G.
—— DIALOGUES (FOR CHAMBER ORCH.)
*2,*2,*2,1 - 1,1,1,0 - timp.,perc.(2) - str.   10:40 Composer.
—— ONCE (IN MEMORIAM MARTIN LUTHER KING, JR.)
(CANTATA FOR SOPRANO, NARRATOR, MIXED CHORUS
AND ENSEMBLE)
0,0,0,0 - 4,3,3,1 - perc.(2) - org. - d.-b.   40:00 Shawnee.
—— SERENADE FOR 14 STRINGS (IN 3 MOVTS.)
str.   20:40 Composer.

BEVERSDORF, S. Thomas
—— CONCERTO FOR TWO PIANOS AND ORCH., OP. 14-A (1951)
    *3,2,*3,2 - 2,2,2,0 - timp. - 2 pf. - str.   18:00 Composer.
—— CONCERTO GROSSO, OP. 8 (FOR OBOE AND CHAMBER
    ORCH.) (1948)
    1. Adagio; 2. Allegro; 3. Largo; 4. Allegro
    1,2,1,1 - 1,1,1,0 - timp. - hp. - str.   15:00 Composer.
—— DANFORTH CONCERTO, OP. 27 (CONCERTO FOR VIOLIN
    AND ORCH.) (1959)
    1. Allegro Moderato; 2. Allegretto
    *3,2,3,*3 - 4,2,1,0 - timp.,perc.(3),bells - hp. - str.
                        28:00 Composer.
—— ESSAY ON MASS PRODUCTION, OP. 3 (ESSAY FOR ORCH.)
    (1945)
    *3,*3,*3,*3 - 4,3,3,1 - timp.,perc. - str.   12:00 Fleisher.
—— GENERATION WITH THE TORCH, OP. 34 (AN OVERTURE
    FOR YOUTH) (1965)
    *3,2,*3,2 - 4,3,3,1 - timp.,perc. - str.   Composer.
—— MEXICAN PORTRAIT, OP. 7 (1947) (IN 3 MOVTS.)
    *3,2(2nd alt. with Eng. hn.),*3,*3 - 4,3,3,1 -
    timp.,perc.(5),mar.,xyl. - hp. - str.   7:00 Fleisher.
—— NEW FRONTIERS, OP. 17 (1953)
    *3,*3,*3,*3 - 4,3,3,1 - timp.,perc.(3) - str.   12:00 Composer.
—— ODE, OP. 15 (1952)
    *3,*3,*3,*3 - 4,3,3,1 - timp.,perc.(2) - hp. - str.   12:00 Fleisher.
—— REFLECTIONS, OP. 5 (1947-1950)
    2(2nd alt. with picc.),2,2,2 - 2,2,2,0 - timp. - hp. - str.
                        7:00 Fleisher.
—— THE ROCK, OP. 26 (ORATORIO) (FOR BASS, MIXED
    CHORUS, MEN'S CHORUS AND ORCH.) (Text: T. S. Eliot
    (1958)
    0,0,0,0 - 0,4,4,0 - org. - str.   28:00 Composer.
—— SERENADE, OP. 22 (1956)
    2(2nd alt. with picc.),2,2,2 - 2,0,0,0 - perc.(1) - hp. - str.
                        8:00 Composer.
—— SUITE FOR CLARINET, CELLO AND STRINGS, OP. 6-B
    (SUITE IN BAROQUE STYLE) (1949)
    cl. - pf. - str.   12:00 Composer.
—— SYMPHONY NO. 1, OP. 4 (1946) (IN 4 MOVTS.)
    *3,2,*3,*3 - 4,3,3,1 - timp.,perc.(3) - str.   21:00 Fleisher.
—— SYMPHONY NO. 2, OP. 10 (1950)
    1. Grave maestoso; 2. Andante cantabile; 3. Vivace; 4. Adagio
    *3,*3,*3,*3 - 4,3,3,1 - timp.,perc.(2) - hp. - pf. - str.
                        28:45 Composer.
—— SYMPHONY NO. 3, OP. 18-B (1954) (IN 4 MOVTS.)
    *3,*3(Eng.hn. alt. with alto sax.),*3,*3 - 4,3,3,1 -
    timp.,perc.(4),bells,xyl. - str.   23:00 Composer.
—— SYMPHONY NO. 4, OP. 29 (1960)
    1. Lento; 2. Rondo; 3. Adagio; 4. Passacaglia (Andante maestoso)
    *3,2,2,2 - 4,3,3,1 - timp.,perc.(4),bells,cel.,xyl. - hp. - str.
                        38:00 Composer.
—— VARIATIONS FOR ORCHESTRA, OP. 31 (THRENODY: THE
    FUNERAL OF YOUTH) (1963)
    *3,2,2,1 alto sax.,0 - 4,3,3,1 - timp.,perc.(4),bells,glock.,xyl. - pf. -
    str.   15:00 Composer.

BEYDTS, Louis
—— A TRAVERS PARIS (6 IMAGES SYMPHONIQUES)
    1,1,1,alto sax.,1 - 1,1,0,0 - perc.,cel. - pf. - str.   15:00 Salabert.
—— CINQ CHANTS D'ORIENT (FOR VOICE AND ORCH.)
                        Salabert.
—— HUE (MORCEAU DE GENRE)
    1,1,1,1 - 1,1,1,0 - perc. - pf. - str.   3:30 Salabert.
—— IL NE FAUT JURER DE RIEN (SUITE) (IN 2 MOVTS.)
    2,2,*3sax.(ad lib.),2 - 3,2,2,0 - timp.,perc. - hp. - str.   14:00 EV.
—— LE VOYAGE DE TCHANG-LI
    1,1,0,1 - 0,0,0,0 - perc.,cel. - cemb. - pf. - str.   Salabert.

BEYER, Frank-Michael
—— CONCERTO FOR FLUTE AND STRINGS (1964)
    fl. - str.   14:00 G. Schirmer.
—— CONCERTO FOR ORCHESTRA (IN 3 MOVTS.)
    2,2,2,2 - 2,2,2,0 - timp. - str.   15:00 Sirius.
—— ODE FOR ORCHESTRA
    *4,*3,3,3 - 4,3,3,1 - timp.,perc. - hp. - str.   18:00 Sirius.
—— RICERCARE NO. 1
    2,0,3,0 - 0,0,0,0 - hp. - str.   11:00 Sirius.
—— SUITE FOR SMALL ORCHESTRA
    2,2,0,2 - 2,0,0,0 - str.   10:00 Sirius.

BEYERMAN-WALRAVEN, Jeanne
—— CONCERT OVERTURE
    2,2,3,2 - 4,3,3,1 - timp.,perc. - hp. - str.   10:00 Henmar.

—— ORKESTSTUK
    4,3,3,4 - 4,3,4,1 - timp.,perc.,cel. - 2hp. - str.   11:00 Henmar.
—— DE ZIEKE BURR ("THE SICK NEIGHBOR") (FOR ALTO AND
    ORCH.) (1922) (Text: François Pauwels)
    4,3,4,4 - 4,3,3,1 - timp.,perc.,cel.   15:00 Henmar.

BHATIA, Vanraj
—— CONCERTO FOR PIANO AND STRINGS (1955) (IN 1 MOVT.)
    pf. - str.   15:00 Novello.

BIALAS, Günter
—— CHAMBER CONCERTO
    hpsc.(or pf.) - str.(7,3,2,1)   18:00 G. Schirmer.
—— CONCERTO FOR CELLO AND ORCH. (1960)
    *3,2,2,2 - 2,2,2,1 - timp.,perc.(3) - hp. - str.   16:00 G. Schirmer.
—— CONCERTO FOR CLARINET AND CHAMBER ORCH. (1961)
    *1,0,1,1 - 1,1,0,0 - timp.,perc.(3) - hp.(ad lib.) - str.
                        14:00 G. Schirmer.
—— CONCERTO FOR VIOLIN AND ORCH. (1948)
    2(2nd alt. with picc.),2,*3,2 - 4,3,3,1 - timp.,perc.(3) - str.
                        27:00 G. Schirmer.
—— CONCERTO LIRICO (FOR PIANO AND ORCH.)(1967)
    *3,2,2,2 - 4,3,3,1 - timp.,perc.(4) - pf. - str.   18:00 G. Schirmer.
—— FOUR SCENES FROM "HERO AND LEANDER" (FOR
    SOPRANO AND ORCH.)(WITH OPTIONAL ADDITIONAL
    VOICES)(1966)
    *3,2,2,2 - 4,3,3,1 - timp.,perc.(5) - hp. - hpsc. - pf. - str.
                        25:00 G. Schirmer.
—— INDIANISCHE KANTATA (FOR SOLO VOICE, SATB
    CHORUS AND ORCH.)
                        Möseler.
—— INTROITUS - EXODUS (FOR ORGAN AND ORCH.)
    *3,2,2,2(2nd alt. with c.-bn.) - 4,3,3,1 - timp.,perc. - hp. - org. -
    str.   26:00 G. Schirmer.
—— INVOCATIONS (1957)
    *3,2,2,*3 - 4,2,3,0 - timp.,perc.(4) - hp. - pf. - str.
                        21:00 G. Schirmer.
—— JAZZ-PROMENADE (FOR PIANO AND ORCH.)
    *3,2,2,2 - 0,3,2,0 - timp.,perc. - pf. - str.   10:00 Modern.
—— JORINDE AND JORINGEL (A MUSICAL FAIRYTALE, FOR 2
    VOICES AND ORCH.)(1963) (Text by: The Brothers Grimm)
    2,1,1,1 - 0,1,1,0 - perc. - hp. - str.(0,3,2,1)   18:00 G. Schirmer.
—— LIEDER AND BALLADS (AFTER POEMS OF FEDERICO
    GARCIA LORCA)(FOR SOPRANO AND ORCH.)(1957)
    2(2nd alt. with picc.),2(2nd alt. with Eng.hn.),1,1 - 1,2,0,0 -
    timp.,perc.,vibra. - str.   9:00 G. Schirmer.
—— MEYERBEER-PARAPHRASE (1971)
    *3,2,2,2 - 4,3,3,1 - timp.,perc.(4) - hp. - pf. - str.
                        23:00 G. Schirmer.
—— MUSIC FOR ELEVEN STRINGS (1969)
    str.(5,3,2,1)   14:00 G. Schirmer.
—— MUSIC IN TWO MOVEMENTS (FOR HARP AND
    STRINGS)(1966)
    hp. - str.   18:00 G. Schirmer.
—— PARTITA FOR 9 WINDS AND DOUBLE BASS (1963)
    1,2,2,2 - 2,0,0,0 - d.-b.   20:00 G. Schirmer.
—— QUODLIBET (1957)
    1(alt. with picc.),1,1,1 - 0,1,0,0 - timp.,perc.(3) - pf. - str.(4,2,2,1)
                        16:00 G. Schirmer.
—— ROMANZERO (1956)
    *3,2,2,*3 - 4,3,3,1 - timp.,perc.(3) - guit. - hp. - hpsc.(or pf.) - str.
                        19:00 G. Schirmer.
—— SERENADE FOR STRINGS (1956)
    str.   6:00 G. Schirmer.
—— SINFONIA PICCOLA (1960)
    fl.,ob.,cl. - str.   15:00 G. Schirmer.

BIANCHINI, Guido
—— THE BRIDGE OF MARVELS (OPERA) % (Text: Giuseppe
    Adami)
    3,3,3,3 - 4,3,3,1 - timp.,perc.(3),cel. - hp. - pf. - str.   Leeds.

BIBALO, Antonio
—— CONCERTO ALLEGORICO (FOR VIOLIN AND ORCH.)
    2,*3,*3,*3 - 1,0,0,0 - timp.,perc.,vibra. - hp. - str.
                        18:00 G. Schirmer.
—— CONCERTO DA CAMERA FOR PIANO AND STRINGS (1964)
    pf. - str.   27:00 G. Schirmer.
—— CONCERTO DA CAMERA, NO. 2 (FOR VIOLIN,
    HARPSICHORD AND STRING ORCH.)
    hpsc. - str.   26:00 G. Schirmer.
—— CONCERTO NO. 1 FOR PIANO AND ORCH. (1955)
    2,2,3,3 - 4,3,3,1 - timp.,perc. - pf. - str.   40:00 G. Schirmer.

—— CONCERTO NO. 2 FOR PIANO AND ORCH. (1971)
    2(2nd alt. with picc.),2(2nd alt. with Eng.hn.),2,2 - 4,3,3,1 -
    timp.,perc.(3) - pf. - str.   25:00 G. Schirmer.
—— ELEGY FOR A SPACE AGE (ELEGIA PER UN'ERA
    SPAZIALE) (FOR SOPRANO, BARITONE, MIXED CHORUS
    AND ORCH.) (Text: Composer; in Italian)
    4,0,0,0 - 0,4,4,1 - timp.,perc. - hp. - hpsc.(amplified) - pf. -
    str.(24,0,0,8)   20:00 G. Schirmer.
—— FANTASY FOR VIOLIN AND ORCH.
    3,3,3,2 - 0,0,0,0 - timp.,perc. - hp. - str.   16:00 G. Schirmer.
—— FOUR BALKAN DANCES (Reduced Orchestration)
    3,3,3,2 - 0,0,0,0 - timp.,perc. - hp. - str.   7:00 G. Schirmer.
—— FOUR BALKAN DANCES
    2,2,2,2 - 4,2,3,0 - timp.,perc.(4),cel. - hp. - pf. - str.
    9:00 G. Schirmer.
—— MARGARITA INFANTE - SERENADE
    8:00 G. Schirmer.
—— OVERTURE TO "THE SERVANT AND TWO MASTERS" (1968)
    2,2,2,2 - 4,3,2,0 - timp.,perc.(4),cel. - hp. - pf. - str.
    9:00 G. Schirmer.
—— OVERTURE TO "THE SERVANT WITH TWO MASTERS"
    (1968) (Reduced Orchestration)
    *2,2,*2,2 - 0,0,0,0 - timp.,perc. - hp. - str.   8:00 G. Schirmer.
—— PINOCCHIO (BALLET) %
    3,3,3,3 - 4,3,3,1 - timp.,perc.,cel. - hp. - str.   110:00 G. Schirmer.
—— PITTURE ASTRATTE (ABSTRACT PICTURES) (Reduced
    Orchestration)
    *2,*2,*2,*2 - 4,3,3,1 - timp.,perc.,xyl. - hp. - pf. - str.
    17:00 G. Schirmer.
—— PITTURE ASTRATTE (IN 4 MOVTS.)
    3,3,3,3 - 4,3,3,1 - timp.,perc. - guit. - hp. - pf. - str.
    12:00 G. Schirmer.
—— SINFONIA NOTTURNA (IN 1 MOVT.) (1968)
    3,3,3,3 - 4,3,3,1 - timp.,perc.,cel. - hp. - str.   22:00 G. Schirmer.
—— THE SMILE AT THE FOOT OF THE LADDER (OPERA) %
    (Text: Composer after Henry Miller's story)
    3,3,3,3 - 4,3,3,1 - timp.,perc.,cel. - mand. - hp. - pf. - str.
    120:00 G. Schirmer.

BIBER, Heinrich Ignaz Franz von - BLAHNIK, Joel
—— BATTALIA (BATTLE MUSIC) (DEDICATED TO BACCHUS,
    YEAR 1673) (IN 7 MOVTS.)
    hpsc. - str.(6,2,2,1)   Arranger.

BIBER, Heinrich Ignaz Franz von - DEBUSMAN, Emil
—— CONCERTO FOR ORCHESTRA (AFTER THE FAMOUS
    VIOLIN SOLO)
    AmerMusEd.

BIEBL, Franz
—— DIVERTIMENTO
    fl. - tpt. - pf. - str.   H.Voggnrtr.

BIELAWA, Herbert
—— ABSTRACTIONS FOR STRINGS (1965) (IN 2 MOVTS.)
    str.   9:00 Composer.
—— BOATS (SUITE) (FOR STRING ORCH.)
    str.   20:00 Composer.
—— CONCERT PIECE FOR ORCHESTRA (1953)
    Composer.
—— CONCERTO FOR ORGAN, STRINGS AND TIMPANI (1961)
    (IN 1 MOVT.)
    timp. - org. - str.   12:00 Composer.
—— DIVERGENTS FOR ORCHESTRA (1969) (IN 3 MOVTS.)
    3(3rd alt. with picc.),*3,*3,*3 - 4,3,3,1 - timp.,perc. - pf. - str.
    25:00 Shawnee.
—— ESSAY FOR STRING ORCHESTRA (1958)
    Composer.
—— OVERTURE FOR ORCHESTRA (1958)
    Composer.

BIELSKI, Michael E.
—— CONCERTO FOR BASSOON AND CHAMBER ORCH. (1969)
    (IN 3 MOVTS.)
    0,0,0,1 - 0,0,0,0 - timp. - str.   21:00 Composer.
—— ELI (FOR OBOE, CLARINET, VIOLIN AND CHAMBER
    ORCH.) (1970) (IN SIX MOVTS.)
    0,1,1,1 - 1,0,0,0 - timp.,perc.(2),xyl. - str.   13:00 Composer.

BIERSACK, Anton
—— OSTINATO SINFONICO
    1,1,2,2 - 2,2,1,1 - timp.,perc. - str.   15:00 SDMV.

BIGGS, John
—— CONCERTO FOR OBOE AND STRING ORCH. (1958)
    ob. - str.   16:30 Composer.
—— PASSACAGLIA (1964)
    2(2nd alt. with picc.),2,2,2 - 4,2,2,1 - timp.,perc.(3),bells - str.
    9:00 Composer.
—— SYMPHONIC ODE (1971)
    *2,*2,2,2 - 4,3,3,1 - timp.,perc.(2),bells - hp. - str. 5:00 Composer.
—— SYMPHONY NO. 1 (1964)
    2(2nd alt. with picc.),2,2,2 - 4,2,2,1 - timp.,perc.(4),glock.- str.
    27:00 Composer.
—— TRIPLE CONCERTO (FOR BRASSES AND STRING ORCH.)
    (1962)
    0,0,0,0 - 1,1,1,0 - str.   18:00 Composer.

BIGGS, Richard K. - JOSEPH, B.
—— PRELUDE ON THE THEME B-A-C-H
    2,*3,2,2 - 4,3,3,1 - timp. - str.   7:00 Leeds.

BIGOT, Eugene
—— IMPROMTOU (FOR TROMBONE AND ORCH.)
    2,2,2,2 - 2,2,1,0 - timp. - hp. - str.   4:30 Baron.
—— JANUS (VARIATIONS CHORÉOGRAPHIQUES)
    3,3,3,3 - 4,3,3,1 - timp.,perc.(4),cel. - str.   25:00 Presser.
—— QUATRE ESQUISSES (FOR SMALL ORCH.)
    1,1,2,1 - 2,2,1,0 - timp.,perc.(3) - str.   14:00 Presser.

BIJL, Theo van der
—— CONCERTO IN F, FOR FLUTE, VIOLIN, VIOLA, HARP AND
    ORCH.
    Henmar.
—— PRELUDIUM EN FUGA
    2,3,2,2 - 4,2,3,0 - timp. - str.   Henmar.
—— ST. FRANCISCUS' ZONNELIED (FOR TENOR, WOMEN'S
    CHORUS AND ORCH.) (1921)
    2,2,2,2 - 4,2,2,1 - timp. - hp. - org. - str.   10:00 Henmar.

BIJVANCK, Henk
—— CONCERTO FOR PIANO AND ORCH.
    3,3,3,3 - 4,3,3,1 - timp.,perc. - pf. - str.   24:00 Henmar.
—— KING DAVID'S HARP SONG ("HARPZANGEN VAN KONIG
    DAVID") (FOR ALTO OR MEZZO-SOPRANO VOICE AND
    ORCH.) (1950-56) (Text: Vondel)
    2,3,3,3 - 4,3,3,2 - timp.,perc. - 2 hp. - str.   20:00 Henmar.
—— LOURDES SYMPHONY (FOR MIXED CHORUS AND ORCH.)
    (1957)
    3,3,3,3 - 4,4,3,5 - timp.,perc. - hp. - str.   35:00 Henmar.
—— SYMPHONIETTA (1952)
    str.   18:00 Henmar.

BILCHICK, Ruth Coleman
—— FIFTH AVENUE (A SYMPHONIC SUITE) (1932) (IN 5
    MOVTS.)
    20:00 Composer.

BILIK, Jerry H.
—— AMERICAN CIVIL WAR FANTASY
    2(2nd alt. with picc.),2,2,2 - 4,3,3,1 - timp.,perc.(4),cannon (ad
    lib.),bells,glock. - str.   8:00 Southern.
—— ASPECTS OF MAN (FOUR THOUGHTS FOR ORCH.)
    *3,*3,2,2 - 4,3,3,1 - timp.,perc.(5),bells,xyl. - str. 12:00 Composer.
—— CONCERT OVERTURE
    *3,*3,*3,2 - 4,3,3,1 - timp.,perc.(5) - str.   7:00 J.Bilik.
—— EPILOGUES (FOR HORN AND STRING ORCH.)
    1hn. - str.   8:00 Composer.
—— INDEPENDENCE (FOR NARRATOR, SATB CHORUS AND
    ORCHESTRA)
    2(2nd alt. with picc.),2,*3,2 -4,3,3,1 - timp.,perc.,bells - str.
    16:00 J.Bilik.
—— OVERTURE BRILLANTE
    *3,*3,*3,*3 - 4,3,3,1 - timp.,perc.(5),glock.,vibra.,xyl. - hp. - str.
    8:00 Composer.
—— THREE PIECES FOR STRINGS
    str.   14:00 J.Bilik.
—— VARIATIONS ON A COLLEGE SONG
    *3,2,2,2 - 4,3,3,1 - timp.,perc. - str.   7:00 J.Bilik.

BILLINGS, William - MAGANINI, Q.
—— CHESTER (FOR PIANO AND STRINGS)
    pf. - str.   5:00 C. Fischer.

BILOTTI, Anton
—— BALLET FOR PIANO AND STRINGS, OP. 40 (IN 4 MOVTS.)
    pf. - str.   30:00 Composer.
—— CONCERTO NO. 1 FOR PIANO AND ORCH. (IN 4 MOVTS.)
    *3,2,*3,*3 - 4,3,3,1 - timp.,perc. - hp. - pf.   30:00 Composer.
—— CONCERTO NO. 2 FOR PIANO AND ORCH. (IN 4 MOVTS.)
    3,3,3,3 - 4hn. - pf. - str.   28:00 Composer.
—— JOAN OF ARC (SUITE) (IN 4 MOVTS.)
    *3,*3,1 E♭cl.,*3,*3 - 4,3,3,1 - timp.,perc. - str.   29:00 Composer.
—— ROMAN SUITE (FOR STRING ORCH.)
    str.   7:00 Composer.
—— SUITE FOR STRINGS, OP. 16 (ON MUSIC OF LULLY,
DANDRIEU, SCHUBERT AND SCARLATTI) (IN 6 MOVTS.)
    str.   18:00 Arranger.

BINDER, A. W.
—— CONCERTANTE FOR STRING ORCH. (IN 3 MOVTS.)
    str.   15:00 Mills.
—— CONCERTINO FOR STRING ORCH. (IN 3 MOVEMENTS)
    str.   18:00 Mills.
—— DYBBUK SUITE
                        Mills.
—— HORA VEHODAYAH (PRAISE AND DANCE) (CHORAL
BALLET) (WITH SOLO VOICES AND SATB CHORUS) %
    2,2,2,2 - 2,2,2,0 - timp.,perc. - hp. - str.   30:00 IsMuPublns.
—— ISRAELI SUITE (IN 3 MOVTS.)
    2,2,2,2 - 4,2,3,1 - timp.,perc. - str.   15:00 Mills.
—— LAMENT
    *3,2,2,2 - 4,2,3,1 - timp.,perc.(3) - hp. - str.   7:00 Mills.
—— THE LEGEND OF ARI
    2,2,2,2 - 2,2,2,0 - timp.,perc. - hp. - str.   30:00 Law-Gould.
—— NIGHT MUSIC (FOR STRING ORCH.)
    str.   Mills.
—— OVERTURE-FANTASY
    *3,2,2,2 - 4,2,3,1 - timp.,perc. - str.   18:00 Mills.
—— POEM TO FREEDOM
                        Mills.
—— RHAPSODY FOR PIANO AND ORCH. ("KING DAVID")
    *3,2,2,2 - 4,2,3,1 - timp.,perc. - pf. - str.   20:00 Mills.

BINET, Jean
—— L' ÎLE ENCHANTÉE (DEUX SUITES POUR GRAND
ORCHESTRE)
    3,3,3,2 - 4,3,3,1 - timp.,perc.,cel.,glock.,xyl.   33:00 S.U.I.S.A.
—— MUSIQUE DE MAI
    *3,*3,*3,2 - 4,3,3,1 - timp.,perc. - hp. - str.   10:00 S.U.I.S.A.
—— L' OR PERDU (POEM FOR SOPRANO OR TENOR WITH
CHAMBER ORCH.)
    2,2,2,2 - 2,2,0,0 - hp. - str.   11:00 Belw-Mills.
—— SUITE D'AIRS ET DE DANSES POPULAIRES SUISSES
                  10:00 Henn.
—— SUITE GRISONNE (BÜNDNER SUITE) (FOR SMALL ORCH.)
    1,1,2,1 - 2,0,0,0 - str.   11:00 Belw-Mills.
—— THREE PIECES FOR STRING ORCH.
    str.   22:00 Swiss M.L.

BINGHAM, Seth
—— CONCERTO FOR ORGAN AND ORCH, OP. 46 (IN 3
MOVEMENTS)
    2tpt.,2trb. - timp.,perc.(2) - org. - str.   19:00 Gray.
—— CONNECTICUT SUITE, OP. 56 (FOR ORGAN AND STRINGS,
WITH OPTIONAL TRUMPET AND TROMBONE)
    tpt.(ad lib.),trb.(ad lib.) - org. - str.   15:00 Gray.
—— PIONEER AMERICA (SECOND SUITE), OP. 23 (IN 4 MOVTS.)
    2(2nd alt. with picc.),2(2nd alt. with Eng.hn.),*3,2 - 4,4,3,1 -
    timp.,perc.(4) - hp. - str.   15:00 Gray.
—— TAME ANIMAL TUNES, OP. 20
    1(alt. with picc.),1,(alt. with Eng.hn.),1,1 - 1,1,0,0 - timp.,perc. -
    str.   Composer.
—— WILDERNESS STONE (CANTATA) (FOR NARRATOR,
SOLOISTS, CHORUS AND ORCH.)
    *3,2(2nd alt. with Eng.hn.),2,2 - 4,3,3,1 - timp.,perc. - hp. - str.
                  80:00 Gray.

BINKERD, Gordon
—— FIVE TRANSCRIPTIONS FOR STRINGS (On works of John
Redford and Girolamo Frescobaldi)
    str.   18:00 Bo. Hawkes.
—— MOVEMENT FOR ORCHESTRA (1964)
    2,2,2,2 - 2,2,0,0 - timp. - str.   11:00 Bo. Hawkes.

—— A PART OF HEAVEN (2 ROMANCES FOR VIOLIN AND
ORCH.) (1972)
    3(1 alt. with picc.),*3,*3,2 - 2,2,2,0 - timp. - hp. - str.
                  16:00 Bo. Hawkes.
—— SUN SINGER (1951)
    *3,*3,*3,*3 - 4,3,3,1 - timp.,perc.(4),xyl. - hp. - str.
                  10:00 Bo. Hawkes.
—— SYMPHONY NO. 1 (1955) (IN 3 MOVTS.)
    *3,*3,*3,*3 - 4,3,3,1 - timp.,perc.(4),glock.,xyl. - hp. - str.
                  24:00 Bo. Hawkes.
—— SYMPHONY NO. 2 (1957)
    1. Allegro; 2. Adagio
    *3(2nd alt. with alto fl.),*3,*3,*3 - 3,3,3,1 - str.
                  30:00 Bo. Hawkes.
—— SYMPHONY NO. 3 (1959) (IN 1 MOVT.)
    *3,2,2,2 - 3,3,3,1 - timp. - str.   15:00 Bo. Hawkes.
—— THREE CANZONAS FOR BRASS CHOIR
    0,0,0,0 - 3,3,3,1   9:00 Bo. Hawkes.

BIRD, Hubert Charles
—— AN AMERICAN OVERTURE
    *2,1,*2,1 - 4,1,1,1 - timp.,perc.(2) - str.   Composer.

BISTRIYZKY, Zinovi
—— IVRIA SUITE (IN 3 MOVTS.)
    2,2,2,2 - 4,3,3,0 - str.   9:00 Transcon.

BITSCH, Marcel
—— CONCERTINO FOR BASSOON AND ORCH.
    2,*2,*2,2 - 2,2,1,0 - timp.,perc. - hp. - str.   8:15 Baron.
—— CONCERTINO FOR PIANO AND SMALL ORCH.
    1,0,1,0 - 0,1,0,0 - pf. - str.   15:00 Baron.
—— CONCERTO FOR PIANO AND 13 WOODWINDS
    2,1,2,2 - 2,2,*2,0 - pf.   19:00 Baron.
—— CONCERTO FOR STRINGS AND TIMPANI
    timp. - str.   17:00 Baron.
—— CONCERTO NO. 2 FOR PIANO AND ORCH.
    2,2,2,2 - 2,2,2,0 - timp.,perc. - pf. - str.   18:00 Baron.
—— LE CHALUMEAU D'OR (SUITE DE BALLET)
    2,2,2,2 - 2,1,1,0 - timp.,perc.,cel.,glock.,xyl. - hp. - str.
                  17:00 Baron.
—— SINFONIETTA
    3,2,2,2 - 2,2,0,0 - timp. - str.   19:00 Baron.
—— SIX SKETCHES
    2,*2,2,2 - 2,1,1,0 - timp.,perc.,cel.,glock.,xyl. - hp. - str.
                  11:00 Baron.

BIZET, Georges
—— CARMEN (4-ACT OPERA) % (Eng. Text: Ruth and Thomas
Martin)
                  G. Schirmer.
—— CARMEN (4-ACT OPERA) % (Engl. Text: John Gutman)
                  G. Schirmer.
—— DJAMILEH (1-ACT OPERA) % (Original French Text: Louis
Gallet; Engl. Text by Jess Perlman)
                  Henmar.
—— LE DOCTEUR MIRACLE (OPÉRA-BOUFFE IN 1 ACT) % (Text:
Available in 3 languages) (Original Text: L. Halevy and L. Battu)
    1(alt with picc.),1,2,1 - 3,2,1,0 - perc.,bells - str. 60:00 Eds. Fran.
Also
    On-stage ensemble: 0,0,1,0 - 0,0,1,0 - perc.(3)
—— JEUX D'ENFANTS (SUITE) (IN 5 MOVTS.)
    2,2,2,2 - 2,2,3,0 - timp.,perc. - str.   9:00 Bo. Hawkes.

BIZET, Georges - BESLY, Maurice
—— CARMEN (CONCERT VERSION, FOR CHORUS AND ORCH.)
    2,2,2,2 - 2,2,3,0 - timp.,perc. - hp. (or pf.) - str.
                  30:00 Bo. Hawkes.

BIZET, Georges - DOUGLAS, R.
—— JEUX D'ENFANTS: SUITE NO. 2
    3,2,2,2 - 4,2,3,1 - timp.,perc. - hp. - str.   8:00 Bo. Hawkes.

BIZET, Georges - FINCK, Herman
—— L' ARLESIENNE SUITE NO. 1
                  14:30 Bo. Hawkes.
—— L' ARLESIENNE SUITE NO. 2
                  17:00 Bo. Hawkes.

BIZET, Georges - LEBOUCHER, M.
—— LES CHANTS DU RHIN (CYCLE OF 6 SONGS)
    2,2,2,2 - 2,0,0,0 - timp. - str.   19:00 Presser.

BIZET, Georges - REIBOLD, Bruno
—— OVERTURE TO "THE PEARL FISHERS"
Fox.

BIZET, Georges - ROBERTS, Charles J.
—— CARMEN (SUITES NOS. 1 AND 2)
C. Fischer.

BIZET, Georges - WAXMAN, Franz
—— CARMEN FANTASIE (FOR VIOLIN AND ORCH.)
2(2nd alt. with picc.),2,2,2 - 4,2,3,0 - timp.,perc.(3) - hp. - str.
9:15 Fidelio.

BIZET, Georges - WEINGARTNER
—— VARIATIONS CHROMATIQUES
2,2,2,2 - 4,2,3,0 - timp.,perc. - hp. - str.
12:00 Henmar.

BIZET, Georges - WILSON, Paul
—— L' ARLESIENNE (SUITES NOS. 1 AND 2)
C. Fischer.

BIZET, Jean
—— LES CHANTS DE LA NUIT
2 cl. - hp. - str.
20:35 Presser.
—— CONCERT FOR ONDES-MARTENOT AND STRINGS
Ondes-martenot - str.
22:00 Presser.
—— CONCERTO NO. 2 ("DA CAMERA") FOR PIANO AND
STRINGS
pf. - str.
Presser.

BJELINSKI, Bruno
—— MEDITERRANEAN SINFONIETTA
Hans Gerig.

BJERNO, Erling D.
—— CHRISTMAS ORATORIO (I HINE DAGE)
K.O.D.A.
—— CIRCULUS VITAE (ORATORIO)
K.O.D.A.
—— COLLAGE CHROMATIC, OP. 109
8:00 K.O.D.A.
—— COLLAGE FOR FLUTE AND ORCH.
K.O.D.A.
—— FORVANDLINGENS TIME (ORATORIO)
K.O.D.A.
—— FRESCOES, OP. 98
26:00 K.O.D.A.
—— GENESIS (ORATORIO)
K.O.D.A.
—— ISHTAR (OPERA) %
K.O.D.A.
—— KONGENS KAMMER (ORATORIO)
K.O.D.A.
—— THE MAN AND THE WOMEN (OPERA) %
K.O.D.A.
—— PASSACAGLIA, OP. 97
ob. - hpsc. - str.
9:00 K.O.D.A.
—— THE SEVEN DAYS, OP. 94 (PASSION)
75:00 K.O.D.A.
—— SISYFOS, OP. 87
12:00 K.O.D.A.
—— SPIL ORD SPILD (OPERA) %
K.O.D.A.
—— SPOON RIVER (OPERA) % (Text in Danish or English)
K.O.D.A.
—— SYMPHONY NO. 1
25:00 K.O.D.A.
—— SYMPHONY NO. 2
25:00 K.O.D.A.
—— SYMPHONY NO. 3
25:00 K.O.D.A.
—— SYMPHONY NO. 4, OP. 84
25:00 K.O.D.A.
—— SYMPOSION
7:00 K.O.D.A.

BJERRE, Jens
—— KAMELIADAMEN (BALLET) (1958) %
25:00 K.O.D.A.
—— MADRIGAL CON VARIAZIONI (1948)
15:00 K.O.D.A.
—— OUVERTURE PARISIENNE (1949)
8:00 K.O.D.A.

—— THE WHITE SUPPER (BALLET) % (1964)
22:00 K.O.D.A.

BJORKANDER, Nils
—— CONCERT FANTASIE (FOR PIANO AND ORCH.)
2,2,2,2 - 3,2,2,0 - timp.,perc. - pf. - str.
20:00 S.T.I.M.

BJORKANDER, Nils - HENNEBERG, A.
—— I HEMMARÖ BY (SUITE FOR ORCH.) (IN 4 MOVTS.)
2,2,2,2 - 2,2,2,0 - timp. - hp. - str.
18:00 S.T.I.M.

BJORKANDER, Nils - MANN, T.
—— POPULARSVIT (IN 4 MOVTS.)
1,1,1,1 - 2,2,0,0 - timp. - str.
14:00 S.T.I.M.
—— SKÄRGÅRDSSKISSER (SUITE)
2,2,2,2 - 2,0,0,0 - timp.,perc. - hp. - str.
9:00 Nordiska.

BJORKANDER, Nils - SKOLD, S.
—— LITEN SVIT (LITTLE SUITE) (IN 3 MOVTS.)
1,1,2,1 - 2,2,1,0 - timp. - str.
10:00 S.T.I.M.

BJÖRKLUND, Steffan
—— PENTATONICS (1970)
1,*1,1,0 - 1,1,0,0 - str.
15:00 Fleisher.

BJÖRKMAN, Rune
—— CONCERTINO FOR CLARINET AND ORCH. (1970)
2,2,3,2 - 2,2,2,0 - timp. - str.
7:00 Fleisher.
—— CONCERTO FOR PIANO AND ORCH. (1972)
2,2,2,2 - 2,2,3,0 - timp. - pf. - str.
20:00 Fleisher.
—— NOCTURNE (FOR TRUMPET AND ORCH.) (1974)
1,1,2,1 - 1,1,0,0 - pf. - str.
4:00 Fleisher.
—— RAPSODISK RESA (1972)
2,2,2,2 - 2,3,2,0 - timp.,perc. - guit. - pf. - str.
10:00 Fleisher.

BJÖRLIN, Ulf
—— EPITAPH FOR LARS GÖRLING (1967)
4,2,3,3 - 4,4,3,1 - timp.,perc. - pf. - str.
10:00 Fleisher.
—— MANDALA I (1974)
1,1,1,1 - 4,0,0,0 - timp.,perc.(3) - hp. - str.(2,1,1,0)
16:00 Fleisher.

BJORNSSON, Arni
—— SUITE FOR STRINGS
str.
Islandia.

BLACK, Stanley
—— OVERTURE TO A COSTUME COMEDY
4:00 Bo. Hawkes.

BLACKBURN, Maurice
—— CONCERTINO IN C MAJOR (FOR PIANO, WOODWIND
AND BRASS) (1948) (IN 3 MOVTS.)
*2,2,2,2 - 2,2,2,0 - pf.
19:40 CanMusCtr.
—— OVERTURE FOR A PUPPET SHOW
3:15 C.A.P.A.C.
—— PETITES RUES DE VIEUX QUEBEC
8:00 C.A.P.A.C.
—— SUITE FOR STRINGS (1960) (IN 5 MOVTS.)
str.
16:00 CanMusCtr.
—— SYMPHONY (IN 1 MOVT.)
15:00 C.A.P.A.C.

BLACKWOOD, Easley, Jr.
—— CHAMBER SYMPHONY FOR 14 WIND INSTRUMENTS, OP. 2
1. Sonata; 2. Romanza; 3. Toccata
2,2,3,3 - 4,0,0,0
17:00 EV.
—— CONCERTO FOR CLARINET AND ORCH., OP. 13 (IN 3
MOVTS.)
4,4,0,2 - 3,3,3,0 - timp. - str.
15:00 G. Schirmer.
—— CONCERTO FOR FLUTE AND STRINGS
fl. - str.
15:00 G. Schirmer.
—— CONCERTO FOR OBOE AND STRINGS, OP. 19 (1966) (IN 3
MOVTS.)
ob. - str.
13:00 G. Schirmer.
—— CONCERTO FOR PIANO AND ORCH.
*3,0,*3,*3 - 3,2,2,0 - timp.,perc. - pf. - str.
23:00 G. Schirmer.
—— CONCERTO FOR VIOLIN AND CHAMBER ORCH.
2 ob. - 2 hn. - str.
15:00 G. Schirmer.
—— SYMPHONIC FANTASY, OP. 17
3,3,3,3 - 4,3,3,1 - timp.,perc. - str.
10:30 G. Schirmer.
—— SYMPHONY NO. 1, OP. 3
4,*3,4,4 - 6,4,3,1 - timp.,perc.,cel. - str.
30:00 EV.

—— SYMPHONY NO. 2, OP. 9
    3,3,3,3 - 4,4,3,1 - timp.,perc. - hp. - str.   24:00 G. Schirmer.
—— SYMPHONY NO. 3, OP. 14 (FOR SMALL ORCH.) (IN 3 MOVTS.)
    2(2nd alt. with picc.),1,2(2nd. alt. with b.-cl.),1, - 2,0,0,0 - str.
                                                         14:30 G. Schirmer.
—— UN VOYAGE À CYTHÈRE, OP. 20 (FOR SOPRANO AND 10 INSTRUMENTS)
    2,1,2,1 - 1,1,1,0 - 1 d.-b.   14:00 G. Schirmer.

BLAINVILLE, C. - BOULAY, L.
—— SYMPHONY NO. 2 (IN 3 MOVTS.)
    hpsc. - str.   9:00 Eds. Fran.

BLAIR, H.
—— ADORAMUS TE (PRELUDE FOR ORCH.)
    2,2,2,3 - 4,2,3,1 - timp.,perc. - hp. - org. - str.   7:00 Novello.
    or:
    2 hn.,2 tpt.,3 trb. - timp. - org. - str.

BLAKE, David
—— THE BONES OF CHUANG TZU
    1(alt. with picc.),1,2,1 - 1,0,0,0 - perc.,cel. - hp. - pf. - str.
                                                         17:00 Novello.
—— CHAMBER SYMPHONY , OP. 7 (1966)
    1(alt.with picc.),1(alt. with Eng.hn.),1,1 - 2,1,0,0 - perc. - str.
                                                         25:00 Novello.
—— METAMORPHOSES
    3,3,3,3- 4,3,3,1 - timp.,perc.,cel. - hp.   22:00 Novello.

BLAKER, Charles R.
—— FUGUE FOR ORCHESTRA (1966)
    2(2nd alt. with picc.),2,2,2 - 4,3,3,1 - timp.,perc.(2),glock. - str.
                                                         5:00 Composer.

BLANCAFORT, Manuel
—— MATI DE FESTA A PUIG-GRACIOS
    2,2,2,2 - 4,2,2,0 - timp.,perc.,cel. - hp. - str.   14:00 Salabert.

BLANCHARD, William G.
—— ENVOY (FOR CHORUS AND ORCH.)
    2,2,3,2 - 4,3,3,1 - timp.,perc.(3) - str.   7:30 Composer.

BLANK, Allen
—— SIX MINIATURES AND A FANTASIA
    3,3,3,3 - 4,3,3,1 - timp.,perc.,cel. - hp. - str.   11:30 C. Fischer.

BLATNÝ, Pavel
—— FOR SYNTHETIC ORCHESTRA (A work for large orch.)
                                                         5:08 Modern.
—— HALEKACKA (ANSWER TO ANSWER)
    1(alt. with picc.),0,1,5 sax.(2 alto, 2 ten., 1 bar.),0 - 0,4,4,0 - pf. - d.-b.
                                                         5:45 Modern.
—— SEHNSUCHT
                                                         8:06 Modern.
—— SONG FOR WALDHORN AND ORCH.
                                                         4:29 Modern.
—— TEN MINUTES AND THIRTY SECONDS
    2(2nd alt. with picc.),2,2,2 - 4,2,1,1 - timp.,perc. - hp. - pf. - str.
                                                         10:30 Modern.

BLEZARD, William
—— SUITE FOR FLUTE AND STRINGS
    fl. - str.   10:00 Novello.

BLICKHAN, Charles T.
—— VARIATIONS-PERMUTATIONS (PLASH AND SILENT ROAR) (1974)
    1,1,1,1 - 1,1,1,0 - perc.(3),bells,vibra.,xyl. - pf.   15:00 Seesaw.

BLISS, Arthur
—— ADAM ZERO (SUITE)
    3,3,2,2 - 4,2,3,1 - timp.,perc.,cel.,glock. - hp. - str.   22:30 Novello.
—— BARAZA (FOR PIANO AND ORCH.)
    2,1,2,2 - 2,2,3,0 - timp.,perc. - pf. - str.   8:00 Novello.
—— THE BEATITUDES (CANTATA) (FOR SOPRANO, TENOR, CHORUS, ORGAN AND ORCH.) (Text: John Ponne and Others)
                                                         Novello.
—— CHECKMATE (FIVE DANCES FROM THE BALLET)
    2,2,2,2 - 4,2,3,0 - timp.,perc.,glock. - hp. - str.   20:00 Novello.
—— A COLOR SYMPHONY (REVISED EDITION) (IN 4 MOVTS.)
    3,3,3,3 - 4,3,3,1 - timp.,perc. - hp. - str.   30:00 Bo. Hawkes.

—— CONCERTO FOR CELLO AND ORCH.
    2(2nd alt. with picc.),1,2,2 - 2,2,0,0 - timp.,cel. - hp. - str.
                                                         26:00 Novello.
—— CONCERTO FOR PIANO AND ORCH.
    2,2,2,2 - 4,2,3,0 - timp. - pf. - str.   30:00 Novello.
—— CONCERTO FOR TWO PIANOS AND ORCH.
    3,3,2,2 - 4,3,3,1 - timp.,perc. - 2pf. - str.   12:00 Oxford.
—— CONCERTO FOR VIOLIN AND ORCH.
                                                         39:00 Novello.
—— CONQUEST OF THE AIR (SUITE FROM THE FILM) (IN 6 MOVTS.)
    2,2,2,2 - 4,2,3,1 - timp.,perc. - hp. - str.   13:00 Bo. Hawkes.
—— DISCOURSE FOR ORCH.
                                                         Novello.
—— INTRODUCTION AND ALLEGRO
    3,3,3,3 - 4,3,3,1 - timp.,perc.,glock.,xyl. - hp. - str.
                                                         12:00 Bo. Hawkes.
—— MEDITATIONS ON A THEME BY JOHN BLOW
                                                         Novello.
—— MÊLÉE FANTASQUE
    3,3,3,3 - 4,3,3,1 - timp.,perc.,glock.,xyl. - str.   G. Schirmer.
—— MIRACLE IN THE GORBALS (SUITE)
    3,3,3,2 - 4,2,3,0 - timp.,perc.,glock. - hp. - str.   20:00 Novello.
—— MUSIC FOR STRINGS
    str.   23:00 Novello.
—— OVERTURE "EDINBURGH"
                                                         Novello.
—— SERENADE FOR BARITONE AND ORCH. (4 SONGS)
    2,1,2,2 - 2,2,1,0 - timp.,perc.,glock. - hp. - str.   24:00 Oxford.
—— THINGS TO COME (SUITE FROM THE FILM)
    2,3,2,2 - 4,3,3,1 - timp.,perc. - 2hp. - str.   17:00 Novello.
—— THE TOWERS (BALLET) %
    2(2nd alt. with picc.),2,2,2 - 2,2,1,0 - timp.,perc.,cel.,glock. - pf. - str.   35:00 Novello.
—— TWO CONTRASTS FOR STRING ORCH. (FROM THE STRING QUARTET NO. 2)
    str.   Novello.
—— VARIATIONS
    3(2nd and 3rd alt. with picc.),3,3,3 - 4,3,3,1 - timp.,perc.,cel.,glock.,vibra. - hp. - str.   35:00 Novello.
—— THE WOMEN OF YEUH (5 SONGS)
    1,1,1,1 - 0,0,0,0 - perc.,glock. - str.   G. Schirmer.

BLITZSTEIN, Marc
—— AIRBORNE, SYMPHONY (FOR NARRATOR, TENOR, BARRITONE, MALE CHORUS AND ORCH.) (IN 3 MOVTS.)
    3(3rd alt. with picc.),3(3rd alt. with Eng.hn.)4(3rd alt. with E♭cl.,4th alt. with b.-cl.),*3 - 4,3,3,1 - timp.,perc.(5),cel.,glock.,xyl. - hp. - pf. - str.   52:00 Chappell.
—— THE CRADLE WILL ROCK (OPERA) %
                                                         Chappell.
—— FREEDOM MORNING (SYMPHONIC POEM, DEDICATED TO THE U.S. ARMY NEGRO TROOPS)
    3(3rd alt.with picc.),3(3rd alt. with Eng.hn.),3(3rd alt. with b.-cl.),*3 - 4,3,3,1 - timp.,perc.(3),glock.,xyl. - hp. - pf. - str.   12:00 Composer.
—— GODS (FOR MEZZO-SOPRANO AND STRINGS)
    str.   8:00 Composer.
—— THE GUESTS (BALLET SUITE)
                                                         Chappell.
—— LEAR - A STUDY
    3,3,4,3 - 4,5,3,1 - timp.,perc. - hp. - str.   Chappell.
—— MOVIE MUSIC (SUITE)
    1(alt. with picc.),1(alt. with Eng.hn.),2(2nd alt. with ten.sax.),1 - 0,2,1,0 - perc. - pf.(alt. with acc.) - str.   30:00 Chappell.
—— REGINA (OPERA) %
                                                         Chappell.
—— SUITE FROM THE FILM "NATIVE LAND" (IN 8 MOVTS.)
    1(alt. with picc.),1(alt. with Eng.hn.),2(2nd alt. with ten.sax.),1 - 0,2,1,0 - timp.,perc.,cel.,xyl. - pf. - str.   20:00 Composer.
—— THIS IS THE GARDEN (A CANTATA FOR N.Y.) (FOR CHORUS AND ORCH.)
    2(2nd alt. with picc.),2(2nd alt. with Eng. hn.),2(2nd alt. with E♭ cl.),2 - 2,2,1,0 - pf.(alt. with harm.) - str.   Chappell.

BLOCH, André J.
—— CONCERTO FOR PIANO AND ORCH.
                                                         S.A.C.E.M.
—— GUIGNOL (BALLET FROM THE OPÉRA BOUFFE) (1949) %
    2,1,2,1 - 2,2,1,0 - timp. - hp. - str.   10:30 Presser.

BLOCH, Ernest

—— AMERICA (EPIC RHAPSODY) (IN 3 MOVTS.)
3(3rd alt. with picc.),*3,*3,*3 - 4-6,3,3,1 - timp.,perc.(5) - 2hp. - org.(ad lib.) - str.   45:00 Western M.L.

—— AVODATH HAKODESH (SACRED SERVICE) (FOR BARITONE, CHORUS AND ORCH.)
*3,*3,*3,*3 - 4,3,3,0 - timp.,perc.(5) - 2hp. - str.   49:00 Broude.

—— BAAL SHEM (THREE PICTURES OF CHASSIDIC LIFE) (FOR VIOLIN AND ORCH.)
2(1 alt. with picc.),2,2,2 - 4,3,0,0 - timp.,perc.(3) - hp. - str.   12:00 C. Fischer.

—— CONCERTINO FOR FLUTE, VIOLA AND ORCH.
*3,2,2,2 - 4,3,3,1 - timp.,perc. - str.   8:00 G. Schirmer.

—— CONCERTO FOR VIOLIN AND ORCH.
2(1 alt. with picc.),*3,*3,*3 - 4,3,3,1 - timp.,perc.(4),cel. - hp. - str.   35:00 Bo. Hawkes.

—— CONCERTO GROSSO (FOR STRING ORCH. AND PIANO OBBLIGATO) (IN 4 MOVTS.)
pf. - str.   22:30 Birchard.

—— CONCERTO GROSSO NO. 2 (FOR STRING ORCH. AND STRING QUARTET CONCERTANTE) (IN 3 MOVEMENTS)
str.   18:00 G. Schirmer.

—— CONCERTO SYMPHONIQUE (FOR PIANO AND ORCH.) (IN 3 MOVEMENTS)
3(3rd alt. with picc.),*3,*3,*3 - 4,3,3,1 - timp.,perc.(3),cel. - pf. - str.   38:00 Bo. Hawkes.

—— EVOCATIONS (SYMPHONIC SUITE) (IN 3 MOVTS.)
3(3rd alt. with picc.),2(2nd alt. with Eng.hn.),2,2 - 4,2,3,1 - timp.,perc.(5),cel.,glock. - hp. - pf. - str.   17:00 G. Schirmer.

—— FOUR EPISODES FOR CHAMBER ORCH.
1,1,1,1 - hn. - pf. - str.   14:00 Western.

—— HELVETIA, THE LAND OF MOUNTAINS, AND ITS PEOPLE (A SYMPHONIC FRESCO)
2picc.,4,*4,*4,*4 - 6,4,3,1 - timp.,perc.(6) - 2hp. - str.   23:00 AmerMusEd.

—— HIVER-PRINTEMPS (WINTER-SPRING) (TWO POEMS)
*3,*3,2,2 - 4,3,3,1 - timp.,perc.(1) - hp. - str.   13:00 G. Schirmer.

—— IN MEMORIAM
2,2,2,2 -3,0,0,0 - timp. - str.   4:00 Broude.

—— IN THE NIGHT (A LOVE POEM)
*4,*3,*3,*3 - 4,3,3,1 - timp.,perc. - hp. - str.   6:00 G. Schirmer.

—— ISRAEL SYMPHONY (FOR TWO SOPRANOS, TWO ALTOS, BASS AND ORCH.)
2(alt. with 2picc.),*4,*4,*4 - 6,4,3,1 - timp.,perc.(5) - 2hp. - str.   30:00 G. Schirmer.

—— JONAH (FOR SOPRANO, TENOR, BASS AND ORCH.)
G. Schirmer.

—— MACBETH: 2 SYMPHONIC INTERLUDES FROM THE OPERA
3,3,3,3 - 4,3,3,1 - timp.,perc.(3) - hp. - str.   11:30 Leeds.

—— MACBETH (3-ACT OPERA, AFTER SHAKESPEARE) %
3,3,3,4 - 4,3,3,1 - timp.,perc. - hp. - str.   Leeds.

—— POEMES D' AUTOMNE (FOR MEZZO-SOPRANO AND ORCH.) (IN 4 MOVTS.)
*4,*3,2,2 - 4,2,3,1 - timp.,cel. - hp. - str.   20:30 G. Schirmer.

—— POEMS OF THE SEA (IN 3 MOVTS.)
3(1 alt. with picc.),*3,*3,*3 - 4,3,3,1 - timp.,perc.(4-5) - hp. - str.   12:00 G. Schirmer.

—— PRELUDE AND TWO PSALMS (FOR SOPRANO AND ORCH.)
3,3,3,2 - 6,2,3,1 - timp.,cel. - 2 hp. - str.   12:00 G. Schirmer.

—— PROCLAMATION (FOR TRUMPET AND ORCH.)
2,2,2,2 - 4,3,0,0 - timp.,perc. - str.   7:00 Broude.

—— PSALM 137 ("BY THE WATERS OF BABYLON")
G. Schirmer.

—— PSALM 22 (FOR BARITONE AND ORCH.)
4(3rd and 4th alt. with 2 picc.),*3,*3(3rd alt. with E♭cl.),*4 - 6,4,3,1 - timp.,perc.(3),cel. - 2 hp. - str.   7:00 G. Schirmer.

—— QUARTET NO. 5 FOR STRINGS (ARR. FOR STRING ORCH.)
str.   30:30 Broude.

—— QUINTET NO. 2 FOR PIANO AND STRINGS (ARR. FOR STRING ORCH.)
pf. - str.   19:30 Broude.

—— SCHELOMO (HEBRAIC RHAPSODY) (FOR CELLO AND ORCH.)
3(3rd alt. with picc.),*3,*3,*3 - 4,3,3,1 - timp.,perc.(4-5),cel. - 2hp. - str.   20:00 G. Schirmer.

—— SCHERZO FANTASQUE (FOR PIANO AND ORCH.)
*3,*3,*3,*3 - 4,3,3,1 - timp.,perc.(3) - hp. - pf. - str.   9:00 G. Schirmer.

—— SINFONIA BREVE (SHORT SYMPHONY)
1. Moderato - Allegro - Calmo; 2. Andante; 3. Allegro molto; 4. Allegro deciso - Calmo
*3,*3,*3,*3 - 4,3,3,1 - timp.,perc.(2-3),cel. - hp. - str.   18:00 G. Schirmer.

—— SUITE FOR VIOLA AND ORCH. (IN 4 MOVEMENTS)
*3,*3,*3,*3 - 4,3,3,1 - timp.,perc.(5) - 2hp. - str.   25:00 G. Schirmer.

—— SUITE HÉBRAÏQUE (FOR VIOLA OR VIOLIN AND ORCH.)
2,2,2,2 - 4,3,0,0 - timp.,perc. - hp. - str.   12:00 G. Schirmer.

—— SUITE MODALE (1956)
fl. - str.   12:00 Broude.

—— SUITE SYMPHONIQUE (IN 3 MOVTS.)
3,3,3,3 - 4,3,3,1 - timp.,perc. - str.   20:00 Bo. Hawkes.

—— SYMPHONY IN E♭
1. Tranquillo - Allegro deciso - Tranquillo; 2. Allegro (Scherzo); 3. Andante; 4. Allegro - Tranquillo
3(3rd alt. with picc.),*3,*3,*3 - 4,3,3,1 - timp.,perc.(2) - str.   24:00 G. Schirmer.

—— SYMPHONY WITH TROMBONE SOLO
1. Maestoso; 2. Agitato; 3. Allegro deciso - Calmo
*3,*3,*3,*3 - 4,3,3,1 - timp.,perc.(3),cel. - hp. - str.   18:00 Broude.

—— TROIS POEMES JUIFS (THREE JEWISH POEMS)
3(3rd alt. with picc.),*3,2,*3 - 4,3,3,1 - timp.,perc.(5),cel.,glock. - hp. - str.   25:00 G. Schirmer.

—— TWO LAST POEMS ("MAYBE"), FOR FLUTE AND ORCH.
3,*3,2,2 - 4,2,0,0 - timp.,perc. - hp. - str.   13:00 Broude.

—— TWO PSALMS FOR SOPRANO AND ORCH. (PRECEDED BY AN ORCHESTRAL PRELUDE)
4(3rd and 4th alt. with 2picc.),*4,*4,*4 - 6,4,3,1 - timp.,perc.(4),cel. - 2hp. - str.   12:30 G. Schirmer.

—— VOIX DANS LA DÉSERT (VOICE IN THE WILDERNESS) (SYMPHONIC POEM, WITH CELLO OBBLIGATO)
3(3rd alt. with picc.),*3,*3,*3 - 4,3,3,1 - timp.,perc.(4),cel. - 2hp. - str.   25:00 G. Schirmer.

BLOCH, Ernest - TALMI, Yoav

—— PSALM 22 (FOR BARITONE AND ORCH.) (Reduced Orchestration)
2(2nd alt. with picc.),1,1,1 - 1,1,0,0 - timp. - pf. - str.   7:00 G. Schirmer.

BLOCH, Joseph

—— SUITE POETIQUE, OP. 26
2,1,2,2 - 2,1,0,0 - timp. - str.   Bo. Hawkes.

BLOCK, David

—— SYMPHONIC POEM (TALE OF A POGROM)
2-3,2,2,2 - 4,3,3,1 - timp.,perc. - str.   7:00 G. Schirmer.

BLOHM, Arthur

—— LITTLE PARTITA FOR STRINGS
str.   12:00 Bo. Hawkes.

BLOHM, Sven

—— CONCERTPIECE IN A MINOR (FOR PIANO AND ORCH.)
2,2,2,2 - 4,2,3,0 - timp.,perc. - str.   15:00 S.T.I.M.

—— HAVET SJUNGER (TWO PIECES FOR VIOLIN AND ORCH.)
2,0,0,0 - 4,0,0,0 - timp.,perc.(2) - hp. - str.   10:00 S.T.I.M.

—— LITEN GRIPSHOLMS-MUSIQUE (SUITE)
2,2,0,2 - 1,0,0,0 - timp. - str.   10:00 S.T.I.M.

—— LITTLE PARTITA IN F MAJOR (IN 3 MOVTS.)
str.   12:00 Gehrmans.

—— PASSACAGLIA
2,2,2,2 - 4,2,3,1 - timp.,perc. - str.   20:00 Gehrmans.

—— PRELUDE TO ACT 3 OF THE OPERA "KARIN MÅNSDOTTER"
2,2,2,2 - 2,1,0,0 - timp. - hp. - str.   S.T.I.M.

—— SINFONIETTA
2,2,2,2 - 2,1,0,0 - timp. - str.   17:00 S.T.I.M.

—— SUITE FROM THE STORY-BALLET "UGGEL-GUGGEL"
2,2,2,2 - 4,2,3,0 - timp.,perc.(2) - str.   10:00 S.T.I.M.

—— VARIATIONER ÖVER VARMLANDSVISAN
perc.(ad lib.) - str.   24:00 S.T.I.M.

—— VISIONER (SYMPHONIC POEM)
2,2,2,2 - 4,0,0,0 - timp.,perc. - hp. - str.   20:00 S.T.I.M.

BLOMBERG, Erik

—— DIALOGUE BETWEEN PIANO AND ORCH (1969)
2,2,2,2 - 2,2,0,0 - timp.,perc.(2) - pf. - str.   8:00 S.T.I.M.

—— FOUR DRAMATIC SKETCHES (1966)
3,3,3,3 - 4,3,3,1 - timp.(3) - str.   20:00 S.T.I.M.

—— INTERLUDE (FOR "A DREAM PLAY" BY AUGUST STRINDBERG)
str.   12:00 Fleisher.

—— SYMPHONY NO. 3 (ASSOCIATIONSKEDJOR) (1971)
2,2,2,0 - 2,2,2,0 - timp.,perc. - str.   23:00 Fleisher.

—— SYMPHONY NO. 4 (1973)
   3,2,2,3 - 3,3,2,0 - timp.,perc. - hp. - str.   31:00 Fleisher.
—— SYMPHONY NO. 5 (1974)
   3,2,2,3 - 2,3,3,1 - timp.,perc.(3) - pf. - str.   35:00 Fleisher.
—— THREE ORCHESTRAL FRAGMENTS (1968)
   4,2,4,2 - 2,2,2,0 - timp.,perc.(3) - str.   7:00 S.T.I.M.
—— THREE STUDIES IN MELODY (1968)
   3,3,3,2 - 4,4,2,1 - timp.,perc.(4) - str.   21:00 S.T.I.M.
—— VILA I RÖRELSE (1970)
   str.   9:00 Fleisher.

BLOMDAHL, Karl-Birger
—— ADAGIO (FROM "VAKNATTEN")
   1,1,0,1 - 2,0,1,0 - str.   6:00 Nordiska.
—— CONCERT OVERTURE
   2,2,2,3 - 4,3,3,0 - timp.,perc. - str.   6:00 S.T.I.M.
—— CONCERTO FOR VIOLA AND ORCH.
   2,2,0,0 - 2,0,0,0 - str.   22:00 S.T.I.M.
—— CONCERTO FOR VIOLIN AND STRING ORCH.
   str.   16:00 S.T.I.M.
—— CONCERTO GROSSO
   1,0,1,1 - 1,0,0,0 - str.   19:00 Nordiska.
—— PASTORAL SUITE (FOR STRING ORCH.)
   str.   19:00 Gehrmans.
—— PRELUDE AND ALLEGRO (FOR STRING ORCH.)
   str.   Nordiska.
—— SYMFONISKA DANSER (1939)
   2,2,2,2 - 4,3,3,0 - str.   25:00 Fleisher.
—— SYMPHONY NO. 1
   3,2,3,2 - 4,3,3,1 - timp. - str.   26:00 S.T.I.M.
—— SYMPHONY NO. 2
   3,2,3,2 - 4,3,3,1 - str.   21:00 S.T.I.M.
—— THEATRE MUSIC NO. 1 ("VAKNATTEN" SUITE)
   2,2,2,2 - 2,2,1,0 - str.   14:00 S.T.I.M.

BLOOM, Robert
—— REQUIEM FOR OBOE AND STRINGS
   ob. - str.   AmerMusEd.

BLOW, John - HARRISON, Julius
—— VENUS AND ADONIS (SHORT SUITE)
   1,1,1,1 - 0,0,0,0 - pf. - str.   10:00 Galaxy.
   or:
   str.

BLOW, John - LEWIS, Anthony
—— AND I HEARD A GREAT VOICE (FOR SATB CHORUS,
ORGAN AND STRINGS)
   org. - str.   10:00 Galaxy.
—— GOD SPAKE SOMETIMES IN VISION (FOR SATB CHORUS,
ORGAN AND STRINGS)
   org. - str.   15:00 Galaxy.
—— THE LORD IS MY SHEPHERD (FOR SATB CHORUS, ORGAN
AND STRINGS)
   org. - str.   12:00 Galaxy.

BLOW, John - SHAW, H. W.
—— THE WHITEHALL SUITE (FOR STRING ORCH.) (IN 4
MOVTS.)
   str.   Oxford.

BLOW, John - VAN HOESEN, Karl D. - HUNT, Frederick
—— OVERTURE TO "VENUS AND ADONIS"
   2,2,2,2 - 4,2,3,0 - timp. - pf. - str.   C. Fischer.

BLOWER, Maurice
—— THE REALM OF FANCY (FOR WOMEN'S SSA CHORUS AND
STRINGS)
   pf. - str.   15:00 Galaxy.

BLUM, Robert
—— CANTATA (FOR SATB CHORUS AND STRING ORCH.)
   str.   12:00 Modern.
—— FANTASY IN THREE PARTS (FOR CHAMBER ORCH.)
   1,1,1,1 - 0,0,0,0 - str.   16:00 Modern.
—— KONZERT FÜR ORCHESTER
   2,2,2,2 - 3,3,2,1 - timp.,perc. - str.   25:00 S.U.I.S.A.
—— KONZERT FÜR VIOLA UND ORCH.
   2,2,2,*3 - 3,3,3,1 - timp.,perc. - str.   35:00 S.U.I.S.A.
—— LAMENTATIO ANGELORUM (FÜR KLEINES ORCH.)
   1,1,1,0 - 1,0,0,0 - str.   18:00 Baerenrtr.
—— MUSIK ÜBER DREI ALTDEUTSCHE VOLKSLIEDER
   cemb. - str.   20:00 Henmar.

—— OUVERTÜRE ZU EINEM BAROCKEN SPIEL (FÜR KLEINES
ORCHESTER)
   2,2,2,2 - 2,2,0,0 - perc. - str.   8:00 Modern.
—— OUVERTÜRE ZU EINER HEROISCHEN TRAGÖDIE
   2,*3,2,*3 - 3,3,3,1 - timp.,perc. - pf. - str.   10:00 S.U.I.S.A.
—— PARTITA II (FOR VIOLIN, VIOLA, CELLO AND SMALL
ORCH.)
   0,1,1,1 - 0,1,1,0 - str.   14:00 Modern.
—— PARTITA III
   2,2,2,2 - 2,2,1,1 - timp. - str.   22:00 Modern.
—— RHAPSODIC SONGS TO THE SEA (FOR TENOR, SATB
CHORUS AND SMALL ORCH.) (Text: Ines Maggi)
   1,1,1,1 - 1,1,1,0 - timp.,perc. - acc. - pf. - str.   18:00 Modern.
—— RONDO FOR ORCH.
   2,2,2,2 - 2,2,1,1 - timp. - str.   9:00 Modern.
—— SELDWYLA-SINFONIE (FÜR KLEINES ORCHESTER)
   2,2,2,2 - 2,2,0,0 - timp. - str.   25:00 S.U.I.S.A.
—— SINFONIE FÜR 16 STREICHER
   str.   15:00 S.U.I.S.A.
—— SONATE FÜR ORCHESTER UND SOLO-VIOLINCELLO (FOR
7 WINDS, PERCUSSION AND 7 STRINGS)
   24:00 S.U.I.S.A.
—— DER STREITER IN CHRISTO JESU (CANTATA) (FOR
SOPRANO AND CHAMBER ORCH.)
   tpt. - perc. - pf. - str.   20:00 Modern.
—— SYMPHONY NO. 5
   1,2,2,1 - 2,0,0,0 - str.   33:00 S.U.I.S.A.
—— SYMPHONY NO. 6
   3,3,3,3 - 4,3,3,1 - timp., perc. - hp. - str.   35:00 S.U.I.S.A.
—— TROPI E CANZONI (FÜR STREICHORCHESTER)
   str.   14:00 S.U.I.S.A.

BLUMENFELD, Harold
—— AMPHITRYON 4: DRAMATIC SYMPHONY, FROM THE
OPERA (FOR MEZZO-SOPRANO, BARITONE, CHORUS AND
ORCH.)
   2,1,2,1 - 3,2,2,0 - timp.,perc.,cel.,xyl. - hp. - str.   M.C.A. Music.
—— AMPHITRYON 4(3-ACT OPERA, AFTER MOLIÈRE) (1956-62)
(FOR 7 PRINCIPAL ROLES, 10 SUPPORTING ROLES,
CHORUS, DANCERS AND ORCH.) % (Text: Composer)
   2(2nd alt. with picc.)1,2,1(alt. with c.-bn.) - 3,2,2,0 - timp.,perc.(6),
cel., vibra., xyl. - hp. - str.   145:00 MCA Music.
—— CONTRASTS FOR ORCHESTRA (1955)
   2(2nd alt. with picc.),2(2nd alt. with. Eng.hn.),2,*3 - 4,2,3,1 -
timp.,perc.(4),cel.,xyl. - str.   12:00 Composer.
—— ELEGY FOR THE NIGHTINGALE (FOR BARITONE, MIXED
CHORUS AND ORCH.) (1954) (Text: Matthew Arnold)
   *3,*3,*3,*3 - 4,2,3,0 - timp.,perc.(3) - str.   16:00 Composer.
—— LOVESCAPES (1971) (FOR SOPRANO AND ENSEMBLE)
   1,1,1,1 - 1,0,0,0 - str.   12:00 Seesaw.
—— MINIATURE OVERTURE (FROM THE OPERA
"AMPHITRYON 4") (1958)
   *2,1,2,1 - 2,0,0,0 - timp.,perc.,cel.,xyl. - hp.(ad lib.) - str.
   4:30 MCA Music.
—— SYMPHONY AMPHITRYON 4 (4 ORCHESTRAL EXCERPTS
FROM THE OPERA "AMPHITRYON 4") (1963)
   2(2nd alt. with picc.),1,2,1(alt. with c.-bn.) - 3,2,2,0 -
timp.,perc.,cel.,xyl. - hp. - str.   18:00 MCA Music.

BLUMER, Theodor
—— BURLESKE FÜR CELLO UND ORCH.
   2,2,2,2 - 4,2,0,0 - timp.,perc. - hp. - str.   16:00 Sikorski.
—— CAPRICIO FANTASTICO (FÜR FLÖTE UND KLEINES
ORCH.)
   1,1,2,2 - 2,1,0,0 - hp. - str.   22:00 Sikorski.
—— CONCERTO GIOCOSO, OP. 98 (FOR FLUTE AND ORCH.)
   1,2,2,2 - 2,2,0,0 - timp.,perc. - hp.(ad lib.) - str.   17:00 Henmar.
—— DIVERTIMENTO IN VARIATION FORM (FOR SMALL
ORCH.), OP. 73
   2,1,1,1 - 1,0,0,0 - timp.,perc. - hp. - str.   14:00 Henmar.
—— EINE MAINACHT, OP. 88
   2,1,2,1 - 2,2,1,0 - perc. - hp.(ad lib.) - str.   18:00 T & J.
—— MUSIKALISCHE BILDER, OP. 69 (FOR FLUTE AND ORCH.)
(IN 5 MOVTS.)
   1,1,1,1 - 1,0,0,0 - timp.,perc. - hp.(ad lib.) - str.   19:30 Henmar.
—— OVERTURE TO A COMEDY, OP. 75
   *3,2,2,2 - 4,3,3,1 - timp.,perc.(4, incl. 3 on timp.) - hp. - str.
   10:00 Henmar.
—— ROMANTISCHE MUSIKA (FOR PIANO AND ORCH.)
   2,2,2,2 - 4,2,3,1 - timp. - pf. - str.   26:00 F. Colombo.
—— SILHOUETTEN, OP. 24 (FOR STRING ORCH.) (IN 5 MOVTS.)
   str.   20:30 Henmar.

—— SINFONISCHE VARIATIONEN ÜBER EINEN BAUERNTANZ, OP. 83
    3,2,2,2 - 4,3,3,1 - timp.,perc. - str.   15:00 Henmar.
—— VAGABOND (SCHERZO FOR ORCH.)
    2,2,2,2 - 2,2,1,0 - timp.,perc. - str.   5:00 F. Colombo.

BLYTON, Carey
—— THE HOBBIT (AN OVERTURE)(1967)
    2,1,2,1 - 2,2,1,0 - perc.(2) - hp.(ad lib) - pf. - str.   5:00 P.R.S.
—— ON HOLIDAY
    str.   6:30 P.R.S.

BOARDMAN, Earle M.
—— ADAGIO MINIQUE (1962)
    1,0,1,1 - 0,3,3,0 - hp. - str.   4:30 Composer.

BOATWRIGHT, Howard
—— VARIATIONS FOR SMALL ORCH.
    1,1,1,1 - 1,1,1,0 - perc. - str.   12:00 Oxford.

BOCCHERINI, Luigi - BARNES, Clifford P.
—— SYMPHONY IN B-FLAT, OP. 22, NO. 1
    ProArtPubs.

BOCCHERINI, Luigi - BAZELAIRE
—— RONDO FOR CELLO AND STRING ORCH.
    str.   Baron.

BOCCHERINI, Luigi - BONELLI
—— SINFONIA IN B FLAT MAJOR, OP. 1, NO. 6
    0,2,0,1 - 2,0,0,0 - str.   13:00 Henmar.
—— SINFONIA, OP. 1, NO. 8
    2ob.,bn. - 2hn. - str.   Henmar.

BOCCHERINI, Luigi - BRUSSELMANS, M.
—— CONCERTO NO. 2 IN D MAJOR, FOR CELLO AND ORCH.
    2,2,2,2 - 2hn. - str.   12:00 Salabert.

BOCCHERINI, Luigi - CARMIRELLI
—— SINFONIA CONCERTANTE IN C MAJOR (FOR CELLO AND STRINGS)
    str.   9:00 Henmar.

BOCCHERINI, Luigi - CASSADO, Gasper
—— CONCERTO FOR GUITAR AND ORCHESTRA
    A.K.M.

BOCCHERINI, Luigi - GALLINI, Franco
—— CONCERTO IN E FLAT FOR CELLO AND ORCH.
    0,2,0,0 - 2,0,0,0 - str.   18:00 Leeds.
—— SYMPHONY IN D MINOR ("LA CASA DEL DIAVOLO")
    0,2,0,0 - 2,0,0,0 - str.   18:00 Leeds.

BOCCHERINI, Luigi - GENDRON, Maurice
—— CONCERTO NO. 3 IN G
    str.   Galaxy.

BOCCHERINI, Luigi - HOECKNER
—— SINFONIA IN B FLAT MAJOR, OP. 22, NO. 1
    2 ob.(or 2 fl.) - 2 hn. - str.   Henmar.

BOCCHERINI, Luigi - SCHÖNHERR, Max
—— LA MUSICA NOTTURNA DI MADRID (FOR SNARE DRUM AND STRING ORCH.)
    sn.dr. - str.   12:00 Bo. Hawkes.

BOCCHERINI, Luigi - SILVA, Luigi
—— CONCERTO NO. 1 IN D MAJOR, OP. 34 (FOR CELLO AND ORCH.)
    2,2,0,2 - 2,0,0,0 - str.   22:00 Ricordi.
—— CONCERTO NO. 2 IN D, FOR CELLO AND ORCH.
    2,2,0,2 - 2,0,0,0 - str.   18:00 Ricordi.

BOCCHERINI, Luigi - TONI, Alceo
—— SONATA CONCERTANTE FOR CELLO AND ORCH.
    2,2,2,2 - 2,2,0,0 - timp. - str.   15:00 Bo. Hawkes.

BODA, John
—— SINFONIA (1960)
    2(2nd alt. with picc.),2(2nd. atl. with Eng. hn.),2,2 - 4,3,3,1 - timp.,perc. - str.   25:00 AmerMusEd.

BODART, Eugen
—— CONCERTINO FOR FLUTE AND ORCH., OP. 45
    1,2,2,1 - 2,2,2,0 - timp. - hp. - str.   6:30 Henmar.
—— CONCERTO FOR BASSOON AND CHAMBER ORCH., OP. 37
    Henmar.
—— DANCE RHAPSODY
    Henmar.
—— EIGHT PIECES FOR SOLO INSTRUMENTS AND STRINGS
    0,1,0,0 - 0,1,0,0 - timp. - hp. - str.   33:15 Henmar.
—— GOLDONI OVERTURE
    Henmar.
—— IMPRESSIONS OF THE TESSIN
    tpt. - perc. - hp. - str.   4:00 Henmar.
—— KONZERTANTE SUITE FOR FLUTE AND ORCH., OP. 23 (IN 4 MOVEMENTS)
    1,2,2,2 - 2,0,0,0 - timp. - str.   15:30 Henmar.
—— OVERTURE TO THE OPERA "DER LEICHTSINNIGE HERR BANDOLIN"
    AhnSimrock.
—— OVERTURE TO THE OPERA "SPANISCHE NACHT", OP. 12
    AhnSimrock.
—— SONATINE FOR ALTO SAXOPHONE AND ORCH.
    2,2,2,alto. sax.,2 - 2,2,2,0 - timp. - hp. - str.   10:30 Henmar.
—— SYMPHONY IN D MINOR (FAREWELL SYMPHONY) (By an anonymous 18th century composer, Arr. by E. Bodart)
    1,2,2,2 - 2,0,0,0 - str.   7:00 Mannheimer.

BOEDIJN, Gerard H.
—— FIVE CONCERTANTE EPIGRAM-SKETCHES, OP. 159 (1959)
    2,2,3,2 - 2,2,0,0 - timp.,perc. - pf.   14:00 Henmar.
—— HOLLAND RHAPSODY, OP. 102
    3,3,3,3 - 4,3,4,1 - timp.,perc. - str.   10:00 Henmar.
—— IN NACHTSCHADUW, OP. 94 (FOR BARITONE AND ORCH.) (1940) (Text: P. C. Boutens)
    1,1,1,1 - 2,1,0,0 - timp.,perc. - str.   10:00 Henmar.
—— LYRIC SUITE NO. 2, OP. 68 (1937)
    pf. - str.   10:00 Henmar.
—— MEI, SINFONIETTA, OP. 104
    3,3,3,3 - 4,3,3,1 - timp. - hp. - str.   27:00 Henmar.
—— PARTITA FOR DOUBLE STRING ORCH., OP. 105-A (1944)
    str.   Henmar.
—— POETIC SUITE (FOR OBOE, STRING ORCH. AND TIMPANI), OP. 90
    0,1,0,0 - 0,0,0,0 - timp. - str.   12:00 Henmar.

BOEHE, Ernst
—— SINFONISCHER EPILOG
    4,4,4,4 - 6,3,2,1 - timp.,perc. - 2hp. - str.   18:00 T & J.

BOEHM, Yohanan
—— SUITE FOR STRINGS
    str.   21:00 IsMuPublns.

BOEHMER, Konrad
—— POSITION (WITH ELECTRONIC AND VOCAL SOUNDS) (1961)
    0,0,5,3 sax.,5 - 3,2,5,3 - perc.,mar. - tape-recorder - 2 hp. - pf. - str.(0,6,5,3)   15:55 Seesaw.
—— VARIATION (1959)
    *2,*2,2,2 sax.,1 - 1,1,2,1 - perc. - guit. - hp. - pf. - str.   14:00 Seesaw.

BOELLMANN, L. - DALLEY, Orien
—— SYMPHONIC VARIATIONS
    3,2,2,2 - 4,3,3,1 - timp.,perc. - str.   Fema.

BOELZA, Igor
—— SYMPHONY NO. 2, OP. 13
    4,3,3,2 - 4,4,3,1 - timp.,perc. - hp. - str.   G. Schirmer.

BOESMANS, Philippe
—— CORRELATIONS (FOR CLARINET AND INSTRUMENTAL ENSEMBLE)
    3 cl. - perc.(2) - 2 hp. - 2 pf. - str.(4,2,2,2)   7:30 Presser.
—— EXPLOSIVES (FOR DIATONIC HARP AND INSTRUMENTAL ENSEMBLE)
    fl.,cl. - perc.(2) - hp. - pf. - str.(2,1,1,1)   6:00 Presser.
—— INTERVALES III (FOR VOICE AND LARGE ORCHESTRA)
    Presser.
—— MULTIPLES (FOR 2 PIANOS AND ORCH.)
    Presser.

—— UPON LA-MI (FOR VOICE, AMPLIFIED HORN AND
INSTRUMENTAL ENSEMBLE)
fl.,cl. - hn.(amplified) - perc.(2) - hp. - pf. - str.(2,1,1,1)
16:00 Presser.

BOGATYRYOV, A.
—— SYMPHONY NO. 1
G. Schirmer.

BOGLER, Georg Josef - BODART, Eugen
—— BALLET SUITE NO. 2 (FROM "KOMISCHEN BALLETTEN")
0,2,0,0 - 2,0,0,0 -str.   11:00 Mannheimer.

BOHM, Yohanen
—— DIVERTIMENTO FOR TEN WIND INSTRS., OP. 20
2,2,2,2 - 2,0,0,0   21:00 IsMuPublns.

BÖHMELT, Harald
—— EIN MANN KOMMT IN DIE STADT (MUSICAL SKETCHES)
2,1,3,1 - 2,2,2,0 - timp.,perc. - hp. - str.   7:30 F. Colombo.

BOHRNSTEDT, Wayne R.
—— CONCERTINO FOR TIMPANI, XYLOPHONE AND ORCH.
(1959)
1. Adagio; 2. Allegro
2(2nd alt. with picc.),2,2,2 - 4,2,2,0 - timp.,xyl. - str.
9:30 Composer.
—— CONCERTINO FOR TROMBONE AND STRINGS (1960) (IN 3
MOVTS.)
0,0,0,0 - 0,0,1,0 - str.   8:00 World Lib.
—— CONCERTO FOR PIANO AND ORCH. (1957) (IN 4 MOVTS.)
2(2nd alt. with picc.),2,2,2 - 4,2,3,1 - timp.,perc.(3),xyl. - pf. - str.
13:00 Composer.
—— CONCERTO FOR TRUMPET AND ORCH. (1951) (IN 3
MOVTS.)
1,1,1,1 - 1,1,0,0 - timp. - str.   13:00 Remick.
—— FESTIVAL OVERTURE (1957)
*2,2,2,2 - 4,3,3,1 - timp.,perc.(3),xyl. - pf. - str.   6:00 Composer.
—— SYMPHONY NO. 1 IN E (1951) (IN 3 MOVTS.)
2(2nd alt. with picc.),2(2nd alt. with Eng. hn.),2,2 - 4,3,3,1 -
timp.,perc.(3),glock.,xyl. - hp. - str.   21:00 Composer.

BOIELDIEU, François-Adrien - DRESCHER
—— CONCERTO IN F MAJOR FOR PIANO AND ORCH.
0,2,0,0 - 2,0,0,0 - pf. - str.   25:00 F. Colombo.

BOIELDIEU, François-Adrien - WINTER, Aubrey
—— OVERTURE TO "THE CALIPH OF BAGDAD"
Orch.   7:30 Bo. Hawkes.
—— OVERTURE TO "THE WHITE LADY"
Orch.   8:00 Bo. Hawkes.

BOIS, Rob du
—— BREUKER CONCERTO (FOR CLARINETS, SAXOPHONES
AND STRING ORCH.) (1968)
23:00 Henmar.
—— ESPACES À REMPLIR
12:00 Henmar.
—— SIMULTANEOUS (1966)
13:00 Henmar.

BOISGALLAIS, Jacques
—— CANTUS TRACTUS
3,0,0,2 - 0,3,3,0 - timp.,perc.,cel. - pf. - str.   9:00 Presser.
—— SYMPHONIE ("LES OMBRES")
3,3,4,3 - 4,3,3,1 - timp.,perc.,cel. - hp. - pf. - str.   24:00 Presser.

BOISSELET, Paul
—— JAZZ-CONCERTO FOR PIANO AND ORCH. (1946)
3,2,3,2 alto sax.,1 ten. sax.,2 - 3,3,3,0 - timp.,perc.(2) - hp. - pf.
6:00 Salabert.
—— SPIRITUALS (HOMAGE TO DUKE ELLINGTON)(1946)
1,1,2(alt. with 2 alto sax. and ten. sax.),1 - 1,4,2,0 - temp., perc. -
guit. - hp. - pf. - str.   10:00 Salabert.

BOLDEMANN, Laci
—— CONCERTO FOR PIANO AND ORCH., OP. 13 (1956)
2,2,2,2 - 4,3,3,1 - timp. - pf. - str.   21:00 S.T.I.M.
—— CONCERTO FOR TRUMPET AND ORCH., OP. 25 (1968)
2,2,2,2 - 4,3,3,1 - timp.,perc.(2) - str.   21:00 S.T.I.M.
—— FANTASIA CONCERTANTE (FOR CELLO AND ORCH.), OP.
12
2,2,2,2 - 2,2,1,0 - timp. - hp. - str.   10:00 S.T.I.M.

—— LYRIC CONCERTO FOR VIOLIN AND ORCH., OP. 15 (1959)
2,2,2,2 - 2,2,1,0 - timp. - str.   19:00 S.T.I.M.
—— NOTTURNO, OP. 14 (1958) (3 SONGS FOR SOPRANO AND
ORCH.) (Text: H. Michaud)
2,2,2,2 - 2,2,1,0 - timp. - hp. - str.   17:00 S.T.I.M.
—— SINFONIETTA FOR STRINGS, OP. 11
str.   12:00 S.T.I.M.
—— SYMPHONY NO. 1, OP. 18 (1962)
2,3,3,3 - 4,3,3,1 - timp.,perc.(2) - str.   23:00 S.T.I.M.

BOLZ, Harriett
—— STAR OVER STAR (2 SONGS FOR BARITONE, CHORUS
AND ORCH.) (1958) (Text: George Cabot Lodge)
2,2,2,2 - 2,2,1,0 - timp.,perc.(2) - str.   5:42 Composer.

BON, Maarten
—— DISTURBING PEACE (1968)
10:00 Henmar.

BON, Willem Frederick
—— CONCERTO FOR STRINGS, OP. 33
str.   Henmar.
—— DIALOGUES AND MONOLOGUES (FOR PIANO AND
ORCH.)
3,2,3,3 - 1,1,1,1 - perc. - pf. - str.   20:00 Henmar.
—— NOCTURNES, OP. 16
str.   Henmar.
—— SKETCHES, OP. 21 (1968)
7:00 Henmar.
—— SYMPHONY NO. 2, OP. 38 ("LES PRÉDICTIONS")
3,3,3,3 - 4,4,3,1 - perc.(4) - hp. - str.   25:00 Henmar.
—— USHER SYMPHONY, OP. 29
3,3,3,2 sax.,3 - 4,4,3,1 - perc. - cemb. - hp. - pf. - str.   Henmar.
—— VARIATIONS ON A THEME BY SWEELINCK, OP. 24
2,2,2,1 - 1,0,0,0 - cemb. - str.   Henmar.

BOND, Richard Capel - FINZI, Gerald
—— CONCERTO NO. 1 IN D MINOR (FOR TRUMPET AND
STRINGS)
tpt. - str.   7:00 Bo. Hawkes.
—— CONCERTO NO. 5 IN G MINOR (FOR STRINGS AND
CONTINUO)
cemb. - str.   14:00 Bo. Hawkes.
—— CONCERTO NO. 6 IN B FLAT (FOR BASSOON AND
STRINGS)
bn. - str.   7:00 Bo. Hawkes.

BOND, Victoria
—— C-A-G-E-D (1972) (IN 3 MOVTS.)
str.   11:00 Seesaw.
—— SONATA FOR ORCHESTRA (1973)
2(2nd alt. with picc.),2,2,2 - 2,2,2,1 - timp.,perc.(2),bells,vibra. -
hp. - str.   5:15 Composer.

BONDEVILLE, Emmanuel
—— L' ÉCOLE DES MARIS (SUITE)
14:00 Henmar.
—— GAULTIER-GARGUILLE
3,*3,3,3 - 4,4,3,1 - timp.,perc.,cel. - 2hps. - pf. - str.   22:00 EV.
—— ILLUMINATIONS (IN 3 MOVTS.)
*3,*3,3,3 - 4,3,3,1 - timp.,perc.(4),cel. - 2hp. - str.   25:00 EV.
—— ILLUSTRATIONS POUR "FAUST" (IN 13 MOVTS.) (FOR
MIXED CHORUS AND ORCH.)
3,2,2,2 - 4,3,2,0 - timp.,cel. - hp. - pf. - org. - str.   28:00 EV.
—— MADAME BOVARY - LES COMICES
2,2,2,2 - 2,2,1,0 - timp.,perc.,xyl. - str.   6:00 Henmar.
—— MADAME BOVARY (THREE SYMPHONIC FRAGMENTS
FROM THE OPERA)
25:00 Henmar.
—— SYMPHONIE CHORÉOGRAPHIQUE
3,3,3,3 - 4,4,3,1 - timp.,perc.(3),xyl. - 2 hp. -str.   30:00 EV.
—— SYMPHONIE LYRIQUE
3,*3,3,3 - 4,4,3,1 - timp.,perc. - str.   35:00 EV.

BONDON, Jacques
—— CONCERT DE PRINTEMPS
tpt. - perc. - str.   16:00 Presser.
—— LA COUPOLE (TABLEAUX FANTASTIQUE D'UN MONDE
ÉTRANGE) (IN 3 MOVTS.)
3,3,3,3 - perc.,cel.,vibra.,xyl. - str.   14:00 Presser.
—— FLEUR DE FEU (SUITE)
2,2,2,2 - 2,2,2,0 - timp.,perc. - Ondes-martenot - hp. - org. - pf. -
str.   28:00 Presser.

—— GIOCOSO (FOR VIOLIN AND STRINGS)
  str.   12:00 Presser.
—— MUSIQUE POUR UN AUTRE MONDE (SUITE FOR ORCH.)
  2,2,2,2 - 2,2,2,0 - perc.(6) - hp. - pf. - str.   18:00 Henmar.
—— LE PAIN DE SERPENT (4 PIECES FOR SOPRANO AND 14
  INSTRS.)
  1,0,1,1 - 0,0,0,0 - perc.(3),cel.,vibra.,xyl. - hp. - pf. - 2 c.,1 d.-b.
                                                        16:00 Presser.
—— SONATE POUR UN BALLET
  1(alt. with picc.),1,1,1 - 1,1,1,0 - perc.(2) - d.-b. 20:00 Henmar.
—— SUITE INDIENNE
  2,2,2,1 - 2,2,2,0 - timp.,perc.,xyl. - hp. - str.   16:00 Presser.
—— LE TAILLIS ENSORCELÉ
  0,0,0,0 - 4,2,2,0 - perc.(2),glock.,vibra. - hp. - pf. - str. (2 str.
  orch.)   14:30 Presser.

BONHEUR, R.
—— POLYPHEME (INCIDENTAL MUSIC) (FOR SOPRANO SOLO,
  FEMALE CHOIR AND ORCH.)
  fl. - bells - str.   Salabert.

BONNEAU, Paul
—— CONCERTO FOR ALTO SAXOPHONE AND ORCH.
  3,3,2,alto sax.,3 - 4,2,2,0 - timp.,perc.,cel. - hp. - str. 15:30 Baron.
—— DIVERTISSEMENT (FOR 4 FLUTES AND ORCH.)
  4,2,2,2 - 3,3,3,0 - timp.,perc.,cel.(ad lib.),glock.,vibra. - guit. - hp. -
  pf. - str.   6:30 Baron.
—— FANTAISIE CONCERTANTE, FOR TRUMPET (OR
  TROMBONE) AND ORCH.
  2,2,2,alto sax.,2 - 3,2-3,3,1-2 - timp.,perc.,cel.,glock.,vibra - hp. -
  str.   5:30 Baron.

BONNER, Eugene
—— TAORMINA (A LITTLE SUITE FOR SMALL ORCH.) (IN 4
  MOVTS.)
  1,1,1,1 - 2,2,1,0 - perc.,cel. - hp. - pf. - str.   J. Fischer.
—— THREE SONGS (FOR MEDIUM VOICE AND ORCH.)
  *3,*3,*3,*3 - 4,3,3,1 - timp.,perc.,cel. - 2hp. - str. G. Schirmer.

BONONCINI, Giovanni Battista - BLANCHARD, Roger
—— SYMPHONY IN D, OP. 3 (FOR STRINGS AND CONTINUO)
  cemb. - str.   4:30 Presser.
—— SYMPHONY NO. 10 (FOR STRINGS AND CONTINUO)
  cemb. - str.   8:00 Presser.

BONPORTI, Francesco Antonio - BARBLAN, Guglielmo
—— CONCERTO IN D, OP. 11, NO. 8
  cemb. - str.   10:00 Bo. Hawkes.
—— CONCERTO IN E, OP. 11, NO. 9
  cemb. - str.   10:00 Bo. Hawkes.
—— CONCERTO IN F, OP. 11, NO. 5 (FOR VIOLIN AND ORCH.)
  (CON IL CELEBRE RECITATIVE)
  cemb. - str.   11:00 Bo. Hawkes.
—— CONCERTO IN F, OP. 11, NO. 6
  cemb. - str.   10:00 Bo. Hawkes.

BONPORTI, Francesco Antonio - TONI, Alceo
—— CONCERTO IN Bb, FOR VIOLIN AND ORCH.
  org. - str.   12:00 Bo. Hawkes.

BONSEL, Adriaan
—— CONCERTO FOR CLARINET AND ORCH.
  1,2,2,2 - 2,0,0,0 - timp.,perc.,cel.,xyl. - 2hp. - str. 15:00 Henmar.
—— DIVERTIMENTO FOR SMALL ORCH.
  2,2,2,2 - 2,2,0,0 - timp.,perc. - str.   12:00 Henmar.
—— GELUCKIG IS HET LAND (CONCERT-STUK)
  2,2,2,2 - 4,3,3,1 - timp.,perc.,cel. - str.   9:00 Henmar.
—— MINNELIEDEREN (6 SONGS) (FOR BARITONE, MIXED
  CHORUS AND ORCH.) (1957)
  3,2,2,0 - 2,2,0,0 - timp.,perc. - str.   25:00 Henmar.
—— SINFONISCH CONCERT
  3,3,3,2 - 4,3,3,1 - timp.,perc. - str.   15:00 Henmar.
—— S.O.S. (OVERTURE) (1962)
  2,2,2,2 - 2,2,1,0 - timp.,perc.,vibra. - str.   8:00 Henmar.
—— SUITE FOR FLUTE AND STRINGS (1946)
  fl. - str.   13:00 Henmar.
—— SYMPHONY NO. 1
  2,3,2,2 - 4,3,3,1 - timp.,perc. - hp. - str.   18:00 Henmar.
—— SYMPHONY NO. 2 (1957)
  2,3,2,2 - 2,2,1,0 - timp. - str.   22:00 Henmar.
—— THREE HYMNS (DRIE HYMNEN) (FOR SPEAKER, MIXED
  CHORUS AND ORCH.) (1948) (Text: H.R.H van der Schalk)
  3,3,3,3 - 4,3,3,1 - timp.,perc. - hp. - str.   27:00 Henmar.

BONTE, Jo
—— JAZZ CONCERTO FOR HORN AND ORCH.
  3,2,2,2 - 5,3,3,0 - timp.,perc. - hp. - str.(incl. 1 jazz d.-b.)
                                                        11:20 Modern.

BONTEMPELLI, Massimo
—— PARTITA ALLA POPOLARE
  1,1,1,1 - 1,0,0,0 - str.   14:00 Bo. Hawkes.

BOONE, Charles
—— CHINESE TEXTS (FOR SOPRANO AND ORCH.) (1971)
  2,2,2,2 - 3,2,2,1 - perc.(3),bells - pf. - str.   15:00 Salabert.
—— THE EDGE OF THE LAND (1968)
  2(alt. with 2 picc.),2,2 Eb cl., 2 - 4,2,2,1 - perc.(4),bells - hp. -
  electric org. (Hammond) - pf. - str.   12:00 Salabert.
—— FIRST LANDSCAPE (1971)
  4,4,4,3 - 4,4,3,0 - perc.(3) - pf. - str.(no vlns.) 15:00 Salabert.
—— LINEA MERIDIANA
                                                        12:00 Salabert.
—— SAN ZENO - VERONA
  1,1,1,*2 - perc. - electric org. - pf. - str.(2,1,1,1) 10:00 Salabert.
—— SECOND LANDSCAPE (FOR CHAMBER ORCH.) (1973)
  1,1,1,1(alt. with cbn.) - 0,2,0,0 - timp.,perc.(2),bells,mar.,vibra. - pf.
  - str.(2,1,1,2)   12:00 Salabert.
—— SHADOW (FOR OBOE AND ORCH.) (1968)
  2,2,2,2 - 4,3,3,1 - timp.,perc. - tape-recorder - str. 6:00 Composer.
  or:
  3,2,3,3 - 4,3,3,1 - timp.,perc. - tape-recorder - str.
—— THE YELLOW BIRD (1967)
  3,2,2,2 - 4,3,3,1 - perc.(4) - pf. - 4-hands - str. 15:00 Composer.

BOOREN, Jo van den
—— L' EPITAPHE VILLON (FOR VOICE AND LARGE ORCH.)
  (1965) (Text: Francois Villon)
                                                        12:00 Henmar.

BOOTH, C. H.
—— THE DIVINE TRAGEDY (DRAMATIC LENTEN CANTATA)
  (FOR FIVE SOLOISTS, CHORUS AND ORCH.)
  2(2nd alt. with picc.),*3,2,*3 - 4,2,3,1 - timp.,perc. - hp. - str.
                                                        Flammer.

BORDES, Charles
—— DIVERTISSEMENT (FOR TRUMPET, WINDS AND PERC.)
  3,2,2,2 - 4,2,3,1 - timp.,perc.(4),cel. - 2hp.   5:00 Salabert.
—— EPITHALAME (FOR VOICE AND ORCH.)
                                                        Salabert.
—— EUSKAL HERRIA (BASQUE FESTIVAL MUSIC) (IN 3
  MOVTS.)
  2,1,1,1 - 1,1,3,0 - timp.,perc. - str.   12:00 Salabert.
—— RAPSODIE BASQUE (FOR PIANO AND ORCH.)
  2,1,2,2 - 2,2,3,0 - timp.,perc. - 2hp. - pf. - str. 15:00 Salabert.

BORDEWIJK-ROEPMAN, Johanna
—— BIERBAUM-LIEDER (4 SONGS) (FOR SOPRANO AND
  ORCH.) (1940)
  3,2,2,2 - 1,1,2,0 - cel. - hp. - str.   12:00 Henmar.
—— CONCERTO FOR PIANO AND ORCH. (1940)
  3,3,2,2 - 4,3,3,1 - timp.,perc. - pf. - str.   20:00 Henmar.
—— EPILOOG
  3,3,2,2 - 4,2,3,1 - timp.,perc. - hp. - str.   16:00 Henmar.
—— LES ILLUMINATIONS (3 SONGS) (FOR SOPRANO AND
  ORCH.) (1940) (Text: Arthur Rimbaud)
  3,3,2,2 - 4,3,3,1 - timp.,perc. - hp. - str. (1938 VERSION)
                                                        20:00 Henmar.
  or:
  2,3,2,2 - 2,2,0,0 - timp.,perc. - hp. - str. (1940 VERSION)
—— DE LENTEWIND (FOR SOPRANO, MIXED CHORUS AND
  ORCH.)(1941) (Text: M. Beversluis)
  2,1,2,2 - 2,0,0,0 - hp. - str.   15:00 Henmar.
—— PLATO'S DOOD (FOR SPEAKER, SOPRANO, TENOR, MIXED
  CHORUS AND ORCH.) (1949) (Text: F. Bordewijk)
  3,3,3,2 - 4,3,3,1 - timp.,perc.,cel. - hp. - str.   75:00 Henmar.
—— SYMPHONIE NO. 1
  3,3,3,2 - 4,3,3,1 - timp.,perc. - hp. - str.   17:00 Henmar.
—— THREE PIECES FOR STRING ORCH. (1936)
  str.   20:00 Heer & Zn.

BORGHI, Luigi - BONELLI
—— CONCERTO IN D MAJOR, FOR CELLO AND SMALL ORCH.
  0,2,0,0 - 2,0,0,0 - str.   17:00 Henmar.

BORGHI, Luigi - RIEGE, Ernest
—— RONDO
    1,1,2,1 - 2,0,0,0 - str.   5:00 F. Colombo.

BORGHI, Luigi - TORREFRANCA, Fausto
—— CONCERTO FOR VIOLIN AND SMALL ORCH.
    0,2,0,0 - 2,0,0,0 - str.   12:00 Bo. Hawkes.

BORGULYA, András
—— CONCERTO BREVE (FOR CELLO AND ORCH.)
        16:00 Bo. Hawkes.

BORISHANSKY, Elliot
—— MUSIC FOR ORCHESTRA
    3,3,3,3 - 4,2,3,0 - timp.,perc. - str.   Chappell.

BOŘKOVEC, Pavel
—— CHAMBER SYMPHONIETTA
    2,2,1,1 - 2,1,0,0 - perc. - pf. - str.   21:00 Bo. Hawkes.
—— CONCERTO FOR CELLO AND ORCH.
    3,2,2,2 - 4,2,3,1 - timp. - str.   32:00 Bo. Hawkes.
—— CONCERTO FOR TWO PIANOS AND ORCH.
        Bo. Hawkes.
—— CONCERTO FOR VIOLIN AND ORCH.
    3,2,2,2 - 4,3,4,0 - timp.,perc. - pf.   25:00 Bo. Hawkes.
—— CONCERTO GROSSO FOR TWO VIOLINS, CELLO AND ORCH., WITH PIANO OBBLIGATO (1942)
    2,2,2,2 - 2,2,0,0 - timp.,perc. - pf. - str.   26:00 Bo. Hawkes.
—— CONCERTO NO. 1 FOR PIANO AND ORCH.
    2,1,2,2 - 2,2,2,0 - timp.,perc. - pf. - str.   20:00 Bo. Hawkes.
—— CONCERTO NO. 2 FOR PIANO AND ORCH.
    3,2,2,2 - 4,2,3,1 - timp.,perc. - pf. - str.   23:00 Bo. Hawkes.
—— PARTITA FOR ORCH.
    3,3,2,2 - 4,3,3,2 - timp.,perc. - hp. - pf. - str.   12:00 Bo. Hawkes.
—— THE PIED PIPER (KRYSAŘ) (MUSIC FROM THE BALLET "THE RATCATCHER") (1939)
    3,2,3,2 - 4,2,3,1 - timp.,perc.,xyl. - mandolin - pf. - str.
        25:00 Bo. Hawkes.
—— START (SYMPHONIC ALLEGRO)
    3,3,3,3 - 6,3,3,1 - timp.,perc. - str.   9:00 Bo. Hawkes.
—— SYMPHONY NO. 1, OP. 6
        Bo. Hawkes.
—— SYMPHONY NO. 2
    3,3,3,3 - 4,3,3,1 - timp.,perc. - hp. - str.   34:00 Bo. Hawkes.
—— SYMPHONY NO. 3
    3,3,3,3 - 4,3,3,1 - timp.,perc. pf. - str.   35:00 Bo. Hawkes.

BORMIOLI, Enrico
—— ALLEGRO DA CONCERTO (CONCERT ALLEGRO) (FOR PIANO AND ORCH.)
    3,1,2,4 sax.,2 - 2,3,2,1 - timp.,perc.,cel.,vibra. - hp. - pf. - str.
        9:00 Leeds.
—— VARIAZIONI SINFONICHE (ON A THEME OF PAGANINI) (FOR PIANO AND ORCH.)
    2,2,2,2 - 2,2,2,0 - hp. - pf. - str.   14:00 Leeds.

BORNSCHEIN, Franz
—— THE CONQUEROR WORM (FOR CHORUS AND ORCH.)
    2,2,2,2 - 4,2,2,0 - timp. - hp. - str.   10:00 Composer.
—— DUNES (CAPE COD IMPRESSIONS) (SYMPHONIC POEM)
    3,2,2,2 - 4,3,3,1 - timp.,perc.(2) - str.   8:00 Composer.
—— THE EARTH SINGS (SYMPHONIC POEM)
    3(3rd alt. with picc.),*3,*3,*3, - 4,3,3,1 - timp.,perc.(3) - hp. - str.
        15:00 Composer.
—— GREMLINS (BURLESQUE OVERTURE)
    3(3rd alt. with picc.),2,2,2 - 4,3,3,1 - timp. - str.   5:00 Composer.
—— LEIF ERICSON (SYMPHONIC POEM)
    3(3rd alt. with picc.),2(2nd alt. with Eng.hn.),2,2 - 4,3,3,1 - timp.,perc.(2) - hp. - str.   12:00 Composer.
—— LOW TIDE
    3,2,2,2 - 4,3,3,1 - timp.,perc.(2) - hp. - str.   7:00 Composer.
—— MIDSUMMER ON SOUTH MOUNTAIN (SYMPHONIC SKETCH)
    2,2,2,2 - 4,3,3,1 - timp. - str.   9:00 Composer.
—— THE MISSION ROAD
    3(3rd alt. with picc.),2(2nd alt. with Eng.hn.),2,2 - 4,3,3,1 - timp.,perc.(3) - hp. - pf. - str.   12:00 Composer.
—— MOON OVER TAOS
    fl. - timp.,perc.(2) - str.   8:00 Composer.
—— ODE TO THE BRAVE
    3,*3,*3,2 - 4,3,3,1 - timp. - hp. - pf. - str.   12:00 Composer.
—— PALESTINIAN LAMENT (AT THE WAILING WALL)
    3,*3,*3,2 - 4,3,3,1 - timp.,perc.(4) - hp. - str.   10:00 Composer.

—— PERSIAN FESTIVALS (IN 3 MOVTS.)
    3(3rd alt. with picc.),2,2,2 - 4,3,3,1 - timp.,perc.(3) - hp. - str.
        30:00 Composer.
—— THE PHANTOM CANOE (INDIAN SUITE) (IN 5 MOVTS.)
    3(3rd alt. with picc.),*3,2,2 - 4,3,3,1 - timp. - hp. - str.
        17:00 Composer.
—— THE SEA GOD'S DAUGHTERS (SYMPHONIC SCHERZO)
    3(3rd alt. with picc.),*3,*3,2 - 4,3,3,1 - timp.,perc.(2) - str.
        13:00 Composer.
—— SOUTHERN NIGHTS (SYMPHONIC POEM)
    3(3rd alt. with picc.),2,2,2 - 4,3,3,1 - timp.,perc. - hp. - str.
        12:00 Composer.
—— SYMPHONIC FANTASY
    3(3rd alt. with picc.),2,*3,*3 - 4,3,3,1 - timp.,perc.(3) - hp. - str.
        24:00 Composer.
—— THEIRS BE THE GLORY
    3(3rd alt. with picc.),*3,*3,*3 - 4,3,3,1 - timp.,perc.(4) - hp. - str.
        10:00 Composer.
—— THE WORD MADE FLESH (CHRISTMAS CANTATA) (FOR SOPRANO, CHORUS AND ORCH.)
    1,1,2,1 - 2,1,1,0 - timp. - str.   20:00 Composer.

BORNUM, Hans
—— SUITE FOR STRING ORCH.
    str.   14:30 S.T.I.M.

BORODIN, Alexander - DEXTER, Harry
—— NOCTURNE (FROM 2ND STRING QUARTET) (ARR. FOR FULL ORCH.)
        7:00 P.R.S.

BORODIN, Alexander - DUBENSKY, A.
—— PETITE SUITE (FOR STRING ORCH.) (IN 3 MOVTS.)
    str.   9:00 Arranger.

BORODIN, Alexander - GLAZOUNOFF, Alexander
—— PETITE SUITE (IN 7 MOVTS.)
    3,2,2,2 - 4,2,3,0 - timp.,perc. - str.   20:00 Baron.
—— SYMPHONY NO. 3 IN A MAJOR (COMPL. AND ORCH. BY GLAZOUNOFF)
    2,2,2,2 - 4,2,3,0 - timp. - str.   15:30 Baron.

BORODIN, Alexander - MOUTON
—— PETITE SUITE (IN 4 MOVTS.)
        14:00 Baron.

BORODIN, Alexander - MOUTON, Henri
—— IN THE STEPPES OF CENTRAL ASIA
        6:00 Bo. Hawkes.

BORODIN, Alexander - SARGEANT, Malcolm
—— NOCTURNE, FROM STRING QUARTET NO. 2 (FOR STRING ORCH.)
    str.   9:00 P.R.S.

BORODIN, Alexander - SCHMID, Adolf
—— POLOVETSIAN DANCES (FROM "PRINCE IGOR")
        G. Schirmer.

BORODIN, Alexander - SEVITZKY, Fabien
—— CHORUS FROM "PRINCE IGOR" (FOR STRING ORCH.)
    str.   C. Fischer.

BORODKIN, Abram E.
—— AN AMERICAN IN ISRAEL (CANTATA), OP. 30 (WITH NARRATOR, CHOIR AND MEZZO-SOPRANO OR ALTO)
    1,0,1,0 - timp.,perc.(2) - pf. - str.   20:00 Belw-Mills.
—— AT SAINT BASIL'S - MOSCOW, 1936 A.D. (FOR STRING ORCH.)
        Mills.
—— FROM BYELORUSSIA (MINSK, 1936), OP. 29 (2 TONE PICTURES)
    *2,2,2,2 - 4,2,3,0 - timp.,perc.(2-3),xyl. - pf. - str.
        10:00 Composer.
—— ISTANBUL (A FANTASY ON 2 TURKISH THEMES)
    2(2nd alt. with picc.),*3,3,2 - 4,4,3,1 - timp.,perc.(3),xyl. - pf. - str.
        6:30 Belw-Mills.
—— JEWISH RHAPSODIE (FOON SHOLOM ALEICHEM'S TZEITN), OP. 28
    1,0,1,0 - timp.,perc. - pf. - str.   12:00 Composer.
—— AN ODYSSEY (FOR STRING ORCH.)
    str.   19:00 Baron.

—— TWO PICTURES FROM MINSK (1961)
  str.   9:00 Composer.

BOROWSKI, Felix
—— ALLEGRO DE CONCERT (FOR ORGAN AND ORCH.)
  3,2,2,2 - 4,2,3,1 - timp. - org. - str.   10:00 Composer.
—— CONCERTO IN D MINOR (FOR PIANO AND ORCH.) (IN 3
  MOVEMENTS)
  2,2,2,2 - 4,2,3,1 - timp. - pf. - str.   20:00 C. Fischer.
—— ECCE HOMO (TONE POEM)
  *3,*3,*3,*3 - 4,3,3,1 - timp.,perc. - hp. - str.   12:00 Composer.
—— ELEGIE SYMPHONIQUE
  3,*3,2,2b.-cl.,*3 - 4,3,3,1 - timp.,perc. - hp. - str.   8:00 Composer.
—— FANFARE FOR THE AMERICAN SOLDIER
  *3,*3,*3,*3 - 4,3,3,1 - timp.,perc. - (2)   5:00 Composer.
—— THE MIRROR
  2,2,2,2 - 4,3,3,1 - perc. - hp. - str.   9:00 Composer.
—— PEINTURES (PAINTINGS) (IN 3 MOVTS.)
  *3,*3,*3,*3 - 4,3,3,1 perc. - hp. - str.   25:00 Composer.
—— LE PRINTEMPS PASSIONNÉ (THE PASSIONATE
  SPRINGTIME) (TONE POEM)
  *3,*3,2,2 - 4,2,3,1 - timp.,perc. - hp. - str.   10:00 Composer.
—— REQUIEM FOR A CHILD
  1(alt. with picc.),2,2,2 - 4,3,3,1 - timp.,perc. - str.   7:00 Composer.
—— SEMIRAMIS (TONE POEM)
  *3,*3,*3,*3 - 4,3,3,1 - perc. - hp. - str.   12:00 Composer.
—— SYMPHONY NO. 1 (IN 3 MOVEMENTS)
  2,*3,*3,*3 - 4,3,3,1 - timp.,perc. - hp. - str.   26:00 Composer.
—— SYMPHONY NO. 2 IN E MINOR (IN 4 MOVEMENTS)
  2(1 alt. with picc.),*3,*3,*3 - 4,3,3,1 - timp.,perc. - hp. - str.   25:00 Composer.
—— SYMPHONY NO. 3 IN G (IN 4 MOVEMENTS)
  3(3rd alt. with picc.),*3,*3,*3 - 4,3,3,1 - timp.,perc. - str.   28:00 Composer.
—— YOUTH (FANTASIE OVERTURE)
  *3,*3,*3,*3 - 4,3,3,1 - timp.,perc. - hp. - str.   12:00 Composer.

BØRRESEN, Hakon
—— CONCERTO IN G MAJOR, FOR VIOLIN AND ORCH.
  2,2,2,2 - 4,2,0,0 - timp. - str.   30:00 G. Schirmer.
—— KADDARA (OPERA) % (1921)
                                        Henmar.
—— MOD DØDEN
  str.   Henmar.
—— PRELUDE TO THE OPERA "THE ROYAL GUEST"
  3,2,2,2 - 4,2,3,1 - timp.,cel. - hp. - str.   8:00 G. Schirmer.
—— SYMPHONY NO. 3
  3,2,2,2 - 4,2,3,1 - timp.,perc. - str.   28:00 Henmar.

BORRIS, Siegfried
—— AEOLIAN SUITE, OP. 31, NO. 2 (IN 6 MOVTS.)
  str.   10:00 Henmar.
—— CONCERTINO FOR ENGLISH HORN AND STRING ORCH.,
  OP. 48 (IN 3 MOVTS.)
  Eng. hn. - str.   10:00 Henmar.
—— CONCERTINO FOR FLUTE AND STRINGS, OP. 71 (IN 5
  MOVTS.)
  fl. - str.   11:00 Henmar.
—— CONCERTO FOR HORN AND ORCH., OP. 89 (IN 3 MOVTS.)
  2,2,2,2 - 1,0,0,0 - str.   20:00 Henmar.
—— CONCERTO FOR ORCH., OP. 112 (IN 1 MOVT.)
  2,2,2,2 - 2,2,3,0 - timp.,perc. - str.   17:00 Henmar.
—— CONCERTO FOR ORGAN, SOLO OBOE, 3 WINDS AND
  STRINGS (IN 3 MOVTS.)
  1,1,1,1 - 0,0,0,0 - org. - str.   21:00 Henmar.
—— CONCERTO FOR PIANO AND SMALL ORCH., OP. 58 (IN 3
  MOVTS.)
  1,0,0,1 - 0,0,0,0 - pf. - str.   25:00 Sirius.
—— CONCERTO FOR SOPRANO SAXOPHONE AND ORCH., OP.
  120 (IN 3 MOVTS.)
  2,2,2,sopr. sax.,2 - 2,2,2,2 - timp.,perc.,vibra. - str.   17:00 Henmar.
—— CONCERTO FOR TWO HARPSICHORDS AND SMALL
  ORCH., OP. 118
  1,1,0,1 - 0,0,0,0 - 2 hpsc. - perc. - str.   15:00 Henmar.
—— CONCERTO FOR VIOLA DA GAMBA AND SMALL ORCH.,
  OP. 87 (IN 3 MOVTS.)
  1,0,1,1 - 0,0,0,0 - str.(incl. vla. da gamba)   22:00 Henmar.
—— DIVERTIMENTO FÜR STREICHORCH. UND 5 BLÄSER
                                        15:00 Sirius.
—— FESTIVE MUSIC (PRELUDE), OP. 39, NO. 1
  2,2,2,2 - 2,2,3,0 - perc. - str.   7:00 Henmar.
—— HANS IM GLÜCK, OP. 40 (RADIO OPERA)
  1,1,1,1 - 0,0,0,0 - str.   28:00 Henmar.

—— HIROTAS UND GERLINDE, OP. 41 (RADIO OPERA)
  2,2,2,2 - 2,2,2,2 - str.   42:00 Henmar.
—— HYMNUS (TE DEUM), FOR OBOE AND ORCH., OP. 110, NO.
  3
  2,1,2,2 - 2,1,0,0 - str.   9:30 Henmar.
—— INTRADA SERENA NO. 1, OP. 57, NO. 1
  1,1,1,1 - 1,1,1,0 - str.   8:00 Henmar.
—— INTRADA SERENA NO. 5 IN D MAJOR, OP. 77, NO. 5
  2,2,2,2 - 2,2,0,0 - str.   8:00 Henmar.
—— INTRADA SERENA NO. 6, OP. 77, NO. 6
  2,2,2,2 - 2,2,2,0 - perc. - str.   10:00 Henmar.
—— KLEINE HOFMUSIK (FROM THE FAIRY-TALE OPERA "DIE
  RÜBE")
  1,1,1,1 - 1,0,0,0 - str.   6:00 Henmar.
—— KONZERT FÜR CEMBALO, FLÖTE, FAGOTT UND
  STREICHORCH.
  fl.,bn. - cemb. - str.   25:00 Sirius.
—— DAS LETZTE SPIEL, OP. 75 %
  2,2,2,2 - 2,2,3,0 - timp.,perc.(4) - str.   35:00 Henmar.
—— NETHERLANDS FOLKSONG SUITE, OP. 69 (FOR SOPRANO,
  TENOR AND SMALL ORCH.)
  1,1,1,1 - 0,0,0,0 - str.   18:00 Henmar.
—— ORCHESTER SUITE, OP. 25
  1. Maestoso; 2. Allegro vivace; 3. Largo; 4. Andante cantabile;
  5. Vivace
  2,2,2,2 - 2,2,3,0 - perc. - str.   11:00 Sirius.
—— RHAPSODY FOR ORCH., OP. 103
                                        Henmar.
—— RUF DES LEBENS, OP. 72 (SCENIC CANTATA) %
  2,2,2,2 - 2,3,3,0 - timp.,perc. - str.   70:00 Henmar.
—— DIE RÜBE, OP. 56 (A HAPPY FAIRY-TALE OPERA, AFTER
  GRIMM)
  1,1,1,1 - 1,0,0,0 - str.   60:00 Henmar.
—— SHAKESPEAREAN SUITE, OP. 39, NO. 3 (IN 9 MOVTS.)
  1,1,0,0-1 - 0,0,0,0 - str.   15:00 Henmar.
—— SPANISH SERENADE, OP. 68
  1,1,1,1 - 0,0,0,0 - perc. - str.   7:45 Henmar.
—— DER STROM, OP. 84 (THE STREAM) (CANTATA) (FOR
  SOPRANO, BARITONE, CHORUS AND ORCH.)
  2,2,2,2 - 2,2,3,0 - perc. - str.   50:00 Henmar.
—— SYMPHONY CONCERTANTE, OP. 58, NO. 1 (IN 3 MOVTS.)
  1,0,0,1 - 0,0,0,0 - str.   25:00 Henmar.
—— SYMPHONY IN A, OP. 29
  2,2,2,2 - 2,2,2,2 - str.   22:00 Sirius.
—— SYMPHONY IN B, OP. 19
  1. Grave- Agitado - Adagio - Allegro moderato - Passacaglia;
  2. Molto adagio; 3. Allegro vivace - Presto
  2,2,2,2(or c.-bn.) - 2,2,3,0 - perc. - str.   21:00 Sirius.
—— SYMPHONY NO. 4 IN E, OP. 60 (IN 3 MOVTS.)
  2,2,2,2 - 2,2,3,0 - timp.,perc. - str.   25:00 Sirius.
—— SYMPHONY NO. 5 IN C SHARP MINOR, OP. 61 (IN 4
  MOVTS.)
  2,2,2,2 - 2,2,3,0 - perc. - str.   23:00 Henmar.
—— TOTENTANZ, OP. 39, NO. 2
  1(alt. with picc.),0,1,1 - 2,2,0,0 - perc. - str.   4:00 Henmar.

BORSARI, Amedée
—— JUVAT (LITTLE SUITE FOR ORCHESTRA)
  2,2,2,2 - 3,3,2,0 - timp.,perc. - pf. - str.   8:00 Presser.

BÖRSCHEL, Erich
—— FOUR MINIATURES (FOR OBOE AND ORCH.)
  1,1,2,1 - 2,0,0,0 - perc. - hp. - str.   7:00 Henmar.
—— NOCTURNE
  2,2,2,1 - 2,3,3,0 - perc.,cel.,vibra. - hp. - pf. - str.
                                        6:00 Mannheimer.

BORTOLOTTI, Mauro
—— TRANSPARENCIAS (1968)
  hpsc. - str.(6,2,2,1)   8:00 MCA Music.

BORTZ, Alfred
—— DIE BLAUE FONTÄNE, OP. 76 (RONDO)
  hp. - pf. - str.   6:00 Henmar.
—— CAPRICCIO, OP. 72
  2,2,2,2 - 4,2,3,0-1 - timp.,perc.(2) - hp.(ad lib.) - str.   5:00 Henmar.
—— HANDWERKER SUITE, OP. 58 (IN 6 MOVTS.)
  2,1,2,2 - 2,2,2,0 - timp.,perc. - hp.(ad. lib.) - str.   20:00 Henmar.
—— HUMORESKE (RONDO)
  2(2nd alt. with picc.),2,2,2 - 4,2,3,0 - timp.,perc. - hp. - str.
                                        4:00 Henmar.
—— SINFONIETTA PASTORALE, OP. 15
  2,2,2,2 - 2,2,2,0 - timp.,perc. - str.   Lengnick.

—— SZENEN EINER MONDNACHT (SUITE) (IN 5 MOVTS.)
str.   20:00 Henmar.

BÖRTZ, Daniel
—— CONCERTO FOR VIOLIN, BASSOON AND CHAMBER
ORCH. (1974)
2,0,2,0 - 2,2,0,0 - timp.,perc. - str.   19:00 Gehrmans.
—— IN MEMORIA DI .... (1968)
2,2,2,2 - 2,2,1,0 - timp.,perc.(5) - pf. - str.   10:00 Fleisher.
—— INSCRIZIONI (1964)
3,3,3,2 - 4,3,3,1 - timp.,perc. - pf. - str.   10:00 Fleisher.
—— SINFONIA NO. 1 (1973)
3,3,3,3 - 4,3,3,1 - timp.,perc. - hp. -str.   17:00 Gehrmans.
—— VOCES (FOR 3 SOPRANOS, TAPE AND ORCH.) (1968)
3,3,4,4 - 4,4,4,1 - timp.,perc.(9, incl. 4 on timp.) - tape-recorder -
str.   24:00 Fleisher.

BORUP-JØRGENSEN, Axel
—— MARIN, OP. 60
23:00 K.O.D.A.
—— NORTHERN SUMMER PASTORALE, OP. 51
2,2,2,0 - 4,0,0,0 - hp. - pf. - str.   12:00 Henmar.

BOSCOVICH, Alexander Uriah
—— CANTO DI MA'ALOT
2,alto. fl.,2,*3,*3 - 4,3,3,1 - timp.,perc.,cel.,vibra.,xyl. - str.
12:00 IsMuPublns.
—— CHANSONS POPULAIRES JUIVES
3,3,2,2 - 4,3,3,1 - timp.,perc.,cel. - hp. - pf. - str.
20:00 IsMuPublns.
—— CONCERTO FOR OBOE AND ORCH.
3,2,3,2 - 2,2,3,0 - timp.,perc.,cel.,xyl. - hp. -pf. - str.
18:00 IsMuPublns.
—— DAUGHTER OF ISRAEL (CANTATA) (FOR TENOR, MIXED
CHORUS AND ORCH.)
3,2(1 alt. with Eng.hn.),2(1 alt. with b.-cl.),2 - 2,2,0,0 - perc.,cel. -
hp. - pf. - str.   13:00 Bo. Hawkes.
—— THE GOLDEN CHAIN (SUITE FOR ORCH.)
3,3,2,sax.,2 - 4,3,3,1 - timp.,perc.,cel. - hp. - pf. - str.
20:00 Bo. Hawkes.
—— LITTLE SUITE (PICCOLA SUITA)
fl. - perc. - str.   12:00 Mills.
—— SEMITIC SUITE
3,3,3,2 - 4,3,3,0 - timp.,perc. - hp. - hpsc. - str. 18:00 IsMuPublns.

BOSMANS, Arthur
—— CYMBALUM (RHAPSODY FOR PIANO AND ORCH.)
2,2,2,3 - 4,3,3,1 - timp. - pf. - str.   12:00 Southern.
—— DANSE BURLESQUE
3,2,3,sax.,2 - 4,2,3,1 - timp.,perc. - hp. - pf. - str. 9:00 Southern.
—— DANSE DRAMATIQUE
3,2,3sax.,2 - 4,2,3,1 - timp.,perc. - str.   9:00 Southern.
—— JAKIANA (SUITE) (IN 3 MOVTS.)
str.   12:00 H. Elkan.
—— SOUTH AMERICAN SUITE
3,3,3,3 - 4,3,3,1 - timp.,perc. - pf. - str.   15:00 Southern.
—— LA VIE EN BLEU (FOR CHAMBER ORCH.) (IN 4 MOVTS.)
2,1,2,1 - 2,2,2,0 - timp.,perc.,cel. - pf.- str. 7:30 Salabert.
—— WISDOM AND DESTINY
3,3,3,3 - 4,3,3,1 - timp.,perc. - str.   15:00 Southern.

BOSMANS, Henriëtte
—— BELSAZER (FOR ALTO AND ORCH.) (1936) (Text: H. Heine)
3,2,2,2 - 4,2,2,0 - timp.,perc.,cel. - hp. - str. 10:00 Henmar.
—— CONCERT PIECE FOR VIOLIN AND ORCH. (1934)
3,2,3,2 - 4,2,2,0 - timp.,perc. - str.   18:00 Henmar.
—— CONCERTINO FOR PIANO AND ORCH.
2,2,2,2 - 4,3,2,0 - perc. - hp. pf. - str.   14:00 Henmar.
—— CONCERTO FOR FLUTE AND CHAMBER ORCH.
1,0,1,sax.,1 - 1,1,1,0 - perc. - pf. - str.   12:00 Henmar.
—— POÈME (FOR CELLO AND ORCH.)
4,3,3,3 - 4,2,3,1 - timp.,perc. - hp. - str.   Henmar.

BOSSEUR, Jean-Yves
—— UN ARRACHE DE PARTOUT (FOR INSTRUMENTAL
ENSEMBLE)
4 tpt.,4 trb.,1 b.-trb. - perc.(2),mar.,vibra.,xyl. - 2 electric guit. -
Hammond org.   25:00 Presser.

BOSSI, Marco Enrico
—— IL CIECO, OP. 112 (POEMETTO) (FOR BARITONE, CHORUS
AND ORCH)
3,3,2,2 - 4,2,3,1 - timp.,perc.,cel. - hp. - str. 23:00 Bo. Hawkes.

—— IN MEMORIAM (FOR STRING ORCH.)
str.   5:00 Bo. Hawkes.
—— INNO DE GLORIA (FOR MIXED CHORUS AND ORCH.)
3,2,2,2 - 4,6,5,1 - timp.,perc. - 1-2 hp. - str. 5:00 Bo. Hawkes.
—— OVERTURE
*2,2,2,2 - 4,2,2,1 - timp. - str.   6:00 Bo. Hawkes.
—— SPOSALIZIO (FOR VIOLIN, CELLO, HARP, ORGAN AND
STRINGS)
hp. - org. - str.   16:00 Bo. Hawkes.
—— TRE MOMENTI FRANCESCANI, OP. 140
3,3,2,2 - 4,2,3,1 - timp.,perc.,cel. - str.   22:00 Bo. Hawkes.
—— TRE PEZZI SINFONICI
3,2,3,2 - 4,3,3,1 - timp. - str.   12:00 Bo. Hawkes.

BOSSI, Renzo
—— FRAMMENTI LIRICI (FOR VOICE AND STRINGS)
str.   10:00 Bo. Hawkes.
—— THE HAPPY PRINCE ("IL PRINCIPE FELICE") (1-ACT RADIO
OPERA AFTER OSCAR WILDE'S STORY) (FOR SPEAKER,
SOPRANO, TENOR AND ORCH.)
2,1,1,1 - 2,2,0,0 - timp.,perc.,cel. - hp. - pf. - str. 33:00 Leeds.
—— MESSA DA REQUIEM, OP. 34 (FOR MIXED CHORUS AND
ORCH.)
3,3,2,2 - 4,3,3,1 - timp.,perc.,bells,cel. - hp. - org. - str.
Bo. Hawkes.
—— PRELUDE TO THE OPERA "ANNO MILLE"
2,2,2,2 - 4,2,3,1 - timp. - hp. - org. - str.   6:00 Bo. Hawkes.
—— RICREAZIONI DI ANTICHE MUSICHE ITALIANA (ARR.
FOR STRING ORCH.)
str.   Bo. Hawkes.
—— SYMPHONY IN A MINOR, OP. 11
*3,*3,*3,2 - 4,2,3,1 - timp.,perc. - hp. - str. 25:00 Bo. Hawkes.
—— TRILOGIA CRISTIANA (FOR CELLO AND ORCH.)
perc. - pf. - str.   29:00 Bo. Hawkes.
—— VIBRAZIONI
2,2,2,2 - 4,2,3,1 - timp.,perc. - hp. - str.   13:00 Leeds.
—— VILLOTTA (VARIAZIONI SU UN TEMA POPOLARE)
3,2,3,2 - 4,3,3,1 - timp.,perc.,cel. - hp. - str. 15:00 Bo. Hawkes.

BOSSLER, Kurt
—— CONCERTINO (FOR 3 RECORDERS AND STRINGS)
3 recorders - str.   Belw-Mills.

BOTHE, Wolfgang
—— SYMPHONIC PROLOGUE
2,2,2,2 - 4,3,3,1 -timp.,perc. - hp. - str.   Tetra.

BOTTENBERG, Wolfgang
—— CONCERTO FOR ORGAN AND ORCH. (1975) (IN 3 MOVTS.)
1,1,1,1 - 2,2,0,0 - timp.,perc.(2) - org. - str. 28:00 CanMusCtr.
—— DUINO CANTATA (FOR BARITONE, MIXED CHORUS AND
CHAMBER ORCH.) (1962) (Text: Traditional)
1,1,1,1 - 1,1,1,0 - timp.,cel.,vibra - str.(no d.-b.)
18:00 CanMusCtr.
—— FANTASIA (FOR TRUMPET AND SMALL ORCH.)
12:00 C.A.P.A.C.
—— FANTASIA SERENA (1973) (IN 1 MOVT.)
1,1,1,1 - 2,0,0,0 - str.   22:00 CanMusCtr.
—— PASSACAGLIA
12:00 C.A.P.A.C.
—— RITUAL (FOR MIXED CHORUS AND ORCH.) (1970)
0,0,0,0 - 2,2,2,2 - timp.,perc.(4),cel. -hp. - pf. - str.
21:00 CanMusCtr.
—— SINFONIETTA FOR ORCH. (1970) (IN 3 MOVTS.)
*3,2,2,2 - 4,2,3,1 - timp.,perc. - str.   15:40 CanMusCtr.
—— A SUITE OF CAROLS (1967)
*3,2,2,2 - 2,3,3,1 - timp. - str.   14:45 CanMusCtr.

BOTTESINI, Luigi - SLATFORD, Rodney
—— BOLERO (FOR DOUBLE BASS AND ORCH.)
1,2,2,2 - 2,2,2,0 - timp. - str.   Galaxy.
—— NEL COR PIÙ (VARIATIONS FOR DOUBLE BASS AND
ORCH.)
Galaxy.

BOUCOURECHLIEV, André
—— CONCERTO FOR PIANO AND ORCH.
21:00 Salabert.

BOUGHTON, Rutland
—— BETHLEHEM (CHORAL DRAMA) (FOR MIXED CHORUS
AND ORCH.)
90:00 G. Schirmer.

—— CONCERTO FOR FLUTE AND STRINGS
fl. - str.   15:00 Bo. Hawkes.
—— CONCERTO NO. 1 FOR OBOE AND STRINGS
ob. - str.   21:00 Bo. Hawkes.
—— CONCERTO NO. 2 FOR OBOE AND STRINGS
ob. - str.   23:00 P.R.S.
—— A CYCLE OF SYMBOL SONGS (FOR VOICE AND ORCH.)
G. Schirmer.

BOUILLON, Jo
—— JAZZ FANTASY NO. 1 (Co-composed with Pierre Guillermain)
2,2,2,5 sax.(2 alto,2 ten.,1 bar.),1 - 4,3,3,0 - timp.,perc. - guit. - hp.
- str.   9:00 Salabert.
—— JAZZ SYMPHONY NO. 1 (3 SHORT PIECES FOR JAZZ
COMBO AND ORCH.) (Co-composed with Pierre Guillermain)
3,2,3,5 sax.(2 alto, 2 ten.,1 bar.),2 - 4,6,6,1 - timp.,perc. - guit. -
hp. - str.   15:00 Salabert.

BOULANGER, Lili
—— FAUST ET HÉLÈNE (LYRIC EPISODE FROM GOETHE) (FOR
VOICES, MEZZO-SOPRANO, TENOR, BARITONE AND
ORCH.)
3,3,3,3 - 4,2 cnt.,3,3,1 - timp.,perc.,cel. - 2 hp. - str.
30:00 Belw-Mills.
—— POUR LES FUNÉRAILLES D'UN SOLDAT (FOR BARITONE,
MIXED CHORUS AND ORCH.)
2,3,3,3 - 4,2 cnt.,3,3,1 - timp.,perc.,bell - 2 hp. - str.
8:00 Belw-Mills.
—— PSALM 129 (FOR BARITONE, CHORUS AND ORCH.)
*3,*3,*3, sarr.,2 - 4,3,3,1 - timp.,perc.,cel. - 2 hp. - str.   12:00 EV.
—— PSALM 130 (DE PROFUNDIS) (FOR SOPRANO OR
CONTRALTO, SATB CHORUS AND ORCH.)
3,3,3,3 - 4,3,4,1 - timp.,perc.(3),cel. - 2 hp. - org. - str.   25:00 EV.
—— PSAUME XXIV (FOR SATB CHORUS AND ORCH.)
0,0,0,0 - 4,3,4,1 - timp. - hp. - org.   5:00 EV.
—— VIEILLE PRIÈRE BOUDDHIQUE (FOR TENOR, SATB
CHROUS AND ORCH.)
2,3,3,3 - 4,3,4,1 - timp.,perc.(3),cel. - 2 hp. - str.   7:00 EV.

BOULEZ, Pierre
—— LIVRE POUR CORDES (1968) (FOR LARGE STRING ORCH.)
str.   7:00 Presser.
—— POLYPHONIE (FOR 18 SOLOISTS)
*2,*2,2,sax.,1 - 1,1,1,0 - str.   20:00 Mercury.
—— LE SOLEIL DES EAUX (2 POEMS OF RENÉ CHAR) (FOR
SOPRANO, TENOR, BASS, MIXED CHORUS AND ORCH.)
2,2,2,2 - 3,2,1,1 - timp.,perc. - hp. - str.   9:30 Presser.
—— LE VISAGE NUPTIAL (FOR SOPRANO, CONTRALTO,
WOMEN'S CHORUS AND ORCH.) (Text: René Char)
*3,2 alto fl.,2,2 Eng.hn.,1 E♭cl.,*4,*4 - 4,3,3,1 - timp.,perc.,2
cel.,glock.,vibra.,xyl. - 2 hp. - str.   22:30 Presser.

BOURGEOIS, Derek
—— JABBERWOCKY (AN EXTRAVAGANZA FOR BARITONE
VOICE, MIXED CHORUS AND ORCH.) (Text: Lewis Carroll)
2,2,2,2 - 4,3,3,1 - timp.,perc.(3) - str.   60:00 Oxford.
—— MAIL TRAIN (OVERTURE)
*2,2,2,2 - 4,3,3,1 - timp.,perc. - hp. - str.   10:00 Oxford.
—— SARABANDE AND SCHERZO (1964)
2,2,2,2 - 4,3,3,1 - timp.,perc. - str.   10:00 P.R.S.
—— SYMPHONIC VARIATIONS
*3,*3,2,2 - 4,3,3,1 - timp.,perc.(5, incl.4 on timp.),cel. - hp. -
org.(ad lib.) - pf. - str.   25:00 Oxford.
—— SYMPHONY IN G MINOR
2,2,2,2 - 4,2,3,1 - timp.,perc.(3-4) - str.   25:00 Oxford.
—— VARIATIONS ON A THEME BY MOZART (FOR TWO
DOUBLE BASSES AND ORCH.)
*2,2,2,2 - 2,0,0,0, - timp.,perc. - str.   15:00 Oxford.

BOURGUIGNON, Francis de
—— ALLEGRO GIOCOSO, OP. 75 (1942)
2,2,2,2 - 4,2-3,2,1 - timp.,perc.,cel.,glock.,xyl. - hp. - str.
6:30 H. Elkan.
—— CONCERTINO FOR PIANO AND CHAMBER·ORCH., OP. 99
(1952)
pf. - str   15:00 H. Elkan.
or:
1,1,0,0 - 0,0,0,0 - pf. - str.
or:
1,1,1,1 -1,0,0,0 - timp.,perc. - pf. - str.
—— CONCERTINO FOR PIANO AND ORCH., OP. 25 (1927)
3,3,2,2 - 4,2,2,1 - timp.,perc.,cel. - pf. - str.   15:00 H. Elkan.

—— CONCERTO FOR PIANO AND ORCH., OP. 89
2,2,2,2 - 4,2,3,1 - timp.,perc.,bells - pf. - str.   18:00 CBDM.
—— CONCERTO FOR VIOLIN AND ORCH., OP. 86
2,2,2,2 - 4,2,3,1 - timp.,perc.,cel.,xyl. - str.   15:00 CBDM.
—— CONCERTO FOR 2 PIANOS AND ORCH., OP. 101 (1953)
2,2,2,2 - 4,2,3,1 - timp.,perc.,cel.,glock. - hp. - 2 pf. - str.
14:30 H. Elkan.
—— CONCERTO GROSSO, OP. 82
S.A.B.A.M.
—— DEUX ESQUISSES SUD-AMÉRICAINES
3,2,3,2 - 4,2,3,1 - timp.,perc.,cel.,xyl. - hp. - str.   10:00 Cranz.
—— FANTASY ON TWO THEMES OF EUGENE YSAYE, OP. 57
(FOR PIANO AND ORCH.) (1938)
2,2,2,2 - 4,2,3,1 - timp.,perc. - pf. - str.   15:00 H. Elkan.
—— FÊTE POPULAIRE (MOUVEMENT SYMPHONIQUE), OP. 34-B
(1929)
3,2,3,2 - 4,3,3,1 - timp.,perc.,cel.,glock.,xyl - hp. - str.
8:00 H. Elkan.
—— JUVENTUS (SYMPHONIC SUITE), OP. 70 (1941)
2,2,2,2 - 4,4,3,1 - timp.,perc.,cel.,glock.,xyl. - hp. - str.
16:00 H. Elkan.
—— OISEAUX DE NUIT (SYMPHONIC POEM), OP. 47 (1936)
2,2,2,2 - 4,3,3,1 - timp.,perc., 2 bells, xyl. -pf. - str.
12:00 H. Elkan.
—— PETITE SUITE (SYMPHONIC SUITE NO. 2) OP. 66 (1940)
2,1,2,1 - 2,2,1,0 - timp.,perc.,cel. - str.   12:00 H. Elkan.
—— PRÉLUDE ET DANSE, OP. 35 (1929)
3,2,2,2 - 4,3,3,1 - timp.,perc.,cel.,glock.,xyl. - hp. - str.
9:00 H. Elkan.
—— PUZZLE (SYMPHONIC SUITE), OP. 58 (1938) (IN 4 MOVTS.)
2,2,2,2 - 4,4,3,1 - timp.,perc.,cel.,xyl. - hp. - str.   21:00 H. Elkan.
—— RECUERDOS: DEUX IMPRESSIONS SUD-AMÉRICAINES, OP.
79
2,2,2,sax.,2 - 4,3,3,1 - timp.,perc.,glock.,cel.,xyl. - hp. - str.
10:00 CBDM.
—— RÉCITATIF ET RONDE (FOR TRUMPET AND ORCH.), OP. 94
(1951)
2,1,2,1 - 2,2,1,0 - timp.,perc., - hp. - str.   8:00 H. Elkan.
—— SINFONIETTA, OP. 62 (1939)
2,1,2,1 - 2,2,1,0 - timp.,perc.,xyl. - str.   15:00 H. Elkan.
—— SUITE DE TROIS DANSES, OP. 96 (1952) (FROM THE
BALLET "JANNAH"))
2,2,2,2 - 4,2,3,1 - timp.,perc.,cel. - hp. - str.   10:00 H. Elkan.
—— SUITE FOR VIOLA AND ORCH., OP. 67 (1940)
1,1,1,1 - 2,2,0,0 - timp.,perc.,glock. - str.   15:00 Hulpiau.
—— SYMPHONIE EN 4 PARTIES, OP. 42 (1924)
2,2,2,2 - 4,3,3,1 - timp.,perc.,bells.,cel.,glock.,xyl. - hp. - str.
22:00 H. Elkan.

BOUTNIKOFF, Ivan
—— LE JARDIN DES CARESSES ("THE GARDEN OF
CARESSES"): SUITE NO. 1, OP. 21 (FOUR PRAYERS FOR
VOICE AND ORCH.) (Text: Franz Toussaint)
2,2,2,2 - 4,2,3,1 - timp.,perc.(2),cel. - hp. - str.   10:00 Composer.
—— LE JARDIN DES CARESSES ("THE GARDEN OF
CARESSES"): SUITE NO. 2, OP. 22 (THREE PRAYERS FOR
VOICE AND ORCH.) (Text: Franz Toussaint)
2(2nd alt. with picc.),2,2,2 - 4,2,3,1 - timp.,perc.(2),cel. - hp. - str.
11:00 Composer.
—— POÈME, OP. 30 (FOR PIANO AND ORCH.)
2(2nd alt. with picc.),2(2nd alt. with Eng.hn.),2,2 - 4,2,3,1 -
timp.,perc.(3) - pf. - str.   18:00 Composer.
—— ROCKET (SYMPHONIC POEM)
2 picc.,2,*4,*4,*4 - 6,4,3,1 - timp.,perc.(4),cel.,glock. - 2 hp. - str.
5:00 Composer.
—— THE SEA (ALBATROSS) (SYMPHONIC POEM)
*3,*3,*3,*3 - 6,3,3,1 - timp.,perc.(3),cel.,glock. - 2 hp. - str.
16:00 Composer.
—— THE SPRING RECITAL (SUITE) (IN 6 MOVTS.)
*3,*3,*3,*3 - 4,3,3,1 - timp.,perc.(4),cel.,glock.,xyl. - hp. - str.
17:00 Composer.
—— SUITE NO. 3 (IN 7 MOVTS.)
2(2nd alt. with picc.),2(2nd alt. with Eng. hn.),2,2 - 4,2,3,1 -
timp.,perc.(3),cel.,glock. - hp. - pf. - str.   17:00 Composer.
—— SYMPHONIC POEM, OP. 10
3(3rd alt. with picc.),*3,*4,2 - 4,3,3,1 - timp.,perc.(4),cel.,glock. -
hp. - str.   14:00 Composer.
—— SYMPHONIC POEM, OP. 9
3,*3,*3,2 - 4,2,3,1 - timp.,perc.(2) - hp. - str.   4:00 Composer.
—— TO PAN (SYMPHONY NO. 1), OP. 16 (SYMPHONIC SUITE
AFTER HOMER) (IN 4 MOVTS.)
3(3rd alt. with picc.),*3,*3(2nd alt. with E♭cl.),*3 - 4,3,3,1 -
timp.,perc.(4),cel.,glock. - 2 hp. - pf. - str.   37:00 Composer.

BOUTRY, Roger
—— CONCERTINO FOR FLUTE AND STRINGS
    fl. - str.   12:00 Baron.
—— CONCERTO FANTASY (FOR 2 PIANOS AND STRING
    ORCH.)
    2 pf. - str.   27:00 Salabert.
—— CONCERTO FOR ORCHESTRA
    4,3,3,alto sax.,3 - 4,4,3,1 - timp.,perc. - 2 hp.   17:00 Salabert.
—— CONCERTO FOR PIANO AND ORCH.
    2,2,2,2 - 2,2,1,0 - timp.,perc. - hp. - pf. - str.   18:00 Salabert.
—— INTERMEZZI (FOR CHAMBER ORCH.)
                           Presser.

    SERIES NO. 1
    tpt. - mar. - pf. - str.   11:30
    SERIES NO. 2
    tpt. - mar. - pf. - str.   14:30
—— PASSACAILLE ET DANSE PROFANE
    3,2,2,3 - 4,3,3,1 - timp.,perc.(3) - hp. - pf. - str.   12:00 Salabert.
—— REFLETS SUR ROME
    3,2,3,alto sax.,2 - 4,3,3,1 - timp.,perc.(3) - str.   15:00 Salabert.
—— SERENADE FOR ALTO SAXOPHONE AND ORCH.
    1,1,1,1 alto sax.,1 - 1,1,1,0 - pf. - str.   14:00 Salabert.

BOUTRY, Roger - ASTORG, Georgette
—— CHAKA (ORATORIO) (FOR SPEAKING VOICE, MEN'S
    CHORUS AND ORCH) (Text: Leopold Senghor)
    2,2,2,alto sax.,3 - 4,3,3,1 - timp., perc.(7),cel. - hp. - pf. - str.
                           60:00 Salabert.
—— LE ROSAIRE DES JOIES (FOR SPEAKING VOICE, SOPRANO,
    SATB CHORUS AND ORCH.) (Text: Marie Noel)
    3,2,3,alto sax.,3 - 4,3,3,1 - timp.,perc.(5) - hp. - str.
                           30:00 Salabert.

BOUVAL, Jules - GOUBLIER, Gustave
—— SUITE
                           11:30 Baron.

BOWLES, Paul
—— CONCERTO FOR TWO PIANOS AND ORCH. (IN 4
    MOVEMENTS)
                      20:00 AmerMusEd.
—— MEDIODIA (NOONDAY) (SUITE OF MEXICAN DANCES)
    1,1,1,1 - 0,1,0,0 - perc. - str.   15:00 AmerMusEd.
—— SCÈNES D'ANABASE (FOR VOICE AND INSTRUMENTAL
    ENSEMBLE)
                      AmerMusEd.
—— SENTIMENTAL COLLOGUY
    2(2nd alt. with picc.),2(2nd alt. with Eng. hn.),2(2nd alt. with
    b.-cl.),1 - 2,2,2,0 - timp.,perc. - hp. - pf. - str.   10:40 Composer.
—— SUITE FROM "PASTORELA" (IN 6 MOVTS.)
    2(2nd alt. with picc.),2(2nd alt. with Eng. hn.),2(2nd alt. with
    b.-cl.),2 - 4,2,3,0 - timp.,perc.,xyl. - pf. - str.   8:32 Composer.
—— SYMPHONIC SUITE (IN 3 MOVTS.)
    2,1,1,1 - 2,2,1,0 - perc. - pf. - str.   12:00 AmerMusEd.
—— THREE PASTORAL SONGS (FOR VOICE, PIANO AND
    STRINGS)
    pf. - str.   AmerMusEd.
—— THE WIND REMAINS (CHAMBER OPERA) %
    1(alt. with picc.),1(alt. with Eng. hn.),1(alt. with b.-cl.),1 - 1,1,1,0 -
    perc. (2) - hp. - 1 vln.,1 d.-b.   16:21 AmerMusEd.

BOYARSKY, Anatoly A.
—— ROMANTIC POEM (FOR VIOLIN AND ORCH.)
                      G. Schirmer.

BOYCE, William - ADLINGTON, Fred
—— SUITE IN A
    pf.(ad lib.) - str.   10:00 Mills.

BOYCE, William - BAUER, Harold
—— YE SWEET RETREAT (FOR STRING ORCH.)
    str.   4:00 G. Schirmer.

BOYCE, William - BRIDGEWATER, Leslie
—— THE SHEPHERD'S LOTTERY (SUITE FOR STRING ORCH.)
    str.   7:00 Bo. Hawkes.

BOYCE, William - BROWN
—— TWO SONATAS (FOR STRING ORCH.)
    str.   Galaxy.

BOYCE, William - FINZI, Gerald
—— ODE FOR HIS MAJESTY'S BIRTHDAY, 1768
    0,2,0,2 - 2,0,0,0, - cemb. - str.   Galaxy.
—— ODE FOR HIS MAJESTY'S BIRTHDAY, 1769
    0,2,0,2 - 2,0,0,0 - cemb. - str.   Galaxy.
—— ODE FOR HIS MAJESTY'S BIRTHDAY, 1775
    0,2,0,2 - 2,0,0,0 - timp. - cemb. - str.   Galaxy.
—— ODE FOR THE NEW YEAR, 1758
    0,2,0,2 - 0,2,0,0 - timp. - cemb. - str.   Galaxy.
—— ODE FOR THE NEW YEAR, 1771
    0,2,0,2 - 0,0,0,0 - cemb. - str.   Galaxy.
—— ODE FOR THE NEW YEAR, 1772
    0,2,0,2 - 0,0,0,0 - cemb. - str.   Galaxy.

BOYCE, William - LAMBERT, Constant
—— OVERTURE IN D MINOR (OVERTURE TO "THE
    CAMBRIDGE ODE")
    0,2,0,2 (ad lib.) - 0,0,0,0 - str.   Oxford.
—— PAN AND SYRINX: OVERTURE
    2 ob. (ad lib.),bn.(ad lib.) - str.   8:00 Oxford.
—— THE POWER OF MUSIC (OVERTURE)
    2 ob. (ad lib.),bn.(ad lib.) - str.   6:00 Oxford.
—— SYMPHONY NO. 1, IN B♭ MAJOR (IN 3 MOVEMENTS)
    2 ob. - str.   5:30 Oxford.
—— SYMPHONY NO. 2, IN A MAJOR
    1. Allegro assai; 2. Vivace; 3. Presto
    2 ob. - str.   Oxford.
—— SYMPHONY NO. 3, IN C MAJOR
    1. Allegro; 2. Vivace; 3. Menvetto - Allegretto
    2 ob. - str.   Oxford.
—— SYMPHONY NO. 4, IN F MAJOR
    1. Allegro; 2. Vivace ma non troppo; 3. Gavot
    2 ob. - 2 hn. - str.   6:00 Oxford.
—— SYMPHONY NO. 5, IN D MAJOR
    1. Allegro ma non troppo; 2. Tempo di Gavotte; 3. Menutto
    2 ob. - 2 tpt. - str.   Oxford.
—— SYMPHONY NO. 6, IN F MAJOR
    1. Largo e sostenuto; 2. Larghetto
    2 ob.(ad lib.) - str.   Oxford.
—— SYMPHONY NO. 7, IN B♭ MAJOR
    1. Andante; 2. Andante moderato; 3. Jigg
    2 fl.(ad lib.),2ob. - str.   Oxford.
—— SYMPHONY NO. 8, IN F MAJOR
    1. Pomposo; 2. Andante; 3. Gavotta
    2 fl.(ad lib.),2 ob. - str.   13:00 Oxford.

BOYCE, William - PLATT, Richard
—— OVERTURE NO. 1, IN D
    0,2,0,0-1 - 0,0,0,0 - cemb. - str.   6:30 Oxford.
—— OVERTURE NO. 2, IN G
    2,2,0,0-1 - 2,0,0,0 - cemb. - str.   7:30 Oxford.
—— OVERTURE NO. 3, IN B FLAT
    0,2,0,0-1 - 0,0,0,0 - cemb. - str.   5:00 Oxford.
—— OVERTURE NO. 4, IN D
    0,2,0,0-1 - 2,2,0,0 - timp. - cemb. - str.   8:00 Oxford.

BOYD, Anne
—— THE VOICE OF THE PHOENIX (1971)
    4(3rd and 4th alt. with piccs.),*3,4(4th alt. with b.-cl.),4 - 4,3,2,1 -
    timp.,perc.(11) - electric guit. - hp.(amplified) - hpsc.(amplified) -
    pf.(amplified) - VCS-3 synthesizer (ad lib.) - str.
                       25:00 G. Schirmer.

BOYER, Jo
—— CHINATOWN, OP. 9 (BALLET SUITE) (1963) (IN 5 MOVTS.)
    2,2,2,2 - 4,3,3,0 - timp.,perc.(4),cel.,glock.,mar.,vibra.,xyl. - 2 pf.(1
    upright) - str.   18:22 Composer.
—— CONCERTINO DA CAMERA, OP. 3 (1955) (IN 1 MOVT.)
    tpt. - timp.,perc.(3),cel.,glock.,xyl. - hp. - pf. - str.
                       10:30 Composer.
—— KOREAN VARIATIONS, OP. 19 (1972)
    3(2nd alt. with alto fl.),3(3rd alt. with Eng. hn.),*3,*3 - 4,3,3,1 -
    timp.,perc.(7),bells,glock.,mar.,vibra.,xyl. - hp. - pf. - str.
                       16:00 Composer.

BOYLE, George
—— CONCERTINO FOR PIANO AND CHAMBER ORCH. (IN 3
    MOVTS.)
    1,1,1,1 - hn. - pf. - str.   16:00 Composer.
—— CONCERTO FOR CELLO AND ORCH.
    2,2,2,2 - 4,2,0,0 - timp. - hp. - str.   23:00 Composer.

—— CONCERTO IN D MINOR, FOR PIANO AND ORCH. (IN 3
MOVEMENTS)
2,2(1 alt. with Eng. hn.),2,2 - 4,2,3,1 - timp. - pf. - str.
25:00 Composer.
—— THE PIED PIPER OF HAMELIN (CANTATA) (FOR
CONTRALTO, TENOR, BARITONE, CHORUS AND ORCH.)
2(1 alt. with picc.),2,2,2 - 4,2,3,1 - perc. - str.   45:00 Chappell.
—— SYMPHONIC FANTASY
2(1 alt. with picc.),2,2,*3 - 4,3,3,1 - timp.,perc. (2) - hp. - str.
15:00 Composer.

BOZAY, Attila
—— KINAI SZELENCE (CANTATA) (FOR SOPRANO AND
ORCH.)
A.R.J.U.S.
—— THE MILL (FOR CHAMBER ORCH.)
22:00 Bo. Hawkes.
—— PEZZO CONCERTATO NO. 2, OP. 24 (FOR CIMBALOM AND
ORCH.)
A.R.J.U.S.
—— PEZZO SINFONICO
*3,*2,2,2 - 4,3,3,1 - perc.,cel. - hp. - pf. - str.   15:16 Bo. Hawkes.

BOŽIČ, Darijan
—— AUDIOGRAPH
0,0,1,0 - 0,0,1,0 - perc. - pf. - str.   10:00 Hans Gerig.
—— AUDIOSPECTRUM
2(2nd alt. with picc.),2(2nd alt. with Eng. hn.),2(2nd alt. with
b.-cl.),2(2nd alt. with c.-bn.) - 4,4,3,1 - timp.,perc.(7) - pf. - str.
8:00 Hans Gerig.
—— AUDIOSTRUCTURAE (FOR PIANO AND ORCH.) (1976)
*3,*3,*3,*3 - 4,3,3,1 - perc.(3) - hp. - pf. - str.   14:00 Hans Gerig.
—— CONCERTO FOR ALTO SAXOPHONE AND ORCH.
1(alt. with picc.),1,2(2nd alt. with b.-cl.),alto sax.,2(2nd alt. with
c.-bn.) - 2,1,1,1 - perc.(2) - hp. - pf. - str.   10:00 Hans Gerig.
—— CONCERTO FOR TROMBONE AND ORCH.
1(alt. with picc.),1,1(alt. with b.-cl. and alto sax.),2 - 2,1,2,1 -
timp.,perc. - hp. - pf. - str.   10:00 Hans Gerig.
—— CONCERTO FOR TRUMPET AND ORCH.
1(alt. with picc.),1,1(alt. with b.-cl. and alto sax.),2 - 2,2,1,1 -
timp.,perc.(5) - pf. - str.   10:00 Hans Gerig.
—— CONCERTO GROSSO IN F
0,0,1,sax.,0 - 0,1,1,0 - timp.,perc.(5),vibra.,xyl. - pf. - d.-b.
12:00 Hans Gerig.
—— ELONGATIONS (FOR PIANO AND 12 INSTRUMENTS)
1,1,1,0 - 1,0,0,0 - hp. - pf. - str.(2,1,1,1)   7:00 Hans Gerig.
—— POLINEIKES (COLLAGE, AFTER DOMENIKA SMOLETA'S
DRAMA "ANTIGONE") (WITH 6 VOICES AND TAPE)
1(alt. with picc. and recorder),0,0,ten. sax.,*1 - 1,2,0,0 - perc.(2) -
tape-recorder - pf. - str.   33:00 Hans Gerig.
—— SYMPHONY (FOR JAZZ COMBO AND ORCH.)
0,0,1,sax.,0 - 0,1,1,0 - perc.(3) - electric guit. - pf. - str.
12:00 Hans Gerig.

BOZZA - PETIOT
—— VOYAGES (IN 5 MOVTS.)
15:00 Baron.

BOZZA, Eugène
—— BALLADE (FOR TROMBONE AND ORCH.)
1,1,1,1 - 2,1,2,0 - timp.,perc. - pf.(or hp.) - str.   9:00 Baron.
—— BEPPO (1-ACT OPERA BUFFA) % (FOR SOLO VOICES,
CHORUS AND ORCH.) (Text: José Bruyr)
2,2,2,2 - 2,2,1,0 - timp.,perc.,xyl. - hp. - pf. - str.   60:00 Baron.
—— CONCERTINO DA CAMERA (FOR CHAMBER ORCH.)
1,1,1,1 - 0,0,0,0 - hp. - str.   15:00 Baron.
—— CONCERTINO FOR ALTO SAXOPHONE AND ORCH.
2,2,2,alto sax.,2 - 2,1,1,0 - timp.,perc.,cel. - str.   15:00 Baron.
—— CONCERTINO FOR BASSOON AND ORCH., OP. 49
1,1,1,1 - 1,1,1,0 - timp.,perc.,cel. - str.   12:00 Baron.
—— CONCERTINO FOR TRUMPET AND SMALL ORCH.
1,1,1,1 - 1,1,0,0 - perc. - str.   15:00 Baron.
—— CONCERTO FOR CELLO AND ORCH., OP. 57
2,1(alt. with Eng. hn.),2,2 - 1,1,0,0 - timp.,perc. - str.
15:00 Baron.
—— CONCERTO FOR CLARINET AND ORCH.
2,1,1,1 - 1,1,1,0 - timp. - str.   16:00 Baron.
—— CONCERTO FOR VIOLIN AND ORCH.
3,3,2,2 - 4,2,3,1 - timp.,perc.(3),glock.,cel. - hp. - str.
16:30 Presser.
—— CONCERTO FOR VIOLIN, VIOLA, CELLO AND ORCH.
2,3,2,2 - 2,1,1,0 - hp. - str.   18:00 Baron.

—— DIVERTISSEMENT FOR VIOLIN AND ORCH.
2,2,2,2 - 2,1,1,0 - cel. - hp. - str.   15:00 Baron.
—— JEUX DE PLAGE (TWO SUITES)
3,3,3,2 alto sax., 3 - 4,3,3,1 - timp.,cel.,glock.,xyl. - guit. - 2 hp. -
pf. - str.   29:00 Baron.
—— LA LÉGENDE DE ROUKMANI (LYRIC FANTASY IN 1 ACT)
% (FOR 3 SOLO VOICES AND ORCH.) (Text: Ch. Clerc.)
3,3,3,3 - 4,3,3,1 - timp.,perc.,bells,cel.,glock. - 2 hp. - str.
24:00 Baron.
—— LÉONIDAS (FRESQUE ANTIQUE) (IN 2 ACTS AND 4
SCENES) % (FOR 3 SOLO VOICES, CHORUS AND ORCH.)
3,3,3,1 alto sax.,3 - 0,0,0,0 - timp.,perc.,bells,cel.,glock. - 2 hp. -
org.(ad lib.) - pf. - str.   Baron.
On Stage: 3 tpt., 3 trb.
—— PAX TRIUMPHANS (POÈME SYMPHONIQUE)
3,3,3,3 - 6(2 ad lib.),4,4,4,1 - timp.,perc.,bells,cel.,glock. - 2 hp. -
org. (ad lib.) - pf. - str.   20:00 Baron.
—— PRELUDE ET PASSACAILLE
3,3,3,3 - 4,3,3,1 - timp.,perc.,xyl. - org. (ad lib.) - pf. - str.
14:00 Baron.
—— RAPSODIE NICOISE (FOR VIOLIN AND ORCH.)
2,2,2,2 - 2,2,0,0 - timp.,perc.,cel. - hp. - str.   16:00 Baron.
—— RHYTMIC (FOR TIMPANI, PERCUSSION AND ORCH.)
2,2,2,2 - 4,3,2,1 - timp.,perc.,cel. - hp. - pf. - str.   7:30 Baron.
—— SHEPHERDS OF PROVENCE (SUITE FOR OBOE, ENGLISH
HORN AND ORCH.)
Baron.
—— SINFONIETTA FOR STRING ORCH.
str.   22:00 Baron.
—— SUITE POUR UN VAUDEVILLE (IN 4 MOVTS.)
2,1,1,1 - 1,1,1,0 - perc. - pf. - str.   7:00 Baron.
—— SYMPHONIE
3,3,3,3 - 4,3,3,1 - timp.,perc.,xyl., - pf. - str.   42:00 Baron.
—— VARIATIONS LIBRES ET FINALE
3,3,3,3 - 4,3,3,1 - timp.,perc. - pf. - str.   5:00 Baron.

BOZZA, Ricard E.
—— CONCERTINO FOR VIOLA AND ORCH.
2,2,2,2 - 4,2,3,0 - timp.,perc.,cel. - hp. - str.   Salabert.

BRAAL, Andries de
—— CHORAL FANTASY ON PSALM 91 (IN OLDEN STYLE) (FOR
TRUMPET AND STRING ORCH.)
tpt. - str.   Henmar.
—— CONCERTINO FOR FLUTE AND STRING ORCH.
fl. - str.   14:00 Henmar.
—— LARGO EN SCHERZO
2,3,2,3 - 3,2,3,1 - timp.,perc. - hp. - str.   15:00 Henmar.
—— STUDY FOR ORGAN, STRING ORCH. AND TIMPANI
timp. - org. - str.   7:00 Henmar.
—— THREE PSALMS (DRIE PSALMEN) (1948) (FOR MIXED
CHORUS AND ORCH.)
3,2,2,3 - 3,3,3,0 -timp.,perc.,cel. - hp. - str.   18:00 Henmar.

BRABANDIERE, J. de
—— ADAGIO IN MEMORIAM JOHANNIS XXIII
str.   12:00 Henmar.

BRADLEY, Desmond
—— SYMPHONY NO. 1 IN C MINOR, OP. 6 (1964)
3,3,3,3 - 5-6,2,3,0 - timp. - hp. - str.   25:00 A.P.R.A.
—— SYMPHONY NO 2, OP. 10
*3,*3,*3,*3 - 5,4,3,1 - timp.,perc.,cel. - 2 hp. - org. - str.
30:00 A.P.R.A.

BRAEIN, Edvard
—— CONCERT POLONAISE
3,2,2,2 - 4,3,3,1 - timp.,perc. - str.   7:00 T.O.N.O.

BRAEIN, Edvard Fliflet
—— ADAGIO FOR STRINGS
str.   7:00 Musikk-Hu.
—— CAPRICCIO FOR PIANO AND ORCH.
1,1,2,1 - 4,2,3,0 - timp.,perc. - pf. - str.   12:00 T.O.N.O.
—— DIVERTIMENTO (FOR FLUTE AND SMALL ORCH.) (IN 3
MOVTS.)
1,1,2,1 - 2,1,0,0 - timp. - str.   16:00 T.O.N.O.
—— INTRATA
3:30 T.O.N.O.
—— LARGO FOR STRINGS
str.   11:30 Musikk-Hu.
—— OVERTURE
2,2,2,2 - 4,2,3,0 - timp.,perc. - str.   6:30 Musikk-Hu.

—— SERENADE (IN 3 MOVTS.)
    1,1,2,1 - 2,1,3,0 - timp.,perc. - str.   12:00 Musikk-Hu.
—— SYMPHONIC PRELUDE
    2,2,2,2 - 4,3,3,0 - perc. - str.   11:00 T.O.N.O.
—— SYMPHONY NO. 1 (IN 4 MOVTS.)
    2,2,2,2 - 4,2,3,0 - timp.,perc. - str.   32:00 T.O.N.O.
—— SYMPHONY NO. 2 (IN 3 MOVTS.)
    2,2,2,2 - 4,3,3,1 - timp.,perc.,cel. - hp. - pf. - str.   24:00 T.O.N.O.
—— SYMPHONY NO. 3
    17:00 T.O.N.O.

BRAEM, Thüring
—— SCHICHTEN (FÜR GROSSES ORCH.)
    10:00 S.U.I.S.A.
—— TEXTURES (FÜR 24 SPIELER IN 6 GRUPPEN)
(KAMMERORCHESTER)
    10:00 S.U.I.S.A.

BRAGA, Antonio
—— LE CARNAVAL DE NAPLES (HOMMAGE À DARIUS
MILHAUD)
    1,2,2,2 - 2,2,1,0 - timp.,perc.(3) - hp. - pf. - str.   5:00 Presser.
—— CONCERTO EXOTIQUE
    2,2,2,2 - 2,2,0,0 - perc.,cel. - pf. - str.   24:00 Choudens.

BRAGGIOTTI, Mario
—— GETTYSBURG CANTATA (FOR BARITONE, MIXED
CHORUS AND ORCH.)
    2(2nd alt. with picc.),*3,*3,2 - 4,3,3,1 - timp.,perc.(2),bells - hp. -
str.   21:00 Composer.
—— PIANORAMA (FANTASY ON A GIVEN THEME FOR PIANO
AND ORCH.) (IN 5 MOVTS.)
    *3,*3,*3,2 - 4,3,3,1 - timp.,perc.(3) - pf. - str.   20:00 Mills.
—— SPANISH RHAPSODY (FANTASY FOR 1 OR 2 PIANOS AND
ORCH.) (IN 3 MOVTS.)
    1(alt. with picc.),*2,*3,1 - 4,3,3,1 - timp.,perc.(2),xyl. - hp. - 1-2pf.
- str.   11:00 Composer.

BRAHMS, Johannes
—— GIPSY SONGS (ZIGEUNERLIEDER), OP. 103 (FOR MIXED
OR WOMEN'S CHORUS AND ORCH. (Edited by W. G.
Whittaker; English text: Albert G. Latham)
    1,1,2,1 - 2,1,1,0 - timp. - str.   18:00 Oxford.

BRAHMS, Johannes - BENZI, Roberto
—— VARIATIONS AND FUGUE ON A THEME OF HANDEL, OP.
24
    2,2,2,2 - 2,2,3,0 - timp.,perc. - hp. - str.   30:00 Presser.
—— VARIATIONS ON A THEME OF SCHUMANN
    3,3,3,3 - 4,3,3,1 - timp. - str.   18:00 Presser.

BRAHMS, Johannes - BOUTNIKOFF, Ivan
—— VARIATIONS AND FUGUE ON A THEME OF HANDEL. OP.
24
    2(2nd alt. with picc.),2(2nd alt. with Eng. hn.),2,2 - 4,2,3,1 -
timp.,perc.,cel.,glock. - hp. - pf. - str.   27:00 Arranger.

BRAHMS, Johannes - DASCH, George
—— SYMPHONY NO. 1 IN C MINOR
    C. Fischer.

BRAHMS, Johannes - DORATI, Antal
—— SEXTET NO. 1 IN B♭ MAJOR, OP. 18
    str.   28:00 A.P.R.A.

BRAHMS, Johannes - GOOSSENS, Eugene
—— SEXTET FOR STRINGS, IN G MAJOR
    str.   32:00 P.R.S.

BRAHMS, Johannes - HAHN, Reynaldo
—— GERMANIA (SUITE OF WALTZES)
    3,2,2,2 - 4,4,0,0 - timp.,perc.(3) - 2 hp. - str.   13:30 Presser.

BRAHMS, Johannes - HOFFMANN, Adolf G.
—— RHAPSODY IN G MINOR, OP. 79, NO. 2
    3,2,3,3 - 4,3,3,1 - timp.,perc. - str.   C. Fischer.

BRAHMS, Johannes - LEINSDORF, Erich
—— CHORALE-PRELUDE: "O GOD, THOU HOLIEST"
    *3,*3,*3,*3 - 4,3,3,1 - str.   6:00 Broude.
—— CHORALE-PRELUDE: "THERE IS A ROSE IN FLOWER"
    3,*3,*3,*3 - 4 hn. - str.   4:00 Broude.

—— FOUR SERIOUS SONGS (FOR BARITONE AND ORCH.)
    3,3,3,3 - 4,3,3,1 - timp. - hp. - str.   20:00 Bo. Hawkes.

BRAHMS, Johannes - MASON, Daniel Gregory
—— CHORALE PRELUDE AND FUGUE (FOR STRING ORCH.)
    str.   Ricordi.

BRAHMS, Johannes - MISCH, Ludwig
—— FOUR SERIOUS SONGS, OP. 121 (FOR BASS AND ORCH.)
    2,2,2,3 - 3,2,3,0 - timp. - hp. - str.   18:00 Lengnick.

BRAHMS, Johannes - RIEGE, Ernst
—— INTERMEZZO IN A MAJOR, OP. 118, NO. 2
    1,1,2,1 - 2,0,0,0 - glock. - hp. - str.   6:30 F. Colombo.

BRAHMS, Johannes - ROBERTS, Charles J.
—— ACADEMIC FESTIVAL OVERTURE
    C. Fischer.

BRAHMS, Johannes - RUBBRA, E.
—— VARIATIONS AND FUGUE ON A THEME BY HANDEL
    2,2,2,2 - 4,2,3,0 - timp. - hp. - str.   26:00 Bo. Hawkes.

BRAHMS, Johannes - SARGENT, Malcolm
—— FOUR SERIOUS SONGS (FOR CONTRALTO OR BARITONE
AND ORCH.)
    2,2,2,2 - 4,2,3,0 - timp. - hp. - str.   20:00 Oxford.

BRAHMS, Johannes - SCHOENBERG, Arnold
—— PIANO QUARTET IN G MINOR
    *3,*3,E♭cl.,*3,*3 - 4,3,3,1 - timp.,perc. - str.   38:00 G. Schirmer.

BRAHMS, Johannes - SEVITZKY, Fabien
—— VIER LIEDER
    Arranger.

    AN EINE AEOLSHARFE, OP. 19, NO. 5 (FOR VOICE AND
STRINGS)
    hp. - str.
    SAPPHISCHE ODE, OP. 94, NO. 4 (FOR VOICE AND
STRINGS)
    hp. - str.
    VERGEBLICHES STÄNDCHEN, OP. 84, NO. 4
    str.
    VON EWIGER LIEBE, OP. 43, NO. 1 (FOR VOICE AND FULL
ORCH.)

BRAHMS, Johannes - SIMON, Eric
—— FOUR SERIOUS SONGS (FOR BARITONE AND ORCH.)
    G. Schirmer.

BRAHMS, Johannes - THOMSON, V.
—— ELEVEN CHORALE PRELUDES, OP. 122
    2(2nd alt. with picc.),2(2nd alt. with Eng. hn.),2,2(2nd alt. with
c.-bn.) - 4,2,3,1 - timp.,perc.(1),glock. - str.   25:30 Bo. Hawkes.

BRAÑA, Pedro
—— FABIOLA (OVERTURE)
    *3,2(2nd alt. with Eng.hn.),2,2 - 4,2,3,0 - timp.,perc. - hp. - str.
    Cranz.

BRANCH, Harold
—— CHAMBER SYMPHONY, OP. 5 (IN 1 MOVT.) (1957)
    1,*2,*3,*2 - 2,1,1,0 - str.   15:00 Composer.

BRAND, Max
—— EINE NACHTMUSIK (FOR CHAMBER ORCH.)
    1,1,1,1 - 1,1,0,0 - perc. - hp. - str.   12:00 Henmar.
—— NIGHT ON THE BAYOUS OF LOUISIANA
    2,2,2,0 - 4,0,0,0 - timp.,cel. - hp. - str.   9:30 Presser.

BRAND, Theo
—— CONCERTINO GIOCOSO
    perc. - str.   13:00 Robbins.

BRANDT-BUYS, Jan
—— TANCRED (CONCERT PIECE FOR CELLO AND ORCH.), OP.
35
    2,2,2,2 - 3,2,0,0 - timp. - str.   Weinberger.

BRANSCOMBE, Gena
—— THE LIGHT (FOR BARITONE, CHORUS AND ORCH.)
    1,1,2,1 - 1,1,1,0 - timp. - org. - str.   12:00 Composer.

—— THE PHANTOM CARAVAN (FOR MEN'S CHORUS AND
CHAMBER ORCH.)
 1,1,1,0 - hn. - timp. - str.   12:00 Church.
—— QUEBEC (SYMPHONIC SUITE)
 *3,2,2,2 - 4,4,3,1 - timp.,perc.(2) - hp. - str. 16:00 Composer.
 or:
 1,0,1,0 - 1,1,0,0 - timp.,perc.(1) - hp. - str.
—— YOUTH OF THE WORLD (FOR WOMEN'S CHORUS AND
ORCH.) (IN 3 MOVTS.)
 2,2,2,2 - 4,2,3,1 - timp.,perc. - hp. - str. 10:00 Composer.

BRANSON, David
—— MEDITERRANEAN
 pf. - str.   6:00 Novello.
—— PARAPHRASES (1942)
 str.   12:00 P.R.S.
—— PAVANE AND TOCCATA (FOR PIANO AND ORCH.)(1944)
 2,3,2,2 - 3,2,3,1 - timp.,perc. - pf. - str. 20:00 P.R.S.

BRANT, Henry
—— AN ADVENTURE
 3,3,3,2 - 4,3,3,0 - perc. - hp. - pf. - str. 5:00 C. Fischer.
—— ANGELS AND DEVILS (CONCERTO FOR FLUTE AND
FLUTE ENSEMBLE) (1931)
 6 fl.,3 picc.,2 alto. fl. 18:00 MCA Music.
—— ANTIPHONY I (FOR 5 ORCHESTRAL GROUPS, WITH 5
CONDUCTORS) (1953)
   12:00 C. Fischer.
—— ATLANTIS (FOR CHORUS, ORCHESTRA, BAND,
PERCUSSION ENSEMBLE, EXTRA BASS GROUP, MALE
SPEAKER AND MEZZO SINGER) (1960)
   23:00 C. Fischer.
—— BARRICADES (FOR TENOR VOICE, SOPRANO SAXOPHONE
AND ENSEMBLE) (1961)
 0,0,1,sopr.sax.,1 - 0,0,1,0 - xyl. - pf. - str.(1,1,1,1)
   12:00 C. Fischer.
—— CEREMONY (FOR SOPRANO, ALTO, TENOR, BASS AND
ANTIPHONAL ENSEMBLE) (1954)
 2,1,2,2 - 0,0,0,0 - perc.(4) - pf.(4-hands) - 1 vln., 1 c.
   9:00 C. Fischer.
—— CONCERTO FOR SAXOPHONE AND ORCH. (1941)
   18:00 C. Fischer.
—— CONCERTO FOR SAXOPHONE (OR TRUMPET) AND NINE
INSTRUMENTS
 1,0,6,sax.(or tpt.),0 - 0,0,0,1 - perc. 20:00 C. Fischer.
—— CONCERTO FOR VIOLIN AND ORCH.
 3,3,3,2 - 2,3,3,2,0 - perc. - hp. - pf. - str. 10:00 C. Fischer.
—— CONCERTO FOR VIOLIN AND ORCH., WITH LIGHTS (1961)
(Projected light patterns)
 1,0,1,0 - 0,1,1,0 - perc. - hp. - str.(1,1,1,1) 20:00 C. Fischer.
—— CONCERTO IN G MINOR FOR CLARINET AND ORCH.
(1938)
 1,1,2,2 - 2,2,1,0 - timp.,perc. - pf. - str. 13:00 C. Fischer.
—— CONCLAVE (FOR 8 WOODWINDS, 2 BRASS, PERCUSSION
AND PIANO) (1955)
   12:00 C. Fischer.
—— COUNTY FAIR (FOR CHORUS AND 10 INSTRUMENTS)
(1949)
   10:00 C. Fischer.
—— DECEMBER (FOR MALE AND FEMALE SPEAKERS,
SOPRANO, SATB CHORUS AND ORCH.)
 0,2,2,2 sax.,0 - 4,4,4,0 - timp.,perc.,bells,glock.,vibra. - org.
   18:00 C. Fischer.
—— DECISION (1940)
   8:00 C. Fischer.
—— DEDICATION (1945)
   8:00 C. Fischer.
—— DIALOGUE IN THE JUNGLE (FOR SOPRANO, TENOR AND
10 WINDS) (1959)
   9:00 C. Fischer.
—— DOWNTOWN SUITE (1942)
 1,1,1,0 - 0,0,0,0 - perc.(ad lib.) - pf. - str.(6 players)
   10:00 C. Fischer.
—— FANTASY AND CAPRICE (FOR VIOLIN AND ORCH.) (1940)
   15:00 Composer.
—— FEUERWERK (FOR FEMALE CHORUS AND ORCH.) (1961)
   4:00 C. Fischer.
—— FIRE IN CITIES (FOR SATB CHORUS AND ORCH.)
 4,0,4,0 - 0,2,2,0 - timp.,perc. - 2 pf. - str. 5:00 C. Fischer.
—— HOMAGE TO IVES (FOR BARITONE AND ORCH.)
 3,3,3,3 - 4-5,3,3,1 - perc. - hp. - pf. - str. 16:00 C. Fischer.

—— KINGDOM COME (FOR STAGE AND BALCONY
ORCHESTRAS, WITH FEMALE VOICE)
 6,3,6,4 sax.,3 - 8,6,6,euph.,3 - timp.,perc.,bells - 2 hp. - str.
   23:00 C. Fischer.
—— LABYRINTH I (1954)
   13:00 C. Fischer.
—— LABYRINTH II (WITH OPTIONAL QUARTET OF WOMEN'S
VOICES) (1955)
 4,4,4,4 - 4,1,0,1 13:00 C. Fischer.
—— MILLENIUM I (1950)
 0,0,0,0 - 0,8(muted),0,0 - perc.(2),bells,glock. 6:00 C. Fischer.
—— MILLENIUM III (1957)
 0,0,0,0 - 0,2,4,0 - perc.(6) 7:00 C. Fischer.
—— MYTHICAL BEASTS (FOR SOPRANO OR MEZZO-SOPRANO,
PLUS 16 INSTRUMENTS) (1958)
   11:00 C. Fischer.
—— NOMADS
 3,3,3,3 - 4,3,3,1 - timp.,perc. - str. 14:00 C. Fischer.
 or:
 3,2,2,2 - 4,3,3,1 - timp.,perc. - str.
—— ODYSSEY-WHY NOT? (FOR FLUTE SOLO, FLUTE
OBBLIGATO AND 4 SMALL ORCHESTRAL GROUPS) (1965)
   18:00 C. Fischer.
—— ON THE NATURE OF THINGS (AFTER LUCRETIUS) (1956)
   13:00 C. Fischer.
—— PROMISED LAND (SYMPHONY NO. 2) (1947)
   23:00 C. Fischer.
—— A REQUIEM IN SUMMER
 2,2,2,2 - 0,0,0,0 - str. 8:00 C. Fischer.
—— SIGNS AND ALARMS (1953)
 *1,0,2,0 - 2,1,1,1 - timp.,xyl. 12:00 C. Fischer.
—— STREET MUSIC (1949)
 *1,0,2,2 sax.,0 - 0,2,2,1 - perc. 7:00 C. Fischer.
—— STRESSES (1953)
 0,0,0,0 - 0,1,0,0 - perc. - pf. - str. 9:00 C. Fischer.
—— SYMPHONY IN B FLAT ("THE 1930'S")
 3,3,3,3 - 4,3,3,1 - perc. - str. 25:00 C. Fischer.
—— TWO CHORAL PRELUDES
 str.   6:00 C. Fischer.
—— TWO LYRIC INTERLUDES (REQUIEM AND IDYLL)
 str.   6:00 C. Fischer.
—— VARIATIONS ON A CANADIAN THEME (1941)
   13:00 C. Fischer.
—— VERTICALS ASCENDING (AFTER THE RODIA TOWERS)
(FOR 2 ORCHESTRAL GROUPS, WITH 2 CONDUCTORS)
(1967)
   8:00 MCA Music.
—— VOYAGE FOUR (TOTAL ANTIPHONY) (WITH 3
CONDUCTORS) (1963)
   28:00 C. Fischer.
—— WHOOPEE IN D MAJOR (1942)
   5:00 C. Fischer.

BRASH, James
—— RHAPSODY (FOR PIANO AND ORCH.)
   A.P.R.A.

BRASSARD, François
—— MARCHE FANTASQUE ET FESTIVAL (1949)
 2(2nd alt. with picc.),2,2,2 - 2,2,0,0 - cel. - hp. - str.
   7:00 CanMusCtr.
—— POÈME D'AMOUR ET DE JOIE (5 SONGS FOR BARITONE
AND ORCH.) (1967) (Text: Hervé Dumont)
 2,2,2,2 - 2,2,0,0 - timp. - hp. - str. 16:00 CanMusCtr.

BRAUN, P. Michael
—— TERMS (FOR CHAMBER ENSEMBLE)
   Hans Gerig.
—— TRANSFER (FOR LARGE ORCH.)
   Hans Gerig.
—— VARIETY (FOR LARGE ORCH.)
   Hans Gerig.

BRAUN, Richard W.
—— INTERMEZZO (FOR STRINGS) (1960)
 pf. - str.   2:30 Ybarra.

BRAUN, Yehezkiel
—— CONCERTO FOR FLUTE AND STRINGS
 fl. - str.   26:00 IsMuPublns.
—— ILLUMINATIONS TO THE BOOK OF RUTH
   19:00 A.C.U.M.

—— MISMOR (PSALM FOR STRINGS)
    Str   15:00 IsMuPublns.
—— SYMPHONY OF DANCES
    2,*3,*3,*3 - 4,2,3,1 - timp.,perc.,xyl. - hp. - str. 19:00 IsMuPublns.

BRAUNFELS, Michael
—— DIVERTIMENTO FOR PIANO AND ORCH.
    2,2,2,2 - 2,2,0,0 - timp.,perc. - pf. - str.   15:30 Henmar.

BRAUNSTEIN, M. - SCHMITT, Florent
—— SYMPHONY: 2ND AND 3RD MOVTS.
                           S.A.C.E.M.

BRÄUTIGAM, Volker
—— CHORALE PARTITA (ON "A MIGHTY FORTRESS IS OUR GOD")
    tpt. - str.   Tetra.

BRAVNIČAR, Matija
—— CONCERTO FOR VIOLIN AND ORCH.
    2(2nd alt. with picc.),2,2,2 - 4,2,3,1 - timp.,perc. - hp. - str.
                                 25:00 Hans Gerig.
—— DANCE CONTRASTS II
    2(2nd alt. with picc.),2,2,2 - 4,2,3,1 - timp.,perc.,cel. - hp. - str.
                                 12:00 Hans Gerig.
—— DIVERTISSEMENTS
    pf. - str.   22:00 Henmar.
—— FANTASIA RHAPSODICA (FOR VIOLIN AND ORCH.)
    2(2nd alt. with picc.),2,2,2 - 4,2,3,1 - timp.,perc.(3),cel. - hp. - pf. - str.
                                 15:00 Hans Gerig.
—— FARONIKA SYMPHONY (FOR CHORUS AND ORCH.)
    2(2nd alt. with picc.),2(2nd alt. with Eng. hn.),2(2nd alt. with b.-cl.),2(2nd alt. with c.-bn.) - 4,3,3,1 - timp.,perc.(5) - hp. - pf. - str.
                                 15:00 Hans Gerig.
—— HYMNUS SLAVICUS (WITH OPTIONAL CHORUS AND OPTIONAL ORGAN)
    2(2nd alt. with picc.),2(2nd alt. with Eng.hn.),2(2nd alt. with b.-cl.),2(2nd alt. with c.-bn.) - 4,3,3,1 - timp.,perc.(3) - org.(ad lib.) - str.
                                   6:00 Hans Gerig.
—— KING MATTHIAS (SYMPHONIC OVERTURE)
    3,2(2nd alt. with Eng. hn.),2,2 - 4,2,3,1 - perc. - str.
                                 25:00 Henmar.
—— KURENT (SYMPHONIC POEM)
    2(2nd alt. with picc.),2,2,2 - 4,3,3,1 - timp.,perc.(3) - str.
                                 7:00 Hans Gerig.
—— SINFONIA STRETTA
    2(2nd alt. with picc.),2(2nd alt. with Eng. hn.),2,2(2nd alt. with c.-bn.) - 4,2,3,1 - timp.,perc.(3) - str. 15:00 Hans Gerig.
—— SYMPHONIC ANTITHESIS
    3,2,2,2 - 4,2,3,1 - perc. - hp. - str.   20:00 Henmar.
—— SYMPHONY NO. 1
    2(2nd alt. with picc.),2(2nd alt. with Eng. hn.),2(2nd alt. with b.-cl.),2(2nd alt. with c.-bn.) - 4,2,3,1 - timp.,perc.(3) - hp. - str.
                                 27:00 Hans Gerig.
—— SYMPHONY NO. 2
    2(2nd alt. with picc.),2(2nd alt. with Eng. hn.),2(2nd alt. with b.-cl.),2(2nd alt. with c.-bn.) - 4,3,3,1 - timp.,perc. - hp. - str.
                                 36:00 Hans Gerig.

BREDOW, Edgar
—— CONCERTINO FOR OBOE AND ORCH.
    0,1,0,0 - 2,0,0,0 - hp. - str.   10:00 Alkor.
—— MUSIC FOR STRING ORCH.
    str.   14:00 Alkor.
—— ORIENTAL SUITE (IN 3 MOVTS.)
                            AstoriaBln.
—— STREIFLICHTER (SUITE) (IN 3 MOVTS.)
    2,1,2,1 - 3,2,3,0 - timp.,perc. - hp. - str. 10:00 Alkor.
—— TÄNZERISCHE PORTRAITS (SUITE) (IN 4 MOVTS.)
                            AstoriaBln.

BRENE, Erling
—— ASPECTS (FOR SOPRANO, TENOR, CHORUS AND ORCH.)(1965)
    2,*2,2,2 - 4,3,3,1 - timp.,perc.,cel. - hp. - pf. - str. 26:00 K.O.D.A.
—— CAPRICCIO (1936)
    2,2,2,sax.,2 - 4,3,3,1 - timp.,perc. - str. 13:00 K.O.D.A.
—— CHAMBER CONCERTO FOR CLARINET AND STRINGS, OP. 81
    cl. - str.   17:00 K.O.D.A.
—— CHAMBER CONCERTO FOR VIOLIN AND STRINGS (1951)
    str.   17:00 K.O.D.A.

—— COMEDY OVERTURE NO. 2 (1950)
    2,2,2,2 - 4,3,3,1 - timp.,perc. - str.   7:00 K.O.D.A.
—— CONCERTO FOR CELLO AND ORCH., OP. 89
    2,2,2,2 - 0,2,2,1 - timp.,perc. - str.   21:00 K.O.D.A.
—— CONCERTO FOR CLARINET AND ORCH. (1935)
    0,0,3,0 - 0,2,2,0 - timp.,perc.,xyl. - str. 18:00 K.O.D.A.
—— CONCERTO FOR FLUTE AND ORCH. (1933)
    1,0,2,1 - 1,0,0,0 - perc. - str.   10:00 K.O.D.A.
—— CONCERTO FOR VIOLIN AND ORCH. (1929)
    1,1,1,1 - 1,0,1,0 - str.   17:00 K.O.D.A.
—— CONCERTO FOR WIND QUINTET AND STRINGS (1947)
    1,1,1,1 - 1,0,0,0 - str.   19:00 K.O.D.A.
—— CONCERTO 1940 FOR CELLO AND ORCH.
    2,2,2,2 - 2,2,0,0 - timp.,perc. - str.   14:00 K.O.D.A.
—— CONCERTO 1945 FOR PIANO AND ORCH.
    2,0,3,2 - 4,2,2,0 - pf. - str.   20:00 K.O.D.A.
—— CONCERTO 1955 FOR PIANO AND ORCH.
    2,2,2,2 - 2,2,0,0 - timp.,perc. - pf. - str. 24:00 K.O.D.A.
—— CONTRASTS (1966)
    2,2,2,2 - 2,2,1,0 - timp.,perc. - pf. - str. 7:00 K.O.D.A.
—— HUMORESQUE (1936)
    2,0,2,2 - 2,2,2,0 - perc. - pf. - str.   5:00 K.O.D.A.
—— NOCTURNE (1936)
    1,2,2,1 - 1,1,1,0 - perc. - str.   5:00 K.O.D.A.
—— OPTIMISTIC PLAY (1959)
    2,*2,2,2 - 4,3,3,1 - timp.,perc. - str.   8:00 K.O.D.A.
—— OVERTURE NO. 1 (1934)
    2,2,2,2 - 4,3,3,1 - perc. - str.   5:00 K.O.D.A.
—— PHASES, OP. 84 (SYMPHONIC PIECES)
    2,2,2,2 - 4,3,3,1 - timp.,perc. - pf. - str. 23:00 K.O.D.A.
—— RHAPSODY (1936)
    2,2,*2,sax.,2 - 2,2,2,0 - timp.,perc. - str. 8:00 K.O.D.A.
—— SUITE CONCERTANTE (1942)
    1,1,1,1 - 2,0,0,0 - str.   15:00 K.O.D.A.
—— SUITE (1928)
    2,1,1,1 - 0,2,1,0 - perc. - str.   18:00 K.O.D.A.
—— SYMPHONY, OP. 77
    2,0,*2,2 - 4,3,3,1 - timp.,perc. - hp. - pf. - str. 18:00 K.O.D.A.
—— SYMPHONY 1941
    2,2,2,2 - 4,3,3,1 - timp.,perc. - str.   25:00 K.O.D.A.
—— SYMPHONY 1948
    3,3,3,3 - 4,3,3,1 - perc. - str.   24:00 K.O.D.A.
—— THREE PIECES FOR CHAMBER ORCH. (1926)
    1,1,1,1 - 2,2,0,0 - pf. - str.   21:00 K.O.D.A.
—— VIGORE (PEZZO PER ORCH.)(1943)
    2,2,2,2 - 4,3,3,1 - timp.,perc. - str.   11:00 K.O.D.A.

BRENET, Thérèse
—— CONCERTO IN THREE MOVEMENTS
    Ondes martenot - pf. - str.   17:00 E.V.
—— SIX SHORT PIECES
    2,2,2,2 - 4,3,3,0 - timp.,perc.,cel. - hp. - str. 14:00 Presser.

BRENNER, Walter
—— ADORATION
    3(3rd alt. with picc.),*3,2,2 - 4,2,3,1 - timp. - hp. - str.
                                 24:00 Composer.
—— ANDANTINO
    1,1,1,0 - 1,0,0,0 - str.   8:00 Composer.
—— THE BIRTH OF VENUS (SYMPHONIC POEM)
    3(3rd alt. with picc.),*3,2,2 - 4,2,3,1 - timp. - hp. - str.
                                 25:00 Composer.
—— CONCERTO NO. 1 FOR PIANO AND ORCH., OP. 25
    3(3rd alt. with picc.),*3,2,2 - 4,2,3,1 - timp. - pf. - str.
                                 35:00 Composer.
—— GOD IS LOVE (FOR MIXED CHORUS AND ORCH.) (Text: Sir John Bowring)
    *3,*3,2,2 - 4,2,3,1 - timp.,perc.(3),cel.,glock.,vibra. - hp. - str.
                                 20:00 Composer.
—— HOME THEY BROUGHT HER WARRIOR DEAD (SYMPHONIC POEM)
    *3,*3,2,2 - 4,2,3,1 - timp. - hp. - str. 17:00 Composer.
—— PROPHECY (INSPIRED BY ISAIAH 27: 6)
    2,2,2,2 - 2,2,0,0 - timp.,perc.(2) - str. 16:00 Composer.
—— ROMANZA
    1,0,1,0 - 0,0,0,0 - str.   14:00 Composer.

BRENTA, Gaston
—— ARIOSO ET MOTO PERPETUO (1940)
    2,2,2,2 - 4,2,3,1 - timp.,perc.,cel.,glock.,xyl. - hp. - str.
                                 8:00 H. Elkan.

—— CANDIDE (ILLUSTRATIONS CHORÉGRAPHIQUES): SUITE
NO. 2 (1955)
3,2,2,2 - 4,2,3,1 - timp.,perc.,cel.,xyl. - hp. - pf. - str.
27:40 H. Elkan.
—— CONCERTINO FOR TRUMPET AND CHAMBER ORCH.
(1958)
tpt. - timp.(ad lib.) - str.   9:30 Baron.
—— CONCERTO FOR PIANO AND ORCH. (1953)
2,2,2,2 - 2,2,1,0 - timp.,perc.,xyl. - hp. - pf. - str.   20:00 CBDM.
—— CONCERTO NO. 2 FOR PIANO AND ORCH. (1968)
2,2,2,2 - 4,2,3,1 - timp.,perc. - pf. - str.   17:30 H. Elkan.
—— FARANDOLE BURLESQUE (1951)
2,2,2,2 - 4,2,3,1 - timp.,perc.,cel.,xyl. - hp. - pf. - str.   8:00 H. Elkan.
—— MATINEE D'ÉTÉ (1967)
3,2,2,2 - 4,2,3,1 - timp.,perc., - str.   10:00 H. Elkan.
—— SYMPHONY
2,2,2,2 - 4,2,3,1 - timp.,perc.,cel.,glock.,xyl. - hp. - str.
20:00 CBDM.
—— WAR MUSIC (1946)
2,2,2,2 - 4,3,3,1 - timp.,perc.,xyl. - str.   6:00 H. Elkan.
—— ZO-HAR (SYMPHONIC POEM, AFTER CATULLE MENDES)
(1929)
3,2,4,3 - 4,3,3,1 - timp.,perc.,cel.,glock.,xyl. - hp. - str.
18:00 H. Elkan.

BRERO, G. Cesare
—— CONCERTO FOR STRING ORCH.
str.   8:00 Bo. Hawkes.

BRESGEN, Cesar
—— CONCERTO FOR HORN AND SMALL ORCH.
Hans Gerig.
—— CONCERTO IN G MINOR FOR TROMBONE AND STRING
ORCH.
trb. - str.   H.Voggnrtr.
—— INTRADA (FOR LARGE ORCH.) (1964)
Hans Gerig.

BRESNICK, Martin
—— INTROIT (1969)
2,2,2,2 - 4,0,2,0   6:00 Composer.

BREUER, Karl Günther
—— ATONALYSE I
cl. - str.   F. Colombo.
—— ATONALYSE II
tpt. - str.   F. Colombo.
—— IMPRESSIONS (3 PIECES FOR LARGE ORCH.)
F. Colombo.

BREVAL, Jean-Baptiste - BROOK, Barry S.
—— SYMPHONIE CONCERTANTE
0,0,1,1 - 1,0,0,0 - str.   FrankMusCp.

BREVAL, Jean Baptiste - DALLEY, Orien
—— CONCERTO FOR ORCHESTRA
2,1,2,1 - 2,2,1,1 - timp.,perc.(2) - pf. - str.   3:00 Fema.

BREVAL, Jean-Baptiste - PEYSSIES, Marcel
—— CONCERTO NO. 1 IN G, FOR CELLO AND ORCH.
0,1,2,0 - 2,0,0,0 - str.   Galaxy.
—— CONCERTO NO. 2 IN D, FOR CELLO AND ORCH.
0,1,2,0 - 2,0,0,0 - str.   Galaxy.

BREVIK, Tor
—— CANTO ELEGICO (1964)
2,2,2,2 - 4,3,3,1 - timp. - str.   7:00 T.O.N.O.
—— CHACONNE
2,2,2,2 - 4,2,3,1 - str.   8:00 T.O.N.O.
—— CHAMBER CONCERTO NO. 1 (IN 3 MOVTS.)
str.   7:30 T.O.N.O.
—— CONCERTINO FOR CLARINET AND STRINGS (IN 3
MOVTS.)
cl. - str.   15:00 T.O.N.O.
—— OVERTURE
2,2,2,2 - 4,2,3,0 - timp. - str.   6:00 T.O.N.O.
—— SERENADE FOR STRINGS (IN 4 MOVTS.)
str.   15:00 T.O.N.O.
—— VAGANTVISE (YOUTH SONG) (FOR MALE CHORUS AND
ORCH.) (Text: Sigmund Skard)
2,1,2,1 - 2,2,2,0 - timp.,perc. - str.   7:00 T.O.N.O.

BREVILLE, Pierre de
—— LES AEGYPANS (EXTRAIT DU BALLET)
5:00 Salabert.
—— EROS VAINQUEUR (BALLET FROM THE OPERA) %~
3,3,3,3 - 4,3,4,0 - timp.,perc.,(2-3),cel. - 2 hp. - str.   Salabert.
—— STAMBOUL
3,3,2,2 - 4,2,3,0 - timp.,perc.,(2-3) - hp. - str.   20:00 Salabert.

BREWER, A. Herbert
—— AGE AND YOUTH
2,2,2,2 - 2,2,3,0 - timp.,perc. - str.   Novello.

BRIAN, Havergal
—— SYMPHONY NO.   2 (1931)
4,4,4,4 - 6,4,4,2 - timp.,perc.,cel. - 2 hp. - org. - 2 pf. - str.
40:00 P.R.S.
—— SYMPHONY NO.   3 (1932)
4,4,4,4 - 8,4,3,2 - timp.,perc.,cel. - 2 hp. - 2 pf. - str.   49:00 P.R.S.
—— SYMPHONY NO.   4 (PSALM OF VICTORY; PSALM 68) (FOR
SOPRANO, SATB CHORUS AND ORCH.) (1933)
6,2,4,4 - 8,4,4,2 - timp.,perc. - 2 hp. - org. - str.   48:00 P.R.S.
—— SYMPHONY NO.   5 (WINE OF SUMMER) (WITH SOLO
VOICE) (1937)
4,2,2,3 - 4,3,3,1 - timp.,perc. - 2 hp. - str.   25:00 P.R.S.
—— SYMPHONY NO.   6 (1948)
3,2,2,3 - 4,4,3,1 - timp.,perc.,cel. - hp. - str.   48:00 P.R.S.
—— SYMPHONY NO.   7 (SINFONICA TRAGICA: DEIDRE OF
THE SORROWS) (1948)
3,2,2,2 - 4,2,3,1 - timp.,perc. - hp. - str.   18:00 P.R.S.
—— SYMPHONY NO. 13 (1959)
4,3,3,4 - 4,4,4,1 - timp.,perc. - 2 hp. - str.   25:00 P.R.S.
—— SYMPHONY NO. 14
4,3,3,4 - 6,4,4,1 - timp.,perc. - hp. - org. - str.   26:00 P.R.S.
—— SYMPHONY NO. 15
4,3,3,4 - 6,4,4,1 - timp.,perc. - 2 hp. - str.   P.R.S.
—— SYMPHONY NO. 16
4,3,3,4 - 6,4,3,1 - timp.,perc. - 2 hp. - str.   P.R.S.
—— SYMPHONY NO. 17
3,3,3,3 - 4,3,3,1 - timp.,perc. - hp. - str.   P.R.S.
—— SYMPHONY NO. 18 (1961)
2,2,2,2 - 4,2,3,1 - timp.,perc. - hp. - str.   P.R.S.
—— SYMPHONY NO. 19
3,2,3,3 - 4,3,3,1 - timp.,perc. - hp. - str.   P.R.S.
—— SYMPHONY NO. 20 (1962)
3,2,2,3 - 4,3,3,2 - timp.,perc. - hp. - str.   P.R.S.
—— SYMPHONY NO. 21
3,2,2,3 - 4,3,3,1 - timp.,perc. - hp. - str.   P.R.S.
—— SYMPHONY NO. 22 (SYMPHONIA BREVIS)(1965)
3,2,2,3 - 4,3,3,1 - timp.,perc. - hp. - str.   P.R.S.
—— SYMPHONY NO. 23
3,2,2,3 - 4,3,3,1 - timp.,perc. - hp. - str.   P.R.S.
—— SYMPHONY NO. 24
3,2,2,3 - 4,3,3,1 - timp.,perc. - str.   P.R.S.
—— SYMPHONY NO. 25, IN A MINOR (1966)
3,2,2,3 - 4,3,3,1 - timp.,perc. - str.   30:00 P.R.S.
—— SYMPHONY NO. 26 (1966)
3,2,2,3 - 4,3,3,1 - timp.,perc. - str.   P.R.S.
—— SYMPHONY NO. 27 (1966)
3,2,2,3 - 4,3,3,1 - timp.,perc. - hp. - str.   P.R.S.
—— SYMPHONY NO. 28 (SINFONIA IN C MINOR)(1967)
3,2,2,3 - 4,3,3,1 - timp.,perc. - hp. - str.   P.R.S.
—— SYMPHONY NO. 29, IN E FLAT (1967)
3,2,2,3 - 4,3,3,1 - timp.,perc. - str.   P.R.S.
—— SYMPHONY NO. 30 (SINFONIA IN B FLAT MINOR)(1967)
2,2,2,2 - 4,2,3,1 - timp.,perc. - 2 hp. - str.   P.R.S.
—— SYMPHONY NO. 31
3,2,2,3 - 4,3,3,1 - timp.,perc. - hp. - str.   P.R.S.
—— SYMPHONY NO. 32, IN A FLAT (1968)
3,2,2,3 - 4,3,3,1 - timp.,perc. - hp. - str.   P.R.S.

BRICCETTI, Thomas
—— CONCERTINO ANTICO (1971) (IN 3 MOVTS.)
*2,*2,2,1 - 2,1,1,0 - timp.,perc.(2),cel.,glock.,mar.,vibra.,xyl. -
str.(8,3,3,2 minimum)   17:00 Bo. Hawkes.
—— CONCERTO FOR VIOLIN AND ORCHESTRA (1967)
*3,*3,*3,*3 - 4,3,3,1 - timp.,perc.(5),bells,cel.,glock. - hp. - str.
28:21 Composer.
—— ECLOGUE NO. 2 (FOR TROMBONE AND STRINGS)
trb. - str.   8:00 Composer.
—— ECLOGUE NO. 3 (FOR STRINGS)
str.   5:00 Composer.

—— FIVE LOVE POEMS (FOR SATB CHORUS AND ORCH.) (1965)
*3,*3,*3,2 - 4,3,3,1 - timp.,perc.(3),bells,glock. - hp. - str.
18:00 Composer.

—— FOUNTAIN OF YOUTH OVERTURE
2,2,3,3 - 4,3,3,1 - timp.,perc. - hp. - pf. - str.   8:00 Bo. Hawkes.

—— FROM THOREAU ("THE MASS OF MEN LEAD LIVES OF QUIET DESPERATION")
2(1st. alt. with picc.),2,2,2 - 2,2,1,0 - timp.,perc.(3),xyl. - hp. - str.
13:00 Composer.

—— OVERTURE TO "THE FOUNTAIN OF YOUTH" (1964)
*3,*3,*3,*3 - 4,3,3,1 - timp.,perc.(4),glock.,xyl. - hp. - pf. - str.
9:00 Bo. Hawkes.

—— LES PRÉNOMBRES (THE MUTE THINGS) (THE SHADOWED THINGS) (MOVEMENT FOR BALLET)
2(2nd alt. with picc.),2,2,2 - 2,2,1,0 - timp.,perc.(3) - hp. - str.
8:00 Composer.

—— SONG OF SOLOMON (CANTICLE OF CANTICLES) (FOR DRAMATIC TENOR OR HIGH VOICE AND ORCH.) (1963)
*3,2(2nd alt. with Eng. hn.),*3,2 - 4,3,3,1 - timp.,perc.(3),glock.,vibra. - hp. - str.   7:00 CMP.

—— SYMPHONY NO. 1 (IN 3 MOVTS.)
2(2nd alt. with picc.),2,2,2 - 2,2,1,0 - timp.,perc.(3),bells,glock.,vibra.,xyl. - hp. - str.   23:00 Composer.

—— TRE TRISTEZZE (THREE SADNESSESS)
str.   6:00 Composer.

BRICKMAN, Joel I.
—— PRELUDE AND DITHYRAMB (CONCERT OVERTURE) (1969)
*3,*3,*3,*3 - 4,3,3,1 - timp.,perc.(4),bells,cel.,glock.,vibra.,xyl. - hp. - pf. - str.   12:00 Composer.

—— SYMPHONY IN THREE MOVEMENTS (1968)
*3,*3,*3,*3 - 4,3,3,1 - timp.,perc.(4),cel.,glock.,xyl. - hp. - pf. - str.   30:00 Composer.

—— THOUSAND OF DAYS (CONCERTO FOR PIANO AND ORCH.) (WITH SOLO SOPRANO) (1970) (Text: Muriel Rukeyser)
*3,*3,*3,*3 - 4,3,3,1 - timp.,perc.(4),cel.,glock.,vibra.,xyl. - hp. - pf. - str.   27:00 Composer.

BRIDEOAKE, Peter
—— MUSIC FOR ORCHESTRA (1971)
2,2(2nd alt. with Eng. hn.),2,2 - 3,2,2,0 - perc. - str.
4:50 A.P.R.A.

—— THREE PIECES FOR LARGE ORCH. (1970)
3(alt. with 3 picc.),2(2nd alt. with Eng. hn.),*3,3(3rd alt. with c.-bn.) - 4,3,2,0 - timp.,perc.(3) - hp. - str.   7:10 A.P.R.A.

BRIDGE, Frank
—— THE CHRISTMAS ROSE (OPERA IN 3 SCENES) %
2,2,2,2 - 2,2,1,0 - timp.,perc. - hp. - str.   45:00 Galaxy.
—— ENTER SPRING (RHAPSODY)
3,3,3,3 - 4,3,3,1 - timp.,perc. - 2 hp. - str.   15:00 G. Schirmer.
—— ISABELLA (SYMPHONIC POEM)
3,3,3,3 - 4,2 cnt.,2,3,1 - timp.,perc. - hp. - str.   20:00 Galaxy.
—— ORATION (CONCERTO ELEGIACO) (FOR CELLO AND ORCH.)
2,2,2,2 - 4,2,3,1 - timp.,perc. - hp. - str.   28:00 Galaxy.
—— PHANTASM (RHAPSODY FOR PIANO AND ORCH.)
2,2,2,2 - 4,2,3,1 - timp.,perc. - hp. - str.   25:00 Galaxy.
—— A PRAYER (FOR SATB CHORUS AND ORCH.)
3(3rd alt. with picc.),2,2,2 - 4,3,3,1 - timp.,perc. - str.
15:00 Galaxy.
—— REBUS OVERTURE
3,3,3,3 - 4,3,3,1 - timp.,perc. - hp. - str.   8:00 Bo. Hawkes.
—— THE SEA
3(3rd alt. with picc.),2(2nd alt. with Eng.hn.),2(2nd alt. with b.-cl.),2(2nd alt. with c.-bn.) - 4,3,3,1 - timp., perc. - hp. - str.
17:00 Galaxy.
—— SUITE FOR STRINGS
str.   24:00 G. Schirmer.
—— SUMMER (TONE POEM)
2(2nd alt. with picc.),2,2,2 - 2,2,0,0 - timp.,perc.,cel. - hp. - str.   12:00 Augener.
—— THERE IS A WILLOW GROWS ASLANT A BROOK
1,1,2,1 - hn. - hp. - str.   8:00 Galaxy.
—— TWO FOLK SONGS (FOR STRINGS)
str.   7:00 Bo. Hawkes.
—— TWO POEMS
3,2,2,2 - 4,2,3,1 - timp.,perc. - hp. - str.   10:00 Augener.
—— VIGNETTES DE DANSE
1,1,2,1 - 2,2,1,0 - timp.,perc. - hp. - str.   10:00 Bo. Hawkes.

BRIDGEWATER, Leslie
—— CONCERTO NO. 1 IN C MINOR, FOR PIANO AND ORCH.
3,3,2,2 - 4,2,3,1 - timp.,perc. - pf.- str.   20:00 Novello.

BRIER, Percy
—— CHORAL FANTASIA (FOR SOPRANO, CHORUS, PIANO AND ORCH.)
A.P.R.A.
—— TWO FANTASY CONCERTOS (FOR PIANO AND ORCH.)
A.P.R.A.

BRIGGS, George Wright, Jr.
—— U.S.A. - 200 (MEDLEY OF NATIONAL AIRS) (ARR. 1973)
*3,*3,*3,*3 - 4,4,3,1 - timp.,perc.(4),bells,glock.,vibra,xyl. - hp. - str.   8:30 Arranger.

BRIGGS, Ralph
—— BURLESQUE (1958)
*3,2,*3(b.-cl. alt. with sopr. sax.),2 - 4,2,3,1 - timp.,perc.(4) - pf. - str.   9:00 Composer.
—— FANTASY FOR ORCHESTRA
*3,2,2,2 - 4,2,3,1 - perc.(5) - hp. - str.   10:00 Composer.
—— PRELUDE, FUGUE AND ARIA WITH VARIATIONS (1960)
1,1,1,1 - 0,0,0,0 - pf. - str.   11:00 Composer.

BRIGHT, Colin Michael
—— TWO MOVEMENTS FOR PIANO AND ORCH., OP. 2 (1974)
2,2,2,0 - 2,2,0,0 - perc.(2) - pf. - str.   12:00 A.P.R.A.

BRIGHT, Robert Houston
—— ISAIAH IN THE TEMPLE (TRILOGY) (FOR SATB CHORUS AND ORCH.) (1961)
2,2,2,1 - 4,3,3,1 - timp.,perc.(2) - str.   12:00 Shawnee.
—— SYMPHONY IN E MINOR (IN 4 MOVTS.)
2(2nd alt. with picc.),*3,*4,*3 - 4,3,3,1 - timp.,perc.(3) - str.
25:50 Composer.

BRINGS, Allen
—— CAPRICCIO (1960)
*3,*3,*3,*3 - 4,3,3,1 - timp.,perc.(3) - hp. - pf. - str.
5:00 Composer.
—— CONCERTO DA CAMERA NO. 1 (FOR PIANO AND CHAMBER ORCH.)
1,1,1,1 - 1,1,1,0 - perc.(2) - pf. - str.   10:00 Seesaw.
—— CONCERTO DA CAMERA NO. 3 (FOR FLUTE AND CHAMBER ORCH.)
14:00 Seesaw.
—— CONCERTO FOR ORCHESTRA (1957)
1. Allegro; 2. Lento
2,2,2,2 - 2,2,1,0 - timp.,perc.(2) - str.   16:00 Composer.
—— NOTTURNO (1960)
*3,*3,*3 - 4,3,3,1 - timp.,perc.(3) - hp. - pf. - str.
5:00 Composer.
—— SONG (FOR MEDIUM VOICE AND ORCH.) (1956) (Text: John Donne)
2,2,2,2 - 2,2,2,0 - hp. - str.   5:00 Composer.
—— SYMPHONY (1964) (IN 3 MOVTS.)
*3,2,2,2 - 4,2,3,0 - timp.,perc.(5),bells,cel.,glock.,xyl. - hp. - pf. - str.   25:00 Composer.
—— TRE SONETTI (FOR SOPRANO AND ENSEMBLE)
1,1,0,0 - 0,0,0,0 - perc. - pf. - str.   8:00 Seesaw.

BRINGUER, Estela
—— LOS BOSQUES DE PALERMO, OP. 21 (1952) (THE FOREST OF PALERMO) (IN 5 MOVTS.)
2,*3,2,2 - 4,3,3,1 - timp.,perc.(3),bells,glock. - str.
28:40 F. Colombo.
—— CANDOMBE, OP. 28 (1966)
2,2,2,2 - timp.,perc.(3) - str.   7:00 Composer.
—— CARNAVAL EN HUMAHUACA, OP. 19 (SUITE FROM THE BALLET) (IN 6 MOVTS.)
2,*3,2,2 - 4,3,3,1 - timp.,perc.(3) - str.   26:40 F. Colombo.
—— CONCERTO NO. 1 IN D, OP. 25 (FOR PIANO AND ORCH.) (1963) (IN 3 MOVTS.)
2,*3,2,2 - 4,3,3,1 - timp.,perc.(2) - pf. - str.   22:00 F. Colombo.
—— ELEGIA, OP. 24 (1960)
str.   10:00 F. Colombo.
—— FANTASIA Y DANZA, OP. 13 (1959)
1,1,1,0 - 1,0,1,0 - str.   17:00 F. Colombo.
—— EL MERCADER INDIGENA, OP. 18 (THE INDIAN MERCHANT) (RHAPSODY) (1949)
2,*3,2,2 - 4,3,3,1 - timp.,perc.(2) - str.   14:00 F. Colombo.

—— MINUETTO, OP. 16
    str.   8:00 Composer.
—— SYMPHONY NO. 1, OP. 20 ("EARTH") (IN 4 MOVTS.)
    2,*3,2,2 - 4,3,3,1 - timp.,perc.(2) - str.   35:00 F. Colombo.
—— SYMPHONY NO. 2, OP. 25 ("SYMPHONY OF THE
    CREATION")
    2,*3,*3,2 - 4,3,3,1 - timp.,perc.,3glock. - str.   30:00 Composer.

BRISCOE, Gerald
—— AUTUMN RHAPSODY, OP. 5 (1956)
    1,1,1,1 - 1,0,0,0 - str.   5:00 P.R.S.
—— CONCERTINO FOR STRING ORCH., OP. 9 (1964)
    str.   8:00 P.R.S.

BRISMAN, Heskel
—— CONCERTO FOR PIANO AND STRINGS (1961)
    pf. - str.   25:00 Composer.
—— NIGHT PIECE NO. 2 (1954)
    1(alt.with picc.),1(alt.with Eng. hn.),1,1 - 2,1,1,0 - timp.,perc.(1) -
    hp. - str.   10:00 Composer.
—— PSALMS FOR SOPRANO AND ORCH. (1968) (Text: Biblical)
    2,2,2,2 - 4,2,2,0 - timp.,perc.(2) - str.   10:00 Composer.
—— SINFONIA BREVE (1956)
    2,2,2,2 - 4,2,3,1 - timp.,perc.(2) - str.   20:00 C. Fischer.

BRITAIN, Radie
—— CACTUS RHAPSODY
    *3,*3,2,2 - 4,3,3,1 - timp.,perc. - str.   Composer.
—— COWBOY RHAPSODY
    3(3rd alt. with picc.),2,2,2 - 4,3,3,1 - perc.(3) - hp. - str.
    8:00 Composer.
—— HEROIC POEM
    2(1 alt. with picc.),*3,*3,*3 - 4,3,3,1 - timp.,perc.(4) - hp. - str.
    13:00 AmerMusEd.
—— INFANT SUITE
    1,1,1,1 - 1,1,0,0 - timp.,perc.(3) - hp. - str.   10:00 Composer.
—— KAMBU
    2,2,2,2 - 4,3,3,1 - timp.,perc. - hp. (or pf.) - str.   8:00 Composer.
—— LAMENT
    1,2,1,2 - 2,0,2,0 - perc.(2) - str.   4:00 Seesaw.
—— LIGHT
    3(3rd alt. with picc.),*3,*3,*3 - 4,3,3,1 - timp.,perc.(4) - hp. - str.
    10:00 Composer.
—— LITTLE PER CENT
    2,1,2,1 - 2,3,3,1 - timp.,perc. - str.   5:00 Composer.
—— NOCTURNE
    1,1,1,1 - 1,1,1,0 - timp.,perc.(3) - hp. - str.   7:00 Composer.
—— ONTONAGON SKETCHES (IN 3 MOVTS.)
    2(1 alt. with picc.),*3,*3,*3 - 4,3,3,1 - timp.,perc.(4) - hp. - pf. -
    str.   20:00 Composer.
—— PHANTASY FOR OBOE AND ORCH.
    1(alt. with picc.),1,2,*3 - 4,3,3,1 - timp.,perc.(3) - str.
    10:00 Seesaw.
—— PRELUDE TO A DRAMA
    2(1 alt. with picc.),*3,*3,*3 - 4,3,3,1 - timp.,perc.(3) - hp. - str.
    6:00 Composer.
—— RHAPSODIC PHANTASY FOR PIANO AND ORCH.
    1(alt. with picc.),2,2,2 - 4,3,3,1 - timp.,perc.(3) - hp. - pf. - str.
    15:00 Composer.
—— SATURNALE
    2(1 alt. with picc.),*3,*3,*3 - 4,3,3,1 - timp.,perc. - hp. - str.
    15:00 Composer.
—— THE SHEPHERD IN THE DISTANCE (BALLET) %
    1(alt. with picc.),2,2,2 - 2,2,2,0 - timp.,perc. - str.   Composer.
—— SOUTHERN SYMPHONY (IN 4 MOVTS.)
    2(1 alt. with picc.),*3,*3,*3 - 4,3,3,1 - timp.,perc.(4) - hp. - str.
    23:00 Composer.
—— SUITE FOR STRINGS (IN 3 MOVTS.)
    timp.,perc. - str.   15:00 Composer.
—— THREE LANDSCAPES
    2(1 alt. with picc.),*3,*3,*3 - 4,3,3,1 - timp.,perc. - hp. - pf. - str.
    15:00 Composer.
—— TWO FRANCISCAN SKETCHES
    2(1 alt. with picc.),*3,*3,*3 - 4,3,3,1 - timp.,perc. - hp. - org. - str.
    20:00 Composer.
—— UBIQUITY (MUSICAL DRAMA) (FOR 10 SOLO VOICES,
    CHORUS AND ORCH.) %
    1(alt. with picc.),2,2,*3 - 4,3,3,1 - timp., perc.(5) - hp. - pf. - str.
    Composer.

BRITTEN, Benjamin
—— ALBERT HERRING, OP. 39 (COMIC OPERA IN 3 ACTS)
    (1947) % (Libretto: Eric Crozier)
    1(alt. with picc. and alto fl.),1(alt. with Eng. hn.),1(alt. with
    b.-cl.),1 - 1,0,0,0 - perc. - hp. - pf. - str.   137:00 Bo. Hawkes.
—— BALLAD OF HEROES, OP. 14
    3,3,3,3 - 4,2,3,1 - timp.,perc. - hp. - str. (optional instruments
    off-stage: 3 tpt. - snare drum)   15:00 Bo. Hawkes.
—— BILLY BUDD, OP. 50 (OPERA IN 2 ACTS) (1960) %
    4(4 alt. with picc.),*3,*3(1st alt. with E♭cl., 2nd alt. with
    b.-cl.),alto sax.,*3 - 4,4,3,1 - timp.,perc. - hp. - str.
    147:00 Bo. Hawkes.
—— THE BUILDING OF THE HOUSE (OVERTURE) (WITH
    OPTIONAL MIXED CHORUS)
    2,2,2,2 - 3,2,0 - 3,1 - timp.,perc. - org.(opt.) - str.
    5:00 G. Schirmer.
—— CANTATA ACADEMICA (CARMEN BASILIENSE), OP. 62
    (FOR SATB SOLOS, MIXED CHORUS AND ORCH.)
    2,2,2,2 - 4,2,3,1 - timp.,perc.(4),cel. - 2 hp. - pf. - str.
    22:00 Bo. Hawkes.
—— CANTATA MISERICORDIUM, OP. 69 (FOR TENOR,
    BARITONE, SMALL CHORUS AND CHAMBER ORCH.)
    timp. - hp. - pf. - str.   19:30 Bo. Hawkes.
—— CHACONNY (ARRANGED FROM STRING QUARTET NO. 2)
    str.   14:00 Bo. Hawkes.
—— CONCERTO NO. 1 FOR PIANO AND ORCH., OP. 13
    (REVISED VERSION) (IN 4 MOVTS.)
    2,2,2,2 - 4,2,3,1 - timp.,perc. - hp. - pf. - str.   31:00 Bo. Hawkes.
—— CONCERTO NO. 1 FOR VIOLIN AND ORCH., OP. 15
    2,2,2,2 - 4,3,3,1 - timp.,perc. - hp. - str.   21:00 Bo. Hawkes.
—— DANCES FROM THE SYMPHONIC SUITE "GLORIANA"
    2,2,2,2 - 4,2,3,1 - timp.,perc. - str.   16:30 Bo. Hawkes.
—— DIVERSIONS FOR PIANO (LEFT HAND ALONE) AND
    ORCH., OP. 21
    2,2,2,sax.(ad lib.),2,c.-bn.(ad lib.) - 4,2,3,1 - timp.,perc. - hp. - pf. -
    str.   25:00 Bo. Hawkes.
—— FOUR SEA INTERLUDES, OP. 33A (FROM "PETER GRIMES")
    2,2,*3 - 4,3,3,1 - timp.,perc. - hp. - str.   15:00 Bo. Hawkes.
—— GLORIANA (OPERA) %
    Bo. Hawkes.
—— LES ILLUMINATIONS, OP. 18 (FOR HIGH VOICE AND
    STRINGS)
    str.   21:00 Bo. Hawkes.
—— KERMESSE CANADIENNE, OP. 19 (CANADIAN CARNIVAL)
    2,2,2,2 - 4,3,3,1 - timp.,perc. - hp. - str.   14:00 Bo. Hawkes.
—— LUTE SONG (FROM THE OPERA "GLORIANA") OP. 53 (FOR
    TENOR OR OBOE SOLO, HARP AND STRINGS)
    ob.(ad lib.) - hp. - str.   5:30 Bo. Hawkes.
—— A MIDSUMMER NIGHT'S DREAM, OP. 64 (3-ACT OPERA) %
    (Text: Composer and Peter Pears, after Shakespeare)
    sopranino recorders,2,1,2,1 - 2,1,1,0 - perc.(2) - 2 hp. - hpsc.(alt.
    with cel.) - str.   140:00 Bo. Hawkes.
—— NOCTURNE, OP. 60 (FOR TENOR, 7 OBBLIGATO
    INSTRUMENTS AND STRINGS)
    1,*1,1,1 - 1,0,0,0 - timp. - hp. - str.   25:00 Bo. Hawkes.
—— NOYE'S FLUDDE (CHESTER MIRACLE PLAY, SET TO
    MUSIC FOR CHILDREN) (FOR NARRATOR, CONTRALTO,
    BASS-BARITONE, CHILDREN'S AND MIXED CHORUSES,
    CHAMBER AND CHILDREN'S ORCH.) %
    Professional Orch. 1 alto recorder - timp. - org. - pf.(4-hands) -
    str.   50:00 Bo. Hawkes.
    Children's (or amateur) Orch.: 2 soprano recorders, 1 alto recoder,
    4 bugles - perc.
—— OUR HUNTING FATHERS (SYMPHONIC CYCLE FOR HIGH
    VOICE AND ORCH.), OP. 8
    2,2,2,sax.,2 - 4,2,3,1 - timp.,perc. - hp. - str.   27:00 Bo. Hawkes.
—— PAS DE SIX (DANCES FROM ACT 3 OF THE BALLET "THE
    PRINCE OF THE PAGODAS")
    2,2,2,2 - 4,3,3,1 - timp.,perc. - hp. - pf. - str.   12:00 Bo. Hawkes.
    or:
    3,3,3,3 - 4,3,3,1 - timp.,perc. - hp. - pf. - str.
—— PASSACAGLIA, OP. 33B (FROM "PETER GRIMES")
    2,2,2,*3 - 4,3,3,1 - timp.,perc.,cel. - hp. - str.   7:00 Bo. Hawkes.
—— PETER GRIMES, OP. 33 (OPERA) % (Libretto: Montagu Slater)
    Main Orch.: 2,2,2,3 - 4,3,3,1 - timp.,perc.,cel. - hp. - str.
    139:00 Bo. Hawkes.
    Off-Stage Orch.: 2 cl. - 1 tu. - perc. - pf. (ad lib.) - vln.,d.-b.
—— PETER GRIMES (OPERA) %
    Bo. Hawkes.
    PETER'S DREAM (FOR TENOR AND ORCH.)
    2,2,2,0 - 2,2,1,0 - hp. - str.   3:00
    EMBROIDERY ARIA (FOR SOPRANO AND ORCH.)
    2,2,0,*3 - 4,3,3,1 - timp.,perc. - hp. - str.   4:00

CHURCH SCENE (FOR SOPRANO AND ORCH.)
2,2,2,2 - 2,2,3,1 - timp.,perc. - hp. - org. (ad lib.) - str.   3:30
—— PRELUDE AND FUGUE FOR 18-PART STRING ORCH., OP. 29
str.   8:30 Bo. Hawkes.
—— THE PRINCE OF THE PAGODAS, OP. 57 (3-ACT BALLET) %
3,3,3, alto sax.,3 - 4,5,3,1 - timp.,perc.(6),cel. - hp. - pf.(4-hands) - str.   125:00 Bo. Hawkes.
—— PSALM 150, OP. 67 (FOR SOPRANO AND ALTO VOICES, WITH VARIABLE GROUP OF INSTRS.)
0-1,0-1,2,0-1 - 1,1(or ob. or harmonica),1,0 - timp.,perc. - cemb. - str. (vla.; add other str. instrs. ad lib.)   5:00 Bo. Hawkes.
—— THE RAPE OF LUCRETIA, OP. 37 (OPERA) % (Text: Ronald Duncan)
1(alt. with picc. and alto fl.),1(alt. with Eng. hn.),1(alt. with b.-cl.),1 - 1,0,0,0 - perc. - hp. - pf. - str.   120:00 Bo. Hawkes.
—— THE RAPE OF LUCRETIA (OPERA) %
Bo. Hawkes.
    THE RIDE (TENOR ARIA)
    picc., 0,1,1,1 -hn. - perc. - hp. - str.   2:00
    THE FLOWER SONG (CONTRALTO ARIA)
    ob., bn. - hp. - str.   2:00
—— SAINT NICOLAS, OP. 41 (CANTATA) (FOR TENOR, CHORUS AND ORCH.)
timp.,perc. - org. - 2 pf. - str.   50:00 Bo. Hawkes.
—— SCOTTISH BALLAD, OP. 26 (FOR 2 PIANOS AND ORCH.)
2,2,2,2-3 - 4,2,3,1 - timp.,perc. - 2 pf. - hp. - str.   13:00 Bo. Hawkes.
—— SERENADE (FOR TENOR, HORN AND STRINGS), OP. 31
hn.,str.   24:00 Bo. Hawkes.
—— A SIMPLE SYMPHONY (FOR STRING ORCH.) (IN 4 MOVTS.)
str.   16:00 Oxford.
—— SINFONIA DA REQUIEM, OP. 20 (IN 3 MOVTS.)
3(3rd alt. with picc. and alto fl.),3, E♭cl.(alt. with b.-cl.),2, alto sax.(ad lib.),*3 - 4-6,3,3,1 - timp.,perc. - 1-2 hp. - str.   20:00 Bo. Hawkes.
—— SINFONIETTA FOR CHAMBER ORCH., OP. 1 (IN 3 MOVTS.)
1,1,1,1 - hn. - str.   15:00 Bo. Hawkes.
—— SIX FRENCH FOLK SONGS (ARR. FOR HIGH VOICE AND ORCH.)
2,2,2,2 - 2,2,0,0 - perc. - hp. - str.   Bo. Hawkes.
—— SPRING SYMPHONY, OP. 44 (FOR 3 SOLO VOICES, MIXED CHORUS, BOY'S CHOIR AND ORCH.)
3,3,3,3 - 4,3, cow horn,3,1 - timp.,perc. - 2 hp. - str.   45:00 Bo. Hawkes.
—— SUITE ON ENGLISH FOLK-TUNES, OP. 90 ("A TIME THERE WAS.....")
2(2nd alt. with picc.),2(2nd alt. with Eng.hn.),2,2 - 2,2,0,0 - timp.,perc.(3) - str.   14:00 G. Schirmer.
—— SYMPHONIC SUITE FROM "GLORIANA", OP. 53A
26:00 Bo. Hawkes.
    I. THE TOURNAMENT
    3,3,3,3 - 4,3,3,1 - timp.,perc. - hp. - str.
    II. THE LUTE SONG (WITH SOLO TENOR OR OBOE)
    ob.(ad lib.) - hp. - str.
    III. THE COURTLY DANCES
    2,2,2,2 - 4,2,3,1 - timp.,perc. - str.
    IV. GLORIANA MORITURA
    3,3,3,3 - 4,3,3,1 - timp.,perc. - hp. - str.
—— SYMPHONY FOR CELLO AND ORCH., OP. 68
2,2,2,2 - 2,2,1,1 - timp.,perc. - str.   31:00 Bo. Hawkes.
—— TE DEUM IN C MAJOR (FOR SOPRANO, MIXED CHORUS AND ORCH.)
8:30 Oxford.
—— THE TURN OF THE SCREW, OP. 54 (OPERA) %
1(alt. with alto fl.),1(alt. with Eng. hn),1(alt. with b.-cl.),1 - 1,0,0,0 - perc. - hp. - pf.(alt. with cel.) - str.   105:00 Bo. Hawkes.
—— VARIATIONS AND FUGUE ON A THEME OF PURCELL (YOUNG PERSON'S GUIDE TO THE ORCH.), OP. 34
3,2,2,2 - 4,2,3,1 - timp.,perc.(3),xyl. - hp. - str.   17:00 Bo. Hawkes.
—— VARIATIONS ON A THEME OF FRANK BRIDGE, OP. 10
str.   25:00 Bo. Hawkes.
—— A WAR REQUIEM (FOR SOPRANO, TENOR, BARITONE, SATB CHORUS, BOY'S CHORUS AND 2 ORCHS.)
Main Orch.: 3(3rd alt. with picc.)*3,3(3rd alt. with E♭cl. and b.-cl.),*3 - 6,4,3,1 - timp.,perc.(4) - harm. - org. - pf. - str.   85:00 Bo. Hawkes.
Chamber Orch.: 1(alt. with picc.),1(alt. with Eng.hn.),1,1 - 1,0,0,0 - timp.,perc. - hp. - str.

BRITTEN, Benjamin - BERKELEY, Lennox
—— MONT JUIC (SUITE OF CATALAN DANCES)
2,2,2,2 sax.(ad lib.), 2 - 4,2,3,1 - timp.,perc. - hp. - str.   12:00 Bo. Hawkes.

BRITTEN, Benjamin - HOLST, Imogen
—— REJOICE IN THE LAMB (FESTIVAL CANTATA), OP. 30
1,1,1,1 - 1,0,0,0 - timp.,perc. - hp. - org. (ad lib.) - str.   16:00 Bo. Hawkes.

BRITTEN, Benjamin - STONE, David
—— THE COURTLY DANCES (FROM "GLORIANA")
9:00 Bo. Hawkes.

BRITTON, Phillip John
—— PASSACAGLIA FOR ORCHESTRA
2,2,3,2 - 4,2,3,1 - timp.,perc. - str.   7:00 S.A.M.R.O.

BROCKT, Johannes Dr.
—— SCHLESISCHE RHAPSODIE
2,0,2,2 sax.,2 - 2,2,2,1 - timp.,perc. - str.   16:00 Weinberger.

BROEKMAN, David
—— CONCERTO FOR PIANO, PERCUSSION AND ORCH.
Composer.
—— CONCERTO FOR VIOLIN AND ORCH.
2,2,*3 - 4,3,3,1 - timp. - str.   31:00 Composer.
—— MANHATTAN FAIRY TALES (IN 4 MOVTS.)
2,*3,*3,4 sax.,2 - 4,3,3,1 - timp.,perc.(3) - hp. - pf. - str.   17:00 Robbins.
—— SYMPHONY NO. 2
*3,*3,*3,*3 - 4,4,3,1 - timp.,perc.(2) - hp. - str.   35:00 Composer.

BROGGER, Reidar
—— FAIRY SUITE ("EAST OF THE SUN AND WEST OF THE MOON")
1,1,1,1 - 2,1,1,0 - timp.,perc. - pf. - org. - str.   25:00 T.O.N.O.
—— MEDITATION (FOR SOPRANO, MIXED CHORUS AND ORCH.)
org. - str.   20:00 T.O.N.O.

BROMAN, Natanael
—— FRITIOF OCH INGEBORG (SYMPHONIC POEM)
2,3,2,2 - 4,2,3,1 - timp. - str.   10:00 S.T.I.M.

BROMAN, Sten
—— CHORAL FANTASY, OP. 17 (1931)
2,2,2,2 - 2,2,2,0 - timp. - str.   17:00 S.T.I.M.
—— GOTISK SUITE (FOR STRING ORCH.) (IN 3 MOVTS.)
str.   S.T.I.M.
—— MUSICA CATHEDRALIS (FOR SOPRANO, BASS, THREE CHORUSES, 2 ORGANS, PRE-TAPED ORGAN AND ORCH.) (1971)
2,2,2,2 - 4,4,4,1 - timp.,perc.(6) - tape-recorder - 2 org. - str.   98:00 Fleisher.
—— SENTENTIA CREVIT (FOR ORCH. AND TAPE)
4,2,2,2 - 4,4,3,1 - timp.,perc.(5) - tape-recorder - str.   13:00 S.T.I.M.
—— SYMPHONY NO. 1 (1962)
3,2,2,3 - 4,4,3,1 - timp.,perc.(7) - str.   28:00 S.T.I.M.
—— SYMPHONY NO. 2 (1963)
3,2,2,3 - 4,4,3,1 - timp.,perc.(9) - str.   33:00 S.T.I.M.
—— SYMPHONY NO. 3 (1964)
4,3,3,3 - 4,4,3,1 - timp.,perc.(5) - hp. - str.   32:00 S.T.I.M.
—— SYMPHONY NO. 4 (1965-66)
4,3,3,3 - 4,4,3,1 - timp.,perc.(5) - 2 hp. - str.   22:00 S.T.I.M.
—— SYMPHONY NO. 5 (WITH SOPRANO) (1967)
4,3,3,3 - 4,4,3,1 - timp.,perc.(5) - hp. - str.   30:00 S.T.I.M.
—— SYMPHONY NO. 6 (1969)
4,3,3,3 - 4,4,3,1 - timp.,perc.(5) - hp. - str.   34:00 S.T.I.M.
—— SYMPHONY NO. 7 (1971)
4,3,3,3 - 4,4,4,1 - timp.,perc.(6),cel. - tape-recorder - hp. - str.   32:00 Fleisher.

BRONS, Carel
—— EPITAPHIUM
2,2,2,2 - 2,2,0,0 - timp.,perc. - str.   8:00 Henmar.
—— MUSIC FOR STRINGS
str.   10:00 Henmar.
—— VARIANTEN (1966)
3,3,3,3 - 4,4,4,1 - timp.,perc. - hp. - str.   11:00 Henmar.

BROTT, Alexander
—— ANALOGY IN ANAGRAM (SUITE) (1955) (IN 3 MOVTS.)
 *3,*3,*3,*3 - 4,4,3,1(alt. with euph.) - timp.,perc. - hp. - str.
              11:00 CanMusCtr.
—— ARABESQUE FOR CELLO AND ORCH.
              15:00 C.A.P.A.C.
—— CENTENNIAL CELEBRATION (FOR WOMEN'S CHORUS,
NARRATOR AND STRINGS) (1967) (Text: Composer)
 str.   22:00 CanMusCtr.
—— CENTENNIAL COLLOQUY (1965) (IN 4 MOVTS.)
 2(2nd alt. with picc.),2,3,basset hn.,*3 - 4,0,0,0 - perc.
            22:55 CanMusCtr.
—— CHARACTERISTIC DANCE (FOR VIOLIN AND ORCH.)
(1940)
 2(2nd alt. with picc.),2,2,2 - 2,2,2,0 - timp.,perc. - hp. - str.
            5:00 CanMusCtr.
—— CONCERTINO FOR VIOLIN AND ORCH. (1950) (IN 3
MOVTS.)
 2(2nd alt. with picc.),2(2nd alt. with Eng. hn.),2(2nd alt. with
 b.-cl.),2 - 2,2,0,0 - timp.,perc. - str. 20:20 CanMusCtr.
—— CONCERTO FOR VIOLIN AND ORCH.
 2,2,2,2 - 2,2,1,0 - timp.,perc.(2) - str. 22:00 C.A.P.A.C.
—— CONCORDIA
 3,3,3,3 - 4,3,3,1 - timp. - str. 20:00 C.A.P.A.C.
—— CRITIC'S CORNER
 perc.(1) - str.   18:00 C.A.P.A.C.
—— CUPID'S QUANDARY (FOR VIOLIN, STRINGS AND
PERCUSSION) (1975) (IN 3 MOVTS.)
 perc. - str.   25:00 CanMusCtr.
—— DELIGHTFUL DELUSIONS (OVERTURE) (1950)
 *3,*3,*3,*3 - 4,4,3,1 - timp.,perc. - hp. - str. 7:00 CanMusCtr.
—— FROM SEA TO SEA (ORCHESTRAL SUITE) (IN 5 MOVTS.)
 3,3,3,3 - 4,3,3,1 - perc.(3) - str. 38:00 C.A.P.A.C.
—— H. B. S. (1975)
 2(2nd alt. with picc.),2,2,2 - 3,2,1,1 - timp.,perc. - pf. - str.
            7:00 CanMusCtr.
—— LAMENT FOR STRINGS
 str.   9:00 C.A.P.A.C.
—— LE CORRIVEAU (BALLET) %
           35:00 C.A.P.A.C.
—— MARTLET'S MUSE
           9:00 C.A.P.A.C.
—— ORACLE
 3,3,3,3 - 4,3,3,1 - perc. - pf. - str. 9:00 C.A.P.A.C.
—— PRELUDE TO OBLIVION (1951)
 1,1,1,1 - 0,3,2,0 - timp.,perc. - hp. - pf. - str. 4:15 CanMusCtr.
—— PROFOUNDUM PRAEDICTUM (FOR VIOLA OR CELLO OR
DOUBLE BASS WITH STRING ORCH.) (1964)
 str.   23:23 CanMusCtr.
—— RITUAL (FOR STRING QUARTET AND STRING ORCH.)
(1942)
 str.   10:00 CanMusCtr.
—— ROYAL TRIBUTE
 3,3,3,3 - 4,4,3,1 - timp.,perc. - str. 11:00 C.A.P.A.C.
—— SONGS OF CONTEMPLATION (FOR VOICE AND STRINGS)
 str.   10:45 C.A.P.A.C.
—— SPHERES IN ORBIT (A FANTASY)
 *3,*3,*3,*3 - 4,4,3,1 - timp.,perc.,cel. - str. 14:30 Huron Press.
—— THREE ASTRAL VISIONS (1959)
 str.   28:45 CanMusCtr.
—— TRIANGLE, CIRCLE, FOUR SQUARES (1963) (IN 3 MOVTS.)
 str.   10:40 CanMusCtr.
—— THE VISION OF DRY BONES (FOR BARITONE, STRINGS
AND PIANO OBBLIGATO) (1944)
 pf. - str.   12:00 CanMusCtr.
—— WAR AND PEACE (SYMPHONIC POEM)
 3,3,3,3 - 4,4,3,1 - timp.,perc. (3) - hp. - pf. - str. 22:00 C.A.P.A.C.

BROUSTET, Edouard
—— LEGENDE LANGUEDOCIENNE
 2,2,2,2 - 2,2,3,1 - timp.,perc. - str. 4:00 Presser.

BROWER, Jay D.
—— CONCERTINO FOR CLARINET AND CHAMBER ORCH.
(1968)
         17:00 Composer.
—— GREENLAND WHALERS (FOR NARRATOR AND ORCH.)
(WITH OPTIONAL BARITONE VOICE) (1967)
 *2,2,2,2 - 2,2,1,1 - timp.,perc.(2),bells - str. 5:15 Fox.

BROWN, Christopher
—— A HYMN TO THE HOLY INNOCENTS (CANTATA) (FOR
TENOR, MIXED CHORUS, TIMPANI AND STRINGS)
 timp. - pf. - str.   16:30 Oxford.
—— CONCERTO FOR TWO PIANOS AND STRINGS (1965)
 2 pf. - str.   14:00 P.R.S.
—— PARTITA FOR CELLO AND ORCH. (1967)
 1,1,2,1 - 2,1,1,0 - timp.,perc.,cel. - str. 17:00 P.R.S.

BROWN, J. C.
—— CONCERTO FOR CHAMBER ORCH.
 2,2,2,2 - 2,2,0,0 - timp.,perc. - str. 18:00 P.R.S.
—— DIVERTIMENTO (1967)
 2,2,2,2 - 4,2,3,1 - timp.,perc. - str. 12:00 P.R.S.

BROWN, James
—— A MINIATURE SYMPHONY
 2,2,2,2 - 2,2,3,0 - timp.,perc. - str. 10:00 P.R.S.
—— SYMPHONY (1956)
 2,2,2,2 - 4,3,3,1 - timp.,perc. - hp. - str. 45:00 P.R.S.

BROWN, Jonathan Bruce
—— LYRIC VARIATIONS (1975)
 tu. - str.   6:00 Composer.
—— THREE PIECES FOR ORCH. ("WARMTH OF DISTANT SUNS")
(IN 3 MOVTS.)
 2(2nd alt. with picc.),2,*3,1 - 2,2,3,1 -
 timp.,perc.(4),bells,mar.,vibra. - str.(min.:2,1,1,1) 12:40 Composer.

BROWN, Keith Crosby
—— LATIN-AMERICAN SUITE (IN 3 MOVTS.)
         12:00 C. Fischer.

BROWN, Keith Crosby - LANGENDOEN, J.
—— BOSTONIA SUITE (IN 3 MOVTS.)
 2,2,2,2 - 4,2,2,0 - timp.,perc. - str. 14:00 C. Fischer.

BROWN, Rayner
—— CONCERTO FOR ORGAN AND ORCH. (IN 3 MOVTS.)
 2,*3,2,2 - 4,3,4,1 - timp.,perc.(3),xyl. - org. - str. 19:00 Composer.
—— SYMPHONY NO. 2 (IN 3 MOVTS.)
 2,2,2,2 - 4,2,3,1 - timp.,perc.(2),xyl. - str. 11:00 Composer.
—— SYMPHONY NO. 3 (IN 4 MOVTS.)
 2,2(2nd alt. with Eng. hn.),2,2 - 4,2,3,1 - timp.,perc.(2) - str.
         14:00 Composer.

BROWNE, Philip
—— CONCERTO FOR STRINGS (1974) (IN 3 MOVTS.)
 str.   8:00 J. Boonin.
—— SERENADE FOR ORCHESTRA (1966)
 1. Adagio; 2. Andante; 3. Allegro
 2,*3,*3,2 - 4,3,3,1 - timp.,perc.(3),bells,glock.,xyl. - pf. - str.
         7:00 Fst. Etling.

BROWNING, Mortimer
—— CONCERTO FOR THEREMIN AND ORCH.
 3,*3,*3,2 - 4,3,3,1 - timp.,perc.(3) - hp. - theremin - str.
         12:00 Composer.
—— KEMPTOWN SUITE (IN 4 MOVEMENTS)
 2,*3,*3,*3 - 4,3,3,1 - timp.,perc.(3) - hp. - str. 16:00 Composer.
—— MARINE CAVALIER (FOR MEN'S CHORUS AND ORCH.)
 tpt. - perc. - pf. - str.   8:00 Gray.
—— RONDO (SCHERZO) FOR VIOLIN AND ORCH.
 3,*3,*3,2 - 4,3,3,1 - timp.,perc. - hp. - str. 10:00 Composer.

BROZA, Elliot
—— A SUITE FOR ANIMALS (IN 4 MOVTS.)
 2,2,2,2 - 4,3,3,0 - perc.,cel. - hp. - str. Fox.

BROZEN, Michael
—— CANTO (1957)
 2(2nd alt. with picc.),2(2nd alt. with Eng. hn.),2,2 - 4,2,3,1 -
 timp.,perc.(2) - str.   14:30 Presser.
—— DARK NIGHT, GENTLE NIGHT (SONG CYCLE FOR
SOPRANO, TENOR AND ORCH.) (1965) (Text: Beaumont and
Fletcher)
 2(2nd alt. with picc.),*2,2(2nd alt. with b.-cl.),2(2nd alt. with
 c.-bn.) - 2,2,1,1 - timp.,perc.(2),cel.(alt. with hpsc.) - hp. - str.
         25:00 Presser.
—— IN MEMORIAM (FOR SOPRANO AND STRING ORCH.)
(1968) (Text: Alfred Lord Tennyson)
 str.   30:00 Presser.

BRUCH, Max - BLACK, Norman
—— KOL NIDREI (FOR SOLO VIOLIN OR CELLO, WITH STRING ORCH.)
    str.   8:00 C. Fischer.

BRUČI, Rudolf
—— CONCERTINO FOR ORCH.
    3,3,3,3 - 4,3,3,1 - timp.,perc.,vibra.,xyl. - pf. - str.
                             16:00 MIC,Zagreb.
—— CONCERTO FOR BASSOON AND ORCH.
    3,3,2,1 - 0,3,3,0 - timp.,perc.,xyl. - hp. - str.   20:00 MIC,Zagreb.
—— CONCERTO FOR CLARINET AND STRINGS
    cl. - str.   22:40 MIC,Zagreb.
—— CONCERTO FOR TROMBONE AND ORCH.
    3,3,3,2 - 4,3,4,1 - timp.,perc. - str.   22:00 S.O.K.O.J.
—— MAN'S ENDLESS VIEW (CANTATA) (FOR CONTRALTO, 2 SPEAKING VOICES, SATB CHORUS AND ORCH.)
    3,2,2,2 - 0,3,3,1 - timp.,perc.,vibra.,xyl. - pf. - str.
                             35:00 S.O.K.O.J.
—— MASKAL (SYMPHONIC SUITE) (1954)
    3,3,3,2 - 4,3,3,0 - perc.(3),cel.,vibra.,xyl. - hp. - pf. - str.
                           20:00 MIC,Zagreb.
—— METAMORPHOSES ON THE NAME OF B-A-C-H
    str.(12,4,4,2)   S.O.K.O.J.
—— RONDO GIOCOSO
    3,3,3,2 - 4,3,3,1 - timp.,perc. - str.   14:00 S.O.K.O.J.
—— SINFONIA LESTA
    3,3,3,3 - 4,3,3,1 - timp.,perc.,cel.,glock.,vibra.,xyl. - hp. - pf. - str.
                             28:00 MIC,Zagreb.
—— SYMPHONY NO. 3
    3,3,3,3 - 4,3,3,1 - timp.,perc.(5),glock.,vibra.,xyl. - hp. - pf. - str.
                             30:00 MIC,Zagreb.
—— VOJVODINA (CANTATA) (FOR SOPRANO, BASS, SATB CHORUS AND ORCH.)
    3,3,3,3 - 4,3,3,1 - timp.,perc. - str.   50:00 S.O.K.O.J.

BRUCKNER, Anton - NOWAK, Leopold
—— SYMPHONY IN F MINOR (STUDIENSYMPHONIE) (1863 VERSION) (URTEXT; ED. POSTH.) (1863 Version)
    2,2,2,2 - 4,2,3,1 - timp. - str.   Henmar.
—— SYMPHONY NO. "ZERO" (URTEXT; ED. POSTH.) (1869 Version)
    2,2,2,2 - 4,2,3,0 - timp. - str.   43:00 Henmar.
—— SYMPHONY NO. 1 (URTEXT; ED. POSTH.) (Linz Version)
    3,2,2,2 - 4,2,3,0 - timp. - str.   48:00 Henmar.
—— SYMPHONY NO. 2 (URTEXT; ED. POSTH.) (1877 Version)
    2,2,2,2 - 4,2,3,0 - timp. - str.   67:00 Henmar.
—— SYMPHONY NO. 3 (URTEXT; ED. POSTH.) (3rd 1889 Version)
    2,2,2,2 - 4,3,3,0 - timp. - str.   65:00 Henmar.
—— SYMPHONY NO. 3 (URTEXT; ED. POSTH.) (2nd 1877 Version, Edited by Oeser and Nowak)
    2,2,2,2 - 4,3,3,0 - timp. - str.   65:00 Henmar.
—— SYMPHONY NO. 4 (URTEXT; ED. POSTH.) ("ROMANTIC") (1874 Version)
    2,2,2,2 - 4,3,3,0 - timp. - str.   72:00 Henmar.
—— SYMPHONY NO. 4 (URTEXT; ED. POSTH.) ("ROMANTIC") (1889 Version)
    2,2,2,2 - 4,3,3,1 - timp. - str.   72:00 Henmar.
—— SYMPHONY NO. 5 (URTEXT; ED. POSTH.) (Original Version)
    2,2,2,2 - 4,3,3,1 - timp. - str.   81:00 Henmar.
—— SYMPHONY NO. 6 (URTEXT; ED. POSTH.) (Original Version)
    2,2,2,2 - 4,3,3,1 - timp. - str.   59:00 Henmar.
—— SYMPHONY NO. 7 (URTEXT; ED. POSTH.) (Original Version)
    2,2,2,2 - 4,4 wagner tubas, 3,3,1 - timp. - str.   65:00 Henmar.
—— SYMPHONY NO 8 (URTEXT; ED. POSTH.) (2nd Version; 1890)
    3,3,3,3 - 8(4 alt. with Wagner tubas),3,3,1 - timp.,perc. - hp. - str.
                             87:00 Henmar.
—— SYMPHONY NO. 8 (URTEXT; ED. POSTH.) (1st Version; 1887)
    2,2,2,2 - 8(4 alt. with Wagner tubas),3,3,1 - timp.,perc. - str.
                             87:00 Henmar.
—— SYMPHONY NO. 9 (URTEXT; ED. POSTH.) (Original Version)
    3,3,3,3 - 8(4 alt. with Wagner tubas),3,3,1 - timp. - str.
                             60:00 Henmar.

BRUMBY, Colin James
—— AEGEAN SUITE (FOR FLUTE AND SMALL ORCH.)
                             12:00 A.P.R.A.
—— ANTIPODEA (1966)
    *3,2,2,2 - 4,2,3,0 - timp.,perc.(3),cel. - hp. - pf. - str.
                             7:00 J. Albert.
—— ANTITHESIS (1964)
    str.   7:00 J. Albert.

—— CONCERTINO FOR VIOLA AND STRINGS (1962)
    str.   10:00 J. Albert.
—— CONCERTO FOR HORN AND STRINGS (1971)
    hn. - str.   13:00 J. Albert.
—— CONCERTO FOR VIOLIN AND ORCH. (1970)
    2,2,2,2 - 2,2,2,2 - timp.,perc.(4, incl. 3 on timp.) - str.
                             30:00 J. Albert.
—— DIVERSION FOR HORN AND ORCH. (1966)
                               J. Albert.
—— ENBRADAS (STRAVINSKY COMMEMORATION) (1968)
                             3:00 J. Albert.
—— FIBONACCI VARIATIONS (1963)
    2,2,2,2 - 4,2,3,0 - timp.,perc.(5, incl. 3 on timp.) - hp. - str.
                          12:25 J. Albert.
—— FIVE DAYS LOST (FOR NARRATOR AND ORCH.) (1969)
    2,2,2,2 - 2,2,3,0 - timp.,perc.(4,incl. 3 on timp.) - hp. - str.
                          10:00 J. Albert.
—— KASTALIA (FOR FLUTE AND SMALL ORCH.)
                             6:00 A.P.R.A.
—— LITANIES OF THE SUN (1971)
    3,3,3,3 - 5,3,3,1 - timp.,perc.(4,incl. 3 on timp.) - hp. - str.
                          25:00 J. Albert.
—— MEDITERRANEAN SUITE (FOR SMALL ORCH.)
                           12:00 A.P.R.A.
—— PAEAN (FOR SMALL ORCH.)
                           12:00 A.P.R.A.
—— PANTOS (1962)
    fl. - str.   7:00 J. Albert.
—— PARTITA (FOR CLARINET AND SMALL ORCH.)
                             A.P.R.A.
—— REALISATIONS (FOR PIANO AND ORCH.) (1966)
    2,0,2,0 - 2,2,2,0 - timp.,perc. - pf. - str.   12:00 J. Albert.

BRUN, Fritz
—— SYMPHONY NO. '2 IN B♭ MAJOR
    *3,2,2,*3 - 4,2,3,1 - timp.,perc. - str.   40:00 Hug.
—— SYMPHONY NO. 7, IN D MAJOR
    *3,2,2,*3 - 4,2,3,0 - timp.,perc. - str.   45:00 S.U.I.S.A.
—— SYMPHONY NO. 10, IN B♭ MAJOR
    *3,2,2,*3 - 4,2,3,1 - timp.,perc. - str.   40:00 S.U.I.S.A.
—— VARIATIONS FOR PIANO AND STRINGS
    pf. - str.   20:00 S.U.I.S.A.

BRÜN, Herbert
—— CONCERTINO FOR ORCHESTRA
    3,3,2,2 - 2,1,1,0 - str.   16:00 IsMuPublns.
—— DEDICATION OVERTURE
    3,3,2,2 - 4,3,2,1 - timp.,perc. - str.   7:00 IsMuPublns.
—— MOBILE (1958)
    *4,*3,4,3 - 4,3,6,2 - timp.(8 drums) - str.   13:00 Seesaw.

BRUNELLI, Louis Jean
—— BURLESCA FOR ORCHESTRA
    3(3rd alt. with picc.),*3,*3,2,1 c.-bn.,(ad lib.) - 4,3,3,1 - timp.,perc.(3),xyl. - hp. - str.   9:00 Wimbledon.
—— TWO GENTLEMEN FROM VERONA (1967)
    2(2nd alt. with picc.),2(2nd alt. with Eng. hn.),*3,2 - 2,2,2,0 - timp.,perc.(2),xyl. - hp. - str.   8:30 Chappell.

BRUNI TEDESCHI, Alberto
—— CIRCULAR DIAGRAM (DRAMATIC ACTION) (WITH CHORUS AND ACTORS) %
    3,0,3,2 sax.,3 - 4,3,3,1 - timp.,perc.(4),bells,cel.,flexaton (variable-pitch steel spring activated by 2 hammers),glock.,mar.,vibra.,xyl. - 2 pf. - str.   Leeds.
    On Stage: 0,0,2,0 - 2,5,2,0
—— CONCERTO FOR PRINCE EUGENE
    2,2,2,2 - 4,3,3,1 - timp.,perc.,bells,cel.,xyl. - pf. - str. 14:00 Leeds.
—— CONCERTO NO. 1 FOR ORCH.
    2,3,2,2 - 2,2,1,0 - timp. - pf. - str.   17:00 Leeds.
—— CONCERTO NO. 2 FOR ORCH.
    3,3,3,3 - 4,4,3,1 - timp.,perc.,cel.,glock.,vibra.,xyl. - hp. - pf. - str.
                                 Leeds.
—— REQUIEM SENZA PAROLE (1970)
    1,1,0,1 sax.,0 - 2,2,2,0 - timp. - pf. - str.   30:00 MCA Music.
—— SYMPHONY IN ONE MOVEMENT
    3,2,2,2 - 2,2,0,0 - timp.,perc. - pf. - str.   12:00 Leeds.
—— VIAGGIO E FINALE (CANTATA TROPICALE) (1967) (FOR TENOR AND ORCHESTRA) (Text: G. Bona)
    2,3,2,1 sax.,2 - 0,2,1,0 - timp.,perc.(9),cel.,glock.,vibra.,xyl. - hp. - pf. - str.   25:00 MCA Music.

BRUNNER, Adolf
—— CONCERTANTE MUSIC FOR ORCH. (REV. 1959)
    2,1,2,sax.,2 - 1,2,2,1 - timp.,perc.(3) - str.   20:00 G. Schirmer.
—— CONCERTO FOR LARGE ORCH. (1956)
    3,3,4,3 - 4,3,3,1 - timp.,perc.(3) - str.   25:00 G. Schirmer.
—— CONCERTO GROSSO (FÜR STREICHORCH. UND PAUKEN)
    timp. - str.   22:00 Baerenrtr.
—— DAS GESPRÄCH JESU MIT NIKODEMUS (SACRED CONCERTO, FOR TENOR, BASS AND CHAMBER ORCH.)(1939)
    ob. - org. - str.   17:00 G. Schirmer.
—— DAS GLEICHNIS VON DEN ZEHN JUNGFRAUEN (Geistliches Konzert, für Vierstimmigen Gemischten Chor, Horn und Streichorch.)
    hn. - str.   10:00 Baerenrtr.
—— PARTITA FÜR KLAVIER UND ORCH.
    2,2,2,*2 - 2,2,0,0 - timp. - str.   17:00 Baerenrtr.

BRUNS, Victor
—— CONCERTO FOR CELLO AND ORCH.
    2,2,3,2 - 4,2,3,1 - timp. - str.   32:00 Tetra.
—— CONCERTO FOR FLUTE AND SMALL ORCH., OP. 51
    2,1,1,1 - 2,0,0,0 - timp.,perc. - str.   Tetra.
—— CONCERTO FOR VIOLIN AND ORCH., OP. 36
    2,2,2,2 - 4,2,3,1 - timp.,perc. - str.   25:00 Tetra.
—— CONCERTO NO. 1 FOR BASSOON AND ORCH., OP. 5
    3,3,2,3 - 4,3,3,1 - timp.,perc. - str.   14:00 Tetra.
—— CONCERTO NO. 3 FOR BASSOON AND ORCH., OP. 41
    1,1,2,1 - 2,2,0,0 - perc. - str.   20:00 Tetra.
—— DAS EDELFRÄULEIN ALS BÄUERIN (BALLET SUITE)
    2,2,2,2 - 4,2,3,0 - perc. - hp. - str.   Tetra.
—— ORCHESTRA PIECE, OP. 19
    3,2,2,2 - 4,3,3,1 - timp.,perc. - str.   15:00 Tetra.
—— DAS RECHT DES HERRN (BALLET SUITES I AND II)
    3,2,2,2 - 4,3,3,1 - timp.,perc. - str.   Tetra.
—— SINFONIETTA, OP. 23
    2,1,2,1 - 3,2,0,0 - perc. - str.   26:00 Tetra.
—— SYMPHONY NO. 4, OP. 47 ("CONCERTANTE") (FOR WIND QUINTET, PERCUSSION AND STRINGS)
    1,1,1,1 - 1,0,0,0 - timp.,perc. - str.   Tetra.

BRUSH, Ruth Jackson
—— RIVER MOONS (AFTER THE POEM BY CARL SANDBURG)
    2(2nd alt. with picc.),2(2nd alt. with Eng. hn.),*3,*3, - 4,0,0,0 - timp.,cel. - hp. - str.   6:00 Composer.

BRUSILOVSKY, Evgenij G.
—— SYMPHONY NO. 7 ("TATTENBET")
    G. Schirmer.

BRUSSELMANS, Michel
—— CONCERTO FOR ORGAN AND ORCH. (1938)
    3,3,3,3 - 4,3,2,1 - timp. - org. - str.   15:00 H. Elkan.
—— HÉLÈNE DE SPARTE (SYMPHONIC POEM) (1914)
    3,3,3,3 - 4,3,3,1 - timp.,perc. - hp. - str.   12:00 H. Elkan.
—— OUVERTURE HÉROÏQUE
    3,3,3,3 - 4,3,3,1 - timp.,perc. - str.   9:00 H. Elkan.
—— RHAPSODIE (FOR HORN AND ORCH.) (1938)
    timp.,perc.,cel. - hp. - str.   12:00 CBDM.
—— SCENES PROVENÇALES
    2,2,2,2 - 2,2,3,1 - timp.,perc.,bells - pf. - str.   12:00 CBDM.
—— SCÈNES BROUGHELIENNES
    3,3,3,3 - 4,3,3,1 timp.,perc.,glock - hp. - str.   14:00 Cranz.
—— SUITE-DIVERTISSEMENT IN G (1937)
    2,1,2,1 - 2,2,2,1 - timp.,perc.,bells,cel.,glock.,vibra.,xyl. - pf. - str.   17:00 H. Elkan.
—— SYMPHONY NO. 2
    3,3,3,3 - 4,3,3,1 - timp.,perc. - pf. - str.   20:00 CBDM.
—— SYMPHONY NO. 3 (1956)
    0,0,0,0 - 4,3,3,1 - timp. - str.   21:00 CBDM.
—— VARIATIONS CONTRAPUNCTIQUES (2ND VERSION) (1935)
    2,2,2,2 - 2,2,1,1 - timp.,perc. - pf. - str.   8:00 H. Elkan.

BRUSSELS, Iris
—— AMERICAN SKETCHES (IN 4 MOVTS.)
    str.   21:00 Composer.
—— SYMPHONY (1946) (IN 4 MOVTS.)
    1,*2,*2,2 - 1,2,3,1 - perc.,cel. - hp. - str.   20:00 Composer.
    or:
    *3,2,*3,2 - 4,2,3,1 - timp.,perc.,bells,cel. - hp. - str.

BRUSTAD, Bjarne
—— CONCERTINO FOR VIOLA AND ORCH. (IN 3 MOVTS.)
    0,2,0,2 - 1,1,0,0 - cembalo(or pf.) - str.   18:00 T.O.N.O.
—— CONCERTO GROSSO FOR ORCH. (A STUDY) (IN 4 MOVTS)
    2,1,2,1 - 2,2,3 0 - str.   15:00 T.O.N.O.
—— CONCERTO NO. 1 FOR VIOLIN AND ORCH.
    23:00 T.O.N.O.
—— CONCERTO NO. 2 FOR VIOLIN AND ORCH. (IN 4 MOVTS.)
    2,2,2,2 - 4,1,0,0 - timp.,perc.,cel. - str.   28:00 T.O.N.O.
—— CONCERTO NO. 4 FOR VIOLIN AND ORCH. (IN 3 MOVTS.)
    2,2,2,2 - 2,2,3,0 - timp.,perc.,cel. - str.   25:00 T.O.N.O.
—— FRAGMENTS FROM THE OPERA "ATLANTIS"
    4,3,5,4 - 6,4,4,0 - timp.,perc.,cel. - hp. - pf. - str.   T.O.N.O.
—— FRENCH SUITE (IN 4 MOVTS.)
    10:00 T.O.N.O.
—— KINDERSPIELE (FRA BARNETS VERDEN) (SUITE) (IN 7 MOVTS.)
    1,1,2,1 - 2,1,1,0 - timp.,perc. - pf. - str.   10:00 T.O.N.O.
—— NORWEGIAN SUITE (IN 5 MOVTS.)
    10:00 T.O.N.O.
—— OVERTURE
    3,2,2,2 -4,3,3,1 - timp.,perc.,cel. - hp. - str.   12:00 T.O.N.O.
—— RHAPSODY FOR VIOLIN AND ORCH.
    3,2,2,2 - 4,2,3,0 - timp.,perc. - hp. - pf. - str.   18:00 T.O.N.O.
—— SUITE NO. 1 (WITH OPTIONAL MALE CHORUS)
    3,3,4,3 - 4,3,3,1 - timp.,perc.,cel. - hp. - str.   10:00 T.O.N.O.
    or:
    2,2,3,3 - 4,3,3,1 - timp.,perc.,cel. - hp. - str.
—— SUITE NO. 2 (IN 4 MOVTS.)
    2,2,2,2 - 4,3,3,1 - timp.,perc.,cel. - hp. - str.   19:00 T.O.N.O.
—— SYMPHONY NO. 3 (IN 3 MOVTS.)
    2,2,2,2 - 4,3,3,0 - timp.,perc.,cel. - pf. - str.   27:00 T.O.N.O.
—— SYMPHONY NO. 4 (IN 4 MOVTS.)
    2,2,2,2 - 4,3,3,0 - timp.,perc. - str.   19:00 T.O.N.O.
—— SYMPHONY NO. 5 (1967) (IN 4 MOVTS.)
    2,2,2,2 - 4,3,3,0 - timp.,perc. - hp.(or pf.) - str.   T.O.N.O.
—— VARIATIONS SÉRIEUSES (ON A THEME BY CORELLI)
    3,2,2,3 - 2,2,3,0 - timp. - str.   10:00 T.O.N.O.

BRYAN, Charles Faulkner
—— THE BELL WITCH (CANTATA) (FOR CHORUS AND ORCH.)
    2,1,2,1 - 4,2,2,0 - timp.,perc. (2) - hp. - str.   28:00 J. Fischer.
—— BIRMINGHAM SUITE (IN 3 MOVTS.)
    2(1 alt. with picc.),1,2,1 - 4,3,2,1 - timp.,perc.(2) - hp. - str.   10:45 Composer.
—— FROM THE TEXTBOOKS (FOUR PART-SONGS) (FOR SOPRANO, SATB CHORUS AND CHAMBER ORCH.)
    1,1,1,0 - 2,0,0,0 - str.   6:30 Belw-Mills.
    or:
    1,0,2,0 - 2,0,0,0 - str.
—— WHITE SPIRITUAL SYMPHONY
    Composer.

BUCCHI, Valentino
—— BALLATA DEL SILENZIO
    2,2,2,2 - 4,3,3,1 - timp.,perc.(2) - str.   11:30 Leeds.
—— CONCERTO GROTTESCO (FOR CONTRABASS AND STRINGS) (1967)
    xyl.(or pf.) - str.   11:00 MCA Music.
—— CONCERTO LIRICO (FOR VIOLIN AND STRING ORCH.)
    str.   12:00 Bo. Hawkes.
—— IL CONTRABASSO (1-ACT GROTESQUE OPERA, AFTER CHEKOV) %
    3,2,2,3 - 4,2,2,0 - timp.,perc.(2),vibra.,xyl. - hp. - str.   Leeds.
    On Stage: Band
—— CORI DELLA PIETÀ MORTA (FOR MIXED CHORUS AND ORCH.) (Text: F. Fortini)
    2,2,2,1 sax.,2 - 4,3,3,1 - timp.,perc.,cel.,vibra.,xyl. - 2 hp. - pf. - str.   22:00 Leeds.
—— IL GIOCO DEL BARONE ("THE BARON'S GAME") (DRAMA WITH SOLO VOICES, SMALL MIXED CHORUS AND ORCH.) %
    2,2,2,2 - 2,2,2,0 - timp.,perc.(3),vibra.,xyl. - 2 d.-b.   Leeds.
—— MIRANDOLINA: BALLET SUITE (IN 8 MOVTS.)
    3,2,2,3 - 4,3,3,0 - timp.,perc.,xyl. - hp. - pf. - str.   20:00 Bo. Hawkes.
—— PIANTO DELLE CREATURE (FOR VOICE AND ORCH.)
    2,2,2,2 - 4,2,2,0 - timp.,perc.,xyl. - pf. - str.   13:00 Bo. Hawkes.
    or:
    perc. - str.

BUCCI, Mark
—— CONCERTO FOR A SINGING INSTRUMENT (FOR ANY MELODIOUS INSTRUMENT, WITH SMALL ORCH.) (IN 3 MOVTS.)
    cel. - hp. - str.   16:37 FrankMusCp.
—— THE DRESS (ONE-ACT COMIC OPERA) %
    1,1(alt. with Eng. hn.),2,1 - 0,1,0,0 - perc. - pf. - str.   Chappell.
—— TALE FOR A DEAF EAR (OPERA) % (Text: M. Bucci and Elizabeth Enright)
    1,1(alt. with Eng. hn.),2(2nd alt. with b.-cl.),1 - 1,1,0,0 - perc.(1) - hp. - pf.(alt. with cel.) - str.   46:00 FrankMusCp.

BUCHANAN, Annabel
—— COME ALL YE FAIR AND TENDER LADIES (FOLK SONG IN DORIAN MODE, ARR. FOR WOMEN'S CHORUS, PIANO AND STRING ORCH.)
    pf. - str.   8:00 J. Fischer.

BUCHAROFF, Simon
—— DEATH SCENE FROM THE OPERA "SAKAHRA"
    2 picc.,2,*4,*5,*4 - 6,4,3,1 - timp.,perc.(5) - 2 hp. - str.
            12:00 Composer.
—— FOUR TONE POEMS
    2picc.,2,2,*3,2,2 c-bn. - 4,4,2,2 - timp.,perc.(5) - 2 hp. - str.
            24:00 Composer.
—— LORD, HEAR MY VOICE (CANTATA FROM SOPRANO, TENOR, BARITONE, CHORUS AND ORCH.)
    *3,*3,*3,*3 - 4,3,3,1 - timp.,perc.(3) - 2 hp. - org - str.
            30:00 Composer.
—— MOSES (RHAPSODIC VARIATIONS)
    2 picc.,2,*3,*3,*4 - 4,4,3,1 - timp.,perc. (5) - 2 hp. - str.
            25:00 Composer.
—— OUR COUNTRY (SYMPHONIC POEM)
    2 picc.,2,*3,*3,2 sax.,*4 - 4,4,3,1 timp.,perc.(6) - 2 hp. - pf. - str.
            30:00 Composer.
—— SCÈNE DE BALLET, FROM "SAKAHRA"
    *3(one alt. with 2nd picc.),*4,2 D cl.,*3,*4 - 6,4,3,1 - timp.,perc.(4) - 2 hp. - str.   8:00 Composer.
—— THE TRUMPETER'S DEATH (FANTASY FOR PIANO AND ORCH.)
    2 picc. 2,*3,*3,*4 - 4,4,3,1 - timp.,perc. - 2 hp. - pf. - str.
            18:00 Composer.
—— THE WANDERER'S SONG (SYMPHONIC POEM)
    2 picc.,2,*3,*3,*4 - 4,4,3,1 - timp.,perc.(4). - 2 hp. - pf. - str.
            Composer.

BUCHT, Gunnar
—— CONCERTO FOR CELLO AND ORCH., OP. 12
    2,2,2,2 - 4,3,3,0 - timp. - str.   18:00 S.T.I.M.
—— COUPLETS ET REFRAINS, OP. 29 (1960)
    2,2,2,2 - 3,2,2,0 - timp.,perc.(3) - str.   16:45 S.T.I.M.
—— DAGEN SVALNAR, OP. 18-B (1956) (FOR SOPRANO AND ORCH.) (Text: Edith Sodergran)
    2,2,2,2 - 3,3,2,1 - timp.,perc.(2) - str.   8:00 S.T.I.M.
—— DIVERTIMENTO, OP. 16 (1956)
    2,2,2,2 - 0,0,0,0 - timp.,perc.(2) - str.   14:00 S.T.I.M.
—— DRAMMA PER MUSICA (1963)
    3,3,3,3 - 4,4,3,1 - timp.,perc.(3) - pf. - str.   10:00 S.T.I.M.
—— ENVAR SIN EGEN PROFESSOR, OP. 19 (1957) (FOR TENOR, MIXED CHORUS AND ORCH.) (Text: Falstaff Fakir)
    2,2,2,2 - 4,3,3,1 - timp.,perc.(3) - pf.   13:00 S.T.I.M.
—— LA FINE DELLA DIASPORA, OP. 22 (1958) (FOR MIXED CHORUS AND ORCH.) (Text: "Auschwitz", by Salvatore Quasimodo)
    2,2,2,2 - 4,2,2,1 - timp.,perc.(4) - str.   15:30 S.T.I.M.
—— INTRODUCTION AND ALLEGRO FOR STRINGS, OP. 4
    str.   7:00 S.T.I.M.
—— PLAY FOR STRINGS (1965)
    str.   4:30 S.T.I.M.
—— SYMPHONIC FANTASY, OP. 13
    2,2,2,2 - 4,3,3,1 - timp.,perc.(3) - hp. - pf. - str.   10:00 S.T.I.M.
—— SYMPHONY NO. 1, OP. 8
    3,3,3,3 - 4,3,3,1 - timp.,perc.,cel. - hp. - pf. - str.   24:00 S.T.I.M.
—— SYMPHONY NO. 2, OP. 9
    3,3,3,3 - 4,4,4,0 - timp.,perc. - str.   16:00 S.T.I.M.
—— SYMPHONY NO. 3, OP. 11
    2,2,2,2 - 4,3,3,0 - timp. - pf. - str.   17:00 S.T.I.M.
—— SYMPHONY NO. 4, OP. 21 (1958)
    2,2,2,2 - 4,4,3,1 - timp.,perc.(2) - str.   18:00 S.T.I.M.
—— SYMPHONY NO. 5, OP. 30 (1960)
    2,2,2,2 - 4,2,2,0 - timp.,perc.(2) - hp. - str.   22:00 S.T.I.M.
—— SYMPHONY NO. 6, OP. 32 (1960-62)
    3,3,3,3 - 4,4,3,1 - timp.,perc.(4),cel. - hp. - str.   34:00 S.T.I.M.

—— SYMPHONY NO. 7 (1971)
    2,2,2,2 - 4,4,3,1 - timp.,perc.(4 incl. 3 on timp.) - hp. - str.
            19:00 Fleisher.
—— VINTERORGEL (1974)
    3,3,3,3 - 5,3,3,1 - timp.,perc.,cel. - hp. - str.   16:00 Fleisher.

BÜCHTGER, Fritz
—— THE CHRISTMAS ORATORIO (IN 3 PARTS)(FOR SOLO VOICES AND ORCH.)(1959)
    fl.,ob. - str.   28:00 G. Schirmer.
—— CONCERTO FOR ORCHESTRA (IN 3 MOVTS.)
    2,2,2,2 - 0,3,2,1 - perc. - str.   14:00 Henmar.
—— CONCERTO FOR STRING ORCH., OP. 42
            Möseler.
—— MUSIC FOR SMALL ORCH., OP. 9
            K & S.

BUCK, Ole
—— CHRISTOPHER COLUMBUS (FOR CHORUS AND ORCH.)
            30:00 G. Schirmer.
—— DECORE (REV. 1970)
    2,0,1,0 - 0,1,0,0 - perc.(3) - str.   12:00 G. Schirmer.
—— ENVOI (FRAGMENTS FOR ORCH.)(1965)
            5:00 G. Schirmer.
—— FAIRIES (1972)
    2,2,2,2 - 2,2,2,0 - timp.,perc.(5) - hp. - pf. - str.   G. Schirmer.
—— FELIX LUNA (BALLET) % (1971)
    3,3,3,2 - 3,3,3,0 - perc. - str.   45:00 G. Schirmer.
—— FOUR PRELUDES (1967)
    1,1,1,1 - 1,1,1,0 - perc. - pf. - str.   7:00 G. Schirmer.
—— GRANULATIONS (1972)
            17:00 G. Schirmer.
—— JEUX D'EAU (DIVERTISSEMENT FOR ORCH.) (1964)
            3:00 G. Schirmer.
—— KALLIGRAFI (FOR SOPRANO AND SMALL ORCH.)
    2,1,1,0 - 0,1,0,0 - perc.(2),cel.,mar.,vibra.,xyl. - hp. - pf. - str.(6,4,2,0)   G. Schirmer.
—— OVERTURE (1966)
    2,2,2,2 - 2,2,0,0 - timp. - str.   6:00 G. Schirmer.
—— PASTORALS FOR ORCH. (1975)
            G. Schirmer.
—— PUNCTUATIONS (1968)
    3,3,3,2 - 3,3,3,0 - timp.,perc.(3) - str.   9:00 G. Schirmer.
—— WHITE FLOWER (MUSIC II FOR ORCH.) (1973)
            12:00 G. Schirmer.

BUCZYNSKI, Walter
—— ADAGIO AND ALLEGRO
            8:30 C.A.P.A.C.
—— BEZTITULA (FOR PIANO AND ORCH.) (1964) (IN 3 MOVTS.)
    2,2,2,2 - 2,2,1,0 - pf. - str.   9:15 CanMusCtr.
—— CONCERTO FOR STRING ORCH.
    str.   15:00 C.A.P.A.C.
—— CONCERTO FOR VIOLIN, CELLO AND ORCH. (1975) (IN 1 MOVT.)
    2,2,2,2 - 4,3,3,1 - timp.,perc. - str.   18:00 CanMusCtr.
—— FOUR MOVEMENTS FOR PIANO AND STRINGS (1969)
    pf. - str.   22:30 CanMusCtr.
—— ISKRY FOR ORCHESTRA (1969)
    *3,*3,2,2 - 4,3,3,1 - timp.,perc.(4) - str.   5:10 CanMusCtr.
—— SCHERZO FOR PIANO AND ORCH.
            12:00 C.A.P.A.C.
—— SEVEN MINATURES FOR ORCH. (1970)
    2,2,2,2 - 2,2,2,0 - timp. - str.   9:00 CanMusCtr.
—— TRYPTYCH FOR ORCHESTRA (1964)
    2,2,2,2 - 4,4,2,1 - timp.,perc. - str.   6:30 CanMusCtr.
—— A WORK FOR DANCE (1970) (IN 4 SECTIONS)
    cl. - perc. - str.   18:40 CanMusCtr.
—— ZEROING IN NO. 2 (1971) (DISTRACTION AND THEN)
    *3,*3,*3,2 - 4,3,3,1 - perc.(4),cel. - str.   12:10 CanMusCtr.
—— ZEROING IN NO. 3 (1973) (PIECE IN PROGRESS) (FOR STRING QUARTET AND ORCH.)
    *3,*3,*3,*3 - 4,3,3,1 - timp.,perc. - str.   15:00 CanMusCtr.
—— ZEROING IN NO. 4 (1972) (INNARDS AND OUTARDS) (FOR SOPRANO, FLUTE, PIANO AND ORCH.)
    *3,*3,*3,*3 - 4,3,3,1 - perc.(3) - pf. - str.   22:05 CanMusCtr.

BUDDE, Kurt
—— DRAMATIC OVERTURE, OP. 28
    3(3rd alt. with picc.),2(2nd alt. with Eng. hn.),2,2 - 4,3,3,1 - timp.,perc.(5, incl. 3 on timp.) - hp. - str.   15:00 Henmar.

BUDER, Ernst Erich
—— FESTIVAL (AN OVERTURE)
6:00 Henmar.

BUDKA, Harry
—— BY THE WATERS OF BABYLON (1950)
2(2nd alt. with picc.)2(2nd alt. with Eng. hn.),*3,1 - 4,3,2,0 -
timp.,perc.(1-2),glock.,xyl. - hp. - str.   6:10 Composer.
—— SEASCAPE (FOR PIANO AND ORCH.) (1969)
2(2nd alt. with Eng. hn.),*3,1 - 4,3,2,0 - timp.,perc.,glock.,xyl. - pf.
- str.   Composer.

BUECHE, Gregory
—— CHORALE FANTASIA (ON "HOLY GOD WE PRAISE THY
NAME") (1943)
*3,2,2,2 - 4,3,3,1 - timp.,perc.(4),bells - hp. - str. 10:00 Composer.
—— THE JUGGLER OF OUR LADY (SYMPHONIC FANTASIA)
(1953)
*3,2,*3,2 - 4,3,3,1 - timp.,perc.(5),bells,xyl. - hp. - str.
10:00 Composer.
—— MASS IN HONOR OF A SPECIAL OCCASION (1962)
org. - str.   25:00 Composer.
or:
*3,2,2,2 - 4,2,3,0 - timp. - org. - str.
—— MELODIE (1961)
Eng. hn. - str.   8:00 Composer.
—— OVERTURE IN E-FLAT (1957)
*3,*3,2,2 - 4,3,3,0 - timp.,perc. - str.   12:00 Composer.
—— PASSACAGLIA FOR VIOLINS (1959)
Vlns.   12:00 Composer.
—— THE FIFTY-EIGHTERS (1858) (OVERTURE-FANTASY) (1957)
*3,2,*3,2 - 4,3,2,1 - timp.,perc.(3) - str.   13:00 Composer.
—— TONE POEM (1952)
*3,2,2,2 - 4,3,3,0 - timp.,perc.(3) - str.   7:30 Composer.

BUECHNER, Margaret
—— THE KEY (AN EASTER BALLET FOR CHILDREN) %
2,2,2,2 - 4,2,3,1 - timp.,perc. - str.   26:00 C. Fischer.
—— THE KEY (SUITE FROM THE BALLET)
2,2,2,2 - 4,3,2,0 - timp.,perc. - str.   15:00 C. Fischer.

BUECHTGER, Fritz
—— CONCERTINO NO. 1, OP. 59 (FOR OBOE, VIOLIN, CELLO
AND STRING ORCH.) (IN 3 MOVTS.)
ob. -str.   15:00 G.E.M.A.
—— CONCERTO FOR ORCHESTRA (IN 3 MOVTS.)
2,2,2,2 - 0,3,3,1 - perc. - str.   14:00 Sirius.
—— THE TRANSFIGURATION (FOR BARITONE, WOMEN'S
VOICES AND STRINGS)
str.   Baerenrtr.

BUGATCH, Samuel
—— TWO DANCES FOR ORCHESTRA
Composer.

CHASSIDIC DANCE
2,2,2,0 - 0,2,2,0 - timp. - str.   5:00
JEWISH DANCE
1,1,2,0 - 0,2,0,0 - perc.(1) - str.   4:00

BÜLAU, Wolfgang
—— SYMPHONION PROTON (SYMPHONY NO. 1)
2,2,2,3 - 4,4,3,1 - timp.,perc. - hp. - pf. - str. 30:00 Sikorski.

BULL, Edvard Hagerup
—— AIR SOLENNEL (HOMMAGE À DARIUS MILHAUD)
2,2,2,2 - 2,2,1,0 - timp.,perc.(3) - hp. - pf. - str. 5:00 Presser.
—— CONCERTO FOR FLUTE, PIANO AND STRINGS
fl. - pf. - str.   17:00 Presser.
—— CONCERTO FOR TROMBONE AND CHAMBER ORCH.
1,1,0,0 - 0,1,1,0 - pf. - str.   14:00 Presser.
—— CONCERTO NO. 1 FOR TRUMPET AND ORCH.
3,3,4,2 - 4,3,3,1 - timp.,perc.,cel. - hp. - pf. - str. 12:00 Presser.
—— CONCERTO NO. 2 FOR TRUMPET AND ORCH.
1,1,0,0 - 1,1,0,0 - perc. - str.   Presser.
—— DIVERTIMENTO FOR PIANO, PERCUSSION AND ORCH.
2,1,1,1 - 2,1,1,0 - timp.,perc.(3) - hp. - str. 16:00 Presser.
—— EPILOGUE FOR STRINGS
str.   13:00 Presser.
—— PETITE SUITE SYMPHONIQUE
1,1,1,1 - 2,1,0,0 - timp.,perc. - hp. - pf. - str. 11:00 Presser.
—— SINFONIA DI TEATRO
3,3,3,3 - 4,3,3,1 - timp.,perc.(3, incl. 2 on timp.) - hp. - pf. - str.
8:00 Presser.

—— SINFONIA HUMANA
2,1,1,1 - 2,1,1,0 - timp.,perc.,cel. - hp. - pf. - str. 21:00 Presser.
—— SIX EPIGRAMMES (FOR SMALL ENSEMBLE)
1,1,1,1 - 1,1,1,0 - perc.(2) - d.-b.   19:00 Presser.
—— TROIS MORCEAUX BREFS (FOR SAXOPHONE AND ORCH.)
2,2,2,sax.,2 - 2,2,0,0 - perc.,cel. - hp. - pf. - str. Presser.

BULL, John - GUERRINI, Guido
—— WALSINGHAM VARIATIONS
S.I.A.E.

BULL, John - HELM, Everett
—— JOHN BULL SUITE
1,1,1,1 - 2,2,1,0 - str.   13:15 C. Fischer.

BUNGE, Sas
—— BALLADE DES PENDUS (FOR ALTO OR BASS VOICE AND
ORCH.) (1944) (Text: François Villon)
2,2,2,2 - 2,0,0,0 - timp.,perc. - hp. - str.   11:00 Henmar.
—— GEBED TOT JEZUS DEN VREDEVORST (FOR WOMEN'S
CHORUS AND STRING ORCH.) (1945) (Text: H. Dullaert)
hp. - str.   9:00 Henmar.

BUNIN, Revol S.
—— SYMPHONY NO. 5
G. Schirmer.

BURGES, Peter
—— SUITE IN E MINOR (FOR STRINGS) (IN 5 MOVTS.)
str.   Novello.

BURGHAUSER, Jarmil
—— CONCERTO FOR WIND QUINTET AND STRINGS
1,1,1,1 - 1,0,0,0 - str.   15:00 Bo. Hawkes.
—— CZECH CANTATA (FOR MIXED CHORUS AND ORCH.)
(Text: Vilem Zavada)
Bo. Hawkes.

BURGON, Geoffrey
—— CHAMBER SYMPHONY (1966)
1,2,0,2 - 2,0,0,0 - str.   15:00 P.R.S.
—— CONCERTO GROSSO (1964)
0,2,0,0 - 2,0,0,0 - str.   24:00 P.R.S.
—— FIVE PIECES FOR STRING ORCH. (1967)
str.   18:00 P.R.S.
—— THE GOLDEN FISH (BALLET) % (1964)
18:00 P.R.S.
—— OPHELIA (BALLET) % (1964)
1,1,1,1 - 1,0,0,0 - str.   16:00 P.R.S.
—— THIS ENDRIS NIGHT (FOR TENOR, SA CHORUS AND
BRASS)
0,0,0,0 - 4,4,2,1 - timp.   30:00 Galaxy.

BURKHARD, Paul
—— STUDIE ZUM PSALM 136
3,3,3,3 - 3,4,4,0 - perc.,cel. - hp. - str. 6:00 Burkhard.Co.

BURKHARD, Willy
—— CANTATA OF PSALMS (FOR SOPRANO, MIXED CHORUS,
ORGAN AND SMALL ORCH.)
Baerenrtr.
—— CONCERTINO FOR TWO FLUTES, HARPSICORD AND
STRING ORCH.
2 fl.,hpsc. - str.   Baerenrtr.
—— CONCERTO FOR ORGAN, STRING AND BRASS
Baerenrtr.
—— CONCERTO FOR VIOLA AND ORCH.
Baerenrtr.
—— FANTASIA MATTUTINA (FOR LARGE ORCH.)
Baerenrtr.
—— DAS GESICHT JESAJAS (THE VISION OF ISAIAH)
(ORATORIUM FUR GEMISCHTEN CHOR, SOPRANO,
TENOR, BASS, ORGEL UND GROSSES ORCH.), OP. 41
4,*3,2,2 - 2,2,2,1 - timp.,perc. - org. - str. 90:00 Hug.
—— HYMNE, OP. 75 (FOR ORGAN AND ORCH.) (1945)
2(2nd alt. with picc.),2,2,2 - 2,2,2,1 - timp. - org. - str. G. Schirmr.
—— MAGNIFICAT, OP. 64 (FOR SOPRANO AND STRING ORCH.)
str.   10:00 Baerenrtr.
—— ORCHESTRAL SUITE FROM "THE BLACK SPIDER"
Baerenrtr.
—— PICCOLA SINFONIA GIOCOSO (FOR SMALL ORCH.)
10:00 Baerenrtr.

—— SINFONIE IN EINEM SATZ, OP. 73
    2,2,*3,*3 - 2,2,2,1 - timp.,perc. - hp. - str.   22:00 Baerenrtr.
—— SOLEMN MASS (FOR SOPRANO, BASS, MIXED CHORUS
AND ORCH.)
        Baerenrtr.
—— SONATA DA CAMERA (FOR STRINGS AND PERCUSSION)
    str.   Baerenrtr.
—— TOCCATA FOR FOUR WIND INSTRUMENTS, STRINGS AND
PERCUSSION, OP. 86
        Baerenrtr.
—— TOCCATA, OP. 55 (FOR STRINGS)
    str.   13:00 Bo. Hawkes.
—— VARIATIONS ON "TILL EULENSPIEGEL", OP. 37 (1932)
    1(alt. with picc.),1,1,1 - 0,1,3,0 - timp.,perc. - str.
    12:00 G. Schirmer.

BURLEIGH, Carl
—— TRILOGY OF SYMPHONIES
    24:00 Fox.

BURLEIGH, Cecil
—— CONCERTO NO. 1 FOR VIOLIN AND ORCH., OP. 25
    *3,2,2,2 - 4,2,3,0 - timp.,perc. - hp. - str.   Composer.
—— CONCERTO NO. 2 FOR VIOLIN AND ORCH., OP. 43 (IN 3
MOVTS.)
    2(2nd alt. with picc.),2,2,2 - 4,2,3,0 - timp. - str.
    15:00 C. Fischer.
—— CONCERTO NO. 3 FOR VIOLIN AND ORCH., OP. 60
    2(2nd alt. with picc.)2,2,2 - 4,2,3,1 - timp., hp. - str.
    18:00 Composer.
—— EVANGELINE, OP. 41
    *3,2(2nd alt. with Eng. hn.),2,3 - 4,2,3,1 - timp.,perc. - hp. - str.
    12:00 C. Fischer.
—— MOUNTAIN PICTURES (SUITE), OP. 42 (IN 4 MOVTS.)
    3(3rd alt. with picc.),2(2nd alt. with Eng. hn.),2,3 - 4,2,3,1 -
timp.,perc. - hp. - str.   13:00 C. Fischer.

BURNARD, Alex
—— L' ALLEGRO (FOR SOPRANO, BARITONE, CHORUS AND
ORCH.)
    55:00 A.P.R.A.
—— AUSTRALIAN FESTIVAL OF SONG (FOR SOPRANO,
CHORUS AND ORCH.)
    A.P.R.A.
—— TE DEUM LAUDAMUS (FOR BARITONE, CHORUS AND
ORCH.)
    15:00 A.P.R.A.
—— THREE SHAKESPEARE SONGETTES (FOR BARITONE AND
ORCH.)
    A.P.R.A.
—— THE VOICES (CORONATION ODE) (FOR SOLO VOICES,
CHORUS AND ORCH.)
    A.P.R.A.

BURRITT, Lloyd
—— ASSASSINATIONS (1968)
    *3,3,*3,*3 - 4,3,3,1 - timp.,perc.(6)(incl. 4 on timp.) -
tape-recorder - hp. - str.   17:25 CanMusCtr.
—— ELECTRIC TONGUE (1969)
    *3,2,2,2 - 4,3,3,1 - timp.,perc.(3) - tape-recorder - str.
    11:15 CanMusCtr.

BURT, George
—— EXIT MUSIC
    1,0,*2,0 - 1,1,b.-trb.,1 - perc.(2) - str.(1,0,1,1)   8:00 Presser.

BURTCH, Mervyn
—— CONCERTO FOR PIANO AND ORCH. (1966)
    2,2,2,2 - 4,2,3,0 - timp.,perc. - pf. - str.   22:00 P.R.S.
—— DANCE SUITE (1960)
    2,2,2,2 - 4,2,3,1 - timp.,perc. - str.   11:00 P.R.S.

BURTON, Eldin
—— BALLADE
    2,2,2,2 - 4,3,3,1 - timp.,perc.(2) - str.   13:00 Composer.
—— CONCERTO FOR FLUTE AND ORCH. (1968)
    2,2,2,2 - 4,2,3,1 - timp. - str.   21:00 C. Fischer.
—— CONCERTO FOR PIANO WITH ORCHESTRA (1971) (IN 3
MOVTS.)
    *4,*3,*3,*3 - 4,3,3,1 - timp.,perc.(2) - pf. - str.   18:15 C. Fischer.

BURTON, Stephen
—— DITHYRAMB
    9:00 Salabert.
—— SONGS OF THE TULPEHOCKEN (FOR BARITONE AND
ORCH.)
    3,3,3,3 - 6,4,3,1 - timp.,perc.(3),cel. - hp. - pf.   53:00 Salabert.
—— STRAVINSKIANA (FOR FLUTE AND SMALL ORCH.) (AN
ORIGINAL WORK IN THE STYLE OF STRAVINSKY)
    13:00 Salabert.
—— SYMPHONY NO. 2 ("ARIEL" SYMPHONY) (FOR VOICE AND
ORCH.) (Text: Sylvia Plath)
    55:00 Salabert.

BUSCH, Adolf
—— PSALM, NO. 6, OP. 70 (FOR CHORUS, ORGAN AND ORCH.)
    17:00 S.U.I.S.A.

BUSCH, Carl
—— INDIAN TRIBAL MELODIES (FOUR NORTH AMERICAN
LEGENDS, FOR STRING ORCH.)
    str.   C. Fischer.

BUSCHMANN, Rainer Glen
—— SERENADE FOR JAZZ QUARTET AND CHAMBER ORCH.
    1(alt. with picc.),0,0,0 - 0,0,0,1 - str.   15:00 Modern.
—— SERENADE FOR JAZZ QUARTET AND CHAMBER ORCH.
    1,0,1,0 - 0,0,0,1 - perc. - guit. - str.(incl. 1 solo d.-b.)
    10:00 Modern.

BUSH, Alan
—— CONCERT SUITE (FOR CELLO AND ORCH.)
    2(2nd alt. with picc.),2(2nd alt. with Eng.hn.),2,2 - 4,2,3,0 -
timp.,perc. - hp. - str.   28:00 Galaxy.
—— CONCERTO FOR PIANO AND ORCH., OP. 18 (WITH
BARITONE SOLO AND MALE CHORUS IN LAST
MOVEMENT)
    3,3,3,3 - 4,3,3,1 - timp. - str.   Galaxy.
—— CONCERTO FOR VIOLIN AND ORCH., OP. 32
    2,2,2,2 - 4,3,3,0 - timp.,perc. - str.   26:00 Galaxy.
—— DANCE OVERTURE, OP. 12
    3,3,3,2 sax.,2 - 4,3,3,1 - timp.,perc. - str.   16:00 P.R.S.
—— DORIAN PASSACAGLIA AND FUGUE, OP. 52 (1959)
    3,1,2,3 - 4,3,3,1 - timp.,perc. - str.   16:00 Novello.
—— ENGLISH SUITE, OP. 28
    str.   25:00 Galaxy.
—— FANTASIA ON SOVIET THEMES
    2,2,2,2 - 4,2,3,0 - timp.,perc. - str.   11:00 Novello.
—— FOR A FESTAL OCCASION (1961)
    2,2,2,2 - 4,2,3,0 - timp.,perc. - org. - str.   6:00 Novello.
—— PARTITA CONCERTANTE (1965)
    2,1,2,1 - 2,2,1,0 - timp.,perc. - str.   13:00 Novello.
—— PIERS PLOWMAN'S DAY (SYMPHONIC SUITE), OP. 30
    27:00 Galaxy.
—— RESOLUTION (OVERTURE), OP. 25
    2,2,2,2 - 4,2,3,0 - perc. - pf. - str.   7:00 Galaxy.
—— SCHERZO FOR WINDS AND PERCUSSION
    4,3,4,3 - 4,2,3,1 - perc.,xyl.   11:00 Novello.
—— SYMPHONY NO. 1, OP. 21
    3,2,3,3 - 4,6,3,1 - timp.,perc. - hp. - pf. - str.   26:00 P.R.S.
—— SYMPHONY NO. 2, OP. 33
    36:00 Galaxy.
—— SYMPHONY NO. 3, OP. 53 ("THE BYRON SYMPHONY") (FOR
BARITONE, SATB CHORUS AND ORCH.) (1960)
    3,3,3,3 - 4,4,3,1 - timp.,perc. - hp. - str.   54:00 P.R.S.
—— TIME REMEMBERED, OP. 67
    1,1,1,1 - 1,0,0,0 - hp. - str.   11:30 P.R.S.
—— VARIATIONS, NOCTURNE AND FINALE ON AN OLD
ENGLISH SEA SONG (FOR PIANO AND ORCH.) (1962)
    2,2,2,2 - 4,2,3,1 - timp.,perc. - pf. - str.   20:00 Novello.
—— THE WINTER JOURNEY (CANTATA) (FOR CHORUS, HARP
AND STRINGS)
    hp. - str.   22:00 Galaxy.

BUSH, Geoffrey
—— CONCERTINO FOR PIANO AND ORCH.
    3,2,2,2 - 4,2,3,0 - timp.,perc. - pf. - str.   18:00 Novello.
—— CONCERTO FOR LIGHT ORCH.
    2,2,2,2 - 4,2,2,1 - timp.,perc. - str.   15:00 Novello.
—— CONCERTO FOR OBOE AND STRINGS
    ob. - str.   15:00 Novello.
—— CONCERTO NO. 1 FOR TRUMPET, PIANO AND STRINGS
    tpt. - pf. - str.   20:00 Galaxy.

—— DIVERTIMENTO FOR STRINGS
str. 22:00 Galaxy.
—— FAREWELL, EARTH'S BLISS (FOR BARITONE AND STRINGS)
str. 16:00 Novello.
—— FINALE FOR A CONCERT (1964)
2,1,2,1 - 2,2,1,0 - timp.,perc. - str. 5:00 Novello.
—— FIVE SONGS (FOR HIGH VOICE AND SMALL ORCH.)
1,1,2,1 - 2,2,1,0 - timp. - str. 10:00 Novello.
—— FOUR SONGS FROM HERRICK'S "HESPERIDES" (FOR BARITONE AND STR.)
str. 8:00 Novello.
—— IF THE CAP FITS (1-ACT OPERA) % (AFTER MOLIERE'S "LES PRECIEUSES RIDICULES") (Text: Composer)
1,1,1,1 - 2,1,1,0 - timp.,perc. - pf. - str. 35:00 Galaxy.
—— IN PRAISE OF MARY (FOR SOPRANO, MIXED CHORUS AND ORCH.)
2(2nd alt. with picc.),2,2,2 - 4,2,3,1 - timp.,perc. - str.
 20:00 Novello.
—— A LITTLE CONCERTO FOR OBOE AND STRINGS
ob. - str. 15:00 Novello.
—— A LITTLE CONCERTO (ON THEMES OF ARNE) FOR PIANO AND STRINGS
pf. - str. 8:00 Novello.
—— MARTINI FANTASIA (AFTER JOHN FIELD)
pf. - str. 10:00 Novello.
—— THE MILLER AND HIS MEN (OVERTURE)
1,2,2,2 - 2,2,1,0 - timp. - str. 7:00 Novello.
—— MUSIC 1967 (FOR STRING QUARTET AND ORCH.)
3(3rd alt. with picc.),2,2,1 - 4,3,2,1 - timp.,perc. - 2 pf. - str.
 14:00 Novello.
—— NATUS EST IMMANUEL (A CHRISTMAS PIECE)
str. 6:00 Novello.
—— NOCTURNE FOR STRING ORCH.
str. Novello.
—— PASTORALE
1,1,1,1 - 2,1,0,0 - str. Novello.
—— THE REHEARSAL (OVERTURE)
2,2,2,2 - 4,2,3,0 - timp.,perc. - str. 6:00 Galaxy.
—— RHAPSODY FOR CLARINET AND STRINGS
cl. - str. 8:00 Novello.
—— SINFONIETTA CONCERTANTE (FOR CELLO AND CHAMBER ORCH.)
1,1,2,1 - 2,1,0,0 - timp. - str. 18:00 Novello.
—— SONGS OF WONDER (FOR HIGH VOICE AND STRING ORCH.) (Text: trad.)
str. 14:00 Novello.
—— THE SPANISH RIVALS (OVERTURE)
2,2,2,2 - 4,2,3,0 - timp. - str. 7:00 Novello.
—— SYMPHONY NO. 1
2,2,2,2 - 2,2,3,1 - timp.,perc.(3) - hp. - str. 28:00 Novello.
—— SYMPHONY NO. 2
2,2,2,2 - 4,3,3,0 - timp.,perc. - str. 32:00 Novello.
—— THREE SONGS (FOR HIGH VOICE AND STRINGS)
str. 7:00 Novello.
—— TWO AUSTRALIAN SKETCHES FOR STRINGS
str. 6:00 Novello.
—— YORICK (OVERTURE FOR ORCH.)
2,2,2,2 - 4,2,3,0 - timp.,perc. - str. 8:00 Novello.

BUSSER, Henri
—— CONCERTINO FOR CELLO AND ORCH.
2,1,2,1 - 2,1,1,0 - timp.,perc. - hp. - str. (8d. - b.) Baron.
—— CONCERTINO FOR CONTRABASS (OR BASSOON) AND CHAMBER ORCH.
2,1,2,1-2 - 2,1,1,0 - timp.,perc. - hp. - 1-2 d.-b. 6:30 Baron.
—— KYRNOS (POÈME CORSE) (3 SYMPHONIC TABLEAUX)
3,3,3,3 - 4,2,3,1 - timp.,perc. - hp. - str. 16:00 Presser.
—— PETITE SUITE, OP. 12
1,1,1,1 - 1,0,0,0 - timp. - hp. - str. 10:00 EV.
—— PIECE IN B♭, FOR OBOE AND ORCH.
2,1,2,1 - 1,0,0,0 - hp. - str. Baron.
—— PIECE IN D, FOR HORN AND ORCH.
1,1,2,1 - 1,1,0,0 - timp. - hp. - str. Baron.
—— PIÈCE DE CONCERT FOR HARP AND ORCH.
1,0,1,0 - 1,0,0,0 - hp. - str. Baron.
—— RÉCIT ET THÈME VARIÉ (FOR BASSOON AND ORCH.)
1,1,1,1 - 1,1,0,0 timp.,perc. - hp. - str. Baron.
—— SUITE FUNAMBULESQUE, OP. 20
2,2,2,2 - 2 hn. - timp.,perc. - hp. - str. 15:00 EV.
—— THREE PIECES (TROIS PIECES) (FOR CELLO AND ORCH.)
 Baron.

—— TOURANGELLES
2,2,2,2 - 2,2,1,0 - timp.,perc.,cel. - 2 hp. - str. 11:00 EV.

BUTLER, Jack H.
—— A CLASSICAL OVERTURE
 Composer.

BUTNIKOFF, Ivan
—— SYMPHONIC POEM, OP. 18
3(3rd alt. with picc.),*3,*3,*3 - 4,3,3,1 - timp.,perc.(2),cel.,glock. - hp. - str. 16:00 Composer.

BUTT, James
—— CONCERTINO FOR PICCOLO AND STRING ORCH. (1957)
picc. - str. 15:00 P.R.S.
—— CONCERTO FOR ORGAN AND STRING ORCH. (1956)
org. - str. 15:00 P.R.S.
—— CONCERTO FOR PIANO AND ORCH. (1962)
2,2,2,2 - 4,0,3,1 - timp.,perc. - pf. - str. 25:00 P.R.S.
—— MINIATURE VARIATIONS (1962)
1,1,1,1 - 0,0,0,0 - timp.,perc. - str. 10:00 P.R.S.

BUTTERLEY, Nigel Henry
—— CANTICLE OF DAVID
str. 17:00 A.P.R.A.
—— CONCERTO FOR VIOLIN AND ORCH. (1970)
*3,*3,*3,*3 - 4,3,3,0 - timp.,perc. - hp. - str. 19:00 J. Albert.
—— EXPLORATIONS (FOR PIANO AND ORCH.) (1970)
*4,*3,2 E♭cl.,*1,0,2 c.-bn. - 0,0,0,0 - timp., perc. - pf. - str.(4,3,3,0) 25:00 J. Albert.
—— FIRE IN THE HEAVENS (1973)
*3,*3,*3,*3 - 4,3,3,1 - timp.,perc.(3) - hp. - pf. - str.
 9:00 J. Albert.
—— FIRST DAY COVERS (FOR NARRATOR AND ORCH.) (1972)
2,2,2,2 - 4,2,3,1 - perc.(3) - hp. - str. 30:00 J. Albert.
—— THE FOUR ELEMENTS (1972)
2,2,2,2 - 4,2,3,0 - timp.,perc.(3) - pf. - str. 16:00 J. Albert.
—— INTERACTION I FOR ORCH. (IMPROVISATION BY COMPOSER, PIANIST AND PAINTER) (1967)
 J. Albert.
—— MEDITATIONS OF THOMAS TRAHERNE (1968)
22 recorders,*3,*3,*3,*3 - 4,3,3,1 - timp.,perc.(3) - hp. - pf. - str.
 J. Albert.
—— PENTAD (FOR 27 WINDS AND ORCH.) (1968)
 12:00 J. Albert.
—— REFRACTIONS (FOR WIND QUARTET AND CHAMBER ORCH.) (1969)
 9:00 J. Albert.

BUTTERWORTH, Arthur
—— CONCERTANTE (1962)
0,2,0,0 - 2,0,0,0 - str. 17:00 P.R.S.
—— DUO CONCERTANTE (FOR OBOE, HARPSICHORD AND STRING ORCH.)
ob. - hpsc. - str. 13:00 P.R.S.
—— ORGAN CONCERTO FOR ORGAN, PERCUSSION AND STRINGS (1965)
perc.(2) - org. - str. 20:00 P.R.S.
—— SUITE FOR SMALL ORCH., (1967)
2,1,2,1 - 2,1,1,0 - timp.,perc. - hp. - str. 14:00 P.R.S.

BUTTERWORTH, George
—— THE BANKS OF GREEN WILLOW
2,2,2,2 - 2,1,0,0 - hp. - str. 4:00 Galaxy.
—— TWO ENGLISH IDYLLS
2(2nd alt. with picc.),2,2,2 - 4,0,0,0 - timp. - hp. - str.
 9:00 Galaxy.

BUTTERWORTH, J. A.
—— A SHROPSHIRE LAD (RHAPSODY)
2,3,3,2 - 4,3,3,1 - timp. - hp. - str. 11:00 Novello.

BUTTERWORTH, Neil
—— RUMPELSTILZKIN (FOR NARRATOR AND CHAMBER ORCH.)
0,0,1,0 - 0,0,0,0 - pf. - str.(no d.-b.) 20:00 Belw-Mills.

BUTTING, Max
—— FIVE SERIOUS PIECES, OP. 92 (FUNF ERNSTE STUCKE) (AFTER DURER)
2,2,3,2 sax.,1 - 4,3,3,2 - timp.,perc. - str. 26:00 F. Colombo.

—— DIE LÜGENGESCHICHTE VOM SCHWARZEN PFERD, OP. 71
(THE LYING STORY OF THE BLACK HORSE) (CANTATA)
(FOR BARITONE, CHAMBER CHOIR AND CHAMBER
ORCH.) (After a Narration by Eckner)
   0,0,1,1, - 1,0,1,0 - timp.,perc. - trautonium(ad lib.) - pf. - str.
          25:00 F. Colombo.

BUXTEHUDE, Dietrich - CAILLIET, Lucien
—— PASSACAGLIA
          12:00 Arranger.

BUXTEHUDE, Dietrich - CHAVEZ, Carlos
—— CHACONNE (IN E MINOR) (ARR. 1937)
   2 piccs,2,*3,2,2 b.-cl.,*3 - 4,4,3,1 - timp., - str.   7:00 Mills.

BUXTEHUDE, Dietrich - EHRET, Walter
—— MAGNIFICAT (FOR SATB CHORUS AND STRINGS)
   str.   14:00 Presser.

BUXTEHUDE, Dietrich - MARGOLA, Franco
—— THREE PIECES FOR STRING ORCH.
   str.   Henmar.

BUXTEHUDE, Dietrich - STONE, Kurt
—— COMMAND THINE ANGEL THAT HE COME ("BEFIEHL
DEM ENGEL, DASS ER KOMM") (CANTATA) (FOR MIXED
CHORUS, CONTINUO AND STRS.)
   org.(or pf.) - str.   8:00 Broude.

BUŽAROVSKI, Dimitrie
—— SYMPHONY NO. 2
   3,3,3,3 - 4,3,3,1 - perc.,cel. - hp. - pf. - str.   30:00 S.O.K.O.J.

BUZZI-PECCIA, Arturo
—— BACCANALE ROMANO
   *3,*3,*3,2 - 4,4,3,1 - timp. - str.   15:00 G. Schirmer.
—— CALMA D'UN NOTTE ESTIVA (CALM OF A SUMMER
NIGHT)
   *3,*3,*3,2 - 2 hn. - timp. - hp. - str.   G. Schirmer.

BYE
—— NETHERLANDS SUITE (PEASANT DANCES)
   str.   Henmar.

BYRD, William - BALES, Richard
—— TWO 16TH CENTURY KEYBOARD PIECES
   1,1,2,1 - 2,2,1,0 - timp. - hp. - str.   Arranger.

BYRD, William - JACOB, Gordon
—— WILLIAM BYRD SUITE (IN 3 MOVTS.)
   3,2,2,2 - 4,2,3,1 - timp.,perc. - hp. - str.   12:00 Bo. Hawkes.

BYRD, William - KIRBY, Percival Robson
—— WALSINGHAM VARIATIONS
   2,2,3,2 - 4,2,3,1 - timp.,perc. - str.   10:00 S.A.M.R.O.

BYRD, William - MACLEAN, Quentin
—— VARIATIONS OF "THE CARMAN'S WHISTLE"
          15:00 C.A.P.A.C.

BYRD, William - RACKLEY, Lawrence
—— FITZWILLIAM SUITE NO. 1 (ARR. 1967) (IN 4 MOVTS.)
   2,2,0,0 - 2,0,0,0 - str.   8:00 Arranger.

BYRNE, Andrew
—— CORONATION OVERTURE, OP. 5 (1953)
   2,2,2,2 - 4,3,3,1 - timp.,perc. - str.   10:00 P.R.S.
—— PROLOGUE FOR ORCH., OP. 12 (1963)
   3,3,3,0 - 2,2,0,0 - timp.,perc. - hp. - pf. - str.   8:00 P.R.S.
—— SYMPHONY IN B FLAT, OP. 9 (1959)
   2,2,2,2 - 4,3,3,1 - timp.,perc. - str.   40:00 P.R.S.
—— TWO PIECES FOR SMALL ORCH., OP. 4 (1951)
   2,2,2,2 - 2,2,0,0 - timp.,perc. - str.   8:00 P.R.S.

C

CAAMANO, Roberto
—— CONCERTO FOR BANDONION AND ORCH.
   2,2,2,2 - 4,2,2,0 - timp.,bandonion(or acc.) - pf. - str.
          20:00 Bo. Hawkes.

—— CONCERTO FOR PIANO AND ORCH.
   3,3,3,3 - 4,3,3,1 - timp.,perc. - pf. - str.   19:00 Bo. Hawkes.
—— MAGNIFICAT (FOR MIXED CHORUS AND ORCH.)
   2,2,2,2 - 4,2,3,1 - timp.,perc. - hp. - str.   20:00 Bo. Hawkes.
—— MUSIC FOR STRINGS, OP. 23
   str.   14:00 Bo. Hawkes.
—— PRELUDE, ADAGIO AND FUGUE
   2,2,2,2 - 4,2,2,0 - timp.,perc. - hp. - pf. - str.   12:00 Bo. Hawkes.
—— PSALM 149 (FOR SOPRANO, MIXED CHORUS AND ORCH.)
   2,2,2,2 - 4,2,3,1 - timp.,perc. - hp. - pf. - str.   15:00 Bo. Hawkes.
—— SUITE FOR STRING ORCH., OP. 9
   str.   18:00 Bo. Hawkes.
—— VARIACIONES AMERICANAS, OP. 16
   2,2,2,2 - 4,3,3,1 - timp.,perc. - hp. - pf. - str.   16:00 Bo. Hawkes.

CABEZON, Felix-Antoine - HALFFTER, Rodolfo
—— VARIATIONS ON "LA GALLARDA MILANESA"
   1,2,2,2 - 2,1,0,0 - perc. - hp. - str.   Salabert.

CABEZON, Felix-Antoine - PITTALUGA, Gustave
—— VARIATIONS ON "EL CANTO DE CABALLERO"
   2,2,2,2 - 2,2,2,0 - str.   6:00 Salabert.

CABLE, Howard
—— NEWFOUNDLAND SKETCHES (SUITE)
   str.   12:00 Canadian.

CACAVAS, John
—— THE DAY THE ORCHESTRA PLAYED (A FANTASY FOR
NARRATOR AND ORCH.)
   3,2,3,2 - 4,3,3,1 - timp.,perc. - hp. - str.   18:00 Bo. Hawkes.

CACCIOLA, Joseph
—— HERO'S DREAM (SYMPHONIC PRELUDE)
   *3,2,*3,2 - 4,3,3,1 - timp.,perc.(3) - hp. - str.   6:00 Composer.
—— POÈME (FOR VIOLIN AND ORCH.)
   3,*3,*3,2 - 4,3,3,1 - timp. - hp. - str.   12:00 Composer.
—— SERENADE AND NOCTURNE (FOR VIOLIN AND ORCH.)
   1,1,2,1 - 2,2,1,0 - timp.,perc. (2),cel.,glock. - hp. - str.   Composer.
—— TWO PIECES FOR STRING ORCH.
   str.   12:00 Composer.

CADMAN, Charles Wakefield
—— AMERICAN SUITE (IN 3 MOVTS.)
   str.   9:35 C. Press.
   or:
   2,2,2,2 - 2,2,2,0 - timp.,perc. - str.
—— AURORA BOREALIS (SYMPHONIC POEM) (FOR PIANO
AND ORCH.)
   *3,*3,2(2nd alt. with b.-cl.),2 - 4,2,3,1 - timp.,perc. (3) - hp. - pf. -
   str.   14:00 Composer.
—— DANCE OF SACRIFICE (FROM "RAMALA")
          Composer.
—— DARK DANCERS OF THE MARDI GRAS (FANTASY)
   *3,2,2,2 sax.(ad lib.),2 - 4,3,3,1 - timp.,perc.(3) - pf. - str.
          10:00 Musicus.
—— THE FAR HORIZION (CANTATA FOR SOPRANO,
BARITONE AND ORCH.)
   *2,1,2,1 - 2,2,1,1 - timp.,perc. - hp. - str.   15:00 Composer.
—— THE FATHER OF WATERS (CANTATA FOR CHORUS AND
ORCH.)
   2,2,2,2 - 2,2,3,1- timp.,perc. (2) - pf. - str.   60:00 Ditson.
—— ORIENTAL RHAPSODY (FROM OMAR KHAYYAM)
   *3,2,2,2 - 4,3,3,1 - timp.,perc. (2) - hp. - str.   9:00 Robbins.
—— SYMPHONY NO. 1 ("PENNSYLVANIA")
   1. Allegretto grazioso; 2. Allegro scherzando - Andante con amore;
   3. Allegro con fuoco- piu maestoso
   3(3rd alt. with picc.),*3,*3,2 - 4,3,3,1 - timp.,perc. (3) - hp. - org. -
   str.   23:00 Composer.
—— THUNDERBIRD (AMERICAN INDIAN SUITE) (IN 5 MOVTS.)
   2,2,2,2 - 4,2,3,1 - timp.,perc. - hp. - str.   18:30 Bo. Hawkes.
—— THE WILLOW TREE (1-ACT OPERA) % (1933)
   1,1,1,1 - 1,1,1,0 - perc.,cel. - pf.(or hp.) - str.   25:00 Presser.

CAGE, John
—— ATLAS ECLIPTICALIS (1962)
   Maximum: *2,alto fl.,*2,*3(incl. 1 cl. or d.-b. cl.),sax.,*3 - 5,3,3,3 -
   timp.(16 drums),perc.(12) - 3 hp. - str.   Henmar.
   or:
   Minimum: 1,1,1,1 - 5,1,3,1 - timp.(4 drums),perc.(2) - hp. - str.

—— CHEAP IMITATION (FOR 24 TO 95 PLAYERS, WITH OR WITHOUT CONDUCTOR)(1972)
(total of 24:) 3(1 alt. with picc.,1 alt. with alto fl.) 2(2nd alt. with Eng. hn.), 2(2nd alt. with b.-cl.), alto sax.,1 - 1,1,1,1 - cel.,glock.,mar. - guit. - str.(2,1,1,1)   Henmar.
or:
(total of 59:) 6(2 alt. with 2 picc.,2 alt. with 2 alto fl.),4(2 alt. with 2 Eng. hn.),4(2 alt. with 2 b.-cl.),2 alto sax.,2 - 2,2,2,2 - timp.,bells,cel.,glock.,mar.,vibra. - guit. - 2 hp. - pf. - str.(12,4,4,3)
or:
(total of 95:) 9(3 alt. with 3 picc., 3 alt. with 3 alto fl.),6(3 alto sax.),3 - 3,3,3,3 - timp.,bells,cel.,glock.,mar.,vibra. - guit. - 3 hp. - pf. - str.(24,9,9,3)
—— CONCERT FOR PIANO AND ORCHESTRA (WITH OPTIONAL VOICE PART)
1(alt. with alto. fl. and picc.),0,1,1(alt. with bar.sax.) - 0,1,1,1 - str.   Henmar.
—— CONCERTO FOR PREPARED PIANO AND CHAMBER ORCH. (IN 3 MOVTS.)
1(alt. with picc.),*2,2,1 - 1,1,2,1 - perc. (4),bells,cel.,glock.,100 misc. perc. inst. - 2pf. - hp. - str.   19:30 Henmar.
—— THE SEASONS (BALLET IN ONE ACT) %
2(2nd alt. with picc.)2(2nd alt. with Eng.hn.),2(1 alt. with E♭ cl.,1 alt. with b.-cl.),2 - 2,2,2,0 - timp.,perc. (3),glock.,xyl. - pf.(alt. with cel.) - str.   15:00 Henmar.

CAGE, John - HARRISON, Lou
—— SUITE FOR TOY PIANO (OR REGULAR PIANO) (1948)
3,3,3,3 - 3,4,4,0 - timp.,perc.,cel. - hp. - pf.(or toy pf.) - str.
8:00 Henmar.

CAHUZAC, Louis
—— VARIATIONS SUR UN AIR DU PAYS D'OC (FOR CLARINET AND ORCH.)
2,2,2,2 - 2,2,3,0 - timp.,glock. - str.   7:00 Baron.

CAILLIET, Lucien
—— A BIRTHDAY FANTASY
*3,*3,*3,2 - 4,3,3,1 - timp.,perc. (3),glock.,xyl. - hp. - str.
4:00 Fox.
—— FANTASY AND FUGUE ON "O SUSANNA"
*3,*3,*3,2 - 4,3,3,1 - timp.,perc. (4),cel.,glock.,xyl. - hp. - str.
7:00 Mills.
—— FANTASY FOR CLARINET AND ORCH.
*3,*3,*3,c.-b. cl.(B♭),2 - 4,3,3,1 - timp.,perc.(3) - hp. - str.
7:00 Composer.
—— FANTASY ON "AULD LANG SYNE"
*3,*3,*3,*3 - 4,3,3,1 - timp.,perc. (3),glock.,xyl. - hp. - str.   Fox.
—— HOMAGE TO AMERICA'S MUSICAL YOUTH (FOR MIXED CHORUS AND ORCH.)
*3,*3,*3,*3 - 4,3,3,1 - timp.,perc. (6),bells,glock.,xyl. - hp. - str.
6:00 Leblanc.
—— OVERTURE ON AN ORIGINAL THEME
*3,*3,*3,*3 - 4,3,3,1 - timp.,perc. (3),glock. - hp. - str.   Composer.
—— RHAPSODY FOR VIOLIN AND ORCH.
*3,*3,*3 - 4,3,3,1 - timp.,perc. (2) - hp. - str.   8:00 Composer.
—— ROMANTIC TONE POEM
*3,2,*3,*3 - 4,3,3,1 - timp.,perc. (3),glock. - hp. - str.
6:00 Composer.
—— SUNDAY MORNING OVERTURE
*3,*3,*3,*3 - 4,3,3,1 - timp.,perc. (3),glock. - str.   Belwin.
—— VARIATIONS ON "POP GOES THE WEASEL"
*3,*3,*3,2 - 4,3,3,1 - timp.,perc. (4),glock. - hp. - str.   7:00 EV.
—— YOUTH WANTS TO LIVE (FOR CHORUS AND ORCH.) (Text: Dr. Emile Cailliet)
*3,*3,1 E♭ cl.,*4,c.-b. cl.,1 - 4,3,3,1 - timp.,perc.(5),bells,glock.,xyl. - hp. - pf. - str.   6:00 LeBlanc.

CAIN, Noble
—— CHRIST IN THE WORLD (CANTATA) (FOR SOPRANO, TENOR, BARITONE, SATB CHORUS, OPTIONAL CHILDREN'S CHORUS AND ORCH.)
2,2,2,2 - 2,2,1,0 - timp.,perc. - str.   40:00 Composer.
—— ODE TO AMERICA (FOR CHORUS AND ORCH.)
*3,2,2,2 - 4,4,3,1 - timp.,perc. - str.   Flammer.

CAIX D'HERVELOIS, Louis de - GAUBERT, P.
—— SUITE NO. 2 (FOR CELLO AND ORCH.)
0,2,2,2 - 2,2,0,0 - perc. - hp. - str.   Galaxy.

CAJA, Alfonso
—— TWO SYRACUSAN IDYLLS (FOR SMALL ORCH.)
2,3,2,2 - 2 hn. - cel. - str.   10:00 Salabert.

CALABRO, Louis
—— CANTILENA (FOR VOICE AND STRINGS)
str.   6:00 EV.
—— SYMPHONY NO. 1 (IN ONE MOVEMENT)
*3,*3,*3,*3 - 4,3,3,1 - timp.,perc.(3),xyl. - str.   20:00 EV.
—— SYMPHONY NO. 2 FOR STRINGS (IN 3 MOVTS.)
str.   20:00 EV.
—— SYMPHONY NO. 3 (IN ONE MOVT.)
*3,*3,*3,*3 - 4,3,3,1 - timp.,perc.(5),bells,cel. - str.   17:00 EV.
—— TEN SHORT PIECES FOR STRING ORCH.
str.   8:30 EV.

CALDWELL, Mary Elizabeth
—— A GIFT OF SONG (CHRISTMAS OPERA) % (FOR 7 SOLO VOICES, MIXED CHORUS AND ORCH.)
1,1,2,1 - 2,1,0,0 - timp.,perc. - hp. - pf. - str.   65:00 Bo. Hawkes.

CALL, Audrey
—— AMERICAN TONE POEM (FOR VIOLIN AND ORCH.)
1(alt. with picc.),1(alt. with Eng.hn.),2(1st alt. with b.-cl.),1 - 2,3,2,1 - timp.,perc.,cel. - hp. - pf. - str.   15:00 Composer.
—— ELEGY
2(2nd alt. with picc.),*3,2,2 - 4,3,3,1 - timp.,perc. (3) - 2 hp. - str.
8:00 Composer.
—— PIECE FOR CHAMBER ORCH.
1,*2,1,1 - hn. - pf. - str.   7:00 Composer.

CALMEL, Roger
—— ALBA OCCITANA (HOMAGE TO DARIUS MILHAUD) (WITH OPTIONAL BASSO)
2,2,2,2 - 2,2,1,0 - timp., perc. - hp. - str.   6:00 Presser.
—— LES CARACTÈRES (SYMPHONIC SUITE)
2,2,2,2 - 2,2,1,0 - timp.,perc.,cel. - str.   17:00 Henmar.
—— CONCERTO FOR CLARINET AND CHAMBER ORCH.
2,1,0,0 - 0,2,0,0 - timp. - str.   17:00 Presser.
—— CONCERTO FOR OBOE AND STRINGS
ob. - str.   16:00 Henmar.
—— CONCERTO FOR ORGAN, PERCUSSION AND STRINGS
timp.,perc.,cel. - org. - str.   20:00 Henmar.
—— CONCERTO FOR 4 SAXOPHONES, PERCUSSION AND STRINGS
4 sax. - timp.,perc. - str.   17:00 Henmar.
—— SYMPHONIE
perc. - str.   19:30 Presser.

CALTABIANO, S.
—— DUE PRELUDI
3,3,3,3 - 4,3,3,1 - timp.,perc.,bells,cel. - 1-2 hp. - str.
17:00 Bo. Hawkes.
—— OVERTURE IN F
2,2,2,2 - 4,2,1,0 - timp. - str.   8:00 Bo. Hawkes.
—— PROMETEO
3,3,3,3 - 4,3,3,1 - timp.,perc. - 1-2 hp. - str.   16:00 Bo. Hawkes.
—— THE VISION OF SAINT MARTIN
*3,*3,*3,*3 - 4,3,3,1 - timp.,perc.cel. - 2 hp. - str.
16:00 Bo. Hawkes.

CAMERLOHER, Placidus von - VOGT, Carl August
—— SINFONIA IN F MAJOR
Bn, - 2hn. - hpsc. - str.   22:00 Mannheimer.

CAMILLERI, Charles
—— CONCERTANTE NO. 4 FOR OBOE AND STRINGS
ob. - str.   Novello.
—— CONCERTO FOR ACCORDION AND STRINGS
acc. - str.   13:00 CanMusCtr.
—— DIARY OF A COWBOY (SUITE) (IN 4 MOVTS.)
15:00 P.R.S.
—— FANTASY FUGUE (1964)
str.   CanMusCtr.
—— MALTA SUITE (IN 5 MOVTS.)
18:00 P.R.S.
—— MALTESE DANCES
2,2,2,2 - 4,2,3,1 - timp.,perc.,glock.,xyl. - hp.   17:00 Novello.
—— MUSIC FOR FLUTE AND STRINGS (1961) (IN 3 MOVTS.)
fl. - str.   9:20 CanMusCtr.
—— ORPHEUS CONTEMPORANIUS
0,0,0,alto sax.,0 - 0,1,0,0 - perc. - pf. - str.   17:00 Novello.
—— QUINTESSA (SONG CYCLE FOR SOPRANO AND CHAMBER ORCH.) (Text: Composer)
13:00 P.McKee.
—— RHAPSODY FOR VIOLIN AND STRINGS (1963)
str.   10:00 CanMusCtr.

—— SUITE FOR SAXOPHONE AND STRINGS (1965)
 alto sax. - hp. - str.   11:00 P.McKee.
—— SYMPHONIC ORE (1963)
 *2,2,*3,2 - 4,3,3,1 - timp.,perc. - str.   CanMusCtr.
—— ZEITGEIST
 2,2,2,2 - 2,2,0,0 - timp.,perc.,xyl. - pf.   15:00 Novello.

CAMINITI, G.
—— CONCERTO IN A FOR CELLO AND ORCH.
 3,3,2,2 - 4,2,3,1 - perc. - hp. - pf. - str.   25:00 Bo. Hawkes.

CAMPAGNOLI, Bartolommeo - SONNTAG, Dieter
—— CONCERTO IN D MAJOR FOR FLUTE AND ORCH., OP. 3, NO. 2
 1,2,0,0 - 2,0,0,0 - str.   29:00 Henmar.

CAMPBELL, Henry C.
—— A FEW THINGS FOR STRINGS (SUITE)
 str.   5:00 Composer.

CAMPBELL, Kenneth
—— CAPITOL CITY SUITE (IN 3 MOVTS.)
        16:00 GVThompson.

CAMPO, Frank
—— ALPINE HOLIDAY OVERTURE, OP. 11 (1955)
 *3,*3,*3,*3 - 4,3,3,1 - timp.,perc.(3) - str.   9:00 Composer.
—— CANTATA NO. 2, OP. 31 (THE WORDS OF AGUR) (1964)
(FOR SATB CHORUS AND ORCH.)
 1,1,*2,0 - 0,1,1,1 - timp.,perc.(2),vibra.,xyl. - 1 c.,1 d.-b.
        12:00 Composer.
—— CONCERTO FOR BASSOON AND STRING ORCH., OP. 34
(1966) (IN 1 MOVT.)
 bn. - str.   15:00 Composer.
—— DUE QUADRI ROMANI (2 ROMAN PORTRAITS), OP. 15
(1957)
 1(alt. with picc.),1,1,1 - 2,1,1,0 - timp.,perc.(3),cel.,xyl. - str.
        16:00 Composer.
—— PARTITA FOR TWO ORCHESTRAS, OP. 45 (IN 7 MOVTS.)
 1,1,*2,1 - 1,0,0,0 - perc. - str.   14:00 Fleisher.
—— SPECTRUM I, OP. 27 (CONCERTO GROSSO FOR ORCH.)
(1961)
 2(2nd alt. with picc.),*2,1 E♭cl.,*2,*2 - 2,2,1,1 -
 timp.,perc.(3),glock.,vibra.,xyl. - str.   10:00 Composer.
—— SYMPHONY FOR CHAMBER ORCH., OP. 9 (1952) (IN 4
MOVTS)
 1,1,1,1 - 2,1,1,0 - timp. - str.   16:00 Composer.
—— SYMPHONY NO. 1, OP. 17 (1958)
 1. Adagio; 2. Allegro scherzando; 3. Moderato; 4. Adagio
 3(3rd alt. with picc.),*3,*3,*3 - 4,3,3,1 - timp.,perc.(3),cel.,xyl. -
 hp. - pf. - str.   24:00 Composer.
—— TRICARNIA, OP. 40
 3(3rd alt. with picc.),3(3rd alt. with Eng. hn.),3,*3 - 4,4,3,1 -
 perc.(5) - hp. - str.   13:00 Fleisher.

CAMUSSI, E.
—— PICCOLA SUITE (IN 4 MOVTS.)
 3,2,2,2 - 2,2,3,1 - timp.,perc.,bells,cel.,xyl. - hp. - str. Bo. Hawkes.

CANINO, Bruno
—— CONCERTO DA CAMERA NO. 2 (FOR 2 PIANOS AND
CHAMBER ORCH.)
 0,3,0,0 - 3,3,0,0 - perc.(2),vibra. - hp. - 2 pf. - 4 vla.,2 d.-b.
        13:30 Leeds.
—— CONCERTO DA CAMERA NO. 3 (FOR OBOE, VIOLIN AND
ORCH.)
        Leeds.

CANNABICH, Johann Christian - BODART, Eugen
—— CONCERTO ALLA PASTORALE, IN C MAJOR
 1,1,0,1 - 1,0,0,0 - str.   7:00 Mannheimer.
—— ENTR'ACTES, NOS. 1 - 13
 2,2,0,1 - 2,0,0,0 - str.   14:00 Mannheimer.
—— PASTORALE NO. 1 IN D MAJOR
 2,2,0,2 - 2,0,0,0 - str.   8:00 Mannheimer.
—— PASTORALE NO. 2 IN D MAJOR
 2,2,0,2 - 2,0,0,0 - org. - str.   6:00 Mannheimer.
—— SINFONIE PASTORALE, IN F MAJOR
 2,2,0,2 - 2,0,0,0 - str.   7:00 Mannheimer.
—— SYMPHONY IN C MAJOR
 0,2,0,0 - 2,0,0,0 - str.   10:00 Mannheimer.

CANNABICH, Johann Christian - HOFMANN, Wolfgang
—— SUITE FROM THE BALLET "LES FÊTES DU SÉRAIL"
 2,2,2,2 - 3,2,0,0 - timp.,perc. - str.   31:00 Mannheimer.
—— SYMPHONIA CONCERTANTE IN F MAJOR (FOR VIOLIN
AND ORCH.)
 0,2,0,2 - 2,0,0,0 - str.   19:00 Mannheimer.

CANNABICH, Johann Christian - VOGT, Carl August
—— SYMPHONY IN A MAJOR
 0,2,0,1 - 2,0,0,0 - str.   15:00 Mannheimer.

CANNING, Thomas
—— FANTASY ON A HYMN BY JUSTIN MORGAN (FOR 2
STRING QUARTETS AND STRING ORCH.)
 str.   9:40 C. Fischer.

CANNON, Philip
—— CONCERTINO FOR PIANO AND STRINGS
 pf. - str.   Novello.
—— ORAISON FUNÈBRE DE L'ÂME HUMAINE
 str.   20:00 Presser.

CANTELOUBE, Marie-Joseph
—— CHANTS D'AUVERGNE (FOR VOICE AND ORCH.)
 *3,2(2nd alt. with Eng. hn.),2,2 - 2,1,0,0 - timp.,perc. - pf. - str.
        Mercury.
—— LAURIERS (THREE PIECES FOR ORCH.) (1931)
 3,3,3,3 - 4,2,3,1 - timp.,perc. - pf. - str.   6:00 Presser.
—— POÈME (FOR VIOLIN AND ORCH.)
 2,2,2,2 - 2,2,2,1 - timp.,perc. - str.   15:00 EV.

CANTELOUBE, Marie-Joseph - KINGSLEY, G.
—— CINQ CHANTS DES PAYS BASQUES
 3,2,2,2 - 2,2,0,0 - timp., perc. - hp. - pf. - str.   15:00 Presser.
—— CINQ CHANTS DU LANGUEDOC
 3,2,2,2 - 2,2,0,0 - timp., perc. (3), cel. - hp. - pf. - str.
        16:00 Presser.

CANTELOUBE, J.
—— TRIPTYQUE (FOR VOICE AND ORCH.)
        Salabert.

CANTU, M.
—— IMPRESSIONI DOLOMITICHE
 3,3,3,2 - 4,3,3,1 - timp.,perc.,cel. - 1-2 hp. - pf. - str.
        16:00 Bo. Hawkes.
—— POEMA LIGURE (IN 3 MOVTS.)
 3,3,3,2 - 4,3,3,1 - timp.,perc.,bells,cel. - 1-2 hp. - pf. - str.
        15:00 Bo. Hawkes.

CAPANNA, Robert
—— CONCERTO FOR CHAMBER ORCH. (1974) (IN 1 MOVT.)
 1(alt. with alto fl.),1(alt. with Eng. hn.),1,1 - 1,1,1,0 -
 perc.(2),bells,glock.,mar.,vibra.,xyl. - hp. - pf. - str.(min.:2,1,1,1)
        13:00 Composer.
—— NAISSANCE (FOR 18 WINDS) (1975) (IN 1 MOVT.)
 *2,1 alto fl.,*2,1 E♭cl.,*2,*2 - 3,2,2,1   13:00 Composer.
—— TRAVELER (FOR BARITONE VOICE AND ORCH.) (1975)
(Text: Composer)
 3(1 alt. with picc.,1 alt. with alto fl.),0,2(1 alt. with b.-cl.),0 -
 0,0,2,0 - perc.(3),bells,glock.,mar.,vibra.,xyl. - 1 vla.,1 c.,1 d.-b.
        15:30 Composer.

CAPDEVIELLE, Pierre
—— LES AMANTS CAPTIFS (OPERA IN 2 ACTS WITH AN
EPILOGUE) % (Text: Paul Guth)
 3,3,4,3 - 4,3,3,1 - timp.,perc.,bells,cel.,glock.,vibra.,xyl. - hpsc.
        120:00 Eds. Fran.
 on stage: 3 tpt. - perc.(3) - 4 ondes Martenot - 4 hp.
—— CONCERTO ("DEL DISPETTO") FOR PIANO AND ORCH.
 2,2,2,2 - 2,2,2,0 - timp.,perc. - pf. - str.   23:00 Baron.
—— ÉPAVES RETROUVÉES
 3,2,2,0 - 4,3,3,1 - timp., perc.(9), cel. - 2 hp. - pf. - str.
        34:15 Presser.
—— INCANTATION POUR LA MORT D'UN JEUNE SPARTIATE
(1931)
 3,2,2,2 - 4,3,3,1 - timp., perc. (5), cel. - 4 hp. - pf. - str.
        21:00 Presser.
—— MOLIERA
 2,1,2,1 - 2,1,1,0 - timp., cel. - hp. - pf. - str.   13:25 Presser.
—— SYMPHONIE DA CAMERA NO. 3
 1,1,1,1 - 2,1,0,0 - hp. - str.   20:00 Presser.

CAPLET, André
—— ÉPIPHANIE (FRESCO FOR CELLO AND ORCH.) (IN 3
MOVTS.)
2(2nd alt. with picc),2,2,2 - 4,2,0,0 - timp.,perc.,cel. - hp. - str.
20:00 EV.
—— LE MIROIR DE JESUS (FOR SOPRANO, MEZZO-SOPRANO,
CONTRALTO, WOMEN'S CHORUS AND STRINGS)
2 hp. - str.   30:00 EV.

CAPUZZI, Antonio - SLATFORD, Rodney
—— CONCERTO IN F, FOR DOUBLE BASS AND ORCH.
0,2,0,0 - 2,0,0,0 - str.   Galaxy.

CARAZO, Castro
—— OVERTURE TO AN IMAGINARY PLAY
8:00 Composer.

CAREY, David
—— SUITE FOR XYLOPHONE AND ORCHESTRA
2,2,2,2 - 2,2,0,1 (ad lib.) - perc., xyl. - str.   8:00 Galaxy.

CARIES, Marc
—— METAPHONIES
2,2,1,1 - 3,3,2,1 - timp., perc.(5) - pf. - str.   14:00 Presser.
—— TROIS CHANTS INCANTATOIRES
alto sax. - str.   14:30 Presser.

CARL, Robert
—— REQUIEM FÜR JOHN F. KENNEDY (FOR SOLO VOICES,
CHORUS AND ORCH.) (Text: Trad. Latin)
55:00 Mvl.R.Carl.

CARLES, Marc
—— CONCERTO FOR VIOLA AND ORCH.
3,3,3,3 - 3,3,2,1 - timp.,cel.,glock.,vibra.,xyl. - ondes Martenot -
str.   20:00 EV.

CARLID, Gote
—— MASS FOR STRING ORCH.
str.   14:00 S.T.I.M.

CARLSEN, Carsten
—— NY PURPURNESEMARSJ
2,2,2,2 - 4,3,3,1 - timp.,perc. - str.   10:00 T.O.N.O.
—— SINFONIETTA
3,3,3,3 - 4,2,3,1 - timp.,perc. - hp. - str.   15:00 T.O.N.O.
—— SUITE NO. 1 (IN 4 MOVEMENTS)
3,2,2,2 - 4,2,3,1 - timp.,perc. - str.   27:00 T.O.N.O.
—— SUITE NO. 2 (PARIS SUITE) (IN 4 MOVTS.)
3,3,3,3 - 4,3,3,1 - timp.,perc. - str.   15:00 T.O.N.O.
—— SUITES FROM THE FILM "TWO LIVING AND ONE DEAD"
(TO LEVENDE OG EN DOD)
2,2,3,3 - 4,3,3,1 - timp.,perc. - pf. - str.   T.O.N.O.
—— SYMPHONY NO. 1 IN B MINOR
3,3,3,3 - 4,2,3,1 - timp.,perc. - str.   45:00 T.O.N.O.
—— SYMPHONY NO. 2 IN C MINOR
3,3,3,3 - 4,2,3,1 - timp.,perc. - hp. - str.   30:00 T.O.N.O.

CARLSON, Bengt
—— AFTER THE STORM (FOR SATB CHORUS AND STRINGS)
(1951)
str.   12:00 FinnMICtr.
—— JUBILEE CANTATA (FOR TENOR, SATB CHORUS AND
ORCH.) (1935)
0,0,0,0 - 0,2,1,0 - org. - str.   22:00 FinnMICtr.
—— MUSIC TO KNUTTILGMAN'S PLAY (THE TREASURE AT
KLINTö" (FOR VOICE AND ORCH.) (1923)
1,0,1,0 - 0,0,0,0 - hp. - str.   31:00 FinnMICtr.
—— MUSIC TO PARUSATER'S PLAY "KING IVAR'S DAUGHTER"
(FOR MALE CHORUS AND ORCH.) (1915)
2,2,2,2 - 2,1,0,0 - timp. - hp. - str.   58:00 FinnMICtr.
—— SUITE (FOR STRINGS) (1925)
str.   12:00 FinnMICtr.
—— SYMPHONIC SUITE (1950) (IN 3 MOVTS.)
2,2,3,2 - 4,3,3,1 - timp., perc. - hp. - str.   35:00 FinnMICtr.
—— THE TEMPLE (CANTATA) (FOR BARITONE, SATB CHORUS
AND ORCH.) (1927)
3,2,2,2 - 4,3,3,1 - timp., perc., bells - 2 hp. - pf. - str.
30:00 FinnMICtr.

CARLSTEDT, Jan
—— SONATA PER ARCHI, OP. 7, NO. 2 (1956)
str.   14:00 S.T.I.M.

—— SYMPHONY NO. 1 IN E MINOR, OP. 1
3,3,3,3 - 4,3,3,1 - timp.,perc. (2) - str.   29:00 S.T.I.M.
—— SYMPHONY NO. 2, OP. 25 (1968)
3,2,3,3 - 5,3,3,1 - timp.,perc.(3) - str.   34:00 S.T.I.M.
—— SYMPHONY OP. 1 (REV. 1960)
3,3,3,3 - 4,3,3,1 - timp.,perc.(3) - str.   35:00 S.T.I.M.

CARMICHAEL, John Russell
—— SUITE FROM "PUPPET SHOW"
2,1,2,1 - 4,2,2,0 - timp.,perc. - str.   9:00 Galaxy.

CARPENTER, John Alden
—— ADVENTURES IN A PERAMBULATOR (IN 6 MOVTS.)
*3,*3,*3,*3 - 4,3,3,1 - timp.,perc. (3) - hp. - pf. - str.
24:00 G. Schirmer.
—— THE BIRTHDAY OF THE INFANTA (BALLET SUITE)
*3,*3,*3,*3 - 4,3,3,1 - timp.,perc. (3) - hp. - pf. - str.
30:00 G. Schirmer.
—— CARMEL CONCERTO
3,3,3,3 - 4,3,3,1 - timp.,perc. - hp. - pf. - str.   17:00 G. Schirmer.
—— CONCERTINO FOR PIANO AND ORCH. (REVISED 1947)
1. Animato; 2. Lento; 3. Allegro
*3,*3,*3,*3 - 4,3,3,1 - timp.,perc. (3) - hp. - pf. - str.
26:00 G. Schirmer.
—— CONCERTO FOR VIOLIN AND ORCH.
*3,*3,2,2 - 4,3,3,1 - timp.,perc. - hp. - pf. - str.
23:00 G. Schirmer.
—— DANCE SUITE (IN 3 MOVTS.)
*3,*3,*3,2 - 4,3,3,1 - timp.,perc.,glock.,xyl. - hp. - pf. - str.
15:00 G. Schirmer.
—— GITANJALI (SONG CYCLE) (FOR MEZZO-SOPRANO AND
ORCH.)
*3,*3,2,2 - 4,2,3,1 - timp.,perc. (3) - hp. - pf. - str.
24:00 G. Schirmer.
—— KRAZY KAT (A JAZZ PANTOMINE) (REVISED 1948) %
2,1,2,sax.,1 - 2,2,1,0 - timp.,perc.,glock.,xyl. - pf. - str. G. Schirmer.
or:
1,1,2,1 - 2,2,1,0, - timp.,perc.,glock. - pf. - str.
—— PATTERNS (CONCERT PIECE FOR PIANO AND ORCH.)
*3,*3,2,2 - 4,3,3,1 - timp.,perc. (2) - hp. - pf. - str.
18:00 G. Schirmer.
—— SEA DRIFT (SYMPHONIC POEM)
*3,*3,2,*3 - 4,3,3,1 - timp.,perc. (3),vibra. - hp. - pf. - str.
15:00 G. Schirmer.
—— THE SEVEN AGES (SUITE)
*3,*3,*3,*3 - 4,3,3,1 - timp.,perc. (3),cel.,glock.,xyl. - hp. - pf. - str.
18:45 G. Schirmer.
—— SKYSCRAPERS (BALLET OF AMERICAN LIFE WITH
SOPRANO AND TENOR SOLOS) (CONCERT VERSION)
*3,*3,*3,*3 - 4,3,3,1 - timp.,perc. (3) - hp. - pf. - str.
15:00 G. Schirmer.
—— SONG OF FAITH (FOR CHORUS AND ORCH.)
*3,*3,2,2 - 4,3,3,1 - timp.,perc. (2) - hp. - org. - pf. - str.
12:00 G. Schirmer.
—— SONG OF FREEDOM (FOR CHORUS AND ORCH.)
*3,2,*3,*3 - 4,3,3,1 - timp.,perc. - hp. - org. - pf. - str.
5:00 G. Schirmer.
—— SYMPHONY NO. 1 (IN 1 MOVT.)
*3,*3,2,*3 - 4,3,3,1 - timp.,perc. (3) - hp. - pf. - str.
18:00 G. Schirmer.
—— SYMPHONY NO. 2 (IN 3 MOVEMENTS)
*3,*3,*3,*3 - 4,3,3,1 - timp.,perc. (3) - hp. - pf. - str.
21:00 G. Schirmer.
—— WAR LULLABY
3,3,2,2 - 4,1,2,0 - timp.,perc.,cel.,glock - hp. - pf. - str.
4:00 G. Schirmer.
—— WATER COLORS (FOUR CHINESE TONE POEMS) (FOR
MEZZO-SOPRANO AND SMALL ORCH.)
*2,1,1,1 - 2,2,0,0 - perc.,cel.,glock. - pf. - str.   G. Schirmer.

CARR, Benjamin - FRANCESCHINI, Romulus
—— FEDERAL OVERTURE (1794)
2(2nd alt. with picc.),2,2,2 - 2,2,2,0 - timp.,perc. - str.
9:00 Fleisher.
—— MELANGE (1815) (IN 11 MOVTS.)
1,1,2,1 - 2,2,0,0 - timp.,perc. - str.   9:00 Fleisher.

CARR, Edwin James Nairn
—— AUBADE FOR CLARINET AND ORCH. (1970)
2,2,3,2 - 4,0,0,0 - hp. - str.   9:00 Belw-Mills.
—— A BLADE CANTATA (FOR 16 CHILDREN'S VOICES AND
SMALL ORCH.)
12:00 A.P.R.A.

—— CONCERTO FOR PIANO AND ORCH. (1961)
3,2,2,2 - 4,3,3,1 - hp. - pf. - str.   20:00 A.P.R.A.
—— ELECTRA (BALLET MUSIC)
17:00 A.P.R.A.
—— FIVE PIECES FOR ORCH. (1966)
3,3,3,*3 - 4,3,3,1 - perc. - hp. - str.   11:00 Belw-Mills.
—— MARDI GRAS (AN OVERTURE) (1950)
3,2,2,2 - 4,3,3,1 - perc. - pf. - str.   4:30 A.P.R.A.
—— NIGHT MUSIC (SCHERZO)
9:00 A.P.R.A.
—— SIX STUDIES FOR STRING ORCH. (1971)
str.   15:00 A.P.R.A.
—— SYMPHONY
str.   20:00 A.P.R.A.
—— THE TWELVE SIGNS (AN ASTROLOGICAL
ENTERTAINMENT) (1974)
3(1 alt. with alto fl.),3,3(1 alt. with E♭ cl. and 1 alt. with b.-cl.),3 - 4,4(incl. tpt. in D),3,1 - perc. - typewriter - hp. - pf
30:00 A.P.R.A.

CARR-BOYD, Anne Kirsten
—— SYMPHONY, OP. 2 (1964) (IN 3 MOVTS.)
1,1,1,1 - 1,1,0,0 - timp. - str.   15:00 AstrlMuCtr.

CARRILLO, Julián
—— CONCERTINO FOR CELLO AND ORCH. (Solo part in quarter-tones and eight-tones)
3,3,2,2 - 4,2,3,1 - timp., perc.(3) - hp. - str.   29:30 Presser.
—— CONCERTO FOR VIOLIN AND ORCH. (Solo part in quarter-tones)
2,2,2,2 - 4,2,3,1 - timp.,perc. - str.   25:00 Presser.
—— HORIZONTES (SYMPHONIC POEM) (FOR VIOLIN, CELLO, HARP AND ORCH.)
3,3,2,2 - 4,2,3,1 - perc. - hp. - str.   17:00 Presser.
—— SYMPHONY NO. 1 IN D MAJOR
3,2,2,2 - 4,2,3,1 - timp., perc. - hp. - str.   35:00 Presser.
—— SYMPHONY NO. 2 IN C MAJOR
3,2,2,2 - 4,2,3,1 - timp., perc. - hp. - str.   38:00 Presser.
—— SYMPHONY NO. 3 ("ATONAL")
3,3,3,3 - 4,2,3,1 - timp., perc. - hp. - str.   30:00 Presser.

CARSE, Adam
—— GEORGIAN TUNES (SIX POPULAR ENGLISH TUNES OF THE 18TH CENTURY)
Augener.
—— HOLIDAY (OVERTURE)
2,2,2,2 - 4,2,3,1 - timp.,perc. - str.   4:45 Galaxy.
—— MINATURE SUITE (BOULOGNE)
Galaxy.
—— MINATURE SYMPHONY IN D
str.   Augener.
—— NORWEGIAN FANTASIA (FOR VIOLIN AND ORCH.)
10:00 Galaxy.
—— SUITE IN C
str.   Augener.
—— SYMPHONY NO. 3 IN F
2,2,2,2 - 4,3,3,1 - timp.,perc. - hp. - str.   24:00 Galaxy.
—— TWO SKETCHES FOR STRING ORCH.
str.   Augener.
—— VARIATIONS ON A THEME
str.   15:00 Galaxy.
—— VARIATIONS ON "BARBARA ALLEN"
str.   Novello.
—— THE WINTON SUITE
str.   Augener.

CARSTE, Hans
—— FESTIVAL OVERTURE AND FINALE (WITH OPTIONAL CHORUS)
3,1,3,0 - 4,3,3,0 - timp.,perc. - guit. - hp. - org.(or chorus) - str.
12:00 F. Colombo.

CARTAN, J.
—— PATER (CANTATA) (FOR SOPRANO, MEZZO-SOPRANO, TENOR, MIXED CHOIR AND ORCH.)
2,2,2,2 - 2,2,3,0 - timp.,perc. - str.   55:00 Salabert.

CARTER, John
—— CANTATA (FOR VOICE AND ORCH.)
2,2,2,2 - 4,3,3,0 - timp.,perc. - hp. - str.   13:30 Southern.

CARWITHEN, Doreen
—— ODTAA, AN OVERTURE
2,2,2,2 - 4,3,3,1 - timp.,perc.(3),glock.,xyl. - hp. - str.   8:00 Oxford.

CASADESUS, Francis
—— LONDON SKETCHES (PETITE SUITE HUMORISTIQUE)
2,2,2,2 - 2,0,0,0   Salabert.
—— SYMPHONIE SCANDINAVE
3,3,3,3 - 4,4,3,1 - timp.,perc. - 2 hp. - str.   27:30 Salabert.

CASADESUS, Marius
—— ET NUNC ET SEMPER (POÈME SYMPHONIQUE) (FOR SOPRANO, CELLO, CHORUS AND ORCH.)
4,3,3,bar. sax.,4 - 4,4,3,1 - timp.,perc. - hp. - str.   30:00 Salabert.

CASADESUS, Robert
—— BALLET SUITE NO. 3 (BASED ON THE NAME OF RAMEAU)
2,2,0,2 - 2,2,0,0 - str.   22:00 C. Fischer.
—— CAPRICCIO, OP. 49 (FOR PIANO AND STRING ORCH.)
pf. - str.   17:00 S.A.C.E.M.
—— CONCERTO FOR CELLO AND ORCH., OP. 43
15:00 S.A.C.E.M.
—— CONCERTO FOR FLUTE AND ORCH., OP. 35
Andraud.
—— CONCERTO FOR PIANO AND ORCH., OP. 37
EV.
—— CONCERTO FOR THREE PIANOS AND STRINGS, OP. 65
3 pf. - str.   14:00 EV.
—— CONCERTO FOR TWO PIANOS AND ORCH.
25:00 S.A.C.E.M.
—— SUITE NO. 2 IN B♭, OP. 26
20:00 S.A.C.E.M.

CASALS, Pablo
—— EL PESEBRE ("THE MANGER") (ORATORIO) (Text: John Alavedra)
3,3,3,3 - 4,3,3,1 - timp.,perc.,cel. - hp. - str.   130:00 Bo. Hawkes.
—— SARDANA (FOR CELLO ORCHESTRA)
cellos   6:00 Tetra.
—— SONG OF THE BIRDS (FOR CELLO AND STRINGS)
str.   3:10 Tetra.

CASANOVA, André
—— ANAMORPHOSES
3,3,3,1 sopr.sax.,3 - 4,3,3,1 - timp.,perc.,(5),cel.,glock.,keyed glock.*,vibra.,xyl. - hp. - str.   24:00 EV.
—— CAPRICCIO (FOR OBOE AND CHAMBER ORCH.)
0,1,0,0 - 2,1,1,0 - str.   24:00 EV.
—— CONCERTINO FOR PIANO AND CHAMBER ORCH.
2,0,2,2 - 1,1,0,0 - timp. - pf. - str.   12:00 EV.
—— CONCERTO FOR VIOLIN AND ORCH.
3,3,3,3 - 4,2,1,1 - timp.,perc.,cel.,xyl. - hp. - str.   27:00 EV.
—— CONCERTO FOR VIOLIN AND ORCH.
3,3,3,3 - 4,3,3,0 - timp., perc. - hp. - str.   27:00 Presser.
—— EPISODES (FOR VIOLIN AND STRINGS)
str.   16:00 Presser.
—— FANTASIA FOR HORN, MARIMBA, 2 TOM-TOMS AND STRINGS
hn. - perc.,mar. - str.   14:00 Boelke-Bo.
—— FIVE IMPROMPTUS FOR ORCH.
3,3,3,3 - 4,3,3,0 - timp.,perc. - hp. - str.   12:00 EV.
—— LE LIVRE DE LA FOI JURÉE (FOR NARRATOR, 3 VOICES AND ORCH.)
3,3,3,2 - 2,2,1,0 - timp., perc.(4), cel. - clavitmbre - str.
75:00 Presser.

CASCARINO, Romeo
—— THE ACADIAN LAND
2,2,2,2 - 2,0,0,0 - perc.(2),cel. - hp. - str.   15:00 Composer.
—— BLADES OF GRASS
Eng.hn. - hp. - str.   7:00 Composer.
—— DIVERTIMENTO (FOR WOODWINDS, HORNS, STRINGS, HARP, CELESTE AND PERCUSSION)
Composer.
—— EPITAPH FOR A SOLDIER
2,*3,2,2 - 4,2,3,1 - timp.,perc. - hp. - str.   15:00 Fleisher.
—— PORTRAIT OF GALATEA
*3,*3,2,2 - 2,2,0,0 - perc.(3),cel. - hp. - str.   10:00 Composer.
—— PRISON INTERLUDE (FROM THE OPERA "WILLIAM PENN")
3,*3,*3,*3 - 4,3,3,1 - timp.,perc. - hp. - str.   4:00 Fleisher.
—— PROSPICE (After the poem by Robert Browning)
*3,2,2,2 - 4,2,2,1 - perc.(5),glock. - hp. - str.   20:00 Composer.

—— PYGMALION (BALLET) %
　　3,*3,2,2 - 4,3,3,1 - perc. - hp. - str.　　　　20:00 Fleisher.
—— SEA INTERLUDE (FROM THE OPERA "WILLIAM PENN")
　　3,*3,*3,*3 - 4,3,3,1 - timp.,perc. - hp. - str.　　5:00 Fleisher.
—— SPRING PASTORALE
　　2,2,2,2 - 2,2,2,0 - timp.,perc. - hp. - str.　　10:00 Fleisher.

CASELLA, Alfredo
—— PAGINE DI GUERRA
　　*4,*3,*4,*4 - 4,3,3,1 - timp.,perc. - hp. - str.　6:00 G. Schirmer.
—— SYMPHONY IN B MINOR, OP. 5
　　3,3,3,4 - 4,3,3,1 - timp.,perc. - str.　　　25:00 Salabert.
—— TRE CANTI SACRI, OP. 67 (3 SACRED SONGS) (FOR
BARITONE AND ORCH.)
　　2,2,2,2 - 3,0,0,1 - timp. - str.(no vlns.)　　10:00 Leeds.
—— TROIS POÈMES (FOR VOICE AND ORCH.)
　　　　　　　　　　　　　　　　　　　　Salabert.

CASHMORE, Donald
—— JERUSALEM (CANTATA) (FOR SOPRANO, TENOR, SATB
CHORUS, ORGAN AND ORCH.)
　　　　　　　　　　　　　　　　　　　　Galaxy.

CASSADO, Joaquin
—— FLORES DE TRIANA (CAPRICHO ESPAÑOL) (FOR VIOLIN
AND ORCH.) (1910)
　　2,2,2,2 - 4,2,3,1 - perc. - str.　　　　　5:00 Salabert.

CASSUTO, Alvaro Leon
—— CIRCLE FOR ORCHESTRA (For Any Number of Instruments)
　　　　　　　　　　　　　　　　　　G. Schirmer.
—— CRO (MO-NO) FONIA (1967)
　　str.　　　　　　　　　　　　　　　　G. Schirmer.
—— EVOCATIONS (1972)
　　2,2,2,2 - 2,2,0,0 - perc.(2) - str.　　　16:00 Seesaw.
—— IN MEMORIAM: PEDRO DE FREITAS BRANCO (1963)
　　　　　　　　　　　　　　　　　　G. Schirmer.
—— SONG OF LONELINESS
　　1,1,1,1 - 1,1,0,0 - perc. - pf. - str.　　13:00 G. Schirmer.
—— TO LOVE AND PEACE
　　3,3,4,3 - 4,4,3,2 - perc.,cel. - pf. - str.　18:00 G. Schirmer.

CASTALDI, Paolo
—— DIECI DISCANTI (FOR CANTUS FIRMUS AND 10 INSTS.)
(1969)
　　0,1,0,1, - 0,1,1,0 - perc.(1) - hpsc. - org. - vla., c., d.-b.
　　　　　　　　　　　　　　　　　33:00 MCA Music.
—— DOKTOR FAUST (1969)
　　0,0,0,0 - 2,0,1,0 - perc.(1) - pf. - str.　13:00 MCA Music.

CASTALDO, Joseph F.
—— FLIGHT (FOR NARRATOR, SOPRANO, SATB CHORUS,
WINDS AND PERC.)
　　4,4,4,4 - 4,4,3,1 - timp.,perc.,cel. - hp. - pf.　30:00 Southern.
—— LACRIMOSA
　　str.　　　　　　　　　　　　　　23:00 Southern.
—— THEORIA (FOR 15 WINDS, PIANO AND PERCUSSION)
(1971)
　　　　　　　　　　　　　　　　15:00 Composer.

CASTELLUCCI, Louis
—— CAPRICCIO (FOR TUBA AND ORCH.)
　　　　　　　　　　　　　　　　5:00 Mills.

CASTELNUOVO-TEDESCO, Mario
—— AN AMERICAN RHAPSODY (BASED ON TWO AMERICAN
FOLK TUNES)
　　*3,2,3,2 - 4,3,3,1 - timp.,perc. (3),xyl. - hp. - pf. - str. 5:00 MGM.
—— THE BIRTHDAY OF THE INFANTA (BALLET SUITE)
　　3(3rd alt. with picc.),*3,3(3rd alt. with b.-cl.),3(3rd alt. with c.-bn.)
　　- 4,3,3,0 - timp.,perc. (3),glock.,xyl. - hp. - pf. - str.　25:00 Feist.
—— CONCERTINO FOR HARP AND CHAMBER ORCH.
　　1,1,1,1 - 0,0,0,0 - hp. - str.　　　　18:00 General.
—— CONCERTINO FOR HARP AND CHAMBER ORCH. (IN 3
MOVTS.)
　　2 cl.,b.-cl. - hp. - str.　　　　　　12:00 General.
　　or:
　　fl.,ob.,cl.,bn. - hp. - str.
—— CONCERTO DA CAMERA (FOR OBOE AND STRINGS)
　　0b. - str.　　　　　　　　　　15:00 Mills.
—— CONCERTO FOR TWO GUITARS AND ORCH., OP. 201
　　2,1,2,1 - 2,1,0,0 - timp.,perc.(4) - 2 guit. - str.　26:00 Presser.

—— CONCERTO NO. 1 IN D FOR GUITAR AND CHAMBER
ORCH.
　　1,1,1,1 - hn. - timp. - guit. - str.　　　21:00 AMP.
—— CONCERTO NO. 2 IN C, FOR GUITAR AND ORCH., OP. 160
(1953)
　　2,1,2,1 - 2,1,0,0 - timp.,perc.(3),bells - guit. - str.
　　　　　　　　　　　　　　　　27:00 Belw-Mills.
—— CONCERTO NO. 2 IN F, FOR PIANO AND ORCH.
　　2,2,*4,2 - 4,3,3,0 - timp.,perc. - pf. - str.　28:00 Forlivesi.
—— FIVE HUMORESQUES ON FOSTER'S THEMES
　　*3,2,3,2 - 4,3,3,1 - timp.,perc. (4),bells,xyl. - hp. - pf.(or cel.) - str.
　　　　　　　　　　　　　　　　13:00 MGM.
—— FOUR DANCES FOR SHAKESPEARE'S "LOVE'S LABORS
LOST"
　　2,1,3,1 - 3,3,3,0 - timp.,perc. (3),glock.,xyl. - hp. - pf. - str.　Mills.
—— THE GIANTS OF THE MOUNTAIN (TWO SYMPHONIC
EPISODES) (FOR CHORUS AND ORCH.)
　　*4,*3,E♭cl.,*4,*3 - 4,4,3,1 - timp.,perc. - 2 hp. - pf. - str.
　　　　　　　　　　　　　　　　20:00 Composer.
—— INDIAN SONGS AND DANCES (BASED ON AMERICAN
INDIAN THEMES) (IN 5 MOVTS.)
　　3(3rd alt. with picc.),*3,3(3rd alt. with b.-cl.),3(3rd alt. with c.-bn.)
　　- 4,3 - 4,3,1 - timp.,perc. (4), xyl.,vibra. - hp. - pf. - str.
　　　　　　　　　　　　　　　　19:00 MGM.
—— LAUDA DI NOSTRA DONNA (IN PRAISE OF OUR LADY),
FROM "SAVONAROLA" (FOR SOPRANO AND ORCH.)
　　3,*3,3,3 - 4,0,3,1 - timp.,perc. - 2 hp. - pf. - str.　3:15 Galaxy.
—— THE LITTLE SIREN AND THE BLUE FISH
　　3(3rd alt. with picc.),*3,3(3rd alt. with b.-cl.),3 - 4,3,3,1 -
　　timp.,perc. - hp. - pf. - str.　　　　10:00 Composer.
—— NAOMI AND RUTH (CANTATA) (FOR SOPRANO, WOMEN'S
CHORUS AND ORCH.)
　　2,2,2,2 - 3,0,0,0 - timp. - hp. - str.　20:00 Belw-Mills.
—— NOAH'S ARK (FOR NARRATOR, CHORUS AND ORCH.)
(FIFTH MOVEMENT FROM GENESIS SUITE)
　　3(3rd alt. with picc.),2(2nd alt. with Eng. hn.),3(3rd alt. with
　　b.-cl.),2(2nd alt. with c.-bn.) - 4,3,3,1 - timp.,perc.,cel.,xyl. - hp. -
　　pf. - str.　　　　　　　　　　10:00 Shilkret.
—— OVERTURE TO A FAIRY TALE (A MIDSUMMER NIGHT'S
DREAM)
　　3(3rd alt. with picc.),*3,*4,2 - 4,3,3,0 - timp.,perc. (3), cel. - 2 hp.
　　- str.　　　　　　　　　　　　8:00 Ricordi.
—— OVERTURE TO "ANTHONY AND CLEOPATRA"
　　3(3rd alt. with picc.),*3,*4,3(3rd alt. with c.-bn.) - 4,3,3,1 -
　　timp.,perc. (3),cel.,xyl. - 2 hp. - str.　15:00 Composer.
—— OVERTURE TO "AS YOU LIKE IT"
　　　　　　　　　　　　　　　　Composer.
—— OVERTURE TO "CORIOLANUS"
　　3(3rd alt. with picc.),*3,3(3rd alt. with b.-cl.),3(3rd alt. with c.-bn.)
　　- 4,3,3,1 - timp.,perc. - pf. - str.　9:45 Composer.
—— OVERTURE TO "KING JOHN"
　　3(3rd alt. with picc.),*3,*4,3(3rd alt. with c.-bn.) - 4,3,3,1 -
　　timp.,perc.,glock. - hp. - pf. - str.　9:00 C. Fischer.
—— OVERTURE TO "MUCH ADO ABOUT NOTHING", OP. 164
　　2,2,2,2 - 4,2,3,1 - timp.,perc. (3) - hp. - pf. - str.　12:00 Ricordi.
—— THE PRINCESS AND THE PEA (MINIATURE OVERTURE,
ON A TALE BY HANS CHRISTIAN ANDERSEN)
　　2,2,3(3rd alt. with b.-cl.),2 - 3,3,3,0 - timp.,perc. (3),cel. (alt. with
　　glock. and xyl.) - hp. - str.　　　8:00 MGM.
—— THE QUEEN OF SHEBA (CANTATA) (FOR SOPRANO,
WOMEN'S VOICES, HARP AND ORCH.)
　　hp. - str.　　　　　　　　　　10:20 Mills.
—— SERENADE FOR GUITAR AND CHAMBER ORCH. (IN 4
MOVTS.)
　　*1,1,2,1 - 1,1,0,0 - timp.,perc. (2) - guit. - str.　20:00 AMP.
—— SIX SCOTTISH SONGS (FOR SOPRANO, TENOR, HARP AND
STRINGS)
　　hp. - str.　　　　　　　　　　30:00 Composer.
—— THREE SEPHARDIC SONGS (FOR MEDIUM VOICE AND
ORCH.) (Text: Composer)
　　1,1,1,1 - 1,0,0,0 - perc. - str.　9:00 IsMuPublns.

CASTERA, Rene de
—— JOUR DE FÊTE AU PAYS BASQUE
　　3,3,3,2 - 4,2,3,0 - timp.,perc. - hp. - str.　16:00 Salabert.

CASTÉRÈDE, Jacques
—— BASKET-BALL (BALLET) %
　　2,2,2,2 - 3,3,2,0 - timp.,perc. - hp. - pf. - str.　20:00 Salabert.
—— THE BOOK OF JOB (ORATORIO) (FOR NARRATOR,
SOLOISTS, MIXED CHORUS AND ORCH.)
　　3,3,3,3 - 4,4,3,1 - timp.,perc.(4) - pf. - str.　75:00 Salabert.

—— LA CHANSON DU MAL AIMÉ (CANTATA) (FOR NARRATOR, BARITONE, 4 WOMEN'S VOICES AND CHAMBER ORCH.)
    1,2,0,0 - 2,1,0,0 - perc.(2) - acc. - guit. - hp. - str.   28:00 Salabert.

—— CONCERTINO (FOR TRUMPET, PIANO, PERCUSSION AND STRING ORCH.)
    0,0,0,0 - 0,1,1,0 - perc. - pf. - str.   13:00 Baron.

—— CONCERTO FOR PIANO AND STRINGS
    pf. - str.   23:00 Salabert.

—— LE DESCENTE DE CROIX
    2,2,2,2 - 2,2,2,0 - timp., perc. - str.   7:00 Presser.

—— LE FIL D'ARIANE (SYMPHONIC POEM)
    2,2,2,2 - 3,2,3,0 - timp.,perc. - str.   18:00 Salabert.

—— FIVE SYMPHONIC DANCES
    3,3,2,2 - 4,3,3,1 - timp.,perc. - hp. - pf. - str.   28:00 Salabert.

—— LA MYTHOMANE (LA FEMME ET SA FABLE) (SUITE FOR ORCH.) (BALLET ET UN TABLEAU) %
    3,2,2,2 - 3,3,3,1 - timp.,perc. - str.   18:00 EV.

—— MUSIC FOR FLUTE, HARP AND STRINGS
    fl. - hp. - str.   22:00 Salabert.

—— MUSIQUE POUR UN CONTE D'EDGAR POE (FOR NARRATOR AND ORCH.)
    3,3(1 alt. with Eng.hn.),3,3 - 4,3,3,1 - timp.,perc.,cel.,vibra.,xyl. - hp. - pf. - str.   25:00 Salabert.

—— PRÉLUDE ET FUGUE POUR CORDES
    str.   12:00 Salabert.

—— SUITE IN THREE MOVEMENTS (IN MEMORY OF ARTHUR HONEGGER)
    0,1,2,2 - 4,3,2,1 - timp.,perc.(4) - str.   12:00 Salabert.

—— SYMPHONY FOR STRINGS
    str.   23:00 Salabert.

—— SYMPHONY NO. 2
    2(1 alt. with picc.),2(1 alt. with Eng.hn.),2,2 - 2,2,2,1 - timp.,perc.(3) - hp. - str.   30:00 Salabert.

—— TROIS FANFARES, POUR DES PROCLAMATIONS DE NAPOLÉON (WITH NARRATOR)
    0,0,0,0 - 4,3,3,1 - timp.,perc.   13:00 Baron.

CASTIGLIONI, Niccolò

—— APRÈSLUDE
    5,4,3,2 - 4,5,3,0 - timp.,perc.(7),bells,cel.,vibra.,xyl. - hp. - pf. - str.   13:00 Leeds.

—— CANTI (SONGS FOR ORCHESTRA)
    2,2,2,2 - 2,2,1,0 - timp.,perc.(3),vibra. - hp. - pf. - str.   8:00 Leeds.

—— DISEGNI (DESIGNS FOR ORCHESTRA)
    2,2,2,2 - 2,2,1,0 - timp.,perc.(2),bells,cel.,vibra.,xyl. - hp. - pf. - str.(no c. or d.-b.)   8:30 Leeds.

—— ELEGIA (ELEGY) (FOR SOPRANO AND 19 INSTS.) (Text: Novalis)
    1,1,1,1 - 1,1,1,0 - vibra. - hp. - pf. - str.(no d.-b.)   Leeds.

—— IMPROMPTUS
    2,2,2,2 - 2,2,1,0 - timp.,cel.,vibra. - hp. - pf. - str.   7:00 Leeds.

—— EINE KLEINE WEINACHTSMUSIK (A LITTLE CHRISTMAS MUSIC)
    2,1,2,1 - 1,2,1,0 - perc. - str.   10:00 Leeds.

—— MOVIMENTO CONTINUATO (FOR PIANO AND 11 INSTS.)
    1,1,1,0 - 0,1,0,0 - cel.,vibra. - hp. - pf. - str.   5:30 Leeds.

—— OVERTURE IN THREE MOVEMENTS
    3,2,2,2 - 2,2,0,0 - timp.,vibra. - pf. - str.   6:00 Leeds.

—— SEQUENZE
    4,3,3,3 - 4,3,3,0 - timp.,perc.,cel.,vibra. - hp. - pf. - str.   8:36 Leeds.

—— SYMPHONY NO. 1 (FOR SOPRANO AND ORCH.) (Text: F. Nietzsche)
    3,3,3,3 - 3,2,2,1 - timp.,xyl. - pf. - str.   20:00 Leeds.

—— SYMPHONY NO. 2
    3,3,3,3 - 4,3,2,1 - timp.,perc.,cel.,vibra.,xyl. - hp. - pf. - str.   20:00 Leeds.

—— SYNCHROMIE
    Leeds.

—— THROUGH THE LOOKING GLASS (ATTAVERSO LO SPECCHIO) (1-ACT RADIO OPERA, AFTER LEWIS CARROLL) (Text: Alberto Ca'Zorzi Noventa)
    4,4,4,4 - 4,4,3,0 - perc.(2),cel.,vibra.,xyl. - hpsc. - 2 hp. - 3 pf. - str.   Leeds.

CASTRO, José Maria

—— CONCERTO FOR PIANO AND ORCH.
    Fleisher.

—— CONCERTO GROSSO FOR SMALL ORCH.
    2,2,2,2 - 2,1,0,0 - str.   12:00 Southern.
    or:
    str.

—— FALARKA BALLET (FOR 16 INSTRUMENTS) %
    Southern.

—— GEORGIA (BALLET) %
    Fleisher.

—— OBERTURA PARA UNA OPERA COMICA
    2,2,2,2 - 3,2,0,0 - timp. - str.   6:00 Southern.
    or:
    str.

—— LA OTRA VOZ: SUITE NO. 1
    2,2,2,2 - 2,2,1,0 - timp.,perc. - pf. - str.   16:00 Bo. Hawkes.

—— LA OTRA VOZ: SUITE NO. 2
    2,2,2,2 - 2,2,1,0 - timp.,perc. - pf. - str.   18:00 Bo. Hawkes.

—— PRELUDE AND TOCCATA, FOR STRING QUARTET AND STRING ORCH.
    str.   Southern.

—— THREE PASTORALES FOR SMALL ORCH.
    2,2,2,2 - 2,2,1,0, - timp. - str.   12:00 Southern.
    or:
    str.

CASTRO, Juan José

—— A UNA MADRE (POEM) (1925)
    3(3rd alt. with picc.),3,3,3 - 4,3,3,1 - timp.,perc.,cel. - hp. - str.   Fleisher.

—— ALLEGRO, LENTO Y VIVACE (1930) (3 TROZOS SINFÓNICOS)
    Fleisher.

—— LA CHELLAH (SYMPHONIC POEM) (1927)
    Fleisher.

—— CONCERTO FOR PIANO AND ORCH.
    3,2,2,2 - 4,2,3,1 - timp.,perc. - pf. - str.   30:00 F. Colombo.

—— DANS LE JARDIN DES MORTS (IN THE GARDEN OF THE DEAD) (1924)
    Fleisher.

—— MÊKHAÑO (BALLET IN 4 ACTS) % (1935)
    3,3,3,3 - 4,3,3,1 - timp.,perc.,cel. - hp. - str.   Fleisher.

—— NANA (PART II FROM THE OPERA "BODAS DE SANGRE") %
    2,2,2,1 - 2,1,0,0 - hp. - str.   Fleisher.

—— PRELUDE Y TOCCATA
    S.A.D.A.I.C.

—— SINFONIA DE LOS CAMPOS
    3,3,3,3 - 4,3,3,1 - timp.,perc.cel. - str.   22:30 S.A.D.A.I.C.

—— SUITE BREVE (FOR SMALL ORCH.)
    2(2nd alt. with picc.),2(2nd alt. with Eng.hn.),2,2 - 2,2,0,0 - perc. - str.   Fleisher.

—— SUITE INFANTIL (CHILDREN'S SUITE) (IN 4 MOVTS.)
    3,2,2,2 - 4,3,3,1 - timp.,perc. - hp. - str.   Fleisher.

—— SUITE INTROSPECTIVA
    S.A.D.A.I.C.

—— LA ZAPATERA PRODIGIOSA: EXCERPTS (FOR VOICE AND ORCH.)
    3,3,2,2 - 4,2,3,1 - timp.,perc.,cel. - hp. - str.   20:00 F. Colombo.

CASTRO, Washington

—— FESTIVAL OVERTURE
    2,1,2,1 - 2,0,0,0 - timp.,trgl. - str.   5:00 Fleisher.

—— SINFONIA BREVE (FOR STRINGS)
    str.   19:00 Bo. Hawkes.

—— TRES PIEZAS (THREE PIECES)
    1,1,1,1 - 4,2,3,0 - timp.,perc. - str.   Bo. Hawkes.

CASTRUCCI, Pietro - KRAMER, A. Walter

—— SONATA (IN 6 MOVTS.)
    str.   15:00 Arranger.

CATOIRE, Georges

—— CONCERTO FOR PIANO AND ORCH., OP. 21
    3,2,2,2 - 0,2,2,3 - timp.,perc. - str.   30:00 Bo. Hawkes.

CATOIRE, Jean

—— SIX VARIATIONS (FOR STRING ORCH.)
    str.   S.A.C.E.M.

CATTINI, U.

—— CINQUE CARMI DI CATULLO (FOR VOICE AND ORCH.)
    2,2,2,2 - 2,2,0,0 - timp. - hp. - str.   11:00 Bo. Hawkes.

—— DIVERTIMENTO
    str.   10:00 Bo. Hawkes.

—— PARTITA
    pf. - str.   12:00 Bo. Hawkes.

CATURLA, Alejandro G.
—— BEMBE (MOUVEMENT AFRO-CUBAIN) (FOR CHAMBER ORCH.)
1,1,*2,1 - 2,1,1,0 - perc. - pf. 10:00 Salabert.
—— THREE CUBAN DANCES
3,3,3,2 - 4,3,3,1 - timp.,perc.,cel. - hp. - pf. - str. 15:00 Salabert.

CAVALLI, Francesco - LEPPARD, Raymond
—— MAGNIFICAT (FOR SSAATTBB CHORUS AND SMALL ORCH.)
2 cornetti(zinken),3 trb. - hpsc. - 1-2 org. - str.
20:00 G. Schirmer.
or:
0,2,2,0 - 0,0,3,0 - hpsc. - 1-2 org. - str.
—— MESSA CONCERTATA (MASS IN C MAJOR) (FOR 8 SOLO VOICES, DOUBLE CHORUS AND ORCH.)
2 Cornetti(Zincken) - 2 trombones - hpsc. - 1-2 org. - str.
50:00 G. Schirmer.

CAZDEN, Norman
—— ADVENTURE, OP. 85 (1963) (FOR 6 SOLO INSTRS. AND ORCH.)
2,0,2,0 - 0,1,1,0 - timp. - str. 7:25 MCA Music.
—— CHAMBER CONCERTO FOR CLARINET AND STRINGS, OP. 94 (1965)
1,1,2,1 - 2,1,0,0 - pf. - str.(0,1,1,0) 20:20 MCA Music.
—— CONCERTO FOR VIOLA AND ORCH., OP. 103 (1972)
2,2,2,2 - 2,2,3,0 - timp.,perc. - hp. - str.(20,9,6,3)
19:00 MCA Music.
—— CONCERTO FOR 10 INSTRUMENTS, OP. 10 (FEATURING PIANO AND VIOLA) (1937)
1,1,1,1 - 2,1,0,0 - pf. - vla.,c. 15:00 MCA Music.
—— PREAMBLE FOR ORCHESTRA, OP. 18 (1938)
*3,2,*3,*3 - 4,3,3,1 - timp.,perc.(3) - pf. - str. 7:45 MCA Music.
—— SIX DEFINITIONS FOR INSTRUMENTAL ENSEMBLE, OP. 25
Variable (minimum: str., no d.-b.) (maximum: 1,2 recorders,*2,3,*2 - 2,1,0,0 - str.) 8:30 Composer.
—— SYMPHONY, OP. 49 (1948)
*3,*3,*3,*3 - 4,3,3,1 - timp. - pf. - str. 30:50 MCA Music.
—— THE TEMPEST, OP. 83 (FOR SOLO VOICES, UNISON CHORUS AND ORCH.) (1964) (Text: Shakespeare)
1 sop. recorder,2 alto recorders,3,1*3,1 - 2,2,2,0 - timp.,perc.(4) - str. 17:15 MCA Music.
—— THREE BALLADS FOR SMALL ORCH., OP. 52 (1949) (ON TRADITIONAL MELODIES FROM THE CATSKILLS) (WITH SOLO VIOLIN, VIOLA AND CELLO)
1,1,2,1 - 2,2,2,0 - timp. - str. 11:45 MCA Music.
—— THREE DANCES FOR ORCHESTRA, OP. 28 (1940)
*3,2,*4,*3 - 4,4,3,1 - timp.,perc.(3) - pf. 10:00 MCA Music.

CECCONI, Monic
—— CORRESPONDANCES (SUITE IN 7 COLORS)
2,2,3,2 - 4,3,3,1 - perc.(6) - hpsc.(amplified) - pf. - str.
26:00 Presser.
—— MÉGARYTHMES
2,2,2,2 - 4,2,2,1 - timp., perc.(4) - pf. - str. 13:00 Presser.

CELIS, Frits
—— DRIE SYMFONISCH BEWEGINGEN, OP. 8 (1969) (IN 3 MOVTS.)
3,3,3,3 - 4,3,3,1 - timp.,perc. - str. 21:00 H. Elkan.
—— ELEGIE, OP. 7 (1966) (IN 2 MOVTS.)
3,3,3,3 - 4,3,3,1 - timp.,perc. - str. 10:00 H. Elkan.
—— MUZIEK VOOR STRIJKERS, OP. 1 (MUSIC FOR STRINGS) (1951) (IN 3 MOVTS.)
str. 12:00 H. Elkan.
—— VARIAZIONI, OP. 11 (FOR CHAMBER ORCH.) (1974)
2,2,2,2 - 2,2,2,0 - timp.,perc. - str. 12:00 H. Elkan.

CERF, Jacques
—— CONCERTO CAPRICIOSO (FOR GUITAR AND ORCH.)
1,1,1,1 - 0,1,1,0 - timp. - guit. - str. 17:00 Presser.
—— CONCERTO MINIATUR, OP. 45, NR. 3 (POUR CLAVECIN ET ORCHESTRE)
1,1,0,0 - 1,1,0,0 - hpsc. - str. 10:00 S.U.I.S.A.
—— CONCERTO MINIATUR, OP. 54, NR. 6 (POUR ORGUE ET ORCHESTRE)
1,1,0,1 - 1,1,1,0 - org. - str. 12:00 S.U.I.S.A.
—— CONTRASTES, OP. 67 (BALLET) %
0,1,1,0 - 0,0,0,0 - timp. - org.(ou vibra.) - pf. - str.
17:00 S.U.I.S.A.

—— TRIPARTITA OP. 39 (QUATRIEME POÈME CHORÉOGRAPHIQUE)
1,1,1,1 - 2,2,3,0 - timp.,perc. - pf. - str. 17:00 S.U.I.S.A.

CERHA, Friedrich
—— ESPRESSIONI FONDAMENTALI (1957)
3(3rd alt. with picc.),*3,*4,*3 - 3,3,3,1 - timp.,perc.(9),cel.,mar.,vibra.,xyl. - hp. - pf. - str.
17:00 G. Schirmer.
—— PHANTASMA '63 (FOR ORGAN AND SMALL ORCH.)
*2,0,3,0 - 2,1,1,1 - perc.(4) - Hammond org.(3 players) Modern.
—— RELAZIONI FRAGILLI (FOR SOPRANO, MEZZO-SOPRANO, HARPSICHORD AND ORCH.)
1,0,*1,0 - 0,1,0,0 - perc.(9),cel. - hp. - hpsc. - str.(1,1,1,0)
20:00 Modern.
—— SYMPHONY IN ONE MOVEMENT
4,4,4,4 - 4,4,3,1 - perc.(9) - pf. - str. 17:00 Modern.

CESANA, Otto
—— MINATURE SYMPHONY FOR STRINGS A GUITAR (IN 4 MOVEMENTS)
guit. - str. 12:00 Composer.

CESTI, M. - STOKOWSKI, Leopold
—— TU MANCAVI A TORMENTARMI CRUDELISSIMA SPERANZA
str. 6:00 Broude.

CHABRIER, Emmanuel - BECKETT, Wheeler
—— ESPANA (FOR GUITAR AND ORCH.) (ARRANGED 1972)
*3,2,2,2 - 4,2,3,1 - timp.,perc. - str.(30,8,8,5) 7:00 Arranger.

CHABRIER, Emmanuel - FRANCAIX, Jean
—— SOUVENIR DE MUNICH (QUADRILLE ON THEMES FROM "TRISTAN AND ISOLDE")
2,2,2,2 - 2,2,2,1 - timp., perc. - str. 7:00 Presser.

CHABRIER, Emmanuel - PERRY, Harold
—— DANSE SLAVE (FROM "LE ROI MALGRE LUI")
6:00 Bo. Hawkes.

CHADWICK, George W.
—— FOUR SYMPHONIC SKETCHES
3,3,3,2 - 4,2,3,0 - timp.,perc.,xyl. - hp. - str. 31:00 G. Schirmer.
—— RIP VAN WINKLE (OVERTURE)
3,2,2,2 - 4,2,3,1 - timp.,perc.,xyl. - str. 10:00 C. Fischer.
—— SINFONIETTA IN D (IN 4 MOVTS.)
3(3rd alt. with picc.),2,2,2 - 4,2,3,0 - timp.,perc. - hp. - str.
40:00 G. Schirmer.
—— TAM O'SHANTER
3,3,4,2 - 4,3,3,1 - timp.,perc.,glock,xyl. - hp. - str. G. Schirmer.

CHAGRIN, Francis
—— BAGATELLES
str. 9:00 Galaxy.
—— CAPRICCIO (1938)
str. 4:00 P.R.S.
—— CONCERTO FOR PIANO AND ORCH.
25:00 Lengnick.
—— ELEGY
str. 7:00 Mills.
—— HELTER SKELTER (COMEDY OVERTURE)
3,2,2,2 - 4,3,3,1 - timp.,perc. - hp. - str. 7:00 Galaxy.
—— LAMENTO APPASSIONATO
str. 11:00 Galaxy.
—— NOCTURNE
2,1,2,1 - 2,1,1,0 - timp.,perc. - hp. - str. 6:00 Belw-Mills.
—— PRELUDE AND FUGUE
2,2,2,2 - 4,2,2,0 - perc. - str. 11:00 Lengnick.
—— RENAISSANCE SUITE FOR STRINGS
str. 8:00 Novello.
—— ROUMANIAN FANTASY (FOR HARMONICA OR VIOLIN WITH ORCH.)(1956)
3,2,2,2 - 4,2,3,0 - timp.,perc.(3),vibra.,xyl. - harmonica(or vln.) - hp. - str. 16:00 Belw-Mills.
—— ROUMANIAN FANTASY (1956)
3,3,2,2 - 4,2,3,0 - timp.,perc. - hp. - str. 16:00 Belw-Mills.
—— SUITE NO. 1 FOR ORCH.
2,2,2,2 - 4,2,2,0 - perc. - str. 17:00 Mills.
—— SYMPHONY NO. 1
3,2(2nd alt. with Eng.hn.),2,2 - 4,3,3,1 - timp.,perc.,vibra.,xyl. - hp. - org. - str. 30:00 Novello.

CHAIKIN, Nikolai
—— CONCERTO FOR BAYAN (CHROMATIC ACCORDIAN) AND ORCH.
2,2,2,2 - 4,2,1,0 - timp.,perc. - accord.(or bayan) - hp.(or pf.) - str.
21:00 G. Schirmer.

CHAILLEY, Jacques
—— PAN ET LA SYRINX (LEGENDARY MORALITY IN 1 ACT, AFTER JULES LAFORGUE) %
1,0,1,1 - 1,1,0,0 - timp.,perc.,cel.,glock.(ad lib.) - pf. - str.
60:00 Baron.
—— SYMPHONIE
Baron.

CHAILLY, Luciano
—— SONATA TRITEMATICA NO. 3
2(2nd alt. with picc.),2,2,2 - 2,2,0,0 - timp.,perc. - str.
12:00 AhnSimrock.
—— SONATA TRITEMATICA NO. 7
str.
20:00 Bo. Hawkes.

CHAJES, Julius
—— BY THE RIVERS OF BABYLON (FOR VOICE AND ORCH.)
2,2,2,*3 - 2,2,1,0 - timp.,perc. - str.
6:00 Transcon.
—— CAPRICCIO
0,0,2,0 - 2,0,0,0 - str.
Composer.
—— CONCERTO FOR CELLO AND ORCH., OP. 13 (IN 3 MOVEMENTS)
2,2,2,2 - 4,1,0,0 - timp. - str.
25:00 Transcon.
—— CONCERTO IN E, FOR PIANO AND ORCH. (IN 3 MOVEMENTS)
2(2nd alt. with picc.),2,2,*3 - 4,3,0,0 - timp.,perc. (2) - str.
26:30 Transcon.
—— EROS (SYMPHONIC POEM)
2,2,2,*3 - 4,3,3,1 - timp.,perc. - str.
10:00 Transcon.
—— FOUR FUGUES, IN MODO ANTICO
str.
12:30 Composer.
—— FUGUE IN A MINOR (BASED ON C-H-A-E-S)
2,2,2,*3 - 4,2,3,0 - str.
or:
str.
6:45 Composer.
—— HEBREW SUITE (IN 3 MOVTS.)
2(2nd alt. with picc.),2,2,2 - 2,2,0,0 - timp.,perc. (1) - str.
10:00 Transcon.
—— MELODY AND DANCE (FOR ENGLISH HORN AND STRINGS)
Eng.hn. - str.
8:30 Transcon.
—— OUT OF THE DESERT - THREE ORCHESTRAL EXCERPTS (1966)
*3,2,2,2 - 2,2,0,0 - perc.(1) - str.
Transcon.
—— THE PROMISED LAND (CANTATA FOR NARRATOR, SOLOISTS, MIXED CHORUS AND ORCH.)
2(2nd alt. with picc.),2,2,*3 - 4,2,3,0 - timp.,perc. - pf. - str.
30:00 Transcon.
—— PSALM 142 (FOR SOLOISTS, MIXED CHORUS AND ORCH.)
2,2,2,2 - 4,2,3,0 - timp. - str.
11:00 Transcon.
—— ROMANTIC FANTASY (FOR PIANO AND ORCH.)
2,2,2,2 - 2,1,0,0 - timp. - pf. - str.
10:00 Composer.
—— SCHERZO (1969)
2,2(2nd alt. with Eng. hn.),2,2 - 2,0,0,0 - timp.,perc.(1) - str.
4:00 Composer.
—— SONG FOR AMERICANS (FOR CHORUS AND ORCH.)
2,2,2,2 - 4,2,3,0 - timp.,perc. - str.
Transcon.
—— SUITE IN D MAJOR FOR STRINGS (FOUR FUGUES) (IN 4 MOVTS.)
str.
10:15 Composer.
—— THEME AND VARIATIONS FOR STRINGS
str.
5:00 Transcon.
—— ZION, RISE AND SHINE (FOR CHORUS AND ORCH.)
2,2,2,2 - 4,2,3,0 - timp. - str.
9:00 Transcon.

CHALLAN, Henri
—— SYMPHONY IN G MAJOR
2,2,2,2 - 4,2,0,0 - timp.,crotales - str.
27:00 EV.

CHALLAN, René
—— CONCERTO FOR ALTO SAXOPHONE AND ORCH.
2,2,2,alto sax.,2 - 2,2,1,0 - timp.,perc.,cel.,xyl. - hp. - str.
20:30 Baron.
—— CONCERTO IN E MINOR FOR VIOLIN AND ORCH.
Henmar.
—— QUE MET-ON DANS MON CORBILLON?
2,2,2,2 - 2,2,2,0 - timp.,perc. - hp. - str.
21:00 Salabert.

—— LA RIVIÈRE
2,2,2,2 - 2,1,2,0 - timp.,perc.(3) - hp. - str.
10:00 Presser.
—— LES SORCIERS (SUITE)
18:00 S.A.C.E.M.
—— SYMPHONY IN F MAJOR
2,2,2,2 - 2,2,2,0 - timp.,perc.(3) - str.
25:00 Presser.

CHAMPAGNE, Claude
—— SUITE CANADIENNE (FOR CHORUS AND ORCH.) (IN 4 MOVTS.)
1,1,1,1 - 2,1,2,0 - timp., perc.(3) - hp. - str.
6:00 EV.

CHANCE, John Barnes
—— FIESTA! (1961)
*3,2,*3,2 - 4,3,3,1 - timp.,perc.(5),xyl. - str.
7:00 Composer.
—— KYRIE AND ALLELUIU (FOR SATB CHORUS AND ORCH.) (1967)
2,2,2,2(2nd alt. with b.-cl.),2 - 4,3,3,1 - timp.,perc.(4) - str.
8:00 Composer.
—— OVERTURE TO A FAIRY TALE (1958)
*3,*3,*3,*3 - 4,0,0,0 - timp.,perc.(3), glock. - hp. - str.
8:45 Composer.
—— SYMPHONY NO. 1 IN C MAJOR (1956)
*3,*3,*3,2 - 4,3,3,1 - timp. - str.
18:00 Composer.

CHANCE, Nancy Laird
—— DARKSONG (FOR SOPRANO AND ENSEMBLE)
2,0,2,0 - 2,0,0,0 - perc.(5) - guit. - pf.
8:00 Seesaw.
—— LYRIC ESSAYS FOR ORCH. (1969)
*3,*3,*3,*3, - 4,3,3,1- timp.,perc.(3),bells,cel.,glock.,xyl. - hp. - pf. - str.
15:00 Seesaw.

CHANDLER, Mary
—— CONCERTO FOR OBOE D'AMORE AND STRINGS
ob. d'amore - str.
12:00 Novello.
—— CONCERTO FOR TRUMPET, PERCUSSION AND STRINGS (1959)
tpt. - perc. - str.
10:00 P.R.S.
—— CONCERTO FOR VIOLA D'AMORE AND STRINGS
str.
P.R.S.
—— DIVERSION
str.
P.R.S.
—— NOCTURNE
3,2,2,2 - 4,2,3,1 - timp. - hp. - str.
7:00 P.R.S.
—— SUITE FOR WOODWIND AND STRINGS (1957)
1,1,1,1 - 0,0,0,0 - str.
10:00 P.R.S.
—— TRIVIA (SUITE)
2,2,2,2 - 4,2,3,1 - timp.,perc. - hp. - str.
6:00 P.R.S.
—— TWO PASTORALS
2,2,2,2 - 2,2,3,1 - perc. - hp. - str.
6:00 P.R.S.

CHARDON, Félix
—— SUITE ROUMAINE (FOR VIOLIN AND ORCH.)
2,2,2,2 - 4,2,3,0 - timp.,perc. - hp.(ad lib.) - str.
9:00 Salabert.

CHARKOVSKY, Willis
—— CONCERTO FOR PIANO AND ORCH. (IN 3 MOVTS.)
0,2,2,2 - 2,2,0,0 - timp. - pf. - str.
20:00 Composer.
—— HARVEST DANCE (FROM THE OPERA "RUTH")
3(3rd alt. with picc.),*3,2,*3 - 4,3,3,1 - timp.,perc.(2),xyl. - hp. - str.
6:00 Composer.
—— SUITE "R.U.R." (IN 4 MOVTS.) (Based on Karel Capek's play "R.U.R.")
3(3rd alt. with picc.),3,3,3 - 4,3,3,1 - timp.,perc.(5),xyl. - hp. - org.(ad lib.) - pf. - str.
16:00 Composer.

CHARPENTIER, Jacques
—— CONCERTO FOR ONDES-MARTENOT AND ORCH.
*3,2,2,2 - 4,3,3,1 - perc.(2),glock. - ondes-Martenot - str.
20:00 Baron.
—— SYMPHONIE BRÈVE
str.
20:00 Baron.

CHARPENTIER, Marc-Antoine - MCDEE
—— PASSACAILLE
Presser.

CHARPENTIER, Marc Antoine - STOKOWSKI, Leopold
—— PASSECAILLE (FROM ACT II OF "MEDEA")
Arranger.

CHARPENTIER, R.
—— SUITE FRANCAISE
    3,2(1 alt. with Eng.hn.),2,2 - 2,2,2,2 - timp. - hp.
          18:00 Eds. Fran.

CHASE, J. Newell
—— CONCERTO FOR LOUISE (CONCERTINO FOR PIANO AND
    ORCH.), OP. 3
    3,*3,*3,*2 - 4,3,3,1 - timp.,perc. (2), cel. - pf. - str.
          9:00 Composer.
—— PAS SEUL FROM "ARIADNE", OP. 1
    2,alto fl.,*3,*3,*3 - 4,3,3,1 - timp.,perc. (2) - 2 hp. - str. Composer.
—— TANGLEWOOD POOL (PASTEL SKETCH), OP. 2
    2,*2,*3,*2 - 4,3,2,0 - timp.,perc. (2),cel. - hp. - pf. - str.   Mills.

CHASINS, Abram
—— CONCERTO NO. 1 FOR PIANO AND ORCH. (IN 3
    MOVEMENTS)
    2(2nd alt. with picc.),2,2,2 - 4,2,3,1 - timp.,perc. (1) - pf. - str.
          28:00 Composer.
—— CONCERTO NO. 2 FOR PIANO AND ORCH.
    2,*3,2,*3 - 4,3,2,1 - timp.,perc. (2) pf. - str.   29:00 Composer.
—— PARADE
    3(3rd alt. with picc.),2,3,*3 - 4,3,3,1 - timp.,perc. (1) - hp. - str.
          7:00 J. Fischer.
—— PERIOD SUITE (IN 6 MOVTS.)
    2(2nd alt. with picc.),2(2nd alt. with Eng. hn.),2(2nd alt. with
    b.-cl.),2 - 2,2,2,0 - timp.,perc. (1) - str.   15:00 Chappell.
—— THREE CHINESE PIECES
          12:00 J. Fischer.

CHATTON, Pierre-André
—— CONCERT À LA MÉMOIRE D'ALOYS FORNEROD (POUR
    PETIT ORCH.)
          14:00 S.U.I.S.A.

CHAUSSON, Ernest - DE FILIPPI, Amedeo
—— JARDINS AUX LILAS (BALLET) %
          Arranger.

CHAVCHAVADZE, George
—— LÉGENDE
    2,2,2,2 - 4,2,3,1 - timp.,perc. - hp. - pf.(alt. with cel.) - str.
          Southern.

CHAVEZ, Carlos
—— BAILE (DANCE) (SYMPHONIC PICTURE)
    3,3,2,3 - 4,2,3,1 - timp.,perc. (3) - pf. - str.   4:10 Composer.
—— CABALLOS DE VAPOR ("H.P.") (BALLET SUITE)
    3,3,4,2 sax.,3 - 4,3,3,1 - timp.,perc. (3) - str.   25:00 Bo. Hawkes.
—— CABALLOS DE VAPOR ("H.P.") (SINFONIA DE BAILE) %
    3,3,4,2 sax.,3 - 4,3,3,1 - timp.,perc. (3) - str.   Bo. Hawkes.
—— CANTO A LA TIERRA (FOR UNISON CHORUS AND ORCH.)
    (1946) (Text: Enrique González Martínez)
    3,3,4,3 - 4,3,3,1 - timp.,perc.(2) - 2 hp. - str.   5:00 Composer.
—— CANTOS DE MEXICO
    *1,1,1 E♭cl.,0,0 - 0,1,0,0 - perc. (7),mar.,2 teponaxtles,1
    huehuetl,1 water gourd - 2 vihuelas - 1 guit. - hp. - str. (vlns.)
          4:00 Composer.
—— CHAPULTEPEC (OBERTURA REPUBLICANA) (3 FAMOUS
    MEXICAN PIECES, ORCH. BY C. CHAVEZ) (1935)
    2 picc.,2,*3,E♭cl.,3,4 sax.(1 sopr., 2 alto,1 ten.),3 - 4,E♭tpt.,3,3,1
    - timp.,perc.(4) - str.   7:20 Mills.
—— CLIO (SYMPHONIC ODE) (1969)
    2(2nd alt. with picc.),*3,2,3(3rd alt. with c-bn.) - 4,3,3,1 -
    timp.,perc.(3) - 2 hp. - str.   17:00 G. Schirmer.
—— CONCERTO FOR FOUR HORNS AND ORCH. (IN 3
    MOVEMENTS)
    0,*1,E♭cl.,*3,3(3rd alt. with c.-bn.) - 4,0,0,0- timp. - str.
          23:00 Mills.
—— CONCERTO FOR PIANO AND ORCH. (IN 3 MOVEMENTS)
    3,3,2,3 - 4,2,3,1 - timp.,perc. (3),cel. - hp. - pf. - str.
          33:00 G. Schirmer.
—— CONCERTO FOR VIOLIN AND ORCH.
    1. Andante - Allegro moderato; 2. Largo - Scherzo - Cadenza -
    Scherzo - Largo; 3. Allegro moderato - Andante, meno mosso di
    prima
    3,3,3,3 - 4,3,3,1 - timp.,perc. (3) - hp. - str.   36:00 Mills.
—— DISCOVERY (DESCUBRIMIENTO) (1969)
    1(alt. with picc.),*2,1,1 - 2,1,0,0 - timp.,perc.(1) - str.
          20:00 G. Schirmer.

—— ELATIO (1967)
    3,3,3,3 - 4,3,3,1 - timp.,perc.(4) - 2 hp. - pf. - str.
          14:00 Composer.
—— EL FUEGO NUEVO (BALLET AZTECA) (FOR WOMEN'S-
    CHORUS AND ORCH.) %
    4,4,6,4 - group of ocarinas - 4,4,4,2 - timp.,perc. (13) - str.
          30:00 Composer.
—— LA HIJA DE COLGUIDE (THE DAUGHTER OF COLCHIS):
    SYMPHONIC SUITE (IN 5 MOVTS.)
    3,3,4,3 - 4,3,3,1 - timp.,perc. (3) - hp. - str.   23:15 Mills.
—— INITIUM (1972)
    3(1 alt. with picc.),*3,*3,*3 - 4,3,3,1 - timp.,perc.(3),
    glock.,mar.,vibra.,xyl. - hp. - str.(30,12,10,8)   18:00 Belw-Mills.
—— JAZZY DANCE (FROM "CABALLOS DE VAPOR") ("H.P.")
    2,2,5,4 - 4,3,3,1 - timp.,perc. - str.   9:00 Bo. Hawkes.
—— LLAMADAS (PROLETARIAN SYMPHONY ON VERSOS
    FROM EL CORRIDO DE LA REVOLUCIÓN) (FOR SATB
    CHORUS AND ORCH.) (1934)
    2 picc.,2,*3,1 E♭cl.*3,3 - 4,4,3,1 - timp.,perc.(5) - str.
          10:00 Composer.
—— MAÑANAS MEXICANAS (MEXICAN MORNINGS) (1974)
    3(1 alt. with picc.),*3,*3,*3 - 4,3,3,1 - timp.,perc.(3),
    glock.,mar.,xyl. - str.   23:00 C. Fischer.
—— LA PALOMA AZUL (FOR MIXED CHORUS AND CHAMBER
    ORCH.)
    *2,1,1 E♭cl.,1,1 - 0,1,1,0 - timp.,perc. (6) - 2 quit. - str.
          8:48 Bo. Hawkes.
—— PIRÁMIDE (4-ACT BALLET) % (WITH SATB CHORUS) (1968)
    (IN 4 MOVTS.)
    3,3,3,3 - 4,3,3,1 - timp.,perc.(4) - tape-recorder - 2 hp. - pf. - str.
          25:00 C. Fischer.
—— PROMETHEUS BOUND (CANTATA) (1956) (English text, after
    Esquilo's tragedy)
    3,3,3,3 - 4,3,3,1 - timp.,perc.(3) - 2 hp. - str.   Belw-Mills.
—— QUATRO NOCTURNOS (FOUR NOCTURNES) (FOR
    SOPRANO, CONTRALTO AND ORCH.) (Text: Xavier
    Villaurrutia)
    *3,*3,*3,*3 - 4,3,3,1 - timp.,perc. (4) - hp. - pf. - str.
          15:00 Composer.
—— LOS QUATRO SOLES (BALLET INDIGEHA) (FOR MIXED
    CHORUS AND ORCH.) %
    3,3,3,2 - 4,3,3,1 - timp.,perc. (4) - str.   30:00 Composer.
    or:
    2,1,2,1 - 2,1,2,0 - timp.,perc. (2) - str.
—— LOS QUATRO SOLES: BALLET SUITE
    3,3,3,2 - 4,3,3,1 - timp.,perc.(4) - str.   22:00 Composer.
    or:
    2,1,2,1 - 2,1,2,0 - timp.,perc. (2) - str.
—— RESONANCIAS (RESONANCES) (1964)
    3,3,3,3 - 4,2,3,1 - timp.,perc.(4) - str.   15:00 Mills.
—— SINFONIA DE ANTIGONA (SYMPHONY NO. 1)
    *2,alto fl.,*2,heck.,E♭cl.,*3,3 - 8,3,0,1 - timp.,perc. (4),glock. - 2
    hp. - str.   11:00 G. Schirmer.
—— SINFONIA INDIA (SYMPHONY NO. 2)
    *4(3rd alt. with 2nd picc.),3,E♭cl.,*3,3 - 4,2,2,0 - timp.,perc.(5) -
    hp. - str.   11:00 G. Schirmer.
    or:
    2,1,3,1 - 2,2,1,0 - timp.,perc.(5) - hp. - str.
—— SINFONIA NO. 7 (1960) (IN 3 MOVTS.)
    3,3,3,3 - 4,3,3,1 timp.,perc.(4) - 2 hp. - str.   Belw-Mills.
—— SINFONIA (1915) (IN 3 MOVTS.) (Un-numbered early work)
    2,2,2,3 - 4,4,3,1 - timp. - str.   Composer.
—— EL SOL (CORRIDO MEXICANO) (FOR MIXED CHORUS
    AND ORCH.)
    2 picc.,2,*3,1 E♭cl.,*3,3 - 4,4,*3,1 - timp.,perc. (3) - str.
          8:00 Mills.
—— SOLI NO. 3 (FOR BASSOON, TRUMPET, TIMPANI, VIOLA
    AND ORCH.) (1965)
    3,3,3,3 - 4,3,3,1 - timp.,perc.(4) - 2 hp. - pf. - str.   16:00 Mills.
—— SONANTE FOR STRING ORCH. (1974)
    str.   15:00 Composer.
—— SYMPHONY NO. 3 (IN 4 MOVTS.)
    3,3,4,3 - 4,3,3,1 - timp.,perc. (3) - hp. - str.   26:00 Bo. Hawkes.
—— SYMPHONY NO. 4 (SINFONIA ROMANTICA) (IN 3
    MOVEMENTS)
    *3,*3,2,3 - 4,2,3,1 - timp.,perc. (3),glock.,xyl. - str.
          23:00 Bo. Hawkes.
—— SYMPHONY NO. 5 (FOR STRINGS) (IN 3 MOVEMENTS)
    str.   18:00 Mills.
—— SYMPHONY NO. 6
    *3,*3,*3,2,*3 - 4,2,3,1 - timp.,perc. - str.   30:00 Mills.
—— TOCCATA FOR ORCHESTRA
    3,3,4,3 - 4,3,3,1 - timp.,perc. (3) - str.   8:00 Composer.

—— THE VISITORS (3-ACT OPERA) % (1953) (Text: Chester
Kallman; Also transl. into Spanish)
3,3,3,3 - 4,3,3,1 - timp.,perc.(4) - hp. - str.   135:00 C. Fischer.
—— XOCHIPILLI-MACUILXOCHITL (AN IMAGINED AZTEC
MUSIC, FOR 4 WINDS AND 7 PERCUSSIONISTS.)
*2,0,1 E♭cl.,0,0 - 0,0,1,0 - perc. (6) as follows: 1. small teponaxtle,
omichicahuaxtli: 2. large teponaxtle, small copper rattles: 3. small
and medium Indian drums, clay rattle: 4. small huehuetl,smooth
rattle: 5. medium huehuetl, clay rattle, large copper rattle: 6. large
huehuetl,omichicahuaxtli   6:00 Mills.

CHAYNES, Charles
—— CONCERTO FOR STRING ORCH.
str.   Baron.
—— CONCERTO FOR TRUMPET AND ORCH.

Baron.
—— DANSES SYMPHONIQUES
2,*2,2(2nd alt. with b.-cl.),2 - 2,2,2,0 - timp.,perc.,cel.,vibra. - hp. -
pf. - str.   12:30 Baron.
—— IRRADIATIONS (FOR VIOLIN, CELLO, HARPISCHORD AND
STRINGS)
hpsc. - str.   25:00 Presser.
—— LIEU DE LUMIÈRE (HOMAGE TO DARIUS MILHAUD)
2,2,2,2 - 2,2,1,0 - perc., cel. - hp. - pf. - str.   6:00 Presser.
—— ODE POUR UNE MORT TRAGIQUE (DRAMATIC
OVERTURE)
2,2,3,2 - 4,2,2,1 - timp.,perc.,cel.,xyl. - hp. - pf. - str. 13:00 Baron.
—— QUATRE ILLUSTRATIONS POUR "LA FLUTE DE JADE"
*1,0,0,0 - 0,0,0,0 - timp.,perc.,cel.,xyl. - hp. - str.   18:00 Baron.
—— SYMPHONY
3,*3,3,3 - 4,3,3,1 - timp.,perc.,bells,cel.,glock.,vibra.,xyl. -
ondes-Martenot(ad lib.) - hp. - pf. - str.   28:30 Baron.

CHEMIN-PETIT, Hans
—— CONCERTO FOR ORGAN, TIMPANI AND STRINGS
(FANTASY AND FUGUE)
timp. - org. - str.   11:00 Henmar.
—— CONCERTO IN D MAJOR, FOR LARGE ORCH.

Henmar.
—— FESTIVE MUSIC (FOR LARGE ORCH.)

Henmar.
—— ORCHESTRAL PROLOGUE

Henmar.
—— SYMPHONY IN A MINOR

Henmar.

CHENOWETH, Wilbur
—— FIESTA (FOR PIANO AND ORCH.)
1 (alt. with picc.),1,3(2nd and 3rd alt. with sax.,3rd al so alt. with
b.-cl.),1 - 2,3,3,0 - perc.(4) - pf. - str.   10:00 G. Schirmer.
—— VARIATIONS ON "LOBE DEN HERRN"
3(3rd alt. with picc.),*3,*3,*3 - 4,3,3,1 - timp.,perc. (2-3),glock. -
hp. - org. (ad lib.) - str.   10:30 Composer.

CHERRY, Richard John
—— CONCERTINO FOR CELLO AND ORCHESTRA
2,2,3,2 - 4,2,3,1 - timp.,perc. - str.   18:00 S.A.M.R.O.
—— FANFARE FOR DURBAN
2,2,3,2 - 4,2,3,1 - timp.,perc. - str.   8:00 S.A.M.R.O.
—— FESTIVAL OVERTURE 1652
2,2,3,2 - 4,2,3,1 - timp.,perc. - str.   13:00 S.A.M.R.O.
—— FUGUE FOR SOUTH AFRICAN VOICES (FOR
MEZZO-SOPRANO, BARITONE, BASS, CHORUS AND
ORCH.) (Text: Percy Baneshik)
2,2,3,2 - 4,2,3,1 - timp.,perc. - str.   60:00 S.A.M.R.O.
—— THE GREAT TREK (FOR CHORUS AND ORCH.) (TEXT:
GEOFFREY BRIDSON) %
2,2,3,2 - 4,2,3,1 - timp.,perc. - str.   60:00 S.A.M.R.O.
—— IN LAUDE REGIS ORIENTALIS (CANTATA) (FOR
BARITONE, CHORUS AND ORCH.)
2,2,3,2 - 4,2,3,1 - timp.,perc. - str.   10:00 S.A.M.R.O.
—— INCIDENTS AT THE BALL (BALLET) %
2,2,3,2 - 4,2,3,1 - timp.,perc. - str.   30:00 S.A.M.R.O.
—— INCIDENTS AT THE BALL (BALLET SUITE)
2,2,3,2 - 4,2,3,1 - timp.,perc. - str.   11:00 S.A.M.R.O.
—— THE LIFE OF GENERAL SMUTS (MUSIC FROM THE RADIO
SERIES) (FOR CHORUS AND ORCH.) (TEXT: SARAH
GERTRUDE MILLIN) %
2,2,3,2 - 4,2,3,1 - timp.,perc. - str.   S.A.M.R.O.
—— LIVINGSTONE (MUSIC FROM THE FILM)
2,2,3,2 - 4,2,3,1 - timp.,perc. - str.   30:00 S.A.M.R.O.

—— PIONEERS O PIONEERS (CANTATA) (FOR CHORUS AND
ORCH.)
2,2,3,2 - 4,2,3,1 - timp.,perc. - str.   20:00 S.A.M.R.O.
—— PONDO STORY (MUSIC FROM THE FILM)
2,2,3,2 - 4,2,3,1 - timp.,perc. - str.   30:00 S.A.M.R.O.
—— RIP VAN WYK (MUSIC FROM THE FILM)
2,2,3,2 - 4,2,3,1 - timp.,perc. - str.   90:00 S.A.M.R.O.
—— SUITE ON SOUTH AFRICAN TUNES (FOR STRING ORCH.)
str.   15:00 S.A.M.R.O.
—— SWIMMING BATH (BALLET) %
2,2,3,2 - 4,2,3,1 - timp.,perc. - str.   30:00 S.A.M.R.O.
—— THIS IS SOUTH AFRICA (FROM THE RADIO SCORE) (FOR
CHORUS AND ORCH.) (Text: Geoffrey Bridson)
2,2,3,2 - 4,2,3,1 - timp.,perc. - str.   60:00 S.A.M.R.O.
—— TRANSVAAL TALE (MUSIC FROM THE FILM)
2,2,3,2 - 4,2,3,1 - timp.,perc. - str.   30:00 S.A.M.R.O.
—— TWO SHORT CHRISTMAS PIECES (FOR SMALL ORCH.)
1,1,2,1 - 3,1,2,1 - perc. - str.   6:00 S.A.M.R.O.
—— VARIATIONS ON A THEME BY ST. SAENS (FOR STRING
ORCH.)
str.   13:00 S.A.M.R.O.

CHERUBINI, Luigi - CONFALONIERI, Giulio
—— REQUIEM IN C MINOR (FOR CHORUS AND ORCH.)
0,2,2,2 - 2,2,3,0 - timp.,gong - str.   50:00 Leeds.

CHERUBINI, Luigi - HERMANN, F.
—— BALLET MUSIC FROM "ALI BABA"
fl. - str.   Galaxy.

CHERUBINI, Luigi - LUALDI, A.
—— SYMPHONY IN D MAJOR
1,2,2,2 - 2,2,0,0 - timp. - str.   30:00 Leeds.

CHERUBINI, Luigi - MAGANINI, Quinto
—— OVERTURE TO "THE PORTUGESE INN"

8:30 Musicus.

CHERUBINI, Luigi - WOJCIECHOWSKI, Johannes
—— TWO SONATAS (CONCERT ETUDES) (FOR HORN OR
ENGLISH HORN AND STRING ORCH.)
hn.(or Eng.hn.) - str.   11:00 F. Colombo.

CHESLOCK, Louis
—— CONCERTO FOR HORN AND ORCH. (1936) (IN 3 MOVTS.)
1,1,1,1 - 3,1,0,0 - timp. - str.   30:00 Composer.
—— CONCERTO FOR VIOLIN AND ORCH. (1921) (IN 3 MOVTS.)
2,2,2,2 - 4,3,3,1 - timp.,perc. - hp. - str.   20:00 Composer.
—— THE LEGEND OF SLEEPY HOLLOW (1936)
*3,*3,2,alto sax.,*3 - 4,2,3,1 - timp.,perc.,cel.,xyl. - hp. - str.
15:00 Composer.
—— RHAPSODY IN RED AND WHITE (AN AMERICAN
DIVERTISSEMENT) (1950)
2(2nd alt. with picc.),2,2,2 - 4,3,3,1 - timp.,perc.,xyl. - hp. - pf. -
str.   10:00 Composer.
—— SET OF SIX (1946)
2,2,2,2 - 2,2,1,1 - timp.,perc. - str.   27:30 Composer.
—— SUITE FROM "DAVID" (FOR TENOR OR BARITONE VOICE,
WITH ORCH.) (1937) (IN 3 MOVTS.) (Text: Biblical)
*3,*3,*3,*3 - 4,2,3,1 - timp.,perc.,bells,cel.,glock. - hp. - str.
16:00 Composer.
—— SYMPHONIC PRELUDE (1925)
3(3rd alt. with picc.),2,2,2 - 4,2,3,1 - timp.,perc. - hp. - str.
12:00 Composer.
—— SYMPHONY IN D MINOR (1932) (IN 4 MOVTS.)
*3,*3,2,2 - 4,2,3,1 - timp.,perc.(3),bells - hp. - str.
40:00 Composer.
—— THREE SCENES (1922)
*3,*3,2,2 - 4,2,3,1 - timp.,perc.,bells,cel. - hp. - pf. - str.
12:30 Composer.

CHEVREUILLE, Raymond
—— BARBE-BLEUE (BLUEBEARD), OP. 42 (1949)
3,3,4,3 - 4,3,3,1 - timp.,perc.,xyl. - hp. - pf. - str. 15:00 H. Elkan.
—— BURLESQUE, OP. 26 (FOR CELLO AND ORCH.) (1941)
2,1,2,1 - 2,2,1,0 - timp.,perc. - str.   6:00 H. Elkan.
—— CONCERTO FOR ALTO SAXOPHONE (OR VIOLA), PIANO
AND ORCH., OP. 34 (1946)
4,2,2,1 alto sax.(ad lib.),2 - 4,2,2,0 - timp.,perc. - str. (cellos and
basses; 1 viola solo ad lib.)   21:00 H. Elkan.
—— CONCERTO FOR CELLO AND ORCH., OP. 16 (1940)
2,2,3,2 - 3,2,3,1 - timp.,perc. - hp. - str.   24:00 CBDM.

—— CONCERTO FOR CLARINET AND STRINGS, OP. 89 (1968)
(IN 3 MOVTS.)
    cl. - timp. - perc. - str.   18:00 H. Elkan.
—— CONCERTO FOR HORN AND ORCH., OP. 43 (1949)
    2,2,2,2 - 2,2,2,0 - timp.,perc. - str.   24:00 CBDM.
—— CONCERTO FOR ORCH., OP. 37 (1947)
    3,3,3,3 - 4,3,3,1 - timp.,perc. - str.   23:00 H. Elkan.
—— CONCERTO FOR TRUMPET AND ORCH., OP. 58
    2,2,2,2 - 3,2,3,0 - timp. - str.   13:00 CBDM.
—— CONCERTO NO. 1 FOR PIANO AND ORCH., OP. 10 (1937)
    3,3,3,3 - 4,3,3,1 - timp.,perc.cel.,xyl. - str. 22:00 H. Elkan.
—— CONCERTO NO. 1 FOR VIOLIN AND ORCH., OP. 19 (1941)
    3,2,3,3 - 4,3,3,0 - timp.,perc.,xyl. - hp. - pf. - str. 30:00 H. Elkan.
—— CONCERTO NO. 2 FOR VIOLIN AND ORCH., OP. 56 (1953)
    2,2,2,2 - 3,2,2,0 - timp. - str.   23:00 CBDM.
—— CONCERTO NO. 3 FOR PIANO AND ORCH., OP. 88 (1968)
(IN 3 MOVTS.)
    2,2,2,2 - 4,2,2,0 - timp.,perc. - pf. - str. 20:00 H. Elkan.
—— CONCERTO NO. 3 FOR VIOLIN AND ORCH., OP. 86 (1965)
    2,2,2,2 - 2,2,0,0 - timp. - str.   25:00 H. Elkan.
—— CONCERTO POUR TRIO D'ANCHES (REED TRIO) AND
ORCH, OP. 29 (1943)
    2,1,3,3 - 4,3,3,1 - timp.,perc. - hp. - pf. - str. 23:00 H. Elkan.
—— DIVERTISSEMENT, OP. 33 (FROM THE BALLET
"CENDRILLION") (1946)
    3,3,3,3 - 4,3,3,1 - timp.,perc.,cel.,xyl. - hp. - pf. - str.
          15:00 H. Elkan.
—— DIVERTISSEMENT, OP. 40 (1948)
    1,0,1,1 - 1,0,0,0 - hp. - str.   15:00 H. Elkan.
—— DOUBLE CONCERTO FOR VIOLA, PIANO AND ORCH., OP.
34 (1946)
    4,2,2,2 - 4,2,2,0 - timp.,perc. - str.   21:00 CBDM.
—— SHORT SYMPHONY (SYMPHONY NO. 4, OP. 54) (1952)
    2,2,2,2 - 4,2,2,0 - timp. - str.   14:00 CBDM.
—— SYMPHONY NO. 1, OP. 14 (1939)
    3,3,3,3 - 4,3,3,1 - timp.,perc.,xyl. - hp. - pf. - str. 30:00 H. Elkan.
—— SYMPHONY NO. 2, OP. 30 (SYMPHONIE DES SOUVENIRS)
(WITH OPTIONAL MIXED CHORUS) (1944) (Text: J.
Weterings)
    3,3,3,3 - 4,3,3,1 - timp.,perc.,cel.,vibra.,xyl. - hp. - pf. - str.
          45:00 H. Elkan.
—— SYMPHONY NO. 3, OP. 47 (1951)
    3,3,4,3 - 4,3,3,1 - timp.,perc.,cel.,xyl. - hp. - pf. - str.
          45:00 CBDM.
—— SYMPHONY NO. 5 ("PRINTANIERE"), OP. 60 (1954)
    2,1,2,1 - 2,2,1,0 - timp.,perc. - str.   18:00 CBDM.
—— SYMPHONY NO. 6, OP. 67 (1957)
    3,3,3,3 - 4,3,3,1 - timp.,perc.,cel.,glock.,vibra.,xyl. - hp. - pf. - str.
          28:00 H. Elkan.
—— SYMPHONY NO. 8, OP. 95 (1970)
    3,2,2,2 - 4,3,3,0 - timp.,perc. - str.   25:00 H. Elkan.

CHIARAMELLO, Giancarlo
—— TRE MOVIMENTI (3 MOVTS. FOR ORCH.) (IN MEMORIAM
JOHN PROCTOR)
          Leeds.

CHIGNELL, Robert
—— THE JACKDAW OF RHEIMS (FOR BASS, SATB CHORUS
ANDORCH.)
    3,2,2,2 - 4,2,3,0 - timp.,perc. - hp. - str. 18:00 Bo. Hawkes.

CHIHARA, Paul
—— CEREMONY III
    1,2,0,1 - 2,0,0,0 - timp.,perc.(2-4) - str. 11:00 Henmar.
—— CEREMONY IV
    3(2nd and 3rd alt. with picc.),3,2, ten. sax.(or b.-cl.),3 - 6,4,4,1 -
    timp.,perc.(4) - hp. - str.   Henmar.
—— CONCERTO FOR VIOLA AND ORCHESTRA (1963) (IN 3
MOVTS.)
    2,1,1,1 - 2,1,1,0 - timp.,perc.(2) - str. 15:00 Wimbledon.
—— FOREST MUSIC (1966)
    3,0,0,3 - 4,3,3,1 - timp.,perc.(3) - str. 10:00 Henmar.
—— GRASS (WITH AMPLIFIED BASS AND OPTIONAL TAPE)
    2(2nd alt. with picc.),1,0,1 - 2,0,3,1 - timp.,perc.(3-4) - tape
    recorder(ad lib.) - d.-b.(amplified) 20:00 Henmar.
—— SHINJU (LOVER'S SUICIDE)
    2(alt. with 2 picc.),2,0,2(2nd alt. with c.-bn.) - 3,3,3,0 -
    timp.,perc.(4) - hp. - pf. - str. 40:00 Henmar.
—— SYMPHONY IN CELEBRATION (CEREMONY V)
    3,3,2,ten. sax.,3 - 6,4,4,1 - perc.(3) - 2 hp. - str. 20:00 Henmar.
—— WIND SONG (FOR CELLO AND ORCH.)
    2,2,2,2 - 3,2,3,0 - timp.,perc. - str. 16:00 Henmar.

CHILCOT, Thomas - LANGLEY, Robin
—— CONCERTO IN A FOR HARPSICHORD AND STRINGS
    hpsc. - str.   Oxford.

CHISHOLM, Eric
—— ADVENTURES OF BABAR (SUITE) (FOR NARRATOR AND
ORCH.)
    ,2,2,2,2 - 2,2,1,0 - timp.,perc - pf. - str. 32:00 Bo. Hawkes.
—— A CELTIC WONDER TALE
    3,2,3,3 - 4,3,3,1 - timp.,perc. - hp. - str. 10:00 Bo. Hawkes.
—— CEOL MOR DANCES
    2,2,2,2 - 4,2,3,0 - timp.,perc. - hp. - str. 12:00 S.A.M.R.O.
—— CONCERTO FOR VIOLIN AND ORCH.
    2,2,3,2 - 4,2,3,1 - timp.,perc. - str. 28:00 Bo. Hawkes.
—— DUNEDIN SUITE (FOR STRING ORCH.)
    str.   12:00 S.A.M.R.O.
—— THE EARTH SHAPERS (BALLET) %
    3,3,3,3 - 4,3,3,1 - timp.,perc. - hp. - str. 40:00 S.A.M.R.O.
—— FEAST OF SAMRAIN (TEXT: COMPOSER) (3-ACT CELTIC
ROMANTIC COMIC OPERA) %
    3,2,2,2 - 4,2,3,0 - timp.,perc. - hp. - str. 135:00 S.A.M.R.O.
—— THE FORSAKEN MERMAID (BALLET) %
    hp. - str.   42:00 McLellans.
—— THE FORSAKEN MERMAID (BALLET SUITE)
    3,2,2,2 - 4,2,3,0 - timp.,perc. - hp. - str. 15:00 S.A.M.R.O.
—— THE INLAND WOMAN (1-ACT OPERA) % (Text: Composer)
    3,2,2,2 - 4,2,3,0 - timp.,perc. - hp. - str. 60:00 S.A.M.R.O.
—— THE MINDE'S MELODIE (FOR CHORUS AND SMALL
ORCH.) (TEXT: BIBLICAL) %
    1,1,2,1 - 3,1,2,0 - str.   30:00 S.A.M.R.O.
—— THE MOODIE (BALLET) %
    perc. - pf. - str.   12:00 S.A.M.R.O.
—— NINE ORCHESTRAL PRELUDES (FROM "THE TRUE EDGE
OF THE GREAT WORLD")
    2,2,2,2 - 4,2,3,0 - timp.,perc. - hp. - pf. - str. 23:00 S.A.M.R.O.
—— OVERTURE FROM "THE FREIRIS OF BERWICK"
    1,1,1,1 - 2,1,1,0 - timp.,perc. - str. 8:00 S.A.M.R.O.
—— PICTURES FROM DANTE
    3,3,3,3 - 4,3,3,1 - timp.,perc.(2) - 2 hp. - org. - pf. - str.
          20:00 S.A.M.R.O.
—— THE PIED PIPER OF HAMELIN (BALLET) %
    1,1,2,1 - 2,2,1,0 - timp.,perc. - pf. - str. 25:00 S.A.M.R.O.
—— PIOBAIREACHD (BURLESQUE BALLET) %
    3,3,3,3 - 4,3,3,1 - timp.,perc. - str. 45:00 S.A.M.R.O.
—— PIOBAIREACHD CONCERTO NO. 1 (FOR PIANO AND
ORCH.)
    2,2,3,2 - 4,2,3,1 - timp.,perc. - pf. - str. 32:00 S.A.M.R.O.
—— THE POLISH WOMAN (BALLET) %
    1,1,2,1 - 2,2,1,0 - timp. - pf. - str. 28:00 S.A.M.R.O.
—— STRALOCH SUITE
    2,2,2,2 - 4,2,3,0 - timp.,perc. - hp. - str. 20:00 S.A.M.R.O.
    or:
    str.
—— SYMPHONY NO. 1 IN C MINOR ("FUNERAL MARCH"
SYMPHONY)
    3,2,2,2 - 4,3,3,0 - str.   35:00 S.A.M.R.O.
—— SYMPHONY NO. 2
    3,2,3,3 - 4,3,3,1 - timp.,perc. - hp. - str. 38:00 S.A.M.R.O.
—— VAN RIEBEECK CONCERTO (FOR PIANO AND ORCH.)
    3,3,3,3 - 4,3,3,1 - timp.,perc. - pf. - str. 20:00 S.A.M.R.O.

CHLUBNA, Osvald
—— ANDANTE FOR VIOLIN AND SMALL ORCH.
    1,1,1,1 - 3,0,0,0 - hp. - str.   11:00 Bo. Hawkes.
—— AUTUMN CARNIVAL
    3,3,3,3 - 4,3,3,1 - timp.,perc.,cel. - hp. - str. 8:00 Bo. Hawkes.
—— COMEDY OVERTURE
    3,3,3,3 - 4,3,3,1 - timp.,perc. - 2 hp. - str. 8:00 Bo. Hawkes.
—— FANTASIA IN C MINOR (FOR VIOLA AND ORCH.)
    3,2,3,3 - 3,2,3,0 - hp. - str. 11:00 Bo. Hawkes.

CHOPIN, Frédéric - AUBERT, Louis
—— LA NUIT ENSORCELÉE (BALLET SUITE)
    3,3,3,3 - 4,4,3,1 - timp.,perc.,cel.,glock. - hp. - str. 20:00 Salabert.

CHOPIN, Frédéric - BOUTNIKOFF, Ivan
—— CHOPINIANA SUITE (IN 7 MOVTS.)
    2(2nd alt. with picc.),2,2,2 - 4,2,3,1 - timp.,perc.(3),glock. - hp. -
    str.   27:00 Arranger.
—— SONATA FOR SYMPHONY ORCH. ("VISIONS FUGITIVES"),
OP. 35 (IN 4 MOVTS.)
    *3,*3,*3,*3 - 4,2,3,1 - timp.,perc.(3),glock. - hp. - str.
          18:00 Arranger.

CHOPIN, Frédéric - DOUGLAS, Roy
—— LES SYLPHIDES
    2,2,2,2 - 4,2,3,0 - timp.,perc. - hp. - str.   26:00 Bo. Hawkes.
    or:
    1,1,2,1 - 2,2,1,0 - timp.,perc. - hp. - pf. - str.

CHOPIN, Frédéric - DUBENSKY, Arcady
—— ETUDE (FOR STRING ORCH.)
    str.   5:00 Ricordi.

CHOPIN, Frédéric - FINCK, Herman
—— CHOPINIANA
    Bo. Hawkes.

CHOPIN, Frédéric - FRANCAIX, Jean
—— TWENTY-FOUR PRELUDES, OP. 28
    3,3,3,3 - 4,3,3,2 - timp., perc.(3, incl. 2 on timp.) - hp. - str.
    25:00 Presser.

CHOPIN, Frédéric - ISAAC, Merle
—— LES SYLPHIDES: MUSIC FROM THE BALLET
    C. Fischer.

CHOPIN, Frédéric - KAY, Hershy
—— THE CONCERT (BALLET) (FOR SOLO PIANO AND ORCH.)
    %
    2,2,2,2 - 4,2,3,1 - timp.,perc. (3) - pf. - str.   Arranger.

CHOPIN, Frédéric - KRAMER, A. Walter
—— FUGUE IN A MINOR (FOR STRINGS)
    str.   Galaxy.

CHOPIN, Frédéric - MESSAGER, A. - VIDAL, P.
—— SUITE DE DANSES (BALLET SUITE)
    4,3,2,3 - 4,4,3,1 - timp., perc. - hp. - str.   25:00 Salabert.

CHOPIN, Frédéric - NICODÉ, J. L.
—— CONCERT ALLEGRO, OP. 46 (FOR PIANO AND ORCH.)
    2,2,2,2 - 4,2,3,0 - timp. - pf. - str.   18:00 Galaxy.

CHOPIN, Frédéric - RIEGE, Ernest
—— SCHERZO IN B MINOR
    3,2,2,3 - 4,2,3,1 - timp.,perc.,xyl. - 2 hp. - str. 12:00 F. Colombo.

CHOPIN, Frédéric - TESSIER, Albert D.
—— FANTAISIE, OP. 49 (FOR PIANO AND ORCH.) (1932)
    *3,*3,2,*3 - 4,3,2,1 - timp. - pf. - str.   17:00 Arranger.

CHOPIN, Frédéric - WILSON, Mortimer
—— TWO PRELUDES (FOR STRINGS)
    hp. (ad lib.) - str.   Witmark.

CHRISTENSEN, Bernhard
—— CONCERT SUITE FOR TENOR SAXOPHONE AND STRING ORCH.
    ten.sax. - str.   13:00 Mannheimer.
—— MUSIC FOR STRING ORCH.
    str.   11:00 Mannheimer.

CHRISTENSEN, James
—— METAMORPHOSIS
    4:00 Almitra.
—— VARIATIONS FOR 2 FLUTES AND STRING ORCH. (1962)
    2 fl. - str.   6:00 Composer.
—— VARIATIONS ON AN ORIGINAL THEME
    5:00 Almitra.

CHRISTIANSEN, Carl
—— I DUR OCH MOLL (SUITE)
    2,2,2,2 - 2,2,1,0 - timp.,perc. - hp. - str   19:00 S.T.I.M.
—— THE TOY BOX
    2,1,2,2 - 2,1,1,0   13:00 Bo. Hawkes.

CHRISTIANSEN, Henning
—— CORRESPONDENCE, OP. 15 (FOR BASS-CLARINET AND ORCH.)
    12:00 K.O.D.A.
—— E. O. S., OP. 6 (CONCERT OVERTURE)
    7:00 K.O.D.A.
—— INFORMATIONS (1965)
    0,4,4,0 - 0,4,4,0   9:00 K.O.D.A.
—— THE MISSING SYMPHONY, OP. 69-C
    17:00 K.O.D.A.

—— OVERTURE NO. 1
    str.   10:00 K.O.D.A.
—— PERCEPTIVE CONSTRUCTIONS II, OP. 28 (FOR CHAMBER ORCH.)
    19:00 Henmar.
—— RHAPSODY FOR CLARINET AND ORCH., OP. 2
    7:00 K.O.D.A.
—— A ROSE TO MISS STEIN, OP. 31
    str.   14:00 K.O.D.A.
—— SPACE AND OBJECT, OP. 23
    7:00 K.O.D.A.
—— TO PLAY TO DAY, OP. 25 (CONCERTO FOR THREE VOICES, PIANO AND ORCH.)
    45:00 K.O.D.A.
—— YOUTH (SUITE)
    Recorder - hpsc. - str.   K.O.D.A.

CHRISTOFF, Dimiter
—— SYMPHONIC EPISODES
    *3,2,2,2 - 3,2,2,0 - perc.,xyl. - pf. - str.   11:35 Modern.

CHRISTOU, Jani
—— ANAPARASTASIS I...ASTRON (1968) (FOR BARITONE AND TWO GROUPS OF INSTRUMENTS)
    10:00 G. Schirmer.
—— ENANTIODROMA (1968)
    6,3,3,0 - 4,4,3,1 - perc.(9) - pf. - str.   15:00 G. Schirmer.
—— MYSTERION (1969) (FOR THREE SATB CHORUSES AND ORCH.)
    3,3,3,0 - 4,4,4,1 - perc.(5),cel. - hpsc. - pf. - str.
    25:00 G. Schirmer.
—— PHOENIX MUSIC
    3,0,2,2 - 4,3,3,1 - timp.,cel.,xyl. - hp. - str. 12:15 Ricordi.
—— SIX SONGS BY T. S. ELIOT
    3,2,3,2 - 4,3,3,1 - timp., perc. - hp. - str.   15:00 Presser.
—— SIX SONGS BY T. S. ELIOT (FOR MEZZO-SOPRANO AND ORCH.)
    2,2,3,2 - 4,3,3,1 - perc. - str.   11:50 Henmar.

CHULAKI, Mikhail
—— SYMPHONY NO. 2
    3,3,3,3 - 4,3,3,1 - timp.,perc.,cel. - 2 hp. - str. 38:00 G. Schirmer.

CIGLIČ, Zvonimir
—— CONCERTINO FOR HARP AND STRING ORCH.
    hp. - str.   13:00 Hans Gerig.
—— LE RIVAGE DES DANCEUSES (CHOREOGRAPHIC SYMPHONIC POEM)
    2(2nd alt. with picc.),2(2nd alt. with Eng. hn.),2(2nd alt. with b.-cl.),2(2nd alt. with c.-bn.) - 4,4,3,1 - timp.,perc.(6),cel. - 2 hp. - pf. - str.   16:00 Hans Gerig.
—— SINFONIA APPASSIONATA
    2(2nd alt. with picc.),2(2nd alt. with Eng. hn.),2(2nd alt. with b.-cl.),2(2nd alt. with c.-bn.) - 4,3,3,1 - timp.,perc.(3) - 2 hp. - pf. - str.   33:00 Hans Gerig.

CIKKER, Ján
—— BATTLE (SYMPHONIC POEM)
    Bo. Hawkes.
—— CAPRICCIO
    Bo. Hawkes.
—— HOMMAGE À BEETHOVEN (1970)
    *3,*3,*3,2 - 4,3,3,1 - timp.,perc.(4) - hp. - str. 13:00 G. Schirmer.
—— MORNING (SYMPHONIC POEM)
    Bo. Hawkes.
—— REMEMBRANCES (1954) (IN 4 MOVTS.)
    1,1,1,1 - 1,0,0,0 - str.   18:00 Bo. Hawkes.
—— SELIG SIND DIE TOTEN (MEDITATION ON A THEME OF HEINRICH SCHÜTZ)(1964)
    *3,2,*3,2 - 4,3,3,1 - timp.,perc.(3) - hp. - str. 11:00 G. Schirmer.
—— SLOVAK SUITE, OP. 22 (1943) (IN 5 MOVTS.)
    Bo. Hawkes.
—— SPRING SYMPHONY (1937)
    Bo. Hawkes.
—— SUMMER (SYMPHONIC POEM)
    Bo. Hawkes.
—— SYMPHONIETTA
    2,3,2,2 - 4,2,3,0 - timp.,perc.,cel. - hp. - str. 14:00 Bo. Hawkes.

CILENŠEK, Johann
—— CONCERTO FOR CELLO AND ORCH.
    2,2,3,2 - 4,2,3,1 - timp. - str.   22:00 Tetra.

—— CONCERTO FOR VIOLIN AND ORCH. (1953)
2,2,2,2 - 4,2,3,0 - timp. - str.   26:00 Tetra.
—— SYMPHONY NO. 1 (1954)
2,2,2,2 - 4,2,3,1 - timp.,perc. - str.   33:00 Tetra.

CIMADOR, Giovanni - SLATFORD, Rodney
—— CONCERTO IN G, FOR DOUBLE BASS AND ORCH.
0,2,0,0 - 2,0,0,0 - str.   Galaxy.

CIMAROSA, Domenico - BENJAMIN, Arthur
—— CONCERTO FOR OBOE (OR CLARINET) AND STRINGS (IN 4 MOVTS.)
ob. (or cl.) - str.   10:00 Bo. Hawkes.

CIMAROSA, Domenico - BORMIOLI, P.
—— OVERTURE TO "IL FANATICO PER GLI ANTICHI ROMANI"
2,2,2,2 - 2,2,0,0 - timp. - str.   8:00 Leeds.
—— OVERTURE TO "LA BELLA GRECA"
2,2,2,2 - 2,2,0,0 - timp. - str.   9:30 Leeds.

CIMAROSA, Domenico - CARSE, A.
—— OVERTURE TO "THE IMPRESARIO"
2,2,0,2 - 2,2,0,0 - timp. - str.   5:00 Galaxy.

CIMAROSA, Domenico - MALIPIERO, G. F.
—— LA CIMAROSIANA (5 SYMPHONIC FRAGMENTS)
*3,2,2,2 - 4,2,0,0 - perc. - str.   12:00 G. Schirmer.

CIMAROSA, Domenico - NAPOLITANO, F. M.
—— OVERTURE TO "I TRACI AMANTI"
2 ob.,bn. - 2 hn. - str.   Henmar.

CIMAROSA, Domenico - OUBRADOUS, Fernand
—— CONCERTANTE FOR 2 FLUTES AND CHAMBER ORCH.
2,0,0,1 - 2,0,0,0 - str.   18:00 Presser.

CIMAROSA, Domenico - RAPALO
—— SINFONIA IN D MAJOR
1,2,0,0 - 2,0,0,0 - str.   8:00 Henmar.

CIMAROSA, Domenico - THILDE, Jean
—— CONCERTO IN B FLAT, FOR OBOE AND STRINGS
ob. - str.   7:35 Presser.
—— CONCERTO IN C, FOR OBOE AND STRINGS
ob. - str.   7:00 Presser.
—— CONCERTO IN G, FOR OBOE AND STRINGS
ob. - str.   7:25 Presser.

CIMAROSA, Domenico - TONI, Alceo
—— OVERTURE TO "ARTEMISIA"
0,2,2,2 - 2,2,0,0 - str.   7:00 Bo. Hawkes.
—— OVERTURE TO "GIANNINA E BERNARDONE"
0,2,0,0 - 2,0,0,0 - timp. - str.   6:00 Bo. Hawkes.
—— OVERTURE TO "IL GIORNO FELICE"
0,2,2,2 - 2,2,0,0 - str.   6:00 Bo. Hawkes.
—— OVERTURE TO "IL MATRIMONIO PER RAGGIRO"
0,2,0,2 - 2,0,0,0 - str.   7:00 Bo. Hawkes.
—— OVERTURE TO "LE ASTUZIE FEMMINILI"
0,2,2,2 - 2,0,0,0 - str.   4:00 Bo. Hawkes.
—— OVERTURE TO "LE TRAME DELUSE"
0,2,0,2 - 2,0,0,0 - str.   7:00 Bo. Hawkes.
—— RONDÒ DI CURIAZIO (FROM "ORAZI E CURIAZI") (FOR TENOR AND SMALL ORCH.)
0,2,2,1 - 2,0,0,0 - str.   8:00 Bo. Hawkes.

CIMAROSA, Domenico - WINTER, Aubrey
—— OVERTURE TO "THE SECRET MARRIAGE"
                                                    8:00 Bo. Hawkes.
—— OVERTURE TO "THE THREE BROTHERS"
                                                    5:30 Bo. Hawkes.

CIPCI, Kruno
—— CONCERTINO FOR OBOE AND STRINGS
ob. - str.   18:00 Hans Gerig.

CIRONE, Anthony J.
—— DOUBLE CONCERTO FOR TWO PERCUSSIONISTS AND ORCH. (IN 1 MOVT.)
2,2,2,2 - 2,2,2,0 - timp.,perc.(2) - str.   7:00 Composer.

CIRRI, Giambattista - BONELLI
—— CONCERTO IN D MAJOR FOR CELLO, CEMBALO AND STRINGS, OP. 14, NO. 6
cemb. - str.   19:00 Henmar.

CIRY, Michel
—— MUSIQUE POUR UN RÉTABLE: "LA CRUCIFIXION"
0,0,1,*2 - 2,2,3,0 - timp.,perc.,xyl. - 2 pf.   7:00 Eds. Fran.
—— STELE POUR UN HEROS
                                                    8:00 S.A.C.E.M.
—— SYMPHONY NO. 6 (Text: Rainer Maria Rilke)
                                                    S.A.C.E.M.

CITROEN, Henk
—— CONCERTO FOR HORN AND ORCH.
2,2,2,2 - 2,2,2,0 - timp.,perc. - hp. - str.   25:00 Henmar.
—— SYMPHONIE NO. 2
2,2,2,2 - 4,2,3,1 - timp.,perc. - hp. - str.   25:00 Henmar.

CLAQUÉ, Yves
—— SEQUENCE 87
2,2,2,2 - 4,3,3,1 - timp.,perc.(3) - hp. - str.   9:00 Salabert.

CLARK, Frank J.
—— LITTLE BLUE OVERTURE
1,1,2,1 - 2,2,2,0 - timp.,perc.(2) - str.   4:10 Composer.

CLARK, Robert Keys
—— THE ANTIC MUSE, OP. 35 (1962) (IN 1 MOVT.)
1,1,1,1 - 0,1,0,0 - perc.(1),glock. - str.   13:00 Composer.
—— ANTIPHON, OP. 20 (1955)
org. - str.   8:00 Composer.
—— CONCERTO FOR VIOLIN, STRINGS AND TIMPANI, OP. 39 (1965) (IN 1 MOVT.)
timp. - str.   22:00 Composer.
—— THE MAGIC TRUMPET, OP. 28 (A MUSICAL FAIRY TALE FOR CHILDREN) % (1957) (Text: After Hans Christian Anderson)
1,1,1,1 - 1,1,0,0 - perc.(1) - str.   60:00 EV.
—— MONUMENT, OP. 51 (1975)
3(alt. with 3 picc.),*3,*3,*3 - 4,3,3,1 - timp.,perc.(3) - str.
                                                    15:30 Composer.
—— REPERCUSSIONS, OP. 46 (STATEMENT FOR ORCH.) (1968) (IN 1 MOVT.)
3(alt. with 3 picc.),3,*3,*3 - 4,3,3,1 - timp.,perc.(4), bells, vibra. - str.
                                                    10:00 Composer.
—— SYMPHONY NO. 1, OP. 10 (1952)
1. Slow; 2. Very fast; 3. Moving
2,2,2,(2nd alt. with b.-cl.),2 - 4,2,2,0 - timp.,perc.(2) - str
                                                    23:00 Composer.
—— SYMPHONY NO. 2, OP. 12 (1953) (IN 3 MOVTS.)
3,*3,*3,*3 - 4,3,3,1 - timp.,perc.(3) - str.   18:00 Composer.
—— SYMPHONY NO. 3, OP. 38 (1963) (IN 4 MOVTS.)
2,2,2,2 - 4,3,3,1 - timp.,perc.(3), bells - str.   18:00 Composer.

CLARKE, Frederick R. C.
—— BEL AND THE DRAGON (SHORT ORATORIO) (FOR SOPRANO, TENOR, BARITONE, MIXED CHORUS AND ORCH.) (1954) (Text: The Apocrypha)
2(2nd alt. with picc.),2,2,2 - 4,2,3,1 - timp.,perc. - str.
                                                    30:00 CanMusCtr.
—— FESTIVAL OVERTURE (1955)
*3,2(2nd alt. with Eng. hn.),2,2 - 4,3,3,1 - timp.,perc. - hp. - str.
                                                    8:00 CanMusCtr.
—— FESTIVAL TE DEUM (FOR MIXED CHORUS AND ORCH.) (1972) (Text: in English)
2,2,2,2 - 4,3,3,1 - timp.,perc. - str.   13:10 CanMusCtr.
—— IMPROMPTU FOR ORCHESTRA (1957)
2,2,2,2 - 4,2,3,1 - timp.,perc. - str.   5:00 CanMusCtr.
—— MINI-SUITE (1971) (IN 3 MOVTS.)
2,2,2,2 - 4,2,3,1 - timp.,perc. - str.   6:00 CanMusCtr.
—— MISSA DE ANGELIS FANTASIA (FOR ORGAN AND STRINGS) (1963)
org. - str.   5:00 CanMusCtr.
—— OVERTURE TO "BEL AND THE DRAGON" (1954)
2(2nd alt. with picc.),2,2,2 - 4,2,3,1 -timp.,perc. - str.
                                                    7:00 CanMusCtr.
—— PASTORALE AND FUGUE OR THE CHRISTMAS HYMN "PUER NOBIS NASCITUR" (FOR STRING ORCH.) (1975)
str.   5:00 CanMusCtr.
—— SONATA FOR ORGAN AND STRINGS (1958) (IN 4 MOVTS.)
org. - str.   17:00 CanMusCtr.

CLARKE, Jeremiah - JACQUES, Reginald
—— TRUMPET VOLUNTARY
    tpt. - str.   5:00 Oxford.

CLAUSEN, Alf. H.
—— WHEN JEREMIAH SANG THE BLUES (1974)
    (CONTEMPORARY ORATORIO FOR NARRATOR, SOLO
    VOICES, SATB CHORUS, JAZZ ENSEMBLE AND ORCH.)
    (Text: Tommy Wolf)
               132:00 Karleigh.

CLEMENTI, Aldo
—— COLLAGE (SUITE FROM THE MUSICAL ACTION)
               13:00 Leeds.
—— COLLAGE (1-ACT MUSICAL ACTION) %
    2,2,3,2 sax.,1 - 2,2,1,0 - perc.,vibra.,xyl. - recorded voice - pf. - str.
               Leeds.
—— EPISODI (EPISODES)
    2,2,3,0 - 3,1,1,1 - timp.,perc.(5),cel.,xyl. - hp. - str.   10:00 Leeds.
—— IDEOGRAMS NO. 1 (FOR 16 INSTRS.)
    2,0,3,1 - 3,2,1,0 - perc.(2),xyl. - pf. - d.-b.   12:00 Leeds.
—— IDEOGRAMS NO. 2 (FOR FLUTE AND 17 INSTRS.)
    1,0,4,4 sax.,0 - 0,2,2,0 - perc.,vibra.,xyl. - pf. - d.-b.   9:00 Leeds.
—— INFORMEL NO. 1 (FOR PERCUSSION AND KEYBOARD; 12
    PLAYERS)
    perc.,bells,cel.,glock.,vibra.,xyl. - pf.   4:00 Leeds.
—— INFORMEL NO. 2 (FOR 15 PLAYERS)
    1,1,1,1 - 1,0,0,0 - glock. - harm. - hp. - pf. (alt. with cel.) - str.
               5:00 Leeds.
—— INFORMEL NO. 3
               Leeds.
—— RETICOLLO: 11 (FOR 11 INSTRUMENTS) (1966)
    hn. - cel.,glock. - guit.,mand. - hpsc. - hp. - 2 vln.,vla.,c.
               MCA Music.
—— SEVEN SCENES (FOR CHAMBER ORCH.)
               Leeds.
—— TRE STUDI (3 STUDIES)
    1,0,2,1 - 2,1,1,0 - xyl. - hp. - pf. - str.(no d.-b.)   10:00 Leeds.
—— VARIANTE B
               Leeds.

CLEMENTI, Muzio - SOPKIN, Henry
—— SONATINA, OP. 36, NO. 1
               C. Fischer.
—— SONATINA, OP. 36, NO. 2
               C. Fischer.

CLEMENTS, Peter J.
—— SESTINA FOR ORCHESTRA (1965)
    *3,*3,*3,*3 - 4,3,3,1 - timp.,perc.(6, incl. 3 on timp.) - hp. - pf. -
    str.   10:00 CanMusCtr.
—— SUITE GROTESQUE (1972) (IN 4 MOVTS.)
    *3,*3,*3,*3 - 4,3,3,1 - timp.,perc.(4) - synthesizer or tape-recorder
    - hp. - pf.(or cel.) - str.   25:00 CanMusCtr.

CLEVE, Halfdan
—— CONCERTO NO. 4 FOR PIANO AND ORCH., OP. 12
    2,2,2,2 - 4,2,3,0 - timp. - pf. - str.   30:00 T.O.N.O.
—— CONCERTO NO. 5 FOR PIANO AND ORCH., OP. 20
    2,2,2,2 - 4,2,3,0 - timp. - pf. - str.   32:00 T.O.N.O.
—— THREE PIECES FOR ORCH., OP. 14
    3,2,2,2 - 4,2,0,0 - timp.,prrc. - hp. - str.   8:00 Norsk Mfl.

CLIFF, Charles Joseph
—— OVERTURE PENTATOMIC (1951)
    3(3rd alt. with picc.),*3,*3,3(3rd alt. with c.-bn.) - 4,3,3,1 -
    timp.,perc.(4),bells,xyl. - hp. - str.   6:00 Composer.
—— PASSACAGLIA FOR ORCHESTRA (1960)
    3(3rd alt. with picc.),*3,*3,3(3rd alt. with c.-bn.) - 4,3,3,1 -
    timp.,perc.(4) - hp. - str.   8:00 Composer.

CLIFFE, F.
—— SYMPHONY IN C MINOR
    2,3,2,2 - 4,2,3,1 - timp. - str.   Novello.

CLIFFORD, Hubert
—— FIVE ENGLISH NURSERY TUNES
    2,2,2,2 - 4,2,3,0 - timp.,perc. - str.   14:00 Bo. Hawkes.
—— FOUR SKETCHES FOR "AS YOU LIKE IT"
    pf.(ad lib.) - str.   10:00 Galaxy.
—— SERENADE FOR STRINGS
    str.   17:00 G. Schirmer.

CLIQUET-PLEYEL, Henri
—— CONCERTO FOR PIANO (RIGHT-HAND) AND ORCH.
    2,2,3,2 - 2,2,2,1 - perc. - hp. - pf. - str.   21:00 EV.
—— CONCERTO FOR PIANO RIGHT-HAND AND ORCH.
    2,2,3,2 - 2,2,2,1 - perc. - hp. - pf. - str.   21:00 EV.
—— SARDANE
    2,2,2,2 - 2,2,2,0 - timp.,perc. - str.   12:00 EV.
—— SCENES DE BALLET
    2,2,2,2 - 2,2,2,0 - perc. - hp. - str.   21:30 EV.

CLIQUET-PLEYEL, Henri - SAUGUET, Henri
—— ELLE AIMÉE (BALLET) % (AFTER "PROMENADES
    ESPAGNOLES")
    1,1,2,1 - 2,1,1,0 - timp.,perc. - pf. - str.   10:00 EV.

CLOKEY, Joseph W.
—— A CANTICLE OF PRAISE (FOR SATB CHORUS AND ORCH.)
    2,2,2,2 - 4,3,3,1 - timp.,perc.,bells - org. - pf.(ad lib.) - str.
               10:00 Belw-Mills.
—— CHILD JESUS (CHRISTMAS CANTATA) (FOR CHORUS AND
    ORCH.)
    1,1,2,1 - 2,2,1,1 - timp.,perc. - str.   25:00 Western.
—— CHRIST CONQUERETH (EASTER ANTHEM) (FOR CHORUS
    AND ORCH.)
    2,2,2,2 - 4,3,3,1 - timp.,perc. (3) - str.   6:00 J. Fischer.
—— FOR HE IS RISEN (EASTER CANTATA) (FOR 4 SOLOISTS,
    CHORUS AND ORCH.)
    2,1,2,1 - 2,2,2,0 - timp.,per. - pf. - str.   30:00 Western.
—— HOW SUMMER CAME (INDIAN LEGEND) (FOR WOMEN'S
    CHORUS AND ORCH.)
    1,0,2,0 - 2,2,2,0 - timp. - pf. - str.   11:00 J. Fischer.
—— THE MARSHES OF GLYN (FOR CHORUS AND ORCH.)
    4 hn. - timp. - str.   10:00 H-McCreary.
—— MILADIE (A CAVALIER SUITE) (FOR MEN'S CHORUS AND
    STRINGS) (IN 5 MOVTS.)
    str.   J. Fischer.
—— NIGHTS (FOR WOMEN'S CHORUS AND ORCH.)
    2(2nd alt. with picc.),2,2,2 - 4,2,3,1 - timp.,perc. (3) - org. (ad lib.)
    - pf. - str.   11:00 J. Fischer.
—— PARTITA IN G MINOR FOR ORGAN AND STRINGS (IN 6
    MOVTS.)
    org. - str. (no. d.-b.)   18:00 Gray.
—— STEADFAST IN FAITH (CANTATA) (FOR BARITONE, SATB
    CHORUS AND SMALL ORCH.)
    2 tpt. - timp. - org. - str.   23:00 Belw-Mills.
—— SYMPHONY IN E
    2(2nd alt. with picc.), 2(2nd alt. with Eng. hn.),2,2 - 4,3,3,1 -
    timp.,perc. (3) - str.   45:00 Composer.
—— THE TEMPLE (ORATORIO) (FOR SATB SOLO VOICES, SATB
    CHORUS AND ORCH.)
    2,2,2,2 - 4,3,3,1 - timp.,perc. - hp. - str.   60:00 Belw-Mills.
—— THE VISION (CHORAL TONE POEM) (FOR ALTO, CHORUS
    AND ORCH.)
    2,1,2,1 - 2,2,2,0 - timp.,perc. (2) - org. (ad lib.) - pf. - str.
               60:00 Gray.
—— WE BEHELD HIS GLORY (SACRED CANTATA) (FOR 4
    SOLOISTS, CHORUS AND ORCH.)
    4 hn., 2 tpt.,3 trb. - org. - str.   60:00 J. Fischer.
—— WHEN THE CHRIST CHILD CAME, OP. 38 (CHRISTMAS
    CANTATA) (FOR 4 SOLOISTS, CHORUS AND ORCH.)
    2 tpt., 2 trb. - org. pf. str.   30:00 Western.

CLOSTRE, Adrienne
—— CONCERTO FOR OBOE AND CHAMBER ORCH.
    1,1,1,1 - 2,1,0,0 - perc.(2) - str.   13:30 Presser.
—— CONCERTO FOR TRUMPET AND STRINGS
    tpt. - str.   12:00 Presser.
—— CONCERTO FOR VIOLIN, FLUTE AND ORCH.
    2,1,1,2 - 2,2,1,0 - perc. - str.   15:30 Presser.

CLOUGH, Robert Arnold
—— BAGDEN LODGE: SUITE (FOR CHAMBER ORCH.)
    1,0,1,1 - 2,0,0,0 - str.   20:00 Cantabile.
—— CONCERTINO 1972 (FOR PIANO AND ORCH.)
    2,1,2,2 - 2,1,1,0 - timp.,perc. - pf. - str.   15:00 Cantabile.
    or:
    *3,*3,2,2 - 4,2,3,1 - timp.,perc. - cel. - hp. - pf. - str.
    or:
    str.
—— PSALM 51 (FOR CHORUS AND ORCH.)
    *3,*3,*3,*3 - 4,2,3,1 - timp.,perc. - str.   5:00 Cantabile.

CLUZEAU-MORTET, Luis
—— LLANURAS (PLAINS) (FIRST NATIVE SYMPHONIC
IMPRESSION) (1932)
3,2,2,2 - 4,4,3,1 - timp.,cel. - hp. - str.   Fleisher.

COATES, Eric
—— CINDERELLA (A FANTASY)
Chappell.
—— THE ENCHANTED GARDEN (BALLET) %
Chappell.
—— FOUR CENTURIES SUITE (IN 4 MOVTS.)
2,2,2-3,3 sax.,2 - 4,3,3,0 - timp.,perc. - hp. - str.
23:30 Bo. Hawkes.
—— FOUR WAYS SUITE
Chappell.
—— FROM MEADOW TO MAYFAIR (SUITE)
Chappell.
—— FROM THE COUNTRYSIDE (SUITE) (IN 3 MOVTS.)
1,2,2,2 - 4,2,3,0 - timp.,perc. - str.   12:00 Bo. Hawkes.
—— JOYOUS YOUTH (SUITE)
Chappell.
—— LONDON AGAIN SUITE (IN 3 MOVEMENTS)
14:30 Chappell.
—— LONDON SUITE (IN 3 MOVTS.)
12:30 Chappell.
—— MINIATURE SUITE (IN 3 MOVTS.)
3,2,2,2 - 2 hn. - timp.,perc. - str.   13:00 Bo. Hawkes.
—— SAXO-RHAPSODY (FOR ALTO SAXOPHONE AND ORCH.)
Chappell.
—— SUMMER DAYS SUITE
Chappell.
—— THE THREE BEARS (FANTASY)
9:30 Chappell.
—— THE THREE ELIZABETHS (SUITE) (IN 3 MOVTS.)
19:30 Chappell.
—— THE THREE MEN (SUITE FROM THE FILM)
Chappell.

COATES, Leon
—— INCIDENTAL MUSIC FOR "OTHELLO" (1956)
2,2,2,2 - 2,2,0,0 - timp. - pf. - str.   15:00 P.R.S.
—— RHAPSODY FOR CLARINET AND STRINGS (1961)
cl. - str.   5:00 P.R.S.

COCACCHI, Stephan
—— SINFONIETTA NO. 2 FOR STRING ORCH., OP. 113
str.   16:00 Mannheimer.

COCKSHOTT, Gerald
—— DIVERTIMENTO (1960)
2,1,2,1 - 2,1,0,0 - timp.,perc. - str.   8:00 P.R.S.

COELHO, Rui
—— PRELUDE ET DANSE DE "LAS BODAS" (FROM THE OPERA
"INES PEREIRA")
2,2,2,2 - 4,2,3,0   6:00 Salabert.

COGNI, Giulio
—— IN TENEBRIS
3,2,2,3 - 4,3,3,0 - timp.,perc.,xyl. - 1-2 hp. - 1-2 pf. - str.
10:00 Bo. Hawkes.

COHEN, David
—— CONCERTINO FOR OBOE AND STRINGS (IN 3 MOVTS.)
ob. - pf. - str.(no d.-b.)   10:30 Composer.
—— ESCAPADE FOR ORCHESTRA
2(2nd alt. with picc.),2,2,2 - 4,2,3,1 - timp.,perc.(3) - pf. - str.
8:00 Composer.
—— OVERTURE FOR STRING ORCH.
str.   8:00 Composer.
—— OVERTURE NO. 1 FOR ORCHESTRA (1951)
2,2,2,2 - 4,2,2,0 - timp. - str.   6:00 Composer.
—— OVERTURE NO. 2 FOR ORCHESTRA (1954)
2,2,*2,2 - 4,2,2,1 - timp. - str.   8:00 Composer.
—— STUDY FOR ORCHESTRA
2,2,2,2 - 4,2,3,0 - timp. - pf. - str.   6:00 Composer.
—— SYMPHONY NO. 1 (1965) (IN 4 MOVTS.)
2(2nd alt. with picc.),2,2,2 - 4,2,3,1 - timp.,cel. - pf. - str.
27:30 Composer.
—— SYMPHONY NO. 2 (1970)
1. Mosaic; 2. Linear
2,2,2,2 - 4,2,3,1 - timp.,perc.(2) - str.   23:30 Composer.

COHEN, Jerome D.
—— BEYOND MIND AND SPEECH (1973)
*3,2,2,2 - 4,3,3,1 - timp. - str.   3:00 Composer.
—— CAPE ANN (CONCERT OVERTURE NO. 2) (1973)
*3,2,2,2 - 4,3,3,1 - timp.,perc.(5-6),glock.,xyl. - str.
13:00 Composer.
—— CONCERT OVERTURE NO. 1
*3,2,*3,2 - 4,3,3,1 - timp.,perc.,glock. - hp.(or pf.) - str.
4:00 Fema.
—— CONCERTO FOR FLUTE AND ORCH. (1957) (IN 3 MOVTS.)
1,2,0,0 - 2,0,0,0 - str.   20:00 Composer.

COHEN, Joel
—— POEM FOR ORCH.
2,2,*3,2 - 4,2,2,1 - timp.,perc.,bells,glock. - str.   5:00 Fema.
—— SUITE FOR OBOE AND ORCH.
2,1,*3,1 - 4,2,1,0 - timp. - str.   7:30 Fema.

COHEN, Joseph Morris
—— CONCERT PIECE, OP. 5
1. Adagio assai; 2. Allegro
2(2nd alt. with picc.),2,*3,2 - 4,3,3,1 - timp.,perc.(3) - str.
18:00 Composer.
—— RHAPSODY FOR THREE, OP. 2 (BALLET IN 3 SCENES) %
*3,*3,*3,2 - 4,3,4,1 - timp.,perc.(3) - pf.(alt. with cel.) - str.
28:00 Composer.

COHEN, Sol B.
—— A BALLAD OF OLYMPUS
3(3rd alt. with picc.),*3,2,2 - 4,2,3,1 - timp.,perc. (2),cel. - hp. -
str.   18:00 Composer.
—— THE LAND OF FANTASY (SUITE IN 4 MOVTS.)
*3,2,2,2 - 4,2,3,1 - timp.,perc. (2),cel. - hp. - str. 15:00 Composer.

COHN, Arthur
—— CONCERTO FOR FLUTE AND ORCH. (IN 4 MOVTS.)
3,3,3,3 - 4,3,3,1 - timp.,perc.,cel. - hp. - str.   45:00 Mills.
—— FOUR PRELUDES, OP. 27
str.   19:00 Mills.
—— FOUR SYMPHONIC DOCUMENTS, OP. 30
3(3rd alt. with picc.),3(3rd alt. with Eng. hn.), ob.
d'amore (ad lib.), 3(3rd alt. with b.-cl.), 3(3rd alt. with c.-bn.) -
4,3,3,1 - timp.,perc. (6) - hp. - str.   32:00 Mills.
—— HISTRIONICS, OP. 32 (FOR STRINGS) (IN 6 MOVTS.)
str.   28:00 Mills.
—— KADDISH FOR ORCHESTRA
2(2nd alt. with picc.),2(2nd alt. with Eng.hn.),2,2 - 4,3,3,1 -
timp.,perc.(3) - str.   7:00 Mills.
—— QUINTUPLE CONCERTO FOR FIVE ANCIENT
INSTRUMENTS AND ORCH., OP. 31
3(3rd alt. with picc.),3(3rd alt. with Eng. hn.),3(3rd alt. with
b.-cl.),3(3rd alt. with c.-bn.) - 4,3,3,1 - timp.,perc. (6) - hp. - hpsc.
- str. (with solo pardessus de viol, viol d'amour, viola da gamba
and basse de viol)   52:00 Mills.
—— RETROSPECTIONS, OP. 11 (SUITE FOR STRING ORCH.) (IN
3 MOVTS.)
str.   17:00 Mills.
—— SUITE FOR ORCHESTRA, OP. 3
3(3rd alt. with picc.),3(3rd alt. with Eng. hn.),2,2 -
timp.,perc.(4),bells - 2 hp. - str.   25:00 Composer.
—— SUITE FOR VIOLA AND ORCH., OP 29A (IN 5 MOVTS.)
3(3rd alt. with picc.),3(3rd alt. with Eng. hn.), 3(3rd alt. with
b.-cl.), 3(3rd alt. with c.-bn.) - 4,3,3,0 - timp.,perc.(4) - hp. - str.
30:00 Mills.
—— SUITE NO. 2 FOR ORCHESTRA
*3,*3,*3,2 - 4,3,3,1 - timp.,perc.(3),xyl. - hp. - str.
22:00 Composer.

COHN, James
—— CONCERTINO IN G SHARP, OP. 8 (FOR PIANO AND
ORCH.) (1946) (IN 4 MOVTS.)
2,2,2,2 - 2,0,0,0 - timp.,perc.(2) - pf. - str.   22:00 Fleisher.
—— CONCERTO IN A FOR CONCERTINA (OR VIOLIN) AND
STRINGS, OP. 44 (1966) (IN 3 MOVTS.)
Concertina (or vln.) - str.   12:00 Fleisher.
—— ENCHANTED JOURNEY, OP. 35 (TWO SCENES FROM A
FAIRY-TALE BALLET) (1961) %
1(alt. with picc.),1,1,1 alto sax.,1 - 1,1,1,0 - timp.,perc.(3),xyl. - hp.
- str.   18:45 Composer.
—— THE FALL OF THE CITY, OP. 17 (1-ACT MUSIC DRAMA)
(1952) % (Text: Archibald MacLeish)
1(alt. with picc.),1,1,1 alto sax.,1 - 1,1,1,0 - timp.,perc.(2) - hp. -
str.   30:00 Composer.

—— HOMAGE, OP. 31 (1959)
1(alt. with picc.),1,1,1 alto sax.,1 - 1,1,1,0 - timp.,perc.(2-3) - str.
6:00 Fleisher.

—— THE LITTLE CIRCUS, OP. 51 (1974)
1(alt. with picc.),0,2,1(alt. with cbn.) - 2,2,1,1 - perc.(1) -
str.(optional)   6:13 Bo. Hawkes.

—— MINIATURES FOR ORCHESTRA, OP. 25-A (1975)
0,1,1,1 - 0,1(alt. with flg.),0,0, - str.   14:07 Composer.

—— MUSIC FOR STRINGS, OP. 14A (1955)
1. Adagio; 2. Allegro; 3. Adagio comodo - Allegro marcato
str.   15:00 Fleisher.

—— THE PEOPLE WILL LIVE ON, OP. 7 (CANTATA) (1946) (Text:
Carl Sandburg)
2(2nd alt. with picc.),2,2,2 - 4,1,3,1 - timp.,perc.(3) - pf. - str.
19:00 Composer.

—— PROMETHEUS - AN OVERTURE, OP. 37 (1962)
1(alt. with picc.),1,1,1 alto sax.,1 - 1,1,1,0 - timp.,perc.(2) - str.
6:10 Composer.

—— SINFONIETTA IN F, OP. 6 (1946) (IN 3 MOVTS.)
1(alt. with picc.),1,2,1 - 2,0,0,0 - timp.,perc.,(2),glock. - str.
13:15 Fleisher.

—— A SONG OF THE WATERS, OP. 53 (VARIATIONS ON THE
FOLKSONG "SHENANDOAH") (1976)
1(alt. with picc.),1,1,1 alto sax.,1 - 1,1,1,0 - timp.,perc.(3) -
str.(min: 9,3,2,1)   6:22 C. Fischer.

—— SYMPHONY NO. 1 IN E FLAT, OP. 11 (1947) (IN 4 MOVTS.)
1(alt. with picc.),1,2,1 alto sax.,1 bar. sax.,*2 - 2,1,2,1 -
timp.,perc.(2),glock. - str.   17:00 Fleisher.

—— SYMPHONY NO. 2 IN F, OP. 13 (1949) (IN 4 MOVTS.)
*2,*2,*3,1 alto sax.,*2 - 2,1,2,1 - timp.,perc.(2),glock. - str.
23:30 Fleisher.

—— SYMPHONY NO. 3 IN G, OP. 27 (1955) (IN 4 MOVTS.)
1(alt. with picc.),1,1,1 alto sax.,1 - 1,1,1,0 - timp.,perc.(2) - str.
21:10 Bo. Hawkes.

—— SYMPHONY NO. 4 IN A, OP. 29 (1956) (IN 3 MOVTS.)
1(alt. with picc.),1,1,1 alto sax.,1 - 1,1,1,0 -
timp.,perc.(3),chime,glock. - str.   15:30 Bo. Hawkes.

—— SYMPHONY NO. 5 IN B FLAT, OP. 32 (1959) (IN 4 MOVTS.)
1(alt. with picc.),1,1,1 alto sax.,1 - 1,1,1,0 - timp.,perc.(3),glock. -
str.   22:30 Bo. Hawkes.

—— SYMPHONY NO. 6 IN B, OP. 43 (1965) (IN 3 MOVTS.)
1(alt. with picc.),1,1,1 alto sax.,1 - 1,1,1,0 - timp.,perc.(2) - str.
18:40 Composer.

—— SYMPHONY NO. 7, IN D, OP. 45 (1967) (IN 4 MOVTS.)
1(alt. with picc.),1,1,1 alto sax.,1,1,1,0 - timp.,perc.(2) - str.
19:32 Composer.

—— VARIATIONS ON "JOHN HENRY", OP. 46-A
*2,1,2,1 alto sax.,2 - 3,1 cnt.(or tpt.),2,3,1 - timp.,perc.(3),glock. -
str.   4:15 C. Fischer.

—— VARIATIONS ON "THE WAYFARING STRANGER", OP. 34
(1960)
1(alt. with picc.),1,1,1 alto sax.,1 - 1,1,1,0 - timp.,perc.(2),chime -
str.   10:51 Bo. Hawkes.

COHON, Baruch J.
—— LET THERE BE LIGHT (YEHI OR) (CANTATA) (FOR
BARITONE VOICE, MIXED CHORUS AND ORCH.) (1953)
(Text: Composer)
*3,*3,2,2 - 4,2,3,1 - timp.,perc.(3),bells,xyl. - pf. - str. 20:00 P.F.J.

COKER, Wilson
—— ANALOGIES
2(2nd alt. with picc.),2,2,2 - 2,1,1,0 - timp.,perc.(3),bells - pf. - str.
6:00 Composer.

—— DECLARATIVE ESSAY ("IS THERE AN EASY ROAD TO
FREEDOM?")
2,*3,*3,2 - 4,3,3,1 - timp.,perc.(5) - hp. - str.   7:00 Presser.

—— LYRIC STATEMENT
2,*3,*3,2 - 4,3,3,1 - timp.,perc.(4) - str.   8:00 Presser.

—— OVERTURE ("GIOCOSO")
*3,*3,*3,*3 - 4,4,3,1 - timp.,perc.(4) - str.   8:00 Presser.

—— PAEAN (FOR SATB CHORUS AND ORCH.)
3,*3,*3, c.-b. cl.,2 - 4,4,3,1 - timp.,perc.(4) - hp. - str.
12:30 Presser.

—— SYMPHONY NO. 1
*3,*3,*3,2 - 4,2,3,1 - timp.,perc.(5) - str.   16:00 Presser.

COLACO, Osorio - SWAAB, Reine
—— DRAMATIC OVERTURE
2,2,2,2 - 4,3,3,1 - timp.,perc. - hp. - str.   Henmar.

COLDING-JOERGENSEN, Henrik
—— SYMPHONY NO. 1 (1965)
14:00 K.O.D.A.

—— TO LOVE THE MUSIC
4,4,4,4 - 6,4,4,1 - timp.,perc.,cel. - hp. - str.   32:00 K.O.D.A.

COLE, Bruce
—— FENESTRAE SANCTAE
0,1,1,1 - 1,1,1,0 - perc. - str.   20:00 Bo. Hawkes.

—— SONGS OF MIMESIS (FOR STRING QUARTET AND ORCH.)
1,1,1,1 - 1,1,0,0 - perc. - str.   12:00 Bo. Hawkes.

COLE, George
—— MOUNT DESERT SUITE (IN 5 MOVTS.)
2,2(2nd alt. with Eng.hn.),2(2nd alt. with b.-cl.),2 - 2,2,2,0 -
timp.,perc.(2),bells,vibra.,xyl. - hp. - str.   22:35 Kimberly.

—— NEPENTHE
2,2,2,2 - 2,2,2,0 - timp.,perc.(2),bells,vibra. - hp. - str.
10:00 Composer.

COLE, Hugo
—— BLACK LION DANCES
2,1,2,1 - 2,2,1,0 - timp.,perc. - str.   12:00 Novello.

COLE, Rossetter G.
—— BALLADE FOR CELLO AND ORCH., OP. 25
2,2,2,2 - 2,2,0,0 - timp. - str.   8:00 Composer.

—— THE MAYPOLE LOVERS (OPERA): SUITE NO. 1, OP. 44 (IN 3
MOVTS.)
3(3rd alt. with picc.),*3,*3,*3 - 4,2,3,1 - timp.,perc. (2) - hp. - str.
18:00 Composer.

—— THE MAYPOLE LOVERS (OPERA): SUITE NO. 2, OP. 45 (IN 3
MOVTS.)
3(3rd alt. with picc.),*3,*3,*3 - 4,2,3,1 - timp.,perc. (2) - hp. - str.
17:00 Composer.

—— PIONEER (OVERTURE) (1818-1918), OP. 35
3(3rd alt with picc.),*3,2,*3 - 4,3,3,1 - timp.,perc. (2),glock. - hp. -
org. - str.   15:00 Composer.

—— RHAPSODY
3(3rd alt. with picc.),*3,*3,*3 - 4,2,3,1 - timp.,perc. (2) - hp. - org.
(ad lib.) - str.   8:00 Composer.

—— SYMPHONIC PRELUDE
3(3rd fl. alt. with picc.),2,2,2 - 4,3,3,1 - timp.,perc. (2) - hp. - org.
(ad lib.) - str.   7:00 Composer.

COLE, Ulric
—— ANDANTE SOSTENUTO (FOR ENGLISH HORN OR CELLO
AND CHAMBER ORCH.)
1,*2,2,0 - 2 hn. - str.   Composer.
or:
Eng.hn. (or c.) - str.

—— CONCERTO NO. 2 FOR PIANO AND ORCH. (IN 3 MOVTS.)
*3,*3,2,2(2nd alt. with c.-bn.) - 4,3,3,1 - timp.,perc. (3) - pf. - str.
22:30 Composer.

—— DIVERTIMENTO FOR TWO PIANOS AND STRINGS (IN 3
MOVTS.)
2 pf. - str.   16:00 J. Fischer.

—— NEVADA
*3,2,2,2 - 4,3,3,1 - timp.,perc. (2), xyl. - str.   12:00 Composer.

—— TWO SKETCHES FOR STRING ORCH.
str.   7:00 Composer.

COLEMAN, Ornette
—— CHAPPAQUA (SYMPHONIC POEM) (1965)
1,1,1,1 - 1,1,1,0 - perc.(1),bells - str.(2,1,1,1)   120:00 Composer.

COLERIDGE-TAYLOR, Avril
—— CEREMONIAL MARCH
3,2,2,3 - 4,3,3,1 - timp.,perc. - str.   8:00 P.R.S.

—— CONCERTO IN F MINOR, FOR PIANO AND ORCH.
2,2,2,2 - 4,2,3,1 - timp.,perc. - pf. - str.   30:00 P.R.S.

—— FROM THE HILLS
2,2,2,2 - 2,2,3,0 - timp.,perc. - hp. - str.   9:00 P.R.S.

—— GOLDEN WEDDING (BALLET SUITE) %
2,2,2,2 - 4,2,3,1 - timp.,perc. - hp. - str.   35:00 P.R.S.

—— HISTORICAL EPISODE (SYMPHONIC IMPRESSION)(FOR
WORDLESS SATB CHORUS, PIANO AND ORCH.)
3,2,2,2 - 4,3,3,1 - timp.,perc. - hp. - pf. - str.   25:00 P.R.S.

—— IN MEMORIAM
2,2,2,2 - 4,2,3,0 - timp.,perc. - str.   5:00 P.R.S.

—— PASTORAL SUITE
str.   12:00 P.R.S.

—— SUNRISE ON THE HILLS (SUSSEX LANDSCAPE NO. 1)
2,2,2,2 - 4,2,3,0 - timp.,perc. - hp. - str.   12:00 P.R.S.
—— SUSSEX LANDSCAPE NO. 2
2,2,2,2 - 4,2,3,0 - timp.,perc. - hp. - str.   4:00 P.R.S.
—— TO APRIL
3,2,2,3 - 4,3,3,1 - timp.,perc. - hp. - str.   8:00 P.R.S.
—— VALSE CAPRICE
2,2,2,2 - 2,2,3,0 - timp.,perc. - hp. - str.   6:00 P.R.S.
—— THE WEEPING FLOWER (A LEGEND)
3,3,3,3 - 4,3,3,1 - timp.,perc. - hp. - str.   P.R.S.
—— WYNDORE (FOR WORDLESS SATB CHORUS AND ORCH.)
1,1,2,2 - 2,1,1,0 - timp.,perc. - hp. - str.   7:00 P.R.S.

COLERIDGE-TAYLOR, Samuel
—— THE BAMBOULA (RHAPSODIC DANCE NO. 1)
3,2,2,2 - 4,2,3,1 - timp.,perc. - str.   8:00 Bo. Hawkes.
—— FAUST: INCIDENTAL MUSIC
15:00 Bo. Hawkes.
—— NERO: INCIDENTAL MUSIC, OP. 62 (IN 4 MOVTS.)
2,2,2,2 - 4,2,3,1 - timp.,perc. - hp. - str.   24:00 Novello.
—— OTHELLO: SUITE (IN 4 MOVTS.)
3,2,2,2 - 4,2,2,1 - timp.,perc. - str.   11:30 Cramer.
—— PETITE SUITE DE CONCERT, OP. 77
14:30 Bo. Hawkes.
—— SAINT AGNES' EVE: SUITE
8:00 Bo. Hawkes.
—— SYMPHONIC VARIATIONS ON AN AFRICAN AIR
3,2(2nd alt. with Eng. hn.),2,2 - 4,2,3,1 - timp.,perc. - str.
20:00 Novello.

COLERIDGE-TAYLOR, Samuel - BAINES, Sydney
—— CHRISTMAS OVERTURE
1,1,2,1 - 4,2,3,0 - perc. - str.   5:00 Bo. Hawkes.

COLERIDGE-TAYLOR, Samuel - SCHENK, Elliott
—— SCENES FROM AN IMAGINARY BALLET (SUITE)
10:30 Bo. Hawkes.

COLGRASS, Michael
—— AS QUIET AS . . . . (1965) (SUITE IN 7 MOVTS.)
*3,*3,*3,*3 - 4,3,3,1 - timp.,perc.(5), bells, cel., glock., vibra - 2
hp. - pf. - str.   15:00 MCA Music.
—— AURAS (FOR HARP AND ORCH.)
2,2,2,2 - 2,2,2,0 - perc.,cel. - hp. - pf. - str.   15:00 C. Fischer.
—— BEST WISHES, U.S.A. (FOR SOLO VOICES, CHORUS,
ORCHESTRA AND JAZZ QUARTET)
2,2,2,2 - 4,3,3,1 - timp.,perc.,cel. - banjo,guit.,ukelele - harmonica -
acc. - hp. - pf.,electric pf. - str.   29:00 C. Fischer.
—— CONCERTMASTERS (FOR 3 VIOLINS AND ORCH.)
2,2,2,2 - 4,3,3,0 - timp.,perc.,cel. - 2 hp. - hpsc. - str.
20:00 C. Fischer.
—— THE EARTH'S A BAKED APPLE (FOR CHORUS AND ORCH.)
(1968) (A MUSICAL CELEBRATION IN HONOR OF MARTIN
LUTHER KING) (Text: Composer)
*2,0,2,*1 - 4,3,3,1 - timp.,perc.(5),bells, cel., glock., xyl. - hp. - pf.
- str.   12:00 MCA Music.
—— IMAGE OF MAN (A CONCERT PIECE FOR CHORUS AND
ORCH.)
3,2,3,3 - 4,3,3,1 - timp.,perc.,cel. - electric pf. - hp. - str.
20:00 C. Fischer.
—— SEA SHADOW (MUSIC FOR A BALLET)
1,1,1,1 - 1,1,1,0 - perc. - hp. - str.   10:00 C. Fischer.
—— SEVENTEEN
3,3,3,3 - 4,3,3,1 - timp.,perc. - str.   8:00 C. Fischer.
—— THEATRE OF THE UNIVERSE (FOR SOLO VOICES, CHORUS
AND ORCH.)
3,3,3,3 - 4,3,3,1 - timp.,perc.,cel. - 2 hp. - pf. - str.
15:00 C. Fischer.

ČOLIĆ, Dragutin
—— PRELUDE, FUGUE, POSTLUDE
3,2,3,2 - 4,3,3,1 - timp.,perc.,xyl. - str.   18:00 MIC,Zagreb.

COLICCHIO, Ralph
—— D-DAY: JUNE 6, 1944
2(2nd alt. with picc.),2,*3,1 - 2,2,2,1 - timp.,perc.(2),cel.(alt. with
pf.),vibra. - hp. - str.   4:00 Composer.
—— THE KINGDOM BENEATH THE SEA (IN 2 MOVTS.)
2,2,*3,1 - 2,2,2,1 - timp.,perc.(2),bells,xyl. - 2 hp. - str.
7:15 Composer.
—— NEW ENGLAND SUITE (IN 6 MOVTS.)
2(2nd alt. with picc.),2,*3,1 - 2,2,2,1 - timp.,perc.(2),bells - str.
17:05 Composer.

—— OAKLAND VALLEY
2,2,2,1 - 2,2,2,1 - timp.,perc. - 2 hp. - str.   4:35 MaxwellWir.

COLLET, Henri
—— POÈME (FOR VIOLIN AND ORCH.)
3,3,3,2 - 4,1,3,1 - hp. - str.   10:00 Salabert.
—— LOS TOREROS (BALLET) %
2,2,2,2 - 3,2,3,1 - timp.,perc. (2) - hp. - pf. (ad lib.) - str.   Salabert.

COLLIER, Ron
—— JAZZ BALLET (FOR FULL 30-PIECE ORCH.) %
7:50 C.A.P.A.C.

COLLINS, Anthony
—— CATHERINE PARR (ONE-ACT OPERA) %
2,2,2,2 - 4,4,0,0 - timp.,perc. - hp. - str.   24:00 Leeds.
—— CONCERTO FOR VIOLIN AND ORCH., OP. 48
2,2,*3,2 - 4,2,3,1 - timp.,perc. - str.   25:00 FDH.
—— THE DANCING MASTER (OVERTURE) (FOR STRING
ORCH.)
str.   7:00 Leeds.
—— FOUR EIGHTEENTH-CENTURY TRANSCRIPTIONS (FOR
STRING ORCH.)
str.   12:00 Bo. Hawkes.
—— HOGARTH SUITE (ARRANGED FROM TRADITIONAL
MUSIC) (FOR OBOE AND STRINGS) (IN 4 MOVTS.)
ob. - str.   18:42 Fox.
—— SIR ANDREW AND SIR TOBY (OVERTURE)
3,2,2,3 - 4,2,3,1 - timp.,perc. - hp. - str.   10:00 Leeds.
—— SPANISH DANCE SUITE (ARRANGED FROM TRADITIONAL
MUSIC)
11:00 Bo. Hawkes.
—— SYMPHONY FOR STRING ORCH. (IN 3 MOVEMENTS)
str.   Novello.
—— SYMPHONY NO. 2 FOR STRINGS
str.   Fox.
—— THRENODY FOR A SOLDIER KILLED IN ACTION (BASED
ON FRAGMENTS LEFT BY MICHAEL HEMING, KILLED AT
EL ALAMEIN)
2,*3,*3,2 - 4,2,3,0 - timp.,perc. (2) - hp. - str.   6:00 Fox.
—— TOPLEY PIKE (A PASTORALE)
2,2,2,2 - 4,3,3,1 - timp.,perc. - hp. - str.   5:00 Bo. Hawkes.

COLLUM, Herbert
—— CONCERTANTE MUSIC NO. 2
str.   22:00 Tetra.
—— CONCERTO IN D MINOR, FOR FLUTE AND CHAMBER
ORCH.
fl. - 2 hn. - str.   24:00 Tetra.
—— CONCERTO IN E FOR STRING ORCH.
str.   24:00 Tetra.

COMARATA, Salvador
—— RHAPSODY FOR E FLAT ALTO SAXOPHONE AND ORCH.
2,1,2,4 sax.(2 alto, 1 ten., 1 bar.),1 - 1,3,3,0 - timp.,perc. - hp. - pf.
- str.   5:00 Belw-Mills.

CONNOLLY, Justin
—— ANTIPHONIES (FOR FIVE GROUPS OF INSTRUMENTS)
2,*2,2,2 - 2,2,2,0 - perc. - str.   13:30 Oxford.
—— OBLIGATI 1, OP. 3
1,1,1,1 - 2,0,0,0 - perc. - pf. - str.   20:00 Novello.
—— OBLIGATI 4, OP. 28
1,0,1,0 - 1,1,1,0 - perc. - pf. - str.(no vlas. or d.-b.) 16:00 Novello.
—— REBUS, OP. 17
3,3,3,3 - 0,0,0,0 - perc. - str.   9:00 Novello.
—— TETRAMORPH, OP. 22
Tape-recorder - str.   20:00 Novello.

CONSTANT, Franz
—— CONCERTINO FOR FLUTE AND STRINGS, OP. 47 (1970)
str.   15:50 H. Elkan.
—— CONCERTINO FOR VIOLIN AND STRINGS, OP. 73 (IN 3
MOVTS.)
str.   H. Elkan.
—— CONCERTO FOR VIOLIN AND ORCH., OP. 48 (1971)
2,2,2,2 - 2,2,1,0 - timp.,perc. - str.   18:00 H. Elkan.
—— EXPRESSIONS FOR VIOLIN, PIANO AND STRINGS, OP. 61
(1973)
1. Quasi Fantasia; 2. Poetico; 3. Ritmo
pf. - str.   17:00 H. Elkan.
—— RHAPSODIE, OP. 54 (1973)
2,2,2,2 - 3,2,1,0 - timp.,perc. - str.   12:00 H. Elkan.

—— VISIONS, OP. 66 (1974)
  3,2,2,2 - 4,2,2,1 timp.,perc. - str.   15:00 H. Elkan.

CONSTANT, Marius
—— CANDIDE (FOR HARPSICHORD AND ORCH.) (1971) (WITH
  CONTACT-MICROPHONES AND AMPLIFICATION FOR
  HARP, 1 VIOLIN AND 1 CELLO)
  3,*3,*4,*3 - 4,3,3,1 - timp.,perc.(5) - 2 hpsc. - hp. - str.(21,0,5,4)
                                           20:00 Salabert.
—— CANDIDE (MIMODRAMA) (FOR 3 MIMES, BALLET
  COMPANY AND ORCH.) % (1970) (WITH
  CONTACT-MICROPHONES AND AMPLIFICATION FOR
  HARP, 1 VIOLIN AND 1 CELLO)
  3,*3,*4,*3 - 4,3,3,1 - timp.,perc.(5),cel. - hp. - hpsc. - str.(21,4,5,4)
                                           60:00 Salabert.
—— CHACONNE ET MARCHE MILITAIRE
  4,4,*5(b.-cl. alt. with d.-b.-cl.),*4 - 4,4,4,1 - timp.,perc.(4), cel.,
  glock., vibra. - 2 hp. - str.   12:00 Salabert.
—— CINQ CHANTS ET UNE VOCALISE (FOR DRAMATIC
  SOPRANO AND ORCH.) (Text: Lou Bruder)
  3,3,*4,*3 - 4,3,3,1 - timp.,perc.(5), cel., mar., vibra. - 2 hp. - pf. -
  str.   28:00 Salabert.
—— CONCERTO FOR TUBA AND STRINGS
  tu. - str.   7:30 Presser.
—— CONCERTO NO. 1 FOR PIANO AND ORCH.
  2,2,2,2 - 2,2,1,0 - timp., perc.(3) - hp. - pf. - str.   17:00 Presser.
—— ÉLOGE DE LA FOLIE (BALLET) % (WITH SOPRANO VOICE)
  1,1,*2(6.-cl.alt.with d.-b.-cl.),1 - 1,2,2,0 - perc.(2) - mandolin - hp.
  - hammond org. - 2 pf.(alt.with cel. and hpsc.) - 1 d.-b.
                                           50:00 Salabert.
—— FACIEBAT ANNO 1972 (FOR 24 VIOLINS AND ORCH.)
  3,*3,*4,*3 - 4,3,3,1 - perc.(4) - str.(24,12,12,10)   20:00 Salabert.
—— THE FLUTE PLAYER (BALLET) %
  2,2,2,2 - 2,2,2,0 - timp.,perc. - hp. - pf. - str.   60:00 Bo. Hawkes.
—— LE JOUEUR DE FLÛTE (THE FLUTE PLAYER): SUITE FROM
  THE BALLET
  2,2,2,2 - 2,2,2,0 - timp.,perc. - hp. - pf. - str.   30:00 Bo. Hawkes.
—— MUSIQUE DE CONCERT (FOR ALTO SAXOPHONE AND 12
  INSTRUMENTS)
  1. Toccata; 2. Aria; 3. Intermezzo; 4. Variazioni; 5. Ostinato
  1,1, alto sax.,0,1 - 1,1,1,0 - perc.,glock.,vibra.,xyl. - pf. - str. (1
  violin, 1 cello, 1 d.-b.)   10:00 Baron.
—— PARADIS PERDU (BALLET) %
  3,3,*4,3 - 4,3,3,0 - timp.,perc.(4),cel.,mar.,vibra. - 2 hp. -
  hammond org. - pf. - 6 c.,4 d - b.   40:00 Salabert.
—— PIANO PERSONNAGE
  1,1,*2,1 - 1,1,1,0 - perc.(2),cel. - guit. - org. - 2 pf.(1 upright) -
  str.(0,1,1,1)   20:00 Salabert.
—— SERENADES
  2,2,2,2 - 2,2,1,0 - timp., perc.(3) - pf. - str.   10:30 Presser.
—— STRINGS
  Electric guit. - str.(7,2,2,1)   12:00 Salabert.
—— TRAITS (FOR VARIABLE ENSEMBLE OF UP TO 25
  MUSICIANS)
                                           8:00 Salabert.
—— TURNER (3 SYMPHONIC ESSAYS)
  2,2,2,2 - 2,2,1,0 - perc. - hp. - pf. - str.   15:00 F. Colombo.
—— WINDS
  2,1,2,1 - 2,2,3,0 - 1 d.-b.   7:30 Salabert.

CONSTANTINESCU, Paul
—— ROMANIAN FOLK DANCE (OLTENEASCA)
  3,2,2,2 - 4,2,3,0 - timp.,perc. - cemb. - hp. - str.   6:00 Templeton.
—— SASH DANCE (BRAUL)
  3,2,2,2 - 4,3,3,1 - timp.,perc. - cemb. - pf. - str.   6:30 Templeton.
—— THE YOUNG SHEPHERD (CIOBANASUL)
  3,2,2,2 - 4,2,0,0 - timp.,perc.,glock.,xyl. - cemb. - str.
                                           4:00 Templeton.

CONTESSE, Henri
—— CINQ CHANSONS DU COEUR (FOR VOICE AND ORCH.)
  2,2,2,2 - 2,2,2,0 - timp.,perc. - hp. - str.   Salabert.

CONTILLI, Gino
—— ESPRESSIONI SINFONICHE
  3,3,3,2 - 4,3,3,1 - timp.,perc.(3),cel.,xyl. - hp. - pf. - str.
                                           15:00 Leeds.
—— IMMAGINI SONORE (FOR SOPRANO AND 11
  INSTRUMENTS)
                                           Leeds.

CONUS, George E.
—— LA FORÊT BRUISSAIT (POÈME SYMPHONIQUE)
  3,2,2,2 - 4,2,3,1 - timp.,perc. - hp. - str.   18:00 Bo. Hawkes.

CONVERSE, Frederick S.
—— CALIFORNIA (TONE POEM)
  3(3rd alt. with picc.),*3, E♭cl.,*3,*3 - 4,3,3,1 - timp.,perc. (4),cel. -
  2 hp. - str.   15:00 Composer.
—— CONCERTINO FOR PIANO AND ORCH.
  3(3rd alt. with picc.),2,2,*3 - 4,3,0,0 - timp. - pf. - str.
                                           10:00 Western.
—— ENDYMION'S NARRATIVE, OP. 10
  *3,*3,2,*3 - 4,3,3,1 - timp.,perc. (3) - str.   15:00 C. Fischer.
—— THE FLIGHT OF THE EAGLE (FOR BARITONE, CHORUS
  AND ORCH.)
  2,1,2,1 - 2,2,1,0 - timp.,perc.,cel. - hp. - str.   15:00 Composer.
—— FLIVVER TEN MILLION (A JOYOUS EPIC)
  3(3rd alt. with picc.),*3,*3,*3 - 4,3,3,1 - timp.,perc. (5) - 2 hp. -
  str.   12:00 C. Fischer.
—— I WILL PRAISE THEE, O LORD (FOR SOPRANO, CHORUS
  AND ORCH.)
  2,2,2,*3 - 4,3,3,1 - timp. - hp. - org. - str.   15:00 Composer.
—— THE MYSTIC TRUMPETER, OP. 19
  3(3rd alt. with picc.),*3,*3,*3 - 4,3,3,1 - timp.,perc.,glock. - hp. -
  str.   20:00 G. Schirmer.
—— ORMAZD, OP 30
  2,*3,3,3 - 6,3,3,1 - timp.,perc. (2) - cel. - hp. - pf. - str.
                                           10:00 Gray.
—— THE PEACE PIPE (FOR BARITONE, CHORUS AND ORCH.)
  2,2,2,2 - 4,2,2,1 - timp.,perc. - str.   30:00 Composer.
—— PROPHECY (TONE POEM FOR SOPRANO AND ORCH.)
                                           P.C.Cabot.
—— SCARECROW SKETCHES (IN 3 MOVTS.)
  3(3rd alt. with picc.),2,3,2 - 4,3,3,1 - timp.,perc. - hp. - pf. - str.
                                           20:00 Ditson.

COOK, John
—— ECLOGUE FOR ORCHESTRA
                                           11:00 C.A.P.A.C.
—— FLOURISH FOR THOSE WHO HAVE FAILED (FOR MIXED
  CHORUS, BRASS AND PERCUSSION) (Text: Walt Whitman)
  0,0,0,0 - 2,3,3,1 - timp.,perc.   7:00 CanMusCtr.
—— A SUITE OF PSALMS (FOR SPEAKING CHORUS AND
  ORCH.) (1960) (IN 7 MOVTS.)
  2,2,2,2 - 4,2,0,0 - timp.,perc.   15:00 CanMusCtr.

COOKE, Arnold
—— CONCERTO FOR CLARINET AND STRINGS
  cl. - str.   25:00 Novello.
—— CONCERTO FOR OBOE AND STRINGS
  ob. - str.   21:00 Novello.
—— CONCERTO FOR SMALL ORCHESTRA
  2,2,2,2 - 2,2,0,0 - timp. - hp. - str.   18:00 Belw-Mills.
—— CONCERTO FOR VIOLIN AND ORCH. (1958)
  2,2,2,2 - 4,3,3,0 - timp.,perc.,cel. - hp. - str.   27:00 Novello.
—— JABEZ AND THE DEVIL (BALLET SUITE)
  2,2,2,2 - 4,3,3,1 - timp.,perc. - hp. - str.   16:30 Oxford.
—— PASSACAGLIA, SCHERZO AND FINALE
  str.   15:00 Oxford.
—— PROCESSIONAL OVERTURE
  2,2,2,2 - 4,3,3,1 - timp.,perc. - str.   8:00 Oxford.
—— SINFONIETTA (FOR 10 PLAYERS)
  1,1,1,1 - 1,1,0,0 - str.(2,1,1,0)   21:00 Belw-Mills.
—— SYMPHONY NO. 2
                                           32:00 Oxford.
—— VARIATIONS ON A THEME BY DUFAY ("CE MOYS DE
  MAI")
  2,2,2,2 - 4,3,1,0 - timp.,perc.,cel. - str.   18:00 Oxford.

COOKE, Greville
—— PRELUDE FOR STRINGS
  str.   Galaxy.

COOKE, James Francis
—— BLACK SWANS AT FONTAINEBLEAU
  1,1,2,2 sax.,1 - 2,2,1,0 - pf. - str.   6:00 Presser.
—— HUNGARIAN ECHOES (IN 4 MOVEMENTS)
  *4,*3, E♭cl.,2,2 - 4,3,3,1 - timp.,perc. - hp. - str.   7:00 Presser.
—— JASMINE AND NIGHTINGALES
  *3,2,2,1 - 3,2,2,1 - timp.,perc. - str.   9:00 Presser.
—— SHADOWS ON LAKE COMO
  1,1,2,0 - 2,2,1,0 - timp.,perc. - str.   11:00 Presser.

—— TWILIGHT AT CARCASSONNE
    1,1,2,1 - 2,2,1,1 - perc. - str.   8:00 Presser.

COOLIDGE, Peggy
—— PIONEER DANCES
    3,2,2,2 - 4,3,3,1 - timp.,perc. - hp. - str.   11:30 Southern.
—— RHAPSODY FOR HARP AND ORCH.
    3,2,2,1 - 4,3,1,0 - timp.,cel.,xyl. - hp. - str.   9:00 Southern.
    or:
    3,1,2,1 - 2,2,1,0 - perc. - hp. - str.

COOLIDGE, Richard A.
—— ELEGY FOR A ROMANTIC COMPOSER (1964)
    pf. - str.   6:00 Composer.
—— FANTASIA FOR PIANO, TIMPANI AND STRINGS (1953)
    timp. - pf. - str.(no d.-b.)   10:00 Composer.
—— SYMPHONY 1963 (IN 3 MOVTS)
    *3,*3,*3,2 - 4,3,4,1 - timp.,perc.(3),vibra. - hp. - str.
        28:00 Composer.

COOPER, John C.
—— SONGS OF THE WOODLANDS (FOR SOPRANO AND
    CHAMBER ORCH.) (Text: Rabindranath Tagore)
    2,2,2,0 - 2,0,0,0 - str.   10:00 Composer.
—— SYMPHONY
    2,2,2,2 - 2,2,2,0 - perc. - str.   20:00 Presser.
—— SYMPHONY NO. 1
    1. Andante molto lirico; 2. Adagio; 3. Lento-Allegro-Lento
    *3,2,1 E♭cl.(alt. with b.-cl.),2,2 - 3,2,2,1 -
    timp.,perc.(3),bells,glock. - hp. - str.   25:00 Composer.
—— SYMPHONY NO. 2 (IN 3 MOVTS.)
    *3,3(3rd alt. with Eng. hn.),*3,2 - 3,2,2,1 -
    timp.,perc.(2),glock.,xyl. - pf. - str.   17:00 Presser.
—— THREE DIVERSIONS, OP. 7
    1,0,1,0 - 1,1,0,0 - str.   4:30 Composer.

COOPER, Paul
—— CANTIGAS (1972) (FOR CHORUS, MALE CHOIR AND
    CHAMBER ORCH.)
    fl.,ob.,cl.,bn. - perc.,cel.(alt. with pf.) - hp. - str.   G. Schirmer.
—— CONCERTO FOR ORCHESTRA (1966)
    1,1,1,1 - 1,1,1,0 - timp.,perc.(3),cel.,xyl. - hp. - str.
        14:00 G. Schirmer.
—— CONCERTO FOR VIOLIN AND ORCHESTRA (1968)
    3,*3,*3,*3 - 4,3,3,1 - timp.,perc.(3),cel.,xyl. - hp. - pf. - str.
        13:00 G. Schirmer.
—— CREDO (FOR 2 SATB CHORUSES AND ORCH.) (1970) (Text:
    Christian Cooper)
    3,3,3,3 - 4,3,3,1 - perc.,cel. - hp. - pf. - str.   25:00 G. Schirmer.
—— GENESIS II (FOR SATB CHORUS AND ORCH. (1970))
        9:00 G. Schirmer.
—— SYMPHONY NO. 3 (LAMENTATIONS) (1971) (IN 5 MOVTS)
    str.   18:00 G. Schirmer.
—— SYMPHONY NO. 4 (LANDSCAPES)
    3,3,3,2 - 4,3,3,1 - perc.,cel.(alt. with pf.) - hp. - str.
        21:00 G. Schirmer.

COOPER, W. Gaze
—— CONCERTO FOR HORN AND ORCH., OP. 88 (1963)
    2,2,2,2 - 3,2,3,0 - timp.,perc. - str.   20:00 P.R.S.
—— CONCERTO FOR VIOLA AND ORCH., OP. 85 (1961)
    2,2,2,2 - 2,2,1,0 - timp.,perc. - str.   25:00 P.R.S.
—— CONCERTO NO. 4 FOR PIANO AND ORCH., OP. 91 (1967)
    2,2,2,2 - 4,2,2,1 - timp.,perc. - pf.- str.   25:00 P.R.S.
—— MY GRANDCHILDREN, OP. 90 (SUITE)
    2,2,2,2 - 2,2,0,0 - timp.,perc. - hp. - str.   17:00 P.R.S.
—— ROMANCE FOR VIOLIN AND ORCH., OP. 44 (1935)
    2,2,2,2 - 2,0,2,0 - timp.,perc. - str.   14:00 P.R.S.
—— THE SCARECROW, OP. 68 (BALLET) %
        20:00 P.R.S.
—— SYMPHONY NO. 7, OP. 82 ("THE SZEZECINIE") (1959)
    3,3,2,2 - 4,3,3,1 - timp.,perc. - hp. - str.   30:00 P.R.S.
—— SYMPHONY NO. 8, OP. 84 (1961)
    3,2,2,2 - 4,2,3,1 - timp.,perc. - hp. - str.   27:00 P.R.S.
—— THE USHABTUE, OP. 69 (BALLET) %
        60:00 P.R.S.

COPE, David
—— CONTRASTS FOR ORCHESTRA
    2,2,2,2 - 4,2,2,1 - timp.,perc. - hp. - str.   6:00 Seesaw.
—— MUSIC FOR BRASS, STRINGS AND PERCUSSION
    0,0,0,0 - 4,2,2,2 - timp.,perc.(2) - hp. - str.   11:00 Seesaw.

—— STREAMS
    3,1,2,1 - 4,3,3,1 - perc.(3) - pf. - str.   14:00 Seesaw.
—— TRAGIC OVERTURE, OP. 5
    timp.(2) - str.   4:00 Seesaw.

COPLAND, Aaron
—— APPALACHIAN SPRING (BALLET FOR MARTHA) %
    2,2,2,2 - 2,2,2,0 - timp.,perc. (2),xyl. - hp. - pf. - str.   Bo. Hawkes.
—— APPALACHIAN SPRING (SUITE FROM THE BALLET) (FOR
    13 INSTRUMENTS; THE ORIGINAL SCORING)
    1,0,1,1 - 0,0,0,0 - pf. - str.   21:00 Bo. Hawkes.
—— APPALACHIAN SPRING (SUITE FROM THE BALLET)
    2,2,2,2 - 2,2,2,0 - timp.,perc. - hp. - pf. - str.   23:00 Bo. Hawkes.
—— BILLY THE KID (BALLET) %
    3,2,2,2 - 4,3,3,1 - timp.,perc. - hp. - pf. - str.   35:00 Bo. Hawkes.
—— BILLY THE KID: SUITE FROM THE BALLET (IN 7 MOVTS.)
    2,2,2,2 - 4,3,3,1 - timp.,perc. (5),glock.,xyl. - hp. - str.
        22:00 Bo. Hawkes.
—— CANTICLE OF FREEDOM (FOR CHORUS AND ORCH.)
    *3,2,2,2 - 4,3,3,1 - timp.,perc. (5),bells,cel.,glock.,vibra.,xyl. - hp. -
    str.   16:00 Bo. Hawkes.
—— CONCERTO FOR CLARINET AND ORCH
    cl. - hp. - pf. - str.   17:00 Bo. Hawkes.
—— CONCERTO FOR PIANO AND ORCH.
    3,3,4,alto sax.,3 - 4,3,3,1 - timp.,perc.,cel. - pf. - str.
        16:00 Bo. Hawkes.
—— CONNOTATIONS FOR ORCHESTRA (1962)
    4,3,4,3 - 6,4,4,1 - timp.,perc.(5),cel. - pf. - str. 19:30 Bo. Hawkes.
—— CORTÉGE MACABRE, FROM THE BALLET "GROHG"
    3,3,4,3 - 4,5,3,1 - timp.,perc.,cel. - 2 hp. - pf. - str.
        8:00 Bo. Hawkes.
—— DANCE PANELS (BALLET) (1959) (IN 7 SECTIONS)
    2,1,2,1 - 2,2,1,0 - timp.,perc. - str.   26:30 Bo. Hawkes.
—— DANCE SYMPHONY
    3,3,4,3 - 4,5,3,1 - timp.,perc.,cel. 2 hp. - pf. - str.
        14:00 Bo. Hawkes.
—— DANZON CUBANO
    3(3rd alt. with picc.),*3,*3,*3 - 4,3,3,1 - timp.,perc. (5),xyl. - pf. -
    str.   6:00 Bo. Hawkes.
—— EIGHT SONGS OF EMILY DICKINSON (FOR VOICE AND
    ORCH.)
    1,1,2,1 - 1,1,1,0 - hp. - str.   21:00 Bo. Hawkes.
—— FANFARE FOR THE COMMON MAN (FOR BRASS AND
    PERCUSSION)
    4 hn., 3 tpt., 3 trb., tu. - timp., perc. (3)   3:00 Bo. Hawkes.
—— FOUR DANCE EPISODES FROM "RODEO"
    *3,2,2,2 - 4,3,3,1 - timp.,perc. (3),xyl. - hp. - pf. - str.
        18:00 Bo. Hawkes.
—— INSCAPE
    3,3,3,2 - 4,3,3,1 - timp.,perc.,cel. - hp. - pf. - str.
        12:00 Bo. Hawkes.
—— JOHN HENRY
    1-2,1-2,2,1-2 - 2,2,1,0 - timp.,perc. - pf. (ad lib.) - str.
        3:30 Bo. Hawkes.
—— LETTER FROM HOME
    3,*3,*3,*3 - 4,3,3,1 - timp.,perc. (2) - hp. - pf. - str.
        7:00 Bo. Hawkes.
—— LINCOLN PORTRAIT (FOR SPEAKER AND ORCH.)
    2,2,*3,*3 - 4,3,3,1 - timp.,perc. (4),cel.,glock. - hp. - str.
        14:00 Bo. Hawkes.
—— MUSIC FOR A GREAT CITY (SUITE)
    3,3,3,3 - 4,3,3,0 - timp.,perc.(5),cel. - hp. - pf. - str.
        25:00 Bo. Hawkes.
—— MUSIC FOR THE MOVIES (SUITE)
    1,1,1,1 - 1,2,1,0 - perc. - hp. - pf. - str.   16:00 Bo. Hawkes.
—— MUSIC FOR THE THEATRE (SUITE FOR SMALL ORCH.) (IN
    4 MOVTS.)
    1,1,1,1 - 0,2,1,0 - perc. - pf. - str.   22:00 Bo. Hawkes.
—— NONET FOR STRINGS (VERSION FOR STRING ORCH.)
    str.(no d.-b.)   18:00 Bo. Hawkes.
—— OLD AMERICAN SONGS: SET NO. 1 (ARR. FOR MEDIUM
    VOICE AND ORCH.)
    1,2,1,1 - 1,1,1,0 - hp. - str.   13:00 Bo. Hawkes.
—— OLD AMERICAN SONGS: SET NO. 2 (FOR MEDIUM VOICE
    AND ORCH.)
    1,1,2,1 - 2,1,1,0 - hp. - str.   11:30 Bo. Hawkes.
—— ORCHESTRAL VARIATIONS
    2,2,2,2 - 4,2,3,1 - timp.,perc. - hp. - str.   12:00 Bo. Hawkes.
—— OUR TOWN: MUSIC FROM THE FILM
    2,*3,*3,2 - 3,3,2,1 - glock. - str.   9:00 Bo. Hawkes.
—— AN OUTDOOR OVERTURE
    *3,2,2,2 - 4,2,3,0 - timp.,perc. (3),cel.xyl. - pf. - str.
        9:30 Bo. Hawkes.

—— PRAIRIE JOURNAL (MUSIC FOR RADIO) (SAGA OF THE PRAIRIE) (1937)
2(1 alt. with picc.),2,2,3 sax.(ad lib.),1-2 - 2-4,2-3,2,1 - timp.,perc.(2),cel. - pf. - str.   12:30 Bo. Hawkes.

—— PREAMBLE FOR A SOLEMN OCCASION (WITH OPTIONAL NARRATOR)
*3,*3,*3,*3 - 4,3,3,1 - timp.,perc. - (3) - hp. - str.
6:00 Bo. Hawkes.

—— THE PROMISE OF LIVING (FROM THE OPERA "THE TENDER LAND") (FOR CHORUS AND ORCH.)
2,2,2,2 - 2,2,2,0 - perc. - hp. - str.   5:00 Bo. Hawkes.

—— THE QUIET CITY
Eng. hn. (or ob.) - tpt. - str.   9:30 Bo. Hawkes.

—— THE RED PONY: SUITE (IN 6 MOVTS.)
2(alt. with 2 piccs.),2(2nd alt. with Eng. hn.),E♭cl. (ad lib.), 3(3rd alt. with b.-cl.),2 - 4,3,3,1 - timp.,perc. (2),cel.,glock.,mar. (ad lib.),vibra.,xyl. - hp. - pf. - str.   23:00 Bo. Hawkes.

—— RODEO (BALLET) %
3,3,3,3 - 4,3,2,1 - timp.,perc.,cel. - hp. - pf. - str.
24:00 Bo. Hawkes.

—— EL SALON MEXICO
*3,*3,e♭cl., *3,*3 - 4,3,3,1 - timp.,perc. - pf. - str.
11:00 Bo. Hawkes.
or:
2,2,2,2 - 4,2,3,1 - perc. - pf. - str.

—— THE SECOND HURRICANE (OPERA) % (Without dialogue)
1(alt. with picc.),1,2,alto sax.,1 - 0,2,1,0 - timp.,perc. - theremin(ad lib.) - pf. - str.   65:00 Bo. Hawkes.

—— THE SECOND HURRICANE (OPERA) % (Including dialogue)
1(alt. with picc.),1,2,alto sax.,1 - 0,2,1,0 - timp.,perc. - theremin (ad lib.) - pf. - str.   90:00 Bo. Hawkes.

—— SHORT SYMPHONY (SYMPHONY NO. 2) (IN 3 MOVEMENTS)
*3,*3,*3,*3 - 4,2,0,0 - pf. - str.   15:00 Bo. Hawkes.

—— SONG OF THE GUERRILLAS, FROM THE FILM "THE NORTH STAR" (FOR BARITONE, MALE CHORUS AND ORCH.)
3,3,3,3 - 4,3,3,1 - timp.,perc. - str.   4:00 Bo. Hawkes.

—— STATEMENTS (IN 6 MOVTS.)
*3,*3,*3,*3 - 4,3,3,1 - timp.,perc. (4) - str.   18:30 Bo. Hawkes.

—— STOMP YOUR FOOT (FROM THE OPERA "THE TENDER LAND") (FOR MIXED CHORUS AND ORCH.)
2,2,2,2 - 2,2,2,0 - perc. - pf. - str.   3:00 Bo. Hawkes.

—— SYMPHONIC ODE (REVISED 1955)
2 picc.,2,*4,1 E♭cl.,*3,*4 - 8,4,3,1 - timp.,perc. (4),bells,cel.,glock.,xyl. - 2 hp. - pf. - str.   21:00 Bo. Hawkes.

—— SYMPHONY FOR ORGAN AND ORCH.
3,3,3, alto sax. (ad lib.),3 - 4,3,3,1 - timp.,perc.,cel. - 2 hp. - org. - str.   25:00 Bo. Hawkes.

—— SYMPHONY NO. 1
3,3,3, alto sax.,3 - 8,5,3,1 - timp.,perc.,cel. - 2 hp. - pf. - str.
25:00 Bo. Hawkes.

—— SYMPHONY NO. 3 (IN 4 MOVEMENTS)
3(2 alt. with picc.),*3,E♭cl.,*3,*3 - 4,4,3,1 - timp.,perc. (5),cel.,glock.,xyl. - 2 hp. - pf. - str.   40:00 Bo. Hawkes.

—— THE TENDER LAND: SUITE FROM THE OPERA
3,2,2,2 - 4,3,3,1 - timp.,perc. - hp. - pf. - str.   18:30 Bo. Hawkes.

—— THE TENDER LAND (3-ACT OPERA) %
2,2,2,2 - 2,2,2,0 - timp.,perc.,cel. - pf.(ad lib.) - str.
100:00 Bo. Hawkes.

—— THREE LATIN-AMERICAN SKETCHES
1,1,1,1 - 1,0,0,0 - perc. - 2 pf. - str.   10:00 Bo. Hawkes.

—— TWO MEXICAN PIECES
1,1,1,1 - 0,1,0,0 - perc. - 2 pf. - str.   6:30 Bo. Hawkes.

—— TWO PIECES FOR STRING ORCHESTRA
str.   11:00 Bo. Hawkes.

—— VARIATIONS ON A SHAKER MELODY (FROM "APPALACHIAN SPRING")
2,2,2,2 - 2,2,2,0 - timp.(ad lib.),perc. - hp.(ad lib.) - pf. - str.
3:30 Bo. Hawkes.

COPLAND, Aaron - BOWDEN, Don
—— FANTASIA MEXICANA
1,1,2,2 - 2,2,3,0 - timp.,perc. - pf. - str.   3:30 Bo. Hawkes.

COPLAND, Aaron - FINE, Irving
—— OLD AMERICAN SONGS: SET NO. 1 (ARR. FOR SOLI, CHORUS AND ORCH.)
1,2,1,1 - 1,1,1,0 - hp. - str.   13:00 Bo. Hawkes.

COPLAND, Aaron - GREEN, Johnny
—— FANTASIA MEXICANA (BASED ON "EL SALON MEXICO")
1,1,2,2 - 2,2,3,0 - timp.,perc.(2) - str.   Bo. Hawkes.

COPPOLA, Piero
—— INTERLUDE DRAMATIQUE
3,3,3,4 - 4,3,3,1 - timp.,perc. - 2 hp. - str.   10:00 Salabert.

—— LA RONDE SOUS LA CLOCHE (SYMPHONIC POEM) (1924)
3,3,3,4 - 4,4,3,1 - timp., perc., bells - 2 hp. - str.   13:00 EV.

—— SYMPHONY IN A MINOR
3,3,3,4 - 4,3,3,1 - timp.,perc.,cel. - 2 hp. - str.   30:00 Salabert.

CORAL, Giampaolo
—— REQUIEM PER JAN PALACH E ALTRI (1969)
2,2,2,1 - 2,2,0,0 - timp. - str.   14:00 MCA Music.

CORELLI, Arcangelo - BARBIROLLI, John
—— CONCERTO FOR OBE AND STRINGS
ob. - str.   10:00 Bo. Hawkes.

—— CONCERTO GROSSO (FROM VIOLIN SONATAS OF ARCANGELO CORELLI) (IN 4 MOVTS.)
str.   18:00 Oxford.

CORELLI, Arcangelo - BAZELAIRE
—— ADAGIO FOR CELLO AND STRING ORCH.
str.   4:30 Baron.

CORELLI, Arcangelo - BROWN, James
—— SONATA DA CAMERA NO. 7
pf. - str.   8:00 Galaxy.

—— SONATA DA CAMERA NO. 8
pf. - str.   6:00 Galaxy.

—— SONATA DA CAMERA NO. 9
pf. - str.   11:00 Galaxy.

—— SONATA DA CAMERA NO. 10
pf. - str.   7:00 Galaxy.

CORELLI, Arcangelo - BRUNI, M.
—— SONATA DA CHIESA, OP. 3, NO. 12 (FOR STRINGS)
str.   Henmar.

CORELLI, Arcangelo - DORATI, Antal
—— CONCERTO GROSSO NO. 1 IN D MAJOR
A.P.R.A.

CORELLI, Arcangelo - DUBENSKY, A.
—— CONCERTO GROSSO IN D MINOR (FOR STRINGS)
str.   14:00 Ricordi.

CORELLI, Arcangelo - FASANO, Renato
—— CONCERTO GROSSO IN D MAJOR, OP. 6, NO. 4
S.I.A.E.

CORELLI, Arcangelo - GOODMAN, Edward
—— THEME AND VARIATIONS
str.   Novello.

CORELLI, Arcangelo - HUNT, Frederick
—— CORELLIANA (SUITE FOR STRING ORCH.)
str.   C. Fischer.

CORELLI, Arcangelo - POLNAUER, Frederick F.
—— SOLO SONATA, OP. V, NO. 8 (ARR. 1969)
str.   12:00 Lyra.

—— TRIO SONATA, OP. I, NO. 4 (ARR. 1969)
str.   12:00 Lyra.

—— TRIO SONATA, OP. I, NO. 5 (ARR. 1968)
str.   12:00 Lyra.

CORELLI, Arcangelo - REGER, Max
—— LA FOLIA (FOR VIOLIN AND ORCH.)
Henmar.

CORELLI, Arcangelo - RHENE-BATON
—— CONCERTO GROSSO NO. 8 IN G MINOR (FOR STRINGS)
str.   15:00 EV.

CORELLI, Arcangelo - TESSON, A.
—— SONATA NO. 6 IN A (FOR HARPSICHORD AND STRINGS)
hpsc. - str.   10:00 Salabert.

CORELLI, Arcangelo - VAN HOESEN, Karl D. - HUNT, Frederick
—— CONCERTO GROSSO NO. 3
2,2,2,2 - 4,2,3,0 - timp. - pf. - str.   C. Fischer.

CORELLI, Arcangelo - WHITTAKER, W. G.
—— CHRISTMAS CONCERTO (CONCERTO GROSSO NO. 8) (FOR
2 VIOLINS, CELLO AND STRINGS)
cemb. (ad lib.) - str.   Oxford.

CORGHI, Azio
—— HOP-FROG (PER CLAVICEMBALO E 10 ARCHI SOLISTI)
(1970)
hpsc. - str.(5,2,2,1)   12:00 MCA Music.

CORIGLIANO, John
—— THE CLOISTERS (FOR VOICE AND ORCH.) (Text: W. H.
Hoffman)
2,2,2,2 - 2,2,0,0 - timp.,perc. - str.   13:00 G. Schirmer.
—— CONCERTO FOR OBOE AND ORCH.
2,2,2,2 - 2,1,1,0 - timp.,perc. - hp. - pf. - str.   25:00 G. Schirmer.
—— CONCERTO FOR PIANO AND ORCH.
2,3,3,2 - 4,3,3,1 - perc. - hp. - pf. - str.   30:00 G. Schirmer.
—— ELEGY
2,2,2,2 - 2,1,1,0 - timp.,perc. - pf. - str.   7:30 G. Schirmer.
—— FERN HILL (Reduced Orchestration)
hp.(ad lib.) - str.   16:00 G. Schirmer.
—— FERN HILL (FOR MEZZO SOPRANO, CHORUS AND ORCH.)
(Text: Dylan Thomas)
2,2,2,2 - 4,2,2,1 - timp.,perc.(2) - hp. - pf. - str.
16:00 G. Schirmer.
—— GAZEBO DANCES
2,2,2,2 - 4,3,3,1 - timp.,perc. - pf. - str.   16:00 G. Schirmer.
—— POEM ON HIS BIRTHDAY (FROM A DYLAN THOMAS
TRILOGY) (FOR BARITONE, SATB CHORUS AND ORCH.)
2(2nd alt. with picc.),2,2(2nd alt. with b.-cl.),2 - 4,2,2,0 -
timp.,perc.(4) - hp. - pf. - str.   30:00 G. Schirmer.

CORINA, John H.
—— GAELIC OVERTURE (FOR YOUTH ORCH.) (1966)
1(alt.with picc.),1,2,1 - 2,2,2,1 - timp.,perc.(3-4),bells,glock.,xyl. -
pf. - str.   6:00 Composer.
—— TWO PIECES FOR OBOE AND STRING ORCH. (1962)
ob. - str.   5:00 Composer.

CORNELIUS, Peter - KRAMER, A. Walter
—— EIN TON (FOR STRINGS)
hp. - str.   Witmark.

CORNIOT, René
—— ONDINE (FOR HARP AND ORCH.)
Henmar.

CORRETTE, Michel - BOULAY, Laurence
—— CONCERTO FOR FLUTE, STRING ORCH. AND CONTINUO
fl. - cemb. - str.   8:30 Presser.
—— CONCERTO NO. 6 IN D MINOR FOR CLAVECIN (OR
ORGAN) (WITH ORCH.)
fl. - hpsc.(or org.) - str.   8:00 Presser.

CORRETTE, Michel - LELOIR, Edmond
—— CONCERTO IN C MAJOR FOR HORN AND ORCH. ("LA
CHOISY") (IN 3 MOVTS.)
0,2,0,1 - 2,0,0,0 - hpsc. - str.   9:00 Henmar.

CORTES, Ramiro
—— THE ETERNAL RETURN: INTRODUCTION AND RONDO
2,3,3,2 - 4,2,2,1 - timp. - str.   11:00 EV.
—— MEDITATION ON "CHRIST LAG IN TODESBANDEN"
str.   6:00 Wimbledon.
—— MISSA BREVIS (FOR WOMEN'S VOICES AND WOODWINDS)
3,2,3,3 - 0,0,0,0   7:30 Presser.
—— MOVEMENTS IN VARIATION (1972)
14:30 Composer.
—— SINFONICA SACRA
Chappell.
—— VARIATIONS FOR ORCHESTRA
2,2,2,2 - 2,1,1,0 - perc. - str.   7:00 Wimbledon.
—— YERMA (SYMPHONIC PORTRAIT OF A WOMAN)
3,*3,4,3 - 4,3,3,1 - timp.,perc. (3), cel. -str.   12:00 EV.

CORTESE, Luigi
—— DAVID (ORATORIO) (FOR SOPRANO OR MEZZO-SOPRANO,
TENOR, BARITONE, MIXED CHORUS AND ORCH.)
3,3,3,4 - 4,4,3,1 - timp.,perc. - 2 hp. - str.   45:00 Leeds.
—— INCLINA, DOMINE, AUREM TUAM (SINFONIA SACRA)
(1967) (FOR MIXED CHORUS AND ORCH.) (Text: Biblical)
3,3,3,4 - 4,4,3,1 - timp.,cel. - hp. - str.   30:00 MCA Music.

—— PRELUDIO E FUGA
2,2,1,2 - 2,2,1,0 - hp. - str.   12:00 Bo. Hawkes.
—— QUATRE ODES DE RONSARD (FOR VOICES AND ORCH.)
2,2,2,2 - 0,0,0,0 - cel. - hp. - str.   13:00 Leeds.
—— SERENATA
3,2,2,2 - 2,2,1,0 - pf. - str.   19:00 Bo. Hawkes.

CORUM, Alfred
—— CAVATINA, OP. 13 (1927)
str.   8:00 P.R.S.
—— CONCERTO FOR VIOLA AND ORCH., OP. 21 (1965)
2,1,2,2 - 4,2,3,1 - timp.,perc. - str.   18:00 P.R.S.
—— CORTÈGE, OP. 16 (1958)
2,3,2,2 - 4,2,3,1 - timp.,perc. - hp. - str.   10:00 P.R.S.
—— FOUR PIECES FOR ORCH., OP. 17 (1960)
2,2,2,2 - 4,2,3,1 - timp.,perc. - hp. - str.   25:00 P.R.S.
—— MINERS DAY, OP. 6 (MARCH RHAPSODY) (1956)
2,2,2,2 - 4,2,3,1 - timp.,perc. - hp. - str.   12:00 P.R.S.
—— A SUITE OF OLD DANCES, OP. 9 (1958)
2,2,2,2 - 2,3,0,0 - timp.,perc. - str.   15:00 P.R.S.
—— SYMPHONIC VARIATIONS, OP. 23
3,3,3,3 - 4,2,3,1 - timp.,perc. - hp. - str.   15:00 P.R.S.
—— SYMPHONY, OP. 22 (1966)
3,3,3,3 - 4,2,3,1 - timp.,perc. - hp. - str.   30:00 P.R.S.
—— THREE ELEGIES, OP. 10 (1926)
2,2,2,2 - 2,2,3,1 - timp.,perc. - hp. - str.   20:00 P.R.S.

COSACCHI, Stephan
—— CONCERTO FOR OBOE AND STRING ORCH., OP. 11-C
ob. - str.   17:00 Mannheimer.
—— LITTLE SUITE FOR ORCHESTRA, OP. 99-C (IN 5 MOVTS.)
Hans Gerig.
—— VALENTIN SUITE, OP. 55 (AFTER 16TH-CENTURY LUTE
COMPOSITIONS OF VALENTIN GREFF-BAKFARK)
3,3,3,3 - 4,3,3,1 - timp.,perc.,cel. - hp. - str.   22:00 F. Colombo.

COSCIA, Silvio
—— CONCERTINO FOR HORN AND ORCH. (IN 3 MOVEMENTS)
1(alt. with picc.),1,2,1 - 1,1,1,0 - timp.,perc. (3) - hp. (or pf.) - str.
15:00 Baron.
—— ECCE HOMO (TONE POEM)
3,*3,*3,2 - 4,2,3,1 - timp.,perc. - (4) - hp. - str.   5:00 Baron.
—— THE EXORCISM (FAUST IN THE FOREST) (SYMPHONIC
POEM)
2(2nd alt. with picc.),2(2nd alt. with Eng. hn.),2,2 - 4,2,3,1 -
timp.,perc. (4) - hp. - str.   17:00 Composer.
—— IDYLL (SYMPHONIC POEM)
2(2nd alt. with picc.),2(2nd alt. with Eng. hn.),2,2 - 4,2,2,1 -
timp.,perc. (3) - hp. - str.   6:00 Baron.
—— IN OLD NAPLES (TONE POEM)
2(2nd alt. with picc.),2(2nd alt. with Eng. hn.),2,2 - 4,2,3,1 -
timp.,perc. - (4),glock. - hp. - pf. - str.   7:00 Composer.
—— INTERMEZZO (A STORY OF LIFE)
3(3rd alt. with picc.),2(2nd alt. with Eng. hn.),*3,2 - 4,3,3,1 -
timp.,perc. (4),cel. - hp. - str.   5:00 Composer.
—— LITTLE SCHERZO OVERTURE
2(2nd alt. with picc.),2,2,2 - 4,2,3,1 - timp.,perc. (2) - hp. - str.
4:30 Composer.
—— VISIONE EROCIA (SYMPHONIC POEM)
2(2nd alt. with picc.),2,2,2 - 4,3,3,1 - timp.,perc. (4) - hp. - str.
10:00 Composer.

COSMA, Edgar
—— POSTLUDE FOR STRINGS
str.   6:30 Salabert.

COSMA, Vladimir
—— OBLIQUE (FOR CELLO AND STRINGS)
str.   9:00 Presser.

COTEL, Morris
—— CONCERTO FOR PIANO AND ORCH. (1968) (IN 1 MOVT.)
0,0,3,3 sax.(2 sopr.,1 alto),0 - 0,3(or 3 cnt.),0,0 -
perc.(9),cel.,glock.,mar.,vibra.,xyl. - pf. - 12 vln., 6 vla.
12:00 Hn. of Gabr.
—— SYMPHONIC PENTAD (WITH CONTRALTO SOLO) (1964)
(Text: Composer)
*3,3E♭cl.,2,*3 - 4,3,3,1 - timp.,perc.(2),cel.,glock.,xyl. - hp. - pf. -
str.   35:00 Hn. of Gabr.
—— VARIATIONS ON A THEME BY HAYDN (1973)
2,2,0,2 - 2,2,0,0 - timp. - str.   10:00 Hn. of Gabr.

—— WHY EVERY FLY MUST (FOR SATB CHORUS AND ORCH.)
(1963) (Text: Composer)
2(2nd alt. with picc.),2,2,2 - 2,2,2,0 - timp.,perc.(2), xyl. - pf. - str.
12:00 Hn. of Gabr.

COULOMBE SAINT-MARCOUX, Micheline
—— HÉTÉROMORPHIE (1970)
*4(1alt. with alto fl.),*3,*3,*3 - 4,3,3,1 - timp.,perc.(4) - 2 hp. - str.
11:15 CanMusCtr.
—— MODULAIRE (POUR ORCHESTRE)
14:00 C.A.P.A.C.

COUPERIN, François - BAZELAIRE
—— PIÈCES EN CONCERT (FOR CELLO AND STRINGS)
str. 10:30 Baron.

COUPERIN, François - BENOY, A. W.
—— EIGHT PIECES
fl.(or recorder) - str. Oxford.

COUPERIN, François - BRIDGEWATER
—— SUITES OF PIECES
pf.(ad lib.) - str. Mills.

COUPERIN, François - BROWN, James
—— FOUR PIECES IN THE FORM OF A SUITE
pf. - str. Galaxy.

COUPERIN, François - DE FILIPPI, Amadeo
—— SUITE FOR ORCHESTRA (IN 7 MOVTS.)
Arranger.

COUPERIN, François - DUBENSKY, A.
—— LE BAVOLET FLOTTANT (FOR STRINGS)
str. Arranger.

COUPERIN, François - HOÉRÉE, A.
—— TROISIÈME LEÇON DES TÉNÈBRES (FOR 2 HIGH VOICES,
SATB CHORUS AND ORCH.)
0,0,0,0 - 0,1,0,0 - hpsc.(or hp.) - org. - str. 18:00 Salabert.
or:
2,2,2,2 - 2,0,0,0

COUPERIN, François - MILHAUD, Darius
—— OVERTURE AND ALLEGRO, FROM "LA SULTANE"
3,3,3,2 - 4,3,3,1 - timp.,perc. - hp. - str. 7:00 EV.

COUPERIN, François - OUBRADOUS, Fernand
—— CONCERTO IN G (HUITIÈME ORDRE) (DANS LE GOUT
THÉATRAL) (IN 8 MOVTS.)
*2,2,0,1 - 0,1,0,0 - timp. - str. 21:00 Presser.
—— CONCERTO NO. 1 - LES GOUTS RÉUNIS
ob.(or vln.), cl.(or vla.), bn.(or c.) - str. 13:00 Galaxy.
—— CONCERTO NO. 6 - LES GOUTS REUNIS
fl. - hpsc.(ad lib.) - str. Galaxy.
—— CONCERTO NO. 6 (FOR TRUMPET AND STRINGS)
pf. - str. Presser.
—— LES GOUTS RÉUNIS - CONCERTO (DIXIÈME ORDRE) (IN 4
MOVTS.)
tpt.(or ob.) - str. 12:00 Presser.

COUPERIN, François - WOOD-HILL, M.
—— LOUIS XIV SUITE (PREMIER CONCERTS ROYAUX) (FOR
CHAMBER ORCH.)
fl.,ob., bn. - cemb. - str. - (no d.-b.) 8:00 Witmark.

COURBOIS, P. - OUBRADOUS, Fernand
—— DOM QUICHOTE (CANTATA) (FOR MEDIUM VOICE AND
ORCH.)
1,0,0,1 - 0,1,0,0 - timp. - str. 15:00 Presser.

COUSINS, M. Thomas
—— FANTASY ON NORTH CAROLINA COLLEGE SONGS
2,2,2,2 - 4,3,3,0 - timp.,perc. (3), bells - str. 6:00 Brodt.
—— HYMN TO THE SUBLIME (FOR MIXED CHORUS, BRASSES
AND PERCUSSION)
0,0,0,0 - 4,3,3,1 - timp.,perc. 6:30 Composer.
—— INTERLUDE FOR TRUMPET AND STRINGS
tpt. - str. 4:30 Composer.
—— OVERTURE, 1962
Composer.

—— SKALD OF FLAT ROCK (A TRIBUTE TO CARL SANDBURG)
(FOR RECITER, SATB CHORUS AND ORCH.) (1968) (Text:
Hal Sieber)
*3,2,*3,2 - 4,3,3,1 - timp.,perc.(4),bells - tape-recorder - str.
16:00 Brodt.

COWELL, Henry
—— CELTIC SUITE (IN 3 MOVTS.)
2,2,2,2 - 2,2,1,1 - timp.,perc. - str. G. Schirmer.
—— CONCERTO FOR PIANO AND ORCH. (IN 3 MOVTS.)
3(1 alt. with picc.),3(1 alt. with Eng. hn.),3,3 - 4,3,3,1 - timp.,perc.
(2) - pf. - str. 18:00 Salabert.

COWEN, Frederick
—— THE MAGIC GOBLET (THE LUCK OF EDENHALL)
2,2,2,2 - 4,2,3,1 - timp.,perc.,cel. - 1-2 hp. - str. 9:00 Bo. Hawkes.
—— MINIATURE VARIATIONS
2,2,2,2 - 4,2,3,0 - timp.,perc. - hp. (ad lib) - str. 6:30 Bo. Hawkes.
—— SUITE OF OLD ENGLISH DANCES: 2ND SET
2,2,2,2 - 4,2,3,1 - timp.,perc.,glock. - str. 25:00 Novello.

COX, David
—— THIS CHILD OF LIFE (CHRISTMAS CANTATA) (FOR SSA
CHORUS AND STRINGS)
str. 20:00 Oxford.
—— THE SUMMER'S NIGHTINGALE (CANTATA) (FOR TENOR,
WOMEN'S CHORUS AND STRINGS) (Text: Marlowe and
Raleigh)
str. 26:00 Oxford.

CRAMER, Franz - VOGT, Carl August
—— CONCERTO IN D MINOR FOR FLUTE AND ORCH. (With
cadenzas by Vogt)
1,2,2,2 - 2,2,0-1,0 - timp. - str. 16:00 Mannheimer.
—— RONDO-CONCERTINO IN C MAJOR (FOR BASSOON AND
ORCH.)
1,0,2,3 - 2,2,0,0 - perc. - str. 12:00 Mannheimer.

CRAMER, Johann Baptist - HOFMANN, Wolfgang
—— CONCERTO IN D MINOR FOR PIANO AND ORCH., OP. 26,
NO. 2
0,2,0,0 - 2,0,0,0 - pf. - str. 24:00 Mannheimer.

CRAS, Jean
—— AMES D'ENFANTS (FOR SMALL ORCH.) (IN 3 MOVTS.)
2,2,2,2 - 3,2,0,0 - timp.,perc. - hp. - str. 15:00 Salabert.
—— CONCERTO FOR PIANO AND ORCH.
2,2,2,2 - 4,2,3,0 - timp.,perc. - pf. - str. 25:00 Salabert.
—— FONTAINES (5 POEMS FOR VOICE AND ORCH.)
Salabert.
—— JOURNAL DE BORD (SYMPHONIC SUITE)
3,3,3,4 - 4,3,3,1 - timp.,perc. - 2 hp. - str. 20:00 Salabert.
—— LEGENDE (FOR CELLO AND ORCH.)
2,2,2,2 - 2,2,0,0 - timp. - hp. - str. 13:00 Salabert.
—— L' OFFRANDE LYRIQUE ("GITANJALI") (FOR VOICE AND
ORCH.)
Salabert.
—— POLYPHÈME: DIVERTISSEMENT (SONGE D'ACIS)
3,3,3,4 - 4,3,3,1 - timp.,perc.,cel. - hp. - str. 10:00 Salabert.
—— POLYPHÈME: INTERLUDE (LE SOMMEIL DE GALATHÉE)
3,3,2,3 - 4,2,0,0 - timp. - hp. - str. 4:30 Salabert.

CRAWFORD, John Charlton
—— ASH WEDNESDAY (ORATORIO) (FOR NARRATOR,
SOPRANO, BARITONE, MIXED CHORUS AND ORCH.)
Oxford.
—— LOB DER MUSIK (IN PRAISE OF MUSIC) (1952)
(VARIATIONS AND FUGUE ON A THEME OF JOHANN
RUDOLF AHLE)
1,1,1,1 - 2,0,0,0 - str. 6:00 ComFacsEd.
—— METRACOLLAGE (1973)
2(2nd alt. with picc.),2,2,2 - 4,2,3,1 - timp.,perc.(2) - str.
8:00 Composer.

CRAWFORD, Paul
—— L' AZUR (1971)
1,1,1,1 - 2,2,2,1 - glock.,cel.,vibra. - str. 12:30 CanMusCtr.

CRÉMONT, Pierre - KANYAN, Joseph M.
—— CONCERTO NO. 1 FOR CLARINET AND ORCH., OP. 4
Salabert.

CRESER, William
—— OLD ENGLISH SUITE
    2,2,2,2 -2,2,3,0 - timp.,perc. - str.   Novello.

CRESTON, Paul
—— AIRBORNE SUITE (IN 4 MOVTS.)
    3,*3,3,*3 - 4,3,3,1 - timp.,perc. - str.   13:00 Shawnee.
—— CHANT OF 1942, OP. 33
    picc. (ad lib.),2,2,2,2 - 2-4,2,3 (ad lib.),1 (ad lib.) - timp.,perc.
    (2-3),xyl. - pf. - str.   10:00 G. Schirmer.
—— CHOREOGRAPHIC SUITE, OP. 86-A
    1,1,1,1 - 2,2,1,0 - perc. - pf. - str.   25:30 Mills.
—— CHOREOGRAPHIC SUITE, OP. 86-B
    2,2,2,2 - 4,2,3,1 - perc. - pf. - str.   25:30 Mills.
—— CONCERTINO FOR MARIMBA AND ORCH., OP. 21 (IN 3
MOVEMENTS)
    2,1,1,1 - 2 hn. - timp.,perc.,mar. - str.   15:00 G. Schirmer.
—— CONCERTO FOR ACCORDIAN AND ORCH., OP. 75 (IN 3
MOVEMENTS)
    2,2,2,2 - 4,2,3,1 - timp. - acc. - str.   20:00 Ricordi.
—— CONCERTO FOR PIANO AND ORCH., OP. 43 (IN 3
MOVEMENTS)
    2(1 alt. with picc.),2,2,2 - 4,2,3,1 - timp. - pf. - str.
        21:00 Templeton.
—— CONCERTO FOR SAXOPHONE AND ORCH., OP. 26 (IN 3
MOVEMENTS)
    *3,2,2, sax.,2 - 4,2,3,1 - timp. - str.   16:00 G. Schirmer.
—— CONCERTO FOR TWO PIANOS AND ORCH., OP. 50 (IN 3
MOVEMENTS)
    *3,2,2,*2 - 4,2,3,1 - timp.,perc. - 2 pf. - str.   21:00 F. Colombo.
—— CONCERTO NO. 1 FOR VIOLIN AND ORCH., OP. 65 (IN 3
MOVEMENTS)
    2(2nd alt. with picc.),2,2,2 - 4,2,3,1 - timp. - str.
        20:00 F. Colombo.
—— CONCERTO NO. 2 FOR VIOLIN AND ORCH., OP. 78 (IN 3
MOVTS.)
    *3,2,2,2 - 4,2,3,1 - timp. - str.   20:30 F. Colombo.
—— CORINTHIANS: XIII (TONE POEM), OP. 82
    3(3rd alt. with picc.),3,3(3rd alt. with b.-cl.),3 - 4,3,3,1,euph.(ad
    lib.) - timp.,perc.(5) - hp. - pf.(alt. with cel.) - str.   14:00 Mills.
—— DANCE OVERTURE, OP. 62
    *4,*3,*3,*3 - 4,3,3,1 - timp.,perc. (3) - str.   12:00 Templeton.
—— DANCE VARIATIONS (FOR COLORATURA SOPRANO AND
ORCH.), OP. 30
    3,2,2,2 - 4,2,3,1 - timp.,perc. (3) - str.   5:00 G. Schirmer.
—— FANFARE FOR PARATROOPERS (FOR BRASS AND
PERCUSSION)
    4 hn., 3 tpt., 3 trb. - perc. (2)   1:00 Bo. Hawkes.
—— FANTASY FOR ACCORDION AND ORCH., OP. 85
    2,1,2,1 - 2,2,1,0 - perc.(2) - str.   7:00 Mills.
—— FANTASY FOR PIANO AND ORCH., OP. 32
    picc. (ad lib.),2,2,2,2 - 2-4,2,2(ad lib.),0 - timp.,perc. (2),xyl. - pf. -
    str.   8:00 G. Schirmer.
—— FANTASY FOR TROMBONE AND ORCH., OP. 42
    2(1 alt. with picc.),2,2,2 - 4,2,3,1 - timp. - str. 10:00 G. Schirmer.
—— FROM THE PSALMIST, OP. 91 (FOR CONTRALTO AND
ORCH.) (1967)
    2,2,2,2 - 4,2,3,1 - perc. - hp. - str.   21:00 Composer.
—— FRONTIERS, OP. 34
    3,*3,*3,*3 - 4,3,3,1 - timp.,perc. (5),glock.,xyl. - pf. - str.
        10:00 G. Schirmer.
—— GREGORIAN CHANT (FROM STRING QUARTET, OP. 8
    str.   6:30 Templeton.
—— HOMAGE (FOR STRING ORCH.)
    str.   3:00 Templeton.
—— INVOCATION AND DANCE, OP. 58
    2,2,2,2 - 4,2,3,1, - timp.,perc.(1-3),glock.,xyl. - pf. - str.
        12:00 G. Schirmer.
    or:
    *3,*3,*3,*3 - 4,3,3,1 - timp.,perc.(1-3),glock.,xyl. - pf. - str.
—— ISAIAH'S PROPHECY (A CHRISTMAS ORATORIO), OP. 80
    2,2,2,2 - 2,2,2,0 - timp.,perc.(2),bells,glock. - hp. - str.
        30:00 F. Colombo.
—— JANUS, OP. 77
    4(4th alt. with picc.),*3,3(3rd alt. with b.-cl.),*3 - 4,3,3,1 -
    timp.,perc.(5) - pf. - str.   12:00 F. Colombo.
—— LEGEND
        6:30 Leeds.
—— LYDIAN ODE, OP. 67
    2(2nd alt. with picc.),2,2,2 - 4,3,3,1 - timp., - str. 12:00 Ricordi.
—— MISSA SOLEMNIS, OP. 44 (FOR CHORUS AND ORCH.) -
    2,2,2,2 - 2,2,2,0 - hp. - str.   20:00 Mills.

—— NOCTURNE, OP. 83 (FOR LYRIC SOPRANO OR LYRIC
TENOR AND ORCH.)
    1,1,1,1 - 1,0,0,0 - pf. - str.   9:00 Mills.
—— OKINAWA (SUITE FOR ORCHESTRA) (IN 9 MOVTS.)
    *2,*2,*3,*2 - 2,2,3,0 - timp.,perc.(2),,xyl. - pf. - str.
        24:00 F. Colombo.
—— OUT OF THE CRADLE, OP. 5 (REVISED 1962)
    2,1,1,1 - 2,1,1,0 - timp.,perc.(2) - pf. - str. 12:00 C. Fischer.
—— PARTITA, FOR FLUTE AND VIOLIN (OR 2 VIOLINS) WITH
STRING ORCH. (IN 5 MOVTS.)
    fl. - str.   16:00 Leeds.
—— PASTORALE AND TARANTELLA, OP. 28
    3(3rd alt. with picc.),2,2,2 - 4,2,3,1 - timp.,perc. (4),xyl. - pf. - str.
        10:00 G. Schirmer.
—— PAVANE VARIATIONS, OP. 89 (1966)
    2,2,2,2 - 2,2,0,0   14:00 G Schirmer.
    or:
    3,*3,*3,*3 - 4,3,3,1 - timp.,perc.(4), bells, xyl. - pf. - str.
—— POEM, OP. 39
    3,2,2,2 - 4,2,3,1 - timp.,perc. (3) - hp. - str. 15:00 G. Schirmer.
—— PRE-CLASSIC SUITE, OP. 71 (IN 3 MOVTS.)
    3,*3,*3,*3, - 2,2,0,0 - str.   10:00 F. Colombo.
—— PRELUDE AND DANCE, OP. 25
    1,1,2,1 - 2,1,1,0 - timp.,perc. (2) - pf. - str. 7:00 G. Schirmer.
—— PSALM XXIII (FOR SATB CHORUS AND ORCH.)
    2,2,2,2 - 4,2,3,1 - timp. - hp. - str.   3:00 G. Schirmer.
—— A RUMOR, OP. 27
    1,1,2,1 - 2,2,1,0 - str.   5:00 G. Schirmer.
—— SYMPHONY NO. 1, OP. 20 (IN 4 MOVEMENTS)
    3(3rd alt. with picc.),2,2,2 - 4,2,3,1 timp.,perc. (1) - str.
        20:00 G. Schirmer.
—— SYMPHONY NO. 3 (THREE MYSTERIES), OP. 48
    3(1 alt. with picc.),*3,*3,*3, - 4,3,3,1 - timp., - hp. - str.
        27:00 Templeton.
—— SYMPHONY NO. 4, OP. 52 (IN 4 MOVEMENTS)
    2(2nd alt. with picc.),2,2,2 - 4,2,3,1 - timp. - str.
        26:00 F. Colombo.
—— SYMPHONY NO. 5, OP. 64 (IN 3 MOVEMENTS)
    *4,*3,1 E♭ cl.,*3,*3 - 4,3,3,1 - timp.,perc. (4),bells,xyl. - str.
        28:00 F. Colombo.
—— THANATOPSIS, OP. 101 (1971)
    2,2(2nd alt. with Eng. hn.),2,2 - 4,2,1,0 - timp.,perc.(2), bells - hp.
    - str.   12:00 Composer.
—— THE NORTHWEST, OP. 98 (FOR CHORUS AND ORCH.)
(1969) (IN 3 MOVTS.)
    *3,2,2,2 - 4,2,3,1 - timp.,perc.(3), xyl. - pf. - str. 14:00 Composer.
—— THRENODY, OP. 16
    3,2,2,2 - 4,2,3,1 - timp.,perc. (2) - hp. - str. 12:00 G. Schirmer.
—— TOCCATA FOR ORCHESTRA, OP. 68
    *4,*3, 1 E♭ cl.,*3,*3 - 4,3,3,1 - timp.,perc. (5),bells,glock.,xyl. - str.
        10:00 G. Schirmer.
—— TWO CHORIC DANCES, OP. 17
    1,1,1,1 - hn. - timp.,perc. (2) - pf. - str. 12:00 G. Schirmer.
    or:
    3(3rd alt. with picc.),2,2,2 - 4,2,3,1 - timp.,perc. (2) - pf. - str.
—— WALT WHITMAN(TONE POEM), OP. 53
    *4,*3,*3,*3 - 4,3,3,1 - timp.,perc. (4),cel.,glock.,xyl. - hp. - str.
        12:00 Ricordi.

CRIST, Bainbridge
—— ABHISARIKA (ORIENTAL POEM)
    *3,*3,*3,*3 - 4,3,3,1 - timp.,perc. (3) - hp. - str. 11:00 C. Fischer.
—— AMERICAN EPIC: 1620 (TONE POEM)
    3(3rd alt. with picc.),*3,*3,*3 - 4,3,3,1 - timp.,perc. (3) - hp. - str.
        13:00 C. Fischer.
—— CHINESE DANCES
    3,3,3,3 - 4,3,3,1 - timp.,perc. - str.   6:00 C. Fischer.
—— CHINESE PROCESSION
    1,1,2,1 - 2,2,1,0 - perc.(4) - str.   3:30 Witmark.
—— CHINESE SKETCHES
    2,*3,*3,*3 - 4,3,3,1 - timp.,perc. (3) - str. 8:00 C. Fischer.
—— COLOURED STARS (4 SONGS FOR VOICE AND ORCH.)
    *3,*3,*3,*3 - 4,3,3,1 - timp.,perc. (1) - hp. - str. 16:15 C. Fischer.
—— EGYPTIAN IMPRESSIONS (SYMPHONIC SUITE) (IN 4
MOVTS.)
    *3,*3,*3,*3 - 4,3,3,1 - timp.,perc. (2) - hp. - str. 12:00 C. Fischer.
—— FAIR AT KARA
    1,1,2,1 - 2,2,1,0 - timp.,perc. (3) - str.   4:45 Composer.
—— FESTIVAL OVERTURE
    3(3rd alt. with picc.),*3,*3,*3 - 4,3,3,1 - timp.,perc. (3) - str.
        8:00 C. Fischer.

—— FINAL DANCE FROM "LE PIED DE LA MOMIE" ("THE MUMMY'S FOOT")
3(3rd alt. with picc.),*3,*3,*3 - 4,3,3,1 - timp.,perc. (4) - hp. - str.
8:00 C. Fischer.

—— HINDU RHAPSODY
3(3rd alt. with picc.),*3,*3,*3 - 4,3,3,1 - timp.,perc. (3) - hp. - str.
12:00 Composer.

—— HYMN TO NEFERTITI (TONE POEM)
3(3rd alt. with picc.),*3,*3,*3 - 4,3,3,1 - timp.,perc. (2) - hp. - str.
15:00 Composer.

—— JAPANESE NOCTURNE (REVISED VERSION)
1,1,2,1 - 2,2,1,0 - timp.,perc. (2) - str.
5:30 Composer.

—— LA MORTE AMOUREUSE
3,2,3,3 - 4,3,3,1 - timp.,perc.,bells,cel.,glock. - hp. - str.
45:00 C. Fischer.

—— NAUTCH DANCE
2,2,2,3 sax.,2 - 4,2,3,1 - timp.,perc. (2) - hp. - pf. - str.
5:00 C. Fischer.

—— NOCTURNE
2,2,2,3 sax.,2 - 4,2,3,1 - timp.,perc. (2) - hp. - pf. - str.
4:00 C. Fischer.

—— LA NUIT REVÉCUE (THE NIGHT REMEMBERED) (TONE POEM)
*3,*3,*3,*3 - 4,3,3,1 - timp.,perc. (2) - hp. - str.   9:00 Composer.

—— ORIENTAL NOCTURNE
1,1,2,1 - 2,2,1,0 - timp.,perc. (2) - str.   4:00 Composer.

—— THE PARTING (POEM FOR VOICE AND ORCH.)
2,*3,*3,*3 - 4,3,3,1 - timp.,perc. (2) - hp. - str.   17:00 C. Fischer.

—— PLACE PIGALLE (SOUVENIR DE MONTMARTRE)
1,1,2,1 - 2,2,1,0 - timp.,perc. (3) - hp. - str.   4:20 C. Fischer.

—— SEVEN CHINESE MOTHER GOOSE RHYMES (FOR WOMEN'S CHORUS AND ORCH.)
*3,*3,*3,*3 - 4,3,3,1 - timp.,perc. (3) - hp. - str.   6:15 C. Fischer.

—— SIX DROLLERIES FROM AN ORIENTAL DOLL'S HOUSE (FOR VOICE AND ORCH.)
3(3rd alt. with picc.),*3,*3,*3 - 4,3,3,0 - timp.,perc. (4) - hp. - str.
5:00 C. Fischer.

—— SOUVENIR DE BALLET (IN 3 MOVTS.)
3(3rd alt. with picc.),2,2,*3 - 4,3(1 alt. with Eng. hn.),3,1 - timp.,perc. (4) - hp. - str.   10:00 Composer.

—— TWO ORIENTAL DANCES
6:00 C. Fischer.

—— VIENNA - 1913
*3,*3,*3,*3 - 4,3,3,1 - timp.,perc. (4) - hp. - str.   6:00 Witmark.

CROLEY, Randell
—— CONCERTO FOR FLUTE AND METAL ORCH. (IN 3 MOVTS.)
1,0,0,0 - 0,0,4,1 - timp.,perc.(4),bells,glock.,mar.,xyl. - pf.(alt. with cel.)   17:30 J. Boonin.

CROSSE, Gordon
—— ARIADNE (CONCERTANTE FOR OBOE AND 12 PLAYERS)
1(alt. with picc.),1,2 (2nd alt. with b.-cl.),0 - 0,1,alto trb.,1,0 - perc. - pf. - str.(1,1,1,1)   23:00 Oxford.

—— CEREMONY FOR CELLO AND ORCH.
2,0,2 Eng.hn.,*2,2 - 2,2,1,1 - perc.,timp. - hp. - pf.(alt. with cel.) - str.   18:00 Oxford.

—— CHANGES (A NOCTURNAL CYCLE) (FOR SOPRANO, BARITONE, OPTIONAL CHILDREN'S CHORUS, MIXED CHORUS AND ORCH.) (Texts: Browne, Blake, Herrick, Hawes, Davenant and Anon.)
2,1,2,2 - 2,2,2,1 - timp.,perc.(4) - pf. - str.   50:00 Oxford.

—— CONCERTO FOR CHAMBER ORCH.
1,1,1,1 - 1,1,1,0 - glock. - str.   15:00 Oxford.

—— ELEGY FOR SMALL ORCH.
1,*2,*2,0 - 1,1,1,0 - str.   8:00 Oxford.

—— EPIPHANY VARIATIONS, OP. 39 (DOUBLE VARIATIONS FOR ORCH.)
3,3,3,3 - 4,3,3,1 - timp.,perc.(5),cel. - hp. - str.   20:00 Oxford.

—— FOR THE UNFALLEN (FOR TENOR, HORN AND STRINGS) (Text: Geoffrey Hill)
hn. - str.   20:00 Oxford.

—— THE GRACE OF TODD (COMIC OPERA) % (Text: David Rudkin)
1,1,2,1 - 0,1,1,0 - perc.(2) - hp. - pf.(alt. with cel., and electronic org.) - str.   75:00 Oxford.

—— MEMORIES OF MORNING: NIGHT (A MONODRAMA) (FOR MEZZO-SOPRANO AND DOUBLE ORCH.)
3(2nd alt. with alto fl.,3rd alt. with picc.),0,0,0 - 1,3,0,0 - timp.,perc.(4) - 2 hp. - pf. - str.(6,1,3,3)   33:00 Oxford.

—— OUVERT CLOS (FOR STRINGS, WITH OPTIONAL WINDS, KEYBOARD, HARP AND PERCUSSION)
8:00 Oxford.

—— PURGATORY (OPERA, AFTER THE PLAY OF WILLIAM BUTLER YEATS) %
1(alt. with picc.),0,2(2nd alt. with b.-cl.)1 - 1,1,1,0 - perc.(2) - hp. - pf.(alt. with cel.) - str.   35:00 Oxford.

—— SINFONIA CONCERTANTE (FOR DOUBLE ORCH.)
3,3,*4,*4 - 4,3,3,1 - timp.,perc.,cel. - hp. - str.   35:00 Oxford.

—— SOME MARCHES ON A GROUND
3,2,3,2 - 4,3,3,1 - timp.,perc.(4),cel. - hp. - str.   12:00 Oxford.

—— THE STORY OF VASCO (OPERA, AFTER GEORGES SCHEHADÉ) % (Text: Ted Hughes)
3,3,*3,3 - 0,3,3,1 - timp.,perc. - cimbalom - hp. - pf.(alt. with cel.) - str.   150:00 Oxford.

—— SYMPHONIES
1(alt. with picc.),2,1(alt. with b.-cl.),0 - 2,0,0,0 - str.   18:00 Oxford.

—— SYMPHONIES FOR CHAMBER ORCHESTRA
Oxford.

—— SYMPHONIES II
str.(9,2,2,1)   15:00 Oxford.

CROSSLEY-HOLLAND, Peter
—— THE SACRED DANCE (CANTATA) (FOR BARITONE, CHORUS AND ORCH.)
2,2,2,2 - 2,2,0,0 - timp.,perc.,cel. - hp. - str.   Lengnick.

CROWE, Peter
—— ELEGY
str.   4:00 A.P.R.A.

CRUFT, Adrian
—— ACTAEON OVERTURE
5:30 Lengnick.

—— CONCERTANTE FOR FLUTE, OBOE, TIMPANI AND STRINGS, OP. 25
fl.,ob. - timp. - str.   9:00 Belw-Mills.

—— DIVERTIMENTO FOR STRINGS, OP. 43
str.   11:00 Novello.

—— DIVERTISSEMENT, OP. 28
3(3rd alt. with picc.),2,2,2 - 4,3,3,1 - timp.,perc.,glock.,vibra.,xyl. - hp. - str.   14:00 Novello.

—— ELEGY FOR HORN AND STRINGS
hn. - str.   8:00 Novello.

—— FANTASY OVERTURE, OP. 39 (PROSPERO'S ISLAND)(1962)
3,3,3,3 - 4,3,3,1 - timp.,perc.(2),cel. - hp. - pf. - str.   11:30 P.R.S.

—— MAGNIFICAT AND NUNC DIMITTIS (FOR SATB CHORUS AND ORCH.)
3,2,2,2 - 4,3,3,1 - timp., - str.   5:30 Bo. Hawkes.

—— PARTITA (FOR SMALL ORCH.)
15:00 Lengnick.

—— TE DEUM LAUDAMUS (FOR SATB CHORUS, PERCUSSION, ORGAN AND STRING ORCH.)
perc. - org. - str.   8:00 P.R.S.

—— TRADITIONAL HORNPIPE SUITE
1(alt with picc.),1,2,1 - 2,1,1,0 - perc. - str.   8:00 Galaxy.

CRUFT, Adrian - BUSH, Geoffrey
—— OXFORD SUITE, OP. 36
3,1,3,1 - 2,2,1,0 - timp.,perc. - str.   11:00 Novello.

CRUGER, J. - BACH, J. S. - CAILLIET, L.
—— NOW THANK WE ALL OUR GOD (FOR CHORUS AND ORCH.)
*3,1,*3,2 - 4,3,3,1 - timp.,perc. (4) - str.   4:00 Bo. Hawkes.

CRUMB, George
—— ECHOES OF TIME AND THE RIVER (ECHOES II) (FOUR PROFESSIONALS FOR ORCHESTRA)
3(alt. with 3 picc.),0,3,0 - 3,3,3,0 - timp.,perc. - mandolin - hp. - 2 pf.(2nd alt. with cel.) - str.   18:00 Belw-Mills.

CRUMP, Peter
—— BIRTHDAY OVERTURE
3,3,3,3 - 4,3,3,1 - timp.,perc. - str.   5:00 P.R.S.

CRUSELL, Bernhard Henrik - MICHAELS, Jost
—— CONCERTO IN F MINOR, OP. 5 (FOR CLARINET AND ORCH.)
1,2,0,2 - 2,2,0,0 - timp. - str.   25:00 F. Colombo.

CRUSIUS, Otto E.
—— CELTIC SUITE (FOR VIOLA, CELLO AND ORCH.)
1,0,1,0 - 2,0,0,0 - hp. - str.   22:00 Mannheimer.

—— CONCERTINO IN D MAJOR, FOR "QUERFLÖTE" AND
STRING ORCH.
 fl. - str.   21:00 Mannheimer.

CSENKI, Imre
—— GYPSIES (SUITE ON ORIGINAL GYPSY THEMES)
 3,2,2,2 - 4,3,3,1 - timp.,perc. - hp. - str. 15:00 Bo. Hawkes.

CUGLEY, Ian
—— CHAMBER SYMPHONY (FOR 11 WIND INSTRUMENTS)
(1971)
 2,2,2,2 - 2,1,0,0   15:00 J. Albert.
—— CONCERTO FOR VIOLIN AND ORCH. (1972)
    24:00 J. Albert.
—— FIVE VARIANTS FOR STRING ORCH. (1968)
 str.   10:30 J. Albert.
—— PAN, THE LAKE (FOR FLUTE, HORN, CELLO, PERCUSSION
AND STRINGS) (1965)
 1,0,0,0 - 1,0,0,0 - perc. - str. 7:30 J. Albert.
—— PRELUDE FOR ORCHESTRA (1965)
 3,3,3,3 - 4,3,3,1 - timp.,perc.(3) - hp. - str. 6:30 J. Albert.
—— THREE PIECES FOR CHAMBER ORCH. (1969)
 1,1,1,1 - 1,0,1,0 - perc. - str. 11:35 J. Albert.

CUI, Cesar
—— SUITE MINATURE (IN 6 MOVTS.)
 2,2,2,2 - 4,2,1,0 - timp. - hp. - str. 12:00 Baron.

CUMAR, R.
—— CINQUE DANZE MODERNE
 0,0,3, sax.,0 - 0,2,1,0 - perc. (1-2) - 1-2 pf. - str.
    11:00 Bo. Hawkes.

CUMMING, Richard
—— THE CROWNE (7 HOLY SONNETS) (FOR BASS OR
BASS-BARITONE AND ORCH.) (Text: John Donne)
 2(2nd alt. with picc.),2(2nd alt. with Eng.hn.),2,2 - 2,2,1,0 -
 timp.,perc.(3),bells, cel.,glock. - hp. - str. 20:00 Composer.

CUNDICK, Robert
—— A FULL HOUSE (SUITE) (FOR PIANO AND CHAMBER
ORCH.) 1961)
 1(alt. with picc.),1(alt. with Eng. hn.),1,1 - 2,1,1,0 - timp.,perc.(2),
 glock. - pf. - str. 14:00 Composer.
—— SONG OF NEPHI (FOR BARITONE VOICE, CHORUS AND
ORCH.) (1954) (IN 5 MOVTS.) (Text: The Book of Mormon)
 2(2nd alt. with picc.),2(2nd alt. with Eng. hn.),2,2 - 3,2,2,0 -
 timp.,perc.(2), glock. - hp. - str. 19:00 Composer.

CUNNINGHAM, Arthur
—— ADAGIO (1954)
 ob. - str.   6:00 CunMusCorp.
—— CONCENTRICS FOR ORCHESTRA (1968)
 2,2,2,1 - 3,3,3,1 - perc. - str. 28:00 Presser.
—— DIALOGUE (FOR PIANO AND CHAMBER ORCH.) (1966)
    10:00 CunMusCorp.
—— DIM DU MIM (TWILIGHT) (FOR OBOE, OR ENGLISH HORN,
AND CHAMBER ORCH.) (1958-9)
    8:00 CunMusCorp.
—— FRAGMENT
 0,0,0,0 - 3,3,3,0 - timp.,perc. 3:00 CunMusCorp.
—— LITANY FOR THE FLOWER CHILDREN (FOR SATB
CHORUS AND ORCH.)
 2,2,3,0 - 2,2,2,0 - perc. - str. 15:00 Presser.
—— LULLABYE FOR A JAZZ BABY (1969)
    7:00 CunMusCorp.
—— NIGHT LIGHTS (1955)
    4:00 Cunmuscorp.
—— NIGHT SONG (FOR VOICES, CHORUS AND ORCH.)
 3,2,*2,0 - 3,3,3,0 - timp., perc. - str. 60:00 Presser.
—— PATADITAS (FOR PIANO AND ORCH.)
 2,2,3,1 - 3,3,3,0 - timp.,perc. - pf. - str. 5:00 Presser.
—— THE PRINCE (FOR BARITONE AND ORCH.)
 3,2,2,2 - 2,2,2,1 - timp.,perc. - str. 30:00 Presser.
—— PROMETHEUS (FOR BASS VOICE AND ORCH.) (1967)
    30:00 CunMusCorp.
—— THEATRE PIECE (1966)
    10:00 Cunmuscorp.
—— THE TWO WORLD SUITE (1971)
    CunMusCorp.
—— WALTON CONCERTO (FOR DOUBLE BASS AND ORCH.)
(1971)
    CunMusCorp.

CUNNINGHAM, Michael G.
—— BALLET IN JAZZ STYLE, OP. 19 (JAZZ BALLET) (1966) %
 1(alt. with picc.),0,2,0 - 0,1,0,0 - perc.(1) - str. 20:00 Composer.
—— CONCERTO FOR PIANO AND ORCH., OP. 26 (1968)
 3(1 alt. with picc.),*3,*3,2 - 4,3,3,1 - hp. - pf. - str.
    20:00 Seesaw.
—— CONCERTO FOR TRUMPET AND ORCH. OP. 23 (1967) (IN 3
MOVTS.)
 2,*3,*3,*3 - 4,1,3,1 - perc.(1) - str. CAP.
—— COUNTER CURRENTS, OP. 16-A (1960)
 3(1 alt.with picc.),*3,*3,*3 - 4,3,3,1 - timp.,perc.(3),cel.,xyl. - hp. -
 str.   6:30 CAP.
—— COUNTER CURRENTS, OP. 16-B (1960)
 str.   6:30 CAP.
—— DIALOGUE FOR ORCH. AND WIND TRIO, OP. 11-A (1959)
(WITH SOLO FLUTE, CLARINET AND BASSOON)
 3(1 alt. with picc.),*3,2,2 - 4,3,3,1 - timp.,perc.(2) - str.
    6:00 Composer.
—— FIGG AND BEAN (OPERA) %
 1,0,1,0 - 1,0,0,0 - str. 60:00 Seesaw.
—— FREE DESIGNS, OP. 45 (1972) (SUITE) (IN 4 MOVTS.)
 3(2 alt.with picc.),2,*3,2 - 4,3,3,1 - perc.(2),glock.,vibra.,xyl. - hp. -
 str.   15:00 Seesaw.
—— IRISH SYMPHONY, OP. 48
 str.   20:00 Seesaw.

CURTIS-SMITH, C.
—— BELLE DU JOUR (BELLS)
 *4,3,3,*4 - 4,4,3,0 - timp.,perc.,cel. - hp. - pf. - str. 18:00 Salabert.

CUSHING, Charles
—— CEREUS (POEM FOR ORCH.)
 3,3,3,2 - 4,2,3,0 - timp.,perc.,cel. - hp. - str. 8:00 Templeton.

CZARNIAWSKI, Cornelius
—— NOTTURNO (FOR PIANO AND ORCH.)
 2,1,2,1 - 3,2,3,1 - timp.,perc. - pf. - str. 6:00 Modern.

CZENSKI, Imre
—— GYPSY SUITE (ON ORIGINAL THEMES)
 3,2,3,2 - 4,3,3,1 - timp.,perc. - hp. - str. 15:00 Bo. Hawkes.

CZERNIK, W.
—— ACHT LIEDER (FÜR MITTLERE STIMME UND ORCH.)
 3,3(1st and 2nd alt. with Eng. hn.),2,2 - 3,2,0,0 - timp.,perc.,cel. -
 hp. - str.   20:45 Henmar.
—— THE BEAUTIFUL CARLOTTA (DIE SCHÖNE CARLOTTI):
BALLET MUSIC IN OLDEN STYLE
 2,2,2,2 - 4,2,3,1 - timp.,perc. - hp. - str. 11:00 F. Colombo.
—— THE BEAUTIFUL CARLOTTA (DIE SCHÖNE CARLOTTI):
ENTR'ACTE MUSIC
 2,2,2,2 - 4,2,3,1 - timp.,perc. - hp. - str. 5:00 F. Colombo.
—— CONCERTINO FÜR FLÖTE UND ORCH.
 1,1,2,2 - 2,2,1,0 - perc. - hp. - str. 9:00 Henmar.
—— DIONYSISCHES FEST (RHAPSODIE FÜR KLAVIER UND
ORCH.)
 1,1,3,1 - 2,3,3,0 - timp.,perc. - hp. - str. 13:00 AhnSimrock.
—— GROSS-STADT BEI NACHT (SUITE) (IN 5 MOVTS.)
 2,2,2,2 - 4,2,3,0 - perc. - hp. - pf. - str. 10:50 Henmar.
—— IN WANDEL DER ZEITEN (SUITE) (IN 3 MOVTS.)
 2,2,2,2 - 4,2,3,0 - perc. - hp. - pf. - str. 9:30 Henmar.
—— EIN KÜNSTLERFEST (OVERTURE)
 2,2,2,2 - 4,2,3,0 - perc. - hp. - pf. - str. 5:00 Henmar.
—— LAUNIGE NACHT (OVERTURE)
 2,2,2,2 - 4,2,3,0 - perc. - hp. - pf. - str. 8:00 Henmar.
—— RÜBEZAHL (SYMPHONIC POEM)
 3(3rd alt. with picc.),2(2nd alt. with Eng. hn.),*3,*3 - 4,3,3,1 -
 timp.,perc.(4),cel. - hp. - str. 26:00 Henmar.
—— VIA VITALIS (SUITE) (IN 3 MOVTS.)
 3(or picc.),2(or Eng. hn.),2,2 - 4,3,3,0 - timp.,perc. - hp. - str.
    23:00 AhnSimrock.

CZERNY, Karl - NEWCATER, Graham
—— CZERNYANA III (BALLET) %
 2,2,3,2 - 4,2,3,1 - timp.,perc. - str. 30:00 S.A.M.R.O.

CZERWONKY, Richard
—— CARNIVAL OF LIFE (A FANTASIA)
 3(3rd alt. with picc.),*3,2,2 - 4,2,3,1 - timp.,perc. - str.
    10:00 C. Fischer.

—— CONCERTO IN D FOR VIOLIN AND ORCH. (IN 3
   MOVEMENTS)
   2(2nd alt. with picc.),2,2,2 - 4,2,3,0 - timp.,perc. - str.
                                          30:00 C. Fischer.
—— EPISODE
   3(3rd alt. with picc.),2,2(2nd alt. with b.-cl.),2 - 4,2,3,1 -
   timp.,perc. - pf. - str.   10:00 C. Fischer.
—— SYMPHONY IN D MINOR
   1. Adagio; 2. Allegro risoluto; 3. Andante con moto; 4. Allegretto
   - Presto; 5. Allegro
   3(3rd alt. with picc.),2,2,2 - 4,2,3,1 - timp.,perc. (3) - hp. - str.
                                          30:00 Composer.
—— TWO MODERN SKETCHES
   3(3rd alt. with picc.),2,2,2 - 4,2,3,1 - timp.,perc. - hp. - str.
                                          8:00 C. Fischer.
—— WELTSCHMERZ (GRIEF)
   3(3rd alt. with picc.),*3,*3,2 - 4,3,3,1 - timp.,perc. - hp. - str.
                                          8:00 C. Fischer.

D

DAETWYLER, Jean
—— ALPEN-SYMPHONIE
   2,2,2,2 - 4,3,3,0 - timp. - hp. - str.   32:00 S.U.I.S.A.
—— CONCERTO FÜR ALPHORN UND ORCH.
   2,2,2,2 - 2,2,alphorn,0,0 - timp.,perc. - str.   25:20 S.U.I.S.A.
—— CONCERTO POUR ORCHESTRE À CORDES ET BATTERIE
   perc. - str.   23:00 S.U.I.S.A.
—— CONCERTO POUR TROMPETTE ET ORCH. DE CHAMBRE
                                          18:00 S.U.I.S.A.
—— CONCERTO POUR VIOLIN ET ORCH.
                                          28:00 S.U.I.S.A.
—— DANSE DE MASQUES ET DANSE MACABRE (FÜR
   STREICHORCH. MIT SCHLAGZEUG)
   perc. - str.   13:00 S.U.I.S.A.
—— KONZERT FÜR VIOLINE UND GROSSES ORCHESTER
                                          28:00 S.U.I.S.A.
—— NOCTURNE, SCHERZO ET PASTORALE (POUR
   VIOLONCELLE ET GRAND ORCH.)
                                          23:00 S.U.I.S.A.
—— SPORT SYMPHONIE (POUR GRAND ORCH.)
                                          22:00 S.U.I.S.A.
—— SYMPHONIE DIALOGUÉE (FÜR GROSSES ORCHESTER)
                                          32:00 S.U.I.S.A.
—— EINE TANZ - SYMPHONIE (DANCES DU TEMPS PRÉSENT)
   (FÜR GROSSES ORCH.)
                                          28:00 S.U.I.S.A.

DAHL, Ingolf
—— ARIA SINFONICA (1965)
   *3,*3,*3,*3 - 4,3,3,1 - timp.,perc.(3) - hp. - pf. - str.
                                          17:00 Composer.
—— CONCERTO FOR SAXOPHONE AND WIND ORCH. (1949)
   *3,*3,*5,1 sax.,*3 - 4,4,3,2 - timp.,perc.(3) - d.-b.-'s
                                          18:30 MCA Music.
—— ELEGY CONCERTO, FOR VIOLIN AND CHAMBER ORCH.
   (Completed 1971 by Donal Michalsky)
                                          14:30 J. Boonin.
—— INTERVALS FOR STRING ORCHESTRA (1970) (IN 4 MOVTS.)
   str.   F. Colombo.
—— QUODLIBET ON AMERICAN FOLKTUNES (THE FANCY
   BLUE DEVIL'S BREAKDOWN) (ORCH. 1965)
   *3,2,*3,2 - 4,3,3,1 - timp.,perc.(2) - pf.(ad lib.) - str. 5:00 Henmar.
—— SYMPHONY CONCERTANTE (FOR 2 CLARINETS AND
   ORCH.) (Revised 1975 by Donal Michalsky)
   *2,*2,2,2 - 2,2,2,0 - timp.,perc.(2) - hp. - str.   18:00 J. Boonin.
—— THE TOWER OF SAINT BARBARA (BALLET) % (1954) (IN 4
   MOVTS.)
   *2,2,2,2 - 4,2,3,1 - timp.,perc.(2) - hp. - str.   23:00 Templeton.
—— VARIATIONS ON A THEME OF C.P.E. BACH (FOR STRINGS)
   str.   14:00 Tetra.

DAHL, Ingolf - MICHALSKY, Donal
—— ELEGY CONCERTO (FOR VIOLIN AND SMALL ORCH.) (IN
   1 MOVT.) (By Ingolf Dahl; completed by Donal Michalsky 1971)
                                          14:00 J. Boonin.

DAHL, Viking
—— INTRODUCTION, DANCE AND FINALE (FROM "MAISON
   DES FOUS")
   2,2,2,2 - 4,2,2,1 - timp.,perc.(3),cel. - pf. - str.   12:00 Fleisher.
—— PRELUDE AND CHORAL
   1,1,1,1 - 2,2,1,0 - str.   S.T.I.M.
—— SUITE ORIENTALE
   3,3,3,2 - 4,3,2,0 - timp.,perc. (2), cel. - hp. - str.   15:00 S.T.I.M.
—— SVENSKA LÅTAR (SUITE)
   1,1,1,1 - 2,2,1,0 - timp.,perc. - str.   15:00 S.T.I.M.
—— UR MAISON DES FOUS
   2,3,3,2 - 4,2,2,0 - timp.,perc. (2) - hp. - str.   10:00 S.T.I.M.
—— UR OPERAN ALLSEGRAREN (RHAPSODY)
   2,2,2,3 sax.,2 - 4,2,2,1 - timp.,perc. (2),cel.,xyl. - hp. - str.
                                          12:00 S.T.I.M.

DAIA, Michael
—— POÈME (FOR VIOLIN AND ORCH.)
                                          S.I.A.E.
—— SYMPHONIC SUITE (IN 18TH CENTURY STYLE)
                                          S.I.A.E.

DALBY, Martin
—— CONCERTO MARTIN PESCATORE (1971)
   str.   13:00 Novello.
—— CONFLICT (THREE EPISODES FOR ORCH.)(1964)
   2,2,2,2 - 4,2,0,0 - timp.,perc. - hp. - str.   13:30 P.R.S.
—— ESTAMPIES
   2,2,2,2 - 4,2,3,1 - timp.,perc. - str.   23:30 P.R.S.
—— OVERTURE ("INTRODUCTION AND RONDO")(1963)
   2,2,2,2 - 4,3,3,1 - timp.,perc.(3) - hp. - str.   10:00 P.R.S.
—— PHYLLIDULA (1964)
   2,2,2,2 - 4,3,2,1 - timp.,perc.(5) - hp. - str.   10:00 P.R.S.
—— SONATA FOR TRUMPET, STRINGS AND TIMPANI
   tpt. - timp. - str.   12:00 P.R.S.
—— SYMPHONY (1969)
   2,2,2,2 - 4,3,3,1 - timp.,perc.(3) - hp. - str.   25:00 P.R.S.
—— SYMPHONY (1970)
   3(2nd and 3rd alt. with picc.),2,2(2nd alt. with b.-cl.),2(2nd alt.
   with c.-bn.) - 4,4,3,1 - timp.,perc.(4) - hp. - pf.(alt. with cel.) - str.
                                          22:00 Novello.
—— THE TOWER OF VICTORY (1973)
   2,2,4(4th alt. with b.-cl.),3 - 4,3(alt. with 3 cnts.),3,2 -
   timp.,perc.(5) - hp. - str.   Novello.
—— WALTZ OVERTURE (1965)
   2,1,2,1 - 1,1,1,0 - perc. - hp. - str.   9:30 P.R.S.

DALE, Gordon
—— BY HOUGHTON MILLS, OP. 7 (1961)
   1,1,1,1 - 0,0,1,0 - perc. - pf. - str.   10:00 P.R.S.
—— CONCERTO FOR PIANO, PERCUSSION AND STRINGS, OP.
   37
   perc. - pf. - str.   14:30 P.R.S.
—— ISLINGTON GREEN, OP. 25 (SUITE) (1966)
   fl. - str.   16:00 P.R.S.
—— A MIDLAND OVERTURE, OP. 36
   3,2,2,2 - 4,2,3,1 - timp.,perc.(3) - str.   14:30 P.R.S.
—— A NIGHT PIECE, OP. 29 (1967)
   3,2,2,2 - 2,2,2,0 - perc.(2) - str.   6:00 P.R.S.
—— SONNET FOR OBOE AND STRINGS, OP. 11 (1962)
   ob. - str.   6:00 P.R.S.
—— THROUGH CHILDHOOD, OP. 9 (FOR PIANO AND ORCH.)
   (1962)
   1,1,1,1 - 0,1,1,0 - perc. - str.   15:00 P.R.S.
—— WOODLAND RIDE, OP. 16 (1963)
   str.   8:00 P.R.S.

DALGLEISH, James
—— STATEMENT FOR ORCH.
                                          Chappell.

DALL'ABACO, E. F. - BONELLI, Ettore
—— CONCERTO DA CHIESA, OP. 2, NO. 4 (FOR STRINGS)
   str.   Henmar.

DALL'ABACO, E. F. - DRESSKELL, Miles A.
—— CONCERTO DA CHIESA
   hpsc.(or pf.) - str.   10:00 C. Fischer.

DALLAPICCOLA, Luigi

—— AN MATHILDE (TO MATHILDE) (CANTATA) (FOR FEMALE VOICE AND ORCH., ON POEMS OF H. HEINE)
1,2,3,1 sax.,1 - 2,1,1,0 - timp.,perc.(3),cel.,glock.,vibra.,xyl. - hp. - str.　　　　15:00 Leeds.

—— CANTI DI LIBERAZIONE (SONGS OF DELIVERANCE) (FOR CHORUS AND ORCH.)
3,3,4,2 sax.,3 - 4,3,3,1 - timp.,perc.(6),bells,cel.,glock.,vibra.,2 xyl. - 2 hp. - str.　　　　30:00 Leeds.

—— CANTI DI PRIGONIA (FOR MIXED CHORUS AND ORCH.) (IN 3 MOVTS.)
timp.,perc.,vibra.,xyl. - 2 hp. - 2 pf. - str.　　　　25:00 Bo. Hawkes.

—— CINQUE FRAMMENTI DI SAFFO (5 FRAGMENTS FROM SAPPHO) (FOR VOICE AND CHAMBER ORCH.)
2,1,3,1 - 1,1,0,0 - cel. - hp. - pf. - str.(no c.)　　　　8:00 Leeds.

—— CONCERTINO PER MURIEL COUVREUX
*3,1,2,1 - 0,2,1,0 - timp.,perc.,xyl. - hp. - pf. - str.　　　　20:00 Bo. Hawkes.

—— CONCERTO PER LA NOTTE DI NATALE DELL'ANNO 1956 (FOR SOPRANO AND CHAMBER ORCH.)
1,1,1,1 sax.,1 - 1,1,0,0 - cel.,glock.,vibra.,xyl. - hp. - pf. - str.　　　　15:00 Leeds.

—— DIALOGHI (DIALOGUES) (FOR CELLO AND ORCH.)
2,2,3,1 sax.,2 - 1,1,1,1 - timp.,perc.(4),cel.,mar.,vibra.,xyl. - hp. - str.　　　　16:00 Leeds.

—— DIVERTIMENTO IN QUATTRO ESERCIZI
1,1,1,0 - 0,0,0,0 - str.　　　　10:00 Bo. Hawkes.

—— DUE PEZZI (TWO PIECES)
2,2,2,2 - 4,3,2,1 - timp.,perc.,cel.,xyl. - hp. - pf. - str.　　11:00 Leeds.

—— JOB - UNA SACRA RAPPRESENTAZIONE (IN 1 ACT) (FOR SOLO VOICES, CHORUS AND ORCH.) %
3,2,3,2 - 2,2,1,1, - timp.,perc.(2),cel.,vibra.,xyl. - hp. - pf. - str.　　　　35:00 Leeds.
on stage: 0,0,0,0 - 2,2,1,0 - org.

—— MARSIA (FRAMMENTI SINFONICI DAL BALLETTO)
4,3,4, sax.,3 - 4,3,3,1 - timp.,perc. - 1-2 hp. - pf. - str.　　　　23:00 Bo. Hawkes.

—— PAROLE DI SAN PAOLO (FOR MEZZO-SOPRANO AND 12 INSTS.)
MCA Music.

—— PARTITA (FOR SOPRANO AND ORCH.) (IN 4 MOVTS.)
*4,*3,*4,*3 - 4,4,3,1 - timp.,perc. (4), cel. - hp. - org. - pf. - str.　　　　26:00 Bo. Hawkes.

—— PREGHIERE (PRAYERS) (FOR BARITONE AND CHAMBER ORCH.) (Text: Murilo Mendes)
1,1,2,1 sax.,2 - 1,1,0,0 - vibra.(alt. with xyl.) - hp. - pf.(alt. with cel.) - str.　　　　8:00 Leeds.

—— IL PRIGIONIERO (THE PRISONER) (1-ACT MUSIC-DRAMA) %
3,2,3,2 sax.,2 - 4,3,3,1 - timp.,perc.,cel.,glock.,vibra.,xyl. - 2 hp. - pf. - str.　　　　50:00 Leeds.
or:
2,2,2,2 - 4,2,2,1 - timp.,perc.(3),cel.,glock.,vibra.,xyl. - hp. - str.
on stage: 0,0,0,0 - 0,2,1,0 - bells - org.

—— QUATTRO LIRICHE DI MACHADO (FOR SOPRANO AND 17 INSTS.)
MCA Music.

—— RAPSODIA (STUDIO PER LA MORTE DEL CONTE ORLANDO) (FOR VOICE AND ORCH.)
1,1,2,1 - 2,3,1,0 - timp.,perc.,cel.,xyl. - hp. - str.　　　　15:00 Bo. Hawkes.

—— REQUIESCANT (FOR CHILDREN'S CHORUS, MIXED CHORUS AND ORCH.)
2,2,3,1 sax.,2 - 1,1,1,1 - timp.,perc.(3),cel.,glock.,vibra.,xyl. - hp. - str.　　　　18:00 Leeds.

—— SEI CORI DI MICHELANGELO BUONARROTI IL GIOVANE: 2ND SERIES (INVENZIONE E CAPRICCIO) (FOR 2 SOPRANOS, 2 CONTRALTOS, FEMALE CHORUS AND 17 INSTRUMENTS)
2,1,2,1 - 2,2,1,1 - pf. - str.　　　　9:00 Bo. Hawkes.

—— SEI CORI DI MICHELANGELO BUONARROTI IL GIOVANE: 3RD SERIES (CIACCONA E GAGLIARDA) (FOR MIXED CHORUS AND ORCH.)
3,3,4, - 1-2 sax.,3 - 4,3,3,1 - timp.,perc.,xyl. - 1-2 hp. - pf. - str.　　　　9:00 Bo. Hawkes.

—— SEX CARMINA ALCAEI (6 POEMS OF ALCAEUS) (FOR VOICE AND 11 INSTRUMENTS)
1,1,1,1 - 1,1,0,0 - hp. - pf. - str.(no d.-b.)　　　　8:00 Leeds.

—— SICUT UMBRA... (FOR CONTRALTO AND 4 INSTRUMENTAL GROUPS) (1970) (Text: J. R. Jimenez)
*2,alto fl.,0,1 E♭cl.,*2,0 - 0,0,0,0, - cel.,vibra. - hp. -vln.,vla.,c.
MCA Music.

—— TRE LAUDI (FOR HIGH VOICE AND CHAMBER ORCH.)
1,1,1,1 - 1,1,0,0 - hp. - pf. - str.　　　　14:00 Bo. Hawkes.

—— TRE STUDI (FOR SOPRANO AND 19 INSTRUMENTS)
2,1,3, sax.,2 - 2,2,0,1 - bells - hp. - pf. - str.　　　　10:00 Bo. Hawkes.

—— ULISSE (ULYSSES) (2-ACT OPERA WITH PROLOGUE, AFTER HOMER, WITH LIBRETTO BY THE COMPOSER) % (1968)
4,3,4,2 sax.3 - 4,4,3,1 - timp.,perc.(6),bells,cel.,glock.,vibra.,xyl. - 2 hp. - org. - pf. - str.　　　　MCA Music.

—— VARIAZIONI
4,3,2,2 - 4,2,3,1 - timp.,perc.(3),cel.,vibra.,xyl. - hp. - str.　　　　14:00 Leeds.

DALLIN, Leon

—— CONCERTO FOR CLARINET AND SMALL ORCH. (IN 3 MOVTS.)
2,2,1,2 - 2,0,0,0 - timp. - str.　　　　14:40 Composer.

—— FILM OVERTURE
*3,2,*3,2 - 4,3,3,1 - timp.,perc.(3) - hp. - pf. - str.　　5:08 Composer.

—— SONGS OF PRAISE (4 SONGS) (FOR CONTRALTO, TENOR, CHORUS AND ORCH.)
2,2,2,2 - 4,3,3,1 - timp. - str.　　　　16:17 Composer.

—— SYMPHONIC SKETCHES (IN 3 MOVTS.)
2(2nd alt. with picc.),2,2,2 - 4,2,3,1 - timp.,perc.(3) - hp. - str.　　　　9:00 Composer.

—— SYMPHONY IN D (IN 3 MOVTS.)
2,2,2,2 - 4,2,3,1 - timp.,perc.(2) - str.　　　　21:20 Composer.

DALMANS, Indulis E.

—— SPRINGTIME SUITE (FOR CHAMBER ORCH.)
G. Schirmer.

DAMAIS, E.

—— LE CHEMIN DE LA CROIX (ORATORIO) (FOR CHORUS AND ORCH.)
Baron.

—— ESQUISSES SYMPHONIQUES
Baron.

DAMAIS, Emile

—— O NUIT (FOR SOPRANO OR TENOR VOICE AND ORCH.)
2,2,2,sop. sax., alto sax., 2 - 2,3,2,1 - timp.,perc. - hp. - str.　　　　10:00 Presser.

DAMASE, Jean-Michel

—— BALANCE À TROIS (BALLET) %
2,2,2,2 - 4,3,2,1 - timp., perc. - hp. - pf.(or cel.) - str.　　　　21:00 Presser.

—— BALLADE (FOR GUITAR AND STRINGS)
guit. - str.　　　　Presser.

—— LA BOUCLE (BALLET) %
2,2,2,2 - 4,3,2,1 - timp., perc., cel. - hp. - pf. - str.　　20:00 Presser.

—— CONCERTINO FOR HARP AND STRINGS
hp. - str.　　　　EV.

—— CONCERTO FOR HARP AND ORCH.
2,2,2,2 - 2,2,2,0 - timp.,perc.,cel. - hp. - str.　　　　20:00 Presser.

—— CONCERTO FOR VIOLIN AND ORCH.
23:00 EV.

—— CONCERTO NO. 1 FOR PIANO AND ORCH.
3,2,2,3 - 4,3,3,1 - timp.,perc.,cel. - 2 hp. - pf. - str.　　24:00 Salabert.

—— CONCERTO NO. 2 FOR PIANO AND ORCH.
2,2,2,2 - 2,2,2,0 - timp., perc., cel. - pf. - str.　　　　20:00 Presser.

—— CONCERTSTÜCK (FOR ALTO SAXOPHONE AND ORCH.)
1,1,1, alto sax.,1 - 1,0,0,0 - hp.- str.　　　　6:00 Baron.

—— DIVERTIMENTO (1954)
2,1,2,1 - 2,2,1,0 - timp. - hp.(or pf.)　　　　12:00 Salabert.

—— DOUBLE CONCERTO FOR FLUTE, HARP (OR HARPSICHORD) AND STRINGS
fl. - hp. (or hpsc.) - str.　　　　Presser.

—— ET LA BELLE SE RÉVEILLA (CONTE LYRIQUE EN 1 ACTE) % (FOR SOPRANO, TENOR, BARITONE AND ORCH.)
2,2,2,2 - 2,2,1,0 - timp.,perc.,cel. - hp. - str.　　22:00 Salabert.

—— UNE LETTRE DE CHARLES BAUDELAIRE (FOR TENOR AND ORCH.) (1965)
2,2,2,2 - 2,2,1,0 - timp.,perc.,cel. - hp. - str.　　22:00 Salabert.

—— PIÈGE DE LUMIÈRE (SUITE FROM THE BALLET)
25:00 EV.

—— PRÉLUDE AU MATIN
1,0,1,1 - 1,1,0,0 - hp. - pf. - str.　　　　7:30 Presser.

—— RHAPSODIE DE PRINTEMPS (FOR PIANO AND ORCH.)
2,2,2,2 - 4,2,2,1 - timp.,perc. - hp. - pf. - str.　　　　17:00 Presser.

—— RHAPSODY FROM THE BALLET "LE PRINCE DU DÉSERT"
2,2,2,2 - 2,2,2,1 - timp.,perc.,cel. - hp. - pf. - str.　　　　12:00 Presser.

—— SYMPHONY
    3,3,3,3 - 4,3,3,1 - timp.,perc.,cel. - 2 hp. - str.   25:00 Salabert.
—— LE TENDRE ÉLÉONORE (OPERA-BUFFA) % (Text: L. Masson)
    2,2,2,2 - 2,2,2,0 - timp.,perc.,cel. - hp. - str.   95:00 Eds. Fran.
—— THREE CHORALES FOR STRINGS
    str.   10:00 Salabert.
—— THREE SONGS OF CHARLES D'ORLÉANS (FOR MEDIUM VOICE AND ORCH.) (1950)
    2,1,2,1 - 2,1,0,0 - cel. - hp. - str.   10:00 Salabert.
—— VARIATIONS ON A THEME BY RAMEAU (FOR HARPSICHORD AND STRINGS)
    hpsc. - str.   17:00 Presser.
—— VARIATIONS ON A THEME OF GILBERT BECAUD (BALLET) %
    2,2,2,2 - 4,3,3,0 - timp., perc., cel. - hp. - str.   22:00 Presser.

DAMM, Sixten
—— BALLET SUITE
    2,2,2,2 - 2,2,0,0 - timp.,perc. - hp. - str.   10:00 S.T.I.M.
—— BYMARKNADEN (SUITE) (IN 5 MOVTS.)
    2,2,2,2 - 2,2,0,0 - timp.,perc. - str.   20:00 S.T.I.M.
—— CONCERTO IN C MINOR, FOR PIANO AND ORCH.
    2,2,2,2 - 4,2,0,0 - timp. - pf. - str.   S.T.I.M.
—— LANTLIG (SUITE)
    ,2,2,2,2 - 4,3,3,1 - timp.,perc. - str.   11:00 S.T.I.M.
—— SAGOSPELS (OVERTURE)
    2,2,2,2 - 2,2,0,0 - timp.,perc. - str.   6:00 S.T.I.M.
—— SKOGS FANTASY (SUITE)
    2,2,2,2 - 2,2,1,0 - timp.,perc. - hp. - str.   10:00 S.T.I.M.
—— SYMPHONIC SUITE
    2,2,2,2 - 4,3,3,1 - timp.,perc. - str.   20:00 S.T.I.M.
—— SYMPHONY IN F MINOR
    2,2,2,2 - 4,3,3,1 - timp.,perc. - str.   S.T.I.M.

DAMROSCH, Walter
—— AN ABRAHAM LINCOLN SONG (FOR BARITONE, CHORUS AND ORCH.)
    2,2,2,2 - 4,3,3,1 - timp.,perc. (3) - hp. - str.   7:00 Witmark.
—— CYRANO (OPERA) %
    Composer.
—— DUNKIRK (BALLAD FOR MEDIUM VOICE, UNISON CHOIR, PIANO, TYMPANI AND STRINGS)
    timp. - pf. - str.   Composer.

DAN, Ikuma
—— THE SILK ROAD (SYMPHONIC SUITE)
    43:00 J.A.S.R.A.C.

DANDELOT, Georges
—— CONCERTO ROMANTIQUE, FOR VIOLIN AND ORCH. (1944)
    3,2,2,2 - 4,3,3,0 - timp., perc., cel. - hp. - str.   27:30 Presser.

DANDELOT, M.
—— CONCERTO FOR PIANO AND ORCHESTRA
    22:15 EV.

D'ANGELO, James
—— CONCERTINO FOR SAXOPHONE QUARTET AND ORCH. (1961) (IN 3 MOVTS.)
    *3,*3,*3,1 alto sax.,2 ten.sax.,1bar.sax.,2 - 4,3,3,1 - timp.,perc.(2) - str.   16:00 Composer.
—— THE FESTIVAL OF ATTIS AND CYBELE (1965) (IN 6 MOVTS.)
    *3,*3,*3,1 alto sax.,*3 - 4,3,3,1 - timp.,perc.(3),vibra.,xyl. - hp. - str.   39:00 Composer.

DANIEL-LESUR
—— L' ANDREA DEL SARTO
    2,2,2,2 - 2,2,2,1 - perc. - hp. - str.   12:00 E.C.Kerby.
—— PASSACAILLE (FOR PIANO AND ORCH.)
    3,3,3,3 - 4,3,3,1 - timp., perc. - 2 hp. - pf. - str.   18:00 Presser.

DANIELS, M. L.
—— CELEBRATION SUITE (1974) (IN 4 MOVTS.)
    *3,2,2,2 - 4,3,3,1 - timp.,perc.,bells - str.   13:00 Composer.
—— FESTIQUE (1970)
    *3,2,2,2 - 4,3,3,1 - timp.,perc. - str.   6:00 Ludwig.
—— THE PROMISE OF AMERICA (A BICENTENNIAL SALUTE) (FOR NARRATOR, SATB CHORUS AND ORCH.) (1975)
    2,1,0,1 - 2,3,3,1 - timp.,perc. - str.(min: 2,1,1,1)   14:00 Composer.

DANIELS, Mabel
—— DEEP FOREST (PRELUDE FOR LITTLE SYMPHONY)
    1,1,1,1 - 1-2,1,1(ad lib.),0 - timp.,perc. - str.   6:00 C. Fischer.
    or:
    2,2,2,2 - 4,2,3,1 - timp.,perc. - hp. - str.
—— PASTORAL ODE, OP. 40
    fl. - str.   9:00 Composer.
—— PIRATES' ISLAND
    *3,2,2,2 - 4,2,3,1 - timp.,perc. (3) - str.   6:00 Composer.
—— A PSALM OF PRAISE (FOR MIXED CHORUS AND ORCH.)
    3 tpt. - timp.,perc. (2) - str.   8:00 Gray.
—— THE SONG OF JAEL, OP. 37 (CANTATA) (FOR SOPRANO, CHORUS AND ORCH.)
    2(2nd alt. with picc.),2(1st alt. with Eng. hn.),2,2 - 4,2,3,1 - timp.,perc (3) - hp. - str.   20:00 J. Fischer.

DANKNER, Stephen
—— SYMPHONY (1970)
    2,2,2,2 - 2,2,2,1 - perc.(5) - str.   23:00 Seesaw.

DANKWORTH, John
—— CONCERTO FOR PIANO AND SMALL ORCH.
    *2,2,0,2 - 2,0,0,0 - pf. - str.   17:00 Novello.
—— ESCAPADE (FOR JAZZ GROUP AND CHAMBER ORCH.)
    2,2,2-*3, sax.(or tpt.),2 - 2,0,0,0 - perc. - pf. - str.   13:00 Oxford.
—— TOM SAWYER'S SATURDAY (FOR NARRATOR AND ORCH.) (Text: Mark Twain)
    2,2,2-3,1-2 - 2,3,2,0 - timp.,perc.(4) - str.   10:00 Oxford.

DANZI, Franz - BODART, Eugen
—— CONCERTO IN E FLAT MAJOR FOR HORN AND ORCH.
    2,2,0,1 - 3,0,0,0 - str.   16:00 Mannheimer.
—— CONCERTO IN E MINOR FOR CELLO AND ORCH.
    1,2,0,2 - 2,2,0,0 - perc. - str.   27:00 Mannheimer.
—— OVERTURE IN E FLAT MAJOR
    2,2,0,1 - 2,0,0,0 - str.   6:00 Mannheimer.

DANZI, Franz - HOFMANN, Wolfgang
—— SINFONIA CONCERTANTE IN B FLAT MAJOR (FOR CLARINET, BASSOON AND ORCH.)
    1,2,1,2 - 2,0,0,0 - str.   20:00 Mannheimer.
—— SYMPHONY IN D MINOR, OP. 24
    1,2,0,2 - 2,2,0,0 - timp. - str.   Mannheimer.

DANZI, Franz - LELOIR, Edmond
—— CONCERTO IN E FLAT MAJOR FOR HORN AND ORCH. (IN 3 MOVTS.)
    2,0,0,0 - 4,0,0,0 - str.   14:00 Henmar.

DAO, Nguyen Thien
—— BA ME VIET NAM
    *1,0,*1,0 - 0,0,2,0 - perc.(3) - Hammond org. - str.(7,0,3,2)   25:00 Salabert.
—— MAU VA HOA
    6,4,6,4(4th alt. with c.-bn.) - 6,4,4,3 - perc.(5) - str. (no vlas.)   30:00 Salabert.

DAOZ, Ram
—— CONCERTINO FOR TREBLE RECORDER AND STRING ORCH.
    Recorder - str.   10:00 A.C.U.M.
—— CONCERTO DA CAMERA (FOR VIOLIN AND STRING ORCH.)
    str.   16:00 IsMuPublns.

DARCY, Robert
—— ANDANTE ET SCHERZO
    2,2,2,2 - 2,0,0,0 - str.   S.A.B.A.M.
—— CAPRICCIO (FOR CHAMBER ORH.)
    1,1,1,1 - 1,0,0,0 - str.   13:30 S.A.B.A.M.
—— CONCERTO FOR FOUR CELLI AND WINDS (1936)
    2,2,3,2 - 2,2,1,0 - 4. c.   S.A.B.A.M.
—— CONCERTO FOR PIANO AND ORCH. (1951)
    2,2,2,1 - 4,2,2,0 - timp. - perc. - pf. - str.   18:00 S.A.B.A.M.
—— CONCERTO FOR SAXOPHONE QUARTET AND ORCH. (1939)
    0,2,2,4 sax.,2 - 2,2,2,0 - timp.,perc. - hp. - str.   S.A.B.A.M.
—— CONCERTO FOR TRUMPET AND ORCH.
    2,2,2,2 - 4,1,2,1 - timp.,perc. - hp. - str.   14:00 S.A.B.A.M.
—— DIVERTISSEMENT
    3,3,3,3 - 4,4,2,1 - timp.,perc. - 2 hp. - str.   S.A.B.A.M.
—— FANTAISIE FOR CELLO AND ORCH.
    2,2,2,2 - 2,2,0,0 - timp.,perc. - hp. - str.   S.A.B.A.M.

—— FANTAISIE FOR CLARINET AND ORCH.
1,1,2,1 - 2,2,1,0 - hp. - str.   S.A.B.A.M.
—— INTRODUCTION ET SCHERZO (1937)
3,3,3,3 - 4,4,2,1 - timp.,perc. - 2 hp. - str.   S.A.B.A.M.
—— PIECE FOR TWO CELLI AND ORCH.
1,1,2,2 - 2,1,1,0 - timp. - hp. - str.   S.A.B.A.M.
—— QUATRE MOUVMENTS
1,1,2,1 - 1,2,1,0 - pf. - str.   S.A.B.A.M.
—— RHAPSODY FOR TRUMPET AND ORCH.
1,1,2,2 - 4,1,1,0 - timp. - hp. - pf. - str.   S.A.B.A.M.
—— SEPT ESQUISSES (FOR SMALL ORCH.)
                                                                   S.A.B.A.M.
—— SIX ESQUISSES (FOR CHAMBER ORCH.)
1,1,2,1 - 1,2,1,0 - pf. - str.   9:00 S.A.B.A.M.
—— SUITE (1935) (FOR WIND INSTRUMENTS)
2,2,3 ten. sax.,2 - 4,2,2,1 - hp.   S.A.B.A.M.
—— SYMPHONY (1953) (IN 4 MOVTS.)
2,3,3,2 - 4,2,3,1 - timp.,perc. - hp. - str.   24:30 S.A.B.A.M.
—— TROIS MARINES
3,3,3,2 - 4,4,3,1 - timp.,perc.,cel. - hp. - str.   S.A.B.A.M.
—— TROIS MOUVEMENTS
1,1,1,1 - 2,0,0,0 - str.   S.A.B.A.M.

DARKE, Harold E.
—— AS THE LEAVES FALL, OP. 26 (CANTATA) (FOR SOPRANO,
WOMEN'S CHORUS AND SMALL ORCH.)
1,0,1,0 - hn. - hp. - str.   Galaxy.
—— AN HYMN OF HEAVENLY BEAUTY (CANTATA) (FOR
SOPRANO, BARITONE, MIXED CHORUS AND ORCH.) (Text:
Edmund Spenser)
                                                          25:00 Oxford.
—— THE LOVE WHICH PASSETH KNOWLEDGE (CANTATA)
(FOR BARITONE, MIXED CHORUS AND ORCH.)
                                                                Oxford.
—— MEDITATION ON "BROTHER JAMES' AIR"
fl.(or vln.) - pf.(ad lib.) - str.   Oxford.
—— RING OUT, YE CRYSTAL SPHERES, OP. 35 (FOR CHORUS
AND ORCH.)
2,2,2,2 - 4,2,3,1 - timp. - org. - str.   Oxford.
—— A SONG OF DAVID (FOR MIXED CHORUS AND ORCH.)
                                                                Oxford.
—— TWO FANTASIAS, OP. 40
str.   11:00 Oxford.

DARLING, David T.
—— JANUARY JOURNEY (1973)
                                                        15:00 Composer.

DARNTON, Christian
—— CANTILENA FOR STRINGS
str.   5:30 Lengnick.
—— CONCERTINO FOR PIANO AND STRINGS
pf. - str.   18:00 Lengnick.
—— SYMPHONY NO. 3 IN D
                                                         30:00 Lengnick.

DAUS, Avraham
—— LEGEND AND SCHERZO
str.   16:00 IsMuPublns.

DAUTREMER, M. R. L.
—— DIVERTISSEMENT (FOR VIOLIN AND ORCH.)
2,2,2,2 - 4,2,1,0 - timp.,perc.,cel. - hp. - str.   17:00 Baron.
—— FÊTE AU PAYS D'AUGE (FOR CELLO AND ORCH.)
2,2,2,2 - 2,2,3,0 - timp.,perc.,cel.,glock.,xyl. - hp. - str. 8:00 Baron.

DAUTREMER, Marcel
—— DUO CONCERTINO (FOR VIOLIN, BASSOON AND
STRINGS)
bn. - str.   14:00 EV.

DAVICO, Vincenzo
—— CANTATA BREVE (FOR BARITONE, CHORUS AND ORCH.)
2,2,2,2 - 2,3,2,1 - timp.,perc.,cel. - hp. - pf. - str.   10:00 Leeds.
—— POLIFEMO (IMPRESSIONE SINFONICA)
*3,*3,*3,*3 - 4,3,3,2 - timp.,perc.,cel. - 2 hp. - str.
                                                      10:00 Bo. Hawkes.
—— REQUIEM PER LA MORTE DI UN POVERO (REQUIEM FOR
THE DEATH OF A POOR MAN) (FOR SOPRANO,
BARITONE, SPEAKER, MIXED CHORUS AND ORCH.)
3,3,3,3 - 4,3,3,1 - timp.,perc.(3),cel.,glock.,xyl. - 2 hp. - pf. - str.
                                                          25:00 Leeds.

    offstage: 0,0,0,0 - 2,2,2,0

—— TRE FACEZIE (FOR VOICE AND ORCH.)
2,2,2,2 - 2,0,0,0 - timp., - hp. - str.   Salabert.

DÁVID, Gyula
—— CONCERTO FOR VIOLA AND ORCH.
2,2,2,2 - 4,2,0,0 - timp. - str.   22:00 Bo. Hawkes.
—— DANCE MUSIC (BASED ON HUNGARIAN FOLK SONGS)
2,2,2,2 - 2,2,0,0, - zimbalon - str.   7:00 Bo. Hawkes.
—— FESTIVE OVERTURE
2,2,2,2 - 4,3,3,1 - perc. - hp. - str.   11:00 Bo. Hawkes.
—— SINFONIETTA
1,1,1,0 - 0,1,0,0 - perc. - str.   11:00 Bo. Hawkes.
—— SYMPHONY NO. 3
2,2,2,2 - 4,3,3,0 - timp.,perc. - hp. - str.   21:00 Bo. Hawkes.
—— SYMPHONY NO. 4
1,1,1,1 - 2,3,0,0 - timp. - str.   18:00 Bo. Hawkes.
—— THEATRE MUSIC
1,1,0,1 - 2,1,0,0 - timp.,perc. - str.   11:00 Bo. Hawkes.

DAVID, Thomas Christian
—— CONCERTO FOR PIANO AND ORCH. (1962)
2,2,2,2 - 2,2,0,0 - timp. - pf. - str.   27:00 Modern.

DAVIDSON, Charles
—— CHASSIDIC SUITE (FOR CHORUS AND ORCH.)
2,2,1,1 - 1,2,1,0 - timp.(ad lib.),perc.(1) - str.   17:00 Composer.
—— FROM THE VALLEY OF JEZREEL
str.   10:00 Composer.
—— I AM THE LORD THY GOD (FOR VOICE AND ORCH.)
1,*2,2,1 - 2,1,0,0 - timp.,perc.(1),cel.,xyl. - hp. - pf. - str.
                                                         7:00 Composer.
—— SHALOM (REFLECTIONS FOR ORCHESTRA)
2,2(2nd alt. with Eng. hn.),1,1 - 1,2,0,0 - timp.(ad lib.),perc.(1) -
str.   12:00 Composer.

DAVIE, Cedric Thorpe
—— BY THE RIVER (FOR SOPRANO, WOMEN'S CHORUS,
STRINGS AND PIANO)
pf. - str.   25:00 Oxford.
—— DIRGE FOR CUTHULLIN (FOR MIXED CHORUS AND
ORCH.)
3,2,*3,*3 - 4,3,3,1 - timp.,perc. - hp. - str.   15:00 Oxford.
or:
pf. - str.
—— REJOICE AND BE MERRY (CHRISTMAS CAROL
SEQUENCE) (FOR BOYS' OR FEMALE VOICES AND
STRINGS)
pf. - str.   15:00 Oxford.
—— REJOICE AND BE MERRY (CHRISTMAS CAROL
SEQUENCE) (FOR BOYS' OR FEMALE VOICES AND
STRINGS)
Pf - str.   15:00 Oxford.

DAVIES, Peter Maxwell
—— FIVE MOTETS (FOR SOLO VOICES, DOUBLE SATB CHORUS
AND INSTRUMENTS)
1,1,1,2 - 0,2,2,0 - 2 org. - str.   18:00 Bo. Hawkes.
—— SEVEN "IN NOMINE"
1,1,1,1 - 1,0,0,0 - hp. - str.   14:00 Bo. Hawkes.
—— THE SHEPHERD'S CALENDAR (FOR SATB CHORUS AND
INSTRUMENTS)
6 recorders,1,1,5,1 - 0,1,1,0 - perc. - str.   21:00 Bo. Hawkes.
—— STONE LITANY ("RUNES FROM A HOUSE OF THE DEAD")
(FOR MEZZO-SOPRANO AND ORCH.)
2,0,3,2 - 2,2,2,1 - timp.,perc. - hp. - str.   23:00 Bo. Hawkes.
—— VENI, SANCTE SPIRITUS (FOR SOPRANO, CONTRALTO,
TENOR, MIXED CHORUS AND ORCH.)
1,1,0,1 - 2,2,2,0 - str.   20:00 Bo. Hawkes.
—— WORLDES BLIS
2,2,3,2 - 4,3,3,1 - timp., perc. - hp. - str.   25:00 Bo. Hawkes.

DAVIES, Victor
—— VARIATIONS (1964)
*3,*3,*3,2 - 4,3,3,1 - timp.,perc.,cel. - str.   11:45 CanMusCtr.

DAVIS, Allan G.
—— A PSALM OF PRAISE (PSALM 148) (FOR MIXED CHOURS,
BRASS AND PERCUSSION) (1969)
0,0,0,0 - 4,4,3,1 - timp.,perc.(2)   6:00 Composer.
—— FESTIVAL CONCERTO (FOR CLARINET AND SMALL
ORCH.)
2,2,1,2 - 2,0,0,0 - timp.,perc. - str.   20:00 Oxford.

—— THE ORDEAL OF OSBERT (1-ACT OPERA) % (1950) (Text: Composer, after P.G. Wodehouse)
1(alt.with picc.),1(alt.with Eng.hn.),1,1 - 1,1,1,0 - timp.,perc.(2),xyl. - pf. - str.   40:00 Bo. Hawkes.
—— THE SAILING OF THE NANCY BELLE (1-ACT COMIC OPERA) %
1,0,0,0 - 0,0,0,0 - perc.,cel.(optional) - pf. - str.
25:00 Bo. Hawkes.
—— THE DEPARTURE (3-ACT OPERA) % (Text: Composer)
1(alt.with picc.),1,1,0 - 1,1,1,0 - timp.,perc.(4),bells,cel.,glock. - hp. - pf. - str.   150:00 Composer.

DAVIS, David H.
—— CYCLES AND CHANGES (QUODLIBET FOR SOPRANO AND 10 INSTS.) (1962) (Text: from Various Hymns)
1,1,1,1 - 1,0,0,0 - pf. - str.   12:00 Composer.
—— DIALOGUE (FOR VIOLA, BASOON AND CHAMBER ORCH.) (1969)
*2,0,*2,1 - 2,0,0,0 - pf. - str.   10:00 Composer.
—— VARIATIONS FOR SMALL ORCH. (1961)
1(alt.with picc.),1,1(alt.with b.-cl.),1 - 1,1,1,0 - timp.,perc.(1) - str.
10:00 Composer.

DAVIS, Jean Reynolds
—— SHENANDOAH HOLIDAY (A BALLET STORY FOR YOUNG PEOPLE) %
*3,2,2(2nd alt. with b.-cl.),2 - 4,3,3,1 - perc.(3),xyl. - pf. - str.
15:00 Presser.
—— SYMPHONY IN ONE MOVEMENT
2 picc.,2,*3,*3,*3 - 4,3,3,1 - timp.,perc.(5) - pf. - str.
10:00 Composer.
—— SYMPHONY NO. 2 (IN 4 MOVTS.)
*3,*3,*3,*3 - 4,3,3,1 - timp.,perc.(6) - pf. - str.   20:00 Composer.

DAVIS, John David
—— THE COVENTRY SUITE, OP. 86
str.   Galaxy.
—— PETITE SUITE ACADÉMIQUE
str.   12:00 Bo. Hawkes.
—— PETITE SUITE SYMPHONIQUE
str.   15:00 Bo. Hawkes.

DAVIS, Katherine K.
—— BURIAL OF A QUEEN
*3,2,2,0 - 4 hn. - timp.,perc. - hp. - str.   10:00 Composer.

DAWNEY, Michael
—— MINTY (MUSIC FOR A FILM)
1,0,1,0 - 0,3,1,0 - timp.,perc. - guit. - str.   20:00 P.R.S.

DAWSON, Ted
—— CONCERTO GROSSO NO. 2 (PELOU-CLAY) (FOR PICCOLO, OBOE, E-FLAT CLARINET, TRUMPET IN D., CELLO AND ORCH.) (1973) (IN 2 MOVTS.)
*1,1,E♭cl.,3,2(2nd alt. with c.-bn.) - 6,1,4,1 - timp.,perc.(6, incl. 3 on timp.) - str.(no vln. or vla.)   12:00 CanMusCtr.

DE BANFIELD, Rafaello
—— QUATRE CHANTS DE RILKE (FOR DRAMATIC SOPRANO AND ORCH.) (1967)
2,1,2,2 - 2,2,2,1 - timp. - hp. - org. - str.   30:00 Salabert.

DE BANFIELD, Raffaello
—— AGOSTINO (BALLET) %
2,1,2,1 - 2,2,1,0 - timp.,perc. - hp. - str.   Ricordi.
—— THE DUEL (LE COMBAT) (BALLET) %
3,3,2,2 - 4,3,3,1 - timp.,perc.,cel. - hp. - str.   Ricordi.
—— QUATUOR (BALLET) %
2,1,2,1 - 2,2,1,0 - timp.,perc. - hp. - str.   Ricordi.

DEBUSMAN, Emil
—— CANTILENA ANGLICA FORTUNAE (AFTER SAMUEL SCHEIDT)
str.   5:00 AmerMusEd.
—— CAPRICCIO FOR STRING ORCH. (AFTER FRESCOBALDI'S "CAPRICCIO PRIMO, SOPRA UT, RE, MI, FA, SOL, LA")
str.   8:00 AmerMusEd.
—— CONCERTO NO. 2 FOR TWO STRING ORCHS. (AFTER JEAN-MARIE LECLAIR'S SONATA IN A MAJOR)
str.   AmerMusEd.
—— FANTASY FOR ORCH.
AmerMusEd.

DEBUSSY, Claude
—— LA BOÎTE À JOUJOUX (BALLET POUR ENFANTS) %
2,*3,2,2 - 2,2,0,0 - timp.,perc.,cel. - hp. - pf. - str.   EV.
—— LA CHAMBRE MAGIQUE (PRELUDE TO ACT II OF "LE MARTYRE DE ST. SÉBASTIEN")
4,3,4,4 - 6,2,3,1 - timp.,perc.,cel. - 3 hp. - str.   2:00 EV.
—— IBÉRIA (IN 3 MOVTS.)
*4(3rd alt. with 2nd picc.),*3,*3,*4 - 4,3,3,1 - timp.,perc.,cel.,xyl. - 2 hp. - str.   18:00 EV.
—— IMAGES POUR ORCHESTRE GIGUES
4,3,ob. d'amour,4,4 - 4,4,3,0 - timp.,perc.,cel. - 2 hp. - str.
4:00 EV.
—— JEUX (BALLET) %
4,4,4,3 sarr. - 4,4,3,1 - timp.,perc.,cel. - 2 hp. - str.   14:00 EV.
—— KHAMMA (BALLET) %
*4,*4,*4,*4 - 4,3,3,1 - timp.,perc.,cel.,glock. - 2 hp. - pf. - str.
22:00 EV.
—— LE MARTYRE DE SAINT SÉBASTIEN (FOR 2 SOPRANOS, 2 CONTRALTOS, MIXED CHORUS, 5 SPEAKING PARTS AND ORCH.)
2 picc.,2,*3,*4,*4 - 6,3,3,1 - timp.,perc.,cel. - 3 hp. - str.
71:00 EV.
—— LE MARTYRE DE SAINT SÉBASTIEN (4 FRAGMENTS SYMPHONIQUES)
2 picc.,2,*3,*4,*4 - 6,4,3,1 - timp.,perc.,cel. - 3 hp. - str.
25:00 EV.
—— ODE À LA FRANCE (FOR SOPRANO, MIXED CHORUS AND ORCH.) (Text: Louis Laloy)
3,*2,*4,*4 - 4,4,3,1 - timp.,perc. - 2 hp. - str.   10:45 Henmar.
—— LA PLUS QUE LENTE
1,0,1,0 - 0,0,0,0 - cimbalom - pf. - str.   4:15 EV.
—— RHAPSODIE (FOR ALTO SAXOPHONE AND ORCH.)
3,3,2, alto sax.,2 - 4,2,3,1 - timp.,perc. - hp. - str.   10:00 EV.
—— RHAPSODY NO. 1 FOR CLARINET AND ORCH.
3,3,2,3 - 4,2,0,0 - perc. - 2 hp. - str.   15:00 EV.
—— RONDES DE PRINTEMPS
3(3rd alt. with picc.),3,3,4 - 4 hn. - timp.,perc.,cel. - 2 hp. - str.
8:00 EV.
—— THREE NOCTURNES (1930; posth. ed. of orig. orchestration, corrected 1964; 16 women's voices required in "Sirènes")
3,2,2,3 - 4,3,3,1 - perc. - hp. - str.   24:00 EV.
—— THREE PRELUDES FROM "LE MARTYRE DE SAINT SÉBASTIEN"
4,3,4,4 - 6,4,3,1 - timp., perc. (3), cel. - 3 hp. - str.   7:20 EV.
—— TROIS BALLADES DE FRANÇOIS VILLON (FOR HIGH OR MEDIUM VOICE AND ORCH.)
3,*3,2,3 - 4 hn. - timp.,perc. - 2 hp. - str.   18:00 EV.
—— TROIS NOCTURNES (RE-ORCHESTRATED BY THE COMPOSER)
3,*3,2,3 - 4,3,3,1 - timp.,perc. - 2 hp. - str.   24:00 EV.
—— TWO FANFARES FROM "LE MARTYRE DE SAINT SÉBASTIEN"
6 hn.,4 tpt.,3 trb.,tu. - timp.   3:00 EV.

DEBUSSY, Claude - ANSERMET, Ernest
—— SIX EPIGRAPHES ANTIQUES
*3(2nd alt. with 2nd picc.),*3(Eng. hn. alt. with ob. d'amour ad lib.),3(3rd alt. with b.-cl.),2,c.-bn. (ad lib.) - 4,3,3,0 - timp.,perc.,cel. - 2 hp. - str.   16:00 EV.

DEBUSSY, Claude - BÜSSER, Henri
—— LA CATHÉDRALE ENGLOUTIE
2,2,2,2 - 4,2,3,1 - timp.,perc. - 2 hp. - str.   6:00 EV.
—— PETITE SUITE (IN 4 MOVTS.)
2(2nd alt. with picc.),2(2nd alt. with Eng. hn.),2,2 - 2,2,0,0 - timp.,perc. - hp. - str.   15:00 EV.
—— LA PUERTA DEL VINO
2,*2,2,2 - 2,2,0,0 - timp.,perc. - hp. - str.   3:00 EV.

DEBUSSY, Claude - CAILLIET, Lucien
—— CLAIR DE LUNE
*3,*3,*3,*3 - 4,3,3,1 - timp.,perc. (3),glock. - hp. - str.   4:30 EV.

DEBUSSY, Claude - CAPLET, Andre
—— THE CHILDREN'S CORNER (SUITE) (IN 6 MOVTS.)
2(2nd alt. with picc.),2,2,2 - 4,2,0,0 - perc. - hp. - str.   15:00 EV.
—— CLAIR DE LUNE
2,2,2,2 - 2 hn. - hp. - str.   4:30 EV.

DEBUSSY, Claude - DE FILIPPI, Amedeo
—— RÊVERIE
3,*3,2,3 - 4,3,3,0 - timp.,perc. (2),cel.,glock. - 2 hp. - str. Arranger.

DEBUSSY, Claude - GLEICHMANN, William
—— CLAIR DE LUNE
    2,3,2,2 - 4,3,3,0 - hp. - str.   4:30 EV.

DEBUSSY, Claude - MILLER, Charles
—— CLAIR DE LUNE (FOR STRINGS)
    str.   4:30 EV.

DEBUSSY, Claude - MOLINARI, Bernardino
—— L' ÎLE JOYEUSE
    3(3rd alt. with picc.),3,4,3 - 4,4,3,1 - timp.,perc.,cel. - 2 hp. - str.
            7:00 EV.

DEBUSSY, Claude - RAVEL, Maurice
—— DANSE
    2,2,2,2 - 2,2,0,0 - timp.,perc. - hp. - str.   6:00 EV.
—— SARABANDE
    2,2,2,2 - 2,1,0,0 - perc. - hp. - str.   6:00 EV.

DEBUSSY, Claude - ROGER-DUCASSE
—— RHAPSODY FOR SAXOPHONE AND ORCH.
            8:00 EV.

DEBUSSY, Claude - STERRETT, Paul
—— CLAIR DE LUNE
            C. Fischer.

DEBUSSY, Claude - STOKOWSKI, Leopold
—— NIGHT IN GRANADA
    4,3,4,3 - 4,3,4,1 - timp.,perc.,cel. - 2 hp. - pf. - str.   Henmar.

DECADT, Jan
—— CONCERTO NO. 1 FOR PIANO AND ORCH. (IN 3 MOVTS.)
    2,2,2,2 - 2,2,2,1 - timp.,perc. - pf. - str.   H. Elkan.

DE CALANDRA, Matilde T.
—— CONCERTO FOR GUITAR AND ORCH.
    3,2,2,2 - 2,2,0,0 - timp.,perc. - hp. - str.   23:00 S.A.D.A.I.C.

DE CEVEE, Alice
—— MEMORABILIA (SUITE FOR SYMPHONY ORCH.) (IN 4
    MOVEMENTS)
    *3,*3,*3,2 - 4,3,3,1 - timp.,perc. (4),bells,cel.,glock.,xyl. - hp. - str.
            15:00 Composer.

DE COLA, Felix
—— CONCERTO FOR PIANO AND ORCH. (IN 1 MOVT.)
            15:00 Composer.

DE CORMIER, Robert
—— REVOLUTIONARY PORTRAIT (FOR SATB CHORUS AND
    ORCH.)
    2,2,2,2 - 2,2,2,1 - perc.(2)   Law-Gould.

DECOUST, Michel
—— ET EE (FOR CHORUS AND ORCH.)
    2,2,2,2 - 4,3,3,0 - timp.,perc.(3) - hp. - str.   20:00 Presser.
—— SI ET SI SEULEMENT
    3,3,3,1 - 4,4,3,1 - perc.(3) - 2 hp. - str.   12:00 Presser.

DECSÉNYI, János
—— CANZONE SOLENNE
    *3,*3,*3,*3 - 3,3,3,1 - timp.,perc.,cel. - cimbalom - hp. - pf. - str.
            12:30 Bo. Hawkes.
—— DIVERTIMENTO FOR HARPSICHORD AND CHAMBER
    ORCH.
    2,0,2,0 - 1,0,0,0 - timp.,perc. - hpsc. - str.   20:00 Bo. Hawkes.
—— FIVE CSONTVÁRY PICTURES
    *3,*3,*3,3 - 4,4,3,1 - timp.,perc.,cel. - 2 hp. - pf. - str.
            29:00 Bo. Hawkes.
—— SINFONIETTA
            Bo. Hawkes.
—— THOUGHTS: BY DAY, BY NIGHT (SONG CYCLE) (FOR
    SOPRANO AND ORCH.)
    *2,2,2,2 - 4,3,3,0 - perc. - 2 hp. - pf. - str.   12:00 Bo. Hawkes.

DEDIEU-PETERS, Madeleine
—— TROIS PETITS PRÉLUDES
    3,2,2,2 - 2,2,2,1 - timp.,perc. - hp. - str.   8:00 Salabert.

DEFAY, Jean-Michel
—— CONCERTINO FOR VIOLIN AND ORCH.
            Baron.

—— CONCERTO FOR TRUMPET, TROMBONE AND STRINGS
    tpt.,trb. - str.   11:00 Baron.
—— DANSES SYMPHONIQUES
    3,2,2,2 - 3,3,3,0 - timp.,perc. - pf. - str.   18:00 Baron.
—— ECHO ET NARCISE (OPERA) % (Text: Claude des Presles)
    1,1,2,2 - 2,1,1,1 - timp.,perc.,vibra. - hp. - str.   25:00 Eds. Fran.

DE FILIPPI, Amedeo
—— BRAZILIAN EXCURSION (IN 4 MOVTS.)
    1(alt. with picc.),2,2,2 - 4,3,3,1 - timp.,perc. (2) - str.
            12:45 Composer.
—— CHILDREN OF ADAM (CANTATA)
            Composer.
—— CONCERTO FOR FLUTE, OBOE, BASSOON, HORN,
    TRUMPET AND STRINGS
    1,1,0,1 - 1,1,0,0 - str.   14:00 Composer.
—— DIVERSIONS FOR STRING ORCH. (IN 4 MOVTS.)
    str.   14:00 Composer.
—— FIVE ARABIAN SONGS (FOR VOICE AND ORCH.)
            Composer.
—— FIVE MEDIEVAL COURT DANCES
    3(3rd alt. with picc.),*3,0,*3 - 4,3,3,1 - hp. - str. 18:00 Composer.
—— FIVE NORMAN SONGS (FOR MEDIUM VOICE AND SMALL
    ORCH.)
    1,1,2,1 - hn.-cel. - hp. - str.   7:00 Composer.
—— THE GREEN COCKATOO (1-ACT OPERA) %
            Composer.
—— MALVOLIO (2-ACT OPERA) %
            Composer.
—— MANHATTAN ISLE (SUITE) (IN 6 MOVTS.)
            TRFMusInc.
—— MUSIC FOR RECREATION (IN 5 MOVTS.)
    str.   Ascher.
—— OVERTURE TO "TWELFTH NIGHT"
    2(2nd alt. with picc.),2,2,2 - 4,2,3,1 - timp. - str.   9:00 Composer.
—— PROVENCAL AIRS (FOR STRING ORCH.)
            15:00 Composer.
—— RAFTMAN'S DANCE (BASED ON TWO FOLKTUNES OF
    THE MISSISSIPPI VALLEY)
    *3,*3,*3,*3 - 4,3,3,1 - timp. - hp. - str.   6:00 Composer.
—— SERENADE
    str.   Composer.
—— SUITE (IN 4 MOVTS.)
    1,1,2,1 - 2,1,1,0 - timp. - str.   12:00 Composer.
—— SYMPHONY
            Composer.
—— THE TESTAMENT OF FRANCOIS VILLON (INTRODUCTION,
    SEVEN INTERLUDES AND EIGHT BALLADES) (FOR
    BARITONE AND SMALL ORCH.)
    1,1,2,1 - 2,1,1,0 - timp. - str.   46:00 Composer.
—— TWO AMERICAN FOLKTUNES
    str.   Composer.
—— TWO SONNETS (FOR VOICE AND ORCH.)
            Composer.
—— VARIATIONS ON "PETER, PETER, PUMPKIN EATER" (FOR
    PIANO AND ORCH.)
            Composer.

DEFOSSEZ, René
—— ADAGIO ET SCHERZO (FOR FLUTE AND ORCH.) (1941)
    2,1,2,1 - 2,2,1,0 - timp.,perc.,cel. - pf.(or hp.) - str. 12:00 Gervan.
—— AMATERASU (SYMPHONIC LEGEND) (1935) (FOR
    SOPRANO AND ORCH.)
    2,2,3,2 - 4,3,3,1 - timp.,perc.,bells,cel. - hp. - pf. - str.
            20:00 H. Elkan.
—— AQUARIUM (3 IMPRESSIONS) (1927)
    1,1,1,1 - 2,1,0,0 - timp.,perc. - pf. - str.   20:00 Henmar.
—— ARIOSO E MOTO PERPETUO
    2,3,3,3 - 4,2,3,1 - timp.,perc. - str.   13:00 H. Elkan.
—— LES BALS DE PARIS (OVERTURE)
    2,2,2,2 - 4,2,3,0 - timp.,perc. - str.   4:00 Bo. Hawkes.
    or:
    2,1,2,1 - 2,0,1,0 - timp.,perc. - str.
—— CONCERTO FOR VIOLIN AND ORCH.
    2,1,2,1 - 2,2,0,0 - timp.,perc. - hp. - str.   28:00 CBDM.
—— CONCERTO FOR 2 PIANOS AND ORCH. (1954)
    2,2,2,2 - 2,2,1,0 - timp.,perc.,xyl. - 2 pf. - str.   21:00 H. Elkan.
—— CONCERTO NO. 1 FOR PIANO AND ORCH. (1951)
    2,2,2,2 - 2,2,1,0 - timp.,perc.,xyl. - pf. - str.   20:00 H. Elkan.
—— CONCERTO NO. 2 FOR PIANO AND ORCH.
    2,2,2,2 - 2,2,1,0 - timp.,perc.,xyl. - pf. - str.   16:00 CBDM.

—— IMAGES SOUS-MARINES
   3,3,3,3 - 4,3,3,1 - timp.,perc.,cel.,glock.,xyl. - hp. - str.
   16:00 CBDM.
—— RECITATIVO ET ALLEGRO (FOR TRUMPET AND ORCH.)
   (1945)
   2,1,2,1 - 2,1,0,0 - timp. - str.   12:00 Gervan.
—— LE RÊVE DE L'ASTRONOME (BALLET) (1950) %
   3,3,3,3 - 4,3,3,1 - timp.,perc.,bells,cel.,glock.,xyl. - hp. - pf. - str.
   27:00 H. Elkan.
—— SINFONIETTA DE PRINTEMPS (1975)
   2,2,2,2 - 4,2,3,1 - timp.,perc. - str.   22:00 H. Elkan.
—— SUITE "MINUTES" (FOR CHAMBER ORCH.)
   2,1,2,1 - 2,2,0,0 - perc. - str.   H. Elkan.
—— SYMPHONIE WALLONNE
   2,2,2,2 - 4,4,3,1 - timp.,perc.,cel.,glock. - hp. - str.   28:00 CBDM.
—— TROIS FARCES (FOR PIANO AND ORCH.) (1937)
   2,1,2,1 - 2,2,1,0 - timp.,perc.,xyl. - hp. - pf. - str.   9:00 H. Elkan.
—— VARIATIONS FOR PIANO AND ORCH. (1938)
   3,3,3,3 - 4,3,3,1 - timp.,perc.,glock.,xyl. - hp. - pf. - str.
   14:00 H. Elkan.

DEGEN, Helmut
—— CONCERTO FOR CELLO AND STRING ORCH.
   str.   Hans Gerig.

DE GRANDIS, Vincenzo - DE GRANDIS, R.
—— L'ESODO DI MOSE' DALL' EGITTO (ORATORIO) (FOR
   SOLO VOICES, CHORUS AND ORCH.) (Text: Giovanbattista
   Giardini)
   2,2,0,2 - 2,2,2,0 - timp. - hp. - hpsc. - org. - str.
   90:00 MCA Music.

DE GREGORIO, M.
—— RURALIA
   2,2,2,2 - 2,2,0,0 - timp.,cel. - hp. - str.   9:00 Bo. Hawkes.
—— TEMA CON VARIAZONI
   2,2,2,2 - 2,280,0 - perc. - str.   11:00 Bo. Hawkes.

DEHNERT, Max
—— DIVERTIMENTO (FOR SMALL ORCH.)
   2,2,2,2 - 2,2,0,0 - str.   17:00 Tetra.
—— FESTIVE MUSIC
   2,2,2,2 - 4,2,2,0 - perc. - str.   6:00 Tetra.

DEJONCKER, Theo.
—— SINFONIE IM KLASSISCHEN STIL
   2,2,2,2 - 2,2,0,0 - timp. - str.   20:00 Alkor.

DELAGE, Maurice
—— SEPT HAÏ-KAÏS (7 HAIKU) (FOR SOPRANO OR TENOR
   VOICE WITH ORCH.)
   1,1,1,0 - 0,0,0,0 - pf. - str.   10:00 EV.
—— TROIS CHANTS DE LA JUNGLE (FOR VOICE AND ORCH.)
   Salabert.

DE LALANDE, Michel-Richard - BOULAY, Laurence
—— SYMPHONIE DES SOUPERS DU ROY (IN 6 MOVTS.)
   2,2,0,2 - 0,1,0,0 - hpsc. - str.   11:00 Eds. Fran.

DE LALANDE, Michel-Richard - CELLER, Alex
—— PSALM 2 ("QUARE FREMUERUNT GENTES") (FOR
   SOLOISTS, CHORUS AND ORCH.)
   2 fl., 2 ob. - org. - str.   27:00 Salabert.

DE LALANDE, Michel-Richard - CELLIER, Alex
—— PSALM 130 ("DE PROFUNDIS") (FOR SOPRANO, ALTO,
   TENOR, BASS, MIXED CHORUS AND ORCH.)
   1,1,0,0 - 0,0,0,0 - org. - str.   35:00 Salabert.
—— PSALM 74 ("CONFITEBIMUR TIBI DEUS") (FOR SOLISTS,
   MIXED CHORUS AND CHAMBER ORCH.)
   ob. - org. - str.   35:00 Salabert.

DE LALANDE, Michel-Richard - SCHROEDER
—— CHRISTMAS SYMPHONY IN C MAJOR
   2 fl.(or 2 ob.),bn.(or. c.) - org. - str.   Henmar.

DE LAMARTER, Eric
—— AT CHRISTMASTIDE (A FANTASY ON CHRISTMAS
   CAROLS)
   2,2,2,2 - 4,3,3,1 - timp.,perc.,glock. - hp. - str.   12:00 EV.
—— THE BLACK ORCHID (IN 7 MOVTS.)
   3(3rd alt. with picc.),*3,*3,*3 - 4,4,3,1 - timp.,perc. (3) - hp. - str.
   15:00 Composer.

—— CLUNY (DIALOGUE FOR VIOLA AND ORCH.)
   2,1,*3,1 - 2,2,0,0 - perc.,mar. - str.   10:00 Composer.
—— CONCERTO NO. 1 IN E, FOR ORGAN AND ORCH. (IN 3
   MOVEMENTS)
   *3,*3,2,2 - 4,3,3,1 - timp.,perc. (3) - org. - str.   22:00 Gray.
—— CONCERTO NO. 2 IN A MAJOR, FOR ORGAN AND ORCH.
   3(3rd alt. with picc.),*3,*3,2 - 4,3,3,1 - timp.,perc. (3), glock. - org.
   - str.   22:00 Gray.
—— THE FABLE OF THE HAPLESS FOLK TUNE (IN 8 MOVTS.)
   3,3,2,2 - 4,2,3,1 - timp.,perc. - hp. - str.   25:30 Composer.
—— THE GIDDY PURITAN (OVERTURE ON TWO EARLY NEW
   ENGLAND HYMN TUNES)
   3(3rd alt. with picc.),*3,2,2 - 4,3,3,1 - timp.,perc. (3) - hp. - str.
   6:00 Composer.
—— HUCKLEBERRY FINN (OVERTURE)
   2,2,2,2 - 4,3,3,1 - timp.,perc. - str.   2:14 Witmark.
   or:
   1,1,2,1 - 2,2,1,0 - timp.,perc. - str.
—— OL' KAINTUCK (OVERTURE)
   2,2,2,2 - 4,3,3,1 - timp.,perc. - str.   Witmark.
   or:
   1,1,2,1 - 2,2,1,0 - timp.,perc. - str.
—— OVERTURE TO "THE FAWN"
   2,2,2,2 - 4,2,3,0 - timp.,perc. - str.   10:00 Witmark.
—— PIETY DOE'S GREMLINS (BALLET FOR WINDS) %
   3(3rd alt. with picc.),1,*3,1 - 2,1,0,1 - hp.   15:00 Witmark.
—— PSALM 144 (FOR VOICE AND ORCH.)
   2,2,2,2 - 2,2,2,0 - timp.,perc. - str.   6:00 C. Fischer.
—— SERENADE (FOR STRING ORCH.) (IN 3 MOVTS.)
   str.   4:30 Witmark.
—— SERENADE NEAR TAOS (IN 4 MOVTS.)
   str.   13:30 Ricordi.
—— SUITE FOR STRING ORCH. (IN 4 MOVTS.)
   str.   Witmark.
—— SUITE FROM "THE BETROTHAL"
   2,*3,2,2 - 4,3,3,1 - timp.,perc. (3) - str.   18:00 SPAM.
—— SYMPHONY NO. 1 IN D (IN 3 MOVEMENTS)
   1,1,*3,1 - 2,2,1,0 - timp.,perc. - str.   15:00 Composer.
—— SYMPHONY NO. 2 (AFTER WALT WHITMAN) (IN 3
   MOVTS.)
   3(3rd alt. with picc.),*3,2,2 - 4,3,3,1 - timp.,perc. (3) - hp. - str.
   20:00 Witmark.
—— SYMPHONY NO. 3 IN E MINOR (IN 4 MOVEMENTS)
   3(3rd alt. with picc.),*3,*3,*3 - 4,4,3,1 - timp.,perc. (3) - hp. - str.
   43:00 Composer.

DE LANEY, Charles
—— AMERICAN WALTZES (1958)
   3(3rd alt.with picc.),2,2,2 - 4,3,3,1 - timp.,perc.(4),bells,cel.,xyl. -
   hp. - str.   15:00 Composer.
—— THE MARSHES OF GLYNN (FOR NARRATOR, CHORUS
   AND ORCH.) (1949) (Text: Sidney Lanier)
   2(2nd alt. with picc.),2,2,2 - 4,3,3,1 - timp.,perc.(3), glock. - hp. -
   str.   14:00 Composer.

DELANNOY, Marcel
—— ABRAHAM ET L'ANGE (CHOREOPERA IN 2 ACTS AND 6
   TABLEAUX) % (Text: M. Sarrazin)
   3,3,3,3 - 4,3,2,1 - timp.,perc.,vibra. - hp. - str.   120:00 Eds. Fran.
—— ABRAHAM ET L'ANGE (PERFORMED AS AN ORATORIO)
   3,3,3,3 - 4,3,2,1 - timp.,perc.,vibra. - hp. - str.   90:00 Eds. Fran.
—— INTRODUCTION ET VALSE HONGROISE
   2,2,2,2 - 4,2,3,0 - timp.,perc. - hp. - pf. - str.   9:00 Henmar.
—— LE MARCHAND DE LUNETTES (SUITE)
   2,2,2,2 - 2,2,2,0 - timp., perc. - hp. - str.   30:00 Presser.
—— LE MOULIN DE LA GALETTE (SYMPHONIC TABLEAU)
   2,2,2,2 - 2,2,2,0 - timp.,perc. - hp. - str.   7:00 Salabert.
—— SYMPHONY
   3,3,3,3 - 4,3,3,1 - timp.,perc. (2) - hp. - pf. (or cel.) - str.
   19:00 Salabert.
—— SYMPHONY NO. 2 FOR STRINGS AND CELESTA, OP. 64
   (1952)
   cel. - str.   28:00 Salabert.
—— VOLPONE (SUITE FROM THE FILM SCORE) (IN 4 MOVTS.)
   2,2,2,2 - 4,2,3,0 - timp.,perc. - hp. - pf. - str.   15:00 Salabert.

DE LARA, Adelina
—— IN THE FOREST (SUITE)
   str.   Galaxy.

DE LA VINA, F.
—— TRES IMPRESSIONES
   3,3,3,3 - 4,3,3,1 - timp.,perc.,cel. - 2 hp. - str.   7:30 Salabert.

DEL BARRIO, R. G.
—— YARAVI
    2,3,3,3 -4,3,2,1 - timp.,perc.,cel. - hp. - str.   11:00 Southern.

DELDEN, Lex van
—— ANTHROPOLIS, OP. 73 (FOR 2 SOLO VOICES, MIXED CHORUS, SPEAKING CHORUS AND ORCH.) (Text: Dr. Jan Wit)
    40:00 Henmar.
—— CANTO DELLA GUERRA, OP. 92 (1967) (FOR SATB CHORUS AND ORCH.) (Text: Erasmus and Composer)
    17:00 Henmar.
—— CONCERTO FOR FLUTE AND ORCH., OP. 85
    1,2,2,2 - 2,1,0,0 - timp.,perc.,cel. - str.   21:00 Henmar.
—— CONCERTO FOR HARP AND ORCH., OP. 32
    2,2,1,2 - 2,1,0,0 - hp. - str.   24:00 Henmar.
—— CONCERTO FOR PERCUSSION, CELESTA, HARP AND STRING ORCH., OP. 94 (1968)
    perc.,cel. - hp. - str.   15:00 Henmar.
—— CONCERTO FOR PIANO AND ORCH., OP. 66 (1960)
    2,2,2,2 - 4,3,3,1 - timp.,perc. - pf. - str.   18:00 Henmar.
—— CONCERTO FOR TRUMPET AND ORCH., OP. 54 (1956)
    2,2,2,2 - 2,1,0,0 - timp.,perc. - str.   18:00 Henmar.
—— CONCERTO FOR TWO OBOES AND ORCH., OP. 64 (1959)
    2,2,2,2 - 2,1,0,0 - timp. - str.   18:00 Henmar.
—— CONCERTO FOR TWO STRING ORCHS., OP. 71 (1961)
    str.   20:00 Henmar.
—— CONCERTO FOR VIOLIN, VIOLA, DOUBLE BASS AND ORCH. (1966)
    15:00 Henmar.
—— CONCERTO FOR 2 SAXOPHONES AND ORCH., OP. 91 (1967) (IN 3 MOVTS.)
    18:00 Henmar.
—— ICARUS, OP. 77 (FOR CHORUS AND ORCH.)
    45:00 Henmar.
—— IN MEMORIAM, OP. 38
    3,2,3,2 - 4,3,3,1 - timp.,perc. - hp. - str.   10:00 Henmar.
—— INTRODUCTION AND ALLEGRO (SMALL CONCERTO FOR VIOLIN, PIANO AND ORCH.), OP. 28
    13:00 Henmar.
—— MUSICA PER ORCHESTRA, OP. 93
    2,3,3,3 - 4,3,3,1 - timp.,perc. - hp. - pf. - str.   20:00 Henmar.
—— MUSICA SINFONICA, OP. 93 (1967)
    20:00 Henmar.
—— OUVERTURE VOOR EEN FEESTDAG, OP. 60 (1958)
    3,3,3,3 - 4,3,3,1 - timp.,perc.,cel.,xyl. - hp. - str.   10:00 Henmar.
—— PICCOLA MUSICA CONCERTATA, OP. 79 (IN 5 MOVTS.)
    0,0,0,0 - 0,0,3,0 - timp. - str.   12:00 Henmar.
—— PICCOLO CONCERTO PER 12 INSTRUMENTI A FIATO, OP. 67 (1960) (LITTLE CONCERTO FOR 12 WIND INSTS.)
    2,2,2,2 - 2,2,0,0 - timp.,perc. - pf.   10:00 Henmar.
—— SINFONIA GIOCOSA, OP. 39
    2,2,2,2 - 2,1,1,0 - timp. - str.   Henmar.
—— SINFONIA NO. 3, OP. 45 ("FACETTEN")
    2,2,3,3 - 4,3,3,1 - timp.,perc.,xyl. - hp. - str.   17:00 Henmar.
—— SINFONIA NO. 4, OP. 56
    2,2,2,2 - 3,2,2,0 - timp.,perc. - str.   31:00 Henmar.
—— SINFONIA NO. 5, OP. 65 (1959)
    3,2,2,2 - 2,2,0,0 - timp.,perc. - pf.   17:00 Henmar.
—— SINFONIA NO. 6, OP. 69-81 (1963)
    2,2,3,2 - 4,3,3,1 - timp.,perc.,xyl. - str.   18:00 Henmar.
—— DE STROOM, MEI 1940, OP. 40 (1954) (SYMPHONY IN 5 PARTS) (FOR SOPRANO, MIXED CHORUS AND ORCH.) (Text: Jan Prins)
    2,2,3,2 - 4,3,3,1 - timp.,perc. - hp. - pf. - str.   31:00 Henmar.
—— SYMPHONY NO. 8, OP. 84 (FOR STRING ORCH.)
    str.   22:00 Henmar.
—— TIJ EN ONTIJ, OP. 52 (BALLET) %
    2,2,2,2 - 2,2,0,0 - timp.,perc. - str.   20:00 Henmar.
—— TRIO FOR STRING ORCH., OP. 44
    str.   13:00 Henmar.

DE LEEUW, Ton
—— DE BIJEN
    17:00 Henmar.
—— BRABANT (SYMPHONIC SONG) (FOR MEDIUM VOICE AND ORCH.) (1959) (Text: Harriet Laurey)
    3,3,3,3 - 4,3,3,1 - timp.,perc. - str.   10:00 Henmar.
—— CONCERTO FOR PIANO AND ORCH.
    3,2,3,2 - 2,2,3,0 - timp.,perc. - pf. - str.   17:00 Henmar.
—— CONCERTO FOR VIOLIN AND ORCH.
    2,2,2,2 - 4,3,3,1 - timp.,perc. - str.   15:00 Henmar.

—— CONCERTO GROSSO
    str.   12:00 Henmar.
—— CONCERTO NO. 2 FOR VIOLIN AND ORCH. (1961)
    2,2,2,2 - 2,2,0,0 - timp.,perc. - str.   20:00 Henmar.
—— HAIKU II (1968) (FOR VOICE AND FULL ORCH.)
    12:00 Henmar.
—— LAMENTO PACIS I (FOR CHORUS AND ORCH.)
    7:00 Henmar.
—— LAMENTO PACIS II (FOR CHORUS AND ORCH.)
    13:00 Henmar.
—— LAMENTO PACIS III (FOR CHORUS AND ORCH.)
    8:00 Henmar.
—— MOUVEMENTS RÉTROGRADES (1957)
    3,3,3,3 - 4,3,3,1 - timp.,perc.,cel. - hp. - pf. - str.   13:00 Henmar.
—— NRITTA (ORCHESTRAL DANCE) (1961)
    3,3,3,1 alto sax.,2 - 4,3,3,1 - timp.,perc.,cel.,vibra. - hp. - str.
    8:00 Henmar.
—— OMBRES (1961)
    3,3,3,1 alto sax.,2 - 2,3,2,1 - timp.,perc.,xyl. - guit. - hp. - str.
    11:00 Henmar.
—— PLUTOS SUITE
    2,2,2,2 -2,2,0,0 - timp.,perc. - str.   12:00 Henmar.
—— SPATIAL MUSIC I (FOR FULL ORCH.)
    24:00 Henmar.
—— SPATIAL MUSIC I (FOR 32 TO 48 PLAYERS)
    24:00 Henmar.
—— SPATIAL MUSIC III (FOR ORCH., DIVIDED INTO 4 GROUPS)
    3,2,2,sax.,2 - 2,2,2,0 - timp. - hp. - str.   Henmar.
—— SPATIAL MUSIC IV (HOMAGE TO IGOR STRAVINSKY) (FOR 12 PLAYERS)
    1,1,1,1 - 1,0,0,0 - perc.(2) - pf. - str.(2,1,1,0)   13:00 Henmar.
—— SYMPHONY FOR STRING ORCH. AND PERCUSSION
    perc. - str.   16:00 Henmar.
—— SYMPHONY FOR STRINGS
    str.   21:00 Henmar.
—— SYNTAXIS II
    4,4,4,4 - 4,4,4,1 - perc.,cel. - hp. - pf. - str.   Henmar.
—— SYNTAXTIS II (1966)
    22:00 Henmar.
—— TREURMUZIEK IN MEMORIAM WILLEM PIJPER
    2,1,1,1 - 2,1,1,0 - timp. - str.   20:00 Henmar.

DE LEONE, Francesco B.
—— GIBRALTAR SUITE (IN 3 MOVTS.)
    *4,*3,3,2 - 4,3,3,1 - timp.,perc. (2) - hp. - str.   12:00 Composer.
—— ITALIAN RHAPSODY
    *3,*3,2,2 - 4,2,3,1 - timp.,perc. (2) - hp. - str.   11:00 Composer.
—— SIX ITALIAN DANCES
    *4,*3,3,2 - 4,3,3,1 - timp.,perc. (3) - hp. - str.   Composer.

DELERUE, Georges
—— CONCERTINO FOR PIANO AND STRINGS
    pf. - str.   11:30 Presser.
—— CONCERTINO FOR TRUMPET AND STRING ORCH.
    tpt. - str.   18:30 Baron.
—— SYMPHONY NO 1 (FOR CHAMBER ORCH.)
    1,2,1,1 - 2,1,0,0 - str.   22:00 Presser.

DELIBES, Leo - BENOY, A. W.
—— SUITE FROM THE OPERA "LE ROI S'AMUSE"
    2,2,2,2 - 2,2,2,0 - perc. - str.   11:00 Oxford.

DELIBES, Leo - ISAAC, Merle
—— MARCH AND PROCESSION OF BACCHUS (FROM "SYLVIA")
    Belwin.

DE LISA, Victor V.
—— CONCERTO NO. 1 IN B♭ MINOR, FOR PIANO AND ORCH. (1949) (IN 3 MOVTS.)
    2,2,2,2 - 2,2,3,0 - timp. - pf. - str.   15:00 Composer.
—— DR. JOSE RIZAL'S LAST FAREWELL (FOR CHORUS AND ORCH.) (Text: Amado Yuzon)
    1,1,2,1 - 2,2,1,0 - timp.,perc. - org. - pf. - str.   15:00 Composer.
—— MOSES, PRINCE OF EGYPT (BALLET IN 10 MOVTS.) % (1951)
    1,1,2,1 - 2,2,1,0 - timp.,perc.,bells.,glock. - str.   90:00 Composer.
—— SUNLIGHT RHAPSODY (FOR ACCORDION AND ORCH.) (1954)
    1,1,2,1 - 2,2,2,0 - timp. - acc. - str.   10:00 Composer.
—— SYMPHONY NO. 1 (THE FOUR SEASONS) (1953)
    1,1,2,1 - 2,2,1,0 - timp. - str.   40:00 Composer.

DELIUS, Frederick

—— AIR AND DANCE (FOR STRING ORCH.)
    str.   7:30 Bo. Hawkes.

—— AN ARABESQUE (FOR BARITONE, CHORUS AND ORCH.)
    3,4,4,4 - 4,3,3,1 - timp.,perc.cel. - hp. - str.   20:00 Bo. Hawkes.

—— CONCERTO FOR CELLO AND ORCH.
    2,2,2,2 - 4,2,3,1 - timp. - hp. - str.   30:00 Bo. Hawkes.

—— CONCERTO FOR PIANO AND ORCH.
    1. Andante - Allegro; 2. Adagio; 3. Andantino; 4. Allegro vivace
    3,3,2,3 - 4,2,3,1 - timp.,perc. - pf. - str.   23:00 Bo. Hawkes.

—— CONCERTO FOR VIOLIN AND ORCH.
    2,*2,2,2 - 4,2,3,1 - timp. - hp. - str.   20:00 Augener.

—— CYNARA (FOR BARITONE AND ORCH.)
    3,*3,4,4 - 4,3,3,1 - timp.,perc.,xyl. - hp. - str.   7:00 Bo. Hawkes.

—— EVENTYR (ONCE UPON A TIME)
    3,*3,4,3 - 4,3,3,1 - sarr. - perc.,cel. - 2 hp. - str.   16:00 Augener.

—— FANTASTIC DANCE
    2,2,2,2 - 4,2,3,1 - timp.,perc. - hp. - str.   Bo. Hawkes.

—— FENNIMORE AND GERDA (OPERA) % (1919)
    3,4,*4,*4 - 4,3,3,1 - timp.,perc. - 2 hp. - str.   Bo. Hawkes.

—— HASSAN (SUITE)
    2,2,2,2 - 4,2,3,1 - timp.,perc. - hp. - str.   17:00 Bo. Hawkes.

—— IDYLL (FOR SOPRANO, BARITONE AND ORCH.)
    2,*3,2,2 - 4,2,3,1 - timp. - hp. - str.   24:00 Bo. Hawkes.

—— IN A SUMMER GARDEN (SYMPHONIC POEM)
            13:00 Bo. Hawkes.

—— INTERMEZZO FROM "FENNIMORE AND GERDA"
    2,2,2,2 - 2,1,0,0 - str.   4:00 Bo. Hawkes.

—— A LATE LARK (FOR TENOR AND ORCH.)
    1,2,2,2 - 2,1,3,0 - str.   4:30 Bo. Hawkes.

—— LIFE'S DANCE (TONE POEM)
    3,*3,*4,*4 - 2,2,3,1 - timp.,perc.,glock. - hp. - str.   12:00 Oxford.

—— A MASS OF LIFE (FOR SOLOISTS, CHORUS AND ORCH.)
    3,4,4,4 - 6,4,3,1 - timp.,perc. - 2 hp. - str.   135:00 Bo. Hawkes.

—— ON HEARING THE FIRST CUCKOO IN SPRING
    2,1,2,2 - 2,0,0,0 - str.   4:00 Oxford.

—— PRELUDE TO "IRMELIN"
    2,2,2-3,2 - 2 hn. - hp. - str.   4:00 Bo. Hawkes.

—— REQUIEM (FOR SOPRANO, BARITONE, CHORUS AND ORCH.)
    3,4,4,4 - 6,3,3,1 - timp.,perc.,cel. - hp. - str.   45:00 Bo. Hawkes.

—— SELECTION FROM "KOANGA"
    2,3,3,2 - 4,2,3,1 - timp.,perc. - banjo - hp. - str.
            11:30 Bo. Hawkes.

—— SERENADE FROM "HASSAN" (FOR HARP AND STRINGS)
    hp. - str.   2:30 Bo. Hawkes.

—— A SONG BEFORE SUNRISE
    2,1,2,2 - 2 hn. - timp. - str.   5:00 Galaxy.

—— A SONG OF SUMMER
    3,*3,*4,*4 - 4,3,3,1 - timp. - hp. - str.   7:00 Bo. Hawkes.

—— SONG OF THE HIGH HILLS (FOR DOUBLE CHORUS AND ORCH.)
            35:00 Bo. Hawkes.

—— SONGS OF FAREWELL (FOR CHORUS AND ORCH.)
    2,3,3,4 - 4,3,3,1 - timp. - hp. - str.   15:00 Bo. Hawkes.

—— SONGS OF SUNSET (FOR SOPRANO, BARITONE, CHORUS AND ORCH.)
    3,3,3,4 - 4,2,3,1 - timp.,perc. - hp. - str.   30:00 Bo. Hawkes.

—— SUMMER NIGHT ON THE RIVER
    2,1,2,2 - 2 hn. - str.   5:00 Oxford.

—— THREE PRELUDES
            Oxford.

DELIUS, Frederick - BEECHAM, Thomas

—— APPALACHIA (VARIATIONS ON AN OLD SLAVE SONG)
    3,4,4,3 - 6,3,3,1 - timp.,perc. - 2 hp. - str.   45:00 Bo. Hawkes.

—— FLORIDA (SUITE)
            Bo. Hawkes.

—— INTERMEZZO AND SERENADE FROM "HASSAN"
    1,1,1,1 - 2,1,0,0 - timp. - hp. - str.   4:00 Bo. Hawkes.

—— IRMELIN (CONCERT SUITE)
    3,*3,*3,3 - 4,2 cnt.,2,3,1 - timp.,perc. - hp. - str.
            15:30 Bo. Hawkes.
    or:
    3,3,3,3 - 4,4,3,1 - timp.,perc. - str.

—— KOANGA (OPERA) (Rev. 1935 %)
    3,3,*4,*4 - 4,2,3,1 - timp.,perc. - str.   Bo. Hawkes.

—— MARCH CAPRICE
    2(2nd alt. with picc.),2,2,2 - 4,2,3,1 - timp.,perc. - str.
            4:00 Galaxy.

—— MASS OF LIFE
            Bo. Hawkes.

—— OVER THE HILLS AND FAR AWAY
    3,2,2,3 - 4,2,3,1 - timp.,perc. - str.   8:00 G. Schirmer.

—— SEA DRIFT (FOR BARITONE, CHORUS AND ORCH.)
    3,4,4,4 - 6,3,3,1 - timp.,perc. - 2 hp. - str.   30:00 Bo. Hawkes.

—— SUMMER EVENING
    3(3rd alt. with picc.),2,2,2 - 4,2,3,1 - timp. - str.   6:00 Galaxy.

—— THE WALK TO THE PARADISE GARDEN (FROM "A VILLAGE ROMEO AND JULIET")
    2,2,2,2 - 4,2,3,0 - timp. - hp. - str.   8:00 Bo. Hawkes.

DELIUS, Frederick - DOUGLAS, Keith

—— THE WALK TO THE PARADISE GARDEN (FROM "A VILLAGE ROMEO AND JULIET")
    2,2,2,2 - 4,2,*2,0 - timp.,perc. (2) - hp. - pf. - (ad. lib.) - str.
            8:00 Bo. Hawkes.

DELIUS, Frederick - FENBY, Eric

—— AIR AND DANCE
    str.   8:00 Bo. Hawkes.

—— LA CALINDA (DANCE FROM "KOANGA")
    2,2,2,2 - 4,2,3,1 (ad lib.) - timp.,perc. - hp. - str.
            3:30 Bo. Hawkes.

—— CAPRICE AND ELEGY (FOR CELLO AND ORCH.)
    1,*2,1,1 - 2 hn. - hp. - str.   8:00 Bo. Hawkes.

—— HASSAN (SUITE)
    2,2,2,2 - 4,2,3,1 - timp.,perc. - hp. - str.   17:00 Bo. Hawkes.

—— LATE SWALLOWS (FROM THE SLOW MOVT. OF THE STRING QUARTET)
    str.   4:00 Galaxy.

—— TWO AQUARELLES
    str.   Bo. Hawkes.

—— A VILLAGE ROMEO AND JULIET (SUITE)
    2,2,3,2 - 4,2,3,1 - timp.,perc.,xyl. - hp. - str.   10:00 Bo. Hawkes.

DELIUS, Frederick - TERTIS, Lionel

—— CONCERTO FOR VIOLIN, VIOLA AND ORCHESTRA
    2,2(2nd alt. with Eng.hn.),2,2(2nd alt. with c.-bn.) - timp. - hp. - str.   18:00 Galaxy.

DELLO JOIO, Norman

—— BALLAD FOR "THE SEVEN LIVELY ARTS" (FOR PIANO AND ORCH.)
    2,2,2,2 - 4,2,3,0 - perc. (3) - pf. - str.   10:00 C. Fischer.

—— CONCERT MUSIC FOR ORCHESTRA
    *3,*3,*3,*3 - 4,3,3,1 - timp.,perc. (4), xyl. - str.   15:00 C. Fischer.

—— CONCERTANTE FOR CLARINET AND ORCH. (IN 2 MOVTS.)
    2(1 alt. with picc.),2(1 alt. with Eng. hn.),2,2 - 2,2,0,0 - timp.,perc. (2),cel. - str.   22:00 C. Fischer.

—— CONCERTO FOR HARP AND ORCH.
    1. Andante; 2. Scherzoso
    2(1 alt. with picc.),2,2(1 alt. with b.-cl.),2 - 2,0,0,0 - timp.,perc. - hp. - str.   18:00 C. Fischer.

—— EPIGRAPH
    *3,2,2,2 - 4,3,3,1 - timp.,perc.,cel.,glock. - hp. - str.
            13:00 C. Fischer.

—— FANTASY AND VARIATIONS (FOR PIANO AND ORCH.)
    *3,2,*3,2 - 4,3,3,1 - timp.,cel. - pf. - str.   22:00 C. Fischer.

—— HERE IS NEW YORK (SUITE)
    2,2,2,2 - 4,2,3,0 - perc. (3) - str.   35:00 C. Fischer.

—— THE LAMENTATION OF SAUL (FOR VOICE AND ORCH.)
    2,*3,2,2b.-cl.,2 - 4,3,3,1 - timp.,perc. (2) - hp. - str.
            18:00 C. Fischer.

—— MAGNIFICAT
    *3,0,2,0 - 4 hn. - timp.,perc. - pf. - str.   16:00 C. Fischer.

—— MEDITATIONS ON ECCLESIASTES (FOR STRINGS)
    str.   22:00 C. Fischer.

—— THE MYSTIC TRUMPETER
            11:00 G. Schirmer.

—— NEW YORK PROFILES (SUITE) (IN 4 MOVTS.)
    2,2,2,2 - 2,2,0,0 - timp.,perc. - str.   20:00 C. Fischer.

—— PSALM OF DAVID (FOR CHORUS AND ORCH.)
    4 hn., 4 tpt., 3 trb., tu. - timp.,perc.,glock. - str.   27:00 C. Fischer.

—— RICERCARI (FOR PIANO AND ORCH.)
    *3,2,2,2 - 4,3,3,1 - timp.,perc. - pf. - str.   20:00 C. Fischer.

—— SERENADE
    3,3,3,2 - 4,3,3,0 - timp.,perc.,cel. (or pf.) - hp. - str.
            16:00 C. Fischer.

—— SINFONIETTA (IN 4 MOVTS.)
    *3,2(1 alt. with Eng.hn),*3,*3 - 4,3,3,1 - timp.,perc.(2) - str.
            22:00 G. Schirmer.

—— SONG OF AFFIRMATION (SYMPHONIC CANTATA FOR CHORUS AND ORCH. (IN 3 MOVTS.)
    *3,2,2,2 b.-cl.,2 - 4,3,3,1 - timp.,perc.,cel.,glock. - str.
    45:00 C. Fischer.
—— SUITE FROM "ON STAGE" (IN 5 MOVTS.)
    *3,*3,2,2 - 4,2,3,1 - timp.,perc.,xyl. - pf. - str. 15:00 G. Schirmer.
—— SYMPHONIC SUITE: "AIR POWER" (IN 4 MOVTS.)
    2,2,2,2 - 4,2,3,0 - perc. (3) - str.
    40:00 C. Fischer.
—— THE TALL KENTUCKIAN (INCIDENTAL MUSIC TO THE PLAY) (FOR SOLO VOICES, MIXED CHORUS AND ORCH.)
    1,1,1,1 - 3,3,3,1 - timp.,perc.,cel. - hp. - str. 17:00 C. Fischer.
—— TO SAINT CECILIA (CANTATA FOR MIXED CHORUS AND TEN BRASSES)
    15:00 C. Fischer.
—— TO ST. CECILIA (FOR CHORUS AND BRASS CHOIR) (Text: John Dryden)
    0,0,0,0 - 3,3,3,1
    15:00 C. Fischer.
—— THE TRIUMPH OF SAINT JOAN (OPERA) %
    *5,*3,*3,2 - 4,3,3,1 - timp.,perc. (2),bells,cel.,glock.,xyl. - str.
    Ricordi.
—— THE TRIUMPH OF SAINT JOAN (SYMPHONY) (IN 3 MOVTS.)
    *3,*3,2,2 - 4,2,3,1 - timp.,perc.,glock. - str.
    30:00 C. Fischer.
—— VARIATIONS, CHACONNE AND FINALE
    3,3,3,3 - 4,3,3,1 - timp.,perc.,xyl. - str.
    21:00 C. Fischer.

DELLO JOIO, Norman - BEGLARIAN, Grant
—— VARIATIONS, CHACONNE AND FINALE (Reduced Orchestration)
    2,2,2,2 - 2,2,1,0 - timp.,perc. - str.
    21:00 C. Fischer.

DEL MAR, Norman
—— CONCERTO FOR FLUTE AND ORCH.
    3,2,2,2 - 3,2,3,0 - timp.,perc. - str.
    16:00 Novello.

DELMAS, Marc
—— DU RÊVE AU SOUVENIR (3 SONGS) (FOR VOICE AND ORCH.) (1919)
    2,1,2,2 - 4,3,3,0 - timp.,perc. - hp. - str.
    Salabert.

DELTOUR, Emile
—— CONCERTINO IN JAZZ (FOR HARP AND ORCH.)
    2,1,2,1 - 2,2,2,0 - timp.,perc. - hp. - pf. - str.
    7:30 EV.

DELTOUR, Emile - DERIDOUX, Edward
—— CONCERTO IN A MINOR FOR ACCORDION AND ORCH.
    picc.,0,2 Eng. hn.,2,2 -0,2,1,0 - perc. (1) - acc. - str. 20:00 FDH.

DEL TREDICI, David
—— ADVENTURES UNDERGROUND (FROM "ALICE IN WONDERLAND") (1973) (FOR AMPLIFIED SOPRANO AND CHAMBER ORCH., WITH SOLO FOLK GROUP OF 2 SAXOPHONES, MANDOLIN, TENOR BANJO AND ACCORDION) (IN TWO MOVEMENTS) (Text: Lewis Carroll)
    20:00 Bo. Hawkes.
—— ANNOTATED ALICE (FANTASCENE ON "TIS THE VOICE OF THE SLUGGARD" AND "THE LOBSTER QUADRILLE") (1976) (FOR AMPLIFIED SOPRANO AND ORCH., WITH SOLO FOLK GROUP OF 2 SAXOPHONES, MANDOLIN, TENOR BANJO AND ACCORDION) (Text: Lewis Carroll)
    28:00 Bo. Hawkes.
—— FINAL ALICE (SETTING OF CONCLUDING CHAPTERS OF "ALICE IN WONDERLAND") (1976) (FOR AMPLIFIED SOPRANO AND ORCH., WITH A SOLO FOLK GROUP OF 2 SAXOPHONES, MANDOLIN, TENOR BANJO AND ACCORDION) (Text: Lewis Carroll)
    40:00 Bo. Hawkes.
—— IN WONDERLAND PART I (A SCENE WITH LOBSTERS) (1969-74) (FOR AMPLIFIED SOPRANO AND ORCH., WITH A SOLO FOLK GROUP OF 2 SAXOPHONES, BANJO AND ACCORDION (IN 3 MOVTS.) (Text: Lewis Carroll)
    22:00 Bo. Hawkes.
—— IN WONDERLAND, PART II (1975) (FOR AMPLIFIED SOPRANO AND ORCH.) (IN 3 MOVTS.) (Text: Lewis Carroll)
    20:00 Bo. Hawkes.
—— THE LAST GOSPEL (FOR AMPLIFIED SOPRANO, SATB CHORUS, ROCK GROUP AND ORCH.) (1967) (Text: Biblical)
    2 picc.0,2,2 Eng. hn.,0,2,2 cbn. - 0,1,1,0 - str. Rock Group: 2 amplified sopr. sax.(1 alt. with ten. sax.),2 electric guit.
    13:00 Bo. Hawkes.

—— THE LOBSTER QUADRILLE (FOR CONCERTANTE GROUP, OPTIONAL SOPRANO OR TENOR VOICE AND ORCH.) (1974) (Text: Lewis Carroll)
    2(alt. with 2 picc.)0,Eᵇcl.,1,2(2nd alt. with c.-bn.) - 4,2,2,1 - perc.(4),mar.,xyl. - str.
    Bo. Hawkes.
    One Concertante Group: 2 sopr. sax. - accord. - banjo,mandolin
—— NIGHT CONJURE - VERSE (FOR SOPRANO, COUNTER-TENOR OR MEZZO-SOPRANO, AND INSTRUMENTS) (1965) (IN 2 MOVTS.) (Text: James Joyce)
    *2,1,*2,1 - 1,0,0,0 - str.
    18:00 Bo. Hawkes.
—— POP-POURRI (FOR AMPLIFIED SOPRANO, SATB CHORUS, ROCK GROUP AND ORCH.) (1968) (IN 5 MOVTS.) (Text: Lewis Carroll, and Litany of the Catholic Mass)
    2(alt. with 2 picc.),2,2(2nd alt. with Eng.hn.),2,2(2nd alt. with cbn.) - 0,2,2,0 - perc.(3),bells - str. Rock group: 2 amplified sopr. sax.(2nd alt. with ten. sax.), 2 electric guit. 28:00 Bo. Hawkes.
—— SCENES AND ARIAS FROM "ALICE IN WONDERLAND" (FOR AMPLIFIED SOPRANO AND ORCH.) (1969) (IN 6 MOVTS.) (Text: Lewis Carroll)
    2(alt. with 2 picc. and alto fl.),2,2(1 alt. with Eᵇcl.),sopr. sax.,2(2nd alt. with cbn.) - 4,2,2,1 - timp.,perc.(5),bells,glock.,mar.,vibra.,xyl. - theremin - accord. - banjo,mandolin - str.
    33:00 Bo. Hawkes.
—— SYZYGY (FOR AMPLIFIED SOPRANO, HORN AND ORCH.) (1966) (IN 2 MOVTS.) (Text: James Joyce)
    1(alt. with picc.),alto fl.(alt. with picc.),2(alt. with 2 Eng.hn.),2(1 alt. with b.-cl.),2(2nd alt. with cbn.) - 2,2,0,0 - perc.(2),bells(many) - str.
    24:00 Bo. Hawkes.
—— VINTAGE ALICE (FANTASCENE ON "A MAD TEA PARTY") (1972) (FOR AMPLIFIED SOPRANO AND CHAMBER ORCH., WITH A SOLO FOLK-GROUP OF 2 SAXOPHONES, MANDOLIN, TENOR BANJO AND ACCORDION) (Text: Lewis Carroll)
    28:00 Bo. Hawkes.

DELVAUX, Albert
—— CONCERTO NO. 2 FOR VIOLIN AND ORCH. (1974) (IN 3 MOVTS.)
    2,2,2,2 - 2,2,0,0 - timp. - str.
    21:00 H. Elkan.
—— INTRODUTTIONE E ALLEGRO (FOR STRING ORCH.) (1971)
    str.
    17:30 H. Elkan.
—— MOUVEMENT SYMPHONIQUE (1966)
    2,2,2,2 - 4,2,3,0 - timp.,perc. - str.
    7:00 H. Elkan.
—— SINFONIA IN D (1968) (IN 4 MOVTS.)
    2,2,2,2 - 4,2,2,1 - timp.,perc. - str.
    25:00 H. Elkan.

DELVINCOURT, Claude
—— BAL VENITIEN (IN 5 MOVTS.)
    2(alt. with 2 piccs.),2,2,2 - 2,2,1,1 - timp.,perc.,cel. - hp. - str.
    24:00 EV.
—— BOCCACERIE (IN 4 MOVTS.)
    2,2,2,2 - 4,2,1,1 - timp.,perc.,cel.,xyl. - hp. - pf. - str. 18:00 Baron.
—— CROQUEMBOUCHES (IN 9 MOVTS.)
    2,1(alt. with Eng. hn.),2,alto sax.,1 - 2,2,1,0 - timp.,perc. - str.
    20:15 Baron.
—— LUCIFER (FOR SOLOISTS, CHORUS AND ORCH.)
    *3,*3,3, sax.,3 - 4,4,2,1 - timp.,perc.,cel. - 2 hp. - org. - str.
    90:00 EV.
—— PAMIR (SUITE)
    3,2,3, sax.,2 - 2,3,3,1 - timp.,perc.,cel. - hp. - pf. - str. 18:00 EV.
—— PRÉLUDE CHORÉGRAPHIQUE
    3,2,2,2 - 2,2,1,1 - timp.,perc.,cel. - hp. - str.
    10:00 EV.
—— RADIO SERENADE
    2,1,2,1 - 1,2,1,1 - timp., perc. (3) - hp. - str.
    20:00 EV.
—— SALUT SOLENNEL (FOR VOCAL QUARTET, CHORUS AND ORCH.) (IN 7 MOVTS.)
    2 tpt., 2 trb. - timp.,perc. - org. - str.
    26:00 EV.

DE MADINA, Francisco
—— BASQUE CHRISTMAS SUITE
    E. F. Kalmus.
—— CHRISTMAS TRIPTYCH
    E. F. Kalmus.
—— ORREAGA (BASQUE SUITE)
    E. F. Kalmus.
—— SUITE FOR HARP AND ORCH.
    E. F. Kalmus.

DEMAREST, Clifford
—— LET FREEDOM RING (OVERTURE)
    2,2,2,2 - 2,2,2,1 - timp.,perc. - str.
    Remick.
—— RHAPSODY FOR PIANO AND ORCH.
    1,1,2,1 - 2,2,1,0 - timp. - pf. - str.
    G. Schirmer.

—— SUNRISE AT SEA (TONE POEM)
2,1,2,2 - 2,3,3,1 - timp.,perc. - str.   Witmark.

DE MARKY, Paul
—— CONCERTO IN B MAJOR FOR PIANO AND ORCH. (IN 4 MOVTS.)
                                        28:30 C.A.P.A.C.

DEMESSIEUX, Jeanne
—— POÈME (FOR ORGAN AND ORCH.)
3,*3,3,3 - 4,2,3,0 - timp.,perc. - org. - str.   15:00 EV.

DE MIDDELEER, Jean
—— CONCERTO FOR PIANO AND ORCH. (1953)
2,2,2,2 - 4,2,3,1 - timp.,perc.,cel.,glock.,xyl. - pf. - str.
                                        14:00 H. Elkan.
—— CONGO SYMPHONY
3,3,3, sax.,0 - 4,3,3,1 - perc.,cel.,glock. - hp. - pf. - str.
                                        25:00 CBDM.
—— POÈME SYMPHONIQUE (1935)
3,3,3,3 - 4,3,3,1 - timp.,perc.,cel.,glock.,xyl. - hp. - str.
                                        7:00 H. Elkan.
—— RONDEAU (JOIE DE VIVRE) (1937)
3,3,3,3 - 4,3,3,1 - timp.,perc.,cel.,glock. - hp. - pf. - str.
                                        6:00 H. Elkan.

DENISOV, Edison
—— SYMPHONY, OP. 28 (FOR 2 STRING ORCHS. AND PERCUSSION)
perc. - str.   15:00 G. Schirmer.

DENT, Edward J. - DENT, E. J.
—— DIDO AND AENEAS: SUITE
cemb. - str.   10:00 Oxford.

DEPELSENAIRE, Jean-Marie
—— CONCERTINO FOR OBOE, ALTO SAXOPHONE AND SMALL ORCH.
2,1,2,alto sax.,0 - 0,0,0,0 - timp. - str.   13:00 Henmar.
—— CONCERTO GROSSO (FOR 2 TRUMPETS, TROMBONE AND STRINGS)
0,0,0,0 - 0,2,1,0 - str.   16:00 Henmar.
—— CONCERTO GROSSO IN E MINOR
1,1,1,0 - 0,0,0,0 - pf. - tr.   12:00 Galaxy.
—— DIALOGUE (FOR TRUMPET, SAXOPHONE AND SMALL ORCH.)
1,1,2,sax.,1 - 0,1,0,0 - str.   6:00 Presser.
—— LES SEPT DERNIÈRES PAROLES DU CHRIST (ORATORIO) (FOR TENOR, BARITONE, BASS, MIXED CHORUS AND ORCH.)
1,1,2,1 - 1,2,2,1 - str.   20:00 Presser.
—— SUITE CONCERTANTE (FOR SAXOPHONE AND ORCH.)
0,0,2,sax.,0 - 1,0,0,0 - str.   Presser.

DEPRAZ, Raymond
—— CONDUCTUS (FOR VIOLA AND INSTRUMENTALISTS)
1,1,0,1 - 1,1,0,1 - timp.,perc.,cel. - vla.   15:00 Presser.
—— ENTELÉCHIES
2,2,2,2 - 2,2,2,0 - timp.,perc.(4),cel. - hp. - pf. - str.   27:00 Presser.
—— LES NAISSANCES (FOR BRASS AND PERCUSSION)
0,0,0,0 - 4,4,4,0 - perc.(6)   15:30 Presser.
—— SUITE QUATROCENTO
str.   21:00 Presser.
—— SYMPHONY NO. 1
0,0,0,0 - 4,4,4,0 - timp.,perc.(6) - str.   23:00 Presser.
—— SYMPHONY NO. 2 (FOR 4 SAXOPHONES AND ORCH.)
4,2,3,4 sax.,2 - 4,3,3,1 - perc.(3),xyl. - pf. - str.   Presser.

DE PUE, Wallace Earl
—— CONCERTO FOR PERCUSSION AND ORCH. (1965) (IN 3 MOVTS.)
2(2nd alt. with picc.),*3,2,2 - 4,2,3,1 - timp.,perc.(5),cel.,glock.,mar.,vibra.,xyl. - hp. - str.
                                        17:00 Composer.
—— PASSACAGLIA FOR ORCHESTRA (1968)
2(2nd alt. with picc.),2,2,2 - 4,2,3,1 - timp.,perc.(2) - str.
                                        7:00 Composer.

DEQEN, Helmut
—— CONCERTO FOR CELLO AND STRINGS
pf. - str.   Robbins.

DERBES, Jean
—— CONCERTO POUR PIANO ET ORCHESTRE
2,2,2,2 - 2,2,2,0 - timp.,perc.(2) - pf. - str.   22:40 S.U.I.S.A.
—— GENÈSE
3,3,3,3 - 4,3,3,0 - timp.,perc.(3),cel. - str.   12:00 S.U.I.S.A.
—— PRAEMONITIO PASSIONIS (PRÉLUDE POUR LA NATIVITÉ)
3,3,3,3 - 4,3,3,0 - timp.,perc.(3),cel. - pf. - str.   17:00 S.U.I.S.A.

DÉRÉ, Jean
—— ESQUISSES (SKETCHES) (10 PETITES PIÈCES)
2,2,2,1 sax.(ad lib.),2 - 2,2,2,1 - str.   16:00 EV.
—— KRISHNA (SYMPHONIC POEM)
3,3,3,3 - 4,3,3,1 - timp.,perc. (3),cel. - 2 hp. - pf. - str.
                                    10:00 Salabert.
—— QUARTRES CHANTS ARABES (FOR VOICE AND ORCH.)
                                    Salabert.
—— QUATRE PETITES PIECES (FOR CHAMBER ORCH.)
1,1,1,1 - 1,1,1,0 - timp.,perc. - hp. (or pf.) - str.   Salabert.

DE ROGATIS, Pascual
—— DANCE FROM THE 1-ACT OPERA "HUEMAC" (1915)
3,3,3,2 - 4,3,3,1 - timp.,perc.,cel. - hp. - str.   8:00 Fleisher.

DERUNGS, Gion Antoni
—— FUORMAS, OP. 43 (PER ORGANO, ORCHESTRA DA CAMERA E PERCUSSION)
                                    12:00 S.U.I.S.A.

DERUNGS, Martin
—— INTERPOLATION (FÜR GROSSES STREICHORCHESTER)
str.   6:00 S.U.I.S.A.

DERVAUX, Pierre
—— DIVERTISSEMENT BURLESQUE (IN 6 MOVTS.)
1,1,2,1 - 2,2,1,0 - timp.,cel. (or vibra.),glock. - pf. - str.
                                    10:00 Baron.
—— SYMPHONY
3,3,3,3 - 4,3,3,1 - timp.,perc. - hp. - pf. - str.   30:00 Salabert.
—— SYMPHONY FOR STRINGS
str.   20:00 Presser.

DESDERI, Ettore
—— FANTASIE ÜBER EIN THEMA VON BEETHOVEN
2,3,3,2 - 2,2,2,0 - timp. - str.   18:00 Alkor.

DESENCLOS, Alfred
—— CONCERTO FOR VIOLIN AND ORCH.
1,1,2,1 - 0,0,0,0 - str.   15:00 Baron.
—— INCANTATION, THRÈNE ET DANSE (FOR TRUMPET AND ORCH.)
2,2,2,2 - 4,0,0,0 - timp.,perc.,cel.,vibra. - hp. - str.   15:00 Baron.
—— MESSE DE REQUIEM (FOR SATB CHORUS AND ORCH.)
2,2,2,1 - 4,0,0,0 - hp. - str.   32:00 EV.

DESORMIERE, Roger
—— CINQ PIÈCES EN SUITE FRANÇAISE DU DIX-HUITIÈME SIÈCLE (FROM A MANUSCRIPT IN THE LIBRARY OF CASSEL)
fl. (ad lib.) - str.   18:00 Salabert.

DE SOUSA, Filipe
—— SUITE DE DANCAS (AUS DEM BALLETT "LUSITANIA")
3,2,3,2 - 4,3,3,1 - timp.,perc. - str.   15:00 Modern.

DESPIĆ, Dejan
—— CONCERTINO IN D, FOR 2 FLUTES AND ORCH.
2,1,1,0 - 0,0,0,0 - hp. - str.   12:20 MIC,Zagreb.
—— DIVERTIMENTO CONCERTANTE IN F, OP. 51 (FOR HORN, TRUMPET AND ORCH.)
2,2(2nd alt. with Eng.hn.),2(2nd alt. with b.-cl.),0 - 1,1,0,0 - timp.,perc.,2 xyl. - pf. - str.   8:50 MIC,Zagreb.

DESPORTES, Yvonne
—— L' EXPLOIT DE LA COULISSE (BALLAD FOR TROMBONE AND ORCH.)
1,1,2,1 - 3,0,1,0 - timp.,perc.(5) - hp. - str.   17:00 Presser.
—— SONATE POUR UN BAPTÊME (SUITE)
2,2,2,alto sax.(ad. lib.),2 - 2,2,1,0 - perc.(2) - pf. - str.
                                    18:00 Presser.

DESPREZ, Josquin - MADERNA, Bruno
—— MAGNIFICAT QUARTI TONI (FOR MIXED CHORUS AND 3 GROUPS OF INSTRUMENTS)
    4,3,0,2 - 2,3,3,0 - timp.,perc.(3),bells,2 vibra. - 2 guit.,mandolin - 2 hp. - str.   9:00 MCA Music.

DESREZ, Maurice
—— ONDINE: ACT I %
    70:00 Baron.
—— ONDINE (LYRIC DRAMA IN 5 ACTS AND 7 TABLEAUX) %
(Text: Jean Bonnerot)
    3,2,2,3 - 4,3,3,0 - timp.,perc. - hp. - str.   180:00 Baron.

DESSAGNES, Gontran
—— FANTASIE-CONCERTANTE (FOR TWO GUITARS AND ORCH.)
    24:00 S.A.C.E.M.

DETERMANN, Gunther
—— CHAMBER CONCERTO FOR HARPSICHORD AND STRING ORCH.
    hpsc. - str.   21:00 Mannheimer.

DETONI, Dubravko
—— ASSONANCE NO. 2 (FOR CELLO AND ORCH.) (1971)
    3,0,*3,alto sax.,*1 - 4,3,3,1 - timp.,perc.(5),cel.,mar.,vibra.,xyl. - guit. - hpsc. - org. - pf. - str.(0,8,1,8)   10:00 MIC,Zagreb.
—— DRAMATIC PROLOGUE (1965)
    3,3,3,*3 - 4,3,3,1 - perc.(4),cel.,vibra. - str.   15:00 MIC,Zagreb.
—— ELUCUBRATIONS (FOR PIANO AND ORCH.) (1969)
    3,3,3(3rd alt. with b.-cl.),3(3rd alt. with c.-bn.) - 4,3,3,1 - perc.(5),cel.,glock. - 2 hp. - hpsc. - pf. - str.   MIC,Zagreb.
—— GRAPHICS NO. 2 (1968)
    1,0,1,sax.,0 - 0,0,0,0 - perc.(2) - org. - pf.(alt. with cel. and hpsc.) - str.   8:00 MIC,Zagreb.
—— GRAPHICS NO. 3 (1970)
    4,0,1(alt. with b.-cl. and sax.),0 - 0,0,0,0 - perc.(3) - tape-recorder - org. - pf.(alt. with hpsc.)   16:00 MIC,Zagreb.
—— GRAPHICS NO. 5 (1972)
    1,0,1(alt. with b.-cl. and sax.),0 - 0,1,1,0 - perc.(2) - org. - pf.(alt. with hpsc.) - str.(1,1,1,0)   12:00 MIC,Zagreb.
—— MONOS NO. 3 (FOR VARIABLE ORCHESTRA) (1972)
    10:00 MIC,Zagreb.
—— MUSIC OR TRACTATE ON THE SUPERFLUOUS (FOR ORGAN, PIANO, PERCUSSION, CLARINET, NARRATING ACTOR AND ORCH.) (1973)
    3,3,4(solo cl. alt. with sax.),3 - 4,3,3,0 - perc.(2-4) - org. - pf. - str.   30:00 MIC,Zagreb.
—— MUSICA À CINQUE (1962)
    str.   10:00 MIC,Zagreb.
—— PASSACAGLIA (1962)
    2 pf. - str.   12:00 MIC,Zagreb.
—— TRANSFIGURATIONS (1963)
    2,2,2,2 - 4,2,2,0 - timp.,perc.(2) - str.   10:00 MIC,Zagreb.

DETT, Nathaniel
—— CHARIOT JUBILEE (FOR TENOR, CHORUS AND ORCH.)
    2,2,2,2 - 4,2,3,1 - timp.,perc. - org. - str.   15:00 Church.
—— ENCHANTMENT SUITE (IN 4 MOVTS.)
    3(3rd alt. with picc.),2,2,2 - 4,2,3,1 - timp.,perc. - hp. - pf. - str.   15:00 Summy-Bir.
—— THE ORDERING OF MOSES (ORATORIO) (FOR SOLOISTS, CHORUS AND ORCH.)
    *3,2,2,2 - 4,2,3,1 - timp.,perc. - hp. - org. - str.   60:00 J. Fischer.

DEUTSCH, Herbert A.
—— MOVEMENTS FOR CHAMBER ORCH. (1967) (IN 4 MOVTS.)
    1(alt. with picc.),0,1(alt. with alto sax.),0 - 0,1,0,0 - timp.,perc.(2),bells,glock.,vibra.,xyl. - pf. - str.   10:00 H. Branch.

DEUTSCH, Peter
—— THE MAGIC PICTURE (CONCERTO FOR PIANO AND ORCH.)
    1,2,1,0 - 2,2,1,0 - timp.,perc. - hp. - str.   10:00 F. Colombo.
—— ROKOKO-MARIONETTEN (OVERTURE)
    1,1,2,1 - 2,2,0,0 - str.   7:00 F. Colombo.

DEVČIĆ, Natko
—— CONCERTINO FOR VIOLIN AND CHAMBER ORCH. (1958)
    Hans Gerig.
—— CONCERTO FOR TENOR AND CHAMBER ENSEMBLE
    Hans Gerig.

—— DIA... (1971)
    *3,2,*3,1 - 4,3,3,0 - perc.(4) - str.   25:00 MIC,Zagreb.
—— PANTA REI (FOR PIANO AND ORCH.) (1973)
    *3,2,*3,2 - 4,3,3,0 - perc.(3) - pf. - str.   11:00 MIC,Zagreb.

DEVIENNE, François - OUBRADOUS, Fernand
—— CONCERTO NO. 7, FOR FLUTE AND ORCH.
    1,2,0,0 - 2,0,0,0 - str.   Presser.

DEVOS, Gerard
—— SINFONIETTA FOR STRINGS
    str.   17:00 EV.

DEVREESE, Frédéric
—— CONCERTO FOR VIOLIN AND ORCH. (1951)
    2,2,2,2 - 2,2,3,0 - str.   23:00 H. Elkan.
—— CONCERTO NO. 1 FOR PIANO AND ORCH. (1949)
    2,2,2,2 - 4,3,3,1 - timp.,perc.,bells,xyl. - pf. - str.   22:00 H. Elkan.
—— CONCERTO NO. 2 FOR PIANO AND ORCH. (1952)
    2,2,2,2 - 4,3,3,1 - timp.,perc. - pf. - str.   22:00 H. Elkan.
—— CONCERTO NO. 3 FOR PIANO AND ORCH. (1956)
    2,2,2,2 - 4,2,3,1 - timp.,perc.,bells - pf. - str.   25:00 H. Elkan.
—— MASQUERADE (SUITE OF THREE DANCES)
    2,2,2,sax.,2 - 4,2,3,1 - timp.,perc.,cel. - str.   12:30 Modern.
—— MOVEMENT LENT (1953)
    str.   7:00 Henmar.
—— SYMPHONY (1953)
    2,2,2,2 - 4,3,3,1 - timp.,perc.,xyl. - hp. - str.   28:00 H. Elkan.

DEVREESE, Godefroid
—— ALLEGRO FOR TRUMPET AND ORCH. (1950)
    2,2,2,2 - 4,3,0,0 - timp.,perc. - str.   5:00 H. Elkan.
—— CONCERTO FOR PIANO AND ORCH. (1938)
    2,2,2,2 - 4,3,3,1 - timp.,perc. - pf. - str.   35:00 H. Elkan.
—— CONCERTO FOR VIOLIN AND ORCH. (1937)
    2,2,2,2 - 4,3,3,1 - timp. - str.   25:00 H. Elkan.
—— GOETHE SYMPHONY (FOR MIXED CHORUS AND ORCH.) (1952)
    2,2,2,2 - 4,3,3,1 - timp.,perc.,glock. - pf. - str.   55:00 H. Elkan.
—— IN MEMORIAM (1928)
    2,2,3,3 - 4,3,3,1 - timp. - hp. - str.   9:00 H. Elkan.
—— POÈME HÉROÏQUE (1923)
    2,2,3,3 - 4,3,3,0 - timp.,perc. - 2 hp. - str.   14:00 H. Elkan.
—— RHAPSODY FOR CLARINET AND ORCH. (1948)
    2,2,3,2 - 2,2,1,0 - str.   8:00 H. Elkan.
—— SUITE (1953)
    2,2,2,2 - 4,3,3,1 - timp.,perc. - str.   18:00 H. Elkan.
—— SYMPHONY NO. 1 ("GOTHIQUE") (1944)
    2,2,2,2 - 4,3,3,1 - timp.,perc. - str.   45:00 H. Elkan.
—— TOMBELÈNE (OLD CELTIC LEGEND) (BALLET-MIMODRAME IN THE FORM OF A DIPTYCH) % (1927)
    3,2,3,3 - 4,3,3,1 - timp.,perc.,cel.,glock.,xyl. - hp. - pf. - str.   20:00 H. Elkan.
—— VARIATIONS SYMPHONIQUES (ON A POPULAR SCOTCH THEME) (1923)
    2,2,2,2 - 4,3,3,1 - timp.,perc.,glock. - hp. - str.   15:00 H. Elkan.

DEVRESSE, Godfried
—— CONCERTO NO. 2 FOR VIOLIN AND ORCH. (1970) (IN 3 MOVTS.)
    2,2,2,2 - 4,2,0,0 - timp.,perc. - str.   25:00 H. Elkan.
—— SYMPHONY NO. 4 (1966) (IN 4 MOVTS.)
    2,2,2,2 - 4,3,3,1 - timp.,perc. - str.   30:00 H. Elkan.

DEVRIES, Yvan
—— ERROMANGO (2-ACT BALLET-CANTATA) (FOR NARRATOR, CONTRALTO, CHORUS AND ORCH.) %
    3,3,3,3 - 4,2,3,1 - timp.,perc.(3),cel. - hp. - pf. - str.   60:00 EV.

DEWANGER, Anton
—— MARCHE SOLENNELLE (1921)
    2,2,2,4 sax.(1 sopr.,2 alto,1 ten.),3 - 4,3,3,1 - timp.,perc. - str.   6:00 Salabert.

DEWAR, Ted Royal
—— LOUISIANA LANDSCAPE (IN 3 MOVTS.)
    3,3,4,2 - 2,3,2,0 - perc. (2), cel. - hp. - pf. - str.   10:00 Composer.

DE ZUCCOLI, G.
—— LA NOTTE DI GETSEMANI
    3,3,3,3 - 4,3,3,1 - timp.,perc.,cel. - hp. - str.   14:00 Bo. Hawkes.

D'HOEDT, Henry-Georges
—— CHRONIQUES BRÈVES DE LA VIE BOURGEOISE (1934)(SUITE) (IN 5 MOVTS.)
3,3,3,3 - 4,3,3,1 - perc. - hp. - str.   26:00 H. Elkan.

DIAMOND, David
—— AHAVAH (SYMPHONIC EULOGY) (FOR NARRATOR AND ORCH.)
3(3rd alt. with picc.),*3,*3,*3 - 4,3,3,1 - timp. (pedal-operated), perc. (3), glock.,xyl. - hp. - pf. - str.   26:00 Witmark.
—— ARIA AND HYMN
3(3rd alt. with picc.),*3, E♭cl.,*3,*3 - 4,3,3,1 - timp.,perc. (5) - hp. - pf. - str.   12:00 Composer.
—— CEREMONIAL FANFARE (FANFARE FOR THE UNITED NATIONS)
0,0,0,0 - 6,4,3,1 - timp.,perc.   1:30 Southern.
—— CONCERT PIECE
2,2,2,2 - 2,3,2,0 - timp.,perc. - pf. - str.   13:00 Southern.
—— CONCERTINO FOR PIANO AND SMALL ORCH.
1,1,1,1 - 2,1,0,0 - timp. - str.   12:00 Southern.
—— CONCERTO FOR CELLO AND ORCH. (IN 3 MOVEMENTS)
3(3rd alt. with picc.),*3,*3,*3 - 4,2,2,1 - timp.,perc. - pf. - str.   20:00 Southern.
—— CONCERTO FOR CHAMBER ORCH. (IN 2 MOVTS.)
1,1,1,1 - 2,1,0,0 - timp.,perc. (1) - str.   15:00 Southern.
—— CONCERTO FOR PIANO AND LARGE ORCH.
3,3,3,2 - 4,2,3,1 - timp.,perc. - pf. - str.   22:00 Southern.
—— CONCERTO NO. 1 FOR VIOLIN AND ORCH. (IN 3 MOVTS.)
3(3rd alt. with picc.),*3, E♭cl. (alt. with sax.),*3,*3 - 4,2,2,1 - timp.,perc. (4) - hp. - pf. - str.   20:00 Southern.
—— CONCERTO NO. 3 FOR VIOLIN AND ORCH.
4(4th alt. with alto fl.),3(3rd alt. with Eng. hn.),4(4th alt. with E♭ cl. and b.-cl.) - 4,3(3rd alt. with picc.tpt.),3,1 - timp.,perc. - hp. - str.   16:15 Southern.
—— DIAPHONY (FOR BRASS, 2 PIANOS, ORGAN AND TIMPANI)
0,0,0,0 - 2,2,2,1 - timp. - 2 pf. - org.   28:00 Harms, Inc.
—— ELEGIES
fl.,Eng. hn. - str.   17:40 Southern.
—— ELEGY IN MEMORY OF RAVEL (FOR STRINGS AND PERCUSSION)
timp.,perc. - str.   7:00 Southern.
—— THE ENORMOUS ROOM
3,3,3,3 - 4,3,3,1 - timp.,perc. - hp. - str.   10:00 Southern.
—— HEROIC PIECE (FOR SMALL ORCH.)
2(2nd alt. with picc.),*2,*2,1 - 2,1,1,1 - perc. (1) - str.   11:00 Southern.
—— THE MARTYR (FOR TTBB CHORUS AND ORCH.)
2,3,3(3rd alt. with E♭cl.),3 - 4,2(2nd alt. with picc.tpt.),3,1 - timp.,perc. pf. - str.   10:00 Southern.
—— MUSIC FOR DOUBLE STRING ORCH., BRASS AND TIMPANI
1. Lento - Allegro vivo; 2. Adagio - Allegro vivace
0,0,0,0 - 4,3,3,1 - timp. - str.   25:00 Composer.
—— MUSIC FOR SHAKESPEARE'S "ROMEO AND JULIET" (IN 5 MOVTS.)
2(2nd alt. with picc.),2(2nd alt. with Eng. hn.),2(2nd alt. with b.-cl.),2 - 2,2,1,0 - timp.,perc. (2),bells,glock.,xyl. - hp. - str.   18:00 Bo. Hawkes.
—— MUSIC (1969) (IN 2 MOVTS.)
2(1st alt. with picc.,2nd alt. with alto fl.),1(alt. with Eng. hn.),1(alt. with E♭cl.),1 - 2,1,1,0 - timp.(pedal),perc.(3),bells(tubular chromatic set),xyl. - hp. - pf. - str.   17:00 Southern.
—— OVERTURE FOR ORCHESTRA
3(3rd alt. with picc.),*3, E♭cl.,*3,*3 - 4,3,3,1 - timp.,perc. (5),xyl. - hp. - str.   4:30 Southern.
—— OVERTURE TO "THE TEMPEST"
3(3rd alt. with picc.),*3,*3,*3 - 4,3,3,1 - timp.,perc.,cel.,glock. - hp. - pf. - str.   4:30 Chappell.
—— PSALM FOR ORCHESTRA
3(3rd alt. with picc.),*3,*3,*3 - 4,3,3,1 - perc. (4),cel.,glock.,xyl. - 2 hp. - pf. - str.   7:00 Southern.
—— ROUNDS FOR STRING ORCHESTRA
1. Allegro, molto vivace; 2. Adagio; 3. Allegro vigoroso
str.   12:00 EV.
—— THIS SACRED GROUND (FOR BARITONE, CHILDREN'S CHORUS, MIXED CHORUS AND ORCH.) (Text: Lincoln's "Gettysburg Address")
3,3,3,3 - 4,3,3,1 - timp.,perc. - hp. - str.   15:00 Southern.

—— SINFONIA CONCERTANTE
1. Allegro aperto; 2. Allegro con brio; 3. Larghetto; 4. Allegro deciso e ben ritmato
*2,*2,1,1 - 1,3,3,1 - timp.,perc. (4),glock.,xyl. - hp. - pf. - str.   23:30 Southern.
—— SINFONIETTA (REFLECTING THE SPIRIT OF AMERICAN LIFE)
1. Allegro; 2. Lento; 3. Allegro
*3,*3,*3,*3 - 4,3,3,1 - timp.,perc. (5) - hp. - pf. - str.   10:00 Robbins.
—— SUITE FROM "TOM"
3(3rd alt. with picc.),*3,*3,*4 - 4,3,3,1 - timp.,perc. (3),cel.,glock.,xyl. - hp. - pf. - str.   30:00 Composer.
—— SYMPHONY NO. 1
1. Allegro con energia; 2. Andante maestoso; 3. Maestoso - Allegro vivo
3(3rd alt. with picc.),*3,*3,*3 - 4,3,3,1 - timp.,perc. (3) - str.   20:00 Southern.
—— SYMPHONY NO. 3
1. Allegro deciso; 2. Andante; 3. Allegro vivo; 4. Adagio; 5. Allegro con impeto
3(3rd alt. with picc.),*3,*3,*3 - 4,4,3,1 - timp.,perc.,xyl. - hp. - pf. - str.   36:00 Southern.
—— SYMPHONY NO. 4
3,3,3,3 - 4 ,3,3,1 - timp.,perc.,xyl. - 2 hp. - pf. - str.   16:00 G. Schirmer.
or:
4(3rd and 4th alt. with picc.),*4,*4,4 - 6,4,3,1 - timp.,perc.,xyl. - 2 hp. - pf. - str.
—— SYMPHONY NO. 5 (1964)
1. Adagio - Allegro energico; 2. Andante - Fuga (Allegretto) - Adagio
*3,*3,1 E♭cl.,*3,*3 - 4,4(incl. 1 D tpt.),3,1 - timp.(2),perc.(4),glock.,xyl. - org. - pf. - str.   17:00 Southern.
—— SYMPHONY NO. 6
*3,*3,1 E♭cl.,*3,*3 - 4,3,3,1 - timp.,perc.,bells,xyl. - pf. - str.   25:00 Harms, Inc.
—— SYMPHONY NO. 7
3,3,4,3 - 4,4,3,1 - timp.,perc. - hp. - pf. - str.   16:00 Southern.
—— SYMPHONY NO. 8
3,3,4,3 - 4,4,3,1 - timp.,perc. - hp. - pf. - str.   28:00 Southern.
—— TIMON OF ATHENS (SYMPHONIC PORTRAIT AFTER SHAKESPEARE)
2(2nd alt. with picc.),2(2nd alt. with Eng. hn.),2,2 - 4,2,3,1 - timp.,perc. (2),glock.,xyl. - pf. - str.   8:30 Leeds.
—— TO MUSIC (CHORAL SYMPHONY) (FOR TENOR, BASS-BARITONE, SATB CHORUS AND ORCH.)
3,3,4,3 - 6,4,3,1 - timp.,perc.(4 incl. 2 on timp.),glock.,xyl. - hp. - pf. - str.   20:00 Southern.
—— VARIATIONS FOR SMALL ORCHESTRA
2(2nd alt. with picc.),*2,*2,2 - 2,1,1,1 - timp.,perc. (2) - pf. - str.   15:00 Composer.
—— THE WORLD OF PAUL KLEE (SUITE) (IN 4 MOVTS.)
*3,*3,*3,2 - 4,2,2,0 - timp.,perc.(2),cel.,glock.,xyl. - hp. - pf. - str.   12:00 Southern.
—— YOUNG JOSEPH (FOR WOMEN'S CHORUS AND STRINGS)
str.   5:30 MusPress.

DI BIASE, Edoardo
—— AN AMERICAN PORTRAIT (OVERTURE)
2,2,2,2 - 4,3,3,1 - timp.,perc. - str.   7:00 Leeds.
—— FANTASIA FOR SOLO CLARINET AND CHAMBER ORCH.
2,1,2,1 - 1,1,1,0 - str.   6:30 Presser.
—— ORIENTAL FANTASY
3,3,3,3 - 4,3,3,1 - timp.,perc.,xyl. - 2 hp. - pf. - str.   9:30 Leeds.

DI BONAVENTURA, Mario
—— TWO MOVEMENTS FOR A FESTIVAL
S.A.C.E.M.

DICK, Marcel
—— ADAGIO AND RONDO
*3,*3,*3,*3 - 4,3,3,1 - timp.,perc.(3),cel.,glock. - hp. - str.   15:00 Presser.
—— CAPRICCIO FOR ORCH.
*3,*3,*3,*3 - 4,3,3,1 - timp.,perc.(3),cel.,glock. - hp. - str.   15:00 Presser.
—— SYMPHONY FOR TWO STRING ORCHS.
str.   20:00 Presser.
—— SYMPHONY (IN 4 MOVTS.)
3(3rd alt. with picc.),*3,*3,*3 - 4,3,3,1 - timp.,perc.(4),cel.,glock.,xyl. - hp. - str.   42:00 Presser.

DICKERSON, Roger D.
—— CONCERT OVERTURE (1957)
2(2nd alt. with picc.),2,2,2 - 4,2,3,1 - timp.,perc.(3) - str.
14:00 Composer.
—— A MUSICAL SERVICE FOR LOUIS (A REQUIEM FOR LOUIS ARMSTRONG) (FOR SATB CHORUS AD LIB. AND ORCH.)
3(3rd alt. with picc.),3(3rd alt. with Eng. hn.),3(3rd alt. with b.-cl.),2 - 4,4,3,1 - timp.,perc.(2)(incl. Jazz set)   15:00 Southern.
—— ORPHEUS AN' HIS SLIDE TROMBONE (FOR NARRATOR AND ORCH.)
3,3,3,3 - 4,3,4,1 - timp.,perc.(2) - hp. - pf. - str.   22:00 Southern.

DICKINSON, Clarence
—— THE REDEEMER (EASTER CANTATA) (FOR SATB SOLO VOICES, SATB CHORUS AND CHAMBER ORCH.)
2,0,0,0 - 0,2,2,0 - timp. - hp. - org. - vln.,c.   60:00 Belw-Mills.
—— STORM KING SYMPHONY (IN 4 MOVTS.)
*3,*3,2,2 - 4,2,3,1 - timp.,perc. (3) - org. - str.   25:00 Gray.

DICKINSON, Peter
—— CONCERTO FOR ORGAN AND ORCH.
2(2nd alt. with picc.),1,2,3 - 4,2,2,0 - timp.,perc.,cel.,vibra.,xyl. - org. - str.   20:00 Novello.
—— FIVE DIVERSIONS
2,2,2,2 - 2,2,2,0 - timp.,perc. - str.   12:00 Novello.
—— TRANSFORMATIONS
3(3rd alt. with picc.),3,3,3 - 4,3,3,1 - timp.,perc.,cel.,glock.,vibra.,xyl. - pf. - str.   17:00 Novello.
—— VITALITUS (BALLET) %
3,2,2,2 - 0,3,3,1 - timp.,perc. - pf. - str.   15:00 Novello.

DIEBEL, Wendel H.
—— LES DANSES GOTHIQUES (1964)
3(3rd alt. with picc.),*3,*3,*3 - 4,3,4,1 - timp.,perc.(3). - 2 hp. - str.   8:00 Composer.
—— FANTASY FOR HARP, STRING ORCH. AND FLUTE (1962)
fl. - hp. - str.   12:45 Lyra.

DIEMENTE, Edward
—— CELEBRATION (1969)
3,3,3,*4 - 4,3,5,2 - perc.(3)   10:00 Seesaw.
—— DIMENSIONS IV
3,3,3,3 - 4,3,3,1 - perc.(3) - tape-recorder   10:00 Seesaw.
—— UNVELOPMENT (1968)
3,3,6,2 - 4,3,4,3 - perc.(2)   12:00 Seesaw.

DIEMER, Emma Lou
—— ANNIVERSARY CHORUSES (FOR MIXED CHORUS AND ORCH.) (1969) (Text: Biblical, Henry Timrod, Archibald Rutledge)
*3,2,2,2 - 4,3,3,1 - timp.,perc.(3) - str.   15:00 C. Fischer.
—— CONCERTO FOR FLUTE AND ORCH. (IN 3 MOVTS.)
*4,2,*3,*3 - 4,3,3,1 - timp.,perc.(3),cel.,xyl. - hp. - pf. - str.   24:00 Composer.
—— CONCERTO FOR HARPSICHORD AND ORCH. (IN 3 MOVTS.)
1,1,1,1 - 4,2,2,1 - timp.,perc.(2) - hpsc. - str.   12:00 Composer.
—— FESTIVAL OVERTURE FOR ORCHESTRA (1961)
*3,2,2,2 - 4,3,3,1 - timp.,perc.(2) - str.   6:00 EV.
—— NINETEEN-SIXTY-TWO OVERTURE
*3,2,2,2 - 4,3,3,1 - timp.,perc.(5) - str.   5:00 Composer.
—— PAVANE FOR STRING ORCHESTRA (1961)
str.   3:12 C. Fischer.
—— RONDO CONCERTANTE
*3,2,2,2 - 4,3,3,1 - timp.,perc.(3) - pf. - str.   4:30 Bo. Hawkes.
—— SUITE FOR ORCH. (IN 3 MOVTS.)
*3,*3,*3,*3 - 4,3,3,1 - timp.,perc.(4),bells,cel.,xyl. - hp. - pf. - str.   20:00 Composer.
—— SYMPHONIE ANTIQUE (SYMPHONY NO. 3) (IN 3 MOVTS.)
*3,2,2,2 - 4,3,3,1 - timp.,perc.(3) - str.   12:00 Composer.
—— SYMPHONY NO. 2 (ON AMERICAN INDIAN THEMES) (IN 3 MOVTS.)
*3,*3,*3,2 - 4,3,3,1 - timp.,perc.(4),bells,cel.,glock.,xyl. - hp. - pf. - str.   15:00 Composer.
—— TO HIM ALL GLORY GIVE (FOR SATB CHORUS AND ORCH.) (Text: Dorothy Diemer Hendry)
*3,2,2,2 - 4,3,3,1 - timp.,perc.(3) - str.   5:00 EV.
—— YOUTH OVERTURE
*3,2,2,2 - 4,3,3,1 - timp.,perc.(3) - str.   5:00 Mills.

DIEPENBROCK, Alphons
—— BALLET SUITE FOR SMALL ORCH.
2,3,3,1 - 1,0,0,0 - timp.,perc. - hp. - str.   Henmar.

—— HYMNE (FOR VIOLIN AND ORCH.) (REVISED VERSION)
2,2,3,2 - 2,3,0,0 - timp. - hp. - str.   16:00 Henmar.
—— LYDISCHE NACHT (FOR BARITONE AND ORCH.) (1913) (Text: B. Verhagen)
2,3,3,2 - 4,3,3,0 - timp.,perc. - hp. - str.   18:00 Henmar.
—— MARSYAS (LA SOURCE ENCHANTÉE) (THE ENCHANTED WELL): SUITE NO. 1 (IN 2 MOVTS.)
1,2,3,2 - 3,0,0,0 - timp.,perc. - str.   16:00 Henmar.
—— MARSYAS (LA SOURCE ENCHANTÉE) (THE ENCHANTED WELL): SUITE NO. 2 (IN 3 MOVTS.)
1,2,3,2 - 3,0,0,0 - timp.,perc. - hp. - str.   Henmar.
—— MUSIC FOR SOPHOKLES' "ELEKTRA" (SUITE)
2,2,3,0 - 0,3,3,0 - timp.,perc. - hp. - str.   17:00 Henmar.
—— DIE NACHT (FOR ALTO OR MEZZO-SOPRANO AND ORCH.) (1911) (Text: F. Holderlin)
2,2,2,2 - 4,1,2,1 - timp.,perc. - hp. - str.   16:00 Henmar.
—— OVERTURE: "DE VOGELS" (THE BIRDS)
3,3,3,2 - 3,3,0,0 - timp.,perc. - str.   9:00 Henmar.
—— TE DEUM LAUDAMUS (FOR SOLI, MIXED CHORUS, PIANO AND ORCH.)
22:00   Henmar.
—— VONDEL'S VAART NAAR AGRIPPINA (FOR BARITONE AND ORCH.) (1914) (Text: J. A. Alberdingk Thijm)
2,3,3,2 - 4,3,3,1 - timp.,perc. - hp. - str.   15:00 Henmar.

DIERCKS, John H.
—— PRELUDE FOR ORCH.
2(2nd alt. with picc.),2,2,2 - 2,2,1,0 - timp.,cel. - hp. - str.   4:00 Composer.
—— SUITE NO. 1 FOR ORCH. (IN 3 MOVTS.)
2(2nd alt. with picc.),2,2,2 - 2,2,1,0 - timp.,perc.(2),cel. - hp. - str.   11:30 Composer.
—— SUITE NO. 2 FOR ORCH. (IN 3 MOVTS.)
2(2nd alt. with picc.),2,2,2 - 4,2,2,1 - timp.,perc.(3),cel.,xyl. - pf. - str.   18:30 Composer.
—— THEMES AND VARIATIONS FOR STRINGS
str.   6:00 Composer.

DIETHELM, Caspar
—— ARKADISCHE WEISEN, OP. 95A FÜR STREICHORCHESTER
str.   18:00 S.U.I.S.A.
—— CONCERTINO FÜR KLARINETTE UND STREICHORCHESTER
cl. - str.   9:00 S.U.I.S.A.
—— CONCERTINO FÜR OBOE UND STREICHORCHESTER OP. 102
ob. - str.   11:00 S.U.I.S.A.
—— DIVERTIMENTO FÜR STREICHORCH.
str.   16:00 S.U.I.S.A.
—— HARLEKINADE (VIOLINKONZERT NR. 5)
6:40 S.U.I.S.A.
—— KONZERT FÜR FAGOTT UND STREICHER
bn. - str.   15:00 S.U.I.S.A.
—— KONZERT FÜR KLARINETTE UND ORCH.
22:00 S.U.I.S.A.
—— KONZERT FÜR POSAUNE UND ORCH., OP. 117
18:00 S.U.I.S.A.
—— KONZERT I FÜR FLÖTE UND ORCH., OP. 84
2,2,2,2 - 0,0,2,2 - str.   18:00 S.U.I.S.A.
—— KONZERT II FÜR FLÖTE UND ORCH., OP. 85
2,2,2,2 - 2,2,0,0 - str.   18:00 S.U.I.S.A.
—— KONZERT NR. 2 FÜR VIOLINE UND KAMMERORCHESTER, OP. 66
15:00 S.U.I.S.A.
—— KONZERT NR. 4 FÜR VIOLINE UND ORCHESTER
18:00 S.U.I.S.A.
—— LUDIBRIUM JOCULATORIS, OP. 101 (10 SPIELWEISEN FÜR STREICHORCH.)
str.   24:00 S.U.I.S.A.
—— OXYMORON I (FÜR FLOTE, KLARINETTE UND STREICHORCHESTER)
fl.,cl. - str.   4:00 S.U.I.S.A.
—— SINFONIETTA I IN C-DUR, OP. 75A (FASSUNG FÜR ORCH.)
2,2,2,2 - 2,2,0,0 - timp. - str.   14:00 S.U.I.S.A.
—— SINFONIETTA I IN C-DUR, OP. 75B
str.   14:00 S.U.I.S.A.
—— SINFONIETTA NR. 2 IN D-DUR, OP. 76
2,2,2,2 - 2,2,0,0 - timp. - str.   20:30 S.U.I.S.A.
—— SINFONIETTA NR. 3 FÜR KAMMERORCHESTER OP. 100
22:00 S.U.I.S.A.
—— SYMPHONISCHER PROLOG, OP. 125 (FÜR GROSSES ORCHESTER)
7:00 S.U.I.S.A.

—— TRIOPRISMA FÜR STREICHER, OP. 91
    str.   10:00 S.U.I.S.A.
—— TRIPARTITA, OP. 120 (FÜR STREICHORCHESTER)
    str.   15:00 Amadeus.
—— VIER FUGEN FÜR STREICHORCHESTER
    str.   14:00 S.U.I.S.A.
—— VIOLINKONZERT NR. 3, OP. 67 (KONZERTANTE
SYMPHONIE FÜR STREICHER)
    str.   17:00 S.U.I.S.A.

DIETRICH, Karl
—— CONCERTINO GIOCOSO FOR STRING ORCH.
    str.   8:00 Tetra.

DIGGLE, Roland
—— CALIFORNIA SUITE, OP. 101 (IN 3 MOVTS.)
    *2,*2,0,0 - 0,0,0,0 - str.   20:00 J. Fischer.
—— CONCERT SKETCH, OP. 120
    2 picc.,2,2,2 - 0,2,2,0 - timp.,perc. - str.   5:00 Composer.
—— FAIRY SUITE, OP. 50 (IN 3 MOVTS.)
    2,2,2, Eng. hn.,2,0 - 0,0,0,0 - timp. - str.   15:00 Composer.
—— FANTASY OVERTURE (LEGEND OF ST. POLYCARP), OP.
150
    2 picc.,2,2,2 Eng. hn.,2,2 - 0,2,2,0 - timp. - str.
                                   20:00 E. H. Morris.

DIJK, Jan H. Van
—— CASSATIO VOOR STRIJKORKEST MET PIANO
    pf. - str.   10:00 Henmar.
—— CONCERTINO FOR ACCORDION AND ORCH. (1962)
                                 10:00 Henmar.
—— CONCERTINO FOR ACCORDION AND STRING ORCH.
(1960)
    acc. - str.   10:00 Henmar.
—— CONCERTINO FOR ALTO RECORDER AND CHAMBER
ORCH. (1958)
    alto recorder - pf. - str.   8:00 Henmar.
—— CONCERTINO FOR ALTO SAXOPHONE AND CHAMBER
ORCH. (1956)
    2,2,2,1 alto sax.,2 - 2,2,0,0 - timp.,perc. - str.   8:00 Henmar.
—— CONCERTINO FOR PIANO AND ORCH.
    2,2,2,2 - 2,2,1,0 - timp.,perc. - hp. - pf. - str.   10:00 Henmar.
—— CONCERTINO FOR TWO PIANOS AND STRINGS
    2pf. - str.   11:00 Henmar.
—— CONCERTINO NO. 2 FOR PIANO AND ORCH.
    0,2,0,0 - 0,0,0,0 - pf. - str.   7:00 Henmar.
—— CONCERTSTUK (FOR PIANO AND ORCH.)
    2,2,3,2 - 3,2,3,0 - timp.,perc. - pf. - str.   8:00 Henmar.
—— FANCY FOR STRINGS (1959)
    str.   5:00 Henmar.
—— FOUR BAGATELLES FOR ORCH. (1960)
    3,2,2,2 - 2,3,3,1 - timp.,perc. - hp. - str.   7:00 Henmar.
—— INTERLUDE FOR FLUTE AND STRINGS
    fl. - str.   5:00 Henmar.
—— MUSIC FOR ORGAN AND SMALL ORCH.
    2,2,0,0 - 0,0,0,0 - org. - str.   Henmar.
—— ORDRE, FOR SMALL ORCH.
    2,2,2,sax.,2 - 2,1,1,0 - perc. - pf. (4 hands) - str.   15:00 Henmar.
—— PETITE SUITE (FOR CHAMBER ORCH.) (1961)
    2,2,2,1 alto sax.,2 - 1,1,0,0 - timp.,perc.,xyl. - str.   3:00 Henmar.
—— PRELUDE AND FUGUE FOR STRINGS
    str.   Henmar.
—— PRELUDE, FUGUE AND POSTLUDIUM
    str.   10:00 Henmar.
—— PRELUDE, MELODY AND RONDO (FOR SAXOPHONE AND
ORCH.) (1959)
    1,0,2,1 sax.,0 - 1,0,0,0 - hp. - str.   6:00 Henmar.
—— SALON SYMPHONIQUE (SUITE FOR ORCH.)
                                   12:00 Henmar.
—— SERENADE FOR WINDS, PERCUSSION AND PIANO (1959)
    3,3,3,2 - 2,2,0,0 - timp.,perc. - pf.   15:00 Henmar.
—— SEVENTEEN PROJECTIONS (FOR CHAMBER ORCH) (1962)
    2,1,0,1 alto sax.,1 ten. sax.,0 - 1,0,2,0 - str.   5:00 Henmar.
—— SINFONIA
    2,2,3,2 - 4,3,3,1 - timp.,perc. - str.   17:00 Henmar.
—— SINFONIA NO. 2
    3,2,3,3 - 4,3,3,1 - perc. - str.   7:00 Henmar.
—— SINFONIA NO. 3
    3,3,3 - 4,3,3,1 - timp.,perc.,xyl. - hp. - pf. - str.   14:00 Henmar.
—— SINFONIETTA
    2,2,3,3 - 4,3,3,1 - timp.,perc.,xyl. - hp. - pf. - str.   18:00 Henmar.
—— SINFONIETTA NO. 2
    1,1,2,2 - 1,2,0,0 - str.   17:00 Henmar.

—— SINFONIETTA NO. 3
    1,2,2,2 - 1,1,0,0 - hp. - str.   5:00 Henmar.
—— SONORITÉS POUR ORCHESTRE
                                   Henmar.
—— SUITE DA SONAR NO. 1
    2,0,2,0 - 1,2,1,0 - str.   9:00 Henmar.
—— SUITE DA SONAR NO. 2
    2,2,2,2 - 2,3,1,0 - st.   10:00 Henmar.
—— SUITE DA SONAR NO. 3 (MUSIQUE POUR ORCHESTRE)
(1958)
    2,2,2,2 - 2,2,0,0 - timp.,perc. - str.   17:00 Henmar.
—— SUITE PASTORALE (FOR OBOE, ENGLISH HORN AND
CHAMBER ORCH.)
    0,*3,1,1 - 0,0,0,0 - str.   8:00 Henmar.
—— SYMPHONY NO. 4 (FOR SATB SOLO VOICES, MIXED
CHORUS AND ORCH.) (IN 3 MOVTS.) (1951)
    4,2,0,0 - 0,0,0,0 - str.   23:00 Henmar.
    Or
    3,3,2,3 - 3,3,3,3 - timp.,perc. - str.
—— TOCCATA FOR STRINGS
    str.   Henmar.

DIJK, Jan Van I
—— BY THE RIVERS OF BABYLON (PSALM 137) (FOR WOMEN'S
CHORUS, ORGAN AND ORCH.)
                                 3:00 Henmar.
—— JARDIN PUBLIC (FOR FLUTE AND ORCH.) (1967)
                                 11:00 Henmar.
—— PROS ROMAIOUS (FOR 2 VOICES, SATB CHORUS,
PERCUSSION AND STRINGS, OR 2 VOICES, SPEAKER, SATB
CHORUS AND FULL ORCH.) (1968)
                                 9:00 Henmar.
—— SIMPLE MUSIC (IN 3 MOVTS.)
    fl. - str.   5:00 Henmar.

DI JULIO, Max J.
—— CONCERTO FOR GUITAR AND ORCH. (IN 1 MOVT.)
                               15:22 Composer.

DILLON, Fannie C.
—— CHINESE SYMPHONIC SUITE, OP. 96 (IN 5 MOVTS.)
    *4,*3,*3,*3 - 4,2,2,1 - timp.,perc.(2),vibra. - 2hp. - str.
                                 25:00 Composer.
—— IN A MISSION GARDEN, OP. 52 (IN 3 MOVTS.)
    *3,*3,*3,2 - 4,2,2,1 - timp.,perc. - hp. - str.   22:00 Composer.

DILLON, Shaun
—— DIVERTIMENTO FOR STRINGS (1965)
    str.   11:00 P.R.S.
—— MEDITATIONS ON A THEME OF WILLIAM BYRD (1966)
    3,2,3,2 - 4,3,3,1 - timp.,perc.(3),cel. - hp. - pf. - str.   12:00 P.R.S.
—— PRELUDE (FILM MUSIC)
    3,0,1,1 - 1,0,3,0 - timp.,perc. - hp. - pf. - str.   10:00 P.R.S.

DI MARTINO, A.
—— IL CANTO DI TERRA D'ORO
    3,2,3,2 - 4,3,4,0 - timp.,perc.,cel.,xyl. - hp. - pf. - str.
                                 11:00 Bo. Hawkes.
—— LA LOCANDIERA (OUVERTURE)
    3,2,2,2 - 4,3,0,0 - timp.,perc.,bells - str.   7:00 Bo. Hawkes.
—— PRELUDIO
    2,2,2,2 - 2,0,0,0 - cel. - hp. - str.   6:00 Bo. Hawkes.

D'INDY, Vincent
—— CHORALE VARIÉE, OP. 55 (FOR ALTO SAXOPHONE,
CELLO, VIOLA AND ORCH.)
    2,2,2,sax.,2 - 4,2,3,0 - timp. - hp. - str.   EV.

DINERSTEIN, Norman
—— CASSATION (FOR CHAMBER ORCH.) (1962) (IN 3 MOVTS.)
    1,1,1,1 - 1,0,0,0 - perc.(1),glock.,xyl. - str.   8:00 C.M.P.
—— CONTRASTO (1968)
    2,2,2,2 - 4,3,3,1 - timp.,perc.(4),bell,glock.,xyl. - str.
                                 11:00 Composer.
—— INTERMEZZO (1964)
    2(alt. with 2 picc.),2,*3,2 - 4,2,3,1 - timp.,perc.(5),cel.,glock.,xyl. -
    hp. - str.   12:00 Composer.
—— REFRAINS (1971) (IN 1 MOVT.)
    3(3rd alt. with picc.),3(3rd alt. with Eng.hn.),*3,*3, - 4,4,3,1 -
    timp.,perc.(5),bells,glock.,vibra.,xyl. - hp. - str.   30:00 Composer.

—— SCHIR HA SCHIRIM (THE SONG OF SONGS) (FOR
SOPRANO, SATB CHORUS AND ORCH.) (1963) (Text: Biblical)
*3,*3,*3,*3 - 4,3,3,1 - timp.,perc.(5),bells,cel.,glock.,xyl. - pf. - str.
Composer.
—— SHORT SUITE FOR YOUNG PLAYERS (1966) (IN 3 MOVTS.)
1,0,1,1 alto sax.,0 - 1,1,0 0 - str.   6:00 C.M.P.
—— THREE MINIATURES FOR STRINGS (1967)
str.   8:00 C.M.P.

DISTLER, Hugo
—— CONCERTO FOR HARPSICHORD AND STRING ORCH., OP.
14
hpsc. - str.   Baerenrtr.
—— KONZERTSTÜCK FÜR KLAVIER UND ORCH., OP. 17
2,2,2,2 - 3,2,2,0 - timp., perc. - str.   15:00 Baerenrtr.

DITTERSDORF, Karl Ditters von - BODART, Eugen
—— CONCERTO IN A MAJOR FOR OBOE D'AMORE AND
ORCH.
ob. d'amore - 2 hn. - str.   16:00 Mannheimer.
—— SINFONIA IN B FLAT MAJOR (DER POSTZUG)
0,2,0,0 - 2,0,0,0 - str.   16:00 Mannheimer.

DITTERSDORF, Karl Ditters von - CARSE, Adam
—— SYMPHONY IN C
2 ob. - 2 hn. - str.   7:00 Galaxy.

DITTERSDORF, Karl Ditters von - KAHN, Emil
—— TOURNAMENT OF THE TEMPERAMENTS (SUITE)
G. Schirmer.

DITTERSDORF, Karl Ditters von - LEBERMANN, Walter
—— CONCERTO IN C MAJOR FOR VIOLIN AND STRING ORCH.
(With cadenzas by Lebermann)
str.   30:00 Henmar.

DITTERSDORF, Karl Ditters von - SCHROEDER, Felix
—— OVERTURE FOR STRINGS (SINFONIA)
2 fl.(or 2 ob.) - hn. - hpsc., - str.   9:40 Mannheimer.

DITTERSDORF, Karl Ditters von - SLATFORD, Rodney
—— SINFONIA CONCERTANTE (FOR DOUBLE BASS, VIOLA
AND ORCH.)
0,2,0,0 - 2,0,0,0 - cemb. - str.   Galaxy.

DI VEROLI, Donato
—— TEMA CON VARIAZIONI
*3,*3,*3,*3 - 4,3,3,0 - timp., perc., cel., glock., xyl. - 2 hp. - pf. -
str.   13:00 Bo. Hawkes.

DJENADER, Dragoje
—— SYMPHONY NO. 1, OP. 32 (IN 3 MOVTS.)
str.   17:00 S.O.K.O.J.

DOBÍAŠ, Václav
—— SONATA
1,1,1,1 - 1,0,0,0 - timp. - pf. - str.   18:00 Bo. Hawkes.
—— SYMPHONIETTA
3,3,3,3 - 4,3,3,1 - timp.,perc. - hp. - str.   17:00 Bo. Hawkes.
—— SYMPHONY NO. 2
4,4,5,4 - 4,4,3,1 - timp.,perc.,cel. - 2 hp. - pf. - str.
53:00 Bo. Hawkes.

DOBOS, Kálmán
—— INTERNAL MOVEMENTS (FOR CHAMBER ORCH.)
Bo. Hawkes.
—— TÖNENDE PHÄNOMENE
0,0,0,0 - 4,1,0,0 - perc.,mar.,vibra. - pf. - str. 5:00 Modern.

DODGSON, Stephen
—— CONCERTO DA CAMERA NO. 1 (1963)
hpsc. - str.   18:00 P.R.S.
—— CONCERTO DA CAMERA NO. 2 (1965)
fl.,cl. - str.   17:00 P.R.S.
—— CONCERTO FOR BASSOON AND SMALL ORCH. (1969)
0,2,0,1 - 2,0,0,0 - str.   19:00 P.R.S.
—— CONCERTO FOR PIANO AND ORCH. (1959)
2,2,2,2 - 4,2,3,1 - timp. - pf. - str.   25:00 P.R.S.
—— CONCERTO FOR VIOLA DA GAMBA AND SMALL ORCH.
(1961)
1,2,1,1 - 2,0,0,0 - str.   15:00 P.R.S.
—— NOCTURNE (1959)
str.   6:00 P.R.S.

—— SINFONIA CONCERTANTE (FOR WIND QUINTET AND
ORCH.)
1,1,1,1 - 1,2,3,1 - timp.,perc. - str.   24:00 P.R.S.
—— SINFONIETTA (1964)
3,2,3,2 - 4,2,3,1 - timp.,perc.(3) - hp. - str.   22:00 P.R.S.
—— VILLANELLE
2,1,2,1- 2,2,1,0 - timp.,perc.(ad lib.) - str.   5:30 Novello.

DÖHL, Friedhelm
—— MELANCOLIA (MAGIC SQUARES) (FOR SOPRANO,
CHORUS AND LARGE ORCH.)
Hans Gerig.

DOHNÁNYI, Ernst von
—— CONCERTO NO. 2 IN B MINOR, FOR PIANO AND ORCH.,
OP. 42
29:00 Lengnick.
—— RURALIA HUNGARICA (FOR VIOLIN AND ORCH.), OP. 32C
2,2,3,1 - 4,0,3,1 - timp. - hp. - pf. - str.   3:00 C. Fischer.
—— SUITE EN VALSE, OPUS 39 (IN 4 MOVTS.)
27:00 Lengnick.
—— SYMPHONY NO. 2 IN E, OP. 40 (REVISED)
55:00 Lengnick.

DOMAŽLICKÝ, František
—— CONCERTO FOR TROMBONE AND ORCH.
Hans Gerig.

DOMINIQUE, Carl-Axel
—— CONCERTO GROSSO (FOR POP GROUP AND SYMPHONY
ORCH.) (1971)
3,2,2,2 - 2,2,2,1 - timp.,perc. - guit. - hp. - Hammond org. -
electric pf. - str.   24:00 Fleisher.

DONAHUE, Robert L.
—— CAPRICCIO FOR PIANO AND ORCH. (1967)
2,2,2,2 - 4,3,3,1 - perc.(3),xyl. - pf. - str.   8:00 Composer.
—— ELEGY FOR ORCHESTRA (1968)
2(2nd alt. with picc.),2,2,2 - 4,2,2,0 - pf. - str. 11:31 Composer.
—— MUSIC FOR ORCHESTRA (1958)
*3,*3,*3,*3 - 4,3,4,0 - timp.,perc.(3) - hp. - str. 11:31 Composer.
—— SYMPHONY FOR STRINGS (SYMPHONY NO. 1) (1960) (IN 3
MOVTS.)
str.   17:35 Composer.
—— SYMPHONY NO. 2 (1963)
1. Largo; 2. Allegro ritmico
3(3rd alt. with picc.),*3,3(3rd alt. with b.-cl.),*3 - 4,3,3,1 -
timp.,perc.(4),glock.,xyl. - hp. - str.   19:15 Composer.

DONATI, P.
—— PASTORALE (FOR VOICE AND ORCH.)
1,1,2,1 - 2,1,0,1 - hp. - str.   11:00 Bo. Hawkes.

DONATO, Anthony
—— ANDANTE (FROM STRING QUARTET NO. 1)
str.   6:00 Presser.
—— CENTENNIAL ODE (1967)
2,2,2,2 - 4,3,3,1 - timp.,perc.(4),vibra.,xyl. - pf. - str.
9:00 Composer.
—— THE CONGO (AFTER VACHEL LINDSEY'S POEM) (1957)
2,2,2,2 - 4,3,3,1 - timp.,perc.,glock.,xyl. - str. 20:00 Composer.
—— DIVERTIMENTO
2,2,*3,2 - 4,2,3,1 - timp., perc. - hp. - str.   16:00 Composer.
—— ELEGY FOR STRINGS
str.   10:00 Composer.
—— EPISODE
3,3,3,3 - 4,3,3,1 - timp., perc. - str.   10:30 Southern.
—— HORIZONS (TWO ORCHESTRAL PIECES)
13:00 C. Press.
—— IMPROVISATION (1966)
*3,2,*3,2 - 4,3,3,1 - timp.,perc.,cel.,vibra.,xyl. - hp. - str.
8:30 Composer.
—— MARCH OF THE HUNGRY MOUNTAINS (FOR CHORUS
AND ORCHESTRA)
2,2,2,2 - 2,2,0,0 - timp. - str.   10:00 Composer.
—— MISSION SAN JOSE DE AQUAYA
2,2,2,2 - 0,0,0,0 - str.   5:00 Composer.
—— PRAIRIE SCHOONER
2,2,2,2 - 4,3,3,0 - timp., perc. - (2) hp. - str. 6:00 Composer.
—— SERENADE FOR SMALL ORCH.
13:02 Composer.
—— SINFONIETTA (IN 3 MOVTS.)
1,1,1,1 - 1,2,1,0 - timp., perc. - hp. - str.   10:30 G. Schirmer.

—— SINFONIETTA NO. 2 (1959) (IN 3 MOVTS.)
2,2,2,2 - 2,2,1,0 - timp.,perc. - hp. - str.   E. B. Marks.
—— SOLITUDE IN THE CITY (FOR NARRATOR AND ORCH.)
*3,*3,*3,*3 - 4,3,3,1 - timp.,perc. (2),xyl. - str.   24:00 Composer.
—— SONNET (FOR VIOLA AND CHAMBER ORCH.)
2,2,2,2 - 2 hn. - str.   5:00 Composer.
—— SUITE FOR STRINGS
str.   9:40 Southern.
—— SYMPHONY NO. 1 (IN 1 MOVT.)
*3,*3,2,*3 - 4,3,3,1 - timp.,perc.(2),cel.,xyl. - hp. - str.
                                              19:00 Composer.
—— SYMPHONY NO. 2
*3,*3,*3,*3 - 4,3,3,1 - timp.perc.(2),glock. - str.   23:00 Composer.
—— THE WALKER THROUGH WALLS (OPERA) % (1964)
1,1,1,1 - 1,1,1,0 - timp.,perc.(3),vibra.,xyl. - str.   53:00 Composer.

DONATONI, Franco
—— ASARD (PER 10 STRUMENTI AD ARCO)
str.   Leeds.
—— BLACK AND WHITE (PER 37 STRUMENTI AD ARCO)
str.   Leeds.
—— DIVERTIMENTO NO. 2 (1965)
str.   11:00 Leeds.
—— DOUBLES II (1970)
3,3,3,3 - 3,3,3,0 - perc.(3) - hp. - hpsc. - pf. - str.(18,9,6,3)
                                              25:00 MCA Music.
—— MOVIMENTO (FOR HARPSICHORD, PIANO AND 9
INSTRUMENTS)
3,0,2,1 - 2,1,0,0 - hpsc. - pf.   5:15 Leeds.
—— ORTS (SOUVENIR NO. 2) (FOR 14 INSTRUMENTS, WITH
OPTIONAL LECTURER) (1969)
1,1,1,1 - 1,1,1,0 - hp. - hpsc. - pf. - str.(2,1,1,0)
                                              10:00 MCA Music.
—— PER ORCHESTRA ("FOR ORCHESTRA") (IN 2 VERSIONS)
4,0,4,0 - 4,4,4,0 - perc.(3) - org.(3 players) - str.   10:00 Leeds.
—— PUPPENSPIEL
2,2,2,2 - 2,2,2,0 - perc.(3) - str.   9:30 Leeds.
—— PUPPENSPIEL NO. 2 (FOR FLUTE AND ORCH.) (1966)
3,2,2,2 - 2,2,2,0 - perc.(3),mar. - str.(12,6,4,2) 14:00 MCA Music.
—— SERENATA (FOR SOPRANO AND CHAMBER ORCH.) (Text:
Dylan Thomas)
3,0,3,0 - 0,1,1,0 - cel.,vibra. - guit. - hp. - mandolin - pf. - vla.,d.-b.
                                              13:00 Leeds.
—— SEZIONI (SECTIONS) (INVENTION FOR ORCH.)
4,4,4,4 sax.,4 - 8,6,4,2 - perc.(5),vibra.,xylomarimba - electric guit.
- hp. - hpsc. - pf. - str.   14:00 Leeds.
—— SINFONIA FOR STRINGS
str.   29:00 Bo. Hawkes.
—— SOLO (FOR 10 BOWED INSTRUMENTS) (1969)
str.(5,2,2,1)   13:00 MCA Music.
—— SOUVENIR (CHAMBER SYMPHONY, OP. 18) FOR 15 INSTS.)
(1967)
1,1,2,1 - 1,1,1,0 - hp. - hpsc. - pf. - str.(1,1,1,1)
                                              14:00 MCA Music.
—— STROPHES
0,4,0,4 - 4,4,3,1 - str.   11:00 Leeds.
—— TO EARLE (FOR CHAMBER ORCH.) (1970)
2,2,2,2 - 2,2,0,0 - str.   MCA Music.

DONIZETTI, Gaetano
—— THE ELIXIR OF LOVE (2-ACT COMIC OPERA) % (Eng. Text:
Ruth and Thomas Martin)
                                              G. Schirmer.

DONIZETTI, Gaetano - PICCIOLI, G.
—— SINFONIA CONCERTATA
1,2,2,2 - 2,2,0,0 - str.   6:00 Bo. Hawkes.

DONIZETTI, Gaetano - TOWNSEND, Douglas
—— AVE MARIA (FOR SOPRANO, SATB CHORUS AND STRING
ORCH.)
str.   4:20 Tetra.

DONNER, Henrik Otto
—— CANTATA PROFANA (FOR SOPRANO, TENOR, BARITONE
AND ORCH.) (1962)
1,0,0,1 - 0,2,0,0 - timp.,perc.(4),mar.,vibra. - pf. - vln.
                                              8:00 FinnMICtr.
—— FOR EMMY II (FOR 3 FEMALE VOICES AND ORCH.) (1963)
0,0,0,ten. sax., 0 - 1,2,2,1 - perc.(3) - acc. - pf. - 2 vln., 1 d.-b.
                                              26:00 FinnMICtr.

—— IDEOGRAMME II (FOR VOICE AND ORCH.) (1963)
1,1,1,sop. sax.,1 - 1,1,1,0 - perc.(4) - tape-recorder - 2 pf. - str.
                                              8:00 FinnMICtr.
—— KINETIQUE (FOR ORCH. AND JAZZ BAND) (1964)
                                              14:00 FinnMICtr.
—— MOONSPRING (AUFFORDERUNG ZUM...) (SYMPHONY NO.
1) (1964)
Hammond org. - str.   12:00 FinnMICtr.
—— TO WHOM IT MAY CONCERN (FOR ORCH. AND JAZZ
COMBO) (1966)
2,1,2,sax.,1 - 3,5,4,1 - perc.(3) - str.   10:00 FinnMICtr.
—— XC (FOR AMPLIFIED SOPRANO, SATB CHORUS AND
ORCH.) (1969) (Text: Ezra Pound)
1,1,1,1 - 1,2,1,1 - timp.,perc.(4) - str.   12:00 FinnMICtr.

DONOVAN, Richard
—— FANTASY ON AMERICAN FOLK BALLADS (FOR MEN'S
CHORUS AND ORCH.)
1(alt. with picc.),2,2,2 - 2-4,2,3,1 - timp.,perc.(2) - pf.(4 hands) -
str.   12:00 J. Fischer.
—— RICERCARE
ob. - str.   6:00 Bo. Hawkes.

DORAN, Matt H.
—— CONCERTO FOR FLUTE AND ORCH. (1953)
1. Adagio; 2. Allegro
2,2,2,2 - 4,3,3,1 - timp. - str.   13:00 Composer.
—— CONCERTO FOR HORN AND ORCH. (1954) (IN 3 MOVTS.)
2,2,2,2 - 4,3,3,1 - timp. - str.   19:00 Composer.
—— OVERTURE: 1957
2,2,2,2 - 4,3,3,1 - timp. - str.   7:00 Composer.
—— OVERTURE: 1964
*3,2,2,2 - 4,3,3,1 - timp., - str.   6:00 Composer.
—— SYMPHONY FOR STRINGS (1959) (IN 3 MOVTS.)
str.   17:00 Composer.

DORATI, Antal
—— CONCERTO FOR CELLO AND ORCH.
                                              A.P.R.A.
—— MADDALENA (7 PIECES FOR ORCH.)
                                              Leeds.
—— NIGHT MUSIC (FOR FLUTE AND ORCH.)
fl. - 2 hn. - hp. - str.   G. Schirmer.
—— SYMPHONY
3,3,3,3 - 4,3,3,1 - timp.,perc.(3) - str.   31:30 Leeds.
—— THE TWO ENCHANTMENTS OF LI TAI PE (FOR BARITONE
AND 14 INSTRUMENTS)
                                              MCA Music.

DORWARD, David
—— COMEDY OVERTURE, OP. 1 ("THE COOPER
O'FIFE")(REVISED VERSION)
3,2,2,3 - 4,3,3,1 - timp.,perc. - str.   8:00 P.R.S.
—— CONCERTO FOR CELLO AND STRINGS, OP. 35 (1966)
str.   35:00 P.R.S.
—— CONCERTO FOR VIOLIN AND STRINGS, OP. 30 (1965)
str.   22:00 P.R.S.
—— FOUR SUMMER INTERLUDES, OP. 12 (1960)
2,2,2,2 - 4,2,3,0 - timp.,perc. - hp. - str.   20:00 P.R.S.
—— LEGEND OF THE MEGALITHS, OP. 42
3,2,2,2 - 4,3,3,1 - timp.,perc. - guit.(ad lib.) - hp. - pf. - str.
                                              13:00 P.R.S.
—— SINFONIETTA, OP. 34 (1966)
str.   10:00 P.R.S.
—— SYMPHONY NO. 1, OP. 13 (1961)
2,2,2,2 - 4,3,3,1 - timp. - hp. - pf. - str.   28:00 P.R.S.
—— VARIATIONS ON AN OLD SCOTS AIR, OP. 22 (1963)
tpt. - str.   15:00 P.R.S.

DOSTAL, Nico
—— GOLDEN SHOES (GOLDENE SCHUHE) (BALLET SUITE) (IN
4 MOVTS.)
2,2,2,2 - 4,3,3,1 - timp.,perc.,cel. - hp. - str. 14:00 F. Colombo.
—— IMPRESSIONS (SUITE) (IN 1 MOVT.)
2,2,2,2 - 4,3,3,1 - timp.,perc. - pf. - str.   12:00 F. Colombo.

DOUBRAVA, Jaroslav
—— DON QUIXOTE (SUITE FROM THE BALLET)
3,3,3,3 - 4,4,3,1 - timp.,perc. - 2 hp. - str. 30:00 Bo. Hawkes.
—— KING LAVRA (SUITE FROM THE BALLET)
3,3,3,3 - 4,3,3,3 - timp.,perc.,cel. - str.   25:00 Bo. Hawkes.
—— SYMPHONY NO. 2
3,3,4,3 - 4,6,3,1 - timp.,perc. - str.   40:00 Bo. Hawkes.

—— SYMPHONY NO. 3
    3,3,3,3 - 6,4,3,1 - timp.,perc. - hp. - pf. - str.   47:00 Bo. Hawkes.

DOUGHERTY, Celius
—— FIVE SEA-CHANTIES (FOR BARITONE AND ORCH.)
    2,2,2,2 - 2,2,3,1 - timp.,perc. - str.   12:00 G. Schirmer.
—— MANY MOONS (1-ACT CHAMBER OPERA, AFTER JAMES THURBER'S STORY) %
    1,1,1(alt. with b.-cl.),1 - 1,1,1,0 - perc.(1) - pf. - str.
        40:00 G. Schirmer.

DOUGLAS, Clive Martin
—— BALLADS OF THE OUTBACK (FOR BARITONE AND ORCH.)
        16:00 A.P.R.A.
—— CARWOOLA
    2,2,2,2 - 4,2,3,1 - timp.,perc. - hp. - str.   12:00 A.P.R.A.
—— COOLAWIDGEE (SUITE) (FOR WOODWINDS AND STRINGS)
        12:00 A.P.R.A.
—— DISCOURSE FOR STRINGS
    str.   15:00 AllansPty.
—— DIVERTIMENTO NO. 2 (FOR 2 PIANOS AND CHAMBER ORCH.) (1962)
    2,2,2,2 - 2,2,0,0 - timp.,perc. - 2 pf. - str.   18:00 AllansPty.
—— ESSAY FOR STRINGS
    str.   A.P.R.A.
—— FANFARE OVERTURE, OP. 82 (1961)
    3,3,3,3 - 4,3,3,1 - timp.,perc. - hp. - str.   8:00 AllansPty.
—— FESTIVAL IN NATAL (RHAPSODY)
        8:00 A.P.R.A.
—— FESTIVAL OF PERTH, OP. 79 (1961)
    2,2,2,2 - 4,2,3,1 - timp. - hp. - str.   17:00 AllansPty.
—— THE LAKES OF TASMANIA (FOR SOPRANO AND SMALL ORCH.)
        12:00 A.P.R.A.
—— MEET THE ORCHESTRA
        15:00 A.P.R.A.
—— NAMATJIRA (POEM)
        17:00 A.P.R.A.
—— OLYMPIC OVERTURE
        8:00 A.P.R.A.
—— OLYMPIC SUITE
    3,2,2,alto sax.,2 - 4,3,3,1 - timp.,perc. - str.   Bo. Hawkes.
—— SINFONIETTA ("FESTIVAL OF PERTH")
        17:00 A.P.R.A.
—— SONG LANDSCAPE (FOR SOPRANO AND SMALL ORCH.)
        12:00 A.P.R.A.
—— STURT 1829 (POEM)
        9:00 A.P.R.A.
—— SYMPHONY NO. 1, OP 48-A
    3(2nd and 3rd alt. with picc.),*3,*3,2 - 4,3,3,1 - perc. - hp. - str.
        34:00 A.P.R.A.
—— SYMPHONY NO. 2 ("NAMATJIRA")
        27:00 A.P.R.A.
—— TERRA AUSTRALIS (FOR NARRATOR, SOPRANO, CHORUS AND ORCH.)
        35:00 A.P.R.A.
—— TERRA AUSTRALIS (POEM)
        16:00 A.P.R.A.
—— THREE FRESCOS, OP. 90 (1969)
    3(3rd alt. with picc.),3(3rd alt. with Eng. hn.),3(3rd alt. with b.-cl.),3(3rd alt. with c.-bn.) - 4,3,3,1 - timp.,perc.(3) - hp. - str.
        21:00 AllansPty.
—— VARIATIONS SYMPHONIQUES
        15:00 A.P.R.A.
—— WONGADILLA (SYMPHONIC SUITE)
    4,3,3,3 - 4,3,3,1 - timp.,perc.,cel. - hp. - str.   Bo. Hawkes.

DOWLAND, John - PUDELKO, Walther
—— FIVE PIECES FOR STRINGS
    str.   7:00 G. Schirmer.

DOWLAND, John - WARLOCK, Peter
—— DANCE SUITE
    str.   Oxford.
—— LACHRIMAE (OR, "SEVEN TEARS") (SUITE)
    cemb.(or lute) - str.   Oxford.

DOWNEY, John
—— ALMOST 12 (FOR CHAMBER ORCHESTRA)
    1,1,1,1 - 1,0,0,0 - perc. - str.   18:30 Presser.
—— SYMPHONIC MODULES FIVE
    5,3,4,3 - 6,4,4,1 - timp.,perc.(6),cel. - hp. - pf. - str.   25:00 Presser.

DOWNS, Hugh
—— ELEGIAC PRELUDE IN A MINOR
    2,2,2,2 - 2,3,3,0 - timp.,perc.(2) - hp. - str.   4:00 Fema.

DOYEN, A.
—— SUITE RUSSE
        8:00 Baron.

DRAGOI, Sabin
—— SUITE POPULAIRE
    1,1,1,1 - 2,1,0,0 - timp., - hp. - str.   18:00 Templeton.

DRAGON, Carmen
—— I AM AN AMERICAN (FOR SATB CHORUS, NARRATOR AND ORCH.)
    2,2,2,2 - 4,3,3,1 - perc. - hp. - pf. - str.   C. Fischer.

DRAGONETTI, Domenico - BAKALEINIKOFF, Vladimir
—— CONCERTO FOR DOUBLE BASS AND ORCH.
        Arranger.

DRAGONETTI, Domenico - ROHE, Robert K.
—— CONCERTO FOR CONTRABASS AND CHAMBER ORCH. (ARR. 1974) (IN 3 MOVTS.)
    2,0,2,0 - 2,0,0,0 - str.   13:15 Arranger.

DRANGOSCH, Ernesto
—— OBERTURA CRIOLLA, OP. 20 (1920)
    3(3rd alt. with picc.),2,2,2 - 4,2,3,1 - timp.,perc. - str.
        7:00 Fleisher.

DREJSL, Radim
—— SYMPHONY FOR STRINGS
    str.   30:00 Bo. Hawkes.

DRESDEN, Sem
—— CARNAVALS CANTATE (FOR SOPRANO, MALE CHORUS AND ORCH.)
        Henmar.
—— CATENA MUSICALE (FOR SOPRANO, WOODWIND QUARTET, STRING TRIO AND ORCH.) (1956)
    5,4,3,3 - 4,3,3,0 - timp.,perc.,cel.,xyl. - hp. - str.   13:00 Henmar.
—— CHORUS SYMPHONICUS (FOR SOLO VOICE, MIXED CHORUS AND ORCH.)
        Henmar.
—— CONCERTO FOR FLUTE AND ORCH.
        23:00 Henmar.
—— CONCERTO FOR OBOE AND ORCH. (1939)
    3,1,2,2 - 3,3,3,0 - timp.,perc.,cel. - str.   20:00 De Wolfe.
—— CONCERTO FOR ORGAN AND ORCH.
    2,2,2,2 - 4,3,3,1 - timp.,perc. - org. - str.   27:00 Henmar.
—— CONCERTO FOR PIANO AND ORCH.
    2,2,2,2 - 3,2,0,0 - timp.,perc. - pf. - str.   20:00 Henmar.
—— CONCERTO NO. 1 FOR VIOLIN AND ORCH.
    2,1,2,2 - 0,3,0,1 - timp.,perc.,xyl. - str.   17:00 Henmar.
—— CONCERTO NO. 2 FOR VIOLIN AND ORCH.
    2,1,2,3 - 3,2,3,0 - timp.,perc.,cel.,xyl - hp. - str.   24:00 Henmar.
—— DANSFLITSEN (DANCE SUITE) (1951)
    3,2,3,1 alto sax.,2 - 3,3,3,0 - timp.,perc.,cel.,xyl. - hp. - str.
        14:00 De Wolfe.
—— FOUR VOCALISES (FOR MEZZO-SOPRANO AND ORCH.) (1935)
    1,0,1,1 - 0,0,0,0 - perc. - pf. - str.(no c. or d.-b.)   10:00 Henmar.
—— PSALM 84 (FOR SOPRANO, TENOR, MIXED CHORUS AND ORCH.) (1954)
    3,3,3,1 alto sax.,3 - 4,3,3,1 - timp.,perc.,xyl. - hp. - str.
        24:00 Henmar.
—— REMBRANDT'S "SAUL AND DAVID" (FOR SOPRANO AND ORCH.)
        Henmar.
—— SAINT GEORGE (FOR NARRATOR, SOPRANO, BARITONE, MIXED CHORUS AND ORCH.)
        Henmar.
—— SYMPHONIETTA FOR CLARINET AND ORCH. (1938)
    2,2,1,2 - 4,3,3,0 - timp.,perc. - str.   20:00 De Wolfe.
—— THE WINES OF BURGUNDY (FOR MIXED CHORUS AND ORCH.) (1954)
    5,1,2,1 - 2,1,0,0 - perc.,xyl. - pf. - str.   20:00 Henmar.

DRESSEL, Erwin
—— ABWANDLUNGEN EINES ALTENGLISCHEN VOLKSLIEDES, OP. 41
    3(3rd alt. with picc.),*3,*3,*3 - 2,2,3,0 - timp.,perc.(3) - hp. - str.
    15:00 Henmar.

—— CAPRICCIO RITMICO (FOR LARGE ORCH.)
    Henmar.

—— CAPRICE FANTASTIQUE
    11:00 Henmar.

—— CASSATION
    16:00 Henmar.

—— CONCERTO FOR CLARINET AND ORCH.
    25:00 Henmar.

—— CONCERTO FOR OBOE, CLARINET, BASSOON AND ORCH.
    2(2nd alt. with picc.),2,2,1 - 2,2,2,0 - timp.,perc.(3) - hp. - str.
    20:00 Henmar.

—— CONCERTO FOR SAXOPHONE AND ORCH., OP. 27
    3,*3,3,sax.,3 - 2,3,2,0 - timp.,perc.,cel. - hp. - str. 30:00 Henmar.

—— CONCERTO IN A MAJOR FOR CLARINET AND ORCH.
    2(2nd alt. with picc.),2(2nd alt. with Eng.hn.),2(2nd alt. with
    b.-cl.),2 - 2,2,1,0 - timp.,perc. - hp. - str. 25:00 Henmar.

—— DANCE MINIATURES (LITTLE SUITE) (IN 5 MOVTS.)
    2,2,2,2 - 2,2,1,0 - perc. - str. 10:00 Henmar.

—— FRENCH OVERTURE
    7:00 Henmar.

—— FREUDIGER AUFKLANG
    2(2nd alt. with picc.),2,2,2 - 4,2,3,0 - timp.,perc. - hp. - str.
    5:00 Henmar.

—— GERMAN FAIRYTALE SUITE, OP. 36 (IN 5 MOVTS.)
    2,2,2,2 - 2,1,1,0 - timp.,perc. - str. 13:00 Henmar.

—— HARLEKINS OUVERTÜRE (OVERTURA BUFFA)
    2(2nd alt. with picc.),2,2,2 - 4,2,3,0 - timp.,perc. - hp. - str.
    5:00 Henmar.

—— IDYLLIC SUITE (IN 3 MOVTS.)
    2(2nd alt. with picc.),*2,2,2 - 2,2,3,0 - timp.,perc. - hp. - str.
    15:00 Henmar.

—— KAPRIOLEN (AN OVERTURE)
    2,2,2,2 - 2,2,1,0 - timp.,perc. - hp. - str. 7:00 Henmar.

—— KUNTERBUNT, OP. 40 (SUITE) (IN 6 MOVTS.)
    2(2nd alt. with picc.),2,2,2 - 2,2,2,1 - timp.,perc. - str.
    18:00 Henmar.

—— LITTLE COMEDY, OP. 63 (SUITE) (IN 4 MOVTS.)
    2(2nd alt. with picc.),2,2,2 - 2,2,2,0 - timp.,perc. - hp. - str.
    16:00 Henmar.

—— LYRIC DANCES, OP. 65 (IN 7 MOVTS.)
    str. 27:00 Henmar.

—— NIGHT MUSIC, OP. 33
    2,2,2,2 - 2,2,0,0 - timp.,perc. - str. 18:00 Henmar.

—— OVERTURE TO A FAIRYTALE PLAY, OP. 47
    Henmar.

—— ROMANTIC SKETCHES (SUITE) (IN 4 MOVTS.)
    Henmar.

—— RONDO BURLESQUE
    7:00 Henmar.

—— SERENADE FOR STRING ORCH., OP. 62 (IN 4 MOVTS.)
    str. 25:00 Henmar.

—— SERENADE NO. 2 IN E FLAT MAJOR (IN 4 MOVTS.)
    str. 14:00 Henmar.

—— SINFONIETTA SERENA
    str. 30:00 Ries-Erler.

—— SUITE DER MASKEN, OP. 57
    2(2nd alt. with picc.),2,2,2 - 2,2,1,0 - timp.,perc.,cel. - hp. - str.
    16:00 Henmar.

—— VARIATIONEN-SERENADE (FOR PIANO AND ORCH.)
    11:00 Henmar.

DREW, James
—— FADING OF THE VISIBLE WORLD (CHAMBER ORATORIO)
    (FOR SOPRANO, TENOR, BASS, SATB CHORUS AND
    CHAMBER ORCH.)
    2,1,2,2 - 2,2,2,1 - perc.(3) - pf. 20:00 Presser.

—— GOTHIC LIGHTS (FOR 11 PLAYERS)
    3 tpt.,3 trb. - perc. - 2 pf. 12:00 Presser.

—— IN MEMORIAM: MARK ROTHKO
    Presser.

—— THE MAZE MAKER (FOR CELLOS ONLY)
    c. section 10:00 Presser.

—— MYSTERIUM (1-ACT OPERA) (FOR SOPRANO, BARITONE
    AND CHAMBER ORCH.) %
    60:00 Presser.

—— OCTOBER LIGHTS
    3,0,1,0 - 2,3,2,1 - perc. - 2 pf. - str. 10:00 Presser.

—— PERSONA MEANS MASCARA (FOR TWO VOICES AND
    INSTRUMENTS)
    3,1,3,1 - 0,3,2,0 - perc. - pf. 12:00 Presser.

—— SAINT MARK CONCERTO (FOR 2 CELLOS AND CHAMBER
    ORCH.)
    2,1,2,2 - 2,2,2,1 - perc.(3) - pf. - 2 c. 15:00 Presser.

—— SYMPHONIES
    4,1,2,1 - 2,3,2,1 - perc. - str. 25:00 Presser.

—— SYMPHONY NO. 1
    20:00 Presser.

—— SYMPHONY NO. 2 (FOR SATB CHORUS AND ORCH.)
    3,1,3,2 - 2,2,1,1 - perc.(4) - hp. - pf. - str. 20:00 Presser.

—— WEST INDIAN LIGHTS
    3,2,3,2 - 4,4,3,1 - timp.,perc.,cel. - hp. - pf. - str. 25:00 Presser.

DREYFUS, George
—— THE GRAND AURORA AUSTRALIS NOW SHOW (1973)
    2,2,2,2 - 3,2,2,1 - timp.,perc. - hp. - org.(ad lib.) - str. AllansPty.

—— JINGLES (1968)
    2,2,2,2 - 4,2,3,1 - timp.,perc. - str. 14:00 AllansPty.

—— MO (FOR BARITONE, STRINGS AND CONTINUO) (1972)
    cemb. - str. 32:00 AllansPty.

DRIESCH, Kurt
—— DREI REIHEN FÜR ORCH.
    2(2nd alt. with picc.),2,2,2 - 2,2,2,1 - timp.,perc. - str.
    15:00 Henmar.

—— EIN FERIENTAG, OP. 72 (A DAY OF VACATION) (SUITE)
    (IN 11 MOVTS.)
    2(2nd alt. with picc.),2,2,2 - 2,2,2,2 - timp.,perc.(3, incl. 2 on
    timp.) - str. 17:00 Henmar.

—— KONZERT FÜR VIOLINE UND ORCH., OP. 50
    2,2,2,2 - 2,2,2,2 - perc. - str. 12:30 Sirius.

—— SINGSPIEL-OUVERTÜRE
    2,1,2,1 - 2,2,1,0 - timp.,perc. - str. 5:30 Henmar.

—— VARIATIONS ON A CHEERFUL THEME (IN 7 MOVTS.)
    2,2,0,2 - 2,1,1,0 - timp.,perc. - str. 9:00 Henmar.

DRIESSLER, Johannes
—— CLAUDIA AMATA (OPERA IN 5 SCENES) %
    Baerenrtr.

—— GAUDIA MUNDANA (ORATORIO) (FOR TENOR, BASS,
    COLORATURA SOPRANO, FIVE-PART CHORUS AND
    LARGE ORCH.)
    Baerenrtr.

—— KONZERT FÜR CELLO UND ORCH., OP. 35
    2,2,2,2 - 0,2,2,0 - timp.,perc. - str. 28:00 Baerenrtr.

—— KONZERT FÜR KLAVIER UND ORCH., OP. 27
    3,3,3,2 - 4,3,2,0 - timp.,perc. - pf. - str. 27:00 Baerenrtr.

—— KONZERT FÜR WALDHORN UND STREICH ORCH., OP. 16
    hn. - str. 17:00 Baerenrtr.

—— SINFONIA BREVE, OP. 5
    3,2,2,2 - 4,2,3,1 - timp.,perc. - str. 15:00 Baerenrtr.

DROGOZ, Philippe
—— ANTINOMIES II
    2,2,2,3 - 3,2,1,0 - perc.(3) - str. 8:00 Presser.

—— ARGOL (FOR 5 INSTRUMENTAL GROUPS)
    3,*2,*3,*3 - 3,2,2,1 - str. 60:00 Presser.

—— ÉCLATEMENT II
    3,3,3,3 - 4,4,3,1 - perc.(3) - 2 hp. - str. 8:30 Presser.

DRUCKMAN, Jacob
—— CONCERTO FOR STRING ORCHESTRA (1951)
    str. Bo. Hawkes.

—— CONCERTO FOR VIOLIN AND SMALL ORCHESTRA (1956)
    Bo. Hawkes.

—— INCENTERS (FOR HORN, TRUMPET, TROMBONE AND
    ORCH.) (1972)
    *3,*3,*3,2 - 4,1,3,1 - perc.(2) - electric org. - pf. - hp. - str.
    14:00 MCA Music.
    or:
    1,1,1,1 - 1,1,1,0 - perc.(1) - electric org. - pf. - str.(1,1,1,1)

—— LAMIA (FOR SOPRANO AND ORCH.) (1974)
    *3,2,*3,2 - 4,3,3,1 - timp.,perc.(3),bells,cel.,glock.,mar.,vibra.,xyl. -
    electric org. - pf. - hp. - str. 16:00 Bo. Hawkes.

—— MIRAGE (FOR 2 ORCHESTRAS)
    3,3,3,2 - 4,3,4,1 - timp.,perc. - hp. - electric org. - electric pf. - str.
    24:00 Bo. Hawkes.

—— MUSIC FOR DANCE (1948)
    Bo. Hawkes.

—— PERFORMANCE (CORTEGE AND DANCE FOR BEING
TOSSED IN A BLANKET) (1960)
Bo, Hawkes.
—— THE SOUND OF TIME (FOR SOPRANO AND ORCH.) (Text:
Norman Mailer)
1(alt. with picc.),2,*2,2 - 2,1,0,0 - perc.(1),glock.,vibra. - pf. - str.
30:00 Bo. Hawkes.
—— VOLPONE (OVERTURE FOR ORCHESTRA) (1953)
Bo Hawkes.
—— WINDOWS (1972)
*3,*3,*3,*3 - 4,3,3,1 - perc.(3) - electric org. pf. - hp. - str.
21:00 MCA Music.

DUBENSKY, Arcady
—— AFTER THE RUBAIYAT OF OMAR KHAYYAM
*3,*3,2,2 - 4,2,3,1 - timp.,perc. - hp. - str.   10:00 Ricordi.
—— THE ALPHABET
*3,2,2,2 - 2,2,1,1 - timp.,perc. - str.   20:00 Composer.
—— ANDANTE AND SCHERZO (FOR FLUTE AND ORCH.)
1,1,1,1 - 1,1,1,0 - timp. - str.   6:00 Composer.
—— ANDANTE RUSSE (FOR STRINGS)
str.   5:00 Ricordi.
—— BALLADE FOR VIOLA AND ORCH.
*3,*3,*3,2 - 4,2,3,1 - timp.,perc. - hp. - str.   15:00 Composer.
—— CONCERTO FOR TROMBONE AND ORCH. (IN 3 MOVTS.)
2,2,2,2 - 4,2,3,1 - timp. - hp. - str.   20:00 Ricordi.
—— CONCERTO GROSSO FOR STRINGS
str.   12:00 Ricordi.
—— CONCERTO GROSSO FOR THREE TROMBONES, TUBA AND
ORCH. (IN 5 MOVTS.)
2,2,2,2 - 0,0,3,1 - timp. - hp. - str.   12:00 Ricordi.
—— ELEGIE (FOR STRINGS)
str.   8:00 Composer.
—— FANFARE (INTRODUCTION TO "THE STAR SPANGLED
BANNER")
0,0,0,4 - 4,4,4,0 - timp.,perc.   Ricordi.
—— FANTASIA FOR TUBA AND ORCH.
2,2,2,2 - 4,3,3,1 - timp.,perc. - str.   10:00 Ricordi.
—— FANTASY ON A NEGRO THEME (FOR TUBA AND ORCH.)
2,2,2,2 - 4,2,3,1 - timp.,perc. - pf. - str.   8:00 Belw-Mills.
—— FIVE IRISH PIECES (17TH CENTURY IRISH FOLKSONGS,
ARRANGED FOR STRINGS)
str.   15:00 Arranger.
—— GOSSIPS (FOR STRINGS)
str.   C. Fischer.
—— LEGEND
*3,*3,*3,*3 - 4,2,3,1 - timp.,perc. - hp. - str.   20:00 Composer.
—— MEDITATION (FOR HARP AND STRINGS)
hp. - str.   5:00 Composer.
—— ON THE HIGHWAY (1-ACT OPERA) %
60:00 F. Colombo.
—— OVERTURE ON CHILDREN'S NAMES
*3,2,2,2 - 4,3,3,0 - timp.,perc. - str.   5:00 Ricordi.
—— OVERTURE TO AN ITALIAN COMEDY
*3,2,2,2 - 4,2,3,1 - timp.,perc. - hp. - str.   10:00 Ricordi.
—— POLITICAL SUITE (IN 4 MOVTS.)
*3,2,2,2 - 2,2,1,0 - timp.,perc. - str.   20:00 Composer.
—— PRELUDE - NOCTURNE (FOR STRINGS)
str.   6:00 Ricordi.
—— PRELUDE AND FUGA LIBERA
*3,*3,*3,*3 - 4,4,3,1 - timp.,perc. - hp. - org. - str.
15:00 Composer.
—— PRELUDE AND FUGUE IN B♭ MINOR
*3,2,2,2 - 4,2,3,1 - timp.,perc. - str.   8:00 Ricordi.
—— PRELUDE, TOCCATA AND FUGUE
2,2,2,2 - 0,0,3,1 - timp.,perc. - hp. - str.   12:00 Ricordi.
—— PSALM (ON A MELODY OF TSAR IVAN THE TERRIBLE)
perc. - str. (with solo d.-b.)   Arranger.
—— THE RAVEN (RECITATION WITH ORCH.)
*3,2,2,*3 - 4,2,3,1 - timp.,perc. - hp. - str.   15:00 Ricordi.
—— RECITATIVO AND FUGA LIBERA
*3,*3,2,*3 - 4,4,3,1 - timp.,bells - hp. - pf. - org. - str.
12:00 Ricordi.
—— ROMANCE WITH DOUBLE-BASS (3-ACT COMIC OPERA) %
90:00 F. Colombo.
—— RONDO AND GIGUE (FOR STRINGS)
str.   10:00 Composer.
—— RUSSIAN BELLS
*3,2,2,2 - 4,3,3,1 - timp.,perc. - hp. - str.   12:00 Ricordi.
—— SECOND SUITE ON STEPHEN FOSTER MELODIES
*3,2,2,2 - 4,2,3,1 - timp.,perc. - hp. - str.   20:00 Ricordi.
—— SERENADE
*2,2,2,2 - 2,2,1,0 - timp.,perc. - str.   10:00 Ricordi.

—— THREE CHORALES FOR BRASS AND PERCUSSION
2 bn. - 5,4,3,1 - timp.,perc.   6:00 Composer.
—— TOM SAWYER (OVERTURE)
*3,2,2,2 - 4,2,3,1 - timp.,perc. - hp. - str.   15:00 Ricordi.
—— TRUMPET OVERTURE (ITALIAN OVERTURE FOR
CHILDREN'S CONCERTS) (FOR STRINGS WITH TOY
TRUMPETS)
5:00 Ricordi.
—— VARIATIONS AND FINALE ON STEPHEN FOSTER THEMES
*3,2,2,2 - 4,2,3,1 - timp.,perc.,cel. - banjo - hp. - str.
15:00 Ricordi.

DUBENSKY, Leo
—— CONCERTO IN D MAJOR, FOR VIOLIN AND ORCHESTRA
3,2,2,2 - 4,2,0,0 - timp. - hp. - str.   25:00 Belw-Mills.
—— THE LIMBERLOST CHORALE, OP. 11 (Text: Dr. Fabies
Sevitzky)
4:00 Composer.
—— PIECE FOR FLUTE AND ORCH., OP. 11 ("THE BLUE HERON
OF CHICONTEAGUE")
2,1,2,2 - 2,0,0,0 - perc.(1) - hp. - str.   5:00 Composer.
—— SCHERZO (FOR VIOLIN AND ORCH.)
1,2,2,2 - 4,2,0,0 - timp.,perc. - str.   4:00 Ricordi.
—— TWO FABLES (FOR NARRATOR AND ORCH.)
Composer.
—— VARIATIONS ON AN ORIGINAL THEME
*3,*3,*3,*4 - 4,3,3,1 - timp.,perc. - hp. - pf. - str.   30:00 Ricordi.

DUBOIS, Pierre Max
—— CAPRICCIO FOR VIOLIN AND ORCH.
1,1,1,1 - 1,1,1,0 - timp.,perc.,cel. - hp. - pf. (ad lib.) - str.
9:00 Baron.
—— CONCERTINO IRONICO (FOR BASSOON AND
ORCHESTRA)
EV.
—— CONCERTO FOR ALTO SAXOPHONE AND STRINGS
alto sax. - str.   18:00 Baron.
—— CONCERTO FOR CELLO AND ORCH.
2,2,2,2 - 2,2,2,0 - timp.,perc.,cel. - hp. - str.   24:00 Baron.
—— CONCERTO FOR FLUTE AND CHAMBER ORCH.
1,0,1,1 - 1,0,0,0 - str.   15:00 Baron.
—— CONCERTO FOR HORN AND CHAMBER ORCH.
1,1,1,1 - 1,1,0,0 - timp. - str.   16:00 Baron.
—— CONCERTO FOR TRUMPET AND CHAMBER ORCH.
2,1,1,1 - 1,1,0,0 - timp.,perc. - hp.(ad lib.) - str.   10:00 Baron.
Or
0,0,0,4 sax.(sopr.,alto,ten.,bar.),0 - 0,1,0,0 - timp.,perc. - hp.(ad
lib.) - str.
—— CONCERTO FOR VIOLIN AND ORCH.
2,2,2,2 - 2,2,2,0 - timp.,perc. - hp. - str.   32:00 Baron.
—— CONCERTO NO. 2 FOR PIANO AND ORCH.
2,2,2,2 - 2,2,2,0-1 - timp.,perc. - hp. - pf. - str.   31:00 Baron.
—— DIVERTISSEMENT (FOR ALTO SAXOPHONE AND ORCH.)
2,2,2, alto sax., 2 - 2,2,1,0 - timp.,perc.,cel. - hp. - str. 9:00 Baron.
—— DOUBLE CONCERTINO (FOR OBOE, BASSOON AND
STRING ORCH.)
0,1,0,1 - 0,0,0,0 - str.   13:00 Baron.
—— POUR MA MIEUX AIMÉE (6 POEMS) (After Kipling's "Just So
Stories")
2,2,2,2 - 2,2,2,0 - timp.,perc.,bells,cel.,glock.,vibra. - hp. - str.
14:30 Baron.
—— SUITE DE DANSES (FOR VIOLA AND STRINGS)
hp.(ad lib.) - str.   8:00 Baron.
—— TEN PRELUDES FOR STRINGS
str.   23:00 EV.

DUBOIS, Theodore
—— FANTASIETTA (FOR FLUTE, HORN, TRUMPET, TIMPANI,
HARP, CELLO AND STRINGS)(1917)
1,0,0,0 - 1,1,0,0 - timp. - hp. - str.   19:00 Presser.

DUBOIS, Theodore - SINNHOLD, Rudolf
—— THE SEVEN LAST WORDS OF CHRIST (CANTATA) (FOR
SOLO VOICES, SATB CHORUS AND ORCH.)
1,1,2,1 - 2,2,1,0 - timp. - hp. - str.   Belw-Mills.

DUCHEMIN, Lucien
—— SYMPHONY
3,3,3,3 - 4,3,3,1 - timp.,perc.(6),cel. - 2 hp. - str.   28:00 Presser.
—— VOCERO
2,2,2,2 - 2,2,2,0 - timp.,perc.(2) - hp. - pf. - str.   10:30 Presser.

DUCK, Leonard
—— CONCERTO FOR OBOE AND STRINGS
ob. - str.   20:00 FDH.

DUCLOS, Pierre
—— DEUX IMAGES CONCERTANTES (FOR PIANO AND
CHAMBER ORCH.)
ob. - hn. - timp. - pf. - str.   20:00 Presser.
—— LES FONTAINES DE VERSAILLES
1,1,1,1 - 3,3,2,0 - timp. - hp. - pf. - str. 8:00 Presser.
—— LES JARDINS DE ROME (SYMPHONIC PRELUDE)
2,2,2,2 - 3,3,3,0 - timp.,perc. - hp. - pf. - str.   6:00 Presser.
—— MACBETH (SYMPHONIC PRELUDE)
2,2,2,2 - 2,2,2,0 - timp. - hp. - str.   12:00 Presser.
—— LE MARCHÉ D'IBIZA (PRELUDE SYMPHONIQUE)
1,1,1,1 - 1,2,1,0 - timp.,perc. - str.   6:00 Presser.
—— OUVERTURE POUR UNE COMÉDIE DE MARIVAUX
2,2,2,2 - 2,2,2,0 - timp. - str.   5:30 Presser.
—— QUATRE DANSES ANCIENNES
str.   10:00 Presser.
—— LE RENDEZ-VOUS (BALLET) %
2,2,2 alto sax.,2 - 4,3,0,1 - timp.,perc. - hp. - pf. - str.
                                              12:00 Presser.
—— SUITE FOR AN ITALIAN COMEDY
1,1,0,1 - 0,1,1,0 - str.   15:00 Presser.
—— EL TORO (BALLET) %
2,2,2,2 - 2,2,2,0 - timp.,perc.(4) - hp. - pf. - str.   25:00 Presser.

DUDDY, John H., Jr.
—— EVANGELINE (SYMPHONIC POEM)
*3,2,2,2 - 4,2,3,1 - timp. - hp. - str.   20:00 Composer.
—— JOMAMBRA (SUITE FOR PIANO AND ORCH. IN 6 MOVTS.)
*3,2,2,2 - 4,2,0,0 - timp. - pf. - str.   15:00 Composer.

DUFF, Arthur
—— IRISH SUITE FOR STRINGS
str.   8:00 Novello.

DUFOURT, Hughes
—— DOWN TO A SUNLESS SEA
str.   Presser.

DUHAMEL, Antoine
—— TERRITOIRES
str.   30:00 Presser.

DUKAS, Paul
—— ARIANE ET BARBE-BLEUE (3-ACT OPERA) %
3,*3,3,4 - 4,3,3,1 - perc. - hp. - str.   EV.
—— LA PÉRI (A DANCE-POEM) %
3(3rd alt. with picc.),3,3,3 - 4,3,3,1 - timp.,perc.,cel.,xyl. - 2 hp. -
str.   EV.

DUKAS, Paul - PICKERING, Norman
—— VILLANELLE
2,2,2,2 - 0,0,0,0 - str.   5:00 Presser.

DUKE, John
—— CAPTAIN LOVELOCK (CHAMBER OPERA) % (FOR
WOMEN'S VOICES AND ORCH.) (Text: Composer)
1,1,1,1 - 2,1,0,0 - str.   35:00 C. Fischer.
—— CARNIVAL OVERTURE
2,2,2,2 - 2,2,3,0 - timp.,perc.(3) - str.   8:00 Composer.
—— CONCERTO FOR PIANO AND STRINGS (IN 3 MOVTS.)
pf. - str.   21:30 Composer.
—— O SING UNTO THE LORD A NEW SONG (FOR CHORUS
AND STRINGS)
str.   8:00 G. Schirmer.
—— OVERTURE IN D MINOR (FOR STRINGS)
str.   10:00 Composer.

DUKELSKY, Vladimir
—— LE BAL DES BLANCHISSEUSES (BALLET-SUITE) (IN 4
MOVTS.)
2(2nd alt. with picc.),2,2,2, 2,2,2,0 - timp.,perc.,xyl. - pf. - str.
                                              18:30 C. Fischer.
—— BALLADE FOR PIANO AND STRINGS, WITH TYMPANI
OBBLIGATO
timp. - pf. - str.   12:00 Composer.
—— CONCERTO FOR CELLO AND ORCH. (IN 3 MOVTS.)
3,3,3,3 - 3,0,1,1 - timp.,perc. - hp. - str. 25:00 C. Fischer.
—— CONCERTO FOR VIOLIN AND ORCH.
3,3,3,3 - 4,0,1,1 - timp.,perc.,cel. - str.   26:00 C. Fischer.

—— DÉDICACES (FOR PIANO AND ORCH., WITH OBBLIGATO
FEMALE VOICE)
3,3,3,3 - 4,3,3,1 - timp.,perc. - hp. - pf. - str.   20:30 Bo. Hawkes.
—— ENTR'ACTE (BALLET SUITE)
2,2,3,2 - 2,2,2,1 - timp.,perc., - hp. - pf. - str.   25:00 Composer.
—— EPITAPH (FOR SOPRANO, CHORUS AND ORCH.)
3,3,3,3 - 2,2,1,1 - timp.,perc. - pf. - str. 10:00 Bo. Hawkes.
—— LENINGRAD (FOR SOLOISTS, CHORUS AND ORCHESTRA)
3,3,4,4 - 6,4,4,1 - timp.,perc.,xyl. - hp. - str.   30:00 Composer.
—— ODE TO THE MILKY WAY
3,3,2,3 - 4,3,3,1 - timp.,perc.,cel.,xyl. - hp. - pf. - str.
                                              14:00 Belw-Mills.
—— PUBLIC GARDENS (OVERTURE)
2,2,2,2 - 2,2,1,0 - xyl. - pf. - str.   17:00 Composer.
—— SOUVENIR DE MONTE CARLO (BALLET FOR ORCH.)
1(alt. with picc.),1(alt. with Eng. hn.),1,1 - 1,1,1,1 - timp.,perc.,cel.
- pf. - str.   15:00 Broude.
—— SYMPHONY NO. 1
3,3,3,3 - 4,4,3,1 - timp.,perc. - pf. - str. 18:00 Bo. Hawkes.
—— SYMPHONY NO. 2, IN D♭ (IN 3 MOVTS.)
4,3(3rd alt. with Eng. hn.),4(3rd alt. with E♭ cl.),3 - 4,4,3,1 -
timp.,perc. - pf. - str.   17:00 Bo. Hawkes.
—— SYMPHONY NO. 3 (IN 3 MOVTS.)
*3,*3,*3,*3 - 4,3,3,1 - timp.,perc.,cel.,glock.,xyl. - pf. - str.
                                              45:00 C. Fischer.
—— VARIATIONS ON AN OLD RUSSIAN CHANT (FOR OBOE
AND STRINGS)
ob. - str.   10:20 Broude.

DUMAS, Louis
—— RHAPSODIE (FOR CELLO AND ORCH.)
2,2,2,2 - 2,2,3,1 - timp.,perc. - str.   13:00 Salabert.

DUMONT, Jacques
—— CINQ PHONIES (FOR STRINGS AND PERCUSSION)
perc. - str.   19:00 Presser.

DUNCAN, Ronald
—— CONCERTO FOR CLARINET, HORN AND STRINGS (REV.
1967)
cl. - hn. - str.   18:00 P.R.S.
—— FESTIVAL OVERTURE (1966)
3,3,3,2 - 4,3,3,1 - perc.(3) - str.   9:00 P.R.S.
—— HIGHLAND RHAPSODY NO. 2 (1965)
3,2,2,2 - 4,3,3,1 - perc.(3) - str.   10:00 P.R.S.
—— ROSE WITHOUT A THORN (SUITE OF INCIDENTAL
MUSIC)(1945)
1,1,1,1 - 0,0,0,0 - str.   10:00 P.R.S.
—— THRENODY (1961)
str.   7:00 P.R.S.
—— VARIATIONS FOR PIANO AND ORCH. (1958)
3,2,2,2 - 4,3,3,1 - perc.(3) - pf. - str.   20:00 P.R.S.

DUNFORD, Benjamin
—— THE PROMISE (EASTER CANTATA) (FOR SATB CHORUS,
BRASS, PERCUSSION AND ORGAN)
0,0,0,0 - 4,3,3,1 - timp.,perc.(5) - org.   30:00 Belw-Mills.
—— PSALM 103 (CANTATA) (FOR BARITONE, SATB CHORUS,
BRASS, PERCUSSION AND ORGAN)
0,0,0,0- 0-2,3,3,1 - timp.,perc. - org.   12:00 Belw-Mills.
—— THE UNSPEAKABLE GIFT (CHRISTMAS CANTATA) (FOR
BARITONE, SAB CHORUS, BRASS, PERCUSSION AND
ORGAN)
0,0,0,0 - 0,3,3,1 - timp.,perc. - org.   25:00 Belw-Mills.

DUNHILL, Thomas F.
—— CHIDDINGFOLD SUITE, OP. 60 (FOR STRINGS) (IN 5
MOVTS.)
str.   15:00 Novello.
—— DANCES IN MINIATURE (FOR STRINGS)
str.   8:00 Bo. Hawkes.
—— IN RURAL ENGLAND (SUITE)
pf.(ad lib.) - str.   8:30 Mills.
—— PASTIME AND GOOD COMPANY (SUITE)
2,2,2,2 - 5,2,3,0 - timp.,perc. - hp.(ad lib.) - str.   10:00 Oxford.
—— THREE PIECES FOR STRINGS WITH ORGAN, OP. 67
org. - str.   19:00 P.R.S.
—— VECTIS (SUITE FOR STRINGS)
str.   7:30 Bo. Hawkes.

DUNN, James P.
—— INTERMEZZO, FROM "THE GALLEON"
*3,*3,*3,2 - 4,3,3,1 - timp.,cel. - hp. - str.   J. Fischer.

—— OVERTURE ON NEGRO THEMES
  3,2,2,2 - 4,2,2,1 - timp.,perc. - hp. - str.   J. Fischer.
—— PASSACAGLIA AND THEME FUGATUM
  *3,*3,*3,*3 - 4,3,3,1 - timp.,perc.,cel.,glock.,xyl. - hp. - str.
                                                        J. Fischer.
—— WE (SYMPHONIC POEM)
  *3,*3,*3,*3 - 4,3,3,1 - timp.,perc.,cel.,glock.,xyl. - hp. - str.
                                                        J. Fischer.

DUPAGE, Florence
—— ALICE IN WONDERLAND (SUITE) (IN 4 MOVTS.)
  3,3,3,2 - 4,3,3,1 - timp. - hp. - str.   18:00 C. Fischer.

DU PAGE, Richard
—— AFGHANISTAN (SYMPHONIC SUITE) (IN 4 MOVTS)
  *4(2nd and 3rd alt. with 2 alto fl.),*3,*4,*5 - 8,4,3,1 -
  timp.,perc.(5) - 2hp. - str.   23:00 C-Ross.
—— ALLEGRO FOR BASSOON AND ORCH.
  2(2nd alt. with picc.),*3,2(2nd alt. with b.-cl.),2 - 4,3,3,1 -
  timp.,perc.(2) - hp. - str.   9:00 C-Ross.
    or:
  2(2nd alt. with picc.),*3,2(2nd alt. with b.-cl.),2 - 2,3,2,0 -
  timp.,perc.(2) - hp. - str.
—— CENTRAL PARK SUITE (IN 5 MOVTS.)
  3(3rd alt. with picc.),3(alt. with bar. sax.),3(alt. with 3
  alto sax.), b.-cl.(alt with ten. sax.),2 - 2,4,3,1 - timp.,perc.(2),
  cel.,xyl. - hp. - 2pf. - str.   20:00 C-Ross.
—— IN THE VALLEY OF MORPHEUS
  3(3rd alt. with picc.),*3,3(2nd and 3rd alt. with 2 b.-cl.),3(3rd alt.
  with c. - bn.) - 4,3,3,1 - timp.,perc.(2), cel. - 2 hp. - str.
                                              8:30 C-Ross.
—— MISSOURI SUITE (IN 4 MOVTS.)
  str.   11:00 C-Ross.
—— SUITE FOR SMALL ORCHESTRA
  1,1(alt. with Eng. hn.),2(2nd alt. with b-cl.),1 - 2 hn. -
  timp.,perc.(2), cel. - hp. - pf. - str.   13:00 C-Ross.
—— VARIATIONS ON AN IRISH THEME
  1(alt. with picc.),1,1,1 - 2,1,0,0 - timp.,perc.(1),cel.,vibra.,xyl. - hp.
  - str.   4:10 C-Ross.
—— THE WOODWIND SUITE
  1. Etude for Flute and Orchestra; 2. Serenade for Oboe and
  Orchestra; 3. Minuet for Clarinet and Orchestra; 4. Allegro for
  Bassoon and Orchestra
  3(1st and 2nd alt. with 2 picc.),3,3,2 - 4,3,3,0 - timp.,perc.(3) - hp.
  - str.   22:30 Composer.
    or:
  3(1st and 2nd alt. with 2 picc.),*4,*4,*3 - 4,3,3,1 - timp.,perc.(3) -
  hp. - str.

DUPARC, Henri
—— AUX ÉTOILES (ENTR'ACTE FROM AN UNPUBLISHED
  DRAMATIC WORK)
  2,2,2,2 - 4,2,0,0 - str.   Salabert.

DUPERIER, Jean
—— IMAGES D'ÉPINAL (IN 5 MOVTS.)
  2,2,2,2 - 4,2,3,0 - xyl. - pf. - str.   16:00 Salabert.

DU PLESSIS, Hubert
—— SERENADE FOR STRINGS
  str.   15:00 Novello.

DUPONT, Gabriel
—— ANTAR (BALLET)(1914) %
  4,4,4,4 - 6,4,3,2 - timp.,cel. - 2 hp. - pf. - str.   16:00 Presser.
—— LE CHANT DE LA DESTINÉE
  3,4,3,4 - 4,4,4,1 - timp.,perc.(3),cel. - 2 hp. - str. 17:30 Presser.
—— SYMPHONIC EXCERPTS FROM "LES HEURES DOLENTES"
  3,3,3,4 - 4,3,3,1 - timp.,perc. - str.   22:00 Presser.
—— TWO EXCERPTS FROM "LA FARCE DU CUVIER" (1912)
  4,3,3,3 - 4,3,3,1 - timp.,perc.(4) - hp. - str. 9:30 Presser.

DU PONT, Jacques
—— LA CLEF DES SONGES (BALLET) %
  timp.,perc.(4),glock.,xyl. - pf. - str.   EV.
—— CONCERTO FOR CELLO AND ORCH.
  2,2,2,2 - 2,2,3,0 - timp.,perc.,cel.,glock. - pf. - str. 27:30 Salabert.
—— CONCERTO FOR PIANO AND ORCH.
  2,2,2,2 - 3,3,3,0 - timp.,perc. - pf. - str. 21:30 Baron.
—— LE DIPTYQUE D'AMDUSCIAS
  2,2,2,2 - 2,2,2,0 - perc. - str.   23:00 Presser.
—— FANTAISIE (FOR PIANO AND ORCH.)
  2,2,2,2 - 2,3,3,0 - timp.,perc.,glock. - pf. - str. 26:00 Salabert.

DUPRÉ, Marcel
—— DE PROFUNDIS (FOR SOLO VOICES, MIXED CHORUS,
  ORGAN AND ORCH.)
  2,2,2,2, - 4,2,3,0 - timp. - hp. - org. - str. 50:00 Baron.
—— FANTAISIE POUR PIANO ET ORCH., OP. 8
  2,2,2,2, - 4,2,3,0 - timp.,perc. - pf. - str. 21:00 Baron.
—— SYMPHONY IN G MINOR FOR ORGAN AND ORCH., OP. 25
  3,3,3,3, - 4,3,3,1 - timp.,perc.,cel.,glock. - hp. - org. - str.
                                              28:00 Salabert.

DUPREIZ, Christian
—— CAPRICE SYMPHONIQUE
  3,3,3,3, - 4,3,3,1 - timp.,perc.,cel.,glock. - hp. - str.
                                              14:00 C. Fischer.

DUPUIS, Sylvain
—— INVOCATION (FOR CELLO OR VIOLIN AND ORCH.)
  1,1,1,1 - 2,1,1,0 - timp., - str.   5:00 Salabert.

DURANTE, Francesco - LUALDI, Adriano
—— CONCERTO NO. 1 IN F, FOR STRINGS
  str.   10:00 Bo. Hawkes.
—— CONCERTO NO. 2 IN G, FOR STRINGS
  str.   10:00 Bo. Hawkes.
—— CONCERTO NO. 3 IN E♭ FOR STRINGS
  str.   7:00 Bo. Hawkes.
—— CONCERTO NO. 4 IN E, FOR STRINGS
  str.   9:00 Bo. Hawkes.
—— CONCERTO NO. 5 IN A, FOR STRINGS
  str.   7:00 Bo. Hawkes.
—— CONCERTO NO. 6 IN A, FOR STRINGS
  str.   8:00 Bo. Hawkes.
—— CONCERTO NO. 7 IN C, FOR STRINGS
  str.   6:00 Bo. Hawkes.
—— CONCERTO NO. 8 IN A ("LA PAZZIA"), FOR STRINGS
  str.   11:00 Bo. Hawkes.

DUREY, Louis
—— SINFONIETTA, OP. 105 (FOR STRINGS)
  str.   18:00 Presser.

DURHAM, Lowell M.
—— PIONEER FOLKSCAPE, OP. 19 (1967)
  2(2nd alt. with picc.),*3,1 E♭cl.,*3,*3 - 4,3,3,1 -
  timp.,perc.(4),bells,cel.,glock.,xyl. - hp. - pf. - str. 12:00 Deseret.
—— PRELUDE AND FUGUE FOR STRING ORCH., OP. 5 (1944)
  str.   9:00 Composer.
—— SUITE FOR STRING ORCH., OP. 2 (1943) (IN 3 MOVTS.)
  str.   11:00 Deseret.
—— SYMPHONY NO. 1, OP. 4 (1945) (IN 4 MOVTS.)
  2(2nd alt. with picc.),2(2nd alt. with Eng.hn.),2,*3 - 4,3,3,1 -
  timp.,perc. - str.   18:00 Deseret.
—— VARIATIONS FOR STRINGS, OP. 9
  str.   10:00 Deseret.

DURKÓ, Zsolt
—— ALTAMIRA (FOR SATB CHORUS AND ORCH.)
                                              9:20 Bo. Hawkes.
—— BALLAD
  *2,2,2,2 - 4,2,2,0 - timp.,perc. - str.   5:30 Bo. Hawkes.
—— CANTATA NO. 1
  *3,1,2,2 - 1,3,3,1 - perc. - hp. - pf. - str. 20:00 Bo. Hawkes.
—— CANTATA NO. 2 (FOR SSAATTBB CHORUS AND ORCH.)
  *3,1,3,*3 - 2,4,4,1 - perc. - hp. - cemb. - pf. - str.
                                              18:00 Bo. Hawkes.
—— CHAMBER MUSIC
  2 pf. - str.   15:00 Bo. Hawkes.
—— EPISODI SUL TEMA B-A-C-H
  2,1,2,2 - 4,3,3,1 - timp.,cel. - hp. - pf. - str. 12:00 Bo. Hawkes.
—— FIORETURE (WITH SMALL CHORUS OF LOW VOICES)
  3,3,3,3 - 3,3,5,2 - timp.,perc. - hp. - hpsc. - str.
                                              10:00 Bo. Hawkes.
—— HUNGARIAN RHAPSODY
  1,0,2,2 - 4,3,3,1 - timp.,perc. - pf. - str. 13:00 Bo. Hawkes.
—— ORGANISMI (FOR VIOLIN AND ORCH.)
                                              12:00 Bo. Hawkes.

DURO, John
—— CONCERTO FOR PIANO AND STRINGS
  pf. - str.   Composer.

DURUFLÉ, Maurice
—— ANDANTE AND SCHERZO, OP. 8
    3,*3,3,2 - 4,3,3,1 - perc. - hp. - str.   13:00 EV.
—— MASS "CUM JUBILO" (FOR BARITONE AND ORCH.)
    2,2,2,2 - 4,3,3,1 - timp.,perc.,glock. - hp. - org. - str.   19:00 EV.
    or:
    org. - str.
—— REQUIEM, OP. 9 (FOR MEZZO-SOPRANO, BARITONE, SATB
    CHORUS AND ORCH.) (Reduced orchestration)
    tpt. - timp. - hp. - org. - str.   40:00 EV.
    or:
    org. - str.
—— REQUIEM, OP. 9 (FOR SOLOISTS, CHORUS AND ORCH.)
    3,*4,3,2 - 4,3,3,1 - timp.,perc.,cel. - hp. - org. - str.   43:00 EV.
—— SCHERZO, OP. 8
    3,*3,3,2 - 4,3,3,1 - timp.,perc.,glock, - 2hp. - str.   7:00 EV.
—— THREE DANCES, OP. 6
    3,*3,3, alto sax.,2 - 4,3,3,1 - timp.,perc.,cel. - 2hp. - str.   14:00 EV.

DUSSEK, Johann L. - PRIEGNITZ, Hans
—— KONZERT-ALLEGRO (FOR PIANO AND ORCH.)
    2,2,2,2 - 2,2,0,0 - pf. - str.   12:00 G. Schirmer.

DUTILLEUX, Henri
—— CINQ MÉTABOLES
    4,4,4,5 - 4,4,3,1 - timp.,perc.(5) - str.   17:00 Presser.
—— DANSE FANTASTIQUE
    3,3,3,3 - 4,3,3,1 - timp.,perc.(5),cel. - hp. - pf. - str.   11:00 EV.
—— LA FILLE DU DIABLE (SUITE TIRÉE DE LA MUSIQUE DU
    FILM)
    2,2,3,alto sax., 2 - 4,3,3,1 - timp.,perc.(2), cel., Ondes-martenot (or
    ob.) - hp. - pf. - str.   15:00 Salabert.
—— FIVE MELODIES (FOR MEDIUM VOICE AND ORCH.)
    11:30 EV.
—— LE LOUP (SYMPHONIC SUITE FROM THE BALLET)
    2,1,2,1 - 2,2,1,1 - timp.,perc.,cel. - hp. - pf. - str.
    20:00 F. Colombo.
—— SALMACIS (POÈME CHORÉOGRAPHIQUE)
    3,2,2,2 - 4,3,3,0-1 - timp.,perc.,cel. - hp.   9:00 Baron.
—— SYMPHONY NO. 1
    *3,*3,3,3, - 4,3,3,1 - timp.,perc.,cel. - hp. - pf. - str.
    31:00 E.C.Kerby.
—— SYMPHONY NO. 2 (FOR 2 ORCHESTRAS)
    Orchestra I (large orch.)3,2,2,2 - 2,2,2,1 - perc. - hp. - str.
    27:00 Presser.
    Orchestra II (small orch.)0,1,1,1 - 0,1,1,0 - timp. - cel. - hps. - 2
    vln., 1 vla., c.
—— TOUT UN MONDE LOINTAIN (CONCERTO FOR CELLO
    AND ORCH.)
    3,2,3,3 - 3,2,2,1 - timp.,perc.,cel. - hp. - str.   26:00 Presser.
—— TROIS TABLEAUX SYMPHONIQUES, D'APRÈS "LES HAUTS
    DE HURLEVENT"
    2,1,2,sax.,2 - 2,2,1,1 - timp.,perc. - hp. - ondes martenot - pf. (alt.
    with cel.) - str.   11:00 Salabert.

DUTTON, Brent
—— CONCERTO NO. 1 FOR TUBA AND ENSEMBLE
    0,0,0,0 - 0,3,3,1 - timp.,vibra. - pf.   15:00 Seesaw.

DVARIONAS, Balys D.
—— CONCERTO FOR VIOLIN AND ORCHESTRA
    3,2,2,2, - 4,2,3,1 - timp.,perc. - str.   30:00 G. Schirmer.

DVORAČEK, Jiří
—— SUITE FOR ORCHESTRA
    3,3,3,3 - 4,3,3,1 - timp.,perc. - hp. - pf. - str.   30:00 Bo. Hawkes.

DVOŘÁK, Antonín - CUMMING, Richard
—— SEVEN GYPSY SONGS (FOR BASS AND ORCH.)
    2,*3,*3,*3 - 4,2,3,1 - timp.,perc.(2) - hp. - str.   12:45 Arranger.

DVOŘÁK, Antonín - ISSACS, Leonard
—— GYPSY SONGS, OP. 55 (FOR LOW VOICE AND ORCH.)
    2,2,2,2 - 2,2,0,0 - timp.,perc. - hp. - str.   14:00 Lengnick.

DVOŘÁK, Antonín - KURZ, V.
—— CONCERTO IN G MINOR FOR PIANO AND ORCH., OP. 33
    (IN 3 MOVTS.)
    2,2,2,2 - 2,2,0,0 - pf. - str.   37:00 Bo. Hawkes.

DVOŘÁK, Antonín - MCKAY, George F.
—— A LITTLE "NEW WORLD SYMPHONY" (TRANSCRIBED
    FROM THE "AMERICAN" STRING QUARTET) (IN 3 MOVTS.)
    (ARR. 1968)
    2,2,2,2 - 4,3,3,0 - timp. - str.   9:00 Arranger.

DVOŘÁK, Antonín - MARSZALEK, Franz
—— BALLADE FOR VIOLIN AND ORCH., OP. 15
    2,2,2,2 - 4,0,0,0 - timp. - hp. - str.   7:00 Mannheimer.

DVOŘÁK, Antonín - OUBRADOUS, Fernand
—— SERENADE
    0,2,2,2 - 3,0,0,0 - c.,d.-b.   Presser.

DVOŘÁK, Antonín - PRIEGNITZ, Hans
—— BAGATELLEN, OP. 47
    3,3,2,2 - 4,2,0,0 - timp.,perc. - str.   18:00 G. Schirmer.

DVOŘÁK, Antonín - SMITH, William Russell
—— GYPSY SONGS (FOR LOW VOICE AND ORCH.) (ARR. 1970)
    (Text: Adolf Heyduk)
    *3,2,2,2 - 4,3,3,1 - timp.,perc.(2),glock. - hp. - str.
    11:00 NewOrl.Phi.

DVOŘÁK, Antonín - SZELL, George
—— SLAVONIC DANCE NO. 1, OP. 46, NO. 1
    3,2,2,2, - 4,2,3,0 - timp.,perc. - str.   3:30 Bo. Hawkes.
—— SLAVONIC DANCE NO. 3, OP. 46, NO. 3
    3,2,2,2, - 4,2,3,0 - timp.,perc. - str.   Bo. Hawkes.
—— SLAVONIC DANCE NO. 4, OP. 46, NO. 4
    4:00 Bo. Hawkes.
—— SLAVONIC DANCE NO. 8, OP. 46, NO. 8
    3,2,2,2, - 4,2,3,0 - timp.,perc. - str.   Bo. Hawkes.
—— SLAVONIC DANCE NO. 10, OP. 72, NO. 2
    2,2,2,2 - 4,0,0,0 - timp.,perc. - str.   Bo. Hawkes.
—— SLAVONIC DANCE NO. 15, OP. 72, NO. 7
    3,2,2,2, - 4,2,3,0 - timp.,perc. - str.   Bo. Hawkes.

DVORAK, Robert J.
—— SONGS OF DELIVERANCE (FOR CHORUS AND ORCH.)
    (1967) (IN 4 MOVTS.) (Text: Biblical)
    0,0,0,0 - 4,3,3,1 - timp.,perc.(4),cel. - hp. - pf. - str.
    19:00 F. Colombo.
—— SUITE ON CZECH THEMES (1970) (IN 4 MOVTS.)
    *3,2(2nd alt. with Eng.hn.),2,2 - 2,2,3,1 -timp.,perc. - str.
    18:30 Composer.

DYCK, V.
—— FÊTES JUIVES (SYMPHONIC SUITE) (IN 3 MOVTS)
    3,3,3,3 - 4,3,3,1 - timp.,perc.(3) - 2hp. - str.   20:00 Salabert.

DYSON, George
—— AT THE TABARD INN (OVERTURE TO "THE CANTERBURY
    PILGRIMS")
    *3,*3,*3,*3 - 4,3,3,1 - timp.,perc.(3) - str.   12:00 Oxford.
    or:
    2,2,2,2 - 4,2,3,1 - timp.,perc.(2) - str.
—— THE CANTERBURY PILGRIMS: CHORAL SUITE (FOR
    WOMEN'S CHORUS AND ORCH.) (Text: Chaucer)
    2,2,2,2 - 4,3,3,1 - timp.,perc. - hp. - org. - str.   18:00 Oxford.
    or:
    2,2,2,2 - 2,1,0,0 - timp.,perc. - str.
    or:
    pf. - str.
—— THE CANTERBURY PILGRIMS (PORTRAITS FROM THE
    PROLOGUE TO CHAUCER'S "CANTERBURY TALES") (FOR
    SOLOISTS, CHORUS AND ORCH.)
    2,2,2,2 - 4,3,3,1 - timp.,perc.(2) - hp. (ad lib.) - org. (ad lib.) - str.
    90:00 Oxford.
—— CONCERTO DA CAMERA
    str.   22:00 Novello.
—— CONCERTO DA CHIESA (FOR STRING QUARTET AND
    STRING ORCH.)
    Novello.
—— CONCERTO FOR VIOLIN AND ORCHESTRA
    2,2,2,2 - 4,2,3,0 - timp. - str.   37:00 Novello.
—— CONCERTO LEGGIERO, FOR PIANO AND STRINGS
    pf. - str.   Novello.
—— IN HONOUR OF THE CITY (FOR MIXED CHORUS AND
    ORCH.) (Text: William Dunbar)
    2,2,2,2 - 4,2,3,1 - timp.,perc. - hp. - str.   16:00 Oxford.
    or:
    2,2,2,2 - 2,1,0,0 - timp.,perc. - str.

or:
    timp. - pf. - str.
—— PRELUDE, PHANTASY AND CHACONNE (FOR CELLO AND ORCH.)
    2,2,2,2 - 2 hn. - timp. - str.   25:00 Novello.
—— SAINT PAUL'S VOYAGE TO MELITA (CANTATA) (FOR TENOR, MIXED CHORUS AND ORCH.)
        25:00 Oxford.
—— SYMPHONY IN G
    2,2,2,2 - 4,2,3,0 - timp. - str.   45:00 Novello.

DZEGELENOK, Aleksandr M.
—— CORTÈGE (ZUG) (FROM "EGYPTIAN SUITE")
    *3,*3,*3,*3 - 4,4,3,1 - timp.,perc.,cel. - hp. - pf. - str.
        15:00 G. Schirmer.
—— IN THE TEMPLE OF AMMON RA (FROM "EGYPTIAN SUITE")
    2,*3,2,2 - 4,2,3,1 - timp.,perc. - hp. - str.   7:00 G. Schirmer.
—— MORNING (FROM "EGYPTIAN SUITE")
    2,3,3,2 - 4,2,3,1 - timp.,perc.,cel. - hp. - pf. - str.
        10:00 G. Schirmer.

DZERZHINSKIJ, Ivan I.
—— AND QUIET FLOWS THE DON (OPERA) %
    3,2,3,2 - 4,3,3,1 - timp.,perc. - hp. - str.   G. Schirmer.

DZIERLATKA, Arié - ANDRÉ, Albert
—— DE PRÈS DE LOIN (CONCERTO POUR 3 PETITS ORCHESTRES ET PIANO SOLISTES)
        26:00 MCA Music.
—— LUMIÈRES
        6:00 S.U.I.S.A.

E

EAGLES, Moneta
—— AUTUMN RHAPSODY (FOR PIANO AND SMALL ORCH.)(1964)
    1,1,1,0 - 1,1,0,0 - perc. - hp. - pf. - str.   5:00 P.R.S.
—— DIVERSIONS FOR PIANO AND ORCH.
        17:00 A.P.R.A.
—— ESSAY FOR ORCH.
        8:00 A.P.R.A.
—— ILLILLIWA (TWO PRELUDES FOR ORCH.)(1965)
    2,2,2,2 - 4,2,2,0 - timp.,perc. - hp. - str.   11:00 P.R.S.
—— SOLILOQUY FOR ORCH. (FOR STRINGS, WOODWIND AND HORNS)
        4:00 A.P.R.A.

EASDALE, Brian
—— THE RED SHOES (BALLET MUSIC) %
    3,2,2,2 - 4,3,3,1 - timp.,xyl.,glock. - hp. - pf. - str. 15:00 Chappell.

EAST, Michael - FELLOWES, Edmund H.
—— WHEN ISRAEL CAME OUT OF EGYPT (ANTHEM) (FOR TENOR, CHORUS AND ORCH.)
        Oxford.

EASTON, Jack
—— SYMPHONY (1951) (IN 4 MOVTS.)
    3(2nd and 3rd alt. with piccs.),*3,*3,*3 - 4,3,3,1 - timp.,perc.(4),bells,cel.(alt. with pf.),glock.,xyl. - hp. - str.
        29:00 Composer.

EASTWOOD, Thomas
—— CHRISTOPHER SLY (OPERA) % (Text: Ronald Duncan)
    2*2,*2,1 - 1,0,0,0 - perc. - pf. - str.   100:00 Oxford.
—— MUSIC TO CELEBRATE
    2,2,2,2 - 4,2,3,1 - timp.,perc. - str.   11:00 Oxford.
—— SYMPHONIC STUDY
    2,2,2,2 - 2,2,1,0 - timp. - str.   9:00 Oxford.
—— SYMPHONY
    2,2,2,2 - 4,2,3,1 - timp.,perc. - str.   30:00 Oxford.

EATON, John
—— THE HOLY SONNETS OF JOHN DONNE (FOR SOPRANO AND ORCH.)
    3,3,1 E♭cl.,3,3 - 4,3,3,1 - perc. - hp. - str.   12:00 Shawnee.

EBEL, Arnold
—— SINFONIETTA GIOCOSA, OP. 39
    3(3rd alt. with picc.),*3,*3,*3 - 4,3,3,1 - timp.,perc.(3) - str.
        35:00 Henmar.

EBEN, Petr
—— SINFONIA GREGORIANO (CONCERTO FOR ORGAN AND ORCH.)
    4 hn.,2 tpt. - timp. - hp. - org. - str.   52:00 Bo. Hawkes.

EBERLIN, Johann Ernst - BARNES, Clifford P.
—— TOCCATA AND FUGUE
        ProArtPubs.

ECKERBERG, Sixten
—— CONCERTINO FOR PIANO AND ORCH. (1962)
    2,2,2,2 - 2,2,0,0 - timp.,perc. - pf. - str.   21:00 Fleisher.
—— CONCERTO NO. 1 FOR PIANO AND ORCH.
    3,2,2,2 - 4,2,3,1 - timp.,perc. (2) - pf. - str.   28:00 S.T.I.M.
—— CONCERTO NO. 2 FOR PIANO AND ORCH.
    2,2,2,2 - 4,2,0,0 - timp. - pf. - str.   35:00 S.T.I.M.
—— CONCERTO NO. 3 FOR PIANO AND ORCH. (1971)
    3,2,2,2 - 4,3,3,1 - timp.,perc. - pf. - str.   20:00 Fleisher.
—— LA DANZE DELLA VITA (1970)
    2,2,2,2 - 4,3,3,1 - timp.,perc. - str.   17:00 Fleisher.
—— FOREST MURMURS (1973)
    2,2,2,2 - 4,2,3,1 - timp.,perc. - hp. - str.   10:00 Fleisher.
—— FRÅN SOMMEN (BILDER FRÅN NATUREN) (SUITE) (IN 4 MOVTS.)
    2,2,2,2 - 2,2,1,0 - timp.,perc. - hp. - str.   19:00 S.T.I.M.
—— SAGAN OM ASARNE (1971)
    2,2,2,2 - 4,2,3,2 - timp.,perc. - hp. - str.   Fleisher.
—— SERENADE (1972)
    2,2,2,2 - 4,2,3,1 - timp.,perc. - str.   20:00 Fleisher.
—— SUB LUNA (SYMPHONIC POEM)
    3,2,2,2 - 4,2,3,1 - timp.,perc. - hp. - str.   11:00 S.T.I.M.
—— SUMMER MUSIC (SUITE) (IN 4 MOVTS.)
    2,2,2,2 - 2,2,1,0 - timp.,perc.,cel. - hp. - str.   21:00 S.T.I.M.
—— SYMPHONIE PASTORALE (1973)
    2,2,2,2 - 4,3,2,0 - timp.,perc. - str.   20:00 Fleisher.
—— SYMPHONY NO. 1
    3,2,2,2 - 4,3,3,1 - timp.,perc. (2) - hp. - str.   36:00 S.T.I.M.
—— SYMPHONY NO. 2
    3,2,2,2 - 4,3,3,1 - timp.,perc. - hp. - str.   41:00 S.T.I.M.
—— SYMPHONY NO. 3 ("AUTUMN SONG")(1965)
    3,2,2,2 - 4,4,4,1 - timp.,perc.(3),cel. - hp. - str.   20:00 Fleisher.
—— VISIONE (1961)
    2,2,2,2 - 4,3,3,1 - timp.,perc.(3),cel. - hp. - str.   10:30 Fleisher.

ECKHARDT-GRAMATTÉ, Sophie
—— CAPRICCIO-CONCERTANTE (1941)
    *3,2,2*3 - 4,3,3,1 - timp,perc. - hp. - pf. - str.   11:25 CanMusCtr.
—— CONCERTINO (FOR STRINGS) (1947) (IN 3 MOVTS.)
    str.   16:30 CanMusCtr.
—— CONCERTO FOR BASSOON AND SMALL ORCH.
        15:00 C.A.P.A.C.
—— CONCERTO FOR ORCHESTRA (1954)
    *3,2,2,*3 - 4,3,3,1 - timp.,perc.,cel. - hp. - pf. - str.
        13:05 CanMusCtr.
—— CONCERTO FOR PIANO AND ORCH. (1946) (IN 3 MOVTS.)
    *3,2,*3,2 - 4,3,3,1 - timp.,perc. - pf. - str.   30:00 CanMusCtr.
—— CONCERTO FOR VIOLIN, CONCERTANTE OF WIND INSTRUMENTS AND ORCH. (1951) (IN 3 MOVTS.)
    *3,*3,*3,*3 - 4,3,3,1 - timp.,perc. - hp. - str.   28:00 CanMusCtr.
—— MARKANTES STÜCK (FOR PIANO, PIANO OBBLIGATO AND ORCH.) (1950) (IN 2 MOVTS.)
    2,2,2,0 - 4,2,2,0 - timp.,perc.(5 incl. 4 or timp.) - hp. - 2 pf. - str.
        14:00 CanMusCtr.
—— SYMPHONY-CONCERTO FOR PIANO AND ORCHESTRA (1967) (IN 3 MOVTS.)
    *3,2,2,2 - 4,3,3,1 - timp.,perc. - hp. - pf. - str.   33:20 CanMusCtr.
—— SYMPHONY IN C (SYMPHONY NO. 1) (1939) (IN 4 MOVTS.)
    *3,2,2,*3 - 4,3,3,1 - timp.,perc. - hp. - str.   40:00 CanMusCtr.
—— SYMPHONY NO. 2 (MANITOBA SYMPHONY)
    *3,2,2,2 - 4,3,3,1 - timp.,perc. - hp. - pf. - str.   34:00 CanMusCtr.

ECKRICH, Willi
—— PASSACAGLIA AND FUGUE FOR STRING ORCH.
    str.   13:00 Mannheimer.

ECKSTEIN, Maxwell
—— CONCERTO FOR YOUNG AMERICANS (FOR PIANO AND ORCH.)
    2,2,1 E♭cl.,3,1 - 4,3,3,1 - timp.,perc. - pf. - str.   8:00 C. Fischer.

EDDLEMAN, David
—— EPISODES FOR ORCHESTRA (1962)
    2(2nd alt. with picc.),2,2,2 - 3,3,3,0 - timp.,perc.(4),xyl. - str.
    9:00 Composer.
—— KADDISH (FOR TENOR, SATB CHORUS AND ORCH.) (1968)
    1(alt. with picc.),0,1,0 - 0,1,0,0 - str.)   9:00 Composer.
—— THE SISTERS' TRAGEDY (1-ACT OPERA) % (1971) (Text: Richard Hughes)
    2(1st alt. with picc.,2nd alt. with alto fl.),*3,*3,*3 - 4,3,3,1 - timp.,perc.(4),cel.,vibra.,xyl. - hp. - str.   40:00 CMP.
—— SKETCH FOR ORCHESTRA (1958)
    2,2,2,2 - 4,0,2,0 - perc.(1) - str.   6:00 Composer.
—— TE DEUM LAUDAMUS (FOR SATB CHORUS AND ORCH.) (1965)
    2(2nd alt. with picc.),1,*3,2 - 1,2,1,0 - timp. - pf. - str.
    10:00 Composer.

EDELSON, Edward
—— PAT A PAN (SUITE ON A BURGUNDIAN CAROL) (IN 3 MOVTS.)
    C. Fischer.

EDER, Helmut
—— ANAMORPHOSE (BALLET) %
    1(alt. with picc.),1,1,1 - 1,1,1,0 - perc. - pf.(or hpsc.) - str.
    30:00 Modern.
—— CONCERTO FOR OBOE AND ORCH. (1962)
    2(2nd alt. with picc.),1,0,alto sax.,1 - 1,1,1,0 - perc.(2) - hpsc. - str.(no vlns.)   11:00 G. Schirmer.
—— CONCERTO FOR VIOLIN AND ORCH., OP. 32
    1,1,1,1 - 1,0,0,0 - str.   17:00 Modern.
—— CONCERTO SEMISERIO, OP. 30 (FOR TWO PIANOS AND ORCH.)(1960)
    1(alt. with picc.),0,1,1 - 2,1,1,0 - perc.(2) - 2 pf. - str.
    16:00 G. Schirmer.
—— DANZA A SOLATIO
    3(3rd alt. with picc.),2,3(3rd alt. with b.-cl.),2 - 4,2,2,1 - perc. - pf. - str.   7:00 Modern.
—— FOUR DIVERTIMENTI (FROM "DIE IRRFAHRTEN DES ODYSSEUS")(1965)
    4(4th alt. with picc.),*4,*3,*3 - 6,4,3,1 - timp.,perc.(6) - pf. - str.
    23:00 G. Schirmer.
—— NAUSIKAA (BALLET SUITE, FROM "DIE IRRFAHRTEN DES ODYSSEUS")(1965)
    *4,*4,*3,*3 - 6,4,3,1 - timp.,perc.(4) - pf. - str. 16:00 G. Schirmer.
—— PEZZO SERENO
    2(2nd alt. with picc.),0,1(alt. with alto sax.),2 - 4,2,2,1 - perc.(3) - pf. - str.   5:00 Modern.
—— SYMPHONY NO. 2, OP. 24
    2(1 alt. with picc.),2,2(1 alt. with alto sax.),2(1 alt. with c.-bn.) - 3,2,2,1 - perc.(4) - pf. - str.   32:00 Modern.
—— SYMPHONY NO. 3, OP. 29 (1959)
    str.   20:00 G. Schirmer.
—— TANZREIHEN (BALLET SUITE)
    3(3rd alt. with picc.),2,2,2 - 4,3,3,1 - timp.,perc. - pf. - str.
    20:00 Modern.

EDGREN, Ole
—— CAVATINA
    2,2,2,2 - 2,0,0,0 - hp. - str.   7:00 FinnMICtr.

EDLER, Robert
—— MANE (1962)
    2,2,2,2 - 4,3,3,0 - perc. - hp. - str.   5:30 Seesaw.
—— MINIATUREN (1972)
    2,2,2,2 - 4,2,3,1 - perc. - hp. - str.   10:10 Seesaw.
—— TEMPORA MUTANTIS (1976) (IN 2 MOVTS.)
    0,0,1,1 - 0,3,3,1 - perc.(3) - pf. - str.   12:14 Seesaw.
—— TUTTE VITA (1959)
    2,2,2,2 - 4,2,3,0 - timp.,perc. - pf. - str.   5:20 Seesaw.

EDLUND, Lars
—— TRACCE (FOR CHAMBER ORCH., HARPSICHORD AND PERCUSSION)(1972)
    22:00 Fleisher.

EDMUNDS, Christopher
—— ENDYMION
    1,1,1,1 - 2,0,0,0 - hp. - str.   5:30 P.R.S.
—— FESTIVAL OVERTURE
    2,2,2,2 - 4,3,3,1 - timp. - hp. - str.   7:30 P.R.S.
—— SYMPHONY NO. 3
    2,2,2,2 - 4,3,3,1 - timp.,perc. - hp. - str.   28:00 P.R.S.
—— THEME AND VARIATIONS (ON AN ENGLISH TUNE)
    2,2,2,2 - 2,2,2,0 - timp.,perc. - hp. - str.   8:00 P.R.S.

EDWARDS, Ross
—— CHOROS (FOR PIANO AND ORCH.) (1972)
    2(alt. with 2 picc.),2,3,2 - 2,2,3,1 - perc. - hp. - pf. - d.-b.
    8:00 J. Albert.
—— ETUDE (1969)
    2(alt. with 2 picc.),*3,3,*3 - 2,2,3,1 - perc.(4),cel. - hp. - str.
    5:00 J. Albert.
—— MOUNTAIN VILLAGE IN A CLEARING MIST (1973)
    2,2,2,2 - 2,2,3,1 - perc.(3) - hp. - pf. - str.   11:00 J. Albert.

EDWARDS, Ryan
—— SEE THE WIND (1-ACT OPERA) % (1956) (Text: Composer)
    1,1,1,1 - 2,0,0,0 - str.(8,3,3,1)   30:00 Composer.

EFFINGER, Cecil
—— AMERICAN MEN (FOR MALE CHORUS AND ORCH.) OP. 16
    *3,2,2,2 - 4,3,3,0 - timp. - str.   5:00 Gray.
—— A CANTATA FOR EASTER, OP. 85 (1971)
    35:00 G. Schirmer.
—— CAPRICCIO FOR ORCH., OP. 91 (1975)
    *3,*3,*3,*3 - 4,3,3,1 - timp.,perc.(4),cel.,glock.,xyl. - hp. - str.
    14:00 G. Schirmer.
—— A CHILD IS BORN (CHRISTMAS CANTATA), OP. 56 (THE SAINT LUKE CHRISTMAS STORY) (IN 4 MOVTS.)
    2 ob. - 2 tpt. - timp.,perc. - org. - str.   35:00 G. Schirmer.
—— CONCERTINO FOR ORGAN AND WIND INSTRUMENTS, OP. 19
    1,1,2,1 - 2,2,0,0 - org.   18:00 Composer.
—— CONCERTO FOR PIANO AND CHAMBER ORCH., OP. 44
    1,1,1,1 - 1,1,0,0 - pf. - str.   15:00 Composer.
—— CONCERTO FOR VIOLIN AND CHAMBER ORCH., OP. 82 (1974) (IN 4 MOVTS.)
    38:00 Composer.
——— CONCERTO GROSSO, OP. 8 (1940) (IN 3 MOVTS.)
    0,2,0,0 - 2,0,0,0 - str.   16:00 Composer.
—— CYRANO DE BERGERAC, OP. 72 (4-ACT OPERA) % (Text: Donald Sutherland, after the play by Rostand)
    2(2nd alt. with picc.),2,2,2,2 - 3,3,3,0 - timp.,perc.(2),glock. - str.
    166:00 Composer.
—— EVENSONG, OP. 59
    *2,2,2,2 - 4,3,3,0 - timp.,perc.(2) - str.   10:00 Composer.
—— THE GENTLEMAN DESPERADO (AND MISS BIRD), OP. 95 (MUSIC-DRAMA) % (1976) (Text: Donald Sutherland)
    1,1,1,1 - 1,1,0,0 - perc.(1) - guit. - str.(2,1,2,1) 108:00 Composer.
—— THE INVISIBLE FIRE, OP. 61 (ORATORIO) (FOR SATB SOLI, SATB CHORUS AND ORCH.) (Text: Tom F. Driver)
    *3,2,2,2 - 4,3,3,1 - timp.,perc.(2) - str.   57:00 Gray.
—— LANDSCAPE, OP. 74 (1966)
    0,0,0,0 - 4,3,3,1 - str.   7:30 Composer.
—— LET YOUR MIND WANDER OVER AMERICA (FOR CHORUS AND ORCH.)
    1,2,*4,2 alto sax. tenor sax.,bar. sax.,2 - 4,3,3,bar.,1 - timp.,perc. - str.   8:00 G. Schirmer.
—— LITTLE SYMPHONY NO. 1, OP. 31
    1 (alt. with picc.),1,2,1 - 2,1,0,0 - str.   14:00 C. Fischer.
—— LITTLE SYMPHONY NO. 2 (IN 4 MOVTS.)
    2,2,2,2 - 2,2,1,0 - str.   12:00 C. Fischer.
    or:
    2,1,2,1 - 2,2,0,0 - str.
—— THE LONG DIMENSION, OP. 83 (FOR BARITONE, SATB CHORUS AND ORCH.) (1970) (Text: Thomas H. Ferril and Composer)
    40:00 Composer.
—— LYRIC OVERTURE, OP. 49
    *3,2,2,2 - 4,3,3,0 - timp. - str.   7:00 Composer.
—— NEW HORIZION, OP. 6 (1939)
    str.   8:00 Composer.
—— NOCTURNE, OP. 3 (1938)
    *3,2,2,2 - 4,3,3,0 - timp. - str.   9:00 Composer.
—— THE OLD CHISHOLM TRAIL, OP. 29 (FOR CHORUS AND ORCH.)
    *3,2,2,2 - 4,3,3,1 - timp.,perc. (2) - str.   7:00 Composer.

—— ONE HUNDRED FIVE DEGREES WEST, OP. 5 (1939) (MUSIC FOR A DANCE)
    1,1,2,1 - 3,2,2,0 - timp. - str.   50:00 Composer.

—— ORCHESTRAL SUITE, OP. 45 (IN 3 MOVTS.)
    *3,*3,*3,*3 - 4,3,3,1 - timp.,perc. (2) - str.   11:00 Composer.

—— OVERTURE, OP. 12
    2,*3,2,2 - 4,3,3,1 - timp. - str.   8:00 Composer.

—— PANDORA'S BOX (A SHORT OPERA FOR YOUNG PEOPLE) % (Text: Sally Monsour)
    1(alt. with picc.),1,1,1 - 1,1,0,0 - timp.,perc.(2),glock. - str.
    15:00 G. Schirmer.

—— PASTORALE FOR OBOE AND STRINGS
    ob. - str.   5:00 Composer.

—— PAUL OF TARSUS (FOR BARITONE, CHORUS, ORGAN AND STRINGS)
    org. - str.   40:00 G. Schirmer.

—— PIECE FOR ORCHESTRA, OP. 1 (1937)
    *3,2,2,2 - 4,3,3,0 - timp. - str.   8:00 Composer.

—— PRELUDE AND FUGUE, OP. 14
    *3,*3,*3,*3 - 4,3,3,1 - timp.,perc. (2) - str.   7:00 Gray.

—— PRELUDE AND TOCCATA, OP. 9 (FOR OBOE AND SMALL ORCH.)
    *2,1,2,1 - 2,1,0,0 - timp. - str.   5:00 Composer.

—— QUIET EVENING, OP. 86 (1972)
    fl. - mar. - str.   7:00 Composer.

—— THE ST. LUKE CHRISTMAS STORY (FOR CHORUS AND INSTRUMENTS)
    2 ob. - 2 tpt. - timp. - str.   35:00 G. Schirmer.

—— A SET OF THREE, OP. 65 (FOR SATB CHORUS AND BRASS) (Text: T. H. Ferril)
    0,0,0,0 - 4,3,3,1   10:00 EV.

—— SING WE MERRILY UNTO GOD, OP. 35 (FOR CHORUS AND ORCH.)
    1(alt. with picc.),2,2,2, - 4,3,3,1 - timp. - str.   6:00 Gray.

—— SUITE FOR CELLO AND CHAMBER ORCH., OP. 32 (IN 4 MOVTS.)
    1(alt. with picc.),2,2,2 - 2,2,0,0 - str.   14:00 Composer.

—— SUITE FOR STRINGS, OP. 18
    str.   12:00 Composer.

—— SYMPHONIC PRELUDE IN D MAJOR (WITH BOY'S VOICES) (Text: Robert Browning)
    *3,*3,*3,*3 - 4,3,3,1 - timp. - str.   19:00 Composer.

—— SYMPHONY CONCERTANTE, OP. 57 (FOR HARP, PIANO AND ORCH.)
    1(alt. with picc.),1,2,1 - 2,2,2,0 - timp. - hp. - pf. - str.
    19:00 Composer.

—— SYMPHONY FOR CHORUS AND ORCH., OP. 54 (IN 3 MOVTS.)
    2,*3,*3,2 - 4,3,3,1 - timp.,perc. (3) - str.   30:00 C. Fischer.

—— SYMPHONY NO. 2 (IN 1 MOVT.)
    *3,*3,*4,2 - 4,3,3,1 - timp.,perc. (2) - str.   17:00 Composer.

—— SYMPHONY NO. 3
    *3,2,2,2 - 4,3,3,1 - timp.,perc. (3), glock. - str.   21:00 Composer.

—— SYMPHONY NO. 5
    *3,2,2,2 - 4,3,3,1 - timp.,perc. (2) - str.   14:00 C. Fischer.

—— TENNESSEE VARIATIONS, OP. 39
    1(alt. with picc.),2,2,2 - 4,3,3,1 - timp.,perc. (2) - str.
    9:00 Composer.

—— THIS WE BELIEVE, OP. 90 (ORATORIO) (1975)
    *3,2,2,2 - 3,3,3,0 - timp. - str.   50:00 BroadmanPr.

—— TONE POEM ON THE SQUARE DANCE
    *3,*3,*3,*3 - 4,3,3,1 - timp.,perc.(2-3) - str.   13:00 Composer.

—— TRIO CONCERTANTE, OP. 71 (FOR HORN, TRUMPET, TROMBONE AND CHAMBER ORCH.)
    1(alt. with picc.),1,1,1 - 1,1,1,0 - timp.,perc.(1) - hp. - str.
    18:00 Composer.

EGGE, Klaus
—— CONCERTO FOR CELLO AND ORCH. (1966) (IN 4 MOVTS.)
    3,2,2,2 - 2,2,1,1 - timp.,perc.,cel.,vibra. - hp. - pf. - str.
    29:00 T.O.N.O.

EGGEN, Arne
—— BJØRGULV SPELEMANN (FROM THE "LITI KERSTI" SUITE)
    2,2,2,2 - 1,0,0,0 - timp. - str.   4:00 Ed. Lyche.

—— CANTATA FOR DRAMMEN'S 100TH ANNIVERSARY (FOR SOLO VOICES, MALE CHORUS AND ORCH.) (Text: Lover Stein)
    T.O.N.O.

—— CIACONNA IN G MINOR
    2,2,2,2 - 4,2,3,1 - timp.,perc. - str.   17:00 T.O.N.O.

—— CYMBELIN (4-ACT OPERA) % (Text: Shakespeare - Norwegian by Henrik Rytter)
    2,2,2,2 - 4,2,3,0 - timp.,perc. - hp. - str.   T.O.N.O.

—— FESTIVAL CHORUS, FROM "CYMBELIN" (FOR MIXED CHORUS AND ORCH.)
    2,2,2,2 - 4,2,3,0 - timp.,perc. - hp.   4:00 T.O.N.O.

—— FRAGMENT FROM ACT I OF "CYMBELIN" (FOR TENOR, BASS AND ORCH.)
    2,2,2,2 - 4,2,3,0 - timp.,perc. - hp. - str.   17:00 T.O.N.O.

—— KING OLAV (ORATORIO) (Text: Olav Gullvag)
    2,3,3,3 - 4,3,3,1 - timp.,perc.,cel. - hp. - org. - str.   90:00 T.O.N.O.

—— MJØSEN (FOR MIXED CHORUS AND ORCH.) (Text: Hulda Garborg)
    2,2,2,2 - 4,2,3,1 - timp.,perc. - hp. - str.   18:00 T.O.N.O.

—— OLAV LILJEKRANS: DANCE SCENES FROM THE OPERA (IN 4 MOVEMENTS)
    2,2,2,2 - 4,2,3,1 - timp.,perc. - hp. - str.   8:00 Ed. Lyche.

—— OLAV LILJEKRANS: FRAGMENT FROM THE OPERA
    2,2,2,2 - 4,2,3,1 - timp.,perc. - str.   20:00 T.O.N.O.

—— OLAV LILJEKRANS: OLAV'S MONOLOGUE AND ARIA (FOR TENOR AND ORCH.) (Text: Henrik Ibsen)
    2,2,2,2 - 4,2,3,1 - timp.,perc. - str.   4:30 T.O.N.O.

—— OLAV LILJEKRANS (OPERA) % (Text: Henrik Ibsen)
    2,2,2,2 - 4,2,3,1 - timp.,perc.,cel. - hp. - str.   T.O.N.O.

—— OLAV'S STORY (FROM ACT I OF "OLAV LILJEKRANS") (FOR TENOR AND ORCH.) (Text: Henrik Ibsen)
    2,2,2,2 - 4,2,1,0 - cel. - hp. - str.   T.O.N.O.

—— SUITE FROM THE PLAY "LITI KERSTI" (IN 4 MOVTS.)
    2,2,2,2 - 4,2,3,1 - timp.,perc. - str.   16:00 T.O.N.O.

—— SYMPHONIC INTERMEZZO FROM "LITI KERSTI"
    2,2,2,2 - 4,2,3,0 - timp.,perc. - str.   T.O.N.O.

EGGLESTON, Anne
—— AUTUMNAL CLOUDS (FOR BARITONE AND ORCH.) (1958) (Text: John Gould Fletcher)
    *3,2,2,2 - 4,3,3,1 - timp.,perc.,cel. - str.   12:30 CanMusCtr.

—— INTERLUDE FOR SMALL ORCHESTRA (1957)
    *2(1 alt. with alto fl.),1,*3,1 - 1,2,3,0 - timp.,perc. - hp.(or pf.) - str.   3:00 CanMusCtr.

—— ON CITADEL HILL (THEME AND SIX VARIATIONS) (FOR STRINGS) (1964)
    str.   5:00 CanMusCtr.

—— THREE PIECES FOR ORCHESTRA (1956)
    2,2,2,2 - 4,2,3,1 - timp.,perc. - str.   10:00 CanMusCtr.

EHLE, Robert
—— SOUND PIECE
    3,3,3,3 -5,3,4,1 - timp.,cel. - hp. - str.   10:00 C. Fischer.

EHRENSPERGER, Carlos
—— PRELUDIO AL SIMPOSIO
    2,2,2,2 - 2,2,0,0 - timp.,perc. - hp. - str.   6:00 S.U.I.S.A.

—— DER SCHWARZE TOD TANZT MIT (MUSIK ZU EINEM BALLETT)
    2,2,2,2 - 4,2,3,1 - timp.,perc.,cel. - hp. - pf. - str.   20:00 S.U.I.S.A.

EHRLICH, Abel
—— BASHRAV (FOR CHOIR OF VIOLINS)
    Vlns.   10:00 IsMuPublns.

—— CONCERTO FOR 10 VIOLINS
    10 vln.   9:00 A.C.U.M.

—— MUSIC FOR CHAMBER ORCHESTRA
    1,1,1,2 - 1,1,0,0 - str.   12:00 A.C.U.M.

—— MUSIC FOR ORCHESTRA
    2,2,2,2 - 4,3,3,1 - perc.(3) - str.   15:00 A.C.U.M.

—— SYMPHONIC BASHRAV
    2,2,*3,2 - 4,3,3,1 - timp.,xyl. - str.   10:00 IsMuPublns.

—— TIME STRUCTURES
    str.   11:00 A.C.U.M.

EHRSTRÖM, Otto
—— BARBARESQUE (1924)
    2,2,2,2 - 2,2,0,0 - timp.,perc. - hp. - str.   8:00 FinnMICtr.

—— HYMNUS JUVENALIS (FOR SATB CHORUS AND ORCH.)
    3,2,2,3 - 6,3,3,1 - timp.,perc.(4),bells - str.   6:00 FinnMICtr.

—— INVOCATION (FROM "IN THE WOODLANDS") (1933)
    2,2,3,3 - 4,3,3,0 - timp.,perc. - str.   9:00 FinnMICtr.

—— MUSIC TO JUHANI AHO'S PLAY "IN THE WOODLANDS" (1925)
    1,1,2,1 - 1,2,1,0 - timp.,perc.,cel. - hp. - str.   20:00 FinnMICtr.

—— PASTORALE (1930)
    1,1,1,1 - 3,2,0,0 - timp.,perc. - hp. - str.   14:00 FinnMICtr.

—— SERENADE TO A YOUNG WITCH (FOR CELLO AND
ORCH.) (1927)
1,1,2,1 - 2,2,0,0 - timp.,perc. - hp. - str.   9:00 FinnMICtr.
—— SUITE CONCERTANTE FOR STRINGS (1928)
str.   27:00 FinnMICtr.
—— SYMPHONY
2,2,2,2 - 4,2,2,0 - timp.,perc. - str.   40:00 FinnMICtr.
—— WENN GOT SICH ERHEBT (FOR 4 SOLO VOICES, SATB
CHORUS AND ORCH.) (Text: Klopstock)
3,2,2,3 - 4,4,3,1 - timp.,perc.(3, incl. 2 on timp.) - 2-6 hp. - org. -
str.   25:00 FinnMICtr.

EICHHEIM, Henry
—— TWO ORIENTAL IMPRESSIONS
                                                      SPAM.

EICHNER, Ernest - ROTHWELL, Evelyn
—— CONCERTO FOR OBOE AND STRINGS
ob. - str.   15:00 Oxford.

EICHNER, Ernst - BODART, Eugen
—— SYMPHONY IN B FLAT MAJOR
0,2,0,0 - 2,0,0,0 - str.   19:00 Mannheimer.
—— SYMPHONY IN C MAJOR
2 fl.(or 2 ob. or 2 cl.) - 2,2,0,0 - timp. - str.   15:00 Mannheimer.
—— SYMPHONY IN E FLAT MAJOR
2,0,2,0 - 2,0,0,0 - str.   17:00 Mannheimer.
—— SYMPHONY IN F MAJOR
2,0,0,0 - 2,0,0,0 - str.   18:00 Mannheimer.
—— SYMPHONY IN G MAJOR
0,2,0,0 - 2,0,0,0 - str.   15:00 Mannheimer.

EICHNER, Ernst - SCHROEDER, Felix
—— CONCERTO IN D MAJOR FOR HARP AND ORCH.
2,0,0,0 - 2,0,0,0 - hp. - str.   26:00 Mannheimer.

EIGER, Walter
—— AMERICAN YOUTH OVERTURE
3,2,2,2 - 4,3,3,1 - timp.,perc. - str.   7:30 Mills.
—— CONCERTO GROSSO FOR SYMPHONY ORCHESTRA AND
JAZZ ENSEMBLE (IN 3 MOVTS.)
Orch.: 2,2,2,2 - 4,2,1,1 - timp.,perc. - str.   28:00 Bourne.
Jazz Ensemble: 2 alto sax., 2 ten. sax., 1 bar. sax. - 4 tpt.,4 trb. -
perc. - guit.(ad lib.) - d.-b.
—— MERRY CHRISTMAS OVERTURE
                                                      5:00 C.A.P.A.C.
—— OVERTURE FANTASY ON CANADIAN FOLK TUNES
3,2,2,2 - 4,3,3,1 - timp.,perc. - str.   7:00 Southern.

EINEM, Gottfried von
—— AN DIE NACHGEGORENEN, OP. 42 (FOR SOLO VOICES,
SATB CHORUS AND ORCH.)
                                                      42:00 Bo. Hawkes.
—— BALLADE FOR ORCHESTRA
3,2,2,2 - 4,3,3,1 - timp. - str.   14:00 G. Schirmer.
—— BRUCKNER DIALOG, OP. 39 ("DIALOG MIT BRUCKNER")
2,2,2,2 - 4,3,3,1 - timp. - str.   14:00 Bo. Hawkes.
—— CONCERTO FOR VIOLIN AND ORCH., OP. 33
2,2,2,2 - 4,2,0,0 - timp.,perc. - hp. - str.   40:00 Bo. Hawkes.
—— HEXAMERON,OP. 37
3,2,2,2 - 4,3,3,1 - timp.,perc. - str.   30:00 Bo. Hawkes.
—— PHILADELPHIA SYMPHONY, OP. 28
3,2,2,2 - 4,3,3,1 - timp. - str.   18:00 Bo. Hawkes.
—— ROSA MYSTICA, OP. 40 (FOR VOICE AND ORCH.) (Text:
H.C. Artmann)
2,2,2,2 - 2,2,1,0 - timp. - str.   18:20 Bo. Hawkes.
—— VON DER LIEBE, OP. 30 (LYRICAL FANTASY, FOR VOICE
AND ORCH.) (Texts: Juan Ramon Jimenez, Bert Brecht and
Gabriela Mistral)
3,2,2,2 - 4,2,2,1 - timp.,perc. - str.   17:30 Bo. Hawkes.
—— DER ZERRISSENE (OPERA) % (Text: G. Von Einem and B.
Blacher)
3,2,2,2 - 4,3,3,1 - perc. - str.   Bo. Hawkes.

EISBRENNER, Werner
—— MUSIK FÜR ORCHESTER
2,*3,*3,*3 - 4,3,3,1 - perc. - hp. - str.   12:00 Henmar.
—— TWO PIECES FOR STRING ORCH. (ALLEGRO AND
ADAGIO)
str.   13:00 Henmar.
—— VORSPIEL ZU EINER KOMÖDIE
2,2,2,2 - 3,3,3,1 - perc. - hp. - str.   5:00 Ries-Erler.

EISENMANN, Rudolf
—— FESTLICHE SUITE FÜR GROSSES ORCHESTER (IN 4
MOVTS.)
3,2,2,2 - 4,3,2,1 - timp.,perc. - hp. - pf. - str.   22:00 Ruhle.

EISENMANN, Will
—— KONFRONTATIONEN, OP. 85 (FÜR FLÖTE UND GROSSES
ORCHESTER)
3,3,3,3 - 2,2,3,1 - timp.,perc. - hp. - pf. - str.   11:00 S.U.I.S.A.
—— THE LITTLE MERMAID (BALLET SUITE, AFTER HANS
CHRISTIAN ANDERSEN)
3,3,3,3 - 2,3,4,1 - timp.,perc. - hp. - str.   6:30 F. Colombo.
—— PRIMAVERA ESPAGNOLA (SINFONISCHE SUITE)
3,2,2,3 - 2,3,3,0 - perc. - pf. - str.   14:00 T & J.

EISENSTEIN, Alfred
—— ADAGIO FOR ORCHESTRA
2,2,2,2 - 4,2,3,1 - timp. - hp. - str.   15:00 P.MusPubCo.
—— IMPROMPTU (TONE POEM)
*3,2,2,2 - 2,3,3,1 - timp.,perc.,cel. - hp. - str.   14:00 P.MusPubCo.
—— MELODIC REFLECTIONS (FOR CELLO AND ORCHESTRA)
2,1,2,1 - 2,0,0,0 - timp.,cel. - hp. - str.   6:00 P.MusPubCo.
—— MOVEMENTS FOR STRING ORCHESTRA
str.   10:00 P.MusPubCo.
—— PETITE SUITE (BALLET) % (IN 4 MOVTS.)
*3,2,2,2 - 4,2,3,1 - timp.,perc.,cel.,glock. - str.   9:10 P.MusPubCo.

EISLER, Hanns
—— FIVE ORCHESTRAL PIECES (1938)
1,1,1,1 - 1,1,1,0 - perc. - str.   13:00 Tetra.
—— DAS VORBILD (THE EXAMPLE) (TRIPTYCH FOR ALTO
AND ORCH.) (Text: Goethe)
1,1,1,1 - 2,0,0,0 - str.   Tetra.

EISMA, Will
—— CONCERTO FOR TWO VIOLINS AND ORCH. (1961)
1,3,2,2 sax.,2 - 4,4,3,1 - timp.,perc.,vibra. - pf. - str.
                                                      14:00 Henmar.
—— CONCERTO NO. 3 FOR ORCHESTRA (1960)
3,3,4,3 - 4,3,3,1 - timp.,perc.,cel.,xyl. - hp. - hpsc. - str.
                                                      15:00 Henmar.
—— TAURUS A (1963)
3,3,3,3 sax.,3 - 4,3,3,1 - timp.,perc.,cel.,vibra.,xyl. - hp. - pf. - str.
                                                      10:00 Henmar.
—— VANBRIDGE CONCERTO (FOR HORN AND ORCH.)
3,1,2,1 - 4,1,1,1 - timp.,perc.,cel. - pf. - str.   Henmar.

EITLER, Esteban
—— SERIE BOLIVIANA (FOR FLUTE AND STRINGS)
fl. - str.   13:00 Henmar.

EK, Gunnar
—— CONCERT-OVERTURE NO. 2
2,2,2,2 - 2,2,1,0 - timp.,perc. - str.   6:30 S.T.I.M.
—— CONCERTINO FOR STRING ORCH. (1971)
str.   10:00 Fleisher.
—— CONCERTO IN B MINOR, FOR PIANO AND ORCH.
2,2,2,2 - 4,2,3,1 - timp.,perc. - pf. - str.   25:00 S.T.I.M.
—— DORIC SUITE (FOR WOODWINDS AND STRINGS)(REV.
1969)
                                                      10:00 Fleisher.
—— FANTASY AND FUGUE FOR STRING ORCH.
str.   11:00 S.T.I.M.
—— FANTASY FOR CELLO AND STRING ORCH.
str.   7:00 S.T.I.M.
—— FANTASY FOR VIOLIN AND ORCH.
2,2,2,2 - 2,2,1,0 - timp. - str.   7:00 Gehrmans.
—— SCHERZO
2,2,2,2 - 4,3,3,1 - timp.,perc.,cel. - str.   5:30 Bo Hawkes.
or:
2,2,2,2 - 2,2,1,0 - timp.,perc.,cel. - str.
—— SUITE FOR ORCH.
2,2,2,2 - 4,2,1,1 - timp. - str.   13:30 S.T.I.M.
or:
2,2,2,2 - 2,2,1,1 - timp. - str.
—— SWEDISH FANTASY
2,2,2,2 - 2,1,1,0 - timp. - str.   6:00 Gehrmans.
—— SYMPHONY NO. 1
2,2,2,2 - 4,2,1,1 - timp.,perc.,cel. - str.   28:00 S.T.I.M.
or:
2,2,2,2 - 2,2,1,0 - timp.,perc.,cel. - str.
—— SYMPHONY NO. 2
2,2,2,2 - 2,2,1,1 - timp.,perc. - str.   28:00 Gehrmans.

or:
2,2,2,2 - 2,2,1,0 - timp.,perc. - str.
—— SYMPHONY NO. 3
2,2,2,2 - 4,2,3,1 - timp.,perc. - str. 26:00 S.T.I.M.
or:
2,2,2,2 - 2,2,1,1 - timp.,perc. - str.
—— VARIATIONER ÖVER ETT KORALTEMA (1969)
str. 9:00 Fleisher.

EKLOF, Ejnar
—— SUITE FOR ORCHESTRA (IN 4 MOVTS.)
2,1,2,1 - 2,2,1,0 - timp.,perc. - str. 15:00 S.T.I.M.

EKLUND, Hans
—— CONCERTO FOR CELLO AND ORCH., OP. 8
(KAMMARMUSIK NR. 1) (1955)
2,2,2,2 - 2,2,0,0 - timp.,perc.(2) - str. 18:30 S.T.I.M.
—— CONCERTO FOR PIANO AND ORCH. (KAMMARMUSIK NR.
4) (1959)
1,1,1,1 - 2,1,0,0 - timp.,perc.(2) - pf. - str. 14:00 S.T.I.M.
—— CONCERTO FOR VIOLIN AND ORCH. (KAMMARMUSIK
NR. 2) (1957)
2,2,2,2 - 2,2,0,0 - timp.,perc.(2) - str. 18:00 S.T.I.M.
—— FACCE (1964)
2,2,2,2 - 2,2,1,0 - timp.,perc.(2) - str. 10:00 S.T.I.M.
—— FANTASIA (FOR CELLO AND STRINGS)(1971)
str. 11:00 Gehrmans.
—— INTERLUDE (1966)
2,2,2,2 - 2,2,1,0 - timp.,perc. - str. 9:00 Gehrmans.
—— INTRODUZIONE ED ALLEGRO (1972)
hpsc. - str. 10:00 Fleisher.
—— KANTAT TILL SANDVIKENS JERNVERKS 100 -
ARSJUBILEUM (FOR BARITONE, MIXED CHORUS AND
ORCH.)
2,2,2,2 - 2,2,1,0 - timp.,perc.(2) - str. 25:00 S.T.I.M.
—— MUSIC FOR ORCHESTRA (1960)
2,2,2,2 - 4,2,3,1 - timp.,perc.(3) - str. 19:00 Gehrmans.
—— MUSICA DA CAMERA, OP. 10 (1956)
tpt. - perc.,xyl. - pf. - str. 22:00 Suecia.
—— MUSICA DA CAMERA VI (FOR OBOE AND SMALL
ORCH.)(1970)
ob. - timp.,perc. - str. 15:00 H.BuschMfl.
—— PASTORAL VARIATIONS (1974)
str. Fleisher.
—— PEZZO ELEGIACO (FOR CELLO AND CHAMBER
ORCH.)(1969)
perc. - str. 10:00 Gehrmans.
—— PRIMAVERA (1967)
str. 8:00 Fleisher.
—— SYMPHONY NO. 1 (SINFONIA SERIA) (1958)
2,2,2,2 - 4,2,3,1 - timp.,perc.(2) - str. 20:00 Gehrmans.
—— SYMPHONY NO. 2 (SINFONIA BREVE)(1964)
2,2,2,2 - 4,2,3,1 - timp.,perc.(3) - str. 16:00 Gehrmans.
—— SYMPHONY NO. 3 (SINFONIA RUSTICA)(1968)
3,2,2,2 - 4,3,3,1 - timp.,perc.(4) - str. 14:00 Gehrmans.
—— SYMPHONY NO. 4 (IN MEMORIAM HJALMAR
BRANTING)(1974)
2,1,2,1 - 4,2,2,1 - timp.,perc. - str. Fleisher.
—— TOCCATA (1966)
2,2,2,2 - 4,2,3,1 - timp.,perc.(2) - str. 8:00 S.T.I.M.

ELGAR, Edward
—— CONCERTO IN B MINOR, OP.61, FOR VIOLIN AND ORCH.
2,2,2,2,c.-bn.(ad lib.) - 4,2,3,0-1 - timp. - str. 50:00 Novello.
—— CONCERTO IN E MINOR, OP. 85, FOR CELLO AND ORCH.
2(2nd alt. with picc.),2,2,2 - 4,2,3,0-1 - timp. - str. 30:00 Novello.
—— THE CROWN OF INDIA (SUITE) (IN 5 MOVTS.)
3,2,2-3,2-3 - 4,3,3,1 - timp.,perc. - hp. - str. 16:30 Bo. Hawkes.
—— FALSTAFF (SYMPHONIC STUDY), OP. 68
3,3,3,3 - 4,3,3,1 - timp.,perc. - 2 hp. - str. 30:00 Novello.
—— FALSTAFF (TWO INTERLUDES)
3,2,2,2 - 2 hn. - hp.(ad lib.) - str. 7:00 Novello.
—— THE KINGDOM: PRELUDE, OP. 51
3,3,3,3 - 3,3,3,1 - timp.,perc. - 2 hp. - org. - str. 9:00 Novello.
—— NURSERY SUITE
2,2,2,2 - 4,2,3,1 - timp.,perc.,glock. - hp. - str. 20:00 Fox.
—— POLONIA (SYMPHONIC PRELUDE)
*3,*3,*3,*3 - 4,3,3,1 - timp.,perc. (6) - 2 hp. - org. - str.
  17:00 Novello.
—— POMP AND CIRCUMSTANCE MARCHES
  Bo. Hawkes.
NO. 4 IN G
3,3,3,3 - 4,3,3,1 - timp.,perc. - hp. - str. 5:00

NO. 5 IN C
3,3,3,3 - 4,3,3,1 - timp.,perc. - str. 5:00
—— ROMANCE FOR BASSOON AND ORCH., OP. 62
2,2,2,2 - 3,0,3,0 - timp. - str. 8:00 Novello.
—— SEA PICTURES (CYCLE OF FIVE SONGS FOR CONTRALTO
AND ORCH.) OP. 37
2,2,2,2 - 4,2,3,1 - timp.,perc. - hp. - str. 12:00 Bo. Hawkes.
—— THE WAND OF YOUTH SUITE NO. 1 (IN 7 MOVTS.)
3,2,2,3 - 4,2,3,1 - timp.,perc. - hp. - str. 18:00 Novello.
—— THE WAND OF YOUTH SUITE NO. 2 (IN 6 MOVTS.)
3,2,2,2 - 4,2,3,1 - timp.,perc. - hp. - str. 18:00 Novello.

ELGAR, Edward - GODFREY, Charles
—— THREE BAVARIAN DANCES
2,2,2,2 - 4,2,3,1 - timp.,perc. - str. 13:30 Bo. Hawkes.

ELGAR, Edward - SCHMID, Adolf
—— CARILLON
*3,*3,*3,*3 - 4,3,3,1 - timp.,perc. (6), glock. - hp. - org. - str.
  Novello.

ELGAR, Edward - YOUNG, Percy M.
—— SUITE FROM "THE SPANISH LADY"
str. Galaxy.

ELIE, Justin - ROBERTS, Charles J.
—— ANCIENT MOUNTAIN LEGEND (SUITE) (IN 2 MOVTS.)
  C. Fischer.
—— BABYLON (SUITE) (IN 4 MOVTS.)
  C. Fischer.
—— KISKAYA (SUITE ABORIGÈNE) (IN 4 MOVTS.)
  C. Fischer.

ELISHA, Haim
—— TEN VARIATIONS FOR ORCHESTRA
3(3rd alt. with picc.),2,*3,*3 - 4,3,3,0 - perc. - pf. - str.
  12:00 Broude.

ELIZALDE, Federico
—— SINFONIE CONCERTANTE (FOR PIANO AND ORCH.)
2,2,2,2 - 2,2,1,0 - perc. - pf. - str. 16:00 G. Schirmer.

ELKUS, Albert I.
—— IMPRESSIONS FROM A GREEK TRAGEDY
  Kalmus.

ELKUS, Jonathan
—— THE MANDARIN (OPERA) %
1,1,2,1 - 2,1,1,0 - perc. - banjo,guit. - str. 105:00 C. Fischer.

ELLBERG, Ernst
—— CONCERT OVERTURE IN F MINOR
2,2,2,2 - 4,2,3,0 - timp. - str. 9:00 S.T.I.M.
—— PRELUDE AND FUGUE IN C MAJOR (FOR STRINGS)
str. 6:00 S.T.I.M.
—— SYMPHONY IN D MAJOR
2,2,2,2 - 4,2,3,0 - timp. - str. 33:00 S.T.I.M.

ELLINGER, Albert
—— CONCERTO FOR CELLO AND ORCH.
2,1,2,1 - 2,2,2,0 - timp. - pf. - str. 22:00 Mannheimer.
—— CONCERTO FOR PIANO AND ORCH.
*3,2,2,2 - 0,3,3,0 - pf. - str. 23:00 Mannheimer.
—— POÉME ÉROTIQUE (FOR CELLO AND STRINGS)
str. 7:00 Mannheimer.
—— SYMPHONIC MUSIC
3,2,2,3 - 4,4,3,1 - timp.,perc. - hp. - str. 30:00 Mannheimer.
—— THREE CANZONE FOR OBOE AND STRINGS
ob. - str. 8:00 Mannheimer.
—— THREE PIECES FOR CELLO AND STRINGS
str. 12:00 Mannheimer.

ELLIS, Merrill
—— CENTRIFUSION (FOR ORCH. AND LIVE ELECTRIC
INSTRUMENTS) (1967)
*3,2,2,2 - 5,3,3,1 - timp.,perc.(5),bells,cel.,xyl. - synthesizer - pf. -
str. 10:00 MCA Music.
—— CHAMBER SYMPHONY (1953) (IN 3 MOVTS.)
2,1,2,2 - 3,2,3,0 - timp.,perc.(3) - str. 12:00 Composer.
—— FESTIVAL OVERTURE (1960)
  11:00 Composer.

—— THE GREAT GIFT (FOR NARRATOR, 4 SOLO VOICES,
CHORUS, ORGAN, PIANO AND ORCH.) (1958)
60:00 Composer.
—— KALEIDOSCOPE (FOR SOPRANO, SYNTHESIZER AND
ORCH.) (1967) (Text: Robert Lockwood)
*3,2,2,2 - 5,3,3,1 - timp.,perc.(6),bells,xyl. - electronic
sound-synthesizer - str. 12:00 MCA Music.
—— RONDO FOR ORCHESTRA (1950)
6:30 Composer.
—— SINFONIETTA NO. 2 (IN 3 MOVTS.) (1956)
*3,2,*3,2 - 4,3,3,1 - timp.,perc.(3),bells - pf. - str.
15:00 Composer.
—— TOCCATA FOR ORCHESTRA (FESTIVE OVERTURE)
*3,2,*3,2 - 4,3,3,1 - timp.,perc.(4),bells - pf. - str. 9:45 Composer.

ELLSASSER, Richard
—— LAMENT OF THE LONELY LAKE (FOR OBOE AND ORCH.)
2,1,2,2 - 2,2,2,0 - timp.,perc.(2),bells,xyl. - hp. - pf.(or cel.) - str.
9:00 Fema.
—— SUNRISE CONCERTO (IN 1 MOVT.)
2,2,2,2 - 4,3,3,1 - timp.,perc.(2) - pf. - str. 8:00 P. Maurice.

ELLSTEIN, Abraham
—— CONCERTO FOR PIANO AND ORCH. ("NEGEV"
CONCERTO)
2,2,2,2 - 4,2,3,1 - timp.,perc. - pf. - str. 18:00 Mills.
—— ODE TO THE KING OF KINGS (CANTATA) (FOR SOPRANO,
BARITONE, SATB CHORUS AND ORCH.)
2,2,2,2 - 4,2,3,1 - timp.,perc. - str. Belw-Mills.
—— PHANTASMATA
*4,*4,*4,*4 - 4,3,3,1 - timp.,perc. - str. 25:00 Mills.

ELMORE, Robert
—— ALL YE SERVANTS OF THE LORD (FOR SATB CHORUS
AND ORCH.)
2,2,2,2 - 2,2,2,0 - timp.,perc. - str. 4:00 Galaxy.
—— CONCERTO IN C MINOR, FOR ORGAN AND ORCH. (IN 3
MOVTS.)
3(3rd alt. with picc.),*3,*3,*3 - 4,4,3,1 - timp. 21:00 Composer.
—— THE LEGEND OF SLEEPY HOLLOW (SUITE) (IN 4 MOVTS.)
2,2,2,2 - 3,2,1,0 - timp.,perc. (3) - str. 17:30 Composer.
—— NARRATIVE FOR HORN AND ORCH.
2(2nd alt. with picc.),2,2,2, - 4,3,2,0 - timp.,perc. (2) - str.
7:00 Composer.
—— THE PRODIGAL SON (A SERMON FOR MEN'S CHORUS
AND ORCH.)
2,2,3,2 - 4,3,2,0 - timp.,perc. (3), cel. - hp. - str. 20:00 Gray.
—— VALLEY FORGE - 1777 (TONE POEM)
3(3rd alt. with picc.),*3,3(3rd alt. with b.-cl.),*3 - 4,4,3,1 -
timp.,perc.(2),cel. - hp. - str. 12:00 Composer.
—— VOCALISE (FOR SATB CHORUS AND ORCH.)
3(3rd alt. with picc.),3(3rd alt. with Eng. hn.)3,(3rd alt. with
b.-cl.),3(3rd alt. with c.-bn.) - 4,4,0,0 - timp.,perc. - hp. - str.
4:00 Composer.

ELOKAS, Ossi
—— THE PHANTOM CASTLE (BALLAD) (FOR SOPRANO,
BARITONE, MALE CHORUS AND ORCH.) (1952)
2,2,2,2 - 3,2,2,0 - timp.,perc. - hp. - str. 15:00 FinnMICtr.
—— PSALM 32 (FOR BARITONE, SATB CHORUS, ORGAN AND
STRINGS) (1948)
org. - str. 6:00 Westerlund.
—— THE WAY TO THE LIGHT (FOR BARITONE, BOYS' CHORUS,
SATB CHORUS AND ORCH.) (1952)
1,1,2,1 - 1,2,2,0 - timp.,perc. - str. 25:00 FinnMICtr.

ELOVAARA, Toivo
—— FAIRY TALE SUITE (1932)
2,2,2,2 - 2,2,1,0 - timp.,perc.(4) - str. 7:00 FinnMICtr.
—— GRAIN OF WISDOM (1938)
1,1,1,1 - 1,2,1,0 - timp.,perc.(3) - str. 25:00 FinnMICtr.
—— MIDSUMMER SUITE (FOR PIANO AND ORCH.)
2,1,1,1 - 1,1,0,0 - timp. - pf. - str. 10:00 FinnMICtr.
—— SINFONIETTA (1935)
str. 15:00 FinnMICtr.
—— SYMPHONIC POEM (1935)
2,3,2,2 - 3,0,1,0 - timp.,perc. - str. 10:00 FinnMICtr.
—— SYMPHONY IN A MINOR (1949)
2,2,2,2 - 4,4,3,0 - timp. - str. 19:00 FinnMICtr.

ELOY, Jean Claude
—— EQUIVALENCES (FOR 18 INSTRUMENTS)
1*2,E^{b}cl.,2,1 - 1,1,1,0 - perc.(6) - hp. - pf.(alt. with cel.)
13:00 Presser.
—— ETUDE III
2,2,2,2 - 2,2,2,0 - perc.(5),cel. - hp. - pf. - str. 20:00 Presser.

ELTON, Antony
—— CONCERTO (FOR BRASS AND PERCUSSION)
13:00 A.P.R.A.
—— MUSIC FOR A YOUNG ORCHESTRA (FOR SMALL ORCH.)
4:30 A.P.R.A.
—— SERENADE NO. 1 (4 DESCRIPTIVE PIECES) (FOR SMALL
ORCH.)
8:00 A.P.R.A.
—— SERENADE NO. 2 (6 DESCRIPTIVE PIECES)
8:00 A.P.R.A.
—— SYMPHONIC SUITE
11:00 A.P.R.A.
—— SYMPHONY, OP. 30 (1964)
2,2,2,2 - 4,3,3,1 - timp., perc. - str. 27:00 P.R.S.

ELWELL, Herbert
—— BLUE SYMPHONY (FOR MEZZO-SOPRANO OR TENOR
AND STRINGS)
str. 20:00 Rochester.
—— CONCERT SUITE FOR VIOLIN AND ORCH. (IN 3 MOVTS.)
*3,2(2nd alt. with Eng. hn.),2,2 - 4,2,3,1 - timp.,perc.(2), cel.,xyl. -
str. 19:00 Rochester.
—— THE FOREVER YOUNG (A RITUAL) (FOR SOLO VOICE
AND ORCH.) (IN 4 MOVTS.)
*3,2(2nd alt. with Eng. hn.),*3,*3 - 4,3,3,1 - timp.,perc. (3),cel., -
str. 24:45 Composer.
—— INTRODUCTION AND ALLEGRO
*3,2,2,2 - 4,3,3,1 - timp.,perc.(2) - hp. - str. 11:30 AmerMusEd.
—— ODE FOR ORCHESTRA
2(2nd alt. with picc.),*3,*3,2 - 4,3,3,1 - timp.,perc. (2), cel. - str.
9:30 Bo. Hawkes.
—— PASTORALE FOR VOICE AND ORCH. (SYMPHONY, AFTER
"SONG OF SOLOMON") (IN 4 MOVTS.)
3(3rd alt. with picc.),*3,*3,*3 - 4,3,3,1 - timp.,perc.(4),bells,cel.,
glock.,xyl. - hp. - str. 33:40 Rochester.
—— SUITE FROM THE BALLET "THE HAPPY HYPOCRITE"
*3,*3,*3,*3 - 4,3,3,1 - timp., perc. (3),cel. - hp. - str.
21:30 C. Fischer.

ELY, Carroll
—— EPITAPH TO BARNEY (FOR STRINGS)
str. G. Schirmer.

EMBORG, Jens Laursøn
—— CONCERTO FOR ORGAN AND ORCH., OP. 92
0,0,0,0 - 0,2,2,0 - timp.,perc. - org. - str. 20:00 G. Schirmer.
—— CONCERTO FOR STRINGS AND PIANO, OP. 72
pf. - str. 12:00 Henmar.
—— THE MOORS OF JUTLAND (DEN JYDSKE HEDE)
*3,2,*3,2 - 4,2,2,1 - timp.,perc. - str. G. Schirmer.
—— THE TWELVE MASKS, OP. 50 (THEME WITH 12
VARIATIONS AND A GIGUE)
3,2,3,2 - 4,2,2,0 - timp.,perc.,cel. - hp. - str. 24:00 Henmar.

ENDERS, Anton
—— CONCERTINO FOR ENGLISH HORN AND STRING ORCH.
Eng. hn. - str. 12:00 Mannheimer.

ENDERS, Harvey
—— DEATH IN HARLEM (NARRATIVE FOR BARITONE AND
ORCH.)
1,1(alt. with Eng. hn.),2(1 alt. with b.-cl.),1 - 2,2,2,1 - timp.,perc.
(2) - hp. - str. 10:00 Composer.

ENDLER, Johann Samuel - VOGT, Carl August
—— OVERTURE NO. 7 IN D MAJOR (FOR VIOLIN AND ORCH.)
0,1,0,1 - 0,3,0,0 - hpsc. - timp. - str. 19:00 Mannheimer.

ENDLER, Johann Samuel - WOJCIECHOWSKI - BUCK
—— SINFONIA CONCERTANTE IN D MAJOR, FOR TRUMPET
(IN D) AND SMALL ORCH.
0,1,0,1 - 2,1,0,0 - timp. - cemb. - str. 20:00 F. Colombo.

ENDO, Ryo
—— RITSU (FOR OBOE AND ORCH.) (1966)
    2,1,2,2 - 2,0,0,0 - timp.,perc.(4),cel.,glock.,vibra.,xyl. - 2 hp. - pf.
                                    10:00 MCA Music.

ENESCO, Georges
—— CONCERT OVERTURE, OP. 32
    3,3,3,3 - 4,4,3,1 - timp.,perc.,cel.,glock. - hp. - pf. - str.
                                      9:00 Salabert.
—— DIXTUOR (SUITE FOR WINDS, IN D MAJOR), OP. 14
    2,*2,2,2 - 2,0,0,0   26:00 Salabert.
—— SUITE NO. 2 IN C MAJOR (IN 6 MOVTS.)
    3,3,2,2 - 4,2,3,1 - timp.,perc.(3),glock. - hp. - pf. - str.
                                    30:00 Salabert.
—— SUITE NO. 3 FOR ORCH., OP. 27 ("SUITE VILLAGEOISE")
    3,3,3,3 - 4,3,3,1 - timp.,perc.,cel.,glock.,xyl. - hp. - pf. - str.
                                    26:00 Salabert.
—— SYMPHONIE DE CHAMBRE
    1,*2,1,1 - 1,1,0,0 - pf. - str.   16:00 Salabert.
—— SYMPHONY NO. 2, OP. 17
    3,3,4,3 - 4,3,3,1 - timp.,perc.,cel. - harm. - pf. - hp. - str.
                                    40:00 Salabert.
—— SYMPHONY NO. 3, OP. 21 (WITH VOICE AND CHORUS)
                                        Salabert.
—— VOX MARIS, OP. 31 (FOR CHORUS AND ORCH.)
    4,4,4,4 - 6,4,3,2 - timp.,perc.(3) - 2 hp. - pf. - str. 20:00 Salabert.

ENGEL, Jehuda
—— RHYTHMS OF YOUTH (SINFONIETTA)
    2,2,2,2 - 2,2,0,0 - timp. - str.   18:00 IsMuPublns.

ENGEL, Joel
—— SUITE FROM "THE DYBBUK"
    cl. - pf. - str.   20:00 Transcon.

ENGEL, Lehman
—— THE SOLDIER (OPERA) %
    1(alt. with picc.),0,1(alt. with b.-cl.),1 1,1,1,0 - timp.,perc. (1) - pf.
    - str.   50:00 Chappell.

ENGELMANN, Hans Ulrich
—— ATALANTIC BALLAD, OP. 14-B (MELODRAMA, FOR ALTO,
    BARITONE, PERCUSSION AND STRING ORCH.) (1955)
    perc. - str.   12:00 AhnSimrock.
—— CONCERTO FOR CELLO AND STRING ORCH., OP. 2-A
    str.   10:00 AhnSimrock.
—— ELEGIA E CANTO, OP. 9 (CONCERT ARIA ON A TEXT OF
    SHAKESPEARE) (FOR SOPRANO, PIANO AND STRING
    ORCH.) (1952)
    pf. - str.   12:00 AhnSimrock.
—— EZRA POUND MUSIC, OP. 21 (1959) (FOR CHAMBER ORCH.)
    1(alt. with picc.),*2,0,1 - 0,0,1,0 - perc. - str.(c. and d.-b. section)
                                9:00 AhnSimrock.
—— FIVE ORCHESTRAL PIECES, OP. 16-B (FROM THE MUSICAL
    DRAMA "MAGOG") (1956)
    2(2nd alt. with picc.),2,2,sax.,*3 - 4,4,3,1 -
    timp.,perc.,cel.,vibra.,xyl. - hp. - pf. - str. 15:00 AhnSimrock.
—— IMPROMPTU (1949)
    1(alt. with picc.),1,1,1 - 4,3,3,1 - timp.,perc. - pf. - str.
                                6:00 AhnSimrock.
—— KALEIDOSCOPE (SUITE FOR ORCH.) (1941)
    1,1,1,sax.,1 - 0,3,3,0 - timp.,perc. - str. 10:00 AhnSimrock.
—— LEOPOLDSKRON (DIVERTIMENTO FOR CHAMBER ORCH.)
    (1949)
    1,1,0,sax.,1 - 0,1,1,0 - timp.,perc. - str. 15:00 AhnSimrock.
—— MUSIC FOR STRINGS, BRASS AND PERCUSSION, OP. 3-A
    (1948)
    0,0,0,0 - 4,3,3,1 - timp.,perc.,vibra.,xyl. - str. 10:00 AhnSimrock.
—— NOCTURNES, OP. 18 (1959) (FOR SOPRANO AND ORCH.)
    1,0,0,1 sax.,0 - 0,0,0,0 - perc.,vibra.,xyl. - guit. - hp. - hpsc. - str.
                                15:00 AhnSimrock.
—— ORCHESTRAL FANTASY, OP. 6 (REV. 1963)
    2,2,2,*3 - 4,3,3,1 - timp.,perc.,cel.,vibra.,xyl. - hp. - pf. - str.
                                15:00 AhnSimrock.
—— PARTITA, OP. 12 (1953) (IN 3 MOVTS.)
    3 tpt. - perc. - str.   10:00 AhnSimrock.
—— POLIFONICA, OP. 17 (WITH SOLO ELECTRIC GUITAR)
    (1957)
    1,*1,0,sax.,1 - 1,1,1,0 - perc.,vibra.,xyl. - electric guit. - hp. - str.
                                8:00 AhnSimrock.

—— STRUCTURES, OP. 15 (DEN TATEN DER NEUEN
    BILDHAUER) (1954) (IN 3 MOVTS.)
    1,1,1,1 - 1,1,1,0 - timp.,perc.,vibra.,xyl - hp.(or cel.) - str.
                                6:00 AhnSimrock.
—— TRIAS, OP. 24 (1962) (FOR PIANO, ORCH. AND
    ELECTRONIC TAPE)
    1,1,1,1 - 1,1,1,1 - perc. - tape-recorder - pf. - str.
                             22:00 AhnSimrock.

ENGER, Elling
—— FESTIVAL OVERTURE (FESTSPEL)
    3,2,2,2 - 4,3,3,1 - timp.,perc. - str.   7:00 T.O.N.O.
—— JUBILEE CANTATA (FOR SOLO VOICES, MIXED CHORUS
    AND ORCH.) (Text: Trygve Bjerkrheim)
    1,1,2,2, - 2,2,2,0 - timp.,perc. - org. - str. 100:00 T.O.N.O.
—— NORWAY - THERE IS MUSIC IN THE NAME (NORGE - DET
    TONAR I NAMNET) (FOR SOLO VOICE, MIXED CHORUS
    AND ORCH.) (Text: Trygve Bjerkrheim)
    2,2,2,2 - 4,3,3,1 - timp.,perc. - str.   12:00 T.O.N.O.

ENGLER, Paul
—— PRELUDIUM AND TOCCATA
                                        G.E.M.A.

ENGLERT, Giuseppe
—— ARIA (POUR TIMBALES ET 13 INSTRUMENTS)
                                  10:00 Henmar.

ENGLISH, George Selwyn
—— BOTANY BAY, 1770
                                  12:00 Southern.
—— FOR A ROYAL OCCASION
                                  12:00 A.P.R.A.
—— IMPRESSIONS FOR ORCHESTRA ("DEATH OF A WOMBAT")
                                  20:00 Southern.
—— SINFONIA (1970)
    *3,2,2,*3 - 4,4,4,1 - timp.,perc.(7, incl. 4 on timp.) - hp. - str.
                                10:000 Southern.

ENGLISH, Granville
—— ALABAMA TWILIGHT
    1,1,2,1 - 2,2,1,0 - timp.,perc. - pf. - str.   4:30 Composer.
—— AMONG THE HILLS (SCHERZO)
    2,2,2,2 - 4,3,3,1 - timp.,perc. (3), glock. - hp. - str.
                                6:30 C. Fischer.
—— COLONIAL PORTRAITS (SUITE) (IN 3 MOVTS.)
    cel. - pf. - str.   12:30 Chappell.
—— EVENING BY THE SEA (TONE PICTURE)
    2,2(2nd alt. with Eng. hn.),2,2 - 4,3,3,1 - timp.,perc. (2), glock. -
    hp. - str.   6:30 C. Fischer.
—— IONIAN SUITE (IN 3 MOVTS.)
    3(3rd alt. with picc.),2(2nd alt. with Eng. hn.),2,2 - 4,3,3,1 -
    timp.,perc. (2) hp. - str.   16:00 Composer.
—— AN ISLAND FESTIVAL (BALLET SUITE) (IN 3 MOVTS.)
    3(3rd alt. with picc.),2,2,2 - 4,2,3,1 - timp.,perc.(3) - hp. - str.
                                  9:00 Composer.
—— THE UGLY DUCKLING (CANTATA) (FOR CHILDREN'S
    CHORUS AND ORCH.)
    3(3rd alt. with picc.),2,2,2 - 4,2,3,1 - timp.,perc.(2) - hp. - str.
                                20:00 Gray.

ENGLUND, Einar
—— CONCERTO FOR CELLO AND ORCH. (1954)
    2,2,2,2 - 2,2,2,0 - timp.,perc. - hp. - str. 20:00 FinnMICtr.
—— CONCERTO FOR PIANO AND ORCH. (1955)
    2,2,2,2 - 2,2,2,0 - timp.,perc. - pf. - str. 18:00 FinnMICtr.
—— CONCERTO NO. 2 FOR PIANO AND ORCH. (IN 3 MOVTS.)
    2,2,2,2 - 4,3,3,0 - timp.,perc.(2) - pf. - str. 23:00 FinnMICtr.
—— EPINIKIA (1947)
    3,3,3,3 - 4,3,3,1 - timp.,perc.(4) - hp. - pf. - str. 6:00 FinnMICtr.
—— FOUR DANCE IMPRESSIONS (1954)
    3,2,2,2 - 4,3,3,1 - timp.,perc.(4) - hp. - str. 14:00 FinnMICtr.
—— THE GREAT WALL OF CHINA (1949)
    3,2,3,2 - 4,3,3,1 - timp.,perc.(4) - hp. - pf. - str. 18:00 FinnMICtr.
—— ODYSSEUS (BALLET) %
    2,2,2,0 - 2,2,2,0 - timp.,perc.(5),cel. - hp. - pf. - str.
                                30:00 FinnMICtr.
—— SYMPHONY NO. 1 (1946)
    3,2,2,2 - 4,3,3,1 - timp.,perc. - hp. - str. 38:00 FinnMICtr.
—— SYMPHONY NO. 2 (1948)
    3,2,2,3 - 4,3,3,1 - timp.,perc.,cel. - 2 hp. - pf. - str.
                              30:00 FinnMICtr.

—— SYMPHONY NO. 3 (1971)
    3,3,3,2 - 4,3,3,1 - timp.,perc. - hp. - pf. - str.   27:00 FinnMICtr.
—— THE WHITE REINDEER (1954)
    2,3,3,2 - 2,2,2,0 - timp.,perc. - hp. - str.   10:00 FinnMICtr.

EPHROS, Gershon
—— AEOLIAN (FOR STRINGS)
    str.   13:30 Fleisher.
—— BIBLICAL SUITE (FOR TENOR, CHORUS AND ORCH.) (IN 3 MOVTS.)
    *3,*2,2,2 - 2,2,2,0 - timp.,perc. - hp. - str.   18:00 Bloch.
—— INTRODUCTION AND FUGUE ON A HEBREW THEME (FOR STRINGS)
    str.   8:00 Composer.
—— S'LICHOS SERVICE (MIDNIGHT PENITENTIAL SERVICE) (FOR SOLO VOICE, CHORUS AND ORCH.) (IN 3 SECTIONS)
    *3,2,*3,2 - 4,3,3,1 - timp.,cymb. - hp. (or pf.) - str.   60:00 AmaMusCo.
—— SUITE HEBRAIQUE
    2(2nd alt. with picc.),2,2(2nd alt. with b.-cl.),2 - 4,3,3,1 - timp.,perc. - str.   Fleisher.
—— SUITE HEBRAÏQUE (IN 4 MOVTS.)
    *3,2,*3,2 - 4,3,3,1 - timp.,perc. - hp.(or pf.) - str. 21:00 Composer.

EPSTEIN, Alvin
—— CONCERTO FOR PIANO AND ORCHESTRA (1968)
    1. Drammatico; 2. Thema and Transformations
    2(2nd alt. with picc.),2,2(2nd alt. with b.-cl.),2 - 4,3,2,1 - timp.,perc.(3-4) - hp. - pf. - str.   33:00 Composer.
—— METAMORPHOSIS (FOR WOODWIND TRIO AND STRINGS) (1961) (THEME AND VARIATIONS)
    1,0,1,1 - 0,0,0,0 - str.   10:00 Composer.
—— MUSIC FOR ORCHESTRA (1955) (IN 5 MOVTS.)
    2,2,*3,*3 - 4,3,3,0 - timp.,perc.(3-4) - hp. - pf. - str.   20:00 Composer.

EPSTEIN, David M.
—— MOVEMENT FOR ORCHESTRA
    2,2(2nd alt. with Eng. hn.),2,2 - 4,2,3,0 - timp. - str.   6:30 C. Fischer.
—— MUSIC FOR THE PLAY "JULIUS CAESAR"
    1,1,1,1 - 1,1,1,0 - timp.,perc. - pf. - str.   13:30 C. Fischer.
—— NIGHT VOICES (FOR NARRATOR, OPTIONAL SMALL CHILDREN'S CHORUS AND ORCH.) (1974) (Text: Anne M. Epstein) (IN 4 MOVTS.)
    2(2nd alt. with picc.),2,2(2nd alt. with Eng.hn.),2(2nd alt. with b.-cl.),2 - 2,2,2,1 - timp.,perc.(4),glock.,mar.,vibra.,xyl. - hp. - str.   13:00 C. Fischer.
—— REFLECTIONS (CYCLE OF 4 SONGS) (FOR SOPRANO, HORN AND STRINGS) (Texts: John Keats and Gerard Manley Hopkins)
    hn. - str.   13:00 Presser.
—— SONORITY-VARIATIONS, FOR ORCH. (1967)
    *3,*3,*3,2 - 4,3,3,1 - timp.,perc.(4-5),bells,cel.,vibra.,xyl. - hp. - pf. - str.   15:00 MCA Music.
—— SYMPHONY NO. 1
    1. Andante non troppo; 2. Scherzo; 3. Recitativo - Adagio - Piu mosso
    2(2nd alt. with picc.),2,*3,2 - 4,3,3,0 - timp.,perc.(2),xyl. - str.   20:00 C. Fischer.
—— VENT-URES
    3,3,3,3 - 4,3,2,1 - timp.,perc.   12:00 C. Fischer.

ERB, Marie Joseph
—— EN ALSACE (IN 3 MOVTS.)
    2,2,2,2 - 2,2,1,0 - timp.,perc.,cel.,bells,glock.,xyl. - hp. - pf. - str.   12:00 Baron.

ERDLEN, Hermann
—— BETWEEN DAY AND DREAM (SOLO CANTATA) (FOR SOPRANO AND ORCH.) (FROM "TAGESLAUF")
    2,2,2,2 - 4,2,3,0 - timp.,perc. - str.   23:00 F. Colombo.
—— FINNISH SUITE (IN 3 MOVTS.)
    K & S.
—— SCHERZO FOR ORCHESTRA
    2,2,2,2 - 4,2,3,1 - timp. - str.   6:30 F. Colombo.
—— THE SILENT WORLD (EVENING MUSIC) (FOR MIXED CHORUS AND STRINGS)
    str.   F. Colombo.
—— TAGESLAUF (THE COURSE OF A DAY) (CANTATA) (FOR SOPRANO, MIXED CHORUS AND ORCH.) (Text: Eichendorff)
    2,2,2,2 - 4,2,3,0 - timp.,perc. - str.   38:00 F. Colombo.
    or:

    1,1,2,1 - 2,1,0,0 - timp.,perc. - str.

ERDMANN, Dietrich
—— CONCERTINO FOR FLUTE AND STRINGS
    fl. - str.   12:00 Robbins.
—— CONCERTINO FOR PIANO AND SMALL ORCH.
    2,0,1,0 - 0,0,0,0 - pf. - str.   15:00 Robbins.
    or:
    1,1,1,0 - 0,0,0,0 - pf. - str.
—— DIVERTIMENTO (FOR ALTO RECORDER AND STRING ORCH.)
    alto recorder - str.   Hans Gerig.
—— SERENATA SERENA (FOR STRING ORCH.)
    str.   Hans Gerig.
—— SUITE FOR SMALL ORCH. (IN 5 MOVTS.)
    1,1,1,1 - 1,1,1,1 - perc. - str.   11:30 Henmar.
—— WOLKENKANTATE (FOR SOPRANO, 3-PART WOMEN'S CHORUS AND STRING ORCH.)
    str.   Hans Gerig.

ERDODY, Leo
—— RUSSIAN RHAPSODY
    2(alt. with 2 piccs.),2(2nd alt. with Eng. hn.),2,2 - 4,2,3,1 - timp.,perc. (3), vibra., xyl. - hp. - pf. - str.   9:00 Leeds.

ERIĆ, Zoran
—— CONCERTO FOR ORCHESTRA
    3,3,3,3 - 4,4,3,1 - timp.,perc.,cel.,vibra. - hp. - pf. - str.   17:00 MIC,Zagreb.
—— IZA SUNČEVIH VRATA (BEHIND THE SUN'S DOOR)
    3,3,3,3 - 4,3,3,1 - timp.,perc.,cel.,xyl. - hp. - pf. - str.   13:00 MIC,Zagreb.

ERICKSON, Frank
—— CHORALE VARIATIONS
    str.   12:00 Composer.
—— OVERTURE TO "THE PICTURE OF DORIAN GRAY"
    2,2,2,2 - 4,3,3,0 - timp.,perc. (3) - hp. - str.   15:00 Composer.
—— A SYMPHONIC POEM
    2,2,2,2 - 4,3,3,1 - timp.,perc.(2) - str.   9:00 Composer.
—— SYMPHONY NO. 2 (MINIATURE)
    2,1,2,1 - 2,2,1,0 - timp.,perc. - str.   17:00 Bourne.

ERIKSON, Åke
—— GROWING (REV. 1975)
    3,2,2,2 - 3,3,2,0 - perc.,bells,cel.,xyl. - pf - str.   12:00 Fleisher.

ERIKSSON, Josef
—— AD TENEBRAS (ANDANTE FOR STRINGS)
    str.   7:30 S.T.I.M.
—— BUKOLIKA (SUITE FOR STRINGS), OP. 27 (IN 5 MOVTS.)
    str.   20:00 S.T.I.M.
—— TVÅ DANSER I FOLKTON, OP. 36 (FOR VIOLIN AND ORCH.)
    2,2,2,2 - 2,0,0,0 - str.   12:00 S.T.I.M.

ERIKSSON, Nils
—— CONCERTO FOR SAXOPHONE AND ORCH.
    2,2,2,sax.,2 - 2,2,2,0 - timp.,perc. - str.   23:00 S.T.I.M.
—— CONCERTO IN B MINOR, FOR BASSOON AND ORCH.
    2,2,2,2 - 2,2,3,0 - timp. - str.   23:00 S.T.I.M.
    or:
    1,1,2,1 - 2,2,1,0 - timp. - str.
—— CONCERTO IN G MINOR, FOR VIOLIN AND ORCH.
    2,2,2,2 - 2,2,3,0 - timp. - str.   24:00 S.T.I.M.
—— ELEGISK SUITE (IN 3 MOVTS.)
    2,2,2,2 - 2,2,2,0 - timp.,perc. - str.   14:00 S.T.I.M.
    or:
    1,1,2,1 - 2,2,1,0 - timp.,perc. - str.
—— LYRIC SUITE (IN 4 MOVTS.)
    2,2,2,2 - 2,2,1,0 - timp.,perc. - hp. - str.   16:00 S.T.I.M.
    or:
    1,1,2,1 - 2,2,1,0 - timp.,perc. - hp. - str.
—— PRELUDIUM AND PASSACAGLIA (OVER ETT KYRIE UR SVENSKA MASSAN)
    2,2,2,2 - 2,2,3,0 - timp. - org. - str.   10:00 S.T.I.M.
—— SHANGHAI (FANTASTIQUE OUVERTURE)
    2,2,2,2 - 2,2,1,0 - timp.,perc. - hp. - str.   8:00 S.T.I.M.

ERÖD, Ivan
—— FOUR PIECES FOR STRING QUARTET (Arranged for String Orch.)
    str.   8:00 Modern.

—— THREE MOVEMENTS FOR CELLO AND CHAMBER ORCH.
   1(alt. with picc.),1,*2,1 - 2,1,1,0 - timp. - hp. - str.(4,3,3,1)
   12:00 Modern.

ESCHER, Rudolf
—— CONCERTO FOR STRINGS, OP. 14
   str.   Henmar.
—— MUSIQUE POUR L'ESPRIT EN DEUIL, OP. 6
   4,4,5,2 sax.,4 - 4,4,3,1 - perc. - 2 hp. - pf. - str.   19:00 Henmar.
—— NOSTALGIES, OP. 21 (4 SONGS FOR TENOR AND ORCH.)
   (1951) (Text: H.J.M. Levet)
   2,0,2,1 - 1,0,0,0 - timp.,perc.,cel. - hp. - str.   15:00 Henmar.
—— SYMPHONIE NO. 1, OP. 26
   4,4,4,sax.,4 - 4,4,3,1 - timp.,perc.,cel. - 2hp. - str.   19:00 Henmar.
—— SYMPHONY NO. 2 (1958)
   2,2,4,2 - 2,2,0,0 - timp.,perc. - hp. - str.   23:00 Henmar.

ESHPAI, André
—— CONCERTO FOR ORCHESTRA (WITH SOLO TRUMPET,
   VIBRAPHONE, PIANO AND DOUBLE BASS)
   G. Schirmer.

ESPOILE, Rául Hugo
—— DANCE AND FINALE, FROM ACT 1 OF THE OPERA
   "FRENOS", OP. 64 (1919)
   3,3,3,basset hn.,3 - 4,2,3,1 - timp.,perc.,cel. - 2 hp. - str.
   8:00 Fleisher.

ESSER, Engelbert István Károly
—— CONCERTO FOR OBOE AND STRING ORCH.
   ob. - str.   10:00 Mannheimer.

ESSYAD, Ahmed
—— DIWAN
   2,2,2,2 - 2,1,1,0 - perc.(3),cel. - hp. - pf. - str.   8:00 Presser.
—— IDENTITY (FOR NARRATOR, SOPRANO, PERCUSSION AND
   13 STRINGS)
   perc. - str.   Presser.
—— SYMPHONY (IN 2 MOVTS.)
   4,4,4,3 - 4,3,3,1 - perc.(2),cel. - hp. - pf. - str.   25:00 Presser.

ETTINGER, Max
—— CANTUS HEBRAICUS (VARIATIONS FOR ORCH.)
   1,1,1,1 - 2,2,0,0 - perc. - hp. - str.   12:00 IsMuPublns.
—— THE SONGS OF MOSES (ORATORIO) (FOR SOLO VOICES,
   SATB CHORUS AND ORCH.)
   2,2,2,2 - 4,3,3,1 - timp.,perc. - hp. - str.   90:00 IsMuPublns.

EVANS, Lindley
—— AN AUSTRALIAN SYMPHONY (FOR CHORUS AND ORCH.)
   16:00 A.P.R.A.
—— IDYLL FOR TWO PIANOS AND ORCH.
   2,2,2,2 - 2,2,3,0 - timp.,perc. - 2 pf. - str.   9:30 A.P.R.A.

EVJE, Johan
—— THE ASCENSION (KRISTI HIMMELFART) (ORATORIO)
   2,2,2,2 - 4,2,3,1 - timp.,perc. - hp. - org. - str.   95:00 T.O.N.O.
—— CHRISTMAS ORATORIO (JULEORATORIUM)
   2,2,2,2 - 4,2,3,1 - timp.,perc. - hp. - org. - str.   T.O.N.O.
—— CONCERTO FOR PIANO AND ORCH.
   2,2,2,2 - 4,2,3,1 - timp.,perc. - hp. - pf. - str.   T.O.N.O.
—— DANCING 'ROUND THE OAK ("ÄNNU GÅR DANSEN
   KRING EKEN") (FOR SOPRANO AND ORCH.) (Text: Gustav
   Frøding)
   2,2,2,2 - 4,2,3,1 - timp.,perc. - hp. - str.   14:00 T.O.N.O.
—— THE NEW JERUSALEM (DET NYE JERUSALEM)
   (ORATORIO)
   2,2,2,2 - 4,2,3,1 - timp.,perc. - hp. - org. - str.   75:00 T.O.N.O.
—— QUO VADIS (DOUBLE FUGUE FOR PIANO AND ORCH.)
   2,2,2,2 - 4,2,3,1 - timp.,perc. - hp. - pf. - str.   25:00 T.O.N.O.
—— SYMPHONY
   2,2,2,2 - 4,2,3,1 - timp.,perc. - hp. - str.   T.O.N.O.

EXTON, John
—— MOVEMENTS FOR ORCH. (1963)
   11:27 A.P.R.A.

EYSER, Eberhard
—— CONCERTINO FOR HORN AND CHAMBER ORCH. (1971)
   1,1,1,1 - 0,0,0,0 - electric guit. - banjo(or hpsc.) - str.(0,2,2,1)
   10:00 Fleisher.

—— CONCERTO FOR PIANO AND CHAMBER ORCH. (TRIPIKO
   I)(1974)
   1,1,1,1 - 1,0,0,0 - timp. - pf. - str.(0,1,1,1)   25:00 Fleisher.
—— GAGLIARDA DI GUSTAV VASA (FROM "HJÄRTER
   KUNG")(FOR ORCH. OF VARIABLE INSTRUMENTATION
   AND SIZE)(1974)
   17:00 Fleisher.
—— LITTLE NOCTURNE (FOR CHAMBER ORCH.)(1972)
   ob. - hpsc. - str.   6:00 Fleisher.
—— STOCHASTA 57-74 (FOR WINDS AND PERCUSSION)(1974)
   1,1,0,3 sax.(sopr.,alto,ten.),1 - 1,2,3,1 - perc.   10:00 Fleisher.
—— SYMPHONIE ORIENTALE (FOR CHAMBER ORCH.)(1974)
   1,1,1,1 - 1,1,1,1 - perc. - 2 cymbaloms(or dulcimers)(1 amplified) -
   2 d.-b.   25:00 Fleisher.
—— TRIGONASMA (1973)
   Tam-tam - str.   9:00 Fleisher.

F

FABINI, Eduardo
—— CAMPO (THE COUNTRY) (SYMPHONIC POEM)
   3,3,3,2 - 4,2,3,1 - timp. - hp. - str.   15:00 F. Colombo.

FAEHNDRICH, Walter
—— DAPHNÉ (BALLET D'APRÉS LES MÉTAMORPHOSES
   D'OVIDE) % (POUR GRAND ORCHESTRE)
   30:00 S.U.I.S.A.
—— DIVERTIMENTO (FÜR GROSSES ORCH.)
   15:00 S.U.I.S.A.
—— ORCHESTERMUSIK
   17:00 S.U.I.S.A.
—— SONATA PER ARCHI
   str.   13:00 S.U.I.S.A.

FAHNESTOCK, Karol
—— CANTO FOR FREEDOM'S MARTYRS (FOR NARRATORS,
   SOLO VOICES, CHORUS AND ORCH.)
   2,2,2,*3 - 4,2,3,1 - timp. - pf. - str.   45:00 EarlhamCol.
—— CONCERTO FOR PIANO AND ORCH. (IN 3 MOVTS.)
   2,2,2,*3 - 4,2,3,1 - timp.,perc. - pf. - str.   45:00 Composer.
—— DIALECTIC NO. 1
   2,2,2,*3 - 4,2,2,0 - timp. - str.   4:00 Fema.
—— DIALECTIC NO. 2
   2,2,2,*3 - 4,2,3,1 - timp. - str.   8:00 Composer.
—— ELEGY FOR ORCHESTRA
   2,*3,2,*3 - 4,2,2,1 - timp. - str.   14:00 Composer.
—— JUBILANT OVERTURE (SYMPHONY)
   2,2,2,*3 - 4,2,3,1 - timp.,xyl. - pf. - str.   15:00 Fema.
—— MISSISSINNEWA (LAMENT FOR ORCHESTRA)
   2,*3,2,*3 - 4,2,2,1 - timp. - str.   15:00 Composer.
—— RHAPSODY IN F MINOR
   2,*3,*3,*3 - 4,2,2,1 - str.   40:00 Composer.
—— STARS (SONGS FOR SOPRANO AND ORCH.) (Text: Pauline
   Hanson)
   2,*3,*3,*3 - 4,2,2,1 - timp. - pf. - str.   30:00 Composer.
—— SYMPHONIC OVERTURE
   2,2,2,*3 - 4,2,2,1 - timp.,xyl. - pf. - str.   6:00 Fema.

FAIRCHILD, Blair
—— DAME LIBELLULE (SYMPHONIC SUITE FROM THE
   BALLET)
   3,3,2,2 - 4,3,0,0 - timp.,perc.,cel. - hp. - str.   25:00 F. Colombo.

FAIRCHILD, Blair - AUBERT, Louis
—— À BEL-EBAT (3 SYMPHONIC TABLEAUX)
   3,3,3,3 - 4,2,3,1 - timp. - hp. - str.   15:30 EV.

FAIRCHILD, Helen
—— THE SON OF THE HIGHEST (CHRISTMAS CANTATA) (FOR
   4 SOLOISTS, CHORUS AND ORCH.)
   1,1,2,1 - 2,2,1,0 - timp. - str.   Flammer.

FAITH, Richard
—— CONCERTO FOR PIANO AND ORCH. (1954) (IN 3 MOVTS.)
   *3,2,2,2 - 4,2,3,1 - timp.,perc.(3),bells,glock. - pf. - str.
   26:30 Composer.
—— ELEGY (1967)
   2(1 alt. with picc.),*3,2,2 - 4,2,3,1 - timp. - str.   6:30 Composer.
—— ODYSSEY (1966)
   *3,*3,2,*3 - 4,2,3,1 - timp. - hp. - str.   8:30 Composer.

—— A PASTORAL OVERTURE (1966)
*3,*3,2,*3 - 4,2,3,1 - timp.,perc.(2),cel.,glock. - hp. - str. Composer.

FAITH, Walter
—— REVANCHE (SUITE AUS DEM BALLETT)
1 (or picc.),1 (or Eng. hn.),*2,sax.(ad. lib.),0 - 0,1,1,0 - perc.(3),
cel. - hp. - str.   25:00 Modern.

FALARO, Anthony
—— COSMOI
Str   12:00 C. Fischer.
—— SUITE FOR STRING ORCHESTRA
str.   10:30 C. Fischer.

FALCONER, Fred - BROWN, James
—— MINIATURE SUITE
str.   P.R.S.

FALLA, Manuel de
—— EL AMOR BRUJO (BALLET SUITE)
2(1 alt. with picc.),1(alt. with Eng. hn.),2,1 - 2,2,0,0 - timp.,perc. -
pf. - str.   20:00 G. Schirmer.
—— HOMENAJES
2(2nd alt. with picc.),2,2,2 - 4,3,3,0 - perc. - hp. - str.
18:00 G. Schirmer.
—— EL RETABLO DE MAESE PEDRO (MASTER PETER'S
PUPPET SHOW) (MARIONETTE OPERA) %
1,*3,1,1 - 2,1,0,0 - timp.,perc.,xyl. - hpsc. - hp. - str.   G. Schirmer.
—— RITUAL FIRE DANCE (FROM "EL AMOR BRUJO")
*3,1,2,1 - 2,2,0,0 - timp. - pf. - str.   14:00 G. Schirmer.
—— SUITE FROM THE OPERA "EL RETABLO DE MAESE
PEDRO" (MASTER PETER'S PUPPET SHOW)
2,2,1,1 - 2 hn., 2 tpt. - timp.,perc. - hp. - pf. - str.
20:00 G. Schirmer.
—— THREE CORNERED HAT (BALLET) %
2(2nd alt. with picc.),2(2nd alt. with Eng.hn.),2,2 - 4,3,3,1 -
timp.,perc.(4),cel. - hp. - pf. - str.   30:00 G. Schirmer.
—— THE THREE CORNERED HAT: SUITE NO. 1 (IN 3 MOVTS.)
*2,*2,2,2 - 2,2,0,0 - perc. - hp. - pf. - str.   14:00 G. Schirmer.
—— THE THREE CORNERED HAT: SUITE NO. 2 (IN 3 MOVTS.)
*3,*3,2,2 - 4,3,3,1 - perc.,cel. - hp. - pf. - str.   12:00 G. Schirmer.

FALLIK, Yu.
—— ORESTEYA (CHOREOGRAPHIC TRAGEDY) %
G. Schirmer.

FANSHAWE, David
—— MEMORIAL TO ABERFAN, OP. 15
2,2,2,2 - 4,4,4,1 - timp.,perc.(4) - tape-recorder - 2 hp. - org.(ad
lib.) - str.   18:00 P.R.S.

FARAGO, Marcel
—— ALLEGRO FOR TUBA AND STRING ORCH., OP. 15-A (1963)
0,0,0,0 - 0,0,0,1 - timp. - str.   Composer.
—— CONCERT OVERTURE, OP. 25 (1967)
*3,*3,2,*3 - 4,4,3,1 - timp.,perc.(3),cel. - hp. - str.   Composer.
—— CONCERTO FOR CELLO AND ORCH., OP. 4
2,*3,2,2 - 4,3,3,1 - timp.,perc. - hp. - str.   9:00 Composer.
—— CONCERTO FOR VIOLIN AND ORCH., OP. 11 (1955) (IN 1
MOVT.)
2,*3,2,2 - 4,2,3,1 - timp. - hp. - str.   32:00 Composer.
—— DIVERTIMENTO FOR ORCH., OP. 17 (1962) (IN 8 MOVTS.)
1,1,1,1 - 1,1,1,0 - timp. - hp. - str.   Composer.
—— FANTAISIE DE CONCERT, OP. 8 (1952)
*3,2,2,2 - 4,3,2,1 - timp.,perc.(2) - str.   12:00 Composer.
—— POEME SYMPHONIQUE, OP. 3 (1941)
2,2,2,2 - 4,4,3,1 - timp. - hp. - str.   8:00 Composer.
—— PRELUDE, INTERLUDE AND POSTLUDE, OP. 10 (1954)
2,*3,2,2 - 4,4,3,1 - timp.,perc.(2) - str.   Composer.
—— SCHERZO FOR 3 FLUTES AND ORCH., OP. 19-B (1967)
3,0,*1,0 - 4,4,0,0 - timp.,perc. - hp. - str.   Composer.
—— A SOLEMN MARCH (1973)
2,2,2,2 - 4,4,3,1 - timp.,perc.(3) - hp. - str.   4:00 Composer.
—— SUITE, OP. 13 (1956) (FOR STRING ORCH.) (IN 4 MOVTS.)
str.   10:00 Composer.
—— SYMPHONY, OP. 20 (ANDANTE AND ALLEGRO) (1968)
*3,*3,*3,*3 - 4,4,3,1 - timp.,perc.(3),cel. - hp. - str.
13:00 Composer.
—— TOCCATA AND SCHERZO, OP. 24 (1967)
str.   7:00 Composer.
—— TOCCATA, SCHERZO AND FINALE, OP. 24 (1966)
str.   10:00 Composer.

FARBERMAN, Harold
—— CONCERTO FOR ALTO SAXOPHONE AND STRING ORCH.
alto. sax. - str.   10:20 General.
—— CONCERTO FOR BASSOON AND STRING ORCH.
bn. - str.   15:00 General.
—— CONCERTO FOR TIMPANI AND ORCH. (IN 1 MOVT.)
*3,*3,*3,2 - 2-4,3,2,1 - timp.,perc.(4),glock.,xyl. - str.
14:00 F. Colombo.
—— CONCERTO FOR VIOLIN AND ORCH. (1972) (IN 1 MOVT.)
*3,*3,*3,*3 - 4,3,3,1 - timp.,perc.(5),bells,glock.,vibra.,xyl. -
tape-recorder - hp. - pf. - str.   20:00 Belw-Mills.
—— DOUBLE CONCERTO FOR SINGLE TRUMPET (WITH
OPTIONAL NARRATION) (Text: Composer)
*3,2(2nd alt. with Eng. hn.),*3(2nd alt. with E^{b}cl.),*3 - 4,3,3,1 -
timp.,perc.(4),glock.,xyl. - str.   14:00 Broude.
—— ELEGY, FANFARE AND MARCH
*3,2,2,2 - 4,3,3,1 - timp.,perc.(5) - str.   9:50 General.
—— EVOLUTION (FOR SOPRANO, HORN, PERCUSSION AND
ORCH.)
17:00 Broude.
—— THE GREAT AMERICAN COWBOY (SUITE)
2,2,2,2 - 4,3,3,1 - timp.,perc.(4) - banjo,guit. - str.
14:00 Belw-Mills.
—— GREEK SCENE (CYCLE OF 5 SONGS) (FOR SOPRANO AND
ORCH.) (Text: Composer)
*3,2,*3,2 - 4,2,2,1 - timp.,perc.(4),bells,xyl. - str.   16:00 General.
—— GREEK SCENE (FOR SOPRANO AND ORCH.)
*3,2,*3,2 - 4,2,2,0 - timp.,perc.(7, incl. 4 on timp.) - str.
25:00 General.
—— IMPRESSIONS (SUITE FOR OBOE, STRINGS AND
PERCUSSION) (IN 4 MOVTS.)
ob. - perc.(1),mar. - str.   14:00 Broude.
—— INITIATION BALLET (FROM THE OPERA "THE LOSERS")
(FOR ORCHESTRA AND JAZZ QUARTET)
3,2,4,alto sax.,0 - 4,4,3,2 - timp.,perc.(8),bells,vibra.,xyl. - electric
guit. - pf. - str.   Belw-Mills.
—— MEDEA (OPERA) %
2(2nd alt. with picc.),2(2nd alt. with Eng.hn.),2(2nd alt. with
b.-cl.),2 - 2,2,2,1 - timp.,perc. - str.   60:00 General.
—— ORCHESTRAL SUITE FROM THE OPERA "MEDEA"
2(2nd alt. with picc.),2,2,2 - 2,2,2,1 - timp.,perc.(3),bells,xyl. - str.
15:00 General.
—— PARAMOUNT CONCERTO (FOR PIANO AND ORCH.)
2,2,2,2 - 4,3,3,1 - perc.(4) - pf. - str.   14:00 Belw-Mills.
—— PROGRESSIONS (FOR FLUTE, PERCUSSION AND ORCH.)
13:50 Broude.
—— SYMPHONY NO. 1 (FOR PERCUSSION AND STRINGS) (IN 3
MOVTS.)
perc.(7),bells,xyl. - str.   20:00 Broude.
—— THERE'S US, THERE'S THEM...TOGETHER? (FOR
VOICE,ORCHESTRA AND JAZZ COMBO)
2,2,3,2 -4,3,3,1 - timp.,perc. - org. - str.   15:00 Belw-Mills.
—— VARIATIONS FOR PERCUSSION, PIANO AND ORCH.
5:00 Broude.
—— WAR CRY ON A PRAYER FEATHER (FOR SOPRANO,
BARITONE AND ORCH.) (1976) (Text: Nancy Wood, after Taos
Indian poems)
2(2nd alt. with picc.),2(2nd alt. with Eng. hn.),2(2nd alt. with
b.-cl.),2 - 4,3,3,1 - timp.,perc. - hp. - 3 org. - str.   20:00 Composer.

FARINA, Carlo - BONELLI, Ettore
—— PAVANA E GAGLIARDA
str.   Henmar.

FARINA, Carlo - HARNONCOURT, Nikolaus
—— CAPRICCIO STRAVAGANTE (AN AMUSING QUODLIBET
FROM "LIBRO DELLE PAVANE", DRESDEN 1626)
cemb. - str.   17:00 Henmar.

FARINA, Guido
—— CORALE
3,3,3,3 - 4,3,3,1 - timp.,perc. - hp. - pf. - str.   6:00 Bo. Hawkes.
—— QUADRI SINFONICI (IN 4 MOVTS)
3,3,3,3 - 4,3,1,0 - timp.,perc.,bells, cel. - 1 - 2 hp. - org. - pf. - str.
31:00 Bo. Hawkes.
—— SEQUENZA AUTUMNALE (IN 3 MOVTS.)
str.   12:00 Bo. Hawkes.
—— SINFONIA DELL' AUTUNNO PAVESE (IN 3 MOVTS.)
pf. - str.   12:00 Bo. Hawkes.
—— TEMPO DI CARNEVALE (OVERTURE)
1,1,2,1 - 2,1,1,0 - timp.,perc. - hp. - pf. - str.   5:00 Bo. Hawkes.

FARIÑAS, Carlos
—— MUROS, REJAS Y VITRALES (1972)
2 picc.,4,*2,*3,*3 - 4,5,3,1 - perc. - pf. - str.　　24:30 Seesaw.

FARINELLO, Orestes
—— ANCHIETA (OVERTURE)
3,3,3,3 - 4,3,3,1 - timp.,perc.,cel. - hp. - str.　10:00 F. Colombo.
—— CREPUSCOLO SERTANEJO
3,3,2,2 - 4,2,2,0 - timp.,perc.,bell,cel. - hp. - str. 7:00 F. Colombo.
—— IMPRESSÕES BRASILEIRAS (SUITE)
3,2,2,3 - 3,2,2,1 - timp.,perc. - str.　　16:00 F. Colombo.
—— SAO PÁULO (SYMPHONIC POEM)
3,2,2,3 - 4,3,3,1 - timp.,perc.,glock. - org.(ad lib.) - pf. - str.
　　15:00 F. Colombo.
—— TOADA (FOR SMALL ORCH.)
1,0,1,1 - 2,0,0,0 - perc. - str.　　6:00 F. Colombo.

FARKAS, Ferenc
—— CANTATA LIRICA (FOR CHORUS AND ORCH.) (Text: Jeno Dsida)
2,2,2,2 - 3,2,1,0 - cel. - hp. - str.　　20:00 Bo. Hawkes.
—— CANTUS PANNONICUS (FOR SOPRANO, SATB CHORUS AND ORCH.)
2,2,2,2 - 4,4,3,1 - timp.,perc.,cel. - guit. - mandolin - hp. - hpsc. - pf. - c.'s,c-b.'s　　20:00 Bo. Hawkes.
—— CARPATHIAN RHAPSODY
1,1,2,1 - 2,2,1,0 - timp.,perc. - hp. - str.　　8:00 Bo. Hawkes.
—— CONCERTO FOR PIANO AND ORCH.
2,2,2,2 - 4,2,3,0 - timp.,perc. - pf. - str.　　15:00 Bo. Hawkes.
—— FESTIVE OVERTURE
*3,2,2,2 - 4,3,3,0 - timp.,perc. - str.　　12:00 Bo. Hawkes.
—— THE MAGIC CUPBOARD: OVERTURE
2,2,2,2 - 4,3,3,1 - timp.,perc. - hp. - str.　　6:00 Bo. Hawkes.
—— THE MARIONETTE'S DANCE (SUITE)
2,1,2,1 - 2,2,1,0 - timp.,perc. - hp. - str.　　20:00 Bo. Hawkes.
—— MUSICA PENTATONICA
str.　　10:00 Bo. Hawkes.
—— PLANCTUS ET CONSOLATIONES
*3,2,2,2 - 4,2,3,1 - timp.,perc. - hp. - pf. - str. 15:00 Bo. Hawkes.
—— PRELUDE AND FUGUE
*3,3(3rd alt. with Eng. hn.),3(3rd alt. with b.-cl.),*3 - 4,2,3,0 - timp.,perc. - str.　　9:00 Mills.
—— SERENADE CONCERTANTE (FOR FLUTE AND STRINGS)
fl. - str.　　14:00 Bo. Hawkes.
—— THE SLY STUDENTS (SUITE)
3,2,2,2 - 4,3,3,1 - timp.,perc. - hp. - str.　　20:00 Bo. Hawkes.
—— SYMPHONIC OVERTURE
*3,*3,*3,*3 - 4,4,3,1 - timp., perc. - hp. - str.　12:00 Bo. Hawkes.
—— TABLE MUSIC
1,1,2,1 - 2,1,1,0 - str.　　9:00 Bo. Hawkes.
—— TRITTICO CONCERTATO (FOR CELLO AND STRINGS)
str.　　15:00 Bo. Hawkes.

FARNABY, Giles - BALES, Richard
—— HOMAGE TO GILES FARNABY, 1560-1640 (1967) (SUITE IN 7 MOVTS., TRANSCRIBED FROM THE FITZWILLIAM VIRGINAL BOOK)
str.　　10:30 Southern.

FÄRNLÖF, Lars
—— HESPERIA (FOR SATB CHORUS, JAZZ GROUP AND ORCH.)(1972)
　　Fleisher.
—— HEUREKA (FOR JAZZ GROUP AND ORCH.)(1969)
2,2,2,2 - 4,2,1,1 - timp.,perc. - 2 pf. - str.　25:00 Fleisher.

FARNON, Robert
—— CASCADES TO THE SEA
　　18:00 Bo. Hawkes.
—— PRELUDE TO "LAKE OF THE WOODS"
2,1,2,2 - 3,2,3,0 - timp.,perc. - hp. - str.　　7:00 Chappell.
—— RHAPSODY FOR VIOLIN AND ORCH.
*3,2,2,2 - 4,2,3,1 - timp.,perc.(2) - hp. - str.　15:00 Chappell.
—— SYMPHONETTE FOR SMALL ORCH.
　　9:00 C.A.P.A.C.
—— SYMPHONY NO. 1, IN D FLAT MAJOR
　　27:00 C.A.P.A.C.
—— SYMPHONY NO. 2 ("OTTAWA")
　　27:00 Chappell.

FARQUHAR, David
—— ANNIVERSARY SUITE NO. 1 (1961)
2,2,2,2 - 2,2,0,0 - timp. - hp. - str.　　15:00 A.P.R.A.

—— ANNIVERSARY SUITE NO. 2 (1965)
2,2,2,2 - 2,2,0,0 - timp. - hp. - str.　　16:00 A.P.R.A.
—— CONCERTINO FOR PIANO AND STRINGS (1960)
pf. - str.　　15:00 A.P.R.A.
—— ELEGY FOR STRINGS (1961)
str.　　6:30 A.P.R.A.
—— EPITHALAMION (FOR SMALL ORCH.)
　　7:00 A.P.R.A.
—— HARLEQUIN
　　7:00 A.P.R.A.
—— RING ROUND THE MOON (DANCE SUITE)(1954)
1,1,1,0 - 1,0,0,0 - perc. - pf. - str.　　18:00 A.P.R.A.
—— SYMPHONY
　　23:00 A.P.R.A.
—— SYMPHONY (1959)
3,2,3,2 - 4,3,3,1 - timp.,perc. - hp. - str.　23:00 A.P.R.A.

FARWELL, Arthur
—— GODS OF THE MOUNTAIN (SUITE), OP. 52 (IN 4 MOVTS.)
3(3rd alt. with picc.),3,*3,*3 - 4,3,3,1 - timp.,perc. - 2 hp. - str.
　　17:00 Composer.

FASCH, Johann Friedrich - KOCH
—— CONCERTO IN G MAJOR
ob.(or fl., or sopr. recorder) - cemb. - str.(no vlas.)　　Henmar.

FASCH, Johann Friedrich - SALLAGAR
—— CONCERTO IN C MAJOR FOR BASSOON, CEMBALO AND STRINGS
bn. - cemb. - str.　　Henmar.

FASCH, Johann Friedrich - SCHROEDER, Felix
—— CONCERTO IN B FLAT MAJOR
2,2,0,1 - 0,0,0,0 - hpsc. - str.　　18:00 Mannheimer.
—— CONCERTO IN D MAJOR FOR 2 FLUTES, HARPSICHORD AND STRING ORCH.
2fl. - hpsc. - str.　　13:00 Mannheimer.

FASCH, Johann Friedrich - WINSCHERMANN - BUCK
—— CONCERTO GROSSO IN D, FOR SMALL ORCH.
2 ob., 2 bn. - 2 hn. - cemb. - str.　　15:00 F. Colombo.
—— CONCERTO GROSSO IN D, WITH 2 SOLO VIOLINS
2 ob. - 2 tpt.(clarino) - timp. - cemb. - str.　17:00 F. Colombo.

FASCH-KESNAR, Maurits
—— OVERTURE
2,2,0,2 - 2,3,0,0 - timp.,perc.(1) - str.　　7:00 Arranger.

FAURÉ, Gabriel-Urbain
—— FANTAISIE, OP. 111 (FOR PIANO AND ORCH.)
2,2,2,2 - 4,1,0,0 - timp. - hp. - pf. - str.　　18:00 EV.
—— MASQUES ET BERGAMASQUES (IN 4 MOVTS.)
2,2,2,2 - 2,2,0,0 - timp. - hp. - str.　　14:00 EV.
—— PRELUDE TO "PENELOPE"
　　Mercury.

FAURÉ, Gabriel-Urbain - INGELBRECHT, D. E.
—— THEME AND VARIATIONS, OP. 73
1,*2,2,1 - 2,1,0,0 - hp. - str.　　16:00 EV.

FAVRE, Georges
—— CONTES D'ARVOR
1,1,1,1 - 2,1,0,0 - timp.,perc.,cel. - hp. - str.　9:50 EV.
—— ÉQUINOXE (TABLEAU SYMPHONIQUE)
*3,*2,*2,*2 - 4,3,3,1 - timp.,perc.,cel.,xyl. - 2 hp. - str. 12:00 EV.
—— SYMPHONIA BREVIS (FOR STRINGS)
str.　　13:00 EV.

FEIGIN, Leonid
—— DON JUAN (SUITE FROM THE BALLET)
　　G. Schirmer.

FEJARD, Simone
—— LE KHENE ENCHANTE (SIX SKETCHES)
　　9:00 EV.

FELCIANO, Richard
—— THE CAPTIVES (FOR CHORUS AND ORCH.) (1965) (Text: Thomas Merton)
3(alt. with 3 picc.),2,*3,1 alto sax.,2 - 4,3,3,1 - timp.,perc.(4),cel.,glock.,xyl. - hp. - pf. - str.　　10:00 Composer.

—— LAMENTATIONS FOR JANI CHRISTOU (FOR 12 PLAYERS AND ELECTRONIC TAPE) (1970)
1,1,0,1 - 1,1,1,1 - perc.(2) - tape-recorder - pf. - c.,d.-b.
9:00 ECSchirmer.

—— MUTATIONS FOR ORCHESTRA (1966)
3(alt. with 3 picc.),2,2,2 - 4,3,3,1 - timp.,perc.,bells,cel. - glock.,mar.(ad lib.),xyl. - hp. - pf. - str.   15:00 Composer.

FELD, Jindřich
—— COMEDY OVERTURE
2,2,2,2 - 2,2,1,0 - timp.,perc. - str.   7:00 Bo. Hawkes.
—— CONCERTO FOR CELLO AND ORCH.
2,2,3,2 - 4,3,3,1 - timp.,perc.,cel. - hp. - pf. - str.
26:00 Bo. Hawkes.
—— CONCERTO FOR CHAMBER ORCH.
2,1,2,1 - 3,3,0,0 - timp. - str.   18:00 Bo. Hawkes.
—— CONCERTO FOR FLUTE, HARP, PIANO, PERCUSSION AND STRING ORCH.
fl. - perc. - hp. - pf. - str.   31:30 General.
—— CONCERTO FOR ORCHESTRA
3,3,4,3 - 4,4,3,1 - timp.,perc. - 2 hp. - pf. - str. 37:00 Bo. Hawkes.
—— DIVERTIMENTO FOR STRINGS
str.   23:00 Bo. Hawkes.
—— RHAPSODY FOR VIOLIN AND ORCH.
3,3,3,3 - 4,3,3,1 - timp.,perc.,xyl. - hp. - str.   11:00 Bo. Hawkes.
—— SERENATA GIOCOSA
2,2,2,2 - 2,1,0,0 - perc. - str.   10:00 Modern.
—— SYMPHONY NO. 1
3(3rd alt. with picc.),2(2nd alt. with Eng.hn.),3(3rd. alt with b.-cl.),3(3rd alt. with c.-bn.) - 4,3,3,1 - timp.,perc. - hp. - str.
21:00 General.

FELDERHOF, Jan
—— CONCERTO FOR FLUTE, PERCUSSION AND STRINGS
fl. - perc. - str.   Henmar.
—— ELEGY (1952) (THEMA MET VERWERKINGEN OVER HET VALERIUSLIED "STORT TRANEN UIT")
2,2,2,2 - 4,3,3,1 - timp.,perc. - hp. - str.   11:00 Henmar.
—— MUSIC FOR 15 WIND AND BRASS INSTRUMENTS, WITH PERCUSSION
2,2,2,sax.,2 - 2,2,1,1 - timp.,perc.   Henmar.
—— OVERTURE
2,2,2,2 - 4,2,3,0 - perc. - pf. - str.   7:00 Henmar.
—— RHAPSODY FOR OBOE AND SMALL ORCH.
1,1,2,1 - 1,1,0,0 - timp.,perc. - str.   6:00 Henmar.
—— SINFONIETTA
2,1,3,2 - 2,2,2,0 - timp.,perc.,xyl. - hp. - str.   10:00 Henmar.
—— SINFONIETTA NO. 2 (FOR SMALL ORCH.) (1962)
1,1,1,1 - 0,1,0,0 - timp.,perc. - str.   12:00 Henmar.
—— SYMPHONIE
2,2,2,2 - 2,2,2,1 - timp.,perc. - str.   21:00 Henmar.
—— TOT WIEN ZULLEN WIJ HENNENGAAN (CANTATA) (FOR SOPRANO, ALTO, BARITONE, MIXED CHORUS AND ORCH.) (1941)
2,2,2,2 - 2,2,1,1 - timp.,perc. - pf. - str.   17:00 Henmar.

FELDSTEIN, Saul
—— SACRED SERVICE (1965) (FOR TENOR, SATB CHORUS AND SMALL ORCH.) (Text: Biblical)
timp. - org. - str.   22:30 Composer.

FELLEGARA, Vittorio
—— CANTATA (FOR 2 WOMEN'S VOICES AND ORCH.) 1966 (Text: G. Leopardi)
3,3,3,3 - 4,4,3,1 - perc.(2) - str.   15:00 MCA Music.
—— CONCERTO BREVE (FOR CHAMBER ORCH.)
2,2,2,2 - 2,2,1,0 - timp.,perc.(2) - str.   14:00 Leeds.
—— CONCERTO FOR ORCHESTRA
3,2,3,3 - 4,3,3,1 - timp.,perc. - str.   15:00 Leeds.
—— FRAMMENTI I
2,2,2,2 - 1,1,1,0 - timp.,perc.(2) - str.   7:00 Leeds.
—— MADRIGALE (FOR 5 VOICES OR SMALL CHORUS WITH CHAMBER ORCH.) (1969) (Text: Anon. Medieval German)
1,1,1,1 - 1,1,1,0 - timp.,perc.(2) - str.(min.:2,1,1,1)
10:00 MCA Music.
—— MUTAZIONI (BALLET) %
3,3,3,3 - 4,4,3,1 - timp.,perc.(3) - str.   35:00 Leeds.
—— MUTAZIONI (4 SYMPHONIC FRAGMENTS FROM THE BALLET)
Leeds.
—— REQUIEM DI MADRID (FOR CHORUS AND ORCH.) (Text: Federico Garcia Lorca)
2,*2,*2,1 sax. - *2 - 2,2,2,1 - timp.,perc.(3) - str.   10:15 Leeds.

—— SERENATA
1,0,1,1(or b.-cl.) - 0,0,0,0 - perc. - pf. - str.(no d.-b.)   8:00 Leeds.
—— SINFONIA 1957
3,3,3,3 - 4,3,3,1 - timp.,perc.(4) - str.   15:00 Leeds.
—— VARIAZIONI (FRAMMENTI II)
2,2,2,2 - 2,0,0,0 - timp.,perc.(3) - str.   10:00 Leeds.

FELTON, William - MCLEAN, Hugh
—— CONCERTO IN B FLAT, OP. 4, NO. 5 (FOR ORGAN AND STRINGS)
org. - str.   Oxford.

FENBY, Eric
—— ROSSINI ON ILKLA MOOR (OVERTURE)
2,2,2,2 - 2,2,1,0 - timp.,perc. - str.   7:30 Bo. Hawkes.

FENNER, Burt
—— CHAMBER SYMPHONY (1958) (IN 4 MOVTS.)
1,1,1,1 - 2,0,0,0 - timp. - str.   17:40 Composer.
—— GIALD (1970)
1,1,E♭cl.,*1,1 - 2,2,2,1 - timp.,perc.(4),vibra.,xyl. - str.
13:00 Composer.
—— SYMPHONY NO. 2 (1961) (IN 3 MOVTS.)
2,2,2(2nd alt. with b.-cl.),2 - 4,3,3,1 - timp.,perc.(2) - str.
22:00 Composer.
—— SYMPHONY NO. 3 (1975) (IN 3 MOVTS.)
2,2,2,2 - 4,3,3,1 - perc.(3) - pf. - str.   24:00 Composer.
—— UNTITLED (IMPROVISATIONAL WORK FOR ANY SIZE ORCH., WITH SYNTHESIZER) (1972)
Composer.
—— VARIATIONS FOR STRING QUARTET AND ORCH. (1961)
2,2,2,2 - 2,2,1,0 - timp. - str.   12:00 Composer.

FENNIMORE, Joseph
—— CONCERTINO FOR PIANO AND ORCH. (1962)
*3,2,2,2 - 4,2,3,0 - timp.,perc.(3) - pf. - str.   9:00 Composer.
—— CONCERTO FOR CELLO AND ORCH. (1973)
3(3rd alt. with picc.),2,2,*3 - 4,2,3,1 - timp.,perc.(3),glock. - str.
21:00 Composer.
—— ECHOES (FOR MEZZO-SOPRANO, TENOR AND ORCH.) (1972)
2,2,0,2 - 2,0,0,0 - perc.(1) - pf. -str.   14:00 Composer.

FENSTOCK, Belle - COX, Clarence
—— AMERICAN RHAPSODY (FOR PIANO AND ORCH.)
2(1st alt. with picc.),2(2nd alt. with Eng. hn.),2(2nd alt. with b.-cl.),3 sax.,2 - 2,3,2,1 - timp.,perc.(1-2), glock.(or bells),xyl.,vibra. - hp. - pf. - str.   12:00 Ditson.

FENSTRÖM, John
—— THE MERCHANT OF VENICE: SUITE NO. 1, OP. 86B
1,1,2,1 - 2,2,1,0 - timp.,perc. - str.   14:00 S.T.I.M.

FERENCZY, Oto
—— ELEGY (FOR CHAMBER ORCH.) (1950)
Bo. Hawkes.
—— FINALE
3,3,3,3 - 4,3,3,1 - timp.,perc. - str.   9:00 Bo. Hawkes.
—— PICTURE OF MY COUNTRY (SYMPHONIC POEM) (1952)
Bo. Hawkes.
—— RONDO (1951)
Bo. Hawkes.

FERGUSON, Howard
—— AMORE LANUEO (FOR TENOR, CHORUS AND ORCH.)
2,2,2,2 - 4,2,3,1 - timp.,perc. - hp. - str.   25:00 Bo. Hawkes.
—— CONCERTO FOR PIANO AND STRINGS
pf. - str.   25:00 Bo. Hawkes.
—— THE DREAM OF THE ROOD (FOR SOPRANO OR TENOR SOLO, MIXED CHORUS AND ORCH.)
2,2,2,2 - 4,2,3,1 - timp.,perc.,cel. - hp. - str.   27:00 Bo. Hawkes.
—— FOUR DIVERSIONS ON ULSTER AIRS
2,2,2,2 - 4,2,3,0 - timp.,perc. - str.   12:00 Bo. Hawkes.
—— OVERTURE FOR AN OCCASION
2,2,2,2 - 4,2,3,0 - timp.,perc. - str.   7:00 Bo. Hawkes.
—— PARTITA
2,3,2,2-3 - 4,3,3,1 - timp.,perc. - hp. - str.   21:00 Bo. Hawkes.
—— SERENADE FOR CHAMBER ORCH.
bn. - hn. - str.   22:00 Bo. Hawkes.

FERNANDEZ, Oscar Lorenzo
—— CONCERTO IN A MAJOR, FOR VIOLIN AND ORCH.
2,3,3,0 - 2,2,0,0 - timp. - str.   14:00 U.B.C.

—— SINFONIA NO. 1
  3,3,3,3 - 6,4,3,1 - timp.,perc.,xyl. - 2 hp. - str.   35:00 U.B.C.
—— SINFONIA NO. 2
  3,3,3,3 - 4,4,3,1 - timp.,perc.,cel.,xyl. - hp. - pf. - str. 40:00 U.B.C.
—— VARIACOES SINFONICAS (FOR PIANO AND ORCH.)
  3,3,3,2 - 4,3,3,1 - perc. - str.   35:00 U.B.C.

FERNSTRÖM, John
—— AMORE STUDIORUM (SYMPHONY) OP. 56
  2,2,2,2 - 4,2,3,1 - timp.,perc. - str.   31:00 S.T.I.M.
—— CHACONNE FOR CELLO AND ORCH., OP. 31
  1,1,2,1 - 2,0,0,0 - str.   6:00 Suecia.
—— CONCERTINO FOR CELLO AND ORCH., OP. 49
  1,1,2,1 - 2,0,0,0 - timp. - str.   12:00 S.T.I.M.
—— CONCERTINO FOR FLUTE, FEMALE CHORUS AND ORCH.,
  OP. 52
  1,0,2,0 - 0,0,0,0 - timp.,perc. - str.   9:00 Suecia.
—— CONCERTO FOR BASSOON AND ORCH., OP. 80
  1,1,2,1 - 2,2,0,0 - timp. - str.   15:00 S.T.I.M.
—— CONCERTO FOR CLARINET AND SMALL ORCH., OP. 30
  cl. - timp. - str.   12:00 S.T.I.M.
—— CONCERTO FOR VIOLA AND ORCH., OP. 34
  1,1,2,1 - 2,2,0,0 - str.   26:00 S.T.I.M.
—— CONCERTO NO. 1 FOR VIOLIN AND ORCH., OP. 5
  2,2,2,2 - 2,2,1,0 - pf. - str.   26:00 S.T.I.M.
—— CONCERTO NO. 2 FOR VIOLIN AND ORCH., OP. 95
  1,1,2,1 - 2,0,0,0 - str.   23:00 S.T.I.M.
—— FOUR INTIMATE MINIATURES FOR STRINGS, OP. 2
  str.   11:00 Suecia.
—— DEN KAPRICLÖSE TRUBADUREN, OP. 21 (SERENADE FOR
  CHAMBER ORCH.) (IN 4 MOVTS.)
  2,1,2,2 - 2,2,1,0 - timp.,perc. - str.   12:00 S.T.I.M.
—— THE MERCHANT OF VENICE: SUITE NO. 2, OP. 86C
  1,1,2,1 - 2,2,1,0 - timp.,perc. - str.   9:00 S.T.I.M.
—— MINIATURE SUITE, OP. 70B (FROM INCIDENTAL MUSIC
  TO "A MIDSUMMER NIGHT'S DREAM") (IN 4 MOVTS.)
  *2,1,2,2 - 2,1,1,1 - timp.,perc. - hp. - str.   8:00 S.T.I.M.
—— OSTINATO FOR STRINGS, OP. 94
  str.   10:00 S.T.I.M.
—— OVERTURE TO THE OPERA "ACHNATON"
  2,2,2,2 - 4,2,3,1 - timp.,perc. - hp. - str.   7:00 S.T.I.M.
  or:
  2,2,2,2 - 2,2,1,0 - timp.,perc. - hp. - str.
—— OVERTURE TO THE OPERA "ISISSYSTRARNAS BRÖLLOP"
  2,2,2,2 - 2,2,3,1 - timp.,perc. - str.   7:00 S.T.I.M.
—— PRELUDE SOLEMNEL, OP. 42
  str.   S.T.I.M.
—— PRELUDE TO STABAT MATER
  str.   4:00 S.T.I.M.
—— RAO-NAI-NAIS SÅNGER (KINESISK RAPSODI), OP. 43
  2,1,2,sax.,2 - 2,2,0,0 - timp.,perc.,xyl. - pf. - str.   11:00 S.T.I.M.
—— SINFONIA BREVE, OP. 61
  2,2,2,2 - 4,2,3,1 - timp.,perc. - str.   18:00 S.T.I.M.
—— SINFONIE DISCRETE, OP. 65
  2,2,2,2 - 2,2,0,0 - timp.,perc.,cel. - hp. - pf. - str.   35:00 S.T.I.M.
—— SINFONIETTA IN FORMA DI SONATA DA CHIESA, OP. 51
  1,1,2,1 - 2,2,1,0 - str.   15:00 S.T.I.M.
—— SKÅNSK RHAPSODY, OP. 13
  2,1,2,2 - 2,2,1,0 - timp.,perc. - str.   11:00 S.T.I.M.
—— SUITE FROM "AROUND THE WORLD IN 80 DAYS", OP. 71B
  2,1,2,1 - 2,2,1,0 - timp.,perc. - str.   17:00 S.T.I.M.
—— SUITE FROM "ISISSYSTRARNAS BRÖLLOP", OP. 58B (IN 4
  MOVTS.)
  2,2,2,2 - 2,2,3,1 - timp.,perc. - str.   19:00 S.T.I.M.
—— SUITE FROM THE BALLET "NI-SI-PLENG", OP. 87B
  1,1,2,1 - 2,2,1,0 - timp.,perc.,cel.,xyl. - hp. - pf. - str.
        11:00 S.T.I.M.
—— SYMPHONIC PROLOGUE, OP. 88
  3,3,3,2 - 4,2,3,1 - timp. - str.   9:00 S.T.I.M.
—— SYMPHONIC VARIATIONS, OP. 17
  2,1,2,2 - 2,2,1,0 - timp.,perc. - str.   12:00 S.T.I.M.
—— SYMPHONY NO. 2 IN D MINOR, OP. 10
  2,2,2,2 - 2,2,1,0 - timp.,perc. - str.   28:00 S.T.I.M.
—— SYMPHONY NO. 3 ("EXOTICA"), OP. 15
  2,2,2,2 - 2,2,3,1 - timp.,perc. - str.   26:00 S.T.I.M.
—— SYMPHONY NO. 4, OP. 20
  2,2,2,sax.,2 - 2,2,3,1 - timp.,perc. - str.   30:00 S.T.I.M.
—— SYMPHONY NO. 5, OP. 27
  2,2,2,2 - 2,2,3,1 - timp.,perc. - str.   26:00 S.T.I.M.
—— SYMPHONY NO. 6, OP. 40
  2,3,3,2 - 4,3,3,1 - timp.,perc. - hp. - str.   34:00 S.T.I.M.
—— SYMPHONY NO. 12, OP. 92
  3,3,2,2 - 2,2,3,1 - timp.,perc.,cel. - str.   33:00 S.T.I.M.

—— UTAN MASK (SYMPHONY), OP. 77
  3,2,2,2 - 4,2,3,1 - timp.,perc. - hp. - str.   38:00 S.T.I.M.

FERRABOSCO, Alfonso - DOLMETSCH, Arnold - GRAINGER, Percy
—— THE FOUR NOTE PAVAN
  str.   G. Schirmer.

FERRAND-TEULET, Denise
—— CONCERTINO FOR TRUMPET, PERCUSSION AND STRINGS
  tpt. - perc. - str.   Presser.

FERRARI, Giorgio
—— ANTIFONE (CONCERTO NO. 2 FOR ORCH.)
  2,3,2,2 - 4,3,3,1 - timp.,perc. - str.   20:00 EV.

FERRARI, Luc
—— FLASHES (FOR 14 INSTRUMENTS)
  *1,1,1,1 - 1,1,1,0 - perc.(2) - str.(2,1,1,1)   16:00 Presser.

FERRARI TRECATE, Luigi
—— CONTEMPLAZIONI (1950)
  3,3,3,2 - 5,3,3,1 - timp.,perc.(5),cel.,xyl. - 2 hp. - org.(ad lib) - pf. -
  str.   13:00 Leeds.
—— UNCLE TOM'S CABIN (LA CAPANNA DELLO ZIO TOM)
  (3-ACT OPERA) (1952) %
  3,3,3,1 sax.,2 - 4,2,3,1 - timp.,perc.(3),cel.,xyl. - hp. - pf. - str.
        Leeds.

FERRARO, Joseph
—— IMPRESSIONES D'ESPAÑA
  *2,*2,2,2 - 4,2,3,1 - timp.,perc. - hp. - pf. - str.   6:00 Composer.

FERRERS, Herbert
—— SONGS OF A ROMAN LEGION (CYCLE FOR BARITONE
  SOLO, MALE CHORUS AND ORCH.) (Text: Kipling)
  2,2,2,2 - 2,2,1,0 - timp. - hp. - str.   18:00 Bo. Hawkes.

FERRIS, William E.
—— THE ANGELIC SALUTATION (FOR CHORUS AND ORCH.)
  (1968) (Text: Biblical)
  0,1,2,0 - 1,2,2,0- timp. - org. - str.   8:00 Composer.
—— BRISTOL HILLS (A REFLECTION FOR STRING ORCH.)
  (1969)
  str.   8:00 Composer.
—— CONCERT PIECE FOR ORGAN AND STRING ORCH. (1963)
  org. - str.   15:00 Composer.
—— CONCERT PIECE FOR TRUMPET, HORN AND STRING
  ORCH. (1960)
  0,0,0,0 - 1,1,0,0 - str.   8:00 Composer.
—— DE PROFUNDIS (FOR SOPRANO, TENOR, SATB CHORUS
  AND ORCH.) (1964)
  2,2,*3,2 - 2,1,2,1 - timp.,perc.(2) - hp. - str.   12:00 Composer.
—— OCTOBER-NOVEMBER (SYMPHONIC MOVEMENT FOR
  ORCH.) (1962)
  *3,*3,*3,*3 - 4,2,3,1 - timp.,perc.(4),xyl. - hp. - str.
        18:00 Composer.

FERROUD, Pierre-Octave
—— AU PARC MONCEAU (SUITE) (IN 4 MOVTS.)
  2,2,2,1 - 2,2,1,0 - timp.,perc.,cel. (or pf.) - hp. - str.
        10:00 Salabert.
—— CHIRURGIE (SUITE)
  3,2,2,2 - 4,3,3,1 - timp.,perc.(4),cel. - 2 hp. - str.   23:00 EV.
—— FOULES
  3,3,3,alto sax.,3 - 4,3,3,1 - timp.,perc.(4),cel.,xyl. - 2 hp. - pf. - str.
        13:00 EV.
—— JEUNESSE (BALLET) %
  3,3,4,3 - 4,4,3,1 - timp.,perc.(5),cel.,glock. - 2 hp. - str.   28:00 EV.
—— JEUNESSE: BALLET SUITE NO. 1
  3,3,4,3 - 4,3,3,1 - timp.,perc.(5),cel.,glock. - 2 hp. - pf. - str.
        14:00 EV.
—— JEUNESSE: BALLET SUITE NO. 2
  3,3,4,3 - 4,4,3,1 - timp.,perc.(5),cel.,glock. - 2 hp. - pf. - str.
        14:00 EV.
—— SERENADE
  2,2,2,2 - 2,2,1,0 - timp.,perc.,cel. - hp. - str.   9:00 EV.
—— SYMPHONY IN A
  3,3,3,3 - 4,3,3,1 - timp. - str.   25:00 EV.
—— TYPES (SUITE) (IN 3 MOVTS.)
  2,2,2,2 - 2,2,1,0 - timp.,perc.,cel. - hp. - pf. - str.   20:00 Salabert.

FERSTL, Erich
—— CONCERTINO FOR GUITAR AND STRING ORCH.
guit. - str.(8,3,2,1) 10:00 Modern.
—— SOL Y SOMBRA
guit. - str. 12:30 Modern.

FESTING, Michael C. - CARSE, Adam
—— CONCERTO IN C MINOR, OP. 3, NO. 2
cemb.(ad lib.) - str. 9:00 Galaxy.

FESTING, Michael C. - PLATT, Richard
—— CONCERTO IN E MINOR, OP. 3, NO 11
fl. - cemb. - str. Oxford.

FETLER, Paul
—— CANTUS TRISTIS (SONG OF SORROW) (IN MEMORY OF
JOHN F. KENNEDY) (1964)
2,1 alto fl.,2,1 E♭cl.,0,0 - 4,3,3,1 - timp.,perc.,bells,glock. - str.
7:00 Composer.
—— A COMEDY OVERTURE
*3,2,2,2 - 4,3,3,1 - timp.,perc.(3), xyl. - str. 7:00 C. Fischer.
—— CONCERTO FOR VIOLIN AND ORCH. (1971) (IN 3 MOVTS.)
1(alt. with picc.),2,0,2 - 2,0,0,0 - timp.,perc.(2),cel. - str.
24:00 Composer.
—— CONTRASTS FOR ORCHESTRA (IN 4 MOVTS.)
*3,*3,*3,*3 - 4,3,3,1 - timp.,perc.(4-5),glock.,xyl. - pf. - str.
22:00 AmerMusEd.
—— GOTHIC VARIATIONS
2(2nd alt. with picc.),2,2,2 - 4,3,3,1 - timp.,perc.(3),xyl. - str.
10:00 Composer.
—— NOTHING BUT NATURE (FOR BARITONE, MIXED CHORUS
AND CHAMBER ORCH.) (1961) (Text: Ogden Nash)
1,1,*2,1 - 1,2,1,0 - timp.,perc.(3),glock. - str. 13:00 Composer.
—— OF EARTH'S IMAGE (CANTATA IN 5 MOVTS.) (FOR
SOPRANO, SATB CHORUS AND ORCH.) (Text: Harriet
Monroe)
*3,2,2,2 - 4,3,3,1 - timp.,perc.(3),bells,glock.,xyl. - str.
18:30 AmerMusEd.
—— SOUNDINGS (SYMPHONY IN 5 MOVTS.)
*3,*3,*3,*3 - 4,3,3,1 - timp.,perc.(3),bells,cel.,glock.,xyl. - pf. - str.
21:00 AmerMusEd.
—— SYMPHONY NO. 3 (IN 3 MOVTS.)
*2,2,2,2 - 4,3,3,1 - timp.,perc.,(3), xyl. - str. 20:00 AMP.
—— SYMPHONY NO. 4 (1967) (IN 2 PARTS, PLAYED WITHOUT
PAUSE)
*3,*3,*3,*3 - 4,3,3,1 - timp.,perc.(3),bells,glock.,xyl. - pf. - str.
22:00 Composer.
—— THIS WAS THE WAY (FOR CHORUS AND ORCH.) (1969)
(Text: Sister Maris Stella)
1,1,*2,1 - 1,0,0,0 - timp.,perc.(3),bells,cel.,glock. - str.
22:00 Composer.
—— THREE POEMS BY WALT WHITMAN (FOR NARRATOR
AND ORCH.)
3(3rd alt. with picc.),*3,*3,*3 - 4,3,3,1 - timp.,perc.,cel.,toy pf. -
pf. - str. 18:00 G. Schirmer.

FÉVRIER, Henri J.
—— APHRODITE: COMPLETE SUITE
2,1,2,1 - 0,1,0,0 - timp.,perc.(2),xyl. - hp. - str. 40:00 Presser.
—— APHRODITE: SUITE NO. 1 (IN 4 MOVTS.)
1,1,2,1 - 0,1,1,0 - perc. - pf. - str. 11:00 Presser.
—— APHRODITE: SUITE NO. 2 (IN 3 MOVTS.)
1,1,2,1 - 0,1,1,0 - perc. - pf. - str. 9:00 Presser.
—— DANSES SICILIENNES (FROM "CARMOSINE")
3,3,2,3 - 4,3,3,0 - timp.,perc.(2) - str. 4:30 Presser.
—— INTERLUDE FROM THE OPERA "GISMONDA"
str. Presser.
—— MONNA VANNA (4-ACT OPERA) %
3,3,3,2 - 4,4,3,1 - timp.,perc.,cel. - hp. - str. 165:00 Presser.
—— PRELUDE TO ACT III OF "MONNA VANNA"
3,3,3,2 - 4,2,3,1 - timp.,perc. - hp. - str. 6:00 Presser.

FICHER, Jacobo
—— CONCERTO FOR VIOLIN AND ORCH., OP. 46 (1942)
2,2,2,2 - 4,2,3,1 - timp. - str. 20:00 Fleisher.
—— HAMLET (FOUR SYMPHONIC MOVEMENTS)
Southern.
—— LOS INVITADOS, OP. 26 ("THE GUESTS") (BALLET) (1933) %
1,0,1,1 alto sax.,1 ten.sax.,0 - 0,2,1,1 - perc. - pf. 17:20 Fleisher.
—— OVERTURE TO THE CANTATA "SALMO DE ALEGRIA", OP.
69
3,3,3,3 - 4,3,3,1 - timp.,perc. - str. Southern.

—— SALMO DE ALEGRIA (CANTATA)
Southern.
—— SEIS FABULAS (6 FABLES), OP. 59
2,2,2,2 - 2,2,2,0 - timp.,perc. - str. 20:00 Southern.
—— SERENATA (FOR STRINGS)
str. 20:00 Southern.
—— SUITE GAUCHO (FOR LARGE ORCH.) (IN 4 MOVTS.)
Southern.
—— SUITE TROPICAL (IN 2 MOVTS.)
I.3,2,2,2 - 2,2,2,1 - timp.,perc. - hp. - str. 20:00 Fleisher.
II.2,2,2,2 - 2,2,2,1 - str.
—— SULAMITA, OP. 8 (SHULAMITE - POEM OF LOVE) (1927)
Fleisher.
—— SYMPHONIC SUITE NO. 2, OP. 6 (1926) (IN 4 MOVTS.)
3,3,3,2 - 4,3,3,1 - timp.,perc. - hp. - str. 23:00 Fleisher.
—— SYMPHONY NO. 1, OP. 20 (SINFONIA DE CAMARA) (1932)
1,1(alt. with Eng.hn.),1,1 - 2,1,0,0 - timp. - str. 15:30 Fleisher.
—— SYMPHONY NO. 2, OP. 24 (1933)
3,3,3,3 - 4,3,3,1 - timp. - hp. - str. 24:00 Fleisher.
—— SYMPHONY NO. 3, OP. 36 (1940) (IN 4 MOVTS.)
3,3,3,3 - 4,3,3,1 - timp. - hp. - str. 32:20 Fleisher.
—— SYMPHONY NO. 7 (EPOPEYA DE MAYO)
3,3,3,3 - 4,3,3,1 - timp.,perc. - hp. - str. 40:00 Southern.
—— THREE SYMPHONIC SKETCHES INSPIRED BY THE
TALMUD, OP. 17
3,3,3,2 - 4,3,3,1 - timp. - str. Fleisher.
—— TWO POEMS, OP. 10 (1928) (Text: Rabindranath Tagore)
1,1,1,1 - 2,0,0,0 - str. 8:00 Fleisher.

FICHTHORN, Claude L.
—— THE EVERLASTING LIGHT (EASTER CANTATA) (FOR 4
SOLO VOICES, MIXED CHORUS AND ORCH.)
1,1,2,1 - 2,2,2,0 - timp. - str. 40:00 Ditson.
—— IN JUDEA'S HILLS (CHRISTMAS CANTATA) (FOR
SOLOISTS, MIXED CHORUS AND ORCH.)
2,2,2,2 - 4,2,3,1 - timp.,glock. - hp. - str. 60:00 Gray.
—— PICTURES OF CALIFORNIA (SYMPHONIC SUITE) (IN 4
MOVTS.)
2(2nd alt. with picc.),2(2nd alt. with Eng. hn.),*3,2 - 4,3,3,1 -
timp.,perc.(3),glock - hp. - pf. - str. 20:00 Composer.
—— THREE SYMPHONIC PIECES (IN 3 MOVTS.)
2(2nd alt. with picc.),*3,*3,2 - 4,3,3,1 - timp.,perc.(3), glock. - hp.
- pf. - str. 25:00 Composer.

FIELD, John - BENOY, A. W.
—— RONDO (FROM THE PIANO SONATA, OP. 1, NO. 1) (FOR
PIANO AND ORCH.)
Oxford.

FIELD, John - BRANSON, David
—— CONCERTO NO. 2 IN A FLAT, FOR PIANO AND ORCH.
(ARR. 1963)
2,0,2,2 - 2,2,0,0 - timp. - pf. - str. 32:00 P.R.S.

FIELD, John - HARTY, Hamilton
—— A JOHN FIELD SUITE (IN 4 MOVTS.)
1,1,1,1 - 1,1,0,0 - timp.,perc. - hp. - str. 18:00 Bo. Hawkes.

FIELD, John - LANGLEY, Robin
—— DIVERTISSEMENT NO.2
pf. - str. Oxford.

FIELD, John - MERRICK, Frank
—— CONCERTO NO. 1 IN E FLAT, FOR PIANO AND ORCH.
1,2,0,2 - 2,2,0,0 - timp. - pf. - str. 18:00 Galaxy.
—— CONCERTO NO. 2 IN A FLAT, FOR PIANO AND ORCH.
1,0,2,2 - 2,2,0,0 - timp. - pf. - str. 30:00 Galaxy.
—— CONCERTO NO. 3 IN E FLAT, FOR PIANO AND ORCH.
2,2,2,2 - 2,2,0,0 - timp. - pf. - str. Galaxy.

FIELD, John - PRIEGNITZ, Hans
—— CONCERTO FOR PIANO AND ORCH. ("IRISH")
2,2,2,2 - 2,2,0,0 - timp. - pf. - str. 18:00 F. Colombo.

FIÉVET, Paul
—— LA PUERTA DEL SOL (ROMANTIC POEM)
3,2,2,2 - 4,3,3,1 - timp.,perc. - 2 hp. - str. 15:00 Salabert.

FILAS, Thomas J.
—— CONCERTO FOR REED DOUBLES
1(alt. with picc.),2,2,2 - 4,3,3,1 - timp.,perc.(2), xyl. - hp. - str.
13:30 C. Fischer.

—— RHAPSODY FOR OBOE, HARP AND STRINGS
    ob. - hp. - str.   6:30 Composer.

FILTZ, Anton - BODART, Eugen
—— CONCERTO IN D MAJOR FOR FLUTE AND ORCH.
    1,2,0,2 - 2,0,0,0 - str.   20:00 Mannheimer.
—— CONCERTO IN G MAJOR FOR FLUTE AND ORCH.
    1,0,0,0 - 2,0,0,0 - str.   21:00 Mannheimer.
—— SYMPHONY IN B FLAT MAJOR, OP. 5, NO. 5
    0,2,0,0 - 2,0,0,0 - str.   11:00 Mannheimer.
—— SYMPHONY IN G MINOR, OP. 2, NO. 2
    0,2,0,0 - 2,0,0,0 - str.   15:00 Mannheimer.

FILTZ, Anton - CARSE, Adam
—— SYMPHONY IN E FLAT
    2 fl. - 2 hn. - str.   10:00 Galaxy.

FILTZ, Anton - HOFMANN, Wolfgang
—— SYMPHONY IN E FLAT MAJOR
    0,2,0,0 - 2,0,0,0 - str.   14:00 Mannheimer.

FILTZ, Anton - SUCHÝ, František
—— CONCERTO IN D MAJOR FOR FLUTE AND ORCH.
    fl. - 2 hn. - str.   22:00 Bo. Hawkes.

FINCH, Ronald
—— CONCERTO FOR OBOE AND STRING ORCH.
    ob. - str.   18:00 Oxford.

FINE, Irving
—— ALICE IN WONDERLAND CHORUSES: I (3 CHORUSES FOR SSA OR SATB CHORUS AND ORCH.)
    6:35 Witmark.
—— BLUE TOWERS
    *3,2,2,2 alto sax.(optional),1 ten. sax.(optional),2 - 4,3,3,1 - timp.,perc. - pf.(optional) - str.   3:00 Mills.
—— DIVERSIONS FOR ORCHESTRA
    2,2(2nd alt. with Eng.hn.),2,2 alto sax.(optional),1 ten. sax.(optional), 1 bar. sax.(optional),2 - 4,3,3,1 - timp.,perc.,cel.(or pf.) - str.   8:15 Mills.
—— MUSIC FOR ORCHESTRA (PARTITA FOR ORCHESTRA)
    3,2,2,2 - 4,3,3,1 - timp.,perc.(3),vibra.,xyl. - str.   MCA Music.
—— NOTTURNO FOR STRINGS AND HARP
    1. Lento; 2. Animato; 3. Adagio
    hp. - str.   14:30 Bo. Hawkes.
—— SERIOUS SONG (A LAMENT FOR STRING ORCH.)
    str.   9:00 Broude.
—— SYMPHONY (1962) (IN 3 MOVTS.)
    *3,*3,*3,*3 - 4,3,3,1 - timp.,perc.(4-5),bells,cel.,glock.,xyl. - hp. - pf. - str.   24:00 Mills.
—— TOCCATA CONCERTANTE (MASQUE)
    *3,*3,*3,3 - 4,2,3,1 - timp.,perc.(3-4) - hp. - pf. - str.   10:30 Bo. Hawkes.

FINE, Vivian
—— ALCESTIS (BALLET SUITE) (1960) (IN 4 MOVTS.)
    2,2(1 alt. with Eng.hn.),2,2 - 2,2,2,0 - timp.,perc.(2),xyl.,vibra.(ad lib) - hp. - pf. - str.   10:45 Composer.
—— CONCERTANTE FOR PIANO AND ORCH. (1944)
    1. Andante con moto; 2. Allegro risoluto
    2,2,2,2 - 2,2,0,0 - timp. - pf. - str.   17:25 Composer.
—— DANCE SUITE (1938) (IN 3 MOVTS.)
    2(2nd alt. with picc.),2,*3,2 - 4,2,2,0 - timp. - 2 hp. - pf. - str.   10:00 Composer.
—— EPITAPH (MY SLEDGE AND HAMMER LY RECLINED) (FOR 4-PART CHORUS AND ORCH.) (1967) (Text: Donald Finkel)
    0,0,0,0 - 0,6,6,0 - timp.(6),perc.(6) - 2 pf. - str.   5:30 Composer.
—— MEETING FOR EQUAL RIGHTS, 1866 (FOR NARRATOR, SOLO VOICES, SATB CHORUS AND ORCH.) (1976)
    2,2,2,2 - 2,2,2,0 - timp.,perc.(2),glock.,xyl. - str.(18,6,5,2)   30:00 Composer.
—— PRELUDE AND ELEGIAC SONG (1937)
    str.   6:30 Composer.
—— THE RACE OF LIFE (BALLET SUITE AFTER DRAWINGS OF JAMES THURBER) (1937) (IN 5 MOVTS.)
    2(2nd alt. with picc.),0,2,1 - 2,2,2,1 - timp.,perc.(2),xyl. - pf. - str.   19:05 Composer.
—— ROMANTIC ODE (FOR VIOLIN, VIOLA, CELLO AND STRING ORCH.) (1976)
    12:00 Composer.

—— VALEDICTIONS (FOR SOPRANO, TENOR, 4-PART CHORUS AND ORCH.) (1959) (Text: John Donne)
    1,1,1,1 - 1,1,0,0 - str.(no d.-b.)   16:00 Composer.

FINGER, Godfrey - BANISTER, John - TILMOUTH, Michael
—— TWO SUITES (FROM "COLLECTION OF MUSICK IN TWO PARTS BY MR. G. FINGER")
    pf. (ad lib.) - str.   Oxford.

FINK, Siegfried
—— CONCERTINO FOR VIBRAPHONE AND STRING ORCH.
    vibra. - str.   10:00 Noack.

FINKE, Fidelio F.
—— BALLET MUSIC FROM THE OPERA "DER ZAUBERFISCH"
    3,2,3,3 - 4,3,3,1 - timp.,perc. - hp. - str.   10:00 Tetra.
—— EIGHT BAGATELLES
    2,2,2,2 - 2,2,3,0 - timp.,perc. - str.   15:00 Tetra.
—— EROS (CANTATA) (FOR SOPRANO, TENOR AND ORCH.) (IN 3 MOVTS.)
    3,3,3,3 - 4,3,3,0 - timp.,perc. - hp. - str.   Tetra.
—— FESTIVE MUSIC
    2,1,1,2 - 1,2,2,0 - timp.,trgl. - str.   Tetra.
—— DER HEIMWEG (ENTR'ACTE FROM THE OPERA "JACOBSFAHRT")
    3,2,2,3 - 4,3,3,1 - timp.,perc. - hp. - pf. - str.   10:00 Tetra.
—— PAN (SYMPHONY FOR LARGE ORCH.)
    4,3,3,4 - 6,3,3,1 - timp.,perc.,cel - hp. - str.   24:00 Tetra.
—— SUITE NO. 2 FOR ORCH.
    2,2,2,3 - 4,3,3,1 - timp.,perc. - hp. - str.   25;00 Tetra.
—— SUITE NO. 3 FOR ORCH.
    3,3,3,3 - 4,3,3,1 - timp.,perc. - hp. - str.   28:00 Tetra.
—— SUITE NO. 4 (FOR 16 WINDS AND PERCUSSION) (IN 3 MOVTS.)
    2,2,2,2 - 2,2,3,1 - timp.,perc.   18:00 Tetra.
—— SUITE NO. 5 (FOR 11 WINDS) (1955)
    1,1,1,1 - 2,2,2,1   19:00 Tetra.
—— SUITE NO. 7 FOR ORCH. (SYMPHONIC MARCHES)
    3,2,3,3 - 4,3,3,1 - timp.,perc. - str.   Tetra.
—— SUITE NO. 8 (FOR WIND QUINTET, TWO PIANOS AND STRING ORCH.)
    1,1,1,1 - 1,0,0,0 - 2 pf. - str.   17:00 Tetra.

FINKELSTEIN, E.
—— TRISTE (FOR 4 VOICES, MEN'S CHORUS AND ORCH.)
    2,2,2,2 - 2,2,2,1 - timp.,perc. - str.   6:00 G. Schirmer.

FINKO, David
—— SYMPHONY NO. 1
    G. Schirmer.

FINLEY, Lorraine
—— A PERSIAN MINIATURE (BALLET PANTOMINE) %
    1,1,1,1 - 2,1,0,0 - perc.(1) - pf. - str.   Composer.

FINN, Father William J.
—— BROTHER ASS AND ST. FRANCIS (FOR HIGH VOICE, CHORUS AND ORCH.)
    2(2nd alt. with picc.),2,2,*3 - 4,2,2,0 - timp. - str.   10:00 Composer.
—— EASTER SERMON OF THE BIRDS (FOR CHORUS AND ORCH.)
    2(2nd alt. with picc.),2,2,2 - 4,2,3,0 - timp. - str.   4:00 Composer.
—— ORCHESTRAL SETTINGS OF FIVE A-CAPPELLA CHORUSES OF THE 16TH CENTURY
    1,2(1st alt. with Eng. hn.),1,2(1 alt. with c.) - hn. - str.   18:00 Summy-Bir.
—— PASCHAL SUITE (IN 5 MOVTS.)
    2(2nd alt. with picc.),2(2nd alt. with Eng. hn),*3,*3 - 4,2,3,1 - timp.,perc.(2) - str.   21:00 Composer.
—— PROLOGUE TO "CAECILIA" (FOR SOPRANO, TENOR, BARITONE, CHORUS, AND ORCH.)
    1(alt. with Eng. hn.),E♭cl.,2,*2 - 4,1,1,0 - timp. - str.   20:00 Composer.
—— QUINTETTE OF CHRISTMAS CAROLS (FOR CONTRALTO, CHORUS AND ORCH.)
    1,1,0,2 - 4,1,2,0 - timp. - str.   12:00 J. Fischer.
—— A RHYTHMIC TRILOGY FOR EASTER (FOR CHORUS AND ORCH.)
    1,1,2,2 - 4,2,2,0 - timp. - str.   9:00 J. Fischer.

FINNEY, Ross Lee

—— BLEHERIS (A MONODY FOR TENOR AND ORCH.)
*3,*3,2,1 - 2,2,3,1 - timp.,perc. (3), cel. - str.   14:00 Henmar.

—— CONCERTINO FOR PIANO AND STRING ORCH. (IN 3 MOVTS.)
pf. - str.   10:00 Composer.

—— CONCERTO FOR ALTO SAXOPHONE ANDD WIND ORCH.
*3,*3,*4,1-3 sax.,*3 - 4,3,2,1-2 - timp.,perc.(3),cel. - hp.   13:30 Henmar.

—— CONCERTO FOR PERCUSSION AND ORCH. (1965) (IN 3 MOVTS.)
*3(2 fl. alt. with 2 picc.),*3,*3,*3 - 4,3,3,1 - timp.,perc.(4-5),bells,cel.,glock.,mar.,vibra.,xyl. - hp. - pf. - str.   15:00 Henmar.

—— CONCERTO FOR VIOLIN AND ORCH. (IN 4 MOVTS.)
2(2nd alt. with picc.),2,2,2 - 4,2,3,1 - timp.,perc.(3) - str.   35:00 Henmar.

—— CONCERTO IN E MAJOR, FOR PIANO AND ORCH. (IN 3 MOVTS.)
2(2nd alt. with picc.),2,2,2 - 4,2,3,1 - timp.,perc. (3) - pf. - str.   18:00 Henmar.

—— CONCERTO NO. 2 FOR PIANO AND ORCH. (1968) (IN 3 MOVTS.)
3(3rd alt. with picc.),*3,*3,*3 - 4,2,3,1 - timp.,perc.,cel.,vibra.,xyl. - hp. - pf. - str.   20:00 Henmar.

—— CONCERTO NO. 2 FOR VIOLIN AND ORCH.
3,3,3,3 - 4,3,3,1 - timp.,perc.(3) - hp. - pf.   15:00 Henmar.

—— HYMN, FUGUING AND HOLIDAY (Formerly: VARIATIONS, FUGUING and RONDO)
3,3,3,3 - 4,3,3,1 - timp.,perc.,glock.,xyl. - pf. - str.   20:00 C. Fischer.

—— LANDSCAPES REMEMBERED (1971)
1(alt. with alto fl. and picc.),0,1,0 - 0,1,1,0 - perc.(1),bells,vibra. - hp. - pf. - str.   16:00 Henmar.

—— THE MARTYR'S ELEGY (FOR TENOR, SATB CHORUS AND ORCH.) (1966) (Text: Percy Bysshe Shelley)
*3,*3,*3,*3 - 4,3,3,1 - timp.,perc.(3-4),glock.,vibra. - hp. - str.   17:30 Henmar.

—— MUSIC TO BE DANCED (IN 3 MOVTS.)
1(alt. with picc.),1,1,1 - 2,1,1,1 - timp.,perc. - pf. - str.   30:00 Composer.

—— THE NUN'S PRIEST'S TALE (FOR SOLO VOICES, CHORUS AND ORCH.)
1(alt. with picc.),1,1,1 - 2,2,2,1 - timp.,perc.(2),bells,glock.,vibra.,xyl. - electric guit. - str.   35:00 Henmar.

—— PILGRIM PSALMS (FOR CHORUS AND ORCH.)
0,0,0,0 - 2,3,2,0 - perc. - str.   28:00 C. Fischer.

—— POLE STAR FOR THIS YEAR (CANTATA) (FOR ALTO, TENOR, CHORUS AND ORCH.)
2,1,2,2 - 2,3,1,0 - timp. - str.   13:00 Composer.

—— THE REMORSELESS RUSH OF TIME (FOR AMPLIFIED NARRATOR, CHORUS AND INSTRUMENTS) (1969) (Text: Composer and Joseph Conrad)
2(alt. with 2 picc.),0,2,0 - 0,2,2,0 - timp.,perc.(2) - pf. - vla.,d.-b.   15:00 Henmar.

—— SPACE (1971) (IN 3 MOVTS.)
3(3rd alt. with picc.),*3,*3,*3 - 4,3 cnt.,0,1 - timp.,perc.(3)bells,cel.,glock.,vibra.,xyl. - 1-2 hp. - pf. - str.(28,12,12,8)   20:00 Henmar.

—— STILL ARE NEW WORLDS (CANTATA) (FOR SPEAKER, TAPE RECORDER, SATB CHORUS AND ORCH.)
*3,*3,*3,*3 - 4,3,3,1 - timp.,perc.(3),bells,cel.,glock.,vibra. - tape-recorder - 2 hp. - str.   24:00 Henmar.

—— SYMPHONY COMUNIQUÉ (IN 4 MOVTS.)
*3,2,*3,*3 - 4,3,3,1 - timp.,perc.(3) - str.   23:00 Henmar.

—— SYMPHONY CONCERTANTE (1967)
3(alt. with 3 picc.),*3,*3,*3 - 4,3,3,1 - timp.,perc.(3),bell,cel.,glock.,vibra.,xyl. - hp. - str.   22:00 Henmar.

—— SYMPHONY FOR STRING ORCH.
str.   25:00 Henmar.

—— SYMPHONY NO. 1
3,3,3,3 - 4,3,3,1 - timp.,perc.(3),cel. - str.   22:00 Henmar.

—— SYMPHONY NO. 2 (IN 4 MOVTS.)
*3,*3,1 E♭cl.,*3,*3 - 4,3,3,1 - timp.,perc.(3),bells,cel.,glock.,vibra.,xyl. - 2 hp. - pf. - str.   21:00 Henmar.

—— SYMPHONY NO. 3 (IN 3 MOVTS.)
*3,*3,*3,*3 - 4,3,3,1 - timp.,perc.(3),bells,cel.,glock.,vibra.,xyl. - 2 hp. - pf. - str.   22:00 Henmar.

—— SYMPHONY NO. 4 (1972) (IN 3 MOVTS.)
3(3rd alt. with picc.),*3,*3,*3 - 4,3,3,1 - timp.,perc.(3),bells,cel.,glock.,vibra.,xyl. - 1-2 hp. - str.(28,12,10,8)   21:00 Henmar.

—— THREE PIECES FOR STRINGS, WIND INSTRUMENTS, PERCUSSION AND TAPE-RECORDER
1(alt. with picc.),1,1,1 - 1,0,0,0 - timp.,perc.(1-2),cel.,vibra.,xyl. - tape-recorder - str.   12:00 Henmar.

—— VARIATIONS FOR ORCHESTRA
3(1 alt. with picc.),*3,*4,*3 - 4,3,3,1 - timp.,perc.(3),bells,cel.,glock.,vibra.,xyl. - hp. - str.   19:00 Henmar.

—— VARIATIONS ON A MEMORY
2,0,2,ten. sax.,o - 2,1,1,0 - perc. - pf.   6:30 Henmar.

FINNISSY, Michael

—— CONCERTO NO. 1 FOR PIANO AND ORCH.
2,2,2,2 - 4,3,3,0 - timp.,perc.(4, incl. 2 on timp.),cel. - hp. - pf. - str.   43:00 Modern.

—— CONCERTO NO. 2 FOR PIANO AND ORCH.
16:00 Modern.

—— FROM THE REVELATIONS OF ST. JOHN THE DIVINE (FOR SOPRANO AND STRINGS)
str.   6:00 P.R.S.

—— HORRORZONE (FOR SOPRANO AND ORCH.)
3,2,0,alto sax.,0 - 0,2,0,0 - perc.(2),cel. - guit. - 2 mandolins - hp. - hpsc. - str.   25:00 P.R.S.

—— JOAN OF ARC (FOR SOPRANO, TENOR, CELLO AND ENSEMBLE)
alto recorder,1(alt. with picc.),alto fl.,0,0,bass sax.,0 - 1,picc. tpt.,0,0 - perc.(4) - guit. - hp. - str.(3,1,2,1)   25:00 Modern.

—— WORLD (FOR 2 SOPRANOS, ALTO, TENOR, BARITONE, BASS AND ORCH.)
2(1 alt. with picc.,1 alt. with alto fl.),2(2nd alt. with Eng. hn.),1,ten. sax.,0 - 1,2,1,1 - perc.(3),cel. - cymbalom - hp. - 2 pf. - str.(2,2,2,2)   18:30 Modern.

FINZI, Gerald

—— CONCERTO FOR CELLO AND ORCH.
2,2,2,2 - 4,2,3,1 - timp.,perc. - str.   36:00 Bo. Hawkes.

—— CONCERTO FOR CLARINET AND STRINGS
cl. - str.   24:00 Bo. Hawkes.

—— DIES NATALIS (FOR HIGH VOICE STRINGS)
str.   20:00 Bo. Hawkes.

—— ECLOGUE FOR PIANO AND STRINGS
pf. - str.   9:00 Bo. Hawkes.

—— THE FALL OF THE LEAF (ELEGY FOR ORCH.)
3,3,2,3 - 4,2,3,1 - timp.,perc. - hp. - str.   9:00 Bo. Hawkes.

—— A FAREWELL TO ARMS (FOR TENOR AND STRINGS)
str.   8:00 Bo. Hawkes.

—— FIVE BAGATELLES FOR CLARINET AND STRINGS
cl. - str.   14:00 Bo. Hawkes.

—— FOR ST. CECILLIA (A CEREMONIAL ODE) (FOR TENOR, CHORUS AND ORCH.)
3,3,3,3 - 4,3,3,1 - timp.,perc.,cel. - 2 hp. - str.   21:00 Bo. Hawkes.

—— GRAND FANTASIA AND TOCCATA
2,2,2,2 - 4,2,3,0 - timp.,perc. - str.   14:00 Bo. Hawkes.

—— IN TERRA PAX (CHRISTMAS SCENE) (FOR SOPRANO, BARITONE, MIXED CHORUS, AND ORCH.)
14:00 Bo. Hawkes.

—— INTERLUDE FOR OBOE AND STRINGS
ob. - str.   8:00 Bo. Hawkes.

—— INTIMATIONS OF IMMORTALITY (FOR TENOR, MIXED CHORUS AND ORCH.)
2,3,2,2 - 4,3,3,1 - timp.,perc. - hp. - str.   43:00 Bo. Hawkes.
or:
3,3,3,3 - 4,3,3,1 - timp.,perc. - hp. - str.

—— INTROIT (FOR VIOLIN AND SMALL ORCH.)
1,*2,2,1 - 2,0,0,0 - str.   9:00 Oxford.

—— LET US GARLANDS BRING (5 SONGS) (FOR VOICE AND STRINGS)
str.   13:15 Bo. Hawkes.

—— LET US NOW PRAISE FAMOUS MEN (FOR 2-PART CHORUS AND STRINGS)
str.   Bo. Hawkes.

—— LO, THE FULL FINAL SACRIFICE (FESTIVAL ANTHEM) (FOR MIXED CHORUS AND ORCH.)
2,2,2,2 - 4,3,2,1 - timp.,perc. - hp.(ad lib.) - org.(ad lib.) - str.   14:00 Bo. Hawkes.

—— MAGNIFICAT (FOR DOUBLE MIXED CHORUS, OPTIONAL SOLO VOICE AND ORCH.)
str. or   9:00 Bo. Hawkes.
2,2,2,2 - 4,2,3,0-1 - timp.,perc. - org.(ad lib.) - str.

—— MUSIC FOR SHAKESPEARE'S PLAY "LOVE'S LABOUR'S
LOST"
2,1,2,1 - 2,1,0,0 - timp.,perc. - str.   23:00 Bo. Hawkes.
—— NEW YEAR MUSIC (NOCTURNE)
2,3,3,3 - 4,3,3,1 - timp.,perc. - hp. - str.   9:30 Bo. Hawkes.
—— PRELUDE
str.   4:00 Bo. Hawkes.
—— ROMANCE FOR STRINGS
str.   6:00 Bo. Hawkes.
—— A SEVERN RHAPSODY
                                                 6:00 P.R.S.

FIOCCO, Joseph H. - BAZELAIRE
—— CONCERTO IN G MAJOR FOR CELLO AND STRINGS
str.   Henmar.

FIOCCO, Joseph-Hector - CAILLIET, Lucien
—— ALLEGRO FOR VIOLIN AND ORCH. (ARR. 1969)
*3,*3,*3,1 d.-b.cl.,*3 - 4,3,3,1 - timp.,perc.(3) - hp. - str.
                                                 5:00 Arranger.

FIORILLO, Federigo - DUBENSKY, Arcady
—— ETUDE FOR VIOLIN AND ORCH.
2,2,2,2 - 4,2,0,0 - timp.,perc. - str.   2:30 Ricordi.

FIRESTONE, Elizabeth
—— CONCERTINO FOR PIANO AND ORCH.
                                                 G. Schirmer.

FIRTICH, Georgij I.
—— LENINGRAD (CANTATA) (FOR SOPRANO, BARITONE,
SATB CHORUS AND ORCH.) (Text: B. Kezhun)
                                                 G. Schirmer.

FISCHER, Ernst
—— FERIENTAGE (SUITE IN 4 MOVTS.)
2,2,2,2 - 4,2,3,0 - perc. - hp. - pf. - str.   16:30 Henmar.
—— FRANÇOIS VILLON SUITE
perc. - cemb.(or mar.) - hp. - str.   10:00 Henmar.
—— JUGENDSTREICHE (A CHEERFUL OVERTURE)
2,2,2,2 - 4,3,3,0 - timp.,perc.,cel. - hp. - str. 7:00 Henmar.
—— PRO MUSICA (DIVERTIMENTO NO. 1)
2,2,2,2 - 4,3,3,0 - timp.,perc. - hp. - pf. - str. 13:30 Bennefeld.
—— THREE PIECES
1,*2,0,0 - 0,0,0,0 - hp. - str.   13:00 Henmar.
—— DER WEG IN DIE LOCKENDE FERNE: OVERTURE
2,2,2,2 - 4,2,3,0 - perc. - hp. - pf. - str.   7:30 Henmar.

FISCHER, Jan F.
—— EUFROSIMA: BALLET SUITE NO. 1
3,3,3,3 - 4,4,3,1 - timp.,perc.,cel.,xyl. - hp. - org. - pf. - str.
                                                 14:00 Bo. Hawkes.
—— EUFROSIMA: BALLET SUITE NO. 2
3,3,3,3 - 4,4,3,1 - timp.,perc.,cel.,xyl. - hp. - org. - pf. - str.
                                                 12:00 Bo. Hawkes.

FISCHER, Johann C. - CARSE, Adam
—— CONCERTO IN C MAJOR FOR OBOE AND STRINGS
ob. - str.   16:00 Galaxy.

FISCHER, William S.
—— CONCERTO GROSSO, BLUES IN D (1968)
2,2,2,4 - 2,2,2,1 - timp.,perc.(2) - str.   30:00 ReadyProds.
—— INTRODUCTION AND SONG
2,2,2,2 - 4,3,2,1 - timp.,perc. - str.   8:00 Composer.
—— STATEMENT (FOR VOICES AND ORCH.) (Text: Composer)
*3,2,2,2 - 4,3,3,1 - timp.,perc.(3),xyl. - str. 10:00 Composer.

FIŠER, Luboš
—— FÜNFZEHN BLÄTTER NACH DÜRER'S "APOKALYPSE"
                                                 Hans Gerig.
—— SYMPHONY
2,2,2,2 - 3,2,0,0 - timp. - str.   19:00 Bo. Hawkes.

FISHMAN, Marian
—— ADAGIO FOR ORCHESTRA (1964)
*3,*3,*3,*3 - 4,3,3,1 - timp.,perc.(4),xyl. - str. 5:21 Composer.

FISKE, Milton
—— SYMPHONY IN E FLAT ("TRANSFIGURATION") (IN 3
MOVTS.)
2,*3,2,2 - 2,2,0,0 - str.   18:00 Composer.

FITCH, Theodore F.
—— ANNE RUTLEDGE (FOR WOMEN'S CHORUS AND ORCH.)
0,0,0,0 - 2,3,2,1 - str.   7:00 Composer.
—— AUGUST, 1939
2,1,2,2 - 4,3,3,0 - timp.,perc.(3) - str.   9:00 Composer.
—— BLUE OXEN (SYMPHONY IN 1 MOVT.)
2,2,2,2 - 4,3,3,0 - timp. - str.   19:00 C. Fischer.
—— COMMENCEMENT OVERTURE
2,1,2,2 - 4,3,3,0 - timp.,perc.(3) - str.   10:30 Composer.
—— CONCERTO FOR PIANO AND ORCH. (IN 3 MOVTS.)
2,2,2,2 - 4,3,3,0 - timp. - pf. - str.   29:00 Composer.
—— CONGO (AN OVERTURE)
2,2,2,2 - 4,2,3,0 - str.   6:00 Composer.
—— A DAY IN JUNE (FOR CHORUS AND ORCH.)
1,1,2,1 - 2,2,2,0 - str.   7:00 Composer.
—— DIVERTIMENTO
1. Allegretto; 2. Adagio; 3. Andante; 4. Allegro; 5. Vivace
1,1,1,1 - 2,1,1,0 - str.   23:00 C. Fischer.
—— HIGHTIDE OF THE YEAR (FOR CHORUS AND ORCH.)
2,2,2,2 - 2,2,2,0 - timp. - str.   20:30 Composer.
—— LENTO MISTERIOSO (REFLECTIONS IN PASTEL)
2,1,2,2 - 4,3,3,0 - timp.,perc.(3) - str.   7:00 Composer.
—— STATE HIGHWAY
3(3rd alt. with picc.),3(3rd alt. with Eng. hn.),*3,*3, - 4,3,3,1 -
timp. - str.   4:00 Composer.
—— TERRA NOVA (OVERTURE)
3,*3,3,*3 - 4,3,3,0 - timp. - str.   10:00 C. Fischer.

FITELBERG, Jerzy
—— CONCERTO NO. 2 FOR PIANO AND ORCH. (NEW
VERSION)
3,3,3,3 - 4,3,3,1 - timp.,perc. - pf. - str.   20:00 Southern.
—— SYMPHONY NO. 2 FOR STRINGS
str.   29:00 Southern.

FITZENHAGEN, Wilhelm K. F. - HALETZKI, Paul
—— PERPETUUM MOBILE (FOR CELLO AND ORCH.)
3(3rd alt. with picc.),2,2,2 - 2,2,0,0 - perc. - hp. - str.
                                                 8:00 Modern.

FITZGERALD, Bernard
—— CONCERTO FOR TRUMPET AND ORCH.
2,2,2,2 - 4,3,3,0 - timp.,perc. - str.   16:00 C. Fischer.

FIUME, O.
—— TRE PEZZI
2,3,2,2 - 2,2,0,0 - perc.,cel. - hp. - str.   10:00 Bo. Hawkes.

FLAGELLO, Nicholas
—— ANIMAL SUITE
*2,*2,2,1 - 2,2,2,0 - timp.,perc.,cel.,glock. - hp. - str.
                                                 20:00 Valentino.
—— CAPRICCIO FOR CELLO AND ORCH.
2(2nd alt. with picc.),2(2nd alt. with Eng.hn.),2,0 - 2,2,1,0 -
timp.,perc.,cel. - hp. - str.   16:00 General.
—— CHORALE AND EPISODE (FOR BRASS ENSEMBLE)
0,0,0,0 - 4,2,3,1   6:00 General.
—— CONCERTINO FOR PIANO, BRASS AND TIMPANI
0,0,0,0 - 4,2,3,1 - timp. - pf.   10:30 General.
—— CONCERTO ANTONIANO (FOR FLUTE AND ORCH.)
1,2,2,2 - 2,1,1,0 - timp.,perc.(2) - hp. - str. 25:45 General.
—— CONCERTO FOR STRING ORCH. (IN 3 MOVTS.)
str.   24:15 General.
—— CONTEMPLATIONS OF MICHELANGELO (4 SONGS FOR
HIGH VOICE AND ORCH.) (Text: Michelangelo)
2(2nd alt. with picc.),2(2nd alt. with Eng.hn.),2,2 - 2,2,1,0 -
timp.,perc.(2),bells,cel.,glock. - hp. - str.   20:35 General.
—— GOLDONI OVERTURE
3,2,2,2 - 4,2,2,1 - timp.,perc.,cel. - hp. - pf. - str. Belw-Mills.
—— L' INFINITO (FOR BASS-BARITONE AND ORCH.) (Text:
Leopardi)
1,1,1,1 - 1,0,0,0 - cel. - pf. - str.   7:30 General.
—— ISLAND IN THE MOON (FOR HIGH VOICE AND ORCH.)
(Text: Blake)
2(2nd alt. with picc.),2,2,2 - 2,0,0,0 - timp.,perc.(1) - hp. - pf.(alt.
with cel.) - str.   16:00 General.
—— THE LAND (6 SONGS FOR BASS-BARITONE AND ORCH.)
(Text: Tennyson)
1,1,1,1 - 1,0,0,0 - timp.,perc.,cel. - pf. - str. 24:00 General.
—— LAUTREC (BALLET SUITE) (1965) (IN 4 MOVTS.)
*3,*3,2,2 - 4,3,3,1 - timp.,perc.(3),cel.,glock. - pf. - str.
                                                 16:30 General.

—— OVERTURE FOR ORCHESTRA
                                         Belw-Mills.

—— THE PASSION OF MARTIN LUTHER KING (FOR BASS-BARITONE, SATB CHORUS AND ORCH.) (Text: Martin Luther King, plus portions of the Mass in Latin)
    3,3,2,2 - 4,3,3,1 - timp.,perc.,cel. - org.(ad lib.) - str.
                                    47:00 Belw-Mills.

—— PROCESSIONAL FOR ORCH.
    2,2,2,2 - 4,3,2,2 - timp.,perc. - str.
                                        Belw-Mills.

—— SERENATA
    1,1,1,1 - 2,0,0,0 - hp. - str.   8:00 General.

—— SUITE FOR AMBER
                                        Belw-Mills.

—— SYMPHONIC ARIA
    4,3,3,3 - 4,3,2,1 - timp.,perc. - hp. - str.   Belw-Mills.

—— SYMPHONY FOR STRINGS (IN 1 MOVT.)
    str.   22:00 General.

—— SYMPHONY NO. 1
    3,3,3,3 - 4,3,3,1 - timp.,perc.,cel. - hp. - pf. - str.
                                        Belw-Mills.

—— SYMPHONY OF THE WINDS
    *3,*3,*3,*3 - 4,3,3,1 - timp.,perc. - pf.(alt. with cel.)
                                    12:00 General.

—— TE DEUM (FOR CHORUS AND ORCH.) (1968) (Text: Liturgical Latin, and John G. Whittier)
    *3,*3,*3,*3 - 4,3,3,1 - timp.,perc.(4),bells,cel.,glock. - hp. - org. - str.
                                17:00 C. Fischer.

—— TE DEUM FOR MANKIND (FOR SATB CHORUS AND ORCH.)
    3,2,3,2 - 4,3,3,1 - timp.,perc. - hp. - org. - str. 15:00 C. Fischer.

—— THEME, VARIATIONS AND FUGUE
    3,3,3,3 - 4,3,3,1 - timp.,perc.,cel.,glock.,xyl. - hp. - org.(ad lib.) - pf. - str.
                                    Belw-Mills.

FLANAGAN, William
—— DIVERTIMENTO FOR ORCH.
    2,2,2,2 - 2,2,0,0 - timp. - str.   16:00 Mills.

FLEISCHER, Willy
—— SUITE FOR STRING ORCH. (IN 5 MOVTS.)
    str.   14:00 Henmar.

FLEMING, Christopher le
—— THE SILVER DOVE, OP. 35 (FOR CHORUS AND ORCH.)
    2,2,2,2 - 4,3,3,1 - timp.,perc. - hp. - str. 26:00 Belw-Mills.

FLEMING, Robert J.
—— AROUND THE HOUSE (NURSERY SUITE)
                                25:00 Oxford.

—— BALLET INTRODUCTION
    *2,2,2,2 - 2,2,3,0 - timp.,perc. - str. 8:05 CanMusCtr.

—— CHAPTER 13 (BALLET MUSIC IN A SATIRICAL VEIN)
                        22:00 C.A.P.A.C.

—— CONCERTO FOR TUBA AND SMALL ORCH. (1966)
    2,1,2,1 - 2,0,0,1 - timp. - str. 13:00 CanMusCtr.

—— CONCERTO '64 (FOR PIANO AND ORCH.) (1964) (IN 3 MOVTS.)
    2,2,2,2 - 4,2,3,1 - timp.,perc.(ad lib.) - hp. - pf. - str.
                              12:00 CanMusCtr.

—— FOUR FANTASIAS ON CANADIAN FOLK THEMES (1966)
    *3,1,*3,3 sax.(alto,ten.,bar.)1 - 3,2,3,0 - timp.,perc. - str.
                              15:20 CanMusCtr.

—— HEXAD (1972)
    2,2(2nd alt. with Eng. hn.),2,2 - 2,2,0,0 - perc. - str.
                              9:30 CanMusCtr.

—— OF A TIMELESS LAND (FOR CONTRALTO AND ORCH.) (1974) (Text: Margaret Fleming)
    2,2,2,2 - 4,2,3,0 - timp.,perc. - str. 15:30 CanMusCtr.

—— OUR MIND WAS THE SINGER (SONG CYCLE) (FOR BARITONE AND ORCH.) (1972) (Text: Robert Finch)
    2,2(2nd alt. with Eng.hn), 2,2 - 2,2,0,0 - perc. - str.
                              15:40 CanMusCtr.

—— RED RIVER COUNTRY
    2,2,2,2 - 2,2,2,1 - pf. - str.   8:00 C.A.P.A.C.

—— SEABOARD SKETCHES
    1,1,1,1 - 1,1,0,0 - pf. - str.   15:00 C.A.P.A.C.

—— SHADOW ON THE PRAIRIE (BALLET) %
                        25:30 C.A.P.A.C.

—— SHADOW ON THE PRAIRIE (SUITE FROM THE BALLET) (1953)
    2(2nd alt. with picc.),2,2,2 - 2,2,2,1 - timp.,perc. - pf. - str.
                            12:40 CanMusCtr.

—— SIX VARIATIONS ON A LITURGICAL THEME (1946)
    str.   8:00 CanMusCtr.

—— THE SON (SUITE)
    2,1,1,1 - 1,0,0,0 - hp. - pf. - str. 6:00 C.A.P.A.C.

—— SUITE FOR STRINGS
    str.   10:00 Oxford.

—— SUMMER SUITE (1957)
    *3,1,*3,1 - 1,3,3,1 - timp.,perc. - str. 8:25 CanMusCtr.

—— THREE CONTRASTS (1964)
                            7:05 CanMusCtr.

—— VARIATIONS ON A LITURGICAL THEME
                        8:00 C.A.P.A.C.

—— YOU NAME IT (SUITE) (1964) (IN 3 MOVTS.)
    str.   5:20 GVThompson.

FLETCHER, H. Grant
—— AN AMERICAN OVERTURE
    2(2nd alt. with picc.),2,2,2 - 4,2,3,1 - timp. - str. 6:00 Mills.

—— THE CARRION CROW (A CHAMBER FOLK OPERA) % (Text: Composer)
    2,2,2,2 - 2,0,0,0 - timp. - str. 43:00 Composer.

—— CINCO DE MAYO (THE FIFTH OF MAY) (BALLET SUITE) (1972)
    2,2,2,2 - 4,2,3,1 - timp.,perc.(5),xyl. - str. 23:00 Composer.

—— CONCERTO FOR PIANO AND ORCH.
    1. Allegro, with spirit; 2. Adagio; 3. Allegro
    2,2,2,2 - 4,2,3,1 - timp. - pf. - str. 35:00 Composer.

—— THE CRISIS (FOR MIXED CHORUS AND ORCH.)
    2(2nd alt. with picc.),2,2,2 - 4,2,3,1 - timp.,perc. (4) str.
                              32:00 Composer.

—— A DICTIONARY OF MUSICAL INSTRUMENTS (1957)
    2,2,2,2 - 2,2,2,0 - timp.,cel. - hp. - str. 8:00 Composer.

—— DIVERSION FOR STRINGS (NO. 3) (1971)
    str.   22:00 Composer.

—— GLYPHS (1968)
    2,2,2,2 - 2,2,0,0 - timp. - str. 17:00 Composer.

—— NOCTURNE
    3(3rd alt. with picc.),*2,2,2 - 4,2,3,1 - timp.,perc.(3) - hp. - str.
                              6:00 Composer.

—— OVERTURE TO "THE CARRION CROW"
    2,2,2,2 - 2 hn. - timp. - str. 4:00 Composer.

—— PANELS FROM A THEATER WALL (SUITE) (IN 5 MOVTS.)
    3(3rd alt. with picc.),2(2nd alt. with Eng - hn.),2,2, - 4,3,3,1 - timp.,perc. (3), xyl. - hp. - pf. - str. 14:15 C. Fischer.

—— POCKET ENCYCLOPEDIA OF THE ORCHESTRA (IN 16 MOVTS.)
    1,1,1,1 - 1,1,0,0 - timp. - str. 15:00 Fema.
    Or
    2,2,2,2 - 2,2,2,0 - timp. - str.

—— REGENCY HOUSE CONCERTO (PIANO CONCERTO NO. 2) (1966)
    pf. - str.   4:30 Composer.

—— RETROSPECTION (RHAPSODY NO. 3) (1965)
    fl. - tape-recorder - str. 12:00 Composer.

—— RHAPSODY FOR FLUTE AND STRINGS
    fl. - str.   12:00 Composer.

—— A RHAPSODY OF DANCES
    2,2,2,2 - 4,2,3,1 - timp.,perc.(3) - str. 8:00 SchmittMC.

—— THE SACK OF CALABASAS (3-ACT OPERA) % (Text: Composer)
                            120:00 Composer.

—— SAILORS' SONGS AND DANCES (FOR STRINGS) (IN 3 MOVTS.)
    str.   10:00 Fema.

—— THE SEVEN CITIES OF CIBOLA
    2(2nd alt. with picc.),2,2,2 - 4,2,3,1 - timp.,perc.(3),xyl. - pf. - str.
                              14:00 Composer.

—— A SONG FOR WARRIORS (VARIATIONS ON A SLAVIC THEME)
    3(3rd alt. with picc.),*3,*3,*3 - 4,3,3,1 - timp.,perc.(5), glock. - str.
                              10:00 Composer.

—— SYMPHONY NO. 1 (IN 3 MOVTS.)
    2,2,2,2 - 4,2,0,0 - timp.,perc. - str. 25:00 Composer.

—— TWO PIECES FOR ORCHESTRA
    2,2,2,2 - 2,2,1,0 - timp.,perc. (1) - str. 12:45 Composer.

FLETCHER, Percy E.
—— CUPID'S GARLAND (A PASTORAL FOR SOPRANO OR TENOR, BARITONE, MALE CHORUS AND ORCH.)
    2,2,2,2 - 3,2,2,2 - timp.,perc. - str. 25:00 Bo. Hawkes.

FLOSMAN, Oldřich
—— CONCERTINO FOR BASSOON AND ORCH.
    2,2,2,3 - 4,2,0,1 - timp.,perc. - str. 18:00 Bo. Hawkes.

—— CONCERTO FOR CLARINET AND ORCH.
2,2,3,2 - 4,2,0,1 - timp.,perc. - pf. - str.   21:00 Bo. Hawkes.

FLÖSSNER, Franz
—— GRÜPPENSPIELMUSIK FOR ORCH.
2,2,2,2 - 4,1,1,1 - hp. - str.   12:00 Alkor.

FLOTHUIS, Marius
—— CANTI E GIUOCHI, OP. 66
1,1,1,1 - 1,0,0,0 - str.   13:00 Henmar.
—— CAPRICCIO, OP. 35, NO. 2
str.   9:00 Henmar.
—— CONCERT OVERTURE, OP. 56
3,2,3,sax.,2 - 4,3,3,1 - timp.,perc. - hp. - str.   8:00 Henmar.
—— CONCERTINO
7:00 Henmar.
—— CONCERTINO FOR OBOE, PERCUSSION AND STRINGS, OP. 70-B
ob. - perc. - str.   Henmar.
—— CONCERTINO FOR SMALL ORCH., OP. 8
1,1,1,sax.,0 - 0,1,0,0 - timp. - pf. - str.   7:00 Henmar.
—— CONCERTO FOR CLARINET AND ORCH., OP. 58 (1957)
2,2,1,2 - 3,2,0,0 - timp.,perc. - hp. - str.   17:00 Henmar.
—— CONCERTO FOR FLUTE AND ORCH., OP. 19
1,0,0,0 - 3,0,0,0 - timp.,cel.,vibra. - str.   22:00 Henmar.
—— CONCERTO FOR HORN AND SMALL ORCH., OP. 24
1,0,2,2 - 1,0,0,0 - timp. - str.   16:00 Henmar.
—— CONCERTO FOR PIANO AND ORCH., OP. 30
1,1,1,1 - 2,0,0,0 - timp. - pf. - str.   16:00 Henmar.
—— CONCERTO FOR VIOLIN AND SMALL ORCH., OP. 39
1,0,2,2 - 2,0,0,0 - timp. - str.   16:00 Henmar.
—— DRAMATIC OVERTURE, OP. 16
3,3,3,3 - 4,3,3,1 - timp.,perc.,cel. - str.   12:00 Henmar.
—— ESPRESSIONI CORDIALI, OP. 63 (7 BAGATELLES) (1963)
str.   12:00 Henmar.
—— FANTASIA FOR HARP AND SMALL ORCH., OP. 51
1,1,1,1 - 1,0,0,0 - timp.,cel. - hp. - str.   13:00 Henmar.
—— FANTASIA QUASI UNA CANTATA, OP. 71 (FOR MEZZO-SOPRANO, HARPSICHORD AND STRING ORCH.) (1969)
hpsc. - str.   6:00 Henmar.
—— FOUR SONGS, OP. 3 (FOR SOPRANO AND ORCH.) (1939) (Text: Chr. Morgenstern)
2,1,2,1 - 2,2,0,0 - timp.,perc.,cel.,vibra. - hp. - str.   8:00 Henmar.
—— FOUR TRIFLES, OP. 33 (FOR HIGH VOICE AND ORCH.) (1950)
1,1,2,1 alto sax.,1 - 1,1,0,0 - timp.,perc.,cel. - hp. - str.   6:00 Henmar.
—— HYMNUS, OP. 67 (FOR SOPRANO AND ORCH.) (1965) (Text: Ingeborg Bachmann)
9:00 Henmar.
—— KLEINE OUVERTURE, OP. 14 (FOR SOPRANO AND ORCH.) (1942) (Text: Chr. Morgenstern)
2,2,3,3 - 3,3,3,1 - timp.,perc.,cel.,vibra. - hp. - str.   7:00 Henmar.
—— SINFONIETTA CONCERTANTE, OP. 55 (FOR CLARINET, ALTO SAXOPHONE AND SMALL ORCH.)
2,0,1,alto sax.,0 - 2,0,0,0 - timp. - pf. - str.   14:00 Henmar.
—— SONNET, OP. 9 (FOR MEZZO-SOPRANO AND ORCH.) (1940) (Text: E. Toller)
2,2,3,2 - 3,3,3,0 - timp.,perc. - pf. - str.   9:00 Henmar.
—— SPES PATRIAE, OP. 62 (SINFONIETTA) (1962) (IN 3 MOVTS.)
2,2,2,2 - 2,2,0,0 - timp.,perc. - str.   13:00 Henmar.
—— SYMPHONIC MUSIC FOR LARGE ORCH., OP. 59 (1957)
3,3,3,3 - 4,3,3,1 - timp.,perc. - 2 hp. - str.   18:00 Henmar.
—— TO AN OLD LOVE, OP. 32 (FOR MEZZO-SOPRANO AND ORCH.) (1948) (Text: E. Marsh)
1,0,3,1 alto sax.,2 - 2,3,2,0 - timp. - hp. - str.   7:00 Henmar.

FLOTOW, F. von - EVANS
—— OVERTURE TO "STRADELLA"
7:00 Bo. Hawkes.

FLOYD, Carlisle
—— IN CELEBRATION: AN OVERTURE FOR ORCHESTRA (1970)
Belw-Mills.
—— INTRODUCTION, ARIA AND DANCE
2,3,3,2 - 4,3,3,1 - timp.,perc. - hp. - str.   16:00 Presser.
—— MARKHEIM (OPERA) %
2,2,2,2 - 4,2,2,1 - timp.,perc. - hp. - str.   Bo. Hawkes.
—— THE MYSTERY (5 SONGS OF MOTHERHOOD) (FOR SOPRANO AND ORCH.) (Text: Gabriela Mistral)
2,2,2,2 - 4,2,2,0 - timp.,perc. - hp. - str.   17:00 Bo. Hawkes.

—— NOCTURNE FOR SOPRANO AND ORCH. ("OUT OF THE CRADLE ENDLESSLY ROCKING")
2,2,2,2 - 4,2,0,0 - timp.,perc. - hp. - str.   10:00 Bo. Hawkes.
—— THE PASSION OF JOHNATHAN WADE (OPERA) %
Bo. Hawkes.
—— PILGRIMAGE (FOR BARITONE AND ORCH.) (ON FIVE BIBLICAL TEXTS)
2,2,2,2 - 4,2,0,0 - timp.,perc.,cel. - str.   20:00 Bo. Hawkes.
—— SLOW DUSK (MUSICAL PLAY IN 1 ACT) %
2,2,2,2 - 2,2,2,0 - timp.,perc. - hp. - str.   40:00 Bo. Hawkes.
—— THE SOJOURNER AND MOLLIE SINCLAIR (1-ACT MUSIC-DRAMA) %
1,1,1,1 - 1,1,1,0 - timp.,perc. - hp. - str.   75:00 Bo. Hawkes.
—— SUSANNAH (OPERA) %
2,2,2,2 - 4,2,3,1 - timp.,perc. - hp. - str.   105:00 Bo. Hawkes.
—— SUSANNAH: SUITE FROM THE OPERA
2,2,2,2 - 4,2,3,1 - timp.,perc. - hp. - str.   19:00 Bo. Hawkes.
—— TWO INTERLUDES FROM THE OPERA "OF MICE AND MEN"
2,2,2,2 - 4,2,2,1 - timp.,perc.,cel. - hp. - str.   Belw-Mills.
—— WUTHERING HEIGHTS (SYMPHONIC SUITE FROM THE OPERA)
2,2,2,2 - 4,2,3,1 - timp.,perc. - hp. - str.   22:00 Bo. Hawkes.
—— WUTHERING HEIGHTS (3-ACT OPERA) %
2,2,2,2 - 3,2,2,0 - timp.,perc. - hp. - str.   130:00 Bo. Hawkes.

FLURY, Richard
—— CAPRICE 1967 (FÜR VIOLINE UND ORCHESTER)
1,1,1,1 - 2,1,1,0 - timp. - str.   10:00 S.U.I.S.A.
—— KONZERT NR. 4 FÜR VIOLINE UND ORCHESTER
22:00 S.U.I.S.A.

FODI, John
—— CONCERTO FOR VIOLA AND TWO WIND ENSEMBLES, OP. 35 (1972)
*2,*2,E♭cl., alto cl.,*3,*2 - 2,2,3,1 - vla.   20:00 CanMusCtr.
—— SYMPARANEKROMENOI, OP. 25 (1971) (IN 5 MOVTS.)
*4,*3,E♭cl.,*4,*3 - 4,3,3,1 - timp.,perc. - hp. - pf. - str.   16:30 CanMusCtr.

FOERSTER, Emanuel A. - LAUSCHMANN
—— CONCERTO IN E MINOR
ob. - cemb. - str.   Henmar.

FOERSTER, Josef Bohuslav
—— EVENING IN BELMONTE, OP. 59
2,3,3,2 - 4,2,3,1 - timp. - 2 hp. - str.   7:00 Bo. Hawkes.
—— FESTIVAL OVERTURE, OP. 70
3,2,2,2 - 4,3,3,1 - timp.,perc. - hp. - str.   10:00 Bo. Hawkes.
—— LEGEND, OP. 83
3,3,3,3 - 4,2,3,0 - timp.,trgl. - hp. - str.   19:00 Bo. Hawkes.
—— SHAKESPERIAN SUITE
3,3,3,3 - 4,3,3,1 - timp. - hp. - str.   28:00 Bo. Hawkes.
—— SYMPHONIC SUITE (JICINSKA), OP. 124
2,3,3,2 - 4,2,3,1 - timp.,perc. - hp. - str.   23:00 Bo. Hawkes.
—— SYMPHONY NO. 5, OP. 141 (1929)
3,3,3,3 - 4,3,3,1 - timp. - 2 hp. - org. - str.   43:00 Bo. Hawkes.

FOGG, Eric
—— CONCERTO FOR BASSOON AND ORCH.
2,0,2,1 - 2,1,0,0 - perc.,cel. - hp. - str.   17:00 Novello.

FONGAARD, Bjørn
—— CONCERTINO FOR PIANO AND STRINGS, OP. 11 (1953)
pf. - str.   11:00 T.O.N.O.
—— FANTASIA FOR STRING ORCH., OP. 69 (1968)
str.   5:00 T.O.N.O.
—— KLANGBILDER, OP. 72 (1968)
str.   16:00 T.O.N.O.
—— KOSMOS, OP. 57 (1968)
perc. - str.   10:00 T.O.N.O.
—— LEGENDE, OP. 68 (1968)
1,1,1,1 - 2,1,2,0 - timp.,perc. - str.   9:00 T.O.N.O.
—— ORAFONI, OP. 37, NO. 1 (FOR MALE SPEAKING CHORUS, PERCUSSION AND STRINGS) (1964)
perc. - str.   5:00 T.O.N.O.
—— ORCHESTRA ANTIPHONALIS, OP. 67 (1968) (WITH ORCH. DIVIDED INTO 2 GROUPS)
1,0,1,3 - 2,2,0,0 - timp.,perc.(2) - str.   10:30 T.O.N.O.
—— SERENADE FOR STRINGS
str.   28:00 T.O.N.O.
—— SINFONIETTA NO. 1, OP. 27 (1950)
2,3,2,2 - 4,2,2,0 - timp.,perc. - str.   20:00 T.O.N.O.

—— SINFONIETTA NO. 2, OP. 71 (1968)
    2,2,2,1 - 4,2,2,0 - timp.,perc. - str.   10:30 T.O.N.O.
—— THREE NOVELETTES, OP. 18 (1954)
    1,1,1,1 - 2,0,0,0 - timp. - str.   14:00 T.O.N.O.
—— THREE PIECES FOR STRINGS, OP. 10 (1953)
    str.   14:00 T.O.N.O.
—— THREE PIECES FOR STRINGS, OP. 22 (1955)
    str.   10:00 T.O.N.O.
—— URANIUM 235 (1963)
    3,2,3,2 - 4,2,2,0 - timp.,perc. - str.   11:00 T.O.N.O.
—— VISION, OP. 59 (1968)
    str.   8:00 T.O.N.O.

FONTYN, Jacqueline
—— GALAXY
    1,1,1,1 - 1,1,1,0 - perc.(2),cel. - hp. - pf. - str.   12:15 Presser.
—— SIX EBAUCHES (SIX SKETCHES)
    2,2,2,2 - 4,3,3,1 - timp.,perc.(4),cel. - hp. - str.   10:00 EV.

FOORT, Reginald
—— CONCERTO FOR ORGAN AND ORCH.
    P.R.S.

FORBES, Sebastian
—— CHACONNE (1967)
    2,2,2,3 - 4,2,3,1 - timp.,perc.(4) - pf. - str.   12:00 P.R.S.
—— PAGEANT OF PAUL (SUITE)(1963)
    2,2,2,2 - 4,2,3,1 - timp.,perc. - hp. - str.   12:00 P.R.S.

FORD, Clifford
—— SUITE FOR ORCHESTRA (1973) (IN 2 MOVTS.)
    *2,alto fl.,2(2nd alt. with Eng. hn.),E♭cl.,*2,2 - 4,2,2,1 -
    timp.,perc.(5), hp. - pf.(or cel.) - str.   13:05 CanMusCtr.

FORDELL, Erik
—— ARNIA, OP. 83 (SUITE)
    str.   FinnMICtr.
—— CANTATA (FOR SATB CHORUS, 2 FLUTES, TRUMPET,
PIANO AND STRINGS) (1968) (Text: U. Kantola)
    2,0,0,0 - 0,1,0,0 - pf. - str.   18:00 FinnMICtr.
—— CANTATA (FOR SATB CHORUS, 4 WOODWINDS, PIANO
AND STRINGS)(1968) (Text: U. Kantola)
    1,1,1,1 - 0,0,0,0 - pf. - str.   24:00 FinnMICtr.
—— CANTATUM PROFANUM, OP. 122 (FOR SOLO VOICES,
CHORUS AND ORCH.)(1970) (Text: U. Kantola)
    FinnMICtr.
—— CHURCH CANTATA (FOR SOLO VOICES, SATB CHORUS,
ORGAN AND ORCH.)(1964)
    2,0,0,0 - 0,1,0,0 - org. - str.   28:00 FinnMICtr.
—— CONCERT OVERTURE, OP. 101 (1969)
    2,2,2,2 - 2,2,3,1 - timp. - str.   12:00 FinnMICtr.
—— CONCERTINO NO. 1 FOR PIANO AND SMALL ORCH., OP.
16 (1961)
    1,1,1,1 - 1,1,0,0 - perc.(2) - pf. - str.   18:00 FinnMICtr.
—— CONCERTO FOR HORN AND ORCH., OP. 46 (1956)
    3,3,2,2 - 1,0,0,0 - str.   34:00 FinnMICtr.
—— CONCERTO NO. 1 FOR VIOLIN AND ORCH., OP. 14 (1955)
    20:00 FinnMICtr.
—— CONCERTO NO. 2 FOR PIANO AND ORCH., OP. 41 (1962)
    1,1,1,1 - 1,1,0,0 - perc.(2) - pf. - str.   20:00 FinnMICtr.
—— CONCERTO NO. 2 FOR VIOLIN AND ORCH., OP. 56 (REV.
1966)
    3,2,2,2 - 2,0,0,2 - str.   30:00 FinnMICtr.
—— CONCERTO NO. 3 FOR PIANO AND ORCH., OP. 42 (1962)
    1,1,1,1 - 1,1,0,0 - perc.(2) - pf. - str.   20:00 FinnMICtr.
—— CONCERTO NO. 4 FOR PIANO AND ORCH., OP. 117 (REV.
1970)
    20:00 FinnMICtr.
—— CONCERTO NO. 4 FOR PIANO AND ORCH., OP. 43 (1962)
    1,1,1,1 - 1,1,0,0 - perc.(2) - pf. - str.   20:00 FinnMICtr.
—— DANCE FANFARE
    15:00 FinnMICtr.
—— LARGE NATURE SYMPHONY, OP. 1-B
    45:00 FinnMICtr.
—— A LITTLE SUITE, OP. 17, NO. 3
    str.   FinnMICtr.
—— MUSIC FOR ORCHESTRA, OP. 13 (1954)
    2,2,2,2 - 2,2,3,1 - timp. - str.   12:00 FinnMICtr.
—— ORATORIUM PROFANUM, OP. 87 (FACTS ABOUT
DICTATORSHIPS OF OUR TIME)(1968) (Text: Composer)
    2,2,2,2 - 2,2,2,0 - timp.,perc.(4, incl. 2 on timp.) - str.
    30:00 FinnMICtr.

—— PRELUDE (FOR STRINGS)
    str.   5:00 FinnMICtr.
—— PRELUDIO EROICO, OP. 123 (1970)
    FinnMICtr.
—— SUITE FOR STRINGS, OP. 59
    str.   FinnMICtr.
—— SUITE NO. 1 FOR STRINGS, OP. 18, NO. 1 (1948)
    str.   20:00 FinnMICtr.
—— SUITE NO. 2 FOR STRINGS, OP. 18, NO. 2 (1948)
    str.   22:00 FinnMICtr.
—— SYMPHONIC TRILOGY, OP. 113 (1970)
    2,2,2,2 - 2,2,0,0 - timp.,perc.(4, incl. 2 on timp.) - str.
    30:00 FinnMICtr.
—— SYMPHONY NO. 1, OP. 15 (1949)
    3,2,2,2 - 4,2,0,3 - timp.(2 players) - str.   28:00 FinnMICtr.
—— SYMPHONY NO. 2, OP. 27 (1949)
    3,2,2,2 - 4,2,0,3 - timp.(2 players) - str.   32:00 FinnMICtr.
—— SYMPHONY NO. 3, OP. 28 (REV. 1964)
    3,2,2,2 - 4,2,0,3 - timp.(2 players) - str.   35:00 FinnMICtr.
—— SYMPHONY NO. 4, OP. 29 (1956)
    3,2,2,2 - 4,2,0,3 - timp.(2 players) - str.   30:00 FinnMICtr.
—— SYMPHONY NO. 5, OP. 31 (REV. 1956)
    3,2,2,2 - 4,2,0,3 - timp.(2 players) - str.   30:00 FinnMICtr.
—— SYMPHONY NO. 6, OP. 32 (REV. 1960)
    3,2,2,2 - 4,2,0,3 - timp.(2 players) - str.   25:00 FinnMICtr.
—— SYMPHONY NO. 7, OP. 33 (1955)
    3,2,2,2 - 4,2,0,3 - timp.(2 players) - str.   45:00 FinnMICtr.
—— SYMPHONY NO. 8 (1955)
    3,2,2,2 - 4,2,0,3 - timp.(2 players) - str.   26:00 FinnMICtr.
—— SYMPHONY NO. 9 (REV. 1964)
    3,2,2,2 - 4,2,0,3 - timp.(2 players) - str.   30:00 FinnMICtr.
—— SYMPHONY NO. 10, OP. 36 (REV. 1964)
    1,1,1,1 - 2,2,3,1 - timp.,perc.(4, incl. 2 on timp.) - str.
    20:00 FinnMICtr.
—— SYMPHONY NO. 11, OP. 37 (1957)
    3,2,2,2 - 4,2,0,3 - timp.(2 players) - str.   25:00 FinnMICtr.
—— SYMPHONY NO. 12, OP. 38 (1957)
    3,2,2,2 - 4,2,0,3 - timp.(2 players) - str.   18:00 FinnMICtr.
—— SYMPHONY NO. 13, OP. 39 (1957)
    3,2,2,2 - 4,2,0,3 - timp.(2 players) - str.   26:00 FinnMICtr.
—— SYMPHONY NO. 14, OP. 40 (1958)
    3,2,2,2 - 4,2,0,3 - timp.(2 players) - str.   32:00 FinnMICtr.
—— SYMPHONY NO. 15, OP. 44 (1961)
    1,1,1,1 - 2,2,3,1 - timp.,perc.(4, incl. 2 on timp.) - str.
    30:00 FinnMICtr.
—— SYMPHONY NO. 16, OP. 63 (REV. 1966)
    1,1,1,1 - 2,2,3,1 - timp.,perc.(4, incl. 2 on timp.) - str.
    30:00 FinnMICtr.
—— SYMPHONY NO. 17, OP. 64 (1966)
    1,1,1,1 - 2,2,3,1 - timp.,perc.(4, incl. 2 on timp.) - str.
    30:00 FinnMICtr.
—— SYMPHONY NO. 18, OP. 65 (REV. 1966)
    1,1,1,1 - 2,2,3,1 - timp.,perc.(4, incl. 2 on timp.) - str.
    30:00 FinnMICtr.
—— SYMPHONY NO. 19, OP. 66 (1967)
    1,1,1,1 - 2,2,3,1 - timp.,perc.(4, incl. 2 on timp.) - str.
    30:00 FinnMICtr.
—— SYMPHONY NO. 20, OP. 84 (1968)
    1,1,1,1 - 2,2,3,1 - timp.,perc.(4, incl. 2 on timp.) - str.
    28:00 FinnMICtr.
—— SYMPHONY NO. 21, OP. 92 (1968)
    1,1,1,1 - 2,2,3,1 - timp.,perc.(4, incl. 2 on timp.) - str.
    30:00 FinnMICtr.
—— SYMPHONY NO. 22, OP. 95 (1969)
    1,1,1,1 - 2,1,3,1 - timp.,perc.(4, incl. 2 on timp.) - str.
    30:00 FinnMICtr.
—— SYMPHONY NO. 23, OP. 96 (1969)
    1,1,1,1 - 2,2,3,1 - timp.,perc.(4, incl. 2 on timp.) - str.
    30:00 FinnMICtr.
—— SYMPHONY NO. 24, OP. 97 (1969)
    1,1,1,1 - 2,2,3,1 - timp.,perc.(4, incl. 2 on timp.) - str.
    30:00 FinnMICtr.
—— SYMPHONY NO. 25, OP. 106 (1969)
    26:00 FinnMICtr.
—— THREE SERIOUS PIECES, OP. 5-B
    str.   FinnMICtr.
—— TRILOGY FOR ORCHESTRA, OP. 108 (1969)
    FinnMICtr.
—— VÄSSI, OP. 8-B
    30:00 FinnMICtr.

FORET, Félicien
—— PÂTRES (FOR OBOE AND ORCH.)
    3,2,2,2 - 2,2,3,1 - timp.,perc. - hp. - str.   6:00 Presser.
—— RYTHMES CHAMPÊTRES (FOR OBOE AND ORCH.)
    3,2,2,2 - 3,2,3,1 - timp.,perc. - hp. - str.   4:35 Presser.

FORSBERG, Roland
—— CANTO ALLA LEGENDA (1964)
    str.   15:00 Fleisher.
—— CONCERTO FOR FLUTE AND STRING ORCH. (1961)
    fl. - str.   10:00 Fleisher.
—— CONCERTO FOR OBOE AND STRING ORCH. (1962)
    ob. - str.   18:00 Fleisher.
—— MUSICA OSTINATA (1960)
    str.   16:00 Fleisher.

FORSSMARK, Karl A.
—— SONATA FOR STRINGS (1946) (IN 3 MOVTS.)
    str.   15:00 Composer.
—— SUMMER NIGHT (1969)
    2,1,2,2 - 4,2,3,0 - timp.,perc.(2) - str.   6:00 Composer.

FORST, Rudolf
—— ADAGIO FOR STRING ORCH.
    str.   7:00 H. Branch.
—— AUBADE MEXICAINE (1938)
    *4,*3,*3,2 - 4,3,3,0 - timp.,xyl. - hp. - str.   5:00 H. Branch.
—— CLASSICAL SYMPHONY (1970) (IN 3 MOVTS.)
    2,2,2,2 - 2,2,0,0 - timp. - str.   21:30 H. Branch.
—— CONCERTO FOR BASSOON AND ORCH. (1970) (IN 3
    MOVTS.)
    2,1,2,2 - 2,0,0,0 - str.   25:00 H. Branch.
—— CONCERTO FOR CELLO AND ORCH. (1939)
    2,1,2,2 - 2 hn. - str.   22:00 H. Branch.
—— CONCERTO FOR ORCHESTRA (1965) (IN 3 MOVTS.)
    *3,*3,*3,2 - 4,3,3,1 - timp.,perc.,bells,cel.,xyl. - hp. - str.
                                                          20:00 H. Branch.
—— DIVERTIMENTO FOR CHAMBER ORCH. (1937) (IN 5
    MOVTS.)
    1(alt. with picc.),1(alt. with Eng. hn.),2,1 - 1,1,0,0 - str.
                                                          22:00 H. Branch.
—— FANTASIA ON AN ELIZABETHAN SONNET (1966) (FOR
    DOUBLE STRING ORCH., WITH OPTIONAL WOODWINDS)
    str.   15:00 H. Branch.
    or:
    2,2,2,2 - 0,0,0,0 - str.
—— FANTASIA ON AN ELIZABETHAN SONNET (1969)
    (VERSION FOR WINDS)
    2,2,*3,2 - 4,0,0,0   15:00 H. Branch.
    or:
    2,2,*3,2 - 4,0,0,0
—— HOMAGE TO CLAUDE DEBUSSY (1946)
    2,1,2,1 - 1,2,0,0 - cel.(ad lib.) - hp.(or pf.) - str. 7:00 H. Branch.
—— HOMAGE TO DELIUS (1946)
    2,1,1,1 - 1,0,0,0 - cel.(ad lib.) - hp.(or pf.) - str. 5:00 H. Branch.
—— MUSIC FOR STRINGS (IN 1 MOVT.) (1943)
    str.   20:00 H. Branch.
—— OZARK RHAPSODY (1937)
    *3,*3,*3,2 - 4,3,3,1 - timp.,perc.(2) - hp. - str.   15:00 H. Branch.
—— SYMPHONIA BREVIS (1933) (IN 3 MOVTS.)
    1,1,2,1 - 3,2,0,0 - timp. - pf. - str.   19:20 H. Branch.
—— SYMPHONY (IN 3 MOVTS.)
    3(3rd alt. with picc.),*3,*3,2 - 4,3,3,1 - timp.,perc.,cel. - hp. - str.
                                                          20:00 Musicus.
—— THRENODY FOR STRINGS (IN MEMORY OF LIDICE) (1945)
    str.   5:00 H. Branch.
—— TWO MOVEMENTS FOR BALLET (1970)
    2,*3,*3,2 - 4,3,3,1 - timp.,xyl. - hp. - str.   20:00 H. Branch.

FORSYTH, Cecil
—— THE LAST SUPPER (FOR BARITONE, SATB CHORUS AND
    SMALL ORCH.)
    fl.(or ob.),cl. - 0,0,0,0 - org. - str.   9:00 Belw-Mills.

FORSYTH, Malcolm
—— ESSAY FOR ORCHESTRA '67 (1967) (VARIATIONS ON A
    GROUND BASS)
    2,2,2,2 - 2,2,3,0 - timp.,perc. - str.   8:15 CanMusCtr.
—— JUBILEE OVERTURE (1966)
    *3,*2,*3,2 - 4,4,3,1 - timp.,perc. - hp. - str.   10:30 CanMusCtr.
    or:
    2(2nd alt. with picc.),2(2nd alt. with Eng.hn.),2,2 - 4,2,3,1 -
    timp.,perc. - hp. - str.

—— SAGITTARIUS (CONCERTO GROSSO FOR BRASS QUINTET
    AND ORCH.) (1975) (IN 3 MOVTS.)
    2(2nd alt. with picc.),2,2,2 - 3,2,1,1 - timp.,perc.(4, incl. 3 on
    timp.) - str.   16:00 CanMusCtr.
—— SKETCHES FROM NATAL (1970) (IN 2 MOVTS.)
    0,2,0,0 - 2,0,0,0 - str.   14:00 CanMusCtr.
—— SYMPHONY (1972) (IN 4 MOVTS.)
    *3,*3,*3,2 - 4,4,3,1 - timp.,perc.(5),cel.(or pf.) - str.
                                                          26:50 CanMusCtr.

FORTIER, Marc
—— BESSARAH (2ND ESSAY FOR CHAMBER ORCH.)
                                                          6:00 Ed. Emmef.
—— UN DOIGT DE LA LUNE (SUITE FOR CHAMBER ORCH. (IN
    3 MOVTS.))
                                                          24:00 Ed. Emmef.
—— QUAND L'ETE REVIENT (3RD ESSAY FOR CHAMBER
    ORCH.)
                                                          5:00 Ed. Emmef.
—— SALAMBO (FIRST ESSAY FOR CHAMBER ORCH.)
                                                          7:00 Ed. Emmef.

FÖRTIG, Peter
—— CONCERT PIECE FOR PIANO AND TWO INSTRUMENTAL
    GROUPS
    1,1,1,1 - 0,0,0,0 - timp.,perc.(3),cel. - pf. - str. 25:00 Modern.

FORTNER, Jack
—— BURLESKE, OP. 5 (FOR 2 CONDUCTORS AND TWO
    CHAMBER ORCHESTRAS) (1965)
    Orch. I: 0,0,1,1 alto sax.,0 - 0,1,1 b.-trb.,0 - perc.(2),vibra. - pf. -
    1 d.-b.   8:00 EV.
    Orch. II: 2,2,0,2 - 2,0,0,0 - str.(6,6,4,4,3)
—— JUNE DAWNS, JULY MOONS, AUGUST EVENINGS
    2,2,2,2 - 2,2,2,0 - perc. - str.   17:00 EV.
—— QUADRI (PICTURES),OP. 8 (1967)
    3(3rd. alt. with picc.),*3,*3(2nd alt. with E♭ cl.),*3 - 4,3,3,1 -
    perc.(4),bells,cell.,glock.,mar.,vibra.,xyl. - hp. - pf. - str. 13:00 EV.
—— VARIATIONS FOR ORCH., OP. 4 (1964)
    3(3rd alt.with picc.),*3,*3(2nd alt.with E♭ cl),*3 - 4,3,3,1 -
    timp.,perc.(5),cel.,glock.,vibra. - hp. - pf. - str. 9:00 EV.

FOSS, Lukas
—— ALLEGRO CONCERTANTE
    2(2nd alt. with picc.),1,1,2 - 2,1,0-1,0 - timp.,perc.(1-2) - str.
                                                          6:00 Composer.
—— BAROQUE VARIATIONS
    3,3,3,2 - 3,3,1,1 - timp.,perc.,cel. - electric guit. - hpsc. - electric
    org. - electric pf. - str.   25:00 C. Fischer.
—— CANTATA DRAMATICA (FOR TENOR, CHORUS AND
    ORCH.)
    2,2,*3,2 - 4,2,3,1 - timp.,perc. (3) - str.   8:00 Composer.
—— CONCERTO FOR CELLO AND ORCH.
    0,0,0,0 - 2,1,2,0 - perc.,vibra. - hp. - org. - pf. - str.
                                                          20:00 C. Fischer.
—— CONCERTO FOR CLARINET AND ORCH.
    2,2,2,2 - 4,2,3,0 - timp.,perc. (3-4) - str.   22:00 Composer.
—— CONCERTO FOR IMPROVISING SOLO INSTRUMENTS AND
    ORCH. (IN 4 MOVTS.)
    2,2,2,2 - 4,3,3,1 - timp.,perc.(3),bells,glock. - str. 21:00 Composer.
—— CONCERTO FOR OBOE AND ORCH.
    1,1,1,1 - 1,1,1,0 - str.   14:30 Southern.
—— CONCERTO NO. 1 FOR PIANO AND ORCH. (IN 3 MOVTS.)
    *3,2,2,2 - 2,2,3,0 - timp.,perc. - pf. - str.   24:00 G. Schirmer.
—— CONCERTO NO. 2 FOR PIANO AND ORCH. (IN 3 MOVTS.)
    *3,2,2,b.-cl(alt. with ten. sax.),*3 - 4,3,1,0 - timp., perc.(2-3),xyl. -
    pf. - str.   39:00 C. Fischer.
—— ELEGY FOR CLARINET AND ORCH.
    2,2,1,2 - 2,2,1,0 - timp.,perc. (2) - str.   8:00 Composer.
—— FANFARE FOR ORCHESTRA
                                                          12:00 Salabert.
—— FOLKSONG (FOR ORCH.)
    3,3,3,3 - 5,3,3,1 - timp.,perc.(4-5) - hp. - pf. - str. 15:00 Salabert.
—— FOR TWENTY-FOUR WINDS
    3,3,4,sax.(ad lib.),3 - 4,3,3,1   12:00 C. Fischer.
—— GEOD (WITH 1 PRINCIPAL CONDUCTOR, 4
    SUB-CONDUCTORS AND FOLK INSTRUMENTS NATIVE TO
    COUNTRY IN WHICH PERFORMANCE TAKES PLACE)
    2,1,3,3 - 4,2,3,0 - 11-12 native instruments - hp. - org. - pf. -
    str.(2,4,8,8,8)   28:00 C. Fischer.
—— GRIFFELKIN (OPERA) %
                                                          120:00 C. Fischer.

—— INTRODUCTIONS AND GOODBYES (OPERA) % (FOR
BARITONE, MIXED CHORUS AND ORCH.) (Text: Gian-Carlo
Menotti)
    1,0,1,1 - 1,1,0,0 - perc.(1),xyl. - hp.(ad lib.) - pf. - str.
             9:00 C. Fischer.
—— THE JUMPING FROG OF CALAVERAS COUNTY (COMIC
OPERA IN ONE ACT, FOR 7 SOLO VOICES, OPTIONAL
CHORUS AND ORCH.) %
             45:00 C. Fischer.
—— ODE
    3,3,3,3 - 4,3,3,0 - timp.,perc. - hp. - pf. - str.   10:00 C. Fischer.
—— ORPHEUS (FOR VIOLIN, VIOLA OR CELLO SOLO WITH
INSTRUMENTS)
    0,2,0,0 - 0,0,0,0 - bells(2) - 2 hp. - pf. - str.   21:00 Salabert.
—— PANTOMINE
    *3,2,2,2 - 4,3,3,1 - timp.,perc.,cel.,xyl. - hp. - pf. - str.
             16:00 Hargail.
—— A PARABLE OF DEATH (EIN MÄRCHEN VOM TOD) (FOR
NARRATOR, TENOR, CHORUS, AND ORCH.)
    2(2nd alt. with picc.),2,2,2 - 2,2,1,0 - timp.,perc.(2), glock., xyl. -
    pf. - str.   31:00 C. Fischer.
—— PHORION (MOVT. III FROM "BAROQUE VARIATIONS")
    3,2,2,sopr. sax.(or E♭cl.),1 - 3,3,1,1 - perc. - electric guit. - electric
    org. - electric pf. - str.   10:00 C. Fischer.
—— THE PRAIRIE (DRAMATIC CANTATA) (FOR 4 SOLO
VOICES, CHORUS AND ORCH.)
    1(alt. with picc.),1(alt. with Eng. hn.),1(alt. with b.-cl.),1(alt. with
    c.-bn.)-1,3,1,0 - timp.,perc. - pf. - str.   G. Schirmer.
—— THE PRAIRIE: SELECTION FROM THE CANTATA
    *3,2,2,2 - 4,3,3,1 - timp.,perc. (2-3) - hp. - pf. - str.
             15:00 G. Schirmer.
—— PSALMS (FOR CHORUS AND ORCH.) (IN 3 MOVTS.)
    *1,0,2,*1 - 2,1,1,0 - timp.,perc. (4), bells,cel.,glock.,xyl. - 1-2 hp. -
    2 pf. - org. - str.   13:00 C. Fischer.
—— RECORDARE (DEDICATED TO GANDHI)
    *3,*3,E♭cl.,*3,*3 - 4,3,3,1 - timp.,perc. (3-4), cel.,xyl. - hp. - pf. -
    str.   10:30 Southern.
—— SONG OF ANGUISH (BIBLICAL CANTATA) (FOR BARITONE
AND ORCH.)
    *3,2,*3,*3 - 4,3,3,1 - timp.,perc. (2), cel.,xyl. - hp - pf. - str.
             19:00 C. Fischer.
—— SONG OF SONGS (BIBLICAL CANTATA) (FOR SOPRANO
AND ORCH.)
    *3,*3,*3,*3 - 2,3,2,0 - timp.,perc. (2-3), glock., xyl. - hp. - str.
             26:45 C. Fischer.
—— SUITE FROM "THE GIFT OF THE MAGI"
    2,2,2,2 - 4,3,3,1 - timp.,perc. (2), cel.,xyl. - hp. - pf. - str.
             16:00 Composer.
—— SUITE TO SHAKESPEARE'S "THE TEMPEST"
    2,2(2nd alt. with Eng. hn.),*3,2 - 2,2,0,0 - perc.(1) - str.
             10:00 Composer.
—— SYMPHONIC MUSIC
    1. Molto tranguillo; 2. Allegro moderato
    *3,2,2,*3 - 4,2,3,1 - timp.,perc. (4) - str.   10:00 Composer.
—— SYMPHONY (IN 4 MOVTS.)
    3,3,3,3 - 4,3,3,0 - timp.,perc. - hp. - pf. - str.   32:00 G. Schirmer.
—— SYMPHONY OF CHORALES
    3,3,3,3 - 4,3,3,1 - timp.,perc. - hp.,mandolin (ad lib.) - pf. - str.
             31:00 C. Fischer.
—— TIME CYCLE (REVISED VERSION) (FOR SOPRANO, SOLO
PIANO, CLARINET, CELLO AND PERCUSSION AND ORCH.)
(IN 4 MOVTS.) (Text: Auden, Foss, Houseman, Kafka, and
Nietzsche)
    2(2nd alt. with picc.),0,2(2nd alt. with b.-cl.),0 - 2,2,1,0 -
    timp.,perc.(3),antique cym.,bells,cel.,vibra.,xyl. - hp. - pf.(alt. with
    cel.) - str.   22:00 C. Fischer.
—— TOYSHOP PARADE (FROM THE OPERA "GRIFFELKIN")
    2,2,2,2 - 2,2,1,1 - timp.,perc. - pf. - str.   C. Fischer.

FOSTER, Anthony
—— CLASSICAL SUITE (1964)
    perc. - org. - str.   15:00 P.R.S.
—— CONCERTINO FOR PIANO AND STRINGS (1962)
    pf. - str.   12:00 P.R.S.
—— SINFONIETTA (1963) (IN 4 MINUTE MOVTS.)
    2,1,2,1 - 2,2,1,0 - timp.,perc. - str.   4:00 P.R.S.
—— SYMPHONIC SKETCHES (FOR PIANO AND ORCH.)(1966)
    3,3,2,2 - 4,2,3,1 - timp.,perc. - hp. - pf. - str.   16:00 P.R.S.

FOSTER, Arnold
—— THE FAIRY ISLE (FOR SA OR CHILDREN'S CHORUS AND
STRINGS)
    str.   18:00 Galaxy.

—— LORD BATEMAN: OVERTURE
    2,2,2,2 - 2,2,0,0 - str.   6:00 Novello.
—— A PLAYFORD SUITE
    1,1,1,0 - 0,0,0,0 - pf. - str.   Galaxy.
    or:
    str.
—— SUITE ON ENGLISH FOLK AIRS
    2,2,2,2 - 4,2,0,0 - timp.,perc. - str.   Novello.
—— THREE FESTIVE CAROLS (FOR SATB CHORUS AND ORCH.)
    2,2,2,2 - 4,2,3,0 - timp.,perc. - str.   10:00 Galaxy.

FOSTER, Stephen - BALES, Richard
—— OLD FOLKS QUADRILLES (FROM "THE SOCIAL
ORCHESTRA", 1853)
    str.   5:00 Arranger.
—— VILLAGE FESTIVAL (FROM "THE SOCIAL ORCHESTRA",
1853)
    str.   5:00 Arranger.

FOSTER, Stephen - JANSSEN, Werner
—— FOSTER SUITE
    1,1,2,1 - 2,2,1,0 - timp.,perc. - str.   10:00 Arranger.

FOUGSTEDT, Nils-Eric
—— ANGOSCIA (VARIAZIONI, CHORALE E FUGA) (1954)
    2,2,2,2 - 4,3,2,1 - perc. - str.   8:00 FinnMICtr.
—— CANZONA (1951)
    str.   6:00 FinnMICtr.
—— CONCERT OVERTURE NO. 1, OP. 20 (1941)
    2,2,2,2 - 2,2,1,0 - timp.,perc. - str.   7:00 FinnMICtr.
—— CONCERT OVERTURE NO. 2, OP. 32-A (1945)
    3,2,2,2 - 4,2,3,1 - timp.,perc. - str.   8:00 FinnMICtr.
—— CONCERTINO FOR VIOLIN AND ORCH., OP. 12 (1937)
    2,2,2,2 - 2,2,0,0 - str.   11:00 FinnMICtr.
—— CONCERTO FOR CELLO AND ORCH., OP. 24 (1942)
    2,2,2,2 - 2,0,0,0 - timp. - str.   18:00 FinnMICtr.
—— CONCERTO IN B MAJOR FOR PIANO AND ORCH., OP. 30
(1944)
    2,2,2,2 - 4,2,3,1 - timp.,perc. - pf. - str.   24:00 FinnMICtr.
—— THE DEFIER, OP. 31 (TONE POEM) (1944)
    2,2,2,2 - 4,3,3,1 - timp.,perc. - str.   8:00 FinnMICtr.
—— FOLK DANCE CYCLE (SUITE)
    1,0,1,0 - 2,1,0,0 - str.   5:00 FinnMICtr.
—— FUGUE IN B FLAT MAJOR, OP. 4, NO. 1 (1933)
    2,2,2,2 - 2,2,1,0 - str.   6:00 FinnMICtr.
—— INTRADA, OP. 37-A (1947)
    str.   6:00 FinnMICtr.
—— A MARITIME RHAPSODY, OP. 7-B (1936)
    str.   6:00 FinnMICtr.
—— PARTITA, OP. 40 (1947)
    2,2,2,2 - 2,2,1,0 - timp.,perc. - str.   12:00 FinnMICtr.
—— PEZZO SINFONICO, OP. 4, NO. 2 (1933)
    2,2,2,2 - 2,2,1,0 - str.   6:00 FinnMICtr.
—— PRELUDE AND CAPRICE, OP. 29-A (FOR VIOLIN AND
ORCH.) (1959)
    1,2,2,2 - 2,0,0,0 - perc. - str.   5:00 FinnMICtr.
—— PRELUDIO E RONDO, OP. 43 (1947)
    3,3,2,2 - 4,3,3,1 - timp.,perc. - str.   8:00 FinnMICtr.
—— PRELUDIO EROICO, OP. 25
    3,3,3,2 - 4,3,2,2 - timp.,perc.(4),cel. - hp. - str.   8:00 FinnMICtr.
—— RHAPSODY FROM UUSIMAA, OP. 22 (1941)
    2,2,2,2 - 2,2,1,0 - timp.,perc. - str.   11:00 FinnMICtr.
—— SCÈNE DRAMATIQUE, OP. 35-B (INTRODUCTION AND
FUGUE) (1946)
    str.   8:00 FinnMICtr.
—— SPRING IS COMING, OP. 16-B (SUITE) (1939)
    2,2,2,2 - 2,2,0,0 - timp.,perc. - str.   11:00 FinnMICtr.
—— SUITE FOR STRINGS, OP. 49 (1949)
    str.   9:00 FinnMICtr.
—— SUITE FROM THE FILM "HELSINKI", OP. 15-A (1939)
    2,2,2,2 - 4,2,3,1 - timp.,perc. - hp. - str.   15:00 FinnMICtr.
—— SUITE IN F MAJOR, OP. 10 (1936)
    2,2,2,2 - 3,2,2,1 - timp. - str.   14:00 FinnMICtr.
—— SYMPHONY NO. 1 IN A MINOR, OP. 13 (1938)
    2,2,2,2 - 4,3,3,1 - timp.,perc. - str.   28:00 FinnMICtr.
—— SYMPHONY NO. 2, OP. 48 (1949)
    3,2,3,2 - 4,3,3,1 - timp.,perc.,xyl. - pf.(or cel.) - str.
             25:00 FinnMICtr.
—— THREE BALLET SCENES, OP. 46
    2,1,2,1 - 2,2,0,0 - timp.,perc. - hp. - str.   6:00 FinnMICtr.
—— THREE MINIATURES (1953)
    str.   4:00 Fazer.

—— THE TINDER-BOX, OP. 50 (FOR NARRATOR, ALTO, BARITONE, CHORUS AND ORCH.) (1950) (Text: Hans Christian Andersen)
1,1,2,1 - 2,2,1,0 - timp.,perc. - hp. - pf. - str.   30:00 FinnMICtr.
—— TRITTICO SINFONICO (1958)
3,3,3,3 - 4,3,3,1 - perc. - str.   15:00 FinnMICtr.
—— TROIS PIÉCES LYRIQUES, OP. 3-A (1933)
2,2,2,2 - 2,2,0,0 - perc. - str.   7:00 FinnMICtr.
—— VARIATIONS ON A FINNISH SOLDIER'S SONG ("JA EIKÄ ME OLLA VELJEKS1Ä"), OP. 27-B (1943)
1,1,2,1 - 1,1,1,0 - timp.,perc. - str.   6:00 FinnMICtr.

FOULDS, John
—— LE CABARET (OVERTURE TO A FRENCH COMEDY)
Mills.

FOURESTIER, Louis
—— À SAINT-VALÉRY
2,2,2,2 - 4,2,0,0 - timp.,perc.(3) - str.   11:00 Presser.
—— POLYNICE (SYMPHONIC POEM)
3,3,3,3 - 4,3,3,1 - timp.,perc.(3) - hp. - str.   30:00 Presser.

FOURNIER, Paul
—— TOCCATA (SYMPHONIC STUDY)
3,2,2,2 - 4,3,3,1 - timp.,perc. - str.   6:00 EV.

FOWLER, Jennifer Joan
—— CHIMES, FRACTURED (1970)
2(2nd alt. with picc.),2,bagpipes,2,2,(2nd alt. with c.-bn.) - 0,0,0,0 - timp.,perc.(7),bells,glock.,vibra. - org.   8:00 A.P.R.A.
—— SCULPTURE IN FOUR DIMENSIONS (1969)
2,2,2,2 - 4,3,3,0 - str.   5:00 A.P.R.A.

FOWLER, Will
—— NOCTURNE
2,*3,2,3 - 4,2,3,0 - timp.,perc.,bells - hp. - str.   7:30 Composer.
—— PASTORAL
2,*3,2,3 - 4,1,0,0 - timp. - hp. - str.   Composer.

FOX, Fred
—— BEC-01 (FOR WIND ENSEMBLE AND PERCUSSION)
4,4,3,1 - 2,3,3,1 - perc.   15:00 MCA Music.
—— BEC-05 (FOR ANY 12 INSTRUMENTS)
9:00 Seesaw.
—— BEC-10 (FOR CHAMBER ORCH.)
1,1,1,1 - 0,1,1,0 - perc. - str.   15:00 Seesaw.
—— CONCERTO FOR VIOLIN AND ORCH. (1971)
3,2,3,2 - 4,3,3,1 - perc.(3) - str.   22:00 Seesaw.
—— CONNEX (1974)
0,0,0,0 - 3,3,3,1 - perc.(4)   12:00 Seesaw.
—— MATRIX FOR VIOLINCELLO AND ENSEMBLE (1972)
perc.(3), cel. - str.   15:00 Seesaw.
—— TERNION (FOR OBOE AND ORCH.)
3,1,0,1 - 2,3,3,0 - timp.,perc.(3) - str.   12:00 Seesaw.
—— VARIABLES 5
3,3,3,2 - 4,3,3,1 - timp.,perc.(4) - str.   19:00 Seesaw.

FRACKENPOHL, Arthur
—— CONCERTINO FOR CLARINET AND ORCH. (IN 3 MOVTS.)
2,2,1,2 - 2,2,1,0 - timp.,snare drum - hp.(or pf.) - str.   7:00 Fleisher.
—— CONCERTINO FOR TUBA AND STRINGS
tu. - str.   8:45 EastonMuCo.
—— DIVERTIMENTO IN F (A LITTLE EVENING MUSIC) (IN 4 MOVTS.)
1,0,1,0 - 1,1,1,0 - str.   Fleisher.
—— DOMESTIC RELATIONS ("TO BEAT OR NOT TO BEAT") (1964) (1-ACT CHAMBER OPERA) % (Text: O. Henry)
1,1,1,1 - 1,1,0,0 - pf. - str.   Composer.
—— A JUBILANT OVERTURE
2,2,2,2 - 4,3,3,1 - timp.,perc.(3),xyl. - str.   8:00 C. Fischer.
—— LARGO AND ALLEGRO
hn. - str.   G. Schirmer.
—— LITTLE SUITE (IN 3 MOVTS.)
str.   4:00 EV.
or:
1,1,2,1 alto sax.,1 ten. sax.,1 - 2,2,2,1 - timp.,perc.(2) - str.
—— THE NATURAL SUPERIORITY OF MEN (CANTATA FOR TREBLE VOICES AND ORCH.) (1959) (Text: Jean Pearson)
2,1,2,1 - 0,0,0,0 - str.   13:50 C. Fischer.
—— RONDO MARZIALE
3,2,3,3 - 4,3,3,1 - timp.,perc. - str.   4:30 Shawnee.

—— SCHERZO FOR STRINGS (FROM "SYMPHONY NO. 2 FOR STRINGS") (1960)
str.   4:00 C. Fischer.
—— SHORT OVERTURE
1,1,2,2 - 2,2,2,1 - timp.,perc.(4),xyl. - str.   4:00 Bo. Hawkes.
—— SONG FOR ORCHESTRA (1965)
2,2,2,2 - 2,1,0,0 - str.   4:45 EV.
—— STAR LAKE SUITE (SERENADE FOR STRINGS) (IN 5 MOVTS.)
str.   Bo. Hawkes.
—— SUITE FOR STRINGS (BASED ON AMERICAN FOLKSONGS) (1952)
str.   6:00 G. Schirmer.
—— SUITE FOR TRUMPET AND STRINGS (1964)
tpt. - str.   8:00 G. Schirmer.
—— SYMPHONY NO. 2
str.   21:00 C. Fischer.

FRAENZL, Ignaz - WUERTZ
—— SINFONIA IN B FLAT MAJOR (FOR STRING ORCH.)
str.   Henmar.

FRAGGI, Hector
—— CHANSONS DES TRAINS ET DES GARES (3 SONGS) (FOR MEDIUM VOICE AND ORCH.) (Text: Franc Nohain)
2,3,2,2 - 4,2,3,1 - timp.,perc.,cel. - hp. - pf. - str.   Salabert.
—— JEUX DE BEAUTÉ (SYMPHONIC POEM)
3,2,2,2 - 4,2,3,1 - timp.,perc.,cel. - 2 hp. - str.   Salabert.
—— TROIS CHANSONS DES TRAINS ET DES GARES
Salabert.

FRAJT, Ludmila
—— ECLOGUE
1,1,1,1 - 1,0,0,0 - perc. - str.   8:00 MIC,Zagreb.

FRANCAIX, Jean
—— L' APOSTROPHE (1-ACT COMIC OPERA, AFTER BALZAC) (1951) %
2,1,2,1 - 2,1,1,0 - timp.,perc. - str.   40:00 Presser.
—— AU MUSÉE GRÉVIN
2,2,3,2 - 4,2,2,1 - timp.,perc. - str.   15:00 Presser.
—— CONCERTO FOR CLARINET AND ORCH.
2,2,2,2 - 2,1,0,0 - timp.,perc. - str.   22:00 Presser.
—— LA DAME DANS LA LUNE (BALLET) %
2,1,2,1 - 2,2,1,1 - perc. - hp. - pf. - str.   25:00 Presser.
—— LE DIALOGUE DES CARMÉLITES (SUITE FROM THE FILM)
2,2,2,2 - 2,2,2,0 - timp. - str.   14:00 Presser.
—— DIVERTIMENTO FOR HORN AND ORCH.
2,0,2,2 - 1,0,0,0 - str.   7:00 Presser.
—— L' HORLOGE DE FLORE (FOR OBOE AND ORCH.)
2,1,2,2 - 2,0,0,0 - str.   16:00 Presser.
—— LES INESTIMABLES CHRONIQUES DU BON GÉANT GARGANTUA (FOR NARRATOR AND STRINGS)
str.   40:00 Presser.
—— ODE SUR LA NAISSANCE DE VENUS
str.   5:30 Presser.
—— QUINZE PORTRAITS D'ENFANTS D'AUGUSTE RENOIR
str.   18:00 Presser.
—— SI VERSAILLES M'ÉTAIT CONTE
2,2,2,3 - 4,4,3,2 - timp.,perc.(2) - str.   28:00 Presser.
—— SIX MARCHES DANS LE STYLE DU PREMIER EMPIRE
2,2,2,1 - 1,2,2,2 - timp.,perc. - str.   14:30 Presser.

FRANCESCHINI, Romulus
—— METAMUSIC 1 (FOR CHAMBER ORCH.) (1966)
7:30 Composer.
—— OMAGGIO A KURT WEILL (WALTZES AND INTERLUDES)
1(alt. with picc. and alto fl.),1,2(2nd alt. with b.-cl.),1 - 2,2,2,1 - timp.,perc. - hp. - str.   9:00 Fleisher.
—— SINFONIA (1970)
perc. - pf.(alt. with cel.) - str.(in 2 groups)   8:00 Fleisher.

FRANCHETTI, Arnold
—— THE BIRDS (1968)
2,2,*3,3 - 2,2,2,1 - perc.(4)   10:00 Seesaw.
—— CANTI (FOR ALTO SAXOPHONE, WINDS AND PERCUSSION)
2,1,5,alto sax.,1 - 4,2,2,1 - perc.(4)   12:00 Seesaw.
—— THREE ITALIAN MASQUES
0,0,0,1(alt. with c.-bn.) - 0,3,2,0 - perc. - pf.   17:00 Galaxy.

FRANCHI, Dorothea
—— CONCERTINO (FOR HARMONICA, HARP AND SMALL ORCH.)
           20:00 A.P.R.A.
—— RHAPSODY (FOR VIOLIN AND SMALL ORCH.)
           18:00 A.P.R.A.

FRANCI, Carlo
—— MUSICA
    timp. - str.   12:00 Leeds.

FRANCK, César - BECKETT, Wheeler
—— PRAYER (PRIÈRE)
    2,*3,*3,2 - 4,2,3,0 - timp.,perc. - str.   10:00 Arranger.

FRANCK, César - DUNN, James P.
—— CHORALE NO. 3
    3,3,3,3 - 4,3,3,0 - timp. - hp. - str.   J. Fischer.

FRANCK, César - GUERRINI, Guido
—— PASTORALE
    2,3,2,2 - 4,0,0,0 - str.   9:00 Bo. Hawkes.

FRANCK, César - HIGGINSON, J. Vincent
—— CHORALE NO. 3
    *3,*3,*3,*3 - 4,3,3,1 - timp. - str.   6:00 Arranger.

FRANCK, César - LOESSER, Arthur
—— CHORALE NO. 1 IN E MAJOR
    2,3,3,2 - 4,3,3,1 - timp. - hp. - str.   13:00 EV.

FRANCK, César - MCKAY, George F.
—— ARIA, CANON AND ALLEGRO
    2,1,2,1 - 2,2,2,0 - timp. - str.   8:00 Galaxy.

FRANCK, César - MEYERS, H. Emerson
—— PIECE HEROIQUE
          Arranger.

FRANCK, Maurice
—— SUITE FOR VIOLA AND ORCH.
    2,2,2,2 - 2,0,0,0 - timp.,perc. - hp. - str.   10:00 Presser.
—— THEME AND VARIATIONS (FOR VIOLA AND ORCH.)
    1,1,1,1 - 4,0,0,0 - timp.,perc. - str.   9:00 EV.

FRANCK, Melchior - SCHERING
—— TWO INTRADAS (1608)
    str.   9:00 Henmar.

FRANCKENSTEIN, Clemens von
—— FESTLICHE MUSIK, OP. 35
    3,3,3,3 - 4,3,3,1 - timp. - 2 hp. - str.   5:00 Bo. Hawkes.

FRANK, Marcel G.
—— THE ARKANSAS TRAVELER (THEME AND VARIATIONS)
    2,2,*3,*3 - 4,3,3,1 - timp.,perc., cel., glock.,xyl. - hp. - str.
        10:00 Composer.
—— CONCERTINO FOR CELLO AND ORCH. (IN 3 MOVTS.)
    *3,1,2,1 - 3,3,2,0 - timp.,perc. - str.   11:00 Mills.
—— CONCERTO IN E FLAT MAJOR, FOR PIANO AND ORCH. (IN 3 MOVTS.)
    *2,2,2,2 - 3,2,2,0 - timp.,perc.(1) - pf. - str.   10:00 H. Elkan.
—— CONCERTO IN G MAJOR, FOR FLUTE AND ORCHESTRA (IN 3 MOVTS.)
    3,1,4,1 - 2,0,0,0 - timp. - str.   8:00 Bourne.
—— THE ENCHANTED ISLAND
    *3,2,*3,2 - 4,2,0,0 - timp.,perc.,cel. - 2 hp. - str. 10:00 Composer.
    or:
    1,2,*3,2 - 4,3,0,0 - perc. (1), bells, cel. - 2 hp. - str.
—— GLORIOUS CREATION (FOR MIXED CHORUS AND ORCH.)
    2,2,2,2 - 4,3,3,1 - timp.,perc. (2) - hp. - str. 8:00 J. Fischer.
—— THE HEATHER HILLS (SYMPHONIC RHAPSODY FOR PIANO AND ORCH.)
    *3,*3,*4,*3 - 4,3,3,1 - timp.,perc. (4), bells, glock. - hp. - pf. - str.
        5:30 C.H.Hansen.
—— SIX NORTH AMERICAN INDIAN IMPRESSIONS
    2,2,2,1 - 2 hn. - timp.,perc. (4), cel. - 2 hp. - pf. - str.
        10:00 Composer.
—— SYMPHONY "BRAZIL"
    2,2,2,2 - 4,3,3,1 - timp.,perc., cel. - hp. - str. 10:00 Composer.
—— SYMPHONY IN E FLAT
    *3,*3,*3,*3 - 4,3,3,1 - timp.,perc. (2), bells,glock. - hp. - str.
        18:00 Composer.

—— SYMPHONY MINIATURE FOR STRING CHOIR (IN 4 MOVTS.)
    cel. - hp. - str.   6:20 Fleisher.
—— SYMPHONY MINIATURE (IN 4 MOVTS.)
    cel. - hp. - str.   6:30 C. Fischer.

FRANK, René
—— AND GOD CAME (A CHRISTMAS ORATORIO), OP. 44 (FOR SOPRANO, BARITONE, SATB CHORUS AND ORCH.)
    1,1,1,1 - 1,3,3,1 - timp. - str.   60:00 Composer.
—— FIVE PSALMS, OP. 3 (FOR VOICE AND ORCH.)
    2,2,2,2 - 4,3,3,1 - timp.,perc.(2) - hp. - str. 20:00 Composer.
—— MUSIC FOR BRASS INSTRUMENTS, OP. 39 (SUITE) (IN 4 MOVTS.)
    0,0,0,0 - 3,4,3,2   15:00 Composer.
—— PASSION SYMPHONY, OP. 38 (IN 3 MOVTS.)
    3(3rd alt. with picc.),2,2,2 - 4,3,3,1 - timp.,perc.(4),xyl. - str.
        27:00 Composer.
—— PILGRIM VARIATIONS, OP. 28 (VARIATIONS ON A GERMAN FOLKSONG)
    2-*3,2,2,2 - 4,3,3,1 - timp.,perc.(2) - str. 13:00 Composer.
—— THE SPITE OF MICHAL (FOR SOPRANO, BARITONE, SSA CHORUS AND CHAMBER ORCH.)
    2 tpt. - pf. - str.   10:00 Transcon.
—— TRIPTYCH OF HEAVENLY LOVE, OP. 43 (FOR VOICE AND ORCH.)
    2,2,2,2 - 2,2,3,1 - timp.,perc.(2) - str. 18:00 Composer.

FRANKEL, Benjamin
—— THE AFTERMATH, OP. 17 (SONG CYCLE) (FOR TENOR AND ORCH.) (Text: Robert Nichols)
    2 tpt. - timp. - str.   24:00 S.U.I.S.A.
—— BAGATELLES FOR 11 INSTRUMENTS, OP. 35
    1,1,1,1 - 1,0,0,0 - hp. - str.   Novello.
—— CATALOGUE OF INCIDENTS, OP. 42
    0,1(alt. with Eng.hn.),2,1 - 1,0,0,0 - perc. - hp. - str.
        20:00 Novello.
—— CONCERTANTE LIRICO, OP. 27
    str.   11:00 Novello.
—— CONCERTO FOR VIOLA AND ORCH., OP. 45
    3(3rd alt. with picc.),3,3,3 - 4,3,3,0 - timp.,perc.,glock.,vibra. - hp. - str.   30:00 Novello.
—— CONCERTO FOR VIOLIN AND ORCH., OP. 24
    2,2,2,2 - 4,3,3,1 - timp.,perc. - hp. - str. 26:00 S.U.I.S.A.
—— KONZERT FÜR JUGENDPUBLIKUM, OP. 48
    3,3,3,3 - 4,3,3,1 - timp. - hp. - str. 15:00 Novello.
—— MAY DAY (A PANORAMA), OP. 22
    2,2,2,2 - 4,3,3,1 - timp.,perc. - hp. - str. 12:00 S.U.I.S.A.
—— MEPHISTOPHELES' SERENADE AND DANCE, OP. 25 (A CARICATURE FOR ORCH.)
    3,3,3,2 - 4,3,3,1 - timp.,perc. - hp. - str. 8:00 S.U.I.S.A.
    or:
    3,3,3,2 - 4,2 cnt.,4,4,1 - timp.,perc. - hp. - str.
—— OVERTURE TO A CEREMONY, OP. 51
    3(3rd alt. with picc.),3,3,3 - 4,3,3,1 - timp.,perc. - hp. - str.
        7:00 Novello.
—— PEZZI MELODICI, OP. 54
    2(2nd alt. with picc.),2,2,2 - 2,0,0,0 - timp.,perc. - str.
        17:00 Novello.
—— SERENATA CONCERTANTE, OP. 37 (FOR VIOLIN, CELLO, PIANO AND ORCH.)
    3,2,2,2 - 4,3,3,0 - timp.,perc.,glock.,xyl. - hp. - str. 14:00 Novello.
—— SYMPHONY NO. 2, OP. 38 (1962)
    5,3,3,3 - 4,3,3,1 - timp.,perc.,cel. - hp. - str. 39:00 Novello.
—— SYMPHONY NO. 3, OP. 40 (1964)
    5,3,3,3 - 4,3,3,1 - timp.,perc. - hp. - str. 20:00 Novello.
—— SYMPHONY NO. 4, OP. 44
    3(3rd alt. with picc.),3,2(2nd alt. with Eng.hn.),3 - 4,3,3,1 - timp.,perc. - hp. - str. 30:00 Novello.
—— SYMPHONY NO. 5, OP. 46
    3,3,3,3 - 4,3,3,1 - timp.,perc.,glock.,vibra. - hp. - str.
        25:00 Novello.
—— SYMPHONY NO. 6, OP. 49
    3,3(3rd alt. with Eng.hn.),3,3 - 4,3,3,1 - timp.,perc.,glock.,vibra.,xyl. - hp. - str. 34:00 Novello.
—— SYMPHONY NO. 7, OP. 50
    3,3,3,3 - 4,3,3,1 - timp.,perc.,glock.,vibra.,xyl. - hp. - str.
        30:00 Novello.
—— SYMPHONY NO. 8, OP. 53
    3(3rd alt. with picc.),3,3,3 - 4,3,3,1 - timp.,perc.,cel.,vibra. - hp. - str. 30:00 Novello.
—— YOUTH MUSIC, OP. 12
    str.   S.U.I.S.A.

FRANKEN, Wim
—— CONCERTINO FOR PIANO AND STRINGS
    pf. - str.   19:00 Henmar.
—— CONCERTO FOR STRING ORCH. (1958)
    str.   15:00 Henmar.
—— DIVERTIMENTO
             19:00 Henmar.
—— HEEDERIK - CANTATA (FOR SATB CHORUS, TAPE AND
ORCH.) (1968) (IN 4 MOVTS.) (Text: Composer)
             13:00 Henmar.
—— RAPSODIA CAMPESTRA (FOR VIOLIN AND ORCH.) (1968)
             14:00 Henmar.
—— SINFONIETTA
    3,2,2,2 - 4,2,3,1 - timp.,perc.,xyl. - hp. - str.   18:00 Henmar.
—— SYMPHONY
    2,2,2,2 - 4,3,3,1 - timp. - str.   26:00 Henmar.

FRANKLIN, Benjamin - CLARK, Frank
—— STRING QUARTET (ARR. FOR STR. ORCH.) (IN 5 MOVTS.)
    str.   6:38 Arranger.

FRANKLIN, Benjamin - DUBENSKY, A.
—— SUITE FOR STRINGS (IN 3 MOVTS.)
    str.   C. Fischer.

FRANKLIN, Benjamin - VINCENT, John
—— BENJAMIN FRANKLIN SUITE (FOR STRINGS, WITH
OBBLIGATO FOR GLASS ARMONICA OR SUBSTITUTE) (IN
5 MOVTS.)
    fl. (or ob., or cl., or bells, or cel., or vibra., or hp., or pf., or vln.) -
    str.   7:00 Arranger.

FRANZÉN, Olov
—— SAIVA (1972)
    2,2,2,2 - 3,2,1,0 - timp.,perc. - str.   10:00 Fleisher.

FRÄNZL, Ferdinand - HOFMANN, Wolfgang
—— SYMPHONY FOR STRINGS IN A MAJOR, OP. 1, NO. 3
    str.   19:00 Mannheimer.
—— SYMPHONY FOR STRINGS IN B FLAT MAJOR, OP. 1, NO. 5
    str.   18:00 Mannheimer.
—— SYMPHONY FOR STRINGS IN C MAJOR, OP. 1, NO. 1
    str.   17:00 Mannheimer.
—— SYMPHONY FOR STRINGS IN G MAJOR, OP. 1, NO. 2
    str.   19:00 Mannheimer.

FRÄNZL, Ignaz - BODART, Eugen
—— SYMPHONY IN D MAJOR
    0,2,0,0 - 2,0,0,0 - str.   13:00 Mannheimer.

FRÄNZL, Ignaz - HOFMANN, Wolfgang
—— CONCERTO IN C, FOR VIOLIN AND ORCH.
    0,2(or 2 cl.),0,0 - 2,0,0,0 - str.   20:00 Mannheimer.

FRÄNZL, Ignaz - WÜRTZ, Roland
—— CONCERTO NO. 7 IN G MAJOR, FOR VIOLIN AND ORCH.
    0,2,0,0 - 2,0,0,0 - str.   22:00 Mannheimer.
—— SYMPHONY IN C MAJOR
    2,0,0,0 - 2,0,0,0 - str.   14:00 Mannheimer.

FRASER, Shena
—— TO HIM GIVE PRAISE (SUITE) (FOR WOMEN'S CHORUS
AND STRINGS) (Texts: George Herbert, William Cornish, John
Clare, Psalm 117)
    pf. - str.   11:00 Oxford.

FRATTURO, Louis M.
—— ANEMONE (EXPECTATION)
    *3,2,2,2 - 4,3,3,1 - timp.,perc.(4),glock. - hp. - str.
             10:00 Composer.

FREDERICKSON, L. Thomas
—— SINFONIA CONCERTANTE (IN 4 MOVTS.)
    2(2nd alt. with picc.),2,*3,2 - 4,3,3,1 - timp.,perc. - str.
             14:06 Composer.

FREDERICK THE GREAT - ERBS, Gustav
—— OVERTURE TO "IL RE PASTORE"
    0,2,0,0 - 2,0,0,0 - str.   5:00 Henmar.

FREDERICK THE GREAT - LENZEWSKI
—— CONCERTO NO. 3 IN C MAJOR FOR FLUTE AND STRINGS
    fl. - cemb. - str.   Henmar.

—— CONCERTO NO. 4 IN D MAJOR FOR FLUTE AND STRINGS
    fl. - cemb. - str.   Henmar.
—— SYMPHONY NO. 1 IN G MAJOR
    cemb. - str.   Henmar.
—— SYMPHONY NO. 2 IN G MAJOR
    cemb. - str.   Henmar.
—— SYMPHONY NO. 3 IN D MAJOR
    2,2,0,1 - 2,0,0,0 - cemb. - str.   Henmar.
—— SYMPHONY NO. 4 IN A MAJOR
    cemb. - str.   Henmar.

FREDRICKSON, Lawrence Thomas
—— SINFONIA NO. 2 (1973) (IN 3 MOVTS.)
    3(3rd alt.with picc.),*3,*3,2 - 4,3,3,1 -
    timp.,perc.(4),bells,cel.,glock.,2 kalimbas,vibra.,xyl. - hp. - pf. -
    str.(30,10,10,8)   15:00 Composer.

FREED, Arnold
—— ALLELUIA FOR ORCHESTRA
    2,2,2,2 - 4,2,3,1 - timp.,perc. - str.   8:30 Bo. Hawkes.
—— THE ZODIAC (MASQUE) (FOR CHORUS, DANCERS,
NARRATOR AND ORCH.) %
    3,2,2,2 - 4,3,3,1 - timp.,perc. - pf. - str.   38:00 Bo. Hawkes.

FREED, Isadore
—— ANTIPHONAL FANTASY
    org. - str.   Gray.
—— APPALACIAN SKETCHES (SUITE ON FOLKTUNES) (IN 4
MOVTS.)
    1,1,2,1 - 2,2,0,0 - timp.,perc.(2), xyl. - str.   11:30 Templeton.
—— BALLAD (FOR PIANO AND CHAMBER ORCH.)
    1,1,1,1 - hn. - pf. - str.   11:00 Composer.
—— BLESS THE LORD, O MY SOUL (PSALM 103) (FOR SATB
CHORUS AND ORCH.)
             3:30 Transcon.
—— CARNIVAL
    3,3,3,3 - 4,3,3,1 - perc. - hp. - str.   7:00 Templeton.
—— CONCERTO FOR CELLO AND ORCH.
             Templeton.
—— CONCERTO FOR VIOLIN AND ORCH.
    1. Moderato quasi recitativo; 2. Andante; 3. Allegro ben rimato
    2,2,2,0 - 4,2,3,1 - timp.,perc. - str.   25:00 Composer.
—— DAREST THOU NOW, O SOUL (FOR WOMEN'S CHORUS
AND ORCH.)
    2,2,2,2 - 4,2,2,0 - timp. - str.   6:00 Gray.
—— ELEGY AND ALLEGRO
    2,2,2,2 - 4,2,3,1 - timp.,perc. - str.   7:00 Templeton.
—— FANFARE AND FUGUE
    2,2,2,2 - 4,2,3,1 - timp. - str.   Transcon.
—— FESTIVAL OVERTURE
    3(3rd alt. with picc.),3(3rd alt. with Eng. hn.),3(3rd alt. with
    b.-cl.),3(3rd alt. with c.-bn.) - 4,3,3,1 - timp.,perc. (4), glock. - hp.
    -str.   12:00 Templeton.
—— HOMO SUM (ONE-ACT OPERA) %
             Templeton.
—— IMPROVISATION AND SCHERZO (FOR HORN, OBOE AND
STRINGS)
    ob. - hn. - str.   Transcon.
—— MUSIC FOR STRINGS (IN 4 MOVTS.)
    str.   20:00 Composer.
—— PASTORALES (SUITE) (IN 9 MOVTS.)
    2(2nd alt. with picc.),2(2nd alt. with Eng. hn.),2(2nd alt. with E♭
    cl.),2 - 4,2,3,1 - timp.,perc.(3) - str.   12:00 Templeton.
—— THE PRINCESS AND THE VAGABOND: SUITE
             Templeton.
—— THE PRINCESS AND THE VAGABOND (2-ACT OPERA) %
             Templeton.
—— THE PROPHECY OF MICAH (ORATORIO)
             14:00 SMP.
—— PSALM 118 ("IN DISTRESS, I CALLED UPON THE LORD")
(FOR BARITONE, CHORUS AND ORCH.)
    2,2,2,2 - 2,2,2,0 - str.   8:00 Transcon.
—— PYGMALION (SYMPHONIC RHAPSODY)
    *3,*3,2,2 - 4,2,3,1 - timp.,perc. (2) - str.   12:00 Composer.
—— RHAPSODY FOR VIOLA AND ORCH.
    2,2,2,2 - 2,2,0,0 - timp. - hp. - str.   9:00 C. Fischer.
—— SYMPHONY NO. 1 ("HORIZONS") (IN 4 MOVTS.)
    3(3rd alt. with picc.),3(3rd alt. with Eng. hn.),3(3rd alt. with
    b.-cl.),3(3rd alt. with c.-bn) - 4,3,3,1 - timp.,perc. (3) - hp. - str.
             24:00 Composer.

—— VIBRATIONS (SUITE IN 6 MOVTS.)
3(3rd alt. with picc.),3(3rd alt. with Eng. hn.),3(3rd alt. with b.-cl.),3(3rd alt. with c.-bn.) - 4,2,3,0 - timp.,perc. (2) - pf. - str.
20:00 Composer.

—— YEMENITE FANTASY
Transcon.

FREEDMAN, Harry
—— ARMANA
11:00 C.A.P.A.C.
—— CHACONNE (1964)
*3,*3,*3,*3 - 4,3,3,1 - str.   5:45 CanMusCtr.
—— CONCERTO FOR VIOLA AND ORCH.
13:00 C.A.P.A.C.
—— DIVERTIMENTO
ob. - str.   15:00 C.A.P.A.C.
—— FANTASIA AND DANCE (FOR VIOLIN AND ORCH.)
3,alto fl.,3,3,2 - 4,3,2,1 - timp.,perc. - hp. - str.   18:00 C.A.P.A.C.
—— FANTASY AND ALLEGRO (1962)
str.   15:40 CanMusCtr.
—— FIVE PIECES FOR STRING ORCH. (1949)
str.   14:00 CanMusCtr.
—— GRAPHIC 1 ("OUT OF SILENCE...") (1971)
*3,*3,3,3 - 4,3,3,0 - timp.,perc.(4) - tape-recorder - hp. - str.
21:00 CanMusCtr.
—— IMAGES
str.   18:00 C.A.P.A.C.
—— KLEE WYCK (THE LAUGHING ONE) (1970)
2(2nd alt. with picc.),2,2,2 - 4,3,3,1 - timp.,perc.(3) - str.
10:05 CanMusCtr.
—— A LITTLE SYMPHONY
*3,2,*3,2 - 4,3,3,1 - timp.,perc. - str.   15:25 MCA Music.
—— MATINEE SUITE (IN 3 MOVTS.)
1,1,1,1 - 0,3,2,0 - timp.,perc. - hp. - str.   9:00 C.A.P.A.C.
—— NOCTURNE 1 (1949)
2,2(2nd alt. with Eng.hn.),2(2nd alt. with b.-cl.),1 - 3,3,0,0 - timp. - hp. - str.
5:25 CanMusCtr.
—— NOCTURNE 2 (1975)
*3,*3,3,3 - 4,3,3,0 - timp.,perc. - hp. - str.   13:00 CanMusCtr.
—— SCENARIO (JAZZ CONCERTINO FOR ALTO SAX., BASS GUITAR AND SYMPHONY ORCH.) (1970) (IN 1 MOVT.)
*3,*3,*3, alto sax.,*3 - 4,3,3,1 - timp.,perc.(4) - b.-guit. - hp. - str.
14:35 CanMusCtr.
—— SYMPHONIC SUITE
2,3,3,2 - 4,3,2,0 - timp.,perc. - str.   15:00 C.A.P.A.C.
—— TANGENTS (SYMPHONIC VARIATIONS) (1967) (IN 1 MOVT.)
*3,*3,*3,*3 - 4,3,3,1 - timp.,perc.(4) - hp. - str.
15:30 MCA Music.
—— TAPESTRY (1973)
2(2nd alt. with picc.),2(2nd alt. with Eng.hn.),2,2 - 2,2,0,0 - timp.,perc.(1) - str.   14:25 CanMusCtr.
—— TROIS POÈMES DE JACQUES PRÉVERT (FOR SOPRANO AND STRING ORCH.) (1962)
str.   13:25 CanMusCtr.

FREEDMAN, Robert M.
—— THE ALLEGORY OF THE SELFISH GIANT (SUITE) (1969) (AFTER THE OSCAR WILDE STORY) (IN 9 MOVTS.)
str.   40:00 Composer.

FRENSEL WEGENER, Emmy
—— RHAPSODY FOR PIANO AND ORCH.
3,3,5,2 sax.,4 - 4,4,4,1 - timp.,perc.,cel.,xyl. - 2 guit. - 2 hp. - pf. - str.   8:00 Henmar.
—— RHAPSODY FOR PIANO AND SMALL ORCH.
2,2,2,1 - 2,1,0,0 - timp.,perc.,cel. - hp. - pf. - str.   Henmar.
—— SUITE (NAAR ILLUSTRATIES VAN WALTER CRANE BIJ FRAGMENTEN VAN SHAKESPEARE)
4,3,5,4 - 6,cnt.,4,3,1 - timp.,perc., cel.,xyl. - 2 hp. - pf. - str.   15:00 Henmar.

FRESCOBALDI, Girolamo - BENVENUTI, Giacomo
—— TOCCATA PER L'ELEVAZIONE (FROM "FIORI MUSICALI")
str.   8:00 Bo. Hawkes.

FRESCOBALDI, Girolamo - BRUNELLI, Louis J.
—— PRELUDIUM AND FUGUE (FROM 2 ORGAN WORKS) (ARR. 1969)
2(2nd alt. with picc.),2(2nd alt. with Eng.hn.),2,2 - 2,2,2,0 - timp. - pf.(ad lib) - str.   4:50 Chappell.

FRESCOBALDI, Girolamo - DUBENSKY, Arcady
—— PRELUDE, CHORALE AND FUGUE (FOR STRINGS)
str.   10:00 Ricordi.

FRESCOBALDI, Girolamo - FELLEGARA, Vittorio
—— PASSACAGLIA
str.   Leeds.
—— TOCCATA E CAPRICCIO
str.   Leeds.

FRESCOBALDI, Girolamo - GIANNINI, Vittorio
—— FRESCOBALDIANA (FREE TRANSCRIPTION OF THREE ORGAN PIECES)
3(3rd alt. with picc.),3(3rd alt. with Eng. hn.),3(3rd alt. with b.-cl.),*3, - 4,3,3,1 - timp.,perc. (2) - str.   15:00 Ricordi.

FRESCOBALDI, Girolamo - KINDLER, Hans
—— TOCCATA (FREELY TRANSCRIBED FOR ORCH.)
2-3,2,*3,2 - 2,3,3,1 - timp.,perc. - str.   5:15 Mills.

FRESCOBALDI, Girolamo - LEONARDI, Leon
—— CONCERTO IN G MINOR, FOR ORCH.
3,2,*3,3 - 4,3,3,1 - timp.,perc. - hp. - str.   10:00 EV.

FRESCOBALDI, Girolamo - RITCHIE, J. A.
—— FIORI MUSICALI
str.   10:00 A.P.R.A.

FRESCOBALDI, Girolamo - SAGUER, Louis
—— FIVE RICERCARI
2,2,2,2 - 4,2,2,1 - str.   16:00 Presser.

FRESCOBALDI, Girolamo - STOESSEL, Albert
—— TOCCATA AND BERGAMASCA, FROM "FIORI MUSICALI"
org. (ad lib.) - str.   G. Schirmer.

FRESCOBALDI, Girolamo - STOKOWSKI, Leopold
—— GAGLIARDA
5:00 Arranger.

FRESCOBALDI, Girolamo - VAN HOESEN, Karl D. - HUNT, Frederick
—— TOCCATA
C. Fischer.

FREUND, Don
—— CANZONA FOR ORCHESTRA (1971)
2,2,2,2 - 2,2,1,0 - hp. - pf. - str.   12:00 Seesaw.
—— CONCERTO FOR PIANO AND ORCH. (1970)
3,3,3,2 - 4,3,3,1 - timp.,perc.(2) - hp. - pf. - str.   20:00 Seesaw.

FRIBEC, Krešimir
—— DANZA DI GIOJA
9:30 Modern.
—— LAMENTO (FOR STRINGS) (1967)
str.   7:00 MIC,Zagreb.
—— PANTA RHEI
1,1,1(alt. with b.-cl.),1 - 0,0,1,0 - perc.(6),vibra.,xyl. - pf. - str.
13:50 Modern.
—— RITMI DRAMMATICI
7:50 Modern.
—— VIBRATIONEN
2(1 alt. with picc.),2(1 alt. with Eng.hn.),2(1 alt. with b.-cl.),2 - 4,2,3,1 - bells,vibra. - hp. - pf. - str.   21:00 Modern.

FRIBOULET, Georges
—— SUITE SANS FIN (FOR STRING ORCH.)
str.   11:00 Eds. Fran.

FRICKER, Peter Racine
—— INTROITUS, OP. 66
2,2,0,2 - 1,2,0,0 - timp. - str.   11:00 G. Schirmer.
—— NOCTURNE, OP. 63
1,2,0,2 - 4,2,0,0 - timp. - str.   9:00 G. Schirmer.
—— THREE SCENES FOR ORCH., OP. 45 (1966)
4,4,4,4 - 6,4,3,1 - timp.,perc. - str.   16:00 P.R.S.

FRID, Géza
—— ABEL ET CAIN, OP. 15 (FOR LOW VOICE AND ORCH.) (1938) (Text: Charles Baudelaire)
3,2,3,3 - 4,3,3,1 - timp.,perc. - 2 hp. - str.   13:00 Henmar.
—— CAECILIA - OVERTURE, OP. 45
3,2,2,2 - 4,3,3,1 - timp.,perc. - str.   8:00 Henmar.

—— CONCERTINO FOR VIOLIN, CELLO, PIANO AND ORCH.,
OP. 63 (1961)
2,2,2,2 - 3,2,2,0 - timp.,perc. - pf. - str.   10:00 Henmar.
—— CONCERTO FOR TWO PIANOS AND ORCH., OP. 55 (1957)
3,2,2,2 - 4,3,3,1 - timp.,perc.,xyl. - 2 pf. - str.   20:00 Henmar.
—— CONCERTO FOR TWO VIOLINS AND ORCH., OP. 40
2,2,2,2 - 1,0,0,0 - timp. - str.   20:00 Henmar.
—— THE DIARY OF ANNE FRANK (MONODRAMA) % (Text:
Géza Frid)
G. Schirmer.
—— DIVERTIMENTO FOR STRINGS, OP. 11
str.   14:00 Henmar.
—— EURIDICE, OP. 61 (BALLET) (1961) %
2,2,2,2 - 3,2,2,0 - timp.,perc. - juke box - str.   27:00 Henmar.
—— ÉTUDES SYMPHONIQUES, OP. 47
3,3,3,3 - 4,3,3,1 - timp.,perc.,cel.,xyl. - 2 hp. - str.   15:00 Henmar.
—— FÊTE CHAMPÊTRE, OP. 38 (SUITE DE DANSES)
perc. - str.   15:00 Henmar.
—— FRAGMENTEN UIT DE OPERA "DE ZWARTE BRUID", OP,
57A(1959)
3,2,2,2 - 3,2,2,0 - timp.,perc. - hp. - str.   20:00 Henmar.
—— HYMNE AAN DE ARBEID, OP. 32 (FOR MALE CHORUS
AND ORCH.) (1951)
3,2,2,2 - 4,3,3,1 - timp.,perc.,xyl. - org. - str.   16:00 Henmar.
—— KERMESSE À CHARLEROI, OP. 44
3,2,2,2 - 4,3,3,1 - timp.,perc. - pf.(alt. with cel.) - str.
7:00 Southern.
—— MUSIC FOR THE BALLET "LUCTOR ET EMERGO", OP. 43A
2,2,2,2 - 4,3,3,1 - timp.,perc. - hp. - str.   25:00 Henmar.
—— NOCTURNES FOR FLUTE, HARP AND STRINGS, OP. 24
fl. - hp. - str.   17:00 Henmar.
—— PARADOU, OP. 28 (FANTASIE SYMPHONIQUE)
3,3,3,2 - 4,3,3,1 - timp.,perc. - hp. - str.   17:00 Henmar.
—— PODIUM - SUITE, OP. 3
2,2,2,2 - 1,1,0,0 - timp.,perc. - str.   12:00 Henmar.
—— RITMISCHE STUDIES VOOR KAMERORKEST, OP. 58 (1959)
1,2,1,2 - 1,0,0,0 - timp. - pf. - str.   10:00 Henmar.
—— ROMANCE AND ALLEGRO, OP. 16 (FOR CELLO AND
ORCH.)
2,2,2,2 - 3,2,0,0 - timp.,perc. - str.   14:00 Henmar.
—— SCHOPENHAUER CANTATA, OP. 22 (FOR
MEZZO-SOPRANO AND ORCH.) (1944)
2,2,2,2 - 1,1,0,0 - timp.,perc. - str.   15:00 Henmar.
—— SERENADE FOR CHAMBER ORCH., OP. 52
2,1,2,1 - 1,0,0,0 - timp. - str.   15:00 Henmar.
—— SEVEN TIMPANI AND BRASS ENSEMBLE, OP. 69
0,0,0,0 - 4,3,3,1 - timp.   10:00 Henmar.
—— DAS SKLAVENSCHIFF, OP. 51 (FOR TENOR, BARITONE,
MALE CHORUS, BRASS AND PERCUSSION) (1956) (Text: H.
Heine)
0,0,0,0 - 4,3,3,1 - timp.,perc.,xyl. - pf.   25:00 Henmar.
—— SOUTH AFRICAN RHAPSODY (ON FOLK MELODIES)
2,2,2,2 - 4,3,2,1 - timp.,perc. - str.   9:00 Henmar.
—— SUITE FOR ORCHESTRA, OP. 6
3,2,2,3 - 4,2,2,1 - timp.,perc. - hp. - pf. - str.   15:00 Henmar.
—— SYMPHONIE, OP. 13
3,3,3,3 - 4,3,3,1 - timp.,perc., cel., xyl. - str.   30:00 Henmar.
—— SYMPHONIETTA, OP. 66 (1963)
str.   10:00 Henmar.
—— THREE ROMANCES, OP. 41-A (FOR SOPRANO AND ORCH.)
(1955) (Text: H. Heine)
2,2,2,2 - 1,0,0,0 - timp.,perc. - hp. - str.   9:00 Henmar.
—— VARIATIONS ON NETHERLANDS FOLK MELODIES
3,2,4,sax.,3 - 4,3,3,1 - timp.,perc. - str.   10:00 Henmar.

FRIDOLFSON, Ruben
—— CONCERTO FOR FLUTE, STRING ORCH. AND TIMPANI
fl. - timp. - str.   Fleisher.

FRIEBE, Wolfgang
—— ROMANTISCHE OUVERTÜRE
2,2,2,2 - 4,2,3,0 - timp.,perc. - hp. - str.   8:00 AhnSimrock.
—— VARIATIONEM ÜBER EIN KINDERLIED
2,2,2,2 - 4,3,3,0 - timp.,perc. - hp. - str.   9:30 AhnSimrock.

FRIEDRICH, Bruno
—— SUITE IN A MINOR, FOR STRING ORCH.
str.   15:00 Mannheimer.

FRIEDRICH, Karl
—— RONDO LEGGIERO
str.   Tetra.

—— TARTUFFE (COMIC OPERA, AFTER MOLIÈRE) %
Tetra.

FRITSCH, Johannes G.
—— CONCERTO BATTUTO
perc. - str.   12:20 Modern.
—— CONCERTO DA CAMERA (FOR AMPLIFIED VIOLIN AND
STRING ORCH.)
str.(incl. 1 vln., amplified)   10:52 Modern.

FRITSCH, Werner
—— RONDO APASSIONATO
2,2,2,2 - 4,3,3,1 - timp.,perc. - pf. - str.   10:00 F. Colombo.

FRITZ, Kaspar - SCHERCHEN
—— SINFONIA NO. 1 IN B FLAT MAJOR
2,0,0,0 - 2,0,0,0 - str.   20:00 Henmar.

FROCK, George
—— CONCERTINO FOR MARIMBA AND ORCH.
2,2,2,2 - 4,2,2,1 - perc.(3),mar. - str.   SouthernTx.

FROMM, Herbert
—— CONCERTO FOR FLUTE AND STRINGS
fl. - str.   22:00 Composer.
—— LIGHT IS SOWN (CANTATA) (FOR MIXED CHORUS AND
ORCH.)
1,1,*2,2 - 1,1,1,0 - hp. - str.   28:00 Transcon.
—— MEMORIAL CANTATA (FOR CHORUS AND ORCH.)
*3,*3,*3,*3 - 4,3,3,1 - timp.,perc. (2) - hp. - str.   19:00 Transcon.
—— PSALM CANTATA (FOR SOPRANO, MIXED CHORUS AND
ORCH.) (1962) (IN 3 MOVTS) (Text: Biblical)
2,2,2,2 - 2,3,3,0 - timp.,perc.(2) - hp. - str.   17:00 Transcon.
—— THE STRANGER (CANTATA) (AFTER A PARABLE BY
BENJAMIN FRANKLIN)
Composer.

FROMMEL, Gerhard
—— CONCERTO IN B MINOR FOR PIANO, CLARINET AND
STRING ORCH.
cl. - pf. - str.   25:00 Henmar.
—— NINE POEMS FROM STEFAN GEORGE'S "SÄNGE EINES
FAHRENDEN SPIELMANNS (FOR VOICE AND CHAMBER
ORCH.)
1,0,1,1 - 1,0,0,0 - str.   25:00 Henmar.
—— VARIATIONS ON AN ORIGINAL THEME
2(2nd alt. with picc.),2,2,2 - 4,2,3,0 - timp.,perc. - hp. - str.
16:00 Henmar.

FROMM-MICHAELS, Ilse
—— MARIAN PASSION (SMALL CHORUS AND CHAMBER
ORCH.)
1,1,0,0 - 1,3,0,0 - pf. - str.   23:00 F. Colombo.
—— MUSICA LARGA
cl. - str.   12:00 F. Colombo.
—— PASSACAGLIA, OP. 16
3(2nd alt. with picc.),2,2,2 - 2,2,2,1 - timp. - str.   15:00 Henmar.
—— SYMPHONY, OP. 19 (IN 1 MOVT.)
3,2,3,2 - 4,3,3,1 - timp.,perc. - str.   23:00 F. Colombo.
—— THREE RILKE SONGS (FOR BARITONE AND ORCH.)
2,1,2,1 - 3,3,2,1 - timp. - pf. - str.   15:00 F. Colombo.

FRÜH, Huldreich
—— PROMENADE (SUITE FROM THE BALLET)
2,2,2,2 - 4,3,3,1 - timp.,perc. - pf. - str.   14:00 Modern.

FRUMERIE, Gunnar de
—— BALLET MUSIC FROM "SINGOALLA"
3,2,2,2 - 4,2,3,1 - timp.,perc. (2), cel. - hp. - str.   6:00 S.T.I.M.
—— CONCERTINO FOR OBOE, STRINGS, HARP AND
PERCUSSION (1960)
ob. - perc. - hp. - str.   15:00 S.T.I.M.
—— CONCERTO FOR CLARINET, STRINGS, HARP AND
PERCUSSION (1958)
cl. - perc. - hp. - str.   16:00 Bo. Hawkes.
—— CONCERTO FOR FLUTE AND ORCH., OP. 67 (1969)
1,0,0,0 - 2,2,0,0 - timp.,perc. - hp. - str.   22:00 Gehrmans.
—— CONCERTO FOR HORN AND ORCH., OP. 70 (1972)
22:00 Gehrmans.
—— CONCERTO FOR TRUMPET AND ORCH. (1959)
2,2,2,2 - 2,1,1,0 - timp.,perc.(3) - hp. - str.   18:00 Gehrmans.
—— CONCERTO FOR TWO PIANOS AND ORCH.
2,2,2,2 - 2,2,1,0 - timp.,perc. (2) - 2 pf. - str.   20:00 S.T.I.M.

—— CONCERTO FOR VIOLIN AND ORCH.
2,3,2,2 - 2,1,0,0 - timp.,perc. - hp. - str.   29:00 S.T.I.M.
—— CONCERTO NO. 1 IN B MINOR, FOR PIANO AND ORCH.
2,2,2,2 - 4,2,3,0 - timp.,perc. - pf. - str.   25:00 S.T.I.M.
—— CONCERTO NO. 2 IN A MINOR, FOR PIANO AND ORCH.
2,2,2,2 - 4,2,3,0 - timp.,perc. - hp. - pf. - str.   40:00 S.T.I.M.
—— DANCE SUITE, OP. 39-B (FROM THE BALLET
"JOHANNESNATTEN")
2,2,2,2 - 4,2,1,1 - timp.   EhrlingFlg.
—— DIVERTIMENTO FOR ORCH. (IN 4 MOVTS.)
3,2,2,2 - 4,2,3,1 - timp.,perc. (2) - hp. - str.   23:00 S.T.I.M.
—— JOHANNESNATTEN, OP. 39 (BALLET) % (1947)
3,2,2,2 - 4,2,3,1 - timp.,perc.(4),xyl. - hp. - pf. - str.   Fleisher.
—— KANTAT TILL STOCKHOLMS UNIVERSITET (FOR
BARITONE, MIXED CHORUS AND ORCH.) (1960) (Text:
Johannes Edfelt)
2,2,2,2 - 4,2,2,0 - timp.,perc.(3) - hp. - pf. - str.   15:00 S.T.I.M.
—— PARTITA FOR STRINGS (IN 4 MOVTS.)
str.   14:00 S.T.I.M.
—— PASTORAL SUITE (FOR FLUTE, HARP AND STRINGS)
fl. - hp. - str.   12:00 Nordiska.
—— SUITE IN OLDEN STYLE (FOR LITTLE ORCH.)
2,2,2,2 - 2,1,0,0 - str.   15:00 S.T.I.M.
—— SYMPHONIC BALLAD (FOR PIANO AND ORCH.)
3,2,2,2 - 4,2,3,1 - timp.,perc. (2) - hp. - pf. - str. 29:00 Gehrmans.
—— SYMPHONIC VARIATIONS
3,2,2,2 - 4,2,3,1 - timp.,perc. (2) - hp. - str.   20:00 Suecia.
—— VARIATIONS AND FUGUE (FOR PIANO AND ORCH.)
2,2,2,2 - 4,2,3,0 - timp.,perc. - hp. - pf. - str.   25:00 Nordiska.
or:
2,2,2,2 - 2,2,1,0 - timp.,perc. - hp. - pf. - str.

FUCHS, Charles Emilio
—— AVENTURAS SINFÓNICAS (INTERMEZZO VENEZOLANO)
2(1 alt. with picc.),*2,2(1 alt. with b.-cl.),2 - 4,3,3,1 -
timp.,perc.(4-5),cel. - hp. - str.   11:00 Composer.
—— CONCERTINO FOR CLARINET, BASS CLARINET, VIOLA,
CELLO AND SMALL ORCH. (IN 3 MOVTS.)
2,2(1 alt. with Eng.hn.),1,2 b.-cl.,0 - 0,1,0,0 - timp.,perc.(2), vibra,
- str.   15:00 Composer.
—— CONCERTO DA CAMERA (FOR 11 INSTRS.) (IN 3 MOVTS.)
*2,*1,*2,0 - 0,0,0,0 - pf. - str.   17:30 Composer.
—— CONCERTO FOR VIOLA AND ORCH. (IN 3 MOVTS.)
2(1 alt. with picc.),1,2(1 alt. with b.-cl.),1 - 2,2,1,0 -
timp.,perc.(2-3),vibra. - hp. - pf.(alt. with cel.) - str.
21:30 Composer.
—— HUNGARIAN SERENADE NO. 1
2,1,2,1 - 2,2,1,0 - timp.,perc.(3) - str.   14:00 Henmar.
—— HUNGARIAN SERENADE NO. 2
2(1 alt. with picc.),2(1 alt. with Eng.hn.),2(1 alt. with b.-cl.),2 -
4,2,3,1 - timp.,perc.(4-5) - hp. - str.   17:00 Composer.
—— IMPROVISATIONS FOR FLUTES, CLARINETS AND STRINGS
(IN 3 MOVTS.)
2,0,*4,0 - 0,0,0,0 - hp. - str.   13:00 Henmar.
—— RHAPSODY NO. 3 FOR ORCH.
3(1 alt. with picc.),2(1 alt. with Eng.hn.),3(1 alt. with b.-cl.),*3 -
4,3,3,1 - timp.,perc.(5-6),cel.,glock.,xyl. - hp. - str.
17:00 Composer.
—— SYMPHONY NO. 2 (IN 4 MOVTS.)
3(3rd. alt. with picc.),2,3(3rd. alt. with b.-cl.),2 - 4,2,3,1 -
timp.,perc.(4-5),xyl. - hp. - str.   32:30 Composer.
—— SYMPHONY NO. 3 (IN MEMORIAM A. FRANCK) (IN 4
MOVTS.)
3(3rd. alt. with picc.),3(3rd. with Eng.hn.),3(3rd. alt. with b.-cl.),2
- 4,2,3,1 - timp.,perc.(5-6) - hp. - pf.(alt. with cel.) - str.
29:45 Composer.
—— SYMPHONY NO. 4 FOR STRINGS (IN 3 MOVTS.)
str.   23:15 Composer.
—— TIBETANA (RHAPSODY NO. 2 FOR ORCH.)
2(1 alt. with picc.),2(1 alt. with Eng.hn.),2(1 alt. with b.-cl.),2 -
4,2,3,1 - timp.,perc.(1-6),xyl. - hp. - str.   19:00 Composer.
—— TURKESTAN (RHAPSODY)
2(1 alt. with picc.),2(1 alt. with Eng.hn.),2,2 - 4,3,3,1 -
timp.,perc.(4) - hp. - str.   10:00 Composer.

FUCHS, Georg Friedrich - HOFMANN, Wolfgang
—— CONCERTO IN B FLAT MAJOR FOR CLARINET AND
ORCH., OP. 14
0,2,1,0 - 2,0,0,0 - str.   16:00 Mannheimer.

FUCHS, Hermann
—— CONCERTO FOR HARPSICHORD AND STRINGS
hpsc. - str.   18:00 G. Schirmer.

FUCHS, Peter Paul
—— SERENADE AT NOON (OPERA) % (1964) (Text: Ann Vermel)
2(2nd alt. with picc.),1,2(2nd alt. with b.-cl.),1 - 2,2,1,0 -
timp.,perc.(2)glock. - pf. - str.   50:00 Presser.
—— SYMPHONY IN C (IN 1 MOVT.) (1938)
3(3rd alt. with picc.),*3,*3,*3 - 4,3,3,1 - timp.,perc.(2) - str.
18:00 Composer.

FUGA, Sandro
—— CONCERTO SACRO (FOR CHORUS AND ORCH.)
3,3,3,3 - 4,3,3,1 - timp.,perc. - pf. - str.   40:00 Leeds.
—— ODE IN MEMORIA
3,2,2,2 - 4,3,3,1 - timp.,perc. - pf. - str.   18:00 Leeds.

FUKUI, Iwao - MITSUI, Sumio
—— FOUR SEASONS OF JAPAN (FOR ENSEMBLE OF JAPANESE
OR WESTERN INSTRUMENTS AND ORCH.)
Ensemble: Yokobue, Shakuhachi, Tsu-Zumi, Uchiwa-Daiko, Kane,
Schamisen, 2 Kotos   24:00 Skidmore.
or: picc.,cl. - bongo,tambourine,gong - banjo - hp. or hpsc.
Orchestra: 2,2,2,2 - 2,3,2,0 - perc. - str.

FUKUSHIMA, Kazuo
—— HI-KYO
10:00 MCA Music.

FULEIHAN, Anis
—— ACCENT ON PERCUSSION (FOR LARGE ORCH.)
4:00 Southern.
—— ACCENT ON PRECISION
2,2,2,3 sax.,2 - 4,2,3,1 - timp.,perc. - str.   4:00 Southern.
—— COMEDY OVERTURE
3,3,3,3 - 4,3,3,1 - timp.,perc. - str.   7:00 Southern.
—— CONCERT ETUDE NO. 1 (MELODY FOR WINDS)
1-2,1-2,1-2,1-2 - 4,3,3,1 - timp.,perc. (2) - pf. (ad lib) - str. Southern.
—— CONCERT ETUDE NO. 2 (STACCATO AND LEGATO)
2,2,2,3 sax.,2 - 4,3,3,1 - timp.,perc. pf. (ad lib) - str.   Southern.
—— CONCERTANTE FOR FLUTE AND STRING ORCH.
fl. - str.   18:00 Bo. Hawkes.
—— CONCERTINO FOR BASSOON AND ORCH. (1965)
1,2,1,2 - 2,2,0,0 - timp. - str.   9:00 Bo. Hawkes.
—— CONCERTINO FOR OUD (LUTE) AND CHAMBER ORCH.
(IN 3 MOVTS.)
1,2,2,1 - 0,0,0,0 - oud(Oriental Lute) - str.   15:00 Composer.
—— CONCERTINO FOR SMALL ORCH.
2,*2,2,1 - 2,0,2,0 - str.   13:00 Southern.
—— CONCERTINO FOR VIOLIN AND ORCH. (1964)
2,2,2,2 - 1,0,0,0 - timp. - str.   14:00 Composer.
—— CONCERTO FOR CELLO AND ORCH. (IN 4 MOVTS.)
2,1 (alt. with Eng. hn.),2,2 - 4,3,3,1 - timp.,perc.(2) - str.
22:00 Composer.
—— CONCERTO FOR FLUTE AND STRINGS (1962)
fl. - str.   Composer.
—— CONCERTO FOR PIANO, VIOLIN AND ORCH.
2,2,2,2 - 3,3,3,1 - timp.,perc. - pf. - str.   20:00 Southern.
—— CONCERTO FOR TWO PIANOS AND ORCH.
2,1(alt. with Eng. hn.),*3,*3 - 4,3,3,1 - timp.,perc.(2) - 2 pf. - str.
22:00 Southern.
—— CONCERTO FOR VIOLA AND ORCH. (1963)
2,2,2,2 - 4,2,1,0 - timp. - str.   20:00 Composer.
—— CONCERTO FOR VIOLIN AND ORCH.
2,2,2,2 - 4,3,3,1 - timp. - str.   20:00 Southern.
—— CONCERTO NO. 1 FOR PIANO AND STRINGS
pf. - str.   21:00 Southern.
—— CONCERTO NO. 2 FOR PIANO AND ORCH. (IN 3 MOVTS.)
*3,*3,2,*3 - 4,3,3,1 - timp. - pf. - str.   21:00 Southern.
—— CONCERTO NO. 2 FOR VIOLIN AND ORCH. (1965)
2,2,2,2 - 4,2,1,0 - timp. - str.   22:00 Composer.
—— CONCERTO NO. 3 FOR PIANO AND ORCH. (1963)
2,2,2,2 - 4,2,2,1 - timp. - pf. - str.   22:00 Composer.
—— CONCERTO NO. 3 FOR VIOLIN AND ORCH. (1967)
2,*3,*3,2 - 4,3,3,1 - timp.,perc.(2) - str.   22:00 Composer.
—— LE CORS ANGLAIS S'AMUSE (DIVERSIONS FOR ENGLISH
HORN AND STRINGS) (1969)
Eng. hn - str.   11:00 Bo. Hawkes.
—— DIVERTIMENTO
0,2,1,1 - 1,1,0,0 - str.   9:00 Southern.
—— DIVERTIMENTO (FOR STRINGS)
str.   10:00 Southern.
—— DIVERTIMENTO NO. 2 (IN 3 MOVTS.)
0,1,0,1 - 1,1,0,0 - str.   Fleisher.

—— DUO CONCERTANTE, FOR VIOLIN, VIOLA AND SMALL
ORCH. (IN 1 MOVT.)
2,2,2,1 - 0,0,0,0 - str.   13:00 Composer.
—— EPITHALAMIUM (VARIATIONS FOR PIANO AND STRING
ORCHESTRA)
pf. - str.   14:00 Southern.
—— ETUDE FOR ORCHESTRA
3(3rd alt. with picc.),2,*3,*3 - 4,2,3,1 - timp. - pf. - str.   Fleisher.
or:
2,2,2,2 - 4,2,3,1 - timp. - str.
—— ETUDE NO. 5 FOR SMALL ORCH. (SHIFTING COLORS)
5:00 Southern.
—— ETUDE NO. 6 FOR SMALL ORCH. (THE PERSISTANT
QUAVER)
6:00 Southern.
—— FANFARE FOR THE MEDICAL CORPS
4 hn., 3 tpt., 3 trb., tu.   Bo. Hawkes.
—— FANTASY FOR THEREMIN AND ORCH.
2,3,2,2 - 4,3,3,1 - timp. - theremin - str.   16:00 Southern.
—— FANTASY FOR VIOLA AND CHAMBER ORCH. (1963)
1,1,1,1 - 1,0,0,0 - str.   9:00 Southern.
—— FANTASY FOR VIOLA AND ORCH.
3,*3,*3,*3 - 4,3,3,1 - timp. - str.   10:00 Composer.
—— FIESTA
3,3,3,3 - 4,3,3,1 - timp.,perc. - str.   8:00 Southern.
—— HELENIC PICTURES
16:00 Bo Hawkes.
—— INVOCATION
3,3,3,3 - 4,2,3,1 - timp.,perc. - str.   7:00 Southern.
—— ISLANDS, FOR ORCHESTRA (1962)
3(3rd alt. with picc.),*3,2,2 - 4,3,3,1 - timp.,perc. - str.
16:00 Composer.
—— MEDITERRANEAN SONGS AND DANCES (1962)
Composer.
—— MEDITERRANEAN (SUITE) (IN 5 MOVTS.)
2 picc.,2,*4,*4,*4 - 4,3,3,1 - timp.,perc. (3) - hp. - str.
13:00 Southern.
—— ODE TO MANKIND (FOR MIXED CHORUS AND ORCH.)
2,1,2,1 - 2,2,2,1 - timp. - str.   9:00 Southern.
—— PIÈCES CONCERTANTES (FOR OBOE AND ORCH.) (1962)
2,*3,2,2 - 4,2,0,0 - timp.,perc. - str.   13:00 Composer.
or:
1,1,1,1 - 2,0,0,0 - str.
—— PREFACE TO A CHILD'S STORY BOOK
3,3,3,3 - 4,2,3,1 - timp.,perc. - hp. - str.   8:00 Southern.
—— PRELUDE, CAPRICE AND EPILOGUE (FOR OBOE, VIOLIN
AND ORCH.) (1964)
2,2,2,1 - 2,0,0,0 - timp. - str.   14:00 Composer.
—— PRELUDE, INTERLUDE AND FINALE
12:00 Bo. Hawkes.
—— QUARTET FOR STRING CHAMBER ORCH.
str.(no d.-b.)   22:00 Southern.
—— RHAPSODY FOR CELLO AND ORCHESTRA
Bo. Hawkes.
—— RHAPSODY FOR CELLO AND STRINGS
str.   18:00 Bo. Hawkes.
—— SCENE FROM "HAMLET" (FOR 2 CELLOS AND ORCH.)
(1964)
1,2,2,2 - 2,1,0,0 - timp. - str.   7:00 Composer.
—— SUITE CONCERTANTE (FOR FLUTE AND STRINGS)
fl. - str.   15:00 Bo. Hawkes.
—— SUITE SUR DES AIRS DE LA VIELLE FRANCE (FOR
SOPRANO AND ORCH.)
2,*2,2,2 - 2,0,0,0 - str.   7:30 Southern.
—— SYMPHONIC CONCERTANTE (FOR STRING QUARTET AND
ORCH.)
3,*3,*3,*3 - 4,3,3,1 - timp. - str.   27:00 Southern.
—— SYMPHONY NO. 1 (IN 4 MOVTS.)
3(1 alt. with picc.),*3,2,b-cl.(alt. with E♭ cl.1,*3 - 4,3,3,1 -
timp.,perc. (2) - str.   23:00 Southern.
—— SYMPHONY NO. 2 (1962) (IN 4 MOVTS.)
*3,*3,2,2 - 4,3,3,1 - timp.,perc.(2) - str.   25:00 Bo. Hawkes.
—— THREE CYPRUS SERENADES
3,3,3,3 - 4,3,3,1 - timp.,perc., cel. - str.   13:00 Southern.
—— TOCCATA FOR PIANO AND ORCH.
2,*3,2,2 - 4,3,3,1 - timp. - pf. - str.   15:00 Composer.
—— VASCO (4-ACT OPERA) %
2,2(1 alt. with Eng.hn.),2,2 - 4,3,2,1 - timp.,perc.(2) - str.
150:00 Composer.

FULKERSON, James
—— CO-ORDINATIVE SYSTEMS NO. 8 (FOR TEN PLAYERS)
alto fl.,0,0,0 - 0,0,0,2 - perc.(1),bells,vibra. - 2 guit. - electric pf. -
str.(0,1,0,2)   8:00 Modern.
—— CONCERTO FOR GUITAR AND ORCH.
1,0,*2,0 - 0,0,1,0 - perc.(3) - guit. - str.(0,0,1,1)   13:00 Modern.
—— FOR WE DON'T SEE ANYTHING CLEARLY
1,1,*1,1 - 0,1,0,1 - timp. - pf. - str.   26:00 Modern.
—— GLOBS (FOR 2 CONDUCTORS AND SMALL ORCH.)
2 tu. - tape-recorder,feedback-board - str.(4,0,4,4)   10:25 Modern.
—— PATTERNS IX (FOR CHAMBER ORCH.)
Modern.
—— TO SEE THINGS CLEARLY (FOR CHAMBER ORCH.)
1,1,1,1 - 0,1,1,1 - timp. - pf. - str.   26:00 Modern.

FULTON, Norman
—— CONCERTO FOR VIOLIN AND ORCH., OP. 38 (1967)
2,2,3,2 - 2,2,3,0 - timp.,perc. - hp. - str.   29:00 P.R.S.
—— DANCE MINIATURES
2,2,2,2 - 4,2,3,0 - timp.,perc.(3) - hp. - str.   8:00 Oxford.
—— SERENADE
str.   16:00 Oxford.
—— SYMPHONIC DANCES, OP. 36 (1965)
3,2,2,2 - 4,3,3,0 - perc.(4) - hp. - str.   P.R.S.
—— WALTZ RHAPSODY FOR PIANO AND ORCH., OP. 29 (1961)
2,2,2,2 - 4,2,3,0 - timp.,perc. - hp. - pf. - str.   10:00 P.R.S.

FURER, Arthur
—— FANTASIE FÜR KLAVIER UND ORCH.
1,1,1,1 - 1,0,0,0 - pf. - str.   12:00 S.U.I.S.A.

FURLOTTI, A.
—— LA SAMARITANA: PRELUDIO
3,3,2,2 - 4,3,3,1 - timp. - str.   Bo. Hawkes.

FURRER, Walter
—— MUSIK FÜR STREICHER
str.   12:00 S.U.I.S.A.

FÜRST, Paul W.
—— CONCERTO FOR 2 PIANOS AND STRING ORCH.
2 pf. - str.   18:00 Mannheimer.

FÜRTWANGLER, Wilhelm
—— SYMPHONISCHES KONZERT FÜR KLAVIER UND ORCH.
3,3,3,3 - 4,3,3,1 - timp.,perc. - pf. - str.   58:00 Alkor.
—— SYMPHONY NO. 2 IN E MINOR
3,3,3,3 - 4,3,3,1 - timp.,perc. - str.   78:00 Alkor.

FURUHJELM, Erik
—— A MODO DI CONCERTO, IN E FLAT MINOR (FOR PIANO
AND ORCH.) (1911)
2,2,2,3 - 3,2,3,0 - pf. - str.   11:00 FinnMICtr.
—— FIVE PICTURES (REV. 1925)
4,3,4,3 - 4,3,3,1 - timp.,perc. - str.   17:00 FinnMICtr.
—— OUVERTURE ROMANTIQUE (1910)
3,3,3,2 - 4,2,3,1 - timp.,perc. - hp. - str.   10:00 FinnMICtr.
—— PHANTASY FOR VIOLIN AND ORCH. (REV. 1926)
3,3,3,2 - 3,2,3,0 - str.   11:00 FinnMICtr.
—— RUSTIC SUITE (1939)
str.   10:00 FinnMICtr.
—— SOLITUDE (1940)
1,0,0,0 - 4,2,0,0 - timp. - str.   6:00 FinnMICtr.
—— SYMPHONY NO. 1, IN D MAJOR (REV. 1911)
3,3,3,2 - 4,3,3,1 - timp.,perc. - hp. - str.   35:00 FinnMICtr.
—— SYMPHONY NO. 2 (REV. 1926)
3,3,3,2 - 4,3,3,1 - timp.,perc.(3, incl. 2 on timp.) - str.
25:00 FinnMICtr.

FUSSELL, Charles C.
—— ARIA OF THE BLESSED VIRGIN, AFTER HENRY PURCELL
1,*2,0,0 - 0,1,0,0 - mandolin - hpsc. - str.(0,2,2,1)   G. Schirmer.
—— FOUR FAIRY TALES, AFTER OSCAR WILDE (1966)
2(2nd alt. with picc.),2,2,1 - 1,2,1,0 -timp.,perc.(4),glock.,vibra - pf.
- str.   12:00 CMP.
—— POEMS FOR CHAMBER ORCH. AND VOICES, AFTER HART
CRANE(IN 5 MOVTS.) (1965) (Text: Hart Crane)
2(1 alt. with picc.),1,1,1 - 2,2,1,0 - perc.(3),glock.,vibra.,xyl. - hp. -
pf.(alt. with cel.) - str.   14:00 CMP.
—— SWEELINCK LIEDVARIATIONEN: "MEIN JUNGES LEBEN"
*2,*2,1,1 - 1,1,1,0 - timp.,mar. - mandolin - hp. - str.
11:00 G. Schirmer.

—— SYMPHONY IN ONE MOVEMENT (SYMPHONY NO. 1)
(1963)
3(2nd and 3rd alt. with piccs.),3(3rd alt. with Eng. hn.),E♭cl.,2(2nd
alt. with b.-cl.),3(3rd alt. with c.-bn.) - 4,3,3,1 -
timp.,perc.(5),bells,glock.,mar.,vibra.,xyl. - hp. - pf. - str.
15:00 CMP.
—— SYMPHONY NO. 2 (FOR SOPRANO AND ORCH.) (1967) (IN
4 MOVTS.) (Texts: Rainer Maria Rilke and C. P. Cavafy)
3(2nd and 3rd alt. with piccs.),3(3rd alt. with Eng. hn.),3(3rd alt.
with b.-cl.),3(3rd alt. with c.-bn.) - 4,3,3,1 -
timp.,perc.(5),bells,mar.,vibra.,xyl. - 2 pf. - str.   46:00 Composer.

FUSTE-LAMBEZAT, Michel
—— SYMPHONY NO. 2
3,2,2,2 - 4,4,3,1 - timp.,perc.(7),cel. - 2 hp. - pf. - str.
28:30 Presser.

FUX, Johann Joseph - HOFMANN, Wolfgang
—— OVERTURE IN D MINOR
hpsc. - str.   22:25 Mannheimer.

G

GAÁL, Jenő
—— ADAGIO
2,2,2,2 - 4,1,0,0 - timp.,perc. - hp. - str.   13:30 Bo. Hawkes.
—— CONCERTINO FOR PIANO AND ORCH.
2,2,2,2 - 4,1,1,0 - timp.,perc. - hp. - pf. - str.   14:00 Bo. Hawkes.

GABAYE, Pierre
—— SUITE GAULOISE
2,1,0,2 alto sax.,2 ten. sax.,1 bar. sax.,0 - 0,4,4,1 -
timp.,perc.(3),cel.,glock.,vibra. - guit. - hp. - 9 c.,1 d.-b. Eds. Fran.
—— SYMPHONIE CONCERTANTE
1,1,0,1 - 1,0,0,0 - str.   16:30 Baron.

GABOLD, Ingolf
—— ARCHETYPON
9:00 K.O.D.A.
—— ATLANTIS (FOR PERCUSSION GROUPS AND SYMPHONY
ORCH.)
23:00 K.O.D.A.
—— SEVEN VISIONS TO ORPHEUS (1-ACT OPERA) %
4,2,4,2 sax.,2 - 4,3,2,1 - perc.,cel. - tape-recorder - hp. - electric
org. - pf. - str.   40:00 G. Schirmer.

GABRIELI, Andrea - CANINO, Bruno
—— EDIPO RE (CHORUSES FOR SOPHOCLES' TRAGEDY
"OEDIPUS REX")
5,4,0,3 - 4,6,3,1 - timp.,perc.(2) - lute,mandolin - hp. - 2 hpsc. -
org. - str.   MCA Music.

GABRIELI, Giovanni - MADERNA, Bruno
—— IN-ECCLESIIS (FROM THE ORIGINAL MOTET FOR 2 SOLO
VOICES, 2 CHORUSES, ORGAN AND ORCH.)
3,3,4,4 - 4,4,4,0 - bells - 2 hp. - str.   7:00 MCA Music.

GABRIELI, Giovanni - NAPOLITANO
—— CANZONA IN A MINOR (FOR DOUBLE STRING ORCH.)
str.   6:00 Henmar.

GABRIELI, Giovanni - STOKOWSKI, Leopold
—— CANZON QUARTI TONI A 15
G. Schirmer.
—— IN ECCLESIIS (FOR SATB CHORUS AND INSTRUMENTS)
0,0,0,0 - 6,4,4,2 - org.   6:00 Broude.
—— SONATA PIAN'E FORTE
*3,*3,*3,*3 - 5,4,4,2 - org.   5:44 Henmar.

GABUNIYA, Nunun
—— SYMPHONY
G. Schirmer.

GABURO, Kenneth
—— ANTIPHONIA (FOR 3 STRING ORCHS.) (IN 3 MOVTS.)
str.   12:00 Composer.
—— ELEGY FOR CHAMBER ORCH.
*2,1(alt. with Eng.hn.),1,0 - 0,2,3,0 - str.   13:00 Presser.
or:
*2,*2,2,0 - 0,2,3,0 - str.

—— ON A QUIET THEME
1(alt. with alto fl. and picc.),1(alt. with Eng. hn.),0,1(alt. with
c.-bn.) - 2,1,1,0 - timp.,perc.(2),cel. - str.   15:00 Chappell.
—— SHAPES AND SOUNDS
*2,1(alt. with Eng.hn.),1(alt. with b.-cl.),0 - 2,1,1,0 -
perc.(2),cel.,xyl. - pf. - str.   25:00 Composer.
—— THE WIDOW (OPERA IN 6 SCENES) % (1960) (Text:
Composer)
*2,1(alt. with Eng.hn.),1(alt. with b.-cl,0 - 0,1,2,0 - cel. -
tape-recorder - str.   55:00 Composer.

GAGNEBIN, Henri
—— ANDANTE AND ALLEGRO (FOR CLARINET AND ORCH.)
2,2,1,2 - 2,0,0,0 - hp. - str.   6:00 Baron.
—— CONCERTO POUR CLARINETTE ET ORCHESTRE, OP. 162
17:00 S.U.I.S.A.
—— CONCERTO POUR HAUTBOIS ET BASSON SOLI,
ORCHESTRE À CORDES, HARPE ET XYLOPHONE, OP. 167
ob.,bn. - xyl. - hp. - str.   17:00 S.U.I.S.A.
—— REQUIEM DES VANITÉS DU MONDE (ORATORIO) (FOR
SOPRANO, BARITONE, MIXED CHORUS, ORGAN AND
ORCH.) OP. 54
3,2,2,2 - 4,3,3,1 - timp.,perc. - hp. - str.   45:00 Henn.
—— SANS BLÂÂÂQUE (SUITE D'ORCH., À LA MÉMOIRE DE
GROCK)
3,2,2,2 - 4,3,0,0 - timp.,perc. - str.   20:00 S.U.I.S.A.
—— SECONDE SUITE D'ORCHESTRE SUR DES PSAUMES
HUGUENOTS
2,2,2,2 - 3,3,2,1 - timp. - str.   19:00 S.U.I.S.A.
—— SUITE POUR LES INSTRUMENTS D'ORCHESTRE, OP. 45
1,1,1,1 - 1,1,0,0 - timp.,perc., xyl. - str.   13:00 Baron.
—— SYMPHONY NO. 3 IN E MAJOR
*3,*3,2,2 - 4,3,3,1 - timp.,perc., cel. - hp. - str.   35:00 S.U.I.S.A.
—— SYMPHONY NO. 4
2,2,2,2 - 4,1,0,0 - timp.,perc. - str.   20:00 S.U.I.S.A.

GAGNIER, Josephat
—— IN THE OLDEN STYLE (SUITE)
16:30 C.A.P.A.C.
—— IN THE SHADE OF THE MAPLES (SUITE)
10:00 C.A.P.A.C.
—— SUITE FOR HARP AND ORCH.
13:00 Fox.
—— THE WIND IN THE LEAFLESS MAPLE (TONE POEM)
8:00 C.A.P.A.C.

GAGNON, Alain
—— ESQUISSE POUR ORCHESTRE (1965)
*3,*3,2,2 - 4,2,3,0 - timp.,perc.,cel. - hp. - str.   8:20 CanMusCtr.
—— PRELUDE POUR ORCHESTRA (1969)
*3,*3,*3,2 - 4,3,3,1 - timp.,perc.,cel. - hp. - str.   8:50 CanMusCtr.

GAILLARD, Marius-François
—— GUYANES (SYMPHONIC SUITE) (FOR WINDS AND
PERCUSSION)
2,2,2,2 - 2,2,0,0 - perc.(2) - pf.   30:00 Presser.
—— SYMPHONY NO. 2 IN E FLAT MAJOR
2,2,3,2 - 4,2,1,0 - timp.,perc. - str.   21:00 Henmar.
—— TOMBEAU ROMANTIQUE (FOR PIANO AND ORCH.)
Henmar.

GAINES, Samuel R.
—— THE CORN SONG (A HARVEST CANTATA) (FOR CHORUS
AND ORCH.)
1,1,2,1 - 2,2,1,0 - timp.,perc. - hp. - str.   7:00 Composer.
—— FANTASY ON A RUSSIAN FOLKSONG (FOR CHORUS AND
ORCH.)
1,1,2,1 - 2,2,1,0 - timp. - str.   J. Fischer.
—— REX GLORIAE (FOR NARRATOR, 4 SOLOISTS, CHORUS
AND ORCH.)
2,2,2,1 - 2,2,1,0 - timp. - str.   8:00 Western.
—— SALUTATION (CHORAL PROLOGUE)
1,1,2,1 - 2,2,1,0 - timp.   J. Fischer.
—— THE VILLAGE BLACKSMITH (CANTATA) (FOR SOPRANO,
BARITONE, CHORUS AND ORCH.)
1,1,2,1 - 2,2,1,0 - timp. - hp. - str.   20:00 Composer.

GAITO, Constantino
—— EL OMBÚ, OP. 31 (SYMPHONIC POEM) (1924)
4,3,4,4 - 6,4,4,1 - timp.,perc.,cel. - hp. - str.   Fleisher.

GÁL, Hans
—— CONCERTINO FÜR VIOLINE UND STREICHORCHESTER
str.   19:00 Alkor.
—— IDYLLIKON, OP. 79
2,2,2,2 - 2,0,0,0 - timp. - str.   23:00 Bo. Hawkes.
—— KALEDONISCHE (SCHOTTISCHE) SUITE (IN 3 MOVTS.)
2,2,2,2 - 2,2,1,0 - perc. - str.   15:00 T & J.
—— LILLIBURLERO (IMPROVISATIONS ON A MARTIAL
MELODY), OP. 48
2,2,2,2 - 3,2,3,0 - timp.,perc. - str. 20:00 Novello.
—— MEANDERS
                                        21:00 Novello.
—— PICKWICKIAN OVERTURE
2,2,2,2 - 2,2,1,0 - timp.,perc. - str. 9:30 Novello.
—— SERENADE FOR STRINGS, OP. 46 (IN 4 MOVTS.)
str.   14:00 Novello.

GÁLININ, Gherman
—— SUITE FOR STRING ORCHESTRA
str.   15:00 G. Schirmer.

GALLA-RINI, Anthony
—— CONCERTO FOR ACCORDION AND ORCH.
2,2,2,2 - 4 hn. - timp. - acc. - str.   22:30 C. Fischer.

GALLEGOS, Romulo - LLOYD, Caroline
—— DOÑA BARBARA (3-ACT OPERA) % (ARR. 1964-67) (Text:
Isaac Chocron; English text by Mordecai Rubin)
2(2nd alt. with picc.),2,2,2 - 2,2,2,0 - timp.,perc.(3),cel. -
tape-recorder - hp. - pf. - str.(12,4,4,2)   150:00 Belw-Mills.

GALLIARD, Johann Ernst - SEVITZY, Fabien
—— SONATA FOR CHAMBER ORCH.
1. Grave; 2. Allegro; 3. Andante temeramente; 4. Allegro spiritoso
                                        Ricordi.

GALLIARD, Johann Ernst - STEINBERG
—— SONATA FOR FLUTE, OBOE, BASSOON AND STRINGS
1,1,0,1 - 0,0,0,0 - str.   Bo. Hawkes.

GALLIERA, Alceo
—— EGLOGA
2,1,2,2 - 2,0,0,0 - timp.,perc.,cel. - 2 hp. - str.   10:00 Bo. Hawkes.

GALLIERA, Arnaldo
—— CHORALE (FROM "SUITE DIONISIACA")
3,3,3,3 - 4,2,3,1 - timp.,perc. - 1-2 hp. - str.   Bo. Hawkes.

GALLO, Gerard
—— CONCERTO FOR PIANO AND ORCH.
2,2,2,2 - 2,2,0,0 - timp.,perc.(4) - pf. - str.   30:00 Presser.

GALLOIS-MONTBRUN, Raymond
—— CONCERTO FOR VIOLIN AND ORCH.
2,2,2,2 - 4,3,3,1 - timp.,perc.,cel.,vibra. - hp. - str.   34:00 Baron.
—— LOUISE DE LA MISÉRICORDE (CANTATA) (FOR 2 SOLO
VOICES AND ORCH.) (Text: Ch. Clerc)
2,2(2nd alt. with Eng.hn.),2,2 - 4,2,2,0 - timp.,perc.,cel. - hp. - str.
                                        21:00 Baron.
—— LE PORT DE DELFT
2,2,2,2 - 2,2,2,1 - timp.,perc.,cel.,vibra. - hp. - pf. (or cel.) - str.
                                        8:30 Baron.
—— SYMPHONIE CONCERTANTE (FOR VIOLIN AND ORCH.)
(IN 3 MOVTS.)
3,2,2,2 - 4,3,3,1 - timp.,perc., cel., xyl. - hp. - str.   32:00 Baron.
—— SYMPHONIE JAPONAISE
3,3,3,2 - 4,3,3,1 - timp.,perc., cel., vibra., xyl. - hp. - pf. - str.
                                        26:00 Baron.

GALLON, Noël
—— SUITE IN D (IN 5 MOVTS)
2,3,2,2 - 4,2,3,1 - timp.,perc. - 2 hp. - str.   Salabert.

GALUN, Andrija
—— HUMORESQUE FOR ORCH.
2,2,2,2 - 2,2,0,0 - str.   5:12 MIC,Zagreb.
—— MUSIC '68 (1968)
3,3,3,3 - 4,3,3,1 - timp.,perc.,cel.,vibra - hp. - str.
                                        12:30 MIC,Zagreb.

GALUPPI, Baldassare - BONELLI
—— SINFONIA (DELLA SERENATA)
2 hn. - str.   Henmar.

—— SINFONIA IN D MAJOR
2 hn. - str.   Henmar.

GALUPPI, Baldassare - BRINCKMANN
—— CONCERTO IN G MAJOR FOR FLUTE AND STRINGS
fl. - cemb. - str.   Henmar.

GALUPPI, Baldassare - ESPOSITO, Michele
—— ADAGIO E GIGA
fl., bn. - timp. - str.   Oxford.

GALUPPI, Baldassare - FARINA
—— CONCERTO IN F MAJOR FOR CEMBALO AND STRINGS
cemb. - str.   14:00 Henmar.

GALUPPI, Baldassare - GENTILI VERONA, Gabriella
—— BEATUS VIR (PSALM 122) (FOR SATB CHORUS AND ORCH.)
0,2,0,0 - 2,0,0,0 - cemb. - str.   30:00 IsMuPublns.

GALUPPI, Baldassare - LUPI
—— OLIMPIADI OUVERTURE
0,2,0,0 - 2,0,0,0 - str.   7:00 Bo. Hawkes.

GALUPPI, Baldassare - MORTARI
—— ARIA OF LENA (FROM THE OPERA "IL FILOSOFA DI
CAMPAGNA") (FOR SOPRANO AND STRINGS)
str.   3:00 Bo. Hawkes.

GALUPPI, Baldassare - SCHROEDER, Felix
—— CONCERTO IN E MINOR
2 fl. - cemb. - str.   Henmar.
—— CONCERTO IN E MINOR FOR TWO FLUTES, STRINGS AND
CONTINUO
2 fl. - cemb. - str.   21:00 Henmar.

GALUPPI, Baldassare - WARRACK, Guy
—— OVERTURE IN D
2 ob. - 2 hn. - str.   5:30 Oxford.

GANDINI, Gerardo
—— CONTRASTES (CONCERTO FOR 2 PIANOS AND SMALL
ORCH.)
2,1,2,0 - 1,1,1,0 - perc.(3) - 1-2 pf. - str.(12,0,0,4)
                                        15:00 Bo. Hawkes.

GANZ, Rudolph
—— ANIMAL PICTURES
3,3,3,3 - 4,3,3,1 - timp.,perc. - hp. - str.   22:00 C. Fischer.
—— CONCERTO FOR E♭, OP. 32, FOR PIANO AND ORCH. (IN 4
MOVTS.)
*3,2,2,2 - 4,2,3,1 - timp.,perc. (3), cel., glock., xyl. - pf. - str.
                                        23:00 C. Fischer.
—— FOUR PIECES, OP. 33
                                        10:00 Mills.
I. BRASSY PRELUDE (FOR BRASS SECTION)
4 hn., 3tpt. 3 trb., tu.
II. STRINGS IN VARIATIONS
hp. - str.
III. WOODY SCHERZO (FOR WOODWIND SECTION)
*3,*3,E♭cl., *3,*3
IV. PERCUSSIONAL MELÉE (FOR PERCUSSION SECTION)
timp.,perc., bells, cel., glock., xyl.
—— SYMPHONIC OVERTURE TO AN UNWRITTEN COMEDY
("LAUGHTER---YET LOVE")
*3,2,2,2 - 4,2,3,1 - timp.,perc. (3), glock., xyl. - str.
                                        7:00 C. Fischer.

GARCES, Vicente
—— MARINADA (BALLET SUITE)
                                        S.G.A.E.

GARCIA, Russell
—— CONCERTO FOR BRASS SECTION AND ORCH.
2,2,2,2 - 4,4,4,0 - timp.,perc. - hp. - str.   42:00 Modern.
—— DREAM SUITE (SUITE OF FIVE DREAMS)
2,2(2nd alt. with Eng. hn.),3(3rd alt. with b.-cl.),3(3rd alt. with
c.-bn.) - 4,4,4,1 - timp.,perc.(3) - hp. - str.   29:30 Modern.

GARCÍA ESTRADA, Juan
—— RURALIA ARGENTINA
                                        65:00 Ricordi.
I. VIDALITA
2,3,2,2 - 3,0,0,0 - perc.,cel.,xyl. - hp. - str.

II. BAILECITO
2,3,2,2 - 3,2,0,0 - timp.,perc.,cel.,guit. - hp. - str.
III. SALTENA
3,3,3,3 - 4,3,3,2 - perc.,cel.,xyl. - hp. - str.
IV. TRISTE
2,3,2,2 - 3,0,0,0 - timp.,perc. - hp. - str.
V. RANCHERA
2,3,2,2 - 4,3,3,1 - timp.,perc.,cel. - hp. - str.
VI. HUELLA
3,3,2,2 - 4,3,3,1 - timp.,perc. - hp. - str.
VII. ESTILO
2,3,2,2 - 3,0,0,0 - timp. - hp. - str.
VIII. PERICON Y GATO
3,3,2,2 - 4,3,3,1 - timp.,perc.,cel.,xyl. - hp. - str.
IX. A LA ORACION
2,3,2,0 - 4,0,0,0 - perc.,cel. - hp. - str.

GARCÍA MORILLO, Roberto
—— CONCERTO FOR PIANO AND ORCH., OP. 6

        Fleisher.
—— RICERCAR CORAL, OP. 19
str.   12:00 Bo. Hawkes.
—— EL TERCER HUESPED (SYMPHONIC MOVEMENT)
3,2,3,2 - 4,2,3,1 - timp.,perc. (6) - pf. - str.   5:00 Southern.
—— VARIACIONES OLIMPICAS
3,3,3,2 - 4,2,3,1 - timp.,perc.,cel.,xyl. - hp. - pf. - str.
    26:00 Bo. Hawkes.

GARDINER, H. Balfour
—— OVERTURE TO A COMEDY
2,2,2,2 - 4,2,3,1 - timp.,perc.,glock. - hp. - str.   7:00 Novello.
—— SHEPHERD FENNEL'S DANCE
3,3,2,3 - 4,2,3,1 - timp.,perc. - hp. - str.   6:00 Bo. Hawkes.

GARDNER, John L.
—— BALLAD OF THE WHITE HORSE (FOR BARITONE, SATB
CHORUS AND ORCH.)
3(3rd alt. with picc.),3(3rd alt. with Eng.hn.),2,2 - 4,2,3,1 -
timp.,perc. - hp. - pf. - str.   45:00 Galaxy.
—— CANTATA FOR CHRISTMAS (SUITE OF 7 SONGS) (FOR
MIXED CHORUS AND SMALL ORCH.)
0,1,0,1 - 1,0,0,0 - str.   24:00 Oxford.
—— CANTIONES SACRA, OP. 12 (FOR SOPRANO, MIXED
CHORUS AND ORCH.))
2,2(2nd alt. with Eng. hn.),2(2nd alt. with b.-cl.),*3 - 4,3,3,1 -
timp.,perc.(2) - hp. - str.   32:00 Oxford.
—— CONCERTO IN C FOR TRUMPET AND STRING ORCH.
tpt. - str.   12:00 Novello.
—— CONCERTO NO. 1 IN B FLAT FOR PIANO AND ORCH., OP.
34
    25:00 Oxford.
—— AN ENGLISH BALLAD, OP. 99
3,3,3,3 - 4,3,3,1 - timp.,perc. - guit. - pf. - str.   12:00 P.R.S.
—— FIVE HYMNS IN POPULAR STYLE (FOR SATB CHORUS
AND SMALL ORCH.)
3 cl. - timp.,perc.(3-4) - 3 guit. - org. - pf.(4-hands) - str.   Oxford.
—— FIVE RYTHMS SUITE, OP. 45
1,1,1,sax.,1 - 1,1,1,0 - str.   15:00 P.R.S.
—— HALF-HOLIDAY OVERTURE
2,2,2,2 - 2,2,1,0 - timp.,perc. - str.   5:00 Novello.
—— HERRICK CANTATA (FOR TENOR SOLO, SATB CHORUS
AND ORCH.)
2,2,2,2 - 4,2,1,0 - trump.,perc.,cel. - hp. - str.   27:00 Galaxy.
—— MIDSUMMER ALE (OVERTURE)
*3,*3,*3,alto sax.,*3 - 4,3,3,1 - timp.,perc.(5) - hp. - pf. - str.
    Oxford.
—— THE NOBLE HEART (FOR SOPRANO, BASS, CHAMBER
CHORUS, FULL CHORUS AND ORCH.)
2,2,2,2 - 4,2,3,1 - timp.,perc.(2) - str.   40:00 Oxford.
—— REFLECTION (BALLET SUITE)
3,3,3,2 - 2,2,3,0 - timp.,perc. - hp. - str.   20:00 Oxford.
—— A SCOTS OVERTURE
*2,*2,2,2 - 4,2,3,1 - timp.,perc., cel.(ad lib.) - hp. - str.
    6:15 Oxford.
—— SEVEN SONGS FOR SATB CHORUS AND SMALL ORCH.
1(alt. with picc.),1,1,1 - 1,0,0,0 - perc. - str.   17:00 Oxford.
—— SINFONIA PICCOLA IN D
str.   15:00 Oxford.
—— SYMPHONY NO. 1 IN D MINOR
3,3,3,3 - 4,3,3,1 - timp.,perc.(2) - str.   40:00 Oxford.
—— VARIATIONS ON A WALTZ OF CARL NIELSEN, OP. 13
2,2,2,3 - 4,3,3,1 - timp.,perc. - hp. - str.   23:30 G. Schirmer.

GARDNER, Samuel
—— BROADWAY (TONE POEM)
*3,*3, E♭ cl., *3,3 sax.,*3 - 4,4,3,1 - perc.(5) - banjo - hp. - org. -
str.   17:00 Composer.
—— CONCERTO IN E MINOR, OP. 18, FOR VIOLIN AND ORCH.
2(1 alt. with picc.),2,2,2 - 4,3,3,1 - perc. - str.   25:00 Composer.
—— COUNTRY MOODS (FOR STRINGS) (IN 3 MOVTS.)
str.   11:00 G. Schirmer.

GÁRDONYI, Zoltán
—— DIVERTIMENTO
2,2,2,2 - 2,2,0,0 - str.   18:00 Bo. Hawkes.
—— FOLK SONG VARIATIONS FOR STRINGS
str.   Bo. Hawkes.

GARLICK, Antony
—— CANTICLE (1971)
3,2,*5,3 - 4,2,3,1 - timp.,perc.   11:00 Seesaw.
—— CANTO (SYMPHONIC POEM)
3,2,2,2 - 2,2,2,1 - timp.,perc.(2) - str.   15:00 Seesaw.

GAROVI, Josef
—— INVENTIONES (FÜR STREICHORCHESTER)
str.   12:00 S.U.I.S.A.

GARRIDO, Pablo
—— CHILEAN RHAPSODY (1937)
1,0,4(2nd and 3rd alt. with alto sax.,4th alt. with ten. sax.),0 -
0,2,1,0 - timp.,perc. - guit. - pf. - str.   18:00 Fleisher.
—— FANTASIA SUBMARINA (1932)
pf. - str.   8:00 Fleisher.

GARRIGUENC, Pierre
—— DREAMLAND, OP. 20 (FOR NARRATOR, SATB CHORUS
AND ORCH.) (1968) (Text: Edgar Allan Poe)
*3,1(alt. with Eng.hn.),*2,2,2 - 3,2,3,1 - perc.(2),cel.,vibra.,xyl. - pf.
- str.   11:00 Composer.
—— SYMPHONY, OP. 14 (IN 4 MOVTS.)
*3,2(2nd alt. with Eng.hn.),2,*3 - 4,3,3,1 - timp.,perc.(4),cel.,glock.
- hp. - pf. - str.   42:18 Composer.
—— SYNTHESIS, OP. 22 (FOR 13 WIND INSTRUMENTS) (1969)
2(2nd alt. with picc.),1(alt. withEng. hn.),*3,2 - 3,1,1,0
  5:00 Composer.

GASANOV, Gotfrid A.
—— CONCERTO NO. 1 FOR PIANO AND ORCH.
3,2,2,2 - 4,2,3,1 - timp.,perc. - pf. - str.   31:00 G. Schirmer.

GASLINI, Giorgio
—— LOGARITHM NO. 3
Bells,xyl. - str.   11:00 Leeds.

GASTYNE, Serge de
—— ATALA (PORTRAIT FOR ORCH.)
3(3rd alt. with picc.),*3,*3,3 - 4,3,3,1 - timp.,perc. (5) - str.
    14:00 EV.
—— ELEGY: IN MEMORIAM MAGYARORSZAG (IN HONOR OF
THE HUNGARIAN REVOLUTION OF 1956)
2,2,2,2 - 3,3,3,0 - timp. - hp. - str.   10:00 Composer.
—— EN BLEU, EN ROSE, EN JAUNE ET NOIR (IN BLUE, IN
PINK, IN YELLOW AND BLACK) (BALLET) %
*3,*3,*3,2 - 4,3,3,1 - timp.,perc.(3),cel., glock. - hp. - str.
    15:00 Composer.
—— GOTHIC MOVEMENT (FOR PIANO AND ORCH.)
*3,*3,*3,*3 - 4,3,3,1 - timp.,perc.(3), cel., glock., xyl. - hp. - pf. -
str.   20:00 Composer.
—— L' ÎLE LUMIERE (THE ISLE OF LIGHT) (IN 5 MOVTS.)
3(3rd alt. with picc.),alto fl.,*4,*4(3rd alt. with E♭cl.),*4 - 4,4,3,1 -
timp.,perc.(5), cel., glock., xyl. - 1-2 hp. - pf. - str.   29:30 EV.
—— ODE FOR ORCHESTRA (HOLLIN HALL) (IN MEMORY OF
ARTHUR HONEGGER)
*3,*3,*3,*3 - 4,4,3,1 - timp.,perc. - hp. - pf. - str.   17:00 EV.
—— THREE ELEGIES (FOR VOICE AND ORCH.)
2,2,2,2 - 3,3,3,0 - timp. - hp. - str.   17:00 EV.

GATES, B. Cecil
—— FESTIVAL OVERTURE
*3,2,3,2 - 4,2,3,1 - timp. - hp. - str.   15:00 Composer.
—— RESSURECTION MORNING (FOR SOPRANO OR TENOR
SOLO, WOMEN'S OR MIXED CHORUS AND ORCH.)
1,1,*3,1 - 2,1,1,0 - timp. - hp. (ad lib.) - pf. (ad lib.) - str.
    32:00 Composer.

—— THE RESTORATION (ORATORIO) (FOR SOPRANO, TENOR, BARITONE, MIXED CHORUS AND ORCH.)
    1,1,2,1 (alt with b.-cl.) - 1,1,1,0 - timp. - hp. org. - pf. - str.
                                       Composer.
—— SYMPHONY IN E MINOR (IN 4 MOVTS.)
    3,2,3,3 - 6,3,3,1 - timp. - hp. - str.   Composer.

GATES, Crawford
—— HERALD OVERTURE ("HIGH ON THE MOUNTAIN TOP"), OP. 27, NO. 3
    2,2,2,2 - 4,3,3,1 - timp.,perc.(4),cel.,glock. - str.   7:00 Pac. Publs.
—— ODE TO ACACIA (CONCERTO FOR PIANO AND ORCH.)
                                         Composer.
—— PORTRAIT OF A GREAT LEADER, OP. 40
    *3,2,2,2 - 4,3,3,1 - timp.,perc.(2),cel.(alt. with pf.) - hp. - str.
                                     Pac. Publs.
—— SUITE NO. 1 FOR ORCH.
                                       Composer.
—— SUITE NO. 3 FOR ORCH.
                                       Composer.
—— SUITE ON LATTER DAY SAINTS HYMNS
    *2(fl. alt. with alto fl. and b.-fl.),*2,0,0 - 2,0,0,0 - cel. - hp. - str.
                                       Composer.
—— SYMPHONIC ALLEGRO
                                       Composer.
—— SYMPHONY NO. 2, OP. 29 (MUSIC TO THE HILL CUMORAH PAGEANT) (SCENES FROM THE BOOK OF MORMON) (FOR NARRATOR, CHORUS AND ORCH.)
    *3,*3,*3,*3 - 4,4,3,1 - timp.,perc.(3-5), cel. - hp. - org. - pf. - str.
                                    77:00 Pac. Publs.
—— SYMPHONY NO. 3
    *3,2,2,2 - 4,3,3,1 - timp.,cel. - hp. - pf. - str.   14:00 Composer.
—— VARIATIONS FOR STRINGS
    str.   Composer.

GATES, Everett
—— PRISMATIC VARIATIONS
    str.   Bo. Hawkes.
—— RAINBOW VARIATIONS
    pf.(ad lib.) - str.   Bo. Hawkes.
—— VARICOLOR VARIATIONS
    str.   Bo. Hawkes.

GATTY, Nicholas
—— THE HASLEMERE SUITE
    str.   Galaxy.

GAUBERT, Philippe
—— AU PAYS BASQUE (SYMPHONIC POEM) (IN 2 MOVTS.)
    4,3,2,2 - 4,3,4,0 - timp.,perc.(2) - hp. - str.   17:30 Presser.
—— LES CHANTS DE LA MER (1929) (3 TABLEAUX SYMPHONIQUES)
    3,3,3,3 - 4,3,4,0 - timp.,perc.,glock. - hp. - str.   15:00 Presser.
—— CONCERTO FOR VIOLIN AND ORCH.
    2,2,2,2 - 2,2,0,0 - str.   14:30 Presser.
—— LE CORTÈGE D'AMPHITRITE
    3,3,3,2 - 4,3,3,1 - timp.,perc. - hp. - str.   14:00 Salabert.
—— DIVERTISSEMENTS SUR UN CHORAL
    1,1,1,1 - 1,1,0,0 - timp.,perc. - str.   10:30 Presser.
—— FANTASY FOR VIOLIN AND ORCH.
    3,2,2,2 - 4,3,3,1 - timp.,perc. - str.   12:00 EV.
—— INSCRIPTIONS POUR LES PORTES DE LA VILLE
                                    25:00 Henmar.
—— JOSIANE (LEGEND) (FOR NARRATOR, SOPRANO, CONTRALTO, WOMEN'S CHORUS AND ORCH.)
    3,3,3,3 - 4,3,3,1 - timp.,perc.,cel. - hp. - str. 20:00 F. Colombo.
—— LAMENTO (FOR CELLO AND ORCH.)
    2,3,2,2 - 4,0,0,0 - hp. - str.   7:00 Presser.
—— QUATRE ESQUISSES (FOR VIOLIN AND ORCH.)
    1,1,2,1 - 2,2,1,0 - perc. - str.   9:30 Presser.
—— SOIR DE NOËL EN BRETAGNE (FROM "CHANTS DE LA TERRE")
    3,4,2,3 - 4,3,3,1 - timp.,perc. - hp. - str.   4:00 Presser.
—— SYMPHONY IN F
    3,3,2,3 - 4,3,2,1 - timp.,perc. - hp. - str.   34:00 Presser.

GAUDIBERT, Eric
—— EPIBOLIE, OP. 10 (POUR FLÛTE SOLO ET ORCH. À CORDES)
    fl. - str.   11:00 S.U.I.S.A.

—— PRELUDE, DANSES ET CHORAL, OP. 12 (POUR VIOLINCELLO SOLO, PETIT ORCHESTRE À CORDES, 2 HAUTBOIS ET 2 BASSONS)
    2 ob., 2 bn. - str.   13:00 S.U.I.S.A.
—— SEVEN TIMES SEVEN PLUS FIVE EQUALS EIGHT (POUR PIANO ET ORCH. À CORDES)
    pf. - str.   15:00 S.U.I.S.A.

GAUDIOSI, Mario
—— SOGNO D'EROE (A HERO'S DREAM)
    3,3,3,3 - 4,3,3,1 - timp.,perc.,vibra. - 2 hp. - str.   Leeds.
—— SUL CAMALDONI (ON THE CAMALDONI) (SYMPHONIC VISION)
    3,2,3,2 - 4,3,3,1 - timp.,perc.(2),cel., vibra.,xyl. - 2 hp. - str.
                                    10:00 Leeds.
—— SYMPHONIC IMPRESSIONS (SENSAZIONI SINFONICHE)
    2,2,2,2 - 2,3,2,0 - timp.,perc.,cel. - hp. - pf. - str. 6:00 Leeds.

GAUL, Harvey B.
—— ALL SOUL'S DAY (TONE POEM)
    *3,*3,2,2 - 4,3,3,1 - timp.,perc. - str.   7:00 Composer.
—— ALONG THE READING PIKE (BASED ON PENNSYLVANIA GERMAN TUNES)
    *3,*3,2,2 - 4,3,3,1 - timp.,perc. - hp. - str.   6:00 Composer.
—— CHARLESTON MADONNA AND CHILD
    fl., cl. - timp.,perc. - hp (or pf.) - str.   10:00 Composer.
—— FATHER GALLITZEN REMEMBERS PRINCE DIMITRI
    str.   J. Fischer.
—— FOUR NEGRO SPIRITUALS (Freely Arranged for Strings)
    str.   12:00 Composer.
—— FROM A CARNEGIE INTERNATIONAL (IN 2 PARTS)
    fl., cl. - hn. - timp., perc. - hp. (or pf.) - str.   10:00 Composer.
—— FROM A PINE CREEK CHURCH-HOUSE
    str.   Composer.
—— FROM AN INDIAN LOG HOUSE (IN 2 PARTS)
    fl. - timp. (ad lib.), perc. - str.   7:00 AmerMusEd.
—— FROM PORTS OF CALL (SUITE) (IN 3 MOVTS.)
    *3,2,2,2 - 2,2,2,1 - timp.,perc. - hp. - pf. - str 16:00 Composer.
—— GRATIOS DEO FOR A NEW YEAR (FOR FULL ORCH.) (BASED ON THE 15TH CENTURY CHORAL "NUN DANKET ALLE GOTT")
                                       Composer.
—— HYMNUS FROM "ORESTES" (FOR CHAMBER ORCH.)
                                       Composer.
—— I HEAR AMERICAN SINGING (CANTATA) (FOR CHORUS AND ORCH.)
    *2,1,2,1 - 2,2,1,0 - timp.,perc. - str.   15:00 Western.
—— MANHATTAN BREATHING SPACES (SUITE FOR STRINGS) (IN 4 MOVTS.)
    str.   21:30 J. Fischer.
—— MISTS ON THE MONONAGAHELA
    2 fl., 2 cl. - hn. - perc. - hp. (or pf.) - str.   10:00 Composer.
—— NEW ENGLAND PRELUDE (BASED ON 2 COLONIAL PSALM TUNES)
    *3,*3,2,2 - 4,3,3,1 - timp.perc. - str.   8:00 Composer.
—— NEW SWEDEN ON THE DELAWARE (BASED ON ANCIENT SWEDISH FOLK SONGS)
    *3,*3,2,*3 - 4,3,3,1 - timp.,perc. - str.   15:00 Composer.
—— NORSE PRELUDE (HOMAGE TO G-A-D-E)
    str.   8:00 Composer.
—— OLD JOHNNY APPLESEED (CANTATA) (FOR SOPRANO, WOMEN'S CHORUS AND ORCH.)
    2,2,2,2 - 4,2,3,1 - timp.,perc. - str.   40:00 Composer.
—— PÈRE MARQUETTE (FOR NARRATOR AND ORCH.)
    *3,*3,2,2 - 4,3,3,1 - timp.,perc. - str.   11:00 Composer.
—— THE SINGERS (CANTATA) (FOR CHORUS AND ORCH.)
    1,1,2,1 - 2,2,1,0 - perc. - str.   Witmark.
—— SUITE ECCLESIASTICUS (IN 3 MOVTS.)
    str.   14:00 J. Fischer.
—— THANKSGIVING (RHAPSODY) (BASED ON "NOW THANK WE ALL OUR GOD")
    timp.,cymb., - org. - str.   8:00 J. Fischer.
—— THREE PALESTINIAN PASTELS
    str.   18:00 J. Fischer.
—— THREE TENNESSEE DEVIL TUNES
    str.   12:30 J. Fischer.
—— TUBAL CAIN (CANTATA) (FOR WOMEN'S CHORUS AND ORCH.)
    2,2,2,2 - 4,2,3,1 - timp. - hp. - str.   30:00 Composer.

GAVAZZENI, Gianandrea
—— CANTI DI OPERAI LOMBARDI
    2,*3,2,2 - 4,3,3,0 - timp.,perc. - str.   11:00 Bo. Hawkes.

—— CONCERTO FOR VIOLIN AND ORCH.
2,2,2,2 - 2,2,0,0 - timp.,perc. - pf. - str.   25:00 Bo. Hawkes.
—— DIALOGO (INTRODUCTION AND INTERLUDE) (FOR
TENOR, BARITONE AND ORCH.)
2,2,2,2 - 2,2,1,0 - timp.,perc. - hp. - pf. - str.   5:00 Bo. Hawkes.
—— IL FURIOSO NELL'ISOLA DI SAN DOMINGO (BALLET
SUITE)
2,2,2,2 - 2,2,1,0 - timp.,perc. - hp. - pf. - str.   13:00 Bo. Hawkes.
—— INTERLUDE FROM THE ORATORIO "CANTI PER SANT'
ALESSANDRO"
3,3,2,3 - 4,3,3,1 - timp.,perc. - hp. - pf. - str.   6:00 Bo. Hawkes.
—— NOTTURNI DI BEVITORI BERGAMASCHI (FOR TENOR
AND ORCH.)
3,3,3,3 - 4,3,3,1 - timp.,perc.(2) - hp. - str.   18:00 Leeds.

GAYFER, James McDonald
—— CANADA THE UNKNOWN (TONE POEM)
20:00 C.A.P.A.C.
—— CANADIAN LANDSCAPE
2(2nd alt. with picc.),2*3,2 - 4,3,3,1 - timp.,perc. - str.
6:00 CanMusCtr.
—— PASTORALE FOR CLARINET (1944)
2,2,1,1 - 3,0,0,0 - timp.,perc. - hp. - str.   8:30 CanMusCtr.
—— SIX CHINESE SONGS (FOR TENOR AND SMALL ORCH.)
fl. - hp. - str.   19:00 Bo. Hawkes.
—— SUITE FOR ORCHESTRA (IN 5 MOVTS.)
8:00 C.A.P.A.C.
—— SYMPHONY IN B FLAT
25:00 C.A.P.A.C.
—— SYMPHONY IN E FLAT
45:00 C.A.P.A.C.

GEARHART, Livingston
—— VARIATIONS ON AN AMERICAN AIR
3,3,3,2 - 4,2,3,0 - timp.,perc. - hp. - str.   11:40 Templeton.

GEBHARDT, Rio
—— FEST DER INFANTIN (EINE MÄRCHEN-OUVERTÜRE)
2,2,2,2 - 4,2,3,0 - perc. - hp. - pf. - str.   7:00 Henmar.
—— FULERO (VORSPIEL)
2,2,2,2 - 4,2,3,0 - perc. - hp. - pf. - str.   5:00 Henmar.
—— IMPROVISATION ÜBER SCHWÄBISCHE VOLKSWEISEN
(FOR SOPRANO, MIXED CHORUS AND STRINGS)
1-2 pf. - str.   5:30 Henmar.
—— KONZERT OVERTURE
2,2,2,2 - 4,3,3,1 - timp.,perc. - hp. - str.   8:30 Henmar.

GEDDES, Maxwell
—— OVERTURE, OP. 6 (1965)
2,2,2,2 - 3,3,3,3 - perc. - hp. - str.   9:00 P.R.S.
—— THREE ORCHESTRAL PIECES (1964)
2,2,2,2 - 3,3,3,0 - perc. - hp. - str.   8:30 P.R.S.

GEEHL, Henry
—— SUITE ESPAGNOLE (IN 4 MOVTS.)
3,2,2,2 - 2,2,3,0 - timp.,perc. - str.   18:00 Novello.

GEFORS, Hans
—— TIDLOSSNING (FOR MARIMBA AND 14 WINDS)(1974)
0,2,2,2 - 3,2,3,0 - mar.   12:00 Fleisher.
—— VISVITER (1973)
str.   10:00 Fleisher.

GEIGER, Emil
—— CHAMBER SYMPHONY, OP. 78
1,1,1,1 - 0,1,0,0 - timp.,glock. - str.   19:00 Mannheimer.
—— SYMPHONY, OP. 89 ("MÄNADE")
*3,2,2,2 - 4,2,3,0 - timp.,perc.,cel. - str.   24:00 Mannheimer.

GEISER, Walther
—— FANTASY NO. 1
Timp- pf. - str.   17:00 Baerenrtr.
—— FANTASY NO. 2 (FOR LARGE ORCH.)
Baerenrtr.
—— FANTASY NO. 3 (FOR STRINGS)
str.   Baerenrtr.
—— FESTLICHES VORSPIEL FÜR GROSSES ORCH., OP. 47
*3,*3,*3,*3 - 4,3,3,1 - timp.,perc. - str.   8:00 Baerenrtr.
—— KONZERTSTÜCK (FOR ORGAN AND CHAMBER ORCH.)
Baerenrtr.
—— OVERTURE TO AN ANTIQUE TRAGEDY, OP. 35
3,3,3,3 - 4,3,3,1 - timp.,perc. - str.   11:00 G. Schirmer.

—— SINFONIE FÜR GROSSES ORCH., OP. 44
*3,*2,*2,*3 - 4,3,3,0 - timp. - str.   17:00 Baerenrtr.
—— STABAT MATER, OP. 23 (FOR BARITONE, MIXED CHORUS,
ORGAN AND ORCH.)
*3,*3,*3,*3 - 4,3,3,1 - timp.,perc., xyl. - 2 hp. - org. - str.
55:00 Baerenrtr.
—— SYMPHONIE II
2,2,2,1 - 3,3,3,0 - timp. - str.   22:00 S.U.I.S.A.

GEISSLER, Fritz
—— THE ADVENTURES OF THE GOOD SOLDIER SCHWEIK
(SYMPHONIC BURLESQUE)
3,3,4,3 - 4,3,3,1 - timp.,perc. - str.   22:00 Tetra.
—— CHAMBER CONCERTO
fl. - hpsc. - str.(3,3,3,1)   Tetra.
—— CHAMBER SYMPHONY (1954)
1,1,1,1 - 0,3,1,0 - timp.,perc. - hp. - str.   14:00 Tetra.
—— CHAMBER SYMPHONY 1970
1,1,1,1 - 1,0,0,0 - perc. - str.   Tetra.
—— DER DOPPELGÄNGER (BALLET COMEDY) %
Tetra.
—— FESTIVAL OVERTURE
3,3,3,3 - 4,4,3,1 - timp.,perc. - pf. - str.   10:00 Tetra.
—— FIVE MINIATURES (FOR SMALL ORCH.)
2,1,1,1 - 2,2,1,0 - timp.,perc. - str.   14:00 Tetra.
—— A MIDSUMMER NIGHT'S DREAM (BALLET, AFTER
SHAKESPEARE) %
Tetra.
—— NOVEMBER 1918 (THREE SYMPHONIC MOVEMENTS)
2,2,2,2 - 4,2,3,0 - timp.,perc. - str.   18:00 Tetra.
—— PRELUDE
2,2,2,2 - 4,3,3,1 - timp.,perc. - str.   8:00 Tetra.
—— SUITE FROM THE BALLET "PIGMENT"
2,2,2(2nd alt. with sax.),2 - 3,3,1,0 - timp.,perc. - hp. - pf. - str.
18:00 Tetra.
—— SYMPHONY CONCERTANTE (FOR WIND QUINTET AND
STRINGS)
1,1,1,1 - 1,0,0,0 - str.   Tetra.
—— SYMPHONY FOR STRINGS (SYMPHONY NO. 4)
str.   18:00 Tetra.
—— SYMPHONY NO. 2
2,2,2,2 - 3,2,2,0 - timp.,perc. - hp. - pf. - str.   27:00 Tetra.
—— SYMPHONY NO. 3
2,2,2,2 - 4,4,3,1 - timp.,perc. - hp. - pf. - str.   25:00 Tetra.
—— SYMPHONY NO. 5
2,2,2,2 - 4,2,3,1 - timp.,perc. - hp. - pf. - str.   Tetra.
—— TWO SYMPHONIC SCENES
2,2,2,2 - 4,2,3,1 - timp.,perc. - hp. - pf. - str.   12:00 Tetra.

GELBRUN, Artur
—— HEDVA (BALLET ON A POPULAR HEBREW TALE) %
3,2,2,1 - 4,3,3,1 - timp.,perc.(3) - hp. - pf. - str.   42:00 Leeds.
—— PICCOLO DIVERTIMENTO
str.   6:00 Bo. Hawkes.
or:
fl. - tpt. - perc. - str.
—— PRELUDIO, PASSACAGLIA E FUGA
3,2,2,2 - 4,3,3,1 - timp.,perc.(2) - str.   39:00 Leeds.
—— SUITE
2,2,2,2 - 4,3,3,1 - timp.,perc. - str.   18:00 Leeds.
—— SYMPHONY NO. 1
3,2,2,2 - 4,3,3,1 - timp.,perc.,glock.,xyl. - hp. - str.   21:00 Leeds.
—— TWO SONGS (FOR VOICE AND CHAMBER ORCH.)
0,1,1,0 - 0,0,0,0 - str.   12:00 A.C.U.M.

GEMINIANI, Francesco - ANTONINI, Alfredo
—— CONCERTO GROSSO IN G MINOR, OP. 3, NO. 2 (FOR
CHAMBER ORCH.)
12:00 Bo. Hawkes.

GEMINIANI, Francesco - BARBLAN
—— CONCERTO GROSSO IN B MINOR (After Corelli's Sonata a tre
da chiesa, Op. 3-a, No. 4)
cemb. - str.   8:00 Henmar.

GEMINIANI, Francesco - CARSE, Adam
—— CONCERTO IN C MINOR, OP. 2, NO. 2
cemb.(ad lib.) - str.   11:00 Galaxy.

GEMINIANI, Francesco - DORATI, Antal
—— CONCERTO GROSSO IN E MINOR
11:00 A.P.R.A.

GEMINIANI, Francesco - ESPOSITO, Michele
—— CONCERTO GROSSO IN C MINOR
    str.   Oxford.

GEMINIANI, Francesco - HARRISON, Julius
—— CONCERTO GROSSO IN E MINOR, OP. 3, NO. 3
    str.   11:00 Bo. Hawkes.

GEMINIANI, Francesco - MORTARI, Virgilio
—— CONCERTO GROSSO NO. 1
    cemb. - str.   10:00 Bo. Hawkes.
—— CONCERTO GROSSO NO. 9
    cemb. - str.   13:00 Bo. Hawkes.
—— CONCERTO GROSSO NO. 12
    cemb. - org. - str.   16:00 Bo. Hawkes.

GEMINIANI, Francesco - UPMEYER
—— CONCERTO GROSSO IN D MINOR, OP. 2, NO. 3
    cemb. - str.   Henmar.

GENTILI, Alberto
—— DANZA JERATICA
    *3,*3,*3,2 - 4,2,2,1 - perc., cel. - hp. - str.   9:00 Bo. Hawkes.
—— PRELUDIO
    2,2,2,2 - 2,1,0,0 - cel. - hp. - str.   6:00 Bo. Hawkes.

GENTILUCCI, Armando
—— FANTASIA NO. 2 (FOR FLUTE, PERCUSSION AND DOUBLE STRING ORCH.) (1968)
    fl. - perc.(1) - str. (8,4,4,2)   10:00 MCA Music.
—— RIFRAZIONI (REFRACTIONS) (1969)
    str.(min. 4,2,1,1)   6:00 MCA Music.

GENZMER, Harald
—— CONCERT SUITE
    2(2nd alt. with picc.),*2,2(2nd alt. with b.-cl.),2 - 4,2,3,1 - timp. - str.   18:00 Henmar.
—— CONCERTO FOR PIANO AND ORCH.
    2(2nd alt. with picc.),2,2,2 - 3,2,0,0 - timp. - pf. - str.
                               20:00 Henmar.
—— CONCERTO FOR TRAUTONIUM AND ORCH.
    2,2,2,2 - 2,2,2,1 - trautonium - str.   20:00 Henmar.
—— DANCE SUITE
    2(2nd alt. with picc.),2(2nd alt. with Eng.hn.),2(2nd alt. with b.-cl.),2 - 4,2,3,1 - timp. - str.   18:00 Henmar.
—— PROLOGUE FOR ORCHESTRA
    2,2,2,2 - 3,2,3,1 - timp.,perc. - str.   11:00 G. Schirmer.
—— SYMPHONIC MUSIC
    2(2nd alt. with picc.),2(2nd alt. with Eng.hn.),2(2nd alt. with b.-cl.),2 - 4,2,3,1 - timp.,perc. - str.   25:00 Henmar.

GEORGE, Earl
—— ABRAHAM LINCOLN WALKS AT MIDNIGHT (FOR MEZZO-SOPRANO, CHORUS AND ORCH.) (Text: Vachel Lindsay)
    2,2,2,2 - 4,2,3,1 - timp.,perc. - pf. - str.   10:00 Composer.
—— CONCERTO FOR PIANO AND ORCH. (IN 3 MOVTS.)
    2(2nd alt. with picc.),0,2,2 - 4,2,3,1 - timp.,perc.(3) - pf. - str.   23:00 Oxford.
—— CONCERTO FOR STRINGS (IN 3 MOVTS.)
    str.   11:00 Composer.
—— CONCERTO IN F, FOR VIOLIN AND ORCH.
                               22:00 Oxford.
—— A CURRIER AND IVES SET (IN 3 MOVTS.)
    1,1,2,1 - 2,2,1,0 - perc.(1) - pf. - str.   10:30 Composer.
—— INTRODUCTION AND ALLEGRO
    3,2,2,2 - 4,3,3,1 - timp.,perc. - str.   7:30 C. Fischer.
—— INTRODUCTION, VARIATIONS AND FINALE
    2(2nd alt. with picc.),2,2,1 - 4,3,3,1 - timp.,perc.(3) - pf. - str.
                               13:00 Composer.
—— MISSA BREVIS (FOR SOPRANO, TENOR, CHORUS AND ORCH.)
    2,2,2,2 - 4,2,3,1 - timp.,perc. - str.   20:00 Composer.
—— A THANKSGIVING OVERTURE
    2,2,2,2 - 4,2,3,1 - timp.,perc. - pf. - str.   5:00 Bo. Hawkes.

GEORGE, Thom Ritter
—— AMERICAN FOLKSONG CYCLE NO. 1, OP. 53 (4 SONGS) (FOR CONTRALTO OR BARITONE AND STRING ORCH.)
    str.   14:00 Arranger.
—— AMERICAN FOLKSONG CYCLE NO. 2, OP. 118-B
    2(2nd alt. with picc.),2(2nd alt. with Eng.hn.),2,2 - 2,0,0,0 - timp. - str.   Arranger.

—— ATAVISM AND TRANSFORMATION, OP. 65 (4 SONGS) (FOR CONTRALTO AND STRINGS) (Text: Henry Malone)
    str.   20:00 Composer.
—— BAL À BOUGIVAL (DANCE AT BOUGIVAL), OP. 245 (1968) (OVERTURE, AFTER A PAINTING BY RENOIR)
    *3,3(3rd alt. with Eng.hn.),3(3rd alt. with b.-cl.),*3 - 4,3,3,1 - timp.,perc.(3),glock.,vibra.,xyl. - hp. - pf. - str.   8:30 Composer.
—— BALLADE FOR ORCHESTRA, OP. 278 (1972)
    *3,2,2,2 - 4,2,3,1 - timp.,perc.(3),glock. - str.   8:30 Composer.
—— LES CHANTS DE NOËL, OP. 200 (FOR SOPRANO, CONTRALTO, TENOR, BARITONE, SATB CHORUS AND ORCH.)
    1(alt. with picc.),1,1,1 - 1,0,0,0 - bells,glock. - hp. - str.
                               20:00 Arranger.
—— CHRISTMAS CANTATA (CANTATA NO. 2), OP. 138 (FOR CONTRALTO, BARITONE, SATB CHORUS AND STRING ORCH.)
    str.   16:00 Rochester.
—— CONCERTINO FOR OBOE AND STRINGS, OP. 190
    1. Pastorale; Andante con moto; 2. Allegro moderato
    ob. - str.   Composer.
—— CONCERTO FOR BASS TROMBONE AND ORCH., OP. 176 (IN 1 MOVT.)
    *3,2,2,2 - 4,3,4,1 - timp.,perc.(3),xyl. - str.   10:00 Rochester.
—— CONCERTO FOR FLUTE AND ORCH., OP. 223-A (1965-6) (IN 3 MOVTS.)
    1,2,0,2 - 0,0,0,0 - str.   8:15 Rochester.
—— CONCERTO FOR PIANO AND ORCH., OP. 144-A (IN 3 MOVTS.)
    2,2,2,2 - 4,3,3,0 - timp. - pf. - str.   18:00 Composer.
—— CONCERTO GROSSO NO. 1 IN G MINOR, OP. 98 (FOR 2 VIOLINS AND STRING ORCH.) (IN 3 MOVTS.)
    hpsc. - str.   10:00 Composer.
—— CONCERTO GROSSO NO. 2, OP. 141 (IN 3 MOVTS.)
    0,0,0,0 - 0,2,2,0 - str.   8:00 Composer.
—— CONCERTO GROSSO NO. 3, OP. 149 (IN 3 MOVTS.)
    trb. - str.   13:00 Composer.
—— CONCERTO GROSSO NO. 4, OP. 159 (FOR VIOLIN AND STRING ORCH.) (IN 3 MOVTS.)
    str.   Composer.
—— CONCERTO GROSSO NO. 5, OP. 168 (IN 3 MOVTS.)
    hn. - str.   Composer.
—— IN MEMORIAM, OP. 177
    2,1,2,2 - 4,0,0,0 - perc. - hp. - str.   6:00 Composer.
—— INCIDENTAL MUSIC TO SHAKESPEARE'S "MACBETH", OP. 60
    4,4,2,2 b.-cl.,2,2 c.-bn. - 8,4,4,2 - timp.,perc.(6),bells - str.
                               Composer.
—— THE NIGHTINGALE, OP. 95-B
    str.   8:00 Composer.
—— SCÈNES DE BALLET, OP. 212 (IN 4 MOVTS.)
    *3,2,2,2 - 4,2,3,1 - timp.,perc.(3),glock.,vibra.,xyl. - str.
                               19:00 Composer.
—— SINFONIETTA, OP. 235 (1967) (IN 4 MOVTS.)
    3(3rd alt. with picc.),2,3,(3rd alt. with b.-cl.),*3 - 4,3,3,1 - timp.,perc.(3),cel.,glock.,vibra.,xyl. - hp. - pf. - str.
                               20:00 Composer.
—— THREE TRADITIONAL CHORALES, OP. 27 (FOR SATB CHORUS AND STRING ORCH.)
    str.   6:00 Arranger.
—— VARIATIONS ON "DRINK TO ME ONLY WITH THINE EYES", OP. 18 (FOR VIOLIN AND STRING ORCH.)
    str.   9:00 Composer.

GERAEDTS, Jaap
—— CONCERTO DA CAMERA (FOR VIOLIN, CELLO, PIANO AND ORCH.) (1956)
    2,2,0,1 - 2,1,0,0 - pf. - str.   23:00 Henmar.
—— DANCE SUITE (FROM THEATRE-MUSIC FOR "KRUSTOCHT")
    2,2,2,1 - 2,1,0,0 - timp.,perc. - str.   9:00 Henmar.
—— GARCIA LORCA SUITE (FROM MUSIC TO THE TRAGEDY "BLOOD WEDDING")
    1,1,1,0 - 1,0,0,0 - timp.,perc. - hp. - str.   10:00 Henmar.
—— DE GRAAF VAN WEET-IK-VEEL (MONSTRUOFONISCHE BALLADE) (FOR SOPRANO, ALTO, BASS, MIXED CHORUS AND ORCH.) (1956) (Text: A. M. G. Schmidt)
    3,1,2,1 - 2,1,0,0 - timp.,perc. - pf. - str.   21:00 Henmar.
—— MEMENTO '45 (TER HERINNERING AAN DE GEVALLENEN VAN HET VERZET) (1960)
    2,3,3,3 - 4,3,3,1 - timp.,perc.,cel. - hp. - org. - str.   10:00 Henmar.
—— ONE TIMES ONE (QUODLIBET-VARIATIONS) (1957)
    3,3,4,3 - 4,3,3,1 - timp.,perc. - hp. - str.   21:00 Henmar.

—— PRELUDIUM EN FUGA (1948)
2,3,2,2 - 4,2,2,0 - timp. - str.   7:00 Henmar.

GERHARD, Fritz Christian
—— CONCERTINO FÜR GEIGE (VIOLIN) UND KAMMEROCH.
1,1,1,1 - 1,0,0,0 - str.   13:00 Alkor.
—— CONCERTO BREVE (FOR ALTO SAXOPHONE AND
STRINGS)
alto. sax. - str.   14:00 G. Schirmer.
—— CONCERTO CON UNISONO (FOR PIANO, TIMPANI AND
STRINGS)
timp. - pf. - str.   11:00 G. Schirmer.
—— SINFONISCHE METAMORPHOSE
2,2,2,2 - 4,2,3,1 - timp.,perc. - str.   12:00 Alkor.
—— SYMPHONIA BREVIS
2,2,2,2 - 4,2,3,1 - timp.,perc. - str.   10:00 Alkor.
—— SYMPHONY IN 3 MOVTS.
3,2,2,2 - 4,3,3,1 - timp.,perc. - str.   23:00 Alkor.
—— SYMPHONY NO. 2
str.   17:00 G. Schirmer.
—— THREE LITTLE PIECES
fl. - pf. - str.   5:00 Robbins.

GERHARD, Roberto
—— ALEGRIAS (SUITE FROM THE BALLET) (DIVERTISSEMENT
FLAMENCO) (IN 2 MOVTS.)
2,2,2,1 - 2,1,1,0 - timp.,perc. - hp. - pf. - str.   13:00 Mills.
—— CONCERTO FOR HARPSICHORD, STRINGS AND
PERCUSSION
perc. - hpsc. - str.   25:00 Mills.
—— CONCERTO FOR ORCHESTRA
3,3,3,3 - 4,4,3,1 - timp.,perc.(4), - hp. - str.   21:00 Oxford.
—— CONCERTO FOR PIANO AND STRING ORCH.
pf. - str.   20:00 Mills.
—— CONCERTO FOR VIOLIN AND ORCH.
*2,*2,*2,*2 - 4,2,2,0 - timp.,perc. - hp. - pf. - str.
                                      28:00 Belw-Mills.
—— DANCES FROM "DON QUIXOTE"
2(2nd alt. with picc.),2,2(2nd alt. with b.-cl.),2 - 4,2,3,0 -
timp.,perc. - pf. - str.   17:30 Mills.
—— DON QUIXOTE (SUITE FROM THE BALLET)
*2,2,2,2 - 2,2,2,0 - timp.,perc. - pf. - str.   26:00 Modern.
—— EPITHALAMION
4,4,3,4 - 4,4,3,1 - timp.,perc. - hp. - pf. - str.   20:00 Oxford.
—— HYMNODY
1,1,1,0 - 1,1,1,1 - perc. - 2 pf.   18:00 Oxford.
—— LEO
1(alt. with picc.),1,0,0 - 1,1,0,0 - perc.(2),cel. - pf. - vln.,c.
                                      20:00 Oxford.
—— METAMORPHOSES (SYMPHONY NO. 2: REVISED VERSION)
4,4,4,4 - 4,4,4,1 - timp.,perc. - hp. - acc. - pf. - str.
                                      28:00 Belw-Mills.
—— THE PLAGUE (FOR SPEAKER, CHORUS AND ORCH.) (Text:
Albert Camus; English translation by Stuart Gilbert)
2 picc.,2 fl.,4(4th alt. with Eng. hn.),*4,*4 - 4,4,4,1 - timp.,perc.(7)
- accord. - pf. - str.   42:00 Oxford.
—— SYMPHONY NO. 1
2(2nd alt. with picc.),*2,2,2 - 4,2,2,1 - timp.,perc. - hp. - pf. - str.
                                      37:00 Mills.
—— SYMPHONY NO. 2
*2,*2,2,2 - 4,2,2,1 - timp.,perc. - hp. - pf. - str.
                                      30:00 Mills.
—— SYMPHONY NO. 3 ("COLLAGES")
*3,*3,*3,*3 - 4,3,3,1 - timp.,perc.(6) - tape-recorder - hp.- pf. - str.
                                      20:00 Oxford.
—— SYMPHONY NO. 4 ("NEW YORK")
4,4,4,*4 - 6,4,4,1 - timp.,perc.(5),cel. - 2 hp. - pf. - str.
                                      25:00 Oxford.

GERMAN, Edward
—— THEME AND SIX DIVERSIONS
3,2,2,2 - 4,2,3,1 - timp.,perc., cel - hp. - str.   17:00 Novello.

GERSHWIN, George
—— AN AMERICAN IN PARIS
*3,*3,*3,3sax.,2 - 4,3,3,1 - timp.,perc. (6) - pf. - str.
                                      16:00 New World.
—— BLUE MONDAY (135TH STREET)(1-ACT OPERA) %
1,*2,0,4 sax.,0 - 1,3,2,1 - timp.,perc. - pf.   20:00 WarnerBros.
—— CATFISH ROW (SUITE FROM "PORGY AND BESS")
2(2nd alt. with picc.),2(2nd alt. with Eng.hn.),4,1 - 3,3,2,1 -
timp.,perc. - banjo - pf. - str.   26:00 Chappell.
—— CONCERTO IN F (FOR PIANO AND ORCH.) (IN 3 MOVTS.)
*3,*3,*3,2 - 4,3,3,1 - timp.,perc. (4) - pf. - str.   30:00 New World.

—— CUBAN OVERTURE
*3,*3,*3,*3, - 5,3,3,1 - timp.,perc. (1) - hp. - str.
                                      11:00 New World.
—— LULLABY (OP. POSTH.) (FOR STRING ORCH.)
str.   WarnerBros.
—— RHAPSODY IN BLUE (FOR PIANO AND ORCH.)
2,2,*3,3sax.,2 - 3,3,3,1 - timp.,perc. (3) - banjo - pf. - str.
                                      16:00 New World.
—— SECOND RHAPSODY (FOR PIANO AND ORCH.)
*3,*3,*3,2 - 4,3,3,1 - timp.,perc. (5) - hp. - pf. - str.
                                      12:14 New World.
—— VARIATIONS ON "I GOT RHYTHM"
1,1,0,4 sax.,1 - 3,3,2,1 - perc. (2) - pf. - str.   8:30 New World.

GERSHWIN, George - BENNETT, Robert Russell
—— GERSHWIN IN HOLLYWOOD
2,2(2nd alt. with Eng.hn.),3,2 - 4,3,3,1 - timp.,perc. - hp. - pf.(alt.
with cel.) - str.   10:00 Chappell.
—— PORGY AND BESS: A SYMPHONIC PICTURE
3(3rd alt. with picc.),*3,*4,2 - 4,3,3,1 - timp.,perc. (3) - 2 hp. - str.
                                      24:00 Gershwin.

GERSHWIN, George - BERKOWITZ, Sol
—— THE REAL MCCOY (BALLET) %
2(2nd alt. with picc.),2,2,alto sax.(alt. with b.-cl.),2 -
timp.,perc.,cel. - str.   18:00 Chappell.

GERSHWIN, George - GOULD, Morton
—— SUITE FROM "PORGY AND BESS"
3,2,3,2 - 4,3,3,1 - perc. - banjo - hp. - str.   Chappell.

GERSHWIN, George - STONE, Gregory
—— PRELUDES (FOR ORCH., OR FOR 2 PIANOS AND ORCH.)
                                      8:30 WarnerBros.

GERSTMAN, Blanche
—— ODE TO SOUTH AFRICA (FOR SOPRANO, VOCAL
QUARTET, CHORUS AND ORCH.) % (Text: Afrikaans - I.D. Du
Plessis; English - Gideon Roos)
2,2,3,2 - 4,2,3,1 - timp.,perc. - str.   21:00 S.A.M.R.O.
—— OUT OF THE CHRISTMAS STOCKING: SUITE
str.   18:00 S.A.M.R.O.
—— OVERTURE: TABLE MOUNTAIN
2,2,3,2 - 4,2,3,1 - timp.,perc. - str.   9:00 S.A.M.R.O.
—— PARAPHRASE ON GRIEG'S 'ICH LIEBE DICH' (FOR
CHAMBER ORCH.)
1,1,2,1 - 3,1,2,0 - str.   5:00 S.A.M.R.O.
—— PRELUDE
2,2,3,2 -4,2,3,1 - timp.,perc. - str.   4:00 S.A.M.R.O.
—— UIT DIE PASSIE (EASTER CANTATA) (FOR CHOIR AND
ORCH.) % (Text: W. E. G. Louw)
2,2,3,2 - 4,2,3,1 - timp.,perc. - str.   23:00 S.A.M.R.O.

GESENSWAY, Louis
—— COMMEMORATION SYMPHONY (1968)
3(1 alt. with picc.),*3,*3,*4 - 4,3,3,1 -
timp.,perc.(5),cel.,glock.,vibra. - 2 hp. - pf. - str.   35:00 Presser.
—— CONCERTO FOR FLUTE AND ORCH. (IN 3 MOVTS.)
1,*3,0,2 - 3,2,1,0 - timp.,perc.(2), cel., xyl - hp. - pf. - str.
                                      26:00 Presser.
—— CONCERTO FOR THIRTEEN BRASS INSTRUMENTS (IN 3
MOVTS.)
4 hn., 4 tpt., 4 trb., tu.   30:00 Presser.
—— A DOUBLE PORTRAIT
*3,*3,*3,*3 - 4,3,4,1 - timp.,perc.(3) - hp. - pf. - str.
                                      12:00 Composer.
—— FIVE RUSSIAN MELODIES (FIVE RUSSIAN PIECES)
2,2,2,2 - 4,2,3,0 - timp.,perc. - hp. - str.   12:30 Composer.
—— THE FOUR SQUARES OF PHILADELPHIA (FOR NARRATOR,
FIVE SPEAKERS AND ORCH.) (IN 6 MOVTS.)
*3,*3,*3,*2 - 4,4,4,1 - timp.,perc., cel., glock., xyl. - 2 hp. - pf. -
str.   28:00 Composer.
—— THE GREAT BOFFO (1-ACT COMIC OPERA) %
1,1,1,1 - 2,1,1,0 - timp.,perc. - pf. - str.   20:00 Presser.
—— NOW LET THE NIGHT BE DARK FOR ALL OF ME (TONE
POEM)
2,*3,*3,*3 - 4,0,0,0 - timp. - hp. - str.   10:00 Composer.
—— ODE TO PEACE
3,alto fl.,3,3,3 - 3,3,1,0 - timp. - hp. - str.   10:00 Presser.
—— A PENNSYLVANIA OVERTURE (1972)
*3,*3,*3,*3 - 4,2,3,1 - timp.,perc.,cel.,glock.,xyl. - str.
                                      18:00 E. Horowitz.

—— REVERY (1966)
    str.   Presser.
—— SUITE ON JEWISH THEMES
    1. Lento; 2. Grazioso; 3. Andante; 4. Allegro vivace
    *3,*3,2,2 - 4,2,2,1 - timp.,perc. (3) - str.   15:00 Presser.
—— THREE MOVEMENTS FOR STRINGS AND PERCUSSION
    timp.,perc.(5), cel.,glock., xyl., vibra. - str.   16:00 Presser.

GESUALDO, Don Carlo - SERLY, Tibor
—— MADRIGAL (Freely Orch. by T. Serly)
    str.   8:00 ModusAssoc.

GESUALDO, Don Carlo - STRAVINSKY, Igor
—— MONUMENTUM PRO GESUALDO DI VENOSA (3
    MADRIGALS, RECOMPOSED FOR INSTRUMENTS)
    0,2,0,2 - 4,2,3,0 - str.(no d.-b.)   7:00 Bo. Hawkes.

GETHEN, Felix
—— CANZONA (FOR ORGAN AND SMALL ORCH.)
                               5:30 A.P.R.A.
—— CAPRICCIO (FOR VIOLIN AND SMALL ORCH.)
                              18:00 A.P.R.A.
—— CONCERTINO (FOR PIANO AND ORCH.)
                              21:00 A.P.R.A.
—— CONCERTO FOR PIANO AND ORCH.
                              21:00 A.P.R.A.
—— DIVERTIMENTO CONCERTANTE
                              10:00 A.P.R.A.
—— ELEGIAC OVERTURE
                              8:00 A.P.R.A.
—— HORATIAN SUITE
                              33:00 A.P.R.A.
—— INTRODUCTION AND RONDO (FOR VIOLIN AND ORCH.)
                              19:00 A.P.R.A.
—— AN IRISH RHAPSODY
                              9:00 A.P.R.A.
—— RHAPSODY (FOR VIOLA AND ORCH.) (1962)
                              11:00 A.P.R.A.
—— SERENADE
    str.   8:30 A.P.R.A.
—— SYMPHONY IN E FLAT
                              24:00 A.P.R.A.
—— TRAGIC OVERTURE
                              8:30 A.P.R.A.

GHEDINI, Giorgio Federico
—— BILLY BUDD (1-ACT OPERA, AFTER MELVILLE'S STORY) %
    (Text: Salvatore Quasimodo)
    2,2,2,2 - 2,2,2,0 - timp.,perc.(3) - str.   Leeds.
—— CONCERTO DELL'ALBATRO (CONCERTO OF THE
    ALBATROSS) (FOR RECITATIVO VOICE, VIOLIN, CELLO,
    PIANO AND ORCH.) (AFTER MELVILLE'S "MOBY DICK")
    1,0,0,0 - 0,0,2,0 - timp.,perc.(2) - pf. - str.   28:00 Leeds.
—— CONCERTO FUNEBRE PER DUCCIO GALIMBERTI (FOR
    TENOR, BASS, AND SMALL ORCH.)
    2 trb. - timp. - str.   23:00 Leeds.
—— CONCERTO GROSSO IN F MAJOR
    1,1,1,1 - 1,0,0,0 - str.   22:00 Leeds.
—— CONCERTO NO. 1 FOR TWO PIANOS AND ORCH.
    2,2,2,2 - 2,2,2,0 - timp.,perc. - 2 pf. - str.   19:00 Leeds.
—— CONCERTO SPIRITUALE (FOR FEMALE CHORUS AND
    CHAMBER ORCH.)
    0,0,0,0 - 1,2,0,0 - timp. - pf. - str.(no vlns.)   18:00 Leeds.
—— CORONA DI SACRE CANZONI, O, LAUDI SPIRITUALI
    (CHAPLET OF SACRED SONGS, OR, SPIRITUAL HYMNS)
    (FOR VOICE, CHORUS, PIANO AND STRINGS)
    pf. - str.   26:00 Leeds.
—— LECTIO LIBRI SAPIENTIAE (READING OF THE BOOK OF
    WISDOM) (SPIRITUAL CANTATA) (FOR VOICE AND
    SMALL ORCH.)
    tpt. - pf. - str.   9:00 Leeds.
—— LA MESSA DEL VENERDI SANTO (GOOD FRIDAY MASS)
    (FOR SOLO VOICES, CHORUS AND ORCH.)
    3,3,3,3 - 4,3,3,1 - timp.,perc.(2) - str.   70:00 Leeds.
—— MUSICA NOTTURNA (NIGHT MUSIC)
    2,2,2,2 - 0,1,0,0 - mandolin - str.   14:00 Leeds.

GHENT, Emmanuel
—— HEX (AN ELLIPSIS FOR TRUMPET, INSTRUMENTS AND
    TAPE) (1966)
    1(alt. with picc.),1,1,1(or*1) - 0,1,0,0 - tape-recorder - 4 vln.,2
    vla.,1 d.-b.   16:00 Composer.

GHEZZO, Dinu
—— THALLA (MUSIC FOR PIANO AND 16 INSTRUMENTS)
    (1974)
    1(alt. with picc.),1(alt. with Eng.hn.),1(alt. with b.-cl.),alto sax.,0 -
    2,2,1,0 - vibra. - pf. - str.(2,1,1,1)   14:00 Seesaw.

GHIONE, F.
—— L' AVVENTO (VISIONE DEL MISTERO) (FOR FEMALE
    CHORUS AND ORCH.)
    3,3,3,3 - 4,3,3,1 - timp.,perc., cel. - 1-2 hp. - org. - pf. - str.
                              20:00 Bo. Hawkes.

GHISI, Federico
—— FANTASIA ALLEGRA (MERRY FANTASY)
    2,3,3,2 - 4,2,2,1 - timp.,perc. - str.   7:30 Leeds.

GIANFERRARI, Vincenzo
—— TRE PRELUDI
    3,3,3,2 - 4,3,3,1 - timp.,perc., cel. - hp. - str.   9:00 Bo. Hawkes.

GIANNEO, Luis
—— BLANCA NIEVES (SUITE)
    3,3,3,3 - 4,3,3,1 - timp. - hp. - str.   10:00 Southern.
—— CONCIERTO AYMARA (FOR VIOLIN AND ORCH.)
    2,2,2,2 - 4,2,3,1 - timp. - str.   25:00 Southern.
—— OBERTURA PARA UNA COMEDIA INFANTIL (FOR WINDS
    AND SOLO STRINGS)
    2(1 alt. with picc.),2,2,2 - 2,1,0,0 - perc., cel. - str. 5:00 Southern.
—— PERICON (FOR LARGE ORCH.)
    2,2,2,2 - 4,3,3,1 - hp. - str.   Southern.
—— SUITE DEL POEMA COREOGRAFICO "ATTIS" (IN 3 MOVTS.)
                                Southern.
—— EL TARCO EN FLOR (POEMA SINFONICO)
    2,2,2,2 - 4,2,1,0 - timp.,perc.(3) - hp. - str.   12:00 Southern.
—— VARIATIONS ON A TANGO MELODY (VARIACIONES
    SOBRE TEMA DE TANGO)
    2,2,2,2 - 2,2,0,0 - timp.,perc. - str.   Southern.

GIANNINI, Vittorio
—— ANTIGONE (MELODRAMA) (FOR SOPRANO AND ORCH.)
    3,3,3,3 - 4,3,2,2 - timp.,perc. - hp. - str.   F. Colombo.
—— APRIL NOCTURNE
    1,*1,1,1 - 2,2,1,0 - timp.,perc. - hp. - pf. - str.   6:00 Composer.
—— BEAUTY AND THE BEAST (RADIO OPERA)
    2,2,2,2 - 4,2,2,1 - timp.,perc.(2),cel. - hp. - str.   Ricordi.
    or:
    1,1,2,1 - 1,2,1,0 - timp.,perc.(2),cel. - hp. - str.
—— BLENNERHASSET (RADIO OPERA)
    *3,2(2nd alt. with Eng. hn.),2,2 - 4,2,2,1 - timp. - hp. - str.
                                27:00 Composer.
—— CANTICLE OF CHRISTMAS (FOR BARITONE, CHORUS AND
    ORCH.)
    3(3rd alt. with picc.),3(3rd alt. with Eng. hn.),3(3rd alt. with
    b.-cl.),2 - 4,3,3,1 - timp.,perc., cel., glock. - hp. - str.
                                28:00 Ricordi.
—— CANTICLE OF THE MARTYRS (FOR BARITONE, CHORUS,
    ORGAN AND ORCH.)
    *3,2,2,2 - 4,3,3,1 - timp.,perc.(1) - str.   21:00 Gray.
—— CONCERTO FOR PIANO AND ORCH. (IN 3 MOVTS.)
    *3,*3,*3,*3 - 4,3,3,1 - timp.,perc(2) - hp. - pf. - str.
                                 25:00 Composer.
—— CONCERTO FOR TRUMPET AND ORCH. (IN 3 MOVTS.)
    2(2nd alt. with picc.),2,2,2 - 4,2,3,1 - timp.,perc. cel - hp. - str.
                                 16:00 Remick.
—— CONCERTO FOR TWO PIANOS AND ORCH. (IN 3 MOVTS.)
    *3,*3,*3,*3 - 4,3,3,1 - timp.,perc.(2) - hp. - 2 pf. - str.
                                 12:00 Composer.
—— CONCERTO FOR VIOLIN AND ORCH.
    2,2,2,2 - 4,2,2,0 - timp.,perc. - str.   15:00 F. Colombo.
—— CONCERTO GROSSO (FOR STRING QUARTET AND STRING
    ORCH.) (IN 3 MOVTS.)
    str.   13:00 EV.
—— DIVERTIMENTO FOR ORCH.
    2(2nd alt. with picc.),2,2,2 - 2,2,1,0 - timp.,perc.(2) - hp. - str.
                                 12:00 Ricordi.
—— DIVERTIMENTO NO. 2
    2,2,2,2 - 2,2,1,0 - timp.,perc. - hp. - str.   15:00 F. Colombo.
—— DIVERTIMENTO NO. 3
    2,0,2,0 - 0,1,1,0 - timp.,perc. - pf. - str.   F. Colombo.
—— THE HARVEST: TWO EXCERPTS FROM THE OPERA (WITH
    OPTIONAL SATB CHORUS) (Text: Karl Flaster)
    3,3,3,3 - 4,3,2,2 - timp.,perc. - hp. - str.   11:00 F. Colombo.

—— LIFE'S SPAN (FOR HIGH VOICE AND STRINGS)
    str.   8:00 Ricordi.
—— LOVE'S LABOUR'S LOST (SUITE FOR ORCH.)
    2,1,1,1 - 2,1,1,0 - perc. - hp. - str.   25:00 F. Colombo.
—— THE MEDEAD (MONODRAMA IN 4 PARTS, FOR SOPRANO
AND ORCH.) (Text: Composer)
    *3,*3,*3,*3 - 4,3,3,1 - timp.,perc.(3) - hp. - str.
          39:00 F. Colombo.
    or:
    2,2,2,2 - 4,2,2,1 - timp.,perc. - hp. - str.
—— AN OPERA-BALLET (IN 4 MOVTS.) %
    3(3rd alt. with picc.),*3,3(3rd alt. with b.-cl.),*3 - 4,3,3,1 -
    timp.,perc.(3) - hp. - pf. - str.   Composer.
—— PRELUDE AND FUGUE FOR STRINGS
    str.   10:30 Chappell.
—— PRELUDE, CHORALE AND FUGUE
    *3,*3,3(3rd. alt. with b.-cl.),*3 - 4,3,3,1 - timp.,perc.(2) - hp. - str.
          18:00 Composer.
—— PRIMAVERA (CANTATA) (FOR SOPRANO, TENOR, CHORUS
AND ORCH.)
    1,1,1,1 - 2,2,1,0 - timp.,perc. - hp. - pf. - str.   60:00 Composer.
—— PSALM 130 (FOR DOUBLE BASS OR CELLO WITH ORCH.)
    *3,2(2nd alt. with Eng.hn.),2,*3 - 4,3,3,1 - timp.,perc.(2) - hp. -
    str.   20:00 Composer.
—— SUITE FOR ORCHESTRA (IN 4 MOVTS.)
    *3,*3,3(3rd alt. with b.-cl),*3 - 4,3,3,1 - timp.,perc. - (3) - hp. - pf.
    - str.   25:00 Composer.
—— SYMPHONY (I.B.M. SYMPHONY)
    *3,*2,2,2 - 4,3,3,1 - timp.,perc.(2) - hp. - pf. - str.   10:00 IBM.
—— SYMPHONY (IN MEMORIAM THEODORE ROOSEVELT) (IN
4 MOVTS.)
    *3,*3,*3,*3 - 4-8,3,3,1 - timp.,perc.(3) - hp. - pf. - str.
          35:00 Composer.
—— SYMPHONY NO. 1
    3,3,3,3 - 4,3,3,1 - timp.,perc. - hp. - str.   Belw-Mills.
—— SYMPHONY NO. 2 (IN 3 MOVTS.)
    *3,2,2,2 - 4,3,3,1 - timp.,perc.(2) - str.   22:00 Chappell.
—— SYMPHONY NO. 4
    3,3,3,3 - 4,3,3,1 - timp.,perc. - hp. - str.   30:00 F. Colombo.
—— SYMPHONY NO. 5
    3,3,3,3 - 4,4,2,2 - timp.,perc. - hp. - pf. - str.   F. Colombo.
—— THE TAMING OF THE SHREW (OPERA) %
          F. Colombo.
—— THE TAMING OF THE SHREW (ORCHESTRAL SUITE FROM
THE OPERA)
    4,4,4,3 - 4,3,3,1 - timp.,perc. - hp. - str.   12:00 F. Colombo.
—— TRYPTICH (FOR SOPRANO AND ORCH.)
    *3,2(2nd alt. with Eng. hn.),2,2 - 4,3,3,1 - timp.,perc.(2) - hp. - str.
          15:00 Composer.

GIANNINI, Walter
—— PRELUDE, CHORALE AND FUGUE
    str.   AmerMusEd.

GIARDINI, Felice - BONELLI, Ettore
—— CONCERTO IN A, FOR VIOLIN AND CHAMBER ORCH.
          Henmar.

GIBBONS, Orlando - CRUFT, Adrian
—— SUITE FOR SOLO TRUMPET AND STRINGS
    tpt. - str.   8:00 Galaxy.

GIBBONS, Orlando - FELLOWES, Edmund H.
—— NINE FANTASIES
    str.   20:00 Galaxy.
—— PAVAN AND GALLIARD
    str.   6:00 Galaxy.

GIBBONS, Orlando - JACOB, Gordon
—— ORLANDO GIBBONS SUITE
          11:00 Galaxy.

GIBBONS, Orlando - KAY, Hershy
—— SUITE FOR ORCHESTRA (IN 3 MOVTS.)
    3,3,3,3 - 4,3,3,1 - timp. - str.   11:00 Bo. Hawkes.

GIBBS, C. Armstrong
—— THE BALLAD OF GIL MORRICE (FOR CHORUS AND
ORCH.)
          25:00 Bo. Hawkes.
—— BEFORE DAWN (FOR MIXED VOICES, PIANO OR ORGAN
AND STRINGS)
    pf. (or org.) - str.   10:00 Bo. Hawkes.

—— BEFORE DAYBREAK (FOR CONTRALTO, WOMEN'S
CHORUS, STRING QUARTET, STRINGS AND PIANO)
    pf. - str.   27:00 Bo. Hawkes.
—— BEHOLD THE MAN (CANTATA FOR PASSIONTIDE) (FOR
TENOR, BARITONE, MIXED CHORUS AND ORCH.) (Text:
Benedict Ellis)
          55:00 Oxford.
—— THE BIRTH OF CHRIST (FOR MIXED CHORUS AND ORCH.)
          G. Schirmer.
—— CONCERTINO FOR PIANO AND STRINGS, OP. 103
    pf. - str.   15:00 Bo. Hawkes.
—— DEBORAH AND BARAK (CANTATA) (FOR CONTRALTO,
BARITONE, CHORUS AND ORCH.)
          25:00 Bo. Hawkes.
—— ESSEX SUITE (FOR STRING QUARTET AND STRINGS) (IN 4
MOVTS.)
    str.   17:00 Bo. Hawkes.
—— THE HIGHWAYMEN, OP. 72 (FOR CHORUS AND ORCH.)
    2,2,2,2 - 4,2,3,1 - timp.,perc. - str.   25:00 Bo. Hawkes.
    or:
    1,1,1,1 - 2,1,0,0 - pf. - str.
    or:
    perc. - pf. - str.
—— IN A DREAM'S BEGUILING, OP. 130 (SUITE) (FOR
MEZZO-SOPRANO OR SEMICHORUS, WOMEN'S CHOIR,
STRINGS AND PIANO)
    pf. - str.   45:00 Bo. Hawkes.
—— A LYRIC GARLAND (FOR WOMEN'S CHORUS AND
STRINGS) (IN 4 MOVTS.) (Text: John Clare, Thomas Hood,
Sydney Dobell. Queen Elizabeth I)
    pf. - str.   12:00 Oxford.
—— MINIATURE DANCE SUITE
    str.   Bo. Hawkes.
—— MUSIC FOR STRINGS (IN 4 MOVTS.)
    str.   17:00 Bo. Hawkes.
—— O PRAISE GOD IN HIS HOLINESS (PSALM 150) (FOR
CHORUS AND ORCH.)
          Oxford.
—— ODYSSEUS, OP. 90 (SYMPHONY IN 4 MOVTS.) (FOR
SOPRANO, BARITONE, CHORUS AND ORCH.)
    2,2,1,2 - 4,2,3,1 - timp.,perc. - pf. - str.   60:00 Bo. Hawkes.
—— OLD WINE IN NEW BOTTLES (4 RESTORATION SONGS)
(FOR BARITONE AND ORCH.)
    2,2,2,2 - 4,2,3,1 - timp. - str.   Bo. Hawkes.
—— PASTORAL SUITE, OP. 123 (FOR BARITONE, MIXED
CHORUS AND ORCH.)
    2,2,2,2 - 4,2,3,0 -timp. - hp. - str.   21:00 Bo. Hawkes.
—— PEACOCK PIE (SUITE) (IN 3 MOVTS.)
    pf. - str.   10:30 Bo. Hawkes.
—— A SAVIOUR BORN (CHRISTMAS CANTATA) (FOR
MEZZO-SOPRANO, WOMEN'S CHORUS, PIANO AND
STRINGS)
    pf. - str.   24:00 Oxford.
—— A SIMPLE CONCERTO (FOR PIANO AND STRINGS)
    pf. - str.   10:00 Oxford.
—— A SIMPLE SUITE
    str.   11:00 Oxford.
—— SIX BRITISH TRADITIONAL TUNES
          15:00 Oxford.
—— SONGS OF CHILDHOOD, OP. 76 (On Traditional Tunes)
    *2,1,1,0 - timp.,perc. - str.   Bo. Hawkes.
    or:
    pf. - str.
—— SPRING GARLAND, OP. 84 (SUITE)
    str.   11:00 Bo. Hawkes.
—— SUITE FOR VIOLIN AND SMALL ORCH.
    2,2,2,0 - 2 hn. - hp. - str.   14:30 Bo. Hawkes.
—— SUITE IN A, OP. 144
    fl. - str.   14:00 Oxford.
—— SYMPHONY NO. 3 IN B♭ ("WESTMORELAND")
    2,*3,2,2 - 4,2,3,1 - timp.,perc. - hp. - str.   31:00 Bo. Hawkes.
—— THREE KINGS (A NATIVITY PLAY) (FOR CHORUS AND
STRINGS) %
    str.   105:00 Bo. Hawkes.

GIBSON, David
—— SYMPHONY (1975) (IN 2 MOVTS.)
    2,2,0,2 - 2,0,0,0 - timp. - str.   26:00 Composer.

GIERLACH, Chester
—— VILLAGE FESTIVAL DANCES
    str.   Mills.

GIESELER, Walter
—— CONCERTO FOR STRING ORCH.
    str.   20:00 Bo. Hawkes.

GIFFORD, Helen Margaret
—— CHIMAERA (1967)
    *4,*3,*3,2 - 3,3,3,0 - timp.,perc.(6),cel. - hp. - hpsc. - str.
        10:00 J. Albert.
—— IMPERIUM (1969)
    3 picc.,3,*4,*4,*3 - 4,3,3,1 - timp.,perc.(6, incl. 3 on
    timp.),glock.,xyl. - str.   10:00 J. Albert.
—— ON REFLECTION (FOR VIOLIN AND STRINGS) (1972)
    str.   8:00 A.P.R.A.
—— PHANTASMA (1963)
    str.   10:00 A.P.R.A.

GILARDI, Gilardo
—— EVOCATIÓN QUICHUA (1929)
    1,1,1,1 - 2,2,1,0 - timp.,perc. - str.   8:00 Fleisher.
—— GAUCHO (CON BOTAS NUEVAS) (HUMORADA SINFONICA PARA ORQUESTA)
    3,3,3,3 - 4,3,3,1 - timp.,perc.,xyl. - pf. - str.   10:00 F. Colombo.
—— NOVIANDO (GETTING MARRIED) (SERIE ARGENTINA NO. 2)
    2,2,2,2 - 4,3,3,1 - timp.,perc. - hp. - str.   Fleisher.

GILBERT, Henry F.
—— RIDERS TO THE SEA (SYMPHONIC PROLOGUE)
    3,2,3,3 - 4,2,3,1 - timp.,perc. - hp. - str.   5:00 G. Schirmer.

GILBOA, Jacob
—— THE TWELVE JERUSALEM CHAGALL WINDOWS (FOR MEZZO-SOPRANO, 5 FEMALE VOICES AND ENSEMBLE)
    6 recorders (or 6 fl) - perc.,cel. - hp. - harm. - 2 pf.(1 prepared) - 4 vla.   18:00 IsMuPublns.

GILLIS, Don
—— THE ALAMO
    2,2(2nd alt. with Eng. hn.),*3,2 - 3,3,3,1 - timp.,perc.(4) - hp. - str.   12:00 Mills.
—— ALICE IN ORCHESTRALIA (FOR NARRATOR AND ORCH.)
        22:00 Mills.
—— AMARILLO (A SYMPHONIC CELEBRATION)
        Composer.
—— ATLANTA (SUITE)
        19:30 Mills.
—— FIVE ACRE POND
    ob. - perc.,cel. - hp. (or pf.) - str.   7:00 Fema.
—— FOUR SCENES FROM YESTERDAY (FOR CHAMBER ORCH.)
    1,1,1,1 - 0,0,0,0 - perc., cel - hp. - pf. - str.   16:00 Bo. Hawkes.
—— THE MAN WHO INVENTED MUSIC (A MUSICAL FABLE) (FOR NARRATOR AND ORCH.)
    2(2nd alt. with picc.),2(2nd alt. with Eng. hn.),*3,2 - 3,3,3,1 - timp.,perc.(3) - hp. (or pf.) - str.   12:30 Mills.
—— THE NEW AMERICA (SYMPHONIC POEM)
        12:00 Composer.
—— NINETEEN HUNDRED AND FIFTY FIVE (A MOMENT IN TIMES' SEARCH FOR BEAUTY)
        14:00 Mills.
—— THE PANHANDLE (SUITE) (IN 6 MVTS.)
    2(2nd alt. with picc.),2(2nd alt. with Eng. hn.), *3,2 - 3,3,3,1 - timp.,perc.(4), cel., xyl. - hp. - str.   16:30 Mills.
—— PAUL BUNYAN (AN OVERTURE TO A LEGEND)
        7:10 Composer.
—— PORTRAIT OF A FRONTIER TOWN (SUITE) (IN 5 MOVTS.)
    2(2nd alt. with picc.),2(2nd alt. with Eng. hn.),*3,2 - 3,3,3,1 - timp.,perc(3) xyl - hp. - str.   17:00 Bo. Hawkes.
—— PRAIRIE POEM
    2(2nd alt. with picc.),2(2nd alt. with Eng. hn.),*3,2 - 3,3,3,1 - timp.,perc.,cel. - hp. - str.   12:00 Mills.
—— THE RAVEN (AN INTERPRETATION OF POE'S POEM) (WITH OPTIONAL NARRATOR)
    1,*2,*3,alto cl., 2 - 3,3,3,1 - timp.,perc.(3) - str.   10:00 Mills.
—— RETROSPECTION (POEM FOR VIOLIN AND CHAMBER ORCH.)
    perc.,cel. - hp. - pf. - str.   5:30 Mills.
—— RHAPSODY (FOR HARP AND ORCH.)
    2(2nd alt. with picc.),2(2nd alt. with Eng.hn.),*3,2 - 3,3,3,1 - timp.,perc.(3) - hp. - str.   14:05 Mills.
—— SHORT OVERTURE TO AN UNWRITTEN OPERA
    2,2,*3,2 - 3,3,3,1 - timp.,perc.,xyl. - str.   4:05 Bo. Hawkes.
—— SOLILOQUY FOR STRINGS
    str.   4:00 Fema.

—— STAR-SPANGLED SYMPHONY (IN 4 MOVTS.)
    str.   22:45 Mills.
—— SYMPHONY NO. 1 (AN AMERICAN SYMPHONY)
    2(2nd alt. with picc.),2(2nd alt. with Eng. hn.),*3,2 - 3,3,3,1 - timp.,perc. - str.   22:00 Composer.
—— SYMPHONY NO. 2 (A SYMPHONY OF FAITH)
    2(2nd alt. with picc.),2(2nd alt. with Eng. hn.),*3,2 - 3,3,3,1 - timp.,perc.(4), xyl. - hp. - str.   20:00 Mills.
—— SYMPHONY NO. 3 (A SYMPHONY OF FREE MEN)
    2(2nd alt. with picc.),2(2nd alt. with Eng. hn.),*3,2 - 3,3,3,1 - timp.,perc.(4), vibra., xyl. - hp. - str.   22:00 Mills.
—— SYMPHONY NO. 4 (THE PIONEERS)
    2(2nd alt. with picc.),2(2nd alt with Eng. hn.),3(3rd alt. with b.-cl.),2 - 3,3,3,1 - timp.,perc.(4),cel., xyl. - hp. - str.   24:00 Mills.
—— SYMPHONY NO. 5 (IN MEMORIAM)
    2(2nd alt. with picc.),2(2nd alt. with Eng. hn.),*3,2 - 3,3,3,1 - timp.,perc. (4), xyl. - hp. - str.   24:00 Mills.
—— SYMPHONY NO. 5 AND ONE HALF (A SYMPHONY FOR FUN) (IN 4 MOVTS.)
    2,2(2nd alt. with Eng. hn.),*3,2 - 3,3,3,1 - timp.,perc.(4), vibra., xyl. - pf. - str.   13:30 Bo. Hawkes.
—— SYMPHONY NO. 6 (MID-CENTURY, U. S. A.)
    2,2(2nd alt. with Eng. hn.),*3,2 - 3,3,3,1 - timp.,perc.(4),xyl. - hp. - str.   23:00 Composer.
—— SYMPHONY NO. 7 (SAGA OF A PRAIRIE SCHOOL) (IN 4 MOVTS.)
    *3,*3,2,2 - 3,2,2,1 - timp.,perc. - hp. - str.   26:00 Chappell.
—— SYMPHONY NO. 8 (DANCE SYMPHONY) (IN 4 MOVTS.)
    2(2nd alt with picc.),2(2nd alt with Eng. hn.),*3,2 - 3,3,3,1 - timp.,perc.(4), cel., xyl. - str.   17:00 Mills.
—— SYMPHONY NO. 10
    2,2,3,2 - 3,3,3,1 - perc. - pf. - str.   19:00 Bo. Hawkes.
—— THE COMING OF THE KING (CANTATA) (FOR NARRATOR, CHORUS AND ORCH.)
        26:00 Mills.
—— THIS IS OUR AMERICA (FOR MEDIUM VOICE, SATB CHORUS AND ORCH.)
    2,2,3,1 - 3,3,2,1 - perc.,bells,cel.,vibra. - org. - pf. - str.   16:00 Belw-Mills.
—— THOMAS WOLFE: AMERICAN (FOR NARRATOR AND ORCH.)
    2(2nd alt. with picc.),2(2nd alt. with Eng. hn.),3,2 - 3,3,3,1 - timp.,perc. - hp. - str.   20:00 Mills.
—— THOUGHTS PROVOKED ON BECOMING A PROSPECTIVE PAPA (SUITE) (IN 5 MOVTS.)
    1(alt. with picc.),1,2,1 - 3,0,0,0 - pf. - str.   15:00 Mills.
    or:
    2(2nd alt. with picc.),2(2nd alt. with Eng. hn.),*3,2 - 3,3,3,1 - timp.,perc.(4),cel.,xyl. - hp. - str.
—— THREE SKETCHES FOR STRINGS
    str.   8:30 Bo. Hawkes.
—— TO AN UNKNOWN SOLDIER
    2(2nd alt. with picc.),2(2nd alt. with Eng. hn.),*3,2 - 3,3,3,1 - timp.,perc.(4) - hp. - str.   9:00 Mills.
—— TULSA (A SYMPHONIC PORTRAIT IN OIL)
    2(2nd alt. with picc.),2,3,2 - 3,3,3,1 - timp.,perc. - pf. - str.   10:00 Mills.
—— TWINKLE TOES (SUITE FROM THE BALLET) (IN 5 MOVTS.)
    2(2nd alt. with picc.),2(2nd alt. with Eng. hn.),3,2 - 3,3,3,1 - timp.,perc. - pf.(alt. with cel.) - str.   16:15 Mills.

GILLMAN, Kurt
—— SCHERZO CHROMATICO
    3,0,2Eng. hn.,3,2 - 4,3,3,1 - timp.,perc. - hp. - str.   10:00 Henmar.

GILMORE, Bernard H.
—— THREE POEMS OF LOVE (FOR SATB CHORUS AND CHAMBER ORCH.) (1970) (IN 3 MOVTS.)
    2,1,2(2nd alt. with b.-cl.),0 - 2,1,1,0 - timp.,perc.(1),bells,cel.,glock. - pf. - str.   10:00 Composer.

GILSE, Jan van
—— EINE LEBENSMESSE (FOR SATB SOLO, CHILDREN'S CHORUS, MIXED CHORUS AND ORCH.) (Text: Richard Dehmel)
    3,3,4,3 - 4,3,3,1 - timp.,perc. - hp. - str.   K & S.
—— SYMPHONY NO. 4 IN A MAJOR, Z.J.
    3,3,2,2 - 4,3,0,0 - timp.,perc. - str.   K & S.
—— THREE DANCE SKETCHES (FOR PIANO AND SMALL ORCH.) (1936)
    2,2,2,1 - 2,1,0,0 - timp.,perc.,cel. - hp. - str.   30:00 Henmar.

—— THREE SONGS FROM R. TAGORE'S "GITANJALI" (FOR SOPRANO AND ORCH.) (1915)
2,3,2,2 - 4,3,3,0 - timp.,perc.,cel. - hp. - str.   14:00 Henmar.

—— THREE SONGS FROM R. TAGORE'S "THE GARDENER" (FOR SOPRANO AND ORCH.) (1923)
3,3,2,2 - 4,3,3,0 - timp.,perc.,cel. - 2 hp. - str.   17:00 Henmar.

GILTAY, Berend
—— CONCERTO FOR ORCHESTRA (1960)
3,2,2,2 - 4,3,3,0 - timp.,perc.,cel. - hp. - str.   20:00 Henmar.
—— SINFONIA PER ORCHESTRA (1956-57)
2,2,2,2 - 0,0,0,0 - timp.,perc. - str.   18:00 Henmar.
—— SYMPHONIC VARIATIONS
22:00 Henmar.

GINASTERA, Alberto
—— BOMARZO, OP. 32 (CANTATA) (FOR BARITONE, NARRATOR AND 18 INSTRUMENTS) (Text: Manuel Mujica Láinez; Engl. by Rolando Costa Picazo)
1(alt. with picc.),1(alt. with Eng. hn.),1(alt. with E♭cl. and b.-bl.),1(alt. with c.-bn.) - 1,1,1,0 - perc. - hp. - hpsc. - pf. - str.(no vlns.)   26:00 Bo. Hawkes.
—— BOMARZO (2-ACT OPERA) % (Text: Manuel Mujica Láinez)
2,2,2,2 - 3,3,3,0 - timp.,perc.(4),cel. - hpsc. - pf. - hp. - mandolin - str.   120:00 Bo. Hawkes.
—— CANTATA PARA AMERICA MAGICA, OP. 27 (FOR SOPRANO, 2 PIANOS AND PERCUSSION)
perc.(12) - 2 pf.   25:00 Bo. Hawkes.
—— LA CAPTIVA (THE CAPTIVE)
3,3,3,3 - 4,4,3,1 - timp.,perc. - str.   30:00 Hawkes.
—— CONCERTO FOR CELLO AND ORCH., OP. 36
3,3,3,3 - 4,4,4,0 - timp.,perc. - str.   28:00 Hawkes.
—— CONCERTO FOR HARP AND ORCH., OP. 25
2,2,2,2 - 2,2,0,0 - timp.,cel. - hp. - str.   22:00 Bo. Hawkes.
—— CONCERTO FOR STRINGS
str.   23:00 Bo. Hawkes.
—— CONCERTO FOR VIOLIN AND ORCH. (1963) (IN 3 MOVTS.)
3,3,4,3 - 4,3,3,1 - timp.,perc.,cel.,mar. - hp. - str.   25:00 Bo. Hawkes.
—— CONCERTO NO. 1 FOR PIANO AND ORCH. (CONCIERTO ARGENTINO)
3,3,4,3 - 4,3,3,1 - timp.,perc.,cel. - hp. - pf. - str.   25:00 Bo. Hawkes.
—— CONCERTO NO. 2 FOR PIANO AND ORCH.
Bo. Hawkes.
—— DON RODRIGO (OPERA) %
Bo. Hawkes.
—— ESTANCIA, OP. 8 (1-ACT BALLET) % (WITH BARITONE VOICE)
2,2,2,2 - 4,2,0,0 - timp.,perc. - pf. - str.   35:00 Bo. Hawkes.
—— ESTUDIOS SINFONICOS, OP. 35
4,4,5,4 - 4,4,4,0 - timp.,perc.,cel. - hp. - pf. - str.   30:00 Bo. Hawkes.
—— FOUR DANCES FROM THE BALLET "ESTANCIA"
2,2,2,2 - 4,2,00 - timp.,perc. - pf. - str.   12:00 Bo. Hawkes.
—— MILENA (CANTATA FOR SOPRANO AND ORCH.) (Text: Franz Kafka)
20:00 Bo. Hawkes.
—— MUSIC FROM THE OPERA "BOMARZO"
2,2,2,2 - 3,2,2,0 - perc.,cel. - hp. - pf. - str.   18:00 Bo. Hawkes.
—— OLLANTAY (SYMPHONIC TRIPTYCH)
3,3,3,2 - 4,3,3,1 - timp.,perc., cel. - hp. - pf. - str.   15:00 Bo. Hawkes.
—— OVERTURE TO "THE CREOLE FAUST"
2,2,2,2 - 4,3,3,1 - timp.,perc. - hp. - pf. - str.   9:00 Bo. Hawkes.
—— PAMPEANA NO. 3
3,2,2,2 - 4,3,3,1 - timp.,perc., cel. - hp. - str.   17:00 Bo. Hawkes.
—— PANAMBI, OP. 1 (CHOREOGRAPHIC LEGEND IN 1 ACT) % (WITH FEMALE CHORUS)
4,4,4,4 - 4,4,3,1 - timp.,perc.,cel. - 2 hp. - pf. - str.   35:00 Bo. Hawkes.
—— PSALM 150, OP. 5 (FOR MIXED CHORUS, OPTIONAL BOY'S CHORUS AND ORCH.)
4,4,4,4 - 4,4,3,2 - timp.,perc.,cel. - 2 hp. - pf. - str.   18:00 Bo. Hawkes.
—— SINFONIA ELEGIACA (SYMPHONY NO. 2)
3,3,3,3 - 4,4,3,1 - timp.,perc. - str.   22:00 Bo. Hawkes.
—— SUITE FROM THE BALLET "PANAMBI", OP. 1-B
4,4,4,4 - 4,4,3,1 - timp.,perc. cel. - 2hp. - pf. - str.   12:00 Bo. Hawkes.

—— SYMPHONY OF DON RODRIGO (FOR DRAMATIC SOPRANO AND ORCH.)
4(3rd. and 4th. alt. with piccs.),4,4(3rd. alt. with E♭cl., 4th. alt. with b.-cl.),4(4th. alt. with c.-bn.) - 6,4,4,1 - timp.(2),perc.(7), 10 bells,cel. - mandolin - hp. - str.   25:00 Bo. Hawkes.
Off Stage: 4-8 hn., 4-8 tpt.
—— TURBAS (FOR CHORUS AND ORCH.) (Text: Biblical, from the Vulgate)
Bo. Hawkes.
—— VARIACIONES CONCERTANTES
2,1,2,1 - 2,1,1,0 - timp., - hp. - str.   21:00 Bo. Hawkes.

GIPPS, Ruth
—— CONCERTO FOR HORN AND ORCH., OP. 58
2,2,2,2 - 4,2,0,0 - timp.,perc.,cel. - str.   18:00 P.R.S.
—— LEVIATHAN, OP. 59 (FOR CONTRABASSOON AND ORCH.)
1,2,2,*2 - 2,0,0,0 - str.   5:00 P.R.S.
—— SYMPHONY NO. 3, OP. 57 (1965)
3,3,3,3 - 4,3,3,1 - timp.,perc. - hp. - str.   34:00 P.R.S.

GIRNATIS, Walter
—— CAPRICCIO FOR OBOE AND ORCH.
2,1,2,2 - 2,2,3,0 - timp.,perc. - hp. - str.   11:00 F. Colombo.
—— CONCERT RETROSPECTIF (FÜR KLAVIER UND ORCH.)
2,2,2,2 - 2,2,1,0 - timp.,perc. - pf. - str.   23:00 Sikorski.
—— COUNTRY DANCE SCENES
2,2,2,2 - 2,2,1,0 - perc. - str.   16:00 F. Colombo.
—— DAINA (LITHUANIAN FANTASY) (FOR BASSOON AND ORCH.)
2,1,2,1 - 2,2,0,0 - timp.,perc. - hp. - str.   7:00 F. Colombo.
—— THE MORRIS DANCES OF ERASMUS GRASSER (SUITE)
2,2,2,2 - 2,2,3,0 - perc. - hp. - str.   15:00 F. Colombo.
—— SCHERZO FANTASTIQUE (RONDO FOR ORCH.)
2,2,2,2 - 2,2,1,0 - timp.,perc. - str.   7:00 F. Colombo.
—— SMALL TOWN PICTURES
2,2,2,2 - 2,1,0,0 - perc. - str.   12:00 F. Colombo.
—— STORTEBEKER BALLAD (VARIATIONS AND FUGUE FOR LARGE ORCH.)
3,2,2,2 - 4,2,3,1 - timp.,perc. - str.   14:00 F. Colombo.
—— WINE CANTATA (FOR MALE CHORUS AND ORCH.)
2,2,2,2 - 2,2,1,0 - timp.,perc. - str.   12:00 F. Colombo.

GIUFFRE, Gaetano
—— INVENZIONE (PER FLAUTO E ORCHESTRA D'ARCHI)
fl. - str.   8:00 S.U.I.S.A.
—— LYRISMES (PER FLAUTO E PICCOLA ORCHESTRA)
9:00 Belw-Mills.
—— LA MANDRACCHINA (DIVERTIMENTO PER CEMBALO E ORCH. D'ARCHI)
cemb. - str.   10:00 Belw-Mills.
—— PRIMORDIA CORCYRAE (SUITE CONCERTANTE PER PIANOFORTE E ORCHESTRA)
32:00 Belw-Mills.

GIULIANI, Mauro - OUBRADOUS, Fernand
—— CONCERTO FOR GUITAR, TIMPANI AND STRINGS, OP. 30
timp. - guit. - str.   Presser.

GIUSTINI, Lodovico - FOREST, Rudolf
—— SONATA DA CAMERA (ARR. 1937) (IN 4 MOVTS.)
str.   17:00 H. Branch.

GIVOTOV, Alexei S.
—— ZAPAD (FOR TENOR, MIXED CHORUS AND ORCH.)
3,2,3,2 - 6,3,3,1 - timp.,perc., xyl. - 2hp. - str.   G. Schirmer.

GJERSTRØM, Gunnar
—— CONCERTO NO. 1 IN F MINOR, FOR PIANO AND ORCH.
2,2,2,2 - 3,2,3,0 - timp. - perc. - pf. - str.   28:00 Norsk Ntk.
—— CONCERTO NO. 2 FOR PIANO AND ORCH. ("SEA MOODS")
3,3,2,2 - 4,2,3,1 - timp. - pf. - str.   20:00 T.O.N.O.
—— NOCTURNE
1,1,1,1 - 2,2,2,0 - hp. - pf. - str.   4:00 T.O.N.O.
—— SUITE NO. 1 IN B MINOR (FOR PIANO AND ORCH.)
1,1,1,0 - 1,1,1,0 - perc. - org. - pf. - str.   14:00 T.O.N.O.
—— SUITE NO. 2 IN D MINOR
2,1,1,1 - 2,2,2,1 - perc. - hp. - org. - pf. - str.   17:00 T.O.N.O.
—— SUITE NO. 3, ON FOLK TUNES FROM KRÖDEREN
1,1,1,1 - 1,1,1,0 - perc. - org. - pf. - str.   12:00 T.O.N.O.

GLASER, Victoria
—— BIRTHDAY FUGUE
*3,2,3,2 - 4,3,2,1 - timp.,perc.(3) - str.   Composer.

or:
1,1,2,1 - 2,1,1,0 - timp.,perc.(2) - str.

GLASER, Werner Wolf
—— ARIOSO AND TOCCATA (FOR PIANO AND ORCH.) (1969)
2,2,0,2 - 2,2,1,0 - timp.,perc.(2) - pf. - str.   9:00 S.T.I.M.
—— CANTO (1970)
sopr. sax. - str.   6:00 Fleisher.
—— CAPRICCIO III (FOR PIANO AND SMALL ORCH.) (1964)
1,1,1,0 - 1,0,0,0 - pf. - str.   20:00 S.T.I.M.
—— CHAMBER MUSIC (FOR WOODWIND QUINTET AND
STRINGS)(1971)
1,1,1,1 - 1,0,0,0 - str.(no d.-b.)   20:00 Fleisher.
—— LES CINQ PAS DE L'HOMME (BALLET) % (1973)
1,0,1,1 - 1,0,0,0 - timp.,perc.(4) - hp. - str.(0,3,2,1) 40:00 Fleisher.
—— CONCERTINO FOR CLARINET AND SMALL ORCH. (1962)
1,1,1,1 - 1,1,0,0 - timp. - str.   20:00 S.T.i.M.
—— CONCERTO FOR FLUTE AND STRING ORCH. (1967)
fl. - str.   25:00 Fleisher.
—— CONCERTO FOR HORN AND ORCH. (1969)
2,2,2,2 - 1,2,3,0 - timp.,perc.,cel. - str.   20:00 Fleisher.
—— CONCERTO FOR OBOE AND ORCH. (1966)
1,2,1, - 1,1,0,0 - timp.,perc.(2) str.   15:00 S.T.I.M.
—— CONCERTO FOR VIOLIN, WINDS AND PERCUSSION (1962)
1,1,3,sax.,2 - 4,4,3,1 - perc. - vln.   25:00 Fleisher.
—— CONCERTO FOR VIOLINO GRANDE AND ORCH. (1964)
2,2,2,2 - 4,3,3,1 - timp.,perc.(2) - str.   30:00 S.T.I.M.
—— CONCERTO FOR 20 WINDS AND PERCUSSION (1966)
1,1,3,sax.,2 - 4,4,3,1 - perc.   20:00 Fleisher.
—— CONCERTO LIRICO (FOR SOPRANO, TIMPANI, PIANO
AND STRINGS)(1971)
timp. - pf. - str.   24:00 Fleisher.
—— CONCERTO PER ORCHESTRA NO. 2 (1957)
2,2,2,2 - 2,2,2,0 - timp.,perc.(2) - str.   20:00 S.T.I.M.
—— CONFLITTI (1966)
2,2,2,2 - 4,4,3,1 - timp.,perc.(2) - str.   25:00 S.T.I.M.
—— FOUR DANCE-SCENES
2,2,2,2 - 4,4,3,0 - timp.,perc.(3) - str.   25:00 S.T.I.M.
—— FÖRVARDLINGAR (FOR PIANO AND ORCH.) (1966)
2,1,0,1 - 2,1,0,0 - timp. - pf. - str.   25:00 S.T.I.M.
—— IDYLL, ELEGY AND FANFARE (1954)
2,2,2,2 - 2,2,2,0 - timp.,perc.(2) - str.   19:00 S.T.I.M.
—— MODI GESTUS (SUITE FOR STRING ORCH.)(1966)
str.   14:00 Fleisher.
—— MUSIC TO METHLING'S "DEN KINESISKA ASKEN"
1,1,1,1 - 1,1,0,0 - perc. - str.   25:00 Fleisher.
—— MUSICA SACRA (1960)
1,0,1,0 - 0,0,0,0 - org. - str.   20:00 Fleisher.
—— OMBRE DIAFANI (1968)
str.   8:00 Fleisher.
—— PARADOSSO (FOR 2 STRING ORCHESTRAS) (1967)
str.   11:00 S.T.I.M.
—— SYRINGA (1966)
3 fl. - str.   10:00 Fleisher.
—— TRE PEZZI (FOR OBOE D'AMORE AND CHAMBER
ORCH.)(1964)
fl.,oboe d'amore - timp.,perc. - hp. - str.   18:00 Fleisher.

GLASS, Louis
—— FANTASY IN F MAJOR, OP. 47 (FOR PIANO AND ORCH.)
2,2,2,2 - 4,2,3,0 - timp.,perc. - pf. - str.   22:30 G. Schirmer.
—— SINFONIA SVASTICA, OP. 57
3,3,3,3 - 4,3,4,1 - timp.,cel. - str.   33:00 G. Schirmer.

GLASS, Paul
—— BALLET MUSIC FOR CHAMBER ORCH.
1,1(alt. with Eng.hn.),1(alt. with b.-cl.),1 - 1,1,1,0 - timp.,perc.(2) -
str.   7:00 Composer.
—— CONCERTO FOR CELLO AND ORCH.
1. Adagio; 2. Allegretto; 3. Moderato; 4. Allegro scherzoso;
5. Adagio
2(2nd alt. with picc.),2(2nd alt. with Eng.hn.),2(2nd alt. with
b.-cl.),2(2nd alt. with c.-bn.) - 2,2,1,0 - timp.,perc.(3) - hp. - str.
16:00 Composer.
—— DRAMATIC MUSIC FOR CHAMBER ORCH.
1,1(alt. with Eng.hn.),1(alt. with b.-cl.),1 - 1,1,1,0 - timp.,perc.(2) -
str.   10:00 Composer.
—— MUSIC FOR BRASS AND PERCUSSION (SUITE)
0,0,0,0 - 4,3,3,1 - timp.   Composer.
—— SUITA SYMFONYCZNA (SYMPHONIC SUITE) (IN 5 MOVTS.)
3(1st and 2nd alt. with 2 picc.),*3,*3,*3 - 4,4,3,1 -
timp.,perc.(5),cel.,vibra.,xyl. - hp. - pf. - str.   18:00 Composer.

—— SYMPHONY (IN 3 MOVTS.)
3(3rd alt. with picc.),*3,*3,*3 - 4,3,3,1 - timp.,perc.(5),glock.,xyl. -
hp. - str.   19:00 Composer.

GLASSER, Stanley
—— PRELUDE, OP. 14 (1967)
2,2,2,2 - 4,3,3,1 - perc.(2) - electric guit. - hp. - pf. - str.
10:00 P.R.S.

GLATZ, Helen
—— BALLET ELECTRIC % (1937)
20:00 P.R.S.
—— BALLET SUITE (FOR SMALL ORCH.)(1952)
10:00 P.R.S.
—— THE BRIDAL GOWN (BALLET) % (1953)
30:00 P.R.S.
—— CHRISTMAS FANTASY (BALLET) % (1954)
15:00 P.R.S.
—— CONCERTINO FOR FLUTE AND STRINGS (1947)
fl. - str.   15:00 P.R.S.
—— DANCE RHAPSODY (FOR HARP AND ORCH.)(1967)
12:00 P.R.S.
—— THE DEMON (BALLET) % (1956)
30:00 P.R.S.
—— ELEGY (1967)
str.   6:00 P.R.S.
—— THE MATCH GIRL (BALLET) % (1954)
35:00 P.R.S.
—— THE MERCHANT OF VENICE (INCIDENTAL MUSIC)(FOR
SMALL ORCH.)(1957)
P.R.S.
—— THE MERRY WIVES OF WINDSOR (INCIDENTAL MUSIC)
(FOR SMALL ORCH.)(1955)
P.R.S.
—— MUCH ADO ABOUT NOTHING (INCIDENTAL MUSIC) (FOR
SMALL ORCH.)(1957)
P.R.S.
—— NURSERY RHYMES (BALLET) % (1956)
P.R.S.
—— PERSEPHONE (BALLET) % (1931)
35:00 P.R.S.
—— PHAETON (BALLET) % (1955)
30:00 P.R.S.
—— ROMEO AND JULIET (INCIDENTAL MUSIC)(FOR SMALL
ORCH.)(1956)
P.R.S.
—— SCHERZO AND TRIO (1932)
10:00 P.R.S.
—— THEME AND VARIATIONS (1948)
17:00 P.R.S.

GLAZOUNOV, Alexander
—— CONCERTO BALLATA FOR CELLO AND ORCH., OP. 108
3,2,2,2 - 4,2,3,0 - timp. - pf. - str.   20:00 Henmar.
—— CONCERTO FOR ALTO SAXOPHONE AND STRINGS, OP.
109 (IN 1 MOVT.)
alto sax. - str.   Baron.
—— CONCERTO NO. 1 IN F MINOR FOR PIANO AND ORCH.,
OP. 92
3,2,2,2 - 4,2,3,1 - timp.,perc. - pf. - str.   27:00 Henmar.
—— CONCERTO NO. 2 IN B FOR PIANO AND ORCH., OP. 100
3,2,2,2 - 4,2,3,1 - timp.,perc. - pf. - str.   17:30 Henmar.
—— KARELIAN LEGEND, OP. 99
3,3,3,3 - 6,3,3,2 - timp.,perc.,cel.,xyl. - 2 hp. - str.
10:00 G. Schirmer.

GLAZOUNOV, Alexander - RICHARDSON
—— THE SEASONS
Bo. Hawkes.

GLEAVES, Ian
—— TUDOR SUITE
2,2,2,2 -2,0,0,0 - str.   20:00 P.R.S.

GLEBOV, Yevgenij A.
—— SUITE NO. 2 FROM THE BALLET "DAYDREAM"
G. Schirmer.

GLICK, Srul Irving
—— DANCE CONCERTANTE NO. 1 (1963)
*2,*2,*2,2 - 2,2,2,0 - perc. - hp. - str.   8:00 CanMusCtr.
—— ELEGY FOR ORCHESTRA (1964)
2,1,2,1 - 1,1,1,0 - timp.,perc. - pf. (or hp.) - str.   5:00 CanMusCtr.

—— FOUR SONGS FOR TENOR AND ORCH. (1973) (Text:
Kenneth Patchen)
*3,*3,*3,3 - 4,3,3,1 - timp.,perc.(4) - guit.,mandolin - str.
27:00 CanMusCtr.
—— GATHERING IN (A SYMPHONIC CONCEPT FOR STRINGS)
(1970) (IN 5 MOVTS.)
str.   22:30 SummitMus.
—— HERITAGE (DANCE SYMPHONY) (1967)
1,1(alt. with Eng. hn.),1,1 - 1,0,0,0 - perc. - pf. - str.
30:30 CanMusCtr.
—— LAMENTATIONS FOR STRING QUARTET AND ORCH.
(SINFONIA CONCERTANTE NO. 2) (1972)
3,*3,*3,2 - 4,3,3,1 - timp.,perc.(4) - hp. - str.   18:15 CanMusCtr.
—— PAN (AN ORCHESTRAL SKETCH) (1966)
2(2nd alt. with picc.),2(2nd alt. with Eng. hn.),2,2 - 2,2,1,0 - perc.
- hp. - str.   4:45 CanMusCtr.
—— PSALM FOR ORCHESTRA (1971)
*3,*3,*3,*3 - 4,3,3,1 - perc.(3) - hp. - pf.(or hpsc.) - str.
11:05 CanMusCtr.
—— SINFONIETTA
20:00 C.A.P.A.C.
—— SONATA FOR STRING ORCH.
str.   10:00 C.A.P.A.C.
—— SUITE HÉBRAÏQUE (1965) (IN 6 MOVTS.)
2(2nd alt. with picc.),2(2nd alt. with Eng.hn.),2,2 - 2,2,2,0 -
timp.,perc. - str.   11:50 CanMusCtr.
or:
str.
—— SYMPHONIA CONCERTANTE (FOR STRING ORCH.) (IN 1
MOVT.) (1961)
str.   11:00 SummitMus.
—— SYMPHONIC DIALOGUES (FOR PIANO AND ORCH) (1963)
*2,2,2,1 alto sax.,2 - 2,2,3,1 - timp.,perc. - pf. - str.
25:55 CanMusCtr.
—— SYMPHONIC ELEGY (1974)
str.   17:15 CanMusCtr.
—— SYMPHONY FOR CHAMBER ORCH. (1966) (IN 4 MOVTS.)
1,1,1,1 - 1,1,1,0 - timp.,perc.(4) - hp. - pf. - str. 36:40 CanMusCtr.
—— SYMPHONY NO. 2
20:00 C.A.P.A.C.
—— TWO ESSAYS FOR ORCH.
12:00 C.A.P.A.C.

GLIÈRE, Reinhold M.
—— THE BRONZE HORSEMAN (BALLET SUITE)
3,3,3,3 - 4,4,3,1 - timp.,perc.,cel.,xyl. - 2 hp. - pf. - str.
40:00 G. Schirmer.
—— DAUGHTER OF CASTILE: EXCERPTS FROM THE BALLET
3,3,3,3 - 4,3,3,1 - timp.,perc. - 2 hp. - pf. - str.   G. Schirmer.
—— THE RED POPPY (BALLET SUITE) (REVISED VERSION)
3,3,3,3 - 4,3,3,1 - timp.,perc.,cel.,xyl. - 2 hp. - pf. - str.
20:00 G. Schirmer.

GLIÈRE, Reinhold M.- FRANK, Marcel G.
—— CONCERTO FOR COLORATURA SOPRANO AND
ORCHESTRA, OP. 82
1. Andante; 2. Allegro
2,2,2,2 - 4,2,0,0 - timp.perc. - hp. - str.   13:30 G. Schirmer.

GLIÈRE, Reinhold M. - SINGER, Joseph
—— CONCERTO FOR HORN AND ORCH., OP. 91
3,2,2,2 - 4,2,3,1 - timp.,perc. - hp. - str.   26:00 G. Schirmer.

GLINKA, Mikhail - GATTI, Carlo
—— RUSSLAN AND LUDMILLA (5-ACT OPERA) %
3,3,2,3 - 4,2,3,0 - timp.,perc.(3) - hp. - pf. - str.   Leeds.
On Stage: trb. - glock. - gong. - acc.

GLINKA, Mikhail - GODFREY, Charles
—— OVERTURE TO "RUSSLAN AND LUDMILLA" (REVISED)
6:00 Bo. Hawkes.

GLINKA, Mikhail - MARKEVITCH, Igor
—— OVERTURE TO "RUSSLAN AND LUDMILLA"
2,2,2,3 - 4,2,3,0 - timp. - str.   10:00 Leeds.

GLINKA, Mikhail - SOPKIN, Henry
—— KAMARINSKAJA
str.   C. Fischer.
—— OVERTURE TO "RUSSLAN AND LUDMILLA"
C. Fischer.

GLUCK, Christoph W. von
—— ORPHEUS AND EURIDICE (4-ACT OPERA) % (Engl. Text:
Walter Ducloux)
G. Schirmer.

**GLUCK, Christoph W. von - ABERT, Anna Amelia - FINSCHER,
Ludwig**
—— OVERTURE TO "ORFEO AND EURIDICE" (1762 VIENNESE
VERSION)
0,2,0,2 - 2,2,0,0 - timp. - cemb. - str.   4:00 G. Schirmer.

GLUCK, Christoph W. von - BAYLIS, Philip
—— ALCESTIS: BALLET MUSIC
2 fl. - pf.(ad lib.) - str.   Oxford.

GLUCK, Christoph W. von - FINSCHER, Ludwig
—— DANCE OF THE BLESSED SPIRITS (FROM "ORFEO AND
EURIDICE")(1774 PARIS VERSION)
2 fl. - str.   7:00 G. Schirmer.
—— DANCE OF THE FURIES (FROM "ORFEO AND
EURIDICE")(1774 PARIS VERSION)
0,2,0,2 - 2,0,2,0 - str.   5:00 G. Schirmer.

GLUCK, Christoph W. von - FRIEDRICH, Paul
—— OVERTURE TO "IPHIGENIA IN AULIS"
2,2,0,2 - 2,2,0,0 - timp. - str.   10:00 G. Schirmer.

GLUCK, Christoph W. von - GERBER, Rudolf
—— BALLET MUSIC FROM "ECHO AND NARCISSUS"
1,2,2,2 - 2,0,0,0 - str.   10:00 G. Schirmer.
—— BALLET MUSIC I FROM "PARIS AND HELEN"
0,2,0,0 - 2,0,0,0 - cemb. - str.   8:00 G. Schirmer.
—— BALLET MUSIC II FROM "PARIS AND HELEN"
0,2,0,2 - 2,2,0,0 - timp. - cemb. - str.   10:00 G. Schirmer.
—— OVERTURE IN D MAJOR (FROM THE OPERA "EURISTEO")
cemb. - str.   5:00 G. Schirmer.
—— OVERTURE TO "ALCESTES"
2,2,0,2 - 2,0,3, 0 - str.   8:00 G. Schirmer.
—— OVERTURE TO "ECHO AND NARCISSUS"
0,2,2,4 - 2,0,0,0 - str.   6:00 G. Schirmer.
—— OVERTURE TO "PARIS AND HELEN"
2,2,0,2 - 2,2,0,0 - timp. - cemb. - str.   5:00 G. Schirmer.
—— SYMPHONY IN F MAJOR
0,0,0,0 - 2,0,0,0 - cemb. - str.   15:00 G. Schirmer.

GLUCK, Christoph W. von - HAUSSWALD, Günter
—— SINFONIA TO "MERLIN'S ISLAND"
2,2,0,0 - 2,0,0,0 - cemb. - str.   4:00 G. Schirmer.

GLUCK, Christoph W. von - HECKMAN, Harald
—— OVERTURE TO "DIE PILGER VON MEKKA"
1,2,0,2 - 2,0,0,0 - cemb. - str.   5:00 G. Schirmer.

GLUCK, Christoph W. von - ISAAC, Merle J.
—— OVERTURE TO "IPHIGENIA IN AULIS"
9:45 C. Fischer.

GLUCK, Christoph W. von - LENGSTORF, Edwald
—— OVERTURE TO "TELEMACH AUF DER INSEL DER CIRCE"
1,2,0,2 - 2,2,0,0 - timp. - str.   4:00 G. Schirmer.

GLUCK, Christoph W. von - MASKE, Hans Herbert Adolf Engelbert
—— DIE KADI (OPERA) %
2,2,3,2 - 4,2,3,1 - timp.,perc. - str.   60:00 S.A.M.R.O.
—— KELDERSPOKE (OPERA) %
2,2,3,2 - 4,2,3,1 - timp.,perc. - str.   60:00 S.A.M.R.O.

GLUCK, Christoph W. von - RICHARDSON
—— OVERTURE
2,1,2,1 - 2,2,2,0 - timp. - str.   9:00 Bo. Hawkes.

GLUCK, Christoph W. von - ROBERTS, Charles J.
—— OVERTURE TO "IPHIGENIA IN AULIS"
C. Fischer.

GLUCK, Christoph W. von - RÜHLMANN, Franz
—— OVERTURE TO "DER BEKEHRTE TRUNKENBOLD"
0,2,0,1 - 2,0,0,0 - cemb. - str.   3:00 G. Schirmer.

GLUCK, Christoph W. von - STRAUSS, Richard
—— IPHIGENIA AUF TAURIS (OPERA) %
3,2,2,2 - 2,2,3,0 - timp.,perc. - str.   Bo. Hawkes.

GLUCK, Christoph W. von - WEINGARTNER, Felix
—— OVERTURE TO "ALCESTE"
S.U.I.S.A.

GNECCO, F.
—— SINFONIA ALL'ITALIANA
1,1,1,1 - 2,1,00 - timp. - str.
Bo. Hawkes.

GOBEC, Radovan
—— BLOOD IN FLAMES (3-ACT OPERA) %
2,2,2,2 - 4,3,3,1 - timp.,perc. - hp. - str.
Hans Gerig.
—— THE DUCAT OF TREMERJE (4-ACT OPERA) %
2,2,2,2, - 2,2,2,1 - timp.,perc. - hp. - str.
Hans Gerig.
—— THE LAST FLOWER (CANTATA) (FOR NARRATOR, SATB CHORUS AND ORCH.) (Text: James Thurber)
2,2,2,2 - 4,3,3,1 - timp.,perc. - hp. - str.
20:00 Hans Gerig.
—— SLOVENE DANCE SUITE
2,2,2,2 - 4,3,3,1 - timp.,perc. - str.
16:00 Hans Gerig.

GODOWSKY, Louis
—— RHAPSODY HUNGARICA (FOR VIOLIN AND ORCH.)
2,2,2,2 - 3,2,2,0 - timp.,perc. - str.
Lengnick.

GODRON, Hugo
—— AMABILE SUITE
cl. - pf. - str.
27:00 Henmar.
—— CONCERT SUITE FOR PIANO AND STRINGS
pf. - str.
24:00 Henmar.
—— CONCERTO FOR SYMPHONY ORCH.
2,2,2,2 - 4,3,3,1 - timp.,perc. - pf. - str.
27:00 Henmar.
—— CONCERTO GROSSO
cl. - str.
17:00 Henmar.
—— FOUR IMPRESSIONS
2,2,2,2 - 2,2,2,0 - timp.,perc., cel., xyl. - str.
12:00 Henmar.
—— HOMMAGES CLASSIQUES
fl. - pf. - str.
15:00 Henmar.
—— MINIATURE SYMPHONY
2,2,2,2 - 2,2,2,0 - timp. - hp. - str.
15:00 Henmar.
—— PROMENADES (SUITE)
3,2,2,2 - 2,2,2,0 - timp.,perc., cel - str.
19:00 Henmar.
—— SEVEN MINIATURES (SCÈNES PÉDAGOGIQUES)
pf. - str.
12:00 Henmar.
—— SÉRÉNADE OCCIDENTALE
2,2,2,2 - 4,1,1,1 - timp.,perc. - pf. - str.
16:00 Henmar.
—— SINFONIETTA FOR SMALL ORCH.
2,1,1,1 - 2,1,1,0 - timp.,perc. - pf. - str.
20:00 Henmar.
—— SUITE FOR STRINGS AND HARPSICHORD
hpsc. - str.
20:00 Henmar.
—— VARIATIONS TRADITIONNELS
2,2,2,2 - 2,2,1,1 - perc.,cel. - str.
20:00 Henmar.

GOEBELS, Behrend
—— SINFONIA IN C FOR STRING ORCH.
str.
18:00 Mannheimer.

GOEDICKE, Alexander - PRATT, F. W.
—— CONCERT ETUDE, OP. 49 (FOR TRUMPET AND ORCH.)
G. Schirmer.

GOETHALS, Lucien
—— CINQ IMPROMPTUS (FOR CHAMBER ORCH.) (1953)
2,1,2,1 - 2,2,1,0 - timp.,perc. - str.
15:00 H. Elkan.
—— CONCERTO (FOR TWO ORCHESTRAS AND PERC.) (1972)
4,3,3,3 - 6,4,3,1 - perc. - str.
H. Elkan.
—— DIALOGOS (FOR STRING ORCH., WIND QUINTET, 2 STRING QUINTETS, PERC., AND TAPE RECORDER) (1963)
1,1,1,1 - 1,0,0,0 - perc. - tape-recorder - str.
H. Elkan.
—— SINFONIA IN GRIS MAYOR (FOR 2 ORCHS.) (1966)
Orch. I :1,1,2,2 - 4,1,1,1 - pf. - perc. - str.
H. Elkan.
Orch. II :2,2,1,1 - 4,2,2,0 - pf. - perc. - str.

GOEYVAERTS, Karel
—— DIAPHONIE (1957) (IN 3 MOVTS.)
2,3,5,2 - 2,1,5,1 - hp. - hpsc. - pf. - str.(24 vlns.,12 d.-b.)
14:30 H. Elkan.
—— OPUS 2 (SERIAL MUSIC FOR 13 INSTRS.) (1951)
*1,2,2, b.-cl.,0 - 0,0,0,0 - pf. - str.
6:30 H. Elkan.
—— OPUS 6, AUX 180 OBJECTS SONORES (SERIAL MUSIC FOR 15 INSTRS.) (1954)
1,1,2,0 - 1,1,0,0 - cel.,xyl. - hp. - guit. - pf. - str.
11:30 H. Elkan.

GOLABOVSKI, Sotir
—— MICRO-SPACES (MIKRO PROSTORI) (5 STUDIES)
1,1,1,1 - 1,0,0,0 - perc. - pf. - str.
50:00 S.O.K.O.J.

GOLD, Ernest
—— AUDUBON, AN OVERTURE
2(2nd alt. with picc.),2,2,2 - 4,3,3,0 - timp.,perc.(2) - hp. - pf. - str.
5:00 Mills.
—— CONCERTO FOR PIANO AND ORCH.
2(2nd alt. with picc.),2(2nd alt. with Eng. hn.),2,2(2nd alt. with c.-bn.) - 4,2,3,1 - timp.,perc.(3) - pf. - str.
27:00 Composer.
—— PAN-AMERICAN SYMPHONY (IN 4 MOVTS.)
3(3rd alt. with picc.),3(3rd alt. with Eng. hn.),3(3rd alt. with b.-cl.),3(3rd alto. with c.-bn.) - 4,3,3,1 - timp.,perc.(4) - str.
18:00 Mills.
—— SONGS OF LOVE AND PARTING (FOR VOICE AND ORCH.)
G. Schirmer.

GOLDBERG, Theo
—— DIVERTISSEMENT NO. 3 IN G, OP. 16 (1957) (IN 4 MOVTS.)
*2,2,2,2 - 2,2,0,0 - timp.,perc. - str.
15:00 CanMusCtr.

GOLDMAN, Edward M.
—— HEBREW SUITE (1965) (IN 3 MOVTS.)
*3,2,2,2 - 4,3,3,1 - timp.,perc.(2) - str.
7:00 Composer.
—— KADDISH (FOR TRUMPET AND ORCH.) (1964)
2,2,2,2 - 4,3,3,1 - timp.,perc.(3) - hp. - pf. - str.
7:00 Composer.
—— SHALOM (PEACE) (1962)
str.
11:00 Composer.
—— SIM SHALOM (GRANT US PEACE, O LORD) (3 DANCE VARIATIONS) (1965)
2,2,2,2 - 2,2,2,1 - timp.,perc.(3) - str.
5:00 Composer.
—— SIMCHAS TORAH (1965)
*3,2,2,2 - 4,3,3,1 - timp.,perc.(3) - str.
6:00 Composer.
—— SYMPHONY NO. 1 ("JOB") (1963) (IN 3 MOVTS.)
*3,2,2,2 - 4,2,3,1 - timp.,perc.(3) - str.
21:00 Composer.
—— SYMPHONY NO. 2 (ROSH HASHONAH) (1964) (IN 3 MOVTS.)
*3,2,2,2 - 4,3,3,1 - timp.,perc.(3) - str.
22:00 Composer.

GOLDMAN, Maurice
—— THE GOLDEN DOOR (CANTATA) (Text: Norman Corwin)
2,1(alt. with Eng.hn.),*3,2 - 2,2,2,0 - timp.,perc.(1),bells - hp. - str.
75:00 Composer.

GOLDMAN, Richard Franko
—— LE BOBINO (SUITE) (IN 3 MOVTS.)
2,1,2,1 - 2,2,1,0 - timp.,perc. - pf. - str.
10:00 Southern.

GOLDMANN, Friedrich
—— ESSAY FOR ORCH., OP. 1
3,2,3,2 - 2,2,2,1 - timp.,perc. - pf. - str.
8:00 Tetra.

GOLDMARK, Rubin
—— REQUIEM
3,3,3,3 - 8,4,3,1 - timp.,perc. - hp. - str.
25:00 G. Schirmer.
—— SAMSON (TONE POEM)
3(3rd alt. with picc.),3,3,4 - 4,4,3,1 - timp. - hp. - str.
22:00 G. Schirmer.

GOLDSCHMIDT, Berthold
—— CONCERTINO FOR HARP AND CHAMBER ORCH.
P.R.S.
—— CONCERTO FOR CELLO AND ORCH.
24:00 P.R.S.
—— MEDITERRANEAN SONGS (1958)
19:35 P.R.S.

GOLESTAN, Stan
—— CONCERTO FOR PIANO AND ORCH. (SUR LES CIMES CARPATHIQUES)
3,*3,3,3 - 4,3,3,0 - timp.,perc., cel. - hp. - pf. - str.
20:00 S.A.C.E.M.
—— CONCERTO MOLDAVE (FOR CELLO AND ORCH.)
2,2,2,3 - 4,2,0,0 - timp.,perc.(5) - hp. - str.
25:00 EV.
—— ELÉGIE ET DANSE RUSTIQUE (FOR OBOE AND ORCH.)
2,1,2,2 - 2,2,0,0 - timp. - hp. - str.
7:00 EV.
—— RUMANIAN CONCERTO (FOR VIOLIN AND ORCH.)
3,3,2,3 - 4,2,3,0 - timp.,perc. - hp. - str.
30:00 Salabert.
—— RUMANIAN RHAPSODY NO. 1
3,*3,2,3 - 4,2,3,0 - str.
EV.

GOLUB, Marta
—— CONCERTO FOR PIANO AND STRING ORCHESTRA
    pf. - str.   12:00 G. Schirmer.

GOLUBEV, Evgenij K.
—— SYMPHONY NO. 6
                                    G. Schirmer.

GOMER, Llewelyn
—— THE SUNKEN VILLAGE (ELEGY FOR WOMEN'S CHORUS
    AND ORCH.)
    3,*2,2,2 - 4,3,3,1 - hp. - str.   Boston.

GOMEZ-CARRILLO, Manuel
—— RAPSODIA SANTIAGUEÑA (ON POPULAR THEMES FROM
    THE REPUBLIC OF ARGENTINA)
                                    Fleisher.

GOODMAN, Joseph
—— CONCERTANTE FOR WIND QUINTET AND ORCH. (1965)
    1. Sostenuto; 2. Allegro molto; 3. Presto
    2(1 alt. with picc.),2,2,2 - 1,2,1,0 - timp.,perc.(4),cel.,glock.,xyl. -
    hp. - pf. - str.   22:00 Composer.
—— CONCERTO FOR ORGAN AND ORCH. (1964) (IN 3 MOVTS.)
    1,1,1,1 - 0,1,2,0 - timp.,perc.(3),cel.glock.,xyl. - org. -
                             22:00 Presser.
—— CONCERTO IN G, FOR FLUTE AND CHAMBER ORCH.
    (1949)
    *3,0,0,0 - 2,0,0,0 - timp.,perc.(2) - str.   15:00 Presser.
—— OF VOICES AND DREAMS (3 SONGS FOR TENOR AND
    ORCH.) (Text: Horace Gregory)
    *3,2,2,2 - 4,2,3,0 - timp.,perc.(4),cel.,glock.,xyl. - str.
                             24:30 Composer.

GOODWIN, Gordon
—— CODES FOR ORCHESTRA (1969) (IN 3 MOVTS.)
    2(2nd alt. with picc.),2,2(2nd alt. with b.-cl.),2 - 4,2,3,1 -
    perc.(3),glock.,vibra.,xyl. - hp. - str.   15:45 Composer.

GOOSSENS, Eugene
—— THE APOCALYPSE (ORATORIO) (FOR SOPRANO,
    MEZZO-SOPRANO, CONTRALTO, 3 TENORS, BARITONE,
    BASS, DOUBLE MIXED CHORUS AND ORCH.)
    4,4,4,4 - 6,4,3,1 - timp.,perc.,cel. - 2hp. - pf.,org. - str.
                           110:00 Bo. Hawkes.
—— BALLET MUSIC FROM "JUDITH"
    *4,*3,*4,*3 - 4,3,3,1 - timp.,perc., cel. - hp. - str.
                              7:30 G. Schirmer.
—— FANFARE FOR THE MERCHANT MARINE (FOR BRASS
    AND PERCUSSION)
    4hn., 3tpt., 3 trb., tu. - timp.,perc.(6)   Bo. Hawkes.
—— FOUR CONCEITS, OP. 20
    *3,2,2,2 - 4,2,3,1 - timp.,perc. cel. - hp. - str.   7:00 G. Schirmer.
—— INTERMEZZO FROM "DON JUAN DE MANARA"
    *4,*3,*4,*3 - 4,3,3,1 - perc., cel. - 2hp. - str. 5:00 G. Schirmer.
—— PASTORALE, OP. 59
                              8:00 Bo. Hawkes.
—— PRELUDE TO "PHILIP II", OP. 23 (FOR SMALL ORCH.)
    1,1,1,1 - 2,1,0,0 - perc. - hp. - str.   9:00 G. Schirmer.
—— SUITE FROM "KALEIDOSCOPE"
    *4,2,2,2 - 4,2,0,0 - perc., cel. - hp. - str.   10:00 G. Schirmer.
—— SYMPHONY NO. 1
    3,3,3,3 - 4,3,3,1 - timp.,perc., cel. - hp. - org. - str.
                              38:00 C. Fischer.
—— SYMPHONY NO. 2 (IN 4 MOVTS.)
    3,3,3,3 - 4,4,4,1 - timp.,perc. - str.   40:00 P.R.S.
—— TAM O'SHANTER (SCHERZO)
    *4,*3,3,*3 - 4,3,3,1 - timp.,perc. - hp. - str.   G. Schirmer.
—— THREE GREEK DANCES (FOR SMALL ORCH.)
                              10:00 G. Schirmer.
—— TWO NATURE POEMS
    2 picc.,2,*3,*3,*3 - 4,3,3,1 - timp.,perc., cel., xyl. - 2 hp. - pf. - str.
                              12:00 G. Schirmer.

GORDELI, Otar
—— CONCERTINO FOR FLUTE AND ORCH., OP. 8
    2,2,2,2 - 4,3,3,1 - timp.,perc.,xyl. - hp. - str.   11:45 G. Schirmer.
—— CONCERTO FOR PIANO AND ORCH.
    3,2,2,2 - 4,2,3,1 - timp.,perc., xyl. - pf. - str.   24:30 G. Schirmer.

GORDON, John Douglas
—— NOCTURNAL FOR STRING ORCH.
    str.   6:30 A.P.R.A.

GORDON, Louis
—— A STORY OF OUR TIME (FOR SINGER AND ORCH.)
    3,3,2,2 - 4,3,3,1 - perc. - Fender b.-guit.(electric) - pf. - str.
                                7:30 Presser.

GORDON, Philip
—— CONCERTINO FOR VIOLIN AND STRING ORCH. (1970) (IN
    1 MOVT.)
    str.   15:00 C. Fischer.
—— FANTASIA ON "WESTRON WYNDE" (1969)
    2 hp. - str.   10:00 Composer.
—— THE SHOE OF LITTLE NOBY (OPERA) % (Text: Composer and
    Marie C. Scanlon)
    3(3rd alt. with picc.),3(3rd alt. with Eng.hn.),3(3rd alt. with
    b.-cl.),3(3rd alt. with c.-bn.) - 4,2,3,1 - timp.,perc.(3) - hp. - str.
                              60:00 Composer.
—— A TALE FROM CHAUCER (OPERA) % (Text: Composer and
    Marie C. Scanlon)
    2(2nd alt. with picc.),2(2nd alt. with Eng.hn.),2(2nd alt. with
    b.-cl.),2(2nd alt. with c.-bn.) - 2,2,1,0 - timp.,perc.(2),cel.,glock. -
    hp. - str.   40:00 Composer.
—— THREE CAMEOS FROM MAINE (1971)
    str.   12:00 Composer.
—— THREE PRELUDES FOR STRINGS (1967)
                                Bourne.
—— TOCCATA FOR ORCHESTRA
    *3,2,3,2 - 4,3,3,1 - timp.,perc.(3),xyl. - str.   Composer.
—— A TRIBUTE OF CAROLS (FOR CHORUS AND ORCH.)
    *3,1,*4,1 - 2,2,3,1 - timp.,perc.(2),bells,glock. - org.(ad lib.) - pf.(ad
    lib.) - str.   Composer.

GORINI, Gino
—— CINQUE STUDI (5 STUDIES)
    perc. - 2 pf. - str.   16:00 Leeds.
—— CONCERTO FOR PIANO AND ORCH.
    3,3,2,2 - 4,3,2,1 - timp.,perc.(2) - hp. - pf. - str. 26:00 Leeds.
—— CONCERTO FOR VIOLIN AND ORCH.
    2,2,0,2 - 4,3,3,1 - timp.,perc. - pf. - str. 27:00 Leeds.
—— DUE INVENZIONI (FOR PIANO AND ORCH.)
    1,1,1,1 - 1,1,0,0 - timp. - hp. - pf. - str. 14:00 Bo. Hawkes.
—— INTRODUZIONE E ARIOSO
    3,3,2,3 - 4,3,3,1 - timp.,perc.(2) - hp. - pf. - str. 12:00 Leeds.
—— SERENATA (1966)
    timp.- hpsc.(or pf.) - str.   18:00 MCA Music.

GORTON, Thomas
—— THE LEGEND OF SLEEPY HOLLOW
    3,2,2,2 - 4,3,3,1 - timp.,perc. - hp. - str.   12:30 C. Fischer.

GOSSEC, Francois - CALMEL, Roger
—— SUITE DE DANSES
    1,1,1,1 - 1,1,0,0 - timp. - str.   12:00 Presser.

GOSSEC, François-Joseph
—— SYMPHONIE CONCERTANTE (DU BALET DE MIRZA)
    0,0,0,0 - 2,0,0,0 - hp. - hpsc. - str.   FrankMusCp.
    or:
    0,0,0,0 - 2,0,0,0 - 2 hp. - str.
    or:
    0,0,0,0 - 2,0,0,0 - 2 hpsc. - str.

GOSSEC, François-Joseph - BODART, Eugen
—— SYMPHONY IN C MAJOR
    2,2,0,2 - 2,2,0,0 - timp. - str.   16:00 Mannheimer.

GOSSEC, François-Joseph - BROOK, Barry S.
—— SYMPHONIE IN D, OP. 3, NO. 6
    0,2,0,0 - 0,0,0,0 - str.   FrankMusCp.
—— SYMPHONIE IN E FLAT, OP. 8, NO. 1
    0,0,2,0 - 2,0,0,0 - str.   FrankMusCp.

GOSSEC, François-Joseph - TOWNSEND, Douglas
—— LA NATIVITÉ (ORATORIO) (FOR SATB SOLO VOICES,
    MIXED CHORUS AND ORCH.) (English Text: Phyllis Mead)
    2,2,2,2 - 4,0,0,0 - timp. - str.   30:00 Tetra.

GOTKOVSKY, Ida
—— CONCERTO FOR ALTO SAXOPHONE AND ORCH.
    2,2,2,alto sax.,2 - 4,2,2,1 - timp.,perc. - hp. - str. 16:30 Presser.
—— CONCERTO FOR CLARINET AND ORCH.
    3,3,3,3 - 4,3,3,1 - timp.,perc. - hp. - str. 23:00 Presser.
—— CONCERTO FOR TRUMPET AND ORCH.
                                    Presser.

—— CONCERTO FOR TRUMPET, TIMPANI AND STRINGS
tpt.(or cnt.) - timp. - str. 7:00 Salabert.
—— VARIATIONS CONCERTANTES (FOR BASSOON AND
ORCH.)
1,1,1,1 - 2,1,0,0 - perc. - hp. - str. Presser.

GOTTLIEB, Jack
—— ARTICLES OF FAITH (FOR ORCH. AND MEMORABLE
VOICES) (1965)
*3(2nd alt. with picc.),*3,*3,2 - 4,1 cnt.,2,2,1 - timp.,perc.(4) bells,
- tape recorder - keyed glock,pf. - str. 13:00 Presser.
—— PIECES OF SEVEN (OVERTURE FOR ORCHESTRA)
*3,2,1 E♭cl.,*3,*3 - 4,2,3,1 - timp.,perc.(3),glock.,xyl. - hp. - str.
8:00 G. Schirmer.
—— SEVEN SONGS OF LONELINESS (FOR VOICE AND ORCH.)
(Text: Constantine Cavafy)
16:05 Composer.
—— THE TEA PARTY (OPERA) %
40:00 Bo. Hawkes.

GOTTSCHALK, Louis Moreau - HATTON, Gaylen
—— NIGHT IN THE TROPICS
3,2,5 bar. sax.(or ophliceid),2 - 4,3,3,euph.,1 - timp.,perc. - str.
Bo. Hawkes.

GOTTSCHALK, Louis Moreau - HUNSBERGER, Donald R.
—— GRANDE MARCHE SOLENELLE
3,2,2,2 - 4,2,3,1 - timp.,perc.(4) - str. MCA Music.

GOTTSCHALK, Louis Moreau - KAY, Hershy
—— CAKEWALK (BALLET SUITE)
2(2nd alt. with picc.)2,2(2nd alt. with b.-cl.),2 - 4,2,3,1 -
timp.,perc., cel. - hp. - pf. - str. 22:00 Bo. Hawkes.
—— GRANDE TARANTELLE (FOR PIANO AND ORCH.)
2,2,2,2 - 2,2,0,0 - timp.,perc. - pf. 7:30 Bo Hawkes.

GOULD, Elizabeth
—— ANDANTE FOR TRUMPET AND STRINGS
tpt. - str. 4:00 EV.
—— CONCERTO FOR PIANO AND ORCH., OP. 7 (IN 3 MOVTS.)
2(2nd alt. with picc.),2,2,2 - 2,2,1,0 - timp. - pf. - str.
16:00 Composer.
—— CONCERTO FOR TRUMPET AND STRINGS
tpt. - str. 13:00 EV.
—— DECLARATION FOR PEACE (FOR CHORUS AND ORCH.)
3,2,3,2 - 4,4,3,1 - perc. - str. 8:00 EV.
—— GAMES (MINIATURE CONCERTO FOR PIANO AND ORCH.)
(IN 3 MOVTS.)
1,1,1,1 - 1,0,0,0 - cel.,xyl. - pf. - str. 6:30 Composer.
—— A MINI-SYMPHONY (WITH AN INTRODUCTION TO THE
INSTRUMENTS OF THE ORCHESTRA) (1973) (IN 3 MOVTS.)
(Text: Composer)
2(1 alt. with picc.),2,2,2 - 4,2,3,1 - timp.,perc.(3),bells,glock.,xyl. -
str. 14:00 Composer.
—— OVERTURE, OP. 6
2,2,2,2 - 4,3,3,0 - timp.,perc.(3) - pf. - str. 6:00 Composer.
—— SALUTATION FOR ORCHESTRA
2(2nd alt. with picc.),2,2,2 - 4,2,3,1 - timp.,perc.(3) - str. 4:00 EV.
—— TWO MOVEMENTS FOR TRUMPET AND STRINGS
tpt. - str. 9:45 Composer.

GOULD, Glenn
—— SO YOU WANT TO WRITE A FUGUE? (FOR SATB CHORUS
AND STRINGS) (Text: Composer)
str. 5:00 G. Schirmer.

GOULD, Morton
—— AMERICAN BALLADS
3,2,3,2 - 4,2-3,3,1 - timp.,perc.(3-4) - hp. - str. 40:00 G & C.
—— AMERICAN CAPRICE
2,2,2,4 sax.,2 - 2,3,2,0 - timp.,perc., cel. - hp. - pf. - str.
5:00 Mills.
—— AMERICAN SALUTE (BASED ON "WHEN JOHNNY COMES
MARCHING HOME")
3(3rd alt. with picc.),3(3rdalt. with Eng. hn.),3(3rd alt. with
b.-cl.),2 - 4,3,3,1 - timp. guit. - hp. - pf. - str. 5:00 Mills.
—— AMERICAN SYMPHONETTE NO. 1 (IN 3 MOVTS)
1,1,1,5 sax.,1 - 2,3,3,0 - timp.,perc.(2) - guit. - pf. - str. 9:00 Mills.
—— AMERICAN SYMPHONETTE NO. 2 (IN 3 MOVTS)
2,2,2,4 sax.,2 -2,3,3,0 - perc. - guit. - hp. - pf. - str. 9:00 Mills.
—— AMERICAN SYMPHONETTE NO. 3 (IN 4 MOVTS)
1(alt. with picc.),1-2 1-2(1 alt. with bar. sax.),3 sax.,1-2 - 4,3,3,1 -
timp.,perc.(3) - hp. - pf. - str. 16:00 Mills.

—— AMERICAN SYMPHONETTE NO. 4 ("LATIN AMERICAN")
(IN 4 MOVTS.)
*3,2,*4,4 sax.,2 - 4,3,3,1 - timp.,perc.(4) - hp. - str. 18:00 Mills.
—— AMERICANA (TWO MOOD SKETCHES)
2,2,*3,3 sax.,1 -2,3,3,1 - perc., cel., vibra., xyl. - banjo - 1-2hp. -
pf. - str. 4:00 C. Fischer.
—— CHORALE AND FUGUE IN JAZZ
2(1 alt. with picc.),2,2,3 sax.,*3 - 4,3,3,1 - timp.,perc.(3), cel. - 2pf.
- str. 14:00 C. Fischer.
—— CINERAMA HOLIDAY (SUITE) (IN 6 MOVTS)
2,1,2,1 - 2,2,2,0 - perc.(1), cel. - hp. - str. 14:30 G & C.
—— COLUMBIA (BROADSIDES FOR ORCH.) (VARIATIONS ON
"HAIL COLUMBIA" AND "COLUMBIA THE GEM OF THE
OCEAN") (1967)
*3,*3,E♭cl.,*3,*3 - 4,3,3,1 - timp.,perc.(4),bells,xyl. - hp. - str.
13:00 G. & C.
—— CONCERTETTE FOR VIOLA AND ORCH. (IN 4 MOVTS.)
2,*3,*3,2 - 4,3,3,1 - timp.,perc.(5) - hp. - str. 12:00 Mills.
—— CONCERTO FOR ORCH. (IN 3 MOVTS.)
3(3rd alt. with picc.),3(3rd alt. with Eng.hn.),E♭cl.,3(3rd alt. with
b.-cl.) - *3-4,3,3,1 - timp.,perc.,vibra.,xyl. - hp. - pf. - str.
18:00 G & C.
—— CONCERTO FOR PIANO AND ORCH. (IN 3 MOVTS.)
1,1,1,1 - 2,2,1,0 - perc.(1) - pf. - str. 20:00 G & C.
—— CONCERTO FOR VIOLA AND ORCH. (IN 3 MOVTS)
2,2,*3,*3 - 4,3,3,1 - timp.,perc. - str. 25:30 Mills.
—— COWBOY RHAPSODY (IN 4 MOVTS.)
3(3rd alt. with picc.), 2-3,3(3rd alt. with b.-cl.),*3 - 6,3,3,1 -
timp.,perc. - guit. - hp. - str. 12:30 Mills.
—— DANCE VARIATIONS (FOR 2 PIANOS AND ORCH.) (IN 4
MVTS.)
2(2nd alt. with picc.),2(2nd alt.with Eng. hn.),2,2 - 4,3,3,1 - perc. -
2 pf. - str. 22:00 G & C.
—— DECLARATION (SUITE FOR ORCH.) (IN 5 MOVTS.)
3(alt. with 3 picc.),2(2nd alt. with Eng. hn.),2,2(2nd alt. ad lib.
with c.-bn.) -4,3,3,1 - timp.,perc. (2-3) - hp. - str. 20:00 G & C.
—— DECLARATION (SYMPHONIC NARRATIVE) (IN 7 MOVTS.
WITH 6 INTERLUDES) (FOR 2 SPEAKERS, ORCH. AND
SPEAKING MALE CHORUS)
3(alt. with 3 picc.),2(2nd alt. with Eng. hn.),2,2(3rd alt. ad lib.
with c.-bn.) - 4,3,3,1 - timp.,perc. (2-3)) - hp. - str. 30:00 G & C.
—— FALL RIVER LEGEND (BALLET SUITE) (IN 6 MOVTS)
1-2(1alt. with picc.),1-2,2,2 - 2,2,2-3,0 - timp.,perc. - pf. - str.
24:00 G & C.
—— FAMILY ALBUM (SUITE) (IN 5 MOVTS.)
2(1 alt. with picc.),*2,2,2 - 4,3,3,1 - timp.,perc.(3),mar.,xyl. - pf.(ad
lib.) - str. 14:40 G & C.
—— FANFARE FOR FREEDOM
2-3,2-3,3,2 - 4,3,2,1 - timp.,perc.(4) 1:30 G & C.
—— FESTIVE MUSIC (SUITE) (IN 3 MOVTS.)
3(2 alt. with picc.),2,3,2 - 4,3(1 off-stage),3,1 - timp.,perc.(3) - hp.
- str. 11:00 G & C.
—— FOLK SUITE (IN 3 MOVTS.)
*3,2,2,2 sax.,2 - 4,3,2,0 - timp.,perc. - hp. - pf.- str. 11:30 Mills.
or:
1,1,2,1 - 2,2,1,0 - timp.,perc. - str.
—— FOSTER GALLERY (THIRTEEN EPISODES, BASED ON
THEMES BY STEPHEN FOSTER)
2(1 alt. with picc.),2(1 alt. with Eng. hn.),*3,*3 - 4,3,3,1 -
timp.,perc.(4) - banjo - hp. - str. 33:00 G & C.
—— FOUR DIALOGUES
pf. - str. 20:00 G & C.
—— FOUR INVENTIONS (FOR 4 PIANOS, WINDS, AND
PERCUSSIONS)
*3,*3,*3,*3 - 4,3,3,1 - timp.,perc. - 4 pf. 17:30 G & C.
—— HARVEST
Vibra - hp. - str. 12:00 G & C.
—— HOLIDAY MUSIC (IN 5 MOVTS.)
2,2,2,2 - 4,3,3,1 - timp.,perc.,cel. - hp. (or pf) - str. 15:00 G & C.
—— A HOMESPUN OVERTURE
3(3rd alt. with picc.),2,3(3rd alt. with b.-cl.),2 - 4,3,3,1 - perc.
-banjo - hp. - str. 5:30 G & C.
—— HOOFER SUITE (FOR TAP DANCER AND ORCH.) (IN 6
MOVTS.)
1(alt. with picc.),1,2,1 - 2,2,2,0-1 - timp.,perc.(1) - str.
11:15 G & C.
—— INTERPLAY (AMERICAN CONCERTETTE FOR PIANO AND
ORCH.) (IN 4 MOVTS.)
2,2,2,2 - 4,3,3,1 - timp.,perc. - pf. - str. 12:00 Mills.
—— JEKYLL AND HYDE VARIATIONS
*3,*3,E♭cl.,*3,*3 - 6,3,3,1 - timp.,perc., cel - hp. - pf. - str.
22:00 G & C.

—— LINCOLN LEGEND
   1(alt. with picc.),2(1 alt. with Eng. hn.),*3-*4,2 - 4,3,3,1 -
   timp.,perc.(3) - hp. - str.   18:00 G & C.
—— LITTLE SYMPHONY (IN 4 MOVTS.)
   3(3rd alt. with picc.),2,*3,4 sax.(ad lib.),*3 - 4,3,3,1 -timp.,perc. (3)
   - hp. - pf. - str.   18:00 G & C.
—— MINSTREL SHOW
   2(2nd alt. with picc.),2,2*3 - 4,3,3,1 - timp.,perc.(4),xyl. - hp. - str.
                                                        8:00 G & C.
—— PHILHARMONIC WALTZES (SUITE)
   *3,2,*3,*3 - 4,3,3,1 - timp.,perc.(5) - hp. - str.   9:00 G & C.
—— REVIVAL (A FANTASY ON 6 NEGRO SPIRITUALS)
   3,2,2,2 - 4,3,2,1 - timp.,perc. - str.   6:00 Mills.
—— RHYTHM GALLERY (FOR NARRATOR AND ORCH)
   2(2nd alt. with picc.),2(2nd alt. with Eng. hn.),2,2 - 3,2,2,1 -
   timp.,perc. (2), glock. - hp. - pf. (alt. with cel.) - str.
                                                        24:00 G & C.
—— RIB OF EVE (BALLET) (IN 6 MOVTS.)
   3(3rd alt. with picc.),2(2nd alt. with Eng. hn.),2,2 - 4,3,3,1 - perc.
   - 2 pf. - str.   G & C.
—— SALUTATIONS (SUITE) (TRIBUTE TO DAVID SARNOFF)
   3(alt.with 3 picc.),0,3,2 - 4,3,3,1 - timp.,perc.(2),cel. - hp.
                                                        14:30 G & C.
—— A SERENADE OF CAROLS (IN 4 MOVTS.)
   2(2nd alt. with picc.),2,*3,2 - 2,2,0,0 - 2 hp. - str.   15:00 G & C.
—— SHOW PIECE (IN 7 MOVTS.)
   *3,*3,E♭cl.,*3,*3 - 6,3,3,1 - timp.,perc.(4), cel., mar., vibra., xyl., -
   hp. - pf. - str.   18:00 G & C.
—— A SONG FOR FREEDOM (FOR NARRATOR, CHORUS AND
   ORCH.)
   *3,*2,*3,2 - 4,3,3,1 - timp.,perc.(5) - guit. - hp. - str.   10:00 Mills.
—— SPIRITUALS FOR STRING CHOIR AND ORCH. (IN 5
   MOVTS.)
   1(alt. with picc.),2,2-3,2 - 2-4,2-3,2-3,1 - timp.,perc.(2-3) - hp. - pf.
   - str.   17:30 Mills.
—— SPIRITUALS FOR STRINGS (SUITE) (IN 6 MOVTS.)
   str.   19:50 G & C.
—— SUITE OF CHRISTMAS HYMNS (IN 3 MOVTS)
                                                        19:30 G & C.
—— SYMPHONY NO. 1 (IN 4 MOVTS.)
   3(3rd alt. with picc.),*3,3,*3 - 6,3,3,1 - timp.,perc. - hp. - str.
                                                        32:00 G & C.
—— SYMPHONY NO. 2 (ON MARCHING TUNES) (IN 4 MOVTS.)
   *3(2nd alt. with 2nd picc.),*3, E♭cl.,3(alt. with b.-cl.),*3 - 4,3,3,1 -
   timp.,perc.(4-5) - hp. - str.   31:00 G & C.
—— SYMPHONY NO. 3 (IN 4 MOVTS.)
   *3,2,*3,*3 - 4,3,3,1 - timp.,perc.(5), cel., xyl - hp. - str.
                                                        35:00 G & C.
—— SYMPHONY OF SPIRITUALS
   3,3,3,3 - 4,3,3,1 - timp.,perc. - hp. - pf. - str.   33:00 G & C.
—— TAP DANCE CONCERTO (FOR TAP DANCER AND ORCH.)
   (IN 4 MOVTS.)
   2,2,2,2 - 2,2,2,0 - timp. - str.   16:00 G & C.
—— VENICE (AUDIOGRAPH FOR DOUBLE ORCH. AND BRASS
   CHOIRS) (1966) (IN 7 MOVTS.)
   Orch. I: 2(1 alt. with picc.),*2,2(1 alt. with b.-cl.),2(1 alt. with
   c.-bn.) - 3,0,0,1 - timp.,perc.(2),bells - hp. - str. Brass Choir
   I,Offstage: 2 tpt.,2 trb. Orch. II: 2(1 alt.with picc.),1,2,1 - 3,0,0,0
   - timp.,perc.(2) - hp. - str. Brass Choir II,Offstage: 2 tpt.,2 trb.
                                                        26:50 G & C.
—— VIVALDI GALLERY (ON VIVALDI THEMES) (FOR DIVIDED
   ORCH. AND STRING QUARTET) (1968) (IN 6 MOVTS.)
   2(alt.with 2 picc.),2,2,2 - 2,2,2,0 - hp. - str.   26:45 G. & C.
—— WINDJAMMER (SUITE FROM THE FILM) (IN 4 MOVTS.)
   2,2,2,2 - 4,3,3,1 - perc.(2),cel. - hp. - str.   12:00 G & C.

GOUNOD, Charles - HARRISON, Julius
—— BALLET MUSIC FROM "FAUST" (WITH SATB CHORUS)
   2,2,2,2 - 4,2,3,1 - timp.,perc. - hp. - str.   16:00 Bo. Hawkes.

GOUNOD, Charles - SUCHOFF, Benjamin
—— BY BABYLON'S WAVE (FOR MIXED CHORUS AND ORCH.)
   *3,2,2,2 - 4,2,3,1 - timp.,perc.(2) - hp. - pf. - str.   8:00 Alfred.

GOW, David
—— SYMPHONY NO. 1
   2,2,2,2 - 4,2,2,1 - timp.,perc. - hp. - str.   22:00 P.R.S.

GRAAP, Lothar
—— CONCERTO BREVE (FOR CHAMBER ORCH.)
   2,1,0,1 - 0,1,0,0 - perc. - str.   Tetra.

GRAAS, John G.
—— SYMPHONY NO. 1 (JAZZ SYMPHONY) (FOR JAZZ SOLOISTS
   AND ORCH.)
   *3,2,*3,3 sax(alto, ten., bar.),2 - 5,3,3,1 - timp., perc. - guit. - pf. -
   str.   26:00 Modern.

GRABNER, Hermann
—— CONCERTO FOR FLUTE, CLARINET, HORN, BASSOON
   AND STRING ORCH., OP. 48
   1,0,1,1 - 1,0,0,0 - str.   K & S.
—— CONCERTO FOR KEYBOARD INSTRUMENT AND STRINGS,
   OP. 60
   cemb. - str.   16:00 Baerenrtr.
—— KONZERT FUR ORGEL UND STREICHER, OP. 59
   org. - str.   20:00 Baerenrtr.

GRABÓCZ, Miklós
—— HUNGARIAN DANCES FOR SMALL ORCH.
   2,0,2,0 - 0,0,0,0 - cymbalom(or hpsc.) - str.   G. Schirmer.

GRAENER, Paul
—— KONZERT FÜR FLÖTE UND ORCH., OP. 116
   1,1,2,1 - 2,0,0,0 - str.   20:00 Henmar.
—— ROMANTIC PHANTASY
   3,3,3,3 - 4,3,3,1 - timp.,perc. - hp. - str.   18:00 G. Schirmer.

GRAENER, Paul - BODART, Eugen
—— SUITE FÜR FLÖTE UND STREICHORCH., OP. 63
   fl. - str.   15:30 Henmar.

GRAFE, Marc L.
—— REVERIE (1970)
   2(2nd alt. with picc.),1,*3,1 - 2,2,2,0 - timp.,perc.(2-3) - str.
                                                        5:15 Composer.

GRAHAM, Robert V.
—— CONCERTO FOR HARPSICHORD AND CHAMBER ORCH.
   (1963)
   1,1,0,0 - 0,0,0,0 - hpsc. - str.   Composer.
—— CONCERTO NO. 1 FOR PIANO AND ORCH. (1949) (IN 4
   MOVTS.)
   2(2nd alt.with picc.),2(2nd alt. with Eng.hn.),2,2 - 4,2,2,1 -
   timp.,perc.(2) - pf. - str.   24:00 Composer.
—— CONCERTO NO. 2 FOR PIANO AND ORCH. (1964) (IN 3
   MOVTS.)
   1,1,1,1 - 2,0,0,0 - timp. - pf. - str.   19:20 Composer.
—— LYON COUNTY (1934) (SUITE) (IN 2 MOVTS.)
   3,*3,*3,*3 - 4,2,2,1 - timp.,perc. - str.   7:00 Composer.
—— OBOOKIAH (AN ORATORIO) (1969) (FOR VOICES, SATB
   CHORUS AND ORCH.)
   1,1,1,1 - 2,0,0,0 - timp.,perc. - org. - str.   90:00 Composer.
—— OILWELLS (1934)
   3,*3,*3,*3 - 4,2,2,1 - timp.,perc.,xyl. - str.   5:00 Composer.
—— SYMPHONY NO. 1 (1952) (IN 4 MOVTS)
   3(2nd alt.with alto fl.,3rd alt. with picc.),2(2nd alt. with
   Eng.hn.),2(2nd alt.with b.-cl.),2(2nd alt.with c.-bn.) - 4,2,2,1 -
   timp.,perc. - pf. - str.   Composer.
—— VOICES OF CHRISTMAS (CANTATA) (FOR MIXED CHORUS
   AND ORCH.) (Text: Joan Sistrunk)
   fl.(ad lib.) - str.   40:00 Southern.

GRAHN, Ulf
—— ANCIENT MUSIC (FOR PIANO AND CHAMBER ORCH.)
   (1970)
   1,1,1,1 - perc. - pf. - str.   14:00 Seesaw.
—— CONCERT FOR SATB SOLO VOICES AND ORCH. (1973) (No
   text)
   1,1,1,1 - 1,2,2,0 - timp.,perc. - hp. - pf. - str.   10:00 Fleisher.
—— A DREAM OF A LOST CENTURY (1971)
   1,1,1,0 - 0,0,0,0 - pf. - str.   15:00 Fleisher.
—— FANCY (1965)
   2,2,2,2 - 2,2,1,0 - timp.,perc.(5, incl. 4 on timp.) - str.
                                                        12:00 Fleisher.
—— HOMAGE TO CHARLES IVES (1968)
   str.   6:00 Seesaw.
—— LAMENTO (1967)
   str.   4:00 Fleisher.
—— SYMPHONY (1967)
   3,2,3,3 - 4,2,3,1 - timp.,perc.(3) - str.   20:00 Fleisher.
—— THE WIND OF DAWN (FOR ORCH. AND TAPE)(1973)
   1,1,1,1 - 0,1,1,0 - perc. - tape-recorder - str.   10:00 Fleisher.

GRAINGER, Percy A.

—— THE BRIDE'S TRAGEDY (FOR CHORUS AND ORCH.)
*3,*3,*3,4 sax.(ad lib.) *3 - 4,3,3,1 - timp.,perc.(2-3) - str.
7:30 G. Schirmer.

—— COLONIAL SONG (A SONG OF AUSTRALIA) (WITH SOPRANO AND TENOR SOLOS AD LIB.)
1-2picc.,2,*3,*3,*3 - 4,3,3,euph.,1 - timp.,perc. (2-3) - pf. - hp. - str.
6:30 G. Schirmer.

—— COUNTY DERRY AIR (BRITISH FOLK-MUSIC SETTINGS NO. 29) (WITH OPTIONAL SSAA OR TB CHORUS)
3,*3,*4,*3 - 1,1,1,euph.,1 - org.(or harm) - str.   5:30 G. Schirmer.

—— DANISH FOLK MUSIC SUITE (IN 4 MOVTS.)
*3,*3,*3,4 sax.(ad lib.),*3 - 4,3,3,euph.,1 - timp.,perc. (5) - hp. - org.(or harm.) - pf. - str.   17:00 G. Schirmer.

—— ENGLISH DANCE (FOR ORCH., ORGAN AND 1 OR MORE PIANOS)
*3,*3,*3,*3, - 4,3,3,euph.,1 - timp.,perc.(6) - org. - pf. - str.
20:00 G. Schirmer.

—— GREEN BUSHES (PASSACAGLIA ON AN ENGLISH FOLKSONG)
picc.(ad lib.),1,1,2,2(2nd alt. with bar. sax) - 2,2(2nd alt. with sop. sax.),0,0 - timp.,perc. (1-2) - pf. - org.(or harm.) - str.
8:30 G. Schirmer.

—— I'M SEVENTEEN COME SUNDAY (FOR MIXED CHORUS AND ORCH.)
G. Schirmer.

—— IN A NUTSHELL (SUITE FOR ORCH., PIANO AND PERCUSSION INSTRUMENTS) (IN 4 MOVTS.)
*3,*3,*3,*3 - 4,3,3,1 - timp.,perc.(11) - hp. - pf. - str.
14:00 G. Schirmer.

—— IRISH TUNE FROM COUNTY DERRY (BRITISH FOLK MUSIC SETTINGS NO. 15)
4 hn.(ad lib.) - str.   5:00 G. Schirmer.

—— KIPLING "JUNGLE BOOK" CYCLE (FOR CHORUS AND ORCH.) (IN 10 MOVTS.)
0,*3,*3,4 sax.,2 - 2,3,3,euph.,1 - str.   28:00 G. Schirmer.
or:
0,*3,*1,2 - 2,0,0,0 - str.

—— THE LADS OF WAMPHRAY (SCOTTISH BORDER BALLAD) (FOR MALE CHORUS AND ORCH.)
*3,*3,*3,*3 - 4,3,3,1 - timp.,perc(2-3) - str.   6:30 C. Fischer.

—— LOVE VERSES FROM "THE SONG OF SOLOMON" (FOR MEZZO SOPRANO OR TENOR, CHORUS AND CHAMBER ORCH.)
2,1,2,2 - 1,1,0,0 - harm. - str.   6:00 G. Schirmer.

—— THE MERRY WEDDING (FOR 9 SOLOISTS, CHORUS AND ORCH.)
2,0,*3,2 - 4,2,3,1 - timp.,perc.(2-3) - org. - str.   6:30 Oxford.

—— MOLLY ON THE SHORE (BASED ON OLD IRISH REELS)
*3,*3,*3,*2 - 4,3,3,1 - timp.,perc.(2-4) - pf. - str.
5:00 G. Schirmer.
or:
str.

—— THE NIGHTINGALE AND THE TWO SISTERS
str.   G. Schirmer.

—— RECESSIONAL (FOR FULL CHORUS AND ORCH.)
4 hn., 3 tpt., 3 trb. - str.   G. Schirmer.

—— SCOTCH STRATHSPEY AND REEL (FOR 4 MALE VOICES AND CHAMBER ORCH.)
picc.(ad lib.),fl., ob., cl., bn. - perc. - English chromatic concertina (or acc. or harm.) - 2 guit. - str.   6:00 G. Schirmer.

—— SHALLOW BROWN (FOR UNISON CHORUS AND CHAMBER ORCH.)
1,0,1,*2 - 2,1,0,euph.,0 - harm. - pf. - str.   G. Schirmer.

—— SIR EGLAMORE (BRITISH FOLK MUSIC SETTINGS NO. 13) (FOR DOUBLE CHORUS AND ORCH.)
0,0,2,2 - 4-6,2-4,3-4, euph.,1 - timp.,perc.(3) - 1-2 hp. - str.
4:00 G. Schirmer.

—— TO A NORDIC PRINCESS (BRIDAL SONG)
*3,*3,*3,*3 - 4,3,3,euph.,1 - timp.,perc. (4-6) harm. - 1-2 hp. - org.(ad-lib) - 1-2 pf. - str.   20:00 G. Schirmer.

—— TRIBUTE TO FOSTER (FOR 5 SOLOISTS, CHORUS AND ORCH.)
*3,*3,*3,*3 - 4,3,3,1 - timp.,perc.(3-6) - hp. - harm. - pf. - str.
9:00 G. Schirmer.

—— THE WARRIORS (MUSIC TO AN IMAGINARY BALLET)
*3,*3,*3,*3 - 4-6,3,3,1 - timp.,perc.(11) - 2 hp. - 3 pf. - str.
18:00 G. Schirmer.

—— YOUTHFUL SUITE (IN 5 MOVTS)
1-2 picc.,2,*3,*3,2,c.-bn. (ad-lib.) - 4,3,3,1 - timp.,perc. (3-8), xyl. (bells, cel.,glock.,mar.,vibra ad lib.) - harm. - hp.(or pf.) - str.
22:30 G. Schirmer.

GRAM, Peder

—— CONCERTO IN D MINOR FOR VIOLIN AND ORCH., OP. 20
2,2,3,2 - 4,2,3,1 - timp. - str.   25:00 G. Schirmer.

—— PROLOG TIL ET DRAMA AF SHAKESPEARE, OP. 27
2,2,2,2 - 2,2,3,0 - perc.(2) - str.   Henmar.

—— SYMPHONY NO. 2, OP. 25 (FOR MEZZO-SOPRANO AND ORCH.)
1,2,3,1 - 2,2,2,0 - perc.(2),cel. - hp. - str.   Henmar.

GRANADLOS, Enrique

—— DANTE, OP. 21 (SYMPHONIC POEM) (WITH MEZZO-SOPRANO SOLO)
3(3rd alt with picc.),3,3,3 - 4,3,3,6 - timp. - 2 hp. - str.
18:00 G. Schirmer.

GRANADOS, Enrique - SCHELLING, Ernest

—— GOYESCAS (SUITE) (IN 4 MOVTS.)
2(2nd alt. with picc.),2,2,2 - 4,2,3,1 - timp.,perc., bells, xyl. - hp.(ad lib.) - str.   17:00 G. Schirmer.

—— THE MAJA AND THE NIGHTINGALE (FOR SOPRANO AND ORCH.)
2,3,2,2 - 4 - hn. - hp. - str.   7:00 G. Schirmer.

GRANDERT, Johnny

—— BARYPET (CONCERTO FOR TRUMPET, BARITONE SAXOPHONE, FLUTES, PERCUSSION AND STRING ORCH.) (1968)
fl.,bar. sax. - tpt. - perc. - str.   19:00 Fleisher.

—— THE D OF B (1967)
4,4,4,2 - 4,4,4,2 - timp.,perc.(4) - str.   8:00 Fleisher.

—— SYMPHONY NO. 1 (1971)
2,0,0,4 - 4,5,4,0 - timp.,perc.(3, incl. 2 on timp.) - str.
20:00 Fleisher.

—— SYMPHONY NO. 2 (1972)
5,5,5,sax.,5 - 4,4,4,1 - timp.,perc. - str.   27:00 Fleisher.

—— SYMPHONY NO. 3 (SINFONIA CALAMAGROSTIS)(1972)
5,5,5,sax.,5 - 5,5,5,1 - timp.,perc. - str.   21:00 Fleisher.

—— SYMPHONY NO. 4 (1974)
5,4,4,4 - 5,5,5,1 - timp.,perc. - hp. - str.   25:00 Fleisher.

GRANDIS, Renato de

—— L' ARLECCHINIANA (REV. 1976)
*3,2,2,2 - 4,3,3,1 - perc.,cel.,mar.,vibra. - hp. - hpsc. - pf. - str.
23:00 Seesaw.

—— CADORÈ (SUITE) (IN 3 MOVTS.) (1963)
2(2 alt. with picc.),0,1,ten. sax.,1 - 2,3,2,0 - perc.(3),cel.,mar.,vibra.,xyl. - harmonica - electric guit. - hp. - electric org. - pf. - str.   26:00 G. Schirmer.

GRANDJANY, Marcel

—— ARIA IN CLASSICAL STYLE (FOR HARP AND STRINGS)
Hp. - org. (ad lib.) - str.   5:00 AMP.

—— POEM FOR HARP, HORN AND ORCH. (LA JEUNE TARENTINE)
3(3rd alt. with picc.),2(2nd alt. with Eng. hn.),2,2 - 4 hn. - timp.,perc.(3) - hp. - str.   14:00 Composer.

—— RHAPSODY FOR HARP AND ORCH.
1,1,1,0 - 1,0,0,0 - hp. - str.   8:00 Baron.

GRANT, Allan

—— CONCERTO IN E MINOR, FOR PIANO AND ORCH. (FANTASY ON ORIGINAL THEMES) (IN 4 MOVTS.)
*3,*3,2,1 - 3,2,2,1 - timp.,perc.(2) - pf. - str.   29:00 Composer.

GRANT, Allan - MADDY, Joseph E.

—— SOUTHLAND SYMPHONY (IN 4 MOVTS.)
2(1 alt. with picc.),*3,*3,2 - 4,2,2,1 - timp.,perc.(2) - 2 hp. - org. - str.   34:00 Composer.

GRANT, Francis

—— WOODSIDE SUITE (1968) (IN 3 MOVTS.)
pf. - str.   6:05 Ludwig.

GRÄSBECK, Gottfrid

—— CONCERTO FOR ORCHESTRA AND TAPE (1964)
14:00 FinnMICtr.

—— LUCIA MUSIC (FOR SOLO VOICES, SATB CHORUS, ORGAN AND ORCH.) (1971)
42:00 Akademiska.

—— SINFONIA DA CAMERA (1969)
2,2,2,2 - 2,2,1,0 - timp.,perc. - str.   20:00 FinnMICtr.

—— TOCCATA DODECAFONICA (1959)
6:00 FinnMICtr.

GRASSI, Ernesta Castellino
—— CINQ MÉLODIES SIAMOISES (FOR VOICE AND ORCH)
                                    Salabert.
—— FÊTE KHMÈRE
    3,3,3,3 - 4,3,3,0 - timp.,perc.,xyl. - 2 hp. - str.   6:00 Salabert.

GRAUN, Johann Gotlieb - TÖTTCHER, Herrmann
—— CONCERTO IN B-FLAT MAJOR FOR BASSOON, STRINGS
    AND BASSO CONTINUO
    bn. - cemb. - str.   F. Colombo.
—— CONCERTO IN C MINOR FOR OBOE, STRINGS AND BASSO
    CONTINUO
    ob. - cemb. - str.   18:00 F. Colombo.

GRAUPNER, Christoph - NOACK, Friedrich
—— CONCERTO IN C MINOR
    bn.(or c.) - cemb. - str.   12:00 G. Schirmer.
—— OVERTURE IN E MAJOR
    fl. - cemb. - str.   21:00 G. Schirmer.

GRAUPNER, Christoph - SCHROEDER, Felix
—— SUITE FOR OBOE D'AMORE, VIOLA D'AMORE (OR VIOLA)
    AND STRING ORCH.
    ob. d'amore - hpsc. - str.   18:00 Mannheimer.

GRAVES, William
—— THE JUGGLER (1-ACT OPERA) % (Text: JeanAnne Lustberg)
    2,1,1,1 - 2,1,1,0 - timp. - hp. - str.   45:00 Bourne.

GRAY, David
—— DIVERTIMENTO NO. 1
    2,2,2,2 - 4,2,2,0 - timp.,perc - str.   13:00 Novello.
—— DIVERTIMENTO NO. 2
    2,2,2,2 - 2,2,1,0 - timp.,perc. - str.   15:00 Novello.

GRAYSON, Denys
—— TWO SKETCHES FOR STRINGS AND PIANO
    pf. - str.   Novello.

GREEF, Arthur de
—— BALLADE (VARIATIONS ON A FLEMISH FOLK SONG)
    str.   Henmar.
—— FOUR OLD FLEMISH SONGS
    *3,*3,2,2 - 2,2,3,1 - timp.,perc. - hp. - str. 16:00 G. Schirmer.

GREEN, Elizabeth A. H.
—— THEME AND VARIATIONS
    str.   4:30 C. Fischer.

GREEN, George
—— PASSACAGLIA (1957)
    2,2,2,2 - 2,2,0,0 - perc. - str.   6:00 Seesaw.
—— PROLOGUE AND FUGUE (1956)
    2,2,2,2 - 4,2,3,1 - timp.,perc. - hp. - pf. - str. 12:00 Seesaw.

GREEN, Philip
—— SAINT PATRICK'S MASS (FOR SATB CHORUS AND
    ORCHESTRA) (IN 10 MOVTS.)
    3,0,5,0 - 4,2,1,0 - perc. - guit. - hp. - str. 33:00 Bourne.

GREEN, Ray
—— THE BIRDS
    2,1,2,1 - 2,2,1,0 - timp.,perc., cel. - str. 20:00 AmerMusEd.
—— CONCERTANTE FOR VIOLA AND ORCH.
    2,1,2,1 - 2,2,1,0 - timp.,perc - hp. - pf.(ad. lib.) - str.
                                20:00 AmerMusEd.
—— CONCERTO BREVIS (FOR VIOLIN AND ORCH.)
    2,1,2,1 - 2,2,1,0 - timp.,perc. - hp. - str. 10:00 AmerMusEd.
—— CONCERTO FOR VIOLIN AND ORCH.
    2,2,2,2 - 4,3,3,0 - timp.,perc - hp. - str. 30:00 AmerMusEd.
—— DANCE SET (IN 3 MOVTS.)
                                  AmerMusEd.
—— DANCE THEME AND VARIATIONS
    2,2,2,2 - 4,2,3,1 - timp.,perc. - hp. - str. 15:00 AmerMusEd.
—— HYMN TUNES FOR STRINGS
    str.   12:00 AmerMusEd.
—— OVERTURE, MARCH AND FINALE (FOR "IPHIGENIA IN
    TAURIS")
    fl., ob., cl., bn. - perc. - str.   15:00 AmerMusEd.
—— PRELUDE AND FUGUE
    2,2,2(1 alt. with b.-cl.),2(1 alt. with c.-bn.) - 4,3,3,1 - timp.,perc. -
    hp. - str.   12:00 AmerMusEd.

—— RHAPSODY FOR HARP AND ORCH.
    2,1,2,1 - 2,2,1,0 - timp.,perc. - hp. - str. 15:00 AmerMusEd.
—— RHAPSODY ON AN APPALACHIAN THEME (FOR HARP
    AND ORCH.)
                                15:00 AmerMusEd.
—— SONATINAS FOR A SYMPHONY ORCH. (IN 4 MOVTS.)
    *2,2,2,2 - 2,2,1,0 - timp.,perc.,cel.(or pf.) - str.
                                10:00 AmerMusEd.
—— SUNDAY SING SYMPHONY (WITH TRIO CONCERTANTE
    OF FLUTE, CLARINET AND BASSOON)
    2,1,1,1 - 2,2,1,0 - timp.,perc. - hp. - str. 22:00 AmerMusEd.
—— SYMPHONY NO. 1 (COUNTRY DANCE SYMPHONY) (IN 4
    MOVTS.)
    2(1 alt. with picc.),1,2,1 - 2,2,1,0 - timp.,perc. - hp. - str.
                                25:00 AmerMusEd.
—— SYMPHONY NO. 2
    *2,1,2,1 - 2,2,1,0 - timp.,perc. - hp. - str. 28:00 AmerMusEd.
—— THREE INVENTORIES ON A TEXAS TUNE
    2,1,2,1 - 2,2,1,0 - timp.,perc.(1-2) - hp. - pf. - str.
                                10:00 AmerMusEd.
—— THREE PIECES FOR A CONCERT
    1,0,2,0 - 0,2,1,0 - perc. - pf.   8:00 AmerMusEd.

GREENBERG, Lionel
—— PRELUDE AND FUGUE FOR ORCH.
    *2,2,2,2 - 4,2,3,1 - timp. - str.   6:30 CanMusCtr.

GREENWOOD, John
—— ALICE IN WONDERLAND (SUITE)(1938)
    2,1,2,2 - 2,0,0,0 - timp.,perc.(3) - hp. - str. P.R.S.
—— FUGUE FOR STRING ORCH. (1950)
    str.   10:00 P.R.S.
—— SALUTE TO GUSTAV HOLST
    1,1,2,1 - 2,1,0,0, - timp. - hp. - str. 15:00 P.R.S.
—— SCHERZANDE (PASTORALE)(1941)
    2,1,2,2 - 2,2,0,0 - timp.,perc.(3) - hp. - str. P.R.S.
—— TWO PIECES FOR STRING ORCH. (1965)
                                9:00 P.R.S.

GREGOR, Cestmir
—— SUITE FOR STRINGS
    str.   20:00 Bo. Hawkes.

GREGORC, Jurij
—— CONCERTO FOR HORN AND STRINGS
    hn. - str.   24:00 Hans Gerig.
—— MELANCHOLY PRELUDE
    str.   7:00 Hans Gerig.
—— SINFONIETTA FOR STRINGS
    str.   19:00 Hans Gerig.
—— SUITE FOR STRINGS
    str.   19:00 Hans Gerig.

GREGSON, Edward
—— MUSIC FOR CHAMBER ORCH.
    0,2,0,2 - 2,0,0,0 - str.   20:00 P.R.S.

GREISSLER, Fritz
—— OVERTURE TO AN ITALIAN COMEDY
    2,2,2,2 - 2,2,1,0 - timp.,perc. - hp. - str. 8:00 Tetra.

GRENZ, Arthur
—— CAPRICCIO ("MANHATTAN CAPRICE") (FOR PIANO AND
    ORCH.)
    3,2,2,2 - 4,2,3,0 - timp.,perc. - str. 12:00 F. Colombo.
—— CONCERTO FOR THREE VIOLINS AND STRINGS (AFTER
    VIVALDI)
    str.   10:00 F. Colombo.
—— KONZERT, OP. 7
    2,2,2,2 - 4,2,4,0 - timp.,perc. - str. 24:00 Sikorski.
—— LEPORELLO (A MERRY OVERTURE)
    2,2,2,2 - 4,3,3,0 - timp.,perc. - hp. - str. 6:00 F. Colombo.
—— LITTLE LEGEND FOR ORCHESTRA
    1,1,2,1 - 2,2,1,0 - perc. - hp. - str. 11:00 F. Colombo.
—— MUSIK FÜR STREICHER, OP. 2
    str.   27:00 Sikorski.
—— SCÈNE PITTORESQUE FOR VIOLIN AND ORCH., OP. 13
    2,2,3,0 - 4,3,0,0 - timp.,perc.,cel. - hp. - org. - str.
                                7:00 F. Colombo.
—— SINFONIETTA, OP. 6
    2,3,2,2 - 2,0,0,0 - str.   22:00 F. Colombo.
—— DER ZAUBERLEHRLING
    3,2,2,2 - 4,4,3,1 - timp.,perc. - hp. - str. 24:00 Sikorski.

GRÉTRY, André Ernest Modeste - BARNES, Clifford P.
—— OVERTURE TO "LUCILE"
              5:00 Ludwig.

GRÉTRY, André Ernest Modeste - BEECHAM, Thomas
—— ZEMIRE ET AZOR (BALLET SUITE)
  2,2,2,2 - 2,0,0,0 - perc. - str.   14:00 Bo. Hawkes.

GRÉTRY, André Ernest Modeste - CARSE, Adam
—— OVERTURE TO "LUCILE"
  0,2,0,2 - 2,2,0,0 - timp. - str.   7:00 Galaxy.

GRÉTRY, André Ernest Modeste - MOTTL, Felix - ROBERTS, Charles J.
—— BALLET SUITE
              C. Fischer.

GRÉTRY, André Ernest Modeste - SONNTAG, Dieter
—— CONCERTO IN C MAJOR FOR FLUTE, 2 HORNS AND
STRINGS
  fl. - 2 hn. - str.   12:00 Henmar.

GREY, Edith
—— PRELUDE IN D, OP. 9 ("IN MEMORIAM")
  str.   Galaxy.

GREY, Frank
—— BALAKLARA OVERTURE
  *3,*3,*3,*3 - 4,2,3,1 - timp.,perc. - hp. - pf. - org. - str. Composer.
—— CONCERTO IN G, FOR PIANO AND ORCH.
  1. Andante non troppo; 2. Moderato; 3. Allegretto
  2,2,2,2 - 4,2,3,1 - timp.,perc.(8) - hp. - pf. - str. 34:00 Composer.

GRIEB, Herbert
—— FESTIVAL TE DEUM (FOR SATB CHORUS AND ORCH.)
  2,2,2,2 - 4,3,3,1 - timp. - str. 10:00 Composer.
—— INTRODUCTION AND ALLEGRO
  2,*3,*3,0 - 4,3,2,1 - timp.,perc.(2) - str. 12:00 Composer.
—— VARIATIONS ON A NEGRO SPIRITUAL
  2,2,2,1 - 4,3,2,1 - timp.,perc.(2),cel. - hp. - str. 18:00 Composer.
—— VARIATIONS ON A NURSERY RHYME
  2,2,2,0 - 2,3,2,1 - timp.,perc.(2) - str. 8:00 Composer.

GRIEG, Edvard - MADDY, Joseph E.
—— SUITE FOR STRINGS (6 SELECTIONS FROM "LYRIC
PIECES")
  str.   Fema.

GRIEG, Edvard - RIEGE, Ernst
—— EIGHT LYRIC PIECES, OP. 12
  1,1,3,1 - 2,2,2,0 - timp.,perc.,cel. - hp. - str. 12:30 F. Colombo.
—— FOUR HUMORESQUES, OP. 6
  2,2,2,2 - 2,2,3,0 - timp.,perc.,glock.,vibra.,xyl. - hp. - str.
          12:00 F. Colombo.

GRIEG, Edvard - ROBERTS, Charles J.
—— PEER GYNT: SUITE NO. 2
             C. Fischer.

—— SIGURD JOSALFAR: SUITE
             C. Fischer.

GRIEND, Jac Koos (van de)
—— CONCERT OVERTURE
  3,3,3,3 - 4,3,3,1 - timp.,perc. - str. 10:00 Henmar.
—— CONCERTINO FOR PIANO AND ORCH.
  1,2,1,1 - 1,1,1,1 - timp. - pf. - str. 15:00 Henmar.
—— CONCERTO FOR CELLO AND ORCH.
  3,3,3,3 - 4,3,0,0 - timp.,perc. - str. 30:00 Henmar.
—— CONCERTO FOR VIOLIN AND ORCH.
  2,2,2,2 - 4,2,3,0 - timp. - pf. - str. 16:00 Henmar.
—— LUCTOR ET EMERGO
  3,3,3,3 - 4,3,3,0 - timp.,perc. - hp. - str. Henmar.
—— OINOE HENA STALAGMON - EEN DRUPPLE WIJNS (FOR
SOPRANO, BARITONE, SPEAKING VOICE, MIXED CHORUS
AND ORCH.) (1947) (Text: J. H. Leopold)
  2,0,0,0 - 0,3,0,1 - timp.,perc. - 3 pf. - str. 29:00 Henmar.
—— REVELATION (FOR TENOR, CHORUS AND ORCH.) (1939)
  4,4,4,4 - 6,4,4,1 - timp.,perc. - 2 hp. - org. - str. 35:00 Henmar.
—— SYMPHONY NO. 1
  3,3,3,3 - 4,3,3,1 - timp.,perc. - str. 25:00 Henmar.
—— SYMPHONY NO. 2 ("ONVOLTTOOID")
  3,3,3,3 - 4,3,3,1 - timp.,perc. - hp. - str. 10:00 Henmar.

—— T ROS BEYAERT DOET SIJN RONDE
  3,3,4,3 - 4,3,3,0 - timp.,perc. - str. 11:00 Henmar.
—— VIER ORKESTSTUKKEN
  3,3,3,3 - 4,3,3,1 - timp.,perc. - 2 hp. - str. 18:00 Henmar.
—— WILLEM VAN NASSOUW (RECITATION WITH ORCH.)
             Henmar.
—— ZES DOORVOERINGEN (FOR SMALL ORCH.)
  2,2,2,0 - 0,2,0,0 - perc. - str. 12:00 Henmar.

GRIESBACH, Karl-Rudi
—— CONCERTANTE MUSIC (FOR PIANO AND CHAMBER
ORCH.)
  2,1,0,0 - 0,0,0,0 - perc. - pf. - str. 10:00 Tetra.
—— SYMPHONY (1967)
  4,3,3,3 - 4,3,3,1 - timp.,perc. - pf. - str. 12:00 Tetra.

GRIFFES, Charles T.
—— BACCHANALE (SCHERZO)
  2picc.,2,*3,*3,*4 - 4,3,3,1 - timp.,perc., cel., glock. - 2hp. - str.
         5:00 G. Schirmer.
—— CLOUDS
  *4,3,*3,3 - 4hns. - perc. - cel. - 2hps. - str. 5:00 G. Schirmer.
—— FIVE OLD CHINESE AND JAPANESE SONGS (FOR VOICE
AND ORCH.)
  *3,*3,2,2 - 1,1,0,0 - perc., cel., glock., xyl. - hp. - str.
         12:00 G. Schirmer.
—— NOCTURNE
  *3,2,*3,*3 - 4,2,3,0 - perc. - hp. - str. 7:00 G. Schirmer.
—— NOTTURNO IN B MAJOR
  2,2,3,2 - 4hn. - timp. - hp. - str. G. Schirmer.
—— THE PLEASURE DOME OF KUBLA KAHN
  *3,*2,*3,3 - 4,3,2,1 - timp.,perc., cel., xyl. - 2hp. - pf. - str.
         14:00 G. Schirmer.
—— POEM FOR FLUTE AND ORCHESTRA
  fl. - 2 hn. - timp. - str. 9:00 G. Schirmer.
—— THREE POEMS OF FIONA MACLEOD (FOR SOPRANO AND
ORCH.)
  2,2,*3,2 - 4,0,3,0 - timp. - hp. - str. 11:00 G. Schirmer.
—— THREE TONE PICTURES FOR CHAMBER ORCH., OP. 5
  1,1,1,1 - hn. - pf. - str. 12:00 G. Schirmer.
—— THE WHITE PEACOCK
  2,2,2,2 - 2,2,2,0 - timp.,perc., cel. - 2 hp. - str. 6:00 G. Schirmer.

GRIFFITHS, Vernon
—— ODE OF THANKSGIVING (FOR SATB CHORUS AND
STRING ORCH.)
  str.   15:00 Novello.
—— THE PASSIONS (FOR SOLO VOICES, CHORUS AND ORCH.)
        40:00 A.P.R.A.
—— PEACE AND WAR (FOR CHORUS AND ORCH.)
        11:00 Bo. Hawkes.
—— SONG OF THE WESTERN MEN (FOR SSA WOMEN'S
CHORUS AND SMALL ORCH.)
        A.P.R.A.

GRIMM, Friedrich Karl
—— JUDITH, OP. 90 (SINFONISCHE DICHTUNG)
  3,3,3,3 - 4,3,4,1 - timp.,perc. - hp. - str. 19:00 AhnSimrock.

GRIMM, Hans
—— DIE WEISE VON LIEBE UND TOD (SYMPHONIC POEM,
AFTER RAINER MARIA RILKE)
  3,2(2nd alt. with Eng. hn.),3,3 - 4,3,3,1 - timp.,perc. - hp. - str.
        19:40 Henmar.

GRIMM, Hans Heinz
—— MARGUERITE AND THE BEAR (RHAPSODIC WALTZ)
  2,2,2,2 - 4,3,3,0 - timp.,perc. - hp. - str. 10:00 Henmar.

GRIMM, Jim
—— ENTROPIEN
  3,3,3,3, - 2,3,2,0 - perc.,vibra.,xylorimba - pf. - str.
        20:00 S.U.I.S.A.

GRIMPE, Alex
—— CARNEVAL, OP. 15
  2,1,2,2 sax.,1 - 2,3,2,0 - timp., perc. - hp. - str. 25:00 SDMV.

GRINBLAT, Romuald S.
—— THE LIFE OF MOLIERE (SUITE FROM INCIDENTAL MUSIC
TO THE PLAY) (FOR HARPSICHORD AND CHAMBER
ORCH.)
        G. Schirmer.

—— SYMPHONY NO. 4

G. Schirmer.

GRISELLE, Thomas
—— A COMEDY OVERTURE (AFTER ARTEMUS WARD)
*3,3(3rd. alt. with Eng. hn.), 3(3rd alt. with b.-cl.),3 - 4,3,3,1 -
timp.,perc. (5) - str. 11:00 Composer.
—— REFLECTIONS
2,2,2,2 - 4,2,3,1 - hp. - str. 4:00 Presser.
or:
1,1,2,1 - 2,2,1,0 - hp. - str.
—— A SUITE OF SERENADES FOR VARIOUS OCCASIONS (IN 5
MOVTS.)
2(alt. with 2 picc.),2,2(2nd alt. with b.-cl.),2 - 4,3,3,1 - timp.,perc.
(3) - str. 6:00 Composer.
—— TWO AMERICAN SKETCHES
2(2nd alt. with picc.),2(2nd alt. with Eng. hn) 2(2nd alt with
b.-cl.),2 - 4,3,3,1 - timp.,perc.(3) - hp. - str. 5:30 Robbins.

GRISEY, Gérard
—— D'EAU ET DE PIERRE (FOR TWO INSTRUMENTAL
GROUPS)
*2(fl. also alt. with picc.),1(alt. with Eng. hn.),1,1 - 1,1,1,1 -
perc.(2) - str.(2,1,1,1) 20:00 Salabert.
—— VAGUES, CHEVAL, LE SOUFFLE (FOR CLARINET AND
DOUBLE ORCH.)
3,3,E^{b}cl.,*3,3 - 4,4,0,1 - perc.(4) - str. 28:00 Presser.

GROFÉ, Ferde
—— AMERICAN BIOGRAPHY: HENRY FORD
*3,*3,*3,*3 - 4,3,3,1 - timp.,perc., bells - hp. - str. 8:00 Robbins.
—— ATLANTIC CROSSING (WITH OPTIONAL NARRATOR AND
MIXED CHORUS)
*3,*3,*3,2 - 4,3,3,1 - timp.,perc.(3), cel., glock., xyl. - hp. - pf. -
str. 28:00 Robbins.
—— AVIATION SUITE (IN 4 MOVTS.)
*3,*3,*3,*3 - 4,3,3,1 - timp.,perc.(4), bells, cel., glock., xyl. - hp. -
str. 20:00 Robbins.
—— CAFE SOCIETY BALLET %
3(3rd alt. with picc.),*3,*3,*3 - 4,3,3,1 - timp.,perc.(3) - hp. - str.
Robbins.
—— DAWN AT LAKE MEAD (SYMPHONIC TONE POEM)
Composer.
—— DEATH VALLEY SUITE (IN 4 MOVTS.)
*3,*3,*3,*3 - 4,3,3,1 - timp.,perc.(4), bells, cel., glock., xyl. - hp. -
str. 16:00 Robbins.
—— GRAND CANYON SUITE (IN 5 MOVTS.)
3(3rd alt. with picc.), *3,*3,*3 - 4,3,3,1 - timp.,perc.(3) - hp. - pf. -
str. 32:00 Robbins.
—— HOLLYWOOD (BALLET SUITE) (IN 5 MOVTS.)
3(3rd alt. with picc.),*3,*3,*3 - 4,3,3,1 - timp.,perc.(3) - hp. - str.
22:00 Robbins.
—— HUDSON RIVER SUITE (IN 4 MOVTS.)
Robbins.
—— KILLARNEY (AN IRISH FANTASY)
3(3rd alt. with picc.),*3,*3,*3 - 4,3,3,1 - timp.,perc.(3) - hp. - str.
9:00 Robbins.
—— MISSISSIPPI SUITE (A TONE JOURNEY IN 4 MOVTS.)
3(3rd alt. with picc.),*3,*3,*3 - 4,3,3,1 - timp.,perc.(3) - hp. - str.
16:00 Feist.
—— NIAGARA FALLS SUITE (IN 4 MOVTS.)
*3,*3,*3,*3 - 4,3,3,1 - timp.,perc.(3),bells,cel. - hp. - pf. - str.
25:00 Robbins.
—— SAN FRANCISCO SUITE (IN 4 MOVTS.)
*3,*3,*3,*3 - 4,3,3,1 - timp.,perc.(3),bells,cel. - hp. - pf. - str.
20:00 Composer.
—— SYMPHONY IN STEEL (SYMPHONIC POEM)
3(3rd alt. with picc.),*3,*3,*3 - 4,3,3,1 - timp.,perc. (3) - hp. - 2
pf. - str. 12:00 Robbins.
—— TABLOID SUITE (IN 4 MOVTS.)
3(3rd alt. with picc.),*3,*3,2 - 4,3,3,1 - timp.,perc. (3) - hp. - str.
20:00 Robbins.
—— VALLEY OF THE SUN (SUITE)
Composer.
—— WORLD'S FAIR SUITE (IN 5 MOVTS.)
*3,*3,*3,*3 - 4,3,3,1 - timp.,perc.(4) - hp. - pf. - str.
35:45 Robbins.

GRØNDAHL, Launny
—— CONCERTO FOR BASSOON AND ORCH.
17:00 Dania.

GRØNDAHL, Launy
—— CONCERTO FOR TROMBONE AND ORCH.
2,2,2,2 - 2,2,1,0 - perc.(1) - pf. - str. Henmar.

GROOT, Cor de
—— CAPRICCIO (FOR PIANO AND ORCH.)
2,2,2,2 - 3,2,3,0 - perc. - pf. - str. 8:00 Modern.
—— CONCERTINO FOR PIANO AND ORCH.
1,1,1,1 - 1,1,0,0 - pf. - str. 14:00 Modern.
—— CONCERTO FOR FLUTE AND ORCH.
2,1,2,2 - 2,1,1,0 - timp.,perc., cel. - str. 20:00 Henmar.
—— CONCERTO FOR VIOLIN AND ORCH.
2,2,2,2 - 0,1,0,0 - str. 16:00 Henmar.
—— DIVERTIMENTO
2,3,2,2 - 3,3,3,1 - timp.,perc. - hp. - pf. - str. 14:00 Henmar.
—— MINIATURE CONCERTO (MINUTENCONCERT), FOR
PIANO AND ORCH. (1950)
1,1,2,1 - 2,2,0,0 - timp.,perc. - pf. - str. 11:00 Henmar.
—— MINUTEN KONZERT (FOR PIANO AND ORCH.)
1,1,2,1 - 0,2,2,0 - perc. - pf. - str. 11:00 Modern.
—— OUVERTÜRE ENERGICO
2,2,2,2 - 4,3,3,1 - timp.,perc., xyl. - str. Henmar.
—— VARIATIONS IMAGINAIRES (FOR PIANO LEFT-HAND AND
ORCH.)
22:00 Henmar.
—— WILHELMUS OUVERTÜRE
3,2,2,2 - 4,3,3,1 - timp.,perc. - str. 11:00 Henmar.

GROSS, Bethuel
—— HYMN TO MUSIC (A TONE POEM) (FOR SOLOISTS,
CHORUS AND ORCH.) (Text: Composer)
*2,1,2,1 - 4,4,3,1 - timp.,perc.(1) - org. - str. 20:00 Composer.
—— MASS OF CHRIST (ORATORIO) (FOR CHORUS AND ORCH.)
(Text: Anna Scott)
*2,1,2,1 - 4,4,3,1 - timp.,perc.(1), bells - org. - str.
100:00 Composer.

GROSS, Eric
—— ANTUBCONSEAS, OP. 11 (1972)
2,2,2,2 - 4,2,3,0 timp.,perc.(3),glock.,xyl. - str. 9:45 MCA Music.
or:
2,1,2,2 - 2,2,0,0 - timp.,perc.(3),glock.,xyl. - str.
—— CONCERT OVERTURE
5:00 A.P.R.A.
—— MOONSCAPE, OP. 32 (FOR STRING QUARTET AND STRING
ORCH.) (1972)
str. 7:00 MCA Music.
—— SINFONIETTA, OP. 9
2,2,3,2 - 0,0,0,0 - cym. - str. 15:00 MCA Music.
or:
1,1,3,1 - 0,0,0,0 - cym. - str.
—— SYMPHONY NO. 1, OP. 20 (FOR SOLO VOICES, SATB
CHORUS AND ORCH.) (1972)
2,2,E^{b}cl.,*3,2 - 4,3,3,1 - timp.,perc.(3),glock.,xyl. - hp. - hpsc.
35:00 MCA Music.
—— VARIATIONS FOR ORCH., OP. 7 (1965)
*3,1,*3,0 - 1,0,0,0 - perc. - hp. - str. 7:40 MCA Music.

GROSS, Paul
—— ADAGIO
2,2,2,2 - 2,2,3,0 - timp. - str. 9:00 Alkor.
—— KONZERT FÜR KAMMERORCH. (MIT OBLIGATEM
KLAVIER)
2,0,1,1 - 2,1,0,0 - timp. - pf. - str. 22:00 Alkor.
—— SINFONIETTA
timp.(ad lib.) - str. 24:00 Mannheimer.

GROSSMAN, Norman
—— MUSIC FOR ORCHESTRA, NO. 1 (1952)
3(3rd alt.with picc.),*3,*3,*3 - 4,4,3,1 - timp.,perc.(4),xyl. - str.
8:30 Composer.
—— MUSIC FOR THE DANCE ("THE DYBBUK") (1951)
1,1,1,1 - 1,1,0,0 - timp. - pf. - str. 10:00 Composer.

GROVEN, Eivind
—— BALLAD (MOT BALLADE) (FOR MIXED CHORUS AND
ORCH) (Text: Hans E. Kinck)
2,2,2,2 - 4,2,3,1 - timp.,perc. - hp. - pf. - str. 16:00 T.O.N.O.
—— BALLAD OF TOSCANALAND (FOR VOICE AND ORCH.)
(Text: Hens E. Kinck)
2,2,2,2 - 4,2,2,0 -timp.,perc. - hp. - str. 8:00 T.O.N.O.

—— THE BRIDEGROOM ("BRUDGOMMEN") (FOR SOLO VOICES, MIXED CHORUS AND ORCH.) (Text: Ingeborg Refling Hagen)
2,2,2,2 - 4,2,3,1 - timp.,perc. - hp. - str.   90:00 T.O.N.O.
—— BY FALLS AND FJORD (VEG FOSS OG FYORD) (FOR MALE CHORUS AND ORCH.) (1966) (Text: H. J. Sandsdalen)
2,2,2,2 - 4,2,3,1 - timp.,perc. - str.   12:00 T.O.N.O.
—— DRAUMKUAEDE (FOR SOPRANO, TENOR, BARITONE, MIXED CHORUS AND ORCH.) (Text: Traditional)
2,2,2,2 - 4,2,3,1 - timp.,perc. - pf. - str.   36:30 T.O.N.O.
—— FALDAFEYKIR
3,2,2,2 - 4,2,3,1 - timp.,perc.,xyl. - pf. - str.   14:00 T.O.N.O.
—— THE FATES ("SKJEBNER") (SYMPHONIC POEM)
2,1,1,1 - 2,2,2,0 - timp. - str.   15:00 T.O.N.O.
—— HISTORICAL VISIONS ("HISTORISKE SYNER") (SYMPHONIC POEM)
2,2,2,2 - 4,2,3,1 - timp. - hp. - str.   20:00 T.O.N.O.
—— IVAR AASEN SUITE (FOR SOPRANO, BASS, MALE CHORUS AND ORCH.) (Text: Ivar Aasen)
2,1,1,1 - 2,2,2,0 - timp.,cel. - str.   30:00 T.O.N.O.
—— RENAISSANCE (SYMPHONIC POEM)
2,2,2,2 - 4,2,3,1 - timp.,perc. - hp. - str.   40:00 T.O.N.O.
—— THE STORY OF A TOWN (SOGA UM EIN BY) (FOR SOPRANO, TENOR, BASS, MIXED CHORUS AND ORCH.) (1956) (Text: H. J. Sandsdalen)
2,2,2,2 - 4,2,3,1 - timp.,perc.,cel. - opt.org.(or pf.) - str.   45:00 T.O.N.O.
—— SYMFONISKE SLÅTTER (3 NORWEGIAN FOLK DANCES)
2,2,2,2 - 4,2,3,1 - timp.,perc. - str.   14:00 T.O.N.O.
—— SYMPHONY NO. 2 ("THE MIDNIGHT HOUR") (MIDNATTSTIMEN)
2,2,2,2 - 4,2,3,1 - timp.,perc. - str.   30:00 T.O.N.O.
—— THE TEMPLE OF NATURE ("NATURENS TEMPEL") (FOR MIXED CHORUS AND ORCH.) (Text: Ragna Groven)
2,1,1,0 - 2,1,0,0 - timp. - str.   10:00 T.O.N.O.
—— TUNES FROM THE HILLS (FJELLTONAR) (SYMPHONIC POEM)
1,1,1,1 - 2,2,2,0 - timp.,perc.,cel.(or pf.) - str.   10:00 T.O.N.O.
—— WEDDING IN THE WOOD (BRYLLUP: SKOGEN) (SYMPHONIC POEM)
2,2,2,2 - 2,2,2,0 - timp.,perc. - str.   10:00 T.O.N.O.

GRUA, Paul - BODART, Eugen
—— ENTR'ACTE
2,2,0,0 - 2,0,0,0 - str.   3:30 Mannheimer.
—— L' ORAGE (THE STORM)
2,2,0,0 - 2,0,0,0 - str.   2:30 Mannheimer.

GRUBER, Georg
—— DIVERTIMENTO IN D MAJOR
str.   24:00 S.A.M.R.O.
—— SUITE IN C MAJOR (FOR FLUTE AND STRINGS)
fl. - str.   30:00 S.A.M.R.O.

GRUENBERG, Louis
—— CONCERTO FOR VIOLIN AND ORCH., OP. 47 (IN 3 MOVTS.)
*3,*3,*3,*3 - 4,3,3,1 - timp.,perc.(3) - hp. - str.   38:00 Composer.
—— THE ENCHANTED ISLE (SYMPHONIC POEM)
*3,*3,*3,2 - 4,3,3,1 - timp.,perc.(4), cel. - hp. - str.   20:00 AmerMusEd.
—— SERENADE TO A BEAUTEOUS LADY
3,3,3,3 - 4,3,2,1 - timp. - hp. - str.   11:30 Composer.

GRÜNAUER, Ingomar
—— SERENADE ET AUBADE (FOR CHAMBER ORCH.)
1,1,1,1 - 0,0,0,0 - perc. - str.(8,4,4,2)   10:05 Modern.

GRUNDMAN, Clare E.
—— POEM AND IMPROMPTU DANCE
2,1,*3,1 - 2,2,2,0 - timp.,perc., (2),glock., xyl. - pf.(ad lib.) - str.   3:30 Bo. Hawkes.
—— THREE SONGS FOR CHRISTMAS (WITH OPTIONAL CHORUS)
1,1,*3,1 - 2,2,2,0 - timp.,perc.(2), bells, glock. - pf. (ad lib.) - str.   4:00 Bo. Hawkes.

GRÜNENWALD, Jean-Jacques
—— CONCERT D'ÉTÉ (FOR PIANO AND STRINGS)
pf. - str.   17:00 Salabert.
—— CONCERTO FOR PIANO AND ORCH.
4,2,2,2 - 4,3,3,0 - timp.,perc. - hp. - pf. - str.   17:00 Salabert.
—— FANTASY IN THE FORM OF A DIALOGUE (FOR ORGAN AND ORCH.)
Hans Gerig.

—— OUVERTURE POUR UN DRAME SACRÉ
3,3,3,3 - 4,3,3,1 - timp.,perc. - hp. - pf. - str.   17:00 Salabert.
—— PSALM 129 (FOR CHORUS AND ORCHESTRA)
2,2,2,2 - 4,3,3,0 - hp. - org. - str.   18:00 Salabert.

GRUNN, Homer
—— CALIFORNIA IDYLS (IN 3 MOVTS.)
fl., cl. - pf. - str.   8:00 Fox.
—— THE LAND OF SIP-O-PHE (FOR PIANO AND ORCH.)
1. Very slowly; 2. Plaintively; 3. Faster
2,1,2,2 - 4,2,2,0 - timp.,perc. - pf. - str.   18:00 Composer.
—— THE PAINTED DESERT (A BALLET OF THE SOUTH-WEST) (IN 3 MOVTS.)
2,2,2,2 - 2,2,2,0 - timp.,perc.(3) - hp. - pf. - str.   Composer.

GRUNN, Homer - LOUD, Walter E.
—— ZUNI INDIAN SUITE (IN 4 MOVTS.)
1,1,2,1 - 2,2,1,0 - timp.,perc.(2) - org. - pf. - str.   25:00 Boston.

GUARINO, Carmine
—— BAGLIORI
2,*3,*3,*3 - 4,3,4,0 - timp.,perc., cel. - hp. - str.   14:00 Bo. Hawkes.

GUARINO, Mario
—— CANTATA (FOR SOPRANO, CHORUS AND ORCH.)
3,3,3,3 - 4,3,3,1 - timp. - hp. - str.   30:00 Leeds.
—— CONCERTO FOR PIANO AND ORCH.
3,3,3,3 - 4,3,4,0 - timp.,perc.(2),cel.,xyl. - hp. - pf. - str.   43:00 Leeds.
—— CONCERTO FOR VIOLIN AND ORCH.
3,3,3,3 - 4,3,3,1 - timp.,perc. - hp. - str.   30:00 Bo. Hawkes.

GUARNIERI, M. Camargo
—— CONCERTO PARA ORQUESTRA DE CORDAS E PERCUSSAO (CONCERTO FOR STRINGS AND PERCUSSION) (IN 3 MOVTS.)
timp.,snare drum - str.   15:00 Broude.
—— ESTUDO (FOR PERCUSSION AND ORCH.)
Broude.

GUASTAVINO, Carlos
—— ROMANCE DE SANTA FÉ (FOR PIANO AND ORCH.)
3,2,2,2 - 4,2,3,1 - timp.,perc. - pf. - str.   13:00 F. Colombo.
—— SUITE ARGENTINA (FOR SOPRANO AND ORCH.)
6:00 F. Colombo.

GUBBY, Roy
—— ANDALUSIAN PIECE NO. 3
2,2,2,2 - 4,2,3,0 - timp.,perc. - str.   4:30 P.R.S.
—— OVERTURE TO THE BALLET "PERRETTE"
2,2,2,2 - 0,2,2,0 - timp.,perc. - pf. - str.   3:30 P.R.S.
—— PERRETTE (BALLET) %
2,2,2,2 - 2,2,2,0 - timp.,perc. - pf. - str.   30:00 P.R.S.
—— THE YOUNG RIDERS (SUITE)
2,2,2,2 - 0,0,0,0 - str.   18:00 P.R.S.

GUBITOSI, Emilia
—— CONCERTO FOR PIANO AND ORCH.
3,3,2,2 - 4,2,4,0 - timp.,perc., bells - hp. - pf. - str.   25:00 Bo. Hawkes.
—— CORAL SINFONICO (FOR ORGAN AND ORCH.)
1,1,0,0 - 0,1,2,0 - bells - org. - pf. - str.   12:00 Bo. Hawkes.
—— SONATA IN BIANCO MINORE (LITTLE POEM FOR 4 FEMALE VOICES AND SMALL ORCH.)
2,1,1,1 - 1,0,0,0 - cel. - hp. - pf. - str.   12:00 Bo. Hawkes.

GUDAUSKAS, Giedra - MILLS, Alvin M.
—— LOS ANGELES SKETCHES (SUITE) (1974) (IN 3 MOVTS.)
15:00 Composer.

GUDMUNDSEN-HOLMGREEN, Pelle
—— CHRONOS, OP. 2 (FOR CHAMBER ORCH.) (1962)
11:00 Henmar.
—— COLLEGIUM MUSICUM CONCERTO (1964)
1,0,1,sax.,1 - 2,2,1,0 - timp.,perc. - str.   10:00 K.O.D.A.
—— FIVE PIECES FOR ORCH.
3,*3,*3,*3 - 4,4,3,1 - perc. - pf. - str.   9:00 K.O.D.A.
—— FRÈRE JACQUES (PIECE FOR CHAMBER ORH.) (1964)
2,1,2,2 - 2,2,2,0 - perc. - pf. - str.   10:00 G. Schirmer.
—— LAMENTO, OP. 1 (1957)
timp.,perc. - str.   7:00 K.O.D.A.

—— MIRROR

32:00 K.O.D.A.

—— OVERTURE (1955)
str. 13:00 K.O.D.A.

—— PIECE BY PIECE (1968)
1,1,*1,1 - 1,1,2,0 - perc. - electric guit.,b.-guit. - pf. - str.(incl.
electric vln.) 17:00 K.O.D.A.

—— RECAPITULATIONS (1967)
*1,1,0,1 - 0,0,3,0 - electric guit.,b.-guit. - hpsc. - pf. - electric
vln.,d.-b. 11:00 K.O.D.A.

—— SIGNALS (FOR ORCH., WITHOUT STRINGS) (1966)
11:00 K.O.D.A.

—— SYMPHONY (REV. 1965)
3,2,3,3 - 4,3,3,1 - timp.,perc.(5) - pf. - str. 14:00 K.O.D.A.

—— THREE MOVEMENTS
Sheep-bells - str. 7:00 K.O.D.A.

—— TRICOLORE I

K.O.D.A.

—— TRICOLORE II (1967)

8:00 K.O.D.A.

—— TRICOLORE III (1967)

8:00 K.O.D.A.

—— TRICOLORE IV (1969)
3,3,3,3 - 4,3,3,0 - str. 12:00 G. Schirmer.

—— VARIATIONS FOR AUNT RIX (1968)
1,1,1,1 - 1,0,0,0 - bells - pf. - str. 8:00 K.O.D.A.

GUERRA PEIXE, César
—— DIVERTIMENTO NO. 2 FOR STRINGS
str. F. Colombo.

—— ISTANTANEOS SINFONICOS NO. 1
2,2,2,2 - 4,3,3,1 - timp.,perc. - str. 6:00 F. Colombo.

—— PEQUEÑO CONCERTO (FOR PIANO AND ORCH.) (1956)
1,1,2,1 - 2,2,2,0 - perc. - pf. - str. 15:00 F. Colombo.

—— SYMPHONIC SUITE NO. 1 (PAULISTA) (1955) (IN 4 MOVTS.)
3,2,2,2 - 4,3,4,1 - timp.,perc.,cel.,xyl. - pf. - str.

25:00 F. Colombo.

—— SYMPHONIC SUITE NO. 2 (PERNAMBUCANA) (1955)
3,2,2,2 - 4,3,4,1 - timp.,perc. - str. F. Colombo.

—— SYMPHONY NO. 1 (1946)
1,1,2,1 - 0,1,0,0 - timp. - pf. - str. 21:00 F. Colombo.

GUERRINI, Guido
—— MISSA PRO DEFUNCTIS (FUNERAL MASS) (FOR SOPRANO,
MEZZO-SOPRANO, TENOR, BASS, CHORUS, ORGAN AND
ORCH.)
4,3,3,3 - 4,4,3,1 - timp.,perc.(3),bells,cel.,xyl. - 2 hp. - org. - str.
90:00 Leeds.

—— NATIVITAS CHRISTI (CANTATA) (FOR SOPRANO,
BARITONE, CHORUS AND ORCH.)

35:00 S.I.A.E.

GUÉZEC, Jean-Pierre
—— ARCHITECTURES COLOREÉS (FOR 15 MUSICIANS) (1964)
1,1,*2,0 - 1,1,1,0 - perc.(3) - str.(2,1,1,1) 8:00 Salabert.

—— ASSEMBLAGES (FOR 28 MUSICIANS) (1967)
*4,*3,1 E♭cl.,*3,*3 - 4,3(1 in D),3,1 - perc.(3) 12:00 Salabert.

—— CONCERT EN TROIS PARTIES (1961)
1,1,1,1 - 0,0,0,0 - perc.(1) - pf. - str.(2,1,1,1) 16:00 Salabert.

—— CONCERTO FOR VIOLIN AND 14 INSTRUMENTS (1960)
1,1,1,1 - 1,1,0,0 - timp.,perc.(2) - hpsc. - str.(3,1,1,1)

11:00 Salabert.

—— ENSEMBLE MULTICOLORE (FOR 18 MUSICIANS) (1965)
1,1,*2,0 - 1,1(in D),1,0 - perc.(3) - str.(3,2,2,1) 15:00 Salabert.

—— FORME-COULEURS (FOR 2 HARPS AND ENSEMBLE) (1969)
2(alt.with 2 picc.),1,*2,0 - 1,1(alt.with piccolo-tpt.),0,0 - perc.(2) -
2 hp. 8:00 Salabert.

—— FORMES (1966)
3,3,3,3 - 4,4,3,1 - perc.(6) - 2 hp. - str. 14:10 Presser.

—— SUCCESSIF-SIMULTANÉ (FOR 12 STRING-PLAYERS) (1968)
str.(7,2,2,1) 13:00 Salabert.

—— TEXTURES ENCHAÎNÉES (FOR 16 MUSICIANS) (1967)
2,1,1 E♭cl.,*2,0 - 2,2,2,0 - perc.(3) - hp. 9:00 Salabert.

GUILMANT, Felix A. - RIEGE, Ernst
—— ALLEGRETTO, OP. 19
2,2,2,2 - 2,2,0,0 - timp.,perc.,cel. - hp. - str. 5:00 F. Colombo.

GUION, David W.
—— PASTORALE
1,1,2,1 -2,1,1,0 - perc. - str. 4:00 G. Schirmer.

—— PRAIRIE SUITE (IN 3 MOVTS.)
2,2,2,2 - 2,2,3,0 - timp.,perc.,bells - hp. - pf. - str.
9:10 G. Schirmer.

—— TEXAS (SYMPHONIC SUITE)
*3,*3,*3,*3, - 4,3,3,1 - timp.,perc.(4),xyl. - phonograph (with
recording of chirping crickets, mocking bird call and coyote's call)
- 2 hp. - str. 48:00 Composer.

—— TEXAS TUNES (FOR VOICE AND ORCH.)

G. Schirmer.

GUION, David W. - GROFÉ, Ferde
—— SHINGANDI (PRIMITIVE AFRICAN BALLET) %
*3,*3,*3,*3 - 4,3,3,1 - timp.,perc.(2), vibra. - hp. - str.
15:00 G. Schirmer.

GUION, David W. - RIEGGER, Wallingford
—— SUITE FOR ORCHESTRA (IN 3 MOVTS.)
2(2nd alt. with picc.),2(2nd alt. with Eng. hn.),2,2 - 4,2,3,1 -
timp.,perc.(3) - str. 9:00 G. Schirmer.

GULBRANSON, Eilif
—— IN MEMORIAM
str. 5:00 Norsk Ntk.
or:
1,1,1,1 - 2,2,1,0 - timp. - str.

—— NORTHWARDS UNDER THE MOUNTAINS ("NORDAN
UNDER FJELLOM")
1,1,1,1 - 2,2,1,0 - timp. - str. 7:00 Norsk Ntk.

GULLIN, Lars
—— JAZZ AMOUR AFFAIR (FOR JAZZ GROUP AND SYMPHONY
ORCH.)
1,*2,1,3 sax.(sopr.,ten.,bar.),1 - 1,mellophone,1,flg.-hn.,1,1 -
timp.,perc. - hp. - pf. - str. 32:00 Fleisher.

GULYÁS, László
—— MUSIC OF SZÉK
cl. - cimbalon - str. 6:20 Bo. Hawkes.

GÜMBEL, Martin
—— CONCERTO FOR ORCH.
2,2,2,2 - 0,0,0,0 - timp.,perc. - pf. - str. 12:00 G. Schirmer.

—— DIVERTIMENTO FOR STRINGS
str. 15:00 G. Schirmer.

GUNAROPULOS, Yrjö
—— ANDANTE RELIGIOSO
str. 6:00 FinnMICtr.

—— BIRD SUITE
1,1,2,0 - 0,2,1,0 - vibra. - org. - str. 8:00 FinnMICtr.

—— CONCERTO FOR PIANO AND ORCH. (1953)
15:00 FinnMICtr.

—— CONCERTO IN D MINOR FOR CELLO AND ORCH. (1942)
24:00 FinnMICtr.

—— CONCERTO NO. 1 IN C MINOR, FOR SAXOPHONE AND
ORCH. (1935)
22:00 FinnMICtr.

—— CONCERTO NO. 2 IN B MAJOR, FOR SAXOPHONE AND
ORCH. (1946)
2,2,2,sax.,2 - 4,2,2,0 - timp. - str. 22:00 FinnMICtr.

—— THE FEBRUARY MANIFESTO (AN OVERTURE) (1963)
2,2,2,1 - 2,2,1,1 - timp.,perc. - hp. - str. 10:00 FinnMICtr.

—— SYMPHONY IN D MAJOR

12:00 FinnMICtr.

GUNDRY, Inglis
—— SYMPHONY (1954)
2,2,2,2 - 4,2,3,0 - timp.,perc. - hp. - str. P.R.S.

GÜRSCHING, Albrecht
—— CONCERTO FOR PIANO AND ORCH.
2,2,2,2 - 1,1,1,0 - perc.(3),xyl. - pf. - str. 16:00 Modern.

—— LUDI (VARIATIONS IRRESPECTUEUSES)
1,2,2,0 - 2,0,0,0 - str. 16:10 Modern.

GUSIKOFF, Michel
—— CONCERTO IN C MAJOR FOR VIOLIN AND ORCH. (1963)
AmerMusEd.

—— CONCERTO NO. 3 FOR VIOLIN AND ORCH.
2(2nd alt. with picc.),2(2nd alt. with Eng. hn.),2,*3 - 3,3,3,0 -
timp.,perc., glock. - hp. - str. 28:00 Composer.

—— FANTASY FOR VIOLA AND ORCH.
2,2,2,2 - 2,2,2,0 - timp. - hp. - str. 13:00 Composer.

GUSIKOFF, Michel - MACHAN, Benjamin
—— AMERICAN CONCERTO (FOR VIOLIN AND ORCHESTRA)
(IN 1 MOVT.)
2(2nd alt. with picc.)*3,*3,4 sax.,2 - 2,2,2,1 - timp.,perc., glock. -
str.   14:00 G. Schirmer.

GUSTAVINO, Carlos
—— TRES ROMANCES ARGENTINOS (FOR LARGO ORCH.)
Southern.

GUTTMAN, Oskar
—— BE-RÊSHIT (IN THE BEGINNING) (CANTATA)
2,2,0,2,2 c.-bn. - 0,2,2,0 - timp. - org. - str.   Transcon.

GUTZEIT, Erich
—— THE OPEN WINDOW (SYMPHONIC IMPRESSION)
10:00 Henmar.

GUY, Barry
—— INCONTRI (FOR CELLO AND ORCH.)
3(3rd alt. with picc.),0,3,0 - 4,3,3,1 - cel.,gong,vibra. - 2 hp. - pf. -
str.   20:00 Novello.

GUYONNET, Jacques
—— SEVEN PORTES DU TEMPS (POUR GRAND ORCHESTRE)
32:00 S.U.I.S.A.
—— SINGLE R (POUR ORCHESTRE DE CHAMBRE ET ALTO
SOLO)
17:00 S.U.I.S.A.
—— DIE WANDLUNG (FÜR GROSSES ORCH.)
28:00 S.U.I.S.A.

GWILT, David
—— ATHLETICS (1967)
2,2,2,2 - 4,3,3,1 - timp.,perc. - str.   15:00 P.R.S.
—— DIALOGUES (1960)
fl.,ob. - str.   15:00 P.R.S.
—— MOVEMENTS FOR BRASS, STRINGS AND PERCUSSION
(1962)
0,0,0,0 - 0,2,3,1 - timp.,perc. - pf. - str.   14:00 P.R.S.
—— VARIATIONS (1956)
str.   14:00 P.R.S.

GYLDMARK, O.
—— VAARBRUD (FESTPRAELUDIUM)
Skand. & Bo.

GYULAI GAÁL, János
—— CONCERTINO FOR PIANO AND ORCH.
2,2,2,2 - 4,2,2,0 - timp.,cel. - hp. - pf. - str.   12:00 Bo. Hawkes.
—— THE SPRING (FOR PIANO AND ORCH.)
3,1,2,1 - 4,3,0,0 - timp. - hp. - pf. - str.   8:00 Bo. Hawkes.

H

HAAPALAINEN, Väinö Ilmari
—— BALLET SCENCES (1963)
1,1,1,1 - 2,1,1,0 - timp.,perc. - pf. - str.   8:00 FinnMICtr.
—— BERTRAND DE BORN (FOR MALE CHORUS AND
ORCH.)(1961) (Text: V. A. Koskenniemi)
1,1,1,1 - 2,2,1,0 - timp.,perc. - str.   15:00 FinnMICtr.
—— BRUMBO AND THE STARS (A MUSICAL FAIRYTALE) (FOR
NARRATOR AND ORCH.)(1957) (Text: Lucie Lundberg)
1,1,2,1 - 2,1,1,0 - timp.,perc. - pf. - str.   25:00 FinnMICtr.
—— CONCERTO NO. 1 IN G MINOR, FOR VIOLIN AND ORCH.
(1944)
2,2,2,2 - 2,2,2,0 - timp.,perc. - str.   20:00 FinnMICtr.
—— CONCERTO NO. 2 IN E MINOR, FOR VIOLIN AND ORCH.
(1954)
2,2,2,2 - 2,2,2,0- timp.,perc. - hp. - str.   25:00 FinnMICtr.
—— COUNTRY SCENES (1944)
2,2,2,2 - 2,2,1,0 - timp.,perc. - str.   12:00 FinnMICtr.
—— FINNISH OVERTURE (1958)
2,2,2,2 - 2,2,2,1 - timp.,perc. - str.   8:00 FinnMICtr.
—— FROM THE LAND OF KALEVA (1957)
2,2,2,2 - 2,2,2,0 - timp.,perc. - str.   7:00 FinnMICtr.
—— INTRODUCTION AND PASSACAGLIA (1964)
2,2,2,2 - 2,2,2,1 - timp.,perc. - str.   15:00 FinnMICtr.
—— LEMMINKÄINEN OVERTURE (1925)
2,2,2,2 - 3,2,3,0 - timp.,perc. - str.   7:00 FinnMICtr.

—— LITTLE LYRICAL SUITE (1954)
1,1,2,1 - 2,1,1,1 - timp.,perc. - str.   8:00 FinnMICtr.
—— LITTLE SUITE FOR ORCH. (1959)
2,2,2,2 - 2,2,2,0 - timp.,perc. - str.   13:00 FinnMICtr.
—— NOCTURNAL VISION (FOR CELLO AND ORCH.) (1930)
2,2,2,1 - 2,2,1,0 - timp.,perc.,cel. - str.   6:00 FinnMICtr.
—— POPULAR SUITE (VARIATIONS) (REV. 1944)
2,2,2,2 - 4,2,3,0 - timp.,perc. - str.   14:00 FinnMICtr.
—— PRELUDIUM (1917)
2,2,2,1 - 4,2,3,0 - timp.,perc. - org. - str.   8:00 FinnMICtr.
—— REPOSAARI (SUITE) (1956)
2,2,2,2 - 2,2,2,0 - timp.,perc. - str.   13:00 FinnMICtr.
—— RHAPSODY SUITE
2,2,4,1 - 4,0,0,0 - timp. - hp. - str.   7:00 FinnMICtr.
—— SIX FINNISH FOLK SONGS (SUITE) (1924)
1,1,1,1 - 1,1,1,0 - pf. - str.   13:00 FinnMICtr.
—— SONG TO LAPLAND (FOR BARITONE, MALE CHORUS AND
ORCH.) (1951)
1,1,1,1 - 2,1,1,1 - timp.,perc. - str.   15:00 FinnMICtr.
—— SPRING'S AWAKENING (1969)
2,1,2,1 - 2,2,1,0 - timp.,perc. - hp. - str.   10:00 FinnMICtr.
—— SUITE FOR CHAMBER ORCH. (1934)
2,2,2,2 - 3,2,3,0 - perc. - pf. - str.   17:00 FinnMICtr.
—— SUITE FOR VIOLA DA GAMBA AND ORCH. (1960)
2,1,2,1 - 2,1,1,0 - timp.,perc. - str.(incl. vla. da gamba)
10:00 FinnMICtr.
—— SYMPHONIC SUITE (1933) (IN 4 MOVTS.)
2,2,2,2 - 3,2,3,0 - perc. - hp. - pf. - str.   19:00 FinnMICtr.
—— SYMPHONY NO. 1 (1948)
2,2,2,2 - 3,2,2,0 - timp.,perc. - str.   25:00 FinnMICtr.
—— SYMPHONY NO. 2 (1953)
2,2,2,2 - 4,3,3,1 - timp.,perc. - hp. - str.   25:00 FinnMICtr.
—— SYMPHONY NO. 3 ("TELJÄ")(1960)
2,2,2,2 - 3,3,2,1 - timp.,perc. - str.   25:00 FinnMICtr.

HAARKLOU, Andreas
—— THE MARRIAGE OF THE KING'S SON ("KONGESØNNENS
BRYLLUP") (FOR MALE CHORUS AND ORCH.) (1936) (Text:
Gunnar Reiss-Andersen)
2,1,1,2 - 2,2,3,0 - timp. - hp. - str.   10:00 T.O.N.O.
—— MOUNTAIN RANGE ("HØIFJELL") (SUITE) (IN 4 MOVTS.)
2,1,2,2 - 2,2,3,0 - timp. - str.   20:00 T.O.N.O.
—— NORWEGIAN SUITE, IN A MINOR (IN 4 MOVTS.)
2,2,2,2 - 2,2,0,0 - timp. - str.   17:00 T.O.N.O.
—— ÕSTRAAT PHANTASY (1936)
1,1,2,2 - 2,2,3,0 - timp. - str.   7:00 T.O.N.O.
—— THREE TONE PICTURES (TRE TONEBILDER) (1959)
2,2,2,2 - 2,2,3,0 - timp. - str.   T.O.N.O.

HAASS, Walter
—— FESTIVE CANTATA (FOR SATB CHORUS AND ORCH.) (Text:
Goethe)
Hans Gerig.

HÁBA, Alois
—— CONCERTO FOR VIOLA AND ORCH., OP. 86
3,3,3,3 - 4,3,3,1 - timp.,perc. - hp. - str.   40:00 Bo. Hawkes.
—— CONCERTO FOR VIOLIN AND ORCH., OP. 83
3,3,3,3 - 4,3,3,1 - timp.,perc. - hp. - str.   30:00 Bo. Hawkes.
—— OVERTURE TO THE OPERA "THE NEW LAND", OP. 47
3,3,4,3 - 4,3,3,1 - timp.,perc.,cel.,xyl. - hp. - pf. - str.
7:00 Bo. Hawkes.
—— WALACHIAN SUITE
3,3,3,3 - 4,3,3,1 - timp.,perc. - hp. - pf. - str. 24:00 Bo. Hawkes.
—— THE WAY OF LIFE (SYMPHONIC FANTASY), OP. 46
3,3,4,3 - 4,3,3,1 - timp.,perc.,cel. - hp. - pf. - str.
29:00 Bo. Hawkes.

HABER, Louis
—— CONCERTO FOR PIANO AND WINDS (1955)
4,*4,*4,*4 - 4,0,0,0 - pf.   18:00 Composer.
—— CONCERTO FOR VIOLIN AND CHAMBER ORCH. (1957)
1,1,1,1 - 2,2,2,0 - timp.,perc.(4),cel.,electric cel., 2 xyl. - pf. - str.
15:00 Composer.
—— CONCERTO FOR VIOLIN AND STRINGS (1956)
str.   15:00 Composer.
—— SONG AND DANCE (SUITE FOR STRINGS) (ON AMERICAN
FOLKSONGS) (1959)
str.   15:00 Arranger.

HABICHT, Günter
—— SINFONIETTA
2,2,2,2 - 0,0,0,0 - timp.,trgl. - str.   11:00 Tetra.

or:
2,2,0,2 - 2,0,0,0 - timp.,trgl. - str.

HADLEY, Henry
—— THE ADMIRAL OF THE SEAS (CANTATA) (FOR TENOR,
CHORUS AND ORCH.)
1,1,2,1 - 2,2,1,0 - timp.,perc. - str.   20:00 Composer.
—— ALMA MATER (OVERTURE)
*3,2,2,2 - 4,3,3,1 - perc. - hp. - str.   8:00 Summy-Bir.
—— CONCERT OVERTURE
*3,2,2,2 - 9,3,3,1 - timp.,perc. - str.   G. Schirmer.
—— CONCERT PIECE FOR CELLO AND ORCH, OP. 61
2,2,2,2 - 4,2,2,b.-trb.(alt with tu.),0 - timp.,perc.,glock. - str.
   G. Schirmer.
—— CONCERTINO FOR PIANO AND ORCH., OP. 131
2,2,2,2 - 4,3,3,1 - timp.,perc. - pf. - str.   12:00 Western.
—— THE CULPRIT FAY (A RHAPSODY), OP. 62
3(3rd alt. with picc.),*3,*3,2 - 4,3,3,1 - timp.,perc. - hp. - str.
   14:00 G. Schirmer.
—— THE ENCHANTED CASTLE (OVERTURE)
2(2nd alt. with picc.),2,2,2,sax.,2 - 4,3,3,1 - timp.,perc. - hp. - str.
   8:00 C. Fischer.
—— HEROD (DRAMATIC OVERTURE)
*3,2,2,2 - 0,2,3,1 - perc. - hp. - str.   C. Fischer.
—— IN BOHEMIA (OVERTURE, OP. 28)
*3,2,2,2 - 4,2,3,1 - timp.,perc., - str.   14:00 G. Schirmer.
—— LUCIFER (TONE POEM), OP. 66
*3,*3,*3,*3 - 4,2,3,1 - perc., cel. - org. - str.   8:00 Composer.
—— MIRTIL IN ARCADIA, OP. 100 (FOR 3 SOPRANOS, TENOR,
BARITONE, BASS, NARRATOR, CHORUS, AND ORCH.)
*4,*3,*3,*3 - 4,3,3,1 - timp.,perc. (5) - hp. - str.   120:00 Composer.
—— THE NIGHTINGALE AND THE ROSE, OP. 54 (FOR WOMENS
CHORUS AND ORCH.)
   G. Schirmer.
—— NORTH, EAST, SOUTH, AND WEST (SYMPHONY NO. 4 IN D
MINOR, OP. 64)
*3,*3,2,2 - 4,2,3,1 - timp.,perc. - hp. - str.   40:00 G. Schirmer.
—— THE OCEAN (A TONE POEM), OP. 99
3,3,3,3 - 4-6,4,3,1 - timp.,perc. - 2 hp. - str.   C. Fischer.
—— OTHELLO (DRAMATIC OVERTURE), OP. 96
*3,2(2nd alt. with Eng. hn.),2,*3 - 4,3,3,1 - timp.,perc. - hp. - str.
   12:00 G. Schirmer.
—— PROPHECY AND FULFILLMENT, OP. 91 (CHRISTMAS
CANTATA) (FOR SOPRANO, ALTO, TENOR, CHORUS, AND
ORCH.)
0,1,0,0 - 3,3,3,0 - timp. - 2 pf.   Flammer.
—— SAN FRANCISCO, OP. 121 (SUITE) (IN 3 MOVTS.)
*3,2,ob. d'amour,*3,2 - 4,3,3,1 - timp.,perc. - hp. - str.
   10:00 AmerMusEd.
—— SCHERZO DIABOLIQUE, OP. 135
*3,*3,*3,*3 - 4,3,3,1 - timp.,perc., xyl. - hp. - str.   6:00 C. Fischer.
—— STREETS OF PEKIN (CHINESE IMPRESSIONS) (IN 7
MOVTS.)
*3,*3,*3,*3 - 4,3,3,1 - timp.,perc., xyl. - hp. - str.   16:00 C. Fischer.
—— SUMMER IDYLL (Completed and Edited by Philip James)
1,1,2,1 - 2,0,0,0 - timp. - hp. - str.   9:45 Presser.
—— SYMPHONIC FANTASIA, OP. 46
3(3rd alt. with picc.) *3,*3,*3 - 4,4,3,1 - timp., - hp. - str.
   11:00 G. Schirmer.
—— SYMPHONY NO. 3 (IN 4 MOVTS.)
*3,2,2,2 - 4,2,3,1 - timp.,perc. - hp. - str.   30:00 C. Fischer.

HAENTJES, Werner
—— CONCERTINO FOR OBOE AND 11 STRINGS
ob. - str.(5,3,2,1)   17:00 Mannheimer.

HAGEMAN, Richard
—— THE CRUCIBLE (FOR 4 SOLOISTS, CHORUS AND ORCH.)
2,*3,2,2 - 4,3,3,1 - timp.,perc. (2) - hp. - str.   55:00 Composer.
—— OVERTURE ("IN A NUTSHELL")
*3,*3,2,2 - 4,3,3,1 - timp.,perc. (3), glock., xyl. - hp. - str.
   5:00 Composer.
—— SUITE MINIATURE (FOR STRINGS)
1. Allegro; 2. Adagio; 3. Presto
str.   12:00 Composer.

HAGEMAN, Richard - CAILLIET, Lucien
—— I HEAR AMERICA CALL (WITH BARITONE OR SATB
CHORUS)
3,3,3,3 - 4,3,3,1 - timp.,perc.,cel. - hp. - str.   11:00 Bo. Hawkes.

HAGEMANN, Philip
—— THE TWO TOWERS OF BABEL (CANTATA) (FOR
BARITONE, MIXED CHORUS AND ORCH.) (Text: Composer)
   20:00 Southern.

HAGERUP BULL, Edvard
—— CASSATION POUR ORCHESTRE DE CHAMBRE (1959) (IN 3
MOVTS.)
1,1,0,0 - 0,1,0,0 - pf. - str.   12:00 T.O.N.O.
—— CONCERTO NO. 1 FOR TRUMPET AND ORCH., OP. 9 (1950)
(IN 3 MOVTS.)
3,2,2,2 - 4,2,3,1 - timp.,perc.,cel. - hp. - pf. - str.   11:00 Billaudot.
—— CONCERTO NO. 2 FOR TRUMPET AND CHAMBER ORCH.
(1960) (IN 3 MOVTS.)
1,1,0,0 - 1,1,0,0 - pf. - str.   12:00 T.O.N.O.
—— CONCERTO POUR TROMBONE ET ORCHESTRE DE
CHAMBRE (1957) (IN 3 MOVTS.)
1,1,0,0 - 0,1,1,0 - pf. - str.   14:00 T.O.N.O.
—— DIALOGUE (1965) (IN 3 MOVTS.)
fl. - pf. - str.   14:00 T.O.N.O.
—— DIVERTIMENTO FOR PIANO AND ORCH. (1954) (IN 3
MOVTS.)
2,1,1,1 - 2,1,1,0 - timp.,perc.,cel. - hp. - pf. - str.   16:00 T.O.N.O.
—— EPILOGUE (HOMMÀGE À LA MÉMOIRE D'UN MONDE
PERDU) (1961) (IN 3 MOVTS.)
str.   13:00 EV.
—— ESCAPADES (SUITE) (1952) (IN 3 MOVTS.)
3,3,2,2 - 4,2,3,1 - timp.,perc.,cel. - hp. - str.   8:00 T.O.N.O.
or:
1,1,0,0 - 0,1,0,0 - pf. - str.
—— MANCHAÜSEN (BALLET SUITE) (1961) (IN 3 MOVTS.)
2,2,2,2 - 4,2,3,1 - timp. - hp. - pf. - str.   15:00 T.O.N.O.
—— MELODIES (2 SONGS FOR SOPRANO AND STRINGS) (1950)
(Text: Gunnar Reiss Andersen)
str.   6:00 T.O.N.O.
—— MORCEAUX RAPSODIQUES (DIVERTISSEMENT) (1950) (IN
3 MOVTS.)
3,2,2,2 - 4,2,3,1 - timp.,perc. - hp. - pf. - str.   10:00 T.O.N.O.
—— PETITE SUITE SYMPHONIQUE (1951) (IN 3 MOVTS.)
1,1,1,1 - 2,1,0,0 - timp.,perc. - hp. - pf. - str.   11:00 EV.
—— SERENADE POUR GRAND ORCHESTRE (1950) (IN 4
MOVTS.)
3,2,2,2 - 4,2,3,1 - timp.,perc. - hp. - pf. - str.   14:00 T.O.N.O.
—— SINFONIA DI TEATRO (PRELUDE SYMPHONIQUE) (1951)
3,3,3,3 - 4,3,3,1 - timp.,perc.,cel. - hp. - pf. - str.   8:00 Billaudot.
—— LE SOLDAT DE PLOMB (THE STEDFAST TIN SOLDIER)
(BALLET SUITE, AFTER HANS CHRISTIAN ANDERSEN'S
STORY) (1949)
3,3,2,3 - 4,2,3,1 - timp.,perc.,cel. - hp. - pf. - str.   15:00 T.O.N.O.
—— SYMPHONY NO. 2 (1958) (IN 4 MOVTS.)
3,3,3,3 - 4,2,3,1 - timp.,perc. - str.   25:00 T.O.N.O.
—— SYMPHONY NO. 3 (SINFONIA ESPRESSIVA) (1964) (IN 4
MOVTS.)
   22:00 T.O.N.O.
—— SYMPHONY NO. 4 (SINFONIA HUMANA) (1968) (IN 4
MOVTS.)
   23:00 T.O.N.O.
—— TROIS MORCEAUX BREFS (FOR ALTO SAXOPHONE AND
ORCH.) (1955)
2,2,2,alto sax.,2 - 2,2,0,0 - timp.,perc.,cel. - hp. - pf. - str.
   12:00 Choudens.
—— TROIS MOUVEMENTS SYMPHONIQUES (SYMPHONY NO. 1)
(1955)
3,3,2,2 - 4,2,3,1 - timp.,perc.,cel. - hp. - pf. - str.   20:00 Choudens.
—— UNDECIM SUMUS (FOR 11 PLAYERS) (1962) (IN 3 MOVTS.)
1,1,1,1 - 1,1,0,0, -perc.(1) - hp. - pf. - 1 c.,1 d.-b.   11:00 T.O.N.O.

HAGERUP BULL, Sverre
—— OVERTURE TO "QUEEN FOR A DAY"
1,1,1,0 - 0,2,1,0 - perc. - pf. - str.   7:00 T.O.N.O.
—— SUITE FROM THE COMIC OPERA "QUEEN FOR A DAY"
(DRONNING FOR EN DAG)
2,1,2,1 - 2,2,1,0 - timp.,perc. - hp. - pf. - str.   16:00 T.O.N.O.
—— TAHOVE (SUITE FROM THE PLAY)
1,1,2,2 - 2,1,0,0 - timp.,perc. - str.   T.O.N.O.

HAHN, Gunnar
—— GOTHIC SUITE
str.   13:30 Nordiska.
—— TILL KIRUNA (FOR SATB CHORUS AND ORCH.)(1968)
1,0,2,1 - 2,2,1,1 - timp. - str.   32:00 Fleisher.

HAHN, Reynaldo
—— LE BAL DE BÉATRICE D'ESTE (SUITE FROM THE BALLET)
2,1,2,2 - 2,1,0,0 - timp.,perc. - 2 hp. - pf. - str.   13:30 Presser.
—— CONCERTO FOR VIOLIN AND ORCH.
2,2,2,2 - 4,2,2,1 - timp.,perc. - hp. - str.   21:00 Presser.
—— CONCERTO IN E MAJOR, FOR PIANO AND ORCH.
2,2,2,2 - 4,2,2,1 - timp.,perc.,glock. - hp. - pf. - str.   31:00 Presser.
—— LA FÊTE CHEZ THÉRÈSE, BALLET SUITE NO. 1 (IN 3 MOVTS.)
4,2,2,1 alto sax.,3 - 4,2 cnt.,2,2,1 - timp.,perc. - 2 hp. - pf. - str.
8:30 Presser.
—— LA FÊTE CHEZ THÉRÈSE, BALLET SUITE NO. 2
4,2,2,1 alto sax.,4 - 4,4,3,0 - timp.,perc.(2) - 2 hp. - pf. - str.
14:20 Presser.
—— THE MERCHANT OF VENICE: INTERLUDE FROM ACT II
3,3,2,1 alto sax.,2 - 4,0,0,0 - timp.,perc.,vibra. - hp. - str.
4:00 Presser.
—— THE MERCHANT OF VENICE: NOCTURNE FROM ACT III
2,2,2,1 alto sax.,2 - 4,2,4,0 - hp. - str.   2:30 Presser.
—— THE MERCHANT OF VENICE (1935) (3-ACT OPERA) %
2,2,2,1 alto sax.,1 - 3,2,2,1 - timp.,perc. - hp. - str.   80:00 Presser.
—— OVERTURE TO "MOZART" (1925)
2,1,1,1 - 2,1,0,0 - pf. - str.   5:00 Presser.

HAHN, Reynaldo - POLLAIN, Fernand
—— CONCERTO INACHEVÉ (FOR CELLO AND ORCH.)
2,2,2,2 - 2,2,0,0 - str.   Salabert.

HAIEFF, Alexei
—— BALLET IN E (IN 3 MOVTS.)
*3,2,2,2 - 4,2,3,1(or c.-bn) - timp.,perc. (2) - str.   22:00 Chappell.
—— BEAUTY AND THE BEAST (BALLET SUITE)
*3,2,2,2 - 4,2,2,0 - timp.,perc. - str.   19:00 Composer.
—— CONCERTO FOR PIANO AND ORCH.
*3,2,2,2 - 4,2,2,0 - timp.,perc. - pf. - str.   22:00 General.
—— CONCERTO FOR PIANO AND SMALL ORCH.
1,2,*1,1 - 4,2,2,0 - timp.,perc. - str.   14:00 General.
—— CONCERTO FOR VIOLIN AND ORCH. (IN 1 MOVT.)
2(2nd alt. with picc.),2,2,2 - 2,2,1,0 - timp.,perc.(2) - str.
16:00 Composer.
—— CONCERTO NO. 1 FOR PIANO AND ORCH.
1. Moderato; 2. Vivace; 3. Lento-Allegro
*3,2,2,2 - 4,2,2,0 - timp.,perc (2) - pf. - str.   24:30 Bo. Hawkes.
—— DIVERTIMENTO (IN 5 MOVTS.)
1(alt. with picc.),1(alt. with Eng. hn.),1,0 - 0,2,2,0 - str.
12:00 Bo. Hawkes.
—— ECLOGUE: LA NOUVELLE HELOÏSE
hp. - str.   12:00 Chappell.
—— SYMPHONY NO. 1 (IN 3 MOVTS.)
*3,*3,*3,3 - 4,2,3,1 - timp. - pf. - str.   25:00 Composer.
—— SYMPHONY NO. 2
2(2nd alt. with picc.),2,2,2 - 4,2,0,0 - timp. - perc. - hp., - str.
21:00 Chappell.
—— SYMPHONY NO. 3
3,2,2,2 - 4,2,3,1 - timp. - hp. - str.   22:00 Chappell.

HAINES, Edmund
—— CONCERTINO FOR SEVEN SOLO INSTRUMENTS AND ORCH. (IN 4 MOVTS.)
3(1 alt. with picc.),2,3,2 - 4,3,3,0 - timp.,perc.(3),xyl - str.
20:00 AmerMusEd.
—— CORONACH
3 tpt.,3 trb. - timp. - str.   9:00 Composer.
—— INFORMAL OVERTURE
2(1 alt. with picc.),2,2,*3 - 4,3,3,1 - timp.,perc. - pf. - str.
7:00 C. Fischer.
—— INTERLUDE FOR STRINGS
str.   6:00 Composer.
—— LANDSCAPE
2,2,2,2 - 2,2,0,0 - timp. - str.   8:00 Composer.
—— RONDINO AND VARIATIONS
2(2nd alt. with picc.),2(2nd alt. with Eng. hn.),2,2, - 4,2,3,0 - timp.,perc. - pf. - str.   15:00 C. Fischer.
—— SCENARIO FOR ORCHESTRA (1966)
*3,2(2nd alt. with Eng. hn.),2,2 - 4,3,3,1 - timp.,perc.(3),cel.xyl. - str.   16:00 Composer.
—— SYMPHONY IN MINIATURE
2,1,2,1 - 2,2,0,0 - str.   10:00 Composer.
—— SYMPHONY NO. 1
2(1 alt. with picc.)2(1 alt. with Eng.hn.),2,2 - 4,3,3,0 - timp.,perc.(2),glock. - str.   21:00 Composer.

—— THREE DANCES FOR ORCHESTRA
2(1 alt. with pic.,),2(1 alt. with Eng. hn.),2,2 - 4,3,3,0 - timp.,perc., xyl - hp. - str.   10:30 C. Fischer.
—— VARIATIONS ON A DORIAN THEME
*3,*3,2,2 - 4,2,3,0 - timp.,perc.,glock. - hp. - str.   12:00 Composer.

HAJDU, Andras
—— GIPSY CANTATA (FOR TENOR, CONTRALTO, MIXED CHORUS AND ORCH.)
3,3,3,3 - 4,3,3,1 - perc. - str.   29:00 Bo. Hawkes.

HAJDU, Mihály
—— CAPRICCIO ALL'ONGARESE (FOR CLARINET AND ORCH.)
*2,2,3,2 - 2,2,0,0 - timp.,perc. - str.   9:00 Bo. Hawkes.

HÅKANSON, Knut
—— CONCERT OVERTURE IN C MAJOR, OP. 10
2,2,2,2 - 2,4,3,1 - timp. - str.   8:00 S.T.I.M.
or:
2,2,2,2 - 2,2,3,1 - timp. - str.
—— DIVERTIMENTO IN C MAJOR, OP. 31
2,2,2,2 - 2,2,0,0 - timp.,perc. - str.   10:00 S.T.I.M.
—— FRÅN HEMBYGDEN, OP. 13
2,2,2,2 - 2,2,3,0 - timp.,perc. - str.   16:00 S.T.I.M.
—— FRÅN KULLABERG, OP. 14
3,2,3,2 - 4,3,0,0 - timp.,perc. - str.   15:00 S.T.I.M.
—— MÄRBOLATAR
2,2,2,2 - 2,2,2,0 - timp.,perc. - str.   14:00 S.T.I.M.
—— SERENADE DRAMATIQUE, OP. 2 (FOR VIOLIN AND ORCH.)
2,2,2,2 - 4,2,2,0 - timp. - str.   10:00 S.T.I.M.
or:
2,1,2,2 - 4,0,0,0 - timp. - str.
—— SERENADE FOR STRINGS, OP. 15
str.   15:00 S.T.I.M.
—— SUITE FROM THE BALLET "MYLITTA", OP. 6
2,2,2,2 - 4,2,3,1 - timp.,perc. - hp. - str.   18:00 S.T.I.M.
—— SWEDISH SUITE NO. 1
2,2,2,2 - 2,2,3,0 - timp. - str.   18:00 Nordiska.
—— SWEDISH SUITE NO. 2, OP. 27
2,2,2,2 - 2,2,0,0 - timp.,perc. - str.   15:00 S.T.I.M.

HALA, Kamil
—— INTENSITY
8:03 Modern.
—— JAZZ SUITE ("GEFÜHLE") (FOR SYMPHONIC JAZZ ORCH.)
0,0,0,5 sax.(2 alto, 2 ten.,bar.),0 - 0,4,4,0 - perc. - pf. - str.(incl. 1 solo d.-b.)   6:00 Modern.

HALASZ, Kalman
—— CONCERTINO FOR STRINGS
str.   16:00 Bo. Hawkes.
—— SUITE
2,2,2,2 - 4,2,0,0 - cymb. - str.   Bo. Hawkes.

HALE, Vernon
—— CONCERTO FOR TRUMPET, TROMBONE, PIANO AND STRINGS (1967)
tpt.,trb. - pf. - str.   9:00 P.R.S.
—— DEUS (1967)
3,3,3,3 - 4,3,3,1 - timp.,perc.(6),cel. - 2 hp. - pf. - str.   9:00 P.R.S.
—— SUITE FOR ORCH. (1967)
0,0,0,0 - 0,3,3,1 - timp.,perc.(6),cel. - org. - pf. - str.   6:00 P.R.S.
—— VISION
str.   12:00 P.R.S.

HALETZKI, Paul
—— BLAUE SYMPHONIE
3,3,3,3 - 6,4,5,0 - timp.,perc. - hp. - str.   18:00 Riccardo.
—— FANTASY FOR PIANO AND SMALL ORCH.
0,1,2(2nd alt. with b.-cl.),1 - 2,0,0,0 - perc. - guit. - hp. - pf.
6:00 Modern.
—— HARFENSPIEL
cel.,glock. - hp. - str.   6:00 Modern.
—— SCHERZO FANTASTICO
3(3rd alt. with picc.),2,2(2nd alt. with b.-cl.),2 - 4,2,3,0 - timp.,perc. - hp. - pf. - str.   5:00 Modern.
—— SERENADE PASTOURELLE
1,1,2,2 - 0,0,0,0 - cel. - hp. - str.   14:40 Riccardo.

HALFFTER, Rodolfo
—— CONCERTO FOR VIOLIN AND ORCH.
2,2,2,2 - 4,2,3,1 - timp.,perc. - str.   18:00 Presser.

—— THREE PIECES FOR STRINGS
  str.   Presser.

HALL, Arthur E.
—— MO 2475 (OVERTURE) (1973)
  2,2,0,2 - 2,0,0,0 - str.   12:00 Composer.
—— MOBILES (IMPRESSIONS AT A CALDER EXHIBITION)
  1,1,2,1 - 2,0,0,0 - str.   10:00 Composer.
—— OVERTURE '72 (FOR CHAMBER ORCH.) (1972)
  pf. - 2,0,0,0 - str.   6:15 Composer.
—— SEVEN PRELUDES TO THE NATIVITY (FOR MIXED
  CHORUS AND ORCH.)
  2,2,2,1 - 2,2,2,0 - timp.,perc.(2) - str.   35:00 Composer.
—— THE SOUNDS OF CHRISTMAS (FOR SATB AND ORCH.)
  (1968)
  2(1 alt. with picc.),*3,*3,*3 - 4,3,3,1 - timp.,perc., bells,cel - hp. -
  str.(20,6,8,6)   36:00 Arranger.
—— THEME AND VARIATIONS FOR STRINGS
  str.   8:00 Composer.
—— THE WEEK (SUITE) (1969)
  2,2,0,2 - 2,0,0,0 - str.   21:55 Composer.

HALL, Charles J.
—— THE CITY IN THE SEA (AFTER THE POEM OF EDGAR
  ALLEN POE) (1970) (IN 3 MOVTS.)
  4(2 alt. with picc.),3(3rd alt. with Eng.hn.),*1,*3 - 4,4,4,2 -
  timp.,perc.(4) - hp.- str.   Composer.
—— FIVE MICROSCOPICS (FOR LARGE ORCH.) (1969)
  *3,*3,*3,*3 - 4,3,3,1 - timp.,perc.(4),glock.,mar.,vibra.,xyl. - 2 hp. -
  str.   12:00 Composer.
—— RECITATIVE FOR ORCHESTRA (1966)
  2,*3,*3,*3 - 4,3,3,0 - timp.,perc.(2) - str. 6:00 Composer.
—— SCHERZO, JUST FOR FUN (1950)
  *3,2,2,2 - 4,3,3,1 - timp. - str.   7:00 Composer.
—— SINFONIETTA FOR SOLO VIOLA AND ORCH. (1970)
  2,2(2nd alt. with Eng.hn.),2(2nd alt. with b.-cl.),2 - 2,2,2,0 -
  timp.,perc.(2),glock.,vibra. - str.   18:00 Composer.
—— ULALUME (FOR NARRATOR, OFFSTAGE MEZZO-SOPRANO
  AND ORCH.) (1968) (Text: Edgar Allen Poe)
  2,0,*3,*2 - 2,0,2,0 - perc.(2),mar.,vibra - hp. - pf. - str.
                                              12:00 Mills.

HALL, John
—— CONCERTO FOR ORGAN AND ORCH.
  0,0,0,0 - 4,4,3,1 - timp. - org. - str.   22:00 P.R.S.
—— SUITE NO. 1 FOR SMALL ORCH.
  2,1,2,1 - 2,2,2,1 - timp.,perc. - hp. - str. 12:00 P.R.S.
—— VARIATIONS FOR ORCH.
  3,2,2,2 - 4,3,3,1 - timp.,perc. - hp. - pf. - str. 16:00 P.R.S.

HALL, Pauline
—— THE MARQUISE (MARKISEN) (BALLET) %
  3,2,3,2 - 4,2,3,1 - timp.,perc. - hp. - str. 20:00 T.O.N.O.
—— THE PRETENDERS (KONGSEMNERNE) (FROM THE
  INCIDENTAL MUSIC TO IBSEN'S DRAMA)
  2,1,2,1 - 2,2,2,0 - timp.,perc. - str.   10:00 T.O.N.O.
—— SUITE FROM MUSIC TO THE PLAY "JULIUS CAESAR" (IN 4
  MOVTS.)
  3,2,2,2 - 4,2,3,1 - timp.,perc. - hp. - str. 10:00 T.O.N.O.
—— THREE SONGS FOR SOPRANO AND CHAMBER ORCH.
  (1957) (Text: Edgar Lee Masters)
  1,1,1,1 - 1,1,0,0, - timp.,perc. - hp. - str. 12:00 T.O.N.O.
—— VERLAINE SUITE (IN 4 MOVTS.)
  3,2,2,2 - 4,2,3,1 - timp.,perc.,cel. - hp. - pf. - str. 23:00 T.O.N.O.

HALL, Reginald
—— ELEGY FOR ORCHESTRA
  2(2nd alt. with picc.),2(2nd alt. with Eng.hn.),2,2 - 4,2,3,1 -
  timp.,perc.(2) - hp. - str.   Chappell.

HALLASTE, Urho
—— LYRICAL SUITE (FOR ENGLISH HORN AND
  STRINGS)(1962)(IN 3 MOVTS.)
  Eng.hn. - str.   14:00 FinnMICtr.
—— PARTITA (1966)
  str.   14:00 FinnMICtr.
—— TEMA CON VARIAZIONI (FOR BASSOON AND ORCH.)
  (1955)
  2,1,1,1 - 1,0,0,0 - timp.,perc. - str.   9.00 FinnMICtr.
—— THREE SCENES (FOR OBOE AND ORCH.)(1951)
  1,2,0,1 - 1,2,0,0 - timp.,perc. - hp. - str. 15:00 FinnMICtr.

HALLBERG, Bengt
—— BEAT RONDO (FOR 6 JAZZ SOLOISTS AND SYMPHONY
  ORCH.)(1971)
  2,2,2,2 - 2,2,1,0 - perc. - str.   16:00 Fleisher.
—— ICELANDIC SOUVENIR (TONE POEM)(FOR JAZZ GROUP
  AND SYMPHONY ORCH.)(1971)
  2,2,2,2 - 2,2,1,0 - timp.,perc. - str.   12:00 Fleisher.
—— LITTLE PROMENADE CONCERTO (FOR PIANO AND
  STRING ORCH.)
  pf. - str.   18:00 Fleisher.
—— LYRIC BALLAD (FOR TWO PIANOS AND ORCH.)(1968)
  2,2,2,2 - 2,2,1,0 - timp.,perc. - hp. - 2 pf. - str. 20:00 Fleisher.
—— MUSIC FOR JAZZ GROUP AND SYMPHONY ORCH. (1969)
  2,2,2,2 sax.,2 - 2,3,1,0 - timp.,perc. - guit. - pf. - str.
                                              30:00 Fleisher.

HALLBERG, Björn Wilho
—— ASPIRATION (1971)
  4,4,4,4 - 5,4,4,1 - str.   14:00 Nordiska.
—— DIE DROHUNG (BALLET) % (1973)
  1,1,3,1 - 1,1,1,1 - perc.(2) - electric guit. - electric d.-b.
                                              30:00 S.T.I.M.
—— ETUDE I
  timp.,perc.,bells(3 sets),cel.,2 mar.,2 vibra.,xyl. - 2 hp. - pf.
                                              10:00 S.T.I.M.
—— ETUDE II
  2,2,2,1 - 1,1,0,0 - hp. - str.(2,1,1,0)   8:00 S.T.I.M.
—— MISSA PRO DEFUNCTIS (FOR SOPRANO, MIXED CHORUS
  AND LARGE ORCH.) (Text: Dag Hammarskjöld)
  4,4,4,4 - 5,5,3,3 - timp.,perc.(9),bells(3 sets),2 mar.,2 vibra.,xyl. -
  tape-recorder - 2 hp. - pf. - str.(26,12,10,7) 50:00 S.T.I.M.
—— NOVELLETTEN (1973)
  1,1,2,1 - 1,1,1,0 - str.   17:00 G. Schirmer.

HALLE, Adam de la - BUCCHI, Valentino
—— LI GIEUS DE ROBIN ET DE MARION (1-ACT OPERA) %
  3,2,0,2 - 0,2,0,0 - perc.,bells,xyl. - hp. - str.(no vlns.) Leeds.

HALLER, Hermann
—— BALLADE FÜR HORN UND STREICHORCHESTER, OP. 38A
  Hn - str.   8:00 Henmar.
—— CONCERTINO IN E FOR STRINGS (IN 3 MOVTS.)
  str.   14:00 Henmar.
—— CONCERTO FOR ORGAN AND STRING ORCH. (IN 3
  MOVTS.)
  org. - str.   21:00 Henmar.
—— CONCERTO FOR STRINGS (CONCERTO PER ARCHI) (IN 3
  MOVTS.)
  str.   Sirius.
—— CONCERTO NO. 1 FOR PIANO AND ORCH. (IN 3 MOVTS.)
  2,2,2,2 - 2,2,2,2 - timp.,perc. - pf. - str. 23:00 Henmar.
—— CONCERTO NO. 2 FOR PIANO, WITH STRING ORCH. (IN 3
  MOVTS.)
  pf. - str.   19:00 Henmar.
—— DOUBLE CONCERTO FOR FLUTE, CLARINET AND STRING
  ORCH. (IN 3 MOVTS.)
  1,0,1,0 - 0,0,0,0 - str.   17:00 Henmar.
—— FIVE LIEDER ON POEMS OF HÖLDERLIN (FOR ALTO OR
  BARITONE AND ORCH.)
  2,2,2,2 - 2,2,3,0 - timp. - str.   17:00 Sirius.
—— PER LA CAMERATA, OP. 47 (FÜR 16 STREICHER)
  str.   11:00 Henmar.
—— PROLOG FÜR ORCHESTER, OP. 41
  2,2,2,1 - 2,2,0,0 - timp.,perc. - str.   8:00 Henmar.
—— SINFONIE, OP. 40 (Nach Gemälden von Max Gubler)
  2,2,2,2 - 2,2,3,0 - timp.,perc. - str.   23:00 Henmar.
—— SONATA CONCERTANTE FOR CHAMBER ORCH.
  3,1,1,0 - 0,0,0,0 - str.   12:30 Henmar.
  or:
  fl. - str.
—— SYMPHONY (AFTER PAINTINGS OF MAX GUBLER) (IN 5
  MOVTS.)
  2,2,2,2 - 2,2,3,0 - timp.,perc. - hp. - str. 24:00 Henmar.

HALLNÄS, Hilding
—— CANTICA LYRICA (1958) (FOR TENOR, MIXED CHORUS
  AND ORCH.) (Text: Horatius)
  2,2,2,2 - 2,2,2,0 - timp.,perc.(3),vibra. - hp. - str.(no vln.)
                                              15:00 S.T.I.M.
—— CONCERTO FOR FLUTE, STRINGS, TIMPANI AND
  PERCUSSION (1958)
  fl. - timp.,perc. - str.   17:00 S.T.I.M.

—— CONCERTO FOR PIANO AND ORCH. (1956)
2,2,2,2 - 2,2,3,0 - timp.,perc.(3) - pf. - str.   19:30 S.T.I.M.
—— CONCERTO FOR STRINGS, TIMPANI AND PERCUSSION
(1959)
timp.,perc. - str.   14:00 S.T.I.M.
—— CONCERTO FOR VIOLIN AND ORCH., OP. 24
2,2,2,2 - 2,2,0,0 - timp.,perc. - hp. - str.   25:00 S.T.I.M.
—— CONCERTO NO. 2 FOR VIOLIN AND ORCH. (1965)
2,2,2,2 - 2,2,2,1 - timp.,perc.(2) - str.   16:00 S.T.I.M.
—— A GREEK TALE (1968)
2,2,2,2 - 2,2,2,0 - timp.,perc.(2) - str.   15:00 S.T.I.M.
—— HORISONT OCH LINJESPEL (1969)
str.   11:00 S.T.I.M.
—— INTRODUCTION TO TWO DANCES (FROM THE BALLET
"IPHIGENIA")(1970)
2,2,2,2 - 2,2,2,1 - timp.,perc. - str.   10:00 Fleisher.
—— INVOCATION (FOR SATB CHORUS AND STRING
ORCH.)(1971)
str.   8:30 Fleisher.
—— LITTLE SYMPHONY FOR STRINGS, OP. 31
str.   20:00 S.T.I.M.
—— METAMORFOSI SINFONICHE IN TRE PARTE (SYMPHONY
NO. 4) (REV. 1960)
3,3,3,3 - 4,3,4,2 - timp. - str.   18:30 S.T.I.M.
—— MOMENTI BUCOLICHI (1969)
ob. - perc. - str.   15:00 S.T.I.M.
—— PASTORALE AND SCHERZO
2,2,2,2 - 2,2,2,0 - timp.,perc.(3) - str.   5:00 Fleisher.
—— A QUITE SMALL SYMPHONY (1973)
2,2,2,2 - 2,2,2,0 - timp.,perc. - str.   11:00 Fleisher.
—— SINFONIA NOTTURNA, OP. 26
3,2,2,2 - 4,3,3,1 - timp.,perc.(2) - str.   26:00 S.T.I.M.
—— SINFONIETTA PASTORALE, OP. 23
2,2,2,2 - 2,2,2,0 - timp. - str.   24:00 S.T.I.M.
—— SYMPHONIC BALLET SUITE (1957)
2,2,2,2 - 2,2,0,0 - timp.,perc.(2) - pf.(ad lib.) - str.   21:00 S.T.I.M.
—— SYMPHONIC METAMORPHOSIS
3,3,3,3 - 4,3,3,1 - timp.,perc.(2) - hp. - str.   15:00 S.T.I.M.
—— SYMPHONIC SUITE FOR STRINGS, OP. 12
str.   16:00 S.T.I.M.
—— SYMPHONY NO. 6 (1966)
perc. - str.   17:00 S.T.I.M.
—— TRIPLE CONCERTO (FOR VIOLIN, CLARINET, PIANO AND
ORCH.)(1973)
2,2,3,2 - 4,2,3,0 - timp.,perc. - pf. - str.   24:00 Fleisher.

HALLNÄS, Lars
—— CHORALE (1970)
2,2,2,2 - 2,3,2,0 - str.   8:00 Fleisher.
—— FROM "SERMONES DE TEMPORE" (FOR SOPRANO AND
STRING ORCH.)(1970)
str.   8:00 Fleisher.

HAMANN, Bernhard
—— CONCERTO FOR CELLO AND ORCH., OP. 5
2(2nd alt. with picc.),2,2,*3 - 4,3,2,1 - timp.,perc. - str.
40:00 Henmar.
—— RONDO CAPRICCIOSO, OP. 2 (FOR VIOLIN AND ORCH.)
1,2,2,2 - 3,0,0,0 - str.   10:00 Henmar.

HAMBRAEUS, Bengt
—— EXPERIMENT X (1969)
2,2,0,0 - 2,2,0,2 - perc.(3) - tape-recorder - hp. - str. 2:30 S.T.I.M.
—— INVOCATION (FOR WINDS AND PERCUSSION)(1971)
0,2,00 - 5,4,3,2 - perc.(3)   7:30 Fleisher.
—— PIANISSIMO IN DUE TEMPI (FOR 20 STRINGS)(1972)
str.   14:00 Fleisher.
—— RENCONTRES (1971)
4,4,4,4 - 6,4,4,0 - timp.,perc.(5) - hp. - str.   23:00 G. Schirmer.
—— ROTA (FOR 3 ORCHESTRAS) (WITH OPTIONAL TAPE)
(1962)
3,3,3,3 - 5,5,5,0 - perc.(1) - tape-recorder(opt.) - 2 hp. - str.
20:00 S.T.I.M.
—— TRANSFIGURATION (1963)
3,3,3,3 - 3,4,3,1 - timp.,perc.(4) - hp - str.   15:00 G. Schirmer.

HAMBURG, Grigory
—— SUITE
3,2,2,2 - 4,2,3,1 - timp.,perc., cel. - hp. - str.   19:00 G. Schirmer.

HAMERIK, Ebbe
—— UN CANTUS FIRMUS (SINFONIA MOLTO BREVE)
2,2,3(1 alt. with B♭sax.),2 - 4,2,3,1 - timp. - hp. - str.
12:00 G. Schirmer.
—— VARIATIONS FOR ORCH. (ON AN OLD DANISH
FOLKTUNE)
3,3,3 alto sax.,3 - 4,3,3,1 - timp.,perc.,xyl. - banjo - hp. - pf. - str.
20:00 Henmar.

HAMILTON, Iain
—— ALASTOR
3,3,3,3 - 4,3,3,1 - timp.,perc. - 2 hp. - pf. - str.   20:00 Presser.
—— AMPHONION (CONCERTO NO. 2 FOR VIOLIN AND
ORCHESTRA)
2,2,2,2 - 4,2,2,0 - perc. - pf. - str.   25:00 Presser.
—— AURORA
3,3,3,3 - 4,3,3,1 - timp.,perc. - hp. - str.   12:00 Presser.
—— CIRCUS (FOR 2 TRUMPETS AND ORCH.)
2,2,2,2 - 4,2,3,1 - timp.,perc. - guit. - hp. - str.   20:00 Presser.
—— COMMEDIA (CONCERTO FOR ORCHESTRA)
3,3,3,3 - 4,3,3,1 - timp.,perc. - hp. - pf. - str.   25:00 Presser.
—— CONCERTO FOR PIANO AND ORCHESTRA (1967 VERSION)
2,2,2,2 - 4,2,3,1 - timp.,perc.,mar. - hp. - pf. - str. 20:00 Presser.
—— PHARSALIA (DRAMATIC COMMENTARY FOR VOICES,
NARRATOR AND ORCH.)
1,0,1,0 - 1,1,1,0 - perc. - hp. - pf. - str.   25:00 Presser.
—— SINFONIA CONCERTANTE (FOR VIOLIN, VIOLA AND
CHAMBER ORCH.)
1,1,1,0 - 2,1,1,0 - hp. - str.   Presser.
—— VOYAGE (FOR HORN AND CHAMBER ORCH.)
1,1,1,0 - 1,2,1,0 - perc. - pf. - str.(single or multiple)
18:00 Presser.

HAMMERSCHLAG, Walter
—— VORSPIEL ZU EINER KOMÖDIE
2,2,2,2 - 4,2,0,0 - timp.,perc. - str.   Riccardo.

HANDEL, Darrell
—— CHAMBER SUITE FOR ORCHESTRA (1965) (IN 3 MOVTS.)
*3,*3,*3,2 - 4,2,3,1 - timp.,perc.,xyl. - hp. - str. 13:00 Fleisher.
—— LAMENT FOR A LOST PRAIRIE (FOR HARP AND ORCH.)
(1970)
*3,*3,*3,2 - 4,3,3,1 - timp.,perc. - 1-2 hp.   6:00 Composer.
—— LOW COUNTRY HAUNTINGS (FOR 4 SOLO VOICES AND
ORCH.) (1975) (Text: Lynn Handel)
2,2,*3,*3 - 5,3,3,1 - timp.,perc.(4),bells,cel.,vibra. - guit. - hp. - pf.
- str.   20:00 Composer.

HANDEL, Georg Frideric - BAINES, Anthony - MACKERRAS, Charles
—— THE MUSIC FOR THE ROYAL FIREWORKS
22:00 Oxford.
—— SUITE FROM "THE WATER MUSIC"
2,2,2,2 - 2,2,3,0 - timp.,perc. - str.   22:00 Oxford.

HANDEL, Georg Frideric - BALES, Richard
—— OVERTURE IN D MINOR (SINFONIA FROM THE 10TH
CHANDOS ANTHEM)
str.   5:00 Arranger.
—— OVERTURE IN G MINOR (SINFONIA FROM THE 9TH
CHANDOS ANTHEM "THE LORD IS MY LIGHT")
str.   4:00 Arranger.
—— SARABANDE AND BOURRÉE
1,1,1,1 - 1,0,0,0 - str.   5:00 Arranger.

HANDEL, Georg Frideric - BANTOCK, Granville
—— OVERTURE FROM "PTOLOMY"
pf.(ad lib.) - str.   6:00 Mills.

HANDEL, Georg Frideric - BARBIROLLI, John
—— CONCERTO FOR CLARINET AND STRINGS
cl. - str.   12:00 Oxford.
—— CONCERTO FOR VIOLA AND STRINGS
str.   15:00 Oxford.

HANDEL, Georg Frideric - BAZELAIRE, P.
—— CONCERTO IN C FOR CELLO AND STRINGS
str.   13:00 Baron.

HANDEL, Georg Frideric - BECKETT, Wheeler
—— LARGO, FROM "XERXES" (ARR. 1967)
2,2,2,2 - 2,0,0,0 - str.   5:30 Arranger.

HANDEL, Georg Frideric - BEECHAM, Thomas
—— AMARYLLIS: SUITE
    2,2,2,2 - 2,2,0,0 - timp. - str.   13:30 Bo. Hawkes.
—— THE FAITHFUL SHEPARD: SUITE (IN 7 MOVTS.)
    2,2,2,2 - 4,2,0,0 - timp.perc. - str.   24:00 Bo. Hawkes.
—— THE GODS GO A-BEGGING (BALLET SUITE)
    2,2,2,2 - 4,2,0,0 - timp.,hp. - str.   21:00 Chappell.
—— THE GREAT ELOPEMENT: SUITE NO. 1
        17:00 P.R.S.
—— THE GREAT ELOPEMENT: SUITE NO. 2
        16:00 P.R.S.

HANDEL, Georg Frideric - BENOY, A. W.
—— CONCERTINO FOR TRUMPET AND STRINGS
    tpt. - pf.(ad lib.) - str.   Oxford.

HANDEL, Georg Frideric - BEST, W. T.
—— CONCERTO NO. 4 IN F, FOR ORGAN AND ORCH.
    2 ob. - org. - str.   Galaxy.
—— CONCERTO NO. 9 IN B FLAT, FOR ORGAN AND ORCH.
        Galaxy.

HANDEL, Georg Frideric - BROWN, James
—— SINFONIETTA IN A
    str.   Galaxy.
—— SUITE OF FIVE PIECES
    str.   Galaxy.
—— TWO OVERTURES ("MESSIAH" AND "SOLOMON")
    Str   Galaxy.

HANDEL, Georg Frideric - CARSE, Adam
—— OVERTURE TO "ESTHER"
    2 ob., 2 bn. - str.   5:00 Galaxy.

HANDEL, Georg Frideric - COLLINS, A.
—— OVERTURE TO "ALEXANDER SEVERUS"
    str.   8:00 Mills.
—— OVERTURE TO "PARNASSO IN FESTA"
    str.   8:00 Robbins.
—— OVERTURE TO "PHARAMOND"
    str.   8:00 Mills.

HANDEL, Georg Frideric - DALLEY, Orien
—— THE ROYAL FIREWORKS SUITE
    2,2,2,2 - 4,2,3,0 - timp. - str.   Fema.

HANDEL, Georg Frideric - DASCH, George
—— GRAND CONCERTO IN B FLAT MAJOR (CONCERTO GROSSO)
    2,2,2,2 - 1,1,1,0 - timp. - pf. - str.   11:00 Presser.

HANDEL, Georg Frideric - DIACK, Michael
—— PASTORAL CANTATA (FOR SA CHORUS AND STRS.)
    str.   40:00 C. Fischer.
—— ST. JOHN PASSION (FOR TWO SOPRANOS, ALTO, TENOR, TWO BARITONES, SATB CHORUS AND STRS.)
    str.   60:00 C. Fischer.
—— SAMSON (ORATORIO)
    1,1,0,1 - 2,1,0,0 - timp. - str.(no c.)   60:00 C. Fischer.
—— SAUL (ORATORIO) (Revised and Abridged)
    2,1,0,1 - 0,4,0,0 - pf. - str.   60:00 C. Fischer.
—— SOLOMON (ORATORIO) (REVISED AND ABRIDGED) (FOR TWO SOPRANOS, BARITONE, BASS, SATB CHORUS AND ORCH.)
    2,1,0,1 - 0,2,0,0 - str.   60:00 C. Fischer.

HANDEL, Georg Frideric - ELGAR, Edward
—— OVERTURE IN D MINOR
    3,3,3,3 - 4,3,3,1 - timp.,perc. - org.(ad lib.) - str.   Novello.

HANDEL, Georg Frideric - FISCHOFF, W.
—— SUITE
        Bo. Hawkes.

HANDEL, Georg Frideric - FROTSCHER
—— OVERTURE AND SUITE FROM THE OPERA "RODRIGO"
    2 ob. - str.   F. Colombo.

HANDEL, Georg Frideric - FROTSCHER, Gotthold
—— OVERTURE AND DANCES FROM THE OPERA "ALMIRA"
    0,2,0,1 - 0,0,0,0 - cemb. - str.   17:00 Henmar.
    or:
    cemb. - str.

HANDEL, Georg Frideric - GEORGE, Thom Ritter
—— THREE SONGS (FOR VOICE AND STRING ORCH.)
    str.   9:00 Arranger.

HANDEL, Georg Frideric - GOLDSBROUGH, Arnold
—— ACIS AND GALATEA (FOR FEMALE VOICES AND STRINGS) %
    pf. - str.   50:00 Oxford.
—— AN AUTUMN DAY (FOR CHORUS OF UPPER VOICES AND STRINGS) (Text: Christopher Hassall)
    Descant recorders (opt.) - pf. - str.   30:00 Oxford.

HANDEL, Georg Frideric - GRANDJANY, Marcel
—— CONCERTO IN B♭, FOR HARP AND ORCH.
        14:00 EV.

HANDEL, Georg Frideric - GUSIKOFF, Michel
—— SONATA IN D MAJOR, FOR VIOLIN AND CHAMBER ORCH.
    fl. - str.   12:00 Arranger.
—— SONATA NO. 4 (FOR VIOLIN AND STRINGS)
    str.   12:00 C. Fischer.

HANDEL, Georg Frideric - HARTY, Hamilton
—— POLONAISE, ARIETTA AND PASSACAGLIA
    3,2,2,2, c.-b. (ad lib.) - 2,3,0,0 - timp. - str.   12:00 Bo. Hawkes.
—— SUITE FROM "THE ROYAL FIREWORKS MUSIC" (IN 4 MOVTS.)
    0,2,0,2 - 4,3,0,0 - timp.,perc. - str.   14:00 Chappell.
—— SUITE FROM "THE WATER MUSIC" (IN 6 MOVTS.)
    2(2nd alt. with picc.),2,2,2, - 4,2,0,0 - timp. - str.   16:00 Chappell.

HANDEL, Georg Frideric - HOLST, A. M.
—— PASTORAL SYMPHONY, FROM THE "MESSIAH"
    fl., cl. - str.   Volkwein.

HANDEL, Georg Frideric - HORROCKS, Herbert
—— A HANDEL SUITE
    pf.(or org.) - str.   9:00 Oxford.

HANDEL, Georg Frideric - HUDSON, Frederick
—— CONCERTO GROSSO IN G MAJOR, OP. 3, NO. 3 (FOR FLUTE OR OBOE, VIOLIN AND STRINGS)
    fl.(or ob.) - cemb. - str.   9:00 G. Schirmer.

HANDEL, Georg Frideric - JACOB, Gordon
—— OVERTURE "THEODORA"
    2(2nd alt. with picc.),2,2,2, c.-bn.(ad. lib.) - 4,2,3,1 - timp. - hp. - str.   12:00 Galaxy.

HANDEL, Georg Frideric - JACQUES, Reginald
—— THE ARRIVAL OF THE QUEEN OF SHEBA (SINFONIA FROM ACT 3 OF "SOLOMON")
    str.   Oxford.
—— OVERTURE TO "ALCINA"
    str.   Oxford.
—— OVERTURE TO "FARAMONDO"
    str.   Oxford.
—— OVERTURE TO "OTTONE"
    2 ob., 2 bn. - str.   11:00 Oxford.
—— SUITE FOR STRINGS
    str.   Oxford.

HANDEL, Georg Frideric - KAHN, Emil
—— WATER MUSIC
        G. Schirmer.

HANDEL, Georg Frideric - KINDLER, Hans
—— PRELUDE AND FUGUE IN D MINOR (FROM CONCERTO GROSSO NO. 5)
        6:00 Mills.

HANDEL, Georg Frideric - LAFOSSE, A. - MEYER, J.
—— CONCERTO IN F MINOR, FOR TROMBONE AND STRING ORCH.
    trb. - str.   10:30 Baron.

HANDEL, Georg Frideric - LAMBERT, Constant
—— CONCERTO IN B♭, FOR PIANO AND SMALL ORCH.
    1. Maestoso; 2. Larghetto; 3. Allegro con brio
    2 ob., 2 hn. - pf. - str.   14:00 Oxford.

HANDEL, Georg Frideric - LEWIS, Anthony
—— ATHALIA (ORATORIO OR SACRED DRAMA) % (FOR SOLO VOICES, MIXED CHORUS AND ORCH.) (Text: Samuel Humphreys)
　　2(or 2 recorders),2,0,2 - 2,2,0,0 - timp. - cemb. - str.
　　　　　　　　　　　　　　　120:00 Oxford.
—— OVERTURE AND DANCES FROM "RODRIGO", SUITES NO. 1 AND 2
　　2 ob., hn. - cemb.(ad lib) - str.　　　　Oxford.
　　or:
　　cemb.(ad lib.) - str.
—— SEMELE (OPERA) % (Text: William Congreve)
　　0,2,0,0, - 2,2,0,0, - timp. - str.　　155:00 Oxford.

HANDEL, Georg Frideric - MAROS, Rudolf
—— LITTLE SUITE
　　str.　　　　　　　　　　　　Bo. Hawkes.

HANDEL, Georg Frideric - MOSS, Lawrence
—— CONCERTO GROSSO NO. 1, IN G. MAJOR (ARR. 1968)
　　hpsc. - str.　　　　　　　20:00 Arranger.

HANDEL, Georg Frideric - NICHOLSON, Ralph
—— CONCERTO IN G MINOR, FOR STRINGS
　　str.　　　　　　　　　　　　Oxford.

HANDEL, Georg Frideric - NOBLE, Robert
—— PASSACAGLIA FOR STRINGS AND CONTINUO (WITH OPTIONAL OBOES AND BASSOONS)
　　　　　　　　　　　　　　　　Novello.

HANDEL, Georg Frideric - ORMANDY, Eugene
—— ANDANTE
　　4,2,*4,*3 - 4,2,3,1 - timp. - str.　　Arranger.
—— CONCERTO IN D MAJOR, FOR ORCH.
　　3,*3,*3,*3 - 4,3,3,1 - timp.,perc. - str.　7:30 C. Fischer.
—— CONCERTO NO. 12 (CONCERTO GROSSO NO. 23 IN B MINOR, OP. 6)
　　2,2,2,2 - 2,3,2,0 - timp. - str.　　16:45 Arranger.
—— CONCERTO NO. 13 IN F, FOR ORGAN AND ORCH.
　　0,2,0,2 - org. - str.　　　　16:45 Arranger.
—— OVERTURE IN D MINOR (FROM CONCERTO GROSSO NO. 5, OP. 3)
　　*3,*3,*3,*3 - 4,4,3,1 - timp.,perc. - str.　5:30 Bo. Hawkes.
—— PASTORAL SYMPHONY, FROM "THE MESSIAH"
　　str.　　　　　　　　　　7:30 C. Fischer.
—— WATER MUSIC: SUITE
　　2,2,2,2(2nd alt. with c.-bn.) - 4,2,0,0 - timp. - str.　17:15 Arranger.

HANDEL, Georg Frideric - OUBRADOUS, Fernand
—— SUITE SÉRÉNADE
　　1,2,0,1 - 2,0,0,0 - str.　　　22:00 Presser.

HANDEL, Georg Frideric - PERRY, Harold
—— SONATA IN F MAJOR
　　1. Adagio; 2. Allegro; 3. Largo; 4. Allegro
　　　　　　　　　　　　　　14:00 Bo. Hawkes.

HANDEL, Georg Frideric - SCHOENBERG, Arnold
—— CONCERTO FOR STRING QUARTET AND ORCH. (IN 5 MOVTS.)
　　2,2,2,2 - 2,2,1,0 - timp.,perc. - hp. - pf. - str.　20:00 G. Schirmer.

HANDEL, Georg Frideric - SEVITZKY, Fabien
—— ALLEGRO, SARABANDE AND GIGUE
　　str.　　　　　　　　　　　Ricordi.
—— CONCERTO FOR STRINGS
　　str.　　　　　　　　　　7:00 Arranger.

HANDEL, Georg Frideric - SKILTON, Charles S.
—— SUITE IN E MINOR (IN 3 MOVTS.)
　　3(3rd alt. with picc.),3,3,3 - 4,3,3,1 - timp.,perc. - str.
　　　　　　　　　　　　　　13:00 C. Fischer.

HANDEL, Georg Frideric - STOESSEL, Albert
—— OVERTURE TO "THE MESSIAH"
　　str.　　　　　　　　　　C. Fischer.
—— SARABANDE AND GIGUE (FROM THE BALLET "TERPSICHORE")
　　str.　　　　　　　　　　C. Fischer.

HANDEL, Georg Frideric - STOKOWSKI, Leopold
—— OVERTURE IN D MINOR
　　　　　　　　　　　　　　　Broude.
—— WATER MUSIC (SUITE) (IN 8 MOVTS.)
　　　　　　　　　　　　19:00 Arranger.

HANDEL, Georg Frideric - STONE
—— THE WATER MUSIC: SUITES I AND II
　　pf. - str.　　　　　　　　Oxford.
　　or:
　　2,1,2,1 - 2,2,3,0 - timp. - pf. - str.

HANDEL, Georg Frideric - THILDE, Jean
—— CONCERTO IN D MINOR (FOR TRUMPET AND STRINGS)
　　tpt. - str.　　　　　　　　Presser.

HANDEL, Georg Frideric - TRINKAUS, George J.
—— SONATA NO. 3 FOR SOLO FLUTE AND STRINGS (IN 4 MOVTS.)
　　fl. - str.　　　　　　　　Arranger.

HANDEL, Georg Frideric - WATTS, Wintter
—— O GRATI ORRORI (RECITATIVE AND AIR FROM "OTTONE")
　　str.　　　　　　　　　5:00 Ricordi.

HANDEL, Georg Frideric - WHITTAKER, W. Gillies
—— ALCINA: SUITE OF DANCES (IN 4 MOVTS.)
　　ob.(ad lib.) - str.　　　　　Oxford.
—— SONATA NO. 6 IN E, FOR STRINGS
　　str.　　　　　　　　12:00 Oxford.

HANDEL, Georg Frideric - WILSON, Mortimer
—— SARABANDE
　　hp.(ad lib.) - str.　　　　　Witmark.

HANFF, Johann Nicholaus - LEONARDI, Leon
—— TWO CHORALE PRELUDES
　　str.　　　　　　　　5:00 EV.

HANKS, Sybil A.
—— THE CREATION: A NEGRO SERMON (CANTATA) (FOR SATB CHORUS AND ORCH.)
　　　　　　　　　　　　　Transcon.

HANNA, James
—— ELEGY (FOR CHAMBER ORCH.)
　　1,1,1,1 - 1,1,0,0 - str.　　　6:30 C. Fischer.

HANNAY, Roger D.
—— ABSTRACTION FOR CHAMBER ORCH.
　　1(alt. with picc.),1,*2,1 - 0,1,1,0 - timp.,perc.(8),cel.,glock.,vibra.,xyl. - guit. - hp. - pf. - 1 vln.,1 c.,1 d.-b.　　　　　7:00 Composer.
—— CELEBRATION (1975)
　　2,2,2,2 - 4,3,3,1 - timp.,perc.(4),bells,cel.,glock.,vibra.,xyl. - tape-recorder(2-channel) - hp. - pf. - str.(20,8,6,4)　7:30 Composer.
—— CONCERTINO FOR ORGAN AND STRINGS (1957)
　　1. Largo; 2. Allegro Vivace
　　org. - str.　　　　　　7:00 Composer.
—— FRAGMENTATION (1969)
　　1,1,*2,1 - 0,1,1,0 - perc.(2) - hp. - pf. - 1 vln.,1 c.,1 d.-b.　　　　9:00 Composer.
—— LAMENT FOR OBOE AND STRINGS (1957)
　　ob. - str.　　　　　　4:00 Rochester.
—— LISTEN (1971)
　　2 picc.,2,*3,*3,*3 - 4,4,3,1 - timp.,perc.(4),bells,mar.,vibra.,xyl. - hpsc. - pf. - str.　　15:00 Composer.
—— OVERTURE
　　*3,2,2,*3 - 3,2,3,1 - timp.,perc.,cel. - hp. - str.　8:00 Composer.
—— REQUIEM ("WHEN LILACS LAST IN THE DOORYARD BLOOM'D") (FOR SOPRANO, CHORUS AND ORCH.) (Text: Walt Whitman)
　　*3,2(2nd alt. with Eng.hn.),2,*3 - 4,3,3,1 - timp.,perc.,cel.,glock. - hp. - str.　　40:00 Composer.
—— SUMMER FESTIVAL OVERTURE
　　*3,2,2,2 - 3,3,3,1 - timp.,perc.,glock. - hp. - str.　5:00 Composer.
—— SYMPHONY NO. 1
　　2,2,2,2 - 2,2,2,0 - timp. - str.　　20:00 Composer.
—— SYMPHONY NO. 2 ("THE LIFE OF LINCOLN") (IN 3 MOVTS.)
　　*3,*3,2,*3 - 4,3,3,1 - timp.,perc.,xyl. - hp. - pf. - str.
　　　　　　　　　　　　25:00 Composer.

HANNIKAINEN, Ilmari

—— CONCERTO IN B FLAT MAJOR, FOR PIANO AND ORCH. (REV. 1919)
2,2,2,2 - 4,3,3,1 - timp.,perc.(3) - pf. - str.   38:00 FinnMICtr.
—— FOUR MINIATURES (1925)
2,2,2,2 - 2,2,2,1 - timp.,perc.(4) - str.   10:00 FinnMICtr.
—— HARVEST DANCE (SUITE)(1932)(IN 5 MOVTS.)
2,2,2,2 - 2,2,2,2 - timp.,perc. - hp. - str.   16:00 FinnMICtr.
—— THREE MINIATURES
1,1,2,1 - 2,2,1,0 - timp.,perc. - pf. - str.   5:00 FinnMICtr.

HANNIKAINEN, Väinö

—— ANIMAL DANCE
1,1,2,1 - 2,2,1,0 - timp.,perc. - hp. - str.   6:00 FinnMICtr.
—— CONCERT PIECE FOR HARP AND ORCH. (1921)
2,2,2,2 - 2,0,0,0 - timp. - 2 hp. - str.   12:00 FinnMICtr.
—— KARELIAN FOLK SONGS FROM KIIHTELYSVAARA: SUITE NO. 1 (FOR SOPRANO AND ORCH.) (1942)
2,1,2,2 - 2,1,0,0 - timp.,perc. - hp. - str.   18:00 Westerlund.
—— KARELIAN FOLK SONGS FROM KIIHTELYSVAARA: SUITE NO 2 (FOR SOPRANO AND ORCH.) (1943)
2,1,2,1 - 2,0,0,0 - timp., - hp. - str.   16:00 Westerlund.
—— KARELIAN FOLK SONGS FROM KIIHTELYSVAARA: SUITE NO. 3 (FOR SOPRANO AND ORCH.) (1946)
2,1,2,2 - 2,0,0,0 - timp. - hp. - str.   16:00 Westerlund.
—— KARELIAN FOLK SONGS FROM KIIHTELYSVAARA: SUITE NO. 4 (FOR SOPRANO AND STRINGS) (1945)
str.   10:00 Westerlund.
—— NORTAMO OVERTURE (1940)
1,1,2,1 - 2,2,1,0 - timp.,perc. - hp. - str.   5:00 FinnMICtr.
—— OVERTURE AND SUITE FROM THE BALLET "THE CASTLE OF HAPPINESS" (1937)
2,2,2,2 - 4,2,3,1 - timp.,perc.(3),cel. - hp. - str.   95:00 FinnMICtr.
—— THE PRODIGAL SON (TONE POEM)(1931)
3,3,3,3 - 4,3,3,1 - timp.,perc.(3),cel. - hp. - str.   16:00 FinnMICtr.
—— SCENES FROM THE KALEVALA (1947)
2,2,2,2 - 2,2,1,0 - timp.,perc. - hp.,kantele - str.   14:00 FinnMICtr.
—— SOUNDS FROM KARELIA (FOR SATB CHORUS AND ORCH.)
2,1,2,1 - 2,1,1,0 - timp.,perc. - kantele - pf. - str.   5:00 FinnMICtr.
—— SUITE FOR ORCHESTRA (1946) (IN 3 MOVTS.)
2,2,2,2 - 2,1,1,0 - timp. - hp. - str   12:00 FinnMICtr.
—— SUITE FROM Z. TOPELIUS' PLAY "ADALMINA'S PEARL" (1932)
1,0,1,0 - 2,1,1,0 - timp.,perc. - hp. - str.   9:00 FinnMICtr.
—— SUITE (1948) (IN 3 MOVTS.)
2,2,2,2 - 2,2,2,0 - timp.,perc. - hp. - str.   11:00 FinnMICtr.
—— VARIATIONS PASTORALES (FOR VIOLIN OR FLUTE AND ORCH.)(1933)
2-3,2,2,2 - 2,2,1,0 - timp.perc. - hp. - str.   14:00 FinnMICtr.

HANSEN, Erik

—— LITTLE NORWEGIAN SUITE
pf. - str.   Bo. Hawkes.

HANSEN, Johannes

—— COMPOSITION FOR MARIMBA, XYLOPHONE AND ORCH., OP. 26
1,1,*2,1 - 0,2,2,0 - timp.,perc.,mar.,xyl. - org. - str.
14:00 K.O.D.A.
—— COMPOSITION FOR ORCH. AND 2 PIANOS, OP. 6
2,*2,*2,2 - 4,2,0,0 - timp.,perc. - 2 pf. - str.   12:00 K.O.D.A.
—— COMPOSITION FOR ORCH., OP. 13
2,*2,*3,2 - 4,2,2,0 - timp.,perc. - str.   7:00 K.O.D.A.
—— COMPOSITION FOR ORCH., OP. 21
*2,*2,*3,*2 - 4,3,2,1 - timp.,perc.,xyl. - str.   7:00 K.O.D.A.
—— PLANKTON, OP. 41
3,0,1,0 - 0,0,0,0 - perc. - 2 pf. - str.   15:00 K.O.D.A.
—— SHORT STORIES, OP. 51
str.   6:00 K.O.D.A.

HANSEN, Ted

—— SYMPHONY NO. 1
2,2,2,2 - 4,3,3,1 - timp. - pf. - str.   35:00 Seesaw.
—— THREE MOVEMENTS FOR ORCHESTRA
3,2,2,2 - 4,3,3,1 - timp.,perc. - str.   19:00 Seesaw.

HANSGÅRDH, Allan

—— FANTASIA PASTORALE (1972)
2,2,2,2 - 2,2,0,0 - timp. - str.   10:00 Fleisher.

HANSON, Gunnar

—— SUITE NO. 1
1,1,1,1 - 1,0,0,0 - str.   8:00 Southern.

HANSON, Howard

—— BOLD ISLAND SUITE (IN 3 MOVTS.)
3,3,2,2 - 4,3,3,1 - timp.,perc.(3) - hp. - pf.(or cel.) - str.
27:30 C. Fischer.
—— CENTENNIAL ODE (FOR CHORUS, NARRATOR AND ORCH.)
27:00 Composer.
—— CHERUBIC HYMN (FOR MIXED CHORUS AND ORCH.)
3,2,2,2 - 4,3,3,1 - timp.,perc. - pf. - str.   12:00 C. Fischer.
—— CONCERTO FOR ORGAN AND ORCH., OP. 27
*3,2,2,*3 - 4,3,3,1 - timp.,perc.(5) - hp. - org. - str.
18:00 Composer.
—— CONCERTO FOR ORGAN, STRINGS AND HARP, OP. 22
hp. - org. - str.   18:00 C. Fischer.
—— CONCERTO FOR PIANO AND ORCH., OP. 36 (IN 3 MOVTS.)
1. Allegro giocoso
*3,2,2,2 - 4,3,3,1 - timp.,perc. (2), xyl. - pf. - str.
20:30 C. Fischer.
—— DIES NATALIS
3,3,3,3 - 4,3,3,1 - timp.,perc. - str.   12:00 C. Fischer.
—— ELEGY, OP. 44 (TO THE MEMORY OF SERGE KOUSSEVITZKY)
2(2nd alt. with picc.),2(2nd alt. with Eng. hn.),2,2 - 4,3,3,1 - timp. - hp. - str.   12:00 C. Fischer.
—— FANFARE FOR THE SIGNAL CORPS (FOR BRASS AND PERCUSSION)
4 hn., 3 tpt., 3 trb., tu. - timp.,perc. (3)   Bo. Hawkes.
—— FANTASY-VARIATIONS ON A THEME OF YOUTH
pf. - str.   12:00 C. Fischer.
—— FOR THE FIRST TIME (SUITE FOR ORCHESTRA)
*2,2,2,2 - 2,0,0,0 - perc. - hp. - pf. - str.   C. Fischer.
—— HEROIC ELEGY (FOR CHORUS AND ORCH.), OP. 28
*2,1,1,*2 - 4,3,3,1 - timp.,perc. (3) - org. - str.   16:00 Composer.
—— THE LAMENT FOR BEOWULF, OP. 25 (FOR CHORUS AND ORCH.)
*3,2,2,*3 - 4,3,3,1 - timp.,perc. (3) - hp. - str.   18:00 C. Fischer.
—— LUX AETERNA, OP. 24 (SYMPHONIC POEM WITH VIOLA OBBIGATO)
*3,2,2,*3 - 4,3,3,1 - timp.,perc. (3), cel. - pf. - str.
15:00 C. Fischer.
—— MOSAICS
*3,*3,*3,*3 - 4,3,3,1 - timp.,perc. (2), cel. - hp. - str.
10:00 C. Fischer.
—— THE MYSTIC TRUMPETER (FOR NARRATOR, SATB CHORUS AND ORCH)
3,3,2,3 - 4,3,3,1 - timp.,perc. - hp. - pf. - str.   16:00 C. Fischer.
—— NORTH AND WEST, OP. 22 (SYMPHONIC POEM)
*3,2,2,*3 - 4,3,3,1 - timp.,perc. (3) - 2 hp. - pf. - str.
18:00 Composer.
—— PAN AND THE PRIEST, OP. 26 (SYMPHONIC POEM)
*3,2(2nd alt. with Eng. hn.),*3 - 4,3,3,1 - timp.,perc. (4) - pf. - str.   10:00 C. Fischer.
—— PASTORALE FOR OBOE AND STRINGS
ob. - hp. - str.   6:00 C. Fischer.
—— SERENADE, OP. 35 (FOR FLUTE, HARP AND STRINGS)
fl. - hp. - str.   6:00 C. Fischer.
—— SINFONIA SACRA (SYMPHONY NO. 5)
*3,*3,2,2 - 4,3,3,1 - timp.,perc. (2) - hp. - str.   16:00 C. Fischer.
—— SONG OF DEMOCRACY (FOR SATB CHORUS AND ORCHESTRA) (Text: Walt Whitman)
2,3,2,2 - 4,3,3,1 - timp.,perc.,cel.,xyl. - hp. - str.   12:00 C. Fischer.
—— SONG OF HUMAN RIGHTS (FOR SPEAKING CHORUS AND ORCH.) (Text: Preamble To Universal Declaration Of Human Rights)
*3,2,2,2 - 4,3,3,1 - timp.,perc. - str.   12:00 C. Fischer.
—— STREAMS IN THE DESERT (FOR SATB CHORUS AND ORCH.)
3,2,2,3 - 4,3,3,1 - timp.,perc. - hp. - pf.- str.   12:00 C. Fischer.
—— SUITE FROM THE OPERA "MERRY MOUNT" (IN 4 MOVTS.)
3(3rd alt. with picc.),*3,2(2nd alt. with b.-cl.),*3 - 4,3,3,1 - timp.,perc. (5), mar., xyl. - 2 hp. - str.   16:00 Harms, Inc.
—— SUMMER SEASCAPE (FROM "BOLD ISLAND SUITE")
3,2,2,2 - 4,3,3,1 - timp. - hp. - str.   12:30 C. Fischer.
—— SUMMER SEASCAPE NO. 2 (1965)
str.   7:00 C. Fischer.
—— SYMPHONY NO. 1 IN E MINOR, OP. 21 ("NORDIC") (IN 3 MOVTS.)
*3,2,2,*3 - 4,3,3,1 - timp.,perc. (2) - hp. - str.   28:00 C. Fischer.

—— SYMPHONY NO. 2, OP. 30 ("ROMANTIC") (IN 3 MOVTS.)
  *3,*3,2,3(3rd alt. with c.-bn.) - 4,3,3,1 - timp.,perc. (2) - hp. - str.
  24:00 C. Fischer.
—— SYMPHONY NO. 3, OP. 33
  1. Andante lamentando - Agitato; 2. Andante tranquillo; 3. Tempo
  scherzando; 4. Largamente e pesante
  *3,*3,*3,*3 - 4,3,3,1 - timp.,perc. - str. 36:00 C. Fischer.
—— SYMPHONY NO. 4, OP. 34 ("REQUIEM") (IN 4 MOVTS.)
  2(2nd alt. with picc.),2,2(2nd alt. with b.-cl.),2(2nd alt. with c.-bn.)
  - 4,3,3,1 - timp. - str. 20:00 C. Fischer.
—— SYMPHONY NO 6
  3,3,3,3 - 4,3,3,1 - timp.,perc. - str. 20:00 C. Fischer.
—— THREE SONGS FROM "DRUM TAPS", OP. 32 (FOR
  BARITONE, CHORUS AND ORCH.)
  *3,*3,*3,*3 - 4,3,3,1 - timp.,perc. (5), xyl. - 2 hp. - str.
  18:00 J. Fischer.
—— TWO PSALMS (PSALMS 121 AND 150) (FOR SATB CHORUS
  AND ORCH.)
  3,2,2,2 - 4,3,3,1 - timp. - str. 9:00 C. Fischer.

HANSON, Howard - BENCRISCUTTO, Frank
—— THE FOREST PLAY: PRELUDE AND BALLET
  1,1,2,1 - 2,0,0,0 - timp. - str. C. Fischer.

HANSON, Raymond
—— CONCERTO FOR PIANO AND ORCH. (1972)
  19:00 A.P.R.A.
—— CONCERTO FOR TROMBONE AND ORCH. (1954)
  20:00 A.P.R.A.
—— CONCERTO FOR TRUMPET AND ORCH., OP. 27 (1948)
  18:00 Southern.
—— CONCERTO FOR VIOLIN AND ORCH., OP. 21 (1947)
  41:00 Southern.
—— GULA (1967)
  13:00 A.P.R.A.
—— NOVELETTE, OP. 22 (1946)
  12:00 A.P.R.A.
—— SYMPHONY, OP. 28 (1952) (IN 1 MOVT.)
  21:13 A.P.R.A.

HANSSEN, Daniel
—— CHURCH CANTATA (KIRKEKANTATE) (FOR SOPRANO,
  BASS, CHORUS, ORGAN AND STRINGS) (Text: Bjarne
  Eriksen)
  org. - str. 45:00 T.O.N.O.
—— HALLVARD AV HUSEBY (DECLAMATION WITH ORCH.)
  (Text: Herman Wildenvey)
  20:00 T.O.N.O.
—— YOUTH CANTATA (UNGDOMSKANTATE) (FOR SOPRANO,
  BARITONE, CHORUS AND ORCH.) (Text: Finn Arbo)
  30:00 T.O.N.O.

HANSSEN, Johannes
—— FESTIVAL MARCH (FESTMARSJ)
  1,1,1,0 - 2,2,1,0 - perc. - str. 7:00 Norsk Ntk.
—— RHAPSODY FROM ØSTERDAL (ØSTERDALSRAPSODI)
  1,1,2,2, - 2,2,2,0 - perc. - pf. - str. 10:00 Musikk-Hu.

HANSSON, C. J. Gunnar
—— FESTIVO
  2,2,2,2 - 4,3,4,1 - timp. - str. 6:00 Southern.

HANUŠ, Jan
—— THE FLAMES (OPERA) (1944) %
  Bo. Hawkes.
—— OTHELLO (BALLET SUITE NO. 1)
  3,3,3,2 - 4,3,3,1 - timp.,perc.,cel. - 2 hp. - str. 26:00 Bo. Hawkes.
—— OTHELLO (BALLET SUITE NO. 2)
  3,3,3,2 - 4,3,3,1 - timp.,perc.,cel. - 2 hp. - str. 36:00 Bo. Hawkes.
—— PETER AND LUCY ("PIERRE ET LUCIE") (SYMPHONIC
  POEM)
  3,3,2,2 - 4,3,3,1 - timp.,perc.,cel. - hp. - str. 19:00 Bo. Hawkes.
—— RONDO CAPRICCIOSO, OP. 3
  3,3,2,2 - 4,3,3,1 - timp.,perc. - hp. - pf. - str. 5:00 Bo. Hawkes.
—— SALT IS WORTH MORE THAN GOLD (BALLET SUITE NO. 1)
  (1953)
  3,3,2,2 - 4,3,3,1 - timp.,perc. - hp. - str. 25:00 Bo. Hawkes.
—— SALT IS WORTH MORE THAN GOLD (BALLET SUITE NO. 2)
  (1953)
  3,3,2,sax.,2 - 4,3,3,1 - timp.,perc.,cel. - hp. - str.
  27:00 Bo. Hawkes.

—— SINFONIA CONCERTANTE FOR ORGAN AND SMALL
  ORCH., OP. 31 (1954) (IN 3 MOVTS.)
  timp. - hp. - org. - str. 22:00 Bo. Hawkes.
—— SONG OF HOPE (CANTATA) (1948)
  Bo. Hawkes.
—— SYMPHONY NO. 2 IN G MAJOR, OP. 26 (1951) (IN 4
  MOVTS.)
  3,2,2,2 - 4,3,3,1 - timp.,perc. - str. 36:00 Bo. Hawkes.
—— SYMPHONY NO. 3, OP. 38
  3,3,3,2 - 4,3,3,1 - timp.,perc. - str. 37:00 Bo. Hawkes.
—— SYMPHONY NO. 4
  3,3,2,2 - 4,3,3,0 - timp.,perc. - pf. - str. 32:00 Bo. Hawkes.

HAQUINIUS, Algot
—— CAROLINIAN SUITE
  2,2,2,2 -4,2,3,1 - timp.,perc. (2) - str. S.T.I.M.
—— CONCERTO IN B MINOR, FOR PIANO AND ORCH.
  S.T.I.M.
—— DIKT (POEM)
  2,2,2,2 - 4,2,3,1 - timp. - str. 15:00 S.T.I.M.
—— FORDOMTIMA ("IN OLDEN TIMES") (SUITE)
  2,2,2,2 - 4,2,3,1 - timp. - str. 28:00 S.T.I.M.
—— LAKE MÄLAR (OVERTURE)
  2,2,2,2 - 2,2,1,0 - timp.,perc. - str. 8:00 S.T.I.M.
—— PASTORALE
  2,2,2,2 - 4,2,2,0 - timp.,perc. - str. 15:00 S.T.I.M.
—— SWEDISH SUITE
  2,2,2,2 - 2,2,1,0 - timp.,perc. - str. 9:00 S.T.I.M.
—— THREE SWEDISH DANCES
  2,2,2,2 - 4,2,3,1 - timp.perc. - str. 15:00 Lundquists.
—— TWO MELODIES FOR STRINGS
  str. 8:00 S.T.I.M.

HARDER, Paul
—— JANUS (OVERTURE FOR ORCH.) (1961)
  3(3rd alt. with picc.),*3,*3,2 - 4,3,3,1 - timp.,perc.(4) - str.
  10:30 Composer.
—— OVERTURE (1959)
  3(3rd alt. with picc.),*3,*3,2 - 4,3,3,1 - timp.,perc.(4) - str.
  9:28 Mills.
—— PANDORA (OVERTURE FOR ORCH.) (1964)
  3(3rd alt. with picc.),*3,*3,2 - 4,3,3,1 - timp.,perc.(4),vibra. - str.
  8:15 Mills.
—— SINFONIETTA (1958) (IN 3 MOVTS.)
  2,2,2,2 - 2,2,1,0 - timp.,perc. - str. 17:35 Composer.
—— A WISP OF TIME (1963)
  str. 5:15 Composer.

HARKNESS, Rebekah
—— AIYOKU (LETTERS FROM JAPAN) (BALLET) %
  Composer.
—— BARCELONA SUITE
  Composer.
—— MACUMBA (SUITE)
  Composer.
—— MEDITERANEAN MOODS (SUITE)
  10:00 Broude.
—— MUSICAL CHAIRS (MUSIC TO THE BALLET "DREAMS OF
  GLORY")
  2,2,2,2 - 2,2,2,1 - timp.,perc. - pf. - str. 30:00 Bo. Hawkes.
  or:
  1,1,1,1 - 1,1,0,0 - timp.,perc. - pf. - str.
—— SAFARI (SUITE) (AFRICAN IMPRESSIONS)
  20:00 Broude.

HÄRKÖNEN, Leo
—— CHRISTMAS CANTATA, OP. 53 (FOR SOPRANO, SATB
  CHORUS, FLUTE, CLARINET AND STRINGS) (1956) (Text:
  Arvo Kippola)
  fl.,cl. - str. 10:00 FinnMICtr.
—— COMMEDIA DELL'ARTE, OP. 35 (SUITE) (1950)
  2,2,2,2 - 2,2,1,0 - timp.(2 players) - str. 10:00 FinnMICtr.
—— CONCERTINO FOR VIOLA AND CHAMBER ORCH., OP. 68
  (1964)
  1,1,2,1 - 2,2,0,0 - str. 12:00 FinnMICtr.
—— DRAMATIC SUITE, OP. 54 (1956)
  2,2,2,2 - 2,2,1,0 - timp. - str. 16:00 FinnMICtr.
—— FANTASY FOR PIANO AND ORCH., OP. 79 (1970)(IN 3
  MOVTS.)
  2,2,2,2 - 4,2,0,0 - pf. - str. 15:00 FinnMICtr.
—— LYRICAL SUITE, OP. 46 (1954)
  1,1,2,1 - 2,2,0,0 - str. 11:00 FinnMICtr.

—— THE MARQUIS OF BOLIBARI, OP. 77 (SUITE) (1969)
  2,2,2,2 - 4,2,1,0 - timp.(2 players) - str.   32:00 FinnMICtr.
—— PIAE CANTIONES, OP. 51 (FOR TWO SOPRANOS,
  BARITONE, SATB CHORUS AND ORCH.) (1956) (Text: V. A.
  Koskenniemi)
  2,2,2,2 - 4,2,3,0 - timp.(2 players) - str.   15:00 FinnMICtr.
—— SYMPHONY NO. 1, OP. 39 (1952)
  2,2,2,2 - 4,2,3,0 - timp.(2 players) - str.   25:00 FinnMICtr.
—— SYMPHONY NO. 2, OP. 49 (1955)
  2,2,2,2 - 4,3,3,1 - timp.(2 players) - str.   27:00 FinnMICtr.
—— SYMPHONY NO. 3, OP. 76 (1968)
  2,2,2,2 - 4,3,3,0 - timp.(2 players) - str.   24:00 FinnMICtr.

HARLINE, Leigh
—— CENTENNIAL SUITE (IN 3 MOVTS.)
                                                          Composer.

HARLING, W. Franke
—— AT THE TOMB OF THE UNKNOWN SOLDIER (SYMPHONIC
  POEM)
  *3,2(1 alt. with Eng. hn.),*3,*3 - 6,6,4,1 - timp.,perc. (4) - str.
                                                    21:00 Composer.
—— BEFORE THE DAWN (PERSIAN IDYL) (FOR TENOR, MEN'S
  CHORUS AND ORCH.)
  2,*2,2,1 - 4,3,3,1 - timp.,perc.(3) - hp. - str.   20:00 Boston.
—— BIBLE TRILOGY (FOR SOLO VOICES, CHORUS AND ORCH.)
                                                          Composer.
—— COLUMBINE'S DREAM (BALLET BANTASTIQUE) %
  *3,*2,2,*2 - 4,3,3,1 - timp.,perc. - hp. - str.   Composer.
—— CONCERTO IN C MINOR FOR PIANO AND ORCH. (IN 3
  MOVTS.)
  *3,*3,*3,*3 - 4,3,3,1 - timp.,perc.(3) - hp. - pf. - str.
                                                    52:00 Composer.
—— THE DEATH OF MINNEHAHA (AN INDIAN PASTORALE)
  (FOR SOPRANO, TENOR, BASS, MEN'S CHORUS AND
  ORCH.)
  1,1(alt. with Eng. hn.),2,*3 - 4,3,3,1 - timp.,perc.(2) - hp. - str.
                                                    24:00 Boston.
—— THE DIVAN OF HAFIZ (FOUR SONGS FOR VOICE AND
  ORCH.)
  2,2(1alt. with Eng. hn.),2,*3 - 4,3,3,1 - timp.,perc. (1) - hp. - str.
                                                    15:00 Boston.
—— THE MIRACLE OF TIME (SYMPHONIC BALLAD) (FOR
  TENOR, DOUBLE CHORUS, CHILDREN'S CHORUS AND
  ORCH.)
  *3,*3,*3,*3 - 4,3,3,4(2 e^b wagner tu.,2 C Wagnertu.) - perc.(4) -
  hp. - str.   28:00 Composer.
—— NOCTURNE FOR STRINGS
  str.   8:00 Composer.
—— REQUIEM ("OH CAPTAIN, MY CAPTAIN") (FOR BARITONE,
  MEN'S CHORUS AND ORCH.)
  2,2(1 alt. with Eng. hn.),*3,*3 - 4,3,3,1 - timp.,perc.(3) - hp. - str.
                                                    6:00 Composer.
—— THE TWENTY-THIRD PSALM OF DAVID (SYMPHONIC
  POEM) (FOR NARRATOR, WOMEN'S CHORUS, ORGAN, 2
  PIANOS AND ORCH.)
  *3,2(1 alt. with Eng. hn.),2,*3 - 4,3,3,1 - timp.,perc.(2) - hp. - org.
  - 2 pf. - str.   18:00 Composer.
—— THE TWO ANGELS (SYMPHONIC BALLAD) (FOR TENOR,
  MEN'S CHORUS AND ORCH.)
  *3,2(1 alt. with Eng. hn.),*3,*3 - 4,3,3,1 - timp.,perc.(2) - hp. - str.
                                                    20:00 Boston.
—— A VENETIAN FANTASY (FOR SOPRANO, TENOR, BASS,
  CHORUS AND ORCH.)
  1,1(alt. with Eng. hn.),2,1 - 4,3,3,1 - timp.,perc.(3) - hp. - str.
                                                    16:00 Composer.
—— WAKE UP, JONATHAN (A MARIONETTE PROLOGUE)
  *2,2,1 - 2,2,1,0 - timp.,perc. - hp. - str.   31:00 Composer.

HARMATI, Sandor
—— PRELUDE TO A MELODRAMA
  *3,*3,*3,*3 - 4,2,2,0 - timp.,perc. (3) - hp. - str.
                                                    12:00 AmerMusEd.

HARPER, Edward
—— BARTÓK GAMES
  2,2,2,2 - 4,2,3,0 - timp.,perc. - pf. - str.   20:00 Bo. Hawkes.
—— CONCERTO FOR VIOLIN AND ORCH. (1964)
  2,2,2,2 - 4,2,3,0 - timp.,perc. - hp. - str.   25:00 P.R.S.
—— SERENADE (1964)
  cl. - str.   13:00 P.R.S.
—— SUITE FOR OBOE AND STRINGS (1966)
  ob. - str.   14:00 P.R.S.

HARRIES, David
—— CONCERTINO FOR CLARINET AND ORCH., OP. 22 (1965)
  2,1,3,1 - 2,2,2,0 - timp.,perc. - str.   8:45 P.R.S.
—— CONCERTO FOR VIOLIN AND ORCH., OP. 18 (1964)
  2,1,2,1 - 2,2,1,0 - timp.,perc. - str.   16:00 P.R.S.
—— PROLEGOMENA, OP. 11 (1960)
  str.   15:00 P.R.S.
—— TWO COMMENTS ON THE TRAGEDY OF ANTIGONE, OP. 3
  (1953)
  0,0,0,1 - 2,0,1,0 - timp. - pf. - str.   8:00 P.R.S.

HARRIS, Albert
—— CONCERTO FOR CELLO AND ORCH.
  1. Andante tranquillo; 2. Allegro comodo; 3. Adagio; 4. Allegro
  moderato
  1,1,2,2 - timp. - str.   18:00 Composer.
—— OVERTURE, WALTZ AND RONDO
  3(3rd alt. with picc.),2,2,3(3rd alt. with picc.) - 4,2,3,1 -
  timp.,perc.(3) cel., glock., xyl. - hp. - str.   20:00 Composer.

HARRIS, Donald
—— FANTASY FOR VIOLIN AND ORCH. (1957)
  2,2,2,2 - 2,2,2,0 - timp.,perc.(2),cel.,xyl. - hp. - str. 7:30 Presser.
—— LUDUS I (1966)
  1,1,1,1 - 1,0,0,0 - str.(2,1,1,1)   8:30 Presser.
—— LUDUS 1 (CHAMBER CONCERTO FOR 10 INSTRUMENTS)
  1,1,1,1 - 1,0,0,0 - str.   10:00 EV.
—— SYMPHONY IN TWO MOVEMENTS (1961)
  3(3rd alt. with picc.),3,4,3 - 4,3,3,1 -
  timp.,perc.(4),cel.,glock.,vibra.,xyl. - hp. - str. 16:00 Presser.
—— SYMPHONY IN 2 MOVEMENTS
  3,3,4,3 - 4,3,3,1 - timp.,perc.(3),cel.,glock.,vibra.,xyl. - hp. - str.
                                                      16:00 EV.

HARRIS, Robert A.
—— ADAGIO FOR STRING ORCHESTRA (1966)
  str.   4:30 Composer.
—— CONCERT PIECE FOR BASSOON AND STRING ORCH.
  (1965)
  2,0,2,1 - 1,0,1 b.-trb.,0 - pf. - str.   5:00 Composer.
—— CONCERT PIECE FOR HORN AND ORCH. (1964)
  2(2nd alt. with picc.),2,2,2 - 3,0,1 b.-trb.,0 - timp. - str.
                                                    5:30 Composer.
—— CONTRASTS (FOR 4 WINDS AND STRING ORCH.) (1966)
  1,0,1,1 - 1,0,0,0 - str.   5:00 Composer.
—— TWO MOODS FOR ORCH. (1969)
  2,2,2,2 - 2,2,2,1 - timp.,perc.(4),bells,cel.,vibra.,xyl. - pf. - str.
                                                    6:30 Composer.

HARRIS, Roy
—— ACCELERATION
  *3,*3,*3,3 - 4,3,3,1 - timp.,perc. (4) - str.   9:00 Mills.
—— AMERICAN CREED (IN 2 MOVTS.)
  *4,*4,E^{b}cl.,*4,4 - 6,4,4,2 - timp.,perc. (4) - str. 18:00 Mills.
—— BLOW THE MAN DOWN (IMPROVISATION FOR
  CONTRALTO, BARITONE, SATB CHORUS AND ORCH.)
  2,2,3,1 - 2,3,3,1 - timp. - hp. - pf. - str.   9:30 C. Fischer.
—— CELEBRATION (VARIATIONS ON A THEME BY HOWARD
  HANSON)
  4,3,3,ten.sax.,4 - 2,3,3,bar.,1 - timp.,perc. - pf. - str.
                                                    10:30 C. Fischer.
—— CHALLENGE, 1940 (FOR MIXED CHORUS AND ORCH.)
                                                          G. Schirmer.
—— CHILDREN'S HOUR
  *3,*3,*3,3 - 4,3,3,0 - timp.,perc. - str.   Mills.
—— CHORALE FOR ORCHESTRA
  2,*1,2,2(ad lib.) - 2,3,3,0 - str.   8:30 Mills.
—— CHORALE FOR STRINGS, OP. 3
  str. (no cl.-b.)   9:00 Flammer.
—— CONCERT MARCH (MARCH IN TIME OF WAR)
  3,3,4,3 - 4,3,3,1 - timp.,perc. - str.   4:00 Belw-Mills.
—— CONCERTO FOR ACCORDIAN AND ORCH. (THEME AND
  VARIATIONS)
  1(alt. with picc.),1(alt. with Eng. hn.),3,sax.,1 - 1,2,2,1 -
  timp.,perc.,vibra. - acc. - str.   17:30 C. Fischer.
—— CONCERTO FOR PIANO AND ORCH.
  *3,1,*5(alt. with 5 sax.),1 - 1,3,3,1 - timp.,perc.(3) - pf. - str.
                                                    14:00 Mills.
—— CONCERTO FOR PIANO AND STRINGS (IN 3 MOVTS.)
  pf. - str.   20:00 G. Schirmer.
—— CONCERTO FOR TWO PIANOS AND ORCH.
  3(3rd alt. with picc.),*3(2nd alt. with 2nd Eng. hn.),3,ten. sax.,3 -
  4,3,3,1 - timp.,perc. - hp. - 2 pf. - str.   25:00 C. Fischer.

—— CONCERTO FOR VIOLIN AND ORCH.
3,3,3,3 - 4,3,3,1 - perc. - hp. - pf. - str.   C. Fischer.
—— CUMBERLAND CONCERTO (FOR ORCH.)
3,3,4,3 - 5,4,3,1 - timp.,perc. - pf. - str.   18:00 F. Colombo.
—— EVENING PIECE
2,1,2,0 - 4,1,1,0 - str.   6:00 Mills.
—— FAREWELL TO PIONEERS
*3,*3,E♭cl.,*3,2 - 4,3,3,1 - timp.,perc. (3) - str.
                                                11:00 G. Schirmer.
—— FOLK RHYTHMS OF TODAY
3,3,4,3 - 4,3,3,1 - timp.,perc. - str.   5:00 Belw-Mills.
—— FOLK SONG SYMPHONY (FOR CHORUS AND ORCH.) (IN 7 MOVTS.)
*3,*3,E♭cl.,*3,3 - 4,3,3,1 - timp.,perc. (4) - pf. - str.
                                                44:00 G. Schirmer.
—— FREEDOM'S LAND (FOR CHORUS AND ORCH.)
1,*2,2,1 - 2,2,1,0 - timp.,perc. (1) - hp. - pf. - str.   5:00 Mills.
—— FROM THIS EARTH (MUSIC FOR THE DANCE)
*2,*2,1,1 - hn. - perc. - pf. - str.   30:00 Mills.
—— KENTUCKY SPRING
3,3,3,3 - 4,3,3,1 - timp.,perc., glock., vibra. - hp. - pf. - str.
                                                10:00 C. Fischer.
—— MELODY
2,3,3,3 - 4,3,3,1 - timp.,perc. - glock., vibra., - hp. - str.
                                                10:00 C. Fischer.
—— MEMORIES OF A CHILD'S SUNDAY (IN 3 MOVTS.)
3,3,3,3 - 2,3,3,1 - timp.,perc., glock., vibra. - hp. - pf. - str.
                                                11:00 C. Fischer.
—— MIRAGE
1,*2,*2,2 - hn. - vibra. - pf. - str.   Mills.
—— ODE TO FRIENDSHIP
0,0,*3,4 sax.,*3 - 2,3,3bar.,1 - timp. - str.   5:00 Mills.
—— ODE TO TRUTH
*3,*3,*3,3 - 4,3,3,1 - timp.,perc. (3) - str.   9:00 Mills.
—— PRELUDE AND FUGUE FOR STRINGS
str. (no. d.-b.)   14:00 G. Schirmer.
—— THE QUEST
3,3,3,sax.,3 - 4,3,3,1 - timp.,perc. - hp. - str. 14:00 C. Fischer.
—— RADIO PIECE (WITH PIANO OBBLIGATO)
*2,*2,*2,2 - 1,1,1,0 - timp.,perc. - pf. - str.   8:00 C. Fischer.
—— RAILROAD MAN'S BALLAD (FOR MEN'S CHORUS AND ORCH.)
*3,*2,*3,3 - 4,3,3,1 - timp.,perc. (2) - str.   10:00 Mills.
—— SYMPHONY NO. 3 (IN 1 MOVT.)
3(3rd alt. with picc.),*3,*3,2 - 4,3,3,2 - timp.,perc. (3), vibra., xyl. - str.   18:00 G. Schirmer.
—— SYMPHONY NO. 5, OP. 55
3(3rd alt. with picc.),3(3rd alt. with Eng. hn.)E♭cl.,*3,ten. sax., *4 - 8,3,2 cnt.,3,bar.,1 - timp.,perc. - pf. - str.   28:00 Mills.
—— SYMPHONY NO. 6, OP. 60 (IN 4 MOVTS.)
*3,*3E♭cl.,*3,ten. sax.,*4 - 4,4,4,1 - timp.,perc. vibra. - hp. - pf. - str.   28:00 Mills.
—— THREE SYMPHONIC ESSAYS
3,3,3,2 -4,3,3,1 - timp.,vibra., xyl. - hp. - pf. - str. G. Schirmer.
—— THREE VARIATIONS ON A THEME
str.   G. Schirmer.
—— TOCCATA FOR ORGAN AND BRASS
2 hn. 3 tpt. 3 trb. - org.   16:00 Mills.
—— WALT WHITMAN SUITE (FOR CHORUS, STRINGS AND 2 PIANOS) (IN 3 MOVTS.)
2 pf. - str.   12:00 Mills.
—— WHEN JOHNNY COMES MARCHING HOME (OVERTURE)
*3,*3,E♭cl.,*3,3 - 6,3,3,2 - timp.,perc. (4) - str. 8:00 G. Schirmer.
—— WORK
*3,*3,*3,3 - 4,3,3,1 - timp. - pf. - str.   10:00 Mills.

HARRIS, Theodore
—— CONCERTO NO. 1 FOR PIANO AND ORCH. (IN 3 MOVTS.)
*3,2,2,0 - 2,2,2,1 - timp.,perc.,xyl. - pf. - str.   20:00 Composer.
—— SYMPHONY NO. 1
1. Slow with expression; 2. Allegro
*3,*3,2,2 - 4,2,2,1 - timp.,perc.(3) - pf. - str.   20:00 Fanfare.

HARRISON, Francis Llewellyn
—— BAROQUE SUITE
                                                25:00 P.R.S.

HARRISON, Julius
—— AUTUMN LANDSCAPE
str.   8:00 Bo. Hawkes.
—— CORNISH HOLIDAY SKETCHES (THEME AND VARIATIONS)
str.   15:00 Bo. Hawkes.

—— FOUR CAVALIER TUNES (FOR TENOR AND ORCH.)
2,2,2,2 - 4,2,3,0 - timp.,perc., cel. - hp. - str.   Bo. Hawkes.
—— FOUR SONGS OF CHIVALRY (FOR TENOR AND ORCH.)
2,2,2,3 - 2,2,3,0 - timp.,perc., cel. - hp. - str.   Bo. Hawkes.
—— MASS IN C MAJOR (FOR SOLO VOICES, CHORUS, ORGAN AND ORCH.)
                                                85:00 Lengnick.
—— PSALM 100 (FOR CHORUS AND ORCH.)
2,2,2,2 - 4,2,3,1 - timp. - org. - str.   Lengnick.
—— REQUIEM MASS (FOR SOLO VOICES, CHORUS, AND ORCHESTRA)
3,2,2,2 - 4,3,3,1 - timp. - hp. - org. - str.   82:00 Lengnick.
—— RHAPSODY FOR BARITONE VOICE AND ORCH.
2,2,2,2 - 4,2,3,0 - timp. - hp. - str.   Bo. Hawkes.
—— RHAPSODY FOR VIOLIN AND ORCH. ("BRENDON HILL")
2,2,2,2 - 4,2,3,1 - timp.,perc. - hp. - str.   12:30 Bo. Hawkes.
—— TROUBADOUR SUITE (FOR STRING ORCH.)
2 hn.(ad lib.) - hp. (or pf.) - str.   10:00 Bo. Hawkes.

HARRISON, Pamela
—— BRIMSTONE DOWN
2,1,2,2 - 0,0,0,0 - str.   P.R.S.
—— A SUITE FOR TIMOTHY
str.   C. Fischer.

HARSÁNYI, Tibor
—— ARIA AND RONDO (FOR CELLO AND ORCH.)
2,2,2,2 - 2,2,0,0 - timp.,perc., glock. xyl. - str.   15:00 Salabert.
—— CANTATE DE NOËL (FOR SOPRANO, MEZZO-SOPRANO, TENOR, BARITONE, AND SMALL ORCHESTRA)
fl. - str.   25:00 Presser.
—— CONCERTINO FOR PIANO AND STRINGS
pf. - str.   25:00 Salabert.
—— CONCERTO FOR VIOLIN AND ORCH.
2,2,2,2 - 4,2,3,0 - timp.,perc. - str.   30:00 Salabert.
—— CONCERTSTÜCK (FOR PIANO AND ORCH.)
3,3,3,2 - 4,2,0,0 - timp.,perc. glock., xyl. - pf. - str. 15:00 Salabert.
—— DANSES VARIÉES
                                                20:00 Mercury.
—— DIVERTIMENTO NO. 1 (CONCERTINO FOR TWO VIOLINS AND CHAMBER ORCH.)
2,1,1,1 - 2,1,0,0 - timp.,perc. - str.   17:00 Salabert.
—— DIVERTIMENTO NO. 2 (SERENADE) (IN 4 MOVTS.)
tpt. - str.   25:00 Salabert.
—— DIVERTISSEMENT FRANÇAIS
2,2,2,2 - 2,2,1,0 - timp.,perc.(3) - str.   10:00 Presser.
—— LA JOIE DE VIVRE (DIVERTISSEMENT)
2,0,4,sax.,1 - 0,3,2,0 - timp.,perc. (3), cel. - hp. - pf. - str.
                                                12:00 Salabert.
—— OUVERTURE SYMPHONIQUE
3,2,3,3 - 4,3,3,1 - timp.,perc. cel. - hp. - str. 7:00 Salabert.
—— RHAPSODIE BURLESQUE
2,2,2,2 - 1,2,1,0 - perc.,cel.,xyl. - hp. - str. 10:00 Presser.
—— SUITE
4,4,4,4 - 4,4,3,1 - timp.,perc., cel., glock., xyl. - 2 hp. - str.
                                                25:00 Salabert.
—— SYMPHONY IN C (IN 4 MOVTS.)
3,3,3,3 - 4,3,3,1 - timp.,perc., glock., xyl. - hp. - str.
                                                30:00 Salabert.
—— TROIS MORCEAUX
4,3,3,2 - 4,3,3,1 - timp.,perc. cel. - hp. - str. 10:00 Salabert.
—— TROIS PIECES DE DANSE
3,3,3,1 alto sax.,1 ten. sax.,3 - 4,3,4,0 - timp.,perc.,cel.,glock.,xyl. - banjo - pf. - str.   7:00 Presser.

HART, Weldon
—— CONCERTO FOR VIOLIN AND ORCH. (IN 3 MOVTS.)
2,2,2,2 - 4,3,3,1 - timp.,perc. (3), glock., xyl. - str.
                                                22:00 Composer.
—— DARLING CORY (STUDY BASED ON A FOLK SONG)
*3,*3,2,2 - 4,2,3,1 - timp.,perc. (4), xyl. - str. 6:30 Composer.
—— JOHN JACOBS NILES SUITE (IN 3 MOVTS.) (LOVE SONGS, CAROLS AND BALLADS)
2(2nd alt. with picc.),2,2,2 - 4,3,3,1 - timp.,perc.(4), bells, xyl. - str.   15:00 G. Schirmer.
—— O SING UNTO THE LORD (FOR MIXED CHORUS AND ORCH.)
2,2,2,2 - 4,3,3,1 - perc. (3), xyl.,- hp. - str. 4:30 C. Fischer.
—— PENNYRILE (A CONCERT OVERTURE)
*3,2,2,2 - 4,3,3,1 - timp.,perc. (3), glock. - str. 6:00 Composer.
—— STATELY MUSIC FOR STRINGS
str.   12:00 C. Fischer.

—— SYMPHONY NO. 1 (IN 3 MOVTS.)
    *3,2,2,2 - 4,3,3,1 - timp.,perc. (4), xyl. - str.   25:00 C. Fischer.
—— THREE WEST VIRGINIA FOLKSONGS (FOR MIXED
CHORUS AND ORCH.)
    2,2,2,2 - 4,3,3,1 - timp.,perc.(3) - hp. - str.   10:00 Arranger.

HARTLEY, Walter S.
—— BALLET MUSIC FOR ORCH. (SUITE) (1949) (IN 6 MOVTS.)
    2(2nd alt. with picc.),2(2nd alt. with Eng.hn.),2,2 - 4,2,3,1 -
    timp.,perc.(2-3) - hp. - str.   13:45 Fema.
—— CHAMBER SYMPHONY (IN 3 MOVTS.)
    1(alt. with picc.),1,1,1 - 2,1,1,0 - hp. - str.   12:30 Galaxy.
—— CONCERT OVERTURE (1954)
    2(2nd alt. with picc.),2,2,2 - 4,2,3,1 - timp.,perc.(2) - str.
    7:30 Fema.
—— CONCERTINO FOR CHAMBER ENSEMBLE (1951)
    1. Andante - Allegro; 2. Lento; 3. Scherzo; 4. Chaconne
    (Andante)
    0,0,1,0 - 0,0,1,0 - perc.(1),glock.,xyl. - pf. - 4 vln.,4 c.
    14:00 Fema.
—— CONCERTO FOR PIANO AND ORCH. (1952) (IN 3 MOVTS.)
    3(3rd alt. with picc.),2(2nd alt. with Eng.hn.),2,2 - 4,3,3,1 -
    timp.,perc.(2) - pf. - str.   19:00 Fema.
—— CONCERTO FOR 23 WINDS (IN 4 MOVTS.)
    3(2nd and 3rd alt. with piccs.),3(3rd alt. with Eng.hn.),3(3rd alt.
    with b.-cl.),3 - 4,3,3,1   17:00 Rochester.
—— DOUBLE CONCERTO, OP. 83 (1969) (FOR ALTO
SAXOPHONE, TUBA AND WIND OCTET)
    1,1,1,1 alto sax.,1 - 1,2,1,1   10:00 J. Boonin.
—— ELEGY FOR STRINGS (1952)
    str.   4:00 Fema.
—— ELIZABETHAN DANCES (1962)
    2,2,2,2 - 2,2,2,0 - timp.,perc.(3) - str.   4:00 Fema.
—— FESTIVE MUSIC FOR ORCH. (1963)
    2,2,2,2 - 4,2,3,1 - timp.,perc.(3) - str.   4:00 Fema.
—— PARTITA FOR CHAMBER ORCHESTRA, OP. 61 (1964) (IN 5
MOVTS.)
    1,1,1,1, - 2,1,0,0 - 1 vln.,1 vla.,1 c.   15:45 Galaxy.
—— PSALM FOR STRINGS, OP. 58 (1964)
    str.   5:00 Presser.
—— SINFONIA NO. 2 FOR ORCH. (1962)
    1. Allegro moderato; 2. Adagio - Allegro molto
    2(2nd alt. with picc.),2,2,2 - 4,3,3,1 - timp.,perc.(2) - str.
    12:00 Fema.
—— TRIPTYCH FOR ORCH. (1951)
    2(2nd alt. with picc.),2(2nd alt. with Eng.hn.),2,2 - 2,2,1,0 -
    timp.,perc.(2-3),xyl.   15:00 Fema.
—— VARIATIONS FOR ORCHESTRA (1973)
    *3,2,2,2 - 4,3,3,1 - timp.,perc.(4) - str.   10:00 Fema.

HARTMANN, Arthur
—— AT THE MID HOUR OF NIGHT (FOR CHORUS AND ORCH.)
    *3,2,2,2 - 4,2,3,1 - timp. - hp. - str.   11:00 Composer.
—— SUITE (IN 3 MOVTS.)
    1,*2,2,1 - 2,1,1,0 - timp.,perc. - pf.(or hp.) - str.   Composer.
—— TIMAR (SYMPHONIC POEM)
    2 picc.,2,*3,*3 - 4,2,3,1 - timp.,perc. - hp. - str.   17:00 Composer.
—— TWO IMPRESSIONS FROM THE BALKANS
    2 picc.,2,*3,2,2 - 4,2,3,1 - timp.,perc. - hp. - str.   14:00 Composer.

HARTMANN, Thomas de
—— AUSONIUS, OP. 13 (FOUR POEMS FOR LOW VOICE AND
ORCH.)
    3,2,2,2 - 4,3,3,1 - timp.,perc. - hp. - str.   12:00 Bo. Hawkes.
—— BABETTE, OP. 49 (BALLET) %
    3,2,2,2 - 4,2,3,1 - timp.,perc.,cel. - hp. - str.   40:00 Bo. Hawkes.
—— CONCERTO (AFTER A CANTATA OF BACH) FOR CELLO
AND STRING ORCH., OP. 73
    str.   18:00 S.A.C.E.M.
—— CONCERTO ANDALUZ, OP. 81
    1 fl. - perc. - hp. - pf. - str.   13:00 Bo. Hawkes.
—— CONCERTO FOR CELLO AND ORCH., OP. 57
    3,2,2,2 - 4,3,1,0 - timp.,perc. - hp. - pf. - str.   28:00 S.A.C.E.M.
—— CONCERTO FOR HARP AND ORCH., OP. 72
    2,2,2,2 - 4,3,1,0 - timp.,perc.,cel. - hp. - str.   22:00 Bo. Hawkes.
—— CONCERTO FOR PIANO AND ORCH., OP. 61
    3,2,2,2 - 4,3,2,1 - timp.,perc.,cel. - hp. - pf. - str.
    23:00 S.A.C.E.M.
—— CONCERTO FOR VIOLIN AND ORCH., OP. 66
    3,2,2,2 - 4,3,1,0 - timp.,perc. - hp. - pf. - str.   29:00 Bo. Hawkes.
—— DANCES FROM ACT III OF THE OPERA "ESTHER", OP. 76
    3,3,3,3 - 4,3,3,1 - timp.,perc. - hp. - pf. - str.
    13:00 Bo. Hawkes.

—— FANTAISIE - CONCERTO FOR DOUBLE BASS AND ORCH.,
OP. 65
    2,2,2,2 - 2,0,0,0 - timp.,perc.,cel. - hp. - str.   12:00 Bo. Hawkes.
—— FEAST IN THE UKRAINE (BALLET) %
    3,2,3,2 - 4,3,3,1 - timp.,perc.,cel. - hp. - str.   30:00 Bo. Hawkes.
—— KOLIADKY (UKRAINIAN CHRISTMAS SONGS), OP. 60
    3,2,2,2 - 4,3,3,1 - timp.,perc.,cel. - hp. - str.   18:00 Beekman.
—— MUSIQUE POUR LA FÊTE DE LA PATRONNE
    *3,2,2,*2 - 4,2,3,1 - timp.,perc. (2) - hp. - pf. - str.   Beekman.
—— SCHERZO FANTASTIQUE, OP. 25
    3,2,3,2 - 4,3,3,1 - timp.,perc.,cel. - hp. - pf. - str.
    18:00 Bo. Hawkes.
—— SUITE FROM THE BALLET "BABETTE", OP. 49
    3,2,3,2 - 4,3,3,1 - timp.,perc.,cel. - hp. - str.   35:00 Bo. Hawkes.
—— SUITE, OP. 62
    3,2,3,2 - 4,3,3,1 - timp.,perc.,cel. - hp. - str.   37:00 Bo. Hawkes.
—— SUITE, OP. 62 (RE-ORCHESTRATED 1952) (IN 3 MOVTS.)
    3,2,2,2 - 4,2,3,1 - timp.,perc. - hp. -pf. - str.   Bo. Hawkes.
—— SYMPHONIE-POÈME, NO. 3, OP. 85
    3,3,3,3 - 4,3,3,1 - timp.,perc. - hp. - pf. - org. - str.   Bo. Hawkes.
—— SYMPHONIE-POÈME, OP. 50 (IN FOUR SECTIONS)
    3,3,4,3 sax.,3 - 4,3,3,1 - timp.,perc.,cel. - hp. - pf. - str.
    54:00 Bo. Hawkes.
—— SYMPHONY NO. 2, OP. 68 ("LE DIT DU SOLEIL")
    3,3,3,3 - 4,3,3,1 - timp.,perc.,cel. - hp. - pf. - str.
    32:00 Bo. Hawkes.
—— SYMPHONY NO. 4, OP. 90: FIRST MOVT.
    2,3,3,3 - 4,3,3,1 - timp.,perc.,cel.,vibra. - hp. - pf. - str.
    12:00 Bo. Hawkes.
—— THREE POEMS OF SHELLEY, OP. 52 (FOR MEDIUM VOICE
AND ORCH.)
    2,2,2,2 - 4,3,1,0 - timp.,perc.,cel. (or pf.) - hp. - str.
    9:00 S.A.C.E.M.
—— TWELVE RUSSIAN FAIRY TALES, OP. 58
    3,3,3,3 - 4,3,3,1 - timp.,perc.,cel. - hp. - pf. - org. - str.
    18:00 Henmar.

HARTWAY, James J.
—— COULEURS (COLORS) (1969) (IN 1 MOVT.)
    2,2,2,2 - 4,4,4,0 - perc.(6),bells - str.   15:00 Composer.
—— DIALOGUE FOR PIANO AND ORCH. (1968) (IN 1 MOVT.)
    2,2,2,2 - 4,4,4,0 - perc.(5),bells - pf. - str.   12:00 Composer.

HARTY, Hamilton
—— THE CHILDREN OF LIR (SYMPHONIC POEM) (WITH
SOPRANO)
    3,3,3,3 - 4,3,3,1 - timp.,perc. - hp. - str.   30:00 Bo. Hawkes.
—— CONCERTO FOR VIOLIN AND ORCH.
    2,2,2,2 - 4,2,3,0 - timp.,perc. - hp. - str.   27:00 Novello.
—— IN IRELAND (FOR FLUTE, HARP AND ORCH.)
    2,2,2,1 - 2 hn. - timp.,perc. - hp. - str.   7:00 Bo. Hawkes.
—— AN IRISH SYMPHONY (IN 4 MOVTS.)
    3,2,2,2 - 4,2,3,1 - timp.,perc. - hp. - str.   27:00 Bo. Hawkes.

HARVANEK, Bohuslav
—— MEDITATION ON THE CHORALE "SVATY VACLAVE"
    6:00 O.S.A.

HARVEY, Eva Noel - ACRES, Harry
—— ESTHER (OPERA) % (Text: Ethel B. Fielding)
    2,2,3,2 - 4,2,3,1 - timp.,perc. - str.   150:00 S.A.M.R.O.

HARVEY, Jonathan
—— BENEDICTUS
    3,3,3,3 - 4,4,3,1 - perc. - 12 music-boxes - electric org. - pf. - str.
    17:00 Novello.
—— LITTLE CONCERTO FOR STRINGS (1961)
    str.   9:00 P.R.S.
—— PERSEPHONE DREAM
    3,3,3,3 - 4,3,3,1 - perc.,cel.,vibra.,xyl. - hp. - str.   16:00 Novello.
—— SYMPHONY (1966)
    2,2,3,2 - 4,2,2,1 - timp.,perc.(4,incl. 3 on timp.) - hp. - str.
    18:00 P.R.S.
—— TWO SYMBOLS (FOR CHAMBER ORCH.)(1963)
    0,2,0,2 - 2,0,0,0 - pf. - str.   8:00 P.R.S.

HARVEY, Vivien
—— RIP VAN WINKLE (SUITE FOR ORCH.)
    3,3,3,2 - 2,3,1,1 - timp.,perc., cel. - 2 hp. - pf. - str. 10:00 Ricordi.

HASELBACH, Josef
—— TRANSTULI
3,3,3,3 - 4,3,3,1 - perc.(6) - 2 hp. - org. - pf. - str.
25:00 S.U.I.S.A.

HASLAM, Herbert
—— AGNUS DEI (FOR MEZZO-SOPRANO AND STRING ORCH.)
str.   10:00 Composer.
—— ANTIMASQUE I (IN 3 MOVTS.)
2,0,2,1 - 0,1,0,0 - str.   6:00 Composer.
—— LAMENT
str.   8:00 Composer.
—— SECTORS (FOR MULTIPLE INSTRUMENTS WITHIN A
CHAMBER ORCH.)
1-*2,0,*2,0-1 - vibra.(ad lib.) - guit. - str.(no d.-b.)   Composer.
—— SPECIAL STARLIGHT (FOR TREBLE VOICES, SATB
CHORUS, NARRATOR AND ORCH.)
3,3,0,0 - 1,2,2,1 - timp.,perc. - pf. - str.   20:00 Presser.
—— SYMPHONY IN ONE MOVEMENT
3(3rd alt. with picc.),*3,*3,*3 - 4,3,3,1 - timp. - str.
20:00 Composer.

HASQUENOPH, Pierre
—— CONCERTINO FOR SAXOPHONE (OR CLARINET) AND
STRING ORCH.
Sax(or cl.) - str.   10:00 Presser.
—— CONCERTINO FOR STRINGS
str.   7:00 Eds. Fran.
—— CONCERTO FOR ORCHESTRA
3,3,3,3 - 4,4,3,1 - timp.,perc.,cel. - 2 hp. - pf. - str.   30:00 Presser.
—— EIGHT INVENTIONS FOR CHAMBER ORCH.
1,1,1,1 ten. sax.(or b.-cl.),1 - 1,1,0,0 - str.   18:00 Presser.
—— SYMPHONY NO. 1, OP. 10
2,2,2,2 - 2,2,2,0 - timp. - str.   21:00 Presser.
—— SYMPHONY NO. 2 (FOR STRINGS AND PERC.)
perc.,bells,xyl. - str.   24:00 Henmar.
—— SYMPHONY NO. 4
3,3,3,3 sax.,3 - 4,3,3,1 - timp.,perc.,cel. - pf. - str.   28:00 Presser.

HASQUENOTH, Pierre
—— STRUCTURES POLYPHONIQUES
str.   23:00 Henmar.
—— SYMPHONY NO. 3
3,3,3,3 - 4,4,3,1 - timp.,perc.,cel. - pf. - str.   24:00 Henmar.
or:
2,2,2,4 sax.,2 - 3,2,2,1 - timp.,perc.,cel. - pf. - str.

HASSE, Johann-Friedrich
—— PROOEMIUM (SYMPHONIC PRELUDE)
3(3rd alt. with picc.),2,2,2 - 4,3,3,1 - timp.,perc. - str.
12:00 Henmar.

HASSLER, Hans Leo - DAVIS, David H.
—— ELEGY: O SACRED HEAD (FOR SATB CHORUS AND
STRING ORCH.) (1967) (Text: 17th Century Hymn Text)
str.   8:00 Arranger.

HASSLER, Hans Leo - SEIBER, Matyas
—— FIVE DANCES
str.   Novello.

HASTINGS, Ross
—— CONCERTO DA CAMERA (FOR CLARINET AND STRINGS)
(1962) (IN 3 MOVTS.)
cl. - str.   12:00 Composer.
—— NOTTURNO (FROM THE "SONATINA FOR ORCH.") (1958)
1,1,2,2 - 0,0,3,0 - hp. or pf. - str.   4:00 C. Fischer.
or:
1,1,*3,1 - 0,0,3,0 - hp. or pf. - str.
—— PRELUDE (FROM THE "SONATINA FOR ORCH.") (1958)
2(2nd alt. with picc.),2,2,2 - 4,3,3,1 - timp.,perc.(6),bells,xyl. - hp.
- str.   3:00 Composer.
—— SCHERZETTO (FROM THE "SONATINA FOR ORCH.") (1958)
2(2nd alt. with picc.),2,2,2 - 4,3,3,1 - timp.,perc.(6), bells,xyl. - hp.
- str.   1:00 Composer.
—— SINFONIA BREVIS (1959) (IN 3 MOVTS.)
3(3rd alt. with picc.),*3,*3,2 - 4,3,3,1 - timp.,perc.(6),bells,xyl. -
hp. - pf. - str.   12:00 Composer.
—— SONATINA CONCERTANTE (FOR 4 CLARINETS AND
STRINGS) (1960) (IN 3 MOVTS.)
0,0*4,0 - 0,0,0,0 - str.   12:00 Composer.

—— SONATINA FOR ORCHESTRA (1958)
1. Prelude; 2. Nocturne; 3. Scherzetto
Composer.

HATZIS, Christos
—— KLEIDOCYMBALON I (1974) (FOR ANY NUMBER OF
INSTRUMENTS)
Seesaw.

HAUBENSTOCK-RAMATI, Roman
—— RECITATIVO ED ARIA (FOR HARPSICHORD AND ORCH.)
2,0,2,0 - 2,0,0,0 - timp.,perc.,cel.,vibra. - hp. - hpsc. - str.
10:00 IsMuPublns.
—— RICERCARI (REVISED 1965 EDITION)
str.   5:00 Is.MuPublns.

HAUBIEL, Charles
—— AMERICAN RHAPSODY (SYMPHONIC POEM)
*3,*3,2,2 - 4,3,3,1 - timp.,perc.(3-4),glock. - hp. - str.
9:35 C. Press.
—— L' AMORE SPIRITUALE (THREE SONGS) (FOR WOMEN'S
CHORUS AND ORCH.)
3(3rd alt. with picc.),2,2,1 - 4,3,0,0 - timp.,perc.(2) - hp. - str.
20:30 C. Press.
—— BERTA ("SUNDAY COSTS FIVE PESOS") (MEXICAN FOLK
OPERA IN 1 ACT) %
2(1 alt. with picc.),2,2,1 - 2,2,1,0 - timp.,perc. (2) - hp. (or pf.) -
str.   C. Press.
—— THE COSMIC CHRIST (FOR HIGH VOICE AND ORCH.)
*3,3,2,1 - 3,2,1,1 - 3 timp.,perc.(2) - hp.(or pf.) - str.
5:00 C. Press.
—— EIGHTEEN SIXTY-FIVE A.D. (SYMPHONIC POEM)
3,3,2,2 - 4,3,3,1 - timp.,perc. - hp. - str.   5:00 C. Press.
—— FATHER ABRAHAM (FOR SATB CHORUS AND ORCH.)
2,1,3,1 - 2,3,3,1 - timp.,perc.(2) - hp.(or pf.) - str.   5:30 C. Press.
—— GOTHIC VARIATIONS (FOR VIOLIN AND ORCH.)
3,3,2,2 - 4,3,3,1 - timp.,perc. - hp. - str.   17:00 C. Press.
—— HEROIC ELEGY (MARCIA SOLEMNE) (FOR SYMPHONY
ORCH.)
3(3rd alt. with picc.),3,3,2 - 4,3,3,1 - timp.,perc. - hp. - str.
13:15 C. Press.
—— KARMA (SYMPHONIC VARIATIONS ON A THEME OF
HANDEL)
4(3rd and 4th alt. with 2 picc.),*4,3(3rd alt. with b.-cl.),*3 -
4-8,4,3,1 - timp.,perc.(3),cel. - 2 hp. - pf. - str.   30:00 C. Press.
—— MARS ASCENDING (SYMPHONIC POEM)
3(3rd alt. with picc.),*3,*3,*3 - 4,4,3,1 - timp.,perc.(3),cel. - 2 hp. -
str.   10:00 C. Press.
—— MINIATURES (BOTH GRAVE AND GAY) (6 PIECES)
*4,1,3,1 - 4,3,3,1 - timp.,perc.(3) - hp. - str.   9:50 C. Press.
or:
str.
—— NUANCES (SUITE) (FOR FLUTE AND STRINGS) (IN 5
MOVTS.)
fl. - str.   10:00 C. Press.
—— OF HUMAN DESTINY (SYMPHONIC VARIATIONS)
4,3,3,3 - 4,3,3,1 - timp.,perc.,cel. - hp. - pf. - str.   30:00 C. Press.
—— PASSACAGLIA TRYPTICH
*4(3rd alt. with 2nd picc.),*4,*4,*3 - 4,3,3,1 - timp.,perc. - hp. -
str.   35:00 C. Press.
—— PIONEERS (A SYMPHONIC SAGA)
3(3rd alt. with picc.),*3,2,2 - 4,3,3,1 - timp.,perc. (3), xyl. - hp. -
str.   17:46 C. Press.
—— PORTALS (A SONG CYCLE)
2(2nd alt. with picc.),1,2,1 - 2,1,1,0 - timp. - hp. - str.
21:20 C. Press.
—— PORTALS (SYMPHONIC SONG CYCLE) (REVISED)
2(2nd alt. with picc.),1,2,1 - 2,1,1,0 - timp.,perc. - hp. - str.
23:30 C. Press.
—— SERENADE (CANTATA FOR SOLOISTS, CHORUS AND
ORCH.)
2,1,2,1 - 4,2,0,0 - hp.   11:45 C. Press.
—— SIX MINIATURES
*4,1,3,1 - 4,3,3,1 - timp.,perc. (3) - hp. - str.   8:00 C. Press.
or:
str.
—— SOLARI (IN 3 MOVTS.)
*4(3rd alt. with 2nd picc.),*4,*4,*3 - 4,3,3,1 - timp.,perc. (3-4) -
hp. - str.   34:30 C. Press.
—— SUITE PASSACAILLE (FOR STRING QUARTET AND ORCH.)
1,1,1,1 - 2,1,1,0 - timp.,perc.(2) - pf. - str.   23:15 C. Press.

—— SYMPHONY NO. 1 (IN FORM OF VARIATIONS) (IN 4
MOVTS.)
*4(3rd alt. with 2nd picc.),*3,*3,*3 - 4,2,3,1 - timp.,perc. - str.
21:30 C. Press.
—— THREE PORTRAITS (RITRATTI)
3(2 alt. with 2 picc.),2,2,2 - 4,3,3,1 - timp.,perc.(3) - hp. - str.
37:30 C. Press.
—— THREE SEA SONGS (FOR MEN'S CHORUS AND ORCH.)
3(3rd alt. with picc.),2,2,1 - 4,3,0,0 - timp.,perc. (2) - hp. - str.
9:00 Gray.
—— THE VISION OF ST. JOAN (A DRAMATIC CANTATA) (FOR
SOPRANO, MEZZO SOPRANO OR CONTRALTO, CHORUS,
OPTIONAL BOY'S CHORUS AND ORCH.)
*3,2,2,2 - 4,3,3,1 - timp.,perc. (3) - hp. - str. 15:00 C. Press.
—— VOX CATHEDRALIS (VOICE OF THE CATHEDRAL) (IN 2
MOVTS.)
3(3rd alt. with picc.),3,*3,3 - 4,3,3,1 - timp. - org.(ad lib.) - str.
18:10 C. Press.
—— YOU 48 STATES (FOR SOPRANO, MALE CHORUS AND
ORCH.)
2(2nd alt. with picc.),1,2,1 - 2,3,2,1 - timp.,perc. (2) - hp. - str.
9:30 Composer.

HAUDEBERT, Lucien
—— ANTIGONE: PRÉLUDE
3,3,3,4 - 4,3,3,1 - timp.,perc. - 2 hp. - str. 8:30 Salabert.
—— LA BATAILLE (FROM "LA FILLE DE JEPHTÉ")
3,3,3,3 - 4,4,3,1 - timp.,perc. - 2 hp. - str. 15:00 Salabert.
—— CHANT DE PÂQUES (SONG OF EASTER) (FOR SOPRANO,
BARITONE, MIXED CHORUS AND ORCH.)
3,2,2,2 - 4,3,3,1 - timp. - org. - str. 6:00 Salabert.
—— DIEU VAINQUEUR (PSALM) (FOR SOPRANO, MEZZO
SOPRANO, BARITONE, MIXED CHORUS AND ORCH.)
2,3,4,3 - 4,4,3,1 - timp.,perc. - 2 hp. - org. - str. 80:00 Salabert.
—— MOÏSE (ORATORIO) (FOR BARITONE, MIXED CHORUS
AND ORCH.)
3,3,3,3 - 4,3,3,1 - timp.,perc. - 2 hp. - str. 55:00 Salabert.
—— NATIVITÉ (FOR MEZZO-SOPRANO OR BARITONE, FEMALE
CHORUS AND ORCH.)
1,1,1,0 - 1,0,0,0 - timp.,perc. - str. 10:00 Salabert.
—— ODE À LA MUSIQUE (FOR FEMALE CHORUS AND ORCH.)
(FOR FEMALE CHORUS AND ORCH.)
2,2,2,3 - 3,2,3,0 - timp. - hp. - str. 9:00 Salabert.
—— LE SACRIFICE D'ABRAHAM (SYMPHONIC POEM)
3,3,3,3 - 4,4,3,1 - timp.,perc. - hp. - str. 13:00 Salabert.
—— SYMPHONIE FRANÇAISE (WITH HIGH AND MEDIUM
VOICES AND MIXED CHORUS)
3,3,3,4 -4,3,3,1 - timp.,perc.,cel. - hp. - pf. - str. 45:00 Salabert.

HAUG, Hans
—— CONCERTINO POUR TROMPETTE ET ORCHESTRE
15:00 S.U.I.S.A.
—— CONCERTO FOR FLUTE AND CHAMBER ORCH.
3,0,2,1 - 1,1,0,0 - perc. - str. 21:00 F. Colombo.
—— CONCERTO POUR FLÛTE, GUITARE ET ORCH.
32:00 S.U.I.S.A.
—— DOPPELKONZERT FÜR OBOE, BRATSCHE UND KLEINES
ORCH.
1,1,2,1 - 2,2,0,0 - timp.,perc. - str. 22:00 S.U.I.S.A.
—— GASTRONOMIC CANTATA (FOR SPEAKING VOICE, SATB
SOLO VOICES, SATB CHORUS AND ORCH.) (French text:
Brillat-Savarin; German text: Hans Haug)
2(2nd alt. with picc.),2(2nd alt. with Eng. hn.),2(2nd alt. with
b.-cl.),2 - 2,2,2,0 - timp.,perc.,cel. - hp. - hpsc.(4 hands) - pf. - str.
35:00 Modern.
—— KONZERT FÜR FLÖTE UND KLEINES ORCH.
1,1,2,1 - 2,2,0,0 - perc. - str. 27:00 Symphonia.
—— OVERTURE TO "DON JUAN IN DER FREMDE"
2,2,2,2 - 4,3,3,1 - timp.,perc. - str. 4:30 Henmar.
—— PASSACAGLIA (AUS "MICHELANGELO")
3,3,3,3 - 4,3,3,1 - timp.,perc. cel. - hp. - str. 11:00 S.U.I.S.A.
—— SYMPHONY IN E ("ROMANTIQUE")
3,3,3,3 - 4,3,3,1 - timp.,perc., cel. - hp. - str. 32:00 S.U.I.S.A.

HAUG, Lukas
—— EIGHT PIECES FOR ORCH. (AFTER JAPANESE POEMS)
2,2,2,2 - 4,2,3,0 - timp.,perc. - str. 12:50 Henmar.

HAUSEGGER, Siegmund von
—— AUFKLÄNGE (SYMPHONIC VARIATIONS) (1919)
3(3rd alt. with picc.),*3,*3,3(3rd alt. with c.-bn.) - 6,3,0,0 -
timp.,perc.(6, incl. 4 on timp.),cel. - 2 hp. - str. 30:00 Henmar.

HAVELKA, Svatopluk
—— SYMPHONY
3,3,3,3 - 4,3,3,1 - timp.,perc. - 2 hp. - pf. - str. 39:00 Bo. Hawkes.

HAWES, Jack
—— AN ENGLISH OVERTURE
2,2,2,2 - 4,2,3,1 - timp.,perc. - str. 15:00 P.R.S.
or:
2,2,2,2 - 2,2,0,0 - timp.,perc. - str.
—— POEM FOR VIOLIN AND ORCH. (REV. 1946)
2,2,2,2 - 4,2,0,0 - timp. - hp. - str. 10:00 P.R.S.

HAWORTH, Frank
—— AVALON (OVERTURE)
5:00 C.A.P.A.C.
—— CALDAY GRANGE SUITE (1958) (IN 3 MOVTS.)
str. 8:31 CanMusCtr.
—— CORNUCOPIA (SUITE FOR HORN AND STRINGS) (1972)
hn. - str. 12:05 CanMusCtr.
—— EDENVALE SUITE (1969)
2,2,2,2 - 2,2,2,0 - timp. - str. 14:00 CanMusCtr.
—— EMELEYA (TONE POEM) (1954)
2,2,2,2 - 2,2,2,0 - timp. - str. 4:30 CanMusCtr.
—— HOLGROVE SUITE (1958) (IN 3 MOVTS.)
2,2,2,2 - 2,2,2,0 - timp. - str. 10:57 CanMusCtr.
—— LOMYRA
2,2,2,2 - 2,2,2,0 - timp. - str. 4:05 CanMusCtr.
—— MACBETH (OVERTURE) (1953)
2,2,2,2 - 2,2,2,0 - timp. - str. 4:02 CanMusCtr.
—— PASTORAL SUITE (1956) (IN 3 MOVTS.)
hn. - str. 3:00 CanMusCtr.
—— ROYCROFT SUITE (1968)
2,2,2,2 - 2,2,2,0 - timp. - str. 6:55 CanMusCtr.

HAWTHORNE-BAKER, Allan
—— THE MINSTREL (CONCERT OVERTURE)
2,2,2,2 - 4,2,3,1 - timp.,perc. - hp. - str. 6:30 P.R.S.
—— PRELUDE TO AN ARTHURIAN DRAMA (1936)
3,2,2,2 - 4,2,3,1 - timp. - hp. - str. 10:00 P.R.S.
—— SYMPHONY NO. 3 IN C (1957)
3,3,3,3 - 4,3,3,1 - timp.,perc. - str. 50:00 P.R.S.
—— TWO POEMS FOR ORCH.
2,2,2,2 - 4,2,3,1 - timp.,perc. - hp. - str. 15:00 P.R.S.

HAYAKAWA, M.
—— THREE MOVEMENTS FOR STRINGS
str. 15:00 Presser.

HAYASHI, Hikaru
—— VARIATIONS FOR ORCHESTRA
3,3,3,3 - 4,3,3,1 - timp., perc.(4) - hp. - str. 18:00 Presser.

HAYDEN, Josef - BAZELAIRE, P.
—— ADAGIO (FOR CELLO AND STRINGS)
str. Salabert.

HAYDEN, Josef - DAHL, Ingolf
—— DIVERTIMENTO (FOR CELLO AND STRINGS) (WITH
OPTIONAL OBOE) (AFTER PIATIGORSKY'S
TRANSCRIPTION)
ob.(ad lib.) - str. 8:30 Presser.

HAYDEN, Josef - DE CAPRIO, Domenico
—— CONCERTO FOR CLARINET AND ORCH.
2,2,2,2 - 2,0,0,0 - str. 28:00 Gam.Hinged.

HAYDEN, Josef - FENDLER, Edvard
—— SYMPHONY NO. 53 IN D
1,2,0,2 - 2,2,0,0 - timp. - str. 17:00 Fox.

HAYDEN, Josef - GÁL, Hans
—— SYMPHONY IN B♭, OP. 10, NO. 2
2 ob. - 2 hn. - hpsc. - str. 10:00 Bo. Hawkes.

HAYDEN, Josef - GEIRINGER, Karl
—— ADAGIO AND PRESTO
fl. - 2 hn. - str. Novello.

HAYDEN, Josef - MOEHLMANN, R. L.
—— GREAT AND GLORIOUS (FOR CHORUS AND ORCH.) (ARR.
1969)
2,2,2,2 - 4,2,3,1 - timp. - str. 7:00 Mills.

HAYDEN, Josef - SEVITZKY, Fabien
—— LARGO FROM QUARTET, OP. 76, NO. 5
    1,*2,1,1 - 2 hn. - str.   5:00 Arranger.

HAYDEN, Josef - SHAW, Robert
—— THE CREATION (ENGLISH TEXT BY ROBERT SHAW AND
    ALICE PARKER)
                             Law-Gould.

HAYDEN, Josef - STOESSEL, Albert
—— THE EMPEROR VARIATIONS (FROM THE STRING
    QUARTET, OP. 76, NO. 3)
    str.   C. Fischer.

HAYDEN, Josef - TERTIS, Lionel
—— CONCERTO IN D FOR VIOLA AND ORCH. (ORIGINALLY
    FOR CELLO AND ORCH.)
    2,2,2,2 - 2 hn. - str.   18:00 Bo. Hawkes.

HAYDN, Franz Josef - BRITTEN, Benjamin
—— CONCERTO IN C FOR CELLO AND ORCH. (With cadenzas by
    B. Britten)
    0,2,0,0 - 2,0,0,0 - str.   25:00 Bo. Hawkes.

HAYDN, Franz Joseph - KIRBY, Percival Robson
—— CONCERTO IN G MAJOR FOR FLUTE AND ORCH.
    2,2,3,2 - 4,2,3,1 - timp.,perc. - str.   15:00 S.A.M.R.O.

HAYDN, Franz Joseph - SWANSON, Walter Donald
—— CONCERTO IN G MAJOR FOR VIOLIN AND ORCH.
    2,2,3,2 - 4,2,3,1 - timp.,perc. - str.   25:00 S.A.M.R.O.

HAYDN, Johann Michael - SCHROEDER, Felix
—— CONCERTO IN C MAJOR FOR OBOE AND ORCH. (With
    cadenzas by F. Schroeder)
    0,3,0,2 - 2,0,0,0 - str.   20:00 Mannheimer.

HAYDN, Josef
—— TE DEUM, 1800 (FOR MIXED CHORUS AND ORCH.) (English
    Text: Ivor Atkins)
    1,2,0,1 - 2,3,0-3,0 - timp. - org. - str.   Oxford.
    or:
    1,0,2,1 - 2,3,0-3,0 - timp. - org. - str.

HAYDN, Josef - BORMANN, Paul
—— CONCERTO FOR VIOLIN, PIANO (OR HARPSICHORD) AND
    STRING ORCH.
    cemb. - str.   Bo. Hawkes.

HAYDN, Josef - COLLINS, Anthony
—— LITTLE SYMPHONY
    str.   Fox.
    or:
    1,1,1,1 - 2,1,0,0 - timp. - str.
—— OPERA OVERTURE
    str.   Fox.
    or:
    2,2,0,2 - 2,0,0,0 - timp. - str.
    or:
    2,0,2,2 - 0,2,0,0 - timp. - str.

HAYDN, Josef - GÁL, Hans
—— OVERTURE TO "ARMIDA"
    2,2,2,2 - 2,2,1,0 - timp. - str.   6:00 Galaxy.
    or:
    1,2,0,2 - 2,0,0,0 - str.

HAYDN, Josef - GÁRDONYI, Zoltán
—— TWELVE SMALL DIVERTIMENTI
                             Bo. Hawkes.

HAYDN, Josef - GEIRINGER, Karl
—— DIVERTIMENTO IN G MAJOR (IN 3 MOVTS.)
    1,1,0,0 - 2,0,0,0 - str.   15:30 Henmar.

HAYDN, Josef - HALL, Ernest
—— CONCERTO FOR TRUMPET AND ORCH.
                       14:00 Bo. Hawkes.

HAYDN, Josef - KODÁLY, Zoltán
—— RONDO (FROM VIOLIN SONATA NO. 5)
    str.   Bo. Hawkes.

HAYDN, Josef - LAKE, M. L.
—— SYMPHONY NO. 15 IN B FLAT MAJOR
                             Ludwig.

HAYDN, Josef - LOTHAR, Mark
—— BALLET MUSIC ("THE TESTING OF HEART AND HEAD")
    FROM THE COMIC OPERA "DIE WELT AUF DEM MONDE"
    2,2,2,2 - 2,2,0,0 - timp. - str.   10:00 Henmar.
—— OVERTURE TO THE COMIC OPERA "DIE WELT AUF DEM
    MONDE"
    2,2,2,2 - 2,2,0,0 - timp. - str.   5:00 Henmar.

HAYDN, Josef - OUBRADOUS, Fernand
—— NOCTURNE NO. 1
    1,1,0,0 - 2,0,0,0 - str.   12:00 Presser.

HAYDN, Josef - PALMER, Edwina - BEST, Agnes
—— HAYDN SUITE
    str.   22:00 Oxford.

HAYDN, Josef - PIATIGORSKY, Gregor
—— DIVERTIMENTO FOR CELLO AND STRING ORCH.
    str.   9:00 EV.

HAYDN, Josef - ROSTROPOVICH, Mstislav L. - BRITTEN, Benjamin
—— CONCERTO IN C MAJOR FOR CELLO AND ORCH.
    0,2,0,0 - 2,0,0,0 - str.   25:00 Bo. Hawkes.

HAYDN, Josef - ROTHWELL, Evelyn
—— CONCERTO IN C FOR OBOE AND ORCH.
    0,3,0,0 - 2,2,0,0 - timp. - str.   21:00 Oxford.

HAYDN, Josef - SCHULTZ, Helmut
—— CONCERTO IN F MAJOR FOR VIOLIN, PIANO AND
    STRINGS
    pf. - str.   Henmar.

HAYDN, Josef - SHAW, Robert
—— SAYINGS OF THE SAVIOR ON THE CROSS (FOR CHORUS
    AND STRING ORCH.) (Engl. Text: Robert Shaw)
    str.   Law-Gould.

HAYDN, Josef - STEVES, Heinz Herbert
—— CONCERTO NO. 1 IN D MAJOR FOR HORN, 2 OBOES AND
    STRINGS
    2 ob. - hn. - str.   14:00 Bo. Hawkes.
—— CONCERTO NO. 2 FOR HORN AND STRINGS
    hn. - str.   15:00 Bo. Hawkes.

HAYDN, Josef - TROWELL, Arnold
—— CONCERTO NO. 2 IN D, FOR CELLO AND ORCH.
    2,2,2,2 - 2,0,0,0 - timp. - str.   22:00 Galaxy.

HAYDN, Josef - WERTHEIM, Gertude
—— CONCERTO IN C FOR CEMBALO AND STRINGS
    2 hn.(ad lib.) - cemb. - str.   11:00 Bo. Hawkes.

HAYDN, Josef - WINTER, Aubrey
—— SYMPHONY NO. 045 IN F SHARP MINOR ("FAREWELL")
                         30:00 Bo. Hawkes.
—— SYMPHONY NO. 085 IN B FLAT ("THE QUEEN")
                         25:00 Bo. Hawkes.
—— SYMPHONY NO. 094 IN G ("SURPRISE")
                         20:00 Bo. Hawkes.
—— SYMPHONY NO. 097 IN C
                         30:00 Bo. Hawkes.
—— SYMPHONY NO. 100 IN G ("THE MILITARY")
                         25:00 Bo. Hawkes.
—— SYMPHONY NO. 101 IN D ("THE CLOCK")
                         25:00 Bo. Hawkes.
—— SYMPHONY NO. 104 IN D ("LONDON")
                         38:00 Bo. Hawkes.
—— TOY SYMPHONY
    perc. (toy instrs.: tpt.,drum,cuckoo, quail, nightingale, rattle, trgl.)
    - pf.(ad lib.) - str.   12:00 Bo. Hawkes.

HAYDN, Josef - WOODHOUSE
—— SYMPHONY NO. 092 IN G ("OXFORD")
                         27:00 Bo. Hawkes.

HAYDN, Michael - KALMÁR, Jenö
—— DIVERTIMENTO
                           Bo. Hawkes.

HAYDN, Michael - OUBRADOUS, Fernand
—— CONCERTO FOR VIOLA, ORGAN, HARPSICHORD AND
STRINGS
hpsc. - org. - str.   Presser.

HAYDN, Michael - SOMFAI, László
—— SYMPHONY IN D MINOR (1774)
0,2,0,2 - 2,2,0,0 - str.   19:00 Bo. Hawkes.

HAYDN, Michael - THILDE, Jean
—— CONCERTO IN C (FOR TRUMPET, STRINGS AND
HARPSICHORD)
tpt. - hpsc. - str.   11:30 Presser.
—— CONCERTO IN E FLAT (FOR TRUMPET AND STRINGS)
tpt. - str.   Presser.

HAYDN, Michael - VÉCSEY, Jenö
—— MYTHOLOGICAL OPERETTA
                                                        Bo. Hawkes.

HAYS, Robert D.
—— MUSIC FOR BRASS (1962) (IN 3 MOVTS.)
0,0,0,0 - 3,3,3,1   17:00 Composer.
—— THE ORACLE OF APOLLO (FOR MOOG SYNTHESIZER,
TAPE AND ORCH.) (1969)
*3,2,*3,2 - 4,3,3,1 - timp.,perc.(2),bells,glock.,2xyl. - tape-recorder
- synthesizer (with heavy-duty amplifier-speaker system) - str.
                                            17:00 Composer.
—— SYMPHONY (1965) (IN 4 MOVTS.)
3(3rd alt. with picc.),2,*3,2 - 4,4,3,1 -
timp.,perc.(3),bells,glock.,mar.,xyl. - hp. - str.   16:27 Composer.
—— TO THE MEMORY OF THE AUTHOR ("WILLIAM
SHAKESPEARE") (FOR TENOR, MIXED CHORUS AND
ORCH.) (1964) (Text: Ben Jonson)
*3,*2,*4,1 - 3,3,3,1 - timp.,perc.bells,xyl. - str.   15:00 Composer.

HAZZARD, Peter
—— FUGUE AND PASTORALE (1971)
str.   5:00 Seesaw.
—— HARWICHPORT INTERLUDE
2,1,3,0 - 1,1,1,0 - timp.,perc. - str.   4:00 Seesaw.

HEAD, Michael
—— DAPHNE AND APOLLO (FOR SOPRANO, BARITONE, SATB
CHORUS AND ORCH.)
2,2,2,2 - 2,2,3,0 - timp.,perc. - hp.(ad lib.)   25:00 Bo. Hawkes.
or:
1,1,2,1 - 2,2,0,0 - timp.,perc. - hp.(ad lib.)

HEADLEE, Bruce J.
—— CONCERTO NO. 1 IN B FLAT MINOR, FOR PIANO AND
ORCH.
*2,2,2,1 - 4,2,3,1 - timp. - pf. - str.   Composer.
—— SYMPHONIC SUITE NO. 1 IN A MINOR, OP. 2 (IN 4
MOVTS.)
*2,2,2,2 - 4,2,3,1 - timp.,perc.(4),bells - str.   18:00 Composer.

HEALEY, Derek
—— VARIATIONS ON "THE THREE GYPSIES"
perc. - org. - str.   P.R.S.

HEARNE, John
—— CONCERTO FOR TRUMPET AND ORCH. (1966)
4,2,3,2 - 4,3,3,1 - timp.,perc. - hp. - pf. - str.   P.R.S.
—— GOSSIP COLUMN (CONCERT OVERTURE) (1960)
3,3,2,2 - 4,3,3,1 - timp.,perc. - hp. - pf. - str.   10:00 P.R.S.
—— SARN HELEN (1965)
0,0,0,0 - 2,2,1,0 a- timp. - str.   7:00 P.R.S.
—— SYMPOSIUM FOR ORCH. (1961)
3,2,2,2 - 4,4,3,1 - timp.,perc. - hp. - pf. - str.   40:00 P.R.S.

HECKMANN, Heinz
—— CONCERTO FOR OBOE, STRINGS AND PERCUSSION
ob. - perc. - str.   22:00 Mannheimer.

HEDDENHAUSEN, Friedel-Heinz
—— DIE LEGENDE VOM FERNEN, FREMDEN LAND (THE
LEGEND OF A STRANGE AND DISTANT LAND)
2,2(2nd alt. with Eng. hn.),2,2 - 4,3,3,1 - timp.,perc. - str.
                                             8:50 Henmar.

HEDLUND, Åke
—— MUSICA SVECICAE NO. 1 (1973)
str.   9:00 Fleisher.

HEDWALL, Lennart
—— CANZONA (1965)
str.   8:00 G. Schirmer.
—— CONCERTO FOR CELLO AND STRING ORCH. (1970)
str.   22:00 Nordiska.
—— CONCERTO FOR OBOE AND ORCH. (1956)
2,1,1,1 - 2,2,0,0 - str.   18:00 S.T.I.M.
—— CONCERTO LIRICO (1969)
str.   15:00 Fleisher.
—— FANTASIA (INTRODUCTION AND PASSACAGLIA ON
"VENI REDEMPTOR GENTIUM")(1972)
str.   9:00 Fleisher.
—— HERREN AR I SITT HELIGA TEMPEL (CANTATA) (FOR
SOPRANO OR BARITONE, MIXED CHORUS AND ORCH.)
(1958)
2,2,0,2 - 2,2,0,0 - org.(ad lib.) - str.   30:00 S.T.I.M.
—— LYRISK MUSIK (LARS ENGLUND IN MEMORIAM) (1959)
(FOR SOPRANO AND ORCH.)
2,2,2,2 - 2,2,1,0 - timp.,perc.(ad lib.) (1-2) - str.   20:00 S.T.I.M.
—— MUSIC NO. 1 FOR STRING ORCH. (1959)
str.   17:00 S.T.I.M.
—— MUSIC NO. 2 FOR STRING ORCH. (1958)
str.   13:00 S.T.I.M.
—— MUSIC NO. 3 FOR STRING ORCH. (1960)
str.   14:00 S.T.I.M.
—— PARTITA FOR 13 WINDS (1961)
2,2,2,2 - 2,2,1,0   18:00 S.T.I.M.
—— THREE SONGS FOR BARITONE AND ORCH. (1954)
2,2,2,2 - 2,2,1,0 - perc.(1) - str.   6:00 S.T.I.M.
—— VARIAZIONI PICCOLI (1958)
2,2,2,2 - 2,2,1,0 - perc.(1) - str.   10:00 S.T.I.M.

HEENAN, Ashley
—— A COLLEGE OVERTURE
                                             12:00 A.P.R.A.
—— SIX MUSICAL PORTRAITS (FOR NARRATOR AND ORCH.)
                                             12:00 A.P.R.A.
—— THREE SEASONS (FOR BARITONE AND ORCH.)
                                             8:30 A.P.R.A.

HEGER, Robert
—— SECHS PARTITEN UND TOCCATA, OP. 41 (ON THE
CHORALE "JAUCHZT ALLE LANDE, GOTT ZU EHREN")
3,2,3,2 - 4,3,3,1 - timp.,perc. - hp. - str.   33:00 G. Schirmer.

HEGNER, Anton
—— AMERICAN FESTIVAL OVERTURE
3,2,2,2 - 4,2,3,1 - perc. - str.   G. Schirmer.

HEIDE, Harald
—— THE SONG OF THE SEA ("HAVETS SANG") (SYMPHONIC
POEM)
3,3,3,3 - 4,2,3,1 - timp.,perc. - hp. - str.   18:00 T.O.N.O.
—— SYMPHONIC ROMANTIQUE
3,2,2,2 - 4,2,3,1 - timp.,perc.,cel. - hp. - str.   37:00 T.O.N.O.

HEIDER, Werner
—— AMERICAN SUITE (FOR HARPSICHORD AND SMALL
ORCH.)
2(2nd alt. with picc.),0,1,0 - perc. - electric guit. - hpsc. - str.
                                             11:00 Modern.
—— CONCERTO FOR TRUMPET, BARITONE SAXOPHONE AND
ORCH.
2(2nd alt. with picc.),2(2nd alt. with Eng.hn.),2(2nd alt. with
b.-cl.),bar.sax.,2(2nd alt. with c.-bn.) - 4,3,3,1 - timp.,perc.(3),cel. -
hp. - str.   9:00 Modern.
—— RITIMICA (SUITE) (FOR JAZZ COMBO AND ORCH.) (IN 7
MOVTS.)
*3,2,2,1 alto sax.,2 - 5,2,4,1 - perc.(2) - hp. - pf. - str.
                                             23:00 AhnSimrock.
—— SIX DROLL STORIES (AFTER BALZAC)
                                             AhnSimrock.
—— TOCCATA FOR ORCHESTRA (1952)
*3,2,2,2 - 4,3,3,0 - timp.,perc. - hp. - str.   8:40 AhnSimrock.
—— TYPEN (FOR ALTO SAXOPHONE AND ORCH.)
2(2nd alt. with picc.),2(2nd alt. with Eng.hn.),2(2nd alt. with
b.-cl.),alto sax.,2 - 4,2,2,0 - perc. - hp. - str.   6:00 AhnSimrock.

HEIFETZ, Vladimir
—— BABI YAR, OP. 81 (FOR SATB CHORUS AND ORCH.) (IN 5 MOVTS.)
1,*2,1,0 - 0,0,0,0 - perc.,bells - pf. - str.   25:00 Composer.
—— PRELUDE AND FUGUE, OP. 52 (ON AN AMERICAN FOLK SONG) (FOR VOICES AND STRING ORCH.)
str.   6:00 Composer.
—— SYMPHONY, OP. 75 ("NEW ERA" - NEW YORK WORLD'S FAIR, 1939) (FOR SOPRANO, ALTO, TENOR, BASS AND ORCH.)
*3,*3,*4,*3 - 4,4,3,1 - timp.,perc.(3),cel.,xyl. - hp. - str.   32:00 Composer.
—— TOCCATA AND FUGUE, OP. 61 (SALUTE TO THE MIGHTY)
*3,*2,2,*3 - 2,3,2,1 - timp.,perc. - str.   7:30 Composer.

HEILMANN, Harald
—— CANTO SINFONICO FÜR ORCH.
2,2,2,2 - 4,2,3,1 - timp. - str.   25:00 Henmar.
—— CONCERTO FOR HARP, CELLO AND STRINGS (IN 3 MOVTS.)
hp. - str.   Henmar.
—— TWO NORWEGIAN BALLADS
str.   14:00 Henmar.

HEIMONEN, Veli
—— CATHEDRAL MUSIC I (1960)
2 fl. - pf. - str.   10:00 FinnMICtr.
—— CATHEDRAL MUSIC II (1960)
2,3,3,2 - 4,2,3,1 - pf. - str.   17:00 FinnMICtr.
—— CATHEDRAL MUSIC III (1961)
2,3,3,2 - 4,2,3,1 - timp.,perc. - pf. - str.   10:00 FinnMICtr.
—— CATHEDRAL MUSIC IV (1961)
2,3,3,2 - 4,2,3,1 - timp.,perc. - pf. - str.   10:00 FinnMICtr.
—— CATHEDRAL MUSIC V (1961)
2,3,3,2 - 4,2,3,1 - pf. - str.   9:00 FinnMICtr.
—— CATHEDRAL MUSIC VI (1962)
2,3,3,0 - 4,2,3,1 - timp.,perc. - pf. - str.   10:00 FinnMICtr.
—— IMPROVISING (1962)
2,3,3,0 - 4,2,3,1 - timp.,perc. - pf. - str.   10:00 FinnMICtr.

HEININEN, Paavo
—— ADAGIO, OP. 12 (CONCERTO FOR ORCHESTRA, IN THE FORM OF VARIATIONS) (REV. 1966)
4,4,4,3 - 6,4,3,0 - perc.(6),cel. - hpsc. - pf. - str.   12:00 FinnMICtr.
—— ARIOSO, OP. 16 (1967)
str.   10:00 Fazer.
—— CANTICO DELLE CREATURE, OP. 17 (FOR BARITONE AND ORCH.) (1968) (Text: St. Francis of Assisi)
2,2,2,1 - 2,2,0,0 - timp. - hp. - str.   15:00 FinnMICtr.
—— CONCERTO FOR STRING ORCH., OP. 6 (REV. 1963)
str.   18:00 FinnMICtr.
—— CONCERTO NO. 1 FOR PIANO AND ORCH., OP. 13 (1964)
3,2,3,2 - 4,2,2,0 - timp.,perc.(3),cel. - hp. - pf. - str.   28:00 FinnMICtr.
—— CONCERTO NO. 2 FOR PIANO AND ORCH., OP. 15 (1966)
3,2,3,2 - 4,2,2,0 - timp.,perc.(3),cel. - hp. - pf. - str.   27:00 FinnMICtr.
—— PREAMBOLO, OP. 4 (AN OVERTURE) (1959)
3,3,3,3 - 4,3,3,0 - timp.,perc. - pf. - str.   10:00 FinnMICtr.
—— SOGGETTO, OP. 10 (FOR 14 SOLO STRINGS AND ORCH.) (1963)
1,1,2,1 - 1,1,0,0 - perc.(2) - pf. - str.(8,3,2,1)   8:00 FinnMICtr.
—— SYMPHONY NO. 1, OP. 3 (REV. 1960)
3,3,3,3 - 4,3,3,1 - timp.,perc.(5) - pf. - str.   24:00 FinnMICtr.
—— SYMPHONY NO. 2, OP. 9 ("PETITE SYMPHONIE JOYEUSE") (1962)
2,2,3,2 - 4,2,2,0 - timp.,perc.(4),cel. - hp. - pf. - str.   24:00 FinnMICtr.
—— SYMPHONY NO. 3, OP. 20 (1969)
3,3,3,2 - 4,3,3,0 - timp.,perc.(3) - hp. - 2 pf. - str.   35:00 FinnMICtr.
—— SYMPHONY NO. 4, OP. 27 (1971)
2,2,2,2 - 2,2,2,0 - timp.,perc.(4) - hp. - pf. - str.   25:00 FinnMICtr.
—— TRIPARTITA, OP. 5 (1959)
3,3,3,2 - 4,3,3,0 - timp.,perc.(3) - hp. - pf. - str.   18:00 FinnMICtr.
or:
2,2,2,2 - 3,2,3,0 - timp.,perc. - hp. - str.

HEINIÖ, Mikko
—— CONCERTO FOR PIANO AND ORCH., OP. 4 (1971)
2,2,2,2 - 4,2,3,0 - timp.,perc.(3) - pf. - str.   25:00 FinnMICtr.

—— SYMPHONY NO. 1, OP. 9 ("THE CREATION") (FOR SOPRANO, BARITONE, SATB CHORUS AND ORCH.) (1972)
4,3,4,3 - 8,4,3,1 - timp.,perc.(6) - 2 hp. - str.   55:00 FinnMICtr.

HEINRICH, Hermann
—— DIE MUSICI (OVERTURE)
2,2,2,2 - 4,3,3,0 - timp.,perc. - hp. - str.   15:00 Henmar.

HEINTZE, Gustaf
—— CONCERT PIECE IN F# MINOR, FOR PIANO AND ORCH.
2,2,2,2 - 2,0,0,0 - pf. - str.   17:00 S.T.I.M.
—— CONCERTO IN A MINOR, FOR 2 PIANOS AND ORCH.
3,2,2,2 - 4,2,3,0 - timp. - 2 pf. - str.   25:00 S.T.I.M.
—— CONCERTO NO. 1 IN B MINOR, FOR VIOLIN AND ORCH.
2,2,2,2 - 4,2,3,1 - timp. - str.   30:00 S.T.I.M.
—— CONCERTO NO. 1 IN F MINOR, FOR PIANO AND ORCH.
2,2,2,2 - 2,2,2,1 - timp. - pf. - str.   30:00 S.T.I.M.
—— CONCERTO NO. 2 IN E MINOR, FOR PIANO AND ORCH.
3,2,2,2 - 4,2,3,0 - timp. - pf. - str.   25:00 S.T.I.M.
—— CONCERTO NO. 2 IN E MINOR, FOR VIOLIN AND ORCH.
2,2,2,2 - 4,2,2,1 - timp. - str.   25:00 S.T.I.M.

HEISS, Hermann
—— BEWEGUNGSSPIELE FÜR ORCH. (1959) (IN 6 MOVTS.)
*2,*1,*2,*2 - 2,2,1,0 - timp.,perc.,xyl. - pf. - str.   20:55 AhnSimrock.
—— CALAMITIES (SCHACHTELGESÄNGE NACH WORTEN VON UDO ESP) (FOR SOPRANO, TENOR AND ENSEMBLE)
0,0,*3,0 - 0,2,1,0 - perc.,mar.,vibra. - pf. - str.(2,1,1,0)   12:00 Modern.
—— DER MANAGER (SUITE FROM THE BALLET)
2,1,3,sax.,2 - 3,3,3,1 - timp.,perc. - acc. - hp. - pf. - str.   40:00 Modern.
—— SIEBEN STÜCKE (7 PIECES)
str.   12:00 G. Schirmer.

HELA, Martti
—— THE CROSS IS BROUGHT TO HÄME, OP. 20 (FOR SATB CHORUS AND ORCH.) (1948) (Text: Lauri Pohjanpää)
2,2,2,2 - 2,2,2,0 - timp.,perc. - str.   12:00 FinnMICtr.
—— PSALM 84 (FOR BARITONE, SATB CHORUS AND ORCH.) (1924)
2,0,2,0 - 2,2,0,0 - str.   14:00 FinnMICtr.
—— SUITE IN THE OLD STYLE (1928)
2,2,0,2 - 4,2,1,1 - timp.,perc. - str.   FinnMICtr.

HELBIG, Otto H.
—— THE PENTAGON (SUITE) (IN 5 MOVTS.)
*3,*3,*3,2 - 4,3,3,1 - timp.,perc.(4),cel.,xyl. - hp. - str.   19:00 Composer.
—— STYLES IN MUSIC (SUITE) (IN 4 MOVTS.)
*3,2,*4,2 - 4,4,3,1 - timp.,perc.(3),bells.,xyl. - str.   9:00 Composer.

HELFER, Walter
—— CHANSON DU VOYAGEUR (FOR CHORUS AND ORCH.)
2,2,2,2 - 4,2,3,0 - timp. - org.(ad lib.) - str.   4:00 Composer.
—— FANTASY ON CHILDREN'S TUNES
1,1,1,1 - 2,1,0,0 - timp.,perc. (2), cel. - pf. - str.   14:00 Composer.
—— OVERTURE
*3,*3,*3,*3 - 4,3,3,1 - timp.,perc. (3) - str.   8:00 Composer.
—— PRELUDE TO "A MIDSUMMER NIGHT'S DREAM"
1,1,1,2 - 1,1,0,0 - timp.(ad lib.) - pf. - str.   14:00 Composer.
—— SUITE FOR CHAMBER ORCH.
1. Prelude; 2. Aria; 3. Fugue
1,1,2,1 - hn. - pf. - str.   15:00 Composer.
—— LE VOYAGEUR (SYMPHONIC FANTASY BASED ON CANADIAN AIRS)
1. Lento; 2. Intermezzo; 3. Allegro moderato
3(3rd alt. with picc.),*3,*4,*4 - 5,3,3,1 - timp.,perc. - hp. - str.   30:00 Composer.

HELLER, Barbara
—— SINFONIETTA FOR STRING ORCH.
str.   21:00 Mannheimer.

HELLER, John
—— DIVERTIMENTO FOR SMALL ORCH. (IN 7 MOVTS.)
2(2nd alt. with picc.),1(alt. with Eng. hn.),1(alt. with b-cl.),1 - 2,1,1,1 - timp.,perc. - str.   12:00 Henmar.

HELLMAN, Ivar
—— CONCERT PIECE FOR VIOLIN AND ORCH.
2,2,2,2 - 4,2,3,1 - timp.,perc. - str.   10:00 S.T.I.M.

or:
2,2,2,2 - 2,2,1,0 - timp. - str.
—— SERENADE FOR STRINGS
str.   23:00 S.T.I.M.
—— SUITE FOR STRINGS, WITH PIANO OBLIGATTO
pf. - str.   20:00 S.T.I.M.
—— SYMPHONIC SUITE (1971)
2,2,2,2 - 4,2,3,0 - timp., - hp. - str.   20:00 Fleisher.
—— TURANDOT (SYMPHONIC POEM)
3,3,3,3 - 4,3,3,1 - timp.,perc. (2) - str.   12:00 S.T.I.M.

HELM, Everett
—— BRASILIANA
4,3,3,3 -4,3,2,1 - timp.,perc. - pf. - str.   12:00 C. Fischer.
—— CONCERTO FOR STRINGS
str.   23:00 Alkor.
—— SUITE FOR SMALL ORCH. (IN 5 MOVTS.)
*2,1,1,1 - 2,2,2,0   14:00 Hargail.

HELY-HUTCHINSON, Victor
—— CAROL SYMPHONY
4,3,3,3 - 4,3,3,1 - timp.,perc. - hp. - str.   26:00 Novello.
—— OVERTURE FOR A THEATRE ORCH.
2(2nd alt. with picc.),1,2,1 - 2,2,3,0 - timp.,trgl. - str.
                                                                     5:00 Novello.
—— THREE FUGAL FANCIES
str.   Novello.
—— THREE NONSENSE SONGS (FOR MEDIUM VOICE AND
ORCH.) (Text: Edward Lear)
1,0,1,1 - 1,0,0,0 - str.   9:00 C. Fischer.
—— THE YOUNG IDEA (RHAPSODY FOR PIANO, WINDS AND
PERCUSSION)
2,1,2,2 - 2,2,1,0 - timp.,perc.(3) - pf.   5:00 Novello.

HEMBERG, Eskil
—— MIGRAINE, OP. 19-B (1973)
1,1,1,1 - 0,0,0,0 - timp. - str.(no d.-b.)   7:00 Fleisher.

HEMEL, Oscar van
—— BALLADE
3,3,3,3 - 4,3,3,1 - timp.,perc. - str.   16:00 Henmar.
—— BALLADE VAN BRABANT (FOR BARITONE, SPEAKER,
BOYS' CHORUS, MALE CHORUS AND ORCH.) (1952) (Text:
Anton van Duinkerken)
2,2,2,2 - 4,3,3,1 - timp.,perc.,cel. - hp. - str. 25:00 Henmar.
—— DE BRUID (FOR SOPRANO, MALE CHORUS AND ORCH.)
(1947) (Text: Jan Prins)
2,2,2,2 - 4,3,3,1 - timp.,perc.,cel. - hp. - str. 15:00 Henmar.
—— CONCERTINO FOR VIOLIN AND ORCH. (1963)
2,2,2,2 - 4,2,3,0 - timp. - str.   13:00 Henmar.
—— CONCERTO DA CAMERA (FOR FLUTE AND STRING
ORCH.) (1962)
fl. - str.   13:00 Henmar.
—— CONCERTO FOR CELLO AND ORCH. (1963)
3,3,2,2 - 4,3,3,1 - timp.,perc.,cel. - hp. - str. 16:00 Henmar.
—— CONCERTO FOR OBOE AND ORCH.
2,1,2,2 - 4,2,0,0 - timp., cel. - str.   18:00 Henmar.
—— CONCERTO FOR PIANO AND ORCH.
2,2,2,2 - 4,3,2,1 - timp. - pf. - str.   20:00 Henmar.
—— CONCERTO FOR VIOLA AND ORCH.
2,2,2,2 - 4,0,3,0 - timp.,perc. - str.   21:00 Henmar.
—— CONCERTO FOR WIND INSTRUMENTS (1960)
3,3,3,3 - 4,3,3,1   13:00 Henmar.
—— CONCERTO NO. 1 FOR VIOLIN AND ORCH. (1946)
2,2,2,2 - 4,1,3,0 - timp. - str.   27:00 H. Elkan.
—— CONCERTO NO. 2 FOR VIOLIN AND ORCH. (4
SCHERZANDI, WITH 4 INSTRUMENTAL GROUPS)
2,2,3,2 - 4,3,3,0 - timp.,perc.,cel. - hp. - str. 13:00 Henmar.
—— DIVERTIMENTO-BALLET FROM THE OPERA "VIVIANE"
2,2,2,2 - 2,2,0,0 - timp.,perc. - str.   7:00 Henmar.
—— DIVERTIMENTO (1964)
str.   17:00 Henmar.
—— FESTIVAL OVERTURE
2,2,2,2 - 4,2,2,1 - timp. - str.   10:00 Henmar.
—— HART VAN NEDERLAND (BALLADE OP HOLLANDS
WATER VAARWEL LAND) (FOR MALE CHORUS, WINDS
AND PERCUSSION) (1952) (Text: B. Aafjes)
1,2,1,1 - 1,2,0,0 - timp.,perc. - pf.(ad lib.)   18:00 Henmar.
—— HERDENKINGSHYMAE (MEMORIAL HYMN) (FOR MIXED
CHOIR, CHILDREN'S CHOIR AND ORCH.)
                                                                     Henmar.

—— HUWELIJKSCANTATE: BEATRIX-CLAUS (FOR MIXED
CHORUS AND ORCH.) (1966) (Text: C. Rijnsdorp)
                                                                     18:00 Henmar.
—— DAT LIET VAN ALIANORA (FOR SOPRANO, MALE
CHORUS AND ORCH.) (1947) (Text: P. C. Boutens)
2,2,2,2 - 4,3,0,0 - timp.,cel. - hp. - str.   12:00 Henmar.
—— MARIA MAGDALENA (CANTATA) (FOR ALTO, TENOR,
MIXED CHORUS AND ORCH.) (1941)
2,1,1,1 - 1,0,0,0 - cel. - hp. - str.   15:00 Henmar.
—— LES MYSTÈRES DU CHRIST (SYMPHONIC HYMN ON
PSALM TEXTS) (FOR ALTO, BARITONE, MALE CHORUS
AND ORCH.) (1958)
2,2,2,3 - 4,4,3,1 - timp.,perc. - hp. - str.   22:00 Henmar.
—— OLOF: SUITE
2,2,2,sax.,2 - 4,2,3,1 - perc., xyl. - str.   17:00 Henmar.
—— PASSACAGLIA AND PSALM 125 (FOR ALTO SOLO AND
LARGE ORCH.)
                                                                     Henmar.
—— SONG OF FREEDOM (FOR MIXED CHORUS, SPEAKING
CHORUS AND FULL ORCH.) (Texts: Socrates, Martin Luther
King)
                                                                     20:00 Henmar.
—— SUITE FOR CHAMBER ORCH.
2,2,0,0 - 0,0,0,0 - pf. - str.   16:00 Henmar.
—— SUITE FOR FLUTE AND CHAMBER ORCH.
1,1,1,1 - 1,0,0,0 - str.   11:00 Henmar.
—— SYMPHONIETTA
2,2,2,2 - 2,0,2,2 - perc. - str.   19:00 Henmar.
—— SYMPHONY NO. 1
3,3,3,3 - 4,3,3,1 - timp.,perc., cel. - str.   14:00 Henmar.
—— SYMPHONY NO. 2
3,3,3,3 - 4,3,3,1 - timp.,perc. - str.   29:00 Henmar.
—— SYMPHONY NO. 4 (1962)
2,2,2,2 - 4,3,3,1 - timp.,perc.,cel.,xyl. - hp. - str. 22:00 Henmar.
—— SYMPHONY NO. 5
                                                                     20:00 Henmar.
—— TE DEUM (1958)
                                                                     Henmar.
—— THEME AND VARIATIONS
2,2,2,2 - 4,3,3,1 - timp.,perc., cel. - hp. - str. 10:00 Henmar.
—— TUIN VAN HOLLAND (FOR SOPRANO, BARITONE, MIXED
CHORUS AND ORCH.) (1958) (Text: G. Stuiveling)
2,2,2,2 - 4,3,3,1 - timp.,perc. - hp. - str.   12:00 Henmar.
—— VARIATIES VOOR ORKEST: "DAAR GING EEN PATERJE
LANGS DE KANT, DIE MEI PLAISANT" (1956)
2,2,2,2 - 4,3,3,0 - timp.,perc.,cel. - hp. - str. 6:00 Henmar.

HEMMER, Eugene
—— CINCINNATI PROFILES (SUITE FOR ORCH.)
                                                                     Composer.
—— CONCERTINO FOR PIANO AND ORCHESTRA (FROM "THE
VOICE OF THE GRAND PIANO")
3,3,3,2 - 4,3,3,1 - timp.,perc.,cel. - hp. - pf. - str. C. Fischer.
—— A FESTIVAL OF SPIRITUALS (FOR BARITONE, SATB
CHORUS AND ORCH.)
1,1,2,1 - 2,2,1,0 - timp. - str.   12:00 C. Fischer.
—— IDYL FOR OBOE AND ORCH.
                                                                     7:00 AmerMusEd.
—— THE MIDNIGHT RIDE OF PAUL REVERE
*3,*3,*3,2 - 4,3,3,1 - timp.,perc. - hp. - str.   5:00 AmerMusEd.
—— THE SCHOOL BUS
*2,2,2,2 - 4,2,3,1 - timp.,perc.,cel. - hp.(or pf.) - str.
                                                                     4:00 AmerMusEd.
—— SUNSHINE GAMES
*2,*2,1,1 - 2,1,1,0 - timp.,perc.,cel.,xyl. - hp. - str.
                                                                     20:00 AmerMusEd.
—— THE VOICE OF THE GRAND PIANO (FOR NARRATOR,
PIANO AND ORCH.)
*3,*3,*3,2 - 4,3,3,1 - timp.,perc.,cel. - hp. - pf. - str.
                                                                     25:00 AmerMusEd.

HENDRIKS, Francis
—— CONCERTO NO. 1 IN E MINOR, FOR PIANO AND ORCH.
(IN 3 MOVTS.)
*3,*3,2,2 - 2,2,2,0 - timp.,perc. (3), cel. - hp. - pf. - str.
                                                                     25:00 Composer.
—— SIX SPANISH DANCES, OP. 46
*3,*3,*3,2 - 4,2,3,1 - timp.,perc. (3), cel., glock. - hp. - str.
                                                                     16:00 Composer.

HENKEMANS, Hans
—— BALLADE (FOR ALTO AND ORCH.) (1936) (Text: Charles d'Orleans)
    2,1,2,0 - 2,0,0,0 - timp. - hp. - str.   8:00 Henmar.
—— BERICHT AAN DE LEVENDEN (FOR SPEAKER, MIXED CHORUS AND ORCH.)
    30:00 Henmar.
—— CONCERTO FOR FLUTE AND ORCH.
    3,3,3,3 - 4,3,3,1 - timp.,perc., cel. xyl. - hp. - str.   16:00 Henmar.
—— CONCERTO FOR HARP AND ORCH.
    18:30 Henmar.
—— CONCERTO FOR PIANO AND ORCH.
    3,3,3,3 - 4,3,3,1 - timp.,perc. - pf. - str.   14:00 Henmar.
—— CONCERTO FOR PIANO AND STRING ORCH. (1967)
    1. Adagio; 2. Adagio molto; 3. Presto
    pf. - str.   12:00 Henmar.
—— CONCERTO FOR PIANO AND STRINGS
    pf. - str.   Henmar.
—— CONCERTO FOR VIOLA AND ORCH.
    3,3,4,3 - 4,3,3,1 - timp.,perc., cel., xyl. - hp. - str.   22:00 Henmar.
—— CONCERTO FOR VIOLIN AND ORCH.
    3,3,3,3 - 4,3,3,1 - timp.,perc., cel., xyl., vibra. - hp. - str.
    26:00 Henmar.
—— DRIEHONDERD WAREN WIJ (FOR MIXED CHORUS AND ORCH.) (1941) (Text: A. den Hoghe)
    2,3,3,3 - 4,3,3,1 - timp.,perc. - pf. - str.   20:00 Henmar.
—— ELEGIES (FOR 4 FLUTES AND ORCH.)
    4,3,3,3 - 4,3,3,1 - timp.,perc.,cel. - hp. - str.   12:00 Henmar.
—— PARTITA PER ORCHESTRA (1960)
    3,3,3,3 - 4,3,3,1 - timp.,perc.,cel.,xyl. - 2 hp. - pf. - str.
    26:00 Henmar.
—— PASSACAGLIA AND GIGUE (FOR PIANO AND ORCH.)
    3,3,3,3 - 4,3,3,1 - timp.,perc., cel., vibra. - hp. - pf. - str.
    15:00 Henmar.
—— PRELUDE
    2,3,3,3 - 4,3,3,1 - timp.,perc. - pf. - str.   Henmar.
—— PRIMAVERA
    1,1,1,0 - 1,0,0,0 - str.   7:00 Henmar.
—— VILLONERIE (1965) (THREE SONGS FOR VOICE AND LARGE ORCH.) (Text: François Villon)
    20:00 Henmar.

HENNAGIN, Michael
—— CONCERTINO FOR OBOE, PIANO AND STRINGS (1961)
    ob. - pf. - str.   7:00 Walton.
—— PASSACAGLIA FOR CHAMBER ORCH (REVISED 1962)
    *2,1,0,1 - 2,3,3,0 - timp.,perc.(3),glock.,cel.,vibra.,xyl. - hp. - pf. - str.   7:00 Composer.
—— A SUMMER OVERTURE
    2(2nd alt. with picc.),2,2,2 - 2,2,2,0 - timp.,perc.(4),glock.,vibra.,xyl. - hp. - pf. - str.   10:00 Composer.

HENNEBERG, Albert
—— BALLET-SCENE FROM "INKA"
    3,3,3,3 - 3,0,0,0 - timp.,perc. - hp. - str.   6:00 S.T.I.M.
—— CAPRICCIO, OP. 13
    2,2,2,2 - 2,2,2,0 - timp. - hp. - str.   10:00 S.T.I.M.
—— CHAMBER SYMPHONY, OP. 11
    1,1,1,1 - 1,0,0,0 - str.   25:00 S.T.I.M.
—— CONCERTINO FOR BASSOON AND STRINGS, OP. 45
    bn. - str.   14:00 S.T.I.M.
—— CONCERTINO FOR CLARINET, PIANO, PERCUSSION AND STRINGS, OP. 46
    0,0,1,0 - 0,0,0,0 - perc. - pf. - str.   S.T.I.M.
—— CONCERTINO FOR FLUTE AND STRINGS, OP. 39
    fl. - str.   13:00 Gehrmans.
—— CONCERTO FOR BASSOON AND ORCH., OP. 28
    2,2,2,2 - 2,2,0,0 - timp.,perc. - str.   15:00 S.T.I.M.
—— CONCERTO FOR CELLO AND ORCH., OP. 41
    1,1,2,1 - 2,0,0,0 - str.   27:00 S.T.I.M.
—— CONCERTO FOR PIANO AND ORCH., OP. 8
    2,2,2,2 - 2,2,2,0 - timp. - pf. - str.   20:00 S.T.I.M.
—— CONCERTO FOR TRUMPET AND ORCH., OP. 21
    2,2,2,2 - 2,1,2,0 - timp. - str.   20:00 S.T.I.M.
—— I DROTTINGHOLMSPARKEN (FROM "BOLLA AND BADIN")
    2,2,2,2 - 2,2,2,1 - timp.,perc. - hp. - str.   5:00 S.T.I.M.
—— GUSTAVIANSKA KAPRISER, OP. 39
    2,2,2,2 - 2,0,0,0 - timp., - str.   22:00 S.T.I.M.
—— I BRYTNINGSTIDER (SYMPHONIC SUITE ON MOTIVES FROM "DEN LYCKLIGA STADEN") OP. 33 (IN 4 MOVTS.)
    2,2,2,2 - 4,2,3,1 - timp.,perc. - hp. - str.   30:00 S.T.I.M.
    or:
    2,2,2,2 - 2,2,1,0 - timp. - hp. - str.

—— INTERMEZZO FROM "INKA"
    2,2,2,2 - 2,0,0,0 - timp. - str.   5:00 S.T.I.M.
—— MANDOM MOD OCH MORSKE MÄN, OP. 7
    2,2,2,2 - 2,2,2,0 - timp. - hp. - str.   10:00 S.T.I.M.
—— MINATYRER (SUITE FOR STRINGS), OP. 27
    str.   10:00 S.T.I.M.
—— NOCTURNE, OP. 2
    2,2,2,2 - 2,2,0,0 - timp. - str.   10:00 S.T.I.M.
—— OVERTURE TO "BOLLA AND BADIN"
    3,2,3,2 - 4,3,3,1 - timp.,perc. - str.   4:00 Suecia.
    or:
    2,2,2,2 - 2,2,1,0 - timp.,perc. - str.
—— PRELUDE TO "HIMLASTENEN", OP. 22A
    3,2,3,3 - 4,3,3,1 - timp.,perc. - hp. - str.   8:00 S.T.I.M.
—— ROSLAGSFJÄRD (SUITE FOR ORCH.), OP. 42 (IN 3 MOVTS.)
    1,0,2,0 - 0,2,1,0 - timp. - hp. - pf. - str.   12:00 S.T.I.M.
—— SERENADE FOR STRINGS. OP. 20
    str.   22:00 Suecia.
—— SOMMAR, OP. 23 (SUITE FOR ORCH.) (IN 4 MOVTS.)
    1,1,2,1 - 2,2,1,0 - timp. - str.   20:00 S.T.I.M.
—— STRIDSMUSIK (FROM "INKA")
    3,3,3,3 - 4,3,3,1 - timp.,perc. - str.   7:00 S.T.I.M.
—— SYMFONISK MELLANAKT ("UR HIMLASFTENEN"), OP. 22B
    3,3,3,3 - 4,3,3,1 - timp.,perc. - hp. - str.   12:00 S.T.I.M.
—— SYMPHONIC SUITE FROM "DER JÄSER I SMÅLAND" (IN 3 MOVTS.)
    2,2,2,2 - 2,2,1,0 - timp.,perc., cel. - hp. - str.   16:00 S.T.I.M.
—— SYMPHONY NO. 1 ("PÅ LEDUNGSFÄRD"), OP. 5
    3,2,3,2 - 4,2,3,1 - timp.,perc. - str.   40:00 S.T.I.M.
—— SYMPHONY NO. 2, OP. 10 (WITH BARITONE SOLO)
    3,2,3,3 - 4,2,3,1 - timp.,perc. - hp. - str.   60:00 S.T.I.M.
—— SYMPHONY NO. 3, OP. 16 ("VÅRVINDAR")
    2,2,2,2 - 2,2,2,0 - timp. - str.   29:00 S.T.I.M.
—— SYMPHONY NO. 4, OP. 19 ("PATHÉTIQUE")
    3,2,3,3 - 4,3,3,1 - timp.,perc. - hp. - org. - str.   35:00 S.T.I.M.
—— SYMPHONY NO. 5, OP. 26
    2,2,2,2 - 4,2,3,1 - timp. - str.   38:00 S.T.I.M.
—— SYMPHONY NO. 6, OP. 44 ("VINTERSKÄRGÅRD")
    2,2,2,2 - 2,2,3,0 - timp. - str.   30:00 S.T.I.M.
—— VALBORGSMÄSSONATT, OP. 15 (SYMPHONIC POEM)
    3,3,3,3 - 4,3,3,1 - timp.,perc. - hp. - str.   15:00 S.T.I.M.
—— VID CHINA SLOTT (FROM "BOLLA AND BADIN")
    2,2,2,2 - 2,2,2,1 - timp.,perc. - hp. - str.   8:00 S.T.I.M.

HENNINGER, Richard, Jr.
—— CATENA (1969)
    3,*3,*3,3 - 4,3,3,1 - timp.,perc.(7, incl. 4 on timp.) - 2 hp. - str.
    14:30 CanMusCtr.

HENRICH, Hermann
—— INNSBRUCK, OP. 43 (SYMPHONIC MUSIC ON A FOLKSONG) (WITH OPTIONAL MEN'S AND BOY'S VOICES)
    2(2nd alt. with picc.),2,2,2 - 4,2,3,1 - timp.,perc.(3, incl. 2 on timp.) - str.   25:00 Henmar.

HEPPENER, Robert
—— AIR ET SONNERIES
    2,2,2,2 - 4,2,3,1 - perc. - hp. - str.   Henmar.
—— CANTICO DELLE CREATURE DI S. FRANCESCO D'ASSISI (FOR HIGH VOICE AND STRING ORCH.) (1955)
    hp. - str.   10:00 Henmar.
—— DERIVAZIONI (1958)
    str.   20:00 Henmar.
—— EGLOGUES
    2,2,2,2 - 2,2,2,0 - timp.,perc. - hp. - str.   18:00 Henmar.
—— SCHERZI PER ARCHI
    str.   Henmar.
—— SCHERZI (1966)
    str.   8:00 Henmar.
—— SINFONIETTA (1961)
    2,2,2,2 - 2,1,0,0 - timp. - str.   14:00 Henmar.
—— SYMPHONY
    3,3,3,3 - 4,2,2,1 - timp.,perc. - pf. - str.   19:00 Henmar.

HERBAGE, Julian
—— THE HUMOURS OF BATH (SUITE)
    pf.(ad lib.) - str.   14:00 Mills.

HERBERGER, Rolf
—— KLEINE KAMMERMUSIK (FOR VIOLA D'AMORE AND STRING ORCH.)
    str.   12:00 Mannheimer.

—— SUITE FOR STRING ORCH.
str.   10:00 Mannheimer.

HERBERIGS, Robert
—— ANTHONY AND CLEOPATRA (SYMPHONIC POEM AFTER
SHAKESPEARE) (1949)
4,4,4,4 - 4,4,3,1 - timp.,perc.,cel. - hp. - str.   25:00 H. Elkan.
—— À LA FONTAINE BELLERIE (SUITE) (1953)
2,2,2,2 - 2,2,2,0 - timp.,perc.,cel.,xyl. - str.   9:00 H. Elkan.
—— LA CHANSON D'ÈVE (SUITE NO. 1) (1955)
3,3,3,3 - 4,3,3,1 - timp.,perc.,cel. - hp. - pf. - str.   22:00 H. Elkan.
—— LA CHANSON D'ÈVE (SUITE NO. 2) (1956)
3,3,3,3 - 4,3,3,1 - timp.,perc.,cel.,glock. - hp. - pf. - str.   27:15 H. Elkan.
—— LE CHANT D'HIAWATHA (POÈME SYMPHONIQUE) (1921)
3,3,3,3 - 4,3,3,1 - timp.,perc., cel., xyl. - hp. - str.   16:00 CBDM.
—— CONCERTO FOR ORGAN AND ORCH. (1957)
1,1,1,1 - 0,0,0,0 - timp.,perc. - org. - str.   15:00 S.A.B.A.M.
—— CONCERTO NO. 1 FOR PIANO AND ORCH.
2,2,2,2 - 4,2,3,1 - timp.,perc. - str.   21:30 CBDM.
—— CYRANO DE BERGERAC (CONCERTO FOR HORN AND
ORCH.) (1912)
2,2,2,2 - 3,2,3,0 - timp.,perc. - str.   25:00 CBDM.
—— DE VROLIJKE VROUNTJES VAN WINDSOR (THE MERRY
WIVES OF WINDSOR) (POÈME SYMPHONIQUE D'APRES
SHAKESPERE) (1950)
3,3,3,3 - 4,3,3,1 - timp.,perc., cel. - str.   17:00 CBDM.
—— ECHOES AND MIRAGES (SUITE) (1954)
2,2,2,2 - 2,2,2,0 - timp.,perc.,cel. - str.   9:00 H. Elkan.
—— ESQUISSES ET IMPROMPTUS (SUITE) (1954)
2,2,2,2 - 2,2,2,0 - timp.,perc.,cel. - str.   11:00 H. Elkan.
—— ODES AUX MUSES (SUITE) (1955)
3,3,3,3 - 4,3,3,1 - timp.,perc.,cel.,xyl. - hp. - str.   23:00 H. Elkan.
—— LA PETITE SIRÈNE (SYMPHONIC LEGEND AFTER
ANDERSEN) (1955)
2,2,2,2 - 2,2,2,0 - timp.,perc.,bells,cel.,glock.,xyl. - str.   21:00 H. Elkan.
—— QUATRE BALLADES (SUITE) (1955)
3,3,3,3 - 4,3,3,1 - timp.,perc.,xyl. - pf. - str.   13:00 H. Elkan.
—— LES QUATRE SAISONS (SUITE) (1956)
2,2,2,2 - 2,2,2,0 - timp.,perc.,bells,cel.,glock.,xyl. - str.   15:00 H. Elkan.
—— RAPSODIA ALLA ZINGARA (1952)
3,3,3,3 - 4,3,3,1 - timp.,perc. - str.   13:00 H. Elkan.
—— SINFONIA BREVE (1947)
3,3,3,3 - 4,3,3,1 - timp.,perc.,cel. - hp. - str.   17:30 H. Elkan.
—— SUITE NO. 1 (FOR BRASS)
0,0,0,0 - 4,3,3,0   10:30 H. Elkan.
—— SUITE NO. 2 (FOR BRASS)
0,0,0,0 - 4,3,3,0   10:00 H. Elkan.
—— VLAANDEREN, O WELIG HUIS (SYMPHONIC POEM) (1949)
2,1,2,1 - 2,2,2,0 - timp.,perc.,bells,cel.,glock. - str. 21:30 H. Elkan.

HERBERT, Victor
—— GRAND FANTASIA ON "NATOMA"
3,3,3,3 - 4,2,3,1 - timp.,perc. - hp. - str.   20:00 G. Schirmer.
—— IRISH RHAPSODY
3,2,2,2 - 4,2,3,1 - timp.,perc. - hp. - str.   10:00 G. Schirmer.
—— PRELUDE TO ACT III OF "NATOMA"
3,3,3,3 - 4,2,3,1 - timp.,perc. - hp. - str.   4:00 G. Schirmer.
—— WESTERN OVERTURE
C. Fischer.

HERCIGONJA, Nikola
—— JAMA (THE CAVERN) (CANTATA) (FOR SOLO VOICES,
SATB CHORUS AND ORCH.)
3,3,3,3 - 4,3,3,1 - timp.,perc.,cel.,vibra. - hp. - pf. - str.   60:00 MIC,Zagreb.

HERMANN, Paul
—— ITALIAN SUITE (FOR STRING ORCH.)
str.   7:00 Henmar.
—— REQUIEM (FOR SPEAKING VOICES, WINDS AND STRINGS)
0,1,1,2 - 1(or Eng. hn.),0,0,0 - str.   Henmar.

HERMANN, Ralph
—— SYMPHONY NO. 3 ("FROM THE SCRIPTURES")
*3,*3,*3,2 - 4,4,3,1 - timp.,perc. - hp. - str.   20:00 Composer.

HERMANS, Nico
—— OUVERTURE JOYEUSE, OP. 6
2,2,2,2 - 3,2,2,1 - perc.,xyl. - pf. - str.   Henmar.

—— SYMPHONY NO. 1, OP. 5 (SINFONIA BREVE) (1948)
3,2,2,2 - 4,3,3,1 - timp.,perc.,cel. - hp. - str.   15:00 Henmar.
—— TWO NOCTURNES, OP. 10 (FOR MEZZO-SOPRANO AND
ORCH.) (1951) (Text: P. C. Boutens)
fl. - str.   8:00 Henmar.

HERMANSON, Åke
—— APPELL I-IV, OP. 10 (1969)
2,2,2,2 - 2,2,1,0 - timp.,perc.(3) - str.   11:00 G. Schirmer.
—— IN NUCE, OP. 7 (1963)
3,2,1,3 - 4,4,3,1 - timp.,perc.(11, incl. 2 on timp.) - pf. - str.   3:00 G. Schirmer.
—— INVOCO PER ARCHI, OP. 4 (1960)
str.   8:00 S.T.I.M.
—— SYMPHONY NO. 1, OP. 9 (1967)
3,3,4,3 - 4,4,3,1 - timp.,perc. - str.   29:00 G. Schirmer.
—— ULTIMA, OP. 13 (1972)
3,3,4,3 - 4,4,3,1 - timp.,perc.(7) - hp. - str.   13:00 Fleisher.

HÉROLD, Louis-Joseph-Ferdinand - LANCHBERY, John
—— LA FILLE MAL GARDEE (BALLET SUITE) (IN 5 MOVTS.)
2,2,2,2 - 4,2,3,1 - timp.,perc. - hp. - str.   16:00 Oxford.

HÉROLD, Louis-Joseph-Ferdinand - SOPKIN, Henry
—— OVERTURE TO "ZAMPA"
C. Fischer.

HÉROLD, Louis-Joseph-Ferdinand - WINTER, Aubrey
—— OVERTURE TO "ZAMPA"
10:00 Bo. Hawkes.

HERRMANN, Bernard
—— FOR THE FALLEN (BERCEUSE)
2,*2,2,2 - 4 hn. - timp. - hp. - str.   7:30 Broude.

HERRMANN, Hugo
—— FEIERMUSIK NO. 1 (MUSIK IN VERWANDLUNGEN ÜBER
EIN ALTES VOLKSLIED)
timp. - str.   12:00 Sikorski.
—— FEIERMUSIK NO. 2 (CONCERTO GROSSO)
2,2,2,2 - 4,2,3,1 - timp.,perc. - str.   Sikorski.
—— SERAPHISCHE MUSIK
3,3,2,3 - 4,2,3,1 - timp.,perc.,cel. - hp. - str.   15:00 Bo. Hawkes.
—— SYMPHONY NO. 3 (WITH TENOR AND BOYS' CHOIR)
3,3,3,2 - 2,3,3,1 - timp.,perc. - 2 hp. - str.   30:00 Bo. Hawkes.
—— SYMPHONY NO. 4 ("PARACELSUS")
2,2,2,2 - 4,2,3,1 - timp.,perc. - str.   15:00 Sikorski.
—— SYMPHONY NO. 5 (TRIPTICHON NACH DANTES
"GÖTTLICHER KOMÖDIE") (IN 3 MOVTS.)
50:00 Sikorski.

HERRMANN, Peter
—— CONCERTO FOR VIOLIN AND ORCH.
2,2,2,2 - 4,2,3,1 - timp.,perc. - pf. - str.   20:00 Tetra.
—— FESTIVAL OVERTURE
3,3,3,3 - 4,3,3,0 - timp.,perc. - str.   Tetra.

HERSCHEL, Lee
—— HOW THE CAMEL GOT HIS HUMP (FOR 4 VOICES,
NARRATOR AND ORCH.) (Text: Kipling, adapted by Leo Paris)
2,1,2,1 - 2,2,1,0 - perc. - hp. - str.   8:43 ReynardPCI.
—— HOW THE WHALE GOT HIS TINY THROAT (FOR 4 VOICES,
NARRATOR AND ORCH.) (Text: Kipling, adapted by Leo Paris)
2,1,2,1 - 2,2,1,0 - perc. - hp. - str.   8:58 ReynardPCI.

HERTEL, Johann Wilhelm - SALLAGAR, Walter Hermann
—— CONCERTO IN A MINOR FOR BASSOON, STRINGS AND
CONTINUO
bn. - cemb. - str.   18:00 Henmar.

HESPOS, Hans-Joachim
—— THE BASS CLEF (CHAMBER MUSIC FOR ORCH.)
1(alt. with picc.),1,ob. d'amore,heck.,picc.heck.,E♭cl.,*2,bassett
hn.,tarogato,*1 - 2,0,picc.cnt.,flg.-hn.,3(incl. 2 b.-trb.),1 - guit. -
d.-b.   20:37 Modern.
—— BLACKOUT
0,1,E♭cl.,*2,*3 - 2,1(picc.B♭),flg.-hn.,2(incl. alto),1 - perc.(2) - pf. -
str.(0,0,3,1)   13:00 Modern.
—— CHE (CH-HHHHH-E)
4(or 4 picc.),*3,heck.,E♭cl.,*3,*4 - 6,3,b.-tpt.,2,d.-b.-trb.,2 -
perc.(6) - str.   22:00 Modern.
—— DSCHEN
ten.sax.(alt. with bar.sax.) - str.   12:00 Modern.

—— KA (FOR BARITONE SAXOPHONE, DOUBLE BASS AND ORCH.)
   1(alt. with picc.),1,E♭cl.,1,bar.sax.,*2 - 2,1,1(alto),1 - str.(6,0,4,0)
   8:30 Modern.
—— KEIME UND MALE (FOR INSTRUMENTAL ENSEMBLE)
   *2,0,2,alto sax.,0 - 0,0,0,0 - perc.(3) - guit. - hp. - str.
   9:00 Presser.
—— MOVEMENTS (VERSION NO. 1)
   *2,1,*3,alto sax.,ten. sax.,1 - 2,3,2,1 - perc.(6),cel. - hp. - pf. - str.(4,4,3,1)   11:00 Modern.
—— MOVEMENTS (VERSION NO. 2)
   *2,1,E♭cl.,*2,alto sax., ten.sax.,1 - 2,3(incl. 1 picc. B♭),2,1 - perc.(6),cel. - hp. - pf. - str.   11:00 Modern.
—— SCAPPA
   1,1,*2,0 - 1,0,1,0 - perc.,cel.,glock.,xylorimba - cymbalom - str.
   4:00 Modern.

HESS, Ernst
—— CONCERTO DA CAMERA, OP. 63 (FOR CELLO AND SMALL ORCH.)(1968)
   1,0,1,1 - 1,0,0,0 - str.   20:00 G. Schirmer.
—— SINFONIETTA, OP. 61
   2,2,2,2 - 2,2,0,0 - timp.,perc. - str.(2,1,1,0)   16:00 S.U.I.S.A.

HESSELBERG, Eyvind
—— ALLEGRETTO GIOCOSO
   3,2,2,2 - 4,3,3,1 - timp.,perc. - hp. - str.   5:00 T.O.N.O.
—— CHORALE ("THE CHURCH IS AN OLD HOUSE") ("KIRKEN DEN ER ET GAMMELT HUS")
   2,2,2,2 - 2,2,3,1 - timp. - pf. - str.   10:00 T.O.N.O.
—— SCHERZO NOTTURNO
   3,2,3,2 - 4,2,1,1 - timp.,perc.,cel. - hp. - str.   6:00 T.O.N.O.
—— THREE SMALL FAIRY-TALE PICTURES (TRE SMÅ EVENTYRBILDER)
   1,1,2,1 - 0,3,1,0 perc. - pf. - str.   4:00 T.O.N.O.
—— TWO MELODIES FOR ORCHESTRA (1929)
   1,1,2,1 - 0,2,1,0 - str.   4:00 T.O.N.O.

HESSENBERG, Kurt
—— CONCERTO FOR ORCH., OP. 70 (1957)
   3(3rd alt. with picc.),2,2(2nd alt. with Eng.hn.),2,*3 - 4,3,3,0 - timp.,perc. - hp. - str.   22:00 G. Schirmer.
—— INTRADA AND VARIATIONS ON A THEME OF JAKOB REGNART, OP. 65 (1955)
   2,*3,2,2 - 4,3,0,0 - timp.,perc. -str.   20:00 G. Schirmer.
—— SINFONIETTA FOR STRING ORCH., OP. 73
   str.   13:00 G. Schirmer.
—— SPIELMUSIK FÜR STREICHER, OP. 61 (SUITE) (IN 4 MOVTS.)
   str.   11:00 G. Schirmer.
—— SYMPHONY, OP. 62
   2,2,2,2 - 3,2,0,0 - timp. - str.   23:00 Wilhmiana.

HEUS, Rudie C. de
—— VIJF BOUTENS LIEDEREN (5 SONGS ON POEMS OF BOUTENS) (FOR SOPRANO, SATB CHORUS AND STRING ORCH.) (1968)
   str.   16:00 Henmar.

HEUSSENSTAMM, George
—— CHAMBER SYMPHONY, OP. 16 (1964) (IN 1 MOVT.)
   1,1,1,1 - 1,1,1,0 - timp.,perc.(1) - str.   15:00 Seesaw.
—— DAS DREIECK
   1,1,1,1 - 1,0,0,0 - perc.(2) - 1 vln.,1 vla.,1 c.   17:00 Seesaw.
—— LITANY OF L. H., OP. 24 (FOR 4 SATB SOLO VOICES, SATB CHORUS AND SMALL ORCH.) (IN 1 MOVT.) (1968) (Text: Anon)
   1(alt. with picc.),1,1,1 - 1,1,1,0 - timp.,perc.(2), bells,cel.,xyl. - 1 vln.,1 c.,1 d.-b.   30:00 Seesaw.
—— SCHERZO
   1,1,1,1 - 1,1,1,1 - perc.(2) - str.   10:00 Seesaw.
—— SEVENTEEN IMPRESSIONS FROM THE JAPANESE
   1,1,1,0 - 1,0,0,0 - timp.,perc.(5) - str.(1,1,1,1)   19:00 Seesaw.

HEWARD, Leslie
—— NOCTURNE
   2,2,2,2 - 2,2,3,0 - timp.,perc. - str.   14:00 Bo. Hawkes.

HEWITT, Harry D.
—— DWELLERS IN THE MIRAGE, OP. 37 NO. 2 (1940)
   8:00 Fleisher.
—— A GOOD-HUMORED OVERTURE, OP. 57 NO. 1 (1947)
   8:00 Fleisher.

—— MOBY DICK, OP. 73 (3-ACT OPERA) % (1950) (Text: Composer, after Herman Melville)
   180:00 Fleisher.
—— PRELUDE TO "SPOON RIVER", OP. 53, NO. 3 (1941)
   5:00 Fleisher.
—— SHADOW OUT OF TIME, OP. 37, NO. 1 (1940)
   Fleisher.
—— SINFONIA FOR CHAMBER ORCH., OP. 40, NO. 1 (1940)
   18:00 Fleisher.
—— SYMPHONY NO. 3, OP. 43 (REVISED 1950)
   30:00 Fleisher.
—— SYMPHONY NO. 8, OP. 103
   30:00 Fleisher.
—— THE TAMING OF THE SHREW (OVERTURE), OP. 53, NO. 6 (1948)
   6:00 Fleisher.
—— TWENTY-FOUR PRELUDES, OP. 19 (1938)
   str.   60:00 Fleisher.
—— YUGEN, OP. 426, NO. 1 (WITH OPTIONAL JAPANESE INSTS.)
   4(2 alt. with 2 picc.) or 4 Sho,2(2nd alt. with Eng.hn),2,2 - 2-4,2,2,1 - timp.,perc.,mar.,vibra. - pf. - str.   Fleisher.
   or:
   2(2 alt. with 2 picc.,2 alt. with Fue),2 Hichiriki (similar to ob.),2,2 - 2-4,2,2,1 - timp.,perc., Ko-Tsume, mar., temple-bells, vibra. - pf. - str.

HEWITT, James
—— THE BATTLE OF TRENTON (A FAVORITE HISTORICAL MILITARY SONATA)
   1,1,2,1 - 2,2,1,0 - timp.,perc. - str.   9:00 Fleisher.
—— MUSIC OF THE AMERICAN REVOLUTION, SUITE NO. 1 (FROM WASHINGTON'S TIME) (IN 6 MOVTS.)
   str.   10:00 Fleisher.
—— MUSIC OF THE AMERICAN REVOLUTION, SUITE NO. 2 (IN 6 MOVTS.)
   str.   10:00 Fleisher.

HEWITT-JONES, Tony
—— CONCERTO FOR OBOE AND SMALL ORCH. (1966)
   1,1,1,1 - 1,0,0,0 - str.   16:00 P.R.S.
—— FIVE PIECES (1963)
   3,2,2,2 - 4,3,3,1 - timp.,perc.(3) - str.   20:00 P.R.S.
—— SINFONIETTA FOR STRINGS(1956)
   str.   15:00 Novello.
—— TE DEUM (FOR ALTO, TENOR, BASS, SOPRANO SEMI-CHORUS, SATB CHORUS AND ORCH.)
   0,0,0,0- 0,3,3,0 - timp. - org. - str.   30:00 Bo. Hawkes.

HEWSON, Richard
—— CONCERTO GROSSO (FOR 4 CELLOS AND ORCH.)
   1,1,1,1 - 2,2,3,0 - perc. - hp. - 4 c.,d.-b.   12:00 P.R.S.
—— SYMPHONY
   2,2,2,2 - 2,0,0,0 - timp. - str.   18:00 P.R.S.

HEYMANN, Werner Richard
—— RHAPSODISCHE SINFONIE (FOR BARITONE AND ORCH.)
   3,3,3,3 - 4,3,2,1 - timp.,perc., cel. - 2 hp. - str.   25:00 Weinberger.

HIDAS, Frigyes
—— CONCERTINO FOR VIOLIN AND ORCH.
   2,2,2,2 - 3,2,0,0 - timp.,perc. - hp. - str.   12:30 Bo. Hawkes.
—— CONCERTO FOR HORN AND ORCH.
   hn. - perc.(5),cel. - hp. - str.   19:57 Bo. Hawkes.
—— CONCERTO FOR OBOE AND ORCH.
   2,1,2,2 - 2,2,0,0 - timp.,cel. - hp. - str.   19:30 Bo. Hawkes.

HIER, Ethel Glenn
—— THREE PIECES FOR ORCH.
   3(2nd and 3rd alt. with 2 picc.),3,2,2 - 4,3,3,1 - timp.,perc. - hp. - str.   10:00 C. Press.

HIGGINSON, J. Vincent
—— THE HOLY KING (FOR CHORUS AND CHAMBER ORCH.)
   fl., cl. - timp. - str.   7:00 Composer.
—— MAGDALEN
   1,*2,1,1 - 1,1,1,0 - timp.,perc. (1) - hp. - str.   7:00 Composer.
—— RONDO SERIEUSE
   1,*2,1,1 - 1,1,1,0 - timp. - str.   Composer.

HILDEBRAND, Camillo
—— FOUR IDYLLS
   1(alt. with picc.),1,2,1 - 2,1,0,0 - timp.,perc. - str.   22:00 Henmar.

HILL, Alfred
—— CONCERTO FOR VIOLA AND ORCH.
    1,1,2,1 - 2,0,0,0 - timp.,trgl. - str.   16:00 Southern.
—— LINTHORPE
    3,2,2,2 - 2,2,3,1 - timp.,perc. - str.   9:00 Bo. Hawkes.
—— OVERTURE OF WELCOME
    3,2,2,2 - 2,2,1,1 - timp.,perc. - hp. - str.   7:00 Bo. Hawkes.

HILL, Edward Burlingame
—— CONCERTINO FOR PIANO AND ORCH. (IN 1 MOVT.)
    3(3rd alt. with picc.),*3,2,*3, - 4,3,3,1 - timp.,perc. (2) - pf. - str.   12:00 G. Schirmer.
—— DIVERSION FOR SMALL ORCH. (IN 4 MOVTS.)
    15:00 Composer.
—— LILACS (POEM FOR ORCH.)
    3-4,2(2nd alt. with Eng. hn.),2(2nd alt. with b.-cl.),2 - 6,3,3,1 - timp., cel. - hp. - pf. - str.   19:00 Bo. Hawkes.
—— NUNS OF THE PERPETUAL ADORATION (FOR WOMEN'S VOICES AND ORCH.)
    *3,2,2,2 - 4,3,3,1 - timp.,perc. - hp. - str.   16:00 Composer.
—— PRELUDE FOR ORCH.
    2,2,3,2 - 2,2,3,0 - timp.,perc. - pf. - str.   6:00 Bo. Hawkes.
—— SINFONIETTA FOR STRINGS, OP. 40A
    str.   16:30 Bo. Hawkes.
—— STEVENSONIANA: SUITE NO. 1 (IN 4 MOVTS.)
    3(3rd alt. with picc.),2,2,2 - 4,3,3,1 - timp.,perc. (2) - hp. - str.   15:00 Composer.
—— STEVENSONIANA: SUITE NO. 2, OP. 29 (IN 3 MOVTS)
    4,3,3,3 - 4,2,3,1 - timp.,perc., cel., glock. - hp. - str.   11:00 G. Schirmer.
—— SYMPHONY NO. 1 IN B FLAT MAJOR, OP. 34
    3(3rd alt. with picc.),*3,*3,2 - 6,3,3,1 - timp.,perc., (2), cel. - pf. - str.   18:00 Composer.
—— SYMPHONY NO. 2 IN C MAJOR (IN 4 MOVTS.)
    3(3rd alt. with picc.),2,3(3rd alt. with b.-cl.),2 - 6,4,3,1 - timp.,perc. - pf. - str.   Composer.
—— SYMPHONY NO. 3 IN G. MAJOR (IN 3 MOVTS.)
    3(3rd alt. with picc.),*3,2,2 - 4,3,3,1 - timp.,perc. (2) - pf. - str.   Composer.

HILL, Jackson
—— CEREMONIES OF SPHERES (CAERIMONIAE SPHAERARUM) (1973)
    3(3rd alt. with picc.),3,3,3 - 4,3,3,1 - timp.,perc.(4),bells,cel.,glock.,vibra. - pf. - str.   20:00 Composer.
—— MOSAICS (1965) (IN 5 MOVTS)
    2,2,2,2 - 4,3,3,1 - timp.,perc.(3),bells,glock.,vibra. - pf. - str.   15:00 Fleisher.
—— PAGANINI SET (1973)
    1,2,0,1 - 2,0,0,0 - str.   7:00 Composer.
—— VARIATIONS FOR ORCHESTRA (1964)
    2,2,2,2 - 4,3,3,1 - timp.,perc.(3) - str.   13:00 Composer.

HILL, Mirrie Irma
—— ABINU MALKENU (FOR VIOLIN AND ORCH.) (1971)
    0,1,1(alt. with b.-cl.),0 - 0,0,0,0 - str.   10:45 J. Albert.
—— ABORIGINAL THEMES (FOR MEZZO-SOPRANO, BARITONE AND ORCH.) (1971)
    1,1,0,0 - 0,0,0,0 - hp. - str.   26:10 A.P.R.A.
—— ANDANTE (1975)
    2,2,2,2 - 2,0,0,0 - hp. - str.   6:20 A.P.R.A.
—— ARNHEM LAND SYMPHONY (1954)
    2(2nd alt. with picc.),2,2,2 - 4,1,3,1 - timp.,perc. - hp. - str.   31:52 A.P.R.A.
—— CARNIVAL NIGHT (1971)
    2(2nd alt. with picc.)2,2,2 - 4,2,3,1 - timp.,perc. - pf.   4:50 A.P.R.A.
—— CINDERELLA SUITE (1925)
    str.   10:00 A.P.R.A.
—— THE LITTLE DREAM (FIVE PIECES FOR ORCH.) (1930)
    2,2,2,2 - 4,2,3,1 - timp.,perc. - hp. - str.   24:00 A.P.R.A.
—— RHAPSODY IN A MAJOR FOR PIANO AND ORCH. (1918)
    21:50 A.P.R.A.
—— THREE ABORIGINAL DANCES (FOR PIANO AND ORCH.) (1950)
    Southern.

HILLER, Lejaren A., Jr.
—— ALGORITHMS I AND II, OP. 38 (1967) (IN 6 MVTS.)
    1,0,1,1 - 0,1,0,0 - perc.(1) - tape-recorder - hp. - vln.c.,d.-b.   18:00 Presser.
—— CONCERTO FOR PIANO AND ORCH., OP. 6 (IN 1 MOVT.)
    2,*3,2,2 - 3,2,3,1 - timp.,perc.(2) - hp. - pf. - str.   15:00 Composer.

—— DIVERTIMENTO FOR CHAMBER ENSEMBLE, OP. 25 (IN 5 MOVTS.)
    1(alt. with picc.),1(alt. with Eng.hn.),1,1 - 1,1,1,0 - timp.,perc.(2-3),cel.,xyl. - guitar - theremin(or ondes Martenot) - 1 d.-b.   36:00 Presser.
—— A PREVIEW OF COMING ATTRACTIONS
    3,3,3,3 - 4,4,3,1 - timp., perc.(4) - hp. - str.   14:00 Presser.
—— SUITE FOR SMALL ORCH., OP. 12 (IN 7 MOVTS.)
    1,2,1,1 - 2,1,1,0 - timp.,perc.(2) - str.   12:30 Composer.
—— SYMPHONY NO. 1, OP. 15 (IN 3 MOVTS.)
    *3,*3,1 E ^{b}cl.,*3,2 - 4,4,3,1 - timp.,perc.(4),cel.,glock.,xyl. - hp. - str.   62:00 Composer.
—— SYMPHONY NO. 2, OP. 27 (IN 4 MOVTS.)
    *3,*3,*3,*3 - 4,2,3,1 - timp.,perc.(4),xyl. - str.   34:00 Presser.
—— THE TIME OF THE HEATHEN, OP. 29 (SUITE FROM THE FILM) (IN 12 MOVTS.)
    1(alt. with picc.),1(alt. with Eng.hn.),1,1 - 2,2,1,1 - timp.,perc.(4),bells, glock.,vibra.,xyl. - tape-recorder - str.   45:00 Composer.
—— A TRIPTYCH FOR HIERONYMUS (FOR MALE SPEAKER, DANCERS, SLIDES AND FILM) % (1966) (Text: Webster Smalley)
    2(1 alt. with picc.),2(1 alt. with Eng.hn.),2-4(2 alt. with alto and ten. sax),1 - 0,2,2,2 - timp.,perc.(3),bells,cel.,glock.,mar.,vibra.,xyl. - tape-recorder - hp. - pf.(alt. with hpsc.,harmonium and org.) - str.   40:00 Presser.

HILSTON, Lucille
—— ONGHIARA (NIAGARA RIVER) (TONE POEM) (1962)
    *3,2,2,2 - 4,3,3,1 - timp.,perc.(1),bells - hp. - pf. - str.   9:00 Composer.

HINES, Jerome
—— I AM THE WAY (OPERA) % (1970)
    2(2nd alt.with picc.),2(2nd alt.with Eng.hn.),2,2 - 2,2,2,1 - timp.,perc.(1) - hp. - str.   2:10 Composer.

HIPMAN, Sylvester
—— RONDEAU FOR PIANO AND ORCH.
    2,2,2,2 - 3,3,2,0 - timp.,perc. - hp. - pf. - str.   5:00 Bo. Hawkes.

HIRAYOSHI, Takekuni
—— VARIAZIONI SINFONICHE
    4,3,3,3 - 4,4,3,1 - perc. - hp. - pf. - str.   Presser.

HIRNER, Teodor
—— SERENADE FOR STRINGS
    str.   21:00 Bo. Hawkes.

HIROSE, Ryôhei
—— CONCERTO FOR CELLO AND ORCH. ("TRISTE")
    2,0,0,0 - 0,1,3,0 - perc.(3) - str.   20:00 Presser.

HJORT ALBERTSEN, Per
—— AKK-A-MEI (ACADEMIC REVUE-OVERTURE)
    1,1,2,1 - 2,3,3,0 - timp.,perc. - pf. - str.   6:00 Ed. Lyche.
—— CHRISTMAS MASS (JULEMESSE), OP. 24 (FOR SOLO VOICES, CHILDREN'S CHORUS AND CHAMBER ORCH.) (Text: Norwegian Hymn-book)
    Bells - org. - str.   NorKomFlg.
—— CONCERTINO FOR FLUTE AND ORCH., OP. 7 (IN 3 MOVTS.)
    1,1,1,1 - 2,0,0,0 - str.   12:00 Henmar.
—— CONCERTO PICCOLO FOR VIOLIN AND STRINGS, OP. 23
    str.   9:00 Ed Lyche.
—— NOTTURNO E DANZA, OP. 22
    2,2,2,2 - 3,3,3,1 - timp.,perc. - str.   9:00 Ed Lyche.
—— PRESENTATION (OVERTURE FOR ORCH.), OP. 20
    2,2,2,2 - 3,3,3,1 - timp.,perc. - str.   10:00 Ed. Lyche.
—— SUMMER MASS (SOMMERMESSE), OP. 28 (FOR SOLO VOICES, 2 MIXED CHORUSES, ORGAN AND ORCH.)
    25:00 NorKomFlg.
—— SYMPHONIC PRELUDE, OP. 10
    2,1,2,2 - 3,3,2,0 - timp.,perc. - str.   7:00 Ed. Lyche.
—— VILLEMANN OG MAGNILL, OP. 8 (BALLAD) (FOR SOPRANO, BARITONE, MALE CHORUS AND ORCH.) (Text: Traditional)
    2,2,2,2 - 3,3,2,1 - timp.,perc. - str.   23:00 Ed Tonika.

HLOBIL, Emil
—— CONCERTO FOR ACCORDION AND ORCH., OP. 54
    1,2,2,2 - 3,2,1,0 - timp.,perc. - acc. - str.   18:00 Bo. Hawkes.

—— CONCERTO FOR VIOLIN AND ORCH.
    2,2,2,2 - 4,2,3,2 - timp.,perc.,xyl. - hp. - str.   30:00 Bo. Hawkes.
—— A FOLK FESTIVAL, OP. 32 (SUITE)
    1,1,2,1 - 0,1,2,0 - perc. - str.   11:00 Bo. Hawkes.
—— IN A WALACHIAN VILLAGE, OP. 39 (SUITE)
    1,1,2,1 - 2,2,1,0 - timp.,perc. - pf. - str.   11:00 Bo. Hawkes.
—— THE PARK OF REST AND RECREATION (SUITE) (1949) (IN 4 MOVTS.)
    20:00 Bo. Hawkes.
—— RHAPSODY FOR CLARINET AND ORCH.
    2,2,4,2 - 4,3,3,0 - timp.,perc. - hp. - str.   11:00 Bo. Hawkes.
—— SERENADE, OP. 49
    2,2,2,2 - 4,2,3,0 - timp.,perc.,cel. - 2 hp. - str.   14:00 Bo. Hawkes.
—— SPRING IN THE GARDENS OF PRAGUE, OP. 35 (SUITE)
    3,2,2,2 - 4,2,3,0 - timp.,perc. - hp. - pf. - str.   21:00 Bo. Hawkes.
—— SUITE FOR ORCHESTRA, OP. 4
    3,3,3,3 - 4,3,1,1 - timp.,perc. - str.   14:00 Bo. Hawkes.
—— SUMMER IN THE GIANT MOUNTAINS, OP. 33 (SUITE)
    3,3,3,2 - 4,3,3,1 - timp.,perc.,cel. - hp. - str.   24:00 Bo. Hawkes.
—— SYMPHONY NO. 1, OP. 31
    3,3,4,3 - 4,3,3,1 - timp.,perc. - 2 hp. - str.   30:00 Bo. Hawkes.
—— SYMPHONY NO. 3
    3,3,3,3 - 4,3,3,1 - timp.,perc. - hp. - str.   29:00 Bo. Hawkes.
—— SYMPHONY NO. 4, OP. 58
    3,3,3,2 - 4,3,3,1 - perc.,trgl. - hp. - str.   24:00 Bo. Hawkes.

HLOUSCHEK, Theodor
—— PRELUDE AND FUGUE (FOR LARGE ORCH.)
    3,3,3,3 - 4,3,3,1 - timp.,perc. - str.   13:00 Tetra.

HNILICKA, Jaromir
—— CARBON DE LUBIDAS
    5 sax.(2 alto, 2 ten., bar.) - 0,4,4,0 - perc. - pf. - d.-b.
    10:00 Modern.

HOAG, Charles K.
—— ENCOUNTER FOR ORCHESTRA (1967)
    2,2,2,2 - 4,2,3,1 - timp.,perc.(1) - str.   11:00 Fleisher.
—— FANTASY ON A BACH CHORALE (1966)
    2(2nd alt. with picc.),2,*3,2 - 4,3,3,1 - timp.,perc.(4),glock. - str.
    12:00 Fleisher.
—— FILIGREES, FROGS AND FANTASIES (1972)
    ob. - perc.(2),cel. - str.   9:00 Composer.
—— FIVE RUNIC DESIGNS (1973)
    *3,2,2,2 - 4,2,3,1 - perc. - str.   7:00 Composer.
—— LEAR'S STORM SOLILOQUY (CONCERT ARIA FOR BASS AND ORCH.) (1970) (Text: Shakespeare)
    2(2nd alt. with picc.), *2,2(2nd alt. with b.-cl.),2 - 2,2,0,0 - timp.,perc.(2),glock, - pf. - str.   9:00 Composer.
—— NOVEMBER 22, 1963
    ob. - str.   6:00 Composer.
—— SYMPHONIC MOVEMENT (1970)
    *3,*3,*3,2 - 4,3,3,1 - perc.,bells - hp. - pf. - str.   8:00 Composer.
—— SYMPHONY (1970) (IN 3 MOVTS.)
    *3,*3,*3,2 - 4,3,3,1 - timp.,perc.(3),bells,glock. - hp. - pf. - str.
    19:00 Composer.
—— A VINLAND NARRATIVE (FOR NARRATOR AND ORCH.) (1971)
    *3,2,*3,2 - 4,2,3,1 - timp.,perc.(3),glock.,vibra. - hp. - str.
    11:00 Composer.
—— ZZZZ! (FOR 30 STRING PLAYERS) (1969)
    str.   6:00 Composer.

HOCH, Francesco
—— IDRIA PER 11 ARCHI
    str.   13:00 MCA Music.
—— L' OGETTO DISINCANTATO (STORIA DI UN'ANALISI) (PER 13 STRUMENTI)
    1,1,1,1 - 1,1,1,0 - pf. - cemb. - str.(2,1,1,0)   12:00 MCA Music.
—— RIFLESSIONI SULLA NATURA DI LACUNI VOCABOLI (FÜR GROSSES ORCHESTER)
    16:00 MCA Music.

HODDINOTT, Alun
—— AUBADE AND SCHERZO
    hn. - str.   Oxford.
—— THE BEACH OF FALESÁ (OPERA) % (Text: Glyn Jones)
    2,2,*3,2 - 4,2,3,1 - timp.,perc.(5) - hp. - str.   120:00 Oxford.
—— CONCERTINO FOR VIOLA AND SMALL ORCH., OP. 14
    18:00 Oxford.
—— CONCERTO FOR CLARINET AND STRINGS
    cl. - str.   15:00 Oxford.

—— CONCERTO FOR HARP AND ORCH., OP. 11
    19:00 Oxford.
—— CONCERTO FOR HORN AND ORCH.
    2,2,2,2 - 4,2,3,0 - timp.,perc. - hp. - str.   12:00 Oxford.
—— CONCERTO FOR OBOE AND STRINGS
    ob. - str.   20:00 Oxford.
—— CONCERTO FOR ORGAN AND ORCH.
    3,*3,*3,2 - 4,3,3,1 - timp.,perc. - org. - str.   16:00 Oxford.
—— CONCERTO FOR VIOLIN AND ORCH.
    25:00 Oxford.
—— CONCERTO GROSSO
    0,2,0,2 - 2,0,0,0 - str.   16:00 Oxford.
—— CONCERTO GROSSO NO. 2
    2,2,2,2 - 4,3,3,0 - timp.,perc. - hp. - str.   16:00 Oxford.
—— CONCERTO NO. 1 FOR PIANO, WINDS AND PERCUSSION
    3,3,3,3 - 4,3,3,1 - timp.,perc.,cel. - pf.   20:00 Oxford.
—— CONCERTO NO. 2 FOR PIANO AND ORCH.
    18:00 Oxford.
—— CONCERTO NO. 3 FOR PIANO AND ORCH.
    3,2,*3,2 - 4,3,3,0 - timp.,perc.,cel. - hp. - pf. - str.   23:00 Oxford.
—— DIVERTIMENTO FOR ORCH., OP. 69
    Oxford.
—— DIVES AND LAZARUS (CANTATA) (FOR SOPRANO, BARITONE, MIXED CHORUS AND ORCH.)
    2,1,2,1 - 0,2,1,0 - timp. - pf. 4-hands - str.   16:00 Oxford.
    or:
    org. - pf. 4-hands - str.
—— FIORITURE
    3,3,3,3 - 4,3,3,1 - timp.,perc. - hp. - str.   20:00 Oxford.
—— THE FLOOR OF HEAVEN
    2,2,0,2 - 4,2,3,0 - timp.,perc. - hp. - str.   6:00 Oxford.
—— FOLK SONG SUITE (ON WELSH FOLKSONGS)
    Oxford.
—— FUGAL OVERTURE
    2,2,2,2 - 2,2,0,0 - timp.,perc. - hp. - str.   10:00 Oxford.
—— THE HAWK IS SET FREE
    14:00 Oxford.
—— INVESTITURE DANCES
    3(3rd alt. with picc.),2,2,2-*3 - 4,2,3,0 - timp.,perc. - hp. - str.
    18:00 Oxford.
—— JACK STRAW (OVERTURE)
    2,2,2,2 - 4,2,3,0 - timp.,perc. - hp.(ad lib) - str.   5:00 Oxford.
—— LANDSCAPES
    20:00 Oxford.
—— MURDER,THE MAGICIAN (OPERA) % (Text: John Morgan)
    1(alt. with picc.),1,1(alt. with b.-cl.),1 - 1,1,1,0 - perc.(2) - str.(0,1,1,1)   25:00 Oxford.
—— NIGHT MUSIC
    2,2,2,2 - 2,0,0,0 - timp.,perc. - str.   10:00 Oxford.
—— NOCTURNE AND DANCE (FOR HARP AND ORCH.)
    2,2,2,2 - 4,2,3,0 - timp.,perc.,cel. - hp. - str.   8:00 Oxford.
—— NOCTURNE, OP. 5
    2,2,2,2 - 2,2,2,0 - timp. - str.   12:00 Oxford.
—— NOCTURNES AND CADENZAS (FOR CELLO AND ORCH.)
    2,2,*3,2 - 3,2,2,0 - timp.,perc.(4) - hp.(ad lib.) - str.   22:00 Oxford.
—— PANTOMIME
    2,2,2,2 - 2-3,2-3,2-3,0 - timp.,perc. - str.   3:00 Oxford.
—— SERENADE FOR STRINGS
    str.   16:00 Oxford.
—— SINFONIA
    Str   12:00 Oxford.
—— SINFONIETTA NO. 1
    2,2,2,2 - 2,2,2,0 - timp.,perc. - str.   12:00 Oxford.
—— SINFONIETTA NO. 2
    3(3rd alt. with picc.),2,2,2 - 4,2,3,0 - timp.,perc. - hp. - str.
    10:00 Oxford.
—— SINFONIETTA NO. 3
    3,2,2,3 - 4,2,3,0 - timp.,perc. - hp. - str.   11:00 Oxford.
—— SINFONIETTA NO. 4
    2,2,2,2 - 4,2,3,0 - timp.,perc. - hp. - str.   10:00 Oxford.
—— THE SUN, THE GREAT LUMINARY OF THE UNIVERSE
    3(3rd alt. with picc.),*3,*3,*3 - 4,3,3,1 - timp.,perc. - hp. - str.
    12:00 Oxford.
—— SYMPHONY NO. 1, OP. 7
    3,3,3,3 - 4,3,3,1 - timp.,perc. - str.   35:00 Oxford.
—— SYMPHONY NO. 2, OP. 29
    3,3,3,3 - 4,3,3,1 - timp.,perc. - hp. - str.   22:00 Oxford.
—— SYMPHONY NO. 3
    *3,*3,*3,*3 - 4,3,3,1 - timp.,perc. - hp. - pf.(alt. with cel.) - str.
    21:00 Oxford.
—— SYMPHONY NO. 4
    *3,*3,*3,*3 - 4,3,3,1 - timp.,perc.(4) - hp. - str.   23:00 Oxford.

—— SYMPHONY NO. 5
    3(3rd alt. with picc.),*3,*3,*3 - 4,3,3,1 - timp.,perc. - hp. - str.
                                  25:00 Oxford.
—— VARIANTS FOR ORCH.
    3(3rd alt. with picc.),*3,3,3 - 4,3,3,1 - timp.,perc.(9, incl. 4 on
    timp.),cel. - hp. - str.   26:00 Oxford.
—— VARIATIONS, OP. 31 (1963)
    2,1,2,1 - 2,2,1,0 - timp.,perc. - str.   10:00 Novello.
—— WELSH DANCES, OP. 15
    2,1-2,2,1-2 - 2-4,2,3,0 - timp.,perc.,cel.(opt.) - hp. - str.
                                  8:00 Oxford.
—— WELSH DANCES: SUITE NO. 2
    2,2,2,2 - 4,2,3,0 - hp. - str.   10:00 Oxford.

HODGE, M. Talbot
—— PASSACAGLIA (FOR STRING ORCH.)
    str.   7:00 Oxford.

HODKINSON, Sidney
—— FRESCO
    3,3,3,3 - 4,3,3,1 - timp.,perc.(4) - electric guit. - hp. - pf. - str.
                                20:00 Presser.
—— STABILE
    3,2,2,2 - 4,3,3,1 - timp.,perc.(3) - pf. - str.   8:30 Presser.
—— VALENCE (FOR CHAMBER ORCH.)
    1,2,1,2 - 2,0,0,0 - pf. - str.   7:00 Presser.

HOEREE, A.
—— LA FAMILLE DE CHARLES IV
    3,3,3,3 - 4,3,3,0 - timp.,perc.(3),cel.,glock. - pf. - str.
                             8:00 Eds. Fran.

HØFFDING, Finn
—— THE ARSENAL AT SPRINGFIELD, OP. 54 (FANTASIA
    SINFONICA) (FOR SOPRANO, ALTO, BARITONE, SATB
    CHORUS AND ORCH.) (Text: H. W. Longfellow)
    3,3,2,2 - 4,3,3,1 - perc.,bells,cel.,xyl. - hp. - org. - str.
                              28:00 Henmar.
—— CONCERTO FOR OBOE AND STRING ORCH., OP. 22
    ob. - str.   17:00 K.O.D.A.
—— CONCERTO GROSSO (FOR 2 VIOLINS, CELLO, PIANO OR
    HARP AND STRING ORCH.)
    pf.(or hp.) - str.   25:00 K.O.D.A.
—— DET ER GANSKE VIST, OP. 37 (SYMPHONIC FANTASY,
    AFTER HANS CHRISTIAN ANDERSEN)
    3,2,2,2 - 4,3,3,1 - perc.(4) - str.   Henmar.
—— FANFARE, OP. 34
    3,2,2,2 - 4,3,4,0 - timp.,perc. - pf. - str.   9:00 K.O.D.A.
—— FANTASIA CONCERTANTE, OP. 67
    3,2,2,2 - 4,3,4,0 - timp.,perc.,cel.,vibra.,xyl. - str. 26:00 K.O.D.A.
—— FOUR PANTOMIMES, OP. 41
    2,2,2,2 - 2,2,0,0 - timp. - str.   15:00 K.O.D.A.
—— MAY-FEAST, OP. 44 (DANCE SUITE)
    3,2,2,2 - 4,2,3,1 - perc.,cel.,xyl. - str. 15:00 G. Schirmer.
—— OVERTURE FOR SMALL ORCH., OP. 18
    fl.,cl. - pf. - str.   Henmar.
—— ROMANCE (FOR VIOLIN AND STRING ORCH.)
    str.   K.O.D.A.
—— SINFONIA CONCERTANTE, OP. 23
    1,1,1,1 - 1,0,0,0 - pf. - str.   20:00 K.O.D.A.
—— THE SPRING JOURNEY (OPERA) %
                        180:00 K.O.D.A.
—— SUITE FROM THE OPERA "THE EMPEROR'S NEW
    CLOTHES"
    3,2,3,2 - 4,3,3,1 - timp.,perc. - hp. - str. 17:00 G. Schirmer.
—— SYMPHONIC FANTASY NO. 1, OP. 31 (EVOLUTION)
    2,2,2,2 - 4,3,3,1 - timp. - str.   14:00 Henmar.
—— SYMPHONIC FANTASY NO. 3, OP. 40 (SPRING-AUTUMN)
    (FOR BARITONE AND ORCH.)
    3,2,2,2 - 4,3,3,1 - timp. - str.   17:00 K.O.D.A.
—— SYMPHONY NO. 1, OP. 3 (SINFONIA IMPETUOSA)
    3,2,*1,0 - 4,3,3,1 - timp.,perc. - str. 35:00 K.O.D.A.
—— SYMPHONY NO. 2, OP. 5 (IL CANTO DE LIBERALE) (FOR
    SOPRANO, CHORUS AND ORCH.)
    3,3,3,3 - 4,3,3,1 - timp.,perc.,glock.,xyl. - pf. - str. 30:00 K.O.D.A.
—— SYMPHONY NO. 3, OP. 12
    2,2,2,2 - 2,2,2,0 - timp.,perc.,xyl. - 2 pf. - str.(10,5,3,3)
                              30:00 Henmar.

HÖFFER, Paul
—— CONCERTO FOR OBOE AND STRING ORCH.
    ob. - str.   K & S.

—— CONCERTO NO. 2 FOR PIANO AND ORCH., OP. 45
                              K & S.
—— SINFONIE DER GROSSEN STADT (FOR LARGE ORCH.)
                              K & S.

HOFFMAN, Adolf G.
—— SARABANDE AND ALLEGRO (FOR CELLO AND ORCH.)
                           C. Fischer.
—— SNAPSHOTS FROM INDIA (SYMPHONIC SUITE)
                          Composer.

HOFFMAN, Richard
—— PRELUDE AND DOUBLE FUGUE FOR STRINGS
    str.   5:00 C. Fischer.

HOFFMANN, Leopold - BODART, Eugen
—— CASSATION IN D MAJOR
    2,0,0,2 - 2,0,0,0 - str.   29:00 Mannheimer.

HOFFMEISTER, Franz Anton - ZOBELEY, Fritz
—— CONCERTO IN B FLAT MAJOR FOR PIANO AND ORCH.,
    OP. 16
    2 ob. - pf. - str.   22:00 Mannheimer.

HOFMAN, Srdjan
—— CONCERTO DINAMICO
    2(2nd alt. with picc.)2(2nd alt. with Eng.hn.),2(2nd alt. with
    b.-cl.),2(2nd alt. with c.-bn.) - 4,3,3,1 - timp.,perc.,xyl. - hp. - pf. -
    str.   21:00 MIC,Zagreb.
—— EPISODI CONCERTANTI (FOR VIOLIN AND ORCH.)
    2,2,2,2 - 2,2,0,0 - timp.,perc.,cel.,vibra.,xyl. - str.
                    17:00 MIC,Zagreb.
—— MOVIMENTO ENERGICO
    2(2nd alt. with picc.),2(2nd alt. with Eng.hn.),2(2nd alt. with
    b.-cl.),2(2nd alt. with c.-bn.) - 4,3,3,1 - timp.,perc.,cel.,xyl. - str.
                    9:00 MIC,Zagreb.
—— SYMPHONY IN TWO MOVEMENTS
    2(2nd alt. with picc.)2(2nd alt. with Eng.hn.),2(2nd alt. with
    b.-cl.),2(2nd alt. with c.-bn) - 4,3,3,1 - timp.,perc.,cel.,xyl. - str.
                    14:00 MIC,Zagreb.
—— ZAKONIK POSLEDOVANJA (THE WORKING LAW) (FOR
    CLARINET AND TWO STRING SEXTETS)
    cl. - str.(6,4,2,0)   14:00 MIC,Zagreb.

HOFMANN, Wolfgang
—— C'EST LE MAI (VARIATIONS ON A FRENCH FOLK SONG)
    (FOR VIOLIN AND STRING ORCH.)
    str.   16:00 Mannheimer.
—— CONCERTINO FOR OBOE AND STRING ORCH. (IN 3
    MOVTS.)
    ob. - str.   10:00 Henmar.
—— CONCERTINO IN A MAJOR FOR PIANO AND SMALL
    ORCH.
    2,0,0,0 - 2,0,0,0 - pf. - str.   12:00 Henmar.
—— CONCERTINO IN D MAJOR FOR VIOLIN AND STRING
    ORCH. (IN 3 MOVTS.)
    str.   14:30 Henmar.
—— CONCERTO FOR CLARINET AND ORCH.
    0,2,1,0 - 2,0,0,0 - str.   15:00 Henmar.
—— CONCERTO FOR VIOLIN AND ORCH. (IN 3 MOVTS.)
    2,2,2,2 - 2,2,0,0 - timp.,perc. - str. 15:00 Henmar.
—— CONCERTO FOR VIOLIN, OBOE AND STRING ORCH.
    ob. - str.   15:00 Mannheimer.
—— CONCERTO IN B FLAT FOR BASSOON AND ORCH.
    2,0,0,1 - 2,0,0,0 - str.   15:00 Mannheimer.
—— CORRESPONDENCE (SUITE) (FOR ENGLISH HORN, VIOLIN
    AND ORCH.)
    2,*1,2,2 - 2,2,1,0 - timp.,perc. - hp. - str. 14:30 Mannheimer.
—— THE DEATH OF THE NIGHTINGALE (BALLET, AFTER
    OSCAR WILDE'S "THE NIGHTINGALE AND THE ROSE") %
    2,2,2,2 - 4,2,3,1 - timp.,perc. - str. 45:00 Mannheimer.
—— DIVERTIMENTO IN A MAJOR FOR VIOLIN AND STRING
    ORCH. (WITH OPTIONAL PIANO)
    pf.(ad lib.) - str.   20:00 Henmar.
—— FANTASIA FILIPINA (FOR VIOLIN AND ORCH.)
    3,0,3,0 - 4,0,0,0 - perc. - hp. 14:00 Mannheimer.
—— FIVE PIECES (FOR STRING ORCH.)
    str.   12:00 Henmar.
—— DER KREISEL (THE TOP) (BALLET) %
    2(2nd alt. with picc.),2(2nd alt. with Eng. hn.),2(2nd alt. with
    b.-cl.),2 - 4,2,3,0 - timp.,perc.(4) - hp. - str. 35:00 Henmar.

—— SINFONIE CONCERTANTE IN D
    3,3,2,2 sax.,3 - 4(alt. with 4 Wagner tu.),3,3,2 - timp.,perc. - str.
                    22:00 Mannheimer.
—— THREE BAGATELLES FOR STRING ORCH.
    str.   6:00 Mannheimer.
—— TWO SKETCHES FOR STRING ORCH.
    str.   6:00 Mannheimer.

HØGENHAVEN, Knud
—— BLUES SINFONICO, OP. 33
                  5:00 K.O.D.A.
—— COLUMBINE AND THE DUCK'S RUMP, OP. 29 (BALLET) %
                  30:00 K.O.D.A.
—— DANCE TRIOMPHALE, OP. 12
    2,2,2,2 - 4,3,3,1 - timp.,perc. - str.   6:00 Henmar.
—— FESTA, OP. 30 (BALLET) %
                  30:00 K.O.D.A.
—— FLITTER, OP. 21 (BALLET) %
                  30:00 K.O.D.A.
—— FRESCO (KALKBILLEDE) %
                  30:00 K.O.D.A.
—— LAMENTO, OP. 9
    str.   5:00 Henmar.
—— MOVEMENT IN F, OP. 37 (FOR PIANO AND ORCH.)
                  10:00 K.O.D.A.
—— NEON (BALLET) %
                  30:00 K.O.D.A.
—— OVERTURE BREVE, OP. 3
                  3:00 K.O.D.A.
—— PRELUDE, OP. 44
                  5:00 K.O.D.A.
—— TEEN-AGE, OP. 27 (BALLET) %
                  20:00 K.O.D.A.

HOHENSEE, Wolfgang
—— DROSSELBART (THRUSHBEARD) (BALLET, AFTER THE BROTHERS GRIMM) %
                  Tetra.
—— DROSSELBART (THRUSHBEARD): SUITE FROM THE BALLET
    3,2,2,2 - 4,2,3,1 - timp.,perc. - pf. - str.   25:00 Tetra.
—— SKLAVEN (SLAVES): SUITE FROM THE BALLET
    3,3,3,3 sax.,0 - 3,3,3,1 - timp.,perc. - hpsc. - pf. - str.(no vlns.)
                  18:00 Tetra.
—— THREE MUSICAL DESIGNS (CONCERTANTE MUSIC) (FOR VARIABLE ORCH., WITH OPTIONAL ACCORDION SOLO)
                  Tetra.

HOIBY, Lee
—— ASCENSION (FOR CHORUS AND ORCH.) (Text: John Donne)
                  Composer.
—— CONCERTO FOR PIANO AND ORCHESTRA, OP. 17
    2,2,2,2 - 4,2,3,1 - timp. - pf. - str.   25:00 G. Schirmer.
—— HEARTS, MEADOWS AND FLAGS (SUITE) (IN 4 MOVTS)
    *3,2(2nd alt. with Eng. hn.),*3,2 - 4,2,2,1 - timp.,perc. (3), cel.,
    glock., xyl. - hp. - pf. - str.   22:00 G. Schirmer.
—— A HYMN OF THE NATIVITY (CANTATA) (FOR SOPRANO, BASS, SATB CHORUS AND ORCH.)
    3,3,3,2 - 2,2,2,1 - timp.,perc. - hp. - str.   30:00 F. Colombo.
—— NATALIA PETROVNA (2-ACT OPERA, AFTER A PLAY OF TURGENEV) % (Text: William Ball)
                  Bo. Hawkes.
—— NOCTAMBULATION, OP. 2
    *3,2,2,2 - 4,3,3,1 - timp. - hp. - str.   5:00 G. Schirmer.
—— OVERTURE TO "TWELFTH NIGHT"
    3,2,2,2 - 4,3,3,1 - timp.,perc. - hp. - str.   7:00 Bo. Hawkes.
—— THE SCARF (1-ACT OPERA, AFTER A STORY BY CHEKOV) % (Text: Harry Duncan)
    1,1,1,1 - 2,1,1,0 - perc. - pf. - str.   45:00 G. Schirmer.
—— STUDY IN DESIGN (FOR STRINGS), OP. 9
    str.   5:00 Composer.
—— SUITE NO. 2 FOR ORCH., OP. 8
    3,3,3,2 - 4,3,3,1 - timp.,perc., cel. - hp. - str.   G. Schirmer.
—— SUMMER AND SMOKE (SUITE FROM THE OPERA)
    2,2,2,2 - 4,2,3,0 - timp.,perc. - guit. - hp. - str.   Belw-Mills.
—— THE TIDES OF SLEEP (SYMPHONIC SONG FOR BASS AND ORCH.) (Text: Thomas Wolfe)
    2,2,3,2 - 4,3,3,1 - timp.,perc. - hp. - str.   17:00 Bo. Hawkes.
—— TWO PASTORAL DANCES FOR FLUTE AND ORCH., OP. 4
    1. Lento; 2. Allegro comodo
    1(alt. with picc.),1,2,1 - 2,1,0,0, - timp. - hp. - str.
                  7:00 G. Schirmer.

HOKANSON, Margarethe
—— FOUR SEASONS IN THE NORTH
    2,2,2,2 - 4,2,2,0 - timp.,perc. - str.   15:00 Composer.
—— NORDIC REVERIE (TONE POEM)
    2,*2,2,2 - 4,2,0,0 - timp. - hp. - str.   7:00 Gray.

HOLBROOKE, Joseph
—— BYRON (POEM NO. 6), OP. 39
    3,2,2,2 - 4,2,3,1 - perc. - hp. - str.   Novello.
—— CONCERTO IN B FLAT (FOR SAXOPHONE OR BASSOON AND ORCH.)
    2,2,2,sax.(or bn.),0 - 2,2,1,0 - perc. - pf. - str.   20:00 P.R.S.
—— DRAMATIC CHORAL SYMPHONY, OP. 1 (FOR MIXED CHORUS AND ORCH.)
                  G. Schirmer.

HOLD, Trevor
—— LUCKY JIM, OP. 11 (AN OVERTURE) (1963)
    3,2,2,alto sax.,2 - 4,2,3,1 - timp.,perc. - hp. - str.   10:00 P.R.S.
—— MY UNCLE SILAS (AN OVERTURE) (1967)
    3,2,2,2 - 2,1,0,0 - timp.,perc. - hp. - str.   5:00 P.R.S.
—— RONDO, OP. 16 (1964)
    str.   30:00 P.R.S.
—— THE TIME-GLASS, OP. 22 (1966)
    3,3,3,3 - 4,2,3,1 - timp.,perc.,cel. - hp. - pf. - str.   25:00 P.R.S.
—— TIME PASSES (1968)
    3,2,2,3 - 4,2,3,1 - timp.,perc.(4) - hp. - str.   12:30 P.R.S.

HOLDEN, David
—— CANTATA ON APPALACHIAN CHRISTMAS CAROLS (FOR MIXED CHORUS AND ORCH.)
    2,2,2,2 - 2,0,0,0 - glock. - hp. - org. - str.   G. Schirmer.
—— MUSIC FOR PIANO AND STRINGS
    pf. - str.   18:00 Presser.

HOLDEN, Oliver - GOINES, Samuel Richard
—— CHORALE PARAPHRASE ON "CROWN OF FREEDOM" (FOR SOPRANO, CHORUS AND ORCH.)
    2,2,2,2 - 3,2,2,0 - timp. - str.   3:00 Summy-Bir.

HOLESOVSKY, Jaroslav P.
—— PROLOGUE, HYMN AND DANCE
    *3,2,2-*3,2 - 4,3,3,1 - timp.,perc.(4),xyl. - pf. - str.   5:00 EV.

HOLEWA, Hans
—— CHAMBER CONCERTO (FOR VIOLA AND 11 STRINGS)(1966)
    str.   12:00 Fleisher.
—— COMPOSITION FOR ORCH. (1966)
    3,3,3,3 - 4,3,4,0 - timp.,perc.(4) - 2 hp. - 2 pf. - str.
                  16:00 Fleisher.
—— CONCERTO FOR PIANO AND ORCH. (1972)
    2,2,2,2 - 4,2,3,1 - timp.,perc.(3) - hp. - pf. - str.   17:00 Fleisher.
—— CONCERTO FOR VIOLIN AND ORCH (1963)
    2,2,2,2 - 4,3,3,1 - timp.,perc.(2) - str.   15:00 S.T.I.M.
—— MOVIMENTO ESPRESSIVO (1971)
    3,3,3,3 - 4,3,4,0 - timp.,perc.(5, incl. 3 on timp.),cel. - hp. - pf. -
    str.   8:00 Fleisher.
—— QUATTRO CADENZE (FOR CELLO AND ORCH.) (1968)
    3,3,3,3 - 4,3,3,1 - timp.,perc.(2) - str.   22:00 S.T.I.M.

HOLLAND, Dulcie Sybil
—— ARIA
    alto sax. - str.   4:30 A.P.R.A.
—— CIVIC OVERTURE (1965)
                  6:00 A.P.R.A.
—— FESTIVAL FLOURISH (1965)
                  12:00 A.P.R.A.
—— MUSIC FOR MY UNWRITTEN PLAY (1975)
                  10:00 A.P.R.A.
—— SYMPHONY FOR PLEASURE (1971)
                  22:20 A.P.R.A.
—— THIS WHITE SHELL STANDING (FOR NARRATOR AND ORCH.) (1973)
                  14:00 A.P.R.A.

HOLLANDER, Ralph
—— ELEGIE
    str.   6:00 Integrity.
—— GALMUD (DESOLATION) (FOR VIOLIN AND ORCH.)
    2(2nd alt. with picc.),2,2,1 - 1,3,2,0 - timp. - str.   7:00 Integrity.
    or:
    2(2nd alt. with picc.),1,2,1 - 2,2,1,0 - timp. - str.

HÖLLER, Karl
—— DIVERTIMENTO, OP. 11
    1,1,0,1 - 0,0,0,0 - hp. - str.   22:00 SDMV.
—— SYMPHONY NO. 1 IN C SHARP MINOR
    3,2,2,3 - 4,3,3,1 - perc., cel - hp. - str.   40:00 Sikorski.

HOLLFELDER, Waldram
—— VARIATIONS FOR CHAMBER ORCH. (ON A THEME OF
JOHANN KRIEGER)
        Tonos Vlg.

HOLLINGSWORTH, Stanley
—— LA GRANDE BRETÈCHE (OPERA) % (1954) (Text: Composer,
after Balzac)
    2(2nd alt. with picc.),2,2,2 - 4,2,3,1 - timp.,perc(2),bells,cel.,xyl. -
    hp. - str.   45:00 Composer.
—— THE MOTHER (1-ACT CHAMBER OPERA) % (1949)
    1(alt. with picc.),1,1,1 - 1,1,0,0 - timp.,perc.(2),cel. - hp. - pf. -
    str.   35:00 F. Colombo.
—— PSALM OF DAVID (FOR TENOR, SATB CHORUS AND
ORCH.) (1962)
    2,2,2,2 - 4,0,3,1 - timp.,perc.,xyl. - hp. - pf. - str. 8:00 Composer.
—— STABAT MATER (FOR SATB CHORUS AND ORCH.) (1958)
    2,2,2,2 - 2,2,1,0 - timp. - hp. - pf. - str.   10:00 G. Schirmer.

HOLLOWAY, Robin
—— CONCERTINO NO. 2
        25:00 Oxford.
—— DOMINATION OF BLACK
        Oxford.
—— EVENING WITH ANGELS
    2(alt. with 2 picc.),*2,2(alt. with 2 E^{b}cl., and 2 b.-cl.),1 - 1,1,1,1 -
    cel. - str.(2,1,1,1)   33:00 Oxford.
—— SEA SURFACE FULL OF CLOUDS (FOR SOLO VOICES, SATB
CHORUS AND ORCH.)
        35:00 Oxford.

HOLM, Mogens Winkel
—— AILOS (SYMPHONY) (FOR 4 ORCHESTRAL GROUPS)
    4,3,3,2 - 4,0,4,0 - glock.,mar. - hp. - pf. - str. 42:00 G. Schirmer.
—— CHAMBER CONCERTANTE, OP. 8 (FOR STRING QUARTET,
BASSOON AND STRING ORCH.)
    bn. - str.   13:00 G. Schirmer.
—— CHRONICLE (OR, THE BOY WHO GOT CURED) (BALLET) %
        40:00 G. Schirmer.
—— CONCERTO PICCOLO, OP. 12
    2,1,3,1 - 4,2,2,1 - timp.,perc. - str.   7:00 K.O.D.A.
—— CUMULUS, OP. 21 (WITH SOLO STRING QUARTET)
    2,1,1,2 - 2,2,2,1 - perc.,vibra. - pf. - str.   7:00 K.O.D.A.
—— GALGARIN (BALLET) %
    2,3,2,3 - 2,2,2,0 - bells, cel. - hp. - pf. - str. 20:00 G. Schirmer.
—— A GHOST STORY, OP. 15 (FOR CHORUS AND ORCH.)
        G. Schirmer.
—— MATES (BALLET) %
    4 c.-bn. - perc.(6) - guit.,mandolin - hp. - acc. - hpsc. - electric
    org. - pf.   16:00 K.O.D.A.
—— RAPPORT (TV BALLET, WITH SOPRANO) %
    4,3,3,2 - 4,0,4,0 - perc.,glock.,mar. - guit. - hp. - pf. - str.
        40:00 G. Schirmer.
—— ST. ANNALAND, OP. 24
    3,0,0,0 - 0,3,0,0 - perc.,cel. - hpsc.,spinet - vla. da gamba
        20:00 K.O.D.A.
—— TROPISMER (BALLET) %
    2,2,2,2 - 3,2,2,1 - timp.,perc. - pf. - str. 25:00 G. Schirmer.

HOLM, Peder
—— CAPRICCIO
        5:00 G. Schirmer.
—— CONCERTINO FOR PIANO AND STRINGS
    pf. - str.   12:00 G. Schirmer.
—— CONCERTINO NO. 2 FOR PIANO AND STRINGS (1967)
    pf. - str.   7:00 G. Schirmer.
—— CONCERTO FOR PIANO AND ORCH. (1953)
        14:00 G. Schirmer.
—— CONCERTO FOR VIOLA AND ORCH. (1954)
        10:00 G. Schirmer.
—— CONCERTO FOR VIOLIN AND ORCH. (1952)
        22:00 G. Schirmer.
—— E. S. A. (1967)
        11:00 G. Schirmer.
—— KHEBEB (FOR 2 PIANOS AND ORCH.)
        13:00 G. Schirmer.

—— PEZZO CONCERTANTE (1964)
    2,2,2,2 - 2,2,3,0 - timp.(3) - str.   7:00 Henmar.
—— STORMSTREET MUSIC (1951)
    str.   4:00 G. Schirmer.
—— SYMPHONIC DANCE (1957)
        5:00 G. Schirmer.
—— SYMPHONY NO. 1 (1955)
        30:00 G. Schirmer.
—— THREE ORCHESTRAL PIECES (1966)
    3,3,4,ten. sax.,3 - 4,3,3,1 - timp.,perc.(4) - str. 19:00 Henmar.
—— TWO SKETCHES (FOR TRUMPET, TROMBONE AND ORCH.)
(1966)
        9:00 G. Schirmer.

HOLMBOE, Vagn
—— BEATUS PARVO, OP. 117
    2,2,2,2 - 2,2,1,0 - timp. - str.   G. Schirmer.
—— CHAMBER CONCERTO NO. 1, OP. 17 (1939)
    timp. - pf. - str.   23:00 K.O.D.A.
—— CHAMBER CONCERTO NO. 10, OP. 40
("WOOD-BRASS-GUT") (1946)
    2,2,2,2 - 2,2,0,0 - timp.,perc. - str.   18:00 Henmar.
—— CHAMBER CONCERTO NO. 11, OP. 44 (FOR TRUMPET AND
ORCH.) (1948)
    0,0,0,0 - 2,1,0,0 - str.   16:00 Henmar.
—— CHAMBER CONCERTO NO. 12, OP. 52 (FOR TROMBONE
AND ORCH.) (1950)
    *3,2,2,2 - 4,3,1,0 - timp.,perc. - str.   22:00 Henmar.
—— CHAMBER CONCERTO NO. 13, OP. 67 (FOR OBOE, VIOLA
AND ORCH.) (1956)
    1,2,1,1 - 2,0,0,0 - str.   23:00 Henmar.
—— CHAMBER CONCERTO NO. 3, OP. 21 (1940)
    0,1,0,0 - 2,2,0,0 - str.   15:00 G. Schirmer.
—— CHAMBER CONCERTO NO. 4 OP. 30 (TRIPLE CONCERTO)
(FOR VIOLIN, CELLO, PIANO AND ORCH.) (1940)
    1,1,2,1 - 2,0,0,0 - pf. - str.   18:00 G. Schirmer.
—— CHAMBER CONCERTO NO. 5, OP. 31 (FOR VIOLA AND
ORCH.) (1943)
    2,2,2,2 - 2,2,0,0 - timp. - str.   21:00 Henmar.
—— CHAMBER CONCERTO NO. 6, OP. 33 (FOR VIOLIN AND
ORCH.) (1943)
    2,2,2,2 - 2,2,0,0 - timp. - str.   20:00 G. Schirmer.
—— CHAMBER CONCERTO NO. 7, OP. 37 (FOR OBOE AND
ORCH.) (1945)
    1,1,2,2 - 2,2,0,0 - timp.,perc. - str.   17:00 Henmar.
—— CHAMBER CONCERTO NO. 9, OP. 39 (FOR VIOLIN, VIOLA
AND ORCH.) (1946)
    2,2,2,2 - 3,3,0,0 - timp.,perc. - str.   18:00 Henmar.
—— CHAMBER SYMPHONY NO. 2, OP. 100 (1968)
    1,1,1,1 - 2,1,0,0 - timp.,perc.,cel.,vibra. - str. 30:00 G. Schirmer.
—— CHAMBER SYMPHONY NO. 3, OP. 103-A ("FRIEZE") (1970)
    1,1,1,1 - 2,2,0,0 - timp.,perc.,vibra.,xyl. - str. 20:00 G. Schirmer.
—— CONCERTINO FOR 4 RECORDERS AND STRINGS (1957)
    4 recorders - str.   G. Schirmer.
—— CONCERTINO NO. 1, OP. 22 (FOR VIOLIN, VIOLA AND
STRINGS) (1940)
    str.   12:00 Henmar.
—— CONCERTINO NO. 2, OP. 24 (FOR VIOLIN AND STRINGS)
(1940)
    str.   K.O.D.A.
—— CONCERTO FOR CELLO AND ORCH., OP. 120 (1974)
        K.O.D.A.
—— CONCERTO FOR CHAMBER ORCH. (1931)
    1,1,1,1 - 1,0,0,0 - str.   K.O.D.A.
—— CONCERTO FOR ORCH. (1929)
    *3,2,2,2 - 4,3,3,2 - timp.,perc. - str.   K.O.D.A.
—— CONCERTO FOR STRINGS (1933)
    str.   K.O.D.A.
—— CONCERTO FOR TUBA AND ORCH., OP. 127
    2,2,2,2 - 4,0,2,1 - perc.,vibra.,xyl. - str.   G. Schirmer.
—— CONCERTO FOR VIOLIN AND ORCH., OP. 14 (1938)
    *3,2,2,2 - 0,2,1,0 - timp.,perc. - str. 30:00 K.O.D.A.
—— CONCERTO NO. 3 FOR CLARINET AND ORCH.
    0,0,1,0 - 2,2,0,0 - str.   18:00 G. Schirmer.
—— CONCERTO NO. 8, OP. 38 (SINFONIA CONCERTANTE)
        Viking Mfl.
—— CONCERTO PER FLAUTO DOLCE ED ORCHESTRA
D'ARCHI, CELESTAE E VIBRAPHONE, OP. 122
    Recorder - cel.,vibra. - str.   G. Schirmer.
—— DANISH SUITE (FOR CHAMBER ORCH.) (1938)
        K.O.D.A.

—— EPILOGUE, OP. 80 (SYMPHONIC METAMORPHOSES)
*3,*3,*3,*3 - 4,3,3,1 - timp.,perc.,cel.,vibra.,xyl. - str.
24:00 G. Schirmer.

—— EPITAPH, OP. 68 (SYMPHONIC METAMORPHOSES) (1956)
3,3,*3,*3 - 4,3,3,1 - timp.,perc.,cel.,vibra.,xyl. - str. 23:00 Henmar.

—— KAMMERCONCERT NO. 2, OP. 20 (FOR FLUTE, VIOLIN
AND CHAMBER ORCH.)
fl. - perc.(3),cel. - str. Henmar.

—— KAMMERSYMFONI, OP. 53
1,1,1,1 - 1,1,0,0 - perc.(1) - str. Viking Mfl.

—— LAVE AND JON (OPERA) % (1948) (Text: Lis Thorbjørnsen)
K.O.D.a.

—— MONOLITH, OP. 76 (SYMPHONIC METAMORPHOSES) (1960)
3,3,2,2 - 4,3,3,1 - timp.,perc.,cel. - hp. - str. 10:00 G. Schirmer.

—— REQUIEM FOR NIETZSCHE, OP. 84 (FOR TENOR,
BARITONE, CHORUS AND ORCH.) (1964) (Text: Thorkild
Bjørnvig)
*3,*3,*3,2 - 4,3,3,1 - timp.,perc.,cel.,vibra.,xyl. - hp. - str. K.O.D.A.

—— RHAPSODY, OP. 5 (FOR FLUTE AND CHAMBER ORCH.)
(1935)
K.O.D.a.

—— ROUMANIAN SUITE FOR CHAMBER ORCH. (1938)
K.O.D.A.

—— ROUMANIAN SUITE FOR PIANO AND CHAMBER ORCH.
(1935)
K.O.D.A.

—— SINFONIA IN MEMORIAM, OP. 65 (1955)
3,2,2,2 - 4,3,3,1 - timp.,perc. - hp. - str. 25:00 K.O.D.A.

—— SINFONIA NO. 1 FOR STRINGS, OP. 73A
str. 12:00 G. Schirmer.

—— SINFONIA NO. 2 FOR STRINGS, OP. 73B
str. 14:30 G. Schirmer.

—— SINFONIA NO. 3, OP. 73-C (1958)
str. 11:00 G. Schirmer.

—— SINFONIA NO. 4, OP. 73-D (1962)
str. 16:00 G. Schirmer.

—— SUITE NO. 1 FOR CHAMBER ORCH., OP. 1 (1935)
1,1,1,1 - 2,1,1,0 - timp.,perc. - str. 15:00 K.O.D.A.

—— SUITE NO. 2 FOR CHAMBER ORCH., OP. 6 (1936)
1,1,1,1 - 0,0,0,0 - perc. - str. K.O.D.A.

—— SUITE NO. 3 FOR CHAMBER ORCH., OP. 11 (1936)
1,1,1,1 - 2,1,0,0 - perc. - pf. - str. K.O.D.A.

—— SUITE NO."A" FOR CHAMBER ORCH. (1932)
1,2,0,0 - 1,1,0,0, - timp. - str. K.O.D.A.

—— SUITE, OP. 32 (FROM "THE CRAZY-MINDED TURK") (1969)
*3,*3,*3,*3 - 4,3,3,1 - timp.,perc.,cel.,vibra.,xyl. - str.
17:00 G. Schirmer.

—— SYMPHONIC OVERTURE, OP. 28 (1941)
*3,2,2,2 - 4,3,3,1 - timp.,perc. - pf. - str. K.O.D.A.

—— SYMPHONY NO. 1, OP. 4 (1935)
1,1,1,1 - 1,1,1,0 - timp.,perc. - str. 16:00 K.O.D.A.

—— SYMPHONY NO. 2, OP. 15 (1939)
*3,*3,*3,*3 - 4,3,3,1 - timp.,xyl. - str. 31:00 K.O.D.A.

—— SYMPHONY NO. 3, OP. 25 (SINFONICA RUSTICA) (1941)
3,2,2,2 - 4,3,3,1 - timp.,perc.,cel. - str. 23:00 K.O.D.A.

—— SYMPHONY NO. 4, OP. 29 (SINFONICA SACRA) (WITH
SPEAKING VOICE AND CHORUS) (1941)
*3,*3,*3,*3 - 4,3,3,1 - timp.,perc. - pf. - str. 32:00 K.O.D.A.

—— SYMPHONY NO. 5, OP. 35
Viking Mfl.

—— SYMPHONY NO. 6, OP. 43
Viking Mfl.

—— SYMPHONY NO. 7, OP. 50
24:00 Viking Mfl.

—— SYMPHONY NO. 8, OP. 56 (SINFONIA BOREALE)
Viking Mfl.

—— SYMPHONY NO. 9, OP. 95 (1968)
3,*3,*3,*3 - 4,3,3,1 - timp.,perc.,cel.,vibra.,xyl. - str.
31:00 G. Schirmer.

—— SYMPHONY NO. 10, OP. 105 (1971)
3,*3,*3,*3 - 4,3,3,1 - timp.,perc.,cel.,vibra.,xyl. - str.
23:00 G. Schirmer.

—— SYMPHONY NO."A" (1927)
2,2,2,3 - 4,2,0,0 - timp.,perc. - str. K.O.D.A.

—— SYMPHONY NO."B" (1927)
K.O.D.A.

—— TEMPO VARIABILE, OP. 108 (SYMPHONIC
METAMORPHOSES) (1972)
3,3,*3,*3 - 4,3,3,1 - timp.,perc.,vibra.,xyl. - str. K.O.D.A.

HOLMES, Paul
—— ADAGIO AND ALLEGRO (1949)
*3,2,2,2 - 4,3,3,1 - timp.,perc.(3) - str. 12:30 Composer.

—— CIBOLA
*3,2,2,2 - 4,3,3,1 - timp.,perc.(2) - str. 12:00 Composer.

—— FABLE (1956)
*3,2,2,2 - 4,3,3,1 - timp.,perc.(3) - str. 8:30 Composer.

—— RUTH (ORATORIO) (FOR SOPRANO, BARITONE,
NARRATOR, SATB CHORUS AND ORCH.) (1960) (Text:
Biblical)
1,1,2,1 - 3,2,2,0 - str. 30:00 Composer.

—— SUITE FOR BRASS (1959) (IN 3 MOVTS.)
0,0,0,0 - 4,3,3,1 6:45 Shawnee.

—— THREE ARCHAIC DANCES
SouthernTx.

HOLMQVIST, Evald
—— DOCKNORAS HERDASPEL, OP. 7
2,2,2,2 - 2,0,0,0 - timp.,perc. 16:00 S.T.I.M.

—— ELEGIAC SYMPHONY, OP. 10
2,1,2,1 - 2,2,1,0 - timp. - str. 40:00 S.T.I.M.

—— FESTIVAL OVERTURE, OP. 14
2,2,2,2 - 4,3,3,1 - timp.,perc. (2) - hp. - str. 9:30 S.T.I.M.

—— ORCHESTRAL SUITE FROM "BERGAKUNGENS BRUD"
2,2,2,2 - 2,2,3,0 - timp.,perc. (2) - hp. - str. 11:00 S.T.I.M.

—— TWO MINIATURES FOR STRINGS, OP. 9
str. 14:00 S.T.I.M.

HOLSCHER, Franz
—— DER TAG VERTREIBT DIE FINSTRE NACHT (THE DAY
EXPELS THE DARK OF NIGHT) (CANTATA) (FOR SOLO
VOICES, MIXED CHORUS, 2 FLUTES AND STRINGS)
2 fl. - str. 9:00 F. Colombo.

HOLST, Gustav
—— BALLET MUSIC FROM "THE PERFECT FOOL", OP. 39
3,3,3,3 - 4,4,3,1 - timp.,perc., cel. - hp. - str. 14:00 Novello.

—— BENI MORA (ORIENTAL SUITE)
3(3rd alt. with picc.),3,2,2 - 4,3,3,1 - timp.,perc. - 2 hp. - str.
16:00 G. Schirmer.
or:
2,2,2,2 - 2,2,1,0 - timp.,perc. - str.

—— BROOK GREEN SUITE
str. G. Schirmer.
or:
1,1,1,0 - 0,0,0,0 - str.

—— CHORAL FANTASIA (FOR CHORUS AND ORCH.)
0,0,0,0 - 0,3,3,1 - timp.,perc. - org. - str. 30:00 G. Schirmer.

—— CHRISTMAS SONG (FOR MIXED CHORUS AND ORCH.)
G. Schirmer.

—— EGDON HEATH, OP. 47
2,3,2,3 - 4,3,3,1 - str. 15:00 Novello.

—— A FESTIVAL CHIME (ON A WELSH MELODY) (FOR
CHORUS AND ORCH.)
2,2,2,2 - 2,3,0,0 - timp., bells - org. (or trb. or tu.) - str. Galaxy.

—— FUGAL CONCERTO, OP. 40, NO. 2 (IN 3 MOVTS.)
fl., ob - str. 10:00 Novello.
or:
str.(incl. 2 solo vlns.)

—— FUGAL OVERTURE, OP. 40, NO. 1
3,3,3,3 - 4,3,3,1 - timp., glock. - str. 6:00 Novello.

—— THE GOLDEN GOOSE (A CHORAL BALLET) (FOR CHORUS
AND ORCH.)
*3,*3,2,2 - 2,2,3,1 - timp.,perc., cel., glock. - str. Oxford.
or:
1,1,1,1 - 1,1,0,0, - pf. - str.

—— HAMMERSMITH (PRELUDE AND SCHERZO), OP. 52
3,3,3,3 - 4,3,3,1 - timp.,perc. - str. 16:30 Bo. Hawkes.
or:
2,2,2,1 - 2,2,3,1 - timp. - str.

—— HECUBA'S LAMENT (FOR MEZZO-SOPRANO, WOMEN'S
CHORUS AND ORCH.)
2,2,2,2 - 2,2,3,0-1 - timp.,perc. (2) - hp. - str. Galaxy.

—— THE HYMN OF JESUS (FOR 2 CHORUSES, SEMI-CHORUS,
PIANO, ORGAN AND ORCH.)
3(2nd alt. with picc.),*3,2,2 - 4,2,3,0 - timp.,perc. cel. - org. - pf. -
str. 20:00 Galaxy.

—— JAPANESE SUITE, OP. 33
2,2,2,2 - 4,2,3,1 - timp.,perc. - hp. - str. 11:00 Bo. Hawkes.

—— LYRIC MOVEMENT FOR VIOLA AND SMALL ORCH.
1,1,1,1 - 0,0,0,0 - str. 10:00 Oxford.

—— THE PLANETS (IN 7 MOVTS) (With Women's Chorus In Last
Movt.)
4(2 alt. with 2 picc. and 1 alto fl.),4(3rd alt. with heckelphone),4,4
- 6,4,3,2 - timp.,perc.,cel.,glock.,xyl. - 2 hp. - org. - str.
55:00 G. Schirmer.

or:
3(3rd alt. with picc.),3,3,2 - 4,3,3,1 - timp.,perc.,cel.,glock.,xyl. - hp. - str.
—— ST. PAUL'S SUITE (FOR STRINGS) (IN 4 MOVTS)
str.   13:00 G. Schirmer.
—— SAVITRI (AN EPISODE FROM THE MAHABBHARATA) (FOR SOPRANO, TENOR, BASS AND ORCH.), OP. 25
2 fl., Eng. hn. - str.   30:00 G. Schirmer.
—— SCHERZO, OP. POSTHUMOUS
3,3,2,2 - 4,3,3,1 - timp.,perc. - hp. - str.   5:30 Bo. Hawkes.
—— A SOMERSET RHAPSODY, OP. 21
2,2,2,2 - 4,2,3,1 - timp.,perc. - str. 8:00 Bo. Hawkes.
—— TE DEUM (FESTIVAL CHORUS)
5:00 Galaxy.
—— TURN BACK, O MAN (FOR CHORUS AND ORCH.)
2,2,2,2 - 2,2,3,0,0 - timp. - org. (or trb. or tu.) - str.   4:00 Galaxy.
—— TWO PSALMS (PSALMS 86 AND 148) (FOR CHORUS, ORGAN AND STRINGS, WITH OPTIONAL BRASS)
12:00 Galaxy.

HOLST, Gustav - HOLST, Imogen
—— CAPRICCIO (1932)
1(alt. with picc.),*2,*2,2 - 2,3,2,1 - perc.(2) - hp. - pf.(alt. with cel.) - str.   6:00 G. Schirmer.
—— THE WANDERING SCHOLAR, OP. 50 (1-ACT CHAMBER OPERA) % (FOR 4 SINGERS AND ORCH.) (Text: Clifford Box)
*2,*2,2,2 - 2,0,0,0 - str.   30:00 G. Schirmer.

HOLST, Gustav - JACOB, Gordon
—— A MOORSIDE SUITE
2,2,2,2 - 4,2,3,1 - timp.,perc. - str. 12:00 Bo. Hawkes.
—— SUITE NO. 1 IN E♭ (IN 3 MOVTS)
2,2,2,2 - 4,2,3,1 - timp.,perc. - str. 11:00 Bo. Hawkes.

HOLST, Gustav - WOODHOUSE, Charles
—— JAPANESE SUITE
Bo. Hawkes.

HOLST, Imogen
—— THE SUN'S JOURNEY (CANTATA) (FOR WOMEN'S VOICES AND SMALL ORCH.) (Text: John Ford andThomas Dekker)
2,0,0,0 - 0,0,0,0 - perc. - pf. - str. 25:00 Oxford.
—— VARIATIONS ON GILES FARNABY'S "LOTH TO DEPART" (FOR STRING QUARTET AND 2 STRING ORCHESTRAS)
str.   Oxford.

HOLSTEIN, Jean-Paul
—— CONCERTINO FOR PIANO AND STRINGS
pf. - str.   17:15 Presser.
—— LA FORCE DU TEMPS
str.   Presser.

HOLZBAUER, Ignaz - CARSE, Adam
—— SYMPHONY IN E FLAT
0,2,0,2 - 2,0,0,0 - str.   16:00 Galaxy.
—— SYMPHONY IN E♭, OP. 4, NO. 3 (IN 4 MOVTS)
0,2,0,2 - 2,0,0,0 - str.   15:00 Augener.

HOLZBAUER, Ignaz Jakob - BODART, Eugen
—— PARTITA IN D MAJOR (FOR STRING ORCH.)
str.   12:00 Mannheimer.
—— SINFONIA (FROM THE ORATORIO "LA BETULIA LIBERATE")
2,2,0,2 - 2,0,0,0 - str.   5:00 Mannheimer.
—— SYMPHONY IN C MAJOR, OP. 4, NO. 1 (FROM "THREE SYMPHONIES, IN WHICH THERE IS THE TEMPEST")
0,2,0,0 - 2,0,0,0 - str.   19:00 Mannheimer.
—— SYMPHONY IN D MAJOR, OP. 4, NO. 2
2,0,0,0 - 2,0,0,0 - str.   16:00 Mannheimer.
—— SYMPHONY IN E FLAT MAJOR (FROM THE STRING QUINTET)
str.   14:00 Mannheimer.
—— SYMPHONY IN E FLAT MAJOR, OP. 4, NO. 3
0,2,0,0 - 2,0,0,0 - str.   17:00 Mannheimer.
—— SYMPHONY IN G MAJOR
0,2,0,0 - 2,0,0,0 - str.   13:00 Mannheimer.

HOLZBAUER, Ignaz Jakob - SCHROEDER, Felix
—— CONCERTO IN E FLAT MAJOR FOR VIOLA, CELLO AND STRING ORCH.
hpsc. - str.   18:00 Mannheimer.

HÖMBERG, Johannes
—— MUSIC FOR STRINGS '67 (1967)
str.   Hans Gerig.

HOMS, Joaquim
—— IMPROMPTU FOR TEN (1970)
1,1,1,0 - 0,1,0,0 - perc. - pf. - str.(2,1,1,0)   8:00 Seesaw.

HONEGGER, Arthur
—— L' AIGLON (OPERA) % (Co-Composed with Jacques Ibert)
Presser.
—— AMPHION (OPERA) % (FOR NARRATOR, BARITONE, 4 WOMEN'S VOICES, MIXED CHORUS AND ORCH.)
3,3,3,3 - 4,3,3,1 - timp.,perc. (4), cel., xyl. - hp. - str.   40:00 Salabert.
—— ANTIGONE (TRAGEDY, AFTER SOPHOCLES) % (FOR SOPRANO, MEZZO-SOPRANO, CONTRALTO, TENOR, 2 BARITONES, 2 BASSES, VOCAL QUARTET, MIXED CHORUS AND ORCH.)
3,3,3,sax,3 - 4,3,3,1 - timp.,perc., cel. - hp. - str.   60:00 Salabert.
—— L' APPEL DE LA MONTAGNE (BALLET) %
Salabert.
—— BALLET MUSIC FROM THE OPERA "L'AIGLON" (Co-composed with Jacques Ibert)
2,2,2,0 - 4,2,2,1 - perc.,cel. - hp. - str.   Presser.
—— BATTLEMENT DU MONDE (FOR WOMAN'S VOICE, CHILD'S VOICE, SATB CHORUS AND ORCH.) (1944) (Text: William Aguet)
2,2,2,2 - 2,2,3,0 - timp. - hp. - pf. - str.   19:00 Salabert.
—— UNE CANTATE DE NOËL (FOR BARITONE SOLO, CHILDREN'S CHORUS, MIXED CHORUS, ORGON AND ORCH.)
2,2,2,2 - 4,3,3,0 - hp. - org. - str.   28:00 Salabert.
—— CANTIQUE DE PÂQUES (FOR THREE WOMEN'S VOICES, WOMEN'S CHORUS AND ORCH.)
2,2,2,2 - 2,2,0,0 - cel. - hp. - str.   9:00 Salabert.
—— LE CANTIQUE DES CANTIQUES (BALLET) (WITH VOICE) %
3,1,3,2 sop. sax.,2 alto sax.,2 - 0,4,5,0 - perc.(3),cel. - ondes Martenot - pf. - c.,d.-b.   43:00 Presser.
—— CHANT DE JOIE
3,3,3,3 - 4,3,3,1 - perc.,cel. - hp. - str.   7:00 Salabert.
—— CHANT DE LIBERATION (FOR BARITONE SOLO, UNISON CHORUS AND ORCH.)
2,2,2,2 - 2,3,3,0 - timp.,perc. - pf. - str.   Salabert.
—— LE CHANT DE NIGAMON
3,3,2,3 - 4,2,3,1 - timp.,perc. - str. 11:00 Salabert.
—— CHRISTOPHE COLOMB (FOR 2 TENORS, SATB CHORUS AND ORCH.) (1940) (Text: William Aguet)
1,1,2,1 - 2,3,3,2,0 - timp.,perc.,bells - hp. - str.   55:00 Salabert.
—— CINQ POÈMES D'APOLLINAIRE (FOR VOICE AND ORCH.)
1,0,0,0 - 2,0,0,0 - cel. - hp. - str.   Salabert.
—— CONCERTINO FOR PIANO AND ORCH.
2,2,2,2 - 2,2,1,0 - pf. - str.   13:00 Salabert.
—— CONCERTO DA CAMERA (FOR FLUTE, ENGLISH HORN AND STRINGS)
fl., Eng. hn. - str.   17:00 Salabert.
—— CONCERTO FOR CELLO AND ORCH.
2,2,2,2 - 2,2,0,1 - timp.,perc. - str. 15:00 Salabert.
—— CRIS DU MONDE (ORATORIO) (FOR SOPRANO, CONTRALTO, BARITONE, MIXED CHORUS AND ORCH.)
3,3,3,3 - 4,3,3,1 - perc. - pf. - str. 55:00 Salabert.
—— LA DANSE DES MORTS (FOR THREE VOICES, MIXED CHOIR AND ORCH.)
2,2,2,2 - 2,2,2,0 - timp.,perc. - org. - pf. - str.   35:00 Salabert.
—— LE DIT DES JEUX DU MONDE (10 DANCES, 2 INTERLUDES AND AN EPILOGUE) (FOR CHAMBER ORCH.)
fl. - pt. - timp.,perc. - str.   50:00 Salabert.
—— LE GRAND BARRAGE (IMAGE MUSICALE)
3,3,3,3 - 4,3,3,0 - timp.,perc., cel. - hp. - str.   6:00 Salabert.
—— HAMLET (FOR NARRATOR, CHORUS AND ORCH.)
0,0,0,0 - 0,3,3,0 - timp.,perc. - ondes Martenot - str.   17:00 Salabert.
—— HORACE VICTORIEUX
3,3,3,3 - 4,3,3,1 - timp.,perc. - hp. - str.   20:00 Salabert.
—— JEANNE D'ARC AU BÛCHER (DRAMATIC ORATORIO) % (FOR 2 SOPRANOS, CONTRALTO, TENOR, BASS, 5 SPEAKING PARTS, CHORUS AND ORCH.)
2(1 alt. with picc.),2,E♭cl.,*2,*3 alto sax.,*4 - 0,1 small tpt. in D,3,3,b.-trb. (or tu.),0 - timp.,perc. (3), cel., ondes Martenot (ad lib.) - 2pf. - str.   80:00 Salabert.
—— JOUR DE FÊTE SUISSE (BALLET-SUITE) (IN 7 MOVTS)
3,3,2,3 - 4,3,3,1 - timp.,perc., cel. - pf. - str.   23:00 Salabert.

—— JUDITH (BIBLICAL DRAMA) % (FOR NARRATOR, SOPRANO, MEZZO-SOPRANO, CHORUS AND ORCH.)
2,2,2,2 - 2,2,2,0 perc. - hp. - pf. - str.   50:00 Salabert.

—— KING DAVID (DRAMATIC PSALM) (FOR NARRATOR, SOPRANO, CONTRALTO, TENOR, MIXED CHORUS AND ORCH.)
2,2,2,2 - 4,2,3,1 - timp.,perc.(3),cel. - 2 hp.,org. - str.   60:00 ECS.

—— MERMOZ: ORCHESTRAL SUITE NO. 1 (LA TRAVERSÉE DES ANDES)
10:00 Henmar.

—— MERMOZ: ORCHESTRAL SUITE NO. 2 (LE/VOL SUR L'ATLANTIQUE)
7:30 Henmar.

—— LES MILLE ET UNE NUITS (FOR SOPRANO, TENOR AND ORCH.) (1937) (Text: Mardrus)
2,2,0,3 sax.,2 - 0,3,3,0 - perc.,cel. - 4 ondes Martenot - hp. - pf. - str.   24:00 Salabert.

—— LES MISÉRABLES (SUITE FROM THE FILM)(1934)
Salabert.

—— MONOPARTITA
2,*3,*3,2 - 4,3,3,0 - timp. - str.   15:00 Salabert.

—— MOUVEMENT SYMPHONIQUE NO. 3
3,3,2,sax.,3 - 4,3,3,1 - perc. - str.   10:00 Salabert.

—— MUSIQUE POUR "LA PHAEDRE" (With optional chorus of 8 contraltos)
2,2,2,2 - 2,2,3,1 - timp.,perc. - str.   18:00 Salabert.

—— LA NOCE MASSACRÉE (FROM "LES MARIÉS DE LA TOUR EIFFEL")
2,2,2,2 - 2,2,3,1 - timp.,perc. - str.   Salabert.

—— NOCTURNE
*3,*3,*3,sax.,3 - 4,3,0,1 - perc. - hp. - str.   9:00 Bo. Hawkes.

—— PACIFIC 231
3,3,3,3 - 4,3,3,1 - perc. (2) - str.   8:00 Salabert.

—— PASTORALE D'ÉTÉ (FOR CHAMBER ORCH.)
1,1,1,1 - hn. - str.   6:00 Salabert.

—— PHAEDRE (SUITE FROM D'ANNUZIO'S PLAY)(1926) (WITH 8 CONTRALTOS AD LIB.)
2,2,2,2 - 2,2,3,1 - timp.,perc. - str.   18:00 Salabert.

—— PRELUDE, ARIOSO AND FUGHETTA ON THE NAME OF B-A-C-H
str.   6:00 Salabert.

—— PRELUDE FOR "AGAVAINE ET SELYSETTE"
1,1,2,2 - 2,1,0,0 - str.   7:00 Salabert.

—— PRELUDE FOR "THE TEMPEST"
2,2,2,2 - 4,2,3,1 - perc. - str.   8:00 Salabert.

—— PRELUDE, FUGUE AND POSTLUDE, FROM "AMPHION"
3,3,3,alto sax.,3 - 4,3,3,1 - timp.,perc., cel. - hp. - str.   13:00 Salabert.

—— REGAIN (MUSIC FOR THE FILM)
1,1,1,alto sax.,1 - 0,2,2,0 - perc. - pf. - str.   16:00 Salabert.

—— RUGBY
3,3,3,3 - 4,3,3,1 - str.   8:00 Salabert.

—— ST. FRANÇOIS D'ASSISE (FOR SPEAKING VOICE, BARITONE, SATB CHORUS AND ORCH.) (1949) (Text: William Aguet)
2,2,2,2 - 0,3,3,0 - perc. - pf. - str.   Salabert.

—— SÉRÉNADE À ANGÉLIQUE (FOR CHAMBER ORCH.)
1,1,1,alto sax.,1 - 2,1,1,0 - perc. - hp. - str.   8:00 Salabert.

—— SIX POÈMES DE GUILLAUME APOLLINARE ("ALCOOLS") (FOR VOICE AND ORCH.)
Salabert.

—— SOUS-MARINE (BALLET MUSIC) %
2,3,2,2 - 4 hn. - perc., cel. - hp. - str.   Salabert.

—— SUITE ARCHAÏQUE (IN 4 MOVTS)
2,2,2,2 - 0,2,2,0 - str.   18:30 Salabert.

—— SUITE FROM "L'IMPÉRATRICE AUX ROCHERS" (IN 5 MOVTS)
3,3,3,3 - 4,3,3,1 - perc., cel. - hp. - str.   20:00 Salabert.

—— SUITE FROM "UN MIRACLE DE NÔTRE DAME" (L'IMPÉRATRICE AUX ROCHERS)
Salabert.

—— SYMPHONY NO. 1
2,2,3,3 - 4,3,3,1 - perc. - str.   22:00 Salabert.

—— SYMPHONY NO. 2
tpt. (ad lib.) - str.   25:00 Salabert.

—— SYMPHONY NO. 3 ("LITURGUIQUE") (IN 3 MOVTS)
3,*3,*3,*3 - 4,3,3,1 - timp.,perc. (2) - pf. - str.   30:00 Salabert.

—— SYMPHONY NO. 4 (DELICIAE BASILIENSES)
2,1,2,1 - 2,1,0,0 - perc., glock. - pf. - str.   32:00 Salabert.

—— SYMPHONY NO. 5 (DI TRE RE)
3(3rd alt. with picc.),*3,*3,3 - 4,3,3,1 - timp. (ad lib.) - str.   27:00 Salabert.

—— TOCCATA
Salabert.

—— TROIS CHANSONS DE "LA PETITE SIRÈNE" D'ANDERSEN (FOR VOICE, FLUTE AND STRINGS)
fl. - str.   Salabert.

HONEGGER, Arthur - HOÉRÉE, A.
—— SIX POÉSIES DE JEAN COCTEAU (FOR VOICE AND STRINGS)
str.   Salabert.

HONGISTO, Mauri
—— CONCERTO FOR VIOLIN AND ORCH., OP. 13 (1954)
2,2,2,2 - 4,2,2,1 - timp.,perc. - str.   20:00 FinnMICtr.

—— CONCERTO NO. 1 FOR PIANO AND ORCH., OP. 21 (1955)
2,2,2,3 - 4,3,4,0 - timp.,perc. - pf. - str.   20:00 FinnMICtr.

—— HIPSUVARVAS AND NÖKÖHAMMAS, OP. 29 (A MUSICAL FAIRY TALE FOR SOPRANO, TENOR, BARITONE, BASS, CHILDREN'S VOICES, SATB CHORUS AND ORCH.) (1958) (Text: Composer)
1,1,2,1 - 2,2,1,0 - timp.,perc.,cel. - hp. - pf. - str.   23:00 FinnMICtr.

—— HYMN TO THE SOIL OF THE EARTH, OP. 31 (FOR WOMEN'S CHORUS AND ORCH.) (1960) (Text: Toivo Lyy)
1,1,2,0 - 2,1,0,0 - timp.,perc. - pf. - str.   17:00 FinnMICtr.

—— INVITATION TO A JOURNEY, OP. 50 (FOR TENOR AND ORCH.) (1963) (Text: Toivo Pekkanen)
2,2,2,1 - 4,2,1,0 - timp.,perc.,cel. - pf. - str.   18:00 FinnMICtr.

—— PIRKANMAA, OP. 62 (VERSION WITHOUT VOICES)
2,2,0,0 - 4,2,2,0 - timp.,perc. - str.   30:00 FinnMICtr.

—— PIRKANMAA, OP. 62 (WITH BARITONE AND MALE CHORUS) (1968) (IN 2 MOVTS.) (Text: Oiva Kulo)
2,2,2,1 - 4,2,2,0 - timp.,perc. - str.   30:00 FinnMICtr.

—— PRELUDE AND FUGUE, OP. 23 (1956)
2,2,2,2 - 4,3,4,0 - timp.,perc. - str.   8:00 FinnMICtr.

—— SONG TO THE TOWN, OP. 80 (CANTATA) (FOR MEZZO-SOPRANO, BARITONE, CHILDREN'S CHORUS, MALE CHORUS AND ORCH.) (1969) (Text: Composer)
1,1,2,0 - 2,2,2,0 - timp.,perc. - pf. - str.   28:00 FinnMICtr.

—— SPRING CANTATA, OP. 49 (FOR SOPRANO, BARITONE, WOMEN'S CHORUS AND ORCH.) (1963) (Text: Composer)
1,1,1,0 - 1,0,0,0 - pf. - str.   15:00 FinnMICtr.

HONNORÉ, L. - WAEL-MUNK
—— MORCEAU DE CONCERT (FOR VIOLA AND STRINGS)
timp. - hp. - str.   5:00 Salabert.

HOOPER, William
—— YEAR OF JUBILEE
2,2,2,2 - 4,3,3,1 - timp.,perc. - str.   30:00 C. Fischer.

HOPKINS, Antony
—— LADY RHOESIA (1-ACT COMIC OPERA) % (7 SINGERS) (Text: Composer)
2,2,2,2 - 4,2,3,1 - timp.,perc. - str.   60:00 G. Schirmer.

HOPKINS, James F.
—— CONCERTO FOR 2 PIANOS AND ORCH. (1964)
*3,2,2,2 - 4,3,3,1 - timp.,perc.,xyl. - hp. - 2 pf. - str.   14:00 Composer.

—— ELEGY AND DITHYRAMB (1963)
3(3rd alt. with picc.),*3,2,2 - 4,3,3,1 - timp.,perc.,bells,glock.,xyl. - hp. - pf. - str.   15:00 Composer.

—— PHANTASMS (FOR SOPRANO AND ORCH.) (1968) (IN 3 MOVTS.) (No Text)
4(alt. with 4 picc. and 1 alt. with alto fl.),*3,*3,*3 - 4,4,4,1 - timp.,perc.(4),bells,cel.,glock.,vibra.,xyl. - 2 hp. - hpsc. - pf. - str.(26,10,10,8)   17:30 Composer.

—— REVELATIONS AND TRANSFORMATIONS (1969)
2(1st alt. with alt. fl., 2nd alt. with picc.),1,1(alt. with b.-cl.),1 - 1,2,3,0 - perc.(2),cel.,glock.,vibra. - hp. - pf. - str.(min.: 6,3,3,2)   13:00 Composer.

—— SYMPHONY NO. 1 (1964) (IN 3 MOVTS.)
4(4th alt. with picc.),3(3rd alt. with b.-cl.),*3 - 4,3,3,1 - timp.,perc.(3),cel.,glock.,xyl. - 2 hp. - pf. - str.   19:00 Composer.

—— THREE PIECES FOR ORCHESTRA (1966)
4(4th alt. with picc.),3(3rd alt. with Eng. hn. and opt. heck.),3,*3 - 4,4,4,1 - timp.,perc.(4),cel.,glock.,vibra.,xyl. - hp. - pf. - str.(26,10,10,8)   9:30 Composer.

—— VARIATIONS FOR ORCHESTRA (1967)
3(3rd alt. with picc.),2(2nd alt. with Eng. hn.),2(2nd alt. with b.-cl.),2 - 4,3,3,1 - perc.,cel. - hp. - pf. - str.   13:00 Composer.

HORDER, Mervin
—— HAMPSHIRE DAYS
    str.   12:00 C. Fischer.

HOROVITZ, Joseph
—— ADAGIO CANTABILE
    1,1,1,0 - 0,0,0,0 - hp. - str.   6:00 Novello.
—— CONCERT SUITE (CONCERTO FOR DANCERS)
    1,1,1,1 - 1,1,1,0 - timp.,perc.(3) - pf. - str.   15:00 P.R.S.
—— CONCERTO FOR CLARINET AND STRING ORCH., OP. 7
    cl. - str.   18:00 Mills.
—— CONCERTO FOR JAZZ HARPSICHORD AND SMALL ORCH.
    perc. - hpsc. - str.   14:00 Novello.
—— CONCERTO FOR TRUMPET AND ORCH.
    2(2nd alt. with picc.),2,2,2 - 4,3,3,0 - timp.,perc.,xyl. - str.
    14:00 Novello.
—— CONCERTO FOR VIOLIN AND STRING ORCH., OP. 11
    str.   18:00 Mills.
—— THE DUCK AND THE KANGAROO (MINIATURE TRIO-CONCERTO)(FOR TENOR OR SOPRANO, CLARINET, CELLO AND ORCH.)
    1,1,2,1 - 0,2,1,0 - timp.,perc. - hp. - str.   4:00 P.R.S.
—— FANTASIA FOR ELEVEN STRINGS (ON A THEME OF COUPERIN)
    str.   13:00 Novello.
—— FOUR DANCES FROM "FEMMES D'ALGER"
    2,2,2,2 - 2,2,3,0 - timp.,perc. - hp. - pf. - str.   10:15 Mills.
—— GENTLEMAN'S ISLAND (1-ACT OPERA BUFFA) % (FOR 2 SINGERS) (Text: Composer)
    1,1,1,1 - 1,0,0,0 - perc. - pf. - str.   30:00 G. Schirmer.
—— GOLDONI OVERTURE
    2(2nd alt. with picc.),2,2,2 - 4,2,3,1 - timp.,perc. - hp. - str.
    6:30 Mills.
—— HORIZON: OVERTURE
    1(alt. with picc.),1,1,1 - 1,1,1,0 - timp.,perc. - str.   5:00 Novello.
—— METAMORPHOSES ON A BED-TIME THEME (FOR SOPRANO, BARITONE AND ORCH.)
    2,2,2,2 - 4,2,3,0 - timp.,perc.(3) - hp. - hpsc. - pf. - str.
    11:00 P.R.S.
—— SINFONIETTA FOR LIGHT ORCH.
    2,2,2,2 - 2,2,3,0 - timp.,perc. - str.   11:00 Novello.
—— A SUITE FOR STRINGS
    pf.(ad lib.) - str.   Galaxy.
—— SUITE FROM "ALICE IN WONDERLAND"
    2,2,2,2 - 2,2,3,0 - timp.,perc.(3) - hp. - pf. - str.   40:00 P.R.S.

HORST, Anthon van der
—— ALIANORA, OP. 57 (1952) (FOR CONTRALTO, BARITONE, SPEAKER, SATB CHORUS AND ORCH.) (Text: P. C. Boutens)
    1,1,1,1 - 0,0,0,0 - guit. - str.   70:00 Henmar.
—— CHOROS I, OP. 20 (1932) (FOR SOPRANO, BARITONE, MIXED CHORUS AND ORCH.) (Text: J. van Ruusbroeck)
    3,3,2,2 - 4,3,3,2 - perc.,cel.,xyl. - hp. - str.   40:00 Henmar.
—— CHOROS III, OP. 72 (1958) (FOR TENOR, MIXED CHORUS AND ORCH.) (Text: Psalms 44 and 45)
    3,2,3,3 - 4,4,4,0 - timp.,perc. - 2 hp. - org.   15:00 Henmar.
—— CHOROS VI, OP. 77 (1957) (FOR TENOR, BOYS' CHORUS, 2 MIXED CHORUSES AND ORCH.) (Text: Wilhelmus)
    6,3,4,3 - zinke(cornetto),6,6,5,2 - perc. - hp. - str.   20:00 Henmar.
—— CONCERTO FOR ORGAN AND ORCH., OP. 58
    2,2,2,2 - 4,3,3,1 - perc. - org. - str.   26:00 Henmar.
—— CONCERTO IN BAROQUE STYLE, OP. 85 (FOR ORGAN AND STRING ORCH.) (1960)
    org. - str.   20:00 Henmar.
—— CONCERTO SPAGNUOLO, OP. 61 (FOR VIOLIN AND ORCH.)
    3,3,2,2 - 4,3,3,0 - timp.,perc., - hp. - str.   17:00 Henmar.
—— DIVEERTIMENTO PITTORALE, OP. 69
    3,3,4,3 - 4,3,3,1 - timp.,perc., xyl. - 2 hp. - str.   27:00 Henmar.
—— NOCTURNE FUNÈBRE, OP. 54
    3,3,3,3 - 4,3,4,0 - timp.,perc. - 2 hp. - str.   15:00 Henmar.
—— ORATORIO, OP. 19A (FOR SOPRANO AND ORCH.) (1942)
    2,3,3,3 - 3,3,3,0 - timp. - 2 hp. - str.   9:00 Henmar.
—— REFLEXIONS SONORES, OP. 99 (1962)
    3,3,3,3 - 4,3,4,1 - perc. - hp. - str.   20:00 Henmar.
—— SEVEN ITALIAN SONGS, OP. 21A (FOR SOPRANO AND ORCH.) (1935)
    3,3,4,2 - 4,2,3,0 - timp.,perc. - 2 hp. - str.   15:00 Henmar.
—— SYMPHONY NO. 3, OP. 84 (1959) (FOR MIXED CHORUS AND ORCH.)
    3,3,2,2 - 2,1,0,0 - perc. - hp. - str.   60:00 Henmar.

—— SYMPHONY, OP. 23 (1937)
    3,3,4,4 - 6,3,3,3 ten.hn.,2 - timp.,perc.,xyl. - 2 hp. - pf. - str.
    30:00 Henmar.
—— TROIS ÉTUDES SYMPHONIQUES, OP. 66
    3,3,4,3 - 4,3,3,2 - timp.,perc. - 2 hp. - str.   Henmar.

HORST, Anton van der
—— CHOROS NO. 2 ("LA NUIT"), OP. 67 (FOR CHORUS AND ORCH.)
    30:00 Henmar.

HORTON, Lewis Henry
—— AN APPALACHIAN NATIVITY (BABE OF BETHLEHEM) (CANTATA) (FOR 4 SOLO VOICES, MIXED CHORUS AND ORCH.)
    2,2,2,2 - 2,2,2,1 - timp.,perc.(1-2),cel. or glock. - hp. - org.(ad lib.) - str.   26:00 Gray.
—— THE WHITE PILGRIM (FOLK-CANTATA) (FOR SOPRANO, ALTO, TENOR, BARITONE, MIXED CHORUS AND STRING ORCH.) (Co-Composed with Buell H. Kazee)
    str.   29:00 Gray.

HORUSITZKY, Zoltán
—— CONCERTO FOR VIOLIN AND ORCH.
    3,3,3,3 - 4,3,0,0 - timp.,perc. - str.   35:00 Bo. Hawkes.
—— CONCERTO NO. 2 FOR PIANO AND ORCH.
    *3,2,2,2 - 4,3,2,1 - timp.,perc. - hp. - pf. - str.   24:00 Bo. Hawkes.
—— SUITE FOR ORCHESTRA
    3,3,3,3 - 4,3,3,1 - timp.,perc. - hp. - str.   15:00 Bo. Hawkes.

HORVÁTH, M.
—— SUITE
    Bo. Hawkes.

HORVIT, Michael
—— ADVENTURE IN SPACE (CHAMBER OPERA FOR CHILDREN) % (1976) (Text: Composer)
    1(alt. with picc.),1,1,1 - 1,1,0,0 - tape-recorder - str.(2,1,1,1)
    50:00 Composer.
—— SYMPHONY (1959) (IN 4 MOVTS.)
    2,2,2,2 - 4,2,3,1 - timp.,perc.(4),cel.,glock.,xyl. - str.
    25:00 Composer.
—— TOCCATINA (1965)
    2(1alt. with picc.),2,2,2 - 2,3,3,0 - timp.,perc.(3),xyl. - str.
    3:00 Shawnee.
—— TOMO (1-ACT OPERA-FANTASY) % (1968) (Text: Composer)
    2(1 alt. with picc.),2,2,2 - 2,1,1,0 - timp.,perc.(3),glock.,xyl. - hp. - str.   50:00 Composer.

HOSKINS, William Barnes
—— ISRAFEL (SYMPHONIC ODE, FOR CHORUS AND ORCH.) (Text: Edgar Allan Poe)
    17:00 Fox.

HOSMER, Lucius
—— SOUTHERN RHAPSODY
    *2,2,2,2 - 4,3,3,1 - timp.,perc. (2) - str.   5:00 C. Fischer.

HOSSEIN, André
—— CONCERTO NO. 2 FOR PIANO AND ORCH.
    2,2,2,2 - 2,2,2,1 - timp.,perc. - pf. - str.   18:00 Presser.
—— CONCERTO NO. 3 FOR PIANO AND ORCH.
    2,2,2,2 - 2,2,2,0 - timp., perc. - pf. - str.   Presser.
—— SYMPHONIE PERSEPOLIS
    3,2,3,3 - 4,3,3,1 - timp., perc.(2) - hp. - str.   Presser.

HOUDY, Pierick
—— LES AVEUGLES DE BREUGHEL
    2,2,2,2 - 2,2,1,1 - timp.,perc. - hp. - str.   7:15 Presser.
—— CONCERTO FOR HARPSICHORD (OR PIANO) AND STRING ORCH.
    hpsc.(or pf.) - str.   13:30 Baron.
—— DEVOIRS DE VACANCES
    2,2,2,2 - 3,3,2,0 - timp.,perc.,cel. - hp. - str.   12:00 Baron.
—— OUVERTURE POUR UN BALLET
    2,2,2,2 - 3,2,2,0 - timp.,perc.,cel.,xyl. - hp. - pf. - str.   4:00 Baron.
—— SIX MUSIQUES SANS PRINCIPE
    2,1,2,3 sax.(alto,ten.,bar.),1 - 0,3,2,0 - vibra. - electric guit.,electric d.-b. - org. - pf. - str.   20:25 Presser.
—— SYMPHONIE
    3,3,3,2 -4,3,2,1 - perc. - pf.(or hp.) - str.   21:00 Baron.

HOVEY, Serge
—— AFRICAN BALLET SUITE (IN 3 MOVTS.)
    2,2,2,2 - 4,2,3,1 - 4,3,1,1 - timp.,perc.(4),cel.glock.,vibra.(or
    African Sansa),xyl. - hp. - pf. - str.   13:00 Templeton.
—— FABLE (IN 3 MOVTS.)
    *3,*3,*3,*3 - 4,4,3,1 - timp.,perc.(2) - str.   15:00 Templeton.
—— OVERTURE ("SIX FOR BURNS")
    3,3,3,3 - 4,3,3,1 - timp.,perc.,cel. - hp. - pf. - str. 4:30 Templeton.
—— ROBERT BURNS RHAPSODY (A SCOTTISH-AMERICAN
    FANTASY) (FOR ALTO, BARITONE, CHORUS, AND ORCH.)
    (IN 5 MOVTS.)
    *3,*3,*3,*3 - 4,3,3,1 - timp.,perc.cel.,glock. - hp. - pf. - str.
    20:00 Templeton.
—— SHOLEM ALEICHEM SUITE (FOR DOUBLE CHORUS AND
    ORCH.)
    32:00 Templeton.
—— WEEKEND, U.S.A.
    3,3,3,3 - 4,3,3,1 - perc. - hp. - pf. - str.   19:00 Templeton.

HOVHANESS, Alan
—— SHEPHERD OF ISRAEL (CANTATA) (FOR TENOR-CANTOR
    AND CHAMBER ORCH.) (Text: Psalm 80)
    Recorder (or fl.) - tpt.(ad lib.) - str.   12:00 IsMuPublns.

HOVLAND, Egil
—— CONCERT OVERTURE, OP. 39-B
    3,3,3,3 - 4,3,3,1 - timp.,perc. - str.   6:00 T.O.N.O.
—— CONCERTINO FOR 3 TRUMPETS AND STRINGS, OP. 23 (IN
    3 MOVTS.)
    0,0,0,0 - 0,3,0,0 - str.   15:00 Ed. Lyche.
—— FANFARE AND CHORAL, OP. 54-B
    3,3,3,3 - 4,3,4,2 - timp.,perc.,cel.,xyl. - str.   8:00 Norsk Mfl.
—— FESTIVAL OVERTURE, OP. 18
    3,2,2,2 - 4,2,3,1 - timp.,perc. - str.   7:00 Ed. Lyche.
—— LILJA, OP. 61 (RECITATION WITH ORCH.) (Text: The Song of
    Songs)
    3,3,2,2 - 2,1,1,0 - perc. - pf.   16:00 T.O.N.O.
—— LITANY, OP. 49 (LITANIVED KRISTI FØDSELSFEST) (FOR
    SPEAKER, SOPRANO, MIXED CHORUS AND ORCH.)
    0,1,0,0 - 2,2,2,0 - perc.,cel. - org. - str.   26:00 T.O.N.O.
—— RORATE, OP. 55 (FOR 5 SOPRANOS AND CHAMBER
    ORCH.) (1967) (IN 3 MOVTS.)
    1,1,0,0 - 0,0,0,0 - perc.(4) - tape-recorder - org. - str.
    24:00 T.O.N.O.
—— SUITE FOR FLUTE AND STRINGS, OP. 31 (IN 5 MOVTS.)
    fl. - str.   20:00 Ed. Lyche.
—— SYMPHONIA VERIS (SYMPHONY OF SPRING), OP. 20 (IN 3
    MOVTS.)
    3,3,3,3 - 4,3,3,1 - timp.,perc.,cel. - hp. - str.   27:00 T.O.N.O.
—— SYMPHONY NO. 2, OP. 24 (IN 1 MOVT.)
    3,2,2,2 - 4,3,3,1 - timp.,perc.,cel. - hp. - str.   16:00 Ed. Lyche.
—— TE DEUM, OP. 41-A (O STORE GUD VI TAKKER DEG) (FOR
    MIXED CHORUS AND ENSEMBLE)
    0,2,0,2 - 0,3,3,1 - org.   15:00 Ed. Lyche.

HOWARD, John Tasker
—— FANTASY ON A CHORAL THEME (CONCERTINO FOR
    PIANO AND ORCH.)
    2,2(1 alt. with Eng. hn.),2,2 - 2,2,0,0 - timp.,perc. - pf. - str.
    15:00 Composer.
—— FOSTER SINFORIETTA (BASED ON STEPHEN FOSTER
    MELODIES) (IN 3 MOVTS.)
    1,1,2,1 - 2,2,1,0 - timp.,perc. (1) - pf. (ad lib.) - str.
    10:00 Composer.
—— INTAGLIO (THREE WALTZES IN MINIATURE)
    str.   5:00 C. Fischer.
—— MOSSES FROM AN OLD MANSE (BALLADE FOR STRINGS)
    5:30 Musicus.
—— OCTOBER AND NOVEMBER (FROM "CALENDAR SUITE")
    2,2,2,2 - 4,3,2-3,1 - timp.,perc. - hp. - str.   6:00 EV.
—— STILL WATERS (REVERIE ON A PSALM TUNE)
    str.   Musicus.

HOWARTH, Elgar
—— CONCERTO FOR TROMBONE AND ORCH.
    2,2,2,2 - 4,2,1,0 - timp. - str.   15:00 P.R.S.
—— CONCERTO FOR TRUMPET AND ORCH.
    2,2,2,2 - 2,1,1,0 - timp. - str.   16:00 P.R.S.

HOWE, Mary
—— AGREEABLE OVERTURE
    *2,*2,2,1 - 2,2,1,0 - timp.,perc., xyl. - str.   8:00 Composer.

—— AMBIANCE (ATMOSPHERE) (FROM "THREE SCORES FOR
    ORCH.")
    2,1,1,1 - 2,2,3,1 - str.   Composer.
—— AMERICAN PIECE (WHAT PRICE GLORY)
    2(1st alt. with picc.),2,2,2 - 4,3,3,1 - timp.,perc. (2) - hp. - str.
    15:00 Composer.
—— ATTENTE (WAITING) (FROM "THREE SCORES FOR
    ORCHESTRA")
    *3,0,1,1 - 3,2,3,1 - timp. - str.   Composer.
—— AXIOM (PASSACAGLIA AND FUGUE)
    1,*2,2,1 - 2,2,1,0 - timp.,perc., bells., cel. - hp. - str.
    12:00 Composer.
—— CANCION ROMANESCA
    str.   5:00 Composer.
—— CASTELLANA (FOR 2 PIANOS AND ORCH.)
    2(1st alt. with picc.),2,2,2 - 4,3,3,1 - timp.,perc. (2) - 2 pf. - str.
    14:00 Composer.
—— CHAIN GANG SONG (WITH MEN'S CHORUS, AND
    OPTIONAL SOPRANO AND ALTO)
    2,2,2,2 - 4,2,3,1 - timp.,perc. - str.   9:00 G. Schirmer.
—— COULENNES (TABLEAU DE GENRE)
    1,1,1,1 - 1,1,0,0 - timp.,perc. (1-2) - str.   10:00 C. Fischer.
—— DIRGE (IN MEMORIAM HAROLD RANDOLPH)
    2,2,2,2 - 4,3,3,1 - timp.,perc. (2) - str.   11:00 G. Schirmer.
—— FIDDLER'S REEL (FOR MIXED CHORUS AND ORCH.)
    *2,2,2,2 - 4,3,3,1 - timp.,perc., cel. - hp. - str.   20:00 Composer.
—— FUGUE FOR STRINGS
    str.   3:30 Composer.
—— OMBRINE (SHADOW-LIGHT) (FROM "THREE SCORES FOR
    ORCHESTRA")
    1,1,1,1 - 2,0,0,0 - str.   Composer.
—— PAEAN
    2(1st alt. with picc.),2,2,sax.,2 - 4,3,3,1 - timp.,perc. (3) - hp. - str.
    11:00 C. Fischer.
—— POEMA (FOR SOPRANO, MEZZO-SOPRANO AND ORCH.)
    2(2nd alt. with picc.),2,2,2 - 4,2,3,1 - timp.,perc. (2) - hp. - str.
    12:00 Composer.
    or:
    1,1,1,0 - hn. - str.
—— POTOMAC (SUITE) (IN 4 MOVTS.)
    2(2nd alt. with picc.),2,2,2 - 4,3,3,1 - timp.,perc.(2) - hp. - str.
    21:00 C. Fischer.
—— PROPHECY (1792) (FROM "A SONG OF LIBERTY") (FOR
    CHORUS AND ORCH.)
    0,2,3,2 - 4,3,3,1 - timp.,perc. - pf. (ad lib.)   12:00 Gray.
—— RIVER
    C. Fischer.
—— ROCK
    *3,2(2nd alt. with Eng. hn.),2,1 - 3,3,3,1 - timp.,perc. (3) - hp. -
    str.   12:00 Galaxy.
—— SONG OF PALMS (FOR WOMEN'S CHORUS AND ORCH.)
    *3,*3,2,2 - 4,3,3,1 - timp.,perc., glock. - hp. - str.
    13:30 C. Fischer.
—— SPRING PASTORAL
    1,1,1,1 - 1,1,0,0 - timp., (ad lib.), perc. (2) - str. 6:00 Composer.
—— STARS AND SAND
    2(2nd alt. with picc.)1,1,1 - 2,1,0,0 - timp.,perc.(1) - hp. - str.
    7:00 Galaxy.

HOWELL, Dorothy
—— LAMIA (SYMPHONIC POEM)
    3,3,3,3 - 4,3,3,1 - timp.,perc. - hp. - str.   15:00 Novello.

HOWELLS, Herbert
—— CONCERTO FOR STRING ORCH.
    str.   25:00 Novello.
—— ELEGY (FOR VIOLA, STRING QUARTET AND STRING
    ORCH.)
    str.   10:00 Bo. Hawkes.

HRISANIDE, Alexandre
—— AD PERPETUAM REI MEMORIAM
    2,2,2,2 - 4,3,3,0 - perc.,xyl. - hp. - pf. - str.   14:50 AhnSimrock.
—— C'ETAIT ISSU STELLAIRE...(CANTATA) (FOR MEN'S
    CHORUS AND ENSEMBLE) (1965) (Text: Stéphane Mallarmé)
    0,0,0,0 - 0,3,4,0 - perc.(5) - org. - pf.   15:00 Salabert.
—— CONCERTO FOR HARPSICHORD AND ORCH.
    Hans Gerig.

HRISTIĆ, Stevan
—— THE LEGEND OF OCHRID (SUITE FROM THE BALLET)
    13:00 S.O.K.O.J.

HRISTIĆ, Zoran
—— DARINKIN DAR (DARINKA'S GIFT) (BALLET) %
 3,3,3,3 - 4,3,3,1 - timp.,perc.,cel.,xyl. - hp. - pf. - str.
 45:00 MIC,Zagreb.
—— GRADILIŠTE 1969 (BUILDING SITE, 1969) (FOR 2 SOLOISTS AND CHAMBER ORCH.)
 18:15 MIC,Zagreb.
—— KAMELEONI (CHAMELEONS) (BALLET) %
 2,2,2,2 - 2,2,1,0 - perc. - pf. - str. 20:00 MIC,Zagreb.
—— KARDIOGRAMI (CARDIOGRAMS) (FOR CHAMBER ORCH.)
 9:45 MIC,Zagreb.
—— OMER I MERIMA (OMER AND MERIMA) (BALLET) %
 2,2,2,2 - 4,2,2,0 - perc. - str. 15:00 MIC,Zagreb.
—— OPOMENA (WARNING) (FOR 3 SOLO VOICES, CHORUS AND ORCH.)
 3,3,3,3 - 4,3,3,1 - timp.,perc.,cel.,vibra.,xyl. - hp. - pf. - str.
 40:00 MIC,Zagreb.
—— PRAZNE ŽICE PA PUNIJE (FROM EMPTY STRINGS TO FULL STRINGS)
 str. 7:00 MIC,Zagreb.

HRUBY, Viktor
—— ELEGIE
 hp. - str. 6:00 Modern.
—— VALSE TRISTE
 vibra. - hp. - str. 10:00 Modern.

HUBAY, Jenö
—— CONCERTO NO. 3 IN G MINOR, OP. 99, FOR VIOLIN AND ORCH. (IN 4 MOVTS.)
 2,2,2,2 - 4,2,3,0 - timp.,perc., bells - hp. - str. 26:00 Henmar.
—— CONCERTO NO. 4 IN A MINOR, OP. 101 ("ALL 'ANTICA"), FOR VIOLIN AND ORCH. (IN 4 MOVTS.)
 18:30 Henmar.
 2,2,2,2 - 3,2,0,0 - timp.,perc. - str.

HUBBELL, Frank Allen
—— CALIFORNIA ELDORADO SUITE (IN 3 MOVTS.)
 2(1st alt. with alto fl.,2nd alt. with picc.),2(2nd alt. with Eng.hn.),2,2 - 4,2,3,1 - timp.,perc.(3-4),bells,cel.,mar. - hp. - str.
 29:10 Composer.
—— CORTÈGE (VERS LE TOMBEAU), OP. 2
 2(alt. with 2 alto fl.),*2,2,2 - 2,2,2,0 - timp.,perc.(3) - hp. - str.
 6:15 Composer.
—— PASSACAGLIA AND SCHERZO, OP. 15
 2(2nd alt. with picc.),2(2nd alt. with Eng.hn.),2,2(2nd alt. with c.-bn.) - 4,2,3,0 - timp.,perc.(2),bells - str. 10:00 Composer.
—— PROCESSION KISMET (ADAGIO FUNÈBRE), OP. 12
 2(2nd alt. with picc.),2,2,2 - 3,2,3,0 - timp.,perc.(2) - hp. - str.
 12:30 Composer.
—— SIERRA SKETCHES (SUITE) (1966) (IN 5 MOVTS.)
 2(2nd alt. with picc.),2(2nd alt. with Eng. hn.),2,2 - 4,3,3,1 - timp.,perc.(4),bells,cel.,vibra.,xyl. - hp. - str. 26:05 Cal-Dorado.
—— THEME, VARIATIONS AND FINALE, OP. 14
 1,1,1,1 - 1,0,0,0 - timp. - str. 14:30 Composer.
 or:
 2,2,2,2 - 2,0,0,0 - timp. - str.

HUBEAU, Jean
—— CONCERTO FOR VIOLIN AND ORCH.
 3,*3,2,2 - 3,2,3,0 - timp.,perc.,cel. - hp. - str. 20:00 EV.
—— CONCERTO HÉROIQUE FOR PIANO AND ORCH.
 2,2,2,2 alto sax.,2 - 4,2,3,1 - timp.,perc.(3),cel. - ondes Martenot(ad lib.) - pf. - str. 25:00 EV.
—— CONCERTO IN A MINOR FOR CELLO AND ORCH.
 2,2,2,2 - 3,2,0,0 - timp.,perc.(3) - str. 18:00 Presser.
—— TROIS TABLEAUX HINDOUS
 2(2nd alt. with picc.),2(2nd alt. with ob. d'amore or Eng. hn.),*3,2 - 4,3,3,0 - timp.,perc., cel., glock., xyl. - hp. - str. 12:30 Baron.

HUBER, Klaus
—— JAMES JOYCE CHAMBER MUSIC (FOR HORN, HARP AND CHAMBER ORCH.)
 2(1 alt. with alto fl.,1 alt. with picc.),*1,*2,1 - 0,1,1,0 - str.
 12:00 G. Schirmer.
—— LITANIA INSTRUMENTALIS
 2,2,2,2 - 2,1,2,0 - timp.,perc. - str. 11:00 G. Schirmer.
—— ORATIO MECHTILDIS (FOR ALTO AND ORCH.)
 2,0,2,2 - 2,1,0,0 - perc.,cel. - str. 25:00 G. Schirmer.

—— SOLILOQUIA AURELII AUGUSTINI (ORATORIO) (FOR SOPRANO, ALTO, TENOR, BARITONE, BASS, SATB CHORUS AND ORCH.)
 3,3,2,3 - 4,3,2,1 - timp.,perc.,cel. - hp. - org.(ad lib.) - pf. - str.
 60:00 G. Schirmer.

HUBER, Nicolaus A.
—— EPIGENESIS III (1969)
 perc.(2) - str. 16:00 G. Schirmer.
—— PARUSIE (1967)
 3(3rd alt. with picc.),3(3rd alt. with Eng.hn.),3(2nd alt. with b.-cl.),3(3rd alt. with c.-bn.) -0,0,0,0 - perc.(2),cel. - tape recorder - banjo - electric guit. - hp. - str. 11:00 G. Schirmer.

HUBER, Paul
—— CONCERTO FOR VIOLIN AND ORCHESTRA
 25:00 S.U.I.S.A.
—— KONZERT FÜR VIOLINE UND STREICHORCHESTER
 str. 23:00 S.U.I.S.A.
—— MARCIA FESTIVA
 1*2,2,2 - 4,2,3,0 - timp.,perc. - str. 6:00 S.U.I.S.A.
—— MUSIK FÜR 10 INSTRUMENTE
 1,1,1,1 - 1,0,0,0 - pf. - 4 str. 22:00 S.U.I.S.A.

HUBER, Walter
—— FANTASIE, OP. 9 (FOR HARP AND ORCH.)
 2,2,2,2 - 4,2,3,0 - timp. - hp. - str. 17:00 Henmar.

HUBER-ANDERACH, Theodor
—— PHANTASTISCHES SCHERZO
 3,3,4,3 - 4,3,3,1 - perc.,cel. - hp. - str. 13:00 T & J.

HÜBNER, Wilhelm
—— KALENDERBLATT-SINFONIE
 str. Tetra.

HÜE, Georges
—— FANTAISIE (FOR FLUTE AND ORCH.)
 *2,*2,2,2 - 2 hn. - timp. - hp. - str. 8:00 Baron.

HUFFMAN, Walter Spencer
—— MARCH, CHORALE AND VARIATIONS
 *3,2,2,2 - 2,2,3,1 - timp.,perc. - str. 22:00 AmerMusEd.
—— SYMPHONY NO. 7
 0,2,0,1 - 2,0,0,0 - str. 20:00 AmerMusEd.
—— SYMPHONY NO. 8 (WITH SOLO WIND QUINTET)
 3,1,3,3 - 3,2,0,0 - timp. - str. 25:00 AmerMusEd.

HUFSCHMIDT, Wolfgang
—— KONTRAFAKTUR I (1972)
 5,4,0,4 - 6,3,3,0 - perc.(5) - hp. - pf. - str. 13:00 G. Schirmer.

HUGHES, Arwel
—— FANTASIA IN A MINOR (FOR STRINGS)
 str. Lengnick.
—— PRELUDE (1945)
 13:00 Lengnick.
—— STUDY: "ANATIAMAROS" (GREAT SOUL)
 12:00 Lengnick.

HUGHES, Mark L.
—— ELEGY FOR CHAMBER ORCHESTRA (1962)
 0,*1,0,0 - 3,0,0,0 - str. 6:30 Composer.
—— REFLECTION (1966)
 3(3rd alt. with picc.),*3,*3,2 - 4,3,3,1 - timp.,perc.(2) - str.
 8:00 Composer.

HUGHES, Robert Watson
—— BALLADE (1969)
 str. 7:30 Chappell.
—— ESSAY FOR ORCHESTRA
 3,3,3,3 - 4,3,3,1 - timp.,perc. - hp. - str. 7:00 Bo. Hawkes.
—— FANTASIA (REV. 1967)
 2(2nd alt. with picc.),2(2nd alt. with Eng.hn.),0,2 - 4,2,3,0 - timp.,perc.(4),cel. - hp. - str. 10:00 Chappell.
—— FARRAGO SUITE
 15:00 A.P.R.A.
—— FESTIVAL OVERTURE
 9:00 A.P.R.A.
—— THE FORBIDDEN RITE (DANCE DRAMA) % (FOR SMALL ORCH.)
 43:00 A.P.R.A.

—— LINN O'DEE (1954)
3(3rd alt. with picc.),3(3rd alt. with Eng.hn.),3(3rd alt. with b.-cl.),3(3rd alt. with c.-bn.) - 4,3,3,1 - timp.,perc.(3),cel. - str.
7:00 AstrlMuCtr.
—— MASQUERADE (OVERTURE) (1956)
2(2nd alt. with picc.),2(2nd alt. with Eng.hn.),2,2 - 4,2,3,0 - timp.,perc.(3) - hp. - str.
6:15 Chappell.
—— SEA SPELL (1973)
4(4th alt. with picc.),*3,3(3rd alt. with b. - cl.),*3 - 4,3,3,1 - timp.,perc.(4),cel. - hp. - str.
10:00 A.P.R.A.
—— SERENADE (FOR SMALL ORCH.)
13:30 A.P.R.A.
—— SINFONIETTA
17:45 Chappell.
—— SYMPHONY NO. 1
30:00 A.P.R.A.
—— SYNTHESIS (1969)
3(3rd alt. with picc.),3(3rd alt. with Eng.hn.),3(3rd alt. with b - cl.),*3 - 4,3,3,1 - timp.,perc.(5),cel. - hp. - str.
10:00 Chappell.
—— XANADU (BALLET SUITE)
2(2nd alt. with picc.),2(2nd alt. with Eng.hn.),2,2 - 4,2,3,1 - timp.,perc.(2) - hp. - str.
18:00 Chappell.

HUGON, Georges
—— ADAGIO (FOR OBOE AND STRINGS)
ob. - str.
6:30 Presser.
—— CONCERTO FOR PIANO AND ORCH.
2,2,2,ten.sax.,2 - 2,1,1,0 - timp.,perc. - hp. - pf. - str.
23:00 Presser.
—— DE LUMIÈRE ET D'OMBRES
3,3,3,3 - 4,3,3,1 - timp.,perc.(4) - 2 hp. - str.   25:12 Presser.
or:
str.
—— LA GENÈSE D'OR (SYMPHONY NO. 2)
3,3,4,4 - 4,3,3,1 - timp.,perc.(5) - 2 hp. - str.   34:00 Presser.
—— SYMPHONY NO. 3
Presser.

HUMEL, Gerald
—— FIVE QUOTATIONS FROM A CZECH FAIRY TALE (FOR CHAMBER ORCH.)
0,0,0,0 - 4,4,4,bar,1 - timp.,perc. - 2 hp.
Mills.

HUMMEL, Bertold
—— PAN 56 (FOR FLUTE AND SMALL ORCH.)
1,1,*2,1 - 1,1,0,0 - perc.,cel. - hp. - str.
4:20 Modern.

HUMMEL, Johann Nepomuk - OUBRADOUS, Fernand
—— CONCERTO IN E FLAT, FOR TRUMPET AND ORCH. (With cadenza by Maurice André)
1,2,0,2 - 2,1,0,0 - timp.(ad lib.) - str.   20:00 Presser.
or:
tpt. - hpsc. - str.
—— FANTAISIE (FOR VIOLA AND ORCH.)
0,0,2,0 - 0,0,0,0 - str.
10:00 Presser.

HUMMEL, Johann Nepomuk - THILDE, Jean
—— CONCERTO IN B FLAT FOR TRUMPET AND ORCH.
1,2,0,2 - 2,1,0,0 - timp. - str.   20:00 Presser.
or:
tpt. - hpsc. - str.

HUMPERDINCK, Englebert - WILHOUSKY, Peter J.
—— EVENING PRAYER AND DREAM PANTOMINE (FROM "HANSEL AND GRETEL") (FOR CHORUS AND ORCH.) (Engl. Text: Lorraine Noel Finley)
C. Fischer.

HUMPERT, Hans
—— MUSIK FÜR ORCH.
2,2,2,2 - 2,2,0,0 - timp.,perc. - str.   27:00 Baerenrtr.
—— SYMPHONIE
2,2,2,2 - 4,2,3,1 - timp.,perc. - str.   30:00 Baerenrtr.

HUMPHRIES, John - LEBELL, L.
—— CONCERTO FOR 2 VIOLINS AND STRINGS
str.
Oxford.

HUNDLEY, Richard
—— NIGHT PIECE (1965)
str.
4:30 Composer.

HUNKINS, Arthur
—— FIVE PIECES FOR ORCH.
3,3,3,3 - 4,3,2,1 - timp.,perc.(4),cel. - hp. - str.   12:00 C. Fischer.

HUNKINS, Eusebia
—— AMERICANA (FOR CHORUS AND ORCH.)
2,2,2,2 - 4,3,1,0 - perc. - str.   9:00 C. Fischer.
—— SPIRIT OWL (WEST INDIAN LEGEND) (WITH SOLO VOICES, CHORUS AND DANCERS) %
2,2,3,2 - 2,2,2,1 - perc. - d.-b.   100:00 C. Fischer.

HUNT, Frederick
—— AIR
2,3,2 alto and ten. sax., 2-4,2,2,0 - timp. - str.   5:00 C. Fischer.
—— FANTASY FOR VIOLIN AND ORCH.
2,2,2,2 - 4 hn. - timp. - str.   7:00 C. Fischer.

HUNT, Michael F.
—— ASYMPTOPIA I (1972)
2(2nd alt. with picc.),2,2,1 - 2,2,3,1 - perc.(3),vibra. - pf. - str.
7:00 Composer.
—— ASYMPTOPIA II (1972)
3(1 alt. with picc.),2,2,1 - 2,2,3,1 - perc.(3),bells,glock.,mar.,vibra. - pf. - str.
7:00 Composer.

HUNT, Wynn
—— BERCEUSE, OP. 56 (1958)
str.
6:00 P.R.S.
—— CONCERTINO FOR PIANO AND STRINGS, OP. 37 (1940)
timp. - pf. - str.
8:00 P.R.S.
—— PANDORA, OP. 60 (1962)
10:00 P.R.S.
—— SOUTHCHURCH HALL, OP. 59 (1961)
str.
6:00 P.R.S.

HURÉ, Jean
—— AU BOIS SACRÉ (BALLET) %
2,2,2,2 - 2,2,3,0 - timp.,perc., bells, cel., glock., xyl. - 2 hp. - mandolin - pf. - str.
Salabert.
—— PRÉLUDE
4,3,3,2 c.-bn. (or sarr.) - 4,3,3,1 - perc.,cel. - 2 hp. - str.   Salabert.
—— QUATRE LETTRES DE FEMMES (FOR VOICE ORCH.)
Salabert.

HURNÍK, Ilja
—— CONCERTO FOR OBOE, CEMBALO AND STRINGS
ob. - cemb. - str.   16:00 Bo. Hawkes.
—— ONDRAS (DANCES FROM THE BALLET)
3,3,3,3 - 4,3,3,1 - timp.,perc. - hp. - pf.   22:00 Bo. Hawkes.

HURUM, Alf
—— BENDIK AND ÅROLILJA (SYMPHONIC POEM)
3,2,2,2 - 4,2,3,1 - timp.,perc. - hp. - str.   16:00 T.O.N.O.
—— EXOTIC SUITE (IN 7 MOVTS.)
3,2,2,2 - 4,2,3,1 - timp.,perc.,cel. - hp. - str.   20:00 T.O.N.O.
—— FAIRYLAND ("EVENTRYLAND") (SUITE) (IN 6 MOVTS.)
3,2,2,3 - 4,2,3,1 - timp.,perc. - hp. - str.   26:00 T.O.N.O.
—— NORSE SUITE, OP. 18 (NORRØN SUITE)
1,1,1,0 - 1,1,1,0 - perc. - str.   11:00 T.O.N.O.
—— SYMPHONY (IN 3 MOVTS.)
3,2,2,2 - 4,2,3,1 - timp.,perc. - str.   T.O.N.O.

HUSTED, Benjamin
—— FUGUE FOR STRINGS
str.
6:15 EV.

HUTCHENS, Frank
—— AIRMAIL, PALESTINE (FOR BARITONE AND ORCH.)
11:00 A.P.R.A.
—— CONCERTO FOR PIANO AND STRING ORCH.
pf. - str.
18:00 A.P.R.A.
—— CONCERTO IN E MINOR, FOR PIANO AND ORCH.
20:00 A.P.R.A.
—— FANTASIE CONCERTO (FOR 2 PIANOS AND ORCH.)
16:00 A.P.R.A.

HUTCHESON, Jere T.
—— NEUTRONS (1963)
*3,*3,*3,*3 - 4,3,3,1 - timp.,perc.,xyl. - hp. - str.   7:00 Composer.
—— SYMPHONY FOR ORCHESTRA (1966)
1. Allegro-Adagio sostenuto; 2. Moderato
*3,2,1 E♭ cl.,*2,*3 - 4,3,3,1 - timp.,perc.(5),cel.,glock.,xyl. - pf. - str.
16:00 Composer.

—— TRANSITIONS FOR ORCHESTRA (1972)
2(2nd alt. with picc.),2,2,2 - 2,2,1,0 - timp.,perc.(2) -
str.(32,12,10,8 or 16,6,4,2)   10:00 Seesaw.

HUTCHINGS, Arthur
—— OVERTURE TO "ORIANA TRIUMPHANS"
                                      Novello.
—— VARIATIONS AND FUGUE ON "PUER NATUS"
str.   Novello.

HUTCHISON, Warner
—— LET US BE GRATEFUL (FOR SATB CHORUS AND ORCH.)
(1965) (Text: John F. Kennedy)
*3,2,*3,2 - 4,3,3,1 - timp.,perc.(2) - str.   7:00 Composer.
—— PRAIRIE SKETCH (1956)
2,1,2,1 - 2,1,1,0 - str.   4:30 Seesaw.
—— PROLOGUE (1959)
*3,2,*3,2 - 2,2,3,1 - timp.,perc.(2) - str.   4:00 Composer.
—— THE SACRILEGE OF ALAN KENT (MONODRAMA) (FOR
BARITONE SOLO, TAPE, ORCH. AND OPTIONAL BALLET)
(1968) (Text: Erskine Caldwell)
*3,2,*3,*3 - 4,3,3,1 - timp.,perc.,bells,cel.,glock.,xyl. -
tape-recorder(stereo) - hp. - str.   30:00 Seesaw.
—— THREE LOVE SONGS (FOR HIGH VOICE AND CHAMBER
ORCH.) (1973) (Text: James Joyce)
*3,1,*3,2 - 2,0,0,0 - bells,cel.,glock.,vibra. - hp. - str.
                                      14:00 Composer.

HUTH, Alfred
—— ZWEI LANDSKNECHTSSCHWÄNKE, OP. 47 (TWO COURT
JESTERS) (FOR MALE CHORUS AND ORCH.)
2,2,2,2 - 4,2,2,1 - timp.,perc. - str.   9:00 F. Colombo.

HUTTEL, Jean
—— L' ARLEQUINADE (FOR 13 INSTRUMENTS)(1931)
1,1,1,1 - 1,1,0,0 - perc. - str.(3,1,1,1)   6:00 Salabert.

HUYBRECHTS, Albert
—— AGAMEMNON (PRELUDE) (1933)
1,1,1,1 - 1,2,2,0 - timp.,perc. - hp. - org. - str.   5:00 H. Elkan.
—— CHANT D'ANGOISSE (1930)
3,3,2,2 - 4,2,3,1 - timp.,perc. - pf. - str.   11:00 CBDM.
—— CHANT FUNÈBRE (FOR CELLO AND ORCH.) (1926)
2,3,3,3 - 4,3,0,0 - timp.,perc.,cel. - hp. - str.   9:00 H. Elkan.
—— CONCERTINO FOR CELLO AND ORCH. (1932)
2,2,2,2 - 2,2,2,1 - timp.,perc. - str.   27:00 CBDM.
—— DAVID (POÈME SYMPHONIQUE) (1923)
3,3,3,3 - 4,3,3,1 - timp.,perc., cel. - 2 hp. - str.   12:00 CBDM.
—— DIVERTISSEMENT (FOR BRASS AND PERCUSSION) (IN 3
MOVTS.)
0,0,0,0 - 4,4,3,1 - timp.,perc.   25:00 H. Elkan.
—— NOCTURNE (1931)
2,2,2,2 - 3,1,1,0 - timp.,perc. - hp. - str.   7:00 H. Elkan.
—— POÈME FÉÉRIQUE (1923)
3,3,3,3 - 4,3,3,1 - timp.,perc., cel., glock. - hp. - str.   20:00 CBDM.
—— SÉRÉNADE EN TROIS MOUVEMENTS (1929)
3,3,3,3 - 4,3,3,1 - timp.,perc., cel., glock. - str.   16:00 CBDM.

HUZELLA, Elek
—— CONCERTINO LIRICO (FOR FLUTE AND STRINGS)
fl. - str.   11:00 Bo. Hawkes.

HYDE, Lewis
—— THE CLOSED ROOM (BALLET) % (FOR SMALL ORCH.)
(1935)
                                      P.R.S.
—— INCIDENTAL MUSIC TO "LE RETOUR DE L'ENFANT
PRODIGUE" (1938)
1,1,1,1 - 0,1,0,0 - harmonica - str.   P.R.S.
—— SYMPHONIC MOVEMENT FOR ORCH. (1936)
2,1,2,2 - 4,3,3,1 - timp.,cel. - hp. - pf.(ad lib) - str.   7:00 P.R.S.

HYDE, Miriam Beatrice
—— ADELAIDE OVERTURE
                                      5:30 A.P.R.A.
—— CONCERTO NO. 1 FOR PIANO AND ORCH.
                                      27:00 A.P.R.A.
—— CONCERTO NO. 2 FOR PIANO AND ORCH.
                                      22:00 A.P.R.A.
—— FANTASY - ROMANTIC (FOR PIANO AND ORCH.)
                                      9:00 A.P.R.A.
—— HAPPY OCCASION (OVERTURE)
                                      4:30 A.P.R.A.

—— HERITAGE (FOR SMALL ORCH.)
                                      31:00 A.P.R.A.
—— HEROIC ELEGY
3,3,2,2 - 4,2,3,1 - timp.,perc. - hp. - str.   9:00 Bo. Hawkes.
—— KELSO OVERTURE, OP. 116 (1959)
3(3rd alt. with picc.),*3,*3,*3 - 4,3,3,1 - timp.,perc.(3) - str.
                                      5:30 A.P.R.A.
—— LENTO IN E MINOR
2,2,2,2 - 4,2,3,0 - timp.,perc. - str.   16:50 A.P.R.A.
—— PRELUDE AND DANCE (FOR SMALL ORCH.)
                                      8:00 A.P.R.A.
—— THE SYMBOLIC GATE (SYMPHONIC POEM)
                                      9:30 A.P.R.A.
—— SYMPHONIC OVERTURE
                                      11:00 A.P.R.A.
—— THEME AND VARIATIONS
                                      15:00 A.P.R.A.
—— VILLAGE FAIR (BALLET) %
                                      12:00 A.P.R.A.

HYE-KNUDSEN, Johan
—— SYMPHONY IN B MINOR
3,3,3,3 - 4,3,3,1 - timp.,perc. - str.   32:00 G. Schirmer.

I

IANNACCONE, Anthony
—— LYSISTRATA (A CONCERT OVERTURE)(1969)
*3,*3,*3,*3 - 4,3,3,1 - timp.,perc.(2),cel.,glock.,xyl. - hp. - pf. - str.
                                      8:00 Seesaw.
—— SYMPHONY NO. 1 (1965) (IN 4 MOVTS.)
*3,*3,*3,*3 - 4,3,3,1 - timp.,perc.(3),cel.,glock.,xyl. - hp. - pf. - str.
                                      60:00 Composer.

IBERT, Jacques
—— LES AMOURS DE JUPITER (BALLET) %
2,2,2,2 - 2,2,1,1 - timp.,perc., cel., glock., xyl. - hp. - pf. - str.
                                      Salabert.
—— ANGÉLIQUE (1-ACT OPERA) % (1927)
2,1,1,1 - 1,1,1,0 - timp.,perc. - pf. - str.   55:00 Presser.
—— BACCHANALE (1958)
3,3,3,4 - 4,3,3,1 - timp.,perc,xyl. - hp. - str.   9:16 Baron.
—— LA BALLADE DE LA GEÔLE DE READING
3,3,3,3 - 4,3,3,1 - timp.,perc., cel., xyl. - 2 hp. - str.   25:00 Baron.
—— BOSTONIANA (1964) (First movt. of an unfinished symphony)
                                      Baron.
—— CAPRICCIO (FOR 10 INSTRUMENTS)
1,1,1,1 - 0,1,0,0 - hp. - str.   10:00 Baron.
—— LE CAVALIER DE FER (INCIDENTAL MUSIC)
                                      Baron.
—— CHANT DE FOLIE (A SONG OF MADNESS) (FOR SOLO
VOICES, MIXED CHORUS AND ORCH.)
3,3,3,3 - 4,3,3,1 - timp.,perc., glock. - hp. - str.   13:00 Baron.
—— LE CHEVALIER ERRANT ("DON QUIXOTE") (EPOPÉE
CHORÉGRAPHIQUE) (ORIG. VERSION, FOR SOLO VOICES,
SPEAKERS, CHORUS AND ORCH.) % (Text: Alex. Arnoux)
3,3,1 alto sax.,4 - 6,4,3,1 - timp.,perc.,bells,cel.,glock.,xyl. - guit.(or
hp.) - 2 hp. - str.   50:00 Baron.
—— LE CHEVALIER ERRANT (ÉPOPÉE CHORÉGRAPHIQUE)
(IN 4 MOVTS.)
3,3,3,alto sax., 4 - 6,4,3,1 - timp.,perc., bells, cel., glock., xyl. -
guit. - 2 hp. - str.   28:00 Baron.
—— CONCERTINO DA CAMERA (FOR ALTO SAXOPHONE AND
11 INSTRUMENTS)
1,1,1,1alto sax., 1 - 1,1,0,0 - str.   Baron.
—— CONCERTO FOR CELLO AND WIND ORCH. (IN 3 MOVTS.)
2(2nd alt., with picc.),2,2,2 - 1,1,0,0 - c.   11:00 Mercury.
—— CONCERTO FOR FLUTE AND ORCH.
1. Allegro; 2. Andante; 3. Allegro scherzardo
2,2,2,2 - 2,1,0,0 - timp. - str.   17:00 Baron.
—— DIANE DE POITIERS (BALLET IN 3 TABLEAUX, WITH OPT.
CHORUS) %
3,3,1 ob. d'amore(ad lib.),3,1 alto cl.(ad lib.),4 - 4,4,3,1 -
timp.,perc.,bells,cel.(or vibra.),glock.,xyl. - 2 hp. - str.
                                      45:00 Baron.
—— DIANE DE POITIERS: SUITE NO. 1 (IN 7 MOVTS)
3(3rd alt. with picc.),*3,ob. d'amore (ad lib.),*3,basset hn. (ad.
lib.),*4-4,4,3,1 - timp.,perc., glock., vibra. (or cel.) - 2 hp. - str.
                                      Baron.

—— DIANE DE POITIERS: SUITE NO. 2 (IN 3 MOVTS)
3(3rd alt. with picc.),*3,ob. d'amore (ad lib.),*3,basset hn (ad. lib.),*4 - 4,4,3,1 - timp., perc., glock., vibra. (or cel.) - 2 hp. - str.
Baron.

—— DIVERTISSMENT (FOR CHAMBER ORCH.) (IN 6 MOVTS)
1,0,1,1 - 1,1,1,0 - perc. - pf. (or cel.) - str.　　8:00 EV.

—— ESCALES (PORTS OF CALL) (IN 3 MOVTS)
*3(2nd alt. with 2nd picc.), *3,2,3 - 4,3,3,1 - timp.,perc. (8), cel., glock. - 2 hp. - str.　　Baron.

—— FÉERIQUE
3,3,3,3 - 4,3,3,1 - timp.,perc.,glock. - 2 hp. - str.　　8:30 Baron.

—— FÉLICIE NANTEUIL (SUITE OF WALTZES)
2,1,2,1 - 2,2,1,0 - timp.,perc. - hp. - str.　　Henmar.

—— GOLGOTHA (SUITE FROM THE FILM)
2,1,1,alto sax.,1 - 2,2,1,0 - timp.,perc., vibra.,xyl. - 2 ondes Martenots - hp. - pf. - str.　　21:00 Baron.

—— GONZAGUE (1-ACT OPERA-BUFFA) % (Text: Renee Kerdyk)
2,2,2,1 alto sax.,2(2nd alt. with c.-bn.) - 1,1,1,0 - timp.,perc.,glock. - hp. - pf. - str.　　55:00 Baron.

—— HOMMAGE À MOZART (RONDO)
2,2,2,2 - 2,2,0,0 - timp. - str.　　5:00 Baron.

—— IMPRESSIONS OF PARIS (IMPRESSIONS PARISIENNES) (SUITE)
11:00 Henmar.

—— LA LICORNE (THE UNICORN, OR, THE TRIUMPH OF CHASTITY) (BALLET) %
1,1,2,alto sax.,1 - 1,1,1,0 - perc. - pf.(alt. with cel.) - str.
25:00 Presser.

—— LOUISVILLE CONCERTO
Baron.

—— MACBETH (MUSIC FROM THE FILM)
20:00 Leeds.

—— OUVERTURE DE FÊTE
3(3rd alt. with picc.), *3,*3,sax,*3 - 4,4,3,1 - timp.,perc. (4), gloc. - 2 hp. - str.　　15:00 Baron.

—— RENCONTRES (BALLET SUITE)
Baron.

—— SARABANDE POUR DULCINÉE
2,3,3,alto sax.,2 - 4,1,2,1 - perc. - hp. - str.　　Baron.

—— SOUVENIR (FOR STRINGS)
str.　　Baron.

—— SUITE ELISABÉTHAINE (IN 9 MOVTS)
2,*2,*2,2 - 3,3,1,0 - timp.,perc.,cel. - hp. - str.　　20:00 Baron.

—— SUITE NO. 1 FROM THE OPERA "PERSÉE ET ANDROMÈDE"
3,3,2,4 - 4,5,3,1 - timp.,perc.(4),cel.,glock.,xyl. - 2 hp. - str.
15:00 EV.

—— SUITE NO. 2 FROM THE OPERA "PERSÉE ET ANDROMÈDE"
3,3,2,4 - 4,5,3,1 - timp.,perc.(4),cel.,glock.,xyl. - 2 hp. - str.
12:00 EV.

—— SYMPHONIE CONCERTANTE (FOR OBOE AND STRINGS)
ob. - str.　　27:00 Baron.

—— TROPISMES POUR DES AMOURS IMAGINAIRES
2,2,2,2 - 2,2,20 - timp., perc. - str.　　25:00 Presser.

IBERT, Jacques - MOUTON, Henri
—— HISTOIRES: SUITE NO. 1 (IN 4 MOVTS)
8:00 Baron.

—— HISTOIRES: SUITE NO. 2 (IN 4 MOVTS.)
13:15 Baron.

IDE, Chester E.
—— SYMPHONY IN A MINOR
3,3,2,2 - 4,2,3,1 - timp.,perc. - str.　　30:00 Musicus.

IFUKUBE, Akira
—— BALLATA SINFONICA
2,2,2,2 - 4,3,3,1 - timp., perc.(4) - hp. - pf. - str.　　Presser.

—— JAPANESE RHAPSODY
3,3,3,3 - 4,2,3,1 - timp.,perc. - 2 hp - pf. - str.　　22:00 Templeton.

IGLESIAS VILLOUD, Hector A.
—— AMANCAY (1-ACT BALLET) %
Fleisher.

IHLAU, Fritz
—— LIEDER
2,2,2,2 - 3,2,2,0 - timp.,perc.,cel. - hp. - str.　　16:00 Riccardo.

IKEBE, Shinichiro
—— SYMPHONY
3,3,3,3 - 4,3,3,1 - timp., perc.(4) - hp. - pf. - str.　　30:00 Presser.

IKENOUCHI, Tomojirô
—— THREE PIECES FROM THE NOH DRAMA "YUYA" (FOR SOPRANO AND ORCHESTRA)
1,1,1,1 - 1,1,1,0 - timp.,perc. - hp. - str.　　13:00 Presser.

IKONEN, Lauri
—— THE BLACK KNIGHT (FOR MALE CHORUS AND ORCH.)
(Text: Bo Bergman)
2,2,2,2 - 4,3,3,1 -timp.,perc. - hp. - str.　　13:00 FinnMICtr.

—— CONCERTINO NO. 2 IN E FLAT MAJOR, FOR PIANO AND ORCH.
2,2,2,2 - 4,3,3,1 - timp.,perc. - pf. - str.　　17:00 FinnMICtr.

—— CONCERTO IN B MINOR, FOR VIOLIN AND ORCH. (1939)
2,2,2,2 - 4,3,3,1 - timp. - str.　　19:00 FinnMICtr.

—— CONCERTO INTIMO (FOR PIANO AND ORCH.)
2,2,2,2 - 4,3,3,0 - timp. - pf. - str.　　13:00 FinnMICtr.

—— CONCERTO MEDITATIVO (FOR CELLO AND ORCH.) (1942)
2,2,2,2 - 4,3,2,0 - timp. - hp. - str.　　15:00 FinnMICtr.

—— INGERMAN SONGS (SUITE) (FOR PIANO AND STRINGS)
pf. - str.　　15:00 FinnMICtr.

—— SINFONIA INORNATA (1922)
2,2,2,2 - 4,3,0,0 - timp - str　　12:00 FinnMICtr.

—— SUITE FOR STRINGS
str.　　13:00 FinnMICtr.

—— SUITE OF THEATRE SCENES
2,2,2,2 - 4,3,3,0 - timp.,perc. - hp. - str.　　15:00 FinnMICtr.

—— SYMPHONY NO. 2, IN D MINOR (1937)
3,2,2,2 - 4,3,3,1 - timp.,perc. - hp. - str.　　25:00 FinnMICtr.

—— SYMPHONY NO. 3 ("THE SON OF LEMMI")(REV. 1959)
3,2,2,2 - 4,3,3,1 - timp.,perc. - hp. - str.　　23:00 FinnMICtr.

—— SYMPHONY NO. 4, IN A MINOR (SINFONIA CONCENTRATA) (1942)
3,2,2,2 - 4,3,3,1 - timp.,perc. - hp. - str.　　24:00 FinnMICtr.

—— SYMPHONY NO. 5, IN C MAJOR (SINFONIA APERTA) (1943)
3,2,2,2 - 4,3,3,1 - timp.,perc. - hp. - str.　　25:00 FinnMICtr.

—— SYMPHONY NO. 6, IN E MINOR
2,2,2,2 - 4,3,3,1 - timp.,perc. - hp. - str.　　25:00 FinnMICtr.

—— THREE FUGUES (1935)
Str　　8:00 FinnMICtr.

—— UNDER THE OPEN SKY
2,2,2,2 - 4,3,3,1 - timp.,perc. - hp. - str.　　10:00 FinnMICtr.

ILLIANSHENKO, Andre
—— TROIS COMPLAINTES POPULAIRES RUSSES (FOR VOICE AND ORCH.)
Salabert.

IMBRIE, Andrew
—— LITTLE CONCERTO FOR PIANO-4-HANDS AND ORCH.
12:00 Templeton.

INCERTI, Bruno
—— CONCERTINO FÜR TROMPETE UND STREICHORCHESTER OP. 27
tpt. - str.　　14:00 S.U.I.S.A.

INCH, Herbert
—— ANSWERS TO A QUESTIONNAIRE (VARIATIONS FOR ORCH.)
2,2,2,2 - 4,3,3,1 - timp.,perc. - hp. - str.　　16:00 EV.

INDY, Vincent d'
—— CONCERTO FOR PIANO, FLUTE, CELLO AND STRINGS, OP. 89
Fl - pf. - str.　　30:00 Salabert.

—— DIPTYQUE MÉDITERRANÉEN, OP. 87
*3,*3,3,3 - 4,3,3,c.-b. trb.,0 - timp., cel. - 2 hp. - str.
20:00 Salabert.

—— FANTASY ON POPULAR FRENCH THEMES, OP. 31 (FOR OBOE AND ORCH.)
3,1,2,2 - 4,2,3,0 timp.,perc. - str.　　EV.

—— LE POÈME DES RIVAGES (SUITE), OP. 77 (IN 4 MOVTS)
3,3,3,4 sax.(ad. lib.),3 - 4,4,4,0 - timp.,cel., xyl. - 2 hp. - pf. - str.
22:00 Salabert.

—— PRELUDE TO ACT III OF "FERVAAL"
4,3,4,4 - 4,4,2 bugle hn.,2 sax.-hns.,4,1 - timp.,perc. - str. 5:00 EV.

—— LA QUESTE DE DIEU (EXCERPT FROM "LA LÉGENDE DE SAINT CHRISTOPHE"), OP. 67
3,3,3,3 - little E♭ bugle,2 B♭ bugles,6,3,3,c.-b.trb.,0 - timp.,xyl. - 2hp. - pf. - str.　　16:00 Salabert.

—— LE RÊVE DE CYNIAS (3-ACT OPERA) (1923) %
Presser.

—— SOUVENIRS, OP. 62 (1907)
3,3,3,3 - 4,3,4,0 - timp. - 2 hp. - str.　　　18:00 EV.
—— SYMPHONY NO. 3, OP. 70 ("SINFONIA BREVIS DE BELLO GALLICO")
3,3,4,3 - 4,4,4,0 - timp.,perc.,xyl. - 2 hp. - str.　28:00 Salabert.

INGENBRAND, Josef
—— BOLERO SINFONICO
2,*3,2,*3 - 4,3,3,1 - timp.,perc.,cel. - hp. - str.　11:00 Henmar.

INGHELBRECHT, Désiré Émile
—— AUTOMNE (SYMPHONIC SKETCH)
2,3,3,2,sarr. - 4,2,3,1 - timp.,perc., cel. - hp. - str.　9:00 Salabert.
—— BALLADE DANS LE GOÛT IRLANDAIS (FOR HARP AND ORCH.)
1,2,1,1 - 1,1,0,0 - perc. - hp. - str.　10:00 Salabert.
—— DERNIÈRES NURSERIES (IN 3 MOVTS.)
1,1,2,1 - 2,1,1,0 - str.　13:00 Salabert.
—— FOUR FANFARES
0,0,0,0 - 4,3,3,1 - timp.,perc.　5:00 Salabert.
—— EL GRECO (SYMPHONIC EVOCATIONS)
3,3,3,3 - 4,3,3,1 - timp.,perc., glock. - 2hp. - str.　15:00 Salabert.
—— IBERIANA (RHAPSODY FOR VIOLIN AND ORCH.)
1,1,1 sax.,1 - 0,0,0,0 - perc. - hp. - str.　10:00 Salabert.
—— LA LÉGENDE DU GRAND SAINT NICOLAS (FOR VOICE AND ORCH.)
7:00 Salabert.
—— LA MÉTAMORPHOSE D'ÈVE (FOR SMALL ORCH.)
1,1,2,1 - 2,1,1,0 - timp.,perc. - hp. - str.　12:00 Salabert.
—— LA NURSERY (FOR SMALL ORCH.)

SUITE NO. 1
2,1,2,1 - 2,1,1,0 - timp.,perc. - hp. - str.　5:30 Salabert.
SUITE NO. 2
2,1,2,1 - 2,1,1,0 - timp.,perc. - hp. - str.　8:30 Salabert.
SUITE NO. 3
1,1,2,1 - 2,1,1,0 - timp.,perc. - hp. - str.　10:30 Baron.
SUITE NO. 4
2,1,2,1 - 2,1,1,0 - timp.,perc. - hp. - str.　6:30 Salabert.
SUITE NO. 5
2,1,2,1 - 2,1,1,0 - timp.,perc. - hp. - str.　4:30 Salabert.
—— PASTOURELLES (FOR CHORUS AND ORCH.)
2,2,2,2 - 4,2,3,0 - timp.,perc. - hp. - pf. - str.　17:00 EV.
—— POUR LE JOUR DE LA PREMIÈRE NEIGE AU VIEUX JAPON
2,3,3,sax.,4 - 4,3,3,1 - timp.,perc., cel., glock., xyl. - 2 hp. - str.　15:00 Salabert.
—— RAPSODIE DE PRINTEMPS
3,3,4,2 - 4,2,3,1 - timp.,perc. - harm. - 2 hp. - pf. str.　10:00 Salabert.
—— REQUIEM (INTROIT AND KYRIE) (FOR SOLO VOICES, CHORUS AND ORCH.) (1940)
2,2,2,2 - 4,2,3,0 - timp.,cel. - 2 hp. - org. - str.　28:00 EV.
—— SINFONIA BREVE NO. 1
1,1,2,1 - 2,1,1,0 - perc. - hp. - str.　15:00 Salabert.
—— LA VALSE RETROUVÉE (SUITE FROM THE BALLET "LA MÉTAMORPHOSE D'ÈVE)(1930)
2,2,2,2 - 4,2,3,1 - timp.,perc. - hp. - str.　9:00 Salabert.
—— VEZELAY (ÉVOCATIONS SYMPHONIQUES) (WITH BARITONE SOLO AND MEN'S CHORUS AD LIB.)
2,2,2,2 - 4,2,3,1 - timp.,perc. (4), cel.,xyl. - 2 hp. - pf. - str.　25:00 Salabert.

INGMAN, Olavi
—— SHEPHERD'S PSALM (FOR SATB CHORUS AND ORCH.) (1943) (Text: Lauri Pohjanpää)
2,2,2,2 - 4,2,0,1 - timp. - org. - str.　7:00 FinnMICtr.

INGRAM, Harold
—— STRATFORD SUITE
pf. (ad lib.) - str.　Bo. Hawkes.

INWOOD, Mary
—— SUITE FOR WINDS AND PERCUSSION (1976) (IN 5 MOVTS.)
2(2nd alt. with picc.),2,*3,1 - 2,2,1,0 - timp.,perc.(1)　10:30 Composer.

IPPOLITOV-IVANOV, M. - FINCK, Herman
—— CAUCASIAN SKETCHES (IN 4 MOVTS.)
22:00 Bo. Hawkes.

IPPOLITOV-IVANOV, M. - ROBERTS, Charles J.
—— CAUCASIAN SKETCHES
C. Fischer.

IRELAND, John
—— CONCERTINO PASTORALE (IN 3 MOVTS.)
str.　19:00 Bo. Hawkes.
—— CONCERTO IN E♭, FOR PIANO AND ORCH.
*3,2,2,2 - 4,2,3,0-1 - perc. - pf. - str.　25:00 G. Schirmer.
—— THE FORGOTTEN RITE (SYMPHONIC PRELUDE)
3(3rd alt. with picc.),*3,3,2 - 4,2,3,0 - timp.,cel. - hp. - str.　8:30 Augener.
—— GREATER LOVE HATH NO MAN (FOR SATB CHORUS AND ORCH.)
2,2,2,2 - 4,3,3,1 - timp. - org. - str.　4:00 Galaxy.
—— A LONDON OVERTURE
2,2,2,2 - 4,3,3,1 - timp.,perc. - str.　12:30 Bo. Hawkes.
—— MAI-DUN (SYMPHONIC RHAPSODY)
3(3rd alt. with picc.),*3,3,2 - 4,3,3,1 - timp.,perc. - str.　13:00 Augener.
—— SATYRICON (OVERTURE)
8:00 Galaxy.
—— THESE THINGS SHALL BE (FOR BARITONE OR TENOR, CHORUS AND ORCH.)
3,3,3,3 - 4,3,3,1 - timp.,cel. - org. - str.　20:00 Bo. Hawkes.
—— TWO PIECES FOR STRINGS
str.　8:00 Bo. Hawkes.

IRGENS JENSEN, Ludvig
—— CANTO D'OMAGGIO (FESTIVAL OVERTURE)
3,2,2,2 - 4,3,3,1 - timp.,perc. - hp. - org. - str.　8:30 T.O.N.O.
—— DER GOTT UND DIE BAJADERE (FOR ALTO, TENOR, BASS, SATB CHORUS AND ORCH.) (Text: Goethe)
2,2,2,2 - 4,3,3,1 - timp.,perc. - hp. - str.　26:00 T.O.N.O.
—— INCIDENTAL MUSIC TO H. STIBOLT'S PLAY "KING BALDWIN'S BRACELET" (KONG BALDVINS ARMRING)
1,0,1,2 sax.,0 - 1,2,1,0 - perc. - harm. - pf. - str.　T.O.N.O.
—— INCIDENTAL MUSIC TO SVERRE HAGERUP BULL'S PLAY "ROBIN HOOD"
1,1,1,1 - 2,2,1,0 - perc. - pf. - str.　T.O.N.O.
—— INCIDENTAL MUSIC TO WERGELAND'S PLAY "THE MAN" (MENNESKET)
2,1,2,1 - 2,2,2,0 - perc. - pf. - str.　T.O.N.O.
—— JAPANISCHER FRÜHLING (JAPANESE SPRING) (9 POEMS, FOR VOICE AND ORCH.)
2,1,2,1 - 2,2,0,0 - perc.,cel. - hp. - str.　22:00 T.O.N.O.
—— PARTITA (SYMPHONIC POEM)
2,2,2,2 - 4,3,3,1 - timp.,cel. - hp. - pf. - str.　18:00 Norsk Mfl.
—— PASSACAGLIA
3,2,3,3 - 4,3,3,1 - timp.,perc. - hp. - str.　22:00 Norsk Mfl.
—— THE RETURN ("HEIMFERD") ("DRAMATIC SYMPHONY") (FOR SOPRANO, ALTO, 3 TENORS, 2 BASSES, SATB CHORUS AND ORCH.) (Text: Olav Gullvåg)
3,2,2,2 - 4,3,3,1 - timp.,perc.,cel. - hp. - str.　90:00 T.O.N.O.
—— SYMPHONY IN D MINOR
3,2,3,3 - 4,3,3,1 - timp.,perc.,cel. - hp. - str.　48:00 T.O.N.O.
—— TEMA CON VARIAZIONI
2,1,2,2 - 4,3,3,1 - timp.,perc.,cel. - hp. - pf. - str.　22:00 Norsk Mfl.

IRVING, Robert
—— MOSAIC NO. 2 (FOR CHAMBER ORCH.)
1,1,1,1 - 0,0,0,0 - glock.,xyl. - str.　A.P.R.A.

ISAAC, Merle J.
—— CAVALIER OVERTURE
C. Fischer.
—— LEGEND (TONE POEM)
C. Fischer.
—— SUITE MODERNE (IN 3 MOVTS.)
2,2,3,2 - 4,2,3,1 - timp.,perc. - str.　10:00 C. Fischer.

ISAAK, Heinrich - MCCOLLIN, Frances
—— CHORALE PRELUDE: "NOW ALL THE WOODS ARE SLEEPING"
str.　4:00 Ricordi.

ISACSSON, Fredrik
—— DESTINY, OP. 25 (AN OVERTURE) (1922)
2,2,2,2 - 4,2,3,1 - timp.,perc. - hp. - str.　15:00 FinnMICtr.
—— EVENING AND NIGHT ON THE STEPPE, OP. 43
2,3,2,2 - 2,2,1,0 - timp.,perc. - str.　16:00 FinnMICtr.
—— HISTORICAL RECOLLECTIONS, OP. 17 (1919)
2,2,2,2 - 4,2,3,1 - timp.,perc. - hp. - str.　20:00 FinnMICtr.
—— IN MEMORIAM (1915)
2,3,2,2 - 3,2,1,0 - timp.,perc. - hp. - str.　30:00 FinnMICtr.

—— LITTLE SUITE NO. 1, OP. 12
    1,2,2,2 - 2,0,0,0 - timp. - hp. - str.   15:00 FinnMICtr.
—— LITTLE SUITE NO. 2
    2,2,2,2 - 2,0,0,0 - timp.,perc. - hp. - str.   15:00 FinnMICtr.
—— LITTLE SUITE NO. 3, OP. 53
    1,1,2,2 - 2,2,0,0 - str.   11:00 FinnMICtr.
—— MARJATTA, OP. 10 (1915)
    3,3,2,2 - 4,2,3,1 - timp.,perc. - str.   13:00 FinnMICtr.
—— MIDSUMMER'S DAY, OP. 20 (SUITE) (1920)
    2,2,2,2 - 4,2,3,1 - timp.,perc. - hp. - str.   20:00 FinnMICtr.
—— PHANTOMS OF THE NIGHT (1923)
    3,2,2,2 - 2,2,1,0 - timp.,perc. - hp. - str.   12:00 FinnMICtr.
—— SYMPHONY NO. 1 IN D MAJOR, OP. 38 (1949)
    2,2,2,2 - 4,3,3,1 - timp.,perc. - str.   26:00 FinnMICtr.
—— SYMPHONY NO. 2, OP. 50 ("AD ASTRA") (1943)
    3,2,2,2 - 3,2,3,0 - timp.,perc. - str.   30:00 FinnMICtr.
—— TWO SCENES FROM THE KALEVALA, OP. 45
    3,3,2,2 - 2,2,1,0 - timp.,perc. - hp. - str.   9:00 FinnMICtr.

ISHII, Maki
—— KYOO (FOR "MULTI-PIANOS", ELECTRONIC SOUNDS AND SMALL ORCH.)
    0,0,0,0 - 3,1,2,0 - perc. (4) - tape-recorder - pf. - str.
    14:00 Presser.
—— SEVEN PIECES (FOR SMALL ORCHESTRA)
    1,0,*1,0 - 0,0,0,0 - perc., cel., vibra. - hp. - pf. - str.   12:00 Presser.

ISHIKETA, Mareo
—— SINFONIA
    3,3,3,3 - 4,3,3,1 - timp.,perc.(5),xyl. - 2 hp. - str.   27:00 Presser.

ISLANDSMOEN, Sigurd
—— CANTATA FOR A CHORUS JUBILEE, OP. 39 (FOR TENOR, MALE CHORUS AND ORCH.) (Text: Thomassen)
    20:00 T.O.N.O.
—— CONCERT OVERTURE, OP. 10
    2,2,2,2 - 4,2,3,1 - timp.,perc. - hp. - str.   10:00 T.O.N.O.
—— ELEGY (FOR FEMALE CHORUS AND STRINGS) (Text: Composer)
    str.   2:00 NorKomFlg.
—— ÉIVIND BOLT (SYMPHONIC POEM), OP. 45
    2,2,2,2 - 4,2,3,1 - timp.,perc. - hp. - str.   60:00 T.O.N.O.
—— ISRAEL IN CAPTIVITY, OP. 14 ("ISRAEL I FANGENSKAP") (ORATORIO) (FOR SOPRANO, ALTO, TENOR, BASS, MIXED CHORUS AND ORCH.)
    2,2,2,2 - 4,2,3,1 - timp.,perc. - hp. - org. - str.   120:00 T.O.N.O.
—— MISSA SOLEMNIS, OP. 56 (FOR SOLO VOICES, CHORUS AND ORCH.)
    75:00 T.O.N.O.
—— MOSSIANA, OP. 40 (CANTATA) (FOR SOLO VOICES, CHILDREN'S CHORUS, MIXED CHORUS AND ORCH.) (Text: Leif Sundsvik)
    35:00 T.O.N.O.
—— NORWEGIAN ALBUM, OP. 19 (SUITE) (IN 7 MOVTS.)
    2,2,1,1 - 2,2,2,0 - timp.,perc. - hp. - org. - pf. - str.
    30:00 T.O.N.O.
—— POLONAISE PATHÉTIQUE, OP. 29
    2,2,2,2 - 4,2,3,1 - timp. - str.   8:00 T.O.N.O.
—— REQUIEM, OP. 42 (FOR SATB SOLO VOICES, MIXED CHORUS AND ORCH.)
    2,2,2,2 - 4,2,3,1 - timp.,perc. - hp. - org. - str.   70:00 Norsk Mfl.
—— RETURN FROM BABEL ("HEIMATT FRÅ BABEL") (ORATORIO), OP. 20 (FOR SOPRANO, ALTO, TENOR, BASS, MIXED CHORUS AND ORCH.)
    2,2,2,2 - 4,2,3,1 - timp.,perc. - hp. - org. - str.   120:00 T.O.N.O.
—— SUITE IN THREE MOVTS., OP. 17
    str.   11:00 T.O.N.O.
—— SYMPHONY NO. 1 IN G MAJOR, OP. 6
    2,2,2,2 - 2,2,0,0 - timp. - str.   35:00 T.O.N.O.
—— SYMPHONY NO. 2 IN F MINOR, OP. 49 (IN 4 MOVTS.)
    40:00 T.O.N.O.
—— TEMA CON VARIAZIONI, OP. 4
    2,2,2,2 - 4,2,3,1 - timp.,perc. - hp. - str.   10:00 T.O.N.O.

ISOZ, Etienne
—— CONCERTO POUR COR DES ALPES
    2,0,2,2 - 2,2,alphorn,0,0 - perc.(3) - str.   20:00 S.U.I.S.A.

ISRAEL-MEYER, Pierre
—— KITSCH-EURYDICE
    2,2,2,2 - 2,2,1,0 - timp.,perc.(3) - pf. - str.   17:20 Presser.

IŠTVAN, Miloslav
—— WINTER SUITE
    timp.,perc.,xyl. - pf. - str.   22:00 Bo. Hawkes.

IVANOV-RADKEVICH, Nikolai
—— RHAPSODY ON UKRAINIAN FOLK THEMES
    3,3,3,3 - 6,3,3,1 - timp.,perc.,xyl. - 2 hp. - pf. - str.   G. Schirmer.
—— RUSSIAN OVERTURE
    *3,2,3,2 - 4,3,3,1 - timp.,perc. - hp. - pf. - str.   8:00 G. Schirmer.

IVES, Charles
—— CENTRAL PARK IN THE DARK (FOR SMALL ORCH.)
    Boelke-Bo.
—— SYMPHONY NO. 2
    1. Andante moderato; 2. Allegro; 3. Adagio cantabile; 4. Lento maestoso; 5. Allegro molto vivace
    *3,2,2,*3 - 4,2,3,1 - timp.,perc. - str.   20:00 Southern.
—— THE UNANSWERED QUESTION (LARGO TO PRESTO)
    Southern.

IVES, Charles - ROCHBERG, George
—— LINCOLN, THE GREAT COMMONER
    2,2,2,2 - 0,2,3,1 - timp.,perc. - str.   11:00 Presser.

IVEY, Jean Eichelberger
—— FORMS IN MOTION
    3,3,3,3 - 4,3,3,1 - timp.,perc. - hp. - pf.(or cel.) - str.
    25:00 C. Fischer.
—— HERA, HUNG FROM THE SKY (FOR MEZZO-SOPRANO AND INSTRUMENTS)
    1,1,1,1 - 1,1,1,0 - perc. - tape-recorder - pf.   12:00 C. Fischer.
—— ODE FOR ORCHESTRA
    3,2,2,2 - 4,2,3,1 - perc. - str.   7:00 C. Fischer.
—— PASSACAGLIA
    1,1,1,1 - 1,1,1,0 - perc. - str.   7:00 C. Fischer.
—— TESTAMENT OF EVE (MONODRAMA) (FOR MEZZO-SOPRANO AND ORCHESTRA)
    2,2,2,2 - 4,2,3,1 - timp.,perc.,cel. - tape-recorder - hp. - str.
    20:00 C. Fischer.
—— TRIBUTE TO MARTIN LUTHER KING (FOR BARITONE AND ORCH.)
    3,3,3,3 - 4,3,3,1 - perc. - str.   28:00 C. Fischer.

J

JACHINO, Carlo
—— PRELUDIO DI FESTA
    3,2,2,2 - 4,3,3,1 - timp.,perc. - hp. - str.   15:00 Salabert.

JACKSON, Hanley
—— CASSANDRA'S DANCE (1967)
    3(1 alt. with picc.),2,*3,0 - 4,2,3,1 - timp.,perc.(3) - str.
    5:00 MCA Music.
—— REQUIEM (FOR SOPRANO, BARITONE, MIXED CHORUS AND ORCH.) (1964)
    3(1 alt. with picc.)3(1 alt. with Eng. hn.),*3,2 - 4,2,3,1 - timp.,perc.(4),bells,cel.,glock.,xyl. - pf. - str.   35:00 Composer.
—— TANGENTS II (FOR ORCHESTRA AND TAPE) (1970)
    2,2,2,2 - 4,3,3,1 - timp.,perc.(5),vibra. - tape-recorder - pf. - str.(no d.-b.)   8:00 MCA Music.

JACOB, Dom Clément
—— LE CHEMIN DE LA CROIX ("THE WAY OF THE CROSS") (FOR NARRATOR AND STRING ORCH.) (Text: Paul Claudel)
    str.   55:00 EV.
—— LE CHEMIN DE LA CROIX (WITHOUT NARRATOR)
    str.   25:00 EV.
—— CONCERTO FOR PIANO AND ORCH.
    2,2,2,2 - 3,3,3,0 - timp.,perc. - hp. - pf. - str.   25:00 EV.
—— SERENADE FOR ORCH.
    2,1,1,1 - 1,1,1,1 - str.   3:00 EV.
—— SIX CHANTS D'EXIL ET DE PEINE
    2,2,2,2 - 2,2,2,0 - timp.,perc. - hp. - str.   14:00 EV.

JACOB, Gordon
—— CHACONNE ON A THEME OF VAUGHAN WILLIAMS
    2(2nd alt. with picc.),*2,2,2 - 2,2,1,0 - timp.,perc.(3),glock. - str.
    6:30 G. Schirmer.

—— COMEDY OVERTURE (THE BARBER OF SEVILLE GOES TO THE DEVIL)
    *2,1,2,1 - 2,2,2,0 - timp.,perc. - hp.(or pf.) - str.   3:30 Oxford.

—— CONCERTINO FOR PIANO AND STRINGS (IN 3 MOVTS.)
    pf. - str.   12:00 Oxford.

—— CONCERTO FOR BASSOON AND STRINGS
    bn. - str.   16:30 Galaxy.

—— CONCERTO FOR CELLO AND STRINGS
    str.   22:00 Galaxy.

—— CONCERTO FOR FLUTE AND STRINGS
    fl. - str.   22:00 Galaxy.

—— CONCERTO FOR HORN AND STRINGS
    hn. - str.   16:00 Galaxy.

—— CONCERTO FOR PIANO (3-HANDS) AND ORCH.
    2,2,2,2 - 2,2,3,0 - timp.,perc.,glock. - pf. (3-hands) - str.   20:00 Novello.

—— CONCERTO FOR TROMBONE AND ORCH.
    18:00 Galaxy.

—— CONCERTO FOR VIOLA AND ORCH. (IN 1 MOVT.)
    2,2,2,2 - 4,3,3,1 - timp. - hp. - str.   17:00 Oxford.

—— CONCERTO FOR VIOLIN AND STRINGS
    str.   20:00 Galaxy.

—— CONCERTO NO. 1 FOR OBOE AND STRINGS
    ob. - str.   22:30 Galaxy.

—— CONCERTO NO. 1 FOR PIANO AND STRINGS
    pf. - str.   18:00 Oxford.

—— CONCERTO NO. 2 FOR OBOE AND STRINGS
    ob. - str.   25:00 Galaxy.

—— CONCERTO NO. 2 FOR PIANO AND ORCH.
    2,2,2,2 - 4,2,3,1 - timp.,perc. - pf. - str.   30:00 Oxford.

—— CONCERTO NO. 2 FOR PIANO AND STRINGS
    pf. - str.   28:00 Oxford.

—— DENBIGH SUITE (FOR STRINGS)
    str.   10:00 Oxford.

—— DIVERSIONS FOR WOODWINDS, HORN AND STRINGS
    23:00 Oxford.

—— DIVERTIMENTO FOR SMALL ORCH. (IN 4 MOVTS.)
    1,1,2,1 - 2,2,1,0 - timp.,perc. - hp. - str.   17:00 Bo. Hawkes.

—— THE DIVERTING HISTORY OF JOHN GILPIN (FOR MIXED CHORUS AND ORCH.) (Text: William Cowper)
    2,2,2,2 - 2,2,3,0 - timp.,perc. - str.   22:00 Oxford.
    or:
    1,1,2,1 - 2,2,0,0 - timp.,perc. - str.

—— FANTASIA ON THE ALLELUIA HYMN
    2,2,2,2 - 4,2,3,1 - timp.,perc. - str.   8:00 Galaxy.
    or:
    2,2,2,2 - 2,2,3,0 - timp.,perc. - str.

—— FANTASIA ON TRADITIONAL TUNES
    3(3rd alt. with picc.),2,2,2 - 4,3,3,1 - timp. - perc. - hp. - str.   17:00 Galaxy.

—— FESTIVAL OVERTURE
    Oxford.

—— A GOODLY HERITAGE (FOR SATB CHORUS, STRINGS AND PIANO)
    pf. - str.   30:00 Galaxy.

—— HIGHWAYS (A CANTATA OF TRAVEL) (FOR BARITONE, MIXED CHORUS AND ORCH.) (Text: Christopher Hassall)
    2,1,2,1 - 2,2,3,0 - timp.,perc.(2) - str.   Oxford.
    or:
    pf. - str.

—— INTRODUCTION AND ALLEGRO
    15:00 Galaxy.

—— LAUDATE DOMINUM (FOR SATB CHORUS AND ORCHESTRA)
    3(3rd alt. with picc.),3(3rd alt. with Eng.hn.),2,3(3rd alt. with c.-bn.) - 4,2,3,1 - timp.,perc. - hp. - str.   20:00 Oxford.

—— A LITTLE CONCERTO (FOR DOUBLE BASS AND STRING ORCH.)
    str.   12:00 Galaxy.

—— LITTLE SYMPHONY
    1,2,0,2 - 2,0,0,0 - str.   20:00 Oxford.

—— THE NEW-BORN KING (CANTATA) (FOR BARITONE SOLO, MIXED CHORUS AND ORCH.)
    32:00 Oxford.

—— A NEW FOREST SUITE
    21:00 Oxford.

—— NEWS FROM NEWTOWN (FOR BARITONE, MIXED CHORUS AND ORCH.) (Text: Christopher Hassell)
    2,2,2,2 - 2,2,3,0 - timp.,perc.(6) - str.   35:00 Oxford.
    or:
    1,1,2,1 - 2,2,0,0 - timp.,perc.(6) - str.

—— A NORTHUMBRIAN OVERTURE
    Oxford.

—— OLD WINE IN NEW BOTTLES (4 OLD ENGLISH TUNES)
    *2,2,2,2-3 - 2,2,0.0   12:00 Oxford.

—— OVERTURE FOR STRINGS
    Oxford.

—— OVERTURE ("FUN FARE")
    Oxford.

—— PASSACAGLIA ON A WELL-KNOWN THEME
    2(2nd alt. with picc.),2,2,2 - 4,2,3,1 - timp.,perc. - hp. - str.   6:00 Galaxy.

—— PRELUDE AND TOCCATA
    3(3rd alt. with picc.),2-*3,2-*3,2 - 4,3,3,1 - timp.,perc. - 1-2 hp. - str.   12:00 Galaxy.

—— RHAPSODY FOR ENGLISH HORN (OR ALTO SAXOPHONE) AND STRINGS
    Eng. hn. (or alto sax.) - str.   9:00 Galaxy.

—— A SEA SONG SUITE (FOR BARITONE, CHORUS AND ORCH.)
    3(3rd alt. with picc.),2,2,2 - 4,3,3,1 - timp.,perc. - str.   20:00 Galaxy.

—— SINFONIETTA NO. 1 FOR SMALL ORCH.
    2,2,2,2 - 2,2,1,0 - timp.,perc. - str.   13:00 Galaxy.

—— SINFONIETTA NO. 3
    2(2nd alt. with picc.),2,2,*3 - 4,3,3,1 - timp.,perc. - hp. - str.   20:00 Galaxy.

—— SINFONIETTA ("THE CEARNE")
    str.   15:00 Novello.

—— THE SPACIOUS FIRMAMENT ON HIGH (FOR CHORUS AND ORCH.) (Text: J. Addison)
    Oxford.

—— SUITE FOR RECORDER AND STRING ORCH.
    Recorder (or fl.) - str.   20:00 Oxford.

—— SUITE IN A, OP. 144
    fl. - str.   14:00 Oxford.

—— SUITE NO. 1 IN F
    13:30 Galaxy.

—— SUITE NO. 2 (SYMPHONIC SUITE) (IN 3 MOVTS.)
    2(2nd alt. with picc.),2,2,2 - 4,3,3,1 - timp.,perc. - hp. - str.   22:00 Galaxy.

—— SUITE NO. 3 (IN 5 MOVTS.)
    2(2nd alt. with picc.),2,2,2 - 4,3,3,1 - timp.,perc. - hp. - str.   22:00 Galaxy.

—— SUITE OF FIVE PIECES (FOR HARMONICA AND STRINGS)
    Harmonica - str.   12:00 Galaxy.

—— SYMPHONY FOR STRINGS (IN 3 MOVTS.)
    str.   20:00 Novello.

—— SYMPHONY NO. 2 IN C MAJOR
    32:00 Galaxy.

—— TWO SKETCHES FOR STRINGS
    str.   11:15 Novello.

—— UNCLE REMUS (BALLET SUITE) (FOR SMALL ORCH.)
    11:00 P.R.S.

—— VARIATIONS ON AN ORIGINAL THEME
    2(2nd alt. with picc.),2,2,3(3rd alt. with c.-bn.) - 4,3,3,1 - timp.,perc. - hp. - str.   23:00 Galaxy.

JACOB, Maxime

—— LE CHEMIN DE LA CROIX (FOR NARRATOR AND STRINGS)
    str.   55:00 Presser.

—— LE CHEMIN DE LA CROIX (FOR STRINGS)
    str.   25:00 Presser.

—— CONCERTO FOR PIANO AND ORCH.
    2,2,2,2 - 3,3,3,0 - timp.,perc. - hp. - pf. - str.   25:00 Presser.

—— SERENADE
    2,1,1,1 - 1,1,1,1 - str.   3:00 Presser.

—— SIX CHANTS D'EXIL ET DE PEINE
    2,2,2,2 - 2,2,2,0 - timp.,perc. - hp. - str.   14:00 Presser.

JACOBI, Frederick

—— AVE ROTA (3 PIECES IN MULTIPLE STYLE) (FOR PIANO AND SMALL OR LARGE ORCH.)
    14:00 Composer.

—— BALLADE CONCERTANTE FOR PIANO AND ORCH.
    *3,2,2,2(1 alt. with c.-bn.) - 4,2,2,1 - timp.,perc.(2) - pf. - str.   7:00 Composer.

—— A CALIFORNIA SUITE
    Composer.

—— CONCERTINO FOR PIANO AND STRINGS
    pf. - str.   17:00 EV.

—— CONCERTO FOR CELLO AND ORCH.
    2,2,2,2 - 2,0,0,0 - timp.,perc.(2) - str.   20:00 AMP.

—— CONCERTO FOR PIANO AND ORCH.
    25:00 Composer.

—— CONCERTO FOR VIOLIN AND ORCH.
*3,2,2,2 - 4,3,3,1 - timp.,perc.(3) - hp. (ad lib.)   24:00 Leeds.
—— THE EVE OF SAINT AGNES (SYMPHONIC POEM)
Composer.
—— FOUR DANCES FROM "THE PRODIGAL SON"
*3,1,2,2 - 4,2,2,0 - timp.,perc.,cel. - hp. - str.   10:15 AmerMusEd.
—— INDIAN DANCES
*3,*3,2,*3 - 3,3,3,1 - timp.,perc.(3) - hp. - pf. - str. 28:00 Western.
—— MUSIC HALL OVERTURE
2(2nd alt. with picc.),2,2,2 - 4,3,3,1 - timp.,perc.(3),xyl. - hp. - pf.
- str.   6:00 Leeds.
—— NIGHT PIECE AND DANCE (FOR FLUTE AND ORCH.)
8:00 Bo. Hawkes.
NIGHT PIECE
1,1,1,2 - 2,0,0,0 - timp.,perc. - hp. str.
DANCE
0,1,0,0 - 0,0,0,0 - timp.,perc. - hp. str.
—— ODE
*3,*3,*3,*3 - 4,3,3,1 - timp.,perc.(2),cel. - hp. - str.
12:00 Bo. Hawkes.
—— THE PIED PIPER (SYMPHONIC POEM)
Composer.
—— THE POET IN THE DESERT (FOR BARITONE, CHORUS AND
ORCH.)
Composer.
—— RHAPSODY FOR HARP AND STRING ORCH.
hp. - str.   9:00 EV.
—— SERENADE FOR PIANO AND ORCH.
10:00 Composer.
—— SYMPHONY IN C (IN 3 MOVTS.)
2(1 alt. with picc.),*3,*3,*3 - 4,3,3,1 - timp.,perc.(3),cel.,xyl. - hp. -
str.   21:00 Composer.
—— TWO ASSYRIAN PRAYERS (FOR VOICE AND ORCH.)
Composer.
—— TWO PIECES IN SABBATH MOOD
1,*2,*2,1 - 2,2,1,0 - timp.,perc.(2) - str.   10:00 Composer.
—— YEIBICHAI (VARIATIONS ON AN AMERICAN INDIAN
THEME)
*3,2(2nd alt. with Eng. hn.),2,*3 - 4,3,3,1 - timp.,perc.(2),cel. - hp.
- pf. - str.   9:00 Leeds.

JACOBI, Wolfgang
—— CAPRICCIO FOR PIANO AND ORCH.
2,2,2,sax.,2 - 0,3,2,1 - timp.,perc. - pf. - str.   15:00 Modern.
—— DIVERTIMENTO FOR ORCH.
2,2,2,2 - 4,3,3,1 - timp.,perc. - hp. - str.   20:00 F. Colombo.
—— DREI BAYERISCHE ZWIEFACHE
perc. - pf. - str.   Hans Gerig.
—— HÖFISCHE TÄNZE NACH LULLY (COURT DANCES, AFTER
JEAN-BAPTISTE LULLY)
perc.,glock. - str.   15:00 Robbins.
—— KLEINE SINFONIE
timp.,perc.,glock.,xyl. - pf.(4 hands) - str.   Robbins.

JACOBSON, Maurice
—— THE HOUND OF HEAVEN (FOR MIXED CHORUS AND
ORCH.)
3,3,3,3 - 4,3,3,1 - timp.,perc. - hp. - str.   58:00 G. Schirmer.
—— THE LADY OF SHALOTT (FOR MIXED CHORUS AND
ORCH.)
35:00 G. Schirmer.
—— LAMENT (FOR STRINGS)
str.   5:00 G. Schirmer.
—— PRELUDE TO A PLAY
5:30 Lengnick.
—— SYMPHONIC SUITE (FOR STRINGS)
str.   16:00 G. Schirmer.
—— THEME AND VARIATIONS
25:00 Lengnick.

JACOBY, Elliott
—— THE BIRTH OF ISRAEL (FOR SOPRANO AND ORCH.) (1948)
(IN 3 MOVTS.) (Text: Traditional Hebrew)
2(alt. with 2 picc.),*2,2,2 - 2,3,2,1 - timp.,perc. - hp. - str.
(15,3,2,2)   14:30 Composer.

JACOBY, Hanoch
—— CAPRICCIO ISRAELIAN
3,3,3,3 - 4,3,3,1 - timp.,perc. - str.   14:00 IsMuPublns.
—— CONCERTO FOR VIOLA AND ORCH.
2,2,2,2 - 2,2,0,0 - timp.,perc. - str.   15:00 IsMuPublns.
—— KING DAVID'S LYRE
1,1,2,2 - 2,2,1,0 - timp.,perc. - str.   11:00 IsMuPublns.

—— LITTLE SUITE
str.   12:00 IsMuPublns.
or:
2,2,2,2 - 4,2,3,1 - timp.,perc. - str.
or:
1,1,2,2 - 2,1,0,0 - timp.,perc. - str.
—— PARTITA ISRAELIANA (FOR STRINGS)
str.   17:00 IsMuPublns.
—— SERIO-GIOCOSO
3,3,3,3 - 4,3,3,1 - timp.,perc. - hp. - str.   10:25 A.C.U.M.
—— SEVEN MINIATURES, OP. 18-B
1,1,2,2 - 2,1,1,0 - timp. - hp. - str.   12:00 IsMuPublns.
—— SINFONIETTA
3,*3,*3,*3 - 4,3,3,1 - timp.,perc. - str.   11:00 IsMuPublns.
—— SUITE POPULAIRE
1,1,2,1 - 2,1,0,0 - timp.,perc. - str.   10:00 IsMuPublns.
—— SYMPHONIC PROLOGUE, OP. 26
2,3,3,3 - 4,2,3,1 - timp.,perc. - str.   12:00 IsMuPublns.
—— SYMPHONY NO. 1
2,2,3,3 - 2,2,3,1 - timp.,perc. - hp. - str.   32:00 IsMuPublns.
—— SYMPHONY NO. 2
3,3,3,3 - 4,3,3,1 - timp.,perc. - hp. - str.   34:00 IsMuPublns.
—— SYMPHONY NO 3
3,*3,*3,*3 - 4,3,3,1 - timp.,perc. - hp. - str.   38:00 IsMuPublns.

JACQUE-DUPONT
—— LA CLEF DES SONGES (DIVERTISSEMENT 48) (FOR PIANO,
PERCUSSION AND STRINGS)
timp.,perc.,glock.,xyl. - pf. - str.   25:00 EV.

JACQUES, Michael
—— THE DEVIL'S DISCIPLE (AN OVERTURE) (1965)
1,1,1,0 - 1,2,2,0 - perc. - pf. - str.   6:00 P.R.S.

JACQUES-DALCROZE, Emile
—— ENTR'ACTE FROM THE OPERA "LES JUMEAUX DE
BERGAME"
2,2,2,2 - 4,2,2,1 - timp.,perc. - pf. - str.   5:00 Presser.

JAGER, Robert E.
—— CONCERTO GROSSO FOR DANCE BAND AND SYMPHONY
ORCH.
Dance band: 0,0,0,2 alto sax.,2 ten.sax.,1 bar.sax.,0 - 0.4,4,0 -
perc.(1) - pf. - 1 d.-b.   15:00 EV.
Orch: *3,2,2,2 - 4,3,3,1 - timp.,perc. - str.
—— DRAMATIC OVERTURE (1965)
2,2,2,2 - 2,2,2,0 - timp.,perc.(4) - str.   7:00 EV.
—— THREE PIECES FOR ORCHESTRA
2,2,2,2 - 2,2,2,0 - timp.,perc. - str.   6:30 EV.

JAMES, Philip
—— BRET HARTE (OVERTURE)
*3,2,2,2 - 4,3,3,1 - timp.,perc.(3) - ten.,banjo - hp. - str.
13:00 Composer.
—— BY THE WATERS OF BABYLON (PSALM 137) (FOR CHORUS,
ORGAN AND ORCH.)
2,1,2,1 - 2,2,1,0 - timp.,perc.(1) - org. - str.   10:00 Gray.
—— CHAUMONT
3,3,2,2 - 2,2,0,0 - timp.,tabor - hp. - str.   10:00 Belw-Mills.
—— FESTAL MARCH: "PERSARE ET PRAESTARE"
3,2,2,2 - 4,3,3,1 - timp.,perc. - str.   6:00 Chappell.
—— GENERAL WILLIAM BOOTH ENTERS INTO HEAVEN
(CANTATA) (FOR TENOR, MEN'S CHORUS AND ORCH.)
1,1,1,sax.,1 - 1,1,1,0 - perc.(1) - org.(ad lib.),2 pf. - str.
14:00 Witmark.
—— GWALIA (A WELSH RHAPSODY)
*3,2(2nd alt. with Eng. hn.),2,2 - 4,2,3,1 - timp.,perc.(3) - hp. - str.
14:00 Mills.
—— THE LIGHT OF GOD, OP. 27 (CANTATA) (FOR CHORUS
AND ORCH.)
1,1,2,1 - 2,2,0,1 - timp.,perc.(1) - org. - str.   20:00 Gray.
—— THE MARSH OF RHUDDLAN
1,1,2,1 - 2,0,0,0 - timp. - str.   10:00 Composer.
—— MINIVER CHEEVY
3,3,2,2 - 2,2,0,0 - timp.,perc. - str.   7:00 Belw-Mills.
—— THE NIGHTINGALE OF BETHLEHEM, OP. 24 (CANTATA)
(FOR SOPRANO, ALTO, BARITONE, CHORUS AND ORCH.)
1,1,2,1 - 2,2,0,0 - timp. - org. - str.   30:00 Gray.
—— THE NUN, OP. 30 (CANTATA) (FOR 2 SOPRANOS, 2 ALTOS,
CONTRALTO AND ORCH.)
2,2(2nd alt. with Eng. hn.),2,2 - 4,0,0,0 - hp. - str.   14:00 Gray.
—— OVERTURE IN OLDEN STYLE, ON FRENCH NOËLS
*3,2,2,2 - 4,2,3,1 - timp.,perc.(2) - str.   8:00 Western.

—— OVERTURE TO A GREEK PLAY
4,2,2,3 - 4,3,3,1 - timp.,perc.,xyl. - hp. - pf. - str.
17:00 Belw-Mills.

—— PASSACAGLIA (ON A CAMBRIAN BASS)
3,2,*3,3 - 4,3,3,1 - timp.,perc. - str.   6:35 C. Fischer.

—— RICHARD CORY
3,2,2,2 - 2,2,0,0 - timp.,perc. - pf. - str.   4:00 Belw-Mills.

—— SEA SKETCHES (CYCLE FOR BASS-BARITONE AND ORCH.)
1. Prologue - Allegro non troppo; 2. Andante sostenuto; 3. Adagio
con gravite; 4. Allegro ma non troppo
2 picc.,2,*3,*3,*3, - 4,3,3,1 - timp.,perc.(3) - hp. - pf. - str.
25:00 Composer.

—— A SEA SYMPHONY (FOR BASS-BARITONE AND ORCH.)
4(3rd and 4th alt. with picc.),3,2,3 - 4,3,3,1 - timp.,perc.,bells,xyl. -
hp. - pf.(alt. with cel.) - str.   20:30 Belw-Mills.

—— SINFONIETTA (IN 3 MOVTS.)
1,1,2,1 - 2,2,1,0 - timp. - hp. - str.   18:00 Templeton.

—— SONG OF THE NIGHT
*3,*3,2,*3 - 4,3,3,1 - timp.,perc.(4) - 2 hp. - pf. (alt. with cel.) -
str.   12:30 Composer.

—— SPRING IN VIENNA (FOR 2 SOPRANOS, ALTO,
CONTRALTO AND ORCH.)
1,1,2,1 - 2,2,1,0 - timp. - str.   14:00 Huntzinger.

—— STABAT MATER SPECIOSA (CHRISTMAS CANTICLE) (FOR
SOPRANO, BARITONE, CHORUS AND ORCH.))
1,1,2,1 - 2,2,1,0 - timp.,perc.(1) - org. - str.   30:00 Gray.

—— STATION WGZBX (A SATIRICAL SUITE) (IN 4 MOVTS.)
*3,2(2nd alt. with Eng hn.),E♭cl. (ad lib.),*3,3 sax.,*3-4,3,3,1 -
timp.,perc.(3) - hp. - pf. (alt. with cel.) - str.   15:00 Composer.

—— SUITE NO. 1 FOR STRINGS (IN 4 MOVTS.)
str.   16:00 Broude.

—— SUITE NO. 2 FOR STRINGS (IN 4 MOVTS.)
str.   14:00 C. Fischer.

—— SYMPHONY NO. 1
1. Andante solenne; 2. Allegro con brio; 3. Tempo di marcia;
4. Allegro spiritoso
3(3rd alt. with picc.),2,2,*3 - 4,3,4,1 - timp.,perc.(3),glock.,xyl. -
hp. - str.   42:00 Mills.

—— SYMPHONY NO. 2 (IN 1 MOVT.)
4(2 alt. with 2 picc.),2,2,*3 - 4,3,3,1 - timp.,perc.(3) - hp. - str.
27:00 Mills.

—— THE VICTORY RIDERS (FOR MEN'S CHORUS AND ORCH.)
*3,2,2,2 - 4,2,3,1 - timp.,perc.(2) - hp. - str.   10:00 Gray.

JAMES, Woodrow
—— TWO SYMPHONIC MOVEMENTS (1960)
2,1,2,1 - 2,2,0,0 - pf. - str.(2,1,1,1)   13:53 Composer.

JAMESON, Robert H.
—— CONCERTO NO. 2 FOR PIANO AND ORCH.
2,2,2,2 - 2,2,2,0 - timp.,cym. - pf. - str.   22:30 MCA Music.

—— A SYMPHONIC AWAKENING (1973)
12:00 Composer.

JAMGOCHIAN, Robert
—— CONCERTO NO. 1 IN A MINOR, FOR PIANO AND ORCH.
2,2,2,2 - 4,2,2,1 - timp.,perc. - pf. - str.   22:30 C. Fischer.

—— CONCERTO NO. 2 IN D MINOR, FOR PIANO AND ORCH.
2,2,2,2 - 4,2,2,1 - timp.,perc. - pf. - str.   23:30 C. Fischer.

—— A SYMPHONIC AWAKENING
2,2,2,2 - 4,2,2,1 - timp.,perc. - str.   10:00 C. Fischer.

JANÁČEK, Leoš
—— BLANÍK BALLAD (SYMPHONIC POEM)
3,2,3,2 - 3,3,3,1 - timp.,perc. - 2 hp. - str. 8:00 Bo. Hawkes.

—— CANTATA NA SOLANI CARTAK (FOR MALE CHORUS AND
ORCH.)
3,3,2,2 - 4,0,0,0 - timp.,perc. - hp. - org. - str.   6:00 Bo. Hawkes.

—— THE FIDDLER'S CHILD (SYMPHONIC POEM)
2,2,3,2 - 3,2,3,1 - timp.,perc. - hp. - str.   12:00 Bo. Hawkes.

—— IDYLL (SUITE FOR STRING ORCH.)
str.   21:00 Bo. Hawkes.

—— JEALOUSY (OVERTURE)
2,3,3,2 - 4,2,3,1 - timp. - hp. - str.   7:00 Bo. Hawkes.

—— LACHIAN DANCES
2,3,3,2 - 4,2,3,0 - timp.,perc. - hp. - org. - str.   18:00 Bo. Hawkes.

—— MORAVIAN DANCES
2,2,2,2 - 4,2,3,0 - timp.,perc. - str.   11:00 Bo. Hawkes.

—— TARAS BULBA (SYMPHONIC RHAPSODY, AFTER GOGOL'S
STORY) (IN 3 MOVTS.)
3,3,2,3 - 4,3,3,1 - timp.,perc. - 2 hp. - org. - str.
23:00 Bo. Hawkes.

—— VECNE EVANGELICUM ("EVERLASTING GOSPEL")
3,3,3,3 - 4,3,3,1 - timp.,perc. - hp. - org. - str.   21:00 Bo. Hawkes.

JANIEWICZ, Felix - PANUFNIK, Andrzej
—— DIVERTIMENTO
str.   15:00 Bo. Hawkes.

JANNOCH, Hans-Peter
—— DIVERTIMENTO (FOR CHAMBER ORCH.)
0,2,0,1 - 2,0,0,0 - str.   Tetra.

JANSEN, Pierre
—— UN VOILE QUI S'ILLUMINE DE SOL (REVERIES FOR 24
STRINGED INSTRUMENTS)
str.   23:00 Presser.

JANSON, Alfred
—— CONSTRUCTION AND HYMN (KONSTRUKSJON OG
HYMNE)
3,3,3,3 - 4-5,3,3,1 - timp.,perc. - str.   10:30 G. Schirmer.

—— CRADLE SONG (VUGGESANG) (FOR 48 STRINGS AND
SOPRANO)
str.   5:00 G. Schirmer.

JANSON, Jean Baptiste - OUBRADOUS, Fernand
—— CONCERTO FOR CELLO AND ORCH.
0,2,0,0 - 2,0,0,0 - str.   20:00 Presser.

JANSON, Johannes
—— ASPIRATION (FOR WINDS, PIANO AND PERCUSSION)(1971)
Fleisher.

—— SITA (1972)
2,1,3,1 - 2,1,1,0 - perc.(3),cel. - pf. - str. 9:00 Fleisher.

JANSSEN, Werner
—— FUGUE ON "DIXIE"
3,2,2,2 - 4,3,3,1 - timp.,perc. - str.   8:00 Henmar.

JÁRDÁNYI, Pál
—— BY THE RIVER TISZA
3,2,2,2 - 4,3,3,1 - timp. - hp. - str.   20:00 Bo. Hawkes.

—— CONCERTINO FOR VIOLIN AND STRINGS
str.   12:00 Bo. Hawkes.

—— CONCERTO FOR HARP AND ORCH.
1,1,2,1 - 2,0,0,0 - timp. - hp. - str.   12:00 Bo. Hawkes.

—— DANCE MUSIC
1,1,1,1 - 2,1,0,0 - timp. - str.   7:00 Bo. Hawkes.

—— SINFONIETTA FOR STRINGSS
str.   11:00 Bo. Hawkes.

—— VIVENTE E MORIENTE
*3,*3,2,2 - 4,3,3,1 - timp. - hp. - str.   13:00 Bo. Hawkes.

—— VÖRÖSMARTY-SYMPHONY
3,2,2,2 - 4,3,3,1 - timp.,perc. - hp. - str.   27:00 Bo. Hawkes.

JÄRNEFELT, Armas
—— THE FACE OF THE FATHERLAND (CANTATA) (FOR
SOPRANO, BARITONE, SATB CHORUS AND ORCH.) (1927)
2,2,2,2 - 4,3,3,1 - timp.,perc.,bells - hp.,kantele - str.
25:00 FinnMICtr.

—— SON OF DAY (CANTATA) (FOR BARITONE, MALE CHORUS
AND ORCH.) (1939) (Text: Eino Leino)
3,2,2,2 - 4,3,3,1 - timp. - str.   14:00 FinnMICtr.

—— THE TEMPLE BUILDERS (CANTATA) (FOR SATB CHORUS
AND ORCH.) (1940) (Text: V. A. Koskenniemi)
3,3,3,3 - 4,3,3,1 - timp. - hp. - str.   30:00 FinnMICtr.

JAROCH, Jiří
—— CHILDREN'S SUITE
O.S.A.

—— SCHERZO FOR ORCH.
3,3,3,3 - 4,3,3,1 - perc.,xyl. - hp. - str.   9:00 Bo. Hawkes.

—— SUITE IN G MAJOR
O.S.A.

—— SYMPHONY NO. 1
3,3,3,3 - 4,3,3,1 - timp.,perc. - hp. - org. - str.   40:00 Bo. Hawkes.

—— SYMPHONY NO. 2
2,2,2,2 - 2,2,0,0, - timp. - str.   28:00 Bo. Hawkes.

JARRE, Jean-Michel - WAKHEVITCH, Igor
—— AOR (FOR LARGE ORCH. AND TAPE) (1971)
Salabert.

JARRE, Maurice
—— CANTATES POUR UNE DÉMENTE (FOR ALTO, SATB CHORUS AND ORCH.)

    3,3,3,3 -4,3,cnt.,3,1 - timp.,perc.(7, incl. 4 on timp.),cel. - electric guit. - hp. - acc. - pf. - str.   12:00 Salabert.

—— FÂCHEUSE RENCONTRE (SYMPHONIC SUITE FROM THE BALLET)

    1,1,1,1 - 1,1,1,0 - perc.,cel. - hpsc. - pf. - str.   15:00 F. Colombo.

    or:
    2,2,2,2 - 2,2,3,1 - timp.,perc. - 2 hp. - pf. - str.

—— MALDOROR (BALLET) (WITH SPEAKING VOICE) % (Text: Lautreamont)

    35:00 Salabert.

—— MOBILES (FOR VIOLIN AND ORCH.)

    3,2,2,2 - 4,3,3,1 - timp.,perc. - hp. - str.   14:00 F. Colombo.

—— NOTRE-DAME DE PARIS (BALLET) %

    4,3,4,4 - 4,3,4,1 - timp.,perc.(11) - 3 hp. - pf. - str.   90:00 Salabert.

—— PASSACAGLIA (IN MEMORY OF ARTHUR HONEGGER)

    2,2,2,2 - 2,1,0,0, - timp.,perc. - str.   14:00 F. Colombo.

—— POLYPHONIES CONCERTANTES (FOR PIANO, TRUMPET, PERCUSSION AND ORCH.)

    2,2,2,2 - 2,3,3,0 - perc. - pf. - str.   15:00 F. Colombo.

—— LA RONDE DE NUIT

    2,2,2,2 - 2,2,2,0 - timp.,perc.(3) - hp. - pf. - str.   7:00 Presser.

JARRETT, Jack M.
—— CHORAL SYMPHONY ON AMERICAN POEMS (FOR SATB CHORUS AND ORCH.)

    3,2,3,2 - 4,3,3,1 - timp.,perc. - hp. - str.   17:00 C. Fischer.

—— FOR UNTO US A CHILD IS BORN (CANTATA) (FOR SATB AND ORCH.) (1959)

    0,0,0,0 - 4,3,3,1 - timp.,perc. - pf. - str.   15:00 Composer.

—— SERENADE FOR STRING ORCH. (1957)

    str.   7:00 Fleisher.

—— SINFONIETTE FOR STRING ORCH. (1965) (IN 3 MOVTS.)

    str.   15:00 Composer.

JAUBERT, Maurice
—— BALLADE

    2,2,2,2 - 2,2,2,0 - perc. - hp. - pf. - str.   9:00 Presser.

JELINEK, Hanns
—— THE DANCES AROUND THE STEEL-BLUE ROSE (IN 11 MOVTS.)

    1,0,1,2 sax.,0 - 0,1,1,0 - cel. - hp. - cemb. - str.   27:00 Modern.

—— HEITERE SYMPHONIE, OP. 8 (SYMPHONY NO. 3) (FÜR BLECHBLASINSTRUMENTE UND SCHLAGWERK)

    0,0,0,sax.,0 - 4,3,3,2 - perc.(3)   25:00 Modern.

—— PRELUDIO SOLENNE, OP. 26

    7:00 A.K.M.

—— RAI BUBA, OP. 34 (ETUDE FOR PIANO AND ORCH.)

    3,3,3,3 - 4,3,3,1 - perc.(6) - hp. - pf. - str.   19:00 Modern.

—— SINFONIA CONCERTANTE, OP. 12 (FOR STRING QUARTET AND ORCH.) (IN 3 MOVTS.)

    27:00 A.K.M.

—— SINFONIA CONCERTANTE, OP. 22 (IN 5 MOVTS.)

    26:00 A.K.M.

—— SINFONIA RITMICA (SYMPHONY NO. 2) (FOR LARGE JAZZ BAND AND ORCH.)

    3,*3,*5,*3 - 4,0,0,1 - Large Jazz Band - perc.(4),cel. - hp. - str.   30:00 Modern.

—— SONATA RITMICA (FOR JAZZ BAND AND LARGE ORCH.) (Rev. 1960)

    2,2,2,2 - 3,0,0,0 - Large Jazz Band - perc.(3) - str.   10:00 Modern.

—— SYMPHONY IN D, OP. 2

    31:00 A.K.M.

JENEY, Zoltán
—— ALEF

    Bo. Hawkes.

—— ROUND (FOR CHAMBER ORCH.)

    Bo. Hawkes.

JENKINS, Cyril
—— CALVARY (FOR CHORUS AND ORCH.)

    2,2,2,2 - 2,2,3,0 - timp.,perc. - org. - str.   G. Schirmer.

JENKINS, Joseph Willcox
—— CHARLES COUNTY - OVERTURE

    Bourne.

—— THE FORTIETH PARALLEL (BALLET) % (1953) (IN 3 MOVTS.)

    2(1 alt. with picc.),2,2,2 - 4,2,3,1 - timp.,perc.(3) - pf. - str.   16:00 Composer.

—— ROUNDS AND SOUNDS IN MEMORY OF MESSRS. PURCELL AND BYRD (SUITE FOR MALE CHORUS, STRINGS AND PERCUSSION)

    perc.(6),bells,xyl. - str.   12:00 Composer.

—— SINFONIA CONCERTANTE FOR STRINGS (FOR 2 STRING QUARTETS AND STRING ORCH.) (IN 3 MOVTS.)

    str.   14:30 Composer.

—— SINFONIA IN C (IN 3 MOVTS.)

    *3,2,*4,3 - 4,3,3,1 - timp.,perc.(3) - str.   11:00 Composer.

—— THE VALIANT WOMAN (CANTATA) (Text: Biblical)

    3(3rd alt. with picc.),2,*4,1 - 4,3,3,1 - timp.,perc.(3) - hp. - org. - pf. - str.   22:00 Composer.

JENNY, Albert
—— KONZERT FÜR OBOE UND STREICHORCH.

    ob. - str.   17:00 S.U.I.S.A.

—— SINFONISCHE MUSIK FÜR GROSSES ORCH.

    *3,*3,2,2 - 4,3,3,1 - timp.,perc. - str.   22:00 S.U.I.S.A.

—— TE DEUM (FÜR GEMISCHTEN CHOR, SOLOQUARTETT UND GROSSES ORCH.)

    2,2,2,2 - 4,2,3,1 - timp., - hp. - org.(ad lib.) - str.   22:00 Hug.

JENTSCH, Walter
—— ASPETTI

    2,2,2,2 - 4,3,3,0 - timp.,perc. - hp. - str.   21:00 F. Colombo.

—— BÄURISCHE FESTMUSIK, OP. 17

    1,1,2,1 - 2,2,1,0 - perc. - str.   11:00 Henmar.

—— KONZERT, OP. 33 (FOR CELLO AND ORCH.)

    2,2,2,2 - 2,2,2,0 - timp.,perc. - str.   30:00 Sikorski.

—— SERENADE CONCERTANTE, OP. 8 (REVISED)

    2,2,2,2 - 2,2,0,0 - timp.,perc. - str.   10:00 Henmar.

JENTZSCH, Wilfried
—— MOBILE (FOR 5 ORCHESTRAL GROUPS)

    Hans Gerig.

—— SONATA FOR STRINGS

    str.   13:00 Tetra.

JEPPESEN, Knud
—— LAVE AND JON (OLD DANISH FOLKSONG) (FOR MALE CHORUS AND ORCH.)

    3,2,2,2 - 4,3,2,1 - timp.,perc. - str.   14:00 G. Schirmer.

—— TE DEUM DANICUM (FOR SATB SOLO VOICES, DOUBLE MIXED CHORUS AND ORCH.)

    3,2,2,2 - 6,5,4,1 - timp.,perc. - org. - str.   30:00 G. Schirmer.

JEPPSON, Kerstin
—— TRE PEZZI MINUTI (1972)

    3,2,4,3 - 3,3,3,0 - perc. - hp. - str.   5:00 Fleisher.

—— TRE SENTENZI

    2,2,2,1 - 2,0,0,0 - perc.(2) - str.   Fleisher.

JEREMIÁŠ, Otakar
—— FANTASY ON AN ANCIENT CZECH CHORALE

    3,3,2,2 - 4,3,3,1 - timp.,perc.,cel. - hp. - org. - str.   7:00 Bo. Hawkes.

—— SPRING OVERTURE

    3,3,3,3 - 4,3,3,1 - timp.,perc. - hp. - str.   8:00 Bo. Hawkes.

JERGENSON, Dale
—— THREE DIALOGUES FOR CHAMBER ORCHESTRA (1962)

    1(alt. with picc.),1(alt. with Eng. hn.),2,1 - 2,2,1,0 - timp.,perc.(2) - str.   14:25 Composer.

JERGER, Wilhelm
—— PARTITA, OP. 21

    2(2nd alt. with picc.),2,2,2 - 2,2,0,0 - timp.,perc. - hp. - str.   12:00 Henmar.

JERNBERG, Johan
—— CONCERTO FOR VIOLIN AND ORCH.

    1,1,1,0 - 1,0,0,0 - str.   Fleisher.

JERSILD, Jørgen
—— ALICE IN WONDERLAND ("ALICE IN EVENTYRLAND") (FOR VOICES, CHORUS AND ORCH.) (Text: Fl. Geill)

    27:00 K.O.D.A.

—— THE BIRTHDAY CONCERT

    2,2,2,2 - 3,2,0,1 - timp.,perc. - str.   12:00 G. Schirmer.

—— CONCERTO FOR HARP AND ORCH. (1972)
2,0,2,1 - 2,0,0,0 - timp. - hp. - str.   16:00 G. Schirmer.
—— LITTLE SUITE
str.   12:00 G. Schirmer.
—— PASTORALE
str.   7:00 G. Schirmer.

JEVTIĆ, Ivan
—— CONCERTO FOR PIANO AND ORCH.
3,3,3,3 - 4,3,3,1 - timp.,perc.,vibra. - pf. - str.   22:00 MIC,Zagreb.
—— CONCERTO FOR TRUMPET AND ORCH.
3,2,2,2, - 4,1,2,0 - timp. - pf. - str.   15:00 Presser.
—— SYMPHONY
2(2nd alt. with picc.),2(2nd alt. with Eng.hn.),2(2nd alt. with b.-cl.),2(2nd alt. with c.-bn.) - 4,3,3,1 - timp.,perc. - str.   26:00 MIC,Zagreb.

JEŽ, Jakob
—— CONCERTINO SEMPLICE (FOR VIOLIN AND STRINGS)
str.   6:00 Hans Gerig.
—— NOMOS (FOR CHAMBER ENSEMBLE)
0,0,0,0 - 1,1,1,0 - perc.(2) - hp. - pf. - str.(2,1,1,1)   6:00 Hans Gerig.
—— STROPHES
ob.,cl. - str.   8:00 Hans Gerig.

JEŽEK, Jaroslav
—— SYMPHONIC POEM
3,2,2,2 - 2,2,2,0 - timp.,perc. - str.   14:00 Bo. Hawkes.

JIRÁK, Karel Boleslav
—— SYMPHONIC VARIATIONS, OP. 40 (1940)
Bo. Hawkes.
—— SYMPHONY NO. 2 (1923)
Bo. Hawkes.
—— SYMPHONY NO. 3, OP. 37 (1938) (IN 3 MOVTS.)
Bo. Hawkes.
—— SYMPHONY NO. 5, OP. 60
Bo. Hawkes.
—— YOUTH (SYMPHONIC OVERTURE), OP. 43 (1946)
Bo. Hawkes.

JIRKO, Ivan
—— CONCERTO IN G MAJOR, FOR PIANO AND ORCH.
2,2,2,2 - 4,2,0,0 - timp.,perc. - pf. - str.   24:00 Bo. Hawkes.
—— SYMPHONY
3,2,3,3 - 4,3,3,1 - timp.,perc. - pf. - str.   28:00 Bo. Hawkes.

JOCHUM, Otto
—— FLORIANER SYMPHONIE, OP. 84
Henmar.
—— GOETHE SYMPHONY, OP. 77 (WITH CHORUS IN THE FINALE)
Henmar.

JOHANSEN, Svend Aaqvist
—— KETJAK, OP. 19 (FOR CHAMBER ORCH.)
2,0,0,0 - 1,2,1,1 - str.(0,0,2,2)   10:00 K.O.D.A.
—— SUMMER MUSIC (FOR SOPRANO, ALTO AND CHAMBER ORCH.)
1,1,0,0 - 1,0,0,0, - perc.(2) - str.   17:00 K.O.D.A.
—— UNITE, OP. 20 (1974)
4,2,4,4 sax.,2 - 4,6,3,3 - timp.,perc.(5),bells,glock. - pf.   11:00 K.O.D.A.

JOHANSON, Martin
—— CONCERTO FOR PIANO AND ORCH.
2,2,2,2 - 4,2,3,1 - timp.,perc. - pf. - str.   20:00 S.T.I.M.
—— PANFESTEN
2,2,2,2 - 2,2,0,0 - timp.,perc. - str.   15:00 S.T.I.M.

JOHANSON, Sven-Eric
—— ASTROFONI (THEME, 12 VARIATIONS AND FUGUE)(1974)
str.   15:00 Fleisher.
—— BORTBYTINGARNA (1-ACT SAGA-OPERA) (1959) %
1,1,1,1 - 1,0,0,0 - timp.,xyl. - str.   60:00 S.T.I.M.
—— CONCERT OVERTURE
2,2,2,2 - 2,1,0,0 - str.   5:00 S.T.I.M.
—— CONCERTO DA CAMERA FOR CELLO AND ORCH. (1958)
1,1,1,1 - 2,1,1,0 - str.   18:00 S.T.I.M.
—— CONCERTO FOR HURDY-GURDY AND STRINGS (1972)
Hurdy-gurdy - str.   10:00 Fleisher.

—— CONCERTO FOR ORGAN AND STRINGS
org. - str.   15:00 S.T.I.M.
—— CONCERTO NO. 3 FOR PIANO AND ORCH. (CONCERTO GOTHENBURGESE)(1970)
2,2,2,2 - 4,2,3,1- timp.,perc. - pf. - str.   30:00 Fleisher.
—— FANTYR (1969)
7,7,7,7 - 9,6,6,1 - timp.,perc. - hp. - str.   3:00 Fleisher.
—— FOTIA (1966)
2,2,2,2 - 2,2,1,0 - timp.,perc.(5) - str.   11:30 S.T.I.M.
—— KUNSKAPENS VIN (1-ACT CHAMBER OPERA) % (Text: Gunnar Möllerstedt)
1,0,1,1 - 1,0,0,0 - perc.(1) - hp. - str.   40:00 S.T.I.M.
—— MASKARAD-DIVERTISSEMENT (SUITE FOR CHAMBER ORCH.) (1958)
1,1,1,1 - 0,1,0,0 - hpsc. - str.   10:00 S.T.I.M.
—— PEZZO PASTORALE (1969)
2,2,2,2 - 0,2,2,0 - perc. - str.   3:30 Fleisher.
—— RELIEVO (1969)
str.   3:00 Fleisher.
—— SERENADE FOR LITTLE ORCH.
1,1,1,0 - 1,0,0,0 - str.   S.T.I.M.
—— SINFONIA ELEGIACA (FOR STRINGS)
str.   S.T.I.M.
—— SINFONIA OSTINATA
3,2,2,2 - 4,3,3,1 - timp.,perc. - pf. - str.   16:00 S.T.I.M.
—— SINFONIA PICCOLA (1974)
str.   15:00 Fleisher.
—— SINFONIETTA CONCERTANTE
1,1,1,1 - 0,0,0,0 - str.   20:00 S.T.I.M.
—— SINFONIETTA PASTORELLA (1972)
2,2,2,2 - 4,2,3,1 - timp.,perc.(4) - hp - str.   15:00 Fleisher.
—— SYMPHONY NO. 3 (1956)
3,2,2,2 - 4,3,3,1 - timp. - hp. - str.   30:00 S.T.I.M.
—— TERRA (1968)
3,3,3,3 - 3,4,4,1 - timp.,perc.(2) - hp. - str.   20:00 S.T.I.M.
—— VAGUES (1965)
2,2,2,2 - 4,3,3,1 - timp.,perc.(2) - str.   12:00 S.T.I.M.
—— VARIATIONS AND FUGUE (ON AN ORIGINAL THEME, IN OSTROGOTHIC STYLE)(1974)
2,2,2,2 - 4,2,3,0 - timp.,perc.(5) - str.   15:00 Fleisher.
—— VIENTOS (1967)
4,4,5,4 - 6,4,4,1 - timp.,perc.(5) - str.   7:00 S.T.I.M.

JOHANSSON, Bengt
—— AQUARELLES (SUITE) (1948)
2,2,2,2 - 2,2,0,0 - timp. - hp. - str.   18:00 FinnMICtr.
—— CANTATA HUMANA (FOR 4 PRE-TAPED SPEAKING VOICES, BARITONE, SATB CHORUS AND ORCH.) (1969) (Text:Dag Hammarskjöld)
3,3,3,2 - 4,3,3,1 - timp.,perc.(5) - tape-recorder - pf. - str.   26:00 FinnMICtr.
—— CONCERTO FOR PIANO AND ORCH. (1951)
2,2,2,2 - 4,2,3,1 - timp.,perc. - pf. - str.   25:00 FinnMICtr.
—— EXPRESSIONS (SUITE FOR STRINGS) (1953)
str.   15:00 FinnMICtr.
—— FESTIVITÀ (AN OVERTURE) (1952)
3,3,2,2, - 4,3,3,1 - timp.,perc. - str.   9:00 FinnMICtr.
—— GRADUALE (FOR BARITONE, SSAATTBB CHORUS, ORGAN AND ORCH.) (1968)
0,0,0,0 - 0,2,0,0 - timp. - org. - str.   6:00 Fazer.
—— MISSA SACRA (FOR TENOR, SATB CHORUS AND ORCH.) (1960)
2,3,2,2 - 4,3,3,1 - timp. - str.   43:00 Westerlund.
—— PETITE SUITE DE BALLET (1948)
3,2,2,2 - 4,2,0,0 - timp.,perc.(3) - hp. - str.   9:00 FinnMICtr.
—— REQUIEM (FOR BARITONE, SSAATTBB CHORUS AND ORCH.) (1966)
0,0,0,0 - 4,3,3,1 - timp.(3) - str.   31:00 FinnMICtr.
—— SERENADE FOR STRINGS (1945)
Str   9:00 FinnMICtr.
—— THEME WITH SEVEN VARIATIONS, IN OLDEN STYLE (FOR CELLO AND ORCH.) (1954)
2,0,2,1 - 2,0,0,0 - str.   17:00 FinnMICtr.

JOHANSSON, Björn
—— CONCERTO FOR ORCH.
2,2,2,2 - 2,2,1,0 - timp.,perc.(3) - str.   40:00 S.T.I.M.
—— CONCERTO FOR PIANO AND ORCH. (1965)
3,3,3,2 - 4,3,3,1 - timp.,perc.(4) - pf.- str.   30:00 Fleisher.
—— UNA PASSEGIATA (1964)
2,2,2,2 - 2,2,1,0 - timp. - str.   16:00 Fleisher.
—— PEZZO SINFONICO (1963)
3,3,3,2 - 4,3,3,1 - timp.,perc. - hp. - str.   30:00 Fleisher.

—— PRIMAVERA (1965)
    3,3,3,2 - 4,3,0,1 - timp.,perc.(2) - hp. - str.   14:00 S.T.I.M.
—— SCAPPATE (1972)
    fl. - str.   25:00 Fleisher.
—— SYMPHONY NO. 2
    3,3,3,3 - 4,3,3,0 - timp.,perc.(2) - hp. - str.   45:00 S.T.I.M.
—— SYMPHONY NO. 3
    3,3,3,3 - 4,3,3,1 - timp.,perc.(3),bells,cel. - hp. - pf. - str. S.T.I.M.
—— SYMPHONY NO. 4
    3,3,3,3 - 4,3,3,1 - timp.,perc.(5) - hp. - pf. - str.   33:00 S.T.I.M.
—— SYMPHONY NO. 5
    3,2,2,2 - 4,3,3,1 - timp.,perc.(2) - hp. - str.   35:00 S.T.I.M.

JOHNER, Hans Rudolf
—— DOUBLE FUGUE FOR 2 TRUMPETS AND STRING ORCH.
    2 tpt. - str.   3:00 Mannheimer.
—— TRIPLE FUGUE FOR STRING ORCH.
    str.   4:00 Mannheimer.

JOHNS, Louis Edgar
—— MEDIEVAL SUITE, OP. 46 (IN 4 MOVTS.)
    str.   10:50 C. Press.

JOHNSEN, Hallvard
—— CONCERTO FOR FLUTE AND STRINGS, OP. 25 (IN 1 MOVT.)
    fl. - str.   14:00 T.O.N.O.
—— CONCERTO FOR TRUMPET AND ORCH., OP. 50
    2,2,2,2 - 2,1,0,1 - timp.,perc. - str.   14:00 T.O.N.O.
—— CONCERTO FOR VIOLIN AND CHAMBER ORCH., OP. 28 (IN 1 MOVT.)
    1,0,1,1 - 2,0,0,0 - str.   14:00 T.O.N.O.
—— CONCERTO FOR VIOLIN AND ORCH., OP. 51
    2,2,2,2 - 2,0,1,1 - timp.,perc.,vibra. - str.   14:00 T.O.N.O.
—— FOUR SONGS, OP. 8 (FOR SOPRANO AND CHAMBER ORCH.) (Text: Ivar Aasen)
    0,0,0,0 - 1,1,1,0 - str.   12:00 T.O.N.O.
—— KROSSPÅSKE (EASTER CANTATA), OP. 39 (FOR BARITONE, MIXED CHORUS AND ORCH.) (Text: Anders Hovden)
    3,2,2,2 - 4,3,3,1 - timp.,perc. - str.   35:00 T.O.N.O.
—— DER LIGGER ET LAND (CANTATA) (FOR TENOR, MALE CHORUS AND ORCH.) (1967) (Text: Bjørnstjerne Bjørnson)
    2,2,2,2 - 4,2,2,1 - timp.,perc. - str.   T.O.N.O.
—— NORSK NATUR (NORWEGIAN NATURE), OP. 21 (FOR MIXED CHORUS AND ORCH.) (1953) (Text: Bjørnstjerne Bjørnson)
    2,2,2,2 - 4,0,0,0 - timp.,perc. - str.   12:00 T.O.N.O.
—— OVERTURA FESTIVO
    2,2,2,2 - 4,3,3,1 - timp.,perc. - str.   8:30 T.O.N.O.
—— SERENADE
    1,1,2,1 - 2,0,0,0 - str.   15:00 T.O.N.O.
—— SINFONIA, OP. 21
    2,2,2,2 - 4,2,3,0 - timp.,perc. - str.   16:00 T.O.N.O.
—— SUITE FOR CHAMBER ORCH. (NORWEGIAN SUITE), OP. 20-A (IN 4 MOVTS.)
    1,1,1,1 - 0,0,0,0 - str.   16:00 T.O.N.O.
—— SYMPHONY NO. 1, OP. 17 (IN 3 MOVTS.)
    2,2,3,2 - 4,2,3,0 - timp.,perc. - str.   28:00 T.O.N.O.
—— SYMPHONY NO. 2 ("PASTORALE"), OP. 22 (1954) (IN 1 MOVT.)
    2,2,2,2 - 4,2,2,1 - timp.,perc. - hp. - str.   18:00 T.O.N.O.
—— SYMPHONY NO. 3, OP. 26 (IN 1 MOVT.)
    2,2,2,2 - 4,2,3,1 - timp.,perc. - str.   20:00 T.O.N.O.
—— SYMPHONY NO. 4, OP. 29 (IN 1 MOVT.)
    3,2,2,2 - 4,3,3,1 - timp.,perc.,cel. - str.   20:00 T.O.N.O.
—— SYMPHONY NO. 5, OP. 32 (IN 1 MOVT.)
    2,2,2,2 - 4,3,3,1 - timp.,perc. - str.   18:00 T.O.N.O.
—— SYMPHONY NO. 6, OP. 35 (IN 1 MOVT.)
    3,2,2,2 - 4,3,3,1 - timp.,perc.,cel. - str.   21:00 T.O.N.O.
—— SYMPHONY NO. 7, OP. 38 (IN 3 MOVTS.)
    3,2,2,2 - 4,3,3,1 - timp.,perc.,cel. - str.   31:00 T.O.N.O.
—— SYMPHONY NO. 8, OP. 42 (1964) (IN 1 MOVT.)
    3,2,2,2 - 4,3,3,1 - timp.,perc. - str.   21:00 T.O.N.O.
—— SYMPHONY NO. 9, OP. 53 (IN 3 MOVTS.)
    2,2,2,2 - 4,3,2,3 - timp.,perc. - str.   38:00 T.O.N.O.

JOHNSON, Carl
—— THE MUNICH PAUL KLEE (SUITE) (IN 3 MOVTS.)
    1,1,1,1 - 1,1,1,0 - perc.(1),xyl. - str.   10:00 G.E.M.A.

JOHNSON, Hall
—— SPIRITUAL MOODS (BASED ON TRADITIONAL NEGRO MELODIES) (FOR MALE CHORUS AND ORCH.)
    2(2nd alt. with picc.),*3,2,*3 - 4,2,2,1 - timp.,perc.(3),bells,cel.,glock. - hp. - str.   25:00 Composer.

JOHNSON, Harold M.
—— MOWIS, OP. 19
    C. Fischer.
—— PASSACAGLIA AND FUGHETTA, OP. 27
    Belwin.
—— PHAON, OP. 18 (MINIATURE SYMPHONIC POEM)
    C. Fischer.
—— ROMANTIC OVERTURE TO A SCOTCH TALE, OP. 37
    C. Fischer.

JOHNSON, Harriet
—— CHUGGY AND THE BLUE CABOOSE (FOR NARRATOR AND ORCH.)
    3,3,3,3 - 2,2,2,1 - timp.,perc. - hp. - str.   16:00 C. Fischer.

JOHNSON, Horace
—— MUSIC FOR STRINGS
    str.   11:00 C. Fischer.
—— STREETS OF FLORENCE (SUITE) (IN 3 MOVTS.)
    2(1 alt. with picc.),*3,2,2 - 4,2,3,0 - timp.,perc.(4),glock.,cdl. - hp. - pf. - str.   10:00 C. Fischer.

JOHNSON, Hunter
—— CONCERTO FOR PIANO AND CHAMBER ORCH.
    1. Maestoso; Allegro moderato - Maestoso; 2. Allegro-Allegro molto
    2,0,2,0 - 0,0,0,0 - pf. - str.   20:00 Composer.
—— ELEGY FOR CLARINET AND STRINGS
    cl. - str.   10:00 Composer.
—— MUSIC FOR STRINGS
    str.   6:30 Galaxy.
—— NORTH STATE (SUITE) (COMMEMORATING THE 1663 CAROLINA CHARTER) (IN 3 MOVTS.)
    3(3rd alt. with picc.),2,*3,2 - 4,3,3,1 - timp.,perc.,xyl. - hp. - str.   15:00 Galaxy.
—— PAST THE EVENING SUN
    2(2nd alt. with picc.),2,2,2 - 4,2,2,0 - timp.,perc.(2),cel. - hp. - str.   9:00 Galaxy.
—— SUITE FROM "LETTER TO THE WORLD"
    1,1,1,1 - 1,0,0,0 - str.   23:00 Galaxy.
    or:
    2,2,2,2 - 2,2,2,0 - timp.,perc. - pf. - str.

JOHNSON, Laurie
—— SYNTHESIS (FOR JAZZ BAND AND SYMPHONY ORCH.)
    3,3,3,4 sax.,3 - 5,8,5,1 - timp.,perc. - guit. - str.   31:00 Novello.

JOHNSON, R. Sherlaw
—— FUGAL STRUCTURES
    2,2,2,2 - 2,2,2,0 - timp.,perc. - str.   20:00 P.R.S.
—— IMPROVISATION IV (TWO ORCHESTRAL PIECES)
    2,2,2,2 - 2,2,3,1 - perc. - str.   10:00 P.R.S.
—— TRIKA (FOR PIANO AND SMALL ORCH.)
    1,1,2,1 - 1,1,0,0 - perc. - pf. - str.   15:00 P.R.S.

JOHNSON, Roger
—— THREE ORCHESTRA PIECES (1971)
    2(2nd alt. with picc.), 2,3(2nd alt. with E♭cl.,3rd alt. with b.-cl.),2 - 4,2,2,1 - timp.,perc.(3),bells,glock.,mar.,vibra.,xyl. - hp. - pf. - str.   13:00 C. Fischer.

JOHNSTON, Ben, Jr.
—— PASSACAGLIA AND EPILOGUE (FROM "ST. JOAN") 1960
    2(1 atl. with picc.),2,2,2 - 3,3,3,1 - timp.,perc.(2),cel.,mar. - hp. - pf. - str.   10:00 Composer.
—— QUINTET FOR GROUPS (1966)
    1(alt. with picc.),1,1,1 alto sax.(alt. with bar. sax.),1, - 3,3,3,1 - timp.,perc.(4) - 2 hp. - 2 pf. - str.   15:00 Composer.

JOHNSTON, Jack R.
—— BUNKER HILL FANTASY
    *3,2,2,2 - 4,3,2,1 - perc. - pf. - str.   4:25 EV.
—— CONCERT MASS (1966)
    25:00 Composer.
—— INVOCATION (1965)
    1,1,1,1 - 2,2,2,1 - str.   6:00 Composer.

—— NOCTURNE (1967)
    1,1,1,1 - 1,0,0,0 - hp. - str.(no d.-b.)   7:30 CMP.
—— PASTORALE AND FUGUE (FOR STRINGS)
    str.   EV.
—— PASTORALE AND FUGUE (1967)
    str.   3:00 EV.
—— SYMPHONIC ELEGY (1966)
     15:00 CMP.

JOHNSTONE, Maurice
—— BANNERS (CELEBRATION OVERTURE)
     6:30 Lengnick.
—— DOVER BEACH (FOR BARITONE AND ORCH.)
    2,2,2,2 - 4,3,2,0 - timp.,perc. - hp. - str.   11:00 Lengnick.
—— THE OAK AND THE ASH (IMPROVISATIONS ON A NORTH COUNTRY SONG)
    3(3rd alt. with picc.),2(2nd alt. with Eng. hn.),2,alto sax.,3 - 4,2,3,1 - timp.,perc. - hp. - str.   18:00 Lengnick.
—— TARN HOWS (CUMBRIAN RHAPSODY)
     15:00 Lengnick.

JOKINEN, Erkki
—— CONCERTO FOR CELLO AND ORCH. (1971)
    2,2,2,2 - 4,2,2,0 - timp.,perc.(3) - str.   20:00 FinnMICtr.

JOKL, George
—— VIER IMPRESSIONEN
    str.   25:00 A.K.M.

JOLAS, Betsy
—— D'UN OPÉRA DE VOYAGE (FOR 22 INSTRUMENTS)
    2,1,4,1 - 1,1,1,0 - perc.(6) - hp. - str.(1,1,1,1)   9:00 Presser.
—— J.D.E. (FOR 14 INSTRUMENTS)
    1,1,2,1 - 1,1,1,0 - hp. - str.(2,1,1,1)   9:00 Presser.
—— MOTET II (FOR SATB CHORUS AND ORCH.)
    2 ob., 2 Eng.hn.,1 bar.ob.,2 bn. - 0,2,3,0 - 6 vla., 4 d.-b.   11:00 Presser.
—— MUSIQUE D'HIVER (FOR ORGAN AND SMALL ORCH.)
    1,1,2,1 - 1,1,1,0 - perc.(3) - hp. - org. - 6 vla.,6 d.-b.   16:00 Presser.
—— POINTS D'AUBE (FOR VIOLA AND 13 WINDS)
    2,0,4,0 - 2,3,3,0 - vla.   12:00 Presser.
—— QUATRE PLAGES (FOR STRINGS)
    str.   7:00 Presser.
—— TROIS RENCONTRES (FOR STRING TRIO AND ORCHESTRA)
    4,4,4,0 - 4,3,3,1 - timp.,perc.(5) - hp. -pf.(alt. with cel.) - str.   28:00 Presser.
—— WELL MET (FOR 12 STRINGS)
    str.   15:00 Presser.

JOLIVET, André
—— ADAGIO FOR STRINGS (1960)
    str.   7:00 Presser.
—— LES AMANTS MAGNIFIQUES (VARIATIONS ON THEMES OF LULLY)
    2,2,0,2 - 2,2,0,0 - timp.,perc. - hp. - hpsc.(pf.) - str.   12:00 Bo. Hawkes.
—— ANDANTE FOR STRINGS
    str.   6:30 Mercury.
—— ARIADNE (BALLET) %
     30:00 Bo. Hawkes.
—— CINQ DANSES RITUELLES
    2,1 alto fl.,*3,*3,*3 - 4,3,3,1 - timp.,perc.(3),cel. - 2 hp. - pf. - str.   25:00 EV.
—— LE COEUR DE LA MATIÈRE
    3,3,3,3 - 4,3,3,1 - timp.,perc. - 2 hp. - str.   30:00 Presser.
—— CONCERTINO FOR TRUMPET AND STRINGS
    tpt. - str.   10:30 EV.
—— CONCERTO FOR BASSOON AND STRINGS
    bn. - str.   13:00 Mercury.
—— CONCERTO FOR CELLO AND ORCH.
    2,2,2,2 - 2,1,1,1 - timp.,perc.(3) - hp. - str.   22:00 Bo. Hawkes.
—— CONCERTO FOR FLUTE AND STRINGS
    Fl - str.   13:00 Mercury.
—— CONCERTO FOR HARP AND ORCH.
    1,1,1,1 - 2,1,0,0 - hp. - str.   17:00 Presser.
—— CONCERTO FOR ONDES MARTENOT AND ORCH.
    *3,*3,2,sax.,2 - 2,3,2,1 - timp.,perc.(2),bells,cel.,vibra.xyl. - hp. - ondes martenot, - str.   22:00 Mercury.
—— CONCERTO FOR PERCUSSION AND ORCH.
    2,2(1 alt. with Eng.hn.),2,1 alto sax.,2 - 2,2,2,1 - perc. - pf. - str.   17:00 Salabert.

—— CONCERTO FOR PIANO AND ORCH.
    3,*2,2,sax.,2 - 2,3,2,1 - timp.,perc.(3).,bells,cel.,vibra.,xyl. - hp. - pf. - str.   23:30 Mercury.
—— CONCERTO FOR VIOLIN AND ORCH.
    2,2,2,2 - 2,2,2,0 - timp.,perc.(3),cel.,vibra. - hp. - str.   30:00 Presser.
—— CONCERTO NO. 2 FOR CELLO, STRING QUINTET AND STRING ORCH.
    str.   21:00 Presser.
—— CONCERTO NO. 2 FOR TRUMPET AND ORCH.
    2,*2,2,sax.,*1 - 1,0,1,0 - perc.(2) - hp. - pf. - str.   12:00 Mercury.
—— DOLORES (1-ACT COMIC OPERA) %
    2,2,2,2 - 2,2,2,1 - timp.,perc.(3) - hp. - str.   60:00 Salabert.
—— LA FLÈCHE DU TEMPS
    str.   Presser.
—— GRAVE AND GIGUE (FOR STRINGS)
    str.   Baron.
—— MADRIGAL (FOR SATB CHORUS AND ORCH.)
    1,1,0,1 - 0,0,0,0 - str.   12;00 Bo. Hawkes.
—— OVERTURE TO "DOLORES"
    2,2,2,2 - 2,2,2,1 - timp.,perc.(2) - hp. - str.   15:00 Salabert.
—— POÈMES INTIMES (FOR MEDIUM VOICE AND CHAMBER ORCH.)
    1,1,1,1 alto sax.,1 - 0,0,0,0 - perc.,cel.,vibra. - hp. - str.   13:00 Presser.
—— SUITE DELPHIQUE (FOR CHAMBER ORCH.)
    1(alt. with picc.),1(alt. with Eng.hn.),1,0 - 2,1,1,0 - ondes Martenot - timp.,perc. - hp.   19:00 Mills.
—— SUITE FROM THE BALLET "ARIADNE"
    2,1,2,1 - 2,1,1,0 - timp.,perc. - pf. - str.   19:00 Bo. Hawkes.
—— SUITE TRANSOCÉANE
    *2,2,2,sax.,2 - 4,2,3,1 - timp.,perc. - hp. - pf. - str.   23:00 Mercury.
—— SYMPHONIE DE DANSES
    2,2,2,2 - 2,2,2,2 - perc. - hp. - pf. - str.   30:00 EV.
—— SYMPHONY FOR STRINGS
    str.   23:00 Bo. Hawkes.
—— SYMPHONY NO. 1
    *3,*3,*3,3 - 4,3,3,1 - timp. - hp. - str.   24:00 Presser.
—— SYMPHONY NO. 2
    3,3,3,3 - 4,3,3,1 - perc.(4) - str.   27:00 Presser.
—— SYMPHONY NO. 3
    3,3,3,alto sax.,ten. sax.,3 - 4,3,3,1 - perc. - str.   25:00 Bo. Hawkes.
—— THREE INTERLUDES (FROM "LA VÉRITÉ DE JEANNE")
    3,3,3,3 - 4,4,3,1 - timp.,perc. - hp. - str.   21:00 Salabert.
—— TWELVE INVENTIONS FOR TWELVE INSTRUMENTS
    1,1,1,1 - 1,1,1,0 - str.(2,1,1,1)   12:00 Presser.
—— LA VÉRITÉ DE JEANNE (ORATORIO)
    3,3,3,3 - 4,4,3,1 - timp.,perc.(3) - hp. - str.   80:00 Salabert.
—— YING-YANG
    str.   Presser.

JOLIVET, André - KELKEL, Manfred
—— TROIS CHANSONS DE MENESTRELS (SONG CYCLE) (FOR MEDIUM VOICE AND ORCH.)
    1,1,1,1 - 2,0,0,0 - timp.,perc. - hp. - str.   10:00 Presser.

JOLY, Suzanne
—— RUPESTRE
    2,2,2,2 - 2,2,2,0 - timp.,perc.(4),cel. - hp. - pf. - str.   16:00 Presser.

JOMMELLI, Niccolo - PICCIOLI, Givseppe
—— CIACONNA (FOR CHAMBER ORCH.)
    0,2,0,0 - 2,1,0,0 - str.   5:00 Bo. Hawkes.

JONES, Charles
—— ALLEGORY FOR ORCHESTRA (1970)
    2(2nd alt. with picc.),2,*3,*3 - 3,2,3,1 - timp.,perc. - str.   10:00 Composer.
—— CASSATION FOR ORCH. (IN 4 MOVTS.)
    2(1 alt. with picc.),*3,*3,*3 - 4,3,3,1 - timp.,perc.(2) - str.   13:00 Composer.
—— CONCERTO FOR 4 VIOLINS AND ORCH. (IN 3 MOVTS.)
    *2,2,*3,2 - 2,2,0,0 - timp.,perc.(2) - str.   20:00 Composer.
—— FIVE MELODIES FOR ORCHESTRA (1945)
    2,*3,*3,*3 - 4,3,3,1 - timp.,perc. - str.   15:00 Piedmont.
—— HYMN FOR ORCHESTRA
    2(1 alt. with picc.),2,*3,2 - 4,3,3,1 - timp.,perc.(2) - str.   10:00 Composer.
—— INTRODUCTION AND RONDO (FOR STRINGS)
    str.   11:45 Henmar.
—— LITTLE SYMPHONY FOR THE NEW YEAR (IN 3 MOVTS.)
    1(alt. with picc.),1,1,1 - 0,3,2,0 - timp.,perc.(2) - pf. - str.   3:45 Beekman.

—— MASQUE (FOR SPEAKER AND 12 INSTRUMENTS) 1968
(Text: Alexander Pope)
 *2,1,1 E♭cl.,*1,1 - 0,1,0,0 - perc.(2) - str.   13:45 Composer.
—— OVERTURE
 *3,2,*3,*3 - 4,3,3,1 - timp.,perc.(2) - str.   4:30 Leeds.
—— PIERS THE PLOWMAN (CANTATA) (FOR TENOR, CHORUS
AND ORCH.) (Text: William Langland, ca. 1377 A.D.)
 1,1,0,1 - 1,1,0,0 - perc.(1) - str.   25:00 Composer.
—— SUITE AFTER A NOTEBOOK OF 1762 (FOR SOPRANO OR
TENOR VOICE AND ORCH.) (1958) (Texts: 18th Century
German)
 1(alt. with picc.),1,0,0 - 0,0,0,0 - str.   11:00 Composer.
—— SUITE FOR SMALL ORCH. (IN 4 MOVTS.)
 1,1,1,1 - 2,1,0,0 - str.   12:30 Composer.
—— SUITE FOR STRINGS
 1. Allegro - Adagio; 2. Allegro agerto
 str.   14:00 Composer.
—— SYMPHONY
 1. Maestoso - Allegro; 2. Allegro moderato
 2(1 alt. with picc.),*3,*3,*3 - 4,3,3,1 - timp. - pf. - str.
   13:00 Henmar.
—— SYMPHONY IN 5 SHORT MOVEMENTS (PASTORAL
SYMPHONY) (1965)
 2(2nd alt. with picc.),2,*3,2 - 3,2,3,1 - timp.,perc.(3),xyl. - str.
   12:02 Composer.
—— SYMPHONY NO. 2 (1957)
 2(2nd alt. with picc.),2,2,2 - 2,3,3,1 - timp.,perc. - str.
   16:00 Composer.
—— SYMPHONY NO. 3 (1962) (IN 3 MOVTS.)
 *2,2,*3,2 - 3,3,3,1 - timp.,perc.(3) - str.   18:00 Composer.

JONES, Daniel
—— ADAR RHIANNON (1961)
 2,1,2,1 - 2,1,0,0 - timp. - hp. - str.   6:00 P.R.S.
—— CAPRICCIO FOR FLUTE, HARP AND STRINGS (1965)
 fl. - hp. - str.   9:00 P.R.S.
—— CONCERT OVERTURE NO. 2 (1951)
 3,3,3,3 - 4,3,3,1 - timp.,perc.(3),cel. - hp. - str.   11:00 P.R.S.
—— CONCERTO FOR VIOLIN AND ORCH. (1966)
 2,2,2,2 - 4,2,3,0 - timp.,perc.(3),cel. - hp. - str.   25:00 P.R.S.
—— CYSTUDDIAU BRANWEN (1938)
 3,3,3,3 - 4,3,3,1 - timp.,perc.(3) - hp. - str.   15:00 P.R.S.
—— SCENES FROM THE MABINOGION (1946)
 3,3,3,3 - 6,3,3,1 - timp.,perc.(3) - hp. - str.   25:00 P.R.S.
—— SYMPHONY NO. 4 (IN MEMORY OF DYLAN THOMAS)
   40:00 P.R.S.
—— SYMPHONY NO. 5 (1958)
 3,2,3,2 - 4,2,3,0 - timp.,perc.(3) - str.   47:00 P.R.S.
—— SYMPHONY NO. 6 (1964)
 3,3,3,3 - 4,3,3,0 - timp.,perc.(3) - str.   30:00 P.R.S.

JONES, (Herbert) Kelsey
—— ADAGIO, PRESTO AND FUGUE (1973) (FOR STRING
QUARTET AND STRING ORCH.)
 str.   18:00 CanMusCtr.
—— CHRISTMAS OVERTURE
   15:00 C.A.P.A.C.
—— JACK AND THE BEANSTALK (FOR CHORUS AND ORCH.)
   13:00 C.A.P.A.C.
—— MIRAMICHI BALLAD (SUITE)
   14:00 Bo. Hawkes.
—— SONGS OF INNOCENCE (FOR SOPRANO AND CHAMBER
ORCH.)
 2,1,1,0 - 0,1,0,0 - pf. - str.   15:45 C.A.P.A.C.
—— SUITE FOR FLUTE AND STRINGS (1954)
 fl. - str.   20:00 CanMusCtr.

JONES, J. Randolph
—— NIGHT SCENE
   11:00 Fox.
—— SYMPHONY NO. 1 IN D♭ MAJOR ("SOUTHERN SCENES")
 3,3,3,2 - 4,2,3,1 - timp.,perc. - hp. - str.   21:30 Fox.

JONES, Kenneth
—— DR. FAUSTUS, OP. 32
 3,3,3,3 - 4,3,3,1 - timp. - perc. - str.   30:00 P.R.S.

JONES, Lewis
—— KING LEAR (SYMPHONIC POEM) (WITH BARITONE)
 2,2,2,2 - 4,3,3,1 - timp. - str.   20:00 P.R.S.
—— MACBETH (SYMPHONIC POEM) (WITH BARITONE)
 2,2,2,2 - 4,2,3,1 - timp. - str.   25:00 P.R.S.

—— SINFONIETTA (1964)
 2,2,2,0 - 2,0,0,0 - timp. - str.   15:00 P.R.S.
—— SYMPHONY ("THE TITANIC") (1957)
 2,2,2,2 - 4,2,3,1 - timp. - str.   40:00 P.R.S.
—— VARIATIONS ("MEDITATIONS ON MURDER") (1965)
 3,3,3,3 - 4,3,3,1 - timp.,perc. - hp. - str.   20:00 P.R.S.
—— VARIATIONS ("THE SEVEN AGES OF MAN") (1964)
 2,2,2,2 - 4,2,3,1 - timp. - str.   20:00 P.R.S.

JONES, Robert W.
—— COMEDY OVERTURE 1960
 *3,2,2,2 - 2,2,2,2 - timp.,perc.(3),xyl. - pf. - str.   6:00 Composer.
—— CONCERTINO FOR STRING ORCH. (1970)
 str.   13:00 Composer.
—— CONCERTO FOR CELLO AND ORCH. (1963) (IN 3 MOVTS.)
 2(2nd alt. with picc.),2,2,2 - 2,0,0,0 - timp.,perc.(3),xyl. - str.
   16:00 Composer.
—— THE GARDEN (OPERA) % (1962) (Text: Joan Woodbury
Wilcoxon)
 1(alt. with alto recorder),1,1,1 - 1,0,0,0 - cel. - hp. - org.(ad lib.) -
 pf. - str.   35:00 Composer.
—— HYMN OF PEACE (FOR SSA CHORUS AND ORCH.) (1966)
(Text: Donald Borenstein)
 2,1,*3,1 - 2,2,2,0 - timp.,perc.(4),bells - str.   10:00 Heritage.
—— NOCTURNE (FOR ALTO FLUTE AND SMALL ORCH.) 1970
 alto fl. - perc.,vibra. - str.   5:30 Composer.
—— PRELUDE AND FUGUE (1965)
 str.   9:00 Composer.
—— SERENADE FOR STRING ORCH. (1967)
 str.   6:00 CMP.
—— THE JUGGLER (MUSIC FOR A BALLET) (1960)
 *3,2,2,2 - 4,3,3,1 - timp.,perc.(3),bells - pf. - str.   14:00 Composer.
—— TO MEN OF GOOD WILL (FOR MIXED CHORUS AND
ORCH.) (1965) (Text: Biblical)
 *3,2,*3,1 - 4,3,3,1 - timp.,perc.(3) - org.(ad lib.) - str.
   7:00 Bourne.

JONES, Roland W.
—— AUTUMN (FANTASY) (TRIO FOR STRING ORCH.) (1969)
 str.(no d.-b.)   Composer.
—— PRELUDE AND SYMPHONY IN D MINOR (1954)
 2,2,2,2 - 3,2,2,0 - str.   Composer.

JONES, Samuel
—— CHACONNE AND BURLESQUE (1960)
 3(3rd alt. with picc.),*3,3(3rd alt. with b.-cl.),*3 - 4,3,3,1 -
 timp.,perc.(4),cel.,glock.,xyl. - hp. - pf. - str.   12:00 C. Fischer.
—— ELEGY FOR STRINGS (1963)
 str.   4:00 Composer.
—— FUGUE AND FINALE ON A THEME OF DAN EMMETT
 2 picc.,1,0,0,0 - 0,1 bass tpt.(or bar.),0,0 - d.-b.'s   2:00 Composer.
—— IN RETROSPECT (1959)
 2(2nd alt. with picc.),2(2nd alt. with Eng. hn.),2,2 - 2,2,1,0 -
 timp.,glock. - str.   C. Fischer.
—— LET US NOW PRAISE FAMOUS MEN
 8(4 off-stage)3,3,3 - 4,3,3,1 - timp.,perc. - hp. - str.
   16:00 C. Fischer.
—— MEDITATION AND SCHERZO (1958)
 *3,*3,*3,*3 - 4,3,3,1 - timp.,perc.(3),glock.,xyl. - hp. - pf. - str.
   12:00 Fleisher.
—— OVERTURE FOR A CITY (1964)
 3(3rd alt. with picc.),*3,3(3rd alt. with b.-cl.),*3 - 4,3,3,1 -
 timp.,perc.(4),glock.,xyl. - hp. - str.   8:30 C. Fischer.
—— SYMPHONY NO. 1 (1960) (IN 4 MOVTS.)
 3(3rd alt. with picc.),*3,3(3rd alt. with b.-cl.),*3 - 4,3,3,1 -
 timp.,perc.(4),cel.,glock.,xyl. - hp. - pf. - str.   27:00 C. Fischer.

JONES, Stephen O.
—— OVERTURE
 *2,1,2,1 - 2,2,2,0 - timp.,perc. - hp. - pf. - str.   3:00 Composer.
—— RONDO APPASIONATA
 *2,1,2,1 - 2,2,1,0 - timp.,perc.(2) - hp. - pf. - str.   8:00 Composer.
—— RONDO À LA BRÈVE
 *2,2,2,2 - 4,3,3,1 - timp.,perc.(2) - hp. - pf. - str.   5:00 Composer.
—— STRING SONATA
 str.   10:00 Composer.

JONG, Marinus de
—— APHORISTISCHE TRYPTIEK, OP. 82
 2,2,2,2 - 2,2,1,0 - timp.,perc. - hp.(or pf.) - str.   11:00 H. Elkan.
—— CONCERTO FOR BASSOON AND ORCH., OP. 146 (1966) (IN
3 MOVTS.)
 2,2,2,3 - 2,2,1,0 - timp.,perc. - str.   16:00 H. Elkan.

—— CONCERTO FOR CELLO AND ORCH., OP. 60 (IN 3 MOVTS.)
2,2,2,2 - 2,2,1,0 - timp.,perc. - str.   25:00 H. Elkan.
—— CONCERTO FOR CLARINET AND ORCH., OP. 148 (1966) (IN 2 MOVTS.)
2,3,2,2 - 2,2,2,0 - timp.,perc. - str.   16:00 H. Elkan.
—— CONCERTO FOR FLUTE AND ORCH., OP. 147 (1967)
3,2,2,2 - 2,2,1,0 - timp.,perc. - str.   16:00 H. Elkan.
—— CONCERTO FOR HORN AND ORCH., OP. 145 (1966) (IN 3 MOVTS.)
2,2,2,2 - 3,2,1,0 - timp.,perc. - str.   16:00 H. Elkan.
—— CONCERTO FOR OBOE AND ORCH., OP. 144(1966) (IN 3 MOVTS.)
2,3,2,2 - 2,2,1,0 - timp.,perc. - str.   16:00 H. Elkan.
—— CONCERTO FOR ORGAN AND ORCH., OP. 168 (1974)
H. Elkan.
—— CONCERTO FOR VIOLIN AND ORCH., OP. 103 (1954)
3,3,3,2 - 4,3,3,0 - timp.,perc. - hp. - str.   23:00 H. Elkan.
—— CONCERTO NO. 1 FOR PIANO AND ORCH., OP. 21 (1924)
2,2,2,2 - 4,2,0,0 - timp. - pf. - str.   21:00 H. Elkan.
—— CONCERTO NO. 2 FOR PIANO AND ORCH., OP. 80 (1952)
3,3,2,2 - 4,3,3,1 - timp.,perc.,cel.,vibra. - hp. - pf. - str.   21:00 H. Elkan.
—— CONCERTO NO. 3 FOR PIANO AND ORCH., OP. 105 (1956)
3,3,3,2 - 4,3,3,1 - timp.,perc. - pf. - str.   18:00 H. Elkan.
—— GRIEKSE RHAPSODIE, OP. 75
2,2,2,2 - 2,2,1,0 - timp.,perc.,glock. - pf.(alt. with cel.) - str.   8:00 H. Elkan.
—— HEIDESTEMMINGEN (IMPRESSIONS DE BRUYÉRE), OP. 39
3,2,2,2 - 4,2,2,0 - timp.,perc.,cel.,glock. - hp. - str.   12:00 H. Elkan.
—— HIAWATHA (SYMPHONIC POEM), OP. 36
3,3,3,3 - 4,3,3,1 - timp.,perc.,cel.,glock. - hp. - str.   12:00 H. Elkan.
—— ID
1,1,1,1 - 0,2,1,0 - timp.,perc.,vibra. - pf. - str.   12:00 H. Elkan.
—— DE KLEINE HAVEN (BALLET), OP. 73 %
2,2,2,2 - 2,2,1,0 - timp.,perc. - pf.(or cel.,or hp.) - str.   9:00 H. Elkan.
—— DE KRINGLOOP (BALLET), OP. 101 %
2,2,2,2 - 2,2,1,0 - timp.,perc.,mar. - pf.(alt. with cel.) - str.   12:00 H. Elkan.
—— SUITE, OP. 79 (IN FORM OF VARIATIONS ON THE SLAVIC MELODY "BOUBLITSCHKY")
2,2,2,2 - 2,2,1,0 - timp.,perc.,glock. - hp. - pf. (alt. with cel.)   12:00 H. Elkan.
—— SYMPHONY NO. 3, OP. 171 (1976)
60:00 H. Elkan.
—— SYMPHONY, OP. 35 (IN 4 MOVTS.)
3,3,2,2 - 4,3,3,1 - timp.,perc.,bells,glock. - hp. - str.   32:00 H. Elkan.
—— VLAAMSE RHAPSODIE NO. 1, OP. 34
3,3,2,2 - 4,3,3,1 - timp.,perc. - hp. - str.   11:00 H. Elkan.
—— VLAAMSE RHAPSODIE NO. 2, OP. 160 (1971)
3,2,2,2 - 4,3,3,1 - timp.,perc. - str.   10:00 H. Elkan.
—— VLAAMSE RHAPSODIE NO. 3, OP. 161 (1971) (FOR PIANO AND ORCH.)
2,2,2,2 - 2,2,1,0 - timp.,perc. - pf. - str.   18:00 H. Elkan.
—— DE VROUWEN VAN ZALONGO, OP. 71 (BALLET, WITH OPTIONAL WOMEN'S CHORUS) %
2,2,2,2 - 2,2,1,0 - timp.,perc. - hp.(or pf.) - str.   9:00 H. Elkan.

JONGEN, Joseph
—— ALLELUIA, OP. 112 (FOR ORGAN AND ORCH.) (1940)
3,3,3,2 - 4,3,3,1 - timp. - org. - str.   7:00 H. Elkan.
—— BALLADE, OP. 136 (HOMAGE TO FRÉDÉRIC CHOPIN) (1949)
3,3,3,2 - 4,3,3,1 - timp.,perc.,cel. - hp. - str.   12:00 H. Elkan.
—— CLAIR DE LUNE ET SOLEIL À MIDI, OP. 33
3,3,2,3 - 4,3,3,1 - timp.,perc.,glock. - hp. - str.   18:00 EV.
—— CONCERTINO FOR TRUMPET AND ORCH., OP. 41 (1913)
2,2,2,2 - 2,1,0-3,0 - str.   10:00 H. Elkan.
—— CONCERTO FOR CELLO AND ORCH., OP. 18
3,2,2,2 - 4,3,3,1 - timp.,perc.(4) - hp. - str.   35:00 EV.
—— CONCERTO FOR HARP AND ORCH., OP. 129 (1944)
2,2,2,2 - 2,0,0,0 - perc.,cel. - hp. - str.   20:00 CBDM.
—— CONCERTO FOR PIANO AND ORCH., OP. 127 (1943)
2,2,2,2 - 4,3,3,0 - timp.,perc.,cel. - pf. - str.   30:00 EV.
—— CONCERTO FOR VIOLIN AND ORCH., OP. 17
2,2,2,2 - 4,2,3,0 - timp. - str.   31:00 EV.
—— DEUX RONDES WALLONNES, OP. 40 (1912)
14:00 EV.
RONDE NO. 1
2,2,2,2 - 2,0,0,0 - hp. - str.

RONDE NO. 2
3,2,2,2 - 4,3,3,1 - timp.,perc.,glock. - hp. - str.
—— EPITHALAME ET SCHERZO, OP. 49 (FOR 3 VIOLINS AND ORCH.) (1917)
2,2,2,2 - 3,0,0,0 - org.(ad lib.) - str.   20:00 H. Elkan.
—— FANTAISIE RHAPSODIQUE, OP. 74 (FOR CELLO AND ORCH.) (1924)
2,2,2,2 - 3,0,0,0 - timp.,perc.,glock. - str.   16:00 Henmar.
—— FANTASY ON TWO POPULAR WALLOON CHRISTMAS CAROLS, OP.24
3,3,2,3 - 4,3,3,1 - timp.,perc. - hp. - str.   15:00 EV.
—— HYMNE, OP. 78 (FOR ORGAN AND STRING ORCH.) (1924)
org. - str.   14:00 H. Elkan.
—— IN MEMORIAM, OP. 133 (1947)
0,1,1,1 - 1,0,0,0 - str.   7:00 H. Elkan.
—— LALLA-ROUKH, OP. 28 (SYMPHONIC TABLEAU, AFTER THOMAS MOORE)
3,3,2,2 - 4,3,3,1 - timp.,perc. - 2 hp. - str.   19:00 G. Schirmer.
—— OVERTURE DE FÊTE, OP. 117 (1941)
3,3,2,2 - 4,3,3,1 - timp.,perc.,cel.,glock. - str.   10:00 H. Elkan.
—— OVERTURE-FANFARE, OP. 110 (1939)
3,3,3,3 - 4,4,3,1 - timp.,perc. - hp.   5:00 H. Elkan.
—— PAGES INTIMES, OP. 55 (1917) (IN 3 MOVTS.)
1,1,1,1 - 1,0,0,0 - perc. - hp. - str.   10:00 G. Schirmer.
—— PASSACAILLE ET GIGUE, OP. 90 (1929)
3,3,2,2 - 4,3,3,1 - timp.,perc.,glock. - hp. - str.   16:00 Southern.
—— PIÈCE SYMPHONIQUE, OP. 84 (FOR PIANO AND ORCH.) (1928)
3,3,2,2 - 4,3,3,1 - timp.,perc.,xyl. - pf. - str.   24:00 H. Elkan.
—— POÈME HÉROÏQUE, OP. 62 (FOR VIOLIN AND ORCH.) (1919)
2,2,2,2 - 3,2,2,0 - timp. - hp. - str.   16:00 Henmar.
—— POÈME NO. 2 (FOR CELLO AND ORCH.), OP. 46 (1914)
2,2,2,2 - 3,0,0,0 - timp. - hp. - str.   15:00 G. Schirmer.
—— PRELUDE AND DANCE, OP. 31 (1907)
2,3,3,2 - 4,3,3,1 - timp.,perc.,glock. - hp. - str.   17:00 G. Schirmer.
—— PRÉLUDE ÉLÉGIAQUE ET SCHERZO, OP. 66 (1920)
3,3,3,3 - 4,3,3,1 - timp.,perc.,bells,cel.,glock. - hp. - str.   25:00 H. Elkan.
—— SUITE SYMPHONIQUE, OP. 48 (SUITE EN DEUX PARTIES) (FOR VIOLA AND ORCH.) (1915)
3,2,2,2 - 4,3,3,0 - timp. - hp. - str.   21:00 EV.
—— SYMPHONIE CONCERTANTE AVEC ORGUE, OP. 81 (1926)
3,3,3,3 - 4,3,3,1 - timp.,perc. - hp. - org. - str.   33:00 Cranz.
—— TABLEAUX PITTORESQUES, OP. 56 (1917)
1,1,1,1 - 1,0,0,0 - perc.,cel.,glock. - hp. - str.   30:00 G. Schirmer.
—— TEN PIECES, OP. 96 (1932)
2,2,2,2 - 2,1,0,0 - timp. - hp. - str.   23:00 H. Elkan.
—— TRIPTYQUE, OP. 103 (1935)
3,3,3,3 - 4,3,3,1 - timp.,perc.,cel.,glock. - hp. - str.   27:00 H. Elkan.
—— TROIS MOUVEMENTS SYMPHONIQUES, OP. 137 (1951)
3,3,3,2 - 4,3,3,1 - timp.,perc.,cel. - hp. - str.   25:00 CBDM.

JONGEN, Léon
—— CAMPEADOR (1932)
3,3,3,4 - 4,3,3,1 - timp.,perc.,cel.,glock. - hp. - str.   9:00 CBDM.
—— DIVERTISSEMENT (IN FORM OF VARIATIONS ON A THEME OF HAYDN) (1956)
2,2,2,alto sax.(ad lib.),2 - 4,2,3,1 - timp.,perc.,cel.,glock.,xyl. - hp. - str.   13:00 H. Elkan.
—— FANTASIA FOR PIANO AND ORCH. (1955)
3,2,2,2 - 4,3,3,1 - timp.,perc.,cel.,glock. - pf. - str.   12:00 H. Elkan.
—— IN MEMORIAM REGIS (1935)
3,3,3,2 alto and 2 ten.sax.(ad lib.),3 - 4,3,3,1 - timp.,perc.,bells - hp. - str.   12:00 EV.
—— MALAISIE (SUITE) (1935) (IN 3 MOVTS.)
4,3,4,4 - 4,3,3,1 - timp.,perc.,cel.,vibra. - hp. - pf. - str.   28:00 CBDM.
—— LE MASQUE DE LA MORT ROUGE (THE MASQUE OF THE RED DEATH) (1-ACT BALLET) (1956) %
2,2,2,2 - 4,3,3,1 - timp.,perc.,cel.,glock.,mar. - pf.(4-hands) - str.   38:00 H. Elkan.
—— MUSIQUE POUR UN BALLET ("LE BAL DES BARRIÈRES") (1954)
3,2,2,2 - 4,3,3,1 - timp.,perc.,cel.,glock.,xyl. - hp. - pf. - str.   18:00 H. Elkan.
—— PRÉLUDE, DIVERTIMENTO ET FINAL, AVEC PIANO SOLO (1937)
3,3,3,3 - 4,3,3,1 - timp.,perc.,cel.,glock. - pf. - str.   18:00 CBDM.
—— RAPSODIA BELGICA (FOR VIOLIN AND ORCH.) (1948)
2,2,2,2 - 4,2,3,1 - timp.,perc.,glock. - hp. - str.   18:00 H. Elkan.

—— RONDE POPULAIRE WALLONNE (1917) (FROM "LE RÊVE
D'UNE NUIT DE NOËL)
3,3,3,3 - 4,3,3,1 - timp.,perc.,glock. - hp. - str.   12:00 H. Elkan.

JONSSON, Josef (Knut)
—— CHAMBER SYMPHONY IN D MINOR, OP. 15B
pf. - str.   38:00 S.T.I.M.
—— CONCERT OVERTURE IN B MAJOR, OP. 12
2,2,2,2 - 4,2,3,0 - timp. - str.   12:30 S.T.I.M.
—— CONCERTO FOR VIOLIN AND ORCH., OP. 56
2,2,2,2 - 2,2,0,0 - timp. - str.   18:00 S.T.I.M.
—— FESTIVAL OVERTURE IN E♭ MAJOR, OP. 28
2,3,3,2 - 4,3,3,0 - timp. - hp. - str.   10:00 S.T.I.M.
—— JULRAPSODI, OP. 44
2,2,2,2 - 2,2,1,0 - timp.,perc. - str.   14:00 S.T.I.M.
—— SUITE FOR WIND INSTRUMENTS AND PERCUSSION, OP.
53
2,2,2,2 - 2,2,2,0 - timp.,perc.   16:00 S.T.I.M.
—— SUITE NO. 1, OP. 9
2,2,2,2 - 2,2,0,0 - timp.,perc. - str.   20:00 S.T.I.M.
—— SUITE NO. 2, OP. 27
2,2,2,2 - 2,2,0,0 - timp.,perc. - str.   21:00 S.T.I.M.
—— SYMPHONY NO. 1 ("NORDLAND"), OP. 23
2,3,3,3 - 4,2,3,0 - timp. - hp. - str.   55:00 S.T.I.M.
—— SYMPHONY NO. 2 IN D MINOR, OP. 34
2,2,2,2 - 4,2,3,0 - timp. - str.   23:00 S.T.I.M.
—— SYMPHONY NO. 3 IN C MINOR, OP. 50
2,2,2,2 - 2,2,3,0 - timp. - str.   27:00 S.T.I.M.
—— THEME, VARIATIONS AND FUGUE, OP. 51B
str.   10:00 S.T.I.M.
—— VIA DOLOROSA, OP. 45 (SUITE FOR STRINGS) (IN 5
MOVTS)
str.   28:00 S.T.I.M.

JOPLIN, Scott - TUROK, Paul
—— GREAT SCOTT! OP. 37 (ORCHESTRAL SUITE AFTER SCOTT
JOPLIN) (1973)
*3,*3,*3,2 - 4,3,3,1 - timp.,perc.(4),glock.,mar.,vibra.,xyl. - hp. -
str.   20:00 G. Schirmer.
—— A SCOTT JOPLIN OVERTURE, OP. 37A (1973)
*3,*3,*3,2 - 4,3,3,1 - timp.,perc.(3),glock.,vibra. - hp. - str.
6:00 G. Schirmer.

JORDAN, Sverre
—— AN MAGRIT (OVERTURE, OP. 72-A) (FROM INCIDENTAL
MUSIC TO JOHAN FALKBERGET'S PLAY)
3,3,2,2 - 4,2,3,0 - timp.,perc. - str.   7:00 T.O.N.O.
—— CONCERTO IN D MINOR FOR CELLO AND ORCH., OP. 51
(IN 3 MOVTS.)
2,2,2,2 - 4,2,0,0 - timp. - str.   21:00 T.O.N.O.
—— CONCERTO IN E MINOR FOR PIANO AND ORCH., OP. 45
(IN 3 MOVTS.)
3,2,2,2 - 4,2,2,1 - timp.,perc. - pf. - str.   30:00 T.O.N.O.
—— CONCERTO IN G MINOR FOR VIOLIN AND ORCH., OP. 82
(IN 3 MOVTS.)
2,2,2,2 - 4,2,2,0 - timp.,perc. - str.   23:00 T.O.N.O.
—— CONCERTO PICCOLO, OP. 77 (FOR PIANO AND ORCH.) (IN
3 MOVTS.)
3,2,2,2 - 4,2,2,0 - timp.,perc. - pf. - str.   17:00 T.O.N.O.
—— CONCERTO ROMANTICO, OP. 63 (FOR HORN AND ORCH.)
(IN 3 MOVTS.)
2,2,2,2 - 4,2,2,0 - timp.,perc. - str.   15:00 T.O.N.O.
—— FESTIVAL OPENING, OP. 67
3,2,2,2 - 4,3,3,1 - timp.,perc. - hp. - str.   5:00 T.O.N.O.
—— FESTIVAL OVERTURE, OP. 46
3,2,2,2 - 4,2,3,1 - timp.,perc. - hp. - str.   4:30 T.O.N.O.
or:
1,1,2,1 - 2,2,1,0 - timp.,perc. - hp. - str.
—— FEVERPOEMS ("FEBERDIKTE") (FOR SPEAKING VOICE
AND ORCH.) (Text: Knut Hamsun)
3,2,2,2 - 2,2,2,1 - timp.,perc. - hp. - str.   20:00 T.O.N.O.
—— HALTE-HULDA, OP. 26 (SUITE FOR VOICE AND ORCH.) (IN
3 MOVTS.)
3,2,2,2 - 4,2,3,1 - timp.,perc. - hp. - str.   15:00 T.O.N.O.
—— HALTE HULDA: SUITE NO. 1, OP. 20 (FROM INCIDENTAL
MUSIC TO BJØRNSTJERNE BJØRNSON'S PLAY) (IN 5
MOVTS.)
2,1,2,1 - 2,2,2,0 - timp.,perc. - hp. - str.   17:00 T.O.N.O.
—— HALTE HULDA: SUITE NO. 2, OP. 26 (IN 3 MOVTS.)
3,2,2,2 - 4,3,3,1 - timp.,perc. - hp. - str.   15:00 T.O.N.O.

—— THE KING (KONGEN), OP. 64 (MELODRAMA, WITH
RECITATION AND CHORAL FINALE) (Text: Nordahl Grieg)
3,3,2,2 - 4,2,3,1 - perc.,cel. - hp. - str.   20:00 T.O.N.O.
—— LEGEND, OP. 78
2,1,2,1 - 2,2,2,0 - timp.,perc. - str.   4:00 T.O.N.O.
—— LYRIC SUITE, OP. 85 (IN 5 MOVTS.)
2,1,2,1 - 2,2,2,0 - timp.,perc. - hp. - str.   14:00 T.O.N.O.
—— MELODRAMA FOR FEMALE VOICE AND ORCH., OP. 20
(RECITATION, FROM BJØRNSTJERNE BJØRNSON'S PLAY
"HALTE HULDA")
1,1,2,1 - 2,0,0,0 - timp. - str.   8:00 T.O.N.O.
—— NORVEGIANA, OP. 22 (IN 5 MOVTS.)
3,2,2,2 - 4,2,2,0 - timp.,perc. - hp. - str.   30:00 Raabe & P.
—— NORWAY ("NORGE"), OP. 32 (FOR SPEAKING VOICE,
SOPRANO, MIXED CHORUS AND ORCH.) (Text: Nordahl
Grieg)
3,2,2,2 - 4,2,3,0 - timp.,perc. - str.   24:00 Norsk Mfl.
—— NORWEGIAN RHAPSODY, OP. 53
3,2,2,2 - 4,2,3,1 - timp.,perc. - str.   10:30 T.O.N.O.
—— NORWEGIAN SUITE, OP. 47 (ON FOLK TUNES FROM
ØSTERDAL)
2,2,2,2 - 2,2,1,0 - timp.,perc. - str.   16:00 T.O.N.O.
—— OVERTURE TO A LYRIC DRAMA, OP. 75
3,2,2,2 - 4,2,3,1 - timp.,perc.,cel. - str.   7:00 T.O.N.O.
—— OVERTURE TO A ROMANTIC PLAY OF SHAKESPEARE, OP.
42
3,2,2,2 - 4,3,3,0 - timp.,perc. - hp. - str.   7:00 T.O.N.O.
—— ROMEO AND JULIET: SUITE, OP. 55-A (FROM INCIDENTAL
MUSIC TO SHAKESPEARE'S PLAY)
2,1,2,1 - 2,2,2,0 - timp.,perc. - hp.(or pf.) - str.   16:00 T.O.N.O.
—— SERENADE FOR STRING ORCH., OP. 68 (IN 5 MOVTS.)
str.   24:00 T.O.N.O.
—— THE SMITH (SMEDEN), OP. 25 (FOR TENOR OR BARITONE,
MIXED CHORUS AND ORCH.) (Text: Olaf Benneche)
3,2,2,2 - 4,2,3,1 - timp.,perc. - hp. - str.   12:00 T.O.N.O.
—— SUITE IN OLDEN SYTLE (SUITE I GAMMEL STIL), OP. 4 (IN
3 MOVTS.)
1,1,1,1 - 2,2,0,0 - timp. - str.   15:00 T.O.N.O.
—— THREE NOCTURNAL SCENES, OP. 66
2,1,2,1 - 2,2,1,0 - timp.,perc. - hp. - str.   13:00 T.O.N.O.
—— THREE WALTZ INTERMEZZI, OP. 58
2,1,2,1 - 2,2,1,0 - timp.,perc. - hp. - str.   15:00 T.O.N.O.
—— TUE BENTSON'S SONGS (TUE BENTSØNS VISER), OP. 44
(FOR TENOR AND ORCH.) (Text: Viggo Stuckenberg)
3,2,2,2 - 4,2,2,0 - timp.,perc.,cel. (ad lib.) - hp. - str.
10:00 T.O.N.O.

JØRGENSEN, Axel
—— SUITE FOR TROMBONE AND ORCH., OP. 22
2,2,2,2 - 4,2,2,1 - timp. - str.   12:30 G. Schirmer.

JØRGENSEN, Erik
—— CONCERTO FOR VIOLIN AND STRING ORCH. (1936)
str.   15:00 K.O.D.A.
—— CONCERTO GROSSO (1935)
1,0,1,1 - 0,0,0,0 - str.   20:00 K.O.D.A.
—— CONFRONTATIONS
3,3,3,3 - 4,3,3,1 - perc. - str.   18:00 K.O.D.A.
—— MODELLO PER ARCHI (1957)
str.   7:00 Henmar.
—— NOTTURNO PER ORCH. (1966)
1,alto fl.,*2,*2,2 - 0,0,0,0 - str.(6,2,2,2)   10:00 Henmar.

JOSEPHS, Wilfred
—— ADAM AND EVE, OP. 61 (FOR NARRATOR AND ORCH.)
1,1(alt. with Eng.hn.),1(alt. with b.-cl.),1 - 1,1,1,1 - timp.,perc. - pf.
- str.   Galaxy.
—— CANZONAS ON A THEME OF RAMEAU, OP. 49
str.   Galaxy.
—— CONCERTO FOR CELLO AND ORCHESTRA
2(2nd alt. with picc.),2(2nd alt with Eng.hn.),2(2nd alt. with
b.-cl.),2 - 2,2,1,0 - timp.,perc.,cel. - hp. - str.   15:00 Galaxy.
—— CONCERTO FOR OBOE, PERCUSSION AND SMALL ORCH.,
OP.58
0,3,0,1 - 2,0,0,0 - perc. - str.   15:00 P.R.S.
—— CONCERTO FOR 2 VIOLINS AND SMALL ORCH., OP. 69
1,2,2,2 - 2,0,0,0 - str.   23:00 P.R.S.
—— CONCERTO NO. 2 FOR PIANO AND ORCH.
1(alt. with picc.),0,2(2nd alt. with b.-cl.),2 - 2,0,0,0 -
timp.,perc.,glock. - pf. - str.   25:00 Novello.
—— THE LAST LAST POST
3,3,4,4 - 5,4,4,0 - timp.,perc. - hp. - str.   6:00 Novello.

—— THE MAGICAL BEING (BALLET) %
          30:00 P.R.S.
—— MEDITATIO DE BEORMUNDO (CONCERTANTE FOR
 VIOLA AND CHAMBER ORCH.)
  0,2,0,0 - 2,0,0,0 - str.(9,3,2,1) 15:00 Bo. Hawkes.
—— MORTALES (1969) (FOR SOPRANO, ALTO, TENOR,
 BARITONE (AD LIB), BASS, CHILDREN'S CHORUS, SATB
 CHORUS AND ORCH.)
  3,3,3,3 - 4,3,3,1 - timp.,perc.(4),cel. - hp. - str. 24:00 G. Schirmer.
—— POLEMIC, OP. 56
  str.   10:00 P.R.S.
—— RAIL, OP. 57
  2(2nd alt. with picc.),2(2nd alt. with Eng.hn.),2,2 - 4,3,3,1 -
  timp.,perc.(3) - hp. - str.   11:00 Galaxy.
—— REQUIEM, OP. 39 (FOR BARITONE, CHORUS, STRING
 QUINTET AND ORCH.)
  2,2,2,2 - 4,2,3,0 - perc. - hp. - str. 50:00 Bo. Hawkes.
—— LA RÉPÉTITION DE PHÈDRE (BALLET) %
          30:00 P.R.S.
—— SINFONIETTA
  2,2,2,2 - 2,2,2,0 - timp. - str. 19:30 Mills.
—— SYMPHONY NO. 2, OP. 42
  3(2 and 3 alt. with picc.),2(2nd alt. with Eng.hn.),2(2nd alt. with
  E♭cl., b.cl.),2 - 4,3,3,1 - timp.,perc.(5),cel. - hp. - str. 25:00 Galaxy.
—— SYMPHONY NO. 3 ("PHILADELPHIA"), OP. 59
          29:00 Presser.
—— SYMPHONY NO. 4, OP. 72 (FOR ALTO, BARITONE AND
 ORCH.)
  3,3,3,3 - 4,3,3,1 - perc. - hp. -str. 38:00 Novello.
—— SYMPHONY NO. 5 ("PASTORALE")
  3(3rd alt. with picc.),2(2nd alt. with Eng. hn.),2(2nd alt. with
  b.cl.),2(2nd alt. with c.-bn.) - 4,3,3,1 - timp.,perc.,cel. - hp. - str.
          35:00 Novello.
—— VARIATIONS ON A THEME OF BEETHOVEN, OP. 68
  3,3,3,3 - 4,3,3,1 - timp.,perc.(4),cel. - hp. - str. 19:00 G. Schirmer.

JOSEPHSON, Harry D.
—— CONCERTO FOR CELLO AND STRING ORCH. (IN 3
 MOVTS.)
  str.   23:00 Composer.
—— CONCERTO FOR VIOLA AND ORCHESTRA (IN 3 MOVTS.)
  2,2,2,2 - 2,0,0,0 - timp.,perc.(2) - str. 23:00 Composer.
—— CONCERTO FOR VIOLIN AND STRING ORCH. (IN 3
 MOVTS.)
  str.   22:00 Composer.
—— FOUR HEBREW PRAYERS (FOR VIOLIN, CELLO AND
 STRING ORCH.)
  str.   15:00 Composer.
—— REVERIE
  fl. - str.   Composer.
—— SYMPHONY (IN 4 MOVTS.)
  *3,2,2,2 - 2,3,3,1 - timp.,perc.(2) - str. 60:00 Composer.
—— TEN MOVEMENTS FOR PIANO AND ORCHESTRA
  *3,2,2,2 - 2,2,3,1 - timp.,perc.(2) - pf. - str. 35:00 Composer.
—— THREE SONGS OF CHICAGO (1939)
  1,0,1,1 - 1,0,0,0 - timp.,perc.(1) - hp. - str. 12:00 Composer.
—— TWO INVENTIONS FOR ORCH.
  2,2,2,2 - 2,0,0,0 - str.   14:00 Composer.
—— TWO MOVEMENTS FOR OBOE AND STRING ORCH.
  ob. - str.   15:00 Composer.
—— VARIATIONS ON A FRESCOBALDI GAGLIARD
  str.   15:00 Composer.

JOSIF, Enriko
—— PTICO NE SKLAPAJ SVOJA KRILA (BIRD, DON'T FOLD
 YOUR WINGS) (BALLET) %
  3,3,3,3 - 4,4,3,1 - timp.,perc.,cel.,xyl. - hp. - str.
         60:00 MIC,Zagreb.
—— SYMPHONIE DI TRE RE
  3,3,3,3 - 4,3,3,1 - timp. - hp. - pf. - str. 25:00 MIC,Zagreb.
—— TEZEJ (CHOREOGRAPHIC POEM) %
  3,3,3,3 - 4,3,3,1 - pf. - str. 4500 MIC,Zagreb.

JOSTEN, Werner
—— BATOULA (SUITE)
          H. Elkan.
—— CANZONA SERIA FOR LOW STRINGS
  str.   H. Elkan.
—— CONCERTO SACRO NO. 1 (IN 2 MOVTS.)
  pf. - str.   20:00 H. Elkan.
—— CONCERTO SACRO NO. 2 (IN 2 MOVTS.)
  pf. - str.   16:00 H. Elkan.

—— SERENADE
          H. Elkan.
—— SYMPHONY FOR STRINGS
  str.   17:00 H. Elkan.
—— SYMPHONY IN F (IN 3 MOVTS.)
  3(2nd and 3rd alt. with picc.),*3,3(3rd alt. with b.cl.),*3 - 4,3,3,1 -
  timp.,perc. - str.   17:00 H. Elkan.

JOUARD, Paul E.
—— CONCERTINO DA CAMERA (IN 3 MOVTS.)
  pf. - str.   20:00 Templeton.
—— ELEGY FOR ORCHESTRA
  2(2nd alt. with picc.),2,*3,*3, - 4,3,3,1 - timp.,perc.(2) - str.
         8:30 Templeton.
—— SINFONIA FOR TROMBONE AND STRINGS (IN 1 MOVT.)
  trb. - str.   15:00 Templeton.
—— VICTORIAN SUITE
  1,1,1,1 - 1,1,0,0, - perc. - pf. - str. 10:00 Templeton.

JOUBERT, John
—— ANTIGONE, OP. 11 (OPERA, AFTER SOPOCHLES) % (Text:
 Rachel Trickett)
  2,2,2,2 - 4,3,3,1 - timp.,perc. - pf. - str. 62:00 Novello.
—— THE BURGHERS OF CALAIS, OP. 12 (CANTATA) (FOR 6
 SOLO VOICES, CHORUS AND ORCH.) (Text: G. K. Hunter)
  1,1,1,1 - 1,1,1,0 - timp.,perc. - pf. - str.(2 vln.,1 vla.,c.,1 d.-b.)
         30:00 Novello.
—— CONCERTO FOR PIANO AND ORCH., OP. 25 (1958)
  2,2,2,2 - 4,2,3,1 - timp.,perc. - pf. - str. 35:00 Novello.
—— CONCERTO, FOR VIOLIN AND ORCH., OP. 13
  2,2,2,2 - 4,2,3,1 - timp.,perc. - str. 26:00 Novello.
—— IN MEMORIAM (1820), OP. 39 (1962)
  3(3rd alt. with picc.),3,3,3 - 4,3,3,1 - timp.,perc.,glock.,xyl. - hp. -
  str.   16:00 Novello.
—— IN THE DROUGHT, OP. 17 (TRAGIC 1-ACT OPERA) % (Text:
 Adolf Wood)
  1,1,1,1 - 1,0,0,0 - timp.,perc. - pf. - str.(2 vln.,1 vla.,1 c.,1 d.-b.)
         40:00 Novello.
—— NORTH COUNTRY OVERTURE, OP. 28 (1957)
  2,2,2,2 - 4,3,3,1 - timp.,perc. - str. 10:00 Novello.
—— OVERTURE, OP. 3
  2,2,2,2 - 4,2,3,1 - timp.,perc. - pf. - str. 8:00 Novello.
—— SILAS MARNER, OP. 31 (3-ACT OPERA, AFTER GEORGE
 ELIOTS' NOVEL) % (Text: Rachel Trickett)
  2,2,2, - 4,2,3,1 - timp.,perc. - hp. - pf. - str. 130:00 Novello.
—— SINFONIETTA FOR CHAMBER ORCH., OP. 38 (1962)
  0,2,0,2 - 2,0,0,0 - str.   19:00 Novello.
—— SYMPHONIC PRELUDE, OP. 9
  2,2,2,2 - 4,2,3,1 - timp. - pf. - str. 8:00 Novello.
—— SYMPHONY NO. 1 OP. 20
  2,2,2,2 - 4,2,3,1 - timp.,perc. - pf. - str. 28:00 Novello.
—— SYMPHONY NO. 2
  3(3rd alt. with picc.),3,4,3 - 4,3,3,1 - timp.,perc. - hp. - pf. - str.
         21:00 Novello.
—— THREE ORCHESTRAL INTERLUDES (FROM "UNDER
 WESTERN EYES")
  3(3rd alt. with picc.),3(3rd alt. with Eng. hn.),3,3 - 4,3,3,1 -
  timp.,perc. - hp. - pf. - str. 15:00 Novello.
—— URBS BEATA, OP. 42 (CANTATA) (FOR TENOR, BARITONE,
 SATB CHORUS AND ORCH.)
  2,2,2,2 - 4,3,3,1 - timp.,perc. - hp. - org. - str. 35:00 Novello.

JUBLER, Ovady
—— PRAYER NO. 2 (FOR 5 SOLO VOICES, MIXED CHORUS,
 ORGAN AND ORCH.) (1960) (Text: Composer)
         80:00 Composer.

JUDD, Magaret
—— TRIESTE (1951)
  str.   5:00 P.R.S.

JULBER, Ovady
—— CONTEMPLATION I
  2(1 alt. with picc.),2(1 alt. with Eng. hn.),2(1 alt. with b.-cl.),2(1
  alt. with c.-bn.) - 4,3,3,1 - timp.,perc.(2),bells,cel.,xyl. - hp. - str.
         12:00 Composer.
—— THE HEART OF A SOLDIER (BALLET) %
  2(1 alt. with picc.),2(1 alt. with Eng. hn.),2(1 alt. with b.-cl.),2(1
  alt. with c.-bn.) - 4,3,3,1 - timp.,perc.(2),bells,cel.glock.,xyl. - hp. -
  str   18:00 Composer.

—— KADESH (FOR BARITONE, SATB CHORUS AND ORCH.)
2(1 alt. with picc.),2(1 alt. with Eng. hn.),2(1 alt. with b.-cl.),2(1 alt. with c.-bn.) - 4,3,3,1 - timp.,perc.,bells,cel.,xyl. - hp. - org. - str.   15:00 Composer.

—— KENNEDY MEMORIAL (FOR 2 SOLO VOICES, MIXED CHORUS, NARRATOR AND ORCH.) (1966) (Text: Composer, John F. Kennedy's Inaugural Address)
3(3rd alt. with picc.),3(3rd alt. with Eng. hn.),3(1 alt. with E♭ cl. and 1 alt. with b.-cl.),*3 - 4,3,3,1 - timp.,perc.(5),bells,cel.,xyl. - 2 hp. - org. - pf. - str.   117:00 Composer.

—— LAMENT
3(3rd alt. with picc.),*3,*3,3(3rd alt. with c.-bn.) - 4,3,3,1 - timp.,perc.(2),bells - hp. - str.   14:00 Composer.

—— POEM IN MOODS
1(alt. with picc.),1(alt. with Eng. hn.),2(1 alt. with b.-cl.),1(alt. with c.-bn.) - 4,2,3,1 - timp.,perc.(2),bells,cel.,glock,xyl. - hp. - str.   14:00 Composer.

—— PRAYER (FOR NARRATOR, SOPRANO, MEZZO-SOPRANO, ALTO, BARITONE, BASS, SATB CHORUS AND ORCH.) (Text: Carl Sandburg)
3(3rd alt. with picc.),*4,*3,*3 - 4,3,3,1 - timp.,perc.(4),bells,cel.,glock,xyl. - hp. - org. - str.   60:00 Composer.

—— REQUIEM IN BLUES (FOR SATB CHORUS AND ORCH.)
3(3rd alt. with picc.),*3,*3,3(3rd alt. with c.-bn.) - 4,3,3,1 - timp.,perc.(3),bells,xyl. - hp. - pf. - str.   12:00 Composer.

—— SYMPHONIE SENTIMENTALE (IN 3 MOVTS.)
2(1 alt. with picc.),2(1 alt. with Eng.hn.),2(1 alt. with b.-cl.),1 soprano sax.,2(1 with c.-bn.) - 0,0,0,0 - timp.,perc.(4),bells,cel.,glock,xyl. - hp. - pf. - str. 40:00 Composer.

—— TANGO DE L'EXTASE TRAGIQUE (BALLET)
2(1 alt. with picc.),2(1 alt. with Eng.hn.),2(1 alt. with b.-cl.),2(1 alt. with c.-bn.) - 4,3,3,1 - timp.,perc.(2),cel.,xyl. - hp. - str.   20:00 Composer.

JULIAN, Joseph
—— CONCEPTION (1975)
*3,*2,*2,*2 - 4,2,3,1 - timp.,perc.(4),bells,cel.,glock.,mar.,vibra.,xyl. - tape-recorder(2-channel) - hp. - str.(24,8,6,4)   Composer.

—— CONCERTO FOR 7 FLUTES AND CHAMBER ORCH. (1971)
7,*2,*2,*2 - 0,1,2,0 - perc.(2),bells,cel.,glock.,mar.,vibra,xyl.   14:00 Seesaw.

JUNGK, Klaus
—— CONCERTINO FOR FLUTE AND STRING ORCH., OP. 44
fl. - str.   13:00 Mannheimer.

—— CONVERSATIONS FOR CLARINET AND STRING ORCH., OP. 53
cl. - str.   8:00 Mannheimer.

—— MUSIC FOR ORCH. (FANTASTIC SCENES), OP. 19
2,2,2,2 - 4,3,3,1 - timp. - str.   9:00 F. Colombo.

—— MUSIC FOR STRING ORCH. AND PERCUSSION, OP. 24
timp. - str.   8:00 Modern.

JUON, Paul
—— SYMPHONY IN A
3,*2,2,3 - 4,2,1,1 - hp. - str.   Boston.

JUROVSKÝ, Šimon
—— GOTTWALD (CANTATA) (FOR SATB CHORUS AND ORCH.) (1951) (Text: Milian Lajciak)
Bo. Hawkes.

—— JOYOUS COMPETITION (SYMPHONIC SCHERZO)
Bo. Hawkes.

—— SYMPHONY NO. 1 (SYMPHONY OF PEACE) (FOR PIANO CONCERTANTE AND STRINGS) (1951) (IN 3 MOVTS.)
pf. - str.   Bo. Hawkes.

JYRKIÄINEN, Reijo
—— EFFATA (BALLET) (WITH SATB CHORUS) % (1963) (CO-COMPOSED WITH ILKKA KUUSISTO)
1,0,2,0 - 2,2,0,0 - timp. - tape-recorder - str.   15:00 FinnMICtr.

K

KABALEVSKY, Dmitri
—— AERO - CITY (FROM THE FILM "AEROGRAD")
*3,*3,E♭ cl.,2,alto sax.,2 - 4,3,3,1 - timp.,perc. - str.   2:30 G. Schirmer.

—— COLAS BREUGNON: SUITE, OP. 24 (IN 4 MOVTS.)
3,3,3,3 - 4,3,3,1 - timp.,perc.,xyl. - hp. - str.   18:00 G. Schirmer.

—— THE COMEDIANS: SUITE (FOR SMALL ORCH.), OP. 26
1,1,2,1 - 2,2,1,1 - timp.,perc.,xyl. - pf. - str.   15:00 G. Schirmer.

—— CONCERTO FOR VIOLIN AND ORCH., OP. 48
1,1,2,1 - 2,1,1,0 - timp.,perc.,xyl. - str.   13:00 G. Schirmer.

—— CONCERTO NO. 1 FOR CELLO AND ORCH., OP. 49
1,1,2,1 - 2,1,1,0 - timp.,perc. - str.   17:00 G. Schirmer.

—— CONCERTO NO. 1 IN A MINOR, FOR PIANO AND ORCH., OP. 9 (IN 3 MOVTS.)
2(2nd alt. with picc.),2,2,2 - 4,2,3,1 - timp.,perc. - pf. - str.   33:00 G. Schirmer.

—— CONCERTO NO. 2 FOR CELLO AND ORCH., OP. 77
2,2,2,alto sax.,3 - 4,2,2,0 - timp.,perc. - hp. - str.   30:00 G. Schirmer.

—— CONCERTO NO. 2 IN G MINOR, FOR PIANO AND ORCH., OP. 23 (IN 3 MOVTS.)
*3,*3,2,2 - 4,3,3,1 - timp.,perc.,xyl. - pf. - str.   23:30 G. Schirmer.

—— CONCERTO NO. 3 ("YOUTH") FOR PIANO AND ORCH., OP. 50
2,2,2,2 - 2,2,2,0 - timp.,perc.,xyl.-hp. - pf. - str.   18:00 G. Schirmer.

—— FÊTE POPULAIRE (FROM "COLAS BREUGNON", OP. 24)
3(3rd alt. with picc.),3,3,3 - 4,3,3,1 - timp.,perc.(5),xyl. - hp. - str.   4:30 G. Schirmer.

—— OVERTURE PATHÉTIQUE, OP. 64
3,3,3,3 - 4,3,3,1 - timp.,perc.,xyl. - pf. - str.   4:00 G. Schirmer.

—— OVERTURE TO "COLAS BREUGNON"
3(3rd alt. with picc.),3,3,3(3rd alt. with c.-bn.) - 4,3,3,1 - timp.,perc.(7),xyl. - hp. - str.   5:00 G. Schirmer.

—— REQUIEM, OP. 72 (FOR MEZZO-SOPRANO, BARITONE, BOY'S CHOIR, MIXED CHORUS AND ORCH.)
3,3,4,3 - 4,3,3,1 - timp.,perc.cel.,xyl. - 2 hp. - pf. - str.   90:00 G. Schirmer.

—— RHAPSODY FOR PIANO AND ORCH., OP. 75
1,1,2,1 - 3,2,1,0 - timp.,perc. - pf. - str.   14:00 G. Schirmer.

—— ROMEO AND JULIET, OP. 56 (MUSIC TO THE PLAY) (IN 10 MOVTS.)
3,3,3,3 - 4,3,3,1 - timp.,perc.,xyl. - hp. - pf. - str.   34:00 G. Schirmer.

—— SPRING, OP. 65 (SYMPHONIC POEM)
3,3,3,3 - 4,2,3,1 - timp.,perc. - hp. - pf. - str.   6:00 G. Schirmer.

—— SYMPHONY NO. 2 IN C MINOR, OP. 19 (IN 3 MOVTS.)
3(3rd alt. with picc.),*3,*3,*3 - 4,3,3,1 - timp.,perc.(5) - str.   25:00 G. Schirmer.

—— SYMPHONY NO. 4
*3,*3,*3,*3 - 4,3,3,1 - timp.,perc.,xyl. - hp. - pf. - str.   39:00 G. Schirmer.

KABALEVSKY, Dmitri - EIGER, Walter
—— SONATINA NO. 1 IN C MAJOR, OP. 13 (IN 3 MOVTS.)
2,2(2nd alt. with Eng. hn.),2,2 - 2,2,2,0 - timp.,perc.(2),cel. - pf. - str.   7:00 G. Schirmer.

—— SONATINA, OP. 13, NO. 1
2,2,3,2 - 2,2,2,0 - timp.,perc. - pf. - str.   4:00 G. Schirmer.

KABALEVSKY, Dmitri - SHELDON, Harold
—— FLÉAU PUBLIQUE (FROM "COLAS BREUGNON" SUITE)
3,3,3,3 - 4,3,3,1 - timp.,perc.,xyl. - hp. - str.   4:00 G. Schirmer.

—— INSURRECTION (FROM "COLAS BREUGNON" SUITE)
3,3,3,3 - 4,3,3,1 - timp.,perc.,xyl. - hp. - str.   5:00 G. Schirmer.

KABELÁČ, Miloslav
—— FANTASY FOR PIANO AND ORCH. (1934)
Bo. Hawkes.

—— THE MYSTERY OF TIME (PASSACAGLIA FOR ORCH.)
3,2,3,3 - 4,3,3,1 - timp. - str.   27:00 Bo. Hawkes.

—— OVERTURE, OP. 17 (1947)
3,2,2,3 - 4,3,3,1 - timp.,perc. - str.   9:00 Bo. Hawkes.

—— SIX CRADLE SONGS, OP. 29 (WITH ALTO AND SATB CHORUS)
fl. - str.   12:00 Bo. Hawkes.

—— SYMPHONIETTA (1931)
Bo. Hawkes.

—— SYMPHONY NO. 1
perc. - str.   30:00 Bo. Hawkes.

—— SYMPHONY NO. 2 (1946)
3,3,3,3 - 6,4,3,1 - timp.,perc. - 2 hp. - org. - str.   35:00 Bo. Hawkes.

—— SYMPHONY NO. 3
0,0,0,0 - 6,4,4,1 - timp. - org.   20:00 Bo. Hawkes.

—— SYMPHONY NO. 4
  2,2,2,2 - 2,2,0,0 - timp. - str.   26:00 Bo. Hawkes.
—— TO THE CHILDREN
  2,2,2,2 - 2,0,0,0 - str.   14:00 Bo. Hawkes.

KADERAVEK, Milan
—— MUSIC FOR ORCHESTRA (1969)
  *3,*3,*3,2 - 4,3,3,1 - timp.,perc.(3) - str.   9:00 Composer.
—— RHAPSODY FOR CELLO AND STRINGS
  str.   10:00 Composer.
—— SINFONIETTA (1958) (IN 3 MOVTS.)
  2(2nd alt. with picc.),2,2,2 - 4,3,3,1 - timp.,perc.(3) - str.
                                                15:30 Composer.

KADOSA, Pál
—— CONCERTINO FOR VIOLA AND ORCH., OP. 27
  1,1,1,1 - 0,1,0,0 - timp. - str.   15:00 Bo. Hawkes.
—— CONCERTINO NO. 2 FOR PIANO AND ORCH. OP. 29
  2,2,2,2 - 2,1,1,0 - timp.,perc. - pf. - str. 17:00 Bo. Hawkes.
—— CONCERTO FOR STRING QUARTET AND CHAMBER
  ORCH., OP. 26
  2,2,2,2 - 2,1,1,0 - timp.,perc. - str.   25:20 Bo. Hawkes.
—— CONCERTO NO. 1 FOR PIANO AND ORCH. OP. 15
  0,0,4,0 - 2,3,1,0 - timp.,perc. - pf. - str. 17:00 Bo. Hawkes.
—— CONCERTO NO. 1 FOR VIOLIN AND ORCH.
  2,2,2,2 - 2,2,0,0 - timp. - str.   25:00 Bo. Hawkes.
—— CONCERTO NO. 2 FOR VIOLIN AND ORCH.
  2,2,2,2 - 2,2,0,0 - timp. - str.   23:00 Bo. Hawkes.
—— CONCERTO NO. 3 FOR PIANO AND ORCH. OP. 47
  2,2,2,2 - 4,3,0,0 - timp.,perc. - pf. - str. 35:00 Bo. Hawkes.
—— CONCERTO NO. 4 FOR PIANO AND ORCH., OP. 63
                                                15:00 Bo. Hawkes.
—— DE AMORE FATALI, OP. 31 (CANTATA) (FOR CHORUS
  AND ORCH.)
  2,2,2,2 - 4,3,3,1 - timp.,perc. - pf. - str. 22:00 Bo. Hawkes.
—— DIVERTIMENTO NO. 1
  2,2,2,2 - 4,2,2,0 - timp.,perc. - pf. - str. 14:00 Bo. Hawkes.
—— DIVERTIMENTO NO. 2, OP. 20-B
  1,1,1,1 - 2,1,1,0 - timp.,perc. - str.   20:00 Bo. Hawkes.
—— FOLKSONGS SUITE
  1,1,1,1 - 2,1,1,0 - timp. - str.   9:00 Bo. Hawkes.
—— HUNGARIAN RHAPSODY (FOR 2 CLARINETS AND ORCH.)
  *2,1,3,*2 - 4,3,*3,1 - timp., perc. - cimbalom - pf. - str.
                                                13:00 Bo. Hawkes.
—— A NOSEGAY OF WILD FLOWERS
  2,2,2,2 - 2,0,0,0 - timp.,perc. - str.   7:00 Bo. Hawkes.
—— PARTITA, OP. 34
  2,2,2,2 - 4,3,3,0 - timp. - str.   30:00 Bo. Hawkes.
—— PIAN É FORTE, OP. 59 (SONATA FOR ORCH.)
  2,2,2,2 - 4,3,3,0 - timp.,perc. - str.   15:30 Bo. Hawkes.
—— SINFONIETTA
                                                     Bo. Hawkes.
—— SUITE
  2,2,2,2 - 2,2,0,0 - timp. - str.   Bo. Hawkes.
—— SUITE FOR THE YOUTH
  2,2,1,1 - 2,2,0,0 - timp. - str.   8:00 Bo. Hawkes.
—— SYMPHONY NO. 1, OP. 33
  2,2,2,2 - 3,3,0,0 - str.   50:00 Bo. Hawkes.
—— SYMPHONY NO. 2 (CAPRICCIO)
  2,2,2,2 - 2,2,3,0 - timp.,perc. - str.   26:00 Bo. Hawkes.
—— SYMPHONY NO. 3, OP. 50
  2,2,2,2 - 4,3,3,0 - timp.,perc. - str.   24:00 Bo. Hawkes.
—— SYMPHONY NO. 4, OP. 53
  str.   Bo. Hawkes.
—— SYMPHONY NO. 5
  1,2,2,2 - 2,2,0,0 - timp.,perc. - str.   16:00 Bo. Hawkes.
—— SYMPHONY NO. 7, OP. 64
  2,2,2,2 - 4,3,3,0 - timp.,perc. - str.   13:20 Bo. Hawkes.
—— SYMPHONY NO. 8, OP. 66
  2,2,2,2 - 4,3,3,0 - timp.,perc. - str.   25:00 Bo. Hawkes.

KAIL, Robert
—— BICENTENNIAL SYMPHONY (1975) (IN 4 MOVTS.)
  2(2nd alt. with picc.),2,2,2 - 4,3,2,1 - perc.(2) - str.
                                                20:00 Composer.
—— CONCERTO NO. 1 FOR SYNTHESIZER ORCH. (1975) (IN 4
  MOVTS.)
  2(2nd alt. with picc.),2,2,2 - 4,3,2,1 - timp. - synthesizer (2-octave
  range) - str.   20:00 Composer.

KAJANUS, Robert
—— ADAGIETTO (1918)
  str.   4:00 FinnMICtr.

—— CANTATA (FOR SOPRANO, SATB CHORUS AND ORCH.)
  (1910)
  2,2,2,2 - 4,2,3,1 - timp. - str.   15:00 FinnMICtr.
—— IMPROMPTU (1926)
  2,2,2,2 - 2,2,3,0 - timp.,perc. - str.   8:00 FinnMICtr.
—— OVERTURA SINFONICA (1926)
  3,3,3,2 - 4,3,3,1 - timp.,perc.,cel. - hp. - str. 9:00 FinnMICtr.
—— SUITE ANCIENNE, IN F MAJOR (1931)
  str.   15:00 FinnMICtr.

KALABIS, Viktor
—— CONCERTO FOR CELLO AND ORCH. (1951) (IN 3 MOVTS.)
  2,2,2,2 - 4,2,3,1 - timp.,perc.,cel. - hp. - str. 37:00 Bo. Hawkes.
—— CONCERTO FOR PIANO AND ORCH. (1954)
  2,2,2,2 - 2,0,0,0 - timp. - pf. - str.   22:00 Bo. Hawkes.
—— CONCERTO FOR TRUMPET AND ORCH.
                                                16:00 General.
—— CONCERTO FOR VIOLIN AND ORCH.
  2,2,2,2 - 4,2,3,1 - timp.,perc.,cel. - str.   20:00 Bo. Hawkes.
—— SYMPHONY
  3,3,3,3 - 4,3,3,1 - timp.,perc. - str.   36:00 Bo. Hawkes.

KALAŠ, Julius
—— CONCERTO IN A MAJOR FOR CELLO AND ORCH., OP. 68
  2,2,2,2 - 4,2,3,1 - timp.,perc.,cel. - hp. - str. 43:00 Bo. Hawkes.
—— CONCERTO IN D MINOR FOR VIOLA AND ORCH., OP. 69
  2,2,2,2 - 3,2,2,0 - timp.,perc. - str.   25:00 Bo. Hawkes.
—— THE NIGHTINGALE AND THE ROSE (FANTASY FOR
  FLUTE AND ORCH.)
  1,1,2,1 - 3,2,1,0 - timp.,perc.,cel. - hp. - str. 25:00 Bo. Hawkes.
—— SERENADE IN E FLAT MAJOR
  str.   27:00 Bo. Hawkes.

KALČIĆ, Josip
—— LJUDSKOJ SOLIDARNOSTI (TO THE SOLIDARITY OF
  HUMANITY) (CANTATA) (FOR SOLO VOICES, SATB
  CHORUS AND ORCH.)
  3,3,3,3 - 4,3,3,1 - timp.,perc.,vibra.,xyl. - hp. - str.
                                                18:00 MIC,Zagreb.
—— MUSIC 1973
  2(2nd alt. with picc.),2(2nd alt. with Eng. hn.),2(2nd alt. with
  b.-cl.),2(2nd alt. with c.-bn.) - 4,3,3,1 - timp.,perc.,vibra. - hp. - pf.
  - str.   10:00 MIC,Zagreb.
—— PRELUDE (1971)
  1,1,1,1 - 1,1,1,0 - perc.(2) - pf. - str.(2,1,1,1) 6:20 MIC,Zagreb.
—— SIMFONIJSKA SLIKA '72 (SYMPHONIC PICTURE 1972)
  3,3,3,2 - 4,4,3,1 - timp.,perc. - pf. - str. 10:00 MIC,Zagreb.
—— STROFE (STROPHE)
  0,0,0,0 - 1,2,1,1 - perc. - hp. - pf. - str. 8:00 MIC,Zagreb.

KALINENKO, Konstantin K.
—— LULLABY (SYMPHONIC POEM FOR MEZZO-SOPRANO,
  BARITONE AND ORCH.) (Text: Yu. Entin)
                                                G. Schirmer.

KALLED, Emil
—— AIR FOR STRING ORCH. (1964)
  str.   4:30 Templeton.
—— CAPRICCIO FOR ORCH.
  3(3rd alt. with picc.),*3,*3,*3 - 4,3,3,1 - timp.,perc. - str.
                                                10:00 Composer.
—— PRELUDE AND FUGUE FOR ORCH.
  3(3rd alt. with picc.),*4,1 E♭cl.,3(3rd alt. with b.-cl.),3(3rd alt.
  with c.-bn.) - 4,3,3,1 - timp.,perc.(3),glock.,xyl. - 2 hp. - str.
                                                13:00 Composer.

KALLSTENIUS, Edvin
—— CONCERTO FOR PIANO AND ORCH., OP. 12 (SINFONIK
  CONCERTATA)
  2,2,2,2 - 4,2,3,1 - timp. - str.   S.T.I.M.
—— DALARAPSODI ("DALECARLIA"), OP. 18
  2,2,2,2 - 2,2,1,0 - timp.,perc. - hp. - str. 15:00 Suecia.
  or:
  2,2,2,2 - 4,2,3,1 - timp.,perc. - str.
—— DIVERTIMENTO DA CAMERA, OP. 29B
  2,2,2,2 - 2,2,0,0 - timp. - str.   15:00 S.T.I.M.
—— GAMMALSVENSK SANGSVIT (IN 4 MOVTS.)
  2,2,2,2 - 2,2,1,0 - timp.,perc. - str.   16:00 T & J.
—— HÖGTID OCH FEST (SYMPHONIC TRILOGY), OP. 26 (IN 3
  MOVTS.)
  2,2,2,2 - 2,2,2,0 - timp.,perc. - str.   21:00 S.T.I.M.
—— KOREOGRAFISK SVIT, OP. 48
  2,2,2,2 - 2-4,2,1,1 - timp.,perc.(2) - str.   S.T.I.M.

—— LITEN FALU-MUSIK (SUITE), OP. 28
2,2,2,2 - 2,2,1,0 - timp.,perc. - str.   12:00 S.T.I.M.
—— MUSICA GIOCONDA (SERENADE), OP. 27 (IN 3 MOVTS.)
str.   17:30 Gehrmans.
—— MUSICA SINFONICA, OP. 42 (VERSION FOR FULL ORCH.)
2,2,2,2 - 2-4,2,1,0 - timp. - str.   18:00 S.T.I.M.
—— PROLOGO SERIALE, OP. 63 (1966)
2,2,2,2 - 2,2,1,0 - timp.,perc. - str.   6:00 Fleisher.
—— ROMANTICO, OP. 24
2,2,2,2 - 4,2,3,1 - timp.,perc. - str.   14:00 S.T.I.M.
or:
2,2,2,2 - 2,2,1,0 - timp.,perc. - str.
—— SAFFO-MINIATURE (SUITE)
1,1,0,0 - 0,0,0,0 - hp. - str.   11:00 S.T.I.M.
—— EN SERENAD I SOMMARNATTEN (SYMPHONIC POEM), OP. 10
2,3,2,2 - 4,3,0,0 - timp.,cel. - hp. - pf. - str.   17:00 Nordiska.
—— SERENADE FROM "CYRANO"
1,2,0,0 - 2,0,0,0 - str.   3:30 Southern.
—— SEVEN MINIATURES (FROM THE FAIRY PLAY "PRINCESS MIRAFLOR")
1,1,2,1 - 2,2,1,0 - timp., - hp. - cemb.(ad lib.) - str.   Gehrmans.
—— SHAKESPEARIAN SUITE (FROM MUSIC FOR "A MIDSUMMER NIGHT'S DREAM")
1,1,0,0 - 1,0,0,0 - str.   16:00 S.T.I.M.
or:
1,0,1,0 - 0,1,0,0 - str.
—— SINFONIETTA NO. 2, OP. 34
2,2,2,2 - 2,2,1,0 - timp. - str.   18:00 S.T.I.M.
or:
2,2,2,2 - 4,2,1,0 - timp. - str.
—— SINFONIETTA NO. 3, OP. 46 ("DODICITONICA")
2,2,2,2 - 2,2,1,1 - timp.,perc.(2) - str.   14:00 S.T.I.M.
—— SINFONIETTA NO. 4 ("SEMI-SERIALE"), OP. 50
2,2,2,2 - 4,3,3,1 - timp. - str.   18:00 S.T.I.M.
—— SISTA STRIDEN (DRAMATIC OVERTURE), OP. 5
2,2,2,2 - 4,2,3,1 - timp.,perc. - str.   16:00 S.T.I.M.
—— SONATA CONCERTANTE FOR CELLO AND ORCH., OP. 40
2,2,2,2 - 2,2,1,0 - timp.,perc. - str.   S.T.I.M.
—— SONG-OFFERING (SANGFOFFER), OP. 32 (CANTATA) (FOR BARITONE AND ORCH.)
2,2,2,2 - 4,2,3,1 - timp. - hp. - str.   17:00 Bo. Hawkes.
—— SUITE FOR ORCHESTRA, OP. 23
1,1,2,1 - 2,1,0,0 - timp. - str.   13:00 S.T.I.M.
—— SUITE FOR 14 WIND INSTRUMENTS AND TYMPANI, OP. 23
2,2,2,2 - 2,2,2,0 - timp.   13:00 S.T.I.M.
—— SWEDISH ROCOCO SUITE (IN 3 MOVTS.)
2,3,0,1 - 2,2,0,0, - timp. - str.   10:00 Southern.
or:
2,1,2,1 - 2,2,0,0 - timp. - str.
—— SYMPHONY NO. 1 IN E♭ MAJOR, OP. 16
2,2,2,2 - 4,3,3,1 - timp. - pf. (ad lib.) - str.   22:00 S.T.I.M.
—— SYMPHONY NO. 2 IN F MINOR, OP. 20
2,3,3,2 - 4,3,3,1 - timp.,perc. - hp. - str.   31:00 S.T.I.M.
—— SYMPHONY NO. 3 IN A MINOR, OP 36
2,2,2,2 - 4,3,3,1 - timp.,perc. - str.   27:00 S.T.I.M.
—— SYMPHONY NO. 4 IN E MINOR, ("SINFONIA A FRESCO"), OP. 43
2,2,2,2 - 4,3,3,1 - timp. - str.   23:00 S.T.I.M.
—— SYMPHONY NO. 5, OP. 52 (SINFONIA ORDINARIA MA SU TEMI 12-TONICI)
2,2,2,2 - 4,3,3,1 - timp.,perc.(2) - str.   22:00 S.T.I.M.
—— THREE DANCE STUDIES, OP. 21
2,2,2,2 - 2,2,1,0 - timp.,perc.,cel. - hp. - pf.(ad lib.) - str.   11:00 S.T.I.M.
—— THREE FANTASIES FOR STRINGS
str.   Ries-Erler.
—— THREE PIECES FOR STRINGS
str.   12:00 S.T.I.M.
—— VIOLINEN OCH DE ONDA MAKTERNA (DRAMATIC PRELUDE)
2,2,2,2 - 2,2,2,1 - timp.,perc. - str.   '6:00 S.T.I.M.
or:
2,2,2,2 - 4,2,3,1 - timp.,perc. - str.

KALMANOFF, Martin
—— CONCERTO NO. 3 FOR PIANO AND ORCH. ("CLIMAX")
*3,2,2,2 - 4,3,3,1 - timp.,perc.(1),cel. - hp. - pf. - str.   Rosarita.
—— THE GREAT STONE FACE (OPERA) %
2,1,1,1 - 2,1,2,0 - timp.,perc. - str.   50:00 C. Fischer.

—— KADDISH FOR A WARRING WORLD (FOR TENOR, BARITONE, CHORUS AND ORCH.) (1970) (Texts: Traditional Jewish Liturgy, Karl Shapiro, Siegfried Sassoon and Allen Ginsberg)
1,1,1,1 - 1,1,1,0 - timp.,perc.,cel.,glock.,xyl. - hp. - str.   35:00 Composer.
—— SYMPHONY IN D
1. Maestoso; 2. Andante moderato; 3. Allegro vivo
*3,*3,2(2nd alt. with E♭ cl.),*3 - 4,2,3,1 - timp.,perc.(2),cel.,xyl. - str.   17:00 Composer.

KALMÁR, László
—— CYCLES (FOR 18 STRINGS)
str.   6:30 Bo. Hawkes.

KALNINS, Janis
—— THE LONG NIGHT (GARA NAKTS) (CANTATA) (FOR MALE CHORUS AND ORCH.) (Text: Velta Toma)
    12:00 C.A.P.A.C.
—— MUSIC FOR STRING ORCH. (1965)
str.   17:00 CanMusCtr.
—— NEW BRUNSWICK RHAPSODY (1966)
*3,2,2,2 - 4,3,3,1 - timp.,perc.,cel. - hp. - str.   13:00 CanMusCtr.
—— SYMPHONY NO. 3 (1973) (IN 3 MOVTS.)
*3,2,2,2 - 4,3,3,1 - timp.,perc. - hp. - str.   26:00 CanMusCtr.
—— SYMPHONY OF THE BEATITUDES (FOR MIXED CHORUS AND ORCH.) (1953)
2,2,2,2 - 4,3,3,1 - timp.,cel. - hp. - str.   32:22 CanMusCtr.

KALOMIRIS, Manolis
—— SYMPHONY NO. 1, OP. 21 ("LA LEVENDIA")
    A.E.P.I.

KAMINSKI, Heinrich
—— APHELIUS (SYMPHONISCHER EPILOG)
3,2,3,3 - 4,4,3,0 - timp.,perc.,cel. - hp. - str.   9:00 Baerenrtr.
—— IN MEMORIAM (FOR VIOLIN, CONTRALTO AND ORCH.)
    Baerenrtr.
—— KING APHELIUS (OPERA) %
    Baerenrtr.
—— PRELUDE FOR ORCH.
    Baerenrtr.
—— PROLOGUE (FOR NARRATOR AND ORCH.)
    Baerenrtr.
—— SYMPHONIC BALLAD (TANZDRAMA)
3(3rd alt. with picc.),2,*3,*3 - 3,3,2,0 - timp.,perc.(5) - str.   15:00 G. Schirmer.

KAMINSKI, Joseph
—— BALLADE FOR HARP AND ORCH.
1,0,1,1 - 1,0,0,0 - perc. - hp. - str.   14:00 IsMuPublns.
—— CONCERTINO FOR TRUMPET AND ORCH.
2,1,1,2 - 2,0,1,1 - timp.,perc. - pf. - str.   15:00 IsMuPublns.
—— CONCERTO FOR VIOLIN AND ORCH.
2,2,2,2 - 4,2,1,1 - timp.,perc. - str.   28:00 Bo. Hawkes.
—— ISRAELI SKETCHES
3,3,2,3 - 4,3,3,1 - timp.,perc.,cel. - hp. - str.   11:00 Bo. Hawkes.
—— OUVERTURE JOYEUSE (OVERTURE COMIQUE)
3,2,2,3 - 4,2,3,1 - timp.,perc. - hp. - str.   10:00 IsMuPublns.

KANCHELI, Georgij A.
—— SYMPHONY NO. 3
    G. Schirmer.

KANITZ, Ernest
—— ABENDFEIER IM RUNDFUNK (EVENING FESTIVAL FOR RADIO) (FOR SOPRANO AND ORCH.) (IN 3 MOVTS.) (Text: Composer)
3(2nd and 3rd alt. with 2 picc.),2(2nd alt. with Eng.hn.),2(alt. with 2 E♭ cl. and 2nd alt. also with b.-cl.),2(2nd alt. with c.-bn.) - 4,3,3,1 - timp.,perc.(3-4), cel.,glock.,xyl. - 2 guit. - mandolin(ad lib) - hp. - 2 pf. - str.   20:00 Composer.
—— CONCERT PIECE FOR TRUMPET AND ORCH.
2,1,2,1 - 2,1,1,0 - timp.,perc. - pf. - str.   9:00 Mills.
—— CONCERTO FOR BASSOON AND ORCH. (IN 3 MOVTS.)
2(2nd alt. with picc.),1,2(2nd alt. with b.-cl.),2(2nd alt. with c.-bn.) - 2,2,2,0 - timp.,perc.(4), cel.,glock.,xyl. - hp. - str.   22:00 Presser.
—— CONCERTO FOR CHAMBER ORCH. (IN 3 MOVTS.)
2(2nd alt. with picc.),1,2,1 - 1,2,1,0 - timp.,perc.(3-4),glock.,xyl. - pf. - str.   14:30 Composer.
—— CONCERTO GROSSO (IN 3 MOVTS.)
1,1,2,1 sopr. sax.,1 - 2,1,0,0 - timp.,perc.(3-4),glock.,xyl. - pf. - str.   14:00 AmMuCtr.

—— GOTTHELF SCHLIGHT (DAS LEBENSLIED EINES
EINFACHEN MENSCHEN) (LIFE-SONG OF A COMMON
MAN) (FOR 5 SOLO VOICES, BOY'S CHORUS, MIXED
CHORUS AND ORCH.) (Text: Wilhelm Alt)
  3(3rd alt. with picc.),3(3rd alt. with Eng. hn.),3(3rd alt. with E♭cl.
  and b.-cl.),3(3rd alt. with c.-bn.) - 4,3,3,1 -
  timp.,perc.(4),cel.,glock.,xyl. - hp. - org.(ad lib.) - pf. - 2 mandolins
  - str.   90:00 Composer.
—— MOTION PICTURE SUITE (IN 3 MOVTS.)
  3(2nd and 3rd alt. with 2.picc.),3(3rd alt. with Eng. hn.),3(3rd alt.
  with b.-cl.),3(3rd alt. with c.-bn.) - 4,3,3,1 - timp.,perc.cel. - hp. -
  pf. - str.   8:00 Composer.
—— SINFONIA SERIA (1963) (IN 3 MOVTS.)
  3(2nd and 3rd alt. with 2 picc.),3(3rd alt. with Eng.hn.),3(3rd alt.
  with E♭cl. and b.cl.),3(3rd alt. with c.-bn.) - 4,3,3,1 -
  timp.,perc.,bells,cel.,glock.,xyl. - hp. - pf. - str.   21:00 Presser.
—— SYMPHONY NO. 2 (1965) (IN 5 MOVTS.)
  3(2nd and 3rd alt. with 2 picc.),3(3rd alt. with Eng.hn.),3(3rd alt.
  with E♭cl.,b.-cl. and alto sax.),3(3rd alt. with c.-bn.) - 4,3,3,1 -
  timp.,perc.(6),cel.,glock.,xyl. - hp. - pf. - str.   30:30 Presser.
—— SYMPHONY NO. 3 (SINFONIA CONCERTANTE) (FOR
VIOLIN CELLO AND ORCH.) (1967) (IN 3 MOVTS.)
  3(3rd alt. with picc.),3(3rd alt. with Eng. hn.),3(3rd alt. with E♭cl.
  and b.-cl.),3(3rd alt. with c.-bn.) - 4,3,3,1 -
  timp.,perc.(6-8),cel.,glock.,xyl. - hp. - pf. - str.   18:30 Presser.
—— VISIONES IN CREPUSCULO (VISIONS AT TWILIGHT) (FOR
MEZZO-SOPRANO OR UNISON WOMEN'S VOICES AND
CHAMBER ORCH.) (1962) (IN 4 MOVTS.)
  fl. - pf. - str.   18:00 Composer.
—— ZEITMUSIK (MUSIC OF THIS TIME) (CANTATA)
(FOR BARITONE, WOMEN'S VOICES AND CHAMBER ORCH.)
  (German Text: Composer; Engl. Text: Hampton Jarrell)
  1(alt. with picc.),0,1(alt. with E♭cl., b.-cl. and alto sax.),0 -
  0,2,0,0 - timp.,perc.(1-2),glock.,xyl. - mandolin(alt. with banjo) -
  pf.(4-hands) - str.   20:00 Composer.

KANTOR, Joseph
—— ARIOSO (FOR OBOE AND SMALL ORCH.)
  3,1,0,0 - 0,0,0,0 - str.   8:00 Composer.
  or:
  2,1,1,0 - 0,0,0,0 - str.
—— ESSAY FOR SMALL ORCH. (IN 3 MOVTS.)
  2,2,2,2 - 2,0,0,0 - timp. - str.   10:00 Composer.
—— MUSIC FOR ORCHESTRA
  2,2,2,2 - 4,2,3,0 - timp.,perc.(2),xyl. - str.   11:00 Composer.
—— PSALM 23 (FOR MEZZO-SOPRANO AND SMALL ORCH.)
  2,2,2,2 - 2,0,0,0 - timp. - str.   5:30 Composer.

KANTUŠER, Božidar
—— CHAMBER SYMPHONY
  timp.,cel.(or pf.) - str.   20:00 Hans Gerig.
—— CONCERTO FOR CELLO AND ORCH.
  2,2,2,1 - 2,1,1,0 - timp.,perc. - str.   18:00 Presser.
—— CONCERTO FOR FLUTE, STRINGS AND PERCUSSION
  fl. - perc. - str.   20:00 Hans Gerig.
—— OUVERTURE DE CONCERT
  2,2,2,2 - 3,2,2,0 - timp. - hp. - str.   8:00 Presser.
—— SIRE HALEWYN (SUITE)
  3,2,3,3 - 4,3,3,1 - timp.,perc.,cel. - hp. - str. 43:00 Presser.
—— SYMPHONY FOR STRINGS
  str.   24:00 Presser.
—— SYMPHONY NO. 3
  *2,2,2,*2 - 4,3,3,1 - perc.,cel. - hp. - str.   24:00 Hans Gerig.

KAPER, Bronislaw
—— THE GLASS SLIPPER (BALLET SUITE FROM THE FILM)
                                                   Robbins.

KAPR, Jan
—— ANDANTE FOR CELLO AND ORCH.
  3,3,3,3 - 2,3,0,0 - timp.,perc. - hp. - str.   10:00 Bo. Hawkes.
—— CONCERTO FOR VIOLIN AND ORCH.,OP. 69 (1955)
  1. Lento tranquillo - Allegro ma non troppo; 2. Allegro con fuoco
  2,1,2,1 - 3,1,0,1 - timp.,perc. - hp. - str.   23:00 Bo. Hawkes.
—— CONCERTO NO. 2 FOR PIANO AND ORCH.
  3,2,2,2 - 4,3,3,1 - timp.,perc. - pf. - str.   36:00 Bo. Hawkes.
—— HARVEST FESTIVAL (RHAPSODY IN FOLK STYLE)
  2,2,2,2 - 4,3,3,1 - timp.,perc.,cel. - hp. - str. 9:00 Bo. Hawkes.
—— SUITE FOR ORCHESTRA
  3,2,3,3 - 4,3,3,1 - timp.,perc.,cel. - hp. - str. 25:00 Bo. Hawkes.
—— SYMPHONY NO. 2
  3,2,3,3 - 4,3,3,1 - timp.,perc.,cel. - hp. - str. 50:00 Bo. Hawkes.

—— SYMPHONY NO. 3 (FOR CHAMBER ORCH.)
  2,1,2,1 - 2,1,0,1 - timp.,perc. - str.   25:00 Bo. Hawkes.

KAPRÁLOVÁ, Vítězslava
—— MILITARY SINFONIETTA
  3,3,4,3 - 6,3,3,i - timp.,perc.,cel. - hp. - pf. - str.
                                                   20:00 Bo. Hawkes.

KARAYEV, Kara
—— OVERTURE TO "LEILY AND MEJNUN"
  3,3,3,2 - 4,3,3,1 - timp.,perc. - hp. - pf. - str.   G. Schirmer.
—— PATH OF THUNDER (BALLET SUITE NO. 1) (WITH
MEZZO-SOPRANO SOLO)
  3(1 alt. with alto fl.),3,4,3 - 4,3,3,1 - timp.,perc.,cel.,xyl. - 2 hp. -
  pf. - str.   23:00 G. Schirmer.
—— THE SEVEN BEAUTIES (BALLET SUITE)
  3,3,3,3 - 4,3,3,1 - timp.,perc.,cel.,xyl. - hp. - pf. - str.
                                                   28:00 G. Schirmer.

KARDOŠ, Dezider
—— CONCERTO FOR ORCHESTRA
  3,3,3,3 - 4,3,3,1 - timp.,perc.,cel. - hp. - pf. - str.
                                                   35:00 Bo. Hawkes.
—— EAST SLOVAKIAN OVERTURE
                                                   Bo. Hawkes.
—— GREETING TO A GREAT LAND, OP. 25 (CANTATA) (FOR
SOPRANO, SATB CHORUS AND ORCH.) (1954)
                                                   22:00 Bo. Hawkes.
—— HEROIC BALLAD
  str.   16:00 Bo. Hawkes.
—— MY HOMELAND (SYMPHONIC OVERTURE)
                                                   Bo. Hawkes.
—— PEACE CANTATA, OP. 21-C (FOR BARITONE, MIXED
CHORUS AND ORCH.) (Text: Pavel Horov)
                                                   Bo. Hawkes.
—— SYMPHONY NO. 1 (1942)
                                                   Bo. Hawkes.

KARJALAINEN, Ahti
—— CERTANTES, OP. 23 (VARIATIONS FOR FLUTE, OBOE AND
ORCH.) (1946)
  2,2,2,2 - 4,2,3,0 - timp. - hp. - str.   10:00 FinnMICtr.
—— CONCERT SUITE FOR BASSOON AND ORCH., OP. 34 (1949)
  2,2,2,2,- 4,2,3,0 - timp. - str.   20:00 FinnMICtr.
—— CONCERTO FOR CELLO AND ORCH., OP. 50 (1956)
  1,1,2,1 - 2,1,1,0 - timp. - str.   20:00 FinnMICtr.
—— CONCERTO FOR TROMBONE AND ORCH., OP. 16 (1942)
  2,2,2,2 - 4,2,2,1 - timp.,perc. - str.   19:00 FinnMICtr.
—— CONCERTO FOR VIOLIN AND ORCH., OP. 40 (1952)
  2,2,2,2 - 2,2,1,0 - timp.,perc. - str.   24:00 FinnMICtr.
—— COUNTERPOINT VARIATIONS, OP. 28 (1947)
  str.   10:00 FinnMICtr.
—— DUO FOR TWO TRUMPETS AND ORCH., OP. 33 (1950)
  1,1,2,1 - 2,4,1,0 - timp. - str.   6:00 FinnMICtr.
—— FOUR WINTER SCENCES, OP. 29 (1948)
  2,2,2,2 - 4,2,3,0 - timp.,perc. - hp. - str.   15:00 FinnMICtr.
—— FROM MORNING TO NIGHT, OP. 8 (A RUSTIC SCENE)
(1937)
  3,3,3,2 - 4,3,3,1 - timp.,perc. - str.   12:00 FinnMICtr.
—— HAKKAA PÄÄLLE, OP. 11 (AN OVERTURE) (1938)
  2,2,2,3 - 4,3,3,1 - timp.,perc.(3) - str.   9:00 FinnMICtr.
—— MERIKOSKI, OP. 7 (1937)
  2,2,3,3 - 4,3,3,1 - timp.,perc.(3) - str.   10:00 FinnMICtr.
—— OVERTURE IN E MAJOR, OP. 5 (1936)
  2,2,2,2 - 4,2,3,0 - timp.,perc. - str.   6:00 FinnMICtr.
—— PARTITA NO. 4, OP. 71 (1961)
  str.   11:00 FinnMICtr.
—— PARTITA NO. 5, OP. 77 (1964)
  fl. - timp, - str.   8:00 FinnMICtr.
—— PARTITA NO. 6, OP. 80 (1965)
  bn. - hn. - timp, - str.   8:00 FinnMICtr.
—— SCHERZO, OP. 12 (FOR TRUMPET, TROMBONE AND
ORCH.) (1940)
  2,2,2,2 - 2,3,2,0 - timp.,perc. - str.   5:00 FinnMICtr.
—— SUITE FOR SMALL ORCH., OP. 76 (1964)
  2,1,2,1 - 2,1,1,0 - timp. - str.   9:00 FinnMICtr.
—— SUMMER SCENES, OP. 18 (SUITE FOR OBOE AND ORCH.)
(1944) (IN 5 MOVTS.)
  2,1,2,2 - 4,3,3,1 - timp. - hp. - str.   18:00 FinnMICtr.
—— SYMPHONY NO. 1 IN C MINOR, OP. 30 (1948)
  3,3,3,3 - 4,3,3,1 - timp.,perc. - hp. - str.   35:00 FinnMICtr.
—— VALMET INC., OP, 85 (A FACTORY SCENE) (1970)
  3,2,2,2 - 4,3,3,1 - timp.,perc.(4),vibra. - str. 10:00 FinnMICtr.

—— VARIATIONS ON A FINNISH SOLDIER'S SONG, OP. 19
(1944)
    2,2,2,2 - 4,2,3,0 - timp.,perc. - str.   10:00 FinnMICtr.

KARKOFF, Maurice
—— CHARACTER PIECES, OP. 109 (PARTES CARACTERIS)(1971)
    2,2,2,1 - 2,0,0,0 - timp.,perc.(4,incl. 3 on timp.) - hp. - str.
    10:00 Fleisher.
—— CONCERTINO FOR ALTO SAXOPHONE, STRINGS AND
PERCUSSION, OP. 15 (1955)
    alto sax. - perc. - str.   13:00 S.T.I.M.
—— CONCERTO DA CAMERA, OP. 56 (FOR 14 WINDS,
PERCUSSION AND DOUBLE BASS)(REV. 1965)
    2,2,2,2 - 2,2,1,1 - timp.,perc.(3) - d.-b   9:30 Fleisher.
—— CONCERTO FOR CELLO AND ORCH., OP. 31 (1958)
    2,2,2,2 - 2,1,1,0 - timp.,perc.(2) - str.   18:00 S.T.I.M.
—— CONCERTO FOR CLARINET AND STRING ORCH.
    cl. - str.   14:00 Mannheimer.
—— CONCERTO FOR HORN AND ORCH., OP. 40 (1959)
    2,1,2,2 - 1,1,0,0 - timp.,perc.(2) - str.   19:00 S.T.I.M.
—— CONCERTO FOR PIANO AND ORCH., OP. 28 (1957)
    2,2,2,2 - 2,2,2,0 - timp.,perc.(3) - pf. - str.   22:00 S.T.I.M.
—— CONCERTO FOR TROMBONE AND ORCH., OP. 35 (1958)
    2,2,2,2 - 3,2,1,0 - timp. - str.   15:00 S.T.I.M.
—— CONCERTO FOR VIOLIN AND ORCH., OP. 22 (1956)
    3,2,2,2 - 4,3,3,0 - timp.,perc.(3),cel. - hp.   26:00 S.T.I.M.
—— CONCERTO NO. 1 FOR ORCH., OP. 70 (1963)
    2,2,2,2 - 2,2,1,0 - timp.,perc.(3) - str.   16:00 S.T.I.M.
—— EPITAFIUM, OP. 93 (FOR CHAMBER ORCH.)(1968)
    1,1,1,1 - 1,0,0,0 - str.   11:00 Fleisher.
—— FIGURE TRANSFORMATE, OP. 78 (1966)
    3,2,2,2 - 4,3,3,1 - timp.,perc. - hp. - str.   13:00 Fleisher.
—— FIVE SUMMER PICTURES, OP. 98 (1969)
    2,0,2,0 - 0,2,0,0 - timp.,perc.(4) - pf. - str.   12:00 Gehrmans.
—— GESANG DES ABGESCHIEDENEN, OP. 48-B (5 SONGS FOR
BARITONE AND ORCH.) (1960) (Text: Georg Trakl)
    2,2,2,2 - 2,2,1,0 - timp.,perc.(2) - str.   12:00 S.T.I.M.
—— HIMMEL OCH JORD, OP. 50 (CANTATA) (FOR
COLORATURA SOPRANO, TTBB CHORUS AND ORCH.)
(1960) (Text: Bo Setterlind)
    2,2,2,2 - 2-4,2,1,1 - timp.,perc.(3) - str.   9:00 S.T.I.M.
—— KORTA VARIATIONER, OP. 9 (FOR STRING ORCH.) (1953)
    str.   14:00 Suecia.
—— LIVET, OP. 41 (SONGS AND RECITATION) (FOR LOW
VOICE AND ORCH.) (1959)
    2,2,2,2 - 2,2,1,0 - str.   12:00 S.T.I.M.
—— LYRIC SUITE NO. 1, OP. 34-A (1958)
    1,1,1,1 - 1,0,0,0 - str.   11:00 Bo. Hawkes.
—— LYRIC SUITE NO. 2, OP. 34-B (1958)
    1,1,1,1 - 1,0,0,0 - str.   10:00 Bo. Hawkes.
—— METAMORFOSI (1967)
    2,0,2,1 - 2,1,1,0 - perc.(2) - str.   12:00 S.T.I.M.
—— NIO AFORISTISKA VARIANTER, OP. 43 (1959)
    2,2,3,2 - 2,2,1,1 - timp.,perc.(2) - hp. - str.   12:00 Gehrmans.
—— ORIENTAL PICTURES, OP. 66-A (1966)
    2,2,2,2 - 2,2,1,0 - perc.(3) - str.   19:00 Gehrmans.
—— PASSACAGLIA FOR STRINGS, OP. 111 (1971)
    str.   8:00 Fleisher.
—— QUATTRO PARTI, OP. 94 (FOR 13 WINDS AND PERC.)(1968)
    0,0,0,0 - 4,4,4,1 - perc.   9:00 Fleisher.
—— SERENADE FOR STRINGS, OP. 6
    str.   10:00 S.T.I.M.
—— SINFONIA DA CAMERA, OP. 72 (1965)
    2,3,2,1 - 2,1,1,0 - str.   16:00 S.T.I.M.
—— SINFONIETTA FOR LITTLE ORCH., OP. 12
    1,1,1,1 - 1,1,1,0 - timp.,perc. - str.   13:00 S.T.I.M.
—— SINFONIETTA GRAVE, OP. 95 (1969)
    2,2,2,2 - 2,2,2,1 - timp.,perc.(4) - str.   12:00 S.T.I.M.
—— SIX ALLVARLIGA SONGS, OP. 14 (FOR LOW VOICE AND
ORCH.) (1955) (Text: Elsa Grave)
    2,2,3,2 - 1,0,0,0 - timp.,perc.(2) - hp. - str.   16:00 S.T.I.M.
—— DET SVENSKA LANDET, OP. 23 (1956) (FESTIVAL
CANTATA) (FOR TENOR OR BARITONE SOLO, TTBB
CHORUS AND ORCH.) (Text: Anders Österling)
    2,2,2,2 - 2,2,1,0 - timp.,perc.(3) - str.   12:30 S.T.I.M.
—— SYMPHONIC REFLECTIONS, OP. 110 (1971)
    2,2,2,2 - 2,2,1,0 - perc.(2) - pf.(or cel.) - str.   15:00 Gehrmans.
—— SYMPHONY NO. 1, OP. 17 (1956)
    3,2,2,2 - 4,3,3,1 - timp.,perc.(2) - str.   21:00 S.T.I.M.
—— SYMPHONY NO. 2, OP. 25 (1957)
    2,2,2,2 - 2,2,2,0 - timp.,perc.(2-4) - str.   20:00 S.T.I.M.

—— SYMPHONY NO. 3, OP. 38 (SINFONIA BREVE) (1959) (IN 1
MOVT.)
    2,2,2,2 - 2,2,1,0 - timp.,perc.(2) - str.   15:00 Gehrmans.
—— SYMPHONY NO. 6, OP. 117 (1973)
    2,2,2,2 - 4,3,3,1 - timp.,perc.(4) - hp. - str.   16:00 Fleisher.
—— TEN JAPANESE SONGS, OP. 45 (FOR HIGH VOICE AND
ORCH.) (1959)
    1,1,1,1 - 2,2,1,0 - timp. - str.   13:00 S.T.I.M.
—— TEXTOM, OP. 87 (1967)
    str.   12:00 S.T.I.M.
—— TRANSFIGURATE MUTATE, OP. 78 (1966)
    3,2,2,2 - 4,3,3,1 - timp.,perc.(2) - hp. - str.   11:00 S.T.I.M.
—— TRIPARTITA, OP. 82 (1967)
    2,2,2,2 - 2,2,1,0 - timp. - str.   12:00 Gehrmans.
—— TRIPTYK, OP. 101 (1970)
    3,2,3,2 - 4,3,3,1 - timp.,perc.(4) - hp. - str.   15:00 Fleisher.
—— VARIATIONS FOR ORCH., OP. 58 (1961)
    2,2,3,2 - 4,3,3,1 - timp.,perc.(4),bells,cel.,vibra. - hp. - str.
    20:00 S.T.I.M.
—— VISION, OP. 79, NO. 1 (1966)
    Recorder,2,0,4,0 - 2,4,2,0 - timp.,perc. - guit. - 2 pf. -str.
    5:00 Gehrmans.

KARKOSCHKA, Erhard
—— CONCERTO FOR VIOLIN AND CHAMBER ORCH. (1955)
    0,2,0,2 - 2,0,0,0 - str.   23:00 G. Schirmer.
—— POLYPHONIC STUDY (1956)
    *4,2,*3,*3 - 4,2,3,1 - pf. - str.   18:00 G. Schirmer.
—— VIER STUFEN
    *4,2,4,*3 - 4,2,3,1 - cel.,2 xyl. - hp. - pf. - str.   23:00 AhnSimrock.

KARLIN, Frederick
—— ADAGIO ("ECHOES OF EDEN")
    1(alt. with picc.),1(alt. with Eng.hn.),1(alt. with b.-cl.),1 - 1,0,0,0 -
    timp.,perc.(1),bells,cel.,xyl. - hp. - pf. - str.   8:00 Troubadour.
—— ON A CHURCH THEME (FOR BRASS ENSEMBLE)
    0,0,0,0 - 4,3,3,1   6:00 Troubadour.

KARTE, Onni
—— AT SUNRISE (1944)
    3,3,2,2 - 4,3,3,1 - timp. - str.   9:00 FinnMICtr.
—— DISTANT SKERRIES (SYMPHONIC POEM) (1936)
    2,3,2,2 - 2,2,1,0 - timp.,perc.(4, incl. 2 on timp.) - hp. - str.
    9:00 FinnMICtr.
—— LYRICAL SUITE NO. 1 (1926)
    2,2,2,2 - 2,2,1,0 - timp.,perc.(5, incl. 2 on timp.) - hp. - str.
    12:00 FinnMICtr.
—— LYRICAL SUITE NO. 2 (1927)
    2,3,2,2 - 4,3,3,1 - timp.,perc.(5, incl. 2 on timp.) - hp. - str.
    15:00 FinnMICtr.
—— MUSIC TO FRANZ WERFEL'S PLAY "PAUL AND THE JEWS"
(FOR CHORUS AND ORCH.) (1936)
    2,2,2,0 - 2,2,2,1 - timp.(2 players) - str.   20:00 FinnMICtr.
—— MUSIC TO HEINRICH VON KLEIST'S PLAY "PRINZ
FRIEDRICH VON HOMBURG" (1936) (IN 4 MOVTS.)
    2,2,2,0 - 2,2,1,0 - timp.(2 players) - str.   22:00 FinnMICtr.
—— MUSIC TO ILMARI VAINIO'S PLAY "THE KEY TO HEARTS"
(FOR SOPRANO, CHORUS AND ORCH.) (1928) (IN 8
MOVTS.)
    1,1,2,0 - 2,2,1,0 - timp.(2 players) - str.   45:00 FinnMICtr.
—— ON THE HIGH SEAS (1930)
    2,3,2,2 - 4,3,3,1 - timp.,perc.(5, incl. 3 on timp.) - hp. - str.
    12:00 FinnMICtr.
—— OVERTURE TO ALEKSIS KIVIS PLAY "LEA" (1934)
    1,1,2,1 - 2,2,1,0 - timp.(2 players) - str.   8:00 FinnMICtr.

KARVONEN, Paul E.
—— CONCERT OVERTURE (1960)
    2,2,2,2 - 4,3,3,0 - timp. - str.   7:30 Composer.

KARYOTAKIS, Theodore
—— KLEINE SYMPHONIE (IN 3 MOVTS.)
    A.E.P.I.

KASKI, Heino
—— FANTASIA APPASSIONATA (FOR VIOLIN AND ORCH.)
(REV. 1954)
    2,2,2,2 - 4,3,3,0 - timp. - hp. - str.   8:00 Fazer.
—— OVERTURE IN E FLAT MAJOR (1922)
    3,2,2,2 - 4,3,3,1 - timp.,perc.,cel. - hp. - str.   7:00 FinnMICtr.
—— RHAPSODY FROM RUSSIAN KARELIA, OP. 44 (1926)
    1,2,2,1 - 2,2,1,0 - timp.,perc. - str.   8:00 Westerlund.
    or:

2,2,2,2 - 2,1,0,0 - pf. - str.
—— SUITE FOR ORCHESTRA, OP. 8 (1913)
2,3,2,2 - 4,2,3,1 - timp.,perc. - hp. - str.   10:00 FinnMICtr.
—— SYMPHONY IN B MINOR, OP. 16 (REV. 1919)
3,3,3,2 - 4,3,3,1 - timp.,perc.,bells,cel. - str.   26:00 FinnMICtr.

KASSCHAU, Howard
—— THE LEGEND OF SLEEPY HOLLOW (CONCERTO FOR
PIANO AND ORCH.) (After the story by Washington Irving)
2,2,2,2 - 4,2,3,0 - timp.,perc. - pf. - str.   10:00 G. Schirmer.

KASSERN, Tadeusz
—— TEEN-AGE PIANO CONCERTO
2,2,2,2 - 4,2,1,0 - pf. - str.   12:00 G. Schirmer.

KASTLE, Leonard
—— DESERET (3-ACT OPERA) % (Text: Anne Howard Bailey)
2,2,2,3 - 4,2,3,1 - timp.,perc.(2),bells,cel. - hp. - str.
135:00 ScudderPro.
—— FROM A WHITMAN READER (CYCLE OF 4 SONGS) (FOR
MEZZO-SOPRANO AND ORCH.) (Text: Walt Whitman)
2,3,3,3 - 4,2,3,1 - timp.,perc.(2),bells,cel.,glock. - hp. - str.
16:00 F. Colombo.
—— THE SWING (ONE-ACT OPERA) %
13:00 Composer.

KATES, Morris
—— SYMPHONIA FOR STRINGS
str.   26:00 C.A.P.A.C.
—— VARIATIONS FOR STRINGS (10 VARS. ON AN ORIGINAL
THEME) (FOR STRING QUARTET AND STRING ORCH.)
str.   18:00 C.A.P.A.C.

KATZ, Paul
—— JOLLY SUITE FOR ISRAEL (IN 3 MOVTS.)
2,2,2,2 - 2,2,1,0 - str.   10:00 Transcon.

KATZER, Georg
—— SONATA NO. 2 FOR ORCH.
2,2,2,2 - 4,3,2,1 - timp.,perc. - hp. - pf. - str.   Tetra.

KAUDER, Hugo
—— CONCERTO FOR HORN AND STRING ORCH. (1930)
hn. - str.   8:00 Seesaw.
—— CONCERTO FOR OBOE AND STRING ORCH. (1928)
ob. - str.   7:00 Seesaw.
—— CONCERTO FOR VIOLIN AND ORCH. (1930)
20:00 A.K.M.

KAUFMANN, Walter
—— ANDHERA (FOR PIANO AND ORCH.)
20:00 C.A.P.A.C.
—— CHIVAREE (OVERTURE)
3:30 C.A.P.A.C.
—— CONCERTINO FOR PIANO AND STRINGS
pf. - str.   18:00 C.A.P.A.C.
—— CONCERTO FOR CELLO AND ORCH.
25:00 C.A.P.A.C.
—— CONCERTO NO. 1 FOR PIANO AND ORCH.
35:00 C.A.P.A.C.
—— CONCERTO NO. 2 FOR PIANO AND ORCH.
C.A.P.A.C.
—— CORONATION CANTATA (FOR CHORUS AND ORCH.)
20:00 C.A.P.A.C.
—— DIRGE
9:00 C.A.P.A.C.
—— DIRGE FOR ORCHESTRA
7:00 C.A.P.A.C.
—— DIVERTIMENTO FOR STRINGS
13:00 C.A.P.A.C.
—— FACES IN THE DARK (SUITE) (1948) (IN 6 MOVTS.)
*3,2,*3,2 - 4,3,3,1 - timp.,perc.,cel. - hp. - str.   CanMusCtr.
—— FANTASY 1949 (FOR PIANO AND ORCH.)
30:00 C.A.P.A.C.
—— FLEET STREET OVERTURE
10:00 Arcadia.
—— FOUR ESSAYS FOR SMALL ORCH.
12:00 C.A.P.A.C.
—— FOUR SKIES (ESSAY FOR ORCH.)
30:00 C.A.P.A.C.
—— FOUR SLAVONIC DANCES FOR PIANO AND ORCH., OP. 33
35:00 Arcadia.

—— KALIF STORY (FAIRY TALE FOR NARRATOR AND ORCH.)
25:00 C.A.P.A.C.
—— MAIN STREET (SUITE FOR STRINGS)
18:00 C.A.P.A.C.
—— NOCTURNE FOR ORCH. (1953)
2,2,2,2 - 4,3,3,0 - timp.,perc. - hp. - str.   12:00 CanMusCtr.
—— ROMANTIC CONCERTO (FOR PIANO AND ORCH.)
C.A.P.A.C.
—— THE ROSE AND THE RING (BALLET) (FOR SMALL ORCH.)
%
70:00 C.A.P.A.C.
—— SHORT SUITE (1953) (IN 3 MOVTS.)
1,1,1,1 - 0,3,2,0 - timp.,perc. - hp. - pf. - str.   5:10 CanMusCtr.
—— SINFONIETTA NO. 1 (1948) (IN 3 MOVTS.)
2,2,2,2 - 3,3,3,0 - str.   10:00 CanMusCtr.
—— SINFONIETTA NO. 2 (1960) (IN 3 MOVTS.)
1,1,1,1 - 2,3,2,0 - str.   12:00 CanMusCtr.
—— SIX INDIAN MINIATURES (1942)
*2,1,2,1 - 2,2,2,0 - timp.,perc. - hp. - pf. - str.   15:00 CanMusCtr.
—— STRANGE TOWN AT NIGHT (VARIATIONS FOR ORCH.)
10:00 C.A.P.A.C.
—— SWANEE RIVER VARIATIONS
15:00 C.A.P.A.C.
—— SYMPHONY NO. 1
str.   15:00 C.A.P.A.C.
—— SYMPHONY NO. 3
C.A.P.A.C.
—— SYMPHONY NO. 5 (SINFONIETTA)
10:00 C.A.P.A.C.
—— SYMPHONY NO. 6
25:00 C.A.P.A.C.
—— THEME, VARIATIONS AND RONDO
20:00 C.A.P.A.C.
—— THREE DANCES FOR AN INDIAN PLAY
8:00 C.A.P.A.C.
—— VARIATIONS FOR STRINGS
str.   15:00 C.A.P.A.C.
—— VISAGES (BALLET MUSIC FOR SMALL ORCH.) %
20:00 C.A.P.A.C.

KAUPPI, Emil
—— THE BANQUET AT THE SUN HILL (OPERA) % (1925) (Text:
Ibsen)
2,2,2,2 - 4,3,3,1 - timp.,perc.(3) - hp. - str.   150:00 FinnMICtr.
—— THE COBBLERS ON THE HEATH (OPERA) % (1930) (Text: A.
Kivi)
2,2,2,2 - 2,2,0,0 - perc.(2) - str.   150:00 FinnMICtr.
—— MUSIC TO J. LINNANKOSKI'S PLAY "SAMSON AND
DELILAH" (FOR SATB CHORUS AND ORCH.) (1911)
1,1,2,1 - 2,2,1,0 - timp.,perc. - hp. - str.   FinnMICtr.
—— MUSIC TO K. LEHTIMAKI'S PLAY "SPARTACUS" (1913)
1,1,2,1 - 2,2,1,0 - timp. - str.   FinnMICtr.
—— MUSIC TO S. RISSANEN'S PLAY "THE TUTOR" (1913)
2,2,2,2 - 2,1,1,0 - timp. - str.   FinnMICtr.

KAVARNALIEVA, Konstantina
—— IDYLLE SUR LA MER (IDYLL ON THE SEA) (1950) (IN 2
MOVTS.)
2,*3,1 E♭cl.,2,2 - 4,2,0,1 - perc.,bells,glock.,xyl. - hp. - str.
21:30 Composer.
—— SYMPHONY IN E♭ MAJOR, OP. 6 ("DOIRAN") (1963) (IN 6
MOVTS.)
*3,*3,1 E♭cl.,*3,*3 - 4,2,3,1 - timp.,perc. - hp. - str.
49:24 Composer.

KAY, Don
—— CONCERT MUSIC FOR VIOLA AND STRING ORCH. (1973)
str.   10:00 .AP.R.A.
—— DANCE EPISODES FOR ORCH. (1973)
2(2nd alt. with picc.),2,2,2 - 2,2,3,1 - timp.,perc. - str.
18:00 A.P.R.A.
—— DANCE MOVEMENT FOR SMALL ORCH. (1968)
3:00 A.P.R.A.
—— THREE PIECES FOR STRING ORCH. (1969)
str.   15:00 A.P.R.A.

KAY, Hershy
—— THE CLOWNS
2,2,2,2 - 4,3,3,1 - timp.,perc. - hp. - str.   25:00 Bo. Hawkes.
—— WESTERN SYMPHONY (IN 4 MOVTS.)
2,2,3,2 - 4,3,3,1 - timp.,perc.,cel.(or pf.) - hp. - str.
27:00 Bo. Hawkes.

KAY, Norman
—— KING HEROD (CANTATA) (FOR SOPRANO, BARITONE, MIXED CHORUS AND ORCH.)
2,2(2nd alt. with Eng.hn.),2,2 - 4,2,3,0 - timp.,perc.(2) - hp. - str.
35:00 Oxford.
—— PASSACAGLIA FOR ORCH.
2,2,2,2 - 4,2,3,0 - timp. - hp. - str.
10:00 Oxford.
—— A SUMMER OVERTURE
Oxford.
—— VARIATIONS ON A THEME OF MICHAEL PRAETORIUS
hpsc. - str.
15:00 Oxford.

KAYN, Roland
—— AGGREGATE
0,0,0,0 - 4,4,4,0 - perc. - str.
15:00 F. Colombo.
—— ALLOTROPIE
Leeds.
—— EVOCATION AND TOCCATA
2,2,2,1 sax.,2 - 4,3,3,1 - timp.,perc.,vibra. - hp. - str.
15:00 F. Colombo.
—— METAMORPHOSES FOR CLARINET AND STRING ORCH.
cl. - str.
F. Colombo.
—— SEQUENZEN (1957)
3,3,3,3 - 6,3,4,1 - perc.(7),cel.,xyl. - hp. - pf. - str.(32,14,12,10)
14:00 MCA Music.
—— SIGNALS (1966)
5,2,4,4 sax.,2 - 6,1 cnt.,4,4,2 - timp.,perc.(12) plus,cel.,2 glock.,2 mar.,vibra.,2 xyl. - 2 electric guit. - electric mand. - 2 hp. - cimbalon - 2 Hammond electric org. - 2 pf. - str.
16:00 MCA Music.
—— VECTORS I (1960)
2,1,2,1 - sax.,1 - 1,1,1,0 - timp.,perc.(6),cle.,vibra. - pf. - str.(5,3,2,1)
7:30 MCA Music.
—— VECTORS II (1960-68)
4,4,4,2 sax.,4 - 6,4,4,0 - 2 hp. - 2 pf. - str.(30,10,10,10)
17:00 MCA Music.

KAYSER, Leif
—— CHRISTMAS ORATORIO (IN NATIVITATE DOMINI) (FOR SOPRANO, BARITONE, BASS, SATB CHORUS AND ORCH.)
2,2,2,2 - 3,3,3,0 - hp. - str.
28:00 Henmar.
—— INNO (HYMN)
3,2,4,2 - 4,3,3,1 - perc.
10:00 K.O.D.A.
—— KING CHRISTIANS STOOD (A CONCERT OVERTURE)
3,0,2,3 - 4,3,3,1 - perc.(2) - str.
9:00 Henmar.

KAZACSAY, Tibor
—— CONCERTO FOR BASSOON AND ORCH.
2,2,2,1 - 2,2,1,0 - timp.,perc. - hp. - str.
14:50 Bo. Hawkes.
—— CONCERTO FOR TRUMPET AND ORCH., OP. 131
18:00 Bo. Hawkes.
—— PRO MEMORIA, OP. 122 (FOR BARITONE AND ORCH.)
20:00 Bo. Hawkes.

KEATS, Albert
—— LA RAMBLA (MEMORIES OF BARCELONA) (1970)
A.P.R.A.

KEATS, Donald
—— CONCERT PIECE FOR ORCH.
2,2,2,2 - 4,2,3,1 - timp.,perc.(2) - str.
12:00 Composer.
—— DIVERTIMENTO FOR WINDS AND STRINGS (IN 3 MOVTS.)
1,1,1,1 - 0,0,0,0 - str.
13:00 Composer.
—— SYMPHONY NO. 1 (1957)
1. Poco adagio; 2. Presto; 3. Andante; 4. Allegro
2,*3,1 e^b cl.,2,*3 - 4,2,3,1 - timp.,perc.(3),xyl. - hp. - str.
21:00 Galaxy.
—— SYMPHONY NO. 2 (AN ELEGIAC SYMPHONY) (1962)
1. Poco adagio - Allegro ma non troppo - Poco adagio; 2. Allegro molto; 3. Adagio
*3,*3,*3,*3 - 4,3,3,1 - timp.,perc.(3),cel.,xyl. - hp. - str.
18:00 Bo. Hawkes.

KECHLEY, Gerald
—— THE BECKONING FAIR ONE (2-ACT OPERA) (1954) % (Text: Elwyn L. Kechley, after a story by Oliver Onions)
1,1,1,1 - 2,1,0,0 - timp.,perc.(1) - hp. - pf. - str.
75:00 Composer.
—— CANTATA FOR ST. CECILIA'S DAY (FOR 2 SOPRANOS, BARITONE, SSAATTBB CHORUS AND ORCH.) (1962) (Text: John Dryden)
1,1,0,1 - 0,1,0,0 - timp.,perc.(2),glock.,xyl. - hp. - str.(no vlas.)
20:00 Composer.

—— DAEDALUS AND THE MINOTAUR (DRAMATIC ORATORIO) (FOR NARRATOR, SOPRANO, MEZZO-SOPRANO, BARITONE, MIXED CHORUS AND ORCH.) (Text: Elwyn Kechley)
*3,*3,*3,*3 - 4,3,3,1 - timp.,perc.(4),cel.,glock.,xyl. - hp. - str.
45:00 Composer.
—— THE DWELLING OF YOUTH (FOR SATB CHORUS AND ORCH.) (Text: Composer, after ancient Sanskrit)
*3,*3,*3,2 - 4,2,2,1 - timp.,perc.,glock. - hp. - str. 9:15 C. Fischer.
—— EIGHT VARIATIONS ON AN ORIGINAL THEME
*3,2,2,2 - 4,3,3,0 - timp.,perc.(2) - str.
18:00 Composer.
—— FOR MEN YET UNBORN (FOR SOPRANO, CHORUS AND ORCH.) (1969) (Texts: Various)
2(2nd alt. with picc.),1,1,1 - 1,2,1,0 - timp.,perc.(3),cel. - hp. - str.
17:00 Composer.
—— THE GOLDEN LION (2-ACT OPERA) (1959) % (Text: Elwyn L. Kechley)
2(2nd alt. with picc.),1,1,1 - 2,1,1,0 - timp.,perc.(2),bells - hp. - pf. - str.
120:00 Presser.
—— INTERLUDE FOR STRINGS
str.
6:00 Composer.
—— MUSIC FOR OBOE AND STRINGS
ob. - str.
6:00 Composer.
—— OVERTURE FOR ORCH.
3(3rd alt. with picc.),2,*3,2 - 4,3,3,1 - timp.,perc. - hp. - pf. - str.
6:00 Composer.
—— PRELUDE AND ALLEGRO
*3,2,2,2 - 2,2,1,0 - timp.,perc.(2) - pf. - str.
7:00 Composer.
—— PROLOGUE - ENACTMENT - EPILOGUE (FOR VIOLIN, OBOE, TRUMPET AND STRING ORCH.) (1972)
0,1,0,0 - 0,1,0,0 - str.
15:00 Composer.
—— SYMPHONY NO. 1
1. Adagio con espressione; 2. Allegretto scherzando; 3. Adagio - Allegro molto energico
2(2nd alt. with picc.),2,2,2 - 2,2,1,0 - timp.,perc.(1) - str.
21:00 Composer.
—— WILL YOU NOT WEEP? (FOR CONTRALTO AND CHAMBER ORCH.) (Text: Yaw-Oh; Korean poem, trans. into Engl.)
cl. - str.
7:00 Composer.

KEETBAAS, Dirk
—— WOODHAVEN (AN ORCHESTRAL OVERTURE)
2,2,2,2 - 2,2,2,0 - timp. - str.
8:45 CanMusCtr.

KEIPER, William
—— HEITERE SUITE (NACH STÜCKEN VON DIABELLI)
2,2,2,2 - 4,3,3,0 - timp.,perc.,cel. - hp. - str.
12:00 Riccardo.

KEISER, Lauren
—— CHROMA (FOR CHAMBER ORCH. OF 28 INSTS.) (1974)
7:04 Composer.

KELKEL, Manfred
—— LE COEUR FROID (SYMPHONIC SUITE FROM THE BALLET) (IN 3 MOVTS.)
2,2,2,2 - 4,2,3,0 - timp.,perc. - hp. - pf. - str. 14:00 F. Colombo.
—— CONCERTINO FOR CELLO AND CHAMBER ORCH.
1,0,0,0 - 0,1,0,0 - pf. - str.
14:00 F. Colombo.
—— CONCERTO FOR BASSOON AND ORCH.
2,2,2,0 - 2,2,2,0 - timp.,perc.,cel. - hp. - pf. - str. 16:30 Presser.
—— HOMMAGE À MOZART (PARAPHRASES ON A MOTIVE FROM "THE MAGIC FLUTE")
str.
9:00 Presser.
—— HUNGARIAN DANCE SUITE (IN 4 MOVTS.)
Presser.
—— MAZEL TOV (OVERTURE ON A THEME OF DARIUS MILHAUD)
2,2,2,2 - 2,2,1,0 - perc.(2) - hp. - pf. - str.
Presser.
—— MUSIQUE FUNÈBRE (FOR OBOE AND ORCH.) (IN MEMORY OF THE INNOCENT VICTIMS OF A WAR)
1,1,2,1 - 2,1,1,0 - perc. - pf. - str. 16:00 F. Colombo.
—— OSTINATO FOR ORCH., OP. 11
2,2,2,2 - 2,2,2,1 - perc.(2),cel. - hp. - pf. - str. 7:00 Presser.
—— OSTINATO FOR WIND ORCH.
3,1,2,3 sax.,0 - 0,4,4,1 - timp.,perc.(3),cel.,glock.,vibra. - guit. - hp. - pf. - c.'s.,d.-b.
7:00 Presser.
—— SUITE OF HUNGARIAN DANCES, OP. 18
2,2,2,2 - 2,0,0,0 - timp.,perc.,cel.,glock. - str. 17:00 Presser.

KELLAM, Ian
—— A STARRE SHON BRIGHT (CHRISTMAS CANTATA) (FOR NARRATOR, SOPRANO, MIXED CHORUS AND ORCH.)
hp. - org. - str.
30:00 Galaxy.

KELLER, Alfred
—— VARIATIONEN ÜBER EIN THEMA VON A. SCHONBERG
(FÜR GR. ORCH.)
        14:00 S.U.I.S.A.

KELLER, Ginette
—— SEPT MOUVEMENTS INCANTATOIRES
3,2,2,2 - 2,2,2,0 - timp.,perc.,cel. - str.   30:00 Presser.

KELLER, Homer
—— CONCERTO FOR PIANO AND ORCH.
2,2,2,2 - 2,1,1,0 - timp.,perc. - str.   15:00 C. Fischer.
—— OVERTURE 1947
3,2,2,2 - 4,3,3,1 - timp.,perc. - str.   3:00 C. Fischer.
—— SERENADE FOR CLARINET AND STRINGS
cl. - str.   6:00 C. Fischer.

KELLER, Walter
—— PRELUDE AND FUGUE, OP. 10
1,2,2,1 - 4,2,3,1 - timp. - org. - str.   13:00 C. Fischer.

KELLEY, Edgar Stillman
—— ALADDIN (SUITE), OP. 10 (IN 4 MOVTS.)
*3,2,2,2 - 4,2,3,1 - timp.,perc.(3),xyl. - hp. - str.
     28:00 AmerMusEd.
—— ALICE IN WONDERLAND (A SERIES OF 6 PANTOMINE
PICTURES)
3(3rd alt. with picc.),*3,3(3rd alt. with b.-cl.),3(3rd alt. with c.-bn.)
- 4,3,3,1 - timp.,perc.,cel. - hp. - str.   30:00 Composer.
—— CONFLUENTIA
str.   G. Schirmer.
—— GULLIVER: HIS VOYAGE TO LILIPUT (SYMPHONY)
3(3rd alt. with picc.),2,2,2 - 4,2,3,1 - timp.,perc. - str.
     30:00 Musicus.
—— SYMPHONY NO. 2 IN B♭ MINOR ("NEW ENGLAND")
3(3rd alt. with picc.),*3,*3,2 - 4,2,3,1 - timp. - hp. - str.
     40:00 Musicus.

KELLY, Bryan
—— CANTICUM FESTIVUM (FOR TENOR, SATB CHORUS AND
ORCH.) (Text: John Dryden)
2,2,2,2 - 4,3,3,1 - timp.,perc. - hp. - org. - pf. - str. 12:00 Oxford.
—— CONCERTO DA CAMERA (FOR OBOE AND STRINGS)
ob. - str.   12:00 Novello.
—— COOKHAM CONCERTINO
1,1,1,1 - 2,0,0,0 - timp.,perc. - hp. - str.   15:00 Novello.
—— IMPROVISATIONS ON CHRISTMAS CAROLS
2,2,2,2 - 4,2,3,1 - timp.,perc. - hp. - str.   12:00 Novello.
—— LATIN QUARTER OVERTURE, OP. 1
3,2,2,2 - 4,2,3,1 - timp.,perc.,xyl. - hp. - str.   6:00 Novello.
—— MISSA BREVIS (FOR SATB CHORUS AND ORCH.)
0,0,0,0 - 4,3,3,1 - timp.,perc. - str.   15:00 Oxford.
—— MUSIC FOR BALLET
2,2,2,2 - 4,3,3,1 - timp.,perc. - hp. - pf. (ad lib.) - str.
     16:00 Novello.
—— TEMPEST SUITE
str.   21:00 Novello.

KELLY, Frederick Septimus
—— SERENADE, OP. 7 (FOR FLUTE OR VIOLIN WITH SMALL
ORCH.)
fl.(or vln.) - hn. - hp. - str.   15:00 Oxford.

KELTERBORN, Rudolf
—— CANTATA PROFANA (NACH KLABUND) (FOR BARITONE,
MIXED CHORUS AND SMALL ORCH.)
1,1,2(1 alt. with b.-cl.),1 - 1,1,1,0 - perc.(1) - str. 22:00 Modern.
—— CANTO APPASSIONATO (1959)
3(3rd alt. with picc.),2,*3,*3 - 4,3,3,1 - timp.,perc.(3) - hp. - str.
     8:00 G. Schirmer.
—— CHAMBER SYMPHONY NO. 1 (FOR VIOLIN, 10 WINDS,
PERCUSSION AND LOW STRINGS)(1960)
2,0,2(2nd alt. with b.-cl.),1 - 2,2,1,0 - perc.(2) - hp. - str.(1,4,3,2)
     15:00 G. Schirmer.
—— CHANGEMENTS POUR GRAND ORCHESTRE (1973)
4(3rd and 4th alt. with picc.),*2,4(3rd alt. with b.-cl.),*2 - 4,4,4,0 -
timp.,perc.(4-5),glock.,vibra. - 2 hp. - str. 12:00 G. Schirmer.
—— COMMUNICATIONS (FOR 6 INSTRUMENTAL
GROUPS)(1972)
3(2 alt. with 2 picc., 1 alt. with alto fl.),2(2 alt. with
Eng.hn.),3(3rd alt. with b.-cl.),1(alt. with c.-bn.) - 3,2,3,0 - perc.(4)
- hp. -str.   16:00 G. Schirmer.

—— CONCERTINO FOR PIANO, PERCUSSION AND STRINGS
(1959)
perc.(2) - pf. - str.   12:00 G. Schirmer.
—— CONCERTO FOR CELLO AND ORCH. (1962) (IN 3 MOVTS)
2,2,2,2 - 2,2,1,0 - timp.,perc.(5,incl. 4 on timp.) - hp. - pf. - str.
     14:10 Henmar.
—— FIVE MADRIGALS (FOR SOPRANO, TENOR AND
ORCH.)(1968)
3(3rd alt. with picc.),3(3rd alt. with Eng.hn.),3(3rd alt. with
b.-cl.),3(3rd alt. with c.-bn.) - 4,3,3,1 - timp.,perc.(4),cel. - hp. -
str.   20:00 G. Schirmer.
—— FOUR NIGHT PIECES (1963)
0,0,2(2nd alt. with b.-cl.),0 - 2,0,0,0 - str. 13:00 G. Schirmer.
—— KOMMUNIKATIONEN (FÜR 6 INSTRUMENTALGRUPPEN
(GROSSES ORCH.)
     15:00 G. Schirmer.
—— LAMENTATIONS (1961)
str.   12:00 G. Schirmer.
—— MASS (FOR SOPRANO, TENOR, SATB CHORUS AND ORCH.)
1,2,2,2 - 2,2,2,0 - perc. - hpsc. - str. 34:00 G. Schirmer.
—— METAMORPHOSES (1960)
3(3rd alt. with picc.),2,2,*3 - 3,3,3,1 - timp.,perc.(4) - hp. - str.
     18:00 G. Schirmer.
—— MUSIC FOR CLARINET AND STRINGS (1965)
cl. - str.   11:00 G. Schirmer.
—— MUSIK FÜR KLARINETTE UND STREICHER
cl. - str.   10:30 G. Schirmer.
—— NUOVI CANTI (PER FLAUTI ED ORCHESTRA DA CAMERA)
1,b.-fl.,2,1,0 - 2,0,0,0 - str.   12:00 G. Schirmer.
—— PHANTASMEN (1966)
*3,*3,3(3rd alt. with b.-cl.),*3 - 4,3,3,1 - timp.,perc.(4) - hp. - str.
     10:00 G. Schirmer.
—— SCÈNES FUGITIVES (FOR RECORDER AND ORCH.)(1961)
Recorder,0,2(2nd alt. with Eng. hn.),2(2nd alt. with b.-cl.),2(2nd
alt. with c.-bn.),1,1,1,0 - timp.,perc.(3) - hp. - str.
     12:00 G. Schirmer.
—— SONATA FOR 15 SOLO STRINGS (Arranged from the Sonata for
16 Solo Strings)
str.(8,3,3,1)   12:00 Modern.
—— SONATA FOR 16 SOLO STRINGS
str.   12:00 Modern.
—— SUITE FOR BRASS, PERCUSSION AND STRING ORCH.
0,0,0,0 - 0,2,2,0 - timp.,perc.(5, incl. 4 on timp.) - str.
     20:00 Modern.
—— SYMPHONY NO. 1 (1967) (IN 3 MOVTS.)
3(3rd alt. with picc.),3(3rd alt. with Eng.hn.),3(3rd alt. with
b.-cl.),*3 - 4,3,3,1 - timp.,perc.(4) - hp. - pf. - str.
     20:00 G. Schirmer.
—— SYMPHONY NO. 2 (1970)
3(3rd alt. with picc.),3(3rd alt. with Eng.hn.),3(3rd alt. with
b.-cl.),3(3rd alt. with c.-bn.) - 4,3,3,1 - timp.,perc.(4), cel. - hp. -
pf. - str.   19:00 G. Schirmer.
—— TABLEAUX ENCADRÉS (7 COMPOSITIONS FOR 13
STRINGS)(1974)
str.(7,3,2,1)   15:00 G. Schirmer.
—— TRAUMMUSIK (6 PIECES FOR SMALL ORCH.)(1971)
1(alt. with picc. and alto fl.),1(alt. with Eng. hn.),1(alt. with
b.-cl.),0 - 1,0,1,0 - perc. - str.   13:00 G. Schirmer.
—— TWO SCENES FOR ORCHESTRA (INTERLUDES FROM THE
OPERA "KAISER JOVIAN")(1965)
2(2nd alt. with picc.),2(2nd alt. with Eng.hn.),2(2nd alt. with
b.-cl.),2(2nd alt. with c.-bn.) - 3,3,3,1 - timp.,perc.(3) - hp. - pf. -
str.   11:00 G. Schirmer.
—— VARIATIONS FOR OBOE AND STRINGS
ob. - str.   S.U.I.S.A.

KEMPE, Harald
—— CONCERTO IN TWO MOVEMENTS FOR STRING ORCH.
(1959)
str.   16:00 S.T.I.M.
—— MALMGORDS MUSIC (DIVERTIMENTO FOR FLUTE AND
STRINGS)
fl. - str.   13:00 S.T.I.M.
—— OBREXIS (CONCERT OVERTURE)
2,2,2,2 - 2,2,2,0 - timp. - str.   6:30 S.T.I.M.
—— PRELUDIO INNOMINATO (CONCERT OVERTURE)
2,2,2,2 - 2,2,3,0 - timp. - str.   7:30 S.T.I.M.
—— SERENADE FOR CELLO AND ORCH.
2,1,2,2 - 2,2,1,0 - timp. - str.   14:00 S.T.I.M.
—— SERENADE FOR OBOE AND STRINGS
ob. - pf.(ad lib.) - str.   11:30 S.T.I.M.
—— SINFONIETTA DA CHIESA
str.   8:00 S.T.I.M.

—— THREE PIECES FOR STRING ORCH. (1928)
str.   7:00 Nordiska.

KEMPFF, Wilhelm
—— ARCADIAN SUITE, OP. 42 (IN 4 MOVTS.)
1,2,0,2 - 0,0,0,0 - trgl. - str.   15:00 Henmar.
—— EPITAPH (SUITE FOR STRING ORCH.)
str.   14:00 Henmar.
—— EIN TOTENTANZ (PIANO CONCERTO IN SUITE FORM,
WITH SATB CHORUS) (IN 9 MOVTS.)
perc. - pf. - str.   20:00 Henmar.

KEMPTER, Lothar
—— CAPRICCIO, OP. 32 (FOR FLUTE AND ORCH.)
1,2,2,2 - 4,2,3,0 - timp. - str.   15:00 Henmar.
—— FANTAISIE PASTORALE, OP. 71 (FOR FLUTE AND ORCH.)
1,2,2,2 - 4,2,3,1 - timp.,perc. - hp. - str.   9:00 Henmar.

KENINS, Talivaldis
—— CHANTS OF GLORY AND MERCY (GLORIA) (FOR
SOPRANO, CONTRALTO, TENOR, BASS-BARITONE, MIXED
CHORUS AND ORCH.) (1970)
2,2,2,2 - 2,2,0,0 - timp.,perc.(5, incl. 4 on timp.) - str.
23:00 CanMusCtr.
—— CONCERTO FOR PIANO AND ORCH.
22:00 C.A.P.A.C.
—— CONCERTO FOR VIOLIN AND ORCH. (1974) (IN 1 MOVT.)
2(2nd alt. with picc.),2(2nd alt. with Eng. hn.),2,2 - 2,2,0,0 -
timp.,perc.(5, incl. 4 on timp.) - hp. - str.   19:20 CanMusCtr.
—— CONCERTO FOR VIOLIN, CELLO AND STRING ORCH.
(1965)
str.   CanMusCtr.
—— DUO FOR PIANO AND ORCH. (IN 2 MOVTS.)
2,3,2,2 - 4,3,3,1 - timp.,perc.(2) - hp. - pf. - str. 14:00 C.A.P.A.C.
—— FOLK DANCE, VARIATIONS AND FUGUE (1964)
2,2,2,2 - 4,3,3,1 - perc. - str.   9:30 CanMusCtr.
—— NAACHAACA (TRANCE) (BALLADE FOR ORCH.) (1975)
*3,2,*3,2 - 4,3,3,1 - timp.,perc.(4) - str.   10:00 CanMusCtr.
—— NOCTURNE AND DANCE (1963)
str.   5:40 Bo. Hawkes.
—— NOCTURNE FOR STRINGS (1963)
str.   3:30 CanMusCtr.
—— SAWAN-OONG (THE SPIRIT OF THE WIND) (SYMPHONIC
CANTATA ON AN OJIBWAY-CREE LEGEND) (FOR MALE
AND FEMALE NARRATORS, BARITONE, MIXED CHORUS
AND ORCH.) (1973) (Text: Uldis Fogels)
2(2nd alt. with picc.),2(2nd alt. with Eng.hn.),2(2nd alt. with
b.-cl.),2 - 2,2,2,1 - timp.,perc.(4) - str.   14:30 CanMusCtr.
—— SCHERZO CONCERTANTE (1953)
1,1,1,1 - 0,1,1,0 - timp.,perc.,cel. - hp. - str.   4:10 CanMusCtr.
—— SYMPHONY FOR CHAMBER ORCH. (1959) (IN 3 MOVTS.)
1,1,2,1 - 1,1,1,0 - timp.,perc. - str.   21:30 CanMusCtr.
—— SYMPHONY NO. 2 (SINFORIA CONCERTANTE) (FOR
FLUTE, OBOE, CLARINET AND ORCH.) (1967) (IN 3
MOVTS.)
*3,3,3,2 - 2,2,2,1 - timp.,perc.(6, incl. 4 on timp.) - str.
19:15 CanMusCtr.
—— SYMPHONY NO. 3 (1970) (IN 3 MOVTS.)
2(2nd alt. with picc.),2(2nd alt. with Eng. hn.),2,2 - 4,3,3,1 -
timp.,perc.(3) - hp. - str.   19:50 CanMusCtr.
—— SYMPHONY NO. 4 (1972) (IN 2 MOVTS.)
1,1,1,0 - 1,1,1,0 - perc. - str.   20:30 CanMusCtr.

KENNAN, Kent
—— ANDANTE FOR OBOE AND ORCH.
2,1,2,2 - 3,0,0,0 - str.   5:00 Composer.
—— BLESSED ARE THEY THAT MOURN (FOR CHORUS AND
ORCH.)
*3,*3,*3,*3 - 4,3,3,1 - timp.,perc.(2) - hp. - pf. - str.
10:00 G. Schirmer.
—— IL CAMPO DEI FIORI (THE MARKETPLACE IN ROME)
2(2nd alt. with picc.),2,2,2 - 2,1,0,0 - timp.,perc.(2) - pf. - str.
Composer.
—— CONCERTINO FOR PIANO AND ORCH.
2(2nd alt. with picc.),1,2,2 - 4,3,3,1 - timp.,perc.(2) - pf. - str.
13:00 Composer.
—— DANCE DIVERTIMENTO

I. PROMENADE
2,2,2,2 - 4,2,3,1 - timp.,perc.(2) - pf. - str. or   1:30 C. Fischer.
2,2,2,2 sax.,2 - 2,2,1,0 - timp.,perc.(2) - pf. - str.
II. AIR DE BALLET
2,2,2,2 - 2,2,0,0 - timp.,perc.(2) - pf. - str.   1:40 Composer.

III. JIG
2,2,2,2 - 2,2,0,0 - timp.,perc.(2) - pf. - str.   1:40 Composer.
—— LAMENT
2,2,2,2 - 2,2,0,0 - perc. - pf. - str.   3:30 Composer.
—— NIGHT SOLILOQUY
fl. - str.   4:00 C. Fischer.
—— NOCTURNE (FOR VIOLA AND ORCH.)
2,2,2,2 - 2 hn. - timp.,perc.(2) - pf. - str.   5:00 Composer.
—— SYMPHONY (IN 3 MOVTS.)
*3,*3,*3,*3 - 4,3,3,1 - timp.perc.(5),glock. - str.   28:00 Composer.

KENNEDY, John Brodbin
—— LYRIC ODE
str.   9:30 Bo. Hawkes.
—— SYMPHONIC FANTASY
*3,*3,*3,*3 - 4,3,3,1 - timp.,perc.(3-4),bells,cel.,glock.,xyl. - hp. -
pf. - str.   14:00 Bo. Hawkes.
—— SYMPHONY IN TWO MOVEMENTS
3,3,3,3 - 4,3,3,1 - timp.,perc.,cel. - pf. - str.   22:00 Bo. Hawkes.
—— TWO SONNETS FROM SHAKESPEARE (FOR CHAMBER
ORCH.)
1,1,1,1 - 0,0,0,0 - str.   10:00 Bo. Hawkes.

KERN, Jerome
—— MARK TWAIN (PORTRAIT FOR ORCH.)
3(3rd alt. with picc.),*3,*3,4 sax.,*3 - 4,3,3,1 -
timp.,perc.(6),cel.,glock.,xyl. - 2 hp. - str.   20:00 T.B.Harms.
—— SCENARIO FOR ORCH. (ON THEMES FROM "SHOWBOAT")
3(3rd alt. with picc.),*3,*3,4 sax.,*3 - 4,3,3,1 -
timp.,perc.,(6),cel.,glock.,xyl. - banjo - guit. harmonica - hp. - str.
20:00 T.B.Harms.

KERNOCHAN, Marshall
—— THE FOOLISH VIRGINS (SACRED CANTATA) (FOR
SOPRANO, ALTO, BARITONE, WOMEN'S CHORUS AND
ORCH.)
*2,1,2,1 - 2,2,1,0 - timp.,perc.(1) - hp. - str.   30:00 Galaxy.
—— OUT OF THE ROLLING OCEAN (FOR BARITONE AND
ORCH.)
2,*3,2,2 - 4,2,3,1 - timp.,perc.(2) - hp. - str.   6:00 Galaxy.

KERSTERS, Willem
—— CAPRICCIO, OP. 59 (1972)
2,2,2,2 - 4,2,2,1 - timp.,perc. - str.   13:00 H. Elkan.
—— CONTRASTEN, OP. 50 (FOR PERCUSSION AND ORCH.)
(1969) (IN 5 MOVTS.)
2,2,2,2 - 4,2,2,1 - perc.,cel. - hp. - str.   10:00 H. Elkan.
—— HALEWIJN, OP. 62 (1974)
3,3,3,3 - 4,4,3,1 - timp.,perc. - str.   H. Elkan.
—— SYMFONIE NO. 3, OP. 39 (1967) (IN 3 MOVTS.)
3,3,3,3 - 4,4,3,1 - timp.,perc. - str.   28:00 H. Elkan.
—— UILENSPIEGEL DE GEUS (1976)
3,3,3,3 - 4,4,3,1 - timp.,perc.,cel. - hp. - str.   H. Elkan.

KESNAR, Maurits
—— INVOCATION
*3,2,2,2 - 4,3,3,1 - timp.,perc. - str.   8:00 Composer.
—— LEGEND
1,1(alt. with Eng. hn.),2,1 - 1,1,1,0 - timp.,perc.(1) - str.
8:00 C. Fischer.
—— POEM
*3,*3,*3,2 - 4,3,3,1 - timp.,perc.(3) - str.   12:00 Composer.
—— ST. NICHOLAS' TREASURE SHIP (THEME AND
VARIATIONS)
3(3rd alt. with picc.),2,2,2 - 2,3,2,0 - timp.,perc. - str.
10:00 J. Fischer.
—— SUNDOWN (FOR SMALL ORCH.)
1,1,2,1 - 1,1,1,0 - timp.(2),glock. - str.   7:00 Composer.
—— SYMPHONIETTA
1,1,2,1 - 1,1,1,0 - timp.,perc.(1) - str.   14:00 Composer.
—— SYMPHONY IN C MINOR
1. Andante-Allegro marciale; 2. Allegro; 3. Andante moderato
*3,*3,*3,2 - 4,3,3,0 - timp.,perc.(2) - str.   35:00 Composer.

KESS, Ludwig
—— CAPRICCIO SCIVOLANDO (GROTESQUE ETUDE)
2,2,2,2 - 4,2,3,0 - timp.,perc. - hp. - str.   6:00 Henmar.

KESSLER, Minuetta Borek
—— ALBERTO CONCERTO (FOR PIANO AND ORCH.)
22:00 C.A.P.A.C.
—— LAKE O'HARA (FOR STRINGS)
str.   13:00 C.A.P.A.C.

—— NEW YORK SUITE (FOR PIANO AND ORCH.) (IN 5 MOVTS.)
16:30 C.A.P.A.C.
—— A WORLD PASSED BY (BALLET) %
C.A.P.A.C.

KETTING, Otto
—— CONCERTINO FOR ORCH. WITH JAZZ QUINTET (1960)
3,2,2,1 sax.,2 - 2,2,1,0 - timp.,perc. - 2 pf. - str.   25:00 Henmar.
—— CONCERTINO FOR TWO TRUMPETS AND ORCH. (1958)
0,0,0,0 - 3,2,0,0 - pf. - str.   14:00 Henmar.
—— DUE CANZONI PER ORCHESTRA (1957)
1,1,2,1 - 2,1,1,0 - perc.,cel. - hp.   11:00 Henmar.
—— INTERIEUR: BALLETMUZIEK (1963) %
2,2,2,1 - 2,3,2,1 - timp.,perc.,cel.,xyl.   17:00 Henmar.
—— INTRADA FESTIVA
0,0,0,0 - 4,3,3,1 - timp.,perc.(3)   5:00 Henmar.
—— KERSTLIEDEREN (3 SONGS FOR MIXED CHORUS AND ORCH.) (1953)
1,1,1,1 - 2,0,0,0 - str.   10:00 Henmar.
—— HET LAATSTE BERICHT: BALLETMUZIEK (1962)
2,2,2,1 - 2,2,2,0 - perc. - hp. - pf. - str.   20:00 Henmar.
—— PAS DE DEUX (CHOREOGRAFISCHE COMMENTAREN) (1961)
3,3,3,1 alto sax.,3 - 4,3,3,1 - timp.,perc.,cel. - hp. - pf. - c.'s
18:00 Henmar.
—— PASSACAGLIA FOR CHAMBER ORCH.
2,2,2,sax.,2 - 2,2,1,0 - timp.,perc. - str.   17:00 Henmar.
—— SINFONIETTA
2,2,2,2 - 2,2,1,0 - timp.,perc. - str.   18:00 Henmar.
—— SYMPHONY NO. 1 (1959)
3,3,3,1 alto sax.,3 - 4,4,3,1 - timp.,perc.,cel. - 2 hp. - str.
16:00 Henmar.
—— VARIAZIONI PER ORCHESTRA (1960)
2,2,3,2 - 2,2,0,0 - per. - hp.   8:00 Henmar.

KETTING, Piet
—— MINNEDEUNTJES (FOR CHORUS AND FULL ORCH.)
32:00 Henmar.
—— SYMPHONY NO. 1 (1928-1929)
3,3,4,1 sax.,3 - 4,4,3,1 - timp.,perc.,cel.,xyl. - hp. - str.
18:00 Henmar.
—— VIER GEDICHTEN (FOR MEZZO-SOPRANO AND CHAMBER ORCH.) (1935) (Text: M. Nijhoff)
2,2,3,0 - 0,0,0,0 - perc. - acc. - pf. - str.(1 vln.,2 vla.,1 c.)
17:00 Henmar.

KEURIS, Tristan
—— QUARTET FOR ORCHESTRA (1967)
3,3,3,alto sax.,0 - 0,3,3,0 - perc. - c.,d.-b.   9:00 Henmar.

KEYES, Nelson
—— CONCERTO GROSSO (FOR STRING QUARTET AND STRING ORCH.) (1962) (IN 3 MOVTS.)
str.   12:45 Composer.
—— DISSERTATION FOR ORCHESTRA (1966) (IN 3 MOVTS.)
3(2 alt. with 2 picc.),3(2 alt. with 2 Eng. hn.),3(3rd alt. with b.-cl.),2(2nd alt. with cbn.) - 4,4,3,1 - timp.,perc.(3),vibra.,xyl. - hp. - pf.(alt. with cel.) - str.   23:00 Composer.
—— ABYSSES, BRIDGES, CHASMS (FOR 10 ROCK JAZZ SOLOISTS AND ORCH.) (IN 1 MOVT.) (1971)
Solo group: 1 alto sax.(alt. with bar. sax.) - 1,2,2,0 - perc..(1) - electric guit. - electric pf.(or electric org.) - elctric d.-b.
24:00 Composer.
Orchestra: 3(3rd alt. with picc.),3(3rd alt. with Eng.hn.),2,3(3rd alt. with cbn.) - 4,3,1,1 - timp.,perc.(2),xyl. - str.   23:00 Composer.
—— LENTO AND ALLEGRO FOR STRING ORCH. (1955)
str.   12:00 Composer.
—— MUSIC FOR MONDAY EVENINGS (1960) (IN 5 MOVTS.)
*3,2,2,2 - 4,3,3,1 - timp.,perc.(3),xyl. - str.   15:00 Composer.

KEYPER, Franz
—— ROMANCE AND RONDO (FOR DOUBLE BASS AND ORCHESTRA)
2,0,0,0 - 2,0,0,0 - str.   9:00 Galaxy.

KEYS, Ivor
—— CONCERTO FOR CLARINET AND STRINGS
cl. - str.   Gray.

KHATCHATURIAN, Aram
—— CONCERTO FOR CELLO AND ORCH.
2,3,3,0 - 4,2,0,0 - timp. - hp. - str.   31:00 G. Schirmer.

—— CONCERTO FOR PIANO AND ORCH. (IN 3 MOVTS.)
2,2,*3,2 - 4,2,3,1 - timp.,perc. - pf. - str.   29:30 G. Schirmer.
—— CONCERTO FOR VIOLIN AND ORCH. (IN 3 MOVTS.)
2,*3,2,2 - 4,3,3,1 - timp. - hp. - str.   35:00 G. Schirmer.
—— CONCERTO-RHAPSODY FOR CELLO AND ORCH.
3,2,2,2 - 4,2,0,0 - timp.,perc.,xyl. - 2 hp. - str.   23:00 G. Schirmer.
—— CONCERTO-RHAPSODY FOR VIOLIN AND ORCHESTRA
3,2,2,2 - 4,0,2,0 - timp.,perc. - hp. - str.   23:00 G. Schirmer.
—— DANCE SUITE (IN 5 MOVTS.)
*3,*3,*3,2 - 4,3,3,1 - timp. - hp. - str.   15:00 G. Schirmer.
—— FUNERAL ODE IN MEMORY OF LENIN
3,3,3,2 - 4,3,3,1 - timp.,perc. - hp. - pf. - str.   10:00 G. Schirmer.
—— GAYNE: BALLET SUITE NO. 1 (IN 3 MOVTS.)
3,3,3,alto sax.,2 - 4,3,3,1 - timp.,perc.,cel.,xyl. - hp. - pf. - str.
8:30 G. Schirmer.
—— GAYNE: BALLET SUITE NO. 1 (IN 8 MOVTS.)
3,3,3,alto sax.,3 - 4,3,3,1 - timp.,perc.,cel.,xyl. - hp. - str.
36:00 G. Schirmer.
—— GAYNE: BALLET SUITE NO. 1A (IN 5 MOVTS.)
3,3,3,alto sax.,2 - 4,3,3,1 - timp.,perc.,cel.,xyl. - hp. - pf. - str.
19:00 G. Schirmer.
—— GAYNE: BALLET SUITE NO. 2 (IN 4 MOVTS.)
3,3,3,2 - 4,3,3,1 - timp.,perc.,xyl. - hp. - str.   17:30 G. Schirmer.
—— GAYNE: BALLET SUITE NO. 3 (IN 6 MOVTS.)
3,3,3,alto sax.,2 - 4,3,3,1 - timp.,perc.,xyl. - hp. - pf. - str.
G. Schirmer.
—— MASQUERADE: SUITE (IN 5 MOVTS.)
*3,2,2,2 - 4,2,3,1 - timp.,perc. - str.   15:00 G. Schirmer.
—— MOURNFUL ODE
3,3,3,2 - 4,3,3,1 - timp.,perc. - hp. - pf. - str.   G. Schirmer.
—— ODE TO JOY (FOR MEZZO-SOPRANO, MIXED CHORUS, VIOLIN AND ORCH.)
3,2,2,2 - 4,2 cnt.,2,3,1 - timp.,perc.,xyl. - 2 hp.- str.
10:00 G. Schirmer.
—— RUSSIAN FANTASY
3,3,2,2 - 4,3,3,1 - timp.,perc. - hp. - pf. - str.   5:00 G. Schirmer.
—— SABRE DANCE (FROM THE BALLET "GAYNE")
3,3,3,alto sax.,2 - 4,3,3,1 - timp.,perc.,cel.,xyl. - hp. - str.
2:15 G. Schirmer.
—— SONG OF STALIN (TONE POEM FOR CHORUS AND ORCH.)
*3,*3,2,2 - 4,3,3,1 - timp.,perc.,glock. - hp. - str.
23:00 G. Schirmer.
—— SPARTACUS (BALLET): SCENE 3 (IN 6 MOVTS.) %
3,3,3,2 - 4,3,3,1 - timp.,perc.,xyl. - hp. - pf. - str.
17:00 G. Schirmer.
—— SPARTACUS (BALLET): SCENE 4 (IN 7 MOVTS.) %
3,3,3,2 - 4,3,3,1 - timp.,perc.,xyl. - hp. - pf. - str.   G. Schirmer.
—— SPARTACUS (BALLET): SCENE 5 (IN 7 MOVTS.) %
3,3,3,2 - 4,3,3,1 - timp.,perc.,xyl. - hp. - pf. - str.   G. Schirmer.
—— SPARTACUS (BALLET): SCENE 9 (SPARTACUS' DEATH) %
3,3,3,1 alto sax.,2 - 4,4,3,1 - timp.,perc.,cel.,xyl. - hp. - pf. - str.
15:00 G. Schirmer.
—— SPARTACUS: BALLET SUITE NO. 1 (IN 5 MOVTS.)
3,3,3,2 - 4,4,3,1 - timp.,perc.,cel.,xyl. - hp. - str.
24:00 G. Schirmer.
—— SPARTACUS: BALLET SUITE NO. 2 (IN 4 MOVTS.)
3,3,3,2 - 4,3,3,1 - timp.,perc.,xyl. - hp. - pf. - str.
20:00 G. Schirmer.
—— SPARTACUS: BALLET SUITE NO. 3 (IN 5 MOVTS.)
3,3,3,2 - 4,3,3,1 - timp.,perc.,xyl. - hp. - pf. - str.
15:00 G. Schirmer.
—— SYMPHONY NO. 1
1. Andante maestoso, con passione; 2. Adagio sostenuto;
3. Allegro risoluto
*3,*3,3,2 - 4,3,3,1 - timp.,perc.,glock.,xyl. - hp. - pf. - str.
25:00 G. Schirmer.
—— SYMPHONY NO. 2
1. Andante maestoso; 2. Allegro risoluto; 3. Andante sostenuto;
4. Andante mosso-Allegro sostenuto-Maestoso
3(3rd alt. with picc.),*3,E♭ cl.,*3,2 - 4,3,3,1 - timp.,perc.,xyl. - hp. - pf. - str.   25:00 G. Schirmer.
—— SYMPHONY NO. 3 (SYMPHONY-POEM)
3,3,2,2 - 4,3,15 solo tpts.,3,1 - timp.,perc. - hp. - org. - str.
26:00 G. Schirmer.
—— THREE ARIAS (FOR HIGH VOICE AND ORCH.)
2,2,2,2 - 4,2,3,1 - timp.,perc. - hp. - str.   21:00 G. Schirmer.
—— TRIUMPHAL POEM (POEMA FESTIVO) (1950)
3,3,3,2 - 4,3,3,1 - timp.,perc.,xyl. - hp. - str.   20:00 G. Schirmer.
—— THE WIDOW OF VALENCIA (SUITE FROM THE MUSIC TO THE LOPE DE VEGA PLAY) (IN 6 MOVTS.)
2,2,2,2 - 4,3,3,1 - timp.,perc.,cel.,xyl. - hp. - str.
27:00 G. Schirmer.

KHOLMINOV, Aleksandr N.
—— CHAPAYEV (3-ACT OPERA) % (Text: A. Kholminov)
G. Schirmer.

KHRENNIKOV, Tikhon N.
—— CONCERTO FOR VIOLIN AND ORCH., OP. 14
3,2,3,3 - 4,3,0,0 - timp.,perc.,cel.,xyl. - hp. - pf. - str.
18:00 G. Schirmer.
—— THE LOW-BORN SON-IN-LAW (2-ACT COMIC OPERA) %
(Text: S. Tsenin)
G. Schirmer.
—— SUITE FROM "MUCH ADO ABOUT NOTHING" OP. 7 (FOR
BARITONE AND ORCH.)
1(alt. with picc.),1,1,1 - 2,2,1,1 - timp.,perc. - hp. - str.
20:00 G. Schirmer.
—— SYMPHONY NO. 2, OP. 9 (IN 4 MOVTS.)
*3,*3,*3,*3 - 4,3,3,1 - timp.,perc. - 2hp. - str. 37:30 G. Schirmer.

KHRENNIKOV, Tikhon N. - SHELDON, Harold
—— SYPHONY NO. 1 IN B FLAT MINOR, OP. 4
3,2,2,2 - 4,2,3,1 - timp.,perc.,cel. - str. 22:00 G. Schirmer.

KIELLAND, Olav
—— ARABESCO PER ORCHESTRA
2,2,2,alto sax.,1 - 2,3,2,0 - timp.,perc. - str. 5:30 T.O.N.O.
—— BRAND: SUITE NO. 1, OP. 9A (FROM THE MUSIC TO
IBSEN'S PLAY) (IN 4 MOVTS.)
1,1,2,1 - 2,2,2,1 - timp. - str. 18:00 T.O.N.O.
—— BRAND: SUITE NO. 2, OP. 9B (IN 5 MOVTS.)
1,1,2,1 - 2,2,2,1 - timp. - str. 27:00 T.O.N.O.
—— CONCERTO FOR VIOLIN AND ORCH., OP. 7 (IN 4 MOVTS.)
1,2,0,1 - 2,2,0,0, - timp. - str. 34:00 T.O.N.O.
—— CONCERTO GROSSO NORVEGESE, OP. 18 (IN 4 MOVTS.)
2 hn. - str. 23:00 Norsk Mfl.
—— MELODIA PER STRUMENTI A CORDA
str. 6:00 T.O.N.O.
—— OVERTURA TRAGICA, OP. 8 (TO IBSEN'S PLAY "BRAND")
2,2,2,2 - 4,2,3,1 - timp.,perc. - str. 12:00 T.O.N.O.
—— SINFONIA NO. 1, OP. 3 (IN 1 MOVT.)
2,2,2,2 - 4,2,3,1 - timp. - str. 23:00 T.O.N.O.
—— SINFONIA NO. 2, OP. 21 (IN 3 MOVTS.)
2,2,2,2 - 4,2,3,1 - timp.,perc. - str. 35:00 T.O.N.O.
—— SIX SIVLE SONGS, OP. 17 (FOR VOICE AND ORCH.) (Text:
Per Sivle)
2,2,3,2 - 4,2,0,0 - timp.,perc. - hp. - str. 20:00 T.O.N.O.
—— SUITE, OP. 5
2,2,2,2 - 4,2,3,1 - timp.,perc. - str. 23:00 T.O.N.O.
—— THE WHITECAPPED MOUNTAINS, OP. 14 (MOT
BLÅSNØHØGDOM) (SUITE FOR HIGH VOICE AND ORCH.)
(IN 3 MOVTS) (Text: Ola Setrom)
2,2,2,2 - 4,2,0,0 - timp. - hp. - str. 23:00 T.O.N.O.

KIENZL, Wilhelm
—— SINFONISCHE VARIATIONEN ÜBER "DAS
STRASSBURGLIED"
3,3,3,2 - 4,3,3,1 - timp.,perc.,xyl. - hp. - str. 30:00 Weinberger.

KIKTA, Valerij G.
—— UKRANIAN KOLYADKAS, SHCHEDRIVKAS AND
VESNYANKAS (CONCERTO FOR ORCHESTRA)
G. Schirmer.

KILADZE, Gregory V.
—— THE HERMIT (SYMPHONIC POEM)
3(3rd alt. with picc.),2(2nd alt. with Eng.hn.),3(3rd alt. with
b.-cl.),3(3rd alt. with c.-bn.) - 4,3,3,1 - timp.,perc.,cel.,glock. - hp. -
str. 28:30 G. Schirmer.

KILLMAYER, Wilhelm
—— DIVERTISSEMENT
3(3rd alt. with picc.),2,2,2 - 2,2,3,1 - timp.,perc.,cel. -. hp. - pf. -
str. 10:00 Modern.

KILPATRICK, Jack Frederick
—— FOUR PIECES FOR STRINGS
str. 14:00 C. Fischer.
—— SONATINA FOR CHAMBER ORCH., OP. 11 (SOUVENIR OF
THE OZARKS)
Chappell.
—— TWO CHEROKEE FOLK TUNES
2,2,3,2 - 4,2,3,1 - timp.,perc. - str. 8:00 C. Fischer.

KILPINEN, Yrjö
—— SONGS OF THE FELLS, OP. 52 (6 SONGS, FOR VOICE AND
ORCH.) (1926)
3,2,1,2 - 2,2,0,0 - timp.,perc. - hp. - str. 18:00 Fazer.

KIM, Byong-Kon
—— SYMPHONY (1967)
3,2,2,2 - 4,3,3,1 - timp.,perc.(2) - str. 25:00 Seesaw.

KIMPTON, Geoffrey
—— CALEDON (AN OVERTURE) (1962)
3,3,3,2 - 4,3,3,0 - timp.,perc.(3) - str. 4:30 P.R.S.
—— PASSACAGLIA AND FUGUE (1962)
str. 8:00 P.R.S.

KINDLER, Hans
—— THREE 17TH CENTURY DUTCH TUNES
3(3rd alt. with picc.),2,2,2 - 4,3,3,1 - timp.,perc.(3),cel. - hp. - pf. -
str. 8:00 C. Fischer.

KING, Harold C.
—— CONCERTO DA CAMERA PER FLAUTO E CORDE (1962)
fl. - str. 17:00 Henmar.
—— CONCERTO FOR ORGAN AND ORCH. (1966)
1. Allegro moderato; 2. Larghetto; 3. Andante
17:30 Henmar.
—— PER ARDUA (SUITE)
2,2,2,2 - 4,2,3,1 - timp.,perc. - str. 35:00 Henmar.
—— PRELUDE DE BALLET
2,2,2,2 - 4,2,3,0 - perc. - hp. - str. 10:00 Henmar.
—— SERENADE FOR STRINGS
str. Henmar.
—— SERENATA
2,2,2,2 -4,2,3,1 - timp.,perc. - hp. - str. 25:00 Henmar.
—— SINFONIETTA (FOR FULL ORCH.) (1955)
22:00 Henmar.

KING, Hial Bancroft
—— FUTURE SHOCK, OP. 2 (1970) (IN 1 MOVT.)
4(2 alt. with picc. and 1 amplified el.),*3,2 E♭cl.,*3,0 - 4,4,3,1 -
timp.,perc.(5),bells,cel.,glock.,xyl. - 2 elec. guit.,1 elec.(Fender)
bass - hp. - pf. - str. 12:15 Composer.
—— MUSIC FOR GAIL, OP. 1 (1968)
2(alt. with 2 picc.),*2,1 E♭cl.,*2,2 - 2,2,2,1 - timp.,perc.(3),bells -
hp. - pf. - str. 7:30 Composer.

KING, Jeffrey
—— FACETS (1968) (IN 3 MOVTS.)
str. 15:00 Composer.

KING, Victor
—— CONCERTO NO. 1 FOR VIOLIN AND ORCH. (1964)
22:00 MuSrvUnltd.
—— GERMAN SUITE (IN 4 MOVTS.) (1965)
18:00 Composer.
—— RHAPSODY FOR VIOLIN AND ORCH.
18:25 MuSrvUnltd.
—— SLAVONIC COUNTRY SUITE (1950) (IN 3 MOVTS.)
28:31 MuSrvUnltd.

KINGMAN, Daniel
—— FIVE EARTHSCAPES WITH BIRDS (FOR SOPRANO AND
ORCH.) (1971) (Text: Robinson Jeffers)
3(3rd alt. with picc.),3(3rd alt. with Eng. hn.),3(3rd alt. with
b.-cl.),3(3rd alt. with cbn.) - 4,4,3,1 -
timp.,perc.(5),bells,cel.,glock.,xyl. - hp. - pf. - str. 25:00 Composer.
—— PASTORALE AND SCHERZO
2(2nd alt. with picc.),2(2nd alt. with Eng.hn.),2,2 - 4,2,3,0 - timp.
- hp. - str. 12:00 Composer.
—— SINFONIA CONCERTANTE (IN 3 MOVTS.)
1,0,0,1 - 0,1,0,0 - str. 15:30 Composer.
—— SYMPHONY NO. 1, OP. 15 (1965) (IN 1 MOVT.)
3(3rd alt. with picc.),*3,*3,*3 - 4,3,3,1 - timp.,perc.(3),glock.,xyl. -
hp. - str. 9:00 Composer.

KINGSFORD, Charles
—— STALINGRAD (FOR CHORUS AND ORCH.)
3(3rd alt. with picc.),*3,*3,*3 - 4,3,3,1 - timp.,perc.(4) - hp. - str.
7:00 Composer.

KINGSLEY, Gershon
—— CONCERTO MOOGO (IN 4 MOVTS.)
  2,2,2,2 - 4,4,3,1 - timp., perc. - 4 Moog synthesizers - str.
  13:00 Bourne.
—— GOD AND ABRAHAM (A MUSICAL CONFRONTATION)
  (FOR NARRATOR, SOPRANO, MEZZO-SOPRANO, TENOR,
  BARITONE, SATB CHORUS AND INSTRS.) (Text: Robert C.
  Larimer)
  1,2,2 (1 alt. with alto sax., 1 alt. with ten. sax.),0 - 1,1,1,0 -
  perc.-Fender b.-guit. - Moog synthesizer - org. - pf.   Bourne.

KIRALY, Ernö
—— REFLECTION NO. 6 (FOR VOICE AND STRING ORCH.)
  (1971)
  str.   10:00 MIC,Zagreb.

KIRBY, Percival Robson
—— IN SUMMERTIME: SUITE
  2,2,3,2 - 4,2,3,1 - timp.,perc. - str.   20:00 S.A.M.R.O.
—— INCIDENTAL MUSIC TO "AGAMEMNON"
  2,2,3,2 - 4,2,3,1 - timp.,perc. - str.   8:00 S.A.M.R.O.
—— INCIDENTAL MUSIC TO "ANTIGONE"
  2,2,3,2 - 4,2,3,1 - timp.,perc. - str.   8:00 S.A.M.R.O.
—— INCIDENTAL MUSIC TO "THE CLOUDS" (FOR VOICES AND
  ORCH.) (Text: Aristophanes andRogers)
  2,2,3,2 - 4,2,3,1 - timp.,perc. - str.   8:00 S.A.M.R.O.
—— INCIDENTAL MUSIC TO "THE FROGS"
  2,2,3,2 - 4,2,3,1 - timp.,perc. - str.   8:00 S.A.M.R.O.
—— INCIDENTAL MUSIC TO "THE TROJAN WOMEN"
  2,2,3,2 - 4,2,3,1 - timp.,perc. - str.   8:00 S.A.M.R.O.
—— SYMPHONIC VARIATIONS ON AN OLD CAPSTAN CHANTY
  (SYMPHONIC VARIATIONS ON "THE MAID OF
  AMSTERDAM")
  2,2,3,2 - 4,2,3,1 - timp.,perc. - str.   20:00 S.A.M.R.O.
—— WILLOW PATTERN: OVERTURE
  2,2,3,2 - 4,2,3,1 - timp.,perc. - str.   8:00 S.A.M.R.O.

KIRK, Theron
—— ADAGIETTO
  1,*1,1,1 - 2,0,0,0 - timp.,cel. - str.   5:30 ProArtPubs.
—— BAILE FRONTERA (DANCE OF THE BORDER) (1963)
  2(2nd alt. with picc.),2,2,2 - 4,3,3,1 - timp.,perc.(3) - str.
  6:00 C. Fischer.
—— BALLET MUSIC (SUITE IN FIVE MOVEMENTS)
  2(2nd alt. with picc.),2,2,2 - 4,3,3,1 - timp.,perc.(3) - str.
  12:00 Composer.
—— CAROL SERVICE WITH NINE LESSONS (FOR SOPRANO,
  SATB CHORUS AND CHAMBER ORCH.)
  2,0,2,0 - 0,2,2,0 - str.   30:00 Belw-Mills.
—— CONCERTO FOR ORCH.
  2(2nd alt. with picc.),2,2,2 - 4,3,3,1 - timp.,perc.(4) - pf. - str.
  12:00 Composer.
—— CONCERTO GROSSO FOR PIANO AND STRINGS
  pf. - str.   11:30 Composer.
—— DIVERTIMENTO
  1,1,1,0 - 2,0,0,0 - timp. - str.   5:00 Composer.
—— FANTASY AND FROLIC (FOR PIANO AND ORCH.)
  2(2nd alt. with picc.),2,2,2 - 2,3,3,1 - timp.,perc.(2) - pf. - str.
  10:00 Composer.
—— FIVE SONGS FROM "PRAYERS FROM THE ARK" (FOR
  MEDIUM VOICE AND CHAMBER ORCH.)
  2,1,2,0 - 2,0,0,0 - hp. - str.   MCA Music.
—— GLORY TO GOD (FOR MIXED CHORUS AND ORCH.)
  1,1,1,0 - 2,0,0,0 - str.   20:00 J. Fischer.
—— INTRADA (AN "OPENING PIECE")
  2(2nd alt. with picc.),2,2,2 - 4,2,3,0 - timp.,perc.(2) - str.
  4:30 C. Fischer.
—— KING DAVID'S DELIVERANCE (FOR MIXED CHORUS AND
  ORCH.)
  2(2nd alt. with picc.),2,2(2nd alt. with b.-cl.),2 - 4,3,3,1 -
  timp.,perc.(2) - str.   11:00 J. Fischer.
—— THE LIB: 393 B.C. (OPERA) %
  3,1,2,0 - 1,2,1,0 - perc.,cel. - str.   52:00 C. Fischer.
—— AN ORCHESTRA PRIMER (FOR NARRATOR AND ORCH.)
  2(2nd alt. with picc.),2,2,2 - 4,3,3,1 - timp.,perc.(2) - str.
  12:30 Oxford.
  or:
  1(alt. with picc.),1,2,1 - 3,2,1,0 - timp.,perc.(2) - str.
—— PRAYERS FROM THE ARK (SONG CYCLE) (FOR SOPRANO,
  TENOR, BASS-BARITONE AND ORCH.)
  3,2,2,2 - 4,3,3,1 - timp.,perc.(3),glock.,xyl. - hp. - str. MCA Music.
—— RESTON OVERTURE (1967)
  *3,2,2,2 - 4,3,3,1 - timp.,perc.(3),xyl. - str.   4:35 Composer.

—— SYMPHONY NO. 1
  1. Andante maestoso; 2. Larghetto; 3. Presto
  2(2nd alt. with picc.),2,2,2 - 3,2,3,1 - timp.,perc.(2),glock. - str.
  21:00 Composer.
—— SYMPHONY NO. 2 ("SAGA OF THE PLAINS")
  2(2nd alt. with picc.),2,2(2nd alt. with b.-cl.),2 - 4,3,3,1 -
  timp.,perc.(3),bells - hp. - str.   20:00 C. Fischer.
—— VIGNETTES (IN 3 MOVTS.)
  2(2nd alt. with picc.),2,2,0 - 4,2,2,0 - timp.,perc.(2) - str.
  6:30 Mills.

KIRKWOOD, Antoinette
—— FANTASIA NO. 1, OP. 13
  2,1,2,1 - 2,2,1,0 - timp. - hp. - str.   4:30 P.R.S.
—— FANTASIA NO. 2, OP. 14
  2,1,2,1 - 2,2,1,0 - timp. - hp. - str.   4:30 P.R.S.
—— FANTASIA NO. 3, OP.18
  2,1,2,1 - 2,2,1,0 - timp. - hp. - str.   4:30 P.R.S.
—— SUITE FOR STRINGS, OP. 5
  str.   18:00 P.R.S.
—— SYMPHONY NO. 1, OP. 8
  2,2,2,2 - 4,3,3,1 - timp. - str.   P.R.S.

KIRNBERGER, Johann - SCARMOLIN, Louis
—— LITTLE BAROQUE SUITE
  3:20 Ludwig.

KJAER, Vilfred
—— CONCERTO IN G MINOR FOR ACCORDION AND ORCH.
  Dacapo Mfl.

KJELDAAS, Arnljot
—— FANTASY ON THE HYMN "VAAR GUD HAN ER SAA FAST
  EN BORG" (FOR MIXED CHORUS, WINDS AND
  PERCUSSION) (1961)
  1,0,3,0 - 4,5,4,1 - perc.   10:00 T.O.N.O.
—— GRY OG GRID (MISERICORDIA), OP. 41 (1960) (FOR
  SPEAKER, TENOR OR BARITONE, MIXED CHORUS AND
  ORCH.) (Text: Stein Mathiesen)
  2,2,2,2 - 4,2,3,1 - timp.,perc. - str.   60:00 T.O.N.O.
—— ROMANCE FOR VIOLIN AND ORCH., OP. 4
  1,1,2,2 - 2,0,0,0 - timp. - str.   4:00 T.O.N.O.
—— SONGS OF MY VALLEY, OP. 31 ("HJEMBYGDENS
  SANGE")(FOR SPEAKING VOICES, TENOR, SATB CHORUS
  AND ORCH.) (1945) (Text: Herman Wildenvey)
  1,1,1,1 - 1,1,1,0 - timp.,cel. - hp. - str.   60:00 T.O.N.O.

KJELDAAS, Gunnar
—— ANDANTE AND SCHERZO
  2,1,2,1 - 1,2,1,1 - perc. - pf. - str.   9:00 T.O.N.O.
—— GREETING TO HOLMESTRAND (HILSEN TIL
  HOLMESTRAND) (OVERTURE)
  1,1,1,1 - 1,1,1,0 - harm. - pf. - str.   10:00 T.O.N.O.
—— IN THE MOUNTAINS (PÅ FJELLET) (SUITE) (IN 6 MOVTS.)
  2,1,2,1 - 1,2,1,1 - perc. - pf. - str.   25:00 T.O.N.O.
—— JUBILEE CANTATA (FOR SOLO VOICES, MALE CHORUS
  AND ORCH.) (Text: Gjertsen andReiss)
  1,0,1,0 - 0,2,1,1 - perc. - harm. - pf. - str.   20:00 T.O.N.O.
—— NORWEGIAN MELODIES
  1,0,1,0 - 0,1,1,0 - pf. - str.   10:00 T.O.N.O.
—— POLONAISE BURLESCA (FOR PIANO AND SMALL ORCH.)
  1,1,1,1 - 1,2,1,0 - perc. - pf. - str.   5:00 T.O.N.O.

KJELL, Erik
—— DALSLANDSVIT
  1,0,1,0 - 0,0,0,0 - perc.- str.   Nordiska.

KJELLSBY, Erling
—— CHACONNE AND FUGUE (ON A NORWEGIAN FOLK
  TUNE)
  2,2,2,2 - 4,2,3,1 - timp.,perc. - str.   8:00 T.O.N.O.
—— NORWEGIAN RHAPSODY
  1,1,2,1 - 2,2,2,0 - timp.,perc. - str.   6:00 T.O.N.O.

KLAAS, Julius
—— AUS GALANTER ZEIT, OP. 10 (DANCE SUITE) (FOR
  CHAMBER ORCH.)
  1,1,0,0 - 0,0,0,0 - str.   22:00 Henmar.
—— DIVERTIMENTO, OP. 66 (IN 6 MOVTS.)
  str.   27:00 Henmar.
—— FESTIVE SUITE, OP. 42 (FOR SMALL ORCH.)
  1,0,1,0 - 1,2,0,0 - timp.,perc. - str.   35:00 Henmar.

—— NACHTMUSIK IN GARTEN, OP. 62 (SERENADE NO. 3) (FOR CHAMBER ORCH.)
1,1,0,0 - 0,0,0,0 - str.   23:00 Henmar.
—— SERENADE NO. 1, OP. 49 (IN 6 MOVTS.)
2,2,2,2 - 0,0,0,0 - timp.,perc. - str.   36:00 Henmar.
—— SERENADE NO. 2, OP. 50 (IN 6 MOVTS.)
2,2,2,2 - 0,0,0,0 - timp.,perc. - str.   24:00 Henmar.
—— SYMPHONIC MUSIC IN 2 MOVTS., OP. 25
2,3,3,1 - 4,3,3,1 - timp. - str.   21:00 Henmar.
—— SYMPHONY NO. 1 IN A MAJOR, OP. 47 (IN 4 MOVTS.)
2,2,2,2 - 4,3,3,1 - timp.,perc. - str.   50:00 Henmar.
—— SYMPHONY NO. 2 IN D MINOR, OP. 51 (IN 3 MOVTS.)
2,2,2,2 - 4,3,3,1 - timp. - str.   36:00 Henmar.

KLAMI, Uuno
—— ALL'OVERTURA (1951)
2,2,2,2 - 4,2,3,1 - timp.,perc. - hp. - str.   8:00 FinnMICtr.
—— AURORA BOREALIS (1946)
4,3,3,3 - 4,3,3,1 - timp.,perc.(3) - 2 hp. - str.   15:00 FinnMICtr.
—— THE COBBLERS ON THE HEATH (AN OVERTURE) (1936)
2,2,2,2 - 2,2,0,0 - timp. - str.   8:00 Fazer.
—— CONCERTINO (1933)
0,1,1,0 - 0,1,0,0 - str.   9:00 FinnMICtr.
—— CONCERTO FOR VIOLIN AND ORCH. (1942)
2,2,2,2 - 4,2,3,1 - timp.,perc. - hp. - str.   33:00 Fazer.
—— CONCERTO NO. 1 FOR PIANO AND ORCH. ("UNE NUIT À MONTMARTRE") (1925)
2,2,2,2 sax.,2 - 4,2,3,1 - timp.,perc.(3) - hp. - pf. - str.   20:00 FinnMICtr.
—— CONCERTO NO. 2 FOR PIANO AND STRINGS (1950)
pf. - str.   29:00 FinnMICtr.
—— THE CYCLIST (1946)
2,2,2,2 - 4,2,3,1 - timp.,perc.(3) - hp. - str.   6:00 Fazer.
—— ELEGY (1936)
str.   5:00 FinnMICtr.
—— FANTAISIE TSCHÉRÉMISSE (FOR CELLO AND ORCH.) (1931)
2,2,2,2 - 4,2,3,1 - timp.,perc.(3),cel. - hp. - pf. - str.   11:00 Fazer.
—— HOMAGE TO HANDEL (1930)
pf. - str.   18:00 Fazer.
—— INTRODUCTION AND STACCATO ETUDE (FOR TRUMPET AND ORCH.)
2,2,2,1 - 2,1,1,0 - timp.,perc.,xyl. - str.   7:00 FinnMICtr.
—— KALEVALA SARJA (SUITE), OP. 23
    29:00 Fazer.
—— KARELIAN DANCES (1935)
2,2,2,2 - 2,2,1,0 - timp.,perc. - str.   6:00 FinnMICtr.
—— KARELIAN MARKET PLACE (1947)
4,4,4,4 - 6,6,3,1 - timp.,perc.(4) - 2 hp. - str.   11:00 FinnMICtr.
—— KARELIAN RHAPSODY
    T.E.O.S.T.O.
—— KING LEAR (AN OVERTURE) (1945)
3,2,3,3 - 4,4,3,1 - timp.,perc.(3) - 2 hp. - str.   15:00 Fazer.
—— LARGO, INTERLUDE, CANTIO
str.   12:00 FinnMICtr.
—— LEMMINKÄINEN (1934)
3,3,3,3 - 4,4,3,1 - timp.,perc.(4) - hp. - str.   12:00 FinnMICtr.
—— MUSIC TO SHAKESPEARE'S PLAY "KING LEAR" (1945)
2,2,2,2 - 2,2,1,0 - timp.,perc. - str.   25:00 FinnMICtr.
—— OPERN REDOUTE (1929)
3,3,3,3 - 4,3,3,1 - timp.,perc.(3) - hp. - str.   12:00 FinnMICtr.
—— PSALMUS (FOR SOPRANO, BARITONE, SATB CHORUS AND ORCH.) (REV. 1936)
2,2,2,2 - 4,2,3,1 - timp.,perc.(3) - org. - str.   55:00 FinnMICtr.
—— RUSTIC SCENES (SUITE NO. 1) (1930)
2,2,2,1 - 2,2,1,0 - perc. - str.   4:00 FinnMICtr.
—— RUSTIC SCENES (SUITE NO. 2) (1930)
3,2,2,2 - 2,2,1,1 - timp.,perc. - pf. - str.   12:00 FinnMICtr.
—— SCENES FROM A PUPPET SHOW (1925)
fl.,cl. - str.   7:00 FinnMICtr.
—— SEA PICTURES (SYMPHONIC POEM) (REV. 1930)
2,2,2,2 - 4,2,3,1 - timp.,perc. - hp. - pf. - str.   23:00 Fazer.
—— SÉRÉNADES ESPAGNOLES (IN 4 MOVTS.) (REV. 1944)
3,3,3,3 - 4,4,3,1 - timp.,perc.(3) - 2 hp. - str.   18:00 FinnMICtr.
—— SÉRÉNADES JOYEUSES (1933)
2,2,2,2 - 2,2,1,0 - timp.,perc.,cel. - pf. - str.   6:00 FinnMICtr.
—— SUITE FOR STRINGS (1937)
str.   15:00 FinnMICtr.
—— SUITE 1945, FOR SMALL ORCH.
2,2,2,2 - 2,2,0,0 - timp. - hp. - str.   15:00 FinnMICtr.
—— SUITE 1946, FOR SMALL ORCH.
2,2,2,2 - 2,2,0,0 - timp.,perc. - hp. - str.   11:00 FinnMICtr.

—— SUOMENLINNA (AN OVERTURE) (1940)
3,2,2,2 - 4,3,3,1 - timp.,perc.(3) - hp. - str.   13:00 Fazer.
—— SYMPHONIE ENFANTINE (1928)
1,2,1,1 - 1,1,0,0 - timp.,perc. - hp. - str.   17:00 FinnMICtr.
—— SYMPHONY NO. 1 (1938)
3,2,2,2 - 4,3,3,1 - timp.,perc. - str.   46:00 FinnMICtr.
—— SYMPHONY NO. 2 (1945)
3,3,3,3 - 4,4,3,1 - timp.,perc.(3) - str.   38:00 FinnMICtr.
—— THEME AND VARIATIONS (FOR CELLO AND ORCH.) (1950)
2,1,1,1 - 2,1,1,0 - timp.,perc. - hp. - str.   15:00 FinnMICtr.
—— VIPUSESSA KAYNTI (FOR BARITONE, MALE CHORUS AND ORCH.)
    LaulMieh.
—— WHIRLS: BALLET SUITE NO. 1 (1960)
2,2,2,2 - 4,3,3,1 - timp.,perc.(3),cel. - hp. - pf. - str.   18:00 FinnMICtr.
—— WHIRLS: BALLET SUITE NO. 2 (1960)
2,2,2,2 - 4,3,3,1 - timp.,perc.(3),cel. - hp. - pf. - str.   22:00 FinnMICtr.

KLATZOW, Peter James Leonard
—— IN MEMORIAM: N. P. VAN WYK LOUW (FOR SOPRANO AND STRING ORCH.) (Text: N. P. van Wyk Louw)
str.   17:00 S.A.M.R.O.
—— INTERACTIONS I (FOR PIANO, PERCUSSION AND CHAMBER ORCH.)
1,1,2,1 - 3,1,2,0 - perc. - pf. - str.   13:00 S.A.M.R.O.
—— MAREOTIS I AND II, OP. 5 (FOR CHAMBER ORCH.)
1,1,2,1 - 3,1,2,0 - perc. - str.   9:00 S.A.M.R.O.
—— NAGSTUK (TONE POEM)
2,2,3,2 - 4,2,3,1 - timp.,perc. - str.   15:00 S.A.M.R.O.
—— OVAMBOLAND (MUSIC FROM THE FILM) (FOR CHAMBER ORCH.)
1,1,2,1 - 3,1,2,0 - perc. - str.   15:00 S.A.M.R.O.
—— STILL LIFE WITH MOONBEAMS
2,2,3,2 - 4,2,3,1 - timp.,perc. - str.   7:00 S.A.M.R.O.
—— SYMPHONY 1972 (PHOENIX SYMPHONY)
2,2,3,2 - 4,2,3,1 - timp.,perc. - str.   21:00 S.A.M.R.O.
—— THE TEMPTATION OF ST. ANTHONY (FOR CELLO AND ORCH.)
2,2,3,2 - 4,2,3,1 - timp.,perc. - str.   15:00 S.A.M.R.O.
—— TIME STRUCTURE II
2,2,3,2 - 4,2,3,1 - timp.,perc. - str.   19:00 S.A.M.R.O.
—— VARIATIONS
2,2,3,2 - 4,2,3,1 - timp.,perc. - str.   15:00 S.A.M.R.O.
—— VARIATIONS (FOR PIANO AND ORCH.)
2,2,3,2 - 4,2,3,1 - timp.,perc. - pf. - str.   6:00 S.A.M.R.O.
—— VARIATIONS, OP. 1
2,2,3,2 - 4,2,3,1 - timp.,perc. - str.   12:00 S.A.M.R.O.

KLAUSS, Noah
—— ANTIPHONAL PRELUDE FOR 12 WINDS (1975)
2,2,*3,1 B^b d.-b.-cl.,2 - 2,0,0,0   4:00 Composer.
—— APOGEE (LUNAR SKETCH FOR ORCH.)
2,2,2,2 - 4,3,3,1 - timp. - hp. - str.   5:50 Composer.
—— CONFIGURATION FOR ORCH. (1972)
2,2,2,2 - 4,3,3,1 - timp.,perc.,bells - electric guit. - electric bass - pf. - str.   9:00 Composer.
—— DAYBREAK (TONE POEM) (1974)
2,2,2,2 - 4,3,3,1 - timp.,perc. - str.   8:40 Composer.
—— DEDICATION (FOR SATB CHORUS AND ORCH.)
2,2,2,2 alto sax.,1 ten. sax.,1 bar. sax., 2 - 4,3,3,1 - timp.,perc.(2),bells - str.   20:00 Composer.
—— DIVERTIMENTO (1972) (IN 3 MOVTS.)
0,0,0,0 - 1,0,0,0 - pf. - str.   7:30 Composer.
—— EVANGELINE (SYMPHONIC POEM)
3(3rd alt. with picc.),3(3rd alt. with Eng.hn.),2,*3 - 4,3,3,1 - timp.,perc.(3) - hp. - str.(15,6,5,5)   33:00 Composer.
—— FANTASY FOR ORCH.
*3,2,2,2 - 4,3,3,1 - timp.,perc.(3) - str.   17:00 Composer.
—— FREE INVENTION FOR ORCHESTRA (1973)
2,2,2,2 - 2,0,0,0 - str.   8:00 Composer.
—— MUSIC FOR LISTENING (1973)
1,1,1,3 sax.(2 alto,1 ten.),1 - 1,1,1,1 - timp. - electronic pf. - str.   12:00 Composer.
—— A NATION PRAYS (FOR SATB CHORUS AND ORCH.) (1970) (Text: Sylvia Klauss)
2,2,2,2 - 4,3,3,1 - perc.(1),bells - str.   7:00 Composer.
—— PRELUDE FOR ORCH.
2,2,2,1 alto sax.(ad lib.), 1 ten. sax.(ad lib.),2 - 4,3,3,1 - timp.,perc.(2) - str.   5:00 ProArtPubs.
—— RHAPSODY FOR ORCHESTRA (1974)
*3,2,*3,2 - 4,3,3,1 - timp.,perc. - str.   11:30 Composer.

—— SUMMER AFTERNOON (TONE POEM) (1965)
  *3,2,*3,2 - 4,3,3,1 - timp.,perc. - pf. - str.   8:40 Composer.
—— SYMPHONY IN ONE MOVEMENT (1969)
  *3,2,2,2 - 4,3,3,1 - timp.,perc. - str.   12:00 Composer.

KLEBANOV, Dmitrij L.
—— UKRAINIAN CONCERTINO
  0,1,1,1 - 1,0,0,0 - pf. - str.   G. Schirmer.

KLEBE, Giselher
—— HERZSCHLÄGE, OP. 57 (3 SYMPHONIC SCENES)(1969)
  0,*3,*3,3 - 2,3,3,1 - timp.,perc.(5) - 3 electric guit. - hp. - pf. - str.
        18:00 G. Schirmer.
—— SCENE AND ARIA, OP. 54 (1967)
  0,0,0,0 - 0,3,3,0 - 2 pf. - 8 c.   12:00 G. Schirmer.
—— SYMPHONY NO. 3, OP. 52 (1966)
  3(3rd alt. with picc.),*3,*4,3 - 4,4,3,1 - perc.(2),cel.(alt. with pf.) -
  hp. - str.   32:00 G. Schirmer.
—— DAS TESTAMENT, OP. 61 (SYMPHONY NO. 4)(A BALLET
  SYMPHONY, AFTER BALLADS OF FRANÇIS VILLON)(1970)
  *2,*2,*2,2 - 4,2,3,1 - perc.(2) - elec. cemb.,org. - 2 pf. - str.
        25:00 G. Schirmer.

KLEGA, Miroslav
—— CONCERTO-PARTITA
  3(3rd alt. with picc.),2,2,*3 - 2,2,2,0 - timp.,perc. - pf. - str.
        12:00 General.

KLEIN, John
—— HORACE THE BEAR (FOR NARRATOR AND ORCH.) (Text:
  Alice Coates)
  1,1,1,1 - 2,1,1,0 - perc. - hp. - pf. - str.   10:00 Mills.

KLEIN, Lothar
—— APPASSIONATO FOR ORCH.
  3(3rd alt. with picc.),2,1 Eᵇcl.,2(2nd alt. with b.-cl.),0 - 4,3,3,1 -
  timp.,perc.(4),glock.,xyl. - hp. - str.   7:00 CanMusCtr.
—— THE BLUEBIRD (SUITE FOR ORCH., AFTER
  MAETERLINCK)
  *3,2,2,2 - 2,2,2,0 - timp. - hp. - pf. - str.   18:00 Composer.
—— CONCERTO FOR WINDS, TIMPANI AND STRINGS (1956)
  (IN 3 MOVTS.) (For abridged version, see Sinfonia Concertante)
  1,1,1,1 - 2,2,2,0 - timp. - str.   28:00 CanMusCtr.
—— DESIGN FOR PERCUSSION AND ORCH. (1970)
  *3,*3,Eᵇcl.,*3,2-3 - 4,3,3,1 - timp.,perc.(4) - tape-recorder - hp. -
  str.   7:25 MCA Music.
—— EPITAPHS (SUITE) (IN 3 MOVTS.)
  2(2nd alt. with picc.),1,2,2 - 4,2,2,0 - timp.,perc.(2),glock.,vibra. -
  hp. - str.   12:00 CanMusCtr.
—— HERBSTLIEDER (6 AUTUMN SONGS) (FOR SOPRANO AND
  23 SOLO INSTS.)
  *2,0,*2,1 d.-b.-cl.,*1 - 2,1,1,0 - perc.(1),glock. - hp. - pf. - str.
        14:00 Composer.
—— INVENTION, BLUES AND CHASE (FOR FREE BASS
  ACCORDION AND STRINGS) (1975)
  B.-acc. - str.   17:00 CanMusCtr.
—— JANIZARY MUSIC (3 PIECES FOR MILITARY ORCH.) (1969)
  3(2 alt. with 2 picc.),2(alt. with 2 Eng. hn.),2,2 - 2,2,2,0 -
  timp.,perc.(2),glock.,xyl. - str.   15:00 AMP.
—— MEDITATIONS ON THE PASSYOUN (FOR ATB CHORUS, 14
  WINDS AND HARP) (IN 5 MOVTS.) (TEXT: RICHARD
  ROLLE) (1961)
        21:00 Composer.
—— MUSIC FOR VIOLIN AND ORCH. (1972) (IN 1 MOVT.)
  2(2nd alt. with picc.),1,2,1 - 2,1,0,0 - perc. - str.
        10:00 CanMusCtr.
—— MUSICA ANTIQUA (ALLEGORY FOR CONSORT AND
  ORCH.) (1975) (IN 2 PARTS OF 4 SECTIONS EACH)
  Consort: 5 player-singers on misc. antique instrs.(with
  amplification ad lib.)   24:10 CanMusCtr.
  Orch: *3,2(2nd alt. with Eng. hn.),Eᵇcl.,*3,*3 - 4,3,3,1 -
  timp.,perc.(3) - pf. (or cel.) - str.
—— MUSIQUE À GO-GO (A SYMPHONIC MÊLÉE) (1966)
  *3,*3,1 Eᵇcl.,*2,*3 - 4,4,3,1 - timp.,perc.(2) - str.   7:15 Presser.
—— ORCHESTRAL SUITE (1971) (IN 3 MOVTS.)
  2(2nd alt. with picc),2(2nd alt. with Eng. hn.),2(2nd alt. with
  b.-cl.),2 - 2,2,0,0 - timp.,perc. - hp. - hpsc. - str.
        17:00 CanMusCtr.
—— PAGANINI COLLAGE (FOR VIOLIN AND ORCH.) (1967) (IN
  1 MOVT.)
  *3,2 Eᵇcl.,*3,2 - 4,2,2,0 - timp.,perc.(3) - str.   17:55 CanMusCtr.

—— PASSACAGLIA OF THE ZODIAC (TWELVE VARIATIONS
  FOR 14 STRS.) (1971)
  str.(8,3,1,1)   15:30 CanMusCtr.
—— THE PHILOSOPHER IN THE KITCHEN (FIVE SONGS FOR
  CONTRALTO AND ORCH.) (1974) (Texts: Composer, after
  Horace and Jean Anthelme Brillat-Savarin)
  *3,2,*3,*3 - 2.,2,2,0 - timp.,perc.(4) - hp. - str.   20:50 CanMusCtr.
—— PRESTO FOR ORCH.
  3(3rd alt. with picc.),2,2,2 - 4,3,3,1 - timp.,perc.(4) - hp. - str.
        6:00 Composer.
—— SGANARELLE, OU, LE COCU IMAGINAIRE
  *3,2,2,2 - 4,2,2,0 - timp.,perc.(3) - str.   5:00 CanMusCtr.
—— SINFONIA CONCERTANTE (FOR WOODWIND QUARTET
  AND ORCH.) (ABRIDGED FROM THE CONCERTO FOR
  WINDS, TIMPANI AND STRINGS) (IN 3 MOVTS.)
  1,1,1,1 - 2,2,2,0 - timp. - str.   12:00 CanMusCtr.
—— SLICES OF TIME (FOR TRUMPET AND STRINGS) (1973) (IN
  1 MOVT.)
  tpt. - str.   9:00 CanMusCtr.
—— SYMMETRIES FOR ORCHESTRA, NOS. 1 AND 4
  (PASSACAGLIA AND VARIATIONS)
  3(3rd alt. with picc.),2,1 Eᵇcl.,*3,0 - 4,3,3,1 -
  timp.,perc.(4),vibra.,xyl. - hp. - str.   20:00 Presser.
—— SYMPHONIC ETUDES (SYMPHONY NO. 3) (1972) (IN 1
  MOVT.)
  *3,*3,Eᵇcl.,*3,*3 - 4,3(incl. tpt. in D),3,1 - timp.,perc.(4) - hp. -
  pf. - str.   17:20 CanMusCtr.
—— SYMPHONY NO. 2 (1965)
  1. Sonata; 2. Rondo Giocoso
  2(alt. with 2 picc.),2,2,2 - 4,2,2,0 - timp. - str.   19:00 Composer.
—— TRIO CONCERTANTE (FOR VIOLIN, VIOLA, CELLO AND
  ORCH.) (IN 2 MOVTS.)
  *3,2(2nd alt. with Eng.hn.),2,2 - 4,2,2,1 - timp.,perc.(2), glock. -
  str.   12:00 CanMusCtr.

KLEIN, Richard Rudolf
—— CHAMBER CONCERTO (FOR 4 SOLO WINDS, TIMPANI
  AND STRING ORCH.)
        Hans Gerig.
—— FANTASY FOR CLARINET AND STRING ORCH.
  cl. - str.   Hans Gerig.
—— PARTITA
  str.   16:00 Robbins.

KLEINE, Werner - HARTMANN, Bruno
—— ROTE ERDE ("THE RED EARTH") (WESTPHALIAN TONE
  POEM)
  3,2,2,3 - 4,3,3,1 - timp.,perc. - hp. - str.   8:00 F. Colombo.

KLEINMAN, Isador
—— FOUR FABLES (FOR NARRATOR AND ORCH.) (Text:
  Composer)
  2,*3,2,2 - 4,2-3,2-3,1,4 shofars (ad lib.) - timp.,perc.(4) - hp. - str.
        18:00 Melomusic.

KLEINSINGER, George
—— ADVENTURES OF A ZOO (FOR NARRATOR AND ORCH.)
  2(1 alt. with picc.),2,2,2 - 4,3,2,1 - timp.,perc.(2),glock.,xyl - str.
        15:00 Rytvoc.
—— ARCHY AND MEHITABEL (A BACK-ALLEY OPERA) %
  1(alt. with picc.),1(alt. with alto sax.),2(alt. with 1 alto and 1 ten.
  sax.)1 - 1,2,2,0 - perc.(1),glock.,xyl. - guit. - pf. - str.(1 vln.,1 d.-b.)
        30:00 Chappell.
—— BROOKLYN BASEBALL CANTATA (FOR SOLOISTS, MIXED
  OR MEN'S CHORUS AND ORCH.)
  1,0,2(2nd alt. with b.-cl.),1 - 0,2,2,0 - timp.,perc.(1),cel.(ad
  lib.),glock. - hp.(ad lib.) - pf. - str.   12:00 Composer.
—— CONCERTO FOR CELLO AND ORCH.
  *3,*3,*3,2 - 4,3,3,1 - timp.,perc.(2),cel.,glock.,xyl. - hp. - str.
        23:00 Janfred.
—— CONCERTO FOR CELLO AND ORCH. (REV. 1964) (IN 3
  MOVTS.)
  *3,2,*3,*3 - 4,3,3,0 - timp.,perc.(2),xyl. - hp. - str.   23:00 Janfred.
—— CONCERTO FOR VIOLIN AND ORCH.
  2(2nd alt. with picc.),2(2nd alt. with Eng.hn.),2(2nd alt. with
  b.-cl.),2 - 2,2,1,0 - str.   15:00 Chappell.
—— CONCERTO FOR 3 PERCUSSIONISTS AND WIND ORCH.
        20:00 Henmar.
—— CONEY ISLAND SUITE (IN 6 MOVTS.)
  *2,2,2,2 - 4,3,3,1 - perc.(2),cel.,glock.,xyl. - pf. - str.
        20:00 Chappell.

—— DAWN TO DAWN (ONCE AROUND THE CLOCK) (A BIG CITY PORTRAIT)
*2,2,2(alt. with sax. and b.-cl.),0 - 3,3,3,1 - timp.,perc.,cel.,glock.,xyl. - hp. - pf. - str.   12:00 Chappell.

—— FANTASY FOR VIOLIN AND ORCH.
1. Lento; 2. Allegro molto
1(alt. with picc.),2,1(alt. with b.-cl.),2 - 4,2,3,1 - timp.,perc.,cel.,xyl. - hp. - pf. - str.   15:00 Composer.

—— FAREWELL TO A HERO (CANTATA) (FOR BARITONE, CHORUS AND ORCH.)
2,2(alt. with Eng.hn.),2,2 - 4,2,3,1 - timp.,perc.(2) - hp. - pf. - str.   10:00 Bo. Hawkes.

—— FURTHER ADVENTURES OF TUBBY THE TUBA (FOR NARRATOR AND ORCH.)
1(alt. with picc.),2,2,1 - 2,2,2,1 - timp.,perc.(2),glock.,xyl. - hp. - str.   14:00 Rytvoc.

—— JACK AND HOMER THE HORSE (FOR NARRATOR AND ORCH.)
1(alt. with picc.),1,1(alt. with b.-cl.),1 - 2,2,2,1 - timp.,perc.(2),cel.,xyl. - str.   13:00 Chappell.

—— JESSE JAMES (FANFARE FOR ORCHESTRA)
3(3rd alt. with picc.),*3,2,b.-cl.(alt. with alto sax. and E♭cl.),2 - 4,3,3,1 - timp.,perc.(4),cel.(or pf.),glock.,xyl. - str.   20:00 Janfred.

—— JOHNNY STRANGER (FOR BARITONE, NARRATOR AND SMALL ORCH.)
1,1,2,3 sax.,1 - 1,2,2,0 - timp.,perc.(1),xyl. - str.   15:00 Bourne.

—— JOIE DE VIVRE (SUITE)
2,2,2,2 - 2,2,2,1 - perc. - str.   9:30 Chappell.

—— THE LITTLE STAR OF BETHLEHEM (FOR NARRATOR, ORCH. AND ORCH. OF ANCIENT INSTS.) (Text: Paul Tripp)
regular orch.: 1(alt.with picc.),1(alt. with Eng. hn.,),1,0 - 1,1,0,0 - perc. - hpsc.(or virginal or pf.) - str.
Orch. of Ancient Instrs.: soprano recoder (alt. with sopranino recorder), tenor recorder, oboe d'amore (alt. with poboe da caccia) - 1 horn, 1 trumpet - perc. - hpsc.(or virginal or pf.) - viols, tenor viols, as viol, d.-b.   18:00 Rytvoc.

—— ONCE UPON AN ORCHESTRA (FOR NARRATOR AND ORCH.)
*2,2,2,1 - 2,2,2,1 - timp.,perc.(2),glock.,xyl. - pf. - str.   15:00 Rytvoc.

—— OVERTURE ON AMERICAN FOLK THEMES
1(alt. with picc.),2,2,2 - 4,2,3,1 - timp.,perc.(2),xyl. - str.   8:00 Chappell.

—— PAN THE PIPER (FOR NARRATOR AND ORCH.)
3(3rd alt. with picc.),2(2nd alt. with Eng.hn.),2(2nd alt. with b.-cl.),2 - 4,3,3,1 - timp.,perc.(2),cel.,glock.,xyl. - hp. - str.   18:00 Fox.

—— PEE WEE THE PICCOLO (FOR NARRATOR AND ORCH.)
1(alt. with picc.),1,1(alt. with b.-cl.),1(alt. with c.-bn) - 2,2,2,1 - timp.,perc.(2),cel.,glock.,xyl. - str.   12:00 Janfred.

—— PLYMOUTH ROCK, 1949 (FOR BARITONE AND ORCH.)
1(alt. with picc. and alto sax.),1(alt. with Eng.hn. and ten.sax.),0,1(alt. with b.-cl.) - 1,1,0,0 - perc. - quit.(alt. with banjo) - str.(no c.)   14:00 General.

—— SCHERZO
1(alt. with picc.),2,1(alt. with b.-cl.),1 - 2,2,2,1 - timp.,perc.(2),xyl. - pf. - str.   6:00 Chappell.

—— SHORT SYMPHONY (IN 3 MOVTS.)
*2,2,*2,2 - 3,3,2,0 - timp.,perc.(2),glock.,xyl. - hp. - str.   20:00 Janfred.

—— THE STORY OF CELESTE (FOR NARRATOR AND ORCH.)
*2,1,1(alt. with b.-cl.),1 - 2,2,2,1 - timp.,perc.(2),cel.,glock.,xyl. - hp. - str.   13:00 Rytvoc.

—— STREET CORNER CONCERTO (FOR HARMONICA OR ALTO SAXOPHONE AND ORCH.) (IN 3 MOVTS.)
2hn.,tpt. - timp.,perc.(1),glock. - harmonica(or alto sax.) - hp. - str.   9:30 Chappell.

—— THE SWALLOW AND THE HAPPY PRINCE (FOR NARRATOR AND ORCH.) (After Oscar Wilde)
2(alt. with 2 picc.),1(alt. with Eng. hn.),2,1 - 2,2,1,0 - timp.,perc.(1),glock. - hp. - str.   15:00 Janfred.

—— SYMPHONY NO. 1
1. Lento; 2. Allegro; 3. Moderato
*3,2(1alt. with Eng.hn.),1(alt. with E♭ cl. and b.-cl.),2 - 4,3,3,1 - timp.,perc.(2),cel.,xyl. - hp. - str.   20:00 Composer.

—— SYMPHONY OF WINDS (FOR NARRATOR AND WIND ORCH.)
15:00 Henmar.

—— THEME AND VARIATIONS ("TUNE AND WORKOUT FOR YOUTHFUL ORCHESTRA")
Chappell.

—— THE TOY BOX (BALLET SUITE) (IN 5 MOVTS.)
3(3rd alt. with picc.),2(2nd alt. with Eng.hn.),0,2 - 4,3,3,1 - perc.(2),cel.(alt. with pf.) - hp. - str.   18:00 Rytvoc.

—— THE TREE THAT FOUND CHRISTMAS (OPERA) %
1(alt. with picc.),2,2,0 - 2,2,2,0 - timp.,perc.(1),bells,glock.,xyl. - hp. - str.   44:00 Helena.

—— TUBBY THE TUBA AT THE CIRCUS (FOR NARRATOR AND ORCH.)
2(2nd alt. with picc.),1(alt. with Eng.hn.),1(alt. with b.-cl.),1 - 2,2,1,1 - timp.,perc.(2) - str.   10:00 Rytvoc.

—— TUBBY THE TUBA (FOR NARRATOR AND ORCH.)
1(alt. with picc.),2,1(alt. with b.-cl.),1 - 2,2,2,1 - timp.,perc.(2),cel.,xyl. - str.   13:00 Rytvoc.

—— UNDER THE CHRISTMAS TREE (FOR ORCH., WITH OPTIONAL NARRATION)
3(3rd alt. with picc.),2(2nd alt. with Eng.hn.),0,2 - 4,3,3,1 - perc.(2),cel.(alt. with pf.) - hp. - str.   19:00 Rytvoc.

—— WESTWARD HO!
*3,2,2,2 - 4,3,3,0 - timp.,perc.(2),glock.,xyl. - str.   8:00 General.

KLEMETTI, Heikki

—— CANTILENA FOR STRINGS (1927)
str.   8:00 Westerlund.

—— JUBILANT PSALM (FOR MEZZO-SOPRANO, SATB CHORUS AND ORCH.) (1926)
1,1,0,0 - 0,0,0,0 - org. - str.   8:00 FinnMICtr.

—— LYRICAL OVERTURE (1930)
2,2,2,2 - 2,2,2,0 - timp. - str.   9:00 FinnMICtr.

—— PRELUDE, AIR AND SCHERZINO (1940)
1,1,1,1 - 1,0,0,0 - str.   FinnMICtr.

—— PSALM 98 (FOR SATB CHORUS AND ORCH.) (1930)
1,1,1,0 - 1,1,1,0 - org. - str.   9:00 FinnMICtr.

—— YELLOW LEAVES (VARIATIONS FOR ORCH.) (1934)
1,2,1,1 - 1,1,0,0 - str.   10:00 FinnMICtr.

KLENAU, Paul von

—— MARION (BALLET PANTOMINE) %
3,2,2,2 - 4,3,3,1 - timp.,perc.,cel. - hp. - pf. - str.   G. Schirmer.

KLENNER, John

—— AIR AND ALLEGRO FOR OBOE AND STRINGS
ob. - str.   6:00 C-Ross.

—— FANTASIA FOR VIOLA AND ORCH.
2,2(2nd alt. with Eng.hn.),2,2 - 2,2,2,0 - timp. - str.   17:00 C-Ross.

—— VARIATIONS FOR STRINGS
str.   8:00 C-Ross.

KLEPPER, Leon

—— CONCERTINO FOR FLUTE, PIANO AND STRINGS
fl. - pf. - str.   14:00 IsMuPublns.

—— CONCERTINO FOR PIANO 4-HANDS AND ORCH.
2(2nd alt. with picc.),2,2,2 - 3,3,3,0 - timp.,perc. - pf. 4-hands - str.   17:00 AhnSimrock.

KLERK, Albert de

—— CONCERTO FOR ORGAN AND ORCH.
3,2,2,2 - 4,2,3,1 - perc. - org. - str.   18:00 Henmar.

—— JAM LUCIS ORTO SIDERE (FOR HIGH VOICE AND ORCH.) (1943)
2,2,2,2 - 2,2,3,0 - timp. - hp. - str.   6:00 Henmar.

—— STABAT MATER (FOR ALTO, TENOR, MIXED CHORUS AND ORCH.)(1952)
1,1,1,1 - 1,1,0,0 - timp.,perc. - str.   35:00 Henmar.

KLEVEN, Arvid

—— LOTUSLAND
2,2,2,2 - 4,0,0,0 - timp.,perc. - hp. - pf. - str.   18:00 Norsk Mfl.

KLEY, Erich

—— MUSIC FOR CHAMBER ORCH., OP. 85
str.   18:00 Tetra.

KLÖSS, Wilfried

—— KAPRIZIÖSES STÄNDCHEN (FOR FLUTE AND SMALL ORCH.)
fl. - hp. - pf. - str.   11:00 F. Colombo.

KLOTZMAN, Dorothy

—— CONCERTO FOR ALTO SAXOPHONE AND ORCH. (IN 3 MOVTS.)
*3,0,2,1 alto sax.,2 - 4,3,3,1 - timp.,perc.(2) - str.   12:00 Composer.

—— VARIATIONS FOR ORCH.
*3,2,2,2 - 4,3,2,1 - timp.,perc.(3) - str.   5:00 Composer.

KLUG, Ernst
—— EIN CHRISTOPHORUS-ZYKLUS (5 STUCKE FÜR
KAMMERORCHESTER)
23:00 S.U.I.S.A.
—— MUSIK FÜR KAMMERORCHESTER (NACH EINEM "VATER
UNSER" VON S. SCHEIDT)
28:00 S.U.I.S.A.
—— SPIELE (3 STUCKE FOR KLEINES ORCHESTER)
6:00 S.U.I.S.A.

KLUSÁK, Jan
—— LYRIC FANTASY (HOMAGE TO GRIEG)
Hans Gerig.

KLUSSMANN, Ernst Gernot
—— SPIELMUSIK I (FIVE VARIATIONS ON A FOLKSONG)
str.   F. Colombo.

KNAAK, Karl
—— BALLETT-SUITE (IN 5 MOVTS.)
2,1,2,2 - 2,2,1,0 - perc. - hp. - str.   T & J.

KNAIFEL, Alexander A.
—— THE CANTERVILLE GHOST (FOR SOPRANO, BASS AND
CHAMBER ORCH.) (Text: T. Kramarova)
G. Schirmer.

KNECHT, Arthur
—— A BOY AND HIS MELODIES (SCENES FROM THE LIFE OF
YOUNG MOZART) (FOR NARRATOR AND ORCH.)
2,2,2,2 - 4,2,3,0 - timp. - hpsc. - str.   13:00 G. Schirmer.
—— DVORAK AND THE NEW WORLD (FOR NARRATOR AND
ORCH.)
3,3,3,3 - 4,2,3,0 - timp.,perc. - str.   16:00 G. Schirmer.
—— MUSICAL DREAMER (SCENES FROM THE LIFE OF
STEPHEN FOSTER) (FOR NARRATOR AND ORCH.)
2,3,2,2 - 4,2,3,1 - perc. - hp. - str.   14:00 G. Schirmer.
—— ON WINGS OF SONG (MENDELSSOHN AND HIS MUSIC)
(FOR NARRATOR AND ORCH.)
2,2,2,2 - 4,2,3,0 - timp.,perc. - hp. - str. 12:00 G. Schirmer.

KNIGHT, Morris
—— ALL NIGHT THE SEA (CYCLE OF 5 SONGS FOR SOPRANO
AND ORCH.) (1960) (Text: Gerald E. Sieg)
*3,2,*3,2 - 4,2,2,0 - timp.,perc.(2) - hp. - str. 25:00 Composer.
—— CONCERTO FOR ALTO SAXOPHONE AND STRINGS (1964)
(IN 1 MOVT.)
alto sax. - str.   11:00 Composer.
—— CONCERTO FOR VIOLIN AND ORCH. (1961) (IN 4 MOVTS.)
*3,*3,*3,*3 - 6,0,0,0 - timp.,perc.(2),cel. - hp. - str.
29:00 Composer.
—— DEL CAMINO (OF THE ROAD) (3 SONGS FOR SOPRANO
AND ORCH.) (1955) (Text: Antonio Machado)
1,1,*3,2 - 2,2,2,0 - timp.,perc. - pf. - str. 9:00 Composer.
—— DESIGN FOR TRUMPET AND STRINGS (1965)
tpt. - str.   4:00 Composer.
—— MINIATURE OVERTURE (1964)
*3,*3,*3,2 - 4,3,3,1 - timp.,perc.,bells,cel. - pf. - str.
3:00 Composer.
—— PROMISE OF YOUTH (OVERTURE) (1960)
2,2,*3,1 - 2,2,2,0 - timp.,perc. - hp. - str. 7:00 Composer.
—— SYMPHONY NO. 1 (1956)
1. Larghetto; 2. Moderato; 3. Adagietto
*3,2,*3,2 - 4,2,2,0 - timp.,perc.(2) - str.   16:00 Composer.
—— SYMPHONY NO. 2 (A CONCISE SYMPHONY) (1961)
1. Lento; 2. Arietta; 3. Allegro
*3,*3,*3,*3 - 4,3,3,1 - timp.,perc.(2) - hp. - pf. - str.
12:00 Composer.
—— SYMPHONY NO. 3 (A CRUCIAL SYMPHONY) (1963) (IN 4
MOVTS.)
*3,*3,*3,*3 - 4,3,3,1 - timp.,perc.,bells,cel.,glock. - pf. - str.
29:00 Composer.
—— SYMPHONY NO. 4 (A SUMMER SYMPHONY) (1966) (IN 1
MOVT.)
3(3rd alt. with picc.),*3,*3,*3 - 4,3,3,1 - timp.,perc.(2),bells,glock. -
pf. - str.   20:00 Composer.
—— THREE CANVASES (1958)
0,0,0,0 - 0,1,1,0 - pf. - str.   22:00 Composer.
—— TO THE SILKEN SWIFT (1965)
*3,*3,*3,*3 - 4,3,3,1 - timp.,perc.(3),cel. - hp. - pf. - str.
10:00 Composer.
—— VARIETIES FOR BRASS ENSEMBLE (1962) (IN 8 MOVTS.)
0,0,0,0 - 4,3,3,1   10:00 Studio Two Twenty-Four.

KNIPPER, Lev K.
—— CONCERTO FOR VIOLIN AND ORCH. (IN 3 MOVTS.)
*2,1,3,1 - 3,0,0,1 - timp. - str.   G. Schirmer.
—— FOUR SOLDIERS' SONGS (SUITE FOR SMALL ORCH.)
4hn.,2tpt. - timp.,perc. - str.   11:00 G. Schirmer.
—— LITTLE CONCERTO FOR ORCH.
3 ob. - 3 tpt. - timp. - 3 hp. - str.   G. Schirmer.
—— LITTLE LYRIC SUITE, OP. 18 (IN 4 MOVTS.)
2(2nd alt. with picc.),1,1,1 - 2 hn. - perc. - hp. - str.
8:30 G. Schirmer.
—— MAKU SUITE (ON IRANIAN THEMES) (IN 4 MOVTS.)
*2,1,1,1 - 2,1,1,1 - timp.,perc. - str.   18:00 G. Schirmer.
—— MOUNTAIN SERENADE (FOR STRINGS)
str.   21:00 G. Schirmer.
—— RADIF (IRANIAN SUITE) (FOR STRING QUARTET AND
STRING ORCH.)
str.   8:00 G. Schirmer.
—— VANCHE (SUITE FOR SMALL ORCH.), OP. 29 (BASED ON
TADJIK MELODIES)
* 1(alt. with picc.),1,1,ten.sax.,1 - 2,1,1,0 - timp.,perc. - str.
22:00 G. Schirmer.

KNOBEL, Theo
—— GOLDENE AKADEMIA (FOUR CENTURIES OF STUDENT
SONGS) (FOR BARITONE, MEN'S CHORUS AND ORCH.)
3,2,2,2 - 4,2,3,0 - timp.,perc. - hp. - str. 35:00 F. Colombo.

KNOX, Charles C.
—— BALLAD SUITE (1961) (IN 3 MOVTS.)
2,2,2,2 - 4,2,3,1 - timp.,perc.(2) - str.   7:00 Composer.
—— CONCERT PIECE FOR BASSOON AND ORCH. (1959)
2,2,2,3 - 4,2,3,1 - timp. - str.   10:00 Composer.
—— CONCERT PIECE FOR ORCH. (1963) (AN ORCHESTRAL
SETTING TO WHICH VARIOUS SOLO PARTS MAY BE
PERFORMED.)
8:00 Composer.
—— OVERTURE IN F (1960)
*3,*3,*3,*3 - 4,3,3,1 - timp.,perc.(3) - str. 6:15 Composer.

KNUSSEN, Oliver
—— CONCERTO FOR ORCHESTRA
3(3rd alt. with picc.),*3,3(1 alt. with E♭cl.,1 alt. with b.-cl.),*3 -
4,2,3,1 - timp.,perc.(5) - pf. - str.   20:00 G. Schirmer.
—— SYMPHONY NO. 1
G. Schirmer.
—— SYMPHONY NO. 2 (FOR SOPRANO AND SMALL ORCH.)
(Texts: Georg Trakl and Sylvia Plath)
2,2,2,2 - 2,0,0,0 - perc. (ad lib.) - str.   17:00 G. Schirmer.
—— SYMPHONY NO. 3 ("THE UNFINISHED")
G. Schirmer.

KOCH, Erland von
—— BALLET OVERTURE
3,2,2,2 - 4,3,3,1 - timp.,perc.(2) - str.   5:00 S.T.I.M.
or:
3,2,2,2 - 4,3,3,1 - timp.,perc. - str.
—— CANTO NORDICO AND RONDO (1973)
ob. - str.   8:00 Fleisher.
—— CINDERELLA: BALLET SUITE NO. 1
3,2,2,2 - 4,3,3,1 - timp.,perc. - hp. - str.   24:00 Nordiska.
—— CONCERT MUSIC (SUITE)
2,2,2,2 - 4,2,3,1 - timp.,perc. - str.   18:00 S.T.I.M.
—— CONCERTINO FOR STRINGS OP. 16
str.   12:00 Gehrmans.
—— CONCERTO FOR CELLO AND ORCH., OP. 49
2,1,2,1 - 2,1,0,0 - timp.,perc. - str.   18:30 S.T.I.M.
—— CONCERTO FOR SAXOPHONE AND STRINGS (1958)
sax. - str.   19:00 Marbot.
—— CONCERTO FOR SMALL ORCH. (1955)
1,1,2,1 - 2,0,0,0 - str.   16:00 Bo. Hawkes.
—— CONCERTO FOR VIOLIN, PIANO AND ORCH. (1974)
2,2,2,2 - 2,2,1,0 - timp.,perc. - pf. - str.   22:00 Fleisher.
—— CONCERTO LIRICO (FOR STRING ORCH.) (1959)
str.   18:00 Marbot.
—— DIVERTIMENTO FOR FLUTE AND STRINGS, OP. 35
fl. - str.   14:00 S.T.I.M.
—— DOUBLE CONCERTO FOR FLUTE, CLARINET AND STRING
ORCH. (1971)
fl.,cl. - str.   18:00 Fleisher.
—— FANTASIA CONCERTANTE (FOR VIOLIN AND
ORCH.)(1969)
2,2,2,2 - 2,1,0,0 - timp.,perc. - str.   12:00 Fleisher.

—— KASPERI (CHILDREN'S BALLET) % (1967)
    2,2,2,2 - 2,1,1,1 - timp.,perc. - str.   10:00 Fleisher.
—— LITTLE COMEDY OVERTURE
    2,2,2,2 - 2,2,1,0 - timp.,perc. - str.   4:00 S.T.I.M.
—— A LITTLE LYRICAL MUSIC (IN 3 MOVTS.)
    2,1,1,1 - 1,0,0,0 - str.   12:00 S.T.I.M.
—— LITTLE SUITE FOR CHAMBER ORCH., OP. 1
    2,2,2,2 - 2,1,0,0 - str.   5:00 S.T.I.M.
—— MIDSOMMARDALEM (1961) (LYRIC SUITE) (FOR
SOPRANO, BARITONE, MIXED CHORUS AND ORCH.) (Text:
Harry Martinson)
    2,2,2,2 - 2,2,1,0 - timp.,perc.(2) - str.   30:00 Gehrmans.
—— MUSICA CONCERTANTE (FOR 8 WINDS, PERCUSSION
AND STRINGS)(1969)
    1,1,1,1 - 1,1,1,1 - timp.,perc.(5, incl. 3 on timp.) - str.
    20:30 S.T.I.M.
—— MUSICA MALINCONICA, OP. 50
    str.   16:00 Bo. Hawkes.
—— NORDIC CAPRICCIO
    2,2,2,2 - 2,2,1,0 - timp. - str.   6:00 Bo. Hawkes.
—— OVERTURE TO "PELLE SVANSLÖS"
    1,1,1,1 - 1,1,1,0 - timp.,perc.(ad lib.) - str.   3:00 S.T.I.M.
—— PELLE SVANSLÖS, OP. 42 (BALLET MUSIC FROM A
CHILDREN'S OPERA)(REV. 1966)
    1,1,1,1 - 1,1,1,0 - timp.,perc.(ad lib.) - str.   13:00 Nordiska.
—— RÖDLUVAN OCH VARGEN (CHILDREN'S BALLET) % (1965)
    1,1,1,1 - 1,1,0,0 - timp.,perc. - str.   10:00 S.T.I.M.
—— RURAL SUITE (FOR STRINGS), OP. 32 (IN 3 MOVTS.)
    str.   14:00 Bo. Hawkes.
—— RUSTIC DANCE
    2,2,2,2 - 4,2,3,1 - timp.,perc. - hp. - str.   10:00 S.T.I.M.
—— SIMSON OCH DELILA (BALLET) % (1963)
    2,2,2,2 - 4,2,3,1 - timp.,perc.(3) - hp. - str.   65:00 Fleisher.
—— SINFONIETTA, OP. 44
    2,2,2,2 - 2,2,1,0 - timp.,perc. - str.   15:00 S.T.I.M.
—— SUITE FROM "PELLE SVANSLÖS", OP. 42
    1,1,1,1 - 1,1,1,0 - timp.,perc.(ad lib.) - str.   13:00 S.T.I.M.
—— SUITE FROM THE BALLET "ASKUNGEN", OP. 24 (IN 3
MOVTS.)
    3,2,2,2 - 4,3,3,1 - timp.,perc.(2) - hp. - str.   14:00 Nordiska.
    or:
    2,1,2,1 - 2,2,1,0 - timp.,perc. - pf. - str.
—— A SWEDE IN NEW YORK (1973)
    2,2,2,2 sax.,2 - 4,3,3,1 - timp.,perc.(5) - pf. - str.   12:00 Fleisher.
—— SYMPHONY NO. 3, OP. 38
    2,2,2,2 - 4,3,3,1 - timp.,perc. - hp. - str.   25:00 S.T.I.M.
—— SYMPHONY NO. 4 ("SINFONIA SERIA"), OP. 51
    2,2,2,2 - 4,2,3,1 - timp.,perc. - str.   25:00 S.T.I.M.
—— SYNCOPERIA (OVERTURE)
    1,1,0,2 sax.,1 - 2,2,1,0 - timp.,perc. - pf. - str.   5:00 S.T.I.M.
—— TAFFELMUSIK (SUITE) (1951) (IN 3 MOVTS.)
    2,2,2,2 - 2,2,1,0 - timp.,perc.(2) - str.   12:00 S.T.I.M.
—— TRIPTYCH FOR VIOLIN AND ORCH., OP. 43
    1,1,1,1 - 1,1,0,0 - timp.,perc. - str.   16:00 S.T.I.M.

KOCH, Frederick
—— CONCERTINO FOR SAXOPHONE AND ORCH.
    2,2,2,sax,2 - 3,2,2,0 - timp.,perc. - hp. - pf. - str.   15:00 Seesaw.
—— DANCE OVERTURE (1971)
    3,2,3,2 - 2,2,1,0 - timp.,perc.(2) - hp. - str.   5:00 Seesaw.
—— MEMORIAL
    2,3,2,2 - 2,2,1,0 - perc.,cel. - str.   5:00 Seesaw.
—— MONADNOCK CADENZAS AND VARIATIONS (1971)
    0,0,1,0 - 0,1,0,0 - perc. - str.   15:00 Seesaw.
—— OVERTURE FOR AMERICA (1974)
    2,2,2,2 - 2,2,2,0 - timp.,perc. - hp. - pf. - str.   8:00 Seesaw.
—— OVERTURE TO A DRAMA, OP. 41
    2,2,2,2 - 2,2,1,0 - timp.,perc.(2),bells,xyl. - mandolin - pf. - str.
    10:00 Composer.
—— RIVER JOURNEY, OP. 24 (SUITE) (IN 3 MOVTS.)
    3(3rd alt. with picc.),*3,2,*3 - 4,3,2,0 - timp.,perc.(3),bells,cel.,xyl.
- hp. - pf. - str.   15:00 Composer.
—— SHORT SYMPHONY NO. 1 (1965)
    2,3,2,2 - 2,2,2,1 - timp.,perc. - hp. - pf. - str.   15:00 Seesaw.
—— SUITE FOR ORCH. AND PIANO, OP. 48 (IN 3 MOVTS.)
    3(3rd alt. with picc.),2,*3,*3 - 4,2,2,1 - timp.,perc.(2),
cel.,glock.,xyl. - hp. - pf. - str.   15:00 Composer.
—— VARIATIONS FOR ORCH. WITH PIANO, OP. 42 (BASED ON
A SOMERSET FOLK SONG)
    3(3rd alt. with picc.),*3,2,*3 - 2,2,2,1 - timp.,perc.(2),cel.,xyl. - hp.
- pf. - str.   7:00 Composer.
—— VELTIN FANTASY (1971)
    ob. - str.   8:00 Seesaw.

KOCH, John Gordon
—— CONCERTO FOR VIOLIN AND ORCH. (1964) (IN 3 MOVTS.)
    2(2nd alt. with picc.),2,2,2 - 2,2,0,0 - timp.,perc.(2) - hp. - str.
    24:45 Composer.
—— CONCERTO NO. 1 FOR PIANO AND ORCH. (1957) (IN 3
MOVTS.)
    2,2,2,2 - 4,3,3,1 - timp. - pf. - str.   22:30 Composer.
—— CONCERTO NO. 2 FOR PIANO AND CHAMBER ORCH.
(1961) (IN 3 MOVTS.)
    2(2nd alt. with picc.),1,2,2 - 2,1,0,0 - perc.(1) - pf. - str.
    20:30 Composer.
—— ELEGY FOR ORCHESTRA (1955)
    2,2(2nd alt. with Eng. hn.),2,2, - 4,3,3,1 - perc.(1) - str.
    10:00 Composer.
—— ELEGY (FOR STRING ORCH.) (1954)
    str.   4:30 Valley.
—— OVERTURE TO A SAD CIRCUS (1955)
    2(2nd alt. with picc.),2,2,2 - 2,2,0,0 - timp.,perc.(2) - str.
    11:00 Composer.
—— SYMPHONY NO. 1 (1962)
    1. Andante sostenuto; 2. Allegro molto; 3. Adagio; 4. Presto
    2(2nd alt. with picc.),2(2nd alt. with Eng. hn.),2,2 - 4,3,3,1 -
timp.,perc.(2) - str.   24:40 Composer.

KOCH, Sigurd von - KOCH, Erland von
—— GAMMALSVENSKA WIJSOR (13 SONGS, TRANSCRIBED
FOR BARITONE AND ORCH. BY ERLAND VON KOCH)
(Text: Wivallius and Lucidor)
    S.T.I.M.

KOCHAN, Günter
—— KARIN LENZ (OPERA) % (Text: Neutsch)
    Tetra.
—— SYMPHONY NO. 2 (IN 1 MOVT.)
    3,2,2,3 - 4,2,3,1 - timp.,perc. - pf. - str.   16:00 Tetra.

KOCHMANN, Spero
—— FREUT EUCH DES LEBENS (OVERTURE)
    2,2,2,2 - 4,2,3,0 - perc. - hp. - pf. - str.   6:00 Henmar.

KODÁLY, Zoltán
—— BALLET MUSIC
    3,2,sax.,2 - 4,3,3cnt.,3,1 - timp.,perc.,cel. - str.   5:00 Presser.
—— CONCERTO FOR ORCHESTRA
    3,2,2,2 - 4,3,3,1 - timp.,perc.(2) - hp. - str.   19:00 Bo. Hawkes.
—— DANCES FROM GALANTA
    2,2,2,2 - 4,2,0,0 - timp.,perc. - str.   15:00 Presser.
—— HARY JANOS: SUITE
    3,2,2,2 - 4,3,3cnt.,3,1 - timp.,perc.,cel. - cimbalom - str.
    21:00 Presser.
—— HUNGARIAN RONDO (ON AN OLD HUNGARIAN
SOLDIER'S TUNE)
    15:00 Bo. Hawkes.
—— INTERMEZZO FROM "HARY JANOS"
    2-3,2,2,2 - 4,2-3,0,0 - timp.,perc. - pf. - str.   4:00 Presser.
—— KADAR KATA (TRANSYLVANIAN FOLK BALLAD) (FOR
CONTRALTO AND CHAMBER ORCH.)
    *2,1,1,0 - 0,0,0,0 - cel. - pf. - str.   8:00 Presser.
—— KALLO FOLK DANCES (FOR CHORUS AND ORCH.)
    3 cl. - 2 cimbalom - str.   8:15 Bo. Hawkes.
—— MAROSSZEK DANCES
    2,2,2,2 - 4,2,0,0 - timp.,perc. - str.   12:00 Presser.
—— MINUETTO SERIO
    2,2,2,2 - 4,2,0,0 - timp. - str.   Bo. Hawkes.
—— MISSA BREVIS (FOR SOLOISTS, MIXED CHORUS AND
ORCH.)
    3,2,2,2 - 4,3,3,1 - timp. - org.(ad lib.) - str.   32:00 Bo. Hawkes.
—— THE PEACOCK (VARIATIONS ON A HUNGARIAN
FOLKSONG)
    3,2,2,2 - 4,3,3,0 - perc. - hp. - str.   24:30 Bo. Hawkes.
—— PSALMUS HUNGARICUS (FOR TENOR, BOY'S CHORUS,
MIXED CHORUS AND ORCH.)
    3,2,2,2 - 4,3,3,0 - timp.,perc. - hp. - org. - str.   23:00 Presser.
—— THE SPINNING ROOM (A PICTURE OF LIFE IN
TRANSYLVANIA) (FOR SOPRANO, 2 CONTRALTOS,
TENOR, 2 BARITONES, MIXED CHORUS AND ORCH.)
    2,2,2,2 - 4,2,3,0 - timp.,perc. - str.(str. quartet)   Presser.
—— SUMMER EVENING
    1,2,2,2 - 2hn. - str.   20:00 Presser.
—— SYMPHONY
    3,2,2,2 - 4,3,3,1 - timp.,perc. - str.   30:00 Bo. Hawkes.
—— TE DEUM (FOR SOLOISTS, CHORUS AND ORCH.)
    2,2,2,2 - 4,3,3,1 - timp. - org.(ad lib.) - str.   21:00 Presser.

—— THEATER OVERTURE
    3,2,2,2 - 4,3,3,1 - timp.,perc. - pf. - str.   12:00 Presser.
—— TWO SONGS, OP. 5 (FOR BASS AND ORCH.)
    3,3,3,3 - 4,2,3,1 - timp.,perc. - hp. - str.   13:00 Bo. Hawkes.

KÖDDERITZSCH, Uwe
—— THIJL UILENSPIEGEL (BALLET) %
                               Tetra.

KOEBNER, Richard
—— FOOTLIGHTS
    2,2,2,2 - 4,3,3,1 - timp.,perc.(3),glock. - str.   6:00 Composer.
—— REVEILLE (TONE POEM)
    2(1 alt. with picc.),*3,2,*3 - 4,3,3,1 - timp.,perc.(3),glock. - hp. - str.   10:00 Composer.
—— SARABANDE (FOR OBOE AND STRINGS)
    ob. - str.   Composer.

KOECHLIN, Charles
—— CHANSONS BRETONNES (FOR CELLO AND ORCH.)
    2,3,2,2 - 2,2,3,1 - timp.,perc.,cel.(or pf.) - hp. - str.   34:00 Salabert.
—— FIVE CHORALES IN THE MEDIEVAL MODES
    3,3,3,3 - 4,4,3,1 - timp. - hp. - pf. - str.   10:00 Salabert.
—— PARTITA FOR CHAMBER ORCH. (IN 5 MOVTS.)
    2,1,2,2 - 1,1,0,0 - ondes Martenot (ad lib.) - str.   15:30 Salabert.

KOEHL, Jean Philippe
—— LA SUITE RHODANIENNE
    2,2,2,2 - 4,3,2,0 - timp.,perc.(3) - ondes Martenot - 2 hp. - str.   25:00 Eds. Fran.

KOENIG, Gottfried Michael
—— ORCHESTERSTÜCK II (1962)
    *3,*3,3,0 - 1,2,2,1 - str.(3,3,6,3)   15:00 Seesaw.

KOERING, René
—— ARCHIGRAMM
    3,3,3,3 - 4,3,3,0 - perc.,2 metronomes - hp. - pf. - str.   12:00 AhnSimrock.
—— CI GIT I (FOR SOPRANO AND INSTRUMENTS)
    fl. - timp.,perc.,cel. - 2 hp. - hpsc. - 2 pf. - vln.   4:00 AhnSimrock.
—— COMBAT T 3 N (FOR PIANO AND ORCH.)
    3(1 alt. with picc.),1 alto fl.,0,*3,0 - 0,3,3,0 - perc.(4) - mandolin - pf. - str.   12:00 AhnSimrock.
—— CONCERTO ZUFRILEDA (FOR VIOLIN AND ORCH.)
    2,1,1,0 - 1,2,2,0 - timp.,perc. - hp. - str.(3,1,1,1)   15:00 AhnSimrock.
—— DYLABY (DYNAMIC LABYRINTH)
    3,3,3,3 - 4,3,3,1 - timp.,perc.(5) - hp. - str.   22:00 Presser.
—— FINN CATAPULTE (FOR PIANO, SOLO PERCUSSION AND ENSEMBLE)
    2 cel.,2 vibra.,2 xylomarimba - 2 hpsc. - 2 pf.   20:00 AhnSimrock.
—— FOUR EXTREMES
    *4,4,4,3 - 5,5,4,0 - perc. - 2 hp. - str.   20:00 AhnSimrock.
—— IMAGE DE COULOIR (FOR VIOLIN AND ORCH.)
    3,3,3,3 - 4,4,4,1 - perc.(3) - str.   16:00 Presser.
—— MUSIQUE POUR UNE PASSION
    2(1 alt. with picc.),2,2(1 alt. with b.-cl.),0 - 3,4,3,1 - perc.,vibra.,xyl. - hp. - pf. - str.   8:00 AhnSimrock.
—— TRAUMA (FOR SMALL ORCH.)
    0,2 picc.,0,2,0 - 6,4,4,1 - perc.   5:00 AhnSimrock.
—— TRIPLE AND TRAJECTORIES (FOR PIANO AND DOUBLE ORCH.)
    3(3rd alt. with picc.),*4,2,3 - 4,4,3,1 - perc.(5),cel. - 2 hp. - electric org. - pf. - org. - str.   16:00 AhnSimrock.
—— VOCERO
    3,2,3,3 - 4,3,3,1 - timp.,perc.(3) - pf. - str.   11:00 Presser.

KOERT, Han Van
—— CONCERTO FOR ORGAN AND ORCH.
    2,2,2,2 - 4,2,2,0 - timp.,perc. - org. - str.   15:00 Henmar.

KOETSIER, Jan
—— ADAGIETTO E SCHERZINO
    2,2,2,2 - 2,2,0,0 - timp. - str.   7:30 Henmar.
—— BAROQUE SUITE IN C (IN 4 MOVTS.)
    2,2,2,2 - 2,2,0,0 - timp. - str.   20:00 Sirius.
—— BAROQUE SUITE IN D MAJOR FOR VIOLIN AND STRING ORCH.
    str.   14:30 Henmar.
—— BAROQUE SUITE IN E, OP. 10, NO. 2 (1935) (FOR CELLO AND 12 WOODWINDS)
    3,3,3,3 - 0,0,0,0 - c.   15:00 Sirius.

—— CONCERTINO FOR PIANO AND ORCH. (IN 3 MOVTS.)
    2,2,2,2 - 2,2,0,0 - perc. - pf. - str.   15:00 Henmar.
—— CONCERTINO FOR VIOLA AND ORCH.
    2,2,2,2 - 2,0,0,0 - perc. - str.   14:00 Henmar.
—— CONCERTINO LIRICO (FOR VIOLIN, CELLO AND STRING ORCH.) (1968) (IN 3 MOVTS.)
                      16:00 Henmar.
—— CONCERTO FOR CELLO AND ORCH.
    1,1,2,1 - 2,1,1,0 - timp. - str.   20:00 Henmar.
—— CONCERTO FOR TRUMPET, TROMBONE AND LARGE ORCH.
                      Henmar.
—— CONCERTO NO. 1 FOR OBOE AND ORCH., OP. 14
    1,1,1,1 - 1,0,0,0 - hp. - str.   15:00 Henmar.
—— DEMETER SYMPHONY, OP. 25 (SYMPHONIC BALLET) (1943) %
    2,3,3,2 - 4,3,3,1 - timp.,perc. - hp. - str.   40:00 Henmar.
—— DIVERTIMENTO, OP. 27
    1,1,2,1 - 2,2,0,0 - timp. - str.   20:00 Henmar.
—— DUO CONCERTANTE FOR FLUTE, VIOLIN AND ORCH., OP. 14, NO. 3
    1,0,2,2 - 0,0,0,0 - str.   Henmar.
—— MUSIC FOR CHAMBER ORCH., OP. 37
    2,2,2,2 - 2,2,0,0 - timp. - cemb. - str.   15:00 Henmar.
—— MUSIC FOR FOUR ORCHESTRAS, OP. 29
    3,3,3,3 - 4,0,0,5 - str.   25:00 Henmar.
—— MUSIC FOR TWO STRING ORCHESTRAS, 3 TRUMPETS, 3 TROMBONES AND TIMPANI, OP. 23
    0,0,0,0 - 0,3,3,0 - timp. - str.   25:00 Henmar.
—— MUSICAL SKETCH (FANTASIA FOR PIANO AND ORCH.)
                      Henmar.
—— OUD-NEDERLANDSE SUITE (ALT-NIEDERLÄNDISCHE SUITE) (IN 6 MOVTS.)
                    18:00 Henmar.
—— OUVERTURE VALERIUS, OP. 22
    3,3,3,3 - 4,3,3,1 - timp.,perc. - str.   12:00 Henmar.
—— SERENATA SERENA
    str.   17:00 Sirius.
—— SICILIANO AND RONDINO (FOR 2 OBOES AND ORCH.)
    0,2,0,0 - 2,0,0,0 - hp. - str.   10:00 Henmar.
—— SYMPHONIC MUSIC, OP. 19
    3,3,3,3 - 4,3,3,1 - timp.,perc. - str.   15:00 Henmar.
—— SYMPHONY NO. 2, OP. 30 (FOR MIXED CHORUS AND ORCH.) (1946)
    3,3,3,3 - 4,2,3,1 - timp.,perc. - 2 hp. - pf. - str.   25:00 Henmar.
—— SYMPHONY NO. 3, OP. 40
                    31:00 Henmar.
—— TRAUERMUSIK
                      Henmar.
—— VISION PASTORALE, OP. 15, NO. 1 (1937)
    Eng. hn. - str.   11:00 Sirius.

KOFF, Charles
—— DESERT CONCERTO ("NEGEV") (IN 2 MOVTS.)
    *3,2,2,2 - 4,2,2,1 - timp.,perc.(2) - str.   7:00 Composer.

KOFFLER, Josef
—— QUINZE VARIATIONS D'APRES UNE SUITE DE DOUZE TONS (1931) (15 VARIATIONS ON A 12-TONE ROW)
    str.   10:00 Salabert.

KOHANIM, Shokrollah
—— HOMAYOUN ("MODERN INVENTION") (1969)
    str.   Composer.
—— THE TRIANGLE CONCERTO (FOR VIOLIN AND ORCH.) (1966) (IN 3 MOVTS.)
    2,2,*3,*3 - 4,2,3,1 - timp.,perc.(3) - hp. - pf. - str.   Composer.

KÖHLER, Ernesto
—— CONCERTO IN G MINOR FOR FLUTE AND ORCH., OP. 97
    2,2,2,2 - 4,2,3,1 - timp. - str.   Henmar.

KOHN, Karl
—— CASTLES AND KINGS (A SUITE FOR CHILDREN) (1958) (IN 6 MOVTS.)
    *3,2,2,2 - 3,2,2,1 - timp.,perc.(4) - str.   8:10 C. Fischer.
—— CENTONE PER ORCHESTRA (1973) (IN 3 MOVTS.)
    *3,*3,*3,*3 - 4,2,3,1 - timp.,perc.(2),glock.,mar.,vibra. - hp. - pf. - str.   28:40 C. Fischer.
—— CONCERT MUSIC FOR TWELVE WIND INSTRUMENTS (1957) (IN 3 MOVTS.)
    2(2nd alt. with picc.),*3,*3,2 - 2,0,0,0   17:00 C. Fischer.

—— CONCERTO FOR HORN AND CHAMBER ORCH. (1974) (IN 3 MOVTS.)
1,1,1,2 - 1,0,0,0 - mar.,vibra. - pf. - str.(14,6,4,4)
25:00 C. Fischer.

—— CONCERTO MUTABILE (FOR PIANO WITH CHAMBER ENSEMBLE OR ORCH.) (1962)
1,1,1,1 - 1,2,3,0 - pf. - str.(min.:2,1,1,1)   13:30 C. Fischer.

—— EPISODES FOR PIANO AND ORCH. (1966)
*2,2,2,2 - 4,2,2,1 - timp.,perc.(3),glock.,vibra. - hp. - pf. - str.
12:00 C. Fischer.

—— ESDRAS - ANTHEMS AND INTERLUDES (1970) (FOR SATB CHORUS, FLUTE, PIANO AND ORCH.) (IN 5 MOVTS.) (Text: Biblical; from the Apocrypha)
5(5th alt. with picc.),2,4,3 sax.,2 - 4,3,3,1 - timp.,perc.(4),bells,glock.,vibra. - hp. - pf. - str.   35:00 C. Fischer.

—— INTERLUDES (1964) (IN 4 MOVTS.)
*3,2,2,2 - 3,2,3,1 - timp.,perc.(3) - str.   12:00 C. Fischer.

—— INTERMEZZO FOR PIANO AND STRING ORCH. (INTERLUDE I FROM "ESDRAS") (1970)
pf. - str.   6:00 C. Fischer.

—— OVERTURE FOR STRING ORCHESTRA (1953)
Str   9:00 Composer.

—— SINFONIA CONCERTANTE (FOR PIANO AND ORCH.) (1951) (IN 3 MOVTS.)
2,2,2,2 - 2,2,3,1 - timp.,perc.(1) - pf. - str.   20:00 Composer.

—— THREE SCENES FOR ORCHESTRA (1958-60)
*3,3,*3,*3 - 4,2,3,1 - timp.,perc.(6),cel.,glock.,mar.,vibra. - hp. - str.
11:30 C. Fischer.

KOHOUT, Josef
—— CONCERTINO FOR HORN AND ORCH.
2,2,2,2 - 1,0,0,0 - perc. - str.   18:00 Mannheimer.

KÓKAI, Rezső
—— CONCERTO FOR VIOLIN AND ORCH.
2,2,2,2 - 4,3,3,1 - timp.,perc.,cel. - hp. - str.   27:00 Bo. Hawkes.

—— KIS VERBUNKOS ZENE
str.   16:00 Bo. Hawkes.

—— RECRUITING SUITE
2,2,2,2 - 4,2,0,0 - timp. - hp. - str.   17:00 Bo. Hawkes.

—— RHAPSODY FROM SZÉK
3,2,2,3 - 4,3,3,1 - timp.,perc. - hp. - str.   14:00 Bo. Hawkes.

—— TWO RONDOS
2,2,2,2 - 2,2,0,0 - timp.,cel. - hp. - pf. - str.   11:00 Bo. Hawkes.

KOKKONEN, Joonas
—— CONCERTO FOR CELLO AND ORCH. (1969)
2,2,3,2 - 4,2,2,0 - timp.,perc.(3) - hp. - str.   21:00 Fazer.

—— THE HADES OF THE BIRDS (3 SONGS FOR MEZZO-SOPRANO AND ORCH.) (1959) (Text: P. Mustapää)
2,2,2,2 - 2,2,0,0 - timp. - str.   15:00 FinnMICtr.

—— INAUGURATIO (1971)
3,3,3,3 - 4,3,3,0 - timp.,perc.(4) - hp. - str.   8:00 FinnMICtr.

—— MUSIC FOR STRINGS (IN 4 MOVTS.)
str.   28:00 T.E.O.S.T.O.

—— OPUS SONORUM (1964)
2,2,3,2 - 4,3,2,0 - pf. - str.   12:00 SuomYRadio.

—— SINFONIA DA CAMERA (1962)
str.(7,2,2,1)   17:00 SuomYRadio.

—— SYMPHONIC SKETCHES (1968)
3,2,3,2 - 4,3,3,0 - timp.,perc.(3) - hp. - str.   14:00 FinnMICtr.

—— SYMPHONY NO. 1 (1960)
3,3,3,3 - 4,3,3,0 - timp. - str.   22:00 FinnMICtr.

—— SYMPHONY NO. 2 (1961)
3,3,3,3 - 4,3,3,0 - timp. - hp. - str.   21:00 FinnMICtr.

—— SYMPHONY NO. 3 (1967)
4,3,3,3 - 4,3,3,0 - timp.,perc.(4) - hp. - str.   18:00 Fazer.

—— SYMPHONY NO. 4 (1971)
1. Moderato; 2. Allegro; 3. Adagio
3,3,3,3 - 4,3,3,0 - timp.,perc.(4) - hp. - str.   21:00 G. Schirmer.

KOLB, Barbara
—— CROSS WINDS (1968)
3(3rd alt. with picc.),*3,*3,sax.,2 - 2,2,2,0 - perc. (4),glock.,mar.
10:00 Bo. Hawkes.

—— SEGUELA (1966)
str.   10:00 C. Fischer.

—— SOUNDINGS (VERSION FOR FULL ORCH., AND WITHOUT TAPE)
3,3,3,3 - 3,0,0,0 - perc.(2) - 2 hp. - str.(24,6,6,0)   14:00 Henmar.

—— SOUNDINGS (1972)
1,1,1,1 - 1,0,0,0 - bells - tape-recorder - hp. - str.   14:00 Henmar.
or:

3,3,3,3 - 3,0,0,0 - bells - tape-recorder - str.

—— TROBAR CLUS (CLOSED CREATION) (1970)
1(alt.with alto fl.),0,0,0 - 0,1,2,0 - perc.(2),bells,mar.,vibra. - guit. - electric pf. - str.(1,2,1,1)   12:00 Bo. Hawkes.

KOLBERG, Kåre
—— ALEXANDER (CHAMBER OPERA) %
0,0,2,0 - 0,2,2,0 - perc. - str.(4,2,2,0)   45:00 T.O.N.O.

—— SUONI PER ORCHESTRA
1,0,1,0 - 0,1,1,0 - timp.,perc.(3),cel. - pf. - str.(4,2,2,1)
12:00 T.O.N.O.

KOMADINA, Vojin
—— COLUMNS (FOR PIANO AND DOUBLE STRING ORCH.)
pf. - str.   10:00 S.O.K.O.J.

—— CONCERT IMPROVISATIONS FOR CHAMBER ORCH.
1,1,1,1 - 0,0,0,0 - perc. - str.   13:00 S.O.K.O.J.

—— CONCERTO FOR PIANO AND ORCH.
2(2nd alt. with picc.),2,*3,2 - 4,2,3,1 - perc. - pf. - str.
17:00 S.O.K.O.J.

—— HAND TO HAND (CHOREOGRAPHIC SUITE) (FOR SOPRANO, SPEAKING VOICE, SATB CHORUS AND ORCH.)
4,0,0,0 - 0,4,4,1 - perc.,vibra.,xyl. - hp. - pf. - str.(0,6,4,2)
27:00 S.O.K.O.J.

—— HASANAGINICA (THE WIFE OF HASSAN-AGA) (BALLET) %
*3,2,*4,2 - 4,2,3,1 - perc.,xyl. - hp. - pf. - str.   90:00 S.O.K.O.J.

—— HEROIC TRIPTYCH (FOR SATB CHORUS AND ORCH.)
2,2,2,2 - 4,2,3,1 - perc. - str.   15:00 S.O.K.O.J.

—— NOCTURNO (FOR STRING ORCH.)
str.   10:00 S.O.K.O.J.

—— SATAN (BALLET) % (WITH SOPRANO AND BARITONE)
4,0,0,0 - 0,4,4,1 - perc.,vibra.,xyl. - hp. - pf. - str.(0,6,4,2)
84:00 S.O.K.O.J.

—— SINFONIETTA FOR STRING ORCH.
str.   15:00 S.O.K.O.J.

—— SPARKS (CANTATA) (FOR SPEAKING VOICE, SATB CHORUS AND ORCH.)
3,3,3,3 - 4,3,3,1 - perc. - str.   10:00 S.O.K.O.J.

—— SUITE OF DANCES
*3,2,2,2 - 4,2,3,1 - perc. - str.   15:00 S.O.K.O.J.

—— SYMPHONY NO. 1 ("THE BRIDGE")
3,3,3,3 - 4,3,3,1 - perc.,vibra.,xyl. - hp. - pf. - str.
14:00 S.O.K.O.J.

KOMIVES, Janos
—— CATÉCHISME DE NUIT (FOR SOPRANO AND ORCH.)
3,3,3,3 - 4,3,3,1 - timp.,perc.(5) - hp. - pf.(alt. with cel.) - str.
16:00 Presser.

—— CONCERTO FOR STRING QUARTET AND ORCH.
3,3,3,3 - 4,3,3,1 - timp.,perc. - hp. - pf.(alt. with cel.) - str.
18:00 Presser.

—— SIENA
3,1,6,1 - timp.,perc.(4) - hp. - 4 c.(or 4 sax.),2 d.-b.   15:00 Presser.

KONIETZNY, Heinrich
—— CONCERTO FOR OBOE AND ORCH.
2(2nd alt. with picc.),1,2,2 - 4,0,0,0 - timp. - str.   17:00 Modern.

KONOYE, Hidemaro
—— ETENRAKU (THE GATES OF HEAVEN)
3,2E^{b}cl.,2,sopr. sax.,2 - 2,2,0,0 - perc.,cel. - hp. - pf. - str.
8:00 Templeton.

KONSTANTINOFF, Konstantin
—— CAPRICCIO, D'APRÈS GOYA
2(2nd alt. with picc.),2(2nd alt. with Eng.hn.),2,2 - 2,2,1-2,0-1 - timp.,perc.(3),cel. - hp. - pf. - str.   12:00 Baron.

—— PICCOLI (SUITE) (IN 3 MOVTS.)
2(2nd alt. with picc.),2(2nd alt. with Eng.hn.),2(2nd alt. with b.-cl.),2,c.-bn.(ad lib.) - 2,2,1-2,0-1 - timp.,perc.(2),cel. - hp. - str.
Baron.

—— PORT SAID (BALLET) %
3,2,2,3 - 4,3,3,1 - timp.,perc.,cel. - hp. - pf. - str.   Bo. Hawkes.

KONT, Paul
—— AMORES PASTORALES (BALLET SUITE)
ob.,cl. - str.   16:00 Modern.

—— DANUBE BALLAD
1(alt. with picc.),1,1,1 - 1,1,1,0 - timp.,perc.,cel. - acc. - hp. - pf. - str.   14:00 Modern.

—— LITTLE SUITE
3,2,3,2 - 2,2,3,1 - perc. - hp. - pf. - str.   9:00 Modern.

KOPELENT, Marek
—— CONTEMPLATION FOR ORCH.

Hans Gerig.

KOPP, Frederick
—— AND THE EARTH SHOOK (1971)
    0,0,0,0 - 3,3,3,1 - timp.,perc.(4)   9:00 Seesaw.
—— DANCE MASS IN LATIN-AMERICAN RHYTHMS (1971)
(WITH CHORUS)
    0,0,4,1 - 0,3,2,0 - perc.(3) - guit. - pf. - str.   40:00 Seesaw.
—— DEEP FOREST (SYMPHONIC POEM)
    2,*2,2,2 - 3,0,3,0 - timp.,perc.(2) - hp. - str.   6:20 Composer.
—— THE DENIAL OF ST. PETER (CANTATA-ORATORIO) (FOR
SOLO VOICES, CHORUS AND ORCH.)
    1,1,2,1 - 2,2,1,0 - timp. - org.(ad lib.) - str.   49:50 Composer.
—— SYMPHONY NO. 1 (IN 1 MOVT.)
    *3,2,2,2 - 4,3,3,0 - timp.,perc.(2) - str.   12:30 Composer.
—— SYMPHONY NO. 2 IN A (SYMPHONY FOR YOUNG PEOPLE)
(IN 4 MOVTS.)
    2,1,2,1 alto sax.(or alto cl.),1 ten. sax.(or b.-cl.),2 - 4,3,3,0 -
    timp.,perc.(3) - pf.(ad lib.) - str.   12:09 Composer.
—— TERROR SUITE
    0,0,3,0 - 3,3,3,1 - timp.,perc.(3) - pf.   12:00 Seesaw.
—— TRILOGY (SUITE) (IN 3 MOVTS.)
    *3,*3,*3,*3 - 3,2,3,0 - timp.,perc.(2) - 2 hp. - pf. - str.
    12:25 Composer.

KOPPEL, Herman D.
—— CAPRICCIO, OP. 23 (FOR VIOLIN AND ORCH.)
    12:00 K.O.D.A.
—— CHAMBER CONCERTO FOR VIOLIN AND STRINGS, OP. 83
    str.   12:00 K.O.D.A.
—— CONCERTINO NO. 1 FOR STRINGS, OP. 32
    str.   17:00 K.O.D.A.
—— CONCERTINO NO. 2 FOR STRINGS, OP. 66
    str.   20:00 Henmar.
—— CONCERTO FOR CELLO AND ORCH., OP. 56
    25:00 G. Schirmer.
—— CONCERTO FOR CLARINET AND ORCH., OP. 35
    20:00 G. Schirmer.
—— CONCERTO FOR FLUTE AND ORCH., OP. 87
    K.O.D.A.
—— CONCERTO FOR OBOE AND ORCH., OP. 82
    2,1,2,2 - 2,0,0,0 - cel.,vibra.,xyl. - hp. - str.   17:00 Henmar.
—— CONCERTO FOR VIOLIN AND ORCH., OP. 4
    15:00 K.O.D.A.
—— CONCERTO FOR VIOLIN, VIOLA AND CHAMBER ORCH.,
OP. 43
    2,0,2,0 - 2,0,0,0 - timp. - hp. - str.   21:00 G. Schirmer.
—— CONCERTO NO. 1 FOR PIANO AND ORCH., OP. 13
    0,0,2,1 - 1,2,0,0 - timp. - pf. - str.   19:00 G. Schirmer.
—— CONCERTO NO. 2 FOR PIANO AND ORCH., OP. 30
    30:00 K.O.D.A.
—— CONCERTO NO. 3 FOR PIANO AND ORCH., OP. 45
    2,2,2,2 - 4,3-4,3,1 - timp. - pf. - str.   ImudicoKbn.
—— CONCERTO NO. 4 FOR PIANO AND ORCH., OP. 69
    22:00 ImudicoKbn.
—— FESTIVAL OVERTURE, OP. 33
    3:00 K.O.D.A.
—— FESTIVAL POLONAISE, OP. 40
    6:00 K.O.D.A.
—— IMMORTALIUS MORTALIUM, OP. 58
    15:00 K.O.D.A.
—— MACBETH (OPERA) %
    K.O.D.A.
—— MOSES, OP. 76 (ORATORIO)
    60:00 K.O.D.A.
—— MUSIC FOR STRINGS, OP. 6
    str.   6:00 K.O.D.A.
—— REQUIEM, OP. 78 (FOR SOLO VOICES, CHORUS AND
ORCH.)
    55:00 K.O.D.A.
—— SINFONIETTA, OP. 41
    20:00 K.O.D.A.
—— THE STOUT MAN, OP. 29 (DEN TYKKE MAND) (BALLET) %
    30:00 K.O.D.A.
—— SUITE FOR CHAMBER ORCH., OP. 52
    16:00 K.O.D.A.
—— SYMPHONY NO. 1, OP. 5
    26:00 K.O.D.A.
—— SYMPHONY NO. 2, OP. 37
    34:00 K.O.D.A.

—— SYMPHONY NO. 3, OP. 39
    2,2,2,2 - 4,2,3,1 - timp. - str.   24:00 G. Schirmer.
—— SYMPHONY NO. 4, OP. 42
    30:00 K.O.D.A.
—— SYMPHONY NO. 5, OP. 60
    2,2,2,2 - 4,3,3,1 - timp.,perc.,cel. - str.   31:00 G. Schirmer.
—— SYMPHONY NO. 7, OP. 70
    29:00 K.O.D.A.
—— THREE PSALMS OF DAVID, OP. 48 (FOR TENOR, CHORUS,
BOY'S CHORUS AND ORCH.)
    30:00 G. Schirmer.
—— TWO BIBLICAL SONGS, OP. 59-B (FOR SOPRANO AND
ORCH.)
    6:00 K.O.D.A.
—— VARIATIONS FOR SMALL ORCH., OP. 27
    12:00 K.O.D.A.

KOPPEL, Thomas
—— PHRASES, OP. 17 (CANTATA) (FOR 2 SOPRANOS, 12
MEZZO-SOPRANOS, 4 SOLO INSTS. AND ORCH.)
    3,2,3,2 - 2,3,2,1 - perc. - hp. - str.   25:00 Henmar.

KORLING, Felix
—— CAUSERIE (SUITE)
    2,2,2,2 - 2,2,3,1 - timp. - str.   6:00 S.T.I.M.
—— DANCES ON KOLDINGHUS
    2,2,2,2 - 2,2,3,1 - timp. - str.   11:00 S.T.I.M.
—— LARS GATHENHJELM (SUITE)
    2,2,2,2 - 2,2,3,1 - timp. - str.   12:00 S.T.I.M.

KORN, Peter Jona
—— CONCERTINO FOR HORN AND STRINGS, OP. 15
    hn. - str.   14:00 Bo. Hawkes.
—— CONCERTO FOR ALTO SAXOPHONE AND ORCH.
    1. Allegro con spirito; 2. Andante sostenuto - Cadenza - Allegretto
    2,2,2 alto sax.,2 - 4,0,0,0 - timp. - str.   23:00 Composer
—— EXORCISM OF A LISZT FRAGMENT
    2,3,3,3 - 4,3,3,1 - timp.,perc.,cel. - hp. - str.   20:00 Bo. Hawkes.
—— IDYLLWILD OVERTURE, OP. 4
    2(2nd alt. with picc.),*3,*3,1 - 4,2,3,0 - timp.,per.(3) - str.
    4:30 Bo. Hawkes.
—— IN MEDIAS RES (OVERTURE)
    2(2nd alt. with picc.),*2,2,2 - 4,2,3,1 - timp.perc.(2),glock. -
    hp.(ad.lib.) - str.   3:30 Bo. Hawkes.
—— DER PFARRER VON CLEVERSULZBACH (4 SONGS FOR
VOICE AND ORCH.)
    Bo. Hawkes.
—— RHAPSODY FOR OBOE AND STRINGS, OP. 14
    ob. - str.   7:30 Bo. Hawkes.
—— ROMANTIC OVERTURE, OP. 1
    2,2(2nd alt. with Eng. hn.),2,2, - 4,2,3,0 - timp. - str.
    10:00 Composer.
—— SYMPHONY NO. 1, OP. 3 (IN 1 MOVT.)
    Composer.
—— SYMPHONY NO. 2, OP. 13
    2,2(2nd alt. with Eng. hn.),2,2 b.-cl.,2 - 6,3,3,1 -
    timp.,perc.(4-5),glock. - str.   36:00 Composer.
—— SYMPHONY NO. 3 (IN 1 MOVT.)
    3(3rd alt. with picc.),*3,*3,*3 - 4,3,3,1 - timp.,perc.(3),cel.,glock. -
    hp. - str.   30:00 Bo. Hawkes.
—— TOM PAINE (OVERTURE)
    *3,2(2nd alt. with Eng. hn.),2(2nd alt. with b.-cl.),2 - 4,2,3,1 -
    timp.,perc.(4-5) - str.   13:00 Bo. Hawkes.
—— VARIATIONS ON A TUNE FROM "THE BEGGAR'S OPERA",
OP. 26
    1(alt. with picc.)1,(alt. with Eng. hn.),2(2nd alt. with b.-cl.),1 -
    2,1,1,0 - timp.,perc.(1),cel.,glock. - str.   27:00 Bo. Hawkes.

KORNAUTH, Egon
—— BALLADE FÜR ORCH., OP. 17 (WITH SOLO CELLO)
    3,*3,*3,2 - 4,2,3,0 - timp.,perc. - hp. - str.   13:00 Henmar.
—— BURLESKE, OP. 11 (FOR FLUTE AND ORCH.)
    2,2,2,2 - 4,1,0,0 - timp.,perc.,cel. - hp. - str.   8:00 Henmar.
—— GROSSE SUITE, OP. 20 (IN 4 MOVTS.)
    3,3,3,2 - 4,3,3,1 - perc. - hp. - str.   25:00 T & J.

KORNGOLD, Erich Wolfgang
—— THE ADVENTURES OF ROBIN HOOD: SUITE (IN 4 MOVTS.)
    *3,2,*3,2 - 4,4,3,1 - timp.,perc.,cel. - guit. - hp. - pf. - str.
    35:00 Harms, Inc.
—— BABY-SERENADE, OP. 24 (IN 5 MOVTS.)
    2(2nd alt. with picc.),1,2(2nd alt. with b.-cl.),3 sax.,1 - 1,3,1,0 -
    perc. - banjo - hp. - pf. - str.   16:00 Modern.

—— CONCERTO IN C, FOR CELLO AND ORCH., OP. 37 (IN 1 MOVT.)
    2(2nd alt. with picc.),2(2nd alt. with Eng. hn.),*3,2(2nd alt. with c-bn.) - 2,2,2,1 - timp.,perc.(3),cel.,glock.,vibra.,xyl. - hp. - pf. - str.
    12:00 AMP.

—— CONCERTO IN D, FOR VIOLIN AND ORCH., OP. 35 (IN 3 MOVTS.)
    2(2nd alt. with picc.),2(2nd alt. with Eng. hn.),*3,2(2nd alt. with c.-bn.) - 4,2,1,0 - timp.,perc.(3),cel.,vibra.,xyl. - hp. str.
    22:00 AMP.

—— PASSOVER PSALM, OP. 30 (FOR SOPRANO, CHORUS AND ORCH.)
    4hn., 3 tpt. - timp.,perc.(2) - hp. - org. - pf. - str.   8:00 Composer.

—— THEME AND VARIATIONS, OP. 42
    2,1,2,1 - 2,2,2,0 - timp.,perc.(3) - hp. - pf. - str.   7:00 Mills.
    or:
    2,0,2,0 - 0,2,2,0 - timp.,perc.(3) - pf. - str.

—— TOMORROW (WHEN YOU ARE GONE) (FOR SOPRANO, WOMEN'S CHORUS AND ORCH.)
    3,2,*3,*3 - 4,3,4,1 - timp.,perc.,cel. - 2 hp. - pf. - str.
    12:00 Witmark.

KORTE, Karl
—— CONCERTATO FOR STRINGS, BRASS AND TIMPANI
    0,0,0,0 - 4,3,3,1 - timp. - str.   10:00 Composer.

—— MASS FOR YOUTH (MISSA ST. DOMINICK) (FOR SSAATTBB CHORUS AND CHAMBER ORCH.) (1963)
    2,2,2,2 - 2,2,2,1 - timp.,perc. - hp. - str.   20:00 Galaxy.

—— MUSIC FOR A YOUNG AUDIENCE (IN 5 MOVTS.)
    1,1,1,1 - 2,2,1,0 - timp.,perc.(1) - str.   9:00 Composer.

—— SONG AND DANCE (FOR DOUBLE STRING ORCH.)
    str.   6:00 Galaxy.

—— SOUTHWEST (A DANCE OVERTURE)
    *3,2,2,2 - 4,3,3,1 - perc.(3),xyl. - hp. - pf. - str.   10:00 Composer.

—— SYMPHONY NO. 2 (IN 1 MOVT.)
    *3,*3,*3,*3, - 4,3,3,1 - timp.,perc.(4),bells,glock. - hp. - str.
    20:00 ECSchirmer.

—— SYMPHONY NO. 3 (1968) (IN 3 MOVTS.)
    *3(2nd alt. with alto fl.),3(3rd alt. with Eng. hn.),3(3rd alt. with b.-cl.),*3 - 4,3,3,1 - timp.,perc.(5),bells,xyl. - hp. - harm. - pf. - str.
    20:00 EV.

KÓSA, György
—— CONCERTO FOR VIOLIN, PIANO AND ORCH.
    perc. - cimbalom - hp. - org. - pf. - str.   30:00 Bo. Hawkes.

—— DANCE SUITE
    2,2,2,1 sax.,3 - 4,2,3,0 - timp. - hp. - str.   16:00 Bo. Hawkes.

—— PETITE SUITE
    2,2,2,2 - 2,2,0,0 - timp.,perc. - str.   Bo. Hawkes.

—— SYMPHONY NO. 8
    3,3,3,3 - 4,3,3,1 - timp.,perc.,cel. - hp. - pf. - str.
    23:40 Bo. Hawkes.

KOSAKOFF, Reuven
—— CONCERTO PALESTINA (FOR PIANO AND ORCH.)
    2,2,2,2 - 4,2,2,0 - timp.,perc. - pf. - str.   12:00 Composer.

—— JACK AND THE BEANSTALK (FOR NARRATOR AND ORCH.)
    2(1 alt. with picc.),2,2,2(1 alt. with c.-bn.) - 4,2,3,1 - timp.,perc.(2),cel.,xyl. - hp. - str.   15:00 Mills.

—— SHIR HASHIRIM (THE SONG OF SONGS) (FOR ALTO AND ORCH.) (IN 5 MOVTS)
    2,*2,2,2 - 4,2,2,0 - timp.,perc.(2) - hp. - str.   15:00 Composer.

—— UNDAUNTED (CANTATA)
    2 tpt. - 2 bass drums - str.   Transcon.

KOSCHINSKY, Fritz
—— ALTBRESLAUER TÄNZE, OP. 15 (IN 5 MOVTS.)
    0,2,0,2 - 2,0,0,0 - str.   13:20 Henmar.

—— BESCHAULICHES LEBEN, OP. 52 (MEDITATIVE LIFE) (SYMPHONY NO. 3)
    1,1,2,1 - 2,2,0,0 - perc. - str.   18:00 Henmar.

—— CONCERTINO FOR FLUTE, 2 HORNS AND STRINGS, OP. 44
    fl. - 2 hn. - str.   9:00 Henmar.

—— CONCERTO IN A MINOR FOR VIOLIN AND ORCH., OP. 51
    1,1,2,1 - 2,2,0,0 - timp. - str.   16:00 Henmar.

—— FOUR PIECES FOR STRING ORCH.
    str.   16:30 Henmar.

—— KLEINE SPIELMUSIK (IN 3 MOVTS.)
    2,2,2,2 - 2,2,0,0 - str.   9:00 Henmar.

—— SYMPHONIC DANCES, OP. 31 (IN 4 MOVTS.)
    2,2,2,2 - 4,2,3,1 - timp.,perc. - hp. - str.   17:50 Henmar.

—— SYMPHONY IN A MAJOR, OP. 23 (SINFONIA BURANA)
    2,2,2,2 - 4,2,3,1 - timp.,perc. - hp. - str.   45:00 Henmar.

—— VARIATIONS AND FUGUE ON A THEME OF WILLIAM BYRD, OP. 55
    0,2,2,2 - 2,2,0,0 - timp. - pf. - str.   12:00 Henmar.

—— VARIATIONS ON A THEME OF MOZART, OP. 49
    0,1,2,1 - 2,0,0,0 - str.   9:00 Henmar.

KOSMA, Joseph
—— CONCERTINO FOR CLARINET AND ORCH.
    2,1,2,2 - 0,1,1,0 - timp.,perc. - pf. - str.   16:00 Presser.

KOTHEN, Axel von
—— KRISTINA WASA (SUITE) (IN 5 MOVTS.)
    2,2,2,2 - 4,2,3,1 - timp. - hp. - str.   FinnMICtr.

—— SYMPHONY NO. 1 IN A MAJOR: 1ST MOVT. (1906)
    2,2,2,2 - 4,2,3,1 - timp. - hp. - str.   8:00 FinnMICtr.

—— SYMPHONY NO. 2 IN E MINOR ("LARGO")
    3,2,2,2 - 4,2,3,1 - timp. - hp. - str.   29:00 FinnMICtr.

—— WASA CANTATA (FOR BARITONE, CHORUS AND ORCH.) (1911) (Text: Hjalmar Procopé)
    1,1,2,1 - 2,1,1,0 - timp. - hp. - org. - pf. - str.   FinnMICtr.

KOTILAINEN, Otto
—— THE PEOPLE OF WÄINÖLÄ (CANTATA) (FOR SOPRANO, BARITONE, BOYS CHORUS, SATB CHORUS AND ORCH.) (1914) (Text: Eino Leino)
    2,2,2,2 - 2,2,2,0 - timp.,perc. - str.   28:00 FinnMICtr.

KÖTSCHER, Edmund
—— SUITE PHANTASTIQUE (IN 3 MOVTS)
    2,2,2,2 - 4,2,3,1 - timp.,perc. - hp. - str.   30:00 Regina.

KOUGUELL, Arkadie
—— COMÈDIE CARNIVALESQUE (BALLET) %
    Composer.

—— CONCERTO FOR CELLO AND ORCH.
    1. Andante; 2. Maestoso - Allegro; 3. Allegro con brio
    2,2,2,2 - 4,2,3,1 - timp. - hp. - str.   16:00 Composer.

—— CONCERTO NO. 1 (QUASI FANTASIA) FOR PIANO AND ORCH., OP. 14
    Composer.

—— CONCERTO NO. 2 IN D MAJOR FOR PIANO AND ORCH., OP. 63 (IN 3 MOVTS.)
    *3,2,2,2 - 4,2,3,0 - timp.,perc.(2) - pf. - str.   17:00 Composer.

—— CONCERTO NO. 3 FOR PIANO (LEFT HAND ALONE) AND ORCH., OP. 74
    Composer.

—— DREAM OF A SHEPHERD (BALLET) %
    Composer.

—— IMPRESSIONS OF DAMASCUS (SUITE) (IN 4 MOVTS.)
    *3,2,2,2 - 2,2,3,1 - timp.,perc.(2),xyl. - pf. - str.   11:00 Salabert.

—— PETITE SUITE
    Composer.

—— POÈME CHORÉOGRAPHIQUE
    *3,2,2,2 - 2,2,2,1 - timp.,perc.(2) - hp. - str.   20:00 Composer.

—— POÈME HEROÏQUE (CANTATA) (FOR BARITONE, SOPRANO, CHORUS AND ORCH.) (Text: guy brière)
    *3,2,2,2 - 4,3,3,1 - timp.,perc.(3),bells,cel. - hp. - str.
    25:00 Composer.

—— SYMPHONIC SUITE (IN 10 MOVTS.)
    *3,2,2,2 - 2,2,3,1 - timp.,perc.,xyl. - str.   25:00 Composer.

—— VERS LA LUMIÈRE ("TOWARDS THE LIGHT") (BALLET) %
    2,2,2,2 - 2,2,2,1 - timp.,perc.(3) - hp. - pf. - str.   30:00 Composer.

—— VOLGA (SYMPHONIC POEM)
    *3,2,2,2 - 4,2,3,1 - timp.,perc.(2) - pf. - str.   6:00 AndrieuFr.

KOUNADIS, Arghyris
—— FIVE COMPOSITIONS FOR ORCH.
    *3,2,*1,*3 - 2,2,1,1 - perc.(2),cel.,vibra.,xyl. - hp. - pf.(4-hands) - str.   22:00 Modern.
    or:
    3,0,3,3, - 2,2,1,1 - vibra.,xyl. - hp. - pf. - str.

KOUNTZ, Richard
—— ABRAHAM LINCOLN (CANTATA) (FOR CHORUS AND ORCH.)
    *2,1,2,0 - 4,2,1,0 - timp.,perc. - str.   35:00 Presser.

—— THE AMERICAN ODE (CANTATA) (FOR CHORUS AND ORCH.)
    1,1,2,1 - 2,2,1,0 - timp. - str.   Witmark.

—— CARAVAN (ÇANTATA) (FOR CHORUS AND ORCH.)
    *2,1,2,1 - 4,2,1,0 - timp. - str   25:00 Witmark.

—— THE HARVEST (CANTATA) (FOR CHORUS AND ORCH.)
*2,1,2,0 - 4,2,1,0 - timp. - str.   20:00 Witmark.
—— IN WOODLAND (CANTATA (FOR WOMEN'S CHORUS AND ORCH.)
1,1,2,1 - 2,2,1,0 - perc. - str.   17:00 Witmark.
—— LIGHT (CANTATA (FOR WOMEN'S CHORUS AND ORCH.)
*2,1,2,1 - 4,2,1,0 - timp.,perc. - str.   Presser.
—— THE SONG OF MAN (CANTATA) (FOR CHORUS AND ORCH.)
*2,1,2,1 - 4,2,1,0 - timp. - str.   12:00 Witmark.
—— SPRING COMETH (CANTATA) (FOR CHORUS AND ORCH)
*2,1,2,1 - 4,2,1,0 - timp. - str.   20:00 Witmark.
—— THE VILLAGE BLACKSMITH (CANTATA)
*2,1,2,1 - 4,2,1,0 - timp. - str.   30:00 Gray.
—— THE WONDROUS STORY (CHRISTMAS CANTATA) (FOR CHORUS AND ORCH.)
*2,1,2,1 - 4,2,1,0 - timp.,perc. - str.   12:00 Witmark.

KOUSSEVITZKY, Serge - MEYER-TORMIN
—— CONCERTO FOR DOUBLE BASS AND ORCH., OP. 3
2,2,3,2 - 3,2,0,0 - timp. - str.   15:00 Henmar.

KOUTZEN, Boris
—— CONCERT PIECE FOR CELLO AND STRINGS (IN 3 MOVTS)
str.   12:00 EV.
—— CONCERTANTE FOR TWO FLUTES AND ORCH. (1965)
2,2,2,2 - 2,2,1,0 - timp.,perc. - pf. - str.   General.
—— CONCERTINO FOR PIANO AND STRINGS
pf. - str.   15:30 General.
—— CONCERTO FOR FIVE SOLO INSTRUMENTS AND STRINGS (IN 3 MOVTS)
1,0,1,1 - 1,0,0,0 - str.(solo c.)   12:00 AmerMusEd.
—— CONCERTO FOR VIOLA AND CHAMBER ORCH. (IN 3 MOVTS)
fl.,cl. - str.   14:00 AmerMusEd.
—— CONCERTO FOR VIOLIN AND ORCH. (IN 3 MOVTS.)
3(3rd alt. with picc.),2,2,2 - 4,2,3,0 - timp.,perc. (3),xyl. - hp. - str.   25:00 Composer.
—— DIVERTIMENTO
2,2,2,2 - 2,2,1,0 - timp.,perc. - hp. - str.   15:00 General.
—— ELEGIAC RHAPSODY
1,1,2,1 - 2,1,1,0 - timp. - str.   11:00 General.
—— FANFARE, PRAYER AND MARCH
2(2nd alt. with picc.),2(2nd alt. with Eng. hn.),2,2 - 2,2,1,0 - timp.,perc.(2) - pf. - str.   12:30 General.
—— THE FATAL OATH (OPERA) % (Text: Composer, after a story of Balzac)
1,1(alt. with Eng. hn.),2,1 - 1,1,1,0 - timp.,perc.(1) - pf. - str.   50:00 Fema.
—— FROM THE AMERICAN FOLKLORE (CONCERT OVERTURE)
3(3rd alt. with picc.),*3,*3,*3 - 4,3,3,1 - timp.,perc.(3),xyl. - str.   8:00 AmerMusEd.
—— AN INVOCATION (FOR SSA WOMEN'S VOICES AND ORCH.) (Text: John Addington Symonds)
2,2,2,0 - 2,2,0,0 - str.   11:00 Presser.
—— MORNING MUSIC (FOR FLUTE AND STRINGS)
Fl - str.   12:00 General.
—— SINFONIETTA (IN 3 MOVTS.)
1,1,1,1 - 1,1,0,0 - pf. - str.   14:00 Composer.
—— SOLITUDE (POEM-NOCTURNE)
*3,*3,2,*3 - 4,2,3,1 - timp.,perc.(4) - 2 hp. - str.   12:00 AmerMusEd.
—— SYMPHONIC MOVEMENT FOR VIOLIN AND ORCH.
3(3rd alt. with picc.),*3,2,2 - 4,2,3,1 - timp.,perc.(3) - hp. - str.   12:00 General.
—— SYMPHONY IN C (IN 4 MOVTS)
3(3rd alt. with picc.),*3,*3,*3 - 4,3,3,1 - timp.,perc. (2) - hp. - str.   27:00 AmerMusEd.
—— VALLEY FORGE (SYMPHONIC POEM)
3(2nd alt. with alto fl., 3rd alt. with picc.),*3,*3(2nd alt. with e^b cl.),*3 - 4,3,3,1 - timp.,perc.,glock. - hp. - str.   12:00 AmerMusEd.
—— YOU NEVER KNOW (1-ACT OPERA) %
1,1,2,1 - 1,1,1,0 - perc.(1) - pf. - str.   30:00 General.

KOVAČ, Ivan
—— CONCERTO FOR PIANO AND ORCH.
2,2,2,2 - 4,2,3,1 - timp.,perc.,cel. - hp. - pf. - str. 18:00 S.O.K.O.J.
—— CONCERTO FOR STRINGS
str.   21:00 S.O.K.O.J.
—— SERENADA BUCOLICA
str.   15:20 S.O.K.O.J.

KOVAČ, Roland
—— WELTRAUM-SUITE (OUTER SPACE SUITE)
    MayaMuRKov.

KOVACH, Andras
—— DANSE SYMPHONIQUE
2,2,2,2 - 4,2,2,0 - timp.,perc. - str. 15:00 K. Neufert.
—— EURYDICE
3,*3,*3,2 - 4,3,2,1 - timp.,perc. - hp. - pf. - str. 15:00 K. Neufert.

KOVAŘÍČEK, František
—— SUITE FOR ORCH.
2,2,2,2 - 2,2,0,0 - timp. - str.   20:00 Bo. Hawkes.

KOX, Hans
—— BALLADE FOR ORCHESTRA (1960)
2,2,1,1 alto sax.,1 - 1,3,2,1 - timp.,perc.,vibra. - hp. - str.   12:00 Henmar.
—— CONCERTANTE MUZIEK (FOR 3 BRASS INSTRUMENTS AND ORCH.)
    Henmar.
—— CONCERTO FOR FLUTE AND ORCH. (1957)
1,0,0,0 - 0,2,3,0 - timp. - str.   22:00 Henmar.
—— CONCERTO FOR PIANO AND ORCH. (1962)
2,2,0,1 alto sax.,0 - 0,3,3,0 - timp.,perc.,vibra.,xyl. - pf. - str.   21:00 Henmar.
—— CONCERTO FOR TWO VIOLINS AND ORCH.
2,2,0,2 - 0,2,2,0 - timp.,perc.(3) - str.   19:00 Henmar.
—— CONCERTO FOR VIOLIN AND ORCH. (1963) (IN 3 MOVTS.)
0,0,*2,0 - 2,2,0,0 - timp.,perc.,vibra. - str.   23:00 Henmar.
—— CYCLOFONIE I (FOR CELLO AND ENSEMBLE)
3 fl. - str.(12,0,1,2)   7:00 Henmar.
—— CYCLOFONIE II (FOR LARGE ORCH.) (1964)
    12:00 Henmar.
—— CYCLOFONIE IV (1965)
alto fl. - str.   8:00 Henmar.
—— CYCLOFONIE V
0,1,1,1 - 0,0,0,0 - str.(13,0,4,2)   7:00 Henmar.
—— LITTLE LETHE SYMPHONY
2,2,2,2 - 2,2,0,0 - timp. - str.   15:00 Henmar.
—— MACBETH (OVERTURE) (1958)
2,2,2,2 - 2,2,0,0 - timp.,perc. - str.   8:00 Henmar.
—— SPLEEN (BALLET) (1960) %
0,1,1,0 - 1,3,2,0 - timp.,perc. - str.   20:00 Henmar.
—— STICHTSE KANTATE (FOR BARITONE, SATB CHORUS AND ORCH.) (1958) (Text: Composer)
2 tpt. - timp. - str.   10:00 Henmar.
—— SYMPHONY NO. 1 FOR STRINGS (1959)
str.   18:00 Henmar.
—— SYMPHONY NO. 2
2,3,3,2 - 4,3,3,1 - timp.,perc. - str.   26:00 Henmar.

KOYAMA, Kiyoshige
—— AINU NO UTA
str.   6:00 Presser.
—— JAPANESE FOLK SONGS (FOR CHAMBER ORCH.)
1,1,*1,1 - 0,0,0,0 - perc. - hp. - pf. - str.   25:00 Presser.
—— KOBIKI-UTA (WOODCUTTER'S SONG) (SYMPHONIC POEM)
2,2,2,ten. sax.,2 - 4,2,3,1 - timp.,perc.(3),cel. - hp. - pf. - str.   10:00 Presser.
—— NOMEN (MASKS FOR A NOH PLAY) (SYMPHONIC SUITE)
2,2,2,2 - 4,2,3,1 - timp.,perc. - hp. - pf. - str.   23:00 Presser.
—— SHINANO-BAYASHI
2,2,2,2 - 4,2,3,1 - timp.,perc. - pf. - str.   13:00 Presser.

KOZINA, Marjan
—— ANTIQUITY (SYMPHONIC POEM)
2(2nd alt. with picc.),2(2nd alt. with Eng. hn.),2(2nd alt. with b.-cl.),2(2nd alt. with c.-bn.) - 4,3,3,1 - timp.,perc.(4) - str.   8:00 Hans Gerig.
—— BALLET SUITE
2(2nd alt. with picc.),2(2nd alt. with Eng. hn.),2(2nd alt. with b.-cl.),2(2nd alt. with c.-bn.) - 4,3,3,1 - timp.,perc.(5),cel.,xyl. - str.   20:00 Hans Gerig.
—— BELA KRAJINA (SYMPHONIC SCHERZO)
2(2nd alt. with picc.),2(2nd alt. with Eng. hn.),2(2nd alt. with b.-cl.),2(2nd alt. with c.-bn.) - 4,4,3,1 - timp.,perc.(5) - str.   12:00 Hans Gerig.
—— THE EQUINOX (4-ACT OPERA) %
*3,2(2nd alt. with Eng. hn.),2(2nd alt. with b.-cl.),*3 - 4,4,3,1 - timp.,perc.(3) - str.   Hans Gerig.

—— MOUNT ILOVA (SYMPHONIC POEM)
2(2nd alt, with picc.),2(2nd alt. with Eng. hn.),2(2nd alt with
b.-cl.),2(2nd alt. with c.-bn.) - 4,4,3,1 - timp.,perc.(6) - str.
15:00 Hans Gerig.
—— TO THE FALLEN (MUSIC FOR MOURNING)
2(2nd alt. with picc.),2(2nd alt. with Eng. hn.),2(2nd alt. with
b.-cl.),2(2nd alt. with c.-bn.) - 4,4,3,1 - timp.,perc.(6) - str.
12:00 Hans Gerig.
—— TOWARDS THE SEA
2(2nd alt. with picc.),2(2nd alt. with Eng. hn.),2(2nd alt. with
b.-cl.),2(2nd alt. with c.-bn.) - 4,4,3,1 - timp.,perc.(5) - str.
16:00 Hans Gerig.

KOZINSKI, David B.
—— A CHILDREN'S SUITE (FIVE MINIATURES)
1(alt. with picc.),1,1,1 - 3,2,2,0 - timp.,perc.(4),xyl. - hp. - str.
15:00 EV.
—— PROJECT PERCUSSION (FOR TIMPANI, PERCUSSION AND
ORCH.)
3,2,3,2 - 2,2,2,1 - timp.,perc. - str.   11:00 Presser.
—— PROLOGUE (PROMENADE) FROM "IMPRESSIONS"
("LONGWOOD")
*3,2(1 alt. with Eng. hn.),3(1 alt. with b.-cl.),2(1 alt. with c.-bn.) -
4,3,3,1 - timp.,perc.(5),bells,xyl. - hp. - pf. - str.   4:00 Composer.
—— A SINFONIA FOR EASTER (IN 3 MOVTS.)
3(3rd alt. with picc.)2,2,2 - 4,2,3,1 - timp.,perc.(2),bells,glock. -
pf.(ad lib.) - str.   7:00 Composer.
—— SUITE FOR STRINGS (IN 3 MOVTS.)
str.   11:30 Composer.
—— TWO DANCES FOR STRINGS
1. Adagio; 2. Allegro
str.   8:30 Composer.
—— VARIATIONS ON A THEME OF ROBERT SCHUMAN (FOR
STRINGS)
str.   19:00 Composer.

KRACKE, Hans
—— PRELUDE AND PASSACAGLIA, AFTER FRESCOBALDI (FOR
STRING ORCH.)
str.   18:00 Henmar.

KRAFT, Leo
—— CONCERTO NO. 1 FOR FLUTE, CLARINET, TRUMPET AND
STRINGS (IN 3 MOVTS.)
1,0,1,0 - 0,1,0,0 - str.   14:00 Composer.
—— CONCERTO NO. 2 (CONCERTO FOR 13 INSTRUMENTS)
(1966)
13:00 Composer.
—— LARGHETTO (IN MEMORY OF KAROL RATHAUS)
timp. - str.   5:00 Presser.
—— NIGHT PIECE
2,2,2,2 - 0,0,0,0 - timp. - hp. - str.   14:00 General.
—— OVERTURE IN G
2,1,2,2 - 2,2,2,0 - timp.,perc. - str.   8:00 Presser.
—— THREE PIECES FOR ORCHESTRA
*3,*3,2,2 - 4,3,3,1 - timp. - str.   14:00 General.
—— VARIATIONS FOR ORCH.
*3,*3,*3,2 - 4,3,3,0 - timp. - str.   20:00 Composer.

KRAFT, William
—— CONCERTO FOR FOUR PERCUSSION SOLOISTS AND
ORCH. (1964) (IN 3 MOVTS.)
2(2nd alt. with picc.),2,2,2(2nd alt. ad lib. with cbn.) - 4,2,2,1 -
timp.,perc.(4),bells,cel.,glock.,vibra.,xyl. - hp. - pf. - str.
18:30 Mills.
—— CONCERTO FOR PIANO AND ORCH. (1973)
22:00 Belw-Mills.
—— CONCERTO GROSSO (FOR FLUTE, BASSOON, VIOLIN,
CELLO AND ORCH.) (IN 3 MOVTS.) (1961)
*3,*4,*4,*3 - 4,3,3,1 - timp.,perc.(5),bells,glock.,xyl. - hp. - pf.(alt.
with cel.) - str.   12:40 Mills.
—— CONFIGURATIONS (CONCERTO FOR FOUR·
PERCUSSIONISTS AND JAZZ ORCH.)
*2,0,1,alto sax.,0 - 2,3,3,1 - perc.(4) - amplified guit. - pf. - d.-b.
15:00 MCA Music.
—— CONTEXTURES (RIOTS DECADE '60) (FOR JAZZ QUARTET
AND ORCH.) (1967) (IN 5 MOVTS.)
Jazz soloists: sopr. sax.,tpt.,perc.(1),d.-b.   MCA Music.
Orch: 4(4th alt. with picc.),*4,4(3rd alt. with E♭ cl.,4th alt. with
b.-cl.and alto sax.),4(4th alt. with cbn.) - 4,4,4,1 -
timp.,perc.(6),mar.,vibra. - hp. - pf. - str.

—— DERIVATIONS (1964)
*3,*3,*3,2 - 4,2,3,1 - timp.,perc.(5),bells,cel.,glock.,vibra.,xyl. - hp.
- pf.(alt. with cel.) - str.   5:30 Mills.
—— THE DREAM TUNNEL: A MAGICAL JOURNEY THROUGH
THE MUSIC OF AMERICA (FOR NARRATOR AND ORCH.)
(Text: Barbara Kraft)
2(2nd alt. with picc.),2(2nd alt with Eng.hn.),2(2nd alt. with
b.-cl.),0 - 2,2-3,2,2 - timp.,perc.(2)   15:00 Composer.
—— GAMES: COLLAGE NO. 1
0,0,0,0 - 8,6,6,2 - perc.(4)   8:10 J. Boonin.
—— MOBILES (FOR 10 OR MORE PLAYERS) (1970)
2(alt. with 2 picc.),1,2 Eng. hn.,3(alt. with 3 b.-cl.),1(or
heckelphone) - 0,0,0,0 - hp. - pf. - 1 vln.,1 c.,1 d.-b.
8:00 MCA Music.
—— SILENT BOUGHS (CYCLE OF 3 SONGS FOR SOPRANO AND
STRINGS) (1963) (Text: Edna St. Vincent Millay)
str.(min.:6,2,2,1)   19:30 Mills.
—— A SIMPLE INTRODUCTION TO THE ORCHESTRA (1958)
*3,2,2,2 - 4,2,2,1 - timp.,perc.(3),bells,glock.,xyl. - str.   3:50 Mills.
or:
*3,*3,*3,3 - 4,3,3,1 - timp.,perc.(3),bells,glock.,xyl. - hp. - pf. - str.
—— SYMPHONY FOR STRINGS AND PERCUSSION (1960) (IN 3
MOVTS.)
timp.,perc.(1),bells,glock.,xyl. - str.   20:15 Mills.
—— THREE MINIATURES FOR PERCUSSION AND ORCH. (1958)
*3,2,*3,*3 - 4,3,3,1 - timp.,perc.(3),bells,glock.,xyl. - str.
4:00 Mills.
or:
2(2nd alt. with picc.),2,2,2 - 2,2,2,0 -
timp.,perc.(1-2),bells,glock.,xyl. - str.
—— TINTINNABULATIONS: COLLAGE NO. 3
3(3rd alt. with picc.),2,2,2 - 4,3,3,1 - timp.,perc.(4),cel.(ad lib.) -
hp.(ad lib.) - str.   10:00 J. Boonin.
—— TRIANGLES (CONCERTO FOR PERCUSSION AND 10
INSTRUMENTS) (1968)
1(alt. with picc.),1,1,1 - 1,1,1,0 -
timp.,perc.(1),bells,glock.,mar.,vibra.,xyl. - 1 vln.,1 vla.,1 c.
18:00 MCA Music.
—— VARIATIONS ON A FOLK SONG (1959)
*3,2,2,2 - 4,3,3,1 - timp.,perc.(3),bells,cel.,glock.,xyl. - hp. - pf. -
str.   5:00 Mills.

KRAMER, A. Walter
—— HUMORESQUE (FOR STRING ORCH.)
str.   Composer.
—— IN ELIZABETHAN DAYS (FOR STRINGS)
str.   C. Fischer.
—— IN NORMANDY, OP. 4G (CYCLE FOR SOPRANO, WOMEN'S
CHORUS AND ORCH.) (IN 4 MOVTS)
2,2,2,2 - 4,2,381 - timp.,perc.(2) - hp. - str.   16:00 J. Fischer.
—— INTERMEZZO
str.   6:00 J. Fischer.
—— MEETING IN SPRING, PARTING IN AUTUMN (FOR
SOPRANO AND ORCH.)
1,1,2,1 - 2,1,0,0 - timp. - str.   9:00 Composer.
—— ROMANCE IN A MAJOR
Composer.
—— SYMPHONIC RHAPSODY IN F MINOR, OP. 35 (FOR VIOLIN
AND ORCH.)
2(2nd alt. with picc.),*3,2,2 - 4,2,3,1 - timp.,perc. hp. - str.
17:00 Composer.
or:
1,1,3,1 - 1,2,1,0 - timp. - hp. - str.
—— TOWARD EVENING (PRELUDE)
str.   4:00 Composer.

KRAMER, Jonathan D.
—— CONCERTO FOR CLARINET AND ORCHESTRA (1965-66)
2,2,3,2 - 0,2,2,0 - timp.,perc.(2) - str.   12:00 Composer.
—— REQUIEM FOR THE INNOCENT (1970)
2,2,*3,2 - 4,3,2,1 - timp.,perc.(2),xyl. - str.   3:00 Composer.

KRANCE, John
—— EPITAPHS FOR ORCHESTRA, OP. 12 (IN 1 MOVT.)
3(3rd. alt. with picc.),*3,2,2 - 4,3,3,1 - timp.,perc.(3),bells,cel.,xyl. -
hp. - cel. - str.   9:00 Composer.
—— SINFONIA (IN 1 MOVT.)
3(3rd alt. with picc.),*3,*3(b.-cl. alt. with E♭ cl.),*3 - 4,3,3,1 -
timp.,perc.,bells,glock.,xyl. - hp. - str.   12:00 Composer.

KRANE, Sherman
—— THE GIANT'S GARDEN (1-ACT CHAMBER OPERA) % (Text:
June Krane, after Oscar Wilde's Fairy Tale)
1,1,1,1 - 1,2,1,0 - timp.,perc.,cel. - pf. - str.   30:00 C. Fischer.

KRAUS, George
—— AN EVENING OF PARODY AND HUMOR (1960)
2,2,2,2 - 4,2,3,1 - timp.,perc. - hp. - str.   100:00 P.R.S.
—— HYMN TO THE NIGHT (FOR BARITONE, CHORUS AND
ORCH.)
15:00 P.R.S.
—— SYDNEY PICTURES (SUITE) (IN 3 MOVTS.)
18:00 P.R.S.
—— THREE PRELUDES
15:00 P.R.S.

KRAUS, Joseph-Martin - BODART, Eugen
—— BALLET SUITE FROM MOLIÈRE'S "AMPHITRYON"
1,2,0,1 - 2,0,0,0 - str.   4:00 Mannheimer.
—— CONCERTO IN C MAJOR FOR VIOLIN AND ORCH.
0,2,0,1 - 2,0,0,0 - str.   27:00 Mannheimer.

KRAUZE, Zygmunt
—— PIECE NO. 1 FOR ORCH.
*4,*4,*4,*4 - 6,4,3,1 - str.   7:00 Modern.

KREBS, Johann Ludwig - URACK, Otto
—— BURLESCA
1,1,2,1 - 0,0,0,0 - str.   5:00 Henmar.

KREISLER, Alexander von
—— DIVERTIMENTO FOR STRINGS
str.   SouthernTx.
—— IN THE FOREST (1938)
str.   8:00 SouthernTx.
—— LEGEND
SouthernTx.
—— OVERTURE FOR ORCHESTRA (1967)
*3,2,2,2 - 4,2,3,1 - timp.,perc.(4),glock.,xyl. - str.
3:00 SouthernTx.
—— PASSACAGLIA
str.   SouthernTx.
—— PRELUDE FOR STRINGS (1967)
str.   3:00 SouthernTx.

KREISLER, Fritz
—— CONCERTO IN C MAJOR, FOR VIOLIN AND STRINGS
str.   8:00 C. Fischer.
—— VIENNESE RHAPSODIC FANTASIETTA
2,2,*3,2 - 4,3,3,1 - timp.,perc. - hp. - str.   8:15 C. Fischer.

KREISLER, Fritz - PIASTRO, Michel
—— PRAELUDIUM AND ALLEGRO (FOR VIOLIN AND ORCH.)
C. Fischer.

KREISLER, Fritz - SEVITZKY, Fabien
—— PRAELUDIUM AND ALLEGRO
*3,*3,*3,*3 - 4,3,3,1 - timp.,perc.,glock. - str.   6:00 C. Fischer.

KREJČÍ, Iša
—— ANTIQUE MOTIFS (THREE SONGS FOR BARITONE AND
ORCH.)
2,2,2,2 - 2,0,0,0 - timp. - hp. - str.   10:00 Bo. Hawkes.
—— FOURTEEN VARIATIONS ON A FOLKSONG
3,2,2,2 - 4,2,3,1 - timp.,perc. - str.   23:00 Bo. Hawkes.
—— LITTLE BALLET %
1,1,2,1 - 0,1,0,0 - timp. - pf. - str.   17:00 Bo. Hawkes.
—— SERENADE FOR ORCH.
3,2,2,2 - 2,2,3,0 - timp.,perc. - pf. - str.   17:00 Bo. Hawkes.
—— SYMPHONY NO. 1 IN D (WITH CHORUS)
3,2,3,2 - 4,2,3,1 - timp.,perc.,cel. - hp. - pf. - str.
25:00 Bo. Hawkes.
—— SYMPHONY NO. 2 IN C SHARP
3,2,2,2 - 4,2,3,1 - timp.,perc. - str.   30:00 Bo. Hawkes.

KREK, Uroš
—— ANCIENT EGYPTIAN STROPHES (FOR HIGH VOICE, 2
HARPS AND STRINGS)
2 hp. - str.   18:00 Hans Gerig.

—— CONCERTINO FOR PICCOLO AND ORCH.
*2,1(alt. with Eng. hn.),1(alt. with b.-cl.),1 - 3,1,0,1 -
timp.,perc.,cel. - hp. - str.   14:00 Hans Gerig.
—— CONCERTO FOR BASSOON AND ORCH.
bn. - timp. - hp. - str.   18:00 Hans Gerig.
—— CONCERTO FOR HORN AND STRINGS
hn. - str.   15:00 Hans Gerig.
—— INVENTIONES FERALES (FOR VIOLIN AND STRINGS)
str.   19:00 Hans Gerig.
—— MOUVEMENTS CONCERTANTS
str.   24:00 Hans Gerig.
—— RHAPSODIC DANCE
2(2nd alt. with picc.),2(2nd alt. with Eng. hn.),2(2nd alt. with
b-cl.),2 - 4,3,3,1 - timp.,perc. - hp. - str.   6:00 Hans Gerig.
—— SINFONIA FOR STRINGS
str.   19:00 Hans Gerig.
—— SINFONIETTA
2(2nd alt. with picc.),2,2,2 - 4,2,3,1 - timp.,perc.(3) - str.
28:00 Hans Gerig.
—— SONATINA FOR STRINGS
str.   14:00 Hans Gerig.

KREMENLIEV, Boris
—— BALKAN RHAPSODY (1965)
2(2nd alt. with picc.),2(2nd alt. with Eng. hn.),2,2 - 4,3,3,1 -
timp.,perc.(4),bells,glock.,xyl. - hp. - str.   14:00 Composer.
—— CRUCIFIXION (SUITE, AFTER A CYCLE OF PAINTINGS BY
RICO LEBRUN) (1952) (IN 4 MOVTS.)
2(alt. with 2 picc. and alto fl.),2(2nd alt. with Eng. hn.),2(2nd alt.
with Eᵇ cl.),2 - 3,4,4,1 bar.,2 - timp.,perc.(4),bells,glock.,xyl. - org.
- pf. - 6 d.-b.   16:30 Composer.
—— ELEGY: JUNE 5, 1968
3(1 alt. with picc., 1 alt. with alto fl. and picc.),3(1 alt. with Eng.
hn.),3(1 alt. with b.-cl.),3(1 alt. with c.-bn.) - 4,2,3,1 -
timp.,perc.(3),bells,glock.,xyl. - str.   8:00 Composer.
—— GRAPES (FOR WOMEN'S SSA VOICES AND STRINGS) (1965)
(Text: Alexander Pushkin)
str.   8:30 Composer.
—— PRAVO HORO (SYMPHONIC DANCE) (1940)
3(1 alt. with picc.),3(1 alt. with Eng. hn.),2,2 - 4,2,3,1 -
timp.,perc.(3),xyl. - hp. - str.   4:30 Composer.
—— SONG FOR PARTING (FOR SSA WOMEN'S CHORUS AND
SMALL ORCH.) (1949) (Text: Elva Kremenliev)
Eng.hn. - str.   8:00 Composer.
—— SYMPHONY NO. 1 (FOR CONTRALTO VOICE AND ORCH.)
(1942) (No. Text)
3(1 alt. with picc.),3(1 alt. with Eng. hn.),3(1 alt. with b.-cl.),3(1
alt. with cbn.) - 4,3,3,1 - perc.(3),bells,cel. - hp. - str.
18:00 Composer.

KREMSKI-PETITGIRARD, Alain
—— APPEL (BALLET) (FOR PIANO AND ORCH.) %
2,1,2,2 - 2,2,2,0 - timp.,perc.(3) - hp. - pf. - str.   15:00 Presser.
—— CONCERTO NO. 1 FOR PIANO AND ORCH.
2,2,2,1 - 2,2,1,0 - perc.(4) - pf. - str.   18:00 Presser.
—— HARMONIE DES MONDES (FOR PIANO AND ORCH.)
3,2,2,2 - 4,3,3,0 - timp.,perc.(5),cel. - 2 hp. - pf. - str.
16:00 Presser.
—— PRÉLUDE POUR UNE FÉE
1,1,2,1 - 2,1,0,0 - perc.,cel. - hp. - pf. - str.   8:00 Presser.
—— TROIS ÉTUDES
2,3,3,3 - 4,4,2,1 - timp.,perc.(5),cel. - hp. - pf. - str.   20:00 Presser.

KRENEK, Ernst
—— SCENES FROM THE WEST (IN 4 MOVTS)
3,1,3,1 - 2,3,2,0 - timp.,perc.(2),glock.,xyl. - pf. - str.   14:00 Mills.
—— SYMPHONIC ELEGY
str.   10:00 EV.

KREUDER, Peter
—— SYMPHONY NO. 1 IN C MAJOR ("THE BRAZILIAN"), OP. 101
3,3,3,3 - 4,3,3,1 - timp.,perc. - hp. - str.   40:00 F. Colombo.

KREUTZ, Arthur
—— ACRES OF SKY (2-ACT OPERA) %
1,1,2,1 - 1,2,1,0 - timp.,perc.(1) - pf. - str.   Composer.
—— CONCERTINO FOR OBOE, FRENCH HORN AND STRINGS
(IN 3 MOVTS.)
ob. - hn.(or Eng. hn.) - str.   15:00 Composer.
—— CONCERTO FOR CLARINET AND ORCH.
2,2,2,2 - 3,3,1,0 - timp.,perc.(2) - hp. - pf. - str.   9:00 Composer.

—— CONCERTO FOR DIXIELAND BAND AND ORCH. (TRIPLE CONCERTO FOR CLARINET, TRUMPET, TROMBONE AND ORCH.) (IN 3 MOVTS.)
1(alt. with picc.)2,2,2 - 2,2,1,0 - timp.,perc. - pf. - str.
12:00 Composer.
—— CONCERTO FOR PIANO AND ORCH. (IN 3 MOVTS)
1(alt. with picc.),2,2,2 - 4,2,1,0 - timp.,perc.(2) - pf. - str.
18:00 Composer.
—— CONCERTO FOR VIOLIN AND ORCH.
2,2,2,2 - 2,2,1,0 - str.
17:00 Composer.
—— CONCERTO NO. 2 FOR VIOLIN AND ORCH. (1965)
2(2nd alt. with picc.),*2,2,1 - 2,2,3,0 - timp.,perc. - pf. - str.
25:00 PhiMuAlpha.
—— DANCE MUSIC FROM "LONG MAY OUR LAND BE BRIGHT"
1(ait. with picc.),1,1,1 - hn. - pf. - str.
13:00 Composer.
—— GETTYSBURG, 1863 (FOR CHORUS AND ORCH.)
4 hn. - timp. - str.
8:00 Composer.
—— JAZZ FUGUE (1965)
*2,1,2,1 - 2,2,2,0 - timp.,perc.(2) - str.
3:30 G. Schirmer.
—— MUSIC FOR SYMPHONY ORCHESTRA (SYMPHONY NO. 1) (IN 3 MOVTS)
2,*3,2,2 - 4,2,3,0 - timp.,perc.(2) - str.
19:00 Composer.
—— PAUL BUNYAN (IN 3 MOVTS.)
2,2,3,2 - 0,3,3,0 - timp.,perc.(3) - pf. - str.
12:30 Composer.
—— SCENES FROM "HAMLET"
1,1,1,1 - 2,2,1,0 - timp.,perc.(2) - pf. - str.
13:00 Composer.
—— SOURWOOD MOUNTAIN (ONE-ACT OPERA) %
1,1,2,1 - 0,2,1,0 - timp.,perc.(1) - pf. - str.
60:00 F. Colombo.
—— SYMPHONIC SKETCH ON THREE AMERICAN FOLK TUNES
2(2nd alt. with picc.),2,2,2 - 2,2,3,0 - perc(1) - pf. - str.
8:00 Composer.
—— SYMPHONY NO. 2 (IN 4 MOVTS.)
2(1 alt. with picc.),*3,*3,2 - 4,2,3,1 - timp.,perc.(3) - str.
27:30 Composer.
—— THREE AMERICAN DANCES
*2,2,2,2 - 2,2,3,0 - timp.,perc.(2) - str.
17:00 Composer.
—— THREE RHODE ISLAND FOLKSONGS (FOR 4 SOLOISTS, CHORUS AND ORCH.) (IN 3 MOVTS)
1(alt. with picc.),1,2,1 - 0,2,3,1 - timp., perc.(2) - str.
13:30 Composer.
—— THREE SHAKESPEARIAN LOVE LYRICS (FOR SOPRANO AND SMALL ORCH.)
1,1,2,1 - 0,0,0,0 - str.
Composer.
—— TRIUMPHANT OVERTURE
1(alt. with picc.),2,2 Eng. hn. 2,2 - 4,3,3,1 - timp.,perc.(3) - str.
10:00 Composer.
—— VERBENA (1-ACT OPERA) % (Text: Zoe Lund Schiller)
Composer.

KREUTZER, Rodolphe - KOUTZEN, Boris
—— OCTAVE STUDY (FOR VIOLIN AND ORCH.)
1,1,2,1 - 2,0,0,0 - str.
General.

KREUZ, Emil
—— CONCERTO IN C FOR VIOLA AND ORCH., OP. 20
2,2,2,2 - 2,2,3,0 - timp.,perc. - str.
Galaxy.
—— SUITE FOR STRING ORCH., OP. 38 (IN 6 MOVTS.)
str.
15:00 Galaxy.

KŘIČKA, Jaroslav
—— THE ADVENT (1921)
3,3,3,3 - 4,2,3,1 - timp.,perc. - 2 hp. - str.
13:00 Bo. Hawkes.
—— THE BLUEBIRD (OVERTURE) (1911)
Bo. Hawkes.
—— HIGHLAND SUITE (1935)
2,2,2,1 sax.,2 - 4,3,3,1 - timp.,perc.,cel. - hp. - str.
18:00 Bo. Hawkes.
—— TO MY NATIVE LAND (3 SONGS FOR CHORUS AND ORCH.) (1939)
Bo. Hawkes.

KRIEGER, Johann Philipp - SCHERING
—— SUITE IN F MAJOR (FROM "LUSTIGE FELDMUSIK")
str.
12:00 Henmar.

KŘIVINKA, Gustav
—— CONCERTO GROSSO NO. 1
pf. - str.
15:00 Bo. Hawkes.

KROHN, Felix
—— ANU AND MIKKO (SUITE) (1940)
3,3,3,2 - 4,2,3,1 - timp. - str.
20:00 FinnMICtr.

—— GREEN GOLD (SUITE) (1939)
3,3,3,2 - 4,2,3,1 - timp. - str.
25:00 FinnMICtr.
—— THE GREEN ROOM AT LINNAINEN (SUITE) (1944)
3,3,3,2 - 4,2,3,1 - timp. - str.
25:00 FinnMICtr.
—— KYLLIKKI (CANTATA) (FOR TENOR, MALE CHORUS AND ORCH.) (1923)
2,2,2,2 - 4,3,3,1 - timp.,perc. - str.
20:00 FinnMICtr.
—— THE MAN FROM SYSMÄ (VARIATIONS FOR ORCH.) (1938)
3,3,3,2 - 4,2,3,1 - timp. - str.
35:00 FinnMICtr.
—— SINFONIA BREVIS ("THE SEASONS") (1921)
2,2,2,2 - 4,2,3,1 - timp. - str.
25:00 FinnMICtr.

KROHN, Ilmari
—— EVERLASTING TREASURES (ORATORIO) (FOR SATB SOLO VOICES, SATB CHORUS AND ORCH.) (REV. 1932) (Text: Hilja Haahti)
3,3,3,2 - 4,3,3,1 - timp.,perc.(4) - hp. - str.
120:00 FinnMICtr.
—— IMPRISONMENT AND FREEDOM (CANTATA) (FOR BARITONE, SATB CHORUS AND ORCH.) (REV. 1933) (Text: Psalms 137 and 126)
1,1,1,1 - 1,1,1,0 - hp. - str.
16:00 FinnMICtr.
—— MIDSUMMER (CANTATA) (FOR SATB SOLO VOICES, SATB CHORUS AND ORCH.) (REV. 1909) (Text: Hilja Haahti)
2,3,3,2 - 4,2,3,1 - timp. - hp. - str.
15:00 FinnMICtr.
—— OMINOUS FLOOD (OPERA) % (REV. 1929) (Text: Hilja Haahti)
3,3,3,2 - 4,3,3,1 - timp.,perc.(4) - str.
150:00 FinnMICtr.
—— THE PASSION ACCORDING TO ST. JOHN (ORATORIO) (FOR SOLO VOICES, SATB CHORUS AND STRINGS) (1940)
org. - str.
60:00 FinnMICtr.
—— THE VICTORS (ORATORIO) (FOR SATB SOLO VOICES, LARGE DIVIDED SATB CHORUS AND ORCH.) (1935)
3,3,3,3 - 4,3,3,1 - timp.,perc.(3) - hp. - org. - str.
120:00 FinnMICtr.

KROLL, William
—— SUITE
*3,1,2,2 - 2,2,2,1 - timp.,perc. (3) - str.
10:00 G. Schirmer.

KRUMPHOLTZ, Johann Baptist - SCHROEDER, Felix
—— CONCERTO IN F MAJOR FOR HARP AND ORCH., OP. 9
1,2,0,0 -2,0,0,0 - hp. - str.
26:00 Mannheimer.

KRUYF, Ton de
—— CHRONOLOGIE II (1967)
24:00 Henmar.
—— CINQ IMPROMPTUS (1958)
5:00 Henmar.
—— DE BLINDE ZWEMMERS (3 FRAGMENTS) (FOR YOUTH-CHOIR AND ORCH.) (1966) (Text: Bert Schierbeek)
25:00 Henmar.
—— POUR FAIRE LE PORTRAIT D'UN OISEAU (FOR VOICE AND ORCH.) (1965) (Text: Jacques Prevert)
14:00 Henmar.

KUBIK, Gail
—— AMERICAN CAPRICE (FOR PIANO AND SMALL ORCH.)
1,1,2,1 - 2,2,1,0 - timp.,perc. - pf. - str.
8:00 Composer.
—— AUDUBON'S CREED (FROM "A MIRROR FOR THE SKY") (FOR BARITONE, SATB CHORUS AND ORCH.)
2,2,2,2 - 2,2,2,1 - perc. - pf. - str.
10:00 MCA Music.
—— BACHATA (CUBAN DANCE PIECE)
2(2nd alt. with picc.),2(2nd alt. with Eng. hn.),2(2nd alt. with b.-cl.),2 - 3,3,3,0 - timp.,perc.(3),glock., xyl. - pf. - str.
5:00 Southern.
—— BENNIE THE BEAVER (A CHILDREN'S TALE) (FOR NARRATOR, PERCUSSION AND 9 INSTRUMENTS)
1(alt. with picc.),1,1,1 - 1,1,0,0 - timp.,perc.(1),bells,glock., xyl. - pf. - str. (1 vla., 1c.)
9:00 MCA Music.
—— CHORUSES FROM THE FOLK-OPERA "MIRROR FOR THE SKY" (FOR SOLOISTS, CHORUS AND ORCH.)
1(alt. with picc.),1(alt. with Eng. hn.),2(1st alt. with E♭cl. and 2nd alt. with b.-cl.),1 - 2,3,2,0 - timp.,perc.(1) - pf. - str.
26:00 MCA Music.
—— A CHRISTMAS SET (FOR SATB CHORUS AND CHAMBER ORCH.)
1(alt. with picc.),1,2,1 - 1,2,1,0 - perc.(2),vibra.,xyl. - hp. - pf. - str.(no vlns.)
10:00 MCA Music.
—— CONCERTO IN D, FOR VIOLIN AND ORCH. (IN 3 MOVTS.)
2(2nd alt. with picc.),2,2,2 - 4,2,3,0 - timp.,perc.(4),cel. - str.
23:00 Chappell.
—— DIVERTIMENTO NO. 1 (FOR 13 PLAYERS)
2,2,2,1 - 1,1,1,0 - perc.,cel. - pf. - str.
16:00 MCA Music.

—— A FESTIVAL OPENING

MCA Music.
—— FOLKSONG SUITE (IN 3 MOVTS.)
    1(alt. with picc.),1(alt. with Eng. hn.),2,1 - 2,2,1,0 -
    timp.,perc.(2),cel.,glock.,xyl. - pf. - str.   12:30 Southern.
—— FRANKIE AND JOHNNIE (BALLET SEQUENCE) (FOR
BARITONE AND SMALL ORCH.)
    5 cl.(alt. with 5 sax., also 1alt. with b.-cl. and 2 alt. with 2 fl.) -
    0,3,3,0 - timp.,perc.(2) - hp. - pf. - str.   Composer.
—— GERALD MCBOING BOING (FOR NARRATOR AND
CHAMBER ORCH.)
    1,1,1,1 - 1,1,0,0 - perc.(1) - pf. - str. (vla., c.)   14:00 Southern.
—— IN PRAISE OF JOHNNY APPLESEED (FOR BASS, CHORUS
AND ORCH.) (IN 3 MOVTS.)
    3(3rd alt. with picc.),*3,3(3rd alt. with b.-cl.)*3 - 4,3,3,1 -
    timp.,perc.(3) - hp. - str.   25:00 F. Colombo.
—— A LITANY AND PRAYER (FOR MEN'S CHORUS, BRASS
AND PERCUSSION)
    0,0,0,0 - 4,3,3,1 - timp.,perc.(2),glock.   12:00 Southern.
—— LYRIC PIECE (FOR VIOLIN AND ORCH.)
    2,2,2,2 - 4,2,3,0 - timp.,perc. - str.   6:00 MCA Music.
—— MEMPHIS BELLE (DRAMATIC EPISODE FOR NARRATOR
AND ORCH.)
    2(2nd alt. with picc.),2(2nd alt. with Eng. hn.),*3,2 - 4,3,3,1 -
    timp.,perc.(4),cel.,glock.,xyl. - pf. - str.   22:15 MCA Music.
—— MEN AND SHIPS
    1(alt. with picc.),1(alt. with Eng. hn.),2(2nd alt. with E♭cl. and
    b.-cl.),1 - 2,2,2,0 - timp.,perc. - hp. - pf. - (or cel.) - str.
    23:00 Composer.
—— A MIRROR FOR THE SKY: CHORAL SUITE NO. 1 (FOR
NARRATOR, MIXED CHORUS AND ORCH.)
    2,2,2,2 - 2,2,2,1 - perc. - pf. - str.   16:00 MCA Music.
—— A MIRROR FOR THE SKY: CHORAL SUITE NO. 2 (FOR
NARRATOR, MIXED CHORUS AND ORCH.)
    2,2,2,2 - 2,2,2,1 - perc. - pf. - str.   16:00 MCA Music.
—— MUSIC FOR DANCING (FOUR SHORT PIECES IN
CLASSICAL STYLE)
    1(alt. with picc.),1,2,1 - 2,2,1,0-1 - timp.,perc.(1),xyl. - pf. - str.
    9:00 Southern.
—— MY LORD'S A FORFENDED PLACE (FROM "MIRROR FOR
THE SKY") (FOR BARITONE, MIXED CHORUS AND ORCH.)
    2,2,2,2 - 2,2,2,1 - perc. - pf. - str.   7:00 MCA Music.
—— NOCTURNE FOR FLUTE AND STRINGS
    fl. - str.   4:00 Composer.
—— OVERTURE FROM "MIRROR FOR THE SKY"
    2(2nd alt. with picc.),2(2nd alt. with Eng. hn. ad lib.),2,2 - 2,2,2,1
    - timp.,perc.,glock.,vibra.,xyl. - pf. - str.   9:00 MCA Music.
—— PARATROOPS
    1,1,2,1 - 2,2,1,0 - perc.,cel. - pf. - str.   8:00 MCA Music.
—— PUCK (A LEGEND OF BETHLEHEM) (FOR NARRATOR
AND CHAMBER ORCH.)
    1,1,1,1 - 1,1,0,0 - str.   8:00 MCA Music.
—— A RECORD OF OUR TIME (CANTATA) (FOR NARRATOR,
SOPRANO, ALTO, TENOR, SATB CHORUS AND ORCH.)
    3,2,2(1st alt. with E♭cl.,2nd alt. with b.-cl.),3 - 4,3,3,1 -
    timp.,perc.(3),glock.,vibra.,xyl. - pf. - str.   40:00 MCA Music.
    Off-stage: small band, live or on tape
—— SCENARIO FOR ORCHESTRA (SUITE ON THEMES FROM
THE FILM "THE DESPERATE HOURS"))
    4,3,4,3 - 4,3,3,1 - perc. - 2 pf. - str.   25:00 Paramount.
—— SCHERZO FOR LARGE ORCH.
    *4,*3,*3,*3 - 4,3,3,1 - timp.,perc.,cel.,glock.,xyl. - pf. - str.
    10:00 MCA Music.
—— SPRING VALLEY OVERTURE
    2(2nd alt. with picc.),2(2nd alt. with Eng. hn.),2(2nd alt. with
    b.-cl.),2 - 4,3,3,0 - timp.,perc.(2) - cel. - str.   6:00 MCA Music.
—— STEWBALL (VARIATIONS ON A SOUTHERN FOLK-TUNE)
    2(2nd alt. with picc.),2(2nd alt. with Eng.hn.),2(2nd alt. with
    b.-cl.),2 - 4,3,3,1 - timp.,perc.(3) - pf. - str.   16:00 Southern.
—— SYMPHONIE CONCERTANTE (FOR TRUMPET, VIOLA,
PIANO AND ORCH.)
    2(2nd alt. with picc.),2,2(2nd alt. with b.-cl.),2(2nd alt. with c.-bn.)
    - 2,1,1,0 - timp.,perc.(2),glock.,xyl. - str.   24:00 Ricordi.
—— SYMPHONY NO. 1 IN E♭
    3(3rd alt. with picc.),*2,*3,*3 - 4,3,3,1 - timp.,perc.(3),cel. - pf. -
    str.   38:00 Southern.
—— SYMPHONY NO. 2 IN F
    2(alt. with 2 picc.),2(2nd alt. with Eng. hn.),2,2 - 4,2,3,1 -
    timp.,perc.(2),cel.,glock.,vibra.,xyl. - pf. - str.   35:00 Ricordi.
—— SYMPHONY NO. 3
    3,3,3,3 - 4,3,3,1 - perc.,cel. - str.   22:00 MCA Music.

—— THUNDERBOLT OVERTURE (TOCCATA)
    2(2nd alt. with picc.),2(2nd alt. with Eng. hn.),2(2nd alt. with
    b.-cl.),2 - 4,3,3,1 - timp.,perc.(3),cel.,glock.,xyl. - pf. - str.
    7:00 Chappell.
—— TOCCATA FOR ORGAN AND STRINGS
    org. - str.   4:00 MCA Music.
—— VARIATIONS ON A 13TH CENTURY TROUBADOUR SONG
    3(3rd alt. with picc.),*3,*3,*3 - 4,3,3,1 - timp.,perc.(3) - str.
    11:00 MCA Music.

KUBÍN, Rudolf
—— CONCERTO FOR ACCORDION AND ORCH.
    Bo. Hawkes.
—— CONCERTO FOR CELLO AND ORCH.
    Bo. Hawkes.
—— CONCERTO FOR CLARINET AND ORCH.
    Bo. Hawkes.
—— CONCERTO FOR TRUMPET AND ORCH.
    Bo. Hawkes.
—— CONCERTO FOR VIOLIN AND ORCH.
    Bo. Hawkes.
—— JULIUS FUČIK (DRAMATIC OVERTURE)
    3,3,3,3 - 4,3,3,1 - timp.,perc. - hp. - str.   12:00 Bo. Hawkes.
—— MARYCKA MAGDONOVA (SYMPHONIC POEM) (1952)
    Bo. Hawkes.
—— OSTRAVA (SYMPHONIC POEM) (1952)
    Bo. Hawkes.
—— SINFONIETTA (1941)
    Bo. Hawkes.
—— SYMPHONY CONCERTANTE (1936)
    Bo. Hawkes.

KUHLAU, Friedrich - FRACKENPOHL, Arthur
—— SONATINA FOR TRUMPET AND STRINGS
    tpt. - str.   G. Schirmer.

KUHLAU, Friedrich - KIRBY, Percival Robson
—— CONCERT MOVEMENT (FOR THREE FLUTES AND ORCH.)
    5,2,3,2 - 4,2,3,1 - timp.,perc. - str.   4:00 S.A.M.R.O.

KUHN, Henry
—— CONCERTO FOR HORN AND ORCH.
    1,1,*2,1 - 1,0,0,0 - timp.,perc. - str.   17:00 Neue Oper.

KUHN, Max
—— VARIATIONEN FÜR ORCHESTER (ÜBER EINE
KANARISCHE MELODIE)
    2,2,2,0 - 3,4,3,1 - perc. - hp. - str.   12:00 S.U.I.S.A.

KUHNAU, Johann - FISHBACK, Horace
—— CHRIST LAG IN TODESBANDEN (CHRIST JESUS LAY IN
DEATH'S STRONG BONDS)(EASTER CANTATA) (FOR SATB
SOLO VOICES, SATB CHORUS AND CHAMBER ORCH.)
    2 cornetti(zinken) - cemb. - str.(4,2,1,1)   Belw-Mills.
—— HOW BRIGHTLY SHINES THE MORNING STAR
(CHRISTMAS CANTATA) (FOR TENOR, SATB CHORUS AND
CHAMBER ORCH.)
    0,0,0,0 - 2,0,0,0 - str.   20:00 Belw-Mills.

KUISMA, Rainer
—— CHAMBER CONCERTO FOR PERCUSSION AND ORCH.
    Nordiska.

KULJERIĆ, Igor
—— BALLADS OF PETRICIA KEREMPUH (WITH SPEAKING
VOICE AND CHORUS) (1972)
    2(2nd alt. with picc.),0,2(2nd alt. with E♭cl.),5 sax.,2 - 4,4,4
    flg.,4,2 ten.tu.,2 bar.,4 - perc.(4) - 2 guit. - electric org. - str.
    20:00 MIC,Zagreb.
—— CONTINUAZIONI (NEW VERSION)
    3(2nd and 3rd alt. with picc.),3(3rd alt. with Eng.hn.),3(2nd alt.
    with E♭cl., 3rd alt. with b.-cl.),3(3rd alt. with c.-bn.) - 4,3,3,1 -
    timp.,perc.(3) - 2 hp. - 2 pf. - str.   10:00 MIC,Zagreb.
—— SOLO-SOLISTI (FOR PIANO AND STRINGS) (1972)
    pf. - str.(7,3,2,1)   11:00 MIC,Zagreb.
—— SOLO-TUTTI (FOR PIANO AND ORCH.) (1972)
    3(2nd and 3rd alt. with picc.),3,3(3rd alt. with b.-cl.),3(3rd alt.
    with c.-bn.) - 4,4,4,1 - timp.,perc.(7) - 2 hp. - org. - pf. - str.
    12:00 MIC,Zagreb.

KULMANN, Alfred
—— POÈME CONCERTANT (FOR PIANO AND ORCH.)
    2,3,2,2 - 4,3,3,0 - perc. - hp. - pf. - str.   12:00 Salabert.

KUNAD, Rainer
—— CONCERTO FOR KEYBOARD INSTRUMENTS, PERCUSSION AND STRINGS, OP. 49
perc.,cel. - hpsc. - ionika - pf. - str.   Tetra.
—— CONCERTO FOR ORGAN, DOUBLE STRING ORCH. AND TIMPANI, OP. 50
timp. - org. - str.   Tetra.
—— CONCERTO FOR STRINGS, OP. 36
str.   18:00 Tetra.
—— DIALOG FOR ORCH., OP. 40
1,0,0,1 - 0,1,1,0 - perc. - hp. - str.   16:00 Tetra.
—— DIVERTIMENTO OP. 43
3,3,2,1 - 4,3,3,0 - timp. - perc.   13:00 Tetra.
—— SINFONIETTA, OP. 44
3,3,3,sax.,3 - 4,3,3,1 - timp.,perc. - hp. - str.   18:00 Tetra.
—— SYMPHONY NO. 2, OP. 38
4,2,2,1 - 4,3,3,0 - timp.,perc. - hp. - pf. - str.   21:00 Tetra.
—— SYMPHONY "64", OP. 32
2,2,2,2 - 4,2,3,0 - timp.,perc. - str.   25:00 Tetra.

KUNERT, Kurt
—— CONCERTO FOR FLUTE AND ORCH., OP. 21
3,2,2,2 - 2,2,0,0 - timp.,perc. - str.   25:00 Tetra.
—— CONCERTO FOR HORN, TRUMPET, TROMBONE AND ORCH.
2,2,2,2 - 3,1,1,0 - timp.,perc. - str.   18:00 Tetra.
—— CONCERTO FOR WIND QUINTET AND ORCH.
1,2,2,2 - 5,2,3,1 - timp.,perc. - str.   17:00 Tetra.
—— SINFONIETTA (1960)
2,2,2,2 - 4,2,3,1 - timp.,perc. - str.   20:00 Tetra.

KÜNNEKE, Eduard
—— CONCERT OVERTURE TO "LADY HAMILTON" ("THE SONG OF THE SEA")
2,1,0,3 sax.,1 - 2,3,1,0 - perc. - hp. - str.   9:00 F. Colombo.
—— CONCERTO IN A FLAT MAJOR FOR PIANO AND ORCH., OP. 36
          R.Birnbach.
—— OVERTURE TO AN ITALIAN COMEDY, OP. 46
          Regina.
—— OVERTURE TO THE OPERA "COEUR AS", OP. 2
          Regina.
—— ROMANTIC OVERTURE
          R.Birnbach.
—— TÄNZERISCHE SUITE, OP. 26 (CONCERTO GROSSO FOR JAZZ BAND AND ORCH.) (IN 5 MOVTS.)
          Regina.

KUNST, Jos
—— INSECTEN (1967)
str.   9:00 Henmar.

KUNZ, Alfred
—— ADAGIO NO. 1
          9:00 C.A.P.A.C.
—— ADAGIO NO. 2
          9:00 C.A.P.A.C.
—— THE BIG LAND (ORATORIO) (1967) (Text: Larry Cummings)
2(2nd alt. with picc.),2,2,2 - 4,3,3,1 - timp.,perc. - pf. - str.   70:00 CanMusCtr.
—— CHRISTMAS KALEIDOSCOPE (FOR MIXED CHORUS, CHAMBER CHORUS AND ORCH.) (1971)
*3,2,2,2 - 4,4,3,1 - timp.,perc. - str.   15:55 CanMusCtr.
—— CONCERTO FOR PERCUSSION AND ORCH. (THEME AND 8 VARIATIONS) (1973)
*3,2,2,2 - 4,2,2,0 - perc.(8) - str.   22:00 CanMusCtr.
—— CONCERTO FOR PIANO AND ORCH. (1975) (IN 3 MOVTS.)
*3,2,2,2 - 4,3,3,1 - timp.,perc.(5, incl. 3 on timp.) - pf. - str.   27:00 CanMusCtr.
—— THE CREATION (FOR NARRATOR, 3 SOPRANOS, ALTO, MIXED CHORUS AND ORCH.) (1972) (Text: Lawrence Cummings)
*3,2,2,2 - 4,4,3,1 - timp.,perc.(4) - pf.(amplified) - str.   30:00 CanMusCtr.
—— EXCURSION NO. 1 (1964)
*4,*3,*3,*3 - 4,4,4,1 - timp.,perc.(4),cel. - pf. - str.   9:00 CanMusCtr.
—— FIVE NIGHT SCENES (1971)
*3,2,2,2 - 2,4,3,1 - timp.,perc.(10, incl. 1 on timp.) - hpsc. - pf. - str.   14:25 CanMusCtr.

—— IN THE PARK OF OCTOBER COLOUR (A SONG OF LOVE) (FOR PIANO, MIXED CHORUS AND ORCH.) (1969) (Text: Composer)
2,2,2,2 - 2,2,2,1 - timp.,perc. - acc. - pf. - str.   16:50 CanMusCtr.
—— A SHORT OVERTURE
          7:00 C.A.P.A.C.
—— SINFONIETTA NO. 1 (1957) (IN 3 MOVTS.)
*2,2,2,2 - 2,2,2,1 - timp.,perc. - str.   17:00 CanMusCtr.
—— SINFONIETTA NO. 2
          20:00 CanMusCtr.
—— TWO MOVEMENTS FOR ORCH.
          8:00 B.-Barclay.
—— THE WILDERNESS (CONCERT CANTATA) (FOR CONTRALTO, CHORUS AND STRING ORCH.)
str.   15:00 C.A.P.A.C.

KUNZ, Ernst
—— CONCERTO DA CAMERA (FÜR STREICHORCHESTER SOLO FLÖTE UND KLAVIER)
fl. - pf. - str.   30:00 S.U.I.S.A.
—— SERENATA STRANA
          13:00 S.U.I.S.A.
—— SINFONIE NR. 5 (FÜR GROSSES ORCH.)
          37:00 S.U.I.S.A.

KUNZEN, Friedrich - FENDLER, Edvard
—— SYMPHONY IN G MINOR
0,2,0,2 - 2,0,0,0 - str.   Bo. Hawkes.

KUOSMANEN, Kari
—— ABACUS (FOR VIOLIN, VIOLA, CELLO AND ORCH.) (1968)
2,0,2,0 - 2,3,1,1, - perc.(3) - str.   25:00 FinnMICtr.

KUPFERMAN, Meyer
—— ADAGIO FOR SMALL ORCH.
ob.,cl. - timp.,perc.(3) - hp. - 2 pf. - str.   10:00 Composer.
—— ATTO
*3,*3,*3,*3, - 4,3,3,1 - timp.,perc.(5, incl. 4 on timp.) - hp. - str.   60:00 General.
—— COMICUS AMERICANUS (A HUMOROUS CANTATA) (FOR NARRATOR, SOPRANO, BARITONE, SATB CHORUS AND ORCH.)
2(2nd alt. with picc.),2(2nd alt. with Eng.hn.),2(2nd alt. with b.-cl.),2(2nd alt. with c.-bn.) - 4,3,3,1 - timp.,perc. - hp. - str.   35:00 General.
—— CONCERTO FOR CELLO, TAPE AND ORCH.
2(2nd alt. with picc.),2(2nd alt. with Eng.hn.),2(2nd alt. with b.-cl.),2 - 4,2,3,1 - timp.,perc.(3) - tape-recorder - hp. - str.   27:00 General.
—— CONCERTO FOR CONDUCTOR AND ORCH.
2(2nd alt. with picc.),2(2nd alt. with Eng. hn.),2(2nd alt. with b.-cl.),2(2nd alt. with c.-bn.) - 4,3,3,1 - timp.,perc.,cel.,xyl. - hp. - str.   20:00 Composer.
—— CONCERTO FOR ORCH.
2(2nd alt. with picc.),2(2nd alt. with Eng.hn.),2(2nd alt. with b.-cl.),2(2nd alt. with c.-bn.) - 4,3,3,1 - timp.,perc.,cel. - hp. - str.   18:00 General.
—— CONCERTO FOR PIANO AND ORCH. (IN 1 MOVT.)
2(2nd alt. with picc.),2(2nd alt. with Eng. hn.),2(2nd alt. with b.-cl.),2(2nd alt. with c.-bn.) - 4,3,3,1 - timp.,perc.(4) - pf. - str.   15:00 General.
—— DIVERTIMENTO FOR ORCH.
2,2,2,2 - 2 hn. - timp. - str.   14:30 General.
—— THE DRAAGENFUT GIRL (COMIC OPERA, IN 2 ACTS) %
*2,1,*2,1 - 1,1,1,0 - timp.,perc.(2),bells,glock. - hp. - pf. - str.   90:00 General.
—— ELECTRA (BALLET TONE-POEM, WITH WOMEN'S CHORUS AND CELLO OBLIGATO)
fl.,ob.,2 cl. - timp.,perc.(3) - hp. - 2 pf. - str.   24:00 Weintraub.
—— FESTIVALS (ORCHESTRAL SUITE FROM THE FILM "HALLELUJAH THE HILLS")
2(2nd alt. with picc.),2(2nd alt. with Eng. hn.),2,2 - 4,2,3,0 - timp.,perc.(3),bells,glock.,xyl. - hp. - str.   12:30 General.
—— FUGUE FOR ORCH.
*3,*3,E♭ cl.,*3,*3 - 4,3,3,1 - timp.,perc.(3) - str.   10:00 Composer.
—— FUGUE ON THE NAME OF B-A-C-H
ob.,cl. - timp.,perc.(2) - hp. - 2 pf. - str.   11:00 Composer.
—— INFINITIES FOURTEEN
1(alt. with picc.),0,2(alt. with 2 b.-cl.),0 - 0,1,0,0 - timp.,perc.(1),bells,vibra.,xyl. - pf. - str.   15:00 General.

—— LIBRETTO (FOR ORCH.)
2(2nd alt. with picc.),2(alt. with Eng.hn.),2(2nd alt. with
b.-cl.),2(2nd alt. with c.-bn.) - 4,3,3,1 - timp.,perc.(7, incl. 4 on
timp.) - electric cel. - str.   12:00 General.

—— LITTLE SYMPHONY
1(alt. with picc.),2,0,2 - 2 hn. - str.   19:00 Weintraub.

—— LYRIC SYMPHONY (IN 1 MOVT.)
2(2nd alt. with picc.),2(2nd alt. with Eng. hn.),2,2 - 4,2,3,1 -
timp.,perc.(2),cel.,glock.,xyl. - hp. - str.   22:43 General.

—— MUSIC FOR ORCH. NO. 1
*4,*4,E♭cl.,*3,*4 - 6,3,3,1 - timp.,perc.(3),xyl - hp. - str.
                                                  6:30 Composer.

—— MUSIC FOR ORCH. NO. 2
*4,*4,E♭cl.,*3,*4 - 6,4,4,1 - timp.,perc.(3),xyl. - pf. - str.
                                                  8:00 Composer.

—— MUSIC FOR ORCH. NO. 3
2,*3,2,2 - 4,2,2,0 - str.   8:30 Composer.

—— OSTINATO BURLESCO (DEVIL DANCE)
picc.,*3,*3,*3 - 4,3,3,0 - timp.,perc. - hp. - pf. - str. 8:20 General.

—— PERSEPHONE (ARIA FOR SOPRANO AND ORCH.) (Text:
Alastair Reid)
2(2nd alt. with picc.),2(2nd alt. with Eng. hn.),2(2nd alt. with
b.-cl.),2 - 2,2,1,0 - timp. - str.   15:00 Composer.

—— PERSEPHONE (BALLET) %
2,*2,2,*2 - 4,2,3,0 - timp.,perc. - hp. - pf. - str. 12:00 General.

—— SCHEMATA : INFINITIES XX
*3,*3,*3,*3 - 4,2,3,0 - timp.,perc.(4) - hp. - str. 15:00 General.

—— SCULPTURES
2(2nd alt. with picc.),2(2nd alt. with Eng.hn.),2(2nd alt. with
b.-cl.),2 - 4,2,3,1 - timp.,perc.(3),hp. - str. 12:00 General.

—— SIX EPILOGUES: INFINITIES XXI
2(2nd alt. with picc.),2(2nd alt. with Eng.hn.),2(2nd alt. with
b.-cl.),2 - 4,2,3,1 - timp.,perc.(3) - hp. - str. 9:00 General.

—— SYMPHONY FOR TWELVE (1974)
1(alt. with picc.),1(alt. with Eng.hn.),1(alt. with b.-cl.),1 - 0,1,1,0 -
perc. - electric hpsc. - str.(1,1,1,1)   20:00.

—— SYMPHONY NO. 1 (IN 3 MOVTS.)
*3,*3,*3,*3 - 4,2,3,1 - timp.,perc.(3),xyl. - pf. - str. 20:00 General.

—— SYMPHONY NO. 4
2(2nd alt. with picc.),2(2nd alt. with Eng. hn.),*3,2 - 4,2,3,1 -
timp.,perc.(3),bells,cel.,glock.,xyl. - hp. - str. 27:00 Weintraub.

—— SYMPHONY NO. 7
2(2nd alt. with picc.),2(2nd alt. with Eng.hn.),2(2nd alt. with
b.-cl.),2(2nd alt. with c.-bn.) - 4,3,3,1 - timp.,perc.(3) - hp. - str.
                                                  24:00 General.

—— SYMPHONY OF THE YIN-YANG
3(1 alt. with picc., 1 alt. with alto fl.),*4, 1 E♭cl.,*2,2(2nd alt. with
c.-bn.) - 6,4,4,2 - timp.,perc.(10),cel.(alt. with pf.) - str.
                                                  40:00 General.

—— SYMPHONY (1950)
*2,*2,*2,*2 - 4,2,3,1 - timp.,perc.,pf. - str.   20:00 General.

—— THREE PIECES FOR SMALL ORCH.
1(alt. with picc.),1(alt. with Eng. hn.),*2,1 - 1,0,1,0 - str.
                                                  6:00 Composer.

—— VARIATIONS FOR ORCH.
2(1 alt. with picc.),2,2,2 - 4,2,3,1 - timp.,perc.(2),cel.,glock.,xyl. -
hp. - str.   12:35 General.

KURKA, Robert
—— BALLAD FOR HORN AND STRINGS, OP. 36
hn. - str.   8:00 Weintraub.

—— CHAMBER SYMPHONY, OP. 3 (IN 3 MOVTS.)
2,2,2,2 - 2,2,0,0 - timp. - str.   20:30 Composer.

—— CONCERTINO FOR TWO PIANOS, TRUMPET AND
STRINGS, OP. 31 (IN 3 MOVTS.)
tpt. - 2 pf. - str.   15:00 Weintraub.

—— CONCERTO FOR MARIMBA AND ORCH, OP. 34 (IN 3
MOVTS.)
2(2nd alt. with picc.),2,2,2 - 2,2,2,0 - timp.,perc.(2)mar. - str.
                                                  20:00 Weintraub.

—— JOHN HENRY, OP. 27 (PORTRAIT FOR ORCH.)
*2,2,2,2 - 2-4,2,2,1 - timp.,perc. - pf. - str. 12:00 Weintraub.

—— JULIUS CAESAR, OP. 28 (SYMPHONIC EPILOGUE, AFTER
SHAKESPEARE'S PLAY)
2(2nd alt. with picc.),2,2,2 - 4,3,2,1 - timp.,perc.(3),glock.,xyl. -
str.   9:00 Weintraub.

—— MUSIC FOR ORCH., OP. 11
3(3rd alt. with picc.),3(3rd alt. with Eng. hn.),3(3rd alt.
withb.-cl.),3(3rd alt. with c.-bn.) - 4,3,3,1 - timp.,perc.(2),cel. - hp.
- str.   15:00 Weintraub.

—— SERENADE FOR SMALL ORCH., OP. 25 (IN 4 MOVTS.)
*2,2,2,2 - 2,2,0,0 - timp. - str.   21:00 Weintraub.

—— SUITE FROM THE OPERA "THE GOOD SOLDIER SCHWEIK",
OP. 22 (FOR WOODWIND, BRASS AND PERCUSSION) (IN 6
MOVTS.)
*2,*2,*2,*2 - 2,2,1,0 - timp.,perc.(2)   21:00 Weintraub.

—— SYMPHONY FOR STRINGS AND BRASS, OP. 7
1. Very slow; 2. Very fast; 3. Very slow
3 hn.,2 tpt.,2 trb.,tu. - str.   17:30 Weintraub.

—— SYMPHONY NO. 1, OP. 17 (IN 4 MOVTS.)
*3,2,2,*3 - 4,3,3,1 - timp.,perc.(3),glock.,xyl. - hp. - str.
                                                  26:00 Composer.

—— SYMPHONY NO. 2, OP. 24 (IN 3 MOVTS.)
*3,*3,*3,*3 - 4;3,3,1 - timp.,perc.(3) - str.   21:00 Weintraub.

—— TWO PIECES FOR ORCH., OP. 15
*2,2,2,2 - 2,2,2,1 - timp.,perc.(3),glock. - str. 13:30 Composer.

—— WHO SHALL SPEAK FOR THE PEOPLE? (FOR TTBB
CHORUS AND ORCH.) (Text: Carl Sandburg)
                                                  6:00 Bo. Hawkes.

KÜRKTSCHIISKI, Krassimir
—— ADAGIO FOR STRINGS
str.   6:30 Modern.

—— DIAPHONIC ETUDE
*3,2,2,2 - 4,3,3,1 - timp.,perc.,xyl. - pf. - str. 12:00 Modern.

KURTÁG, György
—— CONCERTO FOR VIOLA AND ORCH.
2,2,2,2 - 3,2,0,0 - timp. - str.   Bo. Hawkes.

KURTZ, Efrem
—— SYMPHONY NO. 2
3,2,2,2 - 4,3,3,1 - timp.,perc. - hp. - str.   21:00 Bo. Hawkes.

KURTZ, Eugene
—— CHAMBER SYMPHONY FOR THE FOURTH OF JULY
perc.(2) - pf. - str.(2,2,2,1)   15:00 Presser.

—— CONCERT NOCTURNE
1,1,0,0 - 0,0,0,0 - perc. - pf. - str.   12:00 EV.

—— CONVERSATIONS (FOR 12 INSTRUMENTS)
1,1,1,0 - 1,1,0,0 - perc. - pf. - str.(2,1,1,1) 9:00 Presser.

—— ÇA .... (DIAGRAM FOR ORCHESTRA)
4,4,3,2 alto sax.,3 - 0,0,0,0 - timp.,perc.(3),cel.,vibra.,xyl. - hp. -
str.   15:00 Presser.

—— LE MARCHEUR SOLITAIRE (MONOLOGUE FOR ORCH.)
4,4,4,4 - 6,4,3,1 - timp.,perc.,bells,cel.,glock.,vibra.,xyl. - hp. - pf. -
str.   18:00 EV.

—— MÉCANIQUE (FOR LARGE ORCHESTRA)
                                                  Presser.

—— SUITE PARISIENNE (IN 5 MOVTS.)
*2,*2,0,0 - 0,0,0,0 - perc.(1),glock.,vibra.,xyl. - pf. - str. 16:00 EV.
or:
1,1,0,0 - 0,0,0,0 - perc.(1),glock.,vibra.,xyl. - pf. - str.

—— SYMPHONY FOR STRINGS
str.   33:00 EV.

—— THREE SONGS FROM "MEDEA" (TROIS CHANTS DE
MEDEE) (FOR DRAMATIC SOPRANO AND ORCH.) (Text:
Robinson Jeffers)
                                                  9:30 EV.

KURZ, Siegfried
—— CHAMBER CONCERTO, OP. 31 (FOR WIND QUINTET AND
STRING ORCH.)
1,1,1,1 - 1,0,0,0 - str.   18:00 Tetra.

—— CONCERTO FOR PIANO AND ORCH., OP. 32
2,2,2,2 - 4,3,3,1 - timp.,perc.,cel. - hp. - str. 30:00 Tetra.

—— CONCERTO FOR TRUMPET AND STRING ORCH., OP. 23
tpt. - str.   19:00 Tetra.

—— MUSIC FOR ORCH., OP. 30 (1960)
2,2,2,2 - 4,2,3,1 - perc. - str.   12:00 Tetra.

—— MUSIC FOR WOODWINDS, TIMPANI AND STRINGS, OP. 36
2,2,2,2 - 0,3,3,0 - timp. - str.   Tetra.

—— SONATINA FOR ORCH., OP. 35
2,2,2,2 - 2,2,0,0 - timp.,perc.   Tetra.

—— SYMPHONY NO. 1, OP. 28
2,2,2,2 - 4,3,3,1 - timp.,perc.,cel. - hp. - str. 30:00 Tetra.

—— SYMPHONY NO. 2, OP. 29
2,2,2,2 - 4,3,3,1 - timp.,perc. - hp. - str.   25:00 Tetra.

—— VARIATIONS FOR ORCH., OP. 33
2,2,2,2 - 4,2,3,1 - timp.,perc. - hp. - str.   13:00 Tetra.

KURZBACH, Paul
—— SERENADE NO. 3
2,2,2,2 - 2,2,2,0 - timp.,perc. - str.   Tetra.

—— SERENADE NO. 6 FOR STRING ORCH.
    str.   Tetra.

KUSSER, Johann Sigismund - MÖNKEMEYER, Helmut
—— OVERTURE IN C MAJOR (FOR STRING ORCH.)
    str.   8:30 Henmar.

KUSTER, Herbert
—— CAPRIOLEN SUITE (FOR FLUTE AND STRINGS)
    1. Adagio; 2. Allegretto grazioso; 3. Presto
    fl. - str.   10:00 AhnSimrock.

KUUSISTO, Ilkka
—— ANTTI PUUHAARA (1964)
    2,1,1,1 - 2,1,0,0 - perc. - hp. - str.   12:00 FinnMICtr.
—— FROM VANTAA RIVER TO CAP VIRO (1962)
    0,0,2,1 - 2,0,0,0 - perc. - hp. - str.   10:00 FinnMICtr.
—— MUSIC TO THE TV PLAY "THE BAD STATE OF THE
ROADS" (1967)
    str.   13:00 FinnMICtr.

KUUSISTO, Taneli
—— CHRISTMAS NIGHT, OP. 31 (FOR SATB CHORUS AND
ORCH.) (1942) (Text: Ilmari Pimiä)
    2,2,2,2 - 2,2,2,0 - perc. - str.   9:00 FinnMICtr.
—— FINNISH FOLK CHORALES, OP. 30 (FOR SATB CHORUS,
ORGAN AND STRINGS) (1941)
    org. - str.   25:00 FinnMICtr.
—— LAKE LADOGA, OP. 37 (TONE POEM) (1944)
    3,2,2,2 - 4,3,3,1 - timp.,perc. - hp. - str. 11:00 FinnMICtr.
—— LYRICAL SUITE, OP. 35 (FROM THE FILM "THE GLORIFIED
HEART") (1943) (IN 8 MOVTS.)
    3,2,2,2 - 4,2,2,1 - timp.,perc. - hp. - str. 22:00 FinnMICtr.
—— MIRAGES, OP. 39 (4 SONGS FOR MEZZO-SOPRANO AND
ORCH.) (1945) (Text: Elina Vaara)
    2,2,2,2 - 4,2,2,1 - hp. - str.   10:00 Fazer.
—— MUSIC TO THE FILM "PEOPLE IN THE SUMMER NIGHT",
OP. 46 (1948)
    2,2,2,2 - 2,2,2,0 - timp. - hp. - str. 20:00 FinnMICtr.
—— MUSIC TO UNTO SEPPÄNEN'S PLAY "THREE DAYS", OP. 8
(1929)
    str.   7:00 FinnMICtr.
—— NOCTURNE, OP. 29 (FOR CELLO AND ORCH.) (1936)
    2,2,2,2 - 3,0,0,0 - hp. - str.   9:00 Westerlund.
—— PASTORALE, OP. 16 (1934)
    2,2,2,2 - 2,2,2,0 - str.   5:00 FinnMICtr.
—— THE PEARL OF SAIMAA, OP. 47 (CANTATA) (FOR SATB
CHORUS AND ORCH.) (1949) (Text: Ilmari Pimiä)
    3,2,2,2 - 4,2,3,1 - timp.,perc.(5) - hp. - str. 25:00 FinnMICtr.
—— PSALM 40, OP. 27, NO. 1 (FOR BARITONE, SATB CHORUS,
ORGAN AND STRINGS)
    org. - str.   10:00 Fazer.
—— TOCCATA IN C MAJOR, OP. 60 (1953)
    3,2,2,2 - 4,3,3,1 - str.   7:00 FinnMICtr.
—— A WEST-FINNISH OVERTURE, OP. 50 (1948)
    org. - pf. - str.   3:00 FinnMICtr.

KVANDAL, Johan
—— CONCERTO FOR FLUTE AND STRINGS, OP. 22 (IN 4
MOVTS.)
    fl. - str.   13:30 T.O.N.O.
—— DIVERTIMENTO FOR STRINGS, OP. 3 (IN 4 MOVTS.)
    str.   18:00 T.O.N.O.
—— NORWEGIAN OVERTURE, OP. 7
    2,2,2,2 - 4,2,0,0 - timp. - str.   7:00 Musikk-Hu.
—— SINFONIA CONCERTANTE, OP. 29 (IN 3 MOVTS.)
    3,3,2,2 - 4,3,3,1 - timp.,perc.,cel. - str. 17:30 T.O.N.O.
—— SKIPPER WORSE: SUITE NO. 1, OP. 28-A (FROM
INCIDENTAL MUSIC FOR ALEXANDER KIELLAND'S
PLAY) (IN 8 MOVTS.)
    2,2,2,2 - 2,3,2,0 - timp.,perc. - str. 19:00 T.O.N.O.
—— SOLO CANTATA, OP. 10 (FOR HIGH VOICE AND ORCH.)
(Text: Biblical)
    2,2,2,2 - 4,2,0,0 - timp.,perc. - str. 7:30 T.O.N.O.
—— SONG TO STELLA, OP. 6 (FOR SOPRANO AND STRINGS)
(Text: Henrik Wergeland)
    str.   7:00 Musikk-Hu.
—— SYMPHONIC EPOS, OP. 21 (IN 1 MOVT.)
    2,2,2,2 - 4,3,3,1 - timp.,perc.,cel. - str. 18:00 Musikk-Hu.
—— SYMPHONY NO. 1, OP. 18 (IN 3 MOVTS.)
    2,2,2,2 - 4,2,0,0 - timp.,perc. - str. 30:00 T.O.N.O.
—— THEME, VARIATIONS AND FUGUE, OP. 14
    2,2,2,2 - 4,2,3,0 - timp.,perc. - hp. - str. 15:00 T.O.N.O.

KVAPIL, Jaroslav
—— FROM HARD TIMES (SYMPHONIC VARIATIONS)
    3,3,3,3 - 4,2,3,1 - timp.,perc. - hp. - str. 18:00 Bo. Hawkes.

KYNASTON, Trent P.
—— SYMPHONY NO. 1 (1969)
    1. Adagio; 2. Andante; 3. Allegro agitato
    3(3rd alt. with picc.),3(3rd alt. with Eng. hn.),3(3rd alt. with
b.-cl.),3(3rd alt. with c.-bn.) - 8,3,3,1 - timp.,perc.(5),bells,2
glock.,xyl. - hp. - str.   29:00 Composer.

L

LABEY, Marcel
—— LIED (FOR CELLO AND ORCH.)
    2,2,2,2 - 4,0,0,0 - str.   5:30 EV.
—— OUVERTURE POUR UN DRAME
    3,3,3,3 - 4,3,3,1 - timp.,perc. - str. 12:30 EV.

LABROCA, Mario
—— TRE CANTATE SULLA PASSIONE DI CRISTO (3 CANTATAS
ON THE PASSION OF CHRIST) (FOR BASS, CHORUS AND
ORCH.)
    3,3,3,3 - 4,3,3,1 - timp.,perc.(2),cel. - hp. - pf. - str. 35:00 Leeds.

LABUNSKI, Felix
—— CANTO DI ASPIRAZIONE (SONG OF ASPIRATION)
    *3,2,2,*3 - 4,0,0,0 - cel. - hp. - str.   9:30 C. Fischer.
—— ELEGY (IN MEMORY IN IGNACE PADEREWSKI)
    2,2,2,2 - 2,0,0,0 - hp.(or pf.) - str.   3:30 Composer.
—— IMAGES OF YOUTH (CANTATA) (FOR MEZZO-SOPRANO,
BARITONE, CHILDREN'S CHORUS AND ORCH.) (Texts:
Walter De la Mare and David McCord)
    *3,*3,2,2 b.-cl.,*3 - 4,3,3,0 - timp.,perc.(5),cel.,glock.,mar.,xyl. - hp.
- pf. - str.   30:00 C. Fischer.
—— MUSIC FOR PIANO AND ORCHESTRA (IN 1 MOVT.) (1966)
    *3,1 alto fl.,2,2,2 - 4,0,0,0 - timp.,perc.(4),glock.,mar.,xyl. - pf. -
str.   16:00 Composer.
    or:
    *3,2,*3,2 - 4,0,0,0 - timp.,perc.(4),glock.,mar.,xyl. - pf. - str.
—— NOCTURNE
    2,2,2,2 - 3,0,0,0 - hp. - str.   5:00 Composer.
—— POLISH RENAISSANCE SUITE (IN 8 MOVTS.) (1967)
    *3,2,2,2 - 4,3,3,1 - timp.,perc.(4),cel.,glock.,mar. - hp. - pf. - str.
                      14:00 Composer.
—— PRIMAVERA (1973)
    *3,2,*4,*3 - 4,2,3,1 - perc.(3),glock.,mar.,xyl. - hp. - pf. -
str.(34,14,12,10)   11:30 Composer.
—— SALUT A PARIS (SALUTE TO PARIS)(BALLET SUITE)(1968)
(IN 5 MOVTS.)
    *3,2,2,2 - 3,2,0,0 - timp.,perc.(4),glock.,mar.,xyl. - hp. - pf. - str.
                      16:40 Composer.
—— SUITE FOR STRING ORCH. (IN 3 MOVTS.)
    str.   15:00 Composer.
—— SYMPHONIC DIALOGUES
    *3,2,*3(1 alt. with alto fl.),*3 - 4,3,3,1 -
timp.,perc.(4),cel.,glock.,mar.,xyl. - hp. - pf. - str.
                      16:30 C. Fischer.
—— SYMPHONY IN B MAJOR (IN 3 MOVTS.)
    *3,*3,*3,*3 - 4,3,3,1 - timp.,perc.(4),cel.,glock.,mar.,xyl. - hp. - pf.
- str.   24:00 Composer.
—— THERE IS NO DEATH (EASTER CANTATA) (FOR MIXED
CHORUS AND ORCH.) (IN 1 MOVT.) (Text: Joseph Auslander)
    2,2,2 E♭cl.,2,2 - 3,3,3,1 - timp.,perc.,bells,cel.,mar. - hp.(or pf.) -
str.   12:00 Composer.
—— TRIPTYQUE CHAMPÈTRE (PASTORAL TRIPTYCH) (IN 3
MOVTS.)
    *3,*3,*3,*3 - 4,3,0,0 - timp.,perc.,cel. - hp. - str. 13:00 Composer.
—— VARIATIONS FOR ORCH.
    *3,*3,*3,*3, - 4,3,3,1 - timp.,perc.,cel.,glock.,mar.,xyl. - hp. - pf. -
str.   14:00 Composer.
—— XAVERIANA (FANTASY FOR 2 PIANOS AND ORCH.)
    *3,2,2,2 - 4,3,3,1 - timp.,perc.,bells - 2 pf. - str. 12:00 Composer.

LACHENMANN, Helmut
—— AIR (MUSIC FOR PERCUSSION AND LARGE ORCH.)
                             Hans Gerig.
—— NOCTURNE (FOR CELLO AND SMALL ORCH.)
                             Hans Gerig.

—— SOUVENIR (FOR 41 INSTRUMENTS) (1959)

Hans Gerig.

LACOMBE, Paul
—— RAPSODIE SUR DES AIRS DU PAYS D' OC

Enoch.

LADERMAN, Ezra
—— CELESTIAL BODIES (CONCERTO FOR FLUTE AND STRINGS) (IN 3 MOVTS.)
fl. - str.   20:00 Oxford.
—— CONCERTO FOR BASSOON AND STRINGS (1955) (IN 3 MOVTS.)
0,0,0,1 - 0,0,0,0 - str.   18:30 Regaldi.
—— CONCERTO FOR ORCHESTRA (1967) (IN 3 MOVTS.)
*3,*3,*3,*3 - 4,3,3,0 - perc.(5) - hp. - str.   26:00 Regaldi.
—— CONCERTO FOR VIOLIN AND ORCH. (1963) (IN 4 MOVTS.)
*3,*3,*3,2 - 0,0,0,0 - perc.(2) - str.   26:30 Oxford.
—— CONCERTO NO. 1 FOR PIANO AND ORCH. (1940)
20:00 Regaldi.
—— CONCERTO NO. 2 FOR PIANO AND ORCH. (1957)
2,2,2,2 - 2,2,2,0 - perc. - pf. - str.   17:00 Presser.
—— DOUBLE HELIX
fl.,ob. - str.   12:00 Oxford.
—— THE EAGLE STIRRED (ORATORIO) (1961) (Text Clair Roskam)
2,2,2,2 - 2,2,2,0 - timp.,perc.(2) - str.   60:00 Regaldi.
—— THE HUNTING OF THE SNARK (2-ACT OPERA, AFTER THE POEM BY LEWIS CARROLL) %
120:00 Regaldi.
—— MAGIC PRISON (FOR 2 NARRATORS AND ORCH.) (1967) (Text: Emily Dickinson and T. W. Higginson)
2,2,2,2 - 4,3,2,0 - perc.(2) - str.   25:00 Oxford.
Or
2(2nd alt. with picc.),2,3,2 - 4,3,3,0 - timp.,perc.(2) - hp. - str.
—— SATIRE (CONCERTO FOR ORCH.) (IN 3 MOVTS.)
*3,*3,*3,*3, - 4,3,3,1 - timp.,perc.(3),cel. - hp. - str. 24:00 Oxford.
—— A SINGLE VOICE
ob. - str.   10:00 Oxford.
—— STANZAS (FOR CHAMBER ORCH.)
1,1,1 E♭cl.,*2,1 - 1,1,1,1 - perc.(3) - str.(3,1,1,1)   21:00 Oxford.
or:
2,1,2,1 - 1,1,1,1 - timp.,perc. - org. - str.
—— SYMPHONY NO. 1 (1965) (IN 4 MOVTS.)
3(3rd alt. with picc.),*3,*3,*3 - 4,3,4,1 - timp.,perc.(4),cel.,glock.,xyl. - hp. - str.   25:00 Oxford.
—— SYMPHONY NO. 2 ("LUTHER") (1968)
*3,2,2,2 - 4,3,3,1 - perc.(3) - str.   21:30 Oxford.
—— THE TRIALS OF GALILEO (DRAMATIC ORATORIO) (1967) (FOR ALTO, 2 TENORS, COUNTER-TENOR, BARITONE, BASS-BARITONE, BASS, SATB CHORUS AND ORCH.) (Text: Joseph Darion)
2,2,2,2 - 4,3,2,0 - timp.,perc.(3) - hp. - org. - str.   90:00 Oxford.
or:
2,2,2,2 - 2,2,1,1 - timp.,perc.(3) - hp. - org. - str.

LADMIRAULT, Paul
—— EN FORÊT (SYMPHONIC POEM)
24:00 EV.
—— OVERTURE TO THE BALLET "LA PRÉTRESSE DE KORIDWEN"
2,3,2,2 - 4,2-3,3,0 - timp.,perc. - hp. - str.   4:00 Baron.
—— RHAPSODIE GAËLIQUE (IN 6 MOVTS.)
2,3,2,2 - 4,2,3,0 - timp.,perc. - hp. - str.   18:00 Baron.

LAITINEN, Heikki
—— LULLABY TO THE HOUSE OF DEATH (TWO SONGS FOR 3-5 VOICES AND ORCH.) (1970) (Text: The Kanteletar)
2,0,1,1-2 - 0,0,0,0 - str.   11:00 FinnMICtr.

LAJOVIC, Aleksander
—— INTERLUDE (FROM THE BALLET "UNCOMMON DAY")
str.   7:00 Hans Gerig.
—— UNCOMMON DAY (BALLET) %
2(2nd alt. with picc.),2,2(2nd alt. with b.-cl.),2 - 4,3,3,1 - timp.,perc.(3) - hp. - pf. - str.   45:00 Hans Gerig.

LAJTHA, László
—— DIVERTISSEMENT, OP. 25 (IN 5 MOVTS.)
1,0,2,0 - 2,1,0,0 - timp.,perc. - hp. - str.   20:00 Baron.
—— LYSISTRATA, OP. 19 (1-ACT BALLET) %
Baron.
—— OVERTURE TO "LYSISTRATA"
2,2,2,2 - 2,2,2,1 - timp.,perc.,cel. - hp. - str.   6:00 Baron.

—— SINFONIETTA NO. 2, OP. 62
str.   21:00 Baron.
—— SINFONIETTA, OP. 43 (FOR STRINGS)
str.   16:00 Baron.
—— SUITE NO. 2, OP. 38
3,3,3,3 - 4,3,3,1 - timp.,perc.,cel.,xyl. - hp. - str.   28:00 Baron.
—— SUITE NO. 3, OP. 56
2,2,2,2 - 4,2,0,0 - timp.,perc.,cel.,xyl. - 2 hp. - str.   26:10 Baron.
—— SUITE, OP. 19 (IN 4 MOVTS.)
2,2,2,*2 - 2,2,2,1 - timp.,perc.,cel. - hp. - str.   17:00 Baron.
—— SYMPHONY NO. 1, OP. 24
2,2,1,1 - 2,1,1,0 - timp.,perc.,cel. - 2 hp. - str.   25:00 Baron.
—— SYMPHONY NO. 3, OP. 45
2,*2,2,*2 - 4,2,3,1 - timp.,perc.,cel.,glock.,xyl. - hp. - str.   17:00 Baron.
—— SYMPHONY NO. 4 ("LE PRINTEMPS"), OP. 52
2,*2,2,*2 - 4,2,0,0 - timp.,perc.,cel.,glock. - str.   18:00 Baron.
—— SYMPHONY NO. 5, OP. 55
3,3,2,alto sax., 3 - 4,3,3,1 - timp.,perc.,cel.,xyl. - 2 hp. - str.   29:00 Baron.
—— SYMPHONY NO. 6, OP. 61
3,*3,2,1 alto sax.,3 - 4,3,3,1 - timp.,perc.,cel.,xyl. - 2 hp. - str.   29:00 Baron.
—— SYMPHONY NO. 7, OP. 63
3,*3,2,1 alto sax.,3 - 4,3,3,1 - timp.,perc.,xyl. - 2 hp. - str.   26:00 Baron.

LAKE, Mayhew Lester
—— AMERICAN RHAPSODY
*3,2,2,2 - 4,3,4,1 - timp.,perc.(3) - hp. - pf. - str.   10:00 Composer.
—— AMERICANA OVERTURE
*3,2,2,2 - 4,2,3,1 - timp.,perc.(3) - pf. - str.   8:00 C. Fischer.
—— INDIAN SUMMER (SUITE) (IN 4 MOVTS.)
*3,2,2,2 - 2,2,2,1 - timp.,perc.(3) - org. - pf. - str.   12:00 C. Fischer.
—— LOVE (SUITE) (IN 3 MOVTS.)
*3,2,2,2 - 2,2,1,1 - timp.,perc.(3) - org. - pf. - str.   10:00 C. Fischer.
—— THE TEMPEST
*3,2,2,2 - 2,2,2,1 - timp.,perc.(3) - org. - pf. - str.   10:00 C. Fischer.

LAKNER, Yehoshua
—— TOCCATA FOR ORCH.
2,2,2,2 - 0,0,0,0 - pf. - str.   10:00 IsMuPublns.

LALANDE, Michel-Richard de - GENNARO, Marcel
—— DIXIT DOMINUS (PSALM FOR 6 SOLO VOICES, SATB CHORUS AND ORCH.)
2,2,0,3 - 0,2,0,0 - str.   45:00 Presser.

LAMB, Alvin R.
—— DAWN, OP. 3, NO. 2 (1935)
2,2,2,2 - 4,2,3,0 - timp. - str.   5:00 Composer.
—— EVENING, OP. 3, NO. 3 (1936)
2,2,2,2 - 4,2,3,0 - timp. - str.   5:00 Composer.

LAMBERT, Constant
—— AUBADE HEROIQUE
2,*2,2,2 - 2,2,0,0 - perc. - hp. - str.   7:00 Oxford.
—— CONCERTO FOR PIANO AND 9 INSTS.
1,3,0,0 - 0,1,1,0 - perc. - pf. - str.   25:00 Oxford.
—— HOROSCOPE (BALLET SUITE) (IN 5 MOVTS.)
3(2nd and 3rd alt. with picc.),2(2nd alt. with Eng. hn.),2,2 - 4,3,3,1 - timp.,perc.(1-2) - hp. - str.   25:00 Oxford.
—— KING PEST (RONDO BURLESCA)
*3,*3,*3,*3 - 4,3,2 cnt. (or 2 tpt.),3,1 - timp.,perc.(3) - str.   8:30 Oxford.
—— THE MERCHANT SEAMEN (SUITE)
3,3,3,2 - 4,3,3,1 - timp.,perc.,xyl. - hp. - pf. - str.   15:00 Bo. Hawkes.
or:
2,2,2,2 - 3-4,3,3,0-1 - timp.,perc. - hp.(ad lib.) - pf. - str.
—— MUSIC FOR ORCHESTRA
3(2nd and 3rd alt. with picc.),*3,3,*2 - 4,3,3,1 - timp.,perc.(2) - str.   12:00 Oxford.
—— OVERTURE TO "THE BIRD ACTORS"
2,1,2,1 - 2,2,1,0 - perc. - str.   4:00 Oxford.
—— POMONA (BALLET) %
*2,1,2,1 - 2,2,1,0 - timp.,perc. - str.   Oxford.
—— THE RIO GRANDE (FOR CHORUS, PIANO AND ORCH.)
2 tpt.,2 cnt.,3 trb.,tu. - timp.,perc.(3-5), keyed glock.,xyl. - pf. - str.   Oxford.

—— ROMEO AND JULIET (BALLET) %
    1,2,1,1 - 2,2,1,0 - timp.,perc. - str.   30:00 Oxford.
—— SUMMER'S LAST WILL AND TESTAMENT (A MASQUE IN 7
MOVTS.) % (FOR BARITONE, MIXED CHORUS AND ORCH.)
(Text: Thomas Nashe)
    3,*3,*3,*3 - 4,2 cnt.,3,3,1 - timp.,perc.(3) - 2 hp. - str.
                50:00 Oxford.

LAMBRO, Phillip
—— FOUR SONGS (FOR SOPRANO AND ORCH.) (1967) (Text:
Sylvia Plath)
    2,2,2,2(2nd alt. with b.-cl.),1 alto sax.,2 - 4,4,4,1 - timp.,perc.(4),cel.
- electric guit. - hp. - pf. - str.   17:00 Wimbledon.
—— MIRA FLORES (FOR STRING ORCH.)
    str.   5:00 Wimbledon.
—— MUSIC FOR WIND, BRASS AND PERCUSSION
    2,2,2,2 - 4,4,3,1 - perc.(2) - pf.   14:00 Wimbledon.
—— STRUCTURES FOR STRING ORCHESTRA
    str.   9:00 Wimbledon.
—— TWO PICTURES (FOR SOLO PERCUSSIONIST AND ORCH.)
(INSPIRED BY JACKSON POLLOCK PAINTINGS)
    2(2nd alt.with picc.),2,2,2 - 2,2,2,0 - perc.(1) (soloist),cel. - hp. -
pf. - str.   12:00 Wimbledon.

LA MONTAINE, John
—— AMERICA, THE WORKS OF PEACE BE THINE, OP. 45 (FOR
CHORUS AND ORCH.)
                Fredonia.
—— BE GLAD THEN, AMERICA, OP. 43 (A DECENT
ENTERTAINMENT FROM THE 13 COLONIES) (OVERTURE)
                Fredonia.
—— BIRDS OF PARADISE, OP. 34
    *3,*3,2,1 - 4,3,2,1 - perc. - hp. - pf. - str.   12:00 C. Fischer.
—— CANONS FOR ORCH., OP. 10
    2(2nd alt. with picc.),2,2(2nd alt. with b.-cl.),2 - 2-4,2,2,0 -
timp.,perc.,cel. - str.   10:00 C. Fischer.
—— CANTICLE FOR ORCHESTRA, OP. 33
    *3,2,2,2 - 4,3,3,0 - str.   6:00 P. J. Sifler.
—— COLLOQUY FOR STRINGS, OP. 21
    str.   13:00 Fredonia.
—— CONCERTO FOR PIANO AND ORCH., OP. 9 (IN 3 MOVTS.)
    *3,*3,*3,*3 - 4,3,3,0 - timp.,perc.(3),xyl. - pf. - str.   25:00 Galaxy.
—— ERODE THE GREAT, OP. 40 (2-ACT MEDIEVAL
PAGEANT-OPERA) %
                90:00 Fredonia.
—— FRAGMENTS FROM THE SONG OF SONGS, OP. 29 (FOR
SOPRANO AND ORCH.)
    2,2,2,2 - 4,3,3,1 - timp.,perc. - hp. - pf. - str.   30:00 Fredonia.
—— FROM SEA TO SHINING SEA (OVERTURE), OP. 30
    *3,2,2,*3 - 4,3,4,0 - timp.,perc.(3) - str.   7:30 Fredonia.
    or:
    *4,4,4,*4 - 4,4,4,0 - timp.,perc.(3) - str.
    or:
    2,2,2,2 - 4,3,3,1 - timp.,perc.(3) - str.
—— JUBILANT OVERTURE
    *3,2,2,*3 - 4,3,3,1 - timp.,perc.(3) - str.   5:30 C. Fischer.
—— MISSA NATURAE, OP. 37 (MASS FOR NARRATOR, CHORUS
AND ORCH.)
    *3,2(2nd alt. with Eng. hn.),1 E♭cl.,1,*2 - 4,3,3,1 -
timp.,perc.(3),xyl. - hp. - pf. - str.   30:00 P. J. Sifler.
—— NOVELLIS, NOVELLIS (1-ACT MEDIEVAL
PAGEANT-OPERA) %
    2,*3,1,*3 - 0,3,3,0 - timp.,perc. - hp. - hpsc. - org.(ad lib.) - str.
                45:00 Fredonia.
—— ODE FOR OBOE AND ORCH., OP. 11
                7:00 P. J. Sifler.
—— ORCHESTRAL INTERLUDE FROM "THE SONG OF SONGS",
OP. 29-A
    2(2nd alt. with picc.),*2,1,1 - trgl. - hp. - pf. - str.
                5:00 P. J. Sifler.
—— PASSACAGLIA AND FUGUE, OP. 21-A
    str.   9:00 P. J. Sifler.
—— RECITATIVE, ARIA AND FINALE, OP. 16
    str.   12:00 P. J. Sifler.
—— RONDO FOR PIANO AND ORCH.
                6:00 Composer.
—— THE SHEPHARDES PLAYE, OP. 38 (1-ACT MEDIEVAL
PAGEANT-OPERA) %
                60:00 Fredonia.
—— SONGS OF THE ROSE OF SHARON, OP. 6 (FOR SOPRANO
AND ORCH.)
    2,2,2,*3 - 4,2,3,1 - str.   13:00 Broude.

—— A SUMMER'S DAY (SONNET FOR ORCH.), OP. 32
    1,1,1,0 - 1,1,0,0 - hp. - str.   5:00 G. Schirmer.
—— SYMPHONY NO. 1, OP. 28
    2(2nd alt. with picc.),2,2,2 - 2,2,1,0 - perc.(1) - hp. - str.
                20:00 Broude.
—— TE DEUM, OP. 35 (FOR CHORUS, WINDS AND
PERCUSSION)
    *3,2,1 E♭cl.,1,*2 - 2,5,3,1 - timp.,perc.(2-3),bell   7:00 Fredonia.
—— WILDERNESS JOURNAL, OP. 41 (SYMPHONY FOR
BASS-BARITONE, ORGAN AND ORCH.) (1971) (Text: Henry
D. Thoreau)
    *2,2(1 alt. with Eng. hn.),1 E♭cl.,1,1 - 1,2,2,0 -
timp.,perc.(3-4),bells,glock.,xyl. - tape-recorder - hp. - org. - pf. -
str.   45:00 P. J. Sifler.

LA MOTTE, Diether de
—— CONCERTO AVVENTUROSO
    1,1,1,1 - 2,1,0,0 - str.   15:00 G. Schirmer.
—— CONCERTO FOR FLUTE AND ORCH. (1967)
    3(3rd alt. with picc.),1,1,1 - 1,1,1,0 - timp.,perc.(4) - hp. - pf. - str.
                18:00 G. Schirmer.
—— CONCERTO FOR ORCH. (1963)
    *2,2(2nd alt. with Eng.hn.),*2,*2 - 2,2,2,1 - timp.,perc.(3) - hp. -
pf. - str.   15:00 G. Schirmer.
—— ECHO CONCERTO (FOR CELLO AND ORCH.)
    2(2nd alt. with picc.),2,E♭cl.,1,2(2nd alt. with c.-bn.) - 2,2,2,0 -
perc.(1) - str.   18:00 G. Schirmer.
—— KLANG-WEGE (FOR 49 MUSICIANS AND 3
CONDUCTORS)(1971)
    3,3,3,3 - 2,3,2,1 - perc.(2) - str.   G. Schirmer.
—— SYMPHONIC OVERTURE (1966)
    *3,*3,*3,*3 - 2,2,2,1 - timp.,perc. - hp. - str.   9:00 G. Schirmer.
—— SYMPHONY IN 2 MOVTS. (1964)
    *2,2(2nd alt. with Eng.hn.),2(2nd alt. with b.-cl.),2(2nd alt. with
c.-bn.) - 2,2,2,1 - timp.,perc.(5) - hp. - str.   15:00 G. Schirmer.
—— TABLE MUSIC (FOR 7 WOODWINDS, 2 TROMBONES AND 6
HIGH STRINGS)(1972)
                G. Schirmer.

LAMPE, Günter
—— FESTIVAL PRELUDE (FOR SMALL ORCH.)
    2,1,2,2 - 2,2,1,0 - timp.,perc. - str.   6:00 Tetra.

LAMURAGLIA, Nicholas J.
—— SUITE (FOR STRING ORCH., WITH PIANO CONCERTANTE)
    pf. - str.   Fleisher.

LANCE, Le Chevalier de la - SADLER, Helmut
—— CONCERTO IN F MAJOR FOR PIANO AND SMALL ORCH.,
OP. 9
    0,2,0,0 - 2,0,0,0 - pf. - str.   30:00 Mannheimer.

LANCEN, Serge
—— CONCERTO CHAMPÊTRE (FOR HORN AND CHAMBER
ORCH.)
    1,0,0,1 - 1,0,0,0 - str.   12:30 Presser.
—— CONCERTO DA CAMERA (FOR FLUTE AND STRINGS)
    fl. - str.   17:30 Presser.
—— CONCERTO FOR CONTRABASS AND STRING ORCH, OP. 1
    str.   13:30 Presser.
—— SINFONIETTA
    2,2,2,2 - 3,3,3,1 - timp.,perc.(4),cel. - str.   17:30 Presser.

LANDAU, Siegfried
—— KING SOLOMON AND THE COBBLER (FOR NARRATOR
AND ORCH.)
                Composer.

LANDE, Bert
—— ELEGIA HEROICA, OP. 8 (SYMPHONY) (1949)
    3(3rd alt. with picc.),*3,2,*3 - 4,2,3,1 - timp.,perc.(3) - str.
                25:00 Composer.

LANDOWSKI, Marcel
—— CHANT DE SOLITUDE (FOR WOMEN'S VOICES AND
ORCH.)
    2,2,2,2 - 2,2,2,1 - timp.,perc.,bells,cel.,vibra.,xyl. - pf. - str.
                10:00 Henmar.
—— CONCERTO FOR BASSOON AND ORCH.
    1,1,2,1 - 1,1,1,1 - timp.,perc.,cel. - 2 hp. - pf. - str.   14:00 Henmar.
—— CONCERTO FOR CELLO AND ORCH. (1946)
                22:00 Henmar.

—— CONCERTO FOR FLUTE AND STRINGS
    fl. - str.   19:00 Henmar.
—— CONCERTO FOR ONDES MARTENOT, PERCUSSION AND STRINGS
    timp.,perc.,cel. - ondes Martenot - str.   18:00 Henmar.
—— CONCERTO NO. 2 FOR PIANO AND ORCH.
    3,2,2,2 - 2,2,2,1 - timp.,perc.,cel. - pf. - str.   23:00 Henmar.
—— MOUVEMENT (FOR STRING ORCH.)
    str.   8:00 Henmar.
—— LES NOTES DE NUIT (SYMPHONIC SUITE)
    1,1,1,1 - 2,2,1,0 - timp.,perc.,bells,vibra. - str.   17:00 Henmar.
—— PAYSAGE, D'APRÈS "L'ORAGE" DE GIORGIONE
    2,2,2,2 - 2,2,2,1 - perc.(3) - pf. - str.   5:10 Presser.
—— LE PETIT POUCET (SUITE) (1947)
                         10:00 Henmar.
—— POÈME SYMPHONIQUE ("EDINA")
                         Choudens.
—— POÈME (1942) (FOR PIANO AND ORCH.)
                         19:00 Henmar.
—— RHYTHMES DU MONDE
                         42:00 Henmar.
—— SYMPHONY NO. 1 (JEAN DE LA PEUR)
                         25:00 Henmar.
—— SYMPHONY NO. 2
    2,2,2,2 - 4,4,3,1 - timp.,perc. - hp. - pf. - str.   25:00 Henmar.

LANDRÉ, Guillaume
—— ANAGRAMMEN (1960)
    2,2,2,2 - 4,3,3,0 - timp.,perc.,xyl. - str.   12:00 Henmar.
—— BERCEUSE VOOR MOEDE MENSEN (FOR SOPRANO, TENOR, BARITONE, MIXED CHORUS AND ORCH.) (1952) (Text: A. de Vries)
    3,3,3,3 - 4,3,3,1 - timp.,perc.,xyl. - str.   15:00 Henmar.
—— CALEIDOSCOPIO (SYMPHONIC VARIATIONS)
    2,2,2,2 - 4,2,2,1 - timp.,perc.,xyl. - str.   15:00 Henmar.
—— CHAMBER SYMPHONY
    1,1,1,1 - 1,1,0,0 - perc. - hp. - str.   14:00 Henmar.
—— CONCERTANTE FOR BASS CLARINET AND ORCH. (1961)
    1,1,*2,1 - 2,1,0,0 - perc.,xyl. - str.   11:00 Henmar.
—— CONCERTANTE FOR CONTRABASS CLARINET (PEDAL-CLARINET) AND ORCH. (1959)
    1,1,1,1 d.-b. cl.,1 - 2,1,0,0 - perc. - str.   11:00 Henmar.
—— CONCERTO FOR CELLO AND ORCH.
    2,2,2,2 - 4,3,3,1 - timp.,perc. - str.   21:00 Henmar.
—— CONCERTO FOR CLARINET AND ORCH. (1958)
    3,3,2,2 - 4,2,2,1 - timp.,perc. - pf. - str.   20:00 Henmar.
—— CONCERTSTUK
    3,3,3,3 - 4,3,3,1 - timp.,perc.,xyl. - str.   12:00 Henmar.
—— FOUR MINIATURES (FOR CLARINET AND STRINGS)
    cl. - str.   9:00 Henmar.
—— FOUR PIECES FOR ORCH. (1937)
    3,3,3,3 - 4,3,3,1 - timp.,perc. - hp. - str.   12:00 Henmar.
—— FOUR SYMPHONIC MOVEMENTS
    3,3,3,3 - 4,3,3,1 - timp.,perc. - hp. - str.   12:00 Henmar.
—— GROET DER MARTELAREN (FOR BARITONE AND ORCH.) (1944)
    3,2,2,2 - 4,2,3,1 - timp.,perc. - hp. - str.   20:00 Henmar.
—— INTERLUDES DE "LA SYMPHONIE PASTORALE" (1968)
                         22:00 Henmar.
—— PIAE MEMORIAE PRO PATRIA MORTUORUM (FOR MIXED CHORUS AND ORCH.) (1942)
    3,3,3,2 - 4,3,3,1 - timp.,perc. - hp. - str.   20:00 Henmar.
—— SINFONIA SACRA (IN MEMORIAM PATRIS)
    3,3,3,2 - 4,3,3,1 - timp.,perc.,xyl. - hp. - str.   19:00 Henmar.
—— SINFONIETTA
    2,2,2,2 - 3,2,2,1 - timp.,perc. - str.   19:00 Henmar.
—— SONATA FESTIVA (FOR CHAMBER ORCH.)
    1,1,1,1 - 1,1,0,0 - perc. - str.   Henmar.
—— SONATA PER ORCHESTRA DA CAMERA (1961)
    1,1,1,1 - 2,1,0,0 - perc. - str.   13:00 Henmar.
—— SUITE FOR PIANO AND STRINGS
    pf. - str.   13:00 Oiseau Lyre.
—— SYMPHONIC MUSIC FOR FLUTE AND ORCH.
    2,3,3,2 - 3,3,2,1 - timp.,perc.,xyl. - str.   14:00 Henmar.
—— SYMPHONIC PERMUTATIONS (1957)
    3,3,3,2 - 4,3,3,0 - timp.,perc.,xyl. - str.   12:00 Henmar.
—— SYMPHONY NO. 1
    3,3,3,3 - 4,3,3,1 - timp.,perc. - str.   35:00 Henmar.
—— SYMPHONY NO. 2
    3,3,3,2 - 4,2,2,1 - timp.,perc., - str.   30:00 Henmar.
—— SYMPHONY NO. 3
    3,3,3,3 - 4,3,3,1 - timp.,perc.,xyl. - str.   14:00 Henmar.

—— SYMPHONY NO. 4
    3,3,3,3 - 4,3,3,1 - timp.,perc.,xyl. - hp. - str.   24:00 Henmar.
—— VARIAZIONI SENZA TEMA
    3,3,3,3 - 4,3,3,0 - timp.,perc. - hp. - pf. - str.   12:00 Henmar.

LANDRÉ, Willem - LANDRÉ, Guillaume
—— REQUIEM IN MEMORIAM UXORIS (FOR SOLOISTS, CHORUS AND ORCH.)
                         Henmar.

LANE, Eastwood
—— SCENE SAVANNA
    *3,*2,2,2 - 4,4,2,1 - timp.,perc.(2) - hp. - str.   6:30 J. Fischer.
—— SOLD DOWN THE RIVER (AMERICAN BALLET) %
    1,1,2,3 sax.,0 - 2,4,0,1 - timp.,perc.(1) - banjo - hp. - str. J. Fischer.

LANE, Eastwood - SPENCER, H.
—— ADIRONDACK SKETCHES
    * 1,1,2,4 sax.,0 - 2,4,3,1 - timp.perc.(2) - guit. - hp. - str.
                         14:00 Composer.

LANE, Richard B.
—— FERN HILL (FOR TENOR AND ORCH.) (Text: Dylan Thomas)
    2,1,1,1 - 4,3,3,1 - timp.,perc.(2) - hp. - str.   12:00 Composer.
—— FOUR SONGS (FOR MEZZO SOPRANO AND ORCH.)
                      16:00 C. Fischer.
—— PASSACAGLIA
    str.   C. Fischer.

LANG, C. S.
—— LET ALL THE WORLD IN EVERY CORNER SING (FOR MIXED CHORUS AND ORCH.)
                      8:00 Bo. Hawkes.

LÁNG, István
—— CONCERTINO FOR XYLOPHONE AND ORCH.
    *2,2,*3,2 - 4,3,3,1 - timp.,perc.,xyl. - pf. - str.   10:00 Bo. Hawkes.
—— CONCERTO BUCOLICO (FOR HORN AND ORCH.)
    hn. - timp.(3),vibra. - hp. - cemb. - str.   11:00 Bo. Hawkes.
—— CONCERTO FOR STRING ORCH.
    str.   10:00 Mannheimer.
—— MARIO AND THE MAGICIAN (1-ACT DANCE-DRAMA, AFTER THOMAS MANN) %
    *3,*3,*3,*3 - 4,3,3,1 - perc.(4),cel. - hp. - pf. - str.   Mannheimer.
—— THREE SENTENCES FROM "ROMEO AND JULIET"
    str.   14:30 Bo. Hawkes.

LANG, Max
—— CONCERTINO POUR TROMPETTES, CORDES ET BATTERIE
                      18:00 S.U.I.S.A.
—— THE GOLDEN CALF (SUITE FROM THE BALLET)
    1,0,1,0 - 0,0,0,0 - timp.,perc. - hp. - pf. - str.   14:00 Modern.

LANG, Walter
—— CONCERTINO FÜR ORCH., OP. 51
    2,2,2,2 - 2,2,0,0 - timp. - str.   11:00 S.U.I.S.A.
—— FESTIVE SONATA, OP. 25
    str.   6:00 Henmar.
—— KONZERTANTE SUITE (FÜR 2 KLAVIERE STREICHORCH.), OP. 65
    2 pf. - str.   13:00 S.U.I.S.A.
—— SINFONIE FÜR GROSSES ORCH., OP. 45
    3,*3,*3,*3 - 4,3,3,1 - timp.,perc. - hp. - pf. - str.   35:00 S.U.I.S.A.

LANGE, Arthur
—— ANTELOPE VALLEY
    *3,*3,*3,2 - 4,3,3,1 - timp.,perc.(3),cel. - hp. - str.
                         12:00 Composer.
—— ARABESQUE (FOR HARP AND ORCH.)
    1,1,2,1 - 2,2,0,0 - timp.,perc. - hp. - str.   13:00 Composer.
—— BIG TREES
    *3,*3,*3,2 - 4,3,3,1 - timp.,perc.,cel. - hp. - str.   13:00 Composer.
—— THE FISHERMAN AND HIS SOUL (FOUR SYMPHONIC MURALS, FOR NARRATOR AND ORCH.) (BASED ON WILDE'S FAIRY TALE)
    1(alt. with alto fl.),1(alt. with Eng. hn.),1(alt. with b.-cl.),0 - 1,0,0,0 - cel.(alt. with pf.) - str.   23:00 Fox.
—— A GOSLING IN GOTHAM (SYMPHONIC NARRATIVE)
    2(2nd alt. with picc.),1(alt. with Eng. hn.),*3(2 alt. with 2 ten. sax.)2 sax.1 - 2,3,3,1 - timp.,perc. (3),xyl. -guit. - hp. - 2 pf.(2nd alt. with cel.) - str.   23:00 Composer.

—— MOUNT WHITNEY (SYMPHONIC POEM)
2,2(2nd alt. with Eng. hn.),2,2 - 4,3,3,1 - timp.,perc. (3),cel.,vibra.
- hp. - str.   12:00 Composer.
—— SYMPHONY NO. 1 (IN 3 MOVTS.)
*3,2(2nd alt. with Eng. hn.),2,2 - 4,3,3,1 - timp.,perc.(3),cel. - hp. -
str.   29:00 Composer.
—— TWO ORIENTAL MOODS
2,2,2,2 - 4,3,3,0 - timp.,perc. (3),cel, - hp. - str.   8:00 Composer.

LANGER, Ferdinand - CAVALLY, Robert
—— CONCERTO FOR FLUTE AND ORCH.
2,2,2,2 - 2,2,0,0 - timp. - str.   SouthernTx.

LANGER, Hans-Klaus
—— BURLESQUE OVERTURE
2,2,2,2 - 4,2,2,1 - timp.,perc. - str.   11:00 Seesaw.

LANGGAARD, Rued
—— ANGELUS (THE GOLDEN LEGEND) (FOR SOLO VOICES,
CHORUS, ORGAN AND ORCH.) (REV. 1937)
K.O.D.A.
—— BEYOND ALL SEAS (HINSIDES ALLE HAVE) (1950)
K.O.D.A.
—— CARL NIELSEN, OUR GREAT COMPOSER (FOR CHORUS
AND ORCH.) (1948)
K.O.D.A.
—— CONCERTO IN ONE MOVEMENT (FOR VIOLIN AND
ORCH.) (1943)
K.O.D.A.
—— DEATH OF A HERO (HELTEDØD) (1907)
K.O.D.A.
—— DRAPA (1907)
K.O.D.A.
—— THE DREAM (FOR SOLO VOICES, CHORUS, ORGAN AND
ORCH.)(1915)
K.O.D.A.
—— EVENING BELLS (TONE PICTURE)(FOR BARITONE AND
ORCH.)(1915)
K.O.D.A.
—— HERMOD (1947)
K.O.D.A.
—— HVIDBJERG-DRAPA (FOR CHORUS AND ORCH.)(1948)
K.O.D.A.
—— INTERDICT (FOR ORGAN AND ORCH.)(1948)
K.O.D.A.
—— JEPHTA (FOR SOLO VOICES, CHORUS AND ORCH.)(1948)
K.O.D.A.
—— KING VOLMER (FOR MALE CHORUS AND ORCH.)(1908)
G. Schirmer.
—— KREMATIO (A CHURCH OPERA) %
K.O.D.A.
—— LATE SUMMER (TONE PICTURE)(WITH
MEZZO-SOPRANO)(1916)
K.O.D.A.
—— LIGHT OF A WILD STAR (VILDSTJERNELYS)(FOR SOLO
VOICES, CHORUS, ORGAN AND ORCH.) (REV. 1946)
K.O.D.A.
—— MISTERIO (FOR SOLO VOICES, CHORUS AND ORCH.)
K.O.D.A.
—— MUSAE TRIUMPHANTES (FOR SOLO VOICES, CHORUS
AND ORCH.)(1906)
K.O.D.A.
—— THE PHANTOM SHIP (DØDSSEJLEREN)(1932)
K.O.D.A.
—— RES ABSURDA (FOR CHORUS AND ORCH.)
K.O.D.A.
—— SPHEREMUSIC (FOR SOPRANO, 2 ALTOS, SATB CHORUS
AND 2 ORCHS.)
Main Orch.: 4,3,3,3 - 8,3,3,1 - timp.,perc.(9) - org. - str.
20:00 G. Schirmer.
Auxiliary Orch.(in distance): 2,1,2,0 - 1,0,0,0 - timp. - hp. - str.
—— SPHINX (MUSICAL TABLEAU)
3,3,3,3 - 4,3,4,1 - timp.,perc.(3) - str.   9:00 G. Schirmer.
—— SULAMITH (FOR SOLO VOICES, FEMALE CHORUS AND
ORCH.)(1949)
K.O.D.A.
—— SYMPHONY NO. 1 (SINFONIA SONORA) (CLIFF
PASTORALES) (REV. 1911)
K.O.D.A.
—— SYMPHONY NO. 2 (BREAK OF SPRING) (WITH SOPRANO
SOLO) (1913)
K.O.D.A.

—— SYMPHONY NO. 3 (LA MELODIA) (ROAR OF YOUTH)
(WITH SOLO PIANO AND OPTIONAL CHORUS) (1915)
K.O.D.A.
—— SYMPHONY NO. 4 (LEAF-FALL) (1916)
33:00 Henmar.
—— SYMPHONY NO. 5 (STEPPE NATURE) (1918)
K.O.D.A.
—— SYMPHONY NO. 6 (THE HEAVEN-TEARING) (1919)
3,3,3,3 - 4,8,3,1 - timp.,perc.(6 incl. 4 on timp.),cel.,bells,glock. - 2
hp. - org. - str.   23:00 Henmar.
—— SYMPHONY NO. 7
3,3,3,3 - 4,3,3,1 - timp. - str.   20:00 G. Schirmer.
—— SYMPHONY NO. 8 (MEMORIES OF AMALIEN CASTLE)
(1928)
K.O.D.A.
—— SYMPHONY NO. 9 (QUEEN DAGMAR) (1942)
K.O.D.A.
—— SYMPHONY NO. 10 (YON THUNDER DWELLING)(1944)
K.O.D.A.
—— SYMPHONY NO. 11 (IXION)(1945)
K.O.D.A.
—— SYMPHONY NO. 12 (HELSINGEBORG)(1946)
K.O.D.A.
—— SYMPHONY NO. 13 (BELIEF IN MIRACLES)(1947)
K.O.D.A.
—— SYMPHONY NO. 14 (THE MORNING)(1948)
K.O.D.A.
—— SYMPHONY NO. 15 (STORM AT SEA)(1948)
K.O.D.A.
—— SYMPHONY NO. 16 (DELUGE OF SUN)(1951)
K.O.D.A.
—— A THING OF THE PAST (SAGA BLOT)(1917)
K.O.D.A.
—— THE TIME OF THE END (FOR SOLO VOICES, CHORUS AND
ORCH.) (REV. 1939)
K.O.D.A.

LANGLAIS, Jean
—— CONCERTO NO. 1 FOR ORGAN AND ORCH.
2,2,2,2 - 0,0,0,0 - org. - str.   Belw-Mills.
—— CONCERTO NO. 2 FOR ORGAN AND STRING ORCH.
org. - str.   Belw-Mills.

LANGLEY, Bernard Peter Francis
—— CONCERTO FOR CELLO AND ORCH.
2,2,2,2 - 4,2,3,0 - timp.,perc.,cel. - hp. - str.   14:00 S.A.M.R.O.
—— CONCERTO 1962 (FOR CELLO AND ORCH.)
2,2,3,2 - 4,2,3,1 - timp.,perc. - str.   14:00 S.A.M.R.O.
—— SUITE FOR SMALL ORCH.
2,2,2,2 - 3,0,0,0 - timp.,perc. - str.   14:00 S.A.M.R.O.
—— THE TEMPTATIONS OF CHRIST (FOR BARITONE, TENOR,
DOUBLE MIXED CHORUS, STRING QUARTET AND ORCH.)
2,2,3,2 - 4,2,3,1 - timp.,perc. - str.   30:00 S.A.M.R.O.
—— VARIATIONS AND FUGUE ON AN EASTER HYMN (FOR
PIANO AND ORCH.)
2,2,3,2 - 4,2,3,1 - timp.,perc. - pf. - str.   15:00 S.A.M.R.O.

LANGLEY, James
—— CONCERTO FOR STRING QUARTET AND STRING ORCH.
(1965)
str.   14:00 P.R.S.
—— FANTASIA ON CHRISTMAS CAROLS (1960)
2,2,2,2 - 4,2,3,0 - timp.,perc. - str.   12:00 P.R.S.
—— THE IMPORTANCE OF BEING EARNEST (SUITE)(1965)
2,1,2,1 - 2,0,0,0 - timp. - str.   10:00 P.R.S.
—— OVERTURE AND BEGINNERS (1965)
2,2,2,2 - 4,2,3,0 - timp.,perc. - str.   4:30 P.R.S.
—— OVERTURE FOR A RESTORATION COMEDY (1958)
2,2,2,2 - 4,2,3,1 - timp.,perc.   8:00 P.R.S.
—— SINFONIETTA (1960)
2,2,2,2 - 4,3,3,1 - timp. - str.   25:00 P.R.S.
—— VARIAZIONI DA CAMERA (1961)
2,1,2,1 - 2,1,0,0 - str.   23:00 P.R.S.

LANGSTROTH, Ivan
—— INDIAN ROMANCE
2,*3,*3,2 - 2,2,2,0 - timp.,perc. - str.   8:00 Composer.
—— SYMPHONY IN C MAJOR, OP. 31 (IN 4 MOVTS.)
*3,2,2,2 - 4,4,3,1 - timp.,perc.,cel. - pf. - str.   30:00 Composer.

LANJEAN, Marc
—— LE PRINCE TRAVESTI (BALLET) %
1-2,1-2,0,1 - 0,2,0,0 - timp. - hpsc.(or pf.) - str.   15:00 Presser.

—— SCÈNE EN FORÊT
    2,2,2,1 - 2,2,2,0 - timp.,perc. - hp. - str.   12:00 Presser.

LANNIN, Paul
—— GREEK ÈPIPHANY SUITE (IN 4 MOVTS.)
    Composer.

LANNOY, Robert
—— LAMENTO UKRAINIEN
    timp. - str.   11:00 Presser.

LANTIER, Pierre Louis
—— CONCERTINO FOR PIANO AND ORCH.
    1,1,1,1 - 1,1,0,0 - timp. - pf. - str.   14:00 Baron.
—— CONCERTO FOR PIANO AND ORCH.
    24:00 Presser.

LANZA, Alcides
—— CONCERTO FOR PIANO AND ORCH. (1964) (IN 3 MOVTS.)
    2,0,*3,0 - 2,2,2,0 - perc.(5),vibra. - pf.(amplified with contact
    microphones) - str.   15:00 Bo. Hawkes.
—— EIDESIS II (1967)
    0,0,0,0 - 2,0,2,1 - timp.,perc.(3),vibra.,xyl. - 3 c.,2 d.-b.(amplified
    with contact microphones)   11:00 Bo. Hawkes.
—— EIDESIS III (FOR 1 OR 2 ORCHESTRAS AND ELECTRONIC
    SOUNDS) (1971)
    2,*3,2,*3 - 4,2,5,2 - timp.,perc.(8),bells,xyl. - tape-recorder - org. -
    pf. - str.   15:00 Bo. Hawkes.
—— EIDESIS SINFONICA (1963)
    3(3rd alt. with picc.),2,*3,*3 - 2,2,3,1 - timp.,perc.(7),cel. - hp. -
    pf. - str.   11:00 Bo. Hawkes.
—— KRON'KELZ 70 (CHRONICLES 70) (1970) (FOR TWO
    NARRATORS, CHORUS, TAPE, AMPLIFICATION AND
    ORCH.) (Text: Composer)
    *3,*3,1 Eᵇ cl.,*3,*2 - 2,2,2,2 - timp.,perc.,bells,glock.,vibra.,xyl. -
    org. - pf. - str.   15:00 Bo. Hawkes.
—— KRON'KELZ 75 (WITH CONTRALTO, BARITONE,
    ELECTRONIC SOUNDS AND ELECTRONIC EXTENSIONS)
    (1975) (Text: Composer)
    1(alt. with picc. and alto. fl.),1(alt. with Eng. hn.),0,0 - 1,0,0,0 -
    perc.(2),glock.,vibra. - 4 tape-recorders(plus amplification for
    voices) - hp. - pf. - mandolin - 1 c.,1 d.-b.   15:00 Bo. Hawkes.
—— PENETRATIONS V (1970) (INSTRUMENTATION OPTIONAL)
    Maximum: 1,0,*2,*1 - 1,0,2,1 - timp.,perc.,vibra. - org. - pf. - 1
    vla.,1 c.,1 d.-b.   14:00 Bo. Hawkes.

LAPEYRE, Thérèse
—— À JOHN GLENN
    2,2,2,2 - 1,2,1,0 - timp.,perc. - hp. - str.   Presser.

LAPHAM, Claude
—— CONCERTO FOR ALTO SAXOPHONE AND ORCH.
    1. Andante solenne; 2. Andante piangendo; 3. Allegro brilliante
    1,1,2,alto sax.,1 - 4,2,3,1 - timp.,perc. - hp. - str.   28:00 Leeds.

LA PORTA, John D.
—— CONCERTINO FOR ALTO SAXOPHONE AND ORCH. (IN 1
    MOVT.)
    1,1,2,alto sax.,1 - 1,4,3,0 - timp.,perc.(1) - pf. - str.   5:00 Earl.

LAPORTE, André
—— NIGHT MUSIC (FOR LARGE ORCH.)
    Hans Gerig.

LARMANJAT, Jacques
—— SERENADE, OP. 34
    2,2,2,alto sax.,2 - 4,2,0,0 - timp.,perc. - hp. - pf. - str.   10:00 EV.

LA ROTELLA, Pasquale
—— CORSARESCA (SYMPHONIC SUITE) (IN 5 MOVTS.)
    3,3,3,2 - 4,3,3,1 - timp.,perc.,cel.,glock. - hp. - pf. - str.
    29:00 Bo. Hawkes.

LARSON, Sigvard
—— LITTLE SUITE FOR STRINGS AND PIANO
    pf. - str.   9:00 Nordiska.

LARSSON, Lars-Erik
—— ADAGIO
    str.   5:00 Bo. Hawkes.
—— BAROCOCO, OP. 64 (1973)
    2,2,2,2 - 2,2,1,0 - timp.,perc.(3) - str.   Gehrmans.

—— CONCERT OVERTURE NO. 1, OP. 4
    2,2,2,2 - 4,2,3,1 - timp.,perc. - str.   8:00 S.T.I.M.
—— CONCERT OVERTURE NO. 3, OP. 34
    2,2,2,2 - 4,2,3,1 - timp. - str.   8:00 Bo. Hawkes.
—— CONCERTINO FOR BASSOON AND STRINGS, OP. 45, NO. 4
    (1955)
    bn. - str.   11:00 Bo. Hawkes.
—— CONCERTINO FOR CELLO AND STRINGS, OP. 45, NO. 10
    (1956)
    str.   11:00 Bo. Hawkes.
—— CONCERTINO FOR CLARINET AND STRINGS, OP. 45, NO. 3
    (1957)
    cl. - str.   12:30 Bo. Hawkes.
—— CONCERTINO FOR DOUBLE-BASS AND STRINGS, OP. 45,
    NO. 11
    str.   12:00 Bo. Hawkes.
—— CONCERTINO FOR FLUTE AND STRINGS, OP. 45, NO. 1
    (1955)
    fl. - str.   10:00 Bo. Hawkes.
—— CONCERTINO FOR HORN AND STRINGS, OP. 45, NO. 5
    (1955)
    hn. - str.   13:00 Bo. Hawkes.
—— CONCERTINO FOR OBOE AND STRINGS, OP. 45, NO. 2
    (1955)
    ob. - str.   9:30 Bo. Hawkes.
—— CONCERTINO FOR PIANO AND STRINGS, OP. 45, NO. 12
    (1957)
    pf. - str.   17:00 Bo. Hawkes.
—— CONCERTINO FOR TROMBONE AND STRINGS, OP. 45, NO.
    7 (1955)
    trb. - str.   11:00 Bo. Hawkes.
—— CONCERTINO FOR TRUMPET AND STRINGS OP. 45, NO. 6
    (1953)
    tpt. - str.   8:00 Bo. Hawkes.
—— CONCERTINO FOR VIOLA AND STRINGS, OP. 45, NO. 9
    (1956)
    str.   13:30 Bo. Hawkes.
—— CONCERTINO FOR VIOLIN AND STRINGS, OP. 45, NO. 8
    (1956)
    str.   12:30 Bo. Hawkes.
—— CONCERTO FOR CELLO AND ORCH., OP. 37
    1,1,1,1 - 2,1,0,0 - timp. - str.   18:00 S.T.I.M.
—— CONCERTO FOR SAXOPHONE AND STRINGS, OP. 14
    sax. - str.   21:00 Gehrmans.
—— CONCERTO FOR VIOLIN AND ORCH., OP. 37
    1,1,1,1 - 2,1,0,0 - timp. - str.   25:00 Gehrmans.
—— THE DISGUISED GOD (LYRIC SUITE), OP. 24 (FOR
    SOPRANO, BARITONE, CHORUS AND ORCH.)
    2,2,2,2 - 2,2,2,0 - timp. - hp. - str.   31:00 Gehrmans.
—— DUE AUGURI, OP. 62 (1971)
    2,2,2,2 - 4,3,3,0 - timp.(4 players) - hp. - str.   15:00 Gehrmans.
—— EPILOGUE TO A WINTER SAGA, OP. 18 (1938)
    2,2,2,2 - 2,2,1,0 - hp. - str.   4:00 Gehrmans.
—— GUSTAVIAN SUITE, OP. 28
    fl. - cemb. - str.   12:00 S.T.I.M.
—— IN MEMORIAM (1965)
    hp. - str.   6:00 Gehrmans.
—— INVOCATIO, OP. 21 (WITH CHORUS AD LIB)
    2,2,2,2 - 4,2,3,1 - timp. - str.   9:00 S.T.I.M.
—— JORDEN SJUNDER (POEM), OP. 23
    2,2,2,2 - 4,2,3,1 - timp.,perc. - hp. - str.   7:00 S.T.I.M.
—— LINDEN (BALLET) %
    1,1,2,1 - 2,1,0,0 - timp.,perc.(3),cel. - hp. - str.   40:00 S.T.I.M.
—— LYRIC FANTASY, OP. 54 (FOR SMALL ORCH.)(1967)
    1,1,1,1 - 1,0,0,0 - str.   8:30 Gehrmans.
—— MUSIC FOR ORCH., OP. 40
    2,2,2,2 - 4,2,3,1 - timp. - str.   23:00 Bo. Hawkes.
—— OSTINATO, OP. 17
    2,2,2,2 - 4,3,3,1 - timp. - str.   8:00 Bo. Hawkes.
—— PASSACAGLIA FROM THE OPERA "THE PRINCESS OF
    CYPRUS"
    2,2,2,2 - 4,3,3,1 - timp.,perc. - hp. - str.   5:00 S.T.I.M.
—— PASTORAL SUITE, OP. 19
    2,2,2,2 - 2,2,0,0 - timp. - str.   13:00 Gehrmans.
—— SANKTA LUCIA (SUITE), OP. 25
    2,2,2,2 - 2,2,1,0 - timp.,perc. - str.   15:00 S.T.I.M.
—— DET SVENSKA LANDET, OP. 27
    2,2,2,2 - 2,2,1,0 - timp.,perc.   17:00 S.T.I.M.
—— SYMPHONIC SKETCH, OP. 5
    2,2,2,2 - 2,2,0,0 - str.   6:00 S.T.I.M.
—— THREE ORCHESTRA PIECES, OP. 49 (1960)
    2,2,2,3 - 4,2,3,1 - timp. - str.   17:00 Gehrmans.

—— EN VINTERSAGA (THE WINTERS TALE) (SUITE), OP. 18
2,2,2,2 - 2,2,1,0 - timp. - str.   9:00 Bo. Hawkes.

LARSSON, Lars-Erik - GERTLER, Endre
—— CONCERTO FOR VIOLIN AND ORCH., OP. 42 (1952)
28:00 Gehrmans.

LASKER, Henry
—— BEAUTY AND THE BEAST (OPERA) % (Text: Composer)
*3,*3,*3,*3 - 4,3,2,1 - timp.,perc.(3) - hp. - pf. - str. 90:00 Boston.
—— HAVE A HEART (BALLET) % (IN 7 MOVTS.)
*3,*3,*3,*3 - 4,3,2,1 - timp.,perc.(3-4) - hp. - str.   25:00 Boston.
—— JACK AND THE BEANSTALK (A SHORT OPERA, WITH NARRATION) % (Text: Composer)
*3,*3,*3,*3 - 4,3,2,1 - timp.,perc.(3) - pf. - str.   55:00 Boston.
—— THE POWER OF INDUSTRY (BALLET) % (IN 5 MOVTS.)
2,2,2,1 ten. sax.,*3 - 4,2,3,1 - timp.,perc.(3-4),xyl. - pf. - str.   18:00 Boston.
—— SUITE FOR SYMPHONY ORCHESTRA (IN 5 MOVTS.)
*3,*3,*3,*3 - 4,3,2,1 - timp.,perc.(3),cel. - hp. - pf. - str.   16:00 Boston.

LÁSZLÓ, Alexander
—— CHINA (SUITE FOR SOPRANO, CHORUS AND ORCH.)
3(alt. with picc. and alto fl.),1(alt. with Eng. hn.),0,0 - 3,0,bass trb.,0 - timp.,perc.(3),glock.,xyl. - cimbalom - guit. - mandolin - hammond org. (alt. with cel.), theremin - str.   26:00 Guild Cal.
—— CONCERTSTÜCK NO. 2 (FOR PIANO AND ORCH.)
2,2,2,2 - 4,2,3,0 - timp. - perc.(2) - pf. - str.   12:00 Composer.
—— THE GHOST TRAIN OF MARSHALL PASS (AN AMERICAN TALE)
2(1 alt. with picc.),2(2nd alt. with Eng. hn.),3,2 - 4,3,3,1 - timp.,perc.(2-3),glock. - hp. - pf. - str.   7:00 Guild Cal.
—— HOLLYWOOD CONCERTO
2(1 alt. with picc.),2,3,2 - 4,3,3,1 - timp.,perc.(3-4), glock. - hp. - pf. - str.   16:00 Guild Cal.
—— IMPROVISATIONS ON "OH SUSANNAH"
2(2nd alt. with picc.),2,2,2 - 4,2,3,1 - timp.,perc. - hp. - str.   11:00 Guild Cal.
—— LUSTSPIEL OVERTURE (PRELUDE TO A COMEDY), OP. 4
2(2nd alt. with picc.),2,2,2 - 4,2,3,0 - timp.,perc.(2) - str.   10:00 Composer.
—— MANA HAWAII (A SYMPHONIC LEGEND)
25:00 Guild Cal.
—— PACIFIC TRIPTYCH (SUITE) (IN 3 MOVTS.)
*3,2,2,2 - 4,3,3,1 - timp.,perc.,bells,cel.,glock.,vibra.,xyl. - hp. - str.   21:00 Guild Cal.
—— ROULETTE HEMATOLOGIQUE (A FANTASY, IN 3 MOVTS.) (1970)
2,2,2,2 - 4,2,3,1 - timp.,perc.(2),bells,glock.,vibra.,xyl. - hp. - str.   36:00 Guild Cal.

LATHAM, William P.
—— AND THOU, AMERICA (OVERTURE)
3(3rd alt. with picc.),2,2,2 b.-cl.,*3 - 4,3,3,1 - timp.,perc.(2) - hp. - str.   8:00 Composer.
—— FANTASY FOR VIOLIN AND ORCH.
*3,2,*3,*3 - 4,3,3,1 - timp.,perc.(2),cel. - str.   10:00 Composer.
—— THE LADY OF SHALOTT (SYMPHONIC POEM)
*3,*3,2,ten. sax.,2 - 4,3,3,1 - timp.,perc.(3),bells, cel. - hp. - str.   12:00 Composer.
—— A LENTEN LETTER (SOLO CANTATA) (FOR DRAMATIC SOPRANO, STRINGS AND PERCUSSION) (1974) (Texts: Aleksandr Solzhenitsyn and Others)
timp.,perc.(4),bells - str.   10:00 Composer.
—— PEACE (FOR MIXED CHORUS AND ORCH.)
2,*3,*3,*3 - 4,3,3,1 - timp.,perc.(2) - str.   15:00 Composer.
—— A PROPHECY OF PEACE (FOR MIXED CHORUS AND ORCH.)
2(2nd alt. with picc.),2,2,2 - 4,3,3,1 - timp.,perc. - org. - pf. - str.   5:00 Summy-Bir.
—— SINFONIETTA (IN 4 MOVTS.)
2(2nd alt. with picc.),2,2,2 - 2,2,0,0 - timp. - str.   17:00 Presser.

LATTUADA, Felice
—— PRELUDE AND FUGUE IN E FLAT (1946)
3,3,3,3 - 4,3,3,1 - timp.,perc.,cel.,glock. - hp. - pf. - str.   12:00 Leeds.

LAUDENSLAGER, Harold
—— THE CREATION (CANTATA ON GENESIS) (1956)
str.   14:00 Composer.

—— IN MEMORIAM (ELEGY) (FOR ENGLISH HORN AND CHAMBER ORCH.) (1959))
0,*1,0,0 - 0,0,0,0 - timp. - str.   10:00 Composer.
—— LITTLE SUITE (FOR CHAMBER ORCH.) (1958) (IN 5 MOVTS.)
1,*2,0,0 - 0,0,0,0 - pf. - str.   14:00 C. Fischer.
—— THE STRAIGHT (OVERTURE FOR ORCH.) (1963)
*3,*3,*4,*3 - 4,4,3,1 - timp.,perc.(4) - hp. - str.   5:00 C. Fischer.

LAUFER, Beatrice
—— ADAM'S RIB (FOR SOLO VOICES, CHORUS AND ORCH.)
(Text: Biblical and John Milton)
*2,1,*3,2 - 2,2,2,0 - timp.,perc.,bells,xyl. - hp. - str.   15:00 Composer.
—— CONCERTO FOR CHAMBER ORCH. (IN 3 MOVTS.)
1,1,1,1 - 1,0,0,0 - pf. - str.   15:00 Composer.
—— CONCERTO FOR FLUTE, OBOE, TRUMPET AND STRINGS (IN 3 MOVTS.)
1,1,0,0 - 0,1,0,0 - str.   14:00 Composer.
—— CONCERTO FOR VIOLIN AND ORCHESTRA (1966)
*3,*2,*3,*3 - 4,3,3,1 - timp.,perc.(3),bells,xyl. - str.   40:00 Composer.
—— FESTIVAL (FROM "TWO DANCES")
2(2nd alt. with picc.),2,2,2 - 4,2,2,0 - timp., perc. - hp. - str.   6:00 Composer.
—— FROLIC (FROM "TWO DANCES")
2(2nd alt. with picc.),1,2,1 - 2,2,2,0 - timp.,perc.,cel. - hp. - str.   6:00 Composer.
—— ILE ("OIL") (1-ACT OPERA, AFTER EUGENE O'NEILL'S PLAY) %
Composer.
—— MY BROTHER'S KEEPER (2-ACT OPERA) % (1968) (Text: Biblical)
*3,*2,*3,*3 - 4,3,3,1 - timp.,perc.(3),bells,glock.,xyl. - hp. - electric org. - str.   180:00 Composer.
—— OVERTURE FOR ORCHESTRA ("CRUCIBLE")
*3,*3,*3,2 - 4,3,3,1 - timp.,perc.,bells,cel.,xyl. - str.   9:00 Composer.
—— PRELUDE AND FUGUE
*3,2,*3,2 - 4,3,3,1 - timp.,perc.,bells,xyl. - hp. - str.   8:30 Composer.
—— SYMPHONY NO. 1 (IN 3 MOVTS.)
2(1 alt. with picc.),2,*3,2 - 4,2,2,0 - timp.,perc.(2),cel. - hp. - str.   22:00 Composer.
—— SYMPHONY NO. 2 (IN 3 MOVTS.)
*3,2(1 alt. with Eng. hn.),*3,2 - 4,3,3,1 - timp.,perc.,bells,xyl. - hp. - str.   21:00 Composer.

LAUFER, Edward C.
—— VARIATIONS - PART 1 (1967)
2(2nd alt. with picc.),2(2nd alt. with Eng. hn.),2,2 - 2,1,0,0 - timp. - hp. - str.   10:10 CanMusCtr.
—— VARIATIONS - PART 2 (1968)
2(2nd alt. with picc.),2(2nd alt. with Eng. hn.),2(2nd alt. with b.-cl.),2 - 1,1,0,1 - perc. - hp. - str.   9:00 CanMusCtr.

LAUNIS, Armas
—— ANDANTE RELIGIOSO (FROM THE OPERA "THE SORCERER'S SONG")(FOR VIOLIN AND ORCH.)(1932)
3,3,3,2 - 4,3,3,1 - timp.,perc. - hp. - str.   4:00 FinnMICtr.
—— ASLAK HETTA (OPERA) % (1922) (Text: Composer)
3,3,3,2 - 4,3,3,1 - timp.,perc.(3),cel. - hp. - str.   FinnMICtr.
—— FESTIVE CANTATA (FOR SATB CHORUS AND ORCH.) (1910) (Text: Elina Vuorenala)
2,1,2,1 - 2,2,1,0 - timp. - str.   FinnMICtr.
—— JEHUDITH (OPERA) % (1940) (Text: Composer)
3,3,3,2 - 4,3,3,1 - timp.,perc.(3),cel.,xyl. - hp. - str.   FinnMICtr.
—— THE KARELIAN MAGIC KERCHIEF (OPERA) % (1937) (Text: Composer)
3,3,3,2 - 4,3,3,1 - timp.,perc.- hp. - str.   FinnMICtr.
—— KARELIAN SUITE (FROM THE OPERA "ONCE UPON A TIME")(1952)
3,3,3,2 - 4,3,3,1 - timp.,perc.,cel.,xyl. - hp. - str.   7:00 FinnMICtr.
—— KULLERVO (OPERA) % (1917) (Text: A. Kivi, E. Leino and A. Launis)
3,3,3,2 - 4,3,3,1 - timp.,perc.(3),bells,xyl. - hp. - str.   FinnMICtr.
—— NORTHERN SUITE (FOR VIOLIN AND ORCH.)(1950)(IN 4 MOVTS.)
3,3,3,2 - 4,3,3,1 - timp.,perc. - hp. - str.   11:00 FinnMICtr.
—— THE SEVEN BROTHERS (OPERA) % (1913) (Text: A. Kivi and A. Launis)
3,3,3,2 - 4,3,3,1 - timp.,perc.(3) - hp. - str.   FinnMICtr.
—— THE SORCERER'S SONG (OPERA) % (1932) (Text: Composer)
3,3,3,2 - 4,3,3,1 - timp.,perc. - lute - hp. - org. - str.   FinnMICtr.

LAURICELLA, Remo
—— AURORA
    2,2,2,2 - 4,3,3,1 - timp.,perc. - hp. - str.   12:00 P.R.S.
—— BOLIVIANA
    2,1,2,1 - 2,2,3,0 - timp.,perc. - hp. - str.   4:00 P.R.S.
—— CHIAROSCURO
    2,2,2,2 - 4,3,3,1 - timp.,perc. - str.   4:00 P.R.S.
—— CONCERTO FOR VIOLIN AND ORCH.
    2,2,2,2 - 4,2,3,1 - timp.,perc. - hp. - str.   30:00 P.R.S.
—— DIABOLISMES (FOR VIOLIN AND ORCH.)
    2,1,2,1 - 2,2,3,0 - timp.,perc. - hp. - str.   11:30 P.R.S.
—— LONDINIUM
    2,2,2,2 - 4,3,3,1 - timp.,perc. - hp. - str.   12:00 P.R.S.
—— OVERTURE: FLEET STREET
    2(2nd alt. with picc.),1,2,1 - 2,2,3,0 - timp.,perc. - hp. - str.
                                                          6:00 Galaxy.
—— PETITE SUITE
    2,1,2,1 - 2,2,3,0 - timp.,perc. - hp. - str.   13:30 Belw-Mills.
—— PROLEGOMENA ARCHAIA
    2,2,2,2 - 4,3,3,1 - timp.,perc. - hp. - str.   12:00 P.R.S.
—— SINFONIA BREVE
    2,2,2,2 - 4,2,3,2 - timp.,perc. - hp. - str.   16:00 P.R.S.
—— SUITE ROMANTIQUE
    2,1,2,1 - 2,2,3,0 - timp.,perc. - hp. - str.   14:00 P.R.S.

LAURIDSEN, Morten
—— TE DEUM (FOR CHORUS AND ORCH.) (1968) (IN 3 MOVTS.)
    0,0,0,0 - 1,1,1,1 - timp. - str.   15:00 Composer.

LAUSENMEYER - BODART, Eugen
—— SYMPHONY IN D MAJOR
    0,2,0,0 - 2,0,0,0 - str.   14:00 Mannheimer.

LAVAGNE, André
—— CONCERT DANS UN PARC (CONCERTO FOR PIANO AND ORCH.) (IN 4 MOVTS.)
    *3,*3,2,2 - 4,3,3,1 - timp.,perc.,cel.,xyl. - hp. - pf. - str.
                                                          20:00 Presser.
—— CONCERTO ROMANTIQUE (FOR CELLO AND ORCH.)
    3,3,2,2 - 4,3,2,1 - timp.,perc.,cel. - hp. - str.   24:00 Presser.
—— KERMESSE (BALLET SUITE)
    *2,*3,2,2 - 4,3,3,1 - timp.,perc. - str.   Presser.
—— POÈMES D'ADONIS
    2,2,2,2 - 2,2,1,0 - timp.,perc.,cel. - hp. - pf. - str.   20:30 Presser.

LAVAGNINO, F.
—— L' ANNUNCIAZIONE (CONCERTO SACRO PER VIOLINI)
    str.   3:00 Bo. Hawkes.
—— CONCERTO FOR OBOE AND ORCH.
    ob. - perc.,cel. - pf. - str.   14:00 Bo. Hawkes.
—— CONCERTO FOR VIOLIN AND ORCH.
    2,2,2,2 - 4,2,2,0 - timp.,perc.,cel. - hp. - str.   32:00 Bo. Hawkes.
—— OVERTURE TO "LA LOCANDIERA"
    2,2,2,2 - 2,2,0,0 - timp.,perc. - str.   6:00 Bo. Hawkes.
—— TEMPE ALTO (EPISODIO SINFONICO)
    3,3,3,3 - 4,3,3,1 - timp.,perc.,cel. - 1-2 hp. - str.
                                                          18:00 Bo. Hawkes.

LAVIN, Carlos - MUELLER, Fritz A.
—— LAMENTATIONES HUILLICHES (SUITE OF 3 ARAUCANIAN SONGS) (1933)
    2,2(2nd alt. with Eng. hn.),2,2 - 3,3,3,0 - timp.,perc. - str.
                                                          8:00 Fleisher.

LA VIOLETTE, Wesley
—— CHORALE FOR ORCH.
    2,*3,2,2 - 4,2,3,1 - timp.,perc.(2) - hp. - str.   4:30 Composer.
—— COLLEGIANA (FESTIVAL RHAPSODY FOR ORCH.)
    *4,*3(3rd alt. with Eng. hn.),3,*4 - 4,3,3,1 - timp. - str.
                                                          10:00 Composer.
—— CONCERTO FOR STRING QUARTET AND ORCH. (IN 3 MOVTS.)
    *3,*3,2,*4 - 4,2,3,1 - timp.,perc. - str.   23:00 Composer.
—— CONCERTO FOR VIOLIN AND ORCH. (IN 3 MOVTS.)
    2(1st alt. with picc.),2,2,3(3rd alt. with c.-bn.) - 4,2,3,1 - timp.,perc.(4),bells,cel.,glock.,vibra. - hp. - str.   35:00 Composer.
—— LARGO LYRICO
    timp. - hp. - str.   Leeds.
—— NOCTURNE (FOR CHAMBER ORCH.)
    1(alt. with picc.),0,0,2 - 1,1,0,0 - timp.,perc. - str.   9:00 Composer.
—— ODE TO AN IMMORTAL
    3(3rd alt. with picc.),2,2,2 - 4,3,3,0 - timp. - hp. - org. - str.
                                                          12:00 Composer.

—— OSIRIS (AN EGYPTIAN LEGEND)
    *3(1 alt. with alto fl.),3,2,3 - 4,3,3,1 - timp.,cel. - 2 hp. - org. - pf. - str.   19:00 Composer.
—— PENETRELLA (PENETRELLA - TO PENETRATE THE INNER LIFE)
    str.   12:00 Composer.
—— PRELUDE AND ARIA
    2(1st alt. with picc.),*3,0,3(3rd alt. with c.-bn.) - 4,3(1st alt. with flg. hn.),3,bar.,1 - timp.,perc.(4),cel. - 2 hp. - str. 12:00 Composer.
—— THE ROAD TO CALVARY (CANTATA) (FOR NARRATOR, SOPRANO, ALTO, CHORUS AND ORCH.) (Text: Composer)
    1(alt. with picc.),*2,2,2 - 2,2,0,0 - timp.,perc.,cel. - hp. - str.
                                                          27:00 Composer.
—— SAN FRANCISCO OVERTURE ("MUSIC FROM THE HIGH SIERRAS")
    *3,2,2,*4 - 4,2,3,1 - timp.,perc.(4),cel.,vibra.,xyl. - hp. - str.
                                                          14:00 Composer.
—— SUITE FOR CHAMBER ORCH. (IN 5 MOVTS.)
    1(alt. with picc.),2(2nd alt. with Eng. hn.),*3,*2 - 2,1,1,0 - timp. - hp. - str.   11:00 Composer.
—— SYMPHONY (IN 3 MOVTS.)
    *3,*3,2,sax.,*4 - 4,3,3,1 - timp.,perc.(5),vibra. - hp. - str.
                                                          35:00 Composer.
—— SYMPHONY NO. 2 ("TOM THUMB" - A CHILDREN'S SYMPHONY) (IN 3 MOVTS.)
    2,2,2,4 sax.,0 - 0,0,0,0 - timp. - str.   8:00 Composer.

LAVRY, Marc
—— CONCERTO NO. 2 FOR PIANO AND ORCH. (1947)
    3,3,3,3 - 3,3,3,1 - timp.,perc.,cel. - hp. - str.   23:00 IsMuPublns.
—— COUNTRY DANCES OF ISRAEL
    2,2,2,1 - 2,2,1,1 - timp.,perc. - pf. - str.   16:00 IsMuPublns.
—— EMEK (SYMPHONIC POEM)
    2,2,2,2 - 3,3,3,1 - timp.,perc. - hp. - str.   13:00 IsMuPublns.
—— ISRAELI DANCES
    2,2,2,2 - 3,3,3,0 - timp.,perc. - hp. - pf. - str.   18:00 IsMuPublns.
—— KUKIJAH (VARIATIONS ON A PALESTINIAN FOLKSONG)
    2,1,1,1 - 2,1,1,1 - timp.,perc. - hp. - str.   20:00 Salabert.
—— LAKE KINNERET (TONE-POEM)
    2,2,2,2 - 3,3,3,1 - timp.,perc.,xyl. - hp. - str.   13:00 IsMuPublns.
—— SABBATH EVE SERVICE (FOR SOLO VOICES, SATB CHORUS AND ORCH.)
    2,2,2,2 - 4,2,3,0 - timp. - hp. - str.   30:00 SMP.
—— SONG OF SONGS (ORATORIO) (FOR SOLO VOICES, SATB CHORUS AND ORCH.)
                                                          75:00 Bo. Hawkes.
—— TAMAR (BALLET) %
                                                          17:30 A.C.U.M.

LAWERGREN, Bo
—— ENSEMBLES (1967)
    0,2,1,0 - 1,1,1,0 - perc.(11) - pf. - str.(2,1,1,0)   15:00 Composer.

LAWRENCE, Bruce Cassels
—— SALVATOR MUNDI (FOR SOPRANO, TENOR, SATB CHORUS AND ORCH.) (1971)
    1,1,0,0 - 2,0,1,0 - perc. - str.   25:00 A.P.R.A.
—— THREE AYLESBURY SKETCHES (1975)
    *3,2,2,2 - 4,3,3,1 - timp.,perc. - pf. - str.   13:50 A.P.R.A.
—— THREE DANCES FOR TWO FLUTES AND STRINGS
    2fl. - str.   6:00 A.P.R.A.
—— THREE PIECES FOR STRING ORCH.: SET NO. 1 (1968)
    str.   8:00 A.P.R.A.
—— THREE PIECES FOR STRING ORCH.: SET NO. 2 (1970)
    str.   14:00 A.P.R.A.

LAYTON, Billy Jim
—— AN AMERICAN PORTRAIT (SYMPHONIC OVERTURE), OP. 2
    *3,*3,*3,2 - 4,3,3,1 - timp.,perc.(3) - str.   12:30 G. Schirmer.
—— DANCE FANTASY, OP. 7
    3(2nd alt. with alto fl.,3rd alt. with picc.),3(3rd alt. with Eng. hn.),3(3rd alt. with b.-cl.),3(3rd alt. with c.-bn.) - 4,1 cnt.,2,3,1 - timp.,perc.(5),bells,cel.,glock.,mar.,xyl. - hp. - pf. - str.
                                                          26:00 G. Schirmer.

LAZAR, Filip
—— CONCERTO GROSSO NO. 1, OP. 17
    0,2,0,2 - 2,1,0,0 - timp. - str.   22:00 EV.
—— CONCERTO NO. 2 FOR PIANO AND ORCH., OP. 19
    1,1,2,1 - 1,1,1,0 - timp. - pf. - str.   19:00 EV.
—— CONCERTO NO. 4, OP. 24 (CONCERTO DA CAMERA) (FOR PERCUSSIONIST AND 12 INSTRUMENTS)
    1,1,1,1 - 1,1,1,0 - perc. - pf. - str.(2,1,1,0)   20:00 EV.

—— DIVERTISSEMENT
  3,3,3,3 - 4,3,3,1 - timp.,perc.(3) - hp. - str.   12:00 EV.
—— MUSIQUE POUR RADIO
  2,2,2,2 - 2,1,0,0 - str.   9:00 EV.
—— LE RING (A 4-MINUTE ROUND)
  3,3,3,3 - 4,3,3,1 - timp.,perc.(3) - hp. - str.   4:00 EV.
—— TZIGANES (SCHERZO)
  3,3,2,3 sax.(sopr.,ten.,bar.),4 - 4,3,3,1 -
  timp.,perc.(5),cel.,glock.,xyl. - hp. - pf. - str.   18:00 EV.

LAZARUS, Daniel
—— SUITE CONCERTANTE (IN 3 MOVTS.)
  2,0,1,0 - 0,1,0,0 - bells,xyl. - str.   11:30 Eds. Fran.
—— SYMPHONIE AVEC HYMNE (WITH CHORUS) (IN 5 MOVTS.)
  3,3,3,sax.,4 - 4,3,3,1 - timp.,perc.(2),cel.,glock. - hp. - str.
                                                                 28:00 Salabert.

LAZZARI, Sylvio
—— RHAPSODY FOR VIOLIN AND ORCH.
  2,2,2,2 - 4,2,3,1 - timp.,perc. - hp. - str.   20:00 Presser.

LEAHY, Mary Weldon
—— MODERN DANCE RHAPSODY
  str.   5:00 Composer.
—— SUITE FOR STRING ORCH.
  str.   10:00 Composer.
—— SYMPHONY FOR STRINGS
  str.   20:00 Composer.
—— SYMPHONY NO. 1
                                                                 40:00 Composer.

LEBIČ, Lojze
—— KORANT
  3(3rd alt. with picc.),2(2nd alt. with Eng. hn.),3(3rd alt. with
  b.-cl.),2(2nd alt. with c.-bn.) - 4,3,3,1 - perc.(4) - hp. - pf.(alt. with
  cel.) - str.   10:00 Hans Gerig.
—— NICINA
  3(3rd alt. with picc.),2(2nd alt. with Eng. hn.),3(3rd alt. with
  b.-cl.),2(2nd alt. with c.-bn.) - 4,3,3,1 - perc.(4) - hp. - pf.(alt. with
  cel. and electric org.) - str.   12:00 Hans Gerig.
—— SENTENCES (FOR TWO PIANOS AND ORCH.)
  *3,0,3(3rd alt. with b.-cl.),*1 - 4,4,3,0 - perc.(5),cel. - hp. - 2 pf. -
  str.(0,0,4,4)   13:00 Hans Gerig.
—— VOICES (FOR STRINGS, PERCUSSION AND PLUCKING
  INSTRUMENTS)
  perc.(4) - guit.,mandolin - hp. - hpsc. - pf.(alt. with cel.) - str.
                                                                 15:00 Hans Gerig.

LE BORDAYS, Christiane
—— CONCIERTO DE AZUL (FOR GUITAR AND ORCH.)
  1,1,1,1 - 1,1,0,0 - timp.,perc. - guit. - hp.(or pf.) - str.
                                                                 19:00 Presser.

LE BOUCHER, Maurice
—— FANTAISIE CONCERTANTE (FOR OBOE AND ORCH.)
  3,1,2,3 - 2,0,0,0 - timp.,perc.,cel. - hp. - str.   11:00 Baron.
—— TROIS MORCEAUX SYMPHONIQUES
  3,2,2,2 - 4,3,3,1 - timp.,perc.,cel.,xyl. - 2 hp. - str.   12:00 Baron.

LECHNER, Konrad
—— CONTRASTS (1963)
  perc. - hpsc. - str.   Hans Gerig.

LECLAIR, Jean Marie - BOULAY, Laurence
—— CONCERTO FOR FLUTE (OR OBOE), HARPSICHORD AND
  STRINGS
  fl. (or ob.) - hpsc. - str.   17:00 Presser.
—— SCYLLA ET GLAUCUS (SUITE) (FOR STRINGS AND
  CEMBALO)
  cemb. - str.   16:00 Bo. Hawkes.

LECLAIR, Jean Marie - DUBENSKY, Arcady
—— CONCERTO GROSSO (FOR STRINGS)
  1. Andante affetuoso; 2. Intermezzo; 3. Allegro vivace
  str.   15:00 Ricordi.
—— SARABANDE ET TAMBURIN
  1,2,2,1 - 2,1,00 - timp.,perc. - str.   13:30 Belw-Mills.

LECLAIR, Jean Marie - OUBRADOUS, Fernand
—— CONCERTO IN C
  fl.(or ob. or vln.) - str.   20:00 Presser.
—— CONCERTO NO. 6 IN A, FOR VIOLIN AND STRING ORCH.
  str.   20:00 Presser.

LECLAIR, Jean Marie - WAHL, Bernard - BOULAY, Laurence
—— SONATA NO. 3 IN D MINOR
  hpsc. - str.   13:00 Mannheimer.

LEDUC, Jacques
—— CINQ CROQUIS, OP. 34 (1971)
  3,3,3,3 - 4,3,3,1 - timp.,perc. - str.   12:00 H. Elkan.
—— CONCERTO FOR PIANO AND ORCH., OP. 31 (1970)
  2,2,2,2 - 4,2,2,0 - timp.,perc. - pf. - str.   17:00 H. Elkan.
—— DIALOGUE FOR CLARINET AND CHAMBER ORCH., OP. 39
  (1972)
  2,2,3,2 - 2,2,1,0 - timp.,perc. - str.   8:00 H. Elkan.
—— INSTANTANÉS, OP. 37 (SNAPSHOTS) (FOR STRING ORCH.)
  (1972)
  str.   10:00 H. Elkan.
—— OUVERTURE D'ÉTÉ, OP. 28 (1968)
  2,2,2,2 - 2,2,1,0 - timp.,perc. - str.   8:00 H. Elkan.
—— LE PRINTEMPS, OP. 25 (1967)
  2,2,2,2 - 4,2,2,0 - timp.,perc. - str.   11:00 H. Elkan.
—— SYMPHONY, OP. 29 (1969) (IN 4 MOVTS.)
  3,3,3,3 - 4,3,3,1 - timp.,perc. - str.   23:00 H. Elkan.

LEDUC, Simon - OUBRADOUS, Fernand
—— CONCERTO NO. 2 IN C, FOR VIOLIN AND ORCH.
  0,2,0,0 - 2,0,0,0 - str.   14:00 Presser.
—— SYMPHONY IN D
  2,0,0,0 - 2,0,0,0 - str.   14:00 Presser.
  or:
  1,1,0,0 - 2,0,0,0 - str.

LEE, Dai-Keong
—— CANTICLE OF THE PACIFIC (1968)
  *3,2,0,2 - 4,3,3,1 - timp.,perc.,cel.,glock. - str.   15:00 Belw-Mills.
—— CONCERTO FOR VIOLIN AND ORCH. (1958) (IN 3 MOVTS.)
  *3,2,2,2 - 4,3,3,1 - timp.,perc.(1) - str.   24:00 Mills.
—— FESTIVAL ODE
                                                                 8:00 Mills.
—— GOLDEN GATE OVERTURE (ESSAY FOR CHAMBER ORCH.)
  1,1,2,1 - 2,2,1,0 - timp.,perc.(1) - str.   4:00 Mills.
—— HAWAIIAN FESTIVAL OVERTURE
  *4,(3rd alt. with 2nd picc.),*3,2,3 - 4,3,3,1 - timp. - str.
                                                                 6:00 Composer.
—— INTRODUCTION AND ALLEGRO (FOR STRINGS)
  str.   7:30 Leeds.
—— INTRODUCTION AND SCHERZO (FOR CHAMBER ORCH.)
  2,2,2,2 - 2,1,1,0 - timp. - str.   4:30 Mills.
—— MALE OLILI (JOYFUL SONGS) (SCENIC CANTATA OF 15
  POLYNESIAN CHANTS WITH ORCHESTRAL DANCES)
  (1960) (IN 2 MOVTS.) (Text: Traditional)
  *3,2,2,2 - 4,3,3,0 - timp.,perc.(2),glock.,xyl. - str.   44:00 Mills.
—— MUSIC FOR NAUPAKA
  *4(3rd alt. with 2nd picc.),*3,2,3 - 4,3,3,1 - timp., perc. (2) - str.
                                                                 5:00 Composer.
—— OVERTURE FOR CHAMBER ORCH.
  1,1,2,1 - 2,2,1,0 - timp. - str.   7:00 Belw-Mills.
—— OVERTURE IN C
  *3,2,2,2 - 4,3,3,1 - timp.,perc.(3) - str.   6:00 Composer.
—— PACIFIC PRAYER
  *3,2,2,2 - 4,3,3,1 - timp.,perc.(3) - str.   7:00 Composer.
—— PETER AND HIS MAGIC FLUTE (A VARIATION ON A
  THEME OF PROKOFIEFF) (FOR NARRATOR AND ORCH.)
  1,1,2,1 - 2,2,2,1 - perc.,cel. - hp. - str.   10:00 Bo. Hawkes.
—— POLYNESIAN SUITE
  *3,*3,2,*3 - 4,3,3,1 - timp.,perc. - str.   15:00 Mills.
—— PRELUDE AND HULA
  *3,2(2nd alt. with Eng. hn.),2,2 - 4,2,3,0 - timp.,perc.(2) - str.
                                                                 9:00 Mills.
—— SUITE FROM "TEA HOUSE OF THE AUGUST MOON" (IN 3
  MOVTS.)
  *3,2(2nd alt. with Eng. hn),2,2 - 4,3,3,1 - timp.,perc.(3),glock.,xyl.
  - hp. - str.   15:00 Chappell.
—— SYMPHONY NO. 1
  *3,2,2,2 - 4,3,3,1 - timp.,perc. - str.   20:00 Mills.
—— SYMPHONY NO. 2
  *3,2,2,2 - 4,3,3,1 - timp.,perc. - str.   24:00 Chappell.
—— SYMPHONY WITH A TAHITIAN HAPPENING (FOR
  TAHITIAN DANCER AND ORCH.)
  *3,2,2,2 - 4,3,3,1 - timp.,perc.(2),bells.cel.,glock.,xyl. - str.
                                                                 14:00 Composer.
—— THREE PIECES FROM THE PACIFIC (1959)
  *3,2,2,2 - 4,3,3,1 - timp.,perc.(1) - str.   12:00 Mills.
—— WALTZING MATILDA (SUITE FROM THE BALLET)
  3,2,2,2 - 4,3,3,1 - timp.,perc. - str.   15:00 C. Fischer.

LEE, E. Markham
—— RIVERS OF DEVON (SUITE)
    str.   Novello.

LEE, Noël
—— CAPRICCIO (SUR LE RETOUR D'AMIS BIEN-AIMES)
    3,2,2,3 - 4,2,2,1 - timp.,perc. - str.   7:00 Presser.
—— OVERTURE AND LITANY
    str.   17:00 Presser.

LEE, William F.
—— CONCERTO GROSSO FOR BRASS QUINTET AND ORCH. (IN 1 MOVT.)
    *3,3,*3,*3 - 3,1,2,0 - timp.,perc.(4),bells - hp. - str.
                                    12:00 Composer.
—— EIGHT VIGNETTES FOR A FESTIVE OCCASION ("A SIMUL-SENSORY EXPERIENCE") (FOR SOPRANO MEZZO-SOPRANO TENOR BASS, SATB CHORUS, LIQUID LIGHT PROJECTION AND ORCH.)
    4,3,4,3 - 4,4,4,0 - timp.,perc.,cel. - Arp-2600 Synthesizer - electric bass - 2 pf.(1 electric) - str.   55:00 Southern.
—— UNITED NATIONS - EARTH GENESIS
    str.   6:00 Composer.

LEES, Benjamin
—— CONCERTANTE BREVE
    0,1,0,0 - 2,0,0,0 - pf. - str.   15:30 Bo. Hawkes.
—— CONCERTO FOR CHAMBER ORCH. (1966)
    2(2nd alt. with picc.),2,2(2nd alt. with b.-cl.),2 - 2,0,0,0 - timp.,perc. - str.   18:00 Bo. Hawkes.
—— CONCERTO FOR OBOE AND ORCH. (1963)
    2,1,2,2 - 2,0,0,0 - timp.,perc. - str.   17:00 Bo. Hawkes.
—— CONCERTO FOR STRING QUARTET AND ORCH. (1964)
    2,2,2,2 - 4,3,3,1 - timp.,perc. - str.   23:00 Bo. Hawkes.
—— CONCERTO FOR VIOLIN AND ORCH. (1958)
    1. Andante con moto; 2. Adagio; 3. Allegro Giusto
    3(3rd alt. with picc.),3(3rd alt. with Eng.hn.),3(3rd alt. with b.-cl.),3 - 4,3,3,1 - timp.,perc.(4),xyl. - str. 24:00 Bo. Hawkes.
—— CONCERTO FOR WOODWIND QUINTET AND ORCH.
    1,1,1,1 - 3,2,3,0 - perc. - str.   Bo. Hawkes.
—— CONCERTO NO. 1 FOR ORCH. (1959) (IN 3 MOVTS.)
    3(3rd alt. with picc.),3(3rd alt. with Eng. hn.),3(3rd alt. with b.-cl.),*3 - 4,3,3,1 - timp.,perc.(4),cel.,xyl. - pf. - str.
                                    24:00 Bo. Hawkes.
—— CONCERTO NO. 1 FOR PIANO AND ORCH. (IN 3 MOVTS.)
    *3,*3,*3,*3 - 4,3,3,1 - timp.,perc.(3), xyl. - pf. - str.
                                    26:00 Bo. Hawkes.
—— CONCERTO NO. 2 FOR PIANO AND ORCH. (1966)
    2(2nd alt. with picc.),3,3(3rd alt. with b.-cl.),3(3rd alt. with cbn.) - 4,3,3,1 - timp.,perc. - pf. - str. 28:47 Bo. Hawkes.
—— DECLAMATIONS (IN 1 MOVT.)
    pf. - str.   9:30 Weintraub.
—— DIVERTIMENTO BURLESCA (1957) (IN 4 MOVTS.)
    2(2nd alt. with picc.),2(2nd alt with Eng. hn.),2(2nd alt. with b.-cl.),2 - 2,2,1,0 - timp.,perc.(2),glock. - hp. - str.
                                    22:00 Bo. Hawkes.
—— ETUDES FOR PIANO AND ORCHESTRA
                                    Bo. Hawkes.
—— FOUR SONGS OF THE NIGHT (FOR SOPRANO AND 13 INSTS.)
    1,1,1,1 - 1,1,0,0 - timp.,cel. - str.   8:00 Bo. Hawkes.
—— THE GILDED CAGE (3-ACT COMIC OPERA) % (1971) (Text: Alistair Reid)
                                  120:00 Bo. Hawkes.
—— INTERLUDE FOR STRINGS (1960)
    str.   12:00 Bo. Hawkes.
—— THE ORACLE (ONE-ACT OPERA) %
    1,1(alt. with Eng. hn.),1(alt. with b.-cl.),1 - 1,1,0,0 - timp.,perc. - pf. - str.   60:00 Bo. Hawkes.
—— PASSACAGLIA
                                  21:00 Bo. Hawkes.
—— PROFILE
    *3,2,*3,*3 - 4,3,3,1 - timp.,perc.(3),xyl. - str. 7:00 Weintraub.
—— PROLOGUE, CAPRICCIO AND EPILOGUE
    *3,*3,2-*3,2-*3 - 4,3,3,1 - timp.,perc.(4),xyl. - str.
                                  10:30 Bo. Hawkes.
—— SILHOUETTES (1967)
    1(alt. with picc.),1(alt. with Eng. hn.),1,1 - 1,1,1,0 - timp.,perc. - hp. - pf. - str.   15:00 Bo. Hawkes.
—— SPECTRUM (1964)
    2(2nd alt. with picc.),2,2,2 - 2,2,1,0 - perc. - pf. - str.
                                  10:00 Bo. Hawkes.

—— SYMPHONY NO. 1 (IN 3 MOVTS.)
    *3,*3,*3,*3 - 4,3,3,1 - timp.,perc.(3) - pf. - str.   19:30 Templeton.
—— SYMPHONY NO. 2
    2,2,2,2 - 4,3,3,1 - timp.,perc.,xyl. - hp. - str.   22:00 Bo. Hawkes.
—— SYMPHONY NO. 3 (1969) (IN 3 MOVTS., WITH 3 INTERLUDES AND POSTLUDE)
    3(3rd alt. with picc.),3(3rd alt. with Eng. hn.),3(3rd alt. with b.-cl.),1 ten. sax.,3(3rd alt. with c.-bn.) - 5,4,3,1 - timp.,perc.(3-4),cel.,glock. - str.   26:00 Bo. Hawkes.
—— THE TRUMPET OF THE SWAN (FOR NARRATOR AND ORCH.) (1972) (Text: E. B. White)
    2,2,2,2 - 4,3,3,0 - timp.,perc.(4) - hp. - str.   17:00 Bo. Hawkes.
—— VISIONS OF POETS (DRAMATIC CANTATA) (FOR SOPRANO, TENOR, MIXED CHORUS AND ORCH.) (1961) (Text: Walt Whitman)
    *5,3(3rd alt. with Eng. hn.),3(3rd alt. with b.-cl.),3(3rd alt. iwth c.-bn.) - 4,3,3,1 - timp.,perc.(5-6),cel.,glock.,xyl. - hp. - str.
                                  40:00 Bo. Hawkes.

LEFANU, Nicola
—— THE HIDDEN LANDSCAPE
    4(3rd and 4th alt. with picc.),3,4(2nd, 3rd and 4th alt. with b.-cl.),3 - 4,4,3,1 - timp.,perc.(5) - hp. - pf. (or cel.) - str.
                                23:00 Novello.
—— PRELUDIO
    1,1,1,1 - 1,0,0,0 - str.   5:00 Novello.

LEFEBVRE, Claude
—— ETWAS WEITER
    1(alt. with picc.),1,E♭cl.,*2,1 - 2,2,2,0 - perc.(3) - elec. guit. - hp. - pf. - str.(amplified)   12:00 Salabert.

LE FLEM, Paul
—— LA MAGICIENNE DE LA MER (OPERA) %
                                  S.A.C.E.M.
—— SYMPHONY NO. 3
    3,2,3,alto sax.,2 - 4,3,3,1 - timp.,perc. - hp. - str. 20:00 Presser.

LE FLEMING, Christopher
—— RUNE FOR SMALL ORCH., OP. 26
    2,2,1,1 - 1,0,0,0 - str.   3:30 P.R.S.

LEFTWICH, Vernon
—— CONCERTO FOR CELLO AND ORCH.
    3,*3,*3,*3 - 4,3,3,1 - timp.,perc.(1) - str. 30:00 Composer.
—— THE CREMATION OF CARE
    2(1 alt. with picc.),2,2,2 - 4,2,3,1 - timp.,perc.(2) - str.
                                  12:00 Composer.
—— DREAM RIDE (SUITE) (IN 5 MOVTS)
    2(1 alt. with picc.),*3,*3,*3 - 4,3,3,1 - timp.,perc.(2), cel. - hp. - str.   15:00 Composer.
—— ELEGY FOR ORCH.
    2,2,2,2 - 4,3,3,1 - perc.(1) - hp. - str.   5:00 Avant.
—— FESTIVAL OVERTURE
    2(2nd alt. with picc.),*3,2(2nd alt. with b.-cl.),*3 - 4,3,3,1 - timp.,perc. - 1-2 hp. - str.   11:00 Composer.
—— NOCTURNE
    3,*3,*3,*3 - 4,2,2,1 - perc.(2),cel. - hp. - str. 7:00 Composer.
—— REVERIE FOR STRINGS
    str.   10:00 Composer.
—— THE SEVEN AGES (FOR BARITONE AND ORCH.)
    2,2,2,2 - 4,2,3,1 - timp.,perc.(2),glock. - str. 10:00 Composer.
—— SUITE NO. 2
    2,2,2,2 - 2,2,2,0 - timp.,perc.(3) - str.   15:00 Composer.
—— SUNKEN SHIPS (SYMPHONIC POEM)
    2,*3,*3,*3 - 4,3,3,1 - timp.,perc.(2),cel. - hp. - str.
                                  13:00 Composer.
—— SYMPHONIC OVERTURE
    2,2,2,2 - 4,3,3,1 - timp.,perc.(3) - str.   8:00 Composer.
—— SYMPHONY NO. 1 (IN 4 MOVTS.)
    2(1 alt with picc.),*3,*3,*3 - 4,3,3,1 - timp.,perc.(3),glock.,xyl. - hp. - str.   35:00 Composer.
—— WHAT THE MOON SAW
    3(1alt. with picc.),*3,*3,*3 - 4,2,3,1 - timp.,perc.(3),cel.,glock.,xyl. - hp. - str.   17:00 Composer.

LE GALLIENNE, Dorian
—— OVERTURE IN E♭
    3,2,2,2 - 3,2,3,1 - timp.,perc. - hp. - str. 8:00 Bo. Hawkes

LEGLEY, Victor
—— LA CATHÉDRAL D'ACIER (THE STEEL CATHEDRAL), OP.
52 (SYMPHONIC SKETCH, AFTER A PAINTING OF
FERNAND STEVEN) (1958)
    3,3,3,3 - 4,3,3,1 - timp.,perc. - str.   12:00 H. Elkan.
—— CONCERT À TREIZE (CHAMBER SYMPHONY), OP. 17 (1944)
    1,0,1,0 - 0,1,0,0 - pf. - str.   10:00 H. Elkan.
—— CONCERT D'AUTOMNE (FOR ALTO SAXOPHONE AND
ORCHESTRA)
    Presser.
—— CONCERTINO FOR TIMPANI AND ORCH., OP. 49 (1956)
    2,2,2,2 - 2,1,1,0 - timp. - str.   11:00 CBDM.
—— CONCERTINO FOR VIOLIN AND ORCH., OP. 27 (1947)
    2,2,3,3 - 4,2,2,1 - timp. - str.   20:00 CBDM.
—— CONCERTO FOR PIANO AND ORCH., OP. 39(1952)
    3,2,2,3 - 4,2,2,0 - timp. - pf. - str.   15:00 H. Elkan.
—— CONCERTO FOR VIOLA AND ORCH., OP. 78 (1971) (IN 2
MOVTS.)
    2,2,2,2 - 2,1,1,0 - timp.,perc. - str.   32:00 H. Elkan.
—— CONCERTO NO. 2 FOR VIOLIN AND ORCH., OP. 67 (1967)
(IN 3 MOVTS.)
    2,2,2,2 - 2,2,2,0 - timp.,perc. - str.   21:00 H. Elkan.
—— DIVERTIMENTO, OP. 41 (1952)
    2,2,2,2 - 2,2,2,0 - timp. - str.   16:00 H. Elkan.
—— DYPTIQUE, OP. 60
    15:00 S.A.B.A.M.
—— ESPACES, OP. 77 (FOR STRING ORCH.) (1970)
    str.   8:00 H. Elkan.
—— THE GOLDEN RIVER (ESQUISSE SYMPHONIQUE), OP. 30
(1948)
    2,2,2,2 - 2,1,0,0 - timp. - str.   6:00 H. Elkan.
—— MUSIC FOR A GREEK TRAGEDY, OP. 24 (1946)
    3,3,3,3 - 4,3,3,1 - timp.,perc. - 2 hp. - str.   18:00 H. Elkan.
—— MUSIQUE DE MIDI, OP. 33 (1948)
    1,0,1,1 - 1,0,0,0 - str.   24:00 H. Elkan.
—— OVERTURE FOR A COMEDY OF GOLDONI, OP. 53 ("LO
SPIRITO DI CONTRADDIZIONE") (1958)
    2,2,2,2 - 2,2,2,0 - timp. - str.   5:15 H. Elkan.
—— PETITE OUVERTURE DE CARNAVAL (1954)
    2,2,2,2 - 4,3,3,1 - timp.,perc. - str.   4:00 H. Elkan.
—— SERENADE, OP. 44, NO. 2 (1957)
    str.   16:00 H. Elkan.
—— SUITE FOR ORCHESTRA, OP. 18 (1944)
    3,3,4,alto sax.,3 - 4,3,3,1 - timp.,perc.,cel.,glock.,xyl. - 2 hp. - pf. -
str.   24:00 CBDM.
—— SYMPHONIE MINIATURE, OP. 25 (1946)
    2,2,2,1 alto sax.,2 - 2,2,2,1 - timp. - str.   10:00 H. Elkan.
—— SYMPHONY NO. 2, OP. 29 (1947)
    3,3,3,3 - 4,3,3,1 - timp.,perc. - str.   18:00 CBDM.
—— SYMPHONY NO. 3, OP. 42 (1953)
    3,3,3,3 - 4,3,3,1 - timp.,perc.,xyl. - hp. - str.   23:00 CBDM.
—— VARIATIONS SYMPHONIQUES (ON AN OLD FLEMISH
SONG),OP. 6 (1941)
    2,2,2,2 - 4,2,2,1 - timp.,perc. - hp. - str.   13:00 H. Elkan.

LE GRAND, Robert
—— AMADIS ET ORIANE
    3,2,2,2 - 2,2,3,1 - timp.,perc. - hp. - str.   13:00 Salabert.
—— À LA COURT DU ROI PÉTAUD (DIVERSTISSEMENT FOR
BASSOONS, DOUBLE-BASSES AND ORCH.)
    2,2,2,2 - 4,2,3,0 - timp.,perc. - str.   8:00 Salabert.
—— DEUX POÈMES DE LA VILLE ET DES CHAMPS
    6:30 Salabert.
—— DEUX PRÉLUDES CHAMPÊTRES
    2,3,2,2 - 4,2,0,1 - timp.,trgl. - str.   10:00 Salabert.
—— DIMANCHE D'ÉTÉ (SUITE) (IN 3 MOVTS.)
    1,1,2,1 - 2,1,0,0 - timp. - hp. - str.   7:00 Salabert.
—— FANTASY IN A MAJOR (FOR VIOLIN AND ORCH.)
    1,1,2,2 - 2 hn. - timp. - str.   Salabert.
—— LES FESTES D'ATHYS ET DU PRINTEMPS
(DIVERTISSEMENT)
    1,1,0,1 - 2,1,0,0 - timp.,perc. - str.   13:00 Salabert.
—— FOIRE AUX PAINS D'ÉPICES (SCHERZO)
    3,2,2,2 - 4,4,3,1 - timp.,perc. - str.   10:00 Salabert.
—— LA LÉGENDE DE SAINT JULIEN L'HOSPITALIER
    3,2,2,2 - 4,4,3,1 - timp.,perc. - org. - str.   15:00 Salabert.
—— MACBETH ET LES TROIS SORCIÈRES
    3,3,2,2 - 4,4,3,1 - timp.,perc. - str.   8:00 Salabert.
—— POÈMES DE LA VILLE ET DES CHAMPS (IN 3 MOVTS.)
    3,2,2,2 - 4,2,3,0 - timp.,perc. - hp. - str.   10:00 Salabert.
—— SINFONIETTA RUSTICA (PETITE SUITE PASTORALE)
    1,1,2,1 - 2,1,0,0 - timp.,trgl. - hp. - str.   14:00 Salabert.

—— SUITE PASTORALE
    1,1,2,1 - 2,1,0,0 - timp.,perc. - hp. - str.   13:00 Salabert.
—— SYMPHONIE MARITIME
    2,2,2,2 - 4,2,3,1 - timp.,perc. - hp.   19:00 Salabert.
—— TORQUEMADA (SYMPHONIC EPISODE)
    3,3,3,3 - 4,3,3,1 - timp.,perc. - 2 hp. - str.   12:00 Salabert.

LEGRENZI, Giovanni - GANDOLFI
—— SONATA A TRE IN G MAJOR ("LA RASPONA")
    cemb. - str.   7:00 Henmar.

LEGRENZI, Giovanni - SONTAG, Wesley
—— CONCERTO BERNARDI (FOR 2 VIOLINS AND STRING
ORCH.)
    str.   Skidmore.

LE GUILLARD, Albert
—— PRÉLUDE À LA CONTE DE FÉES (OVERTURE TO THE
FAIRY TALE)
    20:00 S.A.C.E.M.

LEHMANN, Hans Ulrich
—— INSTANTS (POUR PIANO ET CORDES)
    pf. - str.   7:00 S.U.I.S.A.

LEHMANN, Kurt
—— CAPRICCIO (FOR SOLO WINDS, PERCUSSION AND STRING
ORCH.)
    1,1,1,1 - 1,0,0,0 - timp.,perc. - str.   13:00 K. Neufert.

LEHMANN, Liza
—— THE GOLDEN THRESHOLD (SONG CYCLE) (WITH SOLO
VOICES AND SATB CHORUS)
    1,1,2,2 - 2,2,1,0 - timp.,perc. - hp.(or pf.) - str. 18:00 Bo. Hawkes.

LEHNER, Franz Xavier
—— SYMPHONY NO. 1
    2,2,*3,2 - 4,2,3,1 - timp.,perc. - str.   30:00 AhnSimrock.

LEHTINEN, Elis
—— ADAGIETTO JUBILOSO (1950)
    str.   5:00 FinnMICtr.
—— ADAGIO RELIGIOSO (1944)
    3,2,2,2 - 4,2,3,0 - timp.,perc. - str.   7:00 FinnMICtr.
—— CONCERTO FOR VIOLA AND ORCH. (1972)
    2,1,2,2 - 4,3,2,0 - timp. - hp. - str.   31:00 FinnMICtr.
—— FESTIVE OVERTURE (1962)
    3,2,2,2 - 4,3,3,1 - timp.,perc. - str.   7:00 FinnMICtr.

LEIBOWITZ, René
—— CHAMBER SYMPHONY FOR 12 INSTRUMENTS
    1(alt. with picc.),1,*2,1 - 1,1,1,0 - str.(2,1,1,1)   17:00 Boelke-Bo.
—— CONCERTINO FOR VIOLA AND CHAMBER ORCH., OP. 35
    19:00 Boelke-Bo.
—— CONCERTO FOR PIANO AND ORCH, OP. 32
    21:00 Boelke-Bo.
—— CONCERTO FOR VIOLIN, PIANO AND ORCH.
    25:00 Boelke-Bo.
—— OVERTURE
    4:20 S.A.C.E.M.
—— SIX PIECES FOR ORCH., OP. 31
    14:00 Boelke-Bo.
—— TOURIST DEATH (FOR SOPRANO AND ORCH.)
    8:00 Boelke-Bo.

LEICHTLING, Alan
—— CONCERTO FOR CHAMBER ORCH. (1966)
    1,0,*2,0 - 1,1,1,0 - perc.(4) - str.   20:00 Seesaw.
—— CONCERTO FOR VIOLA AND ORCH. (1969)
    2,2,3,2 - 4,2,2,1 - timp.,perc.(3) - hp. - str.   47:00 Seesaw.
—— ELEVEN SONGS FROM "A SHROPSHIRE LAD", OP. 50 (FOR
BARITONE AND ORCH.)
    1,1,3,2 - 2,2,2,0 - perc.(3) - hp. - pf. - str.   45:00 Seesaw.
—— ITEM 72-D (MUSIC FOR A FILM)
    1,1,3,2 - 2,0,2,0 - d.-b.   15:00 Seesaw.
—— SCHATTENMUSIK FÜR DREI GRUPPEN (1965)
    1,2,1,1 - 0,0,0,0 - pf.(alt. with cel.) - str.   13:00 Seesaw.
—— SYMPHONY NO. 2 (1966)
    3,3,3,3 - 4,3,3,1 - timp.,perc.(6) - hp. - str.   22:00 Seesaw.
—— THE TEMPEST (OPERA) % (1973) (Text: Gabriela Roepke)
    75:00 Seesaw.

LEIDZEN, Erik
—— FUGUE WITH CHORALE
   3(3rd alt. with picc.),*3,*3,*3 - 4,3,3,1 - timp.,perc.(3) - str.
                                        7:00 Composer.
—— IRISH SYMPHONY
   1. Grave; 2. Scherzo; 3. Larghetto; 4. Allegro energico
   3(3rd. alt. with picc.),*3,*3,*3 - 4,3,3,1 - timp.,perc.(3) - hp. - str.
                                        45:00 Composer.
—— SUITE IN A MINOR (FOR STRINGS) (IN 5 MOVTS.)
   str.   17:00 Composer.
—— SWEDISH RHAPSODY
   2(1 alt. with picc.),*3,*3,*3, - 4,3,3,1 - timp. - hp. - str.
                                        6:00 Composer.
—— SWEDISH SUITE
   pf. (adlib.) - str.   9:30 Composer.

LEIFS, Jón
—— BALDR, OP. 34 (OPERA WITHOUT WORDS) %
                                        Islandia.
—— CANTATA NAZIONALE, OP. 13 (FOR CHOIR AND ORCH)
                                        Islandia.
—— CONCERTO FOR ORGAN AND ORCH., OP. 7
                                        Islandia.
—— EDDA, OP. 20 (ORATORIO) (FOR CHORUS AND ORCH.)
                                        Islandia.
—— ICELAND, OP. 9 (OVERTURE)
                                        Islandia.
—— ICELANDIC DANCES
                                        10:00 Islandia.
—— OVERTURE TO "LOFTR", OP. 10
                                        Islandia.
—— SAGA SYMPHONY, OP. 26
                                        Islandia.
—— SUITE FROM "LOFTR", OP. 6
                                        Islandia.
—— TRILOGIA PICCOLA
                                        Islandia.
—— VARIAZIONI PASTORALI
                                        Islandia.

LEIGH, Walter
—— AGINCOURT (OVERTURE)
   2,2,2,2- 3,2,3,0 - timp.,perc. - hp.(or pf.) - str.   10:00 Oxford.
—— CONCERTINO FOR CEMBALO AND STRINGS
   cemb. - str.   12:00 G. Schirmer.
—— MUSIC FOR STRING ORCH.
   str.   8:00 G. Schirmer.
—— SUITE FOR SMALL ORCH. (FOR SHAKESPEARE'S "A
   MIDSUMMER NIGHT'S DREAM")
   1,0,1,0 - 0,1,0,0 - timp. - hpsc. - str.   12:00 G. Schirmer.

LEIGHTON, Kenneth
—— BURLESQUE, OP. 19 (1957)
   3,2,2,3 - 4,3,3,0 - timp.,perc. - str.   8:00 Novello.
—— CONCERTO FOR CELLO AND ORCH.
   2(2nd alt. with picc.),2,2,2 - 4,3,3,0 - timp.,perc. - str.
                                        32:00 Novello.
—— CONCERTO FOR ORGAN, TIMPANI AND STRINGS
   timp. - org. - str.   21:00 Novello.
—— CONCERTO FOR STRINGS, OP. 39 (1961)
   str.   15:20 Novello.
—— CONCERTO FOR VIOLA, HARP, STRINGS AND TIMPANI
   timp. - hp. - str.   15:00 Novello.
—— CONCERTO FOR VIOLIN AND ORCH.
                                        24:00 Novello.
—— CONCERTO NO. 1 FOR PIANO AND ORCH., OP. 11
   3,2,3,3 - 4,3,3,1 - timp.,perc. - pf. - str.   23:00 Novello.
—— CONCERTO NO. 2 FOR PIANO AND ORCH., OP. 37 (1960)
   3,2,2,3 - 4,3,3,0 - timp.,perc. - pf. - str.   25:00 Novello.
—— CONCERTO NO. 3 FOR PIANO AND ORCH., OP. 57
   2,2,2,3 - 4,3,3,1 - timp.,perc. - hp. - pf. - str.   33:00 Novello.
—— DANCE OVERTURE, OP. 60
   3,2,2,2 - 4,3,3,1 - timp.,perc.,cel.,xyl. - hp. - pf. - str.
                                        9:00 Novello.
—— DANCE SUITE NO. 1, OP. 53
   3,2,2,2 - 4,3,3,1 - timp.,perc. - str.   15:00 Novello.
—— DANCE SUITE NO. 2, OP. 59
   2,2,2,2 - 3,3,2,1 - timp.,perc.,glock.,xyl. - pf. - str.   16:00 Novello.
—— FESTIVE OVERTURE (1962)
   2,1,2,1 - 2,2,1,0 - timp.,perc. - str.   8:00 Novello.
—— PASSACAGLIA, CHORALE AND FUGUE, OP. 18 (1957)
   3,2,2,3 - 4,3,3,0 - timp.,perc. - str.   20:00 Novello.

—— PRIMAVERA ROMANA (OVERTURE)
                                        5:00 Lengnick.
—— SYMPHONY FOR STRINGS
   str.   21:00 Lengnick.
—— SYMPHONY, OP. 42
   2(2nd alt. with picc.),2,2,2 - 4,3,3,1 - timp.,perc. - str.
                                        26:00 Novello.
—— VERIS GRATIA (SUITE) (FOR OBOE, CELLO AND STRING
   ORCH.)
   0,1,0,0 - 0,0,0,0 - str.   26:00 Novello.

LEIVISKÄ, Helvi
—— CONCERTO FOR PIANO AND ORCH., OP. 7 (1935)
   2,2,2,2 - 4,2,3,1 - timp.,perc. - pf. - str.   30:00 FinnMICtr.
—— FOLK DANCE SUITE, OP. 4 (IN 4 MOVTS.)(REV. 1971)
   3,3,2,2 - 4,2,3,1 - timp.,perc. - str.   15:00 FinnMICtr.
—— THE GOBLIN OF DARKNESS, OP. 15 (FOR SATB CHORUS
   AND ORCH.)
   2,2,2,3 - 4,2,3,1 - timp.,perc. - str.   20:00 FinnMICtr.
—— IMPROMPTU ENERGICO, OP. 24 (1948)
   2,2,2,2 - 4,2,3,1 - timp.,perc. - str.   4:00 FinnMICtr.
—— THE LOST CONTINENT, OP. 28 (FOR SOPRANO, TENOR,
   BARITONE, SATB CHORUS AND ORCH.) (1957) (Text: Eino
   Leino)
   3,2,2,2 - 4,2,3,1 - timp.,perc. - hp. - str.   25:00 FinnMICtr.
—— SINFONIA BREVIS, OP. 30 (REV. 1972)
   3,3,3,2 - 4,3,3,1 - timp.,perc. - hp. - str.   13:00 FinnMICtr.
—— SUITE NO. 1, OP. 8 (1934) (IN 3 MOVTS.)
   2,2,2,2 - 4,2,3,1 - timp.,perc. - str.   14:00 FinnMICtr.
—— SUITE NO. 2, OP. 11 (ON THEMES FROM THE FILM "JUHA")
   (1938) (IN 4 MOVTS.)
   2,2,2,2 - 2,2,1,0 - timp.,perc. - str.   20:00 FinnMICtr.
—— SYMPHONY NO. 1 IN B FLAT MAJOR, OP. 23 (1947)
   3,3,3,2 - 4,3,3,1 - timp.,perc. - str.   40:00 FinnMICtr.
—— SYMPHONY NO. 2 IN D MINOR, OP. 27 (1954)
   3,3,3,2 - 4,3,3,1 - timp.,perc. - hp. - str.   26:00 FinnMICtr.
—— SYMPHONY NO. 3, OP. 31 (1971)
   2,2,2,2 - 4,2,3,1 - timp.,perc. - str.   27:00 FinnMICtr.
—— TRIPLE FUGUE, OP. 10 (1935)
   2,2,3,2 - 4,2,3,1 - timp.,perc. - str.   8:00 FinnMICtr.
—— VARIATIONS AND FINALE, OP. 2 (1929)
   2,3,2,2 - 4,2,3,1 - timp.,perc. - str.   15:00 FinnMICtr.

LEJET, Edith
—— MONODRAME (FOR VIOLIN AND ORCH.)
   2,2,2,2 - 2,2,2,1 - timp.,perc. - hp. - str.   20:00 Presser.

LEKEU, Guilliaume
—— FANTAISIE CONTRAPUNTIQUE (FOR CHAMBER ORCH.)
   0,1,1,1 - hn. - str.   9:00 Salabert.

LELEU, Jeanne
—— SUITE POUR UN JOUR D'ÉTÉ (IN 4 MOVTS.)
   3(3rd alt. with picc.),*3,2,alto sax.,1 - 4,3,3,1 - timp.,perc. - str.
                                        27:00 EV.
—— SUITE SYMPHONIQUE (FOR WINDS) (IN 5 MOVTS)
   2,2,1,1 - 1,2,1,0 - perc. - pf.   15:00 Baron.
—— TRANSPARENCES (IN 3 MOVTS)
   2,2,2,alto sax.,2 - 4,2,0,0 - timp.,perc. - 2 hp. - str.   13:30 Baron.
—— TROIS ESQUISSES ITALIENNES
   3,3,3,2 - 4,3,3,1 - timp.,perc.,cel.,xyl. - hp. - str.   16:00 Baron.

LELOIR, Edmond
—— CONCERTO DE SCHWERIN (Anonymous composer; edited by
   Leloir)
   hn. - str.   6:30 Presser.

LEMACHER, Heinrich
—— CONCERT DUO, OP. 149 (FOR PIANO FOUR-HANDS AND
   STRINGS)
   pf. (4 hands) - str.   Robbins.
—— IMPROVISATIONS, OP. 109 (SUITE) (IN 3 MOVTS.)
                                        Hans Gerig.
—— MUSIC FOR STRINGS, OP. 38, NO. 1
   str.   Robbins.
—— MUSIC FOR STRINGS, OP. 38, NO. 2
   str.   10:00 Robbins.
—— MUSICA FESTIVA (FOR FLUTE AND STRING ORCH.)
   fl. - str.   Hans Gerig.
—— OVERTURE, OP. 189 (FOR CHAMBER ORCH.)
                                        Hans Gerig.
—— PARTITA, OP. 20 (FOR STRING ORCH.)
   str.   Hans Gerig.

LEMELAND, Aubert
—— IMPROMPTUS SYMPHONIQUES, OP. 21
    2,2,2,2 - 2,2,1,0 - timp.,cymb. - str.   12:00 Presser.
—— IMPROVISATIONS CONCERTANTES (FOR CLARINET AND STRINGS)
    cl. - str.   13:00 Presser.
—— PARTITA, OP. 27
    str.   Presser.
—— SUITE FOR STRINGS ("L'ARCHE") (IN 3 MOVTS.)
    str.   18:00 EV.

LEMMER, Petrus Johannes
—— SEHNSUCHT (TONE POEM)
    2,2,3,2 - 4,2,3,1 - timp.,perc. - str.   6:00 S.A.M.R.O.

LENDVAY, Kamilló
—— CONCERTINO FOR PIANO, WINDS, PERCUSSION AND HARP
    3,2,3,2 - 4,4,4,1 - timp.,perc. - hp. - str.   10:00 Bo. Hawkes.
—— CONCERTO DA CAMERA (FOR WIND AND STRING QUINTETS)
    1,1,1,1 - 1,0,0,0 - perc. - hp. - pf. - str.(2,1,1,1) 9:35 Bo. Hawkes.
—— CONCERTO FOR VIOLIN AND ORCH.
    *3,*2,*2,*2 - 4,3,3,1 - timp.,perc. - hp. - str.   22:00 Bo. Hawkes.
—— EXPRESSIONS
    str.   11:00 Bo. Hawkes.
—— MAUTHAUSEN (SYMPHONIC POEM)
    3,3,3,2 - 4,3,3,1 - timp.,perc. - hp. - pf. - str.   12:00 Bo. Hawkes.
—— OROGENESIS (ORATORIO) (FOR SOPRANO, CONTRALTO, 2 TENORS, BARITONE, SATB CHORUS AND ORCH.)
    *3,0,*4,*2 - 4,3,3,1 - timp.,perc. - hp. - pf. - str.
        42:00 Bo. Hawkes.
—— TRAGIC OVERTURE
    3,2,2,3 - 4,4,3,1 - timp.,perc.,cel. - 2 hp. - str. 15:00 Bo. Hawkes.

LEO, Leonardo - PASTORE
—— CONCERTO IN D MINOR FOR CELLO AND STRINGS
    str.   13:00 Henmar.

LEO, Leonardo - PICCIOLI, Giuseppe
—— THE DEATH OF ABEL (ORATORIO) (FOR SOLOISTS, MIXED CHORUS AND ORCH.) (Text: Metastasio)
    2 ob. - 2 tpt. - cemb. - org. - str.   90:00 Bo. Hawkes.

LEO, Leonardo - UPMEYER
—— CONCERTO IN D MAJOR FOR 4 VIOLINS AND STRINGS
    cemb. - str.   Henmar.

LEON, Tania
—— HAIKU
    fl.,bn. - perc.(5) - koto - guit. - c.,d.-b. 33:00 DTO Harlem.
—— TONES (BALLET) % (1970) (IN 3 MOVTS.)
    2,1,1,0 - 1,0,0,1 - timp.,perc.,bells,vibra.,xyl. - pf. - str.(16,6,4,2)
        16:11 DTO Harlem.

LEONARD, Beldon C.
—— ELEGY (FOR STRING ORCH.)
    str.   3:00 Composer.
—— NOCTURNE (FOR STRING ORCH.)
    str.   5:00 Composer.
—— POÈME ROMANTIQUE
    *3,2,*3,2 - 4,3,3,1 - timp.,perc.(3),bells - hp. - str. 9:00 Composer.

LEONARD, Stanley S.
—— SOUND SPIRIT (FOR SATB CHORUS, WINDS AND PERCUSSION) (1968) (Text: Composer)
    2,2,*3,*3 - 2,2,3,1 - timp.,perc.(4),bells 12:00 Composer.

LEONCAVALLO, Ruggiero
—— I PAGLIACCI (2-ACT OPERA) % (Eng. text: Joseph Machlis)
    G. Schirmer.

LEPORATTI, Ricardo
—— IL RISVEGLIO (SYMPHONIC POEM)(1923)
    3,2,2,2 - 3,3,0,1 - timp.,perc. - str.   Salabert.

LERCHE, Nils
—— ANDANTE CANTABILE (FOR PIANO AND ORCH.) (1940)
    2,1,2,1 - 2,0,0,0 - pf. - str.   6:00 FinnMICtr.
—— BALLAD FOR PIANO AND ORCH. (1944)
    3,3,2,2 - 4,2,3,1 - timp.,perc. - pf. - str. 11:00 FinnMICtr.
—— CRISTOFORO COLOMBO (BALLET SUITE) (1950)
    2,1,2,1 - 2,2,1,0 - timp.,perc.(3) - hp. - str. 20:00 FinnMICtr.

—— THE DAWN OF SPRING (1943)
    3,3,3,2 - 4,2,3,1 - timp.,perc.(3) - hp. - str. 11:00 FinnMICtr.
—— FAIRY TALE SUITE (FOR FLUTE AND ORCH.) (REV. 1954)
    2,1,2,1 - 2,2,1,0 - timp.,perc. - hp. - str 7:00 FinnMICtr.
—— IN THE VALLEY OF ALFEIO (BALLET) % (1946)
    2,1,2,1 - 2,2,1,0 - timp.,perc.(3) - hp. - str. 12:00 FinnMICtr.
—— LAPPONIA (1943)
    3,3,3,2 - 4,3,3,1 - timp.,perc.(3) - hp. - str. 16:00 A Tempo.
—— PRELUDE IN D MINOR (1940)
    2,3,2,2 - 4,2,3,0 - timp.,perc. - hp. - str. 8:00 FinnMICtr.
—— SCHERZO IN A MINOR (1948)
    3,3,2,2 - 4,2,3,0 - timp.,perc. - str. 7:00 FinnMICtr.
—— S.O.S. (1942)
    3,3,3,3 - 4,3,3,1 - timp.,perc.(3) - hp. - str. 11:00 FinnMICtr.
—— WILDERNESS SUITE (REV. 1954) (IN 4 MOVTS.)
    2,1,2,1 - 2,2,1,0 - timp.,perc. - hp. - str. 8:00 FinnMICtr.

LE ROUX, Maurice
—— LE CERCLE DES MÉTAMORPHOSES
    12:00 Henmar.
—— UN KOAN
    1,2,3,2 - 2,2,1,1 - perc.(2) - hp. - org. - pf. - str. 14:00 Salabert.

LEROUX, Xavier
—— LE NIL
    2,1,2,1 - 2,0,0,0 - timp.,trgl. - hp. - str.   Presser.

LESEMANN, Frederick
—— SYMPHONY IN THREE MOVEMENTS (1971)
    4(2 alt.with 2 picc.),3,3(3rd alt.with b.-cl.),2,2 cbn. - 4,3,3,2 - timp.,perc.(2-3),vibra.,xyl. - hp. - pf. - str. 22:30 Composer.

LE SIEGE, Annette
—— MONTAGE (1975)
    3,3,3,2 - 4,3,3,0 - perc.(4) - str.   15:00 Seesaw.

LESKOVIC, Bogomir
—— MY NATIVE LAND (SYMPHONY IN ONE MOVT.)
    *3,*2,2(2nd alt. with b.-cl.),2 - 4,2,3,1 - timp.,perc. - str.
        35:00 Hans Gerig.
—— PARTITA IN B MINOR
    2,2,0,2 - 2,2,0,0 - str.   24:00 Hans Gerig.
—— STUDY FOR SYMPHONY ORCHESTRA
    *3,*2,2(2nd alt. with b.-cl.),2 - 4,2,3,1 - timp.,perc. - str.
        8:00 Hans Gerig.

LESTER, Thomas William
—— THE LAND OF SOULS (CANTATA) (FOR CHORUS AND ORCH)
    2,2,2,2 - 3,2,3,0 - timp.,perc. - hp. - str. J. Fischer.
—— THE MANGER BABE (CANTATA) (FOR SOLOISTS, CHORUS AND ORCH.)
    1,1,2,2 - 3,3,3,0 - timp. - hp. - str. J. Fischer.
—— THE TALE OF THE BELL (CANTATA) (FOR CHORUS AND ORCH)
    1,1,2,1 - 2,2,1,0 - timp.,perc. - str. J. Fischer.

LESUR, Daniel
—— ANNONCIATION (CANTATA) (FOR NARRATOR, TENOR, SATB CHORUS AND ORCH.)
    2,2,3,1 - 2,1,0,0 - timp.,perc.,cel. - hp. - pf. - str. 25:00 Presser.
—— LE BAL DU DESTIN
    3,3,3,3 - 4,3,3,1 - timp.,perc. - hp. - pf. - str. 23:00 Presser.
—— CONCERTO DA CAMERA (FOR PIANO AND CHAMBER ORCH.)
    1,0,1,0 - 0,0,0,0 - pf. - str. 12:00 F. Colombo.
—— PASSACAILLE (FOR PIANO AND ORCH.)
    Baron.
—— PASTORALE
    1,1,1,1 - 1,1,0,0 - timp. - pf. - str. 9:30 Presser.
—— SÉRÉNADE (FOR STRING ORCH.)
    str.   15:00 F. Colombo.
—— SYMPHONIE DE DANSES
    str.   26:00 F. Colombo.

LETELIER, Alfonso
—— DIVERTIMENTO
    3,2,3,2 - 4,3,3,1 - timp.,xyl. - pf. - str. 20:00 Bo. Hawkes.
—— VITRALES DE LA ANNUNCIACION (FOR WOMAN'S VOICE, WOMEN'S CHORUS AND ORCH.)
    0,2,0,1 - 0,2,0,0 - perc. - pf. - str. 21:00 Bo. Hawkes.

LEVANT, Oscar
—— NOCTURNE
 3(1 alt. with picc.),2(1 alt. with Eng. hn.)*3,*3 - 4,3,3,1 -
 timp.,perc.,cel.,xyl. - hp. - str.   NewMusEd.

LEVENSON, Boris
—— DAVID AND ABSALOM, OP. 79 (DRAMATIC CANTATA)
 (FOR SOLOISTS, CHORUS AND ORCH.)
 *3,*3,2,2 - 4,2,3,1 - timp. - hp. - str. 50:00 Composer.
—— FANTASY ON TWO HEBREW FOLKTUNES, OP. 83
 *3,2(2nd alt. with Eng. hn.),2,2 - 4,2,3,1 - timp.,perc.(3) - hp. - str.
     8:00 Composer.
—— POEM FOR VIOLIN AND ORCH., OP. 89
 *3,*3,*3,*3 - 4,2,3,1 - timp. - hp. - str. 10:00 Composer.

LEVEY, Harold
—— CONCERTO NO. 1 FOR PIANO AND ORCH.
 *3,*3,*3,2 - 4,3,3,1 - timp.,perc.,xyl. - pf. - str. 15:00 Witmark.
—— SUITE NO. 1 FOR ORCH. (THEATRE GUILD SUITE)
 *3,*3,*3,2 - 4,3,3,1 - timp.,perc.,cel.,xyl. - hp. - str.
     15:00 Witmark.

LEVI, Paul Alan
—— SYMPHONIC MOVEMENT
 4,3,3,1 - 2,3,2,1 - timp.,perc. - str. 12:00 EV.

LEVINAS, Michaël
—— APPELS
 1,1,1,1 - 1,0,1 cnt.,1,0 - perc.(2) - pf. - 1 d.-b. 9:00 Salabert.

LEVINE, Jeffrey
—— CHAMBER SETTING NO. 2 (1967)
 1(alt.with alto fl.),1,1(alt.with b.-cl.),1 - 1,1,1,0 - perc.(2),mar.,vibra.
 - 1 d.-b.   15:00 Composer.
—— CONCERTO FOR PIANO AND CHAMBER ORCH. (1971)
 hp. - org. - pf. - str. 17:00 Composer.
—— CRYSTALS (FOR CHAMBER ORCH.) (1975)
 1(alt.with picc.),0,1(alt.with b.-cl.),1 - 0,0,1,0 -
 perc.(2),bells,cel.,glock.,mar.,vibra. - hp. - pf. - str.
     20:00 Composer.
—— DIVERTIMENTO (1974)
 str. 18:00 MCA Music.

LEVITCH, Leon
—— OF PLANTS AND HUMANS, OP. 9 (CANTATA) (FOR
 SOPRANO, TENOR, MIXED CHORUS AND ORCH.) (1956)
 1,1,1,1 - 1,0,0,0 - timp.,perc.(2) - hp. - str. 20:00 Composer.
—— SUITE FOR FLUTE, STRING ORCH., AND HARP, OP. 7 (1955)
 (IN 4 MOVTS.)
 fl. - hp. - str. 20:00 Composer.
—— SYMPHONY NO. 1, OP. 15 (1967) (IN 3 MOVTS.)
 *4,*3,*3,2 - 4,3,3,1 - timp.,perc.(2-3),cel.,xyl. - hp. - str.
     22:30 Composer.

LEVITIN, Yuri
—— CONCERTO FOR CLARINET, BASSOON AND ORCH., OP. 34
 1,1,2,2 - 3,3,1,0 - perc. - hp. - str. 18:00 G. Schirmer.
—— CONCERTO FOR OBOE AND STRING ORCH., OP. 50
 ob. - str. 16:00 G. Schirmer.

LEVY, Ernst
—— CANTATA NO. 3
     30:00 S.U.I.S.A.
—— CONCERTO FOR CELLO AND ORCH. (1947)
 2,2,2,3 - 4,3,3,0 - timp.,perc. - str. 20:00 Seesaw.
—— GAUDEAMUS (KANTATE NO. 4) (1964) (FOR VOICE AND
 ORCH.)
     25:00 S.U.I.S.A.
—— A MUSICAL GATHERING (UNE RÉUNION MUSICALE - EIN
 HAUSKONZERT) (IN 5 TEILEN, FÜR 10 INSTR.)
 1,1,1,1 - 1,0,0,0 - pf. - str. 84:00 S.U.I.S.A.
—— PARTITA CONCERTANTE (FÜR VIOLINE UND ORCH.)
 2,2,2,3 - 2,0,0,0 - timp. - str. 40:00 S.U.I.S.A.
—— SYMPHONY NO. 11
 3,2,3,alto sax.,2 - 4,3,3,0 - timp.,perc. - str. 40:00 Bo. Hawkes.
—— SYMPHONY NO. 15
 2,2,2,1 sax.,2 - 4,3,3,1 - timp.,perc.,cel. - hp. - str. 15:00 Seesaw.

LEVY, Frank
—— DIALOGUE FOR TUBA, HARP, TIMPANI AND STRINGS
 tu. - timp. - hp. - str. 12:00 Seesaw.

—— LAMENT FOR IGNACIO SANCHEZ MEJIAS (FOR
 NARRATOR AND ENSEMBLE)
 0,1,0,0 - 0,0,0,0 - perc. - str. 25:00 Seesaw.
—— SYMPHONY FOR SMALL ORCHESTRA (1969)
 2,1,2,1 - 2,2,2,1 - timp.,perc.(2) - guit. - str. 18:00 Seesaw.

LEVY, Marvin David
—— CARAMOOR FESTIVAL OVERTURE
 2(2nd alt. with picc.),2(2nd alt. with Eng. hn.),2,2 - 4,2,3,1 -
 timp.,perc.(3),bells,xyl. - hp. - str. 12:00 Bo. Hawkes.
—— CONCERTO NO. 1 FOR PIANO AND ORCH. (1969) (IN 1
 MOVT.)
 2(2nd alt. with picc.),2,2,2 - 4,2,3,0 - timp.,perc.,bells,vibra.,xyl. -
 electric guit. - hp. - pf. - str. 28:00 Bo. Hawkes.
—— ESCORIAL (1-ACT OPERA) %
 1(alt. with picc.),1(alt. with Eng. hn.),1(alt. with alto sax.),1(alt.
 with c.-bn.) - 1,1,0,0 - perc. - 2 pf.(1st alt. with cel., 2nd alt. with
 org.) - str. 52:00 Bo. Hawkes.
—— FOR THE TIME BEING (CHRISTMAS ORATORIO) (FOR 6
 SOLO VOICES, NARRATOR, SATB CHORUS AND ORCH.)
 (Text: W. H. Auden)
 3,3,3,3 - 4,5(2 in balcony or box of auditorium),3,1 -
 timp.,perc.,cel. - hp. - org. - pf. - str. 105:00 Bo. Hawkes.
—— IN MEMORIAM W. H. AUDEN
 1,1,1,1 - 1,0,0,0 - electric pf.(or org.) - str.(4,2,2,1)
     22:00 Bo. Hawkes.
—— KYROS (POEM FOR ORCH.)
 2,2,2,2 - 2,1,1,0 - timp.,perc.(1),bells,glock.,xyl. - hp. - str.
     20:00 Bo. Hawkes.
—— MASADA (FOR NARRATOR, TENOR, SATB CHORUS AND
 ORCH.)
 2,2,2,2 - 2,4,3,0 - timp.,perc.,cel. - tape-recorder - hp. - org. - str.
     90:00 Bo. Hawkes.
—— MOURNING BECOMES ELECTRA (OPERA) % (Text: Henry
 Willis Butler)
     Bo. Hawkes.
—— ONE PERSON (CANTATA) (FOR CONTRALTO AND ORCH.)
 (Text: Elinor Wylie)
 2,2,2,2 - 4,2,3,1 - timp.,perc. - hp. - pf. - str. 20:00 Bo. Hawkes.
—— SYMPHONY NO. 1 (IN 4 MOVTS.)
 3-4(3rd alt. with picc.),3-4 (3rd alt. with Eng. hn.),3-4(3rd alt.
 with b.-cl.),3-4(3rd alt. with c.-bn.) - 4,3,3,1 -
 timp.,perc.(5),bells,cel.(alt. with pf.),glock.,xyl. - hp. - pf. - str.
     23:00 Bo. Hawkes.
—— TRIALOGUS I (FOR SYMPHONY ORCHESTRA)
     18:00 Bo. Hawkes.
—— TRIALOGUS II (FOR CHAMBER ORCH. OF 33 PLAYERS)
     20:00 Bo. Hawkes.

LEVY, Michael Maurice
—— LARGO
 str. 7:00 Eds. Fran.

LEWIS, Anthony
—— CANZONA (HOMAGE TO PURCELL)
 2,2,2,2 - 4,2,3,0 - str. 7:30 P.R.S.
—— CITY DANCES
 2,2,2,2 - 4,2,0,0 - str. 20:00 P.R.S.
—— CONCERTO FOR HARPSICHORD AND STRINGS
 hpsc. - str. 23:00 P.R.S.
—— CONCERTO FOR TRUMPET AND ORCH.
     20:00 Lengnick.
—— A RESTORATION SUITE (FOR STRINGS) (ON AIRS AND
 DANCES BY PURCELL AND HIS CONTEMPORARIES)
 str. 13:00 Bo. Hawkes.

LEWIS, John Leo
—— HANNAH'S PRAYER (FOR MIXED CHORUS AND ORCH.)
 2,2,2,2 - 2,2,0,0 - str. 15:00 Composer.
—— PSALM 39 (FOR MIXED CHORUS AND ORCH)
 2,2,2,2 - 2,2,0,0 - str. 15:00 Composer.
—— SYMPHONY IN A MAJOR
 *3,*3,2,*3 - 4,2,3,1 - timp.,perc. - str. 25:00 Composer.

LEWIS, Leon
—— CONCERTO FOR CELLO AND ORCH. (IN 3 MOVTS.)
 *3,*3,2,2 - 4,2,3,1 - timp.,perc.,bells,xyl. - hp. - str.
     25:00 Composer.
—— ISRAELI SUITE
 *3,*3,*3(2nd alt. with E♭ cl.),2 - 4,2,3,1 - timp.,perc.(3),xyl. - hp. -
 str. 18:30 Kelton.

—— JESSICA (A PORTRAIT)
    *3,*3,*3,2 - 4,2,3,1 - timp.,perc.(4),bells,cel.xyl. - 2 hp. - pf. - str.
                       14:00 Composer.
—— LAMENT (FOR CELLO AND ORCH.)
    2,*2,2,2 - 4,2,2,1 - timp.,perc.(2), bells,cel. - hp. - str.
                       9:30 Composer.

LEWIS, Robert Hall
—— CONCERTO FOR CHAMBER ORCH.
    2,2,2,1 - 1,1,1,0 - perc. - hp. - str.   15:00 Presser.
—— DESIGNS
    3,3,3,2- 4,3,3,1 - timp.,perc. - hp. - str.   14:00 Presser.
—— NUANCES II
    3.2,2,2 - 4,2,31 - timp., perc.(5) - tape-recorder - hp. - pf.(alt. with
    cel.) - str.   20:00 Presser.
—— PRELUDE AND FINALE
    1,1,1,1 - 1,1,0,0 - perc. - str.   14:00 Presser.
—— SYMPHONY NO. 2 (1971)
    3,3,3,3 - 4,3,3,1 - timp.,perc.(4) - hp. - pf. - str. 22:00 Seesaw.
—— THREE PIECES FOR ORCHESTRA
    3,3,3,3 - 4,3,3,1 - timp.,perc.,cel. - str.   7:00 Presser.

LEWKOVITCH, Bernhard
—— DANCE SUITE
    2,2,2,2 - 4,2,3,1 - timp.,perc.,xyl. - str.   11:00 G. Schirmer.
—— MASS, OP. 15 (FOR CHORUS AND ORCH.)
    1,*3,0,2 - 0,2,2,0 - hp.   26:00 G. Schirmer.

LHOTKA, Fran
—— SCHERZO
    str.   S.O.K.O.J.

LIBAEK, Sven Erik
—— AUSTRALIAN SUITE (1967)
    2,1,1,alto sax.,ten. sax.,0 - 3,3,2,0 - perc.,vibra. - elec. d.-b - guit. -
    harm. - pf. - str.   50:00 Southern.

LIBBEY, Dee
—— ESSENCE AND DISTRACTIONS
    3,2,3,2 - 4,3,2,1 - timp.,perc. - hp. - pf. - str.   8:00 Bourne.
—— INTROSPECT, OP. 4 (JAZZ SYMPHONY) (IN 3 MOVTS.)
    *3,2,*3,2 - 4,3,3,1 - timp.,perc.(5),xyl. - hp. - pf. - str.
                       12:30 Bourne.
—— LOST FOREST (TONE POEM), OP. 2
    *3,*2,*3,2 - 4,2,3,1 - timp.,perc.(5),bells,glock, - hp. - str.
                       10:30 Composer.

LICHTER, Charles
—— FANTASY ON PAGANINI'S "CARNIVAL OF VENICE" (FOR
    VIOLIN AND ORCH.) (1971)
    2,2,2,2 - 2,0,0,0 - str.(19,6,6,4)   12:00 H. Elkan.
—— VERMONT SUMMER
    3(3rd alt. with picc.),2,3,2 - 4,3,3,0 - timp.,perc.,cel. - pf. - str.
                       9:00 Galaxy.

LIDDLE, Samuel
—— THE MERMAID (CANTATA) (FOR CHORUS AND ORCH.)
                       Bo. Hawkes.

LIDHOLM, Inguar
—— CONCERTO FOR STRINGS
    str.   14:00 S.T.I.M.
—— MUSIC FOR STRINGS
    str.   15:00 S.T.I.M.
—— PEZZO CONCERTANTE (FOR VIOLIN AND ORCH.)
    2,2,2,2 - 4,2,3,1 - timp.,perc. - hp. - pf. - str. 27:00 S.T.I.M.
—— TOCCATA AND CANTO (FOR CHAMBER ORCH.)
    1,1,1,1 - 0,0,0,0 - str.   13:30 S.T.I.M.

LIE, Harald
—— ELEGY, OP. 3 (FOR BARITONE AND ORCH.) (Text: H. H.
    Seedorff)
    2,2,3,2 - 4,2,0,0 - hp. - str.   9:00 T.O.N.O.
—— SYMPHONIC DANCE, OP. 12
    2,2,2,2 - 4,3,3,1 - timp.,perc. - str.   13:30 Musikk-Hu.
—— SYMPHONY NO. 1, OP. 4 (IN 4 MOVTS.)
    2,2,2,3 - 4,2,3,1 - timp. - hp. - str.   46:30 T.O.N.O.
—— SYMPHONY NO. 2, OP. 5 (IN 3 MOVTS.)
    2,2,2,2 - 4,3,3,1 - timp. - str.   35:00 Musikk-Hu.
—— TWO SONNETS OF MICHELANGELO, OP. 9 (FOR VOICE
    AND ORCH.) (German Text: Rainer Maria Rilke)
    2,2,2,2 - 0,0,0,0 - timp. - hp. - str.   11:30 Musikk-Hu.

LIEBERMAN, Fredric
—— SOLITAIRE FOR STRINGS (1964)
    str.   Composer.
—— SYMPHONY FOR SMALL ORCHESTRA
    1,1,1,1 - 0,1,1,0 - str.   8:00 Composer.

LIEBERSON, Goddard
—— HOMAGE TO HANDEL
    str.   14:30 Mills.
—— SUITE FOR 20 INSTRUMENTS
                       Composer.

LIEBERSON, Samuel
—— IN A WINTER GARDEN (SUITE)
    *4,*3,*3,*3 - 4,3,3,1 - timp.,perc.,cel. - 2 hp. - pf. - str.
                       23:00 AmerMusEd.

LIEDBECK, Sixten
—— DIVERTIMENTO FOR FLUTE AND STRINGS
    fl. - str.   12:00 S.T.I.M.
—— RALJANT EFTERSPEL
    2,2,2,2 - 4,3,3,1 - timp.,perc. - str.   Fleisher.
—— SIESTA (1963)
    2,1,2,0 - 1,3,2,0 - timp.,perc.,cel. - str.   5:00 Fleisher.
—— SUITE FOR FLUTE AND ORCH. (1964)
                       Fleisher.
—— SUITE FOR ORCHESTRA
    2,2,2,2 - 4,2,3,0 - timp.,perc.,cel. - str.   9:00 S.T.I.M.
    or:
    1,1,2,1 - 2,2,1,0 - timp.,perc. - str.
—— SUITE FOR STRINGS
    str.   15:00 S.T.I.M.
—— SYMPHONIC DANCES
    2,2,2,2 - 4,2,3,1 - timp.,perc. - hp. - str.   S.T.I.M.

LIER, Bertus Van
—— CANTATA FOR CHRISTMAS
                       Henmar.
—— CANTICUM (FOR WOMEN'S CHORUS AND ORCH.) (1939)
    (Text: P. H. Damsté)
    2 fl. - pf. (4 hands) - str.   8:00 Henmar.
—— CONCERTANTE MUSIC FOR ORCH. (WITH VIOLIN AND
    OBOE SOLOS) (1959)
    4,3,2,2 - 4,3,3,1 - timp.,perc. - pf. - str.   17:00 Henmar.
—— CONCERTO FOR BASSOON AND ORCH.
    4,3,3,2 - 3,3,3,0 - timp.,perc. - pf. - str.   18:00 Henmar.
—— DIVERTIMENTO FACILE (1957)
    2,2,2,2 - 2,2,0,0 - timp.,perc. - str.   10:00 Henmar.
—— THE HOLY SONG (FOR SOPRANO, TENOR, BARITONE,
    SMALL CHORUS AND CHAMBER ORCH.)
    1,1,1,1 - 1,0,0,0 - timp.,perc. - hp. - str.   Henmar.
—— IK SLA DE TROM (FOR MALE CHORUS AND ORCH.) (1948)
    (Text: J. Greshoff)
    3,3,3,2 - 3,3,3,1 - timp.,perc. - 2 hp. - pf. - str. 8:00 Henmar.
—— KATHARSIS (BALLET) %
    3,3,3,2 - 4,3,3,2 - timp.,perc. - str.   27:00 Henmar.
—— O, NETHERLANDS, PAY ATTENTION (O, NEDERLANT, LET
    OP U SAECK) (CANTATA) (FOR CHORUS AND ORCH.)
                       Henmar.
—— SUITE OF MELODIES FROM "HAERLEM'S OUDT
    LIEDT-BOECK" (1716)
                       Henmar.
—— SYMPHONIA (1954)
    2,2,2,2 - 2,0,0,0 - timp., - str.   11:00 Henmar.
—— SYMPHONY NO. 1 (1928)
    4,3,2,3 - 4,3,3,1 - timp.,perc. - str.   13:00 Henmar.
—— SYMPHONY NO. 2 (1931-1945)
    4,3,4,4 - 4,4,3,2 - timp.,perc. - str.   16:00 Henmar.
—— SYMPHONY NO. 3 (1938)
    3,3,4,3 - 4,3,3,1 - timp.,perc. - hp. - str. 23:00 Henmar.
—— SYMPHONY NO. 4 (WITH DOUBLE STRING ORCH.) (1954)
    2,2,2,2 - 2,0,0,0 - str.   11:00 Henmar.

LIEURANCE, Thurlow
—— THE CAMPFIRES (SUITE)
    3,2,2,2 - 4,3,3,0 - timp.,perc. - hp. - pf. - str. 24:00 Composer.
—— COLONIAL EXPOSITION SKETCHES (PARIS, 1931)
    3,2,*3,2 - 4,3,3,1 - timp.,perc.(2) - hp. - pf. - str. 30:00 Composer.
—— CONQUISTADOR (SUITE)
    3,2,2,2 - 4,3,3,1 - timp.,perc. - hp. - pf. - str. 46:00 Composer.
—— FOUR SCENES FROM MEXICO (WITH OPTIONAL CHORUS)
    3,2,*3,2 - 4,3,3,0 - timp.,perc.(3) - hp. - 2 pf. - str.
                       18:00 Composer.

—— MINISA ("RED WATER AT SUNSET") (WITH OPTIONAL
CHORUS) (IN 3 MOVTS.)
3,2,2,1 - 4,3,3,0 - hp. - pf. - str.   30:00 Composer.
—— SCENE ABORIGINAL
*3,2,*3,2 - 4,3,3,0 - timp.,perc.(3) - hp. - pf. - str.   Composer.
—— SCENES SOUTHWEST (WITH OPTIONAL CHORUS)
3,2,*3,0 - 4,3,3,0 - timp.,perc.(2) - hp. - pf. - str.   18:00 Composer.
—— SUITE FROM "TRAILS SOUTHWEST"
3,2,2,2 - 4,3,3,0 - timp.,perc.(2) - pf. - str.   15:00 Composer.
—— TRAILS SOUTHWEST (IN 7 MOVTS.) (WITH OPTIONAL
CHORUS)
3,2,2,2 - 4,3,3,1 - perc. - hp. - pf. - str.   60:00 Composer.

LIFTMANN, Baruch
—— SUITE OF HORAS
str.   10:00 IsMuPublns.

LIGETI, György
—— POÈME SYMPHONIQUE (FOR 10 PLAYERS, EACH
OPERATING 10 METRONOMES)
60:00 G.E.M.A.
—— RUMANIAN CONCERTO
2,2,2,2 - 3,2,0,0 - perc. - str.   10:00 Bo. Hawkes.

LILBURN, Douglas
—— DIVERSIONS FOR STRING ORCHESTRA
12:00 Oxford.
—— FESTIVAL OVERTURE
8:00 A.P.R.A.
—— LANDFALL IN UNKNOWN SEAS (FOR NARRATOR AND
SMALL ORCH.)
16:00 A.P.R.A.
—— SUITE FOR ORCH.
14:00 A.P.R.A.
—— SYMPHONY NO. 2
32:00 A.P.R.A.
—— SYMPHONY NO. 3, (1961)
3(3rd alt. with picc.),3,3(3rd alt. with b.-cl.),*3 - 4,3,3,0 -
timp.,side drum - hp. - str.   16:00 G. Schirmer.

LILIEN, Ignace
—— CONCERT FOR PIANO AND ORCH. (1959)
2,2,2,2 - 4,2,0,0 - timp.,perc.,cel.,xyl. - pf. - str.   20:00 Henmar.
—— CONCERTO ARCADIQUE (FOR 2 FLUTES AND ORCH.)
2,2,2,2 - 2,0,0,0 - timp. - str.   15:00 Henmar.
—— CONCERTO BANSLE STYLE GALATN (FOR CELLO AND
ORCH)
2,2,2,2 - 4,3,3,1 - timp.,perc.,xyl. - hp. - str.   20:00 Henmar.
—— CONCERTO DA CAMERA (1962)
fl. - str.   15:00 Henmar.
—— CONCERTO FOR VIOLIN AND ORCH. (1957)
2,2,2,2 - 4,3,3,1 - timp.,perc.,cel. - hp. - str.   30:00 Henmar.
—— CONCERTO FOR VIOLIN, PIANO AND ORCH.
2,2,2,2 - 2,3,3,0 - timp.,perc. - str.   34:00 Henmar.
—— FIVE NOCTURNES (FOR PIANO AND ORCH.)
2,2,2,2 - 4,2,2,0 - timp.,perc. - hp. - pf. - str.   20:00 Henmar.
—— IN HET ATRIUM DER VESTALINNEN (CANTATA) (FOR
BARITONE, SPEAKING VOICE, WOMEN'S CHORUS AND
ORCH.) (1956) (Text: Bertus Aafjes)
2,2,2,2 - 2,0,0,0 - timp.,perc. - hp. - str.   18:00 Henmar.
—— LÀ-BAS (POÈME SYMPHONIQUE)
3,3,3,3 - 4,3,3,1 - timp.,perc.,cel.xyl. - hp. - str.   12:00 Henmar.
—— LES PALMES DANS LE VENT (ÉTUDE SYMPHONIQUE)
3,2,3,3 - 4,3,3,1 - timp.,perc.,xyl - hp. - pf. - str.   8:00 Henmar.
—— SYMPHONY NO. 1
2,2,2,3 - 4,2,3,0 - timp.,perc. - hp. - str.   20:00 Henmar.
—— SYMPHONY NO. 2
3,3,3,3 - 4,3,3,0 - timp.,perc. - hp. - str.   30:00 Henmar.
—— SYMPHONY NO. 3
2,2,2,2 - 4,2,3,1 - timp.,perc. - hp. - str.   25:00 Henmar.
—— SYMPHONY NO. 4
2,2,2,2 - 4,2,2,1 - timp.,perc. - hp. - str.   23:00 Henmar.
—— TWEE GEDICHTEN (FOR MEDIUM VOICE AND ORCH.)
(1947) (Text: P. van Ostayen)
2,2,2,2 - 4,1,0,0 - timp.,perc.,cel. - hp. - str.   6:00 Henmar.
—— VIER LIEDER VOM GOTT DER BETTLER (FOR MEDIUM
VOICE AND ORCH.) (1925)
2,2,2,2 - 4,2,3,1 - timp.,perc.,cel. - hp. - pf. - str.   25:00 Henmar.
—— VOYAGE AU PRINTEMPS (CONCERTINO IN A MINOR FOR
CHAMBER ORCH.)
2,1,1,1 - 1,1,0,0 - perc. - str.   20:00 Henmar.

LILJA, Bernhard
—— BALLET MUSIC (SUITE) (IN 4 MOVTS.)
2,2,2,2 - 2,1,0,0 - timp.,perc. - str.   12:30 S.T.I.M.
—— SPELMANSVISA
2,2,2,2 - 2,2,1,0 - timp.,perc. - hp. - str.   10:00 S.T.I.M.
or:
2,2,2,2 - 2,2,0,0 - timp. - str.

LILJEFORS, Ingemar
—— BERGET (TONE-POEM), OP. 6
2,2,2,2 - 4,2,3,1 - timp. - str.   15:00 S.T.I.M.
—— BLAND TOMTAR OCH TROLL (RHAPSODY)
2,2,2,2 - 2,2,1,0 - timp.,perc. - str.   S.T.I.M.
—— CONCERTINO FOR PIANO AND ORCH., OP. 22
1,1,2,1 - 2,1,0,0 - timp. - pf. - str.   20:00 S.T.I.M.
—— CONCERTO FOR PIANO AND ORCH., OP. 2
2,2,2,2 - 2,2,1,0 - timp. - pf. - str.   22:00 S.T.I.M.
—— CONCERTO FOR VIOLIN AND ORCH. (1956)
1,1,2,2 - 2,1,0,0 - timp. - str.   19:00 S.T.I.M.
—— DIVERTIMENTO FOR STRINGS, OP. 21
str.   14:00 S.T.I.M.
—— DIVERTIMENTO NO. 2, OP. 23 (FOR STRINGS)
str.   S.T.I.M.
—— DIVERTIMENTO NO. 3 (1968)
str.   12:00 Fleisher.
—— LYRICAL SUITE (FOR SMALL ORCH)
1,1,1,1 - 1,0,0,0 - str.   22:00 S.T.I.M.
—— RHAPSODY FOR PIANO AND ORCH., OP. 5
2,2,2,2 - 2,2,0,0 - timp. - pf. - str.   17:00 S.T.I.M.
—— SINFONIETTA (1961)
2,2,2,2 - 2,2,1,0 - timp. - pf. - str.   18:00 S.T.I.M.
—— SUITE, OP. 2
2,2,2,2 - 2,2,0,0 - timp. - str.   11:00 S.T.I.M.
—— SYMPHONY, OP. 15
2,2,2,2 - 2,2,0,0 - timp. - str.   S.T.I.M.
—— EN TIJDH-SPEGEL (FOR MEZZO-SOPRANO,
BASS-BARITONE, MIXED CHORUS AND ORCH.) (1959)
2,2,2,2 - 2,2,1,0 - timp.,perc.(2) - pf. - str.   45:00 S.T.I.M.
—— TWO INTERMEZZI (1965)
str.   12:00 Fleisher.

LILJEFORS, Ruben
—— FESTIVAL OVERTURE
2,2,2,2 - 4,2,3,1 - timp. - str.   10:00 S.T.I.M.
—— FYRA SMÅSTYCKEN I FOLKTON
2,3,2,2 - 2,2,1,0 - timp. - str.   16:00 S.T.I.M.
—— MARIONETTE OVERTURE
2,2,2,2 - 0,0,0,0 - timp.,glock. - str.   5:00 S.T.I.M.
—— OVERTURE
2,2,2,2 - 4,2,3,0 - 4,2,3,0 - timp. - str.   S.T.I.M.
—— ROMANCE FOR VIOLIN AND ORCH.
2,2,2,2 - 2,2,0,0 - str.   8:00 S.T.I.M.
—— SOMMAR
2,2,2,2 - 2,2,0,0 - timp.,glock. - str.   17:00 S.T.I.M.
—— SYMPHONY IN E♭ MAJOR
2,3,3,2 - 4,2,3,1 - timp.,perc. - hp. - str.   40:00 S.T.I.M.

LINDBERG, Nils
—— LAPPONIAN SUITE (FOR SYMPHONY ORCH. WITH JAZZ
GROUP)(1971)
2,2,2,2 - 4,4,3,1 - timp.,perc. - str.   18:00 Fleisher.

LINDBERG, Oskar
—— DALMÅLNINGAR (IN 3 MOVTS)
2,2,2,2 - 4,2,3,0 - timp. - str.   15:00 S.T.I.M.
or:
2,1,2,1 - 2,2,1,0 - timp. - str.
—— FÄRDEMINNE (IN 3 MOVTS)
2,2,2,2 - 4,2,3,0 - timp. - str.   20:00 S.T.I.M.
—— FLOREZ OCH BLANZEFLOR (SYMPHONIC POEM)
3,3,2,2 - 4,3,3,1 - perc. - hp. - str.   13:30 S.T.I.M.
—— FRÅN DE STORA SKOGARNA (SYMPHONIC POEM)
3,3,3,3 - 4,3,3,2 - timp.,perc. - hp. - str.   15:00 Suecia.
—— GESUNDA (SYMPHONIC POEM)
3,2,2,2 - 4,2,3,1 - timp. - str.   16:00 S.T.I.M.
—— HEMIFRÅN ("AUS DALECARLIEN") (SYMPHONIC POEM)
2,3,2,2 - 4,3,3,1 - timp. - hp. - str.   15:00 S.T.I.M.
—— LEKSANDSSVIT
2,2,2,2 - 4,2,3,0 - timp. - str.   15:00 Nordiska.
—— OVERTURE NO. 1 IN E♭ MAJOR
2,2,2,2 - 4,3,3,1 - timp.,perc. - str.   10:00 S.T.I.M.
—— OVERTURE NO. 2 IN B. MINOR
3,3,2,2 - 4,3,3,1 - perc.(2) - str.   12:00 S.T.I.M.

—— OVERTURE NO. 3 IN D. MAJOR
3,3,2,2 - 4,3,3,1 - perc. - str.   10:00 S.T.I.M.
—— PER SPELMAN HAN SPELTE (RHAPSODY)
2,2,2,2 - 2-4,2,1,0 - timp.,cel. - harm. - hp. - str.   9:30 Suecia.
—— SYMPHONY IN F MAJOR
3,2,2,2 - 4,3,3,1 - timp. - hp. - str.   30:00 S.T.I.M.
—— TWO PIECES FOR STRING ORCH.
str.   13:00 S.T.I.M.
—— VILDMARK (SYMPHONIC POEM)
3,3,3,3 - 4,3,3,1 - timp.,perc. - hp. - str.   15:00 S.T.I.M.

LINDBLAD, Adolf Fredrik
—— SYMPHONY IN C MAJOR
2,2,2,2 - 2,2,0,0 - timp. - str.   30:00 Fleisher.

LINDE, Bo
—— BALLET BLANC (DIVERTISSEMENT, OP. 3) % (1952)
2,2,2,2 - 4,3,3,1 - timp.,perc.,xyl. - hp. - str.   60:00 Fleisher.
—— BARNSLIG UVERTYR
1,1,1,1 - 1,1,0,0 - timp.,perc.(3) - pf. - str.   5:00 S.T.I.M.
—— CONCERTO FOR CELLO AND ORCH., OP. 29 (1964)
2,2,2,2 - 2,2,0,0 - timp.,perc. - str.   31:00 Fleisher.
—— CONCERTO FOR ORCHESTRA, OP. 26 (1962)
3,2,2,3 - 4,3,3,1 - timp.,perc. - pf. - str.   50:00 Fleisher.
—— CONCERTO FOR PIANO AND STRINGS, OP. 12
pf. - str.   23:00 S.T.I.M.
—— CONCERTO FOR VIOLIN AND ORCH., OP. 18
2,2,2,2 - 2,2,0,0 - timp.,perc.(2) - str.   25:00 Bo. Hawkes.
—— CONCERTO NO. 2 FOR PIANO AND ORCH., OP. 17
2,2,2,2 - 4,2,3,1 - timp.,perc.(2) - pf. - str.   28:00 S.T.I.M.
—— GAMMALMODIGSUIT (FOR STRINGS)
str.   S.T.I.M.
—— LITTLE CONCERTO FOR WIND QUINTET AND STRING
ORCH., OP. 35 (1966)
1,1,1,1 - 1,0,0,0 - str.   17:00 Fleisher.
—— MINIATURE SUITE (IN BAROQUE STYLE)
ob. - str.   15:00 S.T.I.M.
—— EN MUNTER UVERTYR, OP. 13
2,2,2,2 - 3,2,1,0 - timp.,perc.(2) - str.   7:00 Bo. Hawkes.
—— PENSIERI SOPRA UN CANTICO VECCHIO (1967)
2,2,2,2 - 2,2,1,0 - timp.,perc.(2) - str.   8:00 S.T.I.M.
—— PEZZO CONCERTANTE, OP. 41 (CONCERTINO FOR BASS
CLARINET AND STRING ORCH.) (1970)
b.-cl. - str.   10:00 Fleisher.
—— PRELUDIO E FINALE
str.   6:00 S.T.I.M.
—— SÅNGEN (FOR MALE CHORUS AND ORCH.) (Text: Olof
Thunman)
2,2,2,2 - 2,2,0,0 - timp.,perc.(2) - str.   13:00 S.T.I.M.
—— SERENATA NOSTALGICA, OP. 30 (FOR 11 STRINGS) (1965)
str.   14:00 Fleisher.
—— SINFONIA FANTASIA, OP. 1
3,3,3,3 - 4,3,3,1 - timp.,perc.(3) - hp. - pf. - str.   20:00 S.T.I.M.
—— SINFONIA, OP. 23 (1960)
3,2,2,3 - 4,3,3,1 - timp.,perc.(2) - hp. - pf. - str.   25:00 S.T.I.M.
—— SUITE BOULOGNE, OP. 32 (1966)
1,1,1,1 - 1,1,1,0 - str.   13:00 S.T.I.M.
—— SUITE FOR ORCH., OP. 21
2,2,2,2 - 2,1,0,0 - timp.,perc.(2) - pf. - str.   25:00 S.T.I.M.

LINDEBERG, Stig
—— DIVERTIMENTO PICCOLO (1960)
str.   15:00 FinnMICtr.
—— FANTASIA PICCOLA (1961)
2,2,2,2 - 4,2,3,1 - timp.,perc. - str.   10:00 FinnMICtr.
—— SUMMER (SUITE) (1958) (IN 4 MOVTS.)
org. - pf. - str.   14:00 FinnMICtr.

LINDEMAN, Osmo
—— AUCTION (BALLET) % (WITH SATB CHORUS AND 6
SPEAKING VOICES) (1967)
4,0,0,0 - 0,0,3,0 - timp.,perc.(4),cel. - hp. - 2 pf. 16:00 FinnMICtr.
—— CONCERTO FOR CHAMBER ORCH. (1966)
1,1,1,1 - 1,1,1,0 - timp.,perc.(4) - hp. - str.   10:00 FinnMICtr.
—— CONCERTO NO. 1 FOR PIANO AND ORCH. (1963)
2,2,2,2 - 4,3,3,0 - timp.,perc.(4) - pf. - str.   14:00 FinnMICtr.
—— CONCERTO NO. 2 FOR PIANO AND ORCH. (1965)
2,2,2,2 - 4,3,3,1 - timp.,perc.(4) - str.   17:00 FinnMICtr.
—— MUSIC FOR CHAMBER ORCH. (1966)
1,1,1,1 - 1,1,1,0 - timp.,perc. - str.   14:00 FinnMICtr.
—— SYMPHONY NO. 1 ("SINFONIA INORNATA") (1958)
2,2,2,2 - 4,3,3,1 - timp.,perc.(3) - str.   20:00 FinnMICtr.

—— SYMPHONY NO. 2 (1964)
2,2,2,2 - 4,3,3,1 - timp.,perc.(4) - str.   20:00 FinnMICtr.
—— VARIABILE (1967)
4,4,4,4 - 4,3,3,1 - timp.,perc.(4) - str.   10:00 FinnMICtr.

LINDEMAN, Signe
—— BURLESCA
2,2,1,2 - 4,2,3,0 - timp.,perc. - str.   7:00 T.O.N.O.
—— FANTASIA ON "HOLY NIGHT" ("GLADE JUL") (FOR BOY'S
CHORUS AND ORCH.)
1,1,1,1 - 2,2,1,0 - bells - str.   6:00 T.O.N.O.
—— FROM ST. HALVARD'S TIME (SUITE) (IN 6 MOVTS.)
str.   16:00 T.O.N.O.
—— KOLLBOTTEN (SYMPHONIC POEM)
2,1,2,1 - 4,2,3,0 - timp.,perc. - str.   5:00 T.O.N.O.
—— THEME AND VARIATIONS
str.   8:00 T.O.N.O.

LINDEN, Nico Van Der
—— IN MEMORIAM F. D. ROOSEVELT
2,2,2,2 - 4,2,3,1 - timp.,perc. - hp. - str.   21:00 Henmar.
—— SCHERZO
2,2,2,2 - 4,2,2,0 - perc. - hp. - str.   6:00 Henmar.

LINDROTH, Henry
—— SYMPHONIC MOVEMENT, OP. 15 (1970)
2,2,2,2 - 4,3,3,1 - str.   Fleisher.

LINEK, Georg Ignaz - GOEBELS, Franzpeter
—— CONCERTO IN F MAJOR (FOR HARPSICHORD AND
SMALL ORCH.)
2 hn. - hpsc. - str.   12:00 Henmar.

LINJAMA, Jaakko
—— THE BUILDERS OF THE COUNTRY (FOR TENOR, BASS,
MALE CHORUS AND ORCH.) (1954) (Text: Einari Vuorela)
2,2,2,2 - 4,2,3,0 - timp.,perc. - str.   17:00 FinnMICtr.
—— CONCERTO BREVIS (FOR VIOLIN AND ORCH.) (1954)
2,2,2,2 - 4,2,3,0 - timp.,perc. - str.   14:00 FinnMICtr.
—— THE DANCE OF DEATH (8 SONGS) (FOR SATB SOLO
VOICES, SATB CHORUS AND ORCH.) (1958)
0,6,0,0 - 0,6,0,0 - timp.,perc.(3),cel. - hp. - str.(12,0,0,8)
    18:00 FinnMICtr.
—— THE GOLDEN APPLE (MELODRAMA) (FOR NARRATOR
AND ORCH.) (1959)
1,1,2,1 - 2,2,1,0 - timp.,perc.(3) - pf. - str.   18:00 FinnMICtr.
—— PRELUDE, ADAGIO AND RONDO (1960)
1,0,1,0 - 2,1,0,0 - str.   12:00 FinnMICtr.

LINJAMA, Jouko
—— CHAMBER ORATORIO ("HOW IT IS") (FOR BARITONE, 6
MALE SINGERS, 3 LOUDSPEAKERS AND ORCH.) (1968)
(Text: Samuel Beckett)
2,2,0,2 - 2,2,2,0 - amplification - org. - str.   45:00 FinnMICtr.
—— A MARK OF RESPECT TO ALEKSIS KIVI (FOR SOPRANO,
BARITONE, SATB CHORUS AND ORCH.) (1971) (Text: Aleksis
Kivi)
3,3,3,3 - 4,3,3,0 - timp.,perc.(3),cel.,vibra. - hp. - str.
    17:00 FinnMICtr.

LINKE, Norbert
—— CONCERTO FOR PIANO AND ORCH.
    Hans Gerig.
—— DIVISIONI (FOR LARGE ORCH.)
    Hans Gerig.
—— KONKRETIONEN V (FOR CHAMBER ORCH.) (1974)
    Hans Gerig.
—— LYRICAL SYMPHONY
    Hans Gerig.
—— PROFIT TOUT CLAIR (FOR CHAMBER ORCH.)
    Hans Gerig.
—— PROLOGUE FOR ORCH.
    Hans Gerig.
—— STRATI FÜR ORCH.
    Hans Gerig.
—— SYMPHONY IN ONE MOVT.
    Hans Gerig.

LINKO, Ernst
—— CONCERTO NO. 1 IN D MINOR, FOR PIANO AND ORCH.
(1916)
2,2,2,2 - 4,2,3,0 - timp. - pf. - str.   17:00 FinnMICtr.

—— CONCERTO NO. 2 IN E MAJOR, FOR PIANO AND ORCH.
(REV. 1920)
3,2,2,2 - 4,2,3,1 - timp. - pf. - str.   23:00 FinnMICtr.
—— CONCERTO NO. 3 IN A MAJOR, FOR PIANO AND ORCH.,
OP. 20 (1931)
2,2,2,2 - 2,2,1,0 - timp. - pf. - str.   24:00 FinnMICtr.
—— CONCERTO NO. 4 IN D MAJOR, FOR PIANO AND ORCH.,
OP. 27 (REV. 1957)
2,2,2,2 - 4,2,0,0 - timp. - pf. - str.   27:00 FinnMICtr.
—— SYMPHONIE CHEVALERESQUE, OP. 25 (1949)
3,2,2,2 - 4,2,3,1 - timp. - str.   30:00 FinnMICtr.

LINLEY, Thomas - CARSE, Adam
—— OVERTURE TO "THE DUENNA"
0,2,0,2 - 2,2,0,0 - timp. - str.   5:00 Galaxy.

LINN, Robert
—— AN ANTHEM OF WISDOM (FOR SATB CHORUS AND
ORCH.) (1958) (Text: Biblical)
2,2,2,2 - 0,3,3,1 - timp. - hp. - str.   8:00 Law-Gould.
—— CONCERTINO (FOR OBOE, HORN, PERCUSSION AND
STRING ORCH.) (IN 4 MOVTS.)
0,1,0,0 - 1,0,0,0 - timp.,perc.(1),bells,glock.,mar.,vibra.,xyl. - str.
19:00 Composer.
—— THE HEXAMERON (VARIATIONS ON A THEME FROM
BELLINI'S I PURITANI) (ARR. 1963) (By the 6 composer-pianists
Chopin, Czerny, Herz Liszt, Pixis and Thalberg)
*3,2,2,2 - 4,2,3,1 - timp.,perc.(3) - 1-6 pf.(ad lib.) - str.
25:00 Arranger.
—— OVERTURE
*3,*3,*3,2 - 4,3,3,1 - timp.,perc.(3) - hp. - str.   9:00 Mills.
—— THE PIED PIPER OF HAMELIN (FOR NARRATOR, TENOR,
SATB CHORUS AND ORCH.) (1968) (Text: Robert Browning)
*3,*3,*3,*3 - 4,3,3,1 - timp.,perc.(4),bells,cel.,glock.,xyl. - hp. - pf.
- str.   28:00 Composer.
—— SYMPHONY FOR STRINGS (1969)
hp. - pf. - str.   20:00 Composer.
—— SYMPHONY IN ONE MOVEMENT (1961)
3(3rd alt. with picc.),*3,*3,2 - 4,3,3,1 -
timp.,perc.(4),cel.,glock.,xyl. - hp. - str.   18:00 Composer.

LINNALA, Eino
—— ANDANTE ELEGIACO
timp. - str.   9:00 FinnMICtr.
—— DANCE SUITE À L'ANCIENNE
1,1,2,2 - 2,2,1,0 - timp.,perc. - str.   14:00 FinnMICtr.
—— ELEGY
timp. - str.   14:00 Westerlund.
—— FINNISH RHAPSODY
2,2,2,2 - 4,2,3,1 - timp.,perc. - str.   10:00 Fazer.
—— FINNISH SUITE (IN 4 MOVTS.)
1,2,2,1 - 2,2,1,0 - timp.,perc. - str.   13:00 SuomenTyMu.
—— MARIA (SYMPHONIC POEM) (FOR BARITONE, SATB
CHORUS AND ORCH.) (1934) (Text: V. A. Koskenniemi)
3,2,2,2 - 4,3,3,1 - timp.,perc.(3) - hp. - str.   15:00 Westerlund.
—— OVERTURE FOR ORCHESTRA
2,2,2,2 - 4,2,3,1 - timp.,perc. - str.   6:00 FinnMICtr.
—— POEM OF HÄME (CANTATA) (FOR SOLO VOICE, SATB
CHORUS AND ORCH.) (Text: Larin-Kyösti)
2,2,2,2 - 2,2,0,0 - timp.,perc. - str.   20:00 FinnMICtr.
—— SONG OF SORROW (3 SONGS FOR VOICE AND ORCH.)
(Text: Li-Tai-Pe)
2,2,2,2 - 4,2,3,0 - timp.,perc. - str.   10:00 FinnMICtr.
—— SUMMER IN THE BLACKWOODS (SUITE) (FOR WOMEN'S
CHORUS AND STRINGS)
str.   12:00 FinnMICtr.
—— SYMPHONY NO. 1 (1927)
3,3,3,3 - 4,3,3,1 - timp.,perc. - str.   38:00 FinnMICtr.
—— SYMPHONY NO. 2 (1935)
2,2,2,2 - 4,3,3,1 - timp.,perc.(3) - str.   22:00 FinnMICtr.

LINSTEAD, George
—— ANGLICAN OVERTURE
2,2,2,2 - 4,2,3,1 - perc.(2) - hp. - str.   15:00 P.R.S.
—— MOTO PERPETUO
2,2,2,2 - 4,2,3,1 - perc.(2) - str.   4:30 P.R.S.
—— OVERTURE IN FRENCH STYLE
2,2,2,2 - 4,2,3,0 - perc.(2) - str.   8:30 P.R.S.
—— SINFONIETTA
2,2,2,2 - 4,2,3,0 - perc. - str.   7:00 P.R.S.
—— VARIATIONS ON A THEME OF MONTEVERDI
str.   14:00 P.R.S.

LINTL, Fritz-Joachim
—— DIE SONNENHYMNEN DES ECHNATON (ICHNATON'S
HYMN TO THE SUN) (FOR MEN'S CHORUS AND ORCH.)
3,2,2,2 - 4,3,3,1 - timp.,perc. - hp. - str.   15:00 Sirius.

LIPAR, Peter
—— DANCE SUITE
str.   7:00 Hans Gerig.

LIPATTI, Dinu
—— DANSES ROUMAINES (FOR PIANO AND ORCH.)
3,3,3,3 - 4,3,3,1 - timp.,perc. - pf. - str.   18:00 Salabert.

LIPKIN, Malcolm
—— CONCERTO NO. 1 FOR VIOLIN AND ORCH. (1952)
2,2,2,2 - 2,2,0,0 - timp. - str.   26:00 P.R.S.
—— DRAMATIC OVERTURE (1955)
2,2,2,2 - 4,2,2,1 - timp. - hp. - str.   7:00 P.R.S.
—— MOSAICS (FOR CHAMBER ORCH.)(1966)
0,2,0,0 - 2,0,0,0 - str.   9:00 P.R.S.

LIPOVŠEK, Marijan
—— CONCERTO FOR TRUMPET AND ORCH.
2,2,2,1 - 2,1,0,0 - timp.,perc.(4),cel. - hp. - str.   13:00 Hans Gerig.
—— MY NATIVE COUNTRY (SYMPHONIC POEM)
2,2(2nd alt. with Eng. hn.),2(2nd alt. with b.-cl.),2 - 4,3,3,1 -
timp.,perc. - hp. - str.   13:00 Hans Gerig.
—— RHAPSODY ON SLOVENE FOLK MOTIFS (FOR VIOLIN
AND ORCH.)
11:00 Hans Gerig.
—— SEVEN MINIATURES FOR STRINGS
str.   10:00 Hans Gerig.
—— SUITE NO. 1 FOR STRINGS
str.   22:00 Hans Gerig.
—— SUITE NO. 2 FOR STRINGS
str.   20:00 Hans Gerig.
—— SUITE NO. 3 FOR STRINGS
str.   21:00 Hans Gerig.
—— SYMPHONY
2(2nd alt. with picc.),2(2nd alt. with Eng. hn.),2(2nd alt. with
b.-cl.),2 - 4,3,3,1 - timp.,perc.(3) - hp. - str.   41:00 Hans Gerig.
—— TOCCATA QUASI APERTURA
2(2nd alt. with picc.),2(2nd alt. with Eng. hn.),2(2nd alt. with
b.-cl.),2(2nd alt. with c.-bn.) - 4,3,3,1 - timp.,perc.(3) - str.
9:00 Hans Gerig.

LIST, Karl
—— GOLDONI SUITE
1(alt. with picc.),1(alt. with Eng. hn.),2(2nd alt. with b.-cl.),1 -
3,3,0,0 - timp.,perc.(3) - hp. - str.   7:50 Modern.

LISZT, Franz - CHARDON, Felix
—— SONATA IN B MINOR (Originally for Piano)
3,2,2,3 - 4,2,3,1 - timp.,perc. - hp. - str.   35:00 Presser.

LISZT, Franz - COLLINS, Anthony
—— CRUCIFIXUS (PASSACAGLIA) (FOR PIANO AND ORCH.)
C. Fischer.

LISZT, Franz - DARVAS, Gábor
—— CONCERTO PATHÉTIQUE (FOR PIANO AND ORCH.)
2,2,2,2 - 2,2,3,1 - timp.,perc. - pf. - str.   18:20 Bo. Hawkes.
—— CZÁRDÁS MACABRE
2,2,2,2 - 4,2,0,2 - timp.,perc. - pf. - str.   6:30 Bo. Hawkes.
—— HUNGARIAN RHAPSODY NO. 2
2,2,2,2 - 4,2,3,1 - timp.,perc. - hp. - str.   10:00 Bo. Hawkes.
—— HUNGARIAN RHAPSODY NO. 6
2,2,2,2 - 4,2,3,1 - timp.,perc. - str.   9:00 Bo. Hawkes.
—— LYON
2,2,2,2 - 4,2,3,1 - timp.,perc. - str.   9:00 Bo Hawkes.

LISZT, Franz - HERMANN, F.
—— HUNGARIAN RHAPSODY NO. 2
str.   Galaxy.

LISZT, Franz - KAY, Hershy
—— FUNERAILLES
3,3,3,3 - 4,3,3,1 - timp.,perc. - hp. - str.   8:30 Bo. Hawkes.

LISZT, Franz - KINDLER, Hans
—— HUNGARIAN RHAPSODY NO. 6
*3,*3,*3,2 - 4,3,3,1 - timp. - hp.(or pf.) - str.   8:30 Mills.

LISZT, Franz - LOTTER, Adolf
—— HUNGARIAN RHAPSODY NO. 2
                    12:00 Bo. Hawkes.

LISZT, Franz - PLESSIS, Hubert Lawrence du
—— VALLÉE DOBERMANN: SYMPHONIC POEM
    2,2,3,2 - 4,2,3,1 - timp.,perc. - str.   15:00 S.A.M.R.O.

LISZT, Franz - ROBERTS, Charles J.
—— HUNGARIAN RHAPSODY NO. 2
                    C. Fischer.

LISZT, Franz - SALABERT, Francis
—— HUNGARIAN RHAPSODY NO. 2
                    Salabert.

LISZT, Franz - WEINER, Leo
—— FOOLISH FIRE ("FUOCHI FATUI") (FROM
TRANSCENDENTAL ETUDE NO. 5)
    2,2,2,2 - 4,2,3,1 - timp.,perc. - str.   4:00 Bo. Hawkes.
—— WEINEN, KLAGEN (VARIATIONS ON A THEME BY BACH)
    2,2,2,2 - 4,3,3,1 - timp.,perc. - str.   14:00 Bo. Hawkes.

LISZT, Franz - WILD, Earl - MCDERMOTT, Wm.
—— ÉTALAGE (A DISPLAY OF BALLETIC MOVEMENT) %
                17:00 WashBalGld.

LISZT, Franz - WINTER, Aubrey
—— HUNGARIAN RHAPSODY NO. 3
                    6:00 Bo. Hawkes.

LITER, Monia
—— MEDITERRANEAN SUITE
    2,1,2,1 - 2,3,3,0 - perc. - guit. - hp. - str.   10:00 Bo. Hawkes.
—— PRELUDE ESPAGNOLE (FOR PIANO AND ORCH.)
    2,2,2,2 - 4,3,3,1 - timp.,perc. - hp. - pf. - str.   6:30 Bo. Hawkes.
—— SCHERZO TRANSCENDENT
    2,2,2,2 - 4,3,3,1 - timp.,perc. - hp. - str.   5:30 Bo. Hawkes.
—— SERENADE FOR STRINGS AND HARP
    hp. - str.   Bo. Hawkes.

LITOLFF, Henry Charles - SWANSON, Walter Donald
—— SCHERZO (FROM THE PIANO CONCERTO)
    2,2,3,2 - 4,2,3,1 - timp.,perc. - pf. - str.   8:00 S.A.M.R.O.

LIUKKO, Eino
—— AUTUMN SUITE (1947)
    2,2,2,2 - 2,2,1,0 - timp.,perc. - str.   19:00 FinnMICtr.
—— BALLAD (FOR ORCH.) (1971)
    3,2,2,2 - 4,3,3,1 - timp. - hp. - str.   7:00 FinnMICtr.
—— CHRISTMAS EVE (1960)
    1,1,2,1 - 2,2,1,0 - timp.,perc. - str.   7:00 FinnMICtr.
—— IN MODO ANTICO (1964)
    str.   12:00 FinnMICtr.
—— LEGEND (1953)
    2,2,2,2 - 2,2,2,0 - timp.,perc. - str.   11:00 FinnMICtr.
—— LYRICAL SUITE (1934)
    2,1,2,1 - 2,2,1,0 - timp.,perc. - str.   14:00 FinnMICtr.
—— MEMORY (FOR VIOLIN AND STRINGS) (1937)
    str.   6:00 FinnMICtr.
—— NORTHERN COMPOSITION (1956)
    str.   6:00 FinnMICtr.
—— NORTHERN WIND (FOR MALE CHORUS AND ORCH.)
(1968) (Text: Naeboe)
    3,2,2,2 - 4,2,3,1 - timp.,perc. - str.   14:00 FinnMICtr.
—— POEM (FOR CELLO AND ORCH.) (1961)
    2,0,2,1 - 1,0,0,0 - str.   9:00 FinnMICtr.
—— PRELUDE ELEGIACO (1959)
    str.   7:00 FinnMICtr.
—— PRELUDE MISTICO (1959)
    str.   6:00 FinnMICtr.
—— PRELUDE (1965)
    org. - str.   5:00 FinnMICtr.
—— SPRING SOUNDS (1938)
    1,1,2,1 - 2,2,1 0 - timp.,perc. - str.   12:00 FinnMICtr.
—— STORM (REV. 1947)
    3,2,2,2 - 4,2,3,0 - timp.,perc. - str.   14:00 FinnMICtr.
—— SUMMER SCENES (SUITE) (1931) (IN 5 MOVTS.)
    2,2,2,2 - 2,2,1,0 - timp.,perc. - str.   18:00 FinnMICtr.
—— SYMPHONY NO. 1 ("SYMPHONIE CLASSIQUE") (1950)
    2,2,2,2 - 2,2,1,0 - timp. - str.   27:00 FinnMICtr.
—— SYMPHONY NO. 2 IN D MAJOR (1955)
    2,2,2,2 - 4,2,3,1 - timp., perc. - str.   35:00 FinnMICtr.

—— SYMPHONY NO. 3 ("SPRING SYMPHONY") (1958)
    1,1,2,1 - 2,1,0,0 - timp.,perc. - str.   30:00 FinnMICtr.

LIVIABELLA, Lino
—— LA MIA TERRA (MY COUNTRY) (SYMPHONIC POEM)
(1942)
    3,3,3,3 - 4,3,3,1 - timp.,perc.(6),cel.,glock.,xyl. - 2 hp. - pf. - str.
                    30:00 Leeds.

LLOYD, Gerald
—— ASSOCIATIONS I
    2,2,2,2 - 2,2,2,1 - timp.,perc.(4) - pf. - str.   MCA Music.
—— CONCERTINO FOR PIANO AND ORCH.
    2,2,2,2 - 4,2,3,1 - timp.,perc.(4) - pf. - str.   18:00 MCA Music.

LLOYD, Norman
—— ALLEGRO FOR STRINGS
    str.   4:00 Composer.
—— INTERLUDE FOR THE INDECENT (EXCERPT FROM A
BALLET)
    1,1,1,1 - 2,2,3,1 - perc.(1) - pf. - str.   3:30 Composer.

LOBEL, Solomon M.
—— SYMPHONY NO. 5 (FOR NARRATOR, SATB CHORUS AND
ORCH.) (Text: Ye. Bukov)
                    G. Schirmer.

LOCATELLI - BONELLI
—— CONCERTO GROSSO, OP. 1, NO. 9 (FOR STRINGS)
    str.   12:00 Henmar.

LOCATELLI - DUBENSKY, Arcady
—— THEME AND VARIATIONS (FOR STRINGS)
    str.   12:00 Arranger.

LOCATELLI, Pietro - EGIDI
—— CONCERTO GROSSO IN C MINOR, OP. 1, NO. 6
    cemb. - str.   Henmar.

LOCATELLI, Pietro - KAHN, Emil
—— INTRODUCTION, GRAVE AND ALLEGRO
                    G. Schirmer.

LOCATELLI, Pietro - SCHERING
—— TRAUER-SYMPHONIE
    cemb. - str.   20:00 Henmar.

LOCKE, Matthew - BUSH, Geoffrey - HARVEY, Francis
—— PSYCHE: SUITE
    str.   Novello.

LOEFFLER, Charles Martin
—— EVOCATION (FOR WOMAN'S CHORUS AND ORCH.)
    3(3rd alt. with picc.),*3,*3,2 sax.,*3 - 4,4,3,1 - timp.,perc.(3),cel. -
2 hp. - pf.(or vibra.) - str.   10:00 AmerMusEd.
—— FIVE IRISH FANTASIES (FOR VOICE AND ORCH)
    2 picc.,3(3rd alt. with picc.),*3,*3,*3 - 4,4,3,1 -
timp.,perc.,cel.,glock.,xyl. - 2 hp. - str.   G. Schirmer.
—— MEMORIES OF MY CHILDHOOD (LIFE IN A RUSSIAN
VILLAGE)
    3(3rd alt. with picc.),*3,*3,*3 - 4,3,3,1 - timp.,perc., cel.,xyl. - 4
harmonicas - 2 hp. - pf. - str.   14:00 G. Schirmer.
—— A PAGAN POEM, OP. 14
    3(3rd alt with picc.),*3,*3,2 - 4,6,3,1 - timp.,perc.,glock. - hp. - pf.
- str.   22:00 G. Schirmer.
—— POEM (LA BONNE CHANSON)
    3(3rd alt. with picc.),*3,*3,3 - 4,3,3,1 - timp.,perc., cel.,glock. - hp.
- str.   17:00 G. Schirmer.

LOEFFLER, Charles Martin - SOKOLOFF, Nikolai
—— QUINTET (TRANSCRIBED FOR STRING ORCH.) (IN 1
MOVT.)
    str.   G. Schirmer.

LOEILLET, Jean-Baptiste - THILDE, Jean
—— CONCERTO IN D MAJOR (FOR TRUMPET AND STRINGS)
    tpt. - str.   6:00 Presser.

LOEVENDIE, Theo
—— CONFLUXUS (FOR JAZZ GROUP AND SYMPHONY ORCH.)
(1966)
                    10:00 Henmar.

—— SCARAMUCCIA (FOR CLARINET AND ORCH.)
2,2,2,0 - 2,1,1,0 - perc. - pf. - str.   10:00 Henmar.

LOEWE, Carl - SCHOENBERG, Arnold
—— DER NOECK (FOR VOICE AND ORCH.) (ARR. 1910)
3,3,3,3 - 4,2,3,1 - perc. - hp. - str.   10:00 Belmont.

LOFER, Hans
—— BALLETTMUSIK AUS "DES KAISERS NEUE KLEIDER"
3,3,3 sax.,3 - 4,3,3,1 - perc. - cemb. - str.   11:30 Alkor.

LÖFGREN, Albert
—— SLÅTTERGILLE (SWEDISH RHAPSODY)
                                                  12:00 G. Schirmer.
—— SWEDISH FANTASY
2,2,2,2 - 2,2,3,0 - timp.,perc. - str.   10:00 S.T.I.M.
—— VASTGÖTARAPSODI
1,2,2,1 - 2,1,1,0 - perc. - str.   14:00 S.T.I.M.

LOGAR, Mihovil
—— BALETSKA FANTAZIJA (BALLETIC FANTASY)
3,3,3,3 - 4,3,3,1 - timp.,perc.,vibra. - hp. - pf. - str.
                                                8:00 MIC,Zagreb.
—— CONCERTO FOR CELLO, WIND QUINTET AND STRINGS
(1971)
1,1,1,1 - 1,0,0,0 - str.(14,4,5,2)   20:00 MIC,Zagreb.
—— CONCERTO MORDENTE (FOR VIOLIN AND ORCH.)
2,2,2,2 - 2,2,0,0 - str.   18:00 MIC,Zagreb.
—— DIVERTIMENTO LIRICO
3,3,3,3 - 4,3,3,1 - timp.,perc.,vibra. - pf. - str.   20:00 MIC,Zagreb.
—— DOUBLE CONCERTO FOR CLARINET, HORN AND ORCH.
2,2,3,2 - 5,3,0,0 - timp.,perc. - str.   15:18 MIC,Zagreb.
—— KANJOŠ MACEDONOVIĆ (PAŠTROVSKI VITEZ) (THE
COUNT OF PAŠTROV)
3,3,3,3 - 4,3,3,1 - timp.,perc.,vibra. - pf. - str. 60:00 MIC,Zagreb.
—— MERMER I ZVUCI (MURMER AND SOUNDS) (OVERTURE)
3,3,3,3 - 4,3,4,0 - perc.,cel. - hp. - str. 4:00 MIC,Zagreb.
—— MINUETTO (FOR VIOLIN AND ORCH.)
2,2,2,2 - 2,2,0,0 - str.   13:00 MIC,Zagreb.
—— OVERTURE TO THE OPERA "THE CONCEITED WIDOW")
                                                  S.O.K.O.J.
—— PARTITA CONCERTANTE
1,1,1,1 - 1,0,0,0 - str.   16:00 MIC,Zagreb.
—— RONDO RUSTICO
2(2nd alt. with picc.),2,2(2nd alt. with b.-cl.),0 - 2-4,3,3,1 -
timp.,perc. - hp. - str.   5:00 MIC,Zagreb.

LOKSHIN, Aleksandr L.
—— SYMPHONY NO. 4 (SINFONIA STRETTA)
                                                  G. Schirmer.
—— SYMPHONY NO. 5 ("SONNETS OF SHAKESPEARE")
                                                  20:00 G. Schirmer.

LOMBARDO, Mario
—— A CITIZEN SONG (FOR SATB CHORUS AND ORCH.)
2,1(alt. with Eng.hn.),2,1 - 2,3,3,1 - perc. - guit. - hp. - str.
                                                  5:00 Chappell.
—— DRAKESTAIL (A SYMPHONIC NARRATIVE FOR
CHILDREN) (FOR NARRATOR AND ORCHESTRA)
3,3,3,2 - 4,3,3,1 - timp.,perc.,cel. - hp. - str. 18:00 Chappell.
—— ROCK 'N RHAPSODY (A PIECE FOR YOUNG AUDIENCES)
2,2,3,2 - 4,3,3,1 - timp.,perc. - guit. - pf. - str. 5:30 Chappell.
—— SYMPHONIC ODE
2,2,3,2 - 4,3,3,1 - timp.,perc. - hp. - str. 7:30 Chappell.
—— VARIATIONS (IN A MOD MOOD)
2,2,3,2 - 4,3,3,1 - timp.,perc. - guit. - pf. - str. 7:30 Chappell.

LONDON, Edwin
—— THE ASSASSINATION OF LINCOLN (A DOCUMENTARY
OPERA) % (FOR 11 VOICES, SATB CHORUS AND ORCH.)
(Text: D. Justice)
2,1,2,1 - 4,2,2,1 - str.   105:00 Composer.
—— THE COMEDY OF ERRORS: SUITE (1956) (IN 4 MOVTS.)
1(alt. with picc.),0,*2,0 - 0,1,0,0 - perc.(1),bells,glock. - str.
                                                  12:00 Composer.
—— GEISTLICHE MUSIK (ADVENT-SURE ON OK CHORALES)
(FOR 4 SOLO VOICES, SSAATTBB CHORUS, CHAMBER
ORCH., AND TAPE) (1972)
1,1,*2,0 - 0,2,2,0 - perc.(1) - tape-recorder - org. - str.
                                                  11:40 Agape.
—— GENESIS 21: 6 (FOR CHAMBER ORCH.) (1972)
1,0,1,1 - 0,1,0,0 - org. - str.   8:00 Agape.

—— THE IRON HAND (AN ORATORIO, FOR 3 SOLO VOICES,
SATB CHORUS AND ORCH.) (Text: D. Justice)
*3,2,Eᵇcl.,*3,2 - 4,4,3,1 - perc.(3) - str.   19:00 Composer.
—— OVERTURE TO "MIDSUMMER NIGHT'S DREAM" (1957)
1,1,1,1 - 0,1,1,0 - perc.(1) - str.   4:00 Composer.
—— OVERTURE TO "TWELFTH NIGHT" (1952)
1,1,1,1 - 0,1,1,0 - perc.(1) - str.   3:30 Composer.
—— PRESSURE POINTS (FOR ALTO SAX. AND ORCH.) (1972)
*3,*3,1 Eᵇcl.,*3,1 alto sax.,3 - 4,3,3,1 - perc.(2) - pf. - str.
                                                  11:00 Composer.
—— SANTA CLAUS (A MIME-OPERA) % (Text: e. e. cummings)
1(alt. with picc.),1,1,1 - 1,1,1,0 - perc.(1) - hp. - pf. - str.
                                                  53:00 Composer.
—— SPELVIN ASSOCIATION (FOR SOPRANO AND 11
INSTRUMENTALISTS) (1975) (Text: Sophocles, Shakespeare,
Heine) (IN 3 MOVTS.)
1(alt. with picc. and sopr. recorder),1(alt. with Eng. hn. and alto
recorder),1(alt. with b.-cl. and ten. recorders),1 - 0,1,1,1 -
timp.,perc.(1),bells,cel. - pf. - vla.,d.-b. 23:00 Composer.
—— TALA OBTUSITIES (A MUSICAL PLAY ON WORDS OF
CHARLES DICKENS) % (1972)
1(alt. with picc.),1(alt. with Eng.hn.),*2,2 sax., 0 - 1,2,1,1 -
perc.(2) - tape-recorder - str.(16,5,5,2)   115:00 Composer.
—— THREE PORTRAITS (OF THREE AMERICAN LADIES)(FOR
NARRATOR, MEZZO-SOPRANO, CHAMBER ORCH. AND
FILM) (1967) (Text: Rosemary Benet)
1(alt. with picc.)1*2(b.-cl. alt. with ten. sax.),0 - 1,2,1,1 -
perc.(2),bells,glock.,xyl. - 1 vln.,1 c.,1 d.-b.   22:00 Henmar.

LONDON, Erwin
—— OVERTURE TO "THE IMAGINARY INVALID" (1959)
1,0,*2,1 - 0,1,0,0 - str.   4:00 J. Boonin.

LONQUE, Georges
—— AFGODEN (IDOLES), OP. 41 (FOR CLARINET AND ORCH.)
(1950)
2,2,2,2 - 2,2,1,0 - timp.,perc. - pf. - str. 10:00 Scherzando.
—— AURA (BALLET AND SYMPHONIC POEM), OP. 13 (1930) %
3,3,3,3 - 4,3,3,1 - timp.,perc.,cel.,glock. - hp. - str. 15:00 Henmar.
—— CONCERTO FOR VIOLIN AND ORCH., OP. 40 (1948)
2,2,2,2 - 4,2,3,1 - timp.,perc. - hp. - str. 29:00 Henmar.
—— IMAGES D'ORIENT, OP. 20 (FOR VIOLA OR ALTO SAX.
WITH ORCH.) (1935)
2,1,2,1 alto sax.(ad. lib.),2 - 2,2,2,1 - timp.,perc. - hp.(or pf.) - str.
                                                  11:00 H. Elkan.
—— POÈME DE LA MER, OP. 19 (FOR VIOLIN AND ORCH)
(1935)
2,2,2,2 - 4,2,3,0 - timp.,perc. - hp. - str. 9:00 H. Elkan.
—— PORCELAINES DE SAXE (PETITE SUITE), OP. 25 (1939)
2,2,2,2 - 4,2,3,1 - timp.,perc. - hp. - str. 10:00 H. Elkan.
or:
2,1,2,1 - 2,2,1,0 - timp.,perc. - hp. - str.
—— PRELUDE ET ARIA, OP. 30 (FOR CELLO AND ORCH.) (1943)
2,1,2,1 - 2,2,1,0 - timp. - hp. - str.   6:00 H. Elkan.

LONQUICH, Heinz Martin
—— CORRISPONDENZA (COMPOSITION FOR ORCH.)
                                                  Hans Gerig.

LOOMIS, Clarence
—— ALBADO SEA ("PRAISE GOD WITH HYMNS") (FOR
BARITONE, CHORUS AND ORCH.)
2,2,*3,2 - 4,2,3,1 - timp. - hp.(or pf.) - str. 35:00 Composer.
—— AMERICA THE ELEVENTH (FOR NARRATOR, CHORUS
AND ORCH)
2(1st alt. with picc.),2(2nd alt. with Eng. hn.),2,2 - 4,2,2,1 -
timp.,vibra. - hp. - pf. - str.   10:00 Composer.
—— AS LIFE SINGS (SONG CYCLE) (FOR DRAMATIC SOPRANO
AND ORCH.)
2,1(alt. with Eng. hn.),2(2nd alt. with b.-cl.),2 - 2,2,2,1 - timp. -
hp. - str.   30:00 Composer.
—— CHORUSES FROM "A NIGHT IN AVIGNON"
2,*3,2(2nd alt. with b.-cl.),2 - 4,3,3,0 - timp. - hp. - str.
                                                  15:00 Composer.
—— CHORUSES FROM "DAVID"
2,2(2nd alt. with Eng. hn.),2(2nd alt. with b.-cl.),2 - 4,3,3,1 -
timp.,perc. - hp. - pf. - str.   7:00 Composer.
—— CHORUSES FROM "THE FALL OF THE HOUSE OF USHER"
*4,2(2nd alt. with Eng. hn.),*4,2 - 4,3,3,1 - timp. - hp. - str.
                                                  30:00 Composer.
—— CHORUSES FROM "YOLANDA OF CYPRUS"
2(1st alt. with picc.),2(2nd alt. with Eng. hn.),2(2nd alt. with
b.-cl.),2 - 2,2,1,0 - timp. - hp. - str.   10:00 Composer.

—— DREAM FANTASY (FOR WOMEN'S CHORUS AND ORCH.)
2,1(alt with Eng. hn.),2,2 - 2,2,1,1 - timp. - hp. - str.
5:00 J. Fischer.
—— ERIN (CHORAL CYCLE)
1(alt. with picc.),1(alt with Eng. hn.),2,1 - 1,2,2,0 - timp. - hp. - pf. - str.
25:00 Composer.
—— THE MELTING POT (AMERICAN DANCES)
3,2,2,4 - 4,3,3,2 - timp. - pf. - str.
16:00 Composer.
—— POTAGANISSING (SYMPHONIC POEM)
2(1st alt. with picc.),2(2nd alt. with Eng. hn.),2(2nd alt. with
b.-cl.),2 - 4,3,3,1 - timp. - hp. - str.
15:00 Composer.
—— SERENADE (FOR TENOR, PIANO AND CHAMBER ORCH.)
2 hn. - timp. - hp. - pf. - str.
10:00 Composer.
—— THE HARP AND THE WILLOW (PSALM 137) (FOR MEDIUM
VOICE AND ORCH.)
*3,1(alt with Eng. hn.),2,2 - 2,2,2,1 - timp. - hp. - str.
7:00 Gam.Hinged.

LOOSER, Rolf
—— ALYSSOS, (5 STÜCKE FÜR STREICHORCHESTER UND
SCHLAGZEUG)
perc. - str.
16:00 S.U.I.S.A.
—— PEZZO PER ORCHESTRA (FOR LARGE ORCH.)
15:00 Henn.
—— PONTI (SEI TEMPI PER ORCH.)
3,2,4.3 - 4,3,3,1 - perc.,cel.,xyl. - hp. - str.
18:00 S.U.I.S.A.

LOOTS, Joyce
—— THREE ORCHESTRAL PIECES
3,2,2,2 - 4,3,3,1 - timp.,perc. - hp. - str.
13:00 P.R.S.

LOOTS, Joyce Mary Ann
—— CONCERTSTUK (FOR PIANO AND ORCH.)
2,2,3,2 - 4,2,3,1 - timp.,perc. - pf. - str.
9:00 S.A.M.R.O.
—— FOUR SOUTH AFRICAN LYRIC PIECES
2,2,3,2 - 4,2,3,1 - timp.,perc. - str.
14:00 S.A.M.R.O.
—— THE GOLDEN THRESHOLD (THREE SONGS) (FOR VOICE
AND ORCH.) (Text: Sarojini Naidu)
2,2,3,2 - 4,2,3,1 - timp.,perc. - str.
9:00 S.A.M.R.O.
—— SUITE FOR STRINGS
str.
20:00 S.A.M.R.O.
—— THREE PIECES FOR ORCHESTRA
2,2,3,2 - 4,2,3,1 - timp.,perc. - str.
20:00 S.A.M.R.O.

LOPATNIKOFF, Nikolai
—— CONCERTINO FOR ORCHESTRA, OP. 30 (IN 3 MOVTS)
2(1 alt. with picc.),2(1 alt. with Eng. hn.),2,2 - 2,2,0,0 -
timp.,perc.(2),glock.,xyl. - pf. - str.
12:00 Leeds.
—— CONCERTO FOR ORCH., OP. 43 (IN 4 MOVTS.)
2(2nd alt. with picc.),2(2nd alt. with Eng.hn.),2(2nd alt. with E♭cl.
and b.-cl.),2 - 4,3,3,1 - timp.,perc.(3),glock.,xyl. - hp. - str.
19:00 Henmar.
or:
*3,*3,*3,2-*3 - 4,3,3,1 - timp.,perc.(2),glock.,xyl. - str.
—— CONCERTO FOR VIOLIN AND ORCH., OP. 26 (IN 3 MOVTS)
2(2nd alt. with picc.),2,2,2 - 3,2,0,0 - timp.,perc.(2),glock.,xyl. -
str.
23:00 AMP.
—— CONCERTO FOR 2 PIANOS AND ORCH., OP. 33 (IN 3 MOVTS)
2(2nd alt with picc.),2,2,2 - 2,2,2,0 - timp.,perc.(2) - 2 pf. - str.
20:00 Leeds.
—— CONCERTO NO. 1 FOR PIANO AND ORCH., OP. 5
3(1 alt. with picc.),3(1 alt. with Eng. hn.),3(1 atl. with b.-cl.),*3 -
4,4,2,1 - timp.,perc.(2),glock.,xyl. - pf. - str.
30:00 Composer.
—— DANTON: CONCERT EXCERPTS FROM THE OPERA (FOR 2
SOLO VOICES AND ORCH.) (IN 5 MOVTS.)
2(2nd alt. with picc.),2(2nd alt. with Eng. hn.),2(2nd alt. with
b.-cl.),2(2nd alt. with c.-bn.) - 4,3,3,1 - timp.,perc.(3),glock.,xyl. -
hp. - str.
25:00 Composer.
—— DIVERTIMENTO FOR ORCHESTRA, OP. 34 (IN 4 MOVTS.)
2(2nd alt. with picc.),2,2,2 - 2,2,0,0 - timp.,perc.(2),glock.,xyl. - pf.
- str.
20:00 Leeds.
—— FESTIVAL OVERTURE, OP. 40
*3,*3,*3,*3 - 4,3,3,1 - timp.,perc.(3),glock.,xyl. - hp. - pf. - str.
11:00 Leeds.
—— INTRODUCTION ET SCHERZO (SCHERZO POUR
ORCHESTRE) OP. 10
*3,2,2,*3 - 3,3,0,0 - timp.,perc.(2),xyl. - str. 8:00 MCA Music.
—— MUSIC FOR ORCHESTRA, OP. 39
2(2nd alt. with picc.),2(2nd alt. with Eng. hn.),2(2nd alt. with
b.-cl.),2 - 4,2,3,1 - timp.,perc.(2),glock. - pf. - str.
14:00 Composer.

—— OPUS SINFONICUM, OP. 21
2(2nd alt. with Eng. hn.),2,2,2(2nd alt. with c.-bn.). - 3,3,2,1 -
timp.,perc.(2) - str.
11:00 Leeds.
—— PARTITA CONCERTANTE, OP. 45 (1969) (IN 4 MOVTS.)
*2,1,*2,1 - 1,1,0,0 - timp.,perc.(1),glock.,xyl. - pf. - str.
22:30 Composer.
—— SINFONIETTA, OP. 27
1(alt. with picc.),1,1,1 - 1,1,0,0 - timp.,perc.(2),glock.,xyl. - pf. -
str.
16:00 AMP.
—— SUITE FROM "DANTON", OP. 20 (FOR MEZZO-SOPRANO
AND ORCH.)
*3,*3,*3,*3 - 4,3,2,1 - timp.,perc.(2),xyl. - hp. - str.
17:00 Composer.
—— SYMPHONY NO. 3 (IN 4 MOVTS.)
2(2nd alt. with picc.),2(2nd alt. with Eng. hn.),2(2nd alt. with
b.-cl.),2(2nd alt. with c.-bn.) - 4,3,2,1 - timp.,perc.(3),glock.,xyl. -
hp. - pf. - str.
36:30 Leeds.
—— SYMPHONY NO. 4, OP. 46 (1971) (IN 4 MOVTS.)
*3,*3,*3,*3 - 4,3,3,1 - timp.,perc.(3),glock.,xyl. - hp. - pf. - str.
38:00 Composer.
—— VARIAZIONI CONCERTANTI, OP. 38 (THEME, 4
VARIATIONS AND FINALE)
2(2nd alt. with picc.),2(2nd alt. with Eng. hn.),2(2nd alt. with
b.-cl.),2(2nd alt. with c.-bn.) - 4,3,3,1 - timp.,perc.(3),glock.,xyl. -
hp. - pf. - str.
24:00 Composer.

LOPES GRAÇA, Fernando
—— PARA UMA CRINÇA QUE VAI NASCER ("FOR A CHILD
ABOUT TO BE BORN") (SUITE)
str.
13:00 EV.
—— SYMPHONY
3,3,3,3 - 4,4,3,1 - timp.,perc.(2) - str.
Leeds.

LO PRESTI, Ronald
—— ELEGY (FOR SATB CHORUS AND ORCH.) (Text: Vachel
Lindsay)
2(2nd alt. with picc.),2,2,2 - 4,3,3,1 - timp. - str. 12:00 Composer.
—— KANSAS OVERTURE
2-*3,2,2,2 - 4,3,3,1 - timp.,perc.(3),xyl. - str. 8:30 C. Fischer.
—— LLANO ESTACADO (THE STAKED PLAIN)
*3,2,2,2 - 4,3,3,1 - timp.,perc.(3),bells - str. 8:00 Composer.
—— THE MASKS (IN 2 MOVTS.)
2(2nd alt. with picc.),2,2,2 - 4,3,3,0 - timp. - str. 8:00 C. Fischer.
—— NOCTURNE FOR SMALL ORCH. (1956)
1,1,1,1 - 2,1,1,0 - timp. - str.
8:00 Composer.
—— NOCTURNE FOR VIOLA AND STRING ORCH. (1960)
str.
C. Fischer.
—— PRELUDE TO THE OPERA "THE BIRTHDAY"
Composer.
—— SUITE FROM "KANZA" (IN 4 MOVTS.)
17:00 Composer.
—— TRIBUTE (FOR SATB CHORUS AND ORCH.) (Text: Walt
Whitman)
*3,2,2,2 - 4,3,3,1 - euph.,1 - timp.,perc. - str. 5:30 C. Fischer.
—— TWO CIVIL WAR SONGS (FOR TTBB CHORUS AND
ENSEMBLE)(1961) (Text: Howard Halgedahl)
2,2,2(2nd alt. with b.-cl.),2 - 0,0,0,0 - timp.,perc.,xyl. - pf.
7:00 Composer.

LORD, Phillip
—— PAGEANT OVERTURE (1963)
2,2,2,2 - 4,3,3,1 - perc.(2) - hp. - str.
4:00 P.R.S.
—— VARIATIONS FOR PIANO AND ORCH. (1957)
2,2,2,2 - 4,2,3,1 - perc.(2) - pf. - str.
20:00 P.R.S.

LORENTZEN, Bent
—— EURYDICE (OPERA) %
1,0,0,0 - 0,0,1,0 - perc. - tape-recorder - 2 pf. - str.(3,3,0,0)
27:00 G. Schirmer.
—— A GARDEN ENCLOSED IS MY BRIDE (FOR SOPRANO,
TAPE AND ORCH.)(1972)
29:00 Tetra.
—— MUSIC FOR MOZART-ORCH. (1967)
2,2,2,2 - 2,2,2,0 - timp. - str.
11:00 G. Schirmer.
—— THE NIGHT (FOR SOPRANO, CHORUS AND ORCH.)
3,3,3,3 - 4,3,3,1 - timp.,perc. - hp. - pf. - str. 35:00 G. Schirmer.
—— SHIFTINGS (1970)
2,2,2,2 - 2,2,2,0 - timp. - str.
12:00 G. Schirmer.
or:
1,1,1,1 - 1,1,1,0 - perc. - str.
—— TIDE (1971)
2,2,2,2 - 2,2,2,0 - perc. - str.
12:00 G. Schirmer.
or:

1,1,1,1 - 1,1,1,0 - perc. - str.
—— THE UNCONSCIOUS (1967)
  2,2,2,2 - 2,2,2,0 - perc. - str.   11:00 G. Schirmer.
  or:
  1,1,1,1 - 1,1,1,0 - perc. - str.
—— VIERGE EN PEAU D'OISEAU
  2,2,2,2 - 2,2,2,0 - perc. - tape-recorder - str.   19:00 G. Schirmer.
  or:
  1,1,1,1 - 1,1,1,0 - perc. - tape-recorder - str.
—— ZYKLUS NO. 4 (FROM "CYCLE FOR STRINGED
INSTRUMENTS") (1966)
  3 "friction instruments" - str.   12:00 G. Schirmer.

LORENZ, Ellen Jane
—— THREE FAIRY TALES (SUITE) (IN 3 MOVTS.)
                                          6:00 Composer.
—— VENITE ADOREMUS DOMINUM (CHURCH SUITE) (FOR
STRINGS) (IN 5 MOVTS.)
  str.   16:00 Lorenz.

LOSH, Werner J.
—— CORONACH (1965)
  3(3rd alt. with picc.),2(2nd alt. with Eng. hn.),2,*3 - 4,3,3,1 -
  timp.,perc.,bells - pf. - str.   9:00 MCA Music.
—— SURSUM CORDA (RAISE UP YOUR HEARTS) (FOR MIXED
CHORUS AND ORCH.) (1950) (Text: Bernard J. Losh)
  2,2,2,2 - 4,2,3,0 - timp. - org. - str.   7:00 Composer.
—— SYMPHONY NO. 1 (1959) (IN 3 MOVTS.)
  2(2nd alt. with picc.),2,2,*3 - 4,3,3,1 - timp.,perc.(3),bells,cel. - hp.
  - pf. - str.   37:30 Mills.
—— SYMPHONY NO. 2 (1962) (IN 4 MOVTS.)
  2 picc.,2,2(2nd alt.with Eng.hn.),2,*3 - 4,4,3,1 -
  timp.,perc.(3),bells,cel. - hp. - pf. - str.   36:12 Mills.

LOTH, Leslie
—— CONCERTO NO. 1 FOR PIANO AND ORCH. (IN FORM OF
VARIATIONS)
  2,2,2,2 - 4,3,3,0 - timp.,perc. - pf. - str.   20:00 Composer.
—— FESTIVAL OVERTURE
  1,1,2,4 sax.,1 - 2,2,1,0 - timp.,perc.(2) - pf. - str.   6:30 Mills.
—— PAEN (SYMPHONIC POEM)
  3(3rd alt. with picc.),*3,*3,*3 - 4,4,3,1 - timp.,perc.(2-3) - hp. - pf.
  - str.   12:00 Composer.
—— SYMPHONIC PRELUDE
  3,2,2,2 - 4,3,3,1 - timp.,perc.(2) - hp. - str.   7:00 Composer.

LOTHAR, Mark
—— CONCERTINO FOR 4 CLARINETS AND SMALL ORCH., OP.
63
  4 cl. - perc. - hp. - str.   22:00 Henmar.
—— EICHENDORFF SUITE, OP. 36 (IN 7 MOVTS.)
  2(2nd alt. with picc.),2(2nd alt. with Eng. hn.),2(2nd alt. with
  b.-cl.),2 - 2,1,1,0 - timp.,perc.(3) - hp. - str.   16:00 Henmar.
—— DIE HIRTENFLÖTE, OP. 50 (THE SHEPHERD'S PIPE)
(DIVERTIMENTO)
                                          J. Oertel.
—— LITTLE THEATRE SUITE, OP. 28 (IN 6 MOVTS.)
  2(2nd alt. with picc.),1,1,1 - 2,2,0,0 - timp.,perc.,cel. - 2
  mandolins(ad lib.) - hp. - str.   15:00 Henmar.
—— LORD SPLEEN (OVERTURE), OP. 17
  2,2,2,2 - 4,3,3,1 - timp.,perc. - harm. - hp. - pf. - str.
                                          6:00 Bo. Hawkes.
—— MITTELALTERLICHE TANZSUITE, OP. 49
  2,2,2,2 - 4,3,3,1 - timp.,perc. - hp. - str.   16:00 Ries-Erler.
—— OLD GERMAN SONGS, OP. 41-A (5 SONGS FOR SOPRANO
AND ORCH.)
  2(2nd alt. with picc.),1,2,2(2nd alt. with c.-bn.) - 2,0,0,0 -
  timp.,perc.,cel. - hp. - str.   14:00 Henmar.
—— SCHNEIDER-WIBBEL (OVERTURE)
  2,2,2,2 - 4,3,3,0 - timp.,perc. - str.   7:00 Sikorski.
—— SONGS OF CHILDHOOD, OP. 38-A (FOR MEDIUM VOICE
AND ORCH.) (Text: Friedrich Bischoff)
  2(2nd alt. with picc.),2(2nd alt. with Eng.hn.),*3,2(2nd alt. with
  c-bn.) - 4,3,3,1 - timp.,perc.(3),cel. - hp. - pf. - str.   12:00 Henmar.
—— SUITE FROM A CHILDREN'S FAIRY TALE, OP. 19 (IN 6
MOVTS.)
  1(alt. with picc.),1,1,1 - 2,1,1,0 - timp.,perc. - pf. - str.
                                          12:00 Henmar.
—— TYLL (3-ACT OPERA, AFTER "TYLL EULENSPIEGEL") %
(Text: Hugo F. Koenigsgarten)
  *3,*3,*3,*3 - 4,3,3,1 - timp.,perc.(4) - hp. - str.   120:00 Henmar.
—— VERWANDLUNGEN EINES BAROCKTHEMAS, OP. 57
  3,2,3,2 - 4,3,3,1 - timp.,perc.,xyl. - hp. - str.   13:00 J. Oertel.

LOTTI, Antonio - PICCIOLI, Giuseppe
—— DIES IRAE (FOR SOLOISTS, MIXED CHORUS AND ORCH.)
  2 ob. - 2 tpt. - org. - str.   50:00 Bo. Hawkes.

LOUCHEUR, Raymond
—— CONCERTINO FOR PERCUSSION AND ORCH.
  3,2,2,2 - 2,2,2,0 - hp. - str.   14:30 Presser.
—— CONCERTINO FOR TRUMPET AND ORCH.
  2,2,2,2 - 2,2,0,0 - timp., perc. - hp. - str.   15:00 Salabert.
—— EN FAMILLE
  1,1,1,1 - 2,1,1,0 - perc. - pf. - str.   11:00 Presser.
—— HOMMAGE À RAOUL DUFY
  1,1,1,1 - 2,1,1,0 - perc.(3),cel. - str.   Presser.
—— HOP-FROG (2 SYMPHONIC SUITES FROM THE BALLET)
  3,3(1 alt. with Eng. hn.),4,3 - 4,4,3,1 - timp.,perc.(4),cel. - 2 hp. -
  pf. - str.   40:00 Salabert.
—— RAPSODIE MALGACHE
  2,2,2,1 - 0,1,1,0 - timp.,perc. - str.   16:00 Salabert.
—— SYMPHONY NO. 2
  3,3,3,3 - 4,3,3,1 - timp.,perc.,cel.,glock. - hp. - str.   25:00 Salabert.

LOUEL, Jean
—— BURLESCA (FOR BASSOON AND ORCH.) (1943)
  2,2,2,3 - 2,1,0,0 - timp. - hp. - str.   9:00 H. Elkan.
—— CONCERTO DA CAMERA (FOR FLUTE AND ORCH.) (1947)
  1,1,1,1 alto sax., 1 - 1,1,0,0 - cel. - hp. - str.   18:00 H. Elkan.
—— CONCERTO FOR VIOLIN AND ORCH. (1950)
  2,2,2,2 - 4,2,3,1 - timp.,perc.,cel.,xyl. - 2 hp. - str.   17:30 CBDM.
—— CONCERTO NO. 2 FOR PIANO AND ORCH. (1949)
  2,2,2,2 - 4,2,3,1 - timp.,perc. - str.   18:00 CBDM.
—— CONCERTO NO. 2 FOR VIOLIN AND ORCH. (1971) (IN 3
MOVTS.)
  2,2,2,2 - 4,3,3,1 - timp.,perc. - str.   18:00 H. Elkan.
—— FANFARES (1948)
  3,4,3,1 - timp.,perc.   8:00 CBDM.
—— FANTAISIE SUR DEUX CHANSONS DE TROUVÈRES (1942)
  3,3,3,3 - 4,4,3,1 - timp.,perc.,cel.,glock.,xyl. - 2 hp. - str.
                                          18:00 H. Elkan.
—— SUITE (FOR CHAMBER ORCH.) (1942)
  1,1,1,1 - 1,0,0,0 - str.   16:00 H. Elkan.
—— SYMPHONY (1968) (FOR STRING ORCH.)
  str.   20:22 H. Elkan.

LOURIÉ, Arthur
—— THE BLACKAMOOR OF PETER THE GREAT (SUITE FROM
THE OPERA)
                                          S.A.C.E.M.
—— THE FEAST DURING THE PLAGUE (SUITE) (FOR SOPRANO,
CHORUS AND ORCH.)
  1,4,2,1 - 4,4,3,1 - timp.,perc. - hp. - str.   26:00 S.A.C.E.M.
—— KORMTCHAIA (SYMPHONY NO. 2)
  4,4,4,4 - 6,4,3,2 - timp.,perc.,cel. - str.   18:00 S.A.C.E.M.
—— LAMENT (FROM DANTE'S "LA VITA NUOVA") (FOR
WOMEN'S CHORUS AND STRINGS)
  str.   6:00 S.A.C.E.M.
—— SINFONIA DIALECTICA
  4,4,4,4 - 4,4,3,1 - timp.,perc. - pf. - str.   15:00 Bo. Hawkes.

LOVEC, Vladimir
—— CONCERTO IN A MINOR, FOR PIANO AND ORCH.
  2(2nd alt. with picc.),2,2,2 - 4,2,3,1 - timp. - pf. - str.
                                          30:00 Hans Gerig.
—— DRAMATIC OVERTURE
  2(2nd alt. with picc.),2,2,2 - 4,3,3,1 - timp.,perc. - str.
                                          9:00 Hans Gerig.

LOVELOCK, William
—— BURLESQUE FOR XYLOPHONE AND ORCH. (1966)
  2,2,2,2 - 4,2,3,0 - perc.,vibra.,xyl. - hp. - str.   10:00 A.P.R.A.
—— CONCERTINO FOR DOUBLE BASS AND ORCH. (1969)
                                          9:00 AllansPty.
—— CONCERTINO FOR TROMBONE AND STRINGS (1965)
  trb. - str.   Chappell.
—— CONCERTO FOR FLUTE AND ORCH. (1961)
  1,2,2,2 - 4,2,0,0 - perc. - str.   15:00 Chappell.
—— CONCERTO FOR PIANO AND ORCH. (1963)
  2,2,2,2 - 4,3,3,1 - perc. - pf. - str.   18:00 A.P.R.A.
—— CONCERTO FOR SAXOPHONE AND ORCH. (1963)
  2,2,2,sax.,2 - 4,2,3,0 - perc. - str.   16:00 AllansPty.
—— CONCERTO FOR SAXOPHONE AND STRINGS (1973)
  sax.(in E♭) - str.   16:00 AllansPty.
—— CONCERTO FOR TRUMPET AND ORCH. (1968)
  2,2,2,2 - 4,1,3,1 - perc. - str.   16:00 Southern.

—— CONCERTO FOR TUBA AND ORCH. (1967)
2,2,2,2 - 4,2,3,1 - perc. - str.   15:00 AllansPty.
—— CONCERTO FOR TWO HARPS AND ORCH. (1965)
1,1,1,1 - 2,1,0,0 - perc.,xyl. - 2 hp. - str.   15:00 A.P.R.A.
—— CONCERTO FOR VIOLA AND ORCH. (1973)
    16:00 A.P.R.A.
—— DIVERTIMENTO FOR STRING ORCH. (1965)
str.   16:00 AllansPty.
—— SINFONIA CONCERTANTE (FOR ORGAN AND ORCH.)
2,2,2,2 - 4,3,3,1 - perc. - org. - str.   20:00 AllansPty.
—— SINFONIETTA FOR ORCH. (1964)
2,2,2,2 - 4,2,3,1 - perc. - hp. - str.   17:00 A.P.R.A.
—— SUITE FOR WINDS AND PERCUSSION (1973)
3,2,2(1 alt. with b.-cl.,1alt. with sax.),3 - 4,3,3,1 - perc.
    17:00 A.P.R.A.
—— SYMPHONY IN C SHARP MINOR (1966)
3,3,3,3 - 4,3,3,1 - perc. - 2 hp. - str.   20:00 A.P.R.A.

LOVINGOOD, Penman, Sr.
—— PRELUDE IN E FLAT
4,2(2nd alt. with Eng.hn.),*3,*3 - 4,2,3,0 - timp. - pf. - str.
    20:00 Composer.
—— VITANIA (SUITE) (IN 6 MOVTS.)
1,2(2nd alt. with Eng. hn.),*3,*3 - 4,2,2,0 - timp. - pf. - str.
    30:00 Composer.

LOVREGLIO, Eleuthere
—— KING-SSE
4,3,6,3 - 4,4,4,1 - timp.,perc.,cel. - 2 hp. - str.   31:00 Presser.
—— SUITE IBÉRIENNE
3,2,2,2 - 4,3,3,0 - timp.,perc.(4),cel. - hp. - str.   19:30 Presser.

LOWE, Jack W.
—— CONCERTO FOR ORGAN AND ORCH. (1938)
*3,2,2,*3 - 4,2,2,1 - timp.,perc.(4),bells - hp. - org. - str.
    11:30 Composer.
—— OVERTURE: SCENE (1938)
*3,2,2,2 - 4,2,3,1 - timp.,perc.(3),glock.,vibra.,xyl. - pf. - str.
    3:50 Composer.
—— SEA-DRIFT (OUT OF THE CRADLE ENDLESSLY ROCKING)
(FOR SOPRANO, BARITONE, CHORUS AND ORCH.) (1939)
(Text: Walt Whitman)
2,2,2,2 - 4,3,3,1 - timp.,perc.(3),glock. - hp. - str. 18:20 Composer.
—— TWO DANCES FOR ORCHESTRA (1937)
*3,*3,*3,2 - 4,0,0,0 - timp.,perc.(2) - hp. - str.   4:10 Composer.

LOWENSTEIN, Gunilla
—— SWEDISH-HUNGARIAN VARIATIONS, OP. 3 (1960)
2,2,2,2 - 2,2,1,0 - timp. - str.   16:00 P.R.S.

LÖWLEIN, Hans
—— CONCERTO FOR ORCH., OP. 14
3,2,3,2 - 4,2,3,1 - timp.,perc. - str.   18:00 Tetra.
—— MUSIC FOR CELLO AND ORCH., OP. 13
2,2,2,2 - 2,2,0,0 - timp.,perc. - pf. - str.   9:00 Tetra.

LU, Yen
—— DAWN (1969)
3(3rd alt. with picc.),3(3rd alt.with Eng.hn.),3(3rd alt.with
b.-cl.)pedal(B♭contrabass) cl.,*3 - 6,4,4,1 -
timp.,perc.(5),bells,cel.,glock.,vibra.,xyl. - pf. - str.
    10:00 Composer.
—— TO A LITTLE WHITE FLOWER (1970)
3(3rd alt. with picc.),3(3rd alt. with Eng.hn.),3(3rd alt. with
b.-cl.),*3 - 4,3,3,1 - timp.,perc.(4),bells,cel.,glock.,vibra.,xyl. - hpsc.
- pf. - str.   12:00 Composer.

LUALDI, Adriano
—— THE MOON OF THE CARIBEES ("LA LUNA DEI CARAIBI")
(1-ACT OPERA, AFTER EUGENE O'NEILL'S DRAMA) %
3,2,2,2 sax.,2 - 2,2,2,0 - timp.,perc.(3),cel.,xyl. - hp. - pf. - str.
    Leeds.

On Stage: tpt.,trb. - perc. - acc.

LUBIC, Sava
—— YOGOSLAV RHAPSODY NO. 1 (1975)
    15:00 Composer.

LUBIN, Ernest
—— DIVERTIMENTO ON AMERICAN THEMES
*3,*3,E♭cl.,*3,*3 - 3,2,3,1 - timp.,perc.(2) - str.   8:30 Fema.
—— FUGHETTA
*3,*2,E♭cl.,2,2 - 4,2,3,1 - timp.,perc.(2),xyl. - str.   Composer.

—— OVERTURE TO A CHILDREN'S PLAY
2(2nd alt. with picc.),2,2,2 - 2,2,0,0 - timp.,perc.(1),glock. - hp. -
str.   3:00 Composer.
—— THE PARDONER'S TALE (1-ACT OPERA) % (Text: Ted Hart)
1,1,2,1 - 2,2,2,0 - timp.,perc.(2),bells - str.   50:00 Composer.
—— SUITE IN THE OLDEN STYLE
str.   D. Gornston.
—— THREE PIECES FOR STRINGS
str.   6:00 Composer.
—— TRAGIC OVERTURE
*3,2,E♭cl.,2,*3 - 4,2,3,1 - timp. - str.   5:00 Composer.
—— TWO SHORT PIECES FROM THE BALLET "FIFTH AVENUE"
*2,1E♭cl.,2,1 - 2,2,0,0 - timp.,perc.(2) - str.   3:00 Composer.
—— VARIATIONS ON A PASTORAL THEME
*3,2,2,2 - 4,2,1,1 - timp.,perc.(1) - str.   8:00 Composer.
—— VARIATIONS ON A THEME OF STEPHEN FOSTER
3(3rd alt. with picc.),2,3(2nd alt. with E♭cl. and 3rd alt. with
b.-cl.),*3 - 4,2,0,0 - timp. - str.   12:00 Composer.

LUDEWIG, Wolfgang
—— SINFONIETTA FOR STRING ORCH.
str.   15:00 Mannheimer.

LUDT, Finn
—— SWEETHEART IN THE WOODS ("KJAERESTEN I SKOGEN")
(BALLET IN 4 MOVTS.) %
1,0,1,0 - 0,0,0,0 - pf. - str.   25:00 T.O.N.O.

LUDWIG, Joachim
—— CONCERTO NO. 1 FOR PIANO AND ORCH.
2,*3,*3,*3 - 2,2,3,1 - timp.,perc.(3) - hp. - pf. - str. 27:00 Modern.

LUENING, Otto
—— SUITE FOR STRINGS
str.   10:00 Bo. Hawkes.

LUETHI, Willy
—— DIVERTIMENTO FÜR KAMMERORCHESTER, OP. 22
    15:00 S.U.I.S.A.

LUKE, Ray E.
—— CONCERTO FOR BASSOON AND ORCH. (1965) (IN 3
MOVTS.)
2(2nd alt. with picc.),2(2nd alt.with Eng.hn.),*3,2 - 4,3,3,1 -
timp.,perc.(2),glock.,mar. - hp. - str.   18:30 Oxford.
—— CONCERTO FOR PIANO AND ORCH. (1968) (IN 3 MOVTS)
*3,*3,*3,*3 - 4,3,3,1 - timp.,perc.(4),glock.,xyl. - hp. - pf. - str.
    20:30 Oxford.
—— EPILOGUE FOR ORCHESTRA
2,2,2,2 - 4,2,3,1 - glock. - hp. - str.   Composer.
—— FANFARE FOR SYMPHONIC WINDS AND PERCUSSION
(1967)
*2,2,2,2 - 4,3,3,1 - timp.,perc.(3)   2:30 Composer.
—— INCANTATION (FOR CELLO, HARP AND STRINGS) (1968)
hp. - str.   8:30 Composer.
—— SUITE FOR ORCHESTRA WOODWINDS (1961) (IN 4 MOVTS.)
*3,*3,*3,*3 - 0,0,0,0   9:30 Composer.
—— SUITE NO. 1 FOR ORCH. (1958) (IN 3 MOVTS.)
*3,2,2,2 - 4,3,3,1 - timp.,perc.(2),glock. - hp. - str.   10:00 Oxford.
—— SUITE NO. 2 FOR ORCH. (1967) (IN 6 MOVTS. PLAYED
WITHOUT INTERRUPTION)
*3,*3,*3,*3 - 4,3,3,1 - timp.,perc.(4),bells,glock.,xyl. - hp. - pf. -
str.   13:00 Oxford.
—— SUMMER MUSIC (AN OVERTURE) (1970)
*3,*3,*3,2 - 4,3,3,1 - timp.,perc.(3),xyl. - hp. - pf. - str.
    9:00 Composer.
—— SYMPHONIC DIALOGUES (FOR VIOLIN, OBOE AND
ORCH.) (1965) (IN 3 MOVTS.)
*2,*2,*2,1 - 0,0,0,0 - timp.,perc.(2),1 bell,xyl. - hp. - pf. - str.
    14:00 Oxford.
—— SYMPHONIC SONGS (FOR MEZZO-SOPRANO AND ORCH.)
(1968) (Text: Wong Mae)
*3,2,*3,2 - 4,0,0,0 - timp.,perc.(3),bells,glock.,vibra.,xyl. - hp. - pf.
- str.   12:00 Composer.
—— SYMPHONY NO. 1 (1959) (IN 4 MOVTS.)
*3,*3,*3,*3 - 4,3,3,1 - timp.,perc.(3) - hp. - str.   20:00 Fleisher.
—— SYMPHONY NO. 2 (1961) (IN 3 MOVTS.)
*3,*3,*3,2 - *3 - 4,3,3,1 - timp.,perc.(3),glock.,2 tuned tomtoms -
hp. - str.   16:30 Oxford.
—— SYMPHONY NO. 3 (1963) (IN 3 MOVTS.)
*3,2(2nd alt. with Eng. hn.),*3,2 - 4,3,3,1 - timp.,perc.(2),glock. -
hp. - pf. - str.   19:30 Oxford.

—— SYMPHONY NO. 4 (IN 1 MOVT.) (1970)
*3,*3,*3,2 - 4,3,3,1 - timp.,perc.(4),glock.,xyl. - hp.- pf. - str.
24:00 Oxford.
—— TWO MINIATURES FOR ORCH. (1957)
Composer.

LULLY, Jean Baptiste - BOULAY, L.
—— SUITE FROM "AMADIS"
2,0,0,0 - 0,2,0,0 - timp. - hpsc. - str.   15:00 Eds. Fran.

LULLY, Jean Baptiste - BROWN, James
—— SIX PIECES
str.   Galaxy.

LULLY, Jean Baptiste - BUSH
—— CHACONNE
1,1,1,0- 2,1,0,0 - str.   8:00 FDH.

LULLY, Jean Baptiste - FENDLER, Edvard
—— CHACONNE
str.   Bo. Hawkes.

LULLY, Jean Baptiste - JACOBI, Wolfgang
—— COURT DANCES, AFTER LULLY (TWO BALLET SUITES)
perc. - str.   Hans Gerig.

LULLY, Jean Baptiste - MURPHY, Arthur L.
—— FRENCH BAROQUE SUITE (FROM "LE BOURGEOIS
GENTILHOMME")
6:45 Witmark.

LULLY, Jean Baptiste - OUBRADOUS, Fernand
—— LA GROTTE DE VERSAILLES
2,2,0,2 - 0,1,0,0 - str.   16:00 Presser.
—— PSYCHE (SELECTIONS FOR SOLO VOICE, MIXED CHORUS
AND ORCH.)
2,2,0,2 - 2,0,0,0 - timp. - pf. - str.   29:00 Presser.
—— SUITE NO. 3 IN B FLAT
0,2,0,1 - 0,0,0,0 - str.   10:00 Presser.
—— SUITE NO. 7 IN G MINOR
0,2,0,1 - 0,0,0,0 - str.   10:00 Presser.
—— SUITE NO. 8 IN C
0,2,0,2 - 2,0,0,0 - timp. - str.   10:00 Presser.

LULLY, Jean Baptiste - ROSENTHAL, Manuel
—— NOCE VILLAGEOISE
2,2,2,2 - 0,0,0,0 - timp. - str.   10:00 EV.

LULLY, Jean-Baptiste - SOLTESZ, L.
—— PSYCHE SUITE
2,2,0,2 - 0,4,0,0 - str.   17:00 Presser.

LUNDBERG, Kjell
—— ÄLVSBORGSRAPSODI
2,2,2,2 - 2,2,3,1 - timp.,perc. - str.   16:00 Fleisher.

LUNDÉN, Lennart
—— DJULÖ SUITE (FOR STRINGS) (IN 3 MOVTS.)
str.   12:00 S.T.I.M.
—— FANTASI ÖVER NYKÖPINGSVISAN
2,1,2,1 - 0,0,0,0 - str.   S.T.I.M.
—— OCH DET HÄHDE SIG.....(CHRISTMAS MUSIC) (FOR SOLO
VOICES, MIXED CHORUS, CHILDREN'S CHORUS AND
ORCH.) (1958)
1,1,2,1 - 1,1,0,0 - perc.(2) - str.   15:00 S.T.I.M.
—— PASTORAL SUITE (IN 8 MOVTS.)
2,2,2,2 - 2,2,1,0 - timp. - str.   26:00 S.T.I.M.
—— SUMMER, 1939 (CONCERT OVERTURE)
2,2,2,2 - 4,2,3,1 - timp. - str.   8:00 S.T.I.M.
—— SYMPHONY IN B MINOR
2,2,2,2 - 4,2,3,0 - timp. - str.   33:00 S.T.I.M.
—— SYMPHONY NO. 2
2,2,2,2 - 4,2,3,1 - timp. - str.   S.T.I.M.
—— SYMPHONY NO. 3 (CHAMBER SYMPHONY)
2,2,2,2 - 2,2,0,0 - str.   20:00 S.T.I.M.
—— THALATTA (OVERTURE-FANTASY) (FOR STRINGS)
str.   14:00 S.T.I.M.
—— VARIATIONER AND FUGA ÖVER ÖRJANSLÅTEN
2,1,2,1 - 2,2,1,0 - timp.,perc. - str.   14:30 S.T.I.M.
—— VARIATIONS ON "PER SPELMAN" (1959)
str.   S.T.I.M.

LUNDKVIST, Per
—— FÖDELSEDAGSBUKETTEN (1951)
1,1,2,1 - 2,0,0,0 - hp. - str.   4:30 Fleisher.
—— HEMBYGDEN (SUITE)
1,1,2,1 - 2,2,0,0 - perc. - str.   9:00 Fleisher.
—— EINE KLEINE MORGENMUSIK (1961)
str.   8:40 Fleisher.
—— THE LAND OF THE MIDNIGHT SUN (SUITE)
2,2,2,2 - 4,2,3,1 - timp. - hp. - str.   12:30 Fleisher.
—— LJUSA SKYAR (SUITE) (1971)
2,2,2,2 - 2,0,0,0 - str.   10:00 Fleisher.
—— MIDNIGHT RHAPSODY (FOR PIANO AND ORCH.) (1974)
2,2,2,2 - 4,2,3,0 - timp.,perc. - pf. - str.   6:30 Fleisher.
—— MOUNTAIN RHAPSODY (FOR PIANO AND ORCH.)
2,2,2,2 - 4,2,3,1 - timp.,perc. - pf. - str.   7:00 Robbins.
—— PEARL DIADEMS (FOR CLARINET AND ORCH.)
1,0,1,0 - 0,3,1,0 - hp. - str.   6:10 Fleisher.
—— RHAPSODY IN RED (FOR PIANO AND ORCH.)
2,1,3,1 - 1,3,3,0 - timp.,perc. - pf. - str.   9:00 Fleisher.
—— I ROSORNAS TID (1971)
2,1,2,1 - 2,0,0,0 - hp. - str.   4:30 Fleisher.
—— EN SAGOKLANG (FOR HORN AND ORCH.) (1962)
1,1,2,1 - 0,0,0,0 - str.   5:40 Fleisher.
—— SILVER FLUTES (FOR FLUTE AND SMALL ORCH.)
1,1,2,1 - 2,0,0,0 - perc. - str.   4:30 Fleisher.
—— SKANSENSVIT
2,2,2,2 - 4,2,3,0 - timp. - hp. - str.   12:00 Fleisher.
—— SKOGEN SUSAR (SUITE) (1971)
2,2,2,2 - 4,0,0,0 - timp. - str.   12:00 Fleisher.
—— SKOGSKLANGER
2,2,2,2 - 4,1,0,0 - timp. - hp. - str.   12:00 Fleisher.
—— STOCKHOLM (AN OVERTURE)
2,2,2,2 - 4,2,3,0 - timp.,perc. - hp. - str.   5:00 Fleisher.
—— SWEDISH PICTURES (SUITE) (1957)
1,1,2,1 - 3,2,1,0 - timp.,perc. - pf.(ad lib.) - str.   13:00 Fleisher.
—— VÄRMLANDSSVIT (1958)
1,1,2,1 - 2,2,1,0 - timp. - hp. - str.   11:30 Fleisher.

LUNDQUIST, Torbjo Aarn
—— DIVERTIMENTO FOR CHAMBER ORCH., OP. 11
1,1,1,1 - 0,0,0,0 - str.   10:00 S.T.I.M.
—— LÅNGT FRÅN VÅRT JORDISKA HEM (CHRISTMAS PLAY)
(FOR SOPRANO, TENOR, BARITONE, BASS, MIXED
CHORUS, CHILDREN'S CHORUS AND ORCH.) % (Text: Bo
Setterlind)
2,1,4,3 sax.(1 alto, 1 ten.,1 bar.),2 - 0,2,1,0 - perc. (1) - pf. - 2 d.-b
20:00 S.T.I.M.
—— TAFFELMUSIK, OP. 2 (FOR FLUTE, CLARINET AND
STRINGS)
fl. - cl. - str.   10:00 S.T.I.M.
—— VARIATIONS SUITE (FOR STRINGS)
str.   6:00 S.T.I.M.

LUNDQUIST, Torbjörn
—— CANZONA, OP. 12
1,1,0,0 - 0,1,0,0 - str.   9:00 S.T.I.M.
—— CHAMBER SYMPHONY, OP. 11
2,2,2,2 - 2,2,2,0 - timp. - str.   19:00 S.T.I.M.
—— CONCERTO DA CAMERA (FOR ACCORDION AND ORCH.)
(1962)
2,2,2,2 - 2,2,1,0 - perc.(1) - acc. - str.   24:00 S.T.I.M.
—— CONCERTO FOR MARIMBA AND ORCH. (1974)
3,3,3,3 - 4,3,3,1 - timp.,perc.(4),mar. - hp. - pf. - str.
20:00 Fleisher.
—— CONCERTO GROSSO (1974)
str.   23:00 Fleisher.
—— CONFRONTATION (1968)
3,3,3,3 - 4,3,4,1 - timp.,perc.(4) - str.   12:00 S.T.I.M.
—— ELEGIER FRÅN BERGEN, OP. 15 (CANTATA) (FOR
TENOR-BARITONE, 3-PART MALE CHORUS AND ORCH.)
(Text: Bo Setterlind)
2,2,2,2 - 2,2,0,0 - timp. - hp.(ad lib.) - pf.(ad lib.) - str.
15:00 S.T.I.M.
—— EVOLUZIONE (1968)
str.   10:00 S.T.I.M.
—— FERVOR (FOR VIOLINO GRANDE AND ORCH.) (1967)
2,2,2,2 - 0,0,0,0 - perc.(2) - str.   15:00 S.T.I.M.
—— GALAX (1971)
3,3,3,3 - 4,4,3,1 - timp.,perc.(3) - 2 hp. - org.(or acc.) - 2 pf. - str.
16:00 Fleisher.
—— HANGAR-MUSIK (FOR PIANO AND ORCH.) (1967)
3,3,3,3 - 4,3,3,1 - timp.,perc.(6) - hp. - pf. - str.   18:00 S.T.I.M.

—— INTARSIA (1968)
acc. - str.　　6:00 S.T.I.M.
—— SOGNO (1968)
ob. - str.　　12:00 S.T.I.M.
—— SOUND ON SOUND (1969)
3,3,3,3 - 4,4,3,1 - timp.,perc.(3) - hp. - str.　　30:00 S.T.I.M.
—— SYMPHONY NO. 1, OP. 11 (CHAMBER SYMPHONY) (REV. 1972)
2,2,2,2 - 2,2,2,0 - timp. - str.　　18:00 Fleisher.
—— SYMPHONY NO. 2 (REV. 1970)
2,2,2,2 - 4,3,3,0 - timp. - hp. - str.　　40:00 EhrlingFlg.
—— VIA TONHETEN (VISIONS) (FOR SOPRANO, BARITONE, MIXED CHORUS, PIANO AND ORCH.) (1960) (Text: Bo Setterlind)
1,1,2,2 - 0,2,1,0 - timp. - pf. - str.　　20:30 S.T.I.M.

LUNDVIK, Hildor
—— LITTLE SUITE (FOR STRINGS)
str.　　10:00 Nordiska.

LUOLAJAN-MIKKOLA, Vilho
—— THREE SONGS (FOR VOICE, HARP AND STRINGS) (1944) (Text: The Kanteletar)
hp. -str.　　9:00 Fazer.

LUPI, Roberto
—— DIVERTIMENTO
1,1,1,1 - tpt. - hp. - str. (no d.-b.)　　6:00 Bo. Hawkes.
—— PSALM 56 (FOR SOLOISTS, MIXED CHORUS AND ORCH.)
3,3,3,3 - 4,3,3,1 - timp.,perc.,cel.,glock. - hp. - str.　　20:00 Bo. Hawkes.
—— STUDI PER UN "HOMUNCULUS" (9 PIECES)
3,3,3,3 - 2,2,2,1 - timp.,perc.,cel.,xyl. - guit. - hp. - pf. - str.　　12:00 Bo. Hawkes.
—— IL VIANDANTE (CONCERTO FOR CELLO AND ORCH.)
3,2,2,2 - 2,2,2,0 - timp.,perc.,cel.,xyl. - hp. - pf. - str.　　22:00 Bo. Hawkes.

LÜRMAN, Ludwig
—— BESCHWINGTES ZWISCHENSPIEL, OP. 27
1,1,2,1 - 2,2,1,0 - timp.,perc. - hp.(or pf.) - str.　　5:00 Henmar.
—— FESTLICHER AUFKLANG, OP. 15 (FESTIVAL PRELUDE)
2,2,2,2-*3 - 4,3,3,1 - timp.,perc. - hp. - str.　　4:00 Henmar.
—— RUF ZUR FREUDE, OP. 20
2,2,2,2-*3 - 4,2,3,1 - timp.,perc. - str.　　6:00 Henmar.
—— SERENADE MUSIC, OP. 25
1,1,2,1 - 2,2,1,0 - timp.,perc. - str.　　14:00 Henmar.

LUSTIG, Moshe
—— KINNERET (FANTASY ON 2 ISRAELI FOLKSONGS)
2,2,2,2 - 2,2,0,0 - timp.,perc.,cel. - hp. - str.　　16:00 IsMuPublns.

LUTECE, Jean
—— CONCERTO FOR ACCORDION AND ORCH.
2,2,2,3 - 2,3,2,0 - timp.,perc. - acc. - hp. - pf. - str.　　25:00 Salabert.
—— RHAPSODY IN SWING
2,2,3,5 sax.(2 alto, 2 ten.,1 bar.),2 - 4,3,2,0 - timp.,perc.(3) - 2 guit. - pf. - str.　　14:00 Salabert.

LUTHER, Martin - MADDY, Joseph E.
—— FESTIVAL FINALE NO. 2 ("A MIGHTY FORTRESS") (FOR MIXED CHORUS AND ORCH.) (Engl. Text: Frederick H. Hedge)　　Fema.

LUTOSLAWSKI, Witold
—— CONCERTO FOR CELLO AND ORCH.
3,3,3,3 - 3,4,3,1 - perc.(3),cel. - hp. - pf. - str.　　24:00 G. Schirmer.
—— CONCERTO FOR ORCHESTRA
3,3,3,3 - 4,4,4,1 - timp.,perc.(4),cel. - 2 hp. - pf. - str.　　29:00 G. Schirmer.
—— DANCE PRELUDES (VERSION NO. 2) (FOR CLARINET AND INSTRUMENTS)
cl. - timp.,perc. - hp. - pf. - str.　　7:00 G. Schirmer.
—— FUNERAL MUSIC
str.　　14:00 G. Schirmer.
—— LITTLE SUITE
3,2,2,2 - 4,3,3,1 - timp.,perc. - str.　　11:00 G. Schirmer.
—— LIVRE POUR ORCHESTRE
3,3,3,3 - 4,1,3,1 - perc.(3),cel. - pf. - str.　　20:00 G. Schirmer.
—— OVERTURE FOR STRINGS
str.　　5:00 G. Schirmer.

—— PAROLES TISSÉES (FOR TENOR, HARP, PIANO, PERCUSSION AND STRINGS)
perc. - hp. - pf. - str.　　16:00 G. Schirmer.
—— PRELUDES AND FUGUES
str.　　34:00 G. Schirmer.
—— SILESIAN TRIPTYCH (FOR SOPRANO AND ORCH.)
3,2,3,2 - 4,3,3,1 - timp.,perc.(4),cel. - hp. - str.　　9:00 G. Schirmer.
—— SYMPHONIC VARIATIONS
3,3,3,3 - 4,3,3,1 - timp.,perc.(4), cel. - hp. - pf. - str.　　9:00 G. Schirmer.
—— SYMPHONY NO. 1
3,3,3,3 - 4,3,3,1 - timp.,perc.(4), cel. - hp. - pf. - str.　　24:00 G. Schirmer.
—— SYMPHONY NO. 2
3,3,3,3 - 4,3,3,1 - perc.,cel. - hp. - pf. - str.　　30:00 G. Schirmer.
—— THREE POSTLUDES
3,3,3,3 - 4,3,3,1 - timp.,perc.(4),cel. - 2 hp. - pf. - str.　　17:00 G. Schirmer.
—— TROIS POÈMES D'HENRI MICHAUX
3,2,3,2 - 2,2,2,0 - timp.,perc.(5),cel. - hp. - 2 pf.　　20:00 G. Schirmer.

LUTYENS, Elisabeth
—— CHAMBER CONCERTO NO. 4, FOR HORN AND SMALL ORCH. (FROM "6 CHAMBER CONCERTOS, OP. 8")
2,1,2,2 - 1,2,1,0 - perc. - str.　　12:00 Mills.
—— CHAMBER CONCERTO, OP. 8, NO. 2
cl.,ten.sax. - pf. - str.　　10:00 Belw-Mills.
—— CHAMBER CONCERTO, OP. 8, NO. 3
bn. - perc. - str.　　10:00 G. Schirmer.
—— CONCERTO FOR VIOLA AND ORCH.　　15:00 Lengnick.
—— DE AMORE, OP. 39 (CANTATA) (FOR SOPRANO, TENOR, MIXED CHORUS AND ORCH.) (Text: Chaucer)
2(1 alt. with picc.),1,2,1 - 2,2 cnt.,2,1,0 - perc.(3) - str.　　35:00 Mills.
—— DIVERTISSEMENT FOR DOUBLE WIND QUINTET
2,2,2,2 - 2,0,0,0　　9:30 Belw-Mills.
—— DIVERTISSEMENT FOR ORCH.
3,2,2,2 - 4,3,3,1 - timp.,perc.,xyl. - str.　　9:30 Belw-Mills.
—— DRAMATIC SCENE ("THE PIT"), OP. 14 (FOR TENOR, BASS, WOMAN'S CHORUS AND ORCH.)　　15:00 Lengnick.
—— EN VOYAGE (SUITE)
2,2,2,2 - 4,2,3,0 - timp.,perc.,xyl. - hp. - str.　　12:00 Belw-Mills.
—— INFIDELIO, OP. 29 (7 SCENES FOR SOPRANO, TENOR AND INSTRUMENTAL ENSEMBLE)　　P.R.S.
—— MUSIC FOR ORCHESTRA, OP. 31 (1954)
2,1,2,2 - 4,2,3,1 - perc. - str.　　19:00 Mills.
—— O SAISONS, O CHÂTEAUX, OP. 13 (CANTATA) (FOR SOPRANO, SOLO VIOLIN AND STRINGS) (1946) (Text: Arthur Rimbaud)
guit.,mand. - hp. - str.　　7:00 Mills.
—— PETITE SUITE　　9:00 Lengnick.
—— QUINCUNX FOR ORCHESTRA, OP. 44 (AFTER SIR THOMAS BROWNE) (WITH OPTIONAL MEZZO-SOPRANO AND BARITONE SOLOS)
2 picc.,2,*3,1 Eᵇcl.,*3,*3 - 3,1 tpt. in D,2,1 b.-tpt.,0,5(2 ten.,2 b.,1d.-b.) - perc.(7),cel. - guit.,mandolin - hp. - pf. - str.　　20:00 Mills.
—— SIX TEMPI FOR TEN INSTS., OP. 42
1,1,1,1 - 1,1,0,0 - pf. - str.(no d.-b.)　　12:00 Mills.
—— SYMPHONIES FOR SOLO PIANO, WIND, HARPS AND PERCUSSION, OP. 46
*3,*3,1 Eᵇcl.,*3,*3 - 4,3,3,1 - perc.(6) - 2 hp. - pf.　　17:00 Mills.
—— THREE PIECES FOR ORCH., OP. 7
3,2,2,2 - 2,1,2,1 - timp.,perc. - str.　　4:00 Belw-Mills.
—— THREE SYMPHONIC PRELUDES　　12:00 Lengnick.

LUTZ, Oswald
—— BREGENZER FESTLICHES VORSPIEL
2(alt. with 2 picc.),2,0,2 b.-cl.,0 - 4,4,2,1 - timp., cymb. - hp. - str.(2,1,1,1)　　10:00 Modern.
—— FOUR BAGATELLES (FOR VIOLIN AND SMALL ORCH.)
1,1,2,1 - 2,0,2,0 - str.　　12:00 Modern.
—— INTERMEZZO ON A THEME OF ROSWITHA ENGELBERGER　　4:30 Modern.
—— RASKOLNIKOFF, OP. 83 (SYMPHONIC POEM)　　16:00 Modern.

—— SCHATTEN IN DER DÄMMERUNG (FOUR DANCE
PICTURES)
  2,2,2,2 - 4,2,3,0 - timp.,perc. - hp. - pf.(ad lib.) - str.
  12:00 Modern.
—— SIEBEN GEDANKEN ÜBER "ES IST EIN SCHNITTER" (FOR
CHAMBER CHORUS AND STRING ORCH.)
  str. 15:00 Modern.
—— SÜDLICHE NACHT (4 MINIATURE FOR ORCH.)
  2,2,2,2 - 4,2,3,0 - timp.,perc. - hp. - str. 10:00 Modern.
—— SYMPHONIC PRELUDE
  2,2,2,2 - 4,2,2,1 - timp.,cymb. - str. 12:00 Modern.
—— TRAUERMUSIK (FOR CHAMBER CHORUS AND STRING
ORCH.)
  str. 12:00 Modern.
—— VARIATIONS ON A THEME OF MOZART
  13:00 Modern.

LYNE, Peter
—— CONTRASTS (1974)
  1,2,1,1 - 2,2,2,1 - timp.,perc.,glock.,vibra. - str. 7:30 Fleisher.

LYNN, George
—— CONCERT PIECE FOR CLARINET AND STRING
ORCHESTRA (1970)
  cl. - str. 12:00 Composer.
—— CONCERTO FOR PIANO AND STRINGS (IN 4 MOVTS.)
  pf. - str. 16:00 Composer.
—— DIVERSIONS FOR STRINGS (IN 4 MOVTS.)
  str. 13:30 Composer.
—— FOUR GREEK FOLKSONGS (FOR CONTRALTO, CHORUS
AND ORCH.)
  2,2,2,2 - 2,0,0,0 - str. 9:00 Arranger.
—— THE GETTYSBURG ADDRESS (FOR BARITONE, CHORUS
AND ORCH.) (Text: Abraham Lincoln)
  *2,2,2,2 - 4,2,3,1 - timp. - str. 8:00 Presser.
—— IDYL FOR VIOLIN AND CHAMBER ORCHESTRA (1956)
  1,0,1,0 - 0,0,0,0 - str. 8:00 Composer.
—— NINE SONGS FOR CHILDREN (FOR CONTRALTO, OR
MEZZO-SOPRANO AND ORCH.) (Text: Aileen Fisher)
  2,2,2,1 - 4,2,2,1 - timp.,perc. - str. Composer.
—— OVERTURE
  2,2,2,2 - 4,3,3,1 - timp.,perc.(2) - str. 8:00 Composer.
—— SYMPHONIC SUITE (IN 3 MOVTS.)
  *3,2,2,2 - 4,2,2,1 - timp.,perc.(3) - str. 15:00 Composer.
—— SYMPHONY NO. 1 (1963) (IN 4 MOVTS.)
  *3,2,2,2 - 4,8,2,1 - timp.,perc. - str. 28:00 Composer.

LYON, A. Laurence
—— FESTIVAL PRELUDE (1963)
  *3,2,2,2 - 4,3,3,1 - timp.,perc.(4),glock.,xyl. - hp. - str.
  4:42 Composer.
—— FESTIVAL SUITE (1964) (IN 4 MOVTS.)
  *3,2,2,2 - 4,3,3,1 - timp.,perc.(4),bells,cel.,glock.,xyl. - hp. - str.
  18:30 Composer.
—— THEME AND VARIATIONS (FOR VIOLA AND ORCH.) (1961)
  2,2,2,2 - 2,2,0,0 - timp. - str. 8:00 Composer.

LYON, David
—— BURLESQUE (AN OVERTURE)
  2,2,2,2 - 4,2,3,0-1 - timp.,perc. - hp. - str. 6:45 P.R.S.
—— CONCERTINO FOR STRINGS
  str. 8:30 P.R.S.
—— CONCERTO FOR PIANO AND ORCH., OP. 5 (IN ONE
MOVT.)(1963)
  3,2,2,2 - 4,2,3,1 - timp.,perc. - pf. - str. 15:00 P.R.S.
—— SERENADE FOR STRING ORCH., OP. 10 (1965)
  str. 15:00 P.R.S.
—— VARIATIONS FOR ORCH., OP. 8 (1964)
  3,3,3,3 - 4,3,3,1 - timp.,perc. - hp. - str. 19:00 P.R.S.

LYON, James
—— BLESSED ARE THE DEAD, OP. 28 (FOR 8-PART CHORUS
AND ORCH.)
  Bo. Hawkes.
—— THE WARDEN OF THE CINQ PORTS, OP. 26 (BALLAD)
(FOR CHORUS AND ORCH.)
  Bo. Hawkes.

M

MAASALO, Armas
—— CHRISTMAS ORATORIO (FOR SOLO VOICE, SATB CHORUS
AND ORCH.) (1945) (Text: J. Rundt)
  2,2,0,0 - 2,2,3,0 - timp.,perc. - cemb. - org. - str. 45:00 Fazer.
—— CONCERTO FOR PIANO AND ORCH. (REV. 1945)
  2,2,2,2 - 4,2,3,1 - timp.,perc. - pf. - str. 33:00 FinnMICtr.
—— KARELIAN SCENES (1920)
  2,2,3,2 - 4,2,3,1 - timp.,perc.,cel. - hp. - str. 15:00 FinnMICtr.
—— PARTITA SERIA (1934)
  str. 12:00 FinnMICtr.
—— THE PATH OF MAN (CANTATA) (FOR VOICE AND ORCH.)
(1926)
  2,0,2,0 - 0,2,2,0 - timp.,perc. -str. 16:00 SuomenTyMu.
—— RICORDANZA (FOR CELLO, PIANO AND ORCH.) (1919)
  2,0,2,2 - 4,2,0,0 - hp. - pf. - str. 7:00 Fazer.
—— SUITE FOR ORGAN AND ORCH. (1945)
  0,2,0,0 - 2,2,3,0 - timp.,perc. - org. - str. 18:00 FinnMICtr.
—— TUNES FROM KARELIA (1918)
  1,1,1,0 - 0,1,1,0 - timp.,perc. - pf. - str. 8:00 FinnMICtr.

MAASZ, Gerhard
—— CONCERTINO FOR OBOE AND STRINGS
  ob. - str. 18:00 F. Colombo.
—— MUSIC NO. 1
  fl.,cl. - str. 12:00 Henmar.
—— MUSIC NO. 2
  1,1,1,1 - 0,0-1,0,0 - str. 15:00 Henmar.

MA'AYANI, Ami
—— CONCERTO DA CAMERA (FOR VIOLIN, WITH STRING
ORCH. OR CHAMBER ORCH.)
  25:00 IsMuPublns.
—— CONCERTO FOR HARP AND ORCH.
  3,3,3,2 - 3,3,0,0 - timp.,perc.,cel. - hp. - str. 25:00 Bo. Hawkes.
—— MISMORIM (FOR HIGH VOICE AND CHAMBER ORCH.)
  1,0,*1,0 - 0,0,0,0 - perc. - hp. - str. 12:00 IsMuPublns.
—— THE SONGS OF SOLOMON (FOR STRING ORCH.)
  Str IsMuPublns.
—— TE'AMIN (CANTILLATION)
  3,2,2,2 - 4,3,3,1 - timp.,perc. - hp. - str. 10:00 IsMuPublns.

MAAZEL, Marvin
—— FANTASIE VARIATIONS ON A PAGANINI THEME, OP. 57
(FOR PIANO AND ORCH.) (1964)
  *3,2,*4,*3 - 4,2,3,1 - timp.,perc.(2) - hp. - pf. - str.
  24:00 Composer.

MCAFEE, Don
—— CHORALE VARIATIONS ("IF THOU BUT SUFFER GOD TO
GUIDE THEE") (FOR SATB CHORUS AND SMALL ORCH.)
  1,1,1,1 - 0,0,0,0 - timp. - org. - str. 18:00 Composer.
—— PSALM 139 (A CHORAL SYMPHONY) (FOR SATB CHORUS
AND SMALL ORCH.) (IN 5 MOVTS.)
  1,1,1,1 - 0,0,0,0 - timp. - org. - str. 20:00 Composer.
—— SERENADE AND SCHERZO
  2,2,1,0 - 0,1,0,0 - pf. - str. (no d.-b.) 8:00 Composer.
—— A SHORT SYMPHONY
  1. Maestoso; 2. Adagio sostenuto; 3. Allegro con brio
  2,2,2,2 - 2,2,2,0 - timp. - org. - pf. - str. 10:00 Composer.

MCBETH, W. Francis
—— ALLEGRO AGITATO
  2(2nd alt. with picc.),2,2,2 - 2,2,1,0 - timp.,perc.(2) - str.
  12:00 Composer.
—— GRACE PRAELUDIUM AND RESPONSE (FOR WINDS AND
PERCUSSION) (1975)
  2,2,0,2 - 4,3,3,1 - timp.,perc.,glock. 7:00 Composer.
—— OVERTURE FOR ORCH.
  *3,2,2,2 - 4,3,3,1 - timp.,perc.(2) - str. 10:00 Composer.
—— PASTORALE AND ALLEGRO
  2(2nd alt with picc.),2,2,2 - 2,2,1,0 - timp.,perc.(2) - str.
  12:00 Composer.
—— QUANAH
  2(2nd alt. with picc.),2,2,2 - 2,2,1,0 - timp.,perc.(2) - hp. - str.
  7:00 Composer.
—— SUITE NO. 1 (SUITE ON A BIBLICAL EVENT)
  *3,2,2,2 - 4,3,3,1 - timp.,perc.(3) - str. 10:00 Composer.
—— SYMPHONY NO. 1 (IN 3 MOVTS.)
  *3,2,2,2 - 4,3,3,1 - timp.,perc.(3) - str. 47:00 Composer.
—— SYMPHONY NO. 2 (IN 1 MOVT.)
  *3,2,2,2 - 4,3,3,1 - timp.,perc. - pf. - str. 15:00 Composer.

—— SYMPHONY NO. 3 (IN 3 MOVTS.)
2(2nd alt. with picc.),2,2,2 - 4,3,3,1 - timp.,perc.(3),xyl. - str.
25:30 Fleisher.
—— SYMPHONY NO. 4 (1970) (IN 4 CONNECTED MOVTS.)
3(3rd alt. with picc.),2,3(3rd alt. with b.-cl.),2 - 4,3,3,1 -
timp.,perc.,bells,glock.,xyl. - str. 13:30 Composer.

MACBRIDE, David
—— ONCE REMOVED (1972)
str. 6:00 Seesaw.
—— PRODUCE (1971)
2,*3,2,*3 - 4,2,2,1 - timp.,perc.(5),vibra.,xyl. - hp. - str.
6:00 Composer.

MCBRIDE, Robert
—— FUGATO ON A WELL-KNOWN THEME
1,1,*3,1 - 2,2,1,0 - timp.,perc.(2) - pf. - str. 5:00 C. Fischer.
—— MEXICAN RHAPSODY
*3,*3,*3(2nd alt. with E♭ cl.),*3 - 4,4,3,1 - timp.,perc.(3) - hp. -
str. 10:30 C. Fischer.

MCCABE, John
—— CHAMBER CONCERTO FOR VIOLA, CELLO AND ORCH.
(1965)
2(2nd alt. with picc.),1,2,2 - 4,2,3,1 - perc.,glock.,vibra.,xyl. - pf.(or
cel.) - str. 31:00 Novello.
—— CONCERTANTE FOR HARPSICHORD AND CHAMBER
ENSEMBLE (1965)
1,1,1,1 - 1,1,0,0 - perc.,glock.,vibra.hpsc. - str. 18:00 Novello.
—— CONCERTANTE FOR PIANO-DUET AND ORCH. (1968)
2,2,2,1 - 2,2,2,0 - timp.,perc.,vibra. - pf. 4 hands - str.
12:00 Novello.
—— CONCERTANTE MUSIC (1968)
3(3rd alt. with picc.),3,3,2 - 4,3,3,0 - timp.,perc.,glock.,xyl. - pf. -
str. 24:00 Novello.
—— CONCERTANTE VARIATIONS (ON A THEME OF
NICHOLAS MAW) (1970)
str. 20:00 Novello.
—— CONCERTO FOR CHAMBER ORCH., OP. 10 (REV. 1968)
1,2,0,2 - 2,0,0,0 - perc. - str. 12:00 Novello.
—— CONCERTO FOR VIOLIN AND ORCH., OP. 2 (SINFONIA
CONCERTANTE) (1959)
3,2,2,2 - 4,2,3,1 - timp.,perc.,xyl. - hp. - str. 30:00 Novello.
—— CONCERTO FUNÈBRE, OP. 11 (FOR VIOLA AND CHAMBER
ORCH.) (1962)
0,2,0,0 - 2,0,0,0 - str. 10:00 Novello.
—— CONCERTO NO. 1 FOR PIANO AND ORCH.
2(2nd alt. with picc.),2,2,2 - 4,2,3,1 - timp.,perc.,glock.,vibra.,xyl. -
hp. - pf. - str. 26:00 Novello.
—— CONCERTO NO. 2 FOR PIANO AND DOUBLE ORCH.
1,2,2,2 - 2,0,0,0 - pf. - str. 22:00 Novello.
—— FIVE ELEGIES (FOR SOPRANO AND ORCH.) (Texts: Nashe,
Jonson, Eliot, Herrick and Dylan Thomas)
1,1,1,1 - 1,0,0,0 - perc.(2) - str. 16:00 Oxford.
—— THE LION, THE WITCH AND THE WARDROBE (SUITE)
1,1,2,1 - 1,2,1,0 - timp.,perc.,xyl. - pf. - str. 15:00 Novello.
—— METAMORPHOSIS FOR HARPSICHORD AND ORCH. (1968)
2(2nd alt. with picc.),2(2nd alt. with Eng.hn.),2,2 - 2,2,2,1 -
perc.,cel.,glock.,vibra. - hp. - hpsc. - str. 22:00 Novello.
—— SUMMER MUSIC (1963)
2,2,2,2 - 2,2,2,0 - timp.,perc.(3) - str. 6:00 P.R.S.
—— SYMPHONY FOR 10 WIND INSTRUMENTS, OP. 33 (1964)
2,2,2,2 - 2,0,0,0 15:00 Novello.
—— SYMPHONY NO. 2 (1971)
3(3rd alt. with picc.),3(3rd alt. with Eng.hn.),3,3 - 4,3,3,1 -
timp.,perc.,glock.,vibra.,xyl. - hp. - pf.(or cel.) - str. 20:00 Novello.
—— VARIATIONS ON A THEME OF KARL AMADEUS
HARTMANN, OP. 28 (1964)
4,3,3,3 - 4,3,3,1 - timp.,perc.,glock.,vibra.,xyl. - hp. - pf. - str.
20:00 Novello.

MCCAULEY, William A.
—— CONCERTO FOR HORN AND ORCH. (1959) (IN 3 MOVTS.)
*2,2,*2,2 - 3,4,3,1 - timp. - hp. - str. 16:30 CanMusCtr.
—— CONCERTO FOR HORN AND ORCH. (1959) (IN 3 MOVTS.)
2(2nd alt. with picc.),2,2(2nd alt. with b.-cl.),2 - 4,3,3,1 -
timp.,perc. - hp. - str. 16:30 CanMusCtr.
—— CONCERTO GROSSO (1973) (FOR BRASS QUINTET AND
ORCH.) (IN 5 MOVTS.)
2(2nd alt.with picc.),2(2nd alt. with Eng.hn.),2,2 - 3,2,2,0 -
timp.,perc. - str. 18:30 MarsegLtd.

—— CONTRASTS (1958)
1,1,2(2nd alt. with b.-cl.),2(2nd alt. with c.-bn.) - 1,1,3,0 -
timp.,perc. - hp. - str. 4:45 CanMusCtr.
—— FIVE MINIATURES FOR BASS TROMBONE, HARP AND
STRINGS (1959)
B.-trb. - hp. - str. 8:00 CanMusCtr.
—— FIVE MINIATURES FOR FLUTE AND STRINGS (1958)
fl. - hp.(ad lib.), - str. 8:25 Leeds.
—— NEWFOUNDLAND SCENE (FROM THE FILM SCORE) (1952)
1,*1,*2,1 - 1,2,2,0 - timp.,perc. - hp. - str. 6:00 CanMusCtr.
—— SASKATCHEWAN SUITE (FROM THE FILM "THE FACE OF
SASKATCHEWAN") (1956) (IN 4 MOVTS.)
1,*1,*2,1 - 1,2,2,0 - timp.,perc. - hp. 12:00 CanMusCtr.
—— THEME AND DEVIATIONS (1960)
*3,*2,*2,*3 - 4,3,3,1 - timp.,perc. - hp. - str. 5:25 Leeds.
—— WILDERNESS (1963) (MUSIC FROM THE FILM
"WILDERNESS")
1(alt. with alto fl.),1(alt. with Eng.hn.),1,0 - 1,0,0,0 - perc. - acc. -
hp. - str. (no vla.) 22:35 CanMusCtr.

MCCLEARY, Fiona
—— OVERTURE
2,2,2,2 - 4,2,2,1 - timp.,perc. - hp. - str. Composer.
—— SERENATA
1,1,1,0 - 1,1,0,0 - timp.,perc. - hp.(or pf.) - str. 5:00 Composer.

MCCLELLAN, Randall
—— VARIATIONS FOR ORCHESTRA (1967)
3,3,3,2 - 4,4,3,1 - timp.,perc. - str. 15:00 Seesaw.

MACCOLL, Hugh F.
—— ARABS (A SYMPHONIC ILLUSTRATION)
*3,*3,2,2 - 4,2,3,1 - timp.,perc.(3) - hp. - str. 6:00 Templeton.

MCCOLLIN, Frances
—— CHRISTMAS FANTASIA
2,*3,2,3 - 4,2,3,1 - timp. - hp. - str. 10:00 Composer.
—— FUGUE IN C MINOR
*3,*3,*3,1 - 4,2,3,1 - timp.,cel. - hp. - str. 5:00 Composer.
—— HEAVENLY CHILDREN AT PLAY (SCHERZO) (FOR
STRINGS)
str. 7:00 Composer.
—— MADRIGAL FOR FLUTE AND ORCH.
2(2nd alt. with picc.),2(2nd alt. with Eng. hn.),2,2 - 4,2,2,0 -
timp.,cel. - hp. - str. 7:00 Composer.
—— NOCTURNE
2,*3,2,2 - 4 hn. - timp.,perc.(2) - hp. - str. 12:00 Composer.
—— PRELUDE AND FUGUE
Composer.
—— RING OUT WILD BELLS (FOR CHORUS AND ORCH.)
2,2,2,2 - 2,2,1,0 - timp.,perc. - hp. - pf. - str. 6:00 EV.
—— SUITE FOR STRINGS (IN 3 MOVTS.)
str. 15:00 Composer.
—— SUITE IN F (IN 5 MOVTS.)
2(2nd alt. with picc.),2(2nd alt. with Eng. hn.),2,2 - 4,2,2,0 -
timp.,cel. - hp. - str. 25:00 Composer.
—— TWO CHORAL PRELUDES
str. Ricordi.
—— TWO SUBURBAN SKETCHES
*3,*3,2,2 - 4,2,1,0 - timp.,perc.(2) - hp. - str. 30:00 Composer.
—— VARIATIONS ON AN ORIGINAL THEME
2,2,2,2 - 2,3,2,0 - timp.,cel. - pf. - str. 9:00 Composer.

MCCOLLIN, Frances - SEVITZKY, Fabien
—— ADAGIO (FOR STRINGS)
str. 7:00 C. Fischer.

MCCORMICK, Clifford
—— SIX SEA SHANTIES (FOR TENOR, BARITONE, MALE
CHORUS AND ORCH.)
1,1,1,1 - 4,1,0,1 - str. 10:00 Arranger.
—— SUITE PROVINCIALE (FOR MIXED CHORUS AND ORCH.)
(IN 4 MOVTS.)
2,1,1,1 - 4,2,0,1 - timp. - str. 15:00 Arranger.

MCCULLOH, Byron
—— CONCERTINO FOR LARGE TROMBONE AND SMALL
ORCH. (1974) (IN 4 MOVTS.)
1(alt. with picc.),1,1(alt. with A cl.),1 - 1,1,1,0 -
perc.(1),bells,glock.,vibra. - hp. -hpsc.(amplified) - str.
15:00 C. Fischer.

—— CONCERTO FOR ORCHESTRA (1951) (IN 3 MOVTS.)
    2,2,2,2 - 4,2,3,1 - timp.,perc.(4),bells,glock.,xyl. - pf. - str.
                            18:00 Composer.
—— CONCERTO FOR TROMBONE AND ORCH. (1949)
    2,2,2,2 - 2,2,1,1 - timp.,perc.(3),xyl. - pf. - str.   8:00 Composer.
—— SINFONIA FOR BRASS AND BATTERY (1974) (IN 3 MOVTS.)
    0,0,0,0 - 4,3,3,1 - timp.,perc.(3),bells,glock.,vibra.,xyl.
                            15:00 C. Fischer.
—— SIX SONGS FOR BARITONE AND CHAMBER ORCH. (1976)
    (Text: Ric Masten)
    1(alt. with picc.),1,1,1 - 1,0,0,0 - perc.(1),glock. - pf. - str.
                            19:30 C. Fischer.
—— SYMPHONY CONCERTANTE (FOR TIMPANIST AND
    ORCH.) (1973) (IN 4 MOVTS.)
    3(3rd alt. with picc.),3(3rd alt. with Eng.hn.),*3,*3 - 4,3,3,1 -
    timp.,perc.(5),bells,cel.,glock.,mar.,vibra.,xyl. - tape-recorder - hp. -
    pf.(alt. with cel.) - str.   25:00 C. Fischer.
—— SYMPHONY NO. 1 (1975) (IN 4 MOVTS.)
    *3,*3,*3,*3 - 4,3,3,1 - timp.,perc.(5),bells,cel.,glock.,mar.,vibra.,xyl.
    - hp. - str.   19:00 C. Fischer.
—— TWO PIECES FOR ORCHESTRA (1953)
    *3,*3,*3,*3 - 4,3,3,1 - timp.,perc.(4),bells,glock.,xyl. - str.
                            11:00 Composer.

MACCUNN, Hamish
—— HIGHLAND MEMORIES, OP. 30 (SUITE) (IN 3 MOVTS.)
    2,2,2,2 - 2,2,0,0 - timp. - str.   13:00 Galaxy.

MACDERMOT, Galt
—— TAKE THIS BREAD (FOR SOPRANO, MEZZO-SOPRANO,
    TENOR, SATB CHORUS, ORCH., AND RHYTHM CONTINUO)
    (Text: William Dumaresque)
                            55:00 Hinshaw.

MCDONALD, Harl
—— CHAMELEON VARIATIONS
    2(1alt. with picc.),2,2,2 - 3,3,3,0 - timp.,perc. - hp. - org.(ad lib.) -
    str.   24:00 EV.
—— CHILDREN'S SYMPHONY (ON FAMILIAR TUNES) (IN 4
    MOVTS.)
    *4,3,3,*3 - 4,3,3,1 - timp.,perc.(4),glock. - hp. - str. 15:00 EV.
—— CONCERTO FOR VIOLIN AND ORCH. (IN 3 MOVTS.)
    2,2,*3,2 - 3,3,0,0 - timp. - str.   22:00 EV.
—— CONCERTO FOR 2 PIANOS AND ORCH. (IN 3 MOVTS.)
    *4,*3,*4,*3 - 4,4,3,1 - timp.,perc. - 2 pf. - str. 23:00 EV.
—— DIRGE FOR TWO VETERANS (FOR WOMEN'S CHORUS
    AND ORCH.)
    2,2,*3,2 - 2,3,2,1 - timp.,perc. - str.   12:00 EV.
—— FESTIVAL OF THE WORKERS
    3,3,3,3 - 3,3,3,1 - timp.,perc. - hp. - str. 15:00 EV.
—— GOD, GIVE US MEN (FOR CHORUS AND ORCH.)
    *3,2,3,2 - 4,3,2,1 - timp.,perc. - str.   9:00 EV.
—— LAMENT TO THE STOLEN (FOR WOMEN'S CHORUS AND
    ORCH.)
    *3,*3,3,*3 - 4,4,3,1 - timp.,perc. - str. 27:00 EV.
—— THE LEGEND OF THE ARKANSAS TRAVELLER
    3(3rd alt. with picc.),*3,2,*3 - 4,4,3,0 - timp.,perc. - str. 4:30 EV.
—— MINIATURE SUITE (AFTER JOHN CHRISTOPHER SMITH,
    1784) (IN 3 MOVTS.)
    2,2,2,2 - 2 hn. - str.   10:00 EV.
—— MY COUNTRY AT WAR (SUITE) (IN 4 MOVTS.)
    *3,*3,*4,*3 - 4,4,3,1 - timp.,perc. - hp. - str. 25:00 EV.
—— SAGA OF THE MISSISSIPPI
    3(3rd alt. with picc.),*3,3,*3 - 4,3,3,0 - timp.,perc.(2) - str.
                            15:00 EV.
—— SAN JUAN CAPISTRANO (TWO NOCTURNES)
    *3,*3,3*3 - 4,4,3,1 - timp.,perc. - hp. - str. 8:00 EV.
—— SCENES FROM CHILDHOOD (SUITE) (IN 3 MOVTS.)
    2,2,3,2 - 3,2,0,0 - timp. - hp. - str. 24:00 EV.
—— SONGS OF CONQUEST (FOR CHORUS AND ORCH.)
    *3,2,2,2 - 4,2,3,1 - timp.,perc. - hp. - str. 14:00 EV.
—— SUITE FOR STRINGS (ON AMERICAN NEGRO THEMES) (IN
    3 MOVTS.)
    str.   12:00 EV.
—— SYMPHONY NO. 1 ("THE SANTA FE TRAIL") (IN 3 MOVTS.)
    *4,*3,*4,*3 - 4,4,3,1 - timp.,perc. - str. 23:00 EV.
—— SYMPHONY NO. 2 ("RHUMBA") (IN 4 MOVTS.)
    *3,*3,3,*3 - 4,4,3,1 - timp.,perc. - 2 hp. - str. 32:00 EV.
—— SYMPHONY NO. 3 ("TRAGIC CYCLE") (FOR SOPRANO,
    CHORUS AND ORCH.) (IN 4 MOVTS.)
    2,*3,2,*3 - 4,4,3,1 - timp.,perc. - str. 33:00 EV.

—— SYMPHONY NO. 4 ("CAKEWALK") (IN 4 MOVTS.)
    3(3rd alt. with picc.),*3,4(4th alt. with b.-cl.),*3 - 4,4,3,1 -
    timp.,perc.(3) - str.   EV.
—— THREE POEMS ON TRADITIONAL ARAMAIC THEMES
    3,*3,3,*3 - 4,4,3,1 - timp.,perc. - hp.(or pf.) - str. 11:15 EV.
—— TWO PIECES "FROM THE DAMARISCOTTA"
    *3,2,3,*3 - 3,3,2,0 - perc. - hp. - str. 12:00 EV.
—— THE WIND IN THE PALM TREES (FOR WOMEN'S CHORUS
    AND STRINGS)
    str.   6:00 EV.

MACDOWELL, Edward - ALTSCHULER, Modest
—— SINFONICA TRAGICA
    3,3,2,2 - 4,3,3,1 - timp.,perc. - hp. - str. 29:00 C. Press.

MCEWEN, John B.
—— SUITE FOR STRINGS (IN 5 MOVTS.)
                              Oxford.

MÁCHA, Otmar
—— INTERMEZZI SINFONICI
    3,2,2,2 - 4,3,3,1 - timp.,perc. - str. 24:00 Bo. Hawkes.
—— THE NIGHT AND HOPE
    4,3,3,3 - 4,3,3,1 - timp.,perc. - str. 12:00 Bo. Hawkes.
—— TESTAMENT OF COMENIUS (FOR SOLOISTS, MIXED
    CHORUS AND ORCH.)
                          45:00 Bo. Hawkes.

MACHAN, Ben
—— NUTMEG SUITE (IN 3 MOVTS.)
                            Composer.

MACHAT, E.
—— IN THE BEGINNING (FANTASY FOR STRINGS)
    str.   12:00 Bo. Hawkes.

MACHAVARIANI, Alexei
—— CONCERTO FOR VIOLIN AND ORCH
                          G. Schirmer.

MÂCHE, François-Bernard
—— LA PEAU DU SILENCE
    4,4,4,4 - 8,4,4,0 - perc.(4) - 2 hp. - 2 pf. - str. 21:50 Presser.
—— RAMBARAMB (FOR PIANO, ORCH. AND TAPE) (1972)
                         15:00 Salabert.
—— RAMBARAMB (FOR 86 PERFORMERS AND TAPE)
    3,3,4,4 - 4,3,3,1 - perc.(4) - tape-recorder - 2 hp. - pf. - str.
                         27:00 Presser.
—— RITUEL D'OUBLI (1969)
    2,0,2 picc.-cl.,*3,1 d.-b.-cl.,2 - 0,3,4,0 - perc.(3) - tape-recorder
    (2-channel stereo)   33:00 Salabert.
—— SYNESPIES
    2,1,2,2 - 2,2,2,0 - perc.(5) - hp. - str. 7:20 Presser.

MCHUGH, Charles R.
—— CONFLUENCE (A SYMPHONY) (FOR 2 VIOLAS AND
    ORCH.) (1975) (IN 3 MOVTS.)
    *3,*3,*3,*3 - 4,3,3,1 - timp.,perc.(4),bells,cel.,glock.,xyl. - hp. - pf.
    - str.   25:00 Composer.
—— FALL MUSIC
    1,1,1,0 - 0,0,0,0 - tape-recorder (2-channel) - 2 pf. - str.
                         26:00 Composer.
—— NOCTURNE
    str.   7:00 Composer.
—— REQUIEM
    1,1,0,0 - 0,2,3,0 - perc.(1),bells,glock.,vibra.,xyl. - tape-recorder
    (2channel) - pf. - str.(1,1,1,0)   25:00 Composer.
—— THEME AND VARIATIONS (1965)
    *3,*3,*3,*3 - 4,3,3,1 - timp.,perc.(5),bells,glock.,xyl - hp. - pf. - str.
                         12:00 Composer.

MACINNIS, Donald
—— DIALOGUES FOR ORCH.
    2,2,2,2 - 2,2,3,1 - timp.,perc.(4),xyl. - pf. - str. 8:00 Piedmont.
—— FOUR MINIATURES FOR STRING ORCH.
    str.   7:10 Piedmont.
—— IN MEMORIAM - JOHN FITZGERALD KENNEDY (AN
    ELEGIAC SONG)
    1,0,1,0 - 2,0,2,0 - timp.,perc.(2) - str. 5:30 Piedmont.
—— INTERSECTIONS (FOR TAPE RECORDER AND ORCH.)
    2,2,2,2 - 2,2,3,1 - timp.,perc.(4),xyl. - stereo tape-recorder - hp. -
    str.   6:00 Piedmont.

—— STUDIES ON REFLECTIVE SURFACES
2,2,2,2 - 2,2,3,1 - timp.,perc.(6),xyl. - hp.   6:00 Composer.

MCINTYRE, Paul P.
—— CONCERTO FOR PIANO AND ORCH.
                                                      22:00 C.A.P.A.C.

—— JUDITH (MELODRAMA-CANTATA)
                                                      28:00 C.A.P.A.C.

—— SONG OF AUTUMN (TONE POEM)
                                                      8:00 C.A.P.A.C.

—— SYMPHONIA SACRA (CHORAL SYMPHONY) (FOR 3 SOLO
VOICES, 2 CHORUSES AND ORCH.)
                                                      40:00 C.A.P.A.C.

—— SYMPHONY "JEAN DE BRÉBEUF" (DRAMATIC SYMPHONY)
(FOR BASS OR BARITONE, AND ORCH.) (1962)
*3,*3,*3,*3 - 4,4,3,1 - timp.,perc.,cel. - hp. - pf. - str.
                                                      40:45 CanMusCtr.

MCKAY, Francis H.
—— ROMANTIC OVERTURE
2(1 alt. with picc.),2,2,2 - 4,3,3,0 - timp.,perc.(3),glock. - hp. - str.
                                                      10:30 Composer.

MCKAY, George F.
—— SINFONIETTA NO. 2 (IN 1 MOVT.)
2,2,2,2,c. - bn.(ad lib.) - 3,3,3,0 - timp.,perc.(2),glock. - str.
                                                      12:00 Composer.

MCKAY, George Frederick
—— THE BIG SKY (SUITE ON WESTERN SUBJECTS) (IN 3
MOVTS.)
2(1 alt. with picc.),1,2,1 - 2,3,2,0 - timp.,perc.(1) - str.
                                                      12:00 Boston.

—— BUFFALO AND CROW (OKLAHOMA INDIAN SUITE) (FOR
STRINGS)
str.   8:00 Composer.

—— CHORAL RHAPSODY, OP. 39 (FOR CHORUS, BRASS AND
TIMPANI)
4 hn., 3 tpt., 3 trb. - timp.   10:00 Western.

—— CONCERTO FOR CHORUS AND ORCH., OP. 58 (IN 3
MOVTS.)
2,2,2,2 - 4,3,3,0 - timp.,perc.(2),cel.,glock.,xyl. - str.
                                                      15:00 Composer.

—— CONCERTO FOR VIOLIN AND ORCH., OP. 49 (IN 3 MOVTS.)
2,2,2,2 - 4,3,3,0 - timp. - str.   23:00 Composer.

—— DOWN TO THE SEA AGAIN (SUITE) (IN 5 MOVTS.)
1,1,1,1 - 1,1,1,1 - hp. - pf. - str.   10:00 Boston.
or:
2,1,2,1 - 3,2,1,0 - timp.,perc.(1) - hp.(or pf.) - str.

—— ETERNAL SONG (ILLUSTRATING THE MELODIC VOICES
OF THE ORCH.)
1,1,1(alt. with Eng.hn.),1 - 1,1,1,1 - timp. - hp. - pf. - str.
                                                      8:00 Boston.

—— FANTASY ON A WESTERN FOLKSONG, OP. 19
2,*1,2,0 - tpt. - str.   11:00 Bo. Hawkes.

—— FROM A MOONLIT CEREMONY (SUITE, ON PACIFIC
NORTHWEST INDIAN SONGS AND DANCES) (IN 4
MOVTS.)
                                                      15:00 Composer.

—— FROM OUTDOOR LIFE (IN 2 MOVTS.)
str.   6:00 Galaxy.

—— FROM THE MAINE WOODS (SUITE) (FOR STRINGS) (IN 3
MOVTS.)
str.   7:00 Birchard.

—— HALYARD AND CAPSTAN (SUITE) (FOR STRINGS) (IN 3
MOVTS.)
str.   4:00 Birchard.

—— HARBOR NARRATIVE, OP. 31 (SUITE)
2,*3,*3,3 sax.,2 - 4,3,3,0 - timp.,perc.(3),xyl. - hp. - pf. - str.
                                                      19:00 Composer.

—— HOMAGE TO STEPHEN FOSTER, OP. 97 (SUITE) (IN 3
MOVTS.)
2,1,2,1 - 2,2,1,0 - timp. - pf. - str.   7:00 J. Fischer.

—— INTROSPECTIVE POEM, OP. 42 (FOR STRINGS)
str.   6:00 Composer.

—— A LANIER PASTORALE, OP. 33B (FOR WOMEN'S CHORUS
AND ORCH.)
3,1,2,1 - 3 hn. - str.   10:00 Composer.

—— LINCOLN LYRICS (CHORAL SUITE) (IN 7 MOVTS.)
2,1,2,1 - 3,3,3,0 - timp.,perc.(2) - str.   25:00 Western.

—— LYRIC POEMS (IN 3 MOVTS.)
2,0,1,0 - 3,0,0,0 - str.   9:00 Composer.

—— MISSOURI HARMONY (SUITE) (FOR STRINGS)
str.   7:00 EV.

—— MOODS, FANTASTIC AND LYRIC, OP. 24 (FOR STRINGS)
(IN 5 MOVTS.)
str.   14:00 Composer.

—— PASTORAL SOLILOQUY
ob. - str.   10:00 Carlvi.

—— PASTORAL SOLILOQUY, OP. 53
2 fl., ob., 2 cl. - str.   4:30 Carlvi.

—— A PIONEER EPIC
2,*3,2,2 - 4,3,3,1 - timp. - pf. - str.   15:00 Composer.

—— PORT ROYAL, 1861, OP. 48 (FOLKSONG SUITE) (FOR
STRINGS) (IN 3 MOVTS.)
str.   8:00 Birchard.

—— A PRAIRIE PORTRAIT, OP. 21
2,2(1 alt. with Eng. hn.),2,2 - 4,3,3,0 - timp. - hp. - str.
                                                      11:00 Composer.

—— ROCKY HARBOUR AND SANDY COVE (NEWFOUNDLAND
SUITE) (FOR STRINGS) (IN 4 MOVTS.)
str.   Birchard.

—— SEA SPRAY (SUITE FOR STRING ORCH.) (IN 3 MOVTS.)
str.   12:00 EV.

—— SINFONIETTA FOR STRINGS (IN 3 MOVTS.)
str.   8:00 Composer.

—— SINFONIETTA NO. 1 ("FROM A MOUNTAIN TOWN") (IN 3
MOVTS.)
2,2,2,1 - 4,2,3,0 - timp.,perc.(3),glock. - hp. - str. 14:00 Composer.

—— SINFONIETTA NO. 3 (IN 3 MOVTS.)
2(1st alt. with picc.),2(2nd alt. with Eng. hn.),*3,2 - 4,3,3,1 -
timp.,perc.(2),glock.,xyl. - harm. - hp. - pf. - str. 21:00 Fox.

—— SINFONIETTA NO. 4 (IN 3 MOVTS.)
2,2,2,2 - 4,3,3,0 - timp.,perc.(2),glock. - str.   14:00 Composer.

—— SONATA (FOR CLARINET OR VIOLIN, WITH STRINGS)
cl.(ad lib.) - str.   7:30 Presser.

—— SONATA FOR TROMBONE AND ORCH.
2,1,2,1 - 4,3,3,0 - timp. - str.   Composer.

—— SONATINE-BALLADE (FOR CLARINET AND STRINGS)
(1968)
cl. - str.   8:00 Composer.

—— SONATINE FOR CLARINET AND STRINGS, OP. 15
1. Moderato; 2. Allegretto
cl. - str.   8:00 Composer.

—— SONATINE FOR FLUTE AND ORCH. (IN 3 MOVTS.)
fl. - str.   9:00 Composer.

—— SONG OVER THE GREAT PLAINS
2,2(2nd alt. with Eng. hn.),2,2 - 4,3,3,0 - timp. - pf. - str.
                                                      12:00 Composer.

—— SUITE FOR VIOLA AND ORCH. (IN 5 MOVTS.)
2,1,2,1 - 4,3,3,0 - timp.,perc.(1) - str.   17:00 Composer.

—— SUITE ON CHILDREN'S THEMES, OP. 57 (FOR STRINGS) (IN
4 MOVTS.)
str.   12:00 Composer.

—— SUITE ON FIDDLERS TUNES, OP. 61
2(alt. with 2 picc.),2,2,2 - 4,3,3,0 - timp.,perc.(2) - str.
                                                      15:00 J. Fischer.

—— SUITE ON NORTHWEST INDIAN SONGS AND DANCES, OP.
66
2,2,2,2 - 4,2,3,0 - timp.,perc.(2) - str.   13:00 Composer.

—— SUITE ON 16TH CENTURY HYMN TUNES (IN 5 MOVTS.)
str.   16:00 Gray.

—— SUZUKI VARIATIONS
str.   Composer.

—— SYMBOLIC ESSAY, OP. 33A
2(alt. with 2 picc.),2(1 alt. with Eng. hn.),2(1 alt. with b.-cl.),2 -
4,3,3,0 - timp.,perc.(2),cel.,glock.,xyl. - hp. - pf. - str.
                                                      12:00 Composer.

—— SYMPHONIE MINIATURE NO. 2 (1967) (IN 3 MOVTS.)
2,2(2nd alt. with Eng.hn),2,0 - 4,3,3,0 -
timp.,perc.(3),cel.,glock.,xyl. - str.   12:00 Composer.

—— SYMPHONIE MINIATURE, OP. 40 (IN 3 MOVTS.)
2,2,2,2 - 4,3,3,0 - timp.,perc.(2),glock. - str.   11:00 Birchard.

—— SYMPHONY ("EVOCATION"), OP. 33C (IN 5 MOVTS.)
2(alt. with 2 picc.),*3,*3,*3 - 4,4,4,0- timp.,perc.(2) - pf. - str.
                                                      26:00 Composer.

—— SYMPHONY NO. 5 (FOR SEATTLE, 1851-1951)
2,2,2,2 - 4,3,3,1 - timp. - str.   24:00 Composer.

—— THLINGET (SUITE, ON ALASKAN INDIAN SONGS AND
DANCES) (IN 6 MOVTS.)
2(2nd alt. with picc.),1,2,1 - 2,2,1,0 - timp.,perc.(2) - pf. - str.
                                                      15:00 Composer.

—— THREE AMERICAN FOLK HYMNS (FOR CHORUS AND
STRINGS)
str.   Composer.

—— THREE LYRIC SOLILOQUIES, OP. 10
    2,1,2,0 - 3 hn. - str.   9:00 Composer.
—— THREE PAWNEE SONGS AND DANCES, OP. 94 (FOR STRINGS)
    str.   6:00 Composer.
—— TO A LIBERATOR, OP. 51 (A LINCOLN TRIBUTE) (FOR CHORUS AND ORCH.)
    2,3,*3,2 - 4,4,4,0 - timp.,perc.(2) - str.   10:00 Bo. Hawkes.
—— VARIANTS ON A TEXAS TUNE, OP. 39
    2,1,2,1 - 2 hn. - str.   11:00 G. Schirmer.
—— VISTAS (SINFONIA)
                    Boston.
—— VIVA SEVITZKY (OVERTURE BRAVA)
    2,2,2,2 - 4,3,3,0 - timp. - str.   1:00 Composer.

MCKAY, Roderick Neil
—— DANCE OVERTURE (1966)
    *3,2,2,2 - 4,3,3,1 - timp.,perc.(5) - hp. - pf. - str.   10:00 Shawnee.
—— FANTASY ON A QUIET THEME
    1(alt. with picc.),1,1,1 - 2,1,1,0 - perc.(1) - hp. - str.
                  7:00 Composer.
—— KALEIDOSCOPE (1971)
    1,1,1,1 - 1,1,1,0 - perc.(2),glock.,vibra. - pf. - str. 8:00 Composer.
—— SYMPHONY NO. 1 (IN 3 MOVTS.)
    *3,2,2,2 - 4,3,3,1 - timp.,perc.(4) - str.   20:00 Kalmus.

MCKAY, Todd
—— CENTRAL PARK SOUTH (FOR PIANO AND ORCH) (1954) (IN 3 MOVTS.)
    2,2,2,2 - 2,3,3,1 - timp.,perc. - hp. - pf. - str.   12:37 Composer.
—— CHILDREN'S SUITE (FOR NARRATOR AND ORCH.) (1954)
    2,2,2,2 - 2,3,3,1 - timp.,perc.(2) - hp. - str.   15:40 Composer.
—— FANTASIA FOR OBOE (AND STRINGS) (1971)
    ob. - str.   7:00 Composer.

MACKEBEN, Theo
—— THE FLANDERS BALLET, FROM THE OPERA "RUBENS" (IN 4 MOVTS.)
                    AhnSimrock.
—— OVERTURE TO THE OPERA "RUBENS"
                    AhnSimrock.
—— RUBENS (BALLET) %
    3(or picc.),2,2,2 - 4,3,3,0 - timp.,perc. - hp. - str.   AhnSimrock.

MCKINLEY, Carl
—— MASQUERADE (AMERICAN RHAPSODY)
    *3,*3,*4,3 - 4,3,3,1 - timp.,perc. - hp. - pf. - str. 9:00 J. Fischer.

MCKINNEY, Howard D.
—— A MYSTERY FOR CHRISTMAS (CHRISTMAS PAGEANT IN THE MEDIAEVAL MANNER) (FOR SOPRANO, BARITONE, SATB CHORUS AND STRINGS)
    str.   Belw-Mills.

MCLEAN, Barton K.
—— METAMORPHOSIS (1972)
    2(1 alt. with picc.),2,2,2 - 4,3,2,0 - timp.,perc.(4),bells,cel.,glock.,vibra.,xyl. - hp. - pk. - str.
                  17:00 Composer.
—— SCHERZO FOR ORCHESTRA (1961)
    2,2(2nd alt. with Eng. hn.),2,2 - 2,3,2,0 - timp.,perc.(2).glock. - str.
                  8:00 Composer.
—— SINFONETTE (IN 1 MOVT.) (1967)
    2(2nd alt. with picc.),2,2,2 - 3,3,2,0 - perc.(4),bells,cel.,glock. - hp. - str.
                  15:00 Composer.
—— SUITE FOR STRINGS (1966)
    str.   20:00 Composer.
—— TRILOGY (CANTATA) (FOR TENOR, SATB CHORUS AND CHAMBER ORCH.) (IN 3 MOVTS.) (1968) (Text: Priscilla Taylor Mclean)
    1,1,1,1 - 0,0,0,0 - perc.(1) - pf. - str.(2,1,1,0)   12:00 Composer.

MCLEAN, Hamilton G.
—— CONCERTINO FOR HORN AND SMALL ORCH. (1958) (IN 3 MOVTS.)
    2,2,2,2 - 2,2,1,0 - timp. - str.   12:00 Composer.
—— THE PILGRIMS' QUEST (CONCERT OVERTURE) (1962)
    2,*3,*3,*3 - 4,3,3,1 - timp.,perc.(2) - hp. - str.   Composer.
—— SERENADE FOR SMALL ORCHESTRA (1951)
    2,*3,2,2 - 0,1,1,0 - timp. - str.   15:00 Composer.
—— SONG OF PRAISE AND JOYOUS DANCE (FROM "SERENADE FOR SMALL ORCH.")
    2,2,2,2 - 4,2,2,1 - timp.perc.(2) - str.   7:30 Composer.

MCLEAN, Priscilla Taylor
—— VARIATIONS AND MOZAICS ON A THEME OF STRAVINSKY (1969)
    *3,*3,2,*3 - 4,3,2,0 - timp.,perc.(3),bells,cel.,xyl. - hp. - str.
                  19:00 Composer.

MACLEAN, Quentin
—— ALGONQUIN LEGEND (1952)
    2,2(2nd alt. with Eng.hn.),2(2nd alt. with b.-cl.),2 - 2,0,3,0 - hp. - str.   6:30 CanMusCtr.
—— CONCERTO FOR PIANO AND ORCH.
                25:00 C.A.P.A.C.
—— CONCERTO PIECE (1932) (FOR ORGAN AND ORCH.)
    0,0,0,0 - 4,3,3,0 - 2 hp. - org. - str.   30:00 CanMusCtr.
—— CONCERTO ROCCOCO FOR VIOLIN AND ORCH. (1957) (IN 3 MOVTS.)
    *3,alto fl.,2(2nd alt. with Eng.hn.),2(2nd alt. with b.-cl.),2 - 0,2,b-tpt. (or valve. trb.),0,0 - timp.,perc. - hp. - str.
                29:00 CanMusCtr.
—— ELECTRIC CONCERTO (IN "POP" STYLE) (FOR 4 ELECTRIC INTS. AND ORCH.)
                20:00 C.A.P.A.C.
—— RHAPSODY ON TWO ENGLISH FOLK TUNES (1938) (FOR HARP AND SMALL ORCH.)
    1,1,2,1 - 2,2,1,0 - timp.,perc. - hp. - str.   19:00 CanMusCtr.
—— RUSTIC RHAPSODY (TONE POEM)
                19:00 C.A.P.A.C.
—— STABAT MATER (1941) (FOR TENOR, BARITONE, MIXED CHORUS AND ORCH.)
    2,*3,*3,alto sax.,*3 - 4,2,0,0 - timp., bells - hp. - str. or
                50:00 CanMusCtr.
    org. - str.
—— THEME AND VARIATIONS
                25:00 C.A.P.A.C.
—— THE WELL-TEMPERED ORCHESTRA (PRELUDE AND FUGUE ON A TUNING FORMULA)
                12:00 C.A.P.A.C.

MACLEOD, Philip
—— VARIATIONS FOR FULL ORCH.
                C.A.P.A.C.

MACMAHON, Desmond
—— CONCERTO FOR OBOE AND STRING ORCH.
    ob. - str.   16:00 Novello.

MACMILLAN, Ernest
—— CONCERT OVERTURE IN A
                12:00 C.A.P.A.C.
—— ENGLAND (ODE) (FOR SOLO VOICES, CHORUS AND ORCH.)
                40:00 Novello.
—— FANTASY ON SCOTTISH MELODIES (1946)
    2,*3,*3,2 - 4,3,3,1 - timp.,perc.(3) - hp. - str.   7:05 CanMusCtr.
—— OVERTURE (1924)
    *3,*3,*3,2 - 4,2,3,1 - timp.,perc. - hp. - str.   CanMusCtr.
—— A SONG OF DELIVERANCE (1944) (FOR MIXED CHORUS AND ORCH.) (Text: Scottish Psalter, 1650)
    2(2nd alt. with picc.),2,2,*3 - 4,3,3,1 - timp.,perc. - hp.(ad lib.) - str.   5:30 CanMusCtr.
—— TE DEUM LAUDAMUS
                8:00 C.A.P.A.C.
—— THERE WAS AN OLD WOMAN (1945) (FOR MEDIUM VOICE AND STRINGS)
    str.   6:45 CanMusCtr.
—— THREE FRENCH-CANADIAN SEA SONGS (1930) (FOR MEDIUM VOICE AND STRINGS)
    str.   8:30 CanMusCtr.
—— TWO SKETCHES (BASED ON FRENCH-CANADIAN AIRS) (FOR STRINGS)
    str.   6:30 Oxford.

MCMULLIN, Robert W.
—— ROCKY MOUNTAIN SKETCHES
                24:00 Anglo.

MCNEIL, James C.
—— IN THE MIST, OP. 15
    2,*3,*3,*3 - 4,3,3,1 - timp.,cel. - hp. - str.   Composer.
—— JUDITH, OP. 3 (SYMPHONIC POEM) (IN 5 MOVTS.)
    *3,*3,2,2 - 4,1,3,1 - timp.,perc.(1),bells,glock. - hp. - str.
                15:00 Composer.

—— MOJAVE, OP. 4 (IN 3 MOVTS.)
2,*2,*3,2 - 4,0,0,0 - timp.,perc.(1)bells - hp. - str.   9:00 Composer.
—— SOUTH CAROLINA SUITE, OP. 2 (IN 3 MOVTS.)
*3,*3,2,*3 - 4,2,3,0 - timp.,perc.(1),cel. - hp. - str.   9:00 Composer.
—— TONE POEM, OP. 1
2,*3,2,2 - 4,2,3,1 - timp.,perc.(1)cel.,glock. - hp. - str.
6:00 Composer.
—— VIGIL, OP. 5 (FOR SOPRANO AND ORCH.) (Text: Benjamin Musser)
2,*3,2,2 - 4,2,3,0 - timp.,perc.(1),glock. - hp. - str.   6:00 Saunders.

MACONCHY, Elizabeth
—— CONCERTINO FOR BASSOON AND STRINGS
bn. - str.   14:00 Lengnick.
—— CONCERTINO FOR PIANO AND SMALL ORCH.
1,1,1,1 - 2,1,0,0 - pf. - str.   16:00 Lengnick.
—— CONCERTINO FOR PIANO AND STRINGS
pf. - str.   14:00 Mills.
—— CONCERTO FOR OBOE, BASSOON AND STRINGS
0,1,0,1 - 0,0,0,0 - str.   14:00 Lengnick.
—— CONCERTO FOR PIANO AND CHAMBER ORCH.
1,1,1,1 - 2,1,0,0 - pf. - str.   16:00 Oxford.
—— DIALOGUE FOR PIANO AND ORCH.
2,2,2,2 - 4,2,2,1 - timp. - pf. - str.   16:00 Lengnick.
—— THE LAND (SUITE)
3,3,3,2 - 4,3,3,1 - timp. - hp. - str.   15:00 Lengnick.
—— NOCTURNE FOR ORCHESTRA
3,3,3,3 - 4,3,3,1 - timp.,perc. - hp. - str.   7:00 Lengnick.
—— PROUD THAMES (OVERTURE)
2,2,2,2 - 4,3,2,1 - timp.,perc. - hp. - str.   11:00 Lengnick.
—— SERENATA CONCERTANTE (FOR VIOLIN AND ORCH.)
2,2,2,2 - 4,3,3,1 - timp.,perc. - hp. - str.   23:00 Oxford.
—— SYMPHONY
24:00 Mills.
—— SYMPHONY FOR DOUBLE STRING ORCH.
str.   23:00 Lengnick.
—— THEME AND VARIATION
str.   16:00 Lengnick.
—— THREE CLOUDSCAPES FOR ORCH. (1968)
2,2,2,2 - 4,3,3,1 - timp.,perc. - hp. - str.   13:00 P.R.S.
—— VARIAZIONI CONCERTANTI (1965)
ob.,cl.,bn. - hn. - str.   15:00 P.R.S.

MADDEN, Edward
—— ANTHEM OF HERITAGE (FOR CHORUS AND ORCH.)
2,2,2,2 - 4,3,3,1 - timp.,perc. - str.   10:00 C. Fischer.

MADERNA, Bruno
—— AMANDA (FOR CHAMBER ORCH.) (1966)
perc.(4),cel.,mar.,xyl. - guit.,mand. - 2 hp. - pf. - str.(6,3,3,3)
12:00 MCA Music.
—— ARIA DA HYPERION (FOR SOPRANO, FLUTE AND ORCH.)
Leeds.
—— COMPOSITION NO. 1
3,3,3,1 sax.,3 - 4,4,3,1 - timp.,perc.(4),cel.,vibra.,xyl. - 2 hp. - pf. - str.   23:00 Leeds.
—— COMPOSIZIONE IN TRE TEMPI (COMPOSITION IN 3 MOVTS.)
3,3,4,3 - 4,4,3,1 - perc.(5),cel.,glock.,mar.,vibra.,xyl. - guit. - mand. - hp. - pf. - str.   14:00 Leeds.
—— CONCERTO FOR PIANO AND ORCH.
5,4,4,3 sax.,3 - 6,5,5,1 - perc.(3),cel.,mar.,vibra.,xyl. - pf. - str.   18:00 Leeds.
—— CONCERTO FOR 2 PIANOS AND CHAMBER ORCH.
timp.,perc.(5),cel.,vibra.,xyl. - 2 hp. - 2 pf.   15:00 Leeds.
—— CONCERTO NO. 2 FOR OBOE AND ORCH. (1967)
0,4,4,0 - 4,0,0,0 - perc.(6),cel. - 2 guit. - 2 hp. - str.(6,3,3,3)
17:00 MCA Music.
—— CONCERTO NO. 3 FOR OBOE AND ORCH.
4(alt. with 4 picc.),4(3rd alt. with Eng. hn.),3(3rd alt. with b.-cl.),3 - 4,5,4,1 - cel.,glock.,mar.,vibra.,xyl. - 2 hp. - str.   15:00 Salabert.
—— DIMENSIONI III (FOR FLUTE AND ORCH.)
Leeds.
—— DON PERLIMPLIN (1-ACT RADIO OPERA, AFTER F. GARCIA LORCA'S PLAY) (Text: Vittorio Bodini)
3,0,1,5 sax.,1 - 1,3,3,0 - timp.,perc.,bells,mar.,vibra. - electric guit. - mandolin - hp. - pf. - str.   Leeds.
—— HYPERION (1-ACT OPERA) %
MCA Music.
—— THE SATYRICON (OPERA, AFTER PETRONIUS) % (Text: William Harrowsmith)
1(alt. with picc.),1(alt. with Eng. hn.),2(2nd alt. with b.-cl.),1 - 1,1,2,1 - perc.,cel. - hp. - pf. - str.   80:00 Salabert.

—— SERENADE NO. 2 (FOR 11 INSTRUMENTS)
1,0,*2,0 - 1,1,0,0 - glock.,vibra.,xyl. - hp. - pf. - str.(no c.)
12:00 Leeds.
—— STELE PER DIOTIMA (1965) (WITH A CADENZA FOR VIOLIN, CLARINET, BASS CLARINET AND HORN)
5,3,4,3 - 3,3,3,2 - timp.,perc.(10),cel.,glock.,2 mar.,2 vibra.,2 xyl. - 3 hp. - 2 pf. - str.(6,3,3,3)   25:00 MCA Music.

MADETOJA, Leevi
—— ASLAK SMAUKKA, OP. 37 (FOR BARITONE, MALE CHORUS AND ORCH.) (1917)
3,2,2,2 - 4,3,3,1 - timp.,perc. - str.   11:00 FinnMICtr.
—— AUTUMN, OP. 68 (6 SONGS FOR VOICE AND ORCH.) (REV. 1940) (Text: L. Onerva)
2,2,3,2 - 3,3,3,1 - timp.,perc. - hp. - str.   17:00 Fazer.
—— COMEDY OVERTURE, OP. 53 (1923)
3,2,3,2 - 4,2,3,1 - timp.,perc. - str.   9:00 Fazer.
—— CONCERT OVERTURE, OP. 7 (1911)
2,2,2,2 - 4,3,3,1 - timp.,perc. - str.   8:00 FinnMICtr.
—— DANCE VISION
2,2,2,2 - 4,2,0,0 - timp.,perc. - hp. - str.   8:00 G. Schirmer.
—— THE GARDEN OF DEATH, OP. 41
3,3,3,2 - 4,2,0,0 - timp.,perc. - hp. - str.   12:00 G. Schirmer.
—— JUHA, OP. 74 (OPERA) % (1934)
2,2,2,2 - 4,3,3,1 - timp.,perc. - str.   FinnMICtr.
—— KULLERVO, OP. 15 (1913)
3,2,3,2 - 4,3,3,1 - timp.,perc. - hp. - str.   16:00 Fazer.
—— LITTLE SUITE, OP. 12 (1912) (IN 5 MOVTS.)
2,2,2,2 - 3,0,0,0 - timp.,perc. - hp. - str.   18:00 Westerlund.
—— LYRIC SUITE, OP. 51 (FOR CELLO AND ORCH.) (REV. 1922) (IN 4 MOVTS.)
2,2,2,2 - 3,2,1,0 - timp. - str.   17:00 Fazer.
—— OESTERBOTTNER, OP. 45 (3-ACT OPERA) % (With Finnish and German Texts)
2,2,2,2 - 4,3,3,1 - timp.,perc. - str.   G. Schirmer.
On Stage: 2 ob., 2 cl. - 2 vln.
—— OKON FUOKO, OP. 58 (BALLET) % (1930)
3,2,2,2 - 4,3,4,1 - timp.,perc.(3),cel.,xyl. - hp. - str.
14:00 FinnMICtr.
—— PASTORAL SUITE, OP. 34 (1916) (IN 4 MOVTS.)
2,2,2,2 - 3,2,2,1 - timp.,perc. - hp. - str.   11:00 Westerlund.
—— THE PLAYING OF VÄINÄMÖINEN (UPON THE KANTELE), OP. 76 (CANTATA) (FOR SOPRANO, BARITONE, SATB CHORUS AND ORCH.) (1935) (Text: The Kalevala)
2,2,2,2 - 4,3,3,1 - timp.,perc. - str.   25:00 FinnMICtr.
—— RUSTIC SCENES, OP. 77 (SUITE FROM THE FILM "THE STRUGGLE FOR THE HOMESTEAD") (1936)
1,1,2,1 - 0,2,0,0 - timp. - str.   11:00 FinnMICtr.
—— SAMMON RYOSTO (THE CAPTURE OF THE SAMPO) (FOR BARITONE, MALE CHORUS AND ORCH.)
Y.Laulajat.
—— THE SPAN OF LIFE, OP. 47 (CANTATA) (FOR SOLO VOICE, SATB CHORUS AND ORCH.) (1920) (Text: V. A. Koskenniemi)
2,2,3,2   4,3,3,1 - timp. - str.   30:00 Fazer.
—— SUITE FROM THE OPERA "OESTERBOTTNER", OP. 45
2,2,2,2 - 4,3,3,1 - timp.,perc.   17:00 G. Schirmer.
—— SUITE FROM THE OPERA "THE OSTROBOTHNIANS", OP. 52 (1923) (IN 5 MOVTS.)
2,2,2,2 - 4,3,3,1 - timp.,perc.   20:00 G. Schirmer.
—— SUITE FROM THE PLAY "CHESS", OP. 5 (1910) (IN 4 MOVTS.)
2,2,2,1 - 2,2,0,0 - timp. - str.   15:00 Fazer.
—— SYMPHONIC SUITE, OP. 4 (1910) (IN 4 MOVTS.)
2,3,3,2 - 4,3,3,0 - timp. - hp. - str.   25:00 Fazer.
—— SYMPHONY NO. 1 IN F MAJOR, OP. 29 (REV. 1916)
3,2,3,2 - 4,3,3,1 - timp.,perc. - hp. - str.   22:00 Fazer.
—— SYMPHONY NO. 2 IN E FLAT MAJOR, OP. 35 (REV. 1918)
3,4,3,2 - 5,3,3,1 - timp.,perc. - str.   45:00 Fazer.
—— SYMPHONY NO. 3 IN A MAJOR, OP. 55 (REV. 1926)
2,2,2,2 - 4,3,3,1 - timp.,perc. - hp. - str.   33:00 Westerlund.
—— TWO SCENES (TRAGIC SCENE AND SHOOTING THE RAPIDS) (FROM THE OPERA "JUHA") (1934)
2,2,2,2 - 4,3,3,1 - timp. - str.   13:00 FinnMICtr.

MADJERA, Gottfried
—— ST. PETERSBURG SKETCHES
2,2,2,2 - 3,2,3,1 - timp.,perc. - str.   13:30 F. Colombo.

MAEGAARD, Jan
—— CHAMBER CONCERTO NO. 1
1,1,1,1 - 0,0,0,0 - str.   25:00 K.O.D.A.
—— CHAMBER CONCERTO NO. 2
1,1,0,1 - 0,0,0,0 - pf.(ad lib.) - str.   Henmar.

—— DUE TEMPI

K.O.D.A.

MAEKELBERGHE, August
—— A CHRISTMAS SUITE (FOR CHORUS, HARP AND STRING
ORCH.) (IN 6 MOVTS.)
hp. - str.   19:00 J. Fischer.
—— FANTASIA
2,*3,0,4 sax.,2 - 4,2,3,1 - timp.,perc. - str.   10:00 J. Fischer.
—— LET ALL MORTAL FLESH KEEP SILENT (SYMPHONIC
POEM)
*3,*3,2,2 - 4,3,3,1 - timp.,perc. - str.   13:00 J. Fischer.

MAES, Jef
—— BURLESCA (FOR BASSOON AND ORCH.) (1957)
2,1,2,1 - 2,2,1,0 - timp.,cel.,xyl. - pf. - str.   7:00 H. Elkan.
—— CONCERTO FOR HARPSICHORD AND STRINGS (1955)
hpsc. - str.   13:30 H. Elkan.
—— CONCERTO FOR PIANO AND ORCH. (1948)
2,2,2,2 - 4,3,3,0 - timp.,perc. - pf. - str.   20:00 H. Elkan.
—— CONCERTO FOR VIOLA AND ORCH. (1943)
2,2,2,2 - 3,3,0,0 - perc. - hp. - str.   16:00 H. Elkan.
—— CONCERTO FOR VIOLIN AND ORCH. (1951)
2,2,2,2 - 4,2,3,0 - timp.,perc. - str.   22:00 H. Elkan.
—— CONCERTSTUK (1938)
3,3,3,3 - 4,3,3,1 - timp.,perc.,glock. - hp. - str.   9:30 H. Elkan.
—— DIALOG FOR VIOLIN AND ORCH. (1973)
2,2,2,2 - 2,2,1,0 - timp.,perc. - str.   7:30 H. Elkan.
—— DRIE RYTHMEN IN DANSVORM (1931)
2,2,2,2 - 4,2,2,0 - timp.,perc. - hp. - pf. - str.   12:00 H. Elkan.
—— OUVERTURE OP EEN BELCANTO THEMA VAN VERDI
(1967)
3,3,2,2 - 4,3,3,1 - timp.,perc. - str.   6:00 H. Elkan.
—— OVERTURA BUFFA (1939)
3,3,3,3 - 4,3,3,1 - timp.,perc.,cel.,glock. - hp. - pf. - str.
                                                      9:30 H. Elkan.
—— PARTITA (FOR STRING ORCH.) (1966) (IN 3 MOVTS.)
str.   14:30 H. Elkan.
—— SYMPHONY NO. 2 (1965) (IN 3 MOVTS.)
3,2,2,3 - 4,3,3,1 - timp.,perc. - str.   13:00 H. Elkan.
—— SYMPHONY NO. 3 (1975) (IN 3 MOVTS.)
3,3,3,3 - 4,3,3,1 - timp.,perc. - str.   18:00 H. Elkan.
—— SYMPHONY (1953)
2,2,2,2 - 4,3,3,0 - timp.,perc. - str.   20:00 H. Elkan.
—— DE VERLOOFDEN (FOR CHAMBER ORCH.) (1969) (AFTER A
PAINTING OF CONSTANT PERMEKE)
1,1,1,1 - 0,0,0,0 - timp.,perc. - str.   10:00 H. Elkan.

MAESCH, LaVahn
—— PASSACAGLIA (1938)
2,2(alt.with Eng.hn.),2,2 - 4,3,3,1 - timp.,perc.(3) - str.
                                                      10:00 Composer.
—— SONATA FOR CHAMBER ORCHESTRA (1950)
1. Slow; 2. Moderately Fast; 3. Swift
1,1,1,1 - 2,1,1,0 - timp.,perc.(2) - pf. - str.   15:00 Composer.
—— SUITE ON CHILDREN'S TUNES (1938) (IN 3 MOVTS.)
2(2nd alt.with picc.),2(2nd alt.with Eng.hn.),2,2 - 4,2,2,0 -
timp.,perc.(3) - hp. - str.   10:30 Composer.
—— SYMPHONY IN E (1942)
1. Slow, with Great Energy; 2. Moderately Fast, in Simple Rustic
Style; 3. Swift, in a lively and sportive manner; 4. Subdued, with
Apprehension
3(3rd alt.with picc.),3(3rd alt.with Eng.hn.),3(3rd alt.with b.-cl.),2 -
4,3,3,1 - timp.,perc.(4),cel.,xyl. - str.   22:00 Composer.
—— TWO CHRISTMAS PIECES ON TRADITIONAL CAROLS
(1938)
2(2nd alt. with picc.),(2nd alt. with Eng.hn.),2,2 - 4,2,3,1 -
timp.,perc.(3),xyl. - str.   8:00 Composer.

MAESSEN, Antoon
—— CONCERTINO FOR PIANO AND ORCH. (1962)
2,2,2,2 - 2,2,2,0 - timp.,perc. - pf. - str.   12:00 Henmar.
—— DIVERTIMENTO FOR BASSOON AND STRINGS (1960)
bn. - str.   16:00 Henmar.
—— HYMNE (TE SAECULORUM PRINCIPEM) (FOR SOPRANO,
MIXED CHORUS AND ORCH.) (1968) (Text: Gabriel Smit)
                                                      12:00 Henmar.
—— DE KINDERKRUISTOCHT (FOR YOUTH CHOIR AND
ORCH.) (Text: M. Nijhoff)
                                                      15:00 Henmar.
—— SYMFONIETTA (1959)
2,2,2,2 - 2,2,2,0 - timp.,perc. - str.   20:00 Henmar.

—— VARIAZIONI SU UNA ELEGIA (FOR CHAMBER ORCH)
1,2,1,1 - 1,1,1,0 - timp.,perc. - str.   17:00 Henmar.

MAGANINI, Quinto
—— AMERICANESE (SUITE ON THREE EARLY AMERICAN
PIECES)
1,1(alt. with Eng. Hn.),2,1 - 2,2,2,0 - timp.,perc.(1) - str.
                                                      11:00 Musicus.
—— THE ARGONAUTS (A CALIFORNIAN TETRALOGY OF
OPERAS) %
                                                      270:00 Musicus.
—— AT THE SETTING OF THE SUN (DANCE SCENE FROM
"THE ARGONAUTS")
                                                      8:30 Musicus.
—— THE CATHEDRAL AT SENS (CONCERTO DA CHIESA) (FOR
SOLO CELLO, CHORUS AND ORCH.)
3,*3,0,0 - 0,0,0,0 - hp. - pf. - str.   8:00 Musicus.
—— CONCERTO IN D. MINOR, FOR STRINGS (IN 3 MOVTS.)
str.   20:00 Musicus.
—— EVEN HOURS (IN 5 MOVTS.)
*4,*3,*3,2 - 4,3,3,1 - timp.,perc.(4) - hp. - pf. - str. 22:00 Musicus.
—— FOUR ORCHESTRAL SONGS (FOR MEDIUM HIGH VOICE
AND ORCH.)
*4,*3,2,2 - 4,3,3,1 - timp.,perc.(4) - str.   20:00 Musicus.
—— GENEVIEVE (RHAPSODY IN VARIATION FORM)
3(3rd alt. with picc.),*3,2,2 - 4,3,3,1 - timp.,perc. (3) - hp. - pf. -
str.   15:00 Musicus.
—— ITALIAN RAILWAY POSTERS (A MUSICAL
ADVERTISEMENT) (FOR VOICE AND ORCH.) (Text: Quinto
Maganini)
*3,*3,2,2 - 3,3,3,0 - timp.,perc.(3) - hp. - str.   12:00 Composer.
—— LADIES OF THE BALLET (SUITE FOR STRINGS)
str.   11:00 Musicus.
—— NAPOLEON I (AN ORCHESTRAL PORTRAIT)
3 picc.,2,*3,*3,2 - 4,4,3,1 - timp.,perc.(4) - hp. - str.
                                                      14:00 Musicus.
—— ORNITHOLOGICAL SUITE, OP. 26 (IN 3 MOVTS.)
*2,2,2,1 - 2,2,1,0 - timp.,perc. - hp. - pf. - str.   17:00 Musicus.
—— OVERTURE TO "TENNESSEE'S PARTNER"
3,2,2,2 - 3,3,3,1 - timp.,perc. - hp. - str.   6:30 Musicus.
—— THE PEACEFUL LAND
2,*3,2,2 - 2 hn. - timp. - str.   5:30 Musicus.
—— THE ROYAL LADIES (SUITE BY LADIES OF ROYALTY) (IN
3 MOVTS.)
                                                      16:00 Musicus.
—— SOUTH WIND
4(2 alt. with 2 picc.),*3,*3,2 - 6,4,3,1 - timp.,perc. (6),cel. - 2 hp. -
str.   18:00 Musicus.
—— SUITE OF MUSIC BY ROYALTY
2(alt. with 2 picc.),2,2,2 - 2,2,2,0 - timp.,perc. - hp. - str.
                                                      17:30 Musicus.
—— SUITE OF RENAISSANCE MUSIC
2(alt. with 2 picc.),2,*3,2 - 2,2,3,1 - perc. - pf. - str.
                                                      15:00 Musicus.
—— SYLVAN SYMPHONY (FOR CHAMBER ORCH.) (IN 4
MOVTS.)
1(alt. with picc.),1(alt. with Eng. hn.),1,1 - 2 hn. - str.
                                                      17:00 Musicus.
—— TANGLEWOOD TALES
2 picc.,3,*4,E♭ cl.,*3,*4 - 4,3,3,1 - timp.,perc.(4) - hp. - pf. - str.
                                                      38:00 Musicus.
—— THREE PIECES FOR SMALL ORCH.
*1,1,2,1 - 2,2,1,0 - timp.,perc.(1) - hp. - pf. - str.
                                                      14:30 C. Fischer.
—— TUOLUMNE
*3,*2,2,2 - 4,4,3,1 - timp.,perc., bells - hp. - str. 17:00 Musicus.

MAGDIĆ, Josip
—— CONCERTANTE GRAVURES (FOR FRENCH HORN AND
ENSEMBLE)
1,0,1,1 - 1,0,1,0 - perc. - hp. - str.(2,1,1,1)   S.O.K.O.J.
—— CONCERTO FOR FLUTE AND ORCH.
1,2,1,1 - 2,2,2,0 - timp.,perc. - str.   13:00 S.O.K.O.J.
—— CONSTELLATION
*3,*3,2,*3 - 4,3,3,1 - timp.,perc.(3) - hp. - pf.   14:00 S.O.K.O.J.
—— HOMMAGE À I.S.
1,1,1,1 - 1,0,0,0 - perc. - hp. - str.(1,1,1,1)   10:00 S.O.K.O.J.
—— LITTLE SUITE (IN 4 MOVTS.)
str.   8:00 S.O.K.O.J.
—— PHANTASM
1,*2,1,*2 - 2,2,2,0 - timp. - pf.   9:00 S.O.K.O.J.
—— RIFLESSIONI (FOR PIANO AND CHAMBER ENSEMBLE)
1,1,0,0 - 0,0,0,0 - perc.(1) - hp. - pf. - str.(2,1,1,1) 8:00 S.O.K.O.J.

—— SINFONIA PROFANA (IN 3 MOVTS.)
*3,*3,2,*3 - 4,3,3,1 - timp.,perc. - pf. - str.   25:00 S.O.K.O.J.
—— SYNTHESIS (FOR FLUTE AND CHAMBER ENSEMBLE)
1,0,*1,0 - 1,0,0,0 - timp.,vibra. - hp. - str.(1,1,1,1)
10:00 S.O.K.O.J.

MAGEAU, Mary Magdalen
—— MONTAGE (1970)
*3,1,1,1 - 2,1,2,1 - timp.,perc.(5),cel.,glock.,vibra. - hp. - str.
9:00 Composer.

MAGENTI CHELVI, Leopoldo
—— ESTAMPAS MEDITERRANEAS (MEDITERRANEAN
SKETCHES)
S.G.A.E.

MAGNARD, Alberic
—— SYMPHONY NO. 4, OP. 21
3,3,3,2 - 4,3,3,0 - timp. - hp. - str.   40:00 Salabert.

MAGNE, Michel
—— LE RENDEZ-VOUS MANGUÉ (BALLET) %
1,1,1,3 sax.(alto, ten., bar.),0 - 1,4,3,1 - perc.(2) - pf. - str.
90:00 Presser.

MAHLER, Gustav
—— BLUMINE (MOVEMENT FROM SYMPHONY NO. 1)
2,2,2,2 - 4,1,0,0 - timp. - hp. - str.   7:40 Presser.
—— DAS LIED VON DER ERDE (THE SONG OF THE EARTH)
(SYMPHONY FOR TENOR, CONTRALTO AND ORCH.) (IN 6
MOVTS.)
*4,3(3rd alt. with Eng. hn.), E♭cl.,*4,3(3rd alt. with c.-bn.) -
4,3,3,1 - timp.,perc.,cel.,glock. - 2 hp. - mandolin - str.
60:00 Presser.
—— LIEDER EINES FAHRENDEN GESELLEN (SONGS OF A
WAYFARER) (FOR SOPRANO AND ORCH.) (IN 4 MOVTS.)
3(3rd alt. with picc.),2(2nd alt. with Eng. hn.),3(3rd alt. with
b.-cl.),2 - 4,2,3,0 - timp.,perc.,glock. - hp. - str. 14:00 Bo. Hawkes.
—— SONGS FROM "THE YOUTH'S MAGIC HORN" ("DES
KNABEN WUNDERHORN") (FOR VOICE AND ORCH.)
3,4,4,4 - 4,3,4,1 - timp.,perc.,glock-hp. - str.   51:00 Presser.
—— SYMPHONY NO. 3 (REVISED BY THE COMPOSER)
4,4,5,4 - 8,4,4,1 - timp.perc.(4, incl.2 on timp.),bells, glock. - 2 hp.
- str.   Presser.
Off-stage: post-hn.
—— SYMPHONY NO. 6 ("TRAGIC")
Presser.
—— SYMPHONY NO. 7 (ORIGINAL VERSION)
4(1 alt. with picc.),3(3rd alt. with Eng.hn.),3(1 alt. with E♭cl., 1
alt. with b.-cl.),3(3rd alt. with c.-bn.) - 4(1 alt. with ten.hn.),3,3,1 -
timp.,perc. - 2 hp. - guit. - mandolin - str.   80:00 AMP.
—— SYMPHONY NO. 8 (WITH SOLO VOICES AND CHORUS)
6,5,6,5 - 8,4,4,1 - timp.,perc.,cel. - 2 hp. - harm. - mandolin - org.
- pf. - str.   90:00 Presser.
—— SYMPHONY NO. 9
5,4,5,4 - 4,3,3,1 - timp.,perc. - 2 hp. - str.   75:00 Presser.
—— WALDMÄRCHEN (FOREST LEGEND)(PART I OF "DAS
KLAGENDE LIED") (FOR SOLO VOICES, SATB CHORUS
AND ORCH.)
3,3,3,3 - 4,4,3,1 - timp.,perc. - 2 hp - str   Belw-Mills.

MAHLER, Gustav - BRITTEN, Benjamin
—— MINUET FROM SYMPHONY NO. 3
2,2,2,2 - 4,3,0,0 - perc. - hp. - str.   8:00 Presser.

MAHLER, Gustav - BYRNS, Harold
—— SIX SONGS (CYCLE FOR BARITONE AND ORCH.)
2,3,3,3 - 4,3,3,1 - timp.,perc.,cel. - hp. - str.   25:00 Belw-Mills.

MAHLER, Gustav - NEUMANN, Alfred. J.
—— FINALE FROM SYMPHONY NO. 2 ("RESURRECTION") (FOR
SOPRANO, ALTO, SATTBB CHORUS AND ORCH.) (ARR.
1973) (Eng. text: A. J. Neumann)
4(4th alt. with picc.),*5,4,*5 - 10,6,4,1 - timp.,perc.(8),bells,cel. - 2
hp. - org. - str.   10:00 C. Fischer.

MAHLER, Gustav - RATZ, Erwin
—— SYMPHONY NO. 4 (REVISED BY E. RATZ) (WITH SOPRANO
SOLO IN 4TH MOVT.)
4,3,3,3 - 4,3,0,0 - timp.,perc.(4),glock. - hp. - str.   Presser.

—— SYMPHONY NO. 6 (Revised Final Version)
5(3 alt. with 3 picc.),5(3 alt. with 3 Eng. hn.),6(3 alt.,1 each, with
D cl., E♭ cl. and b.-cl.),5(1 alt. with c.-bn.) - 8,6,4,1 -
timp.,perc.,cel. - 2 hp. - str.   80:00 Henmar.

MAHLER, Gustav - STEIN, Erwin
—— ANDANTE GROTTESCO (THIRD MOVT. FROM SYMPHONY
NO. 1)
2,2,2,2 - 4,2,3,1 - timp.,perc. - hp. - str.   9:00 Presser.
—— ANDANTE PASTORALE (FROM SYMPHONY NO. 2)
2,2,2,2 - 4,2-3,3,1 - timp.,perc. - hp. - str.   8:30 Presser.

MAILMAN, Martin
—— AUTUMN LANDSCAPE
2,2,2,2 - 2,2,1,0 - timp. - hp. - str.   7:30 Mills.
—— CANTIONES
*3,*3,2,2 - 4,3,3,1 - timp.,perc.(3),glock.,xyl. - str. 8:00 Composer.
—— CHRISTMAS MUSIC (FOR MIXED CHORUS AND ORCH.) (IN
3 MOVTS.)
*3,2,0,2 - 2,2,3,1 - timp.,perc.(4) - hp.(or cel.) - str.   6:30 Mills.
—— GATEWAY CITY OVERTURE
*2,2,2,2 - 4,3,3,1 - timp.,perc.(3),glock.,xyl. - hp. - str. 7:00 Mills.
—— GENESIS RESURRECTED (CANTATA) (FOR NARRATOR,
SPEAKING CHORUS, SINGING CHORUS AND ORCH.)
*3,2,*3,2 - 4,2,3,1 - timp.,perc.(3-4),glock.,xyl. - hp. - str.
20:00 Mills.
—— THE HUNTED (1-ACT OPERA) %
2,2,2,2 - 2,2,2,0 - timp.,perc. - hp. - pf. - str.   55:00 Mills.
—— JUBILATE
*3,2,*3,2 - 4,3,3,1 - timp.,perc.(3),glock.,xyl. - hp. - str.
8:00 Composer.
—— PARTITA FOR STRING ORCH. (IN 3 MOVTS.)
str.   9:00 Mills.
—— PARTITA NO. 4
2,1,2,1 - 1,1,0,0 - timp.,perc.,glock.,xyl. - vln.,d.-b.   Belw-Mills.
—— PRELUDE AND FUGUE NO. 1
*3,2,2,2 - 4,4,3,1 - timp.,perc.(3),glock.,xyl. - hp. - str. 9:00 Mills.
—— PRELUDE AND FUGUE NO. 2
2,2,1,1 - 2,2,2,1 - timp.,perc. - str.   10:00 Mills.
—— SINFONIETTA
3,2,2,2 - 4,3,3,1 - timp.,perc. - hp. - str.   14:00 Belw-Mills.
—— SUITE IN THREE MOVEMENTS
3(3rd alt. with picc.),2*3,2 - 4,3,3,1 - timp.,perc.(3-4),glock.,xyl. -
hp. - str.   12:00 Mills.
—— SYMPHONY NO. 1, OP. 46 (1969) (IN 3 MOVTS.)
3(3rd alt. with picc.),2,*3,1 alto sax.,2 - 4,3,3,1 - timp.,perc.(6-7) -
str.   17:00 Belw-Mills.

MAINARDI, Enrico
—— CONCERTO FOR CELLO AND ORCH.
2,2,2,2 - 4,2,3,0 - timp. - pf. - str.   24:00 Leeds.

MAINGENEAU, Louis
—— PRELUDE TO ACT III OF THE OPERA "NINON DE
LENCLOS"
3,3,2,3 - 4,2,2,1 - timp.,cel. - hp. - str.   Presser.
—— SUITE BRÈVE (FOR BASSOON AND ORCH.)
1,1,2,1 - 2,1,0,0 - timp.,perc. - str.   9:30 EV.
—— SYMPHONY
*3,*3,3,3 - 4,3,3,1 - timp.,perc. - hp. - str.   30:00 EV.

MAIRE, Jacqueline
—— FUGUE ALGERIENNE
P.R.S.
—— I KACHLE MAGNIFIQUE (BALLET) %
P.R.S.

MAJEWSKI, Hans-Martin
—— TWO BUFFOONISH DANCES (ZWEI SKURRILE TÄNZE)
2,2,2,2 - 2,2,2,0 - timp.,perc. - hp. - str.   4:00 Modern.

MAJOROSSY, Aladar
—— TWO SYMPHONIC SKETCHES
5:30 DomoMvl.

MAKRIS, Andreas
—— ANAMNESIS (1971)
1,2,0,2 - 2,0,0,0 - str.   17:00 Mediterran.
or:
1,2,0,2 - 2,2,2,0 - timp. - str.
—— CONCERTINO FOR TROMBONE AND STRINGS (1970)
0,0,0,0 - 0,0,1,0 - str.   10:00 Mediterran.

—— CONCERTO FOR STRINGS (1966) (IN 4 MOVTS.)
    str.   28:00 Composer.
—— CONCERTO FOR VIOLA AND ORCH.
    1,2,0,2 - 2,0,0,0 - str.   26:00 Mediterran.
—— CONCERTO FOR VIOLA AND ORCH. (1970) (IN 3 MOVTS.)
    1,2,0,2 - 2,0,0,0 - str.   26:50 Galaxy.
—— EFTHYMIA (1972)
    *3,*3,*3,*3 - 4,3,3,1 - timp.,perc.(5) - hp. - str.   12:00 Mediterran.
—— FIVE MINIATURES FOR STRINGS
    str.   13:00 Mediterran.
—— LARGO FOR STRINGS
    str.   5:00 Mediterran.
—— SCHERZO FOR VIOLINS (FOR VIOLINS ONLY)
    Vlns.   4:00 Mediterran.
—— SYMPHONIC OVERTURE (1967)
    *4,*3,*4,*3 - 4,3,3,1 - timp.,perc.(5) - str.   12:56 Mediterran.

MAKSIMOVIĆ, Rajko
—— EPPUR SI MUOVE
    3,3,3,3 - 6,3,3,0 - perc. - str.   10:00 MIC,Zagreb.
—— THREE HAIKU (FOR FEMALE CHORUS AND 24 INSTRUMENTS)
    4 fl. - perc. - 2 hp. - pf. - 12 vlns.   9:00 MIC,Zagreb.
—— TO BE OR NOT TO BE
    *3,3,3,3 - 6,3,3,0 - timp.,perc. - pf. - str.   5:30 MIC,Zagreb.

MALDER, Pierre van - BODART, Eugen
—— SYMPHONY IN G MAJOR
    0,2,0,0 - 2,0,0,0 - str.   13:00 Mannheimer.

MALDERE, Pierre van - CARSE, Adam
—— SYMPHONY IN B FLAT, OP. 4, NO. 3
    1. Allegro assai; 2. Andante un poco allegretto
    2 ob. - 2 hn. - str.   10:00 Galaxy.

MALEC, Ivo
—— ARCO - 22 (FOR STRING ORCH.)
    str.(12,4,4,2)   18:00 Salabert.
—— ARCO (FOR 11 STRINGS)
    str.   17:00 Salabert.
—— GAM(M) ES (1971)
    3(3rd alt. with picc.),3(3rd alt. with Eng.hn.),3(3rd alt. with b.-cl.),3(3rd. alt. with c.-bn.) - 6,6,5,1 - timp.,perc.(6) - 2 hp. - pf. - str.(27,12,10,10)   15:00 Salabert.
—— LIED (FOR VOICES AND STRINGS) (1969) (WITH 6 SOPRANOS, 6 MEZZO-SOPRANOS AND 6 TENORS)
    str.   20:00 Salabert.
—— LUMINA (FOR 12 STRINGS AND TAPE) (1968)
    Tape-recorder(stereo) - str. (7,2,2,1)   14:00 Salabert.
—— MOUVEMENT EN COULEUR
    3,1,*1,2 alto sax., 4 ten. sax.,1 bar. sax.,0 - 0,4,4,1 - timp.,perc.(3),bells, vibra. - hp. - pf. - 9 c.,1 - d.b.   11:00 Eds. Fran.
—— ORAL (FOR SPEAKING VOICE AND LARGE ORCH.)
    Hans Gerig.
—— SIGMA (FOR LARGE ORCH.)
    Hans Gerig.
—— TEHRANA
    18:00 Salabert.
—— TUTTI (1962)
    2(2nd alt. with picc.),1,1(alt. with b.-cl.),1(alt. with c.-bn.) - 2,2,1,0 - perc. - tape-recorder - str.(2,1,2,1)   8:00 Salabert.
—— VICTOR HUGO - UN CONTRE TOUS (A MUSICAL POSTER) % (1971) (FOR 2 RECITING COMEDIANS, MIXED CHORUS, TAPE AND ORCH.) (Text: Roger Pillaudin, after Victor Hugo)
    3(3rd alt. with picc.),3(3rd alt. with Eng.hn.),3(3rd alt. with b.-cl.),2(2nd alt. with c.-bn.) - 3,3,3,1 - perc.(3) - hp. - electric org. - str. (15,6,6,3)   90:00 Salabert.
—— VOCATIF FÜR ORCH.
    Hans Gerig.

MALIGE, Fred
—— BEFREIUNG (SYMPHONIC POEM FOR STRING ORCH.)
    str.   9:00 Tetra.
—— CONCERTO FOR CELLO AND ORCH.
    1,1,2,2 - 2,2,1,0 - timp. - str.   25:00 Tetra.
—— CONCERTO FOR CLARINET AND ORCH.
    1,1,3,2 - 2,2,1,0 - timp. - str.   21:00 Tetra.
—— CONCERTO FOR VIOLA AND ORCH.
    1,1,2,1 - 2,2,0,0 - timp. - str.   24:00 Tetra.
—— STRING SYMPHONY (SYMPHONY NO. 2)
    str.   Tetra.

—— SYMPHONY NO. 1
    2,2,2,2 - 4,2,3,1 - timp.,perc. - str.   30:00 Tetra.

MALIN, Don
—— ALL GLORY BE TO GOD ON HIGH (GREGORIAN MELODY) (FOR CHORUS AND ORCH.)
    2,2,2,2 - 4,3,2,0 - timp. - str.   4:30 Western.

MALIPIERO, Gian Francesco
—— ANTONIO E CLEOPATRA: SYMPHONIC FRAGMENTS FROM THE OPERA
    2,2,2,2 - 4,3,3,1 - timp.,perc.,xyl. - hp. - str.   15:00 Leeds.
—— ANTONIO E CLEOPATRA (3-ACT OPERA, AFTER SHAKESPEARE) %
    2,2,2,2 - 4,3,3,1 - timp.,perc.,xyl. - hp. - str.   Leeds.
—— ARMENIA
    3,3,3,2 - 4,2,0,0 - timp.,perc.,cel. - hp. - str.   6:00 Salabert.
—— CANTARI ALLA MADRIGALESCA
    str.   19:00 Henmar.
—— I CAPRICCI DI CALLOT (THE FANCIES OF CALLOT) (3-ACT OPERA) %
    3,3,3,2 - 4,3,3,1 - timp.,perc.(2) - hp. - pf. - str.   Leeds.
—— CONCERTO A TRE (FOR VIOLIN, CELLO, PIANO, AND ORCH.)
    2,2,2,2 - 4,2,0,0 - pf. - str.   15:00 Leeds.
—— CONCERTO FOR CELLO AND ORCH.
    2,2,2,2 - 4,0,0,0 - perc. - str.   14:00 Leeds.
—— CONCERTO FOR VIOLIN AND ORCH.
    3,2,2,2 - 4,1,0,0 - timp.,perc.,cel.,glock. - str.   18:00 Bo. Hawkes.
—— CONCERTO NO. 2 FOR PIANO AND ORCH.
    2,2,2,2 - 4,2,0,0 - pf. - str.   15:00 Leeds.
—— CONCERTO NO. 5 FOR PIANO AND ORCH.
    2,2,2,2 - 4,2,2,1 - perc.(2) - pf. - str.   14:00 Salabert.
—— DITIRAMBO TRAGICO
    2 picc.,2,*3,*3,*3 - 4,3,3,1 - perc.,cel. - hp. - str.   8:00 G. Schirmer.
—— ECUBA ("HECUBA"): SYMPHONIC COMMENTS TO EURIPIDES' TRAGEDY (WITH OPTIONAL FEMALE CHORUS)
    3,3,3,2 - 4,2,3,1 - str.   15:00 Leeds.
—— ECUBA ("HECUBA") (3-ACT TRAGEDY, AFTER EURIPEDES) %
    3,3,3,2 - 4,3,3,1 - timp.,perc.,cel. - 2 hp. - str.   Leeds.
—— LA FESTA DE LA SENSA ("THE FEAST OF THE ASCENSION") (FOR BARITONE, CHORUS AND ORCH.)
    2,2,2,2 - 4,2,3,1 - perc. - pf. - str.   20:00 Leeds.
—— FOUR INVENTIONS
    2,2,2,2 - 2,1,1,0 - perc.(2) - 2pf. - str.   12:00 Bo. Hawkes.
—— GROTTESCO
    1(alt. with picc.),1,1,1 - 1,1,0,0 - perc. - pf. - str.   G. Schirmer.
—— IMPRESSIONI DAL VERO (PART I)
    3,3,3,2 - 4,2,0,0 - timp.,perc. - hp. - str.   8:00 Salabert.
—— IMPRESSIONI DAL VERO (PART 2) (IN 3 MOVTS.)
    2 picc.,3,*3,*3,*3 - 4,3,3,1 - perc.,cel. - hp. - str.   20:00 G. Schirmer.
—— MISSA PRO MORTUIS (FUNERAL MASS) (FOR BARITONE, CHORUS AND ORCH.)
    2,2,2,2 - 4,3,3,1 - perc. - str.   35:00 Leeds.
—— SANTA EUFROSINA ("ST. EUPHROSINE") (A MYSTERY) (FOR SOPRANO, 2 BARITONES, CHORUS AND ORCH.) %
    2,2,3,2 - 4,0,0,0 - hp. - str.   35:00 Leeds.
—— LE SETTE ALLEGREZZE D'AMORE ("THE SEVEN JOYS OF LOVE") (FOR VOICE AND SMALL ORCH.) (Text: Lorenzo de Medici)
    1,*2,1,1 - 0,0,0,0 - hp. - str.   12:00 Leeds.
—— LE SETTE PECATTI MORTALI (THE 7 DEADLY SINS) (FOR CHORUS AND ORCH.)
    2,3,3,2 - 4,2,3,1 - perc. - str.   18:00 Leeds.
—— SEVEN INVENTIONS
    1. Non troppo mosso; 2. Mosso; 3. Non mosso, ma allegro; 4. Lento, ma non troppo; 5. Allegro agitato; 6. Lento, ma non troppo; 7. Allegro
    *3,2,2,*3 - 4,2,3,1 - timp.,perc.(3),cel. - str.   19:00 Bo. Hawkes.
—— SYMPHONY NO. 3 (SINFONIA DELLE CAMPANE) (SYMPHONY OF THE BELLS)
    2,3,3,2 - 4,2,3,1 - timp.,perc.,cel.,glock. - hp. - pf. - str.   18:00 Leeds.
—— LA TERRA ("THE EARTH") (FOR CHORUS AND ORCH.) (Text: Vergilius)
    2,2,2,2 - 4,0,0,0 - perc. - str.   18:00 Leeds.
—— TRE INNI (THREE HYMNS)
    2,2,*3,2 - 4,2,3,1 - timp.,perc.(2) - str.   6:00 Bo. Hawkes.

—— UNIVERSA UNIVERSIS (FOR MALE CHORUS AND
CHAMBER ORCH.)
2,2,0,2 - 4,0,0,0 - pf. - str.(no c.)　　15:00 Leeds.
—— VERGILII AENEIS (HEROIC SYMPHONY) (FOR SOLO
VOICES, CHORUS AND ORCH.)
3,3,3,2 - 4,3,3,1 - timp.,perc.(2),cel. - hp. - pf. - str.　110:00 Leeds.
—— LA VITA È SOGNO (LIFE IS A DREAM) (3-ACT OPERA,
AFTER THE PLAY BY CALDERON DE LA BARCA) %
3,3,3,3 - 4,2,3,1 - timp.,perc.(2),cel. - hp. - str.　　Leeds.

MALIPIERO, Riccardo
—— BATTONO ALLA PORTA ("THEY KNOCK AT THE DOOR")
(1-ACT TELEVISION OPERA) % (Text: Dino Buzzati)
3,3,3,2 - 4,3,3,0 - timp.,perc.(2),glock.,mar.,vibra.,xyl. - hpsc. - hp.
- pf. - str.　　Leeds.
—— CADENCIAS PER ORCHESTRA

Leeds.
—— CANTATA DI NATALE (CHRISTMAS CANTATA) (FOR
SOPRANO, CHORUS AND ORCH.)
2,2,2,2 - 2,2,0,0 - timp.,bells. - str.　　30:00 Leeds.
—— CARNET DE NOTES (1967)
2,2,2,2 - 2,2,0,0 - perc.(3),mar.,vibra. - str.　14:00 MCA Music.
—— CASSAZIONE II (1967)
str.　　16:00 MCA Music.
—— CONCERTO BREVE (FOR BALLERINA AND CHAMBER
ORCH.) %
1,1,1,1 - 2,2,0,0 - str.　　16:00 Leeds.
—— CONCERTO FOR CELLO AND ORCH.
2,2,2,2 - 4,3,3,0 - timp. - str.　　22:00 Leeds.
—— CONCERTO FOR PIANO AND CHAMBER ORCH.
0,2,0,1 - 2,0,0,0 - pf. - str.　　17:00 Leeds.
—— CONCERTO FOR VIOLIN AND ORCH.
2,2,2,2 - 2,2,0,0 - timp.,perc. - str.　　27:00 Leeds.
—— CONCERTO PER DIMITRI (CONCERTO FOR DIMITRI)
(CONCERTO FOR PIANO AND ORCH.)
2,2,2,2 - 4,3,3,0 - timp.,perc. - pf. - str.　25:00 Leeds.
—— LA DONNA È MOBILE ("WOMAN IS INCONSTANT") (1-ACT
OPERA BUFFA, AFTER A COMEDY BY M. BONTEMPELLI)
%
2,2,2,2 - 4,3,3,0 - timp.,perc.,vibra - str.　　Leeds.
On Stage: band
—— MINNIE LA CANDIDA (CANDID MINNIE) (3-ACT OPERA)
% (Text: M. Bontempelli)
2,2,2,2 - 4,3,3,0 - timp.,cel. - hp. - str.　　Leeds.
—— MIRAGES (1966)
3,3,3,3 - 4,4,4,0 - timp.,perc.(4),cel.,mar.,vibra.,xyl. - str.
18:00 MCA Music.
—— MONOLOGO (FOR WOMAN'S VOICE AND STRINGS) (1969)
(Text: G. Leopardi)
str.　　14:00 MCA Music.
—— MOSAICO (MOSAIC) (FOR DOUBLE QUINTET)
1,1,1,1 - 1,0,0,0 - str.　　13:00 Leeds.
—— NYKTEGHERSIA
2,3,3,3 - 4,3,3,0 - timp.,perc.(4),mar.,vibra. - hp. - str.
18:00 Leeds.
—— OVERTURE-DIVERTIMENTO ("DEL RITORNO")
2,2,2,2 - 2,2,0,0 - timp.,perc. - str.　　7:00 Leeds.
—— RHAPSODY FOR VIOLIN AND ORCH. (1967)
3,2,2,2 - 4,4,4,0 - perc.(3),mar.,vibra. - hp. - str.
18:00 MCA Music.
—— SEI POESIE DI DYLAN THOMAS (SIX POEMS OF DYLAN
THOMAS) (FOR SOPRANO AND 10 INSTRUMENTS)
1,1,*1,0 - 0,0,0,0 - perc.,bell,vibra. - str.(no d.-b.)　11:00 Leeds.
—— SERENATA PER ALICE TULLY (FOR CHAMBER ORCH.)
(1969)
1,2,0,1 - 2,2,0,0 - hpsc. - timp.,perc.(1) - str.　13:00 MCA Music.
—— SINFONIA
2,2,2,2 - 4,3,3,0 - timp.,perc. - str.　　25:00 Bo. Hawkes.
—— SINFONIA CANTATA (FOR BARITONE AND ORCH.)
2,3,3,3 - 4,4,3,0 - timp.,perc.,vibra. - hp. - str.　42:30 Leeds.
—— SONATA FOR OBOE AND STRING ORCH.
ob. - str.　　8:00 Leeds.
—— STUDI (STUDIES)
2,2,3,2 - 4,4,4,0 - timp.,perc.,xyl. - str.　14:00 Leeds.
—— SYMPHONY NO. 3
3,3,3,2 - 4,3,3,0 - timp.,perc. - str.　　21:00 Leeds.

MALKO, Nikolai
—— CONCERTO FOR CLARINET AND ORCH.
2,2,1,2 - 3,0,0,0 - str.　　18:00 Bo. Hawkes.

MALMGREN, Jens-Ole
—— DANCING CIRCUS, OP. 15
2,2,2,2 - 2,4,2,0 - perc. - str.　　14:00 K.O.D.A.
—— SAVOYAGES, OP. 13 (SYMPHONY IN TWO MOVEMENTS)
3,3,3,2 - 4,3,3,0 - perc. - str.　　26:00 K.O.D.A.
—— VOYAGES FOR CHAMBER ORCH., OP. 14
1,1,1,1 - 1,0,0,0 - perc. - guit. - hp. - pf. - str.　21:00 K.O.D.A.

MALMSTRÖM, Gunnar
—— GUSTAV VASA (OVERTURE)
2,2,2,2 - 4,2,3,0 - timp. - str.　　8:00 S.T.I.M.
—— PRELUDIO LIRICO
2,2,2,2 - 4,2,3,1 - timp. - str.　　8:30 S.T.I.M.
or:
2,2,2,2 - 2,2,1,1 - timp. - str.

MALOOF, William J.
—— ANTIQUE DANCES FOR STRING ORCH., OP. 14 (1969)
str.　　20:00 Composer.
—— THE CENTURION (2-ACT OPERA) % (1971) (Text: Composer)
2,1,2,1 - 2,2,2,1 - timp.,perc.(3),vibra. - pf. - str.　50:00 Composer.
—— IN CELEBRATION (PRELUDE AND FUGUE FOR BRASS)
(1963)
0,0,0,0 - 0,5,2,0　　4:30 Composer.
or:
0,0,0,0 - 2,3,2,0
—— SINFONIETTA CONCERTANTE, OP. 13 (1969) (IN 3 MOVTS.)
*2,1,*2,1 - 2,2,2,0 - timp.,perc.(2) - str.　24:30 Composer.
—— VARIATIONS FOR ORCHESTRA (1965)
*3,*3,*3,*3 - 4,3,3,1 - timp.,perc.(3) - hp. - str.　17:30 Composer.
—— VOCALISE (1967)
str.　　17:30 Composer.

MAMANGAKIS, Nikos
—— ANARCHY (FOR PERCUSSION AND LARGE ORCH.)
Hans Gerig.
—— SPRACHSYMBOLE 1962 (FOR DRAMATIC SOPRANO, BASS,
CHORUS AND ORCH.)
1,*1,0,0 - 2,1,0,1 - timp.,perc.(3),bells,vibra.,xyl. - str.
25:00 Modern.

MAMIYA, Michio
—— CONCERTO FOR VIOLIN AND ORCHESTRA
2,2,2,2 - 4,2,2,1 - perc.,cel. - hp. - str.　33:00 Presser.
—— CONCERTO NO. 2 FOR PIANO AND ORCH.
3,2,3,3 - 4,2,3,1 - timp., perc. - hp. - pf. - str.　27:00 Presser.
—— DEUX TABLEAUX
3,3,3,alto sax.,3 - 6,3,3,1 - timp.,perc.(8, incl. 2 on timp.) - 2 hp. -
pf. - str.　　21:00 Presser.

MAMORSKY, Morris
—— THE BLUEBIRD (7 SCENES FROM MAETERLINCK) (FOR
NARRATOR AND ORCH.)
14:00 Broude.
—— CONCERTO FOR PIANO AND ORCH.
Broude.
—— INTRODUCTION AND ALLEGRO (FOR TRUMPET, STRINGS
AND PERCUSSION)
tpt. - timp.,perc.(3),vibra. - hp. - str.　　C-Ross.

MANA-ZUCCA
—— CONCERTO FOR PIANO AND ORCH.
*3,2,2,2 - 4,2,2,1 - timp.,perc.(2) - pf. - str.　16:00 Congress.
—— CONCERTO FOR VIOLIN AND ORCH.
28:00 Congress.
—— CONCERTO NO. 2 FOR PIANO AND ORCH.
Congress.
—— HYPATIA (OPERA) %
Congress.
—— THE QUEUE OF KI-LU (OPERA) %
Congress.
—— TONE POEM
6:30 Congress.
—— THE WEDDING OF THE BUTTERFLIES (BALLET) %
16:00 Congress.

MANDER, Francesco
—— VARIAZIONI SINFONICHE
3,2,3,2 - 4,3,3,1 - timp., - str.　　19:00 Leeds.

MANDUELL, John
—— DIVERSIONS
0,2,0,0 - 2,0,0,0 - str.　　15:00 Novello.

—— SUNDERLAND POINT OVERTURE
    *2,2,2,2 - 2,2,0,0 - perc.,glock.,xyl. - str.   4:00 Novello.

MANEN, Juan
—— MINIATURES (FOR STRINGS)
    str.   23:00 Mills.

MANEVICH, Alexander
—— CONCERTO FOR CLARINET AND ORCH.
    2,2,1,2 - 3,1,1,0 - timp.,perc. - hp. - str.   12:30 G. Schirmer.
—— CONCERTO FOR ORGAN, PERCUSSION AND STRINGS
    perc. - org. - str.   24:00 G. Schirmer.

MANFREDINI, Francesco - PAUMGARTNER
—— CONCERTO GROSSO IN G MINOR, OP. 3, NO. 10 (FOR TWO
    VIOLINS AND STRINGS)
    cemb. - str.   12:00 Henmar.

MANFREDINI, Francesco - SCHERING
—— CONCERTO GROSSO IN C MAJOR, OP. 3, NO. 12
    (CHRISTMAS CONCERTO) (FOR TWO VIOLINS AND
    STRINGS)
    cemb. - str.   10:00 Henmar.

MANFREDINI, Francesco - SCHROEDER
—— CHRISTMAS SYMPHONY IN D MAJOR, OP. 2, NO. 12
    cemb. - str.   Henmar.

MANFREDINI, Vincenzo - BONELLI, Ettore
—— CONCERTO GROSSO, OP. 3, NO. 9 (FOR STRINGS)
    str.   Henmar.

MANFREDINI, Vincenzo - TONI, Alceo
—— CONCERTO FOR CEMBALO AND ORCH.
    2,0,0,0 - 2,0,0,0 - cemb. - str.   15:00 Bo. Hawkes.
—— CONCERTO FOR TWO TRUMPETS, ORGAN, CEMBALO
    AND STRINGS
    0,0,0,0 - 0,2,0,0 - cemb. - org. - str.   8:00 Bo. Hawkes.

MANGS, Runar
—— SINFONIETTA (1956)
    perc. - str.   S.T.I.M.

MANIGOLD, Julius
—— CONCERTO IN D MINOR FOR FLUTE AND ORCH., OP. 6
    (IN 3 MOVTS.)
    *3,2,2,2 - 4,2,0,0 - timp.,perc. - hp. - str.   21:00 Henmar.

MANIKOWSKY, Heinrich von
—— CHINESE SONGS (FOR HIGH VOICE AND ORCH.)
    2,2,2,2 - 4,2,3,0 - timp.,perc. - hp. - str.   20:00 F. Colombo.
—— MINIATURE SUITE
    2,2,2,2 - 4,2,3,0 - timp.,perc.,xyl. - hp. - str.   11:00 F. Colombo.

MANKELL, Henning
—— CONCERTO IN D MINOR FOR PIANO AND ORCH
    2,2,2,2 - 4,2,3,0 - timp. - pf. - str.   31:00 S.T.I.M.

MANN, Leslie
—— CONCERTINO IN THE OLD STYLE, OP. 11 (1955)
    1. Largo; 2. Allegro semplice; 3. Larghetto; 4. Allegro moderato
    str.   15:00 CanMusCtr.
—— CONCERTO FOR CLARINET AND ORCH., OP. 24 (1970) (IN
    3 MOVTS.)
    2,2,2,2 - 4,2,3,0 - timp.,perc. - hp. - str.   23:50 CanMusCtr.
—— CONCERTO FOR FLUTE AND ORCH., OP. 21 (1964) (IN 3
    MOVTS.)
    1,2,2,2 - 4,2,3,0 - timp.,perc. - hp. - str.   25:00 CanMusCtr.
—— CONCERTO GROSSO NO. 1, OP. 30 (1972) (IN 4 MOVTS.)
    2,2,2,2 - 2,2,1,0 - str.   19:00 CanMusCtr.
—— FANFARE FOR A FESTIVAL (1971) (WITH OPTIONAL
    SPEAKER) (Text: Mary Elizabeth Bayer)
    0,0,1,1 - 4,2,3,1 - timp.,perc. - c.,d.-b.   4:05 CanMusCtr.
—— INTRODUCTION, PASTORALE AND FUGUE ON A
    FRENCH-CANADIAN AIR, OP. 8 (1954)
    *2,2,2,2 - 2,2,0,0 - timp. - str.   16:00 CanMusCtr.
—— MEDITATIONS ON A CHORALE, OP. 31 (1972) (IN 6
    MOVTS.)
    str.   9:20 CanMusCtr.
—— MY MASTER HATH A GARDEN (CANTATA) (FOR HIGH
    VOICE AND CHAMBER ORCH.) (1963)
    20:00 CanMusCtr.

—— ORCHESTRAL SUITE, OP. 25A (1971) (FROM "THE
    DONKEY'S TALE")
    2(2nd alt. with picc.),2,2,2 - 4,2,3,0 - timp.,perc. - str.
    24:15 CanMusCtr.
—— PRELUDE AND FUGUE, OP. 12
    9:00 C.A.P.A.C.
—— SINFONIA CONCERTANTE FOR BASSOON AND CHAMBER
    ORCH., OP. 27 (1971) (IN 3 MOVTS.)
    2,2,2,2 -2,2,1,0 - perc. - str.   14:15 CanMusCtr.
—— SYMPHONY NO. 1, OP. 32 (1973) (IN 3 MOVTS.)
    2,2,2,2 - 4,2,3,0 - timp.,perc. - hp. - str.   29:55 CanMusCtr.
—— SYMPHONY NO. 2, OP. 35 (1974) (IN 3 MOVTS.)
    2,2,2,2 - 4,2,3,0 - timp.,perc. - hp. - str.   22:25 CanMusCtr.

MANNINO, Franco
—— MARIO E IL MAGO: BALLET SUITE (WITH OPTIONAL
    FEMALE CHORUS)
    3,2,3,1 sax.,3 - 4,4,3,1 - timp.,perc.,cel.,glock.,vibra.,xyl. - hp. - pf.
    - str.   15:40 Leeds.
—— MARIO E IL MAGO ("MARIO AND THE MAGICIAN")
    (BALLET, AFTER THOMAS MANN) %
    4,2,3,1 sax.,3 - 4,4,3,1 - timp.,perc.(3),cel.,glock.,vibra.,xyl. - 2 hp.
    - pf. - str.   Leeds.
—— OMAGGIO A JEAN BABILÉE (HOMAGE TO JEAN BABILÉE)
    (BALLET) %
    1,1,1,1 sax.,1 - 2,2,0,0 - timp.,cel.,vibra. - hp. - pf. - str.   Leeds.
—— SONATINA FOR PIANO AND STRING ORCH.
    pf. - str.   Leeds.
—— TRE TEMPI PER ORCHESTRA (3 MOVTS. FOR ORCH.)
    2,1,2,1 - 3,3,2,1 - timp.,perc.,xyl. - hp. - pf. - str.   12:00 Leeds.

MANSON, Eddy
—— SYMPHONY NO. 1
    22:00 Margery.

MANZIARLY, Marcelle de
—— MUSIQUE POUR ORCHESTRE (IN 3 MOVTS.)
    2,2,2,2 - 2,2,0,0 - str.   14:00 Presser.

MANZONI, Giacomo
—— ATOMTOD (2-ACT OPERA) %
    Leeds.
—— CINQUE VICARIOTE (FOR MIXED CHORUS AND ORCH.)
    3,3,4,1 sax.,3 - 4,2,3,1 - timp.,perc.(3),cel.,glock.,vibra.,xyl. -
    mandolin - hp. - str.   18:00 Leeds.
—— DON CHISCIOTTE ("DON QUIXOTE") (FOR SOPRANO,
    CHORUS AND CHAMBER ORCH.)
    Leeds.
—— INSIEMI (1967)
    3,3,3,3 - 4,3,3,1 - timp.,perc.(7),cel.,glock.,xyl. - hp. -
    str.(24,10,8,6)   20:00 MCA Music.
—— OMBRE (ALLA MEMORIA DI CHE GUEVARA) (FOR
    CHORUS AND ORCH.) (1968)
    4,4,4,4 - 6,0,0,1 - timp.,perc.(3) - str.(30,12,10,8)
    20:00 MCA Music.
—— PARAFRASI CON FINALE (FOR 10 PLAYERS) (1969)
    1,0,1,1 - 1,1,1,0 - perc.(1) - hpsc. - org. - d.-b.
    12:00 MCA Music.
—— SPIEL (FOR 11 STRINGS) (1969)
    str.(6,2,2,1)   8:00 MCA Music.
—— STUDY FOR 24 (STUDIO PER 24)
    2,1,2,1 - 2,1,1,0 - timp.,perc.(2) - mandolin - str.   8:00 Leeds.
—— STUDY NO. 2
    2,2,2,2 - 2,2,1,0 - timp.,perc.(2) - str.   7:00 Leeds.

MARAIS, Marin - BOULAY, Laurence
—— SUITE FROM "SEMELE"
    str.   12:00 Eds. Fran.

MARAIS, Marin - CELLIER, Alex
—— SUITE FROM "ALCYONE"
    2,2,0,1 - 0,0,0,0 - timp.,tambourine - str.   13:00 Presser.

MARAIS, Marin - KORNAUTH, Egon
—— FIVE OLD FRENCH DANCES (FOR VIOLA AND STRING
    ORCH.)
    str.   14:00 A.K.M.

MARC, E.
—— BABYLONE (SYMPHONIC POEM)
    13:00 EV.

—— LA PETITE FILLE AUX ALLUMETTES (THE LITTLE MATCH
GIRL) (BERCEUSE DRAMATIQUE)
10:00 EV.

—— TROIS CONTES D'EDGAR POE
28:00 EV.

MARCEL, Luc-André
—— CANTATE DES CHOSES NUES (FOR SOPRANO, ALTO,
BARITONE, WOMEN'S CHORUS AND STRING ORCH.)
str.   25:00 Presser.
—— CONCERTO NO. 1 FOR PIANO AND ORCH.
2,2,2,2 - 4,2,2,1 - timp.,perc.(5) - str.   35:00 Presser.
—— SCHERZO DI 5 (FOR STRING ORCH.)
str.   5:00 Presser.
—— SYMPHONIE D'ARCHETS
str.   35:00 Presser.

MARCELLI, Nino
—— ODE TO A HERO (A TRIBUTE TO GENERAL PERSHING)
3(3rd alt. with picc.),2,2,2 - 4,3,3,1 - timp.,perc. (4) - hp. - str.
6:00 C. Fischer.
—— SUITE ARAUCANA (IN 4 MOVTS.)
3(3rd alt. with picc.),*3,*3,3(3rd alt. with c-bn.) - 4,3,3,1 -
timp.,perc.(5),cel.,glock.,xyl. - 2 hp. - str.   26:00 Composer.

MARCELLO - LAVAGNINO, Angelo F.
—— PSALM 27 (FOR FEMALE CHORUS AND STRINGS)
str.   20:00 Bo. Hawkes.

MARCELLO, Benedetto - ADLER, Hugo Charles
—— PSALM 19 (FOR SATB CHORUS AND ORCH.)
Transcon.

MARCELLO, Benedetto - BONELLI, Ettore
—— CONCERTO GROSSO IN A MAJOR, OP. 1, NO. 9 (FOR
VIOLIN, CEMBALO AND STRINGS)
cemb. - str.   10:00 Henmar.
—— CONCERTO GROSSO IN B FLAT MAJOR, OP. 1, NO. 6 (FOR
VIOLIN, CEMBALO, AND STRINGS)
cemb. - str.   12:00 Henmar.
—— CONCERTO GROSSO IN B MINOR, OP. 1, NO. 5 (FOR
VIOLIN, CEMBALO, AND STRINGS)
cemb. - str.   13:00 Henmar.
—— CONCERTO GROSSO IN C MAJOR, OP. 1, NO. 10 (FOR
VIOLIN, CEMBALO AND STRINGS)
cemb. - str.   12:00 Henmar.
—— CONCERTO GROSSO IN D MAJOR, OP. 1, NO. 1 (FOR
VIOLIN, CEMBALO AND STRINGS)
cemb. - str   10:00 Henmar.
—— CONCERTO GROSSO IN E MAJOR, OP. 1, NO. 3 (FOR
VIOLIN, CEMBALO AND STRINGS)
cemb. - str.   10:00 Henmar.
—— CONCERTO GROSSO IN E MINOR, OP. 1, NO. 2 (FOR
VIOLIN, CEMBALO AND STRINGS)
cemb. - str.   12:00 Henmar.
—— CONCERTO GROSSO IN F MAJOR, OP. 1, NO. 4 (FOR
STRINGS AND CEMBALO)
cemb. - str.   Henmar.
—— CONCERTO GROSSO IN F MAJOR, OP. 1, NO. 8 (FOR
VIOLIN, CEMBALO AND STRINGS)
cemb. - str.   9:00 Henmar.
—— CONCERTO GROSSO IN F MINOR, OP. 1, NO. 7 (FOR
VIOLIN, CEMBALO AND STRINGS)
cemb. - str.   10:00 Henmar.
—— CONCERTO GROSSO, OP. 1, NO. 11 (FOR VIOLIN,
CEMBALO AND STRINGS)
cemb.- str.   Henmar.
—— CONCERTO GROSSO, OP. 1, NO. 12 (FOR VIOLIN,
CEMBALO AND STRINGS)
cemb. - str.   Henmar.
—— CONCERTO IN C MINOR (FOR OBOE OR VIOLIN AND
STRINGS)
ob. (or vln.) - str.   Henmar.
—— INTRODUZIONE, ARIE E PRESTO (FOR STRINGS AND
CEMBALO)
cemb. - str.   Henmar.
—— PRESTO, ADAGIO E ALLEGRO VIVACE (FOR STRING
ORCH.)
str.   10:00 Henmar.

MARCELLO, Benedetto - DUBENSKY, Arcady
—— CONCERTO GROSSO (FOR STRINGS)
str.   12:00 Arranger.

MARCELLO, Benedetto - LAUSCHMANN
—— CONCERTO IN C MINOR FOR OBOE, CEMBALO AND
STRINGS
ob. - cemb. - str.   10:00 Henmar.

MARCELLO, Benedetto - TOSCANO
—— SONATA IN F MAJOR (FOR CELLO AND STRINGS)
str.   8:00 Henmar.

MARCHAND, Louis - PETIT, J. L.
—— SUITE DE PIÈCES
str.   15:00 Presser.

MARCLAND, P.
—— VARIANTS (FOR 16 INSTRUMENTS)
Presser.

MARCO, Tomas
—— CANTOS DEL POZO ARTESIANO (FOR ACTRESS AND
ENSEMBLE) % (1968)
1,0,0,0 - 1,1,1,1, - perc.(2) - vln. c.,d.-b.   20:00 Salabert.
—— MYSTERIA (1971)
2,2,2,2 - 0,2,0,0 - timp.,perc.(3),cel. - hp. - str.   Salabert.
—— VITRAL (MUSICA CELESTIAL NO. 1) (1969)
org. - str.   13:45 Salabert.

MAREK, Robert
—— OVERTURE FOR A JUBILEE
*3,2,2,2 - 4,3,3,1 - timp.,perc.,xyl. - pf. - str.   6:30 Fema.
—— A SHORT OVERTURE TO A COMEDY (G. B. SHAW'S "ARMS
AND THE MAN")
*3,2,2,2 - 4,3,3,1 - timp.,perc. - pf. - str.   4:00 Fema.

MARESCOTTI, André-François
—— AUBADE
2,2,2,2 - 2,2,0,0 - timp.,perc. - str.   13:00 EV.
—— CONCERT CAROUGEOIS NO. 1
2,2,2,2 - 4,2,1,0 - timp.,perc.,vibra.(or cel.) - str.   18:00 EV.
—— CONCERTO CAROUGEOIS NO. 2
timp.,perc.(2),cel.,xyl. - pf. - str.   21:00 EV.
—— CONCERTO CAROUGEOIS NO. 3
20:00 EV.
—— CONCERTO FOR PIANO AND ORCH. (IN 3 MOVTS.)
2,2,2,2 - 4,2,2,0 - timp.,perc. - pf. - str.   23:00 EV.
—— FESTA (SYMPHONIC OVERTURE)
2*2,2,2 - 4,1,1,0 - timp.,perc.(3) - hp. - pf. - str.   8:00 EV.
—— GIBOULÉES (FANTASY FOR BASSOON AND ORCH.)
2*2,2,2 - 2,2,1,0 - timp.,perc. - pf.(ad lib.) - str.   8:00 EV.
—— HYMNES POUR ORCHESTRE (IN 3 MOVTS.)
2,2,2,2 - 4,2,2,1 - timp.,perc.(3) - hp. - pf. - str.   21:00 EV.
—— INSOMNIES (FOR MEZZO-SOPRANO AND ORCH.)
2,*2,2,2 - 4,2,2,0 - timp.,perc. - hp. - str.   21:00 EV.
—— OVERTURE TO THE RABELAIS COMEDY "THE MAN WHO
MARRIED A MUTE WOMAN"
3,*3,3,2 - 4,2,3,0 - timp.,perc. - 2 hp. - str.   8:00 EV.
—— PRÉLUDE AU GRANDMEAULNES
3,*3,3,2 - 4,2,3,0 - timp.,perc. - 2 hp. - str.   12:00 EV.
—— RONDEAU-CAPRICCIOSO
3,2,3,3 - 4,2,2,1 - timp.,perc.(3),vibra. - str.   10:00 Presser.
—— THREE HYMNS FOR ORCH.
2,2,2,2 - 4,2,2,1 - timp.,perc.(3) - hp. - pf. - str.   21:00 EV.

MARGOLA, Franco
—— ANTICHE MUSICHE DI VIRGINALISTI INGLESI (BASED ON
MELODIES OF PETER PHILLIPS, JOHN BULL, GILES
FARNABY AND WILLIAM BYRD)
str.   Henmar.
—— CONCERTO FOR PIANO AND ORCH.
1,1,1,2 - 2,1,0,0 - timp. - pf. - str.   20:00 Leeds.
—— CONCERTO PER LA CANDIDA PACE
3,3,3,3 - 3,3,3,1 - timp.,perc. - pf. - str.   16:00 Bo. Hawkes.
—— LITTLE CONCERTO FOR OBOE AND STRINGS
ob. - str.   15:00 Bo. Hawkes.
—— PARTITA
str.   Bo. Hawkes.
—— SINFONIA IN QUATTRO TEMPI (DELLE ISOLE)
str.   20:00 Bo. Hawkes.

MARGOLIS, Jerome N.
—— HOMAGE TO SATIE (1970)
2(1 alt.with picc.),1,2,2 - 2,0,0,0 - perc.(1) - hp. - pf. - str.
5:00 Composer.

—— PROLOGUE FOR SPEAKER AND ENSEMBLE (1964) (Text: Composer)
   1,0,2,1 - 0,0,0,0 - timp.,perc.(1) - pf. - str.(1,1,2,0) 5:00 Composer.
—— PYKRON (MUSIC FOR 10 INSTRUMENTS) (1974)
   1,1,2,1 - 0,0,0,0 - timp.,perc.(2),bells,glock. - str.(1,1,1,1)
   15:00 Composer.
—— THE RED BALLOON (CHILDREN'S SUITE FOR NARRATOR AND ORCH., AFTER THE FILM) (1961) (IN 6 MOVTS.) (Text: Composer)
   2,1,*3,1 - 1,3,2,1 - timp.,perc.(2),glock. - str.   15:00 Composer.
—— SYMPHONY NO. 1 (1969) (IN 3 MOVTS.)
   *3,2(1 alt. with Eng. hn.),*3,2 - 3,2,2,1 - timp.,perc.(2),cel.,xyl. - hp. - pf. - str.   24:00 Composer.

MARI, Pierrette
—— DIVERTISSEMENT (FOR FLUTE AND ORCH.)
   2,1,2,2 - 2,1,0,0 - timp.,perc. - str.   Presser.
—— TROIS MOUVEMENTS POUR CORDES
   str.   12:30 AhnSimrock.

MARIE, Gabriel
—— KLEÏS (SYMPHONIC SUITE) (IN 4 MOVTS.)
   2,2,2,2 - 4,2,3,1 - timp.,perc. - 2 hp. - str.   23:00 Salabert.

MARIE, Jean Etienne
—— CONCERTO "MILIEU DIVIN" (FOR TWO ORCHESTRAS)
   2,2,3,3 - 4,4,4,0 - perc.(4) - str.   28:00 Presser.
—— IMAGES THANAÏQUES (FOR ORCHESTRA, ELECTRONIC TAPE AND NARRATOR)
   2,1,3,3 - 4,4,4,0 - timp.,perc.(5),2,xyl. - tape-recorder - pf. - str.
   8:30 Presser.
—— OBEDIENS USQUE AD MORTEM
   0,0,0,0 - 4,3,3,1 - perc.   8:30 Presser.
—— TIALOC
   3,3,3,3- 6,3,4,0 - timp.,perc.(7),bells,cel.(alt. with glock.),xyl.(alt. with vibra.) - pf. - str.   14:00 Presser.

MARINUS, Hector N. C.
—— CONCERTINO FOR PIANO AND ORCH.
   3,3,2,4 - 4,3,3,0 - timp.,perc.,cel.,vibra.,xyl. - hp. - pf. - str.
   30:00 Henmar.
—— CONCERTO FOR VIOLIN AND ORCH.
   3,2,3,bar. sax.,3 - 3,3,3,0 - timp.,perc.,cel.,xyl. - hp. - pf. - str.
   21:00 Henmar.
—— JAVAANSE SUITE
   2,2,2,2 - 3,2,0,0 - timp.,perc.,cel.,xyl. - hp. - 2 pf. - str.   Henmar.
—— LE DORMEUR EVEILLE (SUITE) (FROM "THE THOUSAND AND ONE NIGHTS")
   2,2,3,2 - 3,1,0,0 - timp.,perc.,cel.,xyl. - hp. - pf. - str.   Henmar.

MARINUZZI, Gino
—— CONCERTINO FOR ORCH.
   16:30 Bo. Hawkes.
—— CONCERTO FOR OBOE, SAXOPHONE, PIANO AND STRINGS
   ob.,sax. - pf. - str.   16:30 Bo. Hawkes.
—— CONCERTO FOR ORCH.
   3,3,2,2 - 4,3,2,1 - timp.,cel. - pf. - str.   28:00 Bo. Hawkes.
—— CONCERTO FOR PIANO AND ORCH.
   1,1,1,1 - 2,1,1,0 - timp.,perc. - pf. - str.   25:00 Bo. Hawkes.
—— PICCOLE VARIAZIONI SU FRA MARTINO CAMPANARO
   1,2,2,1 - 2,1,1,0 - timp.,perc.,xyl. - str.   12:00 Bo. Hawkes.

MARIOTTI, Mario
—— LA CATTEDRALE (THE CATHEDRAL) (3-ACT OPERA) %
   (Text: A. De Stefani)
   2,2,2,3 - 4,2 cnt.,1,3,1 - timp.,perc.,cel. - hp. - str.   Leeds.
   on Stage: tpts. - org.

MARKAITIS, Bruno
—— THE BELLS OF VILNIUS (SYMPHONIC CANTATA) (1964)
   (Text: Kazys Bradunas)
   *3,*3,*3,*3 - 4,3,3,1 - timp.perc.(2),bells,xyl. - hp. - str.
   32:00 ChiLitOp.Co.
—— CONCERTINO NO. 1 FOR PIANO, WINDS AND PERCUSSION (1966) (IN 3 MOVTS.)
   *3,*3,*3,*3 - 4,3,3,1 - timp.,perc.(2) - pf.   12:00 Composer.
—— CONCERTO NO. 1 FOR PIANO AND ORCH. (1967) (IN 1 MOVT.)
   *3,*3,*3,*3 - 4,3,3,1 - timp.,perc.(2) - pf. - str.   15:00 Composer.

MARKEVITCH, Igor
—— ICARE (ICARUS)
   3,3,3,3 - 4,3,3,1 - timp.,perc.(4),cel. - pf. - str.   25:00 Bo. Hawkes.
—— LORENZO IL MAGNIFICO (SYMPHONY FOR SOPRANO AND ORCH.)
   3,2,3,3 - 4,2,3,1 - timp.,perc.(2),cel.,glock. - pf. - str.   23:00 Leeds.

MARKOVIĆ, Adalbert
—— STUDY FOR CLARINET AND STRING ORCH. (1970)
   cl. - str.   6:00 MIC,Zagreb.

MAROS, Miklós
—— ASPECTUS (1972)
   1,1,1,1 - 1,0,0,1 - str.   12:00 Fleisher.
—— CONFLUENTIA (1972)
   str.   8:00 Fleisher.

MAROS, Rudolf
—— CONCERTINO FOR BASSOON AND ORCH.
   2,2,2,2 - 4,2,2,0 - timp.,perc.,xyl. - hp. - str.   Bo. Hawkes.
—— EUFONIA NO. 1
   perc. - 2 hp. - str.   11:30 Southern.
—— EUFONIA NO. 2
   3,3,3,3 - 4,4,4,0 - perc. - 2 hp.   13:00 Southern.
—— EUFONIA NO. 3
   3,3,3,3 - 4,4,4,0 - timp.,perc.,glock.2 mar.,2 vibra. - 2 hp. - str.
   11:00 Southern.
—— FIVE STUDIES FOR ORCH.
   Bo. Hawkes.
—— GEMMA (IN MEMORIAM ZOLTAN KODALY)
   1,alto fl.,*2,*2,0 - 4,2,0,0 - str.   12:00 Southern.
—— LANDSCAPES FOR STRING ORCH.
   str.   10:00 Bo. Hawkes.
—— MONUMENTUM (IN MEMORIAM 1945)
   3,3,3,3 - 4,4,4,0 - timp.,perc. - 2 hp. - str.   14:00 Southern.
—— NOTICES
   str.   6:00 Southern.
—— RICERCARE FOR ORCH.
   0,0,0,0 - 0,3,3,0 - timp.,perc.,cel. - hp. - pf. - str.
   7:30 Bo. Hawkes.
—— SINFONIA PER ARCHI
   str.   18:30 Mills.
—— SINFONIETTA NO. 1 (IN 3 MOVTS.)
   Southern.
—— SIRATO (LAMENT) (FOR SOPRANO AND CHAMBER ORCH.)
   0,alt. fl.,1,1,1 - 0,0,0,0 - bells,mar. - hp. - str.   6:00 Southern.
—— A TINY CANTATA (Text: Sandor Weores)
   Southern.

MARSH, Charles
—— A FAIRY SUITE (THREE FAIRY TALES)
   *3,2,2,2 - 4,2,3,1 - timp.,perc.(2) - str.   14:00 Composer.
—— PRAYER OF A SOLDIER IN FRANCE (FOR SOPRANO, CHORUS AND ORCH.)
   1,1,2,1 - 2,2,1,0 - perc.(2) - str.   7:00 Composer.
—— A TROJAN LEGEND (SYMPHONIC POEM)
   *3,2,2,2 - 4,3,3,1 - timp.,perc.(4) - hp. - str.   12:00 Composer.

MARSH, Donald T.
—— PSALM 37 (FOR SATB CHORUS AND ORCH.) (1965)
   2,2,2,0 - 2,2,3,0 - perc.(2),bells,glock.,xyl. - str.   7:00 Composer.

MARSH, Roger
—— DUM'S DREAM (FOR VOICE AND ORCH.)
   6,4,4,3 - 3,4,3,0 - perc. - str.(no vlns.)   14:00 Novello.

MARSHALL, Jack
—— ESSAY FOR GUITAR WITH CHAMBER ORCH.
   1,1,1,1 - 1,0,0,0 - timp.,perc. - guit. - str.   MCA Music.

MARSHALL, Nicholas
—— KALEIDOSCOPE (1963)
   2,2,2,2 - 4,2,3,0 - timp.,perc. - pf. - str.   20:00 P.R.S.

MARSICK, Armand
—— LOUSTICS EN FÊTE (1939)
   1,1,2,2 sax.,1 - 2,2,1,0 - timp.,perc.,xyl. - pf. - str.   8:00 Polfliet.
—— PRELUDE TO ACT II OF "L'ANNEAU NUPTIAL" (1924)
   3,3,3,4 - 4,4,3,1 - timp.,perc. - hp. - str.   4:30 H. Elkan.
—— PRELUDE TO ACT II OF "LARA" (1913)
   3,3,3,3 - 4,3,3,1 - timp.,perc.,glock. - 2 hp. - str.   10:00 CBDM.

—— PRELUDE TO ACT III OF "L'ANNEAU NUPTIAL" (1924)
 3,3,3,4 - 4,4,3,1 - timp.,perc. - hp. - str. 4:00 H. Elkan.
—— SCÈNES DE MONTAGNES (SUITE) (1910)
 3,3,3,2 - 4,2,3,1 - timp.,perc.,cel.,glock. - hp. - str. 28:00 CBDM.
—— LA SOURCE (SYMPHONIC POEM)
 3,3,3,4 - 4,3,3,3 - timp.,perc.,cel.,glock. - hp. - str. 12:00 EV.
—— STÈLE (IN MEMORIAM) (SYMPHONIC POEM)
 3,3,3,2 - 4,3,3,1 - timp.,perc.,bells, glock. - 2 hp. - str.
  15:00 H. Elkan.
—— TABLEAUX DE VOYAGE (1939)
 2,2,2,2 - 2,2,3,0 timp.,perc.,glock. - str. 13:30 De Wolfe.
—— TABLEAUX GRECS (SUITE) (1912)
 3,3,3,2 - 4,4,3,0 - timp.,perc.,glock. - hp. - str. 11:00 Mercury.
—— TROIS MORCEAUX SYMPHONIQUES (1950)
 3,3,3,2 - 4,3,3,1 - timp.,perc.,bells,cel.,glock. - hp. - str.
  26:30 H. Elkan.

MARTELLI, Carlo
—— CONCERTO FOR CLARINET AND STRINGS
 cl. - str. 12:00 Lengnick.
—— FIESTA (OVERTURE)
 *2,*3,2,2 - 4,2,3,1 - timp.,perc. - str. 10:00 Lengnick.
—— SYMPHONY NO. 2, OP. 6
 2,2,2,2 - 4,3,3,1 - timp.,perc. - str. 31:00 Lengnick.

MARTELLI, Henri
—— CONCERTINO FOR WINDS AND STRING ORCH.
 0,1,1,1 - 1,0,0,0 - str. 16:00 F. Colombo.
—— CONCERTO FOR ORCH., OP. 31
 3,2,2,3 - 3,2,2,1 - timp.,perc. - str. 15:00 Ricordi.
—— CONCERTO FOR PIANO AND ORCH., OP. 56 (1948)
  31:00 Henmar.
—— FANTAISIE SUR UN THÈME MALGACHE (FOR PIANO AND ORCHESTRA)
 2,2,2,alto sax.,2 - 4,3,3,1- timp.,perc.(4),cel. - pf. - str.
  19:00 Presser.
—— SCÈNES À DANSER, OP. 98
 2,2,2,2 - 4,3,3,0 - timp.,perc.(3) - str. 15:00 Presser.
—— SINFONIETTA, OP. 70
 1,1,1,1 - 1,1,1,0 - timp.,perc. - pf. - str. 16:00 Presser.
—— SUITE CONCERTANTE (FOR WOODWIND QUINTET AND ORCH.)
  Baron.
—— SUITE NO. 2 FOR ORCHESTRA, OP. 75
 2,1,2,2 - 2,2,1,0 - timp.,perc. - str. 11:00 Presser.
—— SUITE SUR UN THÈME CORSE
 2,3,2,2 - 2,2,2,0 - timp.,perc.(3) - str. 15:00 Presser.
—— SYMPHONY NO. 2, OP. 89
 str. 23:00 F. Colombo.

MARTI, Heinz
—— MASK (FÜR TROMPETE UND 3 ORCH.-GRUPPEN)
  12:00 S.U.I.S.A.

MARTÍN, Edgardo
—— FUGUES FOR STRING ORCHESTRA (FUGAS PARA ORQUESTA DA CUERDA)
 str. 9:30 Southern.
—— SONERAS PARA ORQUESTRA
 3,3,3,2 - 4,3,3,1 - timp.,perc. - hp. - str. 14:00 Southern.

MARTIN, François - BROOK, Barry S.
—— SYMPHONIE IN G. MINOR, OP. 4, NO. 2
 str. FrankMusCP.

MARTIN, Vernon
—— AMERICAN FREEDOM OVERTURE
 2(2nd alt. with picc.),2,2,2 - 2,2,3,0 - timp.,perc.(2) - str.
  9:00 Composer.
—— A CHILDREN'S PIANO CONCERTO
 pf. - str. 5:00 Composer.
—— CONCERTO FOR TUBA AND STRINGS (IN. 3 MOVTS.)
 tu. - hp. (ad lib.) - str. 18:00 Composer.
—— THE MAN WITH THE HOE (TONE POEM)
 2,2,2,2 - 2,2,0,0 - timp. - str. 8:35 Composer.
—— ORCHESTRAL PIECE WITH BIRDS (1968)
 *3,2,2,2 - 4,2,3,1 - timp.,perc.(3),glock. - tape-recorder - hp. - pf.
  7:00 Composer.
—— ORCHESTRAL SET NO. 1 (EQUINOX SET) (IN 4 MOVTS.)
 3(3rd alt. with picc.),3(3rd alt. with Eng.hn.),3(3rd alt. with b.-cl.),3(3rd alt. with c-bn.) - 4,2,3,1 - timp.,perc.(3),bells - pf. - str.
  20:00 Composer.

—— ORCHESTRAL SET NO. 2 (KIOWA SONGS AND DANCES) (IN 3 MOVTS.)
 3,3,3,2 - 4,0,3,1 - timp.,perc.(4) - pf. - str. 12:00 Composer.
—— ORCHESTRAL SET NO. 3 (CENTENNIAL MOTHER) (IN 3 MOVTS.)
 1,2,1,0 - 0,0,0,0 - str. 9:35 Composer.
—— ORCHESTRAL SET NO. 4 (IN 4 MOVTS.)
 2,2,2,2 - 2,2,0,0 - str. 16:00 Composer.

MARTINET, Jean-Louis
—— LE LEÇON D'ANATOMIE
 str. 7:00 Eds. Fran.
—— MOUVEMENT SYMPHONIQUE, OP. 4
 *3,*2,2,*3 - 4,3,3,1 - timp.,perc.,cel. - pf. - str. 12:00 Eds. Fran.
—— MOUVEMENT SYMPHONIQUE, OP. 5
 str. 20:20 Eds. Fran.
—— MOUVEMENT SYMPHONIQUE, OP. 6
 timp.,perc.,bells,cel. - pf. - str. 20:20 Eds. Fran.
—— ORPHÉE (POÈME SYMPHONIQUE) (IN 3 MOVTS.)
 4,*4,4,4 - 8,4,3,2 - timp.,perc. - 2 hp. - pf. - str. 30:00 Mercury.
—— SEPT POÈMES DE RENÉ CHAR (FOR 4 SOLO VOICES AND ORCH.)
 2,1,2,1 - 1,1,0,0 - perc. - hp. - pf. - str. 10:00 Presser.
—— SIX CHANTS (FOR CHORUS AND ORCH.)
 2,2,2,1 alto sax.,2 - 1,1,2,0 - timp.,perc.,cel.,vibra.,xyl. - hp. - org. - pf. - str. 20:00 Presser.
—— LA TRILOGIE DES PROMÉTHÉES
 *2,*3,*3, sax.,*3 - 4,3,3,1 - timp.,perc.(2),bells,cel.,glock.,vibra.,xyl. - hp. - pf. - str. 25:00 Mercury.
—— TROIS POÈMES DE RENÉ CHAR (FOR VOICE AND CHAMBER ORCH.)
 2,1,2,1 - 1,1,0,0 - hp. - pf. - str. 10:00 Presser.

MARTINI, Giambattista - DESDERI
—— CONCERTO IN F MAJOR (FOR CEMBALO AND STRINGS, WITH VIOLIN OBBLIGATO)
 cemb. - str. 13:00 Henmar.
—— CONCERTO IN G MAJOR, FOR CEMBALO AND STRINGS
 cemb. - str. Henmar.
—— SINFONIA A QUATTRO, PER ARCHI
 str. Henmar.

MARTINI, Giambattista - PICCIOLI
—— CONCERTO IN D MAJOR (FOR PIANO AND STRINGS)
 pf. - str. MCA Music.

MARTINI, Giambattista - READ, Gardner
—— PRELUDE, ADAGIO AND FUGUE
 str. 9:00 Arranger.

MARTINI, Gian Mario
—— SALMO FUNEBRE
 1,1,2,2 - 0,0,0,0 - str. 10:00 Bo. Hawkes.

MARTINON, Jean
—— ABSOLVE DOMINE (FOR 4 MALE VOICES AND ORCH.)
  Baron.
—— LA CÈNE (THE LORD'S SUPPER) (SYMPHONIC POEM)
 *3,*3,*3,*3 - 4,2,1,1 - timp.,perc.,cel. - hp. - str. 7:00 Eds. Fran.
—— CONCERTO FOR FLUTE AND ORCH.
 4,3,3,3 - 4,2,3,1 - timp.,perc.(3) - hp. - str. 25:00 Presser.
—— CONCERTO GIOCOSO (FOR VIOLIN AND ORCH.)
  Baron.
—— CONCERTO LYRIQUE (FOR STRING QUARTET AND ORCH.)
  20:00 Baron.
—— DIVERTISSEMENT
 2,1,2,2 - 2,2,1,0 - timp.,perc. - hp. - str. 5:00 Presser.
—— HYMNE, VARIATIONS ET RONDO
 2,2,3(incl. 2 in C) - 4,3,3,1 - timp.,perc.(5),cel. - hp. - pf. - str.
  24:00 Presser.
—— MUSIQUE D'EXIL, OP. 31 (SYMPHONIC MOVEMENT)
  14:00 Henmar.
—— OVERTURE FOR A GREEK TRAGEDY (PRELUDE TO ACT II OF THE OPERA "HERCULE")
  12:00 S.A.C.E.M.
—— PRELUDE AND TOCCATA
  10:00 S.A.C.E.M.
—— PSALM 136 (FOR SOLO VOICES, SATB CHORUS AND ORCH.)
 3,3,4,sopr. sax.,ten. sax.,3 - 6,4,3,1 - perc.(4) - 2 hp. - str.
  38:00 Presser.

—— THE ROSE OF SHARON (ORATORIO) (FOR SOPRANO,
BARITONE, SATB CHORUS AND ORCH.)
    3,*3,*1,1 - 2,2,1,1 - timp.,perc.,cel. - 3 hp. - 2 pf. - str.
                                              80:00 IsMuPublns.
—— SYMPHONIES DE VOYAGE OP. 49, NO. 1
    2,2,*1,1 - 1,1,0,0 - perc. - str.   21:00 Presser.
—— SYMPHONIETTE
    timp. - hp. - pf. - str.   17:00 Salabert.
—— SYMPHONY NO. 1
                                                           Baron.
—— SYMPHONY NO. 2, OP. 37 ("HYMNE À LA VIE") (IN 3
MOVTS.)
                                            30:00 G. Schirmer.
—— SYMPHONY NO. 3, OP. 45 (IRISH SYMPHONY)
                                               28:00 Henmar.
—— SYMPHONY NO. 4 ("ALTITUDES") (IN 3 MOVTS.)
                                               28:00 Presser.
—— SYMPHONY, OP. 17
    3,3,3,3 - 4,4,3,1 - timp.,perc.(3) - 2 hp. - str.   Presser.

MARTINŮ, Bohuslav
—— LA BAGARRE
    3,3,2(2nd alt. with E♭cl.),2 - 4,3,3,1 - timp.,perc. - pf. - str.
                                                      9:00 Baron.
—— BOUQUET OF FLOWERS (KYTICE) (FOR SOLO VOICES,
CHORUS AND ORCH.)
                                               50:00 Bo. Hawkes.
—— THE BUTTERFLY THAT STAMPED (1-ACT BALLET) %
                                                     Bo. Hawkes.
—— COMEDIA DELL' ARTE (BALLET MUSIC) %
    2,2,2,2 - 4,2,2,1 - timp.,perc.,xyl. - pf. - str. 20:00 Bo. Hawkes.
—— COMEDY ON THE BRIDGE (1-ACT OPERA) %
    1,1,1,1 - 2,1,1,0 - timp.,perc. - pf. - str.   Bo. Hawkes.
—— CONCERTINO FOR PIANO AND ORCH.
                                                     Bo. Hawkes.
—— CONCERTINO FOR PIANO (LEFT HAND) AND ORCH.
    1,2,1,2 - 1,0,0,0 - pf. - str.   20:00 Bo. Hawkes.
—— CONCERTO (CONCERTINO) FOR TRIO (VIOLIN, CELLO
AND PIANO AND STRINGS)
    pf. - str.   Bo. Hawkes.
—— CONCERTO FOR FLUTE, VIOLIN AND ORCH.
                                                   G. Schirmer.
—— CONCERTO FOR TWO STRING ORCHESTRAS, PIANO AND
TIMPANI
    timp. - pf. - str.   23:00 Bo. Hawkes.
—— CONCERTO FOR TWO VIOLINS AND ORCH.
    2,2,2,2 - 4,2,3,1 - timp.,perc. - str.   Bo. Hawkes.
—— CONCERTO FOR VIOLA AND ORCH.
                                                        S.U.I.S.A.
—— CONCERTO FOR VIOLIN AND ORCH.
    2,2,2,2 - 4,3,3,1 - timp.,perc. - str.   27:00 Bo. Hawkes.
—— CONCERTO FOR VIOLIN, PIANO AND ORCH. (IN 3
MOVTS.)
    2,2,2,2 - 4,2,3,1 - timp.,perc. (2) - pf. - str. 25:00 Bo. Hawkes.
—— CONCERTO NO. 1 FOR PIANO AND ORCH.
                                                        S.U.I.S.A.
—— CONCERTO NO. 2 FOR PIANO AND ORCH. (REVISED 1944)
    3,2,2,2 - 4,2,3,0 - timp.,perc. - pf. - str. 22:00 Bo. Hawkes.
—— CONCERTO NO. 2 FOR VIOLIN AND ORCH.
                                                     Bo. Hawkes.
—— CONCERTO NO. 3 FOR PIANO AND ORCH.
    2,2,2,2 - 4,2,3,1 - timp.,perc. - pf. - str. 25:00 Bo. Hawkes.
—— CZECH RHAPSODY (FOR SOLO VOICES, MIXED CHORUS,
ORGAN AND ORCH.)
                                                     Bo. Hawkes.
—— DUO CONCERTANTE (FOR TWO VIOLINS AND ORCH.)
                                                        S.U.I.S.A.
—— ESTAMPES (IN 3 MOVTS.)
                                               20:00 Southern.
—— FANTAISIES SYMPHONIQUES (SYMPHONY NO. 6) (IN 3
MOVTS.)
    3(3rd alt. with picc.),3,3,3 - 4,3,3,1 - timp.,perc.(5) - str.
                                               29:00 Bo. Hawkes.
—— FIELD MASS (A MILITARY MASS) (FOR BARITONE, MALE
CHORUS AND SMALL ORCH.)
    2,0,2,0 - 0,3,2,0 - timp.,perc. - harm. - pf.   Bo. Hawkes.
—— HALFTIME (RONDO FOR ORCHESTRA)
    3,3,2,2 - 4,4,3,1 - timp.,perc. - str.   9:00 Bo. Hawkes.
—— INCANTATION (CONCERTO NO. 4 FOR PIANO AND
ORCH.)
    1. Allegro poco; 2. Poco moderato
    *3,2,2,2 - 4,2,3,0 - timp.,perc. - hp. - pf. - str. 20:00 G. Schirmer.

—— INCIDENTAL MUSIC TO GIDE'S "OEDIPUS"
                                                     Bo. Hawkes.
—— INTERMEZZO
    *2,2,2,2 - 4,2,3,0 - timp.,perc.(3) - pf. - str. 10:00 Bo. Hawkes.
—— INVENTIONS
                                                     Bo. Hawkes.
—— ISTAR (BALLET) %
                                                     Bo. Hawkes.
—— JULIETTE (OR, "THE KEY TO DREAMS") (OPERA) %
                                                     Bo. Hawkes.
—— LITTLE SUITE FROM "COMEDY ON THE BRIDGE"
    1,1,1,1 - 2,1,1,0 - timp.,perc. - pf. - str.   6:00 Bo. Hawkes.
—— LA LOCANDIERA (3-ACT OPERA) %
    2,2,2,2 - 4,2,3,0 - timp.,perc. - str.   120:00 S.U.I.S.A.
—— THE MARRIAGE (2-ACT OPERA) %
    *2,2,2,2 - 2,2,0,1 - timp.,perc. - pf. - str. 90:00 Bo. Hawkes.
—— MEMORIAL TO LIDICE
    3,3,3,2 - 4,2,3,1 - timp.,perc. - hp. - pf. - str. 8:00 Bo. Hawkes.
—— THE MIRACLE OF OUR LADY ("PLAYS OF THE HOLY
VIRGIN") (OPERA) %
                                                     Bo. Hawkes.
—— NOVY SPALICEK
                                               16:00 Bo. Hawkes.
—— OVERTURE
    2,2,2,2 - 4,2,0,0 - timp. - str.   8:00 Bo. Hawkes.
—— OVERTURE FOR THE SOKOL FESTIVAL
                                                        S.U.I.S.A.
—— OVERTURE TO THE COMEDY "THE SUBURBAN THEATRE"
                                                     Bo. Hawkes.
—— PARABLES FOR ORCHESTRA ("LES PARABOLES")
    *3,3,3,*4 - 4,3,3,1 - timp.,perc.,glock.,xyl. - hp. - str. G. Schirmer.
—— RHAPSODY (ALLEGRO)
    3,3,2(2nd alt. with E♭cl.) - 4,4,4,1 - timp.,perc. - pf. - str.
                                                     11:00 Baron.
—— RHAPSODY CONCERTO (FOR VIOLA AND ORCH.)
                                                   G. Schirmer.
—— LES RONDES (FOR CHAMBER ORCH.)
                                                     Bo. Hawkes.
—— SALTARELLO (FROM "MIRANDOLINA")(1954)
    *3,2,2,2 - 4,3,3,0 - timp.,perc.(3) - str.   5:00 G. Schirmer.
—— SERENADE NO. 4 (DIVERTIMENTO)
                                                     Bo. Hawkes.
—— SINFONIA CONCERTANTE (FOR VIOLIN, OBOE, BASSOON
AND ORCH.)
    0,1,0-2,1 - 0-2,0,0,0 - pf. - str.   18:00 Bo. Hawkes.
—— SINFONIA FOR TWO ORCHESTRAS
                                                        S.U.I.S.A.
—— SINFONIETTA GIOCOSA (FOR PIANO AND CHAMBER
ORCH.)
    2,2,0,2 - hn. - pf. - str.   22:00 Bo. Hawkes.
—— SINFONIETTA "LA JOLLA" (FOR CHAMBER ORCH.)
    2,2,2,2 - 2,1,0,0 - timp.,perc. - pf. - str. 19:00 Bo. Hawkes.
—— THE SOLDIER AND THE DANCER (OPERA) %
                                                     Bo. Hawkes.
—— SOLEMN OVERTURE
                                                     Bo. Hawkes.
—— SONATA DA CAMERA (FOR CELLO AND CHAMBER
ORCH.)
    1,1,2,2 - 2,0,0,0,0 - str.   Bo. Hawkes.
—— SPALICEK (BALLET-SUITE)
                                                     Bo. Hawkes.
—— SPALICEK: BALLET SUITE NO. 1
    3,2,2,2 - 4,2,2,1 - timp.,perc. - pf. - str. 21:00 Bo. Hawkes.
—— SPALICEK: SUITE NO. 2
    3,2,2,2 - 4,2,2,1 - timp.,perc. - pf. - str. 23:00 Bo. Hawkes.
—— SUITE FROM THE BALLET "REVUE DE CUISINE" (FOR
CHAMBER ORCH.)
                                                           Baron.
—— SYMPHONY NO. 1 (IN 4 MOVTS.)
    3,3,3,3 - 4,3,3,1 - timp.,perc. - hp. - pf. - str. 35:00 Bo. Hawkes.
—— SYMPHONY NO. 2 (IN 4 MOVTS.)
    3,3,3,2 - 4,3,3,1 - timp.,perc. - hp. - pf. - str. 25:00 Bo. Hawkes.
—— SYMPHONY NO. 3
    3,3,3,2 - 4,3,3,1 - timp.,perc. - hp. - pf. - str. 30:00 Bo. Hawkes.
—— SYMPHONY NO. 4 (IN 4 MOVTS.)
    4,4,3,2 - 4,3,3,1 - timp.,perc. - hp. - pf. - str. 34:00 Bo. Hawkes.
—— SYMPHONY NO. 5
    3,3,3,3 - 4,3,3,1 - timp.,perc. - pf. - str. 27:00 Bo. Hawkes.
—— THE THEATRE BEHIND THE GATE (OPERA) %
                                                     Bo. Hawkes.
—— THREE SERENADES FOR CHAMBER ORCH.
                                                     Bo. Hawkes.

—— THREE WISHES (OPERA) %

Bo. Hawkes.

—— THUNDERBOLT P-47
3,3,3,3 - 4,3,3,1 - timp.,perc. - str.   10:00 Bo. Hawkes.

—— TOCCATA AND TWO CANZONE
*1,2,1,1 - 2 tpt. - timp.,perc. - pf. - str.   18:00 Bo. Hawkes.

—— THE TONES' MUTINY (BALLET) %

Bo. Hawkes.

—— TRE RICERCARI (FOR CHAMBER ORCH.)
1,2,0,2 - 2 tpt. - 2 pf. - str. (vlns. and c.) 12:00 Bo. Hawkes.

—— VANISHING MIDNIGHT (FROM "THREE SYMPHONIC
POEMS")

S.U.I.S.A.

—— THE VOICE OF THE FOREST (1-ACT OPERA) %

Bo. Hawkes.

—— WHAT MEN LIVE BY (1-ACT OPERA) %
1-2,2,3,2 - 2,1,1,0 - perc. - pf. - str.   40:00 Bo Hawkes.

—— WHO IS THE MOST POWERFUL IN THE WORLD? (BALLET
OF ANIMALS) %

Bo. Hawkes.

MARTTINEN, Tauno

—— BEATRICE, OP. 57 (BALLET, AFTER DANTE'S "THE DEVINE
COMEDY") % (WITH SATB CHORUS) (1970)
3,3,3,3 - 3,3,3,1 - timp.(2 players),cel. - hp. - pf. - str.
105:00 FinnMICtr.

—— BIRDS OF THE UNDERWORLD, OP. 38 (1964)
3,3,3,3 - 4,3,3,1 - timp.,perc.,cel. - hp. - str.   7:00 FinnMICtr.

—— BORROWING MATCHES, OP. 25 (OPERA) % (REV. 1966)
(Text: Maiju Lassila)
3,2,3,3 - 4,3,3,1 - timp.,perc.(4),cel. - hp. - str. 90:00 FinnMICtr.

—— BURNT ORANGE, OP. 41 (OPERA) % (1968) % (Text:
Eeva-Liisa Manner)
3,3,3,3 - 4,3,3,1 - timp.,perc.(5) - guit. - hp. - pf.(or cel.) - str.
90:00 FinnMICtr.

—— CONCERTO FOR BASSOON AND SMALL ORCH., OP. 40
(REV. 1968)
bn. - cel. - str.   16:00 FinnMICtr.

—— CONCERTO FOR CELLO AND ORCH., OP. 30 ("DALAI
LAMA") (REV. 1966)
3,3,3,3 - 4,3,3,1 - timp.,perc.(3),cel. - hp. - str. 16:00 FinnMICtr.

—— CONCERTO FOR PIANO AND ORCH. (1965)
2,2,2,*1 - 4,4,2,1 - timp. - pf. - str.   22:00 Seesaw.

—— CONCERTO FOR VIOLIN AND ORCH., OP. 13 (REV. 1962)
3,3,3,3 - 4,3,3,1 - timp.,perc.(4),cel. - pf. - str. 21:00 FinnMICtr.

—— DARK LAND, OP. 6 (SONG CYCLE) (FOR ALTO AND
ORCH.) (1960) (Text: Einari Vuorela)
2,2,2,3 - 4,3,3,1 - timp.,perc. - hp. - str.   20:00 FinnMICtr.

—— DREAMS OF DEATH, OP. 32 (SONG CYCLE) (FOR ALTO
AND ORCH.)(1966) (Text: Pirkko Jaakola)
3,2,3,2 - 2,0,0,0 - timp.,perc.,cel.,xyl. - hp. - str. 11:00 FinnMICtr.

—— EAGLE, BIRD OF THE AIR, OP. 1 (FOR MEZZO-SOPRANO
AND ORCH.) (1956) (Text: The Kalevala)
2,2,2,2 - 4,3,3,1 - timp.,perc.(3) - str.   18:00 FinnMICtr.

—— THE ENGAGEMENT, OP. 20 (OPERA) % (1964)
3,2,3,3 - 4,3,3,1 - timp.,perc.(4) - hp. - str. 45:00 FinnMICtr.

—— FAUNI, OP. 26 (1965)
3,3,3,3 - 4,3,3,1 - timp.,perc.(4),cel. - hp. - str 15:00 FinnMICtr.

—— THE FEAST, OP. 10 (SUITE) (FOR SOPRANO, TENOR AND
ORCH.) (1962) (Text: Liisa Heikkerö)
2,2,2,2 - 2,2,2,1 - timp.,perc.,cel. - hp. - str.   8:00 Westerlund.

—— GABBATA, OP. 27 (CANTATA) (FOR NARRATOR, TENOR,
BARITONE, SATB CHORUS AND STRINGS)(1965)
Str   25:00 FinnMICtr.

—— HARMONIA, OP. 60 (1971)
3,3,3,3 - 4,3,3,1 - timp.,perc.(3) - org. - str. 15:00 FinnMICtr.

—— THE HOUSE OF LADY GAMARD, OP. 12 (OPERA) % (REV.
1971) (Text: Balzac)
3,3,3,3 - 4,2,2,1 - timp.,perc.(3),cel. - hp. - str. 55:00 FinnMICtr.

—— THE LADDER, OP. 21 (BALLET, AFTER A STORY BY
HENRY MILLER) % (1964)
3,3,3,3 - 4,3,3,1- timp.,perc.(3),cel. - hp - str. 40:00 FinnMICtr.

—— LEA, OP. 33 (OPERA) % (REV. 1969) (Text: Aleksis Kivi)
3,3,3,3 - 4,3,3,1 - timp.(2 players),cel. - hp. - str.
85:00 FinnMICtr.

—— LEMMINKÄINEN, OP. 37 (CANTATA) (FOR
MEZZO-SOPRANO, ALTO, BARITONE, BASS AND
ORCH.)(REV. 1968) (Text: The Kalevala)
3,3,3,3 - 4,3,3,1 - timp.,perc.(4),cel. - hp. - str. 20:00 FinnMICtr.

—— MASTER PATELIN, OP. 69 (OPERA) % (REV. 1972)
1,1,1,1 - 1,0,0,0 - hpsc. - str.   60:00 FinnMICtr.

—— THE MILKY WAY, OP. 7 (REV. 1961)
4,4,4,4 - 4,4,4,0 - timp.,perc.(4),cel. - hp. - pf. - str.
14:00 FinnMICtr.

—— MONT SAINT MICHEL, OP. 42
2,2,2,2 - 2,2,2,1 - timp.(2 players) - str.   7:00 FinnMICtr.

—— THE NORTH, OP. 67 (1972)
1,1,6,2 - 4,4,3,2 - timp.,perc.   10:00 Seesaw.

—— THE OLD CASTLE, OP. 49 (SUITE) (IN 4 MOVTS.) (REV. 1970)
2,2,2,2 - 2,2,2,0 - timp.,perc. - str.   20:00 FinnMICtr.

—— PANU, THE GOD OF FIRE (1966)
1,1,1,1 - 1,1,1,0 - timp.,perc. - hp. - pf. - str.   9:00 Seesaw.

—— PENTALIA, OP. 50-B (1970)
2,2,2,2 - 2,2,2,0 - timp.,perc. - str.   12:00 FinnMICtr.

—— A PORTRAIT OF DORIAN GRAY, OP. 48 (BALLET) % (1969)
1,1,1,1 - 1,1,1,0 - timp.,perc.,cel. - hp. - pf. - str.
80:00 FinnMICtr.

—— RAHAB, OP. 64 (CANTATA) (FOR MEZZO-SOPRANO,
TENOR, BARITONE, MALE CHORUS AND ORCH.) (1971)
2,1,3,ten. sax.,bar. sax.,1 - 3,2,2,1 - timp.,perc. 35:00 FinnMICtr.

—— REMBRANDT, OP. 11 (FOR CELLO AND ORCH.) (1962)
2,2,2,2 - 2,1,1,0 - hp. - str.   7:00 Fazer.

—— THE SNOW QUEEN, OP. 54 (BALLET, AFTER HANS
CHRISTIAN ANDERSEN) % (WITH 2 SPEAKING VOICES)
(1970)
2,0,1,0 - 1,0,0,0 - timp. - str.   45:00 FinnMICtr.

—— SUITE FOR ORCHESTRA, OP. 5 (1960)
3,3,3,3 - 4,3,3,1 - timp.,cel. - hp. - str.   12:00 FinnMICtr.

—— SYMPHONY NO. 1, OP.2 (REV. 1958)
3,3,3,3 - 4,3,3,1 - timp.,perc.(4),cel. - str. 16:00 FinnMICtr.

—— SYMPHONY NO. 2, OP. 4 (1959)
3,3,3,3 - 4,3,3,1 - timp.,perc.(4),cel. - hp. - str. 18:00 FinnMICtr.

—— SYMPHONY NO. 3, OP. 18 (1963)
3,3,3,3 - 4,3,3,1 - timp.,perc.(4),cel. - hp. - str. 26:00 FinnMICtr.

—— SYMPHONY NO. 4, OP. 31 (1965)
3,3,3,3 - 4,3,3,1 - timp.,perc.(4),cel. - 2 hp. - pf. - str.
30:00 FinnMICtr.

—— SYMPHONY NO. 5, OP. 35 ("THE SHAMAN") (REV. 1972)
2,2,2,2 - 3,2,2,0 - timp.,perc. - str.   22:00 FinnMICtr.

MARTYNOV, Nikolaj A.
—— SYMPHONY NO. 1

G. Schirmer.

MARVIA, Einari
—— SIX SONGS, OP. 30 (FOR SOPRANO OR TENOR AND
ORCH.) (REV. 1952) (Text: Katri Vala)
2,2,2,2 - 4,2,3,0 - timp.,perc. - hp. - str.   17:00 Fazer.

—— VARIATIONS ON A SOUTH OSTROBOTHNIAN FOLK SONG,
OP. 10 (1937)
2,2,2,2 - 4,2,3,1 - timp.,perc. - str.   7:00 FinnMICtr.

MARX, Burle
—— HALLOWE'EN (A REVELER'S PAGEANT IN THE FORM OF
A PASSACAGLIA AND FUGUE)
3(2 alt. with 2 picc.),*3,*3,alto sax.,*3 - 4,3,3,1 - timp.,perc. -
electric guit.(ad lib.) - hp. - pf.(alt. with cel.) - str. 15:00 Fleisher.

—— SAMBA CONCERTANTE
3,2,3,3 - 4,3,3,1 - timp.,perc.,cel.,xyl. - pf. - str. 9:30 Composer.

—— SYMPHONY NO. 3 ("IMPRESSIONS OF MACUMBA")
(GEISTERBESCHWORUNG) (IN 2 MOVTS.)
3(3rd alt. with picc.),3,E♭cl.,3,alto sax.,3 - 4,4(1 in D),3,1 -
timp.,perc. - 2 hp. - pf.(alt. with cel.) - str.   30:00 Fleisher.

—— SYMPHONY NO. 4 (FOR CHAMBER ORCH.)
1(alt. with picc.),2 players on recorders(alt. with
sop.,alto,ten.,bass),1,1,1 - 2,1,0,0 - timp.,perc. - hpsc.(alt. with cel.)
- str.   50:00 Fleisher.

MARX, Hans-Joachim
—— VARIATIONS ON A YUGOSLAVIAN FOLKSONG
3,3,2,2 - 4,4,3,1 - timp.,perc.,glock. - hp. - pf. - str.
15:00 F. Colombo.

MARX, Karl
—— CANTATA: RAUBE DAS LICHT AUS DEM RACHEN DER
SCHLANGE (FOR BARITONE, CHORUS AND ORCH.)

Baerenrtr.

—— CANTATA: UND ENDET DOCH ALLES MIT FRIEDEN (AND
ALL ENDS IN PEACE) (FOR SOLO VOICES, CHORUS AND
ORCH.)

Baerenrtr.

—— CONCERTO IN A MINOR, OP. 5, FOR 2 VIOLINS AND
ORCH.
3,3,3,3 - 4,3,3,1 - timp.,perc.,cel. - hp. - str. 35:00 Baerenrtr.

—— CONCERTO IN E♭ MAJOR, OP. 32, FOR FLUTE AND
STRINGS
 fl. - str.   14:00 Baerenrtr.
—— FESTIVAL PRELUDE
         Baerenrtr.
—— GEBETE DER MÄDCHEN ZUR MARIA, OP. 2 (SONG CYCLE
FOR SOPRANO AND STRINGS) (Text: Rainer Maria Rilke)
 str.   13:00 G. Schirmer.
—— MUSIK NACH ALPENLÄNDISCHEN VOLKSLIEDERN
       16:00 Baerenrtr.
—— PARTITA ÜBER "ES IST EIN ROS ENTSPRUNGEN" (FOR
STRINGS)
 str.   11:00 Baerenrtr.
—— RILKE CANTATA (BOOK OF HOURS) (FOR SOPRANO,
BARITONE, MIXED CHORUS AND ORCH.)
        Baerenrtr.
—— RILKE-KREIS, OP. 8 (FIVE SONGS FOR MEZZO-SOPRANO
AND CHAMBER ORCH.)
 2 fl. - str.   7:00 G. Schirmer.
—— SPIELMUSIK (FOR STRING ORCH.) (IN 3 MOVTS.)
 str.   Möseler.

MASCAGNI, Pietro
—— CAVALLERIA RUSTICANA (1-ACT OPERA) % (Engl. Text:
Joseph Machlis)
       G. Schirmer.

MASELLI, Gianfranco
—— DUE PEZZI (TWO PIECES)
 1,1,2,2 - 1,1,1,0 - cel.,vibra. - hp. - str. 7:00 Leeds.
—— RONDO PER ORCHESTRA
       Leeds.

MASETTI, Enzo
—— SAGRA
 3,3,3,3 - 4,3,3,1 - perc.,cel.,xyl. - hp. - pf. - str. Bo. Hawkes.

MASKE, Hans Herbert Adolf Engelbert
—— CONCERTINO GIOVENTU (FOR TWO VIOLINS, PIANO AND
STRING ORCH.)
 pf. - str.   8:00 S.A.M.R.O.
—— CONCERTO DEI TRE RE (FOR TWO VIOLINS, PIANO,
TIMPANI AND STRING ORCH.)
 timp. - pf. - str.   15:00 S.A.M.R.O.
—— CONCERTO MALGACHE (FOR CLARINET, PERCUSSION
AND STRING ORCH.)
 cl. - perc. - str.   18:00 S.A.M.R.O.
—— MANTIS MOON (BALLET) %
 2,2,3,2 - 4,2,3,1 - timp.,perc. - str. 25:00 S.A.M.R.O.
—— OLIVIER (OPERA) % (Text: Composer)
 1,1,2,1 - 3,1,2,0 - perc. - str. 70:00 S.A.M.R.O.
—— DIE OSSEWA (FOR CHORUS, PERCUSSION AND STRING
ORCH.)
 perc. - str.   10:00 S.A.M.R.O.
—— SINFONIETTA (1969) (FOR PIANO, PERCUSSION AND
STRING ORCH.)
 perc. - pf. - str. 15:00 S.A.M.R.O.

MASON, Daniel Gregory
—— CHANTICLEER (FESTIVAL OVERTURE), OP. 27
 3(3rd alt. with picc.),*3,*3,*3 - 4,3,3,1- timp.,perc. - hp. - str.
       8:00 AmerMusEd.
—— FANNY BLAIR (FOLK SONG FANTASY)
 str.   Oxford.
—— FIVE LOVE SONGS, OP. 15 (FOR SOPRANO AND SMALL
ORCH.)
 2(2nd alt. with picc.),1,2,1- 2,1,0,0 - timp.,perc.(2) - hp. - str.
       15:00 Composer.
—— FIVE SONGS OF THE COUNTRYSIDE, OP. 23 (FOR
SOPRANO, BARITONE, CHORUS AND ORCH.)
 1(alt. with picc.),1,0,0 - 1,1,0,0 - timp.,perc.(1) - pf. - str.
       21:00 Ricordi.
—— PRELUDE AND FUGUE FOR PIANO AND ORCH., OP. 20
 3(3rd alt. with picc.),*3,2,b.-cl.(ad lib.),2,c.-bn.(ad lib.) - 4,3,3,1 -
 timp.,perc. - hp. - pf. - str. 12:00 J. Fischer.
—— RUSSIANS, OP. 18 (FIVE SONG FOR BARITONE AND
ORCH.)
 3(3rd alt. with picc.),*3,2,b.-cl.(ad lib.),2 -2-4,3,3,0-1 - timp.,perc.
 (ad lib.) - hp.(ad lib.) -str. 16:00 G. Schirmer.

—— SCHERZO-CAPRICE, OP. 14A (FOR CHAMBER ORCH.)
 1(alt. with picc.),1,1,1 - hn. - pf. - str. 7:00 SPAM.
—— SUITE AFTER ENGLISH FOLK SONGS, OP. 32 (IN 3 MOVTS.)
 3(3rd alt. with picc.),2,2,2 - 4,3,3,1 - timp.,perc. - hp. - str.
       20:00 G. Schirmer.
—— SYMPHONY NO. 2 IN A, OP. 30 (IN 4 MOVTS.)
 3(3rd alt. with picc.),*3,*3,*3 - 4,3,3,1 - timp.,perc. - hp. - str.
       32:00 Composer.
—— SYMPHONY NO. 3 (A LINCOLN SYMPHONY), OP. 35 (IN 4
MOVTS.)
 3(3rd alt. with picc.),*3,*3,*3 - 4,3,3,1 - timp.,perc. - hp. - str.
       34:00 AmerMusEd.

MASON, Jack
—— CONNECTICUT SUITE (IN 4 MOVTS.)
 1(alt. with picc.),1(alt. with Eng. hn.),*3,1 - 4,3,3,1 -
 timp.,perc.(2),cel.(alt. with pf.) - hp. - str. 16:00 Chappell.

MASSA, Juan Bautista
—— ARGENTINE SUITE NO. 1 (1929) (IN 3 MOVTS.)
 3,3,3,4 - 4,3 cnt.,0,3,1 - timp.,perc.,cel. - hp. - str. F. Colombo.
—— LA MUERTE DEL INCA ("THE DEATH OF THE INCA")
(SYMPHONIC POEM) (1932)
 3(3rd alt. with picc.),3,3,4 - 4,3, cnt.,0,3,1 - timp.,perc.,cel. - hp. -
 str.   F. Colombo.

MASSARANI, Renzo
—— INTRODUZIONE, TEMA E SETTE VARIAZIONI
 1,1,1,1 - 1,1,1,0 - pf. - str. 18:00 Bo. Hawkes.

MASSENET, Jules
—— DON QUICHOTTE: INTERLUDE I (SÉRÉNADE)
 3,3,3,3 - 4,0,0,0 - timp. - hp. - str. 1:30 Presser.
—— DON QUICHOTTE: INTERLUDE II (TRISTESSE DE
DULCINÉE)
 3,0,2,2 - 0,0,0,0 - str. 3:00 Presser.
—— DON QUICHOTTE (5-ACT OPÉRA-COMIQUE) (1910) %
 2,4,3,3, - 4,3,3,1 - timp.,perc. - guit. - hp. - str. 120:00 Presser.
 On Stage: band
—— MANON (5-ACT OPERA) % (Engl. Text: George and Phyllis
Mead)
       G. Schirmer.
—— SAPPHO (5-ACT OPERA) (REVISED VERSION) %
 3,3,2,2 - 4,2,3,1 - timp.,perc. - str. 165:00 Presser.
—— THREE EXCERPTS FROM THE OPERA "ARIANE"
 3,3,3,3 - 4,3,3,0 - timp.,perc.,cel. - hp. - str. 5:15 Presser.

MASSÉUS, Jan
—— CASSAZIONE, OP. 33 (5 DANCES) (1960)
 2,2,2,2 - 2,2,1,0 - timp.,perc. - str. 13:00 Henmar.
—— CONCERTO DA CAMERA, OP. 23 (FOR VIOLIN AND
ORCH.)
 2,2,2,2 - 2,2,0,0 - timp. - str. 18:00 Henmar.
—— CONCERTO FOR PIANO AND ORCH.
 3,2,2,3 - 4,2,2,1 - timp.,perc. - pf. - str. 20:00 Henmar.
—— CONCERTO FOR 2 FLUTES AND ORCH., OP. 29
       Henmar.
—— SYMPHONIC VARIATIONS, OP. 9 (FOR PIANO AND
STRINGS)
 pf. - str.   13:00 Henmar.

MASSIAS, Gérard
—— CONCERT BREF (FOR PIANO AND INSTRUMENTS)
 1,1,2,2 - 2,1,0,0 - perc. - pf. 13:00 Presser.
—— CONCERTO FOR FLUTE AND STRINGS
 fl. - str.   13:00 Presser.
—— FACIES (FOR CHAMBER ORCH.)
 2,0,1,1 - 0,2,1,0 - timp.,perc.,mar.,vibra. - str. 13:00 Presser.
—— LAUDE (FOR CELLO AND STRINGS)
 str.   11:00 Presser.

MASSIMO, Leone
—— CONCERTO FOR VIOLIN AND ORCH.
 1,1,1,2 - 1,1,0,0 - timp. - str. 15:00 Bo. Hawkes.
—— CONCERTO GROSSO
 0,1,1,1 - 0,1,1,0 - timp. - pf. - str. 12:00 Bo. Hawkes.
—— DIVERTIMENTO NO. 1
 *3,*3,*3,*3 - 3,3,1,0 - timp. - str. 17:00 Bo. Hawkes.
—— DIVERTIMENTO NO. 2
 2,2,2,2 - 2,1,1,0 - timp. - str. 18:00 Bo. Hawkes.
—— QUATTRO PEZZI PER ORCHESTRA
 5,3,4,3 - 4,3,2,1 - timp. - hp. - str. 20:00 Bo. Hawkes.

—— SERENATA
   *4,3,E♭ cl.,*3,*4 - 4,3,3,0 - timp. - pf. - str.   16:00 Bo. Hawkes.

MASSIS, Amable
—— BALLADE (FOR VIOLIN, HARP AND WINDS)
   1,*2,2,2 - 2,0,0,0 - hp. - vln.   8:00 Presser.
—— DIVERTISSEMENT CHORÉOGRAPHIQUE (SUITE)
   1,1,2,1 - 3,2,1,0 - timp.,perc.(4),cel. - hp. - str.   18:00 Presser.
—— ENFANTINES (3 PIECES FROM "6 ENFANTINES") (FOR 2-PART CHORUS AND ORCH.)
   2,1,2,2 - 3,2,3,0 - perc.,cel. - str.   9:00 EV.
—— POÈME SYMPHONIQUE (FOR VIOLA AND ORCH.)
   Baron.
—— SONATINE (FOR ORCH.)
   2,1,2,2 - 2,1,0,0 - timp. - hp. - str.   10:00 EV.

MASSON, Gérard
—— BLEU LOIN (1970)
   str.   25:00 Salabert.
—— CANTATA (FOR SATB CHORUS AND ORCH.)
   4,0,6,4 - 4,4,4,3 - perc.(4) - str.   60:00 Presser.
—— DANS LE DEUIL DES VAGUES I (1966)
   4(alt.with 4 picc.),0,4,1 alto sax.,1 ten.sax.,*2 - 0,4,3,1 - electric org.(hammond) - pf. - str.   15:00 Salabert.
—— DANS LE DEUIL DES VAGUES II (1968)
   4 picc.,4,0,4 Eng.hn.,*5,1 alto sax.,1 ten.sax.,*4 - 6,4,3,1 bar.,2 - 2 cel. - str.   18:00 Salabert.
—— PIECES FOR 14 INSTRUMENTS (1965)
   1,1,1,1 alto sax.,1 - 1,1,1,0 - cel.,mar.,vibra. - electric guit. - hp. - c.   7:00 Salabert.
—— QUEST I (FOR 10 INSTRUMENTS) (1967)
   1,0,*2,1 - 0,1,1,0 - hp. - pf. - vln.,c.   15:00 Salabert.
—— QUEST II (FOR MEZZO-SOPRANO AND ENSEMBLE) (1969) (Text: Dominique Fourcade)
   1,*1,*2,1 - 0,1,1,0 - hp. - pf. - str.(2,1,1,0)   25:00 Salabert.

MASSZ, Gerhard
—— SERENATA IRONICA (FOR STRING ORCH.)
   str.   16:00 Modern.

MATĔJ, Josef
—— SONATA FOR OBOE AND CHAMBER ORCH.
   ob. - 2 hn. - timp. - hp. - pf. - str.   26:00 Bo. Hawkes.
—— SYMPHONY NO. 2
   3,3,3,3 - 4,3,3,1 - timp.,perc.,bells - 2 hp. - pf. - str.   35:00 Bo. Hawkes.

MATESKY, Ralph
—— THE MAN WITH THE HOE (FOR SATB CHORUS AND ORCH.) (Text: Edwin Markham)
   *3,*3,2,2 - 4,3,3,1 - timp.,perc.(3) - hp. - str.   20:00 Composer.
—— PRAYER FOR PEACE (FOR CHORUS AND ORCH.)
   2,2,2,3 sax.,1 - 2,3,2,1 - timp.,perc. - str.   12:30 Mills.

MATHER, Bruce (James Mather)
—— CONCERTO FOR PIANO AND CHAMBER ORCH. (IN 1 MOVT.) (1958)
   1,1,1,1 - 1,0,0,0 - pf. - str.   6:00 CanMusCtr.
—— ELEGIE (CONCERTO) (FOR SAXOPHONE AND STRINGS) (1965)
   sax. - str.   7:00 P.McKee.
—— LAMENT FOR PÁSIPHÉ (PART 4 OF THE CANTATA "THE WHITE GODDESS") (1962) (FOR SOPRANO, BARITONE, MIXED CHORUS AND ORCH.) (Text: Robert Graves)
   0,0,0,0 - 4,2,3,1 - perc.,cel. - hp. - pf. - str.   5:00 CanMusCtr.
—— MADRIGAL 5 (1973) (FOR SOPRANO, CONTRALTO AND 17 INSTRS.)
   1(alt. on picc.),1,2(2nd alt. with b.-cl.),0 - 1,1,0,0 - mandolin - hp. - electric org. pf. - str.(2,1,1,1)   23:10 CanMusCtr.
—— MUSIC FOR VANCOUVER (1969)
   0,0,0,0 - 1,1,0,0 - perc.(1-2) - hp. - str.   15:15 CanMusCtr.
—— MUSIQUE POUR ROUEN (1971)
   str.   12:45 CanMusCtr.
—— OMBRES (1967)
   2(2nd alt. with picc.),2,2,2 - 4,2,2,1 - perc.(2) - hp. - pf. - str.   5:30 CanMusCtr.
—— ORCHESTRA PIECE 1967
   *3,*3,E♭ cl.,*4,*3 - 4,3,3,1 - timp.,perc.(8, incl. 4 on timp.) - mandolin - hp. - pf. - str.   14:55 CanMusCtr.
—— THE SONG OF BLODEUWEDD (PART 2 OF THE CANTATA "THE WHITE GODDESS") (1961) (FOR BARITONE AND ORCH.) (Text: Robert Graves)
   timp.,perc. - hp. - pf. - str.   6:00 CanMusCtr.

—— SYMPHONIC ODE (1964)
   *2,2,2,2 - 4,2,2,1 - perc. - hp. - pf. - str.   7:00 CanMusCtr.
—— THREE SONGS TO POEMS OF ROBERT GRAVES (FOR SOPRANO AND STRING ORCH.) (1958)
   str.   13:00 CanMusCtr.
—— THE WHITE GODDESS (CANTATA) (FOR SOPRANO, BARITONE, MIXED CHORUS AND ORCH.) (1962) (Text: Robert Graves)
   2,2,2,2 - 4,2,3,1 - perc.,cel. - hp. - pf. - str.   20:00 CanMusCtr.

MATHER, Martin
—— ANZAC REQUIEM (FOR SOLO VOICES, SATB CHORUS, CHILDREN'S CHORUS AND ORCH.) (1967)
   80:00 A.P.R.A.
—— THE LAST VOYAGE OF MATTHEW FLINDERS (FOR SOPRANO, TENOR, SATB CHORUS AND ORCH.) (1965)
   35:00 A.P.R.A.

MATHEW, David
—— A. T. 70 (ANNUAL TRAINING 1970)
   *3,2,3,2 - 4,3,2,1 - timp.,perc.(8) - str.   7:00 Composer.
—— INTERMEDIA PIECE (FOR 4 SATB SOLO VOICES, CHAMBER ORCH. AND TAPE) (1973) (Text: Composer)
   1,0,1E♭ cl.,0,1 - 1,1,1,0 - timp.,perc.(1) - 2 tape-decks (with amplifiers, loudspeakers and microphones) - str.(2,1,1,0)   10:30 Composer.
—— SIX FOR 27 (SIX MINUTES FOR 27 PLAYERS) (1972)
   2,2,2,2 - 2,1,2,1 - perc.(3),mar. - str.(3,3,2,2)   6:00 CAP.

MATHIAS, William
—— BERCEUSE FOR ORCH., OP. 4 (1956)
   2,2,2,2 - 2,2,2,0 - timp.,perc. - hp. - str.   6:00 P.R.S.
—— CONCERTO FOR CLARINET AND ORCH.
   Oxford.
—— CONCERTO FOR HARP AND ORCH.
   24:00 Oxford.
—— CONCERTO FOR HARPSICHORD, STRINGS AND PERCUSSION
   perc. - hpsc. - str.   Oxford.
—— CONCERTO FOR ORCHESTRA
   3,2,2,*3 - 4,3,3,1 - timp.,perc. - str.   22:00 Oxford.
—— CONCERTO NO. 1 FOR PIANO AND ORCH., OP. 2 (1955)
   2,2,2,2 - 4,3,3,0 - timp.,perc. - pf.- str.   21:00 P.R.S.
—— CONCERTO NO. 2 FOR PIANO AND ORCH.
   2,2,2,2 - 4,3,3,1 - timp.,perc. - pf. - str.   25:00 Oxford.
—— CONCERTO NO. 3 FOR PIANO AND ORCH.
   2,2,2,2 - 4,3,3,1 - timp.,perc.,cel. - pf. - str.   25:00 Oxford.
—— DANCE OVERTURE
   2,2,2,2 - 4,3,3,1 - timp.,perc.(2) - str.   8:00 Oxford.
—— DIVERTIMENTO, OP. 7
   str.   12:00 Oxford.
—— FESTIVAL OVERTURE
   Oxford.
—— HOLIDAY OVERTURE
   Oxford.
—— INTRADA
   ob. - hn. - str.   Oxford.
—— INVOCATION AND DANCE
   2,2,2,2 - 4,3,3,1 - timp.,perc. - hp. - str.   12:30 Oxford.
—— LAUDI
   2,2,2,*3 - 4,2,3,0 - timp.,perc. - pf.(alt. with cel.) - str.   13:00 Oxford.
—— LITANIES
   2,1,2,*3 - 3,2,3,0 - timp.,perc. - hp. - pf.(alt. with cel.) - str.   14:00 Oxford.
—— MUSIC FOR STRINGS, OP. 14
   str.   17:00 Oxford.
—— PRELUDE, ARIA AND FINALE
   str.   10:00 Oxford.
—— SERENADE FOR SMALL ORCH.
   2,2,2,2 - 2,2,2,0 - timp. - hp. - str.   8:00 Oxford.
—— SINFONIETTA
   2,2,2,2 - 4,2,3,0 - timp.,perc. - pf.(alt. with cel.) - str.   15:00 Oxford.
—— SYMPHONY NO. 1
   3,2,2,*3 - 4,3,3,1 - timp.,perc.,cel. - hp. - pf. - str.   28:00 Oxford.

MATHIESON, Muir
—— STIRLING TOWN (A REEL)
   2,2,2,2 - 4,2,3,0 - timp.,perc. - hp. - str.   8:30 Oxford.

MATHIEU, Rodolphe
—— HARMONIE DU SOIR (1918) (FOR HIGH VOICE, VIOLIN AND ORCH.) (Text: Charles Baudelaire)
    1,2,2,1 - 2,0,0,0 - timp.,perc.,cel. - hp. - str.   6:00 CanMusCtr.
—— UN PEU D'OMBRE (1913) (FOR SOPRANO AND ORCH.)
    (Text: Pierre Newton)
    2,2(2nd alt. with Eng. hn.),2,2 - 2,0,0,0 - timp.,cel. - hp. - str.
        5:00 CanMusCtr.
—— TROIS PRÉLUDES (1915)
    *3,*3,2,2 - 2,2,0,0 - timp.,perc. - hp. - str.   3:52 CanMusCtr.

MATIČIČ, Janez
—— SUITE FOR STRINGS
    str.   19:00 Hans Gerig.

MATRAS, Maude
—— BALLADE, OP. 8 (FOR VIOLIN AND ORCH.)
    2,1,2,1 - 2,0,0,0 - hp. - str.   Galaxy.

MATSUDAIRA, Yoriaki
—— CONFIGURATION (FOR CHAMBER ORCH.) (1963)
    2,0,2,0 - 0,0,0,0 - perc.,cel.,glock.,vibra.,xyl. - hp. - pf. - str.(8,3,3,2)   5:30 Leeds.

MATSUDAIRA, Yoritsune
—— BUGAKU
    3,2,3,2 - 2,2,2,0 - perc.(3),cel.,vibra. - hp. - pf. - str. 15:00 Leeds.
—— CONCERTO DA CAMERA (FOR HARP, HARPSICHORD AND INSTRUMENTS) (1964)
    1,1,1,1 - 0,0,0,0 - perc.(2) - hp. - hpsc. - 2 vla.,2 c.
        16:00 MCA Music.
—— DANZA RITUALE E FINALE
        Leeds.
—— DIALOGO COREOGRAFICO (1966)
    2,1,4,1 - 2,0,0,0 - perc.(5),glock.,vibra.,xyl. - hp. - 2 pf.
        13:00 MCA Music.
—— FIGURES SONORES
    2,2,2,1 sax.,1 - 2,0,0,0 - perc.(4),cel.,vibra.,xyl. - 2 hp. - pf. - str.
        18:00 Leeds.
—— KOROMOGAE (LOVE SONG) (FOR SOPRANO AND 19 INSTRUMENTS)
    fl.,ob. - perc.,cel. - hp. - hpsc. - pf. - str.(no vlas.) 8:00 Leeds.
    or:
    fl.,ob. - perc. - 2 hp. - 2 pf. - str.(no vlas.)
—— METAMORFOSI (ON ANCIENT "SAIBARAS") (FOR SOPRANO AND 18 INSTS.)
    fl.,ob. - perc.,cel. - hp. - hpsc. - pf. - str.(no vlas.) Leeds.
    or:
    fl.,ob. - perc. - hp. - hpsc. - 2 pf. - str.(no vlas.)
—— ROEI "JISEI" (TWO STARS IN VEGA) (FOR VOICE AND INSTRUMENTS) (1969)
    fl.,ob. - perc.(3),mar.,vibra. - hp. - pf. - 4 vlns. 7:00 MCA Music.
—— SA-MAI (IN THE STYLE OF JAPANESE "GAGAKU")
    3,2,2,1 sax.,0 - 0,1,0,0 - timp.,perc.(3),cel.,mar.,vibra.,xyl. - hp. - pf. - str. 14:00 Leeds.
—— SERENATA (FOR FLUTE AND 10 INSTRUMENTS)
        MCA Music.
—— SUITE DI DANZE (IN ANCIENT STYLE OF JAPANESE "BUGAKU")
    3,2,2,1 sax.,2 - 2,2,0,0 - perc.(4),cel.,glock.,vibra.,xyl. - hp. - pf. - str. 18:00 Leeds.
—— TEMA E VARIAZIONI (FOR PIANO AND ORCH.)
    3,2,3,1 sax.,3 - 4,2,2,1 - timp.,cel.,glock.,vibra. - 2 hp. - pf. - str.
        15:00 Leeds.
—— TRE MOVEMENTI (3 MOVEMENTS) (FOR PIANO AND ORCH.)
        Leeds.
—— U-MAI (ANCIENT DANCE, IN JAPANESE COURT STYLE)
    1,1,2,1 - 1,1,1,0 - perc.(3),glock.,xyl. - hp. - pf. - str.(no d.-b.)
        12:00 Leeds.

MATSUMURA, Teizo
—— ACHIME (FOR SOPRANO AND INSTRUMENTS)
    1,1,1,alto sax., 1 - 1,1,1,0 - perc. - pf. - c., d.-b. 17:00 Presser.
—— PRELUDE FOR ORCHESTRA
    6,4,4,4 - 6,4,3,1 - perc.(7), cel. - hp. - pf. - str. Presser.
—— SYMPHONY
    3,3,3,3 - 4,4,3,1 - perc.(7) - hp. - pf. - str. Presser.

MATSUSHITA, Shinichi
—— CORRELAZIONI PER TRE GRUPPI
    *2,0,*2,alto sax.,0 - 0,0,0,0 - perc. - clavioline - pf. - str.(1,1,1,1)
        22:00 Presser.

MATTAUSCH, Hans Albert
—— NYMPHENBURGER SCHLOSSMUSIK
    2,1,2,1 - 0,0,0,0 - timp.,perc. - str.   20:00 Ries-Erler.
—— SPITZWEG SUITE (IN 4 MOVTS.)
    str.   20:00 Henmar.

MATTHES, René
—— CONCERTINO FÜR KLAVIER UND ORCHESTER
        14:00 S.U.I.S.A.

MATTHEWS, Donald E.
—— CONCERTO FOR HORN AND CHAMBER ORCH. (FOR 4 WOODWINDS, TIMPANI AND STRINGS) (1960)
        10:00 Composer.
—— ELEGIAC VARIATIONS (1973)
        7:00 Composer.
—— LITTLE SUITE FOR STRINGS (1970)
    str.   4:00 Composer.
—— A MEDITATION ON THE CRUCIFIXION (1964)
    str.   3:00 Composer.
—— PROCLAMATION FOR STRINGS (1964)
    str.   4:00 Composer.
—— SINFONIETTA (1972)
        7:00 Composer.
—— STONEHENGE (1974)
        4:30 Fst. Etling.

MATTHEWS, Ermund
—— CONCERTINO FOR VIOLA AND ORCH.
    2(2nd alt. with picc.),2,2,2 - 4,2,3,0 - timp.,perc. - str.
        14:00 Novello.

MATTHEWS, Harry Alexander
—— BY THE WATERS OF BABYLON (FOR WOMEN'S CHORUS AND STRINGS)
    str.   12:00 EV.
—— THE CONVERSION (CANTATA) (FOR SOLOISTS, CHORUS AND ORCH.)
    2 hn., 2 tpt. - timp. - org. - str.   40:00 G. Schirmer.
—— FAIRY FANTASY
    2,0,0,1 - 2 hn. - hp. - str.   13:00 Ditson.
—— THE RECESSIONAL (FOR CHORUS AND ORCH.)
    2,2,2,2 - 2-4,2,2-3,1 - timp. - org. - str. 12:00 G. Schirmer.
—— THE SLAVE'S DREAM (FOR TENOR, CHORUS AND ORCH.)
    *3,2,2,2 - 4,2,3,1 - timp.,perc. - hp. - str. 14:00 G. Schirmer.
—— SONG OF LIBERTY
    2,2,2,2 - 4,2,3,1 - timp.,perc. - str.   6:30 Gray.
—— THE STORY OF CHRISTMAS (CANTATA) (FOR MIXED CHORUS AND ORCH.)
    1,0,2,0 - 2,2,1,0 - timp. - hp. - str.   G. Schirmer.

MATTHEWS, Holon
—— POEM FOR CELLO AND ORCH.
    2,2,2,2 - 4,3,3,1 - timp. - str.   14:00 Composer.
—— THE PRISONER OF CHILLON
    2,*3,*3,*3 - 4,3,3,1 - timp.,perc. - hp. - str. 14:00 Composer.
—— SYMPHONY NO. 1 (IN 4 MOVTS.)
    *3,*3,*3,*3 - 4,3,3,1 - timp.,perc.(3) - hp. - str. 26:00 Composer.
—— SYMPHONY NO. 2 (IN 4 MOVTS.)
    2,*3,2,2 - 4,3,3,1 - timp.,perc.(3) - hp. - str. 24:00 Composer.
—— SYMPHONY NO. 3
    2,*3,2,2 - 4,3,3,1 - timp.,perc. - hp. - str. Composer.
—— ULALUME
    2,*3,2,2 - 4,3,3,1 - timp. - hp. - str. 12:30 Composer.

MATTHUS, Siegfried
—— CONCERTO FOR PIANO AND ORCH.
    3,3,3,3 - 4,4,3,1 - timp.,perc.,cel. - hp. - str. Tetra.
—— CONCERTO FOR VIOLIN AND ORCH.
    2,2,2,2 - 2,2,2,1 - timp.,perc. - hp. - str. 17:00 Tetra.
—— DRESDEN SYMPHONY
    8,3,3,3 - 4,3,3,1 - timp.,perc.,cel. - hp. - pf. - str. 18:00 Tetra.
—— INVENTIONS FOR ORCH.
    3,3,3,3 - 4,3,3,1 - perc. - hp. - hpsc. - pf. - str. 21:00 Tetra.
—— LITTLE CONCERTO FOR ORCH.
    2,0,0,0 - 0,0,3,0 - perc. - hp. - pf. - str. 9:00 Tetra.
—— TUA RES AGITUR (13 VARIATIONS FOR 15 INSTRUMENTS AND PERCUSSION) (MUSIC TO PETER WEISS' PLAY "THE INVESTIGATION")
    2,2,2,1 - 0,1,1,1 - perc. - str. 15:00 Tetra.

MATTON, Roger
—— CONCERTO FOR SAXOPHONE AND STRINGS
sax. - str.   14:00 C.A.P.A.C.
—— CONCERTO FOR 2 PIANOS AND ORCH. (1964)
*3,2,*3,2 - 4,3,3,0 - timp.,perc. - 2 pf. - str.   20:00 CanMusCtr.
—— ESCAOUETTE (SUITE SUR DES AIRS DE FOLKLORE) (FOR 4
SOLO VOICES, CHORUS AND ORCH.)
10:00 C.A.P.A.C.
—— L' HOROSCOPE (CHOREOGRAPHIC SUITE) (1958) (IN 5
MOVTS.)
*3,2,*3,2 - 4,3,3,1 - timp.,perc. - hp. - pf. - str. 22:00 CanMusCtr.
—— MOUVEMENT SYMPHONIQUE NO. 1 (1960)
*3,2,2,2 - 4,3,3,1 - timp.,perc. - hp. - pf. - str.   13:00 CanMusCtr.
—— MOUVEMENT SYMPHONIQUE NO. 2 (MUSIC FOR A
DRAMA) (1962)
*3,2,*3,2 - 4,3,3,1 - timp.,perc. - hp. - str.   14:30 CanMusCtr.
—— MOUVEMENT SYMPHONIQUE NO. 3 (1974)
3,2,*3,2 - 4,3,3,0 - perc.,cel.,vibra. - hp. - str. 15:00 CanMusCtr.
—— PAX (SYMPHONIC SUITE)
20:00 C.A.P.A.C.
—— SUITE FOR ORCHESTRA, 4 VOICES AND CHORUS
5:00 C.A.P.A.C.
—— TE DEUM (1967) (FOR BARITONE, MIXED CHORUS AND
ORCH.)
*3,2,*3,*3 - 4,3,3,1 - timp.,perc. - tape-recorder - hp. - pf.(or cel.)
- str.   38:50 CanMusCtr.

MATZ, Arnold
—— CONCERTO FOR BASSOON AND ORCH.
0,0,0,1 - 0,3,1,0 - 2 hp. - str.   Tetra.

MAUL, William
—— SACRED SERVICE
2,2,2,1 - 4,2,2,1 - timp.,perc. - str.   Transcon.

MAURICE, P.
—— CONCERTO FOR PIANO AND ORCH.
22:00 EV.
—— SUITE (FOR 2 PIANOS AND ORCH.)
13:20 EV.
—— TABLEAUX DE PROVENCE (FOR SAXOPHONE AND
ORCH.)
12:00 EV.

MAVES, David W.
—— CONCERTO FOR PERCUSSION AND ORCH. (WITH 1 OR
MORE SOLOISTS)
15:00 Composer.
—— GOD'S GRANDEUR (FOR CHORUS AND ORCH.) (Text:
Gerard Manley Hopkins)
11:00 Composer.
—— OVERTURE TO AN OPERA
8:00 Composer.
—— THE STORM IS OVER (FOR CHORUS AND ORCH.) (Text:
Robert Bridges)
15:00 CMP.
—— SYMPHONY IN THREE MOVEMENTS
15:00 Composer.
—— SYMPHONY NO. 3
17:00 Composer.

MAW, Nicholas
—— LIFE STUDIES (FOR TWO STRING GROUPS)
str.   22:00 Bo. Hawkes.
—— ONE-MAN SHOW (2-ACT COMIC OPERA) (1966) % (Text:
Arthur Jacobs)
1(alt. with picc. and alto fl.),1(alt. with Eng.hn.),1(alt. with
b.-cl.),1 - 2,0,0,0 - perc.(1) - hp. - pf.(alt. with cel.) - str.(4,3,2,1
minimum)   120:00 Bo. Hawkes.
—— SCENES AND ARIAS
3,3,3,3 - 4,3,3,1 - timp.,perc.(3) - hp. - str.   29:00 Bo. Hawkes.
—— SCENES AND ARIAS (FOR SOPRANO, MEZZO-SOPRANO,
CONTRALTO AND ORCH.) (1966) (Text: Anon., ca. 1300)
3(2nd alt. with alto fl.,3rd alt. with picc.),3(3rd alt. with
Eng.hn.),*3,*3 - 4,3,3,1 - timp.,perc.,cel.,glock.,vibra.,xyl. - hp. -
str.   35:00 Bo. Hawkes.
—— SINFONIA (1966)
1(alt. with picc.),2(2nd alt. with Eng.hn.),2,2 - 2,0,0,0 - str.
30:00 Bo. Hawkes.
—— SONATA (1967)
2 hn. - str.   17:00 Bo. Hawkes.

MAXWELL, Charles
—— PLYMOUTH ROCK OVERTURE
H. Elkan.
—— PRELUDE AND SCENE (WITH ORATOR) (Text: Shakespeare)
H. Elkan.
—— PUNCH AND JUDY OVERTURE
H. Elkan.
—— STEPHEN FOSTER OVERTURE (ON FOSTER THEMES)
9:00 H. Elkan.
—— U. S. HIGHWAY
*3,2(2nd alt. with Eng. hn.),*3,0 - 4,3,3,1 - timp.,perc. - hp. - str.
12:00 MCA Music.

MAXWELL DAVIES, Peter
—— REVELATION AND FALL (FOR SOPRANO AND
ENSEMBLE) (1965) (Text: Georg Trakl)
1(alt. with picc.),1,1(alt. with b.-cl.),1(alt. with cbn.) - 1,1,1,0 -
timp.,perc.(3),glock. - dulcimer(school model) - hp. - pf.(action
removed) - str.   25:00 Bo. Hawkes.
—— ST. THOMAS WAKE (FOXTROT FOR ORCH., ON A PAVAN
BY JOHN BULL) (1969)
*3,2,*3,*3 - 4,3,3,1 - timp.,perc.(4) - hp.(incl. elec. amplification) -
pf. (upright: action removed) - str. and band-ensemble: 1(alt. with
picc.)0,1,0 - 0,1,1,0 - pf. (out-of-tune: "honky-tonk") -
perc.(1)(jazz) - str.(1,0,1,1)   21:00 min Bo. Hawkes.
—— SHAKESPEARE MUSIC (1964)
alto fl.(alt. with picc.),0,1,*2,1(alt. with cbn.) - 1,0,1,0 - perc.(1) -
quit. - vla.,d.-b.   12:00 Bo. Hawkes.
—— THE SHEPHERDS' CALENDAR (FOR HIGH VOICE, SATB
CHORUS AND ENSEMBLE) (1965) (Text: anon. goliard poets)
6 recorders,1,1,5,1 - 0,1,1,0 - perc.(9), glock.,xyl, - pf. -
str.(2,1,1,0)   21:00 Bo. Hawkes.
—— TAVERNER (2-ACT OPERA) % (1970) (Text: Composer)
2(alt. with 2 picc.),2(2nd alt. with Eng. hn.),2(2nd alt. with
b.-cl.),2 - 4,4,2,2 - timp.,perc.(6) - hp. - str. (plus on-stage
ensemble incl. recorders, early wind insts.,guit.,positive-org., regal
and str.   Bo. Hawkes.
—— VENI SANCTE SPIRITUS (FOR SOPRANO CONTRALTO,
BASS, SATB CHORUS AND ORCH.) (1963)
1,1,0,2 - 2,2,2,0 - str.   20:00 Bo. Hawkes.

MAY, Helmut
—— CONCERTO FOR VIOLIN AND STRING ORCH. (IN 3
MOVTS.)
str.   13:00 Noack.
—— SERENADE PER ARCHI (SERENADE FOR STRINGS) (IN 4
MOVTS.)
str.   9:00 Noack.
—— SUITE IM ALTEN STIL (SUITE IN OLDEN STYLE) (IN 5
MOVTS.)
str.   10:00 Noack.

MAYER, William
—— ANDANTE FOR STRINGS
str.   6:00 Bo. Hawkes.
—— BACK TALK (1969)
1(alt. with picc.),1(alt. with Eng. hn.),1(alt. with b.-cl.),1 - 1,1,1,0 -
timp.,perc.(3),glock.,xyl. - Hohner melodica - pf. - str.(2,1,1,1)
4:30 Presser.
—— BRIEF CANDLE (3-ACT "MICRO-OPERA") % (Text: Milton
Feist)
2(2nd alt. with picc.),1(alt. with Eng.hn.),2(2nd alt. with b.-cl.),1 -
2,2,1,0 - timp.,perc.(1),glock.,xyl. - pf. - str.   6:00 Presser.
—— CONCERT PIECE FOR TRUMPET AND STRINGS
tpt. - timp.,perc.(2),xyl. - str.   9:00 Bo. Hawkes.
—— ESSAY FOR BRASS AND WINDS (IN 2 MOVTS.)
1(alt. with picc.),1,1,1 - 2,2,1,1 - timp. (ad lib.),perc.(1) (ad lib.)
10:30 Presser.
—— THE EVE OF ST. AGNES (FOR CHORUS AND ORCH) (1969)
2,2,2,2 - 2,2,2,0 - timp.,perc.(2),bells,glock.,xyl. - hp. - pf. - str.
11:30 Presser.
—— THE GREATEST SOUND AROUND (THE ANIMAL
CONTEST) (FOR NARRATOR, BARITONE AND ORCH.,
WITH CHORUS DRAWN FROM CHILDREN IN AUDIENCE)
2(1st alt. with picc.),2,2,2 - 2,2,2,0 - timp.,perc.(1) - str.
14:00 Law-Gould.
—— HEBRAIC PORTRAIT
3(3rd alt. with picc.),3(3rd alt. with Eng. hn.),3(3rd alt. with
b.-cl.),2 - 4,3,3,1 - timp.,perc.(2),xyl. - hp. - pf. - str.
11:00 Composer.

—— HELLO WORLD! (AROUND THE WORLD WITH MUSIC)
(FOR BARITONE AND ORCH.)
2(1st alt. with picc.),2(1st alt. with Eng. hn.),2(2nd alt. with
b.-cl.),2(2nd alt. with c.-bn. ad lib.) - 3,2,2,0 -
timp.,perc.(2-5),bells,cel.,glock.,xyl. - pf. - str.   25:00 Bo. Hawkes.
—— LETTERS HOME (FOR NARRATOR, CHORUS AND ORCH.)
(COMPRISED OF AUTHENTIC LETTERS FROM SOLDIERS
FIGHTING IN VIETNAM) (1968)
2(2nd alt. with picc.),2(2nd alt. with Eng. hn.),2(2nd alt. with
b.-cl.),2 - 2,2,2,0 - timp.,perc.(2) - hp. - pf.(alt. with cel.) - str.
9:00 MCA Music.
—— OCTAGON (FOR PIANO AND ORCH.) (1971)
2(2nd alt. with picc.),2(2nd alt. with Eng. hn.),2(2nd alt. with E♭
cl. and b.-cl.),2 - 2,2,2,1 - timp., perc.(4),glock.,vibra.,xyl. - hp. -
org. or harm(ad lib.) - pf. - str.   26:00 MCA Music.
—— ONE CHRISTMAS, LONG AGO (1-ACT OPERA) % (Text:
Composer)
1,1(alt. with Eng.hn.),2(2nd alt. with b. cl.),1 - 2,2,1,0 -
timp.,perc.(1), cel.,glock.,xyl. - hp.(or 2nd pf.) - pf. - str.
60:00 Galaxy.
—— OVERTURE FOR AN AMERICAN (IN MEMORY OF
THEODORE ROOSEVELT)
*3,alto fl. (ad lib.),*3,2(1st alt. with E♭cl. and 2nd alt. with
b.-cl.),*3 - 4,3,3,1 - timp.,perc.(2),cel.glock.,xyl. - hp. - pf. - str.
10:00 Bo. Hawkes.
—— SCENES FROM THE BALLET "THE SNOW QUEEN" (SUITE
IN 3 MOVTS.)
*3,*3,2(2nd alt. with b.-cl.),*3 - 4,3,3,1 - timp.,perc.(2),glock.,xyl. -
hp. - pf. - str.   14:00 Presser.
—— SPRING AND YES FOREVER (3 SONGS) (FOR
MEZZO-SOPRANO, TENOR, BARITONE, SSAATTBB CHORUS
AND ORCH.) (1975)
2(2nd alt. with picc.),2(2nd alt. with Eng. hn.),2,2 - 2,2,2,0 -
timp.,perc.(3),bells,vibra.,xyl. - hp. - pf. - str.   30:00 Composer.
—— TWO PASTELS FOR ORCHESTRA
*3,*3,*3,*3 - 4,3,3,1 - timp.,perc.(3),bells,cel.,glock. - hp. - pf. - str.
11:00 MCA Music.
—— WINTER OVERTURE
2,2,2,2 - 2,2,1,1 - timp.,perc. - hp. - pf. - str.   5:00 Composer.

MAYEUR, Robert G.
—— OVERTURE FOR ORCHESTRA (1964)
*3,2,2,2 - 4,3,3,1 - timp.,perc. - pf. - str.   Composer.

MAYR, Hans
—— KONZERT FÜR OBOE AND ORCH. (1955)
2,2,2,1 - 4,3,3,0 - timp.,cel. - hp. - pf. - str.   24:00 Pacific.

MAYR, Simon Giovan - MOEHN, Heinz
—— OVERTURE TO "I COMMEDIANTI"
2,2,2,2 - 2,2,0,0 - str.   5:00 G. Schirmer.
—— PRELUDE TO ACT II OF "I COMMEDIANTI"
2,2,2,2 - 2,2,0,0 - timp. - str.   4:00 G. Schirmer.

MAZELLIER, Jules
—— POÈME ROMANTIQUE (FOR VIOLIN AND ORCH.)
2,2,2,2 - 2,2,3,1 - timp. - hp. - str.   Baron.

MEAD, Edward G.
—— CONCERT OVERTURE IN C MINOR
3(3rd alt. with picc.),2,2,2 - 4,2,3,1 - timp. - hp. - str.
12:00 Composer.

MEAD, George
—— ANNIVERSARY ANTHEM (FOR CHORUS AND ORCH.)
Composer.
—— THE STORM (FOR MALE CHORUS AND ORCH.)
2,2,2,2 - 4,2,3,0 - timp. - hp. - str.   5:00 Ricordi.
—— WITH INSTRUMENTS OF MUSIC (FOR CHORUS, ORCH.
AND ORGAN)
Composer.

MEALE, Richard
—— CONCERTO FOR FLUTE AND ORCH.
20:00 Bo. Hawkes.
—— HOMAGE TO GARCIA LORCA (FOR DOUBLE STRING
ORCH.)
str.   12:00 Bo. Hawkes.
—— HOMAGE TO RIMBAUD
Bo. Hawkes.
—— IMAGES
2,2,2,2 - 4,3,3,0 - perc. - str.   10:00 Bo. Hawkes.

—— SINFONIA (DIALLAGE) (FOR SMALL ORCH.)
30:00 Bo. Hawkes.
—— VARIATIONS (1970)
2,2,2,2 - 2,2,3,0 - perc. - str.   10:00 Bo. Hawkes.

MECHEM, Kirke
—— AMERICAN MADRIGALS (FOR SATB CHORUS AND ORCH.)
1,0,1,1 - 0,0,0,0 - str.   17:00 C. Fischer.
—— AMERICAN MADRIGALS, OP. 46 (FOR CHORUS AND
CHAMBER ORCH.) (1975) (Text: Trad., adapted by Composer)
17:00 C. Fischer.
—— HAYDN'S RETURN, OP. 18 (FUGUE AND VARIATIONS ON
HAYDN'S "FAREWELL" SYMPHONY)
*3,2,2,2 - 4,3,3,1 - timp.,perc.(3) - hp. - str.   12:30 Presser.
—— THE JAYHAWK, OP. 43 (OVERTURE TO A MYTHICAL
COMEDY) (1974)
3(1 alt.with picc.),2,*3,2 - 4,3,3,1 - timp.,perc.(3),glock.,xyl. - pf. -
str.   8:00 Composer.
—— THE KING'S CONTEST (A COMIC CANTATA), OP. 41 (1973)
(FOR SOPRANO, TENOR, BARITONE, BASS, CHORUS AND
ORCH.) (Text: Composer, adapted from the Apocrypha)
1(alt.with picc.),1,1,1 - 1,0,0,0 - perc.(1),glock. - str.(2,1,1,1) or
27:00 Composer.
3(3rd alt.with picc.),3(3rd alt.with Eng.hn.),3(3rd alt.with b.-cl.),*3
- 4,3,3,1 - timp.,perc. (4), bells,glock.,xyl. - hp. - str.
—— SINGING IS SO GOOD A THING, (AN ELIZABETHEN
RECREATION), OP. 36 (1970) (FOR CHORUS AND ORCH.)
(WITH 4 ELIZABETHAN DANCES) (Text: William Byrd)
1(alt.with picc.),1,0,1 - 0,1,1,0 - perc.(2) - guit. - hpsc. - str.
27:00 Henmar.
—— SPEECH TO A CROWD, OP. 44 (1974) (FOR CHORUS AND
ORCH.) (Text: Archibald Macleish)
*3,2,3(3rd alt.with b.-cl.),2 - 4,3,3,1 - timp.,perc.(4),cel.,glock.,xyl.
- hp. - str.   15:00 NatlMuPubs.
—— SYMPHONY NO. 1, OP. 16 (IN 3 MOVTS.)
*3,2,*3,2 - 4,3,3,1 - timp.,perc.(3) - hp. - str.   21:00 Bo. Hawkes.
—— SYMPHONY NO. 2, OP. 29 (1969) (IN 4 MOVTS.)
*3,*3,3(3rd alt.with b.-cl.),*3 - 4,3,3,1 -
timp.,perc.(5),cel.,glock.,xyl. - hp. - str.   33:00 Bo. Hawkes.

MEDIN, Nino
—— DANZE PER I CINQUE CERCHI (BALLET) %
3,2,2,2 - 4,2,2,0 - timp.,perc. - hp. - str.   18:00 Bo. Hawkes.
—— DIVERTIMENTO NO. 2 (CONCERT VERSION OF "DANZE
PER I CINQUE CERCHI")
3,2,2,2 - 4,2,2,0 - timp.,perc. - hp. - str.   18:00 Bo. Hawkes.
—— INTRODUCTION, ARIA AND FINALE (FOR VIOLIN AND
ORCH.)
1,1,1,1 - 1,1,0,0 - pf. - str.   20:00 Bo. Hawkes.
—— PARTITA
str.   11:00 Bo. Hawkes.

MEDINS, Janis
—— LATVIAN RHAPSODY
11:00 S.T.I.M.

MEESTER, Louis de
—— CAPRICCIO (1948)
2,2,3,2 - 4,2,3,0 - timp.,perc. - hp. - str.   23:00 CBDM.
—— CONCERTO NO. 1 FOR PIANO AND ORCH. (1952)
2,2,2,2 - 2,2,3,0 - timp.,perc. - pf. - str.   20:00 CBDM.
—— MAGREB (FOR VIOLA AND ORCH.) (1946)
2,2,2,2 - 3,3,3,0 - perc. - pf. - str.   13:00 CBDM.
—— MARINE
3,3,3,2 - 4,3,3,0 - timp.,perc. - str.   10:00 H. Elkan.
—— MUSICA PER ARCHI (1955)
str.   18:00 CBDM.
—— SCHERZETTINO (FOR CHAMBER ORCH.) (1971)
1,1,0,0 - 0,0,0,0 - str.   2:00 H. Elkan.
—— SPROOKJES MUZIEK (SUITE FROM "VAN EEN TROTSE
VOGEL") (1948) (IN 4 MOVTS.)
2,2,2,2 - 2,2,1,0 - timp.,perc.,cel.,vibra. - hp. - str. 15:00 H. Elkan.
—— VAN EEN TROSTE VOGEL (CONTE MUSICAL) (1948)
2,2,2,2 - 2,2,1,0 - timp.,perc.,cel.,vibra. - hp. - str. 20:00 H. Elkan.
—— WARAI (FOR STRING ORCH.) (1967)
str.   H. Elkan.

MEFANO, Paul
—— THE CEREMONY (FOR 3 SOLO VOICES, 12-VOICE
SPEAKING CHORUS AND ORCH.) (1969)
4(3 alt. with 3picc.),4(2 alt.with 2 Eng.hn.),4(3 alt.with 3 b.-cl.),0 -
6,5,4,1 - perc.(6),cel. - elec.guit. - electric hp. -
elec.org.(hammond) - 3pf. - str.   25:00 Salabert.

—— INCIDENCES (FOR PIANO AND ORCH.) (1960)
    3(3rd alt.with picc.),3(3rd alt.with Eng.hn.),3(3rd alt.with b.-cl.),0 -
    4,3,3,0 - timp.,perc.(3),bells,mar.,vibra.,xyl. - hp. - pf. - str.
                                                          15:00 Salabert.
—— INTERFERENCES (FOR INSTRUMENTAL ENSEMBLE)
    1,1,1,1 - 1,0,0,0 - perc. - pf. - str.(1,1,1,0)   6:00 Presser.
—— LIGNES (FOR BASSO AND CHAMBER ENSEMBLE)
    0,0,0,1 - 3,3,0,1 - perc.(6) - d.-b.   8:00 Presser.
—— MADRIGAL (FOR 3 WOMEN'S VOICES AND ENSEMBLE)
    (1962)
    fl. - perc.(4) - hp. - pf. - str.(4)   10:00 Salabert.
—— ONDES
    1,b.-fl.,*2,heck.,*2,1 - 1,1,0,0 - timp. - 2 vln.   8:00 Salabert.
—— PARABOLES (FOR DRAMATIC SOPRANO AND ORCH.)
    0,0,2,alto sax.,0 - 0,2,2,1 - perc. - pf. - str.   25:00 Presser.
    or:
    2,2,2,2 - 4,3,3,0 - timp.,perc. - hp. - pf. - str.
—— SIGNES-OUBLI (FOR TWO GROUPS OF INSTRUMENTS)
    *2,*2,E♭cl.,*1,*1 - 1,1(picc.tpt),2,1 - perc. - elec. guit. - Hammond
    org. - str.(2,2,2,2)   7:00 Salabert.

MEHLER, Friedrich
—— CONCERTO NO. 2 FOR VIOLIN AND ORCH. (REV. 1973)
    2,2,2,2 - 0,2,0,0 - timp. - hp. - str.   26:00 Fleisher.
—— SYMPHONY NO. 2 (REV. 1974)
    2,2,2,2 - 2,2,2,0 - timp.(2 players) - str.   30:00 Fleisher.

MÉHUL, Étienne-Nicholas - OUBRADOUS, Fernand
—— SYMPHONY NO. 2 IN D
    2,2,2,2 - 1,0,0,0 - timp. - str.   24:00 Presser.

MEIER, Daniel
—— ODE (FOR STRINGS)
    str.   10:15 Presser.
—— SEMEN (FOR STRING QUINTET AND ORCH.)
    2,2,2,2 - 2,1,2,0 - timp.,perc.(4) - pf. - str.   15:00 Presser.

MEIER, Jost
—— CONCERTO BREVE FÜR VIOLINCELLO UND ORCHESTER
                                                            15:00 S.U.I.S.A.
—— MOUVEMENT DANS I'IMMOBILE (FÜR KLEINES
    ORCHESTER)
    2,1,2,2 - 1,2,0,0 - str.   12:00 S.U.I.S.A.

MEISTER, Karl
—— CHRISTMAS SUITE (WEIHNACHTLICHE SUITE) (WITH
    OPTIONAL VOICE OR CHORUS)
    perc. - pf. - str.   Robbins.

MELARTIN, Erkki
—— AINO, OP. 50 (OPERA) % (1907) (Text: Jalmari Finne)
    2,2,2,2 - 4,3,3,1 - timp.,perc. - hp. - str.   FinnMICtr.
—— THE BLUE PEARL (BALLET SUITE)
    2,2,2,2 - 4,3,0,0 - timp.,perc. - hp. - str.   20:00 FinnMICtr.
—— THE BLUE PEARL, OP. 160 (BALLET) % (1930)
    2,2,2,2 - 4,3,1,0 - timp.,perc.(3) - hp. - pf. - str. FinnMICtr.
—— CONCERTO IN D MINOR FOR VIOLIN AND ORCH., OP. 60
    2,2,2,2 - 4,3,3,0 - timp.,perc. - hp. - str.   29:00 FinnMICtr.
—— DIVERTIMENTO NO. 1, OP. 152 (1928)
    1,1,1,1 - 0,1,1,0 - timp.,perc. - str.   21:00 FinnMICtr.
—— KARELIAN SCENES, OP. 146, NO. 6
    2,2,2,0 - 2,1,1,0 - timp. - pf. - str.   11:00 FinnMICtr.
—— LITTLE SUITE, OP. 76 (1913)
    1,1,2,1 - 2,2,1,0 - timp.,perc. - hp. - str.   8:00 FinnMICtr.
—— LYDIAN SUITE, OP. 102 ("KANDAULES") (1916)
    2,0,2,2 - 0,0,0,0 - timp.,perc. - hp. - str.   12:00 FinnMICtr.
—— LYDIAN SUITE, OP. 102 (1916) (Expanded Orchestration)
    2,1,2,2 - 2,2,0,0 - timp.,perc. - hp. - str.   14:00 FinnMICtr.
—— LYRICAL SUITE NO. 1, OP. 27 (1906)
    2,2,2,2 - 4,2,3,1 - timp.,perc. - hp. - str.   25:00 FinnMICtr.
—— LYRICAL SUITE NO. 2, OP. 56
    2,1,2,1 - 2,2,1,0 - timp.,perc. - hp. - str.   ·9:00 FinnMICtr.
—— LYRICAL SUITE NO. 3, OP. 93 ("IMPRESSIONS DE
    BELGIQUE") (REV. 1917)
    3,3,3,3 - 4,2,3,1 - timp.,perc.,cel. - hp. - harm.(ad lib.) - pf. - str.
                                                           20:00 FinnMICtr.
—— MUSIC TO JOHANNES LINNANKOSKI'S PLAY "THE
    ETERNAL STRIFE", OP. 63 (1909)
    2,1,2,0 - 2,2,1,0 - timp.,perc. - str.   25:00 FinnMICtr.
—— PASTORALE (1909)
    2,1,2,1 - 2,0,0,0 - hp. - str.   12:00 FinnMICtr.

—— PATRIA, OP. 72 (SYMPHONIC STUDY)
    4,3,4,3 - 4,3,3,2 - timp.,perc.(3),cel. - 2 hp. - str.
                                                           16:00 FinnMICtr.
—— SONGS FROM LADOGA, OP. 146-A (SUITE)
    2,0,2,0 - 2,1,1,0 - timp.,perc. - hp. - pf. - str.   13:00 FinnMICtr.
—— SUITE FOR STRING ORCH., OP. 84 (1915)
    timp.,perc. - hp. - str.   10:00 FinnMICtr.
—— SUITE FROM THE PLAY "THE SLEEPING BEAUTY", OP. 22
    (1911)
    2,2,2,2 - 4,2,1,0 - timp.,perc. - hp. - str.   17:00 FinnMICtr.
—— SYMPHONY NO. 3 IN F MAJOR, OP. 40 (1907)
    2,2,2,2 - 4,3,3,1 - timp.,perc. - hp. - str.   38:00 FinnMICtr.
—— SYMPHONY NO. 4, OP. 80 ("SUMMER SYMPHONY") (1912)
    3,3,2,3 - 4,3,3,1 - timp.,perc.,cel. - hp. - str.   36:00 FinnMICtr.
—— SYMPHONY NO. 5 IN A MINOR, OP. 90 ("SINFONIA
    BREVIS") (1916)
    3,2,2,3 - 4,3,1 - timp.,perc.,cel. - str.   34:00 FinnMICtr.
—— TRAUMGESICHT, OP. 70
    3,3,3,3 - 4,3,3,1 - timp.,perc.(3) - 2 hp. - str.   12:00 FinnMICtr.
—— VÄINÄMÖINEN CREATES THE KANTELE (1906)
    2,2,2,2 - 4,2,3,0 - timp. - hp. - str.   9:00 FinnMICtr.

MELARTIN, Frank
—— MARJATTA, OP. 79 (FOR SOLO VOICE AND ORCH.) (1914)
    3,3,3,3 - 4,3,3,1 - timp.,perc.,cel. - hp. - str.   14:00 FinnMICtr.

MELCHERS, Henrik
—— CONCERTO FOR VIOLIN AND ORCH.
    2,2,2,2 - 4,2,0,0 - timp.,perc. - str.   32:00 S.T.I.M.
—— CONCERTO NO. 1 FOR PIANO AND ORCH.
    2,2,2,2 - 4,2,0,0 - timp.,perc. - pf. - str.   30:00 S.T.I.M.
—— CONCERTO NO. 2 FOR PIANO AND ORCH.
    2,2,2,2 - 4,2,0,0 - timp.,perc. - pf. - str.   32:00 S.T.I.M.
—— ELEGY FOR ORCH.
    2,3,2,2 - 4,2,3,1 - timp.,perc.(2) - hp.   10:00 S.T.I.M.
—— LA KERMESSE
    3,3,3,3 - 4,4,3,1 - timp.,perc.(2) - hp. - str.   12:00 S.T.I.M.
—— SWEDISH RHAPSODY
    3,3,3,3 - 4,4,3,1 - timp.,perc.(2) - 2 hp. - str.   14:00 S.T.I.M.
—— SYMPHONY IN D MINOR
    3,3,3,3 - 4,3,3,1 - timp.,perc.(2) - str.   36:00 S.T.I.M.

MELICHAR, Alois
—— BEROCHO (BENEDICTION) (FOR CELLO AND ORCH.)
    2,2,2,2 - 3,2,3,1 - timp.,perc. - hp. - str.   3:00 Modern.
—— SINFONIETTA ITALIANA
    2(2nd alt. with picc.),2,2,2 - 4,3,3,1 - timp.,perc.,cel. - hp. - str.
                                                           23:00 Modern.
—— THREE SONGS (FOR BARITONE AND ORCH.) (Text: Josef
    Weinheber)
    2,2,2,2 - 4,2,3,1 - timp.,perc.,cel.,glock. - hp. - str.   Henmar.

MELIKOV, Arif D.
—— SYMPHONY NO. 3
                                                           G. Schirmer.

MELLERS, Wilfrid
—— ALBA (IN 9 METAMORPHOSES) (FOR FLUTE AND ORCH.)
    1,0,3,2 - 4,2,3,1 - timp.,perc.,cel. - hp. - str.   20:00 Mills.
—— SAMSON AGONISTES (RITUAL MUSIC FOR WOODWIND,
    BRASS AND PERCUSSION)
    3(3rd alt. with picc.),3,3(3rd alt. with alto sax.),2 - 4,3,3,1 -
    timp.,perc. - org.(ad lib.)   18:00 Mills.
—— THE SONG OF RUTH (CANTATA) (FOR SOPRANO,
    MEZZO-SOPRANO, BARITONE, CHORUS AND ORCH.)
                                                           45:00 Lengnick.

MELLNÄS, Arne
—— AURA (1964)
    2,2,2,2 - 2,2,3,0 - timp.,perc.(5),cel.,vibra.,xyl. - pf. - str.
                                                           18:00 G. Schirmer.
—— CHIASMOS (1961)
    3,2,3,3 - 4,3,3,0 - timp.,perc.(2),xyl. - str.   18:00 S.T.I.M.
—— CONCERTO FOR CLARINET AND STRINGS (1957)
    cl. - str.   S.T.I.M.
—— MUSIC FOR ORCH. (1959)
    2,2,2,2 - 2,2,3,0 - timp. - str.   S.T.I.M.
—— TRANSPARENCE (1972)
    4,4,4,4 - 4,4,4,0 - perc.(3),cel. - hp. - str.   14:00 Fleisher.

MENASCE, Jacques de
—— CONCERTO NO. 2 FOR PIANO AND ORCH. (IN 4 MOVTS.)
3(3rd alt. with picc.),2,2,2 - 4,3,2,1 - timp.,perc.,xyl. - hp. - pf. - str.   S.A.C.E.M.
—— DIVERTISSEMENT SUR UNE CHANSON D'ENFANTS
pf. - str.   7:59 Henn.

MENDELSSOHN, Felix
—— A MIDSUMMER NIGHT'S DREAM (CONCERT VERSION FOR CHORUS AND ORCH.) (Adapted by Robert Shaw and Alice Parker)
Law-Gould.

MENDELSSOHN, Felix - BENJAMIN, Arthur
—— PRAELUDIUM IN B MINOR
2,2,3,2 - 4,2,0,0 - timp.,perc. - str.   4:00 Bo. Hawkes.
—— PRELUDE AND FUGUE
2,2,2,3 - 4,2,3,1 - timp.,perc. - str.   7:00 Bo. Hawkes.

MENDELSSOHN, Felix - EVANS
—— FINGAL'S CAVE OVERTURE ("THE HEBRIDES"), OP. 26
8:00 Bo. Hawkes.
—— OVERTURE TO "RUY BLAS"
12:00 Bo. Hawkes.

MENDELSSOHN, Felix - FREUDENTHAL
—— SYMPHONY FOR STRINGS, IN D MAJOR
str.   31:00 Henmar.

MENDELSSOHN, Felix - GODFREY, C.
—— OVERTURE TO "MIDSUMMER NIGHT'S DREAM", OP. 21 (Revised)
10:00 Bo. Hawkes.

MENDELSSOHN, Felix - HERMANN, F.
—— DUO, OP. 38 (ARRANGED FOR STRING ORCH.)
pf. - str.   Galaxy.

MENDELSSOHN, Felix - LEAVIS, R.
—— KYRIE (FOR MIXED CHORUS AND ORCH.)
2,2,2,2 - 2,2,3,0 - timp. - str.   9:00 Oxford.

MENDELSSOHN, Felix - LOTTER, Adolf
—— INTRODUCTION AND SCHERZO (FROM "HYMN OF PRAISE")
6:00 Bo. Hawkes.

MENDELSSOHN, Felix - MILES, Maurice
—— ELIJAH (FOR SOLO VOICES, CHORUS AND ORCH.)
1,1,2,1 - 2,1,1,0 - timp. - str.   Lengnick.

MENDELSSOHN, Felix - MOSCHELES - PRIEGNITZ, Hans
—— PREZIOSA-VARIATIONEN (FOR 2 PIANOS AND ORCH.)
2,2,2,2 - 2,2,0,0 - timp.,perc. - 2 pf. - str.   14:00 F. Colombo.

MENDELSSOHN, Felix - ROBERTS, Charles J.
—— FINGAL'S CAVE OVERTURE
C. Fischer.
—— OVERTURE TO "A MIDSUMMER NIGHT'S DREAM"
C. Fischer.
—— OVERTURE TO "RUY BLAS"
C. Fischer.

MENDELSSOHN, Felix - WINTER, Aubrey - EVANS
—— SYMPHONY NO. 4 IN A MAJOR ("ITALIAN"), OP. 90
Bo. Hawkes.

MENGELBERG, Karel
—— ANION (SYMFONISCHE SCHETS)
3,3,3,3 - 4,3,3,1 - timp.,perc.,cel. - 2 hp. - str.   10:00 Henmar.
—— CONCERTO FOR HORN AND ORCH.
2,2,2,2 - 2,2,0,0 - timp.,perc. - hp. - str.   17:00 Henmar.
—— DIVERTIMENTO
2,2,2,2 - 2,2,0,0 - timp.,perc. - hp.(ad lib.) - str.   19:00 Henmar.
—— REQUIEM FOR ORCHESTRA
2,2,2,sax.,2 - 4,2,3,1 - timp.,perc.,cel. - hp. - str.   3:00 Henmar.
—— ROLAND HOLST-KANTATE (FOR MIXED CHORUS AND ORCH.) (1955) (Text: Henriëtte Roland Holst)
2,2,2,2 - 2,2,0,0 - timp. - str.   18:00 Henmar.
—— SERENADE
str.   10:00 Henmar.
—— SUITE
2,2,2,2 - 2,2,0,0 - timp. - str.   Henmar.

—— THREE SONGS FROM R. TAGORE'S "THE GARDENER" (FOR SOPRANO AND ORCH.) (1925)
2,2,2,2 - 4,3,3,1 - timp.,perc.,bells,cel. - 2 hp. - str.   10:00 Henmar.

MENGELBERG, Micha
—— COMMENTARY (1966)
10:00 Henmar.

MENGELBERG, Rudolf
—— ADORO TE (FOR ALTO AND ORCH.) (1946)
2,3,3,3 - 3,2,0,0 - str.   10:00 Henmar.
—— CAPRICCIO FOR PIANO AND ORCH.
3,2,3,2 - 4,2,3,1 - timp.,perc. - pf. - str.   15:00 Henmar.
—— CONCERTINO FOR FLUTE AND SMALL ORCH.
1,1,2,1 - 2,1,0,0 - str.   15:00 Henmar.
—— MAGNIFICAT (FOR ALTO AND ORCH.) (1942)
2,2,3,2 - 3,1,2,0 - timp. - str.   10:00 Henmar.
—— STABAT MATER (FOR MIXED CHORUS AND ORCH.) (1940)
2,3,3,3 - 4,3,3,1 - timp.,perc. - pf. - str.   17:00 Henmar.
—— SYMPHONIC VARIATIONS FOR CELLO AND ORCH., OP. 15
3,2,2,2 - 3,1,3,0 - timp.,perc.,cel. - hp. - str.   17:00 Henmar.
—— VICTIMAE PASCHALI LAUDES (FOR SOPRANO, MIXED CHORUS AND ORCH.) (1946)
2,2,2,2 - 4,2,2,1 - timp.,perc. - str.   10:00 Henmar.
—— WEINLESE, OP. 17 (CANTATA FOR TENOR, MIXED CHORUS AND ORCH.) (1929) (Text: Wolf Graf Kalckreuth)
3,3,3,2 - 4,2,3,1 - timp.,perc. - hp. - str.   Henmar.

MENNIN, Peter
—— CANTATA DE VIRTUTE (FOR NARRATOR, CHORUS, CHILDREN'S CHORUS AND ORCH.)
4,3,3,3 - 4,3,3,1 - timp.,perc. - str.   40:00 C. Fischer.
—— CANTO FOR ORCH.
*3,*3,*3,2 - 4,3,3,1 - timp.,perc.(2) - str.   9:00 C. Fischer.
—— THE CHRISTMAS STORY (CANTATA) (FOR SOLOISTS, CHORUS AND ORCH.)
2 tpt., 2 trb. - timp. - str.   26:00 C. Fischer.
—— CONCERTATO FOR ORCHESTRA ("MOBY DICK")
*3,*3,*3,2 - 4,3,3,1 - timp.,perc.(4) - str.   11:30 C. Fischer.
—— CONCERTINO FOR FLUTE, STRINGS, AND PERCUSSION
1. Andate moderato; 2. Presto
fl. - timp.,perc.(2) - str.   11:00 Hargail.
—— CONCERTO FOR CELLO AND ORCH. (IN 3 MOVTS.)
*3,2,2,2 - 4,2,3,1 - timp.,perc.(3) - str.   26:30 C. Fischer.
—— CONCERTO FOR PIANO AND ORCH.
*3,2,2,2 - 4,2,3,1 - timp.,perc.(2) - pf. - str.   27:00 C. Fischer.
—— CONCERTO FOR STRINGS (IN 3 MOVTS.)
str.   13:00 Hargail.
—— CONCERTO FOR VIOLIN AND ORCH. (IN 3 MOVTS.)
*3,2,2,2 - 4,3,3,1 - timp.,perc. - str.   21:00 Hargail.
—— FANTASIA FOR STRINGS (IN 2 MOVTS.)
str.   9:00 Hargail.
—— FOLK OVERTURE
2(2nd alt. with picc.),2,2,2 - 4,3,3,1 - timp.,perc.(3) - str.
7:00 Hargail.
—— GINA (GRAND OPERA) % (Text: Maurice Valency)
C. Fischer.
—— SINFONIA (FOR CHAMBER ORCH.)
2,2,2,2 - 2,2,1,0 - timp. - pf. - str.   5:00 C. Fischer.
—— SINFONIA FOR ORCHESTRA (1970)
1. Lento sostento; 2. Allegro vivace
*3,*3,*3,*3 - 4,4,3,1 - timp.,perc.(3) - str.   13:00 C. Fischer.
—— SYMPHONY NO. 1 (IN 4 MOVTS.)
3(2nd alt. with picc.),2,2,2 - 4,3,3,1 - timp.,perc.(3) - pf. - str.
44:00 Composer.
—— SYMPHONY NO. 2 (IN 3 MOVTS.)
3(3rd alt. with picc.),2(1 alt. with Eng. hn.),2,2 - 4,3,3,1 - timp.,perc.(3) - str.   25:00 Harms, Inc.
—— SYMPHONY NO. 3 (IN 3 MOVTS.)
3(3rd alt. with picc.),2,2,2 - 4,3,3,1 - timp.,perc.(3) - str.
20:00 Hargail.
—— SYMPHONY NO. 4 ("THE CYCLE") (FOR CHORUS AND ORCH.)
*3,2,2,2 - 4,3,3,1 - timp.,perc.(2) - str.   23:00 C. Fischer.
—— SYMPHONY NO. 5 (IN 3 MOVTS.)
*3,2,2,2 - 4,3,3,1 - timp.,perc.(3) - str.   22:00 C. Fischer.
—— SYMPHONY NO. 6
*3,*3,2,2 - 4,2,3,1 - timp.,perc.(2) - str.   26:00 C. Fischer.
—— SYMPHONY NO. 7 (VARIATION SYMPHONY) (IN 1 MOVT. OF 5 SECTIONS)
*3,*3,*3,*3 - 4,3,3,1 - timp.,perc.(3) - str.   25:00 C. Fischer.
—— SYMPHONY NO. 8
3,3,3,3 - 4,4,3,1 - timp.,perc. - str.   26:00 C. Fischer.

MENNINI, Louis A.
—— ANDANTE AND ALLEGRO ENERGICO
    *3,2,2,2 - 4,3,3,1 - timp.,perc.(2) - str.   16:00 Composer.
—— CANTILENA
    *3,2,2,2 - 4,3,3,1 - timp.,perc.(2) - str.   9:00 Composer.
—— OVERTURA BREVE
    *3,2,2,2 - 4,3,3,1 - timp.,perc.(2) - str.   6:30 Composer.
—— THE ROPE (OPERA) %
    1,1,2(2nd alt. with b.-cl.),1 - 2,1,0,0 - pf. - str.
     55:00 Composer.
—— SYMPHONY NO. 2 ("DA FESTA") (IN 3 MOVTS.)
    3(3rd alt. with picc.),2,2,2 - 4,3,3,1 - timp.,perc.(1) - str.
     22:00 Composer.
—— THE WELL (OPERA) %
    1,1,1,1 - 2,1,1,0 - timp.,perc.(2) - str.   55:00 Composer.

MENOTTI, Gian Carlo
—— AMAHL AND THE NIGHT VISITORS (OPERA) %
     G. Schirmer.
—— APOCALYPSE (IN 3 MOVTS.)
    *3,*3,*3,*3 - 6,4,3,1 - timp.,perc.,cel. - 2 hp. - pf. - str.
     24:00 G. Schirmer.
—— THE BLACK SWAN (ARIA FROM "THE MEDIUM") (FOR
MEZZO-SOPRANO AND ORCH.)
    1,1,1,1 - hn. - perc. -2 pf. - str.   G. Schirmer.
—— BOB'S ARIA (FROM "THE OLD MAID AND THE THIEF")
(FOR BARITONE AND ORCH.)
    *2,1,1,1 - 2,2,1,0 - timp.,perc.,glock. - str.   Ricordi.
—— CONCERTO FOR VIOLIN AND ORCH.
    2,2,2,2 - 2,2,0,0 - timp.,perc. - hp. - str.   30:00 G. Schirmer.
—— CONCERTO IN F, FOR PIANO AND ORCH. (IN 3 MOVTS.)
    *3,2,2,2 - 4,3,3,1 - timp.,perc.,xyl. - pf. - str.   28:00 Ricordi.
—— THE CONSUL (OPERA) %
     G. Schirmer.
—— THE DEATH OF THE BISHOP OF BRINDISI (DRAMATIC
CANTATA) (FOR MEZZO-SOPRANO, BARITONE,
CHILDREN'S CHORUS, MIXED CHORUS AND ORCH.)
    2,1 alto fl.,2,*3,2 - 4,3,3,1 - timp.,perc.(3) - hp. - 2 pf. - str.
     30:00 G. Schirmer.
—— FANTASIA FOR CELLO AND ORCH.
    *3,*3,*3,2 - 4,2,3,1 - timp.,perc. - hp. - str.   G. Schirmer.
—— INTRODUCTION, MARCH AND SHEPHERD'S DANCE
(FROM "AMAHL AND THE NIGHT VISITORS")
    1,2,1,1 - 1,1,0,0 - perc. - hp. - pf. - str.   10:00 G. Schirmer.
—— LANDSCAPES AND REMEMBRANCES (FOR FOUR
SOLOISTS, SATB CHORUS AND ORCH.)
    2(2nd alt. with picc.),*3,*3,2 - 4,3,3,1 - timp.,perc. - hp. - str.
     45:00 G. Schirmer.
—— THE LAST SAVAGE (3-ACT COMIC OPERA) %
    3,2,3,3 - 4,3,3,1 - timp.,perc. - 2 hp. - pf. - str.
     140:00 F. Colombo.
—— LUCY'S ARIA, FROM "THE TELEPHONE" ("HELLO, HELLO")
(FOR SOPRANO AND ORCH.)
    1,1,1,1 - 1,1,0,0 - perc. - pf. - str.   G. Schirmer.
—— LULLABY, FROM "THE CONSUL"
    1,1,1,1 - 2,1,1,0 - hp. - pf. - str.   G. Schirmer.
—— LULLABY, FROM "THE MEDIUM" (FOR VOICE AND ORCH.)
     G. Schirmer.
—— MAGDA'S ARIA, FROM "THE CONSUL" (FOR SOPRANO
AND ORCH.)
    1,1,1,1 - 2,2,1,0 - perc. - hp. - pf. - str.   G. Schirmer.
—— MARIA GOLOVIN (3-ACT OPERA) %
    3,3,3,2 - 4,3,3,1 - timp.,perc. - hp. - str.   F. Colombo.
—— MARTIN'S LIE (1-ACT OPERA DA CHIESA) %
    1,1,1,1 - 1,2,1,0 - perc. - str.(no vlns.)   50:00 G. Schirmer.
—— THE MEDIUM (2-ACT TRAGIC OPERA) %
    1,1,1,1 - 1,1,0,0 - perc. - pf. - str.   80:00 G. Schirmer.
—— THE MEDIUM'S ARIA, FROM "THE MEDIUM" (CONTRALTO
AND ORCH.)
    1,1,1,1 - 1,1,0,0 - perc. - pf. 4-hands - str.   G. Schirmer.
—— MONICA'S WALTZ, FROM "THE MEDIUM" (FOR VOICE
AND ORCH.)
     G. Schirmer.
—— THE OLD MAID AND THE THIEF (OPERA) %
     Ricordi.
—— PASTORALE
    pf. - str.   G. Schirmer.
—— PRELUDE TO "THE OLD MAID AND THE THIEF"
    *2,1,1,1 - 2,2,1,0 - timp.,perc. - str.   4:30 Ricordi.
—— THE SAINT OF BLEECKER STREET (OPERA) %
     G. Schirmer.

—— SHEPHERD'S CHORUS (FROM "AMAHL AND THE NIGHT
VISITORS") (FOR CHORUS AND ORCH)
    1,2,1,1 - 1,1,0,0 - perc. - hp. - pf. - str.   6:00 G. Schirmer.
—— SUITE FROM THE BALLET "SEBASTIAN" (IN 7 MOVTS.)
    1(alt. with picc.),1(alt. with Eng. hn.),2(2nd alt. with b.-cl.),1 -
    2,2,2,0 - perc.(2),xyl. - hp. - pf. - str.   20:00 Ricordi.
—— SYMPHONY NO. 1 ("HALCYON")
    2(2nd alt. with picc.),*3,*3,2 - 4,2,3,1 - timp.,perc. - hp. - pf. - str.
     G. Schirmer.
—— THE TELEPHONE (OPERA) %
     G. Schirmer.
—— TRIPLO CONCERTO A TRE (FOR 3 SOLO GROUPS AND
ORCH.)
    Solo Group I: perc. - hp. - pf. Solo Group II: ob.,cl.,bn. Solo
    Group III: vln.,vla.,c. tutti: 2,1,1,1 - 2,2,2,1 - str.
     20:00 G. Schirmer.
—— TWO INTERLUDES FROM "THE ISLAND GOD"
    1. Lento; 2. Allegro agitato
    *3,*3,*3,*3 - 4,3,3,1 - timp.,perc.(3),glock.,xyl. - hp. - pf. - str.
     8:00 Ricordi.

MERIKANTO, Aarre
—— THE ABDUCTION OF KYLLIKKI (1935)
    3,2,3,2 - 3,2,3,0 - timp. - pf. - str.   15:00 Fazer.
—— ANDANTE RELIGIOSO (1933)
    1,1,2,1 - 2,2,0,0 - str.   5:00 FinnMICtr.
—— ANDANTE (1956)
    str.   Fazer.
—— CONCERT PIECE FOR CELLO AND CHAMBER ORCH.
(1926)
    1,0,1,0 - 0,0,0,0 - hp. - str.   13:00 FinnMICtr.
—— CONCERTO NO. 1 FOR VIOLIN AND ORCH., OP. 9 (1916)
    2,2,2,2 - 4,2,0,0 - str.   27:00 FinnMICtr.
—— CONCERTO NO. 1 IN F SHARP MINOR FOR PIANO AND
ORCH., OP. 3 (1913)
    2,2,2,2 - 4,2,0,0 - timp. - pf. - str.   20:00 FinnMICtr.
—— CONCERTO NO. 2 FOR CELLO AND ORCH. (1944)
    2,2,2,2 - 3,2,0,0 - str.   21:00 FinnMICtr.
—— CONCERTO NO. 2 FOR PIANO AND ORCH. (1937)
    2,2,2,2 - 3,2,0,0 - timp. - pf. - str.   25:00 FinnMICtr.
—— CONCERTO NO. 2 FOR VIOLIN AND ORCH., OP. 30 (1925)
    3,2,3,2 - 4,1,0,0 - cel. - 2 hp. - str.   15:00 FinnMICtr.
—— CONCERTO NO. 3 FOR PIANO AND ORCH. (1955)
    2,2,2,2 - 2,2,1,1 - timp. - pf. - str.   18:00 FinnMICtr.
—— CONCERTO NO. 4 FOR VIOLIN AND ORCH. (1954)
    2,2,2,1 - 2,1,0,0 - str.   17:00 FinnMICtr.
—— DANCE SUITE (1934) (IN 5 MOVTS.)
    2,2,2,2 - 3,2,2,0 - pf. - str.   9:00 FinnMICtr.
—— FANTASY FOR ORCH. (1923)
    4,4,4,4 - 6,4,3,2 - timp.,perc.(4, incl. 2 on timp.),cel. - 2 hp. - str.
     15:00 FinnMICtr.
—— FOUR COMPOSITIONS FOR ORCH. (1932)
    1,1,2,1 - 2,2,0,0 - cel. - pf. - str.   14:00 FinnMICtr.
—— INTRADA (1936)
    2,2,2,2 - 4,3,3,0 - str.   8:00 Fazer.
—— JUHA (OPERA) (Text: Juhani Aho andAino Ackte)
     LuoSavEd.
—— LEMMINKÄINEN, OP. 10 (1916)
    3,3,2,2 - 4,3,3,1 - timp.,perc.(4) - hp. - str.   17:00 FinnMICtr.
—— MUSIC TO THE SUMMER NIGHT (1942)
    1,1,1,1 - 2,0,0,0 - cel. - hp. - str.   10:00 FinnMICtr.
—— NOTTURNO (1929)
    3,3,3,2 - 4,0,0,0 - str.   9:00 FinnMICtr.
—— PAN (1924)
    3,3,3,2 - 4,1,3,0 - timp.,perc.,cel. - 2 hp. - str.   11:00 FinnMICtr.
—— PARTITA FOR ORCHESTRA (1931) (IN 3 MOVTS.)
    2,2,2,2 - 4,2,2,0 - str.   13:00 FinnMICtr.
—— PRELUDE AND FUGUE (1933)
    2,2,3,2 - 4,3,3,1 - str.   6:00 FinnMICtr.
—— SCHERZO (1937)
    3,2,2,2 - 4,3,3,1 - str.   10:00 FinnMICtr.
—— SERENADE (FOR VIOLIN AND STRINGS) (1914)
    str.   10:00 FinnMICtr.
—— SUITE FOR ORCH. (1924) (IN 3 MOVTS.)
    3,1,2,2 - 4,1,0,0 - cel. - 2 hp. - str.   FinnMICtr.
—— SYMPHONY NO. 1, OP. 5 (1916)
    2,2,2,2 - 4,3,3,1 - timp.,perc. - str.   31:00 FinnMICtr.
—— SYMPHONY NO. 3 (1953)
    3,2,3,2 - 4,4,3,1 - timp. - str.   21:00 FinnMICtr.
—— TEN LITTLE PIECES FOR ORCH. (1930)
    1,1,1,1 - 0,1,1,0 - perc. - harm. - pf. - str.   23:00 Fazer.
—— THEME, FIVE VARIATIONS AND FUGUE, OP. 8 (1915)
    2,2,2,2 - 4,3,3,1 - timp. - str.   23:00 FinnMICtr.

—— THREE MUSICAL IMPRESSIONS (1940)
2,2,2,2 - 4,2,0,0 - str.   9:00 FinnMICtr.
—— TWO ETUDES FOR ORCH. (1936)
*3,2,2,2 - 2,0,0,0 - cel. - 2 hp. - str.(2,1,1,1)   6:00 FinnMICtr.
—— TWO ORCHESTRAL PIECES (1941)
2,2,2,2 - 4,2,1,0 - timp. - str.   10:00 FinnMICtr.

MERIKANTO, Oskar
—— ELINA'S DEATH (OPERA) % (1910) (Text: G. V. Numers and J. Finne)
2,2,2,2 - 2,1,2,0 - timp. - hp. - org. - str.   FinnMICtr.
—— REGINA VON EMMERITZ (OPERA) % (1920) (Text: Z. Topelius and Composer)
2,2,2,2 - 4,2,3,1 - timp.,perc.,bells - hp. - str.   FinnMICtr.
—— TABLEAU MUSIC (1906)
2,1,2,1 - 2,1,1,0 - timp. - str.   12:00 FinnMICtr.

MERILÄINEN, Usko
—— ARIUS (MUSIC FROM THE BALLET "THE PROCESSION OF THE REEDS") % (1960)
3,2,3,3 - 4,3,3,1 - timp.,perc.(3) - pf. - str.   90:00 FinnMICtr.
—— ARIUS: SUITE NO. 1 (1960)
3,2,3,3 - 4,3,3,1 - timp.,perc.(3) - pf. - str.   21:00 FinnMICtr.
—— ARIUS: SUITE NO. 2 (1962)
3,2,3,3 - 4,3,3,1 - timp.,perc.(3) - pf. - str.   22:00 FinnMICtr.
—— CHAMBER CONCERTO (FOR VIOLIN AND SMALL ORCH.) (1962)
timp.,perc. - 2 hp. - str.   18:00 FinnMICtr.
—— CONCERTO FOR ORCHESTRA (1956)
3,2,3,2 - 4,2,3,1 - timp.,perc.(3) - str.   21:00 FinnMICtr.
—— CONCERTO FOR 13 STRINGS (1971)
str.   15:00 FinnMICtr.
—— CONCERTO NO. 1 FOR PIANO AND ORCH. (1956)
3,2,3,2 - 4,2,3,1 - timp.,perc. - pf. - str.   20:00 FinnMICtr.
—— CONCERTO NO. 2 FOR PIANO AND ORCH. (1969)
3,2,3,2 - 4,2,3,1 - timp.,perc.(3) - str.   15:00 FinnMICtr.
—— EROS AND PSYCHE (MUSIC FOR A STATE PRODUCTION) % (1960)
1,1,1,1 - 0,2,1,0 - timp. - tape-recorder - hp. - 1 vla.,1 c.   20:00 FinnMICtr.
—— INTRODUCTION AND VARIATIONS (FROM THE BALLET "ARIUS") (1964)
3,2,3,2 - 4,4,3,1 - timp.,perc.(3) - pf. - str.   12:00 FinnMICtr.
—— MIST (1952)
3,2,3,2 - 4,3,3,1 - timp.,perc. - hp. - str.   10:00 FinnMICtr.
—— MUSIQUE DU PRINTEMPS (1969)
2,2,2,2 - 2,2,2,0 - perc. - str.   10:00 FinnMICtr.
—— SYMPHONY NO. 1 (1955)
2,2,2,2 - 4,2,2,0 - timp.,perc. - str.   22:00 FinnMICtr.
—— SYMPHONY NO. 3
1. Andante; 2. Lento assai; 3. Allegro giocoso
3,2,3,3 - 4,2,3,0 - timp.,perc.(3), cel. - str.   25:00 FinnMICtr.
—— SYMPHONY NO. 3 (1971)
3,2,3,3 - 4,2,3,1 - timp.,perc.(3),cel. - str.   23:00 FinnMICtr.

MERKU, Pavle
—— BAROQUE OVERTURE (FOR DOUBLE STRING ORCH., PIANO AND PERCUSSION)
perc. - pf. - str.   8:00 Hans Gerig.
—— CONCERTINO FOR SMALL ORCH.
1(alt. with picc.),1,1,1 - 1,1,1,0 - timp.,perc.(3) - str.   10:00 Hans Gerig.
—— CONCERTO FOR TRUMPET AND ORCH.
0,1(alt. with Eng. hn.),1(alt. with E♭cl. and b.-cl.),1(alt. with c.-bn.) - 0,1,0,0 - timp.,perc.(2) - str.   13:00 Hans Gerig.
—— CONCERTO FOR VIOLIN AND ORCH.
1(alt. with picc.),1(alt. with Eng. hn.),1(alt. with b.-cl.),1(alt. with c.-bn.) - 4,3,3,1 - timp.,perc. - pf. - str.   10:00 Hans Gerig.
—— CONCERTO LIRICO (FOR CLARINET AND ORCH.)
Leeds.
—— DIVERTIMENTO NO. 1 (SIX SONGS FOR TENOR AND CHAMBER ORCH.)
1,1,1,1 - 1,1,1,0 - perc. - hp. - pf. - str.   9:00 Hans Gerig.
—— DIVERTIMENTO NO. 2 (FOR TENOR AND CHAMBER ORCH.)
1,1,1,1 - 1,1,1,0 - perc. - hp. - pf. - str.   10:00 Hans Gerig.
—— MUSICA PER ARCHI (MUSIC FOR STRINGS)
str.   Leeds.

MERRICK, Frank
—— CELTIC SUITE (1920)
2,2,2,2 - 2,2,0,0 - str.   15:00 P.R.S.

—— CONCERTO NO. 1 IN B FLAT, FOR PIANO AND ORCH. (1906)
2,2,2,2 - 2,2,0,0 - timp. - pf. - str.   30:00 P.R.S.
—— CONCERTO NO. 2 IN E MINOR, FOR PIANO AND ORCH.
2,2,2,2 - 2,2,0,0 - timp.,perc. - pf. - str.   34:00 P.R.S.
—— A DREAM PAGEANT FOR STRINGS
str.   6:00 P.R.S.
—— OVERTURE
2,2,2,2 - 4,2,0,0 - timp. - str.   12:00 P.R.S.
—— SYMPHONY IN D MINOR (1912)
2,2,2,2 - 4,2,3,0 - timp.,perc. - str.   34:00 P.R.S.
—— TWO MOVEMENTS IN SYMPHONIC FORM
2,2,2,2 - 2,2,3,0 - timp. - str.   17:00 Oxford.

MERRIFIELD, Norman L.
—— SYMPHONY IN F MINOR
1. Andante maestoso; 2. Andante sostenuto; 3. Allegretto;
4. Allegro ma non troppo
2,*3,2,2-*3 - 4,2,3,1 - timp.,perc.(2) - hp. - str.   40:00 Composer.

MERSSON, Boris
—— CONCERTO FÜR KLAVIER UND ORCHESTER, OP. 29
2,2,3,2 - 4,3,3,1 - timp.,perc.,cel. - hp. - str.   16:00 S.U.I.S.A.
—— DIVERTIMENTO, OP. 12 (IN 4 MOVTS.)
2(2nd alt. with picc.),1(alt. with Eng. hn.),1,1 - 0,1,0,0 - timp.,perc.,glock.,xyl. - hpsc.(or pf.) - str.   11:00 Modern.
—— EYTAN-RHAPSODY
3,3,3,3 - 2,3,4,0 - timp.,perc.,cel. - hp. - str.   22:00 Riccardo.
—— FLUIDUM II, OP. 26 (FÜR 12 INSTRUMENTE)
11:00 S.U.I.S.A.
—— KONZERT FUR ALTSAXOPHON UND ORCHESTER OP. 25
16:00 S.U.I.S.A.
—— NOCTURNE (FOR VIOLIN AND STRING ORCH.)
str.   6:45 Modern.
—— SNOBISSIMO (DIVERTISSEMENT SYMPHONIQUE)
2,2,2,5 sax., 2 - 2,4,4,1 - timp.,perc. - quit. - cemb. - pf. - hp. - str.   5:10 S.U.I.S.A.

MESRITZ-VAN VELTHUYSEN, Anny
—— LIEDEREN (3 SONGS FOR SOPRANO AND ORCH.) (1938) (Texts: Ch. van Lerberghe)
2,2,2,2 - 2,2,0,0 - cel. - hp. - str.   8:00 Henmar.

MESSIAEN, Olivier
—— L' ASCENSION (4 MEDITATIONS)
3,3,3,3 - 4,3,3,1 - timp.,perc. - str.   30:00 Baron.
or:
2,*2,*2,2 - 4,2,3,1 - timp.,perc.(3) - str.
—— HYMNE
3,*3,3,3 - 4,3,3,0 - timp.,perc. - str.   12:00 Broude.
—— LES OFFRANDES OUBLIÉES (SYMPHONIC MEDITATIONS)
3,*3,3,3 - 4,3,3,1 - perc.,cel.,xyl. - pf. - str.   7:00 EV.
—— POÈMES POUR MI (FOR SOPRANO AND ORCH.)
3,3,3,4 - 4,3,3,1 - timp.,perc. - str.   26:30 EV.
—— REVEIL DES OISEAUX (FOR PIANO AND ORCH.)
*4,*3,4,3 - 2,2,0,0 - perc.,cel.,xyl. - pf. - str.   22:00 EV.
—— LE TOMBEAU RESPLENDISSANT
3,3,3,3 - 4,3,3,1 - timp.,perc.(4) - str.   12:00 EV.
—— TROIS PETITES LITURGIES DE LA PRÉSENCE DIVINE (FOR 3-PART WOMEN'S CHORUS AND SMALL ORCH.)
perc.(3),cel.,vibra - ondes martenot - pf. - str.   35:00 EV.
—— TURANGALILA (SYMPHONY FOR PIANO AND ORCH.)
3,*3,3,3 - 4,5,3,1 - timp.,perc.(5),bells,cel.,vibra. - ondes martenot - pf. - str.   80:00 EV.

MESTRAL, Patrice
—— ALLIAGES (CONCERTO FOR TRUMPET AND 11 INSTRUMENTS)
1,0,1,alto sax.,0 - 0,1,2,0 - org. - pf. - 3 d.-b.   13:00 Presser.
—— BLOCS LUMINEUX (FOR SATB CHORUS AND 16 INSTRUMENTS)
4,0,0,0 - 0,4,2,0 - perc.(6)   12:00 Presser.
—— DISSENSIONS-INSERTIONS
3,3,3,3 - 4,3,3,1 - perc.(7) - 2 hp. - 2 pf. - str.   19:00 Presser.
—— ELEMENTS
3,3,3,3 - 4,3,3,1 - perc.(7) - 2 hp. - pf. - str.   18:00 Presser.
—— RELATIONS II
2,1,0,0 - 0,2,2,0 - perc.(3) - hp. - pf. - str.   11:40 Presser.
—— SURFACES GRANULÉES
2,2,2,2 - 2,2,1,0 - timp.,perc.(2) - hp. - str.   16:00 Presser.

MESTRES-QUADRENY, Josep Maria
—— ARONADA, 1972 (FOR ANY NUMBER AND TYPE OF
INSTRUMENTS)
Seesaw.
—— DOUBLE CONCERTO (FOR ONDES-MARTENOT,
PERCUSSION AND ORCH.) (1970)
3,3,4,3 - 4,3,3,1 - timp.,perc. - ondes-martenot - str. 12:00 Seesaw.
—— FRIGOLI - FRIGOLA (1972) (FOR ANY NUMBER AND TYPE
OF INSTRUMENTS)
Seesaw.
—— LITTLE SUNDAY (1962)
4,2,5,3 - 4,4,4,1 - perc.(3) - str. 15:00 Seesaw.
—— ROBA I OSSOS (THINGS AND BONES)
4,2,3,2 - 2,2,2,1 - perc.(3) - str. 15:00 Seesaw.
—— SUBMERGED VEGETATION
2,2,2,1 - sax.,2 - 2,2,2,1 - tape-recorder - str. 12:00 Seesaw.

METRAL, Pierre
—— CONCERTINO FOR FLUTE, HARP AND STRINGS
fl. - hp. - str. Seesaw.
—— CONCERTINO POUR FLÛTE, HARPE ET ORCHESTRE À
CORDES
fl. - hp. - str. 13:30 S.U.I.S.A.
—— CONCERTO FOR PERCUSSION AND ORCH.
2,2,2,2 - 4,3,3,1 - perc. - hp. - pf. - str. 25:00 Seesaw.
—— VARIATIONS DÉCONCERTANTES SUR "GAMLEC"
0,0,4,0 - 0,3,1,0 - perc.(2) - str. 14:30 S.U.I.S.A.
—— VILLES (1970) (CANTATA) (FOR 3 SOLO VOICES, 4
PERCUSSIONISTS, AND 13 INSTRUMENTS)
16:00 Seesaw.

METZLER, Friedrich
—— CONCERTO FOR FLUTE AND ORCH.
3,1(alt. with Eng.hn.),2,1 - 2,1,0,0 - hp. - str. 17:00 Henmar.
—— O LOVE, SWEET NAME (CANTATA, AFTER THE
MINNESINGERS) (FOR SOLO VOICES, MIXED CHORUS
AND ORCH.)
4,3,2,2 - 4,2,3,1 - timp.,perc. - str. 28:00 F. Colombo.

MEULEMANS, Arthur
—— ACADEMISCHE TRIPTIEK (1955)
2,2,2,2 - 4,2,3,1 - timp.,perc.,glock. - hp. - str. 14:00 H. Elkan.
—— ADAGIO (1939)
str. 10:00 H. Elkan.
—— ADRIAEN BROUWER (OVERTURE) (1935)
3,3,3,3 - 4,3,3,1 - timp.,perc.glock. - hp. - str. 8:00 H. Elkan.
—— ANDANTE SYMPHONIQUE (1939)
2,3,2,2 - 4,3,3,1 - timp.,perc. - hp. - str. 7:00 H. Elkan.
—— BROOSEIND (FROM "TWEE ZOMERPASTORALES") (1941)
2,1,2,1 - 2,2,1,0 - timp.,perc. - hp. - hpsc. - str. 6:00 H. Elkan.
—— CONCERT-IMPROMPTU (FOR PIANO AND ORCH.) (1929)
2,2,2,2 - 2,0,0,0 - timp.,perc. - pf. - str. 5:00 H. Elkan.
—— CONCERTINO FOR PIANO AND ORCH. (1942)
2,2,2,2 - 2,2,2,0 - timp.,perc. - pf. - str. 11:00 H. Elkan.
—— CONCERTINO FOR TROMBONE AND ORCH. (1953)
2,2,2,2 - 2,2,3,0 - timp.,perc.,glock.,xyl. - str. 16:00 H. Elkan.
—— CONCERTO FOR FLUTE AND ORCH. (1942)
2,2,2,2 - 2,2,0,0 - timp.,perc.,glock. - str. 13:00 H. Elkan.
—— CONCERTO FOR HARP AND ORCH. (1953)
2,2,2,1 alto sax.,2 - 2,2,1,0 - timp.,perc.,cel.glock.,xyl. - hp. - str.
20:00 H. Elkan.
—— CONCERTO FOR HARPSICHORD AND ORCH. (1958)
2,2,2,2 - 2,2,1,0 - timp.,perc.,cel.,glock.,xyl. - hp. - hpsc. - str.
20:00 H. Elkan.
—— CONCERTO FOR HORN AND ORCH. (1940)
3,2,2,2 - 4,3,3,0 - timp.,perc.,glock. - hp. - str. 18:00 H. Elkan.
—— CONCERTO FOR OBOE AND ORCH. (1942)
2,*2,2,2 - 2,2,0,0 - timp.,perc. - str. 12:00 H. Elkan.
—— CONCERTO FOR ORCHESTRA (1953)
3,3,3,3 - 4,3,3,1 - timp.,perc.,glock.,cel.,xyl. - 2 hp. - str.
20:00 CBDM.
—— CONCERTO FOR TIMPANI AND ORCH. (1954)
2,2,2,2 - 4,2,3,1 - timp.,perc.,glock. - hp. - str. 18:00 H. Elkan.
—— CONCERTO FOR TRUMPET AND ORCH. (1943)
2,2,2,2 - 4,3,3,0 - timp.,glock. - hp. - str. 15:00 H. Elkan.
—— CONCERTO FOR VIOLA AND ORCH. (1942)
3,2,2,2 - 2,2,0,0 - timp.,perc. - str. 22:00 H. Elkan.
—— CONCERTO GROSSO FOR 4 SAXOPHONES AND ORCH.
(1958)
4 sax. - timp.,perc.,glock. - hp. - str. 18:00 H. Elkan.
—— CONCERTO NO. 1 FOR CELLO AND ORCH. (1920)
2,3,3,2 - 4,3,3,1 - timp.,perc.,cel.,glock. - hp. - str.
15:00 H. Elkan.

—— CONCERTO NO. 1 FOR ORGAN AND ORCH. (1942)
3,3,3,3 - 4,3,3,1 - timp.,perc. - hp. - org. - str. 28:00 H. Elkan.
—— CONCERTO NO. 1 FOR PIANO AND ORCH (1941)
2,2,2,2 - 4,3,3,1 - timp.,perc. - hp. - pf. - str. 20:00 H. Elkan.
—— CONCERTO NO. 1 FOR VIOLIN AND ORCH. (1942)
2,2,2,2 - 4,2,0,0 - timp.,perc. - str. 22:00 H. Elkan.
—— CONCERTO NO. 2 FOR CELLO AND ORCH. (1944)
2,2,2,2 - 3,2,0,0 - timp.,perc. - str. 15:00 H. Elkan.
—— CONCERTO NO. 2 FOR HORN AND ORCH. (1961)
2,2,2,2 - 3,2,2,0 - timp.,perc. - str. 16:00 H. Elkan.
—— CONCERTO NO. 2 FOR ORCH. (1956)
3,3,3,3 - 4,3,3,1 - timp.,perc.,cel.,glock.,xyl. - 2 hp. - str.
25:00 H. Elkan.
—— CONCERTO NO. 2 FOR ORGAN AND ORCH. (1958)
2,2,2,2 - 4,2,3,1 - timp.,perc.glock. - hp. - org. - str.
20:00 H. Elkan.
—— CONCERTO NO. 2 FOR PIANO AND ORCH. (1956)
2,2,2,2 - 4,2,3,1 - timp.,perc.,glock. - hp. - pf. - str.
25:00 H. Elkan.
—— CONCERTO NO. 2 FOR VIOLIN AND ORCH. (1946)
2,2,2,2 - 4,2,1,0 - timp.,perc.,glock. - hp. - str. 22:00 H. Elkan.
—— CONCERTO NO. 3 FOR VIOLIN AND ORCH. (1950)
2,2,2,2 - 4,2,3,1 - timp.,perc.,cel. - hp. - str. 22:00 H. Elkan.
—— DANCE SUITE NO. 1 (1943)
2,1,2,1 - 2,2,1,0 - timp.,perc.,cel.,glock. - hp. - pf. - str.
20:00 H. Elkan.
—— DANCE SUITE NO. 2 (1943)
2,1,2,1 - 2,2,1,0 - timp.,perc.,bells.,cel.,glock.,xyl. - hp. - pf. - str.
18:00 H. Elkan.
—— DIVERTIMENTO (FOR MIXED CHORUS AND ORCH.) (1958)
2,2,2,2 - 4,2,3,1 - timp.,perc.,glock. - pf. - str. 20:00 H. Elkan.
—— EGMONT (OVERTURE) (1944)
3,3,3,2 - 4,3,3,1 - timp.,perc.,cel.,glock. - str. 6:00 H. Elkan.
—— ESQUISSES SYMPHONIQUES (1958)
2,2,2,2 - 4,2,3,1 - timp.,perc.,glock.,xyl. - str. 25:00 H. Elkan.
—— ÉVASIONS (1954)
2,2,2,2,c.-bn.(ad lib.) - 4,3,3,1 - timp.,perc.,glock. - hp. - str.
11:00 CBDM.
—— FOUR SYMPHONIC SKETCHES (1940)
3,3,2,2 - 4,3,3,0 - timp.,perc. - 2 hp. - str. 21:30 H. Elkan.
—— FUSILLÉ À L'AUBE (SYMPHONIC POEM) (1948)
3,3,3,3 - 4,3,3,1 - timp.,perc. bells,cel.,glock.,xyl. - 2 hp. - org. -
str. 15:00 H. Elkan.
—— GYPSY (FOR VIOLIN AND ORCH.) (1927)
2,2,2,3 - 4,3,3,0 - timp.,perc. - hp. - pf. - str. 7:00 H. Elkan.
—— HEIDESCHETSEN (PETITE SUITE) (1922)
2,2,2,2 - 2,1,0,0 - timp.,perc.,cel.,glock.,xyl. - hp. - str.
11:00 H. Elkan.
—— HERTOG JAN VAN BRABANT (SUITE) (FOR BARITONE
AND ORCH.) (1953)
3,2,2,1 alto sax, 2 - 4,3,3,1 - timp.,perc.,bells,cel.,glock.,xyl. - hp. -
str. 20:00 H. Elkan.
—— DE HOOGE MOUW (FROM "TWEE ZOMERPASTORALES")
(FOR VOCAL QUARTET AND ORCH.) (1944)
2,1,1,1 - 1,1,0,0 - perc. - org. - str. 6:00 H. Elkan.
—— IONISATIE (CHOREOGRAPHIC MOVTS.) (1956)
3,3,3,1 alto sax.,3 - 4,3,3,1 - timp.,perc.,cel.,glock.,xyl. - 2 hp. - str.
20:00 H. Elkan.
—— JOSAPHAT PARK (SUITE DE BALLET) (1933)
2,2,2,2 - 4,3,3,1 - timp.,perc.,cel.,glock.,xyl. - hp. - pf. - str.
18:00 H. Elkan.
—— KARNAVAL-SUITE (FOR PIANO AND ORCH.) (1926)
2,2,2,2 - 4,2,3,1 - timp.,perc.,bells,cel.,glock.,xyl. - pf. - str.
20:00 H. Elkan.
—— KERMIS (FANTASY) (1930)
3,2,2,2 - 4,3,3,1 - timp.,perc.,bells,cel.,glock.,xyl. - hp. - str.
5:00 H. Elkan.
—— KLEINE SUITE IN C (1930)
2,1,2,1 alto sax.,1 - 2,2,1,0 - timp.,perc.,bells,cel.,glock.,xyl. - pf. -
str. 7:00 H. Elkan.
—— LYRISCHE SUITE (FOR HARP AND ORCH.) (1939)
2,2,2,2 - 4,3,3,0 - timp.,perc.,xyl. - hp. - str. 8:00 H. Elkan.
—— MEINACHT (1912)
3,3,3,2 - 4,3,3,1 - timp.,perc.,cel.,glock. - 2 hp. - str.
10:30 H. Elkan.
—— METEOROLOGISCH INSTITUUT (1951)
3,3,3,3 - 4,3,3,1 - timp.,perc.,cel.,glock.,xyl. - 2 hp. - str.
20:00 H. Elkan.
—— OP DE DENNENHEUVELEN (PRELUDE) (1948)
3,3,2,2 - 4,3,3,0 - timp.,perc.,glock. - hp. - str. 11:00 H. Elkan.
—— OVERTURA ALLEGRA (1940)
2,2,2,2 - 4,3,3,1 - timp.,perc.,glock.,xyl. - hp. - str. 6:30 H. Elkan.

—— OVERTURE TO THE OPERA "THE VIKINGS" (1934)
3,3,2,2 - 4,3,3,1 - timp.,perc.,cel.,glock. - hp. - str. 8:00 H. Elkan.
—— PETER BREUGHEL (SUITE) (1952)
3,2,2,2 - 4,3,3,1 - timp.,perc.,glock.,xyl. - hp. - str.
15:00 H. Elkan.
—— PLINIUS FONTEIN (1914)
4,3,3,4 - 4,3,3,1 - timp.,perc.,glock.,cel.,xyl. - hp. - str.
18:00 CBDM.
—— PRELUDIËN (PETITE SUITE) (1916)
1,1,1,1 - 1,0,0,0 - perc.,cel.,xyl. - str. 11:00 H. Elkan.
—— RELAIS (SUITE) (1957) (IN 3 MOVTS.)
2,2,3,1 alto sax.,2 - 4,3,3,1 - timp.,perc.,glock.,xyl. - hp. - str.
18:00 H. Elkan.
—— RHAPSODY FOR ALTO SAXOPHONE AND ORCH. (1942)
2,2,2,1 alto sax.,2 - 4,2,3,0 - timp.,perc.,glock. - hp. - str.
5:30 Gervan.
—— RHAPSODY FOR BASSOON AND ORCH. (1942)
2,2,2,2 - 4,2,0,0 - timp.,perc. - hp. - str. 6:00 H. Elkan.
—— RHAPSODY FOR CLARINET AND ORCH. (1932)
2,2,3,2 - 4,2,3,1 - timp.,perc.,cel.,glock.,xyl. - hp. - str.
7:00 Gervan.
—— RHAPSODY FOR TROMBONE AND ORCH. (1941)
2,2,2,2 - 4,2,1,0 - timp.,perc. - hp. - str. 6:00 Gervan.
—— RHAPSODY (1929)
3,3,2,2 - 4,3,3,1 - timp.,perc.,cel.,glock.,xyl. - 2 hp. - str.
7:00 H. Elkan.
—— RONDO SYMPHONIQUE (1954)
2,2,2,1 alto sax.(ad lib.),2 - 4,2,3,1 - timp.,perc.,glock. - hp. - str.
6:00 H. Elkan.
—— SACRALE DANS (FROM THE OPERA "THE VIKINGS") (FOR
MIXED CHORUS AND ORCH.) (1934)
3,3,2,3 - 4,3,3,1 - timp.,perc.,cel.,glock.,xyl. - hp. - org. - str.
7:00 H. Elkan.
—— SERENATA (1929)
2,2,2,3 - 4,3,3,1 - timp.,perc.,cel.,glock.,xyl. - hp. - str.
7:30 H. Elkan.
—— SOCIAL SECURITY (A MASQUERADE) (1954) %
2,2,2,2 - 4,2,3,1 - timp.,perc.,glock.,xyl. - hp. - str. 7:00 H. Elkan.
—— SONATA CONCERTANTE (1948)
cl. - str. 12:00 H. Elkan.
—— STADSPARK (PRELUDE AND SCHERZO) (1928)
3,2,3,3 - 4,4,3,1 - timp.,perc.,bells,cel.,glock.,xyl. - hp. - str.
7:30 Henmar.
—— DE STEEG (L'IMPASSE) (OVERTURE) (1958)
2,2,2,2 - 4,2,3,1 - timp.,perc.,glock.,xyl. - hp. - str.
10:00 H. Elkan.
—— SYMPHONIETTA (1952)
2,2,2,2 - 2,2,2,0 - timp.,perc.,glock. - str. 15:00 H. Elkan.
—— SYMPHONISCHE DANSEN (1957)
2,2,2,1 alto sax.,2 - 4,3,3,1 - timp.,perc.,cel.,glock.,xyl. - 2 hp. - str.
28:30 H. Elkan.
—— SYMPHONISCHE TRIPTIEK (1951)
3,3,2,1 alto sax.,3 - 4,3,3,1 - timp.,perc.,bells,glock.,xyl. - 2 hp. -
str. 19:00 H. Elkan.
—— SYMPHONY NO. 1 (1931)
3,3,3,2 - 4,3,3,1 - timp.,perc.,bells,cel.,glock.,xyl. - hp. - str.
15:30 H. Elkan.
—— SYMPHONY NO. 2 (1933)
3,3,3,2 - 4,3,3,1 - timp.,perc.,bells,cel.,glock.,xyl. - hp. - str.
19:00 H. Elkan.
—— SYMPHONY NO. 3 (DENNENSYMFONIE) (1933)
3,3,3,3 - 4,3,3,1 - timp.,perc.,bells,cel.,glock.,xyl. - 2 hp. - org.(ad
lib.) - pf. - str. 19:00 H. Elkan.
—— SYMPHONY NO. 4 (1935)
3,3,3,3 - 4,3,3,1 - timp.,perc.,bells,cel.,glock.,vibra.,xyl. - str.
15:00 H. Elkan.
—— SYMPHONY NO. 5 (DANSSYMFONIE) (FOR WOMEN'S
CHORUS AND ORCH.) (1939)
3,3,2,1 alto sax.,2 - 4,3,3,1 - timp.,perc.,cel.,glock.,xyl. - 2 hp. -
org. - pf. - str. 27:00 H. Elkan.
—— SYMPHONY NO. 6 (ZEESYMFONIE) (FOR CONTRALTO,
MIXED CHORUS AND ORCH.) (1940) (Text: F. Vercnocke)
3,3,3,3 - 4,3,3,1 - timp.,perc.,cel.,glock.,xyl. - 2 hp. - org. - str.
40:00 PABrussels.
—— SYMPHONY NO. 7 (ZWAHEVEN, EEN SYMFONIE VAN DE
HEIDE) (1942)
3,3,2,2 - 4,3,3,1 - timp.,perc.,cel.,glock.,xyl. - hp. - str.
28:00 H. Elkan.
—— SYMPHONY NO. 8 (HERFSTSYMFONIE) (FOR SOPRANO,
CONTRALTO, TENOR, BARITONE, MIXED CHORUS AND
ORCH.) (1942) (Text: C. S. Adama van Scheltema)
3,3,3,3 - 4,3,3,1 - timp.,perc.,cel.,glock.,xyl. - eoliphone - hp. - org.
- str. 30:00 H. Elkan.

—— SYMPHONY NO. 9 (1943)
3,3,3,3 - 4,3,3,1 - timp.,perc.,cel.,glock. - 2 hp. - str.
30:00 H. Elkan.
—— SYMPHONY NO. 10 (PSALMEN-SYMFONIE) (FOR 5 VOICES,
CHORUS AND ORCH.) (1943)
2,2,2,2 - 4,3,3,1 - timp.,perc.,bells,glock. - hp. - org. - str.
60:00 H. Elkan.
—— SYMPHONY NO. 11 (1946)
3,3,3,3 - 4,3,3,1 - timp.,perc.,cel.,glock.,xyl. - 2 hp. - str.
31:00 H. Elkan.
—— SYMPHONY NO. 12 (1948)
3,3,3,3 - 4,3,3,1 - timp.,perc.,bells,cel.,glock.,xyl. - 2 hp. - org. -
str. 31:00 H. Elkan.
—— SYMPHONY NO. 13 ("REMBRANDT SYMFONIE") (1950)
3,3,3,3 - 4,3,3,1 - timp.,perc.,glock.,cel. - 2 hp. - org. - str.
30:00 CBDM.
—— SYMPHONY NO. 14 (1954)
2,2,2,2-*3 - 4,3,3,1 - timp.,perc.,cel.,glock. - hp. - str.
25:00 H. Elkan.
—— TABLEAUX (1952)
3,3,3,1 alto sax.,3 - 4,3,3,1 - timp.,perc.,glock. - 2 hp. - str.
20:00 H. Elkan.
—— TARTARIN DE TARASCON (OVERTURE) (1955)
2,2,2,2 - 4,2,3,1 - timp.,perc.,glock.,xyl. - hp. - str.
10:00 H. Elkan.
—— UIT HET KINDERLEVEN (1932)
1,1,2,1 - 2,2,1,0 - timp.,perc.,bells,cel.,glock.,xyl. - hp. (or pf.) - str.
10:00 H. Elkan.
—— VARIATIONS FOR PIANO AND ORCH. (1945)
2,3,3,2 - 4,3,3,1 - timp.,perc.,cel.,glock. - pf. - str. 18:00 H. Elkan.
—— VERWORVENHEDEN (SYMPHONIC POEM) (1939)
3,3,3,3 - 4,3,3,1 - timp.,perc.,cel.,glock. - 2 hp. - str.
15:00 H. Elkan.
—— VIJF STUKKEN (FIVE PIECES) (1941)
3,3,3,3 - 4,3,3,1 - timp.,perc.,cel.,glock. - 2 hp. - str.
11:00 H. Elkan.
—— VLAAMSE RAPSODIE (1932)
3,3,3,3 - 4,3,3,1 - timp.,perc.,bells,cel.,glock.,vibra.,xyl. - 2 hp. - str.
10:15 H. Elkan.
—— DE VOGELS (SUITE DE BALLET) (1947)
2,2,2,2 - 4,3,3,0 - timp.,perc.,bells,cel.,glock.,xyl. - hp. - str.
18:00 H. Elkan.
—— DE WITTE (FOR MIXED CHORUS AND ORCH.) (1949)
3,3,3,3 - 4,3,3,1 - timp.,perc.,bells,cel.,glock.,xyl. - 2 hp. - org. -
str. 18:00 H. Elkan.
—— WOUDZANG (FOR VIOLIN AND ORCH.) (1927)
2,2,2,3 - 4,0,0,0 - timp.,perc. - hp. - pf. - str. 6:00 H. Elkan.

MEYER, Ernst H.
—— DIVERTIMENTO CONCERTANTE (1973)
2,3,3,2 - 4,3,3,0 - timp.,perc. - hp. - str. 20:00 Tetra.
—— KLEINE ERÖFFNUNGSMUSIK (A LITTLE INAUGURATION
MUSIC)
cl. - str. Tetra.
—— POEM (FOR VIOLA AND ORCH.)
2,2,2,2 - 4,2,1,0 - timp.,perc. - hp. - str. 14:00 Tetra.
—— SONG OF YOUTH (FOR SOPRANO, SATB CHORUS AND
ORCH., WITH BARITONE OR MEZZO-SOPRANO) (IN 7
MOVEMENTS) (Text: Louis Fürnberg)
2,2,2,2 - 3,3,1,0 - timp.,perc. - hp. - str. Tetra.

MEYER, Pierre
—— POUR 11 (ETUDE CONCERTANTE)
perc.(2) - pf. - str.(1,4,0,3) 17:00 Presser.

MEYERBEER - LAMBERT, Constant
—— LES PATINEURS (BALLET SUITE)
2,2,2,2 - 2,4,2,3 - timp.,perc. - hp. - pf. - str. 12:00 Bo. Hawkes.

MEYERBEER - SAMINSKY, Lazare
—— SCENE FROM "THE PROPHET" (FOR DRAMATIC SOPRANO,
CHORUS AND ORCH.)
6:30 Arranger.

MEYEROVICH, Mikhail
—— THE VIOLIN AND UN POCO NERVOSAMENTE (BALLET
SCENE FOR ORCH.)
G. Schirmer.

MEYEROWITZ, Jan
—— THE GLORY AROUND HIS HEAD (EASTERN CANTATA)
(FOR SOLOISTS, CHORUS AND ORCH.)
2,2,2,2 - 4,3,3,1 - timp.,perc.(2),xyl. - hp. - org. - str.
23:00 Broude.
or:
2,2,2,2 - 2,2,1,0 - timp.,perc.(2),xyl. - hp. - str.
—— MUSIC FOR CHRISTMAS (CANTATA) (FOR SOLOISTS,
CHORUS AND ORCH.)
2,2,2,2 - 4,3,2,1 - timp.,perc.(2),glock.,mar. - hp. - str.
23:00 Broude.
or:
2,2,2,2 - 2,2,2,0 - timp.,perc.(2),glock,mar. - hp. - str.
—— NEW PLYMOUTH CANTATA (FOR SOLOISTS, CHORUS
AND ORCH.)
2,0,2,2 - 2,2,2,1 - timp.,perc.(2),vibra.,xyl. - hp. - str.
20:00 Broude.
—— TWO LITANIES (FOR WOMEN'S CHORUS AND 11 INSTS.)
1,1,2,0 - 0,0,0,0 - hp.(or pf.) - str.
8:00 Broude.

MEYERS, H. Emerson
—— CONCERTINO FOR PIANO AND ORCH. (1949)
23:00 Composer.
—— DOLCEDO (OPERA) % (1959)
28:30 Composer.
—— SARABANDE (1940)
6:00 Composer.
—— SYMPHONY NO. 1 (FOR SMALL ORCH.) (1953)
23:00 Composer.

MEZŐ, Imre
—— VARIATIONS
Bo. Hawkes.

MIARI, Giangiacomo
—— CONCERTO FOR CONTRABASS AND STRING ORCH.
str.
12:00 Henmar.

MIASKOVSKY, Nikolai Y. - SHELDON, Harold
—— SYMPHONY NO. 21, OP. 51 (IN 1 MOVT.)
*3,*3,*3,*3 - 4,3,3,1 - timp. - str.
20:00 G. Schirmer.
—— SYMPHONY NO. 22, OP. 54 (IN 1 MOVT.)
*3,*3,*3 - 4,3,3,1 - timp.,perc.(4) - str.
36:00 G. Schirmer.
—— SYMPHONY NO. 27 IN C MINOR, OP. 85
3,3,3,3 - 4,3,3,1 - timp.,perc. - str.
34:00 G. Schirmer.

MICHAEL, Edward
—— LE FESTIN DES DIEUX, OP. 20
2,2,2,2 - 4,2,2,1 - timp.,perc.(4) - hp. - pf. - str.
6:00 Henmar.
—— INITIATION SUR LES MODES ANCIENS
str.
21:00 Henmar.
—— KAMAAL, OP. 18 (A SYMPHONIC TALE FOR NARRATOR
AND ORCH.) (Text: Composer)
2,2,2,2 - 2,2,2,0 - timp.,perc.,cel.,glock. - hp. - pf. - str.
40:00 Presser.
—— NOCTURE FOR FLUTE AND ORCH.
1,0,2,2 - 2,0,1,0 - trgl.,cel.,glock. - hp. - str.
6:00 Presser.
—— RAPSODIE CONCERTANTE, OP. 17 (FOR VIOLIN AND
ORCH.)
3,2,2,2 - 2,2,2,1 - timp.,perc.(4),cel. - str.
13:00 Henmar.
—— LA REINE DES PLUIES, OP. 19 (CHOREOGRAPHIC POEM) %
2,2,2,3 - 4,2,2,1 - timp.,perc.(5),cel. - hp. - pf. - str. 9:00 Henmar.
—— LE RÊVE D'HIMALEC
2,2,2,2 - 2,2,2,0 - timp.,perc.,cel. - hp. - pf. - str. 14:00 Presser.
—— LES SOIRÉES DE TEDJLAH (WITH OPTIONAL FEMALE
VOICE)
2,1,0,0 - 0,0,0,0 - pf. - str.
20:00 Presser.
—— THREE TABLEAUX FOR ORCH., OP. 11
(STÉRÉOPHONIQUE)
2,2,2,2 - 4,2,2,0 - timp.,perc.(3),cel.,glock. - hp. - str.
11:00 Presser.

MICHAELIDES, Peter
—— FORCES IV (1972)
2,0,2,0 - 4,3,3,1 - perc.(2) - str.
15:00 Seesaw.

MICHAELIDES, Solon
—— DEUX IMAGES SYMPHONIQUES (1959)
2,2,2,1 - 4,2,2,1 - timp.,perc. - hp. - str.
12:00 Seesaw.
—— SUITE ARCHAÏQUE (1955)
1,1,0,0 - 0,0,0,0 - hp. - str.
15:00 Seesaw.

MICHALSKY, Donal
—— FANFARE (AFTER 17TH-CENTURY DANCES OF PAUL
PEURL, JOHANN H. SCHEIN AND ISAAK POSCH) (ARR.
1965) (IN 3 MOVTS.)
2(1 alt. with picc.),*2,2(1 alt. with b.-cl.),2 - 2,1,1,0
6:15 Shawnee.
—— FANTASIA FOR STRING ORCH. (1967)
str.
8:00 Composer.
—— PARTITA (FOR OBOE D'AMORE, STRING TRIO AND
STRING ORCH.) (1956) (IN 4 MOVTS.)
ob. d'amore - str.
15:00 Composer.
—— SINFONIA CONCERTANTE (FOR CLARINET, PIANO AND
ORCH.) (1968) (IN 3 MOVTS.)
20:00 Composer.
—— SIX PIECES FOR CHAMBER ORCH. (1954)
1,1,2,1 - 2,1,0,0 - perc. - hp. - str.
16:00 Composer.
—— SYMPHONY NO. 3 (FOR LARGE ORCH.) (1975)
24:00 Composer.

MICHEELSEN, Hans Friedrich
—— INTRODUCTION, TOCCATA AND PASSACAGLIA (1957)
2(2nd alt. with picc.),2,2,2 - 4,2,3,1 - timp.,perc.(3) - str.
12:00 G. Schirmer.
—— LAND OF MY FATHERS (ORATORIO) (FOR ALTO, MALE
CHORUS AND ORCH.)
1,1,1,1 - 2,1,1,0 - timp.,perc. - str.   60:00 F. Colombo.

MICHEL, Paul-Baudouin
—— LA BOITE DE PANDORE (SUITE FOR ORCH.)
3,3,3,alto. sax.,3 - 4,2,3,1 - timp.,perc. - str.   H. Elkan.
—— CONCATENATION (FOR CHAMBER ORCH.) (1967)
2,1,2,1 - 2,2,1,0 - perc.(2) - str.   16:00 H. Elkan.
—— CONFLUENCES (FOR CHAMBER ORCH.) (1974)
2,1,1,1 - 2,1,1,0 - perc.(2) - pf. - str.   12:00 H. Elkan.
—— HORS-TEMPS (1970)
3,3,4,alto. sax, 3 - 4,2,3,1 - timp.,perc. - tape-recorder - str.
50:00 H. Elkan.
—— TOREUTIQUE IV (1972)
3,3,4,3 - 6,3,3,1 - timp.,perc.(4) - str.   15:30 H. Elkan.

MICHELET, Michel
—— CATHEDRAL WINDOWS (ORATORIO IN 4 PARTS) (FOR 5
SOLO VOICES, CHORUS, ORGAN AND ORCH.) (Text: John
Rufus Sharpe III)
120:00 S.A.C.E.M.

MIDDELEER, Jean De
—— RECITATIVO E ALLEGRO (1970)
2,1,2,1 - 2,2,3,0 - timp.,perc. - str.   H. Elkan.

MIDDLETON, Jean B.
—— SYMPHONY IN C
3,3,3,2 - 4,2,3,1 - timp.,perc., - str.   16:00 Bo. Hawkes.

MIDDLETON, John
—— MUSIC FOR HORN AND STRING ORCH.
hn. - str.   6:30 P.R.S.

MIDDLETON, Owen
—— SYMPHONY IN ONE MOVEMENT (1965)
0,0,0,0 - 4,2,3,1 - timp.,perc.(3),xyl. - str.   18:00 Composer.

MIDGLEY, Charles
—— SYMPHONY NO. 1 IN C MAJOR ("PEACE") (IN 4 MOVTS.)
4(4th alt. with picc.),3(3rd alt. with Eng.hn.),*4,2 - 4,3,3,1 -
timp.,perc.(4),bells,2 church bells - hp. - str.   34:00 Composer.
—— SYMPHONY NO. 2 IN A MINOR ("TEACHER - PUPIL") (IN 4
MOVTS.)
17:00 Composer.
—— SYMPHONY NO. 3 IN G MAJOR ("FOR THE CHILDREN...")
(IN 4 MOVTS.)
18:00 Composer.

MIEG, Peter
—— KONZERT FÜR HARFE UND STREICHORCHESTER
hp. - str.   19:00 Galaxy.
—— KONZERT FÜR VIOLINCELLO UND ORCH.
1,2,0,2 - 2,1,0,0 - timp. - str.   13:15 S.U.I.S.A.
—— THREE MEILENER BALLETTE %
S.U.I.S.A.
NO. 1 (FUR 2 OBOEN, 2 HORNER, CEMBALO UND
STREICHER)
2 ob. - 2 hn. - cemb. - str.   7:00

NO. 2 (FUR STREICHER)
str.   9:00
NO. 3 (FUR STREICHER UND ENGL. HORN)
Eng. hn. - str.   13:00

MIELENZ, Hans
—— DEM GLÜCK ENTGEGEN, OP. 58 (OVERTURE)
                                                    R.Birnbach.
—— OVERTURE TO A COMEDY, OP. 9
*3,*3,*3,*3 - 4,3,3,1 - timp.,perc. - hp. - str.   7:00 Henmar.

MIEREANU, Costin
—— ARES MARES KOUKOUNARES (1972)
0,0,0,0 - 0,1,1,0 - perc.(1) - tape recorder(s) - hpsc. - pf. -
str.(2,1,1,0)   10:00 Salabert.
—— COULEURS DU TEMPS (1966-68)
str.   10:00 Salabert.
—— DANS LA NUIT DES TEMPS (ALEATORIC MUSIC, FOR
VARIABLE-SIZED LARGE ENSEMBLE AND TAPE)
                                                  21:00 Salabert.
—— DANS LA NUIT DES TEMPS (ALEATORIC MUSIC, FOR
VARIABLE-SIZED SMALL ENSEMBLE AND TAPE)
                                                  13:00 Salabert.
—— DONUM SACRUM BRANCUSI (FOR SOPRANO AND ORCH.)
(1965)
2 picc.,1,0,2,1 - 4,3,4,0 - perc.(4) - hp. - electric org. - pf. - str.
                                                  14:00 Salabert.
—— ESPACE AU-DELÀ DU DERNIER (ALEATORIC WORK,
AFTER TEXTS OF JOANNA ANDREESCO) (1968)
1,alto fl. (alt.with picc.),0,1(alt.with b.-cl.),0 - 2,2,2,0 - perc.(1) -
pf. - str.   15:00 Salabert.
—— ESPACE DERNIER (ALEATORIC WORK FOR MIXED
CHORUS, 6 INSTRUMENTAL GROUPS AND TAPE) (1969)
(text: Biblical)   Salabert.
—— ESPACES II (FOR 19 STRINGS, PIANO AND TAPE) (1969)
Tape-recorder - 1-2 pf. - str.(9,4,4,3)   15:00 Salabert.
—— FINIS CORONAT OPUS (FOR PIANIST AND 6
INSTRUMENTAL GROUPS) (1966)
*2,alto fl.,*2,1 ten. sax.,2 - 0,4,4,0 - perc.(4),bells,vibra. - 2 electric
guit. - pf.(alt. with perpared pf.) - str.   21:00 Salabert.
—— MONOSTRUCTURES I (FOR 2 ORCHESTRAS, WITH
OPTIONAL AMPLIFICATION) (1966)
0,0,0,0 - 4,4,4,0 - str.   10:00 Salabert.
—— MONOSTRUCTURES II (1967)
0,0,0,0 - 4,4,4,0 - tape-recorder(optional) - str.   6:00 Salabert.
—— POLYMORPHIE 5 X 7 (FOR VARIABLE-SIZED ENSEMBLES
AND 2 TAPES)
                                                  11:00 Salabert.

MIGNONE, Francisco
—— ALEGRIAS DE NOSSA SENHORA (ORATORIO) (FOR
SOPRANO, BARITONE, MIXED CHORUS AND ORCH.)
2,3,3,2 - 4,3,3,1 - timp.,cel. - hp. - str.   32:00 F. Colombo.
—— ELEGY (FOR STRING ORCH.)
str.   6:00 F. Colombo.
—— FANTASIA BRASILEIRA NO. 2 (1931) (FOR PIANO AND
ORCH.)
                                                        Fleisher.
—— FANTASIA BRASILEIRA NO. 3 (1934) (FOR PIANO AND
ORCH.)
3,2,2,2 - 4,3,3,1 - timp.,perc.,cel. - hp. - pf. -   Fleisher.
—— FESTA DIONISIACA (POEMA)
3,3,3,3 - 4,3,4,0 - timp.,perc.,bells,cel. - hp. - pf. - str.
                                                  20:00 F. Colombo.
—— LENDA SERTANEJA NO. 1
3,3,3,3 - 4,3,3,1 - timp.,perc.,bells,cel. - 2 hp. - pf. - str.
                                                  7:00 F. Colombo.
—— MODINHA IMPERIAL
str.   6:00 F. Colombo.
—— MOMUS (POEMA UMORISTICO)
3,3,3 E♭cl.,3,1 - 4,3,4,1 - timp.,perc.,bells,cel.,xyl. - 2 hp. - pf. -
str.   10:00 F. Colombo.
—— MUSICA NO. 1
3,3,3,2 - 4,3,3,1 - timp. - str.   12:00 F. Colombo.
—— NO SERTÃO (IN THE COUNTRY) (SYMPHONIC POEM)
3,3,3,3 - 4,3,3,1 - timp.,perc.,bells,cel. - 2 hp. - pf. - str.
                                                  10:00 F. Colombo.
—— PLENILUNIO (FULL MOON) (1936)
2,3,2,2 - 4,0,0,0 - cel. - hp. - pf. - str.   Fleisher.
—— SEVEN PRELUDES
3,3,3,3 - 4,3,4,1 - timp.,perc.,bells,cel.,glock. - hp. - pf. - str.
                                                  18:00 F. Colombo.

—— SUITE BRASILEIRA
2,1,3,1 - 2,1,0,0 - cel. - hp. - pf. - str.   18:00 F. Colombo.
—— SUITE CAMPESTRE
3,2,2,2 - 4,2,3,1 - timp.,perc. - str.   20:00 F. Colombo.
—— TUCHO
3,2,2,2 - 4,2,3,1 - timp.,perc. - str.   12:00 F. Colombo.

MIGOT, Georges E.
—— LES AGRESTIDES (TROIS FRESQUES) (SYMPHONY NO. 1)
3,3,3,3 - 4,3,3,0 - timp.,perc.,cel.,xyl. - 2 hp. - str.   40:00 Baron.
—— LA CHUTE D'ICARE (AFTER BREUGHEL)
2,2,2,2 - 2,1,1,0 - perc. - hp. - pf. - str.   7:00 Presser.
—— CONCERTO FOR HARPSICHORD AND CHAMBER ORCH.
1,1,1,1 - 1,0,0,0 - hpsc. - str.   23:00 Presser.
—— CONCERTO FOR PIANO AND ORCHESTRA
1,1,1,1 - 2,1,0,0 - timp. - hp. - pf. - str.   17:00 Presser.
—— UNE DANSE PAR L'ORCHESTRE
2,2,2,2 - 2,2,2,0 - str.   10:00 Presser.
—— DEUX PIÈCES (FOR PIANO, VOICES AND ORCH.)
1,1,*2,1 - 2,1,1,1 - timp.,perc. - pf. - str.   17:00 Baron.
—— DIALOGUE EN QUATRE PARTIES (FOR CELLO AND
ORCH.)
2,1,*2,2 - 2,1,1,1 - timp.,perc.,cel. - str.   13:00 Baron.
—— DIALOGUE EN QUATRE PARTIES (FOR VIOLIN AND
ORCH.)
1,1,1,1 - 1,1,1,0 - perc. - pf. - str.   7:00 Baron.
—— LA FÊTE DE LA BERGÈRE (IN 4 MOVTS.)
1,1,1,1 - 2,1,0,0 - perc. - str.   18:00 Salabert.
—— HAGOROMO (CHOREOGRAPHIC AND LYRIC SYMPHONY
IN 1 SCENE) (FOR CHORUS AND ORCH.) (1922) %
3,3,3,3 - 4,2,2,1 - timp.,perc.,cel. - 2 hp. - str.   40:00 Baron.
—— INTRODUCTION POUR UN CONCERT DE CHAMBRE
1,1,1,1 - 0,0,0,0 - str.   4:00 Presser.
—— LA JUNGLE (POLYPHONIE) (FOR ORGAN AND ORCH.)
3,3,3,3 - 4,3,3,1 - timp.,perc.,cel.,xyl. - 2-3 hp. - org. - pf. - str.
                                                  16:00 Baron.
—— LE LIVRE DES DANCERIES (IN 4 MOVTS.)
3,3,3,3 - 4,2,2,1 - timp.,perc. - pf. - str.   24:00 Baron.
—— LE PARAVENT DE LAQUE AUX CINQ IMAGES
2,2,2,2 - 2,2,0,0 - timp.,perc.,cel. - hp. - pf. - str.   16:30 Baron.
—— LA PASSION (ORATORIO) (IN 12 EPISODES) (FOR SOLO
VOICES, MIXED CHORUS AND ORCH.)
3,3,3,3 - 4,3,2,1 - timp.,perc.,cel. - 2 hp. - str.   110:00 Baron.
—— PRELUDE, SALUT ET DANSE
str.   12:00 Baron.
—— LE ROSSIGNOL EN AMOUR (CHAMBER OPERA) %
1,1,1,1 - 1,0,0,0 - 2 pf. - str.   40:00 Baron.
—— LE SERMON SUR LA MONTAGNE (ORATORIO) (FOR SOLO
VOICES, CHORUS AND CHAMBER ORCH.) (1937)
org. - str.   Baron.
—— SUITE EN CONCERT (FOR HARP AND ORCH.) (IN 3
MOVTS.)
3,2,3,2 - 4,2,2,0 - timp.,perc.,cel.,xyl. - hp. - str.   26:00 Baron.
or:
1,1,2,2 - 2,1,1,0 - timp.,perc.,cel.,xyl. - hp. - str.
—— SUITE FOR PIANO AND ORCH. (IN 3 MOVTS.)
1,1,*2,1 - 2,1,1,1 - timp.,perc. - hp. - pf. - str.   2:00 Baron.
—— SUITE FOR VIOLIN AND ORCH. (IN 5 MOVTS.)
3,3,3,3 - 4,2,2,1 - timp.,perc. - 2hp. - str.   26:00 Baron.
—— SYMPHONIE À LA MEMOIRE DE CHOPIN
2,2,2,2 - 2,2,0,0 - str.   13:00 Baron.
—— SYMPHONY NO. 10
2,2,2,2 - 2,1,1,0 - timp. - str.   25:00 Presser.
—— SYMPHONY NO. 2 (LES NOMBRES)
3,3,3,3 - 4,3,2,1 - timp.,perc.,cel.,xyl. - 2 hp. - pf. - str.
                                                  24:00 Presser.
—— SYMPHONY NO. 3
2,2,2,2 - 2,2,0,0 - str.   23:00 Baron.
—— SYMPHONY NO. 9 FOR STRINGS
str.   28:15 Presser.
—— LE TOMBEAU DE DU FAULT, JOUEUR DE LUTH (IN 3
MOVTS.)
2,2,2,2 - 2,2,1,1 - timp.,perc.,cel. - 2 hp. - str.   12:00 Salabert.
—— TROIS ÉPIGRAMMES
1,1,1,1 - 2,1,0,0, - perc. - hp. - str.   7:00 Salabert.

MIHAJLOVIĆ, Milan
—— UVERTIRA FANTAZIA (OVERTURE-FANTASIA)
2(2nd alt. with picc.),2(2nd alt. with Eng. hn.),2(2nd alt. with
b.-cl.),2(2nd alt. with c.-bn.) - 4,3,3,1 - timp.,perc.,cel.,xyl. - hp. -
pf. - str.   10:00 MIC,Zagreb.

MIHALOVICI, Marcel

—— AUBADE, OP. 89
    str.   14:00 AhnSimrock.
—— BORNE (ACTION SYMPHONIQUE)
    3,3,3,3 - 4,3,3,1 - timp.,perc.(9, incl. 2 on timp.) - pf. - str.
                                         14:00 Presser.
—— CANTILENA (FOR MEZZO-SOPRANO AND CHAMBER
ORCH.)
    1,0,3,0 - 0,0,0,0 - perc. (2-3), cel., mar., vibra. - hp. - str.
                                       23:00 Presser.
—— CASCANDO (INVENTION FOR MUSIC AND VOICE)
    1,0,3,0 - 0,0,0,0 - perc.(2),cel. - hp. - pf. - str.(1,1,1,1)
                                       12:00 Presser.
—— AN EXERCISE FOR STRINGS (ESERCIZIO PER ARCHI)
    str.   13:00 Presser.
—— ÉTUDE (IN TWO PARTS)
    0,0,2,1 - 0,2,1,1 - perc.(2),cel. - pf.   21:00 Mercury.
—— FUGUE (INTERLUDE FROM THE OPERA "PHÈDRE")
    2,2,2,2 - 2,2,2,1 - timp.,perc. - pf. -str.   7:00 Presser.
—— KRAPP ("THE LAST TAPE") (1-ACT OPERA) % (Text: Samuel
Beckett)
    1,1,2,2 - 2,2,0,0 - perc.(3),cel. - pf. - str.   55:00 Presser.
—— OVERTURE TRAGIQUE, OP. 76
    2,2,2,2 - 2,2,2,0 - str.   7:30 Presser.
—— PERIPLES, OP. 93 (FOR SMALL ORCH.)
    1,0,3,0 - 2,0,0,0 - pf.(or cel.) - str.   18:00 Presser.
—— PRÉTEXTES
    0,1,*1,0 - 0,0,0,0 - perc. - pf. - str.   17:00 Presser.
—— RITOURNELLES
    2,2,2,2 - 2,2,1,0 - timp. - pf. - str.   12:00 Mercury.
—— RONDO, OP. 98
    3,3,3,3 - 4,3,3,1 - timp., perc.(7) - pf. - str.   15:00 Presser.
—— SCÈNES DE "THÉSÉE"
    2 picc.,2,2,2,2 - 4,2,3,1 - timp.,perc.(3),cel. - pf. - str.
                                       23:00 Mercury.
—— SÉQUENCE
    1,1,1,1 - 2,2,1,0 - timp.,perc. - str.   15:00 Mercury.
—— SINFONIA CANTATA (FOR BARITONE, SATB CHORUS AND
ORCH.)
    1,1,2,2 - 2,2,1,0 - perc.(3),bells - pf. - str.   40:00 Presser.
—— SINFONIA GIOCOSA
    *2,1,1,1 - 0,0,0,0 - str.   15:00 Mercury.
—— SINFONIA PARTITA (FOR STRINGS)
    str.   26:30 Mercury.
—— SINFONIA VARIATA
    3,3,3,3 - 4,3,3,1 - timp.,perc.(3) - str.   20:00 Presser.
—— SONG NO 1 (FOR TENOR SAXOPHONE AND ORCH.)
    2,1,2,ten. sax.,2 - 2,2,1,0 - perc.(3), cel. - pf. - str.   14:00 Presser.
—— SYMPHONIES POUR UN BALLET (ALTERNAMENTI)
    2,1,2,1 - 2,2,1,1 - perc. - str.   28:00 F. Colombo.
—— SYMPHONY NO. 5 (WITH DRAMATIC SOPRANO)
    3,3,3,3 - 4,3,3,1 - timp.,perc.(7),cel. - 2 hp. - pf. - str.
                                       38:00 Presser.
—— TOCCATA FOR PIANO AND ORCH.
    2,2,2,2 - 2,2,0,0 - pf. - str.   18:00 Mercury.
—— VARIATIONS FOR BRASS AND STRINGS
    2 tpt.,2 trb. - str.   21:00 E.C.Kerby.

MIHÁLY, András

—— CONCERTO FOR CELLO AND ORCH.
    2,2,3,3 - 4,3,3,1 - timp.,perc.,cel. - 2 hp. - str. 35:00 Bo. Hawkes.
—— CONCERTO FOR PIANO AND ORCH.
    2,2,2,3 - 4,3,3,1 - timp.,perc.,cel. - hp. - pf. - str.
                                    23:20 Bo. Hawkes.
—— CONCERTO FOR VIOLIN AND ORCH.
    1,1,2,1 - 2,1,1,0 - timp.,cel. - pf. - str.   15:00 Bo. Hawkes.
—— FANTASY FOR FLUTE, BASSOON, HORN AND STRINGS
    1,0,0,1 - 1,0,0,0 - str.   Bo. Hawkes.
—— FANTASY FOR WIND QUINTET AND STRINGS
    1,1,1,1 - 1,0,0,0 - perc.,cel. - hp. - str.   21:22 Bo. Hawkes.
—— FESTIVAL OVERTURE
    2,2,2,2 - 4,3,3,0 - timp.,perc. - str.   10:00 Bo. Hawkes.
—— SYMPHONY NO. 3
    4(3rd alt. with picc.),*4,*4,*5 - 4,4,4,1 - timp.,perc.,cel. - hp. - str.
                                       25:00 General.

MIHELČIČ, Pavle

—— MODERATO CANTABILE (FOR VIOLA AND 13
INSTRUMENTS)
    2,2,2,2 - 4,0,0,0 - hp. - vla.   4:00 Hans Gerig.
—— TIMBER LINE (FOR CHAMBER ENSEMBLE)
    0,0,0,0 - 1,1,1,0 - perc. - pf. - str.(2,1,1,1)   6:00 Hans Gerig.

MIHELČIČ, Slavko

—— CONCERTINO FOR PIANO AND STRINGS
    pf. - str.   10:00 Hans Gerig.
—— FANTASY FOR PIANO AND STRINGS
    pf. - str.   7:00 Hans Gerig.

MIKI, Minoru

—— CONCERTO FOR MARIMBA AND ORCH. (WITH OPTIONAL
TAPE)
                                         AhnSimrock.
—— HA-NO-KYOKU (CONCERTO FOR KOTO AND ORCH.)
    2,2,2,2 - 4,3,2,0 - perc. (4) - koto - str.   24:00 Presser.

MIKKOLA, Viljo

—— CHILDHOOD MEMORIES (SUITE) (1934)
    2,2,2,2 - 2,2,1,1 - timp.,perc. - hp. - str.   15:00 FinnMICtr.
—— CHRIST (ORATORIO) (FOR SOPRANO, 2 TENORS, BASS,
SATB CHORUS AND ORCH.) (1946)
    2,2,2,2 - 2,2,1,1 - timp.,perc. - str.   150:00 FinnMICtr.
—— EASTER CANTATA (FOR SOPRANO, BARITONE, SATB
CHORUS AND ORCH.) (1920)
    2,2,2,2 - 2,2,1,1 - timp.,perc. - hp. - str.   10:00 FinnMICtr.
—— FINNISH RHAPSODY (1935)
    2,2,2,2 - 2,2,1,0 - timp.,perc. - hp. - str.   10:00 FinnMICtr.
—— HARVEST FEAST (1932)
    2,2,2,2 - 2,2,1,1 - timp.,perc. - hp. - str.   12:00 FinnMICtr.
—— OSTROBOTHNIAN SUITE (1930)
    2,2,2,2 - 2,2,1,1 - timp.,perc. - hp. - str.   20:00 FinnMICtr.
—— SUMMER SCENES FROM FINLAND PROPER (SUITE) (1938)
    2,2,2,2 - 2,2,1,1 - timp.,perc. - hp. - str.   15:00 FinnMICtr.

MILDE-MEISSNER, Hanson

—— CAPRICCIETTO (FOR OBOE AND SMALL ORCH.)
    2,1,2,2 - 2,2,0,0 - timp. - hp. - str.   F. Colombo.
—— FROM MY COUNTRY ("AUS MEINER HEIMAT") (SUITE)
(FOR PIANO AND ORCH.)
    2,2,2,2 - 4,3,3,0 - timp.,perc. - pf. - str.   23:00 F. Colombo.

MILENKOVIĆ, Jelena

—— SYMPHONY
    2(2nd alt. with picc.),2(2nd alt. with Eng. hn.),2(2nd alt. with
    b.-cl.),2(2nd alt. with c.-bn.) - 4,3,3,1 - timp.,xyl. - str.
                                       19:00 MIC,Zagreb.
—— TRI POKRETA (THREE MOVTS.)
    2(2nd alt. with picc.),2(2nd alt. with Eng. hn.),2(2nd alt. with
    b.-cl.),2(2nd alt. with c.-bn.) - 4,3,3,1 - timp.,cel.,xyl. - pf. - str.
                                     15:00 MIC,Zagreb.

MILES, P. Napier

—— HYMN BEFORE SUNRISE (FOR BARITONE, SATB CHORUS
AND ORCH.)
    3,2,3,3 - 4,2,3,1 - timp.,perc. - hp. - str.   14:00 Bo. Hawkes.
—— MUSIC COMES (FOR TENOR, WOMEN'S CHORUS AND
ORCH.)
    2,2,1,1 - 1,0,0,0 - timp. - hp. - str.   12:00 Bo. Hawkes.

MILFORD, Robin

—— ARIEL (PRELUDE FOR SMALL ORCH.)
    2,2,0,2 - 0,0,0,0 - str.   5:30 Oxford.
—— CONCERTO GROSSO, OP. 46
    1,1,1,1 - 2,0,0,0 - str.   22:00 Oxford.
—— THE DARKLING THRUSH, OP. 17 (FOR VIOLIN AND SMALL
ORCH.)
    2,2,2,2 - 2,2,0,0 - timp.(ad lib.) - hp. - str.   12:00 Oxford.
—— EASTER MORNING (A SHORT CANTATA) (FOR SSA
CHORUS AND STRING ORCH.)
    str.   Oxford.
—— FESTIVAL SUITE
                                      11:00 Oxford.
—— FOUR HEAVENLY SONGS (FOR TENOR, MIXED CHORUS
AND ORCH.)
                                      Oxford.
—— MINIATURE CONCERTO IN G (FOR STRINGS)
    str.   8:00 Oxford.
—— THE PILGRIM'S PROGRESS (CANTATA) (FOR SOPRANO,
TENOR, BARITONE, MIXED CHORUS AND ORCH.)
                                    55:00 Oxford.
—— A PROPHET IN THE LAND (CANTATA) (FOR SOPRANO,
TENOR, BARITONE, MIXED CHORUS AND ORCH.)
                                    85:00 Oxford.
—— SIR WALTER'S OVERTURE, OP. 27
    2,2,2,2 - 4,2-3,3,1 - timp.,perc. - str.   7:00 Oxford.

—— SUITE FOR CHAMBER ORCH. (IN 6 MOVTS.)
  2,1,2,2 - 2,0,cnt,0,0 - str.   12:00 Oxford.
—— SUITE IN D MINOR (IN 4 MOVTS)
  ob. - str.   Oxford.
—— THE TWENTY-THIRD PSALM (FOR SOPRANO, CHORUS
  AND STRINGS)
  str.   Oxford.

MILHAUD, Darius
—— ADAGES (FOR 4 VOICES AND SMALL ORCH.)
  1,0,1,1 - 1,0,0,0 - str.   25:00 Salabert.
—— ADAME MIROIR (BALLET SUITE) (IN 5 MOVTS)
  1,1,1,1 - 1,1,1,0 - timp.,perc. - hp. - str.   18:00 Mercury.
—— AGAMENON (FOR SOPRANO, CHORUS AND ORCH.)
                                            Mercury.
—— LES AMOURS DE RONSARD (FOR 4 VOICES AND
  CHAMBER ORCH.)
  fl.,cl.,bn. - hn. - str.   18:00 Salabert.
—— L' ANNONCE FAITE À MARIE (SUITE) (FOR 4 SOLO
  VOICES AND ORCH.)
  2,1,0,2 sax.,0 - 0,0,0,0 - timp.,perc.,vibra. - 2 ondes Martenot -
  org. - pf. 4-hands str.   19:00 Salabert.
—— ASPEN SERENADE
  1,1,1,1 - 0,1,0,0 - str.   16:00 Mercury.
—— AUBADE
  2,2,2,2 - 2,2,2,0 - timp.,perc. - hp. - str.   18:00 Presser.
—— LE BAL MARTINIQUAIS (IN 2 MOVTS.)
  2(2nd alt. with picc.),2,2,2 - 2,2,2,0 - timp.,perc. - hp. - str.
                                       10:00 Leeds.
—— BARBA GARIBO (CHANSONS MENTONAISES) (FOR
  CHORUS AND ORCH.)
  2,2,2,2 - 2,3,2,0 - timp.,perc. - str.   21:00 Mercury.
—— LA BRANCHE DES OISEAUX (MYTHES DE PROVENCE)
  3,3,3,3 - 4,3,2,0 - timp.,perc. - str.   30:00 Presser.
—— CAIN AND ABEL (FOR NARRATOR AND ORCH.) (FOURTH
  MOVT. FROM GENESIS SUITE)
  2,2,2,2 - 2,2,2,0 - timp.,perc. - hp. - str.   5:00 Shilkret.
—— LA CANTATE DE LA CROIX DE CHARITÉ (FOR SOPRANO,
  TENOR, BASS, CHORUS AND ORCH.)
  2,3,3,2 - 2,2,2,0 - timp.,perc. - str.   22:30 Presser.
—— CANTATE DE L'ENFANT ET DE LA MÈRE (FOR
  NARRATOR AND STRINGS)
  pf. - str.   9:15 Presser.
—— CANTATE DE L'INITIATION (FOR MIXED CHORUS AND
  ORCH.)
  2,2,0,2 - 2,2,0,0 - perc. - str.   13:15 Presser.
—— CANTATE NUPTIALE (FOR VOICE AND SMALL ORCH.)
  2,2,2,2 - 2,2,2,0 - perc. - hp. - str.   15:00 Salabert.
—— CANTATE SUR DES POÈMES DE CHAUCER (FOR MIXED
  CHORUS AND ORCH.)
  2,2,2,2 - 2,2,2,0 - timp.,perc. - str.   15:30 Presser.
—— LE CARNAVAL D'AIX (FOR PIANO AND ORCH.)
  2,1,2,1 - 2,2,1,1 - timp.,perc. - pf. - str.   23:00 Mercury.
—— LE CARNIVAL DE LONDRES (SUITE FROM INCIDENTAL
  MUSIC FOR "THE BEGGAR'S OPERA")
  1,1,1,alto sax.,1 - 0,1,1,0 - perc. - hp. - str.   30:00 Salabert.
—— CATALOGUE DE FLEURS (SUR DES POÈMES DE LUCIEN
  DAUDET) (FOR VOICE AND CHAMBER ORCH.)
  1,0,1,1 - 0,0,0,0 - str.   5:00 EV.
—— LES CHOÉPHORES ("THE LIBATION POURERS") (FOR SOLO
  VOICES, CHORUS AND ORCH.)
  3,3,3,4 - 4,3,3,1 - timp.,perc.,cel. - hp. - str.   35:00 Mercury.
—— CINQ CHANSONS DE CHARLES VILDRAC (FOR VOICE
  AND ORCH.)
  1,1,2,1 - 0,2,1,0 - perc. - hp. - pf.   Salabert.
—— CONCERTINO D'AUTOMNE
  1,1,0,0 - 3,0,0,0 - 2pf. - str.   11:00 Mercury.
—— CONCERTINO DE PRINTEMPS (FOR VIOLIN AND ORCH.)
  1,1,1,1 - 1,1,0,0 - timp.,perc. - str.   9:00 Salabert.
—— CONCERTINO D'ÉTÉ
  1,1,1,1 - 1,1,0,0 - str.   10:00 Mercury.
—— CONCERTO FOR CLARINET AND ORCH.
  2,2,2,2 - 2,2,2,1 - timp.,perc. - hp. - str.   12:00 EV.
—— CONCERTO FOR FLUTE, VIOLIN AND ORCH.
  2,2,2,2 - 2,2,2,1 - timp.,perc.,cel. - hp. - str.   18:00 Salabert.
—— CONCERTO FOR HARPSICHORD AND ORCH.
  1,1,1,1 - 0,1,0,0 - timp.,perc.(4) - hp. - hpsc. - str.   17:00 Salabert.
—— CONCERTO FOR MARIMBA, VIBRAPHONE AND ORCH.
                                       28:00 Enoch.
—— CONCERTO FOR OBOE AND ORCH.
  2,1,3,2 alto sax.,2 - 2,2,2,0 - timp.,perc. - hp. - str.   18:30 Presser.
—— CONCERTO FOR PIANO AND ORCH.
  2,2,3,2 - 2,3,2,1 - timp.,perc.,xyl. - hp. - pf. - str.   12:00 Salabert.

—— CONCERTO FOR VIOLIN AND ORCH. (IN 3 MOVTS.)
  2,2,2,2 - 2,2,2,1 - timp.,perc. - hp. - str.   10:00 Mercury.
—— CONCERTO FOR 2 PIANOS AND ORCH. (IN 3 MOVTS.)
  2,2,2,2 - 2,2,2,1 - timp.,perc. - 2pf. - str.   18:00 EV.
—— CONCERTO NO. 1 FOR CELLO AND ORCH.
  2,2,2,2 - 2,2,2,1 - timp.,perc. - hp. - str.   15:00 Salabert.
—— CONCERTO NO. 1 FOR VIOLA AND ORCH.
  2,2,3,2 - 2,2,1,1 - perc. - hp. - str.   15:00 Presser.
  or:
  2,1,2,1 - 1,1,1,1 - perc. - str.(2,1,1,1)
—— CONCERTO NO. 2 FOR PIANO AND ORCH.
  2,2,2,2 - 2,2,2,1 - timp.,perc. - pf. - str.   13:20 Mercury.
—— CONCERTO NO. 2 FOR VIOLA AND ORCH.
  2,2,2,2 - 2,2,2,0 - timp.,perc. - str.   Mercury.
—— CONCERTO NO. 4 FOR PIANO AND ORCH.
                                            Mercury.
—— COURONNE DE GLOIRE (SOLO CANTATA FOR BARITONE
  AND SMALL ORCH.)
  fl. - tpt. - str.   16:30 Presser.
—— LA CUEILLETTE DES CITRONS
  2,2,2,2 - 2,2,2,0 - timp.,perc. - str.   20:00 Mercury.
—— DAVID (5-ACT OPERA)
  2,2,2,2 - 4,3,3,1 - timp.,perc. - hp. - str.   180:00 IsMuPublns.
—— ESTHER DE CARPENTRAS (2-ACT OPERA-BOUFFE) %
  3,2,2,1 - 4,3,3,1 - timp.,perc. - hp. - str.   90:00 Presser.
—— FANTAISIE PASTORALE (FOR PIANO AND ORCH.)
  1,1,1,1 - 1,1,1,1 - perc. - hp. - pf. - str.   10:00 Salabert.
—— FIESTA (1-ACT OPERA) %
  1,1,2,1 alto sax.,1 - 0,1,1,0 - perc. - hp. - str.   23:00 Presser.
—— FOUR POPULAR SONGS OF PROVENCE (FOR VOICE AND
  ORCH.)
                                            Leeds.
—— FOUR SKETCHES
  1,1,1,1 - 1,1,1,0 - perc. - hp. - str.   9:00 Mercury.
—— A FRENCHMAN IN NEW YORK (SUITE)
  3,3,3,3 - 4,3,3,1 - timp.,perc. - hp. - str.   21:00 Salabert.
—— LES FUNERAILLES DE PHOCION (HOMMAGE À
  NICHOLAS POUSSIN)
  3,2,3,3 - 4,3,3,1 - timp.,perc. - str.   9:00 Presser.
—— GLOBE TROTTER SUITE
                                            Mills.
—— THE HOUSEHOLD MUSE
  1,1,1,1 - hn. - str.   24:30 EV.
—— JEUX DE PRINTEMPS (IN 6 MOVTS)
  3,3,3,2 - 4,3,3,1 - timp.,perc. - str.   20:00 Salabert.
—— KENTUCKIANA
  3,2,2,2 - 4,2,2,0 - timp.,perc. - str.   9:00 EV.
—— LITURGIE COMTADINE (5 SONGS FOR ROSH HASHANAH)
  (FOR MEDIUM VOICE AND ORCH.)
  2,1,2,1 - 0,1,0,0 - perc. - hp. - str.   Presser.
—— LES MALHEURS D'ORPHÉE (3-ACT OPERA) %
  1,1,2,1 - 1,0,0,0 - timp.,perc. - hp. - str.   55:00 Presser.
—— MARCHE ET FUGUE DU MASSACRE (FROM "LES MARIÉS
  DE LA TOUR EIFFEL)
  3,2,2,2 - 2,3,3,1 - perc. - str.   Salabert.
—— LE MARIAGE DE LA FEUILLE ET DU CLICHÉ (CANTATA)
  (FOR SOLO VOICES, SATB CHORUS AND ORCH.)
  1,1,1,alto sax.,1 - 0,0,0,0 - timp.,perc. - str.   30:00 Presser.
—— MÉDÉE (OPERA IN 3 SCENES) %
  3,3,3,1 alto sax.,3 - 2,3,3,1 - timp.,perc.,cel. - hp. - str.
                                       75:00 Presser.
—— MIRACLES OF FAITH (FOR MIXED CHORUS AND ORCH.)
                                            G. Schirmer.
—— LA MORT D'UN TYRAN (DEATH OF A TYRAN) (FOR
  CHORUS AND ORCH.)
  *1,0,1,0 - 0,0,0,1 - perc. - str.   11:00 MCA Music.
—— MUSIC FOR BOSTON (FOR VIOLIN AND SMALL ORCH.) (IN
  3 MOVTS.)
  1,0,1,1 - 0,0,0,0 - str.   12:55 EV.
—— L' OISEAU, OP. 181
                                            S.A.C.E.M.
—— OPUS AMERICANUM NO. 2
  2,2,2,2 - 2,2,2,0 - timp.,perc. - hp. - str.   18:00 EV.
—— OUVERTURE MÉDITERRANÉENE
  2,2,2,2 - 4,2,2,0 - timp.,perc. - str.   4:00 Mercury.
—— OVERTURE PHILHARMONIQUE
  3,3,3,3 - 4,3,3,1 - timp.,perc.,cel.,glock.,xyl. - hp. - str.
                                       9:00 Presser.
—— PACEM IN TERRIS (FOR CONTRALTO, BARITONE, SATB
  CHORUS AND ORCH.) (IN 7 MOVTS.) (Text: Pope John XXIII)
  3,2,3,3 - 2,2,3,1 - timp.,perc. - str.   46:00 Salabert.
—— LE PAUVRE MATELOT (1-ACT OPERA) %
  2,2,5,3 - 2,3,2,0 - timp.,perc. - hp. - str.   45:00 Presser.

or:
1,1,1,1 - 1,1,1,0 - perc. - str.
—— POÈME SUR UN CANTIQUE DE CAMARGUE (FOR PIANO
AND ORCH.)
S.A.C.E.M.
—— POLKA (FROM "L'ÉVENTAIL DE JEANNE")
2,2,2,2 - 2,2,0,0 - perc. - str.   2:30 Presser.
—— PRELUDE TO ACT III OF "LES EUMÉNIDES"
3,3,3,4 sax.,4 - 4,4,3,1 - timp.,perc. - hp. - str.   5:00 Presser.
—— PROTÉE (FOR CHORUS AND ORCH.)
EV.
—— QUATRE CHANSONS DE RONSARD (FOR HIGH VOICE
AND ORCH.)
2,2,2,sax.,2 - 2,2,2,0 - timp.,perc. - str.   10:00 Bo. Hawkes.
—— LA ROSE DES VENTS (BALLET) %
2,1,2,1 - 2,2,1,1 - perc. - hp. - pf. - str.   22:00 Salabert.
—— SACRED SERVICE FOR SABBATH MORNING (FOR
BARITONE, MIXED CHORUS AND ORCH.)
2,2,2,2 - 2,2,2,0 - timp.,perc. - hp. - str.   60:00 Ricordi.
—— LA SAGESSE (CANTATA) (FOR NARRATOR, SOLO VOICE,
SATB CHORUS AND ORCHESTRA)
2,3,4,2 sax.,3 - 2,3,3,1 - timp.,perc. - hp. - pf. - str.   60:00 Presser.
—— SALADE (CHORAL BALLET IN 2 ACTS) %
2,1,2,1 - 4 timp.,perc. - str.   33:00 Presser.
—— SCARAMOUCHE (FOR ALTO SAXOPHONE OR CLARINET
AND ORCH.) (IN 3 MOVTS)
2,2,2,sax.,2 - 2,2,2,0 - perc. - str.   8:00 Salabert.
—— SIX CHANTS POPULAIRES HEBRAÏQUES (FOR MEDIUM
VOICE AND ORCH.)
2,2,2,2 - 2,2,2,0 - timp.,perc. - str.   11:00 Presser.
—— LES SONGES (BALLET) %
1,1,1,1 - 1,1,1,0 - perc. - pf. - str.   Salabert.
—— SUITE CAMPAGNARDE
2,2,2,2 - 2,2,2,0 - timp.,perc. - str.   9:00 Mercury.
—— SUITE FOR HARMONICA (OR VIOLIN) AND ORCH. (IN 3
MOVTS)
2,2,2,2 - 2,2,2,1 - timp.,perc. - harmonica - str.
16:30 Bo. Hawkes.
—— SUITE (FOR TWO PIANOS AND ORCH.)
2,2,2,2 - 2,2,3,0 - timp.,perc. - hp. - 2 pf. - str.   18:30 Presser.
—— SUITE FRANÇAISE (IN 5 MOVTS)
2,2,2,2 - 4,3,3,1 - perc. - str.   16:00 Leeds.
or:
2,2,2,2 - 2,2,2,0 - timp.,perc. - str.
—— SUITE PROVENÇALE
2,3,2,2 - 4,3,3,1 - timp.,perc. - str.   16:00 Salabert.
—— SUITE SYMPHONIQUE NO. 2
4,*3,3,4 - 4,3,3,1 - timp.,perc.,cel. - hp. - str.   22:00 EV.
—— SYMPHONIE CONCERTANTE (FOR BASSOON, HORN,
TRUMPET, DOUBLE BASS AND ORCH.)
1,1,1,1 - 1,1,1,0 - timp,perc. - str.   11:00 Presser.
—— SYMPHONIETTE (FOR STRINGS)
str.   9:30 Presser.
—— SYMPHONY NO. 1 (FOR FULL ORCH.)
3,3,3,3 - 4,3,3,1 - timp.,perc. - hp. - str.   28:00 Mercury.
—— SYMPHONY NO. 2 (FOR FULL ORCH.)
*3,*3,*3,*3 - 4,3,3,1 - timp.,perc. - hp. - str.   27:00 Mercury.
—— SYMPHONY NO. 3 (FOR CHORUS AND ORCH)
*3,*3,*3,*3 - 4,3,3,1 - timp.,perc.,xyl. - str.   31:30 Mercury.
—— SYMPHONY NO. 4 (FOR FULL ORCH.) (IN 4 MOVTS.)
3,3,4,2 sax.,3 - 4,4,4,2 - timp.,perc.(3) - str.   30:00 Salabert.
—— SYMPHONY NO. 5 (FOR FULL ORCH.)
*3,2,2,2 - 4,3,3,1 - timp.,perc. - str.   26:00 Mercury.
—— SYMPHONY NO. 6
*3,*3,*3,*3 - 4,3,3,1 - timp.,perc.,cel. - hp. - str.   27:15 Mercury.
—— SYMPHONY NO. 7
*3,*3,*3,*3 - 4,3,3,1 - timp.,perc. - hp. - str.   26:00 Mercury.
—— SYMPHONY NO. 8
*3,*3,*3,*3 - 4,3,3,1 - timp.,perc. - hp. - str.   Mercury.
—— SYMPHONY NO. 9
2,3,2,2 - 4,3,3,1 - timp.,perc. - hp. - str.   16:30 Presser.
—— SYMPHONY NO. 10
3,3,3,3 - 4,3,3,1 - timp.,perc. - hp. - str.   22:00 Presser.
—— SYMPHONY NO. 11 ("ROMANTIQUE")
3,3,3,3 - 4,3,3,1 - timp.,perc.(2) - hp. - str.   26:00 Presser.
—— SYMPHONY NO. 12 ("RURALE")
2,2,3,2 - 2,2,3,1 - timp.,perc. - str.   17:00 Presser.
—— LA TRAGÉDIE HUMAINE (FOR MIXED CHORUS AND
ORCH.)
2,2,3,3 - 2,3,3,1 - timp.,perc. - str.   27:00 Salabert.
—— LE TRAIN BLEU (BALLET MUSIC) %
3,3,3,2 - 4,3,3,1 - timp.,perc. - str.   26:00 Presser.

—— TROIS CHANSONS DE NÉGRESSES (FOR VOICE AND
ORCH.)
1,0,1,alto sax.,0 - 0,2,1,1 - perc. - hp. - str.   6:00 Salabert.
—— TROIS CHANSONS DE TROUBADOUR (FOR VOICE AND
ORCH.)
Salabert.

MILHAUD, Darius - CHAPELIER, S.
—— L' ALBUM DE MADAME BOVARY
Enoch.

MILKEY, Edward T.
—— STRING SECTION SUITE
str.   5:30 Mills.
—— SUITE FOR STRINGS
str.   5:00 Boston.

MILLER, Lewis M.
—— DIRGE AND FUGUE (FOR BRASS ENSEMBLE) (1967)
0,0,0,0 - 4,3,3,1   5:00 Composer.
—— THE IMAGINARY INVALID (OPERA) (1969) % (Text:
Composer andPatrick Goeser, after Moliere)
2,2,2,2 - 4,3,3,1 - timp.,perc.(3),bells,glock.,xyl. - str.
70:00 Composer.
—— INTRODUCTION AND ALLEGRO (1964)
fl. - str.   5:00 Composer.
—— KING HENRY V (OVERTURE) (1962)
*3,*3,2,2 - 4,2,3,1 - timp.,perc.(3),bells,glock. - hp. - str.
9:00 CMP.
—— THE PIED PIPER OF HAMELIN (STAGE WORK FOR
DANCER, BOY SOPRANO, BARITONE SOLO, SATB CHORUS
AND ORCH.) (1960) % (Text: Robert Browning)
1,1,1,1 - 1,1,0,0 - timp.,perc.(2),bells,glock. - str.   30:00 Composer.
—— PRELUDE AND BAROQUE FUGUE (1963)
str.   5:00 CMP.
—— THIS UNIVERSAL FRAME (FOR SATB CHORUS AND
ORCH.) (1962) (Text: John Dryden)
2,2,2,2 -2,2,2,0 - timp.,perc.(1) - pf. - str.   8:00 Composer.
—— TOCCATA FOR ORCHESTRA (1962)
3(3rd alt. with picc.),*3,2,2 - 4,3,3,1 - timp.,perc.(2),glock. - str.
7:00 Composer.

MILLER, Michael R.
—— CAPRICCIO ON THE SEVEN AGES OF MAN (1972)
2(2nd alt. with picc.),2(2nd alt. with Eng.hn.),2,2 - 2,2,2,0 -
timp.,perc.(5-6, incl. - 4 on timp.) - hp. - str.   17:45 CanMusCtr.
—— DANCES OF FANCY (FOR CHAMBER ORCH.)
4:00 Composer.
—— STROPHE, ANTISTROPHE (1971) (SYMPHONY IN 3 MOVTS.,
WITH VIOLA SOLO)
2(2nd alt. with picc.),2(2nd alt. with Eng.hn.),2,2 - 4,3,3,0 -
timp.,perc.(5, incl. 4 on timp.),cel. - pf. - str.   18:00 CanMusCtr.
—— TWO PIECES FOR PIANO AND ORCH. (1975)
2,2,2,2 - 2,2,2,0 - timp.,perc.(5, incl. 4 on timp.) - pf. - str.
13:00 CanMusCtr.

MILLS, Alvin
—— AMERICAN FANFARE (1976)
0,0,0,0 - 3,3,3,0 - timp.,perc.,xyl.   8:00 Composer.
—— AN AMERICAN IN SPAIN (A MUSICAL SUMMARY) (SUITE)
(1970) (WITH 3 SONGS FOR SOPRANO AND ORCH.) (Text:
Composer)
2,2,2,2 - 4,2,2,0 - timp.,perc. - str.   25:00 Composer.
—— ELEGY (1975)
str.   11:30 Composer.
—— SPANISH RHAPSODY (1973)
timp.,perc.(3) - str.   10:00 Composer.
—— SYMPHONY NO. 1 (THE BIG MOUNTAIN) (1960) (IN 3
MOVTS.)
2,2,2,2 - 3,2,0,0 - timp. str.   27:00 Composer.

MILLS, Donn
—— ELEGY FOR STRINGS (1962)
str.   6:00 Composer.
—— FAR HORIZON (WITH OPTIONAL SOPRANO) (1965) (IN 3
MOVTS.)
1,*1,*2,*1 - 1,0,0,0 - perc.(2),bells,glock. - hpsc. - str.
15:00 Composer.
—— MUSIC FOR A FESTIVE OCCASION (1969)
*2,2,2,2 - 4,2,3,1 - timp.,perc.(3),bells,cel.,glock.,xyl. - hp. - str.
5:00 Composer.
—— A NAUTICAL OVERTURE (1960)
*2,2,2,2 - 4,2,3,1 - timp.,perc.(3),glock.,xyl. - str.   7:00 Mills.

—— OVERTURE GIOCOSO (1963)
    *2,2,2,2 - 4,3,3,1 - timp.,perc.(4),bells,cel.,glock.,xyl. - pf. - str.
        7:00 Composer.
—— SUITE FOR STRINGS (1956) (IN 3 MOVTS.)
    str.   15:00 Composer.

MILNER, Anthony
—— BREAK TO BE BUILT, O STONE (ODE FOR SATB CHORUS
    AND ORCH.) (Text: Ursula Vaughan Williams)
    2,2,2,2 - 4,3,3,1 timp.,perc. - org. - str.   7:00 Oxford.
—— SYMPHONY
    3(3rd alt. with picc.),2,3,3 - 4,3,3,1 - timp.,perc.,glock.,vibra.,xyl. -
    2 hp. - str.   25:00 Novello.

MILNER, Arthur
—— DIPTYCH
    2,2,1,2 - 2,0,0,0 - str.   13:00 P.R.S.
—— DIPTYCH (1966)
    str.   9:00 P.R.S.
—— NOCTURNE, ECLOGUE AND PALINDROME (1961)
    str.   10:00 P.R.S.
—— OTTERBURN MOOR (1966)
    2,2,2,2 - 2,0,0,0 - str.   8:00 P.R.S.
—— PASTORALE AND FANTASIA (1960)
    str.   9:00 P.R.S.
—— A SUMMER IDYLL (1940)
    1,1,2,2 - 2,0,0,0 - str.   6:00 P.R.S.
—— VARIATIONS (1965)
    2,2,2,2 - 4,2,3,0 - perc.,cel. - str.   21:00 P.R.S.

MILOŠEVIĆ, Vlado
—— BOSNIAN ELEGY
    *3,2,3,2 - 4,3,3,1 - timp.,perc.,glock.,xyl.   6:10 S.O.K.O.J.
—— BOSNIAN SUITE
    str.   17:00 S.O.K.O.J.
—— CONCERTINO FOR OBOE AND STRINGS
    ob. - str.   17:00 S.O.K.O.J.
—— CONCERTO FOR VIOLIN AND CHAMBER ORCH.
    1,1,1,2 - 2,2,1,0 - timp.,perc.,xyl. - vln.   29:30 S.O.K.O.J.
—— DRAMATIC SYMPHONY
    5,1,1,4 - 8,5,4,0 - perc. - str.   24:30 S.O.K.O.J.
—— SUITE FOR OBOE AND STRINGS
    ob. - str.   14:00 S.O.K.O.J.
—— TREE BALLADS
    *3,2,3,2 - 4,3,3,1 - timp.,perc.,glock.,xyl.   16:10 S.O.K.O.J.
—— VARIATIONS ON A FOLK THEME
    ob. - str.   6:00 S.O.K.O.J.
—— WALKING THROUGH THE TOWN
    1,1,2,1 - 3,1,1,0 - perc. - pf. - str.   11:30 S.O.K.O.J.

MILVEDEN, Ingemar
—— CONCERTO AL FRESCO (FOR CLARINET AND ORCH.)
    (1970)
    2,0,1,2 - 2,1,1,0 - timp.,perc. - str.   15:00 Fleisher.

MILVEDEN, Ingmar
—— SERENADE FOR STRINGS, OP. 7
    str.   13:30 S.T.I.M.

MIMAROGLU, Ilhan
—— IDOLS OF PERVERSITY (FOR VIOLA AND STRINGS (1972)
    str.   9:00 Seesaw.
—— NOCTURNE (FOR STRING ORCH. AND TAPE)
    Tape-recorder - str.   8:00 Seesaw.
—— ROMANCE FOR TROMBONE AND STRINGS (1947)
    trb. - str.   5:00 Seesaw.
—— SEPTEMBER MOON (1967)
        6:00 Seesaw.

MINAMI, Hiroaki
—— BANKA (3 THRENODIES FOR SOPRANO AND ORCH.)
    (1963) (Text: Japanese Poems of 7th and 8th Centuries)
    6,3,3,3 - 4,3,3,1 - timp.,perc.(6),cel.,glock.,vibra.,xyl. - pf. - str.
        12:00 MCA Music.

MINEO, Samuel H.
—— CALIFORNIA RHAPSODY, OP. 5 (CONCERTO FOR PIANO
    AND ORCH.)
    *3,*3,2,b-cl.(alt. with c.-bn.),2 - 4,3,2,0 - timp.,perc.(3),xyl. - pf. -
    str.   16:00 Harrison.
—— EVANGELINE (TONE POEM) (1960)
    *3,*3,*3,*3 - 4,0,3,0 - timp.,perc.(2),cel.,glock. - str.
        29:00 Composer.

—— ROMAN CONCERTO (FOR PIANO AND ORCH.) (IN 1
    MOVT.) (1959)
    *3,*3,1 E♭cl.,*3,*3 - 4,0,3,0 - timp.,perc.(2),glock. - pf. - str.
        11:00 Composer.

MIRANTE, Thomas
—— ARIOSO (1968)
    str.   5:00 Composer.
—— NIGHT SCENE (1966)
    *3,*3,*3,*3 - 4,3,3,1 - timp.,perc.(2),bells,xyl. - pf. - str.
        6:00 Composer.
—— SYMPHONY NO. 1 (1968)
    1. Lento; 2. Adagio; 3. Allegro
    *3,*3,*3,*3 - 4,3,3,1 - timp.,perc.(3),bells,xyl. - hp. - pf. - str.
        19:05 Composer.

MIROGLIO, Francis
—— ESPACES
        Leeds.
—— ESPACES II (FOR CHAMBER ORCH.)
        Leeds.
—— ESPACES III
    str.   Leeds.
—— MAGIES (FOR SOPRANO AND 10 INSTRUMENTS)
        Leeds.

MISSA-ALIPRANDI
—— ESQUISSES PYRÉNÉENNES
    1(alt. with picc.),1(alt. with Eng. hn.),2,1(alt. with c.-bn.) - 1,2,1,0
    - timp.,perc. - hp. - str.   8:20 Eds. Fran.

MISSAL, Joshua M.
—— IN MEMORIAM (FOR VOICE AND ORCH.)
    *3,2,2,*3 - 4,3,3,1 - timp.,perc.(3),bells - str.   11:00 Composer.
—— SYMPHONIETTA (IN 3 MOVTS.)
    2,2,2,2 - 4,2,2,1 - timp.,perc.(2),glock. - hp. - str. 20:00 Composer.
—— THREE KANSAS PORTRAITS (IN 3 MOVTS.)
    *3,2,2,2 - 4,3,3,1 - timp.,perc.(4),glock.,xyl. - hp. - pf. - str.
        11:00 Composer.
—— THRENODY
    fl. - pf. - str.   4:30 Composer.
—— WHEATLAND (CANTATA) (FOR BARITONE, SATB CHORUS
    AND ORCH.) (Text: Dr. Geraldine Hammond)
    *3,2,2,*3 - 4,3,3,1 - timp.,perc.(5),bells,cel. - hp. - pf. - str.
        35:00 Composer.
—— WHEATLAND (SUITE FROM THE CANTATA) (IN 4 MOVTS.)
    *3,2,2,*3 - 4,3,3,1 - timp.,perc.,bells,cel. - hp. - pf.(ad lib.) - str.
        14:00 Composer.

MITCHELL, Lyndol
—— CONCERTO GROSSO (FOR 3 TROMBONES AND ORCH.) (IN
    3 MOVTS.)
    1,1,1,1 - 2,1,3,0 - str.   15:00 Composer.
—— FANTASIA FOR ORCHESTRA
    2(2nd alt. with picc.),2,2,2 - 4,3,3,1 - timp.,perc.(2) - hp. - str.
        10:00 Composer.
—— KENTUCKY MOUNTAIN PORTRAITS (IN 3 MOVTS.)
        13:45 C. Fischer.
—— MELODY FOR STRINGS
    str.   10:00 Composer.
—— OVERTURE "JUBILATION"
    2(2nd alt. with picc.),2,2,2 - 4,2,3,1 - timp.,perc.(2),xyl. - str.
        5:00 Composer.
—— RAILROAD SUITE (IN 3 MOVTS.)
    2(2nd alt. with picc.),2(2nd alt. with Eng. hn.),*3,2 - 4,3,3,1 -
    timp.,perc.(3) - str.   12:00 Shawnee.
—— TOCCATA FOR VIOLIN AND ORCH.
    2(2nd alt. with picc.),2,2,2 - 4,2,3,1 - timp.,perc.(2) - str.
        10:00 Composer.

MITREA-CELARIANU, Mihai Grigore
—— AIN MI
    2(2nd alt. with picc.),2(2nd alt. with Eng. hn.),2,2 - 2,2,3,1 -
    perc.(3-4),mar., vibra. - Hammond org. - str.   14:00 Salabert.
—— CANTATA (FOR MIXED CHORUS AND ORCH.) (1967) (Text:
    Biblical)
    *4(2nd and 3rd fl. also alt. with piccs.), 1 alto fl. in F, *3, 3(3rd
    alt. with b.-cl.),2 - 4,3,3,0 - perc.,glock.,mar.,vibra. - hp. - pf. - str.
        10:00 Salabert.

—— LE CHANT DES ÉTOILES (CANTATA) (FOR SOPRANO OR
MEZZO-SOPRANO AND 20 INSTRUMENTALISTS) (1964)
(Text: Algonquin Indian Poem)
   *2,1 alto fl.,*2,*2,*2,1 - 1,1,1,0 - perc.(3) - elec.guit. - pf. -
   str.(1,1,1,1)   5:00 Salabert.
—— CONVERGENCES III ("IDÉOPHONIE M") (FOR MALE AND
FEMALE SPEAKER, 7-VOICE CHILDREN'S CHORUS AND
ENSEMBLE) (1968) (Text: Michel Empain and Composer)
   2 picc.,1,0,1,1 alto sax.,*2 - 0,1,1, b.-tpt.,1,0 - perc.(2),mar.,vibra. -
   pf. - str.(2,2,0,2)   10:00 Salabert.
—— LA MÉLODIE DES SONS DU TEMPS (A-G) (FOR 17
PLAYERS) (1971)
   Recorder,*2,0,*2,0 - 0,alto bugle,1(alt.with picc.tpt.),1,0 - perc.(2)
   - hpsc. - hammond org. - pf. - str.(2,1,1,1 and alto viola da gamba)
                                              12:00 Salabert.
—— PETITE HISTOIRE D'AVANT-MONDE (1968)
   1,0,*2,1 ato sax.,1 - 0,1,1,0 - perc.(4),bells,mar.,vibra. - hpsc. - pf. -
   d.-b.   14:00 Salabert.
—— SIGNAUX (SUR L'OCÉAN U) (1971)
   *2,0,*2,0 - 0,1,1,1 - perc.(2) - pf. - str.(1,1,0,1)
                                              Salabert.

MITSUKURI, Shukichi
—— SINFONIETTA
   2,2,2,2 - 2,2,1,0 - timp.,perc. - pf. - str.   Templeton.

MIYAGI, Michio
—— SEA OF THE SPRING
                                              7:10 J.A.S.R.A.C.

MIYOSHI, Akira
—— CONCERTO FOR ORCHESTRA
   3,3,3,3 - 6,4,3,1 - timp., perc.(5), cel., xyl. - hp. - pf. - str.
                                              11:00 Presser.
—— CONCERTO FOR VIOLIN AND ORCHESTRA
   2,2,2,2 - 4,2,3,0 - timp., perc.(4), cel., xyl. - str.   25:00 Presser.
—— THREE SYMPHONIC MOVEMENTS
   3,3,3,3 - 4,4,3,1 - timp., perc.(4), bells, cel., xyl. - hp. - pf. - str.
                                              25:00 Presser.

MOENE, Alain
—— CHRONIQUES
   3,3,3,3 - 4,4,3,1 - str.   Presser.
—— KEMMA (FOR STRINGS)
                                              12:00 Presser.

MOERAN, Ernest J.
—— CONCERTO FOR CELLO AND ORCH.
   3,2,2,2 - 4,2,3,0 - timp.,perc. - hp. - str.   26:00 Novello.
—— CONCERTO FOR VIOLIN AND ORCH.
   2,2,2,2 - 4,2,3,0 - timp.,perc. - 2 hp. - str.   32:00 Novello.
—— FARRAGO (SUITE) (IN 4 MOVTS.)
   2,1,2,2 - 2,2,3,0 - timp.,perc. - str.   14:00 P.R.S.
—— IN THE MOUNTAIN COUNTRY
   3(3rd alt. with picc.),2,3,2 - 4,2,3,1 - timp.,perc. - str.
                                              8:00 Oxford.
—— LONELY WATERS
   1,1,1,1 - hn. - perc. - str.   10:00 Novello.
—— OVERTURE FOR A MASQUE
   2,2,3,2 - 4,3,3,0 - timp.,perc. - str.   9:30 Galaxy.
—— RHAPSODY NO. 1
   3,3,3,2 - 4,3,3,1 - timp.,perc. - str.   15:00 Bo. Hawkes.
—— RHAPSODY NO. 2
   3,3,3,2 - 4,3,3,1 - timp.,perc. - hp. - str.   12:00 P.R.S.
   or:
   2,2,2,2 - 4,3,3,1 - timp.,perc. - str.
—— SERENADE
                                              15:00 Novello.
—— SINFONIETTA
   3,2,2,2 - 2,2,0,0 - timp.,perc. - str.   25:00 Novello.
—— SYMPHONY IN G MINOR
   2,2,2,2 - 4,3,3,1 - timp.,perc. - hp. - str.   42:00 Novello.
—— WHYTHORNE'S SHADOW
   1,1,1,0 - 1,0,0,0 - str.   6:00 Novello.

MOERANE, Michael M.
—— CHORALE ETUDE (FOR PIANO AND SMALL ORCH.)
   2,0,3,0 - 0,0,0,0 - pf. - str.   3:00 S.A.M.R.O.
—— FATSE LA HESO (SYMPHONIC POEM)
   2,2,3,2 - 4,2,3,1 - timp.,perc. - str.   10:00 S.A.M.R.O.

MOESCHINGER, Albert
—— AMOR UND PSYCHE (BALLET) %
   3,3,3,3 - 4,3,3,1 - timp.,perc. - str.   40:00 Bo. Hawkes.

—— AMOR UND PSYCHE (SUITE)
   3,3,3,3 - 4,3,3,1 - timp.,perc. - str.   20:00 Bo. Hawkes.
—— BALLADE SYMPHONIQUE, OP. 82
   2,3,3,2 - 4,3,3,1 - timp.,perc.,cel. - hp. - str.   15:00 Bo. Hawkes.
—— CONCERTO FOR PIANO AND ORCH.
   2(2nd alt. with picc.),2,2,2 - 4,2,2,0 - perc.(5),cel. - hp. - pf. - str.
                                              16:00 Modern.
—— CONCERTO FOR TRUMPET AND SMALL ORCH., OP. 77
   0,2,2,2 - 2,0,0,0 - str.   20:00 S.U.I.S.A.
—— CONCERTO FOR VIOLIN AND ORCH., OP. 40
   *2,2,2,2 - 2,2,0,0 - timp.,perc. - str.   20:00 Baerenrtr.
—— CONCERTO LYRIQUE, OP. 83 (FOR SAXOPHONE AND
ORCH.)
   2,1,2 sax.,2 - 2,2,0,0 - timp.,perc.,cel. - hp. - str.
                                              15:00 Bo. Hawkes.
—— ENTRÉE ET SCHERZO INGÉNU
                                              6:00 S.U.I.S.A.
—— FANTAISIE SUR DES LETTRES "SAINTES" B-A-C-H
                                              10:00 S.U.I.S.A.
—— FANTASIE, OP. 84 (FOR STRING ORCH.)
   str.   14:00 Bo. Hawkes.
—— FOUR SHORT PIECES FOR STRING ORCH.
   str.   8:00 Bo. Hawkes.
—— DIE KLEINE SEE JUNGFRAU, OP. 75 (CANTATA) (FOR
SOLO VOICES, MIXED CHORUS AND ORCH.)
   *2,*2,*2,2 - 4,2,0,0 - timp.,perc.,cel. - hp. - pf. - str.
                                              63:00 S.U.I.S.A.
—— PETITE SUITE POUR ORCHESTRE
                                              10:00 S.U.I.S.A.
—— SONATINE PASTORALE (FOR OBOE AND STRINGS)
   ob. - str.   10:00 Bo. Hawkes.
—— STATI D'ANIMO (PASSACAGLIA PER ORCHESTRA)
   2,2,2,2 - 2,2,0,0 - timp.,cel.,vibra.,cymb.,tam. - str. 8:00 S.U.I.S.A.
—— SYMPHONY NO. 2, OP. 73
   1,1,1,1 - 2,0,0,0 - timp.,perc. - str.   25:00 Bo. Hawkes.
—— SYMPHONY NO. 3, OP. 76
   *3,*3,*3,*3 - 4,3,3,1 - timp.,perc. - str.   25:00 Baerenrtr.
—— SYMPHONY NO. 4, OP. 80
   3,3,3,2 - 4,3,3,1 - timp.,perc. - str.   19:00 Bo. Hawkes.
—— TRES CAPRICHOS
   3,2,3,2 - 2,1,2,0 - timp.,perc.,cel.,vibra.,xyl. - hp. - pf. - str.
                                              15:00 S.U.I.S.A.
—— THE VOYAGE (FOR STRING ORCH.)
   str.   12:00 Bo. Hawkes.

MOEVS, Robert
—— ATTIS-PART I (FOR TENOR, SSAT CHORUS AND ORCH.)
(1958) (Text: Catullus)
   3(3rd alt. with picc.),*3,1 E♭cl.,*2,*3 - 4,3,1 b.-tpt.,3,1 -
   timp.,perc.(6),cel.,xyl. - hp. - pf. - str.   20:00 Composer.
—— ATTIS-PART II (FOR SOPRANO, TENOR, SSAT CHORUS
AND ORCH.) (1963) (Text: Catullus)
   3(3rd alt. with picc.),*3,1 E♭cl.,*2,*3 - 4,3,1b.-tpt.,3,1 -
   timp.,perc.(6),cel.,mar.,xyl. - hp. - pf. - str.   15:00 Composer.
—— CONCERTO FOR PIANO, ORCH. AND PERCUSSION (1960)
   3(3rd alt. with picc.),*3,*3(1 alt. with E♭cl.),*3 - 4,3,3,1 -
   timp.,perc.(8-9),bells,xyl. - hp. - pf. - str.   19:00 Composer.
—— ET OCCIDENTUM ILLUSTRA (SHINE ALSO UPON THE
WEST) (FOR MIXED CHORUS AND ORCH.) (1964) (Text:
Dante and Theodore Frelinghuysen)
   *3(2nd alt. with picc.),*3,1 E♭cl.,*2,*3 - 4,3,3,0 -
   timp.,perc.(5-6),bells,glock.,vibra.,xyl. - hp. - pf. - str.
                                              18:30 Piedmont.
—— FOURTEEN VARIATIONS FOR ORCHESTRA (1952)
   3(3rd alt. with picc.),*3,2,*3 - 4,3,3,1 - timp.,perc.(4) - str.
                                              16:00 Composer.
—— MAIN-TRAVELED ROADS (1973)
   2(2nd alt. with picc.),*3,*3,*3 - 4,3,3,1 - timp.,perc.(3) - str.
                                              11:30 Composer.
—— MUSICA DE CAMERA I (MUSIC FOR CHAMBER ORCH.)
(1965)
   1(alt. with picc.),0,1(alt. with E♭cl.),1(alt. with c.-bn.) - 1,0,0,0 -
   perc.(3),glock.,xyl. - 1 hp. - 1 vln.,1 vla.,1 c.   13:00 Piedmont.
—— OVERTURE FOR ORCHESTRA (1950)
   3(3rd alt. with picc.),*3,*3,*3 - 4,3,3,1 - timp.,perc.(3) - 2 hp. - str.
                                              12:30 Composer.

MOHAUPT, Richard
—— BALLET SUITE FROM THE OPERA "DIE BREMER
STADTMUSIKANTEN" ("THE BREMEN TOWN MUSICIANS")
                                              J. Oertel.
—— CONCERTO FOR ORCHESTRA
                                              J. Oertel.

—— CONCERTO FOR PIANO AND ORCH.
J. Oertel.

—— CONCERTO FOR VIOLIN AND ORCH.
J. Oertel.

—— MUCH ADO ABOUT NOTHING (OVERTURE)
2,2,2,2 - 4,2,3,1 - timp. - hp. - pf. - str.   Remick.

—— STADTPFEIFERMUSIK (TOWN PIPER'S MUSIC) (FOR SYMPHONY ORCH.)
J. Oertel.

—— SUITE FROM THE BALLET "DIE GAUNERSTREICHE DER COURASCHE"
J. Oertel.

—— SYMPHONY NO. 1
J. Oertel.

MOHLER, Philipp
—— CONCERTINO FOR ORCHESTRA, OP. 11
Henmar.

—— CONCERTO FOR PIANO AND ORCH., OP. 16
Henmar.

—— FANTASIESTÜCK (FOR CELLO, PIANO AND STRING ORCH.)
pf. - str.   Hans Gerig.

—— SINFONISCHES CAPRICCIO, OP. 40
2,2,3,2 - 4,3,3,1 - timp.,perc.,cel. - hp. - str.   14:00 Sikorski.

MOHR, Gerhard
—— CONCERTO IN B MINOR FOR ACCORDION AND ORCH.
Henmar.

—— MEDITERRANA (SUITE) (IN 5 MOVTS.)
Tonos Vlg.

—— RHAPSODIC CONCERTO (FOR CELLO AND ORCH.)
EdDelicado.

—— SUITE MEDITERRANEA
2,2,2,2 - 4,3,3,0 - timp.,perc. - hp. - str.   17:00 Seesaw.

MOKRANJAC, Vasilije
—— LYRIC POEM
3,3,3,3 - 4,3,3,1 - timp.,perc.,cel. - hp. - pf. - str.
10:00 MIC,Zagreb.

—— SYMPHONY NO. 3 IN E
3,3,3,3 - 4,3,3,1 - timp.,perc.,cel.,vibra. - hp. - pf. - str.
25:00 MIC,Zagreb.

—— SYMPHONY NO. 4
3,3,3,3 - 4,3,3,1 - timp.,perc.,cel.,vibra. - hp. - pf. - str.
23:00 MIC,Zagreb.

MOLINEUX, Allen
—— CONCERTATO FOR ORCHESTRA (1971)
*3,2,*3,2 - 0,3,3,1 - timp.,perc.(2),bells - str.   11:00 Composer.

—— CONCERTO FOR TRUMPET AND ORCH. (1974)
1. Adagio; 2. Allegro; 3. Lento; 4. Presto
3(3rd alt. with picc.),*3,*3,*3 - 4,4,3,1 -
timp.,perc.(5),bells,vibra.,xyl. - hp. - str.   12:00 Composer.

—— SALUTATION (A SHORT PRELUDE FOR ORCH.) (1971)
2,2,2,2 - 4,2,3,1 - timp.,perc.(1) - str.   2:00 Composer.

MOLIQUE, Bernhard - MICHAELS, Jost
—— CONCERTINO IN F MINOR FOR CLARINET AND ORCH.
1,2,1,2 - 2,2,0,0 - timp. - str.   10:00 G. Schirmer.

MÖLLER-HORST, Agnes
—— THREE PORTRAITS OF OLD DENMARK
str.   3:30 Volkwein.

MOMPOU, Federico
—— LOS IMPROPRIOS (FOR BARITONE OR BASS, WITH SATB CHORUS AND ORCH.)
1,1,1,1 - 2,2,0,0 - timp.,perc.,cel. - 2 hp. - str.   30:00 Salabert.

MOMPOU, Federico - ROSENTHAL, Manuel
—— SUBURBIS
2,2,2,2 - 2,2,1,0 - perc.(2) - hp. - str.   13:00 Salabert.

MOMPOU, Federico - TANSMAN, Alexandre
—— SCÈNES D'ENFANTS (SUITE)
2 fl.,ob.,cl. - perc.,cel. - pf. - str.   8:00 Salabert.

MONACO, Richard A.
—— MAGNIFICAT (FOR SOPRANO, TENOR, MIXED CHORUS AND ORCH) (1968)
1(alt.with picc.),1,1,1 - 1,0,0,0 - timp.,perc.(2),cel.,glock.,xyl. - hp. - pf. - str.   40:00 Composer.

—— OVERTURE TO "AS YOU LIKE IT" (1965)
1,1,1,1 - 1,1,0,0 - timp.,perc.(1) - str.   4:30 Composer.

—— SYMPHONY FOR ORCHESTRA (IN 3 MOVTS.) (1960)
2,2,*3,2 - 4,3,3,1 - timp.,perc.(2),cel.,xyl. - hp. - pf. - str.
22:00 Composer.

MONDELLO, Nuncio F.
—— FANTASY FOR ORCHESTRA (1955)
*3,2,2,2 - 4,2,3,1 - timp.,perc.(3),xyl. - str.   16:00 Composer.

—— INTRODUCTION AND ALLEGRO (1959)
alto sax. - str.   7:00 Composer.

—— SUITE FOR STRING ORCH. (1954) (IN 3 MOVTS.)
str.   12:45 Composer.

MONDONVILLE, Jean Joseph - PETIT, J. L.
—— SONATA NO. 1 FOR ORCHESTRA
str.   8:00 Presser.

MONELLE, Raymond
—— DIVERTIMENTO ON LUTE SONGS (1966)
2,2,2,2 - 2,2,0,0 - timp. - str.   18:00 P.R.S.

—— THREE MOVEMENTS FOR STRINGS (1964)
str.   15:00 P.R.S.

MONELLO, Spartaco V.
—— CONCERTO FOR ORCH., OP. 26
2(2nd alt. with picc.),2,2,2 - 2,2,0,0 - timp.,perc.(4) - str.
20:00 Mills.

—— CONCERTO GROSSO, OP. 15
pf. - str.   19:00 Mills.

—— COUNTRY DANCE, OP. 18
*3,2,2,2 - 3,2,2,0 - timp.,perc.(5),xyl. - str.   9:00 Mills.

—— DIVERTIMENTO, OP. 33
3,1,1 E♭cl.,*3,2 sax.(1 alto and 1 ten.),1 - 2,1cnt.,2,3,1 -
timp.,perc.(4),xyl. - str.   5:00 Composer.

—— LAMENT FOR ORCH., OP. 29
2(2nd alt. with picc.),*3,*3,*3 - 4,2,3,1 - timp.,perc.(4) - str.
9:00 Mills.

—— PASSACAGLIA FOR ORCH., OP. 1A
*4,*4,*4,*3 - 4,4,3,1 - timp.,perc.(3),bells - str.   10:00 Composer.

—— SICILIAN SUITE, OP. 25 (IN 4 MOVTS.)
2(2nd alt. with picc.),2,2,2 - 4,2,3,0 - timp.,perc.(4) - str.
22:00 C. Fischer.

—— SINFONIA ACCADEMICA, OP. 31
2(2nd alt. with picc.),2,2,2 - 2,2,3,0 - timp.,perc.(4) - str.
28:00 Mills.

—— SINFONIA FOR ORCH., OP. 6
*3,*3,*3,*3 - 4,4,3,1 - timp.,perc.(4),xyl. - str.   12:00 Composer.

—— SONGS OF FREEDOM (OVERTURE), OP. 8
*3,*3,*3,*3 - 4,4,3,1 - timp.,perc.(5) - str.   10:00 Composer.

—— SYMPHONIC DISCOURSE, OP. 28
*3,*3,2,*3 - 4,3,3,1 - timp.,perc.(6),xyl. - str.   16:00 Composer.

—— SYMPHONY NO. 1, OP. 9
*3,2,2,2 - 4,3,3,1 - timp.,perc.(4) - str.   40:00 Mills.

—— SYMPHONY NO. 2, OP. 11
str.   28:00 Mills.

—— SYMPHONY NO. 3, OP. 22
*3,*3,2,2 - 4,3,3,1 - timp.,perc.(4) - str.   30:00 Composer.

—— SYMPHONY NO. 4, OP. 30
3(3rd alt. with picc.),*3,*4(3rd alt. with E♭cl.),*3 - 4,3,3,1 -
timp.,perc.(5) - str.   45:00 Composer.

MONESTEL, Alexander
—— THE BIRTH OF OUR LORD (CHRISTMAS CANTATA) (FOR SOLO VOICES, SATB CHORUS AND ORCH.)
1,1,2,1 - 2,2,2,0 - timp.,perc. - str.   16:20 C. Fischer.

MONN, Matthias Georg - SCHOENBERG, Arnold
—— CONCERTO FOR CELLO AND ORCH.
1. Allegro moderato; 2. Andante a la marcia; 3. Tempo di minuetto
2(1 alt. with picc.),2,2,2 - 2,2,1,0 - timp.,perc.(2) - hp. - str.
20:00 Belmont.

—— CONCERTO IN G MINOR, FOR CELLO AND STRINGS (ARR. 1912)
cemb. - str.   17:00 Belmont.

MONNIKENDAM, Marius
—— ARBEID (SYMPHONISCHE BEWEGING)
3,3,3,2 sax.,3 - 4,3,3,1 - timp.,perc.,cel.,xyl. - hp. - pf. - str.
13:00 Henmar.

—— BOETPSALMEN (FOR MIXED-CHORUS AND ORCH.) (1934)
2,3,3,3 - 4,3,3,1 - timp.,perc. - pf. - str.   30:00 Henmar.

—— CONCERTO FOR ORGAN AND ORCH.
2,2,2,2 - 4,3,3,0 - timp.,perc.(3, incl. 2 on timp.) - hp.(ad lib.) - org. - 2 d.-b.   17:00 Henmar.
—— CONCERTO FOR ORGAN AND STRINGS (1958)
org. - str.   15:00 Henmar.
—— CONCERTO FOR TRUMPET, HORN AND ORCH.
3,2,2,2 - 1,1,0,0 - timp.,perc. - pf. - str.   17:00 Mills.
—— HYMNE (FOR ALTO, MALE CHORUS AND ORCH.) (1957)
2,2,2,2 - 4,3,3,1 - timp.,perc.,xyl. - org. (ad lib.) - pf.(4 hands) - 2 d.-b.   13:00 Henmar.
—— MAGNIFICAT (FOR SOPRANO, MALE CHORUS AND ORCH.) (1956)
3,2,2,3 - 4,3,3,1 - timp.,perc.,cel.,xyl. - hp. - pf. (4 hands) - 2 d.-b.   18:00 Henmar.
—— MISSA FESTIVA (FOR MIXED CHORUS AND ORCH.) (1956)
2,2,2,2 - 4,2,2,1 - timp.,perc. - hp. - str.   20:00 Henmar.
—— MOUVEMENTS SYMPHONIQUES
3,3,3,3 - 4,3,3,1 - timp.,perc. - 2 hp. - str.   16:00 Henmar.
—— NOE (LA DESTRUCTION DU PREMIER MONDE) (ORATORIO) (FOR SOLO VOICES, CHORUS AND ORCH.)
3,2,2,3 - 4,3,3,1 - timp.,perc.,cel.,xyl. - hp. - pf. - 4-hands - str.   70:00 Henmar.
—— OVERTURE FOR ORGAN AND ORCH. (1960)
2,3,0,2 - 4,3,3,1 - timp.,perc.,cel. - org.   6:00 Henmar.
—— PAASSPEL (FOR MALE CHORUS AND ORCH.)
                    25:00 Henmar.
—— SINFONIA SACRA I (FOR MALE CHORUS AND ORCH.) (1949)
3,3,3,3 - 4,3,3,1 - timp.,perc. - hp. - str.   30:00 Henmar.
—— SINFONIA SACRA II ("DOMINE SALVUM FAC") (FOR BOYS CHORUS, MALE CHORUS AND ORCH.) (1952)
3,2,2,2 - 0,3,3,1 - perc. - str.   18:00 Henmar.
—— SINFONIA SUPER "MERCK TOCH HOE STERCK"
0,0,0,0 - 0,2,2,0 - timp.,perc. - pf. - str.   17:00 Henmar.
—— TROIS PSAUMES POUR LE TEMPS PRÉSENT (FOR SATB SOLO VOICES, CHORUSES AND ORCH.)
2(2nd alt. with picc.),2(2nd alt. with Eng. hn.),2,2 - 3,0,0,0 - timp.,perc. - str.   23:00 Henmar.
—— VAN RIEBEECK-TAFERELEN (FOR 2 SPEAKING VOICES, BOYS CHORUS, MIXED CHORUS AND ORCH.) (1952) (Text: W. A. P. Smit)
2,2,3,3 - 4,3,3,1 - timp.,perc.,cel. - hp. - pf. - str.   30:00 Henmar.
—— VARIATIONS SYMPHONIQUES ON ("MERCK TOCH HOE STERCK")
2,2,2,sax.,3 - 4,3,3,1 - timp.,perc. - hp. - str.   12:00 Henmar.

MONOD, Jacques-Louis
—— CANTUS CONTRA CANTUM (FOR SOPRANO AND 14 INSTRUMENTS) (Texts: Paul Eluard and Jean Sénac)
1,1,*1,1 - 1,0,0,1 - perc.(2) - guit.,mandolin - hp. - pf. - str.(no vla.,or c.)   10:00 Boelke-Bo.

MONONEN, Sakari
—— CONCERTO GROSSO (1970)
2,2,2,2 - 0,0,0,0 - str.   10:00 FinnMICtr.
—— LEGGENDA CON ESPRESSIONE (1971)
2,2,2,2 - 0,0,0,0 - str.   10:00 FinnMICtr.
—— PERSPECTIVES (1972)
2,2,2,2 - 2,2,2,0 - timp., - str.   10:00 FinnMICtr.
—— PRELUDE (1961)
2,2,2,3 - 4,2,3,0 - timp. - str.   18:00 FinnMICtr.
—— SYMPHONY (1961)
2,2,2,3 - 4,3,3,0 - timp. - str.   20:00 FinnMICtr.

MONRAD JOHANSEN, David
—— EPIGRAMS ON NORWEGIAN MOTIFS, OP. 31
2,1,2,1 - 2,2,0,0 - perc. - str.   14:00 T.O.N.O.
—— IGNIS ARDENS, OP. 20 (CANTATA) (FOR SOPRANO, BASS, MIXED CHORUS AND ORCH.) (Text: Olaf Bull)
2,2,2,2 - 4,3,3,1 - timp.,perc. - str.   50:00 T.O.N.O.
—— SIGVAT SKALD, OP. 16 (FOR VOICE AND ORCH.) (Text: Traditional, available in English)
2,2,2,2 - 4,2,3,1 - timp.,perc. - str.   6:00 Ed. Musikk-Hu.
—— SYMPHONIC VARIATIONS, OP. 23
2,2,2,2 - 4,2,0,0 - timp.,perc. - str.   16:00 T.O.N.O.
—— VOLUSPAA, OP. 15 (FOR SOPRANO, ALTO, BARITONE, MIXED CHORUS AND ORCH.) (Text: Traditional, from the "Edda")
3,2,2,2 - 4,2,3,1 - timp.,perc. - str.   42:00 T.O.N.O.

MONTAGUE, Stephen
—— SOUND ROUND
4,3,3,3 - 4,3,3,1 - tape-recorder - str.   22:00 Modern.

—— VARSHAVIAN SPRING (FOR 4 SOPRANOS, 4 ALTOS, 4 TENORS, 4 BASSES AND 16 INSTRUMENTALISTS)
                    9:30 Modern.

MONTANI, Nicola
—— THE BELLS (CANTATA) (FOR WOMEN'S CHORUS AND ORCH.) (IN 4 MOVTS) (Text: Edgar Allan Poe)
2(2nd alt. with picc.),1,2,2 - 4,2,2,1 - timp.,perc.(2) - hp. - pf. - str.   45:00 Gray.
—— MISSA SOLEMNIS (FOR CHORUS AND ORCH.)
1,1,2,1 - 2,2,2,0 - str.   G. Schirmer.

MONTEVERDI, Claudio
—— ORFEO (3-ACT MUSICAL FABLE) % (Engl. Text: Robert Stuart)
3,3,2,2 - 4,2,0,0 - timp.,perc. - hp. - pf. - str.   G. Schirmer.

MONTEVERDI, Claudio - BENVENUTI, Giacomo
—— L' INCORONAZIONE DI POPPEA ("THE CORONATION OF POPPEA") (3-ACT OPERA) %
3,3,3,3 - 4,2,3,1 - timp.,perc. - 2 hp. - str.   Leeds.
On Stage: 2 brass bands

MONTEVERDI, Claudio - DALLAPICCOLA, Luigi
—— IL RITORNO DI ULISSE IN PATRIA ("ULYSSES' RETURN TO HIS HOMELAND") (3-ACT OPERA) %
3,3,4,3 - 4,3,3,1 - timp.,perc.(2) - 2 hp. - hpsc. - str.   Leeds.

MONTEVERDI, Claudio - DE FILIPPI, Amedeo
—— SIX SYMPHONIC FRAGMENTS FROM "THE CORONATION OF POPPEA"
                    Arranger.
—— THREE PIECES FROM "THE CORONATION OF POPPEA"
str.   Arranger.

MONTEVERDI, Claudio - GHEDINI, Giorgio Federico
—— IL COMBATTIMENTO DI TANCREDI E CLORINDA (DRAMATIC MADRIGAL, FROM TASSO'S "JERUSALEM LIBERATED") %
hp. - hpsc. - str.(no vlns.)   25:00 Leeds.
—— MAGNIFICAT (FOR CHORUS AND ORCH.)
2,2,2,0 - 0,3,2,0 - org. - str.   25:00 Leeds.

MONTEVERDI, Claudio - LEPPARD, Raymond
—— L' INCORONAZIONE DI POPPEA (2-ACT OPERA) % (Text: Italian - Francesco Busenello; Engl. - Humphrey Proctor-Gregg)
Lute (alt. with guit. and chitarrone) - hp. - 2 hpsc. - 2 org. - str.   142:00 G. Schirmer.

MONTEVERDI, Claudio - MADERNA, Bruno
—— ORFEO (FAVOLA PASTORALE IN DUE PARTI) % (Text: A. Striggio, Jr.)
3,3,4,3 - 4,3,3,0 - timp.,perc.(4),bells,cel.,vibra. - 2 guit.,mandolin - 2 hp. - hpsc. - org. - str.   MCA Music.

MONTEVERDI, Claudio - MALIPIERO, G. Francesco
—— IL COMBATTIMENTO DI TANCREDI E CLORINDA (DRAMATIC MADRIGAL) % (FOR 3 SINGERS AND SMALL ORCH.) (Original Text: Tasso; Engl. Text: Peter Pears)
hpsc.(or cel.,hp., or pf.) - str.   G. Schirmer.
—— ORFEO (2-ACT FABLE IN MUSIC) (FOR SOLO VOICES, MIXED CHORUS AND ORCH.) % (Text: E. A. Striggio)
2,2,2,2 - 4,0,0,0 - cel. - hp. - pf. - str.   Leeds.

MONTEVERDI, Claudio - MANZONI, Giacomo
—— IL BALLO DELLE INGRATE
2,5,0,2 - 0,0,0,0 - timp.,perc.(4) - hp. - org. - str.(9,7,4,2)   35:00 MCA Music.

MONTEVERDI, Claudio - MEYEROWITZ, Jan
—— CHORUS OF THE PHAEACIANS (FROM THE OPERA "IL RITORNO DE ULISSE IN PATRIA") (FOR MIXED CHORUS AND STRING ORCH.)
str.   4:00 Broude.

MONTEVERDI, Claudio - MORTARI, Virgilio
—— IL COMBATTIMENTO DI TANCREDI E CLORINDA (FOR TWO VOICES, CEMBALO AND STRINGS)
cemb. - str.   25:00 Bo. Hawkes.
—— TEMPRO LA CETRA (FOR VOICE, CEMBALO AND STRINGS)
cemb. - str.   6:00 Bo. Hawkes.

MONTEVERDI, Claudio - PERESS, Maurice
—— OTOCCATA AND RITORNELLI FROM "ORFEO" (IN 1 MOVT.) (ARR. 1967)
2 picc.,1,2,*3,2 - 4,3,3-4,0 - perc.(1) - hp. - str.   4:30 G. Schirmer.

MONTEVERDI, Claudio - SAMUEL, Gerhard
—— TOCCATA (FROM THE OPERA "ORFEO")
2,4,0,0 - 0,3,3,0 - timp. - hp. - str.   4:00 Belw-Mills.

MONTEVERDI, Claudio - SMITHERS, Don
—— MAGNIFICAT A SEI VOCE (FOR CHORUS AND INSTRUMENTS)
3 trb. - str.(2,2,vla. da gamba,1,1)   Law-Gould.

MONTEVERDI, Claudio - STEVENS, Denis
—— IL COMBATTIMENTO DI TANCREDI E CLORINDA (FOR SOPRANO, TENOR, BASS, STRINGS AND CONTINUO) (Text: Tasso)
cemb. - str.   22:00 Oxford.
—— VESPERS (FOR SOLOISTS, DOUBLE CHORUS, ORGAN AND ORCH.)
    65:00 Novello.

MONTEVERDI, Claudio - TONI, Alceo
—— IL COMBATTIMENTO DI TANCREDI E DI CLORINDA (FOR TWO VOICES, NARRATOR AND ORCH.)
0,0,2,2 - 4,3,4,1 - timp.,cel. - hp. - str.   25:00 Bo. Hawkes.
or:
str.

MONTEVERDI, Claudio - WAGNER, Roger
—— MAGNIFICAT PRIMO (FOR CHORUS, ORGAN AND STRINGS)
org. - str.   Law-Gould.

MONTGOMERY, Bruce
—— CONCERTINO FOR STRINGS
str.   16:00 Novello.
—— HERODOTUS FRAGMENTS (FOR SATB CHORUS AND ORCH., OP. 88 (1970) (Text: Herodotus of Halicarnassus)
    30:00 Composer.

MONTSALVATGE, Xavier
—— CINCO CANCIONES NEGRAS (A SONG CYCLE) (FOR VOICE AND ORCH.)
2,2,3,2 - 2,2,2,0 - timp.,perc.,xyl. - hp. - pf. (or cel.) - str.   10:30 Southern.
—— CINCO INVOCACIONES AL CRUCIFICADO (FIVE INVOCATIONS TO THE CRUCIFIED ONE) (FOR VOICE AND ORCH.)
    23:15 Southern.
—— CONCERTO BREVE (FOR PIANO AND ORCH.)
2,2,3,2 - 4,2,3,0 - timp.,perc.,vibra. - str.   24:00 Southern.
—— POEMA CONCERTANTE (FOR VIOLIN AND ORCH.)
2,2,2,2 - 2,2,2,0 - timp.,perc. - hp. - str.   14:00 Southern.
—— TRES DANZAS CONCERTANTES (FOR STRINGS)
str.   8:00 Southern.

MOOR, Emanuel
—— RHAPSODY FOR VIOLIN AND ORCH., OP. 84
2,2,2,2 - 4,2,3,0 - timp. - str.   14:30 Salabert.

MOORE, Donald I.
—— BURLESCA (1949)
*3,2,*3,2 - 4,3,3,1 - timp.,perc.(4) - str.   5:00 Composer.
—— THE GREATNESS OF AMERICA (FOR SSATB CHORUS AND ORCH.) (1968) (Text: Paraphrased from Alexis de Toqueville)
*3,2,*3,2 - 4,3,3,1 - timp.,perc.(4),chimes - str.   6:00 Composer.
—— ORATORY (FOR HORN AND ORCH.)
*3,2*3,2 - 4,3,3,1 - timp.,perc.(4) - str.   7:00 Composer.

MOORE, Douglas
—— THE BALLAD OF BABY DOE (OPERA) %
2(2nd alt. with picc.),1,2,1 - 2,2,2,1 - perc.,cel.,glock. - hp. - pf. - str.   135:00 Chappell.
—— CARRY NATION (OPERA) % (Text: William Jayme)
2(2nd alt. with picc.),2(2nd alt. with Eng.hn.),2,2 - 3,2,3,0 - timp.,perc. - hp. - pf. - str.   120:00 Galaxy.
—— COTILLION (SUITE) (FOR STRINGS)
str.   15:15 C. Fischer.
—— THE DEVIL AND DANIEL WEBSTER (OPERA) %
    Bo. Hawkes.
—— DOWN EAST (SUITE) (FOR VIOLIN AND ORCH.) (IN 3 MOVTS.)
*3,2,2,2 - 2,2,1,0 - timp.,perc.(2),xyl. - str.   15:00 C. Fischer.
—— THE EMPEROR'S NEW CLOTHES (1-ACT OPERETTA) %
2,1,2,1 - 3,3,0,0 - timp.,perc. -str.   12:00 C. Fischer.

—— FARM JOURNAL (SUITE) (IN 4 MOVTS.)
2(1 alt. with picc.),2,2,2 - 2,1,0,0 - perc. - str.   13:00 C. Fischer.
—— GALLANTRY (A "SOAP" OPERA IN 1 ACT) % (Text: Arnold Sundgaard)
2,1,2,1 - 2,2,1,0 - perc. - hp. - str.   35:00 G. Schirmer.
—— GIANTS IN THE EARTH (3-ACT OPERA) (REVISED 1963) % (Text: Arnold Sundgaard)
2(2nd alt. with picc.),1,2,1 - 2,2,2,0 - timp.,perc. - str.   140:00 C. Fischer.
—— THE GREENFIELD CHRISTMAS TREE (OPERA) % (Text: Arnold Sundgaard)
2,2,2,2 - 2,2,2,0 - perc. - hp. - str.   45:00 G. Schirmer.
—— IN MEMORIAM
*3,*3,*3,*3 - 4,4,4,1 - timp.,perc. - hp. - str.   7:00 EV.
—— MARY'S PRAYER (ARIA FROM THE OPERA "THE DEVIL AND DANIEL WEBSTER") (FOR MEZZO-SOPRANO AND ORCH.)
    Bo. Hawkes.
—— OVERTURE ON AN AMERICAN TUNE
    6:00 C. Fischer.
—— THE PAGEANT OF P. T. BARNUM (SUITE)(IN 5 MOVTS.)
*3,*3,*3,*3 - 4,3,3,1 - timp.,perc. - hp. - str.   14:00 C. Fischer.
—— PRAYER FOR THE UNITED NATIONS (FOR CHORUS AND ORCH.) (Text: Stephen Vincent Benet)
    Gray.
—— PUSS IN BOOTS (1-ACT CHILDREN'S OPERETTA) %
1,1,1,1 - 1,1,0,0 - perc. - hp. - str.   15:00 C. Fischer.
—— SYMPHONY NO. 2 IN A MAJOR (IN 4 MOVTS.)
2(1 alt. with picc.),2,*3,2 - 4,3,3,1 - timp.,perc.(3),xyl. - hp. - str.   22:00 G. Schirmer.
—— A SYMPHONY OF AUTUMN (IN 3 MOVTS.)
*3,2(1 alt. with Eng. hn.),2,2 - 4,2,3,1 - timp.,perc.(2),cel. - hp. - str.   22:00 Composer.
—— VILLAGE MUSIC (SUITE)
*2,1,2,1 - 2,2,1,0 - timp.,perc.(2) - str.   9:00 Mercury.
or:
1,0,2,0 - 0,2,1,0 - timp.,perc.(2) - str.
—— THE WINGS OF THE DOVE (OPERA, AFTER HENRY JAMES) % (Text: Ethan Ayer)
2,2,2,2 - 3,2,2,0 - timp.,perc.,cel. - hp.   G. Schirmer.

MOORE, Timothy
—— CONCERTO FOR CLARINET AND STRING ORCH.
cl. - str.   P.R.S.

MOORTEL, Arie van de
—— SYMPHONY, OP. 2 ("SILLY" SYMPHONIE) (1939) (IN 3 MOVTS.)
2,2,2,2 - 2,2,1,0 - timp.,perc. - str.   6:00 H. Elkan.

MOPPER, Irving
—— ALICE IN WONDERLAND (SUITE)
2(2nd alt. with picc.),2(2nd alt. with Eng. hn.),2,2 - 2,2,2,1 - timp.,perc.,cel.,xyl. - hp. - str.   7:00 Boston.
—— CHICAGO (SYMPHONY) (FOR SOLOISTS, MIXED CHORUS AND ORCH.) (IN 4 MOVTS)
3(3rd alt. with picc.),1,2,2 sax.,2 - 4,2,2,1 - timp.,perc.,xyl. - 2pf. - str.   18:00 Composer.
—— THE CREATION (CANTATA) (FOR BASS, CHORUS AND CHAMBER ORCH.)
1(alt. with picc.),0,1(alt. with e♭ cl.),0 - 0,0,0,0 - timp.,perc.(2),xyl. - hp. - pf. - (2 vln., vla., c.)str.   23:00 Composer.
—— THE DOOR (OPERA) %
*3,1,*3,*3 - 4,2,2,1 - timp.,perc.(3) - hp. - str.   45:00 Bo. Hawkes.
—— NERO'S MOTHER (DRAMATIC SCENE FOR VOICE AND ORCH.) (Text: Stephen Phillips)
2(2nd alt. with picc.),1,1,2 - 2,3,1,1 - timp.,perc.(5),cel.,xyl. - hp. - str.   19:00 Composer.
—— THE WONDROUS WORKS OF GOD (CANTATA) (FOR SOLOISTS, MIXED CHORUS AND ORCH.)
1,1,0,1 - hn. - org. - str.   28:00 Composer.

MORALES, Olallo
—— ABU CASEMS TOFFLOR (OVERTURE) (WITH TENOR OR VIOLIN SOLO)
3,3,3,3 - 4,3,3,1 - timp.,perc.,cel. - hp. - str.   10:30 S.T.I.M.
—— CAMACHOS BROLLOP (BALLET SUITE) (IN 6 MOVTS.)
3,3,3,3 - 4,3,3,1 - timp.,perc.(3),cel.,xyl. - guit. - hp. - str.   23:00 S.T.I.M.
—— CONCERTO IN D MINOR FOR VIOLIN AND ORCH.
2,2,2,2 - 4,2,3,0 - timp.,perc.(2) - hp. - str   22:00 S.T.I.M.
—— FORSOMMAR, OP. 10 (CONCERT OVERTURE)
3,2,2,2 - 4,3,3,1 - timp.,perc. - str.   10:00 S.T.I.M.

—— OVERTURE NO. 3 (SOMMARMUSIK)
   3,2,3,2 - 4,3,3,1 - timp.,perc.(2) - hp. - str.   7:00 S.T.I.M.
—— SYMPHONY IN G MINOR, OP. 5
   3,2,2,2 - 4,2,3,1 - timp.,perc. - str.   40:00 S.T.I.M.
—— TRIPTYKON
   3,3,3,2 - 4,3,3,1 - timp.,perc.(2),cel. - hp. - str.   20:00 S.T.I.M.
   or:
   3,2,2,2 - 4,3,3,1 - timp.,perc.(3),cel. - hp. - str.

MORALES, Rosa Mercedes Ayarza de - HOLZMAN, R.
—— LA PENICHOLI
                                                   Fleisher.

MORANÇON, Guy
—— CONCERTO FOR ORGAN AND STRINGS
   org. - str.   20:00 EV.
—— SEQUENCES (FROM THE BALLET "OENOCHOË")
   2,2,2,2 - 3,3,3,1 - timp.,perc.(2),cel. - hp. - str.   20:00 EV.

MORAWETZ, Oskar
—— CAPRICCIO (1960)
   2,2,2,2 - 4,2,2,0 - timp. - str.   8:00 CanMusCtr.
—— CARNIVAL OVERTURE
   3,2,2,2 - 4,2,3,1 - timp.,perc.(2) - hp. - str.   6:00 MCA Music.
—— A CHILD'S GARDEN OF VERSES (1972) (FOR
   MEZZO-SOPRANO OR ALTO OR BARITONE AND ORCH.)
   2(2nd alt. with picc.),2,2,2 - 4,2,3,1 - timp.,perc. - hp. - str.
                                                   15:00 CanMusCtr.
—— CONCERTO FOR BRASS QUINTET AND ORCH.
                                                   25:00 MCA Music.
—— CONCERTO NO. 1 FOR PIANO AND ORCH. (1962) (IN 1
   MOVT.)
   *2,2,2,2 - 4,2,2,1 - timp.,perc. - pf. - str.   18:00 MCA Music.
—— DIRGE
                                                   12:00 C.A.P.A.C.
—— DIVERTIMENTO FOR STRINGS
   str.   9:00 F. Colombo.
—— FANTASY FOR ORCHESTRA
   3,2,2,2 - 4,3,3,1 - timp.,perc. - hp. - str.   11:00 C.A.P.A.C.
—— FOUR SONNETS FROM THE PORTUGUESE
   2,2,2,2 - 4,2,0,0 - timp. - hp. - str.   13:00 C.A.P.A.C.
—— FROM THE DIARY OF ANNE FRANK (1970) (FOR SOPRANO
   OR MEZZO-SOPRANO AND ORCH.)
   2,2,2,2 - 4,2,3,1 - timp.,perc.,cel. - hp. - str.   22:45 CanMusCtr.
—— IMPROVISATION FOR CELLO AND ORCH. (1973)
   2(2nd alt. with picc.),2,2,2 - 4,2,3,1 - timp.,perc.,cel. - hp. - str.
                                                   10:00 CanMusCtr.
—— MEMORIAL TO MARTIN LUTHER KING (1968) (ELEGY FOR
   CELLO AND ORCH.)
   2(2nd alt. with picc.),2,2,2 - 4,3,3,1 - timp.,perc(3),cel. - hp. - pf. -
   d.-b.   10:00 CanMusCtr.
—— OVERTURE TO A FAIRY TALE
   2,2,2,2 - 4,2,0,0 - timp.,perc. - str.   12:00 Bo. Hawkes.
—— PASSACAGLIA ON A BACH CHORALE
   3,*2,2,2 - 4,2,3,1 - timp.,perc. - hp. - str.   5:00 MCA Music.
—— PSALM FOR STRING ORCHESTRA (1971)
   str.   12:00 CanMusCtr.
—— REFLECTIONS AFTER A TRAGEDY (1969)
   2(2nd alt. with picc.),2,2,2 - 4,2,3,0 - timp.,perc.(2) - pf. - str.
                                                   11:50 CanMusCtr.
—— SINFONIETTA FOR WINDS AND PERCUSSION (1965) (IN 3
   MOVTS.)
   *3,*3,*3,*3 - 4,3,3,1 - timp.,perc.(3)   21:30 MCA Music.
—— SYMPHONIC INTERMEZZO (1971)
   2(2nd alt. with picc.),2,2,2 - 3,2,3,0 - timp.,perc. - hp. - str.
                                                   9:00 CanMusCtr.
—— SYMPHONIC SCHERZO
   3,2,2,2 - 4,3,3,1 - timp.,perc.(3) - hp. - str.   10:00 C.A.P.A.C.
—— SYMPHONY NO. 1 (IN 3 MOVTS.)
   3,2,2,2 - 4,3,3,1 - timp.,perc.(3) - hp. - str.   32:00 C.A.P.A.C.
—— SYMPHONY NO. 2 (1959)
   1. Adagio - allegro - adagio; 2. Allegro moderato
   *3,2,2,2 - 4,3,3,1 - timp.,perc. - hp. - str.   23:00 CanMusCtr.
—— TWO PRELUDES FOR VIOLIN AND ORCH. (1972)
   2,2,2,2 - 2,2,0,0 - perc. - str.   9:00 CanMusCtr.

MOREAU, Léon
—— INVOCATION À BOUDHA (IN 4 MOVTS)
   *3,2,2,2 - 4,2,3,1 - timp.,perc.(5) - hp. - str.   Baron.
—— PASTORALE, FOR ALTO SAXOPHONE (OR OBOE) AND
   ORCH. (IN 3 MOVTS.)
   2,2,2,alto sax.,2 - 4,2,3,0 - timp.,perc. - str.   15:00 Baron.

MORGAN, David Sydney
—— CONCERTO FOR CLARINET AND STRINGS (1965)
   cl. - str.   20:00 A.P.R.A.
—— CONCERTO FOR HORN AND SMALL ORCH., OP. 17
   ("ENGLISH SPRING")(1957)
   0,1,1,1 - 1,0,0,0 - str.   15:00 A.P.R.A.
—— CONCERTO FOR VIOLA AND STRING ORCH., OP. 19 (1958)
   str.   18:00 A.P.R.A.
—— CONCERTO FOR VIOLIN AND ORCH., OP. 15 (1957)
   2,2,2,2 - 2,2,2,0 - timp.,perc. - vln.   12:00 A.P.R.A.
—— CONCERTO FOR VIOLIN AND ORCH. (1966)
   3,2,3,2 - 4,4,3,1 - timp.,perc.(5, incl. 4 on timp.),cel. - hp. - str.
                                                   28:00 A.P.R.A.
—— CONCERTO FOR VIOLIN, WOODWIND, BASS AND
   PERCUSSION
                                                   A.P.R.A.
—— DUEL FOR FLUTE AND ORCH., OP. 25 (1966)
   1,0,0,0 - 4,2,3,0 - timp.,perc. - str.(no c.)   2:30 A.P.R.A.
—— FANTASIA ON A CADENCE BY RICHARD ALLWOOD, OP.
   32 (1964)
   str.   9:00 A.P.R.A.
—— FESTIVAL OVERTURE, OP. 2 (1948)
   3,3,3,3 - 4,3,3,0 - timp. - str.   6:00 A.P.R.A.
—— HENDON '64, OP. 29 (AN OVERTURE) (1964)
   3,3,3,3 - 4,3,3,1 - timp.,perc. - str.   8:00 A.P.R.A.
—— MUSIC FOR CHILDREN (1965)
   2,1,2,1 - 2,2,3,0 - timp.,perc. - str.   5:30 A.P.R.A.
—— OVERTURE FOR A FESTIVE OCCASION (1963)
   2,1,2,1 - 2,2,3,0 - timp.,perc. - hp. - str.   8:00 A.P.R.A.
—— RHAPSODY FOR CELLO AND ORCH., OP. 4 (1949)
   2,2,2,2 - 2,2,3,0 - timp. - str.   A.P.R.A.
—— SINFONIETTA, OP. 40 (1965)
   str.   15:00 A.P.R.A.
—— SONG OF PAUMONOK (FOR TENOR, CHORUS AND ORCH.)
   (Text: Walt Whitman)
                                                   A.P.R.A.
—— SYMPHONY NO. 1 IN E MINOR, OP. 5 (REV. 1962)
   2,2,2,2 - 4,2,3,0-1 - timp. - str.   27:00 A.P.R.A.
—— SYMPHONY NO. 2
                                                   23:00 A.P.R.A.
—— SYMPHONY NO. 3 (FOR SMALL ORCH.)
                                                   A.P.R.A.
—— SYMPHONY NO. 4 (FOR SMALL ORCH.)
                                                   A.P.R.A.
—— SYMPHONY NO. 5
                                                   A.P.R.A.
—— SYMPHONY NO. 6, OP. 33 (ENGLISH AUTUMN)(1964)
   0,2,0,2 - 0,0,0,0 - str.   14:00 A.P.R.A.
—— SYMPHONY NO. 7, OP. 45 ("SYMPHONY FOR
   TWELVE")(1966)
   1,1,1,1 - 1,1,1,1 - str.   6:30 A.P.R.A.
—— TRIPLEX, OP. 3 (1948)
   str.   9:00 A.P.R.A.

MORGAN, Robert B.
—— SINFONIETTA (1965) (IN 1 MOVT.)
   3(3rd alt. with picc.),2,3(3rd alt. with b.-cl.),*3 - 5,4,3,1 -
   timp.,perc.(4) - pf. - str.   14:00 Composer.

MORGAN, Thomas - PLATT, Richard
—— LOVE AND HONOR (SUITE)
   cemb. - str.   11:00 Oxford.

MORITZ, Edvard
—— AMERICAN OVERTURE, OP. 107
   2,2,2,2 - 4,3,3,1 - timp.,perc.(8) - hp. - str.   10:00 Composer.
—— THE ANIMATED NINTH, OP. 111 (SCHERZO)
   *3,2,2,2 - 4,3,3,0 - timp.,perc.(8) - str.   5:00 Composer.
—— THE BLUE BIRD, OP. 70
   *3,2,*3,2 - 4,2,3,1 - timp.,pec.(2) - hp. - str.   25:00 Composer.
—— CAVALCADE, OP. 109
   2,2,*3 - 4,2,3,0 - timp.,perc.(2-5) - pf. - str.   10:00 Composer.
—— CHAMBER SYMPHONY, OP. 30
   1(alt. with picc.),1,1,1 - 1,1,0,0 - perc.(2) - hp. - pf. - str.
                                                   22:00 Composer.
—— CONCERTANTE FOR 2 VIOLINS, WINDS, HARP AND
   PERCUSSION, OP. 73 (IN 3 MOVTS.)
   1(alt. with picc),2,2,2 - 4,3,3,1 - timp.,perc.(3) - hp. - str.
                                                   25:00 Composer.
—— CONCERTO FOR PIANO AND ORCH., OP. 135 (IN 4
   MOVTS.)
   2(2nd alt. with picc.),2,2,2 - 4,1,3,0 - timp.,perc.(3),xyl. - pf. - str.
                                                   35:00 Composer.

—— CONCERTO FOR VIOLA AND ORCH.
2,2,2,*3 - 4,3,3,1 - timp.,perc.(2) - str.   35:00 Composer.
—— CONCERTO FOR WIND AND PERCUSSION INSTRUMENTS, OP. 55 (IN 4 MOVTS.)
*3,2,*3,2 - 2,2,1,1 - timp.,perc.(3)   24:00 Composer.
—— CONCERTO GROSSO, OP. 59
2,2,*3,*3 - 4,3,2,1 - timp.,perc.(2) - str.   24:00 Composer.
—— CONCERTO NO. 2 FOR VIOLIN AND ORCH., OP. 117 (IN 3 MOVTS.)
2,2,2,2 - 4,1,0,0 - timp.,perc.(2),glock. - str.   31:30 Composer.
—— DIVERTIMENTO, OP. 63 (FOR WINDS, HARP AND PERCUSSION)
*3,2,2,2 - 4,3,0,0 - timp.,perc.(2) - hp.   15:00 Composer.
—— GITANJALI, OP. 19 (THREE SONGS FOR MEDIUM VOICE AND ORCH.)
2,2,*3,*3 - 4,0,3,1 - timp.,perc.(2) - hp. - str.   27:00 Composer.
—— INTERMEZZO CAPRICCIOSO, OP. 125
*3,2,2,2 - 4,1,3,0 - timp.,perc.(2),glock. - hp. - str.   8:00 Composer.
—— ITALIAN OVERTURE, OP. 67
*3,2,2,2 - 4,2,3,1 - timp.,perc.(1) - str.   7:00 Composer.
—— DER KLINGENDE GARTEN, OP. 65 ("THE RINGING GARDEN") (FOR MEDIUM VOICE AND ORCH.)
*3,2,*3,*3 - 4,3,3,1 - timp.,perc.(2) - hp. - str.   35:00 Composer.
—— DIE LIEDER AN TRISTAN ("SONGS TO TRISTAN") (FOR SOPRANO AND CHAMBER ORCH.)
fl. - hp. - pf. - str.   14:00 Composer.
—— MOLTO ANDANTE, OP. 112
2,2,*3,2 - 4hn. - timp.,perc.(3) - hp. - str.   10:00 Composer.
—— SCHERZO FOR STRINGS, OP. 79
str.   8:00 Composer.
—— SYMPHONY NO. 1 IN C MINOR
*3,*3,*3,1 - 4,3,3,1 - timp.,perc.(1) - str.   35:00 Composer.
—— SYMPHONY NO. 2 IN D MINOR, OP. 108
*3,2,2,*3 - 4,3,3,1 - timp.,perc.(3-7) - hp. - str.   40:00 Composer.
—— SYMPHONY NO. 3 IN A MINOR, OP. 115 (IN 4 MOVTS.)
3(3rd alt. with picc.),2,2,2, - 4,3,3,1 - timp.,perc.(11) - hp. - str.   40:00 Composer.
—— SYMPHONY NO. 4, OP. 127 (IN 4 MOVTS.)
*3,2,*3,2 - 4,3,3,1 - timp.,perc.(3),xyl. - hp. - pf. - str.   39:30 Composer.

MOROI, Makoto
—— COMPOSITION NO. 5 (ODE TO ARNOLD SCHOENBERG) (FOR CHAMBER ORCH.)
1,0,*2,0 - 1,1,1,0 - perc.(3) - guit. - hp. - pf. - str.   Presser.
—— SUITE CONCERTANTE (FOR VIOLIN AND ORCH.)
2,1,2,1 - 2,1,1,0 - timp.,perc.,cel.(alt. with pf.),vibra.,xyl. - hp. - str.   20:00 Presser.
—— TOCCATA, SARABANDE AND TARANTELLA
str.   J.A.S.R.A.C.

MOROSS, Jerome
—— THE BIG COUNTRY (SUITE FROM THE FILM)
3,2,3,2 - 4,3,3,1 - timp.,perc. - hp. - pf. - str.   14:00 Chappell.
—— FRANKIE AND JOHNNY (BALLET SUITE)
2,2,3,2 - 2,2,2,0 - timp.,perc. - pf. - str.   30:00 Composer.
—— THE LAST JUDGMENT (BALLET SUITE)
*3,*2,2,1 - 2,2,1,0 - perc.,cel.(alt. with pf.) - hp. - str.   24:00 Composer.
—— MUSIC FOR THE FLICKS (SUITE)
3,3,3,2 - 4,3,3,1 - timp.,perc. - hp. - pf. - str.   14:00 Chappell.
—— PAEANS
*2,1,1,0 - 2,2,1,0 - timp.,perc.(3),xyl. - pf. - str.   Presser.
—— ROUNDELAY (BALLET SUITE)
2,1,2,1 - 2,2,1,0 - timp.,perc. - hp. - pf. - str.   24:00 Composer.
—— SYMPHONY
3(1 alt. with picc.),3(1 alt. with Eng. hn.),3(1 alt. with b.-cl.),3(1 alt. with c.-bn.) - 4,3,3,1 - timp.,perc. - pf.(alt. with cel.) - str.   20:00 Composer.
—— A TALL STORY
3,2,3,2 - 4,3,3,1 - timp.,perc. - str.   10:00 Composer.
—— VARIATIONS ON A WALTZ
3,3,3,3 - 4,3,3,1 - timp.,perc. - hp. - pf. - str.   15:00 Chappell.

MOROZOV, Igor
—— DOCTOR AIBOLIT: BALLET SUITE NO. 1 (IN 5 MOVTS.)
2,1,2,1 - 3,2,1,1 - timp.,perc. - pf. - str.   G. Schirmer.

MORRICONE, Emilio
—— MUSICA
11 vlns.   6:30 Salabert.

MORRIS, Harold
—— AMERICAN EPIC
*3,*3,2,2 - 4,3,3,1 - timp.,perc. - hp. - str.   14:00 Composer.
—— BALLADE
*3,*3,*3,*3 - 4,3,3,1 - timp.,perc. - str.   8:00 Composer.
—— BALLET MUSIC FOR WOODWINDS
*3,*3,Eᵇcl.,*3,*3   13:00 Composer.
—— CONCERTO FOR VIOLIN AND ORCH. (IN 3 MOVTS.)
2,2,2,2 - 4,2,2,0 - timp.,perc. - str.   27:00 Composer.
—— CONCERTO NO. 1 FOR PIANO AND ORCH. (IN 4 MOVTS.)
2,*3,2,2 - 4,3,3,1 - timp.,perc. - pf. - str.   27:00 Composer.
—— CONCERTO NO. 2 FOR PIANO AND ORCH. (IN 5 MOVTS.)
*3,*3,*3,*3 - 4,3,3,1 - timp.,perc.(4),glock. - pf. - str.   26:00 Composer.
—— DRAMATIC OVERTURE
*3,*3,Eᵇcl.,*3,*3 - 4,3,3,1 - timp.,perc.,xyl. - str.   11:00 Composer.
—— ISOLT OF THE WHITE HANDS (FOR SOPRANO AND ORCH.)
*3,*3,*3,*3 - 4,3,3,1 - timp.,perc.,cel. - str.   20:00 Composer.
—— JOY OF YOUTH
*3,*3,*3,3(3rd alt. with c.-bn.) - 4,3,3,1 - timp.,perc.(4),glock.,xyl. - pf. - str.   10:00 Composer.
—— LONE STAR (A TEXAS SAGA)
*3,*3,*3,*3 - 4,3,3,1 - timp.,perc.,glock. - str.   12:00 Composer.
—— OVERTURE HEROIC
*3,*3,*3,*3 - 4,3,3,1 - timp.,perc.,glock. - pf. - str.   13:00 Composer.
—— PASSACAGLIA AND FUGUE
2,*3,2,2 - 4,3,3,1 - timp.,perc. - str.   16:00 Composer.
—— PASSAGLIA, ADAGIO AND FINALE (FOR SOPRANO AND ORCH.)
*3,*3,*3,*3 - 4,3,3,1 - timp.,perc.,glock.,xyl. - hp. - pf. - str.   20:00 Composer.
—— POEM (AFTER TAGORE'S "GITANJALI")
*4,*2,*2,*2 - 4,3,3,1 - timp.,perc. - hp. - str.   13:00 Composer.
—— PROSPICE (SYMPHONY) (IN 4 MOVTS.)
2-3(1 alt. with picc.),*3,*3,*3 - 4,3,3,1 - timp.,perc.,cel.,glock.,xyl. - pf. - str.   33:00 Musicus.
—— SAM HOUSTON (SUITE) (IN 4 MOVTS.)
*3,*3,*3,*3 - 4,3,3,1 - timp.,perc.,cel.,glock. - pf. - str.   12:00 Composer.
—— SAM HOUSTON (SYMPHONIC WORK IN 1 MOVT.)
*3,*3,Eᵇcl.,*3,*3 - 4,3,3,1 - timp.,perc.,glock. - hp. - pf. - str.   8:00 Composer.
—— STILL DEWS OF QUIETNESS - SPEAK THRU THE EARTHQUAKE, WIND AND FIRE
*3,*3,2,*3 - 4,3,3,1 - timp.,perc. - str.   15:00 Composer.
—— SUITE FOR CHAMBER ORCH. (IN 3 MOVTS.)
1,1,1,1 - 1,1,1,0 - timp.,perc.,glock. - pf. - str.   15:00 Composer.
—— SUITE FOR ORCHESTRA (IN 3 MOVTS.)
*3,*3,*3,*3 - 4,3,3,1 - timp.,perc.,glock. - pf. - str.   15:00 Composer.
—— SUITE FOR PIANO AND STRINGS
pf. - str.   14:00 Composer.
—— SUITE NO. 1 FOR STRINGS
str.   13:00 Composer.
—— SUITE NO. 2 FOR STRINGS (IN 3 MOVTS.)
str.   12:00 Composer.
—— SYMPHONY NO. 2 ("VICTORY") (IN 3 MOVTS.)
*3,*3,*3,*3 - 4,3,3,1 - timp.,perc.,glock. - str.   27:00 Composer.
—— SYMPHONY NO. 3 ("AMARANTH") (IN 4 MOVTS.)
*3,*3,*3,*3 - 4,3,3,1 - timp.,perc.,cel.,glock.,xyl. - pf. - str.   30:00 Composer.
—— SYMPHONY NO. 4 (IN 4 MOVTS.)
2(1 alt. with picc.),*3,*3,*3 - 4,3,3,1 - timp.,perc.,glock. - pf. - str.   25:00 Composer.
—— VARIATIONS ON "I WAS WAY DOWN A-YONDER"
1,1,1,1 - hn. - pf. - str.   14:00 Composer.

MORRIS, Reginald Owen
—— CONCERTO PICCOLO (FOR 2 VIOLINS AND STRINGS)
str.   18:00 Oxford.

MORRISON, Julia
—— THE FAIR IS ON! (SYMPHONY FOR YOUNG PEOPLE) (1969) (IN 3 MOVTS.)
2,1,2 Eng. hn.,2,2 - 4,2,2,1 - timp.,perc.(4),xyl. - hp. - str.   10:35 Composer.
—— LAMENTATIONS OF JEREMIAH, I (FOR SBARB MALE CHORUS AND INSTRUMENTALS) (1969) (Text: Biblical)
Bassoons - baritones - cellos   12:00 Composer.

MORRISSEY, John J.
—— CONCERTO GROSSO FOR 2 TRUMPETS, TROMBONE AND ORCH.
             9:00 Chappell.

MORTARI, Virgilio
—— CONCERTO FOR STRING QUARTET AND CHAMBER ORCH.
 2 hn. - timp. - hp. - str.   24:00 Bo. Hawkes.
—— DUE LAUDE (FOR VOICE AND ORCH.)
 2,1,2,2 - 2,1,0,0 - pf. - str.   11:00 Bo. Hawkes.
—— MUSICA PER ARCHI
 str.   15:00 Bo. Hawkes.
—— MUSICA PER UN BALLETO
 1,1,1,1 - 0,1,0,0 - hp. - str.   10:00 Bo. Hawkes.
—— PICCOLA SERENATA
 str.   8:00 Bo. Hawkes.
—— SARABANDA E ALLEGRO (FOR PIANO AND ORCH.)
 2,2,2,2 - 4,2,1,0 - timp.,xyl. - hp. - pf. - str. 14:00 Bo. Hawkes.
—— STABAT MATER (FOR TWO FEMALE VOICES AND ORCH.)
 2 hn. - timp. - pf. - str.   20:00 Bo. Hawkes.
—— SUITE DAL BALLETTO "L'ALLEGRA PIAZZETTA"
 2,2,2,2 - 2,2,1,0 - timp.,perc. - hp. - pf. - str. 22:00 Bo. Hawkes.
—— TRITTICO (FOR SOPRANO, MEZZO-SOPRANO, OPTIONAL FEMALE CHORUS AND ORCH.)
 3,3,3,2 - 4,3,3,1 - timp.,perc. - hp. - pf. - str. 14:00 Bo. Hawkes.

MORTELMANS, Lodewijk
—— DRIE KLEINE ELEGIËN (1926)
 str.   8:15 H. Elkan.
—— EVANGELISCH DIPTIEK (1934)
 2,3,3,2 - 4,3,3,1 - timp. - str. 10:00 H. Elkan.
—— IN MEMORIAM (ELEGIE NO. 1) (1917)
 2,2,2,2 - 4,2,3,0 - str.   8:00 H. Elkan.
—— MORGENSTEMMING (1922)
 2,2,2,2 - 4,3,3,1 - timp.,perc.,cel. - hp. - str. 13:00 Muz. Fonds.
—— ROMANZA FOR VIOLIN AND ORCH. (1935)
 2,0,2,2 - 2,0,0,0 - str.   6:00 H. Elkan.
—— TREUERDICHT (ELEGY NO. 4) (1925)
 2,2,2,2 - 4,2,3,1 - str.   9:00 Muz. Fonds.

MORTENSEN, Finn
—— CONCERTO FOR PIANO AND ORCH., OP. 25
 3,3,3,3 - 5,3,3,1 - timp.,perc. - pf. - str. 10:00 Norsk Mfl.
—— EVOLUTION, OP. 23
 3,3,3,3 - 4,3,3,1 - timp.,perc. - str. 6:00 Norsk Mfl.
—— FANTASY FOR PIANO AND ORCH., OP. 27
 3,3,3,3 - 4,3,3,1 - timp.,perc. - pf. - str. 13:00 Norsk Mfl.
—— PER ORCHESTRA, OP. 30
 3,3,3,3 - 4,3,3,1 - timp.,perc. - hp. - str. 15:00 T.O.N.O.
—— SYMPHONY, OP. 5 (IN 4 MOVTS.)
 3,3,3,3 - 4,3,3,1 - timp.,perc. - str. 35:00 T.O.N.O.
—— TONE COLORS, OP. 24 (1962)
 3,3,3,3 - 5,3,3,1 - str.   5:00 T.O.N.O.

MORTENSEN, Otto
—— OVERTURE IN G MINOR
 2,2,2,2 - 4,3,3,0 - timp. - str. 8:00 G. Schirmer.

MORTHENSON, Jan W.
—— COLOSSUS (METAMUSIC FOR LARGE ORCH.) (WITH FILM) (1970)
 4,3,3,3 - 6,4,4,5 - perc.(4) -tape-recorder - hp. - pf. - str. 9:30 Nordiska.
—— DECADENZA II (FOR TAPE AND ORCH.)(1970)
         60:00 Tetra.
—— FIVE PIECES FOR ORCH. (1973)
 2,3,2,2 - 2,0,4,0 - timp.,perc.(4) - str. 12:00 Nordiska.
—— SENZA (METAMUSIC FOR STRING ORCH.)(1970)
 str.   Nordiska.
—— SINFONIA DA CAMERA, OP. 1 (1960)
 0,1,2,0 - 1,0,0,0 - timp.,perc.,bells,vibra.,xyl. -str.(no vlns.) 18:00 Fleisher.

MORVAREN, Alex
—— HYMN TO THE DAWN (FROM THE OPERA "QUENTIN DURWARD")
 3,2,3,3 - 4,3,3,1 - timp.,perc. - 1-2 hp. - str. 6:00 Bo. Hawkes.

MOSELEY, Orville
—— CONCERTO FOR PIANO AND ORCH. (1964) (IN 3 MOVTS.)
 2,1,2,4 - 4,2,2,1 - timp.,perc.(2) - pf. - str. 50:00 Composer.
—— FORT MCHENRY (TONE POEM) (1952)
 3(1 alt. with picc.),3(1 alt. with Eng. hn.),2,5(1 alt. with c.-bn.) - 4,3,3,1 - timp.,perc.(3) - str. 15:00 Composer.
—— HOW LONG THE ROAD (OPERA) % (1963) (Text: Chestyn Everett)
 3(1 alt. with picc.),*3,*3,4 sax.,(1 alt. with cbn.) - 4,3,3,1 - timp.,perc.(4),bells,cel.,xyl. - hp. - str. 105:00 Composer.
—— SUITE FOR STRINGS (1947) (IN 5 MOVTS.)
         Composer.

MOSER, Rudolf
—— IL CANTICO DO FRATE SOLE, DI SAN FRANCESCO D'ASSISI, OP. 90 (FOR SOPRANO, ALTO, TENOR, BASS, MIXED CHORUS, ORGAN AND ORCH.)
 2,*2,0,2 - 0,2,0,0 - timp.,cel. - org. - str. 70:00 S.U.I.S.A.
—— CONCERTO FOR OBOE AND STRINGS, OP. 86
 ob. - str.   16:00 S.U.I.S.A.
—— DOUBLE CONCERTO, OP. 74, FOR VIOLA D'AMORE, GAMBA AND STRINGS
 cemb.(ad lib.) - str. 23:00 S.U.I.S.A.
—— VIOLINCELLOKONZERT NR. 2, OP. 71 (FÜR KAMMERORCHESTER)
        20:00 S.U.I.S.A.

MOSS, Barry
—— ESSAY FOR ORCHESTRA
 3,2,2,2 - 4,2,3,1 - timp.,perc. - str. 10:00 Novello.
—— ESSAY FOR STRINGS, OP. 3
 str.   Novello.

MOSS, Lawrence
—— ARIEL (2 SONGS) (FOR SOPRANO AND ORCH.) (1969) (Text: Sylvia Plath)
 3,2,2,2 - 4,2,3,1 - timp.,perc.(3) - hp. - str. 20:00 C. Fischer.
—— PATHS (1971)
 3(3rd alt. with picc.),3,3,3 - 6,3,3,1 - timp.,perc.(5),bells,cel.,glock.,vibra.,xyl. - pf. - str. 10:15 C. Fischer.
—— THE QUEEN AND THE REBELS (3-ACT OPERA) % (AFTER A PLAY BY UGO BETTI) (1965) (Text: Composer)
 2,2,2,2 - 4,2,3,1 - timp.,perc.(2),bells,cel.,glock.,vibra.,xyl. - hp. - pf. - str. 150:00 Composer.
—— SCENES FOR SMALL ORCHESTRA (1961)
 2,2,2,2 - 4,2,0,0 - perc. - str. 8:00 Seesaw.

MOSSMAN, Ted
—— CHICAGO, ILLINOIS (OVERTURE)
 1(alt. with picc.),1,2,1 - 2-4,3,2,0 - timp.,perc.,cel.,xyl. - hp. - str. 15:00 Fanfare.
—— NEW YORK CONCERTO
        16:00 Fanfare.
—— ODE TO GERSHWIN
        Robbins.
—— TEMPLE SCENE (FROM THE BALLET "SALOME")
 *3,2,2,2 - 4,2,3,1 - timp.,perc. - hp. - str. 4:30 Fanfare.

MOSSOLOV, Alexander V.
—— SUITE ON AMERICAN FOLK SONGS
 fl.,cl. - timp.,perc.,xyl. - pf. - str. G. Schirmer.
—— SYMPHONY OF THE MACHINES (THE IRON FOUNDRY), OP. 19
 *3,*3,*3,*3 - 4,3,3,1 - timp.,perc.(5) - str. 10:00 G. Schirmer.

MOSUSOVA, Nadežda
—— INTRODUCTION AND LARGO (FOR STRING ORCH.)
 str.   12:00 MIC,Zagreb.

MOULAERT, Raymond
—— CONCERTINO FOR TRUMPET AND ORCH. (1937)
 2,2,2,2 - 2,1,0,0 - timp.,perc. - str. 5:00 H. Elkan.
—— CONCERTO FOR PIANO AND ORCH. (1938)
 2,2,2,2 - 4,2,3,1 - timp.,perc. - hp. - pf. - str. 22:00 H. Elkan.
—— CONCERTO FOR VIOLIN AND ORCH. (1954)
 2,2,2,2 - 2,2,2,1 - timp.,perc.,cel.,glock.,xyl. - hp. - str. 35:00 CBDM.

—— EROÏCA (FOR HORN AND ORCH.) (1946)
2,2,2,2 - 1,0,0,0 - str.   7:00 H. Elkan.
—— ÉTUDES SYMPHONIQUES (1943)
2,2,2,2 - 4,2,3,1 - timp.,perc.,cel.,glock.,xyl. - hp. - str.
                                            15:00 H. Elkan.
—— LEGEND (FOR FLUTE AND ORCH.) (1951)
1,0,0,1 - 2,2,1,0 - timp. - str.   7:00 H. Elkan.
—— PASSACAILLE (1931)
3,3,3,3 - 4,3,3,1 - timp.,perc.,glock. - hp. - str.   25:00 CBDM.
—— RHAPSODIE ÉCOSSAISE (FOR CLARINET AND ORCH.)
(1940)
2,2,3,2 - 3,0,0,0 - timp.,perc. - hp. - str.   8:00 H. Elkan.
—— SYMPHONIE DE FUGUES (1944)
2,2,2,2 - 4,2,3,1 - timp.,perc. - hp. - org. - str.   30:00 H. Elkan.
—— SYMPHONIE DE VALSES (1936)
2,2,2,2 - 4,3,3,1 - timp.,perc.,glock. - hp. - str.   20:00 H. Elkan.
—— SYMPHONIETTA (1955)
str.   15:00 H. Elkan.
—— THEME AND VARIATIONS (FOR TRUMPET AND ORCH.)
(1910)
2,2,2,2 - 3,1,0,0 - timp. - str.   7:00 H. Elkan.
—— VARIATIONS SYMPHONIQUES (1952)
2,2,2,2 - 4,2,3,1 - timp.,perc. - hp. - str.   20:00 H. Elkan.

MOULE-EVANS, David
—— DIVERTIMENTO FOR STRINGS
str.   20:00 Galaxy.

MOURAVIEFF, Léon
—— NATIVITY (FOR VIOLIN, VIOLA, CELLO AND STRING
ORCH.)
str.   12:00 Henmar.

MOUSSORGSKY, Modest P.
—— BORIS GODUNOV (OPERA) % (Engl. Text: David Lloyd-Jones)
3,2,2,2 - 4,3,3,1 - timp.,perc. - hp. - pf. 4-hands - str.
                                            180:00 Oxford.

MOUSSORGSKY, Modeste P. - DE FILIPPI, Amedeo
—— THE MUSICIAN'S PEEPSHOW (SONG CYCLE) (FOR
BARITONE AND ORCH.)
2,2,2,2 - 4,2,3,0 - timp.,perc.(2),cel. - hp. - str.   Arranger.
—— THE NURSERY (SONG-CYCLE)
2,2,2,2 - 2 hn. - hp. - str.   Arranger.
—— SUNLESS (SONG-CYCLE)
2,1,2,1 - 2,2,0,0 - timp.,perc.(1),glock. - str.   13:30 Arranger.

MOUSSORGSKY, Modeste P. - GOEHR, Walter
—— BORIS GODUNOV (CHORAL SCENES FROM THE OPERA)
(FOR TENOR, BARITONE, MIXED CHORUS AND ORCH.)
2,2,2,2-3 - 4,2,3,1 - timp.,perc. - hp. - str.   50:00 Bo. Hawkes.
—— PICTURES AT AN EXHIBITION
2,2,2,2 - 4,2,3,0 - timp.,perc.,cel.(ad lib.) - hp. - org.(ad lib.) - pf. -
str.   25:00 Bo. Hawkes.

MOUSSORGSKY, Modeste P. - KINDLER, Hans
—— LOVE MUSIC FROM "BORIS GODOUNOV"
                                            Mills.

MOUSSORGSKY, Modeste P. - MAGANINI, Quinto
—— ENTR'ACTE FROM ACT IV OF "KHOVANTCHINA"
                                            Musicus.

MOUSSORGSKY, Modeste P. - MARKEVITCH, Igor
—— SEI MELODIE (6 SONGS) (FOR VOICE AND ORCH.)
3,3,3,2 - 4,2,2,1 - timp.,perc.(2),cel.,xyl. - hp. - str.   23:00 Leeds.

MOUSSORGSKY, Modeste P. - ORMANDY, Eugene
—— BORIS GODUNOV (SYMPHONIC SUITE)
                                            30:00 Arranger.

MOUSSORGSKY, Modeste P. - RAVEL, Maurice
—— PICTURES AT AN EXHIBITION
3(3rd alt. with picc.),3(3rd alt. with Eng. hn.),3,alto sax.,3 - 4,3,3,1
- timp.,perc.,cel. - 2 hp. - - str.   31:00 Bo. Hawkes.

MOUSSORGSKY, Modeste P. - RIMSKY-KORSAKOFF, N.
—— THE DEFEAT OF SENNACHERIB (FOR MIXED CHORUS
AND ORCH.) (Engl. Text: A. W. Cox)
2,2,2,2 - 4,2,3,1 - timp.,perc. - str.   7:00 Bo. Hawkes.

MOUSSORGSKY, Modeste P. - SAMINSKY, Lazar
—— KING SAUL (CANTATA) (FOR MIXED CHORUS AND
ORCH.) (Translation by Lazar Saminsky)
1,0,1,0 - 1,0,0,0 - timp.perc.(2) - str.   C. Fischer.

MOUSSORGSKY, Modeste P. - SEVITZKY, Fabien
—— PICTURES AT AN EXHIBITION
3(3rd alt. with picc.)*3,1 E♭ cl.,*3,*3 - 4,4,3,1 -
timp.,perc.(3),bells,cel.,glock. - hp. - pf. - str.   24:00 Arranger.

MOUSSORGSKY, Modeste P. - SHOSTAKOVICH, Dmitri
—— BORIS GODOUNOV (4-ACT OPERA) %
3,3,4,3 - 4,3,3,1 - timp.,perc.,xyl. - balalaika(opt.),domra(opt.) - 2-4
hp. - pf. - str.   MCA Music.
Plus Stage Band
—— SONGS AND DANCES OF DEATH (FOR SOPRANO AND
ORCH.)
2,2,2,2 - 4,2,3,1 - timp.,perc.,cel. - hp. - pf. - str.   G. Schirmer.

MOUSSORGSKY, Modeste P. - SOPKIN, Henry
—— A NIGHT ON BALD MOUNTAIN
                                            C. Fischer.

MOUSSORGSKY, Modeste P. - STOKOWSKI, Leopold
—— BORIS GODOUNOV (SYMPHONIC SYNTHESIS)
                                            Henmar.
—— ENTR'ACTE FROM "KHOVANTCHINA"
3,2,*3,*3, - 4,2,3,2 - timp.,perc.,bells - str.   4:15 Broude.
—— PICTURES AT AN EXHIBITION
4(2 alt. with 2 picc.),4,5,4 - 8,4,4,1 - timp.,perc.(3-4), cel. - 2 hp. -
org. - str.   29:00 Henmar.

MOUSSORGSKY, Modeste P. - ZILCHER, Heinz Reinhart
—— LIEDER FÜR BARITON UND ORCH. (THE CYCLE
"SUNLESS," AND 3 OTHER SONGS)
3,2,2,3 - 4,3,3,1 - timp.,perc.,cel.,glock.,xyl. - hp. - str.
                                            25:00 F. Colombo.

MOYZES, Alexander
—— CONCERTO FOR VIOLIN AND ORCH.
3,3,3,3 - 4,2,0,0 - timp.,perc.,cel. - hp. - str.   40:00 Bo. Hawkes.
—— DANCES OF GEMER
3,2,2,3 - 4,3,3,1 - timp.,perc.,cel. - hp. - str.   17:00 Bo. Hawkes.
—— DOWN THE VAH RIVER, OP. 26 (SUITE) (REV. 1945) (IN 5
MOVTS.)
                                            Bo. Hawkes.
—— FEBRUARY (OVERTURE) (1948)
4,3,3,3 - 6,4,3,1 - timp.,perc. - hp. - str.   12:00 Bo. Hawkes.
—— JANOSIK'S LADS (OVERTURE) (1934)
                                            Bo. Hawkes.
—— NIKOLA SUHAJ (OVERTURE), OP. 22
                                            Bo. Hawkes.
—— POHRONI DANCES, OP. 43 (DANCE SUITE FOR ORCH.)
(1949)
3,2,2,2 - 4,3,3,1 - timp.,perc.,cel. - hp. - str.   28:00 Bo. Hawkes.
—— SYMPHONY NO. 7, OP. 50 (1954) (IN 4 MOVTS.)
4,3,3,3 - 4,3,3,1 - timp.,perc.,cel. - 2 hp. - str.   45:00 Bo Hawkes.

MOZART, Leopold - KNEUSSLIN
—— CONCERTO IN D MAJOR FOR TRUMPET AND SMALL
ORCH.
0,0,0,0 - 2,1,0,0 - str.   14:00 Henmar.

MOZART, Leopold - KREINER, Viktor
—— CONCERTO IN D MAJOR (FOR D TRUMPET OR CLARINO,
2 HORNS AND STRINGS)
0,0,0,0 - 2,1,0,0 - str.   15:00 Henmar.

MOZART, Leopold - MOENKEMEYER
—— SINFONIA NO. 25 IN G MAJOR
str.   Henmar.

MOZART, Leopold - WHEAR, Paul W.
—— DIVERTIMENTO NO. 3 (ARR. 1969)
str.   6:00 Ludwig.

MOZART, Wolfgang Amadeus
—— THE ABDUCTION FROM THE SERAGLIO (3-ACT OPERA) %
(Engl. Text: George and Phyllis Mead)
                                            Translator.
—— THE ABDUCTION FROM THE SERAGLIO (3-ACT OPERA) %
(Engl. Text: Ruth and Thomas Martin)
                                            Bo. Hawkes.

—— THE ABDUCTION FROM THE SERAGLIO (3-ACT OPERA) %
(Engl. Text: John W. Bloch)

G. Schirmer.

—— COSÌ FAN TUTTE (2-ACT OPERA) % (Engl. Text: Ruth and
Thomas Martin)

G. Schirmer.

—— DON GIOVANNI (2-ACT OPERA) % (Engl. Text: W. H. Auden
and Chester Kallman)

G. Schirmer.

—— DON GIOVANNI (2-ACT OPERA) % (Engl. Text: Edward Dent)

Bo. Hawkes.

—— THE IMPRESARIO (1-ACT COMEDY WITH MUSIC) % (Engl.
Text: Giovanni Cardelli)

G. Schirmer.

—— THE MAGIC FLUTE (2-ACT OPERA) % (Engl. Text: Ruth and
Thomas Martin)

G. Schirmer.

—— THE MARRIAGE OF FIGARO (4-ACT OPERA) % (Engl. Text:
Edward Dent)

Bo. Hawkes.

—— THE MARRIAGE OF FIGARO (4-ACT OPERA) % (Engl. Text:
Ruth and Thomas Martin)

G. Schirmer.

MOZART, Wolfgang Amadeus - BARBIROLLI, John
—— SUITE FOR STRINGS
str.   16:00 Oxford.

MOZART, Wolfgang Amadeus - BAZELAIRE, P.
—— LARGHETTO AND RONDO (FOR CELLO AND STRINGS)
str.   Salabert.

MOZART, Wolfgang Amadeus - BEECHAM, Thomas
—— SYMPHONY NO. 29, IN A
0,2,2,0 - 2 hn. - str.   18:00 Bo. Hawkes.
—— SYMPHONY NO. 38, IN D ("PRAGUE")
2,2,0,2 - 2,2,0,0 - timp. - str.   27:00 Bo. Hawkes.
—— SYMPHONY NO. 41, IN C ("JUPITER")
1-2,2,0,2 - 2-4,2,0,0 - timp. - str. 28:00 Bo. Hawkes.

MOZART, Wolfgang Amadeus - BELLISON, Simeon
—— CONCERTO IN A FOR CLARINET AND ORCH., K 622
2,0,1,2 - 2,0,0,0 - str.   29:00 C. Fischer.
—— CONCERTO-RONDO FOR CLARINET AND ORCH.
1,2,0,2 - 2,2,0,0 - timp.,glock. - str. 9:00 C. Fischer.

MOZART, Wolfgang Amadeus - BUSH, Geoffrey
—— PRELUDE IN THE STYLE OF HANDEL, K. 399
str.   Galaxy.

MOZART, Wolfgang Amadeus - CARNER, Mosco
—— FUGUE IN G MINOR, K. 401
str.   4:00 Galaxy.

MOZART, Wolfgang Amadeus - COLLINS, Anthony
—— FANTAISIE IN F MINOR
*3,*3,*3,*3 - 4,2,3,1 - timp. - str. 11:00 Fox.

MOZART, Wolfgang Amadeus - DIACK, J. Michael
—— BASTIEN AND BASTIENNE (1-ACT OPERETTA) % (Engl.
Text: Arranger)
1,1,0,0 - 2,0,0,0 - str.   30:00 C. Fischer.
—— PAPAGENO (1-ACT OPERETTA, ADAPTED FROM "THE
MAGIC FLUTE") %
1,1,1,1 - 2,0,0,0 - glock. - str.   C. Fischer.

**MOZART, Wolfgang Amadeus - FORBES, Watson - RICHARDSON,
Alan**
—— ADAGIO AND RONDO (FOR VIOLA AND SMALL ORCH.)
2 ob. - 2 hn. - str.   12:30 Oxford.

MOZART, Wolfgang Amadeus - FORST, Rudolf
—— FANTASIA IN F MINOR, K. 594 (ARR. 1941)
str.   12:00 Musicus.

MOZART, Wolfgang Amadeus - FOSS, Lukas
—— DON GIOVANNI: A CONCERT SYNTHESIS

Arranger.

MOZART, Wolfgang Amadeus - GESENSWAY, Louis
—— FANTASIA IN C MINOR
2,2,2,2 - 4,2,2,0 - timp. - str.   6:00 Arranger.

MOZART, Wolfgang Amadeus - GUI, Vittorio
—— IDOMENEO (3-ACT OPERA) %
2,2,2,2 - 4,2,3,0 - timp. - hpsc. - str.   Leeds.

MOZART, Wolfgang Amadeus - HELY-HUTCHINSON, Victor
—— SYMPHONY IN F, K. 497 (FROM THE SONATA FOR PIANO
4-HANDS)
2,2,2,2 - 2,0,0,0 - str.   20:00 Novello.

MOZART, Wolfgang Amadeus - ISAAC, Merle
—— OVERTURE TO "LA FINTA GIARDINIERA"

C. Fischer.

MOZART, Wolfgang Amadeus - JAMES, Philip
—— CONCERTINO FOR PIANO AND CHAMBER ORCH. (IN 3
MOVTS.)
1,1,1,1 - 1,0,0,0 - pf. - str.   9:00 Western.

MOZART, Wolfgang Amadeus - KESZTLER, Lörinc
—— SINFONIETTA (FROM K. 381)

Bo. Hawkes.

MOZART, Wolfgang Amadeus - LEIBOWITZ, René
—— FANTASIA FOR DOUBLE STRING ORCH. (ORIGINALLY
FOR MECHANICAL ORGAN)
str.   Boelke-Bo.

MOZART, Wolfgang Amadeus - LELOIR, Edmond
—— CONCERTO NO. 3 IN Eb FOR HORN AND ORCH., K. 447
15:10 Presser.

MOZART, Wolfgang Amadeus - LOTTER, Adolf
—— SYMPHONY NO. 39 IN E FLAT MAJOR, K. 543
28:00 Bo. Hawkes.

MOZART, Wolfgang Amadeus - MCDONALD, Harl
—— QUARTET IN F MAJOR (FOR OBOE, VIOLIN, VIOLA, CELLO
AND SMALL ORCH.)
0,3,2,0 - 2,0,0,0 - str.   12:00 EV.

MOZART, Wolfgang Amadeus - MORTARI
—— L' OCA DEL CAIRO (OPERA BUFFA) %

Bo. Hawkes.

MOZART, Wolfgang Amadeus - MOUTON, Henri
—— SYMPHONY NO. 40 IN G MINOR, K 550

25:00 Bo. Hawkes.

MOZART, Wolfgang Amadeus - NEGROTTI, Nino
—— SINFONIA IN C
1,2,0,2 - 2,2,0,0 - timp. - str.   13:30 Bo. Hawkes.

MOZART, Wolfgang Amadeus - OUBRADOUS, Fernand
—— ALLEGRO, THEME AND VARIATIONS, K. 212 (FOR STRING
ORCH.)
str.   9:30 Presser.
—— CONCERTO NO. 10 IN A FOR PIANO AND ORCH., K. 414
0,2,0,0 - 2,0,0,0 - pf. - str.   16:00 Presser.

MOZART, Wolfgang Amadeus - PALMER, Edwina - BEST, Agnes
—— FANTASIA (ADAGIO AND ALLEGRO, K. 594)
str.   Oxford.

MOZART, Wolfgang Amadeus - PAUMGARTNER, Bernhard
—— CONCERTO IN C MAJOR, FOR OBOE AND ORCH.
2ob. - 2 hn. - str.   19:00 Bo. Hawkes.

MOZART, Wolfgang Amadeus - ROBERTS, Charles J.
—— OVERTURE TO "LES PETITS RIENS"

C. Fischer.

—— OVERTURE TO "THE IMPRESARIO"

C. Fischer.

—— OVERTURE TO "THE MAGIC FLUTE"

C. Fischer.

MOZART, Wolfgang Amadeus - ROTH, Ernest
—— THE MARRIAGE OF FIGARO (4-ACT OPERA) % (Engl. Text:
Edward Dent)

Bo. Hawkes.

MOZART, Wolfgang Amadeus - SEIBER, Matyas
—— FANTASIA IN F MINOR, K. 608
2,2,2,2 - 2,2,0,0 - timp. - str.   27:00 Novello.

MOZART, Wolfgang Amadeus - SEREDY, Julius S.
—— OVERTURE TO "COSÍ FAN TUTTE"
C. Fischer.

MOZART, Wolfgang Amadeus - SERLY, Tibor
—— FANTASIA AND FUGUE
4,4,4,2 - 4,4,4,2 - timp. - str.   14:00 Southern.
or:
2,2,2,2 - 4,2,2,1 - timp. - str.

MOZART, Wolfgang Amadeus - SONTAG, Wesley
—— OVERTURE TO "MITRIDATE, RE DI PONTO"
2 fl., 2 ob. - str.   6:00 Bo. Hawkes.

MOZART, Wolfgang Amadeus - SWANSON, Walter Donald
—— CONCERTO IN E FLAT MAJOR FOR PIANO AND ORCH., K. 271
2,2,3,2 - 4,2,3,1 - timp.,perc. - pf. - str.   25:00 S.A.M.R.O.

MOZART, Wolfgang Amadeus - SZELL, George
—— CONCERTO IN D FOR CELLO AND ORCH., K. 314
G. Schirmer.

MOZART, Wolfgang Amadeus - SZOKOLAY, Sándor
—— DIVERTIMENTO
Bo. Hawkes.

MOZART, Wolfgang Amadeus - TERTIS, Lionel
—— CONCERTO FOR VIOLA AND ORCH. (FROM THE CLARINET CONCERTO, K. 622)
G. Schirmer.
—— SINFONIA CONCERTANTE IN E FLAT, K. 364 (FOR VIOLIN, VIOLA AND ORCH.) (Edited and with cadenza by L. Tertis)
2 ob. - 2 hn. - str.   35:00 Oxford.

MOZART, Wolfgang Amadeus - TOCH, Ernst
—— VARIATIONS ON GLUCK'S "UNSER DUMMER PÖBEL MEINT" (FOR PIANO AND ORCH.)
12:00 Leeds.

MOZART, Wolfgang Amadeus - VAN HOESEN, Karl D. - HUNT, Frederick
—— SYMPHONY NO. 12
2,2,2,2 - 4,2,3,0 - timp. - pf. - str.   C. Fischer.

MOZART, Wolfgang Amadeus - WAXMAN, Donald
—— VARIATIONS ON "AH, VOUS DIRAI-JE, MAMAN" (FOR PIANO AND ORCH.) (With a cadenza by D. Waxman)
1,0,2,0 - 2,0,0,0 - pf. - str.   7:00 Galaxy.

MOZART, Wolfgang Amadeus - WEINER, Leo
—— SONATA FOR STRINGS (FROM SONATA FOR 4-HANDS, K. 381) (IN 3 MOVTS.)
str.   8:00 EV.

MOZART, Wolfgang Amadeus - WESTCOTT, Frederick
—— SONATA CONCERTANTE (FROM THE PIANO-DUET SONATA IN B FLAT, K. 358)
pf. - str.   12:00 Oxford.

MOZART, Wolfgang Amadeus - WINTER, Aubrey
—— OVERTURE TO "COSÍ FAN TUTTE"
5:00 Bo. Hawkes.
—— OVERTURE TO "DON GIOVANNI"
6:00 Bo. Hawkes.
—— OVERTURE TO "IDOMENEO"
5:30 Bo. Hawkes.
—— OVERTURE TO "L'IMPRESARIO"
3:30 Bo. Hawkes.
—— OVERTURE TO "LUCIO SILLA"
10:00 Bo. Hawkes.
—— OVERTURE TO "THE MAGIC FLUTE"
8:00 Bo. Hawkes.
—— OVERTURE TO "THE MARRIAGE OF FIGARO"
4:00 Bo. Hawkes.
—— OVERTURE TO "THE SERAGLIO"
8:00 Bo. Hawkes.
—— OVERTURE TO "TITUS"
5:00 Bo. Hawkes.
—— THE SHEPHERD KING: OVERTURE
Bo. Hawkes.
—— SYMPHONY NO. 41 IN C MAJOR, K. 551 ("JUPITER")
28:00 Bo. Hawkes.

MSHVELIDZE, Shalva
—— ZVIADOORI (SYMPHONIC POEM)
3,3,3,3 - 4,3,3,1 - timp.,perc.,cel.,xyl. - hp. - pf. - str.
47:00 G. Schirmer.

MUCZYNSKI, Robert
—— CHARADE, OP. 28
2,2,2,2 - 4,3,3,0 - timp.,perc.(4) - str.   7:00 G. Schirmer.
—— CONCERTO NO. 1 FOR PIANO AND ORCH.
3,2,2,2 - 4,3,2,1 - timp.,perc. - hp. - pf. - str.   16:30 Templeton.
—— DANCE MOVEMENTS, OP. 17 (3 MOVTS.)
1,1,1,1 - 1,1,1,0 - timp.,perc.(2),cel. - hp. - str. 14:00 G. Schirmer.
—— DOVETAIL OVERTURE
*3,2,2,2 - 4,3,3,1 - timp.,perc.(3-4),glock.,xyl. - str.
4:30 G. Schirmer.
—— GALENA: A TOWN (SUITE) (IN 3 MOVTS.)
*3,2(2nd alt. with Eng.hn.),1 E♭cl.,2,*3 - 4,2,3,1 - timp.,perc.(3-4),glock.,xyl. - hp. - str.   16:00 Composer.
—— SYMPHONIC DIALOGUES, OP. 20
*3,2,2,2 - 4,3,3,1 - timp.,perc. - hp. - str.   7:30 G. Schirmer.
—— SYMPHONY NO. 1, OP. 5
3,2,2,2 - 4,2,3,1 - timp.,perc.,cel.,xyl. - hp. - pf. - str.
16:00 Templeton.

MUDGE, Richard - FINZI, Gerald
—— CONCERTO NO. 4 IN D MINOR (FOR CONTINUO AND STRINGS)
cemb. - str.   14:00 Bo. Hawkes.
—— CONCERTO NO. 6 IN F, FOR ORGAN, CEMBALO AND STRINGS
org. - cemb. - str.   14:00 Bo. Hawkes.

MUDGE, Richard - WARRACK
—— CONCERTO NO. 2 IN D MINOR
str.   Galaxy.

MUKHATOV, Veli
—— SYMPHONY NO. 1 (IN MEMORY OF MAKHTUMKULI)
G. Schirmer.

MUL, Jan
—— CONCERTO FOR ORCH. (1956)
3,3,3,3 - 4,4,3,1 - timp.,perc. - hp. - str.   28:00 Henmar.
—— CONCERTO FOR PIANO 4-HANDS AND ORCH. (1962)
1,0,0,1 - 0,0,0,0 - perc. - pf.(4-hands) - str.   17:00 Henmar.
—— DIVERTIMENTO (FOR PIANO AND ORCH.)
15:00 Henmar.
—— EGMONDT ONTHALSD (FROM P. D. HOOFT'S "NEDERLANDCHE HISTORIËN") (FOR MIXED CHORUS AND ORCH.) (1938)
1,0,1,0 - 0,1,0,0 - perc. - pf. - str.   10:00 Henmar.
—— INTERVALLEN (6 INVENTIES VOOR ORKEST OVER VERSCHILLENDE INTERVALLEN)
2,3,3,2 - 3,2,2,0 - timp.,perc.,cel. - hp. - str.   12:00 Henmar.
—— OLD FAMILIAR FACES (FOR VOICE AND ORCH.) (1969) (Text: Charles Lamb)
6:00 Henmar.
—— SINFONIETTA
2,3,2,2 - 4,3,1,0 - timp.,perc. - hp. - str.   12:00 Henmar.
—— STABAT MATER (FOR MIXED CHORUS AND ORCH.) (1934)
1,1,1,1 - 1,1,0,0 - timp.,perc. - hp. - str.   10:00 Henmar.
—— TE DEUM LAUDAMUS (FOR MIXED CHORUS AND ORCH.) (1936)
2,2,2,2 - 3,2,3,0 - timp. - str.   10:00 Henmar.

MULDER, Ernest W.
—— CONCERTO FOR PIANO AND ORCH.
2,2,2,2 - 2,2,0,0 - timp. - pf. - str.   Henmar.
—— FUGUE NO. 4 FROM "ARS CONTRAPUNCTICA"
str.   5:00 Henmar.
—— HOLLAND (FOR MIXED CHORUS AND ORCH.) (1942) (Text: Potgieter)
3,3,3,3 - 4,2,3,1 - timp. - str.   8:00 Henmar.
—— REQUIEM (MISSA PRO DEFUNCTIS) (FOR SATB SOLO VOICES, BOYS' CHORUS, MIXED CHORUS AND ORCH.) (1932)
3,2,2,2 - 4,2,3,0 - timp. - str.   30:00 Henmar.
—— STABAT MATER DOLOROSA (IN MEMORIAM J. VAN DEN VONDEL) (FOR SATB SOLO VOICES, MIXED CHORUS AND ORCH.) (1948)
2,2,2,2 - 3,2,3,0 - timp. - str.   37:00 Henmar.

—— SYMPHONIA SACRA I (FOR 2 SOPRANOS, ALTO, TENOR, BARITONE, BASS, MIXED CHORUS AND ORCH.) (1932)
    3,2,2,2 - 2,2,0,0 - timp. - pf. - str.   60:00 Henmar.
—— SYMPHONIA SACRA II (DIALOGUE MYSTIQUE) (FOR BARITONE, MIXED CHORUS AND ORCH.) (1940) (Text: Paul Verlaine)
    2,2,2,2 - 3,3,3,0 - timp.,perc.,cel. - str.   12:00 Henmar.
—— SYMPHONIETTA (FOR MEDIUM VOICE AND ORCH.) (1958) (IN 4 MOVTS.)
    2,2,2,2 - 2,2,0,0 - timp.,perc. - hp. - str.   12:00 Henmar.
—— TE DEUM LAUDAMUS (FOR MIXED CHORUS AND ORCH.) (1951)
    3,3,3,3 - 4,3,3,1 - timp. - hp. - str.   20:00 Henmar.
—— TROIS CHANSONS (FOR SOPRANO AND ORCH.) (1928) (Text: A. Samain)
    1,1,1,1 - 1,0,0,0 - timp. - pf. - str.   20:00 Henmar.

MULDER, Herman
—— CONCERTO FOR PIANO AND ORCH., OP. 3
    2,2,2,2 - 4,3,3,1 - timp. - pf. - str.   Henmar.
—— CONCERTO FOR SYMPHONY ORCHESTRA (OVERTURE, RONDO AND EPILOGUE) (1956)
    3,3,3,3 - 4,4,3,1 - timp.,perc. - hp. - str.   28:00 Henmar.
—— MUZIEK, OP. 140 (FOR VIOLIN AND CHAMBER ORCH.) (1967)
    10:00 Henmar.
—— SUITE, OP. 30
    4,3,3,3 - 4,2,3,0 - timp. - hp. - str.   Henmar.
—— SYMPHONY, OP. 114 (1961)
    3,3,3,3 - 4,4,3,1 - timp.,perc. - 2 hp. - str.   19:00 Henmar.
—— VIER LIEDEREN (4 SONGS, FOR BARITONE AND ORCH.) (Text: M. Vos)
    1,1,1,1 - 1,1,1,0 - timp.,perc. - hp. - str.   10:00 Henmar.

MULÈ, Giuseppe
—— TEMA CON VARIAZIONI (FOR CELLO AND ORCH.)
    1,2,1,1 - 0,0,0,0 - hp. - str.   10:00 Leeds.

MÜLLER, Gerhild
—— FANTASY FOR ORCH.
    3,2,2,2 - 4,3,3,1 - timp.,perc. - hp. - str.   18:00 Tetra.

MÜLLER, Gottfried
—— FANTASY FOR FLUTE AND ORCH.
    1,3,0,1 - 0,3,3,0 - timp. - str.   10:00 F. Colombo.

MÜLLER, Paul
—— CONCERTO FOR TWO VIOLINS AND STRINGS, OP. 61
    Mercurio.
—— KONZERT FÜR CELLO UND ORCH., OP. 55
    2,2,2,2 - 3,2,1,0 - timp.,perc. - str.   24:00 S.U.I.S.A.
—— SYMPHONY IN D, OP. 43
    2,2,*2,2 - 3,3,3,0 - timp.,perc. - hp. - str.   36:00 S.U.I.S.A.
—— SYMPHONY NO. 2 IN E, OP. 53
    fl. - str.   22:00 AhnSimrock.

MÜLLER, Rudolf
—— THEMA UND VARIATIONEN
    str.   10:15 Robbins.

MÜLLER-MEDEK, Tilo
—— RECITATIVE AND ARIA FOR ORCH.
    2,2,2,2 - 2,2,2,0 - timp. - str.   10:00 Tetra.
—— TRIAD FOR ORCH.
    2,2,2,2 - 1,2,2,0 - perc. - hp. - pf. - str.   16:00 Tetra.

MÜLLER VON KULM, Walter
—— CONCERTINO FÜR ALTSAXOPHON UND ORCHESTER, OP. 81
    20:00 S.U.I.S.A.
—— MUSIC FOR STRINGS, OP. 42
    str.   12:00 S.U.I.S.A.
—— PSALM 10, OP. 43 (FOR MEN'S CHORUS AND WINDS)
    1,2,2,*3 - 4,3,3,1 - timp.,perc.   10:00 Hug.
—— VATER UNSER, OP. 52 (ORATORIO) (FOR ALTO,BASS, MIXED CHORUS, CHILDREN'S CHORUS AND ORCH.)
    2,2,2,2 - 2,2,1,0 - timp. - org. - str.   68:00 Hug.

MÜLLER-ZÜRICH, Paul
—— CONCERTO FOR CELLO AND ORCH., OP. 55
    2(2nd alt with picc.),2,2,2 - 2,2,1,0 - timp.,perc. - str.   22:00 AhnSimrock.

—— SINFONIA NO. 1, OP. 40 (1940) (IN 3 MOVTS.)
    str.   23:00 AhnSimrock.
—— SINFONIA NO. 2, OP. 53 (1952) (IN 3 MOVTS.)
    fl. - str.   20:00 AhnSimrock.
—— SONATE FÜR STREICHORCH., OP. 72
    str.   15:00 Ed. Chasen.
—— SONATE NR. 2 FÜR STREICHORCH., OP. 64A
    str.   16:00 Ed. Chasen.
—— SYMPHONY IN D MINOR, OP. 43 (1947) (IN 4 MOVTS.)
    2(2nd alt. with picc.),2(2nd alt. with Eng.hn.),*3,2 - 3,3,3,0 - timp.,perc.,xyl. - hp. - str.   36:00 AhnSimrock.

MUNDY, John - FELLOWS, Edmund H.
—— SING JOYFULLY (ANTHEM) (FOR BASS, MIXED CHORUS AND ORCH.)
    Oxford.

MURADELI, Vano
—— GEORGIAN SYMPHONIC DANCE
    3,3,3,2 - 4,3,3,1 - timp.,perc.,cel.,xyl. - hp. - str. 4:30 G. Schirmer.
—— SYMPHONY NO. 1
    3,3,4,2 - 4,3,3,1 - timp.,perc. - str.   G. Schirmer.
—— SYMPHONY NO. 2
    3,3,4,3 - 4,3,3,1 - timp.,perc.,cel.,xyl. - 2 hp. - str.   40:00 G. Schirmer.

MURADIAN, Vazgen
—— CONCERTO FOR OBOE AND STRING ORCH., OP. 25 (1975) (IN 3 MOVTS.)
    ob. - str.   27:00 Composer.
—— CONCERTO FOR VIOLIN AND ORCH., OP. 52 (1973) (IN 3 MOVTS.)
    2,*3,2,0 - 4,2,0,0 - timp. - str.(23,8,6,6)   35:00 Composer.
—— FOUR SONGS, OP. 39 (FOR VOICE AND STRING ORCH.) (1971)
    str.   15:00 Composer.
—— FOUR SONGS, OP. 40 (FOR VOICE AND ORCH.) (1970) (Texts: Goethe, Byron, Shakespeare)
    2,2,2,2 - 4,0,0,0 - timp. - str.   20:00 Composer.
—— FOUR SONGS, OP. 41 (FOR CHORUS AND STRING ORCH.) (1971)
    str.   29:00 Composer.
—— IF ONE DAY..., OP. 35 (FOR VOICE AND ORCH.) (1962) (Text: Hovanes Toumanian)
    2,*3,2,2 -4,0,0,0 - timp.,perc. - str.   6:30 Composer.
—— PARTITA, OP. 23 (FOR VIOLA D'AMORE AND ORCH.) (1957) (IN 4 MOVTS.)
    0,2,0,0 - 2,0,0,0, - str.   27:00 Composer.
—— THE UNRETURNABLE SPRING, OP. 36 (FOR VOICE AND ORCH.) (1962) (Text: Heghine Muradian)
    2,*3,*3,2 - 4,0,0,0 - timp.,perc. - str.   8:00 Composer.

MURAIL, Tristan
—— ALTITUDE 8000 (FOR ORCH.)
    Presser.
—— AU-DELÀ DU MUR DU SON
    3,3,3,3 - 4,3,3,1 - perc.(4),cel. - 2 hp. - str.   16:30 Presser.
—— COULEUR DE MER (FOR 16 INSTRUMENTS)
    Presser.
—— MÉMOIRE EROSION (FOR HORN AND 9 INSTRS.)
    Presser.

MURAVLEV, Aleksej A.
—— AZOV MOUNTAIN, OP. 10 (TONE POEM)
    3,2,2,2 - 4,3,3,1 - timp.,perc. - hp. - str.   12:30 G. Schirmer.

MURGIER, Jacques
—— CONCERTO FOR ALTO SAXOPHONE AND STRING ORCH.
    alto sax. - str.   30:00 Presser.
—— CONCERTO FOR OBOE AND ORCH.
    15:00 EV.
—— CONCERTO FOR VIOLIN AND STRINGS
    str.   Presser.
—— SPIRALE (BALLET) %
    3,3,2,alto sax.,3 - 4,3,3,1 - timp.,perc. - hp. - str.   Presser.
—— SYMPHONY NO. 1 FOR STRINGS
    str.   22:00 Presser.

MURRAY, Lyn
—— VARIATIONS ON A CHILDREN'S TUNE (FOR STRINGS)
    str.   Bo. Hawkes.

MURRAY, Lyn - STEINER, Frederick
—— RONALD SEARLE SUITE
    2,1,3,1 - 2,0,0,0 - perc.,cel. - pf. - d.-b.   Novello.

MURRILL, Herbert
—— CONCERTO NO. 1 FOR CELLO AND ORCH.
                                      Oxford.
—— CONCERTO NO. 2 FOR CELLO AND ORCH.
    2,2,3,2 - 4,2,3,0 - timp.,perc. - hp. - str.   17:00 Oxford.

MUSGRAVE, Thea
—— BEAUTY AND THE BEAST (BALLET) (FOR CHAMBER
    ORCH. AND TAPE)(1973) %
    1,1,2,1 - 1,2,1,0 - perc.(2) - tape-recorder - str.   100:00 Tetra.
—— CANTATA FOR A SUMMER'S DAY (FOR NARRATOR,
    SOPRANO, ALTO, TENOR, BASS AND ORCH.)
    1 fl., 1 cl. - str.   34:00 G. Schirmer.
—— CONCERTO FOR CLARINET AND ORCH. (1968)
    3,3,2,3 - 4,3,3,1 - timp.,perc.(4) - acc. - hp. - str.
                                    22:00 G. Schirmer.
—— CONCERTO FOR HORN AND ORCH.
    *2,*2,*2,*2 - 5,2,1,0 - perc.(3),cel. - hp. - pf. - str.
                                    22:00 G. Schirmer.
—— CONCERTO FOR ORCHESTRA
    3,3,3,3 - 4,3,3,1 - timp.,perc.(4) - hp. - str.   20:00 G. Schirmer.
—— CONCERTO FOR VIOLA AND ORCH.
    1,1(alt. with Eng.hn.),1(alt. with b.-cl.),1 - 3,2,1,0 - perc. - hp. -
    str.   22:00 Novello.
—— DIVERTIMENTO (FOR STRINGS)
    str.   14:00 G. Schirmer.
—— FESTIVAL OVERTURE (1965)
    2(2nd alt. with picc.),2,2,2 - 4,2,3,0 - timp.,perc. - str.
                                    10:00 G. Schirmer.
—— THE FIVE AGES OF MAN (FOR CHORUS AND ORCH.)
    3,2,2,2 - 4,3,3,1 - timp.,perc. - pf. - str.   27:00 G. Schirmer.
    or:
    3,2,2,2 - 2,2,2,1 - timp.,perc. - pf. - str.
—— MEMENTO VITAE - CONCERTO IN HOMAGE TO
    BEETHOVEN (1970)
    2,2,2,2 - 4,3,3,1 - timp. - str.   18:00 G. Schirmer.
—— NIGHT MUSIC (FOR CHAMBER ORCH.) (1969)
    1,2,0,1 - 2,0,0,0 - str.   18:00 G. Schirmer.
—— NOCTURNES AND ARIAS (1966)
    2(2nd alt. with picc.),2,*3,*3 - 4,3,3,1 - timp.,perc.(3) - hp. - str.
                                    21:00 G. Schirmer.
—— OBLIQUES
    3,2,3,2 - 4,3,3,1 - timp.,perc. - hp. - str.   12:00 G. Schirmer.
—— PERSPECTIVES (1961)
    2(2nd alt. with picc.)2,2,2(2nd alt. with c.-bn.) - 4,3,3,0 -
    timp.,perc. - hp. - str.   8:00 G. Schirmer.
—— SCOTTISH DANCE SUITE (1958)
    3,2,2,2 - 4,2,3,1 - timp.,perc. - hp. - str.   11:00 G. Schirmer.
—— SINFONIA (1963)
    2,*3,2,2 - 4,3,3,1 - timp.,perc. - hp. - str.   16:00 G. Schirmer.
—— A TALE FOR THIEVES (SUITE FROM THE BALLET) (1953)
    2(2nd alt. with picc.),2,2*3 - 4,3,3,1 - timp.,perc. - str.
                                    14:00 G. Schirmer.
—— THEME AND INTERLUDES (1960)
    2,1,3,1 - 2,2,1,0 - timp.,perc.(6) - str.   11:00 G. Schirmer.
—— TRYPTICH (FOR TENOR AND ORCH.) (1959)
    2,2,1,1 - 3,2,0,0 - perc.,cel. - hp. - pf. - str.   10:00 G. Schirmer.

MUSOLINO, Angelo
—— CONCERTO FOR TENOR VIOLIN AND ORCH.
                                  22:00 H. Branch.
—— SERENATA FOR CLASSIC GUITAR AND ORCH.
                                  H. Branch.

MYERS, Robert
—— MOVEMENTS FOR SOPRANO SAXOPHONE AND
    CHAMBER ORCH.
    1,1,2,sax.,1 - 2,2,2,0 - timp.,perc. - pf. - str.   20:00 ArtisnMuPr.

MYERS, Theldon
—— CONCERTINO FOR ORCHESTRA (1960)
    *3,*3,*3,2 - 4,3,3,1 - timp.,perc.(3) - hp. - str.   7:30 CAP.
—— CONFIGURATION (1967)
    *2,*2,*2,2 - 2,2,2,0 - timp.,perc.,vibra.,xyl. - hp. - pf. - str.
                                    4:00 CAP.
—— ELEGY (1966)
    str.   5:30 CAP.

—— SYMPHONY 1969 (IN 3 MOVTS.)
    *3,*3,*3,*3 - 4,3,3,1 - timp.,perc.(7),cel.,glock.,xyl. - hp. - str.
                                    22:00 Composer.

MYROW, Frederic
—— CHAMBER SYMPHONY
    1,1,*2,1 - 2,0,0,0 - perc.(2) - pf. - str.   20:00 Mills.
—— SYMPHONIC VARIATIONS
    *3,*3,*4,*3 - 4,3,3,1 - timp.,perc. - hp. - pf. - str.   25:00 Mills.

MYROW, Joseph - CAMPBELL-WATSON, F.
—— ODE TO A MARINE (FOR BARITONE, CHORUS AND
    ORCH.)
    2,2,*3,2 - 4,4,3,1 - timp.,perc. - str.   7:00 Mills.

MYSLIWEČEK, Josef - FENDLER, Edvard
—— CONCERTO NO. 2 FOR HARPSICHORD AND ORCH. (IN 3
    MOVTS.)
    2 ob. - 2 hn. - hpsc.(or pf.) - str.   16:00 Bo. Hawkes.

N

NABOKOFF, Nicolas
—— CHANTS À LA VIERGE MARIE (FOR VOICE AND ORCH.)
    2,0,0,2 - 0,0,bugle,0,0 - str.   Salabert.
—— COLLECTIONNEUR D'ÉCHOS (FOR SOPRANO, BASS,
    CHORUS AND SMALL ORCH.)
    1,1,1,1 - 0,1,0,0 - perc. - str.   10:00 Bo. Hawkes.
—— CONCERTO CORALE (FOR FLUTE, PIANO AND STRINGS)
    fl. - pf. - str.   17:00 F. Colombo.
—— CONCERTO FOR PIANO AND ORCH.
    2,2,2,2 - 4,2,2,1 - timp.,perc. - pf. - str.   23:00 Bo. Hawkes.
—— LES DANSES DE POLICHINELLE (SUITE)
    3(3rd alt. with picc.),3(3rd alt. with eng. hn.),3,2 sax.,3 - 4,3,3,1 -
    timp.,perc. - hp. - pf. - str.   15:00 Bo. Hawkes.
—— DON QUIXOTE (BALLET) %
    3,3,3,3 - 4,3,3,1 - timp.,perc. - hp. - pf. - str.   Bo. Hawkes.
—— LE FIANCÉ, OP. 9
    2,2,2,2 - 2,2,1,0 - perc. - cel. - str.   6:00 Bo. Hawkes.
—— THE HOLY DEVIL (3-ACT OPERA) % (Text: Stephen Spender)
    2,2,2,2 - 4,2,2,0 - timp.,perc.,cel. - hp. - str.   F. Colombo.
—— LES HOMMAGES (CONCERTO FOR CELLO AND ORCH.)
    2,2,2,2 - 4,1,1,0 - timp.,perc.,cel. - hp. - pf. - str.
                                    22:00 F. Colombo.
—— THE HUNTER'S PICNIC (SYMPHONIC SUITE FROM "DON
    QUIXOTE")
    3,3,3,3 - 4,3,3,1 - timp.,perc. - hp. - pf. - str.   23:00 Seesaw.
—— JOB
    2,1,1,0 - 2,2,2,0 - timp.,perc. - 2 pf. - str.   25:00 Bo. Hawkes.
—— THE LAST FLOWER (SYMPHONIC SUITE FROM THE
    BALLET)
    2,2,2,2 - 4,2,2,0 - timp.,perc. - pf. - str.   30:00 F. Colombo.
—— ODE (FOR 2 VOICES, CHORUS AND ORCH.)
    3,3,3,3 - 4,3,2,1 - timp.,perc. - str.   37:00 Bo. Hawkes.
—— PRELUDE, VARIATIONS AND FINALE ON A THEME OF
    TSCHAIKOWSKY (FOR VIOLIN AND ORCH.)
    2(2nd alt. with picc.),1,2,2 - 4,2,2,0 - timp.,perc.,cel. - hp. - pf. -
    str.   30:00 Henmar.
—— THE RETURN OF PUSHKIN (ELEGY IN 3 MOVTS.) (FOR
    SOPRANO OR TENOR WITH ORCH.)
    2,2,2,2 - 4,3,0,0 - timp. - str.   19:00 F. Colombo.
—— STUDIES IN SOLITUDE (4 MOODS FOR ORCH.)
    2,2,3,1 sax.,2 - 4,1,1,0 - timp.,perc.,cel. - hp. - pf. - str.
                                    15:00 F. Colombo.
—— SYMBOLI CHRESTIANI (FOR BARITONE AND ORCH.)
    2,0,0,2 - 2,2,0,0 - timp.,perc.,cel. - hp. - pf. - str.
                                    17:00 F. Colombo.
—— SYMPHONIC VARIATIONS
    3,3,3,3 - 4,3,3,1 - timp.,perc.,cel. - hp. - pf. - str.   38:00 Henmar.
—— SYMPHONIE BIBLIQUE
    3,3,4,3 - 4,3,3,1 - timp.,perc. - hp. - pf. - str.   25:00 F. Colombo.
—— SYMPHONIE LYRIQUE
    3,3,3,3 - 4,3,3,1 - timp.,perc.(2) - str.   15:00 Bo. Hawkes.
—— SYMPHONY NO. 3 (A PRAYER)
    3,3,3,3 - 4,3,3,1 - timp.,perc. - hp. - pf. - str.   18:00 Henmar.
—— LA VIE DE POLICHINELLE
    3,3,3,3 - 4,3,3,1 - timp.,perc.,cel.,xyl. - hp. - pf. - str.
                                    28:00 Bo. Hawkes.

—— LA VITA NUOVA (CONCERTO FOR SOPRANO, TENOR AND ORCH.)

2,2,2,2 - 4,2,2,1 - timp.,perc. - hp. - pf. - str.   30:00 F. Colombo.

NADELMANN, Leo
—— MUTATIONS

Str   14:00 IsMuPublns.

NAGAN, Zvi
—— MUSIC FOR TWO RECORDERS AND ORCH.

2 recorders(sopr. and alto),0,2,0,2 - 2,1,0,0 - perc. - cemb.- str.(no d.-b.)   18:00 IsMuPublns.
or:
1,3,0,2 - 2,1,0,0 - perc. - cemb. - str.(no d.-b.)

NAGLE, William S. - ZIMMER, Edward
—— THE SOLITARY REAPER (FOR WOMEN'S CHORUS AND ORCH.)

2,1,2,2 - 2,2,2,0 - timp. - hp. - str.   5:00 EV.

NAGOVITSYN, Vjacheslav L.
—— FESTIVE OVERTURE

G. Schirmer.

NAGY, Frederick
—— FESTIVE OVERTURE

1,1,1,1 - 1,1,1,0 - timp.,perc.,bells - str.   7:00 Composer.

NAJERA, Edmund
—— ELEGY FOR STRINGS

str.   16:00 OperaIntl.
—— ELYSE (3-ACT MUSIC-DRAMA) % (1959) (Text: Composer)

2,*3,2(1 alt.with b.-cl.),0 - 1,0,0,0 - timp.,perc.(1),bells,cel. - org. - 2 pf. - str.(optional)   180:00 OperaIntl.
—— THE FREEWAY OPERA (1-ACT COMIC OPERA) % (1967) (Text: John I. Hartley)

1,0,1,0 - 1,1,1,0 - hp. - pf. - str. or   22:00 OperaIntl.
2,0,2,0 - 1,1,1 0 - hp. - pf. - str.
—— ORIENTALE (IN MEMORIAM E. E. CUMMINGS) (FOR EITHER BARITONE, CHORUS AND ORCH. OR ORCH. ONLY) (1960) (IN 4 MOVTS.) (Text: e. e. cummings)

3,(3rd alt. with picc.),*3,*3,*3 - 3,3,2,1 - timp.,perc.(3),bells,cel. - hp. - pf. - str.   34:00 OperaIntl.
—— RHAPSODY FOR PIANO AND ORCHESTRA (1967) (IN 3 MOVTS.)

2,2,2,2 - 2,1,2,0 - timp.,perc.(1) - pf. - str.   19:30 OperaIntl.
—— RHETORICAL SONGS (7 SONGS) (FOR BARITONE AND ORCH.) (1961) (Text: Composer)

2(2nd alt. with picc.),3(3rd alt. with Eng.hn.),0,2(2nd alt. with c.-bn.) - 1,2,1,0 - timp.,perc.(1),cel. - hp. - pf. - str.
20:00 OperaIntl.

NANNY, Edouard
—— CONCERTO FOR DOUBLE BASS AND ORCH.

2,2,0,2 - 2,1,0,0 - str.   12:00 Baron.

NARDINI, Pietro - BONELLI
—— ADAGIO IN E FLAT MAJOR

str.   6:00 Henmar.

NASCIMBENE, Mario
—— ACQUEFORTI DELLA VECCHIA MILANO (QUADRO SINFONICI) (IN 7 MOVTS.)

3,3,3,3 - 4,3,3,1 - timp.,perc.,bells.,cel.,xyl. - hp. - pf. - str.
30:00 Bo. Hawkes.

NAT, Yves
—— CONCERTO FOR PIANO AND ORCH.

2,2,3,3 - 4,3,1,1 - timp.,perc.,cel.,xyl. - 2 hp. - pf. - str.
32:00 Presser.

NATRA, Sergiu
—— MUSIC FOR OBOE AND 14 STRINGS

ob. - str.   12:00 A.C.U.M.
—— SINFONIA FOR STRINGS

str.   20:00 Bo. Hawkes.
—— VARIATIONS FOR PIANO AND ORCHESTRA

20:00 A.C.U.M.

NAUMANN, Siegfried
—— IL CANTICO DEL SOLE (FOR 2 SOLO VOICES, MIXED CHORUS, 10 SOLO INSTS. AND ORCH.) (1966)

0,0,0,0 - 0,3,3,0 - hp. - pf. - str.   28:00 S.T.I.M.

—— IL CIECO DEL PONTE A MORIANO (DIALOGUE FOR TENOR, SATB CHORUS, CELLO AND ORCH.) (1972) (Text: I. Nieri)

2,1,2,2 - 4,4,3,1 - perc.(2) - Hammond org. - acc. - pf. - c.
13:00 Fleisher.
—— ESTATE, OP. 21 (1968)

2,2,2,2 - 2,2,1,0 - perc.(2) - Hammond org. - pf. - str.
30:00 Fleisher.
—— IMPROVVISO (FOR VIOLIN AND ORCH.)

0,2,0,2 - 2,0,0,0 - timp.,perc. - str.   16:00 S.T.I.M.
—— LJUDPOSTER (1970)

3,3,3,4 sax.,3 - 4,4,3,1 - perc.(2) - hammond org. - pf. - str.
11:00 Fleisher.
—— MUSIC FOR 10 INSTRUMENTS, CONTRA-BASSON AND TIMPANI

2,2,2,*3 - 2,0,0,0 - timp.   16:30 S.T.I.M.
—— MUSICA SACRA NO. 2 (FOR 2 FLUTES, TIMPANI AND STRINGS)

2 fl. - timp. - str.   20:00 S.T.I.M.
—— MUSICA SACRA NO. 4 (1958) (FOR BARITONE, MIXED CHORUS AND 2 ORCHESTRAS)

Orch. I: bn. - vla.,c.   20:00 S.T.I.M.
Orch. II: 3 hn.,3 tpt.,3 trb. - d.-b.
—— SPETTACOLO I (FOR SOPRANO AND ORCH.)

4,0,1,0 - 6,6,6,2 - perc.(3) - hp. - 8 d.-b.   12:00 S.T.I.M.
—— SPETTACOLO II (FOR SOPRANO, ALTO, BASS, MIXED CHORUS AND ORCH.) (1969)

4,0,0,0 - 6,6,6,2 - perc.(2) - 2 pf. - 8 d.-b.   16:00 S.T.I.M.
—— SUITE CONCERTANTE (FOR BASSOON AND STRINGS)

bn. - str.   15:00 S.T.I.M.
—— SYMPHONIC PRELUDE

2,2,3,2 - 4,3,3,1 - timp.,perc. - str.   S.T.I.M.
—— SYMPHONY NO. 1

2,2,2,2 - 2,2,0,0 - timp. - str.   32:00 S.T.I.M.
—— SYMPHONY NO. 2

2,2,2,2 - 2,2,3,0 - timp.,perc. - str.   36:00 S.T.I.M.
—— SYMPHONY NO. 3

2,2,2,2 - 4,3,3,1 - timp.,perc. - str.   S.T.I.M.
—— TEATRO STRUMENTALE PER MUSICA NOVA, OP. 22 (FOR STRING QUINTET AND ORCH.)(1971)

1,2,2,1 - 1,1,1,0 - timp.,perc.(3) - guit. - hp. - Hammond org. - pf. - str.   21:00 Fleisher.
—— TRANSFORMAZIONI (1962)

3,3,3,3 - 0,3,3,0 - timp.,perc.(8) - 9 hp. - str.   9:00 S.T.I.M.

NAYLOR, Bernard
—— CANTATA (FOR SOPRANO AND STRINGS)

str.   C.A.P.A.C.
—— FOUR POEMS OF W. H. DAVIES

9:00 C.A.P.A.C.
—— IMAGE OF WISDOM (FOR BARITONE AND ORCH.)

11:00 C.A.P.A.C.
—— THE LIVING FOUNTAIN (1963) (CANTATA FOR TENOR OR SOPRANO AND STRINGS) (Text: Rowland Watkins)

str.   15:00 Novello.
—— MISSA DA CAMERA (1966) (FOR SATB CHORUS OR VOCAL QUARTET AND ORCH.)

0,1,2,2 - 1,0,0,0 - str.   12:00 Novello.
—— THE RESURRECTION ACCORDING TO ST. MATTHEW (1965) (FOR SPEAKERS, SOPRANO, BARITONE, BASS, SATB CHORUS AND ORCH.)

Maximum: 1,1,1,1 - 1,1,1,0 - timp.,cymb. - pf. - str.
15:00 Novello.
or:
str.
—— SING O MY LOVE (1963) (CANTATA FOR BASS-BARITONE, SATB CHORUS AND STRINGS)

str.   9:00 Novello.
—— SPENSER'S MADRIGALS

13:00 C.A.P.A.C.
—— STABAT MATER (1961) (FOR SSAA CHORUS AND ORCH.)

2,2,2,2 - 2,2,0,0 - str.(no d.-b.)   10:00 Novello.
—— WALLENSTEIN (SYMPHONIC POEM)

C.A.P.A.C.

NEANDER, John William
—— ALT DANZIG (SUITE) (IN 5 MOVTS.)

*3,2,2,2(2nd alt. with c.-bn.) - 4,3,3,1 - timp.,perc.,glock. - str.
27:00 Mannheimer.
—— FJORD RHAPSODY

*3,*3,*3,2 - 4,3,3,1 - timp.,perc. - hp. - str.   18:00 Mannheimer.
—— IN HERBST (IN AUTUMN) (CONCERT OVERTURE)

*3,1,2,1 - 4,2,3,0 - timp. - str.   5:00 Mannheimer.

NEAR, Gerald
—— DIVERTIMENTO FOR SMALL ORCHESTRA (1968)
    1,1,1,1 - 0,0,0,0 - str.   12:00 Composer.
—— OVERTURE FOR STRING ORCHESTRA (1969)
    str.   10:00 Composer.

NEEF, Wilhelm
—— SHAKESPEAREANA (BALLET-SUITE) (FOR ORCH. AND
    SOLO JAZZ INSTS.)
    2,2,2,2 - 2,3,3,0 - timp.,perc.,cel. - hpsc. - pf. - str.   32:00 Tetra.

NEGRI, Gino
—— L' ARMONIUM E'UTILE (1-ACT OPERA) %
                                               MCA Music.
—— IL CIRCO MAX ("CIRCUS MAX") (1-ACT OPERA) %
    3,2,2,2 sax.,2 - 2,2,2,0 - timp.,perc. - str.   32:00 Leeds.
—— FINIRO' PER SVEGLIARMI (1-ACT OPERA) %
                                               MCA Music.
—— GIORNO DI NOZZE (1-ACT OPERA) %
                                               MCA Music.
—— IL TESTIMONE INDESIDERATO (1-ACT RADIO OPERA)
                                               MCA Music.
—— MASSIMO ("MAX") (1-ACT CHAMBER OPERA) %
    0,0,1,1 sax.,0 - 0,1,1,0 - perc. - acc. - guit. - org. - pf. - player-pf. -
    d.-b.   30:00 Leeds.
—— SPOON RIVER ANTHOLOGY (FOR SOLO VOICES, CHORUS
    AND ORCH.) (Text: Edgar Lee Masters)
    1,1,1,1 sax.,0 - 1,0,0,0 - bell,cel. - hp - hpsc. - org. - pf. - str.
                                               29:00 Leeds.
—— IL TÈ DELLE TRE ("THE TEA OF THE 3 LADIES") (1-ACT
    CHAMBER OPERA) %
    1,1,0,0 - 1,1,0,0 - perc.,vibra. - pf. - str.(no d.-b.)   30:00 Leeds.
—— VIENI QUI CARLA ("COME HERE, CARLA") (1-ACT OPERA,
    AFTER ALBERTO MORAVIA'S "THE INDIFFERENT") %
    0,0,1,3 sax.,1 - 0,0,0,0 - perc.,vibra. - str.   45:00 Leeds.

NEGRO, Ottavio
—— PASSACAGLIA (1965)
    2,2,2,2 - 2,2,0,0 - timp. - str.   7:00 P.R.S.

NEIKRUG, Marc
—— CIRCA (1975)
    2(2nd alt. with picc.),2(2nd alt. with Eng.hn.),2(2nd alt. with
    b.-cl.),2(2nd alt. with cbn.) - 4,3,3,1 - timp.,perc.(2) - hp. - str.
                                               25:00 Composer.
—— CONCERTO FOR CLARINET AND ORCHESTRA (1968)
    3(3rd alt. with picc.),3(3rd alt. with Eng.hn.),1,1 alto sax., 1
    ten.sax.,3 - 4,3,3,1 - str.   16:00 Baerenrtr.
—— CONCERTO FOR PIANO AND ORCH. (1965)
    2,2,2,2 - 2,0,0,0 - perc.(2) - hp. - pf. - str.   24:00 G. Schirmer.
—— FANTASY FOR ORCHESTRA (1966)
    3(3rd alt. with picc.),3(3rd alt. with Eng.hn.),3,3(3rd alt. with
    c.-bn) - 4,2,1 flg.,3,1 - perc.(2),cel.,vibra. - 2 hp. - str.
                                               12:00 Baerenrtr.
—— MOVEMENT FOR ORCHESTRA (1972)
    2,2,2,2 - 2,2,2,1 - perc.(2),cel.,vibra. - hp. - str.   10:00 Composer.
—— VARIATIONS FOR STRINGS (1971)
    str.   14:00 Composer.

NEJEDLÝ, Vít
—— DAWN (OVERTURE TO "VERHAEREN"), OP. 5
    3,2,4,3 - 4,4,3,1 - timp.,perc. - hp. - pf. - str.   8:00 Bo. Hawkes.
—— FOLK SUITE (1940) (IN 6 MOVTS.)
    1,1,1,1 - 1,1,0,0 - timp.,perc. - str.   22:00 Bo. Hawkes.
—— SYMPHONIC FANTASY (1929)
                                               Bo. Hawkes.
—— SYMPHONIETTA, OP. 13
    2,2,3,2 - 2,2,2,0 - timp.,perc. - str.   20:00 Bo. Hawkes.
—— SYMPHONY NO. 1 (1931)
                                               Bo. Hawkes.
—— SYMPHONY NO. 2, OP. 7 (1934)
    3,3,4,3 - 6,4,3,1 - timp.,perc. - hp. - pf. - str.   35.00 Bo. Hawkes.
—— SYMPHONY NO. 3, OP. 14 (1938)
    3,3,3,3 - 4,4,3,1 - timp.,perc. - org. - pf. - str.   35:00 Bo. Hawkes.

NELHYBEL, Vaclav
—— CANTUS ET LUDUS (FOR SOLO PIANO, 17 WINDS AND
    PERCUSSION)
    3(3rd alt. with picc.),1,*4,d.-b.cl.,1 - 2,2,2,1 -
    timp.,perc.(3),bells,glock.,vibra.,xyl. - pf. -1 d.-b.   16:00 E.C.Kerby.

—— CONCERTINO DA CAMERA (FOR SOLO CELLO, 15 WINDS
    AND PERCUSSION) (1971)
    3(3rd alt. with picc.),alto fl.,*2,*4,d.-b.cl.,2 - 2,0,0,0 -
    perc.(3),bells,cel.,glock.,mar.,vibra. - pf. - 1 c.   11:00 E.C.Kerby.
—— CONCERTINO FOR PIANO AND CHAMBER ORCH.
    1(alt. with picc.),1,1,0 - 0,1,0,0 - pf. - str.   7:40 General.
—— CONCERTO FOR GUITAR AND CHAMBER ORCH.
    2,1,2,0 - 0,0,0,0 - guit. - str.   12:00 General.
—— CONCERTO FOR VIOLA AND ORCH.
    *2,2,2,2 - 3,1,1,0 - perc. - str.   14:00 General.
—— ÉTUDE SYMPHONIQUE (1950)
    *3,*3,*4,*3 - 4,3,3,1 - timp.,perc.(4),bells,glock.,xyl. - pf. - str.
                                               12:00 General.
—— FOUR READINGS (FROM MARLOWE'S "DR. FAUSTUS")
    2,2,2,2 - 2,2,2,0 - perc. - org. - pf. - str.(0,2,2,1)   45:00 General.
—— A MIGHTY FORTRESS (BASED ON THE LUTHER HYMN)
    *3,2,2,2 - 4,3,3,1 - timp.,perc.(4),bells,glock.,xyl. - str.
                                               8:00 E.C.Kerby.
—— MOVEMENT FOR ORCHESTRA (1967)
    *3,2,*4,2 - 4,3,3,1 - timp.,perc.(4),bells,glock.,vibra.,xyl. - str.
                                               9:00 F. Colombo.
—— MUSIC FOR ORCHESTRA (1966)
    4(1 alt. with picc.),0,*3,2 - 4,3,3,1 - timp.,perc.(4),bells,glock.,xyl. -
    str.   8:00 F. Colombo.
—— PASSACAGLIA FOR ORCH. AND PIANO (1965)
    *3,2,*3,2 - 4,3,3,1 - timp.,perc.(3),bells,glock. - pf. - str.
                                               5:00 F. Colombo.
—— POLYPHONIES FOR ORCHESTRA (1972)
    4(1 alt. with picc.),*4,*4,4 - 4,4,4,1 -
    timp.,perc.(5),bells,glock.,vibra.,xyl. - pf. - str.   18:00 E.C.Kerby.
—— SINE NOMINE (FOR SATB SOLO VOICES, SATB CHORUS
    AND ORCH.) (1968)
    2,2 picc.,2,*4,4 sax.,0 - 3,5,5,2 bar., 1 -
    timp.,perc.(7),bells,glock.,vibra.,xyl. - tape-recorder - org. - str.
                                               12:00 F. Colombo.
—— SURPRISE VARIATIONS
    str.   6:30 JC-phrMuCo.
—— THREE MODES FOR ORCHESTRA (1960)
    *2,*2,*4,2 - 3,1,1,0 - timp.,perc.(3),bells,glock.,xyl. - str.
                                               12:30 General.
—— THREE MOVEMENTS FOR STRINGS (1952)
    str.   11:20 General.
—— TOCCATA (FOR HARPSICHORD, 13 WINDS AND
    PERCUSSION) (1972)
    *3,1,*3,1 - 1,2,2,0 - perc.(2),bells,glock.,vibra.,xyl. - hpsc.
                                               8:00 E.C.Kerby.
—— TWO MOVEMENTS FOR CHAMBER ORCH. (WITH SOLO
    PIANO)
    1,1,1,1 - 0,1,1,0 - pf. - str.   8:40 General.

NELLESSEN, Hermann Josef
—— DIVERTIMENTO FOR STRING ORCH. (1960)
    str.   9:00 Tetra.

NELSON, Oliver
—— DIVERTIMENTO
    2,2,2,2 - 2,0,0,0 - d.-b.   12:00 Modern.

NELSON, Paul
—— IN MEMORIAM (FOR MIXED CHORUS AND STRING
    ORCH.) (1959-67) (Text: Alfred Lord Tennyson)
    str.   7:00 Composer.
—— NARRATIVE FOR ORCH.
    1,1,1,1 - 1,1,0,0 - str.   9:00 Modern.
—— QUAD-LIBET (ON TRADITIONAL SONGS OF BROWN
    UNIVERSITY) (FOR MIXED CHORUS AND ORCH.) (1970)
    1(alt. with picc.),1,1,1 - 2,2,3,0 - timp.,perc.(1),bells - hp. - hpsc. -
    str.   20:00 Composer.
—— SINFONIETTA (IN 3 MOVTS.)
    2,2,2,2 - 4,3,3,1 - timp.,perc.(3),glock.,xyl. - str.   21:00 Galaxy.
—— SONGS OF LIFE (FOR MIXED CHORUS, HARP AND
    STRINGS)
    hp. - str.   21:00 C. Fischer.
—— SYMPHONIC THESIS
    2(1st. alt. with picc.),2(2nd alt. with Eng. hn.),2(2nd alt. with
    b.-cl),2 - 4,2,3,1 - timp.,perc.(4),bells,xyl. - hp. - str.
                                               13:00 Composer.
—— THEME AND PASSACAGLIA
    2(1st alt. with picc.),2(2nd alt. with Eng. hn.),2,2 - 4,2-3,3,1 -
    timp.,perc.(2) - hp. - str.   10:00 Composer.
—— TWO CONTRASTS FOR ORCH.
    2,2,2,2 - 4,3,3,1 - timp.,perc. - str.   14:00 Composer.

—— VARIATIONS ON A WESTERN FOLKSONG
1(alt. with picc.),1,1,1 - 2,2,1,1 - timp.,perc.(1) - str.
10:00 Composer.

NELSON, Ron
—— ALL PRAISE TO MUSIC (FANFARE FOR A FESTIVAL) (FOR SATB CHORUS AND ORCH.) (1960) (Text: Walter A. Rodby)
3,2,2,2 - 4,3,3,1 - timp.,perc. - hp. - str.   2:00 Bo. Hawkes.
—— THE BIRTHDAY OF THE INFANTA (1-ACT OPERA, AFTER THE OSCAR WILDE STORY) % (Text: Ron Nelson)
2(2nd alt. with picc.),2,2,2 - 2,2,0,0 -
timp.,perc.(2-3),bells,cel.,glock. - hp. - pf. - str.   56:00 C. Fischer.
—— THE CHRISTMAS STORY (FOR NARRATOR, BARITONE, MIXED CHORUS AND ORCH.)
2,2,2,2 - 2,3,3,1 - timp.,perc.,cel. - hp. - org. - str
31:00 Bo. Hawkes.
—— DANCE IN RUINS (BALLET) % (After the painting by Eugene Berman)
2(2nd alt. with picc.),2(2nd alt. with Eng. hn.),2,2 - 4,3,3,1 -
timp.,perc.(3-4),cel.,glock.,xyl. - hp. - pf. - str.   16:00 Composer.
—— ELEGY FOR ORCHESTRA
2,2,2,2 - 2,2,0,0 - timp.,perc.(2) - hp. - str.   5:00 Composer.
—— FIVE PIECES FOR ORCH. (WITH BARITONE VOICE) (After Paintings by Andrew Wyeth) (1975))
*3,*3,*3,*3 - 4,3,3,1 - timp.,perc.,bells,cel.,glock.,mar.,vibra.,xyl. -
hp. - pf. - str.   24:45 Bo. Hawkes.
—— JUBILEE (PART II OF "THIS IS THE ORCHESTRA")
*3,2,2,2 - 4,3,3,1 - timp.,perc.(3),bells,glock.,xyl. - hp. - str.
6:00 Bo. Hawkes.
—— PRAYER OF THE EMPEROR OF CHINA ON THE ALTAR OF HEAVEN, DEC. 21, 1539 (FOR MIXED CHORUS AND ENSEMBLE) (1972)
*3,2,2,*3 - 0,5,1,0 - timp.,perc.(8-10),cel.,glock.,2 mar.,2 vibra. -
electric org. - 3 pf.(1 electric) - 1 d.-b.   22:00 Bo. Hawkes.
—— PSALM 95 (COME LET US PRAISE YAWEH) (FOR SATB CHORUS AND CHAMBER ORCH.) (1975) (Text: The Jerusalem Bible)
1-3,2,2,0 - 0,0,0,0 - perc.,bells,cel.,glock.,2 mar.,2 vibra. - hp. -
hpsc.,org.,pf.   14:00 Bo. Hawkes.
—— ROCKY POINT HOLIDAY (1966)
2(2nd alt. with picc.),2(2nd alt. with Eng.hn.),2,2 - 4,3,3,1 -
timp.,perc.(2-3),bells,cel.,glock.,vibra.,xyl. - hp. - str.
5:35 Bo. Hawkes.
—— SARABANDE FOR KATHERINE IN APRIL
2,2(2nd alt. with Eng. hn.),2,2 - 2,2,0,0 - perc.(1),cell.,glock. - hp.
- str.   5:00 Bo. Hawkes.
—— SAVANNAH RIVER HOLIDAY
2(2nd alt. with picc.),2,2,2 - 4,3,3,1 -
timp.,perc.(2-3),cel.,glock.,xyl. - hp. - pf.(ad lib.) - str.
8:30 C. Fischer.
—— THIS IS THE ORCHESTRA (FOR NARRATOR AND ORCH.) (IN 2 PARTS)
*3,2,2,2 - 4,3,3,1 - timp.,perc.(3),bells,glock.,xyl. - hp. - str.
22:00 Bo. Hawkes.
—— TOCCATA FOR ORCHESTRA
1(alt. with picc.),2,0,2 - 4,3,3,1 -
timp.,perc.(2-3),bells,cel.,glock.,xyl. - hp. - pf. - str.
7:30 Bo. Hawkes.
—— TRILOGY: JFK - MLK - RFK (FOR SOPRANO 2 ORCH.) (1969)
2(2nd alt. with picc.)2(2nd alt. with Eng.hn.),*2,2 - 2,2,1,1 -
timp.,perc.(3),bells,cel.,glock.,vibra.,xyl. - tape-recorder - hp. - pf. -
str.   26:00 Bo. Hawkes.
—— TRIUMPHAL TE DEUM (FOR SATB CHORUS, BRASS, PERCUSSION AND ORGAN) (1962)
0,0,0,0 - 0,3,3,1 - timp.,perc. - org.   6:30 Bo. Hawkes.
—— WHAT IS MAN? (ORATORIO) (FOR NARRATOR, SOPRANO, BARITONE, MIXED CHORUS, ELECTRONIC TAPE AND ORCH.)
2(2nd alt. with picc.),2(2nd alt. with Eng. hn.),2(2nd alt. with
b.-cl.),2 - 4,3,3,1 - timp.,perc.(2),bells,cel.,glock.,vibra.,xyl. - hp. -
org. - pf. - str.   57:00 Bo. Hawkes.

NEMIROFF, Isaac
—— CONCERTO FOR OBOE AND STRING ORCH. (1954)
ob. - str.   20:00 Josef Marx.
—— SOLO CANTATA (FOR VOICE, FLUTE OBBLIGATO AND STRING ORCH.) (1963) (Text: Frederico Garcia Lorca)
fl. - str.   15:00 Josef Marx.

NEPGEN, Rosa
—— DIE DIEPER REG (CANTATA) (FOR SOLO VOICES, CHORUS AND ORCH.) (TEXT: N.P. VAN WYK LOUW) %
2,2,3,2 - 4,2,3,1 - str.   S.A.M.R.O.

—— DIE PASSIE VAN ONS HEER (CANTATA) (FOR SOLO VOICES, CHORUS AND ORCH.) (TEXT: W.E.G. LOUW) %
2,2,3,2 - 4,2,3,1 - str.   10:00 S.A.M.R.O.

NERO, Paul
—— CONCERTO FOR HOT FIDDLE (AND ORCH.)
0,0,3,4 sax.(ad lib.),2 - 2,3,2,0 - timp.,perc. - guit. - hp. - pf. - str.
16:00 C. Fischer.
—— OVERTURE TO A HORSE OPERA, OP. 69
2,2,*3,2 - 4,3,3,0 - timp.,perc.(2) - pf. - str.   7:30 C. Fischer.
—— PRELUDE AND ALLEGRO (FOR OBOE OR VIOLIN AND STRINGS)
ob.(or vln.) - str.   5:30 Composer.

NERUDA, Johannes - LELOIR, E.
—— CONCERTO FOR HORN AND STRINGS
hn. - str.   13:10 Presser.

NESSLER, Robert
—— CHAMBER CONCERTO FOR PIANO AND SMALL ORCH.
cl. - pf. - str.   20:00 Modern.
—— INTRODUCTION AND ALLEGRO
hpsc. - str.   14:00 Modern.
—— KAMMERKONZERT
cl. - pf. - str.   20:00 Modern.
—— SONNENGESANG DES HEILIGEN FRANZISKUS (FOR SOPRANO AND ORCH.)
2,2,2,2 - 4,2,2,1 - timp.,perc. - str.   12:00 Modern.
—— SYMPHONY NO. 1 (IN 1 MOVT.)
1,1,2(2nd alt. with b.-cl.),0 - 0,0,0,0 - bongos, cel.,vibra.,xyl. - hp. -
str.   15:00 Modern.
—— VARIATIONS ON A THEME OF BACH
2(2nd alt. with picc.),2,2,2(2nd alt. with c.-bn.) - 3,3,3,0 - timp. -
hp. - str.   25:00 Modern.

NESTEROV, Arkadij A.
—— THE STORMY PETREL (POEM-FANTASIA)
G. Schirmer.

NEUBERT, Günter
—— MUSIC FOR ORCHESTRA (ON A THEME OF ROBERT SCHUMANN)
11:00 Tetra.
—— MUSIC FOR STRINGS
str.   11:00 Tetra.

NEWBURY, Kent
—— THE SEPULCHRE OF FAMOUS MEN (FOR CHORUS AND WIND ENSEMBLE)
2,1,*3,2 - 4,3,3,1 - timp.,perc.   G. Schirmer.

NEWCATER, Graham
—— CONCERT OVERTURE, OP. 8
2,2,3,2 - 4,2,3,1 - timp.,perc. - str.   4:00 S.A.M.R.O.
—— CONCERTO GROSSO I, OP. 6
str.   9:00 S.A.M.R.O.
—— JOSEF EN SY BROERS (MUSIC FOR A RADIO PLAY)
2,2,3,2 - 4,2,3,1 - timp.,perc. - str.   11:00 S.A.M.R.O.
—— NOTTURNO PER ORCHESTRA
2,2,3,2 - 4,2,3,1 - timp.,perc. - str.   6:00 S.A.M.R.O.
—— THE RAIN QUEEN (BALLET) %
2,2,3,2 - 4,2,3,1 - timp.,perc. - str.   90:00 S.A.M.R.O.
—— THE RAIN QUEEN: SUITE
2,2,3,2 - 4,2,3,1 - timp.,perc. - str.   28:00 S.A.M.R.O.
—— RAKA (BALLET) %
2,2,3,2 - 4,2,3,1 - timp.,perc. - str.   46:00 S.A.M.R.O.
—— SYMPHONY NO. 1
2,2,3,2 - 4,2,3,1 - timp.,perc. - str.   32:00 S.A.M.R.O.
—— SYMPHONY NO. 2
2,2,3,2 - 4,2,3,1 - timp.,perc. - str.   30:00 S.A.M.R.O.
—— TEMPLE MUSIC
2,2,3,2 - 4,2,3,1 - timp.,perc. - str.   22:00 S.A.M.R.O.
—— VARIATIONS DE TIMBRES
2,2,3,2 - 4,2,3,1 - timp.,perc. - str.   14:00 S.A.M.R.O.

NEWMAN, Eldridge
—— IN DORSET (SUITE) (IN 3 MOVTS.)
*3,2,2,2 - 2,2,*3,0 - timp.,perc.,cel. - hp. - org. - str.   Novello.

NEWMAN, Max
—— ASCAP (CONCERTO FOR PIANO AND STRING ORCH.)
(Dedicated to ASCAP on its 50th Anniversary)
pf. - str.   Composer.

—— THE BEAUTY SALON (COMIC 1-ACT BALLET) %
    0,1,1,0 - 0,2,0,0 - str.   15:00 Composer.
—— CHRISTMAS AROUND THE WORLD, OP. 76 (FOR SSA
    CHORUS AND SMALL ORCH.) (1966) (Text: Composer)
    org. - pf. - str.   10:00 Composer.
—— CONCERTO FOR CELLO AND STRING ORCH. (IN 1 MOVT.)
    pf. - str.   12:00 Composer.
—— CONCERTO FOR VIOLIN AND STRINGS
    1. Sostenuto; 2. Allegretto; 3. Allegro
    pf. - str.   18:00 Composer.
—— CONCERTO FOR VIOLIN AND STRINGS, OP. 6 (1966)
    1. Andante; 2. Moderato; 3. Allegro
    pf. - str.   21:00 Composer.
—— CONCERTO IN G MAJOR FOR PIANO AND ORCH.
    1. Andante; 2. Allegro; 3. Presto
    *2,1,2,0 - 2,2,2,1 - timp.,perc.(1),cel. - pf. - str.   33:00 Composer.
—— CONCERTO NO. 1 IN D MAJOR, FOR PIANO AND ORCH.,
    OP. 78 (1966)
    1. Adagio; 2. Andante sostenuto; 3. Presto
    1,1,1,1 - 2,1,2,1 - timp. - pf. - str.   30:00 Composer.
—— CONCERTO NO. 2 FOR PIANO AND ORCH., OP. 148
    ("PARIS") (1966)
    2 picc.,2,1,1,1 - 2,2,2,0 - timp.,perc. - pf. - str.   30:00 Composer.
—— CONCERTO SENTIMENTO (IN 1 MOVT.)
    ob. - pf. - str.   8:00 Mills.
—— DISCARDED SHOES (1-ACT BALLET) (1966) %
    cl. - tpt. - pf. - str.   20:00 Composer.
—— FUGA NO. 1
    pf. - str.   15:00 Composer.
—— FUGA NO. 2
    str.   12:00 Composer.
—— FUGA REALE A 4 PARTI
    str.   7:00 Composer.
—— FUGO (1966)
    pf. - str.   15:00 Composer.
—— JOHN F. KENNEDY REQUIEM MASS (REQUIEM MASS NO.
    2) (FOR MIXED CHORUS, ORGAN AND ORCH.)
    1,1,1,0 - 2,2,2,1 - timp.,perc. - str.(18,6,6,4)   70:00 Composer.
—— MEDITERRANEAN (1966) (IN 2 MOVTS.)
    str.   15:00 Composer.
—— NOCTURNE FOR PIANO AND STRING ORCH.
    pf. - str.   7:00 Composer.
—— NOCTURNE IN D MINOR
    ob. - pf. - str.   10:00 Composer.
—— OVERTURE, OP. 71 (1966)
    2,1,1,1 - 2,2,2,0 - timp.,perc. - pf. - str.   10:00 Composer.
—— PALMACH CONCERTO (FOR PIANO AND STRING ORCH.)
    (IN 3 MOVTS.)
    pf. - str.   21:00 Composer.
—— PARIS (CONCERTO FOR PIANO AND STRING ORCH.) (IN 2
    MOVTS.)
    pf. - str.   10:00 Composer.
—— PATER NOSTER (FOR CHORUS AND ORCH.)
    org. - pf. - str.   10:00 Composer.
—— POEMA ITALIANA, OP. 75 (1966) (IN 2 MOVTS.)
    pf. - str.   10:00 Composer.
—— PREGHIERA DI NATALE (CHRISTMAS PRAYER,
    DEDICATED TO POPE PIUS XII)
    org. - pf. - str.   12:00 Composer.
—— PRELUDIO, OP. 72 (1966)
    0,1,1,1, - 0,1,0,0 - pf. - str.   10:00 Composer.
—— REQUIEM MASS NO. 1 (FOR MALE CHORUS, ORGAN AND
    ORCH.)
    2,2,2,1 - 0,0,0,0 - org. - str.(18,6,4,2)   60:00 Composer.
—— RESIGNATION (SYMPHONIC PRELUDE)
    pf. - str.   11:00 Composer.
—— SCHERZO
    pf. - str.   10:00 Composer.
—— SYMPHONY FOR STRINGS
    1. Largo cantabile - Allegro; 2. Andante - Vivace
    str.   25:00 Composer.
—— SYMPHONY-POEM
    1. Andante; 2. Allegro
    2,*2,2,0 - 2,2,2,1 - timp.,perc.(1),xyl. - hp. - pf. - str.
        17:00 Composer.
—— TOCCATA FOR PIANO AND STRING ORCH.
    pf. - str.   16:00 Composer.
—— TOCCATA, OP. 73 (1965) (IN 2 MOVTS.)
    pf. - str.   10:00 Composer.
—— VICTORY PRAYER (FOR SOPRANO, WOMEN'S CHORUS
    AND CHAMBER ORCH.)
    org. - pf. - str.   10:00 Composer.

NEWSON, George
—— ALGORITHM (JAZZ BALLET SUITE) (1962)
    3,3,3,4 sax.,3 - 3,3,3,1 - timp.,perc. - guit. - hp. - pf. - str.
        20:00 P.R.S.
—— CONSTRUCTION FOR ORCH. (1957)
    1,1,1,1 - 2,1,1,0 - pf. - str.   7:00 P.R.S.
—— SYMPHONY (1955)
    3,3,3,3 - 4,3,3,1 - perc. - pf. - str.   30:00 P.R.S.
—— VARIATIONS FOR ORCH. (1958)
    3,3,3,3 - 4,3,3,1 - perc. - str.   16:00 P.R.S.

NEZERITIS, Andreas
—— FIVE PSALMS OF DAVID (FOR VOICES AND ORCH.)
        60:00 A.E.P.I.

NGUYEN-THIEN-DAO
—— KOSKOM (1971)
    2 picc., 1 alto fl. 1 b.-fl.,1,2 e^{b}cl.,*1,1 d.-b.-cl.,*1 - 0,2(in
    CandD),3,1 d.-b.-trb.,1 - perc.(4), cel. - str.   30:00 Salabert.
—— THANH-DÔNG-TÔ-QUÔC (FOR SOPRANO, SPEAKER,
    SPEAKING CHORUS AND ENSEMBLE (Text: To-Hun)
    perc.(6) - ondes-Martenot - 4 pf.   10:00 Salabert.
—— THÊ 19 (FOR 4 FEMALE VOICES AND ENSEMBLE) (1969)
    (SEVEN WOODWIND, 7 BRASS 5 PERCUSSION AND ONDES
    MARTENOT)
        8:40 Salabert.

NIBLOCK, James
—— CANTICLE OF MOSES (FOR SATB CHORUS AND CHAMBER
    ORCH.) (1965)
        8:00 Composer.
—— CHAMBER SYMPHONY (IN 4 MOVTS.)
    1,1,1,1 - 2,1,1,0 - timp.,perc.(1) - str.   16:00 Composer.
—— CONCERTO FOR DOUBLE BASS AND ORCH. (1967) (IN 4
    MOVTS.)
    2,2,2,2 - 4,2,2,0 - timp.,perc.(2) - str.   23:00 Composer.
—— CONCERTO FOR VIOLIN AND ORCH. (IN 3 MOVTS.)
    2,2,2,2 - 4,2,2,1 - timp.,perc. - str.   16:00 Composer.
—— ELEGY FOR STRING ORCH.
    str.   8:00 Composer.
—— MIDWESTERN SKETCHES (IN 4 MOVTS.)
    3(3rd alt. with picc.),*3,3(3rd alt with b.-cl.),2 - 4,3,3,1 -
    timp.,perc.(2) - str.   10:00 Composer.
—— OVERTURE
    3(3rd alt. with picc.),3(3rd alt. with Eng. hn.),3(3rd alt. with
    b.-cl.),3 - 4,3,3,1 - timp.,perc.(2) - str.   Composer.
—— SYMPHONY FOR ORCHESTRA
    1. Andante; 2. Allegramente; 3. Adagio; 4. Allegro vivace
    *3,*3,3(3rd alt. with b.-cl.),3 - 4,3,3,1 - timp.,perc.(2) - str.
        25:00 Composer.
—— THREE AMERICAN DANCES
    3(3rd alt. with picc.),*3,3(3rd alt. with b.-cl.),2 - 4,3,3,1 -
    timp.,perc.(2) - str.   12:00 Composer.
—— TRIGON
    str.   Bo. Hawkes.

NICHOLSON, Ralph
—— CONCERTINO FOR OBOE AND STRINGS
    ob. - str.   10:00 Novello.

NICKSON, John Arthur
—— BETWEEN FIVE BELLS (1969)
    3-4,3,*4,0 - 4,2,1,0 - timp.,perc.(3,incl. 2 on timp.) - str.
        5:00 A.P.R.A.
—— HOMAGE TO TSUBOI SHIGEJI (FOR SOPRANO, ALTO AND
    ORCH.) (1970)
    2,1-2,1-2,0 - 0,0,0,0 - glock. - pf. - str.   5:00 J. Albert.
—— JEREMIAD (FOR FLUTE, CLARINET AND STRINGS) (1971)
    1,1,0,0 - 0,0,0,0 - str.   10:00 A.P.R.A.
—— LUNAR MUSIC (FOR BRASS, PERCUSSION AND STRINGS)
    (1972)
        5:00 J. Albert.

NICKSON, Noel John
—— SYMPHONY IN B FLAT (1949)
        30:00 A.P.R.A.

NICODÉ, Jean Louis
—— INTRODUCTION AND SCHERZO, OP. 11 ("THE HUNT
    AFTER FORTUNE")
    2,2,2,2 - 4,2,3,0 - timp. - str.   Galaxy.
—— MARIA STUART, OP. 4 (SYMPHONIC POEM)
    2,2,2,2 - 4,2,3,1 - timp.,perc. - str.   Galaxy.

NICOLAI, Otto
—— THE MERRY WIVES OF WINDSOR (OPERA) % (Engl. Text: Joseph Blatt)

G. Schirmer.

NICOLAI, Otto - ROBERTS, Charles J.
—— OVERTURE TO "THE MERRY WIVES OF WINDSOR"

C. Fischer.

NICOLAI, Otto - WINTER
—— OVERTURE TO "THE MERRY WIVES OF WINDSOR"

9:00 Bo. Hawkes.

NICULESCU, Stefan
—— FORMANTS (FOR 17 STRING PLAYERS, OR 17 PLAYERS ON OTHER INSTRUMENTS) (1968)
     str. (9,4,3,1)   12:00 Salabert.
—— ISON
     1,1,3,1(alt. with c.-bn.) - 1,1,1,0 - str.   Salabert.
—— SCÈNES (1965)
     2(2nd alt. with picc.),*2,2(2nd alt. with b.-cl.),1 - 0,1,1,0 - perc.(4),cel.,vibra.,xyl. - pf. - 2 d.-b.   13:00 Salabert.

NIEDERSTE-SCHEE, Wolfgang
—— CONCERTINO A TRE (FOR CLARINET, VIOLIN, PIANO AND ORCH.)
     1,2,1,2 - 0,2,2,0 - timp.,perc. - pf. - str.   14:00 G. Schirmer.
—— CONCERTINO BURLESCO (FOR PIANO AND STRINGS) (1965)
     pf. - str.   13:00 G. Schirmer.
—— KONZERTANTES SPIEL
     fl.,cl. - str.   13:00 G. Schirmer.

NIËL, Matty
—— OVERTURE, OP. 1-A (FOR 12 WOODWINDS) (1968)

7:00 Henmar.

NIELSEN, Carl
—— ALADDIN (SUITE FROM THE INCIDENTAL MUSIC)
     2,2,2,2 - 4,2,3,1 - perc.(6) - str.   26:00 G. Schirmer.
—— BOHEMIAN DANCE (PARAPHRASE FOR STRING ORCH.) (1928)
     str.   8:00 G. Schirmer.
—— THE COCK'S DANCE (FROM THE OPERA "MASQUERADE")
     3,2,2,2 - 4,3,3,1 - timp.,perc. - str.   5:00 G. Schirmer.
—— CONCERTO FOR CLARINET AND ORCH., OP. 57
     0,0,1,2 - 2,0,0,0 - perc.(1) - str.   27:00 Henmar.
—— CONCERTO FOR FLUTE AND ORCH.
     1,2,2,2 - 2,0,1,0 - perc.(1) - str.   20:00 Henmar.
—— CONCERTO FOR VIOLIN AND ORCH., OP. 33

34:00 G. Schirmer.
—— DREAM OF SAGA, OP. 39
     3,2,2,2 - 4,3,3,1 - timp.,perc. - str.   7:00 G. Schirmer.
—— HELIOS, OP. 17 (OVERTURE)
     3,2,2,2 - 4,3,3,1 - timp. - str.   12:00 G. Schirmer.
—— THE MOTHER: PRELUDE TO SCENE VII OF THE PLAY
     2,2,2,2 - 4,0,3,0 - timp. - str.   3:00 G. Schirmer.
—— OVERTURE TO "AMOR OG DIGTEREN" (1930)
     2(2nd alt. with picc.),2,2,2 - 4,0,0,0 - perc. - str.   5:00 Henmar.
—— OVERTURE TO THE OPERA "MASQUERADE"
     3,2,2,2 - 4,3,3,1 - timp.,perc. - str.   4:00 G. Schirmer.
—— PAN AND SYRINX, OP. 49 (PASTORAL)
     2,2,2,2 - 4,0,0,0 - timp.,perc. - str.   9:00 G. Schirmer.
—— PRELUDE TO ACT II OF "MASQUERADE"
     2,2,2,2 - 4,0,0,0 - str.   4:00 G. Schirmer.
—— PRELUDE TO ACT II OF "SAUL AND DAVID"
     3,2,2,2 - 4,3,3,1 - timp. - str.   6:00 G. Schirmer.
—— PRELUDE TO TABLEAU VII OF "MODERN" ("THE MOTHER")
     2,2,2,2 - 4,0,3,0 - timp. - str.   3:00 G. Schirmer.
—— RHAPSODIC OVERTURE (1927)
     2,2,2,2 - 4,2,3,1 - perc. - str.   10:00 G. Schirmer.
—— SINFONIA ESPANSIVA (SYMPHONY NO. 3), OP. 27
     3,3,3,3 - 4,3,3,1 - timp., - str.   32:00 Henmar.
—— SPRINGTIME ON FUNEN OP. 42, (FYNSK FORÅR) (FOR SOLO VOICES, CHORUS AND ORCH.) (Text in Danish or English)
     2,2,2,2 - 4,2,0,0 - timp.,perc. - str.   19:00 G. Schirmer.
—— SYMPHONY NO. 4, OP. 29 ("THE INEXTINGUISHABLE")
     3,3,3,3 - 4,3,3,1 - timp. - str.   36:00 G. Schirmer.
—— SYMPHONY NO. 5, OP. 50
     3,2,2,3 - 4,3,3,1 - timp.,perc.,cel. - str.   37:00 G. Schirmer.

—— SYMPHONY NO. 6 (SINFONIA SEMPLICE) (1925)
     3,2,2,2 - 4,2,3,1 - timp.,perc. - str.   32:00 Henmar.

NIELSEN, John
—— BAGATELLES, OP. 41
     tu. - str.   11:00 K.O.D.A.
—— BALLET SUITE NO. 1, OP. 28

20:00 K.O.D.A.
—— BALLET SUITE NO. 2, OP. 32

K.O.D.A.
—— CONCERTO DANESE, OP. 51 (FOR TRUMPET AND ORCH.)

17:00 K.O.D.A.
—— CONCERTO FOR VIOLIN AND ORCH., OP. 33 (MARZIALE CON VARIAZIONI)

25:00 K.O.D.A.
—— DIVERTIMENTO FOR TROMBONE AND ORCH., OP. 56

17:00 K.O.D.A.
—— FIFTEEN VARIATIONS FOR ORCH., OP. 40

14:00 K.O.D.A.
—— PROCESSION, OP. 30 (CANON FOR ORCH.)

12:00 K.O.D.A.
—— SEVEN ETUDES, OP. 35
     str.   15:00 K.O.D.A.
—— SYMPHONY NO. 1, OP. 8
     str.   K.O.D.A.
—— SYMPHONY NO. 2

K.O.D.A.
—— TRAGIC FESTIVAL OVERTURE
     str.   K.O.D.A.

NIELSEN, Ludvig
—— CONCERTO FOR ORGAN AND STRINGS, OP. 25 (VARIATIONS AND FUGUE ON THE HYMN OF ST. MAGNUS)
     org. - str.   17:00 T.O.N.O.
—— FAGNADARSONGAR, OP 16 (ORATORIO)
     2,2,2,2 - 3,2,3,0 - timp. - hp. - org. - str.   105:00 T.O.N.O.
—— MASS FOR OLAV'S DAY (MESSEPÅ OLAVSDAGEN), OP. 11 (FOR SATB SOLO VOICES, MIXED CHORUS, AND ORCH.)
     2,2,2,2 - 3,2,3,0 - timp. - hp. - org. - str.   100:00 T.O.N.O.
—— VENI CREATOR, OP. 20-B (CHORAL PARTITA) (FOR MIXED CHORUS AND ORCH.)
     2,2,2,2 - 2,0,0,0 -timp.,cel. - org. - str.   15:00 T.O.N.O.

NIELSEN, Riccardo
—— CAPRICCIO FOR PIANO AND ORCH.
     1,1,1,1 - 0,1,1,0 - timp.,perc.,xyl. - pf. - str.   8:00 Bo. Hawkes.
—— SINFONIA (IN 3 MOVTS.)
     1,1,1,1 - 2,1,1,0 - timp. - str.   21:00 Bo. Hawkes.

NIELSEN, Svend
—— METAMORPHESES (FOR 23 SOLO STRINGS) (1968)
     str.   15:00 G. Schirmer.
—— NUAGES
     3,3,3,3 - 4,3,0,0 - perc. - str.   15:00 G. Schirmer.
—— SONORE

10:00 G. Schirmer.

NIELSEN, Tage
—— BARIOLAGE

8:00 K.O.D.A.
—— THE MAGIC GARDEN
     3,2,3,alto sax.,2 - 4,2,1,1 - perc. - hp. - hpsc. - pf. - str.   10:00 Henmar.

NIELSON, Ludvig
—— TE DEUM, OP. 9 (FOR SOPRANO, ALTO, TENOR, BASS, MIXED CHORUS AND ORCH.)
     2,2,2,2 - 4,2,3,1 - timp. - org. - str.   75:00 Musikk-Hu.

NIETZSCHE, Friedrich - LANG, Max
—— ERMANARICH

8:00 S.U.I.S.A.
—— HYMNUS AUF DIE FREUNDSCHAFT

20:00 S.U.I.S.A.

NIGG, Serge
—— LE CHANT DU DÉPOSSÉDÉ ("SONG OF THE DISPOSSESSED") (FOR BARITONE, NARRATOR AND ORCH.) (Text: Stephane Mallarme)
     3,3,2,3 - 4,3,3,1 - perc.(5),cel. - hp. - pf. - str.   26:00 EV.
—— CONCERTO FOR FLUTE AND STRING ORCH.
     fl. - str.   20:00 EV.

—— CONCERTO FOR PIANO AND ORCH.
2,2,2,2 - 4,2,3,0 - timp.,perc.,cel. - pf. - str.   Leeds.
—— CONCERTO FOR VIOLIN AND ORCH.
2,*2,2,2 - 4,2,3,0 - timp.,perc.,cel. - hp. - str.   30:00 EV.
—— CONCERTO NO. 2 FOR PIANO AND ORCH.
2,2,2,2 - 4,2,3,1 - timp.,perc. - hp. - pf. - str.   22:00 Presser.
—— LA CROISADE DES ENFANTS (ORATORIO) ("THE
CHILDREN'S CRUSADE") (FOR CHILDREN'S CHORUS,
MIXED CHORUS AND ORCH.) (Text: M. Suffran)
*2,1,*2,1 - 1,1,1,0 - perc.(3),bells,cel.,glock.,vibra. - hp. - pf. - 1
vln.,1 c.   34:20 Eds. Fran.
—— FULGUR
3,3,3,3 - 6,4,3,1 - timp.,perc.(5),cel. - 2 hp. - pf. - str.
                                        15:00 Presser.
—— HIERONYMUS BOSCH SYMPHONIE
3,3,3,3 - 4,3,3,1 - timp.,perc.(6),cel. - hp. - pf. - str. 25:00 Presser.
—— MUSIQUE FUNÈBRE
str.   15:00 Presser.
—— SCÈNES CONCERTANTES (FOR PIANO AND STRINGS)
pf. - str.   Presser.
—— THEME AND VARIATIONS (FOR STRINGS)
str.   7:00 Presser.
—— VISAGES D'AXEL (IN 2 MOVTS.)
3,*3,3,3 - 4,4,3,1 - timp.,perc.,cel. - 2 hp. - pf. - str.   21:00 EV.

NIKIPROWETZKY, Tolia
—— ADAGIO FOR STRINGS
str.   5:00 Presser.
—— DIPTYCH FOR STRING ORCH.
str.   13:00 EV.
—— HOMAGE TO ANTONIO GAUDI (SYMPHONIC SUITE)
3,3,3,3 - 4,3,3,1 - timp.,perc.(5) - hp. - pf. - str.   19:00 Presser.
—— SINFONIETTA
2,2,2,2 - 4,2,2,1 - cel. - hp. - str.   12:00 EV.
—— SYMPHONY ("LOGOS 5") (IN 5 MOVTS.)
4,4,4,4 - 4,3,3,1 - timp.,perc.(6) - hp. - str.   30:00 Presser.

NIKOLOVSKI, Mihajlo
—— SUITE FOR STRINGS
str.   18:00 S.O.K.O.J.

NIKOLOVSKI, Vlastimir
—— DIVERTIMENTO, OP. 33
fl.(alt. with picc. and alto fl.) - str.   18:00 S.O.K.O.J.
—— NEI MODI ANTICHI, OP. 8 (SUITE)
2,2,2,2 - 2,1,0,0 - timp.,perc. - pf. - str.   14:00 S.O.K.O.J.
—— OLD DANCES
str.   14:00 S.O.K.O.J.
—— ON THE ROADS, OP. 12 (SONGS FOR ALTO AND ORCH.)
2(2nd alt. with picc.),2,2(2 alt. with Eᵇcl. and b.-cl.),0 - 6,3,3,0 -
timp.,perc. - pf. - str.   11:00 S.O.K.O.J.
—— PASSACAGLIA
*4,2,*2,*3 - 6,3,3,1 - timp.,perc. - acc. - str.   10:00 S.O.K.O.J.
—— SATYR NO. 2, OP. 34 (FOR VOICE AND ORCH.)
1,1,1,1 - 1,1,1,0 - timp.,perc.   12:00 S.O.K.O.J.
—— SYMPHONY NO 3, OP. 34 ("RUSTICA")
*3,2(alt. with zurli),*3(alt. with musettes),*1 - 6,4,3,1 -
timp.,perc.(6) - str.   22:00 S.O.K.O.J.

NILES, John Jacob
—— MARY THE ROSE (FOR CHORUS AND ORCH.) (A MIRACLE
PLAY FOR CHRISTMAS) %
1,1,1,1 - 2,2,2,0 - timp.,perc. - hp. - str.   G. Schirmer.

NILSSON, Bo
—— EXIT (1970) (FOR ORCH AND TAPE)
                                        10:00 Tetra.
—— FOR STRINGS ONLY (1954)
str.   G. Schirmer.
—— FOUR PROLOGUES
0,0,0,0 - 0,4,0,0 - perc.(2),vibra.,2 xylorimbas - tape-recorder - pf. -
str.   G. Schirmer.
—— LITANY OVER THE LOST PERCUSSION
4,4,4,4 - 4,4,4,2 - str.   G. Schirmer.
—— SEANCE (1963)
2,*2,2,2, sax.,1 - 4,4,4,0 - perc.(6) - str.   4:25 Seesaw.

NIXON, Roger
—— CONCERTO FOR VIOLA AND ORCHESTRA
3,3,2,2 - 4,2,3,0 - timp.,perc.,cel. - hp. - str.   30:00 C. Fischer.
—— MOONEY'S GROVE SUITE
2,2,2,2 - 4,3,3,0 - timp.,perc.,cel. - hp. - str.   20:00 Presser.

NOBLE, Harold
—— MASS (FOR SOPRANO, BASS, CHORUS AND ORCH.)
2,2,2,2 - 4,3,3,1 - timp.,perc. - str.   28:00 Lengnick.

NOBLE, T. Tertius
—— SUITE FOR VIOLIN AND ORCH. (IN 3 MOVTS.)
2,2,2,2 - 2 hn. - timp. - hp. - str.   15:00 Composer.

NOBRE, Marlos
—— AUTÓPSIA PARA MINHA SOMBRA, OP. 36-B (BALLET) %
(1971) (AUTOPSY FOR MY SHADOW)
*3,*3,*3,(2nd alt. with Eᵇcl.),*3 - 4,3,3,1 -
timp.,perc.(4),cel.,vibra.,xyl. - hp. - pf. - str.   28:00 G.E.M.A.
—— BIOSFERA, OP. 35 (1970)
str.   12:00 Tonos Vlg.
—— CONCERTINO FOR PIANO AND STRING ORCH., OP. 1
(1959) (IN 3 MOVTS.)
pf. - str.   12:00 Tonos Vlg.
—→CONCERTO BREVE, OP. 33 (FOR PIANO AND ORCH.) (1969)
*3(2nd fl.alt. with picc.),*3,*3,(2nd cl.alt. with Eᵇcl.),*3 - 4,4,4,1 -
timp.,perc.(8),vibra.,xyl. - pf. - str.   13:00 Bo. Hawkes.
—— CONVERGENCIAS, OP. 28 (1968)
2(alt. with 2 picc.),2,2,2 - 4,2,3,1 - timp.,perc.(6),xyl. - str.
                                        12:00 Tonos Vlg.
—— DESAFIO, OP. 31 (DIALOGUE FOR VIOLA AND STRING
ORCH.) (1968)
str.   6:00 Tonos Vlg.
—— DIVERTIMENTO, OP. 14 (FOR PIANO AND ORCH.) (1963)
1. Allegremente; 2. Moderado; 3. Vivo
2(2nd alt. with picc.),1,2,1 - 2,1,1,0 - timp.,perc.(3) - pf. - str.
                                        14:00 G.E.M.A.
—— IN MEMORIAM (1976)
*3,*3,3,3 - 4,3,3,1 - timp.,perc.(7, incl. 6 on timp.) - hp. - str.
                                        18:00 Seesaw.
—— LUDUS INSTRUMENTALIS OP. 34, (FOR CHAMBER ORCH.)
(1969)
1,1,1,0 - 1,1,1,0 - timp.,perc.(4),vibra.,xyl. - pf. - 3 c.,3 d.-b.
                                        10:00 G.E.M.A.
—— MOSAICO, OP. 36 (MOSAIC FOR ORCHESTRA) (1970)
1. Densidades (Densities); 2. Ciclos (Cycles); 3. Jogos (Games)
*3,*3,*3,(2nd alt. with Eᵇcl.),*3 - 4,3,3,1 -
timp.,perc.(4),cel.,vibra.,xyl. - hp. - pf. - str.   15:00 Tonos Vlg.
—— O CANTO MULTIPLICADO, OP. 38 (THE MULTIPLICATE
SONG) (FOR MEZZO-SOPRANO AND STRING ORCH.) (1972)
(Text: Carlos Drummond de Andrade)
str.   12:00 G.E.M.A.
—— RHYTHMETRON (FOR 10 PERCUSSIONISTS)
perc.(10)   16:00 Seesaw.

NOEL-GALLON
—— CONCERTO FOR OBOE, CLARINET, BASSOON AND ORCH.
0,1,1,1 - 2,2,0,0 - timp. - str.   23:00 Baron.
—— FANTAISIE (FOR HARP AND STRINGS)
hp. - str.   14:00 Baron.

NOELTE, Albert
—— SUITE IN EINEM SATZ, OP. 22
timp. - str.   8:00 Henmar.

NOETEL, Konrad
—— CONCERTINO (FOR FLUTE, VIOLIN AND STRINGS)
fl. - str.   25:00 Baerenrtr.
—— KONZERTMUSIK FUR STREICHER
str.   20:00 Baerenrtr.

NOON, David
—— AI, AI ("ALAS"), OP. 20 (BALLET) % (1968)
2(2nd alt. with picc.),1(alt. with Eng.hn.),2(2nd alt. with b.-cl.),2 -
2,2,2,1 - timp.,perc.(3),xyl. - pf. - str.   11:27 Composer.
—— BERCEUSE SECHE (DRY LULLABY), OP. 30 (1972)
3(alt. with 3 picc.),1,2,2 - 0,3,2,0 -
timp.,perc.(2),bells,cel.,vibra.xyl. - pf. - str.   10:20 Composer.
—— CONCERTO, OP. 23 (1969)
2(alt. with 2 picc.),alto fl.,*2,2,1 - 1,0,2,0 - hpsc. - pf. - 1 c.
                                        15:00 Composer.
—— LABYRINTH, OP. 16 (BALLET IN 1 SCENE) %
1(alt. with picc.),1,1,1 - 1,2,1,1 - str.(2,1,1,1)   6:00 C. Fischer.
—— TANGO 1940, OP. 26 (1971)
str.(7,3,4,2)   7:00 Composer.

NORBY, Erik
—— CHACONNE
*3,2,2*3 - 4,3,3,0 - perc.,cel. - str.   8:00 K.O.D.A.

—— CORPS CELESTE

13:00 K.O.D.A.

—— CORTEGE (PASSACAGLIA)

11:00 K.O.D.A.

—— NOCTURNE

*3,2,2,2 - 3,2,0,0 - timp. - str.   8:00 K.O.D.A.

—— THE RAINBOW SNAKE

*3,*4,3,3 - 6,4,3,0 - timp. - str.   18:00 G. Schirmer.

—— SINFONIA DA REQUIEM

*3,2,*2,*3 - 4,3,3,1 - perc.,cel.,vibra. - hp. - pf. - str.

20:00 K.O.D.A.

—— VARIATIONS FOR ORCH.

5:00 K.O.D.A.

NORDAL, Jón

—— CONCERTO GROSSO

Islandia.

NORDEN, Hugo

—— PASSACAGLIA IN F MAJOR

hn. - str.   G. Schirmer.

NORDENSTROM, Gladys

—— EL GRECO FANTASY (FOR ELEVEN STRINGS)(1965)

str.(8,1,1,1)   17:00 G. Schirmer.

—— ELEGY FOR ROBERT F. KENNEDY (1968)

2(2nd alt. with picc.),2,3(3rd alt. with b.-cl.),*3 - 4,3,3,1 - perc.(3),cel.,vibra. - hp. - 2 pf. - str.   G. Schirmer.

—— WORK FOR ORCHESTRA, III (1975)

*3,2,*3,*3 - 4,2,0,0 - timp.,perc. - hp. - pf. - str.   G. Schirmer.

NORDGREN, Erik

—— ARIOSO FOR VIOLA AND ORCH., OP. 2

2,2,2,2 - 2,2,1,0 - timp. - str.   8:30 S.T.I.M.

—— CHAMBER SYMPHONY, OP. 7

2,2,2,2 - 2,2,1,0 - timp.,perc.(2) - str.   13:00 S.T.I.M.

—— CONCERTO FOR BASSOON AND ORCH., OP. 66 (1966)

1,1,2,2 - 2,2,1,0 - timp.,perc.,cel. - hp.- str.   11:30 H.BuschMfl.

—— CONCERTO FOR CLARINET AND ORCH., OP. 26 (1950)

2,2,2,2 - 3,2,1,0 - timp.,perc. - hp. - str.   18:00 H.BuschMfl.

—— DIVERTIMENTO, OP. 16

1,1,2,1 - 2,2,1,0 - timp.,perc. - hp. - str.   11:00 S.T.I.M.

—— ORCHESTRAL VARIATIONS, OP. 68 (1966)

2,2,2,2 - 4,3,3,1 - timp.,perc. - hp. - str.   9:00 Fleisher.

—— OVERTURE, OP. 5

2,2,2,2 - 2,2,3,1 - timp.,perc. - str.   10:00 S.T.I.M.

—— OVERTURE PICCOLA, OP. 13

1,1,2,1 - 2,2,1,0 - timp.,perc. - str.   5:00 S.T.I.M.

NORDGREN, Pehr Henrik

—— AGNUS DEI (SYMPHONY FOR SOPRANO, BARITONE, SATB CHORUS AND ORCH.) (1971) (IN 3 MOVTS.)

4,3,4,3 - 6,4,4,2 - timp.,perc.(10) - 2 hp. - pf. - str.

54:00 FinnMICtr.

—— CONCERTO FOR CLARINET, FOLK INSTRUMENTS AND SMALL ORCH., OP. 14 (1970)

0,0,2,3 - 1,0,1,0 - timp.,perc.(3) - hp.,kantele - two-line acc. - jouhikko(fiddle) - str.   23:00 FinnMICtr.

—— CONCERTO FOR PIANO AND ORCH., OP. 23

3,3,3,3 - 4,3,3,1 - timp.,perc.(6) - hp. - pf. - str. 30:00 FinnMICtr.

—— CONCERTO FOR VIOLA AND ORCH., OP. 12 (1970)

6,0,6,3 - 4,2,2,1 - timp.,perc.(6)cel. - hp. - str. 19:00 FinnMICtr.

—— CONCERTO FOR VIOLIN AND ORCH., OP. 10 (1969)

2,2,3,3 - 4,2,3,1 - timp.,perc.(3),cel. - 2 mandolins - hp. - harm. - str.   26:00 FinnMICtr.

—— ÉPIPHRASE, OP. 4 (1967)

2,2,2,2 - 2,2,2,0 - timp.,perc.(3) - hp. - str.   6:00 FinnMICtr.

—— EUPHONIE I, OP. 1 (1967)

4,4,4,2 - 4,0,1,0 - timp.,perc.(3),cel. - hp. - str. 16:00 FinnMICtr.

—— EUPHONIE II, OP. 5 (1967)

4,3,4,3 - 4,2,2,1 - timp.,perc.(3),cel. - 2 hp. - pf. - str.

20:00 FinnMICtr.

—— EUPHONIE III, OP. 21

2,2,2,2 - 2,2,3,0 - timp.,perc.(3),cel. - pf. - str.   15:00 FinnMICtr.

—— FOUR SCENES OF DEATH, OP. 8 (1968)

1,1,1,1 - 0,1,1,1 - timp.,perc.(3) - str.(2,2,1,1) 17:00 FinnMICtr.

—— MINORE, OP. 6 (1968)

2,2,2,2 - 4,0,0,0 - timp.,perc. - pf. - str.   10:00 FinnMICtr.

—— NIGHTLY WAKE, OP. 3 (SUITE) (1967)

0,0,3,0 - 1,0,0,0 - timp.,perc.(3) - hp. - str.(1,1,1,0)

10:00 FinnMICtr.

—— THE TURNING POINT, OP. 16 (1972)

4,3,4,3 - 4,4,3,2 - timp.,perc.(6),xyl. - 2 hp. - hpsc. - pf. - str.

9:00 FinnMICtr.

NORDHEIM, Arne

—— CANZONA PER ORCHESTRA

3,3,3,3 - 4,3,3,1 - timp.,perc.,cel. - hp. - pf. - str.

12:30 G. Schirmer.

—— ECHO (ECO) (FOR SOPRANO, CHORUS, CHILDREN'S CHORUS AND ORCH.)) (Text: Salvatore Quasimodo)

4,4,4 - 4,4,4,2 - perc.(6) - elec.bass guit. - hp. - 2 pf. - hammond org.(large) - str.(0,12,10,8)   20:00 G. Schirmer.

—— EPITAPH (EPITAFFIO PER ORCHESTRA E NASTRO MAGNETICO)

3,2,2,sax.,1 - 1,1,1,1 - perc.,cel. - tape-recorder(with large amplification system) - guit. - hp. - pf. - str.   11:00 G. Schirmer.

—— EVENING LAND (AFTONLAND) (FOR SOPRANO AND SMALL ORCH.) (CYCLE OF 4 SONGS) (Text: Pär Lagerkvist)

timp.,perc.,cel.,vibra. - hp. - str.(2,1,1,1 min)   13:00 G. Schirmer.

—— FLOATING

4(4th alt. with picc.),2,2 Eng.hn.,2,2 b.-cl.,2,2 c.-bn. - 4,4,4,0 - perc.,cel. - hp. - pf. - str.   12:00 G. Schirmer.

—— GREENING (1973)

4,4,2 Eng.hn.,4,4 - 4,4,4,1 - perc.(5), cel. - electric guit. - electric pf. - 2 hp. - str.   18:00 G. Schirmer.

—— KATHARSIS (BALLET SUITE)

2,2,2,2 - 2,3,3,0 - timp.,perc.,cel. - pf. - str.   15:00 G. Schirmer.

—— KATHARSIS (THE TEMPTATION OF ST. ANTHONY) (BALLET)

2,2,2,2 - 2,3,3,0 - timp.,perc.,cel. - tape-recorder(stereo - pf. - str.

50:00 G. Schirmer.

—— SPUR (FOR ACCORDION AND ORCH.)

G. Schirmer.

—— ZIMBEL

9:30 G. Schirmer.

NORDIO, Cesare

—— FANTASIA NOTTURNA

2,3,2,2 - 4,3,3,0 - timp.,perc.,cel. - 1-2 hp. - str.

12:00 Bo. Hawkes.

—— FESTA LONTANA

2,2,2,2 - 2,2,3,0 - timp.,perc.,cel. - 1-3 hp. - str.

10:00 Bo. Hawkes.

NORDOFF, Paul

—— CONCERTO FOR PIANO AND ORCH.

*3,2(1st alt. with Eng. hn.),2,2 - 4,2,3,0 - timp.,perc.,cel. - pf. - str.

25:00 Composer.

—— CONCERTO FOR PIANO, VIOLIN AND ORCH. (IN 3 MOVTS.)

*3,*3,2,2 - 2,1,0,0 - timp.,perc.(2) - str.   22:00 AmerMusEd.

—— CONCERTO FOR VIOLIN AND ORCH (IN 3 MOVTS.)

2(2nd alt. with picc.),2,2(1st alt. with E♭cl. and 2nd alt. with b.-cl.),2 - 4,2,3,1 - timp.,perc. - hp. - str.   20:00 Composer.

—— THE FROG-PRINCE (FOR NARRATOR AND ORCH.)

1(alt with picc.),1,2,1 - 2,1,1,0 - timp.,perc.(1),cel. - hp. - str.

20:00 AmerMusEd.

—— GOTHIC CONCERTO (FOR PIANO AND ORCHESTRA) (IN 4 MOVTS.)

2(2nd alt. with picc.),2,2,2 - 4,1,3,0 - timp.,perc.(1) - pf. - str.

29:00 AmerMusEd.

—— LANDSCAPE WITH FIGURES

1,1,2,1 - 2,1,1,0 - timp.,perc.(1) - str.   7:00 Composer.

—— LITTLE CONCERTO FOR STRINGS (VIOLIN, VIOLA, CELLO, BASS) AND ORCH.

*2,1(alt. with Eng. hn.),1,1 - 2,1,0,0 - timp.,perc.(2) - str.

8:00 Composer.

—— A LITTLE SYMPHONY

*2,*2,1,1 - 2,1,0,0 - timp.,perc. - str.   12:00 AmerMusEd.

—— LOST SUMMER (FOR MEZZO-SOPRANO AND ORCH.)

1,1,1,1 - 2 hn. - timp. - str.   18:00 Composer.

—— THE MASTERPIECE (OPERA) %

1,1,1,1 - 1,1,1,0 - timp. - pf. - str.   50:00 EV.

—— MR. FORTUNE (THREE-ACT OPERA) %

*3,2 recorders, 2(2nd alt. with Eng. hn.),2 E♭cl.,*2,*3 - 3,1,2,1 - timp.,perc.(3),bells.,cel.,glock.,xyl. - banjo - hp. - str.

165:00 Composer.

—— MORE PERFECT UNION (FOR BARITONE, MIXED CHORUS AND ORCH.)

2,2,2,2 - 4,2,3,1 - timp. - str.   7:00 Composer.

—— PRELUDE AND SMALL FUGUE

1,1,1,1 - 2,1,0,0 - timp.,perc. - pf. - str.   15:00 C. Fischer.

—— PRELUDE AND THREE FUGUES
    1,1(alt. with Eng. hn.)1,1 - 2,1,0,0 - timp. - pf. - str.
                  15:00 AmerMusEd.
    or:
    2(2nd alt. with picc.),2(2nd alt. with Eng. hn.),2,2 - 4,2,2,1 -
    timp.,perc. - str.
—— SECULAR MASS (FOR SOPRANO, CONTRALTO, BARITONE,
    MIXED CHORUS AND ORCH.)
    *3,2(1 alt. with Eng. hn.),2,2 - 4,2,3,0 - timp.,perc.(2),xyl. - 2 hp. -
    str.   35:00 Composer.
—— SUITE
    *3,2(2nd alt. with Eng. hn.),2,2 - 4,2,2,1 - timp.,perc. - hp. - str.
                  17:00 Composer.
—— SUITE FOR CHAMBER ORCH. (IN 5 MOVTS.)
    1(alt. with picc.),1,2,1(alt. with c.-bn.) - 2,1,1,0 - timp.,perc. - pf. -
    str.   15:00 Composer.
—— TRANQUIL SYMPHONY
    1. Andante tranquillo; 2. Allegretto; 3. Lento
    2(2nd alt. with picc.),2(2nd alt. with Eng. hn),2,2 - 4,1,1,0 -
    timp.,perc.(2),cel.,glock. - str.   20:00 AmerMusEd.
—— WINTER SYMPHONY (IN 4 MOVTS.)
    2(2nd alt. with picc.),2(2nd alt. with Eng. hn.),2,2 - 4,2,2,1 -
    timp.,perc. - str.   33:00 AmerMusEd.

NORDQUIST, Gustaf - HENNEBERG, A.
—— SUITE IN OLDEN STYLE
    2,2,2,2 - 2,2,1,0 - timp. - str.   13:00 S.T.I.M.

NORDSTRÖM, Birger
—— SINFONIA SERIA
    2,1,2,2 - 3,2,2,0 - timp.,perc.(4) - str.   Fleisher.

NØRGAARD, Per
—— BABEL (1965) (FOR VOICES, CHORUS, ORCH. AND TAPE)
                  85:00 Tetra.
—— COMPOSITIONS (1966)
    2,2,2,2 - 2,2,0,0 - timp. - pf. - str.   12:00 G. Schirmer.
—— CONCERTO FOR PIANO AND ORCH., OP. 21
    3,2,2,2 - 4,3,3,0 - timp.,perc. - pf. - str.   30:00 G. Schirmer.
—— CONCERTO FOR STRINGS
    str.   22:00 G. Schirmer.
—— CONSTELLATIONS, OP. 22
    str.   22:00 G. Schirmer.
—— FRAGMENT VI (FOR 6 ORCHESTRAL GROUPS)
    2,0,2,1 - 0,3,3,0 - timp.,perc. - hp. - pf.   18:00 G. Schirmer.
    or:
    2,0,3,1 - 0,3,3,0 - timp.,cel.,vibra.,xyl. - hp. - 2 pf.
—— GILGAMESH (OPERA) % (Text: Composer)
    4,1,3,0 - 0,2,1,0 - perc.(3) - str.   105:00 G. Schirmer.
—— IRIS (1967)
    3,3,3,3 - 4,3,3,1 - timp.,perc. - str.   12:00 G. Schirmer.
—— JOUSTING (TURNERING)
    2,1,2,1 - 2,4,2,0 - perc. - pf. - str.   G. Schirmer.
—— THE LABYRINTH (OPERA)(1963) %
    1,ocarina,1,2,2 sax.,1 - 2,2,2,0 - perc. - tape-recorder - 2 guit. -
    acc. - str.   75:00 Tetra.
—— LUNA
    3,2,2,2 - 4,4,4,0 - timp.,cel.,vibra. - hp. - pf. - str.
                  14:00 G. Schirmer.
—— LYSE DANSE, OP. 24 (BRIGHT DANCES)
    1,1,1,1 - 2,1,0,0 - timp. - str.   11:00 G. Schirmer.
—— METAMORFOSI
    str.   10:00 G. Schirmer.
—— MODLYS
    2,2,2(2nd alt. with b.-cl.),2 sopr. sax.,2 - 0,2,4,2 - perc. - 2 pf.
                  13:00 G. Schirmer.
—— NOCTURNES (FOR SOPRANO AND ORCH.)
    1,1,1,1 - 0,1,1,0 - perc. - hp. - pf.   8:00 G. Schirmer.
—— PRISM (JØRGEN SONNE) (1965)
                  8:00 G. Schirmer.
—— RECALL (FOR ACCORDION AND ORCH.)
    2,2,2,2 - 4,3,3,1 - timp.,perc.,cel. - acc. - str.   12:00 G. Schirmer.
—— SINFONIA AUSTÈRA, OP. 13
    3,2,2,2 - 4,3,3,1 - timp.,perc.,cel.,xyl. - str.   35:00 G. Schirmer.
—— SYMPHONY NO. 2 (1970)
    3,2,2,2 - 4,3,3,0 - perc. - hp. - org. - pf. - str.   24:00 G. Schirmer.
—— SYMPHONY NO. 3 (WITH CHORUS)
    3,*3,*3,*3 - 4,3,3,1 - timp.,perc.,cel. - hp. - org. - pf.
                  45:00 G. Schirmer.
—— TANGO CHICANE (BALLET) % (1967)
    3,2,2,2 - 4,3,3,1 - timp.,perc. - str.   12:00 G. Schirmer.

—— THREE LOVE SONGS (FOR CONTRALTO AND ORCH.)
    (1964) (Text: Rimbaud andRilke)
    2,2,2,2 - 2,2,2,0 - timp.,perc. - str.   10:00 G. Schirmer.
—— TRIPTYCHON, OP. 18 (FOR CHORUS AND ORCH.)
    2,1,1,1 - 2,1,1,0 - timp. - str.(0,0,1,1)   15:00 G. Schirmer.
—— VOYAGE INTO THE GOLDEN SCREEN
    2,1,1,1 - 2,2,1,0 - cel.,vibra. - hp. - pf. - str.(8,3,2,1)
                  18:00 G. Schirmer.
—— THE YOUNG MAN IS TO MARRY (BALLET) %
    3,0,3,2 - 2,4,3,0 - timp.,perc.(2-4),vibra.(ad lib.),xyl.(ad lib.) - guit.
    - Hammond org. - str.   40:00 G. Schirmer.

NØRHOLM, Ib
—— AFTER ICARUS, OP. 39 (SUITE)
                  17:00 K.O.D.A.
—— DAY'S NIGHTMARE II, OP. 58 (FOR SOLO VOICES, CHORUS
    AND ORCH.) (Text: Ivan Malinovski)
                  15:00 K.O.D.A.
—— EXIL (1965)
    4,3,3,2 sax.,2 - 4,4,4,2 - timp.,perc.(6) - hp. - pf. - str.
                  14:00 G. Schirmer.
—— FLUCTUATIONS, OP. 25 (DEN USETE PAN)
    guit.,mandolin - 2 hp. - hpsc. - str.   17:00 Henmar.
—— HERETIC HYMN, OP. 62 (FRESCO FOR ORCH.)
    3,*4,3,3 - 4,3,3,0 - perc. - str.   G. Schirmer.
—— KENOTAFIUM, OP. 23 (FOR SOPRANO, CHORUS AND
    ORCH.)
    3,2,2,2 - 4,3,3,1 - perc.,cel. - hp. - str.   22:00 Henmar.
—— SUMMER SCENES (FOR SOPRANO, TENOR, FEMALE
    CHORUS AND ORCH.)
                  20:00 G. Schirmer.
—— SYMPHONY NO. 2, OP. 50 (ISOLA BELLA) (1971)
    3,3,3,3 - 4,3,3,1 - timp.,perc.,cel.,mar.,vibra.,xyl. - pf. - str.
                  60:00 G. Schirmer.
—— SYMPHONY NO. 3, OP. 57 (IN ONE MOVEMENT) (DAY'S
    NIGHTMARE) (1973)
    3,3,3,3 - 4,3,3,1 - timp.,perc.(3),cel. - hp. - str.   15:00 G. Schirmer.
—— TWO RELIEFS, OP. 27
    1,0,1,0 - 0,1,1,0 - perc. - pf. - str.(8,4,2,1)   Henmar.
—— THE YOUN PARK (CHAMBER OPERA) % (1970)
    2,2,2,1 - 1,1,1,0 - perc. - tape-recorder - pf. - str.
                  55:00 G. Schirmer.

NORMAN, Leo
—— POT-POURRI FOR STRING ORCH.
    str.   9:30 P.R.S.

NORMAN, Theodore
—— METAMORPHOSIS (MUSIC FOR A BALLET, AFTER THE
    STORY BY KAFKA) (1951)
    1,*1,0,1 - 0,1,0,0 - timp.,perc. - electric guit.(amplified acoustic
    model) - accord. - 1 vln.,2 d.-b.   18:00 Composer.
—— SYMPHONY (1951) (IN 4 MOVTS.)
    *2,1,1,1 - 1,1,0,0 - timp. - str.   35:00 Composer.

NORTH, Alex
—— THE CITY SINGS FOR MICHAEL (FOR NARRATOR AND
    ORCH.)
    fl.(alt. with picc.),cl.(alt. with E♭cl.) - tpt. - perc.,cel.,glock.,xyl. -
    org. - pf. - str.   12:00 North.
—— CLEOPATRA (SUITE FROM THE FILM)
    3,3,3,3 - 4,3,3,1 - timp.,perc.(4),cel. - hp. - pf. - str.   Robbins.
—— DEATH OF A SALESMAN (SUITE) (IN 5 MOVTS.)
    *3(1 alt. with alto fl.),2(2nd alt. with Eng. hn.),*3,2 - 3,3,3,0 -
    perc.(1),cel.,glock.,vibra.,xyl. novachord - pf. - str.
                  22:00 Columbia.
—— HOLIDAY SET (IN 6 MOVTS.)
    2(alt. with 2 picc.),2,2,2 - 2,2,0,0 - timp.,perc.(2),cel.,glock.,xyl. -
    hp. - pf. - str.   18:00 North.
—— HOMAGE TO VAUDEVILLE
    2(1 alt. with picc.),1,2(1 alt. with b.-cl.),1-1,3,2,0 -
    perc.(2),cel.,glock.,vibra.,xyl. - pf. - str.   11:00 Composer.
—— THE LITTLE INDIAN DRUM (FOR NARRATOR AND ORCH.)
    2(alt. with 2 picc.),0,*3,1 - 3 hn. - timp.,perc.,cel.,glock.,xyl. - hp. -
    str.   7:00 North.
—— A MEMBER OF THE WEDDING (SUITE) (IN 4 MOVTS.)
    2(1st alt. with picc.),2(2nd alt. with Eng.hn.),3(3rd alt. with
    b.-cl.),3 sax.,*3 - 2,3,3,0 - perc.,cel.,glock.,vibra. - hp. - pf. - str.
                  15:00 Columbia.
—— NAMES ON THE LAND (FOR BARITONE, CHORUS AND
    ORCH.)
    2,2,2,2 - 2,2,2,0 - timp.,perc.(2) - pf. -str.   6:00 Mills.

—— QUEST (SUITE) (IN 3 MOVTS.)
2(2nd alt. with picc.),1,*2,1 - 2,2,1,0 - perc.(2), xyl. - pf. - str.
14:00 Mercury.

—— REVUE (FOR CLARINET AND ORCH.) (IN 3 MOVTS.)
3(3rd alt. with picc.),*3,*3,2 - 4,3,3,1 -
timp.,perc.(3),cel.,glock.,vibra.,xyl. - hp. - pf. - str.   15:30 Mills.

—— RHAPSODY FOR PIANO AND ORCH.
2,*2,*3,1 - 2,2,1,0 - perc. - hp. - pf. - str.   12:00 Composer.

—— RHAPSODY U. S. A. (FOR MIXED CHORUS AND ORCH.)
2,2,2,2 - 4,2,2,0 - perc. - str.   6:00 Composer.

—— A STREETCAR NAMED DESIRE (BALLET SUITE)
1(alt. with cl.),0,0,*1 (alt. with alto sax.),0 - 0,1,1,0 -
perc.,glock.,xyl. - pf. - str.   26:00 Witmark.

—— A STREETCAR NAMED DESIRE (SYMPHONIC SUITE) (IN 8
MOVTS.)
2(1st alt. with picc.),2(2nd alt. with Eng. hn.),3(3rd alt. with
b.-cl.),*3 - 4,3,3,0 - timp.,perc.(3),cel.,glock.,xyl. - hp. - novachord
- pf. - str.   30:00 Witmark.

—— SUNDAY IN WALL STREET (BALLET SUITE)
1(alt. with picc.),1,2(alt. with b.-cl.,bar. sax. and b.-sax.),1 - 2,3,2,1
- perc.(2),glock.,vibra.,xyl. - pf. - str.   8:00 Integrity.

—— THREE PIECES FOR CHAMBER ORCH.
1(alt. with picc.),1(alt. with Eng. hn.),*2,*2 - 2,2,1,0 -
timp.,perc.(2),cel.,glock.,xyl. - pf. - str.   12:00 Composer.

—— VIVA ZAPATA (SUITE) (IN 5 MOVTS.)
2(alt. with 2 picc.),3(3rd alt. with Eng. hn.), ob. d'amore,3(3rd alt.
with b.-cl. and E♭ cl.),*3 - 4,3,3,1 -
timp.,perc.(4),cel.,glock.,b.-mar.,xyl. - 2 guit. - 2 mandolins - hp. -
pf. - str.   15:00 Twentieth Cent.

—— THE WALTZING ELEPHANT (FOR NARRATOR AND
ORCH.)
3(3rd alt. with picc.),0,*3,2 sax.,0 - 0,0,0,0 - cel. - pf. - str.
7:00 North.

—— YANK AND CHRISTOPHER COLUMBUS (FOR NARRATOR
AND ORCH.)
2(2nd alt. with picc.),*2,2,2 - 4,3,2,0 - perc.(2),glock.,xyl. - hp. -
pf. - str.   12:00 North.

NORTH, Roger
—— HANSEL AND GRETEL (SUITE)
2,2,2,2 - 2,2,0,0 - cel. - hp. - pf. - str.   15:00 P.R.S.

—— LONDON RIVER (AN OVERTURE)
2,2,2,2 - 4,3,3,1 - timp.,perc. - hp. - str.   10:00 P.R.S.

—— SYMPHONY MOVEMENT
4,4,4,0 - timp.,perc.(3) - 2 pf. - str.   7:30 P.R.S.

—— VARIATIONS ON "OH SUSANNAH"
3,3,3,3 - 4,3,3,1 - timp.,perc. - hp. - str.   9:00 P.R.S.

NOTT, Douglas Duane
—— ADAGIO AND FUGUE, OP. 2 (1973)
2(1 alt. with picc.)2,2,2 - 4,2,2,1 - timp.,perc.(4) - str.
12:00 Composer.

—— CONCERTO FOR ALTO SAXOPHONE AND ORCH., OP. 8
(1971) (IN 1 MOVT.)
*3,2,2,1 alto sax.,2 - 4,3,3,1 - timp.,perc.(4),xyl. - hp. - pf. - str.
10:00 Composer.

NOVÁČEK, Ottokar - STOKOWSKI, Leopold
—— PERPETUAL MOTION (PERPETUUM MOBILE) (FOR
PERCUSSION AND STRINGS)
perc.(4) - str.   4:00 Broude.

NOVÁK, Jan
—— CONCERTO FOR OBOE AND ORCH. (1952) (IN 3 MOVTS.)
3,1,0,0 - 3,0,0,0 - str.   21:00 Bo. Hawkes.

—— CONCERTO FOR PIANO AND ORCH.
Bo. Hawkes.

—— CONCERTO FOR TWO PIANOS AND ORCH.
2,2,2,2 - 4,3,3,1 - timp.,perc. - 2 pf. - str.   29:00 Bo. Hawkes.

—— PHILHARMONIC DANCES
Bo. Hawkes.

—— THE SPECTRE'S BRIDE (BALLET SUITE)
3,3,3,3 - 6,3,3,1 - timp.,perc. - hp. - pf. - str.   25:00 Bo. Hawkes.

NOVÁK, Vítězslav
—— AUTUMN SYMPHONY (WITH MIXED CHORUS)
3,3,3,3 - 6,3,3,1 - timp.,perc. - hp. - mandolin - org. - pf. - str.
35:00 Bo. Hawkes.

—— CONCERTO IN E MINOR, FOR PIANO AND ORCH.
3,3,3,3 - 4,3,3,1 - timp.,perc. - hp. - pf. - str.   27:00 Bo. Hawkes.

—— THE CORSAIR (OVERTURE)
2,2,3,2 - 4,3,3,1 - timp.,perc. - str.   14:30 Bo. Hawkes.

—— DE PROFUNDIS, OP. 67 (SYMPHONIC POEM FOR ORGAN
AND ORCH.) (1941)
Bo. Hawkes.

—— MARYSA (DRAMATIC OVERTURE)
2,3,2,2 - 4,3,3,1 - timp.,perc. - str.   12:00 Bo. Hawkes.

—— MAY SYMPHONY
3,3,3,3 - 6,3,3,1 - timp.,perc. - hp. - str.   55:00 Bo. Hawkes.

—— NIKOTINA, OP. 59 (BALLET IN 7 SCENES) %
Bo. Hawkes.

—— ST. WENCESLAS TRIPTYCH, OP. 70 (FOR ORGAN AND
ORCH.) (1941)
Bo. Hawkes.

—— SIGNORINA GIOVENTU, OP. 58 (BALLET) %
Bo. Hawkes.

—— SLOVAK SUITE
2,2,2,2 - 3,0,0,0 - hp. - org.(ad lib.) - str.   28:00 Bo. Hawkes.

NOWAKOWSKY, Joseph
—— CONCERTINO FOR TROMBONE AND ORCH.
2,2,2,2 - 2,2,1,0 - timp. - str.   10:00 C. Fischer.

NOWKA, Dieter
—— SYMPHONY NO. 2
2,2,2,2 - 4,2,3,0 - timp.,perc. - hp. - str.   30:00 Tetra.

NOWOTNY, Norbert Wilhelm
—— FOCUS (INCIDENTAL MUSIC) (FOR VOICES AND ORCH.)
2,2,3,2 - 4,2,3,1 - timp.,perc. - str.   22:00 S.A.M.R.O.

—— DAS HIMMELREICH IST DER GEWALTSAMEN (CANTATA)
(Text: Angelus Silesius)
2,2,3,2 - 4,2,3,1 - timp.,perc. - str.   12:00 S.A.M.R.O.

NUNES, Emmanuel
—— ES WEBT (FOR TWO ORCHESTRAS)
Presser.

—— PURLIEU (FOR 21 STRINGS)
str.(12,4,3,2)   26:00 Presser.

NUSSIO, Otmar
—— BAGATELLES
fl. - str.   Henmar.

—— BALLERINE (MUSICA DA BALLETTO) (5 DANCES FOR
ORCHESTRA)
2,2,2,0 - 2,2,1,0 - timp.,perc. - hp. - str.   13:00 AhnSimrock.

—— BUKOWINA BALLETT
2,2,2,2 - 2,2,1,0 - timp.,perc. - str.   12:00 AhnSimrock.

—— CANTI E DANZE D'ILLIRIA (IN 3 MOVTS.)
2,2(or Eng. hn.),2,2 - 2,2,1,0 timp.,perc. - hp. - str.
15:00 AhnSimrock.

—— CARNIVAL À MONTMARTRE (SUITE DE BALLET)
2,2,2,2 - 3,2,2,0 - timp.,perc. - hp. - pf. - str.   15:00 Bo. Hawkes.

—— CONCERTO CLASSICO (FOR PIANO AND STRINGS)
pf. - str.   16:00 Bo. Hawkes.

—— CONCERTO FOR FLUTE AND STRINGS
fl. - str.   20:00 Bo. Hawkes.

—— CONCERTO FOR OBOE (OR FLUTE) AND SMALL ORCH.
ob. (or fl.),cl. - tpt. - str.   20:00 Bo. Hawkes.

—— CONCERTO FOR VIOLIN AND STRING ORCH.
str.   20:00 Bo. Hawkes.

—— CONCERTO IN F, FOR PIANO AND ORCH.
2,2,2,2 - 4,2,3,0 - timp. - pf. - str.   22:00 Bo. Hawkes.

—— DANZE DALMATE (IN 3 MOVTS.)
2(or picc.),2(or Eng. hn.),2,2 - 2,2,1,0 - timp.,perc. - str.
14:00 AhnSimrock.

—— DITTICO TICINESE (IN 2 MOVTS.)
2(or picc.),2(or Eng. hn.),2(or b.-cl.),2 - 2,2,2,0 - timp.,perc. - hp. -
pf. - str.   8:15 AhnSimrock.

—— DIVERTIMENTO (FOR CHAMBER ORCH.)
0,0,1,1 - 0,1,0,0 - str.   18:00 Bo. Hawkes.

—— L' EMBARQUEMENT POUR CYTHÈRE
2,2,2,2 - 4,2,2,0 - timp.,perc. - str.   11:00 AhnSimrock.

—— EUROPAISCHER BAROCK (SUITE) (IN 4 MOVTS)
2,2,2,2 - 2,1,1,0 - timp.,perc. - str.   13:00 J. Oertel.

—— FESTE LUGANESI (IN 3 MOVTS.)
2,*3,2,2 - 3,2,2,0 - timp.,perc. - hp. - str.   16:00 AhnSimrock.

—— IMPROMPTU (FOR TRUMPET AND ORCH.)
2(or picc.),2(or Eng. hn.),2,2 - 2,1,1,0 - timp.,perc. - hp. - str.
7:00 AhnSimrock.

—— LADINIA RUSTICA (LADINISCHE BAUERNSPIELE) (SUITE)
2,*2,2,2 - 2,2,2,0 - picc.(3) - str.   6:00 J. Oertel.

—— LEGGENDE DOLOMITICHE (IN 2 MOVTS.)
2(or picc.),2(or Eng. hn.),2,2 - 2,2,2,0 - timp.,perc. - pf.(or cel. and
vibra.) - str.   11:00 AhnSimrock.

—— MONOLOGHI DI VITA E DI MORTE
  2,2,2,2 - 4,2,3,0 - timp.,perc. - hp. - str.   25:00 Bo. Hawkes.
—— MUSICA PER TRE GRAZIE (MUSIC FOR THE THREE
  GRACES) (SUITE) (IN 3 MOVTS.)
  2(1 alt. with picc.),2(1 alt. with Eng.hn.),2,2 - 2,2,1,0 - timp.,perc.
  - hp. - str.   11:45 AhnSimrock.
—— OVERTURE DEL PAN-CHAUD
  2,2,2,2 - 3,2,2,0 - timp.,perc. - harp. - str.   5:00 Bo. Hawkes.
—— OVERTURE TO "LES FOURBERIES DE SCAPIN"
                                                    6:00 Chappell.
—— PAVANE AND BURLESQUE (FOR CELLO AND ORCH.)
  3,2,2,2 - 2,2,1,0 - timp.,perc. - str.   8:00 Bo. Hawkes.
—— PORTRAITS MUSICAUX (IN 2 MOVTS)
  2,2,2,2 - 2,2,1,0 - timp.,perc. - hp. - str.   9:00 AhnSimrock.
—— RUBENSIANA
  fl. - hpsc. - str.   14:00 Bo. Hawkes.
—— SCHWEJK'S LUSTIGE ABENTEUER (SUITE) (IN 5 MOVTS.)
  2,1,2,2 - 3,2,2,0 - timp.,perc. - pf. - str.   11:00 AhnSimrock.
—— SERENADE FOR STRINGS (IN 4 MOVTS.)
  str.   21:00 J. Oertel.
—— SINFONIETTA (IN STILE ANTICO, CON ALCUNE LICENZE)
  (IN 4 MOVTS.)
  2,1,0,1 - 0,2,1,0 - timp.,perc. - str.   15:00 AhnSimrock.
—— SOSTE ITALICHE (SUITE)
  2(or picc.),2(or Eng. hn.),2,2 - 3,2,2,0 - timp.,perc. - hp. - str.
                                                    7:00 AhnSimrock.
—— SUITE BRÈVE (IN 4 MOVTS.)
  1,1,1,1 - 0,0,0,0 - hp. - str.   16:30 Mannheimer.
—— VIRTUOSISMI (FOR FLUTE AND STRINGS)
  fl. - str.   6:30 AhnSimrock.

NXUMALO, Gideon Nathan
—— FANTASIA NO. 2 IN D MINOR (FOR PIANO AND ORCH.)
  2,2,3,2 - 4,2,3,1 - timp.,perc. - pf. - str.   15:00 S.A.M.R.O.

NYSTEDT, Knut
—— AWAKENING OF SPRING, OP. 33 (SOLSONG) (FOR MIXED
  CHORUS AND ORCH.) (Text: Anders Hovden)
  3,2,2,2 - 4,3,3,1 - timp.,perc. - str.   10:00 Henmar.
—— THE BURNT SACRIFICE, OP. 36 (BRENN-OFFERET) (FOR
  SPEAKER, MIXED CHORUS AND ORCH.) (Text: Biblical)
  3,2,2,2 - 4,3,3,1 - timp.,perc.,cel. - pf. - str.   20:05 Walton.
—— COLLOCATIONS, OP. 53
  3,2,2,2 - 4,3,3,0 - timp.,perc.,cel.,vibra.,xyl. - str.   9:00 T.O.N.O.
—— CONCERTINO FOR ENGLISH HORN, CLARINET AND
  STRINGS, OP. 29
  0,*1,1,0 - 0,0,0,0 - str.   19:00 T.O.N.O.
—— FESTIVAL OVERTURE, OP. 25
  3,2,2,2 - 4,3,3,1 - timp.,perc. - str.   9:00 T.O.N.O.
—— THE MOUNTAINS, OP. 8 (HØGFJELL) (SUITE) (IN 4 MOVTS.)
  1,1,1,1 - 2,2,2,0 - timp.,perc. - str.   21:00 T.O.N.O.
—— NORWAY, MY COUNTRY, OP. 15 ("NORGE, MITT LAND")
  (FOR BARITONE, MIXED CHORUS AND ORCH.) (Text: Rolf
  Pande)
  2,2,2,2 - 2,2,2,0 - timp.,perc. - str.   13:00 Norsk Mfl.
—— SYMPHONY, OP. 13
  2,1,2,1 - 2,2,2,0 - timp.,perc. - str.   22:00 T.O.N.O.
—— VIA GRATIAE, OP. 14 (NÅDEVEGEN) (FOR SOPRANO,
  TENOR, BASS, MIXED CHORUS AND ORCH.)
  2,2,2,2 - 4,2,2,0 - timp.,perc. - org. - str.   100:00 T.O.N.O.
—— YOUTH, OP. 41 (UNGDOM) (CANTATA) (FOR SPEAKER,
  BARITONE, MIXED CHORUS AND ORCH.) (Text: Arnold
  Stigum)
  1,1,2,1 - 2,2,2,0 - perc. - str.   23:00 T.O.N.O.

NYSTROEM, Gösta
—— CONCERTO FOR VIOLIN AND ORCH.
  2,1,2,1 - 2,1,1,0 - timp.,perc.(4),cel.,xyl. - hp. - str. 30:00 S.T.I.M.
—— CONCERTO NO. 1 FOR STRINGS
  str.   30:00 S.T.I.M.
—— CONCERTO NO. 2 FOR STRINGS
  str.   28:00 Nordiska.
—— CONCERTO RICERCANTE (1959)
  perc.,cel. - hp. - pf. - str.   24:00 S.T.I.M.
—— HERR ARNES PENNINGAR (OPERA) % (1958) (Text: Selma
  Lagerlöf)
                                                    105:00 S.T.I.M.
—— HOMMAGE À LA FRANCE (CONCERTO FOR VIOLA AND
  ORCH.)
  1,1,1,1 - 2,1,0,0 - timp.,perc. - hp. - str.   20:00 S.T.I.M.
—— ISHAVET (SYMPHONIC POEM)
  3,3,3,3 - 4,3,3,1 - timp.,perc. - 2 hp. - str.   20:00 S.T.I.M.

—— NIGHT-MUSIC AT SEA
  2,1,1,1 - 2,1,1,0 - timp.,perc.,cel. - hp. - str.   18:00 S.T.I.M.
—— OUVERTURE SYMPHONIQUE (1945)
  3,2,2,2 - 4,3,3,1 - timp.,perc.(2) - str.   12:00 S.T.I.M.
—— PARTITA FOR FLUTE, HARP AND STRINGS
  fl. - hp. - str.   16:00 S.T.I.M.
—— REGRETS
  3,3,3,3 - 4,3,0,0 - timp.,perc.,xyl. - 2 hp. - str.   15:00 Salabert.
—— SINFONIA BREVE
  3,3,3,3 - 4,3,3,1 - timp.,perc. - str.   18:00 G. Schirmer.
—— SINFONIA CONCERTANTE (FOR CELLO AND ORCH.)
  2,2,2,2 - 4,2,0,0 - timp. - hp. - pf. - str.   36:00 S.T.I.M.
  or:
  1,1,1,1 - 2,2,0,0 - timp. - hp. - pf. - str.
—— SINFONIA DEL MARE (FOR SOPRANO AND ORCH.)
  3,3,3,3 - 4,3,3,1 - timp.,perc.(4),cel. - pf. - str.   38:00 G. Schirmer.
—— SINFONIA ESPRESSIVA
  2,2,2,2 - 4,3,3,1 - timp.,perc. - str.   31:00 G. Schirmer.
—— SINFONIA NO. 4
  3,3,3,3 - 4,3,3,1 - timp.,perc.(4),cel.,xyl. - hp. - pf. - str.
                                                    37:00 S.T.I.M.
—— SINFONIA TRAMONTANA (1965)
  2,2,2,2 - 4,3,3,1 - timp.,perc.(3) - str.   30:00 S.T.I.M.
—— SUITE FOR LITTLE ORCH.
  2,1,1,1 - 2,1,0,0 - timp.,perc.(3) - hp. - str.   16:30 S.T.I.M.
—— SUITE FROM MUSIC TO "THE MERCHANT OF VENICE" (IN
  4 MOVTS.)
  1,1,1,1 - 0,1,0,0 - timp.,perc. - cemb. - guit. - mandolin - str.
                                                    16:00 Suecia.
—— SUITE NO. 1 FROM MUSIC TO "PA LAGERKVISTS
  KONUNGEN" (IN 5 MOVTS.)
  1,1,1,1 - 2,2,1,0 - timp.,perc.(3),cel. - hp. - pf. - str.   25:00 S.T.I.M.
—— SUITE NO. 1 FROM "THE HUNGARIAN PAGES AND THE
  SIX PRINCESSES"
  3,2,2,3 - 4,3,3,1 - timp.,perc.(3),cel. - hp. - pf. - str.   20:00 S.T.I.M.
—— SUITE NO. 2 FROM MUSIC TO "THE TEMPEST" (WITH
  FEMALE VOICES) (IN 4 MOVTS.)
  2,2,2,2 - 4,3,3,1 - timp.,perc.(3),cel. - hp. - pf. - str.   28:00 S.T.I.M.
—— SUITE NO. 2 FROM "THE HUNGARIAN PAGES AND THE
  SIX PRINCESSES"
  3,2,2,3 - 4,3,3,1 - timp.,perc.(3) - str.   19:00 S.T.I.M.
—— SUMMER MUSIC (FOR SOPRANO AND CHAMBER
  ORCH.)(1964)
  1,1,1,0 - 2,0,0,0 - perc.(2) - hp. - pf. - str.   17:30 Nordiska.

O

OATES, Ernest H.
—— CONCERT OVERTURE (1934)
  3,2,2,2 - 4,2,3,1 - timp.,perc. - str.   11:00 P.R.S.
—— CONCERT PIECE FOR 4 HORNS AND ORCH.
  2,2,2,2 - 4,2,3,1 - timp.,perc. - str.   19:00 P.R.S.
—— CONCERTO IN D MAJOR, FOR HORN AND ORCH. (1967)
  2,2,2,2 - 1,2,3,1 - timp. - str.   20:00 P.R.S.
—— CONCERTO IN D MAJOR, FOR ORGAN AND ORCH. (1942)
  2,2,2,2 - 4,2,3,1 - timp. - org. - str.   20:00 P.R.S.
—— INTRODUCTION AND ALLEGRO, FOR 4 HORNS AND
  ORCH. (1960)
  2,2,2,2 - 4,2,3,1 - timp. - str.   10:00 P.R.S.
—— KING ARTHUR (AN OVERTURE) (1966)
  3,3,3,3 - 5,3,3,1 - timp.,perc. - str.   8:00 P.R.S.
—— LEGEND (1938)
  str.   3:30 P.R.S.
—— SYMPHONY NO. 1 (1933)
  3,2,2,2 - 4,2,3,1 - timp.,perc. - hp. - str.   30:00 P.R.S.
—— THEME AND VARIATIONS FOR CELLO AND ORCH. (1938)
  1,1,2,1 - 3,0,0,0 - timp. - str.   15:00 P.R.S.
—— THEME AND VARIATIONS FOR WIND QUINTET AND
  ORCH. (1951)
  1,1,1,1 - 4,0,0,0 - timp. - str.   20:00 P.R.S.
—— THEME AND VARIATIONS (1965)
  3,3,3,3 - 5,3,3,1 - timp.,perc.,cel. - hp. - str.   20:00 P.R.S.

OBOUSSIER, Robert
—— AMPHYTRION (OPERA) %
                                                    Baerenrtr.
—— ANTIGONE (RECITATIVE, ARIA AND ELEGY) (FOR HIGH
  VOICE AND ORCH.)
  *3,*3,*3,ten. sax.,*3 - 4,3,3,1 - timp.,perc. - hp. - str.
                                                    18:00 Baerenrtr.

—— CONCERTO FOR PIANO AND ORCH.

Baerenrtr.

—— CONCERTO FOR VIOLIN AND ORCH.

2,2,2,2 - 3,2,2,0 - timp. - str. 14:00 Baerenrtr.

—— FUNERAL MUSIC

Baerenrtr.

—— INTROITUS

str. 11:00 Baerenrtr.

—— PSALMEN (FOR SOPRANO, TENOR, MIXED CHORUS AND ORCH)

2,*3,*3,*3, - 2,2,2,0 - timp. - hp. - str. 25:00 Baerenrtr.

—— SUITE IN C MAJOR

Baerenrtr.

—— SYMPHONY FOR LARGE ORCH.

Baerenrtr.

OBRADOVIĆ, Aleksandar

—— EPITAPH H (FOR SYMPHONY ORCH. AND STEREO SYSTEM) (1965)

3,3,3,3 - 4,3,3,1 - timp.,perc.(5-6) - tape-recorder(stereo) - str.

10:00 MIC,Zagreb.

—— MIKROSIMFONIJA (MICRO-SYMPHONY) (SYMPHONY NO. 3) (FOR ORCH. AND TAPE)

3,3,3,3 - 4,3,3,1 - timp.,perc.,bells,xyl. - tape-recorder(stereo) - str.

15:00 MIC,Zagreb.

—— SYMPHONY NO. 4 (IN 2 MOVTS)

3,3,3,3 - 4,3,3,1 - timp.,perc.,cel.,mar.,vibra.,xyl. - pf. - str.

19:00 MIC,Zagreb.

—— SYMPHONY NO. 5

3,3,3,3 - 4,3,3,1 - timp.,perc.,cel.,mar.,vibra.,xyl. - pf. - str

MIC,Zagreb.

OBROVSKÁ, Jana

—— CONCERTO FOR PIANO AND ORCH.

3,2,2,2 - 4,2,3,0 - timp. - pf. - str. 26:00 Bo. Hawkes.

OČENÁŠ, Andrej

—— CONCERTO FOR CELLO AND ORCH.

2,2,2,2 - 4,2,3,1 - timp.,perc. - str. 22:00 Bo. Hawkes.

—— LIBERATED LAND, OP. 6 (PART III OF "PROPHECY", A CYCLE OF SYMPHONIC CANTATAS) (FOR SATB CHORUS, ORGAN AND ORCH.) (1952) (Text: P. O. Hviezdoslav)

Bo. Hawkes.

—— RURALIA SLOVACCA, OP. 19

0,0,2,0 - 2,2,0,0 - timp. - cemb. - str. 8:00 Bo. Hawkes.

O'DONNELL, B. Walton

—— MINIATURE SUITE (IN 3 MOVTS)

pf. - str. 12:00 Bo. Hawkes.

—— SONGS OF THE GAEL (FANTASY)

2,2,2,2 - 4,2,3,1 - timp.,perc. - hp. - str. 19:00 Bo. Hawkes.

—— THREE HUMORESQUES

2,2,2,2 - 4,2,3,1, - timp.,perc. - hp. - str. 14:00 Bo. Hawkes.

OFFENBACH, Jacques - ROSENTHAL, Manuel

—— OFFENBACHIANA

2,2,2,2 - 2,2,3,1 - perc.(3),cel. - hp. - str. 40:00 Presser.

OFFENBACH, Jacques - SOPKIN, Henry

—— OFFENBACHANALIA

2,2,2,2 - 4,3,3,1 - perc. - hp. - str. 16:00 C. Fischer.

ÖFVERLUND, Albin

—— OVERTURE IN FOLK STYLE (1951)

2,2,2,2 - 2,2,3,0 - timp.,perc. - str. 4:00 FinnMICtr.

—— PASTORAL SUITE (1939)

str. 14:00 FinnMICtr.

—— RHAPSODY FROM OSTROBOTHNIA (1927)

2,2,2,2 - 2,2,2,0 - timp., perc. - str. 10:00 FinnMICtr.

OGDON, John

—— CONCERTO FOR PIANO AND ORCHESTRA (CONCERTO OF LOVE)

26:40 Chappell.

OGURA, Rô

—— DANCE SUITE

2,2,2,2 - 3,3,3,0 - timp.,perc.(3),cel. - hp. - pf. - str. 16:00 Presser.

—— SONATINE FOR STRINGS

str. 8:17 Presser.

OHANA, Maurice

—— CANTIGAS

0,3,1,2 - 0,2,3,0 - timp.,perc.(5) - pf. - str. 28:00 Presser.

—— CHIFFRES DE CLAVECIN (FOR HARPSICHORD AND CHAMBER ORCH.) (1968)

1(alt. with picc.),1,*2,1 - 2,1(alt. with tpt. in D),1,0 - perc.(4) - hp. - hpsc. - str.(4,2,2,1) 18:30 Salabert.

—— CONCERTINO FOR TRUMPET AND ORCH.

1,1,1,1 - 2,3,1,0 - perc.(3) - pf. - str. Presser.

—— CONCERTO FOR GUITAR AND ORCHESTRA

E.C.Kerby.

—— LLANTO PUR IGNACIO SANCHEZ MEIJAS (FOR NARRATOR, BARITONE, WOMEN'S CHORUS AND ORCH.) (Text: Federico Garcia Lorca)

1,1,2,1 - 2,1,0,0 - timp.,perc.(4) - hpsc. - str. 39:00 Presser.

—— PROMETHEUS (BALLET) %

1,2,1,1 - 2,2,1,0 - perc. - pf. - str. 28:00 Presser.

—— RECIT DE L'AN ZERO (ORATORIO) (FOR SOLO VOICES, SATB CHORUS AND ORCH.)

1,1,1,1 - 0,0,0,0 - perc.(4) - zither - pf. - str. 35:00 Presser.

—— SILENCIARE (1969)

perc.(6) - str.(7,2,2,1) 17:00 Salabert.

—— SUITE POUR UN MIMODRAME

1,1,1,0 - 0,1,0,0 - perc.(2) - str. 14:30 Presser.

—— THARAN NGO

3,3,4,0 - 4,4,3,1 - timp.,perc.(5) - 2 hp. - pf. - str. 22:00 Presser.

OHKI, Masao

—— FIVE FAIRY TALES (SUITE)

3,*3,alto sax.,3,2 - 4,3,3,1 - timp.,perc.,cel. - hp. - str. 12:00 EV.

—— HIROSHIMA (SYMPHONIC FANTASY)

3,2,2,3 - 4,3,3,1 - timp.,perc.,cel. - str. 50:00 EV.

—— NIGHT MEDITATION

,3,*3,2,2 - 4,3,3,1 - timp.,perc.,cel. - hp. - str. 11:00 EV.

OHLSON, Marion

—— LITTLE CONCERTO FOR PIANO AND ORCH. (IN 3 MOVTS.)

*3,2,2,2 - 2,2,0,0 - timp.,perc.(2),xyl. - hp. - pf. - str.

12:00 Composer.

ÖHRN, Gustav

—— ANDANTE FUNÈBRE

2,2,3,2 - 4,2,3,0 - timp. - str. 15:00 T.O.N.O.

—— SEA CALM (HAVBLIKK)

1,1,2,1 - 1,2,1,0 - timp. - str. 6:00 T.O.N.O.

OHSE, Reinhard

—— SERENADE FOR STRING ORCH.

str. Tetra.

OKKENHAUG, Paul

—— BEFORE THE BATTLE (FØRE SLAGET) (FOR SOPRANO, BARITONE, MALE CHORUS AND ORCH.) (IN 8 MOVTS.) (Text: Olav Gullvåg)

2,2,2,2 - 3,2,2,2 - timp.,perc. - str. 35:00 T.O.N.O.

—— CANTATA FOR LEVANGER'S 100TH ANNIVERSARY (FOR MEZZO-SOPRANO, MIXED CHORUS AND ORCH.)

1,1,1,1 - 2,2,2,0 - timp.,perc. - hp. - str. 35:00 T.O.N.O.

—— LYRIC DANCE

1,1,1,1 - 2,2,2,0 - timp.,perc. - hp. - str. 4:30 T.O.N.O.

—— TUNES FROM TRØNDELAG (TONAR FRÅ TRØNDELAG)

2,2,2,2 - 2,2,2,2 - timp.,perc. - str. 12:00 T.O.N.O.

OKUNEV, Gennedij M.

—— CONCERTO FOR PIANO AND CHAMBER ORCH.

G. Schirmer.

OLAH, Tiberiu

—— COLONNE INFINIE (1962)

*4(2nd and 3rd alt. with piccs.),*3,*3,*3 - 4,4,3,1 - timp.,perc.(8),cel. - hp. - pf. - str. 8:30 Salabert.

—— PERSPECTIVES (FOR 13 INSTRUMENTS) (1970)

1,1(alt. with Eng. hn.),1(alt. with b.-cl.),0 - 1,1,1,0 - perc.(3) - str.(1,1,1,1) 12:00 Salabert.

—— LA PORTE DU BAISER (1967)

2 picc.,3,*4,*4,3 - 4,4,4,1 - perc.(5) - str. 7:00 Salabert.

—— TRANSLATIONS (1969)

str. 12:30 Salabert.

OLDHAM, Arthur

—— CIRCUS PARADE

2,1,2,1 - 2,2,1,0 - timp.,perc.,cel. - hp. - str. 20:00 Bo. Hawkes.

—— DIVERTIMENTO
  str.   14:00 Bo. Hawkes.
—— HYMNS FOR THE AMUSEMENT OF CHILDREN (FOR
  SOPRANO, SATB CHORUS AND ORCH.) (Text: Christopher
  Smart)
  2,1,1,1 - 2,0,0,0 - timp. - str.   11:00 Oxford.
—— VARIATIONS ON A CAROL TUNE
  1,1,1,1 - 1,0,0,0 - perc. - hp. - str.   10:00 Bo. Hawkes.

OLDS, W. B.
—— DESERT DRUMS (FOR SOPRANO, TENOR, CHORUS AND
  ORCH.) (IN 6 MOVTS.)
  1,1,2,1 - 2,2,2,0 - timp. - str.   60:00 Composer.

OLIVER, Harold
—— CONCERTO FOR ORCHESTRA AND CHAMBER ENSEMBLE
  (1971) (IN 3 MOVTS.)
  3(1 alt. with picc.),3,2,1 d.-b.cl.,0 - 4,3,3,1 - timp.,perc.,bells,glock.
  - hp. - str.   27:00 Composer.

OLLI, Arvo
—— DAWN, SUNRISE AND DAY (1968)
  3,3,2,2 - 4,3,3,0 - timp.,perc. - str.   20:00 FinnMICtr.
—— EVENING MOOD (ILTATUNNELMIA) (1967)
  2,2,2,2 - 4,2,2,0 - timp.,perc. - str.   8:00 FinnMICtr.
—— REFLECTIONS (1971)
  2,2,2,2 - 4,2,2,0 - timp.,perc.(3) - str.   8:00 FinnMICtr.
—— SOLITUDE (1972)
  ob. - str.   5:00 FinnMICtr.

OLSEN, Sparre
—— ABOVE ALL THE PEAKS (OVER ALLE TINDAR)
  1,1,1,1 - 2,2,1,0 - str.   3:00 Musikk-Hu.
—— ADAGIO FOR STRINGS, OP. 41A
  str.   8:00 Musikk-Hu.
—— ANDANTE FUNÈBRE (FROM INCIDENTAL MUSIC TO
  NORDAHL GRIEG'S PLAY "THE DEFEAT")
  1,1,2,1 - 2,2,1,0 - timp.perc. - pf. - str.   4:00 T.O.N.O.
—— DE PROFUNDIS SURSUM CORDA, OP. 34 (FREDSKANTATE)
  (FOR SPEAKING VOICES, SOPRANO, TENOR, MIXED
  CHORUS AND ORCH.) (Text: Sigvard Stromme)
  2,2,2,2 - 4,3,3,1 - timp. - pf.(or org.) - str.   55:00 Musikk-Hu.
—— DRAUMKVAEDET, OP. 22 (DREAM SONG) (FOR SPEAKING
  VOICES, SOPRANO OR TENOR, MIXED CHORUS AND
  ORCH.)
  2,2,2,2 - 4,2,3,1 - timp.,perc.,cel. - str.   40:00 Norsk Mfl.
—— FROM TELEMARK: SUITE NO. 1, OP. 31, NO. 1
  1,1,1,0 - 0,1,0,0 - pf. - str.   8:00 Musikk-Hu.
—— FROM TELEMARK: SUITE NO. 2, OP. 31, NO. 2
  1,1,1,0 - 0,1,0,0 - pf. - str.   10:00 Musikk-Hu.
—— LEITOM-SUITE, OP. 33 (IN 6 MOVTS.)
  2,2,2,2 - 4,2,3,1 - timp. - str.   15:00 Musikk-Hu.
—— LITTLE OVERTURE, OP. 7
  1,1,1,2 - 2,2,3,0 - perc. - str.   5:00 Norsk Mfl.
—— NIDAROSDOMEN, OP. 29 (FUGUE AND CHORALE)
  2,2,2,2 - 4,2,3,1 - timp. - str.   5:00 Norsk Mfl.
—— NORWEGIAN SONG, OP. 18 (FOR MALE CHORUS AND
  ORCH.) (Text: Nils Collett Vogt)
  2,2,2,2 - 4,2,2,1 - perc. - str.   8:00 Norsk Mfl.
—— PASTORALE AND DANCE, OP. 40
  2,2,2,2 - 4,2,3,1 - timp.,perc.,cel. - str.   10:00 T.O.N.O.
—— SERENADE FOR FLUTE AND STRING ORCH., OP. 45 (IN 3
  MOVTS.)
  fl. - str.   13:00 Norsk Mfl.
—— THE SPARK (GNEISTEN), OP. 16 (FOR MALE CHORUS AND
  ORCH.) (Text: Olav Aukrust)
  2,2,2,2 - 4,2,3,1 - timp.   6:00 Norsk Mfl.
—— SUITE FROM THE PLAY "ANNE PÅ TORP", OP. 12
  2,2,2,2 - 4,2,3,1 - timp.,perc. - str.   13:00 Musikk-Hu.
—— SYMPHONIC FANTASY NO. 1, OP. 27
  2,3,2,2 - 4,2,3,1 - timp. - str.   29:00 T.O.N.O.
—— SYMPHONIC FANTASY NO. 2, OP. 47
  2,2,2,2 - 4,2,3,1 - timp.,perc. - str.   18:00 Musikk-Hu.
—— VARIATIONS ON AN OLD NORWEGIAN FOLKSONG, OP. 5
  1,1,1,1 - 2,2,2,0 - str.   10:00 Norsk Mfl.
—— VER SANCTUM, OP. 30 (FOR MIXED CHORUS AND ORCH.)
  (Text: Olav Aukrust)
  2,3,2,2 - 4,2,3,0 - timp. - str.   30:00 Musikk-Hu.
—— THE VOICES (RØYSTENE), OP. 21 (FOR SOPRANO, TENOR,
  MIXED CHORUS AND ORCH.) (Text: Tore ørjasaeter)
  1,0,1,0 - 0,1,0,0 - str.   20:00 Norsk Ntk.

OLSSON, Joel
—— ENGLISH SUMMER (SUITE NO. 2 IN G MINOR)
  3,2,2,2 - 2,2,3,1 - timp.,perc. - str.   40:00 S.T.I.M.
  or:
  1,2,2,2 - 2,2,1,0 - timp.,perc. - str.
—— MELODI (SUITE NO. 1 IN D MAJOR)
  3,2,2,2 - 4,2,3,1 - timp.,perc. - str.   35:00 S.T.I.M.
  or:
  1,2,2,2 - 2,2,0,0 - timp.,perc. - str.

O'NEILL, Charles
—— THE ANCIENT MARINER (CONTATA)
                                                        50:00 C.A.P.A.C.
—— A DAY IN JUNE (SUITE) ((IN 4 MOVTS.))
                                                        16:00 C.A.P.A.C.
—— MAJESTY (OVERTURE)
                                                        5:00 Remick.
—— PRELUDE AND FUGUE IN G.
                                                        8:30 C.A.P.A.C.

OOSTVEEN, Klaas van
—— SYMPHONIC VARIATIONS, OP. 31 (IN 3 MOVTS.)
  3,3,3,2 - 4,3,3,1 - timp.,perc.cel.,xyl. - hp. - str. 19:00 Henmar.

ØRBECK, Anne-Marie
—— CONCERTINO FOR PIANO AND ORCH.
  2,2,2,2 - 2,2,1,0 - timp.,perc. - pf. - str.   22:00 T.O.N.O.
—— MINIATURE SUITE (IN 3 MOVTS.)
  1,1,1,1,0 - 0,1,1,0 - harm. - pf. - str.   5:00 T.O.N.O.
—— PASTORALE AND ALLEGRO
  fl. - str.   10:00 T.O.N.O.
—— SYMPHONY
  3,2,2,2 - 4,2,3,1 - timp.,perc. - hp. - str.   31:00 T.O.N.O.

ORBÓN, Julián
—— CONCERTO GROSSO FOR STRING QUARTET AND ORCH.
  2,2,2,2 - 4,3,0,0 - timp.,perc.,cel. - pf. - str.   23:00 Bo. Hawkes.
—— DANZAS SINFONICAS
  3,2,2,2 - 4,3,0,0 - timp.,perc.,cel.,glock. - 2 hp. - pf. - str.
                                                        18:00 Southern.
—— HOMENAJE A LA TONADILLA (DIVERTIMENTO) (ON
  THEMES BY 18TH CENTURY SPANISH COMPOSERS)
  5,5,5,4 - 4,3,3,1 - timp.,perc.,cel. - hp. - str.   16:00 Southern.
—— LAMENTATION OF DAVID (FOR TENOR AND ORCH.)
  (Text: Hebrew)
  2,2,2,2 - 4,3,0,0 - timp.,perc.,cel. - hp. - amplified hpsc. - str.
                                                        17:00 Southern.
—— THREE SYMPHONIC VERSIONS (OF ANCIENT MUSIC)
  4,2,4,4 - 4,4,3,1 - timp.,perc.,cel. - hp. - pf. - str. 23:00 Southern.

O'REILLY, Eric Stephen
—— BABOON (INCIDENTAL MUSIC) (FOR SMALL ORCH.)
  1,1,2,1 - 3,1,2,1 - timp.,perc. - str.   15:00 S.A.M.R.O.
—— THE COMING OF THE BUTTERFLIES (OPERA) % (Text: Cecil
  Jubber)
  2,2,3,2 - 4,2,3,1 - timp.,perc. - str.   59:00 S.A.M.R.O.
—— DAY OF GOOD HOPE (INCIDENTAL MUSIC)
  2,2,3,2 - 4,2,3,1 - timp.,perc. - str.   25:00 S.A.M.R.O.
—— DINGAKA (MUSIC FROM THE FILM)
  2,2,3,2 - 4,2,3,1 - timp.,perc. - str.   25:00 S.A.M.R.O.
—— THE FIVE FACES OF EURYDICE (BALLET) %
  2,2,3,2 - 4,2,3,1 - timp.,perc. - str.   35:00 S.A.M.R.O.
—— NIGHT SEQUENCE (SONG CYCLE) (FOR SOPRANO AND
  SMALL ORCH.) (Text: June Batchelor, Neville Nuttell, Eve Slatter
  and R. M. Titlestad)
  1,1,2,1 - 3,1,2,0 - perc. - str.   16:00 S.A.M.R.O.
—— PARTITA FOR STRINGS
  str.   10:00 S.A.M.R.O.
—— R.U.R. (INCIDENTAL MUSIC)
  2,2,3,2 - 4,2,3,1 - timp.,perc. - str.   20:00 S.A.M.R.O.
—— SONG OF TROY (INCIDENTAL MUSIC)
  2,2,3,2 - 4,2,3,1 - timp.,perc. - str.   20:00 S.A.M.R.O.
—— SOUL OF THE WHITE ANTS (INCIDENTAL MUSIC) (FOR
  SMALL ORCH.)
  1,1,2,1 - 3,1,2,1 - timp.,perc. - str.   20:00 S.A.M.R.O.

O'REILLY, John
—— OLYMPIAN DAWN (BALLET) % (1961)
  *2,*2,2,1 alto sax.,1 - 2,2,2,1 - timp.,perc.(2),bells,xyl., - hp. - str.
                                                        10:00 Composer.
—— PASSACAGLIA FOR STRINGS (1962)
  str.   5:00 Composer.

ORGAD, Ben-Zion
—— BUILDING A KING'S STAGE
　　3,2,2,2 - 3,2,2,0 - timp.,perc. - hp. - pf. - str.　15:00 Bo. Hawkes.
—— HATSVI ISRAEL (SYMPHONY IN 2 MOVTS.) (FOR
　　BARITONE AND ORCH.)
　　2,2,2,2 - 3,2,2,0 - timp.,perc.,cel. - hp. - str.　28:00 Bo. Hawkes.
—— KALEIDOSCOPE
　　3,3,3,3 - 3,3,3,0 - timp.,perc. - hp. - pf. - str.　14:00 A.C.U.M.
—— MIZMORIM (FOR SSATB SOLO VOICES AND CHAMBER
　　ORCH.) (Text: Biblical)
　　1,2,1,1 - 1,0,0,0 - perc.(1) - pf. - str.　35:00 A.C.U.M.
—— MOVEMENTS ON A
　　3,2,2,2 - 3,2,2,0 - timp.,perc.(3),cel. - hp. - str.　18:00 A.C.U.M.
—— MUSIC FOR HORN AND ORCHESTRA
　　3,0,*2,*2 - 1,0,1,0 - timp.,perc.,cel.,vibra.,xyl. - hp. - pf. - str.
　　　　　　　　　　　　　　　　　　　22:00 IsMuPublns.
—— A SOLDIER'S PRAYER (FOR BARITONE AND ORCH.)
　　　　　　　　　　　　　　　　　　　8:00 IsMuPublns.

ORLAND, Henry
—— A CHRISTMAS CANDLE LIGHT PROCESSION, OP. 29 (FOR
　　MIXED CHORUS AND ORCH.) (1964)
　　2,2,2,2 - 2,2,3,0 - timp.,perc. - str.　15:00 Seesaw.
—— A CHRISTMAS LEGEND, OP. 30 (FOR MIXED CHORUS AND
　　ORCH.) (1964)
　　2,*2,2,2 - 2,2,3,0 - timp.,perc. - str.　6:00 Seesaw.
—— ARIADNE, EPISODE AND PSYCHE (SYMPHONY NO. 4), OP.
　　25 (FOR SOPRANO, MALE RECITER AND STRING ORCH.)
　　(1961) (Text: Cecil Day Lewis)
　　str.　40:00 MCA Music.
—— CONCERTO FOR BASSOON AND STRING ORCH., OP. 17
　　(1948)
　　bn. - str.　8:00 MCA Music.
—— DOUBLE CONCERTO, OP. 26 (FOR FLUTE, ENGLISH HORN
　　AND STRING ORCH.) (1962)
　　1,*1,0,0 - 0,0,0,0 - str.　15:00 MCA Music.
—— INITIAL, OP. 33 (1966)
　　2(2nd alt with picc.),2,2,2 - 4,2,3,1 - timp.,perc. - str.
　　　　　　　　　　　　　　　　　　　4:00 Seesaw.
—— ODE, EPITAPH AND DITHYRAMB (SYMPHONY NO. 3), OP.
　　19 (1948)
　　2(2nd alt. with picc.),2(2nd alt. with Eng.hn.),2(1st alt. with E♭
　　cl.,2nd alt. with b.-cl.),2(2nd alt. with cbn.) - 2,2,0,0 - str.
　　　　　　　　　　　　　　　　　　　16:00 MCA Music.
—— PRE-L-TUDE, OP. 32 (1965)
　　str.　4:00 Seesaw.
—— SYMPHONY NO. 3, OP. 19
　　3,3,3,3 - 2,2,0,0 - timp. - str.　MCA Music.

ORLOB, Harold
—— SYMPHONY ("RECREATION") (IN 4 MOVTS.) (WITH
　　OPTIONAL CHORUS)
　　*3,2(2nd alt. with Eng. hn.),2,2 - 4,3,3,1 -
　　timp.,perc.,cel.,glock.,xyl. - pf. - str.　17:00 Orlob.

OROWAN, Thomas F.
—— DIVERTIMENTO FOR LARGE STRING ORCH. (1965) (IN 3
　　MOVTS.)
　　str.　15:00 Composer.
—— SERENADE FOR STRING ORCHESTRA (IN 3 MOVTS.)
　　str.　15:00 Composer.
—— SYMPHONY NO. 1 (A NEW ENGLAND SYMPHONY) (1967)
　　(IN 4 MOVTS.)
　　*4,*3,2,*3 - 4,3,3,1 - timp.,perc.(2),bells,vibra. - str.
　　　　　　　　　　　　　　　　　　　59:00 Composer.

ORR, Robin
—— A FESTIVAL TE DEUM (FOR MIXED CHORUS AND ORCH.)
　　　　　　　　　　　　　　　　　　　Oxford.
—— FULL CIRCLE (ONE-ACT OPERA) % (Text: Sydney Goodsir
　　Smith)
　　　　　　　　　　　　　　　　　　　33:00 G. Schirmer.
—— ITALIAN OVERTURE
　　2,2,0,2 - cemb. - str.　8:00 Oxford.
—— SPRING CANTATA (FOR MEZZO-SOPRANO, MIXED
　　CHORUS, PIANO AND ORCH.) (Text: Helen Waddell and
　　Thomas Nashe)
　　timp.,perc.(1) - pf. - str.　25:00 Oxford.
—— SYMPHONY IN ONE MOVEMENT
　　　　　　　　　　　　　　　　　　　18:30 G. Schirmer.

ORREGO-SALAS, Juan
—— FESTIVAL OVERTURE, OP. 21
　　3,3,3,3 - 4,3,3,1 - timp.,perc. - hp. - str.　9:00 Bo. Hawkes.
—— EL RETABLO DEL REY POBRE, OP. 27 (OPERA-ORATORIO)
　　(1949) %
　　　　　　　　　　　　　　　　　　　Bo. Hawkes.
—— EL UMBRAL DEL SUENO, OP. 30 (BALLET) (1951) %
　　　　　　　　　　　　　　　　　　　Bo. Hawkes.

ORTAKOV, Dragoslav
—— EPTAMERON
　　1,1,1,1 - 1,1,1,0 - timp.,perc. - pf. - str.　21:00 S.O.K.O.J.

ORTHEL, Léon
—— CONCERTINO ALLA BURLA, OP. 12 (FOR PIANO AND
　　ORCH.)
　　3,2,2,2 - 2,2,0,0 - timp.,perc. - pf. - str.　11:00 Henmar.
—— KLEINE BALLET SUITE, OP. 31
　　3,3,3,3 - 4,3,3,1 - perc.,cel. - hp. - str.　11:00 Henmar.
—— NONNENKLAGE, OP. 25A (FOR SOPRANO AND ORCH.)
　　(1942) (Text: R. M. Rilke)
　　2,0,3,0 - 2,0,0,0 - hp. - str.　7:00 Henmar.
—— SCHERZO FOR ORCH., OP. 57
　　　　　　　　　　　　　　　　　　　Henmar.
—— SCHERZO FOR PIANO AND ORCH.
　　2,2,2,2 - 2,2,0,0 - timp. - pf. - str.　7:00 Henmar.
—— SCHERZO NO. 2, OP. 38
　　3,3,3,2 - 4,3,3,0 - timp.,perc. - str.　10:00 Henmar.
—— SYMPHONY NO. 2, OP. 18 (PICCOLA SINFONIA)
　　3,3,3,3 - 4,3,3,1 - timp.,perc. - str.　17:00 Henmar.
—— SYMPHONY NO. 3, OP. 24
　　3,3,3,3 - 4,3,3,1 - timp.,perc. - str.　35:00 Henmar.
—— SYMPHONY NO. 4 OP. 32 (SINFONIA CONCERTANTE) (FOR
　　PIANO AND ORCH.)
　　3,3,3,3 - 4,3,3,1 - timp.,perc. - pf. - str.　23:00 Henmar.
—— SYMPHONY NO. 5, OP. 43 ("MUSICA INIZIALE") (1960)
　　3,3,3,3 - 4,4,3,1 - timp.,perc.,cel. - hp. - str.　15:00 Henmar.
—— SYMPHONY NO. 6, OP. 45 (1961)
　　3,3,3,2 - 4,3,3,1 - timp.,perc.,cel. - hp. - str.　35:00 Henmar.

OSBORNE, Tony
—— BIRTHDAY SUITE (1966)
　　str.　6:30 P.R.S.
—— CONCERTINO FOR OBOE AND STRINGS (1969)
　　ob. - str.　7:00 P.R.S.
—— ESSAY FOR ORCH. (1967)
　　2,2,2,2 - 4,2,3,1 - timp.,perc. - hp. - str.　6:00 P.R.S.
—— THREE PIECES FOR ORCH. (1968)
　　2,2,2,2 - 4,2,3,1 - timp.,perc. - hp. - str.　20:00 P.R.S.

OSIECK, Hans
—— CONCERTINO NO. 1 FOR PIANO AND ORCH.
　　3,2,2,2 - 2,1,1,0 - timp.,perc. - pf. - str.　15:00 Henmar.
—— CONCERTINO NO. 2 FOR PIANO AND ORCH.
　　2,2,2,2 - 2,1,1,0 - timp.,perc.,cel. - pf. - str.　17:00 Henmar.
—— CONCERTO FOR PIANO AND ORCH.
　　2,1,2,2 - 4,2,0,0 - timp.,perc. - pf. - pf. - str.　Henmar.
—— CONCERTO FOR TRUMPET AND ORCH. (1960)
　　2,0,2,2 - 2,1,0,0 - timp.,perc.,xyl. - hp. - pf. - str.　18:00 Henmar.
—— CONCERTO FOR TWO PIANOS AND ORCH
　　3,2,2,2 - 2,1,1,0 - timp.,perc. - 2 pf. - str.　15:00 Henmar.
—— DIVERTIMENTO VOOR KLEIN ORKEST (IN 4 MOVTS.)
　　2,1,1,1 - 1,1,0,0 - timp.,perc. - str.　14:00 Henmar.
—— RENE (ACHT PHASEN UIT "EEN MENSENLEVEN") (SUITE)
　　3,2,2,2 - 4,2,2,0 - timp.,perc.,cel. - str.　12:00 Henmar.
—— RHAPSODY (1962)
　　2,2,2,2 - 4,2,2,0 - timp.,perc. - hp. - pf. - str.　11:00 Henmar.
—— ROMANCE FOR FLUTE, HARP AND STRINGS
　　fl. - hp. - str.　8:00 Henmar.
—— VARIATIONS ON A BAROQUE THEME
　　str.　10:00 Henmar.
—— VARIATIONS ON A FOLK MELODY ("DE BLOEMPJES
　　GINGEN SLAPEN") (FOR PIANO AND ORCH.)
　　3,2,2,2 - 2,1,1,0 - timp.,perc.,cel. - pf. - str.　12:00 Henmar.

OSTERC, Slavko
—— CONCERTO FOR PIANO AND WINDS
　　2(2nd alt. with picc.),1(alt. with Eng. hn.),2(2nd alt. with b.-cl and
　　alto sax.),2 - 4,3,3,1 - timp.,perc. - pf.　20:00 Hans Gerig.
—— SUITE FOR ORCH.
　　1(alt. with picc.),1(alt. with Eng. hn.),2,2 - 4,2,3,1 - timp.,perc. -
　　str.　18:00 Hans Gerig.

—— SYMPHONIC MOVEMENT
  2(2nd alt. with picc.),2(2nd alt. with Eng. hn.),2(2nd alt. with
  b.-cl. and alto sax.),2 - 4,3,3,1 - timp.,perc.(3) - hp. - pf. - str.
  12:00 Hans Gerig.

OSTRČIL, Otakar
—— BALLAD OF A DEAD COBBLER AND A YOUNG DANCER
  (FOR NARRATOR AND ORCH.) (Text: Karel Leger)
  Bo. Hawkes.
—— THE BUD (OPERA) %
  Bo. Hawkes.
—— CALVARY (SYMPHONIC VARIATIONS), OP. 24 (1928)
  3,3,4,3 - 4,3,3,1 - timp.,perc. - 2 hp. - str.   33:00 Bo. Hawkes.
—— IMPROMPTU, OP. 13
  3,3,3,3 - 4,3,3,1 - timp.,perc. - hp. - str.   17:00 Bo. Hawkes.
—— SIMPLE JOHN'S KINGDOM (OPERA) (1933) %
  Bo. Hawkes.
—— SUITE IN C MINOR, OP. 14 (IN 5 MOVTS.)
  3,3,3,3 - 4,3,3,1 - timp.,perc. - str.   26:00 Bo. Hawkes.
—— SUMMER (SYMPHONIC POEM), OP. 23 (1926)
  3,3,4,3 - 4,3,3,1 - timp.,perc. - hp. - str.   17:00 Bo. Hawkes.
—— SYMPHONIETTA, OP. 20 (1921) (IN 5 MOVTS.)
  Bo. Hawkes.

OTT, Joseph
—— DIVERTIMENTO NO. 1 FOR ORCH. (1961)
  2(2nd alt. with picc.),2(2nd alt. with Eng.hn.),2(2nd alt. with
  b.-cl.),2 - 2,2,1,0 - timp.,perc.(3),glock. - str.   13:00 Cl. Benny.
—— DIVERTIMENTO NO. 2 (1967)
  2(2ndalt. with picc.),2(2nd alt. with Eng.hn.),2(2nd alt. with b.-cl.),
  2 - 2,2,2,1 - timp.,perc.(3),xyl. - pf. - str.   Cl. Benny.
—— ELEGY FOR STRINGS
  str.   5:00 Cl. Benny.
—— EXTENSIONS (1972)
  *3,2,2 - 4,3,3,1 - timp.,perc.(3) - tape-recorder(stereo) - pf. - str.
  9:00 Cl. Benny.
—— FIVE DEDUCTIONS IN SYLLOGISTIC FORM (1962)
  3(3rd alt. with picc.),2(2nd alt. with Eng.hn.),2(2nd alt. with
  b.-cl.),2(2nd alt. with c.-bn.) - 4,2,3,1 - timp.,perc.(4),cel. - pf. - str.
  Cl. Benny.
—— FIVE PIECES FOR WOODWIND QUINTET AND STRINGS
  (1961)
  1,1,1,1 - 1,0,0,0 - pf. - str.   11:00 Cl. Benny.
—— FREE VARIATION (1963)
  2(2nd alt. with picc.),2,2,2 - 2,2,1,0 - timp.,perc.(3),glock,xyl. - str.
  8:00 Fleisher.
—— FUGUE FOR ORCHESTRA (1957)
  *3,*3,*3,2 - 4,3,3,1 - timp.,perc.(3),glock. - pf. - str.
  12:00 Composer.
—— MATRIX III (FOR CHAMBER ORCH.) (1969)
  1,2,0,2 - 2,0,0,0 - hpsc. - str.   14:00 Cl. Benny.
—— MUSIC FOR CHAMBER ORCHESTRA (1967)
  1,2,1,2 - 2,0,0,0 - str.   Cl. Benny.
—— ORCHESTRAL VARIATIONS (1958)
  3(3rd alt. with picc.),2,2(2nd alt. with b.-cl.),2 - 4,3,3,1 -
  timp.,perc.(4),glock.,xyl. - str.   18:00 Composer.
—— PREMISE FOR ORCH. (1962)
  2,*3,2,3 - 2,2,3,0 - timp.,perc. - str.   15:00 EV.
—— RHAPSODY FOR ORCHESTRA (1959)
  3(3rd alt. with picc.),2(2nd alt. with Eng.hn.),2(2nd alt. with
  b.-cl.),2 - 4,3,3,1 - timp.,perc.(4),glock.,xyl. - str. 20:00 Cl. Benny.
—— SATIRIC SUITE (1959) (IN 5 MOVTS.)
  2(2nd alt. with picc.),2(2nd alt. with Eng.hn.),2(2nd alt. with
  b.-cl.),2 - 4,3,3,1 - timp.,perc.(3),xyl. - str.   15:30 Cl. Benny.
—— SEVEN HAIKU (FOR SOPRANO AND ORCH.) (1965)
  1,1(alt. with Eng.hn.),1,1 - 2,1,0,0 - perc.(1) - pf. - str.
  10:00 Composer.
—— STUDY IN UNISON, FOR ORCHESTRA (1963)
  3(3rd alt. with picc.),3(3rd alt. with Eng.hn.),*3,2 - 4,3,3,1 -
  timp.,perc.(4),xyl. - pf. - str.   6:00 Composer.
—— THREE STUDIES IN DENSITY (1962)
  2,2,2,2 - 3,2,2,1 - timp.,perc.(3),glock. - str.   12:00 Cl. Benny.
—— TWO DANCES FOR ORCHESTRA (1953)
  *3,*3,*3,2 - 4,3,3,1 - timp.,perc.(2) - str.   8:00 Composer.
—— UNIT 2572 L.A. 64 (FOR SOPRANO AND ORCH.) (1964)
  2(2nd alt. with picc.),2(2nd alt. with Eng.hn.),2(2nd alt. with
  b.-cl.),2 - 4,3,3,1 - timp.,perc.(3),glock.,xyl. - pf. - str.
  16:00 Composer.
—— VARIATIONS FOR ORCHESTRA (1963)
  *3,*3,*3,*3 - 4,4,3,1 - timp.,perc.(3),glock.,xyl. - pf. - str.
  22:00 Composer.

OTTEN, Ludwig
—— ORKESTFANTASIE IN DRIE DELEN (1957)
  3,3,3,2 - 4,3,3,1 - timp.,perc. - hp. - str.   19:00 Henmar.
—— SINFONIE
  3,3,3,2 - 4,3,3,1 - timp.,perc. - hp. - str.   19:00 Henmar.
—— SINFONIETTA
  2,2,2,2 - 2,1,0,0 - timp. - str.   15:00 Henmar.
—— SINFONISCHE MUZIEK IN DRIE DELEN (1959)
  2,2,2,2 - 2,2,2,0 - timp.,perc. - hp. - str.   31:00 Henmar.
—— VIJF STUKKEN (5 PIECES FOR STRING ORCH.) (1967)
  9:00 Henmar.

OTTERLOO, Willem van
—— INTRODUCTION AND ALLEGRO
  3,3,3,3 - 4,4,3,1 - timp.,perc. - str.   14:00 Henmar.
—— SERENADE (DIVERTIMENTO)
  0,0,0,0 - 4,4,3,1 - timp.,perc.,cel. - hp. - pf. - (ad lib.) - str.
  13:00 Henmar.
—— SUITE FOR STRINGS
  str.   10:00 Henmar.
—— SYMPHONIETTA FOR WINDS
  3,3,3,3 - 4,0,0,0   15:00 Henmar.

OTTOSON, David
—— ATIS AND KAMILLA (SYMPHONIC POEM)
  2,2,2,3 - 4,2,3,1 - timp.,perc. - str.   20:00 S.T.I.M.
—— AUTUMN ("HÖST") (SYMPHONIC POEM)
  2,2,2,2 - 2,2,0,0 - timp. - str.   13:00 S.T.I.M.
—— BATSEBA (SYMPHONIC POEM)
  2,2,2,2 - 4,2,0,0 - timp.,perc. - hp. - str.   15:00 S.T.I.M.
—— CONCERT OVERTURE NO. 1
  2,2,2,3 - 4,2,3,1 - timp.,perc. - hp. - str.   15:00 S.T.I.M.
—— CONCERT OVERTURE NO. 2
  2,2,2,2 - 2,2,1,0 - timp.,perc. - hp. - str.   13:00 S.T.I.M.
—— CONCERT PIECE FOR CELLO AND ORCH.
  2,2,2,2 - 2,2,1,0 - timp.,perc. - str.   17:00 S.T.I.M.
—— CONCERTO FOR BASSOON AND ORCH.
  2,2,2,2 - 2,2,0,0, - timp. - str.   18:00 S.T.I.M.
—— CONCERTO FOR CELLO AND ORCH.
  2,2,2,2 - 2,2,0,0 - timp. - hp. - str.   20:00 S.T.I.M.
—— CONCERTO FOR PIANO AND ORCH.
  2,2,2,2 - 2,2,1,0 - timp. - pf. - str.   30:00 S.T.I.M.
—— DIVERTIMENTO FOR STRINGS
  str.   9:30 S.T.I.M.
—— I HAVSBANDET (THE SEA-REEFS)
  2,2,2,2 - 4,2,3,1 - timp.,perc. - hp. - str.   14:00 S.T.I.M.
—— HÄLSINGLAND (SUITE)
  2,2,2,2 - 4,2,3,1 - timp.,perc. - hp. - str.   20:00 S.T.I.M.
—— INTRODUCTION AND FUGUE FOR STRINGS
  str.   6:30 S.T.I.M.
—— ISLOSSNING (SYMPHONIC POEM)
  2,2,2,2 - 4,2,0,0 - timp. - str.   15:00 S.T.I.M.
—— LJUNGBY HORN (LEGEND)
  2,2,3,2 - 4,2,3,1 - timp.,perc. - hp. - str.   15:00 S.T.I.M.
—— LYRIC SUITE
  2,2,2,2 - 4,2,3,1 - timp.,perc. - hp. - str.   20:00 S.T.I.M.
—— MINIATURE SUITE
  2,2,2,2 - 4,2,3,1 - timp.,perc.,cel. - hp. - str.   18:00 S.T.I.M.
—— NORDIC SKETCHES
  2,2,2,2 - 2,2,3,0 - timp.,perc. - str.   14:00 S.T.I.M.
—— NORSELAND RHAPSODY
  32,2,2 - 3,2,3,1 - timp.,perc.(2) - hp. - str.   15:00 S.T.I.M.
—— ORIENTAL SUITE
  2,3,1-3,2 - 4,2,0,0 - timp. - hp. - str.   18:00 S.T.I.M.
—— ROMANCE FOR VIOLIN AND ORCH.
  2,2,2,2 - 2,2,1,0 - timp. - str.   8:00 S.T.I.M.
—— ROMANTIC SUITE
  2,2,2,2 - 2,2,1,0 - timp.,perc. - str.   15:00 S.T.I.M.
—— SWEDISH SUITE
  2,2,2,2 - 1-4,2,3,1 - timp.,perc. - str.   15:00 S.T.I.M.

OUGLITZKY, Paul P.
—— UKRAINA (SYMPHONIC POEM)
  3(3rd alt. with picc.),*3,3(3rd alt. with b.-cl.),*3 - 4,3,3,1 -
  timp.,perc.(5) - hp. - str.   27:00 Baron.

OULIE, Einar
—— ALLEGRETTO SCHERZANDO (FROM STRING QUARTET
  NO. 3, OP. 10)
  2,2,2,2 - 4,2,3,1 - timp.,perc. - str.   9:00 T.O.N.O.
  or:
  1,0,1,4 sax.,0 - 0,2,1,0 - perc. - guit. - str.

—— CONCERTO FOR CELLO AND ORCH. (IN 3 MOVTS.)
  2,2,2,3 - 4,2,3,1 - timp. - hp. - str.   25:00 T.O.N.O.
—— A FAIRY TALE,OP. 21 (ET EVENTYR) (OVERTURE)
  str.   9:30 T.O.N.O.
—— STABAT MATER, OP. 27 (FOR MALE CHORUS AND
  STRINGS) (Text: J. da Todi)
  str.   11:30 T.O.N.O.
—— STIKLESTAD (FOR SOPRANO, TENOR, BARITONE, CHORUS
  AND ORCH.) (Text: Rolf Hjort Schøyen)
  2,2,2,2 - 4,2,3,1 - timp.,perc. - str.   17:00 T.O.N.O.
—— SUITE FOR STRINGS (IN 3 MOVTS.)
  str.   12:00 T.O.N.O.
—— SYMPHONY NO. 1, OP. 19 (IN 3 MOVTS.)
  2,3,2,3 - 4,3,3,1 - timp.,perc. - str.   26:00 T.O.N.O.
—— SYMPHONY NO. 2, OP. 29 (IN 3 MOVTS.)
  2,2,2,2 - 2,2,2,0 - timp.,perc. - hp. - str.   24:00 T.O.N.O.
—— THREE SMALL PIECES
  str.   12:00 T.O.N.O.

OUZOUNOFF, Daniel
—— FIGURES AUDITIVES
  str.   15:00 Presser.

OVANIN, Nikola L.
—— DUSK, OP. 78
  2,2(2nd alt. with Eng.hn.),*3,2 - 4,0,0,0 - hp. - str.
                                                  7:30 Composer.
—— ELEGY (FOR WINDS AND STRINGS)
  1,1,2,1 - 3,0,0,0 - str.   5:00 Composer.
—— ESSAY NO. 1 FOR ORCH., OP. 90
  2,2,1 Eᵇcl.,*3,3 - 4,2,3,1 - timp.,perc.(2) - hp. - str.
                                                  15:00 Composer.
—— ESSAY NO. 2 FOR ORCH.
  2,2,2,2 - 4,2,3,0 - timp.,perc.(3) - hp. - str. 16:00 Composer.
—— POEM FOR STRING ORCHESTRA
  str.   MCA Music.
—— PRELUDE MODERNE
  3,3,3,3 - 4,3,3,1 - timp.,perc. - hp. - str.   5:00 C. Fischer.
—— SINFONIETTA FOR SMALL ORCH. (IN 3 MOVTS.)
  2,1,2,0 - 1,0,0,0 - str.   19:00 Composer.
—— SUITE FOR ORCH. ("PLEIADES") (IN 7 MOVTS.)
  *3,*3,1 Eᵇcl.,*3,2 - 4,3,3,1 - timp.,perc.(4),bells, cel. - hp. - str.
                                                  33:00 MCA Music.
—— SYMPHONY NO. 1 (MARS SYMPHONY), OP. 50 (IN 1
  MOVT.)
  2(2nd alt. with picc.),2,2,3 - 4,2,3,1 - timp.,perc.(2), bells - str.
                                                  20:00 Composer.
—— SYMPHONY NO. 2 (IN 3 MOVTS.)
  *3,*3,1 Eᵇcl.,*3,*3 - 4,3,3,1 - timp.,perc.(3) - hp. - str.
                                                  20:30 Composer.

OVERMAN, Meta
—— THE JESTER (SYMPHONIC POEM)
                                                  7:00 A.P.R.A.
—— SUITE FOR ORCH.
                                                  30:00 A.P.R.A.
—— SUITE OF OLD DANCE FORMS
  str.   12:00 A.P.R.A.

OWEN, Harold
—— CANTICLE OF THE SUN (FOR MIXED CHORUS AND
  ORCH.) (1966) (Text: St. Franics of Assisi)
  1,1,1,1 - 1,1,1,0 - timp. - str.   17:00 Composer.
—— CONCERTO FOR PIANO AND ORCH. (1956)
  2(2nd alt. with picc.),2(2nd alt. with Eng. hn.),2(2nd alt. with
  b.-cl.),2 - 4,2,3,1 - timp.,perc.(2) - pf. - str. 22:00 Composer.
—— VARIATION-SUITE FOR ORCHESTRA (1964)
  2-3(1 alt. with picc.),2(2nd alt. with Eng. hn.),3(3rd alt. with
  b.-cl.),2 - 4,2,3,1 - timp.,perc.(3),xyl. - str. 15:00 Composer.

OWEN, Richard
—— A FISHERMAN CALLED PETER (OPERA) %
  0,1,0,0 - 1,1,0,0 - timp. - org. - str.   60:00 General.

OWENS, Robert - BUCK, Friedrich
—— AMERICAN CARNIVAL (BALLET SUITE)
  3,3,3,3 - 4,3,3,1 - timp.,perc.,cel.,xyl. - hp. - str.
                                                  18:00 F. Colombo.

OXTOBY, Charles Francis
—— DIVERTIMENTO
  str.   10:00 S.A.M.R.O.

—— DROUGHT, OP. 46 (FOR CONTRALTO, CHORUS AND
  ORCH.) (Text: Francis Carey Slater)
  2,2,3,2 - 4,2,3,1 - timp.,perc. - str.   25:00 S.A.M.R.O.
—— FOR UNTO US (FOR CONTRALTO, CHORUS, ORGAN AND
  STRING ORCH.)
  org. - str.   25:00 S.A.M.R.O.
—— HANS ANDERSEN SUITE (FOR NARRATOR AND ORCH.)
  2,2,3,2 - 4,2,3,1 - timp.,perc. - str.   15:00 S.A.M.R.O.
—— INTRODUCTION AND FUGUE IN OLDEN STYLE
  2,2,3,2 - 4,2,3,1 - timp.,perc. - str.   6:00 S.A.M.R.O.
—— JAN VAN RIEBEECK SUITE (FOR OBOE AND STRING
  ORCH.)
  ob. - str.   9:00 S.A.M.R.O.
—— LAND OF THE SETTLERS, OP. 48 (FOR TWO VOICES AND
  ORCH.) (Text: Kingsley Fairbridge and Francis Carey Slater)
  2,2,3,2 - 4,2,3,1 - timp.,perc. - str.   30:00 S.A.M.R.O.
—— MEDITATION FOR ADVENT (PRELUDE FOR STRING
  ORCH.)
  str.   4:00 S.A.M.R.O.
—— SIX SOUTH AFRICAN MINIATURES (FOR SMALL ORCH.)
  1,1,2,1 - 3,1,2,1 - perc. - str.   8:00 S.A.M.R.O.
—— SUITE FOR STRING ORCHESTRA
  str.   7:00 S.A.M.R.O.
—— TWO MINIATURES FOR ORCHESTRA
  2,2,3,2 - 4,2,3,1 - timp.,perc. - str.   4:00 S.A.M.R.O.
—— VARIATIONS ON A NURSERY THEME (FOR OBOE AND
  STRING ORCH.)
  ob. - str.   10:00 S.A.M.R.O.

OZGIJAN, Petar
—— CONCERTO FOR ORCHESTRA (PART II OF "SYMPHONIC
  TRIPTYCH") (1965)
                                                  16:00 MIC,Zagreb.
—— DIFERENCIAS (CONCERTO FOR VIOLIN AND ORCH.)
  3,3,3,3 - 4,3,3,1 - timp.,perc.,cel.,xyl. - hp. - str.
                                                  17:00 MIC,Zagreb.
—— MEDIATIONS (PART I OF "SYMPHONIC TRIPTYCH") (1964)
  perc. - 2 pf. - str.   10:00 MIC,Zagreb.
—— SIGOGIS (PART III OF "SYMPHONIC TRIPTYCH")
  2,2,2,2 - 2,2,2,0 - timp.,perc.,cel.,vibra.,xyl. - 2 hp. - pf. - str.
                                                  10:00 MIC,Zagreb.
—— SYMPHONY '75 (1975)
  3,3,3,3 - 4,4,4,1 - timp.,perc.,cel. - 2 hp. - pf. - str.
                                                  17:00 MIC,Zagreb.

P

PAAP, Wouter
—— BALLET-SUITE VOOR KAMERORKEST
  2,1,2,0 - 2,0,0,0 - timp.,perc. - pf. - str.   11:00 Henmar.
—— GUIRLANDEN VAN MUZIEK
  str.   11:00 Henmar.
—— MUZIEK TER BRUILOFT (FOR TENOR AND ORCH.) (1945)
  (Text: Vondel)
  2,2,2,2 - 2,0,0,0 - timp.,perc. - hp. - str.   14:00 Henmar.
—— OUVERTURE ELECTORA
  3,2,2,2 - 4,3,3,0 - timp.,perc. - hp. - str.   11:00 Henmar.
—— PASSACAGLIA
  2,2,2,2 - 4,3,3,1 - timp.,perc. - hp. - str.   8:00 Henmar.
—— SINFONIETTA FOR CHAMBER ORCH.
  1,1,1,1 - 2,1,1,0 - timp. - pf. - str.   14:00 Henmar.
—— STERRE DER ZEE (FOR SOPRANO, SATB CHORUS AND
  ORCH.) (1937) (Text: J. Engelman)
  2,2,2,2 - 3,2,2,0 - perc. - hp. - str.   20:00 Henmar.

PAASIO, Pekko
—— CHORALE FANTASY (VARIATIONS) (1970)
  1,1,2,1 - 2,2,3,0 - timp. - str.   5:00 FinnMICtr.
—— HEART MUSIC (1970)
  1,2,2,1 - 2,3,3,1 - timp.,perc. - str.   11:00 FinnMICtr.
—— IMPROMPTU (1969)
  1,1,2,1 - 2,3,3,1 - timp. - str.   9:00 FinnMICtr.
—— OVERTURE (1968)
  1,0,2,0 - 0,0,0,0 - 4 kanteles - str.   6:00 FinnMICtr.
—— SPECULATION (1970)
  2,0,0,0 - 0,0,0,0 - str.   6:00 FinnMICtr.

PABLO, Luis de
—— DRUNKEN ELEPHANTS (IN 4 MOVTS., EACH FOR A
DIFFERENT ASSORTMENT OF INSTRUMENTS)
3(3rd alt. with picc.),3(3rd alt. with Eng.hn.),2(2nd alt. with
b.-cl.),ten. sax.,2(2nd alt. with c.-bn.) - 4,3,2,1 - timp.,perc.(4),cel. -
hp. - Hammond org. - pf. - str.   40:00 Salabert.
—— FOUR INVENTIONS FOR ORCH.
*3,2,*3,2 - 0,2,2,0 - perc.,cel. - hp. - str.   12:00 Modern.
—— HETEROGENEO (FOR 2 SPEAKERS, HAMMOND ORGAN
AND LARGE ORCH.) (1968)
4(alt. with picc.),4,4,4 - 4,4,4,2 - timp.,2 cel.,2 xyl. - 2 hp. -
electric org. (Hammond) - 2 pf. - str.   25:00 Salabert.
—— IMAGINARIO II (FOR LARGE ORCH.) (1967)
4,4,4,3 sax.,4 - 4,3,3,2 - timp.,perc.(5) - 2 pf.(3 players) - str.
15:00 Salabert.
—— INICIATIVAS (1966)
*4,*3,4,4 - 4,3,3,1 - timp.,perc.,cel. - 2 hp. - pf. - str.
18:45 Seesaw.
—— JE MANGES, TU MANGES
2,2,2,2 - 2,2,0,0 - timp. - tape-recorder (ad lib.) - str.
20:00 Salabert.
—— LA LIBERTAD SONRIÉ (1971) (FOR 15 WINDS OR
VARIABLE GROUP OF 15 INSTRUMENTS)
20:00 Salabert.
—— MODULOS II (FOR DOUBLE ORCH.) (1966)
3,3,3,3 - 5,3,3,2 - perc. - 2 hp. - pf. - str.(13,9,7,3)   11:05 Seesaw.
—— MODULOS III (FOR 17 INSTRUMENTS) (1967)
0,0,0,0 - 0,4,0,0 - timp.(chromatic),perc.,cel.,glock.,vibra.,2
xyl.(xylorimbas marimba phones) - guit.,mand. - 2 hp. - harm. - 2
pf.   18:00 Salabert.
—— OROÏTALDI (1971)
3,3,3,*3 - 5,4,3,1 - perc.(4),cel. - pf. - str.(24,10,10,8)
20:00 Salabert.
—— PARAFRASIS (ON THEMES OF T. L. DE VITORIA) (FOR 24
INSTRUMENTS) (1968)
2,2,2,2 - 2,2,2,0 - str.(4,2,2,2)   12:00 Salabert.
—— POR DIVERSOS MOTIVOS (1969) (WITH VOICE AND
PROJECTED IMAGES)
0,0,0,0 - 4,3,3,0 - perc.(3) - tape-recorder - pf.(3 players) - 4 vlas,4
d.-b.   30:00 Salabert.
—— PROTOCOLO (OPERA) (1968) %
3 fl. - perc.(4),2 mar. - electric org.(hammond) - pf.(onstage,
played by actor) - 2 vln.(onstage)   35:00 Salabert.
—— QUASI UNA FANTASIA (FOR SOLO STRING SEXTET AND
ORCH.) (1969)
4,4,4,4 - 4,3,3,1 - timp.,perc.(3) - 2 hp. - electric org.(hammond) -
pf. - str.   25:00 Salabert.
—— RADIAL (1960)
1,1,2,2 - 1,1,1,1 - xyl. - hp. - str.   8:00 Seesaw.
—— TOMBEAU (1963)
*3,*3,3,3 - 4,3,0,0 - str.   7:40 Seesaw.

PACHELBEL, Johann - DE LAMARTER, Eric
—— PRAELUDIUM, CHORALE AND FUGUE
str.   Ricordi.

PACHELBEL, Johann - WOODWARD, Henry
—— MAGNIFICAT IN C (FOR MIXED CHORUS AND ORCH.)
Summy-Bir.

PACHERNEGG, Alois
—— ITALIENISCHE LUSTPIEL OUVERTURE "DON CAMILLO
UND PEPPONE"
7:00 Henmar.

PADEREWSKI, Ignace Jan
—— SYMPHONY (1909)
3,3,3,3 - 4,4,4,3 - timp.,perc. - hp. - org. - str.   26:00 Presser.

PADWA, Vladimir
—— ADAGIO "SOLITUDE"
2(2nd alt. with picc.),2(2nd alt. with Eng. hn.),2(2nd alt. with
bl-cl.),2(2nd alt. with c.-bn.) - 4,0,0,0 - timp.,cel. - hp. - str.
6:00 Composer.
—— CONCERTO FOR TWO PIANOS AND STRINGS
2pf. - str.   10:00 Composer.
—— SERENADE IN C
str.   3:00 Composer.
—— SYMPHONY IN D
2(2nd alt. with picc.),2(2nd alt. with Eng. hn.),2,2 - 4,2,3,0 -
timp.,perc.(1) - hp. - str.   23:00 Composer.

—— TOM SAWYER (BALLET SUITE)
2(2nd alt. with picc.),2(2nd alt. with Eng. hn.),2,2 - 4,2,3,0 -
timp.,perc.(2),glock. (ad lib.) - hp. - str.   15:00 Composer.
—— TOM SAWYER (BALLET) (WITH NARRATOR FOR CONCERT
VERSION) %
2,2,2,2 - 4,2,3,0 - timp.,perc.,glock. - hp. - str.   50:00 Composer.

PAËR, F. - TONI, Alceo
—— OVERTURE TO "IL MAESTRO DI CAPPELLA"
2,2,2,2 - 2,0,0,0 - timp.,perc. - str.   8:00 Bo. Hawkes.

PAGANINI, Niccolò - GUSIKOFF, Michel
—— CAPRICES FOR STRING ORCH.
str.   25:00 AmerMusEd.

PAGANINI, Niccolò - KREISLER, Fritz
—— CONCERTO IN D, FOR VIOLIN AND ORCH. (IN 1 MOVT.)
2,2,2,2 - 4,2,0,1 - timp.,perc. - hp. - str.   14:00 C. Fischer.

PAGANINI, Niccolò - MARTINON, Jean
—— MOTO PERPETUO
2,2,2,2 - 4,2,0,0 - perc. - hp. - str.   4:00 Presser.

PAGANINI, Niccolò - POLO, Enrico
—— CONCERTO IN D, FOR VIOLIN AND ORCH. (IN 1 MOVT.)
2,2,2,2 - 2,2,0,0 - timp. - str.   12:00 Bo. Hawkes.

PAGANINI, Niccolò - ROSSI, M.
—— CINQUE CAPRICCI (SUITE)
2,2,2,2 - 4,3,3,0 - timp.,perc. - hp. - str.   18:00 Leeds.

PAGANINI, Niccolò - SOLITO DE SOLIS, Aldo
—— TOCCATA (BASED ON "PERPETUAL MOTION")
2,2,2,2 - 4,2,3,1 - timp. - str.   3:00 Belw-Mills.

PAGANINI, Niccolò - SOPKIN, Henry
—— PERPETUAL MOTION
2,2,2,2 - 4,4,3,1 - timp.,perc. - hp. - str.   11:00 C. Fischer.

PAGANINI, Niccolò - WEINER, L.
—— MOTO PERPETUO
2,2,2,2 - 4,2,3,1 - timp. - str.   11:00 Bo. Hawkes.

PAGE, N. Clifford
—— CAPRICE (IN 5 MOVTS.)
2,2(2nd alt. with Eng. hn.),2,2 - 4,2,3,1 - timp.,perc.(3) - hp. - str.
18:00 Composer.
—— LORD HOWE'S MASQUERADE (BALLAD) (FOR BARITONE,
CHORUS AND ORCH.)
2,2,2,2 - 4,2,3,1 - timp.,perc.(2) - str.   30:00 Ditson.
—— THE PAGEANT OF THE PILGRIMS (FOR SOLOISTS,
CHORUS AND ORCH.) %
2,2,2,2 - 4,2,3,1 - timp.,perc.(2) - str.   Ditson.
—— PETITE SUITE (SIX VILLAGE SCENES IN FRANCE)
3,2,2,2 - 4,2,3,1 - timp.,perc.(3) - str.   Composer.
—— SHANGHAI SKETCHES (MÉLANGE CHINOIS)
3(3rd alt. with picc.),*3,*3,*3 - 4,3,3,4 - timp.,perc.(4) - hp. - str.
13:00 Composer.

PAINTER, Paul
—— PETITE PASTORALE (FOR OBOE AND ORCH.)
2,2,2,2 - 4,2,3,1 - timp.,perc. - str.   6:00 C. Fischer.

PAISIBLE, James - PLATT, Richard
—— SONATA FOR 2 TRUMPETS (OR 2 OBOES) AND STRINGS
2 tpt. (or 2 ob.) - str.   Oxford.

PAISIELLO, Giovanni - BONELLI, Ettore
—— TRE QUARTETTI (FOR STRINGS)
str.   Henmar.

PAISIELLO, Giovanni - DE GUARNIERI, Francesco
—— OVERTURE TO "IL BARBIERE DI SIVIGLIA"
2,2,0,2 - 2,0,0,0 - timp. - str.   6:00 Bo. Hawkes.

PAISIELLO, Giovanni - LUALDI, Adriano
—— CONCERTO IN C FOR PIANO AND ORCH.
2,0,0,1 - 2,0,0,0 - pf. - str.   25:00 Bo. Hawkes.

PAISIELLO, Giovanni - PICCIOLI, Giuseppe
—— NINA: SINFONIA (OVERTURE)
2,0,2,2 - 2 hn. - str.   3:00 Bo. Hawkes.

—— LA SCUFFIARA: SINFONIA (OVERTURE)
2,2,0,2 - 2,2,0,0 - str.   4:00 Bo. Hawkes.
—— SINFONIA FUNEBRE (FOR THE DEATH OF POPE PIUS VI)
2,2,2,2 - 2,2,0,0 - timp. - str.   8:00 Bo. Hawkes.
—— SINFONIA IN TRE TEMPI (FOR CHORUS AND ORCH.) (IN 3 MOVTS.)
2 ob. - 2 hn. - str.   6:00 Bo. Hawkes.

PAKHMUTOVA, Aleksandra N.
—— CONCERTO FOR TRUMPET AND ORCH.
3,2,2,2 - 4,2,3,1 - timp.,perc. - hp. - str.   13:15 G. Schirmer.
—— YOUTH OVERTURE
3,2,2,2 - 4,3,3,1 - timp.,perc. - hp. - str.   6:00 G. Schirmer.

PALANGE, Louis S.
—— THE BEGINNING OF TIME (SUITE) (IN 4 MOVTS.)
*3,*3,*3,*3 - 4,3,3,1 - timp.,perc.(2),xyl. - hp. - pf. - str.
                                            20:00 Composer.
—— CONCERTO NO. 1 FOR VIOLIN AND ORCH.
2,2,2,2 - 4,2,3,1 - timp. - str.   20:00 Composer.
—— CONCERTO NO. 2 FOR VIOLIN AND ORCH.
2,2,2,2 - 4,3,3,1 - timp. - str.   23:00 Composer.
—— EVANGELINE (TONE POEM)
*3,*3,*3,*3 - 4,3,3,1 - timp. - hp. - str.   15:00 Composer.
—— MOTHER NATURE (SUITE) (IN 3 MOVTS.)
*3,*3,*3,*3 - 4,4,3,1 - timp.,perc. - hp. - pf. - str. 15:00 Composer.
—— PICTURES
1,1,1,1 - 1,1,1,0 - str.   10:00 Composer.
or:
fl. - str.
—— THE PLAGUES OF EGYPT (TONE POEM)
*3,*3,2,2 - 4,3,3,1 - timp.,perc.(2) - hp. - str.   26:00 Composer.
—— ROMANTIC CONCERTO FOR PIANO AND ORCH.
2,2,2,2 - 4,3,3,1 - timp. - pf. - str.   30:00 Composer.
—— SYMPHONY IN STEEL (IN 3 MOVTS.)
1(alt. with picc.),1,1,4 sax.,1 - 2,3,3,1 - timp.,perc.(2),xyl. - hp. - pf. - str.   20:00 Presser.
—— SYMPHONY NO. 1 "INVASION"
*3,*3,2,2 - 4,3,3,1 - timp.,perc.(2) - hp. - str.   35:00 Composer.
—— SYMPHONY NO. 2 IN E MINOR
2(2nd alt. with picc.),2,2,2 - 4,3,3,1 - timp. - hp. - str.   30:00 Composer.

PALAU, Manuel
—— TRIPTICO CATEDRALICIO
                                            26:00 S.G.A.E.

PÁLENÍČEK, Josef
—— CONCERTINO FOR CLARINET AND CHAMBER ORCH.
2,1,3,2 - 1,1,0,0 - timp.,perc. - hp. - pf. - str.   14:00 Bo. Hawkes.
—— CONCERTO FOR FLUTE AND ORCH.
2,2,2,2 - 2,2,0,0 - timp.,perc.,cel. - str.   15:00 Bo. Hawkes.
—— CONCERTO FOR SAXOPHONES AND ORCH.
0,0,2,4 sax.,0 - 0,4,4,0 - timp.,perc. - pf. - str.   22:00 Bo. Hawkes.
—— CONCERTO NO. 1 IN C, FOR PIANO AND ORCH.
2,1,0,0 - 0,1,0,0 - timp. - pf. - str.   25:00 Bo. Hawkes.
—— CONCERTO NO. 2 FOR PIANO AND ORCH.
2,2,2,2 - 3,2,2,0 - timp.,perc. - 2 hp. - pf. - str.   31:00 Bo. Hawkes.

PALESTER, Roman
—— ADAGIO FOR STRING ORCH.
str.   Southern.
—— CONCERTO FOR VIOLIN AND ORCH. (REVISED 1966)
3,2,2,2 - 3,3,3,0 - timp.,perc.(4),cel.,vibra.,xyl. - hp. - pf. - str.   21:00 MCA Music.
—— METAMORPHOSES (1967)
4,3,3,3 - 4,4,3,1 - timp.,perc.(5),bells,cel.,glock.,mar.,vibra.,xyl. - guit.mandolin - hp. - pf. - str.   20:00 MCA Music.
—— LA MORTE DI DON GIOVANNI (1-ACT OPERA) (1960) %
3,2,3,1 sax.,2 - 3,3,3,0 - timp.,perc.,bells,cel.,glock.,vibra.,xyl. - guit. - mandolin - hp. - pf. - str.   50:00 Leeds.
—— LA MORTE DI DON GIOVANNI: 3 SYMPHONIC FRAGMENTS
3,2,3,1 sax.,2 - 3,3,3,0 - timp.,perc.,bells,cel.,glock.,vibra.,xyl. - guit. - mandolin - hp. - pf. - str.   15:00 Leeds.
—— NOTTURNO (1949)
str.   10:00 MCA Music.
—— PASSACAGLIA (1953)
3,3,3,3 - 4,3,3,1 - timp.,perc.(2) - 2 hp. - pf. - str.   12:00 Leeds.
—— SYMPHONY NO. 3, FOR 2 STRING ORCHESTRAS (SINFONIA PER DUE ORCHESTRE D'ARCHI) (1950)
str.   24:00 Leeds.

—— SYMPHONY NO. 4 (1951)
3,2,2,2 - 4,3,3,1 - timp.,perc. - 2 hp. - str.   18:00 Leeds.
—— TRE SONETTI A ORFEO (3 SONNETS TO ORPHEUS) (FOR SOPRANO AND CHAMBER ORCH.) (1952)
1,1,*2,0 - 2,1,0,0 - hp. - pf. - str.   14:00 Leeds.
—— VARIAZIONI (FOR CHAMBER ORCH.) (REV. 1968)
3,3,3,2 - 4,3,3,1 - timp.,perc.(5),bells,cel.,mar.,vibra.,xyl. - hp. - pf. - str.   22:00 Leeds.

PALESTRINA, G. P. - STOKOWSKI, Leopold
—— ADORAMUS TE
1-4,*2,*3,*3 - *4,*4 - 4,3,3-4,1 - str.   2:30 Broude.

PALMA, Athos
—— LOS HIJOS DEL SOL ("THE CHILDREN OF THE SUN") (SYMPHONIC POEM) (1927)
                                            Fleisher.

PALMGREN, Selim
—— BALLAD (1930)
2,3,3,2 - 4,3,3,1 - timp.,perc.(3),cel. - hp. - str.   11:00 FinnMICtr.
—— BALLET MUSIC, OP. 105 (1944)
2,2,2,2 - 4,2,0,0 - timp.,perc.(3) - hp. - str.   16:00 Fazer.
—— CHRISTMAS EVE (FOR MALE CHORUS AND ORCH.) (1917)
(Text: J. L. Runeberg)
2,2,2,2 - 4,0,0,0 - timp.,cel. - hp. - str.   15:00 FinnMICtr.
—— COMEDY MUSIC (1937)
2,3,2,2 - 4,2,3,1 - timp.,perc. - pf.(or cel.) - str.   10:00 FinnMICtr.
—— CONCERT FANTASY FOR VIOLIN AND ORCH., OP. 104 (1945)
2,2,2,2 - 4,2,3,1 - timp.,perc.(3) - 2 hp. - str.   15:00 Fazer.
—— CONCERTO NO. 2 FOR PIANO AND ORCH., OP. 33 ("THE RIVER")
2,2,2,2 - 4,2,3,1 - timp.,perc. - pf. - str.   23:00 G. Schirmer.
—— CONCERTO NO. 3 FOR PIANO AND ORCH., OP. 41 ("METAMORPHOSE")
2,2,2,2 - 4,2,3,1 - timp. - pf. - str.   18:00 G. Schirmer.
—— CONCERTO NO. 4 FOR PIANO AND ORCH., OP. 85 ("APRIL")
3,2,2,2 - 4,2,3,1 - timp.,perc. - pf. - str.   18:30 Bo. Hawkes.
—— CONCERTO NO. 5 FOR PIANO AND ORCH., OP. 99 (1941)
2,2,2,2 - 4,2,3,1 - timp.,perc.(3) - pf. - str.   25:00 Fazer.
—— FROM FINLAND, OP. 24 (SUITE) (1908) (IN 4 MOVTS.)
2,2,2,2 - 4,3,3,1 - timp.,perc.(3) - hp. - str.   17:00 Henmar.
—— THE LILY OF TURKU (CANTATA) (FOR SOPRANO, SATB CHORUS AND ORCH.) (1929) (Text: V. A. Koskenniemi)
2,2,2,2 - 4,2,3,1 - timp. - hp. - str.   30:00 FinnMICtr.
—— LITTLE LYRICAL SUITE, OP. 51, NO. 3 (1923)
1,2,2,2 - 2,0,0,0 - timp.,perc. - str.   10:00 FinnMICtr.
—— A PASTORAL IN 3 SCENES, OP. 50
2,2,2,2 - 4,2,0,0 - timp.,perc. - str.   14:00 G. Schirmer.

PALS, Leopold van der
—— RHAPSODIE, OP. 73
3,3,3,2 - 4,3,3,1 - perc. - str.   20:00 T & J.

PANIZZA, Ettore
—— BISANZIO (3-ACT OPERA) (1938) % (Text: G. Marchi)
2,2,2,2 - 4,3,3,1 - timp.,perc. - 2 hp. - str.   Leeds.
On Stage: picc.,3 cl. - perc. - hp.
—— NOTTURNO (NOCTURNE) (1944)
3,2,2,2 - 4,4,3,1 - timp.,perc.,cel.,xyl. - 2 hp. - str.   15:00 Leeds.

PANNAIN, Guido
—— BEATRICE CENCI (3-ACT OPERA) (1941) % (Text: V, Viviani)
3,3,3,2 - 4,3,3,1 - timp.,perc.(2),cel. - 2 hp. - str.   Leeds.

PANNELL, Raymond
—— CONCERTO FOR PIANO AND ORCH. (1961) (IN 3 MOVTS.)
2,2,*3,2 - 3,2,3,0 - timp. - pf. - str.   20:00 CanMusCtr.

PANNI, Marcello
—— AGREMENS (FOR SOLO STRING INSTRUMENTS) (1969)
str.   MCA Music.
—— APRÈS TOUT (SINFONIA CONCERTANTE) (FOR STRING TRIO AND 32 INSTRUMENTS) (1970)
3,0,3,3 - 3,3,3,0 - hpsc. - hamonium - str.(6,2,2,5)   15:00 MCA Music.

PANTILLON, François
—— VISIONES (TROIS TABLEAUX) (POUR ORGUE, ORCHESTRE À CORDES ET PERCUSSION)
perc. - org. - str.   19:00 S.U.I.S.A.

PANUFNIK, Andrzej
—— AUTUMN MUSIC (1965)
    3,0,3,0 - perc.(2),cel. - hp. - pf. - str.(no vlns.) 15:00 Bo. Hawkes.
—— CONCERTO FOR PIANO AND ORCH. (REV. 1970)
    3(3rd alt. with picc.),*3,*3,*3 - 4,3,3,1 - perc.(2) - pf. - str.
        26:00 Bo. Hawkes.
—— CONCERTO FOR VIOLIN AND STRINGS
    str.   23:00 Bo. Hawkes.
—— CONCERTO IN MODO ANTICO (CONCERTO GOTICO)
    tpt. - timp. - 1-2 hp. - hpsc. - str. 15:00 Bo. Hawkes.
—— DIVERTIMENTO FOR STRING ORCH. (AFTER THE STRING
    TRIOS OF FELIX JANIEWICZ, 1762-1848)
    str.   15:00 Bo. Hawkes.
—— ELEGY
    3,2,2,2 - 4,0,0,0 - str.   7:00 Bo. Hawkes.
—— EPITAPH FOR THE VICTIMS OF KATYN
    3,2,2,2 - 0,0,0,0 - timp. - str.   8:00 Bo Hawkes.
—— HEROIC OVERTURE (REV. 1965)
    3(3rd alt. with picc.),2,*3,*3 - 4,3,3,1 - perc. - str.
        6:15 Bo. Hawkes.
—— HOMMAGE À CHOPIN
    fl. - str.   15:00 Bo. Hawkes.
—— JAGIELLONIAN TRIPTYCH (1966)
    str.   7:00 Bo. Hawkes.
—— LANDSCAPE (1965)
    str.   7:00 Bo. Hawkes.
—— LULLABY (REV. 1955)
    2 hp. - str.   8:00 Bo. Hawkes.
—— MISS JULIE (2-ACT BALLET) % (WITH SATB CHORUS)
    3(3rd alt. with picc.),2,3(3rd alt. with b.-cl.),*3 - 4,3,3,1 -
    timp.,perc.(4),cel.,glock. - hp. - pf. - str. 90:00 Bo. Hawkes.
—— NOCTURNE (REVISED 1955)
    3(3rd alt. with picc.),2*3,*3 - 4,3,3,1 - timp., perc. - pf. - str.
        15:00 Bo. Hawkes.
—— OLD POLISH SUITE (IN 3 MOVTS.)
    str.   12:00 Bo. Hawkes.
—— POLONIA (SUITE OF POLISH SONGS AND DANCES) (1959)
    2(2nd alt. with picc.),2,2,2 - 4,2,3,0 - perc.(2) - str.
        20:00 Bo. Hawkes.
—— RHAPSODY (1956)
    *3,*3,*3,*3 - 4,2,1,1 - timp.,perc. - pf. - str. 17:00 Bo. Hawkes.
—— SINFONIA ELEGIACA (SINFONIA PACE) (REVISED 1966)
    *3,*3,*3,*3 - 4,3,3,1 - timp.,perc.(4) - hp. - str.
        24:00 Bo. Hawkes.
—— SINFONIA RUSTICA (REVISED 1955)
    1,2,0,2 - 2,1,0,0 - str.   23:00 Bo. Hawkes.
—— SINFONIA SACRA (1963)
    *3,*3,*3,*3 - 4,4,3,1 - timp.,perc.(4) - str. 22:00 Bo. Hawkes.
—— TRAGIC OVERTURE
    3(3rd alt. with picc.),0,*3,*3 - 4,3,3,1 - perc.(3) - str.
        7:00 Bo. Hawkes.
—— TWO LYRIC PIECES
    0,0,3,1 - 1,1,1,0 - str.   8:00 Bo. Hawkes.
    or:
    0,0,2,0 - 2,0,0,0 - str.

PANULA, Jorma
—— BELLS (A FANTASY) (1965)
    2,2,2,2 - 3,3,3,0 - hp. - str.   5:00 FinnMICtr.
—— CONCERTO FOR VIOLIN AND ORCH. (1954)
    2,2,2,2 - 4,2,3,0 - timp.(2 players) - str. 17:00 FinnMICtr.
—— L' HEURE BLEUE (FOR JAZZ BAND AND ORCH.) (1967)
    2,1,3,ten.,sax.,0 - 4,0,0,0 - perc.,cel. - hp. - pf. - str.
        5:00 FinnMICtr.
—— JAZZ CAPRICCIO (FOR PIANO AND ORCH.) (1965)
    2,2,2,2 - 4,2,3,0 - timp.,perc.(3) - pf. - str. 6:00 FinnMICtr.
—— MUSIC FOR PIANO AND STRINGS (1956)
    pf. - str.   8:00 FinnMICtr.
—— MUSIC FOR STRINGS AND PIANO (1955)
    pf. - str.   5:00 FinnMICtr.
—— MUSIC TO ALEKSIS KIVI'S PLAY "THE SEVEN BROTHERS"
    (1953)
    1,1,2,1 - 2,2,1,0 - str.   15:00 FinnMICtr.
—— MUSIC TO THE PLAY "THE WALTZ OF THE TOREADORS"
    (1954)
    1,1,2,1 - 2,2,1,0 - str.   10:00 FinnMICtr.
—— AN ORCHESTRA GUIDE (1965)
    2,2,2,2 - 3,3,3,0 - hp. - str.   7:00 FinnMICtr.
—— PER ARCHI (1965)
    str.   5:00 FinnMICtr.
—— SAMPANI GALOPPI (FANTASY) (1965)
    2,2,2,2 - 3,3,3,0 - hp. - str.   4:00 FinnMICtr.

—— THE SERVANT OF TWO MASTERS (AN OVERTURE) (1966)
    2,2,2,2 - 4,3,3,0 - timp.,perc. - hp. - hpsc. - str. 5:00 FinnMICtr.
—— SOUTH OSTROBOTHNIAN RHAPSODY (1951)
    1,1,2,0 - 2,2,1,0 - str.   12:00 FinnMICtr.
—— SOUTH OSTROBOTHNIAN SUITE (FOR SATB CHORUS AND
    ORCH.) (1954)
    1,1,1,1 - 1,1,1,0 - str.   15:00 FinnMICtr.
—— STEEL SYMPHONY (FOR SATB CHORUS, WINDS, BRASS
    AND PERCUSSION) (1969) (Text: Paavilainen)
    1,0,3,1 - 0,1,2,0 - perc.(2)   9:00 FinnMICtr.
—— SUITE FROM THE PLAY "DANIEL HJORT" (1957)
    2,2,2,2 - 4,3,3,1 - timp.(2 players) - str. 16:00 FinnMICtr.

PAPAIOANNOU, Yannis A.
—— CONCERTO FOR ORCH.
    1,*2,*2,1 - 4,1,2,1 - timp. - str.   20:00 Modern.

PAPANDOPULO, Boris
—— HOMAGE TO BACH (FOR LARGE ORCH.)
        Hans Gerig.

PAPAVOINE - BOULAY, Laurence
—— SYMPHONY NO. 4 (IN 3 MOVTS.)
    hpsc. - str.   7:00 Eds. Fran.

PAPP, Lajos
—— DIALOGUES FOR PIANO AND ORCH.
        15:00 Bo. Hawkes.

PARAĆ, Frano
—— OBOE SOMMERSO (FOR OBOE, MEZZO-SOPRANO AND
    CHAMBER ENSEMBLE) (1973)
    1,*2,*2,1 - 0,0,0,0 - perc.(2) - guit. - vla.,c. 13:30 MIC,Zagreb.

PARADISI, Pietro Domenico - TONI, Alceo
—— ARIA E TOCCATA
    2,2,2,2 - 2,0,0,0 - str.   7:00 Bo. Hawkes.

PARAY, Paul
—— FANTASY FOR PIANO AND ORCH.
    2,2,2,2 - 4,2,3,1 - pf. - str.   14:00 EV.
—— FANTASY FOR PIANO, WINDS AND PERCUSSION
    2,2,2,2 - 3,1,3,1 - timp.,perc. - pf.   13:00 EV.
—— MASS (FOR SOLO VOICES, CHORUS AND ORCH.)
    3,3,3,3 - 4,3,3,1 - timp. - hp. - org. - str. 36:00 Lemoine.
—— SYMPHONIE D'ARCHETS
    str.   23:00 EV.
—— SYMPHONY NO. 1 IN C
    3,*3,3,3 - 4,3,3,1 - timp.,perc. - 2 hp. - str. 31:00 EV.
—— SYMPHONY NO. 2 IN A MAJOR
        40:00 S.A.C.E.M.

PARCHMAN, Gen Louis
—— ADAGIO FOR STRINGS (1962)
    str.   5:00 Seesaw.
—— CONCERTO FOR MARIMBA AND ORCH., OP. 71 (1969)
    1. Adagio; 2. Allegro; 3. Adagio; 4. Allegro
    *3,*3,*3,*3 - 4,4,3,1 - timp.,perc.(4),mar. - str. 20:00 Mills.
—— CONCERTO FOR ONE PERCUSSIONIST AND ORCH., OP. 80
    (1967)
    1. Adagio; 2. Allegro; 3. Allegro
    *3,*3,*3,*3 - 4,3,3,1 - timp.,perc.(4) - hp. - str. 13:00 Seesaw.
—— CONCERTO FOR PIANO AND ORCH.
    3,3,3,3 - 4,2,3,1 - timp.,perc. - pf. - str. 20:00 Composer.
—— CONCERTO FOR PIANO 4-HANDS AND ORCH. (OR FOR 2
    PIANOS AND ORCH.)
    3,3,3,3 - 4,3,2,1 - timp.,perc.(3) - 1-2 pf. - str. 13:00 Seesaw.
—— CONCERTO FOR SOPRANO (OR TENOR) AND
    ORCHESTRA. (1972)
    3,3,3,3 - 4,4,3,1 - timp.,perc.(4) - hp. - str. 15:00 Seesaw.
—— CONCERTO FOR TIMPANI AND ORCHESTRA, OP. 66 (1963)
    *3,*3,*3,*3 - 4,3,3,1 - timp.,perc.(3) - str. 7:00 Seesaw.
—— CONCERTO NO. 1 FOR PERCUSSION ENSEMBLE AND
    ORCH.
    1. Adagio; 2. Allegretto; 3. Allegro
    *3,*3,*3,*3 - 4,3,3,1 - timp.,perc.(5) - str. 11:00 Seesaw.
—— CONCERTO NO. 2 FOR PERCUSSION ENSEMBLE AND
    ORCH. (1962)
    1. Adagio; 2. Allegretto; 3. Allegro
    3,3,3,2 - 4,3,3,1 - timp.,perc.(7) - str. 11:00 Seesaw.
—— CONCERTO NO. 2 FOR TWO PIANOS AND ORCH. (1963)
        13:00 Seesaw.

—— DRAMATIC OVERTURE (1965)
    3,3,3,3 - 4,4,2,2 - timp.,perc.(4) - str.   5:00 Seesaw.
—— ELEGY FOR ORCHESTRA (1960)
    2,2,2,2 - 4,3,3,1 - perc.(3) - str.   5:00 Seesaw.
—— ESSAY FOR ORCHESTRA (1964)
    3,3,3,3 - 4,4,2,1 - timp.,perc.(4) - str.   5:00 Seesaw.
—— HISTORY OF MUSIC (FOR NARRATOR AND ORCH.) (1965)
(Text: Composer)
    Seesaw.
—— LITTLE FUGUE FOR ORCH. (1962)
    3,2,3,3 - 4,3,4,1 - timp.,perc.(3) - str.   3:00 Seesaw.
—— OVERTURE '56
    2,2,2,2 - 4,2,3,1 - str.   5:00 Composer.
—— PETITE SYMPHONY FOR STRINGS (1962) (SYMPHONY NO. 2 FOR STRINGS)
    str.   9:13 Seesaw.
—— PRELUDE AND FUGUE
    3,2,2,2 - 4,3,3,1 - timp.,perc.(3) - str.   11:00 EV.
    or:
    3,3,3,3 - 4,2,3,1 - str.
—— SONATA FOR LITTLE SYMPHONY
    *2,1,1,1 - 1,1,1,0 - timp.,sn.dr. - str.   16:00 Seesaw.
—— STUDY FOR ORCHESTRA (1968)
    3,3,3,3 - 4,3,3,2 - timp.,perc.(4) - hp. - str.   8:00 Seesaw.
—— SYMPHONY FOR CHORUS AND ORCH., OP. 82 (SPRING SYMPHONY) (1968) (IN 3 MOVTS.) (Text: Dr. Dallas Wiebe)
    *3,*3,*3,*3 - 4,4,3,1 - timp.,perc.(3) - str.   18:00 Seesaw.
—— SYMPHONY FOR CHORUS AND ORCH. (1968)
    3,2,3,3 - 4,4,3,1 - timp.,perc.(4) - hp. - str.   18:00 Seesaw.
—— SYMPHONY FOR STRINGS (1961) (IN 5 MOVTS.)
    str.   20:00 Seesaw.
—— SYMPHONY NO. 3 (1962) (IN 3 MOVTS.)
    *3,*3,3,3 - 4,3,3,1 - timp.,perc. - str.   26:00 Seesaw.
—— TWELVE VARIATIONS ON AN ORIGINAL THEME (FOR 2 PIANOS AND ORCH.)
    2,2,2,2 - 2,3,2,1 - timp.,perc.(3) - 2 pf. - str.   17:00 Seesaw.
—— VIOLIN OVERTURE (FOR VIOLIN AND ORCH.) (1957)
    3,3,3,3 - 4,3,2,1 - timp.,perc.(3) - str.   9:00 Seesaw.
—— WINSEL OVERTURE (REV. 1962)
    *3,*3,*3,*3 - 4,3,3,1 - timp.,perc.(3) - str.   5:00 Seesaw.

PARFREY, Raymond
—— MINIATURE SUITE FOR ORCH. ("TWICE TWO") (1965)
    2,2,2,2 - 2,2,2,0 - timp.,perc. - str.   11:00 P.R.S.
—— TWO HOBBIES (1967)
    2,0-2,2,0-2 - 3,2,2,0 - timp.,perc. - str.   8:00 P.R.S.

PARK, Stephen
—— CONCERTO GROSSO (FOR VIOLIN, CELLO, OBOE AND ORCH.)
    1. Allegro con brio; 2. Allegretto con moto; 3. Adagio
    1,1,0,1 - 1,0,0,0 - timp. - hp. or pf. - str.   23:00 Composer.
—— CONCERTO NO. 1 IN A FLAT, FOR PIANO AND ORCH.
    1. Allegro maestoso; 2. Andante con moto; 3. Andante
    2,1,2,1 - 2,2,1,0 - timp.,perc.(2) - pf. - str.   41:00 Composer.
—— CONCERTO NO. 2 FOR PIANO AND ORCH. (IN 1 MOVT.)
    *3,2,*3,2 - 4,3,3,1 - timp.,perc.(3),glock. - hp. - pf. - str.   21:00 Composer.
—— EGA CIMOTA OVERTURE
    *4,2,2,2 - 4,3,3,1 - timp.,perc.(3),xyl. - pf. - str.   6:30 Composer.
—— FOR THE UNCREATED (A CHORAL SYMPHONY) (FOR SATB SOLO, SATB CHORUS AND ORCH.) (Text: William Daugherty)
    1. Andante moderato; 2. Andante; 3. Andante
    2,*3,2,1 - 4,2,2,0 - timp.,perc.(3) - str.   42:00 Composer.
—— JUBILATE (FOR TWO PIANOS AND ORCH.)
    2,2,2,2 - 4,3,3,1 - timp.,perc.(3),bells,xyl. - 2 pf. - str.   14:00 Composer.
—— SUITE FOR CLARINET AND STRINGS (IN 4 MOVTS.)
    cl. - str.   24:30 Composer.
—— SYMPHONY NO. 1
    1. Lento - Allegro; 2. Allegretto con grazioso; 3. Moderately slow
    2,1,2,1 - 2,2,1,0 - timp. - str.   32:00 Composer.
—— SYMPHONY NO. 3
    1. Adagio - Allegretto - Andante; 2. Andante - Allegro
    *3,*3,*3,2 - 4,3,3,1 - timp.,perc.(4),cel.,xyl. - str.   22:30 Composer.

PARKER, Alice
—— CHRISTMAS MUSIC (FOR MIXED CHORUS AND ORCH.) (IN 3 MOVTS.)
    2,0,2,0 - 0,0,0,0 - str.   30:00 Composer.

—— JOURNEYS (FOR SOPRANO, BARITONE, SATB CHORUS AND ORCH.) (1976) (IN 4 MOVTS.)
    *3,*3,*3,*1 - 4,2,3,1 - timp.,perc.(8,incl. 4 on timp.) - hp. - str.
    plus Jazz Band.   50:00 Hinshaw.
—— SEVEN CAROLS FOR CHRISTMAS (FOR SATB CHORUS AND ORCH.)
    3,2,3,2 - 4,2,2,1 - timp.,perc. - hp. - str.   17:25 C. Fischer.

PARKER, Clifton
—— OVERTURE: "THIEVES' CARNIVAL"
    2,2,2,2 - 2,2,0,0 - timp.,perc. - hp. (ad lib.) - str.   4:00 Oxford.
—— PHANTASY SUITE
    2,2,2,2 sax.,(ad lib.),2 - 4,2,3,0 - timp.,perc.,cel. - pf. - str.
    14:00 Bo. Hawkes.

PARKER, Horatio
—— MONA (OPERA) % (Text: Brian Hooker)
    G. Schirmer.

PARODI, Renato
—— PRELUDIO AD'UNA COMEDIA
    3,2,3,2 - 4,3,3,1 - timp.,perc. - hp. - str.   Salabert.

PARRIS, Herman M.
—— AKIBA SYMPHONY (SYMPHONY NO. 1) (IN 1 MOVT.)
    *3,*3,3,2 - 4,3,3,1 - timp.,perc.(3) - hp. - str.   Composer.
—— CONCERTINO FOR PIANO AND CHAMBER ORCH. (IN 3 MOVTS.)
    1,1,1,1 - 1,1,1,0 - timp. - pf. - str.   15:00 Composer.
—— CONCERTO FOR DOUBLES (SOLOISTS: 1st Movt., alto sax.; 2nd Movt., b.-cl.; 3rd Movt., cl. (alt. with b.-cl.)
    1,1,*5,4 sax.,1(alt. with bar. sax.) - 0,4,3,1 - timp.,perc.(3) - guit. - pf. - str.   Composer.
—— CONCERTO FOR VIOLIN AND ORCH.
    *3,2,2,2 - 4,2,3,1 - timp.,perc.(1) - str.   Composer.
—— CONCERTO NO. 1 FOR PIANO AND ORCH. (IN 1 MOVT.)
    2,2,2,2 - 4,2,3,0 - timp.,perc.(2),xyl. - pf. - str.   Composer.
—— CONCERTO NO. 2 FOR PIANO AND ORCH. (IN 1 MOVT.)
    *3,2,2,2 - 4,2,3,1 - timp.,perc.(2) - pf. - str.   Composer.
—— CONCERTO NO. 3 FOR PIANO AND ORCH. (IN 3 MOVTS.)
    2(2nd alt. with picc.)2(2nd alt. with Eng.hn.),2,2 - 4,2,3,1 - timp.,perc.(3),cel.,glock.,xyl. - pf. - str.   40:00 Composer.
—— CONCERTO NO. 4 FOR PIANO AND ORCH. (IN 1 MOVT)
    *4,*3,*3,*3 - 4,3,3,1 - timp.,perc.(2) - pf. - str.   Composer.
—— CONCERTO NO. 5 FOR PIANO AND ORCH. ("AMERICAN") (IN 3 MOVTS.)
    2,2,2,2 - 4,2,3,1 - timp.,perc.,xyl. - pf. - str.   Composer.
—— CONCERTO NO. 6 FOR PIANO AND ORCH. (IN 3 MOVTS.)
    *3,2,2,2 - 4,2,3,1 - timp.,perc.(2) - pf. - str.   Composer.
—— CONCERTO NO. 7 FOR PIANO AND ORCH.
    H. Elkan.
—— CONCERTO NO. 8 FOR PIANO AND ORCH.
    H. Elkan.
—— DIALOGUE (FOR BASS CLARINET AND CHAMBER ORCH.)
    1,1,*2,1 - 2,1,0,0 - timp. - str.   Composer.
—— ELEGIAC OVERTURE (FOR STRINGS)
    str.   Composer.
—— FOUR ETCHINGS
    2,2,2,2 - 2,2,1,0 - timp.,perc.(2) - str.   Composer.
—— THE HOSPITAL (SUITE)
    2,2,2,2 - 4,3,3,1 - perc. - hp. - str.   12:00 H. Elkan.
—— IN MEMORIAM
    2,*3,2,2 - 4,3,3,1 - timp. - str.   7:00 Composer.
—— INVOCATION AND LAMENTATION (FOR CELLO AND ORCH.)
    2,2,2,2 - 4,2,3,1 - timp. ,perc.(1) - str.   Composer.
—— LAMENT (IN MEMORY OF OLIN DOWNES)
    str.   8:00 H. Elkan.
—— NOCTURNE (FOR BASS CLARINET AND ORCH.)
    2,2,*3,2 - 4,3,3,1 - timp. - str.   Composer.
—— NOCTURNE (FOR CLARINET AND STRINGS)
    cl. - str.   Composer.
—— NOCTURNE FOR STRING ORCH.
    str.   H. Elkan.
—— OVERTURE AMERICA
    3,*3,2,2 - 4,3,3,1 - timp.,perc. - str.   7:00 H. Elkan.
—— RHAPSODY NO. 1 FOR ORCH. (HEBREW RHAPSODY)
    *4,*3,*3,*3 - 4,3,3,1 - timp. - perc. - hp. - str.   Composer.
—— RHAPSODY NO. 2 FOR ORCH. ("HEART RHAPSODY")
    *3,*3*3,2 - 4,3,3,1 - timp.,perc.(2) - str.   Composer.
—— A SHORT STORY
    *3,2,2,2 - 4,2,3,1 - timp.,perc.(2),glock. - str.   Composer.

—— SUITE FOR PIANO AND STRINGS
    pf. - str.   H. Elkan.
—— SUITE FOR STRINGS (IN 5 MOVTS.)
    str.   H. Elkan.
—— SYMPHONY NO. 2
    2,2,2,2 - 4,2,3,1 - timp. - str.   H. Elkan.
—— SYMPHONY NO. 3 (IN 1 MOVT.)
    *3,*3,*3,*3 - 4,3,3,1 - timp.,perc.(2) - hp. - str.   Composer.
—— SYMPHONY NO. 4 (IN 2 MOVTS.)
    *4,*3,*3,*3 - 4,3,3,1 - timp.,perc.(2) - hp. - pf. - str.   Composer.
—— THREE ORCHESTRAL ABSTRACTS
    2,2,2,2 - 4,3,3,1 - timp.,perc.(3),vibra.,xyl. - hp. - pf. - str.
                 20:00 H. Elkan.
—— THE TWENTY-NINTH PSALM OF DAVID (FOR WOMEN'S
  CHORUS AND ORCH.)
                 H. Elkan.

PARRISH, Carl
—— PAGEANT MUSIC
    3,2,2,2 - 4,3,3,1 - timp.,perc. - str.   8:00 C. Fischer.

PARROTT, Ian H.
—— CONCERTO BREVE FOR CELLO AND ORCH. (1961)
    2,3,3,2 - 2,2,1,0 - timp.,perc.,cel. - hp. - pf. - str. 14:00 Novello.
—— CONCERTO FOR ENGLISH HORN AND ORCH.
    3,*2,2,2 - 2,2,1,0 - timp.,perc. - hp. - str.   20:00 Novello.
—— CONCERTO FOR PIANO AND ORCH.
    1,1,1,1 - 2,1,0,0 - timp.,perc.,glock. - pf. - str.   30:00 Novello.
—— EL ALAMEIN (SYMPHONIC PRELUDE)
    2(2nd alt. with picc.),1,1,1 - 4,3,3,1 - timp.,perc. - hp. - str.
                 9:00 Novello.
—— Y FAIR THREE LADIES (SUITE)
    *2,1,2,1 - 2,2,1,0 - timp.,perc.,glock.,xyl. - hp. - str.
                 13:00 Novello.
—— FOUR SHAKESPEARE DANCES
    3,3,2,2 - 4,2,3,1 - timp.,perc.,glock.,xyl. - hp. - str. 12:00 Novello.
—— LUXOR
    2,2,2,2 - 4,3,3,1 - timp.,perc.,cel. - pf. - str. 15:00 Lengnick.
—— PSALM 91 (FOR BASS, CHORUS AND ORCH.)
    2,2,2,2 - 4,3,3,1 - timp.,perc.,cel. - hp. - org.(ad. lib.) - str.
                 15:00 Lengnick.
—— ROMEO AND JULIET (SOLEMN OVERTURE)
    2(2nd alt. with picc.),2,2,2 - 4,2,3,1 - timp.,perc.,cel. - hp. - str.
                 14:00 Novello.
—— SEITHENIN (CONCERT OVERTURE) (1959)
    3,2,2,2 - 4,2,3,0 - timp.,perc.,xyl. - hp. - pf. - str. 8:00 Novello.
—— SOLEMN OVERTURE: "ROMEO AND JULIET"
    2,2,2,2 - 2,2,3,1 - timp.,perc.(3) - hp. - str.   10:00 Novello.
—— SUITE FOR VIOLIN AND ORCH.
    2(2nd alt. with picc.),1,2,2 - 4,2,3,0 - timp.,perc.,glock.,xyl. - hp. - str.
                 9:00 Novello.
—— SYMPHONY NO. 2 ("ROUND THE WORLD") (1960)
    3,3,2,2 - 4,3,3,1 - timp.,perc., cel.,glock.,xyl. - hp. - pf. - str.
                 30:00 Novello.
—— THREE MOORISH PRINCESSES (FOR NARRATOR AND
  ORCH.)
    2,1,2,1 - 2,2,1,0 - timp.,perc.,glock. - str.   17:00 Novello.
—— VARIATIONS ON A THEME OF DUFAY
    3,2,2,2 - 2,3,3,0 - timp.,perc.,cel.,glock.,xyl. - hp. - str.
                 12:00 Novello.

PARRY, C. H. H.
—— AN ENGLISH SUITE (FOR STRINGS)
    str.   14:00 Novello.
—— JERUSALEM (FOR MIXED CHORUS AND ORCH.)
                 G. Schirmer.

PARRY, C. H. H. - FINZI, Gerald
—— CHORAL FANTASIA ON "WHEN I SURVEY THE
  WONDROUS CROSS"
    str.   Novello.

PARRY, Roland
—— ALL FACES WEST (MUSIC-DRAMA) % (Text: Helen Parry)
    2(2nd alt with picc.),2(2nd alt. with Eng.hn),2,2 - 4,3,3,1 -
    timp.,perc.(2),bells,glock. - str.   120:00 Composer.
—— A CHILD IS BORN (A CHRISTMAS MUSIC-DRAMA) %
    2,1,2,2 - 4,3,3,1 - timp.,perc.,bells - 4 pf. - str. 80:00 Composer.
—— SCUM OF THE EARTH (CANTATA) (FOR NARRATOR,
  SOPRANO, TENOR, BARITONE, CHORUS AND ORCH.)
  (Text: Robert H. Schauffler)
    2(2nd alt. with picc.),2(2nd alt. with Eng.hn),2,2 - 4,3,3,1 -
    timp.,perc.(1),bells - str.   20:00 Composer.

PARTOS, Oedoen
—— CANTATA (FOR SOPRANO, MIXED CHORUS AND ORCH.)
  (Text: Ch. N. Bialik)
    3,1,2,1 - 4,3,3,1 - perc.,cel. - hp. - pf. -str. 10:00 Bo. Hawkes.
—— CONCERTINO FOR STRING ORCH.
    str.   9:00 IsMuPublns.
—— CONCERTO FOR VIOLIN AND ORCHESTRA
    3,3,3,2 - 4,3,3,1 - perc.,cel. - hp. - str. 30:00 Bo. Hawkes.
—— CONCERTO NO. 2 FOR VIOLA AND ORCH.
    2,2,2,2 - 3,2,1,0 - timp.,perc. - pf. - str. 22:00 IsMuPublns.
—— EIN GEV (SYMPHONIC FANTASY)
    3,3,3,2 - 4,3,3,1 - timp.,perc. - hp. - str. 15:00 IsMuPublns.
—— IMAGES ("DEMUYOT")
    3,*3,*3,0 - 4,3,3,1 - timp.,perc.,cel.,xyl. - pf. - str.
                 18:00 IsMuPublns.
—— ORIENTAL BALLAD (FOR CELLO OR VIOLA WITH ORCH.)
    2,2,2,2 - 4,2,3,0 - timp.,perc.,cel. - hp. - str. 7:00 IsMuPublns.
—— ORIENTAL BALLAD (FOR VIOLA OR CELLO WITH ORCH.)
    2,2,*3,2 - 4,2,2,1 - timp.,perc.,cel. - hp. - str. 7:00 IsMuPublns.
—— PATHS (NETIVIM)
    3,3,3,3 - 4,3,3,1 - timp.,perc.,cel. - hp. - str. 16:00 Bo. Hawkes.
—— RABAT ISRARUNI (FOR MIXED CHORUS AND CHAMBER
  ORCH.)
    1,1,1,1 - 1,0,0,0 - perc.(1) - pf. - str. 9:00 Bo. Hawkes.
—— SINFONIA CONCERTANTE FOR VIOLA AND ORCH.
    3,3,3,3 - 4,3,3,1 - perc.(4) - hp. - pf. - str. 20:00 Bo. Hawkes.
—— SONG OF PRAISE (CONCERTO FOR VIOLA AND ORCH.)
    3,3,3,2 - 4,3,3,1 - timp.,perc. - hp. - str. 25:00 IsMuPublns.
—— SYMPHONIC MOVEMENTS
    3,3,3,3 - 4,3,3,1 - timp.,perc.(4),cel. - hp. - pf. 16:00 Bo. Hawkes.
—— TEHILIM
    str.(no d.-b.)   22:00 Bo. Hawkes.
—— VISIONS (RECITATIVE, INVOCATION AND DANCE)
    fl. - pf. - str.   16:00 IsMuPublns.
—— YISKOR (IN MEMORIAM) (FOR VIOLA AND STRINGS)
    str.   9:00 IsMuPublns.

PASATIERI, Thomas
—— LA DIVINA (1-ACT OPERA BUFFA) (1965) % (Text: Composer)
    2(2nd alt. with picc.),2(2nd alt. with Eng.hn.),2,2 - 2,1,1,0 -
    timp.,perc.(2),cel. - hp. - pf. - str.   25:00 Presser.
—— INVOCATION FOR ORCHESTRA (1968)
    2(2nd alt. with picc.),2,2,2(2nd alt. with c.-bn.) - 4,2,2,1 -
    timp.,perc.(2) - hp. - str.   12:00 Presser.
—— PADRE VIA (1-ACT LYRIC TRAGEDY) (1966) % (Text:
  Composer)
    1,1,1,1 - 1,1,1,0 - timp.,perc.(2) - hp. - pf. - str. 50:00 Presser.
—— THE PENITENTES (3-ACT OPERA) (1967) % (Text: Anne H.
  Bailey)
    2(2nd alt. with picc.),2(2nd alt. with Eng.hn.),2,2(2nd alt. with
    c.-bn.) - 4,2,2,1 - timp.,perc.(3),bells - hp. - pf. - str.
                 130:00 Belw-Mills.
—— PERMIT ME VOYAGE (SELECTIONS FROM THE WORKS OF
  JAMES AGEE) (FOR SOPRANO, SATB CHORUS AND
  ORCH.)
    *3,*3,*3,*3 - 4,2,2,1 - timp.,perc.(3) - hp. - str. 16:00 Belw-Mills.
—— RITES DE PASSAGE (FOR MEDIUM VOICE AND ORCH.)
    2(2nd alt. ad lib. with picc.),2,2,2 - 2,1,1,0 - timp.,perc. - hp. - str.
                 11:00 Belw-Mills.
—— THE WOMEN (1-ACT CHAMBER OPERA) (1965) % (Text:
  Composer)
    1(alt. with picc.),1,1,1(alt. with c.-bn.) - 1,1,1,0 - timp.,perc.(1) -
    hp. - pf. - str.   14:00 Presser.

PASCAL, André
—— CONCERTINO FOR VIOLIN AND ORCH.
    2,2,2,2 - 2,2,0,0 - timp.,perc.,cel. - hp. - str.   7:00 EV.

PASCAL, Claude
—— CONCERTO FOR CELLO AND ORCH.
    2(1st. alt. with picc.),2(2nd alt. with Eng.hn.),2,2 - 4,3,3,1 -
    timp.,perc.,cel. - hp. - str.   25:00 EV.
—— CONCERTO FOR HARP AND ORCH.
    1,1,1,1 - 2,1,1,0 - timp.,perc.(3) - hp. - str.   19:00 EV.
—— CONCERTO FOR PIANO AND CHAMBER ORCH.
    2 hn. - timp. - pf. - str.   18:00 EV.
—— OVERTURE FOR A FAIRY TALE
    2,2,2,2 - 3,3,3,0 - timp.,perc. - hp. - pf. - str.   4:00 EV.

PASQUALI, N. - CARSE, Adam
—— OVERTURE TO "THE TEMPLE OF PEACE"
    0,2,0,2 - 2,2,0,0 - timp. - str.   5:00 Galaxy.
    or:

2,0,0,2 - 2,2,0,0 - timp. - str.

PASQUET, Jean
—— CONCERTINO IN G MINOR, FOR 2 PIANOS (OR PIANO 4-HANDS) AND ORCH. (IN 3 MOVTS.)
    2,2,2,2 - 2,2,3,1 - timp. - 1-2 pf. - str.   16:00 J. Fischer.
—— EXHORTATION OF THE DAWN (FOR MIXED CHORUS AND ORCH.)
    2,1,2,1 - 2,2,3,0 - timp. - str.   13:00 Composer.
—— LOUISIANA SKETCHES (SUITE) (IN 3 MOVTS.)
    *3,1,2,2 - 2,2,3,0 - hp. - str.   20:00 Composer.

PASSANI, Émile
—— AMOUR ET GRAMMAIRE (SIX SONGS FOR SOPRANO AND ORCH.) (Text: Nino)
    3,2,2,2 - 2,2,3,0 - timp.,perc.,bells,cel.,glock.,xyl. - hp. - str.
     15:00 EV.
—— CONCERTINO FOR OBOE AND ORCH.
    2,1,2,2 - 2,1,0,0 - perc.,bells,cel. - hp. - str.   Presser.
—— CONCERTO FOR CELLO AND ORCH.
     EV.
—— CONCERTO FOR FLUTE AND ORCH.
     Baron.
—— CONCERTO FOR HORN AND STRINGS
    hn. - str.   22:00 Presser.
—— GOURMANDISES PROVENÇALES
    2,1,2,1 - 1,2,1,0 - timp., perc. - str.   20:00 Presser.
—— RAPSODIE PROVENÇALE (FOR PIANO AND ORCH.)
    3,2,2,2 - 3,2,3,1 - timp.,perc.(3),bells,cel. - pf. - str.   10:00 EV.
—— SUITE IN D (IN 4 MOVTS.)
     EV.

PATACHICH, Iván
—— BALKAN SUITE
    2,2,2,2 - 4,3,3,0 - timp.,perc. - hp. - str.   13:00 Bo. Hawkes.
—— CONCERTO FOR HARP AND ORCH.
    2,1,2,1 - 3,2,1,0 - timp.,perc.,cel. - hp. - str.   19:00 Bo. Hawkes.
—— DIVERTIMENTO (PETITE SUITE)
    2,2,2,2 - 4,3,3,0 - timp.,perc. - hp. - pf. - str.   Bo. Hawkes.
—— HUNGARIAN SUITE
    2,2,2,2 - 4,3,3,0 - timp.,perc. - str.   Bo. Hawkes.
—— SERENADE FOR STRING ORCH.
    str.   Bo. Hawkes.

PATIN, Yonel
—— SINFONIA BREVE
    2,2,2,1 alto sax.,2 - 2,2,1,0 - timp. - str.   13:15 Mills.

PATINO ANDRADE, Graciela
—— DOS BOCETOS SINFONICOS
    3,2,3,3 - 4,3,3,1 - timp.,perc. - str.   9:00 Bo. Hawkes.

PATTERSON, Paul
—— THE CIRCULAR RUINS (1975)
    2,2,2,2 - 4,4,3,1 - timp.,perc. - str.   Bo. Hawkes.
—— CONCERTANTE (1970)
    1,1,1,1 - 1,1,1,0 - timp.,perc.(3) - str.   14:00 Bo. Hawkes.
—— CONCERTO FOR HORN AND STRINGS (1971)
    hn. - str.   20:00 Bo. Hawkes.
—— CONCERTO FOR TRUMPET, TIMPANI AND STRINGS (1969)
    tpt. - timp. - str.   15:00 Bo. Hawkes.
—— FIESTA SINFONICA (1972)
    2,2,2,2 - 4,2,3,1 - timp.,perc.(4) - str.   11:00 Bo. Hawkes.
—— FUSIONS (1974)
    2,2,2,2 - 4,3,3,1 - perc.(3) - tape-recorder(stereo) - str.
     10:00 Bo. Hawkes.
—— PARTITA (1970)
    0,2,0,0 - 2,0,0,0 - str.   16:00 Bo. Hawkes.
—— PICCOLA SINFONIA (FOR STRING ORCH.) (1971)
    str.   20:00 Bo. Hawkes.
—— REQUIEM (FOR SATB CHORUS AND ORCH.) (1975)
    2,2,2,2 - 4,3,3,1 - timp.,perc.(5) - str.   46:00 Bo. Hawkes.
—— SONORS (1973)
    2,2,2,2 - 4,3,3,1 - timp.,perc.(5) - str.   12:00 Bo. Hawkes.
—— STRANGE MEETING (1975)
    3,3,3,3 - 4,3,3,1 - timp.,perc.(5) - tape-recorder - str.
     11:00 Bo. Hawkes.
—— SYMPHONIC STUDY NO. 2 (1971)
    2,2,2,2 - 4,2,3,0 - timp.,perc. - hp. - str.   12:00 Bo. Hawkes.

PAUER, Jiří
—— COMEDY SUITE
    1,1,1,1 - 1,1,1,1 - timp.,perc. - hp. - str.   10:00 Bo. Hawkes.

—— CONCERTO FOR BASSOON AND ORCH.
    2,2,2,3 - 2,2,0,0 - timp.,perc.,cel. - str.   28:00 Bo. Hawkes.
—— CONCERTO FOR HORN AND ORCH.
    2,2,2,2 - 4,3,0,0 - timp.,perc.,cel. - str.   16:00 Bo. Hawkes.
—— CONCERTO FOR OBOE AND ORCH.
    2,1,2,2 - 2,0,0,0 - timp. - str.   28:00 Bo. Hawkes.
—— RHAPSODY FOR ORCH.
    2,2,2,2 - 4,3,3,0 - timp.,perc. - hp. - str.   20:00 Bo. Hawkes.
—— SCHERZO FOR ORCH.
    3,2,2,2 - 4,3,3,1 - timp.,perc. - str.   9:00 Bo. Hawkes.
—— SUITE OF YOUTH
    3,2,2,2 - 4,3,3,1 - timp.,perc.,cel. - hp. - str.   17:00 Bo. Hawkes.

PAULSEN, Helmut
—— DORFMUSIK (VILLAGE MUSIC) (IN 4 MOVTS.)
    str.   12:00 Henmar.
—— FEIERMUSIK
    fl. - str.   15:00 Henmar.
—— NORTH GERMAN DANCES
    1,1,1,1 - 1,1,0,0 - timp.,perc. - str.   10:00 Henmar.

PAULSON, Gustaf
—— CONCERTO FOR ALTO SAXOPHONE AND ORCH., OP. 105 (1959)
    2,2,2,1 alto sax.,2 - 2,2,1,0 - timp. - pf. - str.   15:00 S.T.I.M.
—— CONCERTO FOR BASSOON AND ORCH., OP. 130 (1965)
    2,2,2,3 - 2,2,1,0 - timp. - str.   16:00 Fleisher.
—— CONCERTO FOR BASSOON AND STRING ORCH., OP. 101 (1958)
    bn. - str.   12:00 S.T.I.M.
—— CONCERTO FOR HORN AND ORCH., OP. 127 (1964)
    2,2,2,2 - 3,0,2,0 - timp. - str.   Fleisher.
—— CONCERTO FOR TRUMPET AND ORCH., OP. 131 (1965)
    2,2,2,2 - 2,1,0,0 - timp. - str.   18:00 Fleisher.
—— CONCERTO FOR VIOLA AND ORCH., OP. 132 (1965)
    2,2,2,2 - 2,2,1,0 - timp.,perc. - str.   18:00 Fleisher.
—— CONCERTO FOR VIOLIN AND ORCH., OP. 110 (1960)
    2,2,2,2 - 2,2,1,0 - timp.,perc.(2) - pf. - str.   17:00 S.T.I.M.
—— CONCERTO NO. 1 FOR CLARINET AND ORCH., OP. 100 (1958)
    2,2,3,2 - 2,2,2,0 - timp.,perc.(2) - str.   15:00 S.T.I.M.
—— CONCERTO NO. 1 FOR ENGLISH HORN, TIMPANI AND STRING ORCH., OP. 99 (1958)
    Eng.hn. - timp. - str.   12:00 S.T.I.M.
—— CONCERTO NO. 2 FOR CELLO AND ORCH., OP. 90 (1957)
    2,2,2,2 - 3,2,3,0 - pf. - str.   23:00 S.T.I.M.
—— CONCERTO NO. 2 FOR CLARINET AND STRING ORCH., OP. 104 (1959)
    cl. - str.   15:00 S.T.I.M.
—— CONCERTO NO. 2 FOR DOUBLE BASS AND ORCH., OP. 133 (1966)
    2,2,2,2 - 2,2,1,0 - timp. - str.   Fleisher.
—— CONCERTO NO. 2 FOR ENGLISH HORN AND STRING ORCH., OP. 103 (1959)
    Eng. hn. - str.   S.T.I.M.
—— CONCERTO NO. 2 FOR OBOE AND STRING ORCH., OP. 94 (1957)
    ob. - str.   15:00 S.T.I.M.
—— CONCERTO NO. 2 FOR PIANO AND ORCH., OP. 115
    2,2,2,2 - 2,2,1,0 - timp.,perc.(2) - pf. - str.   20:00 S.T.I.M.
—— ETISKA MINIATYRER SUITE (1956)
    2,2,2,2 - 2,2,1,0 - timp.,perc.(2) - str.   17:00 S.T.I.M.
—— PASSION, OP. 114 (FOR CELLO AND ORCH.) (1961)
    2,2,2,2 - 2,2,3,0 - timp.,perc. - str.   17:00 S.T.I.M.
—— SINFONIA FOR STRINGS, OP. 75 ("VÄRLDENS FRÄLSARE KOM HÄR")
    str.   15:00 S.T.I.M.
—— SINFONIA NO. 2 FOR STRINGS, OP. 80 ("SIMEON'S LOVESONG")
    str.   15:00 S.T.I.M.
—— SINFONIETTA, OP. 19
    2,2,2,2 - 2,2,3,1 - timp.,perc. - str.   17:30 S.T.I.M.
—— SKÅNSKT FESTSPEL (1957)
    2,2,2,2 - 2,2,1,0 - timp.,perc.(2) - str.   10:00 S.T.I.M.
—— STABAT MATER, OP. 88 (FOR SOPRANO, ALTO, WOMEN'S CHORUS, TIMPANI AND STRING ORCH.) (1956)
    timp. - str.   50:00 S.T.I.M.
—— SYMPHONY NO. 1, OP. 7
    2,2,2,2 - 2,2,3,1 - timp.,perc. - str.   25:00 S.T.I.M.
    or:
    2,2,2,3 sax.,2 - 2,2,3,1 - timp.,perc. - pf. - str.
—— SYMPHONY NO. 2 IN A MAJOR, OP. 9
    2,2,2,2 - 2,2,3,1 - timp.,perc. - str.   25:00 S.T.I.M.

—— SYMPHONY NO. 3 IN B, OP. 44
    2,2,2,2 - 2,2,1,0 - timp. - str.   16:00 S.T.I.M.
—— SYMPHONY NO. 4, OP. 47 ("UPPSTÅNDELSE") ("ON AN
EASTER THEME")
    2,2,2,2 - 3,2,3,1 - timp.,perc. - str.   34:00 S.T.I.M.
—— SYMPHONY NO. 5, OP. 51 ("IN MEMORIAM ARON
BERGENSON")
    2,2,2,3 - 4,3,3,1 - timp.,perc. - pf. - str.   20:00 S.T.I.M.
—— SYMPHONY NO. 6, OP. 69
    2,2,2,2 - 4,3,3,1 - timp.,perc. - pf. - str.   30:00 S.T.I.M.
—— SYMPHONY NO. 7, OP. 71
    2,2,2,2 - 4,2,3,1 - timp.,perc. - pf. - str.   20:00 S.T.I.M.
—— SYMPHONY NO. 8, OP. 79
    2,2,2,2 - 4,3,3,1 - timp.,perc. - pf. - str.   20:00 S.T.I.M.
—— SYMPHONY NO. 9, OP. 86 (1956)
    2,2,2,2 - 4,3,3,1 - timp.,perc.(2) - pf. - str.   20:00 S.T.I.M.
—— SYMPHONY NO. 10 IN C MAJOR, OP. 93 (1957)
    2,2,2,2 - 2,3,3,1 - timp.,perc.(2) - pf. - str.   30:00 S.T.I.M.
—— SYMPHONY NO. 11 (STABAT MATER), OP. 102 (1959)
    2,2,2,2 - 2,2,1,0 - timp.,perc.(2) - str.   25:00 S.T.I.M.
—— SYMPHONY NO. 13, OP. 135 (1966)
    2,2,2,2 - 2,3,3,1 - timp.,perc. - pf. - str.   Fleisher.
—— VID KORSET, OP. 91 (ORATORIO) (FOR BARITONE, SATB
CHORUS AND STRING ORCH.) (1957)
    str.   50:00 S.T.I.M.

PAULSON, Stephen
—— CONCERTO FOR BASSOON AND ORCH. (1968)
    1. Allegro moderato; 2. Scherzo (Presto); 3. Adagio
    15:00 Presser.

PAULUS, Stephen H.
—— TABLEAUX FROM THE LIFE OF CHRIST (FOR 2
SOPRANOS, BARITONE, SATB CHORUS AND ORCH.) (1974)
(Text: Nikos Kazantzakis)
    *3,2,2,2 - 2,2,2,0 - timp.,perc.(3),xyl. - str.   Composer.

PAUTREMER, Marcel
—— TARTARIN DE TARASCON (SUITE) (IN 5 MOVTS.)
    3,3,2, alto sax.(alt. with ten. sax.),3 - 4,4,3,1 -
    timp.,perc.,cel.,glock. - 2 hp. - str.   17:30 Baron.

PAVIOUR, Paul
—— CAPTAIN BRASSBOUND'S CONVERSION (1947)
    9:00 G. Schirmer.
—— MUSIC FOR A CEREMONIAL (FOR ORGAN AND ORCH.)
(1953)
    12:00 Belw-Mills.

PAYMER, Marvin
—— HOLIDAY OVERTURE (1950)
    *3,2,*3,2 - 4,2,3,1 - timp.,perc.(2) - str.   12:00 Composer.
—— PRELUDE AND VARIATIONS (1957)
    str.   16:00 Composer.

PAYNE, Frank Lynn
—— ASYMPHOMETRIC (1975)
    1,1,1,1 - 2,1,1,1 - timp.,perc. - str.(6,2,2,1)   9:00 Composer.
—— CONCERTO FOR STRING QUARTET AND ORCH. (1968) (IN
3 MOVTS.)
    *3,2,2,2 - 4,2,3,1 - timp.,perc.(5), bells,cel.,xyl. - hp. - str.
    14:05 Composer.

PAZ, Juan Carlos
—— OVERTURE FOR 12 INSTRUMENTS, OP. 19 (OBERTURA
PARA DOCE INSTRUMENTOS)
    1,1,1,1 - 2,1,1,0 - str.(no d.-b.)   Southern.

PECK, Russell
—— THE EMPEROR'S NEW CONCERTO (FOR ELECTRIC
GUITAR, ELECTRIC BASS, JAZZ DRUMS AND ORCH.) (1972)
    *3,2,2,2 - 4,3,3,1 - timp.,perc.(4),bell,glock. - elec.bass,elec.guit., -
    str.   8:00 Studio P/R.
—— JACK AND JILL AT BUNKER HILL (FOR NARRATOR,
ACTOR AND ORCH.) % (Text: Bill Bleich)
    *3,*3,*3,*3 - 4,3,3,1 - timp.,perc.(2) - hp. - str.   38:00 Piedmont.
—— LE TOMBEAU DE L'INCONNU....(THE TOMB OF THE
UNKNOWN...) (1974)
    3,2,3,3 - 4,3,3,1 - str.   12:00 Composer.

—— WHO KILLED COCK ROBIN? (FOR NARRATOR AND
ORCH.) (Co-composed with Kurt Carpenter)(Text: Bill Bleich)
    1*3,3,3(1 alt. with E♭cl.,1 alt. with b.-cl.),*3 - 4,3,3,1 -
    timp.,perc.(2),bells,glock.,mar.,xyl. - hp. - pf. - str.
    17:00 Piedmont.
—— WINTER MUSIC (1968) (IN 3 MOVTS.)
    str.   7:00 Piedmont.

PEDERSEN, Gunnar Møller
—— INSTANT MUSIC FOR ORCH.
    K.O.D.A.
—— SINFONIA I (1967)
    3,3,3,3 - 4,3,3,1 - perc. - hp. - str.   10:00 Henmar.

PEDERSEN, Paul
—— CONCERTO FOR ORCH. (1961) (IN 3 MOVTS.)
    *3,*3,*3,2 - 4,3,3,1 - timp.,perc.(3),vibra. - hp. - str.
    17:00 CanMusCtr.
—— LAMENT (1959)
    *3,*3,*3,*3 - 4,3,3,1 - timp.,perc. - hp. - pf. - str.
    4:00 CanMusCtr.

PEDROLLO, Arrigo
—— L' AMANTE IN TRAPPOLA (1-ACT COMIC OPERA) %
    2,2,2,2 - 0,2,2,1 - timp.,perc. - hp. - str.   35:00 Bo. Hawkes.
—— CONCERTINO FOR OBOE AND STRINGS
    ob. - str.   Henmar.
—— INTERMEZZI PER LA TRAGEDIA "IFIGENIA IN AULIDE"
    2,2,1,1 - 2,2,0,0 - timp., - hp. - str.   14:00 Bo. Hawkes.

PEERSON, M. - BANTOCK, Granville
—— SUITE OF OLD ENGLISH MUSIC
    pf. - str.   6:00 Cramer.

PEERY, Rob Roy
—— GLORY TO GOD (CHRISTMAS CANTATA) (FOR CHORUS
AND STRINGS)
    str.   60:00 Witmark.
—— SYMPHONIC MOVEMENT IN E MINOR
    2,2,2,2 - 2,2,0,0 - timp. - str.   12:00 Composer.

PEETERS, Emil
—— CIACONNA
    3,3,3,3 - 4,3,3,1 - perc. - hp. - str.   10:00 T & J.
—— PRÄLUDIUM UND FUGE
    2,2,3,2 - 4,3,3,1 - timp. - str.   12:00 T & J.

PEETERS, Flor
—— CONCERTO FOR ORGAN AND ORCH., OP. 52 (1958)
    S.A.B.A.M.

PEIKO, Nikolai I.
—— CONCERT FANTASY ON FINNISH FOLK THEMES (FOR
VIOLIN AND ORCH.)
    3,2,2,2 - 4,2,2,0 - timp.,perc. - str.   12:00 G. Schirmer.
—— MOLDAVIAN SUITE (IN 4 MOVTS.)
    3,2,2,2 - 4,3,3,1 - timp.,perc.,xyl. - hp. - str.   20:00 G. Schirmer.
—— SYMPHONY NO. 1
    3,3,3,3 - 4,3,3,1 - timp.,perc.,xyl. - hp. - str.   36:00 G. Schirmer.
—— SYMPHONY NO. 6
    G. Schirmer.
—— YAKUTIAN SUITE (IN 4 MOVTS.)
    2(2nd alt. with picc.),2,2,2 - 4,3,3,1 - timp.,perc. - hp. - pf. - str.
    20:00 G. Schirmer.

PELEMANS, Willem
—— AUTOMNALES (HERFSTGOUD) (SYMPHONIC SUITE FROM
THE BALLET)
    2,2,2,2 - 2,2,2,2 - timp.,perc.,cel.,glock.,xyl. - hp. - str.
    30:00 H. Elkan.
—— BALLADE NO. 1 (1933)
    2,2,2,2 - 2,2,2,0 - timp.,perc. - str.   10:00 H. Elkan.
—— BALLADE NO. 2 (1933)
    2,2,2,2 - 2,2,2,0 - timp. - str.   8:00 H. Elkan.
—— BALLADE NO. 3 (1933)
    2,2,2,2 - 2,2,2,0 - timp. - str.   12:00 H. Elkan.
—— BALLADE NO. 4 (1934)
    2,2,2,2 - 2,2,2,0 - timp. - str.   15:00 H. Elkan.
—— BALLADE NO. 5 (1934)
    2,2,2,2 - 2,2,2,0 - str.   13:00 H. Elkan.
—— BALLADE NO. 6 (1934)
    2,2,2,2 - 2,2,2,0 - timp.,perc. - str.   12:00 H. Elkan.

—— BALLADE NO. 7 (1934)
   2,2,2,2 - 2,2,2,0 - timp.,perc. - pf. - str.   10:00 H. Elkan.
—— BALLADE NO. 8 (1935)
   2,2,2,2 - 2,2,2,0 - timp.,perc.,cel. - pf. - str.   12:00 H. Elkan.
—— CONCERTINO NO. 1 FOR CHAMBER ORCH. (1948)
   0,2,0,0 - 2,0,0,0 - str.   11:00 H. Elkan.
—— CONCERTINO NO. 2 FOR CHAMBER ORCH. (1949)
   1,0,2,1 - 1,2,1,0 - timp.,perc. - hp. - str.   20:00 H. Elkan.
—— CONCERTINO NO. 4 (1957)
   str.   14:00 H. Elkan.
—— CONCERTO FOR VIOLIN AND ORCH. (1954)
   2,2,2,2 - 2,2,2,1 - timp.,perc.,cel.,glock.,xyl. - hp. - str.
                                                         35:00 H. Elkan.
—— CONCERTO NO. 1 FOR ORCHESTRA (1948)
   2,2,2,3 - 4,2,3,1 - timp.,perc.,cel.,glock.,xyl. - hp. - str.
                                                         25:00 H. Elkan.
—— CONCERTO NO. 1 FOR PIANO AND ORCH. (1945)
   2,2,2,2 - 2,2,2,0 - timp.,perc. - pf. - str.   28:00 H. Elkan.
—— CONCERTO NO. 2 FOR CHAMBER ORCH. (1955)
   2,2,2,2 - 2,2,2,1 - timp.,perc.,xyl. - pf. - str.   27:00 H. Elkan.
—— CONCERTO NO. 2 FOR PIANO AND ORCH. (1950)
   2,2,2,2 - 4,3,3,1 - timp.,perc.,glock.,cel.,xyl. - hp. - pf. - str.
                                                         32:00 CBDM.
—— CONCERTO NO. 3 FOR CHAMBER ORCH. (1950)
   1,1,1,1 - 1,1,1,1 - timp.,perc.,bells,cel.,xyl. - pf. - str.
                                                         16:00 H. Elkan.
—— CONCERTO NO. 5 FOR ORCH. (1966) (IN 3 MOVTS.)
   2,2,2,2 - 2,2,2,1 - timp.,perc. - str.   19:00 H. Elkan.
—— MILES GLORIOSUS (BALLET) % (1945)
   2,2,2,2 - 2,2,2,1 - timp.,perc.,cel.,glock. - hp. - str.   CBDM.
—— PAS DE QUATRE (1969) (IN 3 MOVTS.)
   2,2,2,2 - 2,2,2,1 - timp.,perc. - str.   20:00 H. Elkan.
—— SCHETSEN VOOR EEN BUFFA-OPERA (1957)
   1,0,2,1 - 2,1,0,0 - pf. - str.   8:00 H. Elkan.

PELLEGRINI, Ernesto P.
—— MUSIC FOR SIXTEEN INSTRUMENTS AND PERCUSSION
   (1970)
   1(alt. with picc.),1,1,1 - 1,1,1,1 - timp.,perc.(6),bells,cel.,glock.,xyl.
   - hp. - pf. - str.(2,1,1,1)   15:00 Composer.
—— SEVEN STATEMENTS IN THREE-QUARTER TIME (1963)
   *3,*3,*3,*3 - 4,3,3,1 - timp.,perc.(4) - pf. - str.   10:00 Composer.

PENBERTHY, James
—— BALLADE FOR ORCH., OP. 38 (1955)
   2,2,2,2 - 4,2,3,0 - timp. - hp. - str.   5:00 A.P.R.A.
—— BEACH, OP. 50 (PRELUDE AND FUGATO) (1956)
   *3,2,2*3 - 4,2,3,1 - timp. - hp. - str.   9:30 A.P.R.A.
—— BEYOND THE UNIVERSE (NINE SYMPHONIC POEMS, OP.
   140 - 149) (1973) (Duration of each: between 10:00 and 20:00)
   *2,*2,*2,*2 - 4,2,3,1 - timp.,perc. - hp. - str.   A.P.R.A.
—— COLOURS, NUMBERS AND OBJECTS, OP. 116 (1968)
   2,2,3,3 - 4,3,3,1 - timp.(3) - tape-recorder - hp. - org.(ad lib.) - pf.
   - str.   13:50 A.P.R.A.
—— CONCERTO FOR BASSOON AND ORCH., OP. 32
   1,1,2,2 - 2,2,0,0 - perc. - str.   7:00 A.P.R.A.
—— CONCERTO FOR CELLO AND ORCH., OP. 79 (1962)
   2,2,2,2 - 4,2,3,0 - timp. - str.   16:00 A.P.R.A.
—— CONCERTO FOR FLUTE AND ORCH., OP. 37 (1955)
                                                         A.P.R.A.
—— CONCERTO FOR SAXOPHONE AND ORCH., OP. 122 (1970)
   2,2,sax.,2 - 4,3,3,1 - perc.(4) - str.   8:00 A.P.R.A.
—— CONCERTO FOR TROMBONE AND ORCH., OP. 149 (1973)
                                                         10:00 A.P.R.A.
—— CONCERTO FOR TRUMPET AND ORCH., OP. 136 (1972)
   3,3,3,3 - 4,3,3,1 - timp.,perc(4) - hp. - str.   15:00 A.P.R.A.
—— CONCERTO FOR VIOLA AND ORCH., OP. 85 (1963)
   2,2,2,2 - 2,2,2,0 - timp. - str.   17:00 A.P.R.A.
—— CONCERTO NO. 3 FOR PIANO AND ORCH., OP. 154 (1974)
   2,2,2,2 - 4,3,2,1 - timp. - hp. - pf.- str.   17:30 A.P.R.A.
—— DESERT VOYAGE, OP. 30 (1954)
   2,2,2,2 - 4,2,3,0 - timp.(3) - hp. - str.   10:00 A.P.R.A.
—— EDGE OF THE DESERT, OP. 49 (1956)
   2,2,2,*3 - 4,2,3,1 - timp.(2) - str.   6:00 A.P.R.A.
—— EZZE, OP. 10 (1951)
   2,2,2,2 - 4,2,3,0 - 2 hp. - str.   10:00 A.P.R.A.
—— HAPPENING 1970, OP. 118
   2,2,3,3 - 4,2,3,1 - tape-recorder - 2 hp. - pf.   10:00 A.P.R.A.
—— KADJANI AND JULUNGGUL, OP. 52 (1957)
   2,2,*3,0 - 4,2,3,1 - 2 hp. - str.   8:00 A.P.R.A.
—— LAMENT FOR A LOST CHILD, OP. 81(1962)
   str.   3:00 A.P.R.A.

—— LITTLE SYMPHONY (SYMPHONY NO. 7), OP. 104 (1965)
   0,2,0,2 - 0,0,0,0 - str.   13:00 A.P.R.A.
—— MEN AND WOMEN, OP. 121 (1970)
   *3,2,3,sax.,1 - 4,3,3,1 - timp.(3) - hp. - org. - harm. - str.
                                                         20:00 A.P.R.A.
—— ROMANCE FOR VIOLIN AND STRING ORCH., OP. 71 (1960)
   str.   6:00 A.P.R.A.
—— SPHERES, ELLIPSES AND LABYRINTHS, OP. 124 (FOR
   STRING QUARTET AND STRING ORCH.) (1971)
   str.   7:00 A.P.R.A.
—— SQUARES, SPIRALS AND SPHERES, OP. 132 (1972)
   3,3,3,3 - 4,3,3,1 - timp. - tape-recorder - hp. - str. 12:00 A.P.R.A.
—— SUITE FOR ORCH., OP. 23 (1954)
   2,2,2,3 - 4,2,3,0 - timp. - pf. - str.   15:00 A.P.R.A.
—— SUITE, OP. 82 (SAD PIECES FOR STRINGS) (1962)
   str.   A.P.R.A.
—— SYMPHONY NO. 3 ("URANUS"), OP. 40 (1956)
   2,2,2,2 - 4,2,3,1 - timp.,perc. (3) - hp. - pf. - str. 16:00 A.P.R.A.
—— SYMPHONY NO. 4 ("UNDER THE SEA"), OP. 54 (1957)
   2,2,2,2 - 4,2,3,1 - timp.,perc.(2) - hp. - str.   20:00 A.P.R.A.
—— SYMPHONY NO. 6 ("EARTH MOTHER"), OP. 84 (1962)
   3,3,3,3 - 4,2,3,1 - timp.,perc.(3) - hp. - str.   25:00 A.P.R.A.
—— SYMPHONY NO. 8 ("CHORAL"), OP. 133 (FOR CHORUS AND
   ORCH.) (1972)
   3,2,3,3 - 4,3-12,3,1 - timp.,perc.(4) - tape-recorder - hp. - str.
                                                         20:00 A.P.R.A.
—— TWO ENTR'ACTES FOR ORCH., OP. 36 (1955)
   2,2,2,2 - 4,2,3,1 - perc.(3) - str.   6:00 A.P.R.A.
—— VARIATIONS ON A RUSSIAN TUNE, OP. 70 (1960)
   3,3,3,3 - 4,2,3,1 - hp.   10:00 A.P.R.A.

PENDLETON, Edmond
—— CONCERTO ALPESTRE (FOR FLUTE AND ORCH.)
   1,2,2,2 - 2,2,0,0 - timp.,perc.,cel.,glock. - hp. - str. 21:00 Salabert.
—— PRELUDE, FANFARE AND FUGUE
   0,0,0,0 - 0,2,2,0 - timp. - str.   9:00 Salabert.

PENN, William A.
—— DESIGNS (FOR ORCHESTRAL WINDS, JAZZ QUINTET AND
   PERCUSSION) (1972)
   *3,*3,*3,1 sax.,2 - 5,4,3,1 - timp.,perc.(7),bells,xyl. - pf. - 1 d-b.
                                                         14:00 Presser.
—— SOLSTICE: A SYMPHONIC MOVEMENT (1969)
   3(3rd alt.with picc.),2(2nd alt.with Eng.hn.),2,2 - 4,3,3,1 -
   timp.,perc.(6),bells,xyl. - pf. - str.   15:00 Composer.
—— SPECTRUMS, CONFUSIONS AND SOMETIME-MOMENTS
   BEYOND THE ORDER OF DESTINY (1969)
   4(4th alt. with picc.),2,*3,*3 - 4,3,2,1 -
   timp.,perc.(3),glock.,vibra.,xyl. - hp. - 2 pf. - str. 8:00 Presser.
—— ULTRA MENSURAM
   0,0,0,0 - 6,3,3,3   9:00 Seesaw.

PENNARIO, Leonard
—— CONCERTO IN D FLAT, FOR PIANO AND ORCH. (IN 3
   MOVTS.)
   2,*2,*3,2 - 4,2,3,1 - timp.,perc.(2) - str.   19:00 Composer.

PENNISI, Francesco
—— A CANTATA ON MELANCHOLY (FOR SOPRANO AND
   ORCH.) (1967) (Text: Robert Burton)
   2,2,3,1 sax.,3 - 2,2,2,1 - perc.(3),bells,cel.,glock.,vibra.,xyl. - guit. -
   hp. - pf. - str.   15:00 MCA Music.
—— PALERMO, APRILE (FOR 18 INSTRUMENTS) (1965)
   2,2,2,2 - 0,0,0,0 - str.(4,2,2,2)   9:00 MCA Music.

PENTTINEN, Toimi
—— CLOUDS, OP. 2 (SUITE) (1935)
   3,2,3,2 - 4,2,2,0 - timp.,perc. - hp. - str.   11:00 FinnMICtr.
—— CONCERTO FOR ORGAN AND ORCH., OP. 13 (1943)
   1,1,2,1 - 2,2,0,0 - timp. - hp. - org. - str.   25:00 FinnMICtr.
—— ETUDE FOR ORCHESTRA (1935)
   2,2,2,2 - 4,3,0,0 - timp.,perc. - str.   3:00 FinnMICtr.
—— STREET SCENE, OP. 3 (1936)
   3,3,3,2 - 4,2,2,0 - timp. - str.   8:00 FinnMICtr.

PEPIN, André
—— IMPROMPTU (FOR FLUTE AND ORCH.)
   1,1,1,1 - 1,0,0,0 - hp. - str.   9:30 Baron.

PEPIN, Clermont
—— LE CANTIQUE DES CANTIQUES (CANTATA) (FOR CHORUS
   AND STRINGS)
   str.   6:30 C.A.P.A.C.

—— CHROMA (1973)
*3,2,2,2 - 4,3,3,1 - perc.(2) - hp. - pf. - str.   12:00 CanMusCtr.
—— CONCERTO NO. 1 FOR PIANO AND ORCH. (IN 3 MOVTS.)
2,2,2,2 - 4,2,3,1 - pf. - str.   20:00 C.A.P.A.C.
—— CONCERTO NO. 2 IN G# MINOR, FOR PIANO AND ORCH.
(IN 4 MOVTS.)
2,2,2,2 - 4,2,3,1 - perc. - pf. - str.   16:00 C.A.P.A.C.
—— THE GATES OF HELL (BALLET) %
2,2,2,2 - 2,2,2,0 - perc. - str.   C.A.P.A.C.
—— GUERNICA (SYMPHONIC POEM)
3,3,3,3 - 4,2,3,1 - timp.,perc.(4) - str.   17:00 C.A.P.A.C.
or:
2,2,2,2 - 4,2,3,1 - timp.,perc.(4) - str.
—— LA MESSE SUR LE MONDE (1975) (SYMPHONY NO. 4) (FOR
NARRATOR, MIXED CHORUS AND ORCH.) (Text: Teilhard
de Chardin)
3,3,3,3 - 4,3,3,1 - perc.(4),mar.,xyl. - str.   20:00 CanMusCtr.
—— MONADE 3 (1972) (FOR VIOLIN AND ORCH.) (IN 3 MOVTS.)
*3,2,2,2 - 2,2,2,0 - perc.(2) - hp. - str.   10:15 CanMusCtr.
—— MONOLOGUE (1960-61)
2,2,2,2 - 2,2,2,0 - perc. - str.   16:00 CanMusCtr.
—— NOMBRES (FOR 2 PIANOS AND ORCH.) (1962)
2,2,*2,2 - 4,3,3,1 - 2 pf. - str.   12:30 CanMusCtr.
—— L' OISEAU-PHÉNIX (BALLET) %
2,2,2,2 - 3,2,2,0 - timp. - str.   C.A.P.A.C.
—— LE PORT-RÊVE (BALLET) %
C.A.P.A.C.
—— PRISMES ET CRISTAUX (1974) (FOR STRING ORCH.)
str.   13:45 CanMusCtr.
—— QUASARS (SYMPHONY NO. 3)
25:00 MCA Music.
—— LE RITE DU SOLEIL NOIR (SYMPHONIC POEM)
2,2,2,2 - 4,2,3,1 - timp.,perc.(3) - str.   10:00 C.A.P.A.C.
—— SEPT MÉLODIES (SUR DES POÈMES D'ELUARD) (FOR
HIGH VOICE AND STRINGS)
str.   CA.P.A.C.
—— SYMPHONIC VARIATIONS
2,2,2,2 - 4,2,3,1 - perc. - str.   13:00 C.A.P.A.C.
—— SYMPHONY NO. 1 IN B MINOR (IN 3 MOVTS.)
2,2,2,2 - 4,2,3,1 - perc. - str.   18:00 C.A.P.A.C.
—— SYMPHONY NO. 2 (1957)
*2,2,2,2 - 2,2,2,0 - timp.,perc.,mar.,xyl. - str.   22:00 CanMusCtr.
—— THEME AND VARIATIONS
str.   7:30 C.A.P.A.C.
—— THREE MINIATURES FOR STRINGS (1963)
str.   CanMusCtr.

PEPPING, Ernst
—— KONZERT FÜR KALVIER UND ORCH.
2,2,2,2 - 4,2,1,1 - timp. - pf. - str.   22:00 Baerenrtr.
—— O HAUPT VOLL BLUT UND WUNDEN (FOR CONTRALTO
OR BARIOTNE AND ORCH.)
Baerenrtr.
—— SERENADE
2,2,2,2 - 2,2,1,1 - timp.,perc. - str.   26:00 Baerenrtr.
—— SYMPHONY NO. 3
Baerenrtr.
—— TE DEUM (FOR CHORUS, 2 SOLO VOICES AND ORCH.)
Baerenrtr.
—— TWO ORCHESTRAL PIECES ON A CHANSON OF BINCHOIS
(1958)
2(2nd alt. with picc.),2,2,2 - 2,2,1,1 - timp.,perc. - str.
17:00 G. Schirmer.
—— VARIATIONS FOR ORCH.
Baerenrtr.

PEPUSCH, J. C. - AUSTIN, Frederick
—— SELECTIONS FROM "THE BEGGARS OPERA"
fl., ob. - pf. (or hpsc.) - str.   11:30 Bo. Hawkes.

PEPUSCH, J. C. - BRITTEN, Benjamin
—— THE BEGGARS OPERA, OP. 43 (1948) (COMPLETE) % (Text:
John Gay)
1(alt. with picc.),1(alt. with Eng.hn.),1,1 - 1,0,0,0 - perc.,timp. -
hp. - str.   105:00 Bo. Hawkes.

PEPUSCH, J. C. - DENT, E. J.
—— THE BEGGAR'S OPERA (OPERA) % (Text: John Gay)
1,1,1,1 - 2,0,0,0 - hpsc.(or pf.) - str.   90:00 Oxford.

PEPUSCH, J. C. - HORTON, John
—— OVERTURE TO "THE BEGGAR'S OPERA"
2,1,2,0-1 - 0-2,1,0-1,0 - timp. - str.   4:00 Oxford.

PERGAMENT, Moses
—— ADAGIO FOR CLARINET AND STRINGS
cl. - str.   10:00 S.T.I.M.
—— ALMQUISTIANA : SUITE NO. 2
2,2,2,2 - 2,0,0,0 - timp. - str.   13:00 S.T.I.M.
—— CANTO LIRICO (FOR VIOLIN AND ORCH.)
hn. - timp.,perc. - hp. - str.   12:00 S.T.I.M.
—— CONCERTO FOR CELLO AND ORCH.
2,2,2,2 - 4,2,3,1 - timp.,perc. - str.   S.T.I.M.
—— CONCERTO FOR E-VIOLA AND ORCH. (1965)
1,1,1,1 - 1,0,0,0 - timp.,perc. - pf. - str.   Fleisher.
—— CONCERTO FOR PIANO AND ORCH.
2,2,2,2 - 4,2,0,0 - timp.,perc. - hp. - pf. - str.   27:00 S.T.I.M.
—— CONCERTO FOR TWO VIOLINS AND CHAMBER ORCH.
1,1,1,1 - 2,2,0,0 - timp.,perc. - pf. - str.   22:00 S.T.I.M.
—— CONCERTO FOR VIOLIN AND ORCH.
2,2,2,2 - 4,2,0,0 - timp.,perc. - hp. - str.   32:00 S.T.I.M.
—— ELI (RADIO OPERA, AFTER A MYSTERY-PLAY OF NELLY
SACHS)
90:00 S.T.I.M.
—— FANTASIA DIFFERENTE (FOR CELLO AND STRING
ORCH.)(1970)
str.   10:00 Fleisher.
—— FESTIVAL OVERTURE
2,2,2,2 - 4,2,3,1 - timp.,perc.(2) - str.   12:00 S.T.I.M.
—— FOUR POEMS OF EDITH SÖDERGRAN (FOR SOPRANO
AND ORCH.) (1966)
2,2,2,2 - 2,0,0,0 - 2 hp. - str.   20:00 S.T.I.M.
—— JEWISH SONGS ("DEN JUDISKA SANGEN") (FOR SOPRANO,
TENOR, CHORUS AND ORCH.)
3,3,3,2 - 4,3,3,1 - timp.,perc.,cel. - hp. - str.   100:00 S.T.I.M.
—— KOL NIDRE (FOR CELLO AND ORCH.)
2,2,2,2 - 4,0,0,0 - timp.,perc. - str.   13:00 S.T.I.M.
—— PEZZO INTIMO (FOR 16 CELLOS)
16 c.   12:00 S.T.I.M.
—— RHAPSODY EBRAICA
2,2,2,2 - 4,2,3,1 - timp.,perc.(2) - hp. - str.   19:00 S.T.I.M.
—— SONATINA FOR FLUTE AND STRING ORCH. (1973)
fl. - str.   7:00 Fleisher.
—— SUITE FROM "JEWISH SONGS"
3,3,3,2 - 4,3,3,1 - timp.,perc.(3),cel. - hp. - str.   17:00 S.T.I.M.
—— SUITE FROM THE BALLET "KRELANTEMS OCH
ELDELING"
4,4,4,4 - 4,4,4,1 - timp.,perc.(3),cel.,xyl. - hp. - str.   20:00 S.T.I.M.
—— SUITE FROM THE FILM "BARABBAS"
1,1,1,1 - 2,2,0,0, - timp.,perc. - str.   S.T.I.M.
—— SUITE FROM THE FILM "MED LIVET SOM INSATS"
S.T.I.M.
—— SUITE FROM THE FILM "THE MAIDEN AND THE DEVIL"
S.T.I.M.
—— SWEDISH RHAPSODY
2,2,2,2 - 4,2,3,1 - timp.,perc. - hp. - str.   15:00 S.T.I.M.
—— VISION
2,2,2,2 - 2,1,1,0 - timp.,perc. - org.(ad lib.) - str.   10:00 S.T.I.M.

PERGOLESI, Giovanni Battista
—— LA SERVANTE MAÎTRESSE (2-ACT OPÉRA-COMIQUE) (FOR
1 MEZZO-SOPRANO, 1 BARITONE AND 1 MUTE PERSON)
(French text: Baurens)
str.   EV.

PERGOLESI, Giovanni Battista - BARAB, Seymour
—— THE PERFECT WIFE (1-ACT OPERA) % (ARR. 1968)
Bo. Hawkes.

PERGOLESI, Giovanni Battista - BARBIROLLI, John
—— CONCERTO FOR OBOE (OR FLUTE) AND STRINGS
ob.(or fl.) - str.   12:00 Oxford.

PERGOLESI, Giovanni Battista - DE FILIPPI, Amedeo
—— CONCERTO FOR FLUTE AND STRINGS
fl. - str.   9:00 Arranger.

PERGOLESI, Giovanni Battista - FRANKO
—— CONCERTINO IN F MINOR, FOR STRINGS
str.   G. Schirmer.

PERGOLESI, Giovanni Battista - GERELLI, Ennio
—— LO FRATE INNAMMORATO ("IL FRATELLO
INNAMORATO") ("THE FRIAR IN LOVE") (3-ACT OPERA) %
1,2,0,0 - 2,0,0,0 - hpsc. - str.   Leeds.

PERGOLESI, Giovanni Battista - HINNENTHAL, J. P.
—— CONCERTINO NO. 3 IN A MAJOR, FOR STRINGS
cemb. - str.   Baerenrtr.
—— CONCERTINO NO. 4 IN F MINOR, FOR STRINGS
cemb. - str.   Baerenrtr.

PERGOLESI, Giovanni Battista - JACQUES, Reginald - CUDWORTH, Charles
—— CONCERTO NO. 3 FOR STRING ORCH.
str.   Oxford.

PERGOLESI, Giovanni Battista - LACCETTI
—— CONCERTO IN B♭, FOR STRINGS
str.   15:00 Bo. Hawkes.

PERGOLESI, Giovanni Battista - LUALDI, Adriano
—— CONCERTO IN B♭, FOR VIOLIN AND ORCH.
0,2,0,2 - 2 hn. - str.   18:00 Bo. Hawkes.

PERGOLESI, Giovanni Battista - MEYLAND, Raymond
—— CONCERTO IN G, FOR FLUTE, STRINGS AND CEMBALO
fl. - cemb. - str.   10:00 Bo. Hawkes.

PERGOLESI, Giovanni Battista - MORTARI
—— CHI NON ODE (FOR SOPRANO AND STRINGS)
str.   15:00 Bo. Hawkes.

PERGOLESI, Giovanni Battista - SCOTT, C. Kennedy
—— STABAT MATER (FOR 2-PART WOMEN'S CHORUS AND
STRING ORCH.) (Engl. Text: Beatrice E. Bulman)
str.   40:00 Oxford.

PERILHOU, Albert
—— UNE FÊTE PATRONALE EN VÉLAY (SUITE)
3,3,2,2 - 4,2,3,1 - timp. - 2 hp. - str.   12:30 Presser.

PERKINS, Horace James
—— BALLADE ("FROM SOUTHERN SEAS") (1965)
*3,2,2,2 - 4,2,3,1 - timp.,perc. - str.   13:30 A.P.R.A.
—— CONCERTO IN G MINOR FOR VIOLIN AND ORCH. ("THE NIGHTINGALE") (1955)
2,2,2,2 - 2,2,0,0 - timp.,perc. - str.   24:00 A.P.R.A.
—— ELEGIAC SYMPHONY (1951)
*3,*3,*3,*3 - 4,3,3,1 - timp.   38:00 A.P.R.A.
—— PICKWICK SINFONIA (1964)
2(2nd alt. with picc.),2(2nd alt. with Eng.hn.),*3,*3 - 4,2,3,0 -
perc.,xyl.   26:00 A.P.R.A.
—— ROMANTIC SYMPHONY (1960)
2(2nd alt. with picc.),2(2nd alt. with Eng.hn.),2,2 - 4,2,3,0 -
timp.,perc.   28:00 A.P.R.A.

PERL, Lothar
—— CONCERTO FOR VIOLIN AND ORCH. (IN 3 MOVTS.)
2,2,2,2 - 3,2,0,0 - timp.,perc. - str.   23:00 Composer.

PERLE, George
—— CONCERTO FOR CELLO AND ORCH. (IN 3 MOVTS.)
17:00 Presser.
—— SERENADE NO. 1 FOR VIOLA AND SOLO INSTRUMENTS
1,1,1,1 alto sax.,1 - 1,1,1,0 - perc. - 1 vla., 1 d.-b.
13:00 KingsCrown.
—— SERENADE NO. 2 (FOR CHAMBER ORCH.)
18:00 Presser.
—— SERENADE NO. 2 FOR VIOLA AND SOLO INSTRUMENTS
1,1,1,1 alto sax.,1 - 1,1,1,0 - perc.(1),xyl. - 1 vla.   13:00 Presser.
—— SIX BAGATELLES
*3,*3,*3,*3 - 4,3,3,1 - timp.,perc.(3),cel.,xyl. - hp. - str.
5:30 Presser.
—— SONGS OF PRAISE AND LAMENTATION (FOR CHORUS
AND ORCH.) (1974) (IN 3 MOVTS.) (Texts: Biblical, Rainer
Maria Rilke, John Hollander)
40:00 Boelke-Bo.
—— SYMPHONY NO. 2
9:00 C. Fischer.

PERRENOUD, Jean Frédéric
—— CONTRÉES, OP. 31 (THEME VIRGILIEN EN SEPT
MUTATIONS) (POUR ORCH. À CORDES, TIMBALES ET
PIANO)
timp. - pf. - str.   10:00 S.U.I.S.A.
—— FRÈRES HUMAINS, OP. 27 (SYMPHONIE NR. 4)
*3,*2,*2,*2 - 3,2,1,1 - timp.,perc.,cel. - hp. - pf. - str.
25:00 S.U.I.S.A.

—— MOUVANCE, OP. 46 (OUVERTURE ORCHESTRALE)
15:00 S.U.I.S.A.
—— OUTRETERRE (CONCERTO NR. 2 POUR PIANO ET
ORCHESTRE)
*3,*3,*3,*3 - 0,0,0,0 - timp.,perc.,cel. - hp. - pf. - str.
24:00 S.U.I.S.A.

PERRIN, Jean
—— CONCERTO POUR VIOLINCELLE ET ORCHESTRE
2,2,2,2 - 2,2,2,0 - timp.,perc. - str.   28:00 S.U.I.S.A.
—— NOCTURNE POUR ORCHESTRE
1,1,2,1 - 2,2,1,0 - timp.,perc. - str.   7:00 S.U.I.S.A.
—— OUVERTURE POUR UN JOUR DE FÊTE
2,2,2,2 - 2,2,2,0 - timp.,perc. - pf. - str. 6:00 S.U.I.S.A.
—— SYMPHONIE NR. 3
2,2,2,2 - 2,2,0,0 - timp.,perc.(3) - str.   25:25 S.U.I.S.A.

PERRY, Harold
—— CONCERTINO FOR VIOLIN (OR CLARINET) AND ORCH.
2,2,2,2 - 2,2,0,0, - perc. - str.   8:00 Bo. Hawkes.

PERRY, Julia
—— THE CASK OF AMONTILLADO (1-ACT OPERA) %
2,2,4,1 - 2,1,2,1 - timp.,perc. - hp. - pf. - str.   30:00 Southern.
—— CONCERTO FOR VIOLIN AND ORCH.
2,2,2,sax.,2 - 2,2,2,0 - timp.,perc. - hp. - pf. - str.
17:00 C. Fischer.
—— CONCERTO NO. 2 FOR PIANO AND ORCH.
3,2,3,alto sax.,2 - 4,3,2,0 - timp.,perc. - pf. - str.   14:00 Southern.
—— FRAMMENTI DALLE LETTERE DE SANTA CATERINA (FOR
SOPRANO, MIXED CHORUS AND ORCH.)
1,2,2,2 - 1,1,1,0 - timp.,perc. - hp. - str.
10:00 Southern.
—— HOMAGE TO VIVALDI
3,2,2,2 - 4,2,2,bar.,0 - timp.,perc. - hp. - str.   7:30 Southern.
—— SHORT PIECE
2,2,2,2 - 2,2,2,0 - timp.,perc.,cel. - hp. - pf. - str.   8:00 Southern.
or:
3,3,3,3 - 4,3,2,1 - timp.,perc.,cel. - hp. - pf. - str.
—— A SIMPLE SYMPHONY (1973) (IN 1 MOVT.)
0,0,3,0 - 0,3,0,0 - timp.,perc.(3) - str.   6:21 Composer.
—— STABAT MATER (FOR CHORUS AND STRINGS)
str.   17:00 Southern.

PERSICHETTI, Vincent
—— CELEBRATIONS FOR CHORUS AND WIND ENSEMBLE, OP.
103 (IN 9 MOVTS.)
3,2,4,2 - 3,4,3,bar.1 - timp.,perc.(3)   23:00 EV.
—— CONCERTINO FOR PIANO AND ORCH., OP. 16
2,2,2,2 - 2,2,0,0 - timp. - pf. - str.   9:00 EV.
—— CONCERTO FOR PIANO AND ORCH., OP. 90 (IN 3 MOVTS.)
*3,2,*3,2 - 4,3,3,1 - timp.,perc.(3) - pf. - str.   36:00 EV.
—— THE CREATION, OP. 111 (FOR SOPRANO, ALTO, TENOR,
BASS, CHORUS AND ORCH.)
3,3,3,2 - 4,4,3,1 - timp.,perc. - pf. - str.   60:00 EV.
—— DANCE OVERTURE, OP. 20
*3,*3,3,3 - 4,4,3,1 - timp.,perc. - pf. - str. 8:00 EV.
—— FABLES FOR NARRATOR AND ORCH., OP. 23 (IN 6
MOVTS.)
*3,*3,*3,2 - 4,3,3,1 - timp.,perc.(2) - pf. - str.   21:30 C. Fischer.
—— FAIRY TALE
3,3,2,2 - 4,2,3,1 - timp.,perc. - str.   3:30 C. Fischer.
—— THE HOLLOW MEN, OP. 25
tpt. - str.   7:30 EV.
—— INTROIT FOR STRINGS, OP. 96
str.   3:30 EV.
—— A LINCOLN ADDRESS, OP. 124 (FOR NARRATOR AND
ORCH.)
4,3,4,3 - 4,3,3,1 - timp.,perc. - str.   11:00 EV.
—— NIGHT DANCES, OP. 114
3,3,2,2 - 4,3,3,1 - timp.,perc. - str.   22:00 EV.
—— THE PLEIADES (FOR MIXED CHORUS, TRUMPET AND
STRING ORCH.) (Text: Walt Whitman)
tpt. - str.   23:00 EV.
—— SERENADE NO. 1, OP. 1 (FOR TEN WINDS)
1,1,1,1 - 2,2,1,1,   10:00 EV.
—— SERENADE NO. 5, OP. 43
2,2,2,2 - 4,2,3,1 - timp. - str.   10:00 EV.
—— SINFONIA "JANICULUM", OP. 113 (SYMPHONY NO. 9)
4,3,4,3 - 4,3,3,1 - timp.,perc. - hp. - str.   23:00 EV.
—— STABAT MATER, OP. 92 (FOR SATB CHORUS AND ORCH.)
2,2,2,2 - 4,2,3,1 - timp. - str.   28:00 EV.
—— SYMPHONY FOR STRINGS, OP. 61 (IN 1 MOVT.)
str.   18:00 EV.

—— SYMPHONY NO. 1, OP. 18
    1. Lento; 2. Andante con moto
    2,*3,2,*3 - 4,3,3,1 - str.   16:00 Composer.
—— SYMPHONY NO. 2, OP. 19 (IN 3 MOVTS.)
    2,*3,2,2 - 4,2,2,0 - timp. - pf. - str.   18:00 Composer.
—— SYMPHONY NO. 3, OP. 30 (IN 4 MOVTS.)
    *3,*3,*3,*3 - 4,3,3,1 - timp.,perc.(4) - pf. - str.   30:00 EV.
—— SYMPHONY NO. 4, OP. 51
    *3,*3,*3,2 - 4,2,3,1 - timp. - str.   23:00 EV.
—— SYMPHONY NO. 7, OP. 80 ("THE LITURGIC")
    4,*3,4,3 - 4,3,3,1 - timp.,perc.(3) - str.   25:00 EV.
—— SYMPHONY NO. 8, OP. 106 (1967) (IN 4 MOVTS.)
    *3,*3,*3,2 - 4,3,3,1 - timp.,perc.(3) - str.   29:00 EV.
—— TE DEUM, OP. 93 (FOR SATB CHORUS AND ORCH.)
    2,2,2,2 - 4,2,3,1 - timp.,perc. - str.   11:00 EV.

PERT, Morris
—— EILEAN DONNAN, OP. 3
    timp. - str.   20:00 Bo. Hawkes.
—— SUN DRAGON, OP. 12
    3,3,3,3 - 4,3,3,1 - timp.,perc.(5),cel. - tape-recorder - pf. - str.
    17:00 Bo. Hawkes.
—— SYMPHONY IN ONE MOVT., OP. 27
    3,3,3,3 - 5,3,3,1 - timp.,perc.(4),cel. - hp. - pf. - str.   Bo. Hawkes.
—— XUMBU-ATA, OP. 5
    2,2,3,2 - 4,2,3,1 - timp.,perc.(6),cel. - hp. - pf. - str.
    19:00 Bo. Hawkes.

PESKO, Zoltan
—— CONCERTO FOR CELLO AND ORCH.
    Leeds.
—— ICONE D'UNE GRANDE CITTÁ (FRAGMENTS FOR
    SOPRANO AND CHAMBER ORCH.)
    Leeds.
—— RITRATTO DI UNA SANTA (PORTRAIT OF A SAINT) (FOR
    SOPRANO, CHILDREN'S VOICES AND 15
    INSTRUMENTALISTS) (1969)
    1,0,1,1 - 0,1,1,0 - perc.(4),bells,xyl. - hp. - hpsc.(alt. with cel.) - pf.
    - vln.,vla.,c.   10:00 MCA Music.
—— TRASFORMAZIONE (FOR 16 STRING INSTRUMENTS) (1970)
    str.(5,5,3,2,1)   10:10 MCA Music.

PESOLA, Väinö
—— ELEGY (FOR PIANO AND ORCH.)
    1,1,2,1 - 2,2,1,0 - timp.,perc. - pf. - str.   5:00 FinnMICtr.
—— LIGHT SUITE, OP. 25, NO. 2 (1929)
    2,2,2,0 - 2,2,1,0 - timp. - hp. - str.   9:00 FinnMICtr.
—— THE OUTER ISLANDERS (OPERA) % (1950) (Text:
    Larin-Kyösti)
    2,2,2,2 - 4,2,3,1 - timp.,perc. - hp. - str.   FinnMICtr.
—— PIECES FROM YOUTH
    2,2,2,2 - 4,2,3,1 - timp.,perc. - str.   19:00 FinnMICtr.
—— SONG OF THE NEW DAWN, OP. 54 (CANTATA) (FOR
    CHORUS AND ORCH.) (1945) (Text: J. Raitio)
    2,2,2,2 - 4,2,3,1 - timp.,perc. - str.   35:00 FinnMICtr.
—— SUITE FROM SOUTHWEST FINLAND, OP. 29, NO. 1 (1933)
    str.   10:00 FinnMICtr.
—— SUITE FROM VAKKA-SUOMI, OP. 5 (1926) (IN 3 MOVTS.)
    2,2,2,2 - 4,2,3,1 - timp.,perc. - str.   11:00 FinnMICtr.
—— SYMPHONY NO. 1 IN E FLAT MINOR, OP. 26 (1933)
    2,2,2,2 - 4,2,3,1 - timp.,perc. - str.   34:00 FinnMICtr.
—— SYMPHONY NO. 2 IN A MINOR (1944)
    2,2,2,2 - 4,2,3,1 - timp.,perc. - str.   33:00 FinnMICtr.
—— SYMPHONY NO. 3 IN F MINOR (1952)
    2,2,2,2 - 4,2,3,1 - timp.,perc. - str.   22:00 FinnMICtr.

PESONEN, Olavi
—— AWAKENING, OP. 3 (FOR SPEAKING VOICE AND ORCH.)
    (1936)
    3,2,2,2 - 4,1,1,0 - timp. - hp. - str.   25:00 FinnMICtr.
—— FESTIVE OVERTURE (Rev. 1946)
    2,2,2,2 - 3,2,2,0 - timp. - str.   8:00 FinnMICtr.
—— FUGA FANTASTICA, OP. 9 (1948)
    2,2,3,2 - 4,3,3,1 - timp. - str.   8:00 FinnMICtr.
—— GOD! DON'T THROW ME TO YOUR STONES, OP. 26 (6
    SONGS FOR VOICE AND STRINGS) (1953) (Text: Hans
    Schaffen)
    str.   10:00 FinnMICtr.
—— LITTLE SUITE, OP. 4 (1936) (IN 3 MOVTS.)
    2,2,2,2 - 2,3,3,0 - timp. - hp. - str.   12:00 FinnMICtr.
—— SYMPHONY NO. 1, OP. 25 (1949)
    3,2,3,3 - 4,3,3,1 - timp.,perc. - str.   31:00 FinnMICtr.

—— SYMPHONY NO. 2, OP. 27 (1953)
    2,2,2,2 - 4,3,3,1 - timp.,perc.(3) - str.   25:00 FinnMICtr.

PETERSON, Wayne
—— CATACLYSMS (MUSIC FROM A GREEK TRAGEDY) (1967)
    2(2nd alt. with picc.),2(2nd alt. with Eng. hn.)2(2nd alt. with
    b.-cl.),2 - 2,2,2,0 - timp.,perc.(4-5),bells,cel.,glock.,xyl. - hp. -
    str.   14:00 Seesaw.
—— EXALTATION, DITHYRAMB AND CAPRICE (SYMPHONY IN
    3 MOVEMENTS)
    22:00 Bo. Hawkes.
—— FREE VARIATIONS FOR ORCH.
    3,3,3,3 - 4,3,3,1 - timp.,perc.,cel. - pf. - str.   20:00 Bo. Hawkes.

PETERSON-BERGER, Wilhelm
—— CONCERTO FOR VIOLIN AND ORCH.
    2,2,2,2 - 3,3,3,1 - timp.,perc. - hp. - pf. - str.   Lundquists.
—— INTERMEZZO, CHORALE AND FUGUE (FROM "THE
    DOOMSDAY PROPHECIES")
    3,3,3,3 - 4,3,3,1 - timp.,perc. - hp. - org.(ad lib.) - str.
    6:30 Lundquists.
—— ITALIAN SUITE (IN 4 MOVTS.)
    Lundquists.
—— SYMPHONY NO. 1 ("BANERET")
    3,2,2,2 - 3,3,3,1 - timp.,perc. - str.   S.T.I.M.
—— SYMPHONY NO. 2 ("SUNNANFÄRD")
    3,3,3,3 - 4,3,3,1 - timp.,perc. - hp. - str.   45:00 Gehrmans.
—— SYMPHONY NO. 3 ("SAME-ÄTNAM")
    3,3,3,2 - 4,3,3,1 - timp.,perc. - hp. - str.   45:00 E & S.
    or:
    2,1,2,1 - 3,2,3,1 - timp.,perc. - pf. - str.
—— SYMPHONY NO. 4 ("HOLMIA")
    2,2,2,2 - 3,2,3,2 - timp.,perc. - str.   S.T.I.M.
—— SYMPHONY NO. 5 ("SOLITUDO")
    3,2,2,2 - 3,2,3,2 - timp.,perc. - str.   S.T.I.M.
—— TÖRNROSSAGAN (SUITE)
    2,1,2,1 - 3,2,1,0 - timp.,perc. - str.   S.T.I.M.

PETIN, Nikola
—— CONCERTO FOR PIANO AND ORCH.
    3,2,2,2 - 4,3,3,0 - timp.,perc. - pf. - str.   25:00 S.O.K.O.J.
—— SINFONIA BREVIS
    3,3,3,2 - 4,3,3,1 - timp.,perc. - hp. - str.   27:00 S.O.K.O.J.
—— SYMPHONY NO. 3 (ROMANTIQUE)
    3,2,2,2 - 4,3,3,1 - timp.,perc. - str.   26:00 S.O.K.O.J.
—— THREE SYMPHONIC PORTRAITS
    3,3,3,2 - 4,3,3,1 - timp.,perc. - hp. - pf. - str.   25:00 S.O.K.O.J.

PETIOT, André
—— LA CAMARGUAISE (FOR MIXED CHORUS AND ORCH.)
    2,3,3,2 - 4,3,3,0 - timp.,perc.,bells,cel. - hp. - str.   15:00 Baron.

PETIT, Pierre
—— CONCERTINO FOR ORGAN, STRINGS, TIMPANI AND
    PERCUSSION
    timp.,perc. - org. - str.   20:00 Baron.
—— CONCERTINO FOR PIANO AND ORCH.
    Baron.
—— CONCERTO FOR PIANO AND ORCH.
    3,2,3,2 - 4,3,3,1 - timp.,perc. - hp. - pf. - str.   32:00 Salabert.
—— CONCERTO FOR TWO GUITARS AND ORCH.
    2,1,2,2 - 2,2,1,0 - timp.,perc.(3) - 2 guit. - str.   15:30 Presser.
—— SUITE FOR TWO CELLOS AND STRING ORCH. (1966)
    str.   13:00 Salabert.

PETITGIRARD, A.
—— LA LORELEÏ (CANTATA ON A POEM OF APOLLINAIRE)
    *2,*2,2,2 - 2,2,2,1 - timp.,perc.(5),bells,cel.,glock.,vibra.,xyl. - hp. -
    pf. - str.   Eds. Fran.
—— RÊVES POUR UN TEMPS MODERNE (FOR SSA WOMEN'S
    CHORUS AND STRING ORCH.)
    pf. - str.   7:00 Eds. Fran.

PETRASSI, Goffredo
—— CONCERTO FOR FLUTE AND ORCH.
    1,0,2,2 - 4,3,3,0 - perc.(3) - guit. - hp. - c.,d.-b.   16:00 Leeds.
—— CONCERTO FOR PIANO AND ORCH.
    3,3,2,2 - 4,3,3,1 - pf. - str.   25:00 Leeds.
—— CONCERTO NO. 2 FOR ORCH.
    2,2,2,2 - 2,2,0,0 - timp. - str.   17:00 Leeds.
—— CONCERTO NO. 4 FOR STRING ORCH.
    str.   22:00 Leeds.

—— CONCERTO NO. 5 FOR ORCH.
3,3,3,2 - 4,3,3,0 - timp.,perc.(3) - hp. - str.   24:00 Leeds.
—— CONCERTO NO. 7 FOR ORCH.
   Leeds.
—— IL CORDOVANO (1-ACT OPERA, AFTER CERVANTES) %
(Text: E. Montale)
2,2,2,2 - 4,3,3,0 - timp.,perc.,xyl. - hp. - pf. - str.   50:00 Leeds.
or:
2,2,2,1 - 2,1,1,0 - perc.,xyl. - pf. - str.
—— CORO DI MORTI (FOR CHORUS AND ORCH.)
   MCA Music.
—— DUE LIRICHE DI SAFFO (2 POEMS OF SAPPHO) (FOR VOICE AND 11 INSTRS.)
1,1,1,1 - 1,1,0,0 - hp. - str.(no d.-b.)   6:30 Leeds.
—— ESTRI (FOR 15 PLAYERS) (1967)
2,0,2,0 - 1,1,1,0 - perc.(5),cel.,glock.,vibra. - hpsc. - vla.,c.,d.-b.   13:00 MCA Music.
—— LA FOLLIA DE ORLANDO: SYMPHONIC SUITE FROM THE BALLET
3,3,3,3 - 4,3,3,1 - timp.,perc.,xyl. - hp. - hpsc. - str.   20:00 Leeds.
—— LA FOLLIA DI ORLANDO ("THE MADNESS OF ROLAND") (BALLET, WITH BARITONE RECITATIVES ON TEXTS OF ARIOSTO) %
3,3,3,3 - 4,3,3,1 - timp.,perc.,xyl. - hp. - hpsc. - str.   70:00 Leeds.
—— INVENZIONE CONCERTATA (CONCERTO NO. 6 FOR ORCH.)
0,0,0,0 - 4,3,2,1 - perc.(4) - str.   14:00 Leeds.
—— LA MORTE DEL'ARIA (THE DEATH OF THE AIR) (1-ACT OPERA) % (Text: Toti Scialoja)
2,*1,3,1 - 2,1,1,0 - timp.,perc. - harm. - str.(no vlns.)   Leeds.
—— MUSICA DI OTTONI (FOR 13 INSTRUMENTS)
   MCA Music.
—— NOCHE OSCURA ("DARK NIGHT") (CANTATA) (FOR MIXED CHORUS AND ORCH.) (Text: San Juan de la Cruz)
3,3,3,3 - 4,4,3,1 - timp.,perc. - hp. - str.   22:00 Leeds.
—— PROLOGO E CINQUE INVENZIONI
3,2,2,2 - 4,2,3,1 - timp.,perc.(5),xylomarimba - hp. - str.   Leeds.
—— PROPOS D'ALAIN (FOR BARITONE AND 12 INSTRS.)
0,*1,1,0 - 0,0,1,0 - timp.,perc.(2)mar.,xyl. - 2 vla.,2 c.   16:00 Leeds.
—— QUATTRO INNI SACRI (4 SACRED HYMNS) (FOR TENOR, BARITONE, AND ORCH.)
2,2,2,2 - 2,2,0,0 - timp. - str.   19:40 Leeds.
—— RECREATION CONCERTANTE (CONCERTO NO. 3 FOR ORCH.)
2,2,2,2 - 2,1,1,0 - perc.(2) - str.(no d.-b.)   18:00 Leeds.
—— SONATA DA CAMERA (FOR HARPSICHORD AND 10 INSTRS.)
1,1,1,1 - 0,0,0,0 - hpsc. - str.   14:00 Leeds.

PETRESCU, Dinu
—— APOLLO XI (HOMMAGE À CEUX QUI ONT CONQUIS LA LUNE (FOR 52 STRINGS, PERCUSSION, 5 CHILDREN'S VOICES AND TAPE) (1969)
perc. - tape-recorder - str.   12:00 Salabert.
—— MUSIQUE POUR 12 INSTRUMENTISTES (1969)
1,0,1,0 - 0,1,0,0 - perc.(1) - hp. - hpsc. - Hammond org. - pf. - str.(1,1,1,1)   15:00 Salabert.

PETRIĆ, Ivo
—— BURLESQUE POUR LES TEMPS PASSÉS
tpt. - perc. - str.   8:00 Hans Gerig.
—— CONCERT OVERTURE
2,2,2,2 - 4,2,3,1 - timp.,perc.(3) - str.   8:00 Hans Gerig.
—— CONCERTO FOR CLARINET AND ORCH.
1,1,*2,0 - 1,0,0,0 - timp.,perc.(4),vibra. - str.   16:00 Hans Gerig.
—— CONCERTO FOR FLUTE AND ORCH.
*2,0,1,1 - 0,1,0,0 - timp.,perc.(3) - hp. - str.   18:00 Hans Gerig.
—— CONCERTO FOR HARP AND STRINGS
hp. - str.   17:00 Hans Gerig.
—— CONCERTO GROSSO FOR STRING ORCH.
str.   17:00 Hans Gerig.
—— DIALOGUES CONCERTANTS (FOR CELLO AND ORCH.)
0,0,3(3rd alt. with b.-cl.),2 - 0,3,1,0 - perc.(2) - hp. - pf.(alt. with cel.) - str.   17:00 Hans Gerig.
—— DIVERTIMENTO FOR SLAVKO OSTERC
1,1,1,1 - 1,0,0,0 - perc. - hp. - pf. - str.(2,1,1,1) 15:00 Hans Gerig.
—— DIVERTIMENTO (FOR WOODWINDS, BRASS AND PERCUSSION)
*2,*2,2,2 - 4,2,0,0 - timp.,perc.(3)   9:00 Hans Gerig.
—— EPISODES LYRIQUES (FOR OBOE AND CHAMBER ORCH.)
ob. - perc.(3),cel. - guit. - hp. - str.   14:00 Hans Gerig.

—— EPITAPH (FOR CLARINET, HARP, VIOLIN, CELLO, PERCUSSION AND STRING ORCH.)
cl. - hp. - perc. - str.   12:00 Hans Gerig.
—— GEMINI CONCERTO (FOR VIOLIN, CELLO AND ORCH.)
0,2(2nd alt. with Eng. hn.),2(2nd alt. with b.-cl.),0 - 3,0,3,0 - perc.(3),cel. - hp. - pf. - str.   16:00 Hans Gerig.
—— A GOGA SYMPHONY (1954)
2(2nd alt. with picc.),2(2nd alt. with Eng.hn.),2(2nd alt. with b.-cl.),1(alt. with c.-bn.) - 4,3,3,1 - timp.,perc.(5) - hp. - str.   25:00 Hans Gerig.
—— INTAGLIO (FOR WOODWIND TRIO AND CHAMBER ENSEMBLE)
1,0,1,1 - 1,1,1,0 - perc. - str.(2,1,1,1)   13:00 Hans Gerig.
—— INTEGRALS IN COLOR (SOUND-REFLECTIONS ON KOSOVEL'S POETRY)
1(alt. with picc.),1(alt. with Eng. hn.),1(alt. with b.-cl.),1(alt. with c.-bn.) - 1,1,1,0 - perc.(2),vibra. - hp. - pf. - str.   19:00 Hans Gerig.
—— MUSIQUE CONCERTANTE (FOR PIANO AND ORCH.)
3(3rd alt. with picc.),3,3(3rd alt. with b.-cl.),3(3rd alt. with c.-bn.) - 4,3,3,1 - perc.(2),vibra. - hp. - pf.- str.   22:00 Hans Gerig.
—— MUSIQUE CONCERTANTE (FOR WOODWIND QUINTET, TIMPANI AND STRINGS)
1,1,1,1 - 1,0,0,0 - timp. - str.   16:00 Hans Gerig.
—— NOCTURNES AND GAMES (1976)
1(alt. with picc.),1(alt. with Eng. hn.),1(alt. with E♭cl. and b.-cl.),1(alt. with c.-bn.) - 3,3,3,0 - perc.(3),vibra. - hp. - pf.(alt. with cel.) - str.   16:00 Hans Gerig.
—— PETIT CONCERTO DE CHAMBRE (NEW VERSION, FOR OBOE AND STRING ORCH.)
ob. - str.   18:00 Hans Gerig.
—— SUITE CONCERTANTE FOR BASSOON AND STRINGS
bn. - str.   12:00 Hans Gerig.
—— SYMPHONIC FRESCO
*3,2(2nd alt. with Eng. Hn.),2(2nd alt. with b.-cl.),2(2nd alt. with c.-bn.) - 3,3,3,0 - perc.(3) - hp. - pf. - str.   13:00 Hans Gerig.
—— SYMPHONIC MUTATIONS
*3,2(2nd alt. with Eng. hn.),2(alt. with b.-cl. and ten. sax.),2(2nd alt. with c.-bn.) - 4,3,3,1 - timp.,perc.(6),vibra. - hp. - pf. - str.   15:00 Hans Gerig.
—— SYMPHONY NO. 2 (1957)
2(2nd alt. with picc.),2(2nd alt. with Eng. hn.),2(2nd alt. with b.-cl.),2(2nd alt. with c-bn.) - 4,3,3,1 - timp.,perc.(6) - str.   28:00 Hans Gerig.
—— SYMPHONY NO. 3 (1960)
2(2nd alt. with picc.),2(2nd alt. with Eng. hn.),2(2nd alt. with b.-cl.)2,(2nd alt. with c.-bn.) - 4,3,3,1 - timp.,perc.(4) - str.   27:00 Hans Gerig.
—— THREE COMPOSITIONS FOR HORN AND ORCH.
2(2nd alt. with picc.),2(2nd alt. with Eng. hn.),2(2nd alt. with b.-cl.),2(2nd alt. with c.-bn.) - 5,2,3,1 - timp.,perc.(4) - hp. - str.   12:00 Hans Gerig.
—— TROIS IMAGES (CONCERTO FOR VIOLIN AND ORCH.)
3(2 alt. with 2 picc.),*1,3(3rd alt. with b.-cl.),2(2nd alt. with c.-bn.) - 3,1,1,0 - perc.(3) - hp. - pf.(alt. with cel.) - str.   25:00 Hans Gerig.

PETRIDIS, Petro
—— TROIS MELODIES GRECQUES (FOR VOICE AND ORCH.)
   Salabert.

PETROVIĆ, Radomir
—— SYMPHONIC EPITAPH (CANTATA) (FOR SOPRANO, SATB CHORUS AND ORCH.)
3,3,3,3 - 4,3,3,1 - timp.,perc.,cel.,vibra. - hp. - pf. - str.   18:00 MIC,Zagreb.
—— SYMPHONY
3,3,3,3 - 4,3,3,1 - timp.,perc.,cel.,vibra.,xyl. - hp. - pf. - str.   19:00 MIC,Zagreb.

PETROVICS, Emil
—— THE BOOK OF JONAH (ORATORIO) (FOR TENOR, BARITONE, SATB CHORUS AND ORCH.)
*3,*3,*3,*3 - 4,3,3,1 - timp.,perc.,cel. - hp. - cemb. - pf. - str.   43:00 Bo. Hawkes.
—— CANTATA NO. 2 (FOR CHORUS AND ORCH.)
*2,2,2,2 - 4,*3,3,1 - timp.,perc. - str.   12:18 Bo. Hawkes.
—— CONCERTO FOR FLUTE AND ORCH.
3,2,2,2 - 2,2,0,0 - timp.,perc. - hp. - pf. - str.   21:05 Bo. Hawkes.

PETRUSHKA, Shabtai
—— FIVE ORIENTAL DANCES
2,2,2,2 - 4,2,3,0 - timp.,perc. - pf. - str.   10:00 IsMuPublns.

—— THREE MOVEMENTS FOR ORCHESTRA
3,*3,*3,*3 - 4,3,3,1 - timp.,perc. - str.   12:00 IsMuPublns.

PETRŽELKA, Vilém
—— CONCERTO FOR VIOLIN AND ORCH., OP. 40
    Bo. Hawkes.

—— DRAMATIC OVERTURE, OP. 26
    Bo. Hawkes.

—— THE ETERNAL RETURN (SYMPHONIC POEM) (1923)
    Bo. Hawkes.

—— HYMN TO THE SUN (CANTATA) (1921)
    Bo. Hawkes.

—— PARTITA
str.   Bo. Hawkes.

—— PAUL THE MINER (OPERA) (1938) %
    Bo. Hawkes.

—— SINFONIETTA, OP. 38
    Bo. Hawkes.

—— SINFONIETTA (PASTORAL) OP. 51 (1952) (IN 4 MOVTS.)
3,3,2,2 - 4,3,3,1 - timp.,perc. - hp. - str.   20:00 Bo. Hawkes.

PETTERSSON, Allan
—— CONCERTO NO. 1 FOR STRINGS
str.   21:00 S.T.I.M.
—— CONCERTO NO. 2 FOR STRING ORCH. (1956)
str.   22:30 S.T.I.M.
—— CONCERTO NO. 3 FOR STRING ORCH. (1957)
str.   49:00 S.T.I.M.
—— SYMPHONIC MOVEMENT (1973)
2,2,2,2 - 4,3,3,1 - timp.,perc. - str.   11:00 Fleisher.
—— SYMPHONY NO. 2
2,2,2,2 - 2,2,2,0 - timp.,perc.(4),cel. - str.   42:00 S.T.I.M.
—— SYMPHONY NO. 3
3,3,3,3 - 4,3,3,1 - timp.,perc.(3),xyl. - str.   33:30 S.T.I.M.
—— SYMPHONY NO. 4 (1959)
3,3,3,3 - 4,3,3,1 - timp.,perc.(9),cel. - str.   38:00 S.T.I.M.
—— SYMPHONY NO. 5
2,2,2,3 - 4,3,3,1 - timp.,perc.(2) - str.   S.T.I.M.
—— SYMPHONY NO. 6 (1966)
2,2,2,2 - 4,3,3,1 - timp. - str.   55:00 S.T.I.M.
—— SYMPHONY NO. 7 (1967)
3,2,3,3 - 3,4,3,1 - timp.,perc.(4) - str.   42:00 S.T.I.M.
—— SYMPHONY NO. 8 (1968)
3,2,3,3 - 3,4,3,1 - timp.,perc.(4) - str.   S.T.I.M.
—— SYMPHONY NO. 9 (1969)
3,2,3,3 - 3,4,3,1 - timp.,perc.(4) - str.   S.T.I.M.
—— SYMPHONY NO. 10 (1972)
3,2,3,3 - 4,3,3,1 - timp.,perc.(6) - str.   26:00 Fleisher.
—— SYMPHONY NO. 11 (1973)
3,2,3,3 - 3,4,3,1 - timp.,perc.(7) - str.   24:00 Fleisher.
—— SYMPHONY NO. 12 ("DE DÖDA PÅ TORGET")(FOR SATB
CHORUS AND ORCH.)(1974) (Text: Pablo Neruda)
2,2,3,2 - 4,3,3,1 - timp.perc.(5) - str.   Fleisher.

PETTERSSON, Allan - DORATI, Antal
—— ÅTTA BARFOTASÅNGER (1970) (Orch., by A. Dorati)
2,2,2,2 - 4,2,2,0 - timp.,perc. - hp. - str.   Fleisher.

PETYREK, Felix
—— VARIATIONS AND FUGUE ON A THEME FROM VERDI'S
"FALSTAFF"
2,2,2,2 - 3,2,1,0 - timp.,perc. - str.   23:00 Alkor.

PEYROT, Fernande
—— SUITE FOR STRINGS
str.   15:00 S.U.I.S.A.

PEZ, Johann Christoph - HOECKNER
—— CONCERTO PASTORALE IN F MAJOR
2 fl. - cemb. - str.   Henmar.

PEZ, Johann Christoph - SCHROEDER
—— SONATA A 4
cemb. - str.   Henmar.

PEZ, Johann Christoph - SCHULTZ-HAUSER
—— CONCERTO PASTORELLA IN D MAJOR (FOR VIOLIN,
CEMBALO AND STRINGS)
cemb. - str.   8:00 Henmar.

PEZEL, Johann - SCHERING
—— SUITE IN G MINOR
cemb. - str.   14:00 Henmar.

PEZZATI, Romano
—— COMPOSIZIONE (1966)
3,3,3,3 - 4,2,3,1 - timp.,perc.(8),cel.,mar.,vibra.,xyl. - hp. - str.
    17:00 MCA Music.
—— DAILOGHI (FOR PIANO, CHAMBER ORCH. AND
PERCUSSION) (1967)
2,2,2,2 - 2,1,1,0 - timp.,perc.,mar.,vibra. - pf. - str.
    10:00 MCA Music.
—— PUNTI, LINEE, SPESSORI (1968)
2,2,2,2 - 2,2,1,0 - timp.,perc.,mar. - hp. - str.   13:00 MCA Music.

PFANNENSTIEL, Ekkehart
—— MORGENKANTATE ("MORNING CANTATA") (FOR
SOPRANO, BARITONE, MIXED CHORUS, 2 FLUTES AND
STRING ORCH.)
2 fl. - str.   20:00 F. Colombo.

PFIFFNER, Ernst
—— ELEGIE FÜR OBOE UND STREICHER
ob. - str.   9:00 S.U.I.S.A.

PFISTER, Hugo
—— AEGEAN DIARY
ob. - perc. - str.   27:30 Henmar.
—— DUO CONCERTANTE (FÜR VIOLA, VIOLINCELLO UND
STREICHORCHESTER)
str.   16:00 S.U.I.S.A.
—— FANTASY CONCERTANTE
fl. - hn. - hp. - str.   19:30 Henmar.
—— FIVE SKETCHES (FOR PERCUSSION AND ORCHESTRA)
2,2,2,2 - 2,2,2,0 - per. - str.   21:00 S.U.I.S.A.

PFITZNER, Hans
—— DAS CHRISTELFLEIN (2 ACT OPERA) (REVISED) %
2,2,2,2 - 2,1,0,0 - timp.,perc. - hp. - str.   120:00 Bo. Hawkes.
—— CONCERTO IN B MINOR, OP. 34, FOR VIOLIN AND ORCH.
3,3,3,3 - 4,3,3,1 - timp. - hp. - str.   30:00 Bo. Hawkes.
—— CONCERTO IN C MINOR, FOR CELLO AND ORCH., OP. 52
2,2,2,2 - 4,2,0,0 - timp.,perc. - hp. - str.   25:00 J. Oertel.
—— CONCERTO IN E♭, OP. 31, FOR PIANO AND ORCH.
3,3,3,3 - 4,3,3,1 - timp.,perc. - hp. - pf. - str.   40:00 Bo. Hawkes.
—— FANTASIE, OP. 56
3,3,2,2 - 4,2,2,0 - timp.,perc. - str.   17:00 Brockhaus.
—— HOFFEST UND LIEBESMELODIE (FROM "DAS HERZ", OP.
39)
3,3,3,3 - 4,3,3,1 - timp.,cel. - hp. - str.   15:00 Bo. Hawkes.
—— KLEINE SINFONIE, OP. 44
2,2,2,2 - 0,1,0,0 - perc. - hp. - str.   20:00 Brockhaus.
—— OVERTURE TO "DAS CHRIST-ELFLEIN", OP. 20
2,2,2,2 - 2 hn. - timp.,perc. - hp. - str.   12:00 Bo. Hawkes.
—— SYMPHONY NO. 1 IN C# MINOR, OP. 36A (AFTER THE
STRING QUARTET)
2,2,2,2 - 4,3,3,1 - timp. - hp. - str.   45:00 Bo. Hawkes.
—— SYMPHONY NO. 2 IN C, OP. 46 ("AN DIE FREUNDE")
2,2,2,2 - 4,3,3,0 - timp.,perc. - hp. - str.   21:00 Bo. Hawkes.

PHILIDOR - CARSE, Adam
—— OVERTURE TO "LES FEMMES VENGÉES"
2,2,0,2 - 2,2,0,0 - timp. - str.   5:00 Galaxy.

PHILIPPOT, Michel
—— COMPOSITION FOR DOUBLE ORCH. (IN 5 MOVTS.)
Orch. I: *2,*1, E♭cl.,1,1 - 0,1,0,0 - str.   10:40 Eds. Fran.
Orch. II: 1,0,1,1 - 1,0,0,0 - str.
—— COMPOSITION FOR STRINGS
str.   7:30 Eds. Fran.
—— PIÈCE POUR DIX
    5:10 S.A.C.E.M.

PHILLIPS, Burrill
—— CONCERT PIECE FOR BASSOON AND STRINGS
bn. - str.   4:30 C. Fischer.
—— CONCERTO FOR PIANO AND ORCH. (IN 3 MOVTS.)
2,2,2,2 - 4,2,3,1 - timp.,perc. - pf. - str.   18:00 EV.
—— CONCERTO GROSSO FOR STRING QUARTET AND SMALL
ORCH. (IN 3 MOVTS.)
1,1,1,1 - hn. - str.   12:00 Composer.
—— COURTHOUSE SQUARE (SUITE)
3(3rd alt. with picc.),*3,*3,*3 - 4,3,3,1 - timp.,perc. - hp. - str.
    14:00 EV.
—— DANCE OVERTURE
2,2,2,2 sax.,2 - 4,2,3,1 - timp.,perc.(2) - hp. - str.   C. Fischer.

—— DECLARATIVES (FOR WOMEN'S CHORUS AND SMALL ORCH.) (IN 3 MOVTS.)
1,1,2,1 - 2,1,1,0 - perc. - pf. - str.   17:00 EV.

—— DIVERTIMENTO FOR STRINGS (IN 3 MOVTS.)
str.   12:00 Composer.

—— DON'T WE ALL (OPERA BUFFA) (FOR 4 SOLO VOICES AND ORCH.) % (Text: Alberta Phillips)
1,1,2,1 - 2,1,1,0 - timp. - pf. - str.   25:00 Composer.

—— MUSIC FOR STRINGS (IN 3 MOVTS.)
str.   11:00 Composer.

—— PERSPECTIVES IN A LABYRINTH (FOR TRIPLE SRING ORCH.) (1962) (IN 3 MOVTS.)
str.   15:30 Composer.

—— PLAY BALL (BALLET MUSIC) %
2(2nd alt. with picc.),2,2,*3 - 4,2,3,1 - timp.,perc.(2),glock.,xyl. - str.   20:00 Composer.

—— THE RETURN OF ODYSSEUS (FOR NARRATOR, BARITONE, MIXED CHORUS AND ORCH.) (Text: Alberta Phillips)
*3,2,*3,2 - 4,3,3,1 - timp.,perc.(3),glock.,xyl. - str.   25:00 Galaxy.

—— SCENA FOR SMALL ORCH.
1,1,2,1 - 2,2,1,0 - timp. - str.   7:00 Hargail.

—— SCHERZO
*3,2,2,*3 - 4,3,3,1 - timp.,perc. - pf. - str.   10:00 EV.

—— SELECTIONS FROM MCGUFFEY'S READER (IN 3 MOVTS.)
*3,2,2,2 - 4,3,3,1 - timp.,perc.(3),cel. - hp. - str.   16:30 C. Fischer.

—— SOLERIANA CONCERTANTE (FOR CHAMBER ORCH.)
1,1,1,1 - 2,1,1,0 - timp.,perc.(2),xyl. - str.   11:00 Composer.

—— STEP INTO MY PARLOUR (BALLET SUITE)
*3,2,2,2 - 4,2,3,1 - timp.,perc.(3) - str.   20:00 Composer.

—— SYMPHONY CONCERTANTE (IN 3 MOVTS.)
1,1,2(2nd alt. with b.-cl.),1 - 2,1,1,0 - timp. - pf. - str.   14:00 C. Fischer.

—— THEATER DANCES (IN 4 MOVTS.) (1967)
2,2,2,2 - 4,3,3,1 - timp.,perc.(3),mar.,glock. - str. 13:00 Composer.

—— THREE SATIRIC FRAGMENTS
2,2,2,2 - 2,1,1,0 - timp.,perc.(2),glock.,xyl. - str.   6:00 Composer.

—— TOM PAINE OVERTURE
*3,2,2,2 - 4,2,3,1 - timp.,perc.(3) - str.   9:00 Hargail.

—— TRIPLE CONCERTO (FOR PIANO, VIOLA, CLARINET AND ORCH.)
1 (alt. with picc.),1,1,1 - 2,1,1,0 - timp.,perc.(2) - pf. - str.   20:00 Composer.

PHILLIPS, Montague F.
—— SINFONIETTA IN C, OP. 70
2,2,2,2 - 2,2,1,0 - timp.,perc.,glock. - hp. - str.   15:00 Novello.

—— THREE COUNTRY PICTURES
8:00 Galaxy.

PHILLIPS, Robert A. S.
—— MR. WHITTIER (FOR NARRATOR, SATB CHORUS, FLUTE AND STRINGS) (1963) (Text: Winfield Townley Scott)
fl. - str.   15:00 Composer.

—— TROPHIES OF THE SUN (5 SONGS FOR VOICE AND SMALL ORCH.) (1963) (Text: Hart Crane)
1,1,1,1 - 2,0,0,0 - timp.,perc.(2),cel. - hp. - str.   15:00 Composer.

PIAGGIO, Celestino
—— OVERTURE IN C MINOR
2,2,2,2 - 4,2,3,1 - timp.,cymb.,glock. - 2 hp. - str.
12:00 ComNaCulBA.

PIATIGORSKY, Gregor - COHN, Arthur
—— VARIATIONS ON A PAGANINI THEME (FOR CELLO AND ORCH.)
2,2,2,2 - 4,2,2,0 - timp.,perc. - hp. - str.   10:00 EV.

PIAZZOLLA, Astor
—— BUENOS AIRES (3 SYMPHONIC MOVEMENTS)
Southern.

—— CONTEMPLATION AND DANCE (FOR CLARINET AND STRINGS)
Southern.

—— SUITE FOR OBOE AND STRINGS
ob. - str.   Southern.

PICCINNI, Nicolo - NEGROTTI, Nino
—— OVERTURE TO "MOLINARELLA"
2 ob. - 2 tpt. - str.   5:00 Bo. Hawkes.

PICCINNI, Nicolo - PICCIOLI, Giuseppe
—— OVERTURE TO "DIDONE"
2,2,2,0 - 2,2,0,0 - str.   10:00 Bo. Hawkes.

—— OVERTURE TO "MOLINARELLA"
0,2,0,0 - 0,2,0,0 - str.   5:00 Bo. Hawkes.

PICCINNI, Nicolo - SCARMOLIN, A. Louis
—— OVERTURE TO "THE GOOD DAUGHTER"
Ludwig.

PICCIOLI, Giuseppe
—— BURLESCA (FOR PIANO AND ORCH.)
2,2,2,2 - 2,2,1,0 - timp.,perc. - pf. - str.   8:00 Bo. Hawkes.

—— CONCERTO FOR PIANO AND ORCH.
2,2,2,2 - 2,2,1,1 - timp.,perc. - pf. - str.   18:00 Leeds.

—— INTERMEZZI SETTECENTESCHI
1,3,1,2 - 0,0,0,0 - hp. - pf. - str.   8:00 Bo. Hawkes.

—— L' OFFERTA DELLE ROSE (POEMETTO) (FOR VOICE AND ORCH.)
3,3,2,2 - 4,3,3,1 - timp.,perc.,bells,cel. - hp. - pf. - str.
25:00 Bo. Hawkes.

PÍCHA, František
—— INVITATION FOR ORCHESTRA (SYMPHONIC ALLEGRO)
3,3,3,3 - 6,3,2,1 - timp.,perc. - hp. - str.   10:00 Bo. Hawkes.

—— SONG OF COURAGE (SYMPHONIC SCHERZO) OP. 32
3,3,3,3 - 6,3,3,1 - timp.,perc. - hp. - str.   27:00 Bo. Hawkes.

—— STEPANCIKOVO ("SHTEPANCHIK"), OP. 20 (DRAMATIC OVERTURE) (1931)
3,3,3,3 - 6,3,3,1 - timp.,perc. - hp. - str.   8:00 Bo. Hawkes.

—— SUITE FOR SMALL ORCHESTRA, OP. 31
2,2,2,2 - 3,2,0,0 - timp.,perc. - str.   21:00 Bo. Hawkes.

—— SUITE FOR STRING ORCH. AND GONG, OP. 18 (1930) (IN 4 MOVTS.)
Gong - str.   23:00 Bo. Hawkes.

PICHEREAU, Claude
—— NEPENTHES (FOR ONDES MARTENOT AND ORCH.)
3,2,2,0 - 2,2,3,0 - timp.,perc. - ondes Martenot - str.
14:00 Presser.

PICK-MANGIAGALLI, Riccardo
—— CONCERTO FOR PIANO AND ORCH. (1930)
3,2,2,2 - 4,3,3,1 - timp.,perc.(3) - pf. - str.   23:00 Leeds.

—— EVOCAZIONI: SUITE FROM THE BALLET
2,2,2,2 - 4,3,3,1 - timp.,perc.,cel. - hp. - str.   25:00 Leeds.

—— EVOCAZIONI (4 CHOREOGRAPHIC SCENES) (1944) %
2,2,2,2 - 4,3,3,1 - timp.,perc.,cel. - hp. - str.   32:00 Leeds.

—— HUMORESQUE (FOR PIANO AND ORCH.)
*3,2,2,2 - 4,2,2,1 - timp. - pf. - str.   14:00 Bo. Hawkes.

—— INTERMEZZO
2,1,2,0 - hn. - hp. - pf. - str.   9:00 Bo. Hawkes.

—— OMBRE DI SOGNI (IN 3 MOVTS.)
2,2,2,2 - 2,2,1,0 - timp.,perc.(2) - str.   12:00 Bo. Hawkes.

—— PRELUDE AND SYMPHONIC SCHERZO
*3,*3,*3,*3 - 4,3,3,1 - timp.,perc.(3) - hp. - str.
13:00 Bo. Hawkes.

—— RHAPSODIE EPICA
*3,2,*3,*3 - 4,3,3,5 - timp.,perc. - org. - pf. - str.
16:00 Bo. Hawkes.

—— TRE FUGHE (THREE FUGUES) (FOR STRING QUARTET AND STRING ORCH.) (1943)
str.   14:00 Leeds.

PIECHLER, Arthur
—— HYMNE, OP. 32 (FOR MALE CHORUS AND SMALL ORCH.)
1,1,2,1 - 2,2,2,1 - timp.,perc. - str.   Bo. Hawkes.

—— SURSUM CORDA, OP. 18 (HYMNS TO THE CHURCH) (FOR SOLO VOICES, CHORUS AND ORCH.)
1,2,1,2 - 2,2,2,0 - timp.,perc.,cel. - hp. - org. - str.   Bo. Hawkes.

—— DAS TAGEWERK ("THE DAY'S WORK"), OP. 43 (FOR SOPRANO, BARITONE, MIXED CHORUS AND ORCH.)
Bo. Hawkes.

PIERNÉ, Gabriel
—— THE CHILDREN AT BETHLEHEM (FOR MIXED CHORUS AND ORCH.)
2,2,2,3 - 4,2,3,0 - timp.,perc. - 2 hp. - str.   G. Schirmer.

—— THE CHILDREN'S CRUSADE (FOR MIXED CHORUS AND ORCH.)
3,3,3,4 - 4,3,3,1 - timp.,perc.,cel. - 2-4 hp. - str.   G. Schirmer.

—— CYDALISE ET LE CHÈVRE-PIED: BALLET SUITE NO. 1
4,3,4,4 - 4,3,4,0 - perc.(3),cel. - hp. - pf. - str.   18:45 Presser.

—— CYDALISE ET LE CHÈVRE-PIED: BALLET SUITE NO. 2
4,3,4,4 - 4,3,4,0 - perc.(3) - 2 hp. - pf. - str.   14:00 Presser.

—— FRAGONARD (BALLET MUSIC) %
    2,1,2,1 - 2,2,3,0 - timp.,perc. - hp. - str.   Salabert.
—— GIRATION (DIVERTIMENTO CHORÉGRAPHIQUE) (FOR
CHAMBER ORCH.)
    1,0,1,1 - 0,1,1,0 - pf. - str.   8:30 Salabert.
—— PRELUDE TO "LES CATHÉDRALES" (WITH OPTIONAL
MIXED CHORUS)
    2,2,3,2 - 2,3,3,0 - timp.,perc. - harm. - 2 hp. - str. 10:00 Salabert.
—— SOPHIE ARNOULD (1-ACT OPERA) %
    3,2,2,2 - 4,3,3,0 - timp.,perc. - hp. - hpsc. - str. 50:00 Presser.
—— VIENNOISE, OP. 49-B (SUITE)
    3,3,3,3 - 4,3,3,1 - timp.,perc.(2) - hp. - str. 9:00 Salabert.

PIERNÉ, Paul
—— MASQUE DE COMÉDIE (SYMPHONIC POEM) (FOR CELLO
AND ORCH.)
    2,2,2,2 - 2,2,3,1 - timp.,perc. - 2 hp. - str. 20:00 Salabert.
—— REQUIEM
      Baron.

PIERRE-PETIT, Yves
—— LE JEU DE L'AMOUR ET DU HASARD (OPERA) % ("LOVE IS
A GAME")
      Presser.

PIETRI, Giuseppe
—— MARISTELLA (3-ACT OPERA) (1933) %
    3,3,3,2 - 4,2,3,1 - timp.,perc.(3),bells,cel.,glock. - 2 hp. - org. - str.
      Leeds.

On Stage: 3 tpt.

PIHLAJAMAA, Lasse
—— DANCE OF THE WINDS
      T.E.O.S.T.O.

PIJPER, Willem
—— CONCERTO FOR CELLO AND ORCH.
    2,2,3,2 - 3,3,3,0 - timp.,perc. - hp. - str. 14:00 Henmar.
—— CONCERTO FOR PIANO AND ORCH.
    2,2,3(2nd alt. with E^{b}cl.and 3rd alt. with b.-cl.),alto sax.,2 -
    3,3,3,0 - perc.(4) - pf. - str. 17:00 Oxford.
—— CONCERTO FOR VIOLIN AND ORCH.
    2,2,3,3 - 4,3,3,0 - hp. - str. 17:00 Henmar.
—— DEUX BALLADES DE PAUL FORT (FOR WOMEN'S CHORUS
AND ORCH.) (1934)
    1,1,1,0 - 1,0,0,0 - perc. - str. 7:00 Henmar.
—— FÊTES GALANTES (3 SONGS FOR MEZZO-SOPRANO AND
ORCH.) (1916) (Text: P. Verlaine)
    3,2,3,1 - 2,1,0,0 - timp.,perc. - hp. - str. 10:00 Henmar.
—— HYMNE (FOR BASS-BARITONE AND ORCH.) (1943) (Text: P.
C. Boutens)
    2,3,3,3 - 4,3,3,1 - timp.,perc. - hp. - str. 13:00 Henmar.
—— LIEDEREN UIT DE TONEELMUZIEK BIJ "THE TEMPEST"
(FOR MEDIUM VOICE AND ORCH.) (Text: Shakespeare)
    1,0,1,0 - 1,0,0,0 - perc. - pf. - str. 15:00 Henmar.
—— ORKESTSTUK MET PIANO
    3,2,3,2 - 4,2,0,0 - timp.,perc. - hp. - pf. - str. Henmar.
—— ROMANCE SANS PAROLES (C'EST LE CHIEN DE JEAN DE
NIVELLE) (FOR MEZZO-SOPRANO AND ORCH.) (1919)
    3,2,3,1 - 3,3,0,0 - perc.,cel.,xyl. - guit. - 2 mandolins - 2 hp. - pf. -
    str. 10:00 Henmar.
—— SIX ADAGIOS
    2,2,2,3 - 2,3,3,0 - perc. - pf. - str. 11:00 Henmar.
—— SIX SYMPHONIC EPIGRAMS
    4,4,4,4 - 4,4,4,1 - timp.,perc.,cel. - str. 6:00 Henmar.
—— SUITE FROM "THE TEMPEST"
      Henmar.
—— SYMPHONY NO. 1
    3,2,4,3 - 4,3,2,1 - timp.,perc.,cel.,xyl. - 2 hp. - pf. - str.
      15:00 Henmar.
—— SYMPHONY NO. 2
    1. Allegro maestoso; 2. Lento molto rubato - più leggiero - più
    mosso maestoso
    4,4,4,4 - 7, ten. hn.,4,4,1 - timp.,perc.,cel.,xyl. - 4 hp. - 6
    mandolins - org. - 3 pf. - str. 22:00 Henmar.
—— SYMPHONY NO. 3
    4,4,4,ten.sax.,4 - 3, ten. hn.,4,4,1 - timp.,perc. - 2 hp. - mandolin -
    pf.(4 hands) - str. 16:00 Henmar.

PIJPER, Willem - MENGELBERG, Karel
—— SYMPHONY NO. 2 (REV. 1961)
    3,3,3,3 - 4,3,3,1 - timp.,perc.,cel.,vibra.,xyl. - hp. - pf. - str.
      21:00 Henmar.

PIKET, Frederick
—— CONCERTO FOR PIANO AND ORCH. (IN 2 MOVTS.)
    2,2(2nd alt. with Eng. hn.),2,2 - 2,2,0,0 - timp.,perc.(1) - pf. - str.
      14:00 Composer.
—— CONCERTO FOR STRINGS
    1. Allegro moderato; 2. Vivace; 3. Allegro
    str. 14:00 EV.
—— CONCERTO FOR VIOLIN AND ORCH. (IN 3 MOVTS.)
    2(2nd alt. with picc.),2,*3,2 - 4,3,3,1 - timp.,perc.(2) - str.
      23:00 Composer.
—— CROSSROADS
    3,2,3,2 - 4,3,3,1 - timp.,perc.(2) - str. 15:00 Seesaw.
—— FOUR ESSAYS IN RHYTHM
    2,2,2,2 - 2,3,3,0 - timp.,perc.(2) - str. 14:00 Composer.
—— SYMPHONY IN B (WITH TENOR SOLO IN FINALE) (IN 4
MOVTS.)
    2(2nd alt. with picc.),2,*3,2 - 4,3,3,1 - timp.,perc.(2) - str.
      35:00 Composer.
—— VARIATIONS AND FUGUE ON "GO DOWN, MOSES"
    2(2nd alt. with picc.),2,*3,2 - 4,3,3,1 - timp.,perc.(2) - str.
      18:00 Composer.

PILATI, Mario
—— BAGATELLA
    1,1,1,1 - 1,1,0,0 - timp. - hp. - pf. - str. 20:00 Bo. Hawkes.
—— PRELUDE, ARIA AND TARANTELLA
    *3,*3,*3,2 - 4,3,4,0 - timp.,perc.,cel. - hp. - str. 9:00 Bo. Hawkes.

PILLIN, Boris W.
—— SYMPHONY (1964) (IN 3 MOVTS.)
    *3,2,*3,2 - 4,2,3,1 - timp.,perc.,xyl. - hp. - pf. - str.
      30:00 Composer.

PILLNEY, Hermann C.
—— DIVERTIMENTO
    1,1,1,alto sax.,1 - 1,1,1,0 - perc. - pf. - ten. banjo - str.
      14:00 T & J.

PILLOIS, Jacques
—— L'ANÉMONE ET LA ROSE (POÈME LYRIQUE) (FOR 2
SOPRANOS, FEMALE CHORUS AND ORCH.)
    3,3,3,2 - 4,3,3,0 - timp.,perc.,cel. - 2 hp. - str. 13:00 Salabert.

PINCHARD, Max
—— CONCERTO FOR HARPSICHORD AND STRING ORCH.
    hpsc. - str. Galaxy.
—— QUADRUPLE (SYMPHONIC MOVEMENT NO. 1)
    2,2,2,2 - 2,2,1,0 - timp.,perc. - str. 10:00 Presser.
—— SONATA CONCERTANTE (FOR FLUTE AND STRINGS)
    fl. - str. 17:00 Presser.
—— SYMPHONIE DU VERSEAU (SYMPHONY NO. 2)
    str. 22:00 Presser.

PINGOUD, Ernest
—— LE CHANT D'ESPACE (REV. 1938)
    3,3,3,3 - 4,3,3,1 - timp.,perc.(3),bells,cel.,vibra. - 2 hp. - str.
      15:00 FinnMICtr.
—— CHANTECLER, OP. 15 (1919)
    3,3,2,2 - 4,3,3,1 - timp.,perc.(3),cel. - hp. - str. 8:00 FinnMICtr.
—— CONCERTO NO. 1 FOR PIANO AND ORCH., OP. 8 (1917)
    3,2,2,2 - 4,2,2,1 - timp.,perc.,bells - hp. - pf. - str.
      15:00 FinnMICtr.
—— CONCERTO NO. 2 FOR PIANO AND ORCH., OP. 22 (1921)
    2,2,2,2 - 4,2,3,1 - timp.,perc.,bells - hp. - pf. - str.
      16:00 FinnMICtr.
—— CONCERTO NO. 3 FOR PIANO AND ORCH., OP. 23 (1922)
    2,2,2,2 - 4,2,2,1 - timp.,perc.(4),xyl. - hp. - pf. - str.
      20:00 FinnMICtr.
—— CONFESSIONS, OP. 5 (SUITE) (1916) (IN 4 MOVTS.)
    3,3,3,3 - 6,5,3,1 - timp.,perc.(5),bells,xyl. - 2 hp. - pf. - str.
      FinnMICtr.
—— COR ARDENS (1927)
    3,3,3,3 - 4,3,3,1 - timp.,perc.,cel. - hp. - str. 16:00 FinnMICtr.
—— DANSE MACABRE, OP. 10 (BALLET) % (WITH SATB
CHORUS) (1918)
    3,3,3,3 - 4,3,3,1 - timp.,perc.(3),bells,xyl. - 2 hp. - org. - str.
      15:00 FinnMICtr.
—— LA DERNIÈRE AVENTURE DE PIERROT, OP. 6 (1916)
    3,3,4,3 - 6,5,3,1 - timp.,perc.(6),bells,cel.,xyl. - 2 hp. - str.
      10:00 FinnMICtr.
—— DIABLERIES GALANTES ("LE FÉTICHE"), OP. 7 (1917)
    3,3,3,3 - 4-8,4,3,1 - timp.,perc.(5),cel. - 2 hp. - str.
      16:00 FinnMICtr.

—— LA FACE D'UNE GRANDE VILLE (BALLET) % (1937)
3,3,3,3 - 4,3,3,1 - timp.,perc.(3) - hp. - pf. - str.   23:00 FinnMICtr.
—— FIVE SONNETS, OP. 11 (1918)
1,2,2,1 - 1,0,0,0 - str.   12:00 FinnMICtr.
—— FLAMBEAUX ÉTEINTS, OP. 14 (1919)
3,3,3,2 - 4,3,3,1 - timp.,perc.,cel. - hp. - str.   18:00 FinnMICtr.
—— LA FLAMME ÉTERNELLE (FOR ORGAN AND ORCH.) (1939)
3,3,3,3 - 4-8,3,3,1 - timp.,perc.(3),bells - hp. - org. - str.
13:00 FinnMICtr.
—— HYMNS TO THE NIGHT, OP. 9 (1917)
3,3,3,3 - 4,3,3,1 - timp.,perc.(4, incl. 2 on timp.),bells - 2 hp. - str.
17:00 FinnMICtr.
—— THE IDOL (BALLET) %
3,3,3,3 - 4,3,3,1 - timp.,perc.(3) - hp. - pf. - str.   FinnMICtr.
—— THE KNIGHT WITHOUT FEAR AND REPROACH, OP. 12
(AN ADVENTURE FOR ORCH.) (1918) (IN 7 MOVTS.)
3,3,3,3 - 4,2,2,1 - timp.,perc.(3) - hp. - str.   FinnMICtr.
—— MYSTERIUM, OP. 13 (1919)
3,3,3,3 - 4,3,3,1 - timp.,perc.(3),cel. - str.   16:00 FinnMICtr.
—— NARCISSOS (1930)
3,3,3,3 - 4,3,3,1 - timp.,perc.(4),bells,cel. - hp. - str.
19:00 FinnMICtr.
—— PROLOGUE, OP. 4 (1916)
3,3,3,3 - 4,3-4,3,1 - timp.,perc.,bells - 2 hp. - str.   6:00 FinnMICtr.
—— THE PROPHET, OP. 21 (1921)
3,3,3,3 - 4-8,3,3,1 - timp.,perc.(5),bells,cel. - 1-2 hp. - str.
15:00 FinnMICtr.
—— LE SACRIFICE, OP. 17 (1919)
3,3,3,3 - 4,3,3,1 - timp.,perc.(3),bells - 2 hp. - str.
10:00 FinnMICtr.
—— SYMPHONY NO. 1, OP. 18 (1920)
3,3,3,3 - 4,3,3,1 - timp.,perc.(4),bells - hp. - str.   15:00 FinnMICtr.
—— SYMPHONY NO. 2, OP. 20 (1920)
3,3,3,3 - 4,3,3,1 - timp.,perc.(6),bells - 1-2 hp. - org. - str.
20:00 FinnMICtr.
—— SYMPHONY NO. 3, OP. 27 (1927)
3,3,3,3 - 4,3,3,1 - timp.,perc.(3),bells - hp. - str.   20:00 FinnMICtr.

PINOS, Alois
—— CONCERTO FOR ORCHESTRA AND MAGNETIC TAPE
10:00 Modern.
—— ZKRATKY (10 ORCHESTRAL PIECES FOR 19 PLAYERS)
ten. sax. - 2 tpt. - perc.(4) - guit. - 2 hp. - harm. - hpsc. - pf. - str.
16:00 Modern.

PINTO, Octavio
—— MEMORIES OF CHILDHOOD (SCENAS INFANTIS) (IN 5
MOVTS.)
*3,2,2,2 - 4,3,2,1 - timp.,perc.,cel.,glock. - hp. - str.   G. Schirmer.
or:
str.

PISTON, Walter
—— CONCERTO FOR VIOLIN AND ORCH. (IN 3 MOVTS.)
*3,*3,*3,*3 - 4,3,3,1 - timp.,perc. - str.   23:00 Bo. Hawkes.
—— FANFARE FOR THE FIGHTING FRENCH
0,0,0,0 - 4,3,3,1 - timp.,perc.(3)   Bo. Hawkes.
—— SINFONIETTA (IN 3 MOVTS.)
2,2,2,2 - 2 hn. - str.   17:00 Bo. Hawkes.
—— SYMPHONY NO. 1 (IN 3 MOVTS.)
*3,*3,*3,*3 - 4,3,3,1 - timp. - str.   27:00 G. Schirmer.
—— SYMPHONY NO. 3
1. Andantino; 2. Allegro; 3. Adagio; 4. Allegro
*3,*3,*3,*3 - 4,3,3,1 - timp.,perc.(5),glock.,xyl. - 2 hp. - str.
30:00 Bo. Hawkes.
—— TOCCATA
*3,*3,*3,*3 - 4,3,3,1 - timp.,perc.(6) - str.   9:00 Bo. Hawkes.

PITFIELD, Thomas B.
—— CONCERT INTERLUDE
str.   9:30 P.R.S.
—— CONCERTINO FOR PERCUSSION AND FULL ORCH.
*3,1,2,2 - 4,2,3,0 - perc. - str.   10:30 Oxford.
—— CONEY WARREN (OPERA) %
3,0,2,0 - 0,0,0,0 - perc.(3) - pf. - str.   45:00 Seesaw.
—— EILIS A GHRA
2,2,2,2 - 2,3,3,1 - timp.,perc. - hp. - str.   5:00 P.R.S.
—— A KEELE GARLAND (SUITE FOR STRINGS)
str.   11:00 Mills.
—— SINFONIETTA
2,2,2,2 - 4,2,3,0 - timp.,perc. - hp. - str.   21:00 Oxford.
—— THEME AND VARIATIONS
str.   14:00 P.R.S.

PITT, Percy
—— FÊTES GALANTES, OP. 24 (MINIATURE SUITE) (IN 5
MOVTS.)
*3,*3,*3,*3 - 4,2 cnt.,2,3,1 - timp.,perc.,glock. - str.   18:00 Galaxy.

PIZZETTI, Ildebrando
—— CANZONE DI BENI PERDUTI (SONG OF LOST GOODS)
(1950)
2,2,2,2 - 4,3,0,0 - timp.,perc.,cel. - hp. - pf. - str.   14:00 Leeds.
—— CONCERTO IN A FOR VIOLIN AND ORCH. (1945)
2,2,2,2 - 4,3,0,0 - timp. - str.   28:00 Leeds.
—— LA PISANELLA (SUITE)
2,2,2,2 - 4,2,2,0 - timp.,perc.,cel. - 2 hp. - pf. - str.
16:00 Belw-Mills.
—— PRELUDIO A UN ALTRO GIORNO (PRELUDE TO ANOTHER
DAY) (1951)
3,3,2,3 - 4,3,3,1 - timp.,perc.(2) - hp. - str.   11:00 Leeds.
—— SANTA ULIVA (7 CONCERT PIECES) (FOR SOPRANO,
CHORUS AND ORCH.)
3,3,2,3 - 4,3,3,1 - timp.,perc. - 1-2 hp. - org. - str.
26:00 Bo. Hawkes.

PLANEL, Robert
—— CONCERTO FOR TRUMPET AND STRINGS
tpt. - str.   26:00 Presser.

PLATT, Peter
—— SINFONIETTA IN 1 MOVT. (1956)
2,2,2,2 - 2,2,2,0 - timp. - str.   8:00 A.P.R.A.

PLATTI, Giovanni - TORREFRANCA
—— CONCERTO NO. 1 IN G, FOR CEMBALO AND STRINGS
cemb. - str.   16:00 Bo. Hawkes.
—— CONCERTO NO. 2 IN C MINOR, FOR CEMBALO AND
STRINGS
cemb. - str.   16:00 Bo. Hawkes.

PLAYMAN, Gordon
—— BALLET SCORE ON THREE LEVELS (1969)
3(3rd alt.with picc.),2(2nd alt.with Eng.hn.),2(2nd alt.with b.-cl.),2
- 4,3,3,1 - timp.,perc.(3),cel.,glock.,xyl. - hp. - str.
28:30 Composer.
—— CONCERTINO FOR CLARINET AND STRING ORCH.
0,0,1,0 - 0,0,0,0 - hp. - str.   9:00 Composer.
—— DEAR MEN AND WOMEN (FOR SOPRANO, SATB CHORUS
AND STRINGS) (1975) (Text: John Hall Wheelock)
hp. - str.   13:00 Composer.
—— ENCORE NO. 1 (1947)
*3,*3,2,*3, - 4,2,3,1 - timp.,perc.(9),xyl. - pf. - str. 2:00 Composer.
—— ESSAY NO. 1 FOR ORCHESTRA (1966)
3(1 alt.with picc.),3(1 alt.with Eng. hn.),3,2 - 4,3,3,1 -
timp.,perc.(3),cel.,xyl. - hp. - pf. - str.   10:00 Composer.
—— ESSAY NO. 2 FOR ORCH. (1973)
3(3rd alt.with picc.),3(2nd alt.with Eng.hn.),*3,2 - 4,3,3,1 -
timp.,perc.(4),bells,glock.,mar.,xyl. - hp. - str.   13:00 Composer.
—— A LITTLE OVERTURE (1946)
2,2,2,2 - 2,2,0,0 - timp. - str.   7:35 Composer.
—— SYMPHONY NO 1 (1947) (IN 3 MOVTS.)
2(2nd alt.with picc.),2,2,2 - 4,2,3,0 - timp.,perc.(3) - str.
17:15 Composer.
—— SYMPHONY NO. 2 (AFTER ALBERT CAMUS' MYTH OF
SISYPHUS) (1971) (IN 4 MOVTS.)
3(3rd alt.with picc.),2(2nd alt.with Eng.hn.),3(3rd alt.with b.-cl.),2
- 4,3,3,1 - timp.,perc.(2) - str.   25:25 Composer.
—— SYMPHONY NO. 3 (CELEBRATION SYMPHONY) (1972) (IN 4
MOVTS.)
2(2nd alt.with picc.),2(2nd alt.with Eng.hn.),2(2nd alt.with b.-cl.),2
- 4,2,3,1 - timp.,perc.(3),glock.,xyl. - str.   24:45 Composer.
—— THEME AND ALIASES (16 VARIATIONS IN SEARCH OF A
CHARACTER) (1974)
*3,*3,*3,2 - 4,3,3,1 -perc.(3),glock.,vibra.,xyl. - str.
16:00 Composer.
—— TWO SCENES FROM DANTE (1975)
str.   13:30 Composer.

PLESSIS, Hubert Lawrence du
—— DIE DANS VAN DIE REËN, OP. 22 (FOR CHORUS AND
ORCH.) (TEXT: EUGENE MARAIS) %
2,2,3,2 - 4,2,3,1 - timp.,perc. - str.   19:00 S.A.M.R.O.
—— HUBERTA (INCIDENTAL MUSIC) (FOR CHAMBER ORCH.)
1,1,2,1 - 3,1,2,0 - str.   9:00 S.A.M.R.O.
—— MUSIC AFTER THREE PAINTINGS BY HENRI ROUSSEAU
2,2,3,2 - 4,2,3,1 - timp.,perc. - str.   15:00 S.A.M.R.O.

—— SERENADE FOR STRINGS
    str.   13:00 S.A.M.R.O.
—— SLAMSE BEELDE, OP. 21 (FOR CHORUS, CLARINET, HARP AND STRING ORCH.) (Text: Izak David du Plessis)
    cl. - hp. - str.   16:00 S.A.M.R.O.
—— SUID-AFRIKA: NAG EN DAGRAAD (FOR SOPRANO, CHORUS AND ORCH.) (Text: Eugene Marais)
    2,2,3,2 - 4,2,3,1 - timp.,perc. - str.   22:00 S.A.M.R.O.
—— SYMPHONY, OP. 14
    2,2,3,2 - 4,2,3,1 - timp.,perc. - str.   30:00 S.A.M.R.O.
—— TWO GHOSTLY POEMS, OP. 9 (FOR CHORUS, HARP AND STRING ORCH.) (TEXT: THOMAS LOVELL BEDDOES) %
    hp. - str.   10:00 S.A.M.R.O.

PLEYEL, Ignaz J. - BROWN, James
—— SONATINA NO. 1, IN D
    pf. - str.   9:00 Galaxy.
—— SONATINA NO. 2, IN F
    pf. - str.   9:00 Galaxy.

PLEYEL, Ignaz J. - CARSE, Adam
—— SYMPHONY IN C
    2,2,0,2 - 2,2,0,0 - timp. - str.   25:00 Galaxy.
    or:
    2,0,2,2 - 2,2,0,0 - timp. - str.

PLEYEL, Ignaz J. - HALEN, Walter J.
—— SUITE IN C, OP. 8
    str.   SouthernTx.

PLEYEL, Ignaz J. - HERRMANN
—— CONCERTO IN D MAJOR FOR VIOLA AND ORCH., OP. 31
    0,2,0,0 - 2,0,0,0 - str.   33:00 Henmar.

PLEYEL, Ignaz J. - LOTTER, Adolf
—— SYMPHONY MOSAIC IN D
    pf.(ad lib.) - str.   23:00 Bo. Hawkes.

PLEYEL, Ignaz J. - OUBRADOUS, Fernand
—— SYMPHONIE CONCERTANTE NO. 5 (FOR FLUTE, OBOE OR CLARINET, HORN, BASSOON AND ORCH.)
    1,1,0,1 - 2,0,0,0 - str.   22:00 Presser.
    or:
    1,0,1,0 - 2,0,0,0 - str.
—— SYMPHONIE PÉRIODIQUE NO. 6
    2 ob. - 2 hn. - str.   15:00 Presser.
—— SYMPHONY CONCERTANTE NO. 2
    0,2,0,0 - 2,0,0,0 - pf. - str.   22:00 Presser.

PLEYEL, Ignaz J. - PETIT, J. L.
—— SYMPHONIE PÉRIODIQUE NO. 8
    1,2,0,2 - 2,0,0,0 - str.   16:00 Presser.

PLEYEL, Ignaz J. - VOGT, Carl August
—— SERENATE CONCERTANTE, OP. 20 (FOR OBOE, VIOLIN, VIOLA, CELLO, 2 HORNS AND STRING ORCH.)
    ob. - 2 hn. - str.   31:00 Mannheimer.

PLICQUE, Eveline
—— SYMPHONIE CONCERTANTE
    3,2,2,3 - 4,3,3,1 - timp.,perc.,cel. - hp. - str.   16:00 Henmar.

PLUISTER, Simon
—— CANZONA (OVER EEN MELODIE VAN BOURGOIS)
    str.   9:00 Henmar.
—— CONCERTINO QUASI FANTASIA, FOR PIANO AND ORCH. (IN 3 SECTIONS)
    2,2,2,2 - 4,2,3,0 - timp.,perc. - hp. - pf. - str.   21:00 Henmar.
—— CONCERTO DA CHIESA (FOR TENOR, BASS, MIXED CHORUS, ORGAN AND STRING ORCH.) (1953) (Text: E. van Dijk)
    org. - str.   36:00 Henmar.
—— DIVERTISSEMENT FOR STRINGS
    str.   14:00 Henmar.
—— DE EMMAÜSGANGERS (FOR 2 TENORS, BARITONE, BASS, BOY'S CHORUS, MALE CHORUS AND CHAMBER ORCH.) (1953)
    1,1,1,1 - 1,1,1,0 - perc.,cel. - hpsc. - str.   13:00 Henmar.
—— PARTITA PICCOLA
    str.   9:00 Henmar.
—— PSALM 137 (BABYLONISCHE BALLINGSCHAR) (FOR 5 SOLO VOICES, MIXED CHORUS AND ORCH.) (1950)
    4,3,3,3 - 4,3,3,1 - timp.,perc.,cel. - 2 hp. - str.   16:00 Henmar.

—— PSALM 138 (FOR SATB SOLO VOICES, MIXED CHORUS AND ORCH.) (1950)
    3,3,3,3 - 4,3,3,1 - timp.,perc.,cel. - 2 hp. - str.   19:00 Henmar.
—— PUPPET SHOW MUSIC (PUPPENSPIEL-MUSIK) (IN 7 MOVTS.)
    3,3,3,3 - 3,2,2,0 - timp.,perc.,cel. - hp. - str.   20:05 Henmar.
—— SLAAPLIEDEREN VOOR GROTE MENSEN (FOR SOPRANO AND ORCH.) (1952) (Text: P. van Steen)
    2,2,2,2 - 2,2,0,0 - perc. - hp. - str.   10:00 Henmar.
—— SUITE DES FARCES
    2,1,2,1 - 2,1,1,0 - timp.,perc.,cel.,xyl. - clavichord - pf. - str.   Henmar.

PODEŠVA, Jaromír
—— THE KOUNIC STUDENTS' HOSTEL (SYMPHONIC POEM) (PART 1 FROM CYCLE OF 3 SYMPHONIC POEMS "OUR COUNTRY'S PATH")
    3,3,2,3 - 4,2,3,1 - timp.,perc. - str.   12:00 Bo. Hawkes.
—— TRIPLE CONCERTO (FOR VIOLIN, CELLO, PIANO AND ORCH.)
    2,2,2,2 - 4,2,3,0 - timp. - pf. - str.   30:00 Bo. Hawkes.

PODKOVYROV, Petr P.
—— CONCERTO-POEM FOR VIOLIN AND ORCH.
    G. Schirmer.

POIRIER, Joseph M.
—— CHANSON (FOR VIOLIN AND STRING ORCH.) (1956)
    str.   6:30 CanMusCtr.

POLACK, Hans
—— KONZERTSTÜCK, OP. 23 (FOR FLUTE AND CHAMBER ORCH.)
    1,1,2,1 - 0,2,1,0 - timp.,vibra. - str.   5:00 Henmar.

POLACZEK, Dietmar
—— CONCERTINO FOR STRING ORCH.
    str.   8:00 Modern.

POLGÁR, Tibor
—— THE LAST WORDS OF LOUIS RIEL (1967) (CANTATA) (FOR CONTRALTO, BASS, SATB CHORUS AND ORCH.) (Text: John Robert Colombo)
    2(2nd alt. with picc.),2(2nd alt. with Eng. hn.),2(2nd alt. with b.-cl.),2(2nd alt. with c.-bn.) - 4,3,3,1 - timp.,perc.(3) - hp. - pf.(or cel.) - str.   17:15 CanMusCtr.
—— SUITE NO. 2
    3,2,2,2 - 4,3,3,1 - timp.,perc.,cel. - hp. - pf. - str.   22:00 Bo. Hawkes.
—— VARIATIONS ON A HUNGARIAN FOLKSONG (1969)
    timp.(ad lib.) - hp. - str.   9:45 CanMusCtr.

POLIFRONE, Jon
—— PORTRAITS FOR CHAMBER ORCH.
    1,1,1,1 - 0,1,0,0 - str.   9:00 C. Fischer.

POLIN, Claire
—— THE JOURNEY OF OWAIN MADOC (ON THE WELSH DISCOVERY OF AMERICA IN 1170) (1971) (IN 4 MOVTS.)
    0,0,0,0 - 1,2,1,1 - perc.(8-10),glock.,mar.,vibra.,xyl.,amplification system - pf.   15:00 Seesaw.
—— SYMPHONY NO. 1 (IN TWO MOVEMENTS)
    *3,*3,2,2-*3 - 4,3,3,1 - timp.,perc.(4),xyl.(or cel.) - pf. - str.   12:00 Composer.
—— SYMPHONY NO. 2 ("KOREAN") (WITH OPTIONAL NARRATION)
    1. Larghetto; 2. Maestoso marziale; 3. Variati - misterioso
    *3,*3,*3,2 - 4,3,3,1 - timp.,perc.(4-6) - pf. - str.   26:00 Composer.
—— THREE SCENES FROM "GILGAMESH"
    fl. - str.   16:00 Composer.

POLÍVKA, Vladimir
—— OVERTURE IN D MINOR
    3,3,3,3 - 4,3,3,1 - timp.,perc. - str.   13:00 Bo. Hawkes.

POLOVINKIN, Leonid A.
—— IN UNION THERE IS STRENGTH (BALLET SUITE)
    2,1,1,1 - 2,2,1,0 - timp.,perc.,xyl. - hp. - str.   G. Schirmer.
—— OVERTURE TO THE FIRST OF MAY
    4,2,2,2 - 4,3,3,1 - timp.,perc. - hp. - str.   G. Schirmer.
—— SYMPHONY NO. 3 ("ROMANTIC")
    3,3,3,3 - 4,3,3,1 - timp.,perc. - hp. - str.   G. Schirmer.

POLSON, Arthur
—— CONCERTINO FOR VIOLIN AND STRING ORCH. (1957)
    str.   16:00 C.A.P.A.C.
—— CONCERTO FOR BASSOON AND STRINGS (1964)
    bn. - str.   14:00 C.A.P.A.C.
—— CONCERTO FOR ORGAN AND CHAMBER ORCH. (1965)
        28:00 C.A.P.A.C.
—— IMPROVISATION FOR VIOLIN AND ORCH. (1958)
        4:30 C.A.P.A.C.
—— INTRODUCTION AND SCHERZO (FOR CELLO AND ORCH.)
(1959)
        7:00 C.A.P.A.C.
—— TENSIONS NO. 2 (1958)
    ob.(or fl.) - str.   6:00 C.A.P.A.C.

PONCE, Ethel
—— THREE DIALOGUES FOR PIANO AND ORCH.
    *3,*3,*4,3 - 4,3,2,1 - timp.,perc. - hp. - pf. - str. 12:00 Composer.

PONSE, Luctor
—— CONCERTO DA CAMERA, OP. 34 (1962)
    bn. - str.   16:00 Henmar.
—— CONCERTO FOR PIANO AND ORCH., OP. 17
    2,2,2,2 - 4,2,3,1 - timp.,perc.,cel. - pf. - str.   Henmar.
—— CONCERTO FOR TWO PIANOS AND ORCH., OP. 33 (1962)
    3,3,4,3 - 4,4,4,1 - perc.,cel.,vibra.,xyl. - hp. - 2 pf. - str.
        24:00 Henmar.
—— DIVERTISSEMENT FOR STRINGS, OP. 13
    str.   18:00 Henmar.
—— DIVERTISSEMENT FOR TWO PIANOS AND ORCH., OP. 13B
(1946)
    2,2,4,3 - 4,2,4,1 - timp.,perc.,xyl. - 2 pf. - str. 18:00 Henmar.
—— FEESTGERICHT (BALLET), OP. 26 (1957) %
    2,2,2,2 - 2,2,2,0 - timp.,perc. - pf. - str. 28:00 Henmar.
—— SINFONIETTA NO. 2, OP. 29 (1960)
    2,2,2,2 - 2,2,0,0 - perc. - str. 19:00 Henmar.
—— SINFONIETTA NO. 3, OP. 30 (1961)
    2,2,2,1 - 2,2,1,0 - perc.,xyl. - hp. - pf. - str. 18:00 Henmar.
—— SYMPHONIETTA, OP. 15A
    2,2,2,2 - 2,2,2,0 - perc.,cel. - str. 17:00 Henmar.
—— SYMPHONY NO. 2
    3,3,4,3 - 4,3,4,1 - timp.,perc.,cel.,xyl. - hp. - str. Henmar.
—— SYMPHONY, OP. 18
    3,3,3,3 - 4,3,3,1 - timp.,perc.,cel.,xyl. - hp. - str. 31:00 Henmar.
—— TROIS CHANTS (FOR VOICE AND ORCH.) (1950)
    2,2,2,2 - 3,0,0,0 - timp.,perc. - hp. - pf. - str. 8:00 Henmar.

POOT, Marcel
—— BALLADE (FOR CLARINET AND ORCH.) (1941)
    2,1,3,1 - 2,2,1,0 - timp. - str. 10:00 Vriamont.
—— BALLADE SYMPHONIQUE (1976)
    3,3,3,3 - 4,3,3,1 - timp.,perc. - str. 10:00 H. Elkan.
—— CAPRICCIO (CONCERTINO CAPRICCIOSO) (FOR OBOE
AND ORCH.) (1928)
    2,2,2,1 - 2,2,1,0 - timp. - str. 6:00 H. Elkan.
—— CONCERTINO FOR CELLO AND ORCH.
    2,2,2,2 - 2,2,2,0 - timp.,perc. - str. 14:00 H. Elkan.
—— CONCERTINO FOR OBOE AND ORCH.
    2,2,2,2 - 3,3,3,0 - timp.,perc. - str. 7:30 H. Elkan.
—— CONCERTO FOR TRUMPET AND ORCH. (1973)
    2,2,2,2 - 2,3,2,0 - timp.,perc. - str. 15:00 H. Elkan.
—— CONCERTO NO. 2 FOR PIANO AND ORCH. (1975)
    2,2,2,2 - 4,3,3,3,1 - timp.,perc. - pf. - str. 20:00 H. Elkan.
—— DANSE LAUDATIVE
    3,3,3,3 - 4,3,3,1 - timp.,perc. - hp. - str. 7:00 Presser.
—— RONDE DIABOLIQUE
    *3,*3,*3,*3 - 4,3,3,1 - timp.,perc.,glock. - str. 7:00 C. Fischer.
—— SYMPHONY NO. 3 (1952)
    3,3,3,3 - 4,3,3,1 - timp.,perc. - str. 25:00 CBDM.
—— SYMPHONY NO. 4 (1970) (IN 3 MOVTS.)
    3,3,3,3 - 4,3,3,1 - timp.,perc. - str. H. Elkan.
—— SYMPHONY NO. 5 (1974) (IN 3 MOVTS.)
    3,3,3,3 - 4,3,3,1 - timp.,perc. - str. 18:00 H. Elkan.
—— TROIS DANSES (1945)
    2,1,2,1 - 2,2,1,0 - timp.,perc.,cel.,glock. - str. 9:00 H. Elkan.
—— VARIATIONS EN FORME DE DANSES (1923)
    2,2,2,2 - 4,2,3,1 - timp.,perc.,glock. - hp. - str. 9:30 Buyst.

POPESCO, Trajan
—— LITTLE SUITE (FOR STRINGS)
    str.   15:00 Salabert.

POPOVIĆ, Berislav
—— CONCERTO FOR ORCH.
    2,2,3,3 - 4,3,3,1 - timp.,perc.,vibra. - hp. - pf. - str.
        14:00 MIC,Zagreb.
—— MEDIUM TEMPUS (1972)
        7:00 MIC,Zagreb.

PORADOWSKI, Stefan Boleslaw
—— NOCTURNE, OP. 59-B
    fl. - hp. - str.   5:00 AhnSimrock.

PORENA, Boris
—— CADENZE (FOR FLUTE AND 12 INSTS.)
        MCA Music.
—— CADENZE (VERSION FOR VIOLIN AND 13 INSTRUMENTS)
(1965)
    0,2,3,1 - 1,1,1,0 - hp. - str.(2,1,1,0) 7:00 MCA Music.
—— CANTATA DA CAMERA (FOR BASS, CHORUS OF BASSES
AND 10 INSTRUMENTS) (Text: Georg Trakl)
        10:00 Leeds.
—— CANTATA SU VERSI DI ANDREAS GRYPHIUS (FOR 3
WOMEN'S VOICES, MIXED CHORUS AND ORCH.) (1961)
        24:00 Leeds.
—— GOTT UND DIE BAJADERE (FOR SOPRANO, BARITONE,
MIXED CHORUS AND ORCH.) (1957)
    2,2,2,2 - 0,0,4,0 - str. 27:00 Leeds.
—— MUSICA PER ARCHI NO. 2 (1967)
    str.   11:00 MCA Music.
—— MUSICA PER ORCHESTRA NO. 1 (1962)
    3,3,3,3 - 3,3,3,0 - timp.,perc.(5),bells,vibra. - str.
        12:00 MCA Music.
—— MUSICA PER ORCHESTRA NO. 2 (1966)
    3,3,3,3 - 3,3,3,0 - timp.,perc.(2) - str. 15:00 MCA Music.
—— ÜBER ALLER DIESER DEINER TRAUER (CANTATA) (FOR
SOPRANO, BASS, MIXED CHORUS AND ORCH.) (1965) (Text:
Paul Celan and Nelly Sachs)
    3,3,3,3 - 3,4,3,0 - timp.,perc.(4),bells - str. 25:00 MCA Music.

PORRINO, Ennio
—— I CANTI DELL' ESILIO (15 SONGS FOR VOICE AND
CHAMBER ORCH.)
    1,1,1,1 - 0,0,0,0 - perc. - hp. - str. 40:00 Bo. Hawkes.
—— PRELUDIO IN MODO RELIGIOSO E OSTINATO
    1,1,2,1 - 2,1,1,0 - timp.,perc. - pf. - str. 8:00 Leeds.
—— QUATTRO CANTI DI STAGIONE (FOR SOPRANO AND
ORCH.)
    2,1,1,2 - 2,1,1,1 - perc. - hp. - pf. - str. 15:00 Bo. Hawkes.
—— SINFONIA PER UNA FIABA
    *3,*3,*3,*3 - 4,3,3,0 - timp.,perc. - str. 7:00 Bo. Hawkes.
—— SINFONIETTA IN D
    1,1,1,1 - 1,1,0,0 - timp.,glock.,cel. - pf. - str. 10:00 Bo. Hawkes.
—— SONATA DRAMMATICA (FOR PIANO AND ORCH.)
    2,2,2,2 - 4,3,3,1 - timp.,perc.(2) - hp. - pf. - str. 20:00 Leeds.

PORTER, Quincy
—— UKRAINIAN SUITE (FOR STRINGS) (IN 6 MOVTS.)
    str.   13:00 C. Fischer.

PORTO ALEGRE, Walter S.
—— AMAZONAS SYMPHONIE ("BRASILEIA") (IN 3 MOVTS.)
    3,2,2,2 - 4,3,3,1 - timp.,perc.,cel.,xyl. - hp. - str. 20:00 Noack.

POSER, Hans
—— AN SCHWAGER KRONOS (CANTATA) (FOR SOPRANO,
BARITONE, SATB CHORUS AND ORCH.) (Text: Goethe)
    1,0,2,2 - 4,3,3,0 - timp. - str. 12:00 F. Colombo.
—— CONCERTINO FOR PIANO, TRUMPET, STRING ORCH. AND
PERCUSSION, OP. 19
    tpt. - perc. - pf. - str. 17:00 F. Colombo.
—— CONCERTO GRAZIOSO, OP. 34
    str.   14:00 F. Colombo.
—— FESTIVAL SINFONIA, OP. 37 (FOR LOW VOICE AND
STRING ORCH.)
    str.   25:00 F. Colombo.
—— KONZERT FUR ORCH.
    2,2,2,2 - 4,3,3,1 - timp.,perc. - pf. - str. 25:00 Sikorski.
—— THE LAMENTATIONS OF JEREMIAH, OP. 25 (FOR CHORUS
AND ORCH.)
    0,0,0,0 - 3,3,0,0 - timp.,perc. - pf. - c.,d.-b. 20:00 F. Colombo.
—— RENDSBURGER DANCES, OP. 42
    2,2,2,2 - 2,2,2,0 - timp.,perc. - str. 10:00 F. Colombo.

—— TILL EULENSPIEGEL, OP. 35 (CAPRICCIO) (FOR SOPRANO, TENOR, BARITONE, SATB CHORUS AND ORCH.)
2,2,2,2 - 4,2,3,0 - timp.,perc. - str.   80:00 F. Colombo.
—— VARIATIONS ON A CLASSIC THEME, OP. 53
2,2,2,2 - 4,2,3,0 - timp.,perc. - str.   14:00 F. Colombo.
—— VOM FISCHER UND SEINER FRAU, OP. 50 (CONCERNING THE FISHERMAN AND HIS WIFE) (CANTATA) (FOR SOPRANO, BASS, NARRATOR, SATB CHORUS AND ORCH.)
2,2,2,2 - 2,2,2,0 - timp.,perc. - str.   80:00 F. Colombo.

POSER, Hans - EBERT, Wolfgang
—— THREE INTERMEZZI FROM THE CHAMBER OPERA "DIE AUSZEICHNUNG" ("THE REWARD"), OP. 46
2,2,2,1 sax.,2 - 4,3,3,1 - timp.,perc.,xyl. - hp. - str.
10:00 F. Colombo.

POSTON, Elizabeth
—— THE NATIVITY (A SEQUENCE FOR CHRISTMAS) (FOR SOLOISTS, MIXED CHORUS AND STRINGS)
str.   30:00 Oxford.

POTTER, A. J.
—— CEITHRE FICHID LA
2,1,2,1 - 2,3,3,0 - timp.,perc. - hp. - str.   10:00 P.R.S.
—— CONCERTINETTO FOR 2 FLUTES AND ORCH.
2,1,2,1 - 0,0,0,0 - timp.,perc. - hp. - str.   5:00 P.R.S.
—— FONN 'GUS PORT
str.   5:00 P.R.S.
—— PLANXTY LOUIS
str.   5:00 P.R.S.

POULENC, Francis
—— AIRS CHANTÉS (4 SONGS) (FOR SOPRANO AND ORCH.)
2,3,2,2 - 2,0,0,0 - timp. - hp. - str.   8:00 Salabert.
—— AUBADE (CONCERTO CHORÉGRAPHIQUE) (FOR PIANO AND 18 INSTS.) %
2,2,2,2 - 2,1,0,0 - timp. - pf. - str.   Salabert.
—— LE BAL MASQUÉ (SECULAR CANTATA) (FOR BARITONE OR MEZZO-SOPRANO AND CHAMBER ORCH.) (IN 6 MOVTS.)
0,1,1,1 - cnt. - perc. - pf. - str.   17:00 Salabert.
—— LES BICHES (SUITE) (IN 5 MOVTS.)
*3,*3,*3,*3 - 4,3,3,1 - timp.,perc.,cel.,glock. - hp. - str.
15:30 Mercury.
—— CONCERT CHAMPÊTRE (FOR HARPSICHORD OR PIANO AND ORCH.)
2,2,2,2 - 4,2,1,1 - timp. - hpsc.(or pf.) - str.   25:00 Salabert.
—— CONCERTO FOR ORGAN AND ORCH.
timp. - org. - str.   17:00 Salabert.
—— CONCERTO FOR PIANO AND ORCH. (IN 3 MOVTS.)
2,2,1,2 - 2,1,2,1 - timp. - pf. - str.   21:00 Salabert.
or:
2,2,2,2 - 4,2,3,1 - timp. - pf. - str.
—— CONCERTO IN D MINOR, FOR 2 PIANOS AND ORCH. (IN 3 MOVTS.)
2,2,2,2 - 2,2,2,1 - perc. - 2 pf. - str.   19:00 Salabert.
—— LA DAME DE MONTE-CARLO (MONOLOGUE FOR SOPRANO AND ORCH.) (Text: Jean Cocteau)
2,2,2,2 - 2,2,0,0 - timp.,perc. - hp. - str.   7:00 F. Colombo.
—— GLORIA (CANTATA) (FOR SOPRANO, MIXED CHORUS AND ORCH.)
3,3,3,3 - 4,3,3,1 - timp. - hp. - str.   24:00 Salabert.
—— LITANIES À LA VIERGE NOIRE (FOR SOPRANO, MEZZO-SOPRANO, ALTO, STRINGS AND TIMP.)
timp. - str.   8:00 EV.
—— LES MAMELLES DE TIRESIAS (2-ACT OPERA BOUFFE) %
3,3,3,3 - 4,3,3,1 - timp.,perc. - 2 hp. - str.   90:00 Presser.
—— PASTOURELLE (FOR PIANO AND ORCH.) (FROM "L'ÉVENTAIL DE JEANNE")
2,2,2,2 - 2,1,0,0 - timp. - str.   2:00 Presser.
—— PIÈCE BRÈVE SUR LE NOM D'ALBERT ROUSSEL
2,2,2,2 - 2,1,0,0 - timp. - hp. - str.   Baron.
—— POÈMES DE RONSARD (SONG CYCLE) (FOR MEDIUM VOICE AND ORCH.)
2,3,3,2 - 4,2,3,0 - timp.,perc. - hp. - str.   20:00 Presser.
—— QUATRE AIRS CHANTÉS (FOR VOICE AND ORCH.)
Salabert.
—— RAPSODIE NÈGRE (FOR CHAMBER ORCH.) (WITH VOICE AD LIB.)
Salabert.
—— SEPT RÉPONS DES TÉNÈBRES (FOR HIGH VOICE, CHORUS AND ORCH.)
2,2,3,3 - 4,3,3,1 - timp. - hp. - str.   25:00 Salabert.

—— SÈCHERESSES (FOR MIXED CHORUS AND ORCH.)
2,2,2,2 - 4,2,3,1 - timp.,perc.,cel. - hp. - str.   18:00 EV.
—— SINFONIETTA
2,2,2,2 - 2,2,0,0 - timp. - hp. - str.   G. Schirmer.
—— STABAT MATER (FOR SOPRANO, MIXED CHORUS AND ORCH.)
3,3,3,3 - 4,3,3,1 - timp. - 2 hp. - str.   35:00 Salabert.
—— SUITE FRANCAISE (D'APRÈS CLAUDE GERVAISE)
2,0,2,0 - 0,2,3,0 - perc. - pf.   12:00 EV.
—— TWO EXCERPTS ("LA BAIGNEUSE DE TROUVILLE" ET "DISCOURS DU GÉNÉRAL") FROM "LES MARIÉS DE LA TOUR EIFFEL"
3,2,2,2 - 4,2,2,1 - perc. - str.   Salabert.
—— TWO MARCHES AND AN INTERMEZZO
1,1,1,1 - 0,1,0,0 - str.   6:00 Salabert.
—— LA VOIX HUMAINE (1-ACT OPERA) % (Text: Jean Cocteau; Engl. text: Joseph Machlis)
2,2,3,2 - 2,2,1,1 - timp.,perc. - hp. - str.   46:40 F. Colombo.

POULENC, Francis - FRANÇAIX, Jean
—— L' HISTOIRE DE BABAR LE PETIT ÉLÉPHANT (FOR NARRATOR AND ORCH.)
2,2,2,2 - 2,2,1,1 - timp.,perc.(1) - hp. - str.   22:00 G. Schirmer.

POULENC, Francis - MILHAUD, Darius
—— OVERTURE (FOR CHAMBER ORCH.)
2,1,2,1 - 2,2,1,0 - perc. - str.   5:00 G. Schirmer.

POUSSEUR, Henri
—— COULEURS CROISEES (1967)
4,4,4,4 sax.,4 - 6,4,4,1 - timp.,perc.(6),cel.,glock.,vibra. - 2 hp. - hpsc. - 2 pf. - str.   19:00 MCA Music.
—— LES EPHEMERIDES D'ICARE II (FOR PIANO AND INSTRUMENTS) (1970)
2,1,3,1 - 1,1,0,0 - cel.,mar.,vibra. - hp. - hpsc. - pf. - str.(1,1,2,1)   40:00 MCA Music.
—— RIMES POUR DIFFÉRENTES SOURCES SONORES (FOR ORCH. AND MAGNETIC TAPE)
perc.(3),cel.,glock.,vibra. - tape-recorder - hp. - pf. - str.
14:40 Leeds.

POUWELS, Jan
—— CONCERTO FOR FLUTE AND STRINGS (1957)
fl. - str.   13:00 Henmar.
—— CONCERTO FOR ORGAN AND SMALL ORCH.
4 hn. - org. - str.   10:00 Henmar.
—— CONCERTO FOR PIANO AND ORCH. (1967) (IN 3 MOVTS.)
15:00 Henmar.
—— CONCERTO FOR VIOLIN AND ORCHESTRA (1966) (IN 3 MOVTS.)
14:00 Henmar.
—— DE RUYTER FANTASIE (VARIATIES VOOR GRAND ORKEST)
2,3,2,3 - 3,2,3,0 - timp.,perc. - str.   8:00 Henmar.
—— ITALIAANSE OUVERTURE
2,2,2,2 - 2,2,0,0 - timp. - str.   13:00 Henmar.
—— JOB: SUITE NO. 2 FROM THE BALLET (1955)
2,2,2,2 - 3,2,3,0 - timp.,perc. - pf. - str.   22:00 Henmar.
—— OUVERTURE
2,1,2,2 - 3,2,0,0 - timp.,perc. - str.   Henmar.
—— SUITE FOR ORCH.
3,3,3,3 - 4,3,3,1 - timp.,perc.,cel. - str.   24:00 Henmar.
—— SUITE NO. 1 FROM THE BALLET "JOB"
1,2,2,2 - 3,2,3,0 - timp.,perc. - pf. - str.   20:00 Henmar.
—— SYMPHONIC DANCE SUITE (1966) (IN 7 MOVTS.)
14:55 Henmar.
—— SYMPHONIC SUITE NO. 2 (1962)
3,3,3,3 - 4,3,3,1 - timp.,perc. - pf. - str.   16:00 Henmar.
—— SYMPHONY
2,3,2,3 - 4,3,3,1 - timp.,perc. - str.   30:00 Henmar.

POWELL, John
—— AT THE FAIR, OP. 22 (SKETCHES OF AMERICAN FUN)
G. Schirmer.
—— IN OLD VIRGINIA, OP. 28 (OVERTURE)
3(3rd. alt. with picc.),*3,*3,2 - 4,2,3,1 - timp.,perc.(2-3) - hp. - str.   12:00 G. Schirmer.
—— NATCHEZ-ON-THE-HILL, OP. 30 (THREE VIRGINIAN COUNTRY DANCES)
*3,2,2,2 - 4,2,3,1 - timp.,perc.(2-3) - hp. - str.   G. Schirmer.
—— RHAPSODIE NÈGRE (FOR PIANO AND ORCH.)
*3,*3,2,b.-cl.(ad lib.),2 - 4,2,3,1 - timp.,perc.,cel. - hp. - pf. - str.   14:00 G. Schirmer.

—— A SET OF THREE
*3,*3,*3,2 - 4,3,3,1 - timp.,perc.(2-3) - hp. - str.
16:00 G. Schirmer.
—— SYMPHONY IN A
Composer.

POWELL, Laurence
—— CHARIVARI (SUITE) (IN 3 MOVTS.)
1,1,2,1 - 2,1,0,0 - timp.,perc.(3) - str.   15:00 Composer.
—— CONCERTINO FOR ENGLISH HORN AND SMALL ORCH.
15:00 Composer.
—— THE COUNTY FAIR (SUITE)
2,2,2,2 - 2,2,3,1 - timp.,perc.(2),cel.(or glock.) - str.
17:00 AmerMusEd.
—— DEIRDRE OF THE SORROWS (A ROMANTIC PRELUDE)
2,*3,2,2 - 4,2,3,1 - timp. - str.   10:00 Composer.
—— DUO CONCERTANTE (FOR SOPRANO, RECORDER, ALTO RECORDER AND ORCH.)
12:00 Composer.
—— HALCYONE (DRAMATIC POEM) (FOR SOLOISTS, CHORUS AND ORCH.)
15:00 Composer.
—— KELTIC LEGEND
*3,2,2,2 - 4,2,3,1 - timp.,perc.(2) - hp. - str.   12:00 Composer.
—— LEGENDS OF LOSAL (CONCERT PIECE FOR VIOLIN AND ORCH.)
15:00 Composer.
—— THE OGRE OF THE NORTHERN FASTNESS (IN 3 MOVTS.)
*3,*3,2,*3 - 4,2,3,1 - timp.,perc.(3),cel. - hp. - pf. - str.
15:00 Composer.
—— ORACLE (THE OAK OF DODONA)
12:00 Composer.
—— OVERTURE ON FRENCH FOLK SONGS
1,2,1,1 - 2,2,1,0 - timp. - str.   4:00 Studio PR.
—— OVERTURE TO THE CHILDREN'S CANTATA "JACK THE GIANT KILLER" (FOR SMALL ORCH.)
4:00 Galaxy.
—— PENNY OVERTURE
2,1,2,1 - 2,2,1,0 - timp.,perc. - str.   4:00 ConcertMPC.
—— SAM HOUSTON ("IN SHADOW AND IN LIGHT") (TONE POEM)
*3,*3,2,*3 - 4,2,3,1 - timp.,perc.(2) - str.   9:30 Composer.
—— THE SANTA FE TRAIL (SYMPHONIC BALLAD) (FOR NARRATOR, BARITONE, CHORUS AND ORCH.) (Text: John Latham)
40:00 Composer.
—— SUITE FOR STRINGS (IN 3 MOVTS.)
str.   35:00 Composer.
—— SYMPHONY NO. 1 (IN 1 MOVT.)
*3,*3,*3,*3 - 4,3,3,1 - timp. - hp. - str.   40:00 Composer.
—— SYMPHONY NO. 2 (IN 4 MOVTS.)
2(2nd alt. with picc.),2(2nd alt. with Eng. hn.),2,2 - 2,2,3,1 - timp.,perc.(2) - str.   22:00 Composer.
—— VARIATIONS FOR ORCHESTRA
*3,*3,Eᵇcl.(ad lib.),*3,*3 - 4,2,3,1 - timp.,perc.(2),cel.,mar. - hp. - pf. - str.   35:00 Composer.

POWELL, Mel
—— CANTILENA CONCERTANTE (FOR ENGLISH HORN AND ORCH.)
11:00 Templeton.
—— IMMOBILE (FOR TAPE AND DIVERSE INSTRS.)
5:00 G. Schirmer.
—— IMMOBILE V
8:00 G. Schirmer.
—— IMMOBILES (FOR TAPE AND OR ORCH.)
2,2,2,2 - 4,2,3,1 - timp.,perc. - tape-recorder(2-channel) - hp. - str.
12:00 G. Schirmer.
—— INTRADA AND VARIANTS
3,3,3,3 - 4,3,3,1 - timp.,perc. - hp. - pf. - str.   10:00 F. Colombo.
—— SETTING FOR CELLO AND ORCH.
2,2,2,2 - 2,2,0,0 - timp.,perc.,vibra - hp. - str.   6:30 G. Schirmer.
—— STANZAS FOR ORCH.
2,1,2,1 - 2,2,1,0 - perc. - str.   7:00 G. Schirmer.
—— SUITE FOR ORCHESTRA
2,2,2,2 - 4,2,3,1 - timp.,perc. - str.   12:30 Templeton.

POWERS, Maxwell
—— DANCE WORKSHOP (IN 6 MOVTS.)
2,2,2,1 - str.   18:00 Composer.
—— OVERTURE
2,2,2,2 - 2,2,0,0 - timp. - str.   8:00 Composer.

—— PRELUDE AND DANCE
2,2,2,0 - 4,2,2,0 - timp. - str.   10:00 Composer.
—— STRING SUITE (IN 3 MOVTS.)
str.   9:00 Composer.
—— YEARS OF THE MODERN (SYMPHONIC POEM)
2,*3,*3,*3 - 4,2,2,0 - timp.,perc.(2) - str.   15:00 Composer.

POYNTER, Arthur R.
—— CHORAL SUITE NO. 2 (1964) (FOR SSAATTBB CHORUS AND ORCH.) (IN 5 MOVTS.) (Text: Arthur R. Poynter)
*3,2(2nd alt. with Eng. hn.),2,2 - 4,3,3,1 - timp.,perc. - 2 hp. - str.
40:00 CanMusCtr.
—— CHORAL SUITE NO. 3 (CONFEDERATION) (1966) FOR SATB CHORUS AND ORCH. (IN 3 MOVTS.) (Text: Arthur R. Poynter)
*3,2(2nd alt. with Eng. hn.),2,2(2nd alt. with c.-bn.) - 4,3,3,1 - timp.,perc. - 2 hp. - str.   45:00 CanMusCtr.
—— THE GREAT COMMISSION (ORATORIO) (1963) (FOR SOPRANO, ALTO, TENOR, BASS, SSAATTBB CHORUS AND ORCH.) ((IN 2 PARTS)) (Text: Arthur R. Poynter)
3,2,2,alto sax.,2 - 3,3,3,1 - timp. - str.   70:00 CanMusCtr.

POZAJIĆ, Mladen
—— THE BRIDESMAID (DANCE SYMPHONY)
2,2,2,2 - 4,2,3,0 - timp.,perc. - str.   3:00 S.O.K.O.J.
—— LITTLE CONCERTO ON BORROWED THEMES (IN 3 MOVTS.)
str.   17:00 S.O.K.O.J.

POZDRO, John
—— LAMENT (1954)
1,1,2,1 - 2,1,0,0 - timp.,perc. - str.   4:00 Composer.
—— RONDO GIOCOSO (1965)
str.   5:00 Summy-Bir.
—— SYMPHONY NO. 2 (1958) (IN 3 MOVTS.)
3(3rd. alt.with picc.),2,*3,2 - 4,3,3,1 - timp.,perc.(3) - hp. - str.
23:30 Fleisher.
—— SYMPHONY NO. 3 (1959) (IN 4 MOVTS.)
2(2nd alt.with picc.),2(2nd alt.with Eng.hn.),2,2 - 4,2,3,1 - timp.,perc.(3),bells - str.   23:00 Presser.
—— WATERLOW PARK: 1970 (1971)
*3,2,2,2 - 4,3,3,1 - timp.,perc.(3),glock. - hp. - str. 7:00 Composer.

PRAAG, Henri C. van
—— FANTASIA CONCERTANTE (FOR FLUTE, BASSOON AND ORCH.) (1957)
2,2,2,2 - 2,0,0,0 - timp. - str.   20:00 Henmar.
—— FANTASIA SINFONICA (1960)
2,1,2,0 - 0,1,0,0 - timp.,perc. - pf.(4 hands) - str. 16:00 Henmar.
—— FANTASY FOR CELLO AND ORCH.
1,1,1,1 - 2,0,0,0 - str.   9:00 Henmar.
—— HEATON CONCERTO (FOR STRINGS)
str.   Henmar.
—— SINFONIETTA
1,2,1,1 - 2,0,0,0 - str.   10:00 Henmar.
—— DE VIAG UIT HET RAAM (SUITE)
2,2,2,2 - 4,2,2,0 - timp.,perc. - str.   16:00 Henmar.
—— DE VLAG UIT HET RAAM (FOR MIXED CHORUS AND ORCH.) (1953) (Text: J. W. Jacobs)
2,2,2,2 - 4,2,2,0 - timp.,perc. - str.   25:00 Henmar.

PRABHU, Antonio T.
—— GOENCHIM XETAM (THE GREEN FIELDS OF GOA) (OVERTURE) (1953)
2,2,2,1 - 2,3,3,1 - timp.,perc.(3) - str.   10:00 Composer.
—— SOBITH PHOOL GOENCHEM ("BEAUTIFUL FLOWER OF GOA") (SUITE) (FOR SOPRANO, TENOR, CHORUS AND ORCH.) (1955) (IN 3 MOVTS.)
2,2,2,1 - 2,3,3,1 - timp.,perc.(7) - guits.,mands. - pf. - str.
20:00 Composer.
—— SYMPHONY NO. 1 (HAKEEKAT) (1966)
1. Andante; 2. Prestissimo - Allegro - Prestissimo; 3. Allegro
*4,*3,*3,2 - 4,3,3,1 - timp.,perc.(4) - hp. - pf. - str.
12:00 Composer.

PRADO, Almeida
—— AURORA (1975)
2,2,2,2 - 4,3,3,0 - perc.,cel. - str.   18:00 Seesaw.
—— CEREMONIAL (FOR BASSOON AND ORCH.) (1971)
*3,*3,2,1 - 4,2,3,1 - timp.,perc. - hp. - pf. - str.   9:00 Seesaw.
—— CONCERTO FOR VIOLIN AND STRING ORCH. (1976)
str.   18:00 Seesaw.

—— ESTAÇOES (1972)
  *3,*3,2,2 - 4,2,3,1 - timp.,perc. - pf. - str.   11:00 Seesaw.
—— ESTIGMAS (FOR STRING ORCH.)
  str.   11:00 Seesaw.
—— EXOFLORA (FOR PIANO AND ORCH.) (1974)
  1,*2,1,1 - 1,1,1,0 - perc. - pf. - str.   12:30 Seesaw.
—— SYMPHONY NO. 1 (1970)
  *4,*3,2,2 - 4,2,3,1 - timp.,perc. - pf. - str.   20:00 Seesaw.
—— THÉRÈSE (L'AMOUR DE DIEU) (ORATORIO) (FOR 2 SOLO
  VOICES, SATB CHORUS AND ORCH.)
  1,1,1,1 - 2,2,1,0 - perc. - str.   80:00 Seesaw.
—— VARIAÇOES (FOR PIANO AND ORCH.) (1963)
  3,*3,2,3 - 4,2,3,1 - timp.,perc. - pf. - str.   15:00 Seesaw.
—— VILLEGAGNON (ORATORIO) (FOR SOLO VOICES, SATB
  CHORUS AND ORCH.)
  *3,2,2,2 - 4,3,4,0 - perc. - pf. - str.   110:00 Seesaw.

PRATT, Samuel O.
—— CONCERTO NO. 2 IN B MINOR, FOR HARP AND ORCH.
  (1959) (IN 3 MOVTS.)
  1,1,2,1 - 2,0,0,0 - timp.,perc.(1),glock. - hp. - str.   28:00 Fema.

PREGEL, Boris
—— PETITE SUITE
        6:45 S.A.C.E.M.
—— SYMPHONIC POEM
        6:00 S.A.C.E.M.

PREMRL, Stanko
—— FOUR PASTORALES FOR ORCH.: CYCLE NO. 1
  2,2,2,2 - 4,3,3,0 - timp.,perc. - str.   15:00 Hans Gerig.
—— SCHERZO
  2,2,2,2 - 4,2,3,0 - timp. - str.   4:00 Hans Gerig.

PRESLE, Jacques de la
—— ALBUM D'IMAGES
  3,2,2,2 - 4,2,3,1 - timp.,perc. - hp. - str.   12:00 Baron.
—— L' APOCALYPSE DE SAINT JEAN (FOR SOPRANO, TENOR,
  TWO BARITONES, MIXED CHORUS AND ORCH.) (IN 3
  MOVTS.)
  3,2,2,2 - 4,2,3,1 - timp.,perc.(2),cel. - 2 hp. - str.   75:00 Salabert.

PRESS, Jacques
—— DISCONCERTO (FOR PIANO AND SMALL ORCH.)
  1,1,1,1 - 1,2,1,0 - perc. - pf. - str.   6:00 Leeds.
—— HASSENEH ("THE WEDDING") (SUITE)
  3,2,3,3 - 4,3,3,1 - timp.,perc. - str.   20:00 Weintraub.
—— PRELUDE AND FUGUE IN JAZZ
        4:30 Lyra.

PRESSER, William
—— ARCTIC NIGHT
  1,1,2,1 - 2,2,3,1 - timp. - str.   6:00 EV.
—— CONCERTO FOR TENOR SAXOPHONE AND ORCH. (IN 3
  MOVTS.)
  1,1,2,1 - ten.sax.,1 - 2,2,1,0 - str.   19:30 Composer.
—— PATTERNS (SUITE) (IN 3 MOVTS.)
  str.   7:30 Composer.
—— PRELUDE TO A SUMMER'S DAWN
  2,2,2,2 - 2,2,3,1 - timp.,perc. - str.   4:45 Composer.
—— PRELUDE TO AUTUMN
  str.   4:00 Composer.
—— RONDO (FOR SOLO TROMBONE AND STRINGS)
  trb. - str.   5:00 TenutoPbns.
—— SIXTY-SECOND SKETCHES (SUITE) (IN TEN MOVTS.)
  2,2,2,2 - 4,2,3,1 - timp.,perc,(2) - str.   10:00 Composer.
—— SONGS OF DEATH (3 SONGS FOR MEZZO-SOPRANO AND
  STRING ORCH.) (Text: Robert Herrick)
  str.   10:00 Composer.
—— SYMPHONY NO. 1 (IN 4 MOVTS.)
  2,2,2,2 - 4,2,3,1 - timp.,perc.(2) - str.   11:30 Presser.

PREVIN, André
—— CONCERTO FOR CELLO AND ORCHESTRA
  3,2,2,2 - 4,2,2,1 - timp.,perc.,cel. - hp. - str.   26:00 G. Schirmer.
—— CONCERTO FOR GUITAR AND ORCH.
  2(2nd alt. with picc.),2(2nd alt. with Eng.hn.),*3(2nd alt. with E♭
  cl.),2 - 4,2,0,0 - perc.(2)-jazz drums - fender bass - electric guit. -
  guit.- hp. str.   25:00 G. Schirmer.
—— OVERTURE TO A COMEDY
  3,2,3,2 - 4,3,3,1 - timp.,perc.,cel. - hp. - pf. - str.   10:00 Leeds.
—— PORTRAIT FOR STRINGS
  str.   Leeds.

PREVITALI, Fernando
—— DUE PEZZI (TWO PIECES)
  3,3,3,3 - 4,2,3,1 - timp.,perc.,cel. - hp. - pf. - str.
        11:30 Bo. Hawkes.

PREY, Claude
—— LE COEUR RÉVÉLATEUR (THE TELL-TALE HEART)
  (OPERA, AFTER EDGAR A. POE) % (1962) (Text: Phillippe
  Soupault)
  2(2nd alt.with picc.),1 alto fl.,0,*2,1 - 1,1,1,0 - perc.(4) -
  ondes-martenot - hp. - pf.(alt.with cel.) - str.(2,1,1,1)
        45:00 Salabert.
—— LES MOTS CRAISÉS (JEU CONCERTANT) (FOR
  CONTRALTO, TENOR AND 2 INSTRUMENTAL GROUPS)
  (1970)
  1,1,1,1 - 0,1,0,0 - guit.,mand. - vla.,c.,d.-b.(5-str.)   25:00 Salabert.
—— ON VEUT LA LUMIÈRE ALLONS-Y! (OPERA-PARODY IN 2
  TRIAL) % (1967)
  1(alt.with picc.),0,0,0 - 1,0,0,0 - timp.,perc. - hp. - hammond org. -
  pf. - vln.,c.,d.-b.   Salabert.

PRICE, Florence B.
—— CONCERT OVERTURE NO. 1 (BASED ON NEGRO
  SPIRITUALS)
  3,2,2,2 - 4,3,3,1 - timp.,perc.(4-5) - str   10:00 Composer.
—— CONCERT OVERTURE NO. 2 (BASED ON NEGRO
  SPIRITUALS)
  3(1 alt. with picc.),*3,*3,2 - 4,3,3,1 - timp.,perc. - hp. - str.
        12:00 Composer.
—— CONCERTO FOR PIANO AND ORCH. (IN 1 MOVT.)
  1,1,2,1 - 2,2,2,0 - timp.,perc.(2) - pf. - str.   12:00 Composer.
—— CONCERTO IN D MAJOR, FOR VIOLIN AND ORCH.
  2,2,2,2 - 2 tpt. - timp. - str.   16:00 Composer.
—— DANCES IN THE CANEBRAKES (SUITE)
  2,1,*3,3 sax.,2 - 3,3,2,1 - timp.,perc.(2) - hp. - str.   8:15 Mills.
—— MISSISSIPPI RIVER
  *4,*3,*3,*3 - 4,3,3,1 - timp.,perc. - hp. - str.   10:00 Composer.
—— THE OAK (TONE POEM)
  3(1 alt. with picc.),*1,*3,2 - 4,3,3,1 - timp.,perc. - hp. - str.
        7:00 Composer.
—— SONGS OF THE OAK (TONE POEM)
  *4,*3,*3,*3 - 4,3,*4,1 - timp.,perc. (5-6) - hp. - org.(ad lib.) - str.
        12:00 Composer.
—— SYMPHONY IN C MINOR (IN 4 MOVTS.)
  *4,*3,*3,2 - 4,3,3,1 - timp.,perc. - hp. - str.   22:00 Composer.
—— SYMPHONY IN D MINOR (IN 4 MOVTS.)
  *4,*3,*3,2 - 4,3,3,1 - timp.,perc.(3-5) - hp. - str.   20:00 Composer.
—— SYMPHONY IN E MINOR (IN 4 MOVTS.)
  2,2,2,2 - 4,2,3,1 - timp.,perc.(3) - str.   20:00 Composer.
—— SYMPHONY IN G MINOR
  *4,*3,*3,*3 - 4,3,4,0 - timp.,perc.(3) - hp. - str.   25:00 Composer.

PRICE, John E.
—— THE DAMNATION OF DR. FAUSTUS (FOR TENOR, CHORUS
  AND ORCH.) (1963) (Text: Christopher Marlowe)
  1,1,2,0 - 2,1,1,1 - timp.,perc.(3),bells,glock.,xyl. - hp. - str.
        Composer.
—— SCHERZO NO. 1 FOR CLARINET AND ORCH. (1955)
  2(2nd alt. with picc.),*3,2,2 b.-cl.,2 - 4,0,2,1 -
  timp.,perc.,bells,glock.,xyl. - pf. - str.   17:00 Composer.
—— SCHERZO NO. 2 FOR CLARINET AND ORCH. (1957)
  *3,2,*3,2 - 4,3,2,1 - perc.(3),bells,cel.,glock. - hp. - str.   Composer.
—— SUGGESTION FOR THE CENTURY (FOR 4 MALE VOICES
  AND ORCH. (1958) (Text: Composer)
  *3,2,2,2 b.-cl.,0 - 4,3,3,1 - timp.,perc. - hp. - str.   Composer.

PRIEGNITZ, Hans
—— MUSIC FOR PIANO AND ORCH.
  2,2,2,2 - 4,2,3,1 - timp.,perc. - pf. - str.   24:00 G. Schirmer.

PRIESING, Dorothy M.
—— SYMPHONY NO. 1 (IN 1 MOVT.)
  *3,1,*3,1 - 4,3,2,1 - timp. - str.   8:00 Composer.

PROCACCINI, Teresa
—— CONCERTO FOR ORGAN AND ORCH.
  3,2,2,2 - 4,3,0,0 - timp. - org. - str.   27:00 Bo. Hawkes.
—— CONCERTO FOR VIOLIN, CELLO, PIANO AND ORCH. ("I
  FOLLETTI")
  3,2,3,2 - 4,3,0,0 - timp. - pf. - str.   27:00 Bo. Hawkes.

—— DANNAZIONE E PREGHIERA (FROM "SENTIMENTO NEL TEMPO") (FOR MEZZO-SOPRANO AND STRINGS) (Text: G Ungaretti)
str.   13:00 Bo. Hawkes.
—— DIVERTIMENTO
tpt. - pedal timp.,musical saw,xyl.,vibra. - pf. - str.
10:00 Bo. Hawkes.
—— FANTASIA
3,2,3,2 - 4,0,3,1 - timp.,perc.,xyl. - str.   13:00 Bo. Hawkes.
—— IL GIUDIZIO DI SALOMONE (CANTATA) (FOR SOLO VOICES, MIXED CHORUS AND ORCH.)
3,2,3,2 - 4,3,3,1 - timp.,perc. - str.   13:00 Bo. Hawkes.
—— INVENZIONE
fl.,ob.,cl. - str.   7:00 Bo. Hawkes.
—— LA PESTE DI ATENE (FROM "DE RERUM NATURA") (FOR CHORUS AND ORCH.) (Text: L. Caro)
3,2,3,2 - 4,3,3,1 - timp.,perc. - str.   14:00 Bo. Hawkes.
—— SINFONIETTA
2,2,2,2 - 2,2,0,0 - timp. - str.   25:00 Bo. Hawkes.

PROCTOR, Charles
—— CONCERTO IN F MINOR FOR PIANO AND ORCH.
25:00 Lengnick.
—— FOUR SONGS (FOR HIGH VOICES AND STRINGS)
str.   16:00 Lengnick.
—— THREE CHILDREN'S SONGS (FOR HIGH VOICE AND STRINGS)
str.   16:00 Lengnick.
—— VENI CREATOR SPIRITUS (MOTET) (FOR CHORUS AND ORCH.)
11:30 Lengnick.

PROKOFIEFF, Serge
—— ALA ET LOLLY (SCYTHIAN SUITE), OP. 20 (IN 4 MOVTS.) (Ed. by F. H. Schneider)
*4(3rd alt. with alto fl.),*4,*4 (3rd alt. with E♭ cl.),*4 - 8,3-4(3rd alt. with E♭ tpt.),tpt. in F,4,1 - timp.,perc.(6-10),cel.,glock.,xyl. - 2 hp. - pf. - str.
21:30 Bo. Hawkes.
—— ALEXANDER NEVSKY, OP. 78 (CANTATA FOR MEZZO-SOPRANO, CHORUS AND ORCH.) (IN 7 MOVTS.) (Ed. by Harold Sheldon)
*3,*3,*3,sax.,*3 - 4,3,3,1 - timp.,perc.(8),glock.,xyl. - hp. - str.
40:00 G. Schirmer.
—— THE BALLAD OF THE UNKNOWN BOY, OP. 93(CANTATA) (FOR DRAMATIC SOPRANO, DRAMATIC TENOR, CHORUS AND ORCH.)
*3,*3,*3,*3 - 4,3,3,1 - timp.,perc.(5),xyl. - 2 hp. - pf. - str.
G. Schirmer.
—— CHANT SYMPHONIQUE, OP. 57
3,3,3,3 - 4,3,3,1 - timp.,perc. - str.   17:00 Bo. Hawkes.
—— CHOUT (BALLET SUITE), OP. 21A (Ed. by F. H. Schneider)
3,3,3,3 - 4,3,3,1 - timp.,perc.(3-5),xyl. - 2 hp. - pf. - str.
35:00 Bo. Hawkes.
—— CINDERELLA (BALLET), OP. 87 %
3,3,3,3 - 4,3,3,1 - timp.,perc.,cel.,xyl. - hp. - pf. - str. G. Schirmer.
Plus Stage Band
—— CINDERELLA: BALLET SUITE NO. 1, OP. 107 (Ed. by Harold Sheldon)
3,3,3,3 - 4,3,3,1 - timp.,perc.,xyl. - hp. - pf. - str.
30:00 G. Schirmer.
—— CINDERELLA: BALLET SUITE NO. 2, OP. 108
3,3,3,3 - 4,3,3,1 - timp.,perc. - hp. - pf. - str.   17:00 G. Schirmer.
—— CINDERELLA: BALLET SUITE NO. 3, OP. 109
3,3,3,3 - 4,3,3,1 - timp.,perc.,cel.,xyl. - hp. - pf. - str.
27:00 G. Schirmer.
—— CONCERTINO FOR CELLO AND ORCH., OP. 132 (1952) (Edited by Dmitri Kabalevsky and Mstislav Rostropovich)
2,3,2,2 - 4,2,3,1 - timp.,perc. - str.   18:00 G. Schirmer.
—— CONCERTO NO. 1 FOR CELLO AND ORCH., OP. 58
2,2,2,2 - 2,2,0,1 - timp.,perc. - str.   35:00 Bo. Hawkes.
—— CONCERTO NO. 1 IN D♭ FOR PIANO AND ORCH., OP. 10 (IN 1 MOVT.) (Ed. by Gyorgy Sandor)
*3,2,2,*3 - 4,2,3,1 - timp.,glock. - pf. - str.   16:00 G. Schirmer.
—— CONCERTO NO. 1 IN D FOR VIOLIN AND ORCH., OP. 19 (Ed. by F. H. Schneider) (IN 3 MOVTS.)
2,2,2,2 - 4,2,0,1 - timp.,perc. - hp. - str.   22:00 Bo. Hawkes.
—— CONCERTO NO. 1 IN D FOR VIOLIN AND ORCH., OP. 19 (Ed. by Louis Persinger) (IN 3 MOVTS.)
2,2,2,2 - 4,2,0,1 - timp.,perc. - hp. - str.   22:00 G. Schirmer.
—— CONCERTO NO. 2 IN G FOR VIOLIN AND ORCH., OP. 63 (Ed. by Louis Persinger) (IN 3 MOVTS.)
2,2,2,2 - 2,2,0,0 - perc. - str.   24:30 G. Schirmer.

—— CONCERTO NO. 2 IN G FOR VIOLIN AND ORCH., OP. 63 (IN 3 MOVTS.)
2,2,2,2 - 2,2,0,0 - perc. - str.   20:00 Bo. Hawkes.
—— CONCERTO NO. 2 IN G MINOR FOR PIANO AND ORCH., OP. 16 (IN 4 MOVTS.) (Ed. by Harold Sheldon)
2,2,2,2 - 4,2,3,1 - timp.,perc. - pf. - str.   32:00 G. Schirmer.
—— CONCERTO NO. 2 IN G MINOR FOR PIANO AND ORCH., OP. 16 (IN 4 MOVTS.) (Ed. by Albert Spalding)
2,2,2,2 - 4,2,3,1 - timp.,perc. - pf. - str.   25:00 Bo. Hawkes.
—— CONCERTO NO. 3 IN C FOR PIANO AND ORCH., OP. 26 (Ed. by Harold Sheldon) (IN 3 MOVTS.)
2,2,2,2 - 4,2,3,1 - timp.,perc. - pf. - str.   26:00 G. Schirmer.
—— CONCERTO NO. 3 IN C FOR PIANO AND ORCH., OP. 26 (IN 3 MOVTS.) (Ed. by F. H. Schneider)
2(2nd alt. with picc.),2,2,2 - 4,2,3,0 - timp.,perc.(2) - pf. - str.
27:00 Bo. Hawkes.
—— CONCERTO NO. 3 IN C FOR PIANO AND ORCH., OP. 26 (IN 3 MOVTS.) (Ed. by Harold Sheldon)
2,2,2,2 - 4,2,3,1 - timp.,perc. - pf. - str.   26:00 G. Schirmer.
—— CONCERTO NO. 4 FOR PIANO (LEFT HAND ALONE) AND ORCH., OP. 53
2,2,2,2 - 2,1,1,0 - perc. - pf. - str.   23:30 G. Schirmer.
—— CONCERTO NO. 5 IN G FOR PIANO AND ORCH., OP. 55 (IN 5 MOVTS.)
2,2,2,2 - 2,2,2,1 - timp.,perc. - pf. - str.   23:00 Bo. Hawkes.
—— DIVERTIMENTO, OP. 43
2,2,2,2 - 4,2,3,1 - timp.,perc. - str.   14:00 Bo. Hawkes.
—— L' ENFANT PRODIGUE ("THE PRODIGAL SON"), OP. 46 (BALLET) % (1929)
3,3,3,3 - 4,2,3,1 - timp.,perc. - str.   35:00 Bo. Hawkes.
—— THE FLAMING ANGEL (L'ANGE DE FEU), OP. 37 (5-ACT OPERA, AFTER A STORY BY V. BRIOUSSOV) % (1925)
3,*3,3,3 - 4,3,3,1 - timp.,perc. - 2 hp. - str.   Bo. Hawkes.
—— FOUR PORTRAITS FROM "THE GAMBLER", OP. 49
3,3,3,3 - 4,3,3,1 - timp.,perc. - 2 hp. - str.   33:00 Bo. Hawkes.
—— THE GAMBLER ("LE JOUEUR") OP. 24 (4-ACT OPERA, AFTER DOSTOIEVSKY) (REV. 1927) %
3,3,3,3 - 4,3,3,1 - timp.,perc. - 2 hp. - str.   Bo. Hawkes.
—— GYPSY FANTASY (FROM "THE STONE FLOWER")
3,4,3,3 - 4,3,3,1 - timp.,perc.,xyl. - hp. - pf. - str.
8:00 G. Schirmer.
—— THE LOVE FOR THREE ORANGES: SUITE, OP. 33A (Ed. by A. Spalding)
3,3,3,3 - 3,4,3,0 - timp.,perc.,xyl. - 2 hp. - str.   20:00 Bo. Hawkes.
—— THE MEETING OF THE VOLGA AND THE DON, OP. 130 (SYMPHONIC POEM)
3,3,3,3 - 4,3,3,1 - timp.,perc.,cel. - hp. - pf. - str.
15:30 G. Schirmer.
—— NINETEEN FORTY ONE (SUITE), OP. 90 (IN 3 MOVTS.)
*3,*3,*3,*3 - 4,3,3,1 - timp.,perc.(3),xyl. - hp. - str.
12:00 G. Schirmer.
—— ODE TO THE END OF THE WAR, OP. 105
1,*2 E♭ cl.,*2,*2 - 4,3,3,1 - perc. - 8 hp. - 4 pf. - d.-b.
15:00 G. Schirmer.
—— ON GUARD FOR PEACE, OP. 124 (ORATORIO)
2,3,3,3 - 4,2,1,1 - timp.,perc.,cel.,xyl. - hp. - pf. - str. G. Schirmer.
—— OVERTURE IN B FLAT MAJOR, OP. 42
3,3,3,3 - 4,2,3,1 - timp.,perc.,cel. - 2 hp. - pf. - str.
8:00 Bo. Hawkes.
Or
1,1,2,1 - 0.2,1,0 - perc.,cel. - 2 hp. - 2 pf. - str.(c. and d.-b.)
—— OVERTURE TO THE OPERA "THE DUENNA," OP. 86 (1940)
3,3,3,3 - 4,3,3,1 - timp.,perc. - hp. - str.   G. Schirmer.
—— OVERTURE TO THE OPERA "WAR AND PEACE," OP. 91 (REV. 1952)
3,3,3,3 - 4,3,3,1 - timp.,perc. - hp. - str.   5:00 G. Schirmer.
—— LE PAS D'ACIER, OP. 41-B (BALLET SUITE)
3,3,4,3 - 4,4,3,1 - timp.,perc. - str.   14:00 Bo. Hawkes.
—— LE PAS D'ACIER, OP. 41 (BALLET) % (1925)
3,3,4,3 - 4,4,3,1 - timp.,perc. - pf. - str.   35:00 Bo. Hawkes.
—— POEMA FESTIVO, OP. 113 (1947)
2,2,2,2 - 4,2,3,1 - perc. - pf. - str.   G. Schirmer.
—— THE PRODIGAL SON (BALLET), OP. 46 %
35:00 Bo. Hawkes.
—— THE PRODIGAL SON (L'ENFANT PRODIGUE) (BALLET SUITE), OP. 46B
3,3,3,3 - 4,2,3,1 - timp.,perc. - str.   18:00 Bo. Hawkes.
—— PUSHKIN WALTZES, OP. 120
2,3,3,2 - 4,2,3,1 - timp.,perc. - str.   8:00 G. Schirmer.
—— ROMEO AND JULIET (BALLET), OP. 64 %
3,3,3,1 ten. sax., 3 - 6,4,3,1 - timp.,perc.,cel.,xyl. - mand. - 2 hp. - org. - pf. - vla.d'amore (opt.) - str.   G. Schirmer.
Plus Stage Band

—— ROMEO AND JULIET: SUITE NO. 1 (IN 7 MOVTS.)
　　*3,*3,*3,ten. sax.,*3 - 4,cnt.,2,3,1 - timp.,perc.(5),xyl. - hp. - pf. -
　　str.　　　　　　　　　　　　　28:00 G. Schirmer.
—— ROMEO AND JULIET: SUITE NO. 2 (IN 7 MOVTS.)
　　*3,*3,*3,ten. sax.,*3 - 4,cnt.,2,3,1 - timp.,perc.(4) - hp. - pf.(or cel.)
　　- str.　　　　　　　　　　　　31:00 G. Schirmer.
—— ROMEO AND JULIET: SUITE NO. 3, OP. 101 (IN 6 MOVTS.)
　　3,3,3,3 - 4,3,3,1 - timp.,perc.,cel. - hp. - pf. - str.
　　　　　　　　　　　　　　　　20:00 G. Schirmer.
—— RUSSIAN OVERTURE, OP. 72 (Reduced instrumentation)
　　3,3,3,3 - 4,4,3,1 - timp.,perc. - 2 hp. - pf. - str. 14:00 Bo. Hawkes.
—— RUSSIAN OVERTURE, OP. 72
　　*4,4(4th alt. with Eng. hn),*4,*4 - 8,4,3,1 -
　　timp.,perc.(7),glock.,xyl. - 2 hp. - pf. - str.　　12:30 Bo. Hawkes.
—— RUSSIAN OVERTURE, OP. 72 (SOVIET EDITION)
　　*4,4(4th alt. with Eng. hn),*4,*4 - 8,4,3,1 -
　　timp.,perc.(7),glock.,xyl. - 2 hp. - pf. - str.　　12:30 G. Schirmer.
—— SEVEN, THEY ARE SEVEN ("SEPT, ILS SONT
　　SEPT")(CANTATA) (FOR TENOR, CHORUS AND ORCH.), OP.
　　30
　　　4,4,4,4 - 8,4,4,2 - timp.,perc.,cel.,xyl. - 2 hp. - str.
　　　　　　　　　　　　　　　　7:00 Bo. Hawkes.
—— SINFONIA CONCERTANTE, OP. 125 (FOR CELLO AND
　　ORCH.) (CELLO CONCERTO NO. 2)
　　　2,2,2,2 - 4,2,3,1 - timp.,perc.,cel. - str.　　36:00 Bo. Hawkes.
—— SINFONIETTA, OP. 5, NO. 48
　　　2,2,2,2 - 4 hn. - str.　　　　　　　25:00 Bo. Hawkes.
—— SUITE FROM THE OPERA "SEMYON KOTKO", OP. 81 (IN 8
　　MOVTS.)
　　*3,*3,*3,*3 - 4,3,3,1 - timp.,perc. - hp. - str.　40:00 G. Schirmer.
—— SUITE OF WALTZES, OP. 110 (IN 6 MOVTS.)
　　3,3,3,3 - 4,3,3,1 - timp.,perc.,xyl. - hp. - pf. - str.
　　　　　　　　　　　　　　　　26:00 G. Schirmer.
—— SUMMER DAY, OP. 65 (MUSIC FOR CHILDREN)
　　　2,2,2,2 - 2,1,0,0 - timp.,perc.(3) - str.　　11:00 Bo. Hawkes.
—— SUMMER DAY, OP. 65B (SUITE FOR CHILDREN)
　　　2,2,2,2 - 2,2,0,0 - timp.,perc. - str.　　11:00 G. Schirmer.
—— SUMMER NIGHT (SUITE FROM "THE DUENNA"), OP. 123
　　(IN 5 MOVTS.) (1950)
　　3,3,3,3 - 4,3,3,1 - timp.,perc. - hp. - str.　　G. Schirmer.
—— SUR LE BORYSTHÈNE, OP. 51
　　3,3,3,3 - 4,2,3,1 - timp.,perc. - str.　　35:00 Bo. Hawkes.
—— SYMPHONY NO. 2, OP. 40
　　3,2,4,2 - 4,3,3,1 - timp.,perc. - str.　　35:00 Bo. Hawkes.
—— SYMPHONY NO. 3, OP. 44
　　3,3,3,3 - 4,3,3,1 - timp.,perc. - 2 hp. - str.　33:00 Bo. Hawkes.
—— SYMPHONY NO. 4, OP 47 (IN 4 MOVTS.)
　　3,3,3,3 - 4,2,3,1 - timp.,perc. - 2 hp. - str.　23:00 Bo. Hawkes.
—— SYMPHONY NO. 5, OP. 100 (IN 4 MOVTS.)
　　*3,*3,E♭cl.,*3,*3 - 4,3,3,1 - timp.,perc. - hp. - pf. - str.
　　　　　　　　　　　　　　　　40:00 G. Schirmer.
—— SYMPHONY NO. 6, OP. 111 (IN 3 MOVTS.)
　　3,3,4,3 - 4,3,3,1 - timp.,perc. - hp. - pf. - str.　43:00 G. Schirmer.
—— SYMPHONY NO. 7, OP. 131
　　3,3,3,2 - 4,3,3,1 - timp.,perc.,xyl. - hp. - pf. - str.
　　　　　　　　　　　　　　　　32:00 G. Schirmer.
—— THE TALE OF THE STONE FLOWER (BALLET), OP. 118 %
　　3,3,4,3 - 4,3,3,1 - timp.,perc.,xyl. - hp. - pf. - str.　G. Schirmer.
—— A TOAST, OP. 85
　　3,3,3,3 - 4,3,3,1 - timp.,perc.,xyl. - hp. - pf. - str.
　　　　　　　　　　　　　　　　12:30 G. Schirmer.
—— THE UGLY DUCKLING, OP. 18("LE VILAIN PETIT
　　CANARD") (FOR VOICE AND ORCH.)
　　3,2,3,2 - 3,2,3,1 - perc. - hp. - str.　　12:00 Bo. Hawkes.
—— URAL RHAPSODY (FROM THE BALLET "THE STONE
　　FLOWER"), OP. 128 (1951)
　　3,3,4,3 - 4,3,3,1 - timp.,perc.,xyl. - hp. - pf. - str.　G. Schirmer.
—— WAR AND PEACE, OP. 91 (5-ACT OPERA) % (WITH
　　ENGLISH TEXT)
　　3,3,3,3 - 4,3,3,1 - timp.,perc. - hp. - str.　　G. Schirmer.
　　Plus Stage Band
—— WEDDING SUITE (FROM "THE STONE FLOWER"), OP. 126
　　3,3,4,3 - 4,3,3,1 - timp.,perc. - hp. - pf. - str.　15:00 MCA Music.
—— WINTER HOLIDAY, OP. 122 (FOR NARRATOR, BOYS'
　　CHORUS AND ORCH.)
　　2,1,2,1 - 4,2,1,1 - timp.,perc.,cel.,xyl. - hp. - pf. - str.
　　　　　　　　　　　　　　　　20:00 G. Schirmer.
——- SYMPHONY NO. 4, OP. 47 112 (REVISED)
　　3,3,4,3 - 4,3,3,1 - timp.,perc. - hp. - pf. - str.　39:00 G. Schirmer.

PROKOFIEFF, Serge - BARSHAI, R.
—— VISIONS FUGITIVES, OP. 22 (15 PIECES FOR STRING
　　ORCH.)
　　str.　　　　　　　　　　　　18:00 G. Schirmer.

PROKOFIEFF, Serge - BOUTNIKOFF, Ivan
—— PROKOFIEFFIANA (SUITE) (1966) (IN 5 MOVTS.)
　　2(2nd alt. with picc.),2(2nd alt. with Eng. hn.),*3,*3 - 4,3,3,1 -
　　timp.,perc.(4),cel.,glock.,xyl. - hp. - str.　14:00 Arranger.

PROKOFIEFF, Serge - BYRNES, Harold
—— SUITE DIABOLIQUE
　　3,3,3,3 - 4,3,3,1 - timp.,perc. - hp. - str.　12:00 Bo. Hawkes.

PROŠEV, Toma
—— CHAMBER MUSIC NO. 1 (1971)
　　1,1,1,1 - 1,1,1,0 - perc. - pf. - str.(1,1,1,1)　　11:00 MIC,Zagreb.
—— COLORS (FOR 6 SOLO VOICES AND ENSEMBLE) (1967)
　　1,1,1,1 - 1,1,1,0 - perc. - pf. - str.(2,1,1,1)　　40:00 MIC,Zagreb.
—— CONCERTO FOR ONDES-MARTENOT AND ORCH.
　　2,2,2,0 - 1,1,1,0 - perc.(4) - ondes-martenot - str.　20:00 Seesaw.
—— CONCERTO NO. 1 FOR VIOLIN AND ORCH. (1963)
　　*1,1,1,1 - 0,1,0,0 - pf. - str.　　　18:00 MIC,Zagreb.
—— CONCERTO NO. 2 FOR VIOLIN AND STRING ORCH.
　　str.　　　　　　　　　　　25:00 S.O.K.O.J.
—— DIAMETRIA (FOR VOICE AND CHAMBER GROUP) (1965)
　　1,1,1,1 - 1,1,1,0 - perc. - str.(2,1,1,1)　　10:00 MIC,Zagreb.
—— INTEGRALI (FOR PIANO AND CHAMBER ENSEMBLE)
　　(1972)
　　1,1,1,1 - 1,1,1,0 - perc.(1) - pf. - str.(2,1,1,1)　13:00 MIC,Zagreb.
—— SYMPHONY NO. 2
　　str.　　　　　　　　　　　27:00 S.O.K.O.J.
—— TEMPERA II
　　str.　　　　　　　　　　　8:00 S.O.K.O.J.
—— TEMPERA IV
　　str.　　　　　　　　　　　9:00 S.O.K.O.J.

PROSPERI, Carlo
—— INCANTI (FOR DIVERSE INSTRUMENTAL SOLOISTS AND
　　ORCH.) (WITH OFFSTAGE SOPRANO)
　　3,2,0,0 - 4,0,3,0 - perc.(6),mar.,vibra.,xyl. - 2 hp. - org.(alt. with
　　cel.) - pf. - str.　　　　　　14:00 Leeds.
—— MAREZZO (FOR SOPRANO, RECITATIVE VOICE, MIXED
　　CHORUS AND ORCH.)
　　3,1,2,2 sax.,1 - 0,1,1,0 - perc.(5),cel.,vibra.,xyl. - hp. - pf. - vlns.
　　　　　　　　　　　　　　　11:00 Leeds.
—— NOI SOLDA' (UNA MEMORIA) (FOR SOPRANO, SPEAKER,
　　MALE CHORUS AND INSTRUMENTS) (1967) (Text: G.
　　Bedeschi and C. Betocchi)
　　2,0,2,0 - 4,3,0,0 - perc.(4),vibra. - 2 hp. - org. - pf. - 30 vlns.
　　　　　　　　　　　　　　　30:00 MCA Music.
—— TOCCATA E FANFARA (1955)
　　4 tpt. - timp.,perc.(2),vibra.,xyl. - str.　　11:30 Leeds.
—— VARIAZIONI (1951)
　　4,3,4,4 - 4,3,3,1 - timp.,perc.(5),cel.,xyl. - 2 hp. - pf. - str.
　　　　　　　　　　　　　　　15:00 Leeds.

PROTO, Frank
—— AN AMERICAN OVERTURE (1973)
　　2(2nd alt.with picc.),2,2,2 - 2,2,3,1 - timp.,perc.(3),glock. - hp. - pf.
　　- str.　　　　　　　　　　9:00 Liben.
—— CASEY AT THE BAT (AN AMERICAN FOLK TALE) (FOR
　　NARRATOR AND ORCH.) (1973) (Text: Ernest Lawrence
　　Thayer)
　　*3,*3,*3,*3 - 4,3,3,1 - timp.,perc.(5),bells,glock.,vibra.,xyl. -
　　tape-recorder(2-track stereo) - hp. - pf. - str.　13:00 Liben.
—— CONCERTINO FOR PERCUSSION AND STRINGS (1975)
　　perc.(1),xyl. - str.　　　　　　11:00 Liben.
—— CONCERTO FOR DOUBLE BASS AND ORCH. (1968)
　　1. Slowly; 2. Bright; 3. Very Slow (Variations); 4. Moderate
　　3(3rd alt.with picc.),*3,*3,*3 - 4,3,3,1 -
　　timp.,perc.(6),cel.,glock.,vibra.,xyl. - hp. - pf. - str.　30:00 Liben.
—— CONCERTO FOR SAXOPHONE AND ORCH. (1971)
　　*4,*3,*3(1 alt. with E♭cl.),1 sax.,*3 - 4,3,4,1 -
　　timp.,perc.(6),bells,cel.,glock.,xyl. - hp. - pf. - str.　30:00 Liben.
—— CONCERTO FOR VIOLIN, DOUBLE BASS AND ORCH. (1972)
　　(IN 1 MOVT.)
　　2,*3,*4(3rd alt.with E♭cl.),*3 - 4,3,3,1 -
　　timp.,perc.(5),cel.,glock.,vibra.,xyl. - hp. - pf. - str.　15:00 Liben.

—— DEAR FRIENDS AND GENTLE HEARTS (BALLET, ON THE LIFE AND MUSIC OF STEPHEN FOSTER) % (1976)
2(2nd alt. with picc.),2(2nd alt. with Eng.hn.),*3,1 - 2,2,1,1 - timp.,perc.(2),glock.,xyl. - tape-recorder(2-channel) - hp. - pf. - str.
32:00 Liben.

—— DEAR FRIENDS AND GENTLE HEARTS (SUITE FROM THE BALLET) (1976)
3(3rd alt. with picc.),3(3rd alt. with Eng.hn.),3(3rd alt. b.-cl.),3(3rd alt. with c.-bn.) - 4,3,3,1 - timp.,perc. - hp. - pf. - str. 10:00 Liben.

—— DOODLES (AN INTRODUCTION TO THE ORCHESTRA) (1975)
*3,2,*3,2 - 3,2,3,1 - timp.,perc.(2) - hp. - str.(incl.amplified d.-b.)
25:00 Liben.

—— FANTASY FOR DOUBLE BASS AND 20 SOLO STRINGS (1967)
str. 7:00 Liben.

—— FANTASY ON THE PARTITA IN C MINOR OF J. S. BACH (FOR SOLO INSTRUMENTAL QUINTET AND ORCH.) (1970)
3(3rd alt. with picc.),*3,1 E♭cl.,*3,*3 - 4,3,3,1 - timp.,perc.(5), cel.,glock.,vibra.,xyl. - hp. - str. and solo group: 1 tpt.(alt. with E♭ tpt. and flg.-hn.),1 trb.,perc.(1),pf.,1 d.-b.(alt. ad lib. with electric string-bass)
35:00 Liben.

—— HOT ICE (1974)
2(2nd alt.with picc.),2,*2,2 - 4,2,3,1 - timp.,perc.(3),glock. - hp. - pf. - str. 11:30 Liben.

—— SOLAR WIND (AN OVERTURE) (1976)
3(3rd alt. with picc.),2,2,2 - 4,3,3,1 - timp.,perc.(4),cel.,glock.,vibra.,xyl. - hp. - pf. - str. 9:30 Liben.

—— THE SOUNDS OF STRINGS (A DEMONSTRATION PIECE FOR YOUNG AUDIENCES) (1972)
str.(min:8,2,2,2) 15:00 Liben.

—— THREE PIECES FOR PERCUSSION AND ORCH.
4(2 alt. with 2 picc.),4(4th alt. with Eng.hn.),4 cl.(3rd alt. with E♭ cl.,4th alt. with b.-cl.),4(4th alt. with c.-bn.) - 4,4,3,1 - timp.,perc.(4),2 glock.,mar.,vibra. - hp. - pf. - str. 17:30 Liben.

—— TURKEYFOOT (AN OVERTURE FOR ORCH.) (1972)
2,2,2,2 - 2,3,3,1 - timp.,perc.(2) - pf. - str. 9:00 Liben.

—— TWO SONGS FOR ORCHESTRA (1973)
*4,*3,*3,2 - 4,3,3,1 - timp.,perc.(4),glock.,vibra.,xyl. - hp. - pf. - str. 9:00 Liben.

—— VARIATIONS ON "DIXIE" (1973)
3,2 picc.,*3,*3,*3 - 4,3,3,1 - timp.,perc.(4),glock.,vibra.,xyl - hp. - pf. - str. 9:00 Liben.

—— WHAT ARE YOU DOING? (1973)
*3,2,*2,2 - 2,2,0,0 - timp.,perc.(2),glock. - pf. - str. 8:00 Liben.

PROVESI, F. - GERELLI
—— DUE SINFONIE (2 SINFONIAS)
2,2,2,2 - 2,2,0,0 - timp. - str. 13:00 Bo. Hawkes.

PRUDEN, Larry
—— THE ANTIPODES
11:00 A.P.R.A.
—— EVENING MUSIC (FOR SMALL ORCH.)
10:00 A.P.R.A.
—— SOLIQUY FOR STRINGS
str. 11:00 A.P.R.A.

PUCCINI, Giacomo
—— LA BOHÈME (OPERA) % (English Text by Howard Dietz)
Belw-Mills.
—— CAPRICCIO SINFONICO
3,2,2,2 - 4,2,3,1 - timp.,perc. - hp. - str. 18:00 EV.
—— LA BOHÈME (OPERA) % (English Text by Ruth and Thomas Martin)
G. Schirmer.
—— MADAMA BUTTERFLY (OPERA) % (Engl. Text : John Gutman)
G. Schirmer.
—— MESSA DI GLORIA, OP. POSTH. (FOR SOLOISTS, CHORUS AND ORCH.)
*3,2,2,2 - 3,2,3,1 - timp. - str. 42:00 Mills.
—— TOSCA (3-ACT OPERA) % (Engl. Text: John Gutman)
G. Schirmer.

PUCCINI, Giacomo - ANTONINI, Alfredo
—— MADAM BUTTERFLY - A SYMPHONIC SCENARIO
3,3,3,3 - 4,3,3,1 - timp.,perc. - hp. - str. 8:00 Bourne.

PUCCINI, Giacomo - CAILLIET, Lucien
—— LA BOHÈME (CONCERT VERSION FOR CHORUS AND ORCH.)
1,1,2,1 - 2,2,1,0 - perc. - pf. - str. 15:00 Fox.

PUCCINI, Giacomo - HERFURTH, C. Paul
—— LA BOHÈME (SELECTION)
Belw-Mills.

PUCCINI, Giacomo - SPADA, Pietro
—— PRELUDIO SINFONICO
3,2,2,2 - 2,4,3,1 - timp.,perc. - hp. - str. 12:00 EV.

PUETZ, Eduard
—— TAGEBUCHBLÄTTER AUS FRANKREICH
2,2,2,2 - 4,2,3,0 - timp.,perc. - hp. - str. 23:00 Seesaw.

PUIG-ROGET, Henriette
—— RAJOLES
2,2,2,2 - 2,2,1,0 - timp.,perc.(3) - hp. - pf. - str. 12:30 Presser.

PULLI, Jaakko
—— BALLAD TO KARELIA (1970)
str. 30:00 FinnMICtr.
—— FESTIVE MUSIC (1971)
2,2,2,2 - 4,2,3,0 - timp.,perc. - str. 8:00 FinnMICtr.
—— ÖRESUND OVERTURE (1955)
2,2,2,2 - 4,2,3,0 - timp. - str. 16:00 FinnMICtr.
—— PASTORAL SUITE (REV. 1967)
2,2,2,2 - 4,2,3,0 - timp. - str. 10:00 FinnMICtr.
—— SYMPHONY IN G MINOR (1969)
2,2,2,2 - 4,2,3,0 - timp. - str. 36:00 FinnMICtr.

PUNTO, Giovanni - MILLER, James E., ed.
—— CONCERTO NO. 6 IN E-FLAT, FOR HORN AND SMALL ORCH.
0,2,0,0 - 3,0,0,0 - str. 18:00 Presser.

PUNTTILA, Arvi
—— CONCERTO FOR ORCH. (1964)
3,2,2,2 - 4,2,3,1 - timp.,perc. - str. 8:00 FinnMICtr.
—— A DAY AT SEA (FOR ENGLISH HORN AND ORCH.) (1956)
3,*3,2,2 - 2,2,1,0 - timp.,perc. - hp. - str. 16:00 FinnMICtr.
—— A LITTLE THEME AND VARIATIONS (1959)
3,2,2,2 - 3,0,0,0 - timp. - str. 4:00 FinnMICtr.
—— THE OLD AND THE NEW MAN (BALLET) % (1948)
3,3,2,2 - 4,3,3,1 - timp.,perc. - hp. - str. 70:00 FinnMICtr.
—— SUITE DODECAFONIQUE (1962)
2,2,2,2 - 4,2,3,1 - timp.,perc. - str. 7:00 FinnMICtr.
—— SUITE FOR ORCH. (1953)
4,2,2,2 - 2,2,1,0 - timp.,perc. - str. 17:00 FinnMICtr.
—— SYMPHONY NO. 1 IN C MAJOR (1949)
2,2,2,2 - 4,3,3,1 - timp.,perc.,cel. - hp. - str. 36:00 FinnMICtr.
—— THREE POEMS (FOR TENOR AND ORCH.) (1966) (Text: Michelangelo)
2,2,2,2 - 4,3,3,1 - timp.,perc. - str.(0,0,1,1) 7:00 FinnMICtr.
—— THUNDER BIRD (FOR SPEAKING CHORUS AND ORCH.) (1949) (Text: Maxim Gorki)
3,2,2,2 - 4,2,4,1 - timp.,perc. - hp. - str. 7:00 FinnMICtr.

PURCELL, Henry - BARBIROLLI, John
—— CHACONNE IN G MINOR
2,3,1,2 - 4 hn. - org. - str. 8:00 C. Fischer.
—— SUITE FOR STRINGS (FROM THE "DRAMATICK MUSICK")
str. 14:00 Oxford.
Or
2,*1,0,0 - 4 hn. - str.

PURCELL, Henry - BRIDGEWATER, Leslie
—— AYRES FOR THE THEATRE (SUITE) (IN 6 MOVTS.)
pf.(ad lib.) - str. 12:00 Mills.

PURCELL, Henry - BRITTEN, Benjamin
—— CHACONNE IN G MINOR (FOR STRINGS)
str. 7:00 Bo. Hawkes.
—— DIDO AND AENEAS (3-ACT OPERA) % (Realization and Edition by Benjamin Britten and Imogen Holst)
cemb. - str. 50:00 Bo. Hawkes.
—— THE FAIRY QUEEN (FOR SOLOISTS, CHORUS AND ORCH.) (ABRIDGED CONCERT VERSION; DEVISED BY PETER PEARS)
2,3,0,1 - 0,2,0,0 - timp. - hpsc. - str. 120:00 G. Schirmer.
—— THE ORPHEUS BRITANNICUS (6 SONGS FOR HIGH VOICE AND SMALL ORCH.)
2,2,0,1 - 0,1,0,0 - str. 17:30 Bo. Hawkes.
—— WELCOME ODE (FOR CHORUS, STRINGS AND CONTINUO)
cemb. - str. 30:00 Bo. Hawkes.

PURCELL, Henry - BROWN, James
—— SUITE FROM "THE FAIRY QUEEN"
    str.   Galaxy.
—— SUITE NO. 5 IN C
    str.   9:00 Galaxy.

PURCELL, Henry - BUSH, Alan
—— THE RIVAL SISTERS: SUITE
    str.   8:00 FDH.
—— SUITE FROM "THE FAIRY QUEEN"
    2 ob. - 2 tpt. - hpsc. (or pf.) - str.   10:00 Galaxy.
—— THE VIRTUOUS WIFE: SUITE
    str.   8:00 FDH.

PURCELL, Henry - BYRNS, Harold
—— THE FAIRY QUEEN: SUITE
    2,2(2 alt. with Eng.hn.),0,2 - 2,2,0,0 - timp. - str.   12:00 Leeds.

PURCELL, Henry - CAILLIET, Lucien
—— PRELUDE AND PASSACAGLIA (FROM "DIDO AND
AENEAS")
                        5:00 H. Elkan.
—— SUITE FROM "DIDO AND AENEAS"
    *3,*3,*3,*3 - 4,3,3,1 - timp. - hp. - str.   16:00 Arranger.

PURCELL, Henry - CAMPBELL, Arthur
—— OVERTURE IN D MAJOR
    2,1,2,1 - 2,2,2,0 - timp. - str.   6:30 Galaxy.

PURCELL, Henry - COATES, Albert
—— SUITE FROM "THE DRAMATICK MUSICK" (FOR STRINGS)
    str.   10:00 Novello.

PURCELL, Henry - COOPER, Gerald M. - HAYWARD, M.
—— ABDELAZAR: SUITE
    str.   Novello.
—— AMPHITRYON: SUITE
    str.   Novello.
—— WELCOME TO ALL THE PLEASURES: SUITE
    str.   Novello.

PURCELL, Henry - DENT, Edward J.
—— DIDO AND AENEAS (THE COMPLETE OPERA) %
    cemb. - str.   75:00 Oxford.

PURCELL, Henry - DUNHILL, Thomas F.
—— THE OLD BACHELOR: SUITE
    cemb. - str.   Oxford.
—— THE VIRTUOUS WIFE: SUITE
    str.   6:00 Bo. Hawkes.

PURCELL, Henry - EGERTON, Arthur H.
—— REJOICE IN THE LORD ALWAY (THE BELL ANTHEM) (FOR
ALTO OR SEMI-CHORUS, SSA CHORUS AND STRING
ORCH.)
    pf.(ad lib.) - str.   C. Fischer.

PURCELL, Henry - FINNEY, T. M.
—— LAMENT, FROM "DIDO AND AENEAS" (FOR SMALL
ORCH.)
    1,1,1,1 - 0,0,0,0 - str.   Witmark.

PURCELL, Henry - FUSSELL, Charles C.
—— ARIA OF THE BLESSED VIRGIN (ARR. 1967) (FOR
SOPRANO AND CHAMBER ORCH.) (Realization and
instrumentation after Henry Purcell)
    1,*2,0,0 - 0,1,0,0 - mand. - hpsc. - str.(0,2,2,1)   15:00 Arranger.

PURCELL, Henry - HANSON, Howard
—— SUITE OF INCIDENTAL MUSIC FROM "DIOCLESIAN" (IN 4
MOVTS.)
    2,*3,0,2 - 3,3,0,0 - org. - str.   13:35 Arranger.

PURCELL, Henry - HEGER, Robert
—— PURCELL SUITE, OP. 37
    2,3,2,2 - 2,2,0,0 - timp.,perc. - hp. - str.   30:00 G. Schirmer.

PURCELL, Henry - HERBAGE, Julian
—— KING ARTHUR: SUITE (FOR STRINGS)
    str.   11:00 Bo. Hawkes.

PURCELL, Henry - HOLMES, Malcolm
—— DANCE SUITE
    fl. - str.   ECS.

PURCELL, Henry - HOLST, Gustav
—— THE GORDIAN KNOT UNTIED: TWO SUITES (FOR
STRINGS)
    str.   30:00 Novello.
    (SUITE NO. 1 IN 5 MOVTS.)
    (SUITE NO. 2 IN 3 MOVTS.)
—— THE MARRIED BEAU: SUITE (FOR STRINGS)
    str.   20:00 Novello.
—— THE VIRTUOUS WIFE: SUITE (FOR STRINGS)
    str.   15:00 Novello.

PURCELL, Henry - HOLST, Imogen
—— THE RIVAL SISTERS: SUITE (FOR STRINGS)
    str.   Novello.

PURCELL, Henry - LAMBERT, Constant
—— MUSIC FOR THE MASQUE "COMUS"
    2,2,0,2 - 0,2,0,0 - timp. - hp. - str.   15:00 Bo. Hawkes.

PURCELL, Henry - MAITLAND, J.
—— KING ARTHUR (CANTATA) (FOR SOLO VOICES, CHORUS
AND ORCH.)
    2,2,0,0 - 0,2,0,0 - timp. - hpsc. - str.   105:00 Bo. Hawkes.

PURCELL, Henry - MILES, Maurice
—— THE BLESSED VIRGIN'S EXPOSTULATION (FOR VOICE
AND STRINGS)
    str.   Lengnick.

PURCELL, Henry - MÜLLER, Hermann
—— THE FAIRY QUEEN: SUITE (FOR STRING ORCH.)
    str.   F. Colombo.

PURCELL, Henry - NEWTON
—— SONATA FOR TRUMPET AND STRINGS
    tpt. - str.   Oxford.

PURCELL, Henry - NOBLE, Robert
—— TWO OVERTURES, FROM THE ANTHEMS
    cemb. - str.   Oxford.

PURCELL, Henry - O'CONNELL, C.
—— PASSACAGLIA (FROM "DIDO AND AENEAS") (FOR
CHAMBER ORCH.)
    0,*2,0,1 - 0,0,0,0 - str.   2:30 EV.

PURCELL, Henry - REED, William Henry
—— THREE PIECES FOR VIOLIN AND ORCH.
    str.   8:30 Galaxy.

PURCELL, Henry - REED, Wm. L.
—— THE FAIRY QUEEN: SUITE
                        P.R.S.

PURCELL, Henry - SALTER, Lionel
—— TRUMPET OVERTURE (FROM "THE INDIAN QUEEN")
    tpt. - timp. (ad lib) - str.   Oxford.

PURCELL, Henry - SHAW, Watkins
—— DIDO AND AENEAS (SUITE)
    cemb. - str.   Novello.

PURCELL, Henry - STOKOWSKI, Leopold
—— SUITE
                        Arranger.
—— WHEN I AM LAID IN EARTH (FROM "DIDO AND AENEAS")
                    7:00 Arranger.

PURCELL, Henry - VAN HOESEN, Karl D. - HUNT, Frederick
—— DIDO AND AENEAS: SUITE
    2,2,2,2 - 4,2,3,0 - timp. - pf. - str.   C. Fischer.

PURCELL, Henry - WHITTAKER, W. Gillies
—— CHACONNE IN G MINOR
    str.   8:00 Oxford.
—— OVERTURE IN G MAJOR
    cemb. - str.   7:00 Oxford.

PURCELL, Henry - WOOD, Henry J.
—— SUITE (IN 5 MOVTS.)
3,2,2,2 - 4,2,3,0 - timp.,glock. - org. - str.　　11:00 Chappell.

PURSER, John
—— CONCERTO FOR CELLO AND ORCH., OP. 20 (1967)
4,2,2,3 - 4,2,3,1 - timp.,perc.,cel. - str.　　24:00 P.R.S.
—— CONCERTO FOR VIOLA AND STRING ORCH., OP. 14 (1966)
str.　　24:00 P.R.S.
—— EPITAPH, OP. 12 (1966)
3,2,2,3 - 4,3,3,1 - timp.,perc.(3) - hp. - str.　　21:30 P.R.S.
—— INTRADA FOR STRING ORCH., OP. 17 (1966)
str.　　12:00 P.R.S.
—— OPUS 7 (1965)
3,2,2,3 - 4,3,3,1 - timp.,perc. - str.　　12:30 P.R.S.
—— SINFONIETTA, OP. 13 (1966)
3,2,2,3 - 4,2,3,1 - timp.,perc. - str.　　15:00 P.R.S.

PUTSCHE, Thomas
—— THE CAT AND THE MOON (OPERA) % (1958) % (Text:
William Butler Yeats)
1(alt. with picc.)1,1(alt. with b.-cl.),0 - 1,1,1,0 - timp.,perc.(1) - hp.
- str.　　30:00 Seesaw.
—— FANTASY PIECES (1960)
1,1,1,1 - 1,0,0,0 - str.　　12:00 Seesaw.
—— SYMPHONY (1963)
2,2,2,2 - 2,2,2,1 eoph.,1 - str.　　15:00 Composer.
—— THREE BUGS (1965)
3,2,3,2 - 4,2,2,1 - perc.(2),cel. - hp. - str.　　9:00 Seesaw.
—— VERSIONS FOR ORCHESTRA (SUITE) (1968) (IN 5 MOVTS.)
2(1 alt. with picc.),2,2,2 - 4,2,2,0 - cel. - hp. - pf. - str.
14:00 Composer.

PÜTZ, Eduard
—— CONCERTINO FOR FLUTE, PIANO AND STRINGS
fl.(or alto recorder) - pf. - str.　　Hans Gerig.

PYLE, Francis J.
—— OVERTURE TO THE OPERA "THE MAGIC FISHBONE"
2,1,2,1 - 4,3,3,1 - timp.,perc.(2) - str.　　5:18 Composer.
—— PECOS COUNTRY (SUITE) (IN 3 MOVTS.)
*3,1,2,2 - 4,3,3,1 - timp.,perc.(3),bells - str.　　10:00 Composer.
—— PICTURES FOR SUZANNE (SUITE FOR STRING ORCH.) (IN
4 MOVTS.)
str.　　11:15 Mills.
—— SYMPHONY IN D MINOR (IN 3 MOVTS.)
*3,*3,*3,2 - 4,3,3,1 - timp. - str.　　28:00 Composer.

PYLKKÄNEN, Tauno
—— ANDANTE FUNÈBRE, OP. 12 (1940)
str.　　7:00 FinnMICtr.
—— BALLET MUSIC FROM THE OPERA "MARE AND HER SON",
OP. 22-B (SUITE) (WITH SOPRANO) (1943)
2,2,2,2 - 4,2,3,1 - timp.,perc. - str.　　7:00 FinnMICtr.
—— BATHSHEBA AT SAARENMAA, OP. 10 (OPERA) % (REV.
1958)
3,3,2,2 - 4,3,3,1 - timp.,perc. - hp. - str.　　45:00 FinnMICtr.
—— BURNT CLEARING, OP. 40 (1948)
3,3,3,2 - 4,3,3,1 - timp. - hp.,kantele - str.　　12:00 FinnMICtr.
—— CHOREOGRAPHICAL SUITE FROM THE OPERA "IKAROS"
OP. 33-A (1960)
3,3,3,3 - 4,3,3,1 - timp.,perc.(3) - hp. - str.　　16:00 FinnMICtr.
—— CONCERTO FOR CELLO AND ORCH., OP. 48 (1950)
3,2,3,2 - 4,3,3,1 - timp.,perc.(3) - hp. - str.　　25:00 FinnMICtr.
—— IKAROS, OP. 33 (OPERA) % (1960) (Text: Pul Knudsen)
3,3,3,3 - 4,3,3,1 - timp.,perc.(4) - hp. - str.　　120:00 FinnMICtr.
—— IMAGES FROM LAPLAND, OP. 41 (SUITE) (1947)
2,2,2,1 - 3,2,2,0 - timp.,perc. - str.　　9:00 FinnMICtr.
—— INTRODUCTION AND FUGUE, OP. 16 (1940)
3,3,3,2 - 4,3,3,1 - timp.,perc. - str.　　10:00 FinnMICtr.
—— KAARINA, MAUNU'S DAUGHTER, OP. 66 (BALLET) % (1961)
3,3,3,2 - 4,2,2,1 - timp.,perc. - hp. - str.　　50:00 FinnMICtr.
—— KARELIA 39-40 (OVERTURE TO ACT III OF THE OPERA
"OPRI AND OLEKSI") (1957)
3,3,3,2 - 4,3,3,1 - timp.,perc.(3) - hp. - str.　　7:00 FinnMICtr.
—— MARATHON, OP. 38 (AN OVERTURE) (1947)
2,2,2,2 - 4,3,3,1 - timp.,perc. - hp. - str.　　8:00 FinnMICtr.
—— MARE AND HER SON, OP. 22 (OPERA) % (1943) (Text: Aino
Kallas)
2,2,2,2 - 4,2,3,1 - timp.,perc. - str.　　125:00 FinnMICtr.
—— OPRI AND OLEKSI, OP, 61 (OPERA) % (1957) (Text: Kyllikki
Mäntylä)
3,3,3,2 - 4,3,3,1 - timp.,perc.(3) - hp. - str.　　120:00 FinnMICtr.

—— PRELUDIO SINFONICO, OP. 54 (1952)
3,3,3,2 - 4,3,3,1 - timp.,perc. - str.　　7:00 FinnMICtr.
—— THE PRISONERS, OP. 69 (AN OPERA FOR TV) % (1965) (Text:
Arvi Kivimaa)
3,3,3,2 - 4,2,2,1 - timp.,perc. - hp. - str.　　40:00 FinnMICtr.
—— THE SHADOW, OP. 52 (OPERA) % (1952) (Text: Hjalmar
Bergman)
3,3,3,2 - 4,3,3,1 - timp.,perc. - hp. - str.　　50:00 FinnMICtr.
—— SIMO HURTTA, OP. 43 (OPERA) % (1948) (Text: Eino Leino)
3,3,3,3 - 4,3,3,1 - timp.,perc.(3) - hp.,kantele - str.
150:00 FinnMICtr.
—— SINFONIETTA, OP. 25 (1944)
2,2,2,2 - 2,2,1,0 - timp.,perc. - str.　　20:00 FinnMICtr.
—— SUITE FOR OBOE AND STRINGS, OP. 32 (1946)
ob. - str.　　10:00 FinnMICtr.
—— SUMMER IN LAPLAND, OP. 15 (1941)
3,3,3,2 - 4,3,3,1 - timp.,perc. - hp. - str.　　17:00 FinnMICtr.
—— SUMMER SCENES, OP. 60 (1956)
str.　　11:00 FinnMICtr.
—— THE SWAN OF DEATH, OP. 21 (SONG CYCLE) (FOR VOICE
AND ORCH.) (1943)
2,2,3,2 - 3,2,1,0 - timp.,perc. - hp. - str.　　15:00 Fazer.
—— SYMPHONY NO. 1, OP. 30 (1945)
3,3,3,3 - 4,3,3,1 - timp.,perc. - hp. - str.　　45:00 FinnMICtr.
—— THREE SONGS (FOR VOICE AND ORCH.) (1948) (Text: 3
Finnish Poets)
2,2,2,2 - 3,0,0,0 - hp. - str.　　9:00 Fazer.
—— ULTIMA THULE, OP. 45 (1949)
3,3,3,3 - 4,3,3,1 - timp. - pf. - str.　　12:00 FinnMICtr.
—— THE UNKNOWN SOLDIER, OP. 73 (OPERA) % (1967) (Text:
Väinö Linna)
3,3,3,3 - 4,3,3,1 - timp.,perc.(4) - tape-recorder - str.
120:00 FinnMICtr.
—— THE WOLF'S BRIDE, OP. 47 (AN OPERA FOR RADIO) (1950)
(Text: Aino Kallas)
3,3,3,2 - 4,3,3,1 - timp.,perc.(3) - str.　　45:00 FinnMICtr.

Q

QUANTZ, Johann Joachim - FROTSCHER
—— CONCERTO IN B FLAT MAJOR
ob. - cemb. - str.　　Henmar.
—— CONCERTO IN D MINOR
ob. - cemb. - str.　　Henmar.

QUANTZ, Johann Joachim - SONNTAG, Dieter
—— CONCERTO IN C MAJOR
fl. - cemb. - str.　　Henmar.
—— CONCERTO IN C MINOR FOR FLUTE, STRINGS AND
CONTINUO
fl. - cemb. - str.　　16:00 Henmar.

QUEENER, Charles
—— NOCTURNE (1965)
3(3rd alt.with picc.),3(3rd alt.with Eng.hn.),3(3rd alt.with b.-cl.),3 -
4,3,3,1 - timp.,perc.(4) - hp. - str.　　12:00 MCA Music.
—— PRELUDE AND DANCE (1964)
2(2nd alt.with picc.),2(2nd alt.with Eng. hn.),2,2 - 4,2,3,1 -
timp.,perc.(4),xyl. - str.　　13:00 MCA Music.
—— SUITE FOR CHAMBER ORCHESTRA (1962) (IN 3 MOVTS.)
1,1,1,1 - 1,0,0,0 - timp.,perc.(2) - str.　　12:00 MCA Music.
—— SUITE FOR ORCHESTRA (1964) (IN 3 MOVTS.)
2(2nd alt.with picc.),2,2,2 - 4,2,3,1 - timp.,perc.(3),xyl. - str.
12:00 MCA Music.
—— SYMPHONY NO. 2
3(3rd alt. with picc.),2,2,2 - 4,3,3,1 - timp.,perc.(4) - str.
MCA Music.
—— SYMPHONY (1967) (IN 4 MOVTS.)
3(3rd alt.with picc.),3(3rd alt.with Eng.hn.),3(3rd alt.with b.-cl.),*3
- 4,3,3,1 - timp., - hp. - str.　　21:30 MCA Music.
—— TWO ORCHESTRAL DANCES
3,2,2,2 - 4,2,3,1 - timp.,perc. - str.　　11:00 C. Fischer.

QUESNEL, Joseph - RIDOUT, Godfrey
—— OVERTURE TO THE OPERA "COLAS ET COLINETTE" (1964)
2,2,2,2 - 2,0,0,0 - str.　　5:05 GVThompson.

QUILICO, Jack A.
—— EL CHACO (SUITE) (INSPIRED BY AMERICAN INDIAN
HISTORY) (1974) (IN 3 MOVTS.)
3(2 alt. with 2 picc.),*3,*3,*3 - 4,3,3,1 - timp.,perc.(8) - str.
22:00 Composer.

QUILTER, Roger
—— A CHILDREN'S OVERTURE
Chappell.
—— FREEDDOM (FOR CHORUS AND ORCH.)
2,2,2,2 - 2-4,2,3,0-1 - timp. - hp. - str.　　2:00 Bo. Hawkes.
—— NON NOBIS, DOMINE (FOR CHORUS AND ORCH.)
2,2,2,2 - 4,2,3,0 - timp.,perc. - hp. - str.　　18:00 Bo. Hawkes.
—— SUITE FROM "AS YOU LIKE IT" (IN 4 MOVTS.)
1,1,2,1 - 2,2,1,0 - timp.,perc. - hp. - str.　　9:00 Bo. Hawkes.
—— WHERE THE RAINBOW ENDS (SUITE FROM THE PLAY)
1,0,1,0 - 0,2,1,0 - timp. - str.　　12:00 Galaxy.

QUINET, Marcel
—— ALLEGRO DE CONCERT (1958)
3,2,2,2 - 4,2,2,1 - timp.,perc.,cel. - hp. - str.　　5:00 H. Elkan.
—— CONCERTINO FOR VIOLIN AND STRINGS (1970)
str.　　13:00 H. Elkan.
—— CONCERTO FOR PIANO AND ORCH. (1955)
3,2,2,3 - 4,2,2,1 - timp.,cel. - hp. - pf. - str.　　14:00 H. Elkan.
—— CONCERTO NO. 3 FOR PIANO AND STRINGS (1966) (IN
THREE MOVTS.)
pf. - str.　　13:00 H. Elkan.
—— DIALOGUES (FOR 2 PIANOS AND CHAMBER ORCH.) (1975)
2,0,2,1 - 2,1,1,0 - timp.,perc. - 2 pf. - str.　　9:00 H. Elkan.
—— DIPTYQUE (1975)
2,2,2,1 - 2,2,1,0 - timp.,perc. - str.　　9:30 H. Elkan.
—— DIVERTIMENTO (1958)
1,1,1,1 - 2,1,0,0 - timp. - str.　　12:00 H. Elkan.
—— ESQUISSES CONCERTANTES (FOR VIOLIN AND ORCH.)
(1946)
2,2,4,3 - 2,1,1,1 - timp.,perc.,cel. - hp. - str.　　12:00 CBDM.
—— ESQUISSES SYMPHONIQUES (1973) (IN 5 MOVTS.)
3,2,2,3 - 4,2,2,1 - timp.,perc. - str.　　13:00 H. Elkan.
—— GORGONE (1974)
3,2,3,3 - 4,3,3,1 - timp.,perc. - str.　　12:00 H. Elkan.
—— IMPRESSIONI SINFONICHE (1956)
3,2,2,2 - 4,2,2,1 - timp.,perc.,cel. - hp. - str.　　12:00 CBDM.
—— MOVEMENTS (FOR CHAMBER ORCH.) (1973)
1,1,1,1 - 2,1,1,0 - timp. - str.　　12:00 H. Elkan.
—— MUSIQUE (1971)
timp. - str.　　7:30 H. Elkan.
—— LA NÉE DES FOUS (1969)
3,2,2,3 - 4,2,2,1 - timp.,perc. - str.　　30:00 H. Elkan.
—— SEQUENCE (1974)
3,2,3,3 - 4,3,3,1 - timp.,perc. - str.　　12:00 H. Elkan.
—— SERENADE (1956)
str.　　12:00 H. Elkan.
—— THREE PIECES FOR ORCHESTRA (1951)
3,2,2,3 - 4,2,2,1 - timp.,perc.,cel. - hp. - pf.(ad lib.) - str.
13:00 CBDM.
—— VARIATIONS (1956)
3,3,3,3 - 4,2,2,1 - timp.,perc.,cel. - hp. - str.　　17:30 H. Elkan.

R

RAASTED, Niels Otto
—— DIVERTIMENTO, OP. 99
K.O.D.A.
—— HOLBERG OVERTURE, OP. 17
K.O.D.A.
—— IMAGES DE ESPAÑA, OP. 106
K.O.D.A.
—— IN MEMORIAM, OP. 27
K.O.D.A.
—— KUVIA SUOMESTA, OP. 56 (FINNISH SKETCHES) (SUITE)
2,2,2,2 - 4,2,3,1 - perc.(1) - str.　　Henmar.
—— OUR LORD'S NATIVITY, OP. 67 (FOR SOLO VOICES,
CHORUS, ORGAN AND ORCH.) (Text: Edv. Blaumüller)
30:00 Henmar.
—— OVERTURE, OP. 2
K.O.D.A.
—— PASSION MUSIC, OP. 86 (FOR SOLO VOICES, CHORUS,
ORGAN AND STRING ORCH.)
org. - str.　　35:00 Henmar.

—— SINFONIA DA CHIESA, OP. 76
2 tpt.,2 trb. - timp. - org. - str.　　25:00 Henmar.
—— SUITE, OP. 3
str.　　K.O.D.A.
—— SYMPHONIC SUITE, ON MOTIFS OF HANS CHRISTIAN
ANDERSEN
2,2,2,2 - 2,2,2,0 - timp. - str.　　25:00 G. Schirmer.
—— SYMPHONY NO. 2, OP. 73
K.O.D.A.
—— SYMPHONY, OP. 7
K.O.D.A.
—— THEME AND VARIATIONS, OP. 98
K.O.D.A.

RAATS, Jan P.
—— SYMPHONY NO. 3
G. Schirmer.
—— SYMPHONY NO. 7
G. Schirmer.

RABÂUD, Henri
—— EGLOGUE (VIRGILIAN POEM), OP. 7
2,2,2,2 - 2 hn. - timp. - hp. - str.　　5:00 EV.
—— MAROUF (BALLET MUSIC) %
Choudens.
—— PRELUDE AND TOCCATA (FOR PIANO AND ORCH.)
EV.
—— SIXTEENTH CENTURY ENGLISH SUITE NO. 1
1,1,0,1 - 0,2,0,0 - perc. - hp. - hpsc. - str.　　7:00 EV.
—— SIXTEENTH CENTURY ENGLISH SUITE NO. 2
1,1,0,1 - 0,0,0,0 - hpsc. - str.　　7:00 EV.
—— SIXTEENTH CENTURY ENGLISH SUITE NO. 3
1,1,0,1 - 0,1,0,0 - hp. - hpsc. - str.　　10:00 EV.

RACHMANINOFF, Sergei
—— THE BELLS, OP. 35 (FOR SOPRANO, TENOR, BARITONE,
MIXED CHORUS AND ORCH.)
3,3,3,3 - 6,3,3,1 - timp.,perc.,cel. - hp. - pf. - str.
35:00 Bo. Hawkes.
—— CONCERTO NO. 1 IN F SHARP MINOR FOR PIANO AND
ORCH.
2,2,2,2 - 4,2,3,0 - timp.,perc.(2) - pf. - str.　　26:00 Belw-Mills.
—— CONCERTO NO. 4 IN G MINOR FOR PIANO AND ORCH.
2,*3,2,2 - 4,2,3,1 - timp. - pf. - str.　　34:00 Belw-Mills.
—— RHAPSODY ON A THEME OF PAGANINI, OP. 43 (FOR
PIANO AND ORCH.)
*3,*3,2,2 - 4,2,3,1 - timp.,perc.(4) - hp. - pf. - str.
22:00 Belw-Mills.
—— SYMPHONIC DANCES, OP. 45
*3,*3,*3,sax.,*3 - 4 - 4,3,3,1 - timp.,perc. - hp. - pf. - str.
36:00 Belw-Mills.
—— SYMPHONY NO. 3 IN A MINOR, OP. 44
*3,*3,*3,*3 - 4,3,3,1 - timp.,perc.(3) - hp. - str.　　46:00 Belw-Mills.
—— THREE RUSSIAN SONGS, OP.41 (FOR ALTOS, BASSES AND
ORCH.)
3,3,3,3 - 4,3,3,1 - timp.,perc. - hp. - pf. - str.　　13:30 Belw-Mills.
—— VOCALISE (FOR VIOLIN AND ORCH.)
2,*3,*3,2 - 2 hn. - str.　　6:00 Belw-Mills.

RACHMANINOFF, Sergei - CAILLIET, Lucien
—— THREE PRELUDES (ORIGINALLY FOR PIANO)
3,3,4,3 - 4,3,3,1 - timp.,perc. - hp. - str.　　Belw-Mills.

RACHMANINOFF, Sergei - DUBENSKY, Arcady
—— VOCALISE (FOR STRINGS)
str.　　5:00 Belw-Mills.

RACHMANINOFF, Sergei - GOULD, Morton
—— VOCALISE (FOR STRING ORCH.)
str.　　7:25 G. & C.

RACHMANINOFF, Sergei - HOIBY, Lee
—— SUITE NO. 2 FOR PIANO AND ORCH.
2,2,2,2 - 4,2,2,1 - timp.,perc. - pf. - str.　　20:00 Bo. Hawkes.

RACHMANINOFF, Sergei - ORMANDY, Eugene
—— SYMPHONY NO. 1 (IN 4 MOVTS.)
3,2,2,2 - 4,3,3,1 - timp.,perc. - str.　　40:00 Leeds.

RACHMANINOFF, Sergei - RESPIGHI, Ottorino
—— FIVE ETUDES-TABLEAUX
3,3,3,3 - 4,3,1,1 - timp.,perc. - hp. - str.　　25:00 Bo. Hawkes.

RACKLEY, Lawrence
—— CONFLUENCES (1970)
    *3,2,*3,2 - 4,2,3,1 - timp.,perc. - str.   11:00 Composer.
—— DISCOURSE, SOLILOQUY AND CONCOURSE (FOR CELLO
    AND ORCH.) (1969)
    *3,2,*3,2 - 4,2,3,1 - timp.,perc. - str.   19:00 Composer.
—— DIVERTIMENTO (1957)
    1. Adagio; 2. Andante; 3. Allegro; 4. Alla siciliana; 5. Allegro
    *2,0,2,0 - 0,0,0,0 - str.   9:00 CAP.
—— PROLOGUE AND CEREMONIAL DANCE (1968)
    2,1,2,1 - 2,2,2,1 - timp.,perc.(2) - str.   5:30 Composer.
—— SONNET FOR STRINGS (1956)
    str.   4:00 CAP.
—— SYMPHONIC OVERTURE (1956)
    *3,2,2,2 - 4,3,3,1 - timp.,perc.(3) - str.   9:00 Composer.
—— SYMPHONY IN G (1957) (IN 3 MOVTS.)
    *3,2,2,2 - 4,2,3,1 - timp. - pf. - str.   18:15 Composer.
—— VARIATIONS ON A THEME OF HANDEL (1970)
    str.   7:00 CAP.

RADAUER, Irmfried
—— PERSPEKTIVEN AUF B-A-C-H
    1,1,1,1 - 1,1,1,1 - pf. - str.   8:00 Modern.

RADIĆ, Dušan
—— INDEX (FOR SOPRANO, MEZZO-SOPRANO AND
    INSTRUMENTS) (1954)
    0,*3,*1,3 sax.,0 - 0,0,0,0 - perc.(2) - hp. - d.-b. 12:00 MIC,Zagreb.
—— IZ MOJE ZEMLJE (FROM MY HOMELAND)
    (CHOREOGRAPHIC POEM) %
    3,3,3,3 - 4,3,3,1 - timp.,perc.,cel.,vibra.,xyl. - hp. - pf. - str.
        50:00 MIC,Zagreb.
—— METAMORFOZE NESTAJANJA (METAMORPHOSES
    WITHOUT END) (ESSAY FOR CHORUS, ORCH. AND
    DRAMATIC SOLOISTS) %
    3,3,3,3 - 4,3,3,1 - timp.,perc.,cel.,vibra.,xyl. - hp. - pf. - str.
        20:00 MIC,Zagreb.
—— VUKOVA SRBIJA (THE SERBIA OF VUK KARADŽIĆ)
    (CANTATA) (FOR SOLO VOICES, SATB CHORUS AND
    ORCH.)
    4,4,4,4 - 6,4,4,2 - 4c.,2d.-b.   40:00 MIC,Zagreb.

RADICA, Ruben
—— EXTENSIO (FIRST INTEGRAL VERSION) (FOR PIANO AND
    ORCH.) (1973)
    0,2,*4,2 sax.,2 - 2,2,2,0 - perc.,mar.,vibra. - 2 guit. - hp. - pf. - 8
    vlns., 8 c.   12:00 MIC,Zagreb.
—— PROSTRATION (FOR ELECTRIC ORGAN AND ORCH) (1967)
    0,0,0,3 - sax.,0 - 0,1,2,0 - timp.,vibra.,xyl. - electric org. - str.
        12:00 MIC,Zagreb.

RADOVANOVIĆ, Vladan
—— EVOLUTION (FOR 18 STRINGS)
    str.   8:20 MIC,Zagreb.
—— SONORA
    4,4,4,4 - 6,4,4,0 - str.   10:40 MIC,Zagreb.
—— STRINGENT (FOR 15 STRINGS)
    str.(9,4,2,0)   8:00 MIC,Zagreb.

RADULESCU, Horatiu
—— IHI 19 (FOR 19 SPEAKING VOICES, 19 MUSICIANS,
    AMPLIFICATION, TAPE AND 19 DANCERS) %
        57:00 Modern.
—— LAMENTO DI GESU (FOR 7 CHILDREN'S VOICES AND
    ORCH.)
    4,4,4,4 - 6,4,4,1 - perc.(5) - 2 hp. - 7 psalteries - hpsc. - Hammond
    org. - str.   23:00 Modern.
—— MUSIC FOR TAAROA
    2,*3,2,*3 - 3,0,3,1 - perc.(2) - hp. - pf. - str.   20:00 Modern.
—— QN KO'TRO (FOR 11 SPEAKING VOICES, TAPE, CHAMBER
    ORCH. AND 24 STRINGS)
        13:00 Modern.
—— STAR DUST (MUSICA ANGELORUM TO THE "LAMENTO
    DIE JESU") (FOR ORCH. OF 91 PLAYERS, PLUS 7
    PSALTERIES)
        4:00 Modern.

RAGNI, Guido
—— CONCERTO FOR VIOLIN AND ORCH.
    2,2,2,2 - 4,2,3,0 - timp. - str.   25:00 Bo. Hawkes.

RAGUE, Louis-Charles - BROOK, Barry S.
—— SYMPHONIE IN D MINOR, OP. 10, NO. 1
    1,2,0,0 - 2,0,0,0 - str.   FrankMusCp.
—— SYMPHONIE IN F, OP. 10, NO. 2
    0,2,0,0 - 2,0,0,0   FrankMusCp.

RAGWITZ, Erhard
—— DIVERTIMENTO
    timp. - str.   Tetra.
—— FESTIVAL SUITE
    2,2,2,2 - 4,2,3,1 - timp.,perc. - str.   Tetra.
—— THREE MOVEMENTS FOR STRING ORCH., OP. 22
    str.   Tetra.

RAICHL, Miroslav
—— SYMPHONY NO. 2
    3,3,3,3 - 4,3,3,1 - timp.,perc. - pf. - str.   36:00 Bo. Hawkes.

RAITHEL, Hugo
—— SINFONIETTA, OP. 18 (1963)
    2,1,1,2 - 2,2,2,0 - timp.,perc. - str.   24:00 Tetra.

RAITIO, Pentti
—— AUDIENDUM (1967)
    2,2,2,3 - 4,2,2,0 - timp.,perc. - hp. - str.   12:00 FinnMICtr.
—— THIRTEEN (FOR 13 STRINGS) (1964)
    str.(6,2,4,1)   10:00 FinnMICtr.

RAITIO, Väinö
—— ANTIGONE, OP. 23 (1922)
    4,3,3,4 - 3,3,4,1 - timp.,perc.(3),cel. - 2 hp. - str.
        23:00 FinnMICtr.
—— BALLAD (1935)
    2,2,2,2 - 2,2,0,0 - timp.,perc. - str.   9:00 FinnMICtr.
—— LE BALLET GROTESQUE (SUITE) (1943)
    3,3,3,3 - 4,3,3,1 - timp.,perc.(3),cel. - 2 hp. - str.
        15:00 FinnMICtr.
—— CONCERTO FOR PIANO AND ORCH., OP. 6 (1915)
    2,2,2,2 - 4,2,3,1 - timp.,perc. - hp. - pf. - str.   21:00 FinnMICtr.
—— CONCERTO FOR VIOLIN, CELLO AND ORCH. (1936)
    2,2,2,2 - 2,2,0,0 - timp.,perc. - str.   20:00 FinnMICtr.
—— THE DAUGHTER OF JEFTA, OP. 30 (OPERA) % (1929) (Text:
    Johannes Linnankoski and Sulho Ranta)
    3,3,3,3 - 4,3,3,1 - timp.,perc.(3),cel. - hp. - str.   FinnMICtr.
—— FANTASIA ESTATICA, OP. 21 (1921)
    3,3,3,3 - 6,4,3,1 - timp.,perc.(3),cel. - hp. - str.   13:00 FinnMICtr.
—— FANTASIA POETICA, OP. 25 (1923)
    4,3,3,3 - 4,4,3,1 - timp.,perc.(3),cel. - 2 hp. - str.
        10:00 FinnMICtr.
—— FANTASY FOR CELLO, HARP AND ORCH. (1942)
    2,2,2,2 - 2,2,0,0 - timp. - hp. - str.   12:00 FinnMICtr.
—— FOREST IDYLLS (SUITE) (1935)
    2,2,2,2 - 2,2,1,0 - timp.,perc. - pf. - str.   17:00 FinnMICtr.
—— THE KING OF LYDIA (OPERA) % (1937) (Text: Eino Leino,
    after Herodotus)
    3,3,3,3 - 4,3,3,1 - timp.,perc.,cel. - hp. - str.   23:00 FinnMICtr.
—— LEGEND (FOR VIOLIN AND ORCH.) (1935)
    2,2,2,2 - 2,2,0,0 - timp. - str.   8:00 FinnMICtr.
—— MAIDS ON THE HEADLANDS (1935)
    2,2,2,2 - 2,2,1,0 - timp.,perc. - hp. - str.   8:00 FinnMICtr.
—— MOONLIGHT ON JUPITER, OP. 24 (1922)
    3,3,3,3 - 4,4,3,1 - timp.,perc.(4),cel. - 2 hp. - str.
        12:00 FinnMICtr.
—— NOCTURNE (FOR VIOLIN AND ORCH.) (1938)
    2,2,2,2 - 2,2,0,0 - timp.,perc. - str.   10:00 FinnMICtr.
—— NOCTURNE, OP. 17 (1920)
    3,3,3,3 - 4,3,0,0 - timp.,perc.(3),cel. - hp. - str.   8:00 FinnMICtr.
—— OVERTURE AND INTERMEZZO TO THE PLAY "ANTIGONE"
    (1936)
    0,2,2,2 - 2,2,1,0 - timp.,perc.   10:00 FinnMICtr.
—— POEM FOR CELLO AND ORCH., OP. 7 (1915)
    3,3,2,2 - 4,2,0,0 - timp. - pf.(or hp.) - str.   12:00 FinnMICtr.
—— PRINCESS CECILIA (OPERA) % (1933)
    3,3,3,3 - 4,3,3,1 - timp.,perc.(4),bells,cel.,glock. - hp. - harm. - str.
        FinnMICtr.
—— SCHERZO (FELIS DOMESTICA) (1935)
    2,2,2,1 - 2,2,1,0 - perc.,cel. - str.   4:00 Ed.Fennica.
—— SUMMER SCENES (SUITE) (1935)
    2,2,2,2 - 2,2,0,0 - timp.,perc. - pf. - str.   20:00 FinnMICtr.
—— THE SWANS, OP. 15 (1919)
    2,3,3,3 - 4,3,3,1 - timp.,perc.,cel. - str.   8:00 Fazer.
—— SYMPHONIC BALLAD, OP. 9 (1916)
    3,2,2,3 - 4,4,4,1 - timp.,perc. - str.   20:00 FinnMICtr.

—— SYMPHONY IN G MINOR, OP. 13 (1919)
  3,3,3,3 - 4,3,3,1 - timp.,perc.,cel. - str.   35:00 FinnMICtr.
—— THE TWO QUEENS (OPERA) % (1944) (Text: Lauri Haarla)
  3,3,3,3 - 4,3,3,1 - timp.,perc.(3),cel. - hp. - str.   FinnMICtr.
—— WATERSPOUT (BALLET) % (1929)
  3,3,3,3 - 4,3,3,1 - timp.,perc.(3),cel. - hp. - str.   40:00 FinnMICtr.

RAJNA, Thomas
—— CANTILENAS AND INTERLUDES
  2,2,2,2 - 2,0,0,0 - str.   20:00 P.R.S.
—— CONCERTO FOR PIANO AND ORCH. (1961)
  2,2,2,2 - 2,0,0,0 - timp. - pf. - str.   24:00 P.R.S.
—— DANCE (1950)
  3,2,2,3 - 3,4,3,1 - timp.,perc. - hp. - pf. - str.   10:00 P.R.S.
—— DIVERTIMENTO (1957)
  2,2,2,2 - 4,3,3,1 - timp.,perc.,cel. - hp. - str.   17:00 P.R.S.
—— MOVEMENTS FOR STRINGS (1962)
  str.   15:00 P.R.S.
—— SUITE FOR STRINGS (1954)
  str.   17:00 P.R.S.

RAKOV, Nikolai P.
—— MARIISHE SUITE
  3(3rd alt. with picc.),5(5th alt. with Eng.hn.),2,2 - 4,3,3,1 -
  timp.,perc. - hp. - str.   12:00 G. Schirmer.
—— SUITE DANSANTE, OP. 8
  1,1(alt. with Eng. hn.),1,1 - 2,1,1,0 - timp.,perc. - pf. - str.
          13:00 G. Schirmer.
—— SYMPHONY
  2,2,2,2 - 4,2,3,1 - timp.,perc.,xyl. - str.   34:00 G. Schirmer.

RAKSIN, David
—— SUITE FROM THE FILM "STORM WARNING"
  2(1 alt. with picc.),*3,3,sax.,*3 - 4,3,3,1 - timp.,perc.(3) - hp. - pf. -
  str.   12:00 Composer.
—— TOY CONCERTINO (FOR TOY INSTRUMENTS AND ORCH.)
          Broude.

RALF, Richard
—— A DAY IN SANTA BARBARA (SUITE) (IN 4 MOVTS.)
  2,2(1 alt. with Eng. hn.),2,2 - 4,3,3,1 - timp.,perc.(3) - hp. - pf. -
  str.   23:00 G.E.M.A.

RAMANS, Gedert
—— CONCERTO FOR SAXOPHONE, STRING ORCH., PIANO
  AND TIMPANI
  sax. - timp. - pf. - str.   12:00 G. Schirmer.

RAMEAU, Jean-Philippe - DE FILLIPPI, Amedeo
—— SUITE
  2,2,2,2 - 2,2,0,0 - timp. - str.   12:00 Arranger.

RAMEAU, Jean-Philippe - SAVAGE, R. Temple
—— SUITE FOR STRINGS
  str.   15:00 Bo. Hawkes.

RAMEAU, Jean-Phillipe - OUBRADOUS, Fernand
—— SYMPHONIES DES INDES GALANTES (ORCHESTRAL
  SUITE)
  2,2,0,2 - 0,1,0,0 - timp. - str.   20:00 Presser.

RAMEAU, Jean-Phillipe - SKROWACZEWSKI, Stanislaw
—— SUITE FROM "SIX CONCERTS EN SEXTUOR" (FOR
  STRINGS)
  str.   16:00 G. Schirmer.

RAMEAU, Jean-Phillipe - VAUBOURGOIN, Marc
—— ORCHESTRAL SUITE NO. 3 FROM "LES BOREADES"
  2,2,0,4 - 2-4,0,0,0 - str.   13:00 Presser.
—— SUITE D'APRÈS "DAPHNIS ET AEGLE"
  2,4,0,4 - 0,0,0,0 - str.   18:00 Presser.

RAMETTE, Yves
—— PRÉLUDE, FUGUE ET POSTLUDE
  timp. - pf. - str.   11:00 Salabert.
—— SYMPHONY NO. 1
  timp.,perc. - str.   19:00 Salabert.
—— SYMPHONY NO. 2
  3,3(1 alt. with ob. d'amore),3,3 - 4,3,3,1 - timp.,perc.,cel. - pf. -
  str.   24:00 Salabert.
—— SYMPHONY NO. 3 (FOR STRINGS)
  str.   22:00 Salabert.

—— SYMPHONY NO. 4
  3,3,3,3 - 4,3,3,1 - timp.(4),perc.,cel. - hp. - pf. - str.
          25:00 Salabert.
—— SYMPHONY NO. 5 ("HYMN TO LIFE")
  3,3,3,3 - 4,3,3,0 - timp.,perc. - str.   30:00 Salabert.
—— SYMPHONY NO. 6
  3,3,3,3 - 4,3,3,1 - timp.,perc.,cel. - hp. - pf. - str.   32:00 Salabert.

RAMEY, Phillip
—— CONCERT SUITE (FOR PIANO AND ORCH.) (1962) (IN 6
  MOVTS.)
  *3,2,2,2 - 2,2,2,0 - timp.,perc.(2) - pf. - str.   10:00 Composer.
—— CONCERTO NO. 1 FOR PIANO AND ORCH. (1969)
  1. Andante Con Moto; 2. Allegretto
  2(2nd alt.with picc.) ,*3,*3,*3 - 4,3,3,1 - timp.,perc.(3) - pf. - str.
          16:00 Composer.
—— ORCHESTRAL DISCOURSE (1966)
  2(2nd alt.with picc.),*3,2,*3 - 3,2,2,1 - timp.,perc.(2) - hp. - str.
          14:00 Composer.
—— SEVEN, THEY ARE SEVEN (INCANTATION FOR
  BASS-BARITONE AND ORCH.) (1965) (Text: Konstantin
  Balmont)
  2(2nd alt.with picc.),2,2,2 - 3,2,2,1 - timp.,perc.(3) - pf. - str.
          12:00 Composer.
—— WINTER MUSIC (1970)
  2(2nd alt.with picc.),2,2,2 - 2,2,2,0 - timp.,perc.(2) - str.
          12:00 Composer.

RAMIREZ, Luis Antonio
—— FANTASIA SOBRE UN MITO ANTILLANO (1970) (FOR
  DOUBLE BASS, GUITAR, HORN, PERCUSSION AND
  STRINGS)
  hn. - perc. - guit. - str.   26:00 Seesaw.
—— FRAGMENTOS, 1973
          16:00 Seesaw.
—— TRES PIEZAS BREVES (1972)
  0,0,0,0 - 1,2,1,0 - perc. - pf. - str.   7:00 Seesaw.

RAMOUS, Gianni
—— CONCERTO FOR PIANO AND ORCH. (1963)
  2,2,2,2 - 2,2,2,0 - timp. - pf. - str.   12:00 Leeds.
—— LE FATICHE DEL GUERRIERO (1-ACT FARCE) %
  2,2,2,2 - 2,2,2,0 - timp.,perc.(3),xyl. - str.   30:00 Leeds.
—— LETTERA ALLA MADRE (SHORT CANTATA) (FOR
  BARITONE AND STRINGS) (Text: Salvatore Quasimodo)
  hpsc. - str.   6:25 Leeds.
—— POLIMORFIA (1964)
  2,2,2,2 - 2,2,1,0 - timp. - hp. - str.   21:00 MCA Music.

RAMOVŠ, Primož
—— ANTIPARALLELS (FOR PIANO AND ORCH.)
  2(2 alt. with picc.),0,3(3rd alt. with b.-cl.),2(2nd alt. with c.-bn.) -
  4,4,3,1 - timp.,perc.(5) - pf. - str.   14:00 Hans Gerig.
—— CALL (FOR HORN AND CHAMBER ENSEMBLE)
  1,0,1,0 - 1,0,0,0 - hp. - str.(2,1,1,1)   9:00 Hans Gerig.
—— CONCERTINO FOR PIANO AND STRINGS
  pf. - str.   15:00 Hans Gerig.
—— CONCERTO FOR CELLO AND ORCH.
  2(alt. with 2 picc.),2(2nd alt. with Eng. hn.),2(2nd alt. with
  b.-cl.),2(2nd alt. with c.-bn.) - 4,3,3,1 - timp.,perc.(7) - str.
          18:00 Hans Gerig.
—— CONCERTO FOR VIOLIN, VIOLA AND ORCH.
  2(2nd alt. with picc.),2(2nd alt. with Eng. hn.),3(3rd alt. with
  b.-cl.),2(2nd alt. with c.-bn.) - 4,3,3,1 - timp.,perc.(5) - str.
          15:00 Hans Gerig.
—— CONCERTO PICCOLO (FOR BASSOON AND STRING
  ORCH.)
  bn. - str.   11:00 Hans Gerig.
—— CONTRASTS (FOR FLUTE AND ORCH.)
  *3,2(2nd alt. with Eng. hn.),2(2nd alt. with b.-cl.),2(2nd alt. with
  c.-bn.) - 3,3,3,0 - str.   15:00 Hans Gerig.
—— DIVERTIMENTO FOR STRINGS
  str.   20:00 Hans Gerig.
—— DUO (FOR OBOE AND ORCH.)
  2(2nd alt. with picc.),*2,2(2nd alt. with b.-cl.),2(2nd alt. with
  c.-bn.) - 4,0,3,1 - str.   18:00 Hans Gerig.
—— ECHOES (FOR FLUTE AND ORCH.)
  1,0,3(3rd alt. with b.-cl.),0 - 4,0,0,0 - perc.(4) - str.
          15:00 Hans Gerig.
—— INTRADA
  2(2nd alt. with picc.),2(2nd alt. with Eng. hn.),2(2nd alt. with
  b.-cl.),2(2nd alt. with c.-bn.) - 4,3,3,1 - perc.(3) - str.
          8:00 Hans Gerig.

—— MUSIQUE FUNÈBRES
2(2nd alt. with picc.),2(2nd alt. with Eng. hn.),3(3rd alt. with b.-cl.),3(3rd alt. with c.-bn.) - 4,4,3,1 - timp.,perc.(4)- str.
16:00 Hans Gerig.

—— PARALLELS (FOR PIANO AND STRING ORCH.)
pf. - str.
16:00 Hans Gerig.

—— PROFILES FOR ORCH.
2(2nd alt. with picc.),2(2nd alt. with Eng.hn.),2(2nd alt. with b.-cl.),2(2nd alt. with c.-bn.) - 4,3,3,1 - timp.,perc.(7) - str.
22:00 Hans Gerig.

—— SCHERZO (FOR PIANO AND STRINGS)
pf. - str.
3:30 Hans Gerig.

—— SINFONIETTA
1(alt. with picc.),1(alt. with Eng. hn.),1(alt. with b.-cl.),1(alt. with c.-bn.) - 2,2,2,1 - str.
18:00 Hans Gerig.

—— SUITE FOR TWO VIOLINS, CELLO AND STRINGS
str.
20:00 Hans Gerig.

—— SYMPHONIC PORTRAIT
2(2nd alt. with picc.),2(2nd alt. with Eng. hn.),2(2nd alt. with b.-cl.),2(2nd alt. with c.-bn.) - 4,3,3,1 - timp.,perc.(7) - str.
18:00 Hans Gerig.

—— SYMPHONY (BETWEEN PIANO AND ORCH.)
2(2nd alt. with picc.),2(2nd alt. with Eng. hn.),2(2nd alt. with b.-cl.),2(2nd alt. with c.-bn.) - 4,3,3,1 - perc.(7) - pf. - str.
17:00 Hans Gerig.

—— SYMPHONY '68 (1968)
3(3rd alt. with picc.),3(3rd alt. with Eng. hn.),3(3rd alt. with b.-cl.),3(3rd alt. with c.-bn.) - 4,4,3,1 - timp.,perc.(6) - str.
17:00 Hans Gerig.

—— SYNTHESES (FOR HORN AND 3 ORCHESTRAL GROUPS)
2 picc.,2,2,*3,*3 - 2,4,3,1 - perc.(8) - str.   14:00 Hans Gerig.

RAMSIER, Paul
—— DIVERTIMENTO ON A THEME OF COUPERIN (FOR DOUBLE BASS AND ORCH.)
2,2,2(2nd alt. with b.-cl.),2 - 3,1,3,1 - timp.,perc.(2) - hp. - str.
16:00 G. Schirmer.

—— MAN ON A BEARSKIN RUG (1-ACT COMIC OPERA) %
1,1,2,1 - 2,1,1,0 - timp.,perc. - hp. - pf. - str.   30:00 Bo. Hawkes.

—— SIX DANCE DIVERSIONS
2(2nd. alt. with picc.),2,2,2 - 4,2,3,1 - timp.,perc.(2),glock.,xyl. - hp. - pf. - str.   13:00 Bo. Hawkes.

—— SONATA FOR ORCHESTRA (IN 3 MOVTS.)
2,2,2,2 - 2,0,0,0 - timp. - pf. - str.   14:00 Composer.

RAN, Shulamit
—— CAPRICCIO FOR PIANO AND ORCHESTRA (1963)
2(2nd alt. with picc.),1,2,1 - 2,1,1,0 - timp. - pf. - str.
8:00 C. Fischer.

—— CONCERT PIECE FOR PIANO AND ORCHESTRA (1970)
4(2 alt.with 2 picc.),2,4(1 alt.with E♭ cl.,1 alt.with b.-cl.),3(1 alt.with c.-bn.) - 5,4,3,2 - timp.,perc.(4-5),bells,cel.,glock.,mar.,vibra. - pf.(amplified) - str.
12:00 Presser.

—— ENSEMBLE FOR 17 (FOR SOPRANO AND CHAMBER ORCH.) (1975) (IN 2 MOVTS.) (Text: William Shakespeare)
2(1 alt.with picc.),0,2(alt.with E♭ cl.,b.-cl.and sarr.),1 - 1,1,2,0 - perc.(2),bells,mar.,vibra. - pf. - str.(2,1,1,0)   18:00 Presser.

—— ENSEMBLES FOR 17 (FOR AMPLIFIED SOPRANO AND INSTRUMENTS)
2 fl.(1 alt. with picc.,1 alt. with alto fl.),2 cl.(1 alt. with E♭cl., 1 alt. with b.cl., and ad lib. sarr.),bn. - 1,2,2,0 - perc.(2) - pf. - str.(2,1,1,0)
18:00 Presser.

—— FANTASY FOR ORCHESTRA (1967)
*3,*3,3(3rd alt.with b.-cl.),2 - 4,3,3,0 - timp.,perc.(2) - str.
12:00 C. Fischer.

—— HATZRI ISRAEL EULOGY (THE BEAUTY OF ISRAEL-EULOGY) (FOR MEZZO-SOPRANO, FLUTE, HARP AND SMALL STRING ORCH.) (1968) (Text: Biblical)
fl. - hp. - str.   6:30 Composer.

—— MUSIC FOR STRINGS, FLUTE AND HORN (1961)
fl. - hn. - str.   9:00 Composer.

—— SYMPHONIC POEM FOR PIANO AND ORCH. (PIANO CONCERTO) (1966) (IN 4 MOVTS.)
*3,*3,*3,alto sax.,2 - 4,3,3,0 - timp.,perc.(2),vibra.,xyl. - hp. - pf. - str.   20:05 C. Fischer.

—— TEN CHILDREN'S SCENES (1966)
2(2nd alt. with picc.),2,2(2nd alt. with b.-cl.),2 - 2,2,1,0 - timp.,perc.(2),cel. - str.   12:00 C. Fischer.

—— TWO LOVE POEMS (FOR TENOR VOICE, WINDS AND PERCUSSION) (1969) (Text: 16th-Century Japanese Poets)
4(1 alt.with picc.),2,4(1 alt.with b.-cl.),2 - 4,3,3,0 - timp.,perc.(4),bells,cel.,vibra.,xyl.   7:00 Composer.

RANGSTRÖM, Ture
—— BALLADE FOR PIANO AND ORCH.
2,2,2,2 - 2,3,2,1 - timp.,perc. - pf. - str.   17:00 S.T.I.M.

—— DITYRAMB (SYMPHONIC POEM)
2,2,2,2 - 4,3,3,1 - timp.,perc. - str.   19:00 S.T.I.M.

—— DIVERTIMENTO ELEGIACO (FOR STRINGS)
str.   15:00 Nordiska.

—— DRAPA (EULOGY)
2,2,2,2 - 4,3,3,1 - timp.,perc. - pf. - str.   9:00 S.T.I.M.

—— DREI PASTISCHEN
2,2,2,2 - 0,0,0,0 - str.   10:00 Lundquists.

—— GAMLA STOCKHOLM (OVERTURE)
2,2,2,2 - 4,3,2,1 - timp.,perc. - hp. - str.   S.T.I.M.

—— GRAVOFFER (TWO MEDITATIONS) FROM "TILL DAMASKUS" (FOR STRINGS)
str.   6:30 S.T.I.M.

—— HAMLET RHAPSODY (SUITE)
3,2,2,2 - 4,3,2,1 - timp.,perc.(2) - hp. - str.   35:00 S.T.I.M.

—— HAVET SJUNGER (SYMPHONIC POEM)
4,2,3,2 - 6,4,3,2 - timp. - str.
or:
4,3,3,3 - 4,3,3,1 - timp.,perc. - str.   20:00 S.T.I.M.

—— EN HÖSTSÅNG (AUTUMN SONG)
3,3,3,3 - 6,3,3,1 - timp.,perc. - str.   15:00 S.T.I.M.

—— INTERMEZZO DRAMMATICO
2,1,1,1 - 2,1,0,0 - timp.,perc. - str.   15:00 Suecia.

—— KING ERIK'S SONGS (5 SONGS) (FOR VOICE AND ORCH.)
20:00 Nordiska.

—— A LITTLE STOCKHOLM MUSIC (SUITE)
2,2,2,2 - 2,5,2,0 - timp.,perc.(2) - str.   20:00 Nordiska.

—— MÄLARLEGENDER (SUITE)
2,2,2,2 - 2,2,1,0 - timp. - pf. - str.   20:00 Lundquists.

—— ETT MIDSOMMARSTYCKE
2,2,2,2 - 4,3,3,1 - timp.,perc. - str.   15:00 S.T.I.M.

—— EIN NACHTSTÜCK (FOR STRING QUARTET AND STRINGS)
str.   20:00 S.T.I.M.

—— OVERTURA SOLENNE (PRELUDE TO IBSEN'S "BRAND")
2,2,2,2 - 4,3,3,1 - timp.,perc. - pf. - str.   10:00 S.T.I.M.

—— PÅ NORDISK STRÅNG (OVERTURE)
2,2,2,2 - 4,3,0,1 - perc. - str.   6:00 S.T.I.M.

—— POEM-CAPRICCIO AMOROSO (FOR VIOLIN AND ORCH.)
2,1,2,1 - 2,2,0,0 - timp.,perc. - hp. - str.   13:00 S.T.I.M.

—— SHAKESPEARIAN LANDSCAPE (SUITE) (FOR SMALL ORCH.) (IN 3 MOVTS.)
60:00 S.T.I.M.

—— SOTTO VOCE (SYMPHONIC POEM)
2,1,2,1 - 2,2,1,0 - timp.,per. - str.   8:00 S.T.I.M.

—— STADEN SPELAR (SUITE)
2,0,0,0 - 2,2,0,0 - timp.,perc. - str.   20:00 S.T.I.M.

—— SUITE FROM IBSEN'S "BRAND"
2,2,2,1 - 2,1,0,0 - timp.,perc. - 2 pf. - str.   20:00 S.T.I.M.

—— SUITE FROM RACINE'S "ATALIA"
2,2,2,2 - 2,2,2,0 - timp.,perc. - hp. - str.   40:00 S.T.I.M.

—— SUITE FROM "VÄVAREN I BAGDAD"
2,2,2,2 - 2,2,1,0 - timp.,perc.(2) - str.   20:00 S.T.I.M.

—— SYMPHONY NO. 1 IN C SHARP MINOR (IN MEMORIAM AUGUST STRINDBERG)
3,3,3,3 - 4,4,3,1 - timp. - hp. - str.   33:00 Gehrmans.

—— SYMPHONY NO. 2 IN D MINOR ("MITT LAND")
3,2,2,2 - 4,4,3,1 - timp. - str.   38:00 G. Schirmer.

—— SYMPHONY NO. 3 IN D FLAT MAJOR ("SANG UNDER STJÄRNORNA")
3,2,2,2 - 4,3,3,1 - timp.,perc. - pf. - str.   22:00 S.T.I.M.

—— SYMPHONY NO. 4 ("INVOCATIO")
3,2,2,2 - 4,3,3,1 - timp.,perc. - pf. - org. - str.   35:00 S.T.I.M.

—— UPPTAKT
2,2,2,2 - 2,2,1,0 - timp.,perc. - hp. - str.   8:00 S.T.I.M.

—— UR HIMLENS HEMLIGHET (SUITE) (IN 3 MOVTS.)
0,1,0,0 - 0,0,0,0 - timp. - str.   17:00 S.T.I.M.

—— VAUX-HALL (SUITE)
2,2,2,2 - 2,2,2,0 - timp.,perc. - hp. - str.   18:00 S.T.I.M.

—— VÅR STAD (FESTSPEL)
3,3,3,3 - 4,6,3,1 - timp.,perc. - pf. - str.
or:
2,2,2,2 - 4,3,3,1 - timp.,perc. - pf. - str.   20:00 S.T.I.M.

—— VÅRHYMN
2,1,1,1 - 2,2,1,0 - timp.,perc. - str.   S.T.I.M.

RÁNKI, György
—— THE CIRCUS (SYMPHONIC DANCE DRAMA) %
*3,*3,*3,*3 - 4,*3,3,1 - timp.,perc.,cel. - hp. - pf. - str.
39:40 Bo. Hawkes.

—— DON QUIJOTE ET DULCINEA (2 MINIATURES) (FOR OBOE AND SMALL ORCH.)
Bo. Hawkes.

—— FIFTEEN FOURTEEN (FANTASY FOR PIANO AND ORCH.)
2,3,3,3 - 4,3,3,1 - timp.,perc.,cel. - hp. - pf. - str.
21:00 Bo. Hawkes.

—— HEYDUCK DANCE
3,2,2,2 - 4,2,3,1 - timp.,perc. - str.   10:00 Bo. Hawkes.

—— HUNGARIAN DANCES OF THE 16TH CENTURY
1,1,2,1 - 2,0,0,0 - pf. - str.   9:00 Bo. Hawkes.

—— KING POMÁDÉ'S NEW CLOTHES (OPERA) %
3,2,3,2 - 4,3,3,1 - timp.,perc.,cel. - hp. - pf. - str.
Bo. Hawkes.

—— MINIATURES FOR STRINGS
str.
Bo. Hawkes.

—— THE NEW CLOTHES OF KING POMÁDÉ: SUITES NO. 1 AND 2
3,2,3,2 - 4,3,3,1 - perc. - pf. - str.   44:00 Bo. Hawkes.

—— NINETEEN FORTY-FOUR (ORATORIO) (FOR BARITONE, SATB CHORUS AND ORCH.)
timp.,perc. - hp. - str.   18:00 Bo. Hawkes.

RANKL, Karl

—— CHRISTMAS OVERTURE
8:00 Oxford.

—— FOUR SCOTTISH SONGS (FOR VOICE AND ORCH.)
2,2,2,2 - 4,2,3,0 - timp.,perc.,cel. - hp. - str.   12:00 Oxford.

—— SINFONIETTA NO. 1
Oxford.

—— SUITE FOR STRINGS
str.   24:00 Oxford.

—— SUITE FROM THE OPERA "DEIRDRE OF THE SORROWS"
22:00 Oxford.

—— SYMPHONY NO. 1 (FOR VOICES AND ORCH.)
3,3,3,3 - 4,3,3,1 - timp.,perc. - str.   40:00 Oxford.

—— SYMPHONY NO. 2
3,3,3,3 - 4,3,3,1 - timp.,perc. - str.   35:00 Oxford.

—— SYMPHONY NO. 3
2,2,2,2 - 4,3,3,1 - timp. - str.   33:00 Oxford.

—— SYMPHONY NO. 4
3,3,3,3 - 4,3,3,1 - timp.,perc. - str.   30:00 Oxford.

—— SYMPHONY NO. 5
3,3,3,3 - 4,3,3,1 - timp. - str.   29:00 Oxford.

RANTA, Sulho

—— AS THE YEAR ROLLS BY, OP. 45 (A CYCLE OF CHILD EXPRESSIONS) (1933)
2,2,2,1 - 2,2,1,0 - timp.,perc. - str.   13:00 FinnMICtr.

—— THE CHILD AND LIFE, OP. 82-A (5 SONGS) (FOR 2 SOPRANOS AND ORCH.) (1944) (Text: Oiva Paloheimo)
2,2,2,2 - 2,2,1,0 - timp.,perc. - hp. - str.   15:00 FinnMICtr.

—— CONCERTINO FOR PIANO AND STRINGS, OP. 36 (1932)
pf. - str.   7:00 FinnMICtr.

—— CONCERTINO NO. 2 FOR FLUTE, HARP, VIOLA AND STRINGS, OP. 46 (1934)
fl. - hp. - str.   10:00 FinnMICtr.

—— CONCERTO FOR ORCH., OP. 67 (1938) (IN 3 MOVTS.)
3,3,3,3 - 4,3,3,1 - timp.,perc.(4),cel. - hp. - str.   20:00 FinnMICtr.

—— A CYCLE OF FINNISH FOLK POEMS, OP. 49 (FOR VOICE AND ORCH.) (1935)
2,2,2,2 - 2,2,1,0 - timp.,perc.(3) - hp. - str.   8:00 FinnMICtr.

—— THE EVEN, OP. 38 (2 PIECES FOR CLARINET AND ORCH.) (1932)
2,1,2,1 - 2,2,1,0 - timp. - hp. - str.   10:00 FinnMICtr.

—— FAR AWAY THITHER, OP. 91 (4 SONGS FOR VOICE AND ORCH.) (1948) (Text: Kaarlo Sarkia)
2,2,2,2 - 2,2,2,0 - timp.,perc. - hp. - str.   12:00 FinnMICtr.

—— FESTIVAL PRELUDE FOR ORCH., OP. 61 (1937)
2,2,2,1 - 2,2,1,0 - timp. - str.   6:00 FinnMICtr.

—— FESTIVE OVERTURE (1937)
2,2,2,2 - 2,2,1,0 - timp.,perc. - hp. - str.   6:00 FinnMICtr.

—— FOLK TALE, OP. 79 (1940)
3,3,3,3 - 4,3,3,1 - timp.,perc.(4) - hp. - str.   20:00 FinnMICtr.

—— FOREST FOLK (SUITE FROM THE PLAY "THE TOP") (1932)
1,1,2,1 - 2,2,1,0 - timp.,perc. - str.   11:00 FinnMICtr.

—— FROM AN OLD BOWER, OP. 85-A (SUITE) (1943)
2,2,2,2 - 2,2,1,0 - timp.,perc. - hp. - str.   12:00 FinnMICtr.

—— FROM MORNING TO NIGHT, OP. 21 (SUITE OF CHILDHOOD SCENES) (1929)
1,1,2,2 - 2,2,0,0 - timp.,perc. - str.   7:00 FinnMICtr.

—— IMAGES BOREALES, OP. 44 (SUITE) (1933) (IN 3 MOVTS.)
2,2,2,2 - 4,2,3,1 - timp.,perc.(3) - str.   13:00 Fazer.

—— ITALIAN SUITE, OP. 40-B (FROM MUSIC TO THE PLAY "THE MERCHANT OF VENICE") (IN 4 MOVTS.) (1935)
2,1,2,1 - 2,2,1,0 - timp.,perc. - hp. - str.   10:00 FinnMICtr.

—— LITTLE CHINESE SUITE, OP. 26-B (1926)
fl. - timp. - hp. - str.   4:00 FinnMICtr.

—— LITTLE KARELIAN SUITE, OP. 74-D (FROM THE MUSIC TO THE FILM "DEAR FINLAND") (1940)
2,2,2,1 - 2,2,1,0 - timp.,perc. - hp. - str.   13:00 FinnMICtr.

—— A LITTLE SUITE FOR ORCHESTRA, OP. 85-B (1942) (IN 3 MOVTS.)
2,2,2,2 - 2,2,1,0 - timp.,perc. - hp. - str.   12:00 FinnMICtr.

—— PARTITA SINFONICA (1937) (IN 3 MOVTS.)
3,3,3,3 - 4,3,3,1 - timp.,perc.(4) - str.   20:00 FinnMICtr.

—— PETITE SUITE, OP. 22 (THEME AND 3 VARIATIONS) (1929)
3,2,2,2 sax.,2 - 4,2,3,1 - timp.,perc. - hp. - pf. - str.   11:00 FinnMICtr.

—— PSALM 84, OP. 62 (FOR SATB CHORUS, ORGAN AND STRINGS) (1937)
org. - str.   10:00 Fazer.

—— SINFONIA PICCOLA IN D MAJOR, OP. 43 (1932)
2,2,1,2 - 2,2,1,0 - timp.,perc. - hp. - str.   16:00 FinnMICtr.

—— SINFONIA PROGRAMMATICA, OP. 29 (1931) (IN 3 MOVTS.)
3,3,3,3 - 4,3,3,1 - timp.,perc.(4) - hp. - str.   27:00 FinnMICtr.

—— SONG OF THE GRYPHON, OP. 55 (CYCLE OF 4 SONGS FOR BARITONE, WOMEN'S CHORUS AND ORCH.) (REV. 1948) (Text: P. Mustapää)
2,2,2,2 - 4,3,3,0 - timp.,perc. - hp. - org.(ad lib.) - str.   35:00 FinnMICtr.

—— SUITE FROM A. JÄRVENTAUS' PLAY "ONLY ONE IS NECESSARY", OP. 56 (IN 5 MOVTS.) (1935)
2,2,2,2 - 2,2,1,0 - timp.,perc. - hp. - pf. - str.   15:00 FinnMICtr.

—— SUITE FROM THE JAPANESE BALLET "THE CHERRY BLOSSOM FEAST", OP. 24 (1929)
3,2,2,2 - 4,2,2,0 - timp.,perc. - hp. - str.   13:00 FinnMICtr.

—— SUITE FROM THE MUSIC TO MIKA WALTARI'S PLAY "AKHNATON", OP. 65 (1938) (IN 4 MOVTS.)
2,2,2,2 - 4,2,2,0 - timp.,perc. - hp. - str.   16:00 FinnMICtr.

—— SUITE SYMPHONIQUE, OP. 15 (1928)
1,0,1,0 - 1,0,0,0 - pf. - str.   20:00 FinnMICtr.

—— SUMMER CLOUDS, OP. 42 (4 SONGS FOR VOICE AND ORCH.) (1932) (Text: Saima Harmaja)
2,2,2,1 - 2,1,1,0 - timp.,perc. - hp. - str.   14:00 FinnMICtr.

—— SYMPHONY NO. 2 IN A MINOR, OP. 54 ("SEMPLICA") (1936)
3,3,2,2 - 4,3,3,1 - timp.,perc.(3 incl. 2 on timp.) - str.   25:00 FinnMICtr.

—— SYMPHONY NO. 3, OP. 89 ("DELL'ARTE") (1947)
3,2,2,2 - 4,3,3,1 - timp.,perc.(3) - hp. - str.   33:00 FinnMICtr.

—— SYMPHONY NO. 4, OP. 97 ("ORATORIO VOLGARE") (FOR SOPRANO, TENOR, BASS, SATB CHORUS AND ORCH.) (1951) (IN 4 MOVTS.) (Text: P. Mustapää)
3,3,3,3, - 4,3,3,1 - timp.,perc.,bells,xyl. - hp. - str.   45:00 FinnMICtr.

—— THREE CHINESE POEMS, OP. 53 (FOR SOPRANO AND ORCH.) (1936)
2,2,2,1 - 2,2,1,0 - timp. - hp. - str.   11:00 Westerlund.

—— THREE NOCTURNES, OP. 37 (FOR SOPRANO OR TENOR AND ORCH.) (1931) (Text: Elina Vaara)
2,2,2,2 - 4,2,3,0 - timp.,perc. - hp. - str.   15:00 Fazer.

—— THREE SONGS, OP. 30 (FOR VOICE AND ORCH.) (Text: Uuno Kailas)
2,2,2,2 - 2,2,1,0 - timp.,perc. - hp. - str.   9:00 FinnMICtr.

—— TOPELIANA SUITE, OP. 34 (FROM THE PLAY "THE TOP") (1931)
1,1,2,1 - 2,2,1,0 - timp.,perc. - hp. - str.   9:00 FinnMICtr.

—— THE UNKNOWN LAND, OP. 33 (FOR PIANO AND ORCH) (1930)
3,3,2,2 - 4,3,3,1 - timp.,perc.,bells,vibra. - pf. - str.   23:00 FinnMICtr.

—— THE WAY OF THE HEART, OP. 88 (CANTATA) (FOR 2 SOPRANOS, TENOR, SATB CHORUS AND ORCH.) (1946) (Text: A. Kivimaa)
2,2,2,2 - 4,2,3,1 - timp.,perc. - hp. - str.   12:00 FinnMICtr.

RAPHAEL, Günter

—— CONCERTO IN D MINOR FOR ORGAN AND SMALL ORCH., OP. 57
0,0,0,0 - 0,3,0,0 - timp. - org. - str.   26:00 Henmar.

—— CONCERTO NO. 2 FOR VIOLIN AND ORCH., OP. 87
Hans Gerig.

—— SYMPHONY NO. 3 IN F MAJOR, OP. 60
Henmar.

RAPHLING, Sam
—— ABRAHAM LINCOLN WALKS AT MIDNIGHT
(PASSACAGLIA)
2(2nd alt. with picc.),*3,*3,2 - 4,2,3,1 - timp.,perc.,glock.,xyl. - str.
10:00 Composer.
—— CARNIVAL OF THE MIND (8 VARIABLES FOR
ORCHESTRA)
2(2nd alt. with picc.),2,2,2 - 4,3,3,1 - timp. - str.   7:00 General.
—— CONCERTANTE FOR GLOCKENSPIEL AND ORCHESTRA
1,1,1,1 - 1,1,1,0 - glock. - str.   7:00 General.
—— CONCERTINO FOR SEVEN TOY INSTRUMENTS AND
STRINGS
5:30 MCA Music.
—— CONCERTO FOR MARIMBA, VIBRAPHONE, XYLOPHONE
AND WIND ENSEMBLE
1,1,1,1 - 2,2,2,1 - mar.,vibra.,xyl.   12:00 General.
—— CONCERTO FOR PIANO AND STRINGS
pf. - str.   15:00 General.
—— CONCERTO FOR TROMBONE (OR FRENCH HORN) AND
ORCH. (IN 3 MOVTS.)
0,1,0,0 - 0,0,1,0 - str.   10:00 Composer.
—— CONCERTO FOR TRUMPET AND STRINGS
tpt. - str.   10:00 Bourne.
—— CONCERTO NO. 1 FOR PIANO AND ORCH. (IN 3 MOVTS.)
1,0,0,0 - 1,1,0,0 - pf. - str.   11:00 Mills.
—— CONCERTO NO. 2 FOR PIANO AND ORCH. (IN 4 MOVTS.)
2,2(2nd alt. with Eng.hn.),2,2 - 4,2,3,1 - timp. - pf. - str.
28:00 Composer.
—— CONCERTO NO. 3 FOR PIANO AND ORCH. (IN 3 MOVTS.)
2,2,2,2 - 4,2,3,1 - timp. - pf. - str.   19:00 Beekman.
—— CONCERTO NO. 4 FOR PIANO AND ORCH.
2,2,2,2 - 4,2,3,1 - timp. - pf. - str.   14:00 General.
—— DRUM-TAPS (FOR TIMPANI AND ORCH.)
2(2nd alt. with picc.),2,2,2 - 4,3,3,1 - timp. - str.   6:00 Composer.
—— FEATHERTOP (1-ACT OPERA) %
str.   60:00 General.
—— I HEAR AMERICA SINGING (FOR BARITONE, CHORUS
AND ORCH.)
2,2,2,2 - 4,2,3,1 - timp. - str.   16:00 Beekman.
—— ISRAEL (RHAPSODY FOR PIANO AND ORCH.)
2,2,2,2 - 4,3,3,1 - timp. - pf. - str.   16:00 Transcon.
Or
2,2,2,2 - 2,2,0,0 - pf. - str.
—— KIBBUTZ
2,2,2,2 - 4,2,3,0 - timp.,perc. - str.   12:00 General.
—— LIVELY OVERTURE
2,2,2,2 - 4,2,3,1 - timp.,perc.,xyl. - str.   6:00 Composer.
—— MINSTREL RHAPSODY (FOR PIANO AND ORCH.)
2,2,2,2 - 3,2,3,0 - timp.,perc. - pf. - str.   10:00 Mills.
—— THE MYSTIC TRUMPETER (FOR TRUMPET AND ORCH.)
(IN 3 MOVTS.)
2(2nd alt. with picc.),2,2,2 - 4,3,3,1 - timp. - str.   10:00 Composer.
—— NOVELTY SUITE (FOR STRINGS) (IN 3 MOVTS.)
str.   5:00 Mills.
—— PASTORALE FOR OBOE AND STRINGS
ob. - str.   7:00 Musicus.
—— PRELUDE ("TURN, O LIBERTAD")
2(2nd alt. with picc.),2,2,2 - 4,3,3,1 - timp. - str.   Composer.
—— RHAPSODY
0,1,0,0 - 1,0,0,0 - str.   10:00 Belw-Mills.
—— RHAPSODY FOR CLARINET AND ORCH.
2,1,1,1 - 3,2,2,0 - str.   12:00 General.
—— SPOTLIGHT ON THE ORCHESTRA (SCHERZO
CONCERTANTE)
1(alt. with picc.),1,1,1 - 4,1,3,1 - timp.,perc. - hp. - str.
5:00 General.
—— SUITE FOR STRINGS (IN 3 MOVTS.)
str.   13:00 Beekman.
—— SYMPHONY FOR CHAMBER ORCH. (IN 4 MOVTS.)
1,1,1,1 - 1,1,1,0 - timp.,perc. - str.   12:00 Composer.
—— SYMPHONY IN BRASS
0,0,0,0 - 4,4,4,1 - timp.,perc.   8:00 General.
—— SYMPHONY NO. 1 (IN 3 MOVTS.)
*3,2,2,2 - 4,3,3,1 - timp.,xyl. - harmonica - str.   16:00 Composer.
—— SYMPHONY NO. 2 (IN 4 MOVTS.)
2(2nd alt. with picc.),2,*3,2 - 4,3,3,1 - timp.,perc. - str.
10:00 Composer.
—— SYMPHONY NO. 3
2,2,2,2 - 4,2,3,1 - timp.,perc. - str.   12:00 General.
—— WARBLE FOR LILAC TIME
fl. - str.   10:00 Musicus.

—— THE WINDY CITY
2(2nd alt. with picc.),2,2(2nd alt. with alto sax.),2 - 4,2,3,1 - timp.
- str.   8:00 Weintraub.

RASMUSSEN, Karl Aage
—— CORALIS CONSTANTINUS (FOR CHAMBER ORCH.)(1966)
16:00 G. Schirmer.
—— REVIVALS, TEMPTATIONS AND FAIRY-TALES (1968)
3,3,3,3 - 4,3,3,1 - perc.(3),cel. - hp. - Hammond org. - pf. - str.
27:00 G. Schirmer.
—— SYMPHONIE CLASSIQUE
1,2,1,1 - 2,1,1,0 - perc. - electric guit. - hpsc. - Hammond org. -
str.   G. Schirmer.
—— SYMPHONY FOR YOUNG LOVERS (1967)
3,2,2,sax.,1 - 4,3,3,1 - timp.,perc.(4),cel. - hp. - pf. - str.
18:00 G. Schirmer.

RASMUSSEN, Niels Christian
—— LEGEND
perc.(2) - str.(10,4,3,0)   8:00 K.O.D.A.
—— NOCTURNE (FOR SOPRANO, VIOLIN AND ORCH.) (No text)
2,0,1,1 - 1,1,2,0 - perc. - str.   9:00 K.O.D.A.

RASSE, François
—— CONCERTINO FOR TROMBONE (OR TUBA) AND ORCH.
(1921)
2,2,2,2 - 2,2,0-1,0-1 - timp. - str.   8:00 Baron.
—— DOULEUR (POÈME SYMPHONIQUE) (1911)
3,3,3,3 - 4,3,3,1 - timp. - hp. - str.   13:00 CBDM.
—— LA DRYADE (FOR CLARINET AND ORCH.) (1943)
2,2,3,2 - 2,0,0,0 - timp.,perc. - str.   15:00 H. Elkan.
—— ENTRÉE TRIOMPHALE (1929)
3,3,3,3 - 4,3,3,1 - timp.,perc. - str.   12:00 H. Elkan.
—— IMPROVISATA (FOR TRUMPET AND ORCH.) (1928)
2,2,2,2 - 2,1,0,0 - timp. - str.   10:00 H. Elkan.
—— JOIE (POÈME SYMPHONIQUE) (1925)
3,3,3,3 - 4,3,3,1 - timp.,perc. - hp. - str.   15:00 CBDM.
—— LAMENTO (1942)
2,1,1,2 - 2,0,0,0 - timp. - str.   6:00 H. Elkan.
—— LE MAÎTRE À DANSER (BALLET SUITE)
2,2,2,2 - 4,2,3,1 - timp.,perc.,bells - org. - str.   15:00 H. Elkan.
—— POÈME CONCERTANT (FOR PIANO AND ORCH.) (1918)
2,2,2,2 - 4,2,3,1 - timp. - pf. - str.   27:00 H. Elkan.
—— POÈME CONCERTANT (FOR VIOLIN AND ORCH.) (1935)
2,2,2,2 - 2,2,2,0 - timp.,perc. - str.   16:00 H. Elkan.
—— POUR UNE TRAGÉDIE (1929)
2,2,2,2 - 4,2,3,1 - timp.,perc.,bells - hp. - str.   25:00 H. Elkan.

RATEAU, Michel
—— TROIS MUSIQUES POUR ORCHESTRE
3,3,4,3 - 5,4,3,0 - timp. - str.   18:00 Presser.

RATENBACH, A. B.
—— MICROVARIACIONES (FOR TIMPANI AND STRINGS)
timp. - str.   8:00 Bo. Hawkes.

RATHAUS, Karol
—— ALLEGRO CONCERTANTE, OP. 30
tpt. - str.   8:00 Bo. Hawkes.
—— CONCERTO FOR PIANO AND ORCH., OP. 45 (IN 3 MOVTS.)
2(2nd alt. with picc.),2,*3,2 - 4,3,3,0 - timp. - pf. - str.
23:30 Bo. Hawkes.
—— DIAPASON (FOR CHORUS, BARITONE AND ORCH.), OP. 67
(IN 4 MOVTS.)
*3,2,2,2 - 4,3,3,1 - timp.,perc.,glock. - str.   38:00 Queens.
—— INTERMEZZO GIOCOSO
3,2,3,3 - 4,3,3,1 - perc.   7:00 G. Schirmer.
—— LE LION AMOUREUX, OP. 42B (BALLET SUITE) (IN 5
MOVTS.)
3,2,3,3 - 4,3,3,1 - timp.,perc. - hp. - pf. - str.   15:00 Bo. Hawkes.
—— MUSIC FOR STRINGS, OP. 49
str.   15:00 Bo. Hawkes.
—— O JUVENES (CANTATA) (FOR TENOR, CHORUS AND
ORCH.)
2(2nd alt. with picc.),2,2,2 - 4,2,3,0 - timp.,perc.(2),cel.,glock. - str.
12:00 Queens.
—— PRAELUDIUM AND GIGUE, OP. 44
Bo. Hawkes.
—— PRELUDE FOR ORCH., OP. 71
2(2nd alt. with picc.),2,2,2 - 4,2,3,1 - timp. - pf. - str.
12:00 Bo. Hawkes.
—— PSALM 23 (FOR TENOR, WOMEN'S CHORUS AND ORCH.)
2,2,2,2 - 4,2,3,0 - timp. - str.   10:00 Composer.

—— SALISBURY COVE, OP. 65
*3,2,E♭ cl.,2,*3 - 4,3,3,1 - timp.,perc.(2),cel.,glock. - hp. - pf. - str.
15:00 C. Fischer.
—— SINFONIA CONCERTANTE, OP. 68 (IN 3 MOVTS.)
*3,2,*3,*3 - 4,3,3,1 - timp.,perc.,glock. - str.   25:00 Bo. Hawkes.
—— SUITE FROM "URIEL ACOSTA" (IN 4 MOVTS.)
2,2,2,2 - 4,3,3,0 - timp.,perc. - hp. - str.   15:00 IsMuPublns.
—— SYMPHONY NO. 3, OP. 50
3,3,3,3 - 4,3,3,1 - timp.,perc.,cel. - hp. - pf. - str.
30:00 Bo. Hawkes.
—— VISION DRAMATIQUE, OP. 55
2,2,3,2 - 4,3,3,1 - timp.,perc. - pf. - str.   12:00 Bo. Hawkes.

RATHBURN, Eldon
—— ASPECTS OF RAILROAD (1969)
*3,2,2,2 - 4,3,3,1 - timp.,perc.(2) - hp. - str.   11:20 CanMusCtr.
—— CITY OF GOLD SUITE (1967) (FROM THE FILM "CITY OF
GOLD") (IN 5 MOVTS.)
2(2nd alt. with picc.),2,2,2 - 4,3,3,1 - timp.,perc. - harmonica,
Jew's harp. - banjo, guit. - hp. - pf. - str.   17:20 CanMusCtr.
—— GRAY CITY (TONE POEM)
14:45 CanMusCtr.
—— IMAGES OF CHILDHOOD (1950)
*2,2,2,2 - 4,3,2,0 - timp.,perc. - str.   7:50 CanMusCtr.
—— NOCTURNE (1953)
1,1,1,1 - 0,3,2,0 - timp.,perc. - guit. - hp. - pf. - str.
4:00 CanMusCtr.
—— OVERTURE BURLESCA
2,2,2,2 - 4,3,3,1 - timp.,perc.(2) - str.   4:00 C.A.P.A.C.
—— RURAL ROUTE (SUITE) (IN 3 MOVTS.)
2,2,2,2 - 4,2,3,0 - perc. - hp. - str.   7:30 C.A.P.A.C.
—— SYMPHONETTE
20:00 C.A.P.A.C.
—— THREE IRONIES (1975) (FOR BRASS QUINTET AND ORCH.)
10:00 CanMusCtr.

RATHGEBER, Valentin - HESS
—— CONCERTO NO. 15 IN E FLAT MAJOR, OP. 6
2 tpt. - cemb. - str.   Henmar.

RATNER, Leonard
—— SUITE (FOR STRING QUARTET AND STRINGS) (IN 3
MOVTS.)
str.   14:00 Bo. Hawkes.

RAUTAVAARA, Einojuhani
—— ANADYOMENE, OP. 33 (1968)
3,3,3,3 - 4,4,4,1 - timp. - hp. - str.   11:00 Fazer.
—— ARABESCATA, OP. 24 (1963)
3,2,3,2 - 3,3,4,1 - timp.,perc.(6),cel. - hp. - pf. - str.
15:00 FinnMICtr.
—— CANTO NO. 1, OP. 16 (1960)
str.   6:00 FinnMICtr.
—— CANTO NO. 2, OP. 17 (1960)
str.   9:00 FinnMICtr.
—— CANTUS ARCTICUS, OP. 61 (CONCERTO FOR BIRDS AND
ORCH.) (1972)
2,2,2,2 - 2,2,1,0 - timp.,perc.,cel. - tape-recorder - hp. - str.
15:00 Fazer.
—— CONCERTO FOR FLUTES AND ORCH., OP. 69 (IN 4
MOVTS.)
22:00 FinnMICtr.
—— CONCERTO FOR SOPRANO, CHORUS AND ORCH., OP. 49
(1971)
3,3,3,3 - 4,3,3,1 - timp.,perc. - hp. - str.   17:00 FinnMICtr.
—— DITHYRAMBOS, OP. 55
2,0,2,2 - 2,2,0,0 - timp.,perc. - str.   Fazer.
—— FIVE SONNETS TO ORPHEUS, OP. 9 (FOR VOICE AND
ORCH.) (REV. 1960) (Text: Rainer Maria Rilke)
2,2,2,2 - 2,2,2,0 - timp. - hp. - str.   14:00 Fazer.
—— IN MEMORIAM J. K. PAASIKIVI, OP. 38 (1968)
2,2,2,2 - 4,2,2,1 - timp.,perc. - hp. - str.   10:00 FinnMICtr.
—— THE LOVERS, OP. 13 (FOR SOPRANO AND STRINGS) (1959)
(Text: Rainer Maria Rilke)
str.   15:00 FinnMICtr.
—— THE MINE, OP. 15 (OPERA) % (1963) (Text: Composer)
3,3,3,3 - 4,2 Wagner tu.,2,2,1 - timp.,perc.(3),cel. - tape-recorder -
jazz band - hp. - str.   81:00 FinnMICtr.
—— A PORTRAIT OF THE ARTIST AT A CERTAIN MOMENT,
OP. 62 (1972)
str.   15:00 FinnMICtr.

—— REGULAR SETS OF ELEMENTS IN SEMIREGULAR
SITUATION, OP. 60 (1971)
3,0,0,0 - 3,1,0,0 - timp. - pf. - str.(4,0,4,0)   15:00 FinnMICtr.
—— A REQUIEM IN OUR TIMES (FOR 13 BRASSES AND
PERCUSSION)
15:00 Robt. King.
—— SUITE FOR STRING ORCH., OP. 2 (1952)
str.   12:00 FinnMICtr.
—— SYMPHONY NO. 1, OP. 5 (1956)
2,2,2,2 - 4,2,3,1 - timp.,perc.(3) - hp. - str.   26:00 FinnMICtr.
—— SYMPHONY NO. 2, OP. 8 (1957)
1,1,3,1 - 2,1,1,0 - timp.,perc.(3) - str.   20:00 FinnMICtr.
—— SYMPHONY NO. 3, OP. 20 (1961)
2,2,2,2 - 2,4 Wagner tu.,2,3,1 - timp. - str.   30:00 FinnMICtr.
—— SYMPHONY NO. 4, OP. 25 (1964)
2,2,2,2 - 4,3,2,2 - perc. - str.   19:00 Seesaw.
—— THE TEMPTATIONS, OP. 47 (BALLET) % (1969)
2,2,2,2 - 4,3,3,1 - timp.,perc.(3) - 2 hp. - str.   30:00 FinnMICtr.
—— TRUE AND FALSE UNICORN, OP. 58 (FOR SATB CHORUS
AND ORCH.) (1971) (Text: James Broughton)
1,0,1,1 - 2,1,0,0 - timp. - tape-recorder - pf. - str.
45:00 FinnMICtr.
—— THE WATER CIRCLE, OP. 65 (CONCERTO FOR PIANO,
SATB CHORUS AND ORCH.) (1972) (Text: James Broughton)
2,2,2,2 - 4,2,2,0 - timp.,perc. - pf. - str.   20:00 FinnMICtr.

RAUTIO, Matti
—— CONCERTO FOR PIANO AND ORCH. (1971)
3,3,3,3 - 4,3,3,1 - timp.,perc.(7),cel. - hp. - pf. - str.
24:00 FinnMICtr.
—— DIVERTIMENTO (FOR CELLO AND ORCH.) (1955)
2,1,2,2 - 2,2,2,1 - perc.(2) - str.   16:00 FinnMICtr.
—— SUITE FROM THE BALLET "THE BLUE HERON" (1957)
2,1,2,1 - 2,2,2,0 - perc.(2),cel. - pf. - d.-b.   14:00 FinnMICtr.

RAVEL, Maurice
—— BOLERO
*3(2nd alt. with 2nd picc.),3(2nd alt. with ob. d'amore),4,3 sax.,3 -
4,4,3,1 - timp.,perc.,cel. - hp. - str.   11:00 EV.
—— CONCERTO FOR PIANO (LEFT HAND ALONE) AND ORCH.
3,3,4,3 - 4,3,3,1 - timp.,perc. - hp. - pf. - str.   18:00 EV.
—— CONCERTO IN G, FOR PIANO AND ORCH. (IN 3 MOVTS.)
2,2,2,2 - 2,1,1,0 - timp.,perc. - hp. - pf. - str.   20:00 EV.
—— DAPHNIS AND CHLOE: BALLET SUITE NO. 1 (IN 3 MOVTS.)
3(3rd alt. with picc.),alto fl.,3,4,4 - 4,4,3,1 - timp.,perc.,cel. - 2 hp.
- str.   17:00 EV.
—— DAPHNIS AND CHLOE: BALLET SUITE NO. 2 (IN 3 MOVTS.)
3(2 alt. with 2 picc.),alto fl.,3,*4,*4 - 4,4,3,1 - timp.,perc.,cel. - 2
hp. - str.   16:00 EV.
—— DAPHNIS ET CHLOE (BALLET) (WITH OPTIONAL
WORDLESS CHORUS) %
5,*3,4,4 - 4,4,4,1 - timp.,perc.(7),cel. - 2 hp. - str.   50:00 EV.
—— DEUX MÉLODIES HEBRAÏQUES (FOR VOICE AND ORCH.)
2,2,2,2 - 2,0,0,0 - perc. - hp. - str.   7:00 EV.
—— DON QUICHOTTE À DULCINÉE (3 SONGS FOR BARITONE
AND ORCH.) (IN 3 MOVTS.)
2,*2,2,2 -2,1,0,0 - perc. - hp. - str.   12:00 EV.
—— FANFARE TO "L'ÉVENTAIL DE JEANNE"
5:00 Mercury.
—— L' HEURE ESPAGNOLE (ONE-ACT OPERA) %
EV.
—— L'ENFANT ET LES SORTILÈGES ("THE BEWITCHED
CHILD") (CANTATA)
45:00 EV.
—— MA MÈRE L'OYE ("MOTHER GOOSE") (SUITE) (IN 5
MOVTS.)
2(2nd alt. with picc.),2(2nd alt. with Eng. hn.),2,3 - 2 hn. -
timp.,perc.,cel. - hp. - str.   14:00 EV.
—— PIÈCE EN FORME DE HABANERA
2,0,2,2 - 2,1(or ob.),0,0 - perc. - hp.(or pf.) - str.   2:30 Baron.
—— RHAPSODIE ESPAGNOLE (IN 4 MOVTS.)
4,3,3,3,sarr. - 4,3,3,1 - timp.,perc.,cel. - 2 hp. - str.   14:00 EV.
—— SHÉHÉRAZADE, OUVERTURE DE FÉERIE, OP. POSTH.
(1898)
Salabert.
—— SHÉHÉRAZADE (3 SONGS FOR HIGH VOICE AND ORCH.)
(IN 3 MOVTS.)
*3,3,2,2 - 4,2,2,1 - timp.,perc.,cel. - 2 hp. - str.   10:00 EV.
—— LE TOMBEAU DE COUPERIN (SUITE) (IN 4 MOVTS.)
2(2nd alt. with picc.),2(2nd alt. with Eng. hn.),2,2 - 2,1,0,0 - hp. -
str.   19:00 EV.

—— TROIS POÈMES DE STEPHEN MALLARMÉ (FOR VOICE
AND ORCH.)
  3 fl.,2 cl. - timp. - 2 hp. - pf. - str.   EV.
—— TZIGANE (RHAPSODY FOR VIOLIN AND ORCH.)
  2(2nd alt. with picc.),2,2,2 - 2,1,0,0 - perc.,cel. - hp. - str.
                                                      8:00 EV.
—— LA VALSE
  3(3rd alt. with picc.),3(3rd alt. with Eng. hn.),3,3 - 4,3,3,1 -
  timp.,perc. - 2hp. - str.   18:00 EV.
—— VALSES NOBLES ET SENTIMENTALES
  2,3,2,2 - 4,2,3,1 - timp.,perc.,cel. - 2 hp. - str. 14:00 EV.

RAVEL, Maurice - CASTELNUOVO-TEDESCO, Mario
—— LA VALLÉE DES CLOCHES
  3,2,3,2 - 4,2,3,0 - timp.,perc. - cel. - hp. - str.   AMP.

RAVEL, Maurice - HOLMES, Malcolm H.
—— TROIS CHANSONS (FOR CHORUS AND STRING ORCH.)
  str.   6:00 EV.

RAVEL, Maurice - SOPKIN, Henry
—— PIECE IN THE FORM OF A HABANERA
  1,1,2,1 - 2,0,0,0 - timp.,perc.(2) - hp. - str.   7:00 Arranger.

RAWSTHORNE, Alan
—— A CANTICLE OF MAN (CHAMBER CANTATA) (FOR
BARITONE, CHORUS, FLUTE AND STRINGS)
  fl. - str.   Oxford.
—— CARMEN VITALE (FOR SOPRANO, MIXED CHORUS AND
ORCH.)
  3,2,2,2 - 4,3,3,1 - timp.,perc. - hp. - str.   46:00 Oxford.
—— CONCERTANTE PASTORALE
  fl. - hn. - str.   9:00 Oxford.
—— CONCERTO FOR CELLO AND ORCH.
  2,2,2,2 - 4,2,3,1 - timp., perc. - hp. - str.   33:00 Oxford.
—— CONCERTO FOR CLARINET AND STRINGS
  cl. - str.   19:00 Oxford.
—— CONCERTO FOR OBOE AND STRINGS
  ob. - str.   13:00 Oxford.
—— CONCERTO FOR STRING ORCH.
  str.   24:00 Oxford.
—— CONCERTO FOR TEN INSTRUMENTS
  1,1,1,1 - 1,0,0,0 - str.(2,1,1,1)   16:30 Oxford.
—— CONCERTO FOR TWO PIANOS AND ORCH.
  2,2,2,2 - 4,2,3,1 - timp.,perc. - 2 pf. - str.   25:00 Oxford.
—— CONCERTO FOR VIOLIN AND ORCH.
  2,2,2,2 - 4,3,3,0 - timp.,perc. - hp. - str.   30:00 Oxford.
—— CONCERTO NO. 1 FOR PIANO AND ORCH.
  2,2,2,2 - 4,2,3,0 - timp.,perc.(2) - pf. - str.   20:00 Oxford.
  or:
  3,3,3,3 - 4,2,3,1 - timp.,perc.(2) - pf. - str.
—— CONCERTO NO. 2 FOR PIANO AND ORCH.
  2,2,2,2 - 4,2,3,0 - timp.,perc. - pf. - str.   25:00 Oxford.
—— CONCERTO NO. 2 FOR VIOLIN AND ORCH.
                                                    22:00 Oxford.
—— CORTÈGES (FANTASY - OVERTURE)
  2,2,2,2 - 4,2,3,1 - timp.,perc.(3) - hp. - str.   14:30 Oxford.
—— DIVERTIMENTO FOR CHAMBER ORCH.
                                                        Oxford.
—— ELEGIAC FRAGMENTS
  str.   11:00 Oxford.
—— ELEGIAL RHAPSODY FOR STRING ORCHESTRA
                                                        Oxford.
—— THE GOD IN THE CAVE (CANTATA) (FOR MIXED CHORUS
AND ORCH.) (Text: Randall Swingler)
  2,2,2,2 - 4,2,3,1 - timp.,perc. - str.   16:00 Oxford.
—— IMPROVISATIONS ON A THEME BY CONSTANT LAMBERT
  2,2,2,2 - 4,2,0,0 - timp. - str.   12:00 Oxford.
—— MADAME CHRYSANTHÈME (BALLET SUITE)
  2,2,2,2 - 2,2,2,0 - timp.,perc.(3) - hp. - str.   8:00 Oxford.
—— MADAME CHRYSANTHÈME (FOR MEZZO-SOPRANO AND
ORCH.)
  3,1,0,2 - 2,3,0,0 - timp.,perc.,cel. - hp. - pf. - str. 40:00 Oxford.
—— MEDIEVAL DIPTYCH (FOR BARITONE AND ORCH.)
  2(alt. with picc.),2,3,2 - 2,3,2,0 - perc.- str.   Oxford.
—— OVERTURE: HALLE
  2,2,2,2 - 4,3,3,1 - timp.,perc.(3) - str.   7:00 Oxford.
—— PRACTICAL CATS (FOR SPEAKER AND ORCH.)
  2,2,2,2 - 4,2,3,0 - timp.,perc.(2) - str.   24:00 Oxford.
—— STREET CORNER OVERTURE
  2,2,2,2 - 4,2,3,1 - timp.,perc. - str.   5:30 Oxford.
—— SYMPHONIC STUDIES
  3,3,3,3 - 4,2,3,1 - timp.,perc.(2),cel. - hp. - str. 20:00 Oxford.

—— SYMPHONY
  3,3,3,3 - 4,3,3,1 - timp.,perc.(2) - str.   24:00 Oxford.
—— SYMPHONY NO. 2 (PASTORAL) (FOR SOPRANO AND
ORCH.)
  2,2,2,2 - 4,2,3,0 - timp.,perc.(3) - hp. - str.   22:00 Oxford.
—— SYMPHONY NO. 3
  *3,*3,*3,2 - 4,3,3,1 - timp.,perc.,cel. - hp. - str. 29:00 Oxford.
—— THEME, VARIATIONS AND FINALE
  *3,*3,*3,*3, - 4,3,3,0 - timp.,perc. - str.   Oxford.
—— TRIPTYCH FOR ORCHESTRA
  3,*3,3,2 - 4,3,3,1 - timp.,perc.(3) - hp. - str.   16:00 Oxford.

RAXACH, Enrique
—— FLUXION (1962)
  1,1,1,1 - 1,1,1,0 - perc. - harm. - str.   12:50 Seesaw.
—— TEXTURES (1966)
  3,*3,3,3 - 4,4,4,1 - timp.,perc.(5, incl. 4 on timp.),cel. - 2 hp. - str.
                                                    11:45 Seesaw.

RAYMOND, Joseph G.
—— LYRIC SYMPHONY
                                                    13:00 Composer.

RAYMOND, Lewis
—— HIS HALF DOZEN WORDS OF CONSECRATION (FOR
NARRATOR, BARITONE, MIXED CHORUS AND ORCH.)
  (Texts: Abraham Lincoln and John Hay)
  2(2nd alt. with picc.),2,2,2 - 2,2,2,0 - timp.,perc.(3) - hp. - pf. - str.
                                                    7:00 Composer.
—— LENTO AND DANCE (FOR VIOLIN AND ORCH.)
  2,2,2,2 - 2,0,0,0 - cel. - hp. - str.   12:00 Composer.
—— OVERTURE ON EARLY AMERICAN TUNES
  3(3rd alt. with picc.),2,3(3rd alt. with b.-cl.),2 - 4,3,2,1 -
  timp.,perc.,bells - hp. - str.   7:00 KeysMusCal.
—— PASSACAGLIA
  3(3rd alt. with picc.),2(2nd alt. with Eng.hn.),*3,*3 - 4,2,3,1 -
  timp.,perc.(3-4),xyl. - hp. - pf. - str.   13:00 Composer.
—— TODDLER'S SUITE (FOR CHAMBER ORCH.) (IN 6 MOVTS.)
  1,1,*3,0 - 2,2,1,0 - timp.,perc.(2-3),bells,cel.(ad lib.),xyl. - hp. - pf.
  - str.   8:55 Composer.

RAZZI, Fausto
—— IMPROVVISAZIONE I (FOR VIOLA, 18 WINDS AND
TIMPANI) (1965)
  3,2,3,1 - 3,3,3,0 - timp. - vla.   15:00 MCA Music.
—— IMPROVVISAZIONE II (FOR 36-VOICE SATB CHORUS AND
STRINGS) (1966)
  str.   15:00 MCA Music.
—— MOVIMENTO (FOR PIANO AND ORCH.)
                                                        Leeds.
—— MUSIC FOR 10 WINDS (1968)
  0,3,1,2 - 0,2,2,0   7:00 MCA Music.
—— MUSIC FOR 26 INSTRUMENTS (1968)
  0,2,0,2 - 2,2,0,0 - str.(6,5,4,3)   11:00 MCA Music.

READ, Gardner
—— AMERICAN CIRCLE, OP. 52A
  *2,1,2,2, - 4,2,3,0 - timp.,perc.(1) - pf. - str. 4:00 Composer.
—— ARIOSO ELEGIACA, OP. 91 (FOR STRINGS)
  str.   7:30 Henmar.
—— A BELL OVERTURE, OP. 72
  *3,*3,*3,*3 - 4,3,3,1 - timp.,perc.(4-8),cel.,glock. - hp. - str.
                                                    7:30 Southern.
—— DANCE OF THE LOCOMOTIVES, OP. 57A
  3,2,3,2 - 4,2,3,1 - timp.,perc. - pf. - str.   4:00 Seesaw.
—— FESTIVAL FANFARE
  3,2,2,2 - 4,3,3,1 - timp.,perc. - org. - str.   3:00 Composer.
—— FOUR NOCTURNES, OP. 23 (FOR CONTRALTO AND SMALL
ORCH.)
  1,1,1,1 - hn. - hp. - str.   12:00 Composer.
—— FROM A LUTE OF JADE, OP. 36 (3 SONGS FOR MEDIUM
VOICE AND ORCH.)
  2,2,2,2 - 2,0,0,0 - perc.,cel. - hp. - str.   6:00 C. Press.
—— THE GOLDEN JOURNEY TO SAMARKAND (FOR SOPRANO,
CONTRALTO, TENOR, BARITONE, BASS, CHORUS AND
ORCH.), OP. 41
  *3,alto fl.,*3,E♭cl.,*3,*3 - 6,4,4,1 - timp.,perc.(5),cel. - 2 hp. - str.
                                                    26:00 Composer.
—— JEUX DES TIMBRES, OP. 111 (1963)
  3,3,3,3 - 4,3,3,1 - timp.,perc.,cel. - hp. - str. 10:00 Composer.
—— MUSIC FOR PIANO AND STRINGS, OP. 47A (IN 1 MOVT.)
  pf. - str.   21:00 Composer.

—— NIGHT FLIGHT (TONE POEM)
  3,2,3,3 - 4,2,3,1 - timp.,perc.,vibra. - hp. - str.   7:00 Henmar.
—— OVERTURE NO. 1, OP. 58
  3,3,3,3 - 4,3,3,1 - timp.,perc. - hp. - pf. - str.   8:00 C. Press.
—— THE PAINTED DESERT (SUITE), OP. 22 (IN 4 MOVTS.)
  *4,*3,*5,*4, - 4,3,3,1 - timp.,perc.(4),cel. - 2 hp. - str.
        26:00 Composer.
—— PAN E DAFNI, OP. 53 (FOR ALTO FLUTE AND ORCH.)
  2,alto fl.,3,3,3 - 4,0,3,1 - timp.,perc. - hp. - str.   10:00 AMP.
—— PARTITA FOR SMALL ORCH., OP. 70 (IN 3 MOVTS.)
  1,1,1,1 - 1,1,1,0 - timp. - str.   11:00 Southern.
—— PASSACAGLIA AND FUGUE, OP. 34A
  *3,*3,*3,*3 - 4,3,3,1 - timp.,perc.,cel. - hp. - str. 12:00 Belw-Mills.
—— PENNSYLVANIA, OP. 67 (SUITE OF 3 FOLK SONGS FOR
  ORCH.)
  *3-*4,*3,*3,*3 - 4,3,3,1 - timp.,perc.(3) - hp. - pf. - str.
        15:00 F. Colombo.
  or:
  *3,*3,2,2 - 4,3,3,1 - timp.,perc.(3) - str.
—— POEM (FOR HORN, HARP AND STRINGS)
  hn. - hp. - str.   3:00 C. Fischer.
—— PRELUDE AND TOCCATA, OP. 43
  *2,2,2,2 - 2,2,2,0 - timp. - str.   7:00 F. Colombo.
—— THE PROPHET, OP. 110 (FOR MALE NARRATOR, ALTO,
  BARITONE, CHORUS AND ORCH.) (1960) (Text: Kahlil Gibran)
  *3,1 alto fl.,*3,*3,1 d.-b.,cl.,*3 - 4,3,3,1 -
  timp.,perc.(4),cel.,glock.,xyl. - 2 hp. - org. - str.   85:00 Composer.
—— QUIET MUSIC FOR STRINGS, OP. 65
  str.   10:00 Seesaw.
—— THE REVEILLE, OP. 89-B (FOR CHORUS, WINDS, ORGAN
  AND PERCUSSION) (1962)
  0,0,0,2 - 4,4,4,1 - timp.,perc. - org.   8:00 Seesaw.
—— SKETCHES OF THE CITY (SUITE), OP. 26 (IN 3 MOVTS.)
  *4(3rd alt. with alto fl.),*3,*3,*3 - 4,3,3,1 - timp.,perc.(4),cel. - 2
  hp. - str.   15:00 Belw-Mills.
—— SONORIC FANTASIA NO. 2, OP. 123 (FOR VIOLIN AND
  CHAMBER ORCH.) (1965)
  1,1,1,1 - 1,1,1,0 - perc.(2),glock.,vibra. - hp. - str.   10:30 Presser.
—— SUITE FOR ORCHESTRA
        20:00 Composer.
—— SUITE, OP. 33A (IN 4 MOVTS.)
  str.   16:00 Southern.
—— SYMPHONY NO. 1, OP. 30 (IN 4 MOVTS.)
  3(2nd alt. with alto fl. and 3rd alt. with picc.),*3,*3,*3 - 4,3,3,1 -
  timp.,perc.(3),cel. - 2 hp. - str.   38:00 AmerMusEd.
—— SYMPHONY NO. 3, OP. 75 (IN 3 MOVTS.)
  3,3,3,3 - 4,3,3,1 - timp.,perc. - pf. - str.   25:00 F. Colombo.
—— SYMPHONY NO. 4, OP. 92 (IN 2 MOVTS.)
  3,3,3,3 - 4,3,3,1 - timp.,perc. - org. - str.   25:00 Composer.
—— THE TEMPTATION OF ST. ANTHONY (A DANCE
  SYMPHONY), OP. 56
  *3,*3,*3,*3 - 4,3,3,1 - timp.,perc.,cel.,glock. - hp. - str.
        35:00 Composer.
—— THREE SATIRICAL SARCASMS, OP. 29A
  *3,*3,*3,*3 - 3,3,3,1 - timp.,perc.(3) - pf. -.str.   6:00 Composer.
—— THRENODY, OP. 66A
  fl. - hp. - str.   5:00 Seesaw.
—— TOCCATA GIOCOSA, OP. 94
  2(2nd alt. with picc.),2,2,2 - 4,2,3,1 - timp.,perc.(2),glock.,xyl. - hp.
  - str.   7:00 Presser.
—— VERNAL EQUINOX,OP. 96
  2,*2,2,2 - 4,3,3,0 - timp.,perc.(3),cel. - hp. - str.
        10:00 F. Colombo.
—— VILLON, OP. 122 (OPERA IN 3 ACTS AND 11 SCENES) (1967)
  (Text: James Forsyth)
  *3,*3,*3,*3 - 4,3,3,1 - timp.,perc.(4),glock.,xyl. - hp. - org. - str.
        180:00 Composer.

REBNER, Wolfgang
—— FLÖTENTÖNE (FOR FLUTE, HARP AND CHAMBER ORCH.)
  1,0,1,1 - 0,0,0,0 - perc. - hp. - str.   17:00 Modern.
—— PERSONAL NOTES
  2,2,2,2 - 3,3,3,0 - perc.,cel. - hp. - pf. - str.   16:00 F. Colombo.
—— PROVERBIA (FOR SATB CHORUS AND ORCH.)
  2,2,3(1 alt. with b.-cl.,1 alt. with sax.),2 - 3,3,3,0 - timp.,perc. - pf.
  - str.(0,1,1,1)   18:00 Modern.
—— VIRTUOSE LEGENDE (WITH SOLO VIOLA OR CELLO)
  2,2,2,2 - 2,0,0,0 - timp. - str.   9:00 Modern.

RECKOW, Cliff
—— FIVE MINIATURES FOR ORCH. (1964)
  3(3rd alt. with picc.),3(3rd alt. with Eng.hn.),*3,2 - 4,3,3,1 -
  timp.,perc.(3),bells,xyl. - hp. - str.   18:30 Composer.

—— FOUR AMERICAN SKETCHES (1964)
  3(3rd alt. with picc.),3(3rd alt. with Eng.hn.),*3,2 - 4,3,3,1 -
  timp.,perc.,bells,cel. - hp. - str.   16:30 Composer.
—— FOUR LATIN AMERICAN DANCES (1966)
  3(3rd alt. with picc.),3(3rd alt. with Eng.hn.),*3,2 - 4,3,3,1 -
  timp.,perc.(5) - hp. - str.   16:00 Composer.
—— SYMPHONY NO. 1 (1946) (IN 4 MOVTS.)
  3(3rd alt. with picc.),3(3rd alt. with Eng.hn.),*3,2 - 4,3,3,1 -
  timp.,perc.(3),xyl. - hp. - str.   40:00 Composer.

REDDICK, William J.
—— ARMISTICE DAY (FOR TENOR, BARITONE, MEN'S CHORUS
  AND ORCH.)
  2,*3,*3,2 - 4,3,0 0 - timp.,perc. - 2 hp. - str.   18:00 Composer.
—— THE BIOGRAPHY OF ANN BOWERS
  *3,*3,*3,*3 - 4,3,3,1 - timp.,perc.,cel.,xyl. - hp. - str.
        18:00 Composer.

REDMAN, Reginald
—— AWAY ON THE HILLS
  str.   7:00 Oxford.
—— BEAUTY AND THE BEAST
  1,1,1,0 - 0,0,0,0 - perc. - hp. - str.   30:00 P.R.S.
—— THE ELK (BALLET) % (1956)
  2,1,2,1 - 3,3,1,1 - perc. - hp. - str.   35:00 P.R.S.
—— THE EMPEROR'S NIGHTINGALE
  1,1,1,1 - 0,0,0,0 - perc.,cel. - guit. - hp. - str.   30:00 P.R.S.
—— FROM THE HILLS OF A DREAM (FOR TENOR, CHORUS
  AND ORCH.)
        9:00 Lengnick.
—— NIGHT AMONG THE LAKES (FOR CELLO AND STRINGS)
  str.   7:00 P.R.S.

REED, Alfred
—— A FESTIVAL PRELUDE (1968)
  *3,*3,*4,1 B♭ d.-b.-cl.,*3 - 4,3,3,1 - timp.,perc. - str.
        4:45 Piedmont.
—— ODE FOR TRUMPET (FOR B-TRUMPET AND ORCH.)
  3,2,3,2 - 4,4,3,1 - timp.,perc. - hp. - str.   4:47 SouthernTx.
—— RHAPSODY FOR VIOLA AND ORCH.
  3(3rd alt. with picc.),*3,*3,B♭ d.-b. cl.(or c.-bn.),2 - 4,3,3,1 -
  timp.,perc.(4),bell,vibra. - hp. - str.   14:00 Bo. Hawkes.
—— SERENADE FOR B FLAT CLARINET AND ORCH.
  3,2,3,2 - 4,3,3,1 - timp.,bells - hp. - str.   5:00 SouthernTx.
—— SERENADE FOR CLARINET AND ORCH.
  3(3rd alt. with picc.),2,2,2 b.-cl.,2 - 4,3,3,1 - timp.,bells - str.
        5:00 SouthernTx.
—— SYMPHONY FOR BRASS AND PERCUSSION
  0,0,0,0 - 4,4,4,3 - timp.,perc.(4),xyl.   17:00 Fox.
—— TESTAMENT OF AN AMERICAN (FOR NARRATOR,
  CHORUS AND ORCH.) (1974) (Text: Max Winkler)
  3(3rd alt. with picc.),2,*3,2 - 4,3,3,1 - timp.,perc.(2),bells - str.
        6:25 Belw-Mills.
—— TITANIA'S NOCTURNE (1967)
  str.   6:30 Piedmont.

REED, H. Owen
—— CONCERTO FOR CELLO AND ORCH.
  3,2,2,3 - 4,3,3,1 - perc.(5) - str.   19:00 C. Press.
—— EVANGELINE (IN 2 MOVTS.)
  *3,*3,2,2 - 4,3,3,1 - timp.,perc.(5),cel. - hp. - str.   15:00 Fleisher.
—— LA FIESTA MEXICANA
  *3,*3,*3,*3 - 4,3,3,1 - timp.,perc. - hp. - str.   20:00 Mills.
—— LIVING SOLID FACE (BALLET) % (1974) (BASED ON AN
  INDIAN SPIRIT-LEGEND)
  *2,1,1(alt. with b.-cl.),1 - 1,1,1,0 - perc.(4),glock.,mar.,vibra.,xyl. -
  pf. - str.(2,1,1,1)   27:00 Composer.
—— OVERTURE
  2,2,2,2 - 4,3,3,1 - timp.,perc.(3), mar. - str.   6:00 Mills.
—— RIPLEY FERRY
        Mills.
—— SYMPHONIC DANCE
  *3,2,2,2 - 4,2,2,0 - timp.,perc.(3) - pf. - str.   Mills.
—— SYMPHONY NO. 1
  1. Allegro; 2. Largo-Scherzando; 3. Largamente con moto
  *3,*3,*3,2 - 4,3,3,1 - timp.,perc.(3),glock. - str.   20:00 Mills.
—— A TABERNACLE FOR THE SUN (ORATORIO) (FOR MIXED
  CHORUS AND ORCH.) (Text: Dr. Merrick McCarthy)
  *2,2,2,2 - 4,3,3,1 - timp.,perc. - hp. - pf. - str.   18:00 Mills.
—— THE TURNING MIND (1967) (IN 2 MOVTS.)
  3,2,2,2 - 4,3,3,1 - timp.,perc.(5),cel.,bells,mar.,vibra.,xyl. - str.
        11:00 Belw-Mills.

REED, William Henry
—— CALIBAN (SCHERZO FANTASTIQUE)
   3,2,2,2 - 4,2,3,1 - timp.,perc. - hp. - str.   15:00 Novello.
—— CONCERTO IN A MINOR FOR VIOLIN AND ORCH. (IN 1 MOVT.)
   2,2,2,2 - 2,0,0,0 - timp. - str.   15:00 Galaxy.
—— FANTAISIE CAPRICE (FOR FLUTE AND ORCH.)
   1,2,1,1 - 2 hn. - hp. - pf. - str.   8:00 Bo. Hawkes.
—— MERRY ANDREW (OVERTURE)
   *3,2,2,2 - 4,3,3,1 - timp.,perc. - hp. - str.   8:00 Bo. Hawkes.
—— RHAPSODY IN D (FOR VIOLA AND ORCH.)
   2,2,2,2 - 2,2,0,0 - timp. - hp. - str.   Galaxy.
—— SCENES FROM THE BALLET
   3,3,2,2 - 4,2,3,1 - timp.,perc.,glock. - hp. - str.   16:00 Novello.
—— SUITE FOR STRINGS (IN 3 MOVTS.)
   str.   17:00 Novello.
—— SUITE VÉNITIENNE
   3,2,2,2 - 4,2,3,1 - timp.,perc.,glock. - hp. - str.   14:00 Novello.
—— SYMPHONY FOR STRINGS
   str.   17:00 Novello.

REEDER, Haydn Brett
—— ATTRACT AND REPULSE (1972)
   4(alt. with 4 picc.),*4,*4,alto sax.,*4 - 4,4,3,1 - perc.(3),cel. - hp. - pf. - str.   11:00 A.P.R.A.
—— CONCERTO FOR PIANO, HARPSICHORD AND ORCH. (1970) (IN 1 MOVT.)
   Descant recorder,*2,*1,1,1 - 0,2,2,1 - timp.,perc.(4),glock.,vibra. - guit. - hpsc. - pf. - 4 viola da gamba (ten.),4 c., 2 d.-b.   10:00 A.P.R.A.
—— TWO PIECES FOR ORCH. (1971)
   4(3rd alt. with picc.,4 alt. with alto fl.),2,Eᵇcl.,1(alt. with b.-cl. and sax.),2(2nd alt. with c.-bn.) - 4,3,2,0 - timp.,perc. - str.   5:30 A.P.R.A.

REESEN, Emil
—— GAUCHO (SYMPHONIC SUITE FROM THE BALLET)
   3,3,3,3 - 4,3,3,1 - timp.,perc.(4),cel.,glock.,xyl. - hp. bandonen(ad lib) - str.   16:00 Henmar.
—— VARIATIONS FOR ORCH. (ON A THEME OF FRANZ SCHUBERT)
   2,2,2,2 - 4,2,3,0 - timp.,perc. - str.   18:00 Henmar.

REGAMEY, Constantin
—— AUTOGRAPHIE
            14:00 S.U.I.S.A.
—— CHANSONS PERSANES (FOR BARITONE AND ORCH.)
   2,0,*3,2 - 2,2,0,0 - timp.,perc. - pf. - str.   15:00 S.U.I.S.A.
—— CINQ ÉTUDES POUR VOIX DE FEMME ET ORCHESTRE
   2,1,1,1 alto sax.,1 - 2,1,0,0 - perc.,vibra.,xyl. - hp. - pf. - str.   18:00 Presser.
—— MUSIQUE POUR CORDES
   str.   30:00 Mills.
—— VARIAZIONI E TEMA
   *3,*3,*3,alto sax.,2 - 4,3,3,1 - timp.,perc.,cel.,xyl. - 2 hp. - pf. - str.   18:00 Mills.

REGNEY, Noël
—— SLOVENLY PETER AND HIS FRIENDS (FOR BARITONE AND CHAMBER ENSEMBLE)
   1(alt. with picc.),0,1,1 - 1,1 cnt.,1,0 - hp. - pf. - str.   25:00 General.

REIBEL, Guy
—— JEU D'ÉCHANGES (FOR 3 ORCHESTRAS, DIVIDED INTO 5 GROUPS WITH 4 CONDUCTORS)
   3,3,5,3 - 2,2,6,1 - perc. - str.   Presser.
   or:
   2,2,4,2 - 2,1,4,1 - perc. - str.

REICHE, Eugen
—— CONCERTO NO. 2 IN A MAJOR, FOR TROMBONE AND ORCH.
   2,2,2,2 - 4,2,4,0 - timp. - str.   10:30 C. Fischer.

REICHEL, Bernard
—— CONCERTINO FOR PIANO AND ORCH., OP. 68
   *2,*2,2,2 - 2,2,0,0 - timp. - pf. - str.   19:00 Baerenrtr.
—— PASTORALE (POUR PETIT ORCHESTRE)
   1,1,1,1 - 0,2,0,0 - str.   4:00 S.U.I.S.A.
—— PIÈCE CONCERTANTE (FOR FLUTE AND SMALL ORCH.)
   1,2,0,1 - 2 hn. - timp.,cel. - hp. - str.   17:00 S.U.I.S.A.

—— PIÈCE SYMPHONIQUE (FOR ORGAN AND ORCH.)
   *3,*3,0,*3 - 0,0,3,3 - timp.,perc. - org. - str.   20:00 S.U.I.S.A.
—— SUITE POUR ORCHESTRE DE CHAMBRE
   2,1,1,1 - 0,2,0,0 - timp. - str.   12:00 S.U.I.S.A.
—— SUITE SYMPHONIQUE
   *2,*2,2,2 - 4,3,3,1 - timp.,perc. - hp. - str.   22:00 S.U.I.S.A.
—— SYMPHONIE NR. 2
   3,2,2,2 - 2,2,0,0 - timp.,perc.,cel. - hp. - pf. - str.   24:00 S.U.I.S.A.

REIF, Paul
—— ACCUMULATIONS (1970)
   2,2,2,2 - 4,2,3,1 - timp.,perc. - hp. - str.   15:00 Seesaw.
—— AMERICA (1776-1876-1976)
   2,2,2,2 - 2,2,2,1 - timp.,perc. - guit. - str.   28:00 Seesaw.
—— AND BE MY LOVE (5 SONGS FOR VOICE AND ORCH.)
   2(1 alt. with picc.),1,2,1 - 2,2,1,0 - timp.,perc.(2),glock. - hp. - str.   15:00 General.
—— BIRCHES (FOR TENOR AND ORCH.) (Text: Robert Frost)
   2,3,2,2 - 4,2,1,0 - perc. - hp. -.str.   19:00 Bo. Hawkes.
—— EPISODES FOR STRING ORCHESTRA (1971)
   str.   12:00 Seesaw.
—— EULOGY FOR A FRIEND (1969)
   timp.,perc.(2) - str.   15:00 Seesaw.
—— FANFARE AND FUGATO (1969)
   2,2,2,2 - 4,2,3,1 - timp.,perc.(2),bells,glock.,xyl. - hp. - str.   7:00 Seesaw.
—— LINES TO RALPH HODGSON, ESQUIRE (FOR VOICE AND ORCH.)
   2,2,*3,2 - 4,0,0,0 - perc. - hp. - str.   8:00 General.
—— PHILIDOR'S DEFENSE
   2,2,2,2 - 2,0,0,0 - str.   12:45 General.
—— PORTRAIT IN BROWNSTONE (SUITE) (AFTER THE NOVEL BY LOUIS AUCHINCLOSS) (1966) (IN 5 MOVTS.)
   2,2,2,2 - 4,2,3,1 - timp.,perc.(2) - hp. - str.   25:00 Seesaw.
—— TWIN CONCERTOS (A CONCERTO FOR 2 TRUMPETS AND STRINGS AND A CONCERTO FOR 2 VIOLINS AND BRASS ENSEMBLE)
   0,0,0,0 - 4,3,3,1 - str.   35:00 Composer.

REINBERGER, Jiří
—— CONCERTO NO. 2 IN C MAJOR, FOR ORGAN AND ORCH.
   0,0,0,0 - 2,2,2,0 - timp. - org. - str.   34:00 Bo. Hawkes.

REINER, Karel
—— BUTTERFLIES DO NOT LIVE HERE
   2,2,2,2 - 2,2,2,0 - timp.,perc.,cel. - 2 hp. - str.   14:00 Bo. Hawkes.

REINHARDT, Bruno
—— SCHERZO CAPRICCIOSO
   2,2,2,2 - 2,2,2,1 - perc. - str.   6:00 IsMuPublns.

REINHOLD, Otto
—— CONCERTANTE MUSIC (FOR FLUTE, VIOLA AND ORCH.)
   3,2,2,2 - 2,2,2,0 - timp.,perc. - str.   18:00 Tetra.
—— CONCERTO FOR FLUTE, PIANO AND STRINGS, OP. 111
   fl. - pf. - str.   19:00 G. Schirmer.
—— CONCERTO FOR VIOLIN AND ORCH.
   2,2,2,2 - 2,2,2,1 - perc. - str.   30:00 G. Schirmer.
—— TRIPTYCHON
   2,2,2,2 - 2,2,2,1 - timp.,cymb. - str.   19:00 Tetra.

REINL, Franz
—— BERGLAND (FANTASIE) (IN 5 MOVTS.)
   2,2,2,2 - 4,2,3,0 - perc. - hp. - pf. - str.   20:30 Henmar.
—— DESSERT (BALLET SUITE) (IN 3 MOVTS.)
            10:00 Henmar.
—— MIXTUM COMPOSITUM (MERRY MUSIC FOR ORCH.)
            14:00 Henmar.
—— TWO IMPRESSIONS (JOU-JOU)
   2 hp. - timp. - str.   7:00 Henmar.

REISER, Alois
—— CONCERTO FOR CELLO AND ORCH., OP. 9 (IN 3 MOVTS.)
   2,2,*3,2 - 4,2,3,0 - timp. - str.   35:00 Composer.
—— CONCERTO IN D FOR CELLO AND ORCH., OP. 14 (IN 3 MOVTS.)
   *3,2,*3,2 - 4,2,0,0 - timp.,perc. - hp. - str.   40:00 Composer.
—— EREWHON (SYMPHONIC POEM)
   *3,*3,*3,*3 - 4,3,3,1 - timp.,perc. - hp. - str.   30:00 Composer.
—— PRELUDE TO ACT III OF "GOBI"
   2,2,2,2 - 4,2,3,1 - timp. - hp. - str.   8:00 C. Fischer.
—— SLAVIC RHAPSODY
   *3,*3,*3,*3 - 4,3,3,1 - timp.,perc. - hp. - str.   35:00 Composer.

REISFELD, Bert
—— CALIFORNIA CONCERTO (FOR PIANO AND ORCH.)
2,1,2,1 - 4,3,3,0 - timp.,perc. - pf. - str.   10:00 F. Colombo.

REIZENSTEIN, Franz
—— ANNA KRAUS, OP. 30 (1-ACT RADIO OPERA)
2,2,2,2 - 4,2,3,0 - timp.,perc.,cel. - hp. - org. - pf. - str.
63:00 P.R.S.
—— BALLET SUITE
P.R.S.
—— BALLET SUITE, OP. 15 (IN 8 MOVTS.)
2,2,2,2 - 4,3,3,0 - timp.,perc. - hp. - pf. - str.   18:00 Galaxy.
—— CONCERTO FOR PIANO AND ORCH., OP. 16
27:00 Lengnick.
—— CONCERTO FOR STRING ORCHESTRA
G. Schirmer.
—— CONCERTO IN G FOR CELLO AND ORCH., OP. 8
30:00 Lengnick.
—— CONCERTO IN G FOR VIOLIN AND ORCH., OP. 31
2,2,2,2 - 4,3,3,0 - timp.,perc. - hp. - str.   30:00 Lengnick.
—— CONCERTO NO. 2 FOR PIANO AND ORCH.
*3,2,2,2 - 4,2,3,1 - timp.,perc. - pf. - str.   26:00 Lengnick.
—— CYRANO DE BERGERAC (OVERTURE)
12:00 Lengnick.
—— GENESIS, OP. 35 (ORATORIO) (FOR SOPRANO, BARITONE, MIXED CHORUS AND ORCH.)
3,2,3,2 - 4,3,3,1 - timp.,perc. - org. - str.   58:00 Lengnick.
—— PROLOGUE, VARIATIONS AND FINALE, OP. 12A (DANSE FANTASQUE) (FOR VIOLIN AND ORCH.)
3,2,2,2 - 3,2,3,1 - timp.,perc. - hp. - str.   26:00 Bo. Hawkes.
—— SERENADE FOR WIND ENSEMBLE AND DOUBLE BASS, OP. 29
1,2,2,2 - 2,0,0,0 - d.-b.   25:00 Bo. Hawkes.
—— SERENADE IN F, OP. 29A
1,2,2,2 - 2,0,0,0 - timp. - str.   27:00 Bo Hawkes.
—— VOICES OF NIGHT, OP. 27 (CANTATA) (FOR SOPRANO, BARITONE, MIXED CHORUS AND ORCH.)
3,3,3,3 - 4,3,3,1 - timp.,perc.,cel. - hp. - pf. - str.   57:00 Novello.

RENIÉ, Henriette
—— CONCERTO IN C MINOR FOR HARP AND ORCH.
2,2,2,2 - 2 hn. - timp. - str.   25:00 Baron.
—— DEUX PIÈCES SYMPHONIQUES (FOR HARP AND ORCH.)
2,2,2,2 - 4,2,0,0 - timp.,perc. - hp. - str.   16:00 Baron.

RETTICH, William
—— SUITE IN OLD STYLE, OP. 40A (FOR CELLO AND ORCH.)
Novello.
—— SUITE IN OLD STYLE, OP. 40B (FOR VIOLIN AND ORCH.)
Novello.

REULAND, Jacques
—— CONCERTINO (1966)
2 cl. - timp. - hp. - str.   12:00 Henmar.
—— EXPRESSIES (1966)
25:00 Henmar.
—— HYMNI MEDIAVALES (FOR 2 SOLO VOICES, MIXED CHORUS AND ORCH.) (1966) (Text: St. Ambrosius)
25:00 Henmar.

REUTER, Fritz
—— CONCERTO FOR HARPSICHORD, STRINGS AND TIMPANI
timp. - hpsc. - str.   26:00 Tetra.
—— CONCERTO FOR VIOLIN AND ORCH.
2,2,2,2 - 2,2,2,0 - timp. - str.   35:00 Tetra.
—— DAGHESTANISCHE SUITE, OP. 17
3,2,3,3 - 4,2,3,1 - timp.,perc. - hp. - str.   19:00 Ries-Erler.
—— THE RABBIT AND THE HEDGEHOG (A FAIRY-TALE, AFTER THE BROTHERS GRIMM) (FOR NARRATOR AND ORCH.)
2,2,2,2 - 4,2,1,0 - timp.,perc. - pf. - str.   Tetra.

REVEL, Pierre
—— FIVE PIECES FOR FLUTE AND ORCH.
2,2,2,2 - 2,2,0,0 - timp.,perc.,cel. - hp. - str.   12:00 EV.

REVUELTAS, Silvestre
—— ALCANCIAS ("PENNY BANKS")
1,1,2,0 - 1,2,1,0 - timp.,perc. - str.   Southern.
—— CAMINOS ("PATHS")
3,3,4,4 - 4,4,3,1 - timp. - str.   Southern.

—— CINCO CANCIONES DE NIÑOS (FOR VOICE AND ORCH.) (Text: F. García-Lorca)
G. Schirmer.
—— COLORINES
*1,1,E♭cl., 1,1 - 1,1,1,0 - perc.,xyl. - str.   16:00 Southern.
—— LA CORONELA (BALLET FOR ORCHESTRA)
3,3,2,3 - 4,3,3,1 - timp.,perc. - pf. - str.   43:00 Southern.
—— CUAUHNAHUAC
*3,*3,E♭cl.,*3,3 - 4,4,3,1 - timp.,perc.(6),xyl. - str.   11:00 G. Schirmer.
—— DANZA GEOMETRICA (PLANOS)
3,0,5,*3 - 4,4,3,1 - timp.,perc. - 2 pf. - str.   9:00 Southern.
—— DOS PROFANAS (FOR VOICE AND ORCH.) (Text: F. García-Lorca)
G. Schirmer.
—— ESQUINAS
*3,*3,*3,*3, - 4,4,3,1 - timp.,perc.,xyl. - str.   12:00 Southern.
—— HOMENAJE À FEDERICO GARCÍA-LORCA
picc.,e♭cl. - 2 C tpt.,trb.,tu. - tomtom,xyl. - pf. - 2 vln.,d.-b.   13:00 Southern.
—— HORA DE JUNIO (JUNE HOUR) (FOR NARRATOR AND ORCH.)
0,1,3,1 - 2,2,1,1 - perc. - pf. - str.   13:00 Southern.
—— ITINERARIOS ("ITINERARIES")
2,3,3,bar. sax.,1 - 2,3,3,1 - timp.,perc. - hp. - pf. - str.   Southern.
—— JANITZIO
*3,2,2,2 - 4,2,2,1 - perc. - str.   15:00 Southern.
—— MUSICA PARA CHARLAR
1,0,1,1 - 1,2,1,1 - timp.,perc.(2),xyl. - str.   30:00 Southern.
—— NO SÉ FOR QUIEN PIENSES TÚ (FOR VOICE AND CHAMBER ORCH.)
0,0,3,1 - 0,2,1,0 - perc. - 2 vln.,1 d.-b.   Southern.
—— LA NOCHE DE LOS MAYAS ("THE NIGHT OF THE MAYAS") (SUITE FOR SMALL ORCH.) (IN 2 MOVTS.)
2,1,2,1 - 4,1,1,1 - perc. - str.   10:00 Southern.
—— LA NOCHE DE LOS MAYAS("THE NIGHT OF THE MAYAS") (SUITE FOR LARGE ORCH.) (IN 4 MOVTS.)
2,2,3,2 - 4,3,2,1 - timp.,perc.(14) - pf. - str.   35:00 Southern.
—— PAISAJES (LANDSCAPES)
1,0,1,1 - 1,2,1,1 - timp.,perc. - pf. - str.   20:00 Southern.
—— PARIAN (FOR SOPRANO, MIXED CHORUS AND SMALL ORCH.)
1,2,2,0 - 1,2,1,0 - timp.,perc. - str.   15:00 Southern.
—— EL RANACUAJO PASEADOR
*1,0,E♭cl.,1,0 - 0,2,1,0 - perc.(4) - str.(vlns. ad lib., d.-b.)   10:00 G. Schirmer.
—— REDES (WAVES)
2,1,1,1 - 2,2,1,1 - timp.,perc. - str.   18:00 Southern.
—— SENSEMAYA
2 picc.2,*3,E♭cl.,*3,*4 - 4,4,3,1 - timp.,perc.,glock. - pf. - str.   7:00 G. Schirmer.
—— SEVEN CHILDREN'S PIECES (FOR VOICE AND ORCH.)
1,2,0,1 - 1,2,1,1 - timp.,perc. - str.   10:00 Southern.
—— TRES SONETOS (THREE SONNETS)
0,0,3,1 - 1,2,0,1 - perc. - pf.   Southern.
—— TROKA
1,1,2,1 - 1,2,1,1 - timp.,perc. - str.   Southern.
—— VENTANAS ("WINDOWS")
3,3,1,2 - 4,4,3,1 - timp.,perc. - str.   Southern.

REVUTZKY, Lev N.
—— SYMPHONY NO. 2, OP. 12
3,3,3,2 - 4,2,2,1 - timp.,perc. - hp. - str.   G. Schirmer.

REYNOLDS, Alfred
—— OVERTURE FOR A COMEDY
2,2,2,2 - 2,2,3,1 - timp.,perc. - hp. - str.   3:45 P.R.S.

REYNOLDS, Verne
—— ANNIVERSARY FANFARE
7:00 Composer.
—— VENTURES FOR ORCHESTRA (1975)
Composer.

ŘEZÁČ, Ivan
—— OVERTURE TO MAJASKOVSKY'S POEM "THE JUST CAUSE"
3,2,3,2 - 4,3,3,1 - timp.,perc. - pf. - str.   6:00 Bo. Hawkes.
—— SYMPHONY
3,3,3,3 - 4,3,3,1 - timp.,perc.,cel. - str.   30:00 Bo. Hawkes.

REZNÍČEK, Emil Nikolaus von
—— THE GOLDEN CALF (BALLET) % (1935)
3,3,3,3 - 4,3,3,1 - timp.,perc. - str.   Mannheimer.

—— DER GONDOLIERE DES DOGEN (1-ACT OPERA) % (1931)
(Text: Paul Knudsen)
50:00 Henmar.
—— RASKOLNIKOFF (OVERTURE-FANTASY) (1931)
3,3,3,3 - 4,3,3,1 - timp.,perc.,cel. - hp. - str.   23:10 Henmar.

RHENÉ-BATON
—— FANTAISIE ORIENTALE (FOR VIOLIN AND ORCH.)
2,2,2,2 - 4,1,0,0 - timp.,perc.(3),cel. - hp. - str.   10:00 EV.
—— POÈME ÉLÉGIAQUE (FOR CELLO AND ORCH.)
2,2,2,2 - 4,2,3,1 - perc.,glock. - hp. - str.   9:00 EV.
—— POUR LES FUNÉRAILLES D'UN MARIN BRETON
3,2,2,2 - 4,4,3,1 - timp.,perc.(3) - str.   8:00 EV.

RHYS-HERBERT, W.
—— BETHLEHEM (CANTATA) (FOR CHORUS AND ORCH.)
1,1,2,1 - 2,2,1,0 - hp. - str.   Belw-Mills.
—— THE CHRIST-CHILD (CANTATA) (FOR CHORUS, HARP AND STRINGS)
hp. - str.   Belw-Mills.
—— THE NAZARENE (CANTATA) (FOR CHORUS AND ORCH.)
1,1,2,1 - 2,2,1,0 - timp. - str.   Belw-Mills.

RIBÁRI, Antal
—— CLOWN (CANTATA) (FOR TENOR AND CHAMBER ORCH.)
*2,1,1,0 - 1,2,0,0 - timp.,perc. - str.   8:00 General.
—— LA COLOMBE POIGNARDÉE ET LE JET D'EAU
1(alt. with picc.),1,1,1 - 1,1,0,0 - timp.,perc.(9, incl. 4 on timp.) - hp. - 2 pf. - str.   8:00 General.
—— CONCERTO FOR VIOLIN AND ORCH.
*2,1,1,1 - 1,1,1,0 - perc.,cel.,mar.,vibra.,xyl. - pf. - str.(1,0,10,8)   12:00 General.
—— DIALOGUES FOR VIOLA AND ORCH.
3,1,*3,3 - 1,0,0,0 - timp.,perc.,cel. - hp. - pf. - str.   10:00 General.
—— HELLAS (SUITE) (FOR ALTO, TENOR, SATB CHORUS AND ORCH.)
*2,1,1,1 - 2,2,0,0 - timp.,perc. - hp. - pf. - str.   11:00 General.
—— METAMORPHOSES (FOR VOICE AND CHAMBER ENSEMBLE)
1(alt. with picc.),0,1,1 - 0,0,0,0 - perc.,vibra. - pf. - str.   9:00 General.
—— MUSIC FOR STRINGS
str.   10:00 Bo. Hawkes.
—— PANTOMIME
*3,2,2,2 - 4,3,3,0 - timp.,perc.(5, incl. 4 on timp.),cel. - hp. - str.   9:45 General.
—— SYMPHONY NO. 3
3(3rd alt. with picc.),3,3,3 - 4,4,4(4th alt. with tu.),0 - timp. - str.   11:00 General.

RICCARDI, Joseph
—— CONCERTO FOR PIANO AND STRING ORCH. (1966) (IN 3 MOVTS.)
pf. - str.   20:42 Composer.

RICCIOTTI, Carlo - HINNENTHAL, Joh. Phil.
—— CONCERTINO NO. 2 IN G MAJOR (FOR STRING ORCH.)
(Sometimes attributed to Pergolesi)
cemb. - str.   7:00 Baerenrtr.

RICCI-SIGNORINI, Antonio
—— GLI AMORI PASTORALI DATNI E CLOE
2,3,2,4 - 4,4,3,1 - timp.,perc. - 2 hp. - str.   15:00 Bo. Hawkes.
—— BALLATA E DANZA
3,2,2,2 - 4,2,3,0 - timp.,perc. - hp. - str.   9:00 Bo. Hawkes.
—— LA CACCIA DI VERUCCHIO
*4,*3,*3,*4 - 6,4,4,1 - timp.,perc. - 2 hp. - str.   25:00 Bo. Hawkes.
—— CANZONE D'ESTATE DAL TRITTICI (FOR VIOLIN AND ORCH.)
2,2,2,2 - 0,2,0,0 - timp.,perc. - hp. - str.   8:00 Bo. Hawkes.
—— FANTASIA BURLESCA
1,1,1,1 - 2,0,0,0 - perc. - 2 pf. - str.   8:00 Bo. Hawkes.
—— FINALE FARESCO
3,2,2,sax.,2 - 4,2,3,1 - timp.,perc.,xyl. - hp. - str.   6:00 Bo. Hawkes.
—— OUVERTURE GIOCOSA
3,2,2,2 - 4,3,3,1 - timp.,perc. - str.   7:00 Bo. Hawkes.
—— PAPIOL
4,2,2,3 - 4,3,3,1 - timp.,perc. - str.   Bo. Hawkes.
—— POEMA DEL DOLORE (FOR MEZZO-SOPRANO AND ORCH.)
0,1,1,1 - 0,0,0,0 - timp.,perc.,cel. - hp. - str.   10:00 Bo. Hawkes.

—— SUITE NO. 1 (IN 3 MOVTS.)
3,2,2,3 - 4,2,3,1 - timp. - str.   14:00 Bo. Hawkes.
—— SUITE NO. 2 (IN 3 MOVTS.)
*4,2,2,3 - 4,2,3,1 - timp. - hp. - str.   15:00 Bo. Hawkes.

RICE, Thomas
—— CONCERTO FOR TIMPANI AND ORCH.
1,1,1,1 - 1,1,1,1 - timp. - str.   15:00 Seesaw.
—— CONCERTO FOR VIOLIN AND STRING ORCH., OP. 32
str.   10:00 Seesaw.
—— LA CORONA
1,0,1,0 - 0,0,1,0 - perc. - hpsc. - str.   37:00 Seesaw.
—— OVERTURE (1970)
1,1,1,1 - 1,1,1,0 - timp. - pf. - str.   10:00 Seesaw.

RICHARDSON, Darrell E.
—— CAROLINA REGINA (SUITE) (1969) (IN 3 MOVTS.)
2,2,2,2 - 4,3,3,1 - timp.,perc.(2) - hp. - str.   17:11 Composer.
—— SING A NEW SONG OF LOVE (FOR DOUBLE MIXED CHORUS AND ORCH.) (1969) (Text: Biblical)
1,1,1,1 - 1,0,0,0 - pf. - str.   4:10 Composer.
—— SYMPHONY NO. 1, IN D MINOR (1965) (IN 4 MOVTS.)
2,2,2,2 - 4,3,3,1 - timp.,perc.(2),bells - hp. - str.   32:35 Composer.
—— VARIATIONS ON A FOUR-TONE MELODY (1967)
1,1,*2,0 - 1,0,0,0 - timp. - str.   7:22 Composer.

RICHARDSON, Sharon
—— SERENADE FOR VIOLA AND ORCH.
3(1 alt. with picc.),2,*3,2 - 4,3,3,1 - timp.,perc.(6),cel.,glock.,xyl. - hp. - str.   9:00 Composer.

RICHENS, James W.
—— ESCAPE TO MORNING (BALLET) (1971) %
2(2nd alt.with picc.),1,2(2nd alt.with b.-cl.),1 - 2,2,2,0 - timp.,perc.(2),bells,cel.,glock.,xyl. - hp. - pf. - str.   25:00 Composer.
—— WINTERSET (RHAPSODY FOR ENGLISH HORN AND STRINGS (1960)
Eng.hn. - str.   6:00 Composer.

RICHEPIN, Eliane
—— FANTAISIE (FOR PIANO AND ORCH.)
3,3,2,2 - 4,2,3,1 - timp.,perc.,cel. - hp. - str.   12:00 Salabert.

RICHTER, Franz Xaver - BODART, Eugen
—— SYMPHONY IN B FLAT MAJOR
str.   11:00 Mannheimer.
—— SYMPHONY IN C MAJOR
str.   16:00 Mannheimer.
—— SYMPHONY IN D MAJOR
str.   9:00 Mannheimer.
—— SYMPHONY IN E MAJOR
str.   14:00 Mannheimer.
—— SYMPHONY IN G MAJOR
str.   11:00 Mannheimer.
—— SYMPHONY IN G MINOR (WITH FUGUE)
0,2,0,0 - 2,0,0,0 - str.   14:00 Mannheimer.

RICHTER, Franz Xaver - HOECKNER
—— CONCERTO IN E MINOR
cemb. - str.   Henmar.

RICHTER, Franz Xaver - LENZEWSKI
—— SINFONIA IN G MAJOR FOR STRING ORCH.
str.   Henmar.

RICHTER, Franz Xaver - SCHROEDER, Felix
—— SYMPHONY IN D MAJOR (THE TRUMPET SYMPHONY)
tpt. - timp. - cemb. - str.   13:15 Mannheimer.

RICHTER, Marga
—— ABYSS (BALLET) % (1965) (IN 3 MOVTS.)
2(2nd alt. with picc.),1,2,1 - 2-4,1,1,0 - timp.,perc.(2),xyl. - pf. - str.   20:00 Mills.
—— ARIA AND TOCCATA (FOR VIOLA AND STRINGS)
str.   9:00 Mills.
—— BLACKBERRY VINES AND WINTER FRUIT
3,2,2,2 - 4,3,2,1 - timp.,perc.,cel. - hp. - str.   13:00 C. Fischer.
—— CONCERTO FOR PIANO, VIOLAS, CELLOS AND BASSES
pf. - str. (no. vlns.)   20:00 Belw-Mills.
—— EIGHT PIECES FOR ORCH.
*3,*3,*3,*3 - 4,3,3,1 - timp.,perc.(2),cel. - hp. - pf. - str.   6:30 C. Fischer.

—— FRAGMENTS (FIVE PIECES FOR ORCH.)
2,2,2,2 - 2,1,1,1 - timp.,perc.,cel. - hp. - str.   6:30 C. Fischer.
—— LAMENT (FOR STRINGS)
str.   11:00 Broude.
—— LANDSCAPES OF THE MIND I (CONCERTO FOR PIANO AND ORCH.) (1974)
3(3rd alt. with picc.),*3,*3,*3, - 4,4,0,0 - timp.,perc.(2-3),bells,cel.,mar.,vibra. - electric guit.,elec.b.-guit.,elec tamboura(or sitar) - hp. - pf. - str.   29:30 C. Fischer.
—— THE SERVANT (OR: THE TOWER) (BALLET) % (1967)
2(2nd alt.with picc.),1,2,1 - 2,1,1,0 - timp.,perc.(2),cel.,xyl. - hp. - pf. - str. or   27:00 C. Fischer.
2(2nd alt. with picc.),2(2nd alt. with Eng.hn.),2(2nd alt. with b.-cl.),2 - 4,2,2,0 - timp.,perc.(2),cel.,xyl. - hp. - pf. - str.
—— VARIATIONS ON A SARABANDE
2(2nd alt. with picc.),2(2nd alt. with Eng.hn.),2,2 - 4,2,2,1 - timp.,perc.(2),xyl. - hp. - str.   6:00 C. Fischer.

RICHTER, Martin
—— PAGANINI (OUVERTURE)
2,2,2,2 - 4,2,3,0 - perc. - hp. - pf. - str.   12:00 Henmar.

RICHTER, Nico
—— SERENADE (SINFONIETTA NO. 1) (FOR CHAMBER ORCH.)
1,0,1,0 - 0,0,0,0 - guit. - str.   Henmar.

RICKER, Ramon L.
—— GENESIS (FOR JAZZ QUARTET AND ORCH.) (1974) (IN 3 MOVTS.)
*2,1(alt.with Eng.hn.),0,1 sax.(alt.on alto, ten.and bar.),0 -4,4,4,1 - perc.(3) - pf. - str.   30:00 Composer.

ŘÍDKÝ, Jaroslav
—— CONCERTO FOR PIANO AND ORCH., OP. 46 (1952)
3,3,3,2 - 4,3,3,1 - timp.,perc. - hp. - pf. - str.   43:00 Bo. Hawkes.
—— SYMPHONY NO. 7, OP. 47
3,3,3,3 - 6,3,4,1 - timp.,perc. - hp. - str.   48:00 Bo. Hawkes.

RIDOUT, Alan
—— CHRISTMAS ORATORIO (FOR MEZZO-SOPRANO, BARITONE, SATB CHORUS AND ORCH.)
3(3rd alt. with picc.),2,2,2 - 4,2,3,0 - timp.,perc. - str.   45:00 Galaxy.
—— CREATION (FOR CHILDREN'S CHORUS, PIANO AND STRINGS)
perc. - pf. - str.   50:00 Galaxy.
—— THERE'S NEWS, LASSES, NEWS (FOR SA CHORUS AND ORCH.)
2(2nd alt. with picc.),2,2,2 - 2,0,0,0 - timp.,perc. - pf. 4-hands - str.   15:00 Galaxy.

RIDOUT, Godfrey
—— BALLADE (FOR VIOLA AND STRING ORCH.) (1938)
str.   8:30 CanMusCtr.
—— CANTIONES MYSTICAE (FOR SOPRANO AND ORCH.)
2,2,2,2 - 4,3,3,1 - timp. - hp. - str.   16:00 FredHarris.
—— CANTIONES MYSTICAE NO. 3 (THE DREAM OF THE ROOD) (1972) (FOR BARITONE OR TENOR, SATB CHORUS AND ORCH.)
2,2,2,2 - 4,2,3,0 - timp. - org.   22:00 CanMusCtr.
—— COMEDY OVERTURE
6:00 C.A.P.A.C.
—— CONCERTO GROSSO (1974) (FOR VIOLIN, PIANO AND STRINGS) (IN 3 MOVTS.)
pf. - str.   15:00 CanMusCtr.
—— CONSORT, OP. 7 (FOR VIOLIN AND ORCH.)
20:00 C.A.P.A.C.
—— THE DANCE (FOR CHORUS AND ORCH.)
10:00 C.A.P.A.C.
—— DIRGE
7:00 C.A.P.A.C.
—— ESTHER (A DRAMATIC SYMPHONY) (FOR SOPRANO, BARITONE, CHORUS AND ORCH.)
3,3,2,3 - 4,3,3,1 - timp.,perc.(2) - str.   50:00 C.A.P.A.C.
—— FALL FAIR OVERTURE
8:00 CanMusCtr.
—— FESTAL OVERTURE
3,3,3,3 - 4,3,3,1 - timp.,perc.(2) - hp. - str.   6:30 C.A.P.A.C.
—— FOUR SONNETS (FOR MIXED CHORUS AND ORCH.) (1964)
18:00 GVThompson.

—— FRIVOLITÉS CANADIENNES (1973) (BASED ON MELODIES OF JOSEPH VÉZINA)
2(2nd alt. with picc.),2,2,2 - 2,2,3,0 - timp.,perc. - str.   23:00 CanMusCtr.
—— GEORGE THE THIRD, HIS LAMENT (1975) (FIVE VARIATIONS AND FINALE ON A WELL-KNOWN TUNE)
2(2nd alt. with picc.),2(2nd alt. with Eng. hn.),2(2nd alt. with b.-cl.),2 - 2,2,0,0 2 hn.,2 tpt. - timp.,perc. - str. 14:45 CanMusCtr.
—— JUBILEE (1973)
*3,2,2 - *3,2 - 4,3,3,1 - timp.,perc. - str.   10:40 CanMusCtr.
—— MUSIC FOR A YOUNG PRINCE (ORCHESTRAL SUITE) (1959) (IN 4 MOVTS.)
*3,2,2,2 - 4,3,3,1 - timp.,perc. - str.   18:30 CanMusCtr.
—— OVERTURE TO THE BALLET "LA PRIMA BALLERINA" (1967)
2,2,2,2 - 4,3,3,1 - timp.,perc. - str.   5:00 CanMusCtr.
—— LA PRIMA BALLERINA: SUITE NO. 1 (1967)
*3,2,2,2 - 4,3,3,1 - timp.,perc. - hp. - str.   15:25 CanMusCtr.
——*LA PRIMA BALLERINA: SUITE NO. 2 (1967)
*3,2,2,2 - 4,3,3,1 - timp.,perc. - str.   15:00 CanMusCtr.
—— THE ASCENSION (CANTIONES MYSTICAE NO. 2) (FOR SOPRANO, TRUMPET AND STRINGS) (1962)
tpt. - str.   12:00 FredHarris.
—— TWO ETUDES
str.   12:00 Chappell.
—— WHEN AGE AND YOUTH UNITE (1966) (CYCLE OF 3 SONGS) (FOR SATB CHORUS AND ORCH.)
2,1,2,1 - 4,3,3,1 - timp.,perc. - hp. (or pf.) - str.
8:00 GVThompson.

RIEDE, Erich
—— CAPRICCIO FOR PIANO AND ORCH., OP. 19
2,2,2,2 - 2,2,0,0 - timp. - str.   8:30 Alkor.
—— KÖNIG LUSTIK OVERTURE, OP. 11
2,2,2,2 - 4,3,3,1 - timp.,perc. - hp. - str.   7:00 AhnSimrock.
—— SERENADE, OP. 21 (FOR HARP AND STRING ORCH.)
hp. - str.   16:00 AhnSimrock.
—— VARIATIONS AND FUGUE ON A BAROQUE THEME, OP. 25
3(3rd alt. with picc.),2,2,2 - 4,3,3,1 - timp.,perc.,cel. - hp. - str.
28:00 AhnSimrock.

RIEDEL, Georg
—— AD LIBITUM I (FOR ORCH., WITH JAZZ COMBO)
2,2,2,2 - 2,2,1,0 - perc.(2) - str.   5:00 Fleisher.
—— BAXNINGSVISA (FOR STRINGS, WITH JAZZ GROUP)(1970)
str.   6:00 Fleisher.
—— FEM BERÄTTELSER FÖR BARN (FOR JAZZ GROUP AND SYMPHONY ORCH.)(1973)
2,2,2,2 - 4,3,3,1 - perc.(2) - str.   25:00 Fleisher.
—— INTERMITTANT MEDITATION ON MARTIN LUTHER KING (FOR SOPRANO, SATB CHORUS, JAZZ GROUP AND SYMPHONY ORCH.)(1972)
25:00 Fleisher.
—— INTRADA (FOR WINDS AND JAZZ GROUP)(1972)
2,2,2,2 - 4,3,3,1 - timp.,perc.   6:00 Fleisher.
—— SACRIFICIAL DANCE (OFFERDANS)(FOR ORCH. WITH JAZZ COMBO)(1969)
2,2,2,2 - 2,2,1,0 - perc. - str.   7:00 Fleisher.
—— SUMMER NIGHT MUSIC (FOR ORCH. WITH JAZZ COMBO)(1969)
2,2,2,2 - 2,3,1,0 - perc. - str.   12:00 Fleisher.
—— THREE DANCES (FOR ORCH., WITH JAZZ COMBO)(1966)
2,2,2,2 - 3,2,1,0 - str.   17:00 Fleisher.

RIEDT, Friedrich Wilhelm - LELOIR, E.
—— CONCERTO FOR HORN AND STRINGS
hn. - str.   5:00 Presser.

RIEGE, Ernst
—— BURLESQUE
2(2nd alt. with picc.),2,3,2-*3 - 4,3,3,0-1 - timp.,perc.,cel.(ad lib.) - str.   10:00 Henmar.
—— THE COLD HEART (FANTASY-OVERTURE, AFTER WILHELM HAUFF)
2,2,2,2 - 4,2,3,1 - timp.,perc.,xyl. - hp. - str. 18:00 F. Colombo.
—— CONCERTO IN D MINOR, FOR CELLO AND ORCH.
2,2,2,2 - 2,2,0,0 - timp.,perc. - hp. - str. 30:00 F. Colombo.
—— DIVERTIMENTO FOR ORCH. (IN 4 MOVTS.)
1,1,1,1 - 4,2,3,0 - timp.,perc.,cel.,xyl. - hp. - str.
35:00 F. Colombo.
—— FANTASTIC OVERTURE
3,3,3,3 - 4,3,3,1 - timp.,perc.,cel. - hp. - str. 19:00 F. Colombo.

—— MUCH ADO ABOUT NOTHING (AN OVERTURE)
2,3,3,2 - 4,2,3,0 - timp.,perc.,cel. - hp. - str.   14:00 F. Colombo.
—— NOCTURNE FOR CELLO AND SMALL ORCH.
1,1,2,1 - 2,0,0,0 - hp. - str.   7:00 F. Colombo.
—— NOSTALGIA (LEGEND FOR ORCH.)
2,1,2,2 - 2,0,0,0 - perc.,cel. - hp. - str.   8:00 F. Colombo.
—— RHEINSBERGER FESTIVAL MUSIC
1,1,2,1 - 2,2,0,0 - timp.,perc. - str.   12:00 F. Colombo.
—— RONDO GIOCOSO
2,2,2,2 - 2,2,0,0 - timp.,perc.,glock.,xyl. - str.   12:00 F. Colombo.
—— SCHERZO IN E MAJOR
2,2,2,2 - 4,2,3,1 - timp.,perc.,xyl. - hp. - str.   12:00 F. Colombo.
—— SERENADE (IN 5 MOVTS.)
2,2,2,2 - 2,2,0,0 - timp.,perc.,xyl. - hp. - str.   28:00 F. Colombo.
—— SUITE IN B MAJOR (IN 5 MOVTS.)
1,1,2,1 - 2,2,0,0 - timp.,perc.,cel.,glock.,xyl. - hp. - str.
43:00 F. Colombo.
—— VARIATIONS OF AN OLD FOLKSONG
3,3,2,3 - 4,3,3,1 - timp.,perc.,xyl. - str.   27:00 F. Colombo.

RIEGGER, Wallingford
—— IN MEMORIAM
*3,*3,E^{b}cl.,*3,2 - 4,3,3,1 - timp.,perc. - str.   6:00 Leeds.

RIESMAN, Michael
—— CHAMBER CONCERTO
1(alt. with picc.),1,1,1 - 1,0,0,0 - perc. - pf. - str.(2,1,1,1)
G. Schirmer.

RIETHMÜLLER, Helmut
—— CONCERTO FOR PIANO AND ORCH., OP. 34
2,2,2,2 - 4,3,3,0 - timp.,perc. - pf. - str.   23:00 F. Colombo.
—— KINDERLAND SUITE, OP. 50
1,1,1,1 - 2,1,1,0 - timp.,perc. - hp. - str.   12:00 F. Colombo.
—— SINFONIETTA SERENA, OP. 47
2,2,2,2 - 4,3,3,1 - timp.,perc. - str.   12:00 F. Colombo.

RIETI, Vittorio
—— THE CLOCK (OPERA) %
2,2,2,2 - 4,3,3,0 - timp.,perc.,cel. - hp. - str.   90:00 General.
—— CONCERTO FOR CELLO AND 12 INSTRUMENTS
1,1,2,2 - 2,1,0,0 - timp.,perc. - c.,d.-b.   9:00 General.
—— CONCERTO FOR HARPSICHORD AND ORCHESTRA
1,1,1,1 - 0,0,0,0 - hpsc. - pf. - str.   16:00 General.
—— CONCERTO FOR TWO PIANOS AND ORCH.
3,2,2,2 - 4,3,3,1 - timp.,perc. - 2 pf. - str.   20:00 General.
—— CONCERTO FOR VIOLIN AND ORCH.
(2nd alt. with picc.),2,2,2 - 2,2,2,0 - timp.,perc. - str.
21:00 General.
—— CONCERTO NO. 2 FOR CELLO AND ORCH.
2,2,2,2 - 4,2,3,1 - timp.,perc. - str.   15:00 Belw.-Mills.
—— CONCERTO NO. 2 FOR PIANO AND ORCH.
2,2,2,2 - 2,3,2,0 - timp.,perc. - pf. - str.   25:00 General.
—— CONCERTO NO. 3 FOR PIANO AND SMALL ORCH.
3,2,2,2 - 4,3,3,1 - timp.,perc. - pf. - str.   18:00 Belw.-Mills.
—— CONCERTO TRIPLO (TRIPLE CONCERTO) (FOR VIOLIN,
VIOLA, PIANO AND ORCH.)
2(2nd alt. with picc.),2,2,2 - 2,2,2,0 - pf. - str.   20:00 General.
—— FIVE FABLES FROM LA FONTAINE (SUITE)
2,1,2,1 - 2,2,2,0 - timp.,perc. - hp. - str.   21:10 General.
—— MADRIGAL EN QUATRE PARTIES (FOR 12
INSTRUMENTS)(1927)
1,1,1,1 - 1,1,0,0 - pf. - str.(2,1,1,1)   15:00 Salabert.
—— MARYAM THE HARLOT (OPERA) %
2,2,2,2 - 2,2,1,0 - timp.,perc.,cel. - pf. - str.   60:00 General.
—— NOCTURNE (FOR STRINGS) (FROM QUARTET NO. 1)
str.   7:00 Salabert.
—— PARTITA
fl.,ob. - cemb. - str.   22:00 Broude.
—— THE PET SHOP (A MUSICAL FARCE) %
1(alt. with picc.),1,1,0 - 1,1,1,0 - perc. - pf. - str.   35:00 General.
—— SCENES FOR A BALLET
*3,2,2,2 - 4,3,3,1 - timp.,perc. - str.   20:00 General.
—— SERENATA FOR VIOLIN AND CHAMBER ORCH.
1,1,1,2 - tpt. - str.   5:00 Salabert.
—— SETTE LIRICHE SAFFICHE (SEVEN SAPPHIC LYRICS) (FOR
VOICE AND CHAMBER ORCH.)
2,0,2,2 - 0,1,0,0 - hp. - pf. - str.   8:00 General.
—— SINFONIA NO. 6
*3,2,(2nd alt. with Eng.hn.),2,2 - 4,2,3,1 - timp.,perc. - str.
25:00 General.
—— SINFONIETTA
1,1,1,2 - 2,2,2,0 - timp.,perc.(2) - str.   15:00 General.

—— TRIONFO DI BACCO E ARIANNA (FOR SABT CHORUS
AND ORCH.)
2,2,2,2 - 4,2,3,0 - timp.,perc. - str.   25:00 General.

RIETZ, Johannes
—— CONCERTINO IN D FOR OBOE AND STRING ORCH.
ob. - str.   13:00 Mannheimer.
—— CONCERTO FOR ENGLISH HORN, HARP AND STRINGS
Eng.hn. - hp. - str.   20:00 Seesaw.
—— DIVERTIMENTO FOR STRING ORCH.
str.   17:00 Mannheimer.
—— TOCCATA
2,2,2,2 - 4,2,3,1 - timp. - str.   4:25 Seesaw.

RIGACCI, Bruno
—— SCIOFAR (MELODRAMATIC POEM IN 3 PARTS FOR VOICE,
NARRATOR, PIANO AND ORCH.) (Text: Angelo Orvieto)
3,2,2,2 - 4,3,3,1 - timp.,perc. - hp. - pf. - str.   18:00 Bo. Hawkes.

RIGEL, Henri-Joseph - BODART, Eugen
—— SYMPHONY IN D MAJOR
0,2,0,0 - 2,2,0,0 - timp. - str.   13:00 Mannheimer.

RIGEL, Henri-Joseph - BROOK, Barry S.
—— SYMPHONIE IN D MINOR, OP. 21, NO. 2
0,2,0,0 - 2,0,0,0 - str.   FrankMusCp.

RIISAGER, Knudåge
—— AANDELIGT SIUNGEKOR (ON A THEME BY KINGO)
str.   10:00 K.O.D.A.
—— ARCHAEOPTERYX, OP. 51
3,3,2,3 - 4,3,3,0 - perc.,xyl. - hp. - str.   11:00 Henmar.
—— ARLEQUINADE (SUITE)
1,1,0,1 - 0,0,0,0 - str.   11:00 Henmar.
—— BASTA (EPILOGO FESTIVO PER ORCH.)
5:00 K.O.D.A.
—— BOLD PRELUDE (OVERTURE)
5:00 K.O.D.A.
—— BURLESQUE OVERTURE, OP. 60
4:00 K.O.D.A.
—— COMEDY OVERTURE, OP. 21
6:00 K.O.D.A.
—— COMEDY OVERTURE, OP. 27
5:00 K.O.D.A.
—— CONCERTINO FOR TRUMPET AND STRINGS, OP. 29
tpt. - str.   G. Schirmer.
—— CONCERTO FOR ORCH., OP. 24
18:00 K.O.D.A.
—— CONCERTO FOR VIOLIN AND ORCH., OP. 54
30:00 K.O.D.A.
—— DARDUSE (SUITE)
3,2,2,3 - 4,3,3,1 - perc.(7) - hp. - str.   Henmar.
—— ERASMUS MONTANUS, OP. 1 (OVERTURE)
3,2,2,2 - 4,3,3,0 - timp. - str.   10:00 G. Schirmer.
—— ETUDES (BALLET) %
3,3,3,3 - 4,3,3,1 - timp.,perc.,cel. - hp. - pf. - str.   Bo. Hawkes.
—— FOOL'S PARADISE: BALLET SUITE NO. 1, OP. 33
3,2,2,3 - 4,3,3,1 - timp.,perc.,cel. - str.   15:00 G. Schirmer.
—— FOOL'S PARADISE: BALLET SUITE NO. 2, OP. 33
3,2,2,2 - 4,3,3,1 - timp.,perc. - str.   12:00 G. Schirmer.
—— FOR THE CHILDREN'S PARTY (SUITE FROM DANISH
NURSERY RHYMES)
2,2,2,2 - 2,2,1,0 - timp.,perc. - str.   11:30 G. Schirmer.
—— FREDERIK II IN THE DITMARSHES, OP. 39 (VARIATIONS
FOR ORCH.)
K.O.D.A.
—— I ANLEDNING AF..... (CHILDREN'S POEMS FOR ORCH.)
14:00 G. Schirmer.
—— INTRODUZIONE DI TRAVERSO, OP. 10 (AN OVERTURE)
10:00 K.O.D.A.
—— KLODS HANS, OP. 18 (SYMPHONIC PICTURE)
8:00 K.O.D.A.
—— DEN KRØLLEDE FRITS, OP. 43 (A DANISH OVERTURE)
5:00 K.O.D.A.
—— THE LADY FROM THE SEA (BALLET) %
3,3,3,3 - 4,3,3,1 - timp.,perc.,cel. - hp. - pf. - str.   Bo. Hawkes.
—— LAND OF CHILDREN (SUITE FOR SMALL ORCH.)
15:00 K.O.D.A.
—— LITTLE OVERTURE (FOR STRINGS)
str.   5:00 G. Schirmer.
—— MANERENEN (BALLET) %
3,3,3,3 - 4,3,3,1 - timp.,perc.,cel. - hp. - pf. - str.   Henmar.

—— THE MOON REINDEER (BALLET) %
    3,3,3,3 - 4,3,3,1 - timp.,perc.,cel. - hp. - pf. - str.   Bo. Hawkes.
—— PARTITA, OP. 35
    3,2,3,3 - 4,3,3,0 - timp.,perc. - str.   9:00 G. Schirmer.
—— PRIMAVERA, OP. 31 (CONCERT OVERTURE)
    3,2,2,2 - 4,2,3,0 - perc.(4) - str.   Henmar.
—— PRO FISTULIS ET FIDIBUS, OP. 56
    3,2,2,2 - 0,0,0,0 - str.   15:00 Henmar.
—— QUARRTSILUNI ("THE SILENCE OF WAITING FOR
    SOMETHING TO BURST"), OP. 36
    3,2,2,2 - 4,3,3,1 - timp.,perc. - hp. - str.   9:00 G. Schirmer.
—— RONDO GIOCOSO (FOR VIOLIN AND ORCH.)
    2,1,2,1 - 2,2,1,0 - perc. - str.   Henmar.
—— SHROVETIDE, OP. 20 (OVERTURE)
    2,2,2,2 - 4,3,3,1 - timp.,perc. - str.   8:30 G. Schirmer.
—— SINFONIA CONCERTANTE, OP. 34
    str.   14:00 K.O.D.A.
—— SINFONIETTA, OP. 46
    2,1,2,1 - 2,2,1,0 - timp.,perc. - str.   15:00 Bo. Hawkes.
—— SIX DANCES FROM THE BALLET "TWELVE BY THE MAIL,"
    OP. 37
    3,2,2,2 - 4,3,3,1 - timp.,perc. - str.   10:30 G. Schirmer.
—— SPIL OP (OVERTURE)
    K.O.D.A.
—— SUITE DIONYSIAQUE, OP. 6
    17:00 K.O.D.A.
—— SUMMER RHAPSODY
    3,2,2,2 - 4,3,3,0 - timp.,perc. - str.   12:00 G. Schirmer.
—— SYMPHONIC SKETCHES (FOR CHAMBER ORCH.)
    K.O.D.A.
—— SYMPHONY NO. 1, OP. 8
    25:00 K.O.D.A.
—— SYMPHONY NO. 2, OP. 14
    18:00 K.O.D.A.
—— SYMPHONY NO. 3, OP. 30
    19:00 K.O.D.A.
—— SYMPHONY NO. 4, OP. 38 (SINFONIA GAIA)
    20:00 K.O.D.A.
—— SYMPHONY NO. 5, OP. 52 (SINFONIA SERENA)
    timp. - str.   15:00 K.O.D.A.
—— T-DOXC, OP. 13 (POÈME MÉCANIQUE)
    7:00 K.O.D.A.
—— THREE DANISH SONGS FROM THE 16TH CENTURY
    3,2,2,3 - 4,3,3,1 - timp.,perc. - str.   8:00 Henmar.
—— TO APOLLO
    10:00 K.O.D.A.
—— TRITTICO
    2,1,1,1 - 1,3,2,0 - timp.,perc. - d.-b.   12:00 K.O.D.A.
—— VARIATIONS ON A SARABANDE OF CHARLES, DUC
    D'ORLEANS, OP. 53
    str.   26:00 K.O.D.A.
—— VARIATIONS ON A THEME OF C. M. BELLMAN, OP. 45
    (BELLMAN-VARIATIONER)
    2,1,2,1 - 2,2,1,0 - timp.,perc. - str.   10:00 Bo. Hawkes.
—— VARIATIONS ON A THEME OF MEZANGEAU, OP. 12
    2,2,2,2 - 4,2,0,0 - timp.,perc. - str.   20:00 G. Schirmer.

RIMMER, Frederick
—— ESSAY FOR TIMPANI AND STRINGS (1969)
    timp. - str.   8:00 P.R.S.

RIMSKY-KORSAKOFF, Nikolai A.
—— MOZART AND SALIERI (OPERA) % (Engl. Text: Patricia
Neway)
    1,1,1,1 - 0,0,3,0 - timp. - pf.   35:00 Bo. Hawkes.

RIMSKY-KORSAKOFF, Nikolai A. - FOSTER, Arnold
—— CHORAL SUITE FROM "SADKO" (FOR CHORUS AND
ORCH.)
    3,3,3,3 - 4,3,3,1 - timp.,perc. - hp. - pf. - str.   35:00 Bo. Hawkes.
    Or
    2,2,2,2 - 2,2,0-3,0-1 - timp.,perc. - hp. - str.

RIMSKY-KORSAKOFF, Nikolai A. - LUBIN, Ernest
—— PARAPHRASES (IN 5 MOVTS.)
    *3,2,2,2(2nd alt. with c.-bn.) - 4,2,3,1 -
    timp.,perc.(2),bells,cel.,glock.,xyl. - hp. - pf. - str.   8:00 Arranger.

RIMSKY-KORSAKOFF, Nikolai A. - RAVEL, Maurice
—— ANTAR: INCIDENTAL MUSIC AND FIRE DANCE (FOR A
STAGE WORK) %
    3,3,3,3 - 4,3,3,1 - timp.,perc. - 2 hp. - str.   Baron.

RIMSKY-KORSAKOFF, Nikolai A. - ROBERTS, Charles J.
—— CAPRICCIO ESPAGNOLE
    C. Fischer.
—— SCHEHERAZADE
    C. Fischer.

RIMSKY-KORSAKOFF, Nikolai A. - SOPKIN, Henry
—— RUSSIAN EASTER OVERTURE
    C. Fischer.

RIMSKY-KORSAKOFF, Nikolai A. - STONE, Gregory
—— GLORY (WITH OPTIONAL CHORUS)
    4:00 WarnerBros.

RIMSKY-KORSAKOFF, Nikolai A. - WOODHOUSE, Charles
—— CAPRICCIO ESPAGNOL, OP. 34
    15:00 Bo. Hawkes.
—— MLADA (SUITE FROM THE OPERA-BALLET)
    2,2,2,2 - 4,2,3,1 - timp.,perc. - hp. - str.   17:00 Bo. Hawkes.

RINGBOM, Nils-Eric
—— FOUR SONGS (FOR MEZZO-SOPRANO AND ORCH.) (1947)
(Text: Gunnar Björling)
    3,2,2,2 - 4,3,3,1 - timp.,perc.,cel. - hp. - str.   9:00 FinnMICtr.
—— LITTLE SUITE (REV. 1946) (IN 3 MOVTS.)
    3,2,2,2 - 3,0,0,0 - timp.,perc. - hp. - str.   8:00 FinnMICtr.
—— SYMPHONY NO. 1 (1939)
    2,2,2,2 - 4,3,3,1 - timp.,perc. - str.   25:00 FinnMICtr.
—— SYMPHONY NO. 2 (1944)
    3,3,3,3 - 4,3,3,1 - timp.,perc. - hp. str.   30:00 FinnMICtr.
—— SYMPHONY NO. 3 (1948)
    3,2,2,2 - 4,3,3,1 - timp.,perc. - str.   23:00 FinnMICtr.
—— SYMPHONY NO. 4 (1962)
    2,2,2,2 - 4,3,3,1 - timp.,perc. - str.   21:00 FinnMICtr.
—— SYMPHONY NO. 5 (1970)
    3,3,3,3 - 4,3,3,1 - timps.,perc.(3) - str.   18:00 FinnMICtr.
—— THE WANDERER (3 SONGS) (FOR SOPRANO AND ORCH.)
(1942) (Text: Liv Tegengren)
    2,2,2,2 - 2,0,0,0 - timp.,perc. - hp. - str.   9:00 FinnMICtr.

RINGGER, Rolf Urs
—— DUE INVENZIONI PER ORCHESTRA (1961)
    1,*2,*2,1 - 1,1,1,0 - cel.,vibra. - hp. - str.   15:00 Modern.
—— ELOGI PER ORCHESTRA (1961)
    1,*2,*2,1 - 1,1,1,0 - vibra. - hp. - str.   8:00 Modern.
—— RITORNELLI PER ORCHESTRA
    1,2(2nd alt. with Eng. hn.),2(2nd alt. with b.-cl.),1 - 1,1,1,0 -
    timp.,cel.,vibra.,xyl. - hp. - str.   12:00 Modern.
—— VIER LIEDER AUF CHINESISCHE TEXTE (FOR SOPRANO
AND SMALL ORCHESTRA) (1960)
    1,0,*1,0 - 0,0,1,0 - cel. - hp. - str.   6:00 Modern.

RINGWALD, Roy
—— THE SONG OF CHRISTMAS (FOR NARRATOR, SOLOISTS,
CHORUS AND ORCH.)
    17:00 Shawnee.

RIOTTE, Philipp Jakob - MICHAELS, Jost
—— CONCERTO IN B FLAT MAJOR FOR CLARINET AND
ORCH., OP. 24
    1,2,0,2 - 2,2,0,0 - timp. - str.   25:00 F. Colombo.

RIPA, Virgilio
—— RAPSODIA ITALICA (FOR PIANO AND ORCH.)
    1,1,1,0 - 0,2,1,0 - timp. - pf. - str.   Leeds.

RISTIĆ, Milan
—— CONCERTO FOR STRINGS
    str.   17:00 MIC,Zagreb.
—— CONCERTO NO. 2 FOR PIANO AND ORCH.
    3,3,3,3 - 4,3,3,1 - timp.,perc.,cel.,xyl. - pf. - str.
    23:00 MIC,Zagreb.
—— FIVE PIECES FOR CHAMBER ORCH.
    2(2nd alt. with picc.),2(2nd alt. with Eng. hn.),2,2 - 2,2,1,0 - timp.
    - str.   15:00 MIC,Zagreb.
—— SYMPHONY NO. 4
    2(2nd alt. with picc.),2,2,2 - 4,3,3,1 - timp. - hp. - str.
    28:00 MIC,Zagreb.
—— SYMPHONY NO. 5
    3,3,3,3 - 4,4,4,0 - timp.,perc. - str.   30:00 MIC,Zagreb.
—— SYMPHONY NO. 6
    3,3,3,3 - 4,3,3,1 - timp.,perc.,xyl. - hp. - pf. - str.
    27:00 MIC,Zagreb.

—— SYMPHONY NO. 7
    3,3,3,3 - 4,3,3,1 - timp.,perc.,cel.,xyl. - hp. - pf. - str.
                   27:00 MIC,Zagreb.
—— SYMPHONY NO. 8
    3,3,3,3 - 4,3,3,1 - timp.,perc.,cel.,xyl. - hp. pf. - str.
                   19:00 MIC,Zagreb.
—— SYMPHONY NO. 9
    3,3,3,3 - 4,3,3,1 - timp.,perc.,cel.,xyl. - hp. - pf. - str.
                   28:55 MIC,Zagreb.

RITCHIE, John A.
—— CONCERTINO FOR CLARINET AND STRING ORCH.
    cl. - str.   15:00 Novello.
—— CONCERTINO FOR PIANO AND STRINGS
    pf. - str.   12:00 A.P.R.A.
—— SUITE FOR STRINGS
    str.   16:00 A.P.R.A.

RITSCHEL, Johannes - BODART, Eugen
—— CONCERTO IN F MAJOR FOR HARPSICHORD AND ORCH.
    0,2,0,0 - 0,0,0,0 - hpsc. - str.   20:00 Mannheimer.

RITTER, Peter - BODART, Eugen
—— ENTR'ACTE
    2,2,0,0 - 2,0,0,0 - str.   3:00 Mannheimer.

RIVIER, Jean
—— ADAGIO FOR STRING ORCH.
    str.   7:00 Salabert.
—— BURLESQUE (FOR VIOLIN AND ORCH.)
    2,2,2,2 - 4,3,3,1 - timp.,perc. - hp. - str.
                   10:00 Salabert.
—— CHANT FUNÈBRE (SYMPHONIC PRELUDE)
    2,3,3,2 - 4,3,3,1 - timp.,perc.,cel. - hp. - str. 7:00 Salabert.
—— CHRISTUS REX (FOR CONTRALTO, MIXED CHORUS AND
    ORCH.) (1966) (Text: Latin)
    3,*2,3,3 - 4,3,3,1 - timp.,perc.,cel.,vibra. - pf. - str. 24:00 Salabert.
—— CINQ MOUVEMENTS BREFS (FIVE SHORT MOVEMENTS)
    (1931) (FOR SMALL ORCH.)
    2,2,2,2 - 2,2,1,0 - timp.,perc.,cel. - hp. - str. 10:00 Salabert.
—— CONCERT BRÈVE (FOR PIANO AND STRINGS)
    pf. - str.   11:00 Presser.
—— CONCERTINO FOR VIOLA AND ORCH.
    1,1,1,1 - 1,1,1,0 - perc.,cel. - hp. - str. 15:00 Salabert.
—— CONCERTO FOR BASSOON AND STRINGS
    bn. - str.   16:00 Salabert.
—— CONCERTO FOR BRASS, TIMPANI AND STRINGS
    0,0,0,0 - 2,2,2,0 - timp.(3) - str.   28:00 Salabert.
—— CONCERTO FOR CLARINET AND STRINGS
    cl. - str.   17:30 Presser.
—— CONCERTO FOR FLUTE AND STRINGS
    fl. - str.   16:00 EV.
—— CONCERTO FOR OBOE AND STRINGS
    ob. - str.   16:00 Presser.
—— CONCERTO FOR SAXOPHONE, TRUMPET AND STRINGS
    sax. - tpt. - str.   16:30 EV.
—— CONCERTO FOR TRUMPET AND STRINGS
    tpt. - str.   15:00 Presser.
—— CONCERTO FOR VIOLIN AND ORCH.
    2,2,2,2 - 2,2,2,0 - perc.,cel. - hp. - str. 18:00 Salabert.
—— CONCERTO NO. 1 IN C FOR PIANO AND ORCH. (IN 3
    MOVTS.)
    2,2,2,2 - 2,2,2,0 - timp.,perc.,cel. - hp. - pf. - str.
                   Baron.
—— DANSE (D'APRÈS "LE RETOUR DU TCHAD")
    3,3,3,2 - 4,3,3,1 - timp.,perc.,xyl. - hp. - str. 8:00 Salabert.
—— LE DÉJEUNER SUR L'HERBE (MUSICAL ILLUSTRATION,
    AFTER EDOUARD MANET'S PAINTING)
    2,2,2,2 - 2,2,1,0 - timp.,perc. - pf. - str. 8:30 Presser.
—— DIVERTISSEMENT DANS LE STYLE OPERETTE (FOR
    SMALL ORCH.)
    2,2,2,2 - 2,2,1,0 - perc. - str.   11:00 Salabert.
—— DOLOR (FOR SATB CHORUS AND ORCH.)
                   Presser.
—— DRAMES
    2,2,2,2 - 2,2,2,0 - timp.,perc.(1),cel.,vibra.,xyl. - ondes Martenot -
    pf. - str.   22:00 Salabert.
—— HUIT POEMES (FOR VOICE AND ORCH.)
                   Salabert.
—— MUSIC FOR A BALLET (DIVERTIMENTO) (IN 8 MOVTS.)
    2,2,2,2 - 2,2,2,0 - timp.,perc.,glock. - pf. - str. 22:00 Salabert.
—— OUVERTURE POUR UN "DON QUICHOTTE"
    3,2,2,sax.,2 - 4,3,3,1 - timp.,perc. - hp. - pf. - str. 10:00 Salabert.
—— OUVERTURE POUR UN DRAME
    2,2,2,2 - 2,2,2,0 - timp.,perc. - hp. - pf. - str. 10:00 Salabert.

—— OUVERTURE POUR UNE OPÉRETTE IMAGINAIRE
    2,2,2,2 - 2,2,1,0 - timp.,perc. - hp. - str. 6:30 Salabert.
—— RAPSODIE (FOR VIOLIN, CELLO AND ORCH.)
    2,3,2,2 - 4,2,3,0 - timp.,perc. - hp. - str. 14:00 Salabert.
—— RAPSODIE PROVENÇALE
    2,2,2,2 - 2,2,2,0 - timp.,perc. - hp. - pf. - str. 16:00 Salabert.
—— REQUIEM (FOR MEZZO-SOPRANO, BASS, MIXED CHORUS
    AND ORCH.)
    3,3,3,3 - 4,3,3,1 - timp.,perc. - pf. - str. 32:00 Presser.
—— RESONANCES (1967)
    2,2,2,2 - 2,2,2,0 - timp.,perc.(4),cel.,vibra.,xyl. - str.
                   23:00 Salabert.
—— SYMPHONY NO. 1 IN D (IN 3 MOVTS.)
    3,3,3,3 - 4,3,3,1 - timp.,perc.,cel. - hp. - str. 22:30 Salabert.
—— SYMPHONY NO. 3 IN G (FOR STRINGS)
    str.   21:00 Salabert.
—— SYMPHONY NO. 4 (FOR STRINGS) (IN 3 MOVTS.)
    str.   18:00 Salabert.
—— SYMPHONY NO. 5 (IN 4 MOVTS.)
    3,3,3,3 - 4,3,3,1 - timp.,perc.,cel. - hp. - str. 23:00 Salabert.
—— SYMPHONY NO. 6 ("LES PRÉSAGES") (1958)
    3,3,3,3 - 4,3,3,1 - timp.,perc.,cel.,xyl. - pf. - str. 25:00 Salabert.
—— SYMPHONY NO. 7 ("CONTRASTS")
    3,3,3,3 - 4,3,3,1 - timp.,perc.,cel.,xyl. - pf. - str. 22:45 Salabert.
—— THREE PASTORALES (FOR CHAMBER ORCH.)
    2,1,1,1 - 2,1,1,0 - timp.,cel. - hp. - str. 10:00 Salabert.
—— TRIAD (FOR STRINGS)
    str.   18:00 Presser.
—— VÉNITIENNE (1-ACT OPERA-COMIQUE) %
    1,1,1,1 - 0,2,1,0 - timp.,perc. - pf. - str. 29:00 Presser.

RIVILIS, Pavel B.
—— UNISONS (FOUR PIECES FOR ORCHESTRA)
                  G. Schirmer.

RIZO, Marco
—— BROADWAY CONCERTO (FOR PIANO AND ORCH.) (1964)
    (IN 3 MOVTS.)
    *3,2,*3,2 - 4,3,3,1 - timp.,perc.(4),bells - pf. - str.
                   15:40 Composer.
—— SINFONIA CUBANA (1965) (IN 3 MOVTS.)
    *3,2,*3,2 - 4,3,3,0 - timp.,perc.(5) - str. 18:00 Composer.

ROBB, John Donald
—— CONCERTO FOR PIANO AND ORCH., OP. 18 (IN 3 MOVTS.)
    3(2 alt. with 2 picc.),*3,*3,2 - 4,3,3,1 - timp.,perc.,glock. - hp. - pf.
    - str.   26:00 C. Fischer.
—— CONCERTO FOR VIOLA AND ORCH., OP. 24 (IN 3 MOVTS.)
    2,1,2,2 - 2,2,1,1 - timp.,perc.(3),xyl. - str. 14:30 Composer.
—— FREE VARIATIONS ON TWO THEMES, OP. 31
    2,2(2nd alt. with Eng.hn.),2(2nd alt. with b.-cl.),2 - 4,3,3,1 -
    timp.,perc.,cel. - org. - pf. - str. 17:20 Composer.
—— JOY COMES TO DEADHORSE, OP. 28 (MUSICAL PLAY) %
    1(alt. with picc.),0,*4,0 - 0,2,1,bar. hn.,0 - timp.,perc.(3),xyl. - pf. -
    str.   Composer.
—— AN ORCHESTRAL EXCURSION THROUGH FIVE PEACEFUL
    VILLAGES, OP. 10
    2(2nd alt. with picc.),2,2,2 - 4,2,3,1 - perc. - pf. - str.
                   26:45 Composer.
—— SYMPHONY FOR STRINGS, OP. 9 (IN 3 MOVTS.)
    str.   26:30 Composer.
—— SYMPHONY NO. 2 IN C MAJOR, OP. 23 (IN 4 MOVTS.)
    3(3rd alt. with picc.),3,3(3rd alt. with b.-cl.),alto sax.,2 - 4,3,3,1 -
    timp.,perc.,glock.,xyl. - hp. - str. 25:30 Composer.
—— SYMPHONY NO. 3, OP. 34 (IN 1 MOVT.)
    3(1 alt. with picc.),*3,*3,*3 - 4,3,3,1 - timp.,perc.,cel. - hp. - str.
                   12:00 Composer.
—— SYMPHONY NO. 4 (SCENES FROM A NEW MEXICAN
    MOUNTAIN VILLAGE) (IN 4 MOVTS.)
    1,1,2,2 - 1,2,2,1 - perc.(1) - str. 10:15 Composer.

ROBBIANI, Igino
—— ANNA KARENINA: OPERA SUITE NO. 1 (IN 5 MOVTS.)
    3,3,3,3 - 4,3,3,1 - timp.,perc.,bells,cel.,xyl. - hp. - str.
                   23:00 Bo. Hawkes.
—— ANNA KARENINA: OPERA SUITE NO. 2 (IN 2 MOVTS.)
    3,3,3,3 - 4,3,3,1 - timp.,perc.,cel.,xyl. - hp. - str.
                   17:00 Bo. Hawkes.
—— ELEGIA
    2,*3,2,2 - 4 hn. - timp.,perc. - hp. - str. 7:00 Bo. Hawkes.
—— GUIDO DEL POPOLO: FRAMMENTI SINFONICI (IN 2
    MOVTS.)
    3,3,3,3 - 4,3,3,1 - timp.,perc.,cel. - hp. - str. 9:00 Bo. Hawkes.

—— ROMA DEI CESARI
*3,*3,*3,*3 - 4,3,3,1 - timp.,perc.,cel.,xyl. - hp. - str.
15:00 Bo. Hawkes.

—— ROMANTICISMO (FRAMMENTI DELL' OPERA) (IN 3 MOVTS.)
3,3,3,3 - 4,3,3,1 - timp.,perc.,cel. - hp. - str.   22:00 Bo. Hawkes.

—— SUITE NELLO STILE ANTICO (FOR STRINGS) (IN 5 MOVTS.)
str.   22:00 Bo. Hawkes.

ROBERT, Lucie
—— CONCERTO FOR OBOE AND ORCH.
2,2,2,2 - 2,2,0,0 - timp.,perc.,cel. - hp. - str.   18:00 Presser.

—— DOUBLE CONCERTO (FOR ALTO SAXOPHONE, PIANO AND ORCH.)
2,2,2,alto sax.,2 - 2,2,2,1 - timp.,perc.(3) - pf. - str.   27:00 Presser.

ROBERTS, Gordon
—— MARCHE GROTESQUE (1963)
2,2,2,2 - 4,2,2,0 - timp.,perc. - str.   4:00 P.R.S.

—— SUITE FOR STRINGS (1966)
str.   16:00 P.R.S.

—— SUITE (1964)
1,1,1,0 - 0,0,0,0 - pf. - str.   16:00 P.R.S.

ROBERTS, Jeremy Dale
—— CYCLE FOR ORCH. (ARBOR VITAE)(1964)
3,3,3,3 - 4,3,3,1 - timp.,perc.(4) - hp. - str.   30:00 P.R.S.

—— INCIDENTAL MUSIC FOR BJØRNSEN'S "MARY STUART IN SCOTLAND" (1960)
1,1,1,0 - 1,3,0,0 - timp.,perc. - hp. - str.   15:00 P.R.S.

—— SINFONIA DA CACCIA
2,2,2,2 - 2,0,0,0 - timp. - str.   20:00 P.R.S.

—— SUITE FOR FLUTE AND STRINGS
fl. - str.   Novello.

ROBERTSON, Leroy
—— AMERICAN SERENADE (FOR STRINGS) (IN 3 MOVTS.)
str.   16:45 Composer.

—— CONCERTO FOR CELLO AND ORCH. (IN 3 MOVTS.)
3(3rd alt. with picc.),2,2(2nd alt. with b.-cl.),2 - 4,2,3,1 - timp.,perc.(1),glock. - hp. - str.   27:00 Composer.

—— CONCERTO FOR PIANO AND ORCHESTRA (1965-6) (IN 3 MOVTS.)
3(3rd alt. with picc.),2,2,2 - 4,3,3,1 - timp.,perc.(4-5),bells,glock.,xyl. - pf. - str.   28:00 Composer.

—— CONCERTO FOR VIOLIN AND ORCH. (IN 3 MOVTS.)
2(2nd alt. with picc.),2,2,2 - 4,2,3,1 - timp.,perc.(3),glock. - hp. - str.   26:30 Galaxy.

—— DRAMATIC ORATORIOS FROM THE BOOK OF MORMON (FOR BASS-BARITONE, TENOR, MIXED CHORUS, CHILDREN'S CHORUS AND ORCH.)
3(3rd alt. with picc.),2,2,2 - 4,3,3,1 - timp.,perc.(3),glock.,xyl. - hp. - org. - pf. - str.   80:00 Composer.

—— ENDICOTT OVERTURE
3(3rd alt. with picc.),*3,2,*3 - 4,2,3,1 - timp.,perc.(3),glock. - hp. - str.   10:00 Composer.

—— ORATORIO FROM THE BOOK OF MORMON (FOR SOLOISTS, MIXED CHORUS, CHILDREN'S CHORUS AND ORCH.)
3(3rd alt. with picc.),2(2nd alt. with Eng. hn.),2,2(2nd alt. with c.-bn.) - 4,3,3,1 - timp.,perc.(4),cel.(alt. with pf.),glock.,xyl. - hp. - org. - str.   59:00 Composer.

—— PASSACAGLIA
3(3rd alt. with picc.),2, Eng. hn.(ad lib.),2,b.-cl.(ad lib.),2,c.-bn.(ad lib.) - 4,3,3,1 - timp.,perc.(3) - hp. -pf. -str.   12:00 Galaxy.

—— PRELUDE, SCHERZO AND RICERCARE (VARIATIONS ON TWO WESTERN THEMES)
3(3rd alt. with picc.),*3,*3,*3 - 4,3,3,1 - timp.,perc.,glock.,xyl. - hp. - org.(ad lib.) - str.   15:30 EV.

—— PUNCH AND JUDY OVERTURE
3(3rd alt. with picc.),2,2,2 - 4,2,3,0 - timp.,perc.(3) - hp. - str.   6:30 Galaxy.

—— RHAPSODY FOR PIANO AND ORCH.
2(2nd alt. with picc.),2,2,2 - 4,2,3,1 - timp. perc.(3) - pf. - str.   17:00 Composer.

—— TRILOGY
4(2 alt. with 2 picc.),*4,*4(3rd alt. with E♭cl.),*4 - 6,3,3,1 - timp.,perc.(5),cel.,glock.,xyl. - 2 hp. - pf. - str.   33:30 Composer.

—— UNIVERSITY OF UTAH FESTIVAL OVERTURE (1965)
*4,2,2,2 - 4,3,3,1 - timp.,perc.(5),bells,glock.,xyl. - org.(ad lib.) - str.   9:00 Composer.

ROBINSON, Earl
—— ABRAHAM LINCOLN COMES HOME (FOR CHAMBER ENSEMBLES)
2,2,1,1 - 2,3,2,1 - hp. - pf. - vln.,d.-b.   MCA Music.

—— BALLAD FOR AMERICANS (FOR BARITONE, CHORUS AND ORCH.)
2,1(alt. with Eng. hn.),2,2 - 4,3,2,1 - timp.,perc.(2) - hp. - str.   11:00 Robbins.

—— CONCERTO FOR PIANO AND ORCH.
16:00 Composer.

—— CONCERTO FOR 5-STRING BANJO AND ORCH.
25:00 MCA Music.

—— THE COUNTRY THEY CALL PUGET SOUND (FOR TENOR AND ORCH.)
16:00 Templeton.

—— ILLINOIS PEOPLE (CANTATA) (FOR VOICES, CHORUS AND ORCH.) (1968) (Text: Carl Haverlin)
55:00 Composer.

—— IN THE FOLDED AND QUIET YESTERDAYS (FROM "THE PEOPLE, YES") (CANTATA) (FOR SOLO VOICES, CHORUS AND ORCH.) (1942) (Text: Carl Sandburg)
*3,*3,*3,*3 - 2,2,2,1 - perc. - hp. - pf. - str.   8:00 Shawnee.

—— THE LONESOME TRAIN (CANTATA) (FOR NARRATOR, BALLAD SINGER, MIXED CHORUS AND ORCH.)
2,2,2,1 - 2,3,2,3 - timp.,perc. - banjo - guit. - hp. - pf. - str.   50:00 Templeton.

—— PREAMBLE TO PEACE (CANTATA) (FOR NARRATOR AND ORCH.) (1960)
33:00 Composer.

—— RIDE THE WIND (CANTATA) (FOR BARITONE, SPEAKING VOICES, CHORUS AND ORCH.) (1975)
18:00 Composer.

—— TO THE NORTHWEST INDIANS (A SYMPHONIC NARRATIVE) (1974)
30:00 Composer.

ROBINSON, Edward
—— THE STOREKEEPER'S DAUGHTER (SUITE) (IN 3 MOVTS.)
2(2nd alt. with picc.)2,2,2 - 2,2,0,0 - timp.,perc. (1) - str.   14:00 Composer.

ROBISON, Willard
—— CALL THE TRIBE (CANTATA) (FOR MIXED CHORUS AND ORCH.)
2,2,4(1st. alt. with fl.,picc. and bar.sax.,2nd alt. with b.-cl.,picc.,ob.,alto sax. and b-sax.),0 - 0,0,0,0 - perc. - guit. - str.   7:30 Leeds.

—— PEACEFUL VALLEY (CANTATA) (FOR CHORUS AND CHAMBER ORCH.)
0,0,2,0 - 2,2,2,0 - perc.,bells(ad lib.),vibra.(ad lib.) - guit.(ad lib.) - pf. - d.-b.   Leeds.

ROCCA, Lodovico
—— ANTICHE ISCRIZIONI (ANCIENT INSCRIPTIONS) (FOR SOPRANO, BASS, CHORUS AND ORCH.)
3,2,2,2 - 4,3,3,1 - timp.,perc.,cel.,xyl. - hp. - pf. - str.   19:00 Leeds.

—— BIRIBU OCCHI DI RANA (FOR VOICE, PIANO AND STRINGS)
pf. - str.   7:00 Bo. Hawkes.

—— LA CELLA AZZURRA (LEGGENDA)
3,3,3,3 - 4,3,3,1 - timp.,perc.,bells,cel. - hp. - org. - pf. - str.   12:00 Bo. Hawkes.

—— CHIAROSCURI (PETITE SUITE)
3,3,3,2 - 4,3,3,1 - timp.,perc.,bells,cel. - hp. - str.   17:00 Baron.

—— DITTICO (FOR VOICE AND ORCH.)
8:45 Baron.

ROCHBERG, George
—— BALLET MUSIC FOR STRINGS
str.   8:30 Composer.

—— BLACK SOUNDS (MUSIC FOR A BALLET)
2(alt. with 2 picc.),1,2(alt. with E♭cl. and b.-cl.),0 - 2,2,2,1 - timp.,perc.(4),bells,cel.,glock.,xyl. - pf.   12:00 Presser.

—— CHELTENHAM CONCERTO (FOR CHAMBER ORCH.) (1958)
1,1,1,1 - 1,1,1,0 - str.   12:00 Presser.

—— CONCERT PIECE FOR TWO PIANOS AND ORCH.
2(2nd alt. with picc.), 2(2nd alt. with Eng. hn.),2,2 - 4,3,2,1 - timp. - 2 pf. - str.   9:00 Composer.

—— CONCERTO FOR VIOLIN AND ORCHESTRA
3,3,3,3 - 4,3,3,1 - timp.,cel. - 2 hp. - str.   40:00 Presser.

—— DAVID THE PSALMIST (CANTATA FOR TENOR AND ORCH.)
*3,*3,*3,*3 - 4,3,3,1 - timp.,perc. - str.   25:00 Composer.

—— IMAGO MUNDI (IMAGE OF THE WORLD) (1973)
3(3rd alt. with picc.),*3,*3,*3 - 4,3,3,1 - timp.,perc.(4),cel.,glock. -
hp. - str.   22:00 Presser.
—— MUSIC FOR "THE ALCHEMIST" (CONCERT VERSION) (FOR
11 PLAYERS AND INCIDENTAL SOPRANO) (1968)
2(alt. with 2 picc.and 1 alto fl.),0,1 E♭cl.,1,0 - 1,2(1 alt. with
picc.tpt.),0,0 - perc.(2),cel.,glock.,vibra. - hpsc. - pf. - 1 vln.,1 d.-b.
20:00 Presser.
—— MUSIC FOR THE MAGIC THEATER (FOR 15 PLAYERS OR
SMALL ORCH.) (1965)
1(alt. with picc.),1,1(alt. with E♭cl.),1 - 2,1,1,1 - pf. - str.(2,1,1,1)
30:00 Presser.
or:
1(alt. with picc.),1,1,(alt. with E♭cl.),1 - 4,1,1,1 - pf. - str.
—— NIGHT MUSIC
3(3rd alt. with picc.),3(3rd alt. with Eng. hn.),3(3rd alt. with
b.-cl.),3(3rd alt. with c.-bn.) - 4,3,3,1 - timp.,perc.(2) - hp. - str.
11:00 Presser.
—— PHAEDRA (FOR MEZZO-SOPRANO AND ORCH.)
2,2,2,2 - 4,2,3,0 - timp.,perc. - str.   32:00 Presser.
—— SACRED SONGS OF RECONCILIATION (FOR BARITONE
AND ORCH.)
1,1,1,1 - 1,0,1,0 - perc. - 2 pf. - str.   10:00 Presser.
—— SONGS OF INNOCENCE AND EXPERIENCE (BLAKE'S
SONGS) (5 SONGS FOR VOICE AND SMALL ENSEMBLE)
(Text: William Blake)
1,0,*2,0 - perc.(2),cel. - hp. - pf. - str.(2,1,1,0)   12:00 Presser.
—— SUITE FOR ORCHESTRA (IN 4 MOVTS.)
*3,2,2,2 - 4,3,3,1 - timp.,perc.(3) - str.   22:00 Composer.
—— SYMPHONY NO. 1 (IN 4 MOVTS.)
3(3rd alt. with picc.),3(3rd alt. with Eng. hn.),3(3rd alt. with
b.-cl.),3(3rd alt. with c.-bn.) - 4,3,3,1 - timp.,perc.(3) - str.
39:00 Presser.
—— SYMPHONY NO. 2 (IN 1 MOVT.)
3(3rd alt. with picc.),*3,*3,*3 - 4,3,3,1 - timp.,perc.(4),xyl. - hp. -
str.   25:00 Presser.
—— SYMPHONY NO. 3 (FOR DOUBLE CHORUS, CHAMBER
CHORUS, SOLO VOICES AND LARGE ORCH.) (1969) (Text:
Liturgical German andLatin)
8(2 alt. with 2 picc.),7(1 alt. with Eng. hn.),1 E♭cl.,*6,*6 - 8,8,5,3
- timp.,perc.(4-5),bells,cel.,glock.,vibra. - electric org. - org. (pipe) -
str.   40:00 Presser.
—— SYMPHONY NO. 4
3,3,3,3 - 4,3,3,1 - timp., perc., cel., glock. - hp. - str.
48:00 Presser.
—— TABLEAUX (SOUND PICTURES) (FOR SOPRANO AND 11
PLAYERS) (BASED ON "THE SILVER TALONS OF PIERO
KOSTROV") (1968) (Text: Paul Rochberg)
2(1 alt. with picc., 1 alt. with alto fl.),0,1(alt. with E♭cl.),0 -
1,1(alt. with picc. tpt.),1,0 - perc.(2) - str.(2,1,1,1)   30:00 Presser.
—— TIME-SPAN FOR ORCHESTRA (Revised Version)
3,*3,*3,2 - 4,3,3,1 - perc.,bells,cel.,vibra. - pf. - str.   10:00 Leeds.
—— ZODIAC
3(3rd alt. with picc.),*3,1 E♭cl.,*3,*3 - 4,3,3,1 -
timp.,perc.(4),cel.,xyl. - hp. - pf. - str.   14:30 Presser.

RODER, Milan
—— AVE MARIA (FOR HIGH VOICE, CHORUS, ORGAN AND
ORCH.)
2,2(2nd alt. with Eng. hn.),*3,2 - 3,3,3,1 - timp. - org. - str.
6:00 Composer.
—— CAPRICCIO FOR VIOLIN AND ORCH.
2(2nd alt. with picc.),2(2nd alt. with Eng. hn.),*3,2 - 4,3,3,1 -
timp.,perc.(2-3) - hp. - str.   6:30 Composer.
—— FOUR SYMPHONIC SKETCHES
2(2nd alt. with picc.),*2,*3,*3 - 4,3,3,1 - timp.,perc.(3-4),cel.,xyl. -
hp. - str.   16:30 Composer.
—— JELKA'S ARIA (FROM THE OPERA "JELKA") (FOR
SOPRANO AND ORCH.)
2,*3,*3,*3 - 4,3,3,1 - timp.,perc.(2) - hp. - str.   4:00 Composer.
—— MOTO PERPETUO
2(2nd alt. with picc.),*2,*3,2 - 4,3,3,1 - timp.,vibra.,xyl. - pf. - str.
5:00 Composer.
—— OVERTURE TO "JELKA"
*3,*3,*3,*3 - 4,3,3,1 - timp.,perc.(2) - hp. - str.   9:00 Composer.
—— PRAGA (FESTIVAL OVERTURE)
2(2nd alt. with picc.),2,2,2 - 4,2,3,0 - timp.,perc.(2) - hp. - str.
7:00 Composer.
—— ROMANCE SLAV (FOR VIOLIN AND ORCH.)
2(2nd alt. with picc.),2(2nd alt. with Eng. hn.),*3,*3 - 4,3,3,1 -
timp.,perc.,cel. - hp. - str.   8:00 Composer.

—— RONDO CAPRICCIOSO
2(2nd alt. with picc.),*2,*3,2 - 4,3,3,1 - timp.,perc.(2-3) - hp. - str.
6:30 Composer.

RODER, Milan - KRAUSHAAR, Arnold
—— DIN CAVAL (RUMANIAN RHAPSODY WITH SOLO
ENGLISH HORN, TAROGATO OR VIOLA)
2(2nd alt. with picc.),*2,*3,2 - 4,3,3,1 - timp.,perc.(2-3),glock. -
hp. - str.   9:00 Composer.

RODERICK-JONES, Richard
—— BALLADE (1967)
2,2,2,2 - 4,2,3,1 - timp.,perc.,cel. - str.   14:00 P.R.S.
—— CHAMBER CONCERTO FOR 32 INSTRUMENTS (1969)
2,1,2,1 - 2,1,1,0 - str.   20:00 P.R.S.
—— CONCERTO FOR PIANO AND ORCH. (1968)
2,2,2,2 - 4,2,3,1 - timp.,perc.,cel. - pf. - str. 20:00 P.R.S.
—— CONCERTO FOR VIOLA AND ORCH. (1974)
2,1,2,2 - 4,2,3,1 - timp.,perc. - hp. - str.   30:00 P.R.S.
—— PARTITA FOR STRINGS (1968)
str.   16:00 P.R.S.
—— TRIPTYCH FOR CHAMBER ORCH. (1967)
1,1,1,1 - 1,0,0,0 - timp.,cel. - hp. - str.   15:00 P.R.S.

RODGERS, Richard - BENNETT, Robert Russell
—— VICTORY AT SEA: SYMPHONIC SCENARIO
2(2nd alt. with picc.),*3,*3,2 - 4,3,3,1 -
timp.,perc.(2-3),cel.,glock.,xyl. - hp. - pf. - str.   12:00 Williamson.

RODRIGO, Joaquin
—— CINQ PIECES ENFANTINES
3,3,3,2 - 4,3,3,1 - timp.,perc.(4),cel. - 2 hp.   Salabert.
—— CONCERT D'ÉTÉ (FOR VIOLIN AND ORCH.)
2,2,2,2 - 2,2,0,0 - str.   20:00 Presser.
—— CONCERTO ANDALUZ (FOR 4 GUITARS AND ORCH.)
3,2,2,2 - 4,2,0,0 - 4 guit. - str.   30:00 Salabert.
—— CONCERTO IN MODO GALANTE (FOR CELLO AND
ORCH.)
25:00 Salabert.
—— CONCIERTO DE ARANJUEZ (FOR GUITAR AND ORCH.)
21:11 S.G.A.E.
—— CUATRO MADRIGALES AMATORIOS (4 16TH-CENTURY
SPANISH SONGS) (FOR VOICE AND ORCH.)
6:00 G. Schirmer.
—— TRIPTIC DE MOSEN CINTO (FOR HIGH VOICE AND
ORCH.)
2(2nd alt. with picc.),2(2nd alt. with Eng.hn.),1,1 - 2,2,0,0 - cel. -
hp. - str.   8:00 G. Schirmer.

RODRIGUEZ PONS, Francesco
—— EL GITANO GALANTE ("THE GALLANT GYPSY") (SUITE)
18:00 S.G.A.E.

ROE, Christopher
—— CONCERTO FOR VIOLA AND ORCH. (1960)
2,2,2,2 - 4,2,3,1 - perc. - hp. - str.   21:00 P.R.S.
—— FESTIVE MARCH (1962)
2,2,2,2 - 4,2,3,0 - perc. - str.   3:00 P.R.S.
—— A SOMERSET SUITE (1962)
2,1,2,alto sax.,1 - 2,2,3,0 - perc. - hp. - str.   7:30 P.R.S.

ROENTGEN, Johannes
—— AMOR VINCIT (FOR CHORUS, PIANO OR ORGAN AND
STRINGS)
pf.(or org.) - str.   12:00 Henmar.

ROESER, Valentin - HOFMANN, Wolfgang
—— SINFONIA NO. 19 IN G MAJOR
2,0,0,0 - 2,0,0,0 - str.   14:00 Mannheimer.

ROFF, Joseph
—— REVERIE (1949)
ob. - hp. - str.   7:00 Composer.

ROGER, Kurt
—— CONCERTO GROSSO (FOR TRUMPET, TIMPANI AND
STRINGS)
tpt. - timp. - str.   G. Schirmer.

ROGER-DUCASSE, Jean-Jules A.
—— ÉPITHALAME (SYMPHONIC POEM)
3,3,2,3 - 4,5,3,1 - timp.,perc.(5),xyl. - 2 hp. - str.   15:00 EV.

—— INTERLUDE FROM "AU JARDIN DE MARGUERITE"
*3,*3,*3,2 - 4,2,3,1 - timp.,perc.,cel. - 2 hp. - str.   11:00 EV.
—— UN JOLI JEU DE FURET (SYMPHONIC SCHERZO)
3,3,2,3 - 4,3,3,1 - timp.,perc.(4),bells - 2 hp. - str.   5:00 EV.
—— MARCHE FRANÇAISE (SYMPHONIC POEM)
3,3,3,3 - 4,3,3,1 - timp.,perc.(4) - 2 hp. - pf. - str.   8:00 EV.
—— NOCTURNE DE PRINTEMPS
3(3rd alt. with picc.),3,3,2 - 4,2,3,1 - timp.,perc.,cel. - 2 hp. - str.   12:00 EV.
—— ORPHÉE: DEUX FRAGMENTS SYMPHONIQUES
4,4,4,3,sarr. - 4,3,3,1 - timp.,perc. - 2 hp. - str.   8:00 EV.
—— PETITE SUITE
3(3rd alt. with picc.),3,2,2 - 4,3,3,1 - timp.,perc. - hp. - str.   6:00 EV.
—— PRÉLUDE D'UN BALLET
3,3,2,2 - 4,3,0,0 - timp.,perc. - hp. - str.   EV.
—— ROMANCE (FOR VIOLIN, CELLO AND ORCH.)
2,0,2,1 - hn. - str.   EV.
—— SARABANDE (SYMPHONIC POEM) (FOR SAT CHORUS AND ORCH.)
3,3,2,2 - 4,3,3,1 - timp.,perc.(3) - 2 hp. - str.   12:00 EV.
—— SUITE FOR SMALL ORCH.
2,2,2,2 - 2 hn. - timp. - str.   8:00 EV.
—— SUITE FRANCAISE (IN 4 MOVTS.)
3(3rd alt. with picc.),*3(Eng. hn. alt. with ob. d'amore),2,2 - 4,2,3,1 - timp.,perc. - hp. - str.   20:00 EV.
—— SYMPHONIC POEM ON THE NAME OF GABRIEL FAURÉ
3,3,3,2 - 4,3,3,1 - timp.,perc. - hp. - str.   EV.
—— ULYSSE ET LES SIRÈNES (SYMPHONIC POEM) (FOR SOPRANO, CONTRALTO AND ORCH.)
3,3,2,2 - 4,3,3,1 - timp.,perc.(4),cel. - hp. - str.   18:00 EV.
—— VARIATIONS PLAISANTES (ON A SERIOUS THEME)
3(3rd alt. with picc.),3,2,2 - 4,3,3,1 - timp.,perc. - hp. - str.   EV.

ROGER-ROGER
—— CONCERTO-JAZZ NO. 1 (FOR PIANO OR HARP, WITH ORCH.)
2,2,2,4 sax.(2 alto,1 ten.,1 bar.),2 - timp.,perc. - guit. - pf.(or hp.) - str.   8:00 Salabert.
—— CONCERTO-JAZZ NO. 2 ("CONCERTO ROMANTIQUE") (FOR PIANO AND ORCH.)
2,2,3,4 sax.(2 alto, 1 ten. 1 bar.),3 - 0,0,0,0 - perc. - guit. - pf. - str.   14:00 Salabert.

ROGERS, Bernard
—— AFRICA (SYMPHONY IN 2 MOVTS.)
*3,*3,*3,*3 - 4,2,3,1 - timp.,perc.(5),glock.,xyl. - hp. - pf. - str.   14:00 Presser.
—— ALLEGORY
2 fl. - mar. - str.   8:30 Presser.
—— ANZACS
*3,*3,2,2 - 4,3,2,1 - timp.,perc. - hp. - str.   8:00 EV.
—— APPARITIONS (SCENES FROM "THE TEMPTATION OF ST. ANTHONY", AFTER FLAUBERT)
3,3,3,3 - 4,3,3,1 - timp.,perc. - hp. - pf. - str.   MCA Music.
—— THE COLORS OF WAR
3,2,2,2 - 4,2,3,1 - timp.,perc. - hp. - str.   6:00 EV.
—— THE COLORS OF YOUTH
*3,2,*3,*3 - 4,3,3,1 - timp.,perc.(4) - hp. - pf. - str.   10:00 Composer.
—— THE DANCE OF SALOME
*3,*3,*3,*3 - 4,3,3,1 - timp.,perc.(4) - hp. - str.   9:00 EV.
—— DANCE SCENES
2,2,2,2 - 4,2,2,1 - timp.,perc.,glock. - hp. - pf. - str.   14:00 Southern.
—— ELEGY (FROM SYMPHONY NO. 3) (FOR CHAMBER ORCH.)
2 ob., Eng.hn. - str.   5:00 EV.
—— ELEGY (IN MEMORIAM OF FRANKLIN D. ROOSEVELT)
fl. - 2 hn. - timp. - str.   8:00 EV.
—— THE EXODUS (CANTATA) (FOR TENOR, CONTRALTO, BARITONE, CHORUS AND ORCH.)
*3,*3,*3,*3 - 4,3,3,1 - timp.,perc.(3) - hp. - org. - str.   30:00 Composer.
—— THE FAITHFUL (OVERTURE)
*3,*3,*3,*3 - 4,2,3,1 - timp.,perc.(3) - hp. - str.   10:00 Composer.
—— FANTASIA FOR HORN, TIMPANI AND STRINGS
hn. - timp. - str.   11:00 Presser.
—— FANTASY FOR FLUTE, VIOLA AND ORCH.
1,*3,2,2 - 4,2,3,1 - timp.,perc.(2) - hp. - str.   7:00 EV.
—— FOUR CHARACTERS FROM HANS CHRISTIAN ANDERSEN
2(1 alt. with picc.),2,2,2 - 2,2,0,0 - perc. - hp. - pf. - str.   11:00 EV.

—— FUJI IN THE SUNSET GLOW
*3,*3,*3,*3 - 4,3,3,1 - timp.,perc.(3) - hp. - str.   8:00 Composer.
—— LEAVES FROM THE TALE OF PINOCCHIO (WITH OPTIONAL NARRATOR)
1(alt. with picc.),1,1,1(alt. with c.-bn.) - 1,1,1,0 - timp.,perc.(2),glock.,xyl. - hp. - pf. - str.   22:00 Southern.
—— A LETTER FROM PETE (CANTATA) (FOR SOPRANO, TENOR, CHORUS AND ORCH.)
*2,2,2,2 - 4,2,3,1 - timp.,perc.(3),glock.,xyl. - hp. - str.   24:00 Southern.
—— THE LIGHT OF MAN (FOR SOPRANO, ALTO, BASS, SATB CHORUS AND ORCH.)
2,2,2,2 - 4,2,3,1 - timp.,perc.,glock. - pf. - str.   12:30 Presser.
—— THE MUSICIANS OF BREMEN (FOR NARRATOR AND CHAMBER ORCH.)
2,1,1,1 - 1,1,0,0 - timp.,perc. - str.   22:00 Presser.
—— NEW JAPANESE DANCES (IN 4 MOVTS.)
2,3,3,3 - 4,2,3,1 - timp.,perc.,cel. - hp. - pf. - str.   11:30 Presser.
—— THE NIGHTINGALE (OPERA) %
2,1,1,1 - 1,1,1,0 - timp.,perc. - hp. - pf. - str.(ad lib.)   65:00 Southern.
—— ONCE UPON A TIME (5 FAIRY TALES FOR SMALL ORCH.)   22:00 Kalmus.
—— OVERTURE: AMPHITYRON
*3,*3,*3,*3 - 4,3,3,1 - timp.,perc.(4),cel.,glock.,xyl. - 2 hp. - pf. - str.   8:00 Composer.
—— THE PASSION (FOR SOLOISTS, CHORUS AND ORCH.)
*3,*3,*3,*3 - 4,3,3,1 - timp.,perc.(4),cel.,glock.,xyl. - hp. - pf. - str.   75:00 EV.
—— PASTORALE MISTICO (FOR CLARINET AND STRING ORCH.)
cl.,str.   KingsCrown.
—— THE PLAINS (SUITE) (IN 3 MOVTS.)
1(alt. with picc.),1(alt. with Eng. hn.),2,1 - 2,1,0,0 - timp. - str.   14:00 EV.
—— PORTRAIT FOR VIOLIN AND ORCH.
*3,2,2,2 - 4,3,3,1 - timp.,perc.(4),glock.,xyl. - hp. - str.   24:00 Presser.
—— THE PROPHET ISAIAH (FOR SOLO VOICES, CHORUS AND ORCH.)
3,2,2,2 - 4,3,3,1 - timp.,perc. - hp. - pf. - str.   32:00 Southern.
—— PSALM 68 (FOR SOLO BARITONE AND ORCH.)
*3,2,2,*3 - 4,2,3,1 - timp.,perc.(3),glock.,xyl. - hp. - str.   12:00 Southern.
—— THE RAISING OF LAZARUS (CANTATA) (FOR 2 SOPRANOS, TENOR, CHORUS AND ORCH.)
*3,2,2,*3 - 4,2,3,1 - timp.,perc.(3) - hp. - org. - str.   24:00 Composer.
—— SAILORS OF TOULON
*3,*3,*3,*3 - 4,3,3,1 - timp.,perc. - hp. - str.   10:00 EV.
—— THE SILVER WORLD (SUITE) (FOR FLUTE, OBOE AND STRINGS)
fl.(alt. with picc.),ob. - str.   10:00 Southern.
—— SINFONIETTA
str.   20:00 Southern.
—— SOLILOQUY FOR FLUTE AND STRINGS
fl. - str.   5:00 C. Fischer.
—— SOLILQUY NO. 2 (FOR BASSOON AND STRINGS)
bn. - str.   6:00 EV.
—— THE SONG OF THE NIGHTINGALE (SUITE)
3(3rd alt. with picc.),2(2nd alt. with Eng. hn.),*3,*3, - 4,2,3,1 - timp.,perc.(4) - hp. - pf. - str.   19:00 EV.
—— SUITE FROM "THE WARRIOR"
1(alt. with picc.),1(alt. with Eng. hn.),1(alt. with b.-cl.),1(alt. with c.-bn) - 3,2,2,0 - timp.,perc.(3),glock.,xyl. - pf. - str.   9:00 Composer.
—— THE SUPPER AT EMMAUS
*3,*3,*3,*3 - 4,2,3,1 - timp.,perc.cel. - hp. - str.   7:00 EV.
—— SYMPHONY NO. 1 ("ADONAIS")
1. Allegro vehementi; 2. Andante - Lento alla marcia
3(3rd alt. with picc.),*3,*3(2nd alt. with E♭ cl.),*3 - 4,3,3,1 - timp.,perc.(3) - hp. - str.   15:00 EV.
—— SYMPHONY NO. 2 IN A FLAT (IN 1 MOVT.)
2(2nd alt. with picc.),*3,*3,*3 - 4,3,3,1 - timp.,perc.(3) - hp. - str.   12:00 Composer.
—— SYMPHONY NO. 3 ("ON A THANKSGIVING SONG") (IN 4 MOVTS.)
*3,*3,*3,*3 - 4,3,3,1 - timp.,perc.(4) - hp. - str.   40:00 Composer.
—— SYMPHONY NO. 4 (IN 3 MOVTS.)
2(2nd alt. with picc.),2,2(2nd alt. with b.-cl.),2(2nd alt. with c.-bn.) - 4,3,3,1 - timp.,perc.(3) - str.   24:00 Southern.

—— THREE DANCE SCENES
2(2nd alt. with picc.),2,2,2(2nd alt. with c.-bn.) - 4,2,3,1 -
timp.,perc.(3),glock.,xyl. - hp. - pf. - str.   12:00 Southern.
—— THREE DRAWINGS FROM HANS CHRISTIAN ANDERSEN
2,2,2,2 - 4,3,3,1 - timp.,perc.,cel. - hp. - str.   EV.
—— THREE JAPANESE DANCES (WITH MEZZO-SOPRANO SOLO
AD LIB.)
*3,*3,*3,*3 - 4,2,3,1 - timp.,perc.(4) - hp. - str.   12:00 Presser.
—— TO THE FALLEN (DIRGE)
*3,*3,*3,*3 - 4,2,3,1 - timp.,perc.(2) - hp. - str.   8:00 Composer.
—— TWO AMERICAN FRESCOES
*3,*3,*3,*3 - 4,3,1,1 - timp.,perc.(4) - hp. - pf. - str.   11:00 EV.
—— VARIATIONS ON A SONG BY MUSSORGSKY
3(3rd alt. with picc.),*3,*3,*3 - 4,3,3,1 -
timp.,perc.(4),bells,cel.,glock.,xyl. - hp. - pf. - str.   24:00 Presser.
—— THE VEIL (1-ACT OPERA) %
2,1,1,1 - 2,1,1,0 - timp.,perc. - hp. - str.   75:00 Southern.

ROGERS, Bernard - FUSSELL, Charles
—— DIRGE FOR TWO VETERANS (FOR SATB CHORUS AND
STRINGS)
str.   6:30 Presser.
—— PSALM 114 (FOR SATB CHORUS AND STRINGS)
str.   3:00 Presser.

ROGERS, James H. - KERR, Harrison
—— CONCERT OVERTURE IN B MINOR
3(3rd alt. with picc.),*3,*3,*3 - 4,3,3,1 - timp.,perc. - str.
8:00 G. Schirmer.

ROGERS, John E.
—— MOVEMENTS FOR CHAMBER ORCHESTRA (1963) (IN 3
MOVTS.)
1(alt. with picc.),1,1,1 - 1,1,1,0 - timp.,perc.,cel. - pf. - str.
14:00 Composer.
—— SYMMETRIES (TRIPLE CONCERTO, FOR PIANO, ELECTRIC
PIANO, HARPSICHORD AND CHAMBER ORCH.) (1968) (IN
1 MOVT.)
1,1,*2,1 - 1,1,0,1 - perc.(1),cel. - hpsc. - pf. - electric pf. - str.
10:00 Composer.

ROGET, Henriette
—— MONTANYAS DEL ROSELLO (FOR ORGAN AND ORCH.)
3,2,2,2 - 4,2,3,0 - timp.,perc.,glock. - org. - str.   7:30 Baron.
—— SINFONIA ANDORRANA (IN 3 MOVTS.)
34:30 EV.

ROGUE ALSINA, Carlos Maria
—— UEBERWINDUNG (FOR 4 SOLOISTS AND LARGE ORCH.)
(1970)
Soloists: cl.(alt. with fl.,alto sax.,etc.),tpt.(alt.with
alpenhorn,etc.),perc.,pf.   30:00 MCA Music.
Orch.: 4,4,4,4 - 6,4,4,1 - perc.(4),vibra - electric guit - str.

ROHE, Robert K.
—— DATELINE '61 (CIVIL WAR SONGS) (FOR NARRATOR, SATB
CHORUS, WINDS AND PERCUSSION)
3(3rd alt. with picc.),*3,*3,*3 - 4,3,3,1 - timp.,perc.(3),bells,glock.
13:00 Arranger.
—— DUM TEE DUM AND THE VEGETABLE PATCH (A WORK
FOR YOUNG AUDIENCES) (WITH NARRATOR AND 7
SOLOISTS PLAYING TOY BIRD-CALLS)
2(2nd alt. with picc.),2,2,2 - 2,2-3,1,0 - timp.,perc.(3) - hp. - str.
8:30 Bo. Hawkes.
—— THE HOUSE IN THE BEND OF BOURBON STREET (FOR
NARRATOR, TAPE AND ORCH.) (Text: Mrs. Terry Flettrich)
3(3rd alt. with picc.),3(3rd alt. with Eng.hn.),3(3rd alt. with
b.-cl.),3 - 4,3,3,1 - perc.(3),glock.,vibra. - tape-recorder - hp. - str.
15:00 Presser.
—— THE LAND OF BOTTLE (A WORK FOR YOUNG
AUDIENCES) (WITH NARRATOR, AND 4 SOLOISTS
BLOWING ACROSS TOPS OF TUNED WATER-FILLED
BOTTLES)
2(2nd alt. with picc.),2,2(2nd alt. with b.-cl.),2 - 2,2,1,0 -
timp.,perc.(2),glock.,xyl. - str.   18:30 Bo. Hawkes.
—— MAINE-SCAPE (1965)
2,1 alto fl.(alt. with picc.),*3,*3,*3 - 4,3,3,0 - str.   14:00 Composer.
—— A MUSICAL JOURNEY THROUGH TIME (FOR NARRATOR
AND ORCH.) (Text: Composer)
3(alt. with 3 picc.),*3,3(3rd alt. with b.-cl. and Eᵇcl.),*3 - 4,3,3,1 -
timp.,perc.(2) - hp. - str.   16:00 Composer.

—— VARIATIONS ON "HAPPY BIRTHDAY"
3(3rd alt. with picc.),*3,*3,*3 - 4,3,3,1 - timp.,perc.(3),glock.,xyl. -
str.   4:00 Composer.
—— YOHANAN (FOR SOLO CONTRABASS AND ORCH.)
3(3rd alt. with picc.),2(2nd alt. with Eng.hn.),3(3rd alt. with
b.-cl.),2 - 4,3,3,1 - timp.,perc.(3),bells,glock. - hp. - str.
23:00 Composer.

ROHWER, Jens
—— BALLETTINO
2,1,2,1 - 3,0,0,0 - timp.,perc. - str.   8:00 Henmar.
—— CHAMBER CONCERTO FOR VIOLIN, VIOLA AND STRING
ORCH.
str.   Möseler.
—— CONCERTO FOR PIANO AND ORCH.
Möseler.
—— KONZERT FÜR VIOLINE AND ORCH.
2,*2,1,2 - 1,2,2,0 - timp.,perc.,cel. - str.   19:00 Möseler.
—— MIXOLYDISCHES KONZERT
2,*3,*3,0 - 3,3,3,1 - timp.,perc.,cel. - str.   20:00 Möseler.

ROIHA, Eino
—— CONCERTINO FOR PIANO AND ORCH. (1939)
1,1,2,1 - 2,2,1,0 - timp. - pf. - str.   13:00 FinnMICtr.
—— CONCERTINO (REV. 1939)
1,1,1,1 - 2,1,0,0 - str.   15:00 FinnMICtr.
—— FUGUE (1944)
2,2,2,2 - 4,2,3,1 - timp. - str.   6:00 FinnMICtr.
—— OLD-FASHIONED CLASSICAL SUITE (1931) (IN 4 MOVTS.)
str.   9:00 FinnMICtr.
—— SUITE FOR STRINGS AND WOODWINDS (1954)
1,0,1,1 - 0,0,0,0 str.   14:00 FinnMICtr.
—— SUITE PICCOLA PER ORCHESTRA (1946) (IN 4 MOVTS.)
1,1,2,1 - 2,2,2,0 - perc. - str.   12:00 FinnMICtr.

ROIKJER, Kjell
—— ANDANTE AND RONDO, OP. 13 (FOR TRUMPET AND
ORCH.)
2,2,2,2 - 4,1,0,0 - timp.,perc. - str.   K.O.D.A.
—— CONCERTO FOR SAXOPHONE AND ORCH., OP. 25
1,1,2,sax.,1 - 2,2,1,0 - timp.,perc.,xyl. - str.   K.O.D.A.
—— CONCERTO FOR TUBA AND ORCH., OP. 61
K.O.D.A.
—— CONCERTO FOR XYLOPHONE AND ORCH., OP.34
2,2,2,2 - 2,2,1,0 - timp.,perc.,xyl. - str.   15:00 G. Schirmer.
—— CRISS CROSS (FOR MARIMBA AND ORCH.)
K.O.D.A.
—— EVENING MOOD, OP. 21 (FOR SMALL ORCH.)
1,1,1,1 - 2,0,0,0 - str.   5:00 G. Schirmer.
—— GREAT CLAUS AND LITTLE CLAUS (FOR PICCOLO, FLUTE,
BASSOON AND ORCH.) (1937)
K.O.D.A.
—— IMPROMPTU, OP. 27 (FOR ENGLISH HORN AND ORCH.)
5:00 K.O.D.A.
—— JACOB VON THYBO, OP. 6 (HOLBERG OVERTURE)
2,2,2,2 - 4,3,3,1 - timp.,perc. - str.   6:00 K.O.D.A.
—— JERONIMUS AND LEONARD (FOR 2 BASSOONS AND
ORCH.) (1946)
K.O.D.A.
—— PALACE OF TOYS, OP. 12 (SUITE MINIATURE)
2,2,2,2 - 2,2,1,0 - timp.,perc.,cel. - mandolin - hp. - str.
18:00 K.O.D.A.
—— SERENADE ESPAGNOLE (FOR SAXOPHONE AND ORCH.)
(1935)
K.O.D.A.
—— SUITE, OP. 28 (MAGERNES GAVE)
2,2,2,3 sax.,2 - 2,2,1,1 - timp.,perc.,xyl. - guit.   K.O.D.A.
—— THREE PIECES FOR SMALL ORCH., OP. 16
7:00 K.O.D.A.
—— VARIATIONS ON A THEME OF KUHLAU
str.   15:00 K.O.D.A.

ROLAND, Claude
—— ROSSIGNOLET DU BOIS, OP. 50 (1971)
3,3,3,3 - 4,4,3,1 - timp.,perc. - str.   17:00 H. Elkan.

ROLAND-MANUEL, Alexis
—— ISABELLE ET PANTALON (2-ACT OPERA-BUFFA) (1922) %
2,3,2,2 - 2,2,2,1 - timp.,perc.,cel. - str.   60:00 Presser.
—— MUSIC FROM THE BALLET "LE TOURNOI SINGULIER"
2,3,2,2 - 2,2,1,0 - timp.,perc.,cel. - hp. - pf. - str.   7:00 Presser.
—— MUSIC FROM THE BALLET "L'ÉCRAN DES JEUNES FILLES"
4,3,3,4 - 4,3,3,1 - timp.,perc.(3) - pf. - str.   30:00 Presser.

—— OVERTURE TO "ISABELLE ET PANTALON"
2,3,2,2 - 2,2,2,1 - timp.,perc.,cel. - hp. - str.   6:00 Presser.

ROLDÁN, Amadeo
—— HIMNO DEL A.B.C. (WITH TREBLE VOICES AD LIB.)
3,2,2,2 - 4,3,3,1 - timp.,perc. - str.   3:00 Southern.
—— MOTIVOS DE SON (8 CUBAN SONGS) (FOR HIGH VOICE
AND ORCH.)
0,2,0,0 - 0,2,0,0 - perc. - str.   6:30 Presser.
—— LA MUERTE ALEGRE
1,1,1,1 - 0,1,1,0 - hp. - str.   11:00 Southern.
—— OVERTURE ON CUBAN FOLK THEMES (OBERTURA SOBRE
TEMAS POPULARES CUBANOS)
3,3,3,3 - 4,3,3,1 - timp.,perc.,cel. - hp. - str.   Southern.
—— SUITE FROM THE BALLET "LA REBAMBARAMBA"
3,3,3,3 - 4,3,3,1 - timp.,perc. - pf. - str.   8:00 C. Fischer.
—— THREE LITTLE POEMS
3,3,3,2 - 4,3,3,1 - timp.,perc.,cel. - pf. - str.   8:00 C. Fischer.

ROLLA, Alessandro - ABBADO, M.
—— CONCERTO IN A MAJOR FOR VIOLIN AND ORCH.
(REVISED AND WITH NEW CADENZAS)
          Leeds.

ROLLA, Alessandro - BECK, S.
—— CONCERTO FOR VIOLA AND ORCH., OP. 3
0,2,0,0 - 2,0,0,0 - str.   25:00 Belw-Mills.

ROLLA, Alessandro - HERBERGER, Rolf
—— CONCERTO IN F MAJOR FOR VIOLA AND STRING ORCH.
str.   22:00 Mannheimer.

ROLLIN, Jean
—— CONCERTO FOR PIANO AND STRINGS (1951)
pf. - str.   20:00 Salabert.
—— CONCERTO FOR VIOLIN AND ORCH.
1,1,1,1 - 2,1,1,0 - str.   20:00 Salabert.
—— MAGNUS (1950)
3,2,2,2 - 4,2,3,0 - timp.,perc. - hp. - str.   10:00 Salabert.
—— MOSES (ORATORIO) (1943)
          65:00 Salabert.

ROMAN, Johan Helmich - ADORJAN, Andras
—— CONCERTO IN G MAJOR, FOR FLUTE AND ORCH.
          Presser.

ROMAN, Johan Helmich - GENETAY, Claude
—— DROTTNINGHOLM MUSIC
1,2,0,1 - 2,2,0,0 - cel. - str.   24:00 Bo. Hawkes.
—— SINFONIA NO. 16 IN D
2 ob. - pf. - str.   EV.
—— SINFONIA NO. 20 IN E MINOR
pf. - str.   EV.

ROMAN, Johan Helmich - ROSENBERG, Hilding
—— CONCERTO GROSSO IN G MINOR, AFTER GEMINIANI
cemb. - str.   7:00 Bo. Hawkes.
—— CONCERTO IN F MINOR, FOR VIOLIN AND STRINGS
cemb. - str.   12:00 Bo. Hawkes.
—— PARTITA IN C MINOR
ob. - pf. - str.   EV.

ROMAN, Johan Helmich - SÖDERBLOM, Valdemar
—— CONCERTO GROSSO (FOR 2 VIOLINS, CEMBALO AND
STRING ORCH.)
org.(or cemb.) - str.   12:00 Nordiska.

ROMAN, Johan Helmich - SVENSSON, Sven
—— JUBILATE (PSALM 100) (FOR SOLOISTS, MIXED CHORUS
AND ORCH.)
2 ob. - 2 tpt. - org. - str.   Bo. Hawkes.

ROMBERG, Andreas Jakob - WINTER, Aubrey
—— TOY SYMPHONY
perc.(toy instr: cuckoo, quail, nightingale, tpt., rattle, trg.,dr.) - pf.
(ad lib.) - str.   22:00 Bo. Hawkes.

RONNEFELD, Peter
—— CONCERTINO
1,0,1,1 - 1,0,0,0 - str.   12:00 Modern.
—— IMPROVISATION FOR ORCHESTRA
3(3rd alt. with picc.),3(3rd alt. with Eng. hn.),0,3(3rd alt. with
c.-bn.) - 4,3,3,1 - timp.,perc.(5) - hp. - str.   10:00 Modern.

—— LITTLE SUITE FOR ORCH.
2,2,2,0 - 3,2,0,0 - timp. - str.   15:00 Modern.
—— OVERTURE: "NON SCHOLAE, SED VITAE"
1,1,1,1 - 0,0,0,0 - str.   5:50 Modern.
—— QUARTÄR, OP. 5 (CANTATA) (FOR SOPRANO, SPEAKING
VOICE, SPEAKING CHORUS, SATB CHORUS AND ORCH.)
(Text: Gottfried Benn)
3(3rd alt. with picc.),3,3(3rd alt. with b.-cl.),3(3rd alt. with c.-bn.)
- 4,3,3,1 - timp.,perc.(5) - hp. - pf. - str.   23:00 Modern.
—— RONDO FOR ORCH.
3(3rd alt. with picc.),3(3rd alt. with Eng. hn.),3(3rd alt. with
b.-cl.),3(3rd alt. with c.-bn.) - 4,3,3,1 - timp.,perc.(5, incl. 4 on
timp.) - hp. - str.   13:00 Modern.
—— SUITE FROM THE OPERA "DIE AMEISE"
3(3rd alt. with picc.),3(3rd alt. with Eng. hn.),3(3rd alt. with
b.-cl.),3(3rd alt. with c.-bn.) - 4,3,3,1 - timp.,perc.(9-11, incl. 5 on
timp.),cel. - pf. - str.   10:15 Modern.
—— SYMPHONY '52 (DEDICATED TO THE TRITONE)
2,2,2,2 - 2,2,0,0 - timp. - str.   15:00 Modern.
—— TWO EPISODES
1,*1,*1,0 - 0,1,1,0 - perc.,xyl. - str.   12:00 Modern.

ROOPER, Jasper
—— DIVERTIMENTO FOR STRINGS (1967)
str.   10:00 P.R.S.

ROOS, Robert de
—— ADAGIO FOR SMALL ORCH.
1,1,1,1 - 2,1,0,0 - perc. - str.   9:00 Henmar.
—— COMPOSIZIONE PER ORCHESTRA (1962)
3,3,3,3 - 4,3,3,1 - timp.,perc.,cel. - hp. - str.   11:00 Henmar.
—— CONCERTINO FOR VIOLIN AND ORCH.
2,2,3,2 - 3,3,2,0 - timp.,perc. - str.   15:00 Henmar.
—— CONCERTO FOR PIANO AND ORCH. (1944)
2,2,2,2 - 4,3,3,0 - timp.,perc. - hp. - pf. - str.   25:00 Henmar.
—— CONCERTO FOR TWO VIOLINS AND ORCH. (1958)
2,2,3,2 - 4,3,2,0 - timp.,perc. - str.   28:00 Henmar.
—— CONCERTO FOR VIOLA AND ORCH.
2,2,3,1 - 4,3,2,0 - timp.,perc. - str.   20:00 Henmar.
—— CONCERTO FOR VIOLIN AND ORCH.
2,2,3,3 - 4,3,1,0 - timp.,perc. - str.   22:00 Henmar.
—— DANCES FOR FLUTE AND ORCH.
1,1,3,0 - 2,1,0,0 - timp. - str.   15:00 Henmar.
—— LANDELIJKE COMEDIE (DANSPANTOMIME) %
2,2,2,2 - 2,2,2,0 - timp.,perc.,xyl. - hp. - str.   20:00 Henmar.
—— LYRIC SUITE (FOR MIXED CHORUS AND ORCH.) (1938)
1,0,1,1 alto. sax.,0 - 0,0,1,0 - timp.,perc. - str.   20:00 Henmar.
—— MOUVEMENT SYMPHONIQUE
3,2,2,2 - 2,2,2,0 - timp. - str.   9:00 Henmar.
—— OVERTURE TO A TRAGI-COMEDY
3,3,3,3 - 4,3,3,1 - timp.,perc. - hp. - pf. - str.   6:00 Bo. Hawkes.
—— QUO VADIS (SUITE)
3,3,2,3 - 4,3,3,1 - timp.,perc.,xyl. - pf. - str.   15:00 Henmar.
—— SINFONIA IN DUE MOTI (1968)
str.   12:00 Henmar.
—— SINFONIA NO. 2
3,2,3,2 - 4,3,3,1 - timp.,perc. - hp. - str.   22:00 Henmar.
—— SINFONIA ROMANTICA (MUSEUM-SYMPHONIE) (FOR
CHAMBER ORCH.) (1943)
2 ob. - 2 hn. - str.   23:00 Henmar.
—— SINFONIETTA
2,3,2,2 - 4,3,3,1 - timp.,perc.,cel. - hp. - str.   15:00 Henmar.
—— SUGGESTIONI (1961)
2,2,3,3 - 4,2,3,1 - timp.,perc.,cel.,xyl. - hp. - str.   12:00 Henmar.
—— VARIATIONS SÉRIEUSES SUR UN THÈME INGÉNU
3,3,2,2 - 4,2,3,1 - timp.,perc. - str.   15:00 Henmar.

ROOSEVELT, Willard
—— CONCERTO FOR CELLO AND ORCHESTRA
2,2,2,2 - 4,2,3,1 - timp.,perc. - str.   15:00 Presser.

ROOTHAM, Cyril B.
—— PAN: AN ORCHESTRAL RHAPSODY
2,2,3,2 - 4,2,3,1 - timp.,perc.(5) - hp. - str.   12:00 Oxford.
—— PROCESSIONAL (WITH HIGH VOICES AD LIB.)
2,2,2,2 - 4,2,3,1 - timp.,perc. - str.   7:00 Oxford.
—— PSALM OF ADONIS
1,1,2,1 - 1,1,0,0 - str.   10:00 Oxford.
—— RHAPSODY ON THE OLD ENGLISH TUNE "LAZARUS" (FOR
DOUBLE STRING ORCH.)
str.   7:00 Chappell.
—— SAINT JOHN'S SUITE
1,1,2,0 - 1,1(or cnt.),1,0 - perc.(3-4) - str.   10:00 Oxford.

or:
1,*1,2,1 - 1,1(or cnt.),0,0 - perc.(3-4) - str.
or:
perc. - pf. - str.
—— SYMPHONY NO. 1, IN C MINOR
2(2nd alt. with picc.),*2,2,2 - 4,2,3,1 - timp.,perc.(3),cel. - hp. - str.
30:00 Oxford.
—— SYMPHONY NO. 2, IN D MAJOR (WITH WOMEN'S SA CHORUS)
2,*2,2,3 - 4,2,3,1 - timp. - hp. - str.   35:00 Oxford.

ROPARTZ, (Joseph) Guy
—— À MARIE ENDORMIE (SYMPHONIC SKETCH)
2,2,2,2 - 4,2,3,0 - timp. - hp. - str.   6:00 EV.
—— CANTIQUE À SAINTE JEANNE D'ARC (FOR BARITONE, MIXED CHORUS AND ORCH.)
2,2,2,2 - 2,2,0,0 - timp. - str.   8:00 Salabert.
—— LA CHASSE DU PRINCE ARTHUR (SYMPHONIC ETUDE)
3(3rd alt. with picc.),3,3,3 - 4,3,4,0 - timp.,perc. - hp. - str.
10:00 EV.
—— CONCERT EN RÉ MAJEUR
2,2,2,2 - 4,2,3,0 - timp.,perc.(3),cel. - hp. - str.   23:00 EV.
—— DIVERTIMENTO
2,2,2,2 - 2,2,0,0 - timp.,perc. - str.   14:00 Salabert.
—— DIVERTISSEMENT
2,3,2,2 - 4,2,3,0 - timp.,perc. - hp. - str.   11:00 EV.
—— FANTASY IN D MAJOR
3,2,2,2 - 4,2,3,0 - timp. - str.   15:00 Salabert.
—— INDISCREET (1-ACT BALLET) (BASED ON SOPHOCLES' "OEDIPUS AT COLONUS") %
EV.
—— JEUNES FILLES
2,2,2,2 - 4,2,3,0 - timp.,perc.,cel. - hp. - str.   16:00 EV.
—— LITTLE SYMPHONY (FOR CHAMBER ORCH.)
1,1,2,1 - 2,1,1,0 - perc. - str.   18:00 EV.
—— NOCTURNE (FOR SATB CHORUS AND ORCH.)
2,3,2,3 - 4,2,3,0 - timp.,perc.,cel. - hp. - str.   6:00 EV.
—— OEDIPE À COLONE (SUITE)
2,2,2,2 - 2,2,0,0 - timp. - hp. - str.   27:00 EV.
—— PASTORALES
1,1,2,1 - 2,1,0,0 - timp.,perc. - hp. - str.   16:00 EV.
—— PRÉLUDE DOMINICAL ET SIX PIÈCES À DANSER
3,3,3,2 - 4,3,3,0 - timp.,perc.(4),cel.,xyl. - hp. - str. 20:00 EV.
—— PSALM 129 ("DE PROFUNDIS") (FOR BARITONE, SATB CHORUS AND ORCH.)
2,2,2,2 - 4,2,3,0 - str.   8:00 EV.
—— PSALM 136 (FOR MIXED CHORUS, ORGAN AND ORCH.)
2,2,3,2 - 4,2,3,0 - timp. - org. - str.   17:00 Salabert.
—— QUATRE PIÈCES (FROM THE PIANO SUITE "DANS L'OMBRE DE LA MONTAGNE")
3,2,3,2 - 4,2,3,0 - timp. - hp. - str.   18:20 EV.
—— QUATRE POÈMES (FOR VOICE AND ORCH.)
Salabert.
—— REQUIEM (FOR VOICE, CHORUS AND ORCH.)
2,2,2,2 - 4,2,3,0 - timp. - str.   20:00 EV.
—— RHAPSODY FOR CELLO AND ORCH.
2,2,2,1 - 3,1,0,0 - timp.,perc. - hp. - str.   17:00 EV.
—— ROMANZA E SCHERZINO (FOR VIOLIN AND ORCH.)
1,1,1,1 - 2,0,0,0 - timp. - hp. - str.   6:00 EV.
—— SÉRÉNADE CHAMPÊTRE
1,1,2,1 - 2,1,0,0 - timp. - str.   7:00 EV.
—— SOIR SUR LES CHAUMES (SYMPHONIC ETUDE)
3,3,3,2 - 4,3,4,0 - timp. - hp. - str.   14:30 EV.
—— SONS DE CLOCHES (IN 3 MOVTS.)
1,1,1,1 - hn. - timp. - hp. - str.   11:00 Salabert.
—— SYMPHONY NO. 3 (WITH CHORUS)
3,3,3,3 - 4,3,4,0 - timp. - 2 hp. - str.   50:00 Salabert.
—— SYMPHONY NO. 5
2,2,2,2 - 4,2,3,0 - timp.,perc. - hp. - str.   EV.

ROPER, E. Stanley
—— TE DEUM IN G MAJOR (FOR CHORUS AND ORCH.)
Oxford.

ROREM, Ned
—— AIR MUSIC (TEN VARIATIONS FOR ORCHESTRA)
3,3,4,3 - 4,3,3,1 - perc.,cel. - hp. - pf. - str.   20:00 Bo. Hawkes.
—— THE ASCENSION
2,2,2,2 - 2,3,1,1 - timp.   21:00 Bo. Hawkes.
—— ASSEMBLY AND FALL
3,3,3,2 - 4,3,3,1 - timp.,perc. - hp. - str.   25:00 Bo. Hawkes.
—— A CHILDHOOD MIRACLE (1-ACT OPERA) %
1,1,1,1 - 2,1,0,0 - perc. - pf. - str.   Southern.

—— CONCERTO NO. 2 FOR PIANO AND ORCH. (IN 3 MOVTS.)
2,2,2,2 - 2,1,0,0 - timp.,perc.(3),xyl. - hp. - pf. - str.
18:00 Southern.
—— CONCERTO NO. 3 FOR PIANO AND ORCH. (1969) (IN 6 MOVTS.)
3(3rd alt. with picc.),3(3rd alt. with Eng.hn.),3(3rd alt. with Ebcl.),3(3rd alt. with cbn.) - 4,3,3,1 - timp.,perc.(5),bells,cel.,glock.,xyl. - hp. - pf. - str.
27:00 Bo. Hawkes.
—— DESIGN FOR ORCHESTRA
2,2,2,2 - 4,2,2,0 - timp.,perc.,cel. - hp. - pf. - str.
17:30 Bo. Hawkes.
—— EAGLES (SYMPHONIC POEM)
3,3,4,3 - 4,3,3,1 - timp.,perc.,cel.(or pf.) - hp. - str.
8:30 Bo. Hawkes.
—— ELEVEN STUDIES FOR ELEVEN PLAYERS
1(alt. with picc.),1(alt. with Eng.hn.),1,0 - 0,1,0,0 - perc.(2),glock.,xyl. - hp. - pf. - 1 vln.,1 vla.,1 c.
25:00 Bo. Hawkes.
—— IDEAS FOR ORCHESTRA
1,1,1,1 - 2,1,1,0 - timp.,perc. - hp. - pf. - str.   12:00 Bo. Hawkes.
—— IN MEMORIAM
str.   6:00 Southern.
—— LAUDEMUS TEMPUS ACTUM (FOR MIXED CHORUS AND ORCH.) (Text: Composer)
2,2,2,2 - 2,2,2,0 - timp. - hp. - str.   2:30 Bo. Hawkes.
—— LENTO FOR STRINGS
str.   Southern.
—— LETTERS FROM PARIS (FOR MIXED CHORUS AND ORCH.) (Texts: Janet Flanner)
1,1,1,1 - 1,1,1,0- timp.,perc.,cel. - hp. - harm. - pf. - str.
25:00 Bo. Hawkes.
—— LIFT UP YOUR HEADS (FOR MIXED CHORUS, WINDS AND TIMPANI) (Text: John Beaumont)
2,2,2,2 - 2,3,3,1 - timp.   4:00 Bo. Hawkes.
—— LIONS (FOR 4-PIECE COMBO OF ALTO SAXOPHONE, PIANO, DRUMS, DOUBLE BASS AND ORCH.)
3,3,3,alto sax.,2 - 4,3,3,1 - timp.,perc.,cel. - hp. - 2 pf. - str.
14:00 Bo. Hawkes.
—— MISS JULIE (2-ACT OPERA) %
2,2,2,2 - 3,2,2,0 - perc. - hp. - str.   Bo. Hawkes.
—— MOURNING SCENE FROM SAMUEL (FOR VOICE AND STRINGS)
str.   7:00 Henmar.
—— OVERTURE IN C
2(2nd alt. with picc.),2,2,2 - 4,2,3,1 - timp.,perc.(2),xyl. - hp. - pf. - str.   10:00 Chappell.
—— PILGRIMS
str.   5:30 Bo. Hawkes.
—— THE POET'S REQUIEM (FOR SOPRANO, MIXED CHORUS AND ORCH.) (IN 8 MOVTS.)
2,2,2,2 - 2,1,1,0 - timp.,perc.(2),xyl. - hp. - pf. - str.
22:00 Bo. Hawkes.
—— POÈMES POUR LA PAIX (FOR MEDIUM VOICE AND STRING ORCH.) (Texts: Regnier. Ronsard, de Magny, Durat and de Baif)
str.   12:30 Bo. Hawkes.
—— THE ROBBERS (OPERA-MELODRAMA IN 1 SCENE) % (Text: Composer)
1,1,2,1 - 1,0,0,0 - perc. - pf.(or cel.) - str.(2,1,1,1)
28:00 Bo. Hawkes.
—— A SERMON ON MIRACLES (FOR SOLO VOICE, UNISON CHORUS AND STRINGS) (Text: Paul Goodman)
str.   7:00 Bo. Hawkes.
—— SINFONIA FOR 15 WINDS
9:00 Henmar.
—— SIX IRISH POEMS (FOR VOICE AND ORCH.)
2,2,2,2 - 2,0,0,0 - perc.(1) - hp. - str.   15:00 Southern.
—— SIX SONGS FOR HIGH VOICE AND ORCH.
14:00 Henmar.
—— SUN (FOR SOPRANO AND ORCH.) (Texts: Ikhnaton, Byron, Goodman, Blake, Morgan, Shakespeare, Whitman and Roethke)
3,3,2,3 - 4,3,3,1 - timp.,perc. - hp. - pf. - str.   26:00 Bo. Hawkes.
—— SYMPHONY NO. 1
1. Maestoso; 2. Andantino; 3. Largo; 4. Allegro
2(2nd alt. with picc.),2,2,2 - 4,2,2,0 - timp.,perc.(2),xyl. - hp. - str.
25:00 Southern.
—— SYMPHONY NO. 2 (IN 3 MOVTS.)
2(2nd alt. with picc.),2(2nd alt. with Eng. hn.),2,2 - 2,1,1,0 - timp.,perc.(1),xyl. - hp. - pf. - str.   18:00 Bo. Hawkes.
—— SYMPHONY NO. 3 (IN 5 MOVTS.)
*3,*3,3,3 - 4,3,3,1 - timp.,perc.(4),bells,cel.,glock.,xyl. - hp. - pf. - str.   23:30 Bo. Hawkes.

—— WATER MUSIC (FOR CLARINET, VIOLIN AND ORCH.)
    1,1,1,1 - 1,0,0,0 - perc. - hp. - pf. - str.   17:00 Bo. Hawkes.

ROSE, David
—— HOLLYWOOD BOWL SUITE (IN 3 MOVTS.)
    *3,*3,*3,*3 - 2-4,3,3,1 - timp.,perc.(1-2),glock. - hp. - pf.(ad lib.) -
    str.   12:00 E. H. Morris.
—— HOROSCOPE SUITE
    *3,*3,*3,*3 - 4,3,3,1 - timp.,perc.(2-4) - hp. - pf.(ad lib.) - str.
                                                          22:00 B V & C.

ROSE, Griffith Wheeler
—— BLUE BEARD (FOR BARITONE VOICE AND CHAMBER
    ORCH.) (1966) (IN 3 MOVTS.) (Text: Russell Thomas)
    0,0,0,0 - 2,2,2,0 - str.(2,1,1,0)   12:00 Composer.
—— COMPLAINTES (TWO TEXTS OF JULES LAFORGUE) (FOR
    SOPRANO AND CHAMBER ORCH.) (1964)
    2(1 alt. with picc.),0,2(2nd alt. with b.-cl.),0 - 0,0,0,0 -
    perc.(2),glock.,xyl. - pf. - str.(2,1,1,0)   8:00 Presser.
—— CONCERTO FOR VIOLA AND CHAMBER ENSEMBLE (1974)
    (IN 3 MOVTS.)
    1,1,1,1 - 1,1,1,0 - hp. - pf. - str.(2,2,1,1)   11:00 Presser.
—— CONCERTO NO. 2 FOR VIOLA AND ORCH. (1975) (IN 4
    MOVTS.)
    1,1,1,1 - 2,1,1,0 - perc.(2),vibra. - hp. - pf. - str.(2,2,1,1)
                                                          20:00 Presser.
—— CRESCENDO - INTERLUDE - VARIATIONS (1972)
    0,0,0,0 - 4,3,3,1 - 2 pf. - str.(2,1,1,0)   16:00 Presser.

ROSE, John L.
—— CLOUD PHANTASY, OP. 1 (1946)
    2,3,2,2 - 2,2,3,0 - str.   7:30 P.R.S.
—— CONCERTO FOR PIANO AND ORCH., OP. 24 (1965)
    2,3,2,2 - 4,3,3,1 - timp.,perc. - hp. - pf. -str.   31:00 P.R.S.
—— SLOW MUSIC FOR STRINGS AND HARP, OP. 3 (1949)
    hp. - str.   6:00 P.R.S.
—— SUITE NO. 1 FOR SMALL ORCH. OP. 15 (1958)
                                                          P.R.S.
—— SYMPHONIC DANCES FOR ORCH., OP 20 (1962)
    3,3,2,2 - 4,2,3,1 - timp.,perc. - str.   28:00 P.R.S.
—— SYMPHONY NO. 3, OP. 21 (1963)
    3,3,2,2 - 4,2,3,1 - timp. - str.   23:00 P.R.S.

ROSE, Sykes Leonard
—— ETUDE FOR ORCH. (1971)
    1,1,1,1 - 1,0,0,0 - perc. - pf. - str.   8:00 A.P.R.A.

ROSEINGRAVE, Thomas - LAMBERT, Constant
—— OVERTURE IN F
    2,1,0,1 - 2,2,0,0 - str.   7:00 Oxford.

ROSEINGRAVE, Thomas - YOUNG, Percy
—— ARISE, SHINE (FOR SOLOISTS, SATB CHORUS AND ORCH.)
    0,2,0,1(ad lib.) - 0,2,0,0 - timp.(ad lib.) - cemb. - str.
                                                          30:00 Bo. Hawkes.

ROSELL, Lars-Erik
—— MOMENTS OF CHANGING SONORITY (1969)
    Hammond org. - hpsc. - str.   8:15 Fleisher.

ROSENBERG, Hilding
—— BERGSLAGBILDER (SUITE)
    2,1,2,1 - 2,2,1,0 - timp.,perc. - str.   16:00 Nordiska.
—— CONCERTO FOR CELLO AND ORCH.
    2,2,2,2 - 3,3,0,0 - timp.,perc.(2) - str.   22:00 Gehrmans.
—— CONCERTO FOR ORCHESTRA
    3,2,2,2 - 4,3,3,1 - timp.,perc. - hp. - str.   27:00 Gehrmans.
—— CONCERTO FOR PIANO AND ORCH.
    2,2,2,2 - 3,2,0,0 - timp.,perc. - pf. - str.   34:00 Nordiska.
—— CONCERTO FOR TRUMPET AND ORCH.
    2,2,2,2 - 2,1,3,0 - perc.(3) - str.   17:00 S.T.I.M.
—— CONCERTO FOR VIOLA AND ORCH.
    2,2,2,2 - 3,2,0,0 - timp. - hp. - str.   33:00 Nordiska.
—— CONCERTO FOR VIOLA AND STRING ORCH.
    str.   20:00 Nordiska.
—— CONCERTO NO. 1 FOR VIOLIN AND ORCH.
    2,2,2,2 - 3,2,0,0 - timp.,perc. - str.   30:00 Suecia.
—— CONCERTO NO. 2 FOR CELLO AND ORCH.
    2,2,2,2 - 3,3,0,0 - timp.,perc. - str.   27:00 Bo. Hawkes.
—— CONCERTO NO. 2 FOR ORCH.
    3,2,2,2 - 4,3,3,1 - timp.,perc. - str.   27:00 Bo. Hawkes.
—— CONCERTO NO. 2 FOR VIOLIN AND ORCH.
    2,2,2,2 - 3,2,0,0 - timp.,perc. - str.   32:00 Nordiska.

—— CONCERTO NO. 4 FOR STRING ORCH. (1966)
    str.   14:00 Gehrmans.
—— DANCE SUITE (DE TVÅ KONUNGADÖTTRARNA)
    1,1,2,1 - 1,1,0,0 - timp.,perc.,cel. - pf. - str.   11:00 S.T.I.M.
—— DANCE SUITE FROM "MARIONETTER"
    2,2,2,2 - 2,2,0,0 - timp.,perc. - str.   11:00 Nordiska.
—— DJUFAR: SUITE
    2,2,2,1 - 3,2,0,0 - timp.,perc. - pf. - str.   24:00 Nordiska.
—— THE HOLY NIGHT (FOR SOLO VOICES, CHORUS AND
    ORCH.)
    1,1,2,0 - 2,2,0,0 - timp.,perc.,cel. - str.   32:00 G. Schirmer.
—— LENTO (FOR STRING ORCH.)(1956)
    str.   EriksMhflg.
—— THE LOUISVILLE CONCERTO (FOR VIOLIN, VIOLA, CELLO
    AND ORCH.)
    2,2,2,2 - 4,2,3,1 - timp.,perc.(3),cel. - hp. - str. 20:00 S.T.I.M.
—— MARIONETTER: SUITE
    1,1,2,1 - 2,2,0,0 - timp. - hp. - pf. - str.   15:00 Nordiska.
—— METAMORFOSI SINFONICHE I (1963)
    3,3,3,3 - 4,3,3,1 - timp.,perc.(4) - 2 hp. - str.   15:00 S.T.I.M.
—— METAMORFOSI SINFONICHE II (1963)
    3,3,3,3 - 4,3,3,1 - timp.,perc.(4) - 2 hp. - str.   10:00 S.T.I.M.
—— METAMORFOSI SINFONICHE III (1964)
    1,1,1,0 - 0,0,0,0 - pf. - str.   18:00 S.T.I.M.
—— NOCTURNE FROM "ORPHEUS I STA'N"
    2,2,2,2 - 4,3,3,1 - timp.,perc. - hp. - str.   5:00 Nordiska.
—— ORPHEUS IN TOWN ("ORPHEUS I STA'N"): DANCE SUITE
    2,2,2,2 - 4,3,3,1 - timp.,perc.(2) - pf. - str.   12:00 G. Schirmer.
—— OVERTURA PICCOLA (LUSTSPELS OVERTURE)
    2,1,2,sax.,1 - 2,2,1,0 - timp.,perc. - hp. - pf. - str.
                                                          3:30 G. Schirmer.
—— OVERTURE BIANCA-NERA (FOR STRINGS)
    str.   10:00 Nordiska.
—— OVERTURE TO "MARIONETTER"
    2,2,2,2 - 2,2,0,0 - timp.,perc. - str.   6:00 G. Schirmer.
—— PARTITA (SUITE) NO. 3 FROM THE OPERA-ORATORIO
    "JOSEPH AND HIS BROTHERS"
    2,2,2,2 - 4,3,3,1 - timp.,perc.(3) - hp. - str.   16:00 S.T.I.M.
—— PLASTISKA SCENE, FROM "ORPHEUS I STA'N"
    2,2,2,2 - 4,3,3,1 - timp.,perc.(3),cel. - 2 pf. - str. 22:00 S.T.I.M.
—— PRELUDE TO "YTTERSTA DOMEN"
    2,2,2,2 - 4,2,3,1 - timp.,perc.,cel. - pf. - str.   Suecia.
    or:
    3,3,4,3 - 4,3,3,1 - timp.,perc.(3),cel. - hp. - pf. - str.
—— RESA TILL AMERIKA: SUITE
    2,2,2,2 - 4,3,3,1 - timp.,perc.(2) - hp. - str.   20:00 Suecia.
—— RIFLESSIONI NO. 1 (FOR VIOLIN AND STRING ORCH.)
    (1959)
    str.   22:00 Nordiska.
—— RIFLESSIONI NO. 2 (1960)
    str.   25:00 Nordiska.
—— RIFLESSIONI NO. 3 (1960)
    str.   22:00 Nordiska.
—— SCHERZO FROM "ORPHEUS I STA'N"
    2,2,2,2 - 4,3,3,1 - timp.,perc. - hp. - str.   S.T.I.M.
—— SINFONIA DA CHIESA NO. 1
    1,1,1,1 - 2,0,0,0 - timp., - pf. - str.   20:00 S.T.I.M.
—— SINFONIA DA CHIESA NO. 2
    2,2,2,2 - 4,2,0,0 - timp.,perc. - str.   22:00 Nordiska.
—— SINFONIA GRAVE (SYMPHONY NO. 2)
    2,2,2,2 - 4,2,3,1 - timp.,perc.(2) - str.   35:00 S.T.I.M.
—— SUITE IN D MAJOR (FOR VIOLIN AND SMALL ORCH.)
    2,1,2,1 - 0,0,0,0 - str.   17:00 Nordiska.
—— SVIT ÖVER SVENSKA LÅTAR (FOR STRINGS)
    str.   15:00 Nordiska.
—— SYMPHONIE CONCERTANTE (FOR VIOLIN, VIOLA, OBOE,
    BASSOON AND ORCH.)
    0,1,0,1 - 2,2,0,0 - str.   20:00 S.T.I.M.
—— SYMPHONY FOR WIND ORCHESTRA (1966)
    2,2,2,2 - 0,3,3,0 - timp.,perc.(4)   18:00 S.T.I.M.
—— SYMPHONY NO. 1
    2,2,2,2 - 4,3,3,1 - timp.,perc. - str.   35:00 S.T.I.M.
—— SYMPHONY NO. 3
    2,2,2,2 - 4,2,3,1 - timp.,perc. - hp. - str.   35:00 Nordiska.
—— SYMPHONY NO. 4 (THE REVELATION OF ST. JOHN) (FOR
    BARITONE, MIXED CHORUS AND ORCH.)
    2,2,2,2 - 4,4,3,1 - timp.,perc. - str.   70:00 Nordiska.
—— SYMPHONY NO. 5 ("HORTULANUS") (FOR CONTRALTO,
    CHORUS AND ORCH.)
    2,2,2,2 - 4,2,3,1 - timp.,perc. - pf. - str.   45:00 Bo. Hawkes.
—— SYMPHONY NO. 6
    2,2,2,2 - 3,2,3,0 - timp.,perc. - str.   25:00 S.T.I.M.

—— SYMPHONY NO. 7 (1968)
    2,2,2,2 - 4,3,3,1 - timp.,perc.(4) - str.   24:00 S.T.I.M.
—— SYMPHONY NO. 8 ("IN CANDIDUM")(FOR SATB CHORUS AND ORCH.)(1973) (Text: V. Ekelund)
    2,2,2,2 - 4,3,3,1 - timp.,perc.,cel. - hp. - str.   45:00 Fleisher.
—— TAFFLEMUSIK (FOR CHAMBER ORCH.) (IN 4 MOVTS.)
    13:00 Gehrmans.
—— VINDARNAS MUSIC (SUITE FROM "LYCKSALIGHETENS")
    3,2,2,2 - 4,3,3,1 - timp.,perc.(3),cel. - 2 pf. - str.   18:00 S.T.I.M.
—— YTTERSTA DOMEN: SUITE
    3,3,4,3 - 4,3,3,1 - timp.,perc.(2),cel. - hp. - pf. - str.   20:00 Suecia.

ROSENBOOM, David
—— CALIBAN UPON SETEBOS
    2,2,2,sax.,1 - 2,2,2,0 - perc. - pf. - str.   15:00 Seesaw.

ROSENGREN, Frank
—— MARKNADSGYCKEL (CONCERT OVERTURE)(1973)
    2,3,3,3 - 4,3,3,1 - timp.,perc. - str.   5:00 Fleisher.

ROSENMAN, Leonard
—— CHAMBER MUSIC NO. 1 (SUITE FOR 15 INSTRS.)
    24:00 Composer.

ROSENTHAL, Laurence
—— ODE
    3(3rd alt. with picc.),2,2,2 - 4,3,3,1 - timp.,perc.(4),bells,cel.,glock.,vibra. - 2 hp. - pf. - str.   13:00 Composer.
—— OVERTURE IN C
    2(1st alt. with picc.),2,2,2 - 4,3,2,0 - timp.,perc.(2),glock. - pf. - str.   6:00 Composer.

ROSENTHAL, Manuel
—— AEOLUS (FOR WIND QUINTET AND STRINGS)
    1,1,1,1 - 1,0,0,0 - str.   18:00 Presser.
—— AESOPI CONVIVIUM (FOR VIOLIN, PIANO AND ORCH.)
    3,2,2,2 - 2,3,3,1 - timp.,perc. - hp. - pf. - str.   23:00 EV.
—— CHANSONS DU MONSIEUR BLEU (12 SONGS FOR MEZZO-SOPRANO AND ORCH.) (Text: Nino)
    1,1,1,1 sax.,1 - 1,0,0,0 - timp.,perc. - harm. - hp. - str.   28:00 EV.
—— CHRISTMAS CANTATA (CANTATE POUR LE TEMPS DE LA NATIVITÉ) (FOR SOPRANO, CHORUS AND ORCH.)
    2,1,2,2 - 1,0,0,0 - timp.,perc. - str.   35:00 EV.
—— CONCERTO FOR PIANO AND ORCH.
    *3,*3,*3,*3 - 4,3,3,0 - timp.,perc.,cel. - hp. - pf. - str.   27:00 EV.
—— DEUX ÉTUDES EN CAMAÏEU
    timp. - str.   12:00 Presser.
—— DEUX PRIÈRES POUR LES TEMPS MALHEUREUX ("TWO PRAYERS IN TIMES OF HARDSHIP") (FOR BARITONE AND ORCH.)
    2,2,2,2 - 2,2,1,0 - perc. - str.   6:00 EV.
—— DEUX SONNETS DE JEAN CASSOU (FOR SOPRANO AND ORCH.)
    1,1,1,1 - 1,0,0,0 - timp.,perc. - hp. - str.   4:00 EV.
—— LA FÊTE DU VIN
    3,3,3,2 - 4,4,3,1 - timp.,perc.(4),cel.,glock. - hp. - pf. - str.   19:00 Salabert.
—— HOP SIGNOR! (3-ACT LYRIC DRAMA) % (Text: Michel de Ghelderode)
    2,2,2,2 - 2,2,3,1 - timp.,perc.(4) - hp. - str.   135:00 EV.
    On Stage 1,0,2,0 - 2,1,3,1 - perc.
—— JEANNE D'ARC (FOR NARRATOR AND ORCH.)
    3,3,3,3 - 4,4,3,1 - timp.,perc. - 2 hp. - str.   35:00 EV.
—— MAGIC MANHATTAN
    3,*3,3,3 - 4,4,3,1 - timp.,perc. - hp. - pf. - str.   22:00 EV.
—— MUSIQUE DE TABLE (SUITE) (IN 8 MOVTS.)
    *3,*3,*3,*3 - 4,3,3,1 - timp.,perc.,cel. - hp. - str.   25:00 EV.
—— NOCE VILLAGEOISE
    2,2,2,2 - 0,0,0,0 - timp. - str.   15:00 EV.
—— LES PETITS MÉTIERS (AFTER A BALLET BY LULLY)
    *2,2,2,*3 - 2,2,2,1 - timp.,perc.,cel. - hp. - str.   23:00 EV.
—— LA PIETA D'AVIGNON (SIX PRAYERS) (FOR VOCAL QUARTET, STRING ORCH., AND TRUMPET)
    1 tpt. - str.   18:00 EV.
—— ST. FRANCIS OF ASSISSI (SUITE FROM THE ORATORIO) (IN 5 MOVTS.)
    3,3,3,3 - 4,4,3,1 - perc.(8) - ondes Martenot - hp. - str.   27:00 EV.
—— ST. FRANCOIS D'ASSISE (FOR NARRATOR, VOICE, CHORUS AND ORCH.)
    *3,*3,*3,*3 - 4,4,3,1 - timp.,perc.,cel. - 2 hps. - org. - str.   55:00 EV.

—— SIX CHANSONS COLONIALES (SIX SONGS ON POEMS OF NINO) (FOR SOPRANO AND ORCH.)
    1,1,1,1 - 1,1,0,0 - perc.,xyl. - str.   20:00 EV.
—— SYMPHONIES DE NOËL (SUITE)
    3,*3,3,*3 - 4,3,3,1 - timp.,perc.,cel. - hp. - str.   31:00 EV.
—— SYMPHONY IN C MAJOR
    3,*3,*3,3 - 4,3,3,1 - timp.,perc. - hp. - str.   29:00 EV.
—— TROIS BURLESQUES (FOR MIXED CHORUS AND ORCH.)
    2,2,2,2 - 2,2,1,0 - perc.(2) - str.   12:00 EV.
—— TROIS CHANSONS D'AMOUR (FOR SOPRANO AND ORCH.)
    2,1,2,1 - 1,1,0,0 - perc. - str.   7:30 EV.
—— TROIS CHANTS DE FEMMES BERBÈRES (FOR SORPANO, CONTRALTO AND ORCH.)
    2,0,2,2 - 2,0,0,0 - timp.,perc. - str.   6:00 EV.
—— TROIS MÉLODIES (WITH MEZZO-SOPRANO OR TENOR) (Text: Marie Roustan)
    2,2,2,2 - 2,0,0,0 - timp.,perc. - hp. - str.   10:00 EV.
—— TROIS PIÈCES LITURGIQUES (WITH HIGH VOICE OR CHORUS)
    2,1,2,2 - 1,0,0,0 - timp.,perc.(2) - str.   5:00 EV.
—— TROIS PRÉCIEUSES (FOR SOPRANO AND ORCH.)
    2,1,2,1 - 1,1,0,0 - perc. - str.   10:00 EV.

ROSETTI, Antonio - KNEUSSLIN
—— SYMPHONY IN G MINOR
    1,2,0,1 - 2,0,0,0 - str.   Henmar.

RÖSLER, Franz Anton - BODART, Eugen
—— CONCERTO IN D MAJOR FOR OBOE AND ORCH.
    2,1,0,2 - 2,0,0,0 - str.   21:00 Mannheimer.
—— CONCERTO IN E FLAT MAJOR FOR HORN AND ORCH.
    0,2,0,0 - 3,0,0,0 - str.   12:00 Mannheimer.

RÖSLER, Franz Anton - HOFMANN, Wolfgang
—— CONCERTO IN E FLAT MAJOR FOR 2 HORNS AND ORCH.
    2,0,0,0 - 4,0,0,0 - str.   20:00 Mannheimer.
—— SYMPHONY IN C MAJOR, OP. 3, NO. 1
    0,2,0,0 - 2,0,0,0 - str.   25:00 Mannheimer.

RÖSLER, Johann Joseph - PRIEGNITZ, Hans
—— KONZERTSTÜCK, IN D MAJOR (FOR PIANO AND ORCH.)
    1,2,0,2 - 2,2,0,0 - timp. - pf. - str.   12:00 F. Colombo.

ROSS, Walter
—— CONCERTO FOR BRASS QUINTET AND ORCH.
    0,0,0,0 - 3,2,2,2 - timp.,perc.,cel. - hp. - str.   20:00 Bo. Hawkes.
—— CONCERTO FOR TROMBONE AND ORCHESTRA
    2,2,2,2 - 2,2,1,0 - timp.,perc. - str.   13:00 Bo. Hawkes.

ROSSEAU, Norbert
—— CONCERTO FOR HORN AND ORCH. (1967)
    3,3,3,3 - 1,2,3,1 - timp.,perc. - str.   14:00 H. Elkan.
—— CONCERTO FOR ORCH., OP. 37 (1948)
    3,3,3,3 - 4,3,3,1 - timp. - hp. - str.   25:00 S.A.B.A.M.
—— CONCERTSONATE, OP. 64 (1957)
    1,1,1,1 - 2,0,0,0 - str.   18:00 H. Elkan.
—— L' EAU (POÈME SYMPHONIQUE) (1939)
    3,3,3,3 - 4,3,3,1 - timp.,perc.,cel.,glock.,xyl. - hp. - pf. - str.   15:00 CBDM.
—— PIÈCES SYMPHONIQUES, OP. 38
    4,4,4,4 - 6,4,3,1 - timp.,perc.,cel.,glock.,xyl. - 2 hp. - pf. - str.   15:00 CBDM.
—— PRELUDE AND FUGUE (1947)
    org. - str.   7:00 H. Elkan.
—— SUITE AGRESTE, OP. 20 (1936)
    2,2,2,2 - 3,2,2,0 - timp.,perc. - hp. - str.   15:00 CBDM.
—— SYMPHONY, OP. 48 (1954)
    4,4,4,4 - 6,3,3,1 - timp.,perc.,glock. - 2 hp. - str.   30:00 H. Elkan.

ROSSELLINI, Renzo
—— DUE CANTI DI MARZO
    2,3,2,2 - 4,2,2,0 - timp.,perc.,cel. - hp. - pf. - str.   8:00 Bo. Hawkes.

ROSSI, Michaelangelo - TONI, Alceo
—— TOCCATA
    2,*3,*3,2 - 4,3,3,1 - timp. - hp. - str.   6:00 Bo. Hawkes.

ROSSI, Salamone - GRADENWITZ, Peter
—— SUITE OF DANCES
    hp. - str.   12:00 IsMuPublns.

ROSSI, Salomone - FOSS, Lukas
—— SALOMONE ROSSI SUITE

9:00 Salabert.

ROSSINI, Gioacchino
—— THE BARBER OF SEVILLE (OPERA) % (Engl. Text: Ruth and Thomas Martin)

G. Schirmer.
—— AN ITALIAN LADY IN ALGIERS (OPERA) % (Engl. Text: Ruth and Thomas Martin)

G. Schirmer.

ROSSINI, Gioacchino - BRITTEN, Benjamin
—— MATINÉES MUSICALES (SUITE), OP. 24
2,2,2,2 - 2-4,2,3,0-1 - timp.,perc.,cel. - hp. - str.

13:00 Bo. Hawkes.
—— SOIRÉES MUSICALES (SUITE), OP. 9
2,2,2,2 - 2,2,3,0 - timp.,perc. - hp.(or pf.) - str. 11:00 Bo. Hawkes.

ROSSINI, Gioacchino - CASELLA, Alfredo
—— SONATA
str.

12:00 Bo. Hawkes.

ROSSINI, Gioacchino - DAUTEL, J. P.
—— VARIATIONS FOR CLARINET AND STRING ORCH.
(Originally for Clarinet andStrings)
1,2,1,1 - 2,0,0,0 - str.

Presser.

ROSSINI, Gioacchino - GRANDIS, Renato de
—— LA ROSSINIANA (1968)
*3,2,2,2 - 4,2,3,1 - perc. - hp. - pf.(alt. with hpsc.) - str.

15:30 Seesaw.

ROSSINI, Gioacchino - MICHAELS, Jost
—— INTRODUCTION, THEME AND VARIATIONS (FOR CLARINET AND ORCH.)
1,2,0,1 - 2,0,0,0 - str.

17:00 F. Colombo.

ROSSINI, Gioacchino - PERRY, Harold
—— OVERTURE TO "IL SIGNOR BRUSCHINO"

5:00 Bo. Hawkes.
—— OVERTURE TO "LA SCALA DI SETA"

6:30 Bo. Hawkes.

ROSSINI, Gioacchino - PERUZZI
—— VARIAZIONI (FOR CLARINET AND SMALL ORCH.)
1,2,1,1 - 2,0,0,0 - str.

9:00 Henmar.

ROSSINI, Gioacchino - RESPIGHI, Ottorino
—— LA BOUTIQUE FANTASQUE (BALLET SUITE)
*3,*3,2,2 - 4,3,3,1 - perc. - hp. - str.

25:00 G. Schirmer.

ROSSINI, Gioacchino - ROBERTS, Charles J.
—— OVERTURE TO "LA GAZZA LADRA"

C. Fischer.
—— OVERTURE TO "SEMIRAMIDE"

C. Fischer.
—— OVERTURE TO "THE BARBER OF SEVILLE"

C. Fischer.
—— OVERTURE TO "THE ITALIAN IN ALGIERS"

7:05 C. Fischer.
—— OVERTURE TO "WILLIAM TELL"

C. Fischer.

ROSSINI, Gioacchino - STUEBER, Carl
—— DER SCHWAN VON PESARO (BALLET SUITE)
2,2,2,2 - 4,2,3,0 - timp.,perc. - hp. - pf. - str.

37:00 Alkor.

ROSSINI, Gioacchino - TONI, Alceo
—— PRELUDIO RELIGIOSO
2,*3,*3,3 - 4,3,3,1 - str.

6:00 Bo. Hawkes.

ROSSINI, Gioacchino - WINTER, Aubrey
—— OVERTURE TO "SEMIRAMIDE"

12:00 Bo. Hawkes.
—— OVERTURE TO "TANCREDI"

5:30 Bo. Hawkes.
—— OVERTURE TO "THE BARBER OF SEVILLE"

7:30 Bo. Hawkes.
—— OVERTURE TO "THE ITALIAN IN ALGIERS"

7:30 Bo. Hawkes.
—— OVERTURE TO "THE SIEGE OF CORINTH"

9:00 Bo. Hawkes.

—— OVERTURE TO "THE THIEVISH MAGPIE"

9:00 Bo. Hawkes.
—— OVERTURE TO "WILLIAM TELL"

11:00 Bo. Hawkes.

ROSSUM, Frédéric van
—— DER BLAUE REITER (1971)
3,3,3,3 - 4,3,3,1 - timp.,perc. - str.   17:00 H. Elkan.
—— CONCERTO FOR PIANO AND ORCH., OP. 30 (1975)
4,4,4,4 - 4,3,3,0 - timp.,perc. - pf. - str   28:03 H. Elkan.
—— DIVERTIMENTO, OP. 15 (FOR STRINGS) (1967) (IN 4 MOVTS.)
str.   12:00 H. Elkan.
—— DOUZE MINIATURES OP. 13 (1968)
3,3,3,3 - 4,3,3,1 - timp.,perc. - str.   25:00 H. Elkan.
—— EPITAPHE, OP. 25 (FOR STRINGS) (1972)
str.   13:00 H. Elkan.
—— PETITE SUITE RÉACTIONNAIRE, OP. 32 (1975) (IN 4 MOVTS.)
2,2,2,2 - 2,2,2,0 - timp.,perc. - str.   H. Elkan.
—— RÉQUISITOIRE, OP. 28 (FOR BRASS AND PERCUSSION) (1973)
0,0,0,0 - 4,4,4,1 - perc.   H. Elkan.
—— SINFONIETTA
2(2nd alt. with picc.),1,2,1 - 2,0,0,0 - timp.,perc. - str.
18:00 Henmar.
—— SYMPHONIE CONCERTANTE, OP. 11 (1967) (FOR HORN, PIANO, PERC. AND ORCH.) (IN 3 MOVTS.)
3,3,3,3 - 5,3,3,1 - timp.,perc. - pf. - str.   24:00 H. Elkan.

RÖTH, Philipp Jakob - BODART, Eugen
—— CONCERTINO IN F MAJOR FOR BASSET-HORN AND ORCH.
1,2,0,basset-hn.,2 - 2,0,0,0 - str.   15:00 Mannheimer.

ROTHMULLER, Marko
—— DIVERTIMENTO FOR TROMBONE, STRINGS AND TIMPANI
trb. - timp. - str.   9:00 Bo. Hawkes.

ROTONDI, Umberto
—— INTERFERENZE (1969)
2,2,2,2 - 2,2,0,0 - str.(12,4,4,0)   9:00 MCA Music.

RÖTTGER, Heinz
—— CONCERTO FOR PIANO AND ORCH. (1951)
0,1,1,1 - 0,1,0,0 - 2 pf. - str.   Tetra.
—— DESSAU SYMPHONY "65"
2,2,2,2 - 3,3,3,1 - timp.,perc.,cel. - hp. - str.   25:00 Tetra.
—— SINFONIETTA PER ARCHI (1968)
str.   16:00 Tetra.
—— SYMPHONIC MEDITATION 1963
2,2,2,2 - 0,3,3,1 - timp.,perc. - pf. - str.   18:00 Tetra.

ROUS, Fred
—— THE TOTEM POLE SUITE (1957)
*1,*1,*2,0 - 1,1,1,0 - timp.,perc. - pf. - str.   12:15 CanMusCtr.

ROUSSEAU, Jean-Jacques - DUBENSKY, Arcady
—— OVERTURE TO "LE VOISIN DU VILLAGE"
2,2,0,2 - 2 hn. - timp.,perc.(2) - str.   3:00 Belw-Mills.

ROUSSEL, Albert
—— AENEAS (FOR CHORUS AND ORCH.)
3,*3,3,3 - 4,3,3,1 - timp.,perc. - str.   40:00 EV.
—— BACCHUS ET ARIANE, OP. 43: BALLET SUITE NO. 1
3,*3,3,3 - 4,4,3,1 - timp.,perc.,cel. - 2 hp. - str.   17:00 EV.
—— BACCHUS ET ARIANE, OP. 43: BALLET SUITE NO. 2
3,*3,3,2 - 4,4,3,1 - perc.,cel. - 2 hp. - str.   20:00 EV.
—— LE BARDIT DES FRANCS (FOR 4 MEN'S VOICES, BRASS AND PERCUSSION) (Text: Chateaubriand)
0,0,0,0 - 2,2,3,1 - timp.,perc.   6:00 EV.
—— CONCERTINO FOR CELLO AND ORCH., OP. 57
2,2,2,2 - 2,2,0,0 - timp. - str.   12:00 EV.
—— CONCERTO FOR PIANO AND ORCH., OP. 36
3,3,2,2 - 2,2,0,0 - timp.,perc. - pf. - str.   17:00 EV.
—— CONCERTO FOR SMALL ORCH., OP. 34
2(2nd alt. with picc.),2,2,2 - 2,1,0,0 - timp. - str.   14:00 EV.
—— LES ÉVOCATIONS, OP. 15 (CHORAL SYMPHONY) (WITH CONTRALTO, TENOR, BARITONE AND SATB CHORUS IN 3RD MOVT.)
3,3,3,3 - 4,3,3,1 - timp.,perc.(4),cel. - 2 hp. - str.   42:00 EV.

—— LE FESTIN DE L'ARAIGNÉE ("THE SPIDER'S FEAST")
(BALLET) %
    2(2nd alt. with picc),2(2nd alt. with Eng. hn.),2,2 - 2,2,0,0 -
    timp.,perc.,cel. - hp. - str.   20:00 EV.
—— FLEMISH RHAPSODY, OP. 56
    3,3,3,3 - 4,3,3,1 - timp.,perc. - hp. - str.   9:30 EV.
—— LA NAISSANCE DE LA LYRE, OP. 24
    3,3,3,3 - 4,4,3,1 - timp.,perc.(4),cel. - 2 hp. - str.   22:00 EV.
—— OVERTURE TO THE COMIC OPERA "LE TESTAMENT DE
LA TANTE CAROLINE"
    1,1,1,1 - 1,1,1,1 - str.   3:30 EV.
—— PÂDMÂVATÎ, OP. 18 (OPERA-BALLET): SUITE NO. 1 (FOR
TENOR, BARITONE AND ORCH.)
    4,4,4,4 - 4,4,3,1 - timp.,perc.(4),cel. - 2 hp. - str.   17:00 EV.
—— PÂDMÂVATÎ, OP. 18: SUITE NO. 2
    4,4,4,4 - 4,4,3,1 - timp.,perc.(4),cel. - 2 hp. - str.   14:00 EV.
—— PETITE SUITE
    2,2,2,2 - 2,2,0,0 - timp.,perc. - str.   11:00 EV.
—— POÈME DE LA FORÊT (IN 4 MOVTS.)
    3,3,2,2 - 4,2,3,1 - timp. - 2 hp. - str.   36:00 Salabert.
—— POUR UNE FÊTE DE PRINTEMPS, OP. 22
    3,3,2,2 - 4,2,3,1 - timp.,perc.(4) - hp. -str.   12:00 EV.
—— PSALM 80 (FOR TENOR, CHORUS AND ORCH.)
    *3,*3,*3,*3 - 4,4,3,1 - timp.,perc. - hp. - str.   17:00 Summy-Bir.
—— SINFONIETTA
    str.   9:30 EV.
—— SUITE IN F MAJOR, OP. 33
    3(3rd alt. with picc.),3,3,3 - 4,4,3,1 - timp.,perc.,cel. - hp. - str.
    15:00 EV.
—— SYMPHONY NO. 2 IN B FLAT, OP. 23
    3,3,3,4 - 4,4,3,1 - timp.,perc.(4),cel. - hp. - str.   40:00 EV.
—— SYMPHONY NO. 3 IN G MINOR, OP. 42 (IN 4 MOVTS.)
    3(2 alt. with 2 picc.),3,3,3 - 4,4,3,1 - timp.,perc.,cel. - 2 hp. - str.
    25:00 EV.
—— SYMPHONY NO. 4, OP. 53
    3,3,3,3 - 4,4,3,1 - timp.,perc. - hp. - str.   22:30 EV.
—— TROIS EVOCATIONS
    3,*3,3,3 - 4,3,3,1 - perc. - 2 hp. - str.   43:00 EV.

ROUTH, Francis
—— CONCERTO FOR VIOLIN AND ORCH.
    2,2,2,2 - 4,2,3,0 - perc. - str.   22:00 P.R.S.

ROVSING OLSEN, Paul
—— AU FOND DE LA NUIT
    2,2,2,2 - 2,0,1,0 - perc. - pf. - str.   14:00 K.O.D.A.
—— BELISA (OPERA) %
    K.O.D.A.
—— CAPRICCIO, OP. 46
    2,2,2,2 - 2,2,1,0 - perc. - str.   15:00 K.O.D.A.
—— CONCERTO FOR PIANO AND ORCH., OP. 31
    2,2,2,2 - 4,3,2,1 - timp. - pf. - str.   26:00 Henmar.
—— ELEGY, OP. 29-B (FOR CHAMBER ORCH.)
    6:00 K.O.D.A.
—— FESTIVAL OVERTURE, OP. 25
    2,2,2,2 - 2,2,2,0 - timp. - str.   5:00 K.O.D.A.
—— RAGNAROK, OP. 11 (BALLET SUITE)
    2,2,2,2 - 4,3,3,1 - timp.,perc. - hp. - str.   K.O.D.A.
—— RANDERS SUITE, OP. 22
    10:00 K.O.D.A.
—— A RUSSIAN BALL, OP. 52
    1,1,1,1 - 2,0,1,0 - perc. - str.   17:00 K.O.D.A.
—— SYMPHONY NO. 1, OP. 40
    2,2,2,2 - 2,1,0,0 - perc. - hp. - str.   19:00 Henmar.
—— VARIATIONS SYMPHONIQUES, OP. 27 (1953)
    2,2,2,2 - 4,2,2,0 - perc.(2) - hp. - str.   Henmar.

ROWLEY, Alec
—— ANDANTE RELIGIOSO (FOR SMALL ORCH.)
    str.   Novello.
—— THE BOYHOOD OF CHRIST (SUITE) (IN 5 MOVTS.)
    str.   14:00 Novello.
—— BY THE DEEP NINE (NAUTICAL FANTASY) (FOR CHORUS
AND ORCH.)
    18:00 Bo. Hawkes.
—— CONCERTINO FOR ORGAN AND STRINGS
    org. - str.   12:00 Presser.
—— CONCERTO NO. 3 IN F (FOR CEMBALO AND SMALL
ORCH.)
    14:00 Galaxy.
—— COUNTRY IDYLS
    fl.(or ob. or vln.) - str.   10:00 Bo Hawkes.

—— DOWN CHANNEL (NAUTICAL OVERTURE)
    Mills.
—— ENGLISH SUITE (FOR STRINGS)
    str.   10:30 Novello.
—— MINIATURE CONCERTO FOR PIANO AND ORCH.
    2,2,2,2 - 4,2,3,0 - timp.,perc. - pf. - str.   11:00 Bo. Hawkes.
—— MINIATURE CONCERTO FOR VIOLIN AND ORCH.
    2,2,2,2 - 2,2,1,0 - timp. - str.   12:00 Galaxy.
—— NAUTICAL SUITE
    str.   Galaxy.
—— PASTORAL SUITE
    str.   Galaxy.
—— THE RIVER (FOR CHORUS AND ORCH.)
    1,1,1,1 - 2 hn. - hp.(or pf.) - str.   18:00 Bo. Hawkes.
—— SERENATA (FOR STRINGS)
    str.   9:00 Lengnick.
—— SINFONIETTA
    1,1,2,3 sax.,1 - 2,2,1,0 - timp.,perc. - hp. - pf. - str.
    11:00 Bo. Hawkes.
—— THREE ARCADIAN PICTURES
    str.   Galaxy.

ROY, Alphonse
—— KALÉIDOSCOPE (POUR ORCHESTRE DE CHAMBRE)
    13:00 S.U.I.S.A.

ROYCE, Edward
—— FAR OCEAN (SYMPHONIC POEM)
    3,3(3rd alt. with Eng. hn.),3,3 - timp.,perc. - hp. - str.
    7:00 C. Fischer.

ROYER - BOULEY, L.
—— SUITE FROM "ZAÏDE" (IN 6 MOVTS.)
    1,1,0,1 - 1,1,0,0 - timp. - hpsc. - str.   16:00 Eds. Fran.

ROYSE, Mildred Barnes
—— SUITE FOR STRING ORCH. (IN 3 MOVTS.)
    str.   15:23 Composer.

RÓZSA, Miklós
—— BEN-HUR: SUITE FROM THE FILM
    Robbins.
—— CONCERT OVERTURE, OP. 26
    10:00 P.R.S.
—— CONCERTO FOR STRING ORCH. (IN 3 MOVTS.)
    str.   24:00 P.R.S.
—— THE JUNGLE BOOK (SUITE) (FOR NARRATOR AND ORCH.)
    2(2nd alt. with picc.),2(2nd alt. with Eng. hn.),2(2nd alt. with alt.
    sax.),1(alt. with c.-bn.) - 2,2,2,0 - timp.,perc.,cel.(alt. with pf.),xyl. -
    guit.(ad lib) - hp. - str.   24:00 P.R.S.
—— NOTTURNO UNGHERESE, OP. 28
    9:00 P.R.S.
—— QUO VADIS: SUITE
    Robbins.
—— THE RED HOUSE: SUITE FROM THE FILM (WITH AD LIB.)
(FOR 3 SOPRANOS)
    3(alt. with 3 picc.),*3,3(3rd alt. with b.-cl.),*3 - 4,3,3,1 -
    timp.,perc.(5), theremin (or synthesizer) (ad lib.) - str.
    12:30 Broude.
—— SPELLBOUND: CONCERTO
    2,*3,2,2 - 4,3,3,1 - perc.(4),cel. - hp. - pf. - theremin(ad lib.) - str.
    10:00 Chappell.
—— THE THIEF OF BAGDAD: SUITE FROM THE FILM
    20:00 Broude.
—— THE VINTNER'S DAUGHTER (VARIATIONS ON A FRENCH
FOLKSONG)
    15:00 Broude.

RÓŻYCKI, Ludomir
—— MONA LISA GIOCONDA (SYMPHONIC POEM) (1910)
    2,2,2,2 - 4,3,3,1 - perc. - hp. - str.   10:00 G. Schirmer.

RÓŻYCKI, Ludomir - BURT, Julia
—— PAN TWARDOWSKY (BALLET PANTOMIME) %
    3,3,3,3 - 4,3,3,1 - timp.,perc. - hp. - pf. - str.   G. Schirmer.

RUBBRA, Edmund
—— CANTATA IN HONORUM MARIAE MATRIS DEL, OP 97
(FOR SOPRANO, CONTRALTO, CHILDREN'S CHORUS,
MIXED CHORUS AND ORCH.)
    2,2,2,2 - 2,1,0,0 - timp. - hp. - str.   12:00 Lengnick.

—— CONCERTO FOR PIANO AND ORCH., OP. 85
  2,2,2,3 - 4,3,3,1 - timp.,perc.,cel. - hp. - org. - pf. - str.
  26:00 Lengnick.
—— CONCERTO FOR VIOLA AND ORCH., OP. 75
  2,2,2,2 - 4,2,3,1 - timp. - hp. - str.
  25:00 Lengnick.
—— CONCERTO FOR VIOLIN AND ORCH., OP. 103
  3,3,2,2 - 4,2,3,1 - timp.,perc. - str.
  31:00 Lengnick.
—— CONCERTO IN A FOR VIOLA AND ORCH., OP. 75
  23:00 Lengnick.
—— CONCERTO IN G FOR PIANO AND ORCH., OP. 85
  25:00 Lengnick.
—— FESTIVAL OVERTURE, OP. 62
  8:00 Lengnick.
—— FESTIVAL TE DEUM, OP. 71 (FOR SOPRANO, CHORUS AND ORCH.)
  12:00 Lengnick.
—— FIVE SONNETS OF SPENCER (FOR TENOR AND STRINGS), OP.42
  str.
  15:00 Lengnick.
—— FOUR MEDIEVAL LYRICS (FOR BARITONE AND STRINGS), OP.32
  str.
  12:00 Lengnick.
—— IMPROVISATIONS FOR VIOLIN AND ORCH., OP. 89
  3,2,2,2 - 2,2,0,0 - timp.,perc.,cel. - hp. - str. 12:00 Lengnick.
—— IMPROVISATIONS ON VIRGINAL PIECES BY GILES FARNABY, OP. 50
  1-2,1-2,2,1-2 - 2,2,0,0 - timp. - str. 16:00 Lengnick.
—— IN DIE ET NOCTE CANTICUM, OP. 129 (SUITE) (FOR MIXED CHORUS AND ORCH.)
  2,2,2,2 - 2,2,3,0 - timp.,perc. - hp. - str. Lengnick.
—— INSCAPE, OP. 122 (SUITE) (FOR MIXED CHORUS AND STRINGS)
  hp.(or pf.) - str. Lengnick.
—— THE MORNING WATCH, OP. 55 (MOTET) (FOR CHORUS AND ORCH.)
  10:00 Lengnick.
—— ODE TO THE QUEEN, OP. 83 (FOR CONTRALTO AND ORCH.)
  2,2,2,2 - 4,2,3,1 - timp.,perc.,cel. - hp. - str. 14:00 Lengnick.
—— SINFONIA CONCERTANTE, OP. 38 (FOR PIANO AND ORCH.)
  3,3,2,2 - 4,2,3,1 - timp.,perc. - hp. - pf. - str. 28:00 Lengnick.
—— SOLILOQUY FOR CELLO AND SMALL ORCH., OP. 57
  2 hn. - timp. - str. 15:00 Lengnick.
—— SONG OF THE SOUL, OP. 78 (FOR CHORUS, TIMPANI, HARP AND STRINGS)
  timp. - hp. - str. 12:00 Lengnick.
—— SYMPHONY NO. 1 (IN 3 MOVTS.)
  3,3,3,3 - 4,3,3,1 - timp.,perc. - hp. - str. 34:00 Lengnick.
—— SYMPHONY NO. 2, OP. 45
  3,3,3,3 - 4,3,3,1 - timp.,perc. - hp. - str. 36:00 Lengnick.
—— SYMPHONY NO. 3, OP. 49
  2,2,2,2 - 4,2,3,0 - timp. - str. 35:00 Lengnick.
—— SYMPHONY NO. 4, OP. 53
  2,2,2,2 - 4,2,3,1 - str. 28:00 Lengnick.
—— SYMPHONY NO. 5, OP. 63
  30:00 Lengnick.
—— SYMPHONY NO. 6, OP. 80
  2(2nd alt. with picc.),2(2nd alt. with Eng.hn.),*3,2, - 4,2,3,1 - timp.,perc.,cel. - hp. - str. 30:00 Lengnick.
—— SYMPHONY NO. 7 IN C, OP. 88
  2(2nd alt. with picc.),*3,*3,*3, - 4,3,3,1 - timp.,perc.,cel. - hp. - str. 36:00 Lengnick.

RUBINSTEIN, Anton - DUBENSKY, Arcady
—— THREE CHORUSES FROM THE ORATORIO "BABYLON"
  *3,*3,2,2 - 4,0,1,1 - timp. - str. 9:00 Arranger.

RUBINSTEIN, Anton - PRIEGNITZ, Hans
—— RUSSIAN CAPRICE (FOR PIANO AND ORCH.)
  3,2,2,2 - 2,3,0,0 - timp.,perc. - str. 17:00 F. Colombo.

RUCHT, Karl
—— SCHERZO FOR LARGE ORCH.
  10:00 G.E.M.A.

RUCKER, Curt
—— MUSIK FÜR KLAVIER AND ORCH. (1946)
  *3,2,2,2 - 4,2,3,1 - timp.,perc. - pf. - str. 28:00 Henmar.

RUDOLF, Waldemar
—— COMPOSITION FOR CELLO AND ORCH., OP. 12
  2,2,2,2 - 2,2,2,0 - timp. - str. 9:00 S.T.I.M.

—— MUSICA INSTRUMENTALE, OP. 34
  2,2,2,2 - 2,2,2,0 - str. 12:00 S.T.I.M.
—— MUSICA SERIA, OP. 33
  2,2,2,2 - 2,2,2,0 - str. 8:00 S.T.I.M.
—— SINFONIETTA IN E MINOR, OP. 24
  2,2,2,2 - 2,2,2,0 - timp. - str. 16:30 S.T.I.M.
—— SUITE FOR STRINGS IN D MAJOR, OP. 8
  str. 11:30 S.T.I.M.
—— SUITE, OP. 22 (FOR STRINGS)
  str. 10:00 S.T.I.M.
—— SUITE, OP. 25
  1,1,2,1 - 2,1,1,0 - str. 12:00 S.T.I.M.
—— VARIATIONS ON THE MELODY "DRÖMDE MIK EN DRÖM I NAT", OP. 21
  1,1,2,2 - 2,1,1,0 - str. 8:30 S.T.I.M.

RUDZINSKI, Zbigniew
—— MUSIC BY NIGHT
  1,1,1,1 - 1,1,1,0 - perc.(5) - str.(12,0,4,3) 11:00 Modern.

RUEFF, Jeanine
—— CONCERTINO FOR ALTO SAXOPHONE AND ORCH.
  1,1,1,alto sax.,1 - 1,1,0,0 - str. 15:00 Baron.
—— CONCERTINO FOR CLARINET AND ORCH.
  2,2,2,2 - 0,1,0,0 - timp.,perc.,cel. - hp. - str. 8:00 Baron.

RUGE, Filippo - BROOK, Barry S.
—— SYMPHONIE IN D ("LA NOVA TEMPESTA")
  0,0,0,0 - 2,0,0,0 - str. FrankMusCp.
—— SYMPHONIE, OP. 1, NO. 6
  0,0,0,0 - 2,0,0,0 - str. FrankMusCp.

RUGGLES, Carl
—— EVOCATIONS
  4,4,4,4 - 4,3,3,1 - timp.,perc. - pf. - str. 12:00 C. Fischer.
—— MEN AND ANGELS
  5,4,5,4 - 6,6,3,1 - timp.,perc. - 2 hp. - str. 10:00 C. Fischer.
—— MEN AND MOUNTAINS (IN 3 MOVTS.)
  *3,*3,*3,*3 - 4,3,3,1 - perc.(2-3) - pf. - str. 15:00 AmerMusEd.
—— ORGANUM
  *3,*3,Eᵇcl.,*4,*3 - 4,3,3,1 - timp.,perc.(1) - pf. - str.
  8:00 AmerMusEd.
—— PORTALS
  str. 6:00 AmerMusEd.
—— SUN TREADER
  3(2 alt. with 2 picc),3,2 Eng. hn.,Eᵇcl.,*4,*4 - 6,5,5,2 - timp.,perc.(1) - 2 hp. - str. 15:00 AmerMusEd.
—— VOX CLAMENS IN DESERTO
  15:00 AmerMusEd.

RUHLAND, Paul
—— CONCERTO FOR WOODWINDS AND BRASS
  1,0,1,1 alto sax.,0 - 1,3,1,0 - perc. - pf. - d.-b. 16:00 C.A.P.A.C.
—— FANTASY FOR BRASS
  0,0,0,0 - 4,6,4,1 - timp.,perc. - d.-b. 10:00 C.A.P.A.C.

RUPNIK, Ivan
—— NE PRKOSITE SUNCU (DON'T DEFY THE SUN) (SYMPHONIC POEM)
  3,3,4,5 sax.,3 - 8,3,6,0 - timp.,perc.,bells - hp. MIC,Zagreb.

RUSCH, Harold W.
—— MENOMINEE SKETCHES (SUITE) (IN 5 MOVTS.)
  *3,*3,*3,2 - 4,3,3,1 - timp.,perc. - hp. - str. Fema.

RUSH, Loren
—— THE CLOUD MESSENGER (WITH OPTIONAL SA CHORUS) (1970)
  4(1 alt. with picc.),*4,Eᵇcl.,3(1 alt. with b.-cl.),*4 - 4,4,4,1 - perc.(6),bells,cel.,2 glock.,mar.,vibra.,xyl. - guit.(amplified) - 2 hp.(amplified) - hpsc. - pf. - str.(30,10,10,8) (1 d.-b. alt. with electric bass guit.) 18:00 EV.
—— DANS LE SABLE (IN THE SAND) (PART II OF "THE DAY WE ALMOST MADE IT ON THE BEACH") (FOR SPEAKER, SOPRANO, 4 ALTOS AND ORCH.) (1968)
  alto fl.,*1,0,1 - 1,1,1,0 - perc.(2),cel.,vibra. - guit. - hp. - pf. - str.(12,4,4,0 or 2,1,1,0) 20:00 EV.
—— I'LL SEE YOU IN MY DREAMS (FOR AMPLIFIED ORCH. AND TAPE) (1973)
  *4,2,2 Eng.hn.,Eᵇcl.,2,2 - 4,2,2,1 - perc.(3),bells,cel.,vibra. - tape-recorder(stereo) - hp. - pf. - str.(32,12,10,1) 15:00 Composer.

—— NEXUS 16 (1964)
1(alt.with alto fl.),1(alt.with Eng.hn.),1(alt.with b.-cl.),1 - 1,1,1,1 -
timp.,perc.(2),glock.,mar.,vibra.,xyl. - pf.(alt.with cel.) - str.(2,1,1,1)
12:00 EV.
—— SONG AND DANCE
5,4,4,2 - 6,4,2,1 - timp.,perc.(6),cel. - tape-recorder - hp. - pf. - str.
22:00 Presser.

RUSKEEPÄÄ, Raito
—— SUITE FOR ORCHESTRA (TOCCATA, ARIA E FUGA) (1954)
2,2,2,2 - 2,2,1,1 - timp. - str.   11:00 FinnMICtr.

RUSSELL, Alexander - DE LAMARTER, Eric
—— THE BELLS OF ST. ANNE DE BEAUPRÉ
*2,*2,1,*2 - 1,1,1,1 - timp. - hp. - org.(ad lib.) - str.
5:00 Belw-Mills.

RUSSELL, Armand
—— BALLETIC SYMPHONY
*3,2,2,2 - 4,2,3,1 - timp.,perc.(3),glock.,xyl. - str. 25:00 Composer.
—— CONCERTO FOR PERCUSSION AND STRINGS (1961) (IN 5
MOVTS.)
perc.(1),glock.,xyl. - str.   20:00 Composer.
—— CONCERTO NO. 2 FOR PERCUSSION AND ORCH.
("KAWILI") (1971) (IN 4 MOVTS.)
2(2nd alt. with picc.),2,2,2 - 4,2,3,1 - timp.,perc.(4),bells,glock.,xyl.
- str.   26:30 Composer.
—— ECOPHONY, 1974
str.   8:00 Seesaw.
—— FOUR TABLEAUX FOR ORCHESTRA
1,1,1,1 - 1,1,1,0 - timp.,perc.(1),glock.,xyl. - str. 20:00 Composer.
—— GEMINI CONCERTINO (FOR 2 SOLO PERCUSSIONISTS
AND ORCH.) (1973) (IN 3 MOVTS.)
2,2,2,2 - 2,2,1,0 - timp.,perc.(3) - str.   5:40 Composer.
—— HARLEQUIN CONCERTO (FOR DOUBLE BASS AND ORCH.)
2,2,2,2 - 2,0,0,0 - perc.,glock. - str.   20:00 Composer.
—— RONDO FOR PERCUSSION AND ORCH.
*3,2,2,2 - 4,3,3,1 - timp.,perc.(2),glock.,xyl. - str. 10:00 Composer.
—— SCHERZO FOR ORCHESTRA
2(2nd alt. with picc.),2,2,2 - 2,2,1,0 - timp.,perc.(2),glock.,xyl. -
str.   8:00 Composer.
—— SCHERZO FOR PERCUSSION AND STRINGS
perc.(1),glock.,xyl. - str.   5:00 Composer.
—— THEME AND FANTASIA FOR ORCH.
*3,2,2,2 - 4,3,3,1 - timp.,perc.(4),glock.,xyl. - str. 12:00 Composer.

RUSSELL, Robert
—— LITTLE SUITE, OP. 22-A (FOR 10 WIND INSTRUMENTS)
6:00 General.
—— PLACES, OP. 9-A (1968) (IN 7 MOVTS.)
2(2nd alt. with picc.),2,2,1 - 2,1,2,0 - perc.(1),bells(ad
lib.),vibra.,xyl.(ad lib.) - str.   11:00 General.
—— SCENE FROM SHAKESPEARE, OP. 5 (FOR SOPRANO,
TENOR AND SMALL ORCH.) (1960)
2(2nd alt. with picc.),2(2nd alt. with Eng.hn.),2(2nd alt. with
b.-cl.),1 - 2,1,0,0 - hp. - str.   14:00 Composer.
—— SYMPHONIC VARIATIONS, OP. 12 (1964)
2(2nd alt. with picc.),2(2nd alt. with Eng.hn.),2(2nd alt. with
b.-cl.),2 - 4,3,3,1 - timp.,perc.(3),xyl. - hp. - pf.(alt. with cel.) - str.
13:00 General.

RUSSO, William
—— CAROUSEL SUITE, OP. 63 (FOR NARRATOR, CHAMBER
ORCH., AND DANCERS) (1975) %
0,1(alt. with Eng.hn.),1,1 sopr.sax.(alt. with bar.sax.),1 - 1,1,2,0 -
perc.(1),bells,xyl. - pf.(alt with hpsc.) - str.(1,1,1,1)
30:00 Composer.
—— SONGS OF CELEBRATION, OP. 58 (FOR SOLO VOICES,
SATB CHORUS AND ORCH.)
*3,2,*3,*3 - 4,3,3,1 - timp.,perc.(7),xyl. - str. 25:00 Composer.
—— STREET MUSIC, OP. 65 (A BLUES CONCERTO) (FOR
HARMONICA AND ORCH.) (1975) (IN 4 MOVTS.)
*3,3,3,3 - 4,3,3,1 - timp.,perc.(4),mar.,xyl. - harmonica - pf. - str.
20:00 Composer.
—— SYMPHONY NO. 2 IN C, OP. 32 ("TITANS") (IN 4 MOVTS.)
3-4(1 alt. with picc.),*3-4,*3-4,*3-4 - 4,4-5,3-4,4,1 -
timp.,perc.(3),bells,glock. - hp. - pf. - str. 21:00 Bo. Hawkes.
—— THREE PIECES FOR BLUES BAND AND ORCH., OP. 50(1968)
*3,3,3(3rd alt. with Eng. hn.),3(3rd alt. with b.-cl.),3(3rd alt with
c.-bn.) - 4,3,3,1 - timp.,perc.(5),xyl. - hp. - str. and 4 players
(Blues Band)   23:00 Southern.
—— VARIATIONS ON AN AMERICAN THEME, OP. 40
2,2,2,2 - 4,3,3,1 - timp.,perc.(3) - pf. - str. 14:00 Fox.

RUTHEFORD, Paris M., III
—— THREE SCENES FROM EUGENE FIELD (FOR SOPRANO,
SATB CHORUS, 5-PIECE JAZZ COMBO, 3 SYNTHESIZERS
AND ORCH.) (1974) (Text: Eugene Field)
*3,*3,*3,*3 - 4,3,3,1 - timp.,perc.(5) bells - tape-recorder - 3
synthesizers - pf.,str.   17:00 Composer.

RUYNEMAN, Daniel
—— AMATARASU (ODE TO THE SUN GODDESS)
str.   Mills.
—— AMPHITRYON (OVERTURE)
3,2,3,2 - 2,2,2,1 - timp.,perc. - str.   10:00 Henmar.
—— CONCERTO FOR VIOLIN AND ORCH.
3,2,3,2 - 4,2,3,0 - timp.,perc.,xyl. - str.   38:00 Henmar.
—— GILGAMESJ (FOR FULL ORCH.) (1966)
16:00 Henmar.
—— MUSICA PER ORCHESTRA PER UNA FESTA OLANDESE
3,2,2,2 - 3,3,2,1 - timp.,perc.,cel. - hp. - str. 8:00 Henmar.
—— PARTITA FOR STRING ORCHESTRA
str.   15:00 Henmar.
—— SYMPHONY NO. 2
2,2,2,2 - 2,2,2,0 - timp.,perc. - str.   17:00 Henmar.
—— SYMPHONY 1953
3,2,2,2 - 2,2,2,1 - timp.,perc.,xyl. - str.   18:00 Henmar.
—— TROIS CHANSONS DES MAQUISARDS CONDAMNÉS (FOR
ALTO OR BARITONE VOICE AND ORCH.) (1957)
2,3,3,2 - 2,2,2,0 - timp.,perc.,cel. - hp. - str. 10:00 Henmar.
—— VIER LIEDEREN (4 SONGS FOR TENOR AND ORCH.) (1937)
(Text: J. H. Leopold)
2,2,2,1 - 2,0,0,0 - timp.,perc.,cel. - hp. - str. 13:00 Henmar.

RUŽDJAK, Marko
—— DIAPHANA (FOR 8 SOPRANOS, 8 ALTOS, PERCUSSION
AND STRINGS) (1973)
perc.(4) - str.   9:00 MIC,Zagreb.
—— TROIS CHANSONS DE GESTE (FOR BARITONE,
ORCHESTRA AND TAPE) (1972)
2 picc.,0,*2,E♭cl.,*1,*2 - 1,1,1,0 - perc.(4) - tape-recorder - str.
9:20 MIC,Zagreb.

RYAUSOV, Serge
—— CONCERTO FOR FLUTE AND STRINGS
fl. - str.   20:00 G. Schirmer.

RYBRANT, Stig
—— LUSTSPELS OVERTURE
2,2,2,2 - 2,2,1,0 - timp.,perc.(3),cel. - str.   7:00 S.T.I.M.
—— OVERTURE TO A COMEDY ("DER HASARDEUR")
2,2,2,2 - 2,2,1,0 - timp.,perc.(4) - str.   7:30 H.BuschMfl.
—— SUITE DE BALLET
3,3,3,3 - 4,4,3,1 - timp.,perc.(4),cel. - 2 hp. - str. 18:00 S.T.I.M.
—— SYMPHONY NO. 1 IN E MINOR
2,2,2,2 - 4,3,3,1 - timp.,perc. - hp. - str.   37:00 S.T.I.M.
—— SYMPHONY NO. 2 IN A MINOR (SINFONIA BREVE)
2,2,2,2 - 2,2,1,0 - timp. - str.   17:00 S.T.I.M.

RYDMAN, Kari
—— COMPOSITION FOR STRINGS AND SOLO PERCUSSION
(1961)
perc. - str.   6:00 FinnMICtr.
—— DNA (A SYMPHONY) (1970)
3,3,3,3 - 4,3,3,0 - timp.,perc.(3) - electric org. - str.
13:00 FinnMICtr.
—— KHOROS NO. 1 (1964)
3,1,0,0 - 0,0,0,0 - perc. - hp. - str.   6:00 FinnMICtr.
—— KHOROS NO. 2 (1966)
2,1,2,3 sax.,1 - 0,2,2,0 - timp.,perc.(3) - 2 guit. - hp.,kantele - pf. -
str.   7:00 FinnMICtr.
—— RONDOS OF THE LIGHT SUMMER NIGHTS (1966)
2,1,2,1 - 2,1,0,0 - timp.,perc. - hp. - str.   9:00 FinnMICtr.
—— SERENADE TO DJAMILA BOUPACHA (1963)
1,1,2,sax.,1 - 0,0,0,0 - timp.,perc.,bells,vibra. - hp. - pf.- str.
8:00 FinnMICtr.
—— SONATA NO. 9 ("MESTO") (1969)
1,1,1,alto sax.,1 - 0,1,0,0 - timp.,perc. - 2 guit. - acc. - str.
11:00 FinnMICtr.
—— SUITE NO. 1 (FOR SPEAKING VOICE AND ORCH.) (1971)
(Text: Tuomas Anhava)
2,3,3,5 sax.,3 - 2,2,3,0 - timp.,perc. - guit. - hp. - acc. - pf. - str.
20:00 FinnMICtr.
—— SYMPHONY OF THE MODERN WORLDS (1968)
3,3,4,ten. sax.,3 - 4,3,3,0 - timp.,perc.(3) - 2 electric guit. - hp. -
str.   15:00 FinnMICtr.

—— SYRINX (1964)
    2,2,1,1 - 0,0,0,0 - timp.,perc.,cel. - hp. - hpsc. - str.
                                    8:00 FinnMICtr.

RYELANDT, Joseph
—— GETHSEMANI, OP. 42
    2,3,3,2 - 3,3,3,1 - timp. - str.   H. Elkan.
—— GETHSEMANI, OP. 48 (SYMPHONIC POEM) (1908)
    2,3,3,2 - 3,3,3,1 - timp. - str.   12:00 H. Elkan.
—— OUVERTURE JEANNE D'ARC, OP. 78 (1920)
    3,3,3,3 - 4,3,3,1 - timp. - str.   12:00´ H. Elkan.
—— OUVERTURE PATRIA, OP. 69 (1917)
    3,3,4,3 - 4,3,3,1 - timp.,perc. - str.   12:00 H. Elkan.
—— SUITE, OP. 102 (1931) (IN 3 MOVTS.)
    2,2,2,2 - 2,1,0,0 - timp. - str.   10:00 H. Elkan.
—— SYMPHONY IN B♭, OP. 16 (IN 4 MOVTS.)
    2,2,2,2 - 4,2,3,1 - timp.,perc. - str.   H. Elkan.
—— SYMPHONY NO. 2 IN D, OP. 37
    1. Largo; 2. Andante appassionato; 3. Scherzo (Molto allegro);
    4. Adagio Religioso
    2,2,2,2 - 3,2,2,0 - timp.,perc. - str.   H. Elkan.
—— SYMPHONY NO. 3 IN E, OP. 47 (1908) (IN 4 MOVTS.)
    2,3,3,2 - 3,3,3,1 - timp. - str.   30:00 H. Elkan.
—— SYMPHONY NO. 4, OP. 55 (1913) (WITH MIXED CHORUS IN LAST MOVT.)
    2,3,4,*3 - 4,3,3,1 - timp.,perc. - str.   40:00 H. Elkan.
—— SYMPHONY NO. 5 IN A, OP. 108 (1934) (IN 4 MOVTS.)
    2,2,2,2 - 3,2,2,0 - timp. - str.   20:00 H. Elkan.

RYMER, Frantz
—— DAPHNE
    2,0,2,2 - 2,2,0,0 - perc. - str.   20:00 K.O.D.A.

RYTTERKVIST, Hans
—— CINQUE FRAMMENTI (1967)
    1,2,2,1 - 1,1,1,0 - mar.,vibra. - guit. - hp. - hpsc. - pf. - str.
                                   21:00 Fleisher.
—— CONCERTO DA CAMERA (1955)
    1,1,2,2 - 1,1,1,0 - xyl. - pf. - str.   Fleisher.
—— PERMUTE (1972)
    3,3,3,3 - 4,3,3,1 - str.   12:00 Fleisher.
—— RELAZIONI (1973)
    1,2,2,1 - 1,1,1,0 - vibra. - hp. - str.   16:00 Fleisher.
—— SAGGIO (FOR STRING ORCH.)(1967)
    str.   9:40 Fleisher.

S

SAAR, Robert
—— CHOREOPHONIE (FOR DOUBLE STRING ORCH.)
    str.   12:00 Modern.

SAARENPÄÄ, Toivo
—— BALLAD (REV. 1940)
    3,2,2,2 - 2,2,2,1 - timp.,perc. - 2 hp. - str.   SuomSvltjt.
—— FESTIVE MARCH (REV. 1940)
    3,2,2,2 - 2,2,3,1 - timp.,perc. - str. 10:00 SuomSvltjt.
—— KARELIAN DANCE-HUMORESQUE (1920)
    3,2,2,2 - 4,2,3,1 - timp.,perc. - str. 6:00 FinnMICtr.

SACCHINI, Antonio M. G. - CARSE, Adam
—— OVERTURE TO "SEMIRAMIDE"
    0,2,0,2 - 2,2,0,0 - timp. - str.   5:00 Galaxy.
    or:
    2,0,0,0 - 2,2,0,0 - timp. - str.

SACCHINI, Antonio M. G. - NAPOLITANO, F. M.
—— OVERTURE TO "EDIPO A COLONO"
    0,2,0,1 - 2,0,0,0, - timp. - str.   Henmar.

SACCO, John Charles
—— CROSS-COUNTRY (SUITE) (IN 3 MOVTS.)
                                 23:00 Composer.

SACCO, P. Peter
—— CLASSICAL OVERTURE
                           7:00 Ostara.
—— CONCERTO NO. 1 FOR PIANO AND ORCH.
    3(3rd alt. with picc.),*3,*3,*3 - 4,2,3,1 - timp.,perc.(4) - pf. - str.
                                   26:00 Ostara.

—— CONCERTO NO. 1 FOR VIOLIN AND ORCH. (1971) (IN 3 MOVTS.)
    3,*3,*3,*3 - 4,3,3,1 - timp.,perc.(2) - pf. - str. 29:00 Ostara.
—— FOUR SKETCHES ON EMERSON ESSAYS
    2,2,*3,2 - 4,3,3,1 - timp.,perc.(4) - pf. - str. 10:00 Ostara.
—— INTRODUCTION AND ALLEGRO
                           10:00 Ostara.
—— JESU (ORATORIO) (FOR TENOR, SATB CHORUS AND ORCH.)
                           50:00 Ostara.
—— MEDITATION NO. 1
    2,2,2,2 - 2,2,1,0 - timp.,cymb. - str. 6:00 Ostara.
—— MEDITATION NO. 2
    2,2,2,2 - 2,2,1,0 - hp. - str.   4:00 Ostara.
—— MEDITATION NO. 3 (ANDANTE FOR CHAMBER ORCH.)
    2,1,2,0 - 2,2,1,0 - timp.,perc. - str. 4:30 Ostara.
—— MIDSUMMER DREAM NIGHT (FOR NARRATOR, BARITONE, MEN'S CHORUS AND ORCH.) (Text: George B. Harris)
                         60:00 Composer.
—— MR. VINEGAR (OPERA IN 4 SCENES) % (Text: Mrs. P. Peter Sacco)
    2(2nd alt. with picc.),1,2,1 - 2,2,1,0 - timp.,perc.(1-2) - str.(or pf.)
                                 50:00 Ostara.
—— SINFONIETTA FOR STRING ORCH.
    str.   15:00 Ostara.
—— SYMPHONY NO. 1 (IN 1 MOVT.)
    *3,*3,*3,*3 - 4,2,3,1 - timp.,perc. - str. 12:00 Ostara.
—— THANKSGIVING SYMPHONY (SYMPHONY NO. 2, THEMES OF PILGRIM HYMNS) (IN 1 MOVT.)
    3(3rd alt. with picc.),*3,1 D cl.,*3,*3 - 4,4,3,1 - timp.,perc.,cel.,chimes,glock. - pf. - str. 25:00 Ostara.

SADAI, Yizhak
—— NUANCES (FOR CHAMBER ORCH.)
    3 pipes,*1,0,0,0 - 1,1,1,0 - perc.,cel. - guit. - harm. - pf. - str.
                                  9:00 IsMuPublns.
—— RICERCAR SYMPHONIQUE
    3,*3,*3, alto sax.,ten. sax.,*3 - 4,3,2,1 - timp.,perc.,xyl. - hp. - str.
                                9:30 IsMuPublns.

SAEVERUD, Ketil
—— ARISETURO (CONCERTO FOR PERCUSSION) (1966)
    1,1,1,1 - 1,2,1,0 - timp.,perc. 17:00 T.O.N.O.
—— CONCERTINO FOR PIANO AND ORCH.
    3,2,2,2 - 0,2,0,0 - pf. - str. 8:00 T.O.N.O.
—— SINFONIETTA (1963)
    2,2,2,2 - 2,2,2,0 - timp.,perc. - hp. - str. 11:00 T.O.N.O.

SAGUER, Louis
—— BALLI DA "LO SCOLARO" (AFTER ZANETTI)
    2,2,2,2 - 2,2,1,0 - timp.,perc.(3) - hp. - hpsc. - str. 16:00 Presser.
—— CINQUE RICERCARI (AFTER FRESCOBALDI)
    2,2,2,2 - 4,2,2,1 - str. 16:00 Presser.
—— CONCERTO FOR VIOLIN AND ORCH.
                                    EV.
—— MUSIQUE D'APRÈS-MIDI
    2,2,2,2 - 2,2,0,0 - str. 22:00 EV.
—— MUSIQUE D'ÉTÉ
    2,2,2,2 - 2,2,0,0 - timp.,perc.,cel. - hp. - pf. - str.
                            22:00 F. Colombo.
—— MUSIQUE EN SOL (FOR VIOLIN AND ORCH.)
    2,2,2,2 - 2,2,0,0 - timp. - hp. - str. 25:00 Presser.
—— OPHELIA'S MAD SCENE (FOR SOPRANO AND ORCH.)
    2,2,2,2 - 2,2,0,0 - perc.,cel.,glock. - hp. - str. 7:00 EV.
—— SINE NOMINE
    4,3,5,2 - 4,4,3,1 - timp.,perc.(5),cel. - 2 hp. - pf. - str.
                                 18:00 Presser.
—— SUITE SEFARDI
    2,2,2,2 - 2,2,0,0 - str. 14:00 EV.

SAHL, Michael
—— CONCERTO FOR ELECTRIC VIOLIN (1973)
    1,1,1,1 - 1,1,1,0 - perc. - hp. - electric vln. - str. 22:00 Seesaw.

SAIKKOLA, Lauri
—— CHILDHOOD SCENES (1930)
    str. 7:00 FinnMICtr.
—— CONCERTO DA CAMERA (1957)
    1,1,1,1 - 2,2,1,0 - timp. - pf. - str.(0,6,6,4) 15:00 FinnMICtr.
—— CONCERTO DI MINIATURA (FOR CELLO AND ORCH.) (1953)
    1,1,1,1 - 0,0,0,0 - pf. - str.(0,0,7,4) 20:00 FinnMICtr.

—— CONCERTO FOR CLARINET AND STRINGS (1969)
cl. - str.   13:00 FinnMICtr.
—— CONCERTO FOR VIOLIN AND ORCH. (1952)
2,2,2,2 - 4,2,3,1 - timp. - str.   29:00 FinnMICtr.
—— GOING TO HEAVEN, OP. 33 (OPERA) (1950) %
1,1,1,1, - 1,2,1,0 - timp., perc. - pf. - str.   30:00 FinnMICtr.
—— KARELIA IN FLAMES (1940)
2,2,2,2 - 4,2,3,0 - timp.,perc. - str.   10:00 FinnMICtr.
—— KARELIAN SCENES (SUITE) (REV. 1946)
2,2,2,2 - 2,2,1,0 - timp.,perc.(3) - str.   20:00 FinnMICtr.
—— THE MASTER'S SNUFF BOX (OPERA) (1970) % (Text: Robert Kiljander)
2,2,2,2 - 2,2,1,0 - timp.,perc. - hp. - str.   34:00 FinnMICtr.
—— MUSICA PER ARCHI (1950)
str.   10:00 FinnMICtr.
—— MUSICA SINFONICA (1966)
2,2,2,3 - 4,2,3,1 - timp.,perc. - str.   14:00 FinnMICtr.
—— NOCTURNO (FOR CELLO AND ORCH.) (1944)
3,2,2,2 - 4,2,3,1 - timp. - str.   9:00 FinnMICtr.
—— ONE THOUSAND FIVE HUNDRED METERS (A PARODY FOR ORCHESTRA) (1933)
2,2,2,2 - 4,2,3,1 - timp. - str.   6:00 FinnMICtr.
—— OVERTURE DELL'DRAMA (1949)
2,2,2,3 - 4,3,3,1 - timp. - str.   12:00 FinnMICtr.
—— PARTITA (1935)
2,2,2,2 - 4,2,3,1 - timp.,perc. - str.   12:00 FinnMICtr.
—— PASTORALE (1936)
2,2,2,2 - 4,2,3,1 - timp.,perc. - str.   20:00 FinnMICtr.
—— PEZZI PER ARCHI (SUITE) (1965)
str.   20:00 FinnMICtr.
—— RAASEPORI FANTASIA (1971)
2,2,2,2 - 4,3,3,1 - timp.,perc. - str.   13:00 FinnMICtr.
—— RISTIN (OPERA) (1958) % (Text: Lauri Haarla)
2,2,2,2 - 4,2,3,1 - timp.,perc. - str.   75:00 FinnMICtr.
—— SERENATA FOR STRINGS, OP. 34 (1947)
str.   20:00 FinnMICtr.
—— SINFONIA CAMPALE (1938)
3,2,2,3 - 4,2,3,1 - timp.,perc. - str.   35:00 FinnMICtr.
—— SINFONIA TRAGICA (1946)
2,2,2,2 - 4,3,3,1 - timp.,perc. - hp. - str.   30:00 FinnMICtr.
—— SYMPHONY NO. 3 (1949)
3,2,2,3 - 4,3,3,1 - timp.(2 players),cel. - pf. - str.
     21:00 FinnMICtr.
—— SYMPHONY NO. 4 (1951)
3,2,2,3 - 4,3,3,1 - timp.,perc. - pf. - str.   25:00 FinnMICtr.
—— SYMPHONY NO. 5 (1958)
2,2,2,2 - 4,3,3,1 - timp.,perc. - str.   26:00 FinnMICtr.
—— THREE SYMPHONIC SCENES (1932)
3,3,3,3 - 4,2,3,1 - timp.,perc. - str.   30:00 FinnMICtr.

SAINT-GEORGE, Chevalier De - BROOK, Barry S.
—— SYMPHONIE CONCERTANTE IN G (FOR 2 VIOLINS AND STRING ORCH.)
str.   FrankMusCp.

SAINT-GEORGE, George
—— L' ANCIEN RÈGIME: PETITE SUITE NO. 1
pf.(ad lib.) - str.   Galaxy.
—— L' ANCIEN RÈGIME: PETITE SUITE NO. 2, OP. 60
pf.(ad lib.) - str.   Galaxy.

SAINTON, Phillip
—— THE ISLAND (SYMPHONIC POEM)
    19:00 Lengnick.
—— NADIR (SYMPHONIC ELEGY)
    14:00 Lengnick.
—— SERENADE FANTASTIQUE (FOR VIOLA AND ORCH.)
*3,2,2,2 - 4,2,0,0 - timp.,perc. - str.   12:30 G. Schirmer.

SAINT-SAËNS, Camille
—— LE CARNAVAL DES ANIMAUX (THE CARNIVAL OF THE ANIMALS) (With narrator ad lib., using French text by the composer or English text by Ogden Nash)
1(alt. with picc.),0,1,0 - 0,0,0,0 - xyl. - 2 pf. - str.   21:00 EV.
—— LA MUSE ET LE POÈTE, OP. 132 (FOR VIOLIN, CELLO AND ORCH.)
2,2,2,2 - 2,2,3,0- - timp. - hp. - str.   12:30 EV.
—— ODELETTE, OP. 162 (FOR FLUTE AND CHAMBER ORCH.)
1,2,0,2 - 0,0,0,0 - str.   7:30 EV.

SAINT-SAËNS, Camille - CASADESUS, Robert
—— CONCERTO NO. 5 FOR PIANO AND ORCH.
      S.A.C.E.M.

SAINT-SAËNS, Camille - ROBERTS, Charles J.
—— DANSE BACCHANALE (FROM "SAMSON AND DELILAH")
      C. Fischer.
—— SUITE ALGÉRIENNE
      C. Fischer.

SAINT-SAËNS, Camille - TOBANI, Theo. M.
—— PRELUDE TO "THE DELUGE"
      C. Fischer.

SAKAČ, Branimir
—— SOLO I (FOR VIOLIN AND INSTRUMENTS)
1,0,*1,0 - 1,1,1,0 - perc.,mar. - pf.(alt. with cel.) - str.(2,1,1,1)
     12:00 MIC,Zagreb.
—— SPACES (1965)
*3,2,*3,2 ten.sax.,0 - 4,4,4,1 - timp.,perc.,cel.,vibra. - hp. - pf. - str.
     13:50 MIC,Zagreb.

SALIERI, Antonio - NEGROTTI, Nino
—— AXUR RE D'ORMUS: OVERTURE
2,2,2,2 - 2,2,0,0 - timp. - str.   5:00 Bo. Hawkes.

SALIERI, Antonio - WOJCIECHOWSKI
—— TRIPLE CONCERTO IN D MAJOR, FOR OBOE, VIOLIN, CELLO AND ORCH.
0,2,0,1 - 2,0,0,0 - timp. - str.   19:00 F. Colombo.

SALLINEN, Aulis
—— CHAMBER I, OP. 38
str.   13:00 FinnMICtr.
—— CHAMBER II, OP. 41
fl. - str.   10:00 FinnMICtr.
—— CONCERTO FOR CHAMBER ORCH. (1959)
1,1,2,1 - 1,0,0,0 - str.   22:00 FinnMICtr.
—— CONCERTO FOR VIOLIN AND ORCH. (1968)
2,1,1,1 - 1,1,1,0 - perc. - hp. - pf. - str.   16:00 Fazer.
—— FOURTEEN JUVENTAS VARIATIONS (1963)
2,2,2,2 - 2,2,0,0 - perc. - str.   11:00 FinnMICtr.
—— MAUERMUSIK (1962)
3,2,3,2 - 3,2,2,1 - str.   11:00 Fazer.
—— METAMORPHOSES FOR PIANO AND CHAMBER ORCH. (1964)
2,0,2,0 - 0,0,0,0 - pf. - str.   20:00 FinnMICtr.
—— SYMPHONIC DIALOGUE (FOR PERCUSSION AND ORCH.) (1972)
2,2,2,2 - 4,3,3,1 - perc. - hp. - str.   14:00 FinnMICtr.
—— SYMPHONY NO. 3, OP. 35 (IN 3 MOVTS.)
4,3,4,3 - 4,3,3,1 - timp.,perc.(4),cel. - hp. - pf. - str.
     23:00 FinnMICtr.
—— SYMPHONY (1971)
3,3,3,3 - 4,3,3,0 - timp.,perc.(3),cel. - hp. - str.   16:00 FinnMICtr.
—— TWO MYTHICAL SCENES FOR ORCH. (1956)
2,2,3,2 - 3,2,3,0 - timp.,perc. - str.   12:00 FinnMICtr.
—— VARIATIONS FOR CELLO AND ORCH. (1961)
2,1,2,1 - 1,1,1,1 - timp.,perc.(3) - hp. - str.   18:00 FinnMICtr.
—— VARIATIONS ON MALLARMÉ (BALLET) % (1967)
2,2,2,2 - 4,3,2,1 - timp.,perc.(3),cel. - hp. - pf. - str.
     22:00 FinnMICtr.

SALMENHAARA, Erkki
—— LE BATEAU IVRE (1966)
2,0,0,2 - 4,0,0,0 - perc.,cel. - hpsc. - str.   25:00 FinnMICtr.
—— BFK-83 (1967)
2,2,2,2 - 4,2,2,0 - str.   10:00 FinnMICtr.
—— CANZONETTA (1972)
str.   7:00 FinnMICtr.
—— CONCERTO FOR HORN AND ORCH. (IN 3 MOVTS.)
2,2,2,2 - 5,2,3,0 - timp. - str.   10:00 FinnMICtr.
—— THE GIRL IN THE MINI-SKIRT (1967) (LA FILLE EN MINI-JUPE)
3,3,3,2 - 4,2,3,0 - perc. - hp. - pf. - str.   15:00 SuomYRadio.
—— ILLUMINATIONS (1971)
3,3,3,2 - 4,3,3,0 - perc.,cel. - hp. - pf. - str.   12:00 FinnMICtr.
—— REQUIEM PROFANUM (FOR SOPRANO, ALTO, BARITONE, ORGAN, PIANO AND STRINGS) (1969)
org. - pf. - str.   77:00 FinnMICtr.
—— SUOMI-FINLAND (AN UNSYMPHONIC POEM) (1966)
2,2,2,2 - 4,3,3,0 - timp.,perc. - hp. - str.   18:00 FinnMICtr.
—— SYMPHONY NO. 1 ("CRESCENDI") (1962)
3,3,3,3 - 0,2,2,0 - timp.,perc.(5) - str.   17:00 FinnMICtr.
—— SYMPHONY NO. 2 (REV. 1966)
2,2,2,2 - 4,2,2,0 - timp.,perc.(3) - str.   25:00 SuomYRadio.

—— SYMPHONY NO. 3 (1964)
  3,2,2,2 - 4,3,3,0 - timp.,perc.(3) - str.   33:00 FinnMICtr.
—— SYMPHONY NO. 4 ("NEL MEZZO DEL CAMMIN DI
  NOSTRA VITA") (1971)
  3,3,3,2 - 4,3,3,0 - timp. - hp. - str.   23:00 FinnMICtr.
—— THE WOMAN OF PORTUGAL (OPERA) % (1972) (Text: R.
  Musil and Composer)
  3,2,3,2 - 4,2,3,0 - perc.,cel. - hp. - pf. - str.   120:00 FinnMICtr.

SALMHOFER, Franz
—— SUITE FROM THE BALLET "EIN TAUGENICHTS IN WIEN"
  2,2,2,2 - 3,2,1,0 - timp.,perc. - hp. - str.   27:00 Modern.

SALOMON, Karel
—— ARIA ("NIGUN") (FOR VIOLIN AND ORCH.)
  2,1,3,1 - 2,2,0,0 - perc. - hp. - str.   5:00 IsMuPublns.
—— CONCERTO FOR PIANO AND ORCH.
  3,2,3,2 - 2,2,0,0 - timp.,perc. - str.   28:00 IsMuPublns.
—— DAHLIA (DANCE RHAPSODY)
  2,2,3,2 - 2,3,2,1 - timp.,perc. - mandolin - oriental lute(ad lib.) -
  pf. - str.   17:00 IsMuPublns.
—— DAVID AND GOLIATH (MINIATURE OPERA IN 3 SCENES)
  %
  ob. - str.   36:00 IsMuPublns.
—— FOUR TIMES METHUSELAH (OPERA BUFFA IN 1 ACT AND
  2 SCENES) % (Text: Composer)
  2,2,2,2 - 2,2,3,0 - perc.(2) - pf.(alt. with hpsc.) - str.
          60:00 A.C.U.M.
—— ISRAEL LIVES (8 VARIATIONS ON A POPULAR THEME)
  str.   9:00 IsMuPublns.
—— ISRAELI YOUTH SYMPHONY
          16:00 IsMuPublns.
—— NIGHTS OF CANAAN (SYMPHONY)
  3,3,3,3 - 4,3,3,1 - timp.,perc.,cel.,xyl. - hp. - pf. - str.
          22:00 IsMuPublns.
—— PARTITA FOR STRINGS
  str.   26:00 IsMuPublns.
—— SYMPHONIC SUITE ON GREEK THEMES
  3,2,1,sax.,1 - 4,2,3,0 - timp.,perc. - hp.(or pf.) - str.
          18:00 Bo. Hawkes.
—— TWO SONGS OF FAITH (FOR HIGH VOICE AND SMALL
  ORCH.)
  ob., 2 cl., 2 bn. - hp. - str.   6:00 IsMuPublns.

SALONEN, Sulo
—— PASSION CANTATA (1942) (FOR SOPRANO, ALTO. SATB
  CHORUS, ORGAN AND STRINGS)
  org. - str.   13:00 Nordiska.
—— REQUIEM (FOR SATB SOLO VOICES AND ORCH.) (1962)
  0,2,2,2 - 0,2,2,1 - timp.,cel. - str.   50:00 Westerlund.

SALTA, Menotti
—— FOUR CHARACTERISTIC DANCES
  3,3,2,2 - 4,3,3,1 - timp.,perc.,bells,xyl. - hp. - str.
          11:00 Belw-Mills.
—— MIRAGE (SYMPHONIC BALLET)
          Lengnick.
—— NOCTURNE
  2,*2,2,2 - 4,3,3,1 - timp.,perc.,cel.,glock. - hp. - str.   6:00 Ricordi.
—— PRELUDE IN D MINOR (FOR STRINGS)
  str.   Mills.

SALTEN, Alfred
—— MUSICA PER UNA FESTA
  2,2,2,2 - 3,2,0,0 - timp.,perc. - hp. - str.   8:00 Henmar.

SALVIUCCI, Giovanni
—— OVERTURE IN C SHARP MINOR
  3,3,3,0 - 4,3,3,0 - timp. - str.   10:00 Bo. Hawkes.

SALZEDO, Carlos
—— THE ENCHANTED ISLE
  *3,*3,2,*3 - 4,2,3,1 - timp.,perc.,cel.,xyl. - hp. - str.
          13:00 Composer.
—— PRÉAMBULE ET JEUX (FOR CHAMBER ORCH.)
  1,1,0,1 - hn. - hp. - str.   8:30 Composer.

SALZEDO, Carlos - BENNETT, Robert Russell
—— CONCERTO NO. 2 FOR HARP AND ORCH (WITH
  ORCHESTRATION REALIZED FROM COMPOSER'S
  SKETCHES BY BENNETT)
          Lyra.

SALZMAN, Eric
—— CUMMINGS SET (FOR MEDIUM-HIGH VOICE AND ORCH)
  (REVISED 1962) (Text: e. e. cummings)
  *3(1 alt. with alto fl.),*3,1 E♭cl.,*3,*3 - 4,3,3,1 -
  timp.,perc.(3-5),bells,cel.,vibra.,xyl. - hp. - electric org.(ad lib.) -
  str.   18:00 MCA Music.
—— FOXES AND HEDGEHOGS (VERSES AND CANTOS FOR 4
  SOLO SATB VOICES AND SMALL ORCH.) (Text: John Ashberg
  (1964-67))
  1,1,1,1 alto sax.(alt. with ten.sax.),0 - 1,1,1,0 - perc.(2) - pf. -
  str.(1,1,1,1)   35:00 MCA Music.
—— INVENTIONS FOR ORCHESTRA (1957)
  *3,*3,*3,2 - 4,3,3,1 - timp.,perc.(3),xyl. - hp. - str.
          16:00 MCA Music.
—— NIGHT DANCE (1953, REVISED 1960)
  *3,2,2,2 b.-cl.,1 sopr.sax.,2 - 2,2,3,1 - timp.,perc.(5),cel.,vibra.,xyl. -
  hp. - str.   10:00 MCA Music.

SAMAZEUILH, Gustave
—— UNE ÉTUDE SYMPHONIQUE (D'APRÈS "LA NEF" BYELIMIR
  BOURGES)
  3,3,3,3 - 4,3,3,1- timp.,perc.(4) - 2 hp. - str.   18:00 EV.
—— NAÏADES AU SOIR
  2,3,2,2 - 4,2,0,0 - timp.,perc.(3),cel. - hp. - str.   7:00 EV.
—— NUIT
  3,3,3,3 - 4,3,3,1 - timp.,perc.(4),cel. - 2 hp. - str.   9:00 EV.
—— LE SOMMEIL DE CANOPE
  3,3,3,3 - 4,3,3,1 - timp.,perc.(3),cel.,tamb. - 2 hp. - str.   12:00 EV.
—— SUITE IN G (FOR STRINGS)
  str.   23:00 EV.

SAMINSKY, Lazare
—— AUSONIA (ITALIAN PAGES), OP. 39 (IN 4 MOVTS.)
  2(1 alt. with picc.),*3,2,2 - 4,2,0,0 - timp.,perc.(2) - hp. - pf. - str.
          18:00 Salabert.
—— THE DAUGHTER OF JEPHTA (OPERA), OP. 37 %
  3(3rd alt. with picc.),*3,*3,*3 - 4,3,3,1 - timp.,perc.(2-3),cel. - hp. -
  pf. - str.   Salabert.
—— FIVE-PETALLED FLAME (FOR CHORUS AND ORCH.), OP.
  55
  2,2,2,2 - 2,2,0,0 - perc.(1),cel.,glock. - pf. - str.   10:00 Composer.
—— FROM EAST TO WEST (FOR VIOLIN OR CELLO AND
  SMALL ORCH.) (IN 8 MOVTS.)
  1,1,1,1 - 1,1,0,0 - timp.,perc. - str.   28:00 Composer.
—— FROM EAST TO WEST (SEVEN CHANTS AND DANCES)
  3,*3,2,2 - 4,2,3,1 - perc.(2) - hp. - pf.(or cel.) - str.
          20:00 Composer.
—— HASSIDIC SUITE (FOR VIOLIN OR CELLO AND ORCH.), OP.
  24 (IN 3 MOVTS.)
  2,2,2,2 - 4,2,0,0 - timp. - str.   11:00 C. Fischer.
—— HEBREW RHAPSODY (FOR VIOLIN AND ORCH.), OP. 3
  2,2,2,2 - 4,2,0,0 - timp. - str.   5:15 C. Fischer.
—— LITANIES OF WOMEN (FOR SOPRANO OR MEZZO
  SOPRANO AND CHAMBER ORCH.), OP. 34
  2,0,1,0 - hn. - perc.(1),cel.(alt. with pf.) - str.   10:00 Salabert.
—— ORIENTALIA, OP. 7 (IN 4 MOVTS.)
  *3,*3,*3,*3 - 4,2,3,1 - timp.,perc.(2) - hp. - pf. - str.
          17:00 Composer.
—— OUT OF THE DEEP (DE PROFUNDIS) (FOR MIXED CHORUS
  AND ORCH.)
  1,1,1,0 - 1,0,0,0 -str.   6:00 Summy-Bir.
—— OVERTURE, OP. 1
  *3,*3,2,2 - 4,2,3,1 - timp.,perc.(2) - str.   10:00 Composer.
—— THE PLAGUE'S GALLIARD, (OPERA), OP. 29 %
  1,0,1,0 - 1,1,0,0 - timp.,perc.(2),glock. - pf. - str.   Beekman.
—— PSALM 137, OP. 33, NO. 1 ("BY THE RIVERS OF BABYLON")
  (FOR SOPRANO, BARITONE, SATB CHORUS AND ORCH.)
  2,0,2,2 - 2,1,0,0 - perc. - hp. - pf. - str.   6:00 C. Fischer.
—— PUEBLO (A MOON EPIC), OP. 44
  *3,*3,*3,2 - 4,3,3,1 - timp.,perc.(2) - hp. - pf. - str.
          17:00 Composer.
—— RACHEL, LAMENT AND TRIUMPH (BALLET) (WITH SMALL
  WOMEN'S CHORUS), OP. 14 %
  3(3rd alt. with picc.),*3,2,2 - 4,2,3,1 - timp.,perc.(2-3),cel. - hp. -
  str.   30:00 Beekman.
—— REQUIEM IN MEMORY OF A WONDROUS SOUL (FOR
  SOPRANO, CONTRALTO, BARITONE, CHORUS AND
  ORCH.)
  2,*3,*3,2 - 4,2,3,1 - timp.,perc.(2),cel.,glock. - hp. - pf. - str.
          20:00 Composer.
—— RHAPSODY ON THE OLD TUNE "DUNLAP'S CREEK"
  1,1,1,1 - hn. - pf. - str.   C. Fischer.

—— RIVERS AND STANZAS, OP. 56
    2,2,2,2 - 4,2,0,0 - timp.,perc.,cel.,glock. - hp. - pf. - str.
                                                              11:00 Beekman.
—— SONGS OF THREE QUEENS (FOR SOPRANO AND ORCH.), OP. 25
    1,1,1,1 - hn. - pf. - str.   11:00 C. Fischer.
—— STILLED PAGEANT, OP. 48 (IN 2 MOVTS.)
    3,*3,*3,2 - 4,2,0,0 - timp.,perc.(2) - hp. - pf. - str.   9:00 Salabert.
—— SYMPHONY NO. 1 (SYMPHONY OF THE GREAT RIVERS), OP. 10 (IN 3 MOVTS.)
    *3,*3,*3,*3 - 4,3,3,1 - timp.,perc.(2) - str.   30:00 Composer.
—— SYMPHONY NO. 2 (SYMPHONIE DES SOMMETS), OP. 19
    1. Maestoso, marcato; 2. Allegro
    *3,*3,*3,*3 - 4,3,3,1 - timp.,perc.(2) - 2 hp. - pf. - str.
                                            20:00 Salabert.
—— SYMPHONY NO. 5 (JERUSALEM, CITY OF SOLOMON AND CHRIST), OP. 38
    *3,*3,*3,*3 - 4,3,3,1 - timp.,perc.(2) - 2 hp. - org. - pf. - str.
                                          20:00 C. Fischer.
—— THREE OLD AMERICAN AIRS
    1,1,1,1 - hn. - pf. - str.   5:00 Composer.
—— THREE SHADOWS (POEMS FOR ORCH.), OP. 42
    *3,*3,*3,2 - 4,3,3,1 - timp.,perc.(2) - hp. - org. - pf. - str.
                                          8:00 G. Schirmer.
—— TO A YOUNG WORLD (A DITHYRAMB TO SILENCE), OP. 41 (REVISED 1950) (IN 4 MOVTS.)
    *3,2(2nd alt. with Eng. hn.),2,2 - 4,2,3,1 - timp.,perc.,cel.(alt. with piano),glock. - 2 hp. - str.   16:00 Composer.
—— TWO PSALMS, OP. 33 (FOR CHORUS AND ORCH.)
    2,0,2,2 - 2,1,0,0 - timp.,perc.(2) - hp. - pf. - str.   10:30 C. Fischer.
—— THE VISION OF ARIEL (OPERA-BALLET OR ORATORIO WITH DANCE), OP. 16 ½
    3(3rd alt. with picc.),*3,*3,*3 - 4,2,3,1 - timp.,perc.,cel.,glock. - 2 hp. - str.   40:00 Beekman.
—— THE VOW (RHAPSODIC VARIATIONS FOR PIANO AND ORCH.), OP. 15
    2,2,2,2 - 4,2,0,0 - timp.,perc.(2),cel.,glock. - hp. - pf. - str.
                                          10:00 Beekman.
    Or
    2,2(2nd alt. with Eng. hn.),2,2 - 4,2,3,1 - timp.,perc.(2),cel.,glock. - pf. - str.

SAMMARTINI, Giovanni - BONELLI, Ettore
—— SINFONIA FOR STRINGS AND TWO HUNTING HORNS
    2 hn. - str.   Henmar.

SAMMARTINI, Giovanni - CARSE, Adam
—— CONCERTO IN E FLAT, FOR STRING ORCH.
    str.   7:00 Galaxy.

SAMMARTINI, Giovanni - JENKINS
—— CONCERTINO IN G MAJOR
    cemb. - str.   8:00 Henmar.
—— SINFONIA IN F MAJOR
    cemb. - str.   12:00 Henmar.

SAMMARTINI, Giovanni - LANGENDOEN, Jacobus
—— SONATA IN G MAJOR (FOR CELLO, STRINGS AND WINDS)
    2,2,2,2 - 2,0,0,0 - str.   H. Elkan.

SAMMARTINI, Giovanni - SCARMOLIN, A. Louis
—— SYMPHONY IN D MAJOR
                                          Ludwig.

SAMMARTINI, Giovanni - SCHULTZ-HAUSER
—— CONCERTO GROSSO IN D MAJOR, OP. 5, NO. 6 (CHRISTMAS CONCERTO)
    cemb. - str.   15:00 Henmar.

SAMMARTINI, Giovanni - TORREFRANCA, Fausto
—— SINFONIA IN C
    1. Allegro assai; 2. Allegrissimo; 3. Andante
    0,0,1,1 - 2 hn. - timp. - str.   15:00 Bo. Hawkes.
—— SINFONIA NO. 3 IN G
    2,2,0,0 - 2,0,0,0 - cel. - str.   9:00 Bo. Hawkes.

SAMPSON, Godfrey
—— SUITE FOR STRINGS (IN 3 MOVTS.)
    str.   13:00 Novello.
—— SYMPHONIC VARIATIONS (FOR PIANO AND ORCH.)
    2,2,3,2 - 4,2,3,1 - timp.,glock. - pf. - str.   Novello.

SAMSON, François
—— CONCERTO FOR PIANO AND ORCH.
    3,2,2,2 - 4,2,2,1 - timp.,perc. - pf. - str.   20:00 EV.

SAMUEL, Gerhard
—— BEYOND MCBEAM (FOR MEDIUM VOICE AND INSTRUMENTS)
    1,1,1,1 - 1,1,1,0 - perc. - hp. - hpsc. - str.(no vlns.)
                                    12:00 Belw-Mills.
—— COLD WHEN THE DRUM SOUNDS FOR DAWN (FOR CHAMBER ORCH.)
    1(alt. with alto fl. and picc.),*2,0,1 - 2,0,0,0 - perc.,cel.,glock.,mar.,vibra - hpsc. - str.   14:00 Belw-Mills.
—— INTO FLIGHT FROM ....
    3,3,3,3 - 4,3,3,1 - timp.,perc. - str.   13:00 Belw-Mills.
—— LOOKING AT ORPHEUS LOOKING (1971)
    4,4,4,4 - 4,4,3,1 - perc.(4),bells,glock.,vibra. - hpsc.(electric or amplified) - hp. - org. - str.   17:00 Belw-Mills.
—— REFLECTIONS ON A LOVE SONG (1969)
    2,2,2,2 - 2,2,0,0 - perc.(1),bells,vibra - pf. - str.   10:00 Belw-Mills.
—— REQUIEM FOR SURVIVORS ("AND SUDDENLY IT'S EVENING")
    4,4,4,ten. sax.,4 - 0,4.3,1 - timp.,perc.(6, incl. 5 on timp.),perc. - hp. - str.   18:00 Belw-Mills.
—— TO AN END (FOR SATB CHORUS AND ORCH.) (1972) (Text: Sam Blazer)
    2,2,2,2 - 2,2,3,0 - timp.,perc.(4),cel.,glock.,vibra. - hp. - str.
                                    10:00 Belw-Mills.
—— TWELVE ON DEATH AND NO (FOR TENOR, SMALL CHORUS AND CHAMBER ORCH.) (1969) (Text: Ecclesiastes)
    2,2,0,2 - 2,2,1,0 - timp.,perc.(1),vibra. - str.   15:00 Belw-Mills.

SAMUEL, Harry
—— CONCERTINO FOR FLUTE AND STRINGS, OP. 1-B
    fl. - str.   8:00 P.R.S.
—— OBVERSE AND REVERSE, OP. 2
    3,3,3,3 - 5,3,3,1 - timp.,perc.(5) - hp. - str.   36:00 P.R.S.
—— THE ROMANCE OF NUMBERS, OP. 2, NO. 1 (1963)
    2,2,2,2 - 5,3,3(incl. 2 in D),1 - timp.,perc.(5) - hp. - str.
                                    21:00 P.R.S.

SAMUEL-ROUSSEAU, Marcel
—— VARIATIONS À DANSER SUR LE MÊME THÈME (FOR PIANO AND ORCH.)
    3,3,2,2 - 4,2,3,1 - timp.,perc.,cel.,glock.,xyl. - hp. - pf. - str.
                                    14:00 Baron.

SANCAN, Pierre
—— COMMEDIA DELL'ARTE (OVERTURE)
    3,2,3,alto sax.,2 - 3,3,2,1 - timp.,perc.,cel. - hp. - str.   4:30 EV.
—— CONCERTINO FOR PIANO AND CHAMBER ORCH.
    1,1,2,2 - 2,1,0,0 - timp.,perc.(3),cel.,glock.,vibra.,xyl. - pf.
                                    15:00 EV.
—— CONCERTO FOR PIANO AND ORCH.
    2(alt. with 2 picc.),2,2,2 - 3,2,2,1 - timp.,perc.,cel.,xyl. - hp. - pf. - str.   28:00 EV.
—— LES FOURMIS (BALLET) %
    3,3,3,3 - 4,3,2,1 - timp.,perc.(2) - 2 hp. - pf. - str.   30:00 EV.
—— OUVERTURE JOYEUSE
    2,2,2,alto sax.,2 - 2,3,2,0 - timp.,perc.(4),cel. - hp. - str.   8:00 EV.
—— SYMPHONY (FOR STRING ORCH.)
    str.   11:00 EV.

SÁNCHEZ MÁLAGA, Carlos - HOLZMANN, R.
—— PRELUDIO
                                          Fleisher.

SANDAHL, Helge
—— LITTLE SERENADE (FOR STRING ORCH., WITH PIANO)(1964)
    pf. - str.   8:00 Fleisher.

SANDAUER, Heinz
—— VARIATIONS ON "BEAUTIFUL DREAMER" (FOR VIOLIN AND ORCH.)
                                  17:00 Pleasant.
—— VARIATIONS ON "FRÈRE JACQUES"
                                  15:30 Pleasant.

SANDBERG, Sven
—— THE LAKE IN THE WILDERNESS (1964)
    2,2,2,2 - 4,2,2,0 - timp.,perc. - hp. - str.   6:00 FinnMICtr.

—— A SCENE FROM HÄME (1955)
2,2,2,2 - 3,2,2,0 - timp.,perc. - str.   5:00 FinnMICtr.
—— THREE SONGS (FOR VOICE AND ORCH.) (1948) (Text: N. Lenau)
2,2,2,2 - 4,2,0,0 - timp.,perc. - hp. - str.   6:00 FinnMICtr.

SANDER, Peter
—— SYMPHONIC SUITE (IN TWO MOVTS.)
2,2,2,2 - 0,0,0,0 - str.   15:00 P.R.S.
—— SYMPHONIC SUITE ("THE DAY OF A TEENAGER")
2,2,2,2 - 4,3,2,1 - timp.,perc.(3, incl. 2 on timp.) - str.
    25:00 P.R.S.

SANDERS, Robert L.
—— CELEBRATION OF LIFE (CANTATA) (FOR SOPRANO, MIXED CHORUS AND ORCH.)
1,1,2(2nd alt. with b.-cl.),1 - 2,1,0,0 - timp.,perc.(1),glock.,xyl. - hp. - str.   20:00 Composer.
—— CONCERTO IN A MINOR FOR VIOLIN AND ORCH.
1(alt. with picc.),2,2,2 - 4,2,2,0 - timp.,perc.(3) - str.
    30:00 Composer.
—— LITTLE SYMPHONY IN G (IN 3 MOVTS.)
2(2nd alt. with picc.),2,2,2 - 4,2,3,1 - timp.,perc.(1-2) - str.   14:00 Galaxy.
—— LITTLE SYMPHONY NO. 2 IN B FLAT (IN 3 MOVTS.)
1(alt. with picc.),1(alt. with Eng. hn.),2,2 - 4,2,3,1 - timp.,perc.(1-2),glock.,xyl. - hp. - str.   14:00 Belw-Mills.
—— LITTLE SYMPHONY NO. 3 IN D (IN 4 MOVTS.)
1,1,1,1 - 2,1,0,0 - str.   15:10 Galaxy.
—— MUSIC FOR BALLET L'AG'YA %
2(2nd alt. with picc.),2,2,2 - 4,0,3,1 - timp.,perc.(3),cel.,glock.,xyl. - hp. - str.   16:00 Composer.
—— SCENES OF POVERTY AND TOIL
3(1 alt. with picc.),2,2,2 - 4,3,3,1 - timp.,perc.,cel. - org. - str.
    20:00 Am.Mu.Ctr.
—— SYMPHONY IN A
2(2nd alt. with picc.),*3,2,2 - 4,2,3,1 - timp.,perc.(4-5),bells,cel.,glock.,xyl. - str.   27:00 Galaxy.

SANDLOFF, Peter
—— KAPITAL IV (KAIN) (SUITE FROM THE BALLET)
0,0,0,2 alto sax.(1 alt. with b.-cl.),2 ten. sax.,1 bar. sax.,0 - 0,4,4,0 - timp.,perc.(5) - pf. - d.-b.   23:00 Modern.
—— REINEKE FUCHS (SUITE FROM THE BALLET)
1,1,1,1 - 1,1,1,0 - timp.,perc.(3) - hp. - pf. - str.   15:00 Modern.

SANDSTRÖM, Sven-David
—— AROUND A LINE (1971)
2,2,2,2 - 2,2,2,0 - perc.(2) - pf. - str.   12:00 Nordiska.
—— INTRADA (1969)
1,1,1,1 - 1,1,1,0 - perc.(2) - str.   10:00 Fleisher.
—— PICTURES (FOR PERCUSSION AND ORCH.)(1969)
    Fleisher.
—— SJUTTON BILDKOMBINATIONER (FOR WINDS, PERCUSSION, PIANO AND STRINGS)(1969)
    Fleisher.
—— SOUNDS FROM 14 STRINGS (1970)
str.   6:20 Fleisher.
—— THROUGH AND THROUGH (1972)
4,4,4,4 - 6,4,4,1 - timp.,perc.(5, incl. 2 on timp.) - str.
    20:00 Fleisher.
—— TO YOU (1969)
3,3,3,3 - 3,3,3,0 - perc.(4),cel. - hpsc. - 4 pf. - str.   11:00 Fleisher.

SANDVOLD, Arild
—— CANTATA (FOR CONSECRATION OF THE BEKKELAGET CHURCH) (FOR SOLO VOICES, CHORUS AND ORCH.) (Text: Bjarne Engelstad)
2,1,1,1 - 2,1,1,0 - org. - str.   35:00 T.O.N.O.
—— JUBILEE CANTATA (FOR SOPRANO, MIXED CHORUS AND ORCH.)
2,2,2,2 - 4,2,3,1 - timp.,perc. - org. - str.   40:00 T.O.N.O.

SANNER, Lars-Erik
—— CONCERTO FOR THREE TREBLE WOODWINDS AND STRINGS (1948)
1,1,1,0 - 0,0,0,0 - str.   12:00 Fleisher.

SANTA CRUZ, Domingo
—— SINFONIA CONCERTANTE, OP. 21 (FOR FLUTE AND SMALL ORCH.)
1,1,2,1 - 2,1,0,0 - pf. - str.   20:00 Southern.

—— SYMPHONY NO. 2, OP. 25
str.   21:30 Southern.
—— THREE DRAMATIC PRELUDES
3,3,3,3 - 4,3,3,1 - timp.,perc. - 2 hp. - str.   16:00 Southern.

SANTOLIQUIDO, Francesco
—— ASIAN SHRINES (SANTUARI ASIATICI)
3,3,2,3 - 4,3,4,0 - timp.,perc.,glock. - hp. - str. 12:00 F. Colombo.
—— CREPUSCOLO SUL MARE
    10:00 Forlivesi.
—— IL PROFUMO DELLE OASI SAHARIANE ("THE PERFUME OF THE SAHARAN OASES")
*3,*3,2,*4 - 4,3,3,1 - timp.,perc. - hp. - str. 8:00 G. Schirmer.
—— LA SAGRA DEI MORTI (ELEGY)
    Forlivesi.

SANTORO, Claudio
—— CANTATA ELEGIACA (FOR NARRATOR, 2 CHORUSES AND CHAMBER ORCH.)
2,2,2,2 - 2,0,0,0 - perc.(3) - str.   22:00 Presser.
—— INTERAÇOES ASSINTOTICAS
3,3,4,3 - 4,4,3,1 - timp.,perc.(4) - hp. - str.   8:00 Presser.
—— INTERMITENCIAS II (FOR PIANO AND INSTRUMENTS)
1,1,1,1 - 1,1,1,0 - perc.(2) - 1 amplifier,2 microphones - pf. - str.(1,1,1,1)   7:00 Presser.
—— MUSICA 1946
str.   8:00 Composer.
—— SYMPHONY NO. 3
2,2,3,2 - 4,3,3,1 - timp.,perc. - pf. - str.   30:00 Composer.
—— TRES ABSTRAÇOES (FOR STRING ORCH.)
str.   8:00 Presser.

SANTORSOLA, Guido
—— CONCERTINO FOR GUITAR AND ORCH.
2,1,3,1 - 1,1,0,0 - perc.,cel. - guit. - str.   18:00 Southern.
—— CONCERTO FOR BASSOON AND ORCH.
3,2,3,1 - 3,3,3,0 - timp.,perc.,cel. - hp. - str. 25:00 A.G.A.D.U.
—— CONCERTO FOR VIOLA AND ORCH.
1,2,3,1 - 4,1,3,0 - str   25:00 A.G.A.D.U.
or:
Mixed Chorus - 1,2,1,0 - 4,0,0,0 - str.(incl. 2 vla. d'amore)

SANVOLD, Arild
—— MISJONSKANTATE (FOR SOLO VOICES, CHORUS AND ORCH.) (Text: Ronald Fangen)
    99:00 T.O.N.O.

SAPERSTEIN, David
—— PRELUDE FOR ORCHESTRA (1973)
*3(2nd alt.with alto fl.),*2,3,*3 - 4,3,3,1 - perc.(2),cel., vibra - hp. - pf. - str.   3:00 Composer.

SÁRAI, Tibor
—— DIAGNOSIS '69
*2,2,*4,2 - 4,3,3,1 - timp.,perc. - str.   8:00 Bo. Hawkes.
—— SERENADE FOR STRINGS
str.   Bo. Hawkes.
—— SPRING CONCERTO (FOR FLUTE, VIOLA, CELLO AND STRING ORCH.)
fl. - str.   20:10 Bo. Hawkes.
—— SYMPHONY NO. 1
*2,2,2,2 - 4,3,3,1 - timp. - str.   17:00 Bo. Hawkes.
—— SYMPHONY NO. 2
    18:00 Bo. Hawkes.

SARDA, Albert
—— OCHO PIEZAS PARA ORQUESTA
3,3,3,3 - 4,0,3,1 - timp.,perc.,bells,cel.,vibra.,xyl. - 2 hp. - org. - pf. - str.   14:00 Southern.

SÁRKÖZY, István
—— CONCERTO GROSSO
2,2,2,2 - 4,2,3,1 - timp. - str.   15:30 Bo. Hawkes.
—— CONCERTO SEMPLICE (FOR VIOLIN AND ORCH.)
    17:30 Bo. Hawkes.
—— RAPPRESENTAZIONE PROFANA (FOR SOPRANO, SATB CHORUS AND ORCH.)
    28:00 Bo. Hawkes.
—— SINFONIA CONCERTANTE (FOR CLARINET AND ORCH.)
3,3,1,3 - 3,0,0,0 - str.   22:00 Bo. Hawkes.

ŠÁROVÁ, Dagmar
—— SCHERZO FOR ORCH.
    3,2,3,2 - 4,3,3,1 - timp.,perc. - str.   6:00 Bo. Hawkes.

SÁS, Andrés
—— FANTASIA ROMANTICA, OP. 45 (FOR TRUMPET AND ORCH.)
    2,2,2,2 - 2,1,0,0 - hp.(or pf.) - str.   12:00 Southern.
—— INCA RHAPSODY (RAPSODIA INCAICA) (FOR VIOLIN AND ORCH.) (1941)
    Fleisher.
—— PERUVIAN RHAPSODY, OP. 9 (RAPSODIA PERUANA) (FOR VIOLIN AND ORCH.)
    2,2,2,2 - 2,1,1,1 - timp.,perc.,cel. - hp.   13:00 Southern.
—— POEMA INDIO, OP. 39
    2,3,3,3 - 4,3,3,2 - timp. - hp. - str.   14:30 Southern.
—— RECUERDOS (FOR VIOLIN AND ORCH.) (1941)
    2(2nd alt. with picc.),2,2,2 - 2,1,1,1 - timp.,perc.,cel. - hp. - str.
    7:30 Fleisher.
—— TRES ESTAMPAS DEL PERU, OP. 25
    3,3,3,3 - 4,3,3,1 - timp.,perc.,cel. - hp.   19:45 Southern.

SATIE, Erik
—— CINÉMA (ENTR'ACTE FROM THE BALLET "RELÂCHE")
    1,1,1,1 - 3,3,1,0 - perc. - str.   18:00 Salabert.
—— EN HABIT DE CHEVAL (SUITE) (IN 4 MOVTS.)
    2,2,2,3 - 2,2,3,2 - str.   5:00 Salabert.
—— PARADE (BALLET RÉALISTE) %
    3,3,3,2 - 2,3,3,1 - timp.,perc.(3),xyl. - hp. - str.   13:00 Salabert.
—— RELÂCHE (BALLET) %
    1,1,1,1 - 2,1,1,0 - timp.,perc. - str.   22:00 Salabert.

SATIE, Erik - CABY, Robert
—— CINQ MELODIES (FOR HIGH VOICE AND ORCH.)
    2,2,2,2 - 2,1,1,0 - perc. - hp. - str.   10:25 Salabert.
—— THE DREAMING FISH (LE POISSON RÊVEUR) (MUSIC FOR A TALE OF LORD CHEMINOT)
    Salabert.
—— GNOSSIENNE NO. 4
    1,1,1,1 - 1,0,0,0 - cymb. - hp. - str.   3:30 Salabert.
—— GNOSSIENNE NO. 5
    2,1,1,2 - 1,0,0,0 - perc. - hp. - str.   3:30 Salabert.
—— GNOSSIENNE NO. 6
    0,1,1,1 - 0,1,1,0 - perc. - str.   1:25 Salabert.
—— PRELUDE D' ENGINHARD
    2,2,1,2 - 2,1,1,0 - timp.,perc.(3) - str.   2:00 Salabert.
—— US PUD (BALLET) %
    Salabert.

SATIE, Erik - CONSTANT, Marius
—— MESSE DES PAUVRES (MASS FOR THE POOR)
    1,0,*2,1 - 1,1,1,0 - perc.(2) - hp. - pf. - vln.,c.   8:00 Salabert.

SATIE, Erik - DESORMIERE, R.
—— TROIS MORCEAUX EN FORME DE POIRE
    2,3,2,2 - 3,2,2,1 - perc.,cel. - hp. - str.   17:00 Salabert.

SATIE, Erik - DIAMOND, David
—— MESSE DES PAUVRES
    2,2,2,2 - 2,2,0,0 - timp.,perc. - hp. - str.   8:00 Salabert.
—— PASSACAGLIA
    2,3,3,2 - 4,2,3,1 - timp.,perc. - hp. - str.   Salabert.

SATIE, Erik - LANCHBERRY, John
—— GNOSSIENNES, NOS. 1, 2 AND 3
    7:00 Salabert.
—— PRELUDE D' EGINHARD
    2:00 Salabert.

SATIE, Erik - POULENC, Francis
—— TWO POSTHUMOUS PRELUDES AND GNOSSIENNE NO. 3
    2,2,2,2 - 2,2,2,0 - hp. - str.   9:00 Salabert.

SATIE, Erik - ROLAND-MANUEL
—— GYMNOPÉDIE NO. 2
    2,1,1,0 - 4,1,0,0 - perc., cel. - 2 hp. - str.   4:00 Salabert.

SATIE, Erik - ROLAND-MANUEL, Alexis
—— LE FILS DES ÉTOILES
    3,3(1 alt. with Eng.hn.),3,2 - 4,3,3,0 - timp.,perc.,cel. - hp. - str.
    5:00 Salabert.

SATOW, Karl
—— SERENADE FOR STRING ORCH. (IN 4 MOVTS.)
    str.   14:00 Henmar.

SATZ, Ilja
—— THE BLUEBIRD (SUITE) (FOR CHORUS AND ORCH.)
    3,3,2,2 - 4,3,3,1 - timp.,perc. - hp. - str.   17:00 Bo. Hawkes.
—— DANSE DES CHÈVRE-PIEDS
    3,3,3,3 - 4,3,3,1 - timp.,perc. - str.   8:00 Bo. Hawkes.

SAUGUET, Henri
—— L' AS DE COEUR (BALLET-OPERA) (Text: C. Aveline)
    2,2,2,2 - 2,1,1,0 - timp.,perc. - hp. - str.   25:00 Eds. Fran.
—— LE CHARRON (MUSIC FROM THE FILM)
    1,1,1,1 - 1,1,1,0 - timp.,perc.,cel. - pf. - str.   12:00 Henmar.
—— LA CHATTE (BALLET) (1927) %
    3,3,3,3 - 4,3,3,1 - timp.,perc. - str.   22:00 Salabert.
—— LES CINQ ÉTAGES (BALLET) %
    2,2,2,2 - 2,2,2,1 - timp.,perc.,cel. - str.   42:00 Presser.
—— CLOCHEMERLE (MUSIC FROM THE FILM)
    12:00 Henmar.
—— CONCERTO D'ORPHÉE (FOR VIOLIN AND ORCH.)
    picc.,2,*3,2,2 - 2,1,1,0 - timp.,perc.(2),cel.,xyl. - hp. - str.
    25:00 Presser.
—— CONCERTO NO. 3 FOR PIANO AND ORCH. ("CONCERTO FROM THE UNDERWORLD") (1963)
    4,4,3,3 - 4,3,2,1 - timp.,perc.,cel.,glock.,xyl. - hp. - pf. - str.
    30:00 Salabert.
—— LA DAME AUX CAMÉLIAS (SYMPHONIC SUITE FROM THE BALLET)
    2,1,2,1 - 2,1,1,0 - timp.,perc. - hp. - pf. - str.   45:00 F. Colombo.
—— DAVID (BALLET) %
    3,3,3,3 - 4,4,3,1 - timp.,perc.(2),cel.,xyl. - hp. - str.   40:00 Salabert.
—— LES FORAINS (1-ACT BALLET) %
    2,2,2,2 - 2,2,1,1 - timp.,perc.,cel. - pf. - str.   25:00 Salabert.
—— THE GARDEN'S CONCERTO (FOR OBOE OR HARMONICA, WITH CHAMBER ORCH.)
    ob.(or harmonica) - perc.(2),cel. - hp. - str.(2,1,2,0)   16:00 Presser.
—— LES MIRAGES (BALLET) %
    3,3,3,3 - 4,4,4,1 - timp.,perc. - hp. - str.   30:00 Salabert.
—— LA NUIT (BALLET) %
    1,1,2,1 - 2,2,1,0 - timp.,perc. - hp. - str.   12:00 Salabert.
—— L' OISEAU A VU TOUT CELA (FOR BARITONE AND STRING ORCH.)
    str.   17:00 Presser.
—— PARIS (BALLET) (1964) %
    1,1,1,1 - 1,1,1,0 - timp.,perc.(3) - hp. - pf. - str.   40:00 Salabert.
—— LA RENCONTRE
    *2,*2,1,1 - 1,1,1,1 - timp.,perc. - hp. - pf. - str.   22:00 Presser.
—— LA SOLITUDE (SYMPHONIC REVERIE)
    1,1,1,1 - 1,0-1,0,0 - timp.,perc.,cel. - pf.(ad lib.) - str.
    22:00 Presser.
—— SYMPHONIE ALLÉGORIQUE ("LES SAISONS") (FOR SOPRANO, CHORUS AND ORCH.)
    3,3,3,3 -4,3,2,1 - timp. - hp. - pf. - str.   60:00 Presser.
—— SYMPHONIE DE BALLET ("LE CAMÉLÉOPARD")
    2,1,2,1 - 2,2,1,0 - timp.,perc. - hp. - pf. - str.   20:00 F. Colombo.
—— SYMPHONIE EXPIATOIRE
    1. Allegro giusto; 2. Andantino; 3. Allegro alla marcia; 4. Lento quasi adagio
    3,3,3,3 - 4,4,3,1 - timp.,perc. - hp. - str.   45:00 Salabert.
—— SYMPHONIE NO. 3
    3,3,3,2 - 4,3,0,1 - timp.,perc. - hp. - str.   25:00 Salabert.
—— TABLEAUX DE PARIS (SUITE IN 12 MOVTS.)
    2(1 alt. with picc.),2(1 alt. with Eng.hn.),2,1 sax.,1 - 2,2,1,1 - timp.,perc.,cel. - hp. - acc. - pf. - str.   28:30 AhnSimrock.
—— LES TROIS LYS (MOUVEMENT SYMPHONIQUE)
    2,2,2,2 - 2,2,1,1 - timp.,perc. - hp. - str.   8:00 Salabert.
—— TWO MOVEMENTS FOR STRINGS (IN MEMORY OF PAUL GILSON)
    str.   15:30 Presser.
—— LE VOYAGE (SCENE FOR SOPRANO AND CHAMBER ORCH.) (Text: Max Jacob)
    Presser.

SAUNDERS, Max
—— INTERLUDIUM
    str.   8:00 F. Colombo.

SAUTEREAU, Cesar
—— CONCERTO FOR STRING ORCH. (IN 3 MOVTS.)
    str.   16:00 Presser.

SAVINO, Domenico
—— AMERICAN CONCERTO (FOR PIANO AND ORCH.)
                                           Robbins.
—— AUTUMN STORY
    3(3rd alt. with picc.),*3,*3,*3 - 4,3,3,0 - timp.,perc.(3),xyl. - hp. - str.
                                    7:00 Composer.
—— CAVALCADE OF AMERICA (FOR MIXED VOICES, NARRATOR AND ORCH.)
                                           Robbins.
—— CONCERTO FOR PIANO AND ORCH.
    1. Moderato; 2. Allegro vivace
                                  21:00 Consolidtd.
—— CUBAN CONCERTO (FOR PIANO AND ORCH.) (IN 1 MOVT.)
    *2,*3,*3,2 - 4,3,3,0 - timp.,perc.(3) - pf. - str.   7:00 Consolidtd.
—— FOUR IMPRESSIONS
                                        Composer.
—— LATIN AMERICAN OVERTURE
                                    7:00 Robbins.
—— MADRILENA (SYMPHONIC POEM)
    3(3rd alt. with picc.),*3,*3,*3 - 4,3,3,1 - timp.,perc.(4),xyl. - hp. - str.
                                  17:00 Robbins.
—— OVERTURE FANTASY
    *3,*3,*3,*3 - 4,3,3,1 - timp.,perc.(2),xyl. - hp. - str.
                                  8:00 Consolidtd.
—— PANORAMA (SYMPHONIC IMPRESSION)
    3(3rd alt. with picc.),*3,*3,*3 - 4,3,3,1 - timp.,perc.(4),xyl. - hp. - str.
                                  12:00 Robbins.
—— RAPSODIA VESUVIANA
    *3,*3,*3,*3 - 4,3,3,1 - timp.,perc.,cel.,glock.,xyl. - hp. - str.
                                  18:00 Robbins.
—— SYMPHONY NO. 1
    3(3rd alt. with picc.),*3,*3,*3 - 4,3,3,1 - timp.,perc.(4),cel.,xyl. - hp. - str.
                                  30:00 Valentino.
—— VENETIAN SCENES
                                    8:00 Robbins.
—— WORLD OF TOMORROW (FOR HIGH VOICE, MIXED CHORUS, PIANO AND ORCH.)
                                        Robbins.

SAWYER, Wilson
—— TOM SAWYER SUITE (IN 3 MOVTS.)
    2,2,1,1 - 2,2,1,0 - perc.,cel. - banjo - pf. - str.   10:00 Hargail.

SAXE, Serge
—— CONCERTO FOR PIANO AND ORCH. ("THE TEMPEST")
    2,2,2,2 - 4,2,3,1 - timp.,perc. - hp. - pf. - str.   23:00 Southern.

SAXTON, Stanley E.
—— CONCERTO IN A FOR PIANO AND ORCH. (IN 3 MOVTS.)
    1,1,2,2 - 0,0,0,0 - timp.,perc.(2-3) - pf. - org. - str.
                                    22:00 Composer.
    or:
    1,1,2,2 - 4,2,2,1 - timp.,perc.(2-3) - pf. - org. - str.
—— GAY VARIATIONS ON A SOLEMN THEME
    2(2nd alt. with picc.),1,2,1 - 4,2,2,1 - timp.,perc.(2-3) - str.
                                    10:00 Composer.
—— HEROIC OVERTURE
    1,1,2,2 - 2,2,2,1 - timp.,perc.(1-2) - str.   10:00 Composer.
—— MOHAWK SUITE (IN 4 MOVTS.)
                                    22:00 Composer.

SAYGUN, Ahmed Adnan
—— BIR ORMAN MASALI ("A FOREST TALE")
    1,1,1,sax.,1 - 1,1,1,0 - timp.,perc.,cel. - str.   27:00 Southern.
—— CANTATA IN OLD STYLE, OP. 19 (FOR SOPRANO, TENOR, BASS, SATB CHORUS AND ORCH.)
    2,2,2,2 - 0,1,0,0 - str.   16:00 Southern.
—— CONCERTO FOR PIANO AND ORCH.
    2,2,2,2 - 4,3,3,0 - timp.,perc. - pf. - str.   Southern.
—— CONCERTO FOR VIOLIN AND ORCH., OP. 44
    2,2,2,2 - 4,3,3,0 - timp.,perc. - hp. - str.   31:30 Southern.
—— DEYIS (DICTUM), OP. 49
    str.   17:00 Southern.
—— DIVERTIMENTO
    2,3,3,sax.,2,sarr. - 4,2,3,1 - timp.,perc. - str.   11:00 Southern.
—— HALAY (TURKISH FOLK DANCE)
    2,2,3,2 - 2,2,0,0 - timp.,perc. - str.   10:00 Southern.
—— HORON (TURKISH FOLK DANCE)
    2,2,2,2 - 4,3,3,0 - timp.,perc. - str.   5:00 Southern.
—— IMPROVISATION
    0,2,2,2 - 2,0,0,0 - timp.,perc. - hp. - str.   4:00 Southern.

—— INCI'S BOOK (SUITE)
    2,1,1,2 - 2,2,0,0 - perc.,cel. - str.   10:00 Southern.
—— KEREM (3-ACT OPERA) %
    3,3,3,3 - 4,3,3,1 - timp.,perc. - hp. - str.   150:00 Southern.
—— SIKIR RAKSI
    2,2,2,alto sax.,2 - 2,3,3,0 - perc. - pf. - str.   10:00 Southern.
—— SUITE (IN 3 MOVTS.)
    2,3,2,2 - 4,3,3,0 - timp.,perc. - hp. - str.   8:00 Southern.
—— SYMPHONY NO. 1, OP. 29
    1,2,2,2 - 2,0,0,0 - str.   Southern.
—— SYMPHONY NO. 2, OP. 30
    2,2,2,2 - 4,3,3,0 - timp.,perc. - str.   Southern.
—— SYMPHONY NO. 3
    3,3,3,3 - 4,3,4,0 - timp.,perc. - hp. - str.   35:00 Southern.
—— SYMPHONY NO. 4
                                    26:00 Southern.
—— YUNUS EMRE (ORATORIO) (FOR SOLO VOICES, CHORUS AND ORCH.)
    2,2,2,2 - 4,3,3,1 - timp.,perc. - str.   75:00 Southern.

SAYLOR, Bruce
—— CANTILENA (1965)
    Str   5:15 Composer.

SCALERO, Rosario
—— LA DIVINA FORESTA, OP. 32
    2,3,3,3 - 4,3,3,1 - timp. - str.   7:00 Bo. Hawkes.

SCARLATTI, Alessandro - CASTELLINI, John
—— TE DEUM LAUDAMUS (FOR CHORUS AND ORCH.)
    2 ob. - org. - str.   10:00 Presser.

SCARLATTI, Alessandro - LENZEWSKI
—— CONCERTO GROSSO NO. 3 IN F MAJOR
    cemb. - str.   7:00 Henmar.

SCARLATTI, Alessandro - NAPOLITANO, Franco M.
—— CONCERTO NO. 3 IN F MAJOR FOR STRINGS AND CEMBALO
    cemb. - str.   Henmar.
—— PICCOLA SUITE
    str.   10:00 Henmar.

SCARLATTI, Alessandro - PERESS, Maurice
—— SU LA SPONDE DEL MARE (CANTATA) (FOR SOPRANO, STRINGS AND CONTINUO) (ARR. 1960)
    hpsc. - str.   22:00 Arranger.

SCARLATTI, Alessandro - STEIN, Leon
—— TOCCATA NONA
    3,2,2,2 - 4,3,3,1 - timp. - str.   5:00 C. Fischer.

SCARLATTI, Alessandro - UPMEYER
—— CONCERTO GROSSO NO. 1 IN F MINOR
    cemb. - str.   Henmar.
—— CONCERTO GROSSO NO. 2 IN C MINOR
    cemb. - str.   Henmar.

SCARLATTI, Bruno
—— ÉPOQUES (SYMPHONIC SUITE IN 3 PARTS)
    2,2,2,2 - 4,2,2,0 - timp.,perc.,bells - str.   20:00 Henmar.

SCARLATTI, Domenico - BENJAMIN, Arthur
—— CONCERTO FOR FLUTE AND STRINGS
    fl. - str.   12:00 Bo. Hawkes.
—— SUITE FOR FLUTE AND STRINGS
    fl. - str.   20:00 Bo. Hawkes.

SCARLATTI, Domenico - BONELLI, Ettore
—— FIVE SONATAS FOR STRINGS
    str.   Henmar.

SCARLATTI, Domenico - BRYAN, Gordon
—— CONCERTO IN G FOR OBOE AND STRINGS (IN 5 MOVTS.)
    ob. - str.   11:00 G. Schirmer.

SCARLATTI, Domenico - BYRNS, Harold
—— SUITE FOR STRINGS
    str.   8:00 Leeds.

SCARLATTI, Domenico - CASELLA, A.
—— TOCCATA, BOURREE ET GIGUE
    2,1,1,2 - 2,1,0,0 - perc. - str.   12:00 Salabert.

SCARLATTI, Domenico - DE FILIPPI, Amedeo
—— SUITE (IN 4 MOVTS.)
2,2,2,2 - 2,2,0,0 - timp.,perc.,cel. - hp. - str.   17:00 Arranger.

SCARLATTI, Domenico - HARRISON, Julius
—— SUITE FOR STRINGS (IN 3 MOVTS.)
str.   8:15 Novello.

SCARLATTI, Domenico - ROLAND-MANUEL
—— THREE PIECES
2,2,2,2 - 2,2,0,0 - timp. - hp. - str.   11:00 Bo. Hawkes.

SCARLATTI, Domenico - TOMMASINI, Vincenzo
—— THE GOOD-HUMOURED LADIES (BALLET SUITE)
2,2,2,2 - 4 hns.,2 cnt. - perc. - str.   G. Schirmer.

SCARLATTI, Domenico - WARD, Lionel
—— L' HEURE GALANTE (5 HARPSICHORD PIECES)
2,2,2,2 - 2,1,1,0 - str.   10:00 Bo. Hawkes.

SCARMOLIN, A. Louis
—— BREAK OF DAY (TONE POEM), OP. 180
1(alt. with picc.),2,2,2 - 4,2,3,1 - timp.,perc.(3) - str.   Composer.
—— A DRAMATIC TONE POEM
2,2,2,2 - 4,3,3,1 - timp. - hp. - str.   10:00 C. Fischer.
—— FOUR PIECES FOR ORCHESTRA
2,2,2,2 - 4,3,3,1 - timp. - hp. - str.   12:00 Composer.
—— THE GIFTS OF BETHLEHEM (CANTATA) (FOR WOMEN'S CHORUS, ORGAN AND ORCH.), OP. 159
2,2,2,2 - 4,3,3,1 - timp.,perc.(2) - org. - str.   45:00 Composer.
—— INVOCATION
2,2,2,2 - 4,3,3,0 - timp.,cel. - hp. - str.   16:00 Fox.
—— MINIATURE SYMPHONY IN C MAJOR, OP. 171
1. Moderato con grazia; 2. Andantino; 3. Presto
2,2,2,2 - 4,2,3,1 - timp.,perc.(2) - str.   15:00 Ludwig.
—— MINIATURE SYMPHONY NO. 2 IN D MINOR, OP. 176
1. Con moto; 2. Andantino; 3. Allegro
2,2,2,2 - 4,3,3,1 - timp.,perc.(2) - str.   8:00 Composer.
—— NIGHT (A POEM), OP. 156
2,2,2,2 - 4,3,3,1 - timp.,perc.(2) - str.   12:00 Composer.
—— OVERTURE ON A STREET VENDOR'S DITTY, OP. 160
2,2,2,2 - 4,3,3,1 - timp.,perc.(2) - str.   7:00 Composer.
—— PASTORALE, OP. 194
1(alt. with picc.),2,2,2 - 4,3,3,1 - timp.,perc.(2) - hp. - str.   10:00 Fox.
—— SINFONIETTA (FOR STRINGS), OP. 168 (IN 3 MOVTS.)
str.   20:00 Composer.
—— SYMPHONY IN E MINOR, OP. 154 (IN 3 MOVTS.)
2,2,*3,2 - 4,3,3,1 - timp.,perc.(3) - str.   30:00 Fox.
—— THE TEMPTATION ON THE MOUNT (CANTATA) (FOR SOPRANO, BARITONE, MIXED CHORUS, CHILDREN'S OR WOMEN'S CHORUS AND ORCH.), OP. 60
1,1,2,1 - 4,2,3,0 - timp. - str.   30:00 Gray.
—— TWO SYMPHONIC FRAGMENTS, OP. 78
2,2(2nd alt. with Eng. hn.),2,2 - 4,3,3,1 - timp.,perc.(2) - hp. - str.   10:00 Fox.
—— VARIATIONS ON A FOLK SONG, OP. 192 (FOR STRINGS)
str.   9:00 Composer.
—— VISIONS (A SYMPHONIC IMPRESSION), OP. 173
2,2,2,2 - 4,3,3,1 - timp.,perc.(2) - str.   10:00 Composer.

SCHAD, Walter C.
—— A LEGENDARY HERO (OVERTURE)
*3,*3,*3,2 - 4,3,3,1 - timp.,perc.(3) - str.   12:00 Composer.

SCHAEFER, Willis Stewart
—— CONCERT OVERTURE, OP. 5
2,2,2,2 - 4,3,3,0 - timp.,perc.(5),xyl. - str.   8:30 Composer.
—— DESERT POEM, OP. 14
2,2,2,2 (2nd alt. with b.-cl.) - 4,3,3,0 - perc.(3) - hp. - pf. - str.   Composer.

SCHAEUBLE, Hans
—— CONCERTO FOR CELLO AND ORCH., OP. 41
*2,*2,*2,2 - 2,2,2,0 - timp. - str.   19:00 S.U.I.S.A.
—— CONCERTO FOR PIANO AND ORCH. (IN 1 MOVT.), OP. 34
2,2,2,2 - 4,3,3,0 - timp.,perc. - pf. - str.   19:00 S.U.I.S.A.
—— HYMNUS, OP. 29
*2,*2,*2,*2 - 2,3,2,0 - timp. - str.   15:00 S.U.I.S.A.
—— OMBRA ADORATA (KLEINE SINFONIE), OP. 38
2,*2,2,2 - 3,2,1,0 - timp. - str.   21:00 S.U.I.S.A.

SCHÄFER, Gerhart
—— CONCERTO FOR CHAMBER ORCH.
1,1,1,1 - 0,0,0,0 - perc. - str.   17:00 Mannheimer.
—— CONCERTO FOR OBOE AND SMALL ORCH.
2,1,2,2 - 0,0,0,0 - timp. - str.   20:00 Mannheimer.
—— PRELUDE CONCERTANTE
*4,*3,2,2 - 4,3,3,1 - timp. - str.   13:00 Mannheimer.

SCHÄFER, Hermann
—— CONCERTO FOR VIOLIN, VIOLA, CELLO AND STRING ORCH.
str.   21:00 Mannheimer.

SCHÄFER, Karl
—— DIVERTIMENTO ON A THEME OF C. PAUMANN (FOR VIOLA OR VIOLIN, WITH CHAMBER ORCH.)
Hans Gerig.

SCHÄFERS, Anton
—— NINETTE ("DAS MÄDCHEN NINETTE") (BALLET) %
2,2,2,2 - 4,2,4,0 - perc. - pf. - str.   27:00 F. Colombo.

SCHÄFFER, Boguslaw
—— AZIONE A DUE (FOR PIANO AND INSTRUMENTAL ACCOMPANIMENT)
1,*2,*2,ten. sax.,1 - 1,1,1,1 - pf.   4:55 AhnSimrock.
—— EXTREME (FOR 10 INSTRUMENTS)
2 cel.,2 vibra.,2 xyl. - marimbas - 2 hpsc. - 2 pf.   6:20 AhnSimrock.
—— NOCTURNE (MUSIC FOR STRINGS)
str.   8:50 AhnSimrock.
—— PERMUTATIONS FOR 10 INSTRUMENTS
1,1,1,alto sax.,0 - 0,1,1,0 - perc. - hp. - pf. - vla.   6:30 AhnSimrock.
—— SYMPHONY IN NINE MOVEMENTS
4(4th alt. with picc.),4(4th alt. with Eng.hn.),4(1alt. with E♭ cl.,1 alt. with b.-cl.),alto sax.,4(4th alt. with c.-bn.) - 5,3,3,2 - perc.,vibra. - hp. - pf. - str.   17:18 AhnSimrock.

SCHAPIRA, Ilana
—— CONCERTO FOR PIANO AND ORCH.
AC.U.M.

SCHARF, Walter
—— PALESTINE SUITE (IN 5 MOVTS.)
*3,*2,*3,*2 - 4,3,3,1 - perc.(4),cel.,glock. - hp. - str.   18:00 Mills.

SCHAT, Peter
—— CLOCKWISE AND COUNTER-CLOCKWISE
3,3,3,3 - 4,0,0,0   12:00 Henmar.
—— CONCERTO DA CAMERA (1960)
2 cl. - perc. - pf. - str.   15:00 Henmar.
—— CRYPTOGAMEN (FOR BARITONE AND ORCH.) (1959) (Text: Gerrit Achterberg)
3,2,4,3 - 4,3,2,1 - timp.,perc.,cel. - hp. - str.   15:00 Henmar.
—— DANSEN UIT HET LABYRINT (1963)
3,3,3,4 - 4,3,3,2 - perc.,vibra. - hp. - 2 pf. - str.   20:00 Henmar.
—— ENTELECHIE I (FOR 5 INSTRUMENTAL GROUPS) (1961)
1,1,1,1 - 0,2,1,0 - perc.,vibra. - hp. - str.   15:00 Henmar.
—— MOZAÏEKEN (1959)
2,2,2,2 - 2,2,0,0 - timp.,perc.,cel. - hp. - pf. - str.   10:00 Henmar.
—— STEMMEN UIT HET LABYRINT (FOR 3 VOICES AND ORCH.) (Text: composer)
30:00 Henmar.

SCHATT, Leo
—— CONCERTO FOR CELLO AND ORCH.
2,2,2,2 - 2,2,0,0 - timp. - str.   22:00 Mannheimer.
—— SUITE FOR SMALL ORCH.
1,1,1,1 - 2,2,1,0 - timp. - str.   18:00 Mannheimer.

SCHECHTER, Boris S.
—— TURKMENIAN SUITE
1. Allegro giocoso; 2. Lento; 3. Allegro marciale
*3,2(2nd alt. with Eng. hn.),2,2 - 4,2,3,1 - timp.,perc. - str.   15:00 G. Schirmer.

SCHEFFLER, Siegfried
—— BUNTE SUITE (IN 4 MOVTS.)
2,2,2,2 - 2,2,1,0 - perc. - hp. - str.   16:30 Henmar.
—— HANSEATIC SUITE
Henmar.

SCHEIDT, Samuel - LEONARDI, Leon
—— CHORALE-PRELUDE: "VATER UNSER IN HIMMELREICH"
2,3,3,3 - 4,3,3,1 - str.   EV.

SCHEIDT, Samuel - ROCHBERG, George
—— CANTIO SACRA: "WARUM BETRÜBST DU DICH, MEIN HERZ?"
0, 2(2nd alt. with Eng. hn.),0,0 - 0,2,1,0 - str.   17:00 Arranger.

SCHEIN, Johann Hermann - SCHERING
—— SUITE FROM "BANCHETTO MUSICALE"
str.   9:00 Henmar.

SCHELLING, Ernest
—— LEGENDE SYMPHONIQUE
2,*3,2,*3 - 4,2,3,0 - timp. - hp. - str.   15:00 G. Schirmer.
—— MOROCCO (SYMPHONIC TABLEAU)
*3,*3,E♭cl.(alt. with D cl.),*3,*3 - 4,4,3,1 - timp.,perc.,cel.,glock.,xyl. - 2 hp. - pf. - str.   20:00 Composer.
—— SUITE FANTASTIQUE (FOR PIANO AND ORCH.) (IN 5 MOVTS.)
*3,*3,*3,*3 - 4,2,3,1 - timp.,perc. - 2 hp. - str.   Composer.
—— SUITE VARIÉE (IN 7 MOVTS.)
3(3rd alt. with picc.),3(3rd alt. with Eng. hn.),*3,*3 - 4,3,3,1 - timp.,perc.cel.,xyl. - 2 hp. - pf. - str.   26:00 Composer.

SCHENKER, Friedrich
—— CONCERTO FOR BASSOON AND STRINGS
bn. - str.   Tetra.
—— CONCERTO FOR OBOE AND STRINGS
ob. - str.   30:00 Tetra.
—— LITTLE SYMPHONY (FOR STRING ORCH.) (1966)
str.   14:00 Tetra.
—— TRIPLE CONCERTO (FOR OBOE, BASSOON, PIANO, PERCUSSION AND STRINGS)
0,1,0,1 - 0,0,0,0 - perc. - pf. - str.   Tetra.

SCHERBACHEFF, Valadimir V.
—— SUITE NO. 2
3,3,2,3 - 4,3,3,1 - timp.,perc.,cel. - hp. - str.   G. Schirmer.

SCHERER, Frank H.
—— CONTEMPLATION ON THE CRUCIFIXION (ORATORIO) (FOR VOICES, CHORUS AND ORCH.)
2(2nd alt. with picc.),2,2,2 - 4,3,3,1 - timp.,perc.(1) - str.   55:00 Gray.

SCHIASSI, Gaetano Maria - UPMEYER
—— CHRISTMAS SYMPHONY IN D MAJOR
cemb. - str.   Henmar.

SCHIBLER, Armin
—— CONCERTO FOR PERCUSSION AND ORCH., OP. 63 (SCÈNES PHANTASTIQUES)
2,2,2,2 - 3,2,2,1 - perc. - hp. - pf. - str.   27:00 AhnSimrock.
—— CONCERTO FOR VIOLIN AND ORCH., OP. 61
*3,*3,*3,*3 - 4,3,3,1 - perc.,cel. - hp. - pf. - str   22:30 AhnSimrock.
or:
2(2nd alt. with picc.),*2,*2,2(2nd alt. with c.-bn) - 4,2,2,0 - perc.,cel. - hp. - str.
—— CONCERTO, OP. 59 (FOR BRASS, PIANO, PERCUSSION, HARP AND DOUBLE STRING ORCH.) (1959)
0,0,0,0 - 1,1,1,0 - perc. - hp. - pf. - str.   21:00 AhnSimrock.
—— FANTAISIE, OP. 15 (FOR VIOLA AND SMALL ORCH.)
1,0,1,1 - 2,0,0,0 - timp. - str.   12:30 AhnSimrock.
—— FANTAISIE, OP. 12C (FOR OBOE, HARP AND SMALL ORCH.)
1,1,0,1 - 2,0,0,0 - hp. - str.   13:00 AhnSimrock.
—— KONZERTANTE FANTASIE, OP. 31 (FOR CELLO AND ORCH.)
2(or picc.),2,2(b.-cl.),2 - 2-4,1,1,0 - str.   16:00 AhnSimrock.
—— LYRIC MUSIC, OP. 12-C (FOR OBOE AND CHAMBER ORCH.)
                    AhnSimrock.
—— LYRISCHES KONZERT, OP. 40 (FOR FLUTE AND ORCH.)
1,2,2(or b.-cl.),2 - 2,1,1,0 - str.   14:00 AhnSimrock.
—— METAMORPHOSES EBRIETATIS, OP. 75 (LA FÊTE DE DIONYSOS) (BALLET) %
3(3rd alt. with picc.),*3,*3,*3 - 4,3,3,1 - perc. - hp. - pf.(or cel.) - str.   23:00 AhnSimrock.

—— MOONLIGHT, OP. 26 (CANTATA ON A TEXT OF W. BERGENGRUEN) (FOR ALTO AND CHAMBER ORCH.) (1950)
2(2nd alt. with picc.),1(alt. with Eng.hn.),1(alt. with b.-cl.),1 - 2,0,0,0 - hp. - pf. - str.   14:00 AhnSimrock.
—— MUSIC FOR AN IMAGINARY BALLET, OP. 56 (FOR 12 SOLO STRINGS AND HARPSICHORD) (1958)
hpsc. - str.   18:00 AhnSimrock.
—— NACHTMUSIK, OP. 44
*2,*2,*2,*2 - 2,1,1,0 - cel. - hp. - str.   21:00 AhnSimrock.
—— PASSACAGLIA, OP. 24
*3,*3,*3,*3 - 4,3,3,1 - timp.,perc. - hp. - pf. - str.   17:00 G. Schirmer.
—— PRELUDE TO THE BURLESQUE OPERA "BLACKWOOD AND CO.", OP. 46-A
2(2nd alt. with picc.),2,2(2nd alt. with b.-cl.),2(2nd alt. with c.-bn.) - 3,2,2,0 - timp.,perc. - pf.(or cel.) - str.   8:30 AhnSimrock.
—— PROLOGUE, INVOCATION AND DANSE, OP. 47 (FOR HORN AND ORCH.)
2,2,2,2 - 1,1,1,1 - hp. - str.   17:00 AhnSimrock.
—— DER RAUB DES FEUERS, OP. 43 (SYMPHONIC PANTOMIME)
*3,*3,*3,*3 - 4,3,3,1 - timp.,perc.,cel. - hp. - pf. - str.   28:00 AhnSimrock.
—— RHYTHMISCHE METAMORPHOSEN, OP. 35A
*3,*3,*3,*3 - 4,3,3,1 - timp.,perc. - hp. - pf. - str.   20:00 AhnSimrock.
—— SIGNAL, BESCHWÖRUNG UND TANZ, OP. 55 (FOR TROMBONE AND ORCH.)
2,2,2,2 - 4,2,1,1 - perc. - hp. - pf. - str.   15:00 AhnSimrock.
—— SINFONIE, OP. 35
*3,*3,*3,*3 - 4,3,3,1 - timp.,perc. - hp. - pf. - str.   32:00 AhnSimrock.
—— SINFONIE (QUASI UNA FANTASIA), OP. 17
3(or picc.),*3,*3,*3 - 4,3,2,1 - timp.,perc. - str.   21:00 AhnSimrock.
—— SUITE FROM THE BURLESQUE OPERA "BLACKWOOD AND CO.", OP. 46-B (IN 6 MOVTS.)
2(2nd alt. with picc.),2,2(2nd alt. with b.-cl.),2(2nd alt. with c.-bn.) - 3,2,2,0 - timp.,perc. - pf.(or cel.) - str.   23:00 AhnSimrock.

SCHICKELE, Peter
—— CELEBRATIONS WITH BELLS (1960)
2,2,*3,2 - 4,3,3,1 - timp.,perc.(4) - str.   7:00 EV.
or:
2,1,*3,2 sax.,1 - 2,3,2,1 - timp.,perc.(4) - str.
—— CHACONNE À SON GOUT
2,2,2,2 - 2,2,1,0 - str.   6:00 Presser.
—— THE FANTASTIC GARDEN (FOR SINGING ROCK GROUP AND ORCH.)
Orch: 3,3,3,2 - 4,4,4,1 - timp.,perc.(5),cel. - hp. - str.   25:00 EV.
Rock Group(3 Players): electric hpsc., electric org., electric pf. - pf.
—— FANTASY FOR STRING ORCHESTRA (1958) (ON L'HOMME ARMÉ)
str.   3:00 Composer.
—— IN THIS YEAR (CONTATA ON ANGLO-SAXON POEMS) (FOR 2TENORS, GIRL'S CHORUS, MIXED CHORUS, BAND AND STRING ORCH.) (1961) (Text: Trans. into English by Burton Raffel)
1,1,*4,1 alto sax.,1 ten.sax.,1 bar. sax.,1 - 1,3,3,bar.,1 - timp.,perc.(5),bells,glock.,vibra.,xyl. - str.   9:00 Composer.
—— INVENTION FOR ORCHESTRA (1958)
*3,*3,*3,*3 - 4,3,3,1 - timp.,perc. - pf. - str.   8:00 Fleisher.
—— EINE KLEINE NICHTMUSIK
1,1,1, - 1,1,1,0 - str.   12:00 Presser.
—— MAIDEN ON THE MOOR (FOR COUNTER-TENOR OR CONTRALTO WITH CHAMBER ORCH.)
ob. - 2 hn. - finger cymb. - str.   8:00 EV.
—— OVERTURE TO "THE CIVILIAN BARBER" (1953)
0,2,0,2 - 2,0,0,0 - str.   2:30 EV.
—— PENTANGLE (5 SONGS FOR HORN AND ORCH.)
3,2,3,2 - 4,3,3,1 - timp.,perc.,cel. - pf. - str.   25:00 EV.
—— REQUIEM FOR STRING ORCHESTRA (1959)
str.   4:00 Composer.
—— REQUIEM MANTRAS (FOR ROCK GROUP AND ORCH.)
3,2,2,2 - 4,3,3,1 - perc.(3),cel. - pf. - str.   15:00 EV.
—— SERENADE
2(2nd alt. with picc.),2,*3,2 - 4,3,3,0 - timp.,perc.(2) - str.   11:00 EV.
—— THREE GIRLS, THREE WOMEN (FOR MALE SINGING PIANIST AND ORCH.)
2,2,2,2 - 3,2,1,1 - perc.(2),cel. - hp. - pf. - str.   20:00 EV.

—— THREE STRANGE CASES (FOR NARRATOR AND ORCH.)
(Texts: Ogden Nash)
    1,1,1,1 - 0,0,0,0 - perc.(2) - str.   6:00 EV.
—— THE UNBEGUN SYMPHONY
    1,1,1,1 - 1,1,0,0 - str.   9:00 Presser.
—— A ZOO CALLED EARTH (FOR TAPED NARRATION AND
ORCH.) (1970)
    perc.(4),cel. - tape-recorder - str.   14:00 Presser.
—— ZOO PIECE (1961)
    *2,2,2,1 - 1,2,1,0 - perc.(2) - str.   5:00 Composer.

SCHICKHARDT, Johann Christian - BRINCKMANN-MOHR
—— CONCERTO IN G MINOR
    fl.(or alto recorder),2,0,0 - 0,0,0,0 - cemb. - str.   Henmar.

SCHIERBECK, Poul
—— ADRIENNE LECOUVREUR, OP. 49 (RHAPSODY)
    2,2,2,2 - 4,2,3,1 - timp.,perc.,bells,xyl. - pf. - str.   16:00 Henmar.
—— ANDANTE DOLOROSO, OP. 57, NO. 2
    1,0,0,0 - 2,1,0,0 - str.   7:00 G. Schirmer.
—— THE CHINESE FLUTE, OP. 10 (4 SONGS, FOR SOPRANO OR
MEZZO-SOPRANO AND ORCH.)
    2,2,2,2 - 4,3,3,1 - timp.,perc.,cel. - hp. - str.   12:00 G. Schirmer.
—— FÊTE GALANTE, OP. 25 (OPERA) % (Text: Max Lobedanz)
    Henmar.
—— HAEXA, OP. 48 (FOR SOPRANO, ORGAN AND ORCH.)
    2,0,0,0 - 4,2,3,1 - timp., cel. - hp. - org. - str.   7:00 Henmar.
—— LARGO (FROM THE FILM "THE WORD")
    str.   5:00 G. Schirmer.
—— THE NIGHT ("NATTEN"), OP. 41 (SYMPHONIC SCENE FOR
PIANO AND ORCH.)
    2,2,2,2 - 2,2,2,0 - perc.(3) - pf. - str.   Henmar.
—— OVERTURE TO "FÊTE GALANTE"
    2,2,2,2 - 4,2,3,1 - timp.,perc. - str.   8:00 Henmar.
—— QUEEN DAGMAR (FOR NARRATOR, MEZZO-SOPRANO,
TENOR, BARITONE, CHORUS AND ORCH.)
    G. Schirmer.
—— SYMPHONY NO. 1, OP. 15
    3,3,3,3 - 4,3,3,1 - timp.,perc.,cel. - hp. - mandolin - str.
    45:00 G. Schirmer.

SCHILDKNECHT, Bjorn
—— DYNING PÅ DANZIGER GATT (SYMPHONIC POEM)
    2,2,2,2 - 4,2,3,1 - timp. - hp. - str.   12:00 S.T.I.M.
—— LÖRDAGSKVÄLL (SUITE)
    2,2,2,2 - 4,2,3,1 - timp.,perc. - str.   30:00 S.T.I.M.
—— OVERTURE TO "REVISORN"
    1,1,1,0 - 2,2,0,0 - timp. - str.   5:00 S.T.I.M.
—— PRELUDE TO "DEN ITALIENSKA HALMHATTEN"
    2,2,2,2 - 4,2,3,1 - timp.,perc. - str.   5:00 S.T.I.M.
—— PRELUDE TO "OVER EVNE"
    1,1,1,0 - 2,2,0,0 - str.   7:00 S.T.I.M.
—— PRELUDE TO "STOR-KLAS OCH LILL-KLAS"
    1,1,1,0 - 2,2,0,0 - timp. - str.   5:00 S.T.I.M.
—— SUITE NOTTURNO
    3,2,2,2 - 4,2,3,1 - timp.,perc. - hp. - str.   30:00 S.T.I.M.
—— SYMPHONY IN G MINOR
    2,2,2,2 - 4,2,3,1 - timp.,perc. - str.   38:00 S.T.I.M.

SCHILLINGS, Max
—— TWO SYMPHONIC FANTASIAS
    Bo. Hawkes.

    MORNING AT SEA ("SEEMORGEN")
    3,3,3,3 - 4,3,3,1 - timp.,perc. - hp. - str.
    THALATTA ("MEERGRUSS")
    3,3,3,3 - 2,3,3,1 - timp.,perc. - hp. - str.

SCHINDLER, Gerhard
—— CONCERTO GROSSO (FOR 3 TRUMPETS, TIMPANI AND
STRINGS) (IN 3 MOVTS.)
    3 tpt. - timp. - str.   12:15 AhnSimrock.
—— CONCERTO GROSSO NO. 2 ("THE ECHO") (FOR 2
ORCHESTRAS) (IN 3 MOVTS.)
    3,4,0,2 - 4,2,0,0 - timp.,perc. - str.   23:00 AhnSimrock.
    (1st Orch.: 2,2,0,2 - 2,2,0,0 - timp.,perc. - str.)
    (2nd Orch.: 1,2,0,0 - 2,0,0,0 - str.)
—— DAS ZÜNDHOLZMÄDCHEN (BALLET SUITE)
    3,3,3,3 - 4,3,3,1 - timp.,perc. - hp. -str.   20:00 Modern.
—— DIDO UND AENEAS: BALLET SUITE NO. 1 (IN 8 MOVTS.)
    1,2,1,1 - 2,1,1,0 - timp.,perc. - str.   24:00 Modern.
—— DIDO UND AENEAS: BALLET SUITE NO. 2 (IN 6 MOVTS.)
    15:00 Modern.

—— THEATER SUITE (IN 4 MOVTS.)
    2,2,2,2 - 2,2,0,0 - perc. - hp. - str.   17:00 Modern.

SCHINDLER, Walter
—— CONCERTO FOR ORGAN AND SMALL ORCH. (IN 3
MOVTS.)
    0,*3,0,0 - 0,0,0,0 - timp.,perc. - org. - str.   17:00 Henmar.
—— EASTER ORATORIO (FOR SOLO VOICES, CHORUS AND
ORCH.)
    1,3(1 alt. with Eng. hn.),0,1 - 0,3,0,0 - timp.,perc.,glock. - org.(alt.
    with pf.) - str.   62:00 Henmar.

SCHISKE, Karl
—— SYNTHESIS FOR 4 X 4 INSTRUMENTS, OP. 47
    1,1,1,1 - 2,1,1,0 - timp.,perc.(3),xyl. - pf. - str.   20:00 A.K.M.

SCHIUMA, Alfredo Luis
—— PITUNGA (WITH OPTIONAL SOPRANO VOICE) (1928)
    3,3,3,3 - 4,4,4,0 - timp.,perc.,cel. - 2 hp. - str.   Fleisher.

SCHJELDERUP, Gerhard
—— BRAND (SINFONISCHE MUSIK NACH IBSEN)
    3,3,3,3 - 4,4,3,3 - perc. - hp. - str.   35:00 T & J.
—— FRÜHLINGSREIGEN (IN 5 MOVTS.)
    2,2,2,2 - 4,2,0,0 - perc. - hp - str.   20:00 T & J.
—— KLEINE NORWEGISCHE SUITE (IN 5 MOVTS.)
    2,2,2,2 - 4,2,0,0 - perc. - hp. - org. - str.   24:00 T & J.

SCHLEIN, Irving
—— BALLET SUITE
    2,2,2,2 - 2,2,1,0 - timp.,perc.(2),cel. - pf. - str.   15:00 Composer.
—— CONCERT OVERTURE
    3,2,2,2 - 4,3,3,1 - timp.,perc. - hp. - str.   5:00 Chappell.
—— CONCERTINO FOR PIANO AND ORCH.
    2,2,2,2 - 2,2,0,0 - timp.,perc.(2) - pf. - str.   20:00 Composer.
—— FESTIVE DANCE
    *3,2,2,2 - 4,3,3,1 - timp.,perc.(2),xyl. - str.   15:00 Composer.
—— SINFONIA
    2,2,2,2 - 2,1,0,0 - timp.,perc.(2) - str.   8:00 Composer.
—— SONG OF THE BROAD AXE (FOR MIXED CHORUS AND
ORCH.)
    *3,2,2,2 - 4,3,3,1 - timp.,perc.(2) - str.   12:00 Composer.
—— SUITE FOR A SUMMER DAY (IN 3 MOVTS.)
    2,2,2,2 - 2,2,1,0 - timp.,perc.(2),cel.,xyl. - hp. - str.
    20:00 Composer.
—— SUITE FOR ORCHESTRA
    2,2,2,2 - 2,2,0,0 - timp.,perc.(2) - pf. - str.   15:00 Composer.
—— SYMPHONIC TESTAMENT
    *3,*3,*3,*3 - 4,3,2,1 - timp.,perc.(3),cel.,xyl. - hp. - str.
    15:00 Composer.
—— SYMPHONIETTA
    *3,2,2,2 - 4,3,3,1 - timp.,perc.(2) - str.   20:00 Composer.
—— SYMPHONY NO. 2
    1. Lento; 2. Allegro giocoso; 3. Maestoso
    *3,*3,*3,*3 - 4,3,3,1 - timp.,perc.(2) - str.   35:00 Composer.
—— SYMPHONY NO. 8 (IN 3 MOVTS.)
    2,2,2,*3 - 4,3,2,1 - timp.,perc.(2) - str.   15:00 Composer.
—— SYMPHONY NO. 9 (IN 3 MOVTS.)
    *3,2,2,2 - 4,3,2,1 - timp.,perc.(2),cel. - hp. - str.   10:00 Composer.
—— SYMPHONY NO. 10
    1. Andante; 2. Adagio; 3. Andante; 4. Maestoso
    *3,*3,*3,*3 - 4,3,3,1 - timp.,perc.(3),cel.,glock.,xyl. - hp. - str.
    15:00 Composer.
—— THEME AND VARIATIONS
    2,2,2,2 - 4,3,3,1 - timp.,perc.(1) - str.   20:00 Composer.

SCHLEMM, Gustav Adolf
—— SCHWETZINGER SCHLOSSMUSIK
    2,2,2,2 - 2,2,1,0 - timp.,perc.,cel. - hp. - str.   10:50 Seesaw.
—— SYMPHONY NO. 3
    2,*3,2,2 - 4,3,3,1 - timp.,perc. - str.   8:00 Seesaw.

SCHLEMM, Gustave Adolf
—— BALLETTMUSIK
    2,2,2,2 - 2,2,1,0 - timp.,perc. - hp. - str.   10:00 Henmar.
—— SINFONIETTA
    2,2,2,2 - 4,2,3,1 - perc. - str.   30:00 Henmar.

SCHLENSOG, Martin
—— EIN GARTENFEST (SUITE) (IN 7 MOVTS.)
    2,1,1,1 - timp.,trgl. - str.   17:00 Henmar.

SCHLESINGER, Hanan
—— PASTORALE SUITE
    2,2,2,2 - 2,2,0,0 - timp.,perc. - hp.(or pf.) - str. 16:00 IsMuPublns.

SCHLIEPE, Ernst
—— A DANCE RHAPSODY, OP. 27
    2,2,2,2 - 4,2,3,1 - timp.,perc.,cel.(ad lib.) - hp. - str.   12:00 Tetra.

SCHLUMPF, Martin
—— FÜR SOLOVIOLINE UND KAMMERORCHESTER (FÜR SOLOVIOLINE UND KAMMEROCHESTER)
    11:00 S.U.I.S.A.

SCHMALSTICH, Clemens
—— AMOR UND PSYCHE (EINE LIEBESGESCHICHTE IN 5 BILDERN), OP. 103
    2,1,2,1 - 2,2,1,0 - perc. - hp. - str.   16:30 Henmar.
—— AUS EINER KLEINEN STADT (SUITE), OP. 94
    2,1,2,1 - 2,2,1,0 - perc. - hp. - str.   11:30 Henmar.
—— NORDISCHE SUITE, OP. 112 (IN 4 MOVTS.)
    2,*2,2,1 - 2,2,1,0 - perc. - hp. - str.   18:00 Henmar.

SCHMIDEK, Kurt
—— OVERTURE TO A COMEDY
    A.K.M.

SCHMIDT, Friedrich J.
—— PARTITA FOR CHAMBER ORCH.
    2,2,2,2 - 2,2,1,0 - timp.,perc. - cemb. - str.   12:00 Alkor.

SCHMIDT, Kloman
—— SHE PUT A RING IN HIS HANDS (A TRIBUTE TO JOHN F. KENNEDY) (FOR NARRATOR, CONTRALTO AND ORCH.) (Text: Sen. Mike Mansfield)
    2,1,2(2nd alt. with b.-cl.),1 - 2,3,3,0 - timp.,perc.(2), bell - hp. - str.
    5:00 Composer.

SCHMIDT, Ole
—— CONCERTO AND TUBA AND ORCH.
    2,2,2,2 - 4,0,0,1 - timp.,perc. - str.(0,0,8,6)   G. Schirmer.
—— CONCERTO FOR VIOLIN AND CHAMBER ORCH.
    perc.,mar.,vibra. - 2 guit.,mandolin - 2 hp. - hpsc. - vlns.   20:00 G. Schirmer.
—— CONCERTO IN F MAJOR FOR HORN AND ORCH.
    1,1,1,1 - 1,1,1,0 - timp.,perc. - hp. - str.   15:00 G. Schirmer.
—— EXHIBITION (OPERA) % (Text: Klaus Rifbjerg and Jesper Jensen)
    1,1,1,1 - 1,1,1,0 - perc. - hp. - pf. - str.   G. Schirmer.
—— KONZERTSTÜCK, OP. 13 (FOR TRUMPET, TROMBONE AND SMALL ORCH.)
    tpt.,trb. - timp.,perc.,cel. - hp. - pf. - str.   10:00 G. Schirmer.
—— PIÈCE CONCERTANTE, OP. 13
    tpt.,trb. - timp.,perc. - hp. - pf. - str.   10:00 G. Schirmer.
—— SUITE, OP. 21
    fl. - timp. - hp. - str.   16:00 G. Schirmer.
—— SUITE, OP. 23
    fl. - perc. - hp. - str.   14:00 G. Schirmer.
—— SYMPHONIC FANTASY AND ALLEGRO, OP. 20 (FOR ACCORDION AND CHAMBER ORCH.)
    1,1,1,1 - 1,1,0,0 - timp.,perc. - acc. - hp. - str.   14:00 G. Schirmer.

SCHMIDT-WUNSTORF, Rudolf
—— LES ESCALIERS DE PIRANÈSE (PASSACAGLIA)
    3,*3,*3,3 - 3,3,0,0 - hp. - str.   8:00 Henmar.
—— MUSIQUE BOUFFONE
    2,2,2,2 - 3,3,2,0 - timp.,perc. - hp. - pf. - str.   4:00 F. Colombo.

SCHMIT, Camille
—— CONCERTO FOR PIANO AND ORCH. (1955)
    2,2,2,2 - 2,2,2,1 - timp.,perc.,cel.,glock. - pf. - str. 20:00 H. Elkan.
—— MUSIC FOR PIANO AND ORCH. (1949)
    2,2,2,2 - 2,2,2,1 - timp.,perc.,cel.,glock. - pf. - str.   18:00 CBDM.
—— PRÉLUDES JOYEUX (1944)
    1,1,1,1 - 2,1,1,0 - timp.,perc. - str.   10:30 CBDM.
—— TRIPTYQUE (1952)
    2,2,2,2 - 2,2,2,1 - timp.,perc.,cel.,glock. - str.   20:00 CBDM.

SCHMITT, Florent
—— ANDANTE AND SCHERZO (FOR HARP AND STRINGS), OP. 35
    hp. - str.   15:00 Salabert.
—— ANDANTE RELIGIOSO, OP. 109 (1951)
    str.   4:00 EV.

—— ANTOINE ET CLÉOPÂTRE, OP. 69 SUITE NO. 2 (1920) (IN 3 MOVTS.)
    *3,*3,*3(1st alt. with E♭cl.),*3 - 4,3,3,1 - timp.,perc.,cel. - 2 hp. - str.   20:00 EV.
—— ANTOINE ET CLÉOPÂTRE, OP. 69 (6 SYMPHONIC EPISODES, AFTER SHAKESPEARE) SUITE NO. 1 (IN 3 MOVTS.) (1920)
    3(3rd alt. with picc.),*3,*3,*3 - 4,3,3,1 - timp.,perc.,cel. - 2 hp. - str.   20:00 EV.
—— L' ARBRE ENTRE TOUS, OP. 95 (FOR CHORUS AND ORCH.) (1939)
    *3,*3,*3,*3 - 4,3,3,1 - timp.,perc.,bells - 2 hp. - str.   15:00 S.A.C.E.M.
—— CANCUNIK SUITE, OP. 79
    EV.
    LIED (NOCTURNE)
    1(alt. with picc.),1,1,1 - 2,2,2,0 - timp.,perc. - 2 hp. - str.   6:00
    SCHERZO (TARANTELLE)
    2,2,2,2,c.-bn.(ad lib.) - 4,2,3,1 - timp.,perc. - 1-2 hp. - str.   6:00
—— CHANT DE GUERRE, OP. 63 (FOR TENOR, MEN'S CHORUS AND ORCH.) (1914)
    *3,*3,*3,*3 - 4,3,3,1 - timp.,perc.,cel. - 2 hp. - str.   10:00 EV.
—— LE CHANT DE LA NUIT (ODE TO FREDERIC CHOPIN), OP. 120 (FOR MIXED CHORUS AND ORCH.) (1951)
    2,*2,*3,*2 - 4,2,3,1 - timp.,perc. - 2 hp. - str.   10:00 EV.
—— CHANT ELEGIAQUE (FOR CELLO AND ORCH.), OP. 24
    2(2nd alt. with picc.),2,2,2,sarr.(ad lib.) - 4,2,3,1 - timp.,perc. - hp. - str.   15:00 EV.
—— CINQ CHANSONS À QUATRE VOIX, OP. 39
    3,2,2,3 - 4,2,3,1 - timp.,perc. - 1-2 hp. - str.   15:00 Salabert.
—— CINQ CHOEURS EN VINGT MINUTES (5 CHORUSES IN 20 MINUTES), OP. 117 (FOR MIXED CHORUS AND ORCH.) (1951)
    *2,1,1,*2 - 4,1,3,1 - timp.,perc.(3),cel. - 2 hp. - str.   18:00 EV.
—— DANSE D'ABISAG, OP. 75 (1925)
    *2,*2,2,-*3 - 4,2,3,1 - timp.,perc. - 1-2 hp. - str.   8:00 EV.
—— DANSE DES DEVADASIS, OP. 47 (FOR SOPRANO, MIXED CHORUS AND ORCH.) (1908)
    *3,*3,*3,*3 - 4,3,3,1 - timp.,perc.,cel. - 2 hp. - str.   8:00 EV.
—— DEUX MIRAGES, OP. 70
    3,3,3,3 - 4,3,3,1 - timp.,perc.,cel. - 1-2 hp. - str.   EV.
—— EN ÉTÉ, OP. 10
    S.A.C.E.M.
—— ENFANTS, OP. 92 (1938)
    2,1,1,1 - 1,1,0,0 - timp.,perc.(2) - str.   13:00 EV.
—— ENFANTS (8 PIÈCES BREVES) (POUR PETIT ORCH.)
    1,*1,1,1 - 1,1,0,0 - timp.,perc. - str.   EV.
—— FANFARE: "LE CAMP DE POMPÉE (FROM "ANTOINE ET CLEOPATRE")
    4 hn.,3 tpt.,3 trb.,tu. - perc.   EV.
—— FEUILLETS DE VOYAGE, OP. 26 (SUITE) (1913) (IN 5 MOVTS.)
    *3,2(2nd alt. with Eng.hn.),2,2-*3 - 4,2,3,1 - timp.,perc. - hp. - str.   17:00 EV.
—— FÊTE DE LA LUMIÈRE OP. 88(FOR SOPRANO, MIXED CHORUS AND ORCH.) (1936)
    *3,*3,*3,alto sax.,*3 - 4,3,3,1 - timp.,perc.,cel.,glock.,xyl. - ondes Martenot - 2 hp. - str.   S.A.C.E.M.
—— FINALE (FOR CELLO AND ORCH.), OP. 77
    2,2,2,3 - 4,2,3,1 - timp.,perc. - 1-2 hp. - str.   8:00 EV.
—— FIVE MOTETS, OP. 60 (FOR CHORUS AND ORCH.) (1917)
    *3,*3,*3,*3 - 4,3,3,1 - timp.,perc. - 2 hp. - str.   18:00 EV.
—— FONCTIONNAIRE MCMXII OP. 74 (CIVIL SERVANT, 1912) (INACTION IN MUSIC) (1924)
    *2-*3,*3,*3,*2-*3 - 4,2,3,1 - timp.,perc. - 2 hp. - str.   12:00 EV.
—— HABEYSSÉE (A-B-C), OP. 110 (SUITE FOR VIOLIN AND ORCH.) (1948)
    2(2nd alt. with picc.),*2,2,*2 - 4,2,3,1 - timp.,perc. - hp. - str.   15:00 EV.
—— IN MEMORIAM, OP. 72 (1922) (IN 2 MOVTS.)
    *3,*3,*3,*3 - 4,4,3,1 - timp.,perc.(4),cel.,glock. - 1-2 hp. - str.   14:00 EV.
—— INTROÏT, RÉCIT ET CONGÉ, OP. 113 (FOR CELLO AND ORCH.) (1952)
    *3,*3,*3,*3 - 4,3,3,1 - timp.,perc. - 2 hp. - str.   20:00 EV.
—— JANIANA (SYMPHONY FOR STRINGS), OP. 100 (IN 4 MOVTS.)
    str.   20:00 EV.
—— J'ENTENDS DANS LE LOINTAIN, OP. 64, NO. 1 (FROM "OMBRES") (FOR PIANO AND ORCH.) (1917)
    *3,*3,*3,*3 - 4,3,3,1 - timp.,perc. - 2 hp. - pf. - str.   8:00 EV.

—— KERMESSE-VALSE, OP. 80 (FROM "L'ÉVENTAIL DE
JEANNE") (1928)
    3,3,3,3 - 4,3,4,0 - timp.,perc.,glock. - 2 hp. - str.   5:00 Presser.
    or:
    2,2,2,2 - 2,2,1,0 - timp.,perc. - str.
—— KÉROB-SHAL, OP. 67 (THREE SONGS FOR VOICE AND
CHAMBER ORCH.) (1924)
    *2,0,2,0 - 0,0,0,0 - pf. - str.   7:00 EV.
—— LAUDATE, PUERI, DOMINUM, OP. 126 (FOR MIXED
CHORUS AND ORCH.) (1952)
    2,2,2,2 - 4,2,3,1 - timp.,perc. - org.(ad lib.) - str.   7:00 EV.
—— LEGEND FOR VIOLA (OR ALTO SAXOPHONE) AND ORCH.,
OP. 66
    3,3,3,3 - 4,3,3,1 - timp.,perc.,cel. - 1-2 hp. - str.   8:00 EV.
—— LIED ET SCHERZO (FOR HORN AND WINDS), OP. 54
    2,2,2,2 - 3,0,0,0   10:00 EV.
—— MIRAGES, OP. 70 (1921) (IN 2 MOVTS.)
    3,3,3,3 - 4,3,3,1 - timp.,perc.(5),cel.,xyl. - 2 hp. - str.   16:00 EV.
—— ORIANE ET LE PRINCE D'AMOUR, OP. 83 (BALLET) (WITH
VOICES) % (1934)
    *3,*3,*3,*3 - 4,3,3,1 - timp.,perc.,cel.,glock.,xyl. - 2 hp. -
    pf.(4-hands) - str.   55:00 EV.
—— ORIANE ET LE PRINCE D'AMOUR, OP. 83 (SUITE FROM
THE BALLET) (WITH VOICES)
    20:00 EV.
—— LE PETIT ELFE "FERME-L'OEIL": SUITE NO. 1 (IN 3
MOVTS.)
    20:00 EV.
—— LE PETIT ELFE "FERME-L'OEIL": SUITE NO. 2 (IN 4
MOVTS.)
    20:00 EV.
—— LE PETIT ELFE, "FERME-L'OEIL" (UNE SEMAINE DANSÉE),
OP. 73 (BALLET)
    *3,*3,*2,*3 - 4,2,3,1 - timp.,perc.,cel.,glock.,xyl. - hp. - pf. - str.
    40:00 EV.
—— PSALM 47, OP. 38 (FOR SOPRANO, MIXED CHORUS,
ORGAN AND ORCH.)
    3,4,3,4 - 4,3,3,1 - timp.,perc. - 2 hp. - org. - str.   35:00 Salabert.
—— PUPAZZI, OP. 36 (SUITE) (1907) (IN 5 MOVTS.)
    2,2,2,2 - 2,0,0,0 - timp.,perc. - hp. - str.   15:00 Salabert.
—— QUATRE POÈMES DE RONSARD, OP. 100 (FOR VOICE AND
ORCH.) (1942)
    *2,*2,*2,*3 - 2,1,0,0 - timp. - str.   15:00 EV.
—— RAPSODIE PARISIENNE (An early work, without opus number)
    S.A.C.E.M.
—— RÊVES, OP. 63, NO. 1
    3,*3,3,3 - 4,3,2,1 - cel. - 2 hp. - str.   EV.
—— RONDE BURLESQUE, OP. 78 (1927)
    3,2,2,3 - 4,2,4,0 - timp.,perc.(3),cel.,glock. - 2 hp. - str.
    6:30 Presser.
—— SALAMMBÔ, OP. 76 (6 SYMPHONIC EPISODES, AFTER G.
FLAUBERT) (1925)
    *3,*3,*3,*3 - 4,3,3,1 - timp.,perc.,cel.,glock.,xyl. - 1-2hp. - str.
    51:00 EV.
—— SALAMMBÔ: SUITE NO. 1 (IN 2 MOVTS.)
    18:00 EV.
—— SALAMMBÔ: SUITE NO. 2 (IN 2 MOVTS.)
    15:00 EV.
—— SALAMMBÔ: SUITE NO. 3 (IN 3 MOVTS.) (WITH MIXED
CHORUS)
    *3,*3,*3,*3 - 4,3,3,1 - timp.,perc.,cel.,glock.,xyl - org. - str.
    18:00 EV.
—— SCÈNES DE LA VIE MOYENNE, OP. 124(SUITE) (1952) (IN 4
MOVTS.)
    2(2nd alt. with picc.),2(2nd alt. with Eng.hn.),2,2 - 4,2,3,1 -
    timp.,perc. - 2 hp. - str.   18:00 EV.
—— SCHERZO VIF (FOR VIOLIN AND ORCH.) (1910)
    2,2,2,3 - 4,2,3,1 - timp.,perc. - str.   8:00 Salabert.
—— SIX CHORUSES, OP. 81 (FOR 4 WOMEN'S VOICES AND
ORCH.) (1931)
    *3,*3,*3,*3 - 4,3,3,1 - timp.,perc.,cel.,glock.,xyl - 2 hp. - str.
    15:00 EV.
—— SOIRS ("EVENINGS") (7 SHORT PIECES) (FOR SMALL
ORCH.)
    15:00 EV.
—— SUITE FOR FLUTE AND CHAMBER ORCH., OP. 129
    *2,*2,2,2 - 2,0,0,0 - str.   20:00 EV.
—— SUITE FOR TRUMPET AND ORCH., OP. 133 (1955) (IN 3
MOVTS.)
    *3,2(2nd alt. with Eng.hn.),2,2 - 4,1,0,0 - timp.,perc. - hp. - str.
    20:00 EV.

—— SUITE SANS ESPRIT DE SUITE, OP. 89 (1938) (IN 5 MOVTS.)
    3(or*3),3(or*3),*3,*3 - 4,3,3,1 - timp.,perc.(4),cel.,glock. - 2 hp. -
    str.   15:00 EV.
—— SYMPHONIE CONCERTANTE (FOR PIANO AND ORCH.),
OP. 82
    3,3,3,3 - 4,3,3,1 - timp.,perc. - hp. - pf. - str.   30:00 EV.
—— SYMPHONY NO. 2, OP. 137 (1958)
    *3,*3,*3,*3 - 4,3,3,1 - timp.,perc.,cel.,glock.,vibra.,xyl. - 2 hp. - str.
    25:00 EV.
—— THREE DANCES, OP. 86 (1936)
    *3,*3,*3,*3 - 4,3,3,1 - timp.,perc.,cel.,glock. - 2 hp. - str.
    15:00 EV.
—— THREE RHAPSODIES, OP. 53
    EV.
    VIENNOISE
    3,2,2,2,sarr. - 4,2,3,1 - timp.,perc. - hp. - str.   8:00
    POLONAISE
    3,3,2,2,c.-bn.(ad lib.) - 4,2,3,1 - timp.,perc.,cel. - 1-2 hp. - str.
    6:00
    FRANCAISE
    3,2,2,2,c.-bn.(ad lib.) - 4,2,3,1 - timp.,perc. - 1-2 hp. - str.   6:00
—— LA TRAGÉDIE DE SALOMÉ, OP. 50
    3,3,3,2,sarr. - 4,3,3,1 - timp.,perc. - 2 hp. - str.   30:00 EV.
—— TROIS CHANTS AVEC ORCHESTRE, OP. 98 (1943)
    *3,*3,*3,*3 - 4,3,3,1 - timp.,perc.,(3),cel.,glock.,xyl. - 2 hp. - str.
    18:00 EV.
—— TROIS CHANTS EN L'HONNEUR D'AUGUSTE COMTE, OP.
71 (FOR SOLO VOICES, MIXED CHORUS AND STRING
ORCH.) (1921)
    str.   16:00 EV.
—— TROIS TRIOS, OP. 99 (FOR WOMEN'S VOICES AND ORCH.)
(1941)
    *3,*3,*3,*3 - 4,2,3,1 - timp.,perc.,cel.,glock.,xyl. - 2 hp. - str.
    10:00 EV.

SCHMITTBAUER, Josef-Aloys - BODART, Eugen
—— SYMPHONY IN G MAJOR
    0,2,0,0 - 2,2,0,0 - timp. - str.   10:00 Mannheimer.

SCHNEIDER, Urs Peter
—— AUF ANHIEB (FÜR 15 STREICHER)
    str.   S.U.I.S.A.

SCHNEIDER, Willy
—— CONCERTO GROSSO (FOR FLUTE, BASSOON AND
STRINGS)
    1,0,0,1 - 0,0,0,0 - str.   23:30 Henmar.

SCHOECK, Othmar
—— CONCERTO FOR HORN AND STRINGS, OP. 65
    hn. - str.   18:00 Bo. Hawkes.
—— PENTHESILEA (OPERA), OP. 39 %
    90:00 Huni.
—— SOMMERNACHT
    str.   16:00 Swiss M.L.

SCHOEMAKER, Maurits
—— ARC-EN-CIEL (OVERTURE) (1937)
    1,1,1,1 alto sax.,1 - 2,2,1,0 - timp.,perc.,cel.(or vibra),glock.,xyl. -
    hp. - str.   8:00 H. Elkan.
—— CONCERTO FOR BASSOON AND ORCH.
    2,2,2,1 - 2,2,1,0 - timp. - str.   12:00 CBDM.
—— DEUX DANSES FLAMANDES (1944)
    2,2,2,2 - 4,2,3,1 - timp.,perc. - str.   12:00 H. Elkan.
—— DEUX FANTASQUES (1924)
    3,3,4,3 - 4,3,3,1 - timp.,perc.,bells,cel.,glock. - 2 hp. - str.
    9:00 H. Elkan.
—— LE FACÉTIEUX VOYAGE (1914)
    1,1,1,1 - 2,1,1,0 - timp.,perc. - str.   8:00 H. Elkan.
—— FEU D'ARTIFICE (SYMPHONIC POEM) (1924)
    3,3,3,3 - 4,3,3,1 - timp.,perc.,bells,glock.,xyl. - str.   11:00 Henmar.
—— FIVE SKETCHES (FÜNF RHYTHMEN)
    2,1,2,1 - 2,2,1,0 - str.   8:00 Henmar.
—— FLEMISH RHAPSODY
    2,2,2,2 - 4,2,2,1 - timp.,perc. - str.   9:00 Henmar.
—— LÉGENDE DE SIRE HALEWIJN (SYMPHONIC POEMS FOR
CELLO AND ORCH.) (1930)
    3,3,3,3 - 4,3,3,1 - timp.,perc.,cel.,glock.,xyl. - hp. - str.
    17:00 H. Elkan.
—— MARILLA L'ÉPÉE (DRAMATIC PROLOGUE) (1949)
    2,2,2,2 - 4,2,2,0 - timp.,perc. - str.   16:30 H. Elkan.
—— MÉDÉE LA MAGICIENNE (SYMPHONIC POEM) (1936)
    1,1,1,1 - 1,1,1,1 - timp.,perc.,vibra.,xyl. - pf. - str.   10:00 H. Elkan.

—— PAN (SUITE FROM THE BALLET) (1937)
2,2,2,2 - 2,2,1,1 - timp.,perc.,cel.,vibra.,xyl. - hp. - str.
17:00 H. Elkan.

—— PAN (SYMPHONIC PRELUDE) (1921)
3,3,3,3 - 4,3,3,1 - timp.,perc.,cel. - pf. - str.   7:00 H. Elkan.

—— PETITE SUITE DANS LE STYLE ROCCOCO (1936)
1,1,0,1 - 0,0,0,0 - str.   9:00 H. Elkan.

—— PIÈCE CONCERTANTE (FOR TROMBONE AND ORCH.)
(1939)
1,1,2,1 - 2,2,1,0 - timp. - str.   6:00 Gervan.

—— RÉCIT, ARIA ET FINAL (FOR VIOLIN AND ORCH.) (1920)
2,1,2,1 - 2,2,1,0 - timp.,perc. - str.   16:00 H. Elkan.

—— LES ROIS MAGES (1934)
2,2,2,2 - 2,2,2,0 - timp.,perc.,vibra. - str.   6:00 Buyst.

—— ROMANCE FOR CELLO AND ORCH. (1920)
1,1,1,0 - 1,1,1,0 - timp.,vibra.(or cel.) - pf. - str.   5:00 H. Elkan.

—— SCÈNES ESPAGNOLES (1943)
2,2,2,2 - 2,2,1,0 - timp.,perc.,cel. - str.   22:00 CBDM.

—— SINFONIA BREVE (1938)
3,3,3,3 - 4,3,3,1 - timp.,perc.,bells,xyl. - hp. - str.   10:00 H. Elkan.

—— SINFONIA DA CAMERA (FOR VOCAL QUARTET AND
ORCH.) (1929)
1,1,2,4 sax.,1 - 2,1,1,0 - timp.,perc. - str.   20:00 H. Elkan.

—— SWANE-SUITE (WITH OPTIONAL MIXED CHORUS) (1934)
3,3,3,1 alto, sax.,1 ten.sax.,3 - 4,3,3,1 - timp.,perc.,cel.,glock.,xyl. -
2 hp. - str.   23:00 H. Elkan.

—— SYMPHONISCHER SÄTZ
2,2,2,2 - 4,2,2,1 - timp.,perc. - str.   13:00 Alkor.

—— SYMPHONY (1946)
2,2,2,2 - 4,2,3,0 - timp. - str.   30:00 CBDM.

—— VARIATIONS IN A FLEMISH FOLKSONG
3,2,2,2 - 2,2,1,0 - timp.,perc. - str.   10:00 Henmar.

—— VARIAZIONI (FOR HORN AND ORCH.) (1941)
1,1,1,1 - 1,0,0,0 - str.   10:00 H. Elkan.

SCHOENBACH, Dieter
—— CONCERTO IN G MAJOR (AFTER DOMENICO SCARLATTI)
(FOR TRUMPET AND SMALL ORCH.)
2,0,0,1 - 0,1,0,0 - perc. - cemb. - str.   Henmar.

SCHOENBERG, Arnold
—— ACCOMPANIMENT TO A CINEMATOGRAPHIC SCENE, OP.
34
1(alt. with picc.),1,2,1 - 2,2,1,0 - timp.,perc.(2) - pf. - str.
8:00 Henmar.

—— CHAMBER SYMPHONY NO. 1, OP. 9-B (Version for large orch.)
*3,*3,1 E♭ cl.,*2,*3 - 4,2,3,0 - str.   26:00 G. Schirmer.

—— CHAMBER SYMPHONY NO. 1, OP. 9 (ORIGINAL VERSION,
FOR 15 INSTRUMENTS)
1,*2,1 E♭ cl.,*2,*2 - 2,0,0,0 - str.   22:00 Belmont.

—— CHAMBER SYMPHONY NO. 2, OP. 38
1. Molto adagio; 2. Con fuoco
2,2(2nd alt. with Eng. hn.),2,2 - 2,2,0,0 - str.   24:00 G. Schirmer.

—— CONCERTO FOR PIANO AND ORCH., OP. 42
2(1 alt. with picc.),2,2,2 - 4,2,3,1 - timp.,perc.(3),glock.,xyl. - pf. -
str.   24:00 Belmont.

—— CONCERTO FOR VIOLIN AND ORCH., OP. 36
1. Poco allegro; 2. Andante grazioso; 3. Allegro
3(3rd alt. with picc.),3,E♭ cl.,*2,3 - 4,3,3,1 - timp.,perc. - str.
33:00 G. Schirmer.

—— THE DANCE AROUND THE GOLDEN CALF. (FROM
"MOSES AND AARON")
20:00 Belmont.

—— ERWARTUNG, OP. 17 (FOR SOPRANO AND ORCH.)
*4,4(4th alt. with Eng. hn.),1 D cl.,*4,*4 - 4,3,4,1 -
timp.,perc.,cel.,glock.,xyl. - hp. - str.   25:00 Belmont.

—— FIVE PIECES FOR ORCH., OP. 16 (NEW REVISION BY
COMPOSER)
4(incl. 2 picc.),*3, E-flat cl.,*3,*3 - 4,3,3,1 -
timp.,perc.,cel.,glock.,xyl. - hp. - str.   25:00 Henmar.

—— FIVE PIECES FOR ORCH., OP. 16 (ORIGINAL VERSION)
*4(3rd alt. with 2nd picc.),4,5(3rd alt. with cl. in
D),contrabass-cl.,4 - 6,3,4,1 - timp.,perc.,cel. - hp. - str.
27:00 Henmar.

—— FOUR SONGS, OP. 22 (FOR VOICE AND ORCH.) (1916)
5,5(2 alt. with 2 Eng.hn.),6,4(1 alt. with c.-bn.) - 4,1,3,1 -
timp.,perc.,xyl. - hp. - str.   13:00 Belmont.

—— FRIEDE AUF ERDEN, OP. 13 (FOR SATB CHORUS AND
ORCH.)
2,2,2,2 - 2,0,0,0 - str.   8:00 Belmont.

—— DIE GLÜCKLICHE HAND, OP. 18 ("THE LUCKY HAND")
(OPERA) % (1916) (Text: Composer)
*4,*4,1 D cl.,*4,*4 - 4,3,4,1 - timp.,perc.,bells,cel.,glock.,xyl. - hp.
- str.   20:00 Belmont.

—— GURRE-LIEDER (FOR SOLO VOICES, CHORUS AND ORCH.)
8,5,7,5 - 10(incl. 4 tuben;Wagner "tubas"),7,7,1 - timp.,perc.,cel. -
4 hp. - str.   130:00 Belmont.

—— ISRAEL EXISTS AGAIN! (FOR SATB CHORUS AND ORCH.)
Belmont.

—— DIE JAKOBSLEITER (JACOB'S LADDER) (ORATORIO) (1917)
4,*4,E♭ cl.,*4,*4 - 4,3,3,1 - timp.,perc.,cel. - hp. - pf. - str.
40:00 Belmont.

—— KOL NIDRE (JEWISH SERVICE) (FOR RECITER, CHORUS
AND ORCH.), OP. 39
2(2nd alt. with picc.),1,E♭ cl.,*2,1 - 2,2,2,1 - timp.,perc.(3-4),xyl. -
str.   20:00 Boelke-Bo.

—— LIED DER WALDTAUBE (SONG OF THE WOOD DOVE)
(FROM "GURRELIEDER") (FOR MEDIUM VOICE AND
ORCH.) (1922)
3,3,4,3 - 4,3,3,1 - perc. 2 hp. - harm. - pf. - str.   Belmont.
or:
1,2,3,2 - 2,0,0,0 - harm. - pf. - str.

—— MODERNE PSALMEN, OP. 50-C (FOR SPEAKER, SATB
CHORUS AND ORCH.) (Text: Composer)
3,3,3,2 - 2,2,1,0 - perc. - str.   Belmont.

—— MOSES AND AARON (OPERA) %
*4,*4,1 E♭ cl.,*3,*3 - 4,3,3,1 - timp.,perc.,bells,glock.,xyl. - 2 guit. -
2 mand. - hp. - pf. - str.   150:00 Belmont.

—— ODE TO NAPOLEON BONAPARTE, OP. 41-B (FOR
SPEAKING VOICE, PIANO AND STRINGS)
pf. - str.   21:00 Belmont.

—— PELLEAS AND MELISANDE, OP. 5 (SYMPHONIC POEM)
(1903)
4,4,5,4 - 8,4,5,1 - timp.,perc. - 2 hp. - str.   40:00 Belmont.
or:
3,3,3,3 - 4,3,3,1 - timp.,perc. - 2 hp. - str.

—— PRELUDE (FOR CHORUS AND ORCH.), OP. 44 (First
movement from "GENESIS", a work in seven parts by Mario
Castelnuovo-Tedesco, Darius Milhaud, Arnold Schoenberg,
Nathaniel Shilkret, Igor Stravinsky, Alexandre Tansman and Ernest
Toch.)
3(3rd alt. with picc.),3(3rd alt. with Eng. hn.),3(3rd alt. with
b.-cl.),*3 - 4,3,3,1 - perc.,cel.,glock.,xyl. - hp. - str.   5:00 Belmont.

—— SIX SONGS FOR VOICE AND ORCH., OP. 8
3,3,3,3 - 4,3,3,1 - timp.,perc. - hp. - str.   22:00 Belmont.

—— STRING QUARTET NO. 2 (WITH VOICE), OP. 10
(ARRANGED BY COMPOSER FOR VOICE AND STRING
ORCH.) (1921)
str.   29:00 Belmont.

—— SUITE FOR STRING ORCH. (IN 5 MOVTS.)
str.   30:00 G. Schirmer.

—— A SURVIVOR FROM WARSAW (FOR NARRATOR, MEN'S
CHORUS AND ORCH.), OP. 46
2(alt. with 2 picc.),2,2,2 - 4,3,3,1 - timp.,perc.(3),glock.,xyl. - hp. -
str.   12:00 Boelke-Bo.

—— DER TANZ UM DAS GOLDENE KALB (THE DANCE
AROUND THE GOLDEN CALF) (FROM "MOSES UND
ARON")
20:00 Belmont.

—— THEME AND VARIATIONS, OP. 43B
*3,*3,*3,*3 - 4,3,3,1 - timp.,perc.(4),glock.,xyl. - str.
14:00 Belmont.

—— THREE LITTLE ORCHESTRA PIECES (THREE PIECES FOR
ORCH.)
1,1,1,1 - 1,0,0,0 - cel. - org.(or harm.) - str.(2,1,1,1) 3:00 Belmont.

—— TRANSFIGURED NIGHT (VERKLAERTE NACHT) (FOR
STRING ORCH.)
str.(15,8,8,6)   30:00 Belmont.

—— VARIATIONS FOR ORCH., OP. 31
4,4,5,4 - 4,3,4,1 - timp.,perc.,cel.,xyl. - hp. - mandolin - str.
23:00 Belmont.

—— VON HEUTE AUF MORGEN, OP. 32 ("FROM ONE DAY TO
THE NEXT") (1-ACT OPERA) % (Text: Max Blonda)
2(2nd alt. with picc.),2(2nd alt. with Eng.hn.),1 E♭ cl.,*3,1
sop.sax.,1 alto sax.,1 bass sax.,*2 - 2,2,3,1 - timp.,perc. - guit. - -
mandolin - hp. - pf. - str.   60:00 Belmont.

SCHOENBERG, Arnold - GREISSLE, Felix
—— FIVE PIECES FOR ORCHESTRA, OP. 16 (VERSION FOR
CHAMBER ORCH.)
1,1,1,1 - 1,0,0,0 - harm. - pf. - str.   24:00 Henmar.

SCHOENBERG, Arnold - LEIBOWITZ, René
—— THREE SONGS, OP. 48 (FOR LOW VOICE AND ORCH.)
    1,1,*2,1 - 1,1,1,0 - hp. - pf.   7:00 Boelke-Bo.

SCHOENDLINGER, Anton
—— PASSACAGLIA (FOR ORGAN AND DOUBLE STRING
    ORCH.)
    org. - str.   Tetra.

SCHOETTLE, Elmer
—— FANTASY (FOR STRINGS)
    str.   19:00 Presser.

SCHOETTLE, Fritz
—— CONCERTO GROSSO (FOR VIOLIN, PIANO AND ORCH.)
        S.U.I.S.A.

SCHOLIN, C. Albert
—— WESTERN VISTAS (SUITE) (IN 4 MOVTS.)
    *3,1,2,1 - 4,2,3,1 - timp.,perc.(2) - pf. - str.   Composer.

SCHOLZ, Bernd
—— VICTORIA SUITE (AFTER KNUT HAMSUN'S NOVEL) (IN 3
    MOVTS.)
    2,2,2,2 - 4,0,0,0 - timp.,perc.,cel.,glock.,vibra. - hp. - str.
        15:00 F. Colombo.

SCHÖNBACH, Dieter
—— RITORNELLE (7 PIECES FOR ORCH.)
    3,*3,2,*2 - 0,1,3,0 - perc.(4),cel.,mar.,vibra.,xyl. - hp. - pf. - str.
        16:00 Modern.

SCHÖNBERG, Stig Gustav
—— CONCERTINO NO. 1 FOR STRINGS (1966)
    str.   13:00 S.T.I.M.
—— CONCERTINO NO. 2 FOR STRINGS (1966)
    str.   13:00 S.T.I.M.
—— CONCERTINO NO. 3 FOR STRINGS (1966)
    str.   13:00 S.T.I.M.
—— CONCITATO (REV. 1971)
    2,2,2,2 - 4,3,3,1 - str.   17:00 Fleisher.
—— FANTASIA SACRALE (FOR STRING ORCH.)(1967)
    str.   5:00 Fleisher.
—— IMPROMPTU VISIONARIO, OP. 69 (1972)
    2,2,2,2 - 2,2,2,1 - timp.,perc. - pf. - str.   17:00 Fleisher.
—— INTRODUCTION AND ALLEGRO (1959)
    str.   18:00 S.T.I.M.
—— MADELEINE AND KONRAD, OP. 50 (BALLET) % (REV. 1972)
    2,2,2,2 - 4,3,3,0-1 - timp.,perc.,cel. - hp. - str. 35:00 Fleisher.
—— REGINA COELI, OP. 71 (HELIGA BIRGITTA) (CONCERTO
    SPIRITUALE) (FOR SOPRANO, SATB CHORUS AND ORCH.)
    (1973)
    2,2,0,2 - 0,2,2,0 - timp.,perc. - hpsc. - org. - str. 9:00 Fleisher.
—— SINFONIA APERTA (1965)
    2,2,2,2 - 4,3,2,1 - timp.,perc.(2) - str.   35:00 S.T.I.M.

SCHOOP, Paul
—— THE ENCHANTED TRUMPET (DER GLÜCKSTROMPETER)
    (COMIC OPERA) (1937) % (Text: E. Thorsten)
    *2,1,2,*3 - 2,3,3,0 - timp.,perc.(3),bells,glock.,xyl. - hp. - str.
        180:00 Ilse Lahn.
—— FATA MORGANA (SYMPHONIC POEM) (1951)
    *3,*3,*3,*3 - 4,3,3,1 - timp.,perc.(3),bells,xyl. - str.
        10:00 Ilse Lahn.
—— THE LITTLE PIANO THAT LIKED TO PLAY (A MUSICAL
    FANTASY) (FOR NARRATOR AND ORCH.) (1969) (Text:
    David Arkin)
    *3,1,*3,2 - 4,3,3,1 - timp.,perc.(3),xyl. - pf. - str.
        30:00 AccadiaMCo.
—— MARCH BALLET (SATIRE ON THE "RADETZKY MARCH")
    (1951)
    *3,1,2,2 - 2,3,3,0 - timp.,perc.(1),glock.,xyl. - pf. - str.
        3:30 Ilse Lahn.
—— THE WISHING TREE (A MUSICAL FANTASY) (FOR
    NARRATOR AND ORCH.) (1961) (Text: Joyce Parnes)
    1,1,1,1 - 1,1,0,0 - timp.,perc.(2),bells,xyl. - 2 pf. - str.
        25:00 Ilse Lahn.

SCHOUWMAN, Hans
—— FIVE SKETCHES FOR CLARINET AND SMALL ORCH., OP.
    22
    1,1,1,1 - 1,1,0,0 - perc. - str.   13:00 Henmar.

—— FRIESLAND, OP. 44 (4 SONGS FOR LOW VOICE AND
    ORCH.) (1945) (Text: B. Aafjes)
    2,2,2,2 - 1,0,0,0 - perc. - hp. - str.   9:00 Henmar.
—— MEMENTO MORI, OP. 52 (FOR ALTO, MIXED CHORUS
    AND ORCH.) (1947) (Text: D. Buys)
    0,2,0,0 - 2,0,0,0 - str.   12:00 Henmar.

SCHRAMM, Harold
—— CONCERTO DA CAMERA (IN 5 MOVTS.)
    fl. - str.   16:00 Composer.
—— CONCERTO FOR PIANO AND ORCH. (IN 3 MOVTS.)
    2,2,2,2 - 4,2,3,1 - timp.,perc.(2) - pf. - str. 20:00 Composer.
—— CONTOURS (FOR TROMBONE AND CHAMBER ORCH.)
    1,1,1,1 - 1,1,1,0 - str.   9:00 Composer.
—— INVOCATION
    str.   4:30 Leeds.
—— KIRAVANI-RAMAPRIYA (FOR OBOE AND CHAMBER
    ORCH.)
    1,1,2,0 - 1,0,0,0 - timp.,perc.(1-2) - str. 2:00 AmerMusEd.
—— MOGUL SET (IN 2 MOVTS.)
    str.   4:00 Bo. Hawkes.
—— MOVEMENT FOR ORCH.
    3(3rd alt. with picc.),*3,*3,*3 - 4,3,3,1 -
    timp.,perc.(4),cel.,glock.,xyl. - hp. - str. 12:00 Composer.
—— SABHAGANA (CONCERT PIECE) (1965)
    str.   7:00 Composer.
—— SINHALA (CEYLON)
    1,1,1,1 - 2,1,1,1 - timp.,perc.(2),glock.(or pf.) - str.
        3:00 AmerMusEd.
    or:
    2,2,2,2 - 4,2,3,1 - timp.,perc.(2),glock.(or pf.) - str.
—— TOCCATA
    *3,2,2,2(2nd alt. with ten.sax) - 4,3,3,1 - timp.,perc.(4),xyl. - str.
        3:30 Composer.

SCHREIBER, Frederick C.
—— ADAGIO FOR ORCH. (SYMPHONY NO. 9)
    3(3rd alt. with picc.),*3,*3,*3 - 4,3,3,1 - timp.,perc.(3),bells - hp. -
    str.   12:00 Composer.
—— ARISE, SHINE! (FOR CHORUS AND ORCH.)
    3,3(3rd alt. with Eng.hn),0,*3 - 4,3,3,1 - timp.,perc.(2) - hp. - str.
        8:00 Composer.
—— THE BEATITUDES (SYMPHONIC TRILOGY) (FOR CHORUS
    AND ORCH.)
    3(1 alt. with picc.),3,3,*3 - 4,3,3,1 - timp.,perc.(3),cel.,glock. - hp. -
    pf. - str.   42:00 Composer.
—— BIRD CALLS (5 MINIATURES)
    *2,*2,*2,*2 - 3,1,0,0 - timp.,perc. - hp. - str. 8:00 Composer.
—— CHAMBER CONCERTO FOR OBOE, TRUMPET AND
    STRINGS, OP. 57
    ob. - tpt. - str.   15:00 Composer.
—— CHRISTMAS SUITE (FOR CHAMBER ORCH.) (IN 4 MOVTS.)
    1,1,1,0 - 1,1,0,0 - perc.(1),glock. - hp. - str. 12:00 Composer.
—— CHRONOS (SYMPHONIC STATEMENT) (1968)
    3(3rd alt. with picc.),3,3,*3 - 4,3,3,1 - timp.,perc.(4),glock.,xyl. -
    pf. - str.   13:30 Composer.
—— CONCERTINO FOR ORCHESTRA, OP. 68
    2(2nd alt. with picc.),2,2,2(2nd alt. with c.-bn.) -
    timp.,perc.(3),glock. - hp. - str. 13:00 Composer.
—— CONCERTO FOR CELLO AND ORCH., OP. 60
    2(2nd alt. with picc.),2,2,2(2nd alt. with c.-bn.) - 3,1,0,0 -
    timp.,perc.(3),cel.,glock. - hp. - str. 26:00 Composer.
—— CONCERTO FOR CHAMBER ORCHESTRA (1972) (IN 3
    MOVTS.)
    2(2nd alt. with picc.),1,1,1 - 2,1,0,0 - timp.,perc.(3),glock.,xyl. - pf.
    - str.(6,3,4,2)   20:00 Composer.
—— CONCERTO FOR PIANO AND ORCH (1968) (IN 3 MOVTS.)
    3(3rd alt. with picc.),3,3,*3 - 4,3,3,1 - timp.,perc.(3),glock.,xyl. -
    pf. - str.   29:00 Composer.
—— CONCERTO GROSSO FOR COLORATURA SOPRANO, ALTO
    SAXOPHONE, TRUMPET, PIANO AND ORCH., OP. 53
    2(2nd alt. with picc.),2,*3,alto sax.,*2 - 3,1,0,0 - timp.,perc.(3) - pf.
    - str.   24:00 Composer.
—— CONTRASTS (1972)
    3(3rd alt. with picc.),*3,*3,*3, - 4,3,3,1 - timp.,perc.(3),glock.,xyl. -
    hp. - str.   10:00 Composer.
—— DANCE SUITE (IN 5 MOVTS.)
    3(2 alt. with 2 picc.),3,3(3rd alt. with b-cl.),*3 - 4,3,3,1 -
    timp.,perc.(5),glock.xyl. - pf. - str. 23:00 Composer.
—— DE PROFUNDIS (OUT OF THE DEPTHS) (MEDITATION NO.
    1 FOR ORCH.) (1975)
    3(3rd alt. with picc.),*3,*3,*3 - 4,3,3,1 - timp.,perc.(3),glock.,xyl. -
    hp. - pf. - str.   10:00 Composer.

—— DESTINY (A SYMPHONIC EPOS FOR ORCH.) (1975)
3(3rd alt. with picc.),*3,*3,*3 - 4,3,3,1 - timp.,perc.(3),glock.,xyl. - hp. - pf. - str.   13:00 Composer.

—— FAREWELL (SONG CYCLE FOR SOPRANO OR ORCH.) (Text: Christian Morgenstern)
2(2nd alt. with picc.),2,2,2 - 3,1,0,0 - timp.,perc.,cel.,glock. - hp. - str.   14:00 Composer.

—— FIVE PIECES FOR FULL ORCHESTRA (1970)
3(3rd alt. with picc.),3,*3,*3 - 4,3,3,1 - cel.,glock. - hp. - str.   16:00 Composer.

—— FOUR ESSAYS FOR ORCHESTRA (1973)
3(3rd alt. with picc.),*3,*3,*3 - 4,3,3,1 - timp.,perc.(4),cel.,glock.,xyl. - hp. - pf. - str.   16:00 Composer.

—— FOUR SONGS OF FAREWELL (FOR ALTO, OR BARITONE, AND ORCH.) (1970) (Texts: Christina Rossetti, Francis W. Bourdillon, Shelley, Tennyson)
2,2,2,*3 - 4,1,0,0 - timp.,perc.(3),cel.,glock. - hp. - str.   14:00 Composer.

—— THE GETTYSBURG ADDRESS (FOR SATB CHORUS AND ORCH.) (Text: Abraham Lincoln)
3,3,*3,*3 - 4,3,3,1 - timp.,perc.(2) - pf. - str.   6:00 Composer.

—— THE GLORY OF THE LORD (FOR SATB CHORUS AND ORCH.) (1966) (Text: Biblical)
3,3,3,*3 - 4,3,3,1 - timp.,perc.(3),glock. - hp. - str.   9:00 Composer.

—— THE INTANGIBLE (ORATORIO) (FOR SOPRANO, BARITONE, CHORUS AND ORCH.)
3(3rd alt. with picc.),3(3rd alt. with Eng.hn.),3(3rd alt. with b.-cl.),*3 - 4,3,3,1 - timp.,perc.,glock.,xyl. - pf. - str.   27:00 Composer.

—— ITALIAN IMPRESSIONS (SUITE FOR ORCH.) (1970)
*3,*3,*3,*3 - 4,3,0,0 - timp.,perc.(4),cel.,glock - guit. - hp. - str.   19:00 Composer.

—— MAGNIFICAT (FOR SOPRANO, MIXED VOICES, ORGAN AND ORCH.) (1972) (Text: liturgical)
3(3rd alt. with picc.),2,*3,*3 - 4,3,3,1 - timp.,perc.(3),bells,glock. - hp. - org. - str.   11:00 Composer.

—— MEMORIAL (SONG CYCLE) (FOR BARITONE, OR ATO, AND ORCH.) (1968) (Texts: I. Psalm 51; II Christina G. Rossetti; III Trad. Latin)
3,3,3,*3 - 4,3,3,1 - timp.,perc.(3),glock. - pf. - str.   14:00 Composer.

—— MUSIC FOR ORCHESTRA, OP. 54
2(2nd alt. with picc.),2,2(2nd alt. with b.-cl.),2(2nd alt. with c.-bn.) - timp.,perc.(3),xyl. - str.   19:00 Composer.

—— MYSTERION (A SYMPHONIC MEDITATION FOR ORCH.) (1971)
*3,3,*3,*3 - 4,3,3,1 - timp.,perc.(4),bells,cel.,glock.,xyl. - hp. - str.   8:00 Composer.

—— OVERTURE FOR ORCHESTRA (1965)
3(3rd alt. with picc.),3,3,*3 - 4,3,3,1 - timp.,perc.(3),glock. - pf. - str.   8:00 Composer.

—— PROCESSIONAL MARCH FOR ORCHESTRA (1967)
3(3rd alt. with picc.),3,3,*3 - 4,3,3,1 - timp.,perc.,glock. - pf. - str.   9:00 Composer.

—— A PROFILE (1971)
*3,*3,*3,*3 - 4,3,3,1 - timp.,perc.(4),glock.,xyl. - hp. - str.   11:00 Composer.

—— REQUIEM (FOR SOPRANO, ALTO, TENOR, BASS, SATB CHORUS AND ORCH.)
*3,1 alto fl.,*3,*3,*3 - 4,3,3,1 - timp.,perc.(3),glock.,xyl. - hp. - org. - str.   37:00 Composer.

—— THE SEASONS (FOUR POEMS FOR ORCHESTRA) (1969)
3(3rd alt. with picc.),*3,*3,*3 - 4,3,3,1 - timp.,perc.(4),cel.,glock.,xyl. - hp. - org. - str.   19:00 Composer.

—— THE SEVEN LAST WORDS ON THE CROSS (ORATORIO) (FOR 2 TENORS, BARITONE, SATB CHORUS AND ORCH.) (1965)
3,3(3rd alt. with Eng.hn.),3(3rd alt. with b.-cl.),*3 - 4,3,3,1 - timp.,perc.(3) - pf. - str.   28:00 Composer.

—— SEVEN SONGS FOR SOPRANO AND ORCH., OP. 63
*3,*3,*3,*3 - 4,3,3,1 - timp.,perc.(3),bells, glock. - hp. - str.   20:00 Composer.

—— SHORT OVERTURE
3,*3,*3 - 4,3,3,1 - timp.,perc.(3),glock. - hp. - str.   5:00 Composer.

—— SINFONIETTA IN G (IN 3 MOVTS.)
2(2nd alt. with picc.),2,2,2 - 3,1,0,0 - timp.,perc.(3),glock. - pf, - str.   13:30 G. Schirmer.

—— SONATINA NO. 1 FOR ORCHESTRA
2(2nd alt. with picc.),2,2,2(2nd alt. with c.-bn.) - 3,1,0,0 - timp.,perc.(3),cel.,glock. - hp. - str.   10:00 Composer.

—— SONATINA NO. 2 FOR ORCHESTRA (1973) (IN 3 MOVTS.)
2(2nd alt. with picc.),2,2,2 - 3,1,0,0 - timp.,perc.(3),glock.,xyl. - hp. - pf. - str.   12:30 Composer.

—— SUITE FOR CHAMBER ORCH., OP. 61
2(2nd alt. with picc.),2(2nd alt. with Eng. hn.),*2,alto sax.,0 - 2,1,1,0 - timp.,perc.(4),glock.,xyl. - pf. - tenor banjo - str.   19:00 Composer.

—— SYMPHONY NO. 1 IN D MINOR, OP. 42
3(3rd alt. with picc.),3(3rd alt. with Eng. hn.),3(3rd alt. with b.-cl.),*3 - 4,4,3,1 - timp.,perc.,cel.,glock. - 2 hp. - org.(ad. lib.) - str.   45:00 Composer.

—— SYMPHONY NO. 2 OP. 62
3(3rd alt. with picc.),3,3(3rd alt. with b.-cl.),*3 - 4,3,cnt.,3,1 - timp.,perc.(3),glock.,xyl. - hp. - str.   36:00 Composer.

—— SYMPHONY NO. 3, OP. 67
4(4th alt. with picc.),3(3rd alt. with Eng. hn.),*3,*3 - 4,3,3,1 - timp.,perc.(4),glock.,xyl. - 2 hp. - org. - str.   60:00 Composer.

—— SYMPHONY NO. 4 ("FATE AND FAREWELL")
3,3(3rd alt. with Eng. hn.),*3,*3 - 4,3,3,1 - timp.,perc.(4),cel.,glock.,xyl. - hp. - str.   22:00 Composer.

—— SYMPHONY NO. 5
3(3rd alt. with picc.),3(3rd alt. with Eng. hn.),3(3rd alt. with b.-cl.),*3 - 4,3,3,1 - timp.,perc.(4),cel.,glock.,xyl. - hp. - str.   47:00 Composer.

—— SYMPHONY NO. 6
3(3rd alt. with picc.),3(3rd alt. with Eng. hn.)*3,*3 - 4,3,3,1 - timp.,perc.(4),cel.,glock. - hp. - str.   37:00 Composer.

—— SYMPHONY NO. 7 ("DEATH AND ETERNITY") (FOR 4 SOLO VOICES, MIXED CHORUS AND ORCH.) (IN 5 MOVTS.)
3(3rd alt. with picc.),3(3rd alt. with Eng. hn.),3(3rd alt. with b.-cl.),*3 - 4,3,3,1 - timp.,perc.(3),cel.,glock.,xyl. - hp. - str.   30:00 Composer.

—— SYMPHONY NO. 8
3(3rd alt. with picc.),*3,*3,*3 - 4,3,3,1 - timp.,perc.(3),bells,cel.,glock. - hp. - str.   21:30 Composer.

—— THANATOS (DEATH) (MEDITATION NO. 2 FOR ORCH.) (1975)
3(3rd alt. with picc.),*3,*3,*3 - 4,3,3,1 - timp.,perc.(3),cel.,glock.,xyl. - hp. - pf. - str.   11:00 Composer.

—— THEY TRUSTED IN THEE (FOR S.A.T.B. SOLO VOICES, S.A.T.B. CHORUS AND ORCH.) (1967)
3,3,3,*3 - 4,3,3,1 - timp.,perc. - str.   6:00 Composer.

—— THREE IMAGES FOR ORCHESTRA (1971)
*3,3(3rd alt. with Eng.hn.),3(3rd alt.with b.-cl.),*3 - 4,3,3,1 - timp.,perc.(4),glock.,xyl. - hp. - pf. - str.   20:00 Composer.

—— THREE IMPROVISATIONS FOR CHAMBER ORCH. (1966)
1(alt. with picc.),1,1,1 - 1,1,0,1 - timp.,perc.(2),cel.,glock. - 1 vln.,1 vla.,1 c.,1 d.-b.   13:50 Composer.

—— THREE INSTRUMENTAL SONGS FOR ORCHESTRA (1969)
*3,*3,*3,*3 - 4,3,3,1 - timp.,perc.(3),glock. - pf. - str.   17 min. Composer.

—— THREE PIECES FOR ORCHESTRA
3(3rd alt. with picc.),3(3rd alt. with Eng.hn.),*3,*3 - 4,3,3,1 - timp.,perc.(3),xyl. - pf. - str.   14:00 Composer.

—— THRENODY (1973)
3(3rd alt.with picc.),*3,*3,*3 - 4,3,3,1 - timp.,perc.(4),glock.,xyl. - hp. - str.   12:00 Composer.

—— TOCCATA AND FUGUE (1966)
3,2,2,*3 - 3,1,3,1 - timp.,perc.(3),xyl. - pf. - str.   10:00 Composer.

—— VARIATIONS ON A FOLK SONG, OP. 64
3(3rd alt. with picc.),3,*3,*3 - 4,3,3,1 - timp.,perc.(4),glock.,xyl. - hp. - str.   16:30 Composer.

—— VARIATIONS ON A GERMAN FOLKSONG (1974)
*3,*2,2,*3 - 4,1,3,1 - timp.,perc.(3),glock.,xyl. - pf. - str.   11:00 Composer.

—— VARIATIONS ON ONE MOTIF (1968)
3,3,3,*3 - 4,3,3,1 - timp.,perc.,cel.,glock. - pf. - str.   13:00 Composer.

—— VISION (1973)
3(3rd alt.with picc.),2,*3,*3 - 4,3,3,1 - timp.,perc.(3),cel.,glock.,xyl. - hp. - str.   6:00 Composer.

SCHREINER, Alexander

—— CONCERTO IN B MINOR FOR ORGAN AND ORCH. (IN 3 MOVTS.)
2(1 alt. with picc.),2,2,*3 - 4,2,3,1 - timp. - org. - str.   21:00 Composer.

SCHREINER, Alexander - GOODMAN, Saul
—— THE WORRIED DRUMMER (HUMORESQUE FOR SOLO
PERCUSSIONIST AND ORCH.)
2,2,2,2 - 2,2,1,0 - perc. - str.   8:00 Belw-Mills.

SCHREITER, Heinz
—— SERENATA NOTTURNA
1,1,1,1 - 0,0,0,0 - hp. - str.   15:00 Modern.

SCHREKER, Franz
—— CHRISOPHORUS - ODER: DIE VISION EINER OPER (2-ACT
OPERA) % (1932)
2,*2,2,2 - 2,2,2,1 - timp.,perc.,cel. - banjo,guit.,4 mandolins - hp. -
pf. - str.   90:00 Henmar.

SCHRØDER, Walther
—— REBILD HILLS (A DANISH RHAPSODY)
                        G. Schirmer.

SCHROEDER, Hermann
—— CONCERTO FOR VIOLIN AND ORCH.
2 fl. - 2 hn. - perc. - pf. - str.   18:00 Robbins.
—— CONCERTO IN B MAJOR FOR PIANO AND ORCH., OP. 35
                        Hans Gerig.
—— DOUBLE CONCERTO FOR 2 VIOLINS AND ORCH.
                        Hans Gerig.
—— FESTLICHE MUSIK (INTRADA CON PASSAMEZZO) (FOR
PIANO AND STRING ORCH.)
pf. - str.   Robbins.
—— SINFONIA PICCOLA
perc. - pf. - str.   Hans Gerig.
—— VENI, CREATOR SPIRITUS (HYMN FOR LARGE ORCH.)
                        Hans Gerig.

SCHROEDER, William A.
—— THE EMPEROR JONES (SYMPHONIC IMPRESSION)
2(1 alt. with picc.),*2,2,2 - 4,3,3,1 - timp.,perc.(2) - str.
                        7:00 Harms, Inc.
—— JACK AND THE BEAN STALK (SUITE) (IN 3 MOVTS.)
*4,*3,*3,*3 - 4,3,3,1 - timp.,perc. - 2 hp. - str.   17:00 Composer.
—— MINIATURE (CONCERTINO FOR PIANO AND ORCH.)
*3,*3,*3,0 - 4,2,3,0 - timp.,perc.(2) - pf. - str.   Composer.
—— RHAPSODY
*4,*4,*3,2 - 4,3,3,1 - timp.,perc.(2) - 2 hp. - str.   15:00 Composer.

SCHUBACH, Peter
—— CONCERTO FOR CELLO AND ORCH. (1973)
1,1,1,1 - 1,1,0,0 - str.   20:00 Fleisher.

SCHUBART, Mark
—— YVON TO CLAIRE (4 SONGS FOR HIGH VOICE AND
STRINGS)
str.   Leeds.

SCHUBERT, Franz - ABRAHAM, Gerald
—— SCHERZO FOR THE "UNFINISHED" SYMPHONY (Completed
by G. Abraham)
2,2,2,2 - 2,2,3,0 - timp. - str.   7:00 Oxford.

SCHUBERT, Franz - AUSTIN, Richard R.
—— MAY SONATA (AFTER THE PIANO SONATA, D.841)
str.   18:00 P.R.S.
—— SONATA FOR SMALL ORCH. (AFTER THE PIANO SONATA,
D.664)
1,1,2,1 - 2,2,2,0 - timp. - pf. - str.   12:00 P.R.S.

SCHUBERT, Franz - BECKETT, Wheeler
—— HARK! HARK! THE LARK (WITH OPTIONAL VOICE) (Text:
Shakespeare)
2,2,2,2 - 2,2,3,1 - timp.,trgl. - hp.(ad lib.) - str.   6:00 Arranger.
—— WHO IS SYLVIA? (WITH OPTIONAL VOICE) (Text:
Shakespeare)
2,2,2,2 - 2,2,3,0 - timp. - str.   6:00 Arranger.

SCHUBERT, Franz - BUSH, Geoffrey
—— TWO SCHUBERT SCHERZOS
2,2,2,2 - 2,2,3,0 - timp. - str.   12:00 Novello.

SCHUBERT, Franz - COLLINS, Anthony
—— FANTASY, OP. 103
2,2,2,2 - 2,3,3,0 - timp. - str.   Fox.

SCHUBERT, Franz - DASCH, George
—— SYMPHONY NO. 8 IN B MINOR ("THE UNFINISHED")
                        C. Fischer.

SCHUBERT, Franz - DOUGLAS, Roy
—— ROSAMUNDE: BALLET MUSIC (NOS. 1 AND 2)
                        13:30 Bo. Hawkes.

SCHUBERT, Franz - FEKETE, Zóltan
—— SCHNEEWITTCHEN (SUITE)
3,2,2,2 - 4,2,3,0 - timp.,perc. - hp. - str.   21:00 Modern.
or:
2,1,1,1 - 2,2,1,0 - timp. - str.

SCHUBERT, Franz - HARRISON, Julius
—— WINTER AND SPRING (SONG CYCLE FOR CHORUS AND
ORCH.)
2,2,2,2 - 4,2,3,0 - timp. - hp. - str.   22:00 Bo. Hawkes.

SCHUBERT, Franz - KABALEVSKY, Dmitri
—— FANTASY IN F MINOR (FOR PIANO AND ORCH.)
3,2,2,2 - 4,2,3,1 - timp.,perc. - pf. - str.   17:00 G. Schirmer.

SCHUBERT, Franz - KLUG, Heinrich
—— ARPEGGIONE SONATE (FOR CELLO AND STRING
ORCH.)(ARR. 1968)
str.   22:00 G. Schirmer.

SCHUBERT, Franz - LEIBOWITZ, René
—— FANTASIA IN C MAJOR (ORIGINALLY FOR VIOLIN AND
PIANO)
2,2,2,2 - 2,2,3,1 - pf. - str.   Boelke-Bo.
—— FANTASIA IN F MINOR (ORIGINALLY FOR PIANO
4-HANDS)
2,2,2,2 - 2,2,3,1 - timp. - str.   Boelke-Bo.

SCHUBERT, Franz - MEYEROWITZ, Jan
—— TURN YOUR THOUGHTS TO THOSE WHO'RE GONE (FROM
THE CANTATA "LAZARUS") (FOR MIXED CHORUS AND
ORCH.)
                        Broude.
—— WHERE ART AND LOVE OF BEAUTY (FROM THE OPERA
"FIERRABRAS") (FOR MIXED CHORUS AND ORCH.)
                        Broude.

SCHUBERT, Franz - MILLS, Don
—— FANTASY AND FUGUE, OP. 101 (ARR. 1968)
2(2nd alt.with picc.),2,2,2 - 4,2,3,0 - timp.,perc.(2),bells - str.
                        12:00 Arranger.

SCHUBERT, Franz - OESER, Fritz
—— SYMPHONY IN C (AFTER THE GRAND DUO FOR PIANO
4-HANDS, OP. 140)
2,2,2,2 - 2,2,3,0 - timp. - str.   40:00 Henmar.

SCHUBERT, Franz - OTTERLOO, Willem van
—— FANTASIE, OP. 103
2,2,2,1 - 4,2,3,0 - perc. - str.   17:00 Henmar.

SCHUBERT, Franz - PARKER, Alice - SHAW, Robert
—— MASS IN G MAJOR (FOR CHORUS AND CHAMBER ORCH.)
                        G. Schirmer.

SCHUBERT, Franz - PERRY, Harold
—— OVERTURE TO "ROSAMUNDE"
                        11:00 Bo. Hawkes.

SCHUBERT, Franz - ROBERT, Charles J.
—— ROSAMUNDE: BALLET MUSIC AND ENTR'ACTE NO. 2
                        C. Fischer.
—— ROSAMUNDE: BALLET SUITE
                        C. Fischer.
—— ROSAMUNDE: OVERTURE
                        C. Fischer.

SCHUBERT, Franz - ROWLEY, Alec
—— FUGUE IN E MINOR
pf.(ad lib.) - str.   9:00 Galaxy.

SCHUBERT, Franz - SERLY, Tibor
—— SCHERZO (FROM THE "UNFINISHED" SYMPHONY)
(Reconstructed and Orchestrated by T. Serly)
2,2,2,2 - 2,2,3,0 - timp. - str.   6:00 ModusAssoc.

SCHUBERT, Franz - WEAVER, Richard L.
—— OVERTURE TO "ROSAMUNDE"
                               Mills.

SCHUBERT, Franz - WEINER, Leo
—— GRAND RONDEAU IN A, OP. 107
    2,2,2,2 - 2,2,3,0 - timp. - str.   12:00 Bo. Hawkes.

SCHUBERT, Franz - WINTER, Aubrey
—— OVERTURE TO "ALFONSO AND ESTRELLA"
                           6:30 Bo. Hawkes.
—— TWO ENTR'ACTES FROM "ROSAMUNDE"
                        14:00 Bo. Hawkes.

SCHUBERT, Franz - WYK, Arnold van
—— FANTASIA IN F MINOR, OP. 103 (FOR PIANO AND ORCH.)
    2,2,3,2 - 4,2,3,1 - timp.,perc. - pf. - str.   17:00 HAUM.

SCHUBERT, Heinz
—— AMBROSIANISCHES KLAVIERKONZERT
    1,1,0,1 - 0,1,0,0 - pf. - str.   22:00 Alkor.
—— CONCERTANTE SUITE (FOR VIOLIN AND CHAMBER ORCH.)
    2,1,0,0 - 0,0,0,0 - str.   18:00 Henmar.
—— HYMNISCHES KONZERT (SUITE) (WITH SOPRANO AND TENOR) (IN 4 MOVTS.)
    1,1,0,1 - 0,3,0,0 - org. - str.   33:00 Henmar.
—— LYRICAL CONCERTO (FOR VIOLA AND CHAMBER ORCH.)
    0,0,1,0 - 1,0,0,0 - str.(no d.-b.)   27:00 Henmar.
—— PRAELUDIUM AND TOCCATA (FOR VIOLIN, VIOLA, CELLO AND DOUBLE STRING ORCH.)
    str.   13:00 Henmar.
—— SINFONIETTA
    2,2,2,2 - 4,2,0,0 - timp.,perc.(3) - str. 20:00 Henmar.

SCHUBERT, Manfred
—— DANCE STUDIES FOR SMALL ORCH.
    2,1,2,1 - 1,1,1,0 - perc. - pf. - str.   15:00 Tetra.
—— DIVERTIMENTO
    2,1,2,1 - 2,2,1,0 - timp.,perc. - pf. - str.   Tetra.
—— MUSIC FOR ORCHESTRA "66" (PAEAN)
    3,2,2,2 - 4,2,3,1 - timp.,perc. - str.   7:00 Tetra.
—— SUITE FOR ORCHESTRA 1966
    2,2,2,2 - 4,2,3,0 - timp.,perc. - str.   23:00 Tetra.

SCHUETZ, Heinrich - MENDEL
—— THE CHRISTMAS STORY (FOR MIXED CHORUS AND ORCH.)
                            G. Schirmer.

SCHULÉ, Bernard
—— CRESCENDO, OP. 73 (SINFONIE)
                          4:00 S.U.I.S.A.
—— L' ESPRIT ET L'ESPOUSE, OP. 75
    2,2,2,2 - 3,2,1,0 - timp.,perc. - str. 13:00 S.U.I.S.A.
—— GONG AND STRINGS, OP. 81 (POUR CONTREBASSE SOLO ET ORCHESTRE DE CHAMBRE)
                        13:00 S.U.I.S.A.
—— HOMMAGE À L'ACCORD MAJEUR, OP. 98 (CONCERTO GROSSO PER VIOLINO PRINCIPALE E ORCHESTRA)
                        10:00 S.U.I.S.A.
—— HORIZONS D'OR (SUITE), OP. 33
    2,1,2,1 - 2,2,2,0 - timp.,perc. - 2 guit. - hp. - pf. - str.
                        12:00 S.U.I.S.A.
—— MIROIRS CONTRASTES (FOR BARITONE, MIXED CHORUS AND ORCH.), OP. 42
    2,2,2,2 - 2,2,1,0 - timp.,perc. - pf. - str. 22:00 S.U.I.S.A.
—— MUSIQUE DE CONCERT (FOR STRINGS), OP. 14
    str.   18:00 S.U.I.S.A.
—— SÉRÉNADE NO. 2, OP. 80 (POUR FLÛTE, PIANO ET ORCH. À CORDES)
    fl. - pf. - str.   12:00 S.U.I.S.A.
—— SÉRÉNADE POUR ORCHESTRE À CORDES, OP. 5
    str.   10:00 Salabert.
—— SUITE VALAISANNE
    2,2,2,2 - 2,2,1,0 - timp.,perc. - hp. - pf. - str. 14:00 Choudens.
—— SYMPHONIE ("MAGIE DU RAIL")
    2,1,2,2 - 4,3,1,0 - timp.,perc.(3) - hp. - str. 18:00 Eds. Coda.

SCHULHOFF, Ervin
—— DOUBLE CONCERTO FOR FLUTE, PIANO AND ORCH.
    fl. - 2 hn. - pf. - str.   Bo. Hawkes.

—— SYMPHONY NO. 3
    2,2,2,2 - 4,2,2,1 - timp.,perc. - str. 30:00 Bo. Hawkes.
—— SYMPHONY NO. 6
    2,3,2,3 - 8,4,tpt. in d, b.-tpt.,3,2 - timp.,perc. - str.
                          42:00 Bo. Hawkes.

SCHULTZ, Herbert
—— THE SUN DIAL (PROVERBS) (FOR MIXED CHORUS AND STRINGS)
    str.   F. Colombo.

SCHULTZ, Lars Peter
—— CONCERT OVERTURE, OP. 5
    2,1,1,1 - 0,0,0,0 - timp. - str.   10:00 K.O.D.A.

SCHULTZ, Svend S.
—— THE FOUR TEMPERAMENTS (FOR SATB CHORUS AND ORCH.)
                           K.O.D.A.
—— HIOB (SYMPHONIC ORATORIO) (FOR CHORUS, WINDS AND HARPS)
                          Henmar.
—— NORTHERN OVERTURE (1975)
                         G. Schirmer.
—— SERENADE FOR STRING ORCH.
    str.   16:00 G. Schirmer.
—— SINFONIA PICCOLA
    3,2,2,2 - 2,2,2,1 - timp.,perc. - str. 22:00 G. Schirmer.
—— THE STORSTRØM BRIDGE (A SYMPHONIC VISION)
    2,1,2,1 - 2,2,1,1 - timp.,perc. - str. 8:00 Henmar.
—— SYMPHONY NO. 5
                           K.O.D.A.
—— THREE DANISH DANCES
    2,2,2,2 - 2,2,2,0 - timp.,perc. - str. 10:00 G. Schirmer.

SCHULTZE, Norbert
—— BALLETTMUSIK AUS DER OPER "SCHWARZER PETER"
    2,2,2,2 - 2,2,1,0 - timp.,perc. - str. 6:00 Sikorski.
—— OVERTURE TO "DAS KALTE HERZ"
    3,3,3,3 - 4,3,3,0 - timp.,perc. - str. 4:00 F. Colombo.
—— OVERTURE TO "SCHWARZER PETER"
    2,2,2,2 - 2,2,1,0 - timp.,perc. - str. 4:00 F. Colombo.
—— OVERTURE TO "STRUWWELPETER"
    2,2,2,2 - 2,2,0,0 - timp.,perc. - str. 4:00 F. Colombo.
—— SCHWARZER PETER (OPERA) %
                          F. Colombo.
—— STRUWWELPETER (OPERA) %
                          F. Colombo.

SCHULZE, Martin
—— CONCERTO FOR HARPSICHORD AND STRING ORCH.
    hpsc. - str.   20:00 Mannheimer.

SCHULZE, Piet
—— CONCERTO FOR HORN AND STRING ORCH.
    hn. - str.   18:00 Mannheimer.

SCHUMAN, William
—— AMERICAN FESTIVAL OVERTURE
    3(3rd alt. with picc.),*3,*3,2,c.-bn.(ad lib.) - 4,3,3,1 - timp.,perc.(3),xyl. - str.   9:00 G. Schirmer.
—— CIRCUS OVERTURE
    3(2nd and 3rd alt. with picc.),*3,E♭cl.,*3,*3 - 4,3,3,1 - timp.,perc. - pf. - str.   8:00 G. Schirmer.
—— CIRCUS OVERTURE (SIDESHOW) (Reduced Orchestration)
    2,2,3,0 - 2,3,3,1 - timp.,perc. - str. 7:00 G. Schirmer.
—— CONCERTO FOR PIANO AND SMALL ORCH.
    1,1,1,0 - 2,2,1,0 - pf. - str.   20:00 G. Schirmer.
—— A FREE SONG (SECULAR CANTATA NO, 2) (FOR CHORUS AND ORCH.)
    2-3(3rd alt. with picc.),*4,E♭cl.,*4,*4 - 4,3,3,1 - timp.,perc. - str.   22:00 G. Schirmer.
—— JUDITH (CHOREOGRAPHIC POEM) %
    *3,*3,*3,*3 - 4,2,3,1 - timp. - pf. - str. 24:00 G. Schirmer.
—— THE MIGHTY CASEY (A BASEBALL OPERA IN 3 SCENES) %
(Text: Jeremy Gury)
    1,1,2,1 - 0,2,3,0 - perc. - pf. - str. 80:00 G. Schirmer.
—— NEWSREEL (SUITE)
    3(2nd alt. with picc.),*3,*4,3 sax.,*4 - 4,3,3,1 - timp.,perc.,xyl. - pf. - str.   8:00 G. Schirmer.
Or
    2(2nd alt. with picc.),1-2,2-3,1-3 - 2-4,3,3,1 - timp.,perc.,xyl. - str.

—— PRAYER IN TIME OF WAR
    3,3,3,2 - 4,3,3,1 - timp.,perc. - str.   15:00 G. Schirmer.
—— PROLOGUE (FOR CHORUS AND ORCH.)
    3(3rd alt. with picc.),2,2,2 - 2,3,3,1 - timp.,perc. - str.
                                                    7:00 G. Schirmer.
—— SYMPHONY FOR STRINGS, NO. 5
    1. Molto agitato e energico; 2. Larghissimo; 3. Presto
    str.   17:00 G. Schirmer.
—— SYMPHONY NO. 3 (IN 2 MOVTS.)
    2,*3,E^{b}cl.,*3,2 - 4,4,4,1 - timp.,perc.(3),xyl. - pf. - str.
                                     30:00 G. Schirmer.
    or:
    4(3rd and 4th alt. with picc.),*4,E^{b}cl.,*4,*4 - 8,4,4,1 -
    timp.,perc.(3),xyl. - pf. - str.
—— SYMPHONY NO. 4
    3(3rd alt. with picc.),*2-*3,E^{b}cl.,*2-*3, 2-*4 - 4,3,3,1 -
    timp.,perc.(3),glock.,xyl. - str.   24:00 G. Schirmer.
—— SYMPHONY NO. 6
    3,3,3,3 - 4,3,3,1 - timp.,perc. - str.   27:00 G. Schirmer.
—— THIS IS OUR TIME (SECULAR CANTATA NO. 1) (FOR
    CHORUS AND ORCH.) (IN 5 MOVTS.)
    3(3rd alt. with picc.),*3,*3,2 - 4,3,3,1 - timp.,perc. (2 or 3) - str.
                                     30:00 Bo. Hawkes.
—— UNDERTOW (CHOREOGRAPHIC EPISODES) %
    3(2nd and 3rd alt. with picc.),*3,3,3 - 4,2,3,1 - timp.,perc.(3) - pf.
    - str.   25:00 G. Schirmer.

SCHUMANN, Gerhard
—— ADAGIO AND PASSACAGLIA (FROM THE CANTATA
    "NACHT UND MORGEN")
    str.   8:00 Henmar.
—— SERENADE FÜR STREICHER
    str.   7:00 Sirius.

SCHUMANN, Robert - DUMONT, Adolphe
—— NOCTURNAL PIECE
                                       C. Fischer.

SCHUMANN, Robert - KONSTANTINOFF, K.
—— CARNIVAL (SUITE)
    2,2,2,2 - 4,2,3,1 - timp.,perc. - hp. - pf. - str. 25:00 Bo. Hawkes.

SCHUMANN, Robert - KREISLER, Fritz
—— FANTASY, OP. 131 (FOR VIOLIN AND ORCH.)
    2,2,2,2 - 4,2,3,0 - timp. - str.   12:00 C. Fischer.

SCHUMANN, Robert - ORMANDY, Eugene
—— SYMPHONY NO. 2 IN C MAJOR, OP. 61
    2,2,2,2 - 4,3,3,1 - timp. - str.   33:30 Arranger.

SCHUMANN, Robert - VINTER, Gilbert
—— THE POET SPEAKS (SUITE)
    cl. - hp. - str.   16:00 Bo. Hawkes.

SCHÜRMANN, Gerard
—— ATTACK AND CELEBRATION (AN OVERTURE) (1968)
    3,3,3,3 - 4,3,3,1 - str.   8:00 P.R.S.
—— CHUENCH'I (A SONG-CYCLE FROM THE CHINESE) (FOR
    VOICE AND ORCH.) (English Text: Arthur Waley)
                                       Novello.
—— INTRADA FOR STRING ORCH.
    str.   P.R.S.
—— SIX STUDIES OF FRANCIS BACON
    3(alt. with 3 picc.),3(3rd alt. with Eng.hn.),3,3 - 4,3,3,1 -
    timp.,perc.,cel.,glock.,vibra.,xyl. - hp. - pf. - str. 24:00 Novello.
—— VARIANTS
    1(alt. with picc.),2(2nd alt. with Eng.hn.),0,2 - 2,0,0,0 - str.
                                      15:00 Novello.

SCHÜTZ, Heinrich
—— THE SEVEN LAST WORDS FROM THE CROSS (FOR SOLO
    VOICES, MIXED CHORUS, ORGAN AND STRINGS) (English
    text: Nicholas McCabe and Paul Steinitz)
    org. - str.   22:00 Oxford.

SCHÜTZ, Heinrich - GHEDINI, G. F.
—— THE SEVEN WORDS OF CHRIST ON THE CROSS ("LE
    SETTE PAROLE DE CRISTO SULLA CROCE") (FOR SOLO
    VOICES, CHORUS AND ORCH.)
    0,0,0,0 - 0,2,3,0 - org. - str.(no vlns.)   25:00 Leeds.

SCHÜTZ, Heinrich - STEINITZ, Paul
—— GERMAN MAGNIFICAT (FOR DOUBLE MIXED CHORUS,
    ORGAN AND ORCH.)
    0,*3,0,1 - 0,2,alto trb.,2,0 - str.   8:00 Oxford.

SCHÜTZ, Heinrich - STONE, Kurt
—— OUR FATHER ("DAS VATERUNSER") (FOR OPTIONAL
    TENOR SOLO, MIXED CHORUS AND ORCH.) (Engl. Text:
    Julias Elias)
                                          Broude.

SCHUYT, Nico
—— CORTEGGIO (1958)
    3,2,2,2 - 4,3,3,1 - timp.,perc. - hp. - str.   15:00 Henmar.
—— DISCORSI CAPRICCIOSI
    1,2,2,2 - 2,1,1,1 - timp.,perc.   17:00 Henmar.
—— HYMNUS (1966)
                                       10:00 Henmar.
—— NAAR DE MAAN (FOR DOUBLE MIXED CHORUS AND
    ORCH.) (1968) (IN 3 MOVTS.) (Text: Bert Schierbeek)
                                       18:00 Henmar.
—— DE VARKENSHOEDER (OVERTURE) (1959)
    2,2,2,2 - 2,2,0,0 - str.   6:00 Henmar.
—— WIJ ZULLEN EEN MUUR BOUWEN (1952) (FOR MIXED
    CHORUS AND ORCH.) (Text: Nelly Burgdorffer)
    2,2,2,2 - 2,2,0,0 - timp.,perc.,xyl. - hp. - pf. - str. 24:00 Henmar.

SCHWAEN, Kurt
—— FINALE FROM THE BALLET "BALLADE VOM GLÜCK"
    2,2,3,3 - 3,3,3,1 - timp.,perc. - pf. - str.   Tetra.
—— ZWINGERSERENADE
    1,1,1,1 - 0,0,0,0 - str.   9:00 Tetra.

SCHWARTZ, Charles
—— MOTION
    str.   6:30 C. Fischer.
—— PASSACAGLIA
    4,3,3,3 - 4,3,3,1 - timp.,perc.,cel. - hp. - pf. - str. 8:30 C. Fischer.

SCHWARTZ, Elliott
—— CONCERT PIECE FOR TEN PLAYERS (1965) (IN 3 MOVTS.)
    1(alt.with picc.),1,1(alt.with b.-cl.),1 - 1,0,0,0 - perc.(1),glock.,xyl. -
    1 vln.,1 vla.,1 c.,1 d.-b.   14:00 Tetra.
—— CONCERTO FOR BASSOON AND STRING ORCH. (1964) (IN
    3 MOVTS.)
    bn. - str.   14:00 Composer.
—— DREAM OVERTURE (FOR ORCH. AND RECORDED MUSIC)
    (1972)
    2(2nd alt.with picc.),2,2(2nd alt.with b.-cl.),2(2nd alt.with c.-bn.) -
    4,2,2,1 - timp.,perc.(2),vibra. - 2 2-channel tape-recorders -
    phonograph - str.   11:00 Composer.
—— ECLIPSE I (ENIGMA VARIATIONS FOR 10 PLAYERS) (1971)
    0,0,2(2nd alt.with b.-cl.),2(2nd alt.with c.-bn.) - 0,1,1,0 -
    timp.,perc.(1) - pf.(alt.with cel. and hpsc.) - 1 vln.,1 c.
                                12:00 Composer.
—— ECLIPSE III (1975) (FOR CHAMBER ORCH. OF 15 TO 30
    PLAYERS)
    1(alt.with picc.),1,1,1 - 1,1,1,0 - perc.(2),bells,vibra.,xyl. - str.
                                12:00 Tetra.
—— THE HARMONY OF MAINE (ON 4 TUNES FROM SUPPLY
    BELCHER'S 1794 COLLECTION OF THE SAME NAME) (FOR
    SOLO SYNTHESIZER AND ORCH.) (1975)
    2(2nd alt.with picc.),2,2(2nd alt.with b.-cl.),2(2nd alt.with cbn.) -
    4,2,2,1 - timp.,perc.(3),bells,glock.,mar.,vibra. - synthesizer
    (suitable for live performance) - pf. - str.   18:00 C. Fischer.
—— HARUPSPICATING ON VALLEY VIEW FARM (3 SONGS FOR
    BARITONE AND CHAMBER ORCH.) (1964) (Text: Joseph
    Langland)
    1,1,1,1 - 1,0,0,0 - timp. - str.   10:00 Composer.
—— ISLAND (1970)
    2(2nd alt.with picc.),2,2,2(2nd alt.with cbn.) - 4,2,3,1 -
    timp.,perc.(3),bells,glock.,xyl. - 2 tape-recorders (stereo) - pf. - str.
                                12:00 C. Fischer.
—— MAGIC MUSIC (FOR PIANO AND ORCH.) (1968)
    2(2nd alt.with picc.),2,2(1st alt.with b.-cl.,2nd alt.with sax.),2 -
    4,2,3,1 - timp.,perc.(4),glock.,vibra.,xyl. - 2-channel
    tape-recorders - pf.(alt.with org.) - str.   14:00 C. Fischer.
—— MUSIC FOR ORCH. (1965)
    *2,2,2,2 - 4,2,3,0 - timp.,perc.(3),glock.,vibra.,xyl. - tape-recorder -
    pf. - str.   7:00 C. Fischer.
—— PASTORAL (FOR CHAMBER ORCH.) (1964)
    1,1,1,1 - 1,0,0,0 - str.   5:40 Composer.

—— SYMPHONY IN TWO MOVEMENTS (1965)
    1. Slowly; 2. Moderato, but with motion
    2(1 alt. with picc.),1,2,1 - 3,1,2,1 - timp.,perc.(2), bells - str.
                  12:30 Composer.
—— TEXTURE (FOR STRINGS, WINDS AND BRASS) (1966)
    1,1,1,1 - 1,1,1,0 - str.   7:30 Tetra.

SCHWARTZ, Émile
—— POIESIS (1-ACT BALLET) (1910) %
    2,2,2,2 - 4,2,3,1 - timp. - hp. - str.   Salabert.

SCHWARTZ, Francis
—— PLEGARIA (SUPPLICATION) (FOR SOPRANO OR CHILD'S
    VOICE, WITH ORCH.) (1973) (Text: Psalm 26)
    3,2,2,2 - 4,3,3,1 - timp.,perc(3),vibra. - str. 11:00 Southern.
    or:
    2,2,2,2 - 4,2,3,1 - timp.,perc.(3),vibra. - str.
—— THE TROPICAL TREK OF TRISTAN TRIMBLE (FOR SMALL
    ORCH.)
                  8:00 Southern.
—— YO PROTESTO (I PROTEST) (FOR LARGE ORCH.)
                  12:00 Southern.

SCHWARZ, Ira P.
—— CONCERT OVERTURE (1968)
    2,2,*3,2 - 4,3,3,1 - timp.,perc.(3) - str. 9:00 Composer.
—— DIVERTIMENTO FOR STRINGS (1965)
    str.   10:00 Belwin.
—— THE TAR BABY (FOR NARRATOR AND ORCH.) (1960) (Text:
    Traditional American)
    2,2,*3,2 - 4,3,3,1 - timp.,perc.(3) - str. 14:00 Composer.

SCHWARZ, Lev
—— JEWISH SYMPHONY
    3,3,3,3 - 4,3,3,1 - timp.,perc. - hp. - str. Leeds.

SCHWARZ-SCHILLING, Reinhard
—— INTRODUCTION AND FUGUE (FOR STRINGS)
    str.   11:00 Baerenrtr.
—— PARTITA
    2,1,1,2 - 2,2,0,0 - timp.,perc. - hp. - str. 30:00 Baerenrtr.
—— SYMPHONY IN C (1963)
    3(3rd alt. with picc.),*3,*3,3(3rd alt. with c.-bn.) - 3,3,3,0 -
    timp.,perc.(3) - str.   28:00 G. Schirmer.

SCHWEDA, Gerhard
—— SKANDINAVISCHE SKIZZEN (SUITE) (IN 3 MOVTS.)
    2,2,2,2 - 4,2,3,0 - perc. - hp. - str. 13:00 T & J.

SCHWEITZER, Anton - BODART, Eugen
—— SYMPHONY IN D MAJOR
    2,0,0,0 - 2,2,0,0 - str.   8:00 Mannheimer.

SCHWEIZER, Klaus
—— JEU DE VALEURS ET D'INTENSITÉS (1973)
    0,0,0,0 - 0,3,3,0 - cel.,mar.(or vibra.) - hp. - str.
                  12:30 G. Schirmer.

SCHWERTSIK, Kurt
—— FÜR AUDIFAX UND ABACHUM, OP. 8
    3,*3,*2,*3 - 3,4,3,1 - str.   17:00 Modern.

SCHWICKERT, Gustav
—— SINFONIETTA IN C MINOR
    2,2,2,2 - 4,2,3,1 - timp.,perc. - str. 25:00 Ries-Erler.

SCHWINDL, C. F. - CARSE, Adam
—— SYMPHONY IN F
    1. Allegro; 2. Andante; 3. Presto
    2ob.(or 2 fl.) - 2 hn. - str.   11:00 Galaxy.

SCIAMMARELLA, Valdo
—— CANTATA PARA LA FUNDACION DE BUENOS AIRES (FOR
    LOW VOICE, MIXED CHORUS AND ORCH.)
    0,0,2,2 - 0,4,3,1 - timp.,perc. 22:00 S.A.D.A.I.C.
—— CANZONA PARA SOPRANO Y ORQUESTA
    3,2,2,2 - 4,2,3,1 - timp. - hp. - str. 10:00 S.A.D.A.I.C.
—— DIPTICO
    1,1,1,1 - 1,1,1,0 - str.   15:00 Composer.
—— MARIANITA LIMENA (1-ACT CHAMBER OPERA) %
    2,1,2,1 - 0,0,0,0 - perc. - hp. - pf. - str. 45:00 S.A.D.A.I.C.
—— RONDAS
    3,2,3,2 - 4,2,3,1 - timp.,perc. - hp. - pf. - str. 17:00 S.A.D.A.I.C.

—— VARIACIONES CONCERTANTES (FOR PIANO AND ORCH.)
    3,3,3,3 - 4,2,2,1 - timp.,perc.,cel. - hp. - pf. - str.
                  19:00 S.A.D.A.I.C.

SCIANNI, Joseph C.
—— BATIK (1957)
    *2,*2,*3,2 - 4,3,3,1 - timp.,perc.(2),bells - hp. - str.
                  9:00 Composer.
—— SHILOH OVERTURE (1956)
    *3,2,2,2 - 4,3,3,0 - timp.,perc.(2) - str. 5:00 Composer.
—— SINFONIA BREVE (1958) (IN 3 MOVTS.)
    2,2,2,2 - 2,2,1,0 - timp.,perc.(2),bells - str. 12:00 Presser.

SCIORTINO, Patrice
—— CORTÈGES (FOR BRASS, PIANO AND PERCUSSION)
    0,0,0,0 - 4,3,4,1 - perc. - pf. 10:00 Presser.
—— LES MACHINAIRES (FOR HARPSICHORD AND STRINGS)
    hpsc. - str.   Presser.
—— LES NOURRITURES CÉLESTES
    str.   11:00 Presser.

SCLATER, James S.
—— ADAGIO FOR STRING ORCH. (1968)
    str.   4:15 Composer.
—— INTRODUCTION TO THE ORCHESTRA (VARIATIONS ON
    "YANKEE DOODLE") (1975)
    *3,2,*3,2 - 4,3,3,1 - timp.,perc.,bells,glock.,xyl. - hp. - str.
                  6:00 Mt. Salus.
—— SYMPHONY NO. 1 (1975) (IN 2 MOVTS.)
    *3,*3,*3,2 - 4,3,3,1 - timp.,perc.(4),bells,glock.,xyl. - hp. - str.
                  18:00 Composer.
—— THREE PERSONALITY STUDIES (1967)
    1,1,1,1 - 1,1,1,0 - perc.(3),vibra.,xyl. - pf. - str. 14:00 CAP.

SCOLARI, Henri
—— CONCERTO POUR VIOLINCELLE ET ORCHESTRE
    2,2,2,2 - 2,2,0,0 - str.   32:00 S.U.I.S.A.
—— INTÉGRATION (POUR ORCHESTRE ET BANDE
    MAGNÉTIQUE)
    2,2,2,2 - 0,2,2,0 - tape-recorder - str. 19:00 S.U.I.S.A.

SCOTT, Anthony
—— CONCERTO FOR ORGAN AND STRING ORCH. (1959)
    org. - str.   19:00 P.R.S.
—— CONCERTO FOR VIOLIN AND ORCH. (1948)
    2,2,2,2 - 4,2,3,1 - timp. - str. 27:00 P.R.S.
—— FANTASIE FOR STRINGS
    str.   Oxford.
—— INTRODUCTION AND FUGUE FOR ORCH. (1946)
    2,2,2,3 - 4,2,3,1 - timp.,perc. - str. 10:00 P.R.S.
—— PARTITA FOR PIANO AND ORCH. (1964)
    2,2,2,2 - 4,2,3,0 - timp.,perc. - pf. - str. 23:00 P.R.S.
—— PRELUDE AND FUGUE FOR STRINGS
    str.   5:30 Oxford.
—— SERENADE FOR FLUTE AND STRINGS
    fl. - str.   6:00 P.R.S.
—— SINFONIETTA
    str.   Novello.
—— VARIATIONS ON AN OLD GERMAN CHORALE
                  Novello.

SCOTT, Cyril
—— CONCERTINO FOR TWO PIANOS AND ORCH.
    1,0,0,0 - 2,2,3,0 - timp.,perc. - 2 pf. - str. 18:00 P.R.S.
—— CONCERTO FOR OBOE AND STRINGS
    ob. - str.   15:00 Novello.
—— EARLY ONE MORNING (POEM FOR PIANO AND ORCH.)
    2,1,2,2 - 2,0,2,0 - timp.,perc. - pf. - str. 13:30 Bo. Hawkes.
—— FESTIVAL OVERTURE (WITH MIXED CHORUS AD LIB.)
    2-3(2nd alt. with picc.),2-*3,*2-*3,3(3rd alt. with c.-bn.) - 4,2-3,3,1
    - timp.,perc.(4-6),cel.,xyl. - hp. - org.(ad lib.) - pf. - str.
                  12:00 Novello.
—— MIRABELLE (CANTATA) (FOR MIXED VOICES AND
    STRINGS)
    str.   30:00 Bo. Hawkes.
—— MYSTIC ODE (FOR CHORUS AND ORCH.)
    0,0,0,2 - 4,2,3,1 - timp.,perc. - hp. - org. - str. Novello.
—— NEAPOLITAN RHAPSODY
    3,*3,2,3 - 4,3,3,1 - timp.,perc. - hp. - str. 12:00 Bo. Hawkes.
—— SUITE NO. 1 FOR STRINGS
    str.   9:30 Bo. Hawkes.

SCOTT, J. Sebastian
—— CORYDON'S ROUND (A PASTORAL SUITE) (IN 5 MOVTS.)
    pf. - str.   12:00 Bo. Hawkes.

SCOTT, Tom
—— COLLOQUY FOR STRINGS
    str.   12:00 Composer.
—— FANFARE AND CANTILENA
                                        10:00 Charling.
—— FROM THE SACRED HARP (FOR FULL ORCH. OR STRING
    ORCH.)
                                        7:00 Charling.
—— FROM THE SOUTHERN HIGHLANDS (SUITE)
    str.   Composer.
—— SOPHOCLES THE HYENA (FOR NARRATOR AND ORCH.)
    (AFTER A STORY BY JIM MORAN)
                                        23:00 Composer.
—— SYMPHONY NO. 1
                                        30:00 Composer.

SCRIABIN, Aleksandr N. - BOUTNIKOFF, Ivan
—— SCRIABINIANA: SUITE NO. 1 (IN 4 MOVTS)
    3(3rd alt. with picc.),*3,*3,*3 - 4,3,3,1 - timp.,perc.(3),cel.,glock. -
    2 hp. - str.   8:00 Arranger.
—— SCRIABINIANA: SUITE NO. 2 (VERS LA FLAMME) (IN 8
    MOVTS.)
    *3,*3,*3,2 - 4,2,3,1 - timp.,perc.(3),glock. - hp. - str.
                                        25:00 Arranger.

SCRIABIN, Aleksandr N. - STOKOWSKI, Leopold
—— ETUDE IN C SHARP MINOR, OP. 2, NO. 1
    *3, alto fl.,*3,*3,*3 - 4,3,3,1 - timp. - hp. - str.   5:00 Broude.

SCULL, Harold T.
—— CONCERTO IN A MINOR FOR PIANO AND ORCH., OP. 123
    2,2,2,2 - 4,2,3,0 - perc. - pf. - str.   30:00 P.R.S.
—— ENGLISH MINIATURE SUITE, OP. 117
    str.   8:00 P.R.S.
—— LONDON PAGEANTRY, OP. 165
    2,2,2,2 - 4,4,3,1 - hp. - org. - str.   6:30 P.R.S.
—— SOLEMN PRELUDE, OP. 76
    org. - str.   6:00 Galaxy.
—— SUITE IN D, OP. 110
    str.   25:00 P.R.S.
—— A TRUMPET PIECE, OP. 137-A
    2,2,2,2 - 4,2,3,0-1 - timp. - org. - str.   4:30 Galaxy.

SCULTHORPE, Peter
—— THE FIFTH CONTINENT (FOR NARRATOR AND ORCH.)
    (1963)
    0,1,0,0 - 0,1,0,0 - timp.,perc.(3) - hp. - str.   35:00 G. Schirmer.
—— FROM TABUH TABUHAN (1968)
    timp.,perc.,vibra. - str.   5:00 G. Schirmer.
—— IRKANDA IV (FOR VIOLIN, PERCUSSION AND STRINGS)
    perc. - str.   10:00 G. Schirmer.
—— LAMENT (FROM "RITES OF PASSAGE") (1975)
    str.   9:00 G. Schirmer.
—— LOVE 200 (FOR ROCK BAND, 2 SINGERS AND ORCH.)
    (1970)
    Orch.: 2,2,2,3 - 4,3,3,1 - timp.,perc.(4) - str.   20:00 G. Schirmer.
—— MUSIC FOR JAPAN (1970)
    3,3,3,3 - 4,4,3,1 - timp.,perc.(4) - str.   12:00 G. Schirmer.
    or:
    2,2,2,2 - 4,4,3,1 - timp.,perc.(4) - str.
—— OVERTURE FOR A HAPPY OCCASION (1970)
    2,2,2,2 - 2,2,2,1 - timp.,perc. - hp. - str.   4:00 G. Schirmer.
—— RAIN (1970)
    *3,2,2,*3 - 2,2,3,1 - perc.(3) - str.   14:00 G. Schirmer.
—— SMALL TOWN (FROM "THE FIFTH CONTINENT")
    0,1,0,0 - 0,1,0,0 - timp.,perc.(3) - hp. - str.   6:00 G. Schirmer.
—— SUN MUSIC FOR ORCHESTRA I (FOR BRASS, PERCUSSION
    AND STRINGS)
    0,0,0,0 - 4,3,3,1 - perc. - str.   10:00 G. Schirmer.
—— SUN MUSIC II (KETJAK FOR ORCH.)
    2,2,2,2 - 4,2,3,1 - timp.,perc.(4) - amplification(ad lib.) - str.
                                        6:00 G. Schirmer.
—— SUN MUSIC III (ANNIVERSARY MUSIC) (1967)
    2,2,2,2 - 3,2,2,0 - timp.,perc.(3) - str.   12:00 G. Schirmer.
—— SUN MUSIC IV (1967)
    2,2,2,2 - 4,3,3,1 - timp.,perc.(3) - str.   9:00 G. Schirmer.

SEAGRAVE, Malcolm R.
—— SYMPHONY NO. 1
    3,2,2,3 - 4,3,3,1 - timp.,perc. - hp. - str.   Belw-Mills.

SEAR, Walter E.
—— ARSIS AND THESIS (1952)
    *3,2,*3,3 - 4,3,3,1 - timp.,perc. - str.   12:00 Composer.
—— SYMPHONY NO. 2 FOR ORCH. (1953) (IN 4 MOVTS.)
    *3,2,*4,4 - 4,3,3,1 - timp.,perc. - str.   26:00 Composer.

SEARLE, Humphrey
—— CONCERTO IN D MINOR FOR PIANO AND ORCH., OP. 5
                                        24:00 Lengnick.
—— CONTEMPLATIONS, OP. 66 (FOR MEZZO-SOPRANO AND
    CHAMBER ORCH.)
    2,2,2,2 - 2,2,0,0 - timp.,perc. - hpsc. - str.   20:00 G. Schirmer.
—— FUGA GIOCOSA
    *2,*2,*2,*2 - 4,2,3,1 - timp.,perc.,cel. - pf. - str.   4:30 Galaxy.
—— GOLD COAST CUSTOMS (FOR NARRATOR, MEN'S CHORUS
    AND ORCH.)
                                        35:00 Lengnick.
—— HAMLET SUITE (1968) (FOR BARITONE AND ORCH.)
    2,2,2(2nd alt. with b.-cl.),sax.,2(2nd alt. with. c.-bn.) - 4,4,3,1 -
    timp.,perc.(5) - hp. - pf. - str.   15:00 G. Schirmer.
—— LABYRINTH, OP. 56
    3(alt. with 3 piccs, 1 alt. with fl.),3(1 alt. with E♭cl., 1 alt.
    with alto sax., 1 alt. with b.-cl.),*3 - 4,3,3,1 - timp.,perc.(6) - hp. -
    org. - pf. - str.   20:00 G. Schirmer.
—— NIGHT MUSIC (FOR CHAMBER ORCH.)
    1,1,1(alt. with b.-cl.),1 - 1,1,1,0 - timp. - str.   9:00 Galaxy.
—— NOCTURNE NO. 2
    2,1,2,2 - 2,1,1,0 - timp.,perc. - hp. - str.   8:00 Galaxy.
—— OVERTURE TO A DRAMA
    2,2,2,2 - 4,3,3,1 - timp.,perc. - str.   10:00 Galaxy.
—— POEM FOR TWENTY-TWO STRINGS
    str.   10:00 Galaxy.
—— THREE SONGS OF JOCELYN BROOKE
    *2,1,2,1(alt. with c.-bn.) - 1,1,0,0 - hp.(or pf.) - str.
                                        18:00 G. Schirmer.
—— ZODIAC VARIATIONS
    2 ob. - 2 hn. - str.   9:00 G. Schirmer.

SEBESKY, Don
—— WYETH'S WORLD (FOR SOPRANO, TENOR AND CHAMBER
    ORCH.) (1971) (IN 5 MOVTS.) (Text: Nancy Priddy)
    1,1,1,1 - 1,1,0,0 - perc.(1) - hp. - pf. - str.(2,1,1,0)
                                        17:30 Composer.

SECUNDA, Sholom
—— CHASSIDIC SUITE (IN 6 MOVTS.)
    str.   18:00 Composer.
—— CONCERTO IN C, FOR VIOLIN AND ORCH. (1969) (IN 1
    MOVT.)
    2,*3,2,2 - 4,3,3,0 - timp.,perc. - str.   14:00 Ethnic.
—— IF NOT HIGHER (ORATORIO) (FOR NARRATOR,
    MEZZO-SOPRANO, TENOR, BARITONE, SATB CHORUS
    AND ORCH.)
    2,2,2,2 - 4,3,3,0 - timp.,perc. - str.   45:00 Belw-Mills.
—— SULAMITH (GRAND OPERA) %
    2(alt. with 2 piccs.),2(2nd alt. with Eng. hn.),2,2 - 4,2,3,0 -
    timp.,perc.(2) - hp. - org. - str.   Composer.
—— YOM BAIBBUTZ ("A DAY AT A KIBBUTZ") (SYMPHONIC
    POEM)
    *3,*3,2,*3 - 4,3,3,0 - timp.,perc.(2),xyl. - hp. - pf. - str.
                                        18:00 Mills.

SEDSTRÖM, Hugo
—— CONCERT OVERTURE IN G MAJOR
    2,2,2,2 - 4,2,3,0 - timp. - str.   10:00 S.T.I.M.
—— SUITE NO. 1 (IN 4 MOVTS.)
    2,2,2,2 - 4,2,3,0 - timp. - str.   15:30 S.T.I.M.
—— SUITE NO. 2
    2,2,2,2 - 2,2,2,0 - timp. - str.   10:00 S.T.I.M.
—— SUITE NO. 3 (IN 4 MOVTS.)
    2,2,2,2 - 2,2,1,0 - timp. - str.   13:00 S.T.I.M.
—— SUITE NO. 4 ("LYRISKA STYCKEN") (IN 4 MOVTS.)
                                        13:00 Nordiska.

SEEBOTH, Max
—— CONCERTO IN C MAJOR FOR PIANO AND ORCH.
    2,2,2,2 - 4,3,3,1 - timp. - pf. - str.   30:00 Henmar.
—— DIVERTIMENTO NO. 1 (FOR CHAMBER ORCH.)
    0,0,2,0 - 2,0,0,0 - str.   32:00 Henmar.

—— DIVERTIMENTO NO. 2 (FOR STRING ORCH.)
    str.   23:00 Henmar.

SEELY, Scott B.
—— LENTO
    1,1,*2,1 - 1,0,0,0 - timp. - hp. - str.   6:00 S & R.
—— THE SILENT ONES (BALLET) %
    2,*2,*3,*2 - 1,3,2,0 - timp.,perc.(2) - pf. - 2 d.-b.   6:00 S & R.

SEGERSTAM, Leif
—— CAPRICCIO FOR SOPRANINO AND INSTRUMENTS (1968)
    1,1,1,0 - 0,2,0,0 - cel. - str.(1,1,1,1)   7:00 Fazer.
—— CONCERTO SERIOSO (FOR VIOLIN AND ORCH.) (1968)
    2,2,2,2 - 2,3,3,0 - timp.,perc.(4),cel. - hp. - str. 25:00 H.BuschMfl.
—— DIVERTIMENTO (1963)
    str.   12:00 FinnMICtr.
—— EQUILIBRISTIQUUM (1966)
    5,2,4,2 - 2,4,3,1 - timp.,perc. - str.   11:00 FinnMICtr.
—— PANDORA (BALLET) % (1967)
    3,3,3,3 - 4,3,3,1 - timp.,perc.(5),cel. - hp. - str. 23:00 FinnMICtr.
—— PANDORA (ESSAY FOR ORCHESTRA, OR BALLET IN ONE
    ACT)
    3(3rd alt. with picc.),*3,*3,*3 - 4,3,3,1 - timp.,perc.,cel. - hp. - str.
                                     41:00 G. Schirmer.
—— PATRIA
    3,3,3,3 - 4,3,3,1 - timp.,perc.(6),cel. - hp - pf. - str. FinnMICtr.
—— PATRIA
    3(3rd alt. with picc.),*3,*3,*3 - 4,3,3,1 - timp.,perc. - hp. - 2 pf.(1
    alt. with cel.) - str.   G. Schirmer.
—— SEVEN RED MOMENTS (SONG CYCLE FOR SOPRANO AND
    ORCH.) (REV. 1968) (Text: Viola Renwall and Gunnar Björling)
    2,2,2,2 - 2,3,3,0 - timp.,perc.(5),cel. - hp. - str.   20:00 Fazer.
—— SIX SONGS OF EXPERIENCE (FOR SOPRANO AND LARGE
    STEREOPHONICALLY-PLACED ORCHESTRA, WITHOUT
    CONDUCTOR) (1971) (Text: William Blake and W. H. Auden)
    2,2,2,2 - 2,3,3,1 - timp.,perc.(7),cel. - hp. - 2 pf. (amplified) - str.
                                     21:00 FinnMICtr.
—— SIX SONGS OF EXPERIENCE (FOR 5 VIOLINS AND ORCH.)
    2(alt. with 2 picc.),*2,*2,*2 - 2,3,3,1 - timp.,perc.(3) - 2 pf.(or cel.)
    - hp. - str.   G. Schirmer.
—— SKETCHES FROM "PANDORA"
    3(3rd alt. with picc.),*3,*3,*3 - 4,3,3,1 - timp.,perc.,cel. - hp. - str.
                                  20:00 G. Schirmer.
—— THREE PLUS, OR: FOUR NNNOWS (FOR HIGH
    MEZZO-SOPRANO AND CHAMBER ORCH.) (1972) (Text:
    Gunnar Björling)
    1,0,1,0 - 0,0,0,0 - perc.(3),cel. - hp. - str.(1,1,1,1) 7:00 FinnMICtr.
—— TWO; ONWARDS: INWARDS, OUTWARDS, (UPWARDS,
    DOWNWARDS,)...AROUNDWARDS....TOWARDS.... (FOR 2
    PIANOS ORCH. WITH MULTIPLE PERCUSSION AND 2 FULL
    STRING ORCHS.)
    2(2nd alt. with picc.),*2,*2,*2 - 2,3,3,1 - timp.,perc. - hp. 2 pf. -
    str. (min.:44,16,12,8)   G. Schirmer.

SEHLBACH, Erich
—— CONCERTINO FOR FLUTE, 2 OBOES AND ORCH.
    1,2,0,0 - 2,0,0,0 - perc. - str.   T & J.
—— CONCERTINO FOR OBOE AND ORCH., OP. 58
    0,1,2,0 - 2,0,0,0 - timp.,perc. - str.   17:00 Möseler.
—— KONZERTANTE PARTITA, OP. 55
    1,1,1,0 - 1,1,0,0 - timp. - str.   23:00 Möseler.
—— ORCHESTERFANTASIE IN C
    2,2,2,2 - 4,3,3,0 - perc. - str.   20:00 T & J.
—— ORCHESTERFANTASIE IN D
    2,2,2,2 - 4,2,2,0 - perc. - str.   14:00 T & J.
—— VORSPIEL FÜR ORCHESTER
    2,2,2,2 - 3,2,3,0 - perc. - str.   5:00 T & J.

SEIBER, Matyas
—— BESARDO: SUITE NO. 1
    2,2,2,2 - 2,2,2,0 - perc. - hp. - str.   16:00 Galaxy.
—— FAUST (SUITE) (FOR MIXED CHORUS AND ORCH.) (German
    Text: Goethe; Engl. Text: Louis MacNeice)
    2,3,3,1 - 4,3,3,1 - timp.,perc.(3),cel.,vibra.,xyl. - hp. - str.
                               24:00 Leeds.
—— FOUR GREEK FOLK SONGS (FOR HIGH VOICE AND
    STRINGS)
    str.   Bo. Hawkes.
—— TRANSYLVANIAN RHAPSODY
    2,2,2,2 - 4,2,3,1 - timp.,perc. - hp. - str.   9:00 Bo. Hawkes.

SEIBER, Matyas - DORATI, Antal
—— SINFONIETTA (TRANSCRIBED FROM QUARTET NO. 1)
    str.   17:00 Leeds.

SEIDEL, Jan
—— CONCERTO NO. 2 FOR OBOE AND ORCH.
    2,0,2,2 - 2,0,0,0 - hp. - str.   26:00 Bo. Hawkes.
—— PROLOGUE (SYMPHONY FOR ORCH.)
    3,3,4,3 - 4,3,3,1 - timp.,perc. - hp. - str.   45:00 Bo. Hawkes.

SELL, David
—— OSTINATO
    str.   4:00 A.P.R.A.

SEMENOFF, Ivan Kogan
—— CONCERTO FOR VIOLIN AND ORCH.
                          23:00 Henmar.

SEMLER-COLLERY, Jules
—— FANTAISIE ET DANSE EN FORME DE GIGUE (FOR
    CLARINET AND ORCH.)
    2,2,3,2 - 4,0,0,0 - timp. - hp. - str.   8:00 Baron.

SEMPRINI, Alberto
—— SINFONIETTA (FOR PIANO AND ORCH.)
    2,2,2,2 - 4,3,3,1 - timp.,perc. - hp. - pf. - str. 12:00 Bo. Hawkes.

SENAILLE, Jean Baptiste - PARKER, Howard
—— INTRODUCTION AND ALLEGRO SPIRITOSO (FOR
    BASSOON AND ORCH.)
                            Mills.

SENDREY, Albert
—— DIVERTIMENTO FOR CELLO AND ORCH.
    1,1,1,1 - 2,2,2,0 - timp. - hp. - str.   20:00 Composer.
—— JOHNNY APPLESEED OVERTURE
    *3,2,2,2 - 3,3,3,0 - timp.,perc.(4-5),xyl. - hp. - pf. - str.
                                10:00 Composer.
—— SINFONIETTA
    1,1,*2,1 - 2,2,2,0 - perc. - hp. - str.   20:00 EV.
—— SYMPHONY NO. 2 ("INTER-AMERICAN") (IN 4 MOVTS.)
    *3,*3,4,4 - 4,4,3,1 - timp.,perc.(6-7),cel.,glock. - hp. - org. - pf. -
    str.   30:00 Composer.
—— SYMPHONY NO. 3
    *3,*3,*3,*3 - 3,3,3,0 - timp.,perc.(4) - hp. - pf. - str.
                                30:00 Composer.

SENFL, Ludwig - DUBENSKY, Arcady
—— EWIGER GOTT, AUS DEM GEBOT (FOR STRINGS)
    str.   4:00 Arranger.
—— DAS GELÄUT ZU SPEIER ("THE BELLS OF SPEVER") (FOR
    STRINGS)
    str.   Ricordi.

SENIA, Paul A.
—— EPITAPH (FOR BASS VOICE AND ORCH.) (1953) (Text:
    Thomas Gray)
    1,*2,1,1 - 0,0,0,0 - str.(4,1,2,1)   9:00 Composer.
—— LAMENT FOR ORCHESTRA (1954)
    1,1,2,2 - 2,2,0,0 - str.   Composer.
—— ONCE UPON A CHRISTMAS (BALLET) (1969) %
    *3,2,*3,2 - 4,3,2,1 - timp.,perc.(3),bells,cel.,xyl. - hp. - str.
                               Composer.

SENSTIUS, Kai
—— CONCERTINO FOR FLUTE AND ORCH.
    1,1,1,1 - 1,0,0,0 - str.   18:00 Henmar.

SEREBRIER, José
—— POEMA ELEGIACO
                         10:00 Southern.

SERLY, Tibor
—— ALARMS AND EXCURSIONS
    3,*2,*3,3 - 4,3,3,1 - timp.,cel. - str.   8:00 Composer.
—— AMERICAN ELEGY
    3(3rd alt. with picc.),2,2,2 - 4,2,3,1 - timp.,perc.(4) - str.
                             8:00 ModusAssoc.
—— AMERICAN FANTASY OF QUODLIBETS (ON AMERICAN
    FOLKSONGS) (IN 5 MOVTS.)
    2(2nd alt. with picc.),2(2nd alt. with Eng.hn.),2,2 - 4,3,3,0 -
    timp.,perc.(3),bells,glock.,xyl. - str.   11:00 Sam.French.

—— CANONIC FUGUE IN TEN VOICES (IN MODUS LASCIVUS) (1973)
    str.(4,3,2,1)   4:00 J. Bilik.
—— COLONIAL PAGEANT SUITE (IN 3 MOVTS.)
    3(3rd alt. with picc.),2,3(3rd alt. with b.-cl.),*3 - 4,3,3,1 -
    timp.,perc.(2),xyl. - str.   16:00 Southern.
—— CONCERTINO 3 TIMES 3 (IN MODUS LASCIVUS) (FOR PIANO AND ORCH.) (1965) (IN 3 MOVTS.)
    2(2nd alt.with picc.),1(alt.with Eng.hn.),2,1 - 1,1,1,0 -
    timp.,perc.(2),bells,xyl. - pf. - str.   30:00 Fr. & Thos.
—— CONCERTO FOR TROMBONE AND CHAMBER ORCH.
    1. Allegro moderato; 2. Lento parlando; 3. Allegro
    2(2nd alt. with picc.),1,2,1 - 1,0,1,0 - timp.,perc.(2),xyl. - str.
                      16:00 Southern.
—— CONCERTO FOR VIOLA AND ORCH.
    1. Moderato ma risoluto; 2. Andante sostenuto; 3. Allegro
    2,2,2,2 - 2,2,0,0 - timp.,perc.(2),glock. - str. 22:00 ModusAssoc.
—— CONCERTO FOR VIOLIN AND ORCH. (IN 2 MOVTS.)
    *3,2,2,*3 - 4,3,1,0 - timp. - hp. - 1 vln. 14:00 ModusAssoc.
—— CONCERTO FOR 2 PIANOS AND ORCH.
    2,2,2,2 - 2,1,0,0 - 2 pf. - str.   25:00 Composer.
—— CONTRAPUNTAL DIVERTIMENTO FOR WINDS AND PERCUSSION (SYMPHONY IN 2 MOVTS.)
    2,2,2,2 - 2,2,1,0- timp.,perc.(2),glock.,xyl. 11:00 ModusAssoc.
—— FOUR SONGS FROM "CHAMBER MUSIC" (FOR HIGH VOICE AND CHAMBER ORCH.)
    fl.,cl. - hn. - str.   8:00 Composer.
—— FUGUE FOR STRINGS
    str.   4:00 Composer.
—— LAMENT ("HOMAGE TO BELA BARTOK") (FOR STRINGS)
    str.   8:30 Southern.
—— A LITTLE CHRISTMAS CANTATA (FOR AUDIENCE, CHORUS AND ORCH.)
                    7:00 G. Schirmer.
—— MIDNIGHT MADRIGAL (FOR TRUMPET AND ORCH.)
    1,1,2,1 - 2,3,2,0 - timp.,perc. - pf. - str. 5:00 Mills.
—— PAGAN CITY (SYMPHONIC POEM) (Composed with John Klenner)
    3(3rd alt. with picc.),3(3rd alt. with Eng. hn.),3(3rd alt. with
    b.-cl.),*3 - 4,3,3,1 - timp.,perc.(3),cel.,xyl. - hp. - str.
                    15:00 Composer.
—— RHAPSODY FOR VIOLA AND ORCHESTRA
    2,2,2,2 - 2,2,0,0 - timp.,perc.(2),xyl. - str. 10:00 Southern.
—— RHAPSODY ON FOLK SONGS HARMONIZED BY BELA BARTOK (FOR VIOLA AND ORCH.)
    1,1,1,1 - 1,1,0,0 - timp.,perc. - hp. - str. 8:00 Southern.
—— SIX DANCE DESIGNS
    *4,*3,*3(1 alt. with E$\flat$cl.),*3 - 4,3,3,b.-trb.(ad lib.),1 -
    timp.,perc.(4),cel.,vibra.,xyl. - hp. - str. 12:00 ModusAssoc.
—— SONATA CONCERTANTE FOR STRING ORCH.
    1. Moderato; 2. Andante; 3. Vivace
    str.   16:00 ModusAssoc.
—— STRANGE STORY (FOR MEZZO SOPRANO AND ORCH.)
    3(3rd alt. with picc.),2,2,2 - 4,3,3,1 - timp.,perc.(3),xyl. - hp. - str.
                    12:00 Composer.
—— STRING SYMPHONY, FOR YOUNG PEOPLE
    str.   16:00 Composer.
—— SYMPHONIC VARIATIONS (QUODLIBET) (FOR AUDIENCE AND ORCH.)
    *3,2,2,2 - 4,3,3,1 - timp.,perc.(3),xyl. - str. 10:00 G. Schirmer.
—— SYMPHONY FOR WINDS AND PERCUSSION
    1. Slow; 2. Fast
    3(3rd alt. with picc.),2,2,3(3rd alt. with c.-bn.) - 4,3,3,1 -
    timp.,perc.,xyl.   12:00 Southern.
—— SYMPHONY NO. 1 (IN 3 MOVTS.)
    *4,3(3rd alt. with Eng. hn.),3(3rd alt. with b.-cl.),3(3rd alt. with
    c.-bn.) - 4,3,3,1 - timp.,perc.(4),cel.,xyl. - hp. - str.
                    19:00 ModusAssoc.
—— TRANSYLVANIAN SUITE (FOR CHAMBER ORCH.)
    2(2nd alt. with picc.),2,0,0 - 2,1,0,0 - timp. - str.
                    9:00 ModusAssoc.

SERMILÄ, Jarmo
—— EARLY MUSIC (1971)
    2 fl. - str.   11:00 FinnMICtr.
—— HOMAGE TO EV (1971)
    0,0,0,0 - 2,2,3,0 - timp.,perc.(4),xyl. 9:00 FinnMICtr.
—— MIMESIS II
    3,3,3,3 - 4,3,3,0 - timp.,perc.(5) - hp. - str. 14:00 FinnMICtr.

SERRES, L. de
—— SIX POÈMES (FOR HIGH VOICE AND ORCH.)
                    Salabert.

SERRETTE, François
—— MOUVEMENT (FOR ORGAN AND STRINGS)
    org. - str.   Presser.

SERVOZ, H.
—— SYMPHONIC POEM
    3,3,3,3 - 4,3,3,1 - timp.,perc. - hp. - str. 15:00 Salabert.

SESSIONS, Roger
—— SYMPHONY NO. 2
    3,3,3,3 - 4,3,3,1 - timp.,perc. - str. 30:00 G. Schirmer.

SETER STAROMINSKY, Mordecai
—— THE DAUGHTER OF JEPHTHA (BALLET) %
    1,1,1,1 - 1,1,0,0 - perc.(1) - str. 15:00 Bo. Hawkes.
—— ELEGY FOR VIOLA AND STRINGS
    str.   13:00 Bo. Hawkes.
—— FANTASIA CONCERTANTE
    3,3,2,3 - 2,2,3,1 - timp.,perc.,cel. - hp. - str. 23:00 Bo. Hawkes.
—— JUDITH (SYMPHONIC CHACONNE)
    2,2,2,2 - 4,2,3,1 - timp.,perc.,cel. - hp. - pf. - str.
                    20:00 Bo. Hawkes.
—— JUDITH (SYMPHONIC CHACONNE) (1966)
    3,3,3,3 - 4,2,2,1 - timp.,perc.(4),cel. - hp. - pf. - str.
                    22:00 Bo. Hawkes.
—— THE LEGEND OF JUDITH
    2,2,2,2 - 4,2,3,1 - timp.,perc.,cel. - hp. - pf. - str.
                    35:00 Bo. Hawkes.
—— MIDNIGHT VIGIL (ORATORIO) (FOR TENOR, SATB CHORUS AND ORCH.)
    3,3,3,3 - 4,2,3,1 - timp.,perc.,cel. - hp. - pf. - str.
                    40:00 Bo. Hawkes.
—— MIDNIGHT VIGIL (RHAPSODY ON YEMENITE THEMES)
    3,3,2,2 - 2,2,2,0 - timp.,perc.,cel. - hp. - pf. - str.
                    14:00 Bo. Hawkes.
—— RICERCARE
    str.,(no d.-b.)   19:00 Bo. Hawkes.
—— SABBATH CANTATA (FOR SOLO VOICES, CHORUS AND STRING ORCH.)
    str.   31:00 Bo. Hawkes.
—— SINFONIETTA
    3,3,3,3 - 4,2,2,1 - timp.,perc.,cel. - pf. - str. 14:00 Bo. Hawkes.
—— SINFONIETTA (1966)
    3,3,3,3 - 4,2,2,1 - timp.,perc.,cel. - pf. - str. 21:00 Bo. Hawkes.
—— VARIATIONS FOR ORCH.
    2,2,2,2 - 1,1,1,1 - timp.,perc.(2),cel. - hp. - pf. - str.
                    14:00 Bo. Hawkes.
—— YEMENITE SUITE
    1,1,1,1 - 1,0,0,0 - perc.(2) - pf. - str. 17:00 Bo. Hawkes.

SEUEL-HOLST, Marie
—— IN ELFLAND, OP. 26 (MINIATURE CONCERTO FOR PIANO AND STRING ORCH.)
                    Summy-Bir.

SÉVERAC, Déodat de
—— FÊTE DES VENDANGES ET DANSE DES TREILLES (BALLET FROM "COEUR DU MOULIN") %
    3,2,2,2 - 4,4,4,0 - timp.,perc.,xyl. - 2 hp. - str. 12:30 Salabert.

SEVERN, Edmund
—— CONCERTO IN D MINOR FOR VIOLIN AND ORCH.
    1. Allegro energico; 2. Andante espressivo; 3. Allegro
    2(2nd alt. with picc.),2(2nd alt. with Eng. hn.),2,2 - 4,2,3,1 - timp.
    - hp. - str.   25:00 C. Fischer.
—— FROM OLD NEW ENGLAND (SUITE) (IN 4 MOVTS.)
    2,2(2nd alt. with Eng. hn.),2,2 - 4,2,3,1 - timp.,perc. - hp. - str.
                    25:00 Composer.

SEVITZKY, Fabien
—— COLOMBIA OVERTURE
    2,2,2,2 - 4,3,3,1 - timp.,perc. - hp. - str. 8:30 Composer.

SEVIUS, Sven
—— CONCERTINO FOR TRUMPET AND ORCH.
    2,2,2,2 - 2,2,1,0 - timp.,perc. - str. 10:00 Fleisher.

SEYMER, William
—— DALASOMMAR (SUITE)
    2,2,2,2 - 4,2,3,0 - timp.,perc.,cel. - pf. - str. 20:00 S.T.I.M.
—— MINIATYRER (SUITE)
    2,1,2,1 - 2,2,2,0 - timp.,perc. - str. 11:00 S.T.I.M.

SEYMOUR, John L.
—— THE MAID, THE DEMON AND THE SAMURAI, OP. 43
(BALLET SUITE)
*3,*3,*3,*3 - 4,3,3,1 - timp.,perc.(3),glock. - hp. - str.
60:00 Composer.

SEYNES, Georges de
—— PAGES D'ORCHESTRE (IN 3 MOVTS.)
2,2,2,2 - 2,2,3,0 - timp.,perc.(3) - hp. - str.   Baron.

SFETSAS, Kyriacos
—— DOCIMOLOGIE
2,1,0,1 - 0,1,0,0 - perc.(2) - electric guit. - pf. - str.(1,1,1,1)
12:00 Presser.
—— SÉQUENCES PICTURALES
1,1,2,0 - 1,1,2,1 - perc. - electric org. - pf. - str.(2,1,1,1)
14:00 Presser.

SGRIZZI, Luciano
—— CAPRICCIO (FOR FLUTE AND CHAMBER ORCH.)
fl. - timp.,perc.,cel. - pf. - str.   11:40 Leeds.
—— SINFONIETTA ROCOCO FÜR KLEINES ORCH.
1,1,1,1 - 0,0,0,0 - str.   14:00 J. Oertel.
—— SUITE NAPOLETANA (NEAPOLITAN SUITE)
1,1,1,1 - 0,0,0,0 - str.   13:00 Leeds.

SHAFFER, Sherwood
—— ADONIA (TONE POEM)
*3,*3,*3,*3 - 4,2,3,1 - timp.,perc.(4) - hp. - str.   25:00 Composer.
—— CONCERTANTE FOR CELLO AND CHAMBER ORCH. (IN 3
MOVTS.)
1,1,1,1 - 1,0,0,0 - str.   16:00 Composer.
—— CONCERTANTE FOR PIANO AND CHAMBER ORCH. (IN 3
MOVTS.)
1,1,1,1 - 1,0,0,0 - pf. - str.   18:00 Composer.
—— CONCERTO DA CAMERA (FOR VIOLIN AND STRING
ORCH.) (IN 3 MOVTS.)
str.   18:00 Composer.
—— CONCERTO GROSSO FOR STRING ORCH. (IN 3 MOVTS.)
str.   14:00 Composer.

SHAHAN, Paul
—— LAZARROTH (CANTATA) (FOR VOICE AND ORCH.)
2,2,2,2 - 4,3,3,1 - timp.,perc.(4),cel. - str.   8:00 Composer.
—— NOCTURNE FOR FRENCH HORN AND STRING
ORCHESTRA (IN 3 MOVTS.)
hn. - str.   13:00 Composer.
—— SOLILOQUY FOR TRUMPET AND STRING ORCHESTRA
tpt. - str.   6:30 Composer.
—— SYMPHONY NO. 1 (IN 3 MOVTS.)
*3,2,2,2 - 4,3,3,1 - timp.,perc.(4),cel. - str.   26:00 Composer.
—— THREE PORTRAITS FOR ORCHESTRA
*3,2,2,2 - 4,3,3,1 - timp.,perc.(3),xyl. - str.   13:00 Composer.
—— TWO MASKERS (IL PENSEROSO AND L'ALLEGRO)
*3,2,2,2 - 4,3,3,1 - timp.,perc.(3) - str.   14:00 Composer.
—— TWO SYMPHONIC MINIATURES (FOR CHAMBER ORCH.)
2,2,2,2 - 2,1,1,0 - timp.,perc.(2) - str.   10:00 Composer.

SHAKESPEARE, W. - The Composer
—— HAMLET (DRAMATIC OVERTURE)
2,2,2,2 - 4,2,3,0 - timp. - org. - str.   Novello.

SHALLENBERG, Robert
—— DIVISIONS (FOR SMALL ORCH.) (1963) (IN 4 MOVTS.)
2(2nd alt.with picc.),1,2(2nd alt.with b.-cl.),1 - 2,1,1,0 -
timp.,perc.(2),glock.,mar.,vibra.,xyl. - pf. - str.   CMP.

SHANET, Howard
—— SIX VARIATIONS ON A BIZARRE THEME
*2,2,2,2 - 4,2,3,0 - timp.,perc. - pf. - str.   10:00 AmerMusEd.

SHAPERO, Harold
—— CONCERTO FOR ORCH.
1. Maestoso - Allegro; 2. Lento; 3. Allegro risoluto
*3,2,2,*3 - 4,2,3,1 - timp. - str.   27:00 Southern.
—— CREDO FOR SMALL ORCH.
*2,0,2,1 - 1,2,1,1 - timp. - str.   7:00 Southern.
—— NINE-MINUTE OVERTURE
*3,*3,E♭cl.,2,*3 - 4,3,3,1 - timp.,perc.(3) - pf. - str. 9:00 Southern.
—— ON GREEN MOUNTAIN (CHACONNE, AFTER
MONTEVERDI)
1,0,0,1 alto. sax.,1 ten.sax.,1 - 1,1,1,0 - perc.,vibra. - guit. - hp. -
pf. - d.-b.   9:00 Southern.

—— PARTITA IN C, FOR PIANO AND ORCH.
1,1,1,1 - 1,1,1,0 - timp.,perc. - hp. - pf. - str.   17:00 Southern.
—— SERENADE IN D (FOR STRINGS)
1. Adagio - Allegro; 2. Allegretto; 3. Andante; 4. Con moto;
5. Allegro assai
str.   28:00 Southern.
—— SINFONIA IN C MINOR
3,2,2,3 - 4,2,3,0 - timp. - str.   11:00 Southern.
—— SYMPHONY IN B FLAT FOR CLASSICAL ORCH. (IN 4
MOVTS.)
*3,2,2,*3 - 2,2,3,0 - timp. - str.   40:00 Southern.
—— THE TRAVELERS (OVERTURE)
*3,2,2,*3 - 4,2,3,0 - timp. - str.   11:00 G. Schirmer.

SHAPERO, Howard
—— PARTITA IN C (FOR PIANO AND SMALL ORCH.) (IN 8
MOVTS.)
1(alt. with picc.),1(alt. with Eng.hn.),1,1 - 1,1,1,0 -
timp.,perc.(2),glock.,vibra.,xyl. - hp. - pf. - str.   17:00 Southern.

SHAPIRO, Michael Jeffrey
—— CONCERTO FOR TWO GUITARS AND STRINGS (1972) (IN 3
MOVTS.)
2 guit. - str.   17:00 Composer.
—— DUBLIN SONGS (4 SONGS FOR SOPRANO AND ORCH.)
(1972)
2,2,2,2 - 2,1,0,1 - hp. - pf. - str.   7:00 Composer.
—— LAMENTATIONS (1975)
*3,2,2,*3 - 4,3,3,1 - timp.,perc.(3) - hp. - pf. - str. 8:00 Composer.
—— THERE IS THAT IN ME (FOR 3 MEN, 3 WOMEN, SATB
CHORUS, BRASS, PERCUSSION AND PIANO) (1974) (Text:
Walt Whitman)
0,0,0,0 - 4,3,3,1 - timp.,perc.(2) - pf.   7:00 Composer.

SHAPORIN, Yurian
—— ON THE FIELD OF KULIKOVO, OP. 14 (CANTATA)
G. Schirmer.

SHAW, Martin
—— THE EASTER ANTHEMS (CHRIST, OUR PASSOVER) (FOR 2
TENORS, MIXED CHORUS AND ORCH.)
Oxford.
—— GO FORTH WITH GOD! (FOR CHORUS AND ORCH.) (Text:
Barclay Baron)
Oxford.
—— THE REDEEMER (FOR SATB CHORUS AND ORCH.)
2,2,2,2 - 4,2,3,1 - timp. - hp. - str.   48:00 Galaxy.

SHAW, Robert - BENNETT, Robert Russell
—— MANY MOODS OF CHRISTMAS: SUITE NO. 1
*3,*3,*3,*3 - 4,3,3,1 - timp.,perc.(4) - hp. - org. - str.
12:00 Law-Gould.
—— MANY MOODS OF CHRISTMAS: SUITE NO. 2
3(3rd alt. with picc.),*3,*3,*3 - 4,3,3,1 - timp.,perc.(4) - hp. - str.
11:00 Law-Gould.
—— MANY MOODS OF CHRISTMAS: SUITE NO. 3
3(3rd alt. with picc.),*3,*3,*3 - 4,3,3,1 - timp.,perc.(4) - lute - hp. -
str.   13:00 Law-Gould.
—— MANY MOODS OF CHRISTMAS: SUITE NO. 4
3,*3,*3,*3 - 4,3,3,1 - timp.,perc.(4) - hp. - org. - str.
12:00 Law-Gould.

SHCHEDRIN, Rodion
—— CHAMBER SUITE
Accord. - hp. - 20 vln.,2 d.-b.   12:00 G. Schirmer.
—— THE CHIMES
MCA Music.
—— THE HUMPBACKED HORSE (BALLET SUITE)
3,3,3,3 - 4,3,3,1 - timp.,perc.,cel.,xyl. - 2 hp. - pf. - str.
23:00 G. Schirmer.
—— MISCHIEVIOUS MELODIES ("FOLK DITTIES") (A
CONCERTO FOR ORCHESTRA)
3,3,3,3 - 4,4,4,0 - timp.,perc. - hp. - pf. - str.   9:00 G. Schirmer.
—— NOT LOVE ALONE (SYMPHONIC SUITE FROM THE
OPERA) (WITH MEZZO-SOPRANO SOLO)
3,3,3,3 - 4,3,3,1 - timp.,perc.,cel.,xyl. - hp. - pf. - str.
35:00 G. Schirmer.
—— NOT LOVE ALONE (3-ACT OPERA) % (Text: V. Katanyan)
G. Schirmer.
—— SYMPHONY NO. 2 (25 PRELUDES FOR ORCHESTRA)
3,3,4,3 - 4,4,4,1 - timp.,perc.,xyl. - hp. - 2 pf. - str.   G. Schirmer.

SHEBALIN, Vissarion
—— CONCERTO FOR VIOLIN AND ORCH., OP. 21 (IN 3 MOVTS.)
*3,*3,*3,*3 - 4,3,3,1 - timp.,perc. - hp. - str.   35:00 G. Schirmer.
—— SYMPHONY NO. 2, OP. 11
3,3,3,3 - 4,3,3,1 - timp.,perc. - pf. - str.   G. Schirmer.

SHEPHERD, Arthur
—— FANTASY ON "DOWN EAST" SPIRITUALS
3(3rd alt. with picc.),*3,2,2 - 4,3,3,1 - timp.,perc.(3),cel.,glock. -
hp. - pf. - str.   15:00 AmerMusEd.
—— HORIZIONS (SYMPHONY NO. 1) (IN 4 MOVTS.)
3(3rd alt. with picc.),*3,*3,sax.,*3 - 4,D tpt.,4,3,1 - timp.,perc.(4) -
2 hp. - org. - pf. - str.   AmerMusEd.
—— OVERTURE TO A DRAMA
3(1 alt. with picc.),*3,*3,*3 - 4,3,3,1 - timp.,perc. - 2 hp. - str.
12:00 AmerMusEd.
—— TRIPTYCH (FOR HIGH VOICE AND STRINGS)
str.   17:00 SPAM.

SHERIFF, Noam
—— FESTIVAL PRELUDE
3,3,3,3 - 4,3,3,1 - timp.,perc.,cel. - hp. - str.   10:00 IsMuPublns.
—— HEPTAPRISMS (BALLET) %
2,2,2,1 - 1,1,1,0 - perc. - pf. - str.   20:00 Bo. Hawkes.
—— METAMORPHOSIS ON A GALLIARD
3,3,3,3 - 4,3,3,1 - timp.,perc.,cel. - hp. - hpsc. - str.
20:00 A.C.U.M.
—— MUSIC FOR WOODWINDS, TROMBONE, PIANO AND BASS
3,3,3,3 - 0,0,1,0 - pf. - d.-b.   16:00 Bo. Hawkes.
—— SONG OF DEGREES
3,*3,0(2 b.-cl.),0(2 c.-bn.) - 4,3,3,1 - timp.,perc.,cel.,xyl. - hp. - str.
10:00 IsMuPublns.

SHERMAN, Garry
—— IDIOMS (1969)
*3(1 alt. with bass fl. and 1 alt. with alto. fl.),*2,2,1 bar. sax.,0 -
4,3,3,1 - timp.,perc.(4),glock.,trap-drums,xyl. - electric d.-b. -
electric guit. - str.(incl. amplified string quartet)   12:00 Composer.

SHERWOOD, Gordon
—— INTRODUCTION AND ALLEGRO
*3,2,2,2 - 4,2,3,1 - timp.,perc. - pf. - str.   10:00 Chappell.

SHEVITZ, Arnold
—— OVERTURE ("IN AMERICAN STYLE")
2,2,2,2 - 4,3,3,0 - timp.,perc.(2) - pf. - str.(no d.-b.)
6:00 Composer.

SHIBATA, Minao
—— SINFONIA
2,2,2,2 - 3,3,3,0 - perc.(8) - str.   12:00 Presser.

SHILKRET, Nathaniel
—— CHRISTMAS OVERTURE
1(alt. with picc.),1(alt. with Eng. hn.),1(alt. with b.-cl.),2 - 4,3,3,1 -
timp.,perc.(2-3) - hp. - org.(ad lib.) - str.   Shilkret.
—— CONCERTO FOR TROMBONE AND ORCH. (IN 3 MOVTS.)
2(2nd alt. with picc.),*3,*3,2 - 4,3,3,1 - timp.,perc.(3) - str.
18:00 Shilkret.
—— CREATION (FOR NARRATOR, CHORUS AND ORCH.)
(Second movement from "GENESIS", suite)
3(3rd alt. with picc. and 2nd alt. with alto fl.),2(2nd alt. with Eng.
hn.),*3,2(2nd alt. with c.-bn.) - 4,3,3,1 - timp.,perc.,cel.,vibra. - hp.
- novachord (ad lib.) - pf. - str.   10:00 Shilkret.
—— FOUR POEMS FOR VIOLIN AND ORCH.
2,2,2,2 - 4 hn. - timp.,perc.(2) - hp. - str.   Shilkret.
—— NEW YORK BALLET (6: 30 PM TO 6: 30 AM) %
*3,1(alt. with Eng. hn.),*3,0 - 4,3,3,1 - timp.,perc. - hp. - str.
38:00 Shilkret.
—— ODE TO VICTORY
*3,2,*3,2 - 4,3,4,1 - timp.,perc.(3),cel. - hp. - str.   6:30 Mills.
—— SERENADE RHAPSODIC (CONCERTO FOR BANJO AND
ORCH.)
2(1 alt. with picc),*3,*3,2 - 4,3,3,1 - timp.,perc.(4) - banjo - hp. -
str.   8:30 Shilkret.
—— SKYWARD (SYMPHONIC POEM)
1(alt. with picc.),1(alt. with Eng. hn.),*3,2 - 4,3,3,1 -
timp.,perc.(3-4) - hp. - 1-2 pf. - str.   9:00 Shilkret.

SHIMOYAMA, Hifumi
—— REFLECTION (FOR 3 STRING ORCHESTRAS) (1968)
str.(30,15,12,9)   9:00 MCA Music.

SHIRLEY, Henry
—— CONCERTO FOR PIANO AND ORCH.
30:00 A.P.R.A.

SHISHAKOV, Yuri
—— CONCERTO FOR BALALAIKA AND RUSSIAN
FOLK-ORCHESTRA
1,1,0,0 - 0,0,0,0 - timp.,perc. - 6 domra. 2 bayan, 6 balalaikas, 1
gusli   12:00 G. Schirmer.

SHLONSKY, Verdina
—— REFLEXION SYMPHONIQUE
2,1,1,1 - 1,1,1,0 - perc.,cel. - pf. - str.   15:00 A.C.U.M.

SHNAPER, Boris I.
—— SYMPHONY NO. 3 (FOR SMALL ORCH.)
G. Schirmer.

SHORT, Michael
—— BRUTON TOWN (RHAPSODY FOR ORCH.)(1966)
2,2,3,2 - 4,2,3,1 - timp. - str.   15:00 P.R.S.
—— SANS AMOUR ET SANS HAINE (1966)
str.   18:00 P.R.S.

SHOSTAKOVICH, Dmitri D.
—— BALLET RUSSE (SUITE) (1949-50)
2,1,2,1 - 3,2,2,1 - timp.,perc.,cel.,xyl. - pf. - str.
18:00 G. Schirmer.
—— BALLET SUITE NO. 1 (IN 6 MOVTS.)
2,1,2,1 - 3,2,2,1 - timp.,perc.,cel.,xyl. - pf. - str.
20:00 G. Schirmer.
—— BALLET SUITE NO. 2 (IN 6 MOVTS.)
2,1,2,1 - 3,2,2,1 - timp.,perc.,cel.,xyl. - pf. - str.
12:00 G. Schirmer.
—— BALLET SUITE NO. 3
2,2,2,2 - 4,3,3,1 - timp.,perc.,cel.,xyl. - hp. - pf. - str. G. Schirmer.
—— BALLET SUITE NO. 4
3,3,2,3 - 4,3,3,1 - timp.,perc.,cel.,xyl. - hp. - str.
16:00 G. Schirmer.
—— BALLET SUITE NO. 5 (FROM "THE BOLT"), OP. 27-A (IN 8
MOVTS.)
3,3,4,3 - 6,3,3,1 - timp.,perc.,xyl. - str. and Stage Band
27:00 G. Schirmer.
—— CONCERTO FOR VIOLIN AND ORCH., OP. 99
1. Moderato; 2. Allegro; 3. Andante; 4. Allegro con brio
3,3,3,3 - 4,0,0,1 - timp.,perc.,cel. - 2 hp. - str.   35:00 Leeds.
—— CONCERTO IN E FLAT FOR CELLO AND ORCH., OP. 107
(Solo Part Edited by M. Rostropovich)
1. Allegretto; 2. Moderato
2,2,2,2 - 1,0,0,0 - timp.,cel. - str.   27:00 Leeds.
—— CONCERTO NO. 1 FOR PIANO, STRINGS AND TRUMPET,
OP. 35 (Edited by Vivian Rivkin)
1. Allegretto; 2. Lento; 3. Moderato; 4. Allegro con brio
tpt. - pf. - str.   21:00 G. Schirmer.
—— CONCERTO NO. 2 FOR CELLO AND ORCH., OP. 126
2,2,2,3 - 2,0,0,0 - timp.,perc.,xyl. - 2 hp. - str. 37:00 MCA Music.
—— CONCERTO NO. 2 FOR PIANO AND ORCH., OP. 102
*3,2,2,2 - 4,0,0,0 - timp.,perc. - pf. - str.   16:00 Leeds.
—— EIGHT ENGLISH AND AMERICAN FOLKSONGS (FOR
VOICE AND CHAMBER ORCH.)
G. Schirmer.
—— THE EXECUTION OF STEPHAN RAZIN, OP. 119 (POEM FOR
BASS, CHORUS AND ORCH.)
3,3,4,3 - 4,3,3,1 - timp.,perc.,cel. - 2 hp. - pf. - str.
30:00 G. Schirmer.
—— THE FALL OF BERLIN (SUITE FROM THE FILM)
3,3,3,2 - 4,3,3,1 - timp.,perc.,cel.,xyl. - hp. - str.   G. Schirmer.
—— THE GADFLY (SUITE FROM THE FILM), OP. 97-A
3,3,3,3 - 4,4,3,1 - timp.,perc.,cel.,xyl. - hp. - pf. - str.
40:00 G. Schirmer.
—— THE GOLDEN MOUNTAINS (SUITE FROM THE FILM), OP.
30-A (IN 6 MOVTS.)
3,3,3,3 sax.(1 sopr.,1 alto,1 ten.),3 - 8,4,4,2 - timp.,perc.,xyl. -
guit.(hawaiian) - 2 hp. - org. - str.   G. Schirmer.
—— HAMLET (SUITE FROM SHAKESPEARE'S TRAGEDY), OP.
32-A
1,1,1,1 - 2,2,1,1 - timp.,perc. - str.   21:00 G. Schirmer.
—— KATERINA ISMAILOVA: FIVE ENTR'ACTS FROM THE
OPERA
3,3,4,3 - 4,3,3,1 - timp.,perc.,cel.,xyl. - 2 hp. - str. and stage band
15:00 G. Schirmer.

—— KATERINA ISMAILOVA, OP. 29/114 (4-ACT OPERA)(REV. 1962) % (Revised version of "Lady MacBeth of Mtsensk")
  3,3,4,3 - 4,3,3,1 - timp.,perc.,cel.,xyl. - 2 hp. - str.
  135:00 G. Schirmer.
  On stage: 2 alto sax.,2 ten. sax., - 2 tpt.,4 cnt., 2 bar., 2 b.
—— THE NOSE, OP. 15 (SUITE FROM THE OPERA) (IN 3 MOVTS.)
  1,1,1,2 - 1,1,1,0 - perc. - 2 hp. - pf. - str.
  G. Schirmer.
—— THE NOSE (OPERA) %
  G. Schirmer.
—— OVERTURE FESTIVO, OP. 96
  3,3,3,3 - 4,3,3,1 - timp.,perc. - str.
  6:00 G. Schirmer.
—— OVERTURE ON RUSSIAN AND KIRGHIZ FOLK THEMES, OP. 115
  3,2,2,3 - 4,2,3,1 - timp.,perc. - str.
  9:00 G. Schirmer.
—— SONG OF THE FORESTS, OP. 81 (ORATORIO) (FOR MIXED CHORUS, SOLOISTS AND ORCH.)
  3,3,3,2 - 4,3,3,1 - timp.,perc.,cel.,xyl. - hp. - str.
  40:00 G. Schirmer.
—— SYMPHONY NO. 3 ("MAY DAY") FOR CHORUS AND ORCH.), OP. 20 (IN 1 MOVT.) (Edited by Harold Sheldon)
  *3,2,2,2 - 4,2,3,1 - timp.,perc.(4) - str.
  28:00 G. Schirmer.
—— SYMPHONY NO. 4, OP. 43 (REVISED VERSION)
  6 (incl. 2 picc.),4,6,4 - 8,4,3,2 - timp.,perc.,cel.,xyl. - 2 hp. - str.
  60:00 G. Schirmer.
—— SYMPHONY NO. 6, OP. 53 (IN 3 MOVTS.) (Edited by Harold Sheldon)
  *3,*3,*4(3rd alt. with E♭ cl.),3(3rd alt. with c.-bn.) - 4,3,3,1 - timp.,perc.(6),cel.,xyl. - hp. - str.
  33:00 G. Schirmer.
—— SYMPHONY NO. 7, OP. 60 (Ed. by Harold Sheldon)
  1. Allegretto; 2. Moderato (Poco Allegretto); 3. Adagio; 4. Allegro non troppo
  3(3rd alt. with picc.),*3,*4(3rd alt. with E♭ cl.),*3 - 8,6,6,1 - timp.,perc.(5),xyl. - 2 hp. - pf. - str.
  72:00 G. Schirmer.
—— SYMPHONY NO. 8, OP. 65
  1. Adagio; 2. Allegretto; 3. Allegro non troppo; 4. Largo; 5. Allegretto
  2,*3,E♭ cl.,3,3 - 4,3,3,1 - timp.,perc.,xyl. - str. 64:00 G. Schirmer.
—— SYMPHONY NO. 9, OP. 70 (Edited by Harold Sheldon)
  1. Allegro; 2. Moderato; 3. Presto; 4. Largo; 5. Allegretto
  *3,2,2,2 - 4,2,3,1 - timp.,perc. - str. 24:00 G. Schirmer.
—— SYMPHONY NO. 10, OP. 93
  3,3,3,3 - 4,3,3,1 - timp.,perc.,xyl. - str. 50:00 G. Schirmer.
—— SYMPHONY NO. 11, OP. 103
  3,3,3,3 - 4,3,3,1 - perc.,cel.,xyl. - hp. - str. 60:00 G. Schirmer.
—— SYMPHONY NO. 12, OP. 112 ("THE YEAR 1917")
  3(3rd alt. with picc.),3,3,3(3rd alt. with c.-bn.) - 4,3,3,1 - timp.,perc. - str. 40:00 G. Schirmer.
—— SYMPHONY NO. 13, OP. 113 (FOR BASS VOICE, CHORUS AND ORCH.) (Text: Evgeny Evtushenko)
  55:00 MCA Music.
—— SYMPHONY NO. 14, OP. 135
  55:00 MCA Music.
—— SYMPHONY NO. 15, OP. 141
  43:00 MCA Music.
—— THE YOUNG LADY AND THE HOOLIGAN (CHOREOGRAPHIC NOVELLA, AFTER MAYAKOVSKY) %
  3,3,3,3 - 4,3,3,1 - timp.,perc.,cel.,vibra.,xyl. - hp. - pf. - str.
  G. Schirmer.

SHOSTAKOVICH, Dmitri D. - FORST, Rudolf
—— FOUR PRELUDES, OP. 34 (ARR. 1942)
  str. 14:00 H. Branch.
—— THREE FANTASTIC DANCES, OP. 1 (ARR. 1942)
  2,2,2,2 - 2,2,2,0 - timp.,perc. - hp. - pf. - str. 12:00 H. Branch.

SHOSTAKOVICH, Dmitri D. - MAGANINI, Quinto
—— LADY MACBETH OF MZENSK (OPERA): 3 EXCERPTS
  3,2(2nd alt. with Eng. hn.),2,2 - 4,2,3,1 - timp.,perc. - str.
  10:00 Musicus.

SHOSTAKOVICH, Dmitri D. - STOKOWSKI, Leopold
—— PRELUDE IN E FLAT MINOR
  4,*3,*4,*4 - 4,4,4,1 - timp.,perc.(3) - hp. - str. 3:00 Broude.

SHOSTAKOVICH, Dmitri D. - TAYNTON, Jesse C.
—— SYMPHONY NO. 4, OP. 43 (Reduced Orchestration)
  4,4,4,4 - 7,4,3,2 (or 6,4,4,1) - timp.,perc.,cel. - 2 hp. - str.
  60:00 G. Schirmer.

SHUKEN, Leo
—— CINDERELLA (FAIRY TALE IN MUSIC)
  3(2nd alt. with picc.),*3,*3,2 - 4,3,3,1 - timp.,perc.(5),cel.(alt. with pf.),vibra.,xyl. - hp. - str. 13:00 Composer.
—— CONCERTO FOR TRUMPET AND ORCH.
  3(3rd alt. with picc.),*3,*3,*3 - 4,3,3,1 - timp.,perc.(3), xyl. - hp. - pf. - str. 12:00 Columbia.
—— ELEGY FOR ORCHESTRA
  3(3rd alt. with picc.),*3,*3,*3 - 4,3,3,1 - timp.,perc.(2) - hp. - str.
  7:00 Composer.

SHULMAN, Alan
—— CONCERTO FOR CELLO AND ORCH.
  1. Con affetto; 2. Vivace; 3. Moderato
  2,1,2,1 - 2,2,2,0 - timp. - hp. - str. 28:00 Chappell.
—— ELEGY (IN MEMORIAM FELIX SALMOND) (FOR 8-PART CELLO ENSEMBLE) (1971)
  5:30 Composer.
—— FOUR MOODS (FOR STRING ORCH.)
  str. 6:00 Composer.
—— KOL NIDRE (FOR CELLO AND ORCH.) (ARR. 1970)
  2(2nd alt.withicc.),2,2,2 - 3,0,0,0 - str. 7:00 Arranger.
—— A LAURENTIAN OVERTURE
  3(3rd alt. with picc.),3(3rd alt. with Eng. hn.),2(1 alt. with b.-cl.),2 - 4,3,3,1 - timp.,perc.(4),glock.,xyl. - hp. - str. 9:00 Chappell.
—— PASTORALE AND DANCE (FOR VIOLIN AND ORCH.)
  1,1,2,1 - 2,2,2,0 - timp.,perc.(2),glock, - hp. - str. 10:00 Composer.
—— POPOCATAPETL
  3(3rd alt. with picc.),2,2,2 - 4,3,3,1 - timp.,perc.(4) - hp. - str.
  5:30 Templeton.
—— PRELUDE
  2(2nd alt. with picc.),2,*2,2 - 4,2,2,0 - timp.,perc.(2),cel. - hp. - str.
  6:00 Chappell.
—— SUITE FOR STRING ORCH. (ON THEMATIC MATERIAL FROM BENJAMIN FRANKLIN'S STRING QUARTET) (1963) (IN 5 MOVTS.)
  str. 7:34 Composer.
—— SUITE PARISIENNE (FOR CELLO AND STRING ORCH.) (1972) (IN 3 MOVTS.)
  str. 9:35 Composer.
—— THEME AND VARIATIONS (FOR CELLO AND CHAMBER ORCH.) (1966)
  2(2nd alt. with picc.),2,2,2 - 2,1,0,0 - hp. - 1 c.,1 d.-b.
  15:30 Weintraub.
—— THEME AND VARIATIONS (FOR VIOLA WITH FULL OR STRING ORCH.)
  str. 13:00 Chappell.
  or:
  2,2,2,2 - 4,2,3,1 - timp.,perc.(2),glock.,xyl. - hp. - str.
—— THRENODY
  str. 6:00 Tetra.
—— WALTZES FOR ORCHESTRA
  2,2,2,2 - 4,3,3,1 - timp. - hp. - pf.(alt. with cel.) - str.
  8:30 Chappell.

SHURE, R. Deane
—— AMERICAN SYMPHONY (IN 4 MOVTS.)
  3(1 alt. with picc.),*3,2,2 - 4,2,3,1 - timp.,perc. - hp. - str.
  30:00 E. H. Morris.
—— BERKIE SYMPHONY
  3(1 alt. with picc.),*3,2,2 - 4,2,3,1 - timp.,perc.(2) - hp. - str.
  35:00 E. H. Morris.
—— CHORIC SYMPHONY ("THE LIFE OF SIMON GIRTY")
  2(1 alt. with picc.),*3,2,2 - 4,2,3,0 - timp.,perc.(2) - hp. - str.
  25:00 E. H. Morris.
—— THE CIRCLES OF WASHINGTON (IN 4 MOVTS.)
  2(1st alt. with picc.),*3,2,2 - 4,2,3,1 - timp.,perc.(2) - hp. - str.
  25:00 E. H. Morris.

SIBELIUS, Jean
—— ANDANTE FESTIVO
  Southern.
—— ARIOSO (FOR VOICE AND STRING ORCH.)
  str. Southern.
—— FINLANDIA (FOR VOICES AND ORCH.) (Text: Wheeler Beckett)
  5:00 Author.
—— HYMN TO THE EARTH (FOR CHORUS AND ORCH.)
  2,2,2,2 - 4,2,3,0 - timp. - str. 8:00 Southern.
—— OMA MAA (MY OWN LAND), OP. 92 (FOR SATB CHORUS AND ORCH.)
  2,2,2,2 - 4,2,3,0 - timp.,perc. - str. 11:00 Southern.

—— PRELUDE TO SHAKESPEARE'S "THE TEMPEST", OP. 109
    3,2,3,2 - 4,3,3,1 - timp.,perc. - str.   5:00 G. Schirmer.
—— RAKASTAVA (SUITE), OP. 14 (FOR STRINGS)
    str.   12:00 Southern.
—— SCARAMOUCHE, OP. 45 (TRAGIC PANTOMIME) %
    2,2,2,2 - 4,1,0,0 - timp.,perc. - pf. - str.   G. Schirmer.
—— SNÖFRID (MELODRAMA) (FOR MIXED CHORUS AND
    ORCH.)
    2,1,2,1 - 2,3,1,0 - timp.,perc. - str.   13:00 G. Schirmer.
—— THE SONG OF VAÏNÖ, OP. 110 (FOR SATB CHORUS AND
    ORCH.) (Text in Finnish and Swedish)
    2,2,2,2 - 4,3,3,0 - timp.,perc. - str.   8:00 Southern.
—— SUITE CHAMPÊTRE (FOR STRINGS), OP. 98-B (IN 3 MOVTS.)
    str.   9:00 G. Schirmer.
—— SYMPHONY NO. 5, OP. 82
    2,2,2,2 - 4,3,3,0 - timp. - str.   32:30 G. Schirmer.
—— SYMPHONY NO. 6, OP. 104
    2,2,3,2 - 4,3,3,0 - timp. - str.   27:00 G. Schirmer.
—— SYMPHONY NO. 7, OP. 105
    2,2,2,2 - 4,3,3,0 - timp. - str.   20:00 G. Schirmer.
—— THE TEMPEST, OP. 109 (MUSIC TO THE SHAKESPEARE
    PLAY) %
    3,2,4,3 - 4,3,3,1 - timp.,perc. - hp. - org.   G. Schirmer.
—— THE TEMPEST: SUITE NO. 1
    3,2,3,2 - 4,3,3,1 - timp.,perc. - hp. - str. 20:00 G. Schirmer.
—— THE TEMPEST: SUITE NO. 2
    2,2,2,2 - 4,0,0,0 - timp. - hp. - str.   12:00 G. Schirmer.

SIBELIUS, Jean - BURT, Julia
—— SIX HUMORESQUES, FOR VIOLIN AND ORCH.
    2,2,2,2 - 2,0,0,0 - timp. - str.   20:30 G. Schirmer.

SIBELIUS, Jean - MADDY, Joseph E.
—— SYNOPSIS OF SYMPHONY NO. 1
    2,2,2,2 - 4,3,3,1 - timp.,perc. - hp. - str.   Fema.

SIBELIUS, Jean - SOPKIN, Henry
—— FINLANDIA
                                                  C. Fischer.

SICCARDI, Honorio
—— BUENOS AIRES (SYMPHONIC SUITE IN 8 MOVTS.) (WITH
    WORDLESS CONTRALTO SOLO) (1935)
    3,3,3(3rd alt. with b.-cl.),3(3rd alt. with c.-bn.) - 4,3,2-3,0-1 -
    timp.,perc.,cel. - hp. - pf. - str.   Fleisher.
—— CONCERTO FOR VIOLIN AND ORCH. (1942)
    3(3rd alt. with picc.),3(3rd alt. with Eng.hn.),3(3rd alt. with
    b.-cl.),3(3rd alt. with c.-bn.) - 4,2,2,1 - timp.,perc.cel. - hp. - pf. -
    str.   Fleisher.

SICILIANOS, Yeorgo
—— EPISODES, OP. 24 (FOR CHAMBER ORCH.) (1967)
    1,1,2,1 - 0,1,0,0 - perc.(4),cel.,glock.,vibra.,xyl. - hp. - pf. - str.
                                                  10:00 MCA Music.
—— SYMPHONY NO. 1, OP. 14 (IN 4 MOVTS.)
                                                  35:00 S.A.C.E.M.

SIEBERT, Friedrich
—— FESTIVE MUSIC
    2,2,2,2 - 4,2,3,1 - timp.,perc. - hp. - org. - str. 13:40 Henmar.
—— KLEINE ORCHESTERMUSIK (IN 4 MOVTS.)
    2,2,2,2 - 4,2,3,0 - timp.,perc. - hp. - str. 12:00 Henmar.
—— PARTITA NO. 1 (FOR STRING ORCH.) (IN 4 MOVTS.)
    str.   12:00 Henmar.
—— SERENADE FÜR BLÄSER (SERENADE FOR WINDS) (FOR 6
    WOODWINDS, 9 BRASS AND PERCUSSION) (IN 3 MOVTS.)
                                                  9:00 Noack.
—— SYMPHONIC PRELUDE
    2,2,2,2 - 4,2,3,1 - timp.,perc. - str.   5:00 Henmar.

SIEFERT, E.
—— CEUX QUI PIEUSEMENT SONT MORTS POUR LA PATRIE
    (FOR MEZZO-SOPRANO, BARITONE, MIXED CHORUS,
    ORGAN AND ORCH.)
    2,2,2,2 - 3,3,3,0 - timp.,perc.(2) - org.(ad lib.) - str. 8:00 Salabert.

SIEGEL, Paul
—— CONCERTO FOR PIANO AND ORCH. ("TRIPARTITA") (IN 1
    MOVT.)
    *3,2,*3,*3 - 4,3,3,1 - timp.,perc.(3) - pf. - str. 26:00 Sym.House.
—— DREAM OF DARKNESS (4 SONGS FOR BASS AND ORCH.)
    *3,*3,*3,*3 - 4,3,3,1 - timp.,perc.(2) - hp. - str. 10:00 Composer.

—— SYMPHONIC DIARY (1943-1946) (IN 3 MOVTS.)
    *3,2,*3,3 sax.,*3 - 4,3,3,1 - timp.,perc.,cel. - hp. 35:00 Sym.House.
—— SYMPHONY NO. 1 ("BETWEEN TWO WORLDS")
    1. Molto moderato - Allegro piu moderato; 2. Scherzo;
    3. Andante; 4. Allegro con fuoco
    *3,*3,*3,*3 - 4,3,3,1 - timp.,perc.(4),cel.,glock.,vibra.,xyl. - hp. - pf.
    - str.   33:00 Sym.House.

SIEGMEISTER, Elie
—— ABRAHAM LINCOLN WALKS AT MIDNIGHT (1957
    VERSION) (FOR CHORUS AND ORCH.) (Text: Vachel Lindsay)
    1,1,2,1 - 2,2,1,0 - timp.,perc.(2) - str.   7:00 C. Fischer.
—— AMERICAN HOLIDAY (1933)
    2(2nd alt. with picc.),2,2,2 - 3,3,3,1 - timp.,perc.(4),glock. - pf. -
    str.   9:00 C. Fischer.
    or:
    1(alt. with picc.),1,1,1 - 1,1,1,0 - timp.,perc.(3),glock. - pf. - str.
—— CHRISTMAS IS COMING (A FESTIVE CANTATA) (Text:
    Dorothy Ferrante)
    2,0,2,1 - 2,2,1,0 - timp.,perc.(2),bells - str. 24:00 G. Schirmer.
    or:
    2,2,0,0 - 0,0,0,0 - perc. - str.
—— CONCERTO FOR CLARINET AND ORCH. (1956)
    2(2nd alt. with picc.),2,2,2 - 2,2,2,0 - timp.,perc.,cel.(or pf.),xyl. -
    str.   17:00 Fox.
    or:
    1(alt. with picc.),1,*2,1 - 2,2,2,0 - timp.,perc.,cel.(or pf.),xyl. - str.
—— CONCERTO FOR FLUTE AND ORCH. (IN 3 MOVTS.)
    1,1,2,1 - 2,1,1,0 - timp.,perc.(2),vibra.,xyl. - str.
                                                  21:00 MCA Music.
—— CONCERTO FOR PIANO AND ORCH. (1974) (IN 3 MOVTS.)
    2(alt. with 2 picc.),2(2nd alt. with Eng. hn.),2,*3 - 4,2,2,1 -
    timp.,perc.(3),glock.,xyl. - pf. - str.   25:00 C. Fischer.
—— CORDURA (SUITE, FROM THE FILM "THEY CAME TO
    CORDURA") (IN 7 MOVTS.)
    2(2nd alt. with picc.),2(2nd alt. with Eng.hn.),*3,2(2nd alt. with
    c.-bn.) - 4,3,3,1 - timp.,perc.(3),bells,cel.,glock.,xyl. - hp. - pf. - str.
                                                  20:00 Bo. Hawkes.
—— A CYCLE OF CITIES (CANTATA) (FOR SOPRANO, TENOR,
    SATB CHORUS AND ORCH.) (1974) (Texts: Norman Rosten,
    Langston Hughes, Laurence Ferlinghetti)
    2(alt. with 2 picc.),2,2,2(1 alt. with c-bn.) - 4,3,3,1 -
    timp.,perc.(3),bells,glock,vibra.,xyl. - pf. - str. 25:00 C. Fischer.
    or:
    1(alt. with picc.),1,2,1 - 2,2,2,0 - timp.,perc.(3) - pf. - str.
—— DARLING CORIE (1-ACT OPERA) % (Text: Lewis Allan)
    1(alt. with picc.),1,2,1 - 2,2,2,0 - timp.,perc. - pf. - str.
                                                  40:00 C. Fischer.
—— DICK WHITTINGTON AND HIS CAT (A SYMPHONIC
    STORY FOR CHILDREN) (FOR NARRATOR AND ORCH.)
    (1966) (Text: Edward Mabley)
    1,*2,1,1 - 3,1,1,0 - perc.(2),bells,glock.,xyl. - pf. - str.
                                                  19:00 MCA Music.
—— DIVERTIMENTO (IN 4 MOVTS.)
    2(1 alt. with picc.),2(1 alt. with Eng. hn.),2,2 - 2,2,2,0 -
    timp.,perc.(4),glock. - str.   16:00 Templeton.
—— FABLES FROM THE DARK WOOD (1975)
                                                  22:00 C. Fischer.
—— THE FACE OF WAR (SONG-CYCLE) (FOR BARITONE AND
    ORCH.) (1968) (IN 5 MOVTS.) (Text: Langston Hughes)
    2(alt. with 2 picc.),2,2,2 - 2,2,2,0 - timp.,perc.,(2)
    bells,glock.,vibra.,xyl. - hp. - pf. - str.   8:30 C. Fischer.
—— FIVE FANTASIES FOR THE THEATER (1967)
    2-3(2 alt.with 2 picc.)2-3(1 alt.with Eng.hn.),*3(1alt.with Eb
    cl.),2(2nd alt.with c.-bn.) - 4,3,3,1 - timp.,perc.(4),bells,glock.,xyl. -
    hp. - pf. - str.   12:00 MCA Music.
—— FROM MY WINDOW (SUITE)
    2(2nd alt. with picc.),2(2nd alt. with Eng. hn.),2(2nd alt. with
    b.-cl.),2 - 4,3,3,1 - timp.,perc.(3),glock.,vibra.,xyl. - hp. - pf. - str.
                                                  9:00 C. Fischer.
—— FUNNYBONE ALLEY (CHILDREN'S SONGS FOR SOPRANO
    AND STRINGS) (Text: Alfred Kreymborg)
    str.   15:00 C. Fischer.
—— I HAVE A DREAM (CANTATA) (FOR NARRATOR,
    BARITONE, MIXED CHORUS AND ORCH.) (1967) (Text: Dr.
    Martin Luther King, adapted by Edward Mabley)
    2(2nd alt. with picc.),2,2(2nd alt. with alto sax.),2 - 4,2,3,1 -
    timp.,perc.(2),glock.,xyl. - str.   25:00 MCA Music.
—— IN OUR TIME (FOR MIXED CHORUS AND ORCH.) (1965)
    2,2,2,2 - 4,3,3,1 - timp.,perc.(2) - pf. - str. 12:00 C. Fischer.
—— LONESOME HOLLOW
    2(2nd alt. with picc.),2(2nd alt. with Eng. hn.),2(2nd alt. with Eb
    cl.),2 - 4,2,2,0 - timp.,perc.(2),glock. - hp. - str. 7:00 C. Fischer.

—— THE MERMAID IN LOCK NUMBER SEVEN (1-ACT OPERA)
(1958) % (Text: Edward Mabley)
*3,*3,*3,*3 - 4,3,3,1 - timp.,perc.(2),bells,cel.,xyl. - hp. - pf. - d.-b.
50:00 Henmar.
or:
1,1,2,1 - 2,2,1,0 - timp.,perc.,cel. - pf. - d.-b.
—— MIRANDA AND THE DARK YOUNG MAN (1-ACT OPERA)
% (Text: Edward Eager)
1(alt. with picc.),1,2,1 - 2,2,2,0 - timp.,perc.(1),glock. - pf. - str.
60:00 Templeton.
—— THE PLOUGH AND THE STARS (OPERA) (1969) % (Text:
Edward Mabley)
2(1 alt. with picc.),2(1 alt. with Eng.hn.),2,2 - 4,2,3,1 -
timp.,perc.(3),cel.,glock.,xyl. - hp. - 2 pf.(1 off-stage) - str.
140:00 C. Fischer.
or:
1(alt. with picc.),1(alt. with Eng.hn.),2,1 - 2,2,2,0 -
timp.,perc.(3),cel.,glock.,xyl. - hp. - 2 pf.(1 off-stage) - str.
—— PRAIRIE LEGEND (A MIDWESTERN SET) (1944) (IN 3
MOVTS.)
2,*3,*3,2 - 4,3,3,1 - timp.,perc.(3),glock.,xyl. - str.
10:00 C. Fischer.
or:
2,2(2nd alt. with Eng. hn.),2(2nd alt. with b.-cl.),2 - 4,3,3,1 -
timp.,perc.(3),glock.,xyl. - str.
—— SHADOWS AND LIGHT (SUITE) (1975) (IN 5 MOVTS.)
2(1 alt. with picc.),2(2nd alt. with Eng. hn.),2(1 alt. with Eᵇcl.),1
alt. with b.-cl.),2(1 alt. with cbn.) - 4,3,3,1 -
timp.,perc.(5),bells,cel.,glock.,xyl. - hp. - pf. - str.
18:00 C. Fischer.
—— STRANGE FUNERAL IN BRADDOCK (FOR BARITONE AND
ORCH.) (1935) (Text: Michael Gold)
3,3,2,3 - 4,3,3,1 - timp.,perc. - pf. - str.   7:00 Presser.
—— SUMMER NIGHT (1947)
2,2(2nd alt. with Eng. hn.),2(2nd alt. with b.-cl.),2 - 2,2,2,0 - timp.
- hp. - str.   7:00 C. Fischer.
—— SYMPHONY NO. 1 (REVISED 1972) (IN 4 MOVTS.)
3(2 alt. with 2 picc.),*3,Eᵇcl.,*3,*3 - 4,3,3,1 -
timp.,perc.(5),glock.,xyl. - hp. - pf. - str.   27:00 C. Fischer.
—— SYMPHONY NO. 2 (1950)
3(3rd alt. with picc.),*3,2-3(1 alt. with b.-cl.),*3 - 4,2,3,1 -
timp.,perc.(4),cel.,glock.,xyl. - hp. - pf. - str.   27:00 C. Fischer.
—— SYMPHONY NO. 3
2(2nd alt. with picc.),2(2nd alt. with Eng. hn.),2(2nd alt. with Eᵇ
cl.),*3 - 4,2,3,1 - timp.,perc.(3),glock.,xyl. - pf. - str.
18:00 C. Fischer.
—— SYMPHONY NO. 4 (1970) (IN 4 MOVTS.)
3(3rd alt. with picc.),3(3rd alt. with Eng. hn.),*3(1 alt. with Eᵇ
cl.),3(3rd alt. with cbn.) - 4,4,3,1 -
timp.,perc.(4),bells,cel.,glock.,vibra.,xyl. - hp. - pf. - str.
32:00 C. Fischer.
—— SYMPHONY NO. 5 ("VISIONS OF TIME") (1971)
2(alt. with 2 picc.),3(3rd alt. with Eng. hn.),*3,2(2nd alt. with
cbn.) - 4,3,3,1 - timp.,perc.(4),bells,cel.,glock.,xyl. - hp. - pf. - str.
17:30 C. Fischer.
—— THEATER SET (1960) (IN 4 MOVTS.)
2(2nd alt. with picc.),2(2nd alt. with Eng. hn.),*3,2 - 4,3,3,1 -
timp.,perc.(3),cel.,glock.,xyl. - hp. - pf. - str.   12:00 MCA Music.
—— A TOOTH FOR PAUL REVERE (CHORAL PLAY, AFTER THE
STORY BY STEPHEN VINCENT BENET) (1945) % (Text: Hy
Zaret)
1,1,1,1 - 1,1,1,0 - perc. - pf. - str.   23:00 C. Fischer.
—— WESTERN SUITE (1945) (IN 5 MOVTS.)
2(2nd alt. with picc.),2(2nd alt. with Eng. hn.),*3(1 alt. with Eᵇ
cl.),2 - 4,3,3,1 - timp.,perc.(4),cel.,glock.,xyl. - str.
19:30 MCA Music.
—— WILDERNESS ROAD
2(2nd alt. with picc.),2(2nd alt. with Eng. hn.),2(2nd alt. with
b.-cl),2 - 2,2,2,0 - timp.,perc.(3),glock. - str.   6:00 Leeds.

SIENNICKI, Edmund
—— ORCHESTRAL VARIATIONS
2,2,2,1 - 2,4,3,1 - timp.,perc. - str.   6:00 Studio PR.

SIFONIA, Firmino
—— CONCERTO "MCMLVI" (1956) (FOR VIOLA AND ORCH.)
(1963)
3,0,3,0 - 2,2,2,1 - timp.,perc.(4),vibra. - pf. - str.(12,1,4,3)
10:00 MCA Music.

SIGTENHORST MEYER, Bernhard van den
—— DE VERZOEKING VAN BOEDDHA, OP. 8 (FOR SOLO
VOICES, WOMEN'S CHORUS, CELESTA AND STRING
ORCH.) (Text: Rient van Santen)
cel. - 2 hp. - str.   65:00 Henmar.

SIKORSKI, Tomasz
—— FOR STRINGS
str.(9,3,0,0)   4:00 Modern.
—— HOMOPHONIE
0,0,0,0 - 4,4,4,0 - gong - pf.   11:00 Modern.
—— VOX HUMANA (FOR SATB CHORUS AND 22
INSTRUMENTS)
0,0,0,0 - 4,4,4,0 - 4 gongs, 4 tam-tams - 2 pf.   10:00 Modern.

SILBERTA, Rhea
—— THE NIGHTINGALE AND THE ROSE (FOR NARRATOR,
TENOR OR HIGH MEZZO-SOPRANO, CHORUS AND ORCH.)
*3,*3,Eᵇcl.,*2,2 sax.,1 - 4,2,1,1 - timp.,perc.(3) - hp. - pf. - str.
60:00 Composer.

SILVER, Charles
—— LA MÉGÈRE APPRIVOISÉE (4-ACT COMIC OPERA) (1922) %
3,3,2,2 - 4,3,3,0 - timp.,perc.,cel. - guit. - mandolin - hp. - str.
150:00 Presser.

SILVER, Frederick
—— PASSACAGLIA FOR ORCHESTRA (1959)
2 picc.,2,*3,2,2 - 3,3,3,0 - timp. - 2 hp. - str.   10:00 Composer.

SILVER, Mark
—— ARVITH L'SHABBATH (SABBATH EVE SERVICE) (FOR
BARITONE, CHORUS AND ORCH.)
*3,2,2,2 - 4,2,3,1- timp.,perc. - hp. - org. - str.   45:00 Bloch.
—— HANEIROS HOLOLU ("THE KINDLING OF LIGHTS")
(CANTATA) (FOR CHORUS AND ORCH.)
*3,2,2,2 - 4,2,3,1 - timp.,perc. - pf. - str.   7:00 Composer.
—— MARCIA FUNEBRE (SYMPHONIC POEM)
*3,*3,*3,*3 - 4,4,3,1 - timp.,perc. - str.   15:00 Composer.
—— PEACE AND WAR (SYMPHONIC POEM)
*3,*3,*3,*3 - 4,4,3,1 - timp.,perc. - str.   25:00 Composer.
—— PRAISE THE LORD (BIBLICAL CANTATA) (FOR SOLOIST,
CHORUS AND ORCH.)
*3,2,2,2 - 4,2,3,1 - timp.,perc. - hp. - org. - str.   10:00 Transcon.
—— PSALM 99 (FOR TENOR, CHORUS AND ORCH.)
*3,2,2,2 - 4,2,3,1 - timp.,perc. - pf. - str.   12:00 Composer.
—— UNSANE TOKEF (REPENTANCE PRAYER) (FOR VOICE
AND ORCH.)
*3,2,2,2 - 4,2,3,1 - timp.,perc. - str.   12:00 Composer.
—— A ZION FANTASIA (FOR BARITONE, CHORUS AND ORCH.)
*3,2,2,2 - 4,2,3,1 - timp.,perc. - pf. - str.   9:00 Composer.

SILVERMAN, Faye-Ellen
—— MADNESS (FOR NARRATOR AND CHAMBER ORCH.) (1972)
(IN 3 MOVTS.) (Text: Composer)
2(1 alt. with picc.,1 alt. with alto fl.),2,2,2 - 4,2,2,0 - timp.,perc.(1)
5:12 Seesaw.
—— THE MIRACLE OF NEMIROV (OPERA) %
1,1,1,1 - 3,0,0,0 - perc. - tape-recorder - str.   30:00 Seesaw.

SILVESTRI, Constantin
—— MUSIC FOR STRINGS
str.   15:00 Salabert.
—— PRAELUDIUM ET FUGA, OP. 17
4,3,3,3 - 4,4,3,1 - timp.,perc.,cel.,xyl. - hp. - pf. - str.
8:00 Salabert.

SIMILÄ, Martti
—— BALLAD
2,2,2,2 - 2,2,1,0 - timp.,perc. - hp. - str.   6:00 FinnMICtr.
—— THE SHIP "TOIVO" AND OULU TOWN (1944) (FOR SATB
AND ORCH.)
2,2,2,2 - 2,2,0,0 - timp.,perc. - str.   18:00 FinnMICtr.
—— THREE PIECES FOR SMALL ORCH. (1933)
2,2,2,2 - 2,2,1,0 - timp.,perc. - str.   4:00 FinnMICtr.

SIMMONS, Homer
—— CALIFORNIA NIGHTS (FOR PIANO AND ORCH.) (IN 4
MOVTS.)
1,1,2,1 - 2,2,1,0 - timp. - pf. - str.   28:00 Composer.
—— CONCERTO FOR VIOLIN, STRING QUARTET AND ORCH.
2,2,2,*3 - 4 hn. - timp. - str.   35:00 Composer.

—— LITURGY (FOR TWO PIANOS AND STRINGS) (IN 10
MOVTS.)
    2 pf. - str.   67:00 Composer.
—— PARTITA AMERICANA (FOR TWO PIANOS AND ORCH.)
(IN 6 MOVTS.)
    *3,2,2,*4 - 4,4,3,1 - timp.,perc.(6),xyl. - hp. - 2 pf. - str.
               20:00 Composer.
—— PHANTASMANIA (FOR PIANO AND ORCH.)
    *3,*3,*3,*3 - 4,4,3,1 - timp.,perc.(3),vibra. - pf. - str.
               27:00 Composer.

SIMON, Hans
—— SYMPHONY NO. 3 IN D MINOR
    3,*4,*4,*4 - 4,3,3,1 - timp.,perc. - hp. - str.   38:00 Erdmann.

SIMONIS, Jean-Marie
—— L' AUTOMNE, OP. 14 (1967)
    3,3,3,3 - 4,3,3,1 - timp.,perc. - str.   10:00 H. Elkan.
—— PETITE SUITE SATIRIQUE, OP. 31 (FOR ORCH.) (1976)
    3,3,3,3 - 4,3,3,1 - timp.,perc. - hp. - str.   H. Elkan.
—— POLYPHONIES, OP. 27 (FOR STRINGS) (1973)
    1. Lento; 2. Lento esspressivo e rubato; 3. Scherzando
    str.   14:00 H. Elkan.
—— SCHERZETTO, OP. 16 (1968) (FOR CHAMBER ORCH.)
    2,1,2,1 - 2,2,1,0 - timp.,perc. - str.   3:00 H. Elkan.

SIMPSON, Dudley
—— IDILLIO, OP. 3 (1967)
    2,0,2,2 - 2,2,1,0 - perc. - guit. - hp. - str.   13:00 P.R.S.

SIMPSON, Robert
—— ALLEGRO DECISO
    pf.(ad lib.) - str.   11:00 Lengnick.
—— CONCERTO FOR VIOLIN AND ORCH.
    *3,2,2,2 - 4,2,3,0 - timp.,perc. - str.   39:00 Lengnick.
—— SYMPHONY NO. 1
               26:00 Lengnick.
—— SYMPHONY NO. 2
    2,2,2,2 - 2,2,0,0 - timp. - str.   26:00 Lengnick.
—— SYMPHONY NO. 3
    3,2,2,3 - 4,2,3,1 - timp.,perc. - hp. - str.   32:00 Lengnick.

SINCLAIR, John C.
—— EMBRYONIC SKETCHES
               11:00 C.A.P.A.C.
—— PSALM FOR ORCHESTRA
               6:00 C.A.P.A.C.
—— SUITE IN D FOR STRINGS
    str.   9:00 C.A.P.A.C.

SINGER, Lawrence
—— CONCERTO FOR LOTHAR (WITH SOLO OBOE) (1974)
    0,1,0,0 - 0,0,0,0 - timp.,perc.,vibra. - str.(6,4,3,1)
               15:00 MCA Music.
—— SATYR (1974)
    2,2(2nd alt. with Eng. hn.),2,2 - timp.,perc.(2),mar.,vibra. - str.
               12:00 MCA Music.

SIOHAN, Robert
—— CONCERTO FOR VIOLIN AND ORCH.
    2,2,2,2 - 4,3,2,1 - timp.,perc. - str.   9:15 Salabert.

SIPILÄ, Eero
—— FUGUE AND CHACONNE
    str.   12:00 FinnMICtr.
—— TE DEUM LAUDAMUS (FOR ALTO, BARITONE, SATB
CHORUS AND ORCH.)(1969)
    2,3,3,2 - 4,3,3,0 - timp.,perc. - hp. - str.   34:00 FinnMICtr.

SIPPONEN, Erkki
—— HACKAPELITES (FOR SOPRANO, TENOR, BARITONE,
MALE CHORUS AND ORCH.)(1956) (Text: Z. Topelius)
    2,1,2,1 - 2,2,1,0 - timp.,perc. - str.   22:00 FinnMICtr.
—— LAKE SCENES (BALLET) % (1956)
    2,1,2,1 - 0,2,1,0 - perc. - str.   60:00 FinnMICtr.

SIPPONEN, Urho
—— BLACKSMITH LINDBLAD (SONG CYCLE)(FOR VOICE AND
ORCH.)(1968) (Text: P. Mustapää)
    1,1,2,1 - 1,2,1,0 - timp.,perc. - str.   66:00 FinnMICtr.
—— CONCERTO NO. 1 IN F MAJOR, FOR TRUMPET AND
ORCH. (1969)
    2,2,2,2 - 2,2,2,1 - timp.,perc. - str.   27:00 FinnMICtr.

—— CONCERTO NO. 2 FOR PIANO AND ORCH. (1966)
    2,2,2,2 - 3,2,2,1 - timp.,perc. - pf. - str.   27:00 FinnMICtr.
—— ESTONIAN RHAPSODY (1957)
    2,2,2,2 - 4,3,2,1 - timp.,perc. - str.   12:00 FinnMICtr.
—— A FINNISH LANDSCAPE (SUITE)(1967)
    2,1,2,2 - 2,2,2,1 - timp.,perc. - str.   20:00 FinnMICtr.
—— FOUR ELEGIAC COMPOSITIONS (1961)
    str.   21:00 FinnMICtr.
—— KALEVALA RHAPSODY NO. 1 (1970)
    2,1,2,1 - 2,2,1,1 - timp.,perc. - str.   9:00 FinnMICtr.
—— KARELIAN DANCES (1970)
    2,1,2,1 - 2,2,2,1 - perc. - str.   27:00 FinnMICtr.
—— KARELIAN RHAPSODY (1970)
    2,1,2,1 - 2,2,2,1 - timp.,perc. - str.   12:00 FinnMICtr.
—— NIGHTS AT KANNAS (1945)
    2,2,2,2 - 2,2,2,1 - timp.,perc. - str.   8:00 FinnMICtr.
—— SPRING (1943)
    2,2,2,2 - 4,3,2,1 - timp.,perc. - str.   8:00 FinnMICtr.
—— TEN SONGS (FOR VOICE AND ORCH.)(1957) (Text: Mörike)
    1,1,2,1 - 2,2,1,0 - perc. - str.   32:00 FinnMICtr.
—— VIIPURI SUITE (1969)
    2,1,2,1 - 2,2,1,1 - timp.,perc. - str.   29:00 FinnMICtr.

SIRULNIKOFF, Jack
—— CEREMONIAL PIECE (1959) (FOR UNISON VOICES OR
STRINGS OR SOLO TRUMPET)
    4,0,4,0 - 0,1,0,0 - timp.,perc.(6, incl. 3 on timp.) - str.
               4:10 CanMusCtr.
    or:
    str.
—— MOVEMENT FOR ORCHESTRA (1971)
    *3,*3,*3,*3 - 4,3,3,1 - timp.,perc. - hp. - str.   14:00 CanMusCtr.

ŠÍSTEK, V. - LOTTER, Adolf
—— SLAVONIC SCHERZO (FOR STRING ORCH.)
    str.   Bo. Hawkes.

SITSKY, Larry
—— APPARITIONS (1966)
    2,1,2,0 - 2,2,2,1 - timp.,perc. - pf. - str.   Bo. Hawkes.
—— CONCERTO FOR VIOLIN, ORCHESTRA AND FEMALE
VOICES ("MYSTERIUM COSMOGRAPHICUM") (1972)
               35:00 A.P.R.A.
—— CONCERTO FOR WOODWIND QUINTET AND ORCH. (1971)
               25:00 Belw-Mills.
—— FANTASIA CONTRAPPUNTISTICA (1962)
               A.P.R.A.
—— PRELUDE FOR ORCH. (1968)
               4:00 A.P.R.A.

ŠIVIC, Pavle
—— ALTERNATIONS
    *2,*2,*2,2 - 4,3,3,1 - timp.,perc.(4) - pf. - str.   16:00 Hans Gerig.
—— CONCENTRICS (FOR NARRATOR-SINGER AND ORCH.)
    2(2nd alt. with picc.),2(2nd alt. with Eng. hn.),2,2 - 4,3,3,1 -
    timp.,perc.(4) - hp. - str.   26:00 Hans Gerig.
—— CONCERTO FOR CLARINET AND ORCH.
    2(2nd alt. with picc.),2,3,2 - 4,3,3,1 - timp.,perc.(4) - str.
               15:00 Hans Gerig.
—— CONCERTO FOR PIANO AND ORCH.
    2(2nd alt. with picc.),2,2,2 - 4,3,3,1 - perc.(3) - pf. - str.
               16:00 Hans Gerig.
—— CONCERTO FOR VIOLIN AND ORCH.
    *2,2,2,2 - 4,3,3,1 - timp.,perc.(4) - str.   16:00 Hans Gerig.
—— DIALOGUES (FOR OBOE AND STRINGS) (1976)
    ob. - str.   13:00 Hans Gerig.
—— EVENT IN THE TOWN OF GOGA (BALLET, WITH CHORUS)
%
    1(alt. with picc.),2(2nd alt. with Eng. hn.),2(2nd alt. with
    b.-cl.),2(2nd alt. with c.-bn.) - 4,3,3,1 - timp.,perc.(5) - hp. - pf. -
    str.   40:00 Hans Gerig.
—— FLEETING EMOTIONS (BEŽNI VZGIBI) (FOR PIANO AND
CHAMBER ORCH.)
    1,1,1,1 - 1,0,0,0 - perc. - pf. - str.   8:00 Hans Gerig.
—— FOLKSONG AND DANCE FROM MEDJIMURJE
    *2,2,2,2 - 4,3,3,1 - timp.,perc. - hp. - str.   14:00 Hans Gerig.
—— MUSIQUE CONCERTANTE (FOR TROMBONE AND ORCH.)
    2(2nd alt. with picc.),2,2,2 - 4,3,1,0 - timp.,perc.(4) - str.
               15:00 Hans Gerig.
—— THE RETURN OF CORTEZ (OPERA) %
    2(2nd alt. with picc.),2(2nd alt. with Eng. hn.),2,2 - 4,3,3,1 -
    timp.,perc.(4) - hp. - str.   Hans Gerig.

—— SINFONIA DI TRE REGINE (FOR 16 INSTRUMENTS)
1,1,1,1 - 1,1,1,0 - timp.,perc.(4),vibra. - pf. - str.(2,1,1,1)
10:00 Hans Gerig.
—— VON SCHWELLE ZU SCHWELLE (FIVE SONGS FOR
MEZZO-SOPRANO AND STRINGS)
str. 14:00 Hans Gerig.

SJØGREN, Emil - MANN, Tor
—— LEGENDS (FOR STRING ORCH.)
str. 10:00 G. Schirmer.

SJØGREN, Emil - WESTBERG, Eric
—— POEM, OP. 40 (FOR VIOLIN AND ORCH.)
2,2,2,2 - 4,0,0,0 - timp. - str. 8:00 G. Schirmer.

SKEDGELL, Nicholas G.
—— ALLEGRO FOR ORCHESTRA (1974)
5:00 Composer.

ŠKERJANC, Lucijan Marija
—— ALLEGRO DE CONCERT (FOR CELLO AND ORCH.)
16:00 Hans Gerig.
—— CHACONNE ON A FOLK-TUNE
str. 7:00 Hans Gerig.
—— CONCERTANTE RHAPSODY FOR VIOLA AND ORCH.
0,1(alt. with Eng.hn.), 2(2nd alt. with b.-cl.),2 - 2,2,0,0 -
timp.,perc. - hp. - str. 9:00 Hans Gerig.
—— CONCERTINO FOR FLUTE AND SMALL ORCH.
1,0,0,0 - 1,0,0,0 - perc.,cel. - hp. - str. 9:00 Hans Gerig.
—— CONCERTINO FOR PIANO AND STRING ORCH.
pf. - str. 15:00 Hans Gerig.
—— CONCERTO FOR BASSOON, HARP AND STRINGS
bn. - hp. - str. 15:00 Hans Gerig.
—— CONCERTO FOR CLARINET AND SMALL ORCH.
0,0,1,0 - 0,0,0,0 - timp.,perc. - hp. - str. 10:00 Hans Gerig.
—— CONCERTO FOR HARP AND SMALL ORCH.
fl. - hn. - hp. - str. 19:00 Hans Gerig.
—— CONCERTO FOR PIANO AND ORCH.
2,2,2,2 - 4,3,3,1 - timp.,perc.(3) - pf. - str. 25:00 Hans Gerig.
—— CONCERTO FOR PIANO LEFT-HAND AND ORCH.
1,1,1,1 - 2,2,0,0 - timp.,perc.(3) - hp. - pf. - str.
25:00 Hans Gerig.
—— CONCERTO FOR VIOLIN AND ORCH.
2(2nd alt. with picc.),1(alt. with Eng. hn.),1(alt. with b.-cl.),1(alt.
with c.-bn.) - 2,2,0,0 - timp.,perc. - 2 hp. - str. 28:00 Hans Gerig.
—— DRAMATIC OVERTURE
2(2nd alt. with picc.),1(alt. with Eng. hn.),2(2nd alt. with b.-cl.),2 -
4,3,3,1 - timp.,perc.(3) - str. 13:00 Hans Gerig.
—— FANTASIA AND FUGUE (ON MOTIFS BY A. HAJDRIH)
str. 8:00 Hans Gerig.
—— FESTIVE OVERTURE
2(2nd alt. with picc.),2(2nd alt. with Eng. hn.),2(2nd alt. with
b.-cl.),2 - 4,3,3,1 - timp.,perc.(3) - hp. - pf. - str. 7:00 Hans Gerig.
—— GAZELLES (SEVEN POEMS FOR ORCH.)
3,2(2nd alt. with Eng. hn.),2(2nd alt. with b.-cl.),2(2nd alt. with
c.-bn.) - 6,4,3,1 - timp.,perc.(3) - 2 hp. - str. 22:00 Hans Gerig.
—— LYRIC OVERTURE
3,2,2,2 - 4,2,3,1 - timp.,perc.(3) - hp. - pf. - str. 4:00 Hans Gerig.
—— PRELUDE, ARIA AND FINALE
str. 21:00 Hans Gerig.
—— SEVEN DODECAPHONIC FRAGMENTS
str. 16:00 Hans Gerig.
—— SINFONIETTA FOR STRINGS (DIXTUOR)
str.(4,2,3,1) 11:00 Hans Gerig.
—— SOLEMN OVERTURE
3,2,2(2nd alt. with b.-cl.),2 - 4,3,3,1 - timp.,perc.(3) - hp. - str.
10:00 Hans Gerig.
—— SUITE IN OLDEN STYLE (FOR STRING QUARTET AND
STRING ORCH.)
str. 19:00 Hans Gerig.
—— SUITE NO. 2 FOR STRINGS (IN 8 MOVTS.)
str. 15:00 Hans Gerig.
—— SUITE NO. 3 FOR STRINGS (IN 9 MOVTS.)
str. 10:00 Hans Gerig.
—— SYMPHONY NO. 1
2(2nd alt. with picc.),2,2,2 - 4,3,3,1 - timp.,perc.(3) - hp. - str.
14:00 Hans Gerig.
—— SYMPHONY NO. 2
2(2nd alt. with picc.),2,2,2 - 4,3,3,1 - perc. - str.
25:00 Hans Gerig.
—— SYMPHONY NO. 3
2(2nd alt. with picc.),2,2,2 - 4,3,3,1 - perc. - str.
20:00 Hans Gerig.

—— SYMPHONY NO. 4 (FOR STRING ORCH.)
str. 27:00 Hans Gerig.

ŠKERL, Dane
—— CONCERTINO NO. 1 FOR PIANO AND STRINGS
pf. - str. 12:00 Hans Gerig.
—— CONCERTINO NO. 2 FOR PIANO AND STRINGS
pf. - str. 14:00 Hans Gerig.
—— CONCERTO FOR CLARINET AND ORCH.
1,1,1,1 - 2,2,2,0 - timp.,perc. - str. 17:00 Hans Gerig.
—— CONCERTO NO. 1 FOR ORCH.
1(alt. with picc.),1(alt. with Eng. hn.),1,1(alt. with c. bn.) - 2,2,0,0
- timp.,perc. - str. 17:00 Hans Gerig.
—— CONCERTO NO. 2 FOR ORCH.
1(alt. with picc.),1(alt. with Eng. hn.),1(alt. with b.-cl.),1(alt. with
c.-bn.) - 2,2,2,1 - timp.,cel. - hp. - str. 16:00 Hans Gerig.
—— CONTRASTS FOR ORCH.
2(2nd alt. with picc.),2,2,2 - 4,3,3,1 - timp.,perc. - hp. - str.
13:00 Hans Gerig.
—— DIVERTIMENTO PER 24
2(2nd alt. with picc.),2,2,2 - 4,3,3,0 - timp.,perc.(4) - hp. - d.-b.
10:00 Hans Gerig.
—— FIVE PIECES FOR CLARINET AND STRINGS
cl. - str. 9:00 Hans Gerig.
—— INTRADA
2(2nd alt. with picc.),2,2,2(2nd alt. with c.-bn.) - 4,3,3,1 -
timp.,perc.(4) - str. 9:00 Hans Gerig.
—— INVENZIONI (FOR VIOLIN AND STRINGS)
str. 8:00 Hans Gerig.
—— LITTLE SUITE
2(2nd alt. with picc.),1,2,2 - 4,3,3,1 - timp.,perc.(3) - hp. - str.
13:00 Hans Gerig.
—— MUSICA FUNEBRE (FOR TROMBONE AND ORCH.)
2(2nd alt. with picc.),2,2(2nd alt. with b.-cl.),2(2nd alt. with c.-bn.)
- 4,3,1,1 - timp.,perc.(4) - str. 9:00 Hans Gerig.
—— RAVISHING SUMMER (BALLET) %
2(2nd alt. with picc.),2(2nd alt. with Eng. hn.),2(2nd alt. with
b.-cl.),2(2nd alt. with c.-bn.) - 4,3,3,1 - timp.,perc.(4),cel.,vibra.,xyl.
- hp. - str. Hans Gerig.
—— SERENADE FOR STRINGS
str. 16:00 Hans Gerig.
—— SINFONIETTA NO. 3 (FOR WOODWINDS, BRASS AND
PERCUSSION)
10:00 Hans Gerig.
—— SYMPHONY NO. 2 (MONOTHEMATICA) (FOR STRING
ORCH.)
str. 17:00 Hans Gerig.
—— SYMPHONY NO. 3
1(alt. with picc.),1,1,1 - 2,2,2,0 - timp.,perc.(8) - str.
19:00 Hans Gerig.
—— SYMPHONY NO. 4
2(2nd alt. with picc.),2,2,2(2nd alt. with c.-bn.) - 4,4,3,1 -
timp.,perc.(4),cel. - hp. - str. 20:00 Hans Gerig.
—— THREE BAGATELLES
str. 6:00 Hans Gerig.
—— TWO LITTLE STUDIES FOR CHAMBER ORCH.
2,0,2,1 - 0,2,0,0 - perc.(2) - str. 4:00 Hans Gerig.

SKILES, Marlin
—— THE PLAY'S THE THING (FOR BARITONE AND ORCH.)
2(2nd alt. with picc.),2(2nd alt. with Eng. hn.),2,2 - 4,3,3,1 -
timp.,perc.(2),glock.,xyl. - hp. - pf. - str. 8:30 G. Schirmer.

SKILTON, Charles S.
—— THE GUARDIAN ANGEL (A CAROLINA LEGEND)
(ORATORIO) (FOR SOPRANO, ALTO, TENOR, BASS,
CHILDREN'S CHORUS, CHORUS AND ORCH.) (IN 3
MOVTS.)
3(3rd alt. with picc.),*3,*3,*3 - 4,3,3,1 - timp.,perc.(1) - hp. - str.
90:00 Belw-Mills.
—— SUITE IN E MINOR, OP. 4 (IN 3 MOVTS)
3,2,3,3 - 4,3,3,1 - timp.,perc.(2) - str. 9:00 C. Fischer.
—— SUITE PRIMEVAL (BASED ON TRIBAL INDIAN MELODIES)

PART I (IN 2 MOVTS.)
3,*3,Eᵇcl.,2,2 - 4,3,4,1 - timp.,perc.(2) - hp. - str.
10:00 C. Fischer.

PART II (IN 4 MOVTS.)
4,3,3,3 - 4,3,3,1 - timp.,perc.(2) - hp. - str. 25:00 C. Fischer.
—— THE WITCH'S DAUGHTER (CANTATA) (FOR SOPRANO,
BARITONE, CHORUS AND ORCH.)
3,*3,2,2 - 4,3,3,1 - perc.(1) - hp. - str. 33:00 C. Fischer.

SKÖLD, Sven
—— VID ÄLVOM, PÅ BERG OCH I DALOM (SUITE) (IN 8 MOVTS.)
    1,1,2,1 - 2,2,1,0 - timp. - pf. - str.   23:00 S.T.I.M.

SKÖLD, Yngve
—— CONCERT FANTASY FOR PIANO AND ORCH., OP. 21
    3,3,2,2 - 4,2,3,1 - timp. - pf. - str.   20:00 S.T.I.M.
—— CONCERT OVERTURE, OP. 47
    3,2,2,2 - 4,3,3,1 - timp. - str.   8:00 S.T.I.M.
    or:
    2,2,2,2 - 2,2,1,0 - timp. - str.
—— CONCERT PIECE FOR TRUMPET AND ORCH., OP. 37
    1,1,1,1 - 2,1,0,0 - timp. - str.   8:00 S.T.I.M.
—— CONCERTO FOR CELLO AND ORCH, OP. 49
    2,2,2,2 - 2,2,0,0 - timp. - str.   23:00 S.T.I.M.
—— CONCERTO FOR PIANO AND ORCH., OP. 7
    3,2,2,2 - 4,2,3,1 - timp. - pf. - str.   30:00 S.T.I.M.
—— CONCERTO FOR VIOLIN AND ORCH., OP. 40
    2,2,2,2 - 2,2,1,0 - timp.,perc.(2) - str.   28:00 Suecia.
—— CONCERTO FOR VIOLIN, CELLO AND ORCH., OP. 52
    2,2,2,2 - 2,2,1,0 - timp. - str.   28:00 S.T.I.M.
—— CONCERTO NO. 2 FOR PIANO AND ORCH., OP. 46
    2,2,2,2 - 4,2,3,1 - timp. - pf. - str.   30:00 S.T.I.M.
    or:
    2,2,2,2 - 2,2,1,0 - timp. - pf. - str.
—— CONCERTO NO. 3 FOR PIANO AND ORCH. (1969)
    2,2,2,2 - 2,2,2,1 - pf. - str.   30:00 S.T.I.M.
—— DIVERTIMENTO, OP. 53
    2,2,2,2 - 2,2,1,0 - timp. - str.   22:00 S.T.I.M.
—— FANTASY OVERTURE, OP. 56
    2,2,2,2 - 4,2,3,1 - timp. - str.   13:00 S.T.I.M.
    or:
    2,2,2,2 - 2,2,1,0 - timp. - str.
—— POÈME ELÉGIAQUE, OP. 25
    2,3,2,2 - 4,2,3,1 - timp. - hp. - str.   10:00 S.T.I.M.
—— SINFONIA DA CHIESA, OP. 38
    2,2,2,2 - 2,2,1,0 - timp. - org. - str.   24:00 S.T.I.M.
—— SUITE FOR VIOLA AND ORCH., OP. 35
    2,2,2,2 - 2,2,1,0 - timp.,perc. - str.   30:00 S.T.I.M.
—— SUITE NO. 1 FOR STRINGS, OP. 39
    str.   19:00 S.T.I.M.
—— SUITE NO. 1, OP. 30 (IN 5 MOVTS.)
    2,2,2,2 - 2,2,1,0 - timp.,perc. - hp. - str.   16:00 S.T.I.M.
—— SUITE NO. 2 FOR STRINGS, OP. 48
    str.   23:00 S.T.I.M.
—— SUITE NO. 2, OP. 44 (IN 3 MOVTS.)
    2,2,2,2 - 2,2,1,0 - timp.,perc. - str.   26:00 S.T.I.M.
—— SYMPHONY NO. 2, OP. 36
    3,3,2,3 - 4,3,3,1 - timp.,perc. - str.   43:00 S.T.I.M.
—— SYMPHONY NO. 3, OP. 50
    2,2,2,2 - 4,2,3,0 - timp. - str.   31:00 S.T.I.M.
—— SYMPHONY NO. 4, OP. 66 (1966)
    2,2,2,2 - 4,3,3,1 - timp.,perc.(3) - str.   40:00 S.T.I.M.
—— VARIATIONS ON "MODER JORDS VAGGVISA", OP. 51A
    2,2,2,2 - 2,2,1,0 - timp.,perc.,cel. - pf.(ad lib.) - str.   12:00 S.T.I.M.

SKROWACZEWSKI, Stanislaw
—— CONCERTO FOR ENGLISH HORN AND ORCH. (1969) (IN 3 MOVTS.)
    4(4th alt. with picc.),*1,0,0 - 4,4,3,1 - timp.,perc.(3),bell - pf. - str.
    20:00 G. Schirmer.

SLADEK, Paul
—— THE ISLE OF MISTS
    2,1(alt. with Eng.hn.),2,1 - 3,2,3,0 - timp.,perc.(2),vibra or glock. - hp. - pf. - str.   5:00 Volkwein.

SLATER, Joseph Emile
—— RAPSODIE FOR FLUTE AND CHAMBER ORCHESTRA
    2,1,2,1 - 3,1,2,0 - str.   5:00 G. Schirmer.
—— SEPTEMBER EVENING
    str.   7:00 S.A.M.R.O.
—— SUITE FOR ORCHESTRA
    2,2,3,2 - 4,2,3,1 - timp.,perc. - str.   15:00 S.A.M.R.O.
—— THREE MINIATURES FOR STRING ORCHESTRA
    str.   9:00 S.A.M.R.O.

SLATKIN, Leonard
—— THE RAVEN (FOR NARRATOR AND ORCH.)
    3,3,3,3 - 4,4,3,1 - timp.,perc. - 2 hp. - pf. - str. 18:00 G. Schirmer.

SLAVICKY, Klement
—— MORAVIAN DANCE FANTASIAS (SUITE) (IN 5 MOVTS.)
    3,2,2,2 - 4,3,3,0 - timp.,perc. - hp. - str.   24:00 Bo. Hawkes.
—— RHAPSODIC VARIATIONS ON A MORAVIAN THEME
    3,3,2,2 - 4,3,3,0 - timp.,perc. - hp. - str.   30:00 Bo. Hawkes.
—— SINFONIETTA (1940) (IN 3 MOVTS.)
    3,3,3,3 - 4,3,4,0 - timp.,perc. - str.   24:00 Bo. Hawkes.

SLONIMSKIJ, Serge J. M.
—— DRAMATIC SONG
    G. Schirmer.

SLONIMSKY, Nicolas
—— FOUR SIMPLE PIECES
    2(1 alt. with picc.),0,2,0 - 0,2,0,0 - timp.,perc.(1) - str.
    10:00 C-Ross.
—— LITTLE SUITE
    1(alt. with picc.),1,1,1 - 0,1,1,0 - perc.,typewriter,xyl. - str.
    6:00 C-Ross.
—— MUSIC TO "ORESTES"
    tpt. - timp.,perc. - str.   Composer.
—— MY TOY BALLOON (VARIATIONS ON A BRAZILIAN TUNE)
    *3,2,2,2 - 2,2,3,1 - timp.,perc.,cel.(or pf.),xyl. - hp.(or pf.) - str.
    6:00 Templeton.
—— THE PRINCE GOES HUNTING (BALLET SUITE)
    *3,*3,2,2 - 2,2,3,1 - timp.,perc. - hp. - pf. - str.   20:00 Composer.

SLONIMSKY, Sergei M.
—— CONCERTO FOR THREE ELECTRIC GUITARS, SOLO INSTRUMENTS AND ORCHESTRA
    G. Schirmer.

SLY, Allan
—— GOOD WIVES OF PIONEERS (FOR MIXED CHORUS AND ORCH.) (Text: Reuel Denney)
    2,3,2,3 - 4,2,3,1 - timp. - org. - str.   11:00 Bo. Hawkes.
—— HOLIDAY TUNE
    2(2nd alt. with picc.),2,2,2 - 3,2,2,0 - timp.,perc. - str.
    10:00 C. Fischer.
—— MINIATURE SYMPHONY (IN 1 MOVT.)
    3,3,2,3 - 4,2,3,1 - perc. - str.   15:00 C. Fischer.

SMAILOVIĆ, Avdo
—— AD HOMINEM
    3,*3,*3,*3 - 4,3,3,1 - timp.,perc. - hp. - str.   10:00 S.O.K.O.J.
—— DRVAR (TONE POEM)
    cl. - timp. - pf. - str.   15:00 S.O.K.O.J.
—— MOUVEMENT DE CONCERT (FOR FLUTE AND ORCH.)
    1,*2,2,2 - 4,0,0,0 - timp. - hp. - str.   10:00 S.O.K.O.J.
—— UNDER THE IGMAN MOUNTAIN (TONE POEM)
    *3,*3,*3,*1 - 4,3,3,1 - timp.,perc. - hp. - pf. - str. 20:00 S.O.K.O.J.

SMALLEY, Roger
—— BEAT MUSIC (1971) (FOR ORCH., AND FOLLOWING AMPLIFIED INSTRUMENTS: ORGAN, PERCUSSION, VIOLA AND SOPRANO SAX ALTERNATING WITH BASSOON)
    3,3,4sopr. sax.(amplified and alt. with amplified bn.),alto sax.,2 - 3,4,3,1 - perc.(4,incl. 1 amplified) - electric b.-guit. - electric hpsc. - org.(amplified) - electric pf. - str.(incl. 1 amplified vla.)
    20:00 G. Schirmer.
—— GLORIA TIBI TRINITAS
    3,3,3,3 - 4,3,3,1 - timp. - 2 hp. - str.   10:00 G. Schirmer.
—— THE SONG OF THE HIGHEST TOWER (1968) (FOR SOPRANO, BARITONE, CHORUS, BRASS, PERCUSSION AND STRINGS)
    0,0,0,0 - 4,4,3,1 - perc.(3) - str.   35:00 G. Schirmer.
—— STRATA (1971) (FOR STRINGS)
    str.   30:00 G. Schirmer.
—— VARIATIONS FOR STRINGS
    str.   8:00 G. Schirmer.

SMEATON, Bruce
—— FANTASIA FOR ORCHESTRA
    A.P.R.A.

SMETANA, Bedřich
—— THE BARTERED BRIDE (3-ACT OPERA) % (Eng. Text: Marion Farquhar)
    G. Schirmer.

SMETANA, Bedřich - HARRISON
—— THE BARTERED BRIDE (CONCERT VERSION) (FOR
CHORUS AND ORCH.)
3,2,2,2 - 4,2,3,0 - timp.,perc. - str.   80:00 Bo. Hawkes.

SMETANA, Bedřich - LOTTER, Adolf
—— THE BARTERED BRIDE: SUITE
16:00 Bo. Hawkes.
—— THE MOLDAU (VLTAVA)
13:00 Bo. Hawkes.

SMETANA, Bedřich - SZELL, George
—— FROM MY LIFE (STRING QUARTET IN E MINOR) (IN 4
MOVTS.)
3,2,2,2 - 4,2,3,1 - timp.,perc. - hp. - str.   25:00 Bo. Hawkes.

SMETANA, Bedřich - WINTER, Aubrey
—— OVERTURE TO "THE BARTERED BRIDE"
7:00 Bo. Hawkes.

SMIT, Leo - American Composer
—— CAEDMON (FOR MEZZO-SOPRANO, TENOR, BARITONE,
MALE CHORUS AND ORCH.)
3,2,2,2 - 4,3,3,1 - timp. - hpsc. - str.   25:00 C. Fischer.
—— CAPRICCIO (FOR STRING ORCH.)
str.   16:00 C. Fischer.
—— CONCERTO FOR ORCHESTRA AND PIANO
3,0,0,0 - 4,2,2,0 - timp. - pf. - str.   15:00 C. Fischer.
—— FOUR KOOKABURRA MARCHES
2,2,2,2 - 2,2,2,1 - timp. - tape-recorder (ad lib.) - str.
8:00 C. Fischer.
—— THE LAUGHING KOOKABURRAS (A SPACE FABLE IN 3
ACTS) % (1968) (Text: Fred Hoyle)
2(2nd alt. with picc.),2,2,2 - 2,2,3,1 - timp.,perc.(2) - hp. - str.
80:00 Mills.
—— OVERTURE TO "THE PARCAE" (OVERTURE IN C SHARP
MINOR)
*3,2,2,2 - 4,2,3,1 - timp. - str.   7:00 Composer.
—— SUITE FROM THE BALLET "VIRGINIA SAMPLER"
2(2nd alt. with picc.),2,2,2 - 3,2,3,0 - timp.,perc.(3),glock. - hp. -
pf.- str.   16:00 C. Fischer.
—— SYMPHONY NO. 1 IN B FLAT
2(2nd alt. with picc.),2,2,2 - 4,2,2,0 - timp.,perc.(1) - str.
30:00 Bo. Hawkes.
—— SYMPHONY NO. 2 (IN 6 MOVTS.) (1965)
3(3rd alt. with picc.),2,2,*3 - 4,2,3,1 - timp. - hp. - pf. - str.
18:00 Mills.

SMIT, Leo - Dutch Composer
—— CONCERTINO FOR CELLO AND ORCH.
1,1,1,1 - 1,1,0,0 - timp. - str.   15:00 Henmar.
—— CONCERTINO FOR HARP AND ORCH.
2,2,2,2 - 2,3,3,1 - timp.,perc.,hp. - str.   15:00 Henmar.
—— CONCERTO FOR PIANO AND WIND INSTS.
2,2,2,2 - 3,2,1,1 - timp. - pf. - c., d.-b.   16:00 Henmar.
—— CONCERTO FOR VIOLA AND STRINGS
str.   13:00 Henmar.
—— SILHOUETTEN (SUITE)
3,3,3,3 - 4,2,3,0 - timp.,perc.,cel.,xyl. - hp. - str.   17:00 Henmar.
—— SYMPHONY IN C MAJOR
2,2,2,2 - 2,2,0,0 - timp. - str.   21:00 Henmar.

SMITH, David Stanley
—— FALLEN STAR, OP. 26 (FOR CHORUS AND ORCH.)
2,2,2,2 - 4,2,3,1 - timp. - str.   10:00 G. Schirmer.
—— PRINCE HAL, OP. 31 (OVERTURE)
2(1 alt. with picc.),*3,*3,2 - 4,3,3,1 - timp.,perc.(2) - hp. - str.
10:00 G. Schirmer.
—— RHAPSODY OF ST. BERNARD, OP. 38 (FOR SOLO VOICES,
CHORUS AND ORCH.)
2,2(1 alt. with Eng. hn.),2,2 - 4,2,3,1 - timp. - hp. - str.
75:00 G. Schirmer.

SMITH, Geoffrey
—— CONCERTINO FOR PIANO AND STRINGS
pf. - str.   11:00 Lengnick.

SMITH, John Christopher - BUCK, Friedrich
—— ULYSSES: SUITE FROM THE OPERA
0,2,0,1 - 2,0,0,0 - cemb. - str.   16:00 F. Colombo.

SMITH, John Shaffer
—— TEXAS SUITE (IN 4 MOVTS.)
2,2,2,2 - 3,2,3,1 - timp.,perc.(3) - str.   28:00 RejayMuPub.

SMITH, Julia
—— AMERICAN DANCE SUITE
1(alt. with picc.),1(alt. with Eng. hn.),2,1 - 2,2,1,0 - timp.,perc.(1)
- str.   9:30 Mowbray.
—— CONCERTO IN E MINOR, FOR PIANO AND ORCH. (IN 3
MOVTS.)
2,2(2nd alt. with Eng. hn.),2,2 - 4,2,2,1 - timp.,perc.(2) - pf. - str.
22:00 Presser.
—— EPISODIC SUITE
*3,2,2,2 - 4,2,3,1 - timp.,perc.(2),xyl. - hp. - str.   6:00 Mowbray.
—— FOLKWAYS SYMPHONY (IN 4 MOVTS.)
2(2nd alt. with picc.),2,2,sax.,2 - 2,2,1,0 - timp.,perc.(2),xyl. - hp. -
pf.(4-hands) - str.   13:00 C. Fischer.
—— HELLENIC SUITE (IN 3 MOVTS.)
2(2nd alt. with picc.),2(2nd alt. with Eng. hn.),2,2 - 4,2,3,1 -
timp.,perc.(2),glock.,xyl. - hp. - str.   12:00 Presser.
—— THE HERITAGE (FOR CHORUS AND ORCH.)
2(2nd alt. with picc.),2,2,2 - 4,3,3,1 - timp.,perc.(4),bells,glock. -
str.   9:00 Composer.
—— OUR HERITAGE (FOR SATB CHORUS AND ORCH.)
2,2,2,2 - 4,3,3,1 - timp.,perc. - str.   10:00 Presser.
or:
1,1,2,1 - 2,2,1,0 - timp.,perc. - pf. - str.
—— OVERTURE AND MEXICAN DANCES FROM THE OPERA
"THE STRANGER OF MANZANO"
1(alt. with picc.),1(alt. with Eng. hn.),1,1 - 2,2,1,0 -
timp.,perc.(2),cel.(alt. with pf.),xyl. - hp. - str.   13:00 Composer.
—— REMEMBER THE ALAMO! (FOR NARRATOR, OPTIONAL
SATB CHORUS AND ORCH.)
3,3,3,2 - 4,3,3,1 - timp.,perc.(5) - str.   12:30 Presser.

SMITH, Lani
—— PRELUDE AND SCHERZO
0,0,0,0 - 4,3,3,1 - timp. - str.   11:00 C. Fischer.

SMITH, Roger M.
—— OVERTURE "SATURNALIAN"
2(2nd alt. with picc.),2(2nd alt. with Eng. hn.),*3,2 - 4,2,3,1 -
timp.,perc.(3) - str.   8:00 Composer.
—— SUITE FOR CHAMBER ORCH.
1,1,1,1 - 1,1,1,0 - hp. - str.   10:00 Composer.

SMITH, Russell
—— CONCERTO NO. 1 FOR PIANO AND ORCH. (1953) (IN 3
MOVTS.)
1,1,1,1 - 2,0,0,0 - pf. - str.   18:00 Composer.
—— CONCERTO NO. 2 FOR PIANO AND ORCH. (1957) (IN 3
MOVTS.)
2,2,2,*3 - 2,2,2,0 - timp.,perc.(2),glock. - pf. - str.
35:39 Composer.
—— MAGNIFICAT (FOR SOPRANO, CHORUS AND ORCH.)
3,2,3,3 - 4,3,3,1 - timp.,perc. - hp. - pf. - str.   45:00 EV.
—— SINFONIA CONCERTANTE (FOR WOODWIND QUINTET,
HARP AND ORCH.) (1970)
1. Lento - Allegro - Lento; 2. Allegro (Theme andVariations)
3(1 alt. with picc.),3,3,3 - 5,3,3,1 - timp.,perc.(3),glock.,vibra. - hp.
- pf. - str.   25:00 NewOrl.Phi.
—— THE UNICORN IN THE GARDEN (SHORT OPERA, AFTER
JAMES THURBER'S PARABLE) %
1,1,2,1 - 2,1-2,1,0 - timp.,perc. - hp.(ad lib.) - pf. - str.
25:00 G. Schirmer.

SMIT SIBINGA, Th. H.
—— CONCERTO FOR CELLO AND ORCH.
2,2,2,2 - 2,0,3,0 - hp. - str.   18:00 Henmar.
—— CONCERTO FOR GUITAR AND ORCH. (1958)
2,2,2,2 - 2,2,0,0 - timp.,perc. - guit. - str.   21:00 Henmar.
—— KANTJIL - FANTASIE (FOR PIANO AND ORCH.)
2,2,3,3 - 4,3,3,1 - timp.,perc.,cel. - pf. - str.   20:00 Henmar.
—— MOUVEMENT SYMPHONIQUE (1958)
3,2,3,2 - 4,3,3,1 - timp.,perc. - hp. - str.   18:00 Henmar.
—— THREE INDIAN NOCTURNES
3,2,3,2 - 2,2,3,0 - timp.,perc. - cemb. - hp. - str.   14:00 Henmar.
—— VARIAZIONI SU UNA CANZONETTA OLANDESA
2,2,3,2 - 2,2,0,0 - timp.,perc. - hp. - str.   9:00 Henmar.

SMOLANOFF, Michael
—— CANTO FOR TRUMPET AND STRING ORCH., OP. 18 (1964)
tpt. - str.   4:30 Mills.

—— CONCERTINO FOR ALTO SAXOPHONE AND STRING ORCH., OP. 16 (IN 4 MOVTS.)
alto sax. - str.   11:30 EV.

—— CONCERTO FOR ORCHESTRA, OP. 20 (IN 3 MOVTS.)
*4,*3,*3,2 - 4,3,3,1 - timp.,perc.(4),bells,cel.,glock.,xyl. - hp. - pf. - str.   24:00 Composer.

—— CONCERTO FOR PIANO 4-HANDS, STRINGS AND PERCUSSION (1968)
timp.,perc.,bells,vibra.,xyl. - pf. 4-hands - str.   12:00 Seesaw.

—— CONCERTO FOR TROMBONE AND ORCH., OP. 21 (1966) (IN 3 MOVTS.)
2(2nd alt. with picc.),2,3(2nd alt. with b.-cl.),2 - 2,2,1,1 - timp.,perc.(3),cel.,xyl. - hp. - str.   15:00 Mills.

—— CONNOTATIONS FOR STRING ORCH. (1972)
str.   10:00 Seesaw.

—— DAY OF CALM SEA (1972)
1,0,1,1 - 0,0,0,0 - hp. - str.   8:00 Seesaw.

—— ESSAY FOR HORN AND STRING ORCH. (1968)
hn. - str.   4:00 Piedmont.

—— HEAR, O ISRAEL (FOR SATB CHORUS AND STRING ORCH.) (1972)
str.   10:00 Seesaw.

—— SOLILOQUY FOR OCHESTRA, OP. 6
2(2nd alt. with picc.),2,2,2 - 2,2,2,0 - timp.,perc.(2),glock.,xyl. - str.   8:00 EV.

—— VERCINGETORIX (1-ACT OPERA) % (1973) (Text: Frank Mcquilkin)
                                                          55:00 Seesaw.

—— THE WORLD TODAY IS WILD, OP. 33 (FOR BARITONE VOICE, WINDS AND PERCUSSION) (1969) (Text: Rabindranath Tagore)
1,1,1,1 - 2,2,1,1 - perc.(1)   12:00 Seesaw.

SMOLOVER, Raymond
—— WHERE THE RAINBOW ENDS (INTER-FAITH ROCK CEREMONY) (WITH CHORUS, SOLOISTS, DANCERS AND AUDIENCE PARTICIPATION) %
2,1,alto sax.,0 - 0,2,2,1 - timp.,perc. - electric d.-b. - electric org. - pf.   50:00 Belw-Mills.

SØDERLIND, Ragnar
—— PIETÀ, OP. 5 (FOR MEZZO-SOPRANO AND STRINGS) (1965) (Text: Pär Lagerkvist)
str.   5:30 T.O.N.O.

—— POLARIS, OP. 11 (SYMPHONIC VISIONS) (1969)
3,3,3,3 - 6,4,3,1 - perc.(4) - 2 hp. - str.   14:00 T.O.N.O.

—— PRELUDIUM PER OCHESTRA, OP. 4
3,3,3,3 - 4,3,3,1 - timp.,perc.(3) - hp. - pf.(alt. with cel.) - str.   8:45 T.O.N.O.

—— ROKKOMBORRE, (MT. ROKKOMBORRE) OP. 8 (SYMPHONIC POEM)
3,2,3,2 - 4,3,3,1 - perc.(3),cel. - 1-2 hp. - str.   8:00 T.O.N.O.

—— TRAUERMUSIK, OP. 12
3,2,3,2 - 4,3,3,0 - perc.(3) - hp. - org. - str.   7:00 T.O.N.O.

SODERLUND, Gustave Frederic
—— FESTIVAL
2(2nd alt. with picc.),2,2,2 - 4,3,3,1 - timp.,perc.,cel. - str.
                                                          10:00 Composer.

—— SUITE FOR SMALL ORCH. (1964) (IN 5 MOVTS.)
2(2nd alt. with picc.),2,2,2 - 2,2,0,0 - perc.,vibra. - hp. - str.
                                                          22:45 Composer.

—— SYMPHONIC INTERLUDE
2(2nd alt. with picc.)2,2,2 - 4,3,3,1 - timp.,perc.,cel. - str.
                                                          8:00 Composer.

SÖDERLUNDH, Lille Bror
—— ALLEGRO CONCERTANTE (FOR TWO VIOLINS AND STRINGS)
str.   10:00 S.T.I.M.

—— CHRISTINA-MUSIC (SUITE) (FOR STRINGS)
str.   12:00 S.T.I.M.

—— CONCERTO FOR OBOE AND STRINGS
ob. - str.   13:00 S.T.I.M.

—— CONCERTO FOR VIOLIN AND ORCH.
2,1,2,2 - 2,2,2,0 - timp.,perc.,xyl. - str.   24:00 S.T.I.M.

—— FOUR SHORT SUMMER PIECES (FOR STRING ORCH.) (1934)
str.   Nordiska.

—— HAVÄNG-SVIT (FOR PIANO AND STRINGS)
pf. - str.   11:30 S.T.I.M.

—— KEJSARN AV PORTUGALLIEN (BALLET SUITE)
2,2,2,2 - 3,3,2,0 - timp.,perc.(2),xyl. - hp. - cemb. - str.
                                                          20:00 S.T.I.M.

—— PRELUDE NO. 1 FROM "KEJSARN AV PORTUGALLIEN"
2,2,2,2 - 3,3,2,0 - timp.,perc. - hp. - str.   8:00 S.T.I.M.

—— TILL EN KOREOGRAF (SUITE)
1,1,2,1 - 2,2,1,0 - timp.,perc.(2) - hp. - pf. - str.   S.T.I.M.

SODERO, Cesare
—— ELEGY (FOR STRINGS)
str.   Composer.

—— HOLD HIGH THE FRIENDLY LAMP (FOR CHORUS AND ORCH.)
2,2,2,2 - 4,3,3,1 - timp.,perc. - 2 hp. - str.   Composer.

—— INVOCATION (FOR CELLO AND ORCH.)
1,1,2,1 - 2 hn. - pf. - str.   6:00 Composer.

—— NOCTURNE (FOR OBOE AND ORCH.)
1,1,2,1 - 2,0,0,0 - str.   6:00 Composer.

—— PROMETHEUS (SYMPHONIC POEM)
*3,2,2,2 - 4,3,3,1 - timp.,perc. - str.   9:00 Composer.

—— RENATUS ("RETURN TO THE HEARTH") (SYMPHONIC POEM)
3(3rd alt. with picc.),*3,*3,*3 - 4,3,3,1 - timp.,perc. - hp. - str.
                                                          12:00 Composer.

—— THE SINGERS (FOR MEN'S CHORUS AND ORCH.)
*3,*3,*3,*3 - 4,3,3,1 - timp.,perc. - hp. - str.   Composer.

SÖDERSTEN, Gunno
—— CONCERTO NO. 1 FOR ORGAN AND STRING ORCH. (1970)
org. - str.   14:00 Fleisher.

SOHAL, Naresh
—— AALAYKHAM 1
1(alt. with picc.),1(alt. with Eng.hn.),1(alt. with b.-cl.),1 - 1,1,1,0 - perc. - hp. - pf. - str.   14:00 Novello.

—— AALAYKHAM 2
1,1,1,1 - 1,1,1,0 - perc. - guit.,mandolin - hp. - pf. - str.
                                                          22:00 Novello.

—— ASHT PRAHAR (FOR SOPRANO AND ORCH.)
2(alt. with 2 picc.),2(2nd alt. with Eng.hn.),2(2nd alt. with b.-cl.),2(2nd alt. with c.-bn) - 4,4,3,1 - timp.,perc. - 2 hp. - pf. - str.   25:00 Novello.

—— CONCERTO FOR HARMONICA, PERCUSSION AND STRING ORCH.
perc. - harmonica - str.   Novello.

SOINI, Pentti
—— DE PROFUNDIS (1958)
2,3,3,3 - 4,3,3,0 - timp. - str.   7:00 FinnMICtr.

—— LYRICAL OVERTURE (1960)
3,3,3,2 - 4,3,3,0 - timp. - hp. - str.   14:00 FinnMICtr.

—— ORCHESTRAL MUSIC (1957)
2,3,2,3 - 4,3,3,0 - timp.,perc. - pf. - str.   28:00 FinnMICtr.

—— SUITE NO. 1 FOR STRINGS (1959)
str.   19:00 FinnMICtr.

—— SUITE NO. 2 FOR STRINGS (1961)
str.   23:00 FinnMICtr.

—— SUITE NO. 3 FOR STRINGS (1962)
str.   11:00 FinnMICtr.

—— SYMPHONIC SUITE (1958)
3,3,3,3 - 4,3,3,0 - timp. - hp. - str.   26:00 FinnMICtr.

—— SYMPHONY NO. 1 (1958)
2,3,3,2 - 4,3,3,0 - timp.,perc. - str.   31:00 FinnMICtr.

—— SYMPHONY NO. 2 (1961)
2,3,3,2 - 4,3,3,0 - timp.,perc.cel. - str.   41:00 FinnMICtr.

—— SYMPHONY NO. 3 (1963)
2,2,2,2 - 4,3,3,0 - timp.,perc. - pf. - str.   27:00 FinnMICtr.

SOKOLA, Miloš
—— CONCERTO FOR VIOLIN AND ORCHESTRA (1952) (IN 3 MOVTS.)
                                                          Bo. Hawkes.

—— THE PRODIGAL SON (OPERA) %
                                                          Bo. Hawkes.

—— VARIATIONS FOR ORCHESTRA
3,3,3,3 - 4,3,3,1 - timp.,perc. - hp. - pf. - str.   17:00 Bo. Hawkes.

SOKOLOFF, David
—— CARNAVAL ESPAGNOLE (FOR PIANO AND ORCH.)
                                                          Composer.

SOLARES, Enrique
—— PARTITA PARA CUERDAS
str.   12:00 Southern.

SOLBERG, Leif
—— MAIHAUGAN CANTATA (FOR SOLO VOICES, CHORUS
AND STRINGS) (Text: Tore Ørjasaeter)
str.   37:00 T.O.N.O.
—— PASTORALE
2,2,2,2 - 2,2,2,1 - timp.,perc. - str.   10:00 T.O.N.O.
—— SYMPHONY NO. 1
2,2,2,2 - 4,2,3,1 - perc. - hp. - str.   22:00 T.O.N.O.

SOLER, Josep
—— AGAMEMNON (ORATORIO) (1960)
4,3,2,3 - 4,0,3,1 - perc. - 2 hp. - 2 pf. - str.   90:00 Seesaw.
—— CONCIERTO PARA PIANO Y ORQUESTA
16:00 Southern.
—— DANAE
str.   7:00 Southern.
—— LACHRIMAE, 1967
2,0,0,0 - 0,0,0,0 - perc.(2) - guit. - str.   15:00 Seesaw.
—— PASSIO DOMINI NOSTRI JESU CHRISTI, 1968 (ORATORIO)
4,3,3,2 - 0,4,4,0 - perc. - 2 hp. - org. - pf. - str.   120:00 Seesaw.
—— QUETZALCOATL (1966)
1,0,1,0 - 1,0,0,0 - perc.(4) - str,   8:00 Seesaw.
—— SINFONIA (1966)
2,2,2,2 - 5,3,3,1 - timp.,perc.,cel. - 2 hp. - str.   16:00 Seesaw.
—— THE SOLAR CYCLE (1967)
3,3,3,3 - 4,3,3,1 - timp.,perc.,cel. - 2 hp. - pf. - str.   12:00 Seesaw.
—— LA TENTATION DE SAINT ANTOINE (2-ACT OPERA) %
(1967)
4,3,3,2 - 4,3,3,1 - timp.,perc. - hp. - pf. - str.   120:00 Seesaw.
—— THE TRANSFIGURATION
3picc.,2 Eng.hn.,*3,ten.sax.,1 - 4,1,4,1 - perc. - hp. - org. - pf. - str.
11:30 Southern.

SOLHEIM, Karsten
—— CONCERT OVERTURE NO. 1
3,3,2,2 - 4,3,3,1 - timp.,perc. - hp. - str.   13:00 T.O.N.O.
—— CONCERT OVERTURE NO. 2
3,3,2,2 - 4,3,3,1 - timp.,perc. - hp. - str.   18:00 T.O.N.O.
—— ELEGY (FOR VIOLIN AND ORCH.)
1,2,1,1 - 1,1,0,0 - timp. - str.   7:00 T.O.N.O.
—— KING OLAV AND THE KING'S ARMY (KONG OLAV OG
KONGS-HAEREN (FOR SOLO VOICE, MALE CHORUS AND
ORCH.) (Text: S. Skavlan)
2,2,2,2 - 2,2,2,1 - timp.,perc. - str.   8:00 T.O.N.O.
—— ST. OLAV (CANTATA) (KVAD FOR HAILAG OLAG OG DEN
NORSKE KYRKJA) (FOR SOPRANO, ALTO, TENOR, BASS,
MIXED CHORUS AND ORCH.) (Text: Heming Skre)
2,2,2,2 - 4,2,3,1 - timp.,perc. - hp. - org. - str.   120:00 T.O.N.O.
—— ST. OLAV ("HELLIG OLAV") (HISTORICAL LEGEND)
3,2,2,2 - 2,2,3,1 - timp.,perc. - str.   20:00 T.O.N.O.
—— SUITE IN THREE MOVEMENTS
2,2,2,2 - 3,2,3,1 - timp.,perc. - str.   20:00 T.O.N.O.
—— WINTER TIME ("I MØRKETIDEN") (CHRISTMAS CANTATA)
(FOR SOLO VOICE, MIXED CHORUS AND ORCH.)
2,2,2,2 - 2,2,2,1 - timp.,perc. - org. - str.   20:00 T.O.N.O.

SOLITO DE SOLIS, Aldo
—— CADIZ (PORTRAIT OF SPAIN)
3,3,4,3 - 4,4,4,1 - perc.,bells - hp. - str.   5:15 Ricordi.
—— CAPRICCIO ESPAÑOL
3,2,2,2 - 4,3,3,0 - timp.,perc.,bells,xyl. - hp. - str.   4:30 Belw-Mills.
—— TOBALUMI (SYMPHONIC LEGEND)
*3,2,2,2 - 3,3,3,0 - timp.,perc.,bells,cel. - hp. - str.   11:00 Mills.
—— TWO MOODS OF SPAIN
1(alt. with picc.),1,2,1 - 2,2,1,0 - timp.,perc.(2),vibra. - hp. - pf. -
str.   6:00 Mills.

SOLNITZ, Anton Wilhelm - BODART, Eugen
—— SYMPHONY IN C MAJOR, OP. 1, NO. 2
str.   12:00 Mannheimer.
—— SYMPHONY IN D MAJOR, OP. 1, NO. 8
str.   10:00 Mannheimer.
—— SYMPHONY IN E FLAT MAJOR, OP. 1, NO. 10
str.   12:00 Mannheimer.
—— SYMPHONY IN F MAJOR, OP. 1, NO. 11
str.   9:00 Mannheimer.
—— SYMPHONY IN G MAJOR, OP. 1, NO. 1
str.   11:00 Mannheimer.

SOLNITZ, Anton Wilhelm - HOFMANN, Wolfgang
—— SINFONIA IN A MAJOR, OP. 1, NO. 7
str.   10:00 Mannheimer.

—— SINFONIA IN B FLAT MAJOR, OP. 1, NO. 4
str.   8:00 Mannheimer.
—— SINFONIA IN B FLAT MAJOR, OP. 1, NO. 9
str.   9:00 Mannheimer.
—— SINFONIA IN C MINOR, OP. 1, NO. 5
str.   12:00 Mannheimer.
—— SINFONIA IN D MINOR, OP. 1, NO. 3
str.   15:00 Mannheimer.
—— SINFONIA IN E MAJOR, OP. 1, NO. 12
str.   12:00 Mannheimer.
—— SINFONIA IN G MINOR, OP. 1, NO. 6
str.   13:00 Mannheimer.

SOLODUKHO, Jakov S.
—— NINTEEN TWENTY-FOUR (TONE POEM) (FOR BARITONE,
SATB CHORUS AND ORCHESTRA)
G. Schirmer.

SOMARY, Johannes
—— TRIPTYCH
2,2,2,2 - 2,2,0,0 - timp.,perc. - str.   10:00 C. Fischer.

SOMER, Louis
—— BURLESQUE FOR PIANO AND ORCH.
2,2,2,2 - 3,3,3,0 - timp.,perc. - pf. - str.   Henmar.
—— CONCERTO FOR VIOLIN AND ORCH.
3,3,3,2 - 3,3,3,1 - timp.,cel. - hp. - str.   27:00 Henmar.
—— DIVERTIMENTO CONCERTANTE (FOR FLUTE, OBOE,
CLARINET, HARP AND STRINGS)
1,1,1,0 - 0,0,0,0 - hp. - str.   21:00 Henmar.
—— OVERTURE TO "DRIEKONINGENAVOND"
2,3,2,2 - 3,3,3,0 - timp.,perc. - str.   9:00 Henmar.
—— PASSACAGLIA AND FUGUE
3,3,3,2 - 4,4,3,1 - timp.,perc. - str.   17:00 Henmar.
—— SYMPHONIC MUSIC
3,3,2,2 - 4,3,3,1 - timp.,perc. - hp. - str.   10:00 Henmar.
—— VARIATIONS AND FINALE (ON A LIED OF RICHARD HOL)
3,2,3,sax.,2 - 4,3,3,1 - timp.,perc.,cel.,xyl. - hp. - str.   Henmar.
—— VARIATIONS FOR STRINGS
str.   10:00 Henmar.
—— VIJF VOORSPELEN VOOR "GRANIDA"
2,2,2,2 - 3,3,3,1 - timp.,perc. - hp. - str.   20:00 Henmar.

SOMERVELL, Arthur
—— CHRISTMAS (FOR SOLO VOICES, CHORUS AND ORCH.)
1,1,1,1 - 2,1,0,0 - timp. - org. - str.   42:00 Bo. Hawkes.
—— CONCERTO IN G MINOR FOR VIOLIN AND ORCH.
2,2,2,2 - 3,2,3,0 - timp. - str.   30:00 Bo. Hawkes.
—— CONCERTSTÜCK (FOR VIOLIN AND ORCH.)
2,2,2,2 - 4,2,3,1 - timp. - str.   10:00 Galaxy.
—— NORMANDY (SYMPHONIC VARIATIONS FOR PIANO AND
ORCH.)
2,2,*3 - 4,2,3,1 - timp. - pf. - str.   Galaxy.
—— THE PASSION OF CHRIST (FOR SOLO VOICES, MIXED
CHORUS, ORGAN AND STRINGS)
org. - str.   75:00 Bo. Hawkes.
—— SYMPHONY IN D MINOR ("THALASSA")
2,2,2,3 - 4,2,3,1 - timp. - str.   32:30 Bo. Hawkes.
—— THOMAS THE RHYMER (SUITE)
2,2,2,2 - 4,2,0,0 - timp. - hp. - str.   20:00 Bo. Hawkes.
—— TO THE VANGUARD (1914) (FOR SOPRANOS, CHORUS
AND ORCH.)
Bo. Hawkes.
—— VARIATIONS ON AN ORIGINAL THEME
2 pf. - str.   13:30 Galaxy.

SOMMER, Vladimír
—— ANTIGONE (OVERTURE)
3,3,3,3 - 4,4,3,1 - timp.,perc. - str.   13:00 Bo. Hawkes.
—— CONCERTO FOR VIOLIN AND ORCH., OP. 10 (IN 3 MOVTS.)
3,3,3,1 sax.,2 - 4,2,0,0 - timp.,perc. - hp. - str.   28:00 Bo. Hawkes.
—— VOCAL SYMPHONY (FOR ORCH.)
3,3,4,3 - 4,3,3,1 - timp.,perc. - hp. - pf. - str.   32:00 Bo. Hawkes.

SOMMERFELDT, Øistein
—— LITTLE OVERTURE
3,2,2,2 - 4,3,3,1 - timp.,perc. - str.   4:00 Musikk-Hu.
—— MINIATURE SUITE (IN 5 MOVTS.)
1,1,2,1 - 2,1,1,0 - timp.,perc.,cel. - str.   9:00 T.O.N.O.
—— SYMPHONY NO. 1
2,2,2,2 - 4,3,3,1 - timp.,perc. - str.   29:00 T.O.N.O.

SOMMERLATTE, Ulrich
—— FESTLICHER AUFRUF
2,2,2,2 - 4,3,3,1 - timp.,perc. - str.　　　　11:00 Henmar.

SONNINEN, Ahti
—— CONCERTO FOR PIANO AND ORCH., OP. 22 (1945)
2,2,2,2 - 4,2,3,0 - timp. - pf. - str.　　28:00 FinnMICtr.
—— CONCERTO FOR VIOLIN AND ORCH., OP. 16 (1945)
2,2,2,2 - 4,2,3,0 - timp.,perc. - hp. - str.　24:00 FinnMICtr.
—— THE DAUGHTER OF NEPTUNE, OP. 35 (OPERA) % (1949)
(Text: Leo Apo)
2,1,2,1 - 2,2,1,0 - timp.,perc.,cel. - hp. - pf. - str.
　　　　　　　　　　　　　　40:00 FinnMICtr.
—— THE DISTANT GARDEN, OP. 3 (SUITE)(1939)
1,1,1,1 - 2,2,2,0 - perc. - str.　　　13:00 FinnMICtr.
—— EAST KARELIAN SUITE, OP. 15 (1942)
2,1,2,1 - 2,2,2,0 - timp.,perc. - str.　12:00 FinnMICtr.
—— FESTIVAL MUSIC (1961)
0,0,0,0 - 0,2,2,0 - perc. - str.　　　7:00 FinnMICtr.
—— FINALE FURIOSO, OP. 37 (1950)
3,2,3,3 - 4,3,3,1 - timp.,perc.(5),xyl. - hp. - pf. - str.
　　　　　　　　　　　　　　7:00 FinnMICtr.
—— A FINNISH MESSIAH, OP. 67 (FOR SOPRANO, BARITONE, SATB CHORUS, CHILDREN'S CHORUS AND ORCH.) (1972)
1,1,0,1 - 0,2,1,0 - timp.,perc.(3),cel. - hpsc. - str.
　　　　　　　　　　　　　　50:00 FinnMICtr.
—— FIVE SONGS TO WORDS FROM THE BIBLE (FOR SOPRANO AND ORCH.) (1962)
2,0,2,0 - 2,2,1,0 - timp. - hp. - str.　　12:00 Fazer.
—— FOUR PARTITAS, OP. 61 (1958)
str.　　　　　　　　　　25:00 FinnMICtr.
—— FROM THE OLD TESTAMENT, OP. 34-B (SUITE) (REV. 1954)
2,2,0,0 - 1,2,0,0 - perc. - hp. - str.　10:00 FinnMICtr.
—— HAAVRUUVA (OPERA) % (1971) % (Text: Paavo Pitkänen)
2,2,2,2 - 4,3,3,0 - timp.,perc.(5) - str.　100:00 FinnMICtr.
—— IT (BALLET) % (1971)
2,2,2,2 - 4,3,3,0 - timp.,perc.(4),cel. - tape-recorder - hp. - str.
　　　　　　　　　　　　　　30:00 FinnMICtr.
—— LIA'S ARIA (FROM THE OPERA "THE DAUGHTER OF NEPTUNE") (FOR SOPRANO, HARP AND STRINGS) (Text: Leo Apo)
hp. - str.　　　　　　　　　4:00 Fazer.
—— MUSIC TO THE FILM "AUGUST" (1956)
2,2,2,2 - 4,2,3,0 - timp.,perc. - hp. - org. - str.　30:00 FinnMICtr.
—— MUSIC TO THE FILM "THE ENGAGEMENT", OP. 51 (1955)
1,0,1,0 - 1,1,1,0 - timp. - hp. - pf. - str.　10:00 FinnMICtr.
—— MUSIC TO THE FILM "THE UNKNOWN SOLDIER", OP. 54 (1955)
3,2,2,2 - 8,6,6,1 - timp.,perc.(5),cel. - hp. - pf. - str.
　　　　　　　　　　　　　　33:00 FinnMICtr.
—— PARTITA NO. 3 (1961)
str.　　　　　　　　　　FinnMICtr.
—— PARTITA NO. 4 (1961)
str.　　　　　　　　　　FinnMICtr.
—— PESSI AND ILLUSIA, OP. 39 (BALLET) % (1952)
3,2,2,2 - 4,3,3,1 - timp.,perc.(4),cel.,xyl. - hp. - pf. - str.
　　　　　　　　　　　　　　130:00 FinnMICtr.
—— PRELUDE AND ALLEGRO (FOR TRUMPET, TROMBONE AND ORCH.) (1961)
1,0,2,0 - 3,3,1,0 - perc. - str.　　6:00 FinnMICtr.
—— PRELUDE FOR STRING ORCH. (1946)
str.　　　　　　　　　　7:00 FinnMICtr.
—— PRELUDIO FESTIVO, OP. 42 (1953)
2,2,2,2 - 4,3,3,1 - timp. - hp. - str.　7:00 FinnMICtr.
—— REACTIONS, OP. 63 (SUITE)
1,1,1,1 - 1,1,1,0 - perc. - str.　　11:00 FinnMICtr.
—— RHAPSODY, OP. 59 (1957)
2,2,2,2 - 4,3,3,1 - timp.,perc.(4),cel.,xyl. - hp. - str.
　　　　　　　　　　　　　　8:00 FinnMICtr.
—— THE SEVEN BROTHERS, OP. 26 (SUITE) (1948)
2,1,2,1 - 2,2,1,0 - timp.,perc. - hp. - str.　14:00 FinnMICtr.
—— SEVEN SONGS TO HUNGARIAN FOLK POEMS, OP. 14 (FOR SOPRANO AND ORCH.)(1941)
2,2,0,0 - 4,0,0,0 - perc. - str.　　14:00 Westerlund.
—— SYMPHONIC MOMENTS, OP. 29 (1947)
3,2,3,3 - 4,3,3,1 - timp.,perc.(5),cel. - hp. - pf. - str.
　　　　　　　　　　　　　　16:00 Gehrmans.
—— UNDER LAPLAND'S SKY, OP. 49 (SUITE) (1954) (IN 3 MOVTS.)
2,2,2,2 - 4,3,3,1 - timp.,perc.(3),cel.,xyl. - hp. - pf. - str.
　　　　　　　　　　　　　　14:00 FinnMICtr.
—— VILLAGE FESTIVITIES, OP. 31 (1947)
1,0,2,0 - 2,2,1,0 - perc. - pf. - str.　24:00 FinnMICtr.

—— WHEN DOES THE MORNING STAR LIGHT UP? (REV. 1963)
str.　　　　　　　　　　4:00 Fazer.
—— WREATH OF ROSES, OP. 56 (BALLET) % (1956)
2,2,2,2 - 4,2,1,0 - timp.,perc.(3) - hp. - str.　40:00 FinnMICtr.

SØNSTEVOLD, Gunnar
—— CANTATA NO. 1 (FOR SOPRANO, ALTO, SPEAKER AND ORCH.)
2,2,2,2 - 4,3,3,0 - perc. - hp. - pf. - str.　15:00 T.O.N.O.
—— CONCERTO FOR FLUTE, BASSOON AND ORCH.
3,3,3,4 - 4,3,3,1 - timp.,perc.,cel. - hp. - str.　20:30 T.O.N.O.
—— CONCERTO FOR SAXOPHONE AND ORCH.
2,2,2,2 - 4,3,3,1 - timp.,perc. - str.　20:30 T.O.N.O.
—— MUSICAL SPECTACLE (BALLET ON "PEER GYNT") % (1966) (WITH MIXED CHORUS) (Text: H. Ibsen)
2,2,2,3 - 4,3,3,1 - timp.,perc. - hp. - 2 pf. - str.　T.O.N.O.
—— OLD PORTRAITS (GAMLE PORTRETTER)
2,1,2,1 - 2,2,2,0 - timp.,perc.,cel. - hp. - pf. - str.　19:00 T.O.N.O.
—— RITUAL (BALLET) %
3,3,2,2 - 4,2,3,0 - timp.,perc.,cel. - hp. - org. - pf. - str.　T.O.N.O.
—— SINFONIETTA
2,2,2,2 - 4,3,3,1 - timp.,perc. - str.　23:00 T.O.N.O.

SØNSTEVOLD, Maj
—— SIX PAIR OF SHOES (6 PAR SKO) (FOR NARRATOR AND ORCH.)
2,1,2,1 - 2,3,1,1 - timp. - pf. - str.　8:30 T.O.N.O.
—— SØRLANDSSOMMER (SUITE) (IN 4 MOVTS.)
1,1,2,1 - 1,0,0,0 - perc.,cel. - hp. - acc. - pf. - str.　10:00 T.O.N.O.
—— VÅR-VON (BALLAD) (FOR TENOR, 2 MALE CHORUSES AND ORCH.) (1966) (Text: Per Sivle)
2,2,2,2 - 4,3,2,0 - perc.,cel. - hp. - str.　8:00 T.O.N.O.

SONTAG, Wesley
—— FOLK SONG SET
str.　　　　　　　　　　Galaxy.

SONZOGNO, Giulio Cesare
—— L' AMORE DELLE TRE MELARANCE: SUITE FROM THE BALLET
3,2,2,3 - 4,3,3,1 - timp.,perc.,cel.,glock.,xyl. - 2 hp. - pf. - str.
　　　　　　　　　　　　　　14:00 Leeds.
—— L' AMORE DELLE TRE MELARANCE ("THE LOVE FOR THE 3 ORANGES") (BALLET, AFTER CARLO GOZZI'S STORY) %
3,2,2,3 - 4,3,3,1 - timp.,perc.,cel.,glock.,xyl. - 2 hp. - pf. - str.
　　　　　　　　　　　　　　55:00 Leeds.
On stage: buccina
—— DAI NEVAI DELL'ORTLER (FROM THE SNOW GROUNDS OF THE ORTLER) (3 MOVTS. FOR ORCH.)
3,2,2,2 - 4,3,3,1 - timp.,perc.,cel.,glock.,vibra.,xyl. - Hawaiian guit. - 2 hp. - pf. - str.　22:00 Leeds.
—— DITTICO (DIPTYCH) (FOR CELLO AND ORCH.)
timp.,perc.,cel. - hp. - str.　12:00 Leeds.
—— JEDERMANN ("LA LEGGENDA DI OGNUNO")(INCIDENTAL MUSIC FOR HOFFMANSTHAL'S DRAMA) (FOR CHORUS AND ORCH.) %
2,2,2,2 - 4,3,3,1 - timp.,perc.,bells - 2 hp. - org. - pf. - str.　Leeds.
On stage: guit. - mandolas(large lutes) - mandolins
—— LAGO DI BRAIES (3 MOVTS. FOR ORCH.)
3,2,2,2 - 4,3,3,1 - timp.,perc.,cel.,glock.,xyl. - hp. - pf. - str.
　　　　　　　　　　　　　　27:00 Leeds.
—— LEGGENDA SCANDINAVA (BALLET) %
2,2,2,2 - 2,2,2,1 - timp.,perc.,xyl. - str.　30:00 Leeds.
On stage: bells
—— MASS (FOR SOPRANO, TENOR, MIXED CHORUS AND ORCH.)
2,2,2,2 - 4,3,3,1 - timp.,perc.(2) - hp. - str.　45:00 Leeds.
—— PASSEGGERI (1-ACT COMIC OPERA) % (Text: C. Fontana)
3,3,3,3 - 4,3,3,1 - timp.,perc.(2) - hp. - pf. - str.　Leeds.
—— QUADRI RUSTICI (RUSTIC SCENES) (2 MOVTS. FOR SMALL ORCH.)
1,2,1,1 - 2,2,1,0 - cel.,xyl. - hp. - 2 pf. - str.(no d.-b.)　7:00 Leeds.
—— REGINA ULIVA ("QUEEN ULIVA") (3-ACT OPERA) % (Text: Renato Simoni)
3,3,3,3 - 4,3,3,1 - timp.,perc.(2),cel.,xyl. - 2 hp. - pf. - str.　Leeds.
On stage: 0,0,0,0 - 2,3,3,0 - bells - org.

SOPRONI, József
—— CONCERTO FOR CELLO AND ORCH.
*3,2,*3,2 - 4,3,3,1 - timp.,perc.,cel. - hp. - pf. - str.
　　　　　　　　　　　　　　16:20 Bo. Hawkes.
—— CONCERTO FOR STRING ORCH.
str.　　　　　　　　　　Bo. Hawkes.

—— EKLYPSIS
 3,2,*3,2 - 3,4,4,4 - timp.,perc.(4, incl. 3 on timp.),cel. - hp. - pf. - str.   8:00 Bo. Hawkes.

SÖRENSON, Torsten
—— CONCERTO FOR ORGAN AND STRING ORCH., OP. 25
 org.(no pedals) - str.   13:00 S.T.I.M.
—— FIVE SMALL PIECES FOR STRING ORCH. (1967)
 str.   6:00 Gehrmans.
—— ETT LITET BARN SKALL LEDA DEM, OP. 21 (CANTATA)
(FOR SPEAKER, SOLO VOICES, MIXED CHORUS, ORGAN
AND STRINGS) (Text: John Nilsson)
 org. - str.   17:30 Nordiska.
—— PSALM 103, OP. 34 (FOR ALTO, BARITONE, CHILDREN'S
CHORUS, MIXED CHORUS, ORGAN AND ORCH.) (1960)
 2,1,0,1 - 1,2,2,0 - timp. - org. - str.   18:00 S.T.I.M.
—— PSALM 22, OP. 26 (FOR BARITONE, ORGAN AND STRING
ORCH.)
 org. - str.   9:00 S.T.I.M.
—— SINFONIA DA CHIESA NO. 2 (FOR STRING ORCH.) (REV.
1969)
 str.   13:00 Fleisher.
—— SINFONIA DA CHIESA, OP. 32
 str.   14:00 S.T.I.M.
—— SINFONIETTA FOR STRING ORCH., OP. 14 (REV. 1957)
 str.   17:00 S.T.I.M.
—— SYMPHONY FOR CHAMBER ORCH., OP. 29
 1,1,1,1 - 1,1,0,0 - timp.,perc.(2) - str. 21:30 S.T.I.M.
—— EN TACKSÄGELSENS PSALM, OP. 31 (FOR BARITONE,
MIXED CHORUS, ORGAN AND ORCH.)
 1,1,0,0 - 0,1,0,0 - timp. - org. - str.   12:30 S.T.I.M.
—— DEN UNDERBARA KVARNEN, OP. 2 (FOR BARITONE AND
ORCH.) (REV. 1958) (Text: Erik Axel Karlfeldt)
 3,2,2,2 - 2,2,2,1 - timp.,perc.(3),xyl. - hp. - str. 8:30 S.T.I.M.

SORESINA, Alberto
—— L' AMULETO ("THE TALISMAN") (1-ACT OPERA) %
 1,1,1,1 - 2,2,1,0 - timp.,perc.(2),cel.,glock. - hp. - pf. - str. Leeds.
 On stage: 2 tpt.

SORKOZY, Istvan
—— SONGS OF JULIA (CANTATA FOR TENOR, CHORUS AND
ORCH.)
     Bo. Hawkes.

SORRENTINO, Charles
—— ANDANTE FOR ORCH.
 2(1 alt. with picc.),2,2,2 - 2,2,1,0 - timp.,perc.(2) - str.
     5:30 Composer.
—— THE CANDELABRUM (ONE-ACT OPERA) % (Text: W. C.
Harrington)
 1(alt. with picc.),1,2,1 - 2,1,1,0 - timp.,perc.(1) - hp. - pf. - str.
     60:00 Composer.
—— CHRISTOPHER COLUMBUS OVERTURE
 2(1 alt. with picc.),2,2,2 - 2,2,1,0 - timp.,perc.(2),glock. - str.
     4:35 Composer.
—— CONCERTO FOR HARMONICA AND ORCH. (IN 3 MOVTS.)
 *3,2,2,2 - 4,3,2,1 - timp.,perc.(2) - harmonica - str.
     25:00 Composer.
—— CONCERTO FOR VIOLA AND ORCH. (IN 3 MOVTS.)
 *3,2,*3,2 - 4,2,1,0 - timp.,perc.(2),glock. - str. 20:00 Fema.
—— CONCERTO IN A MINOR, FOR VIOLIN AND ORCH. (IN 1
MOVT.)
 2(2nd alt. with picc.),2,2,2 - 2,2,1,0 - perc. - str. 13:00 Composer.
—— CONCERTO IN F MINOR, FOR PIANO AND ORCH. (IN 3
MOVTS.)
 2(2nd alt. with picc.),2,2,2 - timp.,perc.(2) - pf. - str.
     32:00 Composer.
—— DEDICATION (FOR VOICE AND ORCHESTRA) (Text:
Goethe)
 2(1 alt. with picc.),2,2,2 - 2,2,1,0 - timp.,perc.(1) - str.
     12:00 Composer.
—— ETUDE FOR ORCHESTRA (1968)
 *3,2,2,2 - 4,3,3,1 - timp.,perc.(2) - str. 7:00 Composer.
—— THE FERRYMAN (TONE POEM) (1943)
 *3,*3,*3,*3 - 4,3,2,0 - timp.,perc.(3) - hp. - str. 28:00 Composer.
—— FESTIVAL OVERTURE
 1(alt. with picc.),1,2,1 - 2,2,1,0 - timp.,perc. - str. 3:30 Composer.
—— FOR THE YOUNG (SUITE FOR ORCHESTRA) (IN 3 MOVTS.)
 2(2nd alt. with picc.),2,2,2 - 2,2,1,0 - timp.,perc.(2) bell - str.
     9:00 Fema.
—— HIMNO DEL INCA (TONE POEM) (1942)
 *3,*3,*3,*3 - 4,3,2,0 - timp.,perc.(3) - hp. - str. 35:00 Composer.

—— IN RETROSPECT
 1(alt. with picc.),1,2,1 - 2,2,2,0 - timp.,perc.(2) - str.
     5:00 Composer.
—— POÈME (FOR CELLO AND ORCH.)
 2(2nd alt. with picc.),2,2,2 - 4,3,2,0 - timp.,perc.(1),str.
     12:00 Composer.
—— PRELUDE (1942)
 *3,*3,*3,2 - 4,3,3,0 - timp.,perc.(3) - hp. - str. 25:00 Composer.
—— DE PROFUNDIS (1959)
 timp.,perc.,bells - str.   15:00 Composer.
—— SCHERZO ("THE JOLLY WHISTLER")
 2(2nd alt. with picc.),2,2,2 - 2,2,2,1 - timp.,perc. - str. 12:00 Mills.
—— SWANS AND THE JACKAL (BALLET) %
 1,1,1,1 - 1,2,1,0 - timp.,perc.(2) - str. Composer.
—— SYMPHONIETTA (1943)
 str.   36:00 Composer.
—— SYMPHONY IN C MINOR (IN 4 MOVTS.)
 2(2nd alt. with picc.),2,2,2 - 4,3,3,1 - timp.,perc.(2) - str.
     40:00 Composer.
—— THREE PATTERNS FOR ORCHESTRA
 2(2nd alt. with picc.),2,2,2 - 4,2,1,0 - timp.,perc.(2), bells - str.
     20:00 Fema.

SOURIS, André
—— BRUMES (FOR VIOLIN AND ORCH.) (1920)
 2,2,3,2 - 3,3,0,0 - str.   S.A.B.A.M.
—— CALAMI SOLUM (FOR SMALL ORCH.) (1961)
 0,0,0,2 - 2,0,2,0 - str.(no vlns.) 5:00 S.A.B.A.M.
—— LA CHANSON DE ROLAND (1942)
 2,2,2,2 - 4,3,3,1 - timp.,perc. - hp. - pf. - str. S.A.B.A.M.
—— CINQ DANCERIES FLAMANDES (FOR SMALL ORCH.)
(1958)
 1,2,0,2 - 1,2,1,0 - perc. - hp. - str. 7:37 S.A.B.A.M.
—— COLLAGE (1928)
 2,2,3,2 - 4,3,2,1 - timp.,perc. - str. 5:30 S.A.B.A.M.
—— DANSERIES DE LA RENAISSANCE FRANÇAISE (1932)
 2,2,2,2 - 4,2,2,0 - timp.,perc.,cel. - hp. - str. 16:00 H. Elkan.
—— DANSES MOSANES (1943)
 2,1,2,1 - 1,2,1,1 - timp.,perc. - pf. - str. S.A.B.A.M.
—— HUIT CHANSONS ENFANTINES (FOR SMALL ORCH.) (1943)
 2,1,2,1 - 1,2,1,0 - perc. - pf. - str. S.A.B.A.M.
—— OUVERTURE POUR UNE ARLEQUINADE (1962) (FOR
SMALL ORCH.)
 1,1,0,1 - 0,0,0,0 - str.   4:00 S.A.B.A.M.
—— PASSACAILLE (FOR SMALL ORCH.)
 2,2,0,2 - 2,0,0,0 - hp. - str. S.A.B.A.M.
—— PRELUDE (1922)
 2,2,2,2 - 3,2,2,0 - timp. - str. S.A.B.A.M.
—— SCHERZO (1923)
 2,2,2,2 - 4,2,2,0 - timp.,perc. - str. S.A.B.A.M.
—— SEPT PIÈCES D'ISSAC (1963)
 2,3,0,2 - 4,2,3,0 - harp - str. S.A.B.A.M.
—— SOLILOQUE (FOR SMALL ORCH.)
 2,2,2,2 - 0,0,2,0 - perc. - str. S.A.B.A.M.
—— SYMPHONY (1939)
 2,2,3,2 - 4,2,2,1 - timp.,perc.,cel.,glock.,xyl. - str. 14:00 CBDM.

SOUSA, Filipe de
—— SUITE OF DANCES (FROM THE BALLET "LUSITANIA")
 3,2,3,2 - 4,3,3,1 - timp.,perc. - str. 15:00 Modern.

SOUSA, John Philip - KAY, Hershy
—— STARS AND STRIPES (BALLET SUITE)
 *3(alt. with 3 picc.),2,*3(2nd alt. with E♭ cl.),2 - 4,4,3,1 euph.,1 -
 perc.(4),bells,xyl. - hp. - str. 27:00 Bo. Hawkes.

SOUSA, John Philip - TUROK, Paul
—— A SOUSA OVERTURE, OP. 43 (1975)
 *3,*3,*3(incl. E♭ cl. ad lib.),2-*3 - 4,3,3,1 - timp.,perc.(4), glock.,
 xyl. - hp. - str. 8:00 G. Schirmer.

SOWANDE, Fela
—— AFRICAN SUITE
 str.   23:00 Chappell.
—— FOLK SYMPHONY
 2,3,2,2 - 4,2,3,1 - timp.,perc. - hp. - str. 37:00 Leeds.
—— NIGERIAN MINATURES (SUITE)
     20:00 P.R.S.

SOWERBY, Leo
—— THE CANTICLE OF THE SUN (FOR CHORUS AND ORCH.)
 3(3rd alt. with picc.),*3,*3,*3 - 4,3,3,1 - timp.,perc.(3),glock.,xyl. -
 str.   35:00 Gray.

—— CLASSIC CONCERTO (FOR ORGAN AND STRINGS)
org. - str.   16:00 Gray.
—— COMES AUTUMN TIME (OVERTURE)
*3,2,*3,2 - 4,3,3,1 - timp.,perc.(3) - hp. - str.   G. Schirmer.
—— CONCERT OVERTURE
*3,2,2,2 - 4,3,3,1 - perc.(3) - hp. - str.   9:00 Mus.Press.
—— CONCERT PIECE FOR ORGAN AND ORCH.
                                                  7:00 Gray.
—— CONCERTO IN C MAJOR, FOR ORGAN AND ORCH.
3(3rd alt. with picc.),*3,*3,2 - 4,3,3,1 - timp.,perc.(3) - org. - str.
                                                  29:00 Gray.
—— CONCERTO IN E MINOR, FOR CELLO AND ORCH. (IN 3
MOVTS.)
3(3rd alt. with picc.),*3,2,*3 - 4,3,3,1 - timp.,perc.(3) - hp. - str.
                                                  30:00 Composer.
—— CONCERTO IN G MINOR, FOR VIOLIN AND ORCH. (IN 3
MOVTS.)
2(2nd alt. with picc.),2(2nd alt. with Eng. hn.),2,2 - 4,2,3,1 -
timp.,perc.(3) - hp. - str.   31:00 Composer.
—— CONCERTO NO. 1 IN F, FOR PIANO AND ORCH.
*3,*3,2,2 - 4,3,3,1 - timp.,perc.(3) - pf. - str.   30:00 Composer.
—— CONCERTO NO. 2 IN E, FOR PIANO AND ORCH.
2,2,2,2 - 4,3,3,1 - timp.,perc.(4) - pf. - str.   16:00 Composer.
—— FROM THE NORTHLAND (SUITE) (IN 4 MOVTS.)
3(3rd alt. with picc.),*3,E♭cl.,*3,*3 - 4,3,3,1 - timp.,perc.(3) - hp. -
pf. - str.   20:00 SPAM.
—— GREAT IS THE LORD (FOR CHORUS AND ORCH.)
2,2,2,2 - 4,2,3,0 - timp.,perc. - str.   10:00 Gray.
—— KING ESTMERE (BALLAD FOR 2 PIANOS AND ORCH.)
*3,*3,2,3(3rd alt. with c.-bn.) - 4,3,3,1 - timp.,perc.(3) - 2 pf. - str.
                                                  17:00 Composer.
—— MEDIEVAL POEM
1,1(alt. with Eng. hn.),1(alt. with b.-cl.),1 - 2,1,0,0 - timp. - org. -
str.   16:00 C. Fischer.
—— PASSACAGLIA, INTERLUDE AND FUGUE
3(3rd alt. with picc.),*3,*3,*3 - 4,3,3,1 - timp.,perc.(4) - hp. - pf. -
str.   18:00 Composer.
—— POEM FOR VIOLA AND ORCH.
2,2,2,2 - 3,2,0,0 - timp. - str.   14:00 Gray.
—— PRAIRIE (SYMPHONIC POEM)
3(3rd alt. with picc.),*3,*3,*3 - 4,3,3,1 - timp.,perc. - str.
                                                  17:00 C. Fischer.
—— RHAPSODY FOR CHAMBER ORCH.
1,1(alt. with Eng. hn.),2,1 - 2,1,1,0 - perc.(1) - str.
                                                  12:00 Composer.
—— SET OF FOUR (SUITE FOR IRONICS)
*3,*3,*3,2 - 4,3,3,0 - timp.,perc.(3) - hp. - pf. - str.
                                                  14:00 C. Fischer.
—— SINFONIETTA FOR STRING ORCH. (IN 3 MOVTS.)
str.   18:00 Composer.
—— SOLOMON'S GARDEN (CANTATA) (FOR TENOR, SATB
CHORUS AND ORCH.)
1,1,2,1 - 2,1,1,0 - timp.,perc. - org. - str.   Belw-Mills.
—— SYMPHONY NO. 2 IN B MINOR (IN 3 MOVTS.)
*3,*3,*3,*3 - 4,3,3,1 - timp.,perc. - str.   25:00 Composer.
—— SYMPHONY NO. 3 IN F SHARP MINOR (IN 3 MOVTS.)
3(3rd alt. with picc.),*3,*3,*3 - 4,3,3,1 - timp.,perc.(4) - hp. - pf. -
str.   40:00 Composer.
—— SYMPHONY NO. 4
*3,*3,*3,*3 - 4,3,3,1 - timp.,perc.(4) - str.   30:00 Composer.
—— THEME IN YELLOW
2,2(2nd alt. with Eng. hn.),2(2nd alt. with b.-cl.),2 - 4,2,3,1 -
timp.,perc.(3) - hp. - str.   14:00 Composer.
—— THE THRONE OF GOD (A POEM FOR MIXED CHORUS
AND ORCH.)
*3,*3,*3,2 - 4,3,3,1 - timp.,perc.(3) - str.   33:00 Gray.
—— THE VISION OF SIR LAUNFAL (CANTATA) (FOR
CONTRALTO, TENOR, BARITONE, CHORUS AND ORCH.)
2,1,2,1 - 2,1,1,0 - timp.,perc. - str.   60:00 Composer.

SPAGNOLI, Guido
—— SUITE (IN 3 MOVTS.)
3,3,4,3 - 4,3,3,1 - perc.,bells,cel.,xyl. - hp. - pf. - str.
                                                  12:00 Bo. Hawkes.
—— TWO INTERMEZZI (FROM THE LYRIC SYMPHONIC POEM
"I DUE PASTORI")
3,3,2,2 - 4,2,3,0 - timp. - hp. - pf. - str.   6:00 Bo. Hawkes.

SPAIN-DUNK, S.
—— SUITE FOR STRINGS
str.   Galaxy.

SPALDER, Frithjof
—— CANTATA (KANTATE TIL FILADEL FIAMENIGHETENS
NYE LOKALE) (Text: T. B. Barratt)
perc. - org. - str.   30:00 T.O.N.O.
—— CONCERTO FOR ORGAN AND ORCH. (IN 3 MOVTS.)
timp.,perc. - org. - str.   20:00 T.O.N.O.
—— ERLING SKJALGSSON (FOR MALE CHORUS AND ORCH.)
(Text: Per Sivle)
2,2,2,2 - 4,3,3,1 - timp.,perc. - hp. - str.   12:00 T.O.N.O.
—— IN MEMORIAM
2,2,2,2 - 4,3,3,1 - timp.,perc. - str.   5:00 T.O.N.O.
—— JUBILEE CANTATA (FOR MALE CHORUS AND ORCH.)
(Text: M. B. Landstad)
2,2,2,2 - 4,3,3,1 - timp.,perc. - str.   30:00 T.O.N.O.
—— JUBILEE CANTATA (FOR SOLO VOICE, MALE CHORUS
AND CHAMBER ORCH.) (Text: Sverre D. Huseby)
perc. - str.   25:00 T.O.N.O.
—— PASTORALE
1,1,1,0 - 1,1,0,0 - perc.,vibra. - harm. - org. - pf. - str.
                                                  6:00 T.O.N.O.

SPALDING, Albert
—— CONCERTO QUASI FANTASIA (FOR VIOLIN AND ORCH.
IN 3 MOVTS.)
2,2,2,2 - 2,2,2,0 - timp. - str.   25:00 Composer.

SPANNAGEL, Carl
—— CONCERTO GROSSO (FOR 2 VIOLINS, 2 TRUMPETS AND
STRING ORCH.)
2 tpt. - str.   20:00 F. Colombo.

SPEDDING, Frank
—— CONCERTO FOR CELLO AND ORCH. (1964)
2,2,2,alto sax.,2 - 4,3,3,1 - timp.,perc.(3),cel. -guit. - hp. - pf. - str.
                                                  15:00 P.R.S.
—— SINFONIA PICCOLA (1953)
2,2,2,2 - 4,2,3,1 - timp.,perc.(3) - hp. - str.   14:00 P.R.S.
—— SYMPHONY (1959)
2,2,2,2 - 4,2,3,1 - timp.,perc.(4),cel. - hp. - str.   40:00 P.R.S.
—— VARIATIONS ON A WALTZ FROM MONTENEGRO (1958)
3,3,3,3 - 4,3,3,1 - timp.,perc.(3) - hp. - pf. - str.   20:00 P.R.S.

SPELMAN, Timothy M.
—— FIVE BARBARESQUES
2(2nd alt. with picc.),2(2nd alt. with Eng. hn.),2,2 - 2,1,2,0 -
timp.,perc.(4) - hp. - str.   30:00 G. Schirmer.
—— SAINTS' DAYS (4 TONE POEMS)
3(3rd alt. with picc.),*3,*3,2 - 4,3,3,1 - timp.,perc.(4),cel. - hp. -
str.   36:00 G. Schirmer.

SPENCE LYONS, David
—— CONCERTO FOR PIANO AND STRING ORCH. (1968)
pf. - str.   15:00 P.R.S.
—— PARTITA FOR STRING ORCH. (1967)
str.   14:00 P.R.S.

SPENCER, James H.
—— AN AMERICAN DANCE FANTASY
2,1,2,1 - 4,2,3,1 - timp.,perc. - pf. - str.   8:00 Composer.
—— FROM THE ADIRONDACKS (SUITE) (IN 4 MOVTS.)
1,1,2,1 - 2,2,0,0 - timp. - hp. - str.   15:00 Composer.
—— NATIVITY
1,1,2,1 - hn. - pf. - str.   7:00 Composer.
—— THE SONG OF SOLOMON (FOR SOPRANO, ALTO,
BARITONE, CHORUS AND ORCH.)
*3,2,2,2 - 4,3,3,1 - timp.,perc.(2) - hp. - str.   60:00 Composer.
—— SYMPHONY IN D MAJOR (AMERICAN FOLK SYMPHONY)
(IN 3 MOVTS.)
1,1,2,1 - 2,2,1,0 - timp.,perc.(3) - hp. - str.   20:00 Composer.

SPEZZAFERRI, Giovanni
—— CATERINA DA SIENA (CANTATA) (FOR SOPRANO,
CHORUS AND ORCH.) (1947)
2,2,2,2 - 4,2,3,0 - timp.,perc.,cel. - hp. - str.   22:00 Leeds.

SPIALEK, Hans
—— THE TALL CITY (IN 4 MOVTS.)
*3,*3,*4,3 sax.,*3 - 4,4,3,1 - timp.,perc.,cel. - hp. - pf. - str.
                                                  18:00 Harms, Inc.

SPIEGELMAN, Joel
—— TWO MOVEMENTS FOR ORCHESTRA
    2,2,3,3 - 4,3,3,0 - timp.,perc. - hp. - str.   10:00 C. Fischer.

SPIER, Harry R.
—— THE ISLAND (FOR WOMEN'S CHORUS, PIANO AND
    STRINGS)
    pf. - str.   8:00 Composer.

SPIES, Claudio
—— IL CANTICO DI FRATE SOLE (THE CANTICLE OF
    BROTHER SUN) (FOR BASS-BARITONE AND SMALL
    ORCH.) (1958) (Text: St. Francis of Assisi)
    1,1,1,1 - 2,2,2,0 - hp. - str.   Composer.
—— EIGHTS AND FIVES (LXXXV) (FOR STRINGS AND
    CLARINETS)
    21:00 Bo. Hawkes.
—— MUSIC FOR A BALLET (1955) (IN 4 MOVTS.)
    *3,*3,2,2 - 4,2,2,0 - timp. - str.   15:00 Presser.
—— TEMPI (MUSIC FOR 14 INSTRUMENTS)
    0,*2,1 ob.d'amore,*2,0 - 1,0,1 alto trb.,1,0 - cel.,xyl. - hp. - 1 vin.,1
    vla.,1c.   18:00 EV.

SPIES, Leo
—— DER STRALAUER FISCHZUG (BALLET SUITE)
    2,2,2,2 - 4,3,3,1 - timp.,perc. - str.   13:00 Tetra.

ŠPILER, Miroslav
—— INTRODUCTION AND LARGO (FOR CHAMBER ORCH.)
    1,1,1,1 - 2,1,0,0 - timp.,perc.,cel. - hp. - str.   13:00 S.O.K.O.J.
—— OBSESSION
    3(3rd alt. with picc.),*3,*3,*3 - 4,3,3,1 - timp.,perc.,xyl. - pf. - str.
    8:00 S.O.K.O.J.
—— SYMPHONY IN TWO MOVTS.
    3(3rd alt. with picc.),*3,*3,*2 - 4,3,3,1 - timp.,perc.,xyl. - hp. - pf.
    - str.   19:00 S.O.K.O.J.
—— THREE COMPOSITIONS FOR VIOLIN AND CHAMBER
    ORCH.
    1,1,1,1 - 1,0,0,0 - str.   13:00 S.O.K.O.J.

SPINKS, Charles
—— DANCE SUITE
    ob. - str.   8:00 Oxford.
—— SUITE FOR FLUTE AND STRINGS
    fl. - str.   13:00 Lengnick.

SPINNER, Leopold
—— CONCERTO FOR PIANO AND ORCH., OP. 4
    1,1,2,0 - 1,1,1,0 - perc.,xyl. - hp. - pf. - str.   8:00 Bo. Hawkes.
—— PRELUDE AND VARIATIONS FOR ORCH., OP. 18
    1,2,2,0 - 1,1,1,1 - timp.,perc.(2),cel. - hp. - str.   12:00 Bo. Hawkes.

SPIRÉA, André
—— DIVERTIMENTO
    12:00 IsMuPublns.
—— POEM (FOR OBOE AND CHAMBER ORCH.)
    1,1,1,2 - 0,1,0,0 - timp. - str.   12:00 IsMuPublns.
—— SYMPHONIE DE CHAMBRE (FOR VIOLA AND 17
    INSTRUMENTS)
    0,*3,*3,*3 - timp.,perc.,cel.,xyl. - pf. - 1 vla.,2 c., 1 d.-b.
    15:00 IsMuPublns.

SPISAK, Michel
—— CONCERTINO FOR TROMBONE AND ORCH.
    1,1,1,1 - 1,1,1,1 - timp. - str.   10:00 Baron.
—— CONCERTO GIOCOSO (FOR CHAMBER ORCH.)
    2,2,2,2 - 2,2,1,1 - timp.,xyl. - pf. - str.   17:00 Baron.

SPITTA, Heinrich
—— CONCERTO IN G MINOR FOR 4 VIOLINS AND ORCH., OP.
    68
    Möseler.
—— FEIERLICHE MUSIK, OP. 37 (CEREMONIAL MUSIC)
    Möseler.
—— PARTITA FOR ORCH., OP. 25
    Möseler.
—— SINFONIA PASTORALE, OP. 85 (FOR 2 CELLOS AND
    STRING ORCH.)
    Möseler.

SPITZMÜLLER, Alexander
—— CONCERT DANS L'ESPRIT LATIN (FOR PIANO AND
    ORCH.), OP. 37
    1,0,1,1 - 0,1,0,0 - timp.,perc. - pf. - str.   19:00 Bo. Hawkes.
—— CONCERTO NO. 1 FOR PIANO AND ORCH.
    2,2,2,2 - 4,3,3,1 - timp.,perc. - pf. - str.   16:00 Bo. Hawkes.
—— CONCERTO NO. 2 FOR PIANO AND ORCH.
    2,2,2,2 - 4,3,3,1 - timp.,perc. - pf.,str.   25:00 Bo. Hawkes.
—— LES HEURES D'AUTOMNE (FOR WOMEN'S CHORUS AND
    STRING ORCH.)
    str.   12:00 F. Colombo.
—— SYMPHONIE POUR ARCHETS
    str.   20:00 F. Colombo.
—— SYMPHONY, OP. 19
    22:00 A.K.M.
—— TE DEUM, OP. 23 (FOR FEMALE CHORUS, ORGAN AND
    ORCH.)
    25:00 A.K.M.

SPOHR, Louis - HEUSSNER, Horst
—— SYMPHONY NO. 3 IN C MINOR, OP. 78
    2,2,2,2 - 4,2,3,0 - timp. - str.   32:00 G. Schirmer.

SPOHR, Louis - LEINERT
—— CONCERTO IN C MINOR FOR CLARINET AND ORCH., OP.
    26
    2,2,2,2 - 2,2,0,0 - timp. - str.   25:00 G. Schirmer.

SREBOTNJAK, Alojz
—— ANTIPHONY
    2(2nd alt. with picc.),2(2nd alt. with Eng. hn.),2(2nd alt. with
    b.-cl.),2(2nd alt. with c.-bn.) - 4,3,3,0 - timp.,perc.(4) - hp. - str.
    11:00 Hans Gerig.
—— MICROSONGS (FOR VOICE AND 13 INSTRUMENTS)
    1,1,1(alt. with b.-cl.),1 - 1,1,0,0 - perc. - hp. - str.(1,1,1,1)
    12:00 Hans Gerig.

SRNKA, Jiři
—— CONCERTO FOR VIOLIN AND ORCH.
    3,3,3,3 - 4,3,3,0 - timp.,perc. - hp. - pf. - str.   35:00 Bo. Hawkes.

ŠROM, Karel
—— PLIVNÍK (THE GOBLIN) (SCHERZO) (1953)
    3,3,3,3 - 6,3,3,1 - timp.,perc.,cel.,xyl. - 2 hp. - pf. - str.
    15:00 Bo. Hawkes.
—— SUITE FOR ORCHESTRA (1934)
    Bo. Hawkes.
—— SYMPHONY NO. 1 (1930)
    Bo. Hawkes.
—— SYMPHONY NO. 2 (1951)
    3,3,3,3 - 4,3,3,1 - timp.,perc. - hp. - str.   31:00 Bo. Hawkes.

STADLER, Rolf
—— CONCERTO FOR OBOE AND ORCH., OP. 22
    2,1,2,2 - 2,2,0,0 - timp.,perc. - str.   18:00 Tetra.

STAEMPFLI, Edward
—— CONCERT NO. 3 FOR PIANO AND ORCH.
    2,2,*3,*3 - 4,3,3,1 - timp.,perc. - pf. - str.   26:00 S.U.I.S.A.
—— CONCERTINO FOR PIANO AND CHAMBER ORCH.
    1,1,1,1 - 1,1,1,0 - timp. - hp. - pf. - str.   12:00 SDMV.
—— CONCERTO NO. 3 FOR VIOLIN AND ORCH. (1966)
    2,2,*1,2 - 3,2,1,1 - timp.,perc.,vibra. - hp. - pf. - str.
    18:00 Hans Gerig.
—— CONCORDIA DISCORS (FÜR 2 GROSSE ORCHESTER)
    16:00 S.U.I.S.A.
—— GROSSES MOSAIK (FÜR ZWEI SOLOKLAVIERE UND
    INSTRUMENTE)
    10:00 S.U.I.S.A.
—— MUSIK FÜR 16 STREICHER
    str.   12:00 Hans Gerig.
—— NIMMERMEHR (CANTATA) (FOR BARITONE, WOMEN'S
    CHORUS AND SMALL ORCH.)
    1,0,*3,1 - 0,0,3,2 - timp.,perc.,cel.,vibra.,xyl. - hp. - pf. - str.
    22:00 S.U.I.S.A.
—— ORCHESTERSTÜCKE
    *3,*3,*3,*3 - 4,3,3,1 - timp.,perc. - hp. - pf. - str.   15:00 S.U.I.S.A.
—— SÄTZE UND GEGENSÄTZE (FÜR VIBRAPHON, KLAVIER,
    SCHLAGZEUG UND STREICHER)
    perc.,vibra. - pf. - str.   18:00 S.U.I.S.A.
—— TRIPARTITA (FÜR DREI KLAVIERE UND BLASORCHESTER)
    *3,*3,*3,*3 - 4,3,3,1 - 3 pf.   17:00 S.U.I.S.A.

STAJIĆ, Petar
—— SYMPHONY NO. 4
    0,0,1,0 - 4,4,3,1 - timp.,perc. - str.   20:00 MIC,Zagreb.

STALDER, Giuseppe - SCHERCHEN
—— SINFONIA IN E FLAT MAJOR
    0,0,0,0 - 2,0,0,0 - str.   12:00 Henmar.

STALLAERT, Alphonse
—— CONCERTO FOR PIANO AND ORCH.
    3,3,3,3 - 4,4,3,1 - timp.,perc.(3) - pf. - str.   24:00 Presser.

STALLINGS, Kendall
—— ANTIPHONY (1969)
    2,2,2,2 - 4,2,2,0 - perc.(2),glock. - str.   4:00 Composer.
—— CONFLUENCES (1968)
    3(2nd alt. with alto fl.,3rd alt. with picc.),3(3rd alt. with Eng.
    hn.),3(2nd alt. with E♭ cl.,3rd alt. with b.-cl.),3(3rd alt. with c.-bn.)
    - 4,3,3,1 - perc.(6),glock.,mar.,vibra.,xyl. - hp. - str.
        14:00 Composer.

STALVEY, Dorrance
—— CELEBRATION - SEQUENT I (FOR CHAMBER ORCH.)
        13:00 Salabert.
—— POINTS - LINES - CIRCLES
        19:00 Salabert.

STAM, Henk
—— DE RUYTER: OVERTURE
    3,2,2,3 - 4,3,3,1 - timp.,perc.,cel. - str.   Henmar.

STAMITZ, Anton - BODART, Eugen
—— CONCERTO IN E MAJOR FOR VIOLIN AND ORCH.
    0,2,0,1 - 2,0,0,0 - str.   22:00 Mannheimer.

STAMITZ, Anton - SCHULTZ-HAUSER
—— CONCERTO IN G MAJOR FOR VIOLIN, CEMBALO AND
    STRINGS
    cemb. - str.   15:00 Henmar.

STAMITZ, Johann - BODART, Eugen
—— CONCERTO IN B FLAT MAJOR FOR CLARINET AND
    ORCH.
    0,0,1,0 - 2,0,0,0 - str.   18:00 Mannheimer.
—— PASTORALE IN D MAJOR
    2,2,0,2 - 2,0,0,0 - str.   6:00 Mannheimer.
—— PASTORALE IN G MAJOR
    2,2,0,2 - 2,0,0,0 - str.   6:00 Mannheimer.
—— SYMPHONY NO. 8 IN E FLAT MAJOR
    0,2,0,0 - 2,0,0,0 - str.   16:00 Mannheimer.

STAMITZ, Johann - CARSE, Adam
—— SYMPHONY IN G, OP. 3, NO. 3 (IN 3 MOVTS.)
    2 ob. - 2 hn. - str.   8:00 Galaxy.

STAMITZ, Johann - HOFMANN, Wolfgang
—— SYMPHONY IN A MAJOR (SPRING SYMPHONY)
    2,0,0,0 - 2,0,0,0 - str.   16:00 Mannheimer.

STAMITZ, Johann - KOELBEL
—— CONCERTO IN C MAJOR
    fl. - cemb. - str.   25:00 Henmar.

STAMITZ, Johann - LEBERMANN, Walter
—— CONCERTO IN C MAJOR FOR VIOLIN AND STRING ORCH.
    (THE DRESDEN CONCERTO)
    str.   17:00 Henmar.

STAMITZ, Johann - LENZEWSKI
—— SINFONIA IN E FLAT MAJOR
    2 ob.(or 2 fl.) - 2 hn. - str.   Henmar.

STAMITZ, Johann - SCHUBERT, Heino
—— CONCERTO IN C MINOR FOR ORGAN AND STRING
    ORCH.
    org.(or hpsc. or pf.) - str.   12:00 Mannheimer.

STAMITZ, Johann - TÖTTCHER
—— CONCERTO IN C MAJOR, FOR OBOE, STRINGS AND BASS
    CONTINUO
    ob. - cemb. - str.   F. Colombo.

STAMITZ, Johann - UPMEYER
—— SINFONIA PASTORALE IN D MAJOR, OP. 4, NO. 2
    2 ob.(or 2 fl.) - 2 hn. - cemb. - str.   Henmar.

STAMITZ, Karl - BODART, Eugen - HERBERGER, Rolf
—— PERSEPHONE (BALLET) %
    2,3,1,0 - 4,0,0,0 - str.(incl. solo vla. d'amore)   40:00 Mannheimer.
—— SYMPHONY FOR STRINGS IN F MAJOR (FROM THE
    QUARTET, OP. 4, NO. 4)
    str.   12:00 Mannheimer.
—— SYMPHONY IN A MAJOR
    2,0,0,0 - 2,0,0,0 - str.   16:00 Mannheimer.
—— SYMPHONY IN E FLAT MAJOR (THE ECHO SYMPHONY)
    (FOR DOUBLE ORCH.)
    0,1,0,1 - 4,0,0,0 - str.   20:00 Mannheimer.
—— SYMPHONY IN G MAJOR, OP. 6, NO. 3
    0,2,0,0 - 2,0,0,0 - str.   20:00 Mannheimer.
—— SYMPHONY NO. 2, IN E FLAT MAJOR
    0,2,0,0 - 2,0,0,0 - str.   20:00 Mannheimer.
—— SYMPHONY NO. 5, IN F MAJOR
    0,2,0,0 - 2,0,0,0 - str.   17:00 Mannheimer.

STAMITZ, Karl - GRADENWITZ, Peter
—— CONCERTO FOR CLARINET AND STRINGS
    cl. - str.   16:00 Leeds.

STAMITZ, Karl - HERBERGER, Rolf
—— CONCERTO IN D MAJOR FOR VIOLA D'AMORE AND
    STRINGS
    str.   22:00 Mannheimer.

STAMITZ, Karl - HOFMANN, Wolfgang
—— CONCERTO IN D MAJOR FOR VIOLIN AND ORCH.
    0,2,0,0 - 2,0,0,0 - str.   24:00 Mannheimer.

STAMITZ, Karl - KNEUSSLIN
—— SINFONIA CONCERTANTE IN C MAJOR (WITH 2 SOLO
    VIOLINS)
    2 fl.(or 2 ob.) - 2 hn. - str.   25:00 Henmar.
—— SINFONIA CONCERTANTE IN D MAJOR (WITH SOLO
    VIOLIN AND VIOLA)
    2 hn. - str.   22:00 Henmar.

STAMITZ, Karl - LENZEWSKI
—— SINFONIA IN E FLAT MAJOR
    2,0,0,0 - 2,0,0,0 - str.   Henmar.

STAMITZ, Karl - MICHAELS, Jost
—— CONCERTO NO. 10 IN B FLAT MAJOR, FOR CLARINET
    AND ORCH.
    0,2,1,0 - 2,0,0,0 - str.   F. Colombo.

STAMITZ, Karl - SCHROEDER, Felix
—— SINFONIA CONCERTANTE IN D MAJOR (FOR 2 VIOLINS,
    VIOLA AND ORCH.)
    0,2,0,0 - 2,0,0,0 - hpsc. - str.   25:00 Mannheimer.
—— SINFONIA CONCERTANTE IN D MAJOR (SINFONIA XIV)
    (FOR 2 VIOLINS AND ORCH.)
    0,2,0,0 - 2,0,0,0 - str.   15:00 F. Colombo.
—— SINFONIA CONCERTANTE IN E FLAT MAJOR (FOR OBOE,
    VIOLIN, HORN, BASSOON AND STRINGS)
    0,1,0,1 - 3,0,0,0 - hpsc. - str.   25:00 Mannheimer.

STAMITZ, Karl - WOJCIECHOWSKI, Johannes
—— CONCERTO IN B FLAT MAJOR, FOR CLARINET, BASSOON
    AND ORCH.
    0,0,1,1 - 2,0,0,0 - str.   F. Colombo.
—— CONCERTO IN E FLAT MAJOR, FOR CLARINET AND
    ORCH.
    2,0,1,0 - 2,0,0,0 - str.   F. Colombo.
—— CONCERTO IN F MAJOR, FOR BASSOON AND ORCH.
    0,2,0,1 - 2,0,0,0 - str.   F. Colombo.

STANDFORD, Patric
—— ANTITHESES (FOR FIFTEEN STRINGS)
    str.(8,3,3,1)   16:00 Novello.
—— CONCERT OVERTURE (1962)
    2,2,2,2 - 4,2,0,0 - timp. - str.   7:00 P.R.S.
—— CONCERTANTE FOR PIANO AND SMALL ORCH.
    1,1,1,1 - 1,0,0,0 - timp. - pf. - str.   22:00 Novello.
—— NOCTURNE
    2,1,3,0 - 1,0,0,0 - timp. - pf. - str.   8:00 Novello.

—— NOTTE
  1,2,0,1 - 2,0,0,0 - str.   13:00 Novello.
—— PRELUDIO OSTINATO
  2(2nd alt. with picc.),2,2,2 - 4,2,3,1 - timp.,perc. - pf. - str.
                                              6:00 Novello.
—— SARACINESCO SINFONIA III
  3,3,3,3 - 4,2,3,1 - timp.,perc.,xyl. - pf. - str.   17:00 Novello.
—— SUITE
  2,1,2,1 - 2,0,0,0 - str.   17:00 Novello.
—— SUITE NO. 2 FOR SMALL ORCH. (1967)
  2,1,2,1 - 2,1,1,0 - timp. - hp. - pf.(ad lib.) - str.   15:00 P.R.S.
—— SYMPHONY NO. 1
  3,3,4,alto sax.,3 - 4,3,3,1 - timp.,perc.,cel.,glock.,xyl. - hp. - str.
                                              45:00 Novello.
—— THREE STUDIES
  3,2(2nd alt. with Eng.hn.),3,2 - 4,2,3,0 - timp.,perc. - pf. - str.
                                              Novello.

STANFORD, Charles Villiers
—— AT THE ABBEY GATE, OP. 177 (FOR BARITONE, CHORUS
  AND ORCH.)
                                              Bo. Hawkes.
—— FIVE SONGS OF THE FLEET, OP. 117 (FOR BARITONE,
  CHORUS AND ORCH.)
  *3,2,2,b.-cl.(ad lib.),2 - 4,2,3,1 - timp.,perc.(4) - hp. - str.
                                              20:00 Galaxy.
—— IRISH RHAPSODY NO. 6 (FOR VIOLIN AND ORCH.)
  2,2,2,2 - 4,2,3,0 - timp. - str.   12:00 Bo. Hawkes.
—— ODE TO DISCORD (FOR SOPRANO, BARITONE, CHORUS
  AND ORCH.)
                                              Bo. Hawkes.
—— STABAT MATER, OP. 96 (FOR SOLO VOICES, CHORUS AND
  ORCH.)
  3,3,3,3 - 4,3,3,1 - timp.,perc. - hp. - org. - str. 49:00 Bo. Hawkes.
—— WELLINGTON ODE, OP. 100 (CANTATA) (FOR SOPRANO,
  BARITONE, CHORUS AND ORCH.)
                                              Bo. Hawkes.

STANGER, Russell
—— BUFFOONS (A MERRY OVERTURE)
  3,2,3,3 - 4,2,3,1 - timp.,perc. - hp. - str.   6:00 Mills.
—— CHILDHOOD IMAGES (SUITE) (1968)
                                              41:20 Mills.
—— EPISODES '76, OP. 3 (DRAMATIC ORATORIO) % (1976)
  4(2 alt. with 2 picc.),3(3rd alt. with Eng. hn.),3(3rd alt. with E♭ cl.
  and b.-cl.),4(3rd alt. with c.-bn.) - 6,4,4,1 -
  timp.,perc.(6),bells,cel.,glock.,vibra.,xyl. - tape-recorder - 2 hp. -
  org. - pf. - str.(28,8,8,6)   85:00 Composer.
—— ROCK OPUS, OP. 3 (SUITE IN 2 MOVTS.) (WITH OPTIONAL
  ROCK GROUP) (1970)
  3(3rd alt. with picc.),*3,2,2 - 4,3,3,1 - timp.,perc.(3),glock.,xyl. -
  pf. - str.   13:27 Composer.
  or:
  3(3rd alt. with picc.),*3,*3,*3 - 4,3,3,1 - timp.,perc.(4),glock.,xyl. -
  hp. - pf. - str.

STANISLAV, Josef
—— AGAINST ALL (OPERA) %
                                              Bo. Hawkes.
—— SYMPHONY IN G MAJOR
  3,3,4,3 - 4,3,3,1 - timp.,perc.,cel. - 2 hp. - pf. - str.
                                              38:00 Bo. Hawkes.

STANLEY, John - FINZI, Gerald
—— CONCERTO NO. 1 IN D, FOR STRINGS
  str.   8:00 Bo. Hawkes.
  or:
  pf. - str.
—— CONCERTO NO. 2 IN B MINOR, FOR STRINGS
  str.   14:00 Bo Hawkes.
  or:
  cemb.(or org.) - str.
—— CONCERTO NO. 3 IN G, FOR CEMBALO AND STRINGS
  cemb.(or org.) - str.   8:00 Bo. Hawkes.
—— CONCERTO NO. 4 IN D MINOR, FOR CEMBALO AND
  STRINGS
  cemb.(or org.) - str.   9:00 Bo. Hawkes.
—— CONCERTO NO. 5 IN A, FOR CEMBALO AND STRINGS
  cemb.(or org.) - str.   8:00 Bo. Hawkes.
—— CONCERTO NO. 6 IN B FLAT, FOR PIANO AND STRINGS
  pf. - str.   6:00 Bo. Hawkes.

—— PAN AND SYRINX (CANTATA) (FOR SOPRANO, TENOR,
  OBOE AND STRINGS)
  ob. - cemb. - str.   18:00 Bo. Hawkes.

STANLEY, John - LE HURAY, Peter
—— CONCERTO IN C MAJOR FOR ORGAN AND STRINGS
  org. - str.   10:00 Oxford.
—— CONCERTO IN C MINOR, FOR ORGAN AND STRINGS
  org. - str.   12:00 Oxford.

STARER, Robert
—— ARIEL (VISIONS OF ISAIAH) (CANTATA) (FOR SOPRANO,
  BARITONE, MIXED CHORUS, AND ORCH.) (1959)
  2,2,2,2 - 2,2,2,0 - perc.,cel. - str.   27:00 Leeds.
—— BALLADE FOR VIOLIN AND ORCHESTRA
  3,1,2,1 - 2,2,0,0 - perc. - str.   13:00 Presser.
—— CONCERTO A TRE (FOR CLARINET, TRUMPET,
  TROMBONE AND STRINGS)
  0,0,1,0 - 0,1,1,0 - str.   18:00 Leeds.
—— CONCERTO FOR VIOLA, STRINGS AND PERCUSSION (IN 4
  MOVTS.)
  perc.(4),cel.,glock.,xyl. - str.   21:00 Leeds.
—— CONCERTO FOR VIOLIN, CELLO AND ORCH.
  3,2,3,2 - 4,3,3,1 - timp.,perc.(6) - hp. - str.   19:00 MCA Music.
—— CONCERTO NO. 1 FOR PIANO AND ORCH.
  2,2,2,2 - 2,2,2,1 - timp.,perc. - pf. - str.   21:00 Leeds.
—— CONCERTO NO. 2 FOR PIANO AND ORCH.
  2,2,2,2 - 2,2,1,0 - timp.,perc. - pf. - str.   16:00 Leeds.
—— CONCERTO NO. 3 FOR PIANO AND ORCH.
  3,2,2,2 - 2,2,2,1 - timp.,perc.(4) - pf. - str.   MCA Music.
—— DALTON SET (SUITE) (IN 4 MOVTS.) (1960)
  2,1,2,1 alt.sax.,1 ten.sax.,1 - 2,2,1,0 - perc.(2) - pf. - str.   Leeds.
  or:
  2,0,2,0 - 0,2,1,0 - perc.(2) - pf. - str.
—— DIVERTIMENTO (DANCES FROM "ARAMINTHA")
  2,1,2,1 - 2,1,0,0 - perc. - str.   9:00 Templeton.
—— THE DYBBUK (SUITE FROM THE BALLET) (1960)
  2,2,2,2 - 2,2,2,0 - timp.,cel.,xyl. - str.   26:00 Leeds.
—— ELEGY FOR STRINGS
  str.   5:00 Leeds.
—— ESTHER (SUITE FROM THE BALLET)
  1,1,1,0 - 0,1,0,0 - timp.,perc.,xyl. - hp. - vla.,c.
                                              16:00 MCA Music.
—— FANTASY FOR STRINGS
  str.   8:00 Southern.
—— THE INTRUDER (1-ACT OPERA) %
                                              Presser.
—— INVOCATION FOR TRUMPET AND STRINGS (1962)
  tpt. - str.   5:00 EastonMuCo.
—— JOSEPH AND HIS BROTHERS (CANTATA) (FOR
  NARRATOR,OPRANO, TENOR, BASS-BARITONE SATB
  CHORUS AND ORCH.)
  2,2,2,2 - 2,2,0,0 - perc. - hp. - str.   26:00 MCA Music.
—— KOHELET ("ECCLESIASTES") (CANTATA) (FOR SOPRANO,
  BARITONE, MIXED CHORUS AND ORCH.)
  2,2,2,2 - 2,2,1,0 - perc. - pf. - str.   24:00 Leeds.
—— LYRIC MUSIC (FOR VIOLIN, VIOLA AND STRINGS) (1957)
  str.   6:00 Composer.
—— MUTABILI (VARIANTS FOR ORCH.) (1965)
  *3,*3,1 E♭ cl.,*3,*3 - 4,3,3,1 - timp.,perc.(4),xyl. - hp. - pf. - str.
                                              11:00 MCA Music.
—— ORIENTAL RHAPSODY (1946)
                                              5:00 Composer.
—— PANTAGLEIZE (THREE-ACT OPERA) %
                                              MCA Music.
—— PHAEDRA (SUITE FROM THE BALLET) (1962)
  1,1,1,1 - 1,1,1,0 - timp.,perc.,xyl. - hp.   17:00 Leeds.
—— PRELUDE AND DANCE
  3,3,3,3 - 4,3,3,1 - timp.,perc.,cel.,xyl. - hp. - pf. - str.   10:00 Leeds.
—— PRELUDE AND RONDO GIOCOSO
  2,2,2,2 - 2,2,1,0 - timp.,perc. - str.   10:00 Leeds.
—— A PSALM OF DAVID (FOR CHORUS, 2 TRUMPETS AND
  STRINGS) (1959)
  2 tpt. - org.(or pf. ad lib.) - str.   4:30 Presser.
—— SAMSON AGONISTES (SYMPHONIC PORTRAIT) (1961)
  3,3,3,3 - 4,3,3,1 - timp.,perc.,cel.,xyl. - pf. - str.   13:00 Leeds.
  or:
  1,1,1,1 - 1,1,1,0 - timp.,perc.,cel.,xyl. - pf. - str.
—— THE SHIP OF DEATH (FOR SOLO VOICES, CHORUS AND
  ORCH.) (1954)
                                              Composer.
—— SIX VARIATIONS WITH 12 NOTES
  3,3,3,3 - 4,3,3,1 - timp.,perc.(4) - hp. - str.   MCA Music.

—— SYMPHONIC OVERTURE (1948)
    Composer.
—— SYMPHONY NO. 1
    3,3,3,3 - 4,3,3,1 - timp.,perc.,xyl. - hp. - pf. - str.   22:00 Leeds.
—— SYMPHONY NO. 2 (IN 1 MOVT.)
    3,3,3,3 - 4,3,3,1 - timp.,perc. - pf. - str.   12:00 IsMuPublns.
—— SYMPHONY NO. 3
    3,3,4(1 on E♭cl.,1 on b.-cl.),3 - 4,3,3,1 - timp.,perc.(5) - hp. - pf. - str.   MCA Music.

STAROKADOMSKY, Mikhail L.
—— CONCERTO FOR ORCH., OP. 14 (IN 3 MOVTS.) (Ed. by Harold Sheldon)
    *3,*3,E♭cl.,2,*3, - 4,3,3,1 - timp.,perc.(4) - str.   20:00 G. Schirmer.
—— CONCERTO FOR VIOLIN AND ORCH., OP. 20
    2,2,2,2 - 4,3,3,1 - timp.,perc. - str.   G. Schirmer.

STARR, Mark
—— DIVERTIMENTO (1970) (IN 3 MOVTS.)
    2,2,2,2 - 2,2,0,0 - timp.,perc.(2) - str.   23:00 Composer.

STARZER, Josef - LENZEWSKI
—— DIVERTIMENTO IN C MAJOR
    str.   Henmar.

STAVONIN, Gennadij T.
—— OLECO DUNDICI (3-ACT OPERA) % (Text: Ye. Sinitsyn and A. Tarasenko)
    G. Schirmer.

STEEL, Christopher
—— COMEDY OVERTURE, OP. 1 (1960)
    2,2,2,2 - 4,2,3,1 - timp.,perc.(3) - hp. - str.   4:30 P.R.S.
—— CONCERTO FOR CELLO AND ORCH., OP. 3 (1961)
    2,2,2,2 - 4,2,3,1 - timp.,perc.(3) - hp. - str.   18:00 P.R.S.
—— CONCERTO FOR ORGAN AND SMALL ORCH.
    1,1,1,1 - 1,1,1,0 - perc. - org. - str.   13:00 Novello.
—— CONCERTO FOR STRING QUARTET AND ORCH.
    2,2,2,2 - 4,2,3,1 - timp.,perc.,cel.,vibra.,xyl. - str.   17:00 Novello.
—— ISLAND (OVERTURE)
    2,2,2,2 - 4,2,3,1 - timp.,perc.,cel. - hp. - str.   7:00 Novello.
—— SYMPHONY NO. 1, OP. 10 (1962)
    2,2,2,2 - 4,2,3,1 - timp.,perc.(3) - hp. - str.   21:00 P.R.S.
—— SYMPHONY NO. 2
    3,2,2,2 - 4,2,3,1 - timp.,perc.,xyl. - hp. - str.   20:00 Novello.
—— SYMPHONY NO. 4, OP. 37
    3,3,3,3 - 4,2,3,1 - timp.,perc.,cel.,glock.,vibra.,xyl. - hp. - str.   11:00 Novello.

STEENHUIS, François
—— HERDEN KINGSMUZIEK (MEMORIAL MUSIC), OP. 10 (FOR SOPRANO, CHORUS AND ORCH.)
    Henmar.
—— WANG-LI (BALLET PANTOMIME) (1946) %
    2,2,2,2 - 2,2,0,0 - timp.,perc. - hp. - str.   18:00 Henmar.

STEFFANI, Agostino - SCOTT, C. Kennedy
—— STABAT MATER (FOR 6 SOLO VOICES, MIXED CHORUS, ORGAN AND STRINGS) (Engl. Text: Beatrice E. Bulman)
    org. - str.   45:00 Oxford.

STEFFEN, Wolfgang
—— LITTLE SYMPHONY FOR STRING ORCHESTRA (IN 3 MOVTS.)
    str.   13:00 Sirius.
—— SINFONIETTA FOR STRING ORCH., OP. 5 (IN 3 MOVTS.)
    str.   13:00 Henmar.

STEG, Paul O.
—— SYMPHONY ON FOLK SONGS
    Summy-Bir.

STEGER, Werner
—— PRELUDE AND FUGUE FOR STRING ORCH.
    str.   8:00 Mannheimer.
—— SERENADE FOR STRING ORCH.
    str.   12:00 Mannheimer.
—— SUITE FOR STRING ORCH., ON OLD FOLK TUNES
    str.   12:00 Mannheimer.

STEHMAN, Jacques
—— CONCERTO IN A FOR PIANO AND ORCH. (1972) (IN 4 MOVTS.)
    2,2,2,2 - 2,3,2,0 - timp.,perc. - pf. - str.   20:00 H. Elkan.
—— ESCAPADES FOR PIANO AND STRINGS (1968)
    pf. - str.   12:00 H. Elkan.
—— SUITE FOR STRINGS (SUITE POUR CORDES) (1953)
    str.   15:00 H. Elkan.
—— SYMPHONIE DE POCHE (1950)
    2,2,2,2 - 4,2,3,0 - timp.,perc. - str.   14:00 CBDM.

STEIN, Leon
—— PASSACAGLIA
    3,3,3,3 - 4,2,3,1 - perc. - str.   10:00 C. Fischer.
—— SINFONIETTA
    str.   18:00 C. Fischer.
—— THREE HASSIDIC DANCES
    2,2,2,2 - 4,2,3,1 - timp.,perc. - str.   13:30 Transcon.

STEINBERG, Maximilian
—— INTRODUCTION TO "PRINCESS MALEINE", OP. 11 (FOR WOMEN'S CHORUS AND ORCH.)
    *3,*3,2,*3 - 4,3,3,1 - timp.,perc. - hp. - str.   G. Schirmer.
—— SIX FOLK SONGS, OP. 19 (FOR CONTRALTO OR MEZZO-SOPRANO AND ORCH.)
    2(2nd alt. with picc.),2(2nd alt. with Eng.hn.),2,2 - 2,2,0,0 - timp.,perc.,cel.(ad lib.) - hp. - str.   18:00 G. Schirmer.
—— SIX FOLK SONGS, OP. 22 (FOR CONTRALTO AND ORCH.)
    1(alt. with picc.),1,2,1 - 2,2,0,0 - perc.,xyl. - hp. - str.   18:00 G. Schirmer.
—— SIX FOLK SONGS, OP. 27 (FOR CONTRALTO AND ORCH.)
    *2,2(2nd alt. with Eng. hn.),2,2 - 2,2,0,0 - perc. - hp. - str.   18:00 G. Schirmer.
—— SYMPHONY NO. 3, OP. 18 (IN 4 MOVTS.)
    3(3rd alt. with picc.),*3,2,b.-cl.(alt. with D cl.),*3 - 4,3,3,1 - timp.,perc.,cel.,glock. - hp. - str.   40:00 G. Schirmer.
—— SYMPHONY NO. 4 ("TURKSIB", OP. 24 (IN 4 MOVTS.)
    3(3rd alt. with picc.),*3,*3,*3 - 4,3,3,1 - timp.,perc. - 1-2 hp. - str.   G. Schirmer.

STEINER, George
—— RHAPSODIC POEM (FOR VIOLA AND ORCH.)
    2(2nd alt. with picc.),1,*2,1 - 2,2,1,0 - timp.,perc.,xyl. - hp. - str.   11:00 Leeds.

STEINER, Gitta
—— CONCERTO FOR PIANO AND ORCH. (1967)
    2,2,2,2 - 2,2,2,0 - perc.(3) - pf. - str.   15:00 Seesaw.
—— MOVEMENT FOR ELEVEN (1966)
    1,0,2,0 - 1,2,1,1 - 1 vln.,1 vla.,1 c.   5:00 Seesaw.
—— MUSIC FOR STRING ORCHESTRA (1953)
    str.   5:00 Seesaw.
—— SUITE FOR ORCHESTRA (1958)
    3,3,3,2 - 4,3,3,1 - timp.,perc. - str.   6:00 Seesaw.
—— TETRARK FOR STRING ORCH. (1965)
    str.   5:00 Seesaw.

STEINER, Max
—— SYMPHONIE MODERNE
    3,*3,*3,2 sax.,3 - 4,4,3,1 - timp.,perc. - 2 hp. - pf. - str.   7:30 Remick.

STEINERT, Alexander
—— AIR CORPS SUITE
    *3,*2,*5,1 - 4,4,4,1 - timp.,perc.(4) - 2 hp. - str.   7:00 Composer.
—— CONCERTO SINFONICO (FOR PIANO AND ORCH.)
    3(3rd alt. with picc.),*3,*3,*3 - 4,3,3,1 - timp.,perc.(3) - pf. - str.   13:00 Composer.
—— FLIGHT CYCLE (SYMPHONIC POEM)
    *3,*3,*4,2 - 4,4,3,1 - timp.,perc.(3),cel.,glock. - hp. - pf. - str.   17:00 Composer.
—— THE LITTLE HILL (FOR CHAMBER ORCH.) (WITH NARRATOR AD LIB.) (IN 4 MOVTS.)
    1(alt. with picc.),1(alt. with Eng. hn.),1(alt. with b.-cl.),1 - 2,1,1,0 - perc.(1) - hp. - pf. - str.   11:00 Composer.
—— THE NIGHTINGALE AND THE ROSE (FOR NARRATOR AND ORCH.)
    3(3rd alt. with picc.),*3,*3,*3 - 4,3,3,1 - timp.,perc.,cel. - hp. - pf. - str.   18:00 Composer.
—— RHAPSODY FOR CLARINET AND ORCH.
    2,*3,*3,2 - 4,3,3,0 - timp.,perc.(1) - hp. - pf.(ad lib.) - str.   6:00 G. Schirmer.

—— THREE POEMS BY SHELLEY (FOR SOPRANO AND ORCH.)
2,*3,2,2 - 4,2,3,0 - timp.,perc.(2),cel. - hp. - str.   7:00 Salabert.

STEINKE, Greg A.
—— MUSIC FOR BASSOON AND ORCH. (1967)
*2,1, alto fl.,*2,1 E♭ cl.,*2,1 d.-b. cl.,1 - 4,3,3,1 -
timp.,perc.(4),glock.,vibra. - hp. - str.   9:00 Seesaw.
—— PSALM 23 (FOR CHORUS AND CHAMBER ORCH.)
0,1,0,0 - 0,0,0,0 - hp. - str.   5:00 Seesaw.
—— THREE SONNETS FROM WILLIAM SHAKESPEARE (FOR
SOPRANO AND CHAMBER ORCH.) (1962)
fl. - str.(4,2,2,1)   12:00 Seesaw.
—— THRENODY FOR ORCHESTRA (1965)
*3,(2nd alt.with alto. fl.)*3,*3,*3 - 4,3,3,1 - timp.,perc.(3),cel. - 2
hp. - str.   7:00 Seesaw.

STEKEL, Eric Paul
—— ALGER (ÉVOCATION MUSICALE)
3,3,3,3 - 4,4,3,1 - timp.,perc.,cel. - hp. - str.   16:00 Presser.
—— OVERTURE GRENOBLE, OP. 29
      C. Fischer.

STENHAMMAR, Wilhelm
—— EXCELSIOR (SYMPHONIC OVERTURE), OP. 13
3,3,3,3 - 4,3,3,1 - timp. - str.   15:00 S.T.I.M.
—— MUSIC TO AUGUST STRINDBERG'S "ETT DRÖMSPEL", OP.
36
1,1,1,1 - 2,0,0,0 - timp.,perc. - hp. - pf. - str.   S.T.I.M.
—— MUSIC TO CARLO GOZZI'S "TURANDOT", OP. 42
      S.T.I.M.
—— MUSIC TO R. TAGORE'S "CHITRA", OP. 43
      S.T.I.M.
—— MUSIC TO SHAKESPEARE'S "AS YOU LIKE IT", OP. 40
      S.T.I.M.
—— MUSIC TO SHAKESPEARE'S "ROMEO AND JULIET", OP. 45
      S.T.I.M.
—— SERENADE IN F MAJOR, OP. 31 (IN 5 MOVTS.)
2,2,2,2 - 4,2,3,0 - timp.,perc.(2) - str.   33:00 S.T.I.M.
—— SUITE FROM SHAKESPEARE'S "ROMEO AND JULIET"
1,1,0,0 - 0,0,0,0 - guit. - hp. - str.   12:30 S.T.I.M.
—— SUITE FROM THE ROMANTIC COMEDY "LODOLEZZI
SJUNGER", OP. 39
fl. - perc. - guit. - mandolin - str.   S.T.I.M.
—— SYMPHONY NO. 1 IN F MAJOR
3,3,3,3 - 6,3,3,1 - timp. - str.   S.T.I.M.
—— SYMPHONY NO. 2 IN G MINOR, OP. 34
2,2,2,2 - 4,2,3,0 - timp.,perc. - str.   45:00 Bo. Hawkes.

STENHAMMAR, Wilhelm - ROSENBERG, Hilding
—— MUSIC TO STRINDBERG'S PLAY "ETT DRÖMSPEL" ("A
DREAM PLAY") (WITH OPTIONAL NARRATOR)
2,2,2,2 - 4,0,0,0 - timp.,perc. - pf. - str.   Fleisher.

STEPHENS, Ward
—— EIGHT POEMS BY JAMES WHITCOMB RILEY (FOR VOICE
AND ORCH.)
*3,1,1,1 - 2,2,2,0 - timp.,perc. - str.   22:00 Chappell.

STERKEL, Johann Franz Xaver - BODART, Eugen
—— INTRODUCTION AND FINALE
str.   11:00 Mannheimer.
—— SYMPHONY FOR STRINGS, IN G MAJOR
str.   13:00 Mannheimer.
—— SYMPHONY IN D MAJOR
0,2,0,0 - 2,0,0,0 - str.   13:00 Mannheimer.

STERN, Marcel
—— SOUVENIRS DE PROVENCE (IN 5 MOVTS.)
3,2,2,2 - 4,3,1,0 - timp.,perc. - hp. - str.   20:00 Salabert.

STERN, Max
—— SYMPHONY
2,2,2,2 - 4,3,3,1 - timp.,perc. - str.   33:00 C. Fischer.

STERN, Robert L.
—— CAROM (FOR ORCHESTRA AND MAGNETIC TAPE) (1972)
2(2nd alt. with picc.),0,2,0 - 2,2,1,0 - perc.(2),glock.,vibra. -
tape-playback system(2-channel) - str.   8:00 Composer.
—— CREDO FOR ORCHESTRA
3(3rd alt. with picc.),2,2,2 - 4,3,3,1 - timp.,perc.(2) - pf. - str.
      15:00 Composer.

—— FORT UNION (BALLET SUITE) (IN 4 MOVTS.)
3(3rd alt. with picc.),2,2,2 - 4,3,3,1 - timp.,perc.(3),glock.,xyl. - hp.
- pf. - str.   27:00 Composer.
—— GRANT US PEACE (AN ORCHESTRA PRAYER)
2(2nd alt. with picc.),2(2nd alt. with Eng.hn.),2(2nd alt. with
b.-cl.),2 - 4,2,3,1 - timp. - str.   7:00 Composer.
—— HAZKARAH (FOR CELLO AND ORCH.)
3(3rd alt. with picc.),2,2,2 - 4,2,2,0 -
timp.,perc.(3),cel.,glock.,vibra.,xyl. - hp. - pf. - str.
      17:00 Composer.
—— IN MEMORIAM ABRAHAM
str.   7:30 Composer.
—— SYMPHONY (1961) (IN 1 MOVT.)
3(3rd alt. with picc.),2,2,2 - 4,2,2,1 - timp.,perc.(3),vibra.,xyl. - pf.
- str.   18:00 Composer.

STERNBERG, Erich Walter
—— THE STORY OF JOSEPH (SUITE FOR STRING ORCH.)
str.   35:00 Novello.

STERNEFELD, Daniel
—— ELEGIE (1931)
2,2,2,2 - 2,2,2,0 - timp.,perc. - pf. - str.   13:00 H. Elkan.
—— SYMPHONY (1943)
3,3,3,3 - 4,3,3,1 - timp.,perc. - pf. - str.   32:00 H. Elkan.
—— ZANG EN DANS AAN HET HOF VAN MARIA VAN
BOERGONDIE
2,2,2,2 - 2,2,2,0 - timp.,perc. - hp. - str.   H. Elkan.

STEVEN, Donald
—— HARBINGER (1969) (FANTASIA FOR SOPRANO AND
MEDIUM ORCH.)
2(2nd alt. with picc.),1,2(2nd alt. with b.-cl.),0 - perc.(3) - guit.
(alt. with electric guit.) - pf.(or cel.) - str.   11:45 CanMusCtr.

STEVENS, Bernard
—— CHORIAMB, OP. 41
2,2,2,2 - 4,2,3,1 - timp.,perc. - str.   13:00 Novello.
—— CONCERTO FOR CELLO AND ORCH., OP. 18
2,2,2,2 - 4,2,3,1 - timp.,perc. - str.   Lengnick.
—— CONCERTO FOR VIOLIN AND ORCH., OP. 4
2,2,2,2 - 4,2,3,0 - timp.,perc. - str.   32:00 Lengnick.
—— DANCE SUITE, OP. 28
3,2,2,2 - 4,2,3,1 - timp.,perc. - hp. - str.   16:30 Lengnick.
—— EAST AND WEST, OP. 16 (AN OVERTURE)
2,2,3,2 sax.,1 - 0,3,4,1 - timp.,perc.   6:00 P.R.S.
—— ECLOGUE FOR SMALL ORCH., OP. 8
1,1,1,1 - 2,0,0,0 - timp.,perc. - str.   8:00 Lengnick.
—— FUGAL OVERTURE, OP. 9
2,2,2,2 - 4,2,3,1 - timp.,perc. - str.   8:00 Lengnick.
—— PRELUDE AND FINALE, OP. 31
2,1,2,1 - 2,2,1,0 - timp.,perc. - str.   6:00 Novello.
—— RICERCAR FOR STRINGS, OP. 6
str.   12:00 Lengnick.
—— SINFONIETTA FOR STRINGS, OP. 10
str.   Lengnick.
—— SYMPHONY NO. 2, OP. 35
3,2,2,2 - 4,3,3,1 - timp.,perc. - hp. - str.   31:00 P.R.S.
—— SYMPHONY OF LIBERATION, OP. 7
2,2,2,2 - 4,3,3,1 - timp.,perc. - str.   20:00 P.R.S.
—— VARIATIONS FOR ORCH., OP. 36
3,3,3,3 - 5,3,3,1 - timp.,perc. - hp. - str.   19:00 P.R.S.

STEVENS, James
—— CONCERTETTO CONCITATO
1,1,1,1 - 2,2,1,0 - perc. - hp. - pf. - str.   5:30 Modern.
—— CONCERTO CAPRICCIOSO (FOR HARP AND ORCH.)
1(alt. with picc.),1,1,1 - 2,2,1,0 - perc. - hp. - pf. - str.
      8:00 Modern.
—— IN A NUTSHELL (A MINIATURE OVERTURE)
2,1,2,2 - 2,1,0,0 - timp.,perc.,cel. - hp. - str.   3:00 Modern.
—— LION AND UNICORN (A GALA OVERTURE)
2,2,2,2 - 3,3,3,1 - timp.,perc. - hp. - str.   7:30 Modern.
—— SYMPHONY NO. 1 (1949)
3,3,3,3 - 4,4,3,1 - perc.(2) - hp. - pf. - str.   17:30 P.R.S.
—— SYMPHONY NO. 2 (1951)
2,2,2,2 - 4,2,1,0 - perc.(2) - hp. - pf. - str.   25:00 P.R.S.
—— SYMPHONY NO. 3, FOR STRINGS (1953)
str.   25:00 P.R.S.

STEVENS, Leith
—— CONCERTO FOR PIANO AND ORCH.
      Leeds.

STEVENSON, Ronald
—— BERCEUSE SYMPHONIQUE (1951)
    3,2,2,2 - 4,2,3,1 - timp.,perc. - hp. - str.   12:00 P.R.S.
—— JAMBOREE FOR GRAINGER (1960)
    2,2,2,alto sax.,2 - 4,2,3,0 - timp.,perc. - hp. - pf. - str. 6:00 P.R.S.
—— KEENING SONG FOR A MAKAR (IN MEMORIAM FRANCIS
    GEORGE SCOTT)(1963)
    2,2,2,0-3 - 4,2,3,1 - timp.,perc. - hp. - pf. - str. 7:00 P.R.S.
—— PAVAN (AFTER JOHN BULL)(1955)
    1,1,1,1 - 1,0,0,0 - str.   7:00 P.R.S.
—— PRELUDE, FUGUE AND FANTASY (CONCERTO NO. 1 FOR
    PIANO AND ORCH.)
    2,2(2nd alt. with Eng.hn.),2,2 - 4,2,3,0 - timp.,perc. - pf. - str.
    35:00 Novello.
—— SCOTS DANCE TOCCATA (1965)
    2(2nd alt. with picc.),2(2nd alt. with Eng.hn.),2(2nd alt. with
    b.-cl.),2(2nd alt. with c.-bn.) - 4,2,3,0 - timp.,perc. - hp. - pf. - str.
    11:00 Novello.

STEWART, Frank G.
—— THE PHANTOM TRAIN OF MARSHALL PASS (FOR
    NARRATOR, WIND AND PERCUSSION)
    4,0,*4,d.-b.cl.,0 - 0,0,0,0 - perc.,bels,mar. - pf. 10:00 Belw-Mills.

STEWART, Humphrey J.
—— CHRISTMAS (A SACRED CANTATA) (FOR SOPRANO,
    TENOR, BASS, MIXED CHORUS AND ORCH.)
    2,2,3,2 - 0,3,2,0 - perc. - str.   Boston.
—— THE HOUND OF HEAVEN (MUSIC DRAMA) %
    1,1,2,1 - 2,2,1,0 - timp. - org. - str.   J. Fischer.

STEWART, Joseph A.
—— ROMANTIC FANTASY (FOR PIANO AND ORCH.) (1963)
    3(3rd alt.with picc.),*3,*3,2 - 4,3,3,1 - timp.,perc.(3) - pf. - str.
    17:00 Composer.

STIBILJ, Milan
—— CONCERTANT MUSIC (FOR HORN AND ORCH.)
    2,3,2,2 - 3,2,0,0 - str.   12:00 Hans Gerig.
—— CONGRUENCES (FOR PIANO AND ORCH.)
    2(2nd alt. with picc.),0,2(2nd alt. with b.-cl.),2 - 4,2,3,1 - perc.(3) -
    pf. - str.   9:00 Hans Gerig.
—— CONTEMPLATION (FOR OBOE AND STRINGS)(1966)
    ob. - str.   9:00 G. Schirmer.
—— EKTHESIS FOR ORCH. (1968)
    *4,*4,4(4th alt. with b.-cl.),*3 - 4,3,3,1 - perc.(2) - pf. - str.
    10:00 G. Schirmer.
—— THE NIGHTINGALE AND THE ROSE (SYMPHONY)
    2(2nd alt. with picc.),2(2nd alt. with Eng. hn.),2(2nd alt. with
    b.-cl.),2(2nd alt. with c.-bn.) - 4,2,3,1 - timp.,perc.(3) - pf. - str.
    14:00 Hans Gerig.
—— VERSE
    2(2nd alt. with picc.),2,2,2 - 4,2,3,1 - timp.,perc.(5) - str.
    6:00 Hans Gerig.

STIEBER, Hans
—— SYMPHONIC APHORISMS (FOR CHAMBER ORCH.)
    1,2,2,1 - 1,1,0,0 - str.   25:00 Tetra.
—— SYMPHONIC TRILOGY
    2,3,3,3 - 4,3,3,1 - timp.,perc. - str.   30:00 Tetra.

STIEBLER, Ernstalbrecht
—— MODELL (FOR STRING ORCH.)
    str.   14:40 Modern.

STIERLIN, Kuno
—— LA CHASSE (JAGD-STÜCK)
    2,2,2,2 - 4,3,3,1 - timp.,perc. - hp. - str. 5:00 Mannheimer.
—— WARENDORFER-REITER OVERTURE
    2,2,2,2 - 4,3,3,1 - timp.,perc. - hp. - str. 9:00 Mannheimer.

STILL, Robert
—— SYMPHONY NO. 2
    2,2,2,2 - 4,3,3,1 - timp.,perc. - str.   30:00 P.R.S.

STILL, William Grant
—— AFRICA (IN 3 MOVTS.)
    3(3rd alt. with picc.),*3,*4,2 - 4,3,3,1 - timp.,perc.(3),cel.- hp. -
    pf. - str.   30:00 WGS Music.
—— AFRO-AMERICAN SYMPHONY
    1. Moderato assai; 2. Adagio; 3. Animato; 4. Lento, con
    risoluzione
    *3,*3,*4,2 - 4,3,3,1 - timp.,perc.(2) - hp. - str. 24:00 Novello.

—— LOS ALNADOS DE ESPAÑA (THE STEPCHILDREN OF
    SPAIN)(SUITE) (IN 4 MOVTS.)
    3(3rd alt. with picc.),*3,*3,2 - 4,3,3,1 - timp.,perc.,glock. - hp. -
    str.   21:00 WGS Music.
—— THE AMERICAN SCENE: SUITE NO. 1 (THE EAST) (1958)
    (IN 3 MOVTS.)
    3(3rd alt. with picc.),*3,*3,2 - 4,3,3,1 - timp.,perc. (3),bells,cel.,xyl.
    - hp. - str.   6:33 WGS Music.
—— THE AMERICAN SCENE: SUITE NO. 2 (THE SOUTH) (1958)
    (IN 3 MOVTS.)
    3(3rd alt. withpicc.),*3,*3,2 - 4,3,3,1 - timp.,perc.(3),bells,cel. - hp.
    - str.   11:57 WGS Music.
—— THE AMERICAN SCENE: SUITE NO. 3 (THE OLD WEST)
    (1958) (IN 3 MOVTS.)
    (3rd alt. with picc.),*3,2,2 - 4,3,3,1 - timp.,perc.(3),bells,cel. - hp. -
    str.   7:17 WGS Music.
—— THE AMERICAN SCENE: SUITE NO. 4 (THE FAR WEST)
    (1958) (IN 3 MOVTS.)
    3(3rd alt. with picc.),*3,*3,2 - 4,3,3,1 - timp.,perc.,bells,xyl. - hp. -
    str.   7:01 WGS Music.
—— THE AMERICAN SCENE: SUITE NO. 5 (A MOUNTAIN, A
    MEMORIAL AND A SONG) (1958) (IN 3 MOVTS.)
    3(3rd alt, with picc.),*3,*3,2 - 4,3,3,1 - timp.,perc. (3),
    bells,cel.,glock.,xyl. - hp. - str.   14:31 WGS Music.
—— AND THEY LYNCHED HIM ON A TREE (FOR NARRATOR,
    CONTRALTO, DOUBLE CHORUS AND ORCH.)
    2,1(alt. with Eng. hn.),*3,2 - 3,3,2,1 - timp.,perc.(2) - str.
    19:00 WGS Music.
—— ARCHAIC RITUAL (IN 3 MOVTS.)
    3(3rd alt. with picc.),*3,*3,2(2nd alt. with c.-bn.) - 4,3,3,1 -
    timp.,perc.,bells,cel. - hp. - str.   20:00 WGS Music.
—— BELLS
    7:00 Leeds.
    PHANTOM CHAPEL
    2(2nd alt. with picc.)*3,*3,2(2nd alt. with c.-bn.) - 4,3,3,1 -
    timp.,perc.(3) - hp. - pf. - str.
    FAIRY KNOLL
    2(2nd alt. with picc.),*3,*3,2 - hn. - cel. - hp. - pf. - str.
—— BEYOND TOMORROW ("A SONG AT DUSK")
    3(3rd alt. with picc.),*3,*3,2 - 4,3,3,1 - timp.,perc.,cel. - hp. - str.
    9:00 WGS Music.
—— CHOREOGRAPHIC PRELUDE
    2(2nd alt. with picc.),2,2,2 - 3,2,2,1 - timp.,perc. - hp. - str.
    4:30 WGS Music.
—— CHRISTMAS IN THE WESTERN WORLD (FOR SATB
    CHORUS AND STRINGS)
    pf. - str.   15:00 Southern.
—— CUATRO DANZAS DE PANAMA (FOR STRING ORCH.)
    str.   13:00 Southern.
—— DARKER AMERICA
    2,*2,2,2 - 1,1,1,0 - pf. - str.   17:00 C. Fischer.
—— DISMAL SWAMP
    3,*3,*4,*3 - 4,4,3,1 - timp.,perc.vibra. - pf. - str.
    15:00 New Mus Ed.
—— ENNANGA (FOR HARP AND ORCH.) (IN 3 MOVTS.)
    2(2nd alt. with picc.),2(2nd alt. with Eng.hn.),2,2 - 3,2,2,1 -
    timp.,perc.,xyl. - hp. - str.   15:00 WGS Music.
    or:
    hp. - pf. - str.
—— FESTIVE OVERTURE
    3(3rd alt. with picc.),*3,*3,2 - 4,3,3,1 - timp.,perc.(4),cel.,mar.,xyl.
    - hp. - str.   10:00 WGS Music.
—— FIVE SONGS OF SEPARATION (FOR LOW VOICE AND
    ORCH.)
    2,2,2,2 - 4,0,0,0 - timp.,perc.,cel. - hp. - str.   Leeds.
—— FROM A LOST CONTINENT (SUITE)(FOR SATB CHORUS
    AND ORCH.) (IN 4 MOVTS.)
    2,1,2,2 - 0,0,0,0 - timp.,perc. - hp. - str.   15:00 WGS Music.
—— FROM THE BLACK BELT (SUITE)
    2,2,2,2 - 4,3,2,1 - timp.,perc. - hp. - str.   C. Fischer.
—— IN MEMORIAM (THE COLORED SOLDIERS WHO DIED
    FOR DEMOCRACY)
    3(3rd alt. with picc.),*3,*3,2 - 4,3,3,1 - timp.,perc.(3) - hp. - str.
    6:00 Leeds.
—— IN MEMORY OF JAN SIBELIUS (THRENODY)
    2(2nd alt, with picc.),2,2,2 - 3,2,2,1 - timp.,perc.(2),bells - hp. - str.
    4:00 WGS Music.
—— KAINKUCK' (POEM) (FOR PIANO AND ORCH.)
    3(1 alt. with picc.),*3,*3,2 - 4,3,3,1 - timp.,perc. - pf. - str.
    13:00 WGS Music.

—— LENOX AVENUE (CHOREOGRAPHIC STREET SCENE) (FOR NARRATOR, CHORUS AND ORCH.) %
  2(2nd alt. with picc.),2(2nd alt. with Eng. hn.),2,2 - 3,3,2,0 - timp.,perc.(2),bell - pf. - str.   23:00 WGS Music.

—— THE LITTLE RED SCHOOLHOUSE (SUITE) (FOR NARRATOR AND ORCH.) (IN 5 MOVTS.)
  2(2nd alt. with picc.),2(2nd alt. with Eng.hn.),2(2nd alt. with b.-cl.),2 - 3,3,2,1 - timp.,perc.(2),cel. - str.   17:30 Southern.

—— THE LITTLE SONG THAT WANTED TO BE A SYMPHONY (FOR NARRATOR AND ORCH.)
  2,2,2,2 - 3,2,2,0 - timp.,perc.(2),bells,cel.,xyl. - hp. - str.   19:00 C. Fischer.

—— MINIATURE OVERTURE
  3,*3,*3,2 - 4,3,3,1 - timp.,perc.,glock.,xyl. - hp. - str.   3:00 WGS Music.

—— OLD CALIFORNIA
  3(1 alt. with picc.),*3,*3,*3 - 4,3,3,1 - timp.,perc.(2),bells,vibra. - hp. - str.   10:00 WGS Music.

—— OUT OF THE SILENCE
  fl. - pf. - str.   6:30 WGS Music.

—— PAGES FROM A MOTHER'S DIARY (SUITE)
  2(2nd alt. with picc.),2,*3,2 - 4,3,3,0 - timp.,perc.(2),cel. - hp. - str.   14:30 C. Fischer.

—— PAGES FROM NEGRO HISTORY (SUITE)
  2,2,2,2 - 4,2,2,1 - timp.,perc. - hp. - pf. - str.   11:00 C. Fischer.

—— PASTORELA (FOR VIOLIN AND ORCH.)
  3,*3,*3,2 - 4,3,3,1 - timp., - hp. - str.   11:00 Witmark.

—— THE PATH OF GLORY (FOR BASS-BARITONE AND ORCH.) (IN 4 MOVTS.)
  3,*3,*3,2 - 4,3,3,1- timp.,perc. - hp. - str.   15:00 WGS Music.

—— PATTERNS (SUITE) (IN 5 MOVTS.)
  *3,*3,2,2 - 2,0,0,0 - str.   9:00 WGS Music.

—— THE PEACEFUL LAND
  2,2,2,2 - 3,2,2,1 - hp. - str.   10:00 AmerMusEd.

—— PLAIN-CHANT FOR AMERICA (FOR BARITONE AND ORCH., OR SATB CHORUS AND ORCH.)
  3(3rd alt. with picc),*3,*3,2 - 4,3,3,1 - timp.,perc.(2) - hp. - str.   10:00 WGS Music.

—— POEM FOR ORCHESTRA
  3,*3,*3,2(2nd alt. with c-bn.) - timp.,perc.(3),cel. - hp. - str.   15:00 Leeds.

—— A PSALM FOR THE LIVING (FOR SATB CHORUS AND ORCHESTRA) (Text: Verna Arvey)
  2,2,2,2 - 2,2,2,1 - perc. - hp. - str.   8:30 Bourne.

—— RHAPSODY (FOR SOPRANO AND ORCH.) (IN 4 MOVTS.)
  2,2(2nd alt. with Eng.hn.),2,2 - 3,3,2,1 - timp.,perc.,cel. - hp. - str.   15:00 WGS Music.

—— SAHDJI (SUITE FROM THE BALLET)
  2(alt. with 2 picc.)*3,*3,2 - 4,2,2,1 - timp.,perc.(3),bells - hp. - str.   20:30 C. Fischer.

—— SENTIMENTAL SONG
  *3,*3,*3,2 - 4,3,3,1 - timp.,cel. - hp. - str.   10:00 Composer.

—— SERENADE
  fl. - pf. - str.   9:21 WGS Music.
  or:
  2(2nd alt. with picc.),2,2,2 - 3,2,2,1 - timp.,perc.,glock. - hp. - str.

—— SONG OF A CITY (FOR CHORUS AND ORCH.)
  3,*3,*3,2 - 4,3,3,1 - timp.,perc.(2) - hp. - pf. - str.   10:00 Composer.

—— SUITE FOR VIOLIN AND ORCH. (IN 3 MOVTS.)
  *3,*3,*4,*3 - 4,3,3,1 - timp.,perc.(2),bells,cel.,glock,mar. - hp. - str.   15:00 WGS Music.

—— SUMMERLAND (FROM "THREE VISIONS")
  1,1,2,1 - 2,2,1,0 - perc. - pf. - str.   6:00 Composer.

—— SYMPHONY IN G MINOR ("SONG OF A NEW RACE")
  1. Slowly; 2. Slowly and deeply expressive; 3. Moderately fast; 4. Moderately slow
  3(3rd alt. with picc.),*3,*4,2 - 4,3,3,1 - timp.,perc.(2), cel. - hp. - str.   25:00 WGS Music.

—— SYMPHONY NO. 3 ("THE SUNDAY SYMPHONY") (IN 4 MOVTS.)
  3(3rd alt. with picc.),*3,*3,2 - 4,3,3,1 - timp.,perc.(3)bells,cel.,xyl. - hp. - str.   25:00 WGS Music.

—— SYMPHONY NO. 4 ("AUTOCHTHONOUS") (IN 4 MOVTS.)
  3(3rd alt. with picc.),*3,*3,2(2nd alt. with c-bn.) - 4,3,3,1 - timp.,perc.(3),bells,cel.,glock. - hp. - str.   27:00 WGS Music.

—— SYMPHONY NO. 5 ("WESTERN HEMISPHERE") (IN 4 MOVTS.)
  3(3rd alt. with picc.),*3,*3,2(2nd alt. with c.-bn.) - 4,3,3,1 - timp.,perc.,cel. - str.   27:00 WGS Music.

—— THOSE WHO WAIT (FOR SATB CHORUS AND ORCH.)
  *4,*3,*4,2 - 4,3,3,1 - timp.,perc. - hp. - str.   10:00 WGS Music.

—— THREE DANCES FROM "LA GUIABLESSE"
  3(3rd alt. with picc.),3,3,2 - 4,3,3,1 - per. - hp. - str.   8:00 C. Fischer.

—— TROUBLED ISLAND (4-ACT OPERA) %
          Southern.

—— WAILING WOMAN (FOR SOPRANO, CHORUS AND ORCH.)
  3(3rd alt. with picc.),*3,*3,2 - 4,3,3,1 - cel. - hp. - str.   10:00 WGS Music.

—— WOOD NOTES (IN 5 MOVTS.)
  3(3rd alt. with picc.),*3,*3,2 - 4,3,3,1 - timp.,perc.(2),cel. - hp. - str.   27:00 Southern.

STILMAN, Julia
—— CANTATA NO. 1 ("EL ORO INTIMO") (FOR BARITONE VOICE AND CHAMBER ORCH.) (1961) (Text: Amaolo Nerro)
  2,*1,*3,4 sax.(1 sopr.,1 alto,1 ten.,1 bar.),*3 - 0,0,0,0 - perc.(3) - 4 vln.,4 vla.   17:00 Composer.

—— CANTATA NO. 3 ("BARCAROLA") (FOR SOPRANO, MEZZO-SOPR., ALT, TRIPLE SATB CHORUS AND CHAMBER ORCH.) (1973) (Text: Pablo Neruda)
  3,0,1,0 - 0,0,0,0 - perc.(3),cel. - 3 vla.,3 c.,3 d.-b. 13:15 Composer.

STIRES, Ernest M.
—— FANCY FOR PIANO AND ORCHESTRA (1969)
  1,1,1,1 - 1,1,1,0 - xyl. - pf. - str.   Composer.

—— PARTY OF 12 (FOR 12 PLAYERS) (1968)
  1,1,1,1 - 1,1,1,0 - perc.(1)(trap-drums set) - pf.- 1 vln.,1 c., 1 d.-b.   8:00 Composer.

—— SONG AND DANCE FOR ORCHESTRA (1966)
  2(1 alt.with picc.),2,2,2 - 4,2,3,0 - timp.,perc.(2) - str.   10:00 Composer.

STOCKLY, Raymond
—— CONCERTO POUR PIANO ET ORCH.
  2,2,2,2 - 2,2,2,0 - timp.,perc.(2),cel. - pf. - str.   20:00 S.U.I.S.A.

—— RONDES (1973)
  *3,*3,*3,*3 - 4,3,3,1 - timp.,perc.(6) - hp. - str.   12:00 Seesaw.

—— SYMPHONIE NO. 1 ("DELL'ESTATE")
          S.U.I.S.A.

—— A THEATRICAL SET (FÜR KAMMERORCH.)
          12:00 S.U.I.S.A.

STOESSEL, Albert
—— CONCERTO GROSSO FOR PIANO AND STRINGS (IN 4 MOVTS.)
  pf. - str.   22:00 J. Fischer.

—— CYRANO DE BERGERAC (SYMPHONIC PORTRAIT)
  *3,*3,*3,2 - 4,3,3,1 - timp.,perc.(3) - hp. - str. 18:00 AmerMusEd.

—— EARLY AMERICANA (SUITE) (IN 4 MOVTS.)
  *3,*3,*3,*3 - 4,3,3,1 - timp.,perc.(3) - hp. - str.   12:00 Birchard.

—— HISPANIA SUITE (IN 4 MOVTS.)
  *3,*3,*3,2 - 4,3,3,1 - timp.,perc.(3) - hp. - str.   15:00 C. Fischer.

—— SUITE ANTIQUE (FOR 2 VIOLINS AND CHAMBER ORCH.)
  1,1,1,1 - hn. - pf. - str.   13:00 G. Schirmer.

—— SUITE FROM THE OPERA "GARRICK" (IN 5 MOVTS.)
  *3,*3,*3,2 - 4,3,3,1 - timp.,perc.(3) - hp. - str.   15:00 J. Fischer.

STOJKOV, Stojan
—— LETTER (CYCLE OF SONGS FOR MEZZO-SOPRANO AND ORCH.)
  1,b.-fl.,1,1,1 - 1,1,1,0 - timp.,perc. - pf. - str.   12:00 S.O.K.O.J.

—— MUSIQUE CONCERTANTE
  vibra.,xyl. - str.   11:00 S.O.K.O.J.

STOJOWSKI, Sigismond
—— PROLOGUE, SCHERZO AND VARIATIONS, OP. 32 (CONCERTO NO. 2 FOR PIANO AND ORCH.)
  3,3,2,2 - 4,2,3,0 - timp.,perc. - hp. - pf. - str.   32:00 Presser.

STOKER, Richard
—— CHORALE FOR STRINGS
  str.   3:00 Tetra.

—— SERENADE
  1,1,1,1 - 1,0,0,0 - timp. - str.   10:00 P.R.S.

STOKES, Eric
—— A CELEBRATION FOR THE SAINT (MUSIC FOR ST. CECILIA'S DAY)
  1(alt. with picc.),0,0,0 - 0,2,2,0 - timp. - org. - str. 8:00 Composer.
  or:
  2(1 alt. with picc.),0,2,2 - 2,2,2,1 - timp.,xyl. - str.

—— A CENTER HARBOR HOLIDAY (FOR TUBA AND ORCH.)
(1963)
2(2nd alt.with picc.),2,2(2nd alt.with E♭cl.),2 - 4,2,3,1 -
timp.,perc.(4),glock.,xyl. - hp. - pf. - str.   14:30 Composer.
—— THE CONTINENTAL HARP AND BAND REPORT (1974)
(MUSIC IN 9 MOVEMENTS) (FOR WINDS, BRASS,
PERCUSSION, KEYBOARD AND HARP)
3(2 alt.with 2 picc.),3(1 alt.with Eng.hn.),3(1 alt.with E♭cl.,1
alt.with b.-cl. and sopr.sax.),3(1 alt.with cbn.,1 alt.with ten.sax.) -
4,4,4,1 - timp.,perc.(4),bells,cel.,glock.,mar.,vibra.,xyl. - hp. - org. -
pf.   45:00 Composer.
—— DIVERTIMENTO NO. 1
1,0,1,0 - 0,1,0,0 - timp. - str.   6:00 Composer.
—— DIVERTIMENTO NO. 2 (1960)
0,3(3rd alt.with Eng.hn.),0,0 - 0,2,0,0 - timp. - str.
7:00 Composer.
—— FIVE VERBS OF EARTH ENCIRCLED (FOR NARRATOR,
HARMONIUM AND STRINGS) (1973) (IN 6 MOVTS.) (Texts:
Walt Whitman andStephen Vincent Benét)
Harm. - str.(7,3,2,1)   22:00 Composer.
—— HORSPFAL (2-ACT OPERA) % (1968) (Text: Alvin Greenberg)
2(alt.with 2 picc. and 2 sopr.recorders),0,2(alt.with 2 sax.),0 -
0,0,2,0 - timp.,perc.(3),cel.,glock.,mar.,vibra.,xyl. - pf. - str.
110:00 Composer.
—— LAMPYRIDAE (A SUMMER NOCTURNE) (FOR 14 OR MORE
INSTRUMENTS, MOSTLY TREBLE) (1973)
4:23 Composer.
—— ON THE BADLANDS PARABLES (1974) (IN 3 MOVTS.)
1(alt.with picc.),2,1(atl.with E♭cl.),2 - 2,0,0,0 - glock.(ad lib),xyl.(ad
lib.) - tape-recorder(2-channel) - pf. - str.(8,2,3,1)
12:31 Composer.
—— SMOKE AND STEEL (FOR TENOR, MEN'S CHORUS, BRASS
AND LOW STRINGS) (1959) (Text: Carl Sandburg)
0,0,0,0 - 4,0,3,0 - str.(no vlns.)   120:00 Composer.
—— SONATAS (FOR DIVIDED STRING ORCH., SURROUNDING
AUDIENCE) (1967) (IN 1 MOVT.)
str.   9:00 Composer.
—— THREE SIDES OF A TOWN (SUITE) (1964)
*3,2,2,2 - 4,3,3,1 - timp.,perc.(4) - pf. - str.   30:00 Composer.
—— VARIATIONS ON A SPACE AND A QUIET (1973)
0,1,0,0 - 1,0,0,0 - timp.,perc.(1) - str.(4,2,1,1)   9:45 Composer.

STOLLBERG, Sascha von
—— MUSTAFA AND HIS DONKEY (MUSTAFA UND SEIN ESEL)
(BURLESQUE AFTER THE BALLET OF THE SAME NAME)
2(2nd alt. with picc.),2(2nd alt. with Eng. hn.),2,2(2nd alt. with
c.-bn.) - 2,4,3,1 - timp.,perc. - hp. - str.   18:00 Modern.

STÖLZEL, Gottfried Heinrich - THILDE, Jean
—— CONCERTO IN D MAJOR (FOR TRUMPET AND STRINGS)
tpt. - str.   8:30 Presser.

STÖLZEL, Gottfried Heinrich - TÖTTCHER, Hermann
—— CONCERTO IN D MAJOR, FOR OBOE, STRINGS AND
CEMBALO
ob. - cemb. - str.   14:00 F. Colombo.

STOLZENWALD, Otto
—— LITTLE BALLET ETUDE
2,2,2,2 - 4,2,3,0 - timp.,perc. - hp. - str.   4:00 Henmar.
—— STREIFLICHTER (A CHEERFUL CAPRICE)
2,2,2,2 - 4,2,3,0 - timp.,perc.(3) - hp. - str.   5:00 Henmar.

STONE, Gregory
—— CONCERTO FOR 5 CELLI AND ORCHESTRA
3,2,2,2 - 4,2,3,0 - timp.,perc. - c.(5)   15:00 Credo.
—— CONCIERTO VENEZOLANO
16:00 Credo.
—— ELEGY
6:00 Credo.
—— EPITAPH FOR A FRIEND
3,3,3,2 - 4,0,0,0 - str.   6:00 Credo.
—— HORA IN SUON ARMONICI (FOR VIOLIN AND STRINGS)
str.   5:00 Credo.
—— IMPROVISATION BREVE (FOR DOUBLE-BASS AND
STRINGS)
str.   5:00 Credo.
—— INTRODUCTION, PASTORALE AND VIVO ALLA ZINGARA
(FOR HARP, VIOLIN, FLUTE AND STRINGS)
fl. - hp. - str.   14:00 Credo.
—— MATER GLORIOSA
6:00 Credo.

—— MUSIC TO MAX REINHARDT'S "FAUST"
1,1,2,1 - 2,2,1,0 - timp.,perc. - org.   65:00 Credo.
—— PERPETUUM MOBILE SYMPHONIACUM
*3,*3,3,3 - 4,3,1,0 - timp.,perc. - 2 hp. - str.   20:00 Credo.
—— PEZZO APPASSIONATO (FOR TUBA, FLUTE, CLARINET,
HARP AND STRINGS)
fl.,cl. - tu. - hp. - str.   5:00 Credo.
—— ROUMANIAN GYPSY DIVERTISSEMENT (FOR VIOLIN AND
ORCH.)
*3,*3,3,2 - 4,2,3,1 - timp.,perc. - 2 guit. - hp. - str.   22:00 Credo.
—— SKETCHES AT RANDOM (FOR OBOE AND STRINGS)
ob. - str.   10:00 Credo.
—— VARIATIONS CONCERTO (FOR PIANO AND STRINGS)
pf. - str.   25:00 Credo.

STORACE, Stephen - GRAVES, Richard
—— OVERTURE: "MAHMOUD"
2,2,0,2 - 2,2,0,0 - timp. - str.   11:00 Galaxy.

STOUFFER, Paul M.
—— CELEBRATION OVERTURE (1971)
2,2,2,2 - 4,2,1,1 - timp. - str.(12,4,4,3)   3:05 Composer.
—— CONCERTO FOR TWO, OP. 15 (FOR CLARINET, TRUMPET
AND ORCH.) (IN ONE MOVT.)
2,2,2,2 - 4,2,1,0 - timp. - str.   10:00 H. Elkan.
—— FABLE FOR ORCHESTRA, OP. 13
1,1,1,1 - 2,1,1,0 - timp.,perc.(1) - str.   4:00 Composer.

STRADELLA, Alessandro - BONELLI
—— CONCERTO GROSSO NO. 2 IN D MAJOR (FOR 2 VIOLINS,
CELLO AND STRINGS)
str.   7:00 Henmar.

STRADELLA, Alessandro - CRISTIANI
—— ARIA DI CHIESA
ob. - 1-2 hp. - str.   9:00 Bo. Hawkes.

STRADELLA, Alessandro - GENTILI, Alberto
—— SONATA PER TROMBA, CEMBALO E ARCHI
tpt. - hpsc. - str.   MCA Music.
—— SYMPHONY IN G
str.   12:00 Bo. Hawkes.

STRADELLA, Alessandro - OUBRADOUS, Fernand
—— SONATA DE CONCERT (FOR TRUMPET AND STRINGS)
tpt. - str.   7:30 Presser.

STRAESSER, Ewald
—— CONCERT OVERTURE
2,2,2,2 - 2,2,1,0 - timp. - str.   12:00 T & J.
—— SYMPHONY NO. 1 IN G MAJOR, OP. 22
3,2,2,3 - 4,2,3,1 - timp. - str.   40:00 T & J.
—— SYMPHONY NO. 2 IN D MINOR
3,3,3,3 - 4,3,3,1 - perc. - hp. - str.   45:00 T & J.

STRAESSER, Joep
—— CHORAI (1967)
12:00 Henmar.
—— INTERSECTIONS I
16:00 Henmar.
—— MUSIQUE POUR L'HOMME (1968) (FOR 4-PART CHORUS
AND ORCH.) (Text: by the United Nations)
25:00 Henmar.
—— EN RADE (FOR CHORUS AND ORCH.) (1967) (Text: Jan
Engelman)
18:00 Henmar.
—— SUMMER CONCERTO (FOR OBOE AND CHAMBER ORCH.)
2,3,2,2 - 2,2,2,0 - perc. - hp. - str.   11:00 Modern.

STRAIGHT, Willard
—— CONCERTINO FOR OBOE AND SMALL ORCHESTRA
2,1,2,2 - 2,2,0,0 - timp. - perc.   Chappell.
—— CONCERTO FOR PIANO AND ORCH.
2,2,2,2 - 2,2,1,0 - timp.,perc.(2) - pf. - str.   26:10 Chappell.
—— DEVELOPMENT FOR ORCH.
2(2nd alt. with picc.),0,0,0 - 2,2,0,0 - timp.,perc.(1) - str.
9:30 Chappell.
—— PRELUDE, PROCESSION AND PASSACAGLIA (THEMATIC
METAMORPHOSIS FOR ORCH.)
2,2,2,2 - 4,3,3,1 - timp.,perc.(4),cel.,glock. - hp. - str.
17:30 Chappell.

STRANGE, John Allen
—— FORTUNES OF ERE (1966) (IN 4 MOVTS.)
2,1,2,1 - 1,0,0,0 - timp.,perc.(2),mar.,xyl. - pf. - str.
12:30 Composer.

STRANZ, Ulrich
—— DÉJÀ VU (FOR OBOE D'AMORE AND CHAMBER ORCH.)
0,0,oboe d'amore,1,0 - 0,1,0,0 - perc.(2) - hp. - str.
17:00 G. Schirmer.
—— KLANGBILD (SOUND PICTURE FOR ORCH.)
*4,*4,*4,*4 - 6,4,4,1 - timp.,perc.,cel. - hp. - str.
15:00 G. Schirmer.
—— TACHYS (FOR SOLO STRINGS AND ORCH.)(1974)
*3,*3,*3,*3 - 3,3,3,1 - timp.,perc.(6, incl. 4 on timp.),cel. - Aeolian
hp. - hp. - str.
14:00 G. Schirmer.

STRASSBURG, Robert
—— FOUR MANIFESTATIONS (FOR STRINGS)
str.
6:00 Hargail.

STRATEGIER, Herman
—— BALLADE VAN DE MAAGD VAN WOGNUM (FOR CHORUS
AND FULL ORCH.) (1965) (Text: H. L. Prenen)
25:30 Henmar.
—— BOSSCHAGE (BALLET SUITE) (1960)
2,2,2,1 - 1,1,0,0 - timp.,perc. - str.
16:00 Henmar.
—— CONCERTO FOR ACCORDION AND ORCH.
2,2,3,2 - 2,2,0,0 - timp.,perc.(3) - acc. - str.
Henmar.
—— CONCERTO FOR CLARINET AND ORCH.
2,2,1,2 - 2,0,0,0 - perc. - str.
20:00 Henmar.
—— CONCERTO FOR FLUTE AND ORCH.
1,1,1,1 - 2,0,0,0 - timp.,perc. - hp. - str.
20:00 Henmar.
—— CONCERTO FOR PIANO AND ORCH.
2,2,2,2 - 4,2,0,0 - timp.,perc. - pf. - str.
20:00 Henmar.
—— DIVERTIMENTO
1,1,1,1 - 0,0,0,0 - str.
6:00 Henmar.
—— DON RAMIRO (FOR SOPRANO, BARITONE, MALE CHORUS
AND ORCH.) (1943) (Text: H. Heine; Dutch text: B. Verhoeven)
3,2,2,2 - 4,3,3,1 - timp.,perc. - hp. - str.
35:00 Henmar.
—— HAARLEM SUITE
3,3,3,2 - 4,3,3,1 - timp.,perc. - hp. - str.
17:00 Henmar.
—— HENRIC VAN VELDEKE (FOR BARITONE, SPEAKER AND
ORCH.) (1952) (Text: J. Schreurs)
2,2,2,2 - 4,3,3,0 - timp.,perc.,cel. - hp. - str.
20:00 Henmar.
—— HOMMAGE À ANDRIESSEN
2,2,2,2 - 4,3,3,0 - timp.,perc., - str.
7:00 Henmar.
—— INTRADA SINFONICA
3,3,3,2 - 4,3,3,1 - timp.,perc. - cel. - hp. - str.
10:00 Henmar.
—— INTRODUZIONE E PASSACAGLIA
3,3,2,3 - 4,3,3,1 - timp.,perc. - str.
10:00 Henmar.
—— KADULLEN VARIATIES (1958)
1,0,0,1 - 0,0,0,0 - str.
10:00 Henmar.
—— MUSIQUE POUR FAIRE PLAISIR
str.
15:00 Henmar.
—— PARTITA IN MODI ANTICHI
2,2,2,2 - 2,2,0,0 - timp.,perc. - str.
13:00 Henmar.
—— PRAELUDIUM AND FUGA
2,3,3,2 - 4,3,3,0 - timp.,perc. - str.
8:00 Henmar.
—— PSALM FOR ARHHEM (FOR SOLOSTS, CHORUS AND
ORCH.)
Henmar.
—— PSALM 76 (FOR MALE CHORUS AND ORCH.) (1946)
2,2,3,2 - 4,3,3,1 - timp.,perc. - str.
15:00 Henmar.
—— PSALM 118 (FOR BARITONE, ALTO OR MEZZO-SOPRANO
AND ORCH.) (1953)
2,2,2,2 - 3,3,3,0 - timp.,perc.,cel. - hp. - str.
28:00 Henmar.
—— RAMIROSUITE
3,2,2,2 - 4,3,3,1 - timp.,perc. - hp. - str.
20:00 Henmar.
—— RAPSODIA ELEGIACA (1956)
3,3,3,2 - 4,3,3,1 - timp.,perc.,cel. - hp. - str.
17:00 Henmar.
—— REMBRANDT CANTATA (FOR SOLOISTS, CHORUS AND
ORCH.)
22:00 Henmar.
—— SEPTEM CANTICA (FOR MEZZO-SOPRANO AND ORCH.)
(1951) (IN 7 MOVTS.)
1,1,1,1 - 0,0,0,0 - str.
13:00 Henmar.
—— SYMPHONY NO. 1
2,2,3,2 - 4,3,3,1 - timp.,perc. - hp. - str.
27:00 Henmar.
—— TE DEUM (FOR SPORANO, CONTRALTO, CHORUS AND
ORCH.) (1967)
30:00 Henmar.
—— THREE PIECES FOR OBOE AND STRINGS
ob. - str.
10:00 Henmar.

—— THE THREE PUZZLES (FOR CHORUS AND ORCH.)
28:00 Henmar.
—— TURANDOT SUITE (FROM "DE DVIE RAADSELS")
2,1,0,0 - 2,1,0,0 - timp.,perc.,cel.,xyl. - pf. - str.
17:00 Henmar.
—— VANDER MOLLENFEESTE (FOR MIXED CHORUS AND
ORCH.) (1948)
3,0,2,1 - 0,0,0,0 - str.
17:00 Henmar.
—— VIJF MINNELIEDEREN UIT "HENRIC VAN VELDEKEN"
(FOR MEDIUM VOICE AND ORCH.) (1952) (Text: J. Schreurs)
fl. - str.
8:00 Henmar.

STRATTON, George
—— CONCERTO FOR OBOE AND STRING ORCH.
ob. - str.
14:00 Novello.

STRAUSS, Johann, Jr. - DORATI, Antal
—— GRADUATION BALL (BALLET IN 1 ACT) %
2,2,2,2 - 4,2,3,0 - timp.,perc.(4) - hp. - str.
48:00 Mills.

STRAUSS, Johann, Jr. - LUBOSCHUTZ, Pierre
—— THE BAT (A FANTASY ON THEMES FROM "DIE
FLEDERMAUS") (FOR 2 PIANOS AND ORCH.)
9:42 J. Fischer.

STRAUSS, Richard
—— DIE AEGYPTISCHE HELENA: FANTASY FROM THE OPERA
2,2,2,2 - 2,2,3,0 - timp.,perc. - org. - pf. - str.   16:00 Bo. Hawkes.
—— DIE AEGYPTISCHE HELENA, OP. 75 (OPERA) %
150:00 Bo. Hawkes.
HELEN'S SOLO SCENE (FOR SOPRANO AND ORCH.)
4,3,4,3 - 6,6,3,1 - timp.,perc.,cel. - 2 hp. - org. - str.   5:00
—— ARABELLA, OP. 79 (FANTASY FROM THE OPERA)
2,2,2,2 - 4,2,2,' - timp. - hp. - org. - pf. - str.   16:00 Bo. Hawkes.
—— ARABELLA, OP. 79 (OPERA) %
150:00 Bo. Hawkes.
DUET - ARABELLA AND MANDRYKA (FOR SOPRANO,
BARITONE AND ORCH.)
DUET - ARABELLA AND ZDENKA (FOR TWO SOPRANOS
AND ORCH.)
3,3,3,3 - 4,3,3,1 - timp.,perc. - hp. - str.
CLOSING DUET (FOR SOPRANO, BARITONE AND ORCH.)
PRELUDE TO ACT III
3,3,4,3 - 4,3,3,1 - timp.,perc. - hp. - str.   6:00
—— ARIADNE AUF NAXOS, OP. 60 (OPERA) %
100:00 Bo. Hawkes.
ARIADNE'S MONOLOGUE (FOR SOPRANO AND ORCH.)
2,2,2,2 - 2,1,0,2 - harm. - hp. - pf. - str.
ARIETTA OF THE COMPOSER (FOR SOPRANO AND
ORCH.)
DUET - ARIADNE AND BACCHUS (FOR SOPRANO, TENOR
AND ORCH.)
DUET - COMPOSER AND ZERBINETTA (FOR TWO
SOPRANOS AND ORCH.)
OVERTURE AND DANCE SCENE
2,2,2,2 - 2,1,1,0 - timp.,perc.,cel. - harm. - hp. - pf. - str.   10:00
ZERBINETTA'S RECITATIVE AND ARIA (FOR SOPRANO
AND ORCH.)
2,2,2,2 - 2,1,0,0 - timp.,perc. - pf. - str.   10:00
—— CAPRICCIO, OP. 85 (OPERA) %
135:00 Bo. Hawkes.
INTERLUDE
3,3,4,3 - 4,2,3,0 - timp.,perc. - cemb. - 2 hp. - str.   4:00
CLOSING SCENE (FOR SOPRANO AND ORCH.)
3,3,3,3 - 4,2,3,0 - timp.,perc. - cemb. - 2 hp. - str.   15:00
—— CONCERTO FOR OBOE AND SMALL ORCH.
1,*2,2,2 - 0,2,0,0 - str.   23:00 Bo. Hawkes.
—— CONCERTO NO. 2 FOR HORN AND ORCH.
2,2,2,2 - 2,2,0,0 - timp. - str.   25:00 Bo. Hawkes.
—— DAPHNE, OP. 82 (OPERA) %
105:00 Bo. Hawkes.
APOLLO'S ARIA (FOR TENOR AND ORCH.)
3,3,3,3 - 4,3,3,1 - timp.,perc. - 2 hp. - org. - str.   7:00
DAPHNE'S ENTRANCE (FOR SOP. AND ORCH.)
3,3,3,3 - 4,3,3,1 - timp.,perc. - 2 hp. - org. - str.   10:00
DAPHNE'S METAMORPHOSIS (FOR SOPRANO AND ORCH.)
3,3,3,3 - 4,3,3,1 - timp.,perc. - 2 hp. - org. - str.   5:00
MUSIC FOR A CHANGE OF SCENE
3,3,3,3 - 4,3,3,1 - timp.,perc. - 2 hp. - org. - str.   11:00
—— DIVERTIMENTO, OP. 86 (AFTER PIANO PIECES BY
COUPERIN)
2,3,2,2 - 2,1,1,0 - timp.,perc.,cel. - cemb. - hp. - org. - str.
40:00 Bo. Hawkes.

—— DUET CONCERTINO (FOR CLARINET, BASSOON, HARP AND STRINGS)

cl.,bn. - hp. - str.   20:00 Bo. Hawkes.

—— ELEKTRA (OPERA) %

90:00 Bo. Hawkes.

CHRYSOTHEMIS' ARIA (FOR SOPRANO AND ORCH.)

4,4,6,4 - 8,7,4,1 - timp.,perc. - 2 hp. - str.

or:

3,3,4,3 - 4,3,3,1 - timp.,perc. - 2 hp. - str.

DUET - ELEKTRA AND CHRYSOTHEMIS (FOR 2 SOPRANOS AND ORCH.)

ELEKTRA'S ARIA (FOR SOPRANO AND ORCH.)

ELEKTRA'S ARIA (FROM THE DUET) (FOR SOPRANO AND ORCH.)

ELEKTRA'S SOLO SCENE (FOR SOPRANO AND ORCH.)

6:00

GRAND DUET - ELEKTRA AND OREST (FOR SOPRANO, BARITONE AND ORCH.)

—— FESTLICHES PRAELUDIUM, OP. 61

5,4,heck.,5,5 - 8,10,(6 off-stage),4,1 - timp.,perc. - org. - str.

12:00 Bo. Hawkes.

—— FOUR LAST SONGS (FOR SOPRANO AND ORCH.)

Bo. Hawkes.

FRÜHLING

2,3,3,2 - 4,0,0,0 - hp. - str.   4:00

SEPTEMBER

3,3,3,2 - 4,2,0,0 - hp. - str.   4:30

BEIM SCHLAFENGEHEN

4,3,3,2 - 4,2,3,1 - cel. - str.   5:30

IM ABENDROT

2,3,3,3 - 4,3,3,1 - timp. - str.   8:00

—— DIE FRAU OHNE SCHATTEN: INTERLUDES

4,3,5,4 - 6,4,4,3 - timp.,perc.,2 cel. - 2 hp. - str.

20:00 Bo. Hawkes.

Off-Stage: 2 tpt., 2 trb.

—— DIE FRAU OHNE SCHATTEN, OP. 65 (OPERA) %

150:00 Bo. Hawkes.

EMPEROR'S SOLO SCENE (FOR TENOR AND ORCH.)

SYMPHONIC FANTASIA

3,3,3,3 - 4,3,3,1 - timp.,perc.cel. - hp. - str.   18:00

SYMPHONIC FRAGMENT

3,3,3,3 - 4,3,3,1 - timp.,perc.,cel. - hp. - str.   14:00

WATCHMAN'S SONG (FOR VOICE AND ORCH.)

4,4,4,4 - 4,6,4,5 - timp.,perc.,cel. - 2 hp. - str.

—— INTERLUDE FROM ACT 1 OF "INTERMEZZO"

2,2,2,2 - 3,2,2,0 - timp.,perc. - hp. - pf. - str.   7:00 Bo. Hawkes.

—— INTERLUDE IN C MINOR

2,2,2,2 - 4,2,3,0 - str.   8:00 Henmar.

—— INTERMEZZO (OPERA) %

120:00 Bo. Hawkes.

FOUR SYMPHONIC INTERLUDES

2,2,2,2 - 3,2,2,0 - timp.,perc. - hp. - pf. - str.   5:00

WALTZ SCENE

2,2,2,2 - 3,2,2,0 - timp.,perc. - hp. - pf. - str.   10:00

—— JOSEPHSLEGENDE (BALLET) (SYMPHONIC FRAGMENT)

2,2,2,2 - 4,3,3,1 - timp.,perc. - 2 hp. - str.   20:00 Bo. Hawkes.

—— JOSEPHSLEGENDE, OP. 63 (BALLET) %

5,4,4,4 - 6,4,4,2 - timp.,perc.,cel. - 4 hp. - org. - pf. - str.

60:00 Bo. Hawkes.

—— DIE LIEBE DER DANAE; OP. 83 (OPERA) %

Bo. Hawkes.

INTERLUDE AND FRAGMENT

14:00

SYMPHONIC FRAGMENT

3,1,5,4 - 6,3,3,1 - timp.,perc. - 2 hp. - str.   9:00

—— METAMORPHOSEN (STUDY FOR 23 SOLO STRINGS)

str.   30:00 Bo. Hawkes.

—— MÜNCHEN (EIN GEDÄCHTNISWALZER) (2ND VERSION)

3,2,2,3 - 4,3,0,1 - timp.,perc. - hp. - str.   9:30 Bo. Hawkes.

—— OLYMPIC HYMN (FOR MIXED CHORUS AND ORCH.)

3,3,3,3 - 4,10(4 off-stage),6,2 - timp.,perc. - str.   4:00 Bo. Hawkes.

—— PANATHENAENZUG, OP. 74 (PASSACAGLIA FOR PIANO LEFT-HAND AND ORCH.)

3,3,3,3 - 4,3,3,1 - pf. - str.   25:00 Bo. Hawkes.

—— DER ROSENKAVALIER, OP. 59 (OPERA) %

175:00 Bo. Hawkes.

OVERTURE

3,3,4,3 - 4,3,3,1 - timp.,perc.,cel. - hp. - str.   3:00

FIRST SEQUENCE OF WALTZES FROM ACTS I AND II

3,3,3,3 - 4,3,3,1 - timp.,perc. - hp. - str.   12:30

SECOND SEQUENCE OF WALTZES FROM ACT III

2,2,2,2 - 4,2,3,1 - timp.,perc. - hp. - str.   22:00

WALTZ CHAIN FROM ACT III

2,2,2,2 - 4,2,3,1 - timp.,perc. - hp. - str.   12:00

SUITE

3,3,3,3 - 4,3,3,1 - timp.,perc.,cel. - hp. - str.   22:00

DE RIGORI ARMATO (THE ITALIAN TENOR'S ARIA)

DUET - SOPHIE AND OCTAVIAN (FOR SOPRANO, MEZZO-SOPRANO AND ORCH.)

DUET - PRINCESS AND OCTAVIAN (FOR SOPRANO, MEZZO-SOPRANO AND ORCH.)

ENTRY OF THE ROSENKAVALIER (FOR SOPRANO, MEZZO-SOPRANO AND ORCH.)

MONOLOGUE OF THE PRINCESS (FOR SOPRANO AND ORCH.)

TRIO (FOR TWO SOPRANOS, MEZZO-SOPRANO AND ORCH.)

3,3,4,3 - 4,3,3,1 - timp.,perc.,cel. - hp. - str.

CLOSING DUET (FOR SOPRANO, MEZZO-SOPRANO AND ORCH.)

—— SCHLAGOBERS, OP. 70 (BALLET SUITE)

4,3,4,4 - 4,3,3,1 - timp.,perc.,cel. - hp. - pf. - str.

42:00 Bo. Hawkes.

—— SCHLAGOBERS, OP. 70 (ORCHESTRAL SUITE)

4,3,4,4 - 4,3,3,1 - timp.,perc.,cel. - 2 hp. - str.   25:00 Bo. Hawkes.

—— DIE SCHWEIGSAME FRAU ("THE SILENT WOMAN") (OPERA) %

150:00 Bo. Hawkes.

OVERTURE

3,3,4,3 - 4,3,3,1 - timp.,perc.,cel. - hp. - str.   4:00

—— SIX SONGS, OP. 68 (FOR VOICE AND ORCH.)

25:00 Bo. Hawkes.

—— SONATINA NO. 2 IN F (SUITE NO. 2 FOR 16 WINDS)

2,2,4,4 - 4,0,0,0   28:00 Bo. Hawkes.

—— SYMPHONIA DOMESTICA: PARERGON, OP. 73 (FOR PIANO LEFT-HAND AND ORCH.)

2,3,3,3 - 4,2,3,1 - timp. - hp. - pf. - str.   18:00 Bo. Hawkes.

—— SYMPHONY IN E FLAT FOR WINDS (IN 4 MOVTS.)

2,2,*4,basset hn.,*3 - 4 hn.   36:00 Bo. Hawkes.

—— TAILLEFER, OP. 52 (BALLAD FOR SOLO VOICES, CHORUS AND ORCH.)

6,6,7,5 - 8,6,4,2 - timp.,perc. - str.   22:00 Bo. Hawkes.

—— THREE HYMNS, OP. 71 (FOR SOPRANO AND ORCH.)

Bo. Hawkes.

HYMNE AN DIE LIEBE

3,3,4,3 - 3,4,4,1 - timp. - 2 hp. - str.   10:00

RUECKKEHR IN DIE HEIMAT

3,3,3,3 - 4,0,0,0 - timp.,cel. - str.   10:00

DIE LIEBE

3,3,4,3 - 4,2,3,1 - timp. - 2 hp. - str.   9:00

STRAUSS, Richard - CAILLIET, Lucien

—— ENOCH ARDEN (FOR NARRATOR AND ORCH.)

*3,*3,3,3 - 4,4,3,1 - timp.,perc.,cel. - hp. - str.   52:00 EV.

STRAUSS, Richard - DOUGLAS, Roy

—— WALTZ FROM "DER ROSENKAVALIER"

2,2,2,2 - 3,2,3,0 - timp.,perc. - hp. - str.   5:00 Bo. Hawkes.

or:

2,2,2,2 - 2,2,1,0 - timp.,perc. - hp. - str.

STRAUSS, Richard - HAUSSNER, Karl

—— THE DONKEY'S SHADOW (COMIC OPERA) % (Text: Hans Adler; Engl. transl. by Maria Pelikan)

2,2,2,2 - 2,2,2,0 - timp.,perc. - str.   Bo. Hawkes.

STRAUSS, Richard - STEINBERG, William

—— DER ROSENKAVALIER (SUITE FROM THE OPERA)

3,3,4,3 - 4,3,3,1 - timp.,perc.,cel. - 2 hp. - str.   27:00 Bo. Hawkes.

STRAUSS, Wolfgang

—— MUSIC FOR ORCHESTRA 1969

2,2,2,2 - 4,2,3,0 - timp.,perc. - str.   13:00 Tetra.

—— SYMPHONIC SCENE, OP. 47

2,2,2,2 - 4,3,3,0 - timp.,perc. - hp. - str.   7:00 Tetra.

—— SYMPHONY NO. 1, OP. 49

4,3,3,3 - 4,3,3,1 - timp.,perc.,cel. - hp. - str.   20:00 Tetra.

—— SYMPHONY NO. 2

2,2,2,sax.,1 - 1,1,1,1 - timp.,perc. - str.   Tetra.

STRAVINSKY, Igor

—— ABRAHAM AND ISAAC (FOR BARITONE AND CHAMBER ORCH.)

3,2,2,2 - 1,2,2,1 - str.   12:00 Bo. Hawkes.

—— AGON (BALLET) %
    3(3rd alt. with picc.),*3,*3,*3 - 4,4,3,0 - perc. - hp. - mandolin -
    pf. - str.   20:00 Bo. Hawkes.
—— ANNE'S ARIA (FROM "THE RAKE'S PROGRESS") (FOR
    SOPRANO AND ORCH.)
    2,2,2,2 - 2,2,0,0 - str.   7:30 Bo. Hawkes.
—— APOLLON MUSAGÈTE (BALLET SUITE) (1947 VERSION)
    str.   30:00 Bo. Hawkes.
—— BABEL (FOR NARRATOR, CHORUS AND ORCH.) (Seventh
    movement from GENESIS Suite)
    3(3rd alt. with picc.),2,*3,*3 - 4,3,3,0 - timp. - hp. - str.
            5:00 Shilkret.
—— LE BAISER DE LA FÉE (THE COMPLETE BALLET) (REV.
    1950) %
    3,*3,3,2 - 4,3,3,1 - timp.,perc. - hp. - str.   45:00 Bo. Hawkes.
—— CANTICUM SACRUM (FOR TENOR, BARITONE, MIXED
    CHORUS AND ORCH.)
    1,3,0,3 - 0,4,4,0 - hp. - org. - str.(no vlns. or c.)
            17:00 Bo. Hawkes.
—— CAPRICCIO FOR PIANO AND ORCH. (IN 3 MOVTS.)
    3(3rd alt. with picc.),*3,3(2nd alt. with E^{b}cl.),2 - 4,2,3,1 - timp. -
    pf. - str.   20:00 Bo. Hawkes.
—— LE CHANT DU ROSSIGNOL (POÈME SYMPHONIQUE)
    2,2,2,2 - 4,3,3,1 - timp.,perc.,cel. - 2 hp. - pf. - str.
            25:00 Bo. Hawkes.
—— CIRCUS POLKA
    2,2,2,2 - 4,2,3,1 - perc. - str.   6:00 AMP.
—— CONCERTINO FOR TWELVE INSTS.
    1,*2,1,2 - 0,2,2,0 - str.   7:00 G. Schirmer.
—— CONCERTO FOR PIANO AND WIND ORCH.
    1. Lento - Allegro - Lento; 2. Larghissimo; 3. Allegro
    2,2,1,2 - 2,2,2,1 - timp. - harm. - pf. - 4 d.-b.   19:00 Bo. Hawkes.
—— CONCERTO IN D FOR STRINGS (IN 3 MOVTS.)
    str.   12:00 Bo. Hawkes.
—— DIVERTIMENTO FROM THE BALLET "LE BAISER DE LA
    FÉE" (THE FAIRY'S KISS)
    3(3rd alt. with picc.),*3,3(3rd alt. with b.-cl.),2 - 4,3,3,1 -
    timp.,perc. - hp. - str.   20:00 Bo. Hawkes.
—— EBONY CONCERTO
    4sax.(2 alto,2 ten.,1 bar.) - 1,5,3,0 - perc. - guit. - hp. - pf. - d.-b.
            8:00 Bo. Hawkes.
—— EIGHT INSTRUMENTAL MINIATURES (FOR 15 PLAYERS)
    2,2,2,2 - 1,0,0,0 - str.(2,2,2,0)   6:00 G. Schirmer.
—— EPITAPHIUM (À LA MÉMOIRE DE RAOUL DUFY) (FOR
    CHORUS AND ORCH.) (1959)
            Bo. Hawkes.
—— THE FIREBIRD (BALLET SUITE)(1945 VERSION) (IN 6
    MOVTS.)
    *2,2,2,2 - 4,2,3,1 - timp.,perc.,xyl. - hp. - str. 30:00 Leeds.
—— THE FLOOD (A MUSICAL PLAY) (FOR VOICES, CHORUS
    AND ORCH.) %
    4(3rd alt. with picc.),*3,*4,*3 - 4,3,3,2 - timp.,perc.,cel.,mar.,xyl. -
    hp. - pf. - str.   24:00 Bo. Hawkes.
—— FOUR NORWEGIAN MOODS
    2,3,2,2 - 4,2,2,1 - perc. - str.   8:30 AMP.
—— GREETING PRELUDE (BASED ON "HAPPY BIRTHDAY")
    3,2,2,2 - 2,2,2,1 - timp.,perc. - pf. - str. 1:00 Bo. Hawkes.
—— MASS (FOR MIXED CHORUS AND DOUBLE WIND
    QUINTET)
    0,*3,0,2 - 0,2,3,0   17:00 Bo. Hawkes.
—— MAVRA (OPERA IN 1 ACT) % (1922) (Engl. Text: Robert Craft)
    3,*3,3 (incl. E^{b}cl.),2 - 4,4,*3,1 - timp. - str. 25:00 Bo. Hawkes.
—— MOVEMENTS (FOR PIANO AND ORCHESTRA)
    2,*2,2,1 - 0,2,3,0 - cel. - hp. - pf. - str. 10:00 Bo. Hawkes.
—— ODE (IN 3 PARTS)
    *3,2,2,2 - 4,2,0,0 - timp. - str.   10:00 AMP.
—— OEDIPUS REX (OPERA-ORATORIO) %
    3,2,3,2 - 4,3,3,1 - timp.,perc. - hp. - pf. - str. 55:00 Bo. Hawkes.
—— ORPHEUS (BALLET SUITE)
    *3,2(2nd alt. with Eng. hn.),2,2 - 4,2,2,0 - timp. - hp. - str.
            25:00 Bo. Hawkes.
—— PERSEPHONE (FOR FEMALE NARRATOR, TENOR, MIXED
    CHORUS AND ORCH.)
    3,3,3,3 - 4,4,3,1 - timp.,perc. - 2 hp. - pf. - str. 48:00 Bo. Hawkes.
—— PETROUCHKA (BALLET SUITE)(1947 VERSION)
    3(3rd alt. with picc.),*3,3(3rd alt. with b.-cl.),*3 - 4,4,3,1 -
    timp.,perc.,cel.,xyl. - hp. - pf. - str.   42:00 Bo. Hawkes.
—— PULCHINELLA (BALLET) (FOR SOPRANO, TENOR, BASS
    AND ORCH.) %
    2,2,0,2 - 2,1,1,0 - str.   35:00 Bo. Hawkes.
—— PULCHINELLA SUITE (FOR SMALL ORCH.)
    2(2nd alt. with picc.),2,0,2 - 2,1,1,0 - str. 22:00 Bo. Hawkes.

—— QUATRE ÉTUDES
    3(3rd alt. with picc.),3(3rd alt. with Eng.hn.),E^{b}cl. (alt. with
    b.-cl.),3,2 - 4,4,4,1 - timp. -hp. - pf. - str. 12:00 Bo. Hawkes.
—— THE RAKE'S PROGRESS (OPERA) %
            Bo. Hawkes.
—— REQUIEM-CANTICLES (FOR CELLO AND ORCH.)
    3,1 alto fl.,0,0,2 - 4,2,3,0 - timp.,perc.(4),bells,vibra,xyl. - 2 hp. -
    pf. - str.   15:00 Bo. Hawkes.
—— LE ROSSIGNOL (THE NIGHTINGALE) (THE COMPLETE
    OPERA) (REV. 1962) %
    3,2,3,2 - 4,3,3,1 - timp.,perc.,cel. - mandoline - guit. - 2 hp. - pf. -
    str.   45:00 Bo. Hawkes.
—— LE SACRE DU PRINTEMPS (1947 VERSION)
    5,5,5,5 - 8,4,3,2 - timp.,perc. - str. 33:00 Bo. Hawkes.
—— A SERMON, A NARRATIVE AND A PRAYER (FOR
    SPEAKER, ALTO, TENOR, MIXED CHORUS AND ORCH.)
    2,2,2,2 - 4,3,3,1 - perc. - hp. - pf. - str. 17:00 Bo. Hawkes.
—— SOUVENIR DE MON ENFANCE (THREE LITTLE SONGS,
    FOR VOICE AND ORCH.)
    2,2,2,2 - 0,0,0,0 -str.(no d.-b)   3:00 Bo. Hawkes.
—— SUITE NO. 1 FOR SMALL ORCH. (IN 4 MOVTS.)
    *3,1,2,2 - 1,1,1,1 - perc. - str.   6:00 G. Schirmer.
—— SUITE NO. 2 FOR SMALL ORCH. (IN 4 MOVTS.)
    2,1,2,2 - 1,2,1,1 - perc. - pf. - str. 8:00 G. Schirmer.
—— SYMPHONIE DES PSAUMES (FOR MIXED CHORUS AND
    ORCH.)(1948 VERSION)
    5,*5,0,*4 - 4,5,3,1 - timp.,perc. - 2 pf. - str. 23:00 Bo. Hawkes.
—— SYMPHONIES D'INSTRUMENTS À VENT (1947 VERSION)
    3,*3,3,3(3rd alt. with c.-bn.) - 4,3,3,1   12:00 Bo. Hawkes.
—— THREE SELECTIONS FROM THE OPERA "LE ROSSIGNOL"
    (INTRODUCTION, CHANT DU PECHEUR AND AIR DU
    ROSSIGNOL) (FOR VOICE AND ORCH.)
    3,3,3,3 - 4,3,0,0 - timp.,perc.,cel. - hp. - str. 10:00 Bo. Hawkes.
—— THRENI (LAMENTATIONS OF THE PROPHET JEREMIAH)
    (FOR SIX SOLO VOICES, MIXED CHORUS AND ORCH.)
    2,*3,3,0,sarr. - 4,0,flg.-hn.,3,1 - timp.,perc.,cel. - hp. - pf. - str.
            35:00 Bo. Hawkes.
—— TWO SONGS (FOR BARITONE AND ORCH.)
    2,0,2,0 - 2,0,0,0 - str.   4:00 Bo. Hawkes.
—— VARIATIONS (FOR PIANO AND ORCH.)
    3,*3,*3,2 - 4,3,3,0 - hp. - pf. - str.   6:15 Bo. Hawkes.
—— ZVEZDOLILI ("THE STAR-FACED")("LE ROI DES
    ÉTOILES")(CANTATA) (FOR MALE CHORUS AND ORCH.)
    (Text: Constantin Balmont; Engl. text: Nicholas Slominsky)
            6:30 Translator.

STRAVINSKY, Igor - MAGANINI, Quinto
—— PETROUCHKA (BALLET SUITE) (IN 4 MOVTS.)
    2,2,2,2 - 2,2,3,0 - timp.,perc.(3) - hp. - pf. - str. 25:00 Musicus.

STRAVINSKY, Igor - RUDOLF, Robert
—— THE RITE OF SPRING (LE SACRE DU PRINTEMPS)
    3,3,3,3 - 4,3,3,1 - timp.,perc.(3) - str.   Belw-Mills.

STRAVINSKY, Igor - SPALDING, Albert
—— LE CHANT DU ROSSIGNOL (SYMPHONIC POEM)
    2(2nd alt. with picc.),2(2nd alt. with Eng.hn.),2,2 - 4,3,3,1 -
    timp.,perc.,cel. - 2 hp. - pf. - str.   20:00 Bo. Hawkes.

STRECKE, Gerhard
—— KONZERTSTÜCK FÜR VIOLINE UND ORCH.
    3,1,2,1 - 2,1,1,0 - timp.,perc. - str.   7:00 Henmar.
—— A MERRY OVERTURE, OP. 44
    2(2nd alt. with picc.),2,2,2 - 4,2,2,1 - timp.,perc. - str.
            10:00 Henmar.
—— ORCHESTRAL SUITE NO. 2 (IN 5 MOVTS.)
    2(2nd alt. with picc.),1,2,1 - 2,2,1,0-1 - timp.(3),glock.,trgl. - str.
            11:00 Henmar.
—— ORCHESTRAL SUITE NO. 7, OP. 86 (SUITE OF FOLK
    DANCES) (IN 5 MOVTS.)
    1(alt. with picc.),1,2,1 - 2,1,1,0 - timp.,perc. - hp.(or pf.) - str.
            15:00 Henmar.
—— UPPER SILESIAN DANCE SUITE, OP. 43 (IN 4 MOVTS.)
    2,2,2,2 - 2,2,2,1 - timp.,perc. - str.   16:00 Henmar.

STREET, Donald
—— INVENTION NO. 1 (1961)
    1,1,1,0 - 0,0,0,0 - timp.,perc.,cel. - org. - pf. - str. 15:00 P.R.S.
—— KALEIDOSCOPE (SCHERZO)(1960)
    2,2,2,2 - 4,2,0,0 - timp.,perc. - hp. - pf. - str. 5:00 P.R.S.
—— PANOPHONY NO. 1 (1945)
    3,3,3,sax.,3 - 4,3,3,1 - timp.,perc.,cel. - hp. - acc. - org. - pf. - str.
            50:00 P.R.S.

—— THE PETRIFIED CITY (1966)
3,3,3,2 - 4,3,3,1 - str.   5:00 P.R.S.
—— SYMPHONY IN B MINOR (1960)
2,2,2,2 - 4,3,3,1 - timp.,perc.,cel. - pf. - str.   25:00 P.R.S.

STREIFF, Peter
—— RELIEF (FÜR 12 SOLOSTREICHER)
str.   8:00 S.U.I.S.A.

STRENS, Jules
—— ENSORCIANA (1970) (IN 3 MOVTS.)
3,3,3,3 - 4,3,3,1 - timp.,perc. - str.   25:00 H. Elkan.

STRICKLAND, Lily
—— BALLET INDIENNE (IN 4 MOVTS.) %
*2,*2,E♭cl.,*2,*2 - 2-4,1,1,1 - timp.,perc.(2) - hp.(or pf.) - str.
                                                           20:00 Composer.
—— BALLET MUSIC %
1,1,2,1 - 4,2,2,1 - timp.,perc. - hp. - str.   10:00 Composer.
—— CAROLINA (SUITE)(REVISED VERSION) (IN 4 MOVTS.)
*3,*3,E♭cl.,*2,*2 - 4,2,2,1 - timp.,perc.(2) - hp. - str.
                                                           25:00 Composer.
—— CHARLESTON SKETCHES (IN 6 MOVTS.)
*2,1,4,*2 - 4,4,3,1 - timp.,perc.(2) - hp. - org. - str.
                                                           30:00 Composer.
or:
*3,1,2*3 - 2-4,2,2,1 - timp., - hp. - org.(ad lib.) - str.
—— EAST INDIAN NIGHT (SUITE IMPRESSIONISTIC) (IN 3 MOVTS.)
2,2,2,*3 - 4,2,1,1 - timp.,perc.(2) - hp. - str.   30:00 Composer.
—— FLIGHT FANTASY
*2,*2,E♭cl.,*2,*2 - 4,2,2,1 - timp.,perc. - hp.(or pf.) - str.
                                                           20:00 Composer.
—— FOG IN THE HARBOR (TONE POEM) (FOR CHORUS AND ORCH.)
1,*2,E♭cl.,1,*2 - 4,2,1,1 - timp.,perc.(2) - hp. - org(ad lib.) - str.
                                                           15:00 EV.
—— MOORISH DANCE
2,1,2,1 - 4,3,2,1 - timp.,perc. - str.   10:00 Composer.
—— OASIS (SUITE)(REVISED VERSION) (IN 5 MOVTS.)
2,*2,*2(1 alt. with E♭cl.),*2 - 0-4,2,2,1 - timp.,perc.(1) - hp. - pf. - str.
                                                           15:00 Composer.
—— PRELUDE
1,1,2,2 sax.,*2 - 4,2,2,0 - timp. - hp. - str.(no d.-b.)
                                                           15:00 Composer.
—— ST. JOHN THE BELOVED (ORATORIO) (FOR CHORUS AND ORCH.)
2,*2,2,*3 - 4,2,2,1 - timp. - hp. - org. - str.   45:00 J. Fischer.
—— THREE EGYPTIAN SCENES (FOR HARP, PIANO AND STRINGS)
hp. - pf. - str.   20:00 Composer.

STRICKLAND, William
—— THE BOY WHO HATED MUSIC (A STORY IN MUSIC FOR YOUNG CHILDREN) (1973) (Text: Composer)
1,1,1,1 - 1,1,1,0 - timp.,perc.(1)bells - pf. - str.   Consort.
—— CONCERTINO FOR TRUMPET AND STRINGS
tpt. - str.   10:00 Belw-Mills.
—— CONCERTO FOR TWO HAND AND ONE FOOT (A MOCK CONCERTO, FOR PERCUSSIONIST AND ORCH.) (1973)
1,1,1,1 - 1,1,1,0 - perc. (1),bells,xyl. - str.   11:00 Consort.
—— EXCURSION FOR ORCHESTRA (1965)
*3,2,2,2 - 4,3,3,1 - timp.,perc.(4) - str.   11:15 Composer.
—— FOUR DRAWINGS ON A CLASSROOM WALL (A LITTLE SUITE FOR SCHOOL CHILDREN) (1966) (IN 4 MOVTS.)
1,1,1,1 - 2,1,1,0 - timp.,perc.(2),cel. - str.   10:15 Forte.
—— ODYSSEY (FOR NARRATOR AND ORCH.) (1971) (Text: Composer)
1(alt.with sax.),0,*2(alt. with 2 sax.),0 - 2,2,1,0 - timp.,perc.(2),glock.,mar.,vibra.,xyl. - guit - electric bass - hp. - pf.(ad lib.) - str.   Consort.
—— SEPT ET CINQ (SEVEN AND FIVE) (FOR JAZZ TROMBONE AND CHAMBER ENSEMBLE) (1968)
1,0,1,1 ten.sax.,0 - 0,0,1,1 - perc.(1) - guit. - str.   8:00 Alfred.
—— THE TEMPERAMENTAL ORCHESTRA (FOR NARRATOR AND ORCH.) (1971) (Text: Composer)
2(2nd alt.with picc.),2,2,2 - 2,2,0,0 - timp.,perc.(1) - str.
                                                           12:00 Consort.
—— THE TRUMPET SHALL SOUND (THE TRUE ART OF BLOWING THE TRUMPET) (FOR NARRATOR AND ORCH.) (1968)
1,1,1,1 - 2,1 natural tpt.,1 shofar (ram's horn) and several lengths of hose-tubing,0,0 - timp. - str.   10::00 Belw-Mills.

or:
2,2,2,2 - 2(1st alt. with shofar),2(alt. with natural tpts.),0,0 - timp. - str.

STRIEGLER, Kurt
—— SCHERZANDO (RONDO), OP. 40
                                                           9:00 Alte&Neuek.

STRILKO, Anthony
—— CRY OF THE NYMPH TO EROS (FOR MIXED CHORUS AND ORCH.)
3(3rd alt. with picc.),2,*3,2 - 4,2,3,1 - timp.,perc.(3) - hp. - str.
                                                           15:00 Composer.
—— THE LAST PUPPET (1-ACT TRAGIC OPERA) %
2,2,2,2 - 2,2,2,1 - timp.,perc. - hp. - str.   60:00 Presser.
—— MARCH AND FUNERAL MUSIC (IN MEMORIAM JOHN F. KENNEDY) (FOR WINDS AND PERC.)
3,4,4,0 - 4,3(plus 3 cnt. ad lib.),3,1 - timp.,perc - d-b.
                                                           5:00 Presser.
—— OVERTURE FOR ORCHESTRA
2,2,2,2 - 2,2,2,0 - timp.,perc. - str.   6:00 Presser.
—— TWO SONGS ON POEMS OF EDGAR BOGARDUS (FOR SOPRANO AND ORCH.)
1,1,1,1 - 2,1,1,0 - hp. - str.   8:00 Composer.

STRINGFIELD, Lamar
—— FROM THE SOUTHERN MOUNTAINS (SUITE) (IN 4 MOVTS.)
*3,2,2,2 - 4,2,3,1 - timp.,perc.(3) - str.   20:00 C. Fischer.
—— INDIAN LEGEND (SYMPHONIC POEM)
*3,2,2,2 - 4,2,3,1 - timp.,perc.(3) - hp. - str.   10:00 Musicus.
—— THE LEGEND OF JOHN HENRY (SYMPHONIC BALLAD) (IN 3 MOVTS.)
*3,2,2,2 - 4,2,3,1 - timp.,perc.(4) - str.   14:30 J. Fischer.
—— MOUNTAIN DAWN (FOR FLUTE AND STRINGS)
fl. - str.   6:00 Musicus.
—— MOUNTAIN DEW (FROM "THE BLUE RIDGE")
2,1,2,1 - 2,2,0,1 - perc. - str.   6:00 MCA Music.
—— NEGRO PARADE
*3,2,2,2 - 4,4,3,1 - timp.,perc. - str.   8:30 J. Fischer.
—— PASTORAL SCENE (FOR FLUTE AND STRINGS)
fl. - str.   Leeds.
—— THE SEVENTH QUEUE (SYMPHONIC BALLET) %
*3,*3,2,2 - 4,2,3,1 - timp.,perc.(3) - hp. - str.   12:00 Musicus.

STRIPP, Alan
—— CONCERTINO FOR FLUTE (OR OBOE) AND STRINGS, OP. 13 (1965)
fl.(or ob.) - str.   8:00 P.R.S.
—— SERENADE FOR STRINGS, OP. 10 (1961)
str.   8:00 P.R.S.

STROË, Aurel
—— ARCADES (FOR 11 INSTRUMENTAL GROUPS) (1962)
3 picc.,2,0,3,4 sax.(sopr.,alto,ten.,bar.),2 c.-bn. - 4(in E♭),2 cnt.,0,0,4(2 ten.,2 c.-b.) - perc.(6),2 cel.,2 vibra. - 3 ondes-martenot (or 3 elec.org.) - hp. - org. - pf. - str.   9:00 Salabert.
—— CANTO I (FOR 12 INSTRUMENTAL GROUPS) (1967)
3 picc.,0,2,*4,1 ten.sax.,*2 - 2,3,2,2 - 2 elec.org. - str.
                                                           7:00 Salabert.
—— CANTO II (FOR 12 MELO-GROUPS) (1971)
3 picc.,0,2,3,*2 - 3,3,3,2 - 2 ondes-martenot(1 alt.with elec.org.) - str.
                                                           9:06 Salabert.
—— LAUDES I (1966)
str.(14,0,7,7)   8:00 Salabert.
—— LAUDES II (FOR 12 INSTRUMENTAL GROUPS) (1968)
2 picc.,2,2,3,*3 - 0,0,4,2 - perc.(3) - 2 ondes-martenot - 2 elec.org. - str.   10:00 Salabert.
—— MONUMENTUM (FOR MEN'S VOICES AND ORCH.) (1964)
2 picc.,0,2(1 alt.with Eng.hn.),1 E♭cl.,2,*3 - 0,0,4,0 - timp.,perc.(5),vibra.,xyl. - elec.guit. - hpsc. - org. - 8 vla.,1 c.
                                                           12:00 Salabert.
—— MUSIQUE DE CONCERT POUR PIANO, PERCUSSION ET CUIVRES (1964)
0,0,0,0 - 4,4,4,0 - perc.(4) - pf.   13:00 Salabert.
—— LA PAIX (3-ACT OPERA, AFTER ARISTOPHANES) %
0,1,1,1 - 4,3,3,1 - perc.(4) - tape-recorder - pf.(alt. with electric org. and hpsc.) - str.   Salabert.

STRØMHOLM, Folke
—— CONCERTINO FOR PIANO AND STRINGS, OP. 1 (IN 3 MOVTS.)
pf. - str.   14:00 T.O.N.O.

—— CONCERTO FOR PIANO AND ORCH., OP. 12
    1,0,1,1 - 1,1,1,0 - pf. - vins.   9:00 T.O.N.O.
—— INTRADA PER ORCHESTRA
    2,2,2,2 - 4,2,3,1 - timp.,perc. - hp. - str.   13:00 T.O.N.O.
—— SYNTAKS, OP. 14 (FOR BASS VOICE AND ORCH.) (1968)
    (Text: Stein Mehren)
    2,2,2,2 - 4,3,3,1 - timp.,perc. - hp. - str.(min.: 40)
            18:00 T.O.N.O.

STROUSE, Charles
—— NARRATIVE FOR ORCH.
    1(alt. with picc.),2,*3,2 - 2,2,2,1 - timp.,perc.(2),glock.,xyl. - pf. -
    str.   8:30 Leeds.

STRUBE, Gustave
—— PUCK (A COMEDY OVERTURE)
    3,3,3,3 - 4,4,3,1 - timp.,perc.,glock. - str.   8:00 G. Schirmer.
—— SYMPHONY IN B MINOR (IN 4 MOVTS.)
    3(3rd alt. with picc.),*3,*3,*3 - 4,4,3,1 - timp.,perc.,glock. - hp. -
    str.   35:00 G. Schirmer.

STUART, Peggy
—— AMERICAN MOOD
    3,3,3,2 - 4,2,3,1 - timp.,perc.,cel. - hp. - str.   8:00 C. Fischer.
—— DUBLIN TOWN (SUITE FOR ORCHESTRA)
    *2,2,2,2 - 4,3,3,1 - timp.,perc.(4) - hp. - str.   9:00 Wentworth.
—— OUT OF THE NIGHT (RHAPSODY FOR PIANO AND ORCH.)
    2(2nd alt. with picc.),*3,2,2 - 4,3,3,1 - timp.,perc.(2) - hp. - pf. -
    str.   10:00 Wentworth.
—— TWILIGHT CITY (RHAPSODY FOR PIANO AND ORCH.)
    *3,*2,2,2 - 4,3,3,1 - timp.,perc.(2),bells,glock. - hp. - pf. - str.
        8:30 Wentworth.

STUBBS, Thomas
—— L' ARBRE ENCHANTÉ (BALLET) (1955) %
    3,2,2,2 - 4,3,3,1 - timp.,perc. - hp. - pf. - str.   15:00 Salabert.
—— OVERTURE
    3,2,2,2 - 4,2,3,1 - timp.,perc.,cel.,glock. - hp. - pf. - str.
        6:00 Salabert.
—— SUITE CONCERTANTE POUR UN MOIS DE JUILLET
    tpt. - pf. - str.   19:00 Salabert.

STUDER, Hans
—— CONCERTINO FÜR FLÖTE, KLARINETTE UND
    STREICHORCHESTER
    fl.,cl. - str.   18:00 S.U.I.S.A.
—— DREI ORCHESTERSTÜCKE (FÜR STREICHER, 2
    TROMPETEN UND SCHLAGZEUG)
    2 tpt. - perc. - str.   15:00 S.U.I.S.A.
—— EPITAPH (IN MEMORIAM ALFRED ELLENBERGER)
    2,2,2,2 - 2,2,0,0 - perc. - str.   10:00 S.U.I.S.A.
—— KAMMERKONZERT FÜR KLAVIER UND KLEINES ORCH.
    0,0,2,1 - 0,0,0,0 - timp.,perc. - pf. - str.   19:00 Baerenrtr.
—— LITTLE CONCERTO (1951)
    fl.(ad lib.) - pf.(4-hands) - str.   10:00 G. Schirmer.
—— LYRISCHE KANTATE (FOR ALTO, WOMEN'S CHORUS AND
    SMALL ORCH.)
    1,2,0,1 - 2,0,0,0 - hp. - str.   31:00 S.U.I.S.A.
—— VARIATIONEN UND EPILOG (FÜR VIOLONCELLO UND
    STREICHORCHESTER)
    str.   23:00 S.U.I.S.A.

ŠTUHEC, Igor
—— ENTHUSIASMS
    3(3rd alt. with picc.),2(2nd alt. with Eng. hn.),2(2nd alt. with E♭
    cl. and b.-cl.),2(2nd alt. with c.-bn.) - 4,3,3,1 - timp.,perc.(5) - hp.
    - pf. - str.   12:00 Hans Gerig.
—— ENTHUSIASMS BETA
    2(2nd alt. with picc.),2(2nd alt. with Eng. hn.),2(2nd alt. with E♭
    cl. and b.-cl.),2(2nd alt. with c.-bn.) - 4,3,3,1 - timp.,perc.(5) - hp.
    - pf. - str.   12:00 Hans Gerig.
—— FANTASIA CONCERTANTE (FOR HORN AND STRING
    ORCH.)
    hn. - str.   12:00 Hans Gerig.
—— IN MEMORIAM
    2(2nd alt. with picc.),2(2nd alt. with Eng. hn.),2(2nd alt. with E♭
    cl. and b.-cl.),2(2nd alt. with c.-bn.) - 4,3,3,1 - timp.,perc.(6) - hp.
    - pf. - str.   25:00 Hans Gerig.
—— SILHOUETTES FOR CHAMBER ENSEMBLE (WITH SOLO
    VIOLA)
    1(alt. with picc. and alto fl.),1,0,0 - 1,0,0,0 - perc.(4),cel. - pf. -
    str.(2,2,1,1)   6:00 Hans Gerig.

STÜRMER, Bruno
—— FESTLICHES KONZERT, OP. 111
    3tpt. - timp. - org. - str.   20:00 Baerenrtr.
—— KONZERT FOR VIOLIN AND STRING ORCH., OP. 126
    str.   22:00 Baerenrtr.

STURZENEGGER, Richard
—— FRESKE (FÜR STREICHORCHESTER)
    str.   10:00 Henn.
—— KONZERT NR. 4 FÜR VIOLINCELLO UND ORCHESTER
        25:00 S.U.I.S.A.
—— OMAGGIO (SUITE) (FOR HIGH VOICE, FLUTE AND
    STRINGS)
    fl. - str.   25:00 S.U.I.S.A.
—— THIRTEEN (RONDO VARIATO PER ARCHI)
    str.   13:00 S.U.I.S.A.
—— TRIPTYCHON
    *2,2,2,2 - 3,2,3,1 - timp.,perc. - hp. - str.   13:00 S.U.I.S.A.

STUTSCHEWSKY, Joachim
—— CONCERTINO FOR CLARINET AND STRINGS
    cl. - str.   25:00 IsMuPublns.
—— MUSIC FOR STRINGS (1965)
    str.   10:00 Seesaw.
—— PHANTASY FOR OBOE, HARP AND STRING ORCH.
    ob. - hp. - str.   10:00 Seesaw.
—— SAFED (SYMPHONIC POEM) (1960)
    3,3,2,2 - 3,3,3,0 - timp.,perc. - hp. - str.   16:00 Seesaw.

SUBOTNICK, Morton
—— BEFORE THE BUTTERFLY (FOR SOLO INSTRUMENTS AND
    ORCH.)
        MCA Music.
—— LAMINATION I FOR ORCH. AND ELECTRONIC SOUNDS
    (1967)
    2,*3,*2,1 E♭cl.,2 - 4,2,2,1 - timp., perc.(2),glock.,vibra.,xyl. -
    tape-recorder (2-channel) - mandolin - str.   12:00 MCA Music.
—— PLAY! NO. 2 (FOR ORCHESTRA, CONDUCTOR AND TAPE)
    (1965)
    2,2,*3,2 - 3,2,2,0 - perc.(2),glock.,xyl. - tape recorder - str.
        12:00 MCA Music.
—— THE TAROT (FOR 10 INSTRUMENTS) (1964)
    1,1,0,0 - 0,1,1,0 - timp.,perc.(3),bells,cel.,glock.,xyl. - pf. - 1 vla.,1
    d.-b.   10:00 MCA Music.
—— TWO BUTTERFLIES
    1(alt. with picc.),2(2nd alt. with Eng. hn.),3,2(2nd alt. with c.-bn.)
    - 3,3,0,1 - perc. - hp. - str.   MCA Music.

SUCHOŇ, Eugen
—— FANTASY FOR VIOLIN AND ORCH., OP. 7 (1948)
    2,3,3,2 - 4,2,3,1 - timp.,perc. - str.   29:00 Bo. Hawkes.
—— METAMORPHOSES (1952) (IN 5 MOVTS.)
    3,3,3,3 - 4,3,3,1 - timp.,perc. - hp. - pf. - str.   30:00 Bo. Hawkes.
—— SERENADE FOR STRINGS, OP. 5 (IN 5 MOVTS.)
    str.   14:00 Bo. Hawkes.
—— SYMPHONIETTA RUSTICA
    3,2,2,2 - 4,2,3,1 - timp.,perc. - hp. - str.   19:00 Bo. Hawkes.

SUDERBURG, Robert
—— CANTATA I (ON THE REVELATION OF ST. JOHN THE
    DIVINE) (FOR SOPRANO AND ORCH.) (1963) (Text: Biblical)
    1,1,1,1 - 1,1,1,0 - perc.(2),bells,glock.,xyl. - pf. - str. 18:00 Presser.
—— CANTATA II (ON ORIGINAL TEXTS) (FOR TENOR AND
    ORCH.) (1964)
    2,0,1,0 - 2,3,0,0 - pf. - 1 c.,1 d.-b.   12:00 Presser.
—— CHORUSES ON POEMS OF YEATS (FOR SOPRANO, TENOR,
    CHORUS AND ORCH.) (1966) (IN 5 MOVTS.) (Text: William
    Butler Yeats)
    2(2nd alt. with picc.),2(2nd alt. with Eng.hn.),*3,2 - 2,2,2,0 -
    perc.(2),bells,glock. - pf. - str.   35:00 Presser.
—— CONCERTO FOR PIANO AND ORCHESTRA ("WITHIN THE
    MIRROR OF TIME")
    3,3,3,3 - 4,3,3,1 - timp.,perc. - hp. - pf. - str.   25:00 Presser.
—— ORCHESTRA MUSIC I (DRAMATIC MOVEMENTS FOR
    ORCH.) (1969) (FOUR MOVTS.)
    3(1 alt. with alto fl., 2 alt. with 2 picc.),4(1 alt. with
    Eng.hn.),*5(b.-cl. alt. with pedal-cl),*4 - 6,4,4,1 -
    timp.,perc.(4),bells,cel.,glock.,vibra,xyl. - 2 hp. - pf. - str.
        30:00 Presser.
—— WINDS-VENTS
    3,3,3,3 - 4,3,3,1 - perc. - hp. - str.   20:00 Presser.

SUESSE, Dana
—— CONCERTINO FOR PIANO AND ORCH.
2(2nd alt. with picc.),*2,2,1 - 2,3,3,0 - timp.,perc.(3),glock. - hp. -
pf. - str.(20,6,5,4)   10:00 DSMusic.
—— CONCERTO IN E MINOR (FOR 2 PIANOS AND ORCH.)
(1939) (IN 4 MOVTS.)
3(3rd alt. with picc.),*2,2,1 - 4,3,3,1 - timp.,perc.(3),bells,cel.,vibra.
- hp. - 2 pf. - str.   18:30 DSMusic.
—— CONCERTO IN 3 RHYTHMS (FOR PIANO AND ORCH.)
2(2nd alt. with picc.),*2,2,1 - 2,3,3,0 - timp.,perc.(2) - pf. - str.
                                                           15:00 DSMusic.
—— CONCERTO ROMANTICO (FOR PIANO AND ORCH.) (1946)
(IN 3 MOVTS.)
2(2nd alt. with picc.),*2,2,1- 2,3,3,0 - timp.,perc.(3),bells - hp. - pf.
- str.   18:46 DSMusic.
—— JAZZ CONCERTO IN D MAJOR (CONCERTO IN RHYTHM)
(FOR 3-PIECE COMBO AND ORCH.) (1955) (IN 3 MOVTS.)
Solo Group: piano, double bass and jazz drums   21:45 DSMusic.
Orchestra: 2(1 alt. with picc.),*2,2,1 - 2,3,3,0 -
timp.,perc.(3),bells,cel.,vibra. - hp. - str.
—— JAZZ CONCERTO IN D MAJOR (FOR COMBO AND ORCH.)
*3,2,2,1 - 2,3,3,0 - timp.,perc.(4),bells,cel. - hp. - str.
                                                           20:00 DSMusic.
Combo: drums - pf. - d.-b.
—— ODE TO APHRODITE (FOR MEZZO-SOPRANO AND ORCH.)
*3,2,2,1 - 2,3,3,0 - timp.,perc.(4),glock. - hp. - pf. - str.
                                                            5:45 DSMusic.
—— SPINDRIFT (FOR HARP AND ORCH.)
1,1,2,0 - 0,3,2,0 - perc.(2),cel. - guit. - hp. - str.   5:00 DSMusic.
—— THREE CITIES (SUITE FOR ORCH.) (1946)
2(1 alt. with picc.),*2,2,1 - 2,3,3,0 - timp.,perc.(3),bells,cel. - hp. -
pf. - str.   22:35 DSMusic.
—— TWO IRISH FAIRY TALES
2,2,1,1 - 2-3,3,0-1,0 - timp.,perc.(3),bells,cel.,xyl. - pf. - str.
                                                            5:00 DSMusic.
—— YOUNG MAN WITH A HARP (FOR HARP AND ORCH.)
*3,2,2,1 - 2,3,3,0 - timp.,perc.(3),vibra. - hp.   16:30 DSMusic.

SUGÁR, Rezső
—— CONCERTINO FOR FLUTE AND STRINGS
fl. - str.   Bo. Hawkes.
—— CONCERTO (IN MEMORIAM BÉLA BARTÓK)
3(3rd alt. with picc.),*3,*3,*3 - 0,0,0,0 - timp.,perc.,cel. - hp. - pf. -
str.   28:00 General.
—— DIVERTIMENTO FOR STRINGS
str.   Bo. Hawkes.
—— HEROIC SONG (ORATORIO) (FOR SOPRANO, TENOR,
BARITONE, MIXED CHORUS, CHILDREN'S CHORUS AND
ORCH.)
3,3,3,3 - 4,3,3,1 - timp.,perc. - 2 hp. - str.   Bo. Hawkes.
—— KELEMEN, THE MASON (ORATORIO) (FOR SOPRANO,
BARITONE, SATB CHORUS AND ORCH.)
                                                           33:00 Bo. Hawkes.
—— METAMORFOSI
*3,*2,*3,2 - 4,3,3,0 - timp.,perc.,cel. - hp. - pf. - str.
                                                           22:00 Bo. Hawkes.
—— PARTITA FOR STRINGS
str.   26:25 Bo. Hawkes.
—— PASTORALE FOR PIANO AND STRINGS
pf. - str.   6:00 Bo. Hawkes.
—— RÁKÓCZI OVERTURE
2,2,2,2 - 4,3,3,1 timp.,perc. - str.   12:00 Bo. Hawkes.
—— RONDO FOR PIANO AND STRINGS
pf. - str.   Bo. Hawkes.
—— SINFONIA A VARIAZIONE
*3,*3,2,2 - 4,3,3,1 - timp.,perc.,cel. - hp. - pf. - str.
                                                           14:00 Bo. Hawkes.
—— SIX SHORT PIECES
                                                           Bo. Hawkes.
—— SUITE
2,2,2,2 - 4,3,3,1 - timp.,perc. hp. - str.   23:00 Bo. Hawkes.
—— SUITE FOR STRINGS
str.   15:00 Bo. Hawkes.
—— TWO PIECES FOR STRING ORCH.
str.   Bo. Hawkes.
—— VARIATIONS FOR VIOLIN AND STRINGS
pf. - str.   Bo. Hawkes.

SUK, Josef
—— EPILOGUE, OP. 37 (FOR SOPRANO, BARITONE, BASS,
SMALL AND LARGE MIXED CHORUS AND ORCH.) (1929)
(IN 5 MOVTS.)
4,4,4,4 - 6,3,3,1 - timp.,perc. - hp. - str.   41:00 Bo. Hawkes.

—— LEGEND OF THE VICTORIOUS DEAD, OP. 35B (1920)
3,3,3,3 - 6,3,3,1 - timp.,perc. - hp. - str.   8:00 Bo. Hawkes.
—— MEDITATION ON THE ST. WENCESLAS CHORALE, OP. 35
(1951)
str.   8:00 Bo. Hawkes.
—— THE RIPENING, OP. 34 (SYMPHONIC POEM FOR CHORUS
AND ORCH.) (1917)
3,3,4,3 - 6,3,3,1 - timp.,perc.,cel. - 2 hp. - pf. - str.
                                                           41:00 Bo. Hawkes.
—— THE WINTER'S TALE, OP. 9 (REV. 1926)
3,3,3,3 - 4,2,3,1 - timp.,perc. - hp. - str.   15:00 Bo. Hawkes.

SUK, Josef - EIGER, Walter
—— BOHEMIAN SUITE
2,2,2,2 - 4,2,3,1 - timp.,perc. - hp. - str.   Bo. Hawkes.

SULLIVAN, John
—— FANTASIA FOR OBOE AND STRINGS (1964)
ob. - str.   22:00 P.R.S.
—— SINFONIA (1966)
1,1,1,1 - 2,1,0,0 - timp. - str.   P.R.S.
—— VARIATIONS FOR CHAMBER ORCH. (1968)
1,1,1,1 - 2,1,1,0 - str.   12:00 P.R.S.
—— VARIATIONS FOR STRING ORCH. (1965)
str.   20:00 P.R.S.

SULYOK, Imre
—— CONCERTO FOR ORGAN AND ORCH.
                                                           Bo. Hawkes.
—— SUITE
2,2,2,2 - 4,2,3,0 - timp.,perc. - str.   16:00 Bo. Hawkes.

SUMERLIN, Macon D.
—— ANDANTE AND PASSACAGLIA (FOR ORGAN AND ORCH.)
2,2,2,2 - 4,2,3,1 - timp.,perc.(3) - org. - str.   13:00 Composer.
—— MASQUERADE
                                                           Composer.
—— ROMANTIC SYMPHONY (IN 4 MOVTS.)
1,1,1,1 - 1,1,1,0 - timp.,perc.(3) - str.   20:00 Composer.
—— THE SINGERS (FOR CHORUS AND ORCH.)
1,1,2,2 - 3,3,2,0 - timp.,perc.(2) - str.   6:00 Composer.
—— SYMPHONIC SKETCH NO. 1
2,2,2,2 - 4,2,3,1 - timp.,perc.(3) - str.   8:00 Composer.
—— SYMPHONIC SKETCH NO. 2
2,2,2,2 - 4,2,3,1 - timp.,perc.(2) - str.   9:00 Composer.
—— SYMPHONY NO. 3 (IN 3 MOVTS.)
2,2,2,2 - 4,2,3,1 - timp.,perc.(3) - str.   22:00 Composer.
—— SYMPHONY NO. 5 ("DESTINY")(FOR MIXED CHORUS AND
ORCH.) (IN 3 MOVTS.)
2,2,2,2 - 4,3,3,1 - timp.,perc.(3) - str.   24:00 Composer.

SUNDBLAD-HALME, Heidi
—— AT A MARIONETTE THEATRE (1935)
3,2,2,2 - 2,2,2,2, - str.   15:00 FinnMICtr.
—— HUNGARIAN FANTASY ("THE STARRY SKY") (1938)
1,1,1,1 - 1,1,1,0 - timp.,perc. - str.   10:00 FinnMICtr.
—— INTRADA (1945)
1,1,2,0 - 2,2,1,0 - timp.,perc. - hp. - str.   6:00 FinnMICtr.
—— THE MAGIC BELT (BALLET) % (1937)
2,2,2,2 - 4,2,3,1 - timp.,perc. - hp. - str.   70:00 FinnMICtr.
—— PRELUDE AND FUGUE (1941)
2,2,2,2 - 4,3,3,2 - timp.,perc. - hp. - str.   20:00 FinnMICtr.
—— RONDO CARPICCIO (1940)
2,2,2,2 - 4,2,3,0 - timp. - str.   12:00 FinnMICtr.
—— SONGS FOR TELLERVO (FOUR SONGS FOR SOPRANO AND
ORCH.) (1955) (Text: L. Onerva)
1,2,2,0 - 2,2,0,0 - timp. - hp. - str.   14:00 FinnMICtr.
—— SOUTH OSTROBOTHNIAN RHAPSODY, OP. 15 (1932)
3,2,2,2 - 2,4,2,1 - timp.,perc. - str.   17:00 FinnMICtr.
—— SUITE FOR ORCH., OP. 11 (1930)
3,2,2,2 - 2,2,1,1 - timp.,perc. - str.   15:00 FinnMICtr.
—— SUITE FOR STRING ORCH. (1935)
str.   18:00 FinnMICtr.

SUOLAHTI, Heikki
—— LITTLE SYMPHONY (SINFONIA PICCOLA) (IN 4 MOVTS.)
2,2,2,2 - 4,3,3,1 - timp.,perc. - hp. - str.   25:00 Bo. Hawkes.
—— SYMPHONIC OVERTURE IN A MAJOR (1933)
3,3,3,3 - 4,2,3,1 - timp.,perc.,cel. - hp. - str.   5:00 FinnMICtr.

SURDIN, Morris
—— B'RASHEET (IN THE BEGINNING) (FOR MANDOLIN, CLARINET AND STRINGS) (1974)
cl. - mandolin - str.   7:50 CanMusCtr.
—— CONCERTO FOR ACCORDION AND STRINGS (1966)
acc. - str.   16:35 CanMusCtr.
—— CONCERTO FOR MANDOLIN AND STRINGS (1966)
Mandolin - str.   22:50 CanMusCtr.
—— CREDO
                    13:30 C.A.P.A.C.
—— PORTRAIT OF A RIVER (TONE POEM)
                    13:00 C.A.P.A.C.
—— THE REMARKABLE ROCKET (BALLET) % (1960)
1,1,2,1 - 2,2,1,0 - perc.,cel. - hp. - pf. - str.   55:00 CanMusCtr.
—— SOFTLY AS THE FLUTE BLOWS
fl. - str.   10:00 C.A.P.A.C.
—— A SPANISH TRAGEDY (TONE POEM) (FOR SOPRANO ORCH.) (1955)
2,*2,2,2 - 4,3,3,1 - timp.,perc. - str.   12:45 CanMusCtr.
—— THREE EXCERPTS FROM THE BALLET "THE REMARKABLE ROCKET" (1965)
*3,2,2,2 - 4,3,3,1 - perc. - hp. - pf. - str.   5:00 CanMusCtr.
—— TWO SOLITUDES (FOR HORN OR ENGLISH HORN AND STRINGS) (1967)
hn.(or Eng. hn.) - str.   10:00 CanMusCtr.

SUSA, Conrad
—— PASTORALE (FOR STRING QUARTET AND DOUBLE STRING ORCH.)
str.   10:00 ECSchirmer.

SUSSMAN, Ettel
—— LE BIEN AIMÉ (THE SONG OF SONGS) (FOR NARRATOR, HIGH VOICE AND ORCH.)
2,2,2,2 - 3,3,3,1 - perc.,xyl. - hp. - str.   14:00 IsMuPublns.

SÜSSMAYR, Franz Xaver - KECSKEMÉTI, Istvan
—— OVERTURE
                    Bo. Hawkes.

ŠUST, Jiří
—— THE WAY HOME
2,2,3,3 - 4,3,2,1 - timp.,perc.,cel. - hp. - str.   8:00 Bo. Hawkes.

SUTER, Robert
—— DIE BALLADE VON DES CORTEZ LEUTEN (FOR NARRATOR, MIXED CHORUS AND SMALL ORCH.) (1960)
(Text: Berthold Brecht)
1(alt. with picc.),1,*2,0 - 1,1,1,1 - perc.(3) - pf. - str.
                    21:30 Modern.
—— CITY LIGHTS
2(2nd alt. with picc.),1,2,0 - 0,2,1,0 - timp.,perc. - hp. - pf. - str.
                    3:00 Modern.
—— EPITAFFIO (1968)
0,0,0,0 - 3,3,0,0 - timp.,perc. - str.   13:00 G. Schirmer.
—— IMPROMPTU FOR ORCH.
2,2,2,2 - 2,2,2,1 - timp. - str.   10:00 Modern.
—— LYRIC SUITE (FOR CHAMBER ORCH.)
1,1,1,0 - 1,0,0,0 - str.   15:30 Henmar.
—— MUSIKALISCHES TAG BUCH NR. 1 (FOR ALTO AND SMALL ORCH.) (REV. 1960) (IN 11 MOVTS.) (Texts: Hofmannsthal and Trakl)
1,1,0,1 - 0,0,0,0 - str.   32:30 Modern.
—— PETITE SUITE POUR ORCHESTRE
*3,*2,*3,alto sax.,1 - 0,4,2,0 - timp.,perc. - hp. - str.
                    12:00 Modern.
—— SONATA PER ORCHESTRA (1967)
3(3rd alt. with picc.),2(2nd alt. with Eng. hn.),3(3rd alt. with b.-cl.),2(2nd alt. with c-bn.) - 4,3,3,1 - timp.,perc.(4),cel. - hp. - str.
                    18:30 G. Schirmer.
—— SUITE FOR STRINGS (1949)
str.   19:00 Modern.
—— THREE NOCTURNES (FOR VIOLA AND ORCH.) (1969)
1,1,2,2 - 4,0,0,0 - perc.(4),cel. - guit. - hp. - cymbalom - str.
                    30:00 G. Schirmer.

SUTHERLAND, Margaret
—— BALLAD OVERTURE (1948)
*3,2,2,2 - 4,2,3,0 - timp.,perc. - str.   4:00 J. Albert.
—— BUSH BALLAD
*3,2,2,E♭ sax.,2 - 4,2,3,0 - timp.,perc. - str.   6:00 J. Albert.
—— CONCERTANTE (FOR SMALL ORCH.)
                    19:00 A.P.R.A.

—— CONCERTINO FOR PIANO AND ORCH. (1940)
                    16:00 J. Albert.
—— CONCERTO FOR STRINGS
str.   10:00 A.P.R.A.
—— CONCERTO FOR VIOLIN AND ORCH.
                    25:00 J. Albert.
—— CONCERTO GROSSO (FOR VIOLIN, VIOLA, HARPSICHORD AND STRINGS)
hpsc. - str.   21:00 A.P.R.A.
—— DITHYRAMB (1937)
                    4:00 J. Albert.
—— FANTASY FOR VIOLIN AND ORCH.
                    16:00 A.P.R.A.
—— FOUR SYMPHONIC CONCERTS (FOUR SYMPHONIC STUDIES) (1949)
                    J. Albert.
—— HAUNTED HILLS (1950)
2,*2,2,3 - 4,0,3,1 - timp.,perc.,cel. - hp. - str.   15:15 J. Albert.
—— HOMAGE TO J. SEBASTIAN (1947)
2,2,2,2 - 2,2,3,0 - timp. - str.   8:30 J. Albert.
—— MOVEMENT FOR ORCH. (1959)
2,*2,2,3 - 4,2,3,0 - timp. - str.   J. Albert.
—— OPEN AIR PIECE (1953)
*3,*3,2,2 - 4,2,0,0 - timp.,perc. - str.   5:00 J. Albert.
—— OUTDOOR OVERTURE (1958)
*3,2,2,2 - 4,2,3,1 - timp.,perc. - str.   5:00 J. Albert.
—— PAVAN FOR ORCH. (1938)
*3,2,2,2 - 4,2,3,0 - timp.,perc. - str.   4:00 J. Albert.
—— SUITE ON A THEME OF PURCELL (1939)
3(3rd alt. with picc.),*2,2,3 - 4,2,3,0 - timp.,perc. - hp. - str.
                    19:00 J. Albert.
—— THREE TEMPERAMENTS FOR ORCH. (1958)
2,2(2nd alt. with Eng.hn.),*3,2 - 4,2,3,1 - timp.,perc. - hp.
                    11:30 J. Albert.
—— THREESOME (1947)
2,2,2,2 - 2,2,3,0 - timp. - str.   8:30 J. Albert.
—— TRIPTYCH
2,*2,2,*3 - 4,2,3,1 - timp.,perc.(3) - hp. - str.   11:00 J. Albert.
—— VISTAS
                    5:00 J. Albert.

ŠVARA, Danilo
—— CONCERTO GROSSO DODECAFONO (FOR CHAMBER ORCH.)
0,2(2nd alt. with Eng. hn.),0,2 - 1,0,0,0 - str.   17:00 Hans Gerig.
—— OCEAN (OPERA) %
2(2nd alt. with picc.),2(2nd alt. with Eng. hn.),2(2nd alt. with b.-cl.),2(2nd alt. with c.-bn.) - 4,3,3,1 - timp.,perc.(4) - guit. - hp. - org. - str.
                    Hans Gerig.
—— SEVEN ARABESQUES
2(2nd alt. with picc.),2,2(2nd alt. with b.-cl.),2 - 4,2,3,1 - timp.,perc.(4) - str.   20:00 Hans Gerig.
—— SINFONIA DA CAMERA, IN MODO ISTRIANO
str.   25:00 Hans Gerig.

SVENDSEN, Johan S. - DASCH, George
—— ZORAHAYDA (LEGEND), OP. 11
                    C. Fischer.

SVENSSON, Sven E.
—— ADAGIO
2,2,2,1 - 2,2,1,0 - timp. - str.   S.T.I.M.
—— CONCERTO FOR VIOLA AND ORCH.
1,2,2,1 - 2,2,0,0 - str.   15:00 S.T.I.M.
—— CONCERTO FOR VIOLIN, CEMBALO AND STRINGS
cemb. - str.   15:00 S.T.I.M.
—— CONCERTO IN OLDEN STYLE (CONCERTO GROSSO)
1,1,0,1 - 1,1,0,0 - timp. - str.   15:00 S.T.I.M.
—— DIVERTIMENTO FROM MUSIC TO SHAKESPEARE'S "TWELFTH NIGHT"
2,2,2,2 - 2-4,2,3,0 - timp - str.   22:00 S.T.I.M.
—— FANTASIA GOTICA (RICERCARE)
2,3,2,2 - 2,2,0,0 - timp. - pf. - str.   S.T.I.M.
—— FESTIVAL OVERTURE IN E FLAT MAJOR
2,2,2,2 - 4,2,3,1 - timp. - str.   9:00 S.T.I.M.
—— PASSACAGLIA
2,2,2,3 sax.,2 - 4,3,3,1 - timp. - str.   7:00 S.T.I.M.
—— SERENADE FOR TWO STRING ORCH.
str.   11:00 S.T.I.M.
—— SYMPHONY IN E MINOR
2,3,3,3 - 4,3,3,1 - timp. - str.   45:00 S.T.I.M.

SVETLANOV, Yevgenij F.
—— SPANISH PICTURES (RHAPSODY FOR ORCH.)
G. Schirmer.

SVOBODA, Tomas
—— A CHILD'S DREAM, OP. 66 (FOR CHILDREN'S CHORUS AND ORCH.) (1973)
10:00 Composer.
—— CHRISTMAS CONCERTINO, OP. 34 (FOR HARP AND ORCH.) (1961) (IN 1 MOVT.)
12:00 Composer.
—— DOUBLE OCTET, OP. 59 (1971)
8,0,0,0 - 0,0,0,0 - 8 c.   13:00 Composer.
—— DRAMATIC OVERTURE, OP. 26 (1959)
12:00 Composer.
—— ETUDE FOR CHAMBER ORCH., OP. 40 (1963)
3:00 Composer.
—— IN A LINDEN'S SHADOW, OP. 25 (SYMPHONIC POEM) (1958)
55:00 Composer.
—— REFLECTIONS FOR ORCHESTRA, OP. 53 (1968)
1. Moderato; 2. Andante; 3. Moderato - Prestissimo; 4. Molto andante
22:00 Composer.
—— SCHERZO, OP. 8 (FOR 2 EUPHONIUMS AND ORCH.) (1955)
8:00 Composer.
—— SINFONIETTE, OP 60 (À LA RENAISSANCE) (1972)
1. Lento; 2. Molto allegro
20:00 TC Stanglnd.
—— SIX VARIATIONS FOR VIOLIN AND STRING ORCH., OP. 32 (1961)
10:00 Composer.
—— SONNET 44 OF MICHAELANGELO, OP. 51 (FOR ALTO AND 11 INSTRUMENTS) (1967)
13:00 Composer.
—— SYMPHONY NO. 1, OP. 20 ("OF NATURE") (1957) (IN 4 MOVTS.)
45:00 Composer.
—— SYMPHONY NO. 2, OP. 41 (1963) (IN 4 MOVTS.)
28:00 TC Stanglnd.
—— SYMPHONY NO. 3 (FOR ORGAN AND ORCH.), OP. 43 (1965) (IN 1 MOVT.)
30:00 TC Stanglnd.
—— THREE PIECES FOR ORCHESTRA, OP. 45 (1966)
9:00 Composer.
—— THREE STUDIES FOR MEZZO-SOPRANO AND ORCH., OP. 30 (1961)
22:00 Composer.

SWACK, Irwin
—— FANTASIA CONCERTANTE
str.   23:00 C. Fischer.

SWAIN, Freda
—— MINIATURE SUITE (1952)
str.   7:00 P.R.S.
—— PASTORAL FANTASY (1937)
2,2,2,2 - 3,2,0,0 - timp.,perc. - str.   24:00 P.R.S.

SWANSON, Howard
—— CONCERTO FOR ORCHESTRA (1957)
1. Larghetto; 2. Allegro; 3. Largo; 4. Allegro
2,2,2,2 - 4,3,3,1 - timp.,perc.(2) - str.   20:00 Weintraub.
—— FANTASIE PIECE
cl. - str.   Weintraub.
—— MUSIC FOR STRINGS
str.   12:00 Weintraub.
—— NIGHT MUSIC (FOR CHAMBER ORCH.)
1,1,1,1 - 1,0,0,0 - str.   9:00 Weintraub.
—— SHORT SYMPHONY (IN 3 MOVTS.)
2,2,2,2 - 2,2,1,0 - timp. - str.   12:00 Weintraub.
—— SYMPHONY NO. 1
1. Allegro moderato; 2. Andante; 3. Allegro vivo; 4. Moderato maestoso
2(2nd alt. with picc.),2,2,2 - 4,3,3,0 - timp.,perc.(2) - str.
25:00 Weintraub.

SWANSON, Walter
—— ANDANTE SERIOSO
str.   4:30 P.R.S.
—— PINT-SIZE SUITE
1,1,2,1 - 2,1,0,0 - timp. - str.   8:00 P.R.S.

—— SYMPHONY NO. 2, IN E MINOR
2,2,2,2 - 4,2-3,3,1 - timp.,perc. - hp. - str.   29:00 P.R.S.

SWANSON, Walter Donald
—— MAGNIFICAT AND NUNC DIMITTIS (FOR SOPRANO, CHORUS AND ORCH.)
2,2,3,2 - 4,2,3,1 - timp.,perc. - str.   15:00 S.A.M.R.O.
—— OOM PAUL KRUGER: SUITE
2,2,3,2 - 4,2,3,1 - timp.,perc. - str.   7:00 S.A.M.R.O.
—— OVERTURE TO AN UNWRITTEN FARCE
2,2,3,2 - 4,2,3,1 - timp.,perc. - str.   4:00 S.A.M.R.O.
—— SYMPHONY IN B FLAT MAJOR
2,2,3,2 - 4,2,3,1 - timp.,perc. - str.   22:00 S.A.M.R.O.
—— SYMPHONY NO. 2 ("EMINA")
2,2,3,2 - 4,2,3,1 - timp.,perc. - str.   28:00 S.A.M.R.O.
—— DIE WYSE VAN DIE OOSTE: CANTATA (FOR SOPRANO, CHORUS AND ORCH.)
2,2,3,2 - 4,2,3,1 - timp.,perc. - str.   20:00 S.A.M.R.O.

SWEELINCK, Jan P. - FLOTHUIS, Marius
—— PRAELUDIUM
4,4,0,4 - 0,4,4,0 - str.   4:00 Henmar.

SWEELINCK, Jan P. - FUSSELL, Charles C.
—— SWEELINCK LIEDURARIATIONEN: MEIN JUNGER LEBEN HAT EIN END (1965)
*2,*2,1,1 - 1,1,1,0 - timp.,mar. - mand. - hp. - str.   12:00 CMP.

SWEELINCK, Jan P. - HARRIS, Roy
—— FANTASIA
3,3,3,3 - 4,2,3,1 - str.   7:00 G. Schirmer.

SWEELINCK, Jan P. - HORST, Anthon van der
—— RICERCAR SVELATO (FROM THE RICERCAR FOR ORGAN) (ARR. 1963)
0,0,0,0 - 4,3,3,0 - org. - str.   15:00 Henmar.

SWEELINCK, Jan P. - MUL, Jan
—— VARIATIONS ON "MEIN JUNGES LEBEN HAT EIN END" (ARR. 1961)
2,2,2,2 - 1,2,2,0 - timp. - hp. - str.   8:00 Henmar.

SWEELINCK, Jan P. - SIGTENHORST MEYER, Bernhard van den
—— CHROMATIC FANTASY (ARR. 1951)
str.   9:00 Henmar.

SWIFT, Richard
—— CONCERTO FOR VIOLIN AND CHAMBER ORCH. (1968)
1,1,1,1 - 1,1,1,0 - cel. - hp. - mand. - str.   15:00 Composer.
—— A CORONAL (1954)
2(1 alt. with picc.),2,2,2 - 2,2,2,1 - timp.,perc.(2) - pf. - str.
12:00 Composer.
—— DIVERTIMENTO (IN 3 MOVTS.) (1950)
1,1,1,1 - 1,1,0,0 - str.   12:00 Composer.
—— DOMAINS III (FOR 4 GROUPS OF INSTRUMENTS) (1963)
2(1 alt. with picc.),1,*3,1 alto sax.,0 - 1,2,1,1 - perc. (2),cel.,glock.,vibra.,xyl. - hp. - pf. - 1 c.   14:00 Presser.
—— EXTRAVAGANZA, OP. 28 (FOR VIOLIN, VIOLA, CELLO AND ORCH.) (1962) (IN 3 MOVTS.)
*3,*3,*3,2(1 alt. with c.-bn.) - 4,2,3,1 - perc.(3),cel.,glock.,vibra.,xyl. - hp. - pf. - str.   17:00 Presser.
—— SYMPHONY (1970) (IN 2 MOVTS.)
2(2nd alt. with picc.),*2,*2,*2 - 2,2,2,1 - timp.,perc. (2) - pf.(alt. with cel.) - str.   13:00 Composer.
—— THANATOPSIS (1971) (IN 4 MOVTS.)
2(2nd alt. with picc.),*2,*2,*2 - 1,2,2,0 - perc.(2),cel.,glock.
20:00 Composer.
—— TRISTIA (1967)
2,1 alto fl.,2,*3,*2 - 2,2,2,0 - perc.(2),xyl. - pf. - d.-b.
12:00 Composer.

SWINBURNE, Thordur
—— CANADIAN OVERTURE
10:00 C.A.P.A.C.
—— CENTENNARY OVERTURE
10:00 C.A.P.A.C.

SWINSTEAD, Felix
—— SCARLATTI SUITE (FOR PIANO AND STRINGS)
pf. - str.   Novello.

SYBERG, Franz
—— PRELUDE TO STRINDBERG'S DRAMA "A DREAM PLAY"
    2,0,2,2 - 2,2,1,0 - timp.,perc. - str.   6:30 G. Schirmer.

SYDEMAN, William
—— CONCERT PIECE FOR CHAMBER ORCHESTRA (1960)
    1(alt. with picc.),1,1(alt. with b.-cl.),1 - 2,1,0,0 - pf. - str.(6,2,1,1)
    22:00 Seesaw.
—— CONCERT PIECE FOR FRENCH HORN AND STRING ORCH.
(1959)
    hn. - str.   10:00 Seesaw.
—— CONCERTINO FOR OBOE, PIANO AND STRING ORCH.
(1956)
    ob. - pf. - str.   10:00 Seesaw.
—— DIVERTIMENTO FOR FLUTE, CLARINET, BASSOON AND
STRINGS (1957)
    1,0,1,1 - 0,0,0,0 - str.   17:00 Seesaw.
—— DOUBLE CONCERTO (FOR TRUMPET, TROMBONE, BAND
AND STRING ORCH.) (1965)
    13:00 Seesaw.
—— FUGUE FOR STRINGS
    str.   5:00 Seesaw.
—— LARGO FOR CELLO AND STRING ORCH. (1961)
    str.   6:00 Seesaw.
—— MUSIC FOR TEN WOODWINDS (1956)
    15:00 Seesaw.
—— MUSIC FOR VIOLA, WINDS AND PERCUSSION (1965)
    27:00 Seesaw.
—— OECUMENICUS (A CONCERTO FOR ORCH.) (1964)
    4(2 alt. with 2 picc.),4(2 alt. with 2 Eng.hn.),4(2 alt. with E♭cl. and
    b.-cl.),4(1 alt. with cbn.) - 8,4(1 alt. with E♭bass tpt.),3,2 -
    timp.,perc.(5) - str.   55:00 Seesaw.
—— ORCHESTRAL ABSTRACTIONS
    2,2,2,2 - 4,3,3,1 - timp.,perc.,cel. - str.   15:00 Henmar.
—— PROMETHEUS (CANTATA) (FOR 3 MALE VOICES, FEMALE
CHORUS AND ORCH.) (1968)
    25:00 Seesaw.
—— SEVEN MOVEMENTS (1958)
    0,1,1,1 - 0,0,0,0 - str.   12:00 Seesaw.
—— STUDY NO. 1 FOR ORCHESTRA (1959)
    2,2,2,2 - 4,3,3,1 - timp.,perc. - pf. - str.   11:00 Seesaw.
—— STUDY NO. 2 FOR ORCHESTRA (1963)
    2(1 alt.with picc.),2,2(1 alt.with b.-cl.),2 - 4,3,3,1 - timp.,perc. -
    pf.(alt.with cel.) - str.   10:00 Seesaw.
—— TEXTURE STUDIES FOR ORCHESTRA (1969)
    20:00 Seesaw.

SYLVAN, Sixten
—— CONCERTO FOR TRUMPET AND ORCH., OP. 4
    2,2,2,2 - 2,2,1,0 - str.   15:00 S.T.I.M.
—— PASTORAL
    2,2,2,2 - 2,2,0,0 - timp. - str.   8:00 S.T.I.M.
—— SYMPHONY NO. 1, OP. 6
    2,2,2,2 - 4,2,3,1 - timp. - str.   25:00 S.T.I.M.

SYMONDS, Norman
—— AUTUMN NOCTURNE (1960) (FOR TENOR SAXOPHONE
AND STRINGS)
    tenor sax. - str.   7:30 E.C.Kerby.
—— THE DEMOCRATIC CONCERTO (1967) (FOR JAZZ
QUARTET AND ORCH.)
    *3,*3,2,2 - 4,3,3,1 - timp.,perc.(3) - str.   32:25 CanMusCtr.
—— ELEGY FOR STRING ORCH. (1962)
    str.   8:00 CanMusCtr.
—— IMPULSE (1969)
    *3,*3,*3,*3 - 4,3,3,1 - timp.,perc.(4) - str.   10:15 MCA Music.
—— MAYA (1973)
    2,2,2,2 - 2,2,0,0 - perc. - str.   12:00 CanMusCtr.
—— THE NAMELESS HOUR (1966) (FOR IMPROVISED SOLO ON
ANY INSTRUMENT AND STRINGS)
    str. (with a soloist preferably from a jazz background)
    8:50 MCA Music.
—— TENSIONS (A BALLET FOR TV) (FOR JAZZ QUINTET AND
ORCH.) (1962) %
    2(2nd alt. with picc.),2,2,2 - 4,3,3,0 - perc.(2) - hp. - str. Jazz
    Quintet: tenor sax. - trb. - drums - guit. - d.-b. 11:00 CanMusCtr.
—— THREE ATMOSPHERES (1971)
    *3,2,2,2 - 4,3,3,1 - timp.,perc.(4) - hp. - str.   12:50 CanMusCtr.

SZABÓ, Ferenc
—— BALLET MUSIC
    Bo. Hawkes.

—— CONCERTO FOR ORCH. (LE RETOUR)
    3(3rd alt. with picc.),3(3rd alt. with Eng. hn.),3(3rd alt. with
    b.-cl.),*3 - 4,4,3,0 - timp.,perc.,cel. - hp. - pf. - str.
    21:00 Bo. Hawkes.
—— CONFESSION (FOR SATB CHORUS AND INSTRUMENTS)
    0,0,0,0 - 4,4,2,1 - perc.   Bo. Hawkes.
—— IN FURY ROSE THE OCEAN (ORATORIO) (FOR TENOR,
SATB CHORUS AND ORCH.)
    2,2,2,2 - 4,4,3,1 - timp.,perc. - hp. - str.   55:00 Bo. Hawkes.
—— LUDAS MATYI (SUITE)
    2,2,2,2 - 4,3,3,1 - timp.,perc.,cel. - hp. - str.   28:00 Bo. Hawkes.
—— MEMENTO (SYMPHONY)
    2,2,2,2 - 4,3,3,1 - timp.,perc. - hp. - str.   38:00 Bo. Hawkes.
—— MOLDAVIAN RHAPSODY
    2(2nd alt. with picc.),2,*3,*3 - 4,3,0,0 - timp.,perc. - str.
    17:00 Bo. Hawkes.
—— THE RETURN
    3,3,3,2 - 4,4,3,1 - timp.,perc.,cel. - hp. - pf. - str.
    21:00 Bo. Hawkes.
—— SÉRÉNADE OUBLIÉE
    2,2,2,2 - 4,0,2,1 - timp.,perc. - hp. - str.   General.
—— SUITE LYRIQUE (FOR STRINGS) (IN 4 MOVTS.)
    str.   22:00 Bo. Hawkes.
—— SUMMARY (SYMPHONIC PICTURE)
    2,2,2,2 - 4,3,3,1 - timp.,perc. - hp. - pf. - str.   9:00 Bo. Hawkes.

SZALONEK, Witold
—— CONNECTIONS
    1,1,1,1 - 1,0,0,0 - pf. - str.   14:00 Seesaw.
—— FOR STRINGS, 1971
    str.   10:00 Seesaw.
—— PASTORALE FOR OBOE AND ORCH. (1952)
    2,0,2,2 - 2,2,1,0 - timp.,perc.(3) - str.   9:00 Seesaw.
—— SYMPHONIC SATIRE (1956)
    3,3,3,3 - 4,3,3,1 - timp.,perc.(2) - hp. - pf. - str.   16:00 Seesaw.
—— TOCCATA POLIFONICA (1953)
    str.   5:00 Seesaw.

SZALOWSKI, Antoni
—— CONCERTO FOR THREE WOODWINDS AND STRINGS
    0,1,1,1 - 4,3,2,1 - timp. - hp. - str.   20:00 Eds. Fran.
—— MUSIC FOR STRINGS
    str.   20:00 Presser.
—— THE RESURRECTION OF LAZARUS (SYMPHONIC POEM)
    2,2,2,2 - 4,2,1,1 - timp. - hp. - str.   7:00 Eds. Fran.
—— SIX ESSAYS FOR CHAMBER ORCH.
    1,1,2,1 - 1,2,1,0 - perc. - hp. - str.   20:00 Presser.

SZÉKELY, Endre
—— CONCERTO FOR PIANO, PERCUSSION AND STRING ORCH.
    perc. - pf. - str.   20:10 Bo. Hawkes.
—— FANTASMA
    *3,*3,*4,*3 - 4,3,3,1 - timp.,perc.(4 incl. 3 on timp.),cel. - hp. - pf.
    - str.   10:00 Bo. Hawkes.
—— PARTITA NO. 2
    str.   Bo. Hawkes.
—— PETITE SUITE
    2,2,2,2 - 4,3,0,0 - timp.,perc. - str.   Bo. Hawkes.
—— SINFONIA CONCERTANTE (FOR VIOLIN, PIANO AND
ORCH.)
    17:00 Bo. Hawkes.
—— SYMPHONY
    3,2,2,2 - 4,2,3,1 - timp.,perc.,cel. - hp. - str.   25:00 Bo. Hawkes.

SZELÉNYI, István
—— HOMMAGE À BÁRTÓK
    2,2,2,2 - 4,2,2,0 - timp.,perc. - hp. - str.   5:00 Bo. Hawkes.
—— SINFONIETTA A TRE
    Bo. Hawkes.
—— SMALL SUITE FOR 4-PART VIOLIN ENSEMBLE
    Vlns.   Bo. Hawkes.
—— SUMMA VITAE (FOR PIANO AND ORCH.)
    12:00 Bo. Hawkes.

SZERVÁNSZKY, Endre
—— CONCERTO FOR CLARINET AND ORCH.
    2,*1,2,1 - 3,2,2,0 - timp.,perc.,cel. - hp. - str.   14:00 Bo. Hawkes.
—— CONCERTO FOR FLUTE AND ORCH.
    3,2,2,2 - 4,2,0,0 - timp.,perc. - hp. - str.   24:00 Bo. Hawkes.
—— CONCERTO FOR ORCH.
    3,3,3,3 - 4,3,3,1 - timp.,perc. - 2 hp. - str.   41:00 Bo. Hawkes.
—— DIVERTIMENTO NO. 1 FOR STRINGS
    str.   Bo. Hawkes.

—— HUNGARIAN SOLDIER'S CANTATA (FOR TENOR, MALE
CHORUS AND ORCH.)
2,2,2,2 - 4,2,0,0 - timp. - str.   17:00 Bo. Hawkes.
—— ORIENTAL TALE (BALLET SUITE)
3,2,2,2 - 4,3,3,1 - timp.,perc. - hp. - str.   20:00 Bo. Hawkes.
—— RHAPSODY
2,2,2,2 - 4,2,1,0 - timp. - str.   4:00 Bo. Hawkes.
—— SERENADE FOR CLARINET AND ORCH.
    Bo. Hawkes.
—— SERENADE FOR STRINGS
str.   Bo. Hawkes.
—— SIX PIECES FOR ORCH.
2,2,2,2 - 4,3,3,0 - timp.,perc. - hp. - str.   Bo. Hawkes.
—— SUITE FOR STRINGS
str.   Bo. Hawkes.
—— SUITE NO. 1
    Bo. Hawkes.
—— SYMPHONY NO. 1
1,2,2,2 - 4,3,3,1 - timp.,perc. - str.   29:00 Bo. Hawkes.
—— VARIATIONS FOR ORCHESTRA
*3,*3,*3,3 - 4,3,3,1 - timp.,perc.,cel. - 2 hp. - str.
    14:00 Bo. Hawkes.

SZOKOLAY, Sándor
—— CONCERTO FOR PIANO AND ORCH.
2,2,2,2 - 4,3,3,0 - timp.,perc. - hp. - pf. - str.   19:00 Bo. Hawkes.

SZŐLLŐSY, András
—— CONCERTO NO. 3 (FOR 16 STRINGS)
str.   13:00 Bo. Hawkes.
—— CONCERTO NO. 4
2,2,2,2 - 0,2,2,0 - str.   15:00 Bo. Hawkes.
—— MUSICA CONCERTANTE
1,1,*2,1 - 1,0,0,0 - str.   15:00 Bo. Hawkes.
—— TRASFIGURAZIONI
    Bo. Hawkes.

SZŐNYI, Erzsébet
—— ALLEGRO
1,0,2,1 - 2,2,1,1 - timp.,perc. - str.   5:00 Bo. Hawkes.
—— CONCERTO FOR ORGAN AND ORCH.
0,1,2,2 - 2,2,0,0 - timp.,perc. - hp. - org.- str.   18:00 Bo. Hawkes.
—— DIVERTIMENTO NO. 2
2,1,2,1 - 2,2,0,0 - timp.,perc. - hp. - pf. - str.   12:00 Bo. Hawkes.
—— PICCOLA INTRODUZIONE
str.   4:00 Bo. Hawkes.
—— TRIO CONCERTINO (FOR VIOLIN, CELLO, PIANO AND
STRING ORCH.)
pf. - str.   Bo. Hawkes.
—— TWO PIECES FOR ORCH.
2,2,2,2 - 2,2,0,0 - timp.,perc., - hp. - str.   9:00 Bo. Hawkes.

T

TABACHNIK, Michel
—— ALTERNANCES II
    15:00 S.U.I.S.A.
—— CHRYSALIDE (POUR 16 INSTRS.)
    22:00 S.U.I.S.A.
—— PASTEL
1,1,2,1 - 2,2,0,0 - perc.,cel. - 2 hp. - pf. - str.   14:00 Novello.
—— SUPERNOVAE
1,0,1,0 - 0,1,1,0 - perc.,cel.,glock.,vibra.,xyl. - 2 hp. - 2 pf. - str.
    25:00 Novello.

TAFFS, Anthony
—— THE SON OF MAN (SACRED ORATORIO) (FOR SATB SOLO
VOICES, SATB CHORUS AND ORCH.)
2,2,2,2 - 2,2,1,0 - timp.,perc.,glock. - org. - str.   Fema.
—— VICTORY OVERTURE
2,2,2,2 - 4,2,3,1 - timp.,perc. - str.   Fema.

TAGLIAPIETRA, Gino
—— CONCERTINO FOR PIANO AND ORCH.
2,2,2,3 - 2,2,0,0 - pf. - str.   22:00 Bo. Hawkes.

TAHOURDIN, Peter Richard
—— DIVERSIONS FOR ORCH. (1959)
3,3,3,3 - 4,3,3,1 - timp.,perc.(3) - hp. - str.   15:00 A.P.R.A.

—— ILLYRIA (BALLET) % (1965)
2,2,2,2 - 2,2,1,0 - timp.,perc. - str.   26:00 A.P.R.A.
—— PARTITA FOR STRING ORCH. (1962)
str.   21:00 A.P.R.A.
—— SINFONIA CONCERTANTE (FOR CELLO AND ORCH.)
(1966)
2,2,2,2 - 4,2,3,0 - timp.,perc. - str.   22:00 A.P.R.A.
—— SYMPHONY NO. 1 (1960)
3,3,3,3 - 4,3,3,1 - timp.,perc.(3) - hp. - str.   33:00 A.P.R.A.
—— SYMPHONY NO. 2 (1969)
2,2,2,2 - 4,2,3,1 - timp.,perc.(3) - str.   28:00 A.P.R.A.

TAILLEFERRE, Germaine
—— BALLET %
*3,*3,*3,2 - 4,3,3,1 - timp.,perc.(2),cel. - 2 hp. - pf. - str.   Presser.
—— CONCERTINO FOR HARP AND ORCH. (IN 3 MOVTS.)
*3,0,2,0 - 2,2,0,0 - timp.,perc. - 2 hp. - str.   16:00 Presser.
—— CONCERTO FOR PIANO AND ORCH.
2,2,0,2 - 2,1,0,0 - timp. - pf. - str.   12:00 Presser.
—— CONCERTO (FOR SATB CHORUS, 2 PIANOS, SAXOPHONE
QUARTET AND ORCHESTRA)
3,0,3,4 sax.,0 - 0,3,3,1 - timp.,perc.(5) - 2 pf. - str.   22:00 Presser.
—— JEU DE PLEIN AIR
3,3,3,3 - 4,3,3,1 - timp.,perc.(3),cel.,glock. - 2 hp. - pf. - str.
    6:00 EV.
—— LE MAÎTRE (CHAMBER OPERA) % (Text: Eugene Ionesco)
1,1,1,1 - 1,1,1,0 - perc. - hp. - hpsc. - str.   26:00 Eds. Fran.
—— OVERTURE
2,2,1,1 - 4,3,3,1 - timp.,perc.(3),bells.,cel.,xyl. - hp. - str.
    4:15 S.A.C.E.M.
—— LA PETITE SIRÈNE (3 ACT OPERA) % (Text: P. Soupault)
ACT I.: str.   82:45 Eds. Fran.
ACT II: timp. - ondes Martenot - hp. - str.
ACT III: 0,1,1,0 - timp. - perc.,cel.,vibra
—— QUADRILLE ET VALSE DES DEPÊCHES (FROM "LES
MARIÉS DE LA TOUR EIFFEL")
2,2,2,2 - 2,2,3,1 - perc. - hp. - str.   5:50 Salabert.
—— SIX CHANSONS FRANÇAISES (FOR HIGH VOICE AND
ORCH.)
2,3,2,2 - 4,2,2,1 - timp.,perc. - str.   Presser.

TAKÁCS, Jenó
—— CHANT OF CREATION, OP. 44 (FOR CHORUS AND ORCH.)
    16:00 A.K.M.
—— EIGHT MINIATURES, OP. 53
2,2,2,2 - 2,2,1,0 - timp.,perc.,cel. - hp. - pf. - str.   15:00 Leeds.
—— PASSACAGLIA FOR STRING ORCH., OP. 73
str.   A.K.M.

TAKATA, Saburo
—— BALLAD ON FOLKSONGS FROM YAMAGATA (FANTASY
AND FUGUE)
2,2,3,2 - 4,2,0,0 - timp. - str.   12:00 Presser.

TAKAYAMA, Giichi
—— AKEBONO
    J.A.S.R.A.C.

TAKEMITSU, Toru
—— ARC (FOR PIANO AND ORCH.) (1966) (IN 6 MOVTS.)
3,3,3,3 - 4,4,3,1 - perc.(4),cel. - electric guit. - hp. - pf. - str.
    30:00 Salabert.
—— ARC FOR STRINGS (3RD MOVT. FROM "ARC, FOR PIANO
AND ORCH.") (1963)
12 vln.,8 c.   6:00 Salabert.
—— AUTUMN (FOR BIWA, SHAKUHACHI AND ORCH.)
    20:00 Salabert.
—— CASSIOPEIA (FOR PERCUSSIONIST AND ORCH.) (1971)
4(1 alt.with picc.,1 alt.with alto fl.),3(1 alt.with Eng.hn.),4(1
alt.with E♭cl.,1 alt.with b.-cl.),*3 - 4,1 cnt.,2,3,1 -
perc.(6),cel.(5-octave) - electric guit. - 2 hp. - str.   20:00 Salabert.
—— CORAL ISLAND (FOR SOPRANO AND ORCH.) (1962) (Text:
Makoto Ooka)
3(1 alt.with picc.),0,3(1 alt.with b.-cl.),0 - 2,2,2,0 - perc.(5),cel. -
hp. - pf. - str.   17:00 Salabert.
—— CORONA FOR STRINGS (1971)
str.(18,0,4,0)   15:00 Salabert.
—— CROSSING (FOR GUITAR, HARP, PIANO, VIBRAPHONE, 12
WOMEN'S VOICES AND 2 ORCHESTRAS) (1970)
4(1 alt.with picc.,1 alt.with alto fl.),3(1 alt.with Eng.hn.),3(1
alt.with b.-cl.),1 d.-b.-cl.,*3 - 4,4,5,1(5-valve) - perc.(8),cel.,vibra. -
guit. - 2 hp. - pf.(alt.with 5-octave cel.) - str.   10:00 Salabert.

—— DORIAN HORIZON (FOR CHAMBER ORCH.)
Ongaku.

—— EUCALYPTS (1970)
1,1,0,0 - 0,0,0,0 - hp. - str.   11:00 Salabert.

—— GARDEN RAIN (FOR 10 BRASS INSTRUMENTS)
8:00 Salabert.

—— GEMEAUX (FOR OBOE, TROMBONE, 2 ORCHESTRAS AND
2 CONDUCTORS) (1972)
15:00 Salabert.

—— GITIMAYA (FOR MARIMBA AND ORCH.)
16:00 Salabert.

—— REQUIEM (FOR STRING ORCH.) (1957)
str.   Salabert.

—— TEXTURES (1964)
9:00 Salabert.

—— WINTER (1971)
2,2,2,2 - 4,2,3,1 0 perc.(6) - hp. - str.(22,8,6,6)   6:00 Salabert.

TAKTAKSHVILI, Otar V.
—— CONCERTO FOR PIANO AND ORCH.
3,2,2,2 - 4,2,3,1 - timp.,perc. - str.   33:00 G. Schirmer.
—— MEGRELIAN SONGS (CYCLE FOR TENOR, MALE VOCAL
ENSEMBLE AND CHAMBER ORCH.)
G. Schirmer.
—— SYMPHONY NO. 1 (1949)
3,3,3,2 - 4,3,3,1 - timp.,perc.,xyl. - hp. - pf. - str.   G. Schirmer.

TAL, Josef
—— AMNON AND TAMAR (1-ACT OPERA) %
2,2,2,0 - 1,1,1,0 - timp.,perc.,cel.,vibra.,xyl. - hp. - pf. - str.
IsMuPublns.
—— CONCERTO FOR CELLO AND STRING ORCH.
str.   17:00 Bo. Hawkes.
—— CONCERTO FOR VIOLA AND ORCH.
2,2,2,2 - 2,2,0,0 - timp.,perc. - str.   19:00 IsMuPublns.
—— CONCERTO NO. 2 FOR PIANO AND ORCH.
2,2,2,2 - 2,2,0,0 - timp.,perc.,cel.,xyl. - hp. - pf. - str.
22:00 IsMuPublns.
—— CONCERTO NO. 3 FOR PIANO AND ORCH. (WITH TENOR
VOICE)
2,*3,2,1 - 2,2,0,0 - timp.,perc.,cel.,vibra.,xyl. - hp. - pf. - str.
18:00 IsMuPublns.
—— EXODUS (CHOREOGRAPHIC POEM) (WITH BARITONE
VOICE) %
3,3,3,3 - 4,3,3,1 - timp.,perc.,cel.,vibra. - hp. - str.
22:00 IsMuPublns.
—— FESTIVE VISION
3,*3,*4,2 - 3,3,3,1 - timp.,perc.,cel.,vibra. - 2 hp. - pf. - str.
9:00 IsMuPublns.
—— THE MOTHER REJOICES (CANTATA) (FOR CHORUS,
PIANO AND ORCH.)
15:00 IsMuPublns.
—— SAUL AT EN-DOR (FOR VOICE AND ORCH.)
1,*1,0,0 - 2,1,0,0 - timp.,perc. - pf. - str.   32:00 IsMuPublns.
—— SYMPHONY NO. 1
3,2,2,2 - 4,3,3,1 - timp.,perc. - hp. - str.   18:00 IsMuPublns.
—— SYMPHONY NO. 2
3,*3,*3,*3 - 4,3,3,1 - timp.,perc.,cel.,vibra.,xyl. - hp. - pf. - str.
12:30 IsMuPublns.

TALLIS, Thomas - JUREY, Edward B.
—— CANON
Mills.

TALMA, Louise
—— THE ALCESTIAD (3-ACT OPERA) % (Text: Thornton Wilder)
C. Fischer.
—— DIALOGUES FOR PIANO
3,2,2,2 - 4,3,3,1 - timp.,perc. - pf. - str.   21:00 C. Fischer.
—— THE DIVINE FLAME (ORATORIO)
Composer.
—— TOCCATA FOR ORCH.
12:00 C. Fischer.
—— THE TOLLING BELL (FOR BARITONE, SATB CHORUS AND
ORCH.)
2,2,3,3 - 4,3,3,1 - timp.,perc., - hp. - str.   18:00 C. Fischer.

TAMAS, János
—— FEST-OUVERTÜRE
2,2,2,2 - 4,3,3,1 - str.   10:00 S.U.I.S.A.
—— LARGHETTO FÜR VIOLINE UND KLEINES ORCHESTER
10:00 S.U.I.S.A.

TAMKIN, David N.
—— THE DYBBUK (3-ACT OPERA) %
*3,*3,*3,*3 - 4,3,3,1 - timp.,perc.(3),cel.,glock.,xyl. - hp. - str.
120:00 Bo. Hawkes.
—— SUITE FROM "THE DYBBUK" (FOR TENOR, VOICE AND
ORCH.) (IN 8 MOVTS.)
*3,*3,E♭ cl.,*3,*3 - 4,4,3,1 - timp.,perc.(3),cel.,glock.,xyl. - pf. - str.
40:00 Bo. Hawkes.

TANG, Jordan Cho-Tung
—— CONCERTO FOR TIMPANI AND STRINGS (1973) (IN 3
MOVTS.)
timp. - str. (4,2,2,2)   8:00 Seesaw.
—— ELEGY (FOR CELLO AND STRING ORCH.) (1973)
str.   8:00 Composer.
—— PASSACAGLIA (1969)
2,2,2,2 - 2,2,3,0 - timp.,perc.(2) - str.   5:00 Composer.
—— SINFONIA BREVISSIMA (1973) (IN 3 MOVTS.)
2,2,2,2 - 2,2,3,1 - timp.,perc.(2),glock.,vibra.,xyl. - str.
4:00 Composer.
—— A SYMPHONIC MOVEMENT (1971)
1,1,1,1 - 1,1,1,0 - timp.,perc.(1) - str.   10:00 Composer.

TANNER, Jerré E.
—— CANTATA NO. 3 (2 SONGS FOR HIGH VOICE AND ORCH.)
(1966) (Text: Harvey Hess, 3rd and Philip Appleman)
3(3rd alt. with picc.),*3,*3(3rd alt. with b.-cl.),2 - 4,3,3,1 -
timp.,perc.(4),glock.,mar.,vibra. - hp. - str.   16:00 Composer.
—— SINFONIA (1969) (IN 3 MOVTS.)
fl. - hp. - hpsc. - pf. - str.   13:00 Composer.
—— LE TOMBEAU (THE TOMBSITE) (PRELUDE TO PART II OF
CANTATA NO. 3) (1969)
fl. - hp. - hpsc. - pf. - str.   7:30 Composer.

TANSMAN, Alexandre
—— ADAM AND EVE (FOR NARRATOR AND ORCH.) (Third
movement from GENESIS Suite)
*3,2(2nd alt. with Eng. hn.),2(2nd alt. with b.-cl.),2 - 4,3,3,1 -
timp.,perc.,cel.,xyl. - hp. - pf. - str.   10:00 Shilkret.
—— CONCERTO FOR CLARINET AND ORCH.
2,1,2,0 - 2,1,0,0 - perc. - str.   16:00 Presser.
—— DOS ELEGIAS (FOR STRINGS)
str.   Southern.
—— LA LUTTE DE JACOB AVEC L'ANGE
2,2,2,2 - 4,3,3,1 - timp.,perc.(5),cel. - hp. - pf. - str.   7:00 Presser.
—— RICERCARI
3,2,2,2 - 4,3,3,1 - timp.,perc.,cel.,xyl. - pf. -str.   14:30 Leeds.
—— SHORT SUITE
2,2,2,2 - 4,2,3,1 - timp.,perc. - pf. - str.   12:00 Leeds.
—— SIX ÉTUDES POUR ORCHESTRE
2,2,2,2 - 4,4,3,1 - timp.,perc.(5),cel. - hp. - pf. - str. 24:00 Presser.
—— SONATINE TRANSATLANTIQUE (IN 3 MOVTS.)
*3,2(2nd alt. with Eng. hn.),*3,sax.,2 - 3,2,3,1 -
timp.,perc.(4),cel.,xyl. - pf. - str.   Baron.
—— SUITE LÉGÈRE POUR ORCHESTRE SYMPHONIQUE
2,2,2,2 - 3,2,2,1 - timp.,perc.(3),cel. - pf. - str.   16:00 Presser.
—— SYMPHONIE DE CHAMBRE (FOR OBOE, HORN AND
ORCHESTRA)
0,1,0,0 - 1,0,0,0 - timp.,perc.(6) - pf. - str.   16:00 Presser.
—— LE TOMBEAU DE CHOPIN
str.   8:00 Leeds.

TARANU, Cornel
—— DEUX POEMES DE ANA BLANDIANA (FOR SOPRANO,
PIANO AND CHAMBER ORCH.) (Text: Ana Blandiana)
9:10 Salabert.
—— RACCORDS
1,1,1,0 - 1,1,0,0 - perc. - hp. - pf. - str.   9:00 Salabert.

TARCAN, Bülent
—— TURKISH BALLET SUITE, OP. 10 (IN 5 MOVTS.)
3(3rd alt. with picc.),2,3,3 - 4,3,3,1 - perc. - hp. - str.
23:00 Henmar.

TARDOS, Béla
—— CONCERTO FOR PIANO AND ORCH.
2,2,2,2 - 2,3,2,0 - timp.,perc.,cel. - hp. - pf. - str.   31:00 Mills.
—— CONCERTO FOR VIOLIN AND ORCH.
2,2,2,2 - 4,3,3,0 - timp.,perc.,cel.,vibra.,xyl. - hp. - str.
24:00 Bo. Hawkes.
—— FANTASY FOR PIANO AND ORCH.
2,2,2,2 - 2,3,3,0 - timp.,perc.,xyl. - hp. - pf. - str.
12:00 Bo. Hawkes.

—— OVERTURE TO A FAIRY TALE
    3,3,3,3 - 4,3,3,1 - timp.,perc. - hp. - pf. - str.   14:00 Bo. Hawkes.
—— SYMPHONY
    3,3,3,3 - 4,3,3,1 - timp.,perc. - hp. - pf. - str.   23:00 Bo. Hawkes.

TARIVERDIYEV, M.
—— WHO ARE YOU? (2-ACT OPERA) %
                                    G. Schirmer.

TARP, Svend Erik
—— THE BATTLE OF JERICHO, OP. 51
    2,2,2,2 - 4,3,3,0 - perc. - str.   5:00 Henmar.
—— BURLESQUE OVERTURE (1958)
                             3:00 K.O.D.A.
—— THE CIMBRIAN CAMPAIGN (1936)
                             5:00 K.O.D.A.
—— COMEDY OVERTURE NO. 1, OP. 36
    2,2,2,2 - 4,3,3,0 - perc.(5) - str.   Henmar.
—— CONCERTINO FOR FLUTE AND ORCH., OP. 30
    1,2,0,2 - 2,0,0,0 - perc. - str.   11:00 Henmar.
—— CONCERTINO FOR SAXOPHONE AND ORCH. (1932)
                           14:00 K.O.D.A.
—— CONCERTINO FOR VIOLIN AND ORCH., OP. 13
    2,2,2,2 - 2,2,0,0 - timp. - str.   12:00 G. Schirmer.
—— CONCERTO IN C MAJOR FOR PIANO AND ORCH., OP. 39
                         20:00 Engstrøm.
—— CONCERTO (1932)
                         22:00 K.O.D.A.
—— THE DETHRONED ANIMAL TRAINER (BALLET) % (1944)
                         35:00 K.O.D.A.
—— THE DETHRONED ANIMAL TRAINER (SUITE) (1948)
                         12:00 G. Schirmer.
—— DIVERTIMENTO (1954)
                         12:00 K.O.D.A.
—— FRESCOES (FOR CHAMBER ORCH.) (1948)
                         10:00 K.O.D.A.
—— LITTLE DANCE SUITE
                         8:00 K.O.D.A.
—— LITTLE FESTIVAL OVERTURE, OP. 75
    2,2,2,2 - 2,3,1,0 - timp.,perc. - str.   G. Schirmer.
—— LUSTSPIELOUVERTÜRE NO. 2, OP. 53
    1,1,2,1 - 2,2,1,0 - perc. - str.   4:00 Sikorski.
—— LYRIC SUITE (1958)
                         17:00 G. Schirmer.
—— MOSAÏQUE, OP. 31 (MINIATURE SUITE)
    2,2,2,2 - 4,3,1,0 - timp.,perc.,cel. - str.   8:30 G. Schirmer.
—— NORDIC LEGEND
                             F. Colombo.
—— ORANIA SUITE (ON OLD DUTCH FOLKTUNES) (1938)
                         10:00 K.O.D.A.
—— OVERTURE TO A PUPPET PLAY
                             K.O.D.A.
—— OVERTURE (1932)
    str.   6:00 K.O.D.A.
—— PARTITA (1947)
                         14:00 K.O.D.A.
—— PASTORALE (FURESØ) (1955)
                         6:00 K.O.D.A.
—— PRELUDIO FESTIVO
                         3:00 K.O.D.A.
—— PRELUDIO PATETICO
                         3:00 K.O.D.A.
—— THE PRINCESS IN THE DISTANCE (THE FAR-AWAY
    PRINCESS)(OPERA) % (1953)
                         60:00 K.O.D.A.
—— PRO DEFUNCTIS (1945)
                         5:00 G. Schirmer.
—— RHAPSODIC OVERTURE
                         8:00 G. Schirmer.
—— THE SHADOW (BALLET) % (REV. 1959)
                         48:00 K.O.D.A.
—— THE SHADOW (SUITE) % (1961)
                         16:00 K.O.D.A.
—— SINFONIETTA (1931) (FOR CHAMBER ORCH.)
                         12:00 K.O.D.A.
—— SUITE ON OLD DANISH FOLKSONGS
    2,2,2,2 - 2,2,0,0 - timp., - str.   12:00 G. Schirmer.
—— SUITE (1930)
                         4:00 K.O.D.A.
—— SYMPHONY NO. 1 (1945)
                         32:00 K.O.D.A.
—— SYMPHONY NO. 2 IN E FLAT, OP. 50
    3,2,2,2 - 4,3,3,1 - timp.,perc. - str.   23:00 Henmar.

—— SYMPHONY NO. 3, OP. 66 (SINFONIA QUASI UNA
    FANTASIA)
    2,2,2 - 4,3,3,1 - timp. - perc. - pf.(or cel.) - str.   23:00 Henmar.
—— SYMPHONY NO. 4, OP. 77
    2,2,2 - 4,3,3,0 - timp.,perc. - hp. - pf.   24:00 Henmar.
—— TE DEUM, OP. 33 (FOR SATB CHORUS AND ORCH., WITH
    OPTIONAL SOLO VOICES)
                         28:00 Henmar.
—— TOCCATA (1941)
                         5:00 K.O.D.A.

TARTINI, Giuseppe - BAUMGARTNER
—— CONCERTO IN D MINOR (FOR VIOLIN, CEMBALO AND
    STRINGS)
    cemb. - str.   15:00 Henmar.

TARTINI, Giuseppe - BONELLI, Ettore
—— ANDANTE E PRESTO (FROM QUARTET NO. 125 IN D
    MAJOR)
    str.   Henmar.
—— CONCERTO IN F MAJOR, OP. 58 (FOR STRINGS, OBOES
    AND HORNS)
    2 ob. - 2 hn. - str.   Henmar.
—— CONCERTO NO. 57 (FOR VIOLIN AND ORCH.)
    2 hn.,2 tpt. - timp. - str.   Henmar.

**TARTINI, Giuseppe - BRINCKMANN, Johannes von - MOHR,
Wilhelm**
—— CONCERTO À 5 IN G MAJOR
    fl. - cemb. - str.   12:00 F. Colombo.

TARTINI, Giuseppe - DALLAPICCOLA, Luigi
—— TARTINIANA (DIVERTIMENTO FOR VIOLIN AND ORCH.)
    3,1,4,3 - 2,1,0,0 - xyl. - hp. - str.   16:00 Leeds.
—— TARTINIANA NO. 2 (FOR VIOLIN AND ORCH.)
    2,2,3,1 - 1,1,0,0 - timp.,perc.,cel.,glock.,vibra.,xyl. - hp. - str.(no
    d.-b.)   12:00 Leeds.

TARTINI, Giuseppe - FAGOTTO, Virginio
—— SINFONIA A QUATTRO, IN A MAJOR
    cemb. - str.   11:00 Presser.

TARTINI, Giuseppe - GUGLIELMO
—— CONCERTO IN G MINOR (FOR VIOLIN, CEMBALO AND
    STRINGS)
    cemb. - str.   14:00 Henmar.

TARTINI, Giuseppe - JACOB, Gordon
—— CONCERTINO FOR CLARINET AND STRINGS
    cl. - str.   10:00 Bo. Hawkes.

TARTINI, Giuseppe - KREISLER, Fritz
—— SONATA ("THE DEVIL'S TRILL") (FOR VIOLIN AND ORCH.)
    str.   7:00 C. Fischer.
—— VARIATIONS ON A THEME OF CORELLI (FOR VIOLIN
    AND STRINGS)
    str.   6:00 C. Fischer.

TARTINI, Giuseppe - RAVANELLO, Oreste
—— CONCERTO IN A MAJOR FOR CELLO AND STRINGS
    org.(ad lib.) - str.   Henmar.

TARTINI, Giuseppe - ROSTAL, Max
—— CONCERTO IN G MINOR FOR VIOLIN AND STRINGS
    str.   20:00 Novello.

TARTINI, Giuseppe - SCHERCHEN
—— CONCERTO IN E MAJOR FOR VIOLIN AND STRINGS
    str.   12:00 Henmar.

TARTINI, Giuseppe - SCHERING
—— CHRISTMAS SYMPHONY IN D MAJOR (FOR 2 VIOLINS,
    CELLO AND STRINGS)
    cemb. - str.   13:00 Henmar.

TARTINI, Giuseppe - SZIGETI, Joseph
—— CONCERTO IN D MINOR, FOR VIOLIN AND STRING
    ORCH. (With Original Cadenzas by Szigeti)
    str.   11:00 C. Fischer.

TATE, Phyllis
—— CONCERTO FOR SAXOPHONE AND STRINGS
    sax. - str.   22:00 Oxford.

—— DUO CONCERTANTE (FOR TRUMPET, BASSOON AND ORCH.)
2,2,2,2 - 2,1,0,0 - perc. - str.   16:00 Oxford.
—— THE LODGER (OPERA) % (Text: David Franklin)
2,2,2,2 - 4,2,3,0 - timp.,perc.,cel. - pf. - str.   135:00 Oxford.
—— OCCASIONAL OVERTURE
     10:00 Oxford.

TAURIELLO, Antonio
—— CANTI (FOR VIOLIN AND ORCH.) (1967)
2,1,3,2 - 2,0,0,0 - perc.,bells,cel.,glock.,mar.,vibra.,xyl. - hp. - str.
     12:00 Bo. Hawkes.
—— CONCERTO FOR CLARINET AND ORCH.
2,0,1,2 - 2,2,2,0 - timp.,perc. - hp. - pf. - str.   10:00 Bo. Hawkes.
—— CONCERTO FOR PIANO AND ORCH. (1968)
2,2,3,2 - 4,1,3,0 - perc.,cel. - 2 hp. - pf. - str.   16:00 Bo. Hawkes.
—— ILINX (FOR CLARINET AND ORCH.) (1968)
cl. - perc. - pf. - str.   14:00 Bo. Hawkes.
—— MANSIÓN DE TLALOC
3,0,3,0 - 4,3,4,0 - perc. - pf. - str.   12:00 Bo. Hawkes.
—— MÚSICA III (FOR PIANO AND ORCH.) (1966)
3,0,3,0 - 4,3,3,0 - perc. - pf. - str.(9,6,6,0)   12:00 Bo. Hawkes.
—— RICERCARI 1-6
2,1,2,0 - 4,2,3,0 - perc.,cel.,vibra.,xyl. - hp. - pf. - str.(2,1,1,0)
     9:00 Bo. Hawkes.
—— SERENATA
2,2,2,2 - 4,2,2,1 - timp.,perc.,cel. - hp. - pf. - str.
     11:00 Bo. Hawkes.
—— SERENATA I (1964)
3,2,2,2 - 4,2,2,1 - timp.,perc. - cel. - hp. - pf. - str.
     8:00 Bo. Hawkes.
—— SERENATA II (1966)
1,1,1,0 - 0,0,0,0 - perc.(4) - str.(4,4,4,0 or 1,1,1,0)
     8:00 Bo. Hawkes.
—— SINFONIETTA
3,2,2,2 - 4,2,2,0 - timp.,perc. - pf. - str.   14:00 Bo. Hawkes.
—— SYMPHONIC OVERTURE
3,3,3,3 - 4,3,3,2 - timp.,perc. - 2 hp. - pf. - str. 10:00 Bo. Hawkes.
—— TRANSPARENCIAS (FOR 6 INSTRUMENTAL GROUPS) (1964)
3,0,3,0 - 0,3,0,0 - perc.(3) - 6 vlvn.,6 vla.   9:00 Bo. Hawkes.

TAUTENHAHN, Gunther
—— CONCERTO FOR DOUBLE BASS AND ORCH. (1968) (IN 4 MOVTS.)
*2*2*2 - 2,1,1 b.-tpt.,0,0 - timp.,perc.(2),glock. - hp. - str.
     30:00 Seesaw.
—— CONCERTO FOR TRUMPET AND 10 INSTRUMENTS
     12:00 Seesaw.
—— CONCERTO FOR VIOLA AND CHAMBER ORCH. (1969) (IN 2 MOVTS.)
*2,*2,*2,*2 - 2,0,0,0 - timp.,glock. - hp. - 1 vla.   12:00 Seesaw.
—— CONCERTO FOR VIOLIN AND ORCH. (1969) (IN 4 MOVTS.)
*2,*2,*2,*2 - 3,1 cnt.,1,1 b.-tpt.,1,0 - timp.,perc.(2) - str.
     10:00 Composer.
—— DOUBLE CONCERTO, FOR HORN, TIMPANI AND CHAMBER ORCH.(1969) (IN 3 MOVTS.)
0,*3,*1,0 - 1,2,1 b.-tpt.,1 b.-trb.,0 - timp.,perc.(2),xyl. - 2 hp. - 2 pf.   25:00 Seesaw.
—— MONOCHROME OVERTURE (FOR PIANO AND ORCH.) (1970) (IN 1 MOVT.)
1,*2,*2,1 ten.sax.,*2 - 1,1,1,1 - perc.(3),bells, cel.,xyl. - guit. - hp. - pf. - str.(5,4,3,0)   12:00 Composer.
—— PRELUDE FOR CHAMBER ORCH. (1968)
*2,1,*2,*2 - 2,1,1,1 - timp.,perc.(2),glock. - hp. - str.
     7:00 Composer.
—— SYMPHONIC SOUNDS NO. 1 (1971)
     15:00 Seesaw.
—— SYMPHONIC SOUNDS NO. 2 (1973)
     10:00 Seesaw.

TAVARES, Hekel
—— CONCERTO IN BRAZILIAN FORMS FOR PIANO AND ORCH.
3,2,2,2 - 2,3,2,1 - timp.,perc. - pf. - str.   23:00 Bo. Hawkes.

TAVENER, John
—— CAIN AND ABEL (DRAMATIC CANTATA) (FOR SOLO VOICES, CHORUS AND ORCH.)
2,2,2,2 - 3,3,3,1 - timp.,perc. - hp. - str.   20:00 G. Schirmer.
—— CELTIC REQUIEM (1969) (FOR SOPRANO, CHILDREN'S CHORUS, SATB CHORUS AND 3 GROUPS OF INSTRUMENTS)
E♭ picc.,0,0,bagpipes,1,0 - 0,1(alt. with picc. tpt.),2,0 - perc.(6) - b.-guit. - pf. - str.   G. Schirmer.
—— CHAMBER CONCERTO (1968)
2,2,2,2 - 4,3,2,1 - timp.,perc.(5) - hp. - pf. - str.
     13:00 G. Schirmer.
—— CONCERTO FOR ORCHESTRA
2(alt. with 2 picc.),2,2(2nd alt. with b.-cl.),2(2nd alt. with c.-bn.) - 4,2,3,1 - timp.,perc. - hp. - org. - pf. - str.(4,2,2,0)   G. Schirmer.
—— GRANDMA'S FOOTSTEPS (A MUSICAL GAME)
ob.,bn - hn. - 5 Music Boxes - str.   15:00 G. Schirmer.
—— IN ALIUM (FOR SOPRANO AND ORCH.)
perc. - tape-recorder - Hammond org., "Grand" org. - pf. - str.
     14:00 G. Schirmer.
—— LITTLE REQUIEM FOR FATHER MALACHY LYNCH (FOR CHOIR, ORGAN AND CHAMBER ORCH.)
     12:00 G. Schirmer.
—— REQUIEM FOR FATHER MALACHY (FOR SATB CHORUS AND CHAMBER GROUP)
2 fl.(2nd alt. with picc.) - 0,2,2,0 - org. - pf. - str.(2,1,1,0)
     45:00 G. Schirmer.
—— THREE HOLY SONNETS (FOR BARITONE AND ORCH.) (Text: John Donne)
2 hn., 2 trb. - timp. - str.   15:00 G. Schirmer.
—— ULTIMOS RITOS (FOR 5 PRIESTS OR NARRATORS, SOPRANO, ALTO, TENOR, BASS AND ORCH.)
4(incl. 2 amplified alto fl.),4(incl. 2 ob. d'armore),6 recorders, 0,0 - 4,10,4,0 - timp.,perc.(6, incl. 4 on timp.), church bells, Indian bells - chamber-org.(amplified), org. - hpsc.(amplified) - str.
     50:00 G. Schirmer.
—— THE WHALE (FOR BARITONE AND ORCH.)
2(both alt. with picc.),2,2(2nd alt. with b.-cl.),2(nd alt. with c.-bn.) - 4,3,3,1 - timp.,perc.,cel. - tape-recorder - org. - pf. - str.(c. and d.-b. only)   45:00 G. Schirmer.

TAYLOR, Deems
—— BALLET MUSIC FROM "CASANOVA", OP. 22
*2,2,2,2 - 2,2,1,0 - timp.,perc.(2) - str.   6:00 Belw-Mills.
—— THE CHAMBERED NAUTILUS (CANTATA) (FOR CHORUS AND ORCH.), OP. 7
2(2nd alt. with picc.),2(2nd alt. with Eng. hn.),2,2 - 4,3,3,1 - timp.,perc.(2) - hp. - org.(ad lib.) - str.   15:00 Ditson.
—— CIRCUS DAY (EIGHT PICTURES FROM MEMORY), OP. 18
3(3rd alt. with picc.),*3,E♭cl.,2,3 sax.,2 - 4,3,3,1 - timp.,perc.(2),glock.,xyl. - str.   22:00 Belw-Mills.
—— THE DRAGON (OPERA) %
2,2,2,2 - 2,2,2,1 - timp.,perc. - hp. - str.   Fema.
—— ELEGY FOR ORCHESTRA, OP. 27
3(3rd alt. with picc.),*3,*3,2 - 4,3,3,1 - timp.,perc.(2),glock. - hp. - str.   14:00 Belw-Mills.
—— FANTASY ON TWO THEMES, OP. 17
3(3rd alt. with picc.),*3,*3,*3 - 4,3,3,1 - timp.,perc.(3),cel.,glock.,xyl. - hp. - str.   18:00 Belw-Mills.
—— THE HIGHWAY (CANTATA)(FOR BARITONE, CHORUS AND ORCH.), OP. 8
2(2nd alt. with picc.),2(2nd alt. with Eng. hn.),2,2 - 4,3,3,1 - timp.,perc. (2) - hp. - str.   30:00 Ditson.
—— INTRODUCTION AND BALLET MUSIC FROM THE OPERA "RAMUNTCHO", OP. 23
3(3rd alt. with picc.),2(2nd alt. with Eng. hn.),*3,2 - 4,3,3,1 - timp.,perc.(3) - hp. - str.   8:30 Belw-Mills.
—— THE KING'S HENCHMAN (OPERA) %
3(3rd alt. with picc.),*3,*3,3 - 4,3,3,1 - timp.,perc.,cel.,glock.,xyl. - hp. - str.   Belw-Mills.
—— MARCO TAKES A WALK (VARIATIONS), OP. 25
*3,*3,*3,2 - 4,3,3,1 - timp.,perc.(3) - str.   14:00 Belw-Mills.
—— PORTRAIT OF A LADY (RHAPSODY FOR WINDS, PIANO AND STRINGS), OP. 14
1,1,1,1 - hn. - pf. - str.   18:00 Belw-Mills.
—— PROCESSIONAL, OP. 24
2(2nd alt. with picc.),2,*3,2 - 4,3,3,1 - timp.,perc.(2) - str.
     8:00 Composer.
—— RESTORATION SUITE (IN 5 MOVTS.)
2(2nd alt. with picc.),2,*3,2 - 4,3,3,1 - timp.,perc.(6),glock. - str.
     15:00 Composer.
—— THE SIREN SONG (SYMPHONIC POEM), OP. 2
2(2nd alt. with picc.),2(2nd alt. with Eng. hn.),2,2 - 4,2,3,1 - timp.,perc.(2) - hp. - str.   20:00 Belw-Mills.

—— SUITE FROM THE OPERA "PETER IBBETSON", OP. 20 (IN 3 MOVTS.)
3(3rd alt. with picc.),*3,*4,*3 - 4,3,3,1 - timp.,perc. - hp. - str.
14:00 Belw-Mills.
—— THROUGH THE LOOKING-GLASS SUITE , OP. 12 (ORIGINAL VERSION) (IN 3 MOVTS.)
1,1,1,1 - hn. - pf. - str.   Belw-Mills.
—— THROUGH THE LOOKING GLASS SUITE OP. 12 (FOR LARGE ORCH.)
3(3rd alt. with picc.),*3,*3,*3 - 4,3,3,1 - timp.,perc.(2) - pf. - str.
28:00 Belw-Mills.

TAYLOR, Deems - TURNER, Godfrey
—— FANFARE FOR RUSSIA (FOR BRASS AND PERCUSSION)
4 hn.,3 tpt.,3 trb.,tu. - timp.,perc.(4)   Bo. Hawkes.

TAYLOR, Lionel
—— AMERICAN SYMPHONETTE, OP. 9 (SONATINA FOR ORCH.) (IN 3 MOVTS.)
*3,2,*3,*3 - 4,3,3,1 - timp.,perc.(3),bells - hp. - str.
9:30 Composer.
—— CONCERT PIECE FOR PIANO AND ORCH., OP. 7
1,1(alt. with Eng.hn.),1,1 - 4,2,1,0 - timp.,perc.(2) - hp.(optional) - pf. - str.
11:30 Composer.

TCHEMBERDJI, Nikolas K.
—— DANCE SUITE (IN 4 MOVTS.)
3(3rd alt. with picc.),2(2nd alt. with Eng. hn.),2,2 - 4,3,3,1 - timp.,perc. - hp. - str.   19:00 G. Schirmer.

TCHEREPNIN, Alexander
—— BAGATELLES, OP. 5 (FOR PIANO AND ORCH.)
2,2,2,2 - 2,2,0,0 - timp.,perc. - pf. - str.   10:30 Presser.
—— CHOTA ROSTAVELI (BALLET) % (1946)
Bo. Hawkes.
—— CONCERTO NO. 1 IN F MAJOR FOR PIANO AND ORCH.
Presser.
—— CONCERTO NO. 2 FOR PIANO AND ORCH.
2,2,2,2 - 2,2,0,0 - timp.,perc. - pf. - str.   15:00 Presser.
—— CONCERTO NO. 5 FOR PIANO AND ORCH., OP. 96
3,3,3,3 - 4,3,3,1 - timp.,perc. - hp. - pf. - str.   18:00 Henmar.
—— CONCERTO NO. 6 FOR PIANO AND ORCH., OP. 99
3,2,2,2 - 4,2,3,1 - timp.,perc. - hp. - pf. - str.   24:00 Henmar.
—— DEJEUNER SUR L'HERBE (BALLET) (ON THEMES OF LANNER) (1945) %
Bo. Hawkes.
—— L' ENFANCE DE ST. NINO, OP. 69 (1944)
Templeton.
—— EVOCATION
3,*3,3,3 - 4,3,3,1 - hp. - str.   9:00 Templeton.
—— THE FARMER AND THE NYMPH (A LYRIC LEGEND) (OPERA) (FOR NARRATOR, COLORATURA SOPRANO, TENOR AND ORCH.) (1952) %
2,1,2,1 - 2,2,0,0 - timp.,perc. - pf. - str.   35:00 Bo. Hawkes.
—— THE LOST FLUTE, OP. 89 (FOR NARRATOR AND ORCH.)
2,2,2,2 - 2,2,1,0 - timp.,perc. - hp. - str.   41:00 Templeton.
—— RHAPSODY GEORGIENNE (FOR CELLO AND ORCH.)
*3,2,2,2 - 2,2,0,0 - timp.,perc. - str.   16:00 EV.
—— ROMANTIC OVERTURE, OP. 67
3,2,2,2 - 4,2,3,1 - timp.,perc. - hp. - pf. - str.   8:30 G. Schirmer.
—— SONATA FOR TIMPANI AND ORCH. OP. 58
2,2,2,2 - 4,2,3,1 - timp.,perc. - str.   6:00 Bo. Hawkes.
—— STENKA RASINE (BALLET) %
3,3,3,3 - 4,3,3,1 - timp.,perc. - hp. - pf. - str.   45:00 Bo. Hawkes.
or:
2,1,1,1 - 2,2,1,0 - perc. - pf. - str.
—— SYMPHONIC MARCH, OP. 80
3,2,2,2 - 4,3,3,1 - timp.,perc.,cel. - hp. - pf. - str.   5:30 Leeds.
—— SYMPHONIC PRAYER, OP. 93 (1959)
3,3,4,3 - 4,3,3,1 - timp.,perc. - hp. - str.   9:00 Henmar.
—— SYMPHONY NO. 1, OP. 42
3,2,2,2 - 4,2,3,1 - timp.,perc. - str.   20:00 EV.
—— SYMPHONY NO. 3, OP. 83
3,3,3,3 - 4,3,3,1 - timp.,perc. - hp. - pf. - str.   28:00 Templeton.
—— SYMPHONY NO. 4
3,3,4,3 - 4,3,3,1 - timp. - hp. - str.   25:00 Bo. Hawkes.
—— SYMPHONY NO. 4 (IN 3 MOVTS.)
*3,*3,E♭cl.,*3,*3 - 4,3,3,2 - timp. - hp. - str.   28:00 Bo. Hawkes.
—— THE TWELVE ("LES DOUZE"), OP. 73 (FOR NARRATOR AND SMALL ORCH.) (1945) (Text: Peter Ustinov)
timp.,perc. - hp. - pf. - str.   16:00 Henmar.

—— VOM SPASS UND ERNST (FOLK SONG CANTATA) (FOR MEDIUM VOICE AND STRING ORCH.)
str.   Hans Gerig.
—— THE WELL-TEMPERED VIOLONCELLO (FOR CELLO AND STRINGS)
str.   21:00 EV.

TCHEREPNIN, Nicolas N.
—— THE ENCHANTED KINGDOM, OP. 39 (SYMPHONIC SKETCH)
4,3,3,2 - 4,3,3,1 - timp.,perc.,cel.,xyl. - 2hp. - pf. - str.   Leeds.
—— NARCISSUS (BALLET), OP. 40 %
Leeds.

TELEMANN, Georg Philipp - BIRKE
—— CONCERTO IN B FLAT MAJOR
2 recorders (or 2 fl.) - cemb. - str.   Henmar.

TELEMANN, Georg Philipp - BRINCKMANN, Johannes von - MOHR, Wilhelm
—— CONCERTO À 5 IN D MAJOR
fl. - cemb. - str.   17:00 F. Colombo.

TELEMANN, Georg Philipp - COLLINS, Anthony
—— PASSACAGLIA IN E MINOR
Fox.

TELEMANN, Georg Philipp - DORATI, Antal
—— SUITE FOR OBOE AND STRINGS
ob. - str.   A.P.R.A.

TELEMANN, Georg Philipp - FLATTSCHACHER
—— CONCERTO IN G MAJOR, FOR 2 VIOLAS, CEMBALO AND STRINGS
cemb. - str.   Henmar.

TELEMANN, Georg Philipp - KOELBEL
—— CONCERTO IN A MAJOR
2 fl. - cemb. - str.   Henmar.

TELEMANN, Georg Philipp - LELOIR, Edmond
—— CONCERTO IN D MAJOR FOR HORN, STRINGS AND CONTINUO
hn. - cemb. - str.   10:00 Henmar.

TELEMANN, Georg Philipp - LENZEWSKI
—— SUITE IN G MAJOR
cemb. - str.   Henmar.

TELEMANN, Georg Philipp - MÖNKEMEYER, Helmut
—— OVERTURE IN C MAJOR (FOR STRING ORCH.)
str.   8:30 Henmar.

TELEMANN, Georg Philipp - OBERDOERFFER
—— SINFONIA MELODICA IN C MAJOR
2 ob. - cemb. - str.   Henmar.

TELEMANN, Georg Philipp - OUBRADOUS, Fernand
—— SONATE DE CONCERT, IN D
tpt. - hpsc. - str.   12:00 Presser.
—— SUITE IN F
2 hn. - hpsc. - str.   12:00 Presser.

TELEMANN, Georg Philipp - SCHERING
—— SUITE NO. 1 IN A MINOR
cemb. - str.   15:00 Henmar.
—— SUITE NO. 2 IN G MINOR
cemb. - str.   14:00 Henmar.

TELEMANN, Georg Philipp - SCHROEDER, Felix
—— CONCERTO GROSSO FOR 2 TRUMPETS, 2 VIOLINS AND STRINGS
2 tpt. - hpsc. - str.   7:50 Mannheimer.
—— CONCERTO IN D MAJOR FOR VIOLIN, 3 HORNS AND STRINGS ("LA CHASSE")
ob.(ad lib.) - 3 hn. - hpsc. - str.   25:00 Mannheimer.
—— DON QUIXOTE SUITE (BURLESQUE DE QUIXOTE)
cemb. - str.   18:00 Henmar.
—— OVERTURE IN B FLAT MAJOR (WIESBADENER OVERTURE)
hpsc. - str.   16:30 Mannheimer.

—— SINFONIA IN F MAJOR (CONCERTO FOR RECORDER, VIOLA DA GAMBA AND ORCH.)
Recorder - 2,3,0,0 - hpsc. - str.   12:00 Mannheimer.

TELEMANN, Georg Philipp - THILDE, Jean
—— CONCERTO IN B FLAT (FOR TRUMPET AND STRINGS)
tpt. - str.   8:00 Presser.
—— CONCERTO IN B FLAT (FOR 2 TRUMPETS AND STRINGS)
2 tpt. - str.   8:00 Presser.
—— CONCERTO IN C MINOR FOR 2 TRUMPETS (OR OBOE AND TRUMPET) AND STRINGS
ob. - tpt. - str.   10:00 Presser.
or:
2 tpt. - str.
—— CONCERTO IN E FLAT
tpt. - str.   10:00 Presser.

TELEMANN, Georg Philipp - TÖTTCHER, Hermann
—— CONCERTO IN D MINOR
ob. - cemb. - str.   14:00 F. Colombo.
—— CONCERTO IN E MINOR
ob. - cemb. - str.   10:00 F. Colombo.

TELEMANN, Georg Philipp - WHITNEY, Maurice C.
—— AIR AND COURANTE
4:50 Witmark.

TELEMANN, Georg Philipp - WINSCHERMANN, Helmut - BUCK, Friedrich
—— CONCERTO ALLA FRANCESE, IN C MAJOR
2ob.,bn. - cemb. - str.   13:00 F. Colombo.
—— CONCERTO GROSSO IN D MAJOR
2 ob. - 3 tpt. - timp. - cem. - str.   15:00 F. Colombo.
—— CONCERTO GROSSO IN G MINOR
2 ob. - cemb. - str.   14:00 F. Colombo.
—— CONCERTO IN D MAJOR
2 ob. - tpt.(in D) - cemb. - str.   13:00 F. Colombo.
—— THE FRANKFURT PASSION ("DER FÜR DIE SÜNDE DER WELT") (ORATORIO) (FOR SOLI, MIXED CHORUS AND ORCH.)
2,2,0,1 - 2,2,0,0 - cemb. - str.   150:00 F. Colombo.
—— OVERTURE IN C MAJOR (SUITE)
3 ob.,bn. - cemb. - str.   20:00 F. Colombo.
—— OVERTURE IN E MINOR
2 ob. - bn. - cemb. - str.   12:00 F. Colombo.
—— OVERTURE IN F MAJOR ("A MUSICAL JOKE")
2 ob. - 4 hn. - cemb. - str.   15:00 F. Colombo.

TELEMANN, Georg Philipp - WUMMER, John
—— SUITE IN A MINOR (FOR FLUTE AND ORCH.)
SouthernTx.

TEMMINGH, Hendrik
—— MUSIC FOR FLUTE AND ORCHESTRA
3,2,3,2 - 4,2,3,1 - timp.,perc. - str.   5:00 S.A.M.R.O.

TEMMINGH, Roelof Willem
—— BALLADE VAN DIE GRYSLAND (FOR BARITONE, CHORUS AND ORCH.) (Text: D. J. Opperman)
2,2,3,2 - 4,2,3,1 - timp.,perc. - str.   18:00 S.A.M.R.O.
—— LOBOLA
2,2,3,2 - 4,2,3,1 - timp.,perc. - str.   9:00 S.A.M.R.O.
—— MOVEMENT FOR CHAMBER ORCHESTRA
1,1,2,1 - 3,1,2,0 - str.   9:00 S.A.M.R.O.
—— MOVEMENT FOR PIANO AND ORCHESTRA
2,2,3,2 - 4,2,3,1 - timp.,perc. - pf. - str.   10:00 S.A.M.R.O.
—— PRELUDE EN FUGA VIR DIE GIFGOOIERS IN DIE VOORTUIN
str.   10:00 S.A.M.R.O.
—— SCHERZO VIR KLAVIER EN ORKES
2,2,3,2 - 4,2,3,1 - timp.,perc. - pf. - str.   7:00 S.A.M.R.O.

TEMPLETON, Alec
—— CONCERTINO LIRICO (FOR PIANO AND ORCH.)
3,*2,2,2 - 4,3,3,1 - timp.,perc. - str.   18:00 Templeton.
—— GOTHIC CONCERTO (FOR PIANO AND ORCH.)
2(2nd alt. with picc.),2,2,2 - 2,2,0,0 - timp.,perc. - pf. - str.   22:30 Templeton.
—— THE PIED PIPER OF HAMELIN (FOR NARRATOR AND ORCH.)
2,1,1,1 - 2,2,2,0 - cel. - hp. - str.   10:30 Templeton.
—— RHAPSODIE HARMONIQUE (FOR PIANO AND ORCH.)
3,2,2,2 - 4,3,3,1 - timp. - pf. - str.   15:00 Templeton.

—— SUITE FOR STRINGS
str.   10:00 Templeton.

TEPPER, Albert N.
—— CONCERTINO FOR OBOE AND STRINGS (IN 3 MOVTS.)
ob. - str.   7:00 Kalmus.
—— FOUR SKETCHES FROM SHAKESPEARE (1968)
0,2(2nd alt. with Eng. hn.),0,1 - 1,0,0,0 - perc.(1) - str.   13:00 Composer.
or:
0,1,1,1 - 1,0,0,0 - perc.(1) - str.
or:
0,0,2,1 - 1,0,0,0 - perc.(1) - str.
—— OVERTURE TO A CLASSICAL TRAGEDY
2(2nd alt. with picc.),2,2,2 - 2,2,3,0 - timp.,perc.(2) - str.   11:00 Composer.
—— OVERTURE TO THE TUDOR FARCE "JOHN-JOHN"
1(alt. with picc.),1,2(2nd alt. with alto sax.),1 - 2,2,1,0 - timp.,perc.(2) - str.   4:00 Composer.
—— PRELUDE TO A TUDOR COMEDY
*1,0,1,0 - 0,1,0,0 - perc.(1) - str.   3:00 Composer.
—— SONGS OF BLAKE (8 SHORT INSTRUMENTAL MOVEMENTS AND A POSTLUDE, INSPIRED BY POEMS OF WILLIAM BLAKE) (1968)
2,1(alt. with Eng.hn.),2,1 - 2,0,0,0 - 2 vla.,1c.   20:00 Composer.
or:
2,1 (alt. with Eng. hn.),2,1 - 2,0,0,0 - 1 vln., vla.,1 c.
—— SYMPHONY FOR STRINGS (IN 3 MOVTS.)
str.   23:30 Composer.
—— TENT MUSIC (SUITE) (IN 5 MOVTS.)
2(2nd alt. with picc.),*2,2,2 - 4,3,3,1 - perc.(3),xyl. - str.   13:30 Composer.

TERZAKIS, Dimitri
—— COSMOGRAM (1974)
2,2,3,3 - 4,2,2,1 - timp.,perc.(4) - hp. - str.   13:00 G. Schirmer.

TESSARINI, Carlo - THILDE, Jean
—— SONATA IN D
tpt. - str.   7:00 Presser.

TESSIER, Albert Denis
—— CELESTA SYMPHONY (1945) (IN 3 MOVTS.)
*3,*3,*3,*3 - 4,3,3,1 - timp.,perc.(4),bells,cel.,glock.,xyl. - hp. - pf. - str.   35:00 Composer.
—— SYMPHONIC CONCERTO (FOR PIANO AND ORCH.) (1947) (IN 3 MOVTS.)
*3,*3,*3,*3 - 4,3,3,1 - timp.,perc.(3),cel.,glock.,xyl. - hp. - pf. - str.(30,12,10,8)   38:00 Composer.

TEUSCHER, Hans
—— CONCERTO FOR VIOLIN AND ORCH.
2,*3,2,2 - 2,2,3,0 - timp. - str.   28:00 Möseler.

TGETTIS, Nicholas
—— CAPE ANNE SUITE (1967) (IN 5 MOVTS.)
str.   19:00 H. Branch.
—— CLOWNS (SYMPHONIC POEM, AFTER A PAINTING OF ROBERT OWEN) (1971)
*3,*3,*3,*3 - 4,2,3,1 - timp.,perc.(2) - str.   17:00 Composer.
—— INCIDENT AT SALEM BRIDGE, 1775 (CANTATA) (1975)
2,2,2,2 - 2,2,3,1 - timp.,perc.,bells - str.   55:00 Composer.
—— ISAIAH 53 (CANTATA) (FOR SOLO VOICES, SATB CHORUS AND ORCH.) (1971)
*3,3,2,2 - 2,2,3,1 - timp.,perc.(2) - str.   30:00 H. Branch.
—— RHAPSODY FOR PIANO AND ORCH. (1975)
2,2,2,2 - 0,0,0,0 - timp.,perc.(2) - pf. - str.   26:00 Composer.
—— SYMPHONIC FANTASY (1968)
*3,*3,*3,*3 - 4,2,3,1 - timp.,perc.(2) - hp. - str.   12:30 Composer.
—— THREE SONGS FOR SOPRANO AND ORCH. (1973) (Text: Anna Dellamonica)
2,*3,2,2 - 4,3,3,1 - timp. - hp. - str.   16:00 Composer.
—— THE VILLA (SYMPHONIC POEM, AFTER BYRON) (1970)
*3,*3,*3,*3, - 4,2,3,1 - timp.,perc.(2) - hp. - str.   9:00 Composer.

THATCHER, Howard
—— CONCERTO FOR CLARINET AND ORCH.
1,1,1,1 - 2,2,1,0 - timp. - hp. - str.   10:30 Composer.
—— CONCERTO FOR HORN AND ORCH.
2,2,2,2 - 3,2,3,0 - timp. - hp. - str.   12:00 Composer.
—— CONCERTO IN A FOR VIOLIN AND ORCH. (IN 3 MOVTS.)
*3,2,2,2 - 4,3,3,1 - timp.,perc.(2) - hp. - str.   25:00 J. Fischer.

—— ELEGY (FOR 4 CELLOS AND CHAMBER ORCH.)
1,1,2,1 - 2,2,0,0 - timp. - hp. - str.   10:00 Composer.
—— LYRIC SUITE (IN 5 MOVTS.)
*3,*3,*3,*3 - 4,3,3,1 - timp.,perc.(5) - hp. - str.   19:00 Composer.
—— SYMPHONIC FANTASY
*3,*3,*3,*3 - 4,3,3,1 - timp.,perc.(4) - str.   20:00 Composer.

THEODORAKIS, Mikis
—— L' AMOUR ET LA MORT (FOUR POEMS FOR MEDIUM VOICE AND STRINGS)
str.   11:00 Bo. Hawkes.
—— CINQ CHANSONS CRÉTOISES (FOR MIXED CHORUS AND ORCH.)
15:00 S.A.C.E.M.
—— IMAGES D'ANTIGONE (SUITE FROM THE BALLET "ANTIGONE")
3,2,2,2 - 4,3,3,1 - timp.,perc.,cel. - hp. - str.   27:00 Bo. Hawkes.
—— OEDIPUS TYRANNOS (ODE FOR STRINGS)
str.   10:00 Bo. Hawkes.
—— SUITE FOR ORCHESTRA AND PIANO (1960)
3,3,3,3 - 4,4,3,1 - timp.,cel. - hp. - pf. - str.   20:00 Salabert.
—— SUITE NO. 2 FOR ORCH.
3,2,2,2 - 4,3,3,1 - timp.,perc. - hp. - pf. - str.   15:00 Bo. Hawkes.

THIELE, Siegfried
—— CONCERTO FOR ORCH.
2,2,2,2 - 2,1,1,0 - str.   18:00 Tetra.
—— ELEUSIS 62 (PANTOMIME FOR ORCH.)
4,0,4,0 - 0,3,3,1 - timp.,perc. - 2 hp. - str.(0,0,1,1)   21:00 Tetra.
—— FUNERAL MUSIC FOR STRINGS
str.   7:00 Tetra.
—— INTRADA, CANTUS, TOCCATA
2,2,2,2 - 2,2,1,0 - timp.,perc. - str.   12:00 Tetra.
—— INTRODUCTION AND TOCCATA
3,3,3,3 - 4,3,3,1 - timp.,perc. - str.   Tetra.
—— MUSIC FOR ORCH.
3,3,3,3 - 4,3,3,1 - timp.,perc. - hp. - pf. - str.   Tetra.
—— SONATA FOR STRING QUARTET AND SMALL ORCH.
1,1,2,2 - 2,1,1,0 - timp.,perc. - hp. - str.(2,2,1,1)   17:00 Tetra.
—— SYMPHONY (IN 5 MOVTS.)
2,2,2,2 - 4,2,3,0 - timp.,perc. - pf. - str.   25:00 Tetra.

THIEME, Karl
—— MASCHERATA PICCOLA (FOR PIANO AND CHAMBER ORCH.)
1,0,1,1 - 2,1,0,0 - perc. - pf. - str.   14:00 SDMV.

THIERAC, Jacques
—— BALLAD ROMANTIQUE (FOR VIOLIN AND ORCH.)
3,2,2,2 - 2,2,2,0 - timp.,perc. - hp. - pf. - str.   14:00 EV.
—— SYMPHONIE NORMANDE
3,3,2,3 - 4,3,3,1 - timp.,perc.(3),cel.,xyl. - 2 hp. - pf. - str.
30:00 Eds. Fran.

THILMAN, Johannes Paul
—— BALLADE FOR ORCHESTRA
2,2,3,2 - 4,2,2,1 - timp.,perc. - hp. - str.   20:00 Tetra.
—— CONCERTO FOR VIOLIN AND ORCH., OP. 59
2,2,2,2 - 2,2,2,0 - str.   25:00 Tetra.
—— CONCERTO PICCOLO (FOR HARPSICHORD AND SMALL ORCH.)
1,0,2,0 - 0,0,0,0 - perc. - hpsc. - str.   12:00 Tetra.
—— DIVERTIMENTO
2,2,2,2 - 2,2,1,0 - timp.,perc. - str.   Tetra.
—— FESTIVAL OVERTURE, OP. 93
2,2,2,2 - 4,2,2,0 - timp. - str.   10:00 Tetra.
—— IMPULSE
2,3,3,2 - 2,2,2,1 - perc. - hp. - pf. - str.   Tetra.
—— LICHTENBERG CONCERTO (FOR VIOLIN AND STRING ORCH.)
str.   Tetra.
—— MUSIC FOR STRINGS (FOR VIOLINS AND CELLOS) (1960)
str.(no vlas.,no d.-b.)   Tetra.
—— PARTITA PICCOLA, OP. 43 (FOR CHAMBER ORCHESTRA)
0,1,1,2 - 2,1,1,0 - str.(no d.-b.)   12:00 Tetra.
—— SPIEL-SINFONIE
1,1,1,1 - 2,0,0,0 timp. - str.   10:00 Tetra.
—— SYMPHONIC INVENTIONS, OP. 77
2,2,3,2 - 3,2,2,1 - timp.,perc. - str.   22:00 Tetra.
—— SYMPHONIC OVERTURE, OP. 100 (HOMAGE TO ROBERT SCHUMANN)
2,2,2,2 - 4,2,2,0 - hp.(ad lib.) - str.   14:00 Tetra.

—— SYMPHONIC PROLOGUE, OP. 94
2,3,3,2 - 4,3,2,1 - timp.,perc. - str.   12:00 Tetra.
—— SYMPHONY NO. 4 IN D MINOR, OP. 64
2,2,2,2 - 3,2,2,1 - perc. - str.   25:00 Tetra.
—— SYMPHONY NO. 8 IN C MAJOR, OP. 101
2,2,2,2 - 4,2,2,0 - timp.,trgl. - str.   18:00 Tetra.

THIMAN, Eric H.
—— FITTLEWORTH FAIR (SUITE) (IN 4 MOVTS.)
Mills.
—— VARIATIONS ON A THEME OF ELGAR
str.   12:00 Novello.

THIRIET, Maurice
—— LA CHAMBRE NOIRE (BALLET) %
2,2,2,2 - 2,2,2,0 - timp.,perc.(3),cel.,glock.,xyl. - hp. - str.   Presser.
—— CONCERTO FOR FLUTE AND STRINGS
fl. - str.   14:00 Presser.
—— DANCERIES FRANÇAISES
str.   14:00 Presser.
—— LA LOCANDIERA (3-ACT OPERA-BOUFFE) %
2,2,2,2 - 2,2,1,0 - timp.,perc. - hp. - str.   150:00 Presser.
—— MUSIQUE DE COUR
2,2,2,2 - 2,2,2,0 - timp.,cymb. - hp. - hpsc.(alt. with pf.) - str.
18:00 Presser.
—— OEDIPUS REX (INCIDENTAL MUSIC) (Text: Jean Cocteau)
40:00 Henmar.
—— OTHELLO (LE MAURE DE VENISE) (BALLET) %
2,2,2,2 - 2,2,2,0 - timp.,perc.,cel. - hp. - pf. - str.   35:00 Presser.
—— PIÈCE PATHÉTIQUE
10:00 Henmar.
—— SIX CHANSONS DANS LE STYLE POPULAIRE FRANÇAIS (FOR SMALL ORCH.)
1,1,2,1 - 2,2,1,0 - perc. - hp. - str.   10:00 Salabert.
—— LES VISITEURS DU SOIR (SYMPHONIC SUITE FROM THE FILM)
19:00 Henmar.

THOMAS, Ambroise - CLARK, Tom
—— OVERTURE TO THE OPERA "RAYMOND"
G. Schirmer.

THOMAS, Ambroise - ROBERTS, Charles J.
—— OVERTURE TO "MIGNON"
C. Fischer.
—— OVERTURE TO "RAYMOND"
C. Fischer.

THOMAS, Ambroise - WINTER, Aubrey
—— OVERTURE TO "RAYMOND"
7:00 Bo. Hawkes.

THOMPSON, Randall
—— AMERICANA (A SEQUENCE FOR MIXED CHORUS AND ORCH.) (IN 5 MOVTS.)
2,0,2,0 - 2,2,0,0 - str.   E.C.Schirmer.
—— THE LAST WORDS OF DAVID (FOR MIXED CHORUS AND ORCH.)
*3,*3,*3,*3 - 4,3,3,1 - timp.,perc.(3) - hp. - str.   5:00 ECS.
—— THE NATIVITY ACCORDING TO ST. LUKE (A MUSICAL DRAMA IN 7 SCENES) %
1,1,1,1 - 1,1,0,0 - timp.,perc.(1),bells (church bells or recording) - org. - str.   92:15 E.C.Schirmer.
—— O VENUS, REGINA CNIDI PAPHIQUE (FOR MIXED CHORUS AND ORCH.) (Text: Horace)
1,0,2,0 - 0,0,0,0 - perc. - pf. - str.   G. Schirmer.
—— ODE TO THE VIRGINIAN VOYAGE (FOR CHORUS AND ORCH.) (IN 7 MOVTS.)
2(2nd alt. with picc.),2,2,2 - 4,2,3,1 - timp.,perc.(3) - hp. - str.
32:00 ECS.
—— PIERROT AND COTHURNUS (PRELUDE TO "ARIA DA CAPO")
2,*3,2,*3 - 4,2,0,0 - perc.(3) - hp. - str.   11:00 Composer.
—— THE PIPER AT THE GATES OF DAWN
3(3rd alt. with picc.),3(3rd alt. with Eng. hn.),E♭cl., *3,*4 - 4,3,3,1 - timp.,perc.(4) - pf. - 2 hp. - str.   14:00 Composer.
—— REQUIEM (FOR MIXED CHORUS AND STRINGS) (IN 5 MOVTS.)
str.   75:00 E.C.Schirmer.
—— SYMPHONY NO. 1 (IN 3 MOVTS.)
3(3rd alt. with picc.).2(2nd alt. with Eng.hn.),3(3rd alt. with b.-cl.).*3 - 4,3,3,1 - timp.,perc.(4) - hp. - org. - str.
24:00 C. Fischer.

—— SYMPHONY NO. 2 (IN 4 MOVTS.)
  3(3rd alt. with picc.),3(3rd alt. with Eng. hn.),3,3 - 4,3,3,1 -
  timp.,perc. - str.   28:00 C. Fischer.
—— SYMPHONY NO. 3 IN A MINOR (IN 4 MOVTS.)
  3(3rd alt. with picc.),3(3rd alt. with Eng. hn.),2,*3 - 4,3,3,1 -
  timp.,perc.(3) - str.   32:00 C. Fischer.
—— THE TESTAMENT OF FREEDOM (FOR MEN'S CHORUS
  AND ORCH.) (IN 4 MOVTS.)
  2,2,2,2 - 4,3,3,1 - timp.,perc.(4) - str.   25:00 ECS.
—— A TRIP TO NAHANT (FANTASY)
  2,2,2,2 - 4,2,3,0 - perc.,cel.,glock. - hp. - str.   26:00 C. Fischer.

THOMSON, Virgil
—— ACADIAN AIRS AND DANCES (SUITE NO. 2 FROM
  "LOUISIANA STORY")
  2(2nd alt. with picc.),2(2nd alt. with Eng. hn.),2(2nd alt. with
  b.-cl.),2 - 2,2,2,0 - perc.(2),xyl. - acc. - hp. - str.
                                                          14:00-15:00 G. Schirmer.
—— AUTUMN (CONCERTINO FOR HARP, STRINGS AND
  PERCUSSION)
  perc. - hp. - str.   8:00 G. Schirmer.
—— BAYOU (BALLET) % (ARRANGED FROM "ACADIAN AIRS
  AND DANCES")
  2,2,2,2 - 2,2,2,0 - perc.(2) - acc.(or pf.) - hp. - str.
                                                          14:00 G. Schirmer.
—— CANTABILE FOR STRINGS
  str.   4:30 G. Schirmer.
—— COLLECTED POEMS (FOR SOPRANO, BARITONE AND
  SMALL ORCH.) (Text: Kenneth Koch)
  1,1,1,1 - 0,1,0,0 - perc.(1) - pf. - str.   7:00 Composer.
—— CONCERTO FOR CELLO AND ORCH. (IN 3 MOVTS.)
  1(alt. with picc.),1(alt. with Eng. hn.)1(alt. with b.-cl.),1 - 4,2,0,0 -
  timp.,perc.(3),cel.,glock.,xyl. - hp. - str.   22:00 Ricordi.
—— CONCERTO FOR FLUTE, STRINGS, HARP AND
  PERCUSSION
  fl. - perc.(1),cel. - hp. - str.   15:00 Ricordi.
—— CROSSING BROOKLYN FERRY (FOR SATB CHORUS AND
  ORCH.) (Text: Walt Whitman)
  2,2,2,2 - 4,3,3,0 - timp.,perc. - hp. - str.   8:00 Bo. Hawkes.
—— DANCE IN PRAISE (GAUDEAMUS IGITUR) (LET US LIVE
  THEN, AND BE GLAD) (FOR SATB CHORUS AND ORCH.)
  (Engl. Text: John A. Symonds)
  2,2(2nd alt. with Eng.hn.),2,2 - 2,2,0,0 - perc.(3),glock.,xyl. - pf. -
  str.   10:00 G. Schirmer.
—— EIGHT PORTRAITS
  3(2 alt. with picc.),2(1 alt. with Eng.hn.),2,2 - 4,2,4,1 - timp.,perc.
  - str.   27:30 Southern.
—— ELECTION DAY (SUITE FROM THE FILM "TUESDAY IN
  NOVEMBER") (IN 5 MOVTS.)
  *2,1(alt. with Eng. hn.),2,1 - 2,2,2,0 - timp.,perc.(2), glock. - str.
                                                          16:30 AmMuCtr.
—— FANFARE FOR FRANCE (FOR BRASS AND PERCUSSION)
  4 hn.,3 tpt.,3 trb. - perc.(2)   Bo. Hawkes.
—— FANTASY (IN HOMAGE TO AN EARLIER ENGLAND) (IN 4
  MOVTS.)
  2,2(2nd alt. with Eng.hn.),2,2 - 4,2,3,0 - timp.,perc.(2) - str.
                                                          15:00 G. Schirmer.
—— FEAST OF LOVE (FOR BARITONE AND SMALL ORCH.)
  1,1,2,1 - 0,0,0,0 - perc. - hp. - str.   8:00 G. Schirmer.
—— FILLING STATION (BALLET SUITE)
  2(1 alt. with picc.),*1,*1,2 - 4,3,3,1 - timp.,perc.(2-4) - pf. - str.
                                                          20:00 Bo. Hawkes.
—— FIVE SONGS FROM WILLIAM BLAKE (FOR BARITONE
  AND ORCH.)
  1(alt. with picc.),1(alt. with Eng. hn.),2,2 - 4,2,3,1 - timp.,perc.(2)
  - hp. - str.   16:00 Ricordi.
—— FOUR SAINTS IN THREE ACTS (OPERA) %
  1,1,2,1 - 2,1,1,0 - perc.(2) - acc. - harm. - str.   90:00 Beekman.
—— FUGUE AND CHORALE ON "YANKEE DOODLE"
  1,1,3,1 - 2,3,3,0 - perc. - str.   5:00 G. Schirmer.
—— FUGUES AND CANTILENAS (SUITE FROM THE U.N. FILM
  "POWER AMONG MEN") (IN 8 MOVTS.)
  2(alt. with 2 picc.),*2,2 - 4,2,3,1 - timp.,perc.(2),bells,glock.,xyl. -
  hp. - str.   18:15 Bo. Hawkes.
—— THE HARVEST ACCORDING (BALLET) %
  2,2,2,2 - 4,2,3,1 - timp.,perc.(2) - hp. - str.   40:00 Ricordi.
—— JOURNEY TO AMERICA (SUITE FROM THE FILM)
  1(alt. with picc.),1(alt. with Eng.hn.),2(1 alt. with b.-cl.),0 -
  2-4,2,0,0 - perc.(1-2),glock. - str.   15:00 G. Schirmer.
—— LOUISIANA STORY (SUITE FROM THE FILM) (IN 4 MOVTS.)
  2(2nd. alt. with picc.),2(2nd alt. with Eng. hn.),2(2nd alt. with
  b.-cl.),2 - 4,2,3,1 - timp.,perc.(3-4),glock. - hp. - str.
                                                          17:00 G. Schirmer.

—— MASS FOR SOLO VOICE, WITH ORCH.
  2(2nd alt. with picc.),2(2nd alt. with Eng.hn.),2(2nd alt. with
  b.-cl.),2 - 2,2,1,0 - perc.(3),glock.,xyl. - hp. - str.
                                                          10:00 G. Schirmer.
—— MISSA PRO DEFUNCTIS (REQUIEM MASS)
  2(2nd alt. with picc.),3(3rd alt. with Eng.hn.),3(3rd alt. with
  b.-cl.),3 - 4,3,3,1 - timp.,perc.(3),cel.,glock. - hp. - str. 45:00 Gray.
—— THE MOTHER OF US ALL (OPERA) %
  1,1,2,1 - 2,2,1,0 - perc.(2),cel. - hp. - pf. - str.
                                                          120:00 G. Schirmer.
—— THE MOTHER OF US ALL: SUITE (IN 4 MOVTS.)
  2,2(2nd alt. with Eng. hn.),2(2nd alt. with b.-cl.),2 - 2,2,1,0 -
  timp.,perc.(2),cel.,glock.,xyl. - hp. - pf. - str.   20:00 G. Schirmer.
—— ONDINE (INCIDENTAL MUSIC) %
  fl. - perc.,cel. - hp. - str.   18:00 Ricordi.
—— THE PLOUGH THAT BROKE THE PLAINS (SUITE)
  1(alt. with picc.),1(alt. with Eng. hn.),2(alt. with b.-cl. and sax.),1 -
  2,2,2,0 - str. - timp.,perc.(1) - banjo - guit. - str.
                                                          15:00 G. Schirmer.
—— SEA PIECE WITH BIRDS
  3,3,3,3 - 4,3,3,0 - perc. - hp. - str.   5:00 G. Schirmer.
—— THE SEINE AT NIGHT
  *3,*3,*3,*3 - 4,3,3,1 - perc.(1),cel. - 2 hp. - str. 8:00 G. Schirmer.
—— SHIPWRECK AND LOVE SCENE FROM "DON JUAN" (FOR
  TENOR SOLO AND ORCH.)
  4,*4,4,4 - 4,4,4,1 - timp.,perc. - hp. - pf. - str.   14:00 Southern.
—— A SOLEMN MUSIC AND A JOYFUL FUGUE
  3(3rd alt. with picc.),3(3rd alt. with Eng.hn.),3(3rd alt. with
  b.-cl.),3(3rd alt. with c.-bn.) - 4,3,3,1 - timp.,perc.(2-3) - str.
                                                          12:00 G. Schirmer.
—— STABAT MATER (FOR SOPRANO AND STRINGS)
  str.   5:00 Bo. Hawkes.
—— SUITE FROM "THE RIVER" (IN 4 MOVTS.)
  1(alt. with picc.),1(alt. with Eng. hn.),1(alt. with b.-cl.),1 - 2,2,2,0 -
  timp. - banjo - str.   24:00 Southern.
—— SYMPHONY NO. 2 (IN 3 MOVTS.)
  3(3rd alt. with picc.),*3,3,3(3rd alt. with c.-bn.) - 4,2,3,1 -
  timp.,perc.(3-4) - str.   16:00 Leeds.
—— SYMPHONY NO. 3
  2,2,2,2 - 4,2,3,1 - perc. - hp. - str.   20:00 Bo. Hawkes.
—— SYMPHONY ON A HYMN TUNE (IN 4 MOVTS.)
  2(2nd alt. with picc.),2,2,2,c.-bn.(ad lib.) - 4,2,3,1 -
  timp.,perc.(3),glock. - str.   21:00 Southern.
—— WHEAT FIELD AT NOON
  3(3rd alt. with picc.),3(3rd alt. with Eng. hn.),3(3rd alt. with
  b.-cl.),3(3rd alt. with c.-bn.) - 4,3,3,0 - perc.(3-4),xyl. - hp. - pf. -
  str.   6:00 G. Schirmer.

THORARINSSON, Jon
—— OF LOVE AND DEATH (3 ENGLISH SONGS) (FOR
  BARITONE AND ORCH.) (Text: Christina Rosetti)
                                                          12:00 S.T.E.F.

THORARINSSON, Leifur
—— ORO (FOR SMALL ORCH.)
                                                          S.T.E.F.

THYBO, Leif
—— CONCERTO FOR CELLO AND ORCH.
                                                          K.O.D.A.
—— CONCERTO FOR FLUTE AND ORCH.
                                                          K.O.D.A.
—— CONCERTO FOR ORGAN AND ORCH.
                                                          K.O.D.A.
—— CONCERTO FOR PIANO AND ORCH. (1962)
  3,2,2,2 - 4,2,3,1 - timp.,perc. - pf. - str.   22:00 Henmar.
—— CONCERTO FOR VIOLA AND ORCH.
                                                          K.O.D.A.
—— CONCERTO FOR VIOLIN AND ORCH.
                                                          K.O.D.A.
—— CONCERTO PER ARCHI (1957)
  str.   Henmar.
—— THE IMMORTAL STORY (CHAMBER OPERA) %
  2,1,1,0 - cel. - hp. - str.(1,1,1,1)   70:00 G. Schirmer.
—— PROPHETIA (ORATORIO)
                                                          K.O.D.A.
—— TE DEUM (ORATORIO)
                                                          K.O.D.A.

THYRESTAM, Gunnar
—— CONCENTUS GRAVIS (1957) (IN 3 MOVTS.)
  timp. - org. - str.   16:00 S.T.I.M.

—— GAVLE-STAD (SUITE) (1969)
2,2,2,2 - 2,2,2,0 - timp.,perc.(3) - str.　　15:00 Fleisher.
—— MISTINGHÄLLA (1968)
1,1,1,1 - 1,0,0,0 - str.　　12:00 Fleisher.
—— MUSICA GRAVE (4 ORCHESTRAL PIECES) (1956)
1,1,2,1 - 2,2,0,0 - timp. - str.　　12:00 S.T.I.M.
—— OVERTURA BURLESCA (1959)
2,2,2,2 - 2,2,2,0 - timp.,perc.(4) - str.　　8:00 S.T.I.M.
—— SINFONIA OVERTURA (IN 1 MOVT.) (1958)
2,2,2,2 - 2,0,0,0 - timp. - str.　　12:00 S.T.I.M.
—— SUMMER PASTORALE (1969)
fl. - hp. - str.　　4:30 Fleisher.

TIBBITS, George Richard
—— ANTEDILUVIA, OP. 17 (1971)
str.　　28:00 J. Albert.
—— BESIDE THE RIVERING WATERS OF ...., OP. 15 (1969)
*3,2,3,*3 - 4,3,3,1 - timp.,perc.(3) - hp. - str.　　13:00 J. Albert.
—— I THOUGHT YOU WERE ALL GLITTERING WITH THE
NOBLEST OF CARRIAGE, OP. 12 (1969)
*3,2,3,*3 - 4,3,3,1 - timp.,perc.(3),cel. - hp. - str.　　10:00 J. Albert.
—— NEURONIS NEPHRONICUS AND HIS LOWLY QUEEN, OP. 9
(1968)
1,1,1,1 - 1,1,2,0 - str.　　13:00 J. Albert.
—— SERENADE, OP. 14 (1969)
1,1,1,1 - 1,1,1,0 - str.　　15:00 A.P.R.A.

TIENSUU, Jukka
—— LARGO (FOR STRINGS) (1971)
str.　　10:00 FinnMICtr.

TIESSEN, Heinz
—— CONCERTANTE VARIATIONS, OP. 60 (FOR PIANO AND
ORCH.)
2(2nd alt. with picc.),2,2,2 - 4,2,0,0 - timp.,perc.(4) - pf. - str.
23:00 Henmar.
—— HAMLET SUITE, OP. 30 (IN 3 MOVTS.)
3(3rd alt. with picc.),*3,3,*3 - 4,3,3,1 - timp.,perc.(5, incl. 2 on
timp.) - org.(ad lib.,or harm. ad lib.) - str.　　15:00 Henmar.
—— SYMPHONY, OP. 17 ("STIRB UND WERDE")
3(3rd alt. with picc.),*3,3,*3 - 6,3,3,1 - timp.,cymb. - hp. - str.
25:00 Henmar.
—— VISIONEN (TOTENTANZ-SUITE) (FOR VIOLIN AND ORCH.)
2,1,2,2 - 2,1,0,0 - timp.,perc. - str.　　16:00 Ries-Erler.
—— VORSPIEL ZU EINEM REVOLUTIONSDRAMA
2,2,2,3 - 4,2,3,1 - timp.,perc. - str.　　11:00 Ries-Erler.

TIETJENS, Paul
—— CARNIVAL (TONE POEM)
3(3rd alt. with picc.),3,3,3 - 4,3,3,1 - timp.,perc.(2) - str.
8:00 Composer.
—— RUSTIC SKETCHES (JUVENILE SUITE)
2,2,2,2 - 4,3,3,1 - timp.,perc.(2) - str.　　15:00 Composer.
—— SYMPHONY NO. 1 IN E MINOR (IN 3 MOVTS.)
3(2 alt. with 2 picc.),*3,3,3 - 4,3,3,1 - timp. - str.
25:00 Composer.
—— SYMPHONY NO. 2 IN B MINOR (IN 4 MOVTS.)
3(3rd alt. with picc.),3(3rd alt. with Eng. hn.),3,3 - 4,3,3,1 -
timp.,perc.(2) - str.　　40:00 Composer.
—— SYMPHONY NO. 3 IN A MINOR (IN 4 MOVTS.)
*4,*3,*4,*4 - 4,3,3,1 - timp.,perc.(2) - str.　　40:00 Composer.
—— SYMPHONY NO. 4 IN F MINOR
1. Allegro; 2. Andante; 3. Allegro molto; 4. Commodo
*4,*4,*4,*4 - 4,3,3,1 - timp.,perc.(2) - str.　　40:00 Composer.
—— A TOCCATA OF GALUPPI'S (SYMPHONIC POEM)
3(3rd alt. with picc.),3,3,3 - 4,3,3,1 - timp.,perc.(3) - pf. - str.
20:00 Composer.

TIKHOMIROV, Georgij V.
—— SYMPHONY
G. Schirmer.

TINIAKOW, Alexander
—— SUITE, OP. 8 (IN 4 MOVTS.)
3(1 alt. with picc.),*2,3,2 - 4,2,3,1 - timp.,perc. - str.
23:00 Henmar.

TIPTON, Julius R., III
—— JUDAS (2-ACT OPERA) % (1972) (Text: Composer)
2,2,2,1 - 4,3,2,1 - timp.,perc.(3),bells - 2 electric guitars (1 bass, 1
rhythm) - autoharp - hp. - org. - pf. - str.　　75:00 Composer.

—— VARIAZONI DA CHIESA (VARIATIONS ON A SACRED
SONG) (1964)
2(alt.with 2 picc.),2,2(2nd alt.with b.-cl.),*3 - 4,2,2,1 -
timp.,perc.(3),bell - 2 hp. - str.　　4:30 Composer.

TIRRO, Frank
—— THE MASQUE OF THE RED DEATH (BALLET) % (1960)
2(1 alt.with picc.),2,*3,2 - 4,3,3,1 - timp.,perc.(3) - pf. - str.
18:00 Composer.

TISCHHAUSER, Franz
—— CONCERTINO FOR PIANO AND SMALL ORCH.
cl.,bn. - perc. - pf. - str.　　13:00 S.U.I.S.A.
—— DER GEBURTSTAG DER INFANTIN (BALLET) %
*2,*2,*2,2 - 2,2,2,0 - timp.,perc.,cel. - hp. - pf. - str.
21:00 S.U.I.S.A.
—— KONTERTÄNZE FÜR ZWEI ORCHESTER
22:00 S.U.I.S.A.
—— SERENADE FOR STRINGS
str.　　19:00 S.U.I.S.A.

TISCHTSCHENKO, Boris
—— CONCERTO FOR PIANO AND ORCHESTRA
G. Schirmer.

TISNE, Antoine
—— ARBORESCENCES I (PROPHASE-ANAPHASE)
2,2,2,2 - 0,0,0,0 - perc.(4) - hp. - str.　　15:00 Presser.
—— ARBORESCENCES II (METAPHASE-TELOPHASE)
2,2,2,2, - 4,4,4,1 - perc.(4) - hp. - str.　　20:00 Presser.
—— CARACTÈRES
1,1,1,1 - 1,0,0,0 - str.(2,1,1,1)　　22:00 Presser.
—— CHANT DE L'AMOUR ET DE LA MORT
2,2,2,2 - 2,2,2,0 - timp.,perc.(5),cel. - hp. - pf. - str.　22:00 Presser.
—— CONCERTO FOR FLUTE AND STRINGS
fl. - str.　　28:00 Presser.
—— CONCERTO NO. 3 FOR PIANO AND ORCH.
2,2,2,2 - 2,2,2,0 - timp.,perc.(3) - hp. - pf. - str.　　23:00 Presser.
—— DIXTUOR (FOR WIND QUINTET AND STRING QUINTET)
1,1,1,1 - 1,0,0,0 - str.(2,1,1,1)　　18:00 Presser.
—— MOUVEMENTS SYMPHONIQUES
2,2,2,2 - 2,2,2,1 - timp.,perc.(4),cel. - hp. - pf. - str.　17:00 Presser.
—— SÉQUENCES POUR UN RITUEL
str.　　12:00 Presser.
—— SOLSTICES (FOR BASSOON AND STRINGS)
bn. - str.　　19:45 Presser.
—— SYMPHONIE POUR UN GRAND ORCHESTRE
2,2,2,3 - 4,3,3,1 - timp.,perc.(5) - hp. - pf. - str.　　18:00 Presser.

TITTEL, Gerhard
—— CONCERTO FOR VIOLIN AND ORCH.
2,2,0,0 - 0,3,3,0 - timp.,perc.(4, incl. 3 on timp.) - hp. - pf. - str.
18:00 Tetra.

TLIL, Amali
—— CONCERTO FOR VIOLA AND ORCH.
2,2,2,2 - 4,3,2,1 - timp.,perc. - hp. - str.　　25:30 EV.

TOCH, Ernst
—— AN MEIN VATERLAND, OP. 23 ("TO MY FATHERLAND")
(SYMPHONY) (FOR SOPRANO, BOYS' CHORUS, SATB
CHORUS, ORGAN AND ORCH.)
1. Allegro molto vivace; 2. Adagio molto espressivo; 3. Slowly
Composer.
—— CANTATA OF THE BITTER HERBS (FOR SOLOISTS,
CHORUS AND ORCH.)
1,1,2,0 - 1,2,1,0 - timp. - hp. - str.　　50:00 Belw-Mills.
—— THE CHINESE FLUTE, OP. 29 (CHAMBER SYMPHONY FOR
14 SOLO INSTS.)
1(alt. with picc.),0,*2,0 - timp.,perc.(5) - str.　　23:00 Belw-Mills.
—— CIRCUS (OVERTURE)
3(alt. with 3 picc.),2,2,2 - 3,3,3,1 - timp.,perc.(3),glock.,xyl. - pf. -
str.　　5:30 Mills.
—— COMEDY FOR ORCH., OP. 42
3,3,3,2 - 3,2,2,1 - perc.,cel. - hp. - str.　　15:00 Belw-Mills.
—— CONCERTO FOR CELLO AND CHAMBER ORCH., OP. 35
(1925) (IN 4 MOVTS.)
1,1,1,1 - 1,0,0,0 - timp.,perc. - str.　　25:00 Belw-Mills.
—— CONCERTO FOR PIANO AND ORCH., OP. 38
3,2,3,3 - 3,3,3,1 - perc. - org. - pf. - str.　　22:00 Belw-Mills.
—— CONCERTO NO. 2 FOR PIANO AND ORCH., OP. 61
(SYMPHONY FOR PIANO AND ORCH.) (1932) (IN 4 MOVTS.)
2,0,2,2 - 2,2,0,0 - timp.,perc. - pf. - str.　　26:00 Belw-Mills.

—— THE COVENANT (FOR NARRATOR AND ORCH.) (Sixth
movement from GENESIS SUITE)
 3(3rd alt. with picc.),2(2nd alt. with Eng. hn.),3,2 - 4,2,4,0 -
 timp.,perc.,cel.,glock.,vibra. - hp. - str. 4:30 Shilkret.

—— DIVERTIMENTO FOR WIND ORCH., OP. 39
 2,1,5,1 - 4,4,3,1 - perc. 8:00 Belw-Mills.

—— THE FAN ("DER FÄCHER"), OP. 51 (3-ACT OPERA) (1930) %
(Text: Ferdinand Lion)
 2,2,2,1 alto sax.(alt. with sopr.sax.),1 ten. sax. (alt. with b.-cl.),1 -
 2,2,3,1 - timp.,perc.,cel. - hp. - pf.(4-hands) - str. Belw-Mills.
 On Stage: 1 alto sax.(alt. with sopr. sax.) - tpt. - perc.(jazz) - banjo
 - pf. - 2 vln.,1 c.

—— FANAL, OP. 45 (BEACON) (FOR ORGAN AND ORCH.) (1928)
 3,2,3,3 - 4,4,3,1 - timp.,perc. - org. - str. 8:00 Belw-Mills.

—— FIVE PIECES FOR CHAMBER ORCH., OP. 33 (1924)
 2,0,*2,0 - 0,0,0,0 - perc. - str. Belw-Mills.

—— HYPERION (DRAMATIC PRELUDE), OP. 71
 2(1 alt. with picc.),*3,*3,*3 - 3,3,3,1 - timp.,perc.(4),xyl. - hp. - str.
   12:00 Leeds.

—— THE IDLE STROLLER (SUITE) (IN 6 MOVTS.)
 2,2,2,2 - 2,2,3,1 - perc.(3) - hp. - str. 27:00 Composer.

—— JEPTHA - RHAPSODIC POEM (SYMPHONY NO. 5) (1963) (IN
1 MOVT.)
 *3,2,2,2 - 3,3,3,0 - timp.,perc.,bells,glock.,vibra.,xyl. - hp. - str.
   21:00 Belw-Mills.

—— DAS KIRSCHBLÜTENFEST (MUSIK ZU KLABUNDS
SCHAUSPIEL (1928))
 timp.,perc. - harm. - str. 19:00 Belw-Mills.

—— THE LAST TALE ("DAS LETZTE MÄRCHEN"), OP. 88 (1-ACT
OPERA) % (Text: Melchior Lengyel; Engl. Text: Cornel Lengyel)
 3,2,2,2 - 3,3,3,0 - perc.,cel. - hp. - str. Belw-Mills.

—— LITTLE THEATRE SUITE, OP. 54
 3,2,3,2 - 2,2,3,1 - perc. - hp. - str. 16:00 Belw-Mills.

—— MINIATURE OVERTURE (1951)
 2,1,2,1 - 0,2,1,0 - perc. 3:00 Belw-Mills.

—— MOTLEY SUITE, OP. 48
 2,2,2,2 - 2,2,1,0 - perc. - pf. - str. 18:00 Belw-Mills.

—— MUSIC FOR ORCH. AND BARITONE, OP. 60
 2,2,E♭cl.,2,2 - 2,2,2,0 - timp. - str. 18:00 Belw-Mills.

—— NOTTURNO
 *3,2,2,2 - 2,2,3,0 - xyl. - hp. - str. (no d.-b) 11:00 Mills.

—— OVERTURE TO "THE FAN"
 2,0,1,1 - 1,1,0,0 - perc.(4) - str. 5:00 Belw-Mills.

—— OVERTURE TO "THE PRINCESS ON THE PEA"
 2,1,1, - 1,1,0,1 - timp.,perc.(2) - str. 8:00 Belw-Mills.

—— PARAPHRASE ON MOZART'S VARIATIONS OF "UNSER
DUMMER PÖBEL MEINT"(FOR PIANO AND ORCH.)
 2,2,2,2 - 2,2,0,0 - timp.,perc.(2) - pf. - str. 18:00 Belw-Mills.

—— PETER PAN, OP. 76 (A FAIRY TALE FOR ORCH.) (IN 3
MOVTS.)
 *3,2,E♭cl.,2,2 - 4,2,2,0 - timp.,perc.(5),glock., pressure hn., vibra.,
 xyl. - hp. - str. 15:00 Belw-Mills.

—— PHANTASTISCHE NACHTMUSIK, OP. 27
 3,2,2,2 - 4,2,3,0 - perc. - str. 20:00 T & J.

—— PINOCCHIO (A MERRY OVERTURE)
 *3,2,2,2 - 2,2,3,0 - timp.,perc.(2) - str. 7:00 AMP.

—— POEMS TO MARTHA, OP. 66 (FOR MEDIUM VOICE AND
STRINGS) (IN 4 MOVTS.)
 str. 20:00 Leeds.

—— THE PRINCESS ON THE PEA, OP. 43 ("DIE PRINZESSIN AUF
DER ERBSE") (1-ACT OPERA) (1927) % (Text: Benno Elkan;
Eng. Text: Marion Farquhar)
 2,1,1,1 - 1,1,0,0 - timp.,perc. - str. 48:00 Belw-Mills.

—— SHORT STORY
 2,2,2,2 - 2,2,0,0 - timp.,perc. - str. 5:00 Belw-Mills.

—— SINFONIETTA FOR STRINGS, OP. 96
 str. 17:00 Belw-Mills.

—— SINFONIETTA FOR WINDS AND PERCUSSION, OP. 97
 3,2,2,2 - 2,2,0,0 - timp.,perc.,glock.,vibra.,xyl. 12:00 Belw-Mills.

—— SMYPHONY NO. 6
   Belw-Mills.

—— SYMPHONY NO. 1, OP. 72 (IN 4 MOVTS.)
 3,3,3,2 - 3,3,3,1 - perc.,cel. - hp. - str. 40:00 Belw-Mills.

—— SYMPHONY NO. 2, OP. 73 (IN 4 MOVTS.)
 *3,*3,*3,2 - 3,3,3,1 - timp.,perc.(2) - 2 hp. - org. - pf.(4 hands) -
 str. 31:00 AMP.

—— SYMPHONY NO. 3, OP. 75 (IN 3 MOVTS.)
 3(3rd alt. with picc.),*3,E♭cl.,2,*3 - 4,4,3,1 - timp.,perc.(5-6),glass
 harmonica and glass balls (or vibra.),glock.,pressure hn.,xyl. -
 hammond org. - org. - str. 29:00 Mills.

—— SYMPHONY NO. 4 (IN 3 MOVTS.) (WITH SPEAKER AD LIB.)
 2(2nd alt. with picc.),2,2,2(2nd alt. with c.-bn.) - 2,2,2,0 -
 timp.,perc.(3),glock.,vibra.,xyl. - 1-2 hp. - str. 24:00 Mills.

—— SYMPHONY NO. 7
 2(2nd alt. with picc.),2,2,2 - 2,3,3,0 - timp.,perc. - str.
   26:00 Belw-Mills.

—— THREE PANTOMIMES
 2(2nd alt. with picc.),2,2,2 - 2,2,0,0 - timp.,perc.
   15:00 Belw-Mills.

—— DAS WASSER ("THE WATER"), OP, 53 (CANTATA) (FOR
SOLOISTS, NARR., CHORUS, AND SMALL ORCH.)
   25:00 Belw-Mills.

TOEBOSCH, Louis

—— ADAGIO AND ALLEGRO, OP. 69 (1958)
 0,0,0,0 - 2,2,3,0 - timp.,perc. - hp. - str. 11:00 Henmar.

—— AGENA, OP. 96 (1967) (IN 3 MOVTS.)
   19:00 Henmar.

—— ALLEGRO FOR ORGAN AND ORCH., OP. 20
 0,0,0,0 - 4,3,3,1 - timp. - org. - str. 14:00 Henmar.

—— CHANGEMENTS, OP. 98 (1968) (FOR ORGAN AND ORCH.)
(IN 4 MOVTS.)
   15:00 Henmar.

—— CHRISTMAS CANTATA, OP. 73 (KERSTCANTATE) (FOR
SOPRANO, MALE CHORUS AND ORCH.) (1959)
 2,3,3,2 - 2,2,2,0 - str. 12:00 Henmar.

—— CONCERTANTE OUVERTURE, OP. 56
 2,3,2,2 - 4,3,3,1 - timp.,perc.,cel. - hp. - str. 9:00 Henmar.

—— FEESTELIJKE OUVERTURE, OP. 74 (1960)
 2,2,2,2 - 4,3,2,1 - timp.,perc. - str. 9:00 Henmar.

—— PSALM 37, OP. 41 (FOR MALE CHORUS, WINDS AND
PERCUSSION) (1952) (Text: G. Smit)
 2,1,2,1 - 4,2,3,1 - timp.,perc. 19:00 Henmar.

—— PSALM 131 (FOR MALE CHORUS AND ORCH.), OP. 53
   24:00 Henmar.

—— SINFONIETTA NO. 1, OP. 65 (FOR MALE CHORUS AND
ORCH.) (1957)
 2,2,2,2 - 2,2,1,0 - timp. - pf. - str. 18:00 Henmar.

—— SINFONIETTA NO. 2, OP. 78 (1961)
 2,2,2,2 - 4,2,3,1 - timp.,perc. - str. 18:00 Henmar.

—— SUITE NO. 1, OP. 14
 2,3,2,2 - 4,2,3,1 - timp.,perc. - str. 13:00 Henmar.

—— SUITE NO. 2, OP. 30
 2,2,2,2 - 4,2,3,1 - timp.,perc. - str. 20:00 Henmar.

—— TEMA CON VARIAZIONI, OP. 27
 2,2,2,2 - 4,2,0,0 - timp.,perc. - pf. - str. 6:00 Henmar.

—— TRYPTIQUE
 3,3,3,3 - 4,3,3,1 - timp.,perc. - pf. - str. 11:00 Henmar.

—— VARIATIONS FOR ORCH., OP. 68 (1957)
 2,3,2,2 - 2,2,2,0 - timp.,perc.,xyl. - str. 8:00 Henmar.

TOESCHI, Carlo Giuseppe - BODART, Eugen

—— DIVERTIMENTO FOR FLUTE AND STRINGS
 fl. - str. 11:00 Mannheimer.

—— ENTR'ACTES
 0,2,0,0 - 2,0,0,0 - str. 9:00 Mannheimer.

TOESCHI, Carlo Giuseppe - CARSE, Adam

—— SYMPHONY IN D
 0,2,0,0 - 2,0,0,0 - str. 8:00 Galaxy.

TOFFOLETTI, Mario

—— INVENZIONE PER ARCHI
 str. 11:00 Bo. Hawkes.

TOFFOLETTI, Massimo

—— ALTERNANZE (1969)
 2,2,2,2 - 2,2,0,0 - timp.,perc.(2) - pf. - str. 14:00 MCA Music.

TOGNI, Camillo

—— CORO DI T. S. ELIOT, OP. 35 (FOR MIXED CHORUS AND
INSTRUMENTS)
 2 picc.,2 fl. - 2,0,1,1 - timp.,cel.,xyl. 10:30 Leeds.

—— FANTASIA CONCERTANTE
 fl. - str. 9:10 Leeds.

—— GESANG ZUR NACHT ("SONG TO THE NIGHT") (FOR
SOPRANO AND INSTRUMENTS) (Text: G. Trakl)
 1,1,1,1 - 1,0,0,0 - timp. - hp. - pf. - 2 vln. 10:00 Leeds.

—— HELIAN DI TRAKL (FOR SOPRANO AND CHAMBER
ORCH.) (Text: G. Trakl)
 2,1,1,0 - 1,1,1,1 - timp.,cel.,glock.,xyl. - guit. - pf. - str.
   16:00 Leeds.

TOLDI, Julius
—— VARIATIONS ON "YANKEE DOODLE" (WITH OPTIONAL
SPEAKER AND SATB CHORUS)
    3,3,2,2 - 4,4,3,1 - timp.,perc. - hp. - pf. - str.   6:30 C. Fischer.

TOLONEN, Jouko
—— ANDANTE AND RONDO ALLA BURLA (1948)
    2,2,2,2 - 4,2,1,0 - timp.,perc. - str.   10:00 FinnMICtr.
—— ANDANTE FOR PIANO AND STRINGS (1950)
    pf. - str.   7:00 FinnMICtr.
—— KAZAKH-TURKISH SUITE (1949)
    1,1,2,1 - 2,0,0,0 - perc. - str.   8:00 FinnMICtr.
—— SYMPHONY IN ONE MOVEMENT (1952)
    3,2,2,2 - 4,3,3,0 - timp. - str.   22:00 FinnMICtr.
—— THREE ARABESQUES (1953)
    3,2,2,2 - 4,2,2,0 - str.   10:00 FinnMICtr.
—— THREE SONGS BY GOETHE (FOR VOICE AND ORCH.)
(1958)
    2,2,2,0 - 4,0,2,0 - perc. - hp. - str.   7:00 FinnMICtr.

TOLVAS, Ilpo
—— CONCERTINO (1961)
    1,1,1,0 - 0,0,0,0 - str.   7:00 FinnMICtr.
—— FANTASY (1965)
    0,0,0,1 - 0,0,0,0 - timp.,perc.(6) - str.   8:00 FinnMICtr.
—— SUITE (1964)
    2,2,2,0 - 2,2,0,0 - timp.,perc.(4) - str.   12:00 FinnMICtr.

TOMASI, Henri
—— BALLADE FOR ALTO SAXOPHONE AND ORCH.
    2(2nd alt. with picc.),2(2nd alt. with Eng. hn.),2,alto sax.,2 -
    2,2,2,0 - timp.,perc.(3),glock. - hp. - str.   12:00 Baron.
—— CAPRICCIO FOR VIOLIN AND ORCH.
    15:00 EV.
—— CHANSONS DE GEISHAS (4 SONGS, FOR MEDIUM VOICE
AND ORCH.) (Text: R. Dumesnil)
    1,1,1,1 - 1,0,0,0 - perc.,cel. - hp. - str.   12:00 Presser.
—— CHANT POUR LE VIETNAM (SYMPHONIC POEM)
    3,2,2,2 - 4,3,3,1 - timp.,perc.(5) - 2 hp. - pf. - str.   15:00 Presser.
—— CINQ DANSES PROFANES ET SACRÉES (FOR SOLO WIND
INSTRUMENTS AND CHAMBER ORCH.)
    0,1,1,1 - 1,0,0,1(or trb. or B^{b}bass sax-hn.) -
    timp.,perc.,cel.,glock.,mar.,vibra.,xyl. - pf. - str.   11:30 Baron.
—— LE COLIBRI (CHAMBER OPERA) % (Text: F. Didelot)
    3,0,0,4 sax.,0 - 1,3,0,0 - perc.(3) - ondes Martenot - 2 pf. - str.
    30:00 Eds. Fran.
—— CONCERTINO EN E MAJOR, FOR FLUTE AND ORCH.
    1,2,2,2 - 2,2,1,0 - timp. - hp. - str.   13:00 Baron.
—— CONCERTO FOR ALTO SAXOPHONE AND ORCH.
    3,3,3,alto sax.,3 - 4,3,3,1 - timp.,perc.,glock.,xyl. - hp. - str.
    18:30 Baron.
—— CONCERTO FOR BASSOON AND STRING ORCH.
    bn. - hp.(or pf.) - str.   15:00 Baron.
—— CONCERTO FOR CELLO AND ORCH.
    2,2,2,2 - 2,2,0,0 - timp. - hp.(ad lib.) - str.   22:00 Henmar.
—— CONCERTO FOR CLARINET AND STRS.
    cl. - hp.(ad lib.) - str.   22:00 Baron.
—— CONCERTO FOR HORN AND ORCH.
    2,*2,2,2 - 1,1,0,0 - timp.,perc.,cel.(or pf.),glock.,xyl. - hp. - str.
    5:00 Baron.
—— CONCERTO FOR OBOE AND CHAMBER ORCH.
    0,1,1,1 - 0,0,0,0 - pf.(ad lib.) - str.   16:00 Baron.
    or:
    ob. - pf. - str.
—— CONCERTO FOR TROMBONE AND ORCH.
    14:00 Baron.
—— CONCERTO FOR TRUMPET AND ORCH.
    3,2,2,2 - 4,1,3,1 - timp.,perc.,cel.,xyl. - hp. - str.   15:30 Baron.
—— CONCERTO FOR VIOLA AND ORCH.
    2,2,2,2 - 2,2,0,0 - timp.,perc. - hp.(or pf.) - str.   22:00 Baron.
—— CONCERTO IN F, FOR FLUTE AND ORCH.
    2,2,2,2 - 4,3,3,0 - timp.,cel.(or pf.),glock.,xyl. - hp. - str.
    22:00 Baron.
—— CYRNOS (SYMPHONIC POEM)
    17:00 EV.
—— DASSINE (CHOREOGRAPHIC POEM) %
    105:00 EV.
—— DEUX DANSES CAMBODGIENNES
    1,1,0,1 - 2,1,0,0 - perc. - hp. - str.   8:30 EV.
—— DIVERTIMENTO CORSICA (FOR OBOE, CLARINET,
BASSOON AND STRINGS (IN 4 MOVTS.)
    0,1,1,1 - 0,0,0,0 - hp.(ad lib.) - str.   14:00 Baron.

—— DON JUAN DE MANARA (SUITE) (IN 4 MOVTS.)
    2,*2,2,2 - 2,2,1,0 - timp.,perc.,cel.,glock. - hp. - str.
    12:30 Lemoine.
—— FANFARES LITURGIQUES
    0,0,0,0 - 4,3,3-4,1 - perc.   15:30 Baron.
—— FÉERIE LAOTIENNE (SUITE) (IN 5 MOVTS.)
    3,2,3,5 sax.(ad lib.),3 - 4,4,3,1 - timp.,perc.,cel.,glock.,vibra.,2
    xyl.(or pf.) - 2 hp. - str.   20:00 Baron.
—— LES FOLIES MAZARGUAISES (SUITE PROVENÇALE GAIE)
(IN 5 MOVTS.)
    2,*2,2,2 - 4,2,3,1 - timp.,perc.,cel.,glock.,xyl. - hp.(or pf.) - str.
    16:30 Baron.
—— INTRODUCTION ET DANSE (FOR CLARINET OR ALTO
SAXOPHONE AND ORCH.)
    1,0,1(or alto sax.),0 - 0,0,0,0 - hp. - str.   5:00 Baron.
—— JABADAO (SYMPHONIC POEM)
    3,4-8,3,3 - 4,4,3,1 - timp.,perc.,bells,glock.,vibra.,xyl. - 2 hp. - str.
    16:00 Baron.
—— MIGUEL MAÑARA(4-ACT LYRIC DRAMA) % (Text:
Composer)
    3,3,3,3 - 4,3,3,1 d.-b.-trb.,1 - timp.,perc.,bells,cel.,glock.,xyl. - 2 hp.
    - ondes-Martenot(ad lib.) - str.   105:00 Baron.
—— NOA-NOA(3 TAHITIAN POEMS OF PAUL GAUGUIN) (FOR
TENOR OR BARITONE, SMALL MIXED CHORUS AND
ORCH.)
    3,1,*2,0 - 4,3,3,1 - timp.,perc.,mar.,vibra.,xyl. - hp. (or pf.) - str.
    15:00 Baron.
—— LES NOCES DE CENDRES (SUITE) (IN 5 MOVTS.)
    3,3,3,3 - 4,3,3,1 - timp.,perc.,glock.,xyl. - ondes-martenot - 1-2 hp.
    - str.   20:00 Baron.
—— LES NOCES DE CENDRES (2-ACT BALLET) %
    3,3,3,3 - 4,3,3,1 - timp.,perc.,bells,glock.,xyl. - 1-2 hp. -
    ondes-Martenot (ad lib.) - str.   30:00 Baron.
—— LA NUIT OBSCURE DE SAINT JEAN DE LA CROIX (POEME
SYMPHONIQUE) (WITH MEZZO-SOPRANO AND SMALL
CHORUS AD LIB.)
    3,3,3,alto sax.,3 - 4,3,3,1 - timp.,perc.,cel.,glock.,xyl. - hp. - str.
    25:00 Baron.
—— NUITS DE PROVENCE (ÉVOCATIONS SYMPHONIQUES (IN
5 MOVTS.)
    2,*2,2,2 - 4,2,3,1 - timp.,perc.,cel.,glock.,xyl. - hp. - str.
    18:00 Baron.
—— OBSESSIONS (FOR CELLO AND ORCH.)
    12:00 EV.
—— PETITE SUITE MEDIÉVALE (FOR CHAMBER ORCH.)
    1,0,0,1 - 2,1,1,0 - hp. - str.   6:00 EV.
—— PRINCESSE PAULINE (2-ACT OPERA-BUFFA) % (Text: F.
Diderot)
    3,2,2,2 - 4,3,3,1 - timp.,perc.,glock.,xyl. - hp. - pf.   120:00 Presser.
—— LE ROI DE LA NUIT (BALLET) %
    20:00 EV.
—— LA ROSIÈRE DU VILLAGE (SUITE) (IN 3 MOVTS.)
    3,2,2,*2 - 4,2,3,1 - timp.,perc.,cel.,glock.,xyl. - hp. - str.
    13:00 Baron.
—— SCÈNES MUNICIPALES (SUITE)
    7:00 Baron.
—— SINFONIETTA PROVENÇALE ("LE TOMBEAU DE
MIREILLE")
    *1(or Galoubet, a flute or recorder of Provence),1,0,1 - 1,0,0,0 -
    perc.,cel.(ad lib.),vibra,(ad lib.),xyl.(ad lib.) - pf. (or hpsc.) - str.
    18:00 Baron.
—— SYMPHONY IN C
    42:00 EV.
—— TAM-TAM (FOR ORCH)
    25:00 EV.
—— TROIS LETTRES DE MON MOULIN (IMAGES
PROVENÇALES, D'APRÈS ALPHONSE DAUDET)
    2,2(2nd alt. with Eng.hn.),2,2 - 4,3,3,0-1 -
    timp.,perc.,bells,cel.,glock.,vibra.,xyl. - hp. - str.   16:30 Baron.

TOMKINS, Thomas - FELLOWES, Edmund H.
—— FANTASIA
    str.   Galaxy.

TOMLINSON, Ernest
—— ENGLISH PAGEANT (SUITE) (IN 4 MOVTS.)
    3(3rd alt. with picc.),2,2,2 - 4,3,3,1 - timp.,perc. - hp. - str.
    17:00 Mills.
—— MINIATURE SUITE FOR STRINGS (IN 4 MOVTS.)
    pf. - str.   Mills.
—— RHAPSODY AND RONDO (FOR HORN AND ORCH.)
    3,2,2,2 - 4,3,3,1 - timp.,perc.(4),cel. - hp. - str.   11:00 Belw-Mills.
    or:

2,2,2,2 - 4,2,3,0 - timp.,perc.(3),cel. - hp. - str.
—— SUITE OF ENGLISH FOLK DANCES

Novello.

TOMLINSON, Geoffrey
—— ARTOS THE BEAR (CONCERT OVERTURE) (1966)
3,2,2,2 - 2,3,2,0 - timp.,perc. - str.   5:00 P.R.S.
—— DIVERTISSEMENT (1967)
cl. - str.   6:00 P.R.S.
—— DOUBLE CONCERTO, FOR TWO VIOLINS AND STRING
ORCH. (1969)
str.   19:00 P.R.S.
—— OCCASIONAL SUITE (1969)
2,2,2,2 - 4,3,2,1 - perc. - hp. - str.   16:00 P.R.S.
—— PRELUDE, ARIA AND SCHERZO (1968)
str.   12:00 P.R.S.

TOMMASINI, Vincenzo
—— CONCERTO FOR STRING ORCH.
str.   30:00 Leeds.

TONCITCH, Voya
—— CONCERTO FOR TRIANGLE AND ORCH.
        17:00 Modern.
—— DUBLIN, 1969
*1,0,0,1 - 0,0,1,0 - perc.,cel. - str.   3:00 Modern.

TONI, Alceo
—— IL CAVALIERE ROMANTICO (OVERTURE)
3,2,2,2 - 4,2,3,1 - timp.,perc. - str.   11:00 Bo. Hawkes.
—— DUE CANTICHE RELIGIOSE (FOR SOPRANO,
BARITONE,CHORUS AND ORCH.)
3,2,2,3 - 4,3,4,1 - timp. - str.   15:00 Bo. Hawkes.
—— I FANTOCCI RIBELLI (BALLETTO) %
3,2,2,2 - 4,2,3,1 - perc.,cel.,xyl. - hp. - str.   25:00 Bo. Hawkes.
—— INTRODUZIONE E SALTARELLO
3,2,2,3 - 4,4,4,0 - perc.cel. - hp. - pf. - str.   8:00 Bo. Hawkes.
—— NOTTURNO E TARANTELLA
4,3,3,3 - 4,3,2,1 - timp.,perc. - 1-2hp. - str.   9:00 Bo. Hawkes.
—— OVERTURE NO. 2
3,2,2,2 - 4,4,3,1 - timp.,perc. - str.   8:00 Bo. Hawkes.
—— OVERTURE NO. 3
3,2,2,2 - 4,3,4,0 - perc. - str.   6:00 Bo. Hawkes.
—— PARAFRASI SETTECENTESCA
ob. - str.   27:00 Bo. Hawkes.
—— QUADRETTI INFANTILI
2,2,2,3 - 4,3,3,1 - perc.,cel. - str.   14:00 Bo. Hawkes.
—— SINFONIA (IN 3 MOVTS.)
*3,2,2,2 - 4,3,3,1 - timp.,perc.,cel. - hp. - pf. - str.
        35:00 Bo. Hawkes.
—— SUITE IN FORMA DI VARIAZIONI
3,3,3,3 - 4,2,4,1 - timp.,perc.,cel. - 1-2hp. - str. 22:00 Bo. Hawkes.
—— TEMA, VARIAZIONI E FUGA
3,2,2,2 - 4,3,3,1 - timp.,perc.,cel. - hp. - str.   15:00 Bo. Hawkes.
—— TRE SALMI (FOR SOLO VOICES AND ORCH.)
3,3,2,3 - 4,2,3,1 - timp. - hp. - str.   20:00 Bo. Hawkes.

TON-THAT, Tiêt
—— AN TUONG
        Presser.
—— IMAGES LOINTAINES
2,2,2,2 - 4,2,2,0 - timp.,per.(4),cel. - hp. - str.   Presser.
—— MULTICORDI (FOR STRINGS)
str.   Presser.
—— NGU HANH II
3,3,3,3 - 4,3,3,1 - timp., perc.(5) - hp. - org. - pf.(alt. with cel.) -
str.   20:30 Presser.
—— VISION (FOR CELLO AND INSTRUMENTS)
2,2,2,2 - 1,1,1,0 - perc.(2) - pf. - c.   Presser.

TORELLI, Giuseppe - BERGER, Jean
—— SINFONIA CON DUE TROMBE
2 tpt. - hpsc. - str.   15:00 Mannheimer.

TORELLI, Giuseppe - OUBRADOUS, Fernand
—— CONCERTO IN D, FOR TRUMPET AND STRINGS
tpt. - str.   Presser.

TORELLI, Giuseppe - PAUMGARTNER
—— CONCERTO IN E MINOR, OP. 8, NO. 9 (FOR VIOLIN,
CEMBALO AND STRINGS)
cemb. - str.   20:00 Henmar.

TORELLI, Giuseppe - SANTI, Piero
—— CONCERTO IN C MAJOR, OP. 8, NO. 1 (FOR 2 VIOLINS
AND STRINGS)
hpsc. - str.   10:13 Leeds.
—— CONCERTO IN D MINOR, OP. 8, NO. 7 (FOR VIOLIN AND
STRINGS)
hpsc. - str.   9:20 Leeds.
—— CONCERTO IN E MAJOR, OP. 8, NO. 3 (FOR 2 VIOLINS
AND STRINGS)
hpsc. - str.   7:13 Leeds.
—— CONCERTO IN E MINOR, OP. 8, NO. 9 (FOR VIOLIN AND
STRINGS)
hpsc. - str.   14:25 Leeds.

TORELLI, Giuseppe - SCHERING
—— SINFONIA IN E MINOR, OP. 6, NO. 6 (FROM "CONCERTI
MUSICALI")
cemb. - str.   7:00 Henmar.

TORELLI, Giuseppe - THILDE, Jean
—— CONCERTO IN D MAJOR
tpt. - str.   6:00 Presser.

TORJUSSEN, Trygve
—— KARK (FOR TENOR, BASS, FEMALE CHORUS AND ORCH.)
(Text: Kristen Vigdal)
3,2,2,2 - 4,2,3,1 - timp.,perc. - hp. - str.   20:00 T.O.N.O.

TÖRNE, Bengt von
—— BALLAD, OP. 61
2,2,2,2 - 4,3,3,0 - timp. - str.   12:00 FinnMICtr.
—— CONCERTO FOR PIANO AND ORCH., OP. 44
2,2,2,2 - 4,3,3,0 - timp. - pf. - str.   32:00 FinnMICtr.
—— IN MODO ANTICO, OP. 51 (SUITE)
2,2,2,2 - 2,2,0,0 - timp. - str.   14:00 FinnMICtr.
—— INVOCATION, OP. 54
2,2,2,2 - 4,3,3,0 - timp. - str.   12:00 FinnMICtr.
—— OVERTURE, OP. 62 (REV. 1951)
2,2,2,2 - 4,3,3,0 - timp. - str.   10:00 FinnMICtr.
—— REQUIESCAT, OP. 26 (SUITE) (1941)
2,2,2,2 - 3,2,3,0 - timp. - str.   22:00 FinnMICtr.
—— SINFONIA DA CAMERA NO. 1 IN D MAJOR, OP. 64 (1951)
str.   24:00 FinnMICtr.
—— SINFONIETTA "BUCOLICA" IN D MAJOR, OP. 66
2,2,2,2 - 2,2,0,0 - timp. - str.   FinnMICtr.
—— SINFONIETTA NO. 1 IN G MINOR, OP. 33
2,2,2,2 - 2,2,0,0 - timp. - str.   21:00 FinnMICtr.
—— SINFONIETTA NO. 2 IN D MAJOR, OP. 62 (1951)
2,2,2,2 - 2,2,0,0 - timp. - str.   23:00 FinnMICtr.
—— SINFONIETTA NO. 3 IN D MAJOR
2,2,2,2 - 2,2,0,0 - timp. - str.   23:00 FinnMICtr.
—— SYMPHONY NO. 1 IN C MINOR, OP. 31 (1945)
2,2,2,2 - 4,3,3,0 - timp. - str.   34:00 FinnMICtr.
—— SYMPHONY NO. 2 IN A MINOR, OP. 50 (1939)
2,2,2,2 - 4,3,3,0 - timp. - str.   34:00 FinnMICtr.
—— SYMPHONY NO. 3 IN F SHARP MINOR, OP. 53 (1948)
2,2,2,2 - 4,3,3,0 - timp. - str.   36:00 FinnMICtr.
—— SYMPHONY NO. 4 IN G MINOR, OP. 60 (REV. 1954)
2,2,2,2 - 4,3,3,0 - timp. - str.   36:00 FinnMICtr.
—— SYMPHONY NO. 5 IN D MINOR
2,2,2,2 - 4,3,3,0 - timp.,perc. - str.   25:00 FinnMICtr.
—— SYMPHONY NO. 6 IN G MINOR, OP. 68 (1966)
2,2,2,2 - 4,3,3,0 - timp.,perc. - str.   23:00 FinnMICtr.

TORRÁ, Celia
—— SUITE FOR ORCH. (1938) (IN 3 MOVTS.)
3,2,2,2 - 2,2,2,0 - timp.,perc.,cel. - hp. - pf. - str.   19:00 Fleisher.

TORSTENSSON, Klas
—— INTO THE LAYERS (A REPORT FOR ORCH. AND TAPE)
(1974)
2,3,3,bar. sax.,2 - 4,3,3,1 - timp.,perc.(6) - tape-recorder - hpsc. -
pf. - str.   17:00 Fleisher.
—— UND EINE SPRINGFLUT ÜBERSCHWEMMT DEN STILLEN
HORIZONT (FOR STRING ORCH. AND STRING QUARTET)
(1974)
str.   12:00 Fleisher.

TORTANI, Lino
—— MUSIC FOR 12 INSTRUMENTS, NO. 2
3,0,0,3 sax.,o - 0,1,2,0 - timp.,gong. - hp.   5:00 Leeds.

TORTELIER, Paul
—— OFFRANDE
    str.   19:15 Presser.

TOSAR, Hector
—— SYMPHONY NO. 2 (FOR STRINGS)
    str.   25:00 Southern.
—— TE DEUM (FOR BASS, SATB CHORUS AND ORCH.)
    3,3,3,3 - 4,3,3,1 - timp.,perc. - hp. - pf. - str.   23:00 Bo. Hawkes.
—— TOCCATA
    3,3,3,3 - 4,4,3,1 - timp.,glock. - hp. - pf. - str.   6:00 F. Colombo.

TOUMA, Habib
—— REFLEXUS (FOR 12 SOLO STRINGS)
    6:00 IsMuPublns.

TOURNIER, Franz
—— IMAGES (FOR HARP AND STRINGS)
    hp. - str.   EV.
—— SYMPHONY NO. 5
    2,2,2,2 - 2,2,2,0 - timp.,perc.,cel. - str.   40:00 Presser.

TOURNIER, Marcel L.
—— FÉERIE (FOR HARP AND STRINGS)
    hp. - str.   10:00 Baron.

TOVEY, Donald Francis
—— CONCERTO IN C MAJOR FOR CELLO AND ORCH. (IN 4 MOVTS.)
    2(2nd alt. with picc.),2,2,2 - 4,2,3,0 - timp. - str.   60:00 Oxford.

TOWNSEND, Douglas
—— ADAGIO (FOR STRING ORCH.)
    str.   Composer.
—— CHAMBER CONCERTO NO. 2
    trb. - str.   16:00 Presser.
—— CHAMBER SYMPHONY
    Composer.
—— ODE TO LINCOLN (FOR CHAMBER ORCH.)
    Composer.

TOYAMA, Michiko
—— SUITE OF JAPANESE FOLK MUSIC
    1,1,1,1 - 1,0,0,0 - perc. - pf. - str.   C. Fischer.

TOYAMA, Yuzo
—— CONCERTO FOR VIOLIN AND ORCHESTRA
    2,2,2,2 - 4,3,3,1 - timp.,perc.(3) - hp. - str.   13:00 Presser.
—— DIVERTIMENTO
    2,2,2,2 - 2,2,2,0 - timp. - hp. - str.   14:00 Presser.
—— RHAPSODY
    3,2,2,2 - 4,3,3,1 - perc.(3) - hp. - str.   7:00 Presser.

TOZER
—— THE WAY OF THE CROSS
    1,0,2,0 - 0,0,1,0 - perc. - str.   Boston.

TRACK, Gerhard
—— OVERTURE "IN DULCI JUBILO"
    6:40 ProArtPubs.

TRAETTA, Tomaso - BONELLI
—— SINFONIA IN D MAJOR
    0,2,0,0 - 2,0,0,0 - str.   10:00 Henmar.

TRAJKOVIĆ, Vlastimir
—— CONCERTO FOR PIANO AND STRING ORCH.
    pf. - str.   22:00 MIC,Zagreb.
—— DUO FOR PIANO AND ORCH.
    3,3,3,3 - 4,4,3,1 - timp.,perc. - hp. - pf. - str.   9:00 MIC,Zagreb.
—— TEMPORA RETENTA (FOR HORN AND ORCH.)
    3,3,4,3 - 7,4,3,1 - timp.,perc.,xyl. - hp. - pf. - str.
    13:00 MIC,Zagreb.

TRANCHELL, Peter
—— ECLOGUE (1962)
    2,2,2,2 - 2,2,0,0 - timp.,perc. - hp.(ad lib.) - str.   20:00 P.R.S.
—— FESTIVE OVERTURE (1966)
    2,2,2,2 - 4,2,3,1 - timp. - str.   11:00 P.R.S.
—— IMAGES OF LOVE (1964)
    3,3,3,3 - 4,2,3,1 - timp.,perc.(6) - hp. - str.   40:00 P.R.S.
—— NOCTET (1964)
    4,0,0,0 - 0,2,2,0 - org. - 2 pf. - str.   11:00 P.R.S.

—— NOCTURNE (1961)
    0,0,1,0 - 0,1,0,0 - org. - 2 pf. - str.   17:00 P.R.S.
—— SCHERZETTO (1960)
    3,2,2,2 - 4,3,3,1 - timp.,perc.(6) - hp. - str.   11:00 P.R.S.

TRAPP, Max
—— SYMPHONY NO. 6 IN B FLAT MAJOR, OP. 45
    R.Eichmann.

TRAPP, Willy
—— CONCERTINO FOR STRINGS (WITH OPTIONAL WOODWINDS)
    str.   Hans Gerig.

TRAVIS, Roy
—— COLLAGE FOR ORCHESTRA (1968)
    *2,2(2nd alt.with Eng.hn.),2(2nd alt.with b.-cl.),2(2nd alt.with c.-bn.) - 4,2,3,1 - timp.,perc.(3),xyl. - str.   6:20 Oxford.
—— CONCERTO FOR PIANO AND ORCH. (1969) (IN 3 MOVTS.)
    2(2nd alt.with picc.),2,2,2(2nd alt. - c.-bn.) - 2,2,1,0 - timp. - pf. - str.   19:00 Oxford.
—— THE PASSION OF OEDIPUS (2-ACT OPERA) % (1965) (Text: Composer)
    2(2nd alt.with picc.),2(2nd alt.with Eng.hn.),2(2nd alt.with b.-cl.),*3 - 3,2,2,0 - timp.,perc.(3),xyl. - pf. - str.
    135:00 Composer.
—— SONGS AND EPILOGUES
    0,1(alt. with Eng.hn.),0,0 - 2,0,0,0 - str.   12:00 Oxford.
—— SYMPHONIC ALLEGRO (1951)
    *3,2(2nd alt. with Eng. hn.),2(2nd alt.with b.-cl.),*3 - 4,3,3,1 - timp.,perc.(3),xyl. - pf. - str.   8:00 Chappell.

TREBINSKY, Arkady
—— FATA MORGANA
    2 pf. - str.   13:00 Presser.
—— MUSIQUE POUR TOUS, OP. 26 (IN TWO MOVTS.)
    2,2,2,2 - 2,2,2,0 - timp.,perc.,xyl. - hp. - str.   7:30 Presser.
—— OUVERTURE DE "DON QUICHOTTE"
    2,2,2,2 - 2,2,2,1 - timp.,perc.(3) - hp. - str.   13:05 Presser.
—— SUITE FRANÇAISE
    str.   5:30 Presser.
—— SYMPHONIE SYNTHÉTIQUE ("TIME IS MONEY")
    2,2,2,2 - 3,3,3,0 - timp.,perc. - str.   10:00 Salabert.
—— SYMPHONY NO. 2, OP. 23 (FOR STRINGS)
    str.   27:00 Presser.
—— SYMPHONY NO. 3, OP. 27
    3,3,4,4 - 4,3,3,1 - timp.,perc.,cel.,xyl. - 2 hp. - str.   27:00 Presser.
—— TRIANON, OP. 3 (SUITE SYMPHONIQUE)
    2,2,2,2 - 2,2,1,0 - timp.,perc. - hp. - str.   18:00 Presser.

TREDE, Yngve Jan
—— CHAMBER CONCERTO NO. 2 (1971)
    alto recorder,ob. - hpsc. - str.   Henmar.
—— CONCERTO FOR HORN, ORGAN, PERCUSSION AND STRINGS
    hn. - perc. - org. - str.   Henmar.

TREGASKIS, Alan
—— SUITE FOR ORCH. (1974)
    *3,2,2-3,2 - 4,3,3,0 - timp.(2),cymb. - hp.   11:25 J. Albert.

TREHARNE, Bryceson
—— AGAIN IN UNISON WE STAND (FOR CHORUS AND ORCH.)
    *3,*3,2,*3 - 4,2,3,1 - timp.,cel. - hp. - str.   15:00 Boston.
—— THE BANSHEE (BALLAD) (FOR SOPRANO, BARITONE, CHORUS AND ORCH.)
    *3,*3,2,*3 - 4,2,3,1 - timp.,cel. - hp. - str.   35:00 Boston.
—— THE FALL OF JERUSALEM (FOR CHORUS AND ORCH.)
    *3,*3,2,*3 - 4,2,3,1 - timp.,cel. - hp. - str.   20:00 Boston.

TREMAIN, Ronald
—— ALLEGRO FOR STRINGS
    str.   8:00 A.P.R.A.
—— FIVE EPIGRAMS FOR 12 SOLO STRINGS
    str.   8:00 CanMusCtr.
—— SEVEN MEDIEVAL LYRICS (1974) (FOR TENOR, SATB CHORUS AND ORCH.)
    *3,*3,*3,*3 - 4,3,3,1 - timp.,perc. - hp. - str.   28:30 CanMusCtr.
—— THREE MYSTICAL SONGS (FOR MEZZO-SOPRANO AND STRING ORCH.)
    str.   12:00 A.P.R.A.

TREMBLOT DE LA CROIX, Francine
—— CONCERTO FOR ORGAN AND ORCH.
    3,3,3,3 - 4,3,3,1 - timp.,perc. - hp. - org. - str.   15:30 Presser.

TRENKNER, Werner
—— A LITTLE FESTIVAL MUSIC, OP. 29
    2(2nd alt. with picc.),2,2,2 - 2,2,3,0 - timp.,perc. - hp. - str.
        10:00 Henmar.
—— VARIATION AND FUGUE ON A ROMANTIC THEME, OP. 30
    2,2,2,2 - 4,2,3,0 - timp.,perc. - str.   16:00 Henmar.
—— VARIATIONEN-SUITE ÜBER EINE
LUMPENSAMMLERWEISE, OP. 27
    2(2nd alt. with picc.),2,2,2 - 4,2,1,0 - timp.,perc. - str.
        15:00 Henmar.
—— VARIATIONS AND FUGUE ON AN ORIGINAL THEME, OP.
2
    3,2,2,*3 - 4,2,3,0 - timp. - hp. - str.   26:00 Henmar.
—— VARIATIONS ON A THEME FROM "THE MAGIC FLUTE",
OP. 19
    2,2,2,2 - 2,2,0,0 - timp.,cel.(or pf.) - str.   12:00 Henmar.

TREXLER, Georg
—— CONCERTO FOR CELLO AND ORCH. (1952)
    2,3,2,3 - 2,2,0,0 - timp. - str.   18:00 Tetra.
—— CONCERTO FOR OBOE AND CHAMBER ORCH. (REVISED
VERSION)
    2,1,0,2 - 2,0,0,0 - timp. - str.   14:00 Tetra.
—— CONCERTO FOR ORCH. (1962)
    2,2,2,2 - 2,2,0,0 - timp.,perc. - str.   21:00 Tetra.
—— CONCERTO FOR PIANO AND ORCH.
    2,2,2,3 - 2,2,2,1 - timp.,perc. - pf. - str.   18:00 Tetra.
—— LITTLE SUITE (FOR CHAMBER ORCH.) (1954)
    1,1,1,1 - 2,0,0,0 - timp. - str.   15:00 Tetra.
—— METANOEITE (CANTATA, AFTER WERNER
BERGENGRUEN'S "DIES IRAE") (FOR BARITONE, MIXED
CHORUS AND ORCH.) (1951) (IN 9 MOVTS.)
    3,4,4,3 - 4,3,3,1 - timp.,perc. - str.   Tetra.
—— MUSIC FOR ORCHESTRA
    2,2,2,3 - 2,2,0,0 - timp. - str.   25:00 Tetra.
—— SINFONIA BREVE
    2,2,2,3 - 4,2,3,1 - timp.,perc. - str.   23:00 Tetra.
—— SYMPHONIC BURLESQUES (AFTER PAINTINGS OF PIETER
BRUEGHEL)
    3,3,2,3 - 2,2,3,1 - timp.,perc. - str.   25:00 Tetra.
—— THREE SONGS OF PAUL VERLAINE (FOR SOPRANO AND
ORCH.)
    1,2,2,2 - 2,0,0,0 - timp.,trgl. - str.   Tetra.

TRIFUNOVIĆ, Vitomir
—— ANTINOMIJA
    2,0,2,0 - 0,1,0,0 - timp.,perc.,vibra.,xyl. - str.   5:30 MIC,Zagreb.
—— ASOCIJACIJE
    3,3,3,3 - 4,3,3,0 - timp.,perc.,bells,vibra.,xyl. - str.
        15:00 MIC,Zagreb.
—— CONCERTO FOR VIOLIN AND ORCH.
    2,2,2,2 - 2,2,0,0 - timp.,perc.,vibra. - str.   18:00 MIC,Zagreb.
—— IMPULSI (FOR DOUBLE BASS AND ORCH.)
    2,2,2,2 - 2,2,0,0 - timp.,perc.,vibra. - str.   8:00 MIC,Zagreb.
—— PROSPECTS (CANTATA) (FOR SATB CHORUS AND ORCH.)
(1973)
    1,1,1,0 - 2,1,0,0 - timp.,perc.,vibra.,xyl. - str.   15:00 MIC,Zagreb.
—— SINTEZE 4
    3,3,3,3 - 4,3,3,1 - timp.,perc.,cel.,vibra.,xyl. - hp. - pf. - str.
        16:00 MIC,Zagreb.

TRINKHAUS, George J.
—— ARMIDA AND RINALDO (OVERTURE)
    *2,2,2,2 - 2,3,3,1 - timp.,perc.(2) - str.   7:00 Composer.
—— BLOW, WINDS, BLOW! (FROM "THE TEMPEST") (FOR
CHORUS AND ORCH.)
    *2,1,2,1 - 2,2,3,1 - timp. - str.   4:00 Composer.
—— CHAMBER SYMPHONY IN A (IN 3 MOVTS.)
    1,1,1,1 - 1,0,0,0 - pf. - str.   12:00 Composer.
—— THE FOUR WINDS (SUITE)
    1,1,2,1 - 2,2,1,0 - perc.(2) - str.   11:00 Witmark.
—— LAMENT
    1,1,2,1- 2,0,1,0 - timp.,perc. - str.   6:30 Composer.
—— THE MAY QUEEN (OVERTURE IN OLD ENGLISH STYLE)
    1,1,2,1 - 2,2,1,0 - timp.,perc.(2) - str.   4:30 Composer.
—— THE NIGHT VOICES (SUITE)
    1,1,2,1 - 2,2,1,0 - timp.,perc.(2) - str.   7:00 Witmark.
—— THE PHILOSOPHER (OVERTURE)
    *2,1,2,1 - 2,2,3,1 - timp.,perc.(2) - str.   5:00 Composer.

—— POÈME
    1,1,2,1 - 2,2,1,0 - timp. - hp. - str.   6:00 Composer.
—— POSTAGE STAMP SUITE
    *3,2,2,2 - 2,2,3,1 - timp.,perc.(3),bells,glock. - str.
        10:00 Composer.
—— RHAPSODY IN D FOR VIOLIN AND ORCH.
    1,1,2,1 - 2,2,1,0 - timp. - str.   5:00 Composer.
—— SINFONIETTA IN F (IN 3 MOVTS.)
    *3,2,2,2 - 2,2,3,1 - timp.,perc.(2) - str.   11:00 Composer.
—— SONATINA IN G IN OLDEN STYLE (FOR STRINGS) (IN 3
MOVTS.)
    str.   Composer.
—— SOUVENIR DE ROSSINI (OVERTURE IN CLASSICAL STYLE)
    1,1,2,1 - 2,2,1,0 - timp. - str.   6:00 Composer.
—— THE STREETS OF BAGDAD (SUITE)
    1,1,2,1 - 2,2,1,0 - perc.(2) - str.   8:00 Witmark.
—— SYMPHONY IN F (IN 3 MOVTS.)
    *2,2,2,2 - 2,2,3,1 - timp.,perc.(2) - hp. - str.   16:30 Composer.
—— THREE IMPRESSIONS OF THE ORIENT
    1,1,2,1 - 2,2,1,0 - perc.(1) - str.   12:30 Composer.
—— TRIBUTE TO A HERO
    *3,2,2,2 - 4,3,2,1 - timp.,perc. - hp. - str.   3:00 Composer.
—— VISTAS OF SWITZERLAND (IN 3 MOVTS.)
    *2,1,2,1 - 2,2,1,0 - timp.,perc.(2) - hp. - str.   11:00 Composer.

TROJAN, Václav
—— THE CAROUSEL (SUITE FROM THE OPERA)
    3,3,3,2 sax.,3 - 4,3,3,1 - timp.,perc.,cel. - hp. - str.
        24:00 Bo. Hawkes.
—— THE EMPEROR'S NIGHTINGALE (SUITE FROM THE FILM)
    3,3,3,3 - 4,3,3,1 - timp.,perc.,cel. - hp. - mandolin - pf. - str.
        33:00 Bo. Hawkes.

TROTSYUK, Bogdan J. A.
—— CONCERTO-SUITE (FOR PIANO, ORCH. AND JAZZ
ENSEMBLE)
    G. Schirmer.

TRUGLIO, Mario
—— INDIGO (1964) (IN 3 MOVTS.)
    2,2,*3,1 alto sax.,0 - 4,4,0,0 - perc. - str.   15:30 H. Branch.

TRUMBLE, Robert William
—— SUITE NO. 2 FROM "SATURN" (1972)
    0,0,0,0 - 4,2,3,1 - timp.,perc.(3) - str.(0,0,12,4)   10:30 A.P.R.A.
—— SYMPHONY NO. 1 (FOR ORCH. AND TAPE) (1975)
    28:00 A.P.R.A.

TRYTHALL, Richard
—— COMPOSITION FOR PIANO AND ORCHESTRA (1965) (IN 1
MOVT.)
    2(2nd alt. with picc.),2(2nd alt. with Eng.hn.),2(2nd alt. with
b.-cl.),2 - 4,2,3,0 - pf. - str.   10:00 Composer.
—— CONTINUUMS (1968)
    4(3rd alt.with picc.),*4,*4(3rd alt.with E♭cl.),*4 - 4,3,3,1 -
perc.,bells - str.   16:00 Composer.
—— COSTRUZIONE PER ORCHESTRA (CONSTRUCTION FOR
ORCH.) (1967)
    *3,3,3,*3 - 4,3,3,1 - timp.,perc.(3), vibra - pf. - str.
        7:00 Composer.
—— PENELOPE'S MONOLOGUE (CONCERT ARIA FOR
SOPRANO AND ORCH.) (1966) (Text: James Joyce)
    *3,*3,*3,2 - 4,3,3,1 - timp.,perc.(4) - str.   14:00 Composer.

TSCHAIKOVSKY, Peter I.
—— EUGENE ONEGIN (OPERA) % (Eng. Text: Henry Reese)
    G. Schirmer.
—— NUTCRACKER SUITE (WITH NEW VERSES BY OGDEN
NASH)
    L.B. & Co.

TSCHAIKOVSKY, Peter I. - BOGATYRYEV, Semyon
—— SYMPHONY NO. 7 IN E FLAT MAJOR
    3,2,2,2 - 4,2,3,1 - timp.,perc. - hp. - str.   37:23 G. Schirmer.

TSCHAIKOVSKY, Peter I. - BORCH, Gaston
—— EIGHTEEN-TWELVE OVERTURE
    C. Fischer.

TSCHAIKOVSKY, Peter I. - BUKETOFF, Igor
—— EIGHTEEN TWELVE, A FESTIVE OVERTURE (WITH CHORAL PARTS ADDED TO THE ORIGINAL ORCHESTRATION) (ARR. 1967)

16:30 SunburyLtd.

TSCHAIKOVSKY, Peter I. - DORATI, Antal
—— THE NUTCRACKER SUITE

A.P.R.A.

TSCHAIKOVSKY, Peter I. - DOUGLAS, Roy
—— THE SLEEPING BEAUTY: BALLET SUITE NO. 1

10:00 Bo. Hawkes.
—— THE SLEEPING BEAUTY: BALLET SUITE NO. 2

10:30 Bo. Hawkes.

TSCHAIKOVSKY, Peter I. - DUBENSKY, Arcady
—— THE NIGHT (FOR STRING QUARTET AND STRING ORCH.)
str.   6:00 Ricordi.

TSCHAIKOVSKY, Peter I. - FENNIMORE, Joseph
—— CONCERTO IN G MAJOR FOR PIANO AND ORCH. (REV. 1972)
2,2,2,2 - 4,2,3,0 - timp. - pf. - str.   24:00 Arranger.

TSCHAIKOVSKY, Peter I. - GOULD, Morton
—— THE SEASONS ("THE MONTHS")

G & C.

TSCHAIKOVSKY, Peter I. - GRANT, Francis H.
—— FANTASY SUITE (FROM "ALBUM FOR THE YOUNG")
str.   15:00 Studio PR.

TSCHAIKOVSKY, Peter I. - RAPÉE, Erno
—— SYMPHONIE ÉLÉGIAQUE (FROM THE TRIO, OP. 50)

C. Fischer.

TSCHAIKOVSKY, Peter I. - ROBERTS, Charles
—— LE LAC DES CYGNES (BALLET SUITE)

C. Fischer.
—— NUTCRACKER SUITE

C. Fischer.
—— SYMPHONY NO. 6 ("PATHÉTIQUE")

C. Fischer.

TSCHAIKOVSKY, Peter I. - SCHMID, Adolf
—— CAPRICCIO ITALIEN, OP. 45

16:00 Bo. Hawkes.
—— NUTCRACKER SUITE, OP. 71A: PART I (IN 4 MOVTS.)
10:30 Bo. Hawkes.
—— NUTCRACKER SUITE, OP. 71A: PART II (IN 4 MOVTS.)
15:30 Bo. Hawkes.
—— SYMPHONY NO. 6 IN B MINOR, OP. 74("PATHÉTIQUE")
46:30 Bo. Hawkes.

TSCHAIKOVSKY, Peter I. - SOPKIN, Henry
—— CAPRICCIO ITALIEN, OP. 45

C. Fischer.

TSCHAIKOVSKY, Peter I. - TANEIEFF, S.
—— ANDANTE AND FINALE FOR PIANO AND ORCH., OP. 79 (POSTHUMOUS)
3,2,2,2 - 4,2,3,1 - timp.,perc. - pf. - str.   18:30 Bo. Hawkes.

TSCHAIKOVSKY, Peter I. - WINTER, Aubrey
—— SWAN LAKE (BALLET SUITE)

22:00 Bo. Hawkes.

TSCHESNOKOFF
—— LES ESQUISSES DU JOUR
3,3,2,2 - 4,2,3,1 - timp.,perc.,cel. - hp. - str.   Bo. Hawkes.

TSOUYOPOULOS, Georges S.
—— THREE FRAGMENTS (FOR SATB CHORUS AND ORCH.)
(Text: Sophocles and Aeschylus)
3(1 alt. with picc.),*1,3(3rd alt. with b.-cl.),2 - 4,2,2,0 - timp.,perc.(4)   13:00 Modern.
—— TWO MADRIGALS (FOR WOMEN'S VOICES AND ENSEMBLE)
*2,*2,*1,1 - 0,2,1,0 - perc.(4),cel. - hp. - vln.,c.   10:00 Modern.

TUBB, Monte
—— ORCHESTRAMUSIC 72
3,2,3,alto sax.,bar. sax.,2 - 4,4,4,1 - timp.,perc.(5),cel. - guit.,b.-guit. - hp. - pf. - str.   Presser.

TUBIN, Eduard
—— CONCERTO FOR BALALAIKA AND ORCH. (1964)
2,2,2,2 - 4,3,3,0 - timp.,perc.(2) - balalaika - str.   23:00 S.T.I.M.
—— KRATT (SUITE FROM THE BALLET)
2,2,2,1 - 2,2,2,0 - timp.,perc. - hp. - pf. - str.   25:00 Fleisher.
—— MUSIC FOR STRINGS (1963)
str.   14:00 S.T.I.M.
—— SVIT ÖVER ESTNISKA DANSER (FOR VIOLIN AND ORCH.) (1974)
3,3,2,2 - 3,0,0,0 - timp.,perc.(3) - hp. - str.   Fleisher.
—— SYMPHONY NO. 06 (1954)
3,3,3,3 - 4,3,3,1 - timp.,perc.(5) - str.   36:00 S.T.I.M.
—— SYMPHONY NO. 07 (1958)
3,2,2,2 - 2,2,0,0 - timp. - str.   27:00 S.T.I.M.
—— SYMPHONY NO. 08 (1966)
2,2,2,2 - 4,3,3,1 - timp.,perc.(2) - str.   27:00 S.T.I.M.
—— SYMPHONY NO. 09 (SINFONIA SEMPLICE) (1969)
2,2,2,2 - 4,3,2,0 - timp. - str.   21:00 Fleisher.
—— SYMPHONY NO. 10 (1973)
3,3,2,2 - 4,2,3,1 - timp. - str.   27:00 Fleisher.

TUCCI, Terig
—— RAPSODIA IBERO-AMERICANA (FOR GUITAR, CHORUS AND ORCH.)

45:00 Dorian.

TULL, Fisher A., Jr.
—— CAPRICCIO FOR SMALL ORCH., OP. 23 (1966)
2,1,2,1 - 1,1,1,0 - timp. - pf. - str.   10:00 Bo. Hawkes.
—— CONCERTINO FOR OBOE AND STRINGS
ob. - str.   Bo. Hawkes.
—— CONCERTO FOR TRUMPET AND ORCH., OP. 16 (IN 3 MOVTS.)
2(2nd alt. with picc.),2,*3,2 - 4,3,3,1 - timp.,perc.(3-4), glock.,xyl. - pf. - str.   20:00 Bo. Hawkes.
—— CONCERTO NO 2 FOR TRUMPET AND ORCH.
16:00 Bo. Hawkes.
—— THE THREE MUSES (SUITE FOR ORCH.), OP. 15 (IN 3 MOVTS.)
2(2nd alt. with picc.),2,2,2 - 2,2,2,1 - timp.,perc.(3), xyl. - pf. - str.   10:00 Composer.

TUMA, Franz - SCHOENBERG, Arnold
—— SINFONIA

G. Schirmer.
—— SINFONIA A QUATTRO IN E MINOR (Edited by Rudolf Lück)
Hans Gerig.

TUNLEY, David Evatt
—— CONCERTO FOR CLARINET AND STRINGS (1966)
cl. - str.   17:00 A.P.R.A.

TUOMINEN, Harri
—— EPITAPH TO DON ANTONIO MACHADO (FOR MALE CHORUS AND ORCH.) (1972) (Text: Cèsar Lopoz)
2,2,2,2 - 2,2,3,1 - perc.,bells - str.   12:00 FinnMICtr.
—— THE HYADS (1971)
2,2,3,2 - 3,3,2,0 - timp.,perc.(3) - str.   21:00 FinnMICtr.
—— MUSIC FOR INSTRUMENTS (1969)
2,1,2,1 - 1,2,2,0 - timp. - str.   17:00 FinnMICtr.
—— MY LAI (1971) (FOR PERCUSSION AND STRINGS)
timp.,perc.(2) - str.   27:00 FinnMICtr.
—— SURREALISTIC PICTURES (SUITE) (1972)
2,2,2,2 - 2,2,2,1 - timp.,perc. - pf. - str.   16:00 FinnMICtr.

TURCHI, Guido
—— FIVE COMMENTS ON "THE BACCHAE" OF EURIPIDES
2(2nd alt. with picc.),2(2nd alt. with Eng. hn.),*3,2 - 4,2,2,1 - timp.,perc. - str.   20:00 Bo. Hawkes.
—— RAPSODIA (INTONAZIONI SULL 'INNO II DI NOVALIS) (FOR SOPRANO AND ORCH.) (1969)
1,0,2,0 - 1,0,0,0 - bells,mar.,vibra - hp. - pf. - str.
8:00 MCA Music.

TURENKOV, Aleksej
—— SUITE ON BYELO-RUSSIAN FOLK THEMES
3,2,2,sax.,2 - 4,3,3,1 - timp.,perc. - str.   G. Schirmer.

TURINA, Joaquín
—— DANZAS GITANAS (1934)
2,2,2,2 - 2,2,0,0 - perc. - pf. - str.   26:00 Salabert.
—— LA PROCESION DEL ROCIO (IN 2 MOVTS.)
3,3,3,3 - 4,3,3,1 - timp.,perc. - hp. - str.   9:00 Salabert.
—— SCENE ANDALOUSE (FOR VIOLA AND STRINGS)
pf. - str.   11:00 Salabert.

TURINI, Ferdinando - BORMIOLI, Piero
—— SONATA IN D MAJOR (IN 3 MOVTS.)
2,2,2,2 - 2,2,1,0 - timp. - str.   12:00 Bo. Hawkes.

TURINI, Ferdinando - KRANZ, Albert
—— DIVERTIMENTO
1,1,2,1 - 2,2,2,0 - timp. - str.   4:00 Henmar.

TURNER, Charles
—— DARK PASTORALE (Reduced Orch.)
1,1,1,0 - 1,1,0,0 - perc. - pf. - str.   15:00 G. Schirmer.
—— DARK PASTORALE
3,3,3,2 - 4,3,3,1 - timp.,perc. - hp. - str.   15:00 G. Schirmer.
—— ENCOUNTER
3,3,3,2 - 4,2,3,0 - timp.,perc. - hp. - str.   8:00 G. Schirmer.
—— THE MARRIAGE OF ORPHEUS
*3,1 alto fl.,*3,1 E^b cl.,*3,*3 - 4,3,3,1 - timp.,perc.,cel. - guit. - hp. - pf. - str.   18:00 G. Schirmer.

TURNER, Godfrey
—— FANFARE, CHORALE AND FINALE
0,0,0,0 - 4,3,3,1   9:00 Bo. Hawkes.

TURNER, Robert
—— CHAMBER CONCERTO FOR BASSOON AND 17 INSTRUMENTS (1973) (IN 4 MOVTS.)
0,2,0,1 - 2,0,0,0 - str.   16:00 CanMusCtr.
—— CONCERTO FOR TWO PIANOS AND ORCH. (1971) (IN 3 MOVTS.)
2(2nd alt. with picc.),2,2(2nd alt. with b.-cl.),2 - 4,3,3,1 - timp.,perc.(4) - 2pf. - str.   20:00 CanMusCtr.
—— EIDOLONS (1972) (TWELVE IMAGES FOR CHAMBER ORCH.)
2(2nd alt. with picc.),1,1,1 - 1,2,2,0 - timp.(4) - pf.(alt. with cel.) - str.   22:30 CanMusCtr.
—— FOUR SONGS (CYCLE FOR HIGH VOICE AND ORCH.) (1969) (Text: "Friday's Child" by Wilfred Watson)
2(2nd alt. with picc.),2(2nd alt. with Eng. hn.),2,2 - 2,2,2,0 - timp.,perc.,cel. - hp. - str.   10:25 CanMusCtr.
—— THREE EPISODES (1963)
*3,*3,*3,*3 - 4,2,3,1 - timp.,perc.(5) - pf.(alt. with cel.) - str.   15:40 CanMusCtr.
—— VARIATIONS ON "THE PRAIRIE SETTLER'S SONG" (1974)
2(2nd alt. with picc.),2,2,2 - 2,2,0,0 - timp. - str.   22:00 CanMusCtr.

TUROK, Paul
—— ASPECTS OF LINCOLN AND LIBERTY, OP. 20 (VARIATIONS ON AN AMERICAN SONG) (1958)
3(3rd alt. with picc.),*3,*3,2 - 4,3,3,1 - timp.,perc.(2) - hp. - str.   20:00 Composer.
—— CHARTRES WEST, OP. 25 (1968)
3(1 alt.with picc and 1 alt.with alto fl.),3(2 alt.with 2 Eng.hn.),1 E^b cl.,3(3rd alt.with b.-cl.),3(3rd alt.with cbn.) - 6,4,4,1 - timp.,perc.(5),bells,cel.,glock.,vibra.,xyl. - hp. - pf. - str.   8:00 Walkport.
—— CONCERTO FOR VIOLIN AND ORCH., OP. 6 (1953)
*3,*3,*3,2 - 4,2,3,1 - timp.,perc.(3),cel.,glock.,xyl. - hp. - str.   25:00 Seesaw.
—— FOUR STUDIES FOR ORCHESTRA, OP. 21, NO. 5 (1961) (WITH OPTIONAL SATB CHORUS)
2,2,2,2 - 2,2,2,0 - timp. - str.   5:00 Composer.
—— HOMAGE TO BACH, OP. 26 (1969) (IN 5 MOVTS.)
1,*2,*2,1 - 1,1,1,0 - timp.,perc.,vibra - str.(4,2,2,1)   20:00 Walkport.
—— LYRIC VARIATIONS FOR OBOE AND STRINGS, OP. 32 (1971)
ob. - str.   13:00 Walkport.
—— PRELUDE TO "RICHARD III" (1975)
2(1 alt. with picc.),2(1 alt. with Eng.hn.),2(1 alt. with b.-cl.),2 - 2,2,2,0 - timp.,perc.(3),bells,glock.,xyl. - hp. - str.   8:00 Walkport.
—— RICHARD III, OP. 41 (4-ACT OPERA) (1975) % (Text: Shakespeare)
2(1 alt. with picc.),2(1 alt. with Eng.hn.),2(1 alt. with b.-cl.),2 - 2,2,2,0 - timp.,perc.(3),bells,glock.,xyl.hp. - str.   120:00 Walkport.

—— SCENE: DOMESTIC, OP. 12 (1-ACT CHAMBER OPERA) % (1955) (Text: Composer)
1,1,1,1 - 1,1,0,0 - pf. - 2 c.,1 d.-b.   20:00 Composer.
—— SYMPHONY IN TWO MOVEMENTS, OP. 11 (1955)
1. Sinfonia; 2. Variations
*3,*3,*3,2 - 4,2,3,1 - timp.,perc.(3),cel.,vibra.,xyl. - pf. - str.   15:00 Seesaw.
—— TWO PIECES FOR ORCH. (FROM "RICHARD III")
2(1 alt. with picc.),2,2,2 - 4,2,3,1 - timp.,perc.(3),bells,glock.,xyl - hp. - str.   8:00 Walkport.
—— THE YOUNGEST BROTHER, OP. 4 (BALLET IN 2 PARTS) % (1952)
1,0,1,0 - 0,1,1,0 - per.(1) - pf. - str.(1,1,1,1)   20:00 Composer.

TURRIN, Joseph E.
—— ELEGY (FOR TRUMPET AND STRING ORCH.) (1971)
tpt. - str.   5:00 Composer.
—— THE STEADFAST TIN SOLDIER (FOR NARRATOR AND ORCH.) (1972) (Text: Hans Christian Anderson)
2(2nd alt.with picc.),2,*3,2 - 4,2,3,0 - perc.(2) - pf. - str.   15:00 Composer.

TURUNEN, Martti
—— CARRIER PIGEON, OP. 11 (SONGS FOR VOICE AND ORCH.) (Text: Einari Vuorela)
2,2,2,2 - 3,0,0,0 - timp. - hp. - str.   8:00 Westerlund.

TUTHILL, Burnet C.
—— BETHLEHEM (PASTORALE), OP. 8
3,*3,*2-*3(2nd alt. with basset hn. ad lib.),*3 - 4,3,3,1 - timp.,perc.(3) - hp.(ad lib.) - str.   6:00 C. Fischer.
—— BIG RIVER (FOR SOPRANO, WOMEN'S CHORUS AND ORCH.), OP. 22
2(1 alt. with picc.),*3,*3,2 - 4,3,3,1 - timp.,perc.(3) - hp. - str.   15:00 Composer.
—— COME SEVEN (RHAPSODY), OP. 11
2(1 alt. with picc.),2,*3,2 - 4,3,3,1 - timp.,perc.(4) - str.   5:00 Composer.
—— CONCERTO FOR CLARINET AND ORCH., OP. 28 (IN 3 MOVTS.)
2,2,1,2 - 2 hn. - str.   15:00 EV.
—— CONCERTO FOR DOUBLE BASS AND WIND ORCH.
2,2,2,2 - 4,2,3,0 - timp. - d.-b.   9:00 C. Fischer.
—— CONCERTO FOR TENOR SAXOPHONE AND ORCH., OP. 50
0,0,0,1 ten. sax.,0 - 0,3,3,0 - timp.,perc(1) - str. 20:00 SouthernTx.
—— CONCERTO FOR TROMBONE AND ORCH., OP. 54 (1967)
2(2nd alt.with picc.),2,2,2 - 4,3,1,0 - timp. - str.   12:00 EastonMuCo.
—— FLUTE SONG (FOR SMALL ORCH.)
1,0,0,0 - 2,0,0,0 - str.   6:00 SouthernTx.
—— LAURENTIA (SYMPHONIC POEM), OP. 16
2(1 alt. with picc.),*3,*3,d.-b. cl.(ad lib.),*3 - 4,3,3,3 ten. tu. (ad lib.),1 - timp.,perc.(3) - 2 hp. - str.   13:00 Composer.
—— NOCTURNE FOR FLUTE AND STRINGS, OP. 4
fl. - str.   4:30 Composer.
—— REQUIEM, OP. 38 (FOR SOLO VOICES, CHORUS, ORGAN AND ORCH.)
Eng.hn. - 3 trb. - org.- str.   30:00 Composer.
or:
0,*1,2,2 - 2,0,3,0 - str.
—— RHAPSODY FOR CLARINET AND CHAMBER ORCH., OP. 33
1,1,1,1 - 2,1,1,0 - timp. - str.   9:00 Composer.
—— SYMPHONY IN C, OP. 21 (IN 4 MOVTS.)
3,*3,*3,2 - 4,3,3,1 - timp.,perc.(2) - hp. - str.   22:00 Composer.

TUUKKANEN, Kalervo
—— CHRISTMAS SUITE, OP. 41 (FROM WALTER BAUER'S PLAY "THE LAST SHEPHERD") (1955) (IN 6 MOVTS.)
2,2,2,2 - 0,0,0,0 - timp. - hp. - str.   12:00 FinnMICtr.
—— CONCERTO FOR CELLO AND ORCH., OP. 27 (1946)
2,2,2,2 - 4,3,3,0 - timp. - str.   22:00 FinnMICtr.
—— CONCERTO NO. 1 FOR VIOLIN AND ORCH., OP. 20 (1943)
2,2,2,2 - 4,2,2,0 - timp. - str.   31:00 FinnMICtr.
—— CONCERTO NO. 2 FOR VIOLIN AND ORCH., OP. 45 (1956)
2,2,2,2 - 4,0,0,0 - timp. - hp. - str.   21:00 FinnMICtr.
—— HELLENIC FESTIVE MUSIC, OP. 39 (REV. 1967)
2,2,2,2 - 4,3,3,1 - timp. - str.   4:00 FinnMICtr.
—— INDUMATI, OP. 55 (OPERA) % (1962) (Text: Composer)
2,2,2,2 - 4,2,2,0 - timp.,perc.(5),mar. - hp. - str. 50:00 FinnMICtr.
—— THE MINSTRELS, OP. 48 (1955)
2,2,2,2 - 4,3,3,0 - timp.,perc.(3),xyl. - str.   12:00 FinnMICtr.

—— OVERTURE TO TEUVO PAKKALA'S "THE TIMBER
FLOATERS", OP. 1 (REV. 1956)
    2,2,2,2 - 3,2,1,0 - timp. - hp. - str.   6:00 FinnMICtr.
—— SERENATA GIOCOSA, OP. 4 (1937)
    2,2,2,2 - 2,2,1,0 - timp. - str.   22:00 FinnMICtr.
—— SINFONIETTA, OP. 33 (FOR SATB CHORUS AND ORCH.)
(1948) (Text: Aale Tynni)
    2,2,2,2 - 4,3,3,1 - timp.,perc. - str.   15:00 FinnMICtr.
—— SONG OF THE HIGHLANDS, OP. 40 (1953)
    2,2,2,2 - 4,3,3,0 - timp.,perc. - hp. - str.   17:00 FinnMICtr.
—— SYMPHONIC FANTASY, OP. 6 (1939)
    2,2,2,2 - 4,3,3,0 - timp. - str.   26:00 FinnMICtr.
—— SYMPHONY NO. 1, OP. 24 (REV. 1949)
    2,2,2,2 - 4,3,3,1 - timp.,perc. - str.   32:00 FinnMICtr.
—— SYMPHONY NO. 2, OP. 34 (REV. 1949)
    2,2,2,2 - 4,3,3,1 - timp.,perc.(3) - hp. - pf. - str. 20:00 FinnMICtr.
—— SYMPHONY NO. 3, OP. 36 ("THE SEA") (FOR SOPRANO,
TENOR, SATB CHORUS AND ORCH.) (REV. 1953) (Text:
Composer)
    2,2,2,2 - 5,3,3,1 - timp.,perc.(3) - hp. - pf. - str. 34:00 FinnMICtr.
—— SYMPHONY NO. 4, OP. 52 (1958)
    2,2,2,2 - 4,3,3,0 - timp.,perc. - str.   27:00 FinnMICtr.
—— SYMPHONY NO. 5, OP. 54 (1961)
    2,2,2,2 - 4,3,3,0 - timp.,perc. - hp. - str.   18:00 FinnMICtr.
—— THE TALE OF THE PALLID MAIDEN, OP. 2 (1936)
    3,3,3,3 - 4,3,3,1 - timp. - hp. - str.   13:00 FinnMICtr.
—— TEMPUS FESTUM, OP. 53 (1958)
    str.   7:00 FinnMICtr.

TUXEN-BANG, Carlos
—— ABYSSUS
    3,3,3,1 sax.,3 - 4,3,3,1 - timp.,perc.(7) - str. 30:00 Bo. Hawkes.
—— CONCERTO FOR FOUR TRUMPETS AND STRINGS
    4 tpt. - str.   17:00 Bo. Hawkes.
—— SYMPHONIC BALLAD (FOR ORCH.)
    3,3,3,3 - 4,3,3,1 - timp.,perc. - 2 hp. - str.   13:00 Bo. Hawkes.

TVEITT, Geirr
—— BIRGINGU (BALLET IN I ACT) %
    3,2,3,2 - 4,4,3,1 - timp.,perc.,cel. - hp. - str.   18:00 T.O.N.O.
—— CONCERTO FOR STRING QUARTET AND ORCH. (IN 3
MOVTS.)
    2,2,2,2 - 3,3,2,1 - str.   25:00 T.O.N.O.
—— CONCERTO FOR VIOLIN AND ORCH. (IN 3 MOVTS.)
    2,2,2,2 - 2,2,2,2 - perc. - str.   25:00 T.O.N.O.
—— CONCERTO NO. 1 FOR HARDANGER-FIDDLE AND ORCH.,
OP. 163
    2,2,2,2 - 4,3,3,1 - timp.,perc.,cel. - hp. - hardanger fiddle - str.
      30:00 T.O.N.O.
—— CONCERTO NO. 1 FOR PIANO AND ORCH., OP. 5 (IN 3
MOVTS.)
    2,2,2,2 - 4,4,3,1 - timp.,perc. - pf. - str.   25:00 T.O.N.O.
—— CONCERTO NO. 2 FOR HARDANGER-FIDDLE AND ORCH.,
OP. 252 ("THREE FJORDS") (IN 3 MOVTS.)
    2,1,2,1 - 2,2,2,0 - timp.,perc.,cel.,xyl. - hardanger fiddle - str.
      18:00 T.O.N.O.
—— CONCERTO NO. 2 FOR HARP AND ORCH., OP. 170
    3,2,3,2 - 4,3,3,1 - timp.,perc.,cel. - hp. - str.   T.O.N.O.
—— CONCERTO NO. 2 FOR PIANO AND ORCH., OP. 11 (IN 1
MOVT.)
    3,3,3,3 - 4,4,3,1 - timp.,perc.,cel. - hp. - pf. - str. 18:00 T.O.N.O.
—— CONCERTO NO. 3 FOR PIANO AND ORCH. ("HOMAGE TO
BRAHMS") (IN 3 MOVTS.)
    2,2,2,2 - 4,3,3,1 - timp.,perc. - pf. - str.   30:00 T.O.N.O.
—— CONCERTO NO. 4 FOR PIANO AND ORCH. ("NORTHERN
LIGHTS") (IN 3 MOVTS.)
    3,3,3,3 - 4,3,3,1 -timp., perc., cel. - hp. - pf. - str. 35:00 T.O.N..O.
—— CONCERTO NO. 5 FOR PIANO AND ORCH., OP. 156 (IN 3
MOVTS.)
    2,2,2,2 - 4,3,3,1 - timp., perc.,cel. - hp, - pf. - str. 30:00 T.O.N.O.
—— CONCERTO NO. 6 FOR PIANO AND ORCH.
    T.O.N.O.
—— THE DARK NIGHT HAS PASSED (DEN MØRKE NATT
FORGANGEN ER) (FOR SOLO VOICE, CHORUS AND
ORCH.) (Text: Johan Falkberget)
    T.O.N.O.
—— DRAGAREDOKKO (5-ACT OPERA) %
    3,3,3,3 - 4,3,2,1 - timp.,perc.,cel. - hp. - str.   150:00 T.O.N.O.
—— THE DREAMS OF BALDUR (BALDURS DRAUMAR)
(BALLET) (WITH SOPRANO, TENOR AND BASS) %
    3(incl. alto fl.),2,3,3 - 3,3,2,1 -timp.,perc.,cel. - hp. - pf. - str.
      150:00 T.O.N.O.

—— THE DREAMS OF BALDUR (BALDURS DRAUMAR):
CONCERT VERSION
    3,2,3,3 - 3,3,2,1 - timp.,perc.,cel. - hp. - pf. - str. 25:00 T.O.N.O.
—— EIGHT DANCES FOR ORCH.
    3,2,3,2 - 3,3,2,1 - timp.,perc.,cel. - hp. - pf. - str. 50:00 T.O.N.O.
—— EIGHT SONGS TO TEXTS OF ANDERS HOUDEN (FOR
VOICE AND ORCH.)
    T.O.N.O.
—— EIGHT SONGS TO TEXTS OF JOHAN FALKBERGET (FOR
VOICE AND ORCH.)
    T.O.N.O.
—— FROM A TRAVEL-DIARY (FRA EN REISEDAGBOK) (IN 7
MOVTS.)
    22:00 T.O.N.O.
—— THE HOUSEHOLD DEITY (HUSGUDEN) (FOR CHAMBER
ORCH.)
    17:00 T.O.N.O.
—— HUNDRAD HARDINGTONER (100 FOLKTUNES FROM
HARDANGER): SUITE NO. 1, OP. 151
    2,2,2,2 - 4,3,3,1 - timp.,perc.(4),cel. - hp. - str. 30:00 G. Schirmer.
—— INCIDENTAL MUSIC TO THE PLAY "JONSOKNATT" (FOR
ALTO, BASS, AND SMALL ORCH.)
    1,1,1,1 - 1,1,0,0 - pf. - str.   45:00 T.O.N.O.
—— INTRATA ACADEMICA
    12:00 T.O.N.O.
—— JEPPE, OP. 250 (THREE-ACT OPERA, AFTER LUDVIG
HOLBERG'S "JEPPE PÅ BJERGET") % (Text: Composer)
    2,2,2,2 - 4,4,3,1 - timp.,perc. - hp. - pf. - str.   T.O.N.O.
—— NINE SONGS TO TEXTS OF ARNULF ØVERLAND (FOR
VOICE AND ORCH.)
    28:00 T.O.N.O.
—— THE NIXIE (NØKKEN)
    14:00 T.O.N.O.
—— NORTHWEST-SOUTH-NORTHEAST-NORTH (4-ACT OPERA)
%
    3,3,3,3 - 8,6,4,3 - timp.,perc.,cel. - hp. - 2 pf. - str.
      90:00 T.O.N.O.
—— ONE HUNDRED FOLK TUNES FROM HARDANGER, OP.
151: SUITE NO. 1 (NOS. 1-15)
    2,2,2,2 - 4,3,3,1 - timp.,perc.,cel. - hp. - str. 29:00 G. Schirmer.
—— ONE HUNDRED FOLK TUNES FROM HARDANGER, OP.
151: SUITE NO. 2 (NOS. 16-30) (FIFTEEN FJELLSTEV)
    2,2,2,2 - 4,4,3,1 - timp.,perc.cel. - hp. - str.   33:00 T.O.N.O.
—— ONE HUNDRED FOLK TUNES FROM HARDANGER, OP.
151: SUITE NO. 3 (NOS. 31-45)
    T.O.N.O.
—— ONE HUNDRED FOLK TUNES FROM HARDANGER, OP.
151: SUITE NO. 4 (NOS. 46-60)
    3,2,3,3 - 4,3,3,1 - timp.,perc.,cel. - hp. - pf. - str.   T.O.N.O.
—— ONE HUNDRED FOLK TUNES FROM HARDANGER, OP.
151: SUITE NO. 5 (NOS. 61-75) (TROLLTONAR)
    36:00 T.O.N.O.
—— PRILLAR (IN 3 MOVTS.)
    2,2,2,2 - 6,4,3,1 - timp.,perc. - str.   25:00 T.O.N.O.
—— SIX SONGS TO TEXTS OF PER SIVLE (FOR VOICE AND
ORCH.)
    T.O.N.O.
—— SKALDASPILLIRS KVAD: "HÅKONARMÅL" (FOR SOPRANO,
TENOR, BASS, MIXED CHORUS AND ORCH.)
    2,2,2,2 - 4,3,3,1 - timp.,perc. - hp. - str.   43:00 T.O.N.O.
—— SYMPHONY NO. 1, OP. 183
    35:00 T.O.N.O.
—— THREE SONGS TO TEXTS OF KNUT HORVEI (FOR VOICE
AND ORCH.)
    T.O.N.O.
—— VARIATIONS FOR TWO PIANOS AND ORCH.
    2,2,2,2 - 4,2,2,0 - timp.,perc. - 2 pf. - str.   25:00 T.O.N.O.

TWOMBLY, Mary Lynn
—— ALICE IN WONDERLAND (WITH OPTIONAL NARRATOR)
(1960)
    2(2nd alt.with picc.),2,2(2nd alt.with b.-cl.),2 - 3,2,1,1 -
    timp.,perc.,glock. - hp. - pf.(regular, alt.with out-of-tune or
    "honky-tonk" pf.) - str.   34:00 Composer.
—— THE ETERNAL WORD (FOR SOPRANO, TENOR,
NARRATOR, SATB CHORUS AND ORCH) (IN 3 MOVTS)
(1956) (Text: Biblical)
    3(3rd alt.with picc.),*3,*3,*3 - 4,3,3,1 - timp.,perc.(2) - hp. - str.
      27:00 Composer.

TYER, Norma Phyllis
—— FRANZ JOSEF: IMPRESSIONS OF A GLACIER (1971)
3,3,3,3 - 4,3,3,0 - timp.,perc.,glock.,vibra. - pf. - str.
16:20 A.P.R.A.

TZINCOCA, Remus
—— BALLAD FOR STRINGS
str.   10:00 C.A.P.A.C.
—— DOINA (TONE POEM) (FOR CHORUS AND ORCH.)
12:00 C.A.P.A.C.
—— MA TERRE (TONE POEM)
15:00 C.A.P.A.C.

U

UBER, David
—— GRAND ANTIPHONY, OP. 81 (FOR ORGAN AND BRASS
CHOIR) (1969) (IN 3 MOVTS.)
0,0,0,0 - 3,3,2,1 - org.   14:00 Composer.

UDDÉN, Åke
—— COMEDY OVERTURE
2,2,2,2 - 2,2,1,0 - timp. - str.   4:30 S.T.I.M.
—— SUITE (IN 3 MOVTS.)
2,2,2,2 - 2,2,0,0 - timp. - str.   13:00 S.T.I.M.

UGARTE, Florio M.
—— ENTRE LAS MONTAÑAS (BETWEEN THE MOUNTAINS)
(SYMPHONIC POEM)
16:00 S.A.D.A.I.C.
—— ESCENAS INFANTILES (SUITE) (IN 3 MOVTS.)
12:00 S.A.D.A.I.C.
—— INTERLUDE FROM THE OPERA "SAIKA"
8:00 S.A.D.A.I.C.
—— PAISAJES DE ESTIO (SUITE) (IN 3 MOVTS.)
15:00 S.A.D.A.I.C.
—— PRELUDIO EN SOL MENOR
6:00 Ed.Argent.
—— LA REBELIÓN DEL AGUA (THE REBELLION OF THE
WATERS) (SYMPHONIC POEM)
4(3rd and 4th alt. with picc.),4,4,4 - 4,3,3,1 - timp.,perc.,cel. - 2
hp. -str.   25:00 Fleisher.
—— SINFONIA EN LA MAYOR (SYMPHONY IN A MAJOR)
23:00 Ed.Argent.
—— VIDALA
23:00 Fleisher.

UHL, Alfred
—— GILGAMESCH (ORATORISCHES MUSIK-DRAMA) %
100:00 A.K.M.

UKMAR, Vilko
—— THE FIDDLER (BALLET) %
2(2nd alt. with picc.),2,2(2nd alt. with b.-cl.),2 - 4,3,3,0 -
timp.,perc. - hp. - str.   Hans Gerig.
—— SYMPHONY NO. 1 (A POEM)
2,2,2(2nd alt. with b.-cl.),2(2nd alt. with c.-bn.) - 4,3,3,1 - perc.(2)
- str.   29:00 Hans Gerig.
—— SYMPHONY NO. 2 (A POEM)
2(2nd alt. with picc.),2(2nd alt. with Eng. hn.),2(2nd alt. with
b.-cl.),2(2nd alt. with c.-bn.) - 4,3,3,1 - timp.,perc.(5),cel. - hp. -
str.   15:00 Hans Gerig.
—— SYMPHONY NO. 3
2(2nd alt. with picc.),2,2(2nd alt. with b.-cl.),2 - 4,3,3,1 -
timp.,perc.(3),cel. - hp. - str.   21:00 Hans Gerig.
—— TRANSFORMATIONS
perc. - hp. - str.   22:00 Hans Gerig.

ULFRSTAD, Marius Moaritz
—— INCIDENTAL MUSIC TO THE FAIRY-TALE PLAY "POOR
PETER AND THE PRINCESS" ("FATTIGPER OG
PRINSESSEN")
2,2,2,2 - 4,2,3,1 - timp.,perc. - hp. - str.   T.O.N.O.
—— INCIDENTAL MUSIC TO THE PLAY "ELI SJURSDOTTER"
2,2,2,2 - 4,2,3,1 - timp.,perc. - hp. - str.   T.O.N.O.
—— INCIDENTAL MUSIC TO THE PLAY "VENDT, THE MONK"
(MUNKEN VENDT)
2,2,2,2 - 4,2,3,1 - timp.,perc. - hp. - str.   T.O.N.O.

ULIERTE, Enrique de - WATTERS, Cyril
—— SUITE ESPAGNOLA (IN 4 MOVTS.)
Bo. Hawkes.

ULMANN, Helmut von
—— CONCERTO FOR ORCH.
2,2,2,2 - 4,3,3,0 - timp. - cemb. - str.   20:00 F. Colombo.

ULRICH, Boris
—— MULTIPLE VISION (BALLET) % (FOR ORCHESTRA AND 3
TAPES) (1971) %
3(3rd alt. with picc.),3(3rd alt. with Eng.hn.),3(1st alt. with E^b
cl.,3rd alt. with b.-cl.),3(3rd alt. with c.-bn.) - 0,0,0,0 -
timp.,perc.,cel.,vibra. - 3 tape-recorders - org. - pf. - str.
15:00 MIC,Zagreb.

ULRICH, Jürgen
—— EARLY EVENING (1966)
str.   4:00 G. Schirmer.
—— SONATA SERENA (FOR BASSOON AND ORCH.) (1964)
1,1,2,2 - 2,1,1,0 - timp.,perc.,vibra. - str.   15:00 G. Schirmer.
—— SUITE ANCIENNE (1964)
fl. - hpsc. - str.   16:00 G. Schirmer.

UNGER, Hermann
—— CONCERTO FOR ORCH., OP. 61
2,2,2,2 - 4,2,3,1 - perc. - hp. - str. 22:00 T & J.
—— CONCERTO IN D MINOR FOR PIANO AND ORCH., OP. 47
2,2,2,2 - 4,1,3,1 - perc. - hp. - pf. - str.   22:00 T & J.
—— CONCERTO IN E MAJOR FOR VIOLIN AND ORCH., OP. 37
T and J.
—— CONCERTO IN G MAJOR FOR ORGAN AND ORCH., OP. 45
2,2,2,2 - 4,2,3,1 - timp.,perc. - hp. - org. - str.   35:00 T & J.
—— FESTLICHES VORSPIEL, OP. 53A
2,2,2,2 - 4,2,3,1 - perc. - hp. - str. 8:00 T & J.
—— OLD NETHERLANDS SUITE, OP. 77 (IN 4 MOVTS.)
2(2nd alt. with picc.),2(2nd alt. with Eng. hn.),2,2 - 4,2,0,0 -
timp.,perc. - str.   16:00 Henmar.
—— SYMPHONY IN D MINOR, OP. 27
T and J.
—— VIER LANDSCHAFTEN AUS "FAUST II"
2,2,2,2 - 4,1,3,1 - perc.,cel. - hp. - str.   13:00 T & J.

URAY, Ernst Ludwig
—— UNGARISCHE TAENZE
2,2,2,2 - 3,2,3,0 - timp.,perc. - hp. - str.   14:00 Seesaw.

USPENSKY, V.
—— ENGINEER GARIN'S FAILURE (SUITE FROM THE FILM)
G. Schirmer.

V

VAČKÁŘ, Dalibor C.
—— CONCERTO FOR VIOLIN AND ORCH.
2,2,2,2 - 4,2,2,0 - timp.,perc. - hp. - pf. - str.   26:00 Bo. Hawkes.
—— PRELUDES AND METAMORPHOSES
3,3,3,3 - 4,2,3,0 - timp.,perc.,bells,cel. - hp. - str.
23:00 Bo. Hawkes.

VAILLANT, R.
—— AU DELÀ DE L'ABSENCE (FOR MEZZO-SOPRANO AND
INSTRUMENTS)
1,ob. d'amore,*1,0 - 1,1,0,0 - cel., vibra. - hp. - hpsc. - pf. -
str.(2,1,1,0)   Presser.

VAINBERG, Moisei
—— SINFONIETTA NO. 1, OP. 41
3,2,2,2 - 4,3,3,1 - timp.,perc. - hp. - str.   20:00 G. Schirmer.
—— SYMPHONY NO. 7 IN C MINOR, OP. 81
hpsc. - str.   27:00 G. Schirmer.

VALCARCEL, Edgar
—— FISIONES
0,2,2,0 - 0,2,0,1 - 1 vla.,2 c.   11:00 Bo. Hawkes.
—— MONTAJA PARA LUDWIG (IN MEMORIAM LUDWIG VAN
BEETHOVEN) (FOR CLARINET, PIANO AND STRINGS)
cl. - pf. - str.   Seesaw.

VALENTIN, Lucas-Maria
—— EISKUNST-TANZ (SERENADE FÜR 2 FLÖTEN, STREICHER UND PAUKE)
  2 fl. - timp. - str.   11:00 S.U.I.S.A.
—— SCHERZO AUF A (FÜR GROSSES ORCH.)
                                                          11:00 S.U.I.S.A.
—— TESSINER GARTENSERENADE NR. 1 (FÜR 2 FLÖTEN UND STREICHORCH.)
  2 fl. - str.   9:30 S.U.I.S.A.

VALENTINI, Giuseppe - SCHROEDER
—— CHRISTMAS SYMPHONY IN B FLAT MAJOR, OP. 1, NO. 12 (URTEXT)
  cemb. - str.   Henmar.

VALERY, Claude
—— VOYAGE EN ITALIE (EN CINQ VOLETS)
  1,1,1,1 - 1,1,0,0 - timp.,perc. - guit. - hp. - str.   9:17 Henmar.

VALKARE, Gunnar
—— A STUDY IN THE STORY OF HUMAN STUPIDITY (1967)
  4,2,4,2 - 2,4,0,0 - timp.,perc. - str.   7:00 Fleisher.

VALLERAND, Jean
—— CANTATA-ORATORIO (FOR TENOR, CHORUS AND ORCH.)
                                                          12:00 C.A.P.A.C.
—— CONCERTO FOR VIOLIN AND ORCH.
                                                          26:00 C.A.P.A.C.
—— THE DEVIL IN THE BELFRY (SYMPHONIC POEM)
                                                          12:30 C.A.P.A.C.
—— ÉTUDE CONCERTANTE (1969) (FOR VIOLIN AND ORCHESTRA)
  2,2,2,2 - 2,2,0,0 - timp.,perc. - hp. - str.   8:30 CanMusCtr.
—— LE MAGICIEN (1-ACT OPERA) (1961) % (Text: Composer)
  *2,*2,*2(2nd alt. with E♭cl.),1 alto sax.(ad lib.),1 - 1,1,1,0 - perc. - str.   28:00 CanMusCtr.
—— NOCTURNE FOR ORCHESTRA
                                                          25:00 C.A.P.A.C.
—— PRELUDE FOR ORCHESTRA
                                                          13:00 C.A.P.A.C.
—— STRINGS IN MOTION (SUITE) (1961) (IN 6 MOVTS.)
  str.   11:00 CanMusCtr.
—— SYMPHONY (1951) (IN 3 MOVTS.)
                                                          C.A.P.A.C.

VALLIER, Jacques
—— ADAGIO NO. 2 FOR STRINGS
  str.   8:00 Presser.
—— CONCERTINO FOR TRUMPET AND STRINGS
  tpt. - str.   5:30 Presser.

VAMOS, Grace Becker
—— FANTASY CONCERTO (FOR PIANO AND STRING ORCH.) (1951) (IN 3 MOVTS.)
  pf. - str.   23:30 Composer.

VANCEA, Zeno
—— SINFONIETTA
  3,3,3,3 - 4,2,3,1 - timp.,cel. - hp. - pf. - str.   12:00 Templeton.

VAN CLEAVE, Nathan
—— VARIATIONS ON "ALOHA OE"
                                                          Leeds.
—— VARIATIONS ON HAYDN'S "SURPRISE" SYMPHONY
  str.   Bo. Hawkes.

VANDELLE, Romuald
—— SYMPHONIE BRÈVE
  2,2,2,2 - 2,2,2,0 - timp. - pf. - str.   22:00 Bo. Hawkes.

VAN DEN BOGAERDE, Fernand
—— FLEXIBILITÉ DU TEMPS (FOR 2 GROUPS OF INSTRUMENTS AND 2 CONDUCTORS)
  1,1,1,1 - 1,1,1,1 - str.(2,2,2,2)   16:40 Presser.

VANDENBURGH, Mildred
—— CARLSBAD CAVERNS SUITE (1966) (IN 5 MOVTS.)
  2(2nd alt. with picc.),2,2,2 - 4,3,3,1 - timp.,perc.(3),glock.,xyl. - hp. - str.   18:00 Composer.

VANDERMAESBRUGGE, Max
—— DIVERTIMENTO FOR FLUTE AND STRINGS, OP. 29
  Fl - str.   11:10 H. Elkan.

—— HIVER, OP. 31 (1970) (IN 3 MOVTS.)
  3,3,3,3 - 4,3,3,1 - timp.,perc. - str.   7:00 H. Elkan.
—— SINFONIA PER ARCHI, OP. 37 (1972)
  str.   H. Elkan.

VAN DER VELDEN, Renier
—— LES AMOURS DU TORERO (SCÈNE DANSÉE) (1948) %
  1,1,1,1 - 2,0,0,0 - timp. - pf. - str.   7:00 H. Elkan.
—— LES ANCÊTRES (BALLET) (1949) %
  1,1,1,1 - 2,0,0,0 - pf. - str.   20:00 H. Elkan.
—— ARLEQUINADE (BALLET) (1950) %
  2,2,2,2 - 2,2,1,0 -timp.,perc. - pf. - str.   15:00 H. Elkan.
—— CONCERTINO FOR CHAMBER ORCH. (1949)
  0,0,1,1 - 0,0,0,0 - pf. - str.   15:00 H. Elkan.
—— CONCERTO FOR OBOE AND ORCH. (1941)
  1,2,1,1 - 1,0,0,0 - str.   20:00 H. Elkan.
—— DIVERTIMENTO (1938)
  str.   14:00 H. Elkan.
—— DULLE GRIET (BALLET) (1949) %
  2,2,2,2 - 4,3,3,1 - timp.,perc.,cel.,xyl. - str.   30:00 H. Elkan.
—— L' ENLÈVEMENT DE PROSERPINE (BALLET) (1947) %
  1,1,1,1 - 1,0,0,0 - pf. - str.   30:00 H. Elkan.
—— IMPRESSION MARITIME (1930)
  2,2,1,1 - 2,1,0,0 - str.   7:00 H. Elkan.
—— JUDITH (BALLET) % (1953)
  3,2,2,2 - 4,3,3,1 - timp.,perc.,glock.,xyl. - hp. - pf. - str.   30:00 CBDM.
—— KAMMERMUZIEK (FOR VIOLA AND CHAMBER ORCH.) (1956)
  1,0,1,1 - 1,0,0,0 - str.   24:00 H. Elkan.
—— LES MOUCHOIRS (DIVERTISSEMENT CHORÉGRAPHIQUE) (1947) %
  2,2,2,2 - 2,2,1,0 - timp.,perc.,xyl. - hp. - str.   20:00 H. Elkan.
—— SUITE DU BALLET "DULLE GRIET" (1952)
  3,2,2,2 - 4,3,3,1 - timp.,perc. - str.   20:00 CBDM.
—— SYMPHONISCHE SUITE (HOMAGE À RAVEL) (1938)
  3,2,2,2 - 4,2,3,0 - timp.,perc.,glock. - hp. - str.   10:00 H. Elkan.
—— TRIPTIEK (FOR VIOLIN AND ORCH.) (1958)
  2,2,2,2 - 2,1,0,0 - perc. - pf. - str.   17:00 H. Elkan.

VAN DE VATE, Nancy
—— ADAGIO FOR ORCH.
  2,2,2,2 - 4,2,3,1 - timp. - str.   6:00 Mss.Publs.
—— VARIATIONS FOR CHAMBER ORCH.
  1,1,1,1 - 0,0,0,0 - str.   10:00 Composer.

VAN DE WOESTIJNE, David
—— BALLADE FOR PIANO AND ORCH. (1940)
  2,2,2,3 - 4,3,3,1 - timp.,perc. - hp. - pf. - str.   17:00 CBDM.
—— CONCERTO FOR ORCH. (1946)
  2,2,3,3 - 4,3,3,1 - cel. - pf. - str.   12:00 CBDM.
—— CONCERTO FOR VIOLIN AND 12 INSTS. (1945)
  1,0,2,1 - 2,0,0,0 - perc. - hpsc. - str.   13:00 H. Elkan.
—— SERENADES FOR CHAMBER ORCH. (1946)
  1,0,3,3 - 2,1,1,0 - perc. - pf. - 1 d.-b.   13:00 H. Elkan.
—— SYMPHONY (1958)
  3,2,3,3 - 4,3,3,1- timp.,perc. - str.   30:00 H. Elkan.

VÁNDOR, Ivan
—— DANCE MUSIC (MUSICA PER UN BALLETTO NON REALIZZATO) (1969)
  3,3,1,3 - 3,3,1,0 - perc.(5),2 glock. - str.   10:00 MCA Music.
—— MOTI PER ORCHESTRA
                                                          Leeds.

VÁNDOR, Sándor
—— HUNGARIAN SERENADE
  2,2,2,2 - 2,0,0,0 - str.   12:10 Bo. Hawkes.

VANHALL, J. C. - TAUSKY, Vilem
—— CONCERTO FOR OBOE AND STRINGS
  ob. - str.   12:00 Oxford.
—— DIVERTIMENTO FOR STRING ORCH.
  str.   14:00 Oxford.

VAN HULSE, Camil
—— EASTER DAWN (TONE POEM), OP. 87
  2,*3,*3,2 - 4,2,3,1 - timp.,perc.(3),bells,cel. - hp. - str.
                                                          10:00 FitzSimons.

—— NIGHT OF WONDER (CHRISTMAS CANTATA) (FOR SATB
SOLO VOICES, SATB CHORUS, CHILDREN'S CHORUS AND
ORCH.)
    2,2,2,2 - 4,3,3,1 - timp.,perc.,bells,cel.,xyl. - hp.- str.
                  47:00 Belw-Mills.

VAN IDERSTINE, A. P.
—— PASSACAGLIA (1966)
    1,1,2,1 - 2,3,2,1 - xyl. - hp. - str.   6:00 Composer.
—— SYMPHONY IN D MAJOR (1960) (IN 4 MOVTS.)
    1,1,1 E^{b}cl.,*2,1 - 2,3,2,1 - timp.,perc.(3),xyl. - str.
                  14:00 Composer.

VAN KEULEN, Geert
—— CHORDS (FOR 15 WINDS)(1974)
                  10:00 Henmar.

VAN PARYS, Georges
—— LA BELLE DE PARIS (OPERA-BALLET BOUFFE, IN 10
TABLEAUX) %
    2,2,3,2 - 2,3,2,0 - timp.,perc. - hp. - pf. - str.   F. Colombo.

VAN SLYCK, Nicholas
—— CHAMBER CONCERTO (1954)
    tpt. - timp. - str.   15:00 Composer.
—— CHRONICLE OF LIFE (CANTATA) (FOR SOPRANO, BASS,
SATB CHORUS AND CHAMBER ORCH.) (1961) (Text:
Composer)
    0,2,0,0 - 2,0,0,0 - hp. - str.   20:00 Composer.
—— CONCERT MUSIC FOR PIANO AND ORCH. (1954) (IN 4
CONNECTED MOVTS.)
    2,2,2,2 - 4,3,3,1 - timp.,perc.(3) - pf. - str.   19:00 Composer.
—— CONCERTO FOR FLUTE, VIOLIN, HARPSICHORD AND
STRINGS (1949) (IN 3 MOVTS.)
    fl. - hpsc. - str.   15:00 Composer.
—— SYMPHONIC PARAPHRASE NO. 1 (1960) (IN 4 CONNECTED
MOVTS.)
    2,2,2,2 - 4,3,3,1 - timp.,perc.(3) - str.   22:00 Composer.
—— SYMPHONIC PARAPHRASE NO. 2 (1966) (IN 4 MOVTS.)
    2,2,2,2 - 4,3,3,1 - timp.,perc.(2) - str.   17:00 Composer.

VAN VACTOR, David
—— ADAGIO MESTOSO
    str.   7:00 Composer.
—— ANDANTE AND ALLEGRO (1972) (FOR ALTO SAXOPHONE
AND STRINGS)
    alto sax. - str.   8:00 Rog.Rhodes.
—— CANTATA FOR THREE TREBLE VOICES (SSA CHORUS)
AND ORCH. (1947)
    2(2nd alt. with picc.),2,2,2(2nd alt. with c.-bn., ad lib.) - 2,2,0,0 -
    timp.,perc.(1) - str.   21:00 Rog.Rhodes.
—— CHACONNE FOR STRING ORCH. (1928)
    str.   9:00 Rog.Rhodes.
—— CHORALE PRELUDE: "HOLY MADONNA" (1974)
    *3,*3,*3,*3 - 4,3,3,1 - timp.,perc.,bells,glock.,xyl. - hp. - str.
                  7:30 Composer.
—— CHRISTMAS SONGS FOR YOUNG PEOPLE (FOR SSA
CHORUS AND ORCH.) (1961)
    2,2,2,2 - 4,3,3,1 - timp.,perc. - str.   12:00 Rog.Rhodes.
—— COMEDY OVERTURE NO. 1
    *3,2,2,*3 - 4,2,3,1 - timp.,perc. - hp. - str.   10:00 AmerMusEd.
—— COMEDY OVERTURE NO. 2
    *3,2,2,2 - 4,2,3,0 - timp.,perc.(4),bells,glock. - hp. - str.
                  6:00 AmerMusEd.
—— CONCERTO A QUATTRO (CONCERTO GROSSO) (FOR 3
FLUTES, HARP AND ORCH.)(1935)
    3,1,1,1 - 2,0,0,0 - timp. - hp. - str.   15:00 Rog.Rhodes.
—— CONCERTO FOR FLUTE AND ORCH. (1932) (IN 4 MOVTS.)
    1,1,1,1 - 2,0,0,0 - timp.,perc.,bells,cel. - hp. - str.
                  20:00 Rog.Rhodes.
—— CONCERTO FOR VIOLA AND ORCH. (1940) (IN 3 MOVTS.)
    2(2nd alt. with picc.),2,2,2 - 2,2,2,0 - timp.,glock. - str.
                  20:00 Rog.Rhodes.
—— CONCERTO FOR VIOLIN AND ORCH. (1951)
    3(3rd alt. with picc.),1,2,2 - 2,2,1,0 - timp.,perc. - hp. - str.
                  19:00 Rog.Rhodes.
—— CREDO (SECULAR CANTATA) (FOR MEZZO-SOPRANO,
CHORUS AND ORCH.)
    *3,*3,*3,*3 - 4,3,3,1 - timp.,perc.(4),bells - hp. - org.(ad lib.) - str.
                  30:00 Rog.Rhodes.
—— CRUCIFIXUS (EASTER CANTATA) (FOR CHORUS AND
ORCH.) (1976)
                  30:00 Rog.Rhodes.

—— DIVERTIMENTO FOR SMALL ORCH. (1939) (IN 5 MOVTS.)
    1(alt. with picc.),1,1,1 - 1,1,1,0- perc. - pf. - str.
                  20:00 Rog.Rhodes.
—— FANFARE FOR ORCHESTRA (1943)
    *4,*3,*3,*3 - 4,3,3,1 - timp.,perc.(6),bells - str.   4:00 Rog.Rhodes.
—— FANTASIA, CHACONNE AND ALLEGRO (1957)
    *2,*2,*3,2 - 4,2,3,1 - timp.,perc.(1),xyl. - pf. - str.
                  13:00 Rog.Rhodes.
—— FIVE BAGATELLES FOR STRINGS (1938)
    str.   20:00 Rog.Rhodes.
—— FIVE SMALL PIECES FOR LARGE ORCH. (1929)
    2,2,2,2 - 4,2,3,1 - timp. - hp. - str.   17:00 Rog.Rhodes.
—— HOLY MANNA (CHORAL PRELUDE) (1974)
    *3,*3,*3,*3 - 4,3,3,2 - perc. - org. - str.   5:00 Rog.Rhodes.
—— INAUGURATION: FANFARE AND MARCH (1960)
    3,3,3,3 - 4,3,3,1 - timp.,perc.(5) - pf. - str.   6:00 Rog.Rhodes.
—— INTRODUCTION AND PRESTO (1947)
    str.   7:00 Rog.Rhodes.
—— LOUISE (A REQUIESCAT FOR STRING ORCH.) (1970)
    str.   5:00 Rog.Rhodes.
—— THE MASQUE OF THE RED DEATH (1932)
    3,3,3,3 - 4,3,3,1 - timp.,perc. - str.   5:00 Rog.Rhodes.
—— THE NEW LIGHT (CHRISTMAS CANTATA) (1954)
    *3,2,2,2 - 4,3,3,1 - timp.,perc.(4),bells - org. - str.
                  32:00 Rog.Rhodes.
—— OVERTURE TO A CANTATA
    2,2,2,2 - 2,2,0,0 - perc. - str.   4:30 Composer.
—— OVERTURE TO A COMEDY, NO. 1 (1934)
    3,2,2,*3 - 4,2,3,1 - timp.,perc. - str.   10:00 Composer.
—— OVERTURE TO A COMEDY, NO. 2 (1941)
    3,2,2,2 - 4,2,3,0 - timp.,perc. - hp. - str.   6:00 Rog.Rhodes.
—— PASSACAGLIA AND FUGUE IN D MINOR (1933)
    3(3rd alt. with picc.),*3,*3,*3 - 4,3,3,1 - timp. - str.
                  10:00 Rog.Rhodes.
—— PASTORAL AND DANCE (1947)
    fl. - str.   10:00 Rog.Rhodes.
—— THE PLAY ON WORDS
    fl. - timp.,perc.(1),glock.,xyl. - hp. - str.   24:00 Composer.
—— PRELUDE AND FUGUE IN C (1974) (FOR STRINGS)
    str.   4:00 Rog.Rhodes.
—— PRELUDE AND MARCH (1950)
    3,2,2,2 - 4,3,3,1 - timp.,perc. - str.   9:00 Rog.Rhodes.
—— RECITATIVE AND SALTARELLO (1946)
    2,2,2,2 - 2,2,0,0 - timp.,perc. - hp. - str.   16:00 Rog.Rhodes.
—— SARABANDE WITH VARIATIONS (1969) (FOR BRASS
QUINTET AND STRINGS)
                  7:00 Rog.Rhodes.
—— SEWANEE SUITE NO. 1(1963)
    3,alto fl.(ad lib.),3,3,2 - 4,3,3,1 - timp.,perc.(4) - pf. - str.
                  11:00 Rog.Rhodes.
—— SINFONIA BREVE (1964)
    3,3,3,3 - 4,3,3,1 - timp.,perc.(4) - str.   7:00 Rog.Rhodes.
—— SUITE FOR TRUMPET AND SMALL ORCH. (1962)
    1(alt. with picc.),1,1,1 - 0,3,3,1 - perc. - pf. - str.
                  11:00 Rog.Rhodes.
—— SUITE FOR 3 OR 4 TRUMPETS AND ONE TRUMPETER
(1972) (WITH ORCH.) (IN 4 MOVTS.)
    *3,1,*4,contra-alto cl.,1 - 2,1,0,0 - timp. - str.   8:00 Rog.Rhodes.
—— SUITE FOR 3 OR 4 TRUMPETS AND ONE TRUMPETER
(1972) (WITH STRING ORCH.)
    str.   8:00 Rog.Rhodes.
—— SUITE ON CHILEAN FOLK TUNES (1963)
    3,3,3,3 - 4,3,3,1 - timp.,perc.(5),cel. - hp. - pf. - str.
                  13:00 Rog.Rhodes.
—— SYMPHONIC SUITE (IN 4 MOVTS.) (1938)
    3(3rd alt. with picc.),*3,*3,*3 - 4,3,3,1 - timp.,perc. - hp. - org.
    (electric) - str.   19:00 Rog.Rhodes.
—— SYMPHONY NO. 1 IN D (1937) (IN 4 MOVTS.)
    *3,*3,*3,*3 - 4,3,3,1 - timp.,perc.,bells - pf. - str.
                  32:00 Rog.Rhodes.
—— SYMPHONY NO. 2 IN C MAJOR (MUSIC FOR THE
MARINES)(1943) (IN 4 MOVTS.)
    *4,*3,*4,*3 - 4,4,3,1 - timp.,perc.(5),bells,glock. - pf. - str.
                  25:00 Rog.Rhodes.
—— SYMPHONY NO. 3, IN C MAJOR (1958)
    3,3,3,3 - 4,3,3,1 - timp.,perc.(5) - pf. - str.   27:00 Rog.Rhodes.
—— SYMPHONY NO. 5 (1975)
    2(2nd alt. with picc.),2(2nd alt. with Eng.hn.),2(2nd alt. with
    b.-cl.),2 - 4,3,3,1 - timp.,perc. - hp. - str.   18:00 Rog.Rhodes.
—— THREE DANCE SCENES
    2(2nd alt. with picc.),2,2,2(2nd alt. with c.-bn.) - 2,2,0,0 - timp. -
    str.   16:00 Composer.

—— THE TROJAN WOMEN (SUITE) (1959) (IN 3 MOVTS.)
3,3,3,3 - 4,3,3,1 - timp.,perc.(4) - pf. - str.   17:00 Rog.Rhodes.
—— UNITED NATIONS FANFARE (1944)
2,2,3,*3 - 4,3,3,1 - timp.,perc.(4) - hp. - str.   10:00 Rog.Rhodes.
—— VARIAZIONI SOLENNE (1941)
*3,*3,*3,*3 - 4,3,3,1 - timp.,perc.(4) - hp. - str.   9:00 Rog.Rhodes.
—— WALDEN (SYMPHONY NO. 4) (FOR SATB CHORUS AND
ORCH.) (1969) (Text: Henry David Thoreau)
*3,*3,*3,*3, - 4,3,3,1 - timp.,perc .(3) - hp. - str.
22:00 Rog.Rhodes.

VARDELL, Charles, Jr.
—— THE INIMITABLE LOVERS (CANTATA) (FOR SOPRANO,
BARITONE, CHORUS AND ORCH.)
*3,2,2,2 - 4,2,3,1- timp.,perc. - hp. - str.   C. Fischer.
—— JOE CLARK STEPS OUT
3,2,2,2 - 4,2,3,1 - timp.,perc. - str.   5:00 C. Fischer.

VARDI, Emanuel
—— CONCEPTIONS IN RHYTHM (FOR VIOLIN AND ORCH.)
2,2,2,2 - 4,3,3,1 - timp.,perc. - hp. - str.   20:00 Mills.
—— SUITE ON AMERICAN FOLK SONGS (FOR VIOLA AND
ORCH.)
2,2,2,2 - 2,2,0,0 - timp.,perc.glock. - hp. - str.   8:00 G. Schirmer.

VARIOUS
—— L' ÉVENTAIL DE JEANNE (BALLET) % (In 10 movements, 1
each composed by: Georges Auric, Marcel Delannoy, Pierre-Octave
Ferroud, Jacques Ibert, Roland-Manuel, Darius Milhaud, Francis
Poulenc, Maurice Ravel, Albert Roussel and Florent Schmitt)
3,3,3,3 - 4,3,3,1 - timp.,perc.,cel. - 2 hp.   30:00 Presser.
—— GENESIS SUITE (FOR NARRATOR, CHORUS AND ORCH.):
MOVTS. II-VII (By Nathaniel Shilkret, Alexandre Tansman, Darius
Milhaud, Mario Castelnuovo-Tedesco, Ernst Toch and Igor
Stravinsky; further details given in listings for each composer)
44:30 Shilkret.
—— GENESIS SUITE (FOR NARRATOR, CHORUS AND ORCH.):
PRELUDE (MOVT. 1) (By Arnold Schoenberg; Further details
given in listings for "Schoenberg")
5:00 Belmont.
—— GREETING TO KODÁLY (Co-composed by 23 of his former
students and colleagues, including Antal Dorati, Pál Kadosa, Géza
Frid and Ferenc Farkas, all edited and with a finale by the latter)
3,3,3,3 - 4,3,3,1 - timp.,perc.,cel. - hp. - pf. - str.
25:00 Bo. Hawkes.
—— LA GUIRLANDE DE CAMPRA (7 VARIATIONS OR
MEDITATIONS ON A THEME FROM ANDRÉ CAMPRA'S
OPERA "CAMILLE")(1950) (Co-composed by Arthur Honegger,
Daniel Lesur, Roland-Manuel, Germaine Tailleferre, Francis
Poulenc, Henri Sauguet and Georges Auric)
2,2,2,2 - 2,2,0,0 - timp.,perc. - hp. - str.   20:00 Salabert.
—— LES MARIÉS DE LA TOUR EIFFEL (SUITE FOR DOUBLE
ORCH.) (IN 9 MOVTS.) (Co-composed by Georges Auric, Arthur
Honegger, Darius Milhaud, Francis Poulenc and Germaine
Tailleferre)
3,2,2,2 - 4,3,3,1 - timp.,perc. - hp. - str.   19:05 Salabert.
—— SOMBRERITO DE TRES PICOS (SUITE) (1952) (IN 3 MOVTS)
(Co-composed by Albert de Klerk, Jan Mul and Herman Strategier)
2,2,2,2 - 4,3,3,0 - timp.,perc. - str.   15:00 Henmar.
—— SUITE FOR ST. CECELIA'S DAY (1960) (IN 4 MOVTS.) (One
each composed by Geoffrey Bush, Ian Hamilton. Alun Hoddinott
and Thea Musgrave)
3,2,2,2 - 4,2,3,0 - timp.,perc. - str.   11:30 Belw-Mills.
—— SUITE OF FRIENDSHIP (IN 5 MOVTS.) (Co-composed by Kurt
Schwaen, Andrzej Dobrowolski, Eugen Suchoň, Pál Kadosa and Paul
Constantinescu)
2,1,2,1 - 2,2,1,0 - timp.,perc. - str.   Tetra.
—— TATI-TATI (9 PIANO PARAPHRASES OF A CHILDREN'S
TUNE) (Composed variously by Borodine, Cui, Liadoff, Liszt and
Rimsky-Korsakoff, and orchestrated by Nicholas Tcherepnine)
3,3,3,3 - 4,2,3,1 - timp.,perc.,cel. - 2 hp. - 2 pf. - str.
24:00 Bo. Hawkes.
—— UILENSPIEGEL VARIATIONS (FOR 2 VIOLINS AND ORCH.)
(1958) (Composed variously by Hendrik Andriessen, Henk Badings,
Lex van Delden, Marius Flothuis, Géza Frid, Oscar van Hemel,
Hans Henkemans, Hans Kox, Guillaume Landré, Bertus van Lier
and Willem van Otterloo)
3,2,2,2 - 4,3,3,0 - timp.,perc. - hp.(ad lib.) - str.   21:00 Henmar.
—— VARIATIONS ON A THEME OF ALFRED HILL (1970)
(Co-composed by John Antill, Raymond Hanson, Dulcie Sybil
Holland and Miriam Beatrice Hyde)
16:50 A.P.R.A.

—— VARIATIONS ON A THEME OF ZOLTAN KODÁLY (By Antal
Dorati, Oedoen Partos, Sándor Veress, Tibor Serly and Géza Frid)
3(3rd alt. with picc.),3(3rd alt. with Eng. hn.),3(3rd alt. with
b.cl.),3(3rd alt. with c.-bn.) - 4,3,3,1 - timp.,perc.(5),cel.,vibra. - hp.
- pf. - str.   23:00 Bo. Hawkes.
—— VARIATIONS ON "DES WINTERS ALS HET REGENT" (1953)
(Composed variously by Cor de Groot, Jurriaan Andriessen, Herman
Strategier, Marius Flothuis, Karel Mengelberg and Anthon van der
Horst)
2,2,2,2 - 4,3,3,1 - timp.,perc. - hp. - str.   20:00 Henmar.
—— VARIATIONS ON THE ELIZABETHAN THEME
"SELLENGER'S ROUND" (By William Byrd and the six
contemporary British composers Arthur Oldham, Michael Tippett,
Lennox Berkeley, Benjamin Britten, Humphrey Searle and William
Walton)
P.R.S.
—— VARIATIONS SUR LE NOM DE MARGUERITE LONG (1956)
(Co-composed by Jean Françaix, Henri Dutilleux, Darius Milhaud,
Francis Poulenc, Daniel Lesur, Jean Rivier, Henri Sauguet
andGeorges Auric)
3,3,3,3 - 4,3,3,1 - perc.,cel. - hp. - str.   24:00 Salabert.

VARLAY, Rene - HAYMAN, Richard
—— PATRICK HENRY: "GIVE ME LIBERTY OR GIVE ME
DEATH" (FOR NARRATOR AND ORCH.)
*4,*3,*3,*3 - 4,3,3,1 - timp.,perc.(5) - org. - hp. - pf. - str.
10:00 G. Schirmer.

VARVOGLIS, Marios
—— ST. BARBARA ESAGOGI (SYMPHONIC PRELUDE) (1912)
12:00 InFrAthens.
—— SUITE PASTORAL (1910)
str.   A.E.P.I.

VASHAW, Cecile - SMITH, Julia
—— REMEMBER THE ALAMO! (WITH OPTIONAL NARRATOR
AND MIXED CHORUS) (1966) (Texts: Lt. Col. Wm. B. Travis
and Gladys W. Wright)
*3,*3,*3,2 -4,4,3,1 - timp.,perc.(4-5),bells,glock. - str.
12:00 Presser.

VASS, Lajos
—— EVENING IN THE CAMP
2,2,2,2 - 4,3,3,1 - timp.,perc. - hp. - str.   14:00 Bo. Hawkes.
—— MERRY MUSIC
2,2,2,2 - 4,3,3,1 - timp.,perc. - hp. - str.   13:00 Bo. Hawkes.

VASSILENKO, Sergei N.
—— CHINESE SUITE, OP. 60 (IN 6 MOVTS.)
3(3rd alt. with picc.),*3,2,2 - 4,3,3,1 - timp.,perc.,cel.,glock.,xyl. -
hp. - pf. - str.   30:00 G. Schirmer.
—— HINDU SUITE (WITH OPTIONAL CHORUS), OP. 42A (IN 10
MOVTS.)
3(3rd alt. with picc.),*3,E♭cl.(ad lib.),3(3rd alt. with
b.-cl.),2,c.-bn.(ad lib.) - 4,3-6,2 cnt.(ad lib.),3,1 -
timp.,perc.,cel.,glock - 2 hp.,org.(ad lib.) - str.   42:00 G. Schirmer.
—— IN SPRING, OP. 138 (SUITE FOR FLUTE AND ORCH.)
1,0,2,1 - perc. - hp.(or pf.) - str.   16:00 G. Schirmer.
—— LE JARDIN DE LA MORT (SYMPHONIC POEM), OP. 12
3(3rd alt. with picc.),2(2nd alt. with Eng. hn.),*3,*3 - 4,3,3,1 -
timp.,perc.,cel.,glock. - hp. - org.(ad lib.) - str. 18:00 G. Schirmer.
—— MIRANDOLINA (BALLET SUITE), OP. 122
3,3,4, alto sax.,3 - 4,3,3,1 - timp.,perc.,cel.,vibra.,xyl. - mandolin -
2 hp. - str.   30:00 G. Schirmer.
—— SYMPHONY NO. 1 IN G MINOR, OP. 10 (IN 4 MOVTS.)
3(3rd alt. with picc.),2(2nd alt. with Eng.hn.),*3,2 - 4,3,3,1 -
timp.,perc.,xyl. - str.   50:00 G. Schirmer.
—— SYMPHONY NO. 2 IN F, OP. 22 (IN 3 MOVTS.)
3(3rd alt. with picc.),3,3,3 - 4,3,2 cnt.(ad lib.),3,1 - timp.,perc. -
hp. - str.   35:00 G. Schirmer.
—— TURKMENIAN PICTURES, OP. 68 (IN 4 MOVTS.)
3(3rd alt. with picc.),*3,*3,2 - 4,3,3,1 - timp.,perc.,glock. - hp. -
str.   25:00 G. Schirmer.

VASZY, Viktor
—— SUITE NO. 2
3,2,2,2- 4,2,3,1 - timp.,perc. - str.   15:00 Bo. Hawkes.

VAUBOURGOIN, Marc
—— CONCERTO FOR BASSOON AND ORCH.
2,2,2,2 - 4,2,2,0 - timp.,perc.(3),cel.,glock. - hp. - str.
16:30 Presser.

—— CONCERTO FOR HARPSICHORD AND ORCH.
3,2,2,2 - 3,3,0,0 - timp.,perc. - hp. - hpsc. - str.　　20:00 Presser.
—— CONCERTO FOR TRUMPET AND ORCH.
2,2,2,2 - 4,2,2,0 - timp.,perc. - hp. - str.　　23:00 Eds. Fran.
—— SIX SMALL PIECES (FOR ALTO SAXOPHONE AND ORCH.)
2,2,2,alto sax.,2 - 2,2,0,0 - timp.,perc.,cel. - hp. - str.
　　11:00 Presser.
—— SYMPHONY NO. 2
3,2,2,2 - 4,4,3,1 - timp.,perc.(5),cel. - 2 hp. - str.　　Presser.

VAUCLAIN, C.
—— APRIL OVERTURE
2,2,2,2 - 4,2,3,0 - timp.,perc. - str.　　8:00 Southern.
—— CONCERTO FOR VIOLIN AND ORCH.
　　20:00 Southern.
—— NARRATIVE FOR LARGE ORCH.
　　Southern.
—— PRELUDE TO "ENDYMION"
3,2,2,2 - 4,3,3,0 - timp. - str.　　9:00 Southern.
—— SUITE FOR STRINGS AND PIANO
pf. - str.　　18:00 Southern.
—— SYMPHONY FOR STRINGS AND PIANO
pf. - str.　　18:00 Southern.
—— SYMPHONY IN G MINOR
3,3,3,3 - 4,3,3,1 - timp. - str.　　28:00 Southern.
—— SYMPHONY IN 1 MOVT.
3.2,2,2 - 4,3,3,0 - timp. - str.　　15:00 Southern.
—— SYMPHONY NO. 4 FOR LARGE ORCH.
　　Southern.
—— SYMPHONY NO. 5
3,3,3,3 - 4,3,3,1 - timp.,perc.(3) - str.　　25:00 Presser.

VAUGHAN, Clifford
—— BURMESE RHAPSODY
3,3(3rd alt. with Eng. hn.),*4,3(3rd alt. with c.-bn.) - 4,3,3,0 -
perc.,cel. - hp. - str.　　18:00 Composer.
—— CONCERTO FOR ORGAN AND ORCH.
　　Composer.
—— CONCERTO FOR PIANO AND ORCH.
　　Composer.
—— CONCERTO FOR VIOLIN AND ORCH.
2,2(2nd alt. with Eng. hn.),3(3rd alt. with b.cl.),2 - 4,3,3,0 - perc. -
hp. - str.　　40:00 Composer.
—— HINDU RHAPSODY
3,3(3rd alt. with Eng. hn.),*4,*3 - 4,2,2,0 - perc. - hp. - str.
　　18:00 Composer.
—— IMAGINARY DRAMA
3,3(3rd alt. with Eng. hn.),*4,*3 - 4,3,3,1 - perc. - 2 hp. - str.
　　18:00 Composer.
—— SIX ORIENTAL DANCES
fl.,ob.,cl. - perc. - pf. - str.(no d.-b.)　　21:00 Composer.
—— SYMPHONY NO. 1
3,3(3rd alt. with Eng. hn.),3(3rd alt. with b.-cl.),3(3rd alt. with
c.-bn.) - 4,3,3,1 - perc.(2) - 2 hp. - str.　　30:00 Composer.
—— SYMPHONY NO. 2
3,3(3rd alt. with Eng. hn.),3(3rd alt. with b.-cl.),3 - 4,3,3,0 -
perc.(2) - str.　　30:00 Composer.
—— SYMPHONY NO. 3
2,2,*3,1 - 4,2,2,0 - timp. - str.　　25:00 Composer.

VAUGHAN WILLIAMS, Ralph
—— BENEDICTE (FOR SOPRANO, CHORUS AND STRINGS)
str.　　8:00 Oxford.
—— BENEDICTE (FOR SOPRANO, MIXED CHORUS AND
ORCH.) (Text: Biblical and J. Austin)
*3,2,2,2 - 4,2,3,0 - timp.,perc.,cel.(opt.) - pf. - str.　　15:00 Oxford.
or:
2,1,2,1 - 2,1,1,0 - pf. - str.
or:
pf. - str.
—— CAVATINA (3RD MOVT. FROM SYMPHONY NO. 8)
str.　　8:00 Oxford.
—— CHARTERHOUSE SUITE (IN 6 MOVTS.)
str.　　17:00 Galaxy.
—— COASTAL COMMAND: SUITE
2,2,2,2 - 4,2,3,1 - perc.(2) - hp. - str.　　12:00 Oxford.
—— CONCERTO ACCADEMICO (FOR VIOLIN AND STRINGS)
str.　　16:00 Oxford.
—— CONCERTO FOR BASS TUBA AND ORCH.
2(2nd alt. with picc.),1,2,1 - 2,2,2,1 - timp.,perc.(2) - str.
　　18:00 Oxford.
—— CONCERTO FOR OBOE AND STRINGS (IN 3 MOVTS.)
ob. - str.　　17:00 Oxford.

—— CONCERTO FOR PIANO AND ORCH.
2,2,2,2 - 3,2,3,1 - timp. - org.(ad lib.) - pf. - str.　　25:00 Oxford.
—— CONCERTO GROSSO FOR STRINGS
str.　　17:00 Oxford.
—— DONA NOBIS PACEM (CANTATA) (FOR SOPRANO,
BARITONE, CHORUS AND ORCH.)
3(3rd alt. with picc.),2,2,*3 - 4,2-4,3-4,1 - timp.,perc. - hp. - org. -
str.　　34:00 Oxford.
—— THE ENGLAND OF ELIZABETH (SUITE FROM THE FILM)
　　Oxford.
—— EPITHALAMION (CANTATA) (FOR BARITONE, CHORUS
AND SMALL ORCH.)
fl. - pf. - str.　　40:00 Oxford.
—— FANTASIA ON A THEME BY THOMAS TALLIS (FOR
STRING QUARTET AND DOUBLE STRING ORCH.)
str.　　14:00 G. Schirmer.
—— FANTASIA ON "GREENSLEEVES"
1-2 fl.(ad lib.) - hp.(or pf.) - str.　　4:00 Oxford.
—— FANTASIA (QUASI VARIAZIONE) ON THE "OLD 104TH"
PSALM-TUNE (FOR PIANO, MIXED CHORUS AND ORCH.)
　　11:00 Oxford.
—— FESTIVAL TE DEUM (ON TRADITIONAL MELODIES) (FOR
SATB CHORUS AND ORCH.)
　　6:00 Oxford.
—— FIVE TUDOR PORTRAITS (FOR CONTRALTO, BARITONE,
CHORUS AND ORCH.)
3,2,2,3 - 4,0,3,1 - timp.,perc. - hp. - str.　　22:00 Oxford.
—— FIVE VARIANTS OF "DIVES AND LAZARUS"
2 hp. - str.　　10:00 Oxford.
—— FLOS CAMPI (SUITE) (FOR VIOLA, SMALL CHORUS AND
SMALL ORCH.)
1,1,1,1 - 1,1,0,0 - perc.,cel. - hp. - str.　　15:00 Oxford.
—— FLOURISH FOR A CORONATION (FOR MIXED CHORUS
AND ORCH.) (Text: Biblical, Chaucer and other sources)
4,2,3,alto sax.,*3 - 8,6,3,euph.,1 - timp.,perc.(2),bells,glock. - 2 hp.
- org. - pf. - str.　　12:00 Oxford.
or:
2,2,2,2 - 4,2,3,1 - timp. - str.
—— FOLK SONGS OF THE FOUR SEASONS (CANTATA) (FOR
WOMEN'S CHORUS AND STRINGS)
str.　　45:00 Oxford.
—— FOUR HYMNS (FOR TENOR, VIOLA AND STRINGS)
str.　　11:00 Bo. Hawkes.
—— HOUSEHOLD MUSIC (THREE PRELUDES ON WELSH HYMN
TUNES) (FOR SMALL ORCH.)
2,1,2,2 - 2,2,0,0 - timp.,perc. - str.　　15:00 Oxford.
—— IN THE FEN COUNTRY (SYMPHONIC IMPRESSION)
3,*3,*3,2 - 4,2,3,1 - timp. - str.　　14:00 Oxford.
—— IN THE WINDSOR FOREST (CANTATA) (IN 5 MOVTS.)
2(2nd alt. with picc.),2,2,2 - 2,3,1,0 - timp.,perc. - hp.(or pf.) - str.
　　20:00 Oxford.
—— JOB (A MASQUE FOR DANCING) %
3(3rd alt. with picc. and alto fl.),*3,3(3rd alt. with b.-cl. ad
lib.),alto sax.,*3 - 4,3,3,1 - timp.,perc. - 2 hp. - org.(ad lib.) - str.
　　Oxford.
Or
2(2nd alt. with picc.),*2,2,2 - 4,2,3,1 - timp.,perc. - hp. - str.
—— THE LARK ASCENDING (FOR VIOLIN AND ORCH.)
2,1,2,2 - 2,0,0,0 - perc. - str.　　13:00 Oxford.
Or
1,1,1,1 - 1,0,0,0 - perc. - str.
—— LET US NOW PRAISE FAMOUS MEN (FOR MIXED CHORUS
AND ORCH.)
　　G. Schirmer.
—— A LONDON SYMPHONY (SYMPHONY NO. 2)
3(3rd alt. with picc.),*3,*3,*3 - 4,2,2 cnt.,3,1 - timp.,perc.(5),glock.
- 2 hp. - str.　　40:00 Galaxy.
Or
2(2nd alt. with picc.),2(2nd alt. with Eng. hn.),2,2 - 4,2,3,1 -
timp.,perc.(3),glock. - hp. - str.
—— LORD, THOU HAST BEEN OUR REFUGE (FOR CHORUS
AND ORCH.)
2,2,2,2 - 4,2,3,1 - timp. - org. - str.　　G. Schirmer.
—— MAGNIFICAT (FOR CONTRALTO, WOMEN'S CHORUS AND
ORCH.)
3,3,3,2 - 4,2,0,0 - timp. - str.　　15:00 Oxford.
—— OLD KING COLE (BALLET SUITE) (WITH CHORUS AD LIB.)
3,2,2,2 - 4,2,3,1 - timp.,perc.,cel. - hp. - str.　　16:00 G. Schirmer.
Or
1,1,2,2 - 3,2,2,0 - timp.,perc. - hp. - str.

—— ON WENLOCK EDGE (SONG CYCLE FOR TENOR AND ORCH.)
2 picc.,1,*3,2 - 4,2,3,0 - timp.,perc.,cel. - hp. - str.
11:00 Bo. Hawkes.

—— AN OXFORD ELEGY (FOR SPEAKER SMALL CHORUS AND SMALL ORCH.)
25:00 Oxford.

—— PARTITA (FOR DOUBLE STRING ORCH.)
str.
20:00 Oxford.

—— A PASTORAL SYMPHONY (SYMPHONY NO. 3) (IN 4 MOVTS.) (WITH HIGH VOICE AD LIB. IN LAST MOVT.)
3(3rd alt. with picc.),3,3,2 - 4,3,3,1 - timp.,perc.,cel. - hp. - str.
35:00 G. Schirmer.
Or
2,2,2,2 - 4,2,3,1 - timp.,perc.,cel. - hp. - str.

—— PILGRIM'S JOURNEY (CANTATA) (FROM THE SCORE OF THE OPERA "PILGRIM'S PROGRESS") (FOR SOPRANO, TENOR, BARITONE, MIXED CHORUS AND ORCH.)
2,2,2,2 - 4,2,3,0 - timp.,perc. - hp.(or pf.) - str.   40:00 Oxford.
or:
pf. - str.

—— THE PILGRIM'S PROGRESS (OPERA) %
str.
126:00 Oxford.

—— THE POISONED KISS ("THE EMPRESS AND THE NECROMANCER") (OPERA) % (Text: Evelyn Sharp)
120:00 Oxford.

—— PRELUDE AND FUGUE IN C MINOR
3,2,2,*3 - 4,3,0,1 - timp.,perc.(2) - org. - str.   10:00 Oxford.

—— PRELUDE ON AN OLD CAROL TUNE
2,1,2,1 - 2,2,2,0 - timp. - str.   8:00 Oxford.

—— RIDERS TO THE SEA (OPERA) %
Oxford.

—— ROMANCE FOR HARMONICA AND STRING ORCH.
Harmonica - pf. - str.   6:30 Oxford.

—— THE RUNNING SET (FOUNDED ON TRADITIONAL DANCE TUNES)
2,1,2,2 - 1,2,0,0, - perc. - pf.(ad lib.) - str.   5:00 Oxford.

—— SANCTA CIVITAS (FOR MIXED CHORUS AND ORCH.)
4,3,2,3 - 4,3,3,1 - timp. - hp. - pf. - str.   36:00 G. Schirmer.

—— SCHERZO ALLA MARCIA (2ND MOVT. FROM SYMPHONY NO. 8)
1,2,2,2-3 - 2,2,0,0 - timp.,perc. - str.   15:00 Oxford.

—— A SEA SYMPHONY (SYMPHONY NO. 1) (FOR SOPRANO, BARITONE, CHORUS AND ORCH.)
Small scoring for Entire Symphony: 57:00 Galaxy.
2(2nd alt. with picc.),*2,2,2 - 4,3,3,1 - timp.,perc. - hp. - str.
Or
NO. 1."A SONG FOR ALL SEAS, ALL SHIPS
*3,*3,E♭cl.,*3,*3 - 4,3,3,1 - timp.,perc.(4) - 2 hp. - org. - str.
NO. 2."ON THE BEACH AT NIGHT, ALONE"
3,*3,*3,*3 - 4,3,3,1 - timp.,perc.(3) - str.
NO. 3."SCHERZO (THE WAVES)"
*3,*3,E♭cl.,2,*3 - 4,3,3,1 - timp.,perc.(4) - 2 hp. - str.
NO. 4."THE EXPLORERS"
3(3rd alt. with picc.),*3,E♭cl.,*3,*3 - 4,3,3,1 - timp.,perc.(5) - 2 hp. - org. - str.

—— SERENADE TO MUSIC (FOR SPEAKER, SOPRANO, CHILDREN'S CHORUS, CHORUS, AND ORCH.)
3,3,2,2 - 4,2,2,3 - timp.,perc. - str.   14:30 Oxford.
Or
This version for orch. alone: 2,2,2,2 - 4,2,3,1 - timp., perc. - hp. - str.

—— THE SHEPHERDS OF THE DELECTABLE MOUNTAINS (PASTORALE EPISODE) (FOR SOLOISTS, WOMEN'S CHORUS AND ORCH.)
2 fl., 2 ob., 2 tpt., str., soloists, chorus   35:00 Oxford.

—— SINFONIA ANTARCTICA (SYMPHONY NO. 7) (FOR SOPRANO, SMALL WOMEN'S CHORUS AND ORCH.)
3,3,3,3 - 4,3,3,1 - timp.,perc.(3-4),bells,cel.,glock.,vibra.,xyl. - hp. - pf. - org.(ad lib.) - str.   40:00 Oxford.

—— SIR JOHN IN LOVE (4-ACT OPERA) %
Oxford.

—— SIX CHORAL SONGS (FOR UNISON VOICES AND ORCH.)
(Text: Shelley)
2,2,2,*3 - 4,2,3,1 - timp.,perc. - hp. - org. - str.   14:00 Oxford.

—— THE SONS OF LIGHT (CANTATA) (FOR CHORUS AND ORCH.)
25:00 Oxford.

—— THE STORY OF A FLEMISH FARM (SUITE FROM THE FILM)
2,*3,2,*3 - 4,2,3,1 - perc.(2) - hp. - str.   26:00 Oxford.

—— SUITE FOR VIOLA AND ORCH. (IN 3 MOVTS.)
2,1,2,2 - 2,2,0,0, - timp.,perc.,cel. - hp. - str.   23:00 Oxford.

—— SUN, MOON, STARS AND MAN (CHORAL CYCLE FROM "THE SONS OF LIGHT") (FOR UNISON CHORUS, PIANO AND STRINGS)
pf. - str.   Oxford.

—— SYMPHONY NO. 4 IN F MINOR (IN 4 MOVTS.)
3,*4,*3,*3 - 4,2,3,1 - timp.,perc.(2) - str.   32:00 Oxford.
Or
3,*3,2,3 - 4,2,3,1 - timp.,perc.(2) - str.

—— SYMPHONY NO. 5 IN D (IN 4 MOVTS.)
2,*3,2,2 - 2,2,3,0 - timp. - str.   35:00 Oxford.

—— SYMPHONY NO. 6 IN E MINOR
3(3rd alt. with picc.),*3,2, b. -cl.(alt. with ten. sax.),*3 - 4,3,3,1 - timp.,perc.(3) - 1-2 hp. - str.   34:00 Oxford.

—— SYMPHONY NO. 8 IN D MINOR
2,2,2,2 - 2,2,3,0 - timp.,perc.(5),cel.,glock.,vibra.,xyl., 3 tuned gongs (ad lib.) - 1-2 hp. - str.   26:30 Oxford.

—— SYMPHONY NO. 9 IN E MINOR
*3,*3,*3,3 sax.,*3 - 4, flg. - hn.,2,3,1 - timp.(6),perc.,bells,glock.,xyl. - 2 hp. - str.   29:00 Oxford.

—— THANKSGIVING FOR VICTORY (FOR SOPRANO, CHORUS, CHILDREN'S CHORUS AND ORCH.)
2,2,2,2 - 2,2,3,0 - timp.,perc. - hp. - pf. - str.   13:00 Oxford.

—— THIS DAY (CHRISTMAS CANTATA) (FOR SOPRANO, TENOR, BARITONE, CHORUS AND ORCH.)
50:00 Oxford.

VAUGHAN WILLIAMS, Ralph - BROWN, J.
—— CHARTERHOUSE SUITE (FOR STRINGS) (IN 6 MOVTS.)
str.   17:00 Galaxy.

VAUGHAN WILLIAMS, Ralph - DOUGLAS, Roy
—— THE FIRST NOWELL (A NATIVITY PLAY) % (FOR SOLO VOICES, MIXED CHORUS AND SMALL ORCH.)
2,1,2,1 - 2,2,2,0 - timp. - hp. - str.   30:00 Oxford.
or:
org.(or pf.) - str.

—— FOLK SONGS OF THE FOUR SEASONS: SUITE FROM THE CANTATA
2,2,2,2 - 2,2,3,0 - timp.,perc. - hp. - str.   13:30 Oxford.

VAUGHAN WILLIAMS, Ralph - DRESSKELL-ROSENBERG, Earl
—— SINE NOMINE (FOR SATB OR TTBB AND ORCH.)
2,2,2,2 - 2,2,2,0 - timp. - str.   3:37 C. Fischer.

VAUGHAN WILLIAMS, Ralph - FOSTER, Arnold
—— PRELUDE FOUNDED ON THE WELSH HYMN TUNE "HYFRYDOL"
3(3rd alt. with picc.),2(2nd alt. with Eng.hn.),2(2nd alt. with b.-cl.),2(2nd alt. with c.-bn.) - 4,2,3,1 - timp.,perc. - hp. - str.   3:00 Galaxy.

—— PRELUDE ON THE WELSH HYMN TUNE "RHOSYMEDRE"
2,1,2,2 - 2,1,0,0 - str.   3:00 Galaxy.
Or
str.

—— SIX STUDIES IN ENGLISH FOLK SONG (FOR CELLO AND SMALL ORCH.)
2,1,2,2 - 0,0,0,0 - hp. - str.   8:30 Galaxy.
or:
pf. - str.

VAUGHAN WILLIAMS, Ralph - JACOB, Gordon
—— ENGLISH FOLK SONG SUITE (IN 3 MOVTS.)
2,2,2,1 - 2,2,1,0 - perc. - str.   10:00 Bo. Hawkes.
—— VARIATIONS (Originally for brass band)
2,2,2,2 - 4,2,3,1 - timp.,perc.(3) - str.   10:00 Oxford.

VAUGHAN WILLIAMS, Ralph - LAMBERT, Constant
—— JOB (A MASQUE FOR DANCING) %
*3,1,2,sax.,1 - 2,2,1,0 - timp.,perc. - hp. - str.   40:00 Oxford.

VAUGHAN WILLIAMS, Ralph - STORRY, Jean
—— BENEDICITE (FOR SOPRANO, WOMEN'S VOICES AND ORCH.) (Text: Biblical and J. Austin)
*3,2,2,2 - 4,2,3,0 - timp.,perc.,cel,(opt.) - pf. - str.   15:00 Oxford.
or:
2,1,2,1 - 2,1,1,0 - pf. - str.
or:
pf. - str.

VAZZANA, Anthony
—— HARLEQUIN SUITE (IN 5 MOVTS.)
1(alt. with picc.),1,2(2nd alt. with b.-cl.),1 - 2,1,1,0 - timp.,perc.,xyl. - hp. - pf. - str.   16:36 Composer.

—— INTRODUCTION AND ALLEGRO
2,2,2(2nd alt. with b.-cl.),2 - 4,3,3,0 - timp. - str.   8:00 Composer.
—— SUITE FOR STRINGS (IN 3 MOVTS.)
str.   15:00 Composer.
—— SYMPHONIC ALLEGRO
2,2,2,2 - 4,3,3,1 - timp.,perc.(3),xyl. - hp. - pf. - str.
                                                  6:40 Composer.
—— SYMPHONY NO. 1 (IN 3 MOVTS.)
2(2nd alt. with picc.),2(2nd alt. with Eng.hn.),2(2nd alt. with
b.-cl.),2 - 4,3,3,1 - timp.,perc.,bells,xyl. - hp. - str.
                                                  15:00 Composer.

VEALE, John
—— CONCERTO FOR CLARINET AND ORCH.
2,2,2,2 - 4,2,3,0 - timp.,perc. - hp. - str.   12:30 Oxford.
—— KUBLA KHAN (FOR BARITONE, CHORUS AND ORCH.)
3,3,3,3 - 4,3,3,1 - timp.,perc. - hp. - str.   15:00 Lengnick.
—— THE METROPOLIS (OVERTURE)
3,3,3,3 - 4,3,3,1 - timp.,perc. - hp. - str.   11:00 Lengnick.
—— PANORAMA
3,3,3,3 - 4,3,3,1 - timp. - hp. - str.   10:00 Lengnick.
—— SYMPHONY
3,3,3,3 - 4,3,3,1 - timp.,perc.(2) - str.   20:00 Oxford.
—— SYMPHONY NO. 2 (1964)
3,3,3,3 - 4,3,3,1 - timp.,perc.(4) - hp. - str.   40:00 P.R.S.

VÉCSEY, Jenő
—— CONCERTINO FOR PIANO AND ORCH.
2,2,2,2 - 4,3,3,0 - timp.,perc. - hp. - pf. - str.   12:00 Bo. Hawkes.

VELDEN, Renier van der
—— CONCERTO FOR PIANO AND STRINGS (1971)
pf. - str.   15:00 H. Elkan.
—— ETUDE (1969) (FOR CHAMBER ORCH.)
1,1,1,1 - 1,1,1,0 - pf. - str. (0,1,1,1)   10:00 H. Elkan.
—— HULDE AAN LEOS JANACEK (1973) (THREE SHORT PIECES
FOR FLUTE, OBOE AND STRINGS)
fl.,ob. - str.   14:00 H. Elkan.
—— MOUVEMENT (1968)
3,2,2,2 - 4,3,3,0 - timp.,perc. - str.   10:00 H. Elkan.
—— SYMPHONY (1967) (IN 3 MOVTS.)
2,2,2,2 - 2,2,2,0 - timp.,perc. - str.   24:00 H. Elkan.

VELKE, John A., II
—— ADAGIETTO FOR STRINGS
str.   4:00 Composer.
—— CONCERTO GROSSO FOR BRASS SEXTET AND ORCH.
                                               Composer.

VELLONES, Pierre
—— BALLADE (FOR PIANO AND ORCH.)
                                               10:00 EV.
—— CASTILLANNES
3,2,2,1 sax.,3 - 4,3,3,1 - timp.,perc. - 2 hp. - str.   6:00 EV.
—— CINQ ÉPITAPHES (1937) (FOR VOICE AND ORCH.)
2,2,2,2 - 4,2,2,0 - timp.,perc.,cel. - hp. - str.   Salabert.
—— CONCERTO FOR SAXOPHONE AND ORCH.
                                               24:00 EV.
—— RASTELLI (FOR ORCHESTRA)
                                               EV.
—— SUITE CAVALIÈRE
                                               17:00 EV.
—— SUITE D'ORCHESTRE (IN 5 MOVTS.)
                                               EV.

VENÉ, Ruggero
—— AMERICAN LANDSCAPE (FOR STRINGS)
str.   15:00 Composer.
—— ROSSACCIO (A SAILOR WITH REDDISH HAIR)
(SYMPHONIC POEM)
*3,*3,*3,*3 - 4,3,3,1 - timp.,perc. - 2 hp. - pf. - str.
                                               20:00 Composer.

VERACINI, Francesco Maria - BONELLI, Ettore
—— FOUR PIECES FOR STRINGS
str.   Henmar.

VERACINI, Francesco Maria - DAMERINI
—— CONCERTO GRANDE DA CHIESA (FOR VIOLIN AND
ORCH.)
0,2,0,0 - 0,2,0,0 - timp. - org.(or cemb.) - str.   12:00 Henmar.

VERACINI, Francesco Maria - FAGOTTO, Virginio
—— OVERTURE NO. 1 (FOR STRINGS AND CONTINUO)
cemb. - str.   14:50 Presser.

VERACINI, Francesco Maria - MARGOLA, Franco
—— ARIA SCHIAVONA (FOR STRINGS AND CEMBALO)
cemb. - str.   Henmar.

VERACINI, Francesco Maria - RUYSSEN, Pierre
—— CONCERTO FOR VIOLIN AND STRINGS
str.   Galaxy.

VERBESSELT, August
—— ALADIN EN DE WONDERLAMP (1944) (SUITE FOR ORCH.)
2,2,2,2 - 4,2,3,0 - timp.,perc. - str.   11:00 H. Elkan.
—— BALLADE (1956)
2,2,2,2 - 4,2,3,0 - timp.,perc. - str.   H. Elkan.
—— LE BEAU TÉNÉBREUX (1956) (BALLET FOR ORCH.)
1,1,1,1 - 1,2,1,0 - timp.,perc. - pf.   20:00 H. Elkan.
—— CONCERTO FOR FLUTE AND ORCH.
2,1,1,1 - 2,2,1,0 - perc.(2) - hp. - hpsc. - str.   18:00 Presser.
—— CONCERTO FOR ORCH. (1959)
2,2,2,2 - 4,3,3,0 - timp.,perc. - str.   20:00 H. Elkan.
—— DIAGRAMMEN (1972)
2,2,2,2 - 2,2,1,0 - harp,perc. - str.   H. Elkan.
—— GRUPPI DI QUATTRO (FOR CHAMBER ORCH.) (1968)
1,1,0,0 - 0,0,0,0 - perc. - pf. - str.   H. Elkan.
—— MANIPULATIES (FOR BRASS AND PERCUSSION) (1972)
0,0,0,0 - 4,4,4,1 - perc.   H. Elkan.
—— SINFONIETTA (1958)
2,2,2,2 - 2,2,1,0 - timp.,perc. - hp. - str.   H. Elkan.
—— TRIPTIEK (1967)
2,2,2,2 - 4,3,3,0 - timp.,perc. - hp. - str.   H. Elkan.
—— UNIVERSUM (FOR TWO ORCHS. AND TAPE RECORDER)
                                               H. Elkan.
—— DE VEROVERAAR (BALLET FOR ORCH.) (1964)
2,2,2,2 - 4,3,3,0 - timp.,cel. - hp. - pf. - str.   30:00 H. Elkan.

VERCKEN, François
—— POLYTONE
2,2,2,2 - 4,2,2,3 - timp.,perc.(4) - str.   15:30 Presser.

VERDI, Giuseppe
—— AIDA (OPERA) % (Engl. text: Walter Ducloux)
                                               G. Schirmer.
—— FALSTAFF (OPERA) % (Engl. text: Walter Ducloux)
                                               G. Schirmer.
—— THE MASKED BALL (3-ACT OPERA) % (Engl. text: Peter Paul
Fuchs)
                                               G. Schirmer.
—— OTELLO (4-ACT OPERA) % (Engl. text: Walter Ducloux)
                                               G. Schirmer.
—— RIGOLETTO (4-ACT OPERA) % (Engl. text: Ruth and Thomas
Martin)
                                               G. Schirmer.
—— LA TRAVIATA (4-ACT OPERA) % (Engl. text: Ruth and Thomas
Martin)
                                               G. Schirmer.

VERDI, Giuseppe - DAVIS, Katherine K.
—— AVE MARIA (FOR SSA CHORUS, PIANO AND STRING
ORCH.) (Text: Dante; Engl. Text: George Mead)
pf. - str.   4:30 Arranger.

VERDI, Giuseppe - HERFURTH, C. Paul
—— PRELUDE FROM "LA TRAVIATA"
                                               C. Fischer.

VERDI, Giuseppe - JUNGNICKEL, Ross
—— OVERTURE TO "I VESPRI SICILIANI"
                                               Jungnickel.

VERDI, Giuseppe - ROBERTS, Charles J.
—— OVERTURE TO "LA FORZA DEL DESTINO"
                                               C. Fischer.

VEREMANS, Renaat
—— CONCERTO FOR FLUTE AND ORCH. (1962)
                                               H. Elkan.
—— CONCERTO FOR OBOE AND ORCH. (1964)
2,1,2,2 - 2,0,0,0 - timp. - str.   5:20 H. Elkan.
—— CONCERTO FOR TRUMPET AND ORCH. (1960)
2,2,2,2 - 2,1,0,0 - timp. - str.   H. Elkan.

—— MORGENSCHEMER (SYMPHONIC POEM)
2,2,2,2 - 4,2,3,0 - timp.,perc. - str.   H. Elkan.
—— NACHT EN MORGENDONTIWAKER AAN DE NETE
(SYMPHONIC POEM) (1957)
2,2,2,2 - 4,3,3,0 - timp.,perc. - str.   H. Elkan.
—— SYMPHONY NO. 1 (1959)
2,2,2,2 - 4,2,3,1 - timp.,perc. - str.   H. Elkan.
—— SYMPHONY NO. 2 (1961)
2,2,2,2 - 4,2,3,1 - timp.,perc. - str.   H. Elkan.
—— SYMPHONY NO. 3 (1968)
2,2,2,2 - 4,2,3,0 - timp.,perc. - str.   H. Elkan.
—— WOUDTAFERELEN (1961)
2,2,2,2 - 2,2,1,0 - timp.,perc. - str.   H. Elkan.

VERESS, Sándor
—— CONCERTO FOR PIANO, STRINGS AND PERCUSSION
timp.,perc.(3),xyl. - pf. - str.   27:00 Leeds.
—— CONCERTO FOR STRING QUARTET AND ORCH.
2,2,2,2 - 2,2,1,0 - timp.,perc.,cel.,xyl. - hp. - pf. - str. 22:00 Leeds.
—— CONCERTO FOR VIOLIN AND ORCH.
2,2,2,2 - 2,2,0,0 - timp.,perc.(2),xyl. - str.   25:00 Leeds.
—— DIVERTIMENTO
1,1,2,1 - 2,1,0,1 - timp.,perc. - hp. - str.   13:00 S.U.I.S.A.
—— ELEGIA (FOR BARITONE, HARP AND STRINGS)
hp. - str.   18:00 Leeds.
—— EXPOVARE (FOR SMALL ORCH.)
fl.,ob. - str.   3:15 Leeds.
—— HOMMAGE À PAUL KLEE (FANTASIES FOR 2 PIANOS
AND STRINGS)
2 pf. - str.   26:40 Leeds.
—— LAUDATIO MUSICAE (FOR SOPRANO, MIXED CHORUS
AND ORCH.)
1,1,1,1 - 1,1,0,0 - timp.,per.(2),xyl. - hp. - pf. - str.   11:00 Leeds.
—— MUSICA CONCERTANTE (FOR 12 STRINGS) (1966)
str.(7,2,2,1)   15:00 MCA Music.
—— PASSACAGLIA CONCERTANTE
ob. - str.   19;00 Leeds.
—— QUATTRO DANZE TRANSILVANE (FOUR
TRANSYLVANIAN DANCES)
str.   12:00 Leeds.
—— SANCTI AUGUSTINI PSALMUS CONTRA PARTEM DONATI
(FOR BASS, MIXED CHORUS AND ORCH.)
3,3,3,3 - 4,3,3,1 - timp.,perc.(3) - hp. - str.   25:00 Leeds.
—— SINFONIA MINNEAPOLITANA
4,4,3,3 - 4,3,3,1 - timp.,perc.(2),xyl. - hp. - str. 30:00 Leeds.
—— SONATA FOR ORCH.
2,1,2,1 - 2,1,0,0 - timp.,perc.(2) - str.   10:00 Leeds.
—— TERSZILI KATICZA (BALLET, FROM A HUNGARIAN TALE)
%
2,2,2,1 sax.,2 - 6,4,3,1 - perc.,cel.,xyl. - hp. - pf. - str.
                                                     35:00 Leeds.
—— THRENOS (IN MEMORIAM BÉLA BARTÓK)
3,3,3,3 - 4,3,3,1 - timp.,perc.(2) - hp. - str.   11:00 Leeds.

VERETTI, Antonio
—— CONCERTINO FOR FLUTE, PIANO AND STRINGS
fl. - pf. - str.   7:00 Baron.
—— CONCERTO FOR PIANO AND ORCH.
3,2,2,3 - 4,2,3,1 - timp.,perc.(3),cel. - hp. - pf. - str. 38:00 Leeds.
—— FANTASIA FOR CLARINET AND ORCH.
2(2nd alt. with picc.),2(2nd alt. with Eng.hn),3(2nd alt. with
b.-cl.),1 - 1,1,1,1 - timp.,cel.,vibra.,xyl. - hp. - pf. - str.
                                                     14:00 Baron.
—— IL FIGLIUOL PRODIGO ("THE PRODIGAL SON")
(ORATORIO)
2,2,2,2 - 4,2,3,1 - timp.,perc.(2) - hp. - pf. - str. 20:00 Leeds.
—— OUVERTURA DELLA CAMPANA
4,3,4,3 - 4,3,3,1 - timp.,perc.(4),bell,cel.,glock.,xyl. - hp. - pf. - str.
                                                     12:30 Leeds.
—— QUATTRO POESIE DI GIORGIO VIGOLO (FOR SOPRANO
AND ORCH.)
2,2,2,2 - 2,2,0,0, - timp.,perc.,cel.,glock.,xyl. - hp. - pf. - str.
                                                     11:00 Leeds.
—— SINFONIA SACRA (FOR MALE VOICES AND ORCH.)
0,0,0,0 - 4,4,3,1 - timp.,perc.(4),bells,vibra.,xyl. - 2 hp. - 2 pf. - str.
                                                     18:00 Leeds.

VERHAAR, Ary
—— CONCERTO FOR FLUTE AND ORCH.
1,2,2,2 - 2,2,2,0 - timp.,perc.,cel. - hp. - str.   18:00 Henmar.
—— DREI CHINESISCHE LIEDER, OP. 11 (FOR SOPRANO AND
ORCH.) (1939) (IN 3 MOVEMENTS) (German Text: Klabund)
1,0,1,0 - 0,0,0,0 - pf. - str.   10:00 Henmar.

—— DREI GEISHA LIEDER (FOR ALTO AND ORCH.) (1937)
(German Text: Klabund)
1,0,1,0 - 0,0,0,0 - pf. - str.   8:00 Henmar.
—— HAMELN (SYMPHONIC EPISODE), OP. 3
                                                     Henmar.
—— ICHNATON'S ZONNEHYMNE, OP. 5 (FOR SOPRANO,
TENOR, BASS, MIXED CHORUS AND ORCH.) (1933)
1,0,2,3 sax.,0 - 0,1,0,0 - timp.,perc - pf. - str.   30:00 Henmar.
—— KLEINE DAGMUZIEK (AUBADE FOR WINDS) (1959)
2,2,2,2 - 2,2,2,1 - timp.,perc.,cel.(ad lib.) - 2 d.-b.   13:00 Henmar.
—— KLEINE SUITE (FOR SOPRANO AND ORCH.) (1942) (IN 4
MOVTS.)
2,2,2,2 - 2,2,0,0 - timp.,perc.,cel. - hp. - str.   11:00 Henmar.
—— MUSIC FOR CEMBALO AND STRINGS, OP. 4
cemb. - str.   14:00 Henmar.
—— OPUS A (FOR 8 CELLOS AND ORCH.)
2,2,2,2 - 4,2,3,0 - timp.,perc. - hp. - str.   17:00 Henmar.
—— PASSIESPEL, OP. 9 (FOR BOY'S CHORUS, MIXED CHORUS
AND ORCH.) (1942) (Text: Wolbert)
2,2,2,2 - 2,2,4,0 - timp.,perc. - hp. - org. - pf.(or hpsc.) - str.
                                                     20:00 Henmar.
—— PINNEKES-WATER (SYMPHONIC PRELUDE), OP. 39
3,3,2,3 - 4,3,3,1 - timp.,perc. - hp. - str.   8:00 Henmar.
—— A SONG OF JOYS, OP. 14 (FOR BASS, WOMEN'S CHORUS
AND ORCH.) (1938) (Text: Walt Whitman)
1,1,1,1 - 1,0,0,0 - timp. - hp. - pf. - str.   28:00 Henmar.
—— SPIEGEL VAN HET MENSCHELIJKE BEDRIJF NAAR JAN
EN KASPER LUYKEN, OP. 28 (REFLECTIONS UPON THE
MANLY BEHAVIOR OF JAN AND KASPER LUYKEN) (FOR
BOYS' CHORUS, MIXED CHORUS AND ORCH.) (1944)
2,2,2,2 - 2,2,4,0 - timp.,perc. - hp. - org. - pf.(or hpsc.) - str.
                                                     30:00 Henmar.
—— SUITE UIT HET ORATORIUM "GILGAMESJ", OP. 21
3,2,2,2 - 4,3,2,0 - timp.,perc.,cel. - hp. - str.   25:00 Henmar.
—— SYMPHONIETTA VOOR KAMERORKEST, OP. 26
0,1,0,0 - 1,0,0,0 - str.   24:00 Henmar.

VERHEY, Theodor
—— CONCERTO IN A MINOR, FOR FLUTE AND ORCH., OP. 57
(IN 3 MOVTS.)
2(1 alt. with picc.),2,2,2 - 4,2,3,1 - timp.,perc. - str.
                                                     19:00 Henmar.
—— CONCERTO IN A MINOR, FOR VIOLIN AND ORCH., OP. 54
(IN 3 MOVTS.)
2,2,2,2 - 2,2,3,1 - timp. - str.   25:30 Henmar.
—— CONCERTO IN D MINOR, FOR FLUTE AND ORCH., OP. 43
2,2,2,2 - 4,2,3,0 - timp. - str.   15:00 Henmar.
—— CONCERTO IN G MINOR, FOR CLARINET AND ORCH., OP.
47
2,2,2,2 - 4,2,3,0 - timp.,perc. - str.   19:00 Henmar.

VERMEULEN, Matthijs
—— PASSACAILLE ET CORTEGE (UIT "DE VLIEGENDE
HOLLANDER")
3,3,3,3 - 4,3,3,1 - timp.,perc.,xyl. - hp. - str.   12:00 Henmar.
—— SYMPHONIC PROLOGUE (1930)
3,3,3,3 - 4,3,3,0 - timp.,perc.,xyl. - hp. - str.   20:00 Henmar.
—— SYMPHONY NO. 1 ("SYMPHONIA CARMINUM")
2,3,4,3 - 4,4,3,1 - timp.,perc. - str.   14:00 Henmar.
—— SYMPHONY NO. 2 ("PRÉLUDE À LA NOUVELLE JOURNÉE")
4,4,6,4 - 4,6,3,1 - timp.,perc.,xyl. - 2 hp. - str. 26:00 Henmar.
—— SYMPHONY NO. 3 (THRÈNE ET PÉAN) (1922)
4,3,4,1 sopr. sax.,1 alto sax.,4 - 4,4,3,1 - timp.,perc. - 2 hp. - str.
                                                     Henmar.
—— SYMPHONY NO. 4 ("LES VICTORIES")
4,5,6,2 sopr. sax.,4 - 4,3,3,1 - timp.,perc.,xyl. - str. 28:00 Henmar.
—— SYMPHONY NO. 5 ("LES LENDEMAINS CHANTANTS")
4,4,6,3 sax.,4 - 4,4,3,1 - timp.,perc. - 2 hp. - str. 50:00 Henmar.
—— SYMPHONY NO. 6 (LES MINUTES HEUREUSES SUR
LA-DO-RÉ) (1958)
4,4,4,2 sax.,4 - 4,4,3,1 - timp.,perc.,cel. - hp. - str. 24:00 Henmar.
—— SYMPHONY NO. 7 ("DITHYRAMBES POUR LES TEMPS À
VENIR")
4,4,5,alto sax.,4 - 4,4,3,1 - timp.,perc.,cel. - str. 17:00 Henmar.
—— LA VEILLE (FOR MEZZO-SOPRANO AND ORCH.) (1932)
(Text: F. Porché)
3,3,3,2 - 4,3,3,1 - timp.,perc. - hp. - str.   10:00 Henmar.

VERNON, Ashley
—— LU-HSING ("THE JOURNEY") (FOUR SONGS FOR MEDIUM
VOICE AND ORCH.)
3,3,3,2 - 4,3,0,0 - timp.,perc.,cel.,xyl. - hp. - str.
                                                     8:00 MCA Music.

—— RHAPSODY FOR OBOE AND STRINGS
ob. - str.   6:00 EV.

VERNON, W. Knight
—— IN MEMORIAM (FOR NARRATOR AND ORCH.) (1967) (Text: Randall Jarrell)
*3,*3,*3,*3 - 4,3,3,1 - timp.,perc.(6),bells,cel.,glock.,xyl. - hp. - pf. - str.   7:30 Composer.

VERRALL, John
—— SYMPHONY FOR YOUNG ORCHESTRAS
      Boston.

VETESSY, Georg
—— SUITE NO 1 FOR ORCH.
      14:00 A.K.M.

VIANELLO, Hugo
—— CHRISTMAS KALEIDOSCOPE
3,2,2,2 - 4,3,3,1 - timp.,perc.,bells,cel.,glock.,xyl. - org. - str.
      12:00 C. Fischer.

VIBERT, Mathieu
—— EPITAPHE (POUR GRAND ORCHESTRE)
      15:00 S.U.I.S.A.
—— NOCTURNE POUR HAUTBOIS - COR ENGLAIS (1 EXÉCUTANT) ET ORCH.
2,3(1 alt. with Eng. hn.),2,2 - 4,0,0,0 - str.   18:00 S.U.I.S.A.

VIC, Claude Henri
—— JESUS (CANTATA) (FOR SATB CHORUS AND ORCHESTRA) (IN 12 MOVTS.)
2,1,2,3 sax.(alto,ten.,bar.),2 - 1,1,4,0 - perc. - 2 guit., b.-guit. - hp. - org. - str.   30:00 Bourne.

VICK, Lloyd
—— THE STORY OF UDAIPORE (FOR FEMALE CHORUS AND ORCH.)
      30:00 A.P.R.A.

VICTORIA, Tomas Luis - STOKOWSKI, Leopold
—— JESU DULCIS MEMORIA
      3:00 Broude.

VICTORY, Gerard
—— BALLADE, OP. 27 (1963)
3,3,3,3 - 4,3,3,1 - perc.(3) - hp. - str.   17:30 P.R.S.
—— CONCERTO FOR PIANO AND ORCH., OP. 8 (1954)
2,2,2,2 - 4,3,3,0 - perc.(2) - pf. - str.   22:00 P.R.S.
—— FAVOLA DI NOTTE, OP. 41 (1966)
3,2,3,2 - 4,3,3,1 - timp.,perc.(4) - hp. - pf. - str.   13:00 P.R.S.
—— PARIAH - MUSIC, OP. 29 (1964)
1,0,1,1 - 0,1,00 - perc.(3) - pf. - str.   12:00 P.R.S.
—— SHORT SYMPHONY, OP. 19 (1961)
2,2,2,2 - 4,3,3,1 - perc.(2) - hp. - str.   22:00 P.R.S.

VIDAL, Paul - MAZELLIER
—— DEUXIÈME SOLO DE CONCERT (FOR TROMBONE AND ORCH.)
2,2,2,2 - 2,2,1,0 - timp. - str.   5:30 Baron.

VIDAS, Raoul
—— ANDROMEDA (OPERA) % (1930) (Text: Minna Katheryn Breid)
*4,*3,*4,*4 - 4,3,3,1 - timp.,perc. - 4 hp. - org. - str.
      90:00 Composer.
—— OVERTURE IN F MAJOR ("SOMEWHAT IN IRISH STYLE") (1965)
*4,*3,*4,*4 - 4,3,3,1 - timp. - hp. - str.   12:00 Composer.
—— RESURRECTION AT SUNDOWN (GRAND OPERA) % (1948) (Text: Gemma d'Auria)
*4,*3,*4,*4 - 4,3,3,1 - timp.,cym. - 2 hp. - str.   210:00 Composer.
—— STEPHEN FOSTER SYMPHONY (FOR SOLO VOICES, SATB CHORUS AND ORCH.) (Text: Minna Katheryn Breid)
*4,*4,*4,2 alto cl.,1 d.-b.-cl.,*5 - 7,2 cnt.,3,4,1 - timp.,perc. - 2 hp. - org. - str.   90:00 Composer.

VIERNE, Louis
—— ADAGIO, OP. 28 (FOR ORGAN AND ORCHESTRA) (FROM THE SYMPHONY NO. 3)
2,3,3,2 - 2,0,0,0 - str.   4:15 EV.
—— BALLADE FOR VIOLIN AND ORCHESTRA
      EV.

—— SOIRS ÉTRANGERS (SUITE FOR CELLO AND ORCH.) (IN 5 MOVTS.)
      EV.

VIERU, Anatol
—— CONCERTO FOR CELLO AND ORCH. (1962)
2,2,2,2 - 2,2,1,0 - perc.(3), cel. - pf. - str.   14:00 Salabert.
—— ECRAN (1970)
3,2,*3,*3 - 4,3,3,1 - perc.(6),glock.,mar.,vibra. - elec. guit. - str.
      15:00 Salabert.
—— JEUX (FOR PIANO AND ORCH.) (1963)
*2,1,*2,3 sax.,0 - 0,3,3,0 - perc.(5),glock.,mar - pf. - str.
      17:00 Salabert.
—— MUSEUM MUSIC (1968)
hpsc.(or electric hpsc.) - str.(7,2,2,1)(also alt. with perc.)
      11:00 Salabert.
—— ODE AU SILENCE (1967)
3,0,0,0 - 0,3,3,0 - perc.(6),glock. - tape-recorder - str.
      18:00 Salabert.

VIINHOLT-NIELSEN, Bendt
—— RUIN
4,0,0,0 - 4,3,3,1 - timp.,perc. - hpsc. - pf. - str.   5:00 K.O.D.A.

VILLA-LOBOS, Heitor
—— BACHIANAS BRASILEIRAS NO. 3 (FOR 2 PIANOS AND ORCH.)
3,3,3,3 - 4,1,4,1 - timp.,xyl. - 2 pf. - str.   25:00 Belw-Mills.
—— BACHIANAS BRASILEIRAS NO. 4
3,3,3,3 - 4,3,2,1 - timp.,cel.,xyl. - str.   20:00 Belw-Mills.
—— CIRANDA DAS SETE NOTAS (FOR BASSOON AND STRINGS)
bn. - str.   10:00 Southern.
—— FANTASIA DE MOVIMENTOS MIXTOS (FOR VIOLIN AND ORCH.)
3,3,3,3 - 4,2,2,1 - timp.,perc. - hp. - str.   25:00 Southern.
—— FANTASIA (FOR SOPRANO OR TENOR SAXOPHONE AND ORCH.)
sax. - 3 hn. - str.   14:00 Southern.
—— ODYSSEY OF A RACE (SYMPHONIC POEM)
3,3,3,3 - 4,3,3,1 - timp.,perc.,cel.,xyl. - 2 hp. - pf. - str.
      MCA Music.
—— SINFONIA NO. 2 ("ASCENCAO")
4,3,3,3 - 4,4,4,1 - timp.,perc.,cel. - 2 hp. - str.   55:00 Belw-Mills.
—— SINFONIA NO. 3 ("AGUERRA")
4,3,3,4 - 4,4,4,1 - timp.,perc.,cel.(3) - 2 hp. - str.
      20:00 Belw-Mills.
—— SINFONIA NO. 4 ("VICTORIA")
4,3,3,2 sax.,4 - 4,4,4,1 - timp.,perc.,cel. - 2 hp. - str.
      25:00 Belw-Mills.
—— SINFONIA NO. 6 ("MONTANHAS DO BRAZIL")
4,3,3,3 - 4,4,4,1 - timp.,perc.,cel. - 2 hp. - str.   20:00 Ricordi.
—— SINFONIA NO. 7 ("ODEISSEIA DE PAZ")
5,4,4,4 - 6,4,4,1 - timp.,perc.,cel.,vibra.,xyl. - novachord - 2 hp. - str.   35:00 Ricordi.
—— SINFONIETTA NO. 1
2,2,2,2 - 2,2,2,0 - timp. - str.   15:00 Southern.
—— SINFONIETTA NO. 2
1,1,1,alto sax.,1 - 2,1,1,1 - timp.,perc. - hp. - str.   15:00 Southern.

VILLETTE, Pierre
—— CONCERTO FOR VIOLIN AND ORCH.
2,2,2,2 - 4,2,3,1 - timp.,perc.(3),cel. - hp. - str.   28:30 EV.
—— THREE PRELUDES FOR STRINGS
str.   8:00 Presser.

VINCENT, John
—— BAROQUE ALBUM (16 PIECES) (ON WORKS OF BACH, COUPERIN, J. K. F. FISCHER, HANDEL, MONTEVERDI AND VIVALDI)
pf. - str.   24:00 Curlew.
—— CONSORT (A SYMPHONY FOR PIANO AND STRING ORCH.) (1975) (IN 3 MOVTS.)
pf. - str.   26:00 Curlew.
—— THE HOUSE THAT JACK BUILT (FOR NARRATOR AND ORCH.) (FROM THE BALLET "THE THREE JACKS")) (Text: Henry Reese)
2(alt. with picc.),2(2nd alt. with Eng.hn.),2(2nd alt. with b.-cl.),2 - 2,1,1,0 - timp.,perc.(2) - str.   17:00 Mills.
—— LA JOLLA CONCERTO (IN 4 MOVTS.)
2(alt. with 2 picc.),2(1 alt. with Eng.hn.),2,2 - 2,1,1,0 - timp.,perc. - str.   12:00 Mills.

—— NUDE DESCENDING THE STAIRCASE (AFTER MARCEL DUCHAMP'S PAINTING)
xyl. - str.   8:00 Composer.
—— OVERTURE TO THE OPERA "LORD ARLING"
2(alt. with 2 picc.),2,2,2 - 4,3,3,1 - timp.,perc.(2),xyl. - str.
8:00 Mills.
—— THE PHOENIX (FABULOUS BIRD) (SYMPHONIC POEM) (1966)
2,2,*3,*3 - 4,3,3,1 - timp.,perc. - str.   17:00 Belw-Mills.
or:
3,3,*3,*3 - 4,3,3,1 - timp.,perc. - str.
—— PRIMEVAL VOID (1-ACT OPERA BUFFA) % (1972)
1,1,2,1 - alto sax.,1 - 2,1,1,0 - timp.,perc.(2) - pf. - str.
27:00 Curlew.
—— QUARTET (FOR STRING ORCH.) (IN 4 MOVTS.)
str.   26:00 Mills.
—— RONDO RHAPSODY (1965)
*3,2,E♭cl.,*3,2 - 4,3,3,1 - timp.,perc.(2),glock.,xyl. - str.
9:00 Belw-Mills.
—— SOLILOQUY AND DANCE
str.   16:00 Mills.
—— SUITE FROM THE BALLET "THE THREE JACKS" (IN 3 MOVTS.)
*3,*3,*3,0 - 4,2,3,0 - timp.,perc.(3),glock.,xyl. - str.   15:00 Mills.
or:
3,3,3,3 - 4,3,3,1 - timp.,perc.(3) - str.
—— SYMPHONIC POEM AFTER DESCARTES (IN 2 MOVTS.)
3(2nd and 3rd alt. with piccs.),*3,*3,2 - 4,3,3,1 -
timp.,perc.(3),bells,cel. - hp. - str.   15:00 Mills.
—— SYMPHONIC STRUCTURE
2(2nd alt. with picc.),2,2,2 - 4,2,3,0 - timp.,perc.(2) - str.
15:00 Composer.
—— SYMPHONIC SUITE (IN 3 MOVTS.)
2,2,2,2 - 4,3,3,0 - timp.,perc.(2) - str.   13:00 Mills.
—— SYMPHONY IN D (FESTIVAL SYMPHONY) (IN 1 MOVT.)
2(2nd alt. with picc.),2,2,2 - 4,3,3,1 - timp.,perc.(2) - str.
18:00 Mills.
—— THE THREE JACKS (BALLET) %
2(2nd alt. with picc.),2(2nd alt. with Eng. hn.),2(2nd alt. with
b.-cl.),2 - 2,1,1,0 - timp.,perc.(2),glock.,xyl. - str.   30:00 Mills.

VINCZE, Imre
—— AFORISMO
str.   10:00 Bo. Hawkes.
—— CONCERTINO
1,1,1,1 - 1,1,1,0 - timp.,perc. - pf. - str.   8:30 Bo. Hawkes.
—— MOVIMENTO SINFONICO
2,2,2,1 sax.,2 - 4,3,3,1 - timp.,perc. - hp. - str. 18:30 Bo. Hawkes.
—— RAPSODIA CONCERTANTE (FOR PIANO AND ORCH.)
*3,2,2,2 - 4,2,3,1 - timp.,perc. - pf. - str.   13:00 Bo. Hawkes.
—— SYMPHONY NO. 1
2,2,2,2 - 4,3,3,1 - timp.,perc. - hp. - str.   25:00 Bo. Hawkes.
—— SYMPHONY NO. 2
3,3,2,2 - 4,3,3,1 - timp.,perc. - hp. - str.   Bo. Hawkes.

VINCZE, Ottó
—— FANTASTIC DANCES
2,2,2,2 - 4,2,2,0 - timp.,perc. - hp. - pf. - str.   Bo. Hawkes.
—— MERRY LITTLE OVERTURE
2,2,2,2 - 4,2,0,0 - timp.,perc. - hp. - str.   5:00 Bo. Hawkes.

VINTER, Gilbert
—— DIVERTIMENTO FOR STRINGS
str.   14:00 Galaxy.
—— HUNTER'S MOON (FOR HORN AND ORCH.)
2,1,2,1 - 1,0,0,0 - perc. - hp.(or pf.) - str.   6:00 Bo. Hawkes.
—— NEW LAMPS FOR OLD (SUITE)
3,3,2,2 - 4,2,3,0 - perc. - hp. - str.   10:30 Bo. Hawkes.

VINTER, Gilbert - PERRY
—— CONCERTINO FOR CLARINET AND ORCH.
1,1,2,1 - 2,0,0,0 - timp.,perc.,cel. - str.   7:30 Bo. Hawkes.

VIOTTI, G. B. - QUARANTA, Felice
—— SINFONIA CONCERTANTE NO. 1 (FOR 2 VIOLINS AND ORCH.)
0,2,0,0 - 2,0,0,0 - str.   20:00 Bo. Hawkes.
—— SINFONIA CONCERTANTE NO. 2 (FOR TWO VIOLINS AND ORCH.)
2,2,2,2 - 2,2,0,0 - str.   20:00 Bo. Hawkes.

VIOTTI, G. B. - SGRIZZI, Luciano
—— VIOTTIANA
3,3,2,2 - 2,2,1,0 - timp.,perc. - str.   18:00 Leeds.

VISÉE, Robert de - KELKEL, M.
—— PETITE SUITE IN E MINOR
1,1,0,1 - 1,0,0,0 - str.   10:00 F. Colombo.

VISKI, János
—— CONCERTO FOR CELLO AND ORCH.
3,2,2,3 - 4,3,3,1 - timp.,perc. - str.   26:00 Bo. Hawkes.
—— CONCERTO FOR PIANO AND ORCH.
3,2,2,3 - 4,3,3,1 - timp.,perc. - hp. - pf. - str.   27:00 Bo. Hawkes.
—— CONCERTO FOR VIOLIN AND ORCH. (IN 3 MOVTS.)
3(alt. with 3 picc.),2(2nd alt. with Eng. hn.),2,2 - 4,3,3,1 -
timp.,perc.,xyl. - hp. - str.   30:00 Bo. Hawkes.

VITALI, Giovanni Battista - GUERRINI
—— CIACONNA (FOR VIOLIN, ORGAN AND STRINGS)
org. - str.   18:00 Henmar.

VITALI, Giovanni Battista - LENZEWSKI
—— CAPRICCIO IN F MAJOR
str.   Henmar.

VITALI, Giovanni Battista - SONTAG, Wesley
—— CONCERTO IN D MINOR
str.   Fox.

VITALI, Tommaso - AKON, Alfred
—— CIACONNA
3,3,3,2 - 4,3,3,1 - timp.,perc.,cel.(ad lib.),glock. - hp. - str.
12:00 Belw-Mills.

VITALI, Tommaso - FARINA, Guido
—— CIACCONA
2,*3,2,*3 - 4,3,3,1 - timp. - hp. - org. - str.   10:00 Bo. Hawkes.

VITALI, Tommaso - LAVIGNE, Jean
—— CHACONNE
S.A.C.E.M.

VITALIS, George
—— GREEK FANTASY
2(2nd alt. with picc.),*1,*3,*3 - 4,2,3,1 - timp.,perc.(3), cel. - hp. -
str.   6:30 Mills.

VITO-DELVAUX, Berthe di
—— CONCERTO FOR HORN AND ORCH., OP. 93 (1963)
2,1,2,1 - 3,2,2,0 - timp.,perc. - hp. - str.   H. Elkan.
—— CONCERTO FOR PIANO AND ORCH., OP. 120 (1969)
2,2,2,2 - 4,2,4,1 - timp.,perc. - pf. - str.   H. Elkan.
—— LE MIROIR (1974) (BALLET FOR ORCHESTRA)
2,2,2,2 - 4,2,3,1 - timp.,perc. - hp. - str.   H. Elkan.
—— NEILOVIM, OP. 123 (FOR TRUMPET AND ORCH.) (1970)
2,1,2,1 - 2,3,1,0 - timp.,perc. - hp. - str.   H. Elkan.
—— PIÈCE CONCERTANTE, OP. 105 (FOR ENGLISH HORN AND ORCH.)
H. Elkan.

VITTORIA, Mario
—— CONCERTINO FOR STRINGS
str.   17:00 Henmar.
—— SYLLEPSES (SYMPHONIE CONCERTANTE)
2,2,2,2 - 2,2,1,0 - timp.,perc.(3) - pf. - str.   20:00 Presser.
—— TRIPTYQUE ANACOLUTHE (FOR VIOLA AND ORCH.)
2,2,2,2 - 2,2,1,0 - timp.,perc. - hp. - str.   25:00 Presser.

VITTORIO, Ezio
—— PRELUDIO E ALLEGRO
str.   10:00 Bo. Hawkes.

VIVALDI, Antonio - ASLANIAN, Vahe, ed.
—— CHAMBER MASS (FOR CHORUS, WINDS, ORGAN
CONTINUO AND DOUBLE STRING ORCH.)
0,2,0,0 - 0,1,0,0 - org. - str.   Law-Gould.

VIVALDI, Antonio - ALLARD, Maurice
—— CONCERTO IN B FLAT MAJOR (FOR BASSOON AND ORCH.)
10:10 Presser.
—— CONCERTO IN F MAJOR (FOR BASSOON AND ORCH.)
8:15 Presser.

VIVALDI, Antonio - BACH, Johann Sebastian - FASANO, Renato
—— CONCERTO IN G MAJOR, FOR CELLO, STRINGS AND
CEMBALO
cemb. -str.   S.I.A.E.
—— CONCERTO NO. 1, IN C MAJOR
org.(or hpsc.) - str.   4:45 Presser.
—— CONCERTO NO. 2, IN A MAJOR
org.(or hpsc) - str.   Presser.
—— CONCERTO NO. 3, IN C MAJOR
org.(or hpsc.) - str.   12:00 Presser.
—— CONCERTO NO. 4, IN G MAJOR
org.(or hpsc.) - str.   9:00 Presser.

VIVALDI, Antonio - BAZELAIRE, Paul
—— CONCERTO IN E MINOR, FOR CELLO AND STRINGS
str.   14:00 Baron.

VIVALDI, Antonio - BEHREND, Siegfried
—— CONCERTO FOR GUITAR AND STRINGS
(LAUTENKONZERT) (Originally for Lute and Ensemble)
guit. - str.   Henmar.
—— CONCERTO IN D MAJOR, FOR GUITAR AND STRINGS
(After the A Major Sonata for Lute, Violin and Continuo)
guit. - str.   12:00 F. Colombo.

VIVALDI, Antonio - BLANCHARD, Roger
—— LA GLORIA E IMENEO (FOR 2 WOMEN'S VOICES, STRINGS
AND CONTINUO)
cemb. - str.   50:00 Presser.
—— INTRODUZIONE AL GLORIA E IMENEO (FOR SOPRANO,
ALTO, TENOR, SATB CHORUS AND ORCH.)
0,2,0,0 - 0,1,0,0 - hpsc.(or org.) - str.   30:00 Presser.

VIVALDI, Antonio - BONELLI, Ettore
—— CONCERTO GROSSO IN F MAJOR, FOR 3 VIOLINS AND
STRINGS
str.   Henmar.
—— CONCERTO IN B MINOR, OP. 3, NO. 10 (FOR 4 VIOLINS,
STRINGS AND CEMBALO)
cemb. - str.   11:00 Henmar.

VIVALDI, Antonio - BROWN
—— SONATA DA CAMERA IN E MINOR
str.   Galaxy.

VIVALDI, Antonio - BRUNI, M.
—— SINFONIA FROM THE OPERA "IL GIUSTINO"
cemb. - str.   6:00 Bo. Hawkes.

VIVALDI, Antonio - CASELLA, Alfredo
—— CONCERTO ("ALLA RUSTICA") (FOR STRINGS)
str.   5:00 Bo. Hawkes.
—— CONCERTO IN C, FOR ORCH.
2,1,0,0 - 0,2,0,0 - cel. - 1-2 hp. - mandolin - str.
                                                       14:00 Bo. Hawkes.
—— CONCERTO NO. 3 ("LA CETRA") (FOR VIOLIN AND
STRINGS)
str.   10:00 Bo. Hawkes.
—— DUE ARIE DALL' OPERA "ERCOLE SUL TERMODONTE"
cemb. - str.   7:00 Bo. Hawkes.
—— STABAT MATER (FOR CONTRALTO, ORGAN AND
STRINGS)
org. - str.   13:00 Bo. Hawkes.

VIVALDI, Antonio - CHAVEZ, Carlos
—— CONCERTO IN G MINOR FOR VIOLIN AND ORCH., OP. 6,
NO. 1 (IN 3 MOVTS.)
3,3,3,3 - 4,3,3,1 - timp.,perc.(2) - pf. - str.   14:00 Arranger.

VIVALDI, Antonio - COMPANY, Alvaro
—— CONCERTO IN D MAJOR (FOR GUITAR AND STRING
ORCH.)
guit. - str.   8:00 MCA Music.

VIVALDI, Antonio - COURTE, Robert
—— CONCERTO IN B FLAT MINOR, FOR VIOLA AND STRING
ORCH.
str.   C. Fischer.
—— CONCERTO IN E FOR VIOLA AND STRING ORCH.
str.   C. Fischer.

VIVALDI, Antonio - DALLEY, Orien
—— CONCERTO GROSSO, OP. 3, NO. 11
2,2,2,2 - 2,2,3,1 - timp. - str.   Fema.

VIVALDI, Antonio - ESPOSITO, M.
—— CONCERTO IN B MINOR FOR STRINGS
str.   Oxford.

VIVALDI, Antonio - FASANO, Renato
—— CONCERTO IN G FOR STRINGS AND CEMBALO ("ALLA
RUSTICA")
cemb. - str.   S.I.A.E.
—— THE FOUR SEASONS (CONCERTI FROM OP. 8) (FOR
VIOLINS, CEMBALO AND STRING ORCH.)
cemb. - str.   S.I.A.E.

VIVALDI, Antonio - FEDER, Edgard
—— CONCERTO FOR CELLO AND STRINGS
str.   17:00 EV.

VIVALDI, Antonio - FRANKO, Sam
—— CONCERTO GROSSO IN D MINOR FOR STRINGS
str.   G. Schirmer.
—— CONCERTO IN A MINOR FOR STRINGS
str.   G. Schirmer.
—— CONCERTO IN G MINOR (LA STRAVAGANZA, NO. 6;
ORIGINALLY FOR VIOLIN)
pf. - str.   10:00 C. Fischer.
—— CONCERTO IN G MINOR, OP. 4, NO. 6 (FOR VIOLIN,
CEMBALO AND STRINGS)
cemb. - str.   Henmar.

VIVALDI, Antonio - FRENKEL, Stefan
—— CONCERTO IN B FLAT MAJOR (La Stravaganza, No. 1;
Originally for Violin)
pf. - str.   13:00 C. Fischer.
—— CONCERTO IN B FLAT MAJOR, OP. 4, NO. 1 (FOR VIOLIN
AND STRINGS)
str.   Henmar.

VIVALDI, Antonio - GIANNINI, Vittorio
—— CONCERTO GROSSO IN D MINOR
3(3rd alt. with picc.),3(3rd alt. with Eng. hn.),3(3rd alt. with
b.-cl.),*3 - 4,3,3,1 - timp.,perc. (2) - str.   9:00 EV.

VIVALDI, Antonio - GRENZ, Artur
—— CONCERTO FOR 3 VIOLINS AND STRING ORCH.
str.   10:00 F. Colombo.

VIVALDI, Antonio - JOHN
—— CONCERTO FOR MANDOLIN AND STRING ORCH. (IN 3
MOVTS.)
Mandolin - str.   9:00 Noack.

VIVALDI, Antonio - KNIESEL, Franz - DAMROSCH, Frank
—— CONCERTO IN D, OP. 3, NO. 10 (FOR 4 VIOLINS AND
STRING ORCH.)
pf. - str.   C. Fischer.

VIVALDI, Antonio - KOGAN, Leonid
—— CONCERTO IN G MINOR, FOR VIOLIN AND STRINGS
str.   8:30 Presser.

VIVALDI, Antonio - KUECHLER-HERRMANN
—— CONCERTO IN G MAJOR, OP. 3, NO. 3 (FOR VIOLIN AND
STRINGS)
str.   10:00 Henmar.

VIVALDI, Antonio - MATESKY, Ralph
—— CONCERTO GROSSO IN G MAJOR
                                                          F. Colombo.

VIVALDI, Antonio - MORTARI, Virgilio
—— CONCERTO IN C FOR 2 VIOLINS AND STRINGS
str.   15:00 Bo. Hawkes.
—— OLIMPIADE: SINFONIA (FOR STRINGS)
str.   6:00 Bo. Hawkes.

VIVALDI, Antonio - OUBRADOUS, Fernand
—— CONCERTO NO. 1, IN F (FOR VIOLIN AND ORCH.)
0,2,0,1 - 2,0,0,0 - str.   12:00 Presser.
—— CONCERTO NO. 2, IN C
2 fl. - str.   9:00 Presser.

or:
fl.,ob. - str.
—— CONCERTO NO. 3, IN G
2 mandolins(or 2 guit.) - org.(or cemb.) - str.   12:30 Presser.
—— CONCERTO NO. 4, IN C MINOR (FOR CELLO AND STRINGS)
str.   12:30 Presser.
—— CONCERTO NO. 5, IN F (FOR OBOE AND STRINGS)
ob. - str.   10:30 Presser.
—— CONCERTO NO. 6, IN G MINOR (FOR FLUTE AND ORCH.)
1,0,0,1 - 0,0,0,0 - str.   12:00 Presser.
—— CONCERTO NO. 7, IN G MINOR ("FOR THE ORCHESTRA OF DRESDEN")
2,2,0,1 - 0,0,0,0 - str.   11:00 Presser.
—— CONCERTO NO. 8, IN A (FOR STRING ORCH.)
str.   10:00 Presser.
—— CONCERTO NO. 9, IN C MINOR (FOR VIOLIN AND STRINGS)
str.   12:30 Presser.
—— CONCERTO NO. 10, IN C MINOR (FOR STRING ORCH.)
str.   7:00 Presser.
—— CONCERTO NO. 11, IN D MINOR (FOR STRINGS AND CLAVECIN)
cemb. - str.   10:00 Presser.
—— CONCERTO NO. 12, IN C MAJOR (ORIGINALLY FOR VIOLIN AND ORCH.) (With cadenzas by Robert Veyron-Lacroix)
2,*2,0,0 - 0,2,0,0 - hpsc. - str.   10:00 Presser.
—— CONCERTO NO. 13, IN C
picc. - str.   10:00 Presser.
—— CONCERTO NO. 14, IN E ("SPRING", FROM " THE SEASONS") (FOR VIOLIN AND STRINGS)
str.   10:00 Presser.
—— CONCERTO NO. 15, IN G MINOR ("SUMMER", FROM " THE SEASONS") (FOR VIOLIN, CEMBALO AND STRINGS)
cemb. - str.   10:00 Presser.
—— CONCERTO NO. 16, IN F ("AUTUMN", FROM "THE SEASONS") (FOR VIOLIN AND STRINGS)
str.   10:00 Presser.
—— CONCERTO NO. 17, IN F MINOR ("WINTER", FROM "THE SEASONS") (FOR VIOLIN AND STRINGS)
str.   10:00 Presser.
—— CONCERTO NO. 18, IN F (FOR 2 OBOES, BASSOON, 2 HORNS, VIOLIN AND STRINGS)
0,2,0,1 - 2,0,0,0 - cemb.(ad lib.) - str.   15:00 Presser.
—— CONCERTO NO. 19, IN A (FOR VIOLA AND STRINGS)
hp.(ad lib.) - str.   10:00 Presser.
—— CONCERTO NO. 20
2 hn. - cemb.(ad lib.) - str.   10:00 Presser.
—— CONCERTO NO. 21, IN C MAJOR
2 ob.,2 bn. - cemb.(ad lib.) - str.   10:00 Presser.
—— CONCERTO NO. 22, IN G MAJOR
ob.,hn. - cemb.(ad lib.) - str.   10:00 Presser.
—— CONCERTO NO. 23, IN C MAJOR (FOR 2 GUITARS AND STRINGS) (With cadenzas by Amable Massis)
2 guit. - cemb.(ad lib.) - str.   10:00 Presser.
—— CONCERTO NO. 24, IN G MINOR (FOR 2 CELLOS AND STRINGS)
str.   10:00 Presser.
—— CONCERTO NO. 25, IN G MINOR (WITH SOLO FLUTE, OBOE AND BASSOON)
fl.,ob.,bn. - str.   8:00 Presser.
—— CONCERTO NO. 26, IN E FLAT MAJOR (FOR CELLO, STRINGS AND KEYBOARD)
cemb. - str.   10:00 Presser.

VIVALDI, Antonio - STOKOWSKI, Leopold
—— CONCERTO GROSSO IN D MINOR, OP. 3, NO. 11
   Arranger.

VIVALDI, Antonio - THILDE, Jean
—— CONCERTO IN B FLAT
tpt. - str.   8:35 Presser.
—— CONCERTO IN C MAJOR FOR TRUMPET AND STRINGS
tpt. - str.   10:00 Presser.
—— CONCERTO IN C MAJOR FOR 2 TRUMPETS AND STRINGS
2 tpt. - str.   9:30 Presser.
—— CONCERTO IN D MINOR (FOR TRUMPET AND STRINGS)
tpt. - str.   8:00 Presser.
—— CONCERTO IN G MINOR
tpt. - str.   5:00 Presser.
—— CONCERTO NO. 2 IN B FLAT (FOR TRUMPET AND ORCH.)
   5:30 Presser.

VIVALDI, Antonio - TONI, Alceo
—— LE STAGIONI ("THE SEASONS") (IN 4 MOVTS.)
ob. - pf. - str.   46:00 Bo. Hawkes.

VIVALDI, Antonio - TORREFRANCA, Fausto
—— CONCERTO IN B FOR CEMBALO AND STRINGS
cemb. - str.   15:00 Bo. Hawkes.

VIVALDI, Antonio - UPMEYER, Walter
—— CONCERTO IN A MAJOR, OP. 3, NO. 5 (FOR TWO VIOLINS AND STRINGS) (FROM "L'ESTRO ARMONICO")
cemb. - str.   7:00 G. Schirmer.
—— CONCERTO IN B MINOR, OP. 3, NO. 10 (FOR FOUR VIOLINS AND STRINGS) (FROM "L'ESTRO ARMONICO")
cemb. - str.   10:00 G. Schirmer.
—— CONCERTO IN D MAJOR, OP. 3, NO. 1 (FOR FOUR VIOLINS AND STRINGS) (FROM "L'ESTRO ARMONICO")
cemb. - str.   10:00 G. Schirmer.
—— CONCERTO IN E MINOR, OP. 3, NO. 4 (FOR FOUR VIOLINS AND STRINGS) (FROM "L'ESTRO ARMONICO")
cemb. - str.   8:00 G. Schirmer.
—— CONCERTO IN F MAJOR, OP. 3, NO. 9 (FOR FOUR VIOLINS AND STRINGS) (FROM "L'ESTRO ARMONICO")
cemb. - str.   7:00 G. Schirmer.

VIVALDI, Antonio - VENE, Ruggero
—— CONCERTO NO. 2 IN A MINOR FOR FLUTE, OBOE, BASSOON AND STRINGS (IN 3 MOVTS.)
1,1,0,1 - 2,0,0,0 - str.   15:00 Ricordi.

VIVALDI, Antonio - VINCENT, John
—— CONCERTO IN G MINOR (IN 3 MOVTS.)
pf. - str.   9:00 Curlew.

VIVALDI, Antonio - YEPES, Narciso
—— CONCERTO IN D MAJOR (With cadenzas by Narciso Yepes)
guit.(or lute) - str.   11:00 Presser.

VLAD, Roman
—— LE CIEL EST VIDE ("THE SKY IS EMPTY") (FOR MIXED CHORUS AND ORCH.)
4,3,3,3 - 4,4,3,1 - timp.,perc.(3),cel.,vibra.,xyl. - hp. - pf. - str.   25:00 Leeds.
—— CINQUE ELEGIE SU TESTI BIBLICI (FOR VOICE AND STRING ORCH.)
str.   17:30 Leeds.
—— DE PROFUNDIS (FOR MIXED CHORUS AND ORCH.)
3,3,3,3 - 4,3,3,1 - timp.,perc.(2) - 2 hp. - pf. -str.   26:30 Leeds.
—— DIVERTIMENTO FOR ELEVEN INSTS.
1,1,1,1 - 0,0,0,0 - hpsc. - str.   15:00 Bo. Hawkes.
—— IL DOTTORE DI VETRO ("THE GLASS DOCTOR") (1-ACT RADIO OPERA, AFTER PHILIPPE QUINAULT) (Text: M. L. Spaziani)
2,2,2,2 - 2,2,2,0 - perc.,cel.,vibra.,xyl. - hp. - pf. - str.   Leeds.
—— MASQUES OSTENDAIS ("HOMMAGE Á ENSOR") (BALLET, AFTER M. DE GHELDERODE) %
1,1,1,1 sax.,1 - 0,1,1,0 - perc.,vibra.,xyl. - 2 pf. - str.   20:00 Leeds.
—— MUSIC FOR STRINGS (MELORITMI)
str.   15:00 Leeds.
—— MUSICA CONCERTATA (FOR HARP AND ORCH.)
3,3,3,3 - 4,3,3,1 - timp.,perc.(2) - hp. - str.   25:00 Leeds.
—— SERENATA (FOR 12 INSTRUMENTS)
1,2,2,2 - 2,0,0,0 - cel. - 2 vla.   16:30 Leeds.
—— SINFONIA ALL'ANTICA
3,3,3,3 - 4,3,3,1 - timp.,perc.(3) - pf. - str.   Leeds.
—— STORIA D'UNA MAMMA (1-ACT OPERA, AFTER HANS CHRISTIAN ANDERSEN) %
2,2,2,2 - 4,3,3,1 - timp.,perc.,vibra.,xyl. - hp. - pf. - str.   30:00 Leeds.
—— LA STRADA SUL CAFFÈ ("THE STREET OVER THE CAFE") (BALLET) %
4,3,4,1 sax.,3 - 4,4,3,1 - timp.,perc.(3),cel.,glock.,vibra.,xyl. - acc. - hp. - pf. - str.   30:00 Leeds.
—— LA STRADA SUL CAFFÈ("THE STREET OVER THE CAFE") (SUITE FROM THE BALLET)
   Leeds.
—— VARIAZIONI CONCERTANTI (FOR PIANO AND ORCH.) (ON A 12-NOTE ROW FROM MOZART'S "DON GIOVANNI")
2,2,2,2 - 2,2,2,1 - timp. - pf. - str.   30:00 Leeds.

VLAG, Harrend
—— BULGAARSCHE RHAPSODIE
2,2,2,2 - 4,3,3,1 - timp.,perc. - str.   12:00 Henmar.

VLAJIN, Milan
—— BALKAN (SYMPHONIC POEM)
2(2nd alt. with picc.),2(2nd alt. with Eng.hn.),2(2nd alt. with b.-cl.),2 - 4,3,3,1 - timp.,perc. - 2 hp. - str.   30:00 MIC,Zagreb.

VLASOV, Vladimir
—— ANAR (BALLET SUITE) (Composed with Vladimer Fehre)
3,3,3,3 - 4,2,3,1 - timp.,perc. - hp. - str.   G. Schirmer.
—— PATRIOTS (OVERTURE) (Composed with Vladimer Fehre)
2,2,2,3 - 4,3,3,1 - timp.,perc.,cel. - hp. - str.   G. Schirmer.

VLIJMEN, Jan Van
—— GRUPPI (FOR 20 INSTRUMENTS AND PERCUSSION) (1962)
1,1,1,1 - 1,1,1,1 - perc.,vibra.,xyl. - hp. - str.   13:00 Henmar.
—— MYTHOS (FOR VOICE AND ORCH.) (Text: Paul van Ostayen)
13:00 Henmar.
—— PER DICIASSETTE
3,3,2,ten. sax.,4 - 4,0,0,0   19:00 Henmar.
—— SERENATA I (FOR 12 INSTRUMENTS AND PERCUSSION)
2,2,2,2 - 2,0,2,0 - perc.   Henmar.
—— SERENATA II (FOR FLUTE AND 4 INSTRUMENTAL GROUPS)
1,1,4,ten. sax.,2 - 1,2,1,0 - timp.,perc. - guit. - hp. - str.   13:00 Henmar.
—— SONATA FOR PIANO AND ORCH. (1966)
17:00 Henmar.
—— SONATA FOR PIANO AND 3 INSTRUMENTAL GROUPS
2,2,2,2 - 2,2,2,0 - perc.,cel. - hp. - pf. - str.   16:00 Henmar.
—— SPOSTAMENTI
4,3,3,3 - 6,3,3,2 - perc. - 2 hp. - str.   9:00 Henmar.

VOCHT, Louis de
—— CONCERTO FOR VIOLIN AND ORCH. (IN 3 MOVTS.)
2,2,2,2 - 4,2,3,0 - timp. - str.   27:00 Salabert.

VOGEL, Ernst
—— MUSIC FOR CONTRABASS AND CHAMBER ORCH.
2(2nd alt. with picc.),2(2nd alt. with Eng. hn.),1,2(2nd alt. with c.-bn.) - 2,1,1,0 - timp.,perc. - str.   12:00 Modern.
—— SPIEGELUNGEN
*2,*3,*3,0,2 c.-bn. - 4,2,3,1 - perc. - str.   20:00 Modern.

VOGEL, Helmut
—— CONCERTO FOR VIOLIN AND CHAMBER ORCH.
1,1,1,1 - 0,0,0,0 - str.   15:00 Mannheimer.
—— MEPHISTO (BALLET SUITE)
2,2,3,2 - 4,2,3,1 - timp.,perc.,cel.,glock.,vibra.,xyl. - pf. - str.   32:00 F. Colombo.

VOGEL, Johann Christoph - WOJCIECHOWSKI, Zbigniew
—— CONCERTO IN C MAJOR, FOR BASSOON AND ORCH.
0,2,0,1 - 2,0,0,0 - str.   15:00 F. Colombo.

VOGEL, Wladimir
—— ABSCHIED (FÜR STREICHORCHESTER)
str.   8:00 S.U.I.S.A.
—— AUS DER EINHEIT - DIE VIELFALT, IN DER VIELFALT - DIE EINHEIT (HÖRFORMAN FÜR KLAVIER UND STREICHORCHESTER)
pf. - str.   16:00 S.U.I.S.A.
—— CANTIQUE EN FORME D'UN CANON À QUATRE VOIX (POUR GRAND ORCH.)
6:00 S.U.I.S.A.
—— CONCERTO FOR CELLO AND ORCH.
2,2,3,2 - 0,2,2,0 - timp.,perc.(2) - str.   24:00 Leeds.
—— GOETHE APHORISMEN (FOR SOPRANO AND STRING ORCH.)
str.   Leeds.
—— HÖRFORMEN, HEFT II
3,3,4,3 - 4,3,3,1 - str.   20:00 S.U.I.S.A.
—— MELOFORMEN (FÜR STREICHORCHESTER)
str.   12:00 S.U.I.S.A.

VOGLER, Ernst
—— CONCERTO FOR CLARINET, TRUMPET AND STRING ORCH.
cl. - tpt. - str.   14:00 Mannheimer.

VOGLER, Georg Josef - BODART, Eugen
—— BALLET SUITE NO. 1 (FROM "KOMISCHEN BALLETTEN")
2,2,0,2 - 2,0,0,0 - timp. - perc.   8:00 Mannheimer.

—— LA BROULLERIE ENTRE MARI ET FEMME (THE MARITAL QUARREL) (CONCERTO FOR PIANO AND STRING ORCH.)
pf. - str.   10:00 Mannheimer.

VOGT, Hans
—— CONCERTO FOR PIANO AND ORCH.
2,2,2,2 - 3,2,2,1 - timp.,perc. - hp. - pf. - str.   29:00 Alkor.
—— KONZERT FÜR MEHRCHÖRIGES ORCH. (CONCERTO GROSSO)
3,3,2,3 - 3,3,3,1 - timp.,perc. - hp. - str.   23:00 Alkor.
—— MONOLOGUE (FOUR PIECES FOR ORCH.)(1964)
3(3rd alt. with picc.),3(3rd alt. with Eng. hn.),3(3rd alt. with b.-cl.),3(3rd alt. with c.-bn.) - 2-4,3,3,1 - timp.,perc.(6),cel.,glock.,mar.,vibra.,xyl. - electric guit. - hp. - hpsc. - pf. - str.   17:00 G. Schirmer.
—— RHYTHMISCHE SUITE (FOR STRINGS)
str.   21:00 Alkor.
—— ROMANTISCHE SUITE (BALLETT-MUSIK FÜR GROSSES ORCHESTER)
27:50 Mozart Ed.
—— SINFONIE NR. 2
2,2,3,3 - 4,3,3,1 - timp.,perc. - hp. - str.   28:00 S.U.I.S.A.
—— SONATA FOR 17 INSTS.
2,2,2,1 - 0,1,1,0 - 1 sax. - perc.(2) - hp. - pf. - vln.,c.,d.-b.   22:00 Alkor.
—— SUITE NO. 2 FOR ORCH.
3,3,3,3 - 3,3,3,1 - timp.,perc.,cel. - hp. - pf. - str.   18:00 Alkor.

VOGT, Hellmuth
—— HEITERES VORSPIEL
2,2,2,2 - 4,2,1,0 - perc. - hp. - str.   5:00 Henmar.

VOLKONSKY, André
—— CONCERTO ITINÉRANT (FOR SOPRANO VOICES AND ORCH.)
fl. - hp. - perc. - str.   60:00 Salabert.

VOLPE, Arnold - DUBENSKY, Arcady
—— PRELUDE AND FUGUE NO. 10, IN D MINOR
2,2,2,2 - 4,2,0,0 - timp. - str.   10:00 U.MiamiSo.

VON HALLBERG, Gene
—— CONCERTO IN B FLAT, FOR CLARINET, BASS CLARINET AND ORCH. (IN 3 CONNECTED MOVTS.)
2(2nd alt. with picc.),2(2nd alt. with Eng.hn.),*2,2 - 4,3,3,1 - timp.,perc.(2),bells,glock. - hp. - str.   14:00 Composer.

VON KOCH, Erland
—— ARIOSO E FURIOSO (1967)
str.   9:00 S.T.I.M.
—— ECI (1965)
3,3,3,3 - 4,3,3,1 - timp.,perc.(4) - str.   14:00 S.T.I.M.
—— IMPULSI (1964)
3,3,3,3 - 4,3,3,1 - timp. - str.   12:00 S.T.I.M.
—— POLSKA SVEDESE (1968)
3,2,2,2 - 4,3,3,1 - timp.,perc.(4) - hp. - str.   9:00 S.T.I.M.
—— RITMI (1966)
2,2,2,2 - 4,3,3,1 - timp.,perc.(3) - str.   10:00 S.T.I.M.

VOORMOLEN, Alexander
—— ARETHUZA (SYMPHONISCHE MYTH)
3,3,3,3 - 4,4,3,1 - timp.,perc.,cel. - 2 hp. - org. - str.   13:00 Henmar.
—— BARON HOP (SUITE NO. 1) (1949) (IN 4 MOVTS.)
22:00 Henmar.
—— BARON HOP (SUITE NO. 2) (IN 4 MOVTS.)
22:00 Henmar.
—— CHACONNE AND FUGUE
15:00 Henmar.
—— CONCERTO FOR OBOE AND ORCH.
2,1,2,2 - 2,2,0,0 - timp. - str.   20:00 Henmar.
—— CONCERTO FOR 2 CEMBALOS AND STRINGS
2 cemb. - str.   15:00 Henmar.
—— CONCERTO FOR 2 OBOES AND ORCH.
2,2,2,2 - 2,2,0,0 - timp. - str.   25:00 Henmar.
—— DRIE GEDICHTEN (FOR SOPRANO AND ORCH.) (1932) (IN 3 MOVTS) (Text: L. Luyken)
2,1,2,2 - 2,0,0,0 - perc.,cel. - pf. - str.   10:00 Henmar.
—— DE DRIE RUITERTJES (VARIATIONS ON A DUTCH SONG) (1927)
3,3,3,3 - 4,3,3,1 - timp.,perc.,cel. - 2 hp. - str.   16:00 Henmar.

—— KLEINE HAAGSCHE (PETITE SUITE HAGUENOISE) (IN 7 MOVTS.)
2,1,1,1 - 1,0,0,0 - perc.,cel. - str.   12:00 Henmar.
—— EEN NIEUWE LENTE OP HOLLANDS ERF (FOR SOPRANO AND ORCH.) (1936) (Text: P. C. Boutens)
3,2,2,2 - 4,3,3,0 - timp.,perc. - hp. - org. - str.   9:00 Henmar.
—— OUVERTURE, UIT LE BARON HOP SUITE
3,2,2,3 - 4,3,3,0 - timp.,perc.,cel. - str.   5:00 Henmar.
—— SINFONIA CONCERTANTE, FOR CLARINET, HORN AND STRINGS
0,0,1,0 - 1,0,0,0 - str.   19:00 Henmar.
—— LA SIRÈNE (ROMANCE FOR SAXOPHONE AND ORCH.) (1949)
2,3,0,1 sax.,0 - 2,1,0,0 - timp.,perc.,cel. - hp. - str.   8:00 Henmar.
—— LA SIRÈNE (1949) (FOR VOICE AND ORCH.) (Text: Jules von der Becke)
2,1,3,0 - 2,1,0,0 - timp.,cel. - hp. - str.   8:00 Henmar.
—— SPIEGELSUITE (BALLETMUZIEK BIJ LANGENDIJKS SPIEGEL DER VADERSLANDSCHE KOOPLIEDEN) (1943)
0,2,0,0 - 2,0,0,0 - pf. - str.   25:00 Henmar.
—— STANZAS OF CHARLES II (FOR VOICE AND ORCH.) (1966)
6:00 Henmar.

VORLOVÁ, Sláva
—— CONCERTO FOR OBOE AND ORCH.
Bo. Hawkes.
—— CONCERTO FOR TRUMPET AND ORCH., OP. 31 (IN 3 MOVTS .)
3,2,2,2 - 4,4,3,1 - timp.,perc. - str.   19:00 Bo. Hawkes.
—— CONCERTO FOR VIOLIN AND ORCH.
Bo. Hawkes.
—— THE GOLDEN BIRD (OPERA) %
Bo. Hawkes.
—— ROZMARYNKA (FOLK OPERA) %
Bo. Hawkes.
—— THREE CZECH DANCES
3,2,2,2 - 2,2,3,1 - timp. - str.   11:00 Bo. Hawkes.

VOSTRÁK, Zbynek
—— THREE SHAKESPEARE SONNETS, OP. 33 (FOR BASS AND CHAMBER ORCH.)
Hans Gerig.

VRANKEN, Jaap
—— CONCERTERENDE MUSIEK (FOR CELLO AND WINDS)
2,2,2,1 - 2,1,1,0 - c.   14:00 Henmar.
—— KORAALVARIATIES EN TRIPELFUGA
3,3,2,2 - 4,3,3,1 - str.   12:00 Henmar.
—— SUITE
1,2,2,1 - 2,1,1,0 - timp. - str.   7:00 Henmar.

VREDENBURG, Max
—— HORIZONS HOLLANDAIS
1,1,1,1 - 2,2,1,0 - timp. - hp. - str.   6:00 Henmar.

VREMŠAK, Samo
—— SONATINA FOR STRINGS
str.   14:00 Hans Gerig.
—— SYMPHONY NO. 2
2,2(2nd alt. with Eng. hn.),2(2nd alt. with b.-cl.),2 - 4,2,3,1 - timp. - str.   20:00 Hans Gerig.

VRETBLAD, Patrik
—— DALALÅTAR (TWO SUITES)
2,0,2,1 - 0-1,1,0,0 - str.   12:00 S.T.I.M.
—— DALASVIT (SUITE)
2,2,2,2 - 4,2,2,1 - timp.,perc. - str.   12:00 S.T.I.M.
—— INTRODUCTION, FUGUE AND CHORAL
2,2,2,2 - 4,2,3,1 - timp. - str.   15:00 S.T.I.M.
—— LITEN DALASVIT
1,0,1,0 - 1,0,0,0 - str.   11:00 Lundquists.

VREULS, Victor
—— POÈME NO. 2 FOR CELLO AND ORCH.
3,3,2,2 - 4,2,3,1 - timp.,perc. - hp. - str.   13:30 Salabert.

VRIEND, Jan
—— DIAMANT (1967)
13:00 Henmar.
—— HUANTAN (1969)
13:00 Henmar.
—— PAROESIE (1967)
15:00 Henmar.

—— TRANSFORMATION I ("ON THE WAY TO HALLELUJA") (FOR CHORUS AND ORCH.)
18:00 Henmar.
—— WATERMUZIEK (FOR ELECTRONIC MUSIC AND ORCH.) (1966)
12:00 Henmar.

VRIES ROBBÉ, Willem de
—— BALLADE
3,2,2,2 - 4,2,3,1 - timp.,perc. - hp. - str.   9:00 Henmar.
—— CONCERTINO FOR FLUTE AND STRING ORCH. (1966) (IN 3 MOVTS.)
fl. - str.   12:00 Henmar.
—— CONCERTO FOR FLUTE, HARP AND ORCH.
3,2,2,2 - 4,2,2,1 - perc. - hp. - str.   Henmar.
—— CONCERTO PASTORALE (FOR FLUTE AND ORCH.) (1962)
4,2,3,2 - 4,3,3,0 - timp.,perc.,cel. - hp. - str.   15:00 Henmar.
—— NOCTURNE
2,2,2,2 - 4,3,0,0 - timp. - str.   8:00 Henmar.
—— PASTORALE AND DANCE
2,2,2,2 - 2,2,0,0 - hp. - str.   10:00 Henmar.

VUATAZ, Roger
—— ÉPOPÉE ANTIQUE, OP. 89 (GRANDE FRESQUE SYMPHONIQUE D'APRÈS "MOISE")
*2,*2,*2,*2 - 4,2,3,1 - timp.,perc.,cel. (pf. opt.) - hp., pf.(cel. opt.) - str.   S.U.I.S.A.
SUITE NO. 1
18:00
SUITE NO. 2
24:00
—— HUIT POÈMES D'ORIENT, OP. 17 (FOR SOPRANO AND ORCH.)
*3,*3,*3,*3 - 3,2,2,1 - timp.,perc. - hp. - pf.(ad lib.) - str.   18:00 S.U.I.S.A.
—— JÉSUS (ORATORIO), OP. 85 (FOR SPEAKERS, 5 SOLOISTS, DOUBLE MIXED CHORUS AND ORCH.)
*3,*4,*4,*4 - 4,3,3,1 - timp.,perc.,cel. - 2 hp. - pf. - str.   120:00 S.U.I.S.A.
—— PETIT CONCERT, OP. 39
1,1,1,1 - 2,1,1,0 - timp.,perc.,cel. - hp. - str.   14:00 Bo. Hawkes.
—— POUR UNE FÊTE DE JEUNESSE
4,3,4,4 - 4,3,3,1 - timp.,glock. - str.   9:00 Bo. Hawkes.
—— SUITE NO. 2 SUR DES THÈMES POPULAIRES, OP. 53
str.   17:00 S.U.I.S.A.
—— TROIS FANTAISIES, OP. 123 (CONCERTO POUR HARPE ET ORCH.)
23:00 S.U.I.S.A.

VUILLEMIN, Louis
—— EN KERNEO, OP. 23
3,3,3,3 - 4,3,3,0 - timp.,perc.(3),bells,cel.,xyl. - hp. - str.   16:00 EV.

VYCPÁLEK, Ladislav
—— AWAKING, OP. 17 (TWO SONGS FOR SOPRANO AND ORCH.)
Bo. Hawkes.
—— BLESSED IS THE MAN, OP. 34 (CANTATA) (FOR SOLO VOICE, MIXED CHORUS AND ORCH.)
Bo. Hawkes.
—— CONCERNING THE LAST THINGS OF MAN, OP. 16 (CANTATA) (FOR SOLO VOICE, MIXED CHORUS AND ORCH.)
Bo. Hawkes.
—— SURSUM CORDA (TWO FANTASY VARIATIONS ON A HUSSITE HYMN)
2,3,3,2 - 4,2,2,1 - timp.,perc. - str.   6:00 Bo. Hawkes.

W

WAGENAAR, Bernard
—— CANZONE SINFONICA (CONCERTO FOR VIOLIN AND ORCH.) (IN 1 MOVT.)
2,2,2,*3 - 4,2,3,1 - timp.,perc.(2) - hp. - str.   18:00 Composer.
—— CONCERT OVERTURE
2(2nd alt. with picc.),2,2,2 - 2,2,0,0 - timp.,perc.(2) - hp. - str.   7:00 Templeton.
—— DIVERTIMENTO NO. 1 (IN 4 MOVTS.)
*3,2,*3,*3 - 4,3,3,1 - timp.,perc.(3),cel. - hp. - str.   20:00 C. Fischer.

—— DIVERTIMENTO NO. 2
2(2nd alt. with picc.),2(2nd alt. with Eng.hn.),2,2 - 2,2,0,0 -
timp.,perc.(3) - hp. - str. 15:00 Templeton.
—— FANFARE FOR AIRMEN (FOR BRASS AND PERCUSSION)
4 hn.,3 tpt.,3 trb.,tu. - timp.,perc.(2) 1:00 Bo. Hawkes.
—— FANTASIETTA ON BRITISH-AMERICAN THEMES (FOR
CHAMBER ORCH.) (IN 3 MOVTS.)
1,1,2,1 - 2,2,1,0 - timp.,perc.(1) - str. 4:00 Composer.
—— FEUILLETON
*3,2,2,*3 - 4,3,3,1 - timp.,perc.(3),glock. - str. 5:00 Composer.
—— FIVE TABLEAUX FOR CELLO AND ORCH.
2(2nd alt. with picc.),2,2,*3 - 4,3,3,1 - timp.,perc.(3) - hp. - str.
14:00 Templeton.
—— PIECES OF EIGHT (2-ACT CHAMBER OPERA) %
1(alt. with picc.),1,2,1 - 2,2,1,0 - timp.,perc.(2),glock. - guit.(ad
lib.) - harmonica(ad lib.) - hp. - pf.(ad lib.) - str.
105:00 Composer.
—— SINFONIETTA
1,1,1,1 - 1,1,1,1 - timp.,perc. - hp. - pf. - str. 25:00 Bo. Hawkes.
—— SONG OF MOURNING (A REFLECTION UPON THE SLAIN
DUTCH PATRIOTS)
1,1,1,0 - 2,2,0,0 - perc(2) - hp. - str. 6:00 C. Fischer.
—— SYMPHONY NO. 2 (IN 4 MOVTS.)
*3,alto fl.,*4,E♭cl.,*4, sax.,*4 - 6,ten. hn.,*4,3,1 - timp.,perc.(5) -
guit. - 2 hp. - pf. - str. 25:00 Composer.
—— SYMPHONY NO. 3 (IN 3 MOVTS.)
*3,*3,*3,*3 - 4,3,3,1 - timp.,perc.(4) - hp. - pf. - str.
22:00 Composer.
—— SYMPHONY NO. 4 (IN 5 MOVTS.)
*3,2(2nd alt. with Eng.hn.),*3,*3 - 4,3,3,1 -
timp.,perc.(3),cel.,glock. - hp. - pf. - str. 24:00 Chappell.
—— TRIPLE CONCERTO, FOR FLUTE, HARP, CELLO AND
ORCH. (IN 3 MOVTS.)
*3,*3,*3,*3 - 4,2,3,1 - timp.,perc.(3) - hp. - str. 35:00 Composer.

WAGNER, Alfred
—— KLEINSTADTBILDER, OP. 24
2,2,2,2 - 4,2,3,0 - timp.,perc. - hp. - str. 17:00 Schuberth.

WAGNER, Joseph
—— AMERICAN JUBILEE
*3,2,2,2 - 4,3,3,1 - timp.,perc.(3) - hp. - str. 6:00 Composer.
—— BALLAD OF BROTHERHOOD (FOR CHORUS AND ORCH.)
*3,2,2,2 - 4,3,3,1 - timp.,perc.(3) - str. 7:00 EV.
—— CONCERTINO FOR HARP AND ORCH. (IN 3 MOVTS.)
2,2,2,2 - 2,2,0,0 - timp.,perc.(2),cel. - hp. - str. 15:00 Lyra.
—— CONCERTINO IN G MINOR FOR PIANO AND ORCH.
1,1,2,1 - 2,2,0,0 - timp.,perc.(3) - pf. - str. 12:00 MCA Music.
—— CONCERTO FOR ORGAN, BRASS AND PERCUSSION (1963)
(IN 1 MOVT.)
0,0,0,0 - 4,3,3,1 - timp.,perc.(3),bells,glock. - org.
20:00 Composer.
—— CONCERTO FOR VIOLIN AND ORCH.
3(3rd alt. with picc.),2(2nd alt. with Eng. hn.),2(2nd alt. with
b.-cl.),2 - 4,2,0,0 - timp. - hp. - str. 30:00 Composer.
—— DANCE DIVERTISSEMENT (FIVE ABSTRACTIONS WITH A
PROLOGUE)
2,2,2,2 - 2,2,2,0 - timp.,perc. - str. 14:00 Composer.
—— FANTASY IN TECHNICOLOR (FOR PIANO AND ORCH.)
*3,2,2,2 - 4,3,3,1 - timp.,perc.(3) - pf. - str. 15:00 Composer.
—— FESTIVAL PROCESSIONS (A CHOREOGRAPHIC EPISODE)
*3,*3,*3,*3 - 4,3,3,1 - timp.,perc.(3) - pf. - str. 9:00 Southern.
or:
2,2,2,2 - 4,3,3,1 - timp.,perc.(3) - pf. - str.
—— FOUR MINIATURES
1(alt. with picc.),2,2,2 - 2,2,0,0 - timp.,perc.(3) - str.
10:00 Southern.
—— A FUGAL TRIPTYCH (FOR PIANO, PERCUSSION AND
STRINGS) (IN 3 MOVTS.)
timp.,perc.(2),xyl. - pf. - str. 17:00 Composer.
—— GLORIA IN EXCELSIS (CHRISTMAS CAROL) (FOR
SOPRANO, CHORUS AND ORCH.)
1,0,1,0 - 0,0,0,0 - pf. - str. 10:00 Composer.
—— HUDSON RIVER LEGEND (BALLET) % (1941)
30:00 Composer.
—— HUDSON RIVER LEGEND (SUITE FROM THE BALLET) (IN 5
MOVTS.)
3,2,2,2 - 4,3,3,1 - timp.,perc.,cel. - pf. - str. 8:10 Composer.
or:
1,1,2,1 - 2,2,1,0 - timp.,perc.,cel. - pf. - str.
—— INTRODUCTION AND RONDO (FOR FLUTE AND STRINGS)
fl. - str. 9:00 Composer.

—— INTRODUCTION AND RONDO (FOR TRUMPET AND
ORCH.)
2,2,2,2 - 2,1,0,0 - timp.,perc. - str. 8:00 Chappell.
—— INTRODUCTION AND SCHERZO (FOR BASSOON AND
STRINGS)
bn. - str. 8:00 SouthernTx.
—— LITANY FOR PEACE (FOR STRINGS)
str. 12:00 Composer.
—— MISSA SACRA (FOR CHORUS AND ORCH.)
2(2nd alt. with picc.),*2,2,2 - 3,2,3,0 - timp. - str. 30:00 Ricordi.
—— MUSIC OF THE SEA (TWO SEA PIECES) (FOR STRINGS)
str. 10:00 Composer.
—— NEW ENGLAND SAMPLER (1-ACT OPERA) % (1964) (FOR
SOPRANO, TENOR, BARITONE AND ORCH.) (Text: Jean
Karsavina)
1,1,2,1 alto sax.,1 - 2,1,1,0 - timp.,perc.(1),bell,glock.,xyl. - pf. -
str. 30:00 Composer.
—— NORTHLAND EVOCATION (LANDSCAPE) (FOR SOPRANO
AND ORCH.)
3,2,3(3rd alt. with b.-cl.,),2 - 4,3,3,0 - timp.,perc.(3),cel. - str.
13:00 Southern.
—— PASTORAL COSTARRICENSE
2,*2,2,2 - 2,0,0,0 - cel.(or pf.) - str. 10:00 Composer.
or:
1,1,1,1 - 2,0,0,0 - timp.,perc.(1),bells,cel.(or pf.) - str.
—— PSALM 29 (FOR MALE CHORUS AND ORCH.)
*3,2,2,2 - 4,3,3,1 - timp.,perc.(2) - str. 11:00 Composer.
—— RADIO CITY SNAPSHOTS
*3,2,2,3 sax.,2 - 4,3,3,1 - timp.,perc.(3), cel., xyl. - hp. - str.
7:00 Mills.
—— RHAPSODY FOR CLARINET, PIANO AND STRINGS
cl. - pf. - str. 10:00 Bo. Hawkes.
—— SINFONIETTA NO. 1 (IN 3 MOVTS.)
2,2,2,2 - 2,2,0,0 - timp., perc.(2),xyl. - pf. - str. 15:00 Southern.
—— SINFONIETTA NO. 2 (FOR STRINGS)
1. Allegro energico - scherzando; 2. Allegro risoluto; 3. Andante
maestoso
str. 15:00 Southern.
—— SONG OF ALL SEAS, ALL SHIPS (FOR BARITONE, CHORUS
AND ORCH.)
3,2,2,2 - 4,3,3,1 - timp.,perc.(3) - str. 9:00 Composer.
—— THE STORY OF A PRINCESS (MUSICAL FABLE) (FOR
NARRATOR, MIXED CHORUS AND ORCH.)
3,2,2,2 - 4,3,3,1 - timp.,perc. - str. 15:00 Mills.
or:
1,1,2,1 - 2,2,1,0 - timp., perc. - str.
—— SYMPHONY NO. 1 (IN 3 MOVTS.)
3(3rd alt. with picc.),3(3rd alt. with Eng. hn.),3(3rd alt. with
b.-cl.),3(3rd alt. with c.-bn.) - 4,3,3,1 - timp.,perc.(3),glock.,xyl. -
hp. - pf. - str. 22:00 MCA Music.
—— SYMPHONY NO. 2 (IN 4 MOVTS.)
*3,2,2,2 - 4,3,3,1 - timp.,perc.(3),xyl. - pf. - str. 28:00 Composer.
—— SYMPHONY NO. 3 (IN 1 MOVT.)
3(1 alt. with picc.),2,2,2 - 4,3,3,1 - timp.,perc.(2) - str.
25:00 Composer.
—— TWO MOMENTS MUSICALES (FOR STRING ORCH.)
str. 9:00 MCA Music.
—— VARIATIONS ON AN OLD FORM
*3,2,2,2 - 3-4,3-4,3,1 - timp.,perc.(3) - org.(ad lib.) - str.
10:00 Composer.
—— THE VOICE OF THE LORD (PSALM 29) (FOR TTBB CHORUS
AND ORCH.)
Composer.
—— WHOM SHALL I FEAR (A PSALM OF FAITH) (FOR VOICE
AND ORCH.)
2(1 alt. with picc.),*2,*3,2 - 4,3,0,0 - timp.,perc. - hp. - str.
12:00 Composer.

WAGNER, Richard
—— LOHENGRIN (3-ACT OPERA) % (Engl. Text: Stewart Robb)
G. Schirmer.

WAGNER, Richard - BOWDON, David
—— SIEGFRIED'S JOURNEY TO THE RHINE
3,3,3,3 - 4,3,3,1 - timp.,perc. - hp. - str. 12:30 Lengnick.

WAGNER, Richard - GODFREY, Charles
—— OVERTURE TO "RIENZI"
12:00 Bo. Hawkes.

WAGNER, Richard - HERFURTH, C. Paul
—— OVERTURE TO "RIENZI"
C. Fischer.

WAGNER, Richard - HERTZ, Alfred
—— OVERTURE TO "TANNHAUSER"

C. Fischer.

WAGNER, Richard - OUBRADOUS, Fernand
—— ADAGIO (FOR CLARINET AND STRINGS)
cl. - str.   5:00 Presser.

WAGNER, Richard - ROBERTS, Charles J.
—— PRELUDE TO "DIE MEISTERSINGER"

C. Fischer.
—— THE RIDE OF THE VALKYRIES (FROM "DIE WALKÜRE")

C. Fischer.

WAGNER, Richard - SEVITZKY, Fabien
—— THE RING OF THE NIBELUNGEN (SYMPHONIC SUITE)
(INSTRUMENTAL VERSION)
3,*3,*3,2,2 c.-bn. - 6,4,3,1 - timp.,perc. (3) - hp. - str.
80:00 F. Colombo.
—— THE RING OF THE NIBELUNGEN (SYMPHONIC SUITE,
WITH DRAMATIC SOPRANO, LYRIC SOPRANO, TENOR,
BARITONE AND BASS)
3,*3,*3,2,2 - c.-bn. - 6,4,3,1 - timp.,perc.(3) - hp. - str.
92:00 F. Colombo.

WAGNER, Richard - STOKOWSKI, Leopold
—— PARSIFAL: SCENES FROM ACT 3
2,2 picc.,*4,*4,*4 - 5,4,3,1 - timp.,perc.(2),bells - str.
17:30 Henmar.

WAGNER, Richard - WEAVER, Richard L.
—— INTRODUCTION TO ACT III OF "LOHENGRIN"

Mills.

WAGNER, Richard - WINTER, Aubrey
—— OVERTURE TO "TANNHAUSER"

12:30 Bo. Hawkes.

WAGNER, Roger
—— THE CHRISTMAS STORY ACCORDING TO ST. LUKE (FOR
NARRATOR AND ORCH.)
2,2,*3,2 - 2,3,3,1 - timp.,perc.(3),cel.,glock. - hp. - str. Law-Gould.
—— HERITAGE OF FREEDOM (FOR SATB CHORUS AND
ORCH.) (Text: Joseph Auslander)
1,1,1,0 - 2,2,2,0 - timp.,perc. - str.   4:45 C. Fischer.
—— A MEDLEY OF AMERICAN SONGS (1973)
*3,*3,*3,2 - 4,0,3,1 - timp.,perc.,bells - str.   3:00 Arranger.

WAGNER, Siegfried
—— SYMPHONIE
3,2,2,2 - 4,3,3,1 - timp. - hp. - str.   55:00 Brockhaus.

WAGNER, Thomas S.
—— CONCERTO FOR PIANO AND ORCH. (IN 3 MOVTS.)
2(1 alt. with picc.),2,2,1 alto sax.,2 - timp.,perc.(3) - pf. - str.
40:00 Bo. Hawkes.
—— CONCERTO FOR TWO PIANOS AND ORCH.
18:00 Composer.
—— THE CROCODILE (1-ACT OPERA, AFTER DOSTOIEVSKY) %
(Text: Composer)
1(alt. with picc.),1(alt. with Eng.hn.),1(alt. with b.-cl.),1(alt. with
alto sax.) - 1,1,0,0 - timp.,perc.(1),xyl. - pf. - str. 45:00 Composer.
—— INTRODUCTION AND DANCE (FOR VIOLIN AND ORCH.)
2,2(1 alt. with Eng.hn.),2(1 alt. with b.-cl.),2 - 2,2,1,0 -
timp.,perc.(2) - hp. - str.   15:00 Composer.
—— MADRIGAL CONCERTO (CONCERTO GROSSO FOR 6 SOLO
VOICES AND ORCH.) (IN 4 MOVTS.) (Text: Harold G.
Henderson)
2,2,2,2 - 4,2,2,0 - timp.,perc.(2-3) - hp. - str.   25:00 Bo. Hawkes.

WAHLBERG, Rune
—— AFRODITE (SYMPHONIC POEM)
3,2,2,2 - 2,3,3,1 - timp.,perc. - hp. - str.   12:00 S.T.I.M.
—— ALLMOGE (SUITE) (IN 6 MOVTS.)
2,2,2,2 - 2,2,1,0 - timp.,perc. - str.   17:30 S.T.I.M.
—— BALLAD FOR PIANO AND ORCH.
2,2,2,2 - 3,2,1,0 - timp.,perc. - pf. - str.   14:00 S.T.I.M.
—— CARNIVAL (FOR 2 PIANOS AND ORCH.)
2,2,2,3 sax.,2 - 2,2,1,1 - timp.,perc. - 2 pf. - str. 16:00 S.T.I.M.
—— CONCERT FANTASY FOR PIANO AND ORCH. (1967)
1,1,2,2 - 2,2,1,0 - timp.,perc. - pf. - str.
10:00 Fleisher.
—— CONCERT OVERTURE NO. 1 IN F MAJOR
2,2,2,2 - 4,2,3,1 - timp.,perc. - str.   6:00 S.T.I.M.

or:
2,2,2,2 - 2,2,1,0 - timp.,perc. - str.
—— CONCERT OVERTURE NO. 2 ("VÅRBRYTNING") (1972)
2,2,2,2 - 2,3,1,0 - timp.,perc. - str.   6:00 Fleisher.
—— CONCERT SUITE (1961) (IN 3 MOVTS.)
str.   13:30 S.T.I.M.
—— CONCERTO BAROCCO FOR VIOLIN AND STRING ORCH.
(1960)
str.   12:00 S.T.I.M.
—— CONCERTO FOR BASS CLARINET AND ORCH. (1961)
1,1,*3,2 - 2,0,0,0 - str.   13:30 S.T.I.M.
—— CONCERTO FOR CELLO AND ORCH. (1961)
2,2,2,2 - 2,2,1,0 - timp. - str.   15:00 S.T.I.M.
—— CONCERTO FOR PIANO AND ORCH.
2,2,2,2 - 3,2,1,1 - timp.,perc.,glock. - pf. - str. 22:00 S.T.I.M.
—— CONCERTO FOR VIOLIN AND ORCH. (1958)
2,2,2,2 - 2,2,1,0 - timp. - str.   22:00 S.T.I.M.
—— FESTIVO (SUITE FOR A STRING ORCH.) (1964)
str.   9:00 Fleisher.
—— FESTSPIEL
3,2,2,alto sax.,2 - 4,3,3,1 - timp.,perc. - str.   8:00 G. Schirmer.
or:
2,2,2,alto sax.,2 - 2,2,1,0 - timp.,perc. - str.
—— NORDIC SUITE
2,2,2,2 - 2,2,3,1 - timp.,perc. - str.   21:00 S.T.I.M.
or:
2,2,2,2 - 2,2,1,0 - timp.,perc. - str.
—— NORDLAND (FOR MALE CHORUS AND ORCH.) (1958) (Text:
Arvid Mörne)
2,2,2,2 - 2,2,1,0 - timp.,perc.(2) - str.   9:30 S.T.I.M.
—— PRELUDE, LARGHETTO AND FUGUE IN D MAJOR
2,2,2,2 - 2,2,1,1 - timp.,perc. - str.   15:00 S.T.I.M.
—— SAGOLAND (SUITE) (IN 5 MOVTS.)
2,2,2,2 - 2,2,1,0 - timp.,perc. - hp.(ad lib.) - str. 18:00 S.T.I.M.
—— SINGOALLA (SYMPHONIC POEM)
2,2,2,2 - 4,2,2,1 - timp.,perc. - hp. - str.   10:00 S.T.I.M.
—— SPELMANS BLOMSTER (Text: Emil Hagström)
str.   11:00 S.T.I.M.
—— SYMPHONY NO. 1 IN F MAJOR
3,2,2,2 alto sax.,3 - 4,3,3,1 - timp.,perc. - hp. - str. 33:00 S.T.I.M.
—— SYMPHONY NO. 2 IN E MAJOR
2,2,2,alto sax.,2 - 2,3,1,0 - timp.,perc. - pf. - str. 23:00 S.T.I.M.
—— SYMPHONY NO. 3 IN D MAJOR
1,1,1,1 - 1,1,0,0 - timp. - str.   21:00 S.T.I.M.
—— SYMPHONY NO. 4, IN C MAJOR (1959)
2,2,2,2 - 2,2,1,0 - timp. - str.   20:00 S.T.I.M.

WAL-BERG
—— CAPRICCIO FOR PIANO AND ORCH.
2,2,2,2 - 2,2,3,0 - timp.,perc. - hp. - str.   9:00 S.A.C.E.M.
—— CONCERTO FOR TRUMPET AND ORCH.
2,2,3,2 - 2,2,3,0 - timp.,perc.,cel. - hp. - str.   9:30 Leeds.
—— CONCERTO TZIGANE
2,2,2,2 - 4,2,4,0 - timp.,perc.,cel. - hp. - str.   9:00 Riccardo.
—— KONZERT FÜR DIE EINZIGE
2,2,3,2 - 4,3,4,0 - timp.,perc. - hp. - str.   10:00 Riccardo.

WALDENMAIER, August Peter
—— DREI ORCHESTERSTÜCKE
3,2,2,2 - 4,3,3,1 - timp.,perc. - hp. - str.   16:00 Alkor.

WALDROP, Gid
—— ANDANTE FOR STRINGS
str.   10:00 Bo. Hawkes.
—— FROM THE SOUTHWEST (SUITE)
3,3,2,2 - 4,2,3,1 - timp.,perc. - hp. - pf. - str. 11:00 Bo. Hawkes.
—— PRELUDE AND FUGUE
3,2,2,2 - 4,3,3,1 - timp.,perc. - str.   11:00 Bo. Hawkes.
—— PRESSURES
str.   9:00 Bo. Hawkes.
—— SYMPHONY NO. 1
3,3,2,2 - 4,3,3,1 - timp.,perc. - str.   21:00 Bo. Hawkes.

WALKER, Ernest
—— FANTASIA - VARIATIONS ON A NORFOLK FOLKSONG, OP.
45
2,2,2,2 - 2,1,0,0 - timp. - str.   11:00 Oxford.

WALKER, George T.
—— ADDRESS FOR ORCH. (IN 3 MOVTS.) (1966)
*3,*3,*3,*3 - 4,2,2,1 - timp.,perc.(2),bells,cel.,glock.,xyl. - hp. - str.
20:00 MCA Music.

—— ANTIFONYS (1968)
*2,1,1,1 - 1,1,1,0 - perc. - str.   5:00 General.
—— CONCERTO FOR PIANO AND ORCHESTRA
1,2,*3,*3 - 4,3,3,1 - timp.,perc.(4) - hp. - pf. - str.   21:00 General.
—— CONCERTO FOR TROMBONE AND ORCH. (1957) (IN 3 MOVTS.)
*3,*3,*3,*3 - 4,2,2,1 - timp.,perc.,cel.,glock.,xyl. - hp. - str.
18:00 General.
—— DIALOGUS FOR CELLO AND ORCH. (1975)
*3,alto fl.,*3,*3,*3 - 4,4,3,1 -
timp.,perc.,bells,cel.,glock.,mar.,vibra.,xyl. - hp. - pf. - str.
14:00 General.
—— LYRIC FOR STRINGS
str.   6:00 General.
—— PASSACAGLIA (3RD MOVT. FROM "ADDRESS FOR ORCHESTRA")
4,4,4,3 - 4,2,3,1 - timp.,perc.(5),bells,xyl. - hp. - str.   MCA Music.
—— SPIRITUALS FOR ORCHESTRA
*3,2,2,2 - 4,3,3,1 - timp.,perc.,cel.,glock.,xyl.   9:00 General.
—— SYMPHONY (1961) (IN 4 MOVTS.)
*3,*3,*3,*3 - 4,4,3,1 - timp.,perc.(2),glock.,vibra.,xyl. - hp. - str.
20:00 General.
—— VARIATIONS FOR ORCHESTRA (1972)
*3,*3,*3,*3 - 4,3,3,1 - timp.,perc.,glock. - str.   22:00 General.

WALKER, Mark F.
—— A BAROQUE OVERTURE (ON WORKS OF DENIS GAULTIER AND GIOVANNI LEGRENZI)
2,2,2,2 - 2,2,2,0 - timp.,perc.(3) - str.   4:30 Arranger.
—— BUTLER CENTENNIAL OVERTURE
*3,*3,*3,*3(3rd alt. with c.-bn.) - 4,3,3,1 - timp.,perc.(4) - hp. - str.
8:00 Composer.
—— RICERCAR FOR ORCHESTRA (1971)
3(3rd alt. with picc.),*3,*3,3(3rd alt. with c.-bn.) - 4,3,3,1 -
timp.,perc.(4),glock.,vibra.,xyl. - str.   5:00 Composer.
—— SYMPHONIC SUITE (IN 5 MOVTS.)
2(2nd alt. with picc.),2,2,2 - 2,2,2,0 - timp.,perc.(4) - str.
28:00 Composer.
—— THEME AND VARIATIONS
3(3rd alt. with picc.),*3,3(3rd alt. with b.-cl.),3(3rd alt. with c.-bn.)
- 4,3,3,1 - timp.,perc.(4),bells,cel.,glock. - hp. - str.   Composer.

WALKER, William S.
—— THE GETTYSBURG ADDRESS (FOR BARITONE AND ORCH.) (Text: Abraham Lincoln)
2,*3,*3,2 - 4,3,3,0 - timp.,perc. - str.   4:35 AdverMuInc.
—— RETURN TO SHENANDOAH (WITH CHORUS AND OR MALE VOCALIST)
*3,*3,*3,2 - 4,3,3,1 - timp.,perc.(4) - str.   5:10 AdverMuInc.

WALLACE, William
—— CELEBRATIONS (1974) (IN 3 MOVTS.)
2(2nd alt. with picc.),2,2,2 - 4,2,3,0 - timp.,perc.(4, incl. 3 on timp.),cel. - str.   15:00 CanMusCtr.
—— CEREMONIES (1974)
2(2nd alt. with picc.)2(2nd alt. with Eng. hn.),2(2nd alt. with b.-cl.) 2 - 4,3,3,1 - timp.,perc.(5,incl. 4 on timp.) - str.
15:55 CanMusCtr.
—— ELEGY (1963) (FOR CELLO AND ORCH.)
2,2,2,2 - 4,2,3,0 - timp. - str.   10:00 CanMusCtr.

WALLBANK, Newell
—— CONCERTO GROSSO FOR STRINGS
str.   16:00 Lengnick.
—— PARTITA IN E FOR STRINGS
str.   17:00 Lengnick.

WALTER, Arnold
—— CONCERTO FOR ORCHESTRA (1958) (IN 3 MOVTS.)
*3,*3,*3,*3 - 4,3,3,1 - timp.,perc. - str.   22:30 CanMusCtr.
—— FOR THE FALLEN (CANTATA)
16:00 C.A.P.A.C.
—— MUSIC FOR HARPSICHORD AND STRINGS
hpsc. - str.   10:00 C.A.P.A.C.
—— SYMPHONY IN G MINOR (1942) (IN 4 MOVTS.)
2,*3,*3,2 - 4,3,3,1 - timp. - str.   33:00 CanMusCtr.

WALTER, Fried
—— BALLETT SZENE
hp. - str.   5:00 Henmar.
—— BERGSOMMER SUITE (IN 4 MOVTS.)
2,*2,2,2 - 3(3rd alt. with 1 trb. ad lib.),0,0,0 - cel.(or pf.) - hp.(or pf.) - str.   17:00 Henmar.

—— BREMER CAPRICCIO (1951)
3,2,2,2 - 4,3,3,1 - timp.,perc. - hp. - str.   9:00 Henmar.
—— CONCERTINO FOR PIANO AND CHAMBER ORCH.
1,2,0,2 - 2,0,0,0 - pf. - str.   15:00 AhnSimrock.
—— CONCERTINO PICCOLO FOR VIOLIN AND SMALL ORCH.
AhnSimrock.
—— DIVERTIMENTO (FOR PIANO AND ORCH.) (IN 3 MOVTS.)
2(or picc.),2(or Eng. hn.),2,2 - 4,3,3,0 - timp.,perc. - pf. - str.
16:30 AhnSimrock.
—— FANTASIE UND RONDO (FOR VIOLIN AND ORCH.)
2(or picc.),2,2,2 - 4,2,3,0 - timp.,perc.,vibra. - hp. - pf. - str.
12:00 AhnSimrock.
—— HYMNUS, TOCCATA UND FUGE, OP. 32
*3,2,2,2 - 2-4,2,1-3,0-1 - timp.,cel. - 2 hp. - str.   5:00 Henmar.
—— KASKADEN NACH CZERNY (FOR PIANO AND ORCH.)
AhnSimrock.
—— KLEINE BAROCKMUSIK (FOR PIANO OR HARPSICHORD, WITH ORCH.) (IN 3 MOVTS.)
0,2,0,2 - 0,2,2,0 - pf.(or hpsc.) - str.   11:00 AhnSimrock.
—— KLEINE SINFONIE (IN B MAJOR)
2,2,2,2 - 4,3,3,0 - timp.,perc. - str.   24:00 Henmar.
—— LEGEND
ob. - hp. - str.   AhnSimrock.
—— LUSTSPIEL OUVERTURE
2,2,2,2 - 4,2,3,0 - timp.,perc. - hp. - str.   3:30 Henmar.
—— DER PARADIESVOGEL (FANTASIESTÜCK) (FOR FLUTE, HARP AND STRINGS)
fl. - hp. - str.   7:30 Henmar.
—— DER PFEIL: BALLET SUITE NO. 1
2,2,2,2 - 4,3,3,1 - timp.,perc. - hp. - str.   15:00 Henmar.
—— DER PFEIL: BALLET SUITE NO. 2
3,*3,4 sax.,*3 - 4,3,3,1 - timp.,perc. - hp. - str.   12:00 Henmar.
—— DER PFEIL: BALLET SUITE NO. 3
3,*3,*3,4 sax.,*3 - 4,3,3,1 - timp.,perc. - hp. - str.   15:00 Henmar.
—— DIE REISE NACH VENEDIG (ITALIENISCHE OUVERTURE)
2,2,2,2 - 4,3,3,0 - timp.,perc. - hp. - pf. - str.   9:00 Ries-Erler.
—— SCHAUSPIEL OUVERTURE, OP. 28
2,2,2,2 - 2-4,2,1-3,1-3,0 - timp.,perc. - hp. - str.   8:00 Henmar.
—— DIE TAGESZEITEN (SUITE)
2,2,2,2 - 2-4,2,1-3,0 - timp.,perc. - hp. - str.   12:00 Henmar.
—— TANZ-SUITE IM LEICHTEN STIL (FOR VIOLIN AND ORCH.)
2,2,2,2 - 2,2,1,0 - perc. - hp. - str.   18:00 Henmar.
—— THREE BAGATELLES (FOR LARGE ORCH.)
AhnSimrock.
—— VARIATIONS ON THE HILDEBRANDLIED
AhnSimrock.
—— DER WALD (SUITE FOR ORCH.)
2(1 alt. with picc.),2(1 alt. with Eng. hn.),2(1 alt. with b.-cl.),2(1 alt. with c.-bn.) - 4,3,3,1 - timp.,perc.,cel. - hp. - str.
18:30 AhnSimrock.
—— ZIRKUS-SUITE
2(or picc.),2,2,2 - 4,3,3,1 - timp.,perc. - hp. - pf. - str.
14:00 AhnSimrock.

WALTER, Ludwig
—— FESTIVAL MUSIC (1958)
str.   14:00 Tetra.

WALTERHAUSEN, H. W. von
—— APOKALIYPTISCHE SINFONIE, OP. 19
3,3,3,3 - 6,3,4,1 - perc. - 2 hp. - org. - str.   45:00 T & J.
—— HERO UND LEANDER, OP. 22
3,3,3,3 - 4,3,3,1 - perc.,cel. - 2 hp. - str.   32:00 T & J.

WALTERS, Gareth
—— DIVERTIMENTO FOR STRINGS (IN 5 MOVTS.)
str.   14:30 Oxford.

WALTHEW, Richard H.
—— JOHN-A-DREAMS (CANTATA FOR SOLO VOICES, CHORUS AND ORCH.)
27:00 Bo. Hawkes.
—— THE MASQUERADERS (SUITE) (IN 7 MOVTS.)
2,2,2,2 - 2,1,2,0 - perc. - hp. - str.   11:00 Galaxy.
—— ODE TO A NIGHTINGALE (FOR BARITONE, CHORUS AND ORCH.)
9:00 Bo. Hawkes.

WALTON, Kenneth
—— MICHELANGELO SUITE (IN 3 MOVTS.)
2(2nd alt. with picc.),2,2,2(2nd alt. with c.-bn.) - 4,3,2,1 - timp.,perc.(2) - hp. - str.   11:00 Leeds.

WALTON, William
—— THE BEAR (1-ACT OPERA, AFTER CHEKHOV) % (Text: Paul Dehn)
  *2,1(alt. with Eng.hn.),1(alt. with b.-cl.),1 - 1,1,1,0 - timp.,perc. - hp. - str.   42:00 Oxford.
—— BELSHAZZAR'S FEAST (FOR BARITONE, CHORUS AND ORCH.)
  *3,2,Eng.hn.(or E♭ sax.), E♭cl.)2(2nd alt. with b.-cl.),*3, - 4,9,9,3 - timp.,perc.,glock.,xyl. - 2 hp. - org. - pf. - str.   38:00 Oxford.
—— CAPRICCIO BURLESCO
  *3,*3,*3,*3 - 4,3,3,1 - timp.,perc.(4) - hp. - str.   7:00 Oxford.
—— CONCERTO FOR CELLO AND ORCH. (IN 3 MOVTS.)
  2,2,2,2 - 4,2,3,1 - timp.,perc.,cel. - hp. - str.   26:00 Oxford.
—— CONCERTO FOR VIOLA AND ORCH. (IN 3 MOVTS.)
  3(3rd alt. with picc.),3,3,3 - 4,3,3,1 - timp. - str.   23:00 Oxford.
—— CONCERTO FOR VIOLIN AND ORCH. (IN 3 MOVTS.)
  2,2,2,2 - 4,2,3,0 - timp.,perc.(2) - str.   30:00 Oxford.
—— CORONATION "TE DEUM" (FOR DOUBLE CHORUS, ORGAN AND ORCH.)
  3,3,3,3 - 4,3,3,1 - timp.,perc. - hp. - org. - str.   8:30 Oxford.
—— CROWN IMPERIAL (CORONATION MARCH)
  3,3,3,3 - 4,3,3,0 - timp.,perc.(2) - hp. - org.(ad lib.) - str.   9:00 Oxford.
  or:
  1,1,2,2 sax.(ad lib.),1 - 2,2,1,0 - perc. - pf. - str.
—— ESCAPE ME NEVER (BALLET FROM THE MOTION PICTURE) %   Oxford.
—— FACADE ENTERTAINMENT (FOR SPEAKER AND ORCH.) (Text: Dame Edith Sitwell)   Oxford.
—— FACADE: SUITE NO. 1
  2(alt. with 2 picc.),2(2nd alt. with Eng. hn.),2,alto sax.(ad lib.),2 - 4,2,1,1 - timp.,perc. - str.   17:00 Oxford.
—— FACADE: SUITE NO. 2
  2(2nd alt. with picc.),*3,2,alto sax.,2 - 2,2,1,0 - perc. - str.   9:00 Oxford.
—— FANTASY OVERTURE   8:00 Oxford.
—— FUNERAL MARCH FROM "HAMLET"
  2,2,2,2 - 4,2,3,0-1 - timp.,perc. - hp. - str.   5:30 Oxford.
—— GLORIA (FOR CONTRALTO, TENOR, BASS, MIXED CHORUS AND ORCH.)
  3,3,3,3 - 4,3,3,1 - timp.,perc. - hp. - org.(ad lib.) - str.   19:00 Oxford.
—— HAMLET AND OPHELIA (A POEM FOR ORCH.)
  2,2,2,2 - 4,2,3,0 - timp.,perc.,cel. - hp. - str.   13:00 Oxford.
—— HENRY V: SUITE (FOR CHORUS AND ORCH.)
  3,3,3,3 - 4,3,3,1 - timp.,perc. - hp. - hpsc. - str.   12:15 Oxford.
—— HENRY V: SUITE (REVISED 1963)   Oxford.
—— IMPROVISATION ON AN IMPROMPTU OF BENJAMIN BRITTEN
  *3,*3,*3,*3 - 4,3,3,1 - timp.,perc.(4) - hp. - str.   14:00 Oxford.
—— IN HONOUR OF THE CITY OF LONDON (FOR MIXED CHORUS AND ORCH.)
  *3,2,2,2 - 4,3,3,1 - timp.,perc. - hp. - str.   16:00 Oxford.
—— JOHANNESBURG FESTIVAL OVERTURE
  3,*3,3,3 - 4,3,3,1 - timp.,perc. - hp. - str.   7:30 Oxford.
—— MUSIC FOR CHILDREN (SUITE)
  2,*3,2,2 - 4,2,3,1 - timp.,perc.(2) - hp. - str.   14:00 Oxford.
—— ORB AND SCEPTRE (CORONATION MARCH)
  3,3,3,3 - 4,3,3,1 - timp.,perc.(4) - hp. - org.(ad lib.) - str.   8:00 Oxford.
—— PARTITA FOR ORCHESTRA
  3,3,3,3 - 4,3,3,1 - timp.,perc(4),cel. - hp. - str.   15:00 Oxford.
—— PORTSMOUTH POINT OVERTURE
  *3(2nd alt. with picc.),*3,*3,*3 - 4,3,3,1 - timp.,perc.(2-3),xyl. - str.   6:00 Oxford.
—— THE QUEST (BALLET SUITE)   Oxford.
—— SCAPINO (COMEDY OVERTURE)
  3,3,3,2 - 4,4,3,1 - timp.,perc.(3),xyl. - hp. - str.   10:00 Oxford.
—— A SHAKESPEARE SUITE (FROM "RICHARD III")   12:00 Oxford.
—— SIESTA FOR SMALL ORCH.
  1,1,2,1 - 2,0,0,0, - str.   5:00 Oxford.
—— SINFONIA CONCERTANTE (FOR PIANO AND ORCH.)
  *3,*3,2,2 - 4,3,3,1 - timp.,perc.(2) - pf. - str.   19:00 Oxford.
—— SONATA FOR STRING ORCH. (FROM THE 1947 STRING QUARTET)
  str.   28:00 Oxford.

—— SPITFIRE (PRELUDE AND FUGUE)
  1,1,2,1 - 4,2,3,1 - timp.,perc. - hp. - str.   8:00 Oxford.
—— SYMPHONY NO. 1 (1935)
  1. Allegro assai; 2. Presto con malizia; 3. Andante con malincolia; 4. Maestoso
  2(2nd alt. with picc.),2,2,2 - 4,3,3,1 - timp.,perc.(3) - str.   43:00 Oxford.
—— SYMPHONY NO. 2 (IN 4 MOVTS.)
  3,3,3,3 - 4,3,3,1 - timp.,perc.(4),cel. - 2 hp. - pf. - str.   27:00 Oxford.
—— THREE ARIAS FROM "TROILUS AND CRESSIDA" (FOR SOPRANO AND ORCH.)
  *3,*3,*3,*3 - 4,2,3,1 - timp.,perc. - 2 hp. - str.   14:30 Oxford.
—— TROILIUS AND CRESSIDA (OPERA) %   Oxford.
—— THE TWELVE (AN ANTHEM FOR THE FEAST OF ANY APOSTLE) (FOR MIXED VOICES AND ORCH.) (Text: W. H. Auden)
  2,2,2,2 - 4,2,3,1 - timp.,perc. - hp. - str.   11:00 Oxford.
—— TWO PIECES FOR STRINGS (FROM "HENRY V")
  str.   5:00 Oxford.
—— VARIATIONS ON A THEME OF HINDEMITH
  3,*3,3,3 - 4,3,3,1 - timp.,perc. - hp. - str.   23:00 Oxford.

WALTON, William - DOUGLAS, Roy
—— FACADE SUITE (FOR HARMONICA AND ORCH.)
  2,1,2,1 - 2,0,1,0 - timp.,perc. - str.   8:00 Oxford.
—— ORB AND SCEPTRE (CORONATION MARCH) (Reduced Orchestration)
  2,2,2,2 - 2-4,2,3,0-1 - timp.,perc. - hp. - str.   8:30 Oxford.

WALTON, William - LAMBERT, Constant
—— PORTSMOUTH POINT (AN OVERTURE) (Reduced Orchestration)
  *2,1,2,1 - 2,2,1,0 - timp.,perc.(1-2) - str.   6:00 Oxford.

WALTON, William - MATHIESON, Muir
—— HENRY V (ORCHESTRAL SUITE FROM THE FILM)
  2(alt. with 2 picc.),2,2,2 - 4,2,3,0-1 - timp.,perc. - hp. - str.   15:30 Oxford.
—— PRELUDE TO "RICHARD III"
  2,2,2,2 - 4,2,3,0-1 - timp.,perc.(2) - hp. - str.   7:00 Oxford.

WALTON, William - TAUSKY, Vilem
—— CROWN IMPERIAL: CORONATION MARCH (Reduced Orchestration)
  2,*2,2,2 - 4,2,3,0-1 - timp. - hp. - str.   7:00 Oxford.
—— JOHANNESBURG FESTIVAL OVERTURE (Reduced Orchestration)
  2,2(2nd alt. with Eng.hn.),2,2 - 4,2,3,0-1 - timp.,perc. - hp. - str.   14:00 Oxford.
—— THE QUEST (BALLET SUITE) (IN 4 MOVTS.)
  2,2,2,2 - 4,2,3,0 - timp.,perc.(1-2),cel.,keyed glock. - hp. - str.   15:00 Oxford.

WANGENHEIM, Volker
—— CONCERTO PER ARCHI
  str.   20:00 Bo. Hawkes.
—— SINFONIA NOTTURNA
  2,2,2,2 - 4,2,3,1 - perc. - str.   35:00 Bo. Hawkes.
—— SINFONIETTA CONCERTANTE
  2,2(2nd alt. with Eng. hn.),2,2 - 2,2,2,0 - perc. - str.   20:00 Bo. Hawkes.
—— SONATINA FOR ORCHESTRA
  2,2,2,2 - 2,2,0,0 - timp. - str.   9:00 Bo. Hawkes.

WANHAL, Johann Baptist - BODART, Eugen
—— SYMPHONY IN B FLAT MAJOR
  0,2,0,0 - 2,0,0,0 - str.   14:00 Mannheimer.
—— SYMPHONY IN D MINOR
  0,2,0,2 - 2,0,0,0 - str.   14:00 Mannheimer.
—— SYMPHONY IN F MAJOR
  2(or 2 ob.),0,0,0 - 2,0,0,0 - str.   14:00 Mannheimer.

WANHAL, Johann Baptist - HOFMANN, Wolfgang
—— SYMPHONY FOR STRINGS IN C MAJOR
  str.   21:00 Mannheimer.
—— SYMPHONY FOR STRINGS IN F MAJOR
  str.   23:00 Mannheimer.

WANHAL, Johann Baptist - KNEUSSLIN
—— SYMPHONY IN A MINOR
  2 ob.(or 2 fl.) - 2 hn. - str.   15:00 Henmar.

WARD, William R.
—— SATIRE (1954)
    2,2,2,2 - 2,0,0,0 - timp.,perc.(2) - str.   4:00 Composer.
—— SYMPHONY NO. 3 (1954) (IN 3 MOVTS.)
    2(2nd alt. with picc.),2,*3,2 - 4,3,3,1 - timp.,perc.(4),bells,cel. - str.
    18:00 Composer.

WARE, Harriet
—— SIR OLUF (CANTATA) (FOR SOPRANO, BARITONE, WOMEN'S CHORUS AND ORCH.)
    2,2,2,2 - 4,2,3,0 - timp. - hp. - str.   20:00 G. Schirmer.
—— UNDINE (TONE POEM) (FOR SOPRANO, TENOR, WOMEN'S CHORUS AND ORCH.)
    2,*3,*3,*3 - 2 trb. - timp.,perc. - pf. - str.   40:00 Presser.

WARLOCK, Peter
—— CAPRIOL SUITE
    2,2,2,2 - 2,2,3,1 - perc. - str.   10:00 G. Schirmer.
—— CAPRIOL SUITE (VERSION FOR STRINGS)
    str.   10:00 G. Schirmer.
—— SERENADE FOR STRINGS
    str.   7:30 Oxford.
—— SIX ENGLISH TUNES FROM THE 16TH AND EARLY 17TH CENTURIES
    str.   Oxford.
—— SIX ITALIAN DANCES (FOR STRING ORCH.)
    str.   Oxford.

WARNER, H. Waldo
—— THE BROAD HIGHWAY (SEVEN SKETCHES FROM A TRAMP'S DIARY), OP. 47A
    1(alt. with picc.),1,1,1 - 2,2,1,0 - timp. - pf. - str.   24:00 J. Fischer.
—— PHANTASY, OP. 35
    3,3,2,3 - 4,2,3,1 - timp.,perc.,cel. - hp. - str.   P.R.S.
—— SUITE IN THE OLDEN STYLE, OP. 34 (FOR STRINGS) (IN 4 MOVTS.)
    str.   12:00 J. Fischer.

WARNER, Philip
—— CONCERTO FOR PIANO AND ORCH. (IN 4 MOVTS.)
    2,*3,2,2 - 4,3,3,1 - timp.,perc.(3),glock. - hp. - pf. - str.
    15:00 Composer.
—— CROKIPO SUITE
    2,2,2,2 - 4,3,3,0 - timp.,perc.,cel. - hp. - str.   9:15 Composer.
—— GREAT LAKES SUITE (IN 4 MOVTS.)
    3(3rd alt. with picc.),2(2nd alt. with Eng. hn.),2,0 - 4,3,3,1 - timp.,perc.,glock. - hp. - str.   16:00 Composer.
—— GREEN MANSIONS (SUITE)
    3(3rd alt. with picc.),*2,*3,*3 - 4,3,3,1 - timp.,perc.(3),cel.,glock. - hp. - str.   12:00 Composer.
—— GREGORIAN POEM
    3(3rd alt. with picc.),*3,*3,*3 - 4,3,3,1 - timp.,perc.,glock. - hp. - str.   6:15 Composer.
—— PERELANDRA
    3(3rd alt. with picc.),2(2nd alt. with Eng. hn.),2,2 - 4,4,3,1 - timp.,perc.(3),glock.,xyl. - hp. - str.   12:00 Composer.
—— SARABANDE-CHACONNE (FOR FLUTE AND ORCH.)
    1,2,2,2 - 2,3,2,0 - timp. - hp. - str.   4:00 Witmark.
—— SINFONIETTA (IN 4 MOVTS.)
    3,2,2,2 - 4,3,3,1 - timp.,perc.,glock. - hp. - str.   16:30 Composer.
—— SYMPHONIC SUITE (IN 4 MOVTS.)
    3(3rd alt. with picc.),*3,2,2 - 4,3,3,1 - timp.,perc.(3),cel. - hp. - str.   16:00 Composer.
—— THUMBNAIL SKETCHES OF CHICAGO
    3(3rd alt. with picc.),*3,*3,*3 - 4,3,3,1 - timp.,perc.(3),cel.,glock.,xyl. - pf. - str.   14:00 Composer.
—— YOUTH (OVERTURE)
    2,*3,2,2 - 4,3,3,1 - timp.,perc. - hp. - str.   13:00 Composer.

WARRACK, Guy
—— DIVERTIMENTO PASTICCIATO
    3,2,2,2 - 4,2,3,0 - timp.,perc.,cel. - str.   13:00 Bo. Hawkes.
—— MUSICA BELLICOSA
    1,1,0,0 - 0,1,0,0 - str.   12:00 Galaxy.
—— SYMPHONY IN C MINOR
    2,2,2,2 - 4,2,3,1 - timp.,perc. - str.   45:00 Galaxy.
—— VARIATIONS FOR ORCH.
    2,2,2,2 - 4,2,3,1 - timp.,perc. - str.   18:00 Galaxy.

WARREN, Elinor Remick
—— ABRAM IN EGYPT (CANTATA) (FOR BARITONE, MIXED CHORUS AND ORCH.)
    2(alt. with picc.),2(2nd alt. with Eng. hn.),2,2(2nd alt. with c.-bn.) - 4,2,3,1 - timp.,perc.(2),bells,cel.,xyl. - hp. - str.
    23:00 Gray.
—— ALONG THE WESTERN SHORE (3 SKETCHES FOR ORCH.)
    2(2nd alt. with picc.),2(2nd alt. with Eng. hn.),*3,2(2nd alt. with c.-bn.) - 4,2,3,1 - timp.,perc.(3),cel. - hp. - str.   10:45 C. Fischer.
—— THE CRYSTAL LAKE
    2,2,2,2 - 4,2,3,0 - timp.,perc.,cel. - hp. - str.   9:00 C. Fischer.
—— THE DARK HILLS
    2(2nd alt. with picc.),2,*3,2(2nd alt. with c.-bn.) - 4,2,3,1 - timp.,perc.(3) - hp. - str.   5:00 C. Fischer.
—— FOUR SONNETS FOR SOPRANO AND STRINGS (Text: Edna St. Vincent Millay)
    str.   12:30 C. Fischer.
—— GOOD MORNING, AMERICA (FOR NARRATOR, CHORUS AND ORCH.)
    3,3,2,2 - 2,2,2,0 - timp.,perc.,cel. - pf. - str.   16:00 C. Fischer.
—— THE HARP WEAVER (FOR BARITONE, WOMEN'S CHORUS AND ORCH.)
    2(2nd alt. with picc.),*3,2,2 - 4,2,3,1 - timp.,perc.(3) - hp. - str.   16:00 Gray.
—— INTERMEZZO FROM "THE LEGEND OF KING ARTHUR"
    2,2,*3,2 - 4,3,3,1 - timp.,perc.(2) - hp. - str.   5:30 Gray.
—— KING ARTHUR'S FAREWELL (FOR TENOR OR BARITONE AND ORCH.) (FROM "THE LEGEND OF KING ARTHUR")
    2,2,2,2 - 4,2,3,0 - timp. - hp. - str.   6:00 Gray.
—— THE LEGEND OF KING ARTHUR (CHORAL-SYMPHONIC POEM) (FOR CHORUS AND ORCH.)
    3(3rd alt. with picc.),*3,*3,2(2nd alt. with c.-bn.) - 4,3,3,1 - timp.,perc.(4) - hp. - org. - str.   60:00 Gray.
—— REQUIEM (FOR CHORUS AND ORCH.)
    2,2,2,2 - 4,2,3,1 - timp.,perc.,cel. - hp. - str.   53:00 Law-Gould.
—— SEA RHAPSODY
    2,2,2,2 - 4,2,3,1 - timp.,perc. - hp. - str.   4:00 C. Fischer.
—— SINGING EARTH (FOR HIGH VOICE AND ORCH.)
    2(2nd alt. with picc.),2,2,2 - 4,3,3,1 - timp.,perc.(2),cel.,glock. - hp. - str.   18:00 Presser.
—— SLEEPING BEAUTY (FOR SOLO VOICES, CHORUS AND ORCH.) (IN 5 MOVTS.)
    2(2nd alt. with picc.),1,2,1 - 2,2,3,0 - timp.,perc.(3),bells, glock. - pf. - str.   20:00 Gray.
—— SUITE FOR ORCHESTRA (IN 4 MOVTS.)
    2(2nd alt. with picc.),2,2,2 - 4,2,3,1 - timp.,perc.(3),bells,cel.,glock.,xyl. - hp. - str.   17:30 C. Fischer.
—— SYMPHONY IN ONE MOVEMENT (1970)
    2(2nd alt. with picc.),2(2nd alt. with Eng. hn.),2,2 - 4,2,3,1 - timp.,perc.(2),cel.,glock.,xyl. - hp. - str.   17:00 C. Fischer.
—— TRANSCONTINENTAL (FOR BARITONE, MIXED CHORUS, AND ORCH.)
    2,1,2,1 - 2,2,2,0 - timp.,perc. - pf. - str.   25:00 Presser.

WARREN, Raymond
—— CONCERTO FOR VIOLIN AND ORCH.
    2(2nd alt. with picc.),2,2(2nd alt. with b.-cl.),2 - 2,2,2,0 - perc.,xyl. - hp. - str.   25:00 Novello.
—— MAGNIFICAT FANFARE FOR TRUMPET, CLARINET AND PIANO (WITH STRINGS AND PERCUSSION)(1965)
    cl. - tpt. - perc. - pf. - str.   9:00 P.R.S.
—— NOCTURNE FOR ORCH. (1964)
    3,2,2,2 - 4,3,3,1 - timp.,perc.(3) - hp. - pf. - str.   10:00 P.R.S.
—— PROCESSIONS (AN OVERTURE)
    2,2,2,2 - 2,2,0,0 - timp. - str.   14:00 P.R.S.
—— SYMPHONY NO. 1 (1965)
    3,2,3,2 - 4,3,3,1 - timp.,perc.(3),cel. - pf. - str.   33:00 P.R.S.
—— SYMPHONY NO. 2
    2,2,2,2 - 2,2,0,0 - timp. - str.   18:00 P.R.S.
—— WEXFORD BELLS (SUITE)
    2,2,2,2 - 2,2,1,0 - timp.,perc. - hp. - str.   12:00 Novello.

WASHBURN, Robert
—— CONCERTINO FOR TWO WIND QUINTETS (CONCERTINO FOR WOODWIND AND BRASS QUINTETS) (1966) (IN 2 MOVTS.)
    1,1,1,1 - 2,2,1,1   10:00 Oxford.
—— ELEGY (1974)
    2,2,2,2 - 4,3,3,1 - timp.,perc.(2),bells - hp. - str.(12,5,5,4)
    6:50 Composer.
—— EXCURSION FOR ORCHESTRA (1970)
    2(2nd alt. with picc.),2,2,2 - 4,3,3,1 - timp.,perc.(3),bells,xyl. - str.   5:00 Oxford.

—— FESTIVE OVERTURE (1960)
*2,2,2,2 - 4,2,3,1 - timp.,perc.(3),glock.,xyl. - str.   7:00 Oxford.

—— NORTH COUNTRY SKETCH (1969)
2(2nd alt. with picc.),2,2,2 - 4,3,3,1 - timp.,perc.,bells,xyl. - str.
6:00 Composer.

—— ODE TO FREEDOM (FOR CHORUS AND ORCH.) (Text:
Composer)
2(2nd alt. with picc.),2,2,2 - 4,3,3,1 - timp.,perc. - str.
6:30 Oxford.

—— PASTORALE FOR HORN AND STRINGS (1949)
hn. - str.   6:00 Composer.

—— PASTORALE SKETCH (1954)
ob. - str.   5:00 Composer.

—— PROLOGUE AND DANCE (1970)
2(2nd alt. with picc.),2,2,0 - 4,3,3,1 - timp.,perc.(3),bells,xyl. - str.
7:00 Oxford.

—— ST. LAWRENCE OVERTURE
2(2nd alt. with picc.),2,2,2 - 2,2,2,1 - timp.,perc.(3),bells,xyl. - str.
11:05 Bo. Hawkes.

—— SERENADE FOR STRINGS
str.   8:00 Oxford.

—— SET FOR TWO WIND QUINTETS (IN 3 MOVTS.) (1966)
1,1,1,1 - 2,2,2,1   9:00 Oxford.

—— SINFONIETTA FOR STRING ORCH. (IN 4 MOVTS.)
str.   14:00 Oxford.

—— SUITE FOR STRINGS (IN 4 MOVTS.)
str.   11:00 Oxford.

—— SYMPHONY NO. 1 (IN 3 MOVTS.)
2(2nd alt. with picc.),2,2,2 - 4,2,3,1 - timp.,perc.(3),bells - str.
18:00 Oxford.

—— SYNTHESIS FOR ORCH.
2(2nd alt. with picc.),2,2,2 - 4,2,3,1 - timp.,perc.(3),bells,xyl. - str.
6:00 Shawnee.

—— THREE PIECES FOR SMALL ORCH.
*2,2,2,2 - 2,2,1,0 - timp.,perc. - str.   5:00 Oxford.

—— TRIPLEX FOR ORCH.
2(2nd alt. with picc.),2,2,2 - 4,2,3,1 - timp.,perc.(3),bells,xyl. - str.
5:00 Shawnee.

WASLOHN, Alvin
—— A BALLET FANTASY ("RIDE A CELLOPHANE PEGASUS")
0,0,0,1 alto sax.,1 bar. sax.,0 - 0,1,1,0 - perc.(2) - hp. - str.
18:00 Composer.

—— SCENES OF CHILDHOOD REVISITED (1956)
2,0,2,2 - 4,3,2,0 - timp.,perc.(5),glock. - hp. - pf. - str.
6:15 Composer.

WATANABE, Urato
—— YAJIN (SUITE)
21:00 Fox.

WATERS, James
—— CONCERTINO FOR STRING QUARTET AND STRING ORCH.
(1967) (IN 3 MOVTS.)
str.   11:30 Composer.

—— THREE HOLY SONNETS OF JOHN DONNE (FOR
BASS-BARITONE AND ORCH.) (1966)
2(2nd alt. with picc.),2(2nd alt. with Eng. hn.),2(2nd alt. with
b.-cl.),2 - 4,2,2,0 - timp.,perc.(3),glock. - str.   20:00 Composer.

—— TWO PIECES FOR SMALL ORCH. (1966)
2(2nd alt. with picc.),2(2nd alt. with Eng. hn.),2,2 - 2,2,1,0 -
timp.,perc.(3),xyl. - str.   10:00 Composer.

WATKINS, Michael Blake
—— CONCERTANTE
1(alt. with picc.),1(alt. with Eng.hn.),1,0 - 1,1,0,0 - perc. - pf. -
str.(no d.-b.)   30:00 Novello.

—— DOUBLE CONCERTO ("AFTER PSALLEIN") (FOR OBOE,
GUITAR AND ORCH.)
2(2nd alt. with picc.),1,2,0 - 1,2,1,0 - perc.,cel.,glock.,vibra.,xyl. -
guit. - str.   27:00 Novello.

—— PROEM
3,3,3,3 - 4,3,3,1 - timp.,perc.,cel.,glock.,xyl. - hp. - str.
11:00 Novello.

WATSON, Walter
—— CELEBRATION (FOR PIANO AND ORCH.) (1963)
*2,1,2,2 - 2,3,3,1 - timp.,perc.(3),xyl. - pf. - str.   6:00 Composer.

—— CONCERTO FOR GUITAR AND CHAMBER ORCH. (1975) (IN
3 MOVTS.)
1,1,1,1 - 1,0,0,0 - timp.,perc.(1) - guit. - pf. - str.(8,3,2,1)
15:00 Ludwig.

—— ECLOGUE FOR ORCH., OP. 5 (1961)
*3,2,2,2 - 2,2,3,1 - timp. - str.   10:00 Composer.

—— OZARK OVERTURE (1966)
*3,2,2,2 - 4,2,3,1 - timp. - str.   6:00 Composer.

—— SYMPHONY NO. 1 (1965) (IN 3 MOVTS.)
*3,2,*3,*3 - 4,4,3,1 - timp.,perc.(3) - str.   25:00 Composer.

—— SYMPHSIS (1972)
*3,2,2,2 - 4,3,3,1 - timp.,perc.(2) - hp. - str.   5:00 Composer.

—— VARIATIONS ON A SOUTHERN MOUNTAIN TUNE (1965)
2,2,2,2 - 4,2,3,1 - timp.,perc.(4),xyl. - pf. - str.   3:30 Shawnee.

WATTERS, Lorrain
—— AMERICA'S HERITAGE (FOR SATB CHORUS AND ORCH.)
(Co-composed with Frederick Beckman)
3,2,2,3 - 4,3,3,1 - timp., perc. - str.   9:00 C. Fischer.

WAXMAN, Donald
—— FOUR SONGS OF FAITH (FOR TENOR AND ORCH.)
2,2,2,2 - 0,0,0,0 - str.   Composer.

—— OVERTURE TO "SERENADE CONCERTANTE"
1,1,1,1 - 1,0,0,0 - str.   6:00 Galaxy.

—— A PARIS OVERTURE (1965)
*3,2,2,2 - 2,2,2,1 - timp.,perc.(3) - str.   7:00 Composer.

WAXMAN, Franz
—— ATHANEAL THE TRUMPETER (COMEDY OVERTURE) (FOR
TRUMPET AND ORCH.)
3,2,*3,*3 - 4,4,3,1 - timp.,perc.(3),glock.,xyl. - hp. - str.
6:00 Fidelio.

—— ELEGY FOR STRINGS
hp. - str.   5:00 Composer.

—— JOSHUA (DRAMATIC ORATORIO) (FOR NARRATOR, SOLO
VOICES, MIXED CHORUS, AND ORCH.) % (Text: James
Forsyth)
3,3,3,1 ten. sax.,3 - 4,3,3,1 - timp.,perc. - hp. - pf. - str.
80:00 F. Colombo.

—— SINFONIETTA FOR TIMPANI AND STRINGS (1955) (IN 3
MOVTS.)
timp. - str.   14:00 Bo. Hawkes.

—— THE SONG OF TEREZIN (CANTATA) (FOR
MEZZO-SOPRANO, MIXED CHORUS, CHILDREN'S CHORUS
AND ORCH.)
3(3rd alt. with picc.),2(2nd alt. with Eng.hn.),3(3rd alt. with
b.-cl.),2 - 4,3,3,1 - timp.,perc.(4) - pf.(alt. with cel.) - str.
45:00 Presser.

—— SUITE FROM "REBECCA"
2,*3,*3,2 - 4,3,3,1 - timp.,perc.(2) - hp. - pf. - str.
13:00 Composer.

—— SYMPHONIC FANTASY ON "A MIGHTY FORTRESS IS OUR
GOD"
2,*3,*3,2 - 4,3,3,1 - timp.,perc.(3) - hp. - pf. - str.   9:00 Composer.

WAYDITCH, Gabriel von
—— BALLET MUSIC FROM THE OPERA "HORUS"
2,*3,*3,*3 - 4,*5,3,1 - perc.(2) - hp. - str.   8:00 GWMusFndtn.

—— FINALE TO ACT I OF THE OPERA "MARIA TESZTVER"
7:00 GWMusFndtn.

—— SUITE FROM THE OPERA "OPIUM DREAMS" (IN 2 PARTS)
2,*3,*3,*3 - 4,*5,3,1 - perc.(2) - hp. - str.   40:30 GWMusFndtn.

WEAVER, Powell
—— DANCE OF THE SAND-DUNE CRANES (SYMPHONIC
POEM) (FOR PIANO AND ORCH.)
2,*3,2,2 - 3,0,3,1 - timp.,perc.(2) - hp. - pf. - str.   17:00 Composer.

—— THE FAUN (SUITE) (IN 3 MOVTS.)
2,*3,*3,1 - 2 hn. - perc.(2),cel.,xyl. - hp. - pf. - str.
12:00 Composer.

—— FUGUE FOR STRINGS
str.   8:00 Composer.

—— THE VAGABOND (SYMPHONIC POEM)
3(3rd alt. with picc.),3(3rd alt. with Eng. hn.),3(3rd alt. with
b.-cl.),*3 - 4,3,3,1 - timp.,perc. - 2 hp. - pf. - str.   14:00 Composer.

WEAVER, Thomas W.
—— IKARUS (A SYMPHONIC POEM) (1960)
3(3rd alt. with picc.),3(3rd alt. with Eng. hn.),3(3rd alt. with
b.-cl.),*3 - 4,4,3,1 - timp.,perc.(2),glock. - hp. - str.
17:00 Composer.

WEBER, Alain
—— D'APRÈS WOLS (AQUARELLES FOR CELLO AND ORCH.)
2,2,2,2 - 2,2,2,0 - timp.,perc.(4),cel. - str.   19:00 Presser.

—— LINÉAIRE I (FOR SAXAPHONE AND ORCH.)
    2,2,2,sax.,2 - 2,2,1,0 - perc.(2),cel. - str.   17:00 Presser.
—— SCHERZO BURLESQUE
    2,2,2,2 - 2,2-3,2,0 - timp.,perc.,xyl. - hp. - pf. - str.   3:30 Baron.
—— SUITE POUR UNE PIÈCE VUE
    2,2,2,2 - 3,3,1,0 - timp.,perc.,xyl. - hp. - pf. - str.   14:00 Baron.
    or:
    2,2,2,2 - 2,2,2,0 - timp.,perc. - hp. - pf. - str.

WEBER, Carl Maria von - EDER, Helmut
—— DIVERTISSEMENT (FROM PART II OF THE BALLET
    "MODERN DREAM")
    2,2,2,2 - 2,2,2,1 - perc. - hp. - str.   15:00 Modern.
—— MODERN DREAM (MODERNER TRAUM) (SUITE FROM
    THE BALLET)
    2(2nd alt. with picc.),2,2(2nd alt. with alto sax.),2(2nd alt. with
    c.-bn.) - 2,2,2,1 - timp.,perc.(5) - hp. - str.   35:00 Modern.

WEBER, Carl Maria von - EVANS
—— OVERTURE TO "PETER SCHMOLL"
    8:30 Bo. Hawkes.

WEBER, Carl Maria von - KAY, Hershy
—— THE THIEF WHO LOVED A GHOST (BALLET) %
    2(2nd alt. with picc.),2(2nd alt. with Eng. hn.),2(2nd alt. with
    b.-cl.),2 - 2,2,1,0 - timp.,perc.(3),xyl. - hp. - pf. - str.
    27:00 Arranger.

WEBER, Carl Maria von - LAKE, Mayhew Lester
—— CONCERTINO FOR CLARINET AND ORCH., OP. 26
    C. Fischer.

WEBER, Carl Maria von - LINK, Helmut
—— SYMPHONY NO. 2 IN C MAJOR
    2,2,0,2 - 2,2,0,0 - timp. - str.   23:00 Mannheimer.

WEBER, Carl Maria von - ROBERTS, Charles J.
—— OVERTURE TO "DER FREISCHUTZ"
    C. Fischer.
—— OVERTURE TO "OBERON"
    C. Fischer.

WEBER, Carl Maria von - SOPKIN, Henry
—— OVERTURE TO "OBERON"
    C. Fischer.

WEBER, Carl Maria von - SZELL, George
—— PERPETUUM MOBILE
    3,2,2,*4 - 4,2,3,1 - timp.,perc.,cel.(ad lib.) - str. 5:00 Bo. Hawkes.

WEBER, Carl Maria von - WARRACK, Guy
—— ANDANTE, THEME AND VARIATIONS (FOR CELLO AND
    ORCH.)
    1-2,2,0,2 - 2,0,0,0 - str.   12:00 Bo. Hawkes.

WEBER, Carl Maria von - WINTER, Aubrey
—— OVERTURE TO "DER FREISCHUETZ"
    10:00 Bo. Hawkes.
—— OVERTURE TO "EURYANTHE"
    8:00 Bo. Hawkes.
—— OVERTURE TO "OBERON"
    9:00 Bo. Hawkes.
—— OVERTURE TO "SILVANA"
    7:00 Bo. Hawkes.

WEBER, Sven F.
—— CONCERTO FOR PIANO AND SMALL ORCH., OP. 2
    ("ACADEMIC ESSAY")(1957)
    2,2,2,2 - 2,0,0,1 - timp. - pf. - str.   18:00 P.R.S.
—— VARIATIONS ON A GROUND BASS BY BACH, OP. 4 (1959)
    3,3,3,3 - 4,2,3,1 - timp. - str.   7:30 P.R.S.

WEBERN, Anton von
—— IM SOMMERWIND (IDYLL FOR LARGE ORCH.)
    3,*3,4,1 - 6,2,0,0 - timp.,perc. - 2 hp. - str.   C. Fischer.
—— ORCHESTRA PIECES (1913)
    3,3,4,3 - 4,3,3,1 - cel. - guit. - hp. - harm. - str. 5:00 C. Fischer.
—— THREE ORCHESTRAL SONGS (WITH SOPRANO)
    1,2,2,0 - 1,1,2,0 - timp., perc., cel. - guit. - hp. - harm. - str.
    4:45 C. Fischer.

WEDDINGTON, Maurice
—— SEUL ENSEMBLE
    4 picc.,0,heck.,4,d.-b.-cl.,bar. sax.,sarr. - 4,4 picc. tpt.,0,4 - perc.(4)
    - 2 hp. - str.   38:00 Modern.
—— WHEN THE SUNSET
    2 picc.,2,2,2 sopr. sax.,ten. sax.,bass sax. - 2,2,0,2 - perc.(2) -
    str.(10,4,4,2)   22:00 Modern.

WEDIG, Hans
—— CONCERTO IN B FLAT MINOR FOR PIANO AND ORCH.,
    OP. 7
    2,2,2,2 - 2,2,3,0 - perc. - pf. - str.   25:00 T & J.
—— KLEINE SINFONIE, OP. 5
    2,2,2,2 - 2,2,3,0 - perc. - hp. - str.   23:00 T & J.
—— SUITE, OP. 3 (IN 3 MOVTS.)
    2,2,2,2 - 2,2,0,0 - perc. - str.   13:00 T & J.

WEEGENHUISE, Johan
—— CONCERTO FOR ALTO RECORDER (OR FLUTE) AND
    STRING ORCH. (1959)
    alto recorder (or fl.) - str.   16:00 Henmar.
—— PETITE SÉRÉNADE (1967) (IN 5 MOVTS.)
    7:00 Henmar.
—— SUITE FOR ORCH. (1960)
    3,2,2,2 - 2,2,0,0 - timp.,perc. - str.   15:00 Henmar.
—— VARIATIONS IN OLD STYLE (ON "MERCK TOCH HOE
    STERCK")
    Henmar.

WEEKS, Richard
—— SHADES OF AGORA (1975)
    3,2,2,1 - 4,3,3,1 - timp.,perc.(4) - hp. - str.   5:00 Seesaw.

WEGELIN, Arthur Willem
—— ADAGIO (FOR STRING ORCH.) (A 12-MINUTE WORK)
    str.   12:00 S.A.M.R.O.
—— ADAGIO FOR STRINGS (A 6-MINUTE WORK)
    str.   6:00 S.A.M.R.O.
—— ARIA SINFONICA (CONCERTO FOR VIOLIN AND ORCH.)
    2,2,3,2 - 4,2,3,1 - timp.,perc. - str.   22:00 S.A.M.R.O.
—— DRIE KOORSTUKKE (FOR CHORUS AND SMALL ORCH.)
    (Text: Boerneef, Ingrid Jonker and Abraham de Vries)
    1,1,2,1 - 3,1,2,0 - perc. - str.   8:00 S.A.M.R.O.

WEGNER, August
—— ICE-NINE (FOR PREPARED PIANO AND ENSEMBLE)
    1,0,2,0 - 1,1,1,0 - pf.(prepared) - str.   10:00 Seesaw.

WEHDING, Hans Hendrick
—— VARIATIONS FOR ORCHESTRA (ON AN ENGLISH SCHOOL
    SONG)
    4,3,4, sax.,3 - 4,3,3,1 - perc.,cel. - hp. - pf. - str.   27:00 Tetra.
    or:
    2,2,2,2 - 4,3,3,1 - perc. - str.

WEHLE, Gerhard F.
—— GROSSTADT (SYMPHONIC CANTATA NO. 17) (FOR
    BARITONE, MEN'S CHORUS AND ORCH.)
    2(2nd alt. with picc.),2,2,2 - 2,2,2,0 - timp.,perc.(3, incl. 2 on
    timp.) - str.   25:00 Henmar.

WEILL, Kurt
—— THE BALLAD OF THE MAGNA CARTA (CANTATA) (FOR
    SOLO VOICES, CHORUS AND ORCH.)
    2,1,4,sax.,1 - 0,3,2,0 - timp.,perc.(2) - guit. - hp. - pf. - str.
    20:00 Chappell.
—— BERLINER SINFONIE
    2,1,3,3 - 2,1,1,0 - perc. - str.   20:00 Presser.
—— CONCERTO FOR VIOLIN AND WINDS, OP. 12
    2,1,2,2 - 2,1,0,0 - perc. - vln.,d.-b.   33:00 AMP.
—— FINALE FROM DIVERTIMENTO, OP. 7 (FOR UNISON MALE
    CHORUS AND SMALL ORCH.)
    1 hn.,2 tpt. - str.   Composer.
—— LINDBERGHFLUG ("LINDBERG'S FLIGHT") (FOR TENOR,
    BARITONE, BASS MIXED CHORUS AND ORCH.)
    2,0,2,2 - 2,2,0,0 - perc. - pf. - str.   25:00 Harms, Inc.
—— DER NEUE ORPHEUS (CANTATA) (FOR SOPRANO, VIOLIN
    AND ORCH.)
    2,2,2,2 - 0,2,2,0 - perc. - hp. - str.   18:00 Hampshire.
—— PARISER SINFONIE
    2,2,2,2 - 2,2,0,0 - timp.,perc.(2) - str.   25:00 Presser.
—— QUODLIBET
    2,2,2,2 - 2,2,2,0 - perc.,glock. - str.   20:00 Hampshire.

—— DIE SIEBEN TODSÜNDEN ("THE 7 DEADLY SINS") (FOR
SOPRANO, MALE CHORUS AND ORCH.)
2,1,2,1 - 2,2,1,1 - perc. - banjo - pf. - str.   35:00 Composer.
—— SYMPHONY NO. 2
2,2,2,2 - 2,2,2,2 - timp. - str.   28:00 Presser.
—— THREE WALT WHITMAN SONGS (FOR BARITONE AND
ORCH.)
2,1,2,1 - 2,2,2,0 - perc. - hp. - ukulele - str.   15:00 Chappell.

WEINBERG, Henry
—— CANTUS COMMEMORABILIUS I (FOR CHAMBER ORCH.)
1,1,1,0 - 1,1,1(tenor-bass),0 - perc.(2) - pf. - str.   MCA Music.

WEINBERG, Jacob
—— CONCERT PIECE FOR PIANO AND ORCH., OP. 9
*3,*3,2,2 - 4,3,3,1 - timp.,perc.(2) - pf. - str.   15:00 Composer.
—— FANTASY ON RUSSIAN THEMES, OP. 2 (FOR PIANO AND
ORCH.)
*3,*3,*3,*3 - 4,2,3,1 - timp.,perc.(2) - pf. - str.   10:00 Composer.
—— THE GETTYSBURG ADDRESS (FOR CHORUS AND SMALL
ORCH.)
1,0,2,0 - 2,2,1,0 - timp. - str.   6:30 Transcon.
—— THE GETTYSBURG ADDRESS (SYMPHONIC ODE) (FOR
BARITONE, CHORUS AND ORCH.), OP. 36
*3,*3,*4,*3 - 4,4,3,1 - timp.,perc.(2) - 2 hp. - org. - pf. - str.
                                                     12:00 Witmark.
—— THE LIFE OF MOSES, OP. 57 (ORATORIO) (FOR SOLOISTS,
MIXED CHORUS AND ORCH.)
2,2,2,2 - 2,2,2,1 - timp.,perc.(3),bells,glock. - hp. - org. - str.
                                                     86:00 SMP.
—— PURIM (CARNIVAL IN ISRAEL)
cl. - tpt. - pf. - str.   12:00 Transcon.
—— SABBATH EVE SERVICE (SERVIZIO PENTATONICO), OP. 35
(FOR BARITONE, CHORUS AND STRINGS)
str.   40:00 Transcon.
—— YEMENITE RHAPSODY
                                                     J. Fischer.

WEINBERG, Moisej
—— SINFONIETTA ON JEWISH THEMES, OP. 41 (1948)
3,2,2,2 - 4,3,3,1 - timp.,perc. - str.   G. Schirmer.

WEINBERGER, Jaromir
—— THE BIRDS' OPERA: SUITE (IN 4 MOVTS.)
3,2,2,ten. sax.,2 - 4,3,3,1 - timp.,perc. - hp. - 2 pf. - str.
                                                     30:00 Southern.
—— CONCERTO FOR ALTO SAXOPHONE AND ORCHESTRA
(1940)
                                                     SouthernTx.
—— CZECH RHAPSODY
*3,2,2,2 - 4,3,3,1 - timp.,perc.(2) - str.   9:00 Mercury.
—— THE LEGEND OF SLEEPY HOLLOW (SUITE) (IN 4 MOVTS.)
3,2,2,2 - 4,3,3,1 - timp.,perc.(2) - str.   24:00 Shilkret.
—— LINCOLN SYMPHONY (IN 4 MOVTS.)
3,*3,*3,*3 - timp.,perc.(4) - org. - str.   45:00 C. Fischer.
—— PRELUDE AND FUGUE ON "DIXIE"
3,2,2,2 - 4,3,3,1 - timp.,perc. - hp. - org. - str.   18:00 Bo. Hawkes.
—— PRÉLUDES RELIGIEUX ET PROFANES (IN 3 SECTIONS)
3,2,2,2 - 4,3,3,0 - timp.,perc. - hp. - str.   40:00 Bo. Hawkes.

WEINER, László
—— CONCERTO FOR PIANO, FLUTE, VIOLA AND STRING
ORCH.
fl. - pf. - str.   Bo. Hawkes.

WEINER, Lawrence
—— ELEGY FOR STRING ORCHESTRA (1957)
str.   SouthernTx.
—— PROLOGOS SYNKRETISMOS (1970)
3(3rd alt. with picc.),*3,*3,2 - 4,3,3,1 -
timp.,perc.(6),bells,glock.,xyl. - str.   11:00 Composer.

WEINER, Lazar
—— AMOS (FOR TENOR, BARITONE, SATB CHORUS AND
ENSEMBLE)
1,2,1,1 - 2,1,1,1 - org. - pf.   10:00 Bourne.
—— FUGUE AND POSTLUDE
*3,*3,*3,*3 - 4,3,3,1 - timp.,perc.,xyl. - str.   11:00 Composer.
—— THE LAST JUDGMENT (CANTATA) (FOR SOLO VOICES,
SATB CHORUS AND ORCH.)
2,2,2,2 - 2,2,1,0 -perc. - str.   40:00 Belw-Mills.
—— LEGEND OF TOIL (CANTATA) (FOR CHORUS AND ORCH.)
2,2,2,2 - 2,2,1,0 - timp.,perc. - str.   30:00 Transcon.

—— PRELUDE
*3,2,*3,*3 - 4,2,2,1 - timp.,perc. - hp. - str.   8:00 Transcon.
—— TO THEE, AMERICA (FOR CHORUS AND ORCH.)
2,2,2,2 - 4,2,2,0 - timp.,perc. - str.   15:00 Transcon.

WEINER, Leo
—— BALLAD FOR CLARINET AND ORCH., OP. 28
                                                     Bo. Hawkes.
—— CSONGER AND TÜNDE, OP. 10-B
2,2,2,2 - 4,2,3,0 - timp.,perc. - hp. - str.   24:00 Bo. Hawkes.
—— DIVERTIMENTO NO. 1, OP. 20 (AFTER OLD HUNGARIAN
DANCES)
str. (with opt. picc., hn., tpt. in movement 4)   9:00 Bo. Hawkes.
or:
picc. - hn.,tpt. - str.
—— DIVERTIMENTO NO. 2, OP. 24 (HUNGARIAN FOLK
MELODIES) (FOR STRING ORCH.) (IN 4 MOVTS.)
str.   13:00 Bo. Hawkes.
—— DIVERTIMENTO NO. 3, OP. 25 (IN 5 MOVTS.)
2(2nd alt. with picc.),2,2,2 - 4,2,3,0 - timp.,perc.,glock. - hp. - str.
                                                     14:00 Leeds.
—— DIVERTIMENTO NO. 4, OP. 38
                                                     Bo. Hawkes.
—— HUNGARIAN FOLK-DANCES, OP. 18
2,2,2,2 - 4,2,3,1 - timp.,perc.,cel. - hp. - str.   24:00 Bo. Hawkes.
—— PASSACAGLIA FOR ORCH., OP. 44
                                                     Bo. Hawkes.
—— PASTORALE, PHANTASY, AND FUGUE, OP. 23 (FOR
STRING ORCH.)
str.   7:00 Bo. Hawkes.
—— ROMANCE FOR CELLO, HARP AND STRINGS
hp. - str.   7:00 Bo. Hawkes.
—— VARIATIONS ON A HUNGARIAN FOLK SONG, OP. 30
2,2,2,2 - 4,2,3,0 - timp. - str.   6:00 Bo. Hawkes.

WEINER, Stanley
—— CONCERTO FOR HORN AND STRING ORCH. (1965)
hn. - str.   15:00 MCA Music.
—— CONCERTO FOR OBOE AND ORCH. (1966)
2,2,2,2 - 2,2,2,0 - timp.,perc. - str.   18:00 S.A.B.A.M.
—— CONCERTO FOR STRING ORCHESTRA (1967)
str.   16:00 S.A.B.A.M.
—— CONCERTO NO. 1 FOR VIOLIN AND ORCH. (1961)
2,2,2,2 - 4,3,2,0 - timp.,perc. - str.   26:00 MCA Music.
—— CONCERTO NO. 2 FOR VIOLIN AND STRING ORCH. (1963)
str.   22:00 S.A.B.A.M.
—— CONCERTO NO. 3 FOR VIOLIN AND STRING ORCH.
(CONCERTO DA CAMERA) (1964)
str.   17:00 S.A.B.A.M.
—— SYMPHONY NO. 1
4,3,3,4 - 4,3,3,1 - timp.,perc.(4) - str.   MCA Music.

WEINGARDEN, Louis
—— GHIRLANDE (GARLANDS) (FOR DRAMATIC SOPRANO,
PERCUSSION AND STRINGS) (1970) (Text: Michelangelo)
timp.,perc.(5),bells,cel.,glock.,mar.,vibra. - pf. - str.   7:30 Oxford.
—— THE SORROWS OF DAVID (FOR SATB SOLO VOICES, SATB
CHORUS AND ORCH.) (1967) (IN 3 MOVTS.) (Text: Biblical)
4(4th alt. with picc.),*4,*4,*3 - 4,3,3,1 -
timp.,perc.(5),bells,cel.,vibra. - hp. - pf. - str.   25:00 Oxford.

WEINGERL, Albin
—— PAYSAGE SYMPHONIQUE
1,1,1,1 - 2,2,2,1 - timp. - harm. - pf. - str.   9:00 Hans Gerig.
—— SUITE FOR PIANO AND STRINGS
pf. - str.   8:00 Hans Gerig.

WEINZWEIG, John Jacob
—— CONCERTO FOR HARP AND CHAMBER ORCH. (1967) (IN 1
MOVT.)
1,1,1,1 - 1,0,0,0 - hp. - str.   17:30 MCA Music.
—— CONCERTO FOR PIANO AND ORCHESTRA
                                                     15:00 C.A.P.A.C.
—— CONCERTO FOR VIOLIN AND ORCH. (IN 3 MOVTS.)
2,2,2,2 - 2,2,0,0 - timp. - str.   27:00 C.A.P.A.C.
—— DIVERTIMENTO NO. 1 FOR FLUTE AND STRINGS
fl. - str.   11:00 Bo. Hawkes.
—— DIVERTIMENTO NO. 2 FOR OBOE AND STRINGS
ob. - str.   14:00 Bo. Hawkes.
—— DIVERTIMENTO NO. 3 (1959) (IN 3 MOVTS.)
bn. - str.   15:00 Leeds.

—— DIVERTIMENTO NO. 4 (1968) (FOR CLARINET AND
STRINGS)
cl. - str.   13:30 CanMusCtr.
—— DIVERTIMENTO NO. 5 (FOR TRUMPET, TROMBONE AND
WINDS)
3(3rd alt. with picc.),3,3,3 - 4,3,3,1 - timp.,perc.(4),glock.,vibra.
                                             12:30 MCA Music.
—— DIVERTIMENTO NO. 6 (1972) (FOR ALTO SAXOPHONE
AND STRINGS)
alto sax. - str.   13:10 CanMusCtr.
—— DUMMIYAH (SILENCE) (1969)
*3,*3,*3,*3 - 4,3,3,1 - timp.,perc.(7, incl.4 on timp.) - hp. - str.
                                             15:30 CanMusCtr.
—— EDGE OF THE WORLD
2,2,2,2 - 2,2,2,0 - timp.,perc.(1) - str.   10:00 Leeds.
—— THE ENCHANTED HILL (TONE POEM)
                                             10:00 C.A.P.A.C.
—— INTERLUDE IN AN ARTIST'S LIFE (1943)
str.   7:25 Leeds.
—— OUR CANADA (SUITE)
2,2,2,1 - 0,2,2,0 - timp.,perc.(1) - str.   11:00 C.A.P.A.C.
—— RHAPSODY FOR ORCHESTRA
3,3,3,2 - 4,2,3,1 - timp.,perc. - str.   9:00 C.A.P.A.C.
—— SUITE FOR ORCHESTRA
                                             7:00 C.A.P.A.C.
—— SUITE FROM THE BALLET "RED EAR OF CORN" (IN 3
MOVTS.)
2,2,2,1 - 2,2,2,0 - timp.,perc.(1) - str.   15:00 C.A.P.A.C.
—— SYMPHONIC ODE (1958)
*3,*3,*3,2 - 4,3,3,1 - timp.,perc.,xyl. - str.   10:00 Leeds.
—— SYMPHONY NO. 1
                                             30:00 C.A.P.A.C.
—— TALE OF TUOMOTU (TONE POEM) (FOR BASSOON AND
ORCH.)
                                             22:00 C.A.P.A.C.
—— WINE OF PEACE (FOR SOPRANO AND ORCH.)
3,3,3,alto sax.,2 - 4,3,3,1 - timp.,perc.(4) - str. 17:00 C.A.P.A.C.

WEIS, Flemming
—— INTRODUCTIONE GRAVE
pf. - str.   7:00 G. Schirmer.

WEISGALL, Hugo
—— ATHALIAH (OPERA) % (1963) (Text: Richard Franko Goldman)
2(1 alt. with picc.),2(2nd alt. with Eng. hn.),2(1st alt. E♭ cl., 2nd
alt. with b.-cl.),2(2nd alt. with c.-bn.) - 2,2,3,0 - timp.,perc.(3) -
str.   120:00 Presser.
—— GRAVEN IMAGES (SUITE) (1966)
1,1,1,1 - 2,1,2,0 - timp.,perc. - pf. - str. 36:00 Presser.
—— NINE RIVERS FROM JORDAN (3-ACT OPERA WITH
PROLOGUE) % (1968) (Text: Denis Johnston)
3(3rd alt. with picc.),3(3rd alt. with Eng. hn.),3(3rd alt. with
b.-cl.),3(3rd alt. with c.-bn.) - 4,3,3,1 - timp.,perc.(3) - hp. - pf. -
str.   Composer.
—— OUTPOST (DANCES FROM THE BALLET)
3,3,2,2 - 4,3,3,1 - timp.,perc.(2) - pf. - str. 16:00 Presser.
—— OVERTURE IN F
*3,*3,2,2 - 4,3,3,1 - timp.,perc.(2),xyl. - pf. - str. 10:00 Presser.
—— QUEST (SUITE FROM THE BALLET)
3,3,2,2 - 4,3,3,1 - timp.,perc.(2) - hp. - str. 13:30 Presser.

WEISGARBER, Elliot
—— AUTUMNAL MUSIC (1973) (FOR ENGLISH HORN AND
STRINGS)
Eng. hn. - str.   15:00 CanMusCtr.
—— KYŌTO LANDSCAPES (LYRICAL EVOCATIONS FOR VOICE
AND ORCH.) (1972)
*3,2,*3,2 - 2,2,0,0 - timp.,perc.(incl. several Japanese instrs.) - hp.
- pf. - str.   32:10 CanMusCtr.
—— MUSICA SERENA (1974) (IN 3 MOVTS.)
1(alt. with picc.),1,1,1 - 1,0,0,0 - str.   8:35 CanMusCtr.
—— NETORI: A FANTASIA (1974) (FOR ALTO SAXOPHONE AND
ORCH.)
alto sax. - 2 hn. - timp.,perc.(4) - hp. - str. 12:00 CanMusCtr.
—— A PACIFIC TRILOGY (1974)
*3,*3,*3,*3 - 4,3,3,1 - timp.,perc. - hp. - str. 18:00 CanMusCtr.

WEISMANN, Julius
—— KONZERT, OP. 106
fl.,cl.,bn. - tpt. - timp. - str.   23:00 T & J.
—— RHAPSODY (IN 3 MOVTS.), OP. 56
2,3,2,3 - 4,2,3,0 - perc. - hp. - str.   30:00 T & J.

WEISS, Flemming
—— CHACONNE
                                             15:00 K.O.D.A.
—— CONCERTINO FOR CLARINET AND STRINGS (1934)
cl. - str.   15:00 K.O.D.A.
—— CONCERTINO FOR STRING ORCH. (1960)
str.   16:00 Henmar.
—— IN TEMPORIS VERNALIS (1947)
                                             8:00 K.O.D.A.
—— MUSIKANTISK OUVERTURE (1949)
                                             5:00 G. Schirmer.
—— PRELUDE AND INTERMEZZO (FOR OBOE AND ORCH.)
                                             8:00 K.O.D.A.
—— QUINTUPLE FORM III (1963)
1,1,1,1 - 2,1,1,0 - timp.,perc.,cel. - str. 11:00 Henmar.
—— SINE NOMINE
                                             14:00 K.O.D.A.
—— SYMPHONY NO. 1 (1943)
                                             24:00 K.O.D.A.
—— SYMPHONY NO. 2 (1948)
                                             18:00 K.O.D.A.

WEISS, Manfred
—— PRELUDE, MEDITATION AND HYMN
3,3,3,3 - 4,3,3,1 - timp.,perc.,cel. - hp. - pf. - str. 12:00 Tetra.
—— TOCCATA FOR ORCH.
2,2,2,2 - 4,2,3,0 - timp.,perc. - pf. - str. 10:00 Tetra.

WEISSBERG, Julia L.
—— AT NIGHT (SYMPHONIC POEM), OP. 10
3(3rd alt. with picc.),*3,*3,*3 - 4,3,3,1 - timp.,glock. - hp. - str.
                                             8:00 G. Schirmer.
—— BALLADE, OP. 12
*3,*3,*3,*3 - 4,3,3,1 - timp.,perc.,glock. - hp. - str.
                                             12:00 G. Schirmer.
—— A FAIRY TALE, OP. 13
*3,*3,3,2 - 4,2,3,1 - timp.,perc.,cel.,glock. - 2 hp. - str.
                                             17:00 G. Schirmer.

WEISSENSTEINER, Raimund
—— DAS GROSSE MYSTERIUM (ORATORIO)
                                             105:00 Oberon.
—— SINFONISCHE FANTASIE
                                             26:00 Oberon.
—— SINFONISCHE SUITE
                                             35:00 A.K.M.
—— SYMPHONY NO. 1
                                             95:00 A.K.M.
—— SYMPHONY NO. 2
                                             75:00 A.K.M.
—— SYMPHONY NO. 3
                                             70:00 A.K.M.
—— SYMPHONY NO. 4
                                             45:00 A.K.M.
—— SYMPHONY NO. 5
                                             57:00 A.K.M.
—— SYMPHONY NO. 7
                                             45:00 A.K.M.
—— SYMPHONY NO. 8
                                             43:00 Oberon.
—— SYMPHONY NO. 9
                                             85:00 Oberon.
—— VARIATIONEN UBER EINEN GREGORIANISCHEN CHORAL
                                             28:00 A.K.M.

WELANDER, Svea
—— SCHERZANDO (FOR STRING ORCH.)
str.   Fleisher.

WELANDER, Waldemar
—— CONCERTO DA CAMERA (FOR PIANO AND ORCH.)
1,1,2,1 - 2,0,0,0 - timp. - pf. - str.   22:00 S.T.I.M.
—— DIVERTIMENTO FOR STRINGS
str.   10:00 S.T.I.M.
—— DIVERTIMENTO NO. 3 (1958)
str.   S.T.I.M.
—— DUE PEZZI (1966)
2,2,2,2 - 4,2,3,0 - timp. - str.   25:00 Fleisher.
—— PASSACAGLIA (1967)
1,1,1,1 - 2,1,2,0 - str.   Fleisher.
—— SINFONIA BREVE
2,2,2,2 - 4,2,3,1 - timp. - str.   25:00 S.T.I.M.

—— SINFONIA GRAVE
    2,2,2,2 - 4,2,3,1 - timp. - str.   30:00 S.T.I.M.
—— SINFONIA MODESTA
    2,2,2,2 - 2,2,2,0 - timp. - str.   40:00 S.T.I.M.
—— SINFONIA PICCOLA (FOR STRINGS)
    str.   27:00 S.T.I.M.
—— SUITE FOR CHAMBER ORCH.
    ob. - 2 hn. - str.   25:00 S.T.I.M.
—— THREE PIECES FOR STRINGS
    str.   12:00 S.T.I.M.

WELCHER, Dan
—— CONCERTO DA CAMERA (FOR BASSOON AND SMALL
    ORCH.)
    1,1,1,1 - 1,1,0,0 - perc. - pf. - str.   20:00 EV.
—— CONCERTO FOR FLUTE AND ORCH. (1974) (IN 2 MOVTS.)
    2,1,2,1 - 2,2,1,0 - timp.,perc.,cel. - hp. - pf. - str.
         25:00 C. Fischer.
—— EPISODES FOR ORCHESTRA (1971)
         Composer.

WELIN, Karl-Erik
—— PEREO (FOR STRING ORCH.) (1964)
    str.   10:00 G. Schirmer.

WELLEJUS, Henning
—— CONCERTO DE DANSE, OP. 21
         18:00 K.O.D.A.
—— CONCERTO FOR OBOE AND ORCH., OP. 32
         10:00 K.O.D.A.
—— CONCERTO FOR VIOLIN AND ORCH., OP. 10
         20:00 K.O.D.A.
—— CONCERTO PICCOLO, OP. 29
         10:00 K.O.D.A.
—— COPENHAGEN RHAPSODY, OP. 37
    2,2,2,2 - 4,3,3,1 - timp.,perc. - str.   7:00 G. Schirmer.
—— A DANISH SUMMER, OP. 17 (PASTORALE)
         6:00 Henmar.
—— THE DREAM, OP. 31 (BALLET) %
         18:00 K.O.D.A.
—— EPITAPH
         K.O.D.A.
—— FESTIVAL PRELUDE, OP. 18
         K.O.D.A.
—— FREEDOM OVERTURE, OP. 13 ("HASTE IS NOT FOR HIM
    THAT BELIEVETH")
    2,2,2,2 - 4,3,3,0 - timp.,cymb. - str.   10:00 Henmar.
—— THE HISTORY OF THE YEAR, OP. 22 (SYMPHONIC
    FANTASY)
         13:00 K.O.D.A.
—— OVERTURE, OP. 16 (POSTVOGNEN RULLER)
         K.O.D.A.
—— PASSACAGLIA, OP. 19
    2,2,2,2 - 4,3,3,1 - timp.,perc. - str.   9:00 G. Schirmer.
—— SOMMERPASTORALE
    2,2,2,2 - 2,0,0,0 - timp. - str.   5:45 Henmar.
—— SUEÑOS ESPAÑOLES, OP. 9 (SUITE)
         K.O.D.A.
—— SUITE, OP. 1
    str.   12:00 K.O.D.A.
—— THE SWAN: SUITE, OP. 15
         14:00 G. Schirmer.
—— THE SWAN: SUITE, OP. 20
         14:00 K.O.D.A.
—— SYMPHONY NO. 1, OP. 24
         18:00 K.O.D.A.
—— SYMPHONY NO. 2, OP. 27
         17:00 K.O.D.A.
—— SYMPHONY NO. 3, OP. 35
         27:00 K.O.D.A.

WELLESZ, Egon Joseph
—— CONCERTO FOR VIOLIN AND ORCH., OP. 84
    3(3rd alt. with picc.),2(2nd alt. with Eng. hn.),2(2nd alt. with
    b.-cl.),2 - 2,2,3,1 - timp.,perc. - hp. - str.   31:00 Henmar.
—— SYMPHONY NO. 2, OP. 65 (1948)
    3,3,3,2 - 4,3,3,1 - timp.,perc. - str.   47:00 Lengnick.
—— SYMPHONY NO. 3, OP. 68 (1951)
    2,2,2,2 - 4,3,3,1 - timp.,perc. - str.   39:00 Lengnick.
—— SYMPHONY NO. 4, OP. 70 ("SINFONIA AUSTRIACA")
    3,3,3,2 - 4,3,3,1 - timp.,perc. - str.   26:00 Sikorski.
—— SYMPHONY NO. 5, OP. 75
    2,3,3,2 - 4,3,3,1 - timp.,perc. - str.   35:00 F. Colombo.

WENDEL, Martin
—— CONCERTO FOR VIOLIN, PIANO AND STRING ORCH.
    pf. - str.   16:00 Mannheimer.
—— DREI KONZERTANTE SKIZZEN (FÜR FLÖTE UND
    KLAVIER, MIT STREICHORCHESTER)
    fl. - pf. - str.   10:00 S.U.I.S.A.
—— MUSIK FÜR KLAVIER UND ORCH.
    2,2,2,2 - 2,2,2,0 - perc.(3),cel. - pf. - hp. - str.   14:00 S.U.I.S.A.

WENDELBURG, Norma R.
—— ANDANTE AND ALLEGRO
    *3,2,2,2 - 4,3,3,0 - timp.,perc.(3) - str.   11:00 Composer.
—— SYMPHONY NO. 1 (1967) (IN 3 MOVTS.)
    2(2nd alt. with picc.),2,2(2nd alt. with b.-cl.),2 - 4,3,3,1 -
    timp.,perc.(3),bells,cel.,glock.,xyl. - hp. - str.   20:45 Composer.
—— TRIPTYCH (1961)
    2(2nd alt. with picc.),2,2,2 - 2,2,1,1 -
    timp.,perc.(3),bells,cel.,glock.,xyl. - hp. - str.   16:10 Composer.

WENNIG, Hermann
—— DREI ORCHESTERSTÜCKE MIT SOLO-INSTRUMENTEN, OP.
    36
    2,2,2,2 - 2,2,1,0 - timp. - str.   18:00 Schuberth.

WENZEL, Eberhard
—— SUITE IN B FLAT MINOR (IN 4 MOVTS.)
    2,2,2,2 - 2,2,2,1 - perc. - str.   26:00 T & J.

WEPRIK, Alexander M.
—— DANCES AND SONGS OF THE GHETTO, OP. 12
    *3,3(3rd alt. with Eng. hn.),3(3rd alt. with b.-cl.),3(3rd alt. with
    c.-bn.) - 4,3,3,1 - timp.,perc.,cel.,xyl. - hp. - pf. - str.
         15:00 G. Schirmer.
—— FIVE PIECES, OP. 17
    1,2,2,1 - 2,2,2,0 - timp.,perc. - str.   G. Schirmer.

WERDER, Felix
—— ABSTRACT 67 (FOR ORCH. DIVIDED INTO 3 GROUPS)
    (1967)
         6:37 AllansPty.
—— ABSTRACTIONS
         12:00 A.P.R.A.
—— ACTOMOS, OP. 5 (ELEGY FOR STRINGS)
    str.   A.P.R.A.
—— LA BELLE DAME SANS MERCI (1973)
         A.P.R.A.
—— BRAND (SYMPHONIC POEM)
         12:00 A.P.R.A.
—— CONCERT MUSIC FOR FLUTE, STRINGS AND
    PERCUSSION, OP. 15 (1970)
    fl. - perc. - str.   15:30 A.P.R.A.
—— CONCERTO FOR CLARINET AND ORCH., OP. 47 (1962)
         A.P.R.A.
—— CONCERTO FOR PIANO AND ORCH.
         25:00 A.P.R.A.
—— CONCERTO FOR VIOLA AND ORCH., OP. 53 (1963)
         A.P.R.A.
—— CONCERTO FOR VIOLIN AND ORCH.
         25:00 A.P.R.A.
—— CONCERTO NO. 2 FOR VIOLIN AND ORCH., OP. 72 (1966)
         A.P.R.A.
—— DON GIOVANNI RETIRED, OP. 116 (EPILOGUE FOR ORCH.)
    (1971)
         A.P.R.A.
—— DRAMATURGIE, OP. 73 (1966)
         A.P.R.A.
—— FIVE ACTS OF CORIOLANUS, OP. 110 (1970)
         19:40 A.P.R.A.
—— LA GAMME D'AMOUR, OP. 94 (AFTER WATTEAU) (FOR
    VIOLIN AND ORCH.) (1961)
    2,2,1,0 - 2,2,2,0 - timp.,perc.(3),vibra. - mandolin - hp. - str.
         9:57 AllansPty.
—— HEXASTROPHE, OP. 40 (1961)
         A.P.R.A.
—— KLANG BILDER, OP. 105 (1960)
         A.P.R.A.
—— KONZERT MUSIK, OP. 60 (FOR 10 SOLO INSTRUMENTS)
    (1964)
         A.P.R.A.
—— DIE KRANISCHE DER IBICUS, OP. 77 (1967) (FOR ORCH.)
         A.P.R.A.
—— MONOSTROPHE, OP. 43 (1961)
         A.P.R.A.

—— MORGEN ROT, OP. 84 (FOR VIOLIN AND CHAMBER
ORCH.) (1968)
A.P.R.A.
—— MUSIC FOR STRING ORCH., OP. 57 (1964)
str. A.P.R.A.
—— LA PRIMAVERA, OP. 26 (TONE POEM) (1957)
A.P.R.A.
—— PROM GOTHIC, OP. 122 (FOR ORGAN AND ORCH.) (1972)
A.P.R.A.
—— THE SECOND PAISAGO, OP. 93 (1968)
A.P.R.A.
—— SOUND CANVAS FOR ORCH., OP. 101 (1969)
A.P.R.A.
—— SYMPHONY NO. 2
30:00 A.P.R.A.
—— SYMPHONY NO. 3 OP. 67 ("THE LAOCOON") (1965)
24:00 AllansPty.
—— SYMPHONY NO. 4, OP. 108 (1970)
A.P.R.A.
—— SYMPHONY NO. 5, OP. 118 (1971)
A.P.R.A.
—— TOWER CONCERTO, OP. 92 (FOR ORCH. DIVIDED INTO 3
GROUPS) (1968)
8:03 J. Albert.
—— TRIPLE MEASURE FOR ORCH., OP. 108 (1970)
A.P.R.A.
—— TRISTROPHE FOR ORCH., OP. 58 (1964)
A.P.R.A.
—— LA TROBE, OP. 104 (REVISED VERSION) (1969)
A.P.R.A.

WERLE, Floyd E.
—— CONCERTO NO. 1 FOR TRUMPET AND ORCHESTRA (IN 3
MOVTS.)
2,2,2,2 - 4,4,3,1 - timp.,perc. - str. 20:00 Bourne.
—— CONCERTO NO. 2 FOR TRUMPET AND ORCHESTRA (IN 4
MOVTS.)
3,3,3,2 - 4,4,3,1 - timp.,perc. - str. 20:00 Bourne.
—— WE HOLD THESE TRUTHS (FOR SPEAKER AND
ORCHESTRA) (Text: Thomas Jefferson)
2(alt. with 2 picc.), *3,*3,2 - 4,4,4,1 - timp.,perc.(5) - hp. - str.
11:00 Bourne.
—— WESTWARD HO! (FOR NARRATOR, MALE CHORUS AND
ORCHESTRA)
2(alt. with 2 picc.),*3,*3,2 - 4,4,4,1 - timp.,perc.(5) - hp. - str.
16:40 Bourne.

WERLE, Lars Johan
—— SINFONIA DA CAMERA (1961)
1,1,1,1 - 1,1,1,0 - timp.,perc.(2) - pf. - str. 15:00 S.T.I.M.
—— SUMMER MUSIC 1965 (FOR PIANO AND STRING ORCH.)
pf. - str. 7:30 G. Schirmer.
—— ZODIAC, OP. 5 (BALLET) % (1966)
3,3,3,3 - 4,3,3,1 - timp.,perc. - hp. - pf. - str. 50:00 Nordiska.

WERNER, Eric
—— REQUIEM SYMPHONY
2,2,2,2 - 2,2,1,0 - str. S.U.I.S.A.

WERNER, Fritz
—— SUITE CONCERTANTE
tpt. - perc. - str. 19:40 Presser.

WERNER, Gregor Joseph - VÉCSEY, Jenő
—— CONCERTANT PIECES FOR HARPSICHORD (OR ORGAN)
AND CHAMBER ORCH.
Bo. Hawkes.

WERNER, Jean-Jacques
—— CAPRICCIO
2,2,2,2 - 4,3,2,1 - perc. - hp. - str. 11:30 Presser.
—— CONCERTO FOR PIANO AND ORCH.
3,2,2,2 - 4,2,3,0 - timp.,perc. - hp. - pf. - str. 26:00 Presser.
—— L'OISEAU INAUGURAL (CANTATA) (FOR SOPRANO OR
TENOR, WITH CHAMBER ORCH.)
1,0,1,1 - 0,1,0,0 - perc. - pf. - str.(no vlns.) 13:00 Presser.
—— POUR DES FRAGMENTS D'HERACLITE
str. Presser.
—— TROIS GATHAS
2,2,2,2 - 2,2,1,0 - perc. - hp. - str. 10:00 Presser.

WERNER, Sven Erik
—— COMBINATIONS (FOR WINDS AND PERCUSSION)
2,2,2,2 - 2,2,2,0 - perc. 10:00 G. Schirmer.
—— EPHICURE III (FOR SATB CHORUS AND ORCH.)
K.O.D.A.
—— MASS (FOR ORCH., SATB CHORUS, CHILDREN'S CHORUS
AND 28 SOLOISTS)
K.O.D.A.
—— MODULUS (FOR 14 WINDS AND 3 PERCUSSION)
8:00 K.O.D.A.
—— RONDO (1968)
13:00 K.O.D.A.

WERNICK, Richard
—— AEVIA
4,2,3,2 - 4,3,3,1 - timp.,perc.(5) - str. 12:00 Presser.
—— HEXAGRAMS FOR CHAMBER ORCH. (IN 2 MOVTS.)
2,2,2,2 - 2,0,0,0 - str. 10:00 Mills.
—— VISIONS OF TERROR AND WONDER (FOR
MEZZO-SOPRANO AND ORCH.)
4,4,4,4 - 4,3,3,1 - timp.,perc.(7, incl. 2 on timp.),cel. - str.
30:00 Presser.

WERTHEIM, Rosy
—— CONCERTO FOR PIANO AND ORCH.
2,2,2,2 - 3,2,2,0 - timp.,perc. - pf. - str. 16:00 Henmar.
—— DIVERTIMENTO
1,1,1,1 - 2,1,1,0 - str. 14:00 Henmar.
—— OVERTURE
2,2,2,2 - 4,3,3,1 - timp.,perc. - hp. - str. 10:00 Henmar.

WESLEY, Samuel - PLATT, Richard
—— SYMPHONY NO. 5 IN A MAJOR
0,0,0,0 - 2,0,0,0 - str. 15:00 Oxford.

WESSMAN, Harri
—— PIECE FOR SYMPHONY ORCH. (1969)
2,2,2,2 - 3,2,3,0 - timp.,perc.,xyl. - str. 7:00 FinnMICtr.
—— SCORPIUS, A CONSTELLATION (FOR CELLO AND
STRINGS) (1971)
str. 7:00 FinnMICtr.

WESTBERG, Eric
—— BALLET SCENE
2,2,2,2 - 4,2,3,0 - timp. - str. 10:00 S.T.I.M.
—— GASK ("KNEIPE") (SYMPHONIC POEM)
2,1,2,2 sax.,1 - 2,2,1,0 - timp.,cel. - banjo - hp. - str. 13:00 Suecia.
—— LUSTSPELS OVERTURE
2,2,2,2 - 2,2,3,1 - timp. - str. 9:00 Suecia.
—— NENIA (SYMPHONIC POEM)
str. 13:00 Suecia.
—— SYMPHONY NO. 1 IN E FLAT MAJOR
2,2,2,2 - 4,2,3,1 - timp.,perc. - str. 30:00 S.T.I.M.
—— SYMPHONY NO. 2
2,2,2,2 - 4,3,3,1 - timp.,perc. - str. 35:00 S.T.I.M.
—— SYMPHONY NO. 3
2,2,2,2 - 4,2,3,1 - timp.,perc. - str. 32:00 S.T.I.M.

WESTERGAARD, Svend
—— CAPRICCIO PER VIOLINO SOLO ED ORCH. D'ARCHI, OP.
23
10:00 G. Schirmer.
—— CONCERTO FOR CELLO AND ORCH., OP. 26
30:00 G. Schirmer.
—— L'HOMME ARMÉ, OP. 22 (CANZONA PER 16
INSTRUMENTI)
1,*1,*2,0 - 1,0,0,0 - perc. - hp. - str. 18:00 G. Schirmer.
—— PEZZO CONCERTANTE, OP. 27
2,2,2,2 - 4,2,3,0 - timp.,perc. - pf. - str. 9:00 G. Schirmer.
—— PEZZO SINFONICA, OP. 20
14:00 K.O.D.A.
—— SINFONIA DA CAMERA, OP. 29
G. Schirmer.
—— SINFONIA, OP. 21
3,2,2,2 - 4,3,3,1 - timp.,perc.(3) - hp. - pf. - str. 30:00 Henmar.
—— SYMPHONIC VARIATIONS FOR WINDS AND PERCUSSION
G. Schirmer.
—— SYMPHONY NO. 1, OP. 21
3,3,2,2 - 4,3,3,1 - timp. - hp. - pf. - str. 30:00 Henmar.
—— VARIAZIONE SINFONICHE, OP. 25
str. 18:00 G. Schirmer.

WESTIN, Karl Otto
—— DUET FOR FOUR ("LA VIE DIABOLIQUE"), OP. 61 (BALLET)
% (1964) (IN 3 MOVTS.)
*2,2,2,2 -4,3,3,1 - timp.,perc.(3) - hp. - pf. - str.   16:00 Composer.
—— TWILIGHT CONCERTO, OP. 53 (FOR PIANO AND ORCH.)
*2,2,2*3 - 4,4,3,1 - timp. - pf. - str.   17:00 Fox.

WETTSTEIN, Peter
—— DREI GESÄNGE (FÜR STREICHORCH.)
str.   17:00 S.U.I.S.A.
—— KONZERT FÜR STREICHORCHESTER
str.   16:00 S.U.I.S.A.
—— ZWEI SZENEN FÜR ORCHESTER
13:00 S.U.I.S.A.

WETZLER, Robert P.
—— OUR ASCENDED KING (A CANTATA) (FOR CONTRALTO,
TENOR, BASS, SATB CHORUS AND ORCH.) (IN 6 PARTS)
(1966) (Text: Various)
2,2,2,2 - 1,2,1,0 - timp. - str.   30:00 Composer.

WHEAR, Paul W.
—— CATHARSIS SUITE (1967)
*3,*3,*3,2 - 4,3,3,1 - timp.,perc. - hp. - str.   15:00 Ludwig.
—— CATSKILL LEGEND (AN OVERTURE) (1962)
2,1,2,0 - 2,2,3,0 - timp.,perc.,glock.,xyl. - str.   6:00 EV.
or:
2,2,2,2 - 4,3,3,1 - timp.,perc.(5),glock.,xyl. - str.
—— DECADE OVERTURE (1968)
*3,2,2,2 - 4,2,3,1 - timp.,perc. - str.   7:00 Ludwig.
—— THE DOOR (SUITE FROM THE OPERA) (1963) (IN 4 MOVTS.)
1,1,1,1 - 2,1,1,0 - timp.,perc.(2),glock. - str.   12:15 Ludwig.
—— THE DOOR (1-ACT COMIC OPERA) % (1959) (Text: Phillip
Stevick)
1,1,1,1 - 2,1,0,0 - timp.,perc.(1),glock. - str.   45:00 Ludwig.
—— FROM SHAKESPEARE (FOR BARITONE AND ORCH.) (1973)
(IN 4 MOVTS.)
2,2,2,2 - 2,0,0,0 - timp.,perc.(1),tabor(with drum) - hp. - str.
17:55 Composer.
—— IN MEMORIAM: RALPH VAUGHAN WILLIAMS (FROM
SYMPHONY NO. 2) (1970)
8:30 Ludwig.
—— OLYMPIAD (CONCERTINO FOR STRING ORCH.) (1964) (IN
3 MOVTS.)
str.   8:40 EV.
—— PASTORAL LAMENT (1954)
hn. - str.   6:00 Ludwig.
—— PRELUDE AND PASSACAGLIA (1963)
*3,2,*3,2 - 4,3,3,1 - timp.,perc.(4),bells,glock.,xyl. - str.
12:00 Composer.
—— PRELUDE TO "THE TEN COMMANDMENTS" (1954)
2,2,2,2 - 2,2,0,0 - timp. - hp. - str.   3:20 Ludwig.
—— QUINTET CONCERTANTE (FOR FLUTE, OBOE, CLARINET,
BASSOON, TRUMPET AND ORCH.) (1968)
*3,2,2,2 - 4,3,3,1 - timp.,perc. - hp. - str.   11:30 Ludwig.
—— RENAISSANCE SUITE (1957) (IN 3 MOVTS.) (With
mezzo-soprano in 2nd Movt.)
*3,2,2,2 - 4,2,3,0 - timp.,perc.(3) - str.   17:00 Ludwig.
—— THE SEASONS (CANTATA) (FOR BARITONE, SSAATTBB
CHORUS AND ORCH.) (1965) (Text: Ralph Stutzman)
2,2,2,2 - 4,3,3,0 - timp.,perc.(2),glock.,vibra. - str.   25:00 Ludwig.
—— SOLILOQUY (FOR VIOLIN AND ORCH.) (1949)
3,2,2,2 - 4,3,3,0 - timp.,perc.(2) - str.   4:30 Fema.
—— SYMPHONY NO. 2 ("THE BRIDGE") (1970)
*3,*3,*3,*3 - 4,3,3,1 - timp.,perc. - hp. - str.   31:00 Ludwig.
—— THREE FOUR TWO - THREE FIVE SIX ZERO (A
TOUCH-TONE TELEPHONE TUNE) (1969)
*3,2,2,2 - 4,3,3,1 - timp.,perc. - amplified touch-tone telephone -
str.   5:00 Ludwig.
—— UNITAS (1962)
*3,2,2 Eng. hn.,2,2 - 4,3,3,1 - timp.,perc.(4),bells,glock. - str.
9:30 Ludwig.

WHEELER, Joe
—— CONCERT MUSIC FOR ORCH. (REV. 1966)
2,2,2,2 - 4,2,3,1 - timp.,perc.(3) - str.   9:00 P.R.S.
—— ERDGEIST (EARTH SPIRIT)(FOR FLUTE AND ORCH.)(1958)
0,3,4,3 - 4,3,3,1 - timp.,perc.(3) - str.   8:00 P.R.S.
—— RITRATTINO AND SCHERZO (1964)
tpt. - str.   5:30 P.R.S.
—— SINFONIETTA (1957)
1,1,2,1 - 2,1,1,0 - timp.,perc. - str.   10:00 P.R.S.

—— SYMPHONY FOR ORCH. ("FRED")(1961)
2,2,3,2 - 4,3,3,1 - timp.,perc. - str.   12:00 P.R.S.
—— SYMPHONY IN G MINOR (1963)
3,3,3,3 - 4,3,3,1 - timp.,perc.(4, incl. 3 on timp.) - str.
15:00 P.R.S.

WHITE, Clarence Cameron
—— BANDANNA SKETCHES, OP. 12 (IN 4 MOVTS.)
*3,*3,Eb cl.,*3,*3 - 2,2,2,1 - timp.,perc.(2) - pf. - str.
15:00 C. Fischer.
—— DANCE RHAPSODY
Composer.
—— DIVERTIMENTO
2,*3,2,2 - 4,2,3,1 - timp.,perc.(2) - str.   6:00 Fox.
—— ELEGY
1,2,2,2 - 2 hn. - timp. - str.   4:00 C. Fischer.
—— FROM THE COTTON FIELDS, OP. 18 (IN 3 MOVTS.)
*3,2,2,2 - 2,2,2,1 - timp.,perc.(2) - pf. - str.   12:00 C. Fischer.
—— HERITAGE (A MUSICAL STATEMENT) (FOR SOPRANO OR
TENOR, SPEAKING CHORUS, MIXED CHORUS AND
ORCH.) (Text: Countee Cullen)
10:00 Composer.
—— KUTAMBA ("KWTAMBA"), OP. 50
3,3,3,3 - 4,2,3,1 - timp.,perc. - hp. - pf. - str.   10:00 Fox.
—— PANTOMIME, OP. 36
2,2,2,2 - 2,2,2,0 - timp.,perc.(2) - hp. - pf. - str.   15:00 Composer.
—— PIECE FOR STRINGS AND TIMPANI
timp. - str.   10:00 Fox.
—— POÈME
9:00 Composer.
—— PRELUDE TO "OUANGA"
*3,2,2,2 - 2,2,2,1 - timp.,perc.(2) - hp. - str.   12:00 Composer.
—— SERENADE
C. Fischer.
—— SUITE ON NEGRO FOLK TUNES (IN 4 MOVTS.)
2,2,3,2 - 4,2,3,1 - timp.,perc. - hp. - str.   15:00 Composer.
—— TAMBOUR, OP. 34 (HAITIAN DANCE)
1,1,2,1 - 2,2,1,0 - timp.,perc.(2) - pf. - str.   8:00 Fox.

WHITE, Donald H.
—— ANDANTE FOR OBOE, HARP AND STRINGS
ob. - hp. - str.   7:30 Composer.
—— CONCERTO FOR CELLO AND ORCH. (IN 3 MOVTS.)
*3,2,2,2 - 4,3,3,1 - timp.,perc.(2) - hp. - str.   25:00 Composer.
—— DIVERTISSEMENT NO. 2 FOR STRING ORCH. (1968) (IN 3
MOVTS.)
str.   8:45 Composer.
—— KENNEBEC (A SUITE FOR ORCHESTRA) (IN 3 MOVTS.)
*3,2,2,2 - 4,2,3,1 - timp.,perc.(3) - str.   8:30 Composer.
—— OVERTURE FOR ORCH.
*3,2,2,2 - 4,3,3,1 - timp.,perc.(2) - str.   8:05 Composer.
—— SAGAN (OVERTURE FOR ORCH.)
*3,2,2,2 - 4,2,3,1 - timp.,perc.(3) - str.   7:00 Composer.
—— SERENADE NO. 1 FOR ORCH. (IN 5 MOVTS.)
*3,2,2,2 - 4,3,3,1 - timp.,perc.(4) - str.   14:00 Composer.

WHITE, John
—— SYMPHONY NO. 2 (1960)
23:00 Rochester.
—— THREE MADRIGALS (FOR CHORUS AND ORCH.)
2,2,2,2 - 2,2,2,0 - perc. - hp. - pf. - str.   20:00 G. Schirmer.

WHITE, John D.
—— CONCERTO FOR CELLO AND CHAMBER ORCH. (IN 3
MOVTS.)
2,2,2,1 - 0,0,0,0 - perc.(2) - str.(no vlns.)   15:00 Composer.

WHITE, Joseph
—— CONCERTO FOR VIOLIN AND ORCHESTRA
2,2,2,2 - 2,2,0,0 - timp. - str.   20:00 Belw-Mills.

WHITE, Louie L.
—— REJOICE! EMMANUEL SHALL COME (CANTATA) (FOR
SATB CHORUS AND ORCH.)
2 ob. - 2 hn. - hp. - str.   30:00 Galaxy.

WHITE, Michael
—— THE DIARY OF ANN FRANK (2 SONGS FOR SOPRANO
AND ORCH.)
2(1 alt. with picc.),2,2,2 - 4,2,2,0 - timp.,perc.(2-3),bells,glock.,xyl.
- hp. - str.   18:00 Composer.
—— THE DYBBUK (OPERA) % (Text: George Bluestone)
120:00 Composer.

—— GLORIA (FOR CHORUS AND ORCH.)
    *3,2,2,2 - 4,4,4,1 - timp.,perc.(3),bells,glock.,xyl. - str.
                    18:00 G. Schirmer.
—— PRELUDE AND OSTINATO
    str.   8:00 G. Schirmer.
—— REQUIEM FOR STRINGS
    str.   4:00 Composer.
—— SUITE FOR ORCHESTRA (IN 3 MOVTS.)
    2(2nd alt. with picc.),2,2,2 - 2,2,1,0 - timp.,perc.(2),glock.,xyl. -
    str.   20:00 Composer.
—— TENSIONS (IN 4 MOVTS.)
    2(alt. with 2 picc.),2,2,2 - 2,2,2,0 - perc. - hp. - str. 20:00 Fleisher.
—— THROUGH THE LOOKING GLASS (2-ACT OPERA) (1965) %
    (Text: George Bluestone)
    *3,*3,*4,2 - 4,3,2,1 - timp.,perc.(2-3),bells,cel.,glock.,xyl. - hp. - pf.
    - str.   120:00 Composer.

WHITE, Paul
—— ANDANTE AND RONDO (FOR CELLO AND ORCH.)
    2(2nd alt. with picc.),1,1,1 - hn. - timp.,perc.(2),cel.,glock. - hp. -
    str.   9:00 EV.
—— FIVE MINIATURES
    1(alt. with picc.),1(alt. with Eng. hn.),1,1,c.-bn.(ad. lib.) - 2,2,3,0 -
    perc.(2),vibra. - hp. - str.   6:00 EV.
—— FOUR SPOKES FROM THE HUB, OP. 3
    *3,2,2,2 - 4,3,3,1 - timp.,perc.(2),cel. - hp. - pf. - str.
                 9:00 C. Fischer.
—— IMPROVISATION TO J. WHITCOMB RILEY (FOR CHAMBER
    ORCH.)
    2,2,2,0 - 0,0,0,0 - cel. - hp. - str.   7:00 EV.
—— LAKE PLACID SCENES, OP. 17 (IN 4 MOVTS.)
    3(3rd alt with picc.),2(2nd alt. with Eng. hn.),2*3 - 4,3,3,1 -
    timp.,perc.(4),cel.,glock.,xyl. - hp. - str.   16:00 EV.
—— LAKE SPRAY, OP. 13
    3(3rd alt. with picc.),2,2,2 - 4,4,3,1 - timp.,perc.(4),cel.,glock.,xyl. -
    hp. - str.   8:00 EV.
—— LITTLE TUNE AND VARIATIONS
    2,1,2,2 - 2,2,0,0 - timp.,perc. - hp. - str.   EV.
—— LYRIC OVERTURE, OP. 1
    2,2,*3,*3 - 4,3,3,1 - timp.,perc.(3) - hp. - str. 8:00 Composer.
—— MINIATURE OVERTURE (1965)
    2,1,2,2 - 4,2,3,1 - timp.,perc. - hp. - str. 1:00 Composer.
—— OVERTURE TO YOUTH
    3(3rd alt. with picc.),2,2,2 - 4,3,3,1 - timp.,perc.(2) - hp. - str.
                 8:00 Composer.
—— PAGAN FESTIVAL OVERTURE
    *3,2,2,2 - 4,3,3,1 - timp.,perc. (2-3) - hp. - str. 4:30 EV.
—— SEA CHANTY, OP. 16 (FOR HARP AND STRINGS) (IN 3
    MOVTS.)
    hp. - str.   15:00 EV.
—— SINFONIETTA FOR STRING ORCH., OP. 8 (IN 3 MOVTS.)
    str.   18:00 EV.
—— SUITE IN OLD FASHIONED STYLE
    . str.   EV.
—— SYMPHONY NO. 1 IN E MINOR
    2(alt. with 2 picc.),*3,2,2 - 4,3,3,1 - timp.,perc.(3) - hp. - str.
                 18:00 EV.
—— THE VOYAGE OF THE MAYFLOWER, OP. 3 (BALLAD, WITH
    CHORUS AD LIB.)
    3(3rd alt. with picc.),2,3,*3 - 4,3,3,1 - timp.,perc.(3),cel. - hp. -
    org.(ad. lib.) - pf. - str.   12:00 EV.

WHITEFIELD, Bernard
—— DAKOTA FANTASY
    *3,*2,2,1 - 3,2,2,0 - timp.,perc.(3) - str. 5:00 Musicus.
    or:
    *3,*2,2,1 - 3,4,4,0 - timp.,perc.(3) - str.
—— ODE TO A NIGHTINGALE (FOR SOPRANO, BASS, FULL
    CHORUS AND STRINGS)
    str.   16:00 G.E.M.A.

WHITEHOUSE, Stanley David
—— CELEBRATION OVERTURE
    1,1,2,2 - 2,2,2,1 - timp.,perc. - str. 4:30 A.P.R.A.
—— CONCERTINO FOR RECORDER AND ORCH. (1967)
    Recorder,0,0,0,0 - 0,2,3,0 - perc. - str. 9:00 A.P.R.A.
—— DANCE PARODY FOR STRINGS (1967)
    str.   20:00 A.P.R.A.

WHITHORNE, Emerson
—— THE AEROPLANE (1920)
    3,3,4,3 - 4,3,3,1 - timp., perc., cel. - hp. - str. 4:00 C. Fischer.

—— THE DREAM PEDDLER, OP. 50 (SYMPHONIC POEM)
    3(3rd alt. with picc.),*4,*4,*4 - 4,3,3,1 - timp.,perc.(3),cel. - hp. -
    str.   16:00 Composer.
—— FATA MORGANA, OP. 44 (SYMPHONIC POEM)
    3(3rd alt. with picc.),*3,*3,*3 - 4,3,3,1 - timp.,perc.(2),cel. - hp. -
    str.   25:00 Composer.
—— NEW YORK DAYS AND NIGHTS (SUITE), OP. 40 (IN 5
    MOVTS.)
    3(3rd alt. with picc.),*3,2,*3 - 4,3,4,1 - timp.,perc.,cel.,xyl. - hp. -
    str.   20:00 C. Fischer.
—— POEM FOR PIANO AND ORCH., OP. 43
    *3,*3,*3,*3 - 4,3,3,1 - timp.,perc.(2) - pf. - str. 20:00 C. Fischer.
—— RANGA (SYMPHONIC PHANTASY), OP. 26
                 C. Fischer.
—— SATURDAY'S CHILD (FOR MEZZO SOPRANO, TENOR AND
    ORCH.), OP. 42
    1(alt. with picc. and alto fl.),1,1,1 - hn. - timp.,perc.(2) - pf. - str.
               20:00 Composer.
—— SIERRA MORENA (SYMPHONIC POEM), OP. 59
    3(3rd alt. with picc.),*3,*3,*3 - 4,3,3,1 - timp.,perc.(3) - hp. - str.
              6:00 C. Fischer.
—— SOONER AND LATER (DANCE SATIRE), OP. 30 (FOR
    CHORUS AND CHAMBER ORCH.) %
                 C. Fischer.
—— SYMPHONY NO. 2, OP. 56
    3(3rd alt. with picc.),*3,*3,*3 - 4,3,3,1 - timp.,perc.(3),cel. - hp. -
    str.   33:00 C. Fischer.
—— SYMPHONY NO. 3, OP. 57
                 C. Fischer.

WHITLOCK, E. Florence
—— CONCERTO IN B, OP. 9 (FOR 2 VIOLINS AND SMALL
    ORCH.) (1963)
    2,0,1,0 - 0,0,0,0 - str.   30:00 P.R.S.
—— CONCERTO NO. 2 IN F SHARP, OP. 14 (FOR VIOLIN AND
    STRING ORCH.)
    str.   25:00 P.R.S.
—— PHANTASIAS FOR STRINGS, OP. 17
    str.   P.R.S.

WHITLOCK, Percy
—— CONVERSATION PIECE (FOR ORGAN AND ORCH.)
               10:00 Oxford.
—— THE FEAST OF ST. BENEDICT (CONCERT OVERTURE)
    2,2,3,2 - 4,3,3,1 - timp.,perc. - hp. - org. - str. 11:00 Oxford.
    or:
    2,1,2,2 - 2,2,3,1 - timp.,perc. - str.
—— PRELUDE, AIR AND FUGUE (FOR ORGAN AND ORCH.)
               15:00 Oxford.
—— SYMPHONY IN G MINOR (FOR ORGAN AND ORCH.)
               37:00 Oxford.

WHITNEY, Maurice C.
—— CHACONNE
               4:30 Witmark.
—— DEIRDRE OVERTURE
    2,2,2,2 - 4,3,3,1 - timp.,perc.(3) - str. 5:00 Witmark.
—— VARIATIONS ON A THEME OF HANDEL
               Witmark.

WHITTAKER, Howard
—— TWO MURALS FOR ORCH.
    *3,2,*3,*3 - 4,3,3,1 - timp.,perc.,xyl. - str. 8:00 Galaxy.

WHYTE, Ian
—— AIRS AND DANCES FROM THE SCOTTISH PAST (FOR
    STRINGS)
    str.   Bo. Hawkes.
    FIRST SERIES (IN 5 MOVTS.)
               15:00
    SECOND SERIES (IN 5 MOVTS.)
               16:00

WIBLE, Michel
—— ELÉGIE (POUR COR ANGLAIS ET ORCHESTRE À CORDES)
    Eng. hn. - str.   4:00 S.U.I.S.A.
—— INTRADA POUR INSTRUMENTS À VENT, TIMBALES ET
    ORGUE
    0,*2,0,2 - 0,3,2,0 - timp.(3) - org. 4:30 S.U.I.S.A.
—— OUVERTURE DE CONCERT
    3,3,3,3 - 4,3,3,1 - timp.,perc. - hp. - pf. - str. 7:00 S.U.I.S.A.

—— RÉSONNANCES ("MUSICA 71") (POUR COR ANGLAIS SOLO
ET ORCH.)
2,*2,2,1 - 0,1,0,0 - perc. - str.   16:00 S.U.I.S.A.
—— VARIATIONS CONCERTANTES
2,2,2,2 - 2,2,2,0 - timp.,perc. - pf. - str.   16:00 S.U.I.S.A.

WICKENS, Dennis
—— DOUBLE CONCERTO FOR HARMONICA AND VIOLIN,
WITH STRINGS AND PERCUSSION (1968)
perc. - harmonica - str.   23:00 P.R.S.
—— FIVE SONGS FOR TENOR AND ORCH. (1962)
1,1,1,1 - 1,0,0,0 - cel. - pf. - str.   22:00 P.R.S.

WIDDOES, Lawrence
—— A FESTIVE OVERTURE (REVISED 1971)
*3,2,*3,2 - 4,3,3,1 - timp.,perc.(1),bells,glock.,xyl. - hp. - str.
                                                  10:00 Composer.
—— GREENERY (OVERTURE) (1961)
2,2,2,2 - 4,4,3,1 - timp.,perc.(2),bells,xyl. - str. 7:00 CMP.
—— JOURNEY (1970) (IN 5 MOVTS.)
*3,2(1 alt. with Eng. hn.),2(1 alt. with b.-cl.),2(1 alt. with c.-bn.) -
4,3,3,1 - perc.(2),bells,cel.,glock.,xyl. - hp. - pf. - str.
                                                  30:00 Composer.
—— QUIET MUSIC FOR STRINGS (1962)
str.   6:00 CMP.
—— SHORT OVERTURE (REV. 1967)
2(2nd alt. with picc.),2,2,2 - 2,2,2,0 - timp.,perc.(1) - hp. or pf. -
str.   4:00 CMP.
—— SUITE NO. 1 FOR STRINGS
str.   5:00 CMP.

WIDMER, Ernst
—— CELLOKONZERT
1,0,2,1 - 2,0,0,0 - str.   24:15 S.U.I.S.A.
—— CONCERTO DA CAMERA FOR VIOLIN AND STRING
ORCH.
str.   19:00 Henmar.
—— DIUTURNO FÜR ORCH.
3,3,3,3 - 4,3,3,1 - perc.(4) - str.   14:30 S.U.I.S.A.
—— DIVERTIMENTO VI FÜR STREICHER
str.   25:00 S.U.I.S.A.
—— PRISMEN (FÜR KLAVIER UND ORCH.)
1,1,1,1 - 1,1,0,0 - perc.(2) - pf. - str.   21:00 S.U.I.S.A.
—— QUASARS, OP. 69
3,3,3,3 - 4,3,3,1 - perc.(5) - hp. - pf. - str.   13:45 S.U.I.S.A.

WIDOR, Charles Marie
—— OVERTURE TO THE OPERA "NERTO" (1924)
3,3,3,3 - 4,4,3,1 - timp.,perc. - str.   6:30 Presser.

WIENER, Jean
—— CADENCES (FOR PIANO AND ORCH.) (IN 4 MOVTS.)
2,2,2,2 - 4,2,3,1 - perc. - pf. - str.   16:00 Salabert.
—— CONCERTO FOR ACCORDION AND ORCH.
0,0,0,0 - 0,3,3,0 - timp. - acc. - str.   20:00 Presser.
—— CONCERTO FOR PIANO AND ORCH.
1,3,0,1 - 0,3,2,0 - pf. - str.   20:00 Presser.
—— CONCERTO FOR 2 GUITARS AND ORCH.
1,2,0,1 - 0,2,1,0 - 2 guit. - str.   20:00 Presser.
—— LEXIQUE (BALLET) %
2,2,2,2 - 2,3,2,0 - timp.,perc. - hp. - str.   28:00 Salabert.
—— SUITE DE DANSES (FOR TRUMPET AND SMALL ORCH.)
0,0,1,0 - 0,1,0,0 - pf. - str.   18:00 Mercury.

WIENER, Karl
—— IN MEMORIAM M. H. (KAMMERSTÜCK, OP. 7) (FOR 12
PLAYERS)
0,1,1(alt. with b.-cl.),1 - 2,0,0,0 - timp. - hp. - str.(2,1,1,1)
                                                  6:30 Henmar.

WIENIAWSKI, Henri - NITSCHKE, Manfred
—— SCHERZO-TARANTELLA (FOR VIOLIN AND ORCH.)
2,2,2,2 - 2,2,0,0 - timp.,perc. - hp. - str.   6:00 F. Colombo.

WIESLANDER, Ingvar
—— CONCERTO FOR STRING ORCH. (1961)
str.   15:00 S.T.I.M.
—— DANS I MIDSOMMARTID
2,2,2,2 - 4,2,3,1 - timp.,perc.(2) - hp. - str.   12:00 S.T.I.M.
—— DIVERTIMENTO FOR STRINGS
str.   12:30 S.T.I.M.

—— FRÖKNARNA I PARKEN (CHAMBER OPERA FOR RADIO)
(Text: Erland Josephson)
1,0,1,1 - 1,0,0,0 - hp. - str.   45:00 S.T.I.M.
—— DE FYRA ÅRSTIDERNA (4 SONGS FOR SOPRANO AND
ORCH.)
2,2,2,2 - 4,2,3,0 - timp. - hp. - str.   12:25 S.T.I.M.
—— FYRA SÖRMLANDSLÅTÅR
str.   10:00 S.T.I.M.
—— LITTLE SUITE FOR CHAMBER ORCH.
1,0,1,1 - 0,0,0,0 - str.   7:30 S.T.I.M.
—— NORDIC SAGA (SUITE FROM THE BALLET
"SKYMNINGSLEKAR")
2,2,2,2 - 4,3,3,0 - timp.,perc.(2) - hp. - str.   23:00 S.T.I.M.
—— OVERTURE GIOCOSA (1958)
1,1,1,1 - 0,0,0,0 - str.   5:00 S.T.I.M.
—— OVERTURE TO THE OPERA "SKÅLKNALLEN"
2,2,2,2 - 2,2,1,0 - str.   S.T.I.M.
—— SINFONIA DA CAMERA
2,2,2,2 - 2,2,1,0 - str.   16:00 S.T.I.M.
—— SINFONIA NOTTURNA
3,3,3,3 - 4,3,3,1 - timp.,perc. - hp. - str.   35:00 S.T.I.M.
—— SINFONIA PICCOLA
2,2,2,2 - 4,3,3,0 - timp.,perc.(2) - hp. - str.   25:30 S.T.I.M.
—— SINFONIA SERIA
2,2,2,2 - 4,2,3,1 - timp.,perc.(2) - str.   17:00 S.T.I.M.
—— SKÅLKNALLEN (KOKA SOPPA PÅ EN SPIK) (OPERA) %
(Libretto: Lars-Levi Laestadius)
2,2,2,2 - 2,2,1,0 - timp. - hp. - str.   37:00 S.T.I.M.
—— SUITE FROM "ATT SÖKA SIN GENIUS"
fl. - str.   11:30 S.T.I.M.
—— SUITE FROM "EN VINTERSAGA"
2,2,2,2 - 4,2,3,1 - timp.,perc.(3) - hp. - str.   14:00 S.T.I.M.
—— SUITE FROM "SOM NI BEHAGER"
1,1,1,1 - 0,0,0,0 - str.   11:00 S.T.I.M.
—— SUITE NO. 1
2,2,2,2 - 4,2,3,0 - timp.,perc. - cemb. - hp. - str. S.T.I.M.
—— SUITE NO. 2
2,2,2,2 - 4,2,3,0 - timp.,perc.(2) - hp. - str.   11:00 S.T.I.M.
—— SYMPHONY IN D
2,2,2,2 - 4,3,3,0 - timp.,perc. - str.   34:00 S.T.I.M.
—— THREE INTERLUDES FROM THE OPERA "FRÖKNARNA I
PARKEN"
1,1,1,1 - 1,0,0,0 - hp. - str.   9:00 S.T.I.M.
—— THREE PIECES FOR ORCH.
1,1,2,2 - 2,2,1,0 - timp. - hp. - str.   15:30 S.T.I.M.

WIJDEVELD, Wolfgang
—— CONCERTSTUK VOOR KAMERORKEST
1,1,1,1 - 1,0,0,0 - str.   15:00 Henmar.
—— PSALM 150 (FOR SOPRANO, MIXED CHORUS AND
ORCHESTRA) (1950)
2,2,2,2 - 4,2,3,1 - timp.,perc. - str.   13:00 Henmar.

WIKANDER, David
—— INTRODUCTION AND FUGUE FOR STRINGS
str.   8:00 S.T.I.M.

WIKLUND, Adolf
—— CONCERT OVERTURE
2,2,2,2 - 4,2,3,1 - str.   12:00 S.T.I.M.
—— CONCERT PIECE FOR PIANO AND ORCH.
2,2,2,2 - 4,2,3,1 - timp. - pf. - str.   25:00 S.T.I.M.
—— CONCERTO NO. 1 FOR PIANO AND ORCH.
3,2,2,2 - 4,3,3,1 - timp. - pf. - str.   33:00 G. Schirmer.
—— CONCERTO NO. 2 FOR PIANO AND ORCH.
3,2,2,3 - 4,2,3,1 - timp. - pf. - str.   27:00 G. Schirmer.
—— LITTLE SUITE
2,2,2,2 - 4,2,1,0 - timp.,perc. - hp. - str.   16:00 S.T.I.M.
—— SOMMARNATT OCH SOLUPPGÅNG (SYMPHONIC POEM)
3,2,4,2 - 4,3,3,1 - timp. - hp. - str.   14:00 S.T.I.M.
—— SYMPHONIC PROLOGUE
3,3,3,3 - 4,2,3,1 - timp. - str.   10:00 S.T.I.M.
—— SYMPHONY, OP. 20
3,3,3,3 - 6,3,3,1 - timp. - str.   30:00 S.T.I.M.
—— THREE PIECES FOR HARP AND STRINGS
hp. - str.   20:00 Suecia.

WILD, Earl
—— REVELATION (ORATORIO) (FOR 5 SOLO VOICES, MIXED
CHORUS AND ORCH.) (Text: William Lewis)
*3,*3,*3,2 - 4,3,3,1 - timp.,perc.,bells,cel. - 2 hp. - pf. - str.
                                                  50:00 Cap. Press.

WILDBERGER, Jacques
—— CONCERTO FOR OBOE AND ORCH. (IN 3 MOVTS.)
    0,1,0,0 - 0,0,0,0 - perc.,cel.,vibra. - hp. - hpsc. - str.
            14:00 AhnSimrock.
—— CONTRATEMPI (FÜR 1 SOLO FLÖTE UND 4
ORCHESTERGRUPPEN)
    0,0,*1,*1 - 2,2,4,0 - perc.(4),cel. - hp. - guit. - mand. - str.
            18:00 Hans Gerig.
—— DIVERTIMENTO FOR PIANO AND ORCH.
    1,1,1,1 - 0,2 mellophones,1,0,0 - perc. - org. - pf. - str.
            7:00 Modern.
—— ÉPITAPHE POUR ÉVARISTE GALLOIS (FOR SOPRANO,
BARITONE, SPEAKING VOICE, SPEAKING CHORUS AND
ORCH.)
    *3,*3,*3,*2 - 4,3,3,1 - perc.(6) - tape-recorder(4-channel) - pf. -
    str.(2,1,1,1)   55:00 Modern.
—— IHR MEINT, DAS LEBEN SEI KURZ.....(CANTATA ON
JAPANESE HAIKU) (FOR SATB CHORUS AND ENSEMBLE)
(German text: Anna von Rottauscher)
    1,0,*2,0 - 0,0,0,0 - perc.,cel. - hp. - pf. - str.(2,1,0,1)
            23:00 Modern.
—— IN MY END IS MY BEGINNING (CANTATA) (FOR
SOPRANO, TENOR AND CHAMBER ORCH.) (Text: T. S.
Eliot)
            Hans Gerig.
—— INTENSIO - CENTRUM - REMISSIO
    *2,*2,E♭cl.,*2,1 - 2,1,1,1 - perc.(4) - hp. - hpsc. - pf. - str.
            10:00 Modern.
—— MOVEMENTS FOR ORCHESTRA
    3(3rd alt. with picc.),*3,*3,3(3rd alt. with c.-bn.) - 4,3,3,1 -
    perc.,vibra. - hp. - str.   10:45 AhnSimrock.
—— MUSIC FOR 22 SOLO STRINGS
    str.   12:00 AhnSimrock.
—— TRE MUTAZIONI
    *2,*2,E♭cl.,*2,1 - 0,2,2,0 - perc.(4) - hp. - hpsc. - pf. - str.
            14:00 Modern.

WILDER, Alec
—— THE LOWLAND SEA (1-ACT OPERA) % (Text: Arnold
Sundgaard)
    1,1,2,1 - 2,2,2,0 - perc. - pf. - str.(no vla.)   55:00 G. Schirmer.
—— SUNDAY EXCURSION (1-ACT OPERA) % (Text: Arnold
Sundgaaard)
    1,1,2,1 - 1,1,0,0 - perc. - pf. - str.   25:00 G. Schirmer.

WILDMAN, Charles
—— SWEDISH RHAPSODY (FOR PIANO AND ORCH.)
    2,2,3,3 - 4,2,3,1 - timp.,perc. - hp. - pf. - str.   8:00 Leeds.

WILHELMI, Tobias
—— CONCERTO FOR VIOLIN AND ORCH.
    3,2,2,2 - 4,2,3,0 - timp. - hp. - str.   30:00 Nordiska.
—— GITANJALI (SYMPHONIC POEM)
    3,3,2,2 - 4,2,3,0 - timp. - hp. - str.   11:00 S.T.I.M.
—— LITTLE SUITE FOR OBOE AND ORCH.
    1,1,2,2 - 2,2,1,0 - str.   13:00 S.T.I.M.
—— ÖSTERGÖTLAND (SUITE) (IN 4 MOVTS.)
    2,2,2,2 - 2,2,1,0 - timp.,perc. - str.   18:30 S.T.I.M.
—— SUITE FOR STRINGS
    str.   26:00 S.T.I.M.
—— SYMPHONY NO. 1
    3,3,3,3 - 4,3,3,1 - timp.,perc. - str.   25:00 S.T.I.M.
—— SYMPHONY NO. 2
    2,2,2,2 - 4,3,3,0 - timp.,perc. - str.   45:00 S.T.I.M.
—— SYMPHONY (POSTHUMOUS)
    2,2,2,2 - 2,1,2,1 - timp. - str.   S.T.I.M.

WILKINSON, Philip
—— SHAKESPEAREAN SUITE (1958)
    2,2,2,2 - 2,2,0,0 - timp.,perc. - str.   Novello.

WILKINSON, Stephen, ed.
—— VARIATIONS ON "GO FROM MY WINDOW, GO" (Attributed
to Orlando Gibbons)
    pf.(ad lib.) - str.   6:45 Oxford.

WILLAN, Healey
—— THE MYSTERY OF BETHLEHEM (CHRISTMAS CANTATA)
(FOR SOPRANO, BARITONE, SATB CHORUS AND SMALL
ORCH.)
    0,1,0,0 - 4,2,3,0 - timp.,glock. - hp. - org.   30:00 Belw-Mills.
—— SYMPHONY NO. 1
    2,3,2,2 - 4,3,3,1 - timp.,perc. - hp. - str.   40:00 C. Fischer.

WILLEMZE, Theo
—— L' HOMME HEUREUX, OP. 24 (1960)
    3,3,3,3 - 4,3,3,1 - timp.,perc.,cel.,xyl. - hp. - str.   10:00 Henmar.

WILLIAMS, Alberto
—— SYMPHONY NO. 3 IN F MAJOR, OP. 58 (THE SACRED
FOREST) (1911)
            Fleisher.
—— SYMPHONY NO. 4 IN E FLAT, OP. 98 (NIGHT BIRD) (1935)
            Fleisher.
—— SYMPHONY NO. 5 IN E FLAT, OP. 100 ("THE HEART OF A
DOLL") (1936)
            Fleisher.
—— SYMPHONY NO. 7 IN D, OP. 103 ("ETERNAL REST")
            Fleisher.
—— SYMPHONY NO. 8 IN F MINOR, OP. 104 ("THE SPHINX")
            Fleisher.
—— SYMPHONY NO. 9 IN B FLAT MAJOR ("THE TADPOLES"; A
HUMORESQUE) (1939)
    3,3,3,3 - 4,4,4,2 - timp.,perc.,cel. - hp. - str.   Fleisher.

WILLIAMS, David McKay
—— CANTATE DOMINO (FOR CHORUS, BRASS, PERCUSSION
AND ORGAN)
            8:00 Gray.
—— IN THE YEAR THAT KING UZZIAH DIED (FOR CHORUS
AND ORCH.)
    2,1,2,0 - 2,2,2,0 - timp.,perc. - org. - str.   10:00 Gray.
—— WHISPERS OF HEAVENLY DEATH (FOR CHORUS AND
ORCH.) (IN 2 MOVTS.)
    2,1,2,2 - 4,2,2,0 - timp. - hp. - str.   17:00 Gray.

WILLIAMS, David Russell
—— AIR FOR OBOE AND STRINGS, OP. 45 (1965)
    ob. - str.   5:30 Composer.
—— CONCERTO FOR PIANO 4-HANDS AND ORCH., OP. 39
(1964) (IN 3 MOVTS.)
    *3,2,2,2 - 2,2,1,0 - timp.,perc.(3) - pf. 4-hands - str.
            17:00 Composer.
—— FIVE STATES OF MIND, OP. 42 (SUITE) (1965)
    2(2nd alt. with picc.),2,2,2 - 2,2,1,0 - perc.(1) - str.
            8:30 C. Fischer.
—— SINFONIA (SYMPHONY IN E, OP. 14) (1956)
    1. Slowly - Moderately; 2. Slowly
    2(2nd alt. with picc.),2(2nd alt. with Eng. hn.),2,2 - 2,2,2,0 -
    timp.,perc.(3) - str.   12:00 Composer.

WILLIAMS, Grace
—— BALLADS FOR ORCH.
    2,2,2,2 - 4,2,3,1 - timp.,perc.(3) - hp. - str.   14:00 P.R.S.
—— CARILLONS (FOR OBOE AND ORCH.)(1965)
    0,1,0,0 - 2,2,3,0 - perc.,cel. - hp. - str.   9:00 P.R.S.
—— CONCERTO FOR TRUMPET AND ORCH. (1963)
    2,2,2,2 - 4,1,3,1 - timp. - hp. - str.   13:00 P.R.S.
—— THE DANCERS (A CHORAL SUITE) (FOR SOPRANO,
WOMEN'S CHORUS AND STRINGS) (Texts: Hilaire Belloc,
Chatterton, May Sarton and Kathleen Raine)
    hp.(or pf.) - str.   16:00 Oxford.
—— FANTASIA ON WELSH NURSERY TUNES
    2,2,2,2 - 4,2,3,0 - timp.,perc.(2),glock. - hp. - str.   10:30 Oxford.
—— PENILLION (SUITE)
            12:00 Oxford.
—— PROCESSIONAL (1962)
    2,2,2,2 - 4,2,3,1 - timp.,perc.(3) - hp. - str.   9:00 P.R.S.
—— SEA SKETCHES (FOR STRINGS)
            17:00 Oxford.

WILLIAMS, James Clifton
—— FESTIVAL
            8:00 Summy-Bir.
—— LEGEND
            Composer.
—— RONDO CONCERTANTE
            Composer.
—— A SOUTHWESTERN OVERTURE
            Composer.
—— SOUTHWESTERN SUITE
    str.   Summy-Bir.
—— SYMPHONY FOR YOUNG PEOPLE
            2:00 WarnerBros.
—— TRILOGY FROM THE "SONG OF SOLOMON" (FOR
SOPRANO AND STRINGS)
    str.   Composer.

WILLIAMS, Kimberley Lynton

—— AND STILL IT'S THERE (1974)
3(3rd alt. with picc.),2(2nd alt. with Eng. hn.),3,2 - 2,4,2,1 -
perc.(2),cel.,glock.,mar. - hp. - str.   16:00 AstrlMuCtr.

WILLIAMSON, Malcolm

—— THE BRILLIANT AND THE DARK (CHORAL OPERATIC
SEQUENCE) (FOR WOMEN'S VOICES AND ORCH.) (Text:
Ursala Vaughan Williams)
2,2,2,2 - 3,2,2,0 - timp.,perc.(3) - hp. - 4 pf.(8 hands) - str.
66:00 Bo. Hawkes.

—— CONCERTO FOR ORGAN AND ORCHESTRA
1(alt. with picc.),0,*2,1(alt. with c.-bn.) - 4,3,3,1 - timp.,perc.(4) -
org. - 2 hp. - str.   20:00 Bo. Hawkes.

—— CONCERTO FOR PIANO AND STRINGS
pf. - str.   16:00 Chappell.

—— CONCERTO FOR TWO PIANOS AND STRINGS (1973)
2 pf. - str.   19:00 Weinberger.

—— CONCERTO FOR VIOLIN AND ORCH.
2,2,2,2 - 4,3,3,1 - perc. - hp. - str.   26:00 Bo. Hawkes.
or:
1,1,1,1 - 1,0,0.0 - str.

—— CONCERTO GROSSO
3,3,3,3 - 4,4,3,1 - timp.,perc.(3) - hp. - str.   10:30 Bo. Hawkes.

—— CONCERTO NO. 1 FOR PIANO AND ORCH.
2,2,2,2 - 3,2,3,1 - timp.,perc. - pf. - str.   19:00 Bo. Hawkes.

—— THE DISPLAY (A DANCE SYMPHONY) (BALLET) % (IN 4
MOVTS.)
2,2,2,2 - 4,3,3,1 - timp.,perc. - pf. - str.   40:00 Bo. Hawkes.

—— THE DISPLAY (CONCERT SUITE FROM THE BALLET) (IN 3
MOVTS.)
2,2,2,2 - 4,3,3,1 - timp.,perc. - pf. - str.   25:00 Bo. Hawkes.

—— ELEVAMINI (A SYMPHONY)
2,2,2,2 - 4,3,3,1 - timp.,perc. - str.   26:30 Bo. Hawkes.

—— EPITAPHS FOR EDITH SITWELL
str.   7:00 Bo. Hawkes.

—— FOUR NORTH COUNTRY SONGS (WITH SOLO VOICE AND
OPTIONAL SATB CHORUS)
1,2,0,2 - 2,0,0,0 - perc. - hpsc. - str.   9:00 Bo. Hawkes.

—— THE GROWING CASTLE: FINAL SCENE FROM THE OPERA
(FOR SOPRANO AND ORCH.) (Text: Composer, after
Strindberg's "Dream Play")
2,2,2,2 - 4,3,3,1 - timp.,perc. - hp. - str.   5:00 Bo. Hawkes.

—— THE HAPPY PRINCE (1-ACT OPERA, FOR CHILDREN'S
AND FEMALE VOICES, AFTER OSCAR WILDE'S
FAIRY-TALE) % (Text: Composer)
perc.(1-4) - pf. 4-hands - str.(2,1,1,1)   40:00 Bo. Hawkes.

—— THE ICY MIRROR (FOR SOPRANO, MEZZO-SOPRANO, 2
BARITONES, SATB CHORUS AND ORCH.) (Text: Ursala
Vaughan Williams)
2,2,2,2 - 4,3,3,1 - perc. - hp. - pf. - str.   29:00 Bo. Hawkes.

—— JULIUS CAESAR JONES (2-ACT OPERA, FOR CHILDREN'S
VOICES WITH 3 ADULTS) % (Text: Geoffrey Dunn)
1,1,1,1 - 1,0,0,0 - perc. - hp. - pf. - str.(2,1,1,1)
60:00 Bo. Hawkes.

—— LUCKY-PETER'S JOURNEY (OPERA) (A COMEDY WITH
MUSIC) % (Text: Edmund Tracey, after Strindberg's fairy-tale play)
2(1 alt. with picc.),2(1 alt. with Eng. hn.),2(1 alt. with b.-cl.),2(1
alt. with c-bn.) - 4,3,3,1 - timp.,perc.(3) - hp. - str.   Bo. Hawkes.

—— ODE TO MUSIC (FOR CHORUS, ECHO CHORUS AND
ORCH.) (Text: Ursala Vaughan Williams)
2,2,2,2 - 4,3,3,0 - perc. - hp. - str.   Bo. Hawkes.

—— OUR MAN IN HAVANA (ORCHESTRAL SUITE FROM THE
OPERA)
2,2,2,2 - 4,3,3,0 - perc.(2) - hp. - str.   18:00 Bo. Hawkes.

—— OUR MAN IN HAVANA (SUITE FROM THE OPERA) (WITH
SOPRANO, TENOR, BASS AND SATB CHORUS) (Text: Sidney
Gilliat)
2,2,2,2 - 4,2,3,0 - perc. - guit. - hp. - str.   31:00 Bo. Hawkes.

—— OUR MAN IN HAVANA (3-ACT OPERA) % (Text: Sidney
Gilliat, after Graham Greene's novel)
1(alt. with picc.),1(alt. with Eng. hn.),1(alt. with b.-cl.),sax.,1(alt.
with c.-bn.) - 1,1,2,0 - perc.,cel. - guit. - hp. - pf. - str. Bo. Hawkes.

—— SANTIAGO DE ESPADA (OVERTURE)
2,2,2,2 - 3,2,3,1 - timp.,perc. - str.   6:30 Bo. Hawkes.

—— SERENADE AND AUBADE (MOVTS. II AND III FROM
"SYMPHONIC VARIATIONS")
1,1,1,1 - 1,0,0,0 - hp. - str.   10:00 Bo. Hawkes.

—— SINFONIA CONCERTANTE
3 tpt. - pf. - str.   16:30 Bo. Hawkes.

—— SINFONIETTA
2,2,2,2 - 4,3,3,1 - perc.(3) - hp. - str.   18:00 Bo. Hawkes.

—— SIX ENGLISH LYRICS (FOR LOW VOICE AND STRING
ORCH.) (Texts: Waller, Tennyson, Rossetti, Leigh Hunt)
str.   10:00 Bo. Hawkes.

—— THE STONE WALL (CASSATION FOR AUDIENCE AND
ORCH.) (MINIATURE OPERA) %
2,2,2,2 - 4,3,3,1 - perc. - hp. - str.   6:00 Bo. Hawkes.

—— SUN INTO DARKNESS (3-ACT BALLET) %
2,2,2,2 - 2,2,2,0 - timp.,perc. - hp. - pf. - str.   93:00 Bo. Hawkes.

—— SYMPHONIC VARIATIONS
3,3,3,3 - 4,4,3,1 - perc.(2) - hp. - pf. - str.   42:00 Bo. Hawkes.

—— SYMPHONY NO. 2
3,3,3,3 - 4,3,3,1 - timp.,perc.(4) - hp. - str.   20:00 Bo. Hawkes.

—— THE VIOLINS OF SAINT-JACQUES (THREE-ACT OPERA) %
(Text: Wm. Chappell, after Patrick Leigh Fermor's novel)
3,3,3,3 - 4,4,3,1 - timp.,perc.(4) - 2 hp. - org. - str.   Bo. Hawkes.
Plus On-Stage: 1,0,1,0 - 2,4,0,0 - str.(3,0,0,1)

WILLIS, Richard

—— CONCERTINO FOR PIANO AND ORCH. (1953)
2,1,2,2 - 3,2,2,0 - timp.,perc.(4),glock.,xyl. - hp. - pf. - str.
15:00 Composer.

—— EVOCATION (1967)
*3,2,*3,2 - 4,3,3,1 - timp.,perc.(3),glock.,vibra.,xyl. - hp. - pf.(alt.
with cel.) - str.   9:30 Composer.

—— THE PLAYGROUND (A SUITE FOR ORCH.) (1965) (IN 7
MOVTS.)
*3,*3,*3,*3 - 4,3,3,1 - str.   23:00 Composer.

—— PRELUDE AND DANCE (1956)
1,2,2,1 - 2,2,0,0 - timp.,perc.(3) - pf. - str.   15:00 Composer.

—— RECITATIVE AND DANCE (1963)
fl. - pf. (alt. with cel.) - str.   9:00 Presser.

—— SOLILOQUY (1957)
1,1,2,1 - 2,1,1,0 - timp. - hp. - str.   10:00 Composer.

—— SONANTS (FOR 15 WINDS AND 2 PERCUSSION)
*3,2(2nd alt. with Eng. hn.), 2(2nd alt. with b.-cl.),2 - 2,2,2,0 -
perc.(2)   9:00 Composer.

—— SYMPHONY NO. 1 (1953) (IN 3 MOVTS.)
*3,2,2,2 - 4,2,3,1 - timp.,perc.(3) - str.   23:00 Composer.

—— SYMPHONY NO. 2 (1964) (IN 3 MOVTS.)
*3,2,2,2 - 4,3,3,1 - timp.,perc.(3),xyl. - hp. - str.   23:00 Composer.

WILLISEGGER, Hansruedi

—— GESANG AN DIE SONNE (VIER STÜCKE)
*3,3,*3,*3 - 4,3,3,1 - perc.,cel. - hp. - str.   15:00 S.U.I.S.A.

WILLNER, Arthur

—— SUITE FOR STRINGS AND PIANO
pf. - str.   5:30 Novello.

WILLS, Arthur

—— CONCERTO FOR ORGAN, STRINGS AND TIMPANI
timp. - org. - str.   26:00 Bo. Hawkes.

WILLSON, Meredith

—— THE JERVIS BAY
*3,*3,*3,*3 - 4,4,4,1 - timp.,perc.(3), cel. - hp. - pf. - str.
14:00 Composer.

—— SYMPHONIC VARIATIONS ON AN AMERICAN THEME
2(1 alt. with picc.),*3,*4,*3 - 4,3,3,1 - timp.,perc.(3),cel.,glock.,xyl.
- hp. - pf. - str.   24:30 Composer.

—— SYMPHONY NO. 1 IN F MINOR ("A SYMPHONY OF SAN
FRANCISCO") (IN 4 MOVTS.)
2(1 alt. with picc),*3,*3,4 sax.,*3 - 4,3,3,1 - timp.,perc.(3) - hp. -
str.   38:00 Composer.

—— SYMPHONY NO. 2 ("MISSIONS OF CALIFORNIA") (IN 4
MOVTS.)
2(2nd alt. with picc.),*3,*3,2 - 4,3,3,1 - perc.(2),bells,cel. - str.
20:30 FrankMusCp.

WILSON, Charles M.

—— THE ANGELS OF THE EARTH (1966) (ORATORIO) (FOR 2
NARRATORS, SOPRANO, BARITONE, SATB CHORUS AND
ORCH.) (IN 2 PARTS) (Text: Wilson MacDonald)
*3,*3,*3,2 - 4,3,3,0 - timp.,perc.(7) hp - str.   135:00 CanMusCtr.

—— CANTATA (ON THE MORNING OF CHRIST'S NATIVITY)
(1963) (FOR SOPRANO, TENOR, BARITONE, SATB CHORUS
AND ORCH.)
1,1,1,1 - 0,2,1,0 - str.   25:00 CanMusCtr.

—— CRISTO PAREMUS CANTICAM (1973) (FOR SATB CHORUS
AND ORCH.) (Text: Thomas Traherne)
2,2,*3,2 - 4,2,3,1 - timp.,perc. - hp. - str.   25:00 CanMusCtr.

—— DAVID'S LAMENT OVER SAUL AND JONATHAN (FOR CHORUS AND ORCH.)
15:00 C.A.P.A.C.

—— DIVERTIMENTO FOR CLARINET AND STRINGS
cl. - str.   12:00 C.A.P.A.C.

—— LAMENT (FOR CHORUS AND ORCH.)
20:00 C.A.P.A.C.

—— SINFONIA (1972) (FOR DOUBLE ORCH.) (IN 1 MOVT. OF 2 SECTIONS)
2,2,2,2 - 2,2,2,0 - timp.,perc.(3) - hp. - str.   12:45 CanMusCtr.

—— SONATA DA CHIESA (1960) (FOR OBOE AND STRINGS) (IN 3 MOVTS.)
ob. - str.   18:10 CanMusCtr.

—— SYMPHONIC PERSPECTIVES (KINGSMERE) (IN 1 MOVT.)
2,2,2,2 - 2,2,2,0 - timp. - str.   20:00 CanMusCtr.

—— SYMPHONY IN A
25:00 C.A.P.A.C.

—— TONE POEM
12:00 C.A.P.A.C.

WILSON, George Balch
—— CONCATENATIONS (FOR 12 INSTRUMENTS) (1969)
1,0,*2,0 - 1,1,1,0 - perc.(1) - guit.(amplified) - accord.(amplified) - 1 vln.,1 c., 1 d.-b.   7:00 EV.

WILSON, Mortimer
—— CONCERTO GROSSO FOR STRING QUARTET, HARP AND STRING ORCH., OP. 13 (IN 4 MOVTS.)
hp. - str.   Composer.

—— EUTERPEAN LYRICS, OP. 28 (IN 5 MOVTS.)
str.   J. Fischer.

—— MY COUNTRY (A SCENIC FANTASY), OP. 70
*3,2,2,2 - 4,3,3,1 - timp.,perc. - hp. - str.   J. Fischer.

—— NEW ORLEANS ("MARDI GRAS")
2(2nd alt. with picc.),2,2,2 - 4,3,3,0 - timp.,perc. - hp. - str.   9:00 Composer.

—— OVERTURE "1849", OP. 71
2(2nd alt. with picc.),2,2,2 - 4,3,3,1 - timp.,perc. - hp. - str.   J. Fischer.

—— SYMPHONY NO. 3 ("THE QUAKER"), OP. 18 (IN 4 MOVTS.)
Composer.

—— THREE ELIZABETHAN AIRS
1,1,2,1 - 2,2,1,0 - timp.,perc.(1) - str.   J. Fischer.

WILSON, Olly W.
—— AKWAN (FOR PIANO AND ORCH.)(1972)
3(1 alt. with picc.),2,*3,*3 - 4,3,3,1 - timp.,perc.(4) - pf.(alt. with electronic pf.) - str.   17:00 Composer.

—— THREE MOVEMENTS FOR ORCHESTRA (1964)
*3,2,*3,*3 - 4,2,3,1 - timp.,perc.(4),bells,glock.,vibra.,xyl. - hp. - pf. - str.   Composer.

—— VOICES (1970)
3(1 alt. with picc.),*3,*3,*3 - 4,3,3,1 - timp.,perc.(5),glock.,xyl. - pf. - str.   10:00 Composer.

WILSON, Richard
—— FANTASY AND VARIATIONS FOR CHAMBER ORCH. (1966)
1,0,1,1 - 0,1,1,0 - timp.,perc.(2),bells,glock,xyl. - str.(1,1,1,1)   10:00 Composer.

WILSON, Thomas B.
—— ANTIPHON (1957)
str.   15:00 P.R.S.

—— CONCERTINO FOR PIANO AND STRING ORCH. (1949)
pf. - str.   25:00 P.R.S.

—— CONCERTO FOR CLARINET AND STRING ORCH. (1951)
cl. - str.   25:00 P.R.S.

—— CONCERTO FOR ORCH. (1967)
3,3,3,3 - 4,3,3,1 - timp.,perc.,cel. - hp. - pf. - str.   18:00 P.R.S.

—— SINFONIETTA (1949)
1,1,1,1 - 0,0,0,0 - str.   25:00 P.R.S.

—— SYMPHONY NO. 1 (1956)
2,2,2,2 - 4,2,3,1 - timp.,perc. - hp. - str.   35:00 P.R.S.

—— SYMPHONY NO. 2 (1966)
3,2,2,2 - 4,2,3,1 - timp.,perc.,cel. - hp. - pf. - str.   23:00 P.R.S.

—— TOCCATA
3,2,2,2 - 4,2,3,1 - timp.,perc.,cel. - hp. - pf. - str.   9:00 Novello.

—— TOUCHSTONE (PORTRAIT FOR ORCH.)
G. Schirmer.

—— VARIATIONS
3,3,3,3 - 4,3,3,1 - timp.,perc.,cel. - hp. - pf. - str.   18:00 Novello.

WIMBERGER, Gerhard
—— AUGUSTINE VARIATIONS (LOGA-RHYTHMS)
2(2nd alt. with picc.),*3,*3,*3 - 4,3,3,1 - timp.,perc. - hp. - str.   8:45 Modern.

—— MULTIPLAY (CANONIC REFLECTIONS FOR 23 PLAYERS)(1973)
13:00 G. Schirmer.

—— PAS D'ILLUSION (SUITE FROM THE BALLET "DER HANDSCHUH" OR "THE GLOVE")
*2,1,*2,alto sax.,1 - 0,0,1,0 - perc. - pf. - str.   23:00 Modern.

WINKLER, Karl
—— SYMPHONY NO. 2 IN D, OP. 47 ("MAIENSYMPHONIE" OR "SPRING SYMPHONY")
40:00 A.K.M.

WINNEBERGER, Paul Anton - BODART, Eugen
—— SYMPHONY IN F MAJOR
2,2,0,2 - 2,0,0,0 - str.   19:00 Mannheimer.

WINNUBST, Johan
—— LA DIVINA COMEDIA (FOR SOPRANO AND ORCH.) (Text: Dante)
2,2,2,2 - 4,3,3,0 - timp. - hp. - str.   9:00 B.U.M.A.

—— ECCE SACERDOS MAGNUS (FOR SATB SOLO VOICES, MIXED CHORUS AND ORCH.) (1933)
3,3,3,3 - 4,3,3,1 - timp. - str.   B.U.M.A.

—— KLEINE SERENADE
1,1,1,1 - 1,0,0,0 - hp. - str.   20:00 Henmar.

—— OPHELIA (OVERTURE-FANTASY) (FOR MIXED CHORUS AND ORCH) (1912)
2,2,3,2 - 4,3,3,1 - timp.,perc. - hp. - str.   B.U.M.A.

—— PRIESTER HYMNE (FOR SOPRANO, TENOR, BASS, BOYS' CHORUS, MIXED CHORUS AND ORCH.) (1924) (Text: Bern. Verhoeven)
3,3,3,3 - 4,3,3,1 - timp. - hp. - str.   B.U.M.A.

—— SYMPHONY NO. 1
3,3,3,3 - 4,3,3,1 - timp. - hp. - str.   17:00 Henmar.

WINSTEAD, William
—— THE MOONSINGERS (FOR NARRATOR AND ORCH.)
3,2,3,2 - 4,2,2,1 - timp.,perc. - str.   19:00 Presser.

WINTER, Peter von - BODART, Eugen
—— ENTR'ACTE AND DIVERTIMENTO
2,2,0,0 - 2,0,0,0 - str.   13:00 Mannheimer.

—— OVERTURE TO THE OPERA "DAS UNTERBROCHENE OPFERFEST"
2,2,2,2 - 4,2,0,0 - timp. - str.   Mannheimer.

WINTER, Peter von - MICHAELS
—— CONCERTINO IN E FLAT MAJOR, FOR CLARINET, CELLO AND ORCH.
cl. - 2 hn. - str.   20:00 F. Colombo.

WINTERS, Geoffrey
—— ACTION, REACTION, INTERACTION (1969)
3,3,3,3 - 4,3,3,1 - timp.,perc. - str.   13:00 P.R.S.

—— PAGEANT (1968)
2,2,3,1 - 2,2,3,1 - timp.,perc. - str.   12:00 P.R.S.

—— A YORKSHIRE SUITE (1950)
3,3,2,2 - 4,3,3,1 - timp.,perc. - str.   25:00 P.R.S.

WIRÉN, Dag
—— BALLET SUITE, OP. 24A
2,2,2,2 - 4,2,3,1 - timp.,perc.(2) - str.   14:00 Bo. Hawkes.

—— CONCERT OVERTURE NO. 1, OP. 2
2,2,2,2 - 2,2,1,0 - timp.,perc. - str.   8:00 S.T.I.M.

—— CONCERT OVERTURE NO. 2, OP. 16
2,2,2,2 - 4,2,3,1 - timp.,perc. - str.   5:00 S.T.I.M.

—— CONCERTINO FOR FLUTE AND SMALL ORCH., OP. 44 (1972)
3,2,2,2 - 2,2,0,0 - str.   13:40 Gehrmans.

—— CONCERTO FOR CELLO AND ORCH., OP. 10
2,2,2,2 - 2,2,1,0 - timp. - str.   16:00 Bo. Hawkes.

—— CONCERTO FOR PIANO AND ORCH., OP. 26
2,2,2,2 - 4,2,1,0 - timp.,perc. - pf. - str.   19:00 Bo. Hawkes.

—— CONCERTO FOR VIOLIN AND ORCH., OP. 23
2,2,2,2 - 4,2,3,1 - timp.,perc. - hp. - str.   21:00 EV.

—— DIVERTIMENTO, OP. 29
2,2,2,2 - 2,2,1,0 - timp.,perc.(2) - str.   S.T.I.M.

—— DEN ELAKA DROTTNINGEN, OP. 34 (BALLET) %
2,2,2,2 - 4,3,2,0 - timp.,perc.(3),cel. - hp. - pf. - str.   30:00 S.T.I.M.

—— LITTLE SUITE, OP. 17
    2,2,2,2 - 2,2,1,0 - timp.,perc. - str.   11:00 Bo. Hawkes.
—— LUSTSPELS OVERTURE, OP. 21
    2,2,2,2 - 2,2,1,0 - timp.,perc. - str.   4:00 S.T.I.M.
—— MUSIC FOR STRING ORCH., OP. 40
    str.   12:00 Bo. Hawkes.
—— OSCARSBALEN, OP. 24 (BALLET) %
    2,2,2,2 - 4,2,3,1 - timp.,perc.(3) - hp. - str.   Gehrmans.
—— OVERTURE JOYEUSE
        4:00 S.T.I.M.
—— ROMANTIC SUITE FROM "THE MERCHANT OF VENICE",
OP. 22
    1,1,1,1 - 1,0,0,0 - str.   12:00 Gehrmans.
—— SCHERZO NO. 2, OP. 7-B
    2,2,2,2 - 2,2,1,0 - timp. - str.   4:00 Bo. Hawkes.
—— SERENADE FOR STRINGS, OP. 11
    str.   15:00 Southern.
—— SYMPHONY NO. 2, OP. 14
    2,2,2,2 - 2,2,3,1 - timp.,perc. - str.   29:00 S.T.I.M.
    or:
    2,2,2,2 - 2,2,1,0 - timp.,perc. - str.
—— SYMPHONY NO. 3, OP. 20
    2,2,2,2 - 4,2,3,1 - timp.,perc.(2) - str.   23:00 Bo. Hawkes.
—— SYMPHONY NO. 4
    2,2,2,2 - 4,2,3,1 - timp.,perc.(2) - str.   18:00 Bo. Hawkes.
—— SYMPHONY NO. 5, OP. 38 (1964)
    2,2,2,2 - 4,3,3,1 - timp.,perc. - str.   22:00 Bo. Hawkes.
—— TRIPTYCH FOR SMALL ORCH., OP. 33
    1,1,1,1 - 0,0,0,0 - str.   14:00 MusKonFor.

WIRTH, Carl Anton
—— DIVERSIONS IN DENIM (5 PIECES FOR STRINGS)
    str.   24:00 Composer.
—— ELEGY ON AN APPALACHIAN FOLK SONG
    2,2,2,2 - 4,2,3,1 - timp.,perc.(2) - str.   9:00 Composer.
—— ICHABOD CRANE SUITE (IN 4 MOVTS.)
    2,2(2nd alt. with Eng. hn.),2(2nd alt. with b.-cl.),2 - 4,3,3,1 -
    timp.,perc.(3),glock. - str.   14:00 Composer.
—— IDLEWOOD CONCERTO (FOR SAXOPHONE AND ORCH.)
(IN 3 MOVTS.)
    2(2nd alt. with picc.),2,2,alto sax.,2 - 4,3,3,1 - timp.,perc.(3),glock.
    - str.   6:00 EV.
—— JEPHTHA (INVOCATION AND DANCE, FOR 2
SAXOPHONES AND ORCH.)
    1 sopr. sax.(or cl.),1 alto sax. - perc.(1) - pf. - str.
        10:00 Composer.
—— PORTALS (PRELUDE) (FOR STRINGS)
    str.   Composer.
—— RHAPSODY FOR PIANO AND ORCH.
    2,2,2,2 - 4,3,3,1 - timp.,perc.(3) - pf. - str.   10:00 Composer.
—— SERENADE FOR SOLO WOODWINDS AND STRINGS
    1(alt. with picc.),1,1,1 - 0,0,0,0 - str.   10:00 Composer.

WISHART, Peter
—— COME, HOLY GHOST (CANTATA) (FOR CONTRALTO,
WOMEN'S CHORUS AND STRINGS)
    str.   24:00 Oxford.
—— CONCERTO FOR PIANO AND ORCH.
    0,2,0,1 - 2,0,0,0 - pf. - str.   20:00 Galaxy.
—— CONCERTO FOR VIOLIN AND ORCH.
    0,*3,0,2 - 0,2,3,0 - str.   17:00 Galaxy.
—— CONCERTO FOR VIOLIN AND WINDS
    0,3(3rd alt. with Eng. hn.),0,2 - 0,2,3,0 - vln.   17:00 Galaxy.
—— CONCERTO NO. 2 FOR VIOLIN AND ORCH., OP. 61
    2,2,2,2 - 2,2,0,0 - str.   24:00 P.R.S.
—— A CYCLE OF SEVEN SONGS (FOR TENOR AND SMALL
ORCH.)
    1,0,1,1 - 0,0,0,0 - hp. - str.   17:00 Oxford.
—— DIVISIONS
    2(2nd alt. with picc.),2(2nd alt. with Eng.hn.),2,2 - 4,2,3,0 -
    timp.,perc. - hp. - str.   20:00 Galaxy.
—— FIVE PIECES FOR STRING ORCH.
    str.   15:00 Galaxy.
—— MEDITATIONS AND MYSTERIES (FOR MEZZO-SOPRANO,
SATB CHORUS AND STRINGS)
    str.   20:00 Galaxy.
—— SERENADE IN D
    1,2,0,2 - 2,0,0,0 - str.   18:00 Galaxy.
—— SYMPHONY NO. 2
    3(3rd alt. with picc.),3(3rd alt. with Eng.hn.),3(3rd alt. with
    b.-cl.),3(3rd alt. with c.-bn.) - 4,2,3,1 - timp.,perc. - pf. - str.
        20:00 Galaxy.

WISSE, Jan
—— SETTE AFORISMI (7 APHORISMS) (1956)
    2,2,2,2 - 2,2,0,0 - str.   3:00 Henmar.

WISSMER, Pierre
—— ANTHONY AND CLEOPATRA (SYMPHONIC SUITE)
    2,2,2,2 - 4,3,2,0 - timp.,perc.(3) - hp. - str.   22:00 EV.
—— CASSATION (FOR CHAMBER ORCH.)
    1,1,1,1 - 2,1,0,0 - str.   15:00 Presser.
—— CHRISTINA ET LES CHIMÈRES: SUITE NO. 1
    2,1,2,2 - 2,2,1,0 - timp.,perc.,cel. - pf. - str.   31:00 Presser.
—— CHRISTINA ET LES CHIMÈRES: SUITE NO. 2
    2,1,2,2 - 2,2,1,0 - timp.,perc.,cel. - pf. - str.   26:00 Presser.
—— CHRISTINA ET LES CHIMÈRES: SUITE NO. 3
    2,1,2,2 - 2,2,1,0 - timp.,perc.,cel. - pf. - str.   21:00 Presser.
—— CLAMAVI (TRIPTYQUE SYMPHONIQUE)
    2,2,2,2 - 4,3,3,1 - timp.,perc.,cel. - hp. - str.   15:00 F. Colombo.
—— CONCERTINO-CROISIÈRE (POUR FLÛTE, ORCHESTRE À
CORDES ET PIANO)
    fl. - pf. - str.   11:00 Presser.
—— CONCERTO FOR GUITAR AND ORCH.
    2,2,2,2 - 2,2,0,0 - timp.,perc. - guit. - str.   21:00 Presser.
—— CONCERTO NO. 2 FOR PIANO AND ORCH.
    2,2,2,2 - 4,3,3,1 - timp.,perc.(3),cel. - hp. - pf. - str.   26:00 Presser.
—— CONCERTO NO. 2 FOR VIOLIN AND ORCH.
    2,2,2,2 - 4,2,3,0 - timp.,perc.(3),cel. - hp. - str.   23:00 Presser.
—— CONCERTO VALCROSIANO
    3,3,3,3 - 4,3,3,1 - timp.,perc.,cel.,vibra.,xyl. - hp. - pf. - str.
        33:00 E.C.Kerby.
—— DIVERTIMENTO
    2,2,2,2 - 4,2,3,0 - timp.,perc.,xyl. - hp. - pf. - str.   14:00 EV.
—— L' ENFANT ET LA ROSE (THEME AND VARIATIONS)
        25:00 F. Colombo.
—— FUGUE IN G MINOR (AFTER J. OXINAGAS)
    2 ob., 2 bn. - str.   3:00 Presser.
—— LA MANDRELLINA (OVERTURE)
        E.C.Kerby.
—— MOUVEMENT (FOR STRINGS)
    str.   EV.
—— LE QUATRIÈME MAGE (ORATORIO)
    2,2,2,2 - 4,3,3,1 - timp.,perc.(3),cel. - hp. - pf. - str. 52:00 Presser.
—— STELE (POUR ORCHESTRE À CORDES)
    str.   6:30 E.C.Kerby.
—— SYMPHONY NO. 2
    2,2,2,2 - 4,2,3,0 - timp.,perc.,xyl. - hp. - pf. - str.   22:00 Ricordi.
—— SYMPHONY NO. 3
    str.   24:00 EV.
—— SYMPHONY NO. 5
    3,3,3,3 - 4,3,3,1 - timp.,perc.(4),cel.,vibra.,xyl. - hp. - pf. - str.
        35:00 Presser.

WISZNIEWSKI, Zbigniew
—— CONCERTO FOR CLARINET AND STRINGS
    cl. - str.(7,4,3,1)   13:00 Modern.
—— KAMMERMUSIK II
    str.(4,3,2,1)   10:00 Modern.

WITKIN, Beatrice
—— COMBINATIONS FOR 13 INSTRUMENTS (1965)
        11:00 Composer.
—— TWELVE-TONE VARIATIONS ON QUOTES BY THE
BEATLES (1967)
        12:00 MCA Music.

WITKOWSKI, Georges-Martin
—— INTRODUCTION AND DANCES (FOR VIOLIN AND ORCH.)
    2,2,2,2 - 2,2,0,0 - timp.,perc. - hp. - str.   13:00 Salabert.
—— MON LAC (PRELUDE, VARIATIONS AND FINALE) (FOR
PIANO AND ORCH.)
    3,3,3,2 - 4,3,4,0 - timp.,perc.,cel. - hp. - pf. - str.   23:00 Salabert.
—— LE POÈME DE LA MAISON (POÈME LYRIQUE) (FOR SOLO,
MIXED CHORUS AND ORCH.) (IN 5 MOVTS.)
    3,3,3,3 - 4,4,4,0 - timp.,perc.(3), cel. - 2 hp. - pf. - str.
        86:00 Salabert.
—— QUATRE POÈMES, OP. 25 (FROM "COEUR INNOMBRABLE")
(FOR SOLO VOICES, MIXED CHORUS AND ORCH.) (Text:
Comtesse de Noailles)
        18:00 Salabert.

WITTELSBACH, Rudolf
—— CONCERTINO FÜR KAMMERORCH.
    1,1,1,1 - 0,1,0,0 - str.   17:00 S.U.I.S.A.

—— CONCERTO FOR PIANO AND ORCH., OP. 8
    2,2,2,2 - 0,1,0,0 - pf. - str.   18:00 S.U.I.S.A.
—— DIVERTIMENTO FÜR KAMMERORCH.
    1,1,1,1 - 0,1,0,0, - timp. - str.   18:00 S.U.I.S.A.
—— MUSIK FÜR ORCH.
    2,2,2,2 - 4,2,0,0 - str.   12:00 S.U.I.S.A.

WITTMER, Eberhard Ludwig
—— MUSIK FÜR STREICHORCH.
    str.   20:00 SDMV.
—— SINFONIETTA
    2,2,2,2 - 2,2,2,1 - timp.,perc. - str.   24:00 SDMV.

WOHLFAHRT, Frank
—— CONCERTO FOR HARPSICHORD AND CHAMBER ORCH.
    (IN 3 MOVTS.)
    0,1,0,1 - 1,1,1,0 - hpsc. - str.   20:00 F. Colombo.
—— GOTT UND WOLF (SCENIC ORATORIO) (FOR NARRATOR
    AND ORCH.) %
    3,2,2,2 - 3,3,3,0 - timp. - str.   80:00 F. Colombo.
—— SYMPHONY IN 5 MOVTS. (AFTER THE SCENIC ORATORIO
    "GOTT UND WOLF") %
    3,2,2,2 - 3,3,3,0 - timp. - str.   39:00 F. Colombo.

WOHLFART, Karl
—— CONCERT PIECE FOR PIANO AND ORCH.
    2,2,2,2 - 4,2,4,0 - timp. - pf. - str.   25:00 S.T.I.M.
—— SWEDISH RHAPSODY
    3,2,2,2 - 4,2,4,0 - timp.,perc. - str.   12:00 S.T.I.M.

WOLF, Hugo
—— THE CORREGIDOR (OPERA) % (Engl. text: George and Phyllis
Mead)
          Translator.

WOLF, Hugo - GÁL, Hans
—— DER CORREGIDOR: SUITE (IN 5 MOVTS.)
    3,2,2,2 - 4,2,3,1 - timp.,perc. - str.   16:00 Bo. Hawkes.

WOLF, Hugo - JANCIK
—— ITALIAN SERENADE (Urtext of version for small orch.)
    2,2,2,2 - 2,0,0,0 - str.   15:00 Henmar.

WOLF, Hugo - STRAVINSKY, Igor
—— TWO SACRED SONGS (FROM THE "SPANISCHES
LIEDERBUCH") (FOR VOICE AND 10 INSTS.)
    0,0,3,0 - 2,0,0,0 - str.(2,1,1,1)   Bo. Hawkes.

WOLF, Jaroslav J.
—— INTEGRALE
    3(3rd alt. with picc.),3(3rd alt. with Eng. hn.),3(1 alt. with E♭cl.,1
    alt. with b.-cl.),3(3rd alt. with c.-bn.) - 4,3,3,1 - timp.,perc.(5) - hp.
    - str.   18:00 Modern.
—— TRANSZENDENZ II (FOR VARIABLE SIZE ORCH.)
          Modern.

WOLF, Winfried
—— CONCERTO FOR PIANO AND ORCH., OP. 13 (IN 3 MOVTS.)
    2,2,2,2 - 2,2,3,1 - timp.,perc. - pf. - str.   Bo. Hawkes.

WOLFE, Jacques
—— JOHN HENRY (OPERA) % (Text: Roark Bradford)
          Composer.

WOLFE, Stanley
—— CANTICLE FOR STRINGS, OP. 12
    str.   10:00 Composer.
—— FIRST OVERTURE, OP. 5
    2(2nd alt. with picc.),2,2,2 - 4,3,3,1 - timp.,perc.(2),xyl. - str.
        8:00 Composer.
—— KING'S HEART, OP. 10 (BALLET) %
    *2,1,1,1 - 2,2,2,1 - timp.,perc.(2) - str.   19:00 Composer.
—— LINCOLN SQUARE OVERTURE, OP. 13
    2(2nd alt. with picc.),2,2,2 - 4,3,3,1 - timp.,perc.(2),bells - str.
        9:00 Composer.
—— SYMPHONY NO. 1, OP. 6
    2(2nd alt. with picc.),2,2,2 - 4,3,3,1 - timp.,perc.(2),glock. - str.
        14:00 Composer.
—— SYMPHONY NO. 2, OP. 8
    2(2nd alt. with picc.),2(2nd alt. with Eng.hn.),2(2nd alt. with
    b.-cl.),*3 - 4,3,3,1 - timp.,perc.(2),glock. - pf. - str.
        18:00 Composer.

—— SYMPHONY NO. 3, OP. 14 (IN 3 MOVTS.)
    2(2nd alt. with picc.),2,2,2 - 4,3,3,1 - timp.,perc.(2-3),bells,glock. -
    str.   28:00 Bo. Hawkes.

WOLFF, Albert
—— CONCERTO FOR FLUTE AND ORCH.
    3,2,2,2 - 4,2,3,0 - timp.,perc. - hp. - str.   24:00 Henmar.
—— RANDONNÉE DE L'ÂME DÉFUNTE (SYMPHONIC POEM)
    3,3,3,3 - 4,3,3,1 - timp.,perc.(4) - hp. - str.   18:00 EV.

WOLFF, S. Drummond
—— FESTIVAL TE DEUM (FOR CHORUS AND ORCH.)
    2,2,2,2 - 4,3,3,1 - timp.,perc.(3) - org.(ad lib.) - str.
        12:00 Composer.
—— PRELUDE ON "GREENSLEEVES"
    2,2,0,2 - 0,0,0,0 - str.   5:00 Composer.

WOLF-FERRARI, Ermanno
—— L' AMORE MEDICO (DR. CUPID) (OPERA) %
          Bo. Hawkes.
—— THE JEWELS OF THE MADONNA (OPERA) %
          Bo. Hawkes.
—— THE JEWELS OF THE MADONNA: SUITE FROM THE
OPERA
    3,2,2,3 - 4,3,2,1 - timp.,perc. - hp. - pf. - str.   Bo. Hawkes.
—— OVERTURE TO "LE DONNE CURIOSE" ("THE INQUISITIVE
WOMEN")
    3,2,2,2 - 2,2,0,0 - timp. - hp. - str.   Bo. Hawkes.
—— OVERTURE TO "THE SECRET OF SUZANNE"
    3,2,2,2 - 4,2,3,0 - timp. - hp. - str.   Bo. Hawkes.
—— THE SCHOOL FOR FATHERS (OPERA) % (DIE VIER
GROBIANE) (I QUATTRO RUSTEGHI)
          Bo. Hawkes.
—— THE SECRET OF SUZANNE (1-ACT OPERA) % (Engl. text:
Claude Aveling)
    3,2,2,2 - 4,2,3,0 - timp.,cel. - hp. - pf. - str.   Bo. Hawkes.
    or:
    2,1,1,1 - 2,2,1,0 - timp.,cel. - hp. - pf. - str.

WOLPE, Stefan
—— CANTATA FOR THREE VOICES AND 10 INSTRUMENTS
          Josef Marx.
—— CHAMBER PIECE NO. 1 (PIECE FOR CHAMBER ORCH.)
(FOR 14 PLAYERS)
    1,*2,1,1 - 1,1,1,0 - pf. - str.   10:00 Josef Marx.
—— FOR PIANO AND SIXTEEN PLAYERS
    2,1,1,1 bar. sax.(or b.-cl.),0 - 2,2,0,1 - perc. - electric guit. - hp. -
    pf. - str.(1 vln.,1 vla.,1 c.)   11:00 Josef Marx.
—— THE MAN FROM MIDIAN (BALLET) % (1942)
    3(2 alt. with 2 picc.),*3,*3,alto sax.,ten. sax.,*3 - 4,3,2,1 -
    timp.,perc.(1),glock.,xyl. - hp. - pf. - str.   40:00 Josef Marx.
—— THE MAN FROM MIDIAN (SUITE NO. 1 FROM THE
BALLET) (IN 8 MOVTS.)
    3(2nd alt. with 2 picc.),*3,*3,1 alto sax.,1 ten. sax.,*3 - 4,3,2,1 -
    timp.,perc.(2),glock.,xyl. - hp. - pf. - str.   Josef Marx.
—— PASSACAGLIA FOR ORCHESTRA (1936)
    3,*4,*4,*4 - 4,3,3,1 - timp.,perc.(1),glock. - 2 hp. - pf. - str.
        12:00 Josef Marx.
—— PIECE IN THREE PARTS FOR PIANO AND 16
INSTRUMENTS (1961)
    2,1,1,1 bar. sax.,0 - 2,2,0,1 - timp.,perc.(3) - electric guit. - hp. -
    pf. - str.(1,1,1,0)   13:00 Josef Marx.
—— SYMPHONY NO. 1 (1955) (IN 3 MOVTS.)
    3,3(3rd alt. with Eng. hn.),*4,*4 - 4,3,3,1 -
    timp.,perc.(3),cel.,glock.,xyl. - hp. - pf. - str.   25:00 Josef Marx.
—— YIGDAL (FOR BARITONE, MIXED CHORUS AND ORCH.)
(1945) (Text: Moses Maimonides)
        20:00 Composer.

WOLPERT, Franz Alfons
—— BANCHETTO MUSICALE II (FOR PIANO AND ORCH.) (IN 3
MOVTS.)
    1,2,0,0 - 2,0,0,0 - timp. - pf. - str.   25:00 Henmar.

WOOD, Arthur
—— CONCERTINO FOR FLUTE AND ORCH.
    1,1,2,1 - 2,2,3,0 - timp. - hp. - str.   10:00 G & T.

WOOD, Haydn
—— AMERICAN RHAPSODY (FOR MIXED CHORUS AND
ORCH.)
    2,1-2,2,2 - 2-4,2,3,0 - timp.,perc. - hp. - org.(ad lib.) - str.
        9:00 Bo. Hawkes.

—— APOLLO OVERTURE
2,2,2,2 - 2-4,2,3,0 - timp.,perc. - str.   9:00 Bo. Hawkes.
—— CONCERTO IN A MINOR, FOR VIOLIN AND ORCH.
2,2,2,2 - 2-4,2,3,0 - hp. - str.   24:00 Bo. Hawkes.
—— CONCERTO IN D MINOR, FOR PIANO AND ORCH.
2,2,2,2 - 4,2,3,1 - timp.,perc. - pf. - str.   26:00 Bo. Hawkes.
—— EGYPTA (SUITE)
10:00 Bo. Hawkes.
—— FRESCOES (SUITE)
16:00 Bo. Hawkes.
—— HARVEST TIME (SUITE)
8:30 Bo. Hawkes.
—— KING ORRY (A MANX RHAPSODY)
2,2,2,2 - 2-4,2,3,0 - timp.,perc. - hp. - org - str.
10:00 Bo. Hawkes.
—— MANNIN VEEN ("DEAR ISLE OF MAN") (MANX TONE POEM)
2,2,2,2 - 2-4,2,3,0 - timp.,perc.- str.   10:00 Bo. Hawkes.
—— A MANX OVERTURE ("THE ISLE OF MOUNTAINS AND GLENS")
2,2,2,2 - 2-4,2,3,0 - timp.,perc. - str.   9:00 Bo. Hawkes.
—— A MAY DAY OVERTURE
2,2,2,3 sax.(ad lib.),2 - 2,2,3,0 - timp.,perc. hp. - str.
8:00 Bo. Hawkes.
—— ODE TO GENIUS (FOR CHORUS AND ORCH.)
7:30 Bo. Hawkes.
—— PHILHARMONIC VARIATIONS (FOR CELLO AND ORCH.)
2,2,2,2 - 2-4,2,3,0 - timp. - hp. - str.   18:00 Bo. Hawkes.
—— PICTURES IN THE FIRE (SUITE)
2,2,2,2 - 4,2,3,0 - timp. - hp. - str.   16:30 Bo. Hawkes.
—— SEAFARER (A NAUTICAL RHAPSODY)
8:30 Bo. Hawkes.
—— THREE FAMOUS PICTURES (SUITE)
10:00 Bo. Hawkes.
—— TORCH OF FREEDOM (FOR CHORUS AND ORCH.)
2,2,2,2 - 4,2,2,1 - timp.,perc. - str.   Bo. Hawkes.
—— VIRGINIA (A SOUTHERN RHAPSODY)
5:00 Chappell.

WOOD, R. W. (Ralph Wood)
—— CELEBRAZIONE
2,2,2,2 - 4,2,3,1 - timp.,perc. - hp. - str.   13:00 P.R.S.
—— CONCERTINO FOR WIND QUINTET AND SMALL ORCH. (1962)
3,3,3,3 - 3,0,0,0 - timp.,perc. - str.   16:00 P.R.S.
—— CONCERTO FOR PIANO AND ORCH.
24:00 P.R.S.
—— CONCERTO FOR STRINGS
str.   30:00 P.R.S.
—— FIVE DRAMATIC STUDIES
14:00 P.R.S.
—— OENONE
13:00 P.R.S.
—— RESURRECTION OF MARTYRES
8:00 P.R.S.
—— SUITE FOR SMALL ORCH.
24:00 P.R.S.
—— SYMPHONY NO. 3 (1966)
2,2,2,2 - 4,2,3,0 - timp.,perc. - hp. - str.   21:00 P.R.S.

WOODGATE, Leslie
—— ENGLISH DANCE SUITE
str.   9:00 Novello.
—— MARGINALE, OP. 16 (SIX CHORAL PICTURES FOR SOLO VOICES, MIXED CHORUS AND ORCH.)
1,1,1,1 - 2,0,0,0 - perc. - hp. - str.   17:00 Bo. Hawkes.
or:
2,2,2,2 - 4,2,3,0 - perc. - hp. - str.

WOOD-HILL, Mabel
—— AESOP'S FABLES (SUITE)
1,1,1,1 - hn. - timp. - hp. - str.   10:00 J. Fischer.

WOODS, Donald James
—— AFRICAN OVERTURE
2,2,3,2 - 4,2,3,1 - timp.,perc. - str.   15:00 S.A.M.R.O.

WOODS, F. Cunningham
—— THE GRESSENHALL (SUITE FOR STRINGS AND PIANO)
pf. - str.   9:30 Bo. Hawkes.

WOOLDRIDGE, David
—— CONCERTO FOR VIOLA AND ORCH.
1,1,1,1 - 2,1,0,0 - timp.,perc.,cel. - hp. - str.   21:00 MCA Music.
—— THE ELIZABETHANS (CONCERT OVERTURE)
11:00 P.R.S.

WOOLDRIDGE, John
—— THE CONSTELLATIONS (SYMPHONIC POEM)
2,2,3,2 - 4,3,3,1 - timp.,perc. - str.   Bo. Hawkes.

WOOLLETT, Henry
—— MAURES ET GITANES (BALLET SUITE)
2,2,2,2 - 4,3,3,1 - timp.,perc. - hp. - str.   15:00 Salabert.
—— SENTIER COUVERT
2,3,4,2 - 4,3,0,0 - timp.,trgl. - hp. - pf. - str.   6:00 Salabert.

WORDSWORTH, William
—— CONCERTO FOR CELLO AND ORCH., OP. 73 (1963)
2,2,2,2 - 4,2,3,0 - timp.,perc.,cel. - hp. - str.   28:00 P.R.S.
—— CONCERTO FOR VIOLIN AND ORCH., OP. 60
2,2,2,2 - 4,3,3,1 - timp.,perc. - str.   38:00 Lengnick.
—— CONCERTO IN D MINOR FOR PIANO AND ORCH., OP. 28
25:00 Lengnick.
—— CONFLICT, OP. 86 (AN OVERTURE)
2,2,2,2 - 4,3,3,0 - timp.,perc. - hp. - str.   9:00 P.R.S.
—— DIVERTIMENTO IN D, OP. 58
2,2,2,2 - 4,3,3,1 - timp.,perc. - str.   25:00 Lengnick.
—— A HIGHLAND OVERTURE, OP. 76 (1964)
2,2,2,2 - 4,2,3,0 - timp.,perc.,cel. - hp. - str.   9:00 P.R.S.
—— HYMN OF DEDICATION, OP. 26 (FOR CHORUS AND ORCH.)
9:00 Lengnick.
—— IN NO STRANGE LAND, OP. 49 (FOR CHORUS AND STRINGS) (Text: Francis Thompson)
pf. - str.   6:00 Lengnick.
—— JUBILATION, OP. 78 (A FESTIVITY FOR FULL ORCHESTRA) (1965)
2,2,2,2 - 4,2,3,0 - timp.,perc.,cel. - hp. - str.   10:00 P.R.S.
—— SINFONIA IN A MINOR, OP. 6 (FOR STRINGS)
str.   22:00 Lengnick.
—— SINFONIA SEMPLICE, OP. 87
str.   12:00 P.R.S.
—— SINFONIETTA, OP. 62 (1957)
1,1,1,1 - 2,1,0,0 - timp.,perc. - str.   25:00 P.R.S.
—— SYMPHONIC STUDY, OP. 53
str.   12:00 Lengnick.
—— SYMPHONY NO. 1 IN F, OP. 23
32:00 Lengnick.
—— SYMPHONY NO. 2 IN D, OP. 34
35:00 Lengnick.
—— SYMPHONY NO. 3, OP. 48
2,2,2,2 - 4,3,3,0 - timp.,perc.,cel. - str.   23:00 Lengnick.
—— SYMPHONY NO. 4, OP. 54
2,2,2,2 - 4,3,3,1 - timp.,perc. - str.   26:00 Lengnick.
—— SYMPHONY NO. 5 IN A MINOR, OP. 68 (1960)
3,3,3,3 - 4,3,3,1 - timp.,perc.,cel. - hp. - str.   36:00 P.R.S.
—— THEME AND VARIATIONS FOR SMALL ORCH., OP. 19
15:00 Lengnick.
—— THREE PASTORAL SKETCHES, OP. 10
22:00 Lengnick.
—— TWO SCOTTISH SKETCHES, OP. 83
1,1,1,1 - 1,1,0,0 - perc. - hp. - pf. - str.   8:00 P.R.S.
—— VALEDICTION, OP. 82-A
2,3,2,3 - 4,3,3,0 - timp.,perc. - hp. - pf. - str.   8:00 P.R.S.
—— VARIATIONS ON A SCOTTISH THEME, OP. 72 (1962)
0,1,1,1 - 1,0,0,0 - perc. - str.   12:00 P.R.S.

WORK, John Wesley
—— PICTURE SUITE FROM THE SOUTH (IN 4 MOVTS.)
2(2nd alt. with picc.),2(2nd alt. with Eng. hn.),2,2 - 4,2,3,1 - timp.,perc.(2) - str.   15:00 Composer.
—— THE SINGERS (FOR CHORUS AND ORCH.)
2,2,2,2 - 0,0,0,0 - timp. - str.   8:00 Mills.
—— TALIAFERO (OVERTURE)
2,2,2,2 - 4,2,3,0 - timp.,perc.(2) - str.   11:00 Composer.
—— YENVALOU (SUITE ON HAITIAN THEMES)
2,2,2,2 - 4,2,3,0 - timp.,perc.(2) - str.   8:00 Galaxy.

WORK, Julian C.
—— MYRIORAMA BY NIGHT (SUITE) (IN 4 MOVTS.)
. 3(3rd alt. with picc.),*3,*3,*3 - 4,3,3,1 - timp.,perc.(3),bells - hp. - str.   16:20 Composer.

WORMSER, André
—— FANTAISIE, THÈME ET VARIATIONS (FOR TRUMPET OR CORNET AND ORCH.)
2,1-2,2,2 - 2-4,1(or cnt.),3,0 - timp. - str.　　　7:00 Baron.

WORONOFF, Wladimir
—— TRIPARTITA FOR VIOLA AND ORCH. (1970) (IN 3 MOVTS.)
2,1,2,1 - 2,2,1,0 - timp.,perc. - str.　　28:00 H. Elkan.

WRIGHT, Geoffrey
—— SYMPHONY
2,2,2,2 - 4,2,3,0 - perc.(2) - hp. - str.　　27:00 P.R.S.

WRIGHT, John
—— CONCERTO FOR VIOLIN AND ORCH. (1969)
2,2,2,2 - 4,2,3,0 - timp.,perc. - str.　　31:00 P.R.S.
—— DIVERTIMENTO FOR OBOE AND STRINGS
ob. - str.　　　　　　　　　　P.R.S.
—— ENDYMION (FANTASIE CONCERTANTE)(1967)
ob. - hn. - str.　　　　　　15:00 P.R.S.

WRIGHT, Kenneth
—— OVERTURE (THE GOLDEN ROSE)
　　　　　　　　　　　　　P.R.S.

WRIGHT, M. Searle
—— FANTASY ON "WAREHAM" (FOR CHORUS, ORGAN AND ORCH.)
　　　　　　　　　　　5:15 Gray.
—— THE GREEN BLADE RISETH (EASTER CANTATA) (FOR SOPRANO, ALTO, BARITONE, SATB CHORUS AND ORCH.)
3,2,2,2 - 4,3,3,1 - timp.,perc.,bells,cel.,glock.,xyl. - hp. - org. -str.
　　　　　　　　　　　Belw-Mills.

WRIGHT, Rayburn
—— PATTERNS
　　　　　　　　　　10:00 T. English.
—— REGENERATION (CONCERTO FOR JAZZ QUARTET, ROCK ENSEMBLE AND ORCH.)
　　　　　　　　　　20:00 T. English.
—— THE WAR FOR THE UNION (SYMPHONIC SUITE) (FOR MALE CHORUS AND ORCH.)
　　　　　　　　　　30:00 Composer.

WUENSCH, Gerhard
—— BALLAD, OP. 19 (FOR TRUMPET AND ORCH.)
　　　　　　　　　　8:00 C.A.P.A.C.
—— CONCERTO FOR PIANO AND CHAMBER ORCH., OP. 57 (1971) (IN 3 MOVTS.)
2,2,2,2 - 2,0,0,0 - timp. - pf. - str.　　24:40 CanMusCtr.
—— LABYRINTH, OP. 6 (BALLET FOR ORCH.)
　　　　　　　　　　25:00 C.A.P.A.C.
—— NOCTURNE, OP. 6 (1956)
2(2nd alt. with picc.),2,2,2 - 4,2,2,1 - timp.,perc.,cel. - hp. - str.
　　　　　　　　　　8:00 CanMusCtr.
—— NOCTURNE, OP. 7
　　　　　　　　　　8:00 C.A.P.A.C.
—— IL POMO D'ORO, OP. 9 (BALLET FOR ORCH.)
　　　　　　　　　　25:00 C.A.P.A.C.
—— VARIATIONS, OP. 10
　　　　　　　　　　10:00 C.A.P.A.C.

WURTZLER, Aristid von
—— MODERN SKETCHES (FOR HARP AND STRING ORCH.) (1969) (IN 3 MOVTS.)
Hp - str.(8,2,2,1)　　　　12:00 Southern.

WÜSTHOFF, Klaus
—— CONCERTINO FOR PIANO AND ORCH.
　　　　　　　　　　R.Birnbach.

WYK, Arnold van
—— AUBADE
2,2,2,2 - 4,2,0,0 - perc. - str.　　9:00 S.A.M.R.O.
—— CONCERTINO FOR PIANO AND ORCHESTRA
2,2,3,2 - 4,2,3,1 - timp.,perc. - pf. - str.　10:00 S.A.M.R.O.
—— INCIDENTAL MUSIC TO 'BECKET'
2,2,3,2 - 4,2,3,1 - timp.,perc. - str.　25:00 S.A.M.R.O.
—— KERSKANTATE (FOR SOLO VOICES, CHORUS AND ORCH.) (Text: W. E. G. Louis)
2,2,3,2 - 4,2,3,1 - timp.,perc. - str.　　65:00 HAUM.
—— MASQUERADE
2,2,3,2 - 4,2,3,1 - timp.,perc. - str.　17:00 S.A.M.R.O.

—— PRIMAVERA: SYMPHONIC SUITE
2,2,3,2 - 4,2,3,1 - timp.,perc. - str.　25:00 HAUM.
—— RHAPSODY FOR ORCHESTRA
2,2,3,2 - 4,2,3,1 - timp.,perc. - str.　10:00 S.A.M.R.O.
—— SAUDADE (FOR VIOLIN AND ORCH.)
2,2,3,2 - 4,2,3,1 - timp.,perc.,cel. - str.　13:00 S.A.M.R.O.
—— SECOND SYMPHONY
2,2,3,2 - 4,2,3,1 - timp.,perc. - str.　18:00 S.A.M.R.O.
—— SYMPHONY NO. 1 IN A MINOR
2,2,3,2 - 4,2,3,1 - timp.,perc. - str.　19:00 Haum.
—— VIER GEBEDE BY JAARGETYE IN DIE BOLAND
2,2,3,2 - 4,2,3,1 - timp.,perc. - str.　15:00 S.A.M.R.O.

WYKES, Robert
—— ADEQUATE EARTH (A SYMPHONIC SETTING OF THE POEM BY DONALD FINKEL) (FOR 2 NARRATORS, BARITONE, 3 SATB CHORUSES AND ORCH.)
3(1 alt. with picc.,1 alt. with alto fl.),*3,*3,*3 - 4,0,3,1 - timp.,perc.(4),2 glock.,cel.,mar. - hp. - pf. - str.　67:00 Composer.
—— CONCERTINO FOR FLUTE, OBOE, PIANO AND STRINGS (IN 3 MOVTS.)
1,1,0,0 - 0,0,0,0 - pf. - str.　　12:00 Composer.
—— DANCE OVERTURE
*3,2,*3,2 - 4,3,3,0 - timp.,perc.,glock. - hp. - str.　6:00 Composer.
—— DENSITY III
0,2,*3,*3 - 2,2,3,1 - timp.,perc.(2),glock.,xyl. - hp. - str.
　　　　　　　　　　4:00 Presser.
—— FANFARE: TIME OF THE WEST
*3,2,*3,2 - 4,2,3,1 - timp.,perc.(3),glock. - str.　1:00 Composer.
—— HORIZONS (SUITE) (IN 3 MOVTS.)
2(2nd alt. with picc.),2,2(2nd alt. with b.-cl.),2(2nd alt. ad lib. with c.-bn.) - 2,2,1,0 - timp.,perc.(2),glock.,xyl. - hp. - str.
　　　　　　　　　　10:09 Composer.
—— LETTER TO AN ALTO MAN (FOR SATB CHORUS, HARP, PIANO, PERCUSSION SOLOIST AND ORCH.) (1966-67) (Text: Donald Finkel)
3(3rd alt. with picc.),*3,*3,*3 - 4,3,3,1 - timp.,perc.(3),glock.,mar.,xyl. - hp. - pf. - str.　12:25 Presser.
—— RESONANCES (1971) (IN 2 MOVTS.)
3(3rd alt. with picc.),*3,2,2 - 4,3,3,1 - timp.,perc.(3),bells,glock.,vibra. - hp. - pf. - str.　12:00 Composer.
—— A SHADOW OF SILENCE (1972)
3(3rd alt. with picc.),2,2,2 - 4,3,3,0 - timp.,perc.(4),glock.,vibra. - pf. - str.　9:00 Composer.
—— THE SHAPE OF TIME (WITH 2 ANTIPHONAL PERCUSSION AND DOUBLE-BASS GROUPS)
*3(2nd alt. with 2nd picc.),*3,1 e^{b}cl.,2,1 e^{b}d.-b. cl.,*3 - 4,3,3,1 - 8 timp.,perc.(6),2 b.dr.,2 glock.,2 mar.,2 xyl. - hp. - pf. - str.
　　　　　　　　　　17:00 Presser.
—— TOWARD TIME'S RECEDING (1972)
3(3rd alt. with picc.),*3,2,2 - 4,3,3,1 - timp.,perc.(4),2 glock.,vibra. - hp. - pf. - str.　17:00 Composer.
—— WAVE FORMS AND PULSES
*3,2,*3,2 - 4,2,3,1 - timp.,perc.(3),mar.,xyl. - pf. - str.
　　　　　　　　　　7:30 Presser.

WYLIE, Ruth Shaw
—— CONCERTINO FOR CLARINET AND ORCH., OP. 24, NO. 1 (1967)
1. Recitative - Adagio; 2. Allegro moderato
2,2,2,2 - 4,3,2,1 - timp.,perc.(3) - str.　7:00 Composer.
—— CONCERTO GROSSO, OP. 15 (1952) (IN 3 MOVTS.)
2,1,2,2 - 0,0,0,0 - str.　　18:00 Composer.
—— ECHO, OP. 22 (FOR WOMEN'S CHORUS AND STRING ORCH.) (1965) (Text: Christina Rosetti)
str.　　　　　　　　　5:00 Composer.
—— HOLIDAY OVERTURE, OP. 14 (1951)
*3,2,2,2 - 4,3,3,1 - timp.,perc.(3),mar. - str.　7:00 Composer.
—— INCUBUS, OP. 28 (FOR FLUTE, CLARINET, PERCUSSION AND CELLO ENSEMBLE) (1973)
1,1,0,0 - 0,0,0,0 - perc.(4),bells,mar. - c.(8-24)　5:00 Composer.
—— INVOLUTION, OP. 24, NO. 2 (1967)
2,1,2,2 - 0,2,2,0 - perc.(4),bells,mar.,xyl. - str.　8:00 Composer.
—— THE LONG LOOK HOME, OP. 30, NO. 2 (SUITE) (1975) (IN 5 MOVTS.)
2(1 alt. with alto fl.),1 alt. with picc.),2(1 alt. with Eng.hn.),2,2 - 4,2,1,1 - timp.,perc.(3) - str.　23:00 Composer.
—— THE RAGGED HEART, OP. 21 (BALLET) % (1961)
2,0,2,0 - 0,2,1,0 - perc.(3) - pf.　20:00 Composer.
—— SUITE FOR CHAMBER ORCH., OP. 3 ("FOR A LITTLE NEPHEW") (1942) (IN 3 MOVTS.)
1,1,1,1 - 2,1,0,0 - str.　　10:00 Composer.

—— SYMPHONY NO. 1 ("ARCHAIC"), OP. 6 (1943)
   1. Allegro ma non troppo; 2. Allegretto; 3. Presto (Scherzo);
   4. Adagio
   2,2,2,2 - 4,3,2,1 - timp. - str.   30:00 Composer.
—— SYMPHONY NO. 2, OP. 11 (1948) (IN 4 MOVTS.)
   *3,2,2,*3 - 4,3,3,1 - timp.,perc.(3) - str.   36:00 Composer.

WYMAN, Dann Coriat
—— ODE TO THE VIOLA (FOR VIOLA AND STRING ORCH.)
   pf. - str.   6:00 Seesaw.

WYNNE, David
—— CONCERTO FOR TWO PIANOS (3-HANDS) AND ORCH.
   (1961)
   2,2,2,2 - 4,3,3,0 - timp.,perc. - 2 pf. - str.   18:00 P.R.S.
—— CYMRIC RHAPSODY (1966)
   2,2,2,2 - 4,3,3,1 - timp.,perc. - hp. - str.   7:30 P.R.S.
—— FANTASIA CONCERTO (FOR VIOLA AND ORCH.)(1964)
   2,2,2,2 - 4,3,3,1 - timp.,perc.(3) - hp. - str. 19:00 P.R.S.
—— FANTASIA NO. 2 (1961)
   2,2,2,2 - 2,2,2,0 - timp.,perc. - pf. - str.   9:00 P.R.S.
—— SINFONIETTA (1958)
   str.   21:00 P.R.S.
—— SYMPHONY NO. 3 (1963)
   2,2,2,2 - 4,3,3,1 - timp.,perc.(3) - hp. - str. 25:00 P.R.S.
—— A WELSH SUITE (1960)
   2,2,2,2 - 4,3,3,0 - timp.,perc.(3) - hp. - str. 20:00 P.R.S.

X

XENAKIS, Yannis
—— AKRATA
   1,1,3,3 - 2,3,2,1   11:00 Bo. Hawkes.
—— AMORSIMA-MORSIMA
   0,0,2,0 - 2,0,0,0 - perc. - hp. - str.   5:00 Bo. Hawkes.
—— ANTIKHTHON (1971) (With contact-microphones and
   amplification)
   *4,3,3,*4 - 4,3,3,1 - timp.,perc.(3) - str. 23:00 Salabert.
—— AROURA (1971)
   str.(7,2,2,1)   11:00 Salabert.
—— ATRÉES
   1,0,*2,0 - 1,1,1,0 - perc.(3) - str.(2,0,1,0) 15:00 Salabert.
—— CENDRÉES (FOR SATB CHOURS AND ORCH.) (1974)
   2(2nd alt. with picc.),2,2(2nd alt. with b.-cl.),2 - 2,2,2,1 - str.
      25:00 Salabert.
—— DUEL (MUSICAL GAME FOR 2 CONDUCTORS AND 2
   ORCHS.) (1959)
   Two identical groups as follows: 10:00 Salabert.
   *1,1,1, E♭cl.,*1,*2 - 0,2,1,0 - perc.(1) - str.(12,0,4,2)
—— EMPREINTES
      12:00 Salabert.
—— ERIDANOS (1973)
   0,0,0,0 - 2,2,2,2 - str.   15:00 Salabert.
—— ERIKHTHON (CONCERTO FOR PIANO AND ORCH.) (1974)
   3(3rd alt. with picc.),3,*4,*4 - 4,4,4,1 - timp. - pf. - str.
      15:00 Salabert.
—— HIKETIDES (THE SUPPLICANTS): INSTRUMENTAL SUITE
   (1964)
   0,0,0,0 - 0,2,2,0 - str.   10:00 Salabert.
—— HIKETIDES (THE SUPPLICANTS) (WITH CHORUS OF 50
   ALTOS OR MEZZO-SOPRANOS PLAYING PERCUSSION
   INSTRUMENTS)
   0,0,0,0 - 0,2,2,0 - (perc.) - str.(2,0,2,2) 30:00 Salabert.
—— MEDEA (SUITE) (FOR ORCH., WITH CHOIR OF MEN'S
   VOICES)
      Salabert.
—— METASTASEIS
   2,2,1,0 - 3,2,2,0 - timp.,perc. - str. 8:00 Bo. Hawkes.
—— NOMOS GAMMA (FOR ORCH. OF 98 DISPERSED AMONG
   THE AUDIENCE) (1968)
   *3,3,1 E♭cl.,1,1 d.-b.cl.,2,3 cbn. - 6,5,4,1 - timp.,perc.(8) - str.
      15:00 Salabert.
—— THE ORESTEIA (FOR SATB CHORUS AND INSTRUMENTS)
   1,1,2,1 - 1,2,1,1 - perc. - c. 100:00 Bo. Hawkes.
—— THE ORESTEIA (SUITE) (FOR SATB CHORUS AND
   INSTRUMENTS)
   1,1,2,1 - 1,2,1,1 - perc. - c. 50:00 Bo. Hawkes.
—— PHLEGRA
   1(alt. with picc.),1,1(alt. with b.-cl.),1 - 1,1,1,0 - str.
      15:00 Salabert.

—— PITHOPRAKTA
   2 trb. - perc.,xyl. - str.   10:00 Bo. Hawkes.
—— POLLA TA DINA (FOR CHILDREN'S CHORUS AND ORCH.)
   (Text: Sophocles) (in Greek or English)
   *2,2,*2,*2 - 2,2,2,0 - timp.,perc. - str. 7:30 Modern.
—— POLYTOPE (FOR 4 IDENTICAL ORCHESTRAS)
   4,0,8,4 - 0,4,4,0 - perc. - str.   6:00 Bo. Hawkes.
—— ST-10 - 1,080262
   0,0,2,0 - 2,0,0,0 - perc. - hp. - str. 12:00 Bo. Hawkes.
—— ST-48 - 1,240262
   2,2,2,2 - 2,2,2,0 - timp.,perc. - str. 11:00 Bo. Hawkes.
—— STRATÉGIE (GAME FOR 2 ORCHESTRAS)
   4,2,6,4 - 4,4,4,2 - perc. - str.   2:00 Bo. Hawkes.
—— SYRMOS (FOR 18 STRING PLAYERS) (1959)
   str.(12,0,4,2)   15:00 Salabert.
—— TERRETEKTORH (FOR ORCH. OF 88 MUSICIANS
   DISPERSED AMONG THE AUDIENCE) (1959) (Each musician
   should have a woodblock, whip, maracas and an Acme siren,
   available from the publisher)
   *3,3,1 E♭cl.,*2,*3 - 4,4,4,1 - perc.(3) - str.(30,12,10,8)
      20:00 Salabert.
—— WINDUNGEN (FOR 12 CELLOS)
   12 c.   8:00 Salabert.

Y

YAMPILOV, Baudorzhei B.
—— THE WONDERFUL TREASURE (3-ACT OPERA) %
      G. Schirmer.

YANG, Johann Y.
—— EIGHT CHINESE FOLK SONGS (8 CHINESE SKETCHES)
   (1955)
   *3,2(2nd alt. with Eng. hn.),2,2 - 4,2,3,1 - timp.,perc.(5),cel. - hp. -
   str.   18:00 Composer.
—— THE PASSION AND RESURRECTION (SYMPHONIC POEM,
   AFTER MATTHEW, 26-29) (1954)
   *3,2(2nd alt. with Eng. hn.,),2,2 - 4,2,3,1 - timp.,perc.(4) - hp. -
   str.   15:00 Composer.

YARDUMIAN, Richard
—— ARMENIAN SUITE
   *4,*4,*3(2nd alt. with D cl.),*4 - 6,4,4,1 -
   timp.,perc.(3),bells,glock. - hp. - str. 17:00 EV.
—— CANTUS ANIMAE ET CORDIS ("SONG OF THE SOUL AND
   HEART")
   str.   15:00 EV.
—— CHORALE-PRELUDE ON THE PLAINSONG "VENI, SANCTE
   SPIRITUS"
   2,*3,2,2 - 2,2,2,0 - hp. - str.   9:00 EV.
—— CONCERTO FOR VIOLIN AND ORCH. (IN 2 MOVTS.)
   3(3rd alt. with picc.),3(3rd alt. with Eng. hn.),3(3rd alt. with
   b.-cl.),*3 - 4,4,4,0 - timp.,perc.(3),glock. - 2 hp. - str. 17:00 EV.
—— CONCERTO FOR VIOLIN AND ORCHESTRA
   3,3,3,3 - 4,4,4,0 - timp.,perc. - 2 hp. - str. 24:00 EV.
—— DESOLATE CITY (IN 2 MOVTS.)
   *4,*3,*4,*4 - 4,4,4,1 - timp.,perc.(3) - 2 hp. - str. 20:00 EV.
—— EPIGRAM: WILLIAM F. KINCAID (FOR FLUTE AND
   STRINGS)
   fl. - str.   6:00 EV.
—— MASS ("VENI, CREATOR SPIRITUS") ("COME, CREATOR
   SPIRIT") (FOR CONTRALTO, CHORUS AND ORCH.)
   2,*3,2,3 - 2,3,2,0 - timp.,perc.(4) - hp. - str. 42:00 EV.
—— ORATORIO: ABRAHAM (FOR SOLO VOICES, SATB CHORUS
   AND ORCHESTRA)
   3,*3,3,3 - 4,4,4,1 - timp.,perc.(3) - hp. - str. 68:00 EV.
—— PASSACAGLIA, RECITATIVE AND FUGUE (CONCERTO
   FOR PIANO AND ORCH.)
   3,*3,3,3 - 4,4,3,1 - timp.,perc. - hp. - pf. - str. 18:00 EV.
—— SYMPHONIC SUITE (IN 3 MOVTS.)
   *3,*3,*3,*3 - 4,4,3,1 - timp.,perc.(2) - hp. - pf. - str. 14:00 EV.
—— SYMPHONY NO. 1
   *4,*3,*4,*4 - 6,4,4,1 - timp.,perc. - 2 hp. - str. 24:00 EV.
—— SYMPHONY NO. 1 (REVISED) (IN 3 MOVTS.)
   *4,*4,*4,*4 - 4,4,4,1 - timp.,perc.,cel. - 2 hp. - str. 24:00 EV.
—— SYMPHONY NO. 2 (PSALMS) (FOR CONTRALTO AND
   ORCH.)
   *4,*4,*4,*4 - 4,4,4,1 - timp.,perc.,cel. - 2 hp. - str. 30:00 EV.
—— THREE PICTOGRAPHS
   *4,*4,*4,*4 - 4,4,4,1 - timp.,perc.(2) - 2 hp. - str. 18:00 EV.

YASHIRO, Akio
—— CONCERTO FOR CELLO AND ORCHESTRA
    2,1,2,2 - 4,2,3,0 - timp., perc., cel., vibra. - hp. - str.
                                            22:00 Presser.
—— CONCERTO FOR PIANO AND ORCHESTRA
    3,2,2,0 - 4,2,3,1 - timp., perc.(3), vibra. - pf. - str.   28:00 Presser.
—— SYMPHONY
    3,3,3,3 - 4,3,3,1 - timp., perc.(7) - 2 hp. - pf. - str.   35:00 Presser.

YELLIN, Gleb
—— ROUMANIAN FANTASY
    *3,*3,*3,*3 - 4,3,3,1 - timp.,perc.(4), cel.,glock.,xyl. - hp. - str.
                                            18:00 Composer.

YEVLAKHOV, Orest A.
—— TRIPTYCH
                                          G. Schirmer.

YON, Pietro
—— CONCERTINO FOR OBOE AND ORCH. (IN 2 MOVTS.)
    ob. - 4 hn. - str.   8:00 Composer.
—— CONCERTO GREGORIANO (FOR ORGAN AND ORCH.) (IN 4 MOVTS.)
    0,0,0,0 - 4,2,3,0 - timp. - 2 hp. - org. - str.   20:00 J. Fischer.
—— THE TRIUMPH OF SAINT PATRICK (ORATORIO) (FOR CHORUS, ORGAN AND ORCH.)
    1,1,1,1 - 4,2,3,0 - timp.,perc. - 2 hp. - org. - str.   120:00 Ricordi.

YOSHIOKA, Emmett
—— ARIOSO FOR ALTO SAXOPHONE, HARP AND STRINGS
    alto. sax. - hp. - str.   6:00 ArtisnMuPr.

YOUNG, Derek
—— CONCERTO FOR TRUMPET AND ORCH. (1959)
    3,2,2,2 - 4,3,3,1 - timp.,perc. - str.   28:00 P.R.S.

YOUNG, Douglas
—— AUBADE (1972)
    2(alt. with 2 picc.),1,1,1 - 2,2,1,0 - timp.,perc. - hp.(ad lib.) - str.
                                      10:00 G. Schirmer.
—— DEPARTURE (1970)
    *3,*3,*3,*3 - 4,3,3,1 - timp.,perc.(4, incl. 2 on timp.) - hp. - pf. - str.   17:00 G. Schirmer.
—— OF BIRDS AND BEASTS (1969) (FOR SATB CHORUS AND ORCH.)
    3,3,3,3 - 4,3,3,1 - timp.,perc.(7) - 2 pf. - str.   25:00 G. Schirmer.
—— PASIPHAE (1969) (FOR 3 SOPRANOS AND ORCH.)
    1,1,1,0 - 1,1,1,0 - timp.,perc.(3),cel. - chamber-org. - hp. - pf. - str.   25:00 G. Schirmer.

YOUNG, Victor
—— SCHERZETTO
    *3,*3,*3,*3 - 4,3,3,1 - timp.,perc.(2-3) - pf. - str.   5:30 Composer.

Z

ZACHOW, Friedrich Wilhelm - LENZEWSKI
—— FANTASY (FOR STRING ORCH)
    str.   Henmar.

ZÁDOR, Eugene
—— ARIA AND ALLEGRO (1966)
    0,0,0,0 - 4,3,3,0 - str.   9:15 MCA Music.
—— ARIA AND TOCCATA FOR ORGAN AND STRINGS (1966)
    org. - str.   14:00 Composer.
—— BIBLICAL TRIPTYCH (IN 3 MOVTS.)
    2(2nd alt. with picc.),2(2nd alt. with Eng. hn.),2(2nd alt. with b.-cl.),*3 - 4,3,3,1 - timp.,perc.(3),glock.,xyl. - hp. - str.
                                      20:00 Composer.
—— A CHILDREN'S SYMPHONY
    2(2nd alt. with picc.),2(2nd alt. with Eng. hn.),2,2 - 2,2,0,1 - timp.,perc.,cel.(or pf.) - hp. - pf. - str.   13:00 Mills.
—— CHILDREN'S SYMPHONY (REVISED) (IN 4 MOVTS.)
    *2,2,2,2 - 2,2,0,1 - timp.,perc.(2),bells - hp. - pf. - str.   13:00 Mills.
—— CHRISTMAS OVERTURE
    3(3rd alt. with picc.),2,2,*3 - 4,3,3,1 - timp.,perc.(2) - hp. - org.(ad lib.) - str.   8:00 Mills.
—— CONCERTO FOR ACCORDION AND ORCH. (1972) (IN 3 MOVTS.)
    timp.,perc.(3),bells,xyl. - accordion - str.   14:00 Ars Nova.

—— CONCERTO FOR HARP AND STRING ORCH. (1975) (IN 3 MOVTS.)
    hp. - str.   15:00 Composer.
—— CONCERTO FOR OBOE AND STRING ORCH. (1975) (IN 3 MOVTS.)
    ob. - str.   15:00 Composer.
—— CONCERTO FOR TROMBONE AND ORCH. (1966) (IN 3 MOVTS.)
    *2,2,2,2 - 2,2,1,0 - timp.,perc.(2-3),xyl. - hp. - pf. - str.
                                  14:00 MCA Music.
—— DANCE OVERTURE (1965)
    *3,2,2,2 - 4,3,3,1 - timp.,perc.(3),bells - pf. - str.   9:00 Composer.
—— DIVERTIMENTO FOR STRINGS
    str.   12:00 Eulenberg.
—— ELEGIE FOR ORCHESTRA
    2,2,2,2 - 4,0,3,0 - timp. - hp. - str.   8:00 Composer.
—— ELEGY AND DANCE
    2,2(2nd alt. with Eng. hn.),2,2 - 4,3,3,1 - timp.,perc.(3),glock.,xyl. - hp. - pf. - str.   12:00 Composer.
—— FANTASIA HUNGARICA (FOR CONTRABASS AND ORCH.) (1970)
    *2,1,2,2 - 4,0,0,0 - timp;perc.(2) - str.   15:00 Composer.
—— FANTASY ON THEMES FROM "THE INSPECTOR GENERAL" (1973)
    2,2,2,2 - 3,3,3,0 - timp.,perc.,bells, glock. - hp. - str.
                                      12:00 Composer.
—— FESTIVAL OVERTURE
    *3,2,3,*3 - 4,3,3,1 - timp.,perc.(3) - hp. - pf. - str.   10:00 Mills.
—— FIVE CONTRASTS FOR ORCH. (1963)
    3(3rd alt. with picc.),2,3(3rd alt. with Eb cl.),3(3rd alt. with c.-bn.) - 4,4,3,1 - timp.,perc.(3-4),cel.,mar. or vibra(ad lib.) - acc. - hp. - pf. - str.   16:00 Henmar.
—— FUGUE-FANTASIA (1958)
    *3,2,2,*3 - 4,3-4,3,1 - timp.,perc.(2) - str.   15:00 Henmar.
—— HUNGARIAN RHAPSODY
                                        8:00 Composer.
—— HUNGARIAN SCHERZO (1975)
    *3,2,2,2 - 4,3,3,1 - timp.,perc. - hp. - pf. - str.   11:00 Composer.
—— THE JUDGMENT (ORATORIO) (FOR CHORUS, BRASS AND PERCUSSION) (1974) (Text: Patrick Mahony)
    0,0,0,0 - 3,3,3,0 - timp.,perc.,glock.,xyl   14:30 Composer.
—— MACHINE MAN (BALLET SUITE)
    *3,2,2,*3 - 4,3,3,1 - timp.,perc.(2) - hp. - pf. - str.
                                      20:00 Composer.
—— THE MAGIC CHAIR (1-ACT COMIC OPERA) (Text: George Jellinek)
                                      25:00 Mills.
—— MINIATURE OVERTURE (1965)
    2,2,2,2 - 4,3,3,1 - timp.,perc.(2) - str.   2:00 Composer.
—— MUSIC FOR CLARINET AND STRINGS (1970) (IN 3 MOVTS.)
    cl. - str.   13:00 Composer.
—— ODE TO PEACE
    *3,2,2,2 - 4,6,3,1 - timp.,perc.(3) - hp. - pf. - str.   7:00 Composer.
—— THE REMARKABLE ADVENTURES OF HENRY BOLD (A FAIRY TALE) (FOR NARRATOR AND ORCH.) (Text: Basil Swift)
    2(2nd alt. with picc.),2(2nd alt. with Eng.hn.),2,2(2nd alt. with c.-bn.) - 3,3,3,0 - timp.,perc.(2),cel.,glock. - hp. - pf. - str.
                                      15:00 Mills.
—— RHAPSODY FOR ORCHESTRA
    *3,2,3,*3 - timp.,perc.(3),glock. - hp. - str.   12:00 Henmar.
—— STUDIES FOR ORCHESTRA
    3,2,2,2 - 4,3,3,1 - timp.,perc.(5) - hp. - pf. - str.   MCA Music.
—— VARIATIONS ON A MERRY THEME
    3(3rd alt. with picc.),2,3(1st. alt. with alto sax.),*3 - 4,4,3,1 - timp.,perc.(3-4),bells - pf. - str.   18:00 Mills.
—— YEHU (A CHRISTMAS LEGEND) (FOR 6 SOLO VOICES, SSA CHORUS AND ORCH.) (1974) (Text: Anna Egyud)
    *2,1,2,1 - 2,2,2,0 - timp.,perc.,glock.,xyl. - hp. - pf. - str.(10,3,3,2 or 5,2,2,1)   31:00 C. Fischer.

ZAFRED, Mario
—— SYMPHONY NO. 3
    2,2,2,2 - 4,3,3,1 - timp.,perc.,cel.,xyl. - str.   Leeds.

ZAGWIJN, Henri
—— AUFERSTEHUNG ("OSTERGLOCKEN") (PRELUDE)
    3,3,3,3 - 4,3,3,1 - timp.,perc.,cel. - 2 hp. - org. - str.
                                      18:00 Henmar.
—— CONCERTANTE FOR FLUTE AND ORCH.
    1,2,2,2 - 2,1,0,0 - timp.,cel. - hp. - str.   15:00 Henmar.
—— CONCERTANTE NO. 1 FOR PIANO AND ORCH.
    2,3,2,2 - 2,2,1,0 - timp.,perc.,cel. - hp. - pf. - str.   13:00 Henmar.

—— CONCERTANTE NO. 2 FOR PIANO AND ORCH.
3,3,2,2 - 4,2,1,0 - timp.,perc.,cel. - 2 hp. - pf. - str. 18:00 Henmar.
—— CONCERTO FOR HARP AND ORCH.
2,2,2,2 - 2,0,0,0 - hp. - str. 16:00 Henmar.
—— CONCERTSTUK VOOR GROOT ORKEST
3,3,1,3 - 4,3,3,1 - timp.,perc. - str. 12:00 Henmar.
—— ELEGIA AND CAPRICCIO (FOR HARP AND ORCH.)
2,3,3,2 - 2,2,1,0 - timp. - hp. - str. 15:00 Henmar.
—— FRÜHLING (FOR MIXED CHORUS AND ORCH.) (1941) (IN 5
MOVTS.) (Text: R. Steiner)
2,0,1,0 - 0,0,0,0 - harm. - str. 30:00 Henmar.
—— DIE FUSSWASCHUNG (FOR SOPRANO AND ORCH.) (1927)
(Text: Chr. Morgenstern)
1,1,1,1 - 1,0,0,0 - timp.,perc.,cel. - harm. - pf. - str.
10:00 Henmar.
—— ODE AAN SAPPHO (FOR SATB SOLO VOICES, MIXED
CHORUS AND ORCH.) (1949) (Text: P. C. Boutens)
2,3,2,2 - 4,2,1,0 - timp.,perc.,cel. - hp. - str. 35:00 Henmar.
—— ODE (FOR ALTO AND ORCH.) (1949) (Text: B. Voeten)
2,3,2,2 - 4,2,1,0 - timp.,perc. - str. 7:00 Henmar.
—— PASTORALE ET HYMNE
3,3,3,3 - 4,3,3,1 - timp.,perc.,cel. - 2 hp. - str. 10:00 Henmar.
—— DER PILGER UND DIE SARAZENIN (FOR SOPRANO,
TENOR, BASS, WOMEN'S CHORUS AND ORCH.) (1938) (Text:
C. F. Meyer)
2,2,2,2 - 1,1,1,0 - str. 35:00 Henmar.
—— SCENES DE BALLET (SUITE EN DEUX IMAGES)
3,3,3,3 - 4,3,3,1 - timp.,perc. - str. 18:00 Henmar.
—— SUITE SYMPHONIQUE
3,3,3,3 - 4,3,3,1 - timp.,perc.,cel. - 2 hp. - str. 30:00 Henmar.
—— TEMA CON VARIAZIONI, PER VIOLINI E VIOLONCELLI
str. 10:00 Henmar.
—— VOM JAHRESLAUF (FOR MIXED CHORUS AND ORCH.)
(1938) (Text: R. Steiner)
3,3,3,3 - 4,3,3,1 - timp.,perc.,cel. - 2 hp. - str. 30:00 Henmar.
—— WEIHNACHT (PRELUDE)
3,3,3,3 - 4,3,3,1 - timp.,perc. - 2 hp. - org. - str. 18:00 Henmar.
—— WINTER (2 SONNETS FROM P. C. BOUTENS'
"TUSSENSPELEN") (FOR MIXED CHORUS AND ORCH.)
(1942)
2,3,2,2 - 2,1,1,0 - timp.,cel. - hp. - str. 10:00 Henmar.
—— ZONNEGANG (FOR TENOR, BASS, MALE CHORUS AND
ORCH.) (1952) (Text: Rene de Clerq)
2,3,2,2 - 4,3,3,0 - timp.,perc. - str. 22:00 Henmar.

ZAHRADNICK, Zdenek
—— SUITE FOR STRING ORCH.
str. 13:00 Mannheimer.

ZAIDEL, Jeanne
—— KALEIDOSCOPE FOR WIND INSTRUMENTS AND
PERCUSSION
1,1,2,1 - 3,1,2,1 - perc. 15:00 S.A.M.R.O.

ZANDER, Hans - BUCHHOLD, Heinz
—— FANTASTIC INTERMEZZO (BALLET SCENE)
Mannheimer.

ZANETTI, Gasparo - SAGUER, Louis
—— BALLI DA LA SCOLARO
2,2,2,2 - 2,2,1,0 - timp.,perc.(3) - hp. - hpsc. - str. 16:00 Presser.

ZANINELLI, Luigi
—— THE TALE OF PETER RABBIT (FOR NARRATOR AND
ORCH.)
2,2,2,2 - 4,3,3,1 - timp.,perc.,bells,cel.,vibra.,xyl. - str.
40:00 Shawnee.

ZANON, Sante
—— IDILLI PAESANI (RURAL IDYLLS)
3,3,3,2 - 4,2,2,1 - timp.,perc. - hp. - str. 12:00 Leeds.
—— PRELUDIO EROICO
3,3,2,2 - 4,3,3,1 - timp. - hp. - str. 10:00 Bo. Hawkes.
—— SANTA CATERINA DA SIENA (SACRA
RAPPRESENTAZIONE) %
2,2,2,2 - 4,3,3,1 - timp.,perc.,cel. - hp. - pf. - str. 90:00 Leeds.
—— SINFONIA IN QUATTRO TEMPI
2,2,1,1 - 4,2,1,1 - timp.,perc. - hp. - pf. - str. 15:00 Bo. Hawkes.

ZBINDEN, Julien-François
—— ÉTHIOPIQUES (FOR NARRATOR AND ORCH.) (Text: L. S.
Senghor)
2,2,2,2 - 2,2,0,0 - perc. - hp. - str. 20:00 Presser.

—— LEMANIC 70, OP. 48 (OUVERTURE POUR GRAND
ORCHESTRE)
12:00 ECSchirmer.

ŽEBRE, Demetrij
—— ALLEGRO RISOLUTO MARCIALE
*2,2(2nd alt. with Eng. hn.),2(2nd alt. with b.-cl.),2 - 4,3,3,1 -
timp.,perc.(4) - str. 12:00 Hans Gerig.
—— AWAKENING
2,1(alt. with Eng. hn.),2,2 - 3,2,1,0 - hp. - str. 7:00 Hans Gerig.
—— BACCHANALE
3(3rd alt. with picc.),2(2nd alt. with Eng. hn.),*3,2(2nd alt. with
c.-bn.) - 4,3,3,1 - timp.,perc.(4),cel. - hp. - str. 25:00 Hans Gerig.
—— CONCERTINO FOR PIANO AND ORCH.
1,1,1,1 - 2,1,0,0, - pf. - str. 22:00 Hans Gerig.
—— MOURNING MUSIC
2(2nd alt. with picc.),2(2nd alt. with Eng. hn.),2(2nd alt. with
b.-cl.),2(2nd alt. with c.-bn.) - 4,3,3,1 - timp.,perc.(5) - hp. - str.
7:00 Hans Gerig.
—— THE RUN (SYMPHONIC PICTURE)
2(2nd alt. with picc.),2,2,2 - 4,3,3,1 - timp.,perc.(4) - str.
8:00 Hans Gerig.
—— SUITE FOR SMALL ORCH.
2,1,2,2 - 0,2,1,1 - perc.(2) - pf. - str. 8:00 Hans Gerig.
—— THREE VISIONS
*2,1(alt. with Eng. hn.),2,2 - 3,2,1,0 - hp. - str. 21:00 Hans Gerig.
—— TOCCATA
2(2nd alt. with picc.),2(2nd alt. with Eng. hn.),2(2nd alt. with
b.-cl.),2(2nd alt. with c.-bn.) - 4,3,3,1 - timp.,perc.(4) - str.
8:00 Hans Gerig.
—— TOWARDS LIBERTY (SYMPHONIC POEM)
2(2nd alt. with picc.),2(2nd alt. with Eng. hn.),2,2 - 4,3,3,1 -
timp.,perc.(4) - str. 12:00 Hans Gerig.

ZECHLIN, Ruth
—— CONCERTINO FOR FLUTE AND CHAMBER ORCH.
1,1,0,0 - 0,1,1,0 - timp.,perc. - pf. - str. 16:00 Tetra.
—— CONCERTO FOR VIOLIN AND ORCH. (1963)
3,2,2,2 - 4,2,2,0 - timp.,perc. - str. 16:00 Tetra.
—— ORCHESTRA PIECE NO. 1 ("DIE WOLKEN") (VERSION FOR
SOPRANO AND ORCH.) (Text: Günther Deike)
1,1,0,0 - 0,1,0,0 - perc.,xyl. - hp. - str. 10:00 Tetra.
—— ORCHESTRA PIECE NO. 1 (VERSION FOR VIOLIN AND
ORCH.) (1965)
1,1,0,0 - 0,1,0,0 - perc. - hp. - str. 10:00 Tetra.
—— SYMPHONY NO. 1
3,2,2,3 - 4,3,3,0 - timp.,perc. - str. 32:00 Tetra.
—— THOUGHTS ON A PIANO PIECE OF PROKOFIEFF (FOR
PIANO AND 10 INSTS.)
1,1,1,1 - 0,1,0,0 - perc. - pf. - str.(1,1,1,1) 10:00 Tetra.

ZEHNDER, Max
—— CANTATA FOR ALTO VOICE AND SMALL ORCH.
1,1,2,1 - 2,1,1,0 - timp. - str. 26:00 S.U.I.S.A.
—— CONCERTO FOR FLUTE, OBOE AND STRINGS
fl.,ob. - str. 14:00 S.U.I.S.A.
—— MEDIA VITA
*2,*2,2,2 - 3,2,3,1 - timp.,perc.,xyl. - str. 20:00 S.U.I.S.A.
—— PRELUDE AND CHACONNE, FOR STRINGS
str. 11:00 S.U.I.S.A.
—— TOCCATA
*3,2,2,2 - 4,3,3,1 - timp.,perc. - str. 12:00 S.U.I.S.A.

ZEISL, Eric
—— CANTATA OF VERSES (FOR MIXED CHORUS AND ORCH.)
(IN 4 MOVTS.)
2,2,2,2 - 2,2,2,1 - perc.(2) - pf. - str. 15:00 Composer.
—— CONCERTO IN C FOR PIANO AND ORCH. (IN 3 MOVTS.)
2,1,0,1 - 2,2,2,0 - timp.,perc.(2),xyl. - pf. - str. 26:00 Composer.
—— FOUR SONGS FOR "THE DAUGHTER OF JEPHTA"
(WORDLESS SONGS FOR WOMEN'S CHORUS AND
CHAMBER ORCH.)
tpt. - timp.,perc.(1),glock. - hp. - str. 18:00 J. Fischer.
—— MOON PICTURES (FOR BARITONE AND ORCH.) (IN 4
MOVTS.)
3(3rd alt. with picc.),2(2nd alt. with Eng. hn.),3,3 - 4,3,3,1 -
timp.,perc.(2),cel.,glock.,xyl. - hp. - pf. - str. 18:00 Composer.
—— MUSIC FOR CHRISTMAS (VARIATIONS AND FUGUE ON
CHRISTMAS CAROLS)
2(alt. with 2 picc.),2,2,2 - 4,3,3,0 - timp.,perc.,cel.,glock.,xyl. - hp.
- str. 10:00 Composer.

—— OVERTURE AND DANCE OF THE COSSACKS, FROM "JOB"
2(2nd alt. with picc.),2(2nd alt. with Eng. hn.),2,2 - 4,2,3,1 -
timp.,perc.(2),glock.,xyl. - hp. - pf. - str.   10:00 Composer.
—— PASSACAGLIA
3(2nd alt. with picc.),2(2nd alt. with Eng. hn.),3,3 - 4-6,3-4,3-4,1 -
timp.,perc.(2),cel.,glock. - hp. - str.   13:00 Composer.
—— PIERROT IN THE FLASK (BALLET SUITE)
3(2nd alt. with picc.),2(2nd alt. with Eng. hn.),2,2 - 4,3,3,1 -
timp.,perc.(2) - hp. - pf. - str.   25:00 Composer.
—— REQUIEM EBRAICO (FOR SOLOISTS, CHORUS AND
CHAMBER ORCH.)
1(alt. with picc.),1,1,0 - 1,1,1,0 - timp.,perc.,glock. - hp. - org. -
str.   23:00 Transcon.
—— RETURN OF ULYSSES (SUITE) (FOR CHAMBER ORCH.) (IN
4 MOVTS.)
1(alt. with picc.),1(alt. with Eng. hn.),2,2 - 2,2,1,0 - hp. - str.
13:00 Composer.
—— ROMANTIC COMEDY SUITE
2(2nd alt. with picc.),2(2nd alt. with Eng. hn.),2,2 - 2,2,1,0 - hp. -
str.   18:00 Composer.
—— SUITE FOR STRINGS (IN 3 MOVTS.)
str.   20:00 Composer.
—— TO THE PROMISED LAND (SUITE) (IN 4 MOVTS.)
1(alt. with picc.),1(alt. with Eng. hn.),2,1 - 2,2,1,0 - timp.,perc. -
pf. - str.   14:00 Transcon.
—— URANIUM 235 (SYMPHONIC BALLET) %
2(2nd alt. with picc.),2(2nd alt. with Eng. hn.),2(2nd alt. with
b.-cl.),2(2nd alt. with c.-bn.) - 4,2,3,1 -
timp.,perc.(3),cel.,glock.,xyl. - hp. - pf. - str.   Carlvi.

ZELENKA, István
—— BIAIS
1,*2,*2,1 - 1,1,1,0 - str.   14:15 Modern.
—— DECORS
1,0,*2,0 - 2,1,1,0 - hp. - hpsc. - str.(2,3,4,1)   10:00 Modern.
—— VOLS POUR ORCHESTRE
3 picc.(1 alt. with fl., 1 alt. with alto fl.),0,*2,*2 - 2,2,1,0 - bells -
hp. - pf. - str.   10:00 Modern.

ZELJENKA, Ilja
—— DRAMATIC OVERTURE
3,2,2,3 - 4,3,3,1 - timp.,perc.,cel. - str.   10:00 Bo. Hawkes.

ZENTNER, Johannes
—— CONCERTO FÜR CELLO AND STREICHORCHESTER
str.   18:00 S.U.I.S.A.
—— KONZERT IN D, FÜR VIOLINE UND STREICHORCHESTER
str.   10:00 S.U.I.S.A.
—— SINFONIETTA FÜR STREICHORCHESTER
str.   11:00 Henmar.
—— SINFONIETTA FÜR VIOLINE UND STREICHORCHESTER
str.   15:00 Henmar.

ZHIGANOV, Nazib G.
—— SYMPHONY NO. 3 (THE LYRICAL)
G. Schirmer.

ZHUBANOVA, Giziza A.
—— SYMPHONY (ZHIGER)
G. Schirmer.

ZICH, Jaroslav
—— RHAPSODY FOR CELLO AND ORCH.
2,2,3,2 - 4,2,3,1 - timp.,perc. - hp. - str.   22:00 Bo. Hawkes.

ZICH, Otakar
—— OVERTURE TO THE OPERA "LES PRÉCIEUSES RIDICULES"
3,2,4,2 - 4,2,0,1 - timp.,perc. - str.   8:00 Bo. Hawkes.

ZIERITZ, Grete von
—— PICTURES FROM THE FAIR (BILDER VOM JAHRMARKT)
(FOR FLUTE AND ORCH.) (IN 4 MOVTS.)
3,2,2,2 - 2,0,0,0 - timp.,perc.(5, incl. 3 on timp.) - hp. - str.
14:00 Henmar.
—— LE VIOLON DE LA MORT (DANSES MACABRES) (FOR
VIOLIN AND ORCH.) (IN 5 MOVTS.)
2(2nd alt. with picc.),2(2nd alt. with Eng.hn.),2(2nd alt. with
b.-cl.),2 - 4,3,3,2,0 - timp.,perc.(7, incl. 4 on timp.) - str.
26:00 Henmar.

ZIFFRIN, Marilyn J.
—— THE DEATH OF MOSES (CANTATA) (1954) (FOR
NARRATOR, SOLO VOICES, SATB CHORUS AND ORCH.)
(Text: Falasha Anthology, translated by Wolf Leslau)
2,2,*3,*3 - 4,2,3,1 - timp.,perc.(3) - str.   30:00 Composer.
—— A SMALL SUITE FOR STRING ORCH. (1963) (IN 3 MOVTS.)
str.   5:15 Composer.
—— XIII (FOR CHAMBER ENSEMBLE) (1969) (IN 3 MOVTS.)
2,0,1,2 - 2,0,1,0 - timp.,perc.(1) - str. (2,1,1,0)   13:45 Composer.

ZIINO, Ottavio
—— TOCCATA E FUGA
3,3,3,2 - 4,3,3,1 - str.   12:00 Bo. Hawkes.

ZILCHER, Hermann
—— KAMMERKONZERT, OP. 102
1,1,1,1 - 1,1,0,0 - timp.,perc. - pf. - str.   27:00 SDMV.
—— MUSICA BUFFA (ZUR "KOMÖDIE DER IRRUNGEN" VON
SHAKESPEARE) (IN 10 MOVTS.)
2,1,1,1 - 1,1,0,0 - perc. - str.   30:00 Henmar.
—— MUSIK ZU "WIE ES EUCH GEFÄLLT" VON SHAKESPEARE,
OP. 33 (IN 6 MOVTS.)
2,1,1,1 - 2,1,0,0 - perc. - str.   14:00 Henmar.
—— SKIZZEN AUS DEM ORIENT, OP. 18 (FOR VIOLIN AND
ORCH.) (IN 2 MOVTS.)
2(1 alt. with picc.),2,2,2 - 2,2,0,0 - timp.,perc. - str.
14:00 Henmar.
—— SYMPHONY NO. 4 IN F SHARP MINOR, OP. 84
3,2,2,2 - 4,2,3,1 - timp.,perc. - hp. - str.   36:00 SDMV.
—— SYMPHONY NO. 5 IN C MINOR, OP. 112
3,2,2,2 - 4,2,3,1 - timp.,perc. - hp. - str.   30:00 SDMV.

ZILLIG, Winfried
—— CONCERTO FOR CELLO AND WINDS (REV. 1952)
2(2nd alt. with picc.),2(2nd alt. with Eng.hn.),*3,2(2nd alt. with
c.-bn.) - 4,2,2,1 - c.   43:00 G. Schirmer.
—— CONCERTO FOR ORCH.
Baerenrtr.
—— CONCERTO FOR VIOLIN AND ORCH. (1955)
*3,*3,*3,*3 - 4,3,3,1 - timp.,cel. - hp. - pf. - str.
42:00 G. Schirmer.
—— DANCE SYMPHONY (1938)
*2,2(2nd alt. with Eng.hn.),*3,2 - 4,3,3,1 - timp.,perc.(3),cel. - hp.
- pf. - str.   25:00 G. Schirmer.
—— EIGHT SONGS ON POEMS OF GABRIELE D'ANNUNZIO
(FOR LOW VOICE AND ORCH.)
*3,alto fl.,*3,*3,*3 - 4,4,4,1 - timp.,perc.(3),cel.(ad lib.) - hp. - str.
31:00 G. Schirmer.
—— FANTASIA LIRICA FOR HARP AND STRINGS (1953)
hp. - str.   20:00 G. Schirmer.
—— FANTASIA PASSACAGLIA AND FUGUE (ON THE
"MEISTERSINGER" CHORALE)(1963)
*3,*3,*3,*3 - 4,4,3,1 - timp.,perc.(5),cel. - hp. - pf.(ad lib.) - str.
32:00 G. Schirmer.
—— FIVE SONGS ON TEXTS OF GEORG TRAKL (FOR LOW
VOICES AND CHAMBER ORCH.)(1954)
1,1,2,1 - 2,1,1,0 - timp.,perc. - str.   19:00 G. Schirmer.
—— LUSTSPIELSUITE
1,1,2,1 - 2,2,1,0 - timp.,perc. - str.   17:30 Alkor.
—— MUSIC FOR AN ABSTRACT FILM (1954)
1,0,0,0 - 0,1,0,0 - timp.,perc.(4) - hp. - pf. - str. 8:00 G. Schirmer.
—— OSTERKONZERT (FOR STRING QUARTET AND ORCH.)
2,2,2,2 - 2,2,1,0 - timp.,perc. - pf. - org.(ad lib.) - str. 27:00 Alkor.
—— OVERTURE (1928)
*3,*3,*4,*3 - 4,4,3,1 - timp.,perc.(4),cel. - hp. - str.
5:00 G. Schirmer.
—— PRAGER BAROCK (1943)
1,1,2,1 - 2,2,1,0 - timp.,perc. - str.   G. Schirmer.
—— PRELUDE TO STRINDBERG'S "A DREAM PLAY" (1929)
0,0,*3,0 - 0,1,0,1 - perc. - pf.(or cel.) - str.(2,1,1,1)
5:00 G. Schirmer.
—— SERENADE IV (1952)
1,1,1,1 - 1,1,0,0 - timp.,perc.,cel. - hpsc. - str.(2,0,1,1,1)
23:00 G. Schirmer.
—— SEVEN SONNETS OF EICHENDORFF (FOR HIGH VOICE
AND ORCH.)
2,2,3,2 - 4,0,0,0 - timp. - pf. - str.   21:00 G. Schirmer.
—— SIX SONGS FROM GOETHE (FOR HIGH VOICE AND
ORCH.)(1951)
2,2,2(2nd alt. with b.-cl.),2 - 4,2,0,0 - timp. - str.
16:00 G. Schirmer.
—— SIX SONGS FROM GOETHE (FOR LOW VOICE AND ORCH.)
2,2,2,2 - 4,2,0,0 - timp. - str.   17:00 G. Schirmer.

—— SUITE NO. 1 FROM THE FILM "TRAUMSTRASSE DER WELT"

    1,1,2,1 - 3,3,3,0 - perc.(2) - polychord - hp. - str.

            15:00 G. Schirmer.

—— SUITE NO. 2 FROM THE FILM "TRAUMSTRASSE DER WELT"

    1,1,2,1 - 3,3,3,0 - perc.(2) - polychord - hp. - str.

            16:00 G. Schirmer.

—— VERGESSENE WEISEN (AFTER POEMS OF PAUL VERLAINE) (FOR HIGH VOICE AND ORCH.) (German Text: Stefan George)

    2,2,2,2 - 2,1,1,0 - cel. - hp. - pf. - str.   20:00 G. Schirmer.

ZIMBALIST, Efrem, Sr.

—— AMERICAN RHAPSODY

    3(3rd alt. with picc.),*3,*3,*3 - 4,3,3,1 - timp.,perc.(3),cel. - 2 hp. - str.   11:00 G. Schirmer.

ZIMMER, Ján

—— CONCERTO FOR ORGAN AND ORCH.

    perc. - org. - str.   25:00 Bo. Hawkes.

ZIMMER, Lowell Jay

—— THE CHINESE NIGHTINGALE (1961)

    2,1,2,1 - 2,3,0,0 - timp.,perc(3) - str.   15:00 Composer.

—— ESSAY FOR ORCHESTRA (1963)

    2,1,2,1 - 3,3,3,1 - timp.,perc.(3) - str.   8:00 Composer.

—— ETUDE FOR ORCHESTRA (1962)

    2,1,2,1 - 3,0,0,0 - timp. - str.   8:00 Composer.

—— IMPRESSIONS (1965)

    2,1,2,1 - 3,3,3,1 - timp.,perc.(2) - str.   10:00 Composer.

—— JOY (1964)

    2,1,2,1 - 3,3,3,1 - timp.,perc.(3) - str.   10:00 Composer.

—— PRELUDE AND FUGUE (1964)

    str.   6:00 Composer.

—— SPRING BALLET (1962)

    2,1,2,1 - 3,0,0,0 - timp. - str.   10:00 Composer.

ZIMMERMANN, Bernd Alois

—— ANTIPHONEN (FOR VIOLA AND SMALL ORCH.) (1961)

    3 fl.(alt. with 3 picc. and 1 alt. with alto fl.) - 3 trb.(1 alt. with alto trb., 2 alt. with ten.-E♭ b.-trb.) - perc. - hp. - str.(0,1,7,5)

            18:00 Modern.

—— IMPROMPTU FOR ORCH.

    3,*3,*3,alto sax.,*3 - 4,0,0,0 - perc.(4) - hp. - pf. - str.

            7:00 Modern.

—— MUSIQUE POUR LES SOUPERS DU ROI UBU (MUSIC FOR THE SUPPERS OF KING UBU) (SUITE)

    *4,*4,*4,1 ten.sax.,3 - 4,3,3,1 - timp.,perc.,cel. - guit.,mandolin,electric bass - hp. - org. - pf. - 4 d.-b.   Baerenrtr.

ZIMMERMANN, Rolf

—— SERENADE (IN 4 MOVTS.)

    pf. - str.   Tetra.

ZIMMERMANN, Udo

—— MUSIC FOR STRINGS (1968)

    str.   14:00 Tetra.

—— SIEH, MEINE AUGEN (REFLECTIONS FOR CHAMBER ORCH., AFTER ERNST BARLACH)

    2,1,2,0 - 2,3,2,0 - timp.,perc.,cel. - hp. - pf. - str.(0,0,1,1,0)   Tetra.

ZINGARELLI, Nicola A. - MAIONE

—— SINFONIA NO. 7 IN C MAJOR, OP. 22, NO.3

    2,2,2,2 - 2,0,0,0 - timp. - str.   7:00 Henmar.

ZINSSTAG, Dolf

—— LÉGENDE ORIENTALE, OP. 86 (POUR GRAND ORCHESTRE)

            4:00 S.U.I.S.A.

—— SUITE HELVÉTIQUE, OP. 85 (POUR GRAND ORCHESTRE)

            14:00 S.U.I.S.A.

ZIPP, Friedrich

—— CHAMBER CONCERTO, OP. 15 (FOR PIANO, CLARINET, CELLO AND CHAMBER ORCH.)

    cl. - 2 hn.(ad lib.) - pf. - str.   Hans Gerig.

—— MUSIK FÜR ORCH., OP. 9

    1,1,1,1 - 0,0,0,0 - timp. - str.   10:00 Möseler.

ŽIVKOVIĆ, Mirjana

—— METAMORPHOSES CONCERTANTS (FOR PIANO AND ORCH.)

    3,3,3,3 - 4,3,3,1 - timp.,perc.,cel. - pf. - str.   17:00 MIC,Zagreb.

—— O ŽIVOTU I SMRTI (OF LIFE AND DEATH) (CANTATA) (FOR SOPRANO, BARITONE, SATB CHORUS AND ORCH.)

    2,2,2,2 - 4,2,2,0 - perc. - hp. - str.   30:00 MIC,Zagreb.

—— SIMFONIJSKI TORZO

    3,2,3,2 - 4,2,3,0 - timp.,perc. - str.   11:35 MIC,Zagreb.

ZOGRAFSKI, Tomislav

—— BITTER LAKE (FOR SOPRANO, PIANO AND STRINGS) (1968)

    pf. - str.(12,6,4,4)   8:00 MIC,Zagreb.

ZOLL, Paul

—— HESSISCHE SPIELMUSIK

    1,0,1,0 - 0,2,0,0 - str.   12:00 Baerenrtr.

ZOLTAI, Matthew

—— SUMMER EVENING AT LAKE BALATON (SUITE) (IN 4 MOVTS.)

    3(3rd alt. with picc.),2(2nd alt. with Eng. hn.),3(alt. with b.-cl.and2 sax.),3 - 4,3,3,1 - timp.,perc.,cel.,vibra.,xyl. - hp. - pf. - str.   23:00 J. Fischer.

ZUCKERT, León

—— DIVERTIMENTO ORIENTALE (BALLET SUITE) (1965) (IN 4 MOVTS.)

    ob. - str.   25:00 CanMusCtr.

—— DNIEPR (SYMPHONIC POEM) (FOR SATB CHORUS AND ORCH.)

    *3,*3,*3,*3 - 4,3,3,1 - timp.,perc. - str.   35:00 CanMusCtr.

    or:

    *3,3,3,3 - 4,2,2,1 - timp.,perc. - str.

—— FANTASIA ON UKRAINIAN THEMES (1973) (IN 1 MOVT.)

    2(2nd alt. with picc.),2,2,2 - 4,2,3,1 - timp.,perc. - hp. - str.   18:30 CanMusCtr.

—— IMPRESSIONS OF TENERIF (SUITE) (1970)

    2(2nd alt. with picc.),2,2,2 - 2,2,2,0 - timp.,perc. - hp. - str.   34:55 CanMusCtr.

—— IN THE GLEAM OF NORTHERN LIGHTS (1974) (CHOREOGRAPHIC ORATORIO) (FOR SATB CHORUS AND ORCH.) (Text: Ella Bobrow)

    timp.,perc. - 2 pf. - str.   45:00 CanMusCtr.

—— QUETICO (SUITE FROM THE FILM) (1957) (IN 10 MOVTS.)

    *3,*3,*3,*3 - 4,3,2,1 - timp.,perc.,cel.,vibra.(ad lib.) - hp. - pf. - str.   25:00 CanMusCtr.

—— SONG IN BRASS (FOR VOICE, VIOLA, BRASS AND PERCUSSION) (1964)

    0,0,0,0 - 4,2,3,1 - timp.,perc.   28:00 CanMusCtr.

—— SYMPHONY NO. 1 (IN 3 MOVTS.)

            45:00 C.A.P.A.C.

—— SYMPHONY NO. 2 (1962)

    *3,*3,*3,*3 - 4,3,3,1 - timp.,perc. - str.   45:00 CanMusCtr.

—— TWO MOODS IN ONE (1968) (FOR STRINGS)

    str.   11:10 CanMusCtr.

ZUPKO, Ramon

—— BALLADE FOR ORCHESTRA (1957)

    *3,*3,*3,*3 - 4,2,3,1 - timp.,perc. - hp. - str.   4:30 Composer.

—— CENTROIDS (1963) (IN 5 MOVTS.)

    2(1st alt. with picc. and 2nd alt. with alto fl.),2,2(2nd alt. with b.-cl.),*1 - 0,0,0,0 - perc.(8),cel.,glock.,xyl. - electric guit. - hp. - pf. - str.   17:30 Composer.

—— CONCERTO FOR VIOLIN AND ORCHESTRA (1962) (IN 3 MOVTS.)

    *3,2,2,2 - 4,3,3,1 - timp.,perc.(4),bells,xyl. - hp. - pf. - str.   29:20 Belw-Mills.

—— ELEGY FOR STRING ORCHESTRA (1957)

    str.   5:00 Composer.

—— GILGAMESH (2-ACT BALLET FOR DANCERS AND CHAMBER ORCHESTRAL GROUPS) % (1963)

    2(2nd alt. with picc.),1 alto fl.,3(3rd alt. with Eng. hn.),3(2nd alt. with E♭ cl.,3rd alt. with b.-cl.),1 alto sax.,1 ten. sax.,1 bar. sax.,3(3rd alt. with c.-bn.) - 0,3,3,0 - timp.,perc.(6),cel.,glock.,vibra.,xyl. - guit. - hp. - pf. - str.   95:00 Composer.

—— PRELUDE AND BAGATELLE (1961)

    str.   4:30 EV.

—— PROLOGUE, ARIA AND DANCE (1961)

    hn. - str.   8:00 Composer.

—— RADIANTS (1971)
    3(1 alt. with picc.),3(3rd alt. with Eng. hn.), *4(1 alt. with E^{b}cl.),2
    - 4,4,3,1 - timp.,perc.(6),mar.,vibra.,xyl. - str.   12:00 Composer.
—— THIS IS THE GARDEN (FOR MIXED CHORUS AND SMALL
ORCH.) (1962) (Text: E. E. Cummings)
    1,1,1,0 - 0,1,0,0 - timp.,perc.,glock. - str.   9:00 Composer.
—— TRANSLUCENTS (1967)
    str.   9:00 Composer.
—— VARIATIONS FOR ORCHESTRA (1961)
    *3,2,2,2 - 4,3,3,1 - timp.,perc.(2) - str.   6:50 Composer.

ZVANKIN, Peter
—— POEM FOR ORCHESTRA (1936)
    2,2,2,2 - 4,3,3,1 - timp.,perc. - hp. - str.   10:00 CanMusCtr.

ZWILICH, Ellen Taafe
—— SYMPOSIUM FOR ORCHESTRA
    3,3,4,3 - 4,3,3,1 timp.,perc. - 2 hp. - str.   12:00 EV.

ZYKAN, Otto M.
—— KRYPTOMEMNIE
    1(alt. with picc.),1,1,1 - 2,3,2,1 - perc.(3) - pf.   12:00 Modern.

KEY TO PUBLISHERS'
ABBREVIATIONS AND ADDRESSES

When a publisher's name is in parentheses (   ) and is followed by the symbol c/o and the name of another publisher, it means that the latter has representation *for the United States* of the first publisher's symphonic catalog.

When the source of availability of a work is shown as composer or arranger or translator, ASCAP's address is given. This means that a letter addressed to one of those parties will be forwarded by the Society. *Do not write* the Society directly requesting score and/or parts as we do not maintain a library of our members' works.

A Tempo
A-Tempo-Verlag
Lindengasse 10, Wien 7, Austria

AccadiaMCo
Accadia Music Co.
9961 1/2 Durant Dr., Beverly Hills, CA 90212

A.C.U.M.
A.C.U.M., Ltd. (Société des Auteurs, Compositeurs et Editeurs de Musique en Israel)
P.O.B. 11201, Tel-Aviv, Israel

AdverMuInc
Advertiser's Music, Inc.
124 W. Kinzie St., Chicago, IL 60610

A.E.P.I.
A.E.P.I. (Société Anonyme Héllénique Pour la Protection De la Propriété Intellectuelle)
14 Rue Deliyianni, Athens (148), Greece

A.G.A.D.U.
A.G.A.D.U. (Asociacion General de Autores del Uruguay)
Calle Canelones No. 1130, Montevideo, Uruguay

Agape
Agape Music
c/o Don Norville, 1636 N. Cahuenga, No. 207, Los Angeles, CA 90028

AhnSimrock
Ahn & Simrock Musikverlag
Widenmayerstrasse 6, 8000 Munich 22, West Germany

Akademiska
Akademiska Musikförlaget
Piispank 17, 20500 Turku 50, Finland

A.K.M.
A.K.M. (Staatlich Genehmigte Gesellschaft der Autoren, Komponisten und Musikverleger)
Baumannstrasse 8, 1031 Wien, Austria

Alfred
Alfred Publishing Co., Inc.
75 Channel Drive, Port Washington, NY 11050

Alkor
Edition Alkor, GMBH
Heinrich-Schütz-Allee 29, 35 Kassel-Wilhelmshöhe, West Germany

AllansPty
Allans Music (Aust.), Pty., Ltd.
Box 513J, G.P.O. Melbourne, Vic. 3001, Australia

Almitra
Almitra Music Co., Inc.
Delevan, NY 14042

Alsbach
(G. Alsbach & Co.)
c/o Henmar Press, Inc., 373 Park Ave. South, New York, NY 10016

Alte&NeueK
Alte & Neue Kunst Verlag
Rheingaustr. 3, 1 Berlin 41, West Germany

Amadeus
Amadeus Verlag
c/o S.U.I.S.A., Bellariastrasse 82, 8038 Zurich, Switzerland

AmaMus.Co.
AMA Music Co., Suite 301
1650 Broadway, New York, NY 10019

AmerMusEd
American Music Edition
c/o Carl Fischer Inc., 62 Cooper Sq., New York, NY 10003

Am.Mu.Ctr
American Music Center, Suite 626-7
250 W. 57th St., New York, NY 10019

AMP
Associated Music Publishers, Inc.
c/o G. Schirmer, Inc., 866 Third Ave., New York, NY 10022

Andraud
(Albert J. Andraud, Wind Instrument Music Library)
c/o Southern Music Co., 1100 Broadway, P.O. Box 329, San Antonio, TX 78206

AndrieuFr.
(Andrieu Frères c/o Billaudot)
c/o Theodore Presser Co., Presser Place, Bryn Mawr, PA 19010

Anglo
(Anglo-Canadian Music Co., Ltd.)
c/o Canadian Music Sales Corp., Ltd., 58 Advance Rd., Toronto, Ont., M8Z 2T8, Canada

Anton Böhm
Anton Böhm & Sohn KG Musikverlag
D-8900 Augsburg 1, West Germany

A.P.R.A
A.P.R.A. (Australasian Performing Right Association Ltd.)
P.O. Box 291, Crows Nest, N.S.W., Australia 2065

Arcadia
Arcadia Music Publishing Co., Ltd.
10 Sherlock Mews, Baker St., London W1M 3RH, England

A.R.J.U.S.
A.R.T.I.S.J.U.S. (Bureau Hongrois Pour la Protection Des Droits D'Auteur)
Vörösmarty Tér 1, Budapest V, Hungary

Arranger
(Name of Individual)
c/o A.S.C.A.P., 1 Lincoln Plaza, New York, NY 10023

Ars Nova
(Ars Nova, Calif.) c/o Music Graphics Press
Attn: Donald Balestrieri, 117 Washington St., San Diego, CA 92103

ArtisnMuPr
Artisan Music Press
176 Furnace Dock Rd., Peekskill, NY 10566

Ascher
Emil Ascher, Inc.
666 Fifth Ave., New York, NY 10022

AstoriaBln
Astoria Verlag GmbH
Brandenburgischestrasse 22, D-1000 Berlin, West Germany

AstrlMuCtr
Australia Music Center, Ltd.
P.O. Box N9, Grosvenor St., The Rocks, Sydney, N.S.W. 2000, Australia

Augener
(Augener, Ltd.)
c/o Galaxy Music Corp., 2121 Broadway, New York, NY 10023

Augsburg
Augsburg Publishing House
426 South Fifth St., Minneapolis, MN 55415

Author
(Name of Individual)
c/o A.S.C.A.P., 1 Lincoln Plaza, New York, NY 10023

Avant
Avant Music
2859 Holt Ave., Los Angeles, CA 90034

B.-Barclay
Barger & Barclay
1325 Orange Isle, Ft. Lauderdale, FL 33315

B V & C
Bregman, Vocco & Conn, Inc.
Attn: Mr. Herbert N. Eisenman, 8544 Sunset Blvd., Hollywood, CA 90069

Baerenrtr
(Bärenreiter Verlag)
c/o G. Schirmer, Inc., 866 Third Ave., New York, NY 10022

Baron
M. Baron Co.
P.O. Box 149, Oyster Bay, NY 11771

Beekman
(Beekman Music, Inc.)
c/o Theodore Presser Co., Presser Place, Bryn Mawr, PA 19010

Belmont
Belmont Music Publishers
P.O. Box 49961, Los Angeles, CA 90049

Belw-Mills
Belwin-Mills Publishing Corp.
16 W. 61st St., New York, NY 10023

Belwin
(Belwin)
c/o Belwin-Mills Publishing Corp., 16 W. 61st St., New York, NY 10023

Bennefeld
Bennefeld Mvlg.
Schopenhauerstr. 23, 1 Berlin 38, West Germany

Billaudot
(Edition Billaudot, Paris)
c/o Theodore Presser Co., Presser Place, Bryn Mawr, PA 19010

Birchard
(C. C. Birchard)
c/o Summy-Birchard Co., 1834 Ridge Ave., Evanston, IL 60204

BizetMuPrd
Bizet Music Productions, Inc.
c/o Paris Music Co., Inc., 157 W. 57th St., New York, NY 10019

BKJ
BKJ Publications
Box 324, Astor Station, Boston, MA 02123

Bloch
Bloch Publishing Co.
31 W. 31st St., New York, NY 10001

Bo. Hawkes
Boosey & Hawkes, Inc.
30 W. 57th St., New York, NY 10019

Boelke-Bo.
Boelke-Bomart, Inc.
Hillsdale, NY 12529

Boston
Boston Music Co.
116 Boylston St., Boston, MA 02116

Bourne
Bourne Co.
1212 Avenue of the Americas, New York, NY 10036

BroadmanPr
Broadman Press
127 Ninth Ave. North, Nashville, TN 37203

Brockhaus
Max Brockhaus Musikverlag
Oskar-Gretherstrasse 13, D-7850 Lörrach III, West Germany

Brodt
Brodt Music Co.
P.O. Box 1207, Charlotte, NC 28231

Broude
Broude Brothers, Ltd.
56 W. 45th St., New York, NY 10036

B.U.M.A.
B.U.M.A. (Het Bureau Voor Muziek-Auteursrecht)
Marius Bauerstraat 30, Amsterdam 17, Netherlands.

Burkhard.Co.
Burkhard Co.
c/o S.U.I.S.A., Bellariastrasse 82, 8038 Zurich, Switzerland

Buyst
Mme. Vve. Buyst-Rijckmans M. Th.
142 Boulevard Guillaume van Haelen, Forest-Brussels 19, Belgium

C. Fischer
Carl Fischer, Inc.
62 Cooper Sq., New York, NY 10003

C. Press
The Composers Press, Inc.
4941 Ambrose Ave., Los Angeles, CA 90027

C-Ross
Coleman-Ross Co.
550 Fifth Ave., New York, NY 10036

Cal-Dorado
Cal-Dorado Music
Attn: Mrs. Thelma Lee Hubbell, 4331 Lake Washington Blvd. N.E., Suite 7307, Kirkland, WN 98033

Canadian
Canadian Music Sales Corp., Ltd.
58 Advance Rd., Toronto, Ont. M8Z 2T8, Canada

CanMusCtr
Canadian Music Center
1263 Bay St., Toronto, Ont. M5R 2C1, Canada

Cantabile
Cantabile Music Co.
c/o S.A.M.R.O., P.O. Box 9292, Johannesburg, South Africa

CAP
Composers Autograph Publications
P.O. Box 671, Hamilton, OH 45012

Cap. Press
Capital Press
c/o Mr. Ralph Hermann, Music Department, American Broadcasting Co., 7 W. 66th St., New York, NY 10023

C.A.P.A.C.
C.A.P.A.C. (Composers, Authors and Publishers Assoc. of Canada, Ltd.)
1240 Bay St., Toronto, Ont. M5R 2C2, Canada

Carlvi
Carlvi Music Co., Apt. 403
511 S. Mariposa Ave., Los Angeles, CA 90005

CBDM
(Centre Belge De Documentation Musicale)
c/o Henri Elkan Music Publisher, 1316 Walnut St., Philadelphia, PA 19107

Chappell
Chappell & Co., Inc.
c/o Theodore Presser Co., Inc., 111 W. 57th St., New York, NY 10019
For materials which Chappell & Co., Inc. sells or rents as agent for other firms, contact Chappell & Co., Inc., 810 Seventh Ave., New York, N.Y. 10019

Charling
(Charling Music Corp.)
c/o Edwin H. Morris & Co., Inc., 810 Seventh Ave., New York, NY 10019

C.H.Hansen
Charles H. Hansen Music & Books, Inc.
1842 West Ave., Miami Beach, FL 33139

ChiLitOpCo
(Chicago Lithuanian Opera Co.) Mr. Bruno Markaitis
c/o A.S.C.A.P, 1 Lincoln Plaza, New York, NY 10023

Choudens
(Editions Choudens)
c/o Henmar Press, Inc., 373 Park Ave. South, New York, NY 10016

Church
The John Church Co.
Bryn Mawr, PA 19010

Cl. Benny
(Claude Benny Press) Mr. Joseph Ott
c/o A.S.C.A.P, 1 Lincoln Plaza, New York, NY 10023

CMP
Contemporary Music Project
c/o M.E.N.C., 1902 Association Dr., Reston, VA 22091

Columbia
Columbia Pictures Music Corp.
10 E. 53rd St., New York, NY 10022

ComFacsEd
(Composers' Facsimile Edition)
c/o Carl Fischer Facsimile Edition, 62 Cooper Sq., New York, NY 10003

ComNaCulBA
Comisión Nacional de Cultura
Avenida Alvear 1690, Buenos Aires, Argentina

Composer
(Name of Individual)
c/o A.S.C.A.P., 1 Lincoln Plaza, New York, NY 10023

ConcertMPC
Concert Music Publishing Co.
224 S. Lebanon St., Lebanon, IN 46052

Congress
Congress Music Publications, Suite 501
Flagler Federal Building, 111 Northeast First St., Miami, FL 33132

Consolidtd
(Consolidated Music Publishers, Inc.)
c/o Music Sales Corp., 33 W. 60th St., New York, NY 10023

Consort
(Consort Music, Inc.)
c/o Real Time Productions, Inc., 54 William St., Hempstead, NY 11550

Cousins
Editions Cousins
116 Ave. Franklin Roosevelt, Brussels 5, Belgium
Attn: M. René Defossez

Cramer
J. B. Cramer & Co., Ltd.
99 St. Martin's Lane, London WC2N 4AZ, England

Cranz
(Albert Cranz)
c/o New Music Corp., 30, Rue St. Christophe, B-1000 Brussels, Belgium

Credo
Credo Music Co.
2750 Sherwood Pl., Reno, NE 89502

CunMusCorp
Cunningham Music Corp.
4 N. Pine St., Nyack, NY 10960

Curlew
Curlew Music Publishers, Inc.
Attn: Herman Langinger, 1311 N. Highland Ave., Hollywood, CA 90028

D. Gornston
David Gornston
117 W. 48th St., New York, NY 10036

Dacapo Mfl.
Dacapo Mfl.
Pilestraede 2, Copenhagen K, Denmark

Dania
(Edition Dania) (Dan Fog)
c/o Henmar Press, Inc., 373 Park Ave. South, New York, NY 10016

De Wolfe
De Wolfe, Ltd.
80-88 Wardour St., London W1V 3LF, England

Deseret
(Deseret Music Publishers) Mr. Lowell M. Durham
c/o A.S.C.A.P., 1 Lincoln Plaza, New York, NY 10023

Ditson
Oliver Ditson Co.
Bryn Mawr, PA 19010

DomoMvl.
Domo Musikverlag
c/o G.E.M.A., Herzog-Wilhelmstrasse 28, D-8000 Munich 2, West Germany

Dorian
Dorian Music Publishers, Inc.
40 E. 49th St., New York, NY 10017

DSMusic
Dana Suesse Music Co.
P.O. Box 2088, Frederiksted, St. Croix, VI

DTO Harlem
Dance Theatre of Harlem, Inc.
c/o Tania Leon, 35-20 Leverich St., Apt. B-430, Jackson Heights, NY 11372

E & S
Elkan & Schildknecht
Sveavägen 45, Stockholm C, Sweden

E. B. Marks
Edward B. Marks Music Corp.
1790 Broadway, New York, NY 10019

E. F. Kalmus
See Kalmus

E. H. Morris
Edwin H. Morris & Co., Inc.
c/o Chappell & Co., Inc., 810 Seventh Ave., New York, NY 10019

E. Horowitz
E. Horowitz (Agent)
626 Spruce St., Philadelphia, PA 19103

Earl
Earl Music Co.
c/o Mr. Earl S. Shuman, Suite 3-B, 111 E. 88th St., New York, NY 10028

EarlhamCol
Department of Music, Earlham College
Richmond, IN

EastonMuCo
Easton Music Co.
c/o Robert King, 112-A Main St., North Easton, MA 02356

E.C.Kerby
E.C.Kerby, Ltd.
198 Davenport Rd., Toronto, Ont., M5R 1J2, Canada

ECS
See ECSchirmer

ECSchirmer
E. C. Schirmer Music Co.
112 South St., Boston, MA 02111

Ed. Chasen
Edition Chasen
c/o S.U.I.S.A., Bellariastrasse 82, 8038 Zurich, Switzerland

Ed. Emmef
Editions Emmef Enrg.
516 Rue Ste. Hélène, Longueuil, Quebec J4K 3R5, Canada

Ed. Lyche
(Harald Lyche & Cos., Forlag)
c/o Henmar Press, Inc., 373 Park Ave. South, New York, NY 10016

Ed. Musikk-Hu.
See Musikk-Hu.

Ed·Tonika
Edition Tonika
c/o T.O.N.O., Postboks 1666, Vika, Oslo 1, Norway.

Ed.Argent
Editorial Argentina de Musica Internacional
Lavalle 1494, Buenos Aires, Argentina

EdDelicado
Edition Delicado (Lydia Mohr)
D-6200 Wiesbaden, West Germany

Ed.Fennica
Edition Fennica
Runebergink. 15 A, 00100 Helsinki 10, Finland

Eds. Coda
Editions Coda
Brunnwiesenstrasse 26, CH-8049 Zurich, Switzerland

Eds. Fran.
(Editions Françaises De Musique) Theodore Presser Co.
Presser Pl., Bryn Mawr, PA 19010

EhrlingFlg
A.B. Ehrlingförlagen
Linnegatan 9/11, S-102 45 Stockholm, Sweden

Engstrøm
(Engstrøm & Sødring)
c/o Henmar Press, Inc., 373 Park Ave. South, New York, NY 10016

Enoch
Enoch & cie.
27 Boulevard des Italians, 75002 Paris, France

Erdmann
Musikverlag Rudolph Erdmann
Adolfallee 34, D-6200 Wiesbaden, West Germany

EriksMhflg
Eriks Musikhandel-Förlag A.B.
c/o S.T.I.M., Tegnerlunden 3, S-111 85 Stockholm, Sweden

Ethnic
Ethnic Music Publications, Inc.
263 Veterans Blvd., Carlstadt, NJ 07072

Eulenberg
(Ernst Eulenberg, Ltd.)
c/o Henmar Press, Inc., 373 Park Ave. South, New York, NY 10016

EV
Elkan-Vogel Co., Inc.
Presser Place, Bryn Mawr, PA 19010

F. Colombo
(Franco Colombo, Inc.)
c/o Belwin-Mills Publishing Corp., 16 W. 61st St., New York, NY 10023

Fanfare
Fanfare Music Co.
1337 N. Orange Dr., Hollywood, CA 90028

Fazer
Fazer Musiikki Oy
Aleksanterinkatu 11, 00100 Helsinki 10, Finland

FDH
(Francis, Day & Hunter, Ltd.)
c/o Robbins Music Corp., 729 Seventh Ave., New York, NY 10019

Feist
Leo Feist, Inc.
729 Seventh Ave., New York, NY 10019

Fema
Fema Music Publications
c/o Crescendo Music Sales Co., P.O. Box 395, 8 Bunting Lane, Naperville, IL 60540

Fidelio
Fidelio Music Publishing Co.
c/o Kelman, Greenberg & Co., 7060 Hollywood Blvd., Hollywood, CA 90028

Finale
Finale Bühnen und Musikverlag
Schwalbeneck 13, 89 Augsburg, West Germany

FinnMICtr
Finnish Music Information Center
Runeberginkatu 15 A1, SP-00100 Helsinki 10, Finland

FitzSimons
H. T. FitzSimons Co., Inc.
615 N. LaSalle St., Chicago, IL 60610

Flammer
(Harold Flammer, Inc.)
c/o Shawnee Press, Inc., Delaware Water Gap, PA 18327

Fleisher
The Edwin A. Fleisher Collection of Orchestral Music
c/o The Free Library of Philadelphia, Logan Sq., Philadelphia, PA 19107

Forlivesi
(Casa Editrice Di Musica - A. Forlivesi & Cia.)
c/o Belwin-Mills Publishing Corp., 16 W. 61st St., New York, NY 10023

Forte
Forte Music, Inc.
157 W. 57th St., New York, NY 10019

Fox
Sam Fox Publishing Co., Inc.
P.O. Box 850, Valley Forge, PA 19482

Fr. & Thos
Forrell & Thomas, Inc.
157 W. 57th St., New York, NY 10019

FrankMusCp
Frank Music Corp.
119 W. 57th St., New York, NY 10019

FredHarris
The Frederick Harris Music Co., Ltd.
P.O. Box 670, Oakville, Ont. L6J 5C2, Canada

Fredonia
Fredonia Press
3947 Fredonia Dr., Hollywood, CA 90028

Fst. Etling
Forest R. Etling, Publisher
1790 Joseph Court, Elgin, IL 60120

G & C
(G & C Music Corp.)
c/o G. Schirmer, Inc., 866 Third Ave., New York, NY 10022

G & T
Goodwin & Tabb, Ltd.
c/o P.R.S., 29/33 Berners St., London W1P 4AA, England

G. Schirmer
G. Schirmer, Inc.
866 Third Ave., New York, NY 10022

Galaxy
Galaxy Music Corp.
2121 Broadway, New York, NY 10023

Gam.Hinged
(Gamble Hinged Music Co.)
c/o Carl Fischer, Inc., 62 Cooper Sq., New York, NY 10003

Gate
(Gate Music Co.)
c/o Sam Fox Publishing Co., P.O. Box 850, Valley Forge, PA 19482

Gehrmans
Carl Gehrmans Musikförlag
P.O. Box 505, S-101 26 Stockholm, Sweden

KEY TO PUBLISHERS' ABBREVIATIONS

G.E.M.A.
G.E.M.A. (Gesellschaft für Musikalische Aufführungs und Mechanische Vervielfältigungsrechte)
Herzog-Wilhelm-Strasse 28, D-8000 Munich 2, West Germany

General
(General Music Publishing Co., Inc.: for Serious Music Only)
c/o G. Schirmer, Inc., 866 Third Ave., New York, NY 10022

Gershwin
Gershwin Publishing Corp.
c/o Chappell Music Co., Inc., 810 Seventh Ave., New York, NY 10019

Gervan
Edition Gervan
496-F Chaussée de Waterloo, Brussels 6, Belgium
Attn: Melle. Germaine Blaton

Gray
(H. W. Gray Co., Inc.)
c/o Belwin-Mills Publishing Corp., 16 W. 61st St., New York, NY 10022

Guild Cal.
Guild Publications of California
c/o Alexander Publications, 1711 Margate St., No. 314, Encino, CA 91316

GVThompson
Gordon V. Thompson, Ltd.
29 Birch Ave., Toronto 7, Ont., Canada

GWMusFndtn
Gabriel von Wayditch Music Foundation, Inc.
80-61 Lefferts Blvd., Kew Gardens, NY 11415

H & G
Hüllenhagen & Griehl
Loogestr. 28, 2 Hamburg 20, West Germany

H. Branch
Harold Branch Publishing, Inc.
42 Cornell Dr., Plainview, NY 11803

H. Elkan
Henri Elkan, Music Publisher
1316 Walnut St., Philadelphia, PA 19107

H-McCreary
Schmitt, Hall & McCreary Co.
110 N. Fifth St., Minneapolis, MN 55403

Hampshire
Hampshire House Publishing Corp., Suite 1406
10 Columbus Circle, New York, NY 10019

Hans Gerig
(Hans Gerig Musikverlag) MCA Music (A Division of MCA, Inc.)
c/o Belwin-Mills Publishing Corp., 16 W. 61st St., New York, NY 10023

Hänssler
Hänssler-Verlag Friedrich Hänssler KG
D-7303 Neuhausen, West Germany

Hargail
Hargail Music Press
28 W. 38th St., New York, NY 10018

Harmonia
(Harmonia-Uitgave)
c/o Henmar Press, Inc., 373 Park Ave South, New York, NY 10016

Harms, Inc.
Harms, Inc.
c/o Warner Bros. Music Publications, 14th Floor, 75 Rockefeller Plaza, New York, NY 10019

Harrison
Harrison Music Corp.
6380 Hollywood Blvd., Hollywood, CA 90028

HAUM
Hollandsch Afrikaansche Uitgevers Maatschappij
c/o S.A.M.R.O., P.O. Box 9292, Johannesburg, South Africa

Hawlik
Friedrich Hawlik
Neubaugasse 7, Wien 7, Austria

H.BuschMfl
Hans Busch's Musikförlag AB
Stubbstigen 3, S-181 46 Lidingö, Sweden

Heer & Zn.
Joh. de Heer & Zoon
Jensiusstraat 58, Rotterdam, Netherlands

Helena
Helena Music Corp.
c/o Mr. Joe Darion, 110 Riverside Dr., New York, NY 10024

Henmar
Henmar Press, Inc.
373 Park Ave. South, New York, NY 10016

Henn
Editions Henn
c/o Fanfan Music, rue de Hesse 8-10, CH-1211 Geneva 11, Switzerland

Heritage
Heritage Music Press
c/o Lorenz Industries, 501 E. Third St., Dayton, OH 45401

Hinshaw
Hinshaw Music Inc.
P.O. Box 470 Chapel Hill, NC 27514

Hn. of Gabr.
(Horn of Gabriel Music Publications, Inc.) Mr. Morris Cotel
c/o A.S.C.A.P., 1 Lincoln Plaza, New York, NY 10023

Hug
(Hug & Co.)
c/o Henmar Press, Inc., 373 Park Ave. South, New York, NY 10016

Hulpiau
Gabrielle C. M. Hulpiau
122 rue De la Clinique, Anderlecht-Brussels, Belgium

Humphries
(Bruce Humphries)
c/o Boston Music Co., 116 Boylston St., Boston, MA 02116

Huni
Musikhaus Hüni, Helbing & Co.
Haus Melodie, 8604 Volketswil, Switzerland

Huntzinger
R.L.Huntzinger, Inc.
c/o The Willis Music Co., 7380 Industrial Rd., Florence, KY 41042

Huron Press
Huron Press
Box 3083, London 12, Ont., Canada

H.Voggnrtr
Verlag Heinrich Voggenreiter
D-5300 Bonn-Bad Godesberg 10, West Germany

IBM
International Business Machines
590 Madison Ave., New York, NY 10022

Ilse Lahn
Ilse Lahn
c/o Paul Kohner Agency, Inc., 9169 Sunset Blvd., Beverly Hills, CA 90069

ImudicoKbn
Imudico Musikforlaget A/S
Colbjørnsensgade 19, DK-1652 Copenhagen V, Denmark

InFrAthens
Institut Français D'Athènes
Athens, Greece

Integrity
Integrity Music Corp., Apt. 14-A
1050 Fifth Ave., New York, NY 10028

Islandia
Islandia Edition
Freyjugata 3, Reykjavík, Iceland

IsMuPublns
(Israeli Music Publications)
c/o Tetra Music Corp., 225 W. 57th St., New York, NY 10019

J. Albert
J. Albert & Son Pty., Ltd.
139 King St., Sydney, NSW 2000, Australia

J. Bilik
Jerry Bilik Music, Inc.
2635 W. Delhi Rd., Ann Arbor, MI 48103

KEY TO PUBLISHERS' ABBREVIATIONS

J. Boonin
Joseph Boonin, Inc.
P.O. Box 2124, South Hackensack, NJ 07606

J. Fischer
(J. Fischer & Bro.)
c/o Belwin-Mills Publishing Corp., 16 W. 61st St., New York, NY 10023

J. Oertel
Johannes Oertel
Prinzregenten Str. 64, 8 Munich 8, West Germany

Janfred
Janfred Music
c/o Mr. George Kleinsinger, Hotel Chelsea, 222 W. 23rd St., New York, NY 10011

J.A.S.R.A.C.
J.A.S.R.A.C. (The Japanese Society of Rights of Authors and Composers)
JASRAC House, 7-13, 1-Chome Nishishimbashi, Minato-Ku, Tokyo 105, Japan

JC-phrMuCo
J. Christopher Music Co.
Attn: Vaclav Nelhybel, R.F.D. 4, Hi Barlow Rd., Newtown, CT 06470

Josef Marx
Josef Marx Music Co., Apt. 706
201 W. 86th St., New York, NY 10024

Jungnickel
(Ross Jungnickel, Inc.)
c/o Chappel & Co., Inc., 810 Seventh Ave., New York, NY 10019

K & S
Fr. Kistner & C. F. W. Siegel
Postfach 101, 5 Köln 7, West Germany

K. Neufert
Kurt Neufert
Oppelner Str. 9, 69 Heidelberg-Kirchheim, West Germany

Kalmus
Edwin F. Kalmus & Co.
Miami-Dade Industrial Park, P.O. Box 1007, Opa-Locka, FL 33054

Karleigh
Karleigh Music Co.
c/o Mr. Alf H. Clausen, 12652 Tiara St., North Hollywood, CA 91607

Kelton
(Kelton, Inc.)
c/o Pleasant Music Publishing Corp., 3505 S. Ocean Dr., Apt. 1421, Hollywood, FL 33019

KeysMusCal
Keystone Music Co. of California
9615 Helen Ave., Sunland, CA 91040

Kimberly
Kimberly Music Corp.
Schillings Crossing Rd., Canaan, NY 12029

KingsCrown
Kings Crown Music Press (Div. of Columbia University Press)
c/o Galaxy Music Corp., 2121 Broadway, New York, NY 10023

K.O.D.A.
K.O.D.A. (Selskaber Til Forvaltning af Internationale Komponistrettigheder I Danmark)
Rosenvaengets Hovedvej 14, 2100 Copenhagen O, Denmark

LaulMieh
Laulu-Miehet
Hietaniemenkatu 2, Helsinki, Finland

Law-Gould
Lawson-Gould Music Publishers, Inc.
866 Third Ave., New York, NY 10022

L.B. & Co.
Little, Brown & Co. (Publishers of TEXTS ONLY)
34 Beacon St., Boston, MA 02116

Leblanc
Leblanc Publications, Inc.
7019 30th Ave., Kenosha, WI 53140

Leeds
(Leeds Music Corp.) MCA Music (A Division of MCA, Inc.)
c/o Belwin-Mills Publishing Corp., 16 W. 61st St., New York, NY 10023

Lemoine
(Henri Lemoine & Cie.)
c/o Elkan-Vogel, Inc., Presser Pl., Bryn Mawr, PA 19010

Lengnick
(Alfred Lengnick & Co., Ltd.)
c/o The Frederick Harris Music Co., Ltd., Box 670, Oakville, Ont. L6J 5C2, Canada

Liben
Liben Music Publishers
Attn: Mr. Frank Proto, 6265 Dawes Drive, Cincinnati, OH 45230

Lorenz
Lorenz Industries
501 E. 3rd St., Dayton, OH 45401

Louis Lane
Mr. Louis Lane
c/o Dallas Symphony Assn., Inc., P.O. Box 26207, Dallas, TX 75226

Ludwig
Ludwig Music Publishing Co.
557 E. 140th St., Cleveland, OH 44110

Lundquists
Abr. Lundquists Musikförlag AB
Katarina Baganta 17, S-116 25 Stockholm, Sweden

LuoSävEd
Louvan Säveltaiteen Edistämissäätiö
Runeberginkatu 15-A, 00100 Helsinki 10, Finland

Lyra
Lyra Music Co.
133 W. 69th St., New York, NY 10023

McLellans
McLellan's
c/o S.A.M.R.O., P.O. Box 9292, Johannesburg, South Africa

Mannheimer
Mannheimer Musik-Verlag, GMBH
Postfach 1504, D-6800 Mannheim 1, West Germany

Marbot
(Edition Marbot, GMBH)
c/o Southern Music Publishing Co., Inc., 1740 Broadway, New York, NY 10019

Margery
Margery Music, Inc.
c/o Mr. Eddy L. Manson, 2616 N. Beachwood Dr., Hollywood, CA 90068

MarsegLtd
Marseg, Ltd.
18 Farmstead Rd., Willowdale, Ont. M2L 2G2, Canada

MaxwellWir
(Maxwell-Wirges Publications)
c/o Shawnee Press, Inc., Delaware Water Gap, PA 18327

MayaMuRKov
Maya-Music Dr. Roland Kovác
Attn: Dr. Roland Kovác, D-2000 Hamburg 70, West Germany

MCA Music
MCA Music (A Division of MCA Inc.)
c/o Belwin-Mills Publishing Corp., 16 W. 61st St., New York, NY 10023

Mediterran
Mediterranean Press
Attn: Mr. A. Makris, 11204 Oakleaf Dr., Silver Spring, MD 20901

Melomusic
Melomusic Publications, Inc.
c/o Fred Barovick, 20 Coles St., River Edge, NJ 07661

Mercurio
Mercurio, S.R.L.
Via Stoppani 10, Rome, Italy

Mercury
(Mercury Music Corp.)
c/o Theodore Presser Co., Bryn Mawr, PA 19010

MGM
(Metro Goldwyn Mayer Corp. Library)
c/o Robbins Music Corp., 729 Seventh Ave., New York, NY 10019

MIC,Zagreb
(Muzički Informativni Centar)
c/o Z.A.M.P., Ul. 8 maja 37, Yu 41000 Zagreb, Yugoslavia

Mills
(Mills Music, Inc.)
c/o Belwin-Mills Publishing Corp., 16 W. 61st St., New York, NY 10023

Modern
Edition Modern, Hans Wewerka Musikverlage
Franz-Josephstrasse 2, D-8000 Munich 40, West Germany

ModusAssoc
Modus Associates
Attn: Mr. Jerry H. Bilik, 1510 Plymouth Rd., Ann Arbor, MI 48105

Möseler
Möseler-Verlag
Hoffman-von-Fallersleben-Str. 8, 334 Wolfenbüttel, West Germany

Mowbray
(Mowbray Music Publishers)
c/o Theodore Presser Co., Presser Place, Bryn Mawr, PA 19010

Mozart Ed.
Mozart Edition
c/o S.T.I.M., Box 1539, S-111 85 Stockholm, Sweden

Mss.Publs.
Manuscript Publications
c/o David Berlin, 4809 Baptist Rd., Pittsburgh, PA 15227

Mt. Salus
Mount Salus Music
c/o James S. Sclater, 709 E. Leake St., Clinton, MS 39056

Musicus
Edition Musicus - New York, Inc.
P.O. Box 1341, Stamford, CT 06904

Musikk-Hu.
Musikk-Huset A/S
Karl Johansgaten 45, Oslo 1, Norway

MusKonFor
Musikaliska Konstföreningen
Floragat 15 B, Stockholm Ö, Sweden
Attn: Jan Carlstedt

Mus.Press
(Music Press)
c/o Theodore Presser Co., Presser Place, Bryn Mawr, PA 19010

MuSrvUnltd.
Music Services, Unlimited
c/o Dr. Victor King, 2414 Lake Ave., Cheverly, MD 20785

Muz. Fonds
Het Muziekfonds Uitgave
c/o Metropolis, 5 Van Ertbornstr., B-2000 Antwerp, Belgium

Mvl.R.Carl
Musikverlag Robert Carl
c/o G.E.M.A., Herzog-Wilhelm-Strasse 28, D-8000 Munich 2, West Germany

Nagel
(Adolf Nagel)
c/o Bärenreiter Verlag, Heinrich Schütz-Allee 35, D-3500 Kassel-Wilhelmshöhe 1, West Germany

NatlMuPubs
National Music Publishers Corp.
P.O. Box 1000, Newark, NJ 07101

Neue Oper.
(Die Neue Operette)
c/o Kurt Neufert Verlag, Oppelner Str. 9, Heidelberg-Kirchheim, West Germany

New Mus. Ed.
(New Music Edition)
c/o Theodore Presser Co., Presser Place, Bryn Mawr, PA 19010

New SW MuP
The New Southwest Music Publications
P.O. Box 4552, Santa Fe, NM 87502

New World
(New World Music Corp.)
c/o Warner Bros. Music Publications, 14th Fl., 75 Rockefeller Plaza, New York, NY 10019

NewOrl.Phi
New Orleans Philharmonic Symphony Orch., Suite 903
203 Carondelet St., New Orleans, LA 70130

Noack
Walter Noack Verlag
Moselstr. 20, 62 Wiesbaden-Schierstein, West Germany

Noetzel
(Noetzel Mvlg.)
c/o Henmar Press, Inc., 373 Park Ave. South, New York, NY 10016

Nordiska
Nordiska Musikförlaget AB
P.O. Box 745, Drottninggatan 37, S-101 30 Stockholm 1, Sweden

NorKomFlg
Norske Komponisters Forlag
c/o T.O.N.O., Klingenbergaten 5, Oslo 1, Norway

Norsk Mfl.
Norsk Musikforlag A/S
Karl Johansgaten 39, Oslo 1, Norway

Norsk Ntk.
(Norsk Notestikk & Forlag)
c/o Norsk Musikforlag A/S, Karl Johansgaten 39, Oslo 1, Norway

North
(North & Son Music, Inc.)
c/o Shapiro, Bernstein & Co., Inc., 10 E. 53rd St., New York, NY 10022

Novello
(Novello & Co., Ltd.: for RENTALS ONLY)
c/o Belwin-Mills Publishing Corp., 16 W. 61st St., New York, NY 10023
Novello Publications, Inc. (FOR NON-RENTAL MATERIALS)
Attn: Mr. Frank Moore, 145 Palisade St., Dobbs Ferry, NY 10522

Oberon
Edition Oberon
Roosevelt-Platz 8, Wien 9, Austria

Oiseau Lyre
Editions Oiseau Lyre
2 rue des Ramparts, Monte Carlo, Monaco

Ongaku
(Ongaku-No-Tomo-Sha)
c/o Theodore Presser Co., Presser Pl., Bryn Mawr, PA 19010

OperaIntl.
(Opera International) Mr. Edmund Najera
c/o A.S.C.A.P., 1 Lincoln Plaza, New York, NY 10023

Orlob
Orlob Music Co.
636 W. 174th St., New York, NY 10033

O.S.A.
O.S.A. (Ochranný Svaz Autorský)
Bubeneč, Třída Čs. Armády 20, 160-56 Prague 6, Czechoslovakia

Ostara
Ostara Press, Inc.
1092 Skyline Drive, Daly City, CA 94015

Oxford
Oxford University Press, Inc.
Attn: Music Dept., 200 Madison Ave., New York, NY 10016

P. J. Sifler
(Paul J. Sifler)
c/o Fredonia Press, 3947 Fredonia Dr., Hollywood, CA 90028

P. Maurice
The Peter Maurice Music Co., Ltd.
65 W. 55th St., New York, NY 10019

PABrussels
Palais des Académies
Brussels, Belgium

Pac. Publs.
Pacific Publications
University Station 8, Provo, UT 84601

Pacific
Edition Pacific (Inh. Michael Wilke)
Herzog-Wilhelmstr. 27, 8 Munich 2, West Germany

Paramount
Paramount Music Corp.
c/o Mr. Sidney Herman, 1 Gulf & Western Plaza, New York, NY 10023

P.C.Cabot
Paul C. Cabot
225 Franklin St., Boston, MA 02110

P.F.J.
Publications for Judaism
1237 S. Crescent Heights Blvd., Los Angeles, CA 90035

Phil Or Assn.
Philadelphia Orchestra
1420 Locust St., Philadelphia, PA 19102

PhiMuAlpha
Phi Mu Alpha Sinfonia Foundation
c/o National Office, Phi Mu Alpha Sinfonia, Lyrecrest, 10600 Old State Rd., Evansville, IN 47711

Piedmont
Piedmont Music Co., Inc.
1790 Broadway, New York, NY 10019

Pleasant
Pleasant Music Publishing Corp., Apt. 1421
3505 S. Ocean Ave., Hollywood, FL 33019

P.McKee
Peter McKee Music Co., Ltd.
3 Regina St. North, Waterloo, Ont., Canada

P.MusPubCo
Pops Music Publishing Co.
c/o Alfred Eisenstein, 18900 N.E. 14th Ave., North Miami, FL 33162

Polfliet
J. Polfliet, Fa. van Rosmalen & Zn.
Rosendaalselaan 18, Velp bij Arnhem, Netherlands

Presser
Theodore Presser Co.
Presser Place, Bryn Mawr, PA 19010

ProArtPubs
Pro Art Publications, Inc.
469 Union Ave., Westbury, NY 11590

P.R.S.
P.R.S. (The Performing Right Society, Ltd.)
29-33 Berners St., London W1P 4AA, England

Queens
Music Dept., Queens College
65-30 Kissena Blvd., Flushing, NY 11367

Raabe & P.
(Ed. Raabe & Plothow)
c/o N. Simrock, Werderstrasse 44, D-2000 Hamburg 13, West Germany

R.Birnbach
Musikverlag Richard Birnbach KG
D-1000 Berlin 45, West Germany

ReadyProds
Ready Productions, Inc.
500 W. 122nd St., Apt. 62, New York, NY 10027

Regaldi
Regaldi Music Co.
279 Warwick Ave., Teaneck, NJ 07666

Regina
Regina-Verlages-Wrede
Schumannstr. 35-A, 62 Wiesbaden, West Germany

R.Eichmann
Rudolf Eichmann Musikverlag
D-1000 Berlin 33, West Germany

RejayMuPub
Rejay Music Publishers
5052 Berkeley Ave., Westminster, CA 92683

Remick
(Remick Music Corp.)
c/o Warner Bros. Music Publications, 14th Fl., 75 Rockefeller Plaza, New York, NY 10019

ReynardPCI
Reynard Publishing Co., Inc.
Attn: Howard T. Pachner, P.O. Box 850, Valley Forge, PA 19482

Riccardo
Riccardo-Ton
c/o Hans Gerig Musikverlage, Drususgasse 7-11, D-5000 Köln 1, West Germany

Ricordi
(G. Ricordi & Co.)
c/o Belwin-Mills Publishing Corp., 16 W. 61st St., New York, NY 10023

Ries-Erler
(Ries & Erler Mvlg.)
c/o Henmar Press, Inc., 373 Park Ave. South, New York, NY 10016

Robbins
Robbins Music Corp.
729 Seventh Ave., New York, NY 10019

Robt. King
Robert King Music Co.
112-A Main St., North Easton, MA 02356

Rochester
Rochester Music Publishers, Inc.
358 Aldrich Rd., Fairport, NY 14450

Rog.Rhodes
Roger Rhodes Music, Ltd.
P.O. Box 855, Radio City Station, New York, NY 10019

Rosarita
(Rosarita Music, Inc.)
c/o Chappell & Co., Inc., 810 Seventh Ave., New York, NY 10019

Ruhle
(Robert Rühle)
c/o Siegel Musikverlage, Pelargonienweg 41, D-8000 Munich 70, West Germany

Rytvoc
Rytvoc, Inc.
39 W. 54th St., New York, NY 10019

S & R
S & R Music Publishing Co.
6533 Hollywood Blvd., Hollywood, CA 90028

S.A.B.A.M.
S.A.B.A.M. (Société Belge des Auteurs, Compositeurs et Editeurs)
61 rue de la Loi, B-1040 Brussels, Belgium

S.A.C.E.M.
S.A.C.E.M (Société des Auteurs, Compositeurs et Editeurs de Musique)
225 Avenue Charles De Gaulle, 92521 Neuilly s/Seine Cedex, France

S.A.D.A.I.C.
S.A.D.A.I.C. (Sociedad Argentina De Autores Y Compositores De Musica)
Lavalle 1547, Buenos Aires, Argentina

Salabert
Editions Salabert, Inc.
575 Madison Ave., New York, NY 10022

Sam.French
Samuel French, Inc.
25 W. 45th St., New York, NY 10036

S.A.M.R.O.
S.A.M.R.O. (South African Music Rights Organisation, Ltd.)
P.O. Box 9292, Johannesburg, South Africa

Saunders
Saunders Publications, Inc.
119 W. 57th St., New York, NY 10019

Scherzando
Scherzando Uitgave
Attn: M. Georges De Heer Follman, 41 Transvaalstraat, Berchm-Antwerp, Belgium

Schirmer
See G. Schirmer

SchmittMC
Schmitt Music Center, Inc.
110 N. Fifth St., Minneapolis, MN 55403

Schuberth
J. Schuberth & Co.
Schliessfach 1053, 62 Wiesbaden, West Germany

ScudderPro
Scudder Productions
P.O. Box 13, Bondville, VT 05340

SDMV
(Süddeutscher-Musikverlag)
c/o Henmar Press, Inc., 373 Park Ave. South, New York, NY 10016

Seesaw
Seesaw Music Corp.
1966 Broadway, New York, NY 10023

S.G.A.E.
S.G.A.E. (Sociedad General de Autores de España)
Calle Fernando VI, Madrid 4, Spain

Shawnee
Shawnee Press, Inc.
Delaware Water Gap, PA 18327

Shilkret
Nathaniel Shilkret Music Co., Inc.
P.O. Box 38, Malverne, NY 11565

S.I.A.E.
S.I.A.E (Societa Italiana degli Autori ed Editori)
Viale della Letteratura N. 30, Rome (E.U.R.), Italy

Sikorski
(Hans Sikorski Musikverlag)
c/o Belwin-Mills Publishing Corp., 16 W. 61st St., New York, NY 10023

Sirius
(Sirius Verlag, c/o Heinrichshofen Verlag)
c/o Henmar Press, Inc., 373 Park Ave. South, New York, NY 10016

Skand & Bo
(Scandinavisk Musikforlag, c/o Wilhelm Hansen Musikvorlag)
c/o G. Schirmer, Inc., 866 Third Ave., New York, NY 10022

Skidmore
(Skidmore Music Co., Inc.)
c/o Shapiro, Bernstein & Co., Inc., 10 E. 53rd St., New York, NY 10022

SMP
Sacred Music Press of the Hebrew Union College - Jewish Institute of Religion
40 W. 68th St., New York, NY 10023

S.O.K.O.J.
S.O.K.O.J. (Sojuz na Kompozitorite na Jugoslavija)
Mišarska 12, Belgrade, Yugoslavia

Southern
Southern Music Publishing Co., Inc.
1740 Broadway, New York, NY 10019

SouthernTx
Southern Music Co.
1100 Broadway, P.O. Box 329, San Antonio, TX 78292

SPAM
(Society for the Publication of American Music)
c/o Theodore Presser Co., Presser Place, Bryn Mawr, PA 19010

S.T.E.F
S.T.E.F. (Samband Tónskálda og Eigenda Flutningsréttar)
Laufásvegi 40, Reykjavík, Iceland

S.T.I.M.
S.T.I.M. (Société Suédoise des Compositeurs, Auteurs et Editeurs de Musique, Tegnérlunden 3, 1185 Stockholm, Sweden); Agent for U.S.A.:The Edwin A. Fleisher Collection of Orchestral Music
c/o The Free Library of Philadelphia, Logan Square, Philadelphia, PA 19107

Studio P/R
Studio P/R, Inc.
224 S. Lebanon St., Lebanon, IN 46052

Studio Two Twenty-Four
See Studio P/R

Suecia
(Edition Suecia); Agent for U.S.A.: The Edwin A. Fleisher Collection of Orchestral Music
c/o The Free Library of Philadelphia, Logan Square, Philadelphia, PA 19107

S.U.I.S.A.
S.U.I.S.A. (Société Suisse des Auteurs et Editeurs)
Bellariastrasse 82, 8038 Zurich, Switzerland

SummitMus
Summit Music, Ltd.
497 Eglington Ave. West, Toronto, Ont. M5N 1A8, Canada

Summy-Bir.
Summy-Birchard Publishing Co.
1834 Ridge Ave., Evanston, IL 60204

SunburyLtd
Sunbury Music, Ltd.
155/57 Oxford St., London W1, England

SuomenTyMu
Suomen Työväen Musiikkiliitto
Hallituskatu 19, 33200 Tampere 20, Finland

SuomSvltjt
Suomen Säveltäjätry (Society of Finnish Composers)
Runeberginkatu 15-A, 00100 Helsinki 10, Finland

SuomYRadio
Suomen Yleisradio (Finnish Broadcasting Co.)
Unioninkatu 16, 00130 Helsinki 13, Finland

Swiss M.L.
The Swiss Music Library
c/o Mrs. M. Staehelin, 1 Lincoln Plaza, New York, NY 10023

Sym.House
Symphony House Music Publishers Corp.
Tauentzien Str. 16, 1 Berlin 30, West Germany

Symphonia
(Symphonia Verlag. A.G.)
c/o Belwin-Mills Publishing Corp., 16 W. 61st St., New York, NY 10023

T & J
Tischer & Jagenberg
Nibelungenstrasse 48, D-8000 Munich 19, West Germany

T. English
Thomas English Music Publishing Co., Inc.
Attn: Rayburn Wright, 69 Sunset Blvd., Pittsford, NY 14534

T.B.Harms
T.B.Harms Co., Suite 700
100 Wilshire Blvd., Santa Monica, CA 90401

TC Stanglnd
Thomas C. Stangland Co.
3200 S.W. Dolph Court, Apt. 7, Portland, OR 97219

Templeton
(Templeton Publishing Co., Inc.)
c/o Shawnee Press, Inc., Delaware Water Gap, PA 18327

TenutoPbns
(Tenuto Publications)
c/o Theodore Presser Co., Presser Place, Bryn Mawr, PA 19010

T.E.O.S.T.O.
T.E.O.S.T.O. (Säveltäjäin Tekijänoikeustoimisto)
Lauttasaarentie 1, 00200 Helsinki 20, Finland

Tetra
Tetra Music Corp.
225 W. 57th St., New York, NY 10019

Third Stream
Third Stream Music, Inc.
Attn: Paul Schwartz, Suite 810, 200 W. 57th St., New York, NY 10019

T.O.N.O.
T.O.N.O. (Norsk Komponistforenings Internasjonale Musikkbyrå)
Postboks 1666, Vika, Oslo 1, Norway

Tonos Vlg.
Tonos Verlag Franz König
D-6100 Darmstadt, West Germany

Transcon
Transcontinental Music Publications
1674 Broadway, New York, NY 10019

KEY TO PUBLISHERS' ABBREVIATIONS

Translator
(name of individual)
c/o A.S.C.A.P., 1 Lincoln Plaza, New York, NY 10023

TRFMusInc.
(T.R.F. Music, Inc.)
c/o Dorian Music Publishers, Inc., 501 Madison Ave., New York, NY 10022

Troubadour
Troubadour Publishing Co.
Attn: Fred Karlin, 605 Funchel Rd., Los Angeles, CA 90024

Twentieth Cent.
(Twentieth Century Music Corp.)
c/o Robbins Music Corp., 729 Seventh Ave., New York, NY 10019

U.B.C.
U.B.C. (União Brasileira de Compositores)
Rua Visconde de Inhaúma No. 134-7 Andar, Rio De Janeiro, Brazil

U.MiamiSo
University of Miami Symphony Orchestra
c/o Music Dept., University of Miami, Coral Gables, FL 33124

Valentino
Thomas J. Valentino, Inc.
151 W. 46th St., New York, NY 10036

Valley
Valley Music Press
c/o Smith College, Northampton, MA 01060

Viking Mfl.
(Viking Musikforlag, c/o Engstrøm & Sødring's Musikforlag A/S)
c/o Henmar Press, Inc., 373 Park Ave. South, New York, NY 10016

Volkwein
Volkwein Bros., Inc.
117 Sandusky St., Pittsburgh, PA 15212

Vriamont
M. Georges Vriamont
25 Rue de la Régence, Brussels 1, Belgium

W-Levant
(Weaner-Levant)
c/o Theodore Presser Co., Presser Place, Bryn Mawr, PA 19010

Walkport
Walkport Associates, Apt. 601
170 W. 74th St., New York, NY 10023

Walton
Walton Music Corp.
17 W. 60th St., New York, NY 10023

WarnerBros
Warner Bros. Music Publications, Inc., 14th Fl.
75 Rockefeller Plaza, New York, NY 10019

WashBalGld
Washington Ballet Guild
3515 Wisconsin Ave. N.W., Washington, DC

Weinberger
Josef Weinberger, Ltd.
10-16 Rathbone St., London W1P 2BJ, England

Weintraub
Weintraub Music Co.
33 W. 60th St., New York, NY 10023

Wentworth
Wentworth Music Co.
c/o Mr. Felix C. Ziffer, 22nd Fl., 641 Lexington Ave., New York, NY 10022

Westerlund
(R.E. Westerlund)
c/o Fazer Musiikki Oy, Aleksanterinkatu 11, 00100 Helsinki 10, Finland

Western
(Western Music Library)
c/o H. T. FitzSimons Co., Inc., 615 N. LaSalle St., Chicago, IL 60610

Western M.L.
See Western

WGS Music
William Grant Still Music
1262 Victoria Ave., Los Angeles, CA 90019

Wilhmiana
Wilhelmiana Musikverlag
Eschersheimer Landstr. 12, 6 Frankfurt-am-Main, West Germany

Williamson
(Williamson Music, Inc.)
c/o Chappell & Co., Inc., 810 Seventh Ave., New York, NY 10019

Wimbledon
(Wimbledon Music Co.)
c/o Tetra Music Corp., 225 W. 57th St., New York, NY 10019

Witmark
(M. Witmark & Sons)
c/o Warner Bros. Music Publications, 14th Fl., 75 Rockefeller Plaza, New York, NY 10019

World Lib
World Library Publications, Inc.
2145 Central Parkway, Cincinnati, OH 45214

Ybarra
Ybarra Music
P.O. Box 665, Lemon Grove, CA 92045

Y.Laulajat
Ylioppilaskunnan Laulajat
Vanha Ylioppilastalo, 00100 Helsinki 10, Finland

DO NOT REMOVE

SLIP FROM POCKET